ANTHOLOGY OF AMERICAN LITERATURE

FOURTH EDITION

[**VOLUME II**

Realism to the Present]

GENERAL EDITOR

GEORGE MCMICHAEL   *California State University, Hayward*

ADVISORY EDITORS

FREDERICK CREWS   *University of California, Berkeley*

J. C. LEVENSON   *University of Virginia*

LEO MARX   *Massachusetts Institute of Technology*

DAVID E. SMITH   *Hampshire College*

Macmillan Publishing Company

NEW YORK

Macmillan Publishing Company
866 Third Avenue, New York, New York 10022

Library of Congress Cataloging-in-Publication Data
Anthology of American Literature.

Includes index.
Contents: —v. 2. Realism to the present.
1. American Literature. I. McMichael, George L., 1927–   . II. Crews, Frederick C.
PS507.A68   1989   810'.8   88-8413
ISBN 0-02-379622-7 (v. 2)

Printing: 1 2 3 4 5 6 7   Year: 9 0 1 2 3 4 5

Acknowledgments

Atheneum Publishers, Inc. W. S. MERWIN. "The Dry Stone Mason," "The Asians Dying," "Fly," from *The Lice*. Copyright © 1966, 1967 by W. S. Merwin. "The Dry Stone Mason" and "The Asians Dying" appeared originally in *The New Yorker*. "Fly" appeared originally in *The Atlantic Monthly*. "Noah's Raven" from *The Moving Target*. Copyright 1963 by W.S. Merwin. "Direction" from *Opening the Hand*. Copyright 1983 by W.S. Merwin. Reprinted by permission of Atheneum Publishers.

Gwendolyn Brooks. "Kitchenette Building," "The Mother," "Sadie and Maude" copyright 1945 by Gwendolyn Brooks. "The Vacant Lot" from *The Bean Eaters*. Copyright 1960 by Gwendolyn Brooks. "The Children of the Poor" Copyright 1949 by Gwendolyn Brooks. "The Lovers of the Poor" from *The Bean Eaters*. Copyright 1960 by Gwendolyn Brooks. "Beverly Hills, Chicago" from *Annie Allen*. Copyright 1949 by Gwendolyn Brooks. "We Real Cool. The Pool Players. Seven at the Golden Shovel." Copyright © 1959 by Gwendolyn Brooks. "The Chicago Defender Sends a Man to Little Rock." Copyright © 1960 by Gwendolyn Brooks. "The Blackstone Rangers: As Seen by Disciples. The Leaders. Gang Girls." Copyright © 1968 by Gwendolyn Brooks Blakely. All selections reprinted from *The World of Gwendolyn Brooks* by Gwendolyn Brooks by permission of the author.

Corinth Books, Inc. IMAMU AMIRI BARAKA (LEROI JONES). "In Memory of Radio," "The Bridge," "Notes for a Speech" from *Preface to a Twenty-Volume Suicide Note*. Copyright © 1961 by LeRoi Jones. Reprinted by permission of Corinth Books.

Delacorte Press. TILLIE OLSEN. "I Stand Here Ironing" from *Tell Me a Riddle* by Tillie Olsen. Copyright 1956, 1957, 1960, 1961 by Tillie Olsen. Reprinted by arrangement with Delacorte Press/Seymour Lawrence.

The Dial Press. JAMES BALDWIN, "Sonny's Blues." Copyright © 1957 by James Baldwin. From

Going to Meet the Man by James Baldwin. Reprinted by permission of the publisher, The Dial Press. Originally appeared in *Partisan Review.*

Elizabeth H. Dos Passos. JOHN DOS PASSOS, "Preface to *U.S.A.*," "Proteus" from *42nd Parallel,* "Newsreel XLIII," "The Body of an American" from *1919,* "Newsreel LXVI," "The Camera Eye (50)," "Newsreel LXVII," "Vag" from *Big Money.* All selections from *U.S.A.*, originally published by Houghton Mifflin Company. Copyright held by Elizabeth H. Dos Passos. Reprinted by permission of Elizabeth H. Dos Passos.

Doubleday & Company, Inc. JAMES DICKEY. "Diabetes" from *The Eye Beaters.* Copyright 1968, 1969, 1970 by James Dickey. Reprinted by permission of Doubleday & Company, Inc. THEODORE ROETHKE. "Dolor," copyright © 1960 by Modern Poetry Association, Inc.; "Open House," "On the Road to Woodlawn," "The Lost Son," "Cuttings," "Cuttings (Later)," and "The Waking," copyright 1941, 1947, 1948, 1953 by Theodore Roethke; "Root Cellar," copyright 1943 by Modern Poetry Association, Inc.; "Big Wind," copyright 1947 by The United Chapter of Phi Beta Kappa; "My Papa's Waltz," copyright 1942 by The Hearst Magazine, Inc.; "Four for Sir John Davies," copyright 1952 by The Atlantic Monthly Company; "In a Dark Time" and "Wish for a Young Wife," copyright © 1960, 1963 by Beatrice Roethke, Administratrix of the Estate of Theodore Roethke. From the book *The Collected Poems of Theodore Roethke* by Theodore Roethke. Reprinted by permission of Doubleday & Company, Inc.

The Dreiser Trust. THEODORE DREISER. "Nigger Jeff" from *Free and Other Stories* by Theodore Dreiser. Copyright 1918 by Boni & Liveright, Inc.; copyright renewed 1945 by Theodore Dreiser. Reprinted by permission of The Dreiser Trust, Harold J. Dies, Trustee.

The Ecco Press. LOUISE GLÜCK. "The Drowned Children" "Mock Orange" copyright © 1985 by Louise Glück, from *The Triumph of Achilles* by Louise Glück. Published by The Ecco Press in 1985. "The Garden" "The Reproach" copyright © 1976, 1977, 1978, 1979, 1980 by Louise Glück, from *Descending Figure* by Louise Glück. Published by The Ecco Press in 1980. "Hesitate to Call," "The Chicago Train," "The Edge," "My Neighbor in the Mirror," and "Thanksgiving" copyright © 1968 by Louise Glück, from *From Born* by Louise Glück. All reprinted by permission.

Farrar, Straus & Giroux Inc. DONALD BARTHELME. "The School" from *Amateurs* by Donald Barthelme. Copyright © 1974, 1976 by Donald Barthelme. Reprinted by permission of Farrar, Straus & Giroux, Inc. This piece originally appeared in *The New Yorker.* ELIZABETH BISHOP. "A Miracle for Breakfast," "Roosters," "The Fish," "Visits to St. Elizabeths," "The Prodigal," "The Armadillo," "In the Waiting Room" and "Over 2,000 Illustrations and a Complete Concordance" from *The Complete Poems 1927–1979* by Elizabeth Bishop. Copyright © 1979, 1983 by Alice Helen Methfessel. Reprinted by permission of Farrar, Straus and Giroux, Inc. RANDALL JARRELL. "Losses," "The Death of the Ball Turret Gunner," "A Camp in the Prussian Forest," "Seele im Raum," "A Girl in a Library," from *The Complete Poems* by Randall Jarrell. Copyright © 1945, 1948, 1950, 1951, 1955, 1969 by Mrs. Randall Jarrell. Copyright renewed © 1972, 1973, 1975, 1977 by Mrs. Randall Jarrell. Reprinted by permission of Farrar, Straus & Giroux, Inc. ROBERT LOWELL. "Commander Lowell," "Memories of West Street and Lepke," "Skunk Hour," "Waking in the Blue," from *Life Studies* by Robert Lowell. Copyright © 1956, 1959 by Robert Lowell. "For the Union Dead," "The Public Garden," "Lady Ralegh's Lament" from *For the Union Dead* by Robert Lowell. Copyright © 1956, 1960, 1961, 1962, 1963, 1964 by Robert Lowell. "Waking Early Sunday Morning," "For Theodore Roethke" and "Near the Ocean" from *Near the Ocean* by Robert Lowell. Copyright © 1963, 1965, 1966, 1967 by Robert Lowell. Reprinted by permission of Farrar, Straus & Giroux, Inc.

Harcourt Brace Jovanovich, Inc. E. E. CUMMINGS. "this little bride and groom are" from *E. E. Cummings, Complete Poems, 1913–1962,* copyright 1980. Reprinted by permission of Harcourt Brace Jovanovich, Inc. "anyone lived in a pretty how town," "my father moved through dooms of love," copyright 1940 by E. E. Cummings, copyright 1968 by Marion Morehouse Cummings. "a salesman is an it that stinks Excuse," "pity this busy monster,manunkind," copyright 1944 by E. E. Cummings. All reprinted from his volume *Poems*

Inc.; renewed 1953 by Ida M. Cullen. "From the Dark Tower" from *On These I Stand* by Countee Cullen. Copyright 1927 by Harper & Row, Publishers, Inc.; renewed 1955 by Ida M. Cullen. "Heritage," "Incident" and "Scottsboro, Too, Is Worth Its Song," from *On These I Stand* by Countee Cullen. Copyright 1925 by Harper & Row, Publishers, Inc.; renewed 1953 by Ida M. Cullen. All selections reprinted by permission of Harper & Row, Publishers, Inc. ZORA NEALE HURSTON. *The Gilded Six-Bits.* Copyright 1937. Reprinted by permission of Harper & Row. ALLEN GINSBERG. "Mugging" copyright © 1974 by Allen Ginsberg, "American Change" and "To Aunt Rose" copyright © 1958 by Allen Ginsberg, "America" copyright © 1956, 1959 by Allen Ginsberg, "Sunflower Sutra," "A Supermarket in California," and "Howl" copyright © 1955 by Allen Ginsberg. From *Collected Poems 1947–1980* by Allen Ginsberg. Reprinted by permission of Harper & Row, Publishers, Inc. SYLVIA PLATH. "The Hanging Man," "Morning Song," and "The Applicant" from *Collected Poems of Sylvia Plath.* Copyright 1981 by Ted Hughes. Reprinted by permission of Harper & Row. "Lady Lazarus," copyright © 1963 by Ted Hughes; "Ariel" copyright © 1965 by Ted Hughes; "Daddy" copyright © 1963 by Ted Hughes; "Fever 103°" copyright © 1963 by Ted Hughes; all from *The Collected Poems of Sylvia Plath* edited by Ted Hughes. MARK TWAIN. "Whittier's Birthday Dinner Speech" from *Mark Twain's Speeches* by Mark Twain. Copyright 1923 by Mark Twain Company; renewed 1951 by Mark Twain Company. "The War Prayer" (pages 394–398) from *Europe and Elsewhere* by Mark Twain. Copyright 1923 by Mark Twain Company; renewed 1951 by Mark Twain Company. Both selections reprinted by permission of Harper & Row, Publishers, Inc.

Harvard University Press. EMILY DICKINSON. "Success is counted sweetest," "These are the days when birds come back," "A wounded deer—leaps highest," "The thought beneath so slight a film," "I taste a liquor never brewed," "Wild nights—Wild nights!" "There's a certain slant of light," "I felt a funeral, in my brain," "The soul selects her own society," "It sifts from Leaden Sieves," "Nature—sometimes sears a sapling," "A Bird came down the Walk," "'Twas like a Maelstrom, with a notch," "Much madness is divinest sense," "I died for beauty—but was scarce," "I heard a Fly buzz—when I died," "I would not paint—a picture," "I started early—took my dog," "Mine—by the right of the White Election!" "The Heart Seeks Pleasure—first—" "The brain, within it's groove," "I measure every Grief I meet," "I like to see it lap the miles," "The Brain—is wider than the sky," "I cannot live with You," "Pain—has an element of Blank," "One need not be a chamber—to be haunted," "Because I could not stop for death," "Renunciation—is a piercing virtue—" "my life had stood—a Loaded Gun—" "Presentiment—is that long shadow—on the lawn," "A narrow fellow in the grass," "Crumbling is not an instant's act," "Further in summer than the birds," "Tell all the truth but tell it slant," "As imperceptibly as grief," "Those—dying then," "Apparently with no surprise," "My life closed twice before its close," "To make a prairie is to take a clover and one bee," and "Elysium is as far as to" all reprinted by permission of the publishers and the Trustees of Amherst College from *The Poems of Emily Dickinson*, edited by Thomas H. Johnson, Cambridge, Mass.: The Belknap Press of Harvard University Press. Copyright 1951, © 1955, 1979, 1983 by the President and Fellows of Harvard College.

Henry Holt and Company. ROBERT FROST. "The Tuft of Flowers," "Mending Wall," "Home Burial," "After Apple-Picking," "The Wood Pile," "The Road Not Taken," "An Old Man's Winter Night," "Birches," "The Oven Bird," "Putting in the Seed," "The Witch of Coös," "For Once, Then, Something," "Fire and Ice," "Dust of Snow," "Design," "Nothing Gold Can Stay," "Stopping by Woods on a Snowy Evening," "Once by the Pacific," "Acquainted with the Night," "West-Running Brook," "Desert Places," "Neither Far Out Nor In Deep," "Provide, Provide," "The Silken Tent," "The Most of It," "The Gift Outright," "Directive," and "Forgive, O Lord," all from *The Poetry of Robert Frost* edited by Edward Connery Lathem. Copyright © 1969 by Holt, Rinehart and Winston, Inc. Copyright © 1962 by Robert Frost. Copyright © 1975 by Lesley Frost Ballantine. Reprinted by permission of Henry Holt and Company, Inc.

Houghton Mifflin Company. HENRY ADAMS. Chapter XXV, "The Dynamo and the Virgin," from *The Education of Henry Adams*. Copyright 1918 by the Massachusetts Historical Society. Reprinted by permission of Houghton Mifflin Company. RAYMOND CHANDLER. "Red Wind" from *The Midnight Raymond Chandler* by Raymond Chandler. Copyright © 1971 by Helga Greene, Executrix. Reprinted by permission of Houghton Mifflin Company. PHILIP ROTH, "The Conversion of the Jews" from *Goodbye Columbus* by Philip Roth. Copyright © 1959 by Philip Roth. Reprinted by permission of Houghton Mifflin Company. Anne Sexton. "Her Kind," "Us," and Rowing" from *Complete Poems* by Anne Sexton. Copyright 1981 by Anne Sexton. "The Farmer's Wife" and "Ringing the Bells" from *Bedlam and Part Way Back* by Anne Sexton. Copyright 1960 by Anne Sexton. "All My Pretty Ones," "For God While Sleeping," and "The Truth the Dead Know" from *All My Pretty Ones* by Anne Sexton. Copyright 1962 by Anne Sexton. "And One for My Dame" and "The Addict" from *Live or Die* by Anne Sexton. Copyright 1966 by Anne Sexton. All reprinted by permission of Houghton Mifflin Company.

International Creative Management. JOHN CHEEVER, "The Swimmer" from *The Brigadier and the Golf Widow*, published by Harper & Row. Reprinted by permission of International Creative Management. First appeared in *The New Yorker*. Copyright © 1964 by John Cheever.

Jargon Press. DENISE LEVERTOV. "Pure Products" from *Overland to the Islands*. Copyright © 1958 by Denise Levertov. Reprinted by permission of the author and the publishers.

Little, Brown and Company. EMILY DICKINSON, "The robin's my criterion for tune," "A clock stopped—," "After great pain, a formal feeling comes," "This was a poet—it is that," "I dwell in possibility," "Publication—is my auction," "The Bible is an antique volume," "In winter in my room" all from *The Complete Poems of Emily Dickinson* edited by Thomas H. Johnson. Copyright 1914, 1929, 1935 by Martha Dickinson Bianchi; copyright renewed 1942 by Martha Dickinson Bianchi; copyright renewed © 1957, 1963 by Mary L. Hampson. Reprinted by permission of Little, Brown and Company.

Liveright Publishing Corporation. HART CRANE. "Black Tambourine," "Chaplinesque," "At Melville's Tomb," "Voyages I, II, III," "To Brooklyn Bridge," "Powhatan's Daughter: The Harbor Dawn, Van Winkle, The River, The Dance, Indiana," "The Tunnel," "Atlantis," and "The Broken Tower," all reprinted from *The Complete Poems and Selected Letters and Prose of Hart Crane*, edited by Brom Weber, with the permission of Liveright Publishing Corporation. Copyright 1933, © 1958, 1966 by Liveright Publishing Corporation. E. E. CUMMINGS. "in Just—," "O sweet spontaneous," "Buffalo Bill's defunct," "the Cambridge ladies who live in furnished souls," copyright 1923, 1951 by E. E. Cummings. Reprinted by permission of Liveright Publishing Corporation. "nobody loses all the time," "next to of course god America I," "my sweet old etcetera," copyright 1926 by Horace Liveright; copyright 1954 by E. E. Cummings. Reprinted by permission of Liveright Publishing Corporation. "i sing of Olaf glad and big" copyright 1931, 1959 by E. E. Cummings. Reprinted by permission of Liveright Publishing Corporation. "r-p-o-p-h-e-s-s-a-g-r" from *No Thanks* by E. E. Cummings, edited by George James Firmage, by permission of Liveright Publishing Corporation. Copyright 1935 by E. E. Cummings; copyright © 1968 by Marion Morehouse Cummings. Copyright © 1973, 1978 by The Trustees for the E. E. Cummings Trust. Copyright © 1973, 1978 by George James Firmage. JEAN TOOMER. "Blood Burning Moon" from *Cane* by Jean Toomer, Copyright 1923 by Boni & Liveright, Inc. Copyright renewed 1951 by Jean Toomer. Reprinted by permission of Liveright Publishing Corporation.

Macmillan Publishing Company. RANDALL JARRELL. "In Montecito" from *The Lost World* by Randall Jarrell. Copyright © 1963, 1965 by Randall Jarrell. Originally appeared in *The New Yorker*. Reprinted by permission of Macmillan Publishing Company. "A Well-to-Do Invalid" from *The Lost World* by Randall Jarrell. Copyright © 1964, 1965 by Randall Jarrell. Reprinted by permission of Macmillan Publishing Company. MARIANNE MOORE. "To a Steam Roller," "The Monkeys," "The Fish," "Poetry," and "No Swan So Fine," from *Collected Poems* by Marianne Moore and T. S. Eliot. Copyright 1941 by Marianne Moore; renewed 1969 by Marianne Moore. Reprinted by permission of Macmillan Publishing

"The Knife of the Times" and "The Use of Force" from *The Farmer's Daughters* by William Carlos Williams. Copyright 1932, 1938 by William Carlos Williams. Reprinted by permission of New Directions Publishing Corporation.

W. W. Norton & Company, Inc. A. R. AMMONS. "So I Said I Am Ezra," "Apologia Pro Vita Sua," "Gravelly Run," "Coon Song," "Unsaid," "Corsons Inlet," "The Unifying Principle," "The City Limits," all from *Collected Poems, 1951–1971* by A. R. Ammons. Copyright © 1972 by A. R. Ammons. Reprinted by permission of W. W. Norton & Company, Inc. ADRIENNE RICH. "The Celebration in the Plaza," "Two Songs [Sex, as they harshly call it]," "Charleston in the 1860's," and "Planetarium" all reprinted from *Poems, Selected and New, 1950–1974* by Adrienne Rich. Copyright © 1975, 1973, 1971, 1969, 1966 by W. W. Norton & Company, Inc. Copyright © 1967, 1963, 1962, 1961, 1960, 1959, 1957, 1956, 1955, 1954, 1953, 1952, 1951 by Adrienne Rich. Reprinted by permission of W. W. Norton & Company, Inc. "The Trees" and "Breakfast in a Bowling Alley in Utica, New York" reprinted from *Necessities of Life, Poems 1962–1965* by Adrienne Rich. Copyright © 1966 by W. W. Norton & Company, Inc. Reprinted by permission of W. W. Norton & Company, Inc. "Integrity" from *A Wild Patience Has Taken Me This Far*. Copyright 1981 by W. W. Norton & Company, Inc. Reprinted by permission of W. W. Norton & Company, Inc.

Harold Ober Associates. SHERWOOD ANDERSON. "Death in the Woods" by Sherwood Anderson, first published in *The American Mercury*. Copyright 1926 by The American Mercury, Inc.; copyright renewed 1953 by Eleanor Copenhavor Anderson. Reprinted by permission of Harold Ober Associates Incorporated. LANGSTON HUGHES. "On the Road" from *Laughing to Keep from Crying* by Langston Hughes. Copyright 1952 by Langston Hughes; copyright renewed 1980 by George Houston Bass. Reprinted by permission of Harold Ober Associates Incorporated. "Dream Boogie" and "Harlem" from *Montage of a Dream Deferred*. Copyright 1951 by Henry Holt. Reprinted by permission of Harold Ober Associates.

G. P. Putnam's Sons. EDWARD ALBEE. *The Zoo Story* by Edward Albee. Copyright © 1960 by Edward Albee. Reprinted by permission of Coward-McCann, Inc. from *The Zoo Story* by Edward Albee. NORMAN MAILER. "The White Negro" from *Advertisements for Myself* by Norman Mailer. Copyright © 1959 by Norman Mailer. *The Armies of the Night* from Parts II and III. Copyright 1986 by Norman Mailer. All reprinted by permission of G. P. Putnam's Sons.

Random House and Alfred A. Knopf, Inc. ANN BEATTIE. "The Lawn Party" from *Secrets and Surprises* by Ann Beattie. Copyright 1976, 1977, 1978 by Ann Beattie. Reprinted by permission of Alfred A. Knopf, Inc. WILLA CATHER. "Neighbor Rosicky" from *Obscure Destinies* by Willa Cather. Copyright 1930 by Willa Cather; renewed 1958 by the Executors of the Estate of Willa Cather. Reprinted by permission of Alfred A. Knopf, Inc. AMY CLAMPITT. "The Kingfisher," "Marginal Employment," and "Berceuse" from *The Kingfisher* by Amy Clampitt. Copyright 1983 by Amy Clampitt. "Witness" and "Burial in Cypress Hills" from *What the Light Was Like* by Amy Clampitt. Copyright 1985 by Amy Clampitt. "Man Feeding Pigeons" and "Archaic Figure" from *Archaic Figure* by Amy Clampitt. Copyright 1987 by Amy Clampitt. All reprinted with permission of Alfred A. Knopf, Inc. RALPH ELLISON. Chapter 1 from *Invisible Man* by Ralph Ellison. Copyright 1947 by Ralph Ellison. Reprinted by permission of Random House, Inc. WILLIAM FAULKNER. "That Evening Sun" from *Collected Stories of William Faulkner*. Copyright 1931 and renewed 1959 by William Faulkner. Reprinted by permission of Random House, Inc. "A Rose for Emily" from *Collected Stories of William Faulkner*. Copyright 1930 and renewed 1958 by William Faulkner. Reprinted by permission of Random House, Inc. "Barn Burning" from *Collected Stories of William Faulkner*. Copyright 1939 and renewed 1967 by Estelle Faulkner and Jill Faulkner Summers. Reprinted by permission of Random House, Inc. LANGSTON HUGHES. "The Weary Blues," "The Negro Speaks of Rivers" copyright 1926 by Alfred A. Knopf and renewed 1954 by Langston Hughes. "Young Gal's Blues" copyright 1927 by Alfred A. Knopf, Inc. and renewed 1955 by Langston Hughes. "Note on Commercial Theatre" copyright 1948 by Alfred A. Knopf, Inc. "I, Too" copyright 1926 by Alfred A. Knopf, Inc. and renewed 1954 by Langston Hughes. All reprinted from *Selected Poems of Langston*

Hughes by permission of Alfred A. Knopf, Inc. ROBINSON JEFFERS. "Boats in a Fog," copyright 1925 and renewed 1953 by Robinson Jeffers; "Hurt Hawks" and "Shine, Perishing Republic" copyright 1928 and renewed 1956 by Robinson Jeffers; "The Purse-Seine" copyright 1937 and renewed 1965 by Donnan Jeffers and Garth Jeffers; all reprinted from *The Selected Poetry of Robinson Jeffers* by permission of Random House, Inc. EUGENE O'NEILL. "The Hairy Ape" copyright 1922 and renewed 1950 by Eugene O'Neill. Reprinted from *Nine Plays* by Eugene O'Neill by permission of Random House, Inc. SYLVIA PLATH. "All the Dead Dears" copyright © 1962 by Sylvia Plath; "Two Views of a Cadaver Room" copyright © 1962 by Sylvia Plath. Both reprinted from *The Colossus and Other Poems* by Sylvia Plath, by permission of Alfred A. Knopf, Inc. JOHN CROWE RANSOM. "Here Lies a Lady," "Bells for John Whiteside's Daughter," and "Captain Carpenter" copyright 1924 by Alfred A. Knopf, Inc.; renewed 1952 by John Crowe Ransom. Reprinted from *Selected Poems, Third Edition, Revised and Enlarged,* by John Crowe Ransom, by permission of Alfred A. Knopf, Inc. "Blue Girls," "Piazza Piece," and "The Equilibrists" copyright 1927 and renewed 1955 by John Crowe Ransom. Reprinted from *Selected Poems, Third Edition, Revised and Enlarged* by John Crowe Ransom by permission of Alfred A. Knopf, Inc. GERTRUDE STEIN. "The Gentle Lena" from *Three Lives* by Gertrude Stein. Copyright 1909 by Random House, Inc. WALLACE STEVENS. "Peter Quince at the Clavier," "Disillusionment at Ten O'Clock," "Sunday Morning," "Domination of Black," "The Death of a Soldier," "Anecdote of the Jar," "The Snow Man," "A High-Toned Old Christian Woman," all copyright 1923, renewed 1951 by Wallace Stevens. Reprinted from *The Collected Poems of Wallace Stevens* by permission of Alfred A. Knopf, Inc. "The Plot Against the Giant," copyright 1923, 1951 by Wallace Stevens; "The Idea of Order at Key West," copyright 1936 by Wallace Stevens, renewed 1964 by Holly Stevens; "The Blue Buildings in the Summer Air," copyright 1942 by Wallace Stevens; "No Possum, No Sop, No Taters," copyright 1947 by Wallace Stevens; "Final Soliloquy of the Interior Paramour," copyright 1951 by Wallace Stevens; "The Plain Sense of Things," copyright 1952 by Wallace Stevens; all reprinted from *The Collected Poems of Wallace Stevens* by permission of Alfred A. Knopf, Inc. "Dry Loaf," copyright 1942 by Wallace Stevens, and reprinted from *The Collected Poems of Wallace Stevens* by permission of Alfred A. Knopf, Inc. "Of Modern Poetry" copyright 1942 by Wallace Stevens and renewed 1970 by Holly Stevens. Reprinted from *The Collected Poems of Wallace Stevens* by permission of Alfred A. Knopf, Inc. "The Course of a Particular" from *Opus Posthumous* by Wallace Stevens. Copyright 1957 by Elsie Stevens and Holly Stevens. Reprinted by permission of Alfred A. Knopf, Inc. JOHN UPDIKE. "Flight" copyright © 1962 by John Updike. Reprinted from *Pigeon Feathers and Other Stories* by John Updike by permission of Alfred A. Knopf, Inc. Originally appeared in *The New Yorker* in another version. TENNESSEE WILLIAMS. *The Glass Menagerie* by Tennessee Williams. Copyright 1945 by Tennessee Williams, renewed 1973 by Tennessee Williams. Reprinted by permission of Random House, Inc.

Adrienne Rich. "At a Bach Concert," "Living in Sin," "Lucifer in the Train" copyright 1951, 1955 by Adrienne Rich. Reprinted by permission of the author.

Concepción G. Rivera. TOMÁS RIVERA. "and the earth did not part." Reprinted by permission of Concepción G. Rivera.

Charles Scribner's Sons. F. SCOTT FITZGERALD. *The Great Gatsby.* Copyright 1925 by Charles Scribner's Sons; copyright renewed 1953 by Frances Scott Fitzgerald Lanahan. Reprinted with the permission of Charles Scribner's Sons, an imprint of Macmillan Publishing Company. ERNEST HEMINGWAY. "Big Two-Hearted River," "The Capital of the World," and "The Short Happy Life of Francis Macomber" from *The Complete Short Stories of Ernest Hemingway,* 1987. "Big Two-Hearted River" parts 1 & 2 from *In Our Time.* Copyright 1925 Charles Scribner's Sons; copyright renewed 1953 Ernest Hemingway. Reprinted with the permission of Charles Scribner's Sons, an imprint of Macmillan Publishing Company. "The Capital of the World" and "The Short Happy Life of Francis Macomber" from *The Short Stories of Ernest Hemingway.* Copyright 1936 with the Ernest Hemingway; copyright renewed 1964 by Mary Hemingway. Reprinted with the permission of Charles Scribner's

Sons, an imprint of Macmillan Publishing Company. RING LARDNER. "Some Like Them Cold" from *How to Write Short Stories* by Ring Lardner. Copyright 1924 by Charles Scribner's Sons, an imprint of Macmillan Publishing Company. EDWIN ARLINGTON ROBINSON. "Luke Havergal," "When Annandale Went Out," "Richard Cory," "Cliff Klingenhagen" from *The Children of the Night* by Edwin Arlington Robinson. Copyright under the Berne Convention. Reprinted with the permission of Charles Scribner's Sons, an imprint of Macmillan Publishing Company. "Miniver Cheevy" and "For a Dead Lady" from *The Town Down the River* by Edwin Arlington Robinson. Copyright 1910 by Charles Scribner's Sons; copyright renewed 1938 by Ruth Nivison. Reprinted with the permission of Charles Scribner's Sons, an imprint of Macmillan Publishing Company. THOMAS WOLFE. "Only the Dead Know Brooklyn" from *From Death to Morning*. Reprinted by permission of Charles Scribner's Sons Co. First published in *The New Yorker*. "The Far and Near" from "From Death to Morning." Copyright 1935 by International Magazine Company. First published under the title "The Cottage by the Tracks." Both selections reprinted by permission of Charles Scribner's Sons.

Simon & Schuster, Inc. JOSEPH HELLER. "XLI Snowden," from *Catch-22* by Joseph Heller. Copyright © 1955, 1961 by Joseph Heller. Reprinted by permission of Simon & Schuster, Inc., a Division of Gulf & Western Corp.

The Sterling Lord Agency, Inc. IMAMU AMIRI BARAKA (LEROI JONES). "An Agony as Now," "A Poem for Democrats," "A Poem for Speculative Hipsters" all from *The Dead Lecturer* by LeRoi Jones. Copyright © 1964 by LeRoi Jones. "Dutchman" from *Dutchman and the Slave* by LeRoi Jones. Copyright © 1964 by LeRoi Jones. All selections reprinted by permission of The Sterling Lord Agency, Inc.

Mrs. James Thurber. JAMES THURBER. "The Secret Life of Walter Mitty" from *My World and Welcome to It* by James Thurber, published by Harcourt Brace Jovanovich. Copyright © 1942 by James Thurber. Originally appeared in *The New Yorker*. Reprinted by permission of Mrs. James Thurber and Harcourt Brace Jovanovich, Inc.

University of Chicago Press. HOWARD NEMEROV. "The Pond," "The Vacuum," "The Goose Fish," "The Town Dump," and "Boom!" from *New and Selected Poems* by Howard Nemerov. Copyright 1960 by the University of Chicago Press. Reprinted by permission of the University of Chicago Press. "Thirtieth Anniversary Report of the Class of '41" and "Figures of Thought" from *The Collected Poems of Howard Nemerov*. Copyright 1977 by the University of Chicago Press. Reprinted by permission of the University of Chicago Press.

The University Press of Virginia. STEPHEN CRANE. "The Open Boat," "The Red Badge of Courage" from *Tales of Adventure* edited by Fredson Bowers. Used by permission.

Vanguard Press, Inc. JOYCE CAROL OATES. "How I Contemplated the World from The Detroit House of Correction and Began My Life Over Again" from *The Wheel of Love* by Joyce Carol Oates. Copyright © 1970 by Joyce Carol Oates. Reprinted by permission of the publisher, Vanguard Press, Inc.

Viking Penguin, Inc. SAUL BELLOW. *Seize the Day*. Copyright © 1956 by Saul Bellow. All rights reserved. Reprinted by permission of Viking Penguin, Inc. MARIANNE MOORE. "Apparition of Splendor" from *The Complete Poems of Marianne Moore*. Copyright 1952 by Marianne Moore. Reprinted by permission of Viking Penguin, Inc. JOHN STEINBECK, "Flight" from *The Long Valley* by John Steinbeck. Copyright 1938, renewed 1986 by John Steinbeck. Reprinted by permission of Viking Penguin Inc.

Wesleyan University Press. JAMES DICKEY. "The Lifeguard" copyright © 1961 by James Dickey. Reprinted from *Drowning with Others* by permission of Wesleyan University Press. "The Lifeguard" first appeared in *The New Yorker*. "Reincarnation" copyright © 1964 by James Dickey. Reprinted from *Buckdancer's Choice* by permission of Wesleyan University Press. "Reincarnation" first appeared in *The New Yorker*. "In the Mountain Tent" copyright © 1961 by James Dickey. Reprinted from *Drowning with Others* by permission of Wesleyan University Press. "In the Mountain Tent" first appeared in *The New Yorker*. "Cherrylog Road" copyright 1964 by James Dickey. Reprinted from *Helmets* by permission of Wesleyan University Press. "The Shark's Parlor" copyright © 1965 by James Dickey. Reprinted from

Buckdancer's Choice by permission of Wesleyan University Press. "The Shark's Parlor" first appeared in *The New Yorker.* JAMES WRIGHT. "Autumn Begins in Martin's Ferry, Ohio" copyright © 1962; "Depressed by a Book of Bad Poetry . . ." copyright © 1961, 1962, 1963 by James Wright; "A Prayer to Escape from the Market Place" copyright © 1963; "A Blessing" copyright © 1961 by James Wright; all reprinted from *The Branch Will Not Break* by James Wright by permission of Wesleyan University Press. "Confession to J. Edgar Hoover" and "In Response to a Rumor . . ." copyright © 1960, 1966 by James Wright. Reprinted from *Shall We Gather at the River* by James Wright by permission of Wesleyan University Press.

Ellen Wright. RICHARD WRIGHT. "The Man Who Was Almost a Man," from *Eight Men.* Reprinted by permission of Ellen Wright.

Preface

Fifteen years lie between this fourth edition of *Anthology of American Literature* and the appearance of the first edition. Those years have added approximately four percent to the period of American literature, but they have added even more in changes to the cultural perspective by which American literature is viewed. In 1974, the contributions of women and minorities to the American literary tradition lacked the secure recognition with which we regard them now, and the confirmation of that recognition has altered the face of the American literary canon. To assume that this change renders the traditional canon obsolete, however, is to suggest that we must apply special standards to accommodate new authors; whereas writers such as Anne Bradstreet, Louisa May Alcott, Frederick Douglass, Kate Chopin, Zora Neale Hurston, Tillie Olsen, and Alice Walker are truly significant when measured by the standards generations of scholars have applied to Nathaniel Hawthorne, Herman Melville, Walt Whitman, Henry James, Stephen Crane, Robert Frost, Eugene O'Neill, and F. Scott Fitzgerald. It is as fruitless as it is unjust to ignore any one component of the canon in favor of another.

Stating a principle is always easier than applying one, and the application of a literary principle is particularly difficult when the body of literature is constantly and rapidly enlarging while the confines of a literary survey course—and of the volumes designed to serve it—remain unchanged. Some of the principles that informed previous editions of *Anthology of American Literature* had to be retained for the fourth: the representation of individual authors by substantial samplings of their works; the inclusion of many landmark long works in their entireties rather than in excerpts; the reliance on literary significance as a criterion of selection; and the provision of generous editorial explanation for the benefit of the reader in period introductions, headnotes, and footnotes. To these we have added the principle of increasing the representation of women and minority authors in the American literary tradition. Among the innovations reflecting the last principle in the fourth edition are the additions of Hannah Webster Foster, Louisa May Alcott, Charlotte Perkins Gilman, Gertrude Stein, Hilda Doolittle, Zora Neale Hurston, Louise Glück, Amy Clampitt, Tillie Olsen, Alice Walker, and Ann Beattie. The anthology continues to include complete long works such as Franklin's *Autobiography*, Cooper's *The Prairie*, Tyler's *The Contrast*, Emerson's *Nature*, Hawthorne's *The Scarlet Letter*, Melville's *Billy Budd*, Thoreau's *Walden*, Chopin's *The Awakening*, Twain's *Huckleberry Finn*, James's *Daisy Miller*, Crane's *The Red Badge of Courage* and *Maggie*, Eugene O'Neill's *Hairy Ape*, Chandler's *Red Wind*, and Bellow's *Seize the Day*. We have added the complete *The Great Gatsby* by F. Scott Fitzgerald and increased the representation of Ernest Hemingway to three stories: "The Short Happy Life of Francis Macomber," "Big Two-Hearted River," and "The Capital of the World." Numerous other adjustments within the selections for various authors are based on the advice of many users of previous editions of the anthology.

The same source of information persuaded us to maintain the practice of including the Walt Whitman selections at the end of Volume I and repeating them in their entirety at the beginning of Volume II. Harriet Beecher Stowe is moved from Volume II to Volume I. We have also retained and added to the chronological schematic at the end of each volume to help readers associate literary works with events in the technological, political, and cultural history of the United States.

Authors and works in the anthology follow a generally chronological order. In deciding on a standard text from among the various editions available for many of the selections, the editors have chosen, whenever possible, that edition most respected by modern scholars. The text reprinted is identified at the end of each author's headnote. Spelling and punctuation are, in some instances, regularized and modernized to correct obvious errors and to suit the reader's convenience. An editorial excision of less than one paragraph is indicated by an ellipsis thus: . . .; excisions of a paragraph or more are indicated by a centered ellipsis thus:

· · ·

For each author and for each of the five literary periods, brief introductory notes summarize historical and critical information. The date on the left immediately following each selection indicates the date of composition, when known; dates on the right indicate the date or dates of publication.

George McMichael of California State University, Hayward, prepared the manuscript of this fourth edition; Frederick Crews of the University of California, Berkeley; J. C. Levenson of the University of Virginia; Leo Marx of the Massachusetts Institute of Technology; and David E. Smith of Hampshire College reviewed the entire work. The editors and publisher are grateful also to Rex Burbank, Robert Lee, and the following persons for advice on the preparation of this fourth edition: Gary Aday, Virginia Highlands Community College; Carl L. Anderson, Duke University; Beulah B. Baker, Taylor University; Martha Banta, University of California, Los Angeles; Vincent Betz, Palm Beach Junior College; Stephen G. Bolger, Rosemont College; Frank Bonjione, Seminole Community College; Anthony Bradley, University of Vermont; Robert Brien, Madison Area Technical College; Joe S. Britton, Kentucky Wesleyan University; William M. Burke, Northern Arizona University; Dean Cantrell, Berry College; Miriam Cheikin, Nassau Community College; James Childs, Middlesex Community College; Randolph Chilton, College of St. Francis; Mary Cimerelli, Richland College; Peter Clarke, Herkimer Community College; Hubert Cloke, Georgetown University; Arthur B. Coffin, Montana State University; Clare Colquitt, San Diego State University; Sandra Corse, Georgia Institute of Technology; James Dalil, West Georgia College; Donald A. Daiker, Miami University; John H. Davis, Chowan College; Francine Dempsey, S. S. J., College of St. Rose; James P. Dougherty, The University of Notre Dame; Fae Dremock, Northeast Louisiana University; Greg Eliot, Blue Mountain Community College; Hans Feldmann, Susquehanna University; Frank M. Flack, Los Angeles Pierce College; Rosemary M. Fisk, Samford University; Benjamin Franklin, V, University of South Carolina; Hood Frazier, Southside Virginia Community College; Peter A. Fritzell, Lawrence University; Peggy L. Garrett, Kutztown University; Sharon K. George, Texas A&I University; Russell B. Gill, Elon College; Willard Giuggerich, University of Texas, El Paso; Lawrence J. Gorman, East–West University; Susette Graham, Nazareth College; Rich Gray, Montreat–Anderson College; Judith Green, University of Wisconsin; George Grella, The University of Rochester; Kelley Griffith, The University of North Carolina, Greensboro; Darlene Harbur Unrue, University of Nevada; Howard Harrison, The Hebrew University of Jerusalem, Israel; John Hattman, West Liberty State College; Glen Hayden, Valencia Community College; Jonathan Hershey, Floyd Junior College; Tim Hirsch, University of Wisconsin, Eau Claire; Robert B. Howells, Baldwin–Wallace College; Kathleen Hulley, University of North Dakota; John Humma, Georgia Southern College; John Husbands, Dodge City Community College; Jack Locher, Gettysburg, College; Helen Lojek, Boise State University; Karen Kalinevitch, St. Louis Community College; D. G. Kehl, Arizona State University; Cynthia Kimand, Indiana University, Bloomington; David Kirby, Florida State University; Kenneth Kupier, Calvin College; M. Loomis, Northeast Louisiana University; Ada M. Lord, University of Wisconsin, La Crosse; Joseph P. Lovering, Cenisius College; James Marshall, The University of Rhode Island; Ronald Martin, University of Delaware; Bob Mielke, Northern Missouri State University; Herbert Miller, New York Technical College; Randall Miller, Ricks College; Stuart A. Millner, Suffolk University; Neil Nakadate, Iowa State University; Cameron Nickels, James Madison University; Alma E. Nugent, Goucher College; Pat Onion, Colby College; William Osborne, Baptist Bible College; Lawrence Parker, Mt. San Antonio College; Alice Hall Petry, Rhode Island School of Design; Kenneth P. Prines, Alice Lloyd College; Ann Rayson, University of Hawaii; Jerome Rosenberg, Miami University; James Sanderson, Odessa College; Robert Sandler, University of Miami; Wayne Scheer, Atlanta Junior College; Neil Schmitz, SUNY Buffalo; Virginia L. Shields, University of Georgia, John Simms, Clemson State University; Louis N. Soloani, Anna Maria College; Raymond A. St. John, Bob Jones University; Frank Stallings, Northern Kentucky University; Gary Storhoff, University of Connecticut; Stephen Tatum, University of Utah; Dawn Trouard, University of Akron; Edward Uehling, Valparaiso University; Peter Von Egmond, University of Maryland; Clarence Walhout, Calvin College; Elizabeth Walquist, Brigham Young University; Emily Watts, University of Illinois; H. Wehringer, Hawthorne College; Mary A. Witt, Georgia Southwestern College; Fred Wood, Cleveland State Community College; Joan C. Young, Palm Beach Junior College; and Lawrence E. Ziewacz, Michigan State University.

THE PUBLISHER

Contents

The Age of Realism   1

MARY E. WILKINS FREEMAN   183
(1852–1930)

SARAH ORNE JEWETT   191
(1849–1909)

BRET HARTE   199
(1836–1902)

GEORGE WASHINGTON CABLE   206
(1844–1925)

CHARLES WADDELL CHESNUTT   219
(1858–1932)

JOEL CHANDLER HARRIS   228
(1848–1908)

MARK TWAIN   237
(1835–1910)

Contents

Twentieth-Century Literature   961

ROBERT FROST   981
(1874–1963)

CARL SANDBURG   1006
(1878–1967)

WALLACE STEVENS   1240
(1879–1955)

WILLIAM CARLOS WILLIAMS   1257
(1883–1963)

THEODORE ROETHKE   1657
(1908–1963)

RANDALL JARRELL   1669
(1914–1965)

ELIZABETH BISHOP   1679
(1911–1979)

The Age of Realism

BY THE END of the Civil War (1861–1865), powerful forces had emerged that would dominate life in twentieth-century America. The industrial North had triumphed over the agrarian South, and from that victory came a society based on mass labor and mass consumption. Steam power began to replace water power, and machines driven by steam engines supplanted traditional hand labor in factories and on farms. Thomas Jefferson had hoped that the majority of Americans would never be "occupied at a work bench, for those who labor in the earth are the chosen people of God." But after 1865, the United States ceased to be the simple agrarian democracy that Jefferson had cherished. It became instead the most heavily industrialized nation in the world, and its people in ever greater numbers ceased to "labor in the earth" and moved to towns and cities to labor on the machines of new industries.

As industrialism spread, the nature of labor changed. Machines displaced more than half of the hand labor previously required in manufacturing. Independent, skilled handcraftsmen became obsolete, unable to compete with machines operated by semiskilled laborers twenty-four hours a day, seven days a week. And the machines, with their great cost and high efficiency, came to be seen by mill owners and factory managers as far more useful and valuable than the workers who tended them. As a result, traditional relationships between employers and craftsmen altered, grew more impersonal. In giant corporations employing hundreds, even thousands, workers no longer knew their customers, no longer even saw their employers. Nonetheless, great numbers of men, women, and children—native-born and foreign—flocked to American cities, drawn by hopes for steady factory work and high factory pay.

In the cities—swollen with growing numbers of the poor, the ignorant, and the unskilled—great political change was taking place. As the lower classes sought, and found, greater power at the polls, the centers of political power shifted. Traditional political alliances weakened, and new political groups emerged, taking their power from, and proclaiming their devotion to, the laboring classes.

Amid the political upheavals of the time, the art of political patronage and graft rose to new heights in the United States, causing the first grand age of American political corruption. Confused and ignorant voters, new to the ballot box, elected political bosses and their henchmen who flourished on kickbacks and fraud, boldly collected their boodle, and scoffed at the law. In six years, during the 1860s and 1870s, New York's "Boss" William Tweed and his "Tweed Ring" of municipal crooks cost the city of New York an estimated two hundred

1

million dollars, the equivalent of two billion dollars in the 1980s. And during the presidency of Ulysses S. Grant (1869–1877) the crimes of high federal officials were exposed in scandals unequaled in the history of the United States. The actions of the president in protecting his political cronies and ignoring their blatant misdeeds led many Americans to conclude that the president of the United States was himself a common thief. Never before had American government, at all levels, seemed so overrun with rascals. Never before had civic virtue seemed to have fallen so low.

During the Civil War the power of the federal government dramatically expanded. For the first time the federal government intruded directly into the lives of the majority of the people. The war brought the first national conscription laws; the first federal income taxes were levied, and the first national currency was issued—paper money backed by the federal government rather than by individual states and local banks. Rapid growth of federal power brought benefits and troubles. In 1865 the first official step toward nationwide racial equality was made when the Thirteenth Amendment to the Constitution was adopted, abolishing slavery within the United States. And the federal government used its powers to encourage business growth and the exploitation of natural resources, creating vast new wealth.

But great riches and economic power were increasingly concentrated in the hands of the few: bankers and industrialists who seemed to represent the benefits of "business and bustle," luminaries who symbolized the virtues of self-help. The laudatory term "Captain of Industry" was coined in the 1880s as business and financial tycoons came for the first time to be celebrated as national heroes, as models for young men who hoped to rise in the world through luck and pluck. It was the beginning of what Mark Twain called "The Gilded Age," an age of extremes: of decline and progress, of poverty and dazzling wealth, of gloom and bouyant hope—an age of gaudy excesses that one historian described as "The Great Barbecue."

In the last half of the nineteenth century, Americans ceased to be isolated from the world and from each other. Coast-to-coast overland mail service began in 1858—a letter could be sent from St. Louis to San Francisco in as little as four weeks. In 1860 the Pony Express cut that time to ten and a half days. And within a year a message could be sent from New York to San Francisco in seconds, on the new telegraph line that spanned the nation in 1861. A transatlantic telegraph cable joined America and Europe in 1866; ten years later, Alexander Graham Bell patented his invention of the telephone. By 1900 the United States had 1,356,000 telephones, twice as many as all Europe.

If the telegraph and the telephone helped to bring Americans closer together, the United States were finally "united" by the railroads. The first railroad, the Baltimore and Ohio, began operation in 1830 with thirteen miles of track. In 1869 the first transcontinental railroad was completed, linking the Atlantic and the Pacific. Five years later railroad mileage exceeded 74,000 miles, and the United States had the most extensive railroad system in the world. By 1889, the trip across the continent that had taken as much as five months by wagon during the Gold Rush of 1849 could now be made in trains (with Pullman sleepers and dining cars) in 108 hours—little more than four days.

With the building of the railroads came vast commercial development. New lands reached by rail lines were put under the plow, bringing enormous increases in farm goods. The production of livestock and wheat doubled, tripled, and quadrupled. New Yorkers began to eat beef shipped in newly invented refrigerator cars all the way from the slaughterhouses of Chicago, and Floridians began to buy flour from mills in Minneapolis.

Enterprising merchants like Richard Sears and Montgomery Ward created nationwide retail organizations that could undersell local shopkeepers. The clothing, household goods, and farm equipment once made locally by costly handwork were replaced by inexpensive, mass-produced goods made from standardized patterns in centralized factories. The nation was becoming a single giant marketplace, and retail stores that sold ready-made clothes and packaged foods began to resemble those of modern America, where the same goods, displayed in the same ways, can be seen from one end of the land to the other.

The coming of the railroads changed how Americans worked, where they lived, how they ate, how they dressed. In 1883 the railroads even changed the way Americans kept time when the more than fifty-six time zones in the United States were reduced to four, to promote greater efficiency in scheduling railroad traffic.

As transportation became better and cheaper, the nation's people became increasingly mobile. In the last surge of westward expansion, Americans, lured by the promise of free land, settled the Great Plains and the mountain states. The states of the nation now ran from the Atlantic to the Pacific. Vast areas were no longer unknown, unexplored; by 1890 the frontier—the westward-moving line of settlement begun three hundred years before on the Atlantic Coast—ceased to exist, although its influence would long remain, shaping the life of the nation and inspiring the legends, novels, and western movies by which the world would come to know America.

With the turn of the century, the pace of growth and change quickened. It became a time of steel and steam, electricity and oil. From the Civil War to World War I, steel production in the United States increased more than six hundred times, and steelmaking became the nation's dominant industry. Alternating electrical current was introduced (1886). Incandescent lamps illuminated the cities with electricity provided by giant, steam-driven dynamos. The tallow candles and whale-oil lamps of rural America were replaced by lanterns filled with inexpensive kerosene made from crude oil. The American petroleum industry began, and with it came the age of the automobile.

From 1870 to 1890 the total population of the United States doubled. Villages became towns, towns became cities, and cities grew to a size and with a speed that would have astonished the Founding Fathers. From 1860 to 1910 the population of Philadelphia tripled; that of New York City more than quadrupled, while the population of Chicago increased twenty times to two million, making it the nation's second largest city.

As the population doubled, the national income quadrupled, and by the mid-1890s the United States could boast 4,000 millionaires. The rich prospered mightily, and prodigious fortunes were piled up by industrial and banking magnates such as John D. Rockefeller, Andrew Carnegie, and J. Pierpont Morgan. The growth of big business and big industry also widened further the gulf between the rich and the poor, giving rise to reform movements and labor unions that voiced the grievances of debt-ridden farmers and of immigrant workers who lived in city slums and labored in giant, impersonal factories. Yet it was also an age of optimism; little heed was given to such gloomy skeptics as Henry Adams, who saw America as a land of unbridled power and flamboyant greed. It was a time of glowing visions, a time of radiant prospects, when ministers preached (and congregations believed) a gospel of wealth, suggesting

3

that riches were at last in league with virtue, that an age of unlimited progress had finally dawned.

Immigration dropped sharply during the Civil War, but after the 1880s a rising tide of foreigners, beckoned by the American promise of jobs and political freedom, came to the New World at such a rate that by 1910 more than a third of the population of America's largest cities was foreign-born. Large-scale immigration and technical advancements in industry and agriculture increased the need for literacy, creating a demand for widespread public education. In the fifty years following the Civil War, the number of high schools in the United States increased thirty-five times. Colleges were established for women: Vassar in 1861, Wellesley in 1870, Smith in 1871. Higher education ceased to be a privilege limited to children of the well-to-do. Under the Morrill Act of 1862, millions of acres of federal land were given to the states for the establishment of public "land-grant" universities for "the liberal and practical education of the industrial classes."

Increased wealth, and the desire for its conspicuous display, gave rise to a gingerbread era of American design whose prime function was to attract attention. American millionaires built Gothic and Romanesque mansions and decorated them with towers, domes, columns, stained-glass windows, and ornamental gimcracks of wood and iron. Their rooms were filled with art imported from Europe, as were most symbols of culture. Well-to-do Americans adopted European dress styles and manners, sent their sons to Europe for an education, and eagerly married off their daughters to European noblemen, many of them impoverished, some of them bogus.

America remained culturally dependent on Europe for drama and music. Companies of touring English actors, playing in tents and "opera houses" throughout America, presented European plays and dramatizations of popular European novels. Symphony orchestras, which had begun to appear in the United States after mid-century, limited their repertoires almost wholly to European music. The nation lacked first-rate composers of serious music until the 1900s. And even in the twentieth century, America's greatest contributions to the world of music remained its folk songs, its Negro spirituals, and the jazz music that spread from New Orleans around the world, after World War I.

After 1865, a strong native tradition in painting began to develop, apparent in the work of such artists as Thomas Eakins, who realistically portrayed the America he saw around him and who urged his students "to remain in America, to peer deeper into the heart of American life." But numerous artists saw opportunity elsewhere and preferred to lead expatriate lives in Europe. Among them were the most renowned American painters of the period: James McNeill Whistler and John Singer Sargent. In a land of triumphant materialism, high culture had little impact on the mass of the people, who sought and found their entertainment in circuses, in vaudeville shows, in the new professional sports, and, after the 1890s, in motion-picture theaters named "nickelodeons" after their five-cent admission fee.

In the latter half of the nineteenth century, women became the nation's dominant culture force, a position they have never relinquished. Ladies' journalism began to flourish. In 1891, *The Ladies Home Journal* (founded in 1883) became the first American magazine to exceed a circulation of half a million; by 1905 its circulation had reached a full million. A new generation of women authors appeared whose poetry and fiction enlivened the pages of popular ten-cent monthly and weekly magazines. The greatest woman writer of the age, Emily Dickinson, was almost completely unknown; her first collection of poetry

4

was not published until 1890, four years after her death. But Harriet Beecher Stowe, the author of *Uncle Tom's Cabin* (1852), had become an American institution and the most famous literary woman in the world. The American reading public's appetite for sentiment and sensation was constantly fed by such inexhaustible writers as Mrs. E. D. E. N. Southworth, who spilled forth novels seething with romantic extravagance: ancestral curses, sudden passions, villains blasted, and heroes triumphant. Sales of such "molasses fiction" far exceeded the sales of works by such highly regarded writers as William Dean Howells, Edith Wharton, Henry James, and even Mark Twain.

Although Americans continued to read the works of Irving, Cooper, Hawthorne, and Poe, the great age of American romanticism had ended. By the 1870s the New England Renaissance had waned. Hawthorne and Thoreau were dead; Emerson, Lowell, Longfellow, Holmes, and Whittier had passed their literary zeniths. Melville, living in obscurity, had ceased to publish his fiction. Only Whitman continued to offer a new literary vision to the world, issuing a fifth edition of *Leaves of Grass* in 1870 and publishing *Democratic Vistas* in 1871. As New England's cultural dominance waned, New York replaced Boston as the nation's literary center, drawing writers from New England, the South, and the West to the publishing houses and periodicals of the nation's largest city.

Reductions in the cost of paper and printing, new methods of illustration, and growing profits from national advertisers encouraged the establishment of low-cost, general-interest magazines. From 1865 to 1905 the total number of periodicals published in the United States increased from about seven hundred to more than six thousand, all trying to satisfy the appetites of a vast new reading audience that was hungry for articles, essays, fiction, and poems.

A host of new writers appeared, among them Bret Harte, William Dean Howells, Hamlin Garland, and Mark Twain, whose background and training, unlike those of the older generation they displaced, were middle-class and journalistic rather than genteel or academic. Influenced by such Europeans as Zola, Flaubert, Balzac, Dostoyevsky, and Tolstoy, America's most noteworthy new authors established a literature of realism. They sought to portray American life as it really was, insisting that the ordinary and the local were just as suitable for artistic portrayal as the magnificent and the remote.

As in most literary rebellions, the new literature rose out of the authors' desire to renovate the literary theories of a previous age. Realists had grown scornful of artistic ideals that had been trivialized, worn thin by derivative writers eager to supply the "great popular want" for sentiment, adventure, and "tingling excitement." In contrast, the realists had what Henry James called "a powerful impulse to mirror the unmitigated realities of life." Earlier in the nineteenth century, James Fenimore Cooper had insisted on the author's right to avoid representations of "squalid misery" and to present instead an idealized and "poetic" portrait of life. But by the end of the nineteenth century the realists, and the literary naturalists who followed them, had turned from the portrayal of idealized characters and events. Instead, they sought to describe the wide range of American experience and to present the subtleties of human personality, to portray characters who were not simply all good or all bad.

Realism had originated in France as *réalisme*, a literary doctrine that called for "reality and truth" in the depiction of ordinary life. "Realism" first appeared in the United States in the literature of local color, an amalgam of romantic plots and realistic descriptions of things immediately observable: the dialects, customs,

5

sights, and sounds of regional America. Bret Harte in the 1860s was the first American writer of local color to achieve wide popularity. He presented stories about western mining towns involving colorful gamblers, outlaws, and scandalous women. Thereafter editors—ever sensitive to public taste—demanded, and such writers as Harte, Harriet Beecher Stowe, Kate Chopin, Joel Chandler Harris, and Mark Twain provided, regional stories and tales of the life of America's Westerners, Southerners, and Easterners. Local-color fiction reached its peak of popularity in the 1880s, but by the turn of the century it had begun to decline as its limited resources were exhausted and as its most popular writers grew tediously repetitious or turned to other literary modes.

The arbiter of nineteenth-century literary realism in America was William Dean Howells. He defined realism as "nothing more and nothing less than the truthful treatment of material," and he best exemplified his theories in such novels as *A Modern Instance* (1882), *The Rise of Silas Lapham* (1885), and *A Hazard of New Fortunes* (1890). Howells spoke for a generation of writers who attempted to sustain an objective point of view and who found their subject matter in the experiences of the American middle class, describing their houses, families, and jobs, their social customs, achievements, and failures. The bulk of America's literary realism was limited to optimistic treatment of the surface of life. Yet the greatest of America's realists, Henry James and Mark Twain, moved well beyond a surface portrayal of nineteenth-century America. James probed deeply into the individual psychology of his characters, writing in a rich and intricate style that supported his intense scrutiny of complex human experience. Twain, breaking out of the narrow limits of local-color fiction, described the breadth of American experience as no one had ever done before, or since, and he created, in *Huckleberry Finn* (1884), a masterpiece of American realism that is one of the great books of world literature.

In the 1880s, Howells spoke out against the writing of a bleak fiction of failure and despair. He called for the treatment of the "smiling aspects of life" as being the more "American," insisting that America was truly a land of hope and of possibility that should be reflected in its literature. But at the end of the century came a generation of writers whose ideas of the workings of the universe and whose perception of society's disorders led them to naturalism, a new and harsher realism. America's literary naturalists scorned the idea that literature should present comforting moral truths. Instead, naturalist writers attempted to achieve extreme objectivity and frankness, presenting characters of low social and economic classes who were dominated by their environment and heredity. In presenting the extremes of life, the naturalists sometimes displayed an affinity to the sensationalism of early romanticism, but unlike their romantic predecessors, the naturalists emphasized that the world was amoral, that men and women had no free will, that their lives were controlled by heredity and the environment, that religious "truths" were illusory, that the destiny of humanity was misery in life and oblivion in death.

Naturalism, like realism, had come from Europe. In America it had been shaped by the Civil War, by the social upheavals that undermined the comforting faith of an earlier age, and by the disturbing teachings of Charles Darwin. Darwinism seemed to stress the animality of man, to suggest that people are dominated by the irresistible forces of evolution. The pessimism and deterministic ideas of naturalism pervaded the works of such writers as Stephen Crane, Frank Norris, Jack London, Henry Adams, and Theodore Dreiser. They wrote detailed descriptions of the lives of the downtrodden and of the abnormal; they offered frank treatment of human passion and sexuality; they portrayed men and women overwhelmed by the blind forces of nature; and the works of such literary naturalists still exert a powerful influence on modern writers.

Although realism and naturalism were products of the nineteenth century, their final triumph came in the twentieth century, with the popular and critical successes of such writers as Edwin Arlington Robinson, Willa Cather, Sherwood Anderson, Robert Frost, and William Faulkner. But the triumph of realism, even in the twentieth century, did not bring an end to the extremes of romanticism, for romanticism in all its varieties still abounds, in popular novels, movies, and television shows about heroes and heroines of unspotted virtue and dazzling accomplishments. Nonetheless, the coming of realism, with all its limitations and in all of its forms, permanently transformed American culture. By depicting a "real" America, by commemorating the lives of ordinary men and women, by celebrating the commonplace truths of the land, realistic writers and artists in the nineteenth century showed the diversity and the amplitude of the nation and validated its democratic spirit. And in the twentieth century, realism still remains a fundamental and pervading part of the national life, helping to bring social and artistic changes that have vitalized and enriched modern America.

Walt Whitman   *1819–1892*

In 1855, after first reading Leaves of Grass, *Ralph Waldo Emerson wrote to Walt Whitman, "I am not blind to the worth of the wonderful gift of* Leaves of Grass. *I find it the most extraordinary piece of wit and wisdom that America has yet contributed. . . . I greet you at the beginning of a great career, which yet must have had a long foreground somewhere, for such a start."*

Whitman was thirty-six years old, and nothing in his "long foreground" suggested that he would write the greatest single book of poetry in America's literary history. He had been born in 1819 in a rural village on Long Island, New York. His parents were semiliterate and could give him little more than a sympathy for political liberalism and a deistic faith shaped by the teachings of Quakerism. He had only five or six years of formal schooling, but he was a voracious reader of nineteenth-century novelists, English romantic poets, the "classics" of European literature, and the New Testament. His teachers characterized him as a "dreamy and impractical youth," and he drifted through a series of jobs as an office boy, a printer, and a country schoolteacher. He had a natural talent for journalism. For a short time he edited a Long Island weekly newspaper, and when he was twenty-two and attracted to the Bohemian life of Manhattan he went to New York City.

In New York, Whitman worked as a printer, as an editor, and as a freelance journalist contributing essays, short stories, and poems to the popular newspapers and magazines of the 1840s. When he was twenty-seven he became editor of the Brooklyn Daily Eagle, but after only two years he was dismissed because of his radically liberal political views. He next made a brief visit to New Orleans, but he soon returned to New York City, where he opened a printing office and stationery store and began to write his greatest poetry.

In 1855 he published the first edition of Leaves of Grass. It contained twelve poems which Whitman himself reportedly had set in type and printed at his own expense. Few copies of his slim book of poetry were sold, yet those who read it were rarely indifferent. His apparently formless free-verse departures from poetic convention, his incantations and boasts, his sexuality, and his exotic and vulgar language caused critics steeped in the gentilities of the nineteenth century to label his work a "poetry of barbarism" and warn that it was "not to be read aloud to a mixed audience." At best, the reviewers judged the poems "gross yet elevated," "superficial yet profound," a "mixture of Yankee transcendentalism and New York rowdyism." At worst, Whitman's "leaves" were called "noxious weeds," "spasmodic idiocy," "a mass of stupid filth." Emerson found the poetry "extraordinary"; Whittier judged it "loose, lurid, and impious" and threw his gift-copy into the fireplace.

From 1857 to 1859 Whitman edited the Brooklyn Times, and, undaunted by the critical response to the first edition, he reworked Leaves of Grass, publishing expanded second and third editions in 1856 and 1860. When the Civil War began, he traveled south to Washington, D.C., where he obtained an appointment as a government clerk and worked as a volunteer nurse, a "wound-dresser," in nearby military hospitals. While living in Washington he published Drum-Taps (1865), Civil War poems that he gathered into the fourth edition of Leaves of Grass (1867).

By the appearance of the fifth edition (1871), Whitman's poetry had begun to receive increasing critical recognition in England and America. He had come to see his work as a single "poem" to be revised and improved through a lifetime, but in 1873, when he was fifty-four, he suffered a paralytic stroke. He moved from Washington, D.C., to his brother's home in Camden, New Jersey, and there, declining in his poetic abilities and cared for by a small group of devoted friends, Whitman spent most of the remaining nineteen years of his life, revising successive editions of Leaves of Grass until the final version was published shortly before his death in 1892.

The more than four hundred poems that had appeared in the nine editions of Leaves of Grass *printed in Whitman's lifetime were unprecedented in American literature. They were a compound of commonplaces, of disorganized and raw experience, of sentimentalism, and of true poetic inspiration. They were filled with "barbaric yawps." They had ecstatic perceptions of man and nature, united and divine. Whitman had an expansive oceanic vision, an urgent desire to incorporate the entire American experience into his life and into poetry. He aspired to be a cosmic consciousness, to experience and glorify all humanity and all human qualities, including "sex, womanhood, maternity, lusty animations, organs, acts."*

He had yearned to be the "bard of democracy," a public poet celebrated by democratic men "en-masse," but while he lived, the bulk of his poetry was read only by the literary enthusiasts and intellectuals. In his final years, Whitman's devoted followers solemnized him as "The Good Gray Poet." He became a national figure, America's whiskery sage, but the wide popularity he had yearned to have nonetheless escaped him. He was defeated in his greatest literary ambitions, yet his poems came to exert more influence on modern American poetry than the work of any other writer. Whitman had been a radically new poet, had made his own rhythms, created his own mythic world, and in writing his sprawling epic of American democracy he helped make possible the free-verse unorthodoxies and the private literary intensities of a twentieth-century world that would one day come to honor him as one of the great poets of all time.

FURTHER READING: *The Complete Writings of Walt Whitman,* ed. R. Bucke, T. Harned, and H. Traubel, 10 vols., 1902; *The Collected Writings of Walt Whitman,* 18 vols., ed. G. Allen et al., 1961–   ; G. Allen, *The Solitary Singer, A Critical Biography of Walt Whitman,* 1955, 1967; R. Asselineau, *The Evolution of Walt Whitman,* 2 vols., 1960, 1962; J. Kaplan, *Walt Whitman, A Life,* 1980; R. Chase, *Walt Whitman Reconsidered,* 1955; J. Miller, *A Critical Guide to "Leaves of Grass,"* 1957; *The Americanness of Walt Whitman,* ed. L. Marx, 1960; H. Waskow, *Whitman, Explorations in Form,* 1966; E. Miller, *Walt Whitman's Poetry,* 1968, 1969; *A Century of Whitman Criticism,* ed. E. Miller, 1969; G. Allen, *A Reader's Guide to Walt Whitman,* 1970; J. Rubin, *The Historic Whitman,* 1973; F. Stovall, *The Foreground of Leaves of Grass,* 1974; S. Black, *Whitman's Journey into Chaos,* 1975; G. Allen, *The New Walt Whitman Handbook,* 1975; S Giantvalley, *Walt Whitman, 1838–1839, A Reference Guide,* 1981; P. Zweig, *Walt Whitman, The Making of the Poet,* 1984; J. Miller, *Walt Whitman,* 1986; T. Wynn, The *Lunar Light of Whitman's Poetry,* 1987.

TEXTS: *The Collected Writings of Walt Whitman: The Early Poems and the Fiction,* Vol. II, ed. F. Stovall, 1964; *Leaves of Grass, Comprehensive Reader's Edition,* ed. H. Blodgett and S. Bradley, 1965.

PREFACE TO THE 1855 EDITION OF
LEAVES OF GRASS[1]

America does not repel the past or what it has produced under its forms or amid other politics or the idea of castes or the old religions. . . . accepts the lesson with calmness . . . is not so impatient as has been supposed that the slough[2] still sticks to opinions and manners and literature while the life which served its requirements has passed into the new life of the new forms . . . perceives that the corpse is slowly borne from the eating and sleeping rooms of the house . . . perceives that it waits a little while in the door . . . that it was fittest for its days . . . that its action has descended to the stalwart and wellshaped heir who approaches . . . and that he shall be fittest for his days.

The Americans of all nations at any time upon the earth have probably the fullest poetical nature. The United States themselves are essentially the greatest poem. In the history of the earth hitherto the largest and most stirring appear tame and orderly to their ampler largeness and stir. Here at last is something in the doings of man that corresponds with the broadcast doings of the day and night. Here is not merely a nation but a teeming nation of nations. Here is action untied from strings necessarily blind to particulars and details magnificently moving in vast masses. Here is the hospitality which forever indicates heroes. . . . Here are the roughs and beards and space and ruggedness and nonchalance that the soul loves. Here the performance disdaining the trivial unapproached in the tremendous audacity of its crowds and groupings and the push of its perspective spreads with crampless and flowing breath and showers its prolific and splendid extravagance. One sees it must indeed own the riches of the summer and winter, and need never be bankrupt while corn grows from the ground or the orchards drop apples or the bays contain fish or men beget children upon women.

Other states indicate themselves in their deputies. . . . but the genius of the United States is not best or most in its executives or legislatures, nor in its ambassadors or authors or colleges or churches or parlors, nor even in its newspapers or inventors . . . but always most in the common people. Their manners speech dress friendships—the freshness and candor of their physiognomy—the picturesque looseness of their carriage . . . their deathless attachment to freedom—their aversion to anything indecorous or soft or mean—the practical acknowledgment of the citizens of one state by the citizens of all other states—the fierceness of their roused resentment—their curiosity and welcome of novelty—their self-esteem and wonderful sympathy—their susceptibility to a slight—the air they have of persons who never knew how it felt to stand in the presence of superiors—the fluency of their speech—their delight in music, the sure symptom of manly tenderness and native elegance of soul . . . their good temper and openhandedness—the terrible significance of their elections—the President's taking off his hat to them not they to him—these too are unrhymed poetry. It awaits the gigantic and generous treatment worthy of it.

The largeness of nature or the nation were monstrous without a corresponding largeness and generosity of the spirit of the citizen. Not nature nor swarming

[1]The first (1855) edition of *Leaves of Grass* contained a dozen poems and a Preface in which Whitman declared his literary philosophy. Later editions omitted the 1855 Preface, but portions were incorporated in poems subsequently added to the text. The marks of ellipsis (. . .) are Whitman's, as are the eccentric spellings.
[2]Dead tissue, such as the cast-off skin of a snake.

states nor streets and steamships nor prosperous business nor farms nor capital nor learning may suffice for the ideal of man . . . nor suffice the poet. No reminiscences may suffice either. A live nation can always cut a deep mark and can have the best authority the cheapest . . . namely from its own soul. This is the sum of the profitable uses of individuals or states and of present action and grandeur and of the subjects of poets.—As if it were necessary to trot back generation after generation to the eastern records! As if the beauty and sacredness of the demonstrable must fall behind that of the mythical! As if men do not make their mark out of any times! As if the opening of the western continent by discovery and what has transpired since in North and South America were less than the small theatre of the antique or the aimless sleepwalking of the middle ages! The pride of the United States leaves the wealth and finesse of the cities and all returns of commerce and agriculture and all the magnitude of geography or shows of exterior victory to enjoy the breed of fullsized men or one fullsized man unconquerable and simple.

The American poets are to enclose old and new for America is the race of races. Of them a bard[3] is to be commensurate with a people. To him the other continents arrive as contributions . . . he gives them reception for their sake and his own sake. His spirit responds to his country's spirit. . . . he incarnates its geography and natural life and rivers and lakes. Mississippi with annual freshets and changing chutes, Missouri and Columbia and Ohio and Saint Lawrence with the falls and beautiful masculine Hudson, do not embouchure[4] where they spend themselves more than they embouchure into him. The blue breadth over the inland sea of Virginia and Maryland and the sea off Massachusetts and Maine and over Manhattan bay and over Champlain and Erie and over Ontario and Huron and Michigan and Superior, and over the Texan and Mexican and Floridian and Cuban seas and over the seas off California and Oregon, is not tallied by the blue breadth of the waters below more than the breadth of above and below is tallied by him. When the long Atlantic coast stretches longer and the Pacific coast stretches longer he easily stretches with them north or south. He spans between them also from east to west and reflects what is between them. On him rise solid growths that offset the growths of pine and cedar and hemlock and liveoak and locust and chestnut and hickory and limetree and cottonwood and tuliptree and cactus and wildvine and tamarind and persimmon. . . . and tangles as tangled as any canebrake or swamp. . . . and forests coated with transparent ice and icicles hanging from the boughs and crackling in the wind. . . . and sides and peaks of mountains. . . . and pasturage sweet and free as savannah or upland or prairie. . . . with flights and songs and screams that answer those of the wildpigeon and highhold[5] and orchard oriole and coot and surf-duck and redshouldered-hawk and fish-hawk and white-ibis and indianhen and cat-owl and water-pheasant and qua-bird and pied-sheldrake and blackbird and mockingbird and buzzard and condor and night-heron and eagle. To him the hereditary countenance descends both mother's and father's. To him enter the essences of the real things and past and present events—of the enormous diversity of temperature and agriculture and mines—the tribes of red aborigines—the weatherbeaten vessels entering new ports or making landings on rocky coasts—the first settlements north or south—the rapid stature and muscle—the haughty defiance of '76,[6] and the war and peace and formation of the constitution. . . . the union always surrounded by blatherers and always calm and impregnable—the perpetual coming of immigrants—the wharf hem'd cities

---

[3]The poet-singer of a tribe or nation.   [4]Pour out, as from a river mouth.
[5]Woodpecker.   [6]The Declaration of Independence.

and superior marine—the unsurveyed interior—the loghouses and clearings and wild animals and hunters and trappers. . . . the free commerce—the fisheries and whaling and golddigging—the endless gestation of new states—the convening of Congress every December,[7] the members duly coming up from all climates and the uttermost parts. . . . the noble character of the young mechanics[8] and of all free American workmen and workwomen. . . . the general ardor and friendliness and enterprise—the perfect equality of the female with the male. . . . the large amativeness[9]— the fluid movement of the population—the factories and mercantile life and laborsaving machinery—the Yankee swap[10]—the New-York firemen and the target excursion[11]—the southern plantation life—the character of the northeast and of the northwest and southwest—slavery and the tremulous spreading of hands to protect it, and the stern opposition to it which shall never cease till it ceases or the speaking of tongues and the moving of lips cease. For such the expression of the American poet is to be transcendant and new. It is to be indirect and not direct or descriptive or epic. Its quality goes through these to much more. Let the age and wars of other nations be chanted and their eras and characters be illustrated and that finish the verse. Not so the great psalm of the republic. Here the theme is creative and has vista. Here comes one among the wellbeloved stonecutters and plans with decision and science and sees the solid and beautiful forms of the future where they are now no solid forms.

Of all nations the United States with veins full of poetical stuff most need poets and will doubtless have the greatest and use them the greatest. Their Presidents shall not be their common referee so much as their poets shall. Of all mankind the great poet is the equable man. Not in him but off from him things are grotesque or eccentric or fail of their sanity. Nothing out of its place is good and nothing in its place is bad. He bestows on every object or quality its fit proportions neither more nor less. He is the arbiter of the diverse and he is the key. He is the equalizer of his age and land. . . . he supplies what wants supplying and checks what wants checking. If peace is the routine out of him speaks the spirit of peace, large, rich, thrifty, building vast and populous cities, encouraging agriculture and the arts and commerce—lighting the study of man, the soul, immortality—federal, state or municipal government, marriage, health, freetrade, intertravel by land and sea. . . . nothing too close, nothing too far off . . . the stars not too far off. In war he is the most deadly force of the war. Who recruits him recruits horse and foot[12] . . . he fetches parks[13] of artillery the best that engineer ever knew. If the time becomes slothful and heavy he knows how to arouse it . . . he can make every word he speaks draw blood. Whatever stagnates in the flat[14] of custom or obedience or legislation he never stagnates. Obedience does not master him, he masters it. High up out of reach he stands turning a concentrated light . . . he turns the pivot with his finger . . . he baffles the swiftest runners as he stands and easily overtakes and envelopes them. The time straying toward infidelity and confections and persiflage he withholds by his steady faith . . . he spreads out his dishes . . . he offers the sweet firmfibred meat that grows men and women. His brain is the ultimate brain. He is no arguer . . . he is judgment. He judges not as the judge judges but as the sun falling around a helpless thing. As he sees the farthest he has the most faith.

[7]In the nineteenth century the Congress of the United States convened in December.
[8]Manual workers, artisans.
[9]Phrenological term signifying a capacity for loving others.   [10]Bargain.
[11]Trip to a shooting meet.   [12]Horse soldiers (cavalry) and foot soldiers (infantry).
[13]Depots, assembly areas.   [14]Shoal, marsh.

His thoughts are the hymns of the praise of things. In the talk on the soul and eternity and God off of his equal plane he is silent. He sees eternity less like a play with a prologue and denouement. . . . he sees eternity in men and women . . . he does not see men and women as dreams or dots. Faith is the antiseptic of the soul . . . it pervades the common people and preserves them . . . they never give up believing and expecting and trusting. There is that indescribable freshness and unconsciousness about an illiterate person that humbles and mocks the power of the noblest expressive genius. The poet sees for a certainty how one not a great artist may be just as sacred and perfect as the greatest artist. . . . . . The power to destroy or remould is freely used by him but never the power of attack. What is past is past. If he does not expose superior models and prove himself by every step he takes he is not what is wanted. The presence of the greatest poet conquers . . . not parleying or struggling or any prepared attempts. Now he has passed that way see after him! there is not left any vestige of despair or misanthropy or cunning or exclusiveness or the ignominy of a nativity or color or delusion of hell or the necessity of hell. . . . . and no man thenceforward shall be degraded for ignorance or weakness or sin.

The greatest poet hardly knows pettiness or triviality. If he breathes into any thing that was before thought small it dilates with the grandeur and life of the universe. He is a seer. . . . he is individual . . . he is complete in himself. . . . the others are as good as he, only he sees it and they do not. He is not one of the chorus. . . . he does not stop for any regulation . . . he is the president of regulation. What the eyesight does to the rest he does to the rest. Who knows the curious mystery of the eyesight? The other senses corroborate themselves, but this is removed from any proof but its own and foreruns the identities of the spiritual world. A single glance of it mocks all the investigations of man and all the instruments and books of the earth and all reasoning. What is marvellous? what is unlikely? what is impossible or baseless or vague? after you have once just opened the space of a peachpit and given audience to far and near to the sunset and had all things enter with electric swiftness softly and duly without confusion or jostling or jam.

The land and sea, the animals fishes and birds, the sky of heaven and the orbs, the forests mountains and rivers, are not small themes . . . but folks expect of the poet to indicate more than the beauty and dignity which always attach to dumb real objects . . . . they expect him to indicate the path between reality and their souls. Men and women perceive the beauty well enough . . probably as well as he. The passionate tenacity of hunters, woodmen, early risers, cultivators of gardens and orchards and fields, the love of healthy women for the manly form, seafaring persons, drivers of horses, the passion for light and the open air, all is an old varied sign of the unfailing perception of beauty and of a residence of the poetic in outdoor people. They can never be assisted by poets to perceive . . . some may but they never can. The poetic quality is not marshalled in rhyme or uniformity or abstract addresses to things nor in melancholy complaints or good precepts, but is the life of these and much else and is in the soul. The profit of rhyme is that it drops seeds of a sweeter and more luxuriant rhyme, and of uniformity that it conveys itself into its own roots in the ground out of sight. The rhyme and uniformity of perfect poems show the free growth of metrical laws and bud from them as unerringly and loosely as lilacs or roses on a bush, and take shapes as compact as the shapes of chestnuts and oranges and melons and pears, and shed the perfume impalpable to form. The fluency and ornaments of the finest poems or music or orations or recitations are not independent but dependent. All beauty comes from beautiful blood and a beautiful brain. If the greatnesses are in conjunction in a man or woman it is enough. . . . the fact will prevail through the universe. . . . but the gaggery[15] and gilt of a million years will not prevail. Who troubles himself about his ornaments or fluency is lost. This is what you shall do: Love the earth and sun and the animals, despise riches, give alms to every one that asks, stand up for the stupid and crazy, devote your income and labor to others, hate tyrants, argue not concerning God, have patience and indulgence toward the people, take off your hat to nothing known or unknown or to any man or number of men, go freely with powerful uneducated persons and with the young and with the mothers of families, read these leaves in the open air every season of every year of your life, re-examine all you have been told at school or church or in any book, dismiss whatever insults your own soul, and your very flesh shall be a great poem and have the richest fluency not only in its words but in the silent lines of its lips and face and between the lashes of your eyes and in every motion and joint of your body. . . . . The poet shall not spend his time in unneeded work. He shall know that the ground is always ready ploughed and manured. . . . others may not know it but he shall. He shall go directly to the creation. His trust shall master the trust of everything he touches. . . . and shall master all attachment.

The known universe has one complete lover and that is the greatest poet. He consumes an eternal passion and is indifferent which chance happens and which possible contingency of fortune or misfortune and persuades daily and hourly his delicious pay. What balks or breaks others is fuel for his burning progress to contact and amorous joy. Other proportions of the reception of pleasure dwindle to nothing to his proportions. All expected from heaven or from the highest he is rapport with in the sight of the daybreak or a scene of the winter woods or the presence of children playing or with his arm round the neck of a man or woman. His love above all love has leisure and expanse. . . . he leaves room ahead of himself. He is no irresolute or suspicious lover . . . he is sure . . . he scorns intervals. His experience and the showers and thrills are not for nothing. Nothing can jar him. . . . suffering and darkness cannot—death and fear cannot. To him complaint and jealousy and envy are corpses buried and rotten in the earth. . . . he saw them buried. The sea is not surer of the shore or the shore of the sea than he is of the fruition of his love and of all perfection and beauty.

The fruition of beauty is no chance of hit or miss . . . it is inevitable as life. . . . it is exact and plumb as gravitation. From the eyesight proceeds another eyesight and from the hearing proceeds another hearing and from the voice proceeds another voice eternally curious of the harmony of things with man. To these respond perfections not only in the committees that were supposed to stand for the rest but in the rest themselves just the same. These understand the law of perfection in masses and floods . . . that its finish is to each for itself and onward from itself . . . that it is profuse and impartial . . . that there is not a minute of the light or dark nor an acre of the earth or sea without it—nor any direction of the sky nor any trade or employment nor any turn of events. This is the reason that about the proper expression of beauty there is precision and balance . . . one part does not need to be thrust above another. The best singer is not the one who has the most lithe and powerful organ . . . the pleasure of poems is not in them that take the handsomest measure and similes and sound.

Without effort and without exposing in the least how it is done the greatest poet brings the spirit of any or all events and passions and scenes and persons

---

[15]Sham.

some more and some less to bear on your individual character as you hear or read. To do this well is to compete with the laws that pursue and follow time. What is the purpose must surely be there and the clue of it must be there.... and the faintest indication is the indication of the best and then becomes the clearest indication. Past and present and future are not disjoined but joined. The greatest poet forms the consistence of what is to be from what has been and is. He drags the dead out of their coffins and stands them again on their feet.... he says to the past, Rise and walk before me that I may realize you. He learns the lesson.... he places himself where the future becomes present. The greatest poet does not only dazzle his rays over character and scenes and passions ... he finally ascends and finishes all... he exhibits the pinnacles that no man can tell what they are for or what is beyond.... he glows a moment on the extremest verge. He is most wonderful in his last half-hidden smile or frown ... by that flash of the moment of parting the one that sees it shall be encouraged or terrified afterward for many years. The greatest poet does not moralize or make applications of morals... he knows the soul. The soul has that measureless pride which consists in never acknowledging any lessons but its own. But it has sympathy as measureless as its pride and the one balances the other and neither can stretch too far while it stretches in company with the other. The inmost secrets of art sleep with the twain. The greatest poet has lain close betwixt both and they are vital in his style and thoughts.

The art of art, the glory of expression and the sunshine of the light of letters is simplicity. Nothing is better than simplicity ... nothing can make up for excess or for the lack of definiteness. To carry on the heave of impulse and pierce intellectual depths and give all subjects their articulations are powers neither common nor very uncommon. But to speak in literature with the perfect rectitude and insousiance[16] of the movements of animals and the unimpeachableness of the sentiment of trees in the woods and grass by the roadside is the flawless triumph of art. If you have looked on him who has achieved it you have looked on one of the masters of the artists of all nations and times. You shall not contemplate the flight of the graygull over the bay or the mettlesome action of the blood horse or the tall leaning of sunflowers on their stalk or the appearance of the sun journeying through heaven or the appearance of the moon afterward with any more satisfaction than you shall contemplate him. The greatest poet has less a marked style and is more the channel of thoughts and things without increase or diminution, and is the free channel of himself. He swears to his art, I will not be meddlesome, I will not have in my writing any elegance or effort or originality to hang in the way between me and the rest like curtains. I will have nothing hang in the way, not the richest curtains. What I tell I tell for precisely what it is. Let who may exalt or startle or fascinate or sooth[17] I will have purposes as health or heat or snow has and be as regardless of observation. What I experience or portray shall go from my composition without a shred of my composition. You shall stand by my side and look in the mirror with me.

The old red blood and stainless gentility of great poets will be proved by their unconstraint. A heroic person walks at his ease through and out of that custom or precedent or authority that suits him not. Of the traits of the brotherhood of writers savans[18] musicians inventors and artists nothing is finer than silent defiance advancing from new free forms. In the need of poems philosophy politics mechanism science behaviour, the craft of art, an appropriate native

[16]Insouciance, lack of concern.   [17]Changed to "soothe" in later texts.
[18]Savants, sages.

grand-opera, shipcraft, or any craft, he is greatest forever and forever who contributes the greatest original practical example. The cleanest expression is that which finds no sphere worthy of itself and makes one.

The messages of great poets to each man and woman are, Come to us on equal terms, Only then can you understand us, We are no better than you, What we enclose you enclose, What we enjoy you may enjoy. Did you suppose there could be only one Supreme? We affirm there can be unnumbered Supremes, and that one does not countervail another any more than one eyesight countervails another . . . and that men can be good or grand only of the consciousness of their supremacy within them. What do you think is the grandeur of storms and dismemberments and the deadliest battles and wrecks and the wildest fury of the elements and the power of the sea and the motion of nature and of the throes of human desires and dignity and hate and love? It is that something in the soul which says, Rage on, Whirl on, I tread master here and everywhere, Master of the spasms of the sky and of the shatter of the sea, Master of nature and passion and death, And of all terror and all pain.

The American bards shall be marked for generosity and affection and for encouraging competitors . . They shall be kosmos[19] . . without monopoly or secresy[20] . . glad to pass any thing to any one . . hungry for equals night and day. They shall not be careful of riches and privilege . . . . they shall be riches and privilege. . . . they shall perceive who the most affluent man is. The most affluent man is he that confronts all the shows he sees by equivalents out of the stronger wealth of himself. The American bard shall delineate no class of persons nor one or two out of the strata of interests nor love most nor truth most nor the soul most nor the body most. . . . and not be for the eastern states more than the western or the northern states more than the southern.

Exact science and its practical movements are no checks on the greatest poet but always his encouragement and support. The outset and remembrance are there . . . there the arms that lifted him first and brace[21] him best . . . . there he returns after all his goings and comings. The sailor and traveler . . the anatomist, chemist, astronomer, geologist, phrenologist, spiritualist, mathematician, historian and lexicographer are not poets, but they are the lawgivers of poets and their construction underlies the structure of every perfect poem. No matter what rises or is uttered they sent the seed of the conception of it . . . of them and by them stand the visible proofs of souls . . . . . always of their fatherstuff[22] must be begotten the sinewy races of bards. If there shall be love and content between the father and the son and if the greatness of the son is the exuding of the greatness of the father there shall be love between the poet and the man of demonstrable science. In the beauty of poems are the tuft and final applause of science.

Great is the faith of the flush of knowledge and of the investigation of the depths of qualities and things. Cleaving and circling here swells the soul of the poet yet it[23] president of itself always. The depths are fathomless and therefore calm. The innocence and nakedness are resumed . . . they are neither modest nor immodest. The whole theory of the special and supernatural and all that was twined with it or educed[24] out of it departs as a dream. What has ever happened . . . . what happens and whatever may or shall happen, the vital laws enclose all . . . . they are sufficent[25] for any case and for all cases . . . none to be hurried or retarded . . . . any miracle of affairs or persons inadmissible in the vast clear scheme where every motion and every spear of grass and the frames

---

[19]Cosmos.   [20]Changed to "secrecy" in later texts.
[21]Changed to "braced" in later texts.   [22]Seminal fluid.
[23]Corrected to "is" in later texts.   [24]Brought.   [25]Changed to "sufficient" in later texts.

and spirits of men and women and all that concerns them are unspeakably perfect miracles all referring to all and each distinct and in its place. It is also not consistent with the reality of the soul to admit that there is anything in the known universe more divine than men and women.

Men and women and the earth and all upon it are simply to be taken as they are, and the investigation of their past and present and future shall be unintermitted and shall be done with perfect candor. Upon this basis philosophy speculates ever looking toward the poet, ever regarding the eternal tendencies of all toward happiness never inconsistent with what is clear to the senses and to the soul. For the eternal tendencies of all toward happiness make the only point of sane philosophy. Whatever comprehends less than that . . . whatever is less than the laws of light and of astronomical motion . . . or less than the laws that follow the thief the liar the glutton and the drunkard through this life and doubtless afterward. . . . . . or less than vast stretches of time or the slow formation of density or the patient upheaving of strata—is of no account. Whatever would put God in a poem or system of philosophy as contending against some being or influence is also of no account. Sanity and ensemble characterise the great master . . . spoilt in one principle all is spoilt. The great master has nothing to do with miracles. He sees health for himself in being one of the mass . . . . he sees the hiatus in singular eminence. To the perfect shape comes common ground. To be under the general law is great for that is to correspond with it. The master knows that he is unspeakably great and that all are unspeakably great . . . . that nothing for instance is greater than to conceive children and bring them up well . . . that to be is just as great as to perceive or tell.

In the make of the great masters the idea of political liberty is indispensible. Liberty takes the adherence of heroes wherever men and women exist. . . . but never takes any adherence or welcome from the rest more than from poets. They are the voice and exposition of liberty. They out of ages are worthy the grand idea . . . . to them it is confided and they must sustain it. Nothing has precedence of it and nothing can warp or degrade it. The attitude of great poets is to cheer up slaves and horrify despots. The turn of their necks, the sound of their feet, the motions of their wrists, are full of hazard to the one and hope to the other. Come nigh them awhile and though they neither speak or advise you shall learn the faithful American lesson. Liberty is poorly served by men whose good intent is quelled from one failure or two failures or any number of failures, or from the casual indifference or ingratitude of the people, or from the sharp show of the tushes[26] of power, or the bringing to bear soldiers and cannon or any penal statutes. Liberty relies upon itself, invites no one, promises nothing, sits in calmness and light, is positive and composed, and knows no discouragement. The battle rages with many a loud alarm and frequent advance and retreat . . . . the enemy triumphs . . . . the prison, the handcuffs, the iron necklace and anklet, the scaffold, garrote and leadballs do their work . . . . the cause is asleep . . . . the strong throats are choked with their own blood . . . . the young men drop their eyelashes toward the ground when they pass each other . . . . and is liberty gone out of that place? No never. When liberty goes it is not the first to go nor the second or third to go . . it waits for all the rest to go . . it is the last . . . When the memories of the old martyrs are faded utterly away . . . . when the large names of patriots are laughed at in the public halls from the lips of the orators . . . . when the boys are no more christened after the same but christened after tyrants and traitors instead . . . . when the laws of the free are

[26]Tusks, teeth.

grudgingly permitted and laws for informers and bloodmoney are sweet to the taste of the people . . . . when I and you walk abroad upon the earth stung with compassion at the sight of numberless brothers answering our equal friendship and calling no man master—and when we are elated with noble joy at the sight of slaves . . . . when the soul retires in the cool communion of the night and surveys its experience and has much extasy over the word and deed that put back a helpless innocent person into the gripe of the gripers or into any cruel inferiority . . . when those in all parts of these states who could easier realize the true American character but do not yet—when the swarms of cringers, suckers,[27] doughfaces,[28] lice of politics, planners of sly involutions for their own prefer- ment to city offices or state legislatures or the judiciary or congress or the presidency, obtain a response of love and natural deference from the people whether they get the offices or no . . . . when it is better to be a bound booby[29] and rogue in office at a high salary than the poorest free mechanic or farmer with his hat unmoved from his head and firm eyes and a candid and generous heart . . . . and when servility by town or state or the federal government or any oppression on a large scale or small scale can be tried on without its own punishment following duly after in exact proportion against the smallest chance of escape . . . . or rather when all life and all the souls of men and women are discharged from any part of the earth—then only shall the instinct of liberty be discharged from that part of the earth.

As the attributes of the poets of the kosmos concentre in the real body and soul and in the pleasure of things they possess the superiority of genuineness over all fiction and romance. As they emit themselves facts are showered over with light . . . . the daylight is lit with more volatile light . . . . also the deep between the setting and rising sun goes deeper many fold. Each precise object or condition or combination or process exhibits a beauty . . . . the multiplication table its—old age its—the carpenter's trade its—the grand-opera its . . . . the hugehulled cleanshaped New-York clipper at sea under steam or full sail gleams with unmatched beauty . . . . the American circles and large harmonies of gov- ernment gleam with theirs . . . . and the commonest definite intentions and actions with theirs. The poets of the kosmos advance through all interpositions and coverings and turmoils and strategems to first principles. They are of use . . . . they dissolve poverty from its need and riches from its conceit. You large proprietor they say shall not realize or perceive more than any one else. The owner of the library is not he who holds a legal title to it having bought and paid for it. Any one and every one is owner of the library who can read the same through all the varieties of tongues and subjects and styles, and in whom they enter with ease and take residence and force toward paternity and mater- nity, and make supple and powerful and rich and large. . . . . These Amer- ican states strong and healthy and accomplished shall receive no pleasure from violations of natural models and must not permit them. In paintings or mould- ings or carvings in mineral or wood, or in the illustrations of books or newspa- pers, or in any comic or tragic prints, or in the patterns of woven stuffs or any thing to beautify rooms or furniture or costumes, or to put upon cornices or monuments or on the prows or sterns of ships, or to put anywhere before the human eye indoors or out, that which distorts honest shapes or which creates unearthly beings or places or contingencies is a nuisance and revolt. Of the human form especially it is so great it must never be made ridiculous. Of ornaments to a work nothing outre[30] can be allowed . . but those ornaments can

[27]Blackmailing politicians.   [28]Pliable, unprincipled men.
[29]A political hack controlled by special interests.   [30]Extravagant.

be allowed that conform to the perfect facts of the open air and that flow out of the nature of the work and come irrepressibly from it and are necessary to the completion of the work. Most works are most beautiful without ornament . . . Exaggerations will be revenged in human physiology. Clean and vigorous children are jetted[31] and conceived only in those communities where the models of natural forms are public every day. . . . . Great genius and the people of these states must never be demeaned to romances. As soon as histories are properly told there is no more need of romances.

The great poets are also to be known by the absence in them of tricks and by the justification of perfect personal candor. Then folks echo a new cheap joy and a divine voice leaping from their brains: How beautiful is candor! All faults may be forgiven of him who has perfect candor. Henceforth let no man of us lie, for we have seen that openness wins the inner and outer world and that there is no single exception, and that never since our earth gathered itself in a mass have deceit or subterfuge or prevarication attracted its smallest particle or the faintest tinge of a shade—and that through the enveloping wealth and rank of a state or the whole republic of states a sneak or sly person shall be discovered and despised . . . . and that the soul has never been once fooled and never can be fooled . . . . and thrift without the loving nod of the soul is only a fœtid puff . . . . and there never grew up in any of the continents of the globe nor upon any planet or satellite or star, nor upon the asteroids, under the fluid wet of the sea, nor in that condition which precedes nor in any part of the ethereal space, nor in the midst of density, nor the birth of babes, nor at any time during the changes of life, nor in that condition that follows what we term death, nor in any stretch of abeyance or action afterward of vitality, nor in any process of formation or reformation anywhere, a being whose instinct hated the truth.

Extreme caution or prudence, the soundest organic health, large hope and comparison and fondness for women and children, large alimentiveness and destructiveness and causality,[32] with a perfect sense of the oneness of nature and the propriety of the same spirit applied to human affairs . . these are called up of the float[33] of the brain of the world to be parts of the greatest poet from his birth out of his mother's womb and from her birth out of her mother's. Caution seldom goes far enough. It has been thought that the prudent citizen was the citizen who applied himself to solid gains and did well for himself and his family and completed a lawful life without debt or crime. The greatest poet sees and admits these economies as he sees the economies of food and sleep, but has higher notions of prudence than to think he gives much when he gives a few slight attentions at the latch of the gate. The premises of the prudence of life are not the hospitality of it or the ripeness and harvest of it. Beyond the independence of a little sum laid aside for burial-money, and of a few clapboards around the shingles overhead on a lot[34] of American soil owned, and the easy dollars that supply the year's plain clothing and meals, the melancholy prudence of the abandonment of such a great being as a man is to the toss and pallor of years of moneymaking with all their scorching days and icy nights and all their stifling deceits and underhanded dodgings, or infinitessimals of parlors, or shameless stuffing while others starve . . and all the loss of the bloom and odor of the earth and of the flowers and atmosphere and of the sea and of the true taste of the women and men you pass or have to do with in youth or middle age, and the issuing sickness and desperate revolt at the close of a life without

---

[31]I.e., produced by a jet of seminal fluid.

[32]Phrenological terms meaning an appetite for food, an interest in destruction, and a tendency to trace effects to their causes.   [33]Flow or fluid.   [34]Small plot of land.

elevation or naivete, and the ghastly chatter of a death without serenity or majesty, is the great fraud upon modern civilization and forethought, blotching the surface and system which civilization undeniably drafts, and moistening with tears the immense features it spreads and spreads with such velocity before the reached kisses of the soul . . . Still the right explanation remains to be made about prudence. The prudence of the mere wealth and respectability of the most esteemed life appears too faint for the eye to observe at all when little and large alike drop quietly aside at the thought of the prudence suitable for immortality. What is wisdom that fills the thinness of a year or seventy or eighty years to wisdom spaced out by ages and coming back at a certain time with strong reinforcements and rich presents and the clear faces of wedding-guests as far as you can look in every direction running gaily toward you? Only the soul is of itself . . . . all else has reference to what ensues. All that a person does or thinks is of consequence. Not a move can a man or woman make that affects him or her in a day or a month or any part of the direct lifetime or the hour of death but the same affects him or her onward afterward through the indirect lifetime. The indirect is always as great and real as the direct. The spirit receives from the body just as much as it gives to the body. Not one name of word or deed . . not of venereal sores or discolorations . . not the privacy of the onanist[35] . . not of the putrid veins of gluttons or rumdrinkers . . . not peculation[36] or cunning or betrayal or murder . . no serpentine poison of those that seduce women . . not the foolish yielding of women . . not prostitution . . not of any depravity of young men . . not of the attainment of gain by discreditable means . . not any nastiness of appetite . . not any harshness of officers to men or judges to prisoners or fathers to sons or sons to fathers or of husbands to wives or bosses to their boys . . not of greedy looks or malignant wishes . . . nor any of the wiles practised by people upon themselves . . . ever is or ever can be stamped on the programme but it is duly realized and returned, and that returned in further performances . . . and they returned again. Nor can the push of charity or personal force ever be any thing else than the profoundest reason, whether it bring arguments to hand or no. No specification is necessary . . to add or subtract or divide is in vain. Little or big, learned or unlearned, white or black, legal or illegal, sick or well, from the first inspiration down the windpipe to the last expiration out of it, all that a male or female does that is vigorous and benevolent and clean is so much sure profit to him or her in the unshakable order of the universe and through the whole scope of it forever. If the savage or felon is wise it is well . . . . if the greatest poet or savan is wise it is simply the same . . . if the President or chief justice is wise it is the same . . . if the young mechanic or farmer is wise it is no more or less . . if the prostitute is wise it is no more nor less. The interest will come round . . all will come round. All the best actions of war and peace . . . all help given to relatives and strangers and the poor and old and sorrowful and young children and widows and the sick, and to all shunned persons . . all furtherance of fugitives and of the escape of slaves . . all the self-denial that stood steady and aloof on wrecks and saw others take the seats of the boats . . . all offering of substance or life for the good old cause, or for a friend's sake or opinion's sake . . . all pains of enthusiasts scoffed at by their neighbors . . all the vast sweet love and precious suffering of mothers . . all honest men baffled in strifes recorded or unrecorded . . . . all the grandeur and good of the few ancient nations whose fragments of annals we inherit . .

[35]In the nineteenth century the sin for which the Lord slew Onan (Genesis 38:9) was thought to have been masturbation.   [36]Embezzlement.

and all the good of the hundreds of far mightier and more ancient nations unknown to us by name or date or location .... all that was ever manfully begun, whether it succeeded or no .... all that has at any time been well suggested out of the divine heart of man or by the divinity of his mouth or by the shaping of his great hands .. and all that is well thought or done this day on any part of the surface of the globe .. or on any of the wandering stars or fixed stars by those there as we are here .. or that is henceforth to be well thought or done by you whoever you are, or by any one—these singly and wholly inured at their time and inure now and will inure always to the identities from which they sprung or shall spring ... Did you guess any of them lived only its moment? The world does not so exist .. no parts palpable or impalpable so exist ... no result exists now without being from its long antecedent result, and that from its antecedent, and so backward without the farthest mentionable spot coming a bit nearer the beginning than any other spot. .... Whatever satisfies the soul is truth. The prudence of the greatest poet answers at last the craving and glut of the soul, is not contemptuous of less ways of prudence if they conform to its ways, puts off nothing, permits no let-up for its own case or any case, has no particular sabbath or judgment-day, divides not the living from the dead or the righteous from the unrighteous, is satisfied with the present, matches every thought or act by its correlative, knows no possible forgiveness or deputed atonement .. knows that the young man who composedly periled his life and lost it has done exceeding well for himself, while the man who has not periled his life and retains it to old age in riches and ease has perhaps achieved nothing for himself worth mentioning .. and that only that person has no great prudence to learn who has learnt to prefer real longlived things, and favors body and soul the same, and perceives the indirect assuredly following the direct, and what evil or good he does leaping onward and waiting to meet him again—and who in his spirit in any emergency whatever neither hurries or avoids death.

The direct trial of him who would be the greatest poet is today. If he does not flood himself with the immediate age as with vast oceanic tides ..... and if he does not attract his own land body and soul to himself and hang on its neck with incomparable love and plunge his semitic[37] muscle into its merits and demerits ... and if he be not himself the age transfigured .... and if to him is not opened the eternity which gives similitude to all periods and locations and processes and animate and inanimate forms, and which is the bond of time, and rises up from its inconceivable vagueness and infiniteness in the swimming shape of today, and is held by the ductile anchors of life, and makes the present spot the passage from what was to what shall be, and commits itself to the representation of this wave of an hour and this one of the sixty beautiful children of the wave—let him merge in the general run and wait his development. ....
Still the final test of poems or any character or work remains. The prescient poet projects himself centuries ahead and judges performer or performance after the changes of time. Does it live through them? Does it still hold on untired? Will the same style and the direction of genius to similar points be satisfactory now? Has no new discovery in science or arrival at superior planes of thought and judgment and behavior fixed him or his so that either can be looked down upon? Have the marches of tens and hundreds and thousands of years made willing detours to the right hand and the left hand for his sake? Is he beloved long and long after he is buried? Does the young man think often of him? and

[37]Seminal.

the young woman think often of him? and do the middleaged and the old think of him?

A great poem is for ages and ages in common and for all degrees and complexions and all departments and sects and for a woman as much as a man and a man as much as a woman. A great poem is no finish to a man or woman but rather a beginning. Has any one fancied he could sit at last under some due authority and rest satisfied with explanations and realize and be content and full? To no such terminus does the greatest poet bring . . . he brings neither cessation or sheltered fatness and ease. The touch of him tells in action. Whom he takes he takes with firm sure grasp into live regions previously unattained . . . . thenceforward is no rest . . . . they see the space and ineffable sheen that turn the old spots and lights into dead vacuums. The companion of him beholds the birth and progress of stars and learns one of the meanings. Now there shall be a man cohered out of a tumult and chaos . . . . the elder encourages the younger and shows him how . . . they two shall launch off fearlessly together till the new world fits an orbit for itself and looks unabashed on the lesser orbits of the stars and sweeps through the ceaseless rings and shall never be quiet again.

There will soon be no more priests. Their work is done. They may wait awhile . . perhaps a generation or two . . dropping off by degrees. A superior breed shall take their place . . . . the gangs of kosmos and prophets en masse shall take their place. A new order shall arise and they shall be the priests of man, and every man shall be his own priest. The churches built under their umbrage[38] shall be the churches of men and women. Through the divinity of themselves shall the kosmos and the new breed of poets be interpreters of men and women and of all events and things. They shall find their inspiration in real objects today, symptoms of the past and future. . . . They shall not deign to defend immortality or God or the perfection of things or liberty or the exquisite beauty and reality of the soul. They shall arise in America and be responded to from the remainder of the earth.

The English language befriends the grand American expression . . . . it is brawny enough and limber and full enough. On the tough stock of a race who through all change of circumstance was never without the idea of political liberty, which is the animus of all liberty, it has attracted the terms of daintier and gayer and subtler and more elegant tongues. It is the powerful language of resistance . . . it is the dialect of common sense. It is the speech of the proud and melancholy races and of all who aspire. It is the chosen tongue to express growth faith self-esteem freedom justice equality friendliness amplitude prudence decision and courage. It is the medium that shall well nigh express the inexpressible.

No great literature nor any like style of behaviour or oratory or social intercourse or household arrangements or public institutions or the treatment by bosses of employed people, nor executive detail or detail of the army or navy, nor spirit of legislation or courts or police or tuition or architecture or songs or amusements or the costumes of young men, can long elude the jealous and passionate instinct of American standards. Whether or no the sign appears from the mouths of the people, it throbs a live interrogation in every freeman's and freewoman's heart after that which passes by, or this built to remain. Is it uniform with my country? Are its disposals without ignominious distinctions? Is it for the evergrowing communes of brothers and lovers, large, well-united, proud

---

[38]Shadow.

beyond the old models, generous beyond all models? Is it something grown fresh out of the fields or drawn from the sea for use to me today here? I know that what answers for me an American must answer for any individual or nation that serves for a part of my materials. Does this answer? or is it without reference to universal needs? or sprung of the needs of the less developed society of special ranks? or old needs of pleasure overlaid by modern science and forms? Does this acknowledge liberty with audible and absolute acknowledgment, and set slavery at nought for life and death? Will it help breed one goodshaped and wellhung man, and a woman to be his perfect and independent mate? Does it improve manners? Is it for the nursing of the young of the republic? Does it solve[39] readily with the sweet milk of the nipples of the breasts of the mother of many children? Has it too the old ever-fresh forbearance and impartiality? Does it look with the same love on the last born and on those hardening toward stature, and on the errant, and on those who disdain all strength of assault outside of their own?

The poems distilled from other poems will probably pass away. The coward will surely pass away. The expectation of the vital and great can only be satisfied by the demeanor of the vital and great. The swarms of the polished deprecating and reflectors and the polite float off and leave no remembrance. America prepares with composure and goodwill for the visitors that have sent word. It is not intellect that is to be their warrant and welcome. The talented, the artist, the ingenious, the editor, the statesman, the erudite . . they are not unappreciated . . they fall in their place and do their work. The soul of the nation also does its work. No disguse can pass on it . . no disguse can conceal from it. It rejects none, it permits all. Only toward as good as itself and toward the like of itself will it advance half-way. An individual is as superb as a nation when he has the qualities which make a superb nation. The soul of the largest and wealthiest and proudest nation may well go half-way to meet that of its poets. The signs are effectual. There is no fear of mistake. If the one is true the other is true. The proof of a poet is that his country absorbs him as affectionately as he has absorbed it.

1855

---

[39]Dissolve.

from *INSCRIPTIONS*

ONE'S-SELF I SING

One's-Self I sing, a simple separate person,
Yet utter the word Democratic, the word En-Masse.

Of physiology from top to toe I sing,
Not physiognomy[1] alone nor brain alone is worthy for the Muse, I
     say the Form complete is worthier far,
The Female equally with the Male I sing.

Of Life immense in passion, pulse, and power,
Cheerful, for freest action form'd under the laws divine,
The Modern Man I sing.

                                                      1867, 1871[2]

WHEN I READ THE BOOK

When I read the book, the biography famous,
And is this then (said I) what the author calls a man's life?
And so will some one when I am dead and gone write my life?
(As if any man really knew aught of my life,
Why even I myself I often think know little or nothing of my real life,
Only a few hints, a few diffused faint clews and indirections
I seek for my own use to trace out here.)

                                                      1867, 1871

BEGINNING MY STUDIES

Beginning my studies the first step pleas'd me so much,
The mere fact consciousness, these forms, the power of motion,
The least insect or animal, the senses, eyesight, love,
The first step I say awed me and pleas'd me so much,
I have hardly gone and hardly wish'd to go any farther,
But stop and loiter all the time to sing it in ecstatic songs.

                                                      1865, 1871

STARTING FROM PAUMANOK[1]

1

Starting from fish-shape Paumanok where I was born,
Well-begotten, and rais'd by a perfect mother,

[1]Facial features, as indications of character.
[2]The first date following each of Whitman's poems indicates its first appearance in print. The second, publication in its final form.
[1]Indian name for Long Island, New York.

After roaming many lands, lover of populous pavements,
Dweller in Mannahatta[2] my city, or on southern savannas,
Or a soldier camp'd or carrying my knapsack and gun, or a miner in
  California,
Or rude in my home in Dakota's woods, my diet meat, my drink
  from the spring,
Or withdrawn to muse and meditate in some deep recess,
Far from the clank of crowds intervals passing rapt and happy,
Aware of the fresh free giver the flowing Missouri, aware of mighty
  Niagara,
Aware of the buffalo herds grazing the plains, the hirsute and
  strong-breasted bull,
Of earth, rocks, Fifth-month[3] flowers experienced, stars, rain, snow,
  my amaze,   10
Having studied the mocking-bird's tones and the flight of the
  mountain-hawk,
And heard at dawn the unrivall'd one, the hermit thrush from the
  swamp-cedars,
Solitary, singing in the West, I strike up for a New World.

                              2

Victory, union, faith, identity, time,
The indissoluble compacts, riches, mystery,
Eternal progress, the kosmos, and the modern reports.

This then is life,
Here is what has come to the surface after so many throes and
  convulsions.

How curious! how real!
Underfoot the divine soil, overhead the sun.   20

See revolving the globe,
The ancestor-continents away group'd together,
The present and future continents north and south, with the
  isthmus between.

See, vast trackless spaces,
As in a dream they change, they swiftly fill,
Countless masses debouch upon them,
They are now cover'd with the foremost people, arts, institutions,
  known.

See, projected through time,
For me an audience interminable.   30

With firm and regular step they wend, they never stop,
Successions of men, Americanos, a hundred millions,
One generation playing its part and passing on,

[2]Indian word from which "Manhattan" was derived.
[3]A Quaker term for May.

Another generation playing its part and passing on in its turn,
With faces turn'd sideways or backward towards me to listen,
With eyes retrospective towards me.

3

Americanos! conquerors! marches humanitarian!
Foremost! century marches! Libertad![4] masses!
For you a programme of chants.

Chants of the prairies,   40
Chants of the long-running Mississippi, and down to the Mexican
    sea,
Chants of Ohio, Indiana, Illinois, Iowa, Wisconsin and Minnesota,
Chants going forth from the centre from Kansas, and thence
    equidistant,
Shooting in pulses of fire ceaseless to vivify all.

4

Take my leaves America, take them South and take them North,
Make welcome for them everywhere, for they are your own
    offspring.
Surround them East and West, for they would surround you,
And you precedents, connect lovingly with them, for they connect
    lovingly with you.

I conn'd[5] old times,
I sat studying at the feet of the great masters,   50
Now if eligible O that the great masters might return and study me.

In the name of these States shall I scorn the antique?
Why these are the children of the antique to justify it.

5

Dead poets, philosophs,[6] priests,
Martyrs, artists, inventors, governments long since,
Language-shapers on other shores,
Nations once powerful, now reduced, withdrawn, or desolate,
I dare not proceed till I respectfully credit what you have left wafted
    hither.
I have perused it, own it is admirable, (moving awhile among it,)
Think nothing can ever be greater, nothing can ever deserve more
    than it deserves,   60
Regarding it all intently a long while, then dismissing it,
I stand in my place with my own day here.

Here lands female and male,
Here the heir-ship and heiress-ship of the world, here the flame of
    materials,
Here spirituality the translatress, the openly-avow'd,

----

[4]Spanish: liberty.   [5]Studied.   [6]Philosophers.

The ever-tending, the finalè of visible forms,
The satisfier, after due long-waiting now advancing,
Yes here comes my mistress the soul.

6

The soul,
Forever and forever—longer than soil is brown and solid—longer
    than water ebbs and flows.   70

I will make the poems of materials, for I think they are to be most
    spiritual poems,
And I will make the poems of my body and of mortality,
For I think I shall then supply myself with the poems of my soul
    and of immortality.

I will make a song for these States that no one State may under any
    circumstances be subjected to another State,
And I will make a song that there shall be comity[7] by day and by
    night between all the States, and between any two of them,
And I will make a song for the ears of the President, full of weapons
    with menacing points,
And behind the weapons countless dissatisfied faces;
And a song make I of the One form'd out of all,
The fang'd and glittering One[8] whose head is over all,
Resolute warlike One including and over all,   80
(However high the head of any else that head is over all.)

I will acknowledge contemporary lands,
I will trail the whole geography of the globe and salute courteously
    every city large and small,
And employments! I will put in my poems that with you is heroism
    upon land and sea,
And I will report all heroism from an American point of view.

I will sing the song of companionship,
I will show what alone must finally compact these,
I believe these are to found their own ideal of manly love, indicating
    it in me,
I will therefore let flame from me the burning fires that were
    threatening to consume me,
I will lift what has too long kept down those smouldering fires,   90
I will give them complete abandonment,
I will write the evangel-poem of comrades and of love,
For who but I should understand love with all its sorrow and joy?
And who but I should be the poet of comrades?

7

I am the credulous man of qualities, ages, races,
I advance from the people in their own spirit,
Here is what sings unrestricted faith.

[7]Friendliness, social harmony.   [8]Whitman's term for the American flag.

Omnes![9] omnes! let others ignore what they may,
I make the poem of evil also, I commemorate that part also,
I am myself just as much evil as good, and my nation is—and I say
    there is in fact no evil,   100
(Or if there is I say it is just as important to you, to the land or to
    me, as any thing else.)

I too, following many and follow'd by many, inaugurate a religion, I
    descend into the arena,
(It may be I am destin'd to utter the loudest cries there, the winner's
    pealing shouts,
Who knows? they may rise from me yet, and soar above every thing.)

Each is not for its own sake,
I say the whole earth and all the stars in the sky are for religion's
    sake.

I say no man has ever yet been half devout enough,
None has ever yet adored or worship'd half enough,
None has begun to think how divine he himself is, and how certain
    the future is.

I say that the real and permanent grandeur of these States must be
    their religion,   110
Otherwise there is no real and permanent grandeur;
(Nor character nor life worthy the name without religion,
Nor land nor man or woman without religion.)

                                      .8
What are you doing young man?
Are you so earnest, so given up to literature, science, art, amours?
These ostensible realities, politics, points?
Your ambition or business whatever it may be?

It is well—against such I say not a word, I am their poet also,
But behold! such swiftly subside, burnt up for religion's sake,
For not all matter is fuel to heat, impalpable flame, the essential life
    of the earth,   120
Any more than such are to religion.

                                      9
What do you seek so pensive and silent?
What do you need camerado?[10]
Dear son do you think it is love?
Listen dear son—listen America, daughter or son,
It is a painful thing to love a man or woman to excess, and yet it
    satisfies, it is great,
But there is something else very great, it makes the whole coincide,
It, magnificent, beyond materials, with continuous hands sweeps and
    provides for all.

[9]Latin: all.   [10]Comrade.

10

Know you, solely to drop in the earth the germs of a greater
    religion,
The following chants each for its kind I sing.   130

My comrade!
For you to share with me two greatnesses, and a third one rising
    inclusive and more resplendent,
The greatness of Love and Democracy, and the greatness of
    Religion.

Melange[11] mine own, the unseen and the seen,
Mysterious ocean where the streams empty,
Prophetic spirit of materials shifting and flickering around me,
Living beings, identities now doubtless near us in the air that we
    know not of,
Contact daily and hourly that will not release me,
These selecting, these in hints demanded of me.

Not he with a daily kiss onward from childhood kissing me,   140
Has winded and twisted around me that which holds me to him,
Any more than I am held to the heavens and all the spiritual world,
After what they have done to me, suggesting themes.

O such themes—equalities! O divine average!
Warblings under the sun, usher'd as now, or at noon, or setting,
Strains musical flowing through ages, now reaching hither,
I take to your reckless and composite chords, add to them, and
    cheerfully pass them forward.

11

As I have walk'd in Alabama my morning walk,
I have seen where the she-bird the mocking-bird sat on her nest in
    the briers hatching her brood.

I have seen the he-bird also,   150
I have paus'd to hear him near at hand inflating his throat and
    joyfully singing.

And while I paus'd it came to me that what he really sang for was
    not there only,
Nor for his mate nor himself only, nor all sent back by the echoes,
But subtle, clandestine, away beyond,
A charge transmitted and gift occult for those being born.

12

Democracy! near at hand to you a throat is now inflating itself and
    joyfully singing.

[11]Mixture.

Ma femme![12] for the brood beyond us and of us,
For those who belong here and those to come,
I exultant to be ready for them will now shake out carols stronger
    and haughtier than have ever yet been heard upon earth.

I will make the songs of passion to give them their way,   160
And your songs outlaw'd offenders, for I scan you with kindred
    eyes, and carry you with me the same as any.

I will make the true poem of riches,
To earn for the body and the mind whatever adheres and goes
    forward and is not dropt by death;
I will effuse egotism and show it underlying all, and I will be the
    bard of personality,
And I will show of male and female that either is but the equal of
    the other,
And sexual organs and acts! do you concentrate in me, for I am
    determin'd to tell you with courageous clear voice to prove you
    illustrious,
And I will show that there is no imperfection in the present, and can
    be none in the future,
And I will show that whatever happens to anybody it may be turn'd
    to beautiful results,
And I will show that nothing can happen more beautiful than death,
And I will thread a thread through my poems that time and events
    are compact,   170
And that all the things of the universe are perfect miracles, each as
    profound as any.

I will not make poems with reference to parts,
But I will make poems, songs, thoughts, with reference to ensemble,
And I will not sing with reference to a day, but with reference to all
    days,
And I will not make a poem nor the least part of a poem but has
    reference to the soul,
Because having look'd at the objects of the universe, I find there is
    no one nor any particle of one but has reference to the soul.

                                  13
Was somebody asking to see the soul?
See, your own shape and countenance, persons, substances, beasts,
    the trees, the running rivers, the rocks and sands.

All hold spiritual joys and afterwards loosen them;
How can the real body ever die and be buried?   180

Of your real body and any man's or woman's real body,
Item for item it will elude the hands of the corpse-cleaners and pass
    to fitting spheres,
Carrying what has accrued to it from the moment of birth to the
    moment of death.

[12]French: My woman. Whitman's term of address for Democracy.

Not the types set up by the printer return their impression, the
  meaning, the main concern,
Any more than a man's substance and life or a woman's substance
  and life return in the body and the soul,
Indifferently before death and after death.

Behold, the body includes and is the meaning, the main concern,
  and includes and is the soul;
Whoever you are, how superb and how divine is your body, or any
  part of it!

14

Whoever you are, to you endless announcements!

Daughter of the lands did you wait for your poet?   190
Did you wait for one with a flowing mouth and indicative hand?
Toward the male of the States, and toward the female of the States,
Exulting words, words to Democracy's lands.

Interlink'd, food-yielding lands!
Land of coal and iron! land of gold! land of cotton, sugar, rice!
Land of wheat, beef, pork! land of wool and hemp! land of the
  apple and the grape!
Land of the pastoral plains, the grass-fields of the world! land of
  those sweet-air'd interminable plateaus!
Land of the herd, the garden, the healthy house of adobie!
Lands where the north-west Columbia winds, and where the south-
  west Colorado winds!
Land of the eastern Chesapeake! land of the Delaware!   200
Land of Ontario, Erie, Huron, Michigan!
Land of the Old Thirteen! Massachusetts land! land of Vermont and
  Connecticut!
Land of the ocean shores! land of sierras and peaks!
Land of boatmen and sailors! fisherman's land!
Inextricable lands! the clutch'd together! the passionate ones!
The side by side! the elder and younger brothers! the bony-limb'd!
The great women's land! the feminine! the experienced sisters and
  the inexperienced sisters!
Far breath'd land! Arctic braced! Mexican breez'd! the diverse! the
  compact!
The Pennsylvanian! the Virginian! the double Carolinian!
O all and each well-loved by me! my intrepid nations! O I at any rate
  include you all with perfect love!   210
I cannot be discharged from you! not from one any sooner than
  another!
O death! O for all that, I am yet of you unseen this hour with
  irrepressible love,
Walking New England, a friend, a traveler,
Splashing my bare feet in the edge of the summer ripples on
  Paumanok's sands,

Crossing the prairies, dwelling again in Chicago, dwelling in every
   town,
Observing shows, births, improvements, structures, arts,
Listening to orators and oratresses in public halls,
Of and through the States as during life, each man and woman my
   neighbor,
The Louisianian, the Georgian, as near to me, and I as near to him
   and her,
The Mississippian and Arkansian yet with me, and I yet with any of
   them,   220
Yet upon the plains west of the spinal river, yet in my house of
   adobie,
Yet returning eastward, yet in the Seaside State or in Maryland,
Yet Kanadian[13] cheerily braving the winter, the snow and ice
   welcome to me,
Yet a true son either of Maine or of the Granite State, or the
   Narragansett Bay State, or the Empire State,[14]
Yet sailing to other shores to annex the same, yet welcoming every
   new brother,
Hereby applying these leaves to the new ones from the hour they
   unite with the old ones,
Coming among the new ones myself to be their companion and
   equal, coming personally to you now,
Enjoining you to acts, characters, spectacles, with me.

15

With me with firm holding, yet haste, haste on.

For your life adhere to me,   230
(I may have to be persuaded many times before I consent to give
   myself really to you, but what of that?
Must not Nature be persuaded many times?)

No dainty dolce affettuoso[15] I,
Bearded, sun-burnt, gray-neck'd, forbidding, I have arrived,
To be wrestled with as I pass for the solid prizes of the universe,
For such I afford whoever can persevere to win them.

16

On my way a moment I pause,
Here for you! and here for America!
Still the present I raise aloft, still the future of the States I harbinge[16]
   glad and sublime,
And for the past I pronounce what the air holds of the red
   aborigines.   240

---

[13]Whitman's spelling of "Canadian."   [14]Vermont, Rhode Island, New York.
[15]Italian: sweet, loving man.   [16]Foretell.

The red aborigines,
Leaving natural breaths, sounds of rain and winds, calls as of birds
and animals in the wood, syllabled to us for names,
Okonee, Koosa, Ottawa, Monongahela, Sauk, Natchez,
Chattahoochee, Kaqueta, Oronoco,
Wabash, Miami, Saginaw, Chippewa, Oshkosh, Walla-Walla,
Leaving such to the States they melt, they depart, charging the water
and the land with names.

17

Expanding and swift, henceforth,
Elements, breeds, adjustments, turbulent, quick and audacious,
A world primal again, vistas of glory incessant and branching,
A new race dominating previous ones and grander far, with new
contests,
New politics, new literatures and religions, new inventions and arts.   250

These, my voice announcing—I will sleep no more but arise,
You oceans that have been calm within me! how I feel you,
fathomless, stirring, preparing unprecedented waves and storms.

18

See, steamers steaming through my poems,
See, in my poems immigrants continually coming and landing,
See, in arriere,[17] the wigwam, the trail, the hunter's hut, the flat-boat,
the maize-leaf, the claim, the rude fence, and the backwoods village,
See, on the one side the Western Sea and on the other the Eastern
Sea, how they advance and retreat upon my poems as upon their
own shores,
See, pastures and forests in my poems—see, animals wild and tame—
see, beyond the Kaw,[18] countless herds of buffalo feeding on short
curly grass,
See, in my poems, cities, solid, vast, inland, with paved streets, with
iron and stone edifices, ceaseless vehicles, and commerce,
See, the many-cylinder'd steam printing-press—see, the electric
telegraph stretching across the continent,
See, through Atlantica's[19] depths pulses American Europe reaching,
pulses of Europe duly return'd.   260
See, the strong and quick locomotive as it departs, panting, blowing
the steam-whistle,
See, ploughman ploughing farms—see, miners digging mines—see,
the numberless factories,
See, mechanics busy at their benches with tools—see from among
them superior judges, philosophs, Presidents, emerge, drest in
working dresses,
See, lounging through the shops and fields of the States, me well-
belov'd, close-held by day and night,
Here the loud echoes of my songs there—read the hints come at last.

[17]French: in retrospect, in the past.   [18]The Kaw River in Kansas.
[19]Whitman's name for the Atlantic Ocean.

19

O camerado close! O you and me at last, and us two only.
O a word to clear one's path ahead endlessly!
O something ecstatic and undemonstrable! O music wild!
O now I triumph—and you shall also;
O hand in hand—O wholesome pleasure—O one more desirer and
    lover!   270
O to haste firm holding—to haste, haste on with me.

                                                                   1860, 1881

SONG OF MYSELF

1

I celebrate myself, and sing myself,
And what I assume you shall assume,
For every atom belonging to me as good belongs to you.

I loafe and invite my soul,
I lean and loafe at my ease observing a spear of summer grass.

My tongue, every atom of my blood, form'd from this soil, this air,
Born here of parents born here from parents the same, and their
    parents the same,
I, now thirty-seven years old in perfect health begin,
Hoping to cease not till death.

Creeds and schools in abeyance,   10
Retiring back a while suffic'd at what they are, but never forgotten,
I harbor for good or bad, I permit to speak at every hazard,
Nature without check with original energy.

2

Houses and rooms are full of perfumes, the shelves are crowded
    with perfumes,
I breathe the fragrance myself and know it and like it,
The distillation would intoxicate me also, but I shall not let it.

The atmosphere is not a perfume, it has no taste of the distillation, it
    is odorless,
It is for my mouth forever, I am in love with it,
I will go to the bank by the wood and become undisguised and
    naked,
I am mad for it to be in contact with me.   20
The smoke of my own breath,
Echoes, ripples, buzz'd whispers, love-root, silk-thread, crotch and
    vine,
My respiration and inspiration, the beating of my heart, the passing
    of blood and air through my lungs,

The sniff of green leaves and dry leaves, and of the shore and dark
  color'd sea-rocks, and of hay in the barn,
The sound of the belch'd words of my voice loos'd to the eddies of
  the wind,
A few light kisses, a few embraces, a reaching around of arms,
The play of shine and shade on the trees as the supple boughs wag,
The delight alone or in the rush of the streets, or along the fields
  and hill-sides.
The feeling of health, the full-noon trill, the song of me rising from
  bed and meeting the sun.

Have you reckon'd a thousand acres much? have you reckon'd the
  earth much?   30
Have you practis'd so long to learn to read?
Have you felt so proud to get at the meaning of poems?

Stop this day and night with me and you shall possess the origin of
  all poems,
You shall possess the good of the earth and sun, (there are millions
  of suns left,)
You shall no longer take things at second or third hand, nor look
  through the eyes of the dead, nor feed on the spectres in books,
You shall not look through my eyes either, nor take things from me,
You shall listen to all sides and filter them from your self.

3

I have heard what the talkers were talking, the talk of the beginning
  and the end,
But I do not talk of the beginning or the end.

There was never any more inception than there is now,   40
Nor any more youth or age than there is now,
And will never be any more perfection than there is now,
Nor any more heaven or hell than there is now.

Urge and urge and urge,
Always the procreant urge of the world.

Out of the dimness opposite equals advance, always substance and
  increase, always sex,
Always a knit of identity, always distinction, always a breed of life.

To elaborate is no avail, learn'd and unlearn'd feel that it is so.

Sure as the most certain sure, plumb in the uprights, well entretied,[1]
  braced in the beams,
Stout as a horse, affectionate, haughty, electrical,   50
I and this mystery here we stand.

Clear and sweet is my soul, and clear and sweet is all that is not my
  soul.

[1] A carpenter's term meaning supported, braced.

Lack one lacks both, and the unseen is proved by the seen,
Till that becomes unseen and receives proof in its turn.

Showing the best and dividing it from the worst age vexes age,
Knowing the perfect fitness and equanimity of things, while they
    discuss I am silent, and go bathe and admire myself.

Welcome is every organ and attribute of me, and of any man hearty
    and clean,
Not an inch nor a particle of an inch is vile, and none shall be less
    familiar than the rest.

I am satisfied—I see, dance, laugh, sing;
As the hugging and loving bed-fellow[2] sleeps at my side through the
    night, and withdraws at the peep of the day with stealthy tread.   60
Leaving me baskets cover'd with white towels swelling the house with
    their plenty,
Shall I postpone my acceptation and realization and scream at my
    eyes,
That they turn from gazing after and down the road,
And forthwith cipher[3] and show me to a cent,
Exactly the value of one and exactly the value of two, and which is
    ahead?

4

Trippers and askers[4] surround me,
People I meet, the effect upon me of my early life or the ward and
    city I live in, or the nation,
The latest dates, discoveries, inventions, societies, authors old and
    new,
My dinner, dress, associates, looks, compliments, dues,
The real or fancied indifference of some man or woman I love,   70
The sickness of one of my folks or of myself, or ill-doing or loss or
    lack of money, or depressions or exaltations,
Battles, the horrors of fratricidal[5] war, the fever of doubtful news,
    the fitful events;
These come to me days and nights and go from me again,
But they are not the Me myself.

Apart from the pulling and hauling stands what I am,
Stands amused, complacent, compassionating, idle, unitary,
Looks down, is erect, or bends an arm on an impalpable certain rest,
Looking with side-curved head curious what will come next,
Both in and out of the game and watching and wondering at it.

Backward I see in my own days where I sweated through fog with
    linguists and contenders,
I have no mockings or arguments, I witness and wait.   80

[2]In the 1855 edition the "bed-fellow" is identified as God.   [3]Calculate.
[4]I.e., travelers and beggars.   [5]Brother killing brother.

5

I believe in you my soul, the other I am must not abase itself to you,
And you must not be abased to the other.

Loafe with me on the grass, loose the stop from your throat,
Not words, not music or rhyme I want, not custom or lecture, not
  even the best,
Only the lull I like, the hum of your valvèd voice.

I mind how once we lay such a transparent summer morning,
How you settled your head athwart my hips and gently turn'd over
  upon me,
And parted the shirt from my bosom-bone, and plunged your
  tongue to my bare-stript heart,
And reach'd till you felt my beard, and reach'd till you held my feet.   90

Swiftly arose and spread around me the peace and knowledge that
  pass all the argument of the earth,
And I know that the hand of God is the promise of my own,
And I know that the spirit of God is the brother of my own,
And that all the men ever born are also my brothers, and the women
  my sisters and lovers,
And that a kelson[6] of the creation is love,
And limitless are leaves stiff or drooping in the fields,
And brown ants in the little wells beneath them,
And mossy scabs of the worm fence,[7] heap'd stones, elder, mullein
  and poke-weed.

6

A child said *What is the grass?* fetching it to me with full hands;
How could I answer the child? I do not know what it is any more
  than he.   100

I guess it must be the flag of my disposition, out of hopeful green
  stuff woven.

Or I guess it is the handkerchief of the Lord,
A scented gift and remembrancer designedly dropt,
Bearing the owner's name someway in the corners, that we may see
  and remark, and say *Whose?*

Or I guess the grass is itself a child, the produced babe of the
  vegetation.

Or I guess it is a uniform hieroglyphic,
And it means, Sprouting alike in broad zones and narrow zones,
Growing among black folks as among white,
Kanuck, Tuckahoe, Congressman, Cuff,[8] I give them the same, I
  receive them the same.

[6]Keelson, ship timbers that brace the keel.   [7]A zigzag rail fence.
[8]Canuck: a French-Canadian; Tuckahoe: a Virginian of the coastal lowlands; Cuff: a Negro.

And now it seems to me the beautiful uncut hair of graves.   110

Tenderly will I use you curling grass,
It may be you transpire from the breasts of young men,
It may be if I had known them I would have loved them.
It may be you are from old people, or from offspring taken soon out
    of their mothers' laps,
And here you are the mothers' laps.

This grass is very dark to be from the white heads of old mothers.
Darker than the colorless beards of old men,
Dark to come from under the faint red roofs of mouths.

O I perceive after all so many uttering tongues,
And I perceive they do not come from the roofs of mouths for
    nothing.   120

I wish I could translate the hints about the dead young men and
    women,
And the hints about old men and mothers, and the offspring taken
    soon out of their laps.

What do you think has become of the young and old men?
And what do you think has become of the women and children?

They are alive and well somewhere,
The smallest sprout shows there is really no death,
And if ever there was it led forward life, and does not wait at the
    end to arrest it,
And ceas'd the moment life appear'd.

All goes onward and outward, nothing collapses,
And to die is different from what any one supposed, and luckier.   130

7

Has any one supposed it lucky to be born?
I hasten to inform him or her it is just as lucky to die, and I know it.

I pass death with the dying and birth with the new-wash'd babe, and
    am not contain'd between my hat and boots.
And peruse manifold objects, no two alike and every one good,
The earth good and the stars good, and their adjuncts all good.

I am not an earth nor an adjunct of an earth,
I am the mate and companion of people, all just as immortal and
    fathomless as myself,
(They do not know how immortal, but I know.)

Every kind for itself and its own, for me mine male and female,
For me those that have been boys and that love women,   140
For me the man that is proud and feels how it stings to be slighted,

For me the sweet-heart and the old maid, for me mothers and the
  mothers of mothers,
For me lips that have smiled, eyes that have shed tears,
For me children and the begetters of children.

Undrape! you are not guilty to me, nor stale nor discarded,
I see through the broadcloth and gingham whether or no,
And am around, tenacious, acquisitive, tireless, and cannot be shaken
  away.

8

The little one sleeps in its cradle,
I lift the gauze and look a long time, and silently brush away flies
  with my hand.

The youngster and the red-faced girl turn aside up the bushy hill,   150
I peeringly, view them from the top.

The suicide sprawls on the bloody floor of the bedroom,
I witness the corpse with its dabbled hair, I note where the pistol has
  fallen.

The blab of the pave,[9] tires of carts, sluff of boot-soles, talk of the
  promenaders,
The heavy omnibus, the driver with his interrogating thumb, the
  clank of the shod horses on the granite floor,
The snow-sleighs, clinking, shouted jokes, pelts of snow-balls,
The hurrahs for popular favorites, the fury of rous'd mobs,
The flap of the curtain'd litter, a sick man inside borne to the
  hospital,
The meeting of enemies, the sudden oath, the blows and fall,
The excited crowd, the policeman with his star quickly working his
  passage to the centre of the crowd,   160
The impassive stones that receive and return so many echoes,
What groans of over-fed or half-starv'd who fall sunstruck or in fits,
What exclamations of women taken suddenly who hurry home and
  give birth to babes,
What living and buried speech is always vibrating here, what howls
  restrain'd by decorum,
Arrests of criminals, slights, adulterous offers made, acceptances,
  rejections with convex lips,
I mind them or the show or resonance of them—I come and I
  depart.

9

The big doors of the country barn stand open and ready,
The dried grass of the harvest-time loads the slow-drawn wagon,
The clear light plays on the brown gray and green intertinged,
The armfuls are pack'd to the sagging mow.   170

[9] The talk of the streets.

I am there, I help, I came stretch'd atop of the load,
I felt its soft jolts, one leg reclined on the other,
I jump from the cross-beams and seize the clover and timothy,
And roll head over heels and tangle my hair full of wisps.

10

Alone far in the wilds and mountains I hunt,
Wandering amazed at my own lightness and glee,
In the late afternoon choosing a safe spot to pass the night,
Kindling a fire and broiling the fresh-kill'd game,
Falling asleep on the gather'd leaves with my dog and gun by my
    side.

The Yankee clipper is under her sky-sails,[10] she cuts the sparkle and
    scud,[11]   180
My eyes settle the land, I bend at her prow or shout joyously from
    the deck.

The boatman and clam-diggers arose early and stopt for me,
I tuck'd my trowser-ends in my boots and went and had a good time;
You should have been with us that day round the chowder-kettle.

I saw the marriage of the trapper in the open air in the far west, the
    bride was a red girl,
Her father and his friends sat near cross-legged and dumbly
    smoking, they had moccasins to their feet and large thick blankets
    hanging from their shoulders,
On a bank lounged the trapper, he was drest mostly in skins, his
    luxuriant beard and curls protected his neck, he held his bride by
    the hand,
She had long eyelashes, her head was bare, her coarse straight locks
    descended upon her voluptuous limbs and reach'd to her feet.

The runaway slave came to my house and stopt outside,
I heard his motions crackling the twigs of the woodpile,   190
Through the swung half-door of the kitchen I saw him limpsy[12] and
    weak,
And went where he sat on a log and led him in and assured him,
And brought water and fill'd a tub for his sweated body and bruis'd
    feet,
And gave him a room that enter'd from my own, and gave him some
    coarse clean clothes,
And remember perfectly well his revolving eyes and his
    awkwardness,
And remember putting plasters on the galls of his neck and ankles;
He staid with me a week before he was recuperated and pass'd
    north,
I had him sit next me at table, my fire-lock[13] lean'd in the corner.

11

Twenty-eight young men bathe by the shore,
Twenty-eight young men and all so friendly;   200

---

[10]Upper sails.   [11]Sea foam.   [12]Limp.   [13]Gun.

Twenty-eight years of womanly life and all so lonesome.

She owns the fine house by the rise of the bank,
She hides handsome and richly drest aft the blinds of the window.

Which of the young men does she like the best?
Ah the homeliest of them is beautiful to her.

Where are you off to, lady? for I see you,
You splash in the water there, yet stay stock still in your room.

Dancing and laughing along the beach came the twenty-ninth bather,
The rest did not see her, but she saw them and loved them.

The beards of the young men glisten'd with wet, it ran from their
    long hair, 210
Little streams pass'd all over their bodies.

An unseen hand also pass'd over their bodies,
It descended tremblingly from their temples and ribs.

The young men float on their backs, their white bellies bulge to the
    sun, they do not ask who seizes fast to them,
They do not know who puffs and declines with pendant and
    bending arch,
They do not think whom they souse with spray.

12

The butcher-boy puts off his killing-clothes, or sharpens his knife at
    the stall in the market,
I loiter enjoying his repartee and his shuffle and break-down.[14]

Blacksmiths with grimed and hair chests environ the anvil,
Each has his main-sledge, they are all out, there is a great heat in the
    fire. 220

From the cinder-strew'd threshold I follow their movement,
The lithe sheer[15] of their waists plays even with their massive arms,
Overhand the hammers swing, overhand so slow, overhand so sure,
They do not hasten, each man hits in his place.

13

The negro holds firmly the reins of his four horses, the block swags[16]
    underneath on its tied-over-chain,
The negro that drives the long dray[17] of the stone-yard, steady and
    tall he stands pois'd on one leg on the string-piece,[18]
His blue shirt exposes his ample neck and breast and loosens over
    his hip-band,

[14]Popular dance steps.   [15]Curve.   [16]Sways, sags heavily.
[17]A sledge or wagon used for hauling heavy loads.   [18]A long, support timber.

His glance is calm and commanding, he tosses the slouch of his hat
    away from his forehead,
The sun falls on his crispy hair and mustache, falls on the black of
    his polish'd and perfect limbs.

I behold the picturesque giant and love him, and I do not stop there,   230
I go with the team also.

In me the caresser of life wherever moving, backward as well as
    forward sluing,[19]
To niches aside and junior[20] bending, not a person or object missing,
Absorbing all to myself and for this song.

Oxen that rattle the yoke and chains or halt in the leafy shade, what
    is that you express in your eyes?
It seems to me more than all the print I have read in my life.

My tread scares the wood-drake and wood-duck on my distant and
    day-long ramble,
They rise together, they slowly circle around.

I believe in those wing'd purposes,
And acknowledge red, yellow, white, playing within me,   240
And consider green and violet and the tufted crown[21] intentional,
And do not call the tortoise unworthy because she is not something
    else,
And the jay in the woods never studied the gamut,[22] yet trills pretty
    well to me,
And the look of the bay mare shames silliness out of me.

14

The wild gander leads his flock through the cold night,
Ya-honk he says, and sounds it down to me like an invitation,
The pert[23] may suppose it meaningless, but I listening close,
Find its purpose and place up there toward the wintry sky.

The sharp-hoof'd moose of the north, the cat on the house-sill, the
    chickadee, the prairie-dog,
The litter of the grunting sow as they tug at her teats,   250
The brood of the turkey-hen and she with her half-spread wings,
I see in them and myself the same old law.

The press of my foot to the earth springs a hundred affections.
They scorn the best I can do to relate them.

I am enamour'd of growing out-doors,
Of men that live among cattle or taste of the ocean or woods,
Of the builders and steerers of ships and the wielders of axes and
    mauls, and the drivers of horses,
I can eat and sleep with them week in and week out.

[19]Turning, twisting.   [20]Smaller.   [21]Of the drake.
[22]Musical scale.   [23]Self-assured, cocky.

What is commonest, cheapest, nearest, easiest is Me,
Me going in for my chances, spending for vast returns, 260
Adorning myself to bestow myself on the first that will take me,
Not asking the sky to come down to my good will,
Scattering it freely forever.

15

The pure contralto sings in the organ loft,
The carpenter dresses his plank, the tongue of his foreplane whistles
    its wild ascending lisp,
The married and unmarried children ride home to their
    Thanksgiving dinner,
The pilot seizes the king-pin,[24] he heaves down with a strong arm,
The mate stands braced in the whale-boat, lance and harpoon are
    ready,
The duck-shooter walks by silent and cautious stretches,
The deacons are ordain'd with cross'd hands at the altar, 270
The spinning-girl retreats and advances to the hum of the big wheel,
The farmer stops by the bars[25] as he walks on a First-day loafe[26] and
    looks at the oats and rye,
The lunatic is carried at last to the asylum a confirm'd case,
(He will never sleep any more as he did in the cot in his mother's
    bed-room;)
The jour[27] printer with gray head and gaunt jaws works at his case,[28]
He turns his quid of tobacco while his eyes blurr with the
    manuscript;
The malform'd limbs are tied to the surgeon's table,
What is removed drops horribly in a pail;
The quadroon[29] girl is sold at the auction-stand, the drunkard nods
    by the bar-room stove,
The machinist rolls up his sleeves, the policeman travels his beat, the
    gate-keeper marks who pass, 280
The young fellow drives the express-wagon, (I love him, though, I
    do not know him;)
The half-breed straps on his light boots to compete in the race,
The western turkey-shooting draws old and young, some lean on
    their rifles, some sit on logs,
Out from the crowd steps the marksman, takes his position, levels his
    piece;
The groups of newly-come immigrants cover the wharf or levee,
As the wooly-pates[30] hoe in the sugar-field, the overseer views them
    from his saddle,
The bugle calls in the ball-room, the gentlemen run for their
    partners, the dancers bow to each other,
The youth lies awake in the cedar-roof'd garret and harks to the
    musical rain,
The Wolverine[31] sets traps on the creek that helps fill the Huron,
The squaw wrapt in her yellow-hemm'd cloth is offering moccasins
    and bead-bags for sale, 290

[24]An extended spoke on a ship's pilot wheel.   [25]Fence rails.
[26]A Sunday (from Quaker terminology) time of ease.   [27]Journeyman, trained.   [28]Type case.
[29]Of one-quarter black ancestry.   [30]Blacks.   [31]Inhabitant of Michigan.

The connoisseur peers along the exhibition-gallery with half-shut
    eyes bent sideways,
As the deck-hands make fast the steamboat the plank is thrown for
    the shore-going passengers,
The young sister holds out the skein while the elder sister winds it
    off in a ball, and stops now and then for the knots,
The one-year wife is recovering and happy having a week ago borne
    her first child,
The clean-hair'd Yankee girl works with her sewing machine or in
    the factory or mill,
The paving-man[32] leans on his two-handed rammer, the reporter's
    lead flies swiftly over the note-book, the sign-painter is lettering
    with blue and gold,
The canal boy trots on the tow-path,[33] the book-keeper counts at his
    desk, the shoemaker waxes his thread,
The conductor beats time for the band and all the performers follow
    him,
The child is baptized, the convert is making his first professions,
The regatta is spread on the bay, the race is begun, (how the white
    sails sparkle!)   300
The drover watches his drove sings out to them that would stray,
The pedler sweats with his pack on his back, (the purchaser
    higgling[34] about the odd cent;)
The bride unrumples her white dress, the minute-hand of the clock
    moves slowly,
The opium-eater reclines with rigid head and just-open'd lips,
The prostitute draggles her shawl, her bonnet bobs on her tipsy and
    pimpled neck,
The crowd laugh at her blackguard[35] oaths, the men jeer and wink
    to each other,
(Miserable! I do not laugh at your oaths nor jeer you;)
The president holding a cabinet council is surrounded by the great
    Secretaries,
On the piazza walk three matrons stately and friendly with twined
    arms,
The crew of the fish-smack pack repeated layers of halibut in the
    hold,   310
The Missourian crosses the plains toting his wares and his cattle,
As the fare-collector goes through the train he gives notice by the
    jingling of loose change,
The floor-men are laying the floor, the tinners are tinning[36] the roof,
    the masons are calling for mortar,
In single file each shouldering his hod pass onward the laborers;
Seasons pursuing each other the indescribable crowd is gather'd, it is
    the fourth of Seventh-month,[37] (what salutes of cannon and small
    arms!)
Seasons pursuing each other the plougher ploughs, the mower
    mows, and the winter-grain falls in the ground;

[32]Street-repair man.   [33]Canal-side path for the draft animals that tow canal barges.
[34]Bargaining.   [35]Rude, abusive.   [36]I.e., tinsmiths are sealing the sheet-metal roof.
[37]July.

Off on the lakes the pike-fisher watches and waits by the hole in the
    frozen surface,
The stumps stand thick round the clearing, the squatter strikes deep
    with his axe,
Flatboatmen make fast towards dusk near the cotton-wood or pecan-
    trees,
Coon-seekers go through the regions of the Red river[38] or through
    those drain'd by the Tennessee, or through those of the Arkansas,   320
Torches shine in the dark that hangs on the Chattahooche or
    Altamahaw,[39]
Patriarchs sit at supper with sons and grandsons and great-grandsons
    around them,
In walls of adobie, in canvas tents, rest hunters and trappers after
    their day's sport,
The city sleeps and the country sleeps,
The living sleep for their time, the dead sleep for their time,
The old husband sleeps by his wife and the young husband sleeps by
    his wife;
And these tend inward to me, and I tend outward to them,
And such as it is to be of these more or less I am,
And of these one and all I weave the song of myself.

16

I am of old and young, of the foolish as much as the wise,   330
Regardless of others, ever regardful of others,
Maternal as well as paternal, a child as well as a man,
Stuff'd with the stuff that is coarse and stuff'd with the stuff that is
    fine,
One of the Nation of many nations, the smallest the same and the
    largest the same,
A Southerner soon as a Northerner, a planter nonchalant and
    hospitable down by the Oconee[40] I live,
A Yankee bound my own way ready for trade, my joints the
    limberest joints on earth and the sternest joints on earth,
A Kentuckian walking the vale of the Elkhorn[41] in my deer-skin
    leggings, a Louisianian or Georgian,
A boatman over lakes or bays or along coasts, a Hoosier, Badger,
    Buckeye;[42]
At home on Kanadian snow-shoes or up in the bush, or with
    fishermen off Newfoundland,
At home in the fleet of ice-boats, sailing with the rest and tacking,   340
At home on the hills of Vermont or in the woods of Maine, or the
    Texas ranch,
Comrade of Californians, comrade of free North-Westerners, (loving
    their big proportions,)
Comrade of raftsmen and coalmen, comrade of all who shake hands
    and welcome to drink and meat,
A learner with the simplest, a teacher of the thoughtfullest,
A novice beginning yet experient of[43] myriads of seasons,

---

[38]Along the Oklahoma-Texas border.   [39]Rivers in Georgia.   [40]River in Georgia.
[41]River in Nebraska.   [42]An inhabitant of Indiana, of Wisconsin, of Ohio.
[43]I.e., one who has experienced.

Of every hue and caste am I, of every rank and religion,
A farmer, mechanic, artist, gentleman, sailor, quaker,
Prisoner, fancy-man,[44] rowdy, lawyer, physician, priest.

I resist any thing better than my own diversity,
Breathe the air but leave plenty after me,   350
And am not stuck up, and am in my place.

(The moth and the fish-eggs are in their place,
The bright suns I see and the dark suns I cannot see are in their
    place,
The palpable is in its place and the impalpable is in its place.)

17

These are really the thoughts of all men in all ages and lands, they
    are not original with me,
If they are not yours as much as mine they are nothing, or next to
    nothing,
If they are not the riddle and the untying of the riddle they are
    nothing,
If they are not just as close as they are distant they are nothing.

This is the grass that grows wherever the land is and the water is,
This the common air that bathes the globe.   360

18

With music strong I come, with my cornets and my drums,
I play not marches for accepted victors only, I play marches for
    conquer'd and slain persons.

Have you heard that it was good to gain the day?
I also say it is good to fall, battles are lost in the same spirit in which
    they are won.

I beat and pound for the dead,
I blow through my embouchures[45] my loudest and gayest for them.

Vivas[46] to those who have fail'd!
And to those whose war-vessels sank in the sea!
And to those themselves who sank in the sea!
And to all generals that lost engagements, and all overcome heroes!   370
And the numberless unknown heroes equal to the greatest heroes
    known!

19

This is the meal equally set, this the meat for natural hunger,
It is for the wicked just the same as the righteous, I make
    appointments with all,
I will not have a single person slighted or left away,
The kept-woman, sponger, thief, are hereby invited,

[44]A whore's pimp.   [45]Mouthpieces of musical instruments.   [46]Salutes.

The heavy-lipp'd slave is invited, the venerealee[47] is invited;
There shall be no difference between them and the rest.

This is the press of a bashful hand, this the float and odor of hair,
This the touch of my lips to yours, this the murmur of yearning,
This the far-off depth and height reflecting my own face,   380
This the thoughtful merge[48] of myself, and the outlet again.

Do you guess I have some intricate purpose?
Well I have, for the Fourth-month[49] showers have, and the mica on
    the side of a rock has.

Do you take it I would astonish?
Does the daylight astonish? does the early redstart twittering through
    the woods?
Do I astonish more than they?

This hour I tell things in confidence,
I might not tell everybody, but I will tell you.

20

Who goes there? hankering, gross, mystical, nude,
How is it I extract strength from the beef I eat?   390

What is a man anyhow? what am I? what are you?

All I mark as my own you shall offset it with your own,
Else it were lost listening to me.

I do not snivel that snivel the world over,
That months are vacuums and the ground but wallow and filth.

Whimpering and truckling fold with powders for invalids,[50]
    conformity goes to the fourth-remov'd,[51]
I wear my hat as I please indoors or out.

Why should I pray? why should I venerate and be ceremonious?

Having pried through the strata, analyzed to a hair, counsel'd with
    doctors and calculated close,
I find no sweeter fat than sticks to my own bones.   400

In all people I see myself, none more and not one a barley-corn less,
And the good or bad I say of myself I say of them.

I know I am solid and sound,
To me the converging objects of the universe perpetually flow,
All are written to me, and I must get what the writing means.

---

[47]One crazed by sexual desire or disease.   [48]Union, convergence.   [49]April.
[50]I.e., whimpering and knuckling under are suited to combine with medicines for invalids.
[51]Those distantly separated, far removed from others.

I know I am deathless,
I know this orbit of mine cannot be swept by a carpenter's compass,
I know I shall not pass like a child's carlacue cut with a burnt stick at
    night.[52]

I know I am august,
I do not trouble my spirit to vindicate itself or be understood,   410
I see that the elementary laws never apologize,
(I reckon I behave no prouder than the level I plant my house by,
    after all.)

I exist as I am, that is enough,
If no other in the world be aware I sit content,
And if each and all be aware I sit content.

One world is aware and by far the largest to me, and that is myself,
And whether I come to my own to-day or in ten thousand or ten
    million years,
I can cheerfully take it now, or with equal cheerfulness I can wait.

My foothold is tenon'd and mortis'd[53] in granite,
I laugh at what you call dissolution,   420
And I know the amplitude of time.

21

I am the poet of the Body and I am the poet of the Soul,
The pleasures of heaven are with me the pains of hell are with me,
The first I graft and increase upon myself, the latter I translate into
    a new tongue.

I am the poet of the woman the same as the man,
And I say it is as great to be a woman as to be a man,
And I say there is nothing greater than the mother of men.

I chant the chant of dilation or pride,
We have had ducking and deprecating about enough,
I show that size is only development.   430

Have you outstript the rest? are you the President?
It is a trifle, they will more than arrive there every one, and still pass
    on.

I am he that walks with the tender and growing night,
I call to the earth and sea half-held by the night.

Press close bare-bosom'd night—press close magnetic nourishing
    night!
Night of south winds—night of the large few stars!
Still nodding night—mad naked summer night.

[52]A momentary pattern (a curlicue) made in the dark by waving a glowing stick or ember.
[53]Carpenter's term meaning fastened together by a strong, interlocked joint.

Smile O voluptuous cool-breath'd earth!
Earth of the slumbering and liquid trees!
Earth of departed sunset—earth of the mountains misty-topt! 440
Earth of the vitreous[54] pour of the full moon just tinged with blue!
Earth of shine and dark mottling the tide of the river!
Earth of the limpid gray of clouds brighter and clearer for my sake!
Far-swooping elbow'd earth—rich apple-blossom'd earth!
Smile, for your lover comes.

Prodigal, you have given me love—therefore I to you give love!
O unspeakable passionate love.

22

You sea! I resign myself to you also—I guess what you mean,
I behold from the beach your crooked inviting fingers,
I believe you refuse to go back without feeling of me, 450
We must have a turn together, I undress, hurry me out of sight of
  the land,
Cushion me soft, rock me in billowy drowse,
Dash me with amorous wet, I can repay you.

Sea of stretch'd ground-swells,
Sea breathing broad and convulsive breaths,
Sea of the brine of life and of unshovell'd yet always-ready graves,
Howler and scooper of storms, capricious and dainty sea,
I am integral with you, I too am of one phase and of all phases.

Partaker of influx and efflux I, extoller of hate and conciliation,
Extoller of amies[55] and those that sleep in each others' arms. 460

I am he attesting sympathy,
(Shall I make my list of things in the house and skip the house that
  supports them?)

I am not the poet of goodness only, I do not decline to be the poet
  of wickedness also.

What blurt is this about virtue and about vice?
Evil propels me and reform of evil propels me, I stand indifferent,
My gait is no fault-finder's or rejecter's gait,
I moisten the roots of all that has grown.

Did you fear some scrofula[56] out of the unflagging pregnancy?
Did you guess the celestial laws are yet to be work'd over and
  rectified?

I find one side a balance and the antipodal side a balance, 470
Soft doctrine as steady help as stable doctrine,
Thoughts and deeds of the present our rouse and early start.

[54]Glassy.   [55]French: friends, lovers.   [56]A disease of the lungs and glands.

This minute that comes to me over the past decillions,[57]
There is no better than it and now.

What behaved well in the past or behaves well to-day is not such a
    wonder,
The wonder is always and always how there can be a mean man or
    infidel.

23

Endless unfolding of words of ages!
And mine a word of the modern, the word En-Masse.

A word of the faith that never balks,
Here or henceforward it is all the same to me, I accept Time
    absolutely.   480

It alone is without flaw, it alone rounds and completes all,
That mystic baffling wonder alone completes all.

I accept Reality and dare not question it,
Materialism first and last imbuing.

Hurrah for positive science! long live exact demonstration!
Fetch stonecrop[58] mixt with cedar and branches of lilac,
This is the lexicographer, this the chemist, this made a grammar[59] of
    the old cartouches,[60]
These mariners put the ship through dangerous unknown seas,
This is the geologist, this works with the scalpel, and this is a
    mathematician.

Gentlemen, to you the first honors always!   490
Your facts are useful, and yet they are not my dwelling,
I but enter by them to an area of my dwelling.

Less the reminders of properties told my words,
And more the reminders they of life untold, and of freedom and
    extrication,
And make short account of neuters and geldings, and favor men and
    women fully equipt,
And beat the gong of revolt, and stop with fugitives and them that
    plot and conspire.

24

Walt Whitman, a kosmos, of Manhattan the son,
Turbulent, fleshy, sensual, eating, drinking and breeding,
No sentimentalist, no stander above men and women or apart from
    them,
No more modest than immodest.   500

[57]The number 1 followed by thirty-two zeros.
[58]An herb used in folk medicine.   [59]I.e., deciphered.
[60]Oval borders within which Egyptian hieroglyphs were inscribed.

Unscrew the locks from the doors!
Unscrew the doors themselves from their jambs!

Whoever degrades another degrades me,
And whatever is done or said returns at last to me.

Through me the afflatus[61] surging and surging, through me the
    current and index.

I speak the pass-word primeval, I give the sign of democracy,
By God! I will accept nothing which all cannot have their
    counterpart of on the same terms.

Through me many long dumb voices,
Voices of the interminable generations of prisoners and slaves,
Voices of the diseas'd and despairing and of thieves and dwarfs,   510
Voices of cycles of preparation and accretion,
And of the threads that connect the stars, and of wombs and of the
    father-stuff,
And of the rights of them the others are down upon,
Of the deform'd, trivial, flat, foolish, despised,
Fog in the air, beetles rolling balls of dung.

Through me forbidden voices,
Voices of sexes and lusts, voices veil'd and I remove the veil,
Voices indecent by me clarified and transfigur'd.

I do not press my fingers across my mouth,
I keep as delicate around the bowels as around the head and heart,   520
Copulation is no more rank to me than death is.

I believe in the flesh and the appetites,
Seeing, hearing, feeling, are miracles, and each part and tag of me is
    a miracle.

Divine am I inside and out, and I make holy whatever I touch or am
    touch'd from,
The scent of these arm-pits aroma finer than prayer,
This head more than churches, bibles, and all the creeds.

If I worship one thing more than another it shall be the spread of
    my own body, or any part of it,
Translucent mould of me it shall be you!
Shaded ledges and rests it shall be you!
Firm masculine colter[62] it shall be you!   530
Whatever goes to the tilth[63] of me it shall be you!
You my rich blood! your milky stream pale strippings of my life!
Breast that presses against other breasts it shall be you!
My brain it shall be your occult convolutions!

[61]Divine spirit, poetic inspiration.
[62]Iron blade at the front of a plow.   [63]Cultivation.

Root of wash'd sweet-flag![64] timorous pond-snipe! nest of guarded
    duplicate eggs! it shall be you!
Mix'd tussled hay of head, beard, brawn, it shall be you!
Trickling sap of maple, fibre of manly wheat, it shall be you!
Sun so generous it shall be you!
Vapors lighting and shading my face it shall be you!
You sweaty brooks and dews it shall be you!   540
Winds whose soft-tickling genitals rub against me it shall be you!
Broad muscular fields, branches of live oak, loving lounger in my
    winding paths, it shall be you!
Hands I have taken, face I have kiss'd, mortal I have ever touch'd, it
    shall be you.

I dote on myself, there is that lot of me and all so luscious,
Each moment and whatever happens thrills me with you,
I cannot tell how my ankles bend, nor whence the cause of my
    faintest wish,
Nor the cause of the friendship I emit, nor the cause of the
    friendship I take again.

That I walk up my stoop, I pause to consider if it really be,
A morning-glory at my window satisfies me more than the
    metaphysics of books.

To behold the day-break!   550
The little light fades the immense and diaphanous shadows,
The air tastes good to my palate.

Hefts[65] of the moving world at innocent gambols silently rising,
    freshly exuding,
Scooting obliquely high and low.

Something I cannot see puts upward libidinous prongs,
Seas of bright juice suffuse heaven.

The earth by the sky staid with, the daily close of their junction,
The heav'd challenge from the east that moment over my head,
The mocking taunt, See then whether you shall be master!

25

Dazzling and tremendous how quick the sun-rise would kill me,   560
If I could not now and always send sun-rise out of me.

We also ascend dazzling and tremendous as the sun,
We found our own O my soul in the calm and cool of the day-break.

My voice goes after what my eyes cannot reach,
With the twirl of my tongue I encompass worlds and volumes of
    worlds.

[64]The calamus, a plant with green flowers and aromatic roots.   [65]Mass, main parts.

Speech is the twin of my vision, it is unequal to measure itself,
It provokes me forever, it says sarcastically,
Walt you contain enough, why don't you let it out then?

Come now I will not be tantalized, you conceive too much of
    articulation,
Do you not know O speech how the buds beneath you are folded?   570
Waiting in gloom, protected by frost,
The dirt receding before my prophetical screams,
I underlying causes to balance them at last,
My knowledge my live parts, it keeping tally with the meaning of all
    things,
Happiness, (which whoever hears me let him or her set out in search
    of this day.)

My final merit I refuse you, I refuse putting from me what I really
    am,
Encompass worlds, but never try to encompass me,
I crowd your sleekest and best by simply looking toward you.

Writing and talk do not prove me,
I carry the plenum[66] of proof and every thing else in my face,   580
With the hush of my lips I wholly confound the skeptic.

26

Now I will do nothing but listen,
To accrue what I hear into this song, to let sounds contribute toward
    it.

I hear bravuras of birds, bustle of growing wheat, gossip of flames,
    clack of sticks cooking my meals,
I hear the sound I love, the sound of the human voice,
I hear all sounds running together, combined, fused or following.
Sounds of the city and sounds out of the city, sounds of the day and
    night,
Talkative young ones to those that like them, the loud laugh of
    work-people at their meals,
The angry base[67] of disjointed friendship, the faint tones of the sick,
The judge with hands tight to the desk, his pallid lips pronouncing a
    death-sentence
The heave'e'yo of stevedores unlading ships by the wharves, the   590
    refrain of the anchor-lifters,
The ring of alarm-bells, the cry of fire, the whirr of swift-streaking
    engines and hose-carts with premonitory tinkles and color'd lights,
The steam-whistle, the solid roll of the train of approaching cars,
The slow march play'd at the head of the association marching two
    and two,
(They go to guard some corpse, the flag-tops are draped with black
    muslin.)

[66]Fullness.   [67]Bass.

I hear the violoncello, ('tis the young man's heart's complaint,)
I hear the key'd cornet, it glides quickly in through my ears,
It shakes mad-sweet pangs through my belly and breast.

I hear the chorus, it is a grand opera,
Ah this indeed is music—this suits me.   600

A tenor large and fresh as the creation fills me,
The orbic flex of his mouth is pouring and filling me full.

I hear the train'd soprano (what work with hers is this?)
The orchestra whirls me wider than Uranus[68] flies,
It wrenches such ardors from me I did not know I possess'd them,
It sails me, I dab with bare feet, they are lick'd by the indolent
      waves,
I am cut by bitter and angry hail, I lose my breath,
Steep'd amid honey'd morphine, my windpipe throttled in fakes[69] of
      death,
At length let up again to feel the puzzle of puzzles,
And that we call Being.   610

27

To be in any form, what is that?
(Round and round we go, all of us, and ever come back thither,)
If nothing lay more develop'd the quahaug[70] in its callous shell were
      enough.

Mine is no callous shell,
I have instant conductors all over me whether I pass or stop,
They seize every object and lead it harmlessly through me.

I merely stir, press, feel with my fingers, and am happy,
To touch my person to some one else's is about as much as I can
      stand.

28

Is this then a touch? quivering me to a new identity,
Flames and ether making a rush for my veins,   620
Treacherous tip of me reaching and crowding to help them,
My flesh and blood playing out lightning to strike what is hardly
      different from myself,
On all sides prurient provokers stiffening my limbs,
Straining the udder of my heart for its withheld drip,
Behaving licentious toward me, taking no denial,
Depriving me of my best as for a purpose,
Unbuttoning my clothes, holding me by the bare waist,
Deluding my confusion with the calm of the sunlight and pasture-
      fields,
Immodestly sliding the fellow-senses away,

---

[68]Planet with a large orbit.   [69]Coils of rope.   [70]An Atlantic clam.

They bribed to swap off with touch and go and graze at the edges of
    me,
No consideration, no regard for my draining strength or my anger, 630
Fetching the rest of the herd around to enjoy them for a while,
Then all uniting to stand on a headland and worry me.

The sentries desert every other part of me,
They have left me helpless to a red marauder,
They all come to the headland to witness and assist against me.

I am given up by traitors,
I talk wildly, I have lost my wits, I and nobody else am the greatest
    traitor,
I went myself first to the headland, my own hands carried me there.

You villain touch! what are you doing? my breath is tight in its
    throat, 640
Unclench your floodgates, you are too much for me.

29

Blind loving wrestling touch, sheath'd hooded sharp-tooth'd touch!
Did it make you ache so, leaving me?

Parting track'd by arriving, perpetual payment of perpetual loan,
Rich showering rain, and recompense richer afterward.

Sprouts take and accumulate, stand by the curb profile and vital,
Landscapes projected masculine, full-sized and golden.

30

All truths wait in all things,
They neither hasten their own delivery nor resist it,
They do not need the obstetric forceps of the surgeon,
The insignificant is as big to me as any, 650
(What is less or more than a touch?)

Logic and sermons never convince,
The damp of the night drives deeper into my soul.

(Only what proves itself to every man and woman is so,
Only what nobody denies is so.)

A minute and a drop of me settle my brain,
I believe the soggy clods shall become lovers and lamps,
And a compend[71] of compends is the meat of a man or woman,
And a summit and flower there is the feeling they have for each
    other,
And they are to branch boundlessly out of that lesson until it 660
    becomes omnific,[72]
And until one and all shall delight us, and we them.

[71]Compendium, epitome.   [72]All-creating, all-inclusive.

31

I believe a leaf of grass is no less than the journey-work of the stars,
And the pismire[73] is equally perfect, and a grain of sand, and the
  egg of the wren,
And the tree-toad is a chef-d'oeuvre[74] for the highest,
And the running blackberry would adorn the parlors of heaven,
And the narrowest hinge in my hand puts to scorn all machinery,
And the cow crunching with depress'd head surpasses any statue,
And a mouse is miracle enough to stagger sextillions[75] of infidels.

I find I incorporate gneiss,[76] coal, long-threaded moss, fruits, grains,
  esculent roots,   670
And am stucco'd with quadrupeds and birds all over,
And have distanced what is behind me for good reasons,
But call any thing back again when I desire it.

In vain the speeding or shyness,
In vain the plutonic rocks[77] send their old heat against my approach,
In vain the mastodon retreats beneath its own powder'd bones,
In vain objects stand leagues off and assume manifold shapes,
In vain the ocean settling in hollows and the great monsters lying
  low,
In vain the buzzard houses herself with the sky,
In vain the snake slides through the creepers and logs,   680
In vain the elk takes to the inner passes of the woods,
In vain the razor-bill'd auk sails far north to Labrador,
I follow quickly, I ascend to the nest in the fissure of the cliff.

32

I think I could turn and live with animals, they are so placid and
  self-contain'd,
I stand and look at them long and long.

They do not sweat and whine about their condition,
They do not lie awake in the dark and weep for their sins,
They do not make me sick discussing their duty to God,
Not one is dissatisfied, not one is demented with the mania of
  owning things,
Not one kneels to another, nor to his kind that lived thousands of
  years ago,   690
Not one is respectable or unhappy over the whole earth.

So they show their relations to me and I accept them,
They bring me tokens of myself, they evince them plainly in their
  possession.

I wonder where they get those tokens,
Did I pass that way huge times ago and negligently drop them?

[73]Ant.   [74]French: masterpiece.   [75]The number 1 followed by twenty-one zeros.
[76]Coarse-grained rock with light and dark mineral layers, found in the United States from New
England to the Rocky Mountains.
[77]Once-molten rock formed deep within the earth.

Myself moving forward then and now and forever,
Gathering and showing more always and with velocity,
Infinite and omnigenous,[78] and the like of these among them,
Not too exclusive toward the reachers of my remembrancers,
Picking out here one that I love, and now go with him on brotherly
    terms. 700

A gigantic beauty of a stallion, fresh and responsive to my caresses,
Head high in the forehead, wide between the ears,
Limbs glossy and supple, tail dusting the ground,
Eyes full of sparkling wickedness, ears finely cut, flexibly moving.

His nostrils dilate as my heels embrace him,
His well-built limbs tremble with pleasure as we race around and
    return.

I but use you a minute, then I resign you, stallion,
Why do I need your paces when I myself out-gallop them?
Even as I stand or sit passing faster than you.

33

Space and Time! now I see it is true, what I guess'd at, 710
What I guess'd when I loaf'd on the grass,
What I guess'd while I lay alone in my bed,
And again as I walk'd the beach under the paling stars of the
    morning.

My ties and ballasts[79] leave me, my elbows rest in sea-gaps,[80]
I skirt sierras, my palms cover continents,
I am afoot with my vision.

By the city's quadrangular houses—in log huts, camping with
    lumbermen,
Along the ruts of the turnpike, along the dry gulch and rivulet bed,
Weeding my onion-patch or hoeing rows of carrots and parsnips,
    crossing savannas,[81] trailing in forests,
Prospecting, gold-digging, girdling the trees of a new purchase, 720
Scorch'd ankle-deep by the hot sand, hauling by boat down the
    shallow river,
Where the panther walks to and fro on a limb overhead, where the
    buck turns furiously at the hunter,
Where the rattlesnake suns his flabby length on a rock, where the
    otter is feeding on fish,
Where the alligator in his tough pimples sleeps by the bayou,
Where the black bear is searching for roots or honey, where the
    beaver pats the mud with his paddle-shaped tail;
Over the growing sugar, over the yellow-flower'd cotton plant, over
    the rice in its low moist field,

[78]Of all kinds.
[79]The ropes and heavy weights that limit the ascent of a passenger balloon.
[80]Inlets, bays.
[81]Flat, tropical grasslands.

Over the sharp-peak'd farm house, with its scallop'd scum and
    slender shoots from the gutters,[82]
Over the western persimmon, over the long-leav'd corn, over the
    delicate blue-flower flax,
Over the white and brown buckwheat, a hummer and buzzer[83] there
    with the rest,
Over the dusky green of the rye as it ripples and shades in the
    breeze;   730
Scaling mountains, pulling myself cautiously up, holding on by low
    scragged[84] limbs,
Walking the path worn in the grass and beat through the leaves of
    the brush,
Where the quail is whistling betwixt the woods and the wheat-lot,
Where the bat flies in the Seventh-month eve, where the great
    goldbug[85] drops through the dark,
Where the brook puts out of the roots of the old tree and flows to
    the meadow,
Where cattle stand and shake away flies with the tremulous
    shuddering of their hides,
Where the cheese-cloth hangs in the kitchen, where andirons
    straddle the hearth-slab, where cobwebs fall in festoons from the
    rafters;
Where trip-hammers crash, where the press is whirling its cylinders,
Wherever the human heart beats with terrible throes under its ribs,
Where the pear-shaped balloon is floating aloft, (floating in it myself
    and looking composedly down,)   740
Where the life-car[86] is drawn on the slip-noose, where the heat
    hatches pale-green eggs in the dented sand,
Where the she-whale swims with her calf and never forsakes it,
Where the steam-ship trails hind-ways its long pennant of smoke,
Where the fin of the shark cuts like a black chip out of the water,
Where the half-burn'd brig[87] is riding on unknown currents,
Where shells grow to her slimy deck, where the dead are corrupting
    below;
Where the dense-starr'd flag is borne at the head of the regiments,
Approaching Manhattan up by the long-stretching island,
Under Niagara, the cataract falling like a veil over my countenance,
Upon a door-step, upon the horse-block[88] of hard wood outside,   750
Upon the race-course, or enjoying picnics or jigs or a good game of
    base-ball,
At he-festivals, with blackguard gibes, ironical license, bull-dances,[89]
    drinking, laughter,
At the cider-mill tasting the sweets of the brown mash, sucking the
    juice through a straw,
At apple-peelings wanting kisses for all the red fruit I find,

---

[82]Pointed roof with sediment washed into patterns by the rain and with grass sprouting from soil
deposited in the roof gutters.
[83]Hummingbird and bee.   [84]Stunted.   [85]A beetle.
[86]Watertight rescue vessel pulled by rope from ship to shore.
[87]Sailing ship.   [88]Mounting step.
[89]Dances where men, lacking female partners, dance with each other.

At musters,[90] beach-parties, friendly bees,[91] huskings, house-raisings;
Where the mocking-bird sounds his delicious gurgles, cackles,
    screams, weeps,
Where the hay-rick stands in the barn-yard, where the dry-stalks are
    scatter'd, where the brood-cow waits in the hovel,
Where the bull advances to do his masculine work, where the stud to
    the mare, where the cock is treading the hen,
Where the heifers browse, where geese nip their food with short
    jerks,
Where sun-down shadows lengthen over the limitless and lonesome
    prairie,   760
Where herds of buffalo make a crawling spread of the square miles
    far and near,
Where the humming-bird shimmers, where the neck of the long-
    lived swan is curving and winding,
Where the laughing-gull scoots by the shore, where she laughs her
    near-human laugh,
Where bee-hives range on a gray bench in the garden half hid by the
    high weeds,
Where band-neck'd partridges roost in a ring on the ground with
    their heads out,
Where burial coaches enter the arch'd gates of a cemetery,
Where winter wolves bark amid wastes of snow and icicled trees,
Where the yellow-crown'd heron comes to the edge of the marsh at
    night and feeds upon small crabs,
Where the splash of swimmers and divers cools the warm noon,
Where the katy-did works her chromatic reed[92] on the walnut-tree
    over the well,   770
Through patches of citrons[93] and cucumbers with silver-wired leaves,
Through the salt-lick or orange glade, or under conical firs,
Through the gymnasium, through the curtain'd saloon, through the
    office or public hall;
Pleas'd with the native and pleas'd with the foreign, pleas'd with the
    new and old,
Pleas'd with the homely woman as well as the handsome,
Pleas'd with the quakeress as she puts off her bonnet and talks
    melodiously,
Pleas'd with the tune of the choir of the whitewash'd church,
Pleas'd with the earnest words of the sweating Methodist preacher,
    impress'd seriously at the camp-meeting;
Looking in at the shop-windows of Broadway the whole forenoon,
    flatting the flesh of my nose on the thick plate glass,
Wandering the same afternoon with my face turn'd up to the clouds,
    or down a lane or along the beach,
My right and left arms round the sides of two friends, and I in the   780
    middle;
Coming home with the silent and dark-cheek'd bush-boy,[94] (behind
    me he rides at the drape,[95] of the day,)

---

[90]Gatherings.   [91]Parties where friends gather to work, like bees.
[92]I.e., sounds colorful harmonies in her throat.
[93]A variety of watermelon.
[94]Wilderness boy.   [95]Close.

Far from the settlements studying the print of animals' feet, or the
   moccasin print,
By the cot in the hospital reaching lemonade to a feverish patient,
Nigh the coffin'd corpse when all is still, examining with a candle;
Voyaging to every port to dicker and adventure,
Hurrying with the modern crowd as eager and fickle as any,
Hot toward one I hate, ready in my madness to knife him,
Solitary at midnight in my back yard, my thoughts gone from me a
   long while,
Walking the old hills of Judæa with the beautiful gentle God by my
   side,   790
Speeding through space, speeding through heaven and the stars,
Speeding amid the seven satellites and the broad ring,[96] and the
   diameter of eighty thousand miles,
Speeding with tail'd meteors, throwing fire-balls like the rest,
Carrying the crescent child[97] that carries its own full mother in its
   belly,
Storming, enjoying, planning, loving, cautioning,
Backing and filling, appearing and disappearing,
I tread day and night such roads.

I visit the orchards of spheres and look at the product,
And look at quintillions[98] ripen'd and look at quintillions green.

I fly those flights of a fluid and swallowing soul,   800
My course runs below the soundings of plummets.

I help myself to material and immaterial,
No guard can shut me off, no law prevent me.

I anchor my ship for a little while only,
My messengers continually cruise away or bring their returns to me.

I go hunting polar furs and the seal, leaping chasms with a pike-
   pointed staff, clinging to topples[99] of brittle and blue.

I ascend to the foretruck,[100]
I take my place late at night in the crow's-nest,
We sail the arctic sea, it is plenty light enough,
Through the clear atmosphere I stretch around on the wonderful
   beauty,   810
The enormous masses of ice pass me and I pass them, the scenery is
   plain in all directions,
The white-topt mountains show in the distance, I fling out my
   fancies toward them,
We are approaching some great battle-field in which we are soon to
   be engaged,

[96]The eight major planets, including Saturn with its minute surrounding particles that appear as
a broad ring.
[97]The bright, crescent portion of a new (full) moon partially lighted by the setting sun.
[98]The number 1 followed by eighteen zeros.
[99]Fallen ice.   [100]Platform on the head of a foremast.

We pass the colossal outposts of the encampment, we pass with still
    feet and caution,
Or we are entering by the suburbs some vast and ruin'd city,
The blocks and fallen architecture more than all the living cities of
    the globe.

I am a free companion, I bivouac by invading watchfires,
I turn the bridegroom out of bed and stay with the bride myself,
I tighten her all night to my thighs and lips.

My voice is the wife's voice, the screech by the rail of the stairs,   820
They fetch my man's body up dripping and drown'd.

I understand the large hearts of heroes,
The courage of present times and all times,
How the skipper saw the crowded and rudderless wreck of the
    steam-ship, and Death chasing it up and down the storm,
How he knuckled tight and gave not back an inch, and was faithful
    of days and faithful of nights,
And chalk'd in large letters on a board, *Be of good cheer, we will not
    desert you;*
How he follow'd with them and tack'd with them three days and
    would not give it up,
How he saved the drifting company at last,
How the lank loose-gown'd women look'd when boated from the side
    of their prepared graves,
How the silent old-faced infants and the lifted sick, and the sharp-
    lipp'd unshaved men;   830
All this I swallow, it tastes good, I like it well, it becomes mine,
I am the man, I suffer'd, I was there.[101]

The disdain and calmness of martyrs,
The mother of old, condemn'd for a witch, burnt with dry wood, her
    children gazing on,
The hounded slave that flags in the race, leans by the fence, blowing,
    cover'd with sweat,
The twinges that sting like needles his legs and neck, the murderous
    buckshot and the bullets,
All these I feel or am.

I am the hounded slave, I wince at the bite of the dogs,
Hell and despair are upon me, crack and again crack the marksmen,
I clutch the rails of the fence, my gore dribs,[102] thinn'd with the ooze
    of my skin,   840
I fall on the weeds and stones,
The riders spur their unwilling horses, haul close,
Taunt my dizzy ears and beat me violently over the head with whip-
    stocks.

[101]The shipwreck episode is based on an actual sea disaster reported in newspapers in January
1854.   [102]Drips.

Agonies are one of my changes of garments,
I do not ask the wounded person how he feels, I myself become the
   wounded person,
My hurts turn livid upon me as I lean on a cane and observe,

I am the mash'd fireman with breast-bone broken,
Tumbling walls buried me in their debris,
Heat and smoke I inspired,[103] I heard the yelling shouts of my
   comrades,
I heard the distant click of their picks and shovels,   850
They have clear'd the beams away, they tenderly lift me forth.

I lie in the night air in my red shirt, the pervading hush is for my
   sake,
Painless after all I lie exhausted but not so unhappy,
White and beautiful are the faces around me, the heads are bared of
   their fire-caps,
The kneeling crowd fades with the light of the torches.

Distant and dead resuscitate,
They show as the dial or move as the hands of me, I am the clock
   myself.

I am an old artillerist, I tell of my fort's bombardment,
I am there again.

Again the long roll of the drummers,   860
Again the attacking cannon, mortars,
Again to my listening ears the cannon responsive.

I take part, I see and hear the whole,
The cries, curses, roar, the plaudits for well-aim'd shots,
The ambulanza[104] slowly passing trailing its red drip,
Workmen searching after damages, making indispensable repairs,
The fall of grenades through the rent roof, the fan-shaped
   explosion,
The whizz of limbs, heads, stone, wood, iron, high in the air.

Again gurgles the mouth of my dying general, he furiously waves
   with his hand,
He gasps through the clot *Mind not me—mind—the entrenchments.*   870

34

Now I tell what I knew in Texas in my early youth,[105]
(I tell not the fall of Alamo,
Not one escaped to tell the fall of Alamo,
The hundred and fifty are dumb yet at Alamo,)
'Tis the tale of the murder in cold blood of four hundred and twelve
   young men.

[103]Inhaled.   [104]Military ambulance.
[105]Whitman was never in Texas. The episode described below was drawn from reports of a massacre
of Texans by Mexicans in the Revolution of 1836.

Retreating they had form'd in a hollow square with their baggage for
    breastworks,
Nine hundred lives out of the surrounding enemy's, nine times their
    number, was the price they took in advance,
Their colonel was wounded and their ammunition gone,
They treated for an honorable capitulation, receiv'd writing and seal,
    gave up their arms and march'd back prisoners of war.
They were the glory of the race of rangers,   880
Matchless with horse, rifle, song, supper, courtship,
Large, turbulent, generous, handsome, proud, and affectionate,
Bearded, sunburnt, drest in the free costume of hunters,
Not a single one over thirty years of age.

The second First-day morning they were brought out in squads and
    massacred, it was beautiful early summer,
The work commenced about five o'clock and was over by eight.

None obey'd the command to kneel,
Some made a mad and helpless rush, some stood stark and straight,
A few fell at once, shot in the temple or heart, the living and dead
    lay together,
The maim'd and mangled dug in the dirt, the new-comers saw them
    there,
Some half-kill'd attempted to crawl away,   890
These were despatch'd with bayonets or batter'd with blunts of
    muskets,
A youth not seventeen years old seiz'd his assassin till two more came
    to release him,
The three were all torn and cover'd with the boy's blood.

At eleven o'clock began the burning of the bodies;
That is the tale of the murder of the four hundred and twelve
    young men.

35
Would you hear of an old-time sea-fight?
Would you learn who won by the light of the moon and stars?
List to the yarn,[106] as my grandmother's father the sailor told it to
    me.

Our foe was no skulk in his ship I tell you, (said he,)   900
His was the surly English pluck, and there is no tougher or truer,
    and never was, and never will be;
Along the lower'd eve he came horribly raking[107] us.

We closed with him, the yards entangled, the cannon touch'd,
My captain lash'd fast[108] with his own hands.

[106]Whitman's description is based on a letter from John Paul Jones to Benjamin Franklin (September
1779) telling of the sea battle (1779) between the British ship *Serapis* and the American ship *Bonhomme
Richard* commanded by John Paul Jones, whose words "I have not yet begun to fight" are paraphrased
below.

[107]Sweeping the length of the ship with gunfire.

[108]Jones reported that he "made both ships fast" when they came together.

We had receiv'd some eighteen pound shots under the water,
On our lower-gun-deck two large pieces had burst at the first fire,
   killing all around and blowing up overhead.

Fighting at sun-down, fighting at dark,
Ten o'clock at night, the full moon well up, our leaks on the gain,
   and five feet of water reported,[109]
The master-at-arms loosing the prisoners confined in the after-hold
   to give them a chance for themselves.

The transit to and from the magazine[110] is now stopt by the
   sentinels,   910
They see so many strange faces they do not know whom to trust.

Our frigate takes fire,
The other asks if we demand quarter?[111]
If our colors are struck[112] and the fighting done?

Now I laugh content, for I hear the voice of my little captain,
We have not struck, he composedly cries, *we have just begun our part of
   the fighting.*

Only three guns are in use,
One is directed by the captain himself against the enemy's mainmast,
Two well serv'd with grape and canister[113] silence his musketry and
   clear his decks.

The tops[114] alone second the fire of this little battery, especially the
   main-top,   920
They hold out bravely during the whole of the action.

Not a moment's cease,
The leaks gain fast on the pumps, the fire eats toward the powder-
   magazine.

One of the pumps has been shot away, it is generally thought we are
   sinking.

Serene stands the little captain,
He is not hurried, his voice is neither high nor low,
His eyes give more light to us than our battle-lanterns.

Toward twelve there in the beams of the moon they surrender to us.

36

Stretch'd and still lies the midnight,
Two great hulls motionless on the breast of the darkness,   930

---

[109]Jones reported that during the battle, the destructive fire from the British *Serapis* caused the
Bonhomme Richard to take "five feet of water in the hold."
  [110]Gunpowder storage room.   [111]Ask for clemency.
  [112]During the battle, the flag of the *Bonhomme Richard* was shot away, causing the British to think
the flag had been lowered as a sign of surrender.
  [113]Charges of large (grape) or small (canister) iron balls.
  [114]The platforms on the mastheads from which sharpshooters fired onto the enemy's deck below.

Our vessel riddled and slowly sinking, preparations to pass to the
   one we have conquer'd,
The captain on the quarter-deck coldly giving his orders through a
   countenance white as a sheet,
Near by the corpse of the child that serv'd in the cabin,
The dead face of an old salt with long white hair and carefully curl'd
   whiskers,
The flames spite of all that can be done flickering aloft and below,
The husky voices of the two or three officers yet fit for duty,
Formless stacks of bodies and bodies by themselves, dabs of flesh
   upon the masts and spars,
Cut of cordage, dangle of rigging, slight shock of the soothe of
   waves,
Black and impassive guns, litter of powder-parcels, strong scent,
A few large stars overhead, silent and mournful shining,   940
Delicate sniffs of sea-breeze, smells of sedgy grass and fields by the
   shore, death-messages given in charge to survivors,
The hiss of the surgeon's knife, the gnawing teeth of his saw,
Wheeze, cluck, swash of falling blood, short wild scream, and long,
   dull, tapering groan,
These so, these irretrievable.

37

You laggards there on guard! look to your arms!
In at the conquer'd doors they crowd! I am possess'd!
Embody all presences outlaw'd or suffering,
See myself in prison shaped like another man,
And feel the dull unintermitted pain.

For me the keepers of convicts shoulder their carbines and keep
   watch,   950
It is I let out in the morning and barr'd at night.

Not a mutineer walks handcuff'd to jail but I am handcuff'd to him
   and walk by his side,
(I am less the jolly one there, and more the silent one with sweat on
   my twitching lips.)

Not a youngster is taken for larceny but I go up too, and am tried
   and sentenced.

Not a cholera patient lies at the last gasp but I also lie at the last
   gasp,
My face is ash-color'd, my sinews gnarl, away from me people
   retreat.

Askers embody themselves in me and I am embodied in them,
I project[115] my hat, sit shame-faced, and beg.

38

Enough! enough! enough!
Somehow I have been stunn'd. Stand back!   960

[115]Hold forth.

Give me a little time beyond my cuff'd head, slumbers, dreams,
     gaping.
I discover myself on the verge of a usual mistake.

That I could forget the mockers and insults!
That I could forget the trickling tears and the blows of the
     bludgeons and hammers!
That I could look with a separate look on my own crucifixion and
     bloody crowning.

I remember now,
I resume the overstaid fraction,
The grave of rock multiplies what has been confided to it, or to any
     graves,
Corpses rise, gashes heal, fastenings roll from me.

I troop forth replenish'd with supreme power, one of an average
     unending procession,   970
Inland and sea-coast we go, and pass all boundary lines,
Our swift ordinances on their way over the whole earth,
The blossoms we wear in our hats the growth of thousands of years.

Eleves,[116] I salute you! come forward!
Continue your annotations, continue your questionings.

39
The friendly and flowing savage, who is he?
Is he waiting for civilization, or past it and mastering it?

Is he some Southwesterner rais'd out-doors? is he Kanadian?
Is he from the Mississippi country? Iowa, Oregon, California?
The mountains? prairie-life, bush-life? or sailor from the sea?   980

Wherever he goes men and women accept and desire him,
They desire he should like them, touch them, speak to them, stay
     with them.

Behavior lawless as snow-flakes, words simple as grass, uncomb'd
     head, laughter, and naiveté,
Slow-stepping feet, common features, common modes and
     emanations,
They descend in new forms from the tips of his fingers,
They are wafted with the odor of his body or breath, they fly out of
     the glance of his eyes.

40
Flaunt of the sunshine I need not your bask—lie over!
You light surfaces only, I force surfaces and depths also.

Earth! you seem to look for something at my hands,
Say, old top-knot,[117] what do you want?   990

[116]French: students.   [117]Indian, from the tuft of hair used to ornament the head.

Man or woman, I might tell how I like you, but cannot,
And might tell what it is in me and what it is in you, but cannot,
And might tell that pining I have, that pulse of my nights and days.

Behold, I do not give lectures or a little charity,
When I give I give myself.

You there, impotent, loose in the knees,
Open your scarf'd chops[118] till I blow grit[119] within you,
Spread your palms and lift the flaps of your pockets,
I am not to be denied, I compel, I have stores plenty and to spare,
And any thing I have I bestow.   1000

I do not ask who you are, that is not important to me,
You can do nothing and be nothing but what I will infold you.

To cotton-field drudge or cleaner of privies I lean,
On his right cheek I put the family kiss,
And in my soul I swear I never will deny him.

On women fit for conception I start bigger and nimbler babes,
(This day I am jetting the stuff of far more arrogant republics.)

To any one dying, thither I speed and twist the knob of the door,
Turn the bed-clothes toward the foot of the bed,
Let the physician and the priest go home.   1010

I seize the descending man and raise him with resistless will,
O despairer, here is my neck,
By God, you shall not go down! hang your whole weight upon me.

I dilate[120] you with tremendous breath, I buoy you up,
Every room of the house do I fill with an arm'd force,
Lovers of me, bafflers of graves.

Sleep—I and they keep guard all night,
Not doubt, not decease shall dare to lay finger upon you,
I have embraced you, and henceforth possess you to myself,
And when you rise in the morning you will find what I tell you is so.   1020

41

I am he bringing help for the sick as they pant on their backs,
And for strong upright men I bring yet more needed help.

I heard what was said of the universe,
Heard it and heard it of several thousand years;
It is middling well as far as it goes—but is that all?

[118]Lined and wrinkled cheeks, jaws.   [119]Strength of spirit, courage.
[120]Inflate, expand.

Magnifying and applying come I,
Outbidding at the start the old cautious hucksters,[121]
Taking myself the exact dimensions of Jehovah,
Lithographing Kronos, Zeus his son, and Hercules his grandson,
Buying drafts of Osiris, Isis, Belus, Brahma, Buddha,   1030
In my portfolio placing Manito loose, Allah on a leaf, the crucifix
    engraved,
With Odin and the hideous-faced Mexitli[122] and every idol and
    image,
Taking them all for what they are worth and not a cent more,
Admitting they were alive and did the work of their days,
(They bore mites as for unfledg'd birds who have now to rise and fly
    and sing for themselves,)
Accepting the rough deific[123] sketches to fill out better in myself,
    bestowing them freely on each man and woman I see,
Discovering as much or more in a framer framing a house,
Putting higher claims for him there with his roll'd-up sleeves driving
    the mallet and chisel,
Not objecting to special revelations, considering a curl of smoke or a
    hair on the back of my hand just as curious as any revelation,
Lads ahold of fire-engines and hook-and-ladder ropes no less to me
    than the gods of the antique wars,   1040
Minding their voices peal through the crash of destruction,
Their brawny limbs passing safe over charr'd laths, their white
    foreheads whole and unhurt out of the flames;
By the mechanic's wife with her babe at her nipple interceding for
    every person born,
Three scythes at harvest whizzing in a row from three lusty angels
    with shirts bagg'd out at their waists,
The snag-tooth'd hostler[124] with red hair redeeming sins past and to
    come,
Selling all he possesses, traveling on foot to fee lawyers for his
    brother and sit by him while he is tried for forgery;
What was strewn in the amplest strewing the square rod about me,
    and not filling the square rod then,
The bull and the bug never worshipp'd half enough,
Dung and dirt more admirable than was dream'd,
The supernatural of no account, myself waiting my time to be one of
    the supremes,   1050
The day getting ready for me when I shall do as much good as the
    best, and be as prodigious;
By my life-lumps![125] becoming already a creator,
Putting myself here and now to the ambush'd womb of the shadows.

42

A call in the midst of the crowd,
My own voice, orotund sweeping and final.

[121]Peddlers.
[122]Whitman's list of gods includes those from Greek, Egyptian, Babylonian, and Norse mythology
and from Judaism, Christianity, Hinduism, Buddhism, and Islam. Manito was a nature god of the
Algonquian Indians; Mexitli, an Aztec god of war.
[123]Divine.   [124]Stableman.   [125]Testicles.

Come my children,
Come my boys and girls, my women, household and intimates,
Now the performer launches his nerve, he has pass'd his prelude on
the reeds within.

Easily written loose-finger'd chords—I feel the thrum of your climax
and close.

My head slues round on my neck,   1060
Music rolls, but not from the organ,
Folks are around me, but they are no household of mine.

Ever the hard unsunk ground,
Ever the eaters and drinkers, ever the upward and downward sun,
ever the air and the ceaseless tides,
Ever myself and my neighbors, refreshing, wicked, real,
Ever the old inexplicable query, ever that thorn'd thumb, that breath
of itches and thirsts,
Ever the vexer's *hoot! hoot!* till we find where the sly one hides and
bring him forth,
Ever love, ever the sobbing liquid of life,
Ever the bandage under the chin, ever the trestles[126] of death.

Here and there with dimes on the eyes[127] walking,   1070
To feed the greed of the belly the brains liberally spooning,
Tickets buying, taking, selling, but in to the feast never once going,
Many sweating, ploughing, thrashing, and then the chaff for
payment receiving,
A few idly owning, and they the wheat continually claiming.

This is the city and I am one of the citizens,
Whatever interests the rest interests me, politics, wars, markets,
newspapers, schools,
The mayor and councils, banks, tariffs, steamships, factories, stocks,
stores, real estate and personal estate.

The little plentiful manikins skipping around in collars and tail'd
coats,
I am aware who they are, (they are positively not worms or fleas,)
I acknowledge the duplicates of myself, the weakest and shallowest is
deathless with me,   1080
What I do and say the same waits for them,
Every thought that flounders in me the same flounders in them.

I know perfectly well my own egotism,
Know my omnivorous lines and must not write any less,
And would fetch you whoever you are flush with myself.

[126]Supports for coffins.
[127]Whitman refers both to the dead (whose eyelids are held shut by coins) and to the greedy.

Not words of routine this song of mine,
But abruptly to question, to leap beyond yet nearer bring;
This printed and bound book—but the printer and the printing-
    office boy?

The well-taken photographs—but your wife or friend close and solid
    in your arms?
The black ship mail'd with iron, her mighty guns in her turrets—but
    the pluck of the captain and engineers?   1090
In the houses the dishes and fare and furniture—but the host and
    hostess, and the look out of their eyes?
The sky up there—yet here or next door, or across the way?
The saints and sages in history—but you yourself?
Sermons, creeds, theology—but the fathomless human brain,
And what is reason? and what is love? and what is life?

43

I do not despise you priests, all time, the world over,
My faith is the greatest of faiths and the least of faiths,
Enclosing worship ancient and modern and all between ancient and
    modern,
Believing I shall come again upon the earth after five thousand
    years,
Waiting responses from oracles, honoring the gods, saluting the sun,   1100
Making a fetich[128] of the first rock or stump, powowing with sticks in
    the circle of obis,[129]
Helping the llama[130] or brahmin as he trims the lamps of the idols,
Dancing yet through the streets in a phallic procession, rapt and
    austere in the woods a gymnosophist,[131]
Drinking mead from the skull-cup, to Shastas and Vedas[132]
    admirant,[133] minding the Koran,
Walking the teokallis,[134] spotted with gore from the stone and knife,
    beating the serpent-skin drum,
Accepting the Gospels, accepting him that was crucified, knowing
    assuredly that he is divine,
To the mass kneeling or the puritan's prayer rising, or sitting
    patiently in a pew,
Ranting and frothing in my insane crisis, or waiting dead-like till my
    spirit arouses me,
Looking forth on pavement and land, or outside of pavement and
    land,
Belonging to the winders of the circuit of circuits.   1110

One of that centripetal and centrifugal gang I turn and talk like a
    man leaving charges before a journey.

Down-hearted doubters dull and excluded,
Frivolous, sullen, moping, angry, affected, dishearten'd, atheistical,
I know every one of you, I know the sea of torment, doubt, despair
    and unbelief.

---

[128]Fetish, an object of worship.   [129]Magic charms.
[130]Lama, a Tibetan high priest.   [131]A Hindu ascetic.
[132]Hindu religious writings.   [133]French: admiring.
[134]Aztec temple with sacrificial altar.

How the flukes[135] splash!
How they contort rapid as lightning, with spasms and spouts of
    blood!

Be at peace bloody flukes of doubters and sullen mopers,
I take my place among you as much as among any,
The past is the push of you, me, all, precisely the same,
And what is yet untried and afterward is for you, me, all, precisely
    the same.
        1120

I do not know what is untried and afterward,
But I know it will in its turn prove sufficient, and cannot fail.

Each who passes is consider'd, each who stops is consider'd, not a
    single one can it fail.

It cannot fail the young man who died and was buried,
Nor the young woman who died and was put by his side,
Nor the little child that peep'd in at the door, and then drew back
    and was never seen again,
Nor the old man who has lived without purpose, and feels it with
    bitterness worse than gall,
Nor him in the poor house tubercled by rum and the bad
    disorder,[136]
Nor the numberless slaughter'd and wreck'd, nor the brutish
    koboo[137] call'd the ordure[138] of humanity,
Nor the sacs merely floating with open mouths for food to slip in,   1130
Nor any thing in the earth, or down in the oldest graves of the
    earth,
Nor any thing in the myriads of spheres, nor the myriads of myriads
    that inhabit them,
Nor the present, nor the least wisp that is known.

44

It is time to explain myself—let us stand up.

What is known I strip away,
I launch all men and women forward with me into the Unknown.

The clock indicates the moment—but what does eternity indicate?

We have thus far exhausted trillions of winters and summers,
There are trillions ahead, and trillions ahead of them.

Births have brought us richness and variety,   1140
And other births will bring us richness and variety.

I do not call one greater and one smaller,
That which fills its period and place is equal to any.

---

[135]The tail of a whale.   [136]Syphilis.
[137]Primitive native of Sumatra.   [138]Filth, excrement.

Were mankind murderous or jealous upon you, my brother, my
    sister?
I am sorry for you, they are not murderous or jealous upon me,
All has been gentle with me, I keep no account with lamentation,
(What have I to do with lamentation?)

I am an acme of things accomplish'd, and I am encloser of things to
    be.

My feet strike an apex of the apices[139] of the stairs,
On every step bunches of ages, and larger bunches between the
    steps,   1150
All below duly travel'd, and still I mount and mount.

Rise after rise bow the phantoms behind me,
Afar down I see the huge first Nothing, I know I was even there,
I waited unseen and always, and slept through the lethargic mist,
And took my time, and took no hurt from the fetid carbon.

Long I was hugg'd close—long and long.

Immense have been the preparations for me,
Faithful and friendly the arms that have help'd me.

Cycles ferried my cradle, rowing and rowing like cheerful boatmen,
For room to me stars kept aside in their own rings,   1160
They sent influences to look after what was to hold me.

Before I was born out of my mother generations guided me,
My embryo has never been torpid, nothing could overlay it.

For it the nebula cohered to an orb,
The long slow strata piled to rest it on,
Vast vegetables gave it sustenance,
Monstrous sauroids[140] transported it in their mouths and deposited it
    with care.

All forces have been steadily employ'd to complete and delight me,
Now on this spot I stand with my robust soul.

45

O span of youth! ever-push'd elasticity!   1170
O manhood, balanced, florid and full.

My lovers suffocate me,
Crowding my lips, thick in the pores of my skin,
Jostling me through streets and public halls, coming naked to me at
    night,
Crying by day *Ahoy!* from the rocks of the river, swinging and
    chirping over my head,

---

[139]Plural of "apex," the highest point.   [140]Prehistoric reptiles.

Calling my name from flower-beds, vines, tangled underbrush,
Lighting on every moment of my life,
Bussing[141] my body with soft balsamic[142] busses,
Noiselessly passing handfuls out of their hearts and giving them to
   be mine.

Old age superbly rising! O welcome, ineffable grace of dying days!   1180

Every condition promulges[143] not only itself, it promulges what
   grows after and out of itself,
And the dark hush promulges as much as any.

I open my scuttle[144] at night and see the far-sprinkled systems,
And all I see multiplied as high as I can cipher edge but the rim of
   the farther systems.

Wider and wider they spread, expanding always expanding,
Outward and outward and forever outward.

My sun has his sun and round him obediently wheels,
He joins with his partners a group of superior circuit,
And greater sets follow, making specks of the greatest inside them.

There is no stoppage and never can be stoppage,   1190
If I, you, and the worlds, and all beneath or upon their surfaces,
   were this moment reduced back to a pallid float,[145] it would not
   avail in the long run,
We should surely bring up again where we now stand,
And surely go as much farther, and then farther and farther.

A few quadrillions of eras, a few octillions[146] of cubic leagues, do not
   hazard the span or make it impatient,
They are but parts, any thing is but a part.

See ever so far, there is limitless space outside of that,
Count ever so much, there is limitless time around that.

My rendezvous is appointed, it is certain,
The Lord will be there and wait till I come on perfect terms,
The great Camerado,[147] the lover true for whom I pine will be there.   1200

46

I know I have the best time and space, and was never measured and
   never will be measured.

I tramp a perpetual journey, (come listen all!)
My signs are a rain-proof coat, good shoes, and a staff cut from the
   woods,

---

[141]Kissing.   [142]Fragrant with the aroma of balsam.
[143]Generates.   [144]An opening in a house roof.
[145]I.e., returned to a primordial state where all life is suspended as particles in water.
[146]The number 1 followed by twenty-seven zeros.   [147]Comrade.

No friend of mine takes his ease in my chair,
I have no chair, no church, no philosophy,
I lead no man to a dinner-table, library, exchange,[148]
But each man and each woman of you I lead upon a knoll,
My left hand hooking you round the waist,
My right hand pointing to landscapes of continents and the public
   road.

Not I, not any one else can travel that road for you,   1210
You must travel it for yourself.

It is not far, it is within reach,
Perhaps you have been on it since you were born and did not know,
Perhaps it is everywhere on water and on land.

Shoulder your duds dear son, and I will mine, and let us hasten
   forth,
Wonderful cities and free nations we shall fetch[149] as we go.

If you tire, give me both burdens, and rest the chuff[150] of your hand
   on my hip,
And in due time you shall repay the same service to me,
For after we start we never lie by again.

This day before dawn I ascended a hill and look'd at the crowded
   heaven.   1220
And I said to my spirit *When we become the enfolders of those orbs, and
   the pleasure and knowledge of every thing in them, shall we be fill'd and
   satisfied then?*
And my spirit said, *No, we but level that lift[151] to pass and continue
   beyond.*

You are also asking me questions and I hear you,
I answer that I cannot answer, you must find out for yourself.

Sit a while dear son,
Here are biscuits to eat and here is milk to drink,
But as soon as you sleep and renew yourself in sweet clothes, I kiss
   you with a good-by kiss and open the gate for your egress[152]
   hence.

Long enough have you dream'd contemptible dreams,
Now I wash the gum from your eyes,
You must habit yourself to the dazzle of the light and of every
   moment of your life.   1230

Long have you timidly waded holding a plank by the shore,
Now I will you to be a bold swimmer,
To jump off in the midst of the sea, rise again, nod to me, shout,
   and laughingly dash with your hair.

---

[148]Stock exchange.   [149]Reach.   [150]Heel.
[151]Rising ground.   [152]Exit.

47

I am the teacher of athletes,
He that by me spreads a wider breast than my own proves the width
    of my own,
He most honors my style who learns under it to destroy the teacher.

The boy I love, the same becomes a man, not through derived
    power, but in his own right,
Wicked rather than virtuous out of conformity or fear,
Fond of his sweetheart, relishing well his steak,
Unrequited love or a slight cutting him worse than sharp steel cuts,   1240
First-rate to ride, to fight, to hit the bull's eye, to sail a skiff, to sing a
    song or play on the banjo,
Preferring scars and the beard and faces pitted with small-pox over
    all latherers,
And those well-tann'd to those that keep out of the sun.

I teach straying from me, yet who can stray from me?
I follow you whoever you are from the present hour,
My words itch at your ears till you understand them.

I do not say these things for a dollar or to fill up the time while I
    wait for a boat,
(It is you talking just as much as myself, I act as the tongue of you,
Tied in your mouth, in mine it begins to be loosen'd.)

I swear I will never again mention love or death inside a house,   1250
And I swear I will never translate myself at all, only to him or her
    who privately stays with me in the open air.

If you would understand me go to the heights or water-shore,
The nearest gnat is an explanation, and a drop or motion of waves a
    key,
The maul, the oar, the hand-saw, second my words.

No shutter'd room or school can commune with me,
But roughs and little children better than they.

The young mechanic is closest to me, he knows me well,
The woodman that takes his axe and jug with him shall take me with
    him all day,
The farm-boy ploughing in the field feels good at the sound of my
    voice,
In vessels that sail my words sail, I go with fishermen and seamen
    and love them.   1260

The soldier camp'd or upon the march is mine,
On the night ere the pending battle many seek me, and I do not fail
    them,
On that solemn night (it may be their last) those that know me seek
    me.

My face rubs to the hunter's face when he lies down alone in his
  blanket,
The driver thinking of me does not mind the jolt of his wagon,
The young mother and old mother comprehend me,
The girl and the wife rest the needle a moment and forget where
  they are,
They and all would resume what I have told them.

48

I have said that the soul is not more than the body,
And I have said that the body is not more than the soul,   1270
And nothing, not God, is greater to one than one's self is,
And whoever walks a furlong without sympathy walks to his own
  funeral drest in his shroud,
And I or you pocketless of a dime may purchase the pick of the
  earth,
And to glance with an eye or show a bean in its pod confounds the
  learning of all times,
And there is no trade or employment but the young man following it
  may become a hero,
And there is no object so soft but it makes a hub for the wheel'd
  universe,
And I say to any man or woman, Let your soul stand cool and
  composed before a million universes.

And I say to mankind, Be not curious about God,
For I who am curious about each am not curious about God,
(No array of terms can say how much I am at peace about God and
  about death.)   1280

I hear and behold God in every object, yet understand God not in
  the least,
Nor do I understand who there can be more wonderful than myself.

Why should I wish to see God better than this day?
I see something of God each hour of the twenty-four, and each
  moment then,
In the faces of men and women I see God, and in my own face in
  the glass,
I find letters from God dropt in the street, and every one is sign'd by
  God's name.
And I leave them where they are, for I know that wheresoe'er I go,
Others will punctually come for ever and ever.

49

And as to you Death, and you bitter hug of mortality, it is idle to try
  to alarm me.

To his work without flinching the accoucheur[153] comes,   1290
I see the elder-hand[154] pressing receiving supporting,
I recline by the sills of the exquisite flexible doors,
And mark the outlet, and mark the relief and escape.

[153]Midwife, obstetrician.   [154]Left hand.

And as to you Corpse I think you are good manure, but that does
    not offend me,
I smell the white roses sweet-scented and growing,
I reach to the leafy lips, I reach to the polish'd breasts of melons.

And as to you Life I reckon you are the leavings of many deaths,
(No doubt I have died myself ten thousand times before.)

I hear you whispering there O stars of heaven,
O suns—O grass of graves—O perpetual transfers and promotions,   1300
If you do not say any thing how can I say any thing?

Of the turbid pool that lies in the autumn forest,
Of the moon that descends the steeps of the soughing[155] twilight,
Toss, sparkles of day and dusk—toss on the black stems that decay in
    the muck,
Toss to the moaning gibberish of the dry limbs.

I ascend from the moon, I ascend from the night,
I perceive that the ghastly glimmer is noonday sunbeams reflected,
And debouch[156] to the steady and central from the offspring great
    or small.

50
There is that in me—I do not know what it is—but I know it is in
    me.

Wrench'd and sweaty—calm and cool then my body becomes,   1310
I sleep—I sleep long.

I do not know it—it is without name—it is a word unsaid,
It is not in any dictionary, utterance, symbol.

Something it swings on more than the earth I swing on,
To it the creation is the friend whose embracing awakes me.

Perhaps I might tell more. Outlines! I plead for my brothers and
    sisters.

Do you see O my brothers and sisters?
It is not chaos or death—it is form, union, plan—it is eternal life—it
    is Happiness.

51
The past and present wilt—I have fill'd them, emptied them,
And proceed to fill my next fold of the future.   1320

Listener up there! what have you to confide to me?
Look in my face while I snuff[157] the sidle[158] of evening,
(Talk honestly, no one else hears you, and I stay only a minute
    longer.)

[155]Sighing, moaning.   [156]Emerge.
[157]Extinguish.   [158]Fading light.

Do I contradict myself?
Very well then I contradict myself,
(I am large, I contain multitudes.)

I concentrate toward them that are nigh, I wait on the door-slab.

Who has done his day's work? who will soonest be through with his
    supper?
Who wishes to walk with me?

Will you speak before I am gone? will you prove already too late?   1330

52
The spotted hawk swoops by and accuses me, he complains of my
    gab and my loitering.

I too am not a bit tamed, I too am untranslatable,
I sound my barbaric yawp[159] over the roofs of the world.

The last scud[160] of day holds back for me,
It flings my likeness after the rest and true as any on the shadow'd
    wilds,
It coaxes me to the vapor and the dusk.
I depart as air, I shake my white locks at the runaway sun,
I effuse[161] my flesh in eddies, and drift it in lacy jags.

I bequeath myself to the dirt to grow from the grass I love,
If you want me again look for me under your boot-soles.   1340

You will hardly know who I am or what I mean,
But I shall be good health to you nevertheless,
And filter and fibre your blood.

Failing to fetch me at first keep encouraged,
Missing me one place search another,
I stop somewhere waiting for you.

                                                              1855, 1881

from *CHILDREN OF ADAM*

FROM PENT-UP ACHING RIVERS

From pent-up aching rivers,
From that of myself without which I were nothing,
From what I am determin'd to make illustrious, even if I stand sole
    among men,
From my own voice resonant, singing the phallus,

---

[159]Loud cry, yell.   [160]Wind-driven clouds or mist.   [161]Pour out.

Singing the song of procreation,
Singing the need of superb children and therein superb grown
     people,
Singing the muscular urge and the blending,
Singing the bedfellow's song, (O resistless yearning!
O for any and each the body correlative attracting!
O for you whoever you are your correlative body! O it, more than all
     else, you delighting!)
From the hungry gnaw that eats me night and day,
From native moments, from bashful pains, singing them,   10
Seeking something yet unfound though I have diligently sought it
     many a long year,
Singing the true song of the soul fitful at random,
Renascent with grossest Nature or among animals,
Of that, of them and what goes with them my poems informing,
Of the smell of apples and lemons, of the pairing of birds,
Of the wet of woods, of the lapping of waves,
Of the mad pushes of waves upon the land, I them chanting,
The overture lightly sounding, the strain anticipating,
The welcome nearness, the sight of the perfect body,   20
The swimmer swimming naked in the bath, or motionless on his
     back lying and floating,
The female form approaching, I pensive, love-flesh tremulous
     aching,
The divine lust for myself or you or for any one making,
The face, the limbs, the index from head to foot, and what it
     arouses,
The mystic deliria, the madness amorous, the utter abandonment,
(Hark close and still what I now whisper to you,
I love you, O you entirely possess me,
O that you and I escape from the rest and go utterly off, free and
     lawless,
Two hawks in the air, two fishes swimming in the sea not more
     lawless than we;)
The furious storm through me careering, I passionately trembling,   30
The oath of the inseparableness of two together, of the woman that
     loves me and whom I love more than my life, that oath swearing,
(O I willingly stake all for you,
O let me be lost if it must be so!
O you and I! what is it to us what the rest do or think?
What is all else to us? only that we enjoy each other and exhaust
     each other if it must be so;)
From the master, the pilot I yield the vessel to,
The general commanding me, commanding all, from him permission
     taking,
From time the programme hastening, (I have loiter'd too long as it
     is,)
From sex, from the warp and from the woof,[1]
From privacy, from frequent repinings alone,   40
From plenty of persons near and yet the right person not near,

---

[1]Interwoven vertical and horizontal threads of a fabric.

From the soft sliding of hands over me and thrusting of fingers
    through my hair and beard,
From the long sustain'd kiss upon the mouth or bosom,
From the close pressure that makes me or any man drunk, fainting
    with excess,
From what the divine husband knows, from the work of fatherhood,
From exultation, victory and relief, from the bedfellow's embrace in
    the night,
From the act-poems of eyes, hands, hips and bosoms,
From the cling of the trembling arm,
From the bending curve and the clinch,   50
From side by side the pliant coverlet off-throwing,
From the one so unwilling to have me leave, and me just as unwilling
    to leave,
(Yet a moment O tender waiter, and I return,)
From the hour of shining stars and dropping dews,
From the night a moment I emerging flitting out,
Celebrate you act divine and you children prepared for,
And you stalwart loins.

                                                               1860, 1881

OUT OF THE ROLLING OCEAN THE CROWD

Out of the rolling ocean the crowd came a drop gently to me,
Whispering *I love you, before long I die,*
I have travel'd a long way merely to look on you to touch you,
For I could not die till I once look'd on you,
For I fear'd I might afterward lose you.

Now we have met, we have look'd, we are safe,
Return in peace to the ocean my love,
I too am part of the ocean my love, we are not so much separated,
Behold the great rondure,[1] the cohesion of all, how perfect!
But as for me, for you, the irresistible sea is to separate us,   10
As for an hour carrying us diverse, yet cannot carry us diverse
    forever;
Be not impatient—a little space—know you I salute the air, the ocean
    and the land,
Every day at sundown for your dear sake my love.

                                                               1865, 1881

ONCE I PASS'D THROUGH A POPULOUS CITY

Once I pass'd through a populous city imprinting my brain for
    future use with its shows, architecture, customs, traditions,

[1]Gracefully rounded curve.

Yet now of all that city I remember only a woman I casually met
   there who detain'd me for love of me,
Day by day and night by night we were together—all else has long
   been forgotten by me,
I remember I say only that woman who passionately clung to me,
Again we wander, we love, we separate again,
Again she holds me by the hand, I must not go,
I see her close beside me with silent lips sad and tremulous.

                                    1860, 1867

FACING WEST FROM CALIFORNIA'S SHORES

Facing west from California's shores,
Inquiring, tireless, seeking what is yet unfound,
I, a child, very old, over waves, towards the house of maternity,[1] the
   land of migrations, look afar,
Look off the shores of my Western sea, the circle almost circled;
For starting westward from Hindustan,[2] from the Vales of
   Kashmere,[3]
From Asia, from the north, from the God, the sage, and the hero,
From the south, from the flowery peninsulas and the spice islands,[4]
Long having wander'd since, round the earth having wander'd,
Now I face home again, very pleas'd and joyous,
(But where is what I started for so long ago?   10
And why is it yet unfound?)

                                    1860, 1867

AS ADAM EARLY IN THE MORNING

   As Adam early in the morning,
   Walking forth from the bower refresh'd with sleep,
   Behold me where I pass, hear my voice, approach,
   Touch me, touch the palm of your hand to my body as I pass,
   Be not afraid of my body.

                           1861, 1867

from *CALAMUS*[1]

IN PATHS UNTRODDEN

In paths untrodden,
In the growth of margins of pond-waters,

---

[1]I.e., Asia, thought to be the place of man's origin.
[2]India.   [3]Mountain region of northern India.
[4]The islands of Indonesia.
[1]Whitman wrote that Calamus "is the very large and aromatic grass, or rush, growing about water-ponds . . . spears about three feet high."

Escaped from the life that exhibits itself,
From all the standards hitherto publish'd, from the pleasures,
    profits, conformities,
Which too long I was offering to feed my soul,
Clear to me now standards not yet publish'd, clear to me that my
    soul,
That the soul of the man I speak for rejoices in comrades,
Here by myself away from the clank of the world,
Tallying and talk'd to here by tongues aromatic,
No longer abash'd, (for in this secluded spot I can respond as I
    would not dare elsewhere,)   10
Strong upon me the life that does not exhibit itself, yet contains all
    the rest,
Resolv'd to sing no songs to-day but those of manly attachment,
Projecting them along that substantial life,
Bequeathing hence types of athletic love,
Afternoon this delicious Ninth-month[1] in my forty-first year,
I proceed for all who are or have been young men,
To tell the secret of my nights and days,
To celebrate the need of comrades.

                                                            1860, 1867

SCENTED HERBAGE OF MY BREAST

Scented herbage of my breast,
Leaves from you I glean, I write, to be persued best afterwards,
Tomb-leaves,[1] body-leaves growing up above me above death,
Perennial roots, tall leaves, O the winter shall not freeze you delicate
    leaves,
Every year shall you bloom again, out from where you retired you
    shall emerge again;
Or I do not know whether many passing by will discover you or
    inhale your faint odor, but I believe a few will;
O slender leaves! O blossoms of my blood! I permit you to tell in
    your own way of the heart that is under you,
O I do not know what you mean there underneath yourselves, you
    are not happiness,
You are often more bitter than I can bear, you burn and sting me,
Yet you are beautiful to me you faint tinged roots, you make me
    think of death,   10
Death is beautiful from you, (what indeed is finally beautiful except
    death and love?)
O I think it is not for life I am chanting here my chant of lovers, I
    think it must be for death,
For how calm, how solemn it grows to ascend to the atmosphere of
    lovers,

[1]September.
[1]Probably an allusion derived from a contemporary illustration of an Egyptian mummy from
which were sprouting leaves of grain.

Death or life I am then indifferent, my soul declines to prefer,
(I am not sure but the high soul of lovers welcomes death most,)
Indeed O death, I think now these leaves mean precisely the same as
  you mean,
Grow up taller sweet leaves that I may see! grow up out of my
  breast!
Spring away from the conceal'd heart there!
Do not fold yourself so in your pink-tinged roots timid leaves!
Do not remain down there so ashamed, herbage of my breast!   20
Come I am determin'd to unbare this broad breast of mine, I have
  long enough stifled and choked;
Emblematic and capricious blades I leave you, now you serve me not;
I will say what I have to say by itself,
I will sound myself and comrades only, I will never again utter a call
  only their call,
I will raise with it immortal reverberations through the States,
I will give an example to lovers to take permanent shape and will
  through the States,
Through me shall the words be said to make death exhilirating,
Give me your tone therefore O death, that I may accord with it,
Give me yourself, for I see that you belong to me now above all, and
  are folded inseparably together, you love and death are,
Nor will I allow you to balk me any more with what I was calling life,   30
For now it is convey'd to me that you are the purports essential,
That you hide in these shifting forms of life, for reasons, and that
  they are mainly for you,
That you beyond them come forth to remain, the real reality,
That behind the mask of materials you patiently wait, no matter how
  long,
That you will one day perhaps take control of all,
That you will perhaps dissipate this entire show of appearance,
That may-be you are what it is all for, but it does not last so very
  long,
But you will last very long.

1860, 1881

FOR YOU O DEMOCRACY

Come, I will make the continent indissoluble,
I will make the most splendid race the sun ever shone upon,
I will make divine magnetic lands,
  With the love of comrades,
   With the life-long love of comrades.

I will plant companionship thick as trees along all the rivers of
  America, and along the shores of the great lakes, and all over the
  prairies,
I will make inseparable cities with their arms about each other's
  necks,
  By the love of comrades,
   By the manly love of comrades.

For you these from me, O Democracy, to serve you ma femme![1]   10
For you, for you I am trilling these songs.

1860, 1881

THE BASE OF ALL METAPHYSICS

And now gentlemen,
A word I give to remain in your memories and minds,
As base and finalè too for all metaphysics.

(So to the students the old professor,
At the close of his crowded course.)

Having studied the new and antique, the Greek and Germanic
    systems,
Kant having studied and stated, Fichte and Schelling and Hegel,[1]
Stated the lore of Plato, and Socrates greater than Plato,
And greater than Socrates sought and stated, Christ divine having
    studied long,
I see reminiscent to-day those Greek and Germanic systems,
See the philosophies all, Christian churches and tenets see,
Yet underneath Socrates clearly see, and underneath Christ the
    divine I see,
The dear love of man for his comrade, the attraction of friend to
    friend,
Of the well-married husband and wife, of children and parents,
Of city for city and land for land.

1871, 1871

RECORDERS AGES HENCE

Recorders ages hence,
Come, I will take you down underneath this impassive exterior, I will
    tell you what to say of me,
Publish my name and hang up my picture as that of the tenderest
    lover,
The friend the lover's portrait, of whom his friend his lover was
    fondest,
Who was not proud of his songs, but of the measureless ocean of
    love within him, and freely pour'd it forth,
Who often walk'd lonesome walks thinking of his dear friends, his
    lovers,

[1]French: my woman.
[1]Immanuel Kant (1724–1804), Johann Fichte (1762–1814), Friedrich Schelling (1775–1854),
Georg Wilhelm Hegel (1730–1831), German philosophers whose speculations were metaphysical,
based on philosophy and pure reasoning rather than scientific experiment.

Who pensive away from one he lov'd often lay sleepless and
   dissatisfied at night,
Who knew too well the sick, sick dread lest the one he lov'd might
   secretly be indifferent to him,
Whose happiest days were far away through fields, in woods, on
   hills, he and another wandering hand in hand, they twain apart
   from other men,
Who oft as he saunter'd the streets curv'd with his arm the shoulder
   of his friend, while the arm of his friend rested upon him also.   10

1860, 1867

I SAW IN LOUISIANA A LIVE-OAK GROWING

I saw in Louisiana a live-oak growing,
All alone stood it and the moss hung down from the branches,
Without any companion it grew there uttering joyous leaves of dark
   green,
And its look, rude, unbending, lusty, made me think of myself,
But I wonder'd how it could utter joyous leaves standing alone there
   without its friend near, for I knew I could not,
And I broke off a twig with a certain number of leaves upon it, and
   twined around it a little moss,
And brought it away, and I have placed it in sight in my room,
It is not needed to remind me as of my own dear friends,
(For I believe lately I think of little else than of them,)
Yet it remains to me a curious token, it makes me think of manly
   love;
For all that, and though the live-oak glistens there in Louisiana   10
   solitary in a wide flat space,
Uttering joyous leaves all its life without a friend a lover near,
I know very well I could not.

1860, 1867

I HEAR IT WAS CHARGED AGAINST ME

I hear it was charged against me that I sought to destroy institutions,
But really I am neither for nor against institutions,
(What indeed have I in common with them? or what with the
   destruction of them?)
Only I will establish in the Mannahatta[1] and in every city of these
   States inland and seaboard,
And in the fields and woods, and above every keel little or large that
   dents the water,

[1]Manhattan, New York City.

Without edifices or rules or trustees or any argument,
The institution of the dear love of comrades.

1860, 1867

HERE THE FRAILEST LEAVES OF ME

Here the frailest leaves of me and yet my strongest lasting,
Here I shade and hide my thoughts, I myself do not expose them,
And yet they expose me more than all my other poems.

1860, 1871

CROSSING BROOKLYN FERRY[1]

1

Flood-tide below me! I see you face to face!
Clouds of the west—sun there half an hour high—I see you also face
   to face.

Crowds of men and women attired in the usual costumes, how
   curious you are to me!
On the ferry-boats the hundreds and hundreds that cross, returning
   home, are more curious to me than you suppose,
And you that shall cross from shore to shore years hence are more
   to me, and more in my meditations, than you might suppose.

2

The impalpable sustenance of me from all things at all hours of the
   day,
The simple, compact, well-join'd scheme, myself disintegrated, every
   one disintegrated yet part of the scheme,
The similitudes[2] of the past and those of the future,
The glories strung like beads on my smallest sighs and hearings, on
   the walk in the street and the passage over the river,
The current rushing so swiftly and swimming with me far away,   10
The others that are to follow me, the ties between me and them,
The certainty of others, the life, love, sight, hearing of others.

Others will enter the gates of the ferry and cross from shore to
   shore,
Others will watch the run of the flood-tide,
Others will see the shipping of Manhattan north and west, and the
   heights of Brooklyn to the south and east,
Others will see the islands large and small;
Fifty years hence, others will see them as they cross, the sun half an
   hour high,

[1]Originally titled "Sun-Down Poem."   [2]Similarities.

A hundred years hence, or ever so many hundred years hence,
  others will see them,
Will enjoy the sunset, the pouring-in of the flood-tide, the falling-
  back to the sea of the ebb-tide.

3

It avails not, time nor place—distance avails not,   20
I am with you, you men and women of a generation, or ever so
  many generations hence,
Just as you feel when you look on the river and sky, so I felt,
Just as any of you is one of a living crowd, I was one of a crowd,
Just as you are refresh'd by the gladness of the river and the bright
  flow, I was refresh'd,
Just as you stand and lean on the rail, yet hurry with the swift
  current, I stood yet was hurried,
Just as you look on the numberless masts of ships and the thick-
  stemm'd pipes of steamboats, I look'd.

I too many and many a time cross'd the river of old,
Watched the Twelfth-month[3] sea-gulls, saw them high in the air
  floating with motionless wings, oscillating their bodies,
Saw how the glistening yellow lit up parts of their bodies and left the
  rest in strong shadow,
Saw the slow-wheeling circles and the gradual edging toward the
  south,   30
Saw the reflection of the summer sky in the water,
Had my eyes dazzled by the shimmering track of beams,
Look'd at the fine centrifugal spokes of light round the shape of my
  head in the sunlit water,
Look'd on the haze on the hills southward and south-westward,
Look'd on the vapor as it flew in fleeces tinged with violet,
Look'd toward the lower bay to notice the vessels arriving,
Saw their approach, saw aboard those that were near me,
Saw the white sails of schooners and sloops, saw the ships at anchor,
The sailors at work in the rigging or out astride the spars,
The round masts, the swinging motion of the hulls, the slender
  serpentine pennants,   40
The large and small steamers in motion, the pilots in their pilot-
  houses,
The white wake left by the passage, the quick tremulous whirl of the
  wheels,
The flags of all nations, the falling of them at sunset,
The scallop-edged waves in the twilight, the ladled cups, the
  frolicsome crests and glistening,
The stretch afar growing dimmer and dimmer, the gray walls of the
  granite storehouses by the docks,
On the river the shadowy group, the big steam-tug closely flank'd on
  each side by the barges, the hay-boat, the belated lighter,[4]

[3]December.   [4]Barge used in loading and unloading cargo ships.

On the neighboring shore the fires from the foundry chimneys
    burning high and glaringly into the night,
Casting their flicker of black contrasted with wild red and yellow
    light over the tops of houses, and down into the clefts of streets.

                      4
These and all else were to me the same as they are to you,
I loved well those cities, loved well the stately and rapid river,   50
The men and women I saw were all near to me,
Others the same—others who look back on me because I look'd
    forward to them,
(The time will come, though I stop here to-day and to-night.)

                      5
What is it then between us?
What is the count of the scores or hundreds of years between us?

Whatever it is, it avails not—distance avails not, and place avails not,
I too lived, Brooklyn of ample hills was mine,
I too walk'd the streets of Manhattan island, and bathed in the
    waters around it,
I too felt the curious abrupt questionings stir within me,
In the day among crowds of people sometimes they came upon me,   60
In my walks home late at night or as I lay in my bed they came upon
    me,
I too had been struck from the float forever held in solution,
I too had receiv'd identity by my body,
That I was I knew was of my body, and what I should be I knew I
    should be of my body.

                      6
It is not upon you alone the dark patches fall,
The dark threw its patches down upon me also,
The best I had done seem'd to me blank and suspicious,
My great thoughts as I supposed them, were they not in reality
    meagre?
Nor is it you alone who know what it is to be evil,
I am he who knew what it was to be evil,   70
I too knitted the old knot of contrarity,
Blabb'd, blush'd, resented, lied, stole, grudg'd,
Had guile, anger, lust, hot wishes I dared not speak,
Was wayward, vain, greedy, shallow, sly, cowardly, malignant,
The wolf, the snake, the hog, not wanting[5] in me,
The cheating look, the frivolous word, the adulterous wish, not
    wanting,
Refusals, hates, postponements, meanness, laziness, none of these
    wanting,
Was one with the rest, the days and haps[6] of the rest,
Was call'd by my nighest[7] name by clear loud voices of young men as
    they saw me approaching or passing,

[5]Lacking.   [6]Chance events.   [7]Shortest or most familiar.

Felt their arms on my neck as I stood, or the negligent leaning of
   their flesh against me as I sat,
Saw many I loved in the street or ferry-boat or public assembly, yet
   never told them a word,
Lived the same life with the rest, the same old laughing, gnawing,
   sleeping,
Play'd the part that still looks back on the actor or actress,
The same old role, the role that is what we make it, as great as we
   like,
Or as small as we like, or both great and small.

80

7

Closer yet I approach you,
What thought you have of me now, I had as much of you—I laid in
   my stores in advance,
I consider'd long and seriously of you before you were born.

Who was to know what should come home to me?
Who knows but I am enjoying this?
Who knows, for all the distance, but I am as good as looking at you
   now, for all you cannot see me?

90

8

Ah, what can ever be more stately and admirable to me than mast-
   hemm'd Manhattan?
River and sunset and scallop-edg'd waves of flood-tide?
The sea-gulls oscillating their bodies, the hay-boat in the twilight,
   and the belated lighter?
What gods can exceed these that clasp me by the hand, and with
   voices I love call me promptly and loudly by my nighest name as I
   approach?
What is more subtle than this which ties me to the woman or man
   that looks in my face?
Which fuses me into you now, and pours my meaning into you?

We understand then do we not?
What I promis'd without mentioning it, have you not accepted?
What the study could not teach—what the preaching could not
   accomplish is accomplish'd, is it not?

100

9

Flow on, river! flow with the flood-tide, and ebb with the ebb-tide!
Frolic on, crested and scallop-edg'd waves!
Gorgeous clouds of the sunset! drench with your splendor me, or the
   men and women generations after me!
Cross from shore to shore, countless crowds of passengers!
Stand up, tall masts of Mannahatta! stand up, beautiful hills of
   Brooklyn!
Throb, baffled and curious brain! throw our questions and answers!
Suspend here and everywhere, eternal float of solution!
Gaze, loving and thirsting eyes, in the house or street or public
   assembly!

Sound out, voices of young men! loudly and musically call me by my
    nighest name!
Live, old life! play the part that looks back on the actor or actress!   110
Play the old role, the role that is great or small according as one
    makes it!
Consider, you who peruse me, whether I may not in unknown ways
    be looking upon you;
Be firm, rail over the river, to support those who lean idly, yet haste
    with the hasting current;
Fly on, sea-birds! fly sideways, or wheel in large circles high in the
    air;
Receive the summer sky, you water, and faithfully hold it till all
    downcast eyes have time to take it from you!
Diverge, fine spokes of light, from the shape of my head, or any
    one's head, in the sunlit water!
Come on, ships from the lower bay! pass up or down, white-sail'd
    schooners, sloops, lighters!
Flaunt away, flags of all nations! be duly lower'd at sunset!
Burn high your fires, foundry chimneys! cast black shadows at
    nightfall! cast red and yellow light over the tops of the houses!
Appearances, now or henceforth, indicate what you are,   120
You necessary film, continue to envelop the soul,
About my body for me, and your body for you, be hung our divinest
    aromas,
Thrive, cities—bring your freight, bring your shows, ample and
    sufficient rivers,
Expand, being than which none else is perhaps more spiritual,
Keep your places, objects than which none else is more lasting.

You have waited, you always wait, you dumb, beautiful ministers,
We receive you with free sense at last, and are insatiate
    henceforward,
Not you any more shall be able to foil us, or withhold yourselves
    from us,
We use you, and do not cast you aside—we plant you permanently
    within us,
We fathom you not—we love you—there is perfection in you also,   130
You furnish your parts toward eternity,
Great or small, you furnish your parts toward the soul.

                                1856, 1881

from *SEA-DRIFT*

OUT OF THE CRADLE ENDLESSLY ROCKING

Out of the cradle endlessly rocking,
Out of the mocking-bird's throat, the musical shuttle,
Out of the Ninth-month[1] midnight,

---
[1]September.

Over the sterile sands and the fields beyond, where the child leaving
    his bed wander'd alone, bareheaded, barefoot,
Down from the shower'd halo,
Up from the mystic play of shadows twining and twisting as if they
    were alive,
Out from the patches of briers and blackberries,
From the memories of the bird that chanted to me,
From your memories sad brother, from the fitful risings and fallings
    I heard,
From under that yellow half-moon late-risen and swollen as if with
    tears,   10
From those beginning notes of yearning and love there in the mist,
From the thousand responses of my heart never to cease,
From the myriad thence-arous'd words,
From the word stronger and more delicious than any,
From such as now they start the scene revisiting,
As a flock, twittering, rising, or overhead passing,
Borne hither, ere all eludes me, hurriedly,
A man, yet by these tears a little boy again,
Throwing myself on the sand, confronting the waves,
I, chanter of pains and joys, uniter of here and hereafter,   20
Taking all hints to use them, but swiftly leaping beyond them,
A reminiscence sing.

Once Paumanok,[2]
When the lilac-scent was in the air and Fifth-month[3] grass was
    growing,
Up this seashore in some briers,
Two feather'd guests from Alabama, two together,
And their nest, and four light-green eggs spotted with brown,
And every day the he-bird to and fro near at hand,
And every day the she-bird crouch'd on her nest, silent, with bright
    eyes,
And every day I, a curious boy, never too close, never disturbing
    them,   30
Cautiously peering, absorbing, translating.

Shine! shine! shine!
Pour down your warmth, great sun!
While we bask, we two together.

Two together!
Winds blow south, or winds blow north,
Day come white, or night come black,
Home, or rivers and mountains from home,
Singing all time, minding no time,
While we two keep together.   40

[2]Indian name for Long Island.   [3]May.

Till of a sudden,
May-be kill'd, unknown to her mate,
One forenoon the she-bird crouch'd not on the nest,
Nor return'd that afternoon, nor the next,
Nor ever appear'd again.

And thenceforward all summer in the sound of the sea,
And at night under the full of the moon in calmer weather,
Over the hoarse surging of the sea,
Or flitting from brier to brier by day,
I saw, I heard at intervals the remaining one, the he-bird,   50
The solitary guest from Alabama.

Blow! blow! blow!
Blow up sea-winds along Paumanok's shore;
I wait and I wait till you blow my mate to me.

Yes, when the stars glisten'd,
All night long on the prong of a moss-scallop'd stake,
Down almost amid the slapping waves,
Sat the lone singer wonderful causing tears.

He call'd on his mate,
He pour'd forth the meanings which I of all men know.   60

Yes my brother I know,
The rest might not, but I have treasur'd every note,
For more than once dimly down to the beach gliding,
Silent, avoiding the moonbeams, blending myself with the shadows,
Recalling now the obscure shapes, the echoes, the sounds and sight
      after their sorts,
The white arms out in the breakers tirelessly tossing,
I, with bare feet, a child, the wind wafting my hair,
Listen'd long and long.

Listen'd to keep, to sing, now translating the notes,
Following you my brother.   70

Soothe! soothe! soothe!
Close on its wave soothes the wave behind,
And again another behind embracing and lapping, every one close,
But my love soothes not me, not me.

Low hangs the moon, it rose late,
It is lagging—O I think it is heavy with love, with love.

O madly the sea pushes upon the land,
With love, with love.

O night! do I not see my love fluttering out among the breakers?
What is that little black thing I see there in the white?   80

Loud! loud! loud!
Loud I call to you, my love!
High and clear I shoot my voice over the waves,
Surely you must know who is here, is here,
You must know who I am, my love.

Low-hanging moon!
What is that dusky spot in your brown yellow?
O it is the shape, the shape of my mate!
O moon do not keep her from me any longer.

Land! land! O land!
Whichever way I turn, O I think you could give me my mate back again if
    you only would,
For I am almost sure I see her dimly whichever way I look. 90

O rising stars!
Perhaps the one I want so much will rise, will rise with some of you.

O throat! O trembling throat!
Sound clearer through the atmosphere!
Pierce the woods, the earth,
Somewhere listening to catch you must be the one I want.

Shake out carols!
Solitary here, the night's carols! 100
Carols of lonesome love! death's carols!
Carols under that lagging, yellow, waning moon!
O under that moon where she droops almost down into the sea!
O reckless despairing carols.

But soft! sink low!
Soft! let me just murmur,
And do you wait a moment you husky-nois'd sea,
For somewhere I believe I heard my mate responding to me,
So faint, I must be still, be still to listen,
But not altogether still, for then she might not come immediately to me. 110

Hither my love!
Here I am! here!
With this just-sustain'd note I announce myself to you,
This gentle call is for you my love, for you.

Do not be decoy'd elsewhere,
That is the whistle of the wind, it is not my voice,
That is the fluttering, the fluttering of the spray,
Those are the shadows of leaves.

O darkness! O in vain!
O I am very sick and sorrowful. 120

O brown halo in the sky near the moon, drooping upon the sea!
O troubled reflection in the sea!
O throat! O throbbing heart!
And I singing uselessly, uselessly all the night.

O past! O happy life! O songs of joy!
In the air, in the woods, over fields,
Loved! loved! loved! loved! loved!
But my mate no more, no more with me!
We two together no more.

The aria sinking,   130
All else continuing, the stars shining,
The winds blowing, the notes of the bird continuous echoing,
With angry moans the fierce old mother incessantly moaning,
On the sands of Paumanok's shore gray and rustling,
The yellow half-moon enlarged, sagging down, drooping, the face of
    the sea almost touching,
The boy ecstatic, with his bare feet the waves, with his hair the
    atmosphere dallying,
The love in the heart long pent, now loose, now at last tumultuously
    bursting,
The aria's meaning, the ears, the soul, swiftly depositing,
The strange tears down the cheeks coursing,
The colloquy there, the trio, each uttering,   140
The undertone, the savage old mother incessantly crying.
To the boy's soul's questions sullenly timing, some drown'd secret
    hissing.
To the outsetting bard.

Demon or bird! (said the boy's soul,)
Is it indeed toward your mate you sing? or is it really to me?
For I, that was a child, my tongue's use sleeping, now I have heard
    you,
Now in a moment I know what I am for, I awake,
And already a thousand singers, a thousand songs, clearer, louder
    and more sorrowful than yours,
A thousand warbling echoes have started to life within me, never to
    die.

O you singer solitary, singing by yourself, projecting me,   150
O solitary me listening, never more shall I cease perpetuating you,
Never more shall I escape, never more the reverberations,
Never more the cries of unsatisfied love be absent from me,
Never again leave me to be the peaceful child I was before what
    there in the night,
By the sea under the yellow and sagging moon,
The messenger there arous'd, the fire, the sweet hell within,
The unknown want, the destiny of me.

O give me the clew! (it lurks in the night here somewhere,)
O if I am to have so much, let me have more!

A word then, (for I will conquer it,) 160
The word final, superior to all,
Subtle, sent up—what is it?—I listen:
Are you whispering it, and have been all the time, you sea-waves?
Is that it from your liquid rims and wet sands?

Whereto answering, the sea,
Delaying not, hurrying not,
Whisper'd me through the night, and very plainly before daybreak,
Lisp'd to me the low and delicious word death,
And again, death, death, death, death,
Hissing melodious, neither like the bird nor like my arous'd child's
    heart,
But edging near as privately for me rustling at my feet, 170
Creeping thence steadily up to my ears and laving me softly all over,
Death, death, death, death, death.

Which I do not forget,
But fuse the song of my dusky demon and brother,
That he sang to me in the moonlight on Paumanok's gray beach,
With the thousand responsive songs at random,
My own songs awaked from that hour,
And with them the key, the word up from the waves,
The word of the sweetest song and all songs, 180
That strong and delicious word which, creeping to my feet,
(Or like some old crone rocking the cradle, swathed in sweet
    garments, bending aside,)
The sea whisper'd me.

                                        1859, 1881

AS I EBB'D WITH THE OCEAN OF LIFE

1

As I ebb'd with the ocean of life,
As I wended the shores I know,
As I walk'd where the ripples continually wash you Paumanok,
Where they rustle up hoarse and sibilant,
Where the fierce old mother endlessly cries for her castaways,
I musing late in the autumn day, gazing off southward,
Held by this electric self out of the pride of which I utter poems,
Was seiz'd by the spirit that trails in the lines underfoot,
The rim, the sediment that stands for all the water and all the land
    of the globe.

Fascinated, my eyes reverting from the south, dropt, to follow those
    slender windrows,[1]
Chaff, straw, splinters of wood, weeds and the sea-gluten,[2] 10

---

[1] Rows heaped up by the wind or waves.   [2] Thick, sticky plant substance.

Scum, scales from shining rocks, leaves of salt-lettuce, left by the
    tide,
Miles walking, the sound of breaking waves the other side of me,
Paumanok there and then as I thought the old thought of likenesses,
These you presented to me you fish-shaped island,
As I wended the shores I know,
As I walk'd with that electric self seeking types.[3]

2

As I wend to the shores I know not,
As I list to the dirge, the voices of men and women wreck'd,
As I inhale the impalpable breezes that set in upon me,   20
As the ocean so mysterious rolls toward me closer and closer,
I too but signify at the utmost a little wash'd-up drift,
A few sands and dead leaves to gather,
Gather, and merge myself as part of the sands and drift.

O baffled, balk'd, bent to the very earth,
Oppress'd with myself that I have dared to open my mouth,
Aware now that amid all that blab whose echoes recoil upon me I
    have not once had the least idea who or what I am,
But that before all my arrogant poems the real Me stands yet
    untouch'd, untold, altogether unreach'd,
Withdrawn far, mocking me with mock-congratulatory signs and
    bows,
With peals of distant ironical laughter at every word I have written,   30
Pointing in silence to these songs, and then to the sand beneath.

I perceive I have not really understood any thing, not a single object,
    and that no man ever can,
Nature here in sight of the sea taking advantage of me to dart upon
    me and sting me,
Because I have dared to open my mouth to sing at all.

3

You oceans both, I close with you,
We murmur alike reproachfully rolling sands and drift, knowing not
    why,
These little shreds indeed standing for you and me and all.

You friable[4] shore with trails of debris,
You fish-shaped island, I take what is underfoot,
What is yours is mine my father.   40

I too Paumanok,
I too have bubbled up, floated the measureless float, and been
    wash'd on your shores,
I too am but a trail of drift and debris,
I too leave little wrecks upon you, you fish-shaped island.

[3] I.e., seeking "likenesses" of himself.   [4] Crumbling.

I throw myself upon your breast my father,
I cling to you so that you cannot unloose me,
I hold you so firm till you answer me something.

Kiss me my father,
Touch me with your lips as I touch those I love,
Breathe to me while I hold you close the secret of the murmuring I
    envy.

50

4

Ebb, ocean of life, (the flow will return,)
Cease not your moaning you fierce old mother,
Endlessly cry for your castaways, but fear not, deny not me,
Rustle not up so hoarse and angry against my feet as I touch you or
    gather from you.

I mean tenderly by you and all,
I gather for myself and for this phantom looking down where we
    lead, and following me and mine.

Me and mine, loose windrows, little corpses,
Froth, snowy white, and bubbles,
(See, from my dead lips the ooze exuding at last,
See, the prismatic colors glistening and rolling,)
Tufts or straw, sands, fragments,
Buoy'd hither from many moods, one contradicting another,
From the storm, the long calm, the darkness, the swell,
Musing, pondering, a breath, a briny tear, a dab of liquid or soil,
Up just as much out of fathomless workings fermented and thrown,
A limp blossom or two, torn, just as much over waves floating,
    drifted at random,
Just as much for us that sobbing dirge of Nature,
Just as much whence we come that blare of the cloud-trumpets,
We, capricious, brought hither we know not whence, spread out
    before you,
You up there walking or sitting,
Whoever you are, we too lie in drifts at your feet.

60

70

1860, 1881

ON THE BEACH AT NIGHT ALONE

On the beach at night alone,
As the old mother sways her to and fro singing her husky song,
As I watch the bright stars shining, I think a thought of the clef[1] of
    the universes and of the future.

A vast similitude interlocks all,
All spheres, grown, ungrown, small, large, suns, moons, planets,

[1]Key.

All distances of place however wide,
All distances of time, all inanimate forms,
All souls, all living bodies though they be ever so different, or in
    different worlds,
All gaseous, watery, vegetable, mineral processes, the fishes, the
    brutes,
All nations, colors, barbarisms, civilizations, languages,   10
All identities that have existed or may exist on this globe, or any
    globe,
All lives and deaths, all of the past, present, future,
This vast similitude spans them, and always has spann'd,
And shall forever span them and compactly hold and enclose them.

                                                                1856, 1881

from *BY THE ROADSIDE*

WHEN I HEARD THE LEARN'D ASTRONOMER

When I heard the learn'd astronomer,
When the proofs, the figures, were ranged in columns before me,
When I was shown the charts and diagrams, to add, divide, and
    measure them,
When I sitting heard the astronomer where he lectured with much
    applause in the lecture-room,
How soon unaccountable I became tired and sick,
Till rising and gliding out I wander'd off by myself,
In the mystical moist night-air, and from time to time,
Look'd up in perfect silence at the stars.

                                                                1865, 1865

THE DALLIANCE OF THE EAGLES

Skirting the river road, (my forenoon walk, my rest,)
Skyward in air a sudden muffled sound, the dalliance[1] of the eagles,
The rushing amorous contact high in space together,
The clinching interlocking claws, a living, fierce, gyrating wheel,
Four beating wings, two beaks, a swirling mass tight grappling,
In tumbling turning clustering loops, straight downward falling,
Till o'er the river pois'd, the twain yet one, a moment's lull,
A motionless still balance in the air, then parting, talons loosing,

[1]In the sense of amorous play and mating.

Upward again on slow-firm pinions, slanting, their separate diverse
　flight,
She hers, he his, pursuing.　　　　　　　　　　　　　　　　　　　10
　　　　　　　　　　　　　　　　　　　　　　　　1880, 1881

from *DRUM-TAPS*

BEAT! BEAT! DRUMS!

Beat! beat! drums!—blow! bugles! blow!
Through the windows—through doors—burst like a ruthless force,
Into the solemn church, and scatter the congregation,
Into the school where the scholar is studying;
Leave not the bridegroom quiet—no happiness must he have now
　with his bride,
Nor the peaceful farmer any peace, ploughing his field or gathering
　his grain,
So fierce you whirr and pound you drums—so shrill you bugles
　blow.

Beat! beat! drums!—blow! bugles! blow!
Over the traffic of cities—over the rumble of wheels in the streets;
Are beds prepared for sleepers at night in the houses? no sleepers
　must sleep in those beds,
No bargainers' bargains by day—no brokers or speculators—would　　10
　they continue?
Would the talkers be talking? would the singer attempt to sing?
Would the lawyer rise in the court to state his case before the judge?
Then rattle quicker, heavier drums—you bugles wilder blow.

Beat! beat! drums!—blow! bugles! blow!
Make no parley—stop for no expostulation,
Mind not the timid—mind not the weeper or prayer,
Mind not the old man beseeching the young man,
Let not the child's voice be heard, nor the mother's entreaties,
Make even the trestles to shake the dead where they lie awaiting the
　hearses,　　　　　　　　　　　　　　　　　　　　　　　　20
So strong you thump O terrible drums—so loud you bugles blow.
　　　　　　　　　　　　　　　　　　　　　　　　1861, 1867

CAVALRY CROSSING A FORD

A line in long array where they wind betwixt green islands,
They take a serpentine course, their arms flash in the sun—hark to
　the musical clank,
Behold the silvery river, in it the splashing horses loitering stop to
　drink,

Behold the brown-faced men, each group, each person a picture, the
  negligent rest on the saddles,
Some emerge on the opposite bank, others are just entering the
  ford—while,
Scarlet and blue and snowy white,
The guidon flags[1] flutter gayly in the wind.

                                                                    1865, 1871

BIVOUAC ON A MOUNTAIN SIDE

I see before me now a traveling army halting,
Below a fertile valley spread, with barns and the orchards of
  summer,
Behind, the terraced sides of a mountain, abrupt, in places rising
  high,
Broken, with rocks, with clinging cedars, with tall shapes dingily
  seen,
The numerous camp-fires scatter'd near and far, some away up on
  the mountain,
The shadowy forms of men and horses, looming, large-sized,
  flickering,
And over all the sky—the sky! far, far out of reach, studded,
  breaking out, the eternal stars.

                                                                    1865, 1871

VIGIL STRANGE I KEPT ON THE FIELD ONE NIGHT

Vigil strange I kept on the field one night;
When you my son and my comrade dropt at my side that day,
One look I but gave which your dear eyes return'd with a look I
  shall never forget,
One touch of your hand to mine O boy, reach'd up as you lay on the
  ground,
Then onward I sped in the battle, the even-contested battle,
Till late in the night reliev'd to the place at last again I made my
  way,
Found you in death so cold dear comrade, found your body son of
  responding kisses, (never again on earth responding,)
Bared your face in the starlight, curious the scene, cool blew the
  moderate night-wind,
Long there and then in vigil I stood, dimly around me the battle-
  field spreading,
Vigil wondrous and vigil sweet there in the fragrant silent night,   10
But not a tear fell, not even a long-drawn sigh, long long I gazed,
Then on the earth partially reclining sat by your side leaning my
  chin in my hands,

---

[1]Military flags or pennants.

Passing sweet hours, immortal and mystic hours with you dearest
  comrade—not a tear, not a word,
Vigil of silence, love and death, vigil for you my son and my soldier,
As onward silently stars aloft, eastward new ones upward stole,
Vigil final for you brave boy, (I could not save you, swift was your
  death,
I faithfully loved you and cared for you living, I think we shall
  surely meet again,)
Till at latest lingering of the night, indeed just as the dawn appear'd,
My comrade I wrapt in his blanket, envelop'd well his form,
Folded the blanket well, tucking it carefully over head and carefully
  under feet,
And there and then and bathed by the rising sun, my son in his   20
  grave, in his rude-dug grave I deposited,
Ending my vigil strange with that, vigil of night and battle-field dim,
Vigil for boy of responding kisses, (never again on earth
  responding,)
Vigil for comrade swiftly slain, vigil I never forget, how as day
  brighten'd,
I rose from the chill ground and folded my soldier well in his
  blanket,
And buried him where he fell.

1865, 1867

A MARCH IN THE RANKS HARD-PREST,
AND THE ROAD UNKNOWN

A march in the ranks hard-prest, and the road unknown,
A route through a heavy wood with muffled steps in the darkness,
Our army foil'd with loss severe, and the sullen remnant retreating,
Till after midnight glimmer upon us the lights of a dim-lighted
  building,
We come to an open space in the woods, and halt by the dim-lighted
  building,
'Tis a large old church at the crossing roads, now an impromptu
  hospital,
Entering but for a minute I see a sight beyond all the pictures and
  poems ever made,
Shadows of deepest, deepest black, just lit by moving candles and
  lamps,
And by one great pitchy torch stationary with wild red flame and
  clouds of smoke,
By these, crowds, groups of forms vaguely I see on the floor, some
  in the pews laid down,   10
At my feet more distinctly a soldier, a mere lad, in danger of
  bleeding to death, (he is shot in the abdomen,)
I stanch the blood temporarily, (the youngster's face is white as a
  lily,)
Then before I depart I sweep my eyes o'er the scene fain to absorb it
  all,

Faces, varieties, postures beyond description, most in obscurity, some
    of them dead,
Surgeons operating, attendants holding lights, the smell of ether, the
    odor of blood,
The crowd, O the crowd of the bloody forms, the yard outside also
    fill'd,
Some on the bare ground, some on planks or stretchers, some in the
    death-spasm sweating,
An occasional scream or cry, the doctor's shouted orders or calls,
The glisten of the little steel instruments catching the glint of the
    torches,
These I resume as I chant, I see again the forms, I smell the odor,   20
Then hear outside the orders given, *Fall in, my men, fall in;*
But first I bend to the dying lad, his eyes open, a half-smile gives he
    me,
Then the eyes close, calmly close, and I speed forth to the darkness,
Resuming, marching, ever in darkness marching, on in the ranks,
The unknown road still marching.

1865, 1867

A SIGHT IN CAMP IN THE DAYBREAK
GRAY AND DIM

A sight in camp in the daybreak gray and dim,
As from my tent I emerge so early sleepless,
As slow I walk in the cool fresh air the path near by the hospital
    tent,
Three forms I see on stretchers lying, brought out there untended
    lying,
Over each the blanket spread, ample brownish woolen blanket,
Gray and heavy blanket, folding, covering all.

Curious I halt and silent stand,
Then with light fingers I from the face of the nearest the first just
    lift the blanket;
Who are you elderly man so gaunt and grim, with well-gray'd hair,
    and flesh all sunken about the eyes?
Who are you my dear comrade?   10

Then to the second I step—and who are you my child and darling?
Who are you sweet boy with cheeks yet blooming?

Then to the third—a face nor child nor old, very calm, as of
    beautiful yellow-white ivory;
Young man I think I know you—I think this face is the face of the
    Christ himself,
Dead and divine and brother of all, and here again he lies.

1865, 1867

THE WOUND-DRESSER

1

An old man bending I come among new faces,
Years looking backward resuming in answer to children,
Come tell us old man, as from young men and maidens that love me,
(Arous'd and angry, I'd thought to beat the alarum, and urge
    relentless war,
But soon my fingers fail'd me, my face droop'd and I resign'd
    myself,
To sit by the wounded and soothe them, or silently watch the dead;)
Years hence of these scenes, of these furious passions, these chances,
Of unsurpass'd heroes, (was one side so brave? the other was equally
    brave;)
Now be witness again, paint the mightiest armies of earth,
Of those armies so rapid so wondrous what saw you to tell us?   10
What stays with you latest and deepest? of curious panics,
Of hard-fought engagements or sieges tremendous what deepest
    remains?

2

O maidens and young men I love and that love me,
What you ask of my days those the strangest and sudden your
    talking recalls,
Soldier alert I arrive after a long march cover'd with sweat and dust,
In the nick of time I come, plunge in the fight, loudly shout in the
    rush of successful charge,
Enter the captur'd works[1]—yet lo, like a swift-running river they
    fade,
Pass and are gone they fade—I dwell not on soldiers' perils or
    soldiers' joys,
(Both I remember well—many the hardships, few the joys, yet I was
    content.)

But in silence, in dreams' projections,   20
While the world of gain and appearance and mirth goes on,
So soon what is over forgotten, and waves wash the imprints off the
    sand,
With hinged knees returning I enter the doors, (while for you up
    there,
Whoever you are, follow without noise and be of strong heart.)

Bearing the bandages, water and sponge,
Straight and swift to my wounded I go,
Where they lie on the ground after the battle brought in,
Where their priceless blood reddens the grass the ground,
Or to the rows of the hospital tent, or under the roof'd hospital,
To the long rows of cots up and down each side I return,   30
To each and all one after another I draw near, not one do I miss,

---

[1]Fortifications.

An attendant follows holding a tray, he carries a refuse pail,
Soon to be fill'd with clotted rags and blood, emptied, and fill'd
  again.

I onward go, I stop,
With hinged knees and steady hand to dress wounds,
I am firm with each, the pangs are sharp yet unavoidable,
One turns to me his appealing eyes—poor boy! I never knew you,
Yet I think I could not refuse this moment to die for you, if that
  would save you.

                                    3
On, on I go, (open doors of time! open hospital doors!)
The crush'd head I dress, (poor crazed hand tear not the bandage
  away,)   40
The neck of the calvalry-man with the bullet through and through I
  examine,
Hard the breathing rattles, quite glazed already the eye, yet life
  struggles hard,
(Come sweet death! be persuaded O beautiful death!
In mercy come quickly.)

From the stump of the arm, the amputated hand,
I undo the clotted lint, remove the slough, wash off the matter and
  blood,
Back on his pillow the soldier bends with curv'd neck and side-falling
  head,
His eyes are closed, his face is pale, he dares not look on the bloody
  stump,
And has not yet look'd on it.

I dress a wound in the side, deep, deep,   50
But a day or two more, for see the frame all wasted and sinking,
And the yellow-blue countenance see.

I dress the perforated shoulder, the foot with the bullet-wound,
Cleanse the one with a gnawing and putrid gangrene, so sickening,
  so offensive,
While the attendant stands behind aside me holding the tray and
  pail.

I am faithful, I do not give out,
The fractur'd thigh, the knee, the wound in the abdomen,
These and more I dress with impassive hand, (yet deep in my breast
  a fire, a burning flame.)

                                    4
Thus in silence in dreams' projections,
Returning, resuming, I thread my way through the hospitals,
The hurt and wounded I pacify with soothing hand,   60
I sit by the restless all the dark night, some are so young,
Some suffer so much, I recall the experience sweet and sad,

(Many a soldier's loving arms about this neck have cross'd and
    rested,
Many a soldier's kiss dwells on these bearded lips.)

1865, 1881

LONG, TOO LONG AMERICA

Long, too long America,
Traveling roads all even and peaceful you learn'd from joys and
    prosperity only,
But now, ah now, to learn from crises of anguish, advancing,
    grappling with direst fate and recoiling not,
And now to conceive and show to the world what your children en-
    masse really are,
(For who except myself has yet conceiv'd what your children en-
    masse really are?)

1865, 1881

GIVE ME THE SPLENDID SILENT SUN

1

Give me the splendid silent sun with all his beams full-dazzling,
Give me juicy autumnal fruit ripe and red from the orchard,
Give me a field where the unmow'd grass grows,
Give me an arbor, give me the trellis'd grape,
Give me fresh corn and wheat, give me serene-moving animals
    teaching content,
Give me nights perfectly quiet as on high plateaus west of the
    Mississippi, and I looking up at the stars,
Give me odorous at sunrise a garden of beautiful flowers where I
    can walk undisturb'd,
Give me for marriage a sweet-breath'd woman of whom I should
    never tire,
Give me a perfect child, give me away aside from the noise of the
    world a rural domestic life,
Give me to warble spontaneous songs recluse by myself, for my own
    ears only,   10
Give me solitude, give me Nature, give me again O Nature your
    primal sanities!

These demanding to have them, (tired with ceaseless excitement, and
    rack'd by the war-strife,)
These to procure incessantly asking, rising in cries from my heart,
While yet incessantly asking still I adhere to my city,
Day upon day and year upon year O city, walking your streets,
Where you hold me enchain'd a certain time refusing to give me up,

Yet giving to make me glutted, enrich'd of soul, you give me forever
  faces;
(O I see what I sought to escape, confronting, reversing my cries,
I see my own soul trampling down what it ask'd for.)

2

Keep your splendid silent sun,   20
Keep your woods O Nature, and the quiet places by the woods,
Keep your fields of clover and timothy, and your corn-fields and
  orchards,
Keep the blossoming buckwheat fields where the Ninth-month bees
  hum;
Give me faces and streets—give me these phantoms incessant and
  endless along the trottoirs![1]
Give me interminable eyes—give me women—give me comrades and
  lovers by the thousand!
Let me see new ones every day—let me hold new ones by the hand
  every day!
Give me such shows—give me the streets of Manhattan!
Give me Broadway, with the soldiers marching—give me the sound
  of the trumpets and drums!
(The soldiers in companies or regiments—some starting away, flush'd
  and reckless,
Some, their time up, returning with thinn'd ranks, young, yet very
  old, worn, marching, noticing nothing;)   30
Give me the shores and wharves heavy-fringed with black ships!
O such for me! O an intense life, full to repletion and varied!
The life of the theatre, bar-room, huge hotel, for me!
The saloon of the steamer! the crowded excursion for me! the
  torchlight procession!
The dense brigade bound for the war, with high piled military
  wagons following;
People, endless, streaming, with strong voices, passions, pageants,
Manhattan streets with their powerful throbs, with beating drums as
  now,
The endless and noisy chorus, the rustle and clank of muskets, (even
  the sight of the wounded,)
Manhattan crowds, with their turbulent musical chorus!
Manhattan faces and eyes forever for me.   40

1865, 1881

RECONCILIATION

Word over all, beautiful as the sky,
Beautiful that war and all its deeds of carnage must in time be
  utterly lost,
That the hands of the sisters Death and Night incessantly softly wash
  again, and ever again, this soil'd world;

[1]French: sidewalks.

For my enemy is dead, a man divine as myself is dead,
I look where he lies white-faced and still in the coffin—I draw near,
Bend down and touch lightly with my lips the white face in the
   coffin.

from *MEMORIES OF PRESIDENT LINCOLN*

WHEN LILACS LAST IN THE DOORYARD BLOOM'D

1

When lilacs last in the dooryard bloom'd,
And the great star[1] early droop'd in the western sky in the night,
I mourn'd, and yet shall mourn with ever-returning spring.

Ever-returning spring, trinity sure to me you bring,
Lilac blooming perennial and drooping star in the west,
And thought of him I love.

2

O powerful western fallen star!
O shades of night—O moody, tearful night!
O great star disappear'd—O the black murk that hides the star!
O cruel hands that hold me powerless—O helpless soul of me!   10
O harsh surrounding cloud that will not free my soul.

3

In the dooryard fronting an old farm-house near the white-wash'd
   palings,
Stands the lilac-bush tall-growing with heart-shaped leaves of rich
   green,
With many a pointed blossom rising delicate, with the perfume
   strong I love,
With every leaf a miracle—and from this bush in the dooryard,
With delicate-color'd blossoms and heart-shaped leaves of rich green,
A sprig with its flower I break.

4

In the swamp in secluded recesses,
A shy and hidden bird is warbling a song.

Solitary the thrush,   20
The hermit withdrawn to himself, avoiding the settlements,
Sings by himself a song.

Song of the bleeding throat,
Death's outlet song of life, (for well dear brother I know,
If thou wast not granted to sing thou would'st surely die.)

[1]Venus.

5

Over the breast of the spring, the land, amid cities,
Amid lanes and through old woods, where lately the violets peep'd
  from the ground, spotting the gray debris,
Amid the grass in the fields each side of the lanes, passing the
  endless grass,
Passing the yellow-spear'd wheat, every grain from its shroud in the
  dark-brown fields uprisen,
Passing the apple-tree blows[2] of white and pink in the orchards,   30
Carrying a corpse to where it shall rest in the grave,
Night and day journeys a coffin.[3]

6

Coffin that passes through lanes and streets,
Through day and night with the great cloud darkening the land,
With the pomp of the inloop'd flags with the cities draped in black,
With the show of the States themselves as of crape-veil'd women
  standing,
With processions long and winding and the flambeaus[4] of the night,
With the countless torches lit, with the silent sea of faces and the
  unbared heads,
With the waiting depot, the arriving coffin, and the sombre faces,
With dirges through the night, with the thousand voices rising strong
  and solemn,   40
With all the mournful voices of the dirges pour'd around the coffin,
The dim-lit churches and the shuddering organs—where amid these
  you journey,
With the tolling tolling bells' perpetual clang,
Here, coffin that slowly passes,
I give you my sprig of lilac.

7

(Not for you, for one alone,
Blossoms and branches green to coffins all I bring,
For fresh as the morning, thus would I chant a song for you O sane
  and sacred death.

All over bouquets of roses,
O death, I cover you over with roses and early lilies,   50
But mostly and now the lilac that blooms the first,
Copious I break, I break the sprigs from the bushes,
With loaded arms I come, pouring for you,
For you and the coffins all of you O death.)

8

O western orb sailing the heaven,
Now I know what you must have meant as a month since I walk'd,
As I walk'd in silence the transparent shadowy night,

[2]Blossoms.
[3]Following Lincoln's assassination in April 1865, his body was carried on a funeral train from
Washington, D.C., to Springfield, Illinois, for burial.
[4]Burning torches.

As I saw you had something to tell as you bent to me night after
   night,
As you droop'd from the sky low down as if to my side, (while the
   other stars all look'd on,)
As we wander'd together the solemn night, (for something I know
   not what kept me from sleep,)
As the night advanced, and I saw on the rim of the west how full
   you were of woe,
As I stood on the rising ground in the breeze in the cool transparent
   night,
As I watch'd where you pass'd and was lost in the netherward black
   of the night,
As my soul in its trouble dissatisfied sank, as where you sad orb,
Concluded, dropt in the night, and was gone.

9

Sing on there in the swamp,
O singer bashful and tender, I hear your notes, I hear your call,
I hear, I come presently, I understand you,
But a moment I linger, for the lustrous star has detain'd me,
The star my departing comrade holds and detains me.

10

O how shall I warble myself for the dead one there I loved?
And how shall I deck my song for the large sweet soul that has
   gone?
And what shall my perfume be for the grave of him I love?

Sea-winds blown from east and west,
Blown from the Eastern sea and blown from the Western sea, till
   there on the prairies meeting,
These and with these and the breath of my chant,
I'll perfume the grave of him I love.

11

O what shall I hang on the chamber walls?
And what shall the pictures be that I hang on the walls,
To adorn the burial-house of him I love?

Pictures of growing spring and farms and homes,
With the Fourth-month[5] eve at sundown, and the gray smoke lucid
   and bright,
With floods of the yellow gold of the gorgeous, indolent, sinking sun,
   burning, expanding the air,
With the fresh sweet herbage under foot, and the pale green leaves
   of the trees prolific,
In the distance the flowing glaze, the breast of the river, with a wind-
   dapple here and there,
With ranging hills on the banks, with many a line against the sky,
   and shadows,

[5]April.

And the city at hand with dwellings so dense, and stacks of
  chimneys,
And all the scenes of life and the workshops, and the workmen
  homeward returning.

12

Lo, body and soul—this land,
My own Manhattan with spires, and the sparkling and hurrying
  tides, and ships,   90
The varied and ample land, the South and the North in the light,
  Ohio's shores and flashing Missouri,
And ever the far-spreading prairies cover'd with grass and corn.

Lo, the most excellent sun so calm and haughty,
The violet and purple morn with just-felt breezes,
The gentle soft-born measureless light,
The miracle spreading bathing all, the fulfill'd noon,
The coming eve delicious, the welcome night and the stars,
Over my cities shining all, enveloping man and land.

13

Sing on, sing on you gray-brown bird,
Sing from the swamps, the recesses, pour your chant from the
  bushes,   100
Limitless out of the dusk, out of the cedars and pines.

Sing on dearest brother, warble your reedy song,
Loud human song, with voice of uttermost woe.

O liquid and free and tender!
O wild and loose to my soul—O wondrous singer!
You only I hear—yet the star holds me, (but will soon depart,)
Yet the lilac with mastering odor holds me.

14

Now while I sat in the day and look'd forth,
In the close of the day with its light and the fields of spring, and the
  farmers preparing their crops,
In the large unconscious scenery of my land with its lakes and
  forests,   110
In the heavenly aerial beauty, (after the perturb'd winds and the
  storms,)
Under the arching heavens of the afternoon swift passing, and the
  voices of children and women,
The many-moving sea-tides, and I saw the ships how they sail'd,
And the summer approaching with richness, and the fields all busy
  with labor,
And the infinite separate houses, how they all went on, each with its
  meals and minutia of daily usages,
And the streets how their throbbings throbb'd, and the cities pent—
  lo, then and there,

Falling upon them all and among them all, enveloping me with the
    rest,
Appear'd the cloud, appear'd the long black trail,
And I knew death, its thought, and the sacred knowledge of death.

Then with the knowledge of death as walking one side of me,   120
And the thought of death close-walking the other side of me,
And I in the middle as with companions, and as holding the hands
    of companions,
I fled forth to the hiding receiving night that talks not,
Down to the shores of the water, the path by the swamp in the
    dimness,
To the solemn shadowy cedars and ghostly pines so still.

And the singer so shy to the rest receiv'd me,
The gray-brown bird I know receiv'd us comrades three,
And he sang the carol of death, and a verse for him I love.

From deep secluded recesses,
From the fragrant cedars and the ghostly pines so still,   130
Came the carol of the bird.

And the charm of the carol rapt me,
As I held as if by their hands my comrades in the night,
And the voice of my spirit tallied the song of the bird.

Come lovely and soothing death,
Undulate round the world, serenely arriving, arriving,
In the day, in the night, to all, to each,
Sooner or later delicate death.

Prais'd be the fathomless universe,
For life and joy, and for objects and knowledge curious,
And for love, sweet love—but praise! praise! praise!   140
For the sure-enwinding arms of cool-enfolding death.

Dark mother always gliding near with soft feet,
Have none chanted for thee a chant of fullest welcome?
Then I chant it for thee, I glorify thee above all,
I bring thee a song that when thou must indeed come, come unfalteringly.

Approach strong deliveress,
When it is so, when thou hast taken them I joyously sing the dead,
Lost in the loving floating ocean of thee,
Laved in the flood of thy bliss O death.   150

From me to thee glad serenades,
Dances for thee I propose saluting thee, adornments and feastings for thee,
And the sights of the open landscape and the high-spread sky are fitting,
And life and the fields, and the huge and thoughtful night.

The night in silence under many a star,
The ocean shore and the husky whispering wave whose voice I know,
And the soul turning to thee O vast and well-veil'd death,
And the body gratefully nestling close to thee.

Over the tree-tops I float thee a song,
Over the rising and sinking waves, over the myriad fields and the prairies
*   wide,*   160
Over the dense-pack'd cities all and the teeming wharves and ways,
I float this carol with joy, with joy to thee O death.

15

To the tally of my soul,
Loud and strong kept up the gray-brown bird,
With pure deliberate notes spreading filling the night.

Loud in the pines and cedars dim,
Clear in the freshness moist and the swamp-perfume,
And I with my comrades there in the night.

While my sight that was bound in my eyes unclosed,
As to long panoramas of visions.   170

And I saw askant[6] the armies,
I saw as in noiseless dreams hundreds of battle-flags,
Borne through the smoke of the battles and pierc'd with missiles I
    saw them,
And carried hither and yon through the smoke, and torn and
    bloody,
And at last but a few shreds left on the staffs, (and all in silence,)
And the staffs all splinter'd and broken.

I saw battle-corpses, myriads of them,
And the white skeletons of young men, I saw them,
I saw the debris and debris of all the slain soldiers of the war,
But I saw they were not as was thought,   180
They themselves were fully at rest, they suffer'd not,
The living remain'd and suffer'd, the mother suffer'd,
And the wife and the child and the musing comrade suffer'd,
And the armies that remain'd suffer'd.

16

Passing the visions, passing the night,
Passing, unloosing the hold of my comrades' hands,
Passing the song of the hermit bird and the tallying song of my soul,
Victorious song, death's outlet song, yet varying ever-altering song,
As low and wailing, yet clear the notes, rising and falling, flooding
    the night,
Sadly sinking and fainting, as warning and warning, and yet again   190
    bursting with joy,

[6]Sideways, out of the corner of the eye, with mistrust.

Covering the earth and filling the spread of the heaven,
As that powerful psalm in the night I heard from recesses,
Passing, I leave thee lilac with heart-shaped leaves,
I leave thee there in the dooryard, blooming, returning with spring.

I cease from my song for thee,
From my gaze on thee in the west, fronting the west, communing
  with thee,
O comrade lustrous with silver face in the night.

Yet each to keep and all, retrievements out of the night,
The song, the wondrous chant of the gray-brown bird,
And the tallying chant, the echo arous'd in my soul,   200
With the lustrous and drooping star with the countenance full of
  woe,
With the holders holding my hand nearing the call of the bird,
Comrades mine and I in the midst, and their memory ever to keep,
  for the dead I loved so well,
For the sweetest, wisest soul of all my days and lands—and this for
  his dear sake,
Lilac and star and bird twined with the chant of my soul,
There in the fragrant pines and the cedars dusk and dim.

1865–1866, 1881

from AUTUMN RIVULETS

THERE WAS A CHILD WENT FORTH

There was a child went forth every day,
And the first object he look'd upon, that object he became,
And that object became part of him for the day or a certain part of
  the day,
Or for many years or stretching cycles of years.

The early lilacs became part of this child,
And grass and white and red morning-glories, and white and red
  clover, and the song of the phœbe-bird,
And the Third-month lambs and the sow's pink-faint litter, and the
  mare's foal and the cow's calf,
And the noisy brood of the barnyard or by the mire of the pond-
  side,
And the fish suspending themselves so curiously below there, and
  the beautiful curious liquid,
And the water-plants with their graceful flat heads, all became part
  of him.   10

The field-sprouts of Fourth-month and Fifth-month became part of
  him,
Winter-grain sprouts and those of the light-yellow corn, and the
  esculent roots of the garden,

And the apple-trees cover'd with blossoms and the fruit afterward,
    and wood-berries, and the commonest weeds by the road,
And the old drunkard staggering home from the outhouse of the
    tavern whence he had lately risen,
And the schoolmistress that pass'd on her way to the school,
And the friendly boys that pass'd, and the quarrelsome boys,
And the tidy and fresh-cheek'd girls, and the barefoot negro boy and
    girl,
And all the changes of city and country wherever he went.

His own parents, he that had father'd him and she that had
    conceiv'd him in her womb and birth'd him,
They gave this child more of themselves than that,   20
They gave him afterward every day, they became part of him.

The mother at home quietly placing the dishes on the supper-table,
The mother with mild words, clean her cap and gown, a wholesome
    odor falling off her person and clothes as she walks by,
The father, strong, self-sufficient, manly, mean, anger'd, unjust,
The blow, the quick loud word, the tight bargain, the crafty lure,
The family usages, the language, the company, the furniture, the
    yearning and swelling heart,
Affection that will not be gainsay'd, the sense of what is real, the
    thought if after all it should prove unreal,
The doubts of day-time and the doubts of night-time, the curious
    whether and how,
Whether that which appears so is so, or is it all flashes and specks?
Men and women crowding fast in the streets, if they are not flashes
    and specks what are they?   30
The streets themselves and the façades of houses, and goods in the
    windows,
Vehicles, teams, the heavy-plank'd wharves, the huge crossing at the
    ferries,
The village on the highland seen from afar at sunset, the river
    between,
Shadows, aureola and mist, the light falling on roofs and gables of
    white or brown two miles off,
The schooner near by sleepily drooping down the tide, the little boat
    slack-tow'd astern,
The hurrying tumbling waves, quick-broken crests, slapping,
The strata of color'd clouds, the long bar of maroon-tint away
    solitary by itself, the spread of purity it lies motionless in,
The horizon's edge, the flying sea-crow, the fragrance of salt marsh
    and shore mud,
These became part of that child who went forth every day, and who
    now goes, and will always go forth every day.

                                                                          1855, 1871

PASSAGE TO INDIA

1

Singing my days,
Singing the great achievements of the present,
Singing the strong light works of engineers,
Our modern wonders, (the antique ponderous Seven[1] outvied),
In the Old World the east the Suez canal[2]
The New by its mighty railroad spann'd,[3]
The seas inlaid with eloquent gentle wires,[4]
Yet first to sound, and ever sound, the cry with thee O soul,
The Past! the Past! the Past!

The Past—the dark unfathom'd retrospect!
The teeming gulf—the sleepers and the shadows!
The past—the infinite greatness of the past!

For what is the present after all but a growth out of the past?
(As a projectile form'd, impell'd, passing a certain line, still keeps on,
So the present, utterly form'd, impell'd by the past.)

2

Passage O soul to India!
Eclaircise[5] the myths Asiatic, the primitive fables.

Not you alone proud truths of the world,
Not you alone ye facts of modern science,
But myths and fables of eld,[6] Asia's, Africa's fables,
The far-darting beams of the spirit, the unloos'd dreams,
The deep diving bibles and legends,
The daring plots of the poets, the elder religions;
O you temples fairer than lilies pour'd over by the rising sun!
O you fables spurning the known, eluding the hold of the known,
    mounting to heaven!
You lofty and dazzling towers, pinnacled, red as roses, burnish'd
    with gold!
Towers of fables immortal fashion'd from mortal dreams!
You too I welcome and fully the same as the rest!
You too with joy I sing.

Passage to India!
Lo, soul, seest thou not God's purpose from the first?
The earth to be spann'd, connected by network,
The races, neighbors, to marry and be given in marriage,
The oceans to be cross'd, the distant brought near,
The lands to be welded together.

[1]The Seven Wonders of the Ancient World.
[2]Completed in 1867, formally opened in 1869.
[3]The transcontinental railroad was completed at Promontory, Utah, in 1869.
[4]A transatlantic cable was laid in 1866.
[5]Clarify, explain.   [6]Antiquity.

A worship new I sing,
You captain, voyages, explorers, yours,
You engineers, you architects, machinists, yours,
You, not for trade or transportation only,
But in God's name, and for thy sake O soul.   40

3

Passage to India!
Lo soul for thee of tableaus twain,
I see in one the Suez canal initiated, open'd,
I see the procession of steamships, the Empress Eugenie's[7] leading
    the van,
I mark from on deck the strange landscape, the pure sky, the level
    sand in the distance,
I pass swiftly the picturesque groups, the workmen gather'd,
The gigantic dredging machines,
In one again, different, (yet thine, all thine, O soul, the same,)
I see over my own continent the Pacific railroad[8] surmounting every
    barrier,
I see continual trains of cars winding along the Platte carrying
    freight and passengers,   50
I hear the locomotives rushing and roaring, and the shrill
    steamwhistle,
I hear the echoes reverberate through the grandest scenery in the
    world,
I cross the Laramie plains, I note the rocks in grotesque shapes, the
    buttes,
I see the plentiful larkspur and wild onions, the barren, colorless,
    sage-deserts,
I see in glimpses afar or towering immediately above me the great
    mountains, I see the Wind river and the Wahsatch mountains,
I see the Monument mountain the Eagle's Nest, I pass the
    Promontory, I ascend the Nevadas,
I scan the noble Elk mountain and wind around its base,
I see the Humboldt range, I thread the valley and cross the river,
I see the clear waters of Lake Tahoe, I see forests of majestic pines,
Or crossing the great desert, the alkaline plains, I behold enchanting
    mirages of waters and meadows,   60
Marking through these and after all, in duplicate slender lines,
Bridging the three or four thousand miles of land travel,
Tying the Eastern to the Western sea,
The road between Europe and Asia.

(Ah Genoese[9] thy dream! thy dream!
Centuries after thou art laid in thy grave,
The shore thou foundest verifies thy dream.)

[7]Empress of France, wife of Napoleon III. She was aboard the ship leading the procession at the formal opening of the Suez Canal.
[8]The transcontinental railroad linked the Atlantic and the Pacific oceans in 1869. Below, Whitman lists sites, from Nebraska to California, along the route of the railroad.
[9]Christopher Columbus.

4

Passage to India!
Struggles of many a captain, tales of many a sailor dead,
Over my mood stealing and spreading they come,   70
Like clouds and cloudlets in the unreach'd sky.

Along all history, down the slopes,
As a rivulet running, sinking now, and now again to the surface
    rising,
A ceaseless thought, a varied train—lo, soul, to thee, thy sight, they
    rise,
The plans, the voyages again, the expeditions;

Again Vasco de Gama[10] sails forth,
Again the knowledge gain'd, the mariner's compass,
Lands found and nations born, thou born America,
For purpose vast, man's long probation fill'd,
Thou rondure[11] of the world at last accomplish'd,   80

5

O vast Rondure, swimming in space,
Cover'd all over with visible power and beauty,
Alternate light and day and the teeming spiritual darkness,
Unspeakable high processions of sun and moon and countless stars
    above,
Below the manifold grass and waters, animals, mountains, trees,
With inscrutable purpose, some hidden prophetic intention,
Now first it seems my thought begins to span thee.

Down from the gardens of Asia descending radiating,
Adam and Eve appear, then their myriad progeny after them,
Wandering, yearning, curious, with restless explorations,   90
With questionings, baffled, formless, feverish, with never-happy
    hearts,
With that sad incessant refrain, *Wherefore unsatisfied soul?* and *Whither
    O mocking life?*

Ah who shall soothe these feverish children?
Who justify these restless explorations?
Who speak the secret of impassive earth?
Who bind it to us? what is this separate Nature so unnatural?
What is this earth to our affections? (unloving earth, without a throb
    to answer ours,
Cold earth, the place of graves.)

Yet soul be sure the first intent remains, and shall be carried out,
Perhaps even now the time has arrived.   100

[10]Vasco da Gama. Portuguese navigator, first European to sail (1497–1498) from Europe, around
Africa's Cape of Good Hope, to India.
[11]Encirclement, circumnavigation.

After the seas are all cross'd, (as they seem already cross'd,)
After the great captains and engineers have accomplish'd their work,
After the noble inventors, after the scientists, the chemist, the
   geologist, ethnologist,
Finally shall come the poet worthy that name,
The true son of God shall come singing his songs.

Then not your deeds only O voyagers, O scientists and inventors,
   shall be justified,
All these hearts as of fretted children shall be sooth'd,
All affection shall be fully responded to, the secret shall be told,
All these separations and gaps shall be taken up and hook'd and
   link'd together,
The whole earth, this cold, impassive, voiceless earth, shall be
   completely justified,   110
Trinitas[12] divine shall be gloriously accomplish'd and compacted by
   the true son of God, the poet,
(He shall indeed pass the straits and conquer the mountains,
He shall double the cape of Good Hope to some purpose,)
Nature and Man shall be disjoin'd and diffused no more,
The true son of God shall absolutely fuse them.

6

Year at whose wide-flung door I sing!
Year of the purpose accomplish'd!
Year of the marriage of continents, climates and oceans!
(No mere doge of Venice now wedding the Adriatic,)[13]
I see O year in you the vast terraqueous globe given and giving all,   120
Europe to Asia, Africa join'd, and they to the New World,
The lands, geographies, dancing before you, holding a festival
   garland,
As brides and bridegrooms hand in hand.

Passage to India!
Cooling airs from Caucasus[14] far, soothing cradle of man,
The river Euphrates[15] flowing, the past lit up again,

Lo soul, the retrospect brought forward,
The old, most populous, wealthiest of earth's lands,
The streams of the Indus and the Ganges[16] and their many affluents,
(I my shores of America walking to-day behold, resuming all,)   130
The tale of Alexander[17] on his warlike marches suddenly dying,
On one side China and on the other side Persia and Arabia,
To the south the great seas and the bay of Bengal,
The flowing literatures, tremendous epics, religions, castes,
Old occult Brahma interminably far back, the tender and junior
   Buddha,

[12]Whitman's approximate Spanish for "the Holy Trinity."
[13]The Doge (chief magistrate of the city-state of Venice, 697–1797) symbolized the union of Venice
and the sea by annually casting a gold ring into the Adriatic.
[14]Area in Russia between the Black and Caspian seas.
[15]River flowing from Turkey to the Persian Gulf.
[16]Rivers in India.   [17]Alexander the Great (356–323 B.C.).

Central and southern empires and all their belongings, possessors,
The wars of Tamerlane,[18] the reign of Aurungzebe,[19]
The traders, rulers, explorers, Moslems, Venetians, Byzantium, the
    Arabs, Portuguese,
The first travelers famous yet, Marco Polo,[20] Batouta the Moor,[21]
Doubts to be solv'd, the map incognita,[22] blanks to be fill'd,   140
The foot of man unstay'd, the hands never at rest,
Thyself O soul that will not brook a challenge.

The mediæval navigators rise before me,
The world of 1492, with its awaken'd enterprise,
Something swelling in humanity now like the sap of the earth in
    spring,
The sunset splendor of chivalry declining.

And who art thou sad shade?
Gigantic, visionary, thyself a visionary,
With majestic limbs and pious beaming eyes,
Spreading around with every look of thine a golden world,   150
Enhuing it with gorgeous hues.

As the chief histrion,[23]
Down to the footlights walks in some great scena,[24]
Dominating the rest I see the Admiral[25] himself,
(History's type[26] of courage, action, faith,)
Behold him sail from Palos[27] leading his little fleet,
His voyage behold, his return, his great fame,
His misfortunes, calumniators, behold him a prisoner, chain'd,
Behold his dejection, poverty, death.

(Curious in time I stand, noting the efforts of heroes,   160
Is the deferment long? bitter the slander, poverty, death?
Lies the seed unreck'd[28] for centuries in the ground? lo, to God's
    due occasion,
Uprising in the night, it sprouts, blooms,
And fills the earth with use and beauty.)

7
Passage indeed O soul to primal thought,
Not lands and seas alone, thy own clear freshness,
The young maturity of brood and bloom,
To realms of budding bibles.

O soul, repressless, I with thee and thou with me,
Thy circumnavigation of the world begin,   170
Of man, the voyage of his mind's return,
To reason's early paradise,
Back, back to wisdom's birth, to innocent intuitions,
Again with fair creation.

---

[18]Mongol conqueror (1336?–1405).   [19]Emperor of Hindustan (1618–1707).
[20]Venetian (1254–1324), early traveler to China.   [21]Explorer of Africa and Asia (1303–1377).
[22]Unknown.   [23]Actor.   [24]Scene.   [25]Columbus.
[26]Symbol, model.   [27]Spanish seaport from which Columbus sailed, August 1492.
[28]Unnoticed.

8

O we can wait no longer,
We too take ship O soul,
Joyous we too launch out on trackless seas,
Fearless for unknown shores on waves of ecstasy to sail,
Amid the wafting winds, (thou pressing me to thee, I thee to me, O
    soul,)
Caroling free, singing our song of God,   180
Chanting our chant of pleasant exploration.

With laugh and many a kiss,
(Let others deprecate, let others weep for sin, remorse, humiliation,)
O soul thou pleasest me, I thee.

Ah more than any priest O soul we too believe in God,
But with the mystery of God we dare not dally.

O soul thou pleasest me, I thee,
Sailing these seas or on the hills, or waking in the night,
Thoughts, silent thoughts, of Time and Space and Death, like waters
    flowing,
Bear me indeed as through the regions infinite,   190
Whose air I breathe, whose ripples hear, lave me all over,
Bathe me O God in thee, mounting to thee,
I and my soul to range of thee.

O Thou transcendent,
Nameless, the fibre and the breath,
Light of the light, shedding forth universes, thou centre of them,
Thou mightier centre of the true, the good, the loving,
Thou moral, spiritual fountain—affection's source—thou reservoir,
(O pensive soul of me—O thirst unsatisfied—waitest not there?
Waitest not haply for us somewhere there the Comrade perfect?)   200
Thou pulse—thou motive of the stars, suns, systems,
That, circling, move in order, safe, harmonious,
Athwart the shapeless vastnesses of space,
How should I think, how breathe a single breath, how speak, if, out
    of myself,
I could not launch, to those, superior universes?

Swiftly I shrivel at the thought of God,
At Nature and its wonders, Time and Space and Death,
But that, I, turning, call to thee O soul, thou actual Me,
And lo, thou gently masterest the orbs,
Thou matest Time, smilest content at Death,   210
And fillest, swellest full the vastnesses of Space.

Greater than stars or suns,
Bounding O soul thou journeyest forth;
What love than thine and ours could wider amplify?
What aspirations, wishes, outvie thine and ours O soul?
What dreams of the ideal? what plans of purity, perfection, strength?
What cheerful willingness for others' sake to give up all?
For others' sake to suffer all?

Reckoning ahead O soul, when thou, the time achiev'd,
The seas all cross'd, weather'd the capes, the voyage done, 220
Surrounded, copest, frontest God, yieldest, the aim attain'd,
As fill'd with friendship, love complete, the Elder Brother found,
The Younger melts in fondness in his arms.

9

Passage to more than India!
Are thy wings plumed indeed for such far flights?
O soul, voyagest thou indeed on voyages like those?
Disportest thou on waters such as those?
Soundest below the Sanscrit and the Vedas?[29]
Then have thy bent[30] unleash'd.

Passage to you, your shores, ye aged fierce enigmas!
Passage to you, to mastership of you, ye strangling problems! 230
You, strew'd with the wrecks of skeletons, that, living, never reach'd
  you.

Passage to more than India!
O secret of the earth and sky!
Of you O waters of the sea! O winding creeks and rivers!
Of you O woods and fields! of you strong mountains of my land!
Of you O prairies! of you gray rocks!
O morning red! O clouds! O rain and snows!
O day and night, passage to you!

O sun and moon and all you stars! Sirius and Jupiter![31] 240
Passage to you!

Passage, immediate passage! the blood burns in my veins!
Away O soul! hoist instantly the anchor!
Cut the hawser—haul out—shake out every sail!
Have we not stood here like trees in the ground long enough?
Have we not grovel'd here long enough, eating and drinking like
  mere brutes?
Have we not darken'd and dazed ourselves with books long enough?

Sail forth—steer for the deep waters only,
Reckless O soul, exploring, I with thee, and thou with me,
For we are bound where mariner has not yet dared to go, 250
And we will risk the ship, ourselves and all.

O my brave soul!
O farther farther sail!
O daring joy, but safe! are they not all the seas of God?
O farther, farther, farther sail!

1871, 1881

[29]Hindu scriptures, written in Sanskrit.   [30]Force, energy.
[31]Sirius: the brightest star in the sky. Jupiter: the largest planet.

THE SLEEPERS

1

I wander all night in my vision,
Stepping with light feet, swiftly and noiselessly stepping and
    stopping,
Bending with open eyes over the shut eyes of sleepers,
Wandering and confused, lost to myself, ill-assorted, contradictory,
Pausing, gazing, bending, and stopping,

How solemn they look there, stretch'd and still,
How quiet they breathe, the little children in their cradles.

The wretched features of ennuyés,[1] the white features of corpses, the
    livid faces of drunkards, the sick-gray faces of onanists,
The gash'd bodies on battle-fields, the insane in their strong-door'd
    rooms, the sacred idiots, the new-born emerging from gates, and
    the dying emerging from gates,
The night pervades them and infolds them.   10

The married couple sleep calmly in their bed, he with his palm on
    the hip of the wife, and she with her palm on the hip of the
    husband,
The sisters sleep lovingly side by side in their bed,
The men sleep lovingly side by side in theirs,
And the mother sleeps with her little child carefully wrapt.

The blind sleep, and the deaf and dumb sleep,
The prisoner sleeps well in the prison, the runaway son sleeps,
The murderer that is to be hung next day, how does he sleep?
And the murder'd person, how does he sleep?

The female that loves unrequited sleeps,
And the male that loves unrequited sleeps,   20
The head of the money-maker that plotted all day sleeps,
And the enraged and treacherous dispositions, all, all sleep.

I stand in the dark with drooping eyes by the worst-suffering and
    the most restless,
I pass my hands soothingly to and fro a few inches from them,
The restless sink in their beds, they fitfully sleep.

Now I pierce the darkness, new beings appear,
The earth recedes from me into the night,
I saw that it was beautiful, and I see that what is not the earth is
    beautiful.

I go from bedside to bedside, I sleep close with the other sleepers
    each in turn,
I dream in my dream all the dreams of the other dreamers,   30
And I become the other dreamers.

[1]French: bored, vexed people.

I am a dance—play up there! the fit is whirling me fast!

I am the ever-laughing—it is new moon and twilight,
I see the hiding of douceurs,[2] I see nimble ghosts whichever way I
    look,
Cache[3] and cache again deep in the ground and sea, and where it is
    neither ground nor sea.

Well do they do their jobs those journeymen divine,
Only from me can they hide nothing, and would not if they could,
I reckon I am their boss and they make me a pet besides,
And surround me and lead me and run ahead when I walk,
To lift their cunning covers to signify[4] me with stretch'd arms, and
    resume the way;
Onward we move, a gay gang of blackguards! with mirth-shouting
    music and wild-flapping pennants of joy!

I am the actor, the actress, the voter, the politician,
The emigrant and the exile, the criminal that stood in the box,[5]
He who has been famous and he who shall be famous after to-day,
The stammerer, the well-form'd person, the waster or feeble person.

I am she who adorn'd herself and folded her hair expectantly,
My truant lover has come, and it is dark.

Double yourself and receive me darkness,
Receive me and my lover too, he will not let me go without him.

I roll myself upon you as upon a bed, I resign myself to the dusk.

He whom I call answers me and takes the place of my lover,
He rises with me silently from the bed.

Darkness, you are gentler than my lover, his flesh was sweaty and
    panting,
I feel the hot moisture yet that he left me.

My hands are spread forth, I pass them in all directions,
I would sound up the shadowy shore to which you are journeying.

Be careful darkness! already what was it touch'd me?
I thought my lover had gone, else darkness and he are one,
I hear the heart-beat, I follow, I fade away.

2

I descend my western course,[6] my sinews are flaccid,
Perfume and youth course through me and I am their wake.

[2]Delights, pleasures.   [3]Hide.   [4]Signal.
[5]Courtroom dock, where the accused stands during a criminal trial.
[6]I.e., grow old.

It is my face yellow and wrinkled instead of the old woman's,
I sit low in a straw-bottom chair and carefully darn my grandson's
  stockings.

It is I too, the sleepless widow looking out on the winter midnight,
I see the sparkles of starshine on the icy and pallid earth.

A shroud I see and I am the shroud, I wrap a body and lie in the
  coffin,
It is dark here under ground, it is not evil or pain here, it is blank
  here, for reasons.

(It seems to me that every thing in the light and air ought to be
  happy,
Whoever is not in his coffin and the dark grave let him know he has
  enough.)

3

I see a beautiful gigantic swimmer swimming naked through the
  eddies of the sea,   70
His brown hair lies close and even to his head, he strikes out with
  courageous arms, he urges himself with his legs,
I see his white body, I see his undaunted eyes,
I hate the swift-running eddies that would dash him head-foremost
  on the rocks.

What are you doing you ruffianly red-trickled waves?
Will you kill the courageous giant? will you kill him in the prime of
  his middle age?

Steady and long he struggles,
He is baffled, bang'd, bruis'd, he holds out while his strength holds
  out,
The slapping eddies are spotted with his blood, they bear him away,
  they roll him, swing him, turn him,
His beautiful body is borne in the circling eddies, it is continually
  bruis'd on rocks,
Swiftly and out of sight is borne the brave corpse.   80

4

I turn but do not extricate myself,
Confused, a past-reading, another, but with darkness yet.

The beach is cut by the razory ice-wind, the wreck-guns[7] sound,
The tempest lulls, the moon comes floundering through the drifts.

I look where the ship helplessly heads end on, I near the burst as
  she strikes, I hear the howls of dismay, they grow fainter and
  fainter.

[7]Guns that fire a lifeline to wrecked ships.

I cannot aid with my wringing fingers,
I can but rush to the surf and let it drench me and freeze upon me.

I search with the crowd, not one of the company is wash'd to us
    alive,
In the morning I help pick up the dead and lay them in rows in a
    barn.

5

Now of the older war-days, the defeat at Brooklyn,[8]   90
Washington stands inside the lines, he stands on the intrench'd hills
    amid a crowd of officers,
His face is cold and damp, he cannot repress the weeping drops,
He lifts the glass perpetually to his eyes, the color is blanch'd from
    his cheeks,
He sees the slaughter of the southern braves[9] confided to him by
    their parents.

The same at last and at last when peace is declared,
He stands in the room of the old tavern,[10] the well-belov'd soldiers
    all pass through,
The officers speechless and slow draw near in their turns,
The chief encircles their necks with his arm and kisses them on the
    cheek,
He kisses lightly the wet cheeks one after another, he shakes hands
    and bids good-by to the army.

6

Now what my mother told me one day as we sat at dinner together,   100
Of when she was a nearly grown girl living home with her parents
    on the old homestead.

A red squaw came one breakfast-time to the old homestead,
On her back she carried a bundle of rushes for rush-bottoming
    chairs,
Her hair, straight, shiny, coarse, black, profuse, half-envelop'd her
    face,
Her step was free and elastic, and her voice sounded exquisitely as
    she spoke.

My mother look'd in delight and amazement at the stranger,
She look'd at the freshness of her tall-borne face and full and pliant
    limbs,
The more she look'd upon her she loved her,
Never before had she seen such wonderful beauty and purity,
She made her sit on a bench by the jamb of the fireplce, she cook'd
    food for her,   110
She had no work to give her, but she gave her remembrance and
    fondness.

[8]British victory over American forces at the Battle of Brooklyn Heights, August 1776.
[9]Revolutionary soldiers from the southern colonies.
[10]Fraunces Tavern, New York City, where Washington bid farewell to his troops, in 1783.

The red squaw staid all the forenoon, and toward the middle of the
    afternoon she went away,
O my mother was loth[11] to have her go away,
All the week she thought of her, she watch'd for her many a month,
She remember'd her many a winter and many a summer,
But the red squaw never came nor was heard of there again.

7

A show of the summer softness—a contact of something unseen—an
    amour of the light and air,
I am jealous and overwhelm'd with friendliness,
And will go gallivant with the light and air myself.

O love and summer, you are in the dreams and in me,   120
Autumn and winter are in the dreams, the farmer goes with his
    thrift,
The droves[12] and crops increase, the barns are well-fill'd.

Elements merge in the night, ships make tacks in the dreams,
The sailor sails, the exile returns home,
The fugitive returns unharm'd, the immigrant is back beyond
    months and years,
The poor Irishman lives in the simple house of his childhood with
    the well-known neighbors and faces,
They warmly welcome him, he is barefoot again, he forgets he is well
    off,
The Dutchman voyages home, and the Scotchman and Welshman
    voyage home, and the native of the Mediterranean voyages home,
To every port of England, France, Spain, enter well-fill'd ships,
The Swiss foots it towards his hills, the Prussian goes his way, the
    Hungarian his way, and the Pole his way,   130
The Swede returns, and the Dane and Norwegian return.

The homeward bound and the outward bound,
The beautiful lost swimmer, the ennuyé, the onanist, the female that
    loves unrequited, the money-maker,
The actor and actress, those through with their parts and those
    waiting to commence,
The affectionate boy, the husband and wife, the voter, the nominee
    that is chosen and the nominee that has fail'd,
The great already known and the great any time after to-day,
The stammerer, the sick, the perfect-form'd, the homely,
The criminal that stood in the box, the judge that sat and sentenced
    him, the fluent lawyers, the jury, the audience,
The laugher and weeper, the dancer, the midnight widow, the red
    squaw,
The consumptive, the erysipalite,[13] the idiot, he that is wrong'd,   140
The antipodes,[14] and every one between this and them in the dark,

---

[11]Reluctant.   [12]Herds of animals.
[13]One suffering from erysipelas, infected and inflamed skin.
[14]Those living on the opposite side of the earth.

I swear they are averaged now—one is no better than the other,
The night and sleep have liken'd them and restored them.

I swear they are all beautiful,
Every one that sleeps is beautiful, every thing in the dim light is
    beautiful,
The wildest and bloodiest is over, and all is peace.

Peace is always beautiful,
The myth of heaven indicates peace and night.

The myth of heaven indicates the soul,
The soul is always beautiful, it appears more or it appears less, it
    comes or it lags behind,   150
It comes from its embower'd garden and looks pleasantly on itself
    and encloses the world,
Perfect and clean the genitals previously jetting, and perfect and
    clean the womb cohering,
The head well-grown proportion'd and plumb, and the bowels and
    joints proportion'd and plumb.

The soul is always beautiful,
The universe is duly in order, every thing is in its place,
What has arrived is in its place and what waits shall be in its place,
The twisted skull waits, the watery or rotten blood waits,
The child of the glutton or venerealee waits long, and the child of
    the drunkard waits long, and the drunkard himself waits long,
The sleepers that lived and died wait, the far advanced are to go on
    in their turns, and the far behind are to come on in their turns,
The diverse shall be no less diverse, but they shall flow and unite—
    they unite now.   160

8

The sleepers are very beautiful as they lie unclothed,
They flow hand in hand over the whole earth from east to west as
    they lie unclothed,
The Asiatic and African are hand in hand, the European and
    American are hand in hand,
Learn'd and unlearn'd are hand in hand, and male and female are
    hand in hand,
The bare arm of the girl crosses the bare breast of her lover, they
    press close without lust, his lips press her neck,
The father holds his grown or ungrown son in his arms with
    measureless love, and the son holds the father in his arms with
    measureless love,
The white hair of the mother shines on the white wrist of the
    daughter,
The breath of the boy goes with the breath of the man, friend is
    inarm'd by friend,
The scholar kisses the teacher and the teacher kisses the scholar, the
    wrong'd is made right,

The call of the slave is one with the master's call, and the master
    salutes the slave,   170
The felon steps forth from the prison, the insane become sane, the
    suffering of sick persons is reliev'd,
The sweatings and fevers stop, the throat that was unsound is sound,
    the lungs of the consumptive are resumed, the poor distress'd
    head is free,
The joints of the rheumatic move as smoothly as ever, and smoother
    than ever,
Stiflings and passages open, the paralyzed become supple,
The swell'd and convuls'd and congested awake to themselves in
    condition,
They pass the invigoration of the night and the chemistry of the
    night, and awake.

I too pass from the night,
I stay a while away O night, but I return to you again and love you.

Why should I be afraid to trust myself to you?
I am not afraid, I have been well brought forward by you,   180
I love the rich running day, but I do not desert her in whom I lay so
    long,
I know not how I came of you and I know not where I go with you,
    but I know I came well and shall go well.

I will stop only a time with the night, and rise betimes,
I will duly pass the day O my mother, and duly return to you.

1855, 1881

from *WHISPERS OF HEAVENLY DEATH*

CHANTING THE SQUARE DEIFIC

1

Chanting the square deific, out of the One advancing, out of the
    sides,
Out of the old and new, out of the square entirely divine,
Solid, four-sided, (all the sides needed,) from this side Jehovah am I,
Old Brahm[1] I, and I Saturnius[2] am;
Not Time affects me—I am Time, old, modern as any,
Unpersuadable, relentless, executing righteous judgments,
As the Earth, the Father, the brown old Kronos,[3] with laws,
Aged beyond computation, yet ever new, ever with those mighty laws
    rolling,
Relentless I forgive no man—whoever sins dies—I will have that
    man's life;

[1]Brahma, chief Hindu god.   [2]Saturn, a chief Roman god.
[3]Kronos, ancient Greek god and father of Zeus.

Therefore let none expect mercy—have the seasons, gravitation, the
   appointed days, mercy? no more have I,   10
But as the seasons and gravitation, and as all the appointed days that
   forgive not,
I dispense from this side judgments inexorable without the least
   remorse.

2

Consolator most mild, the promis'd one advancing,
With gentle hand extended, the mightier God am I,
Foretold by prophets and poets in their most rapt prophecies and
   poems,
From this side, lo! the Lord Christ gazes—lo! Hermes[4] I—lo! mine is
   Hercules' face,
All sorrow, labor, suffering, I, tallying it, absorb in myself,
Many times have I been rejected, taunted, put in prison, and
   crucified, and many times shall be again,
All the world have I given up for my dear brothers' and sisters' sake,
   for the soul's sake,
Wending my way through the homes of men, rich or poor, with the
   kiss of affection,   20
For I am affection, I am the cheer-bringing God, with hope and all-
   enclosing charity,
With indulgent words as to children, with fresh and sane words,
   mine only,
Young and strong I pass knowing well I am destin'd myself to an
   early death;
But my charity has no death—my wisdom dies not, neither early nor
   late,
And my sweet love bequeath'd here and elsewhere never dies.

3

Aloof, dissatisfied, plotting revolt,
Comrade of criminals, brother of slaves,
Crafty, despised, a drudge, ignorant,
With sudra[5] face and worn brow, black, but in the depths of my
   heart, proud as any,
Lifted now and always against whoever scorning assumes to rule me,   30
Morose, full of guile, full of reminiscences, brooding, with many
   wiles,
(Though it was thought I was baffled and dispel'd, and my wiles
   done, but that will never be,)
Defiant, I, Satan, still live, still utter words, in new lands duly
   appearing, (and old ones also,)
Permanent here from my side, warlike, equal with any, real as any,
Nor time nor change shall ever change me or my words.

4

Santa Spirita,[6] breather, life,
Beyond the light, lighter than light,
Beyond the flames of hell, joyous, leaping easily above hell,

[4]Messenger of the Greek gods.   [5]Lowest of the four Hindu castes.
[6]The Holy Spirit.

Beyond Paradise, perfumed solely with mine own perfume,
Including all life on earth, touching, including God, including
   Saviour and Satan,   40
Ethereal, pervading all, (for without me what were all? what were
   God?)
Essence of forms, life of the real identities, permanent, positive,
   (namely the unseen,)
Life of the great round world, the sun and stars, and of man, I, the
   general soul,
Here the square finishing, the solid, I the most solid,
Breathe my breath also through these songs.

                                               1865–1866, 1881

A NOISELESS PATIENT SPIDER

A noiseless patient spider,
I mark'd where on a little promontory it stood isolated,
Mark'd how to explore the vacant vast surrounding,
It launch'd forth filament, filament, filament, out of itself,
Ever unreeling them, ever tirelessly speeding them.

And you O my soul where you stand,
Surrounded, detached, in measureless oceans of space,
Ceaselessly musing, venturing, throwing, seeking the spheres to
   connect them,
Till the bridge you will need be form'd, till the ductile anchor hold,
Till the gossamer thread you fling catch somewhere, O my soul.   10

                                               1868, 1881

from *NOON TO STARRY NIGHT*

TO A LOCOMOTIVE IN WINTER

Thee for my recitative,[1]
Thee in the driving storm even as now, the snow, the winter-day
   declining,
Thee in thy panoply,[2] thy measur'd dual throbbing and thy beat
   convulsive,
Thy black cylindric body, golden brass and silvery steel,
Thy ponderous side-bars, parallel and connecting rods, gyrating,
   shuttling at thy sides,
Thy metrical, now swelling pant and roar, now tapering in the
   distance,
Thy great protruding head-light fix'd in front,
Thy long, pale, floating vapor-pennants, tinged with delicate purple,

---

[1] A rhythmically free, vocal narration, a recitation.   [2] Suit of armor.

Thy dense and murky clouds out-belching from thy smoke-stack,
Thy knitted frame, thy springs and valves, the tremulous twinkle of
    thy wheels,   10
Thy train of cars behind, obedient, merrily following,
Through gale or calm, now swift, now slack, yet steadily careering;
Type of the modern—emblem of motion and power—pulse of the
    continent,
For once come serve the Muse and merge in verse, even as here I
    see thee,
With storm and buffeting gusts of winds and falling snow,
By day the warning ringing bell to sound its notes,
By night thy silent signal lamps to swing.

Fierce-throated beauty!
Roll through my chant with all thy lawless music, thy swinging lamps
    at night,
Thy madly-whistled laughter, echoing, rumbling like an earthquake,
    rousing all,   20
Law of thyself complete, thine own track firmly holding,
(No sweetness debonair of tearful harp or glib piano thine,)
Thy trills of shrieks by rocks and hills return'd,
Launch'd o'er the prairies wide, across the lakes,
To the free skies unpent and glad and strong.

                                              1876, 1881

from *SANDS AT SEVENTY*

AS I SIT WRITING HERE

    As I sit writing here, sick and grown old,
    Not my least burden is that dulness of the years, querilities,
    Ungracious glooms, aches, lethargy, constipation, whimpering
        ennui,[1]
    May filter in my daily songs.

                                   1888, 1888–1889

from *GOOD-BYE MY FANCY*

L. OF G.'S PURPORT

Not to exclude or demarcate, or pick out evils from their formidable
    masses (even to expose them,)
But add, fuse, complete, extend—and celebrate the immortal and the
    good.

[1] French: weariness, dissatisfaction.

Haughty this song, its word and scope,
To span vast realms of space and time,
Evolution—the cumulative—growths and generations.

Begun in ripen'd youth and steadily pursued,
Wandering, peering, dallying with all—war, peace, day, and night
  absorbing,
Never even for one brief hour abandoning my task,
I end it here in sickness, poverty, and old age.

I sing of life, yet mind me well of death: 10
To-day shadowy Death dogs my steps, my seated shape, and has for
  years—
Draws sometimes close to me, as face to face.

                                                                 1891, 1891–1892

from *DEMOCRATIC VISTAS*

America, filling the present with greatest deeds and problems, cheerfully accepting the past, including feudalism, (as, indeed, the present is but the legitimate birth of the past, including feudalism,) counts, as I reckon, for her justification and success, (for who, as yet, dare claim success?) almost entirely on the future. Nor is that hope unwarranted. To-day, ahead, though dimly yet, we see, in vistas, a copious, sane, gigantic offspring. For our New World I consider far less important for what it has done, or what it is, than for results to come. Sole among nationalities, these States have assumed the task to put in forms of lasting power and practicality, on areas of amplitude rivaling the operations of the physical kosmos, the moral political speculations of ages, long, long deferr'd, the democratic republican principle, and the theory of development and perfection by voluntary standards, and self-reliance. Who else, indeed, except the United States, in history, so far, have accepted in unwitting faith, and, as we now see, stand, act upon, and go security for, these things?

But preluding no longer, let me strike the key-note of the following strain. First premising that, though the passages of it have been written at widely different times, (it is, in fact, a collection of memoranda, perhaps for future designers, comprehenders,) and though it may be open to the charge of one part contradicting another—for there are opposite sides to the great question of democracy, as to every great question—I feel the parts harmoniously blended in my own realization and convictions, and present them to be read only in such oneness, each page and each claim and assertion modified and temper'd by the others. Bear in mind, too, that they are not the result of studying up in political economy, but of the ordinary sense, observing, wandering among men, these States, these stirring years of war and peace. I will not gloss over the appalling dangers of universal suffrage in the United States. In fact, it is to admit and face these dangers I am writing. To him or her within whose thought rages the battle, advancing, retreating, between democracy's convictions, aspirations, and the people's crudeness, vice, caprices, I mainly write this essay. I shall use the words America and democracy as convertible[1] terms. Not an ordinary one is

[1]Equivalent.

the issue. The United States are destined either to surmount the gorgeous history of feudalism, or else prove the most tremendous failure of time. Not the least doubtful am I on any prospects of their material success. The triumphant future of their business, geographic and productive departments, on larger scales and in more varieties than ever, is certain. In those respects the republic must soon (if she does not already) outstrip all examples hitherto afforded, and dominate the world.

Admitting all this, with the priceless value of our political institutions, general suffrage, (and fully acknowledging the latest, widest opening of the doors,) I say that, far deeper than these, what finally and only is to make of our western world a nationality superior to any hitherto known, and outtopping the past, must be vigorous, yet unsuspected Literatures, perfect personalities and sociologies, original, transcendental, and expressing (what, in highest sense, are not yet express'd at all,) democracy and the modern. With these, and out of these, I promulge new races of Teachers, and of perfect Women, indispensable to endow the birth-stock of a New World. For feudalism, caste, the ecclesiastic traditions, though palpably retreating from political institutions, still hold essentially, by their spirit, even in this country, entire possession of the more important fields, indeed the very subsoil, of education, and of social standards and literature.

I say that democracy can never prove itself beyond cavil,[2] until it founds and luxuriantly grows its own forms of art, poems, schools, theology, displacing all that exists, or that has been produced anywhere in the past, under opposite influences. It is curious to me that while so many voices, pens, minds, in the press, lecture-rooms, in our Congress, &c., are discussing intellectual topics, pecuniary dangers, legislative problems, the suffrage, tariff and labor questions, and the various business and benevolent needs of America, with propositions, remedies, often worth deep attention, there is one need, a hiatus the profoundest, that no eye seems to perceive, no voice to state. Our fundamental want today in the United States, with closest, amplest reference to present conditions, and to the future, is of a class, and the clear idea of a class, of native authors, literatuses, far different, far higher in grade than any yet known, sacerdotal,[3] modern, fit to cope with our occasions, lands, permeating, the whole mass of American mentality, taste, belief, breathing into it a new breath of life, giving it decision, affecting politics far more than the popular superficial suffrage, with results inside and underneath the elections of Presidents or Congresses—radiating, begetting appropriate teachers, schools, manners, and, as its grandest result, accomplishing (what neither the schools nor the churches and their clergy have hitherto accomplish'd, and without which this nation will no more stand, permanently, soundly, than a house will stand without a substratum,) a religious and moral character beneath the political and productive and intellectual bases of the States. For know you not, dear, earnest reader, that the people of our land may all read and write, and may all possess the right to vote—and yet the main things may be entirely lacking?—(and this to suggest them.)

View'd, to-day, from a point of view sufficiently over-arching, the problem of humanity all over the civilized world is social and religious, and is to be finally met and treated by literature. The priest departs, the divine literatus comes. Never was anything more wanted than, to-day, and here in the States, the poet of the modern is wanted, or the great literatus of the modern. At all times, perhaps, the central point in any nation, and that whence it is itself really sway'd

[2]Argument, question   [3]Priestly.

the most, and whence it sways others, is its national literature, especially its archetypal[4] poems. Above all previous lands, a great original literature is surely to become the justification and reliance, (in some respects the sole reliance,) of American democracy.

Few are aware how the great literature penetrates all, gives hue to all, shapes aggregates and individuals, and, after subtle ways, with irresistible power, constructs, sustains, demolishes at will. Why tower, in reminiscence, above all the nations of the earth, two special lands, petty in themselves, yet inexpressibly gigantic, beautiful, columnar? Immoral Judah[5] lives, and Greece immortal lives, in a couple of poems.

Nearer than this. It is not generally realized, but it is true, as the genius of Greece, and all the sociology, personality, politics and religion of those wonderful states, resided in their literature or esthetics, that what was afterwards the main support of European chivalry, the feudal, ecclesiastical, dynastic world over there—forming its osseous[6] structure, holding it together for hundreds, thousands of years, preserving its flesh and bloom, giving it form, decision, rounding it out, and so saturating it in the conscious and unconscious blood, breed, belief, and intuitions of men, that it still prevails powerful to this day, in defiance of the mighty changes of time—was its literature, permeating to the very marrow, especially that major part, its enchanting songs, ballads, and poems.

To the ostent[7] of the senses and eyes, I know, the influences which stamp the world's history are wars, uprisings or downfalls of dynasties, changeful movements of trade, important inventions, navigation, military or civil governments, advent of powerful personalities, conquerors, &c. These of course play their part; yet, it may be, a single new thought, imagination, abstract principle, even literary style, fit for the time, put in shape by some great literatus, and projected among mankind, may duly cause changes, growths, removals, greater than the longest and bloodiest war, or the most stupendous merely political, dynastic, or commercial overturn.

In short, as, though it may not be realized, it is strictly true, that a few first-class poets, philosophs, and authors, have substantially settled and given status to the entire religion, education, law, sociology, &c., of the hitherto civilized world, by tinging and often creating the atmospheres out of which they have arisen, such also must stamp, and more than ever stamp, the interior and real democratic construction of this American continent, to-day, and days to come. Remember also this fact of difference, that, while through the antique and through the mediæval ages, highest thoughts and ideas realized themselves, and their expression made its way by other arts, as much as, or even more than by, technical literature, (not open to the mass of persons, or even to the majority of eminent persons,) such literature in our day and for current purposes, is not only more eligible than all the other arts put together, but has become the only general means of morally influencing the world. Painting, sculpture, and the dramatic theatre, it would seem, no longer play an indispensable or even important part in the workings and mediumship of intellect, utility, or even high esthetics. Architecture remains, doubtless with capacities, and a real future. Then music, the combiner, nothing more spiritual, nothing more sensuous, a god, yet completely human, advances, prevails, holds highest place; supplying in certain wants and quarters what nothing else could supply. Yet in the civilization of to-day it is undeniable that, over all the arts, literature dominates, serves beyond all—shapes the character of church and school—or, at any rate,

[4]Original, upon which others are based.   [5]Ancient kingdom in Palestine.
[6]Bony, skeletal.   [7]Appearance.

is capable of doing so. Including the literature of science, its scope is indeed unparallel'd.

Before proceeding further, it were perhaps well to discriminate on certain points. Literature tills its crops in many fields, and some may flourish, while others lag. What I say in these Vistas has its main bearing on imaginative literature, especially poetry, the stock of all. In the department of science, and the specialty of journalism, there appear, in these States, promises, perhaps fulfillments, of highest earnestness, reality, and life. These, of course, are modern. But in the region of imaginative, spinal and essential attributes, something equivalent to creation is, for our age and lands, imperatively demanded. For not only is it not enough that the new blood, new frame of democracy shall be vivified[8] and held together merely by political means, superficial suffrage, legislation, &c., but it is clear to me that, unless it goes deeper, gets at least as firm and as warm a hold in men's hearts, emotions and belief, as, in their days, feudalism or ecclesiasticism, and inaugurates its own perennial sources, welling from the centre forever, its strength will be defective, its growth doubtful, and its main charm wanting. I suggest, therefore, the possibility should some two or three really original American poets, (perhaps artists or lecturers,) arise, mounting the horizon like planets, stars of the first magnitude, that, from their eminence, fusing contributions, races, far localities, &c., together, they would give more compaction and more moral identity, (the quality to-day most needed,) to these States, than all its Constitutions, legislative and judicial ties, and all its hitherto political, warlike, or materialistic experiences. As, for instance, there could hardly happen anything that would more serve the States, with all their variety of origins, their diverse climes, cities, standards, &c., than possessing an aggregate of heroes, characters, exploits, sufferings, prosperity or misfortune, glory or disgrace, common to all, typical of all—no less, but even greater would it be to possess the aggregation of a cluster of mighty poets, artists, teachers, fit for us, national expressers, comprehending and effusing for the men and women of the States, what is universal, native, common to all, inland and seaboard, northern and southern. The historians say of ancient Greece, with her ever-jealous autonomies, cities, and states, that the only positive unity she ever own'd or receiv'd, was the sad unity of a common subjection, at the last, to foreign conquerors. Subjection, aggregation of that sort, is impossible to America; but the fear of conflicting and irreconcilable interiors, and the lack of a common skeleton, knitting all close, continually haunts me. Or, if it does not, nothing is plainer than the need, a long period to come, of a fusion of the States into the only reliable identity, the moral and artistic one. For, I say, the true nationality of the States, the genuine union, when we come to a mortal crisis, is, and is to be, after all, neither the written law, nor, (as is generally supposed,) either self-interest, or common pecuniary or material objects—but the fervid and tremendous IDEA, melting everything else with resistless heat, and solving all lesser and definite distinctions in vast, indefinite, spiritual, emotional power.

It may be claim'd, (and I admit the weight of the claim,) that common and general worldly prosperity, and a populace well-to-do, and with all life's material comforts, is the main thing, and is enough. It may be argued that our republic is, in performance, really enacting to-day the grandest arts, poems, &c., by beating up the wilderness into fertile farms, and in her railroads, ships, machinery, &c. And it may be ask'd, Are these not better, indeed, for America, than any utterances even of greatest rhapsode,[9] artist, or literatus?

---

[8]Given life.   [9]A singer of poems.

I too hail those achievements with pride and joy: then answer that the soul of man will not with such only—nay, not with such at all—be finally satisfied; but needs what, (standing on these and on all things, as the feet stand on the ground,) is address'd to the loftiest, to itself alone.

Out of such considerations, such truths, arises for treatment in these Vistas the important question of character, of an American stock-personality, with literatures and arts for outlets and return-expressions, and, of course, to correspond, within outlines common to all. To these, the main affair, the thinkers of the United States, in general so acute, have either given feeblest attention, or have remain'd, and remain, in a state of somnolence.

For my part, I would alarm and caution even the political and business reader, and to the utmost extent, against the prevailing delusion that the establishment of free political institutions, and plentiful intellectual smartness, with general good order, physical plenty, industry, &c., (desirable and precious advantages as they all are,) do, of themselves, determine and yield to our experiment of democracy the fruitage of success. With such advantage as present fully, or almost fully, possess'd—the Union just issued, victorious, from the struggle[10] with the only foes it need ever fear, (namely, those within itself, the interior ones,) and with unprecedented materialistic advancement—society, in these States, is canker'd, crude, superstitious, and rotten. Political, or law-made society is, and private, or voluntary society, is also. In any vigor, the element of the moral conscience, the most important, the verteber[11] to State or man, seems to me either entirely lacking, or seriously enfeebled or ungrown.

I say we had best look our times and lands searchingly in the face, like a physician diagnosing some deep disease. Never was there, perhaps, more hollowness at heart than at present, and here in the United States. Genuine belief seems to have left us. The underlying principles of the States are not honestly believ'd in, (for all this hectic glow, and these melodramatic screamings,) nor is humanity itself believ'd in. What penetrating eye does not everywhere see through the mask? The spectacle is appaling. We live in an atmosphere of hypocrisy throughout. The men believe not in the women, nor the women in the men. A scornful superciliousness rules in literature. The aim of all the *littérateurs*[12] is to find something to make fun of. A lot of churches, sects, &c., the most dismal phantasms I know, usurp the name of religion. Conversation is a mass of badinage. From deceit in the spirit, the mother of all false deeds, the offspring is already incalculable. An acute and candid person, in the revenue department in Washington, who is led by the course of his employment to regularly visit the cities, north, south and west, to investigate frauds, has talk'd much with me about his discoveries. The depravity of the business classes of our country is not less than has been supposed, but infinitely greater. The official services of America, national, state, and municipal, in all their branches and departments, except the judiciary, are saturated in corruption, bribery, falsehood, mal-administration; and the judiciary is tainted. The great cities reek with respectable as much as non-respectable robbery and scoundrelism. In fashionable life, flippancy, tepid amours, weak infidelism, small aims, or no aims at all, only to kill time. In business, (this all-devouring modern word, business,) the one sole object is, by any means, pecuniary gain. The magician's serpent in the fable ate up all the other serpents; and money-making is our magician's serpent, remaining to-day sole master of the field. The best class we show, is but a mob

[10]The American Civil War (1861–1865).   [11]Vertebrae.
[12]I.e., literary dilettantes, superficial critics.

of fashionably dress'd speculators and vulgarians. True, indeed, behind this fantastic farce, enacted on the visible stage of society, solid things and stupendous labors are to be discover'd, existing crudely and going on in the background, to advance and tell themselves in time. Yet the truths are none the less terrible. I say that our New World democracy, however great a success in uplifting the masses out of their sloughs, in materalistic development, products, and in a certain highly-deceptive superficial popular intellectuality, is, so far, an almost complete failure in its social aspects, and in really grand religious, moral, literary, and esthetic results. In vain do we march with unprecedented strides to empire so colossal, outvying the antique, beyond Alexander's, beyond the proudest sway of Rome. In vain have we annex'd Texas, California, Alaska, and reach north for Canada and south for Cuba. It is as if we were somehow being endow'd with a vast and more and more thoroughly-appointed body, and then left with little or no soul.

Let me illustrate further, as I write, with current observations, localities, &c. The subject is important, and will bear repetition. After an absence, I am now again (September, 1870) in New York city and Brooklyn, on a few weeks' vacation. The splendor, picturesqueness, and oceanic amplitude and rush of these great cities, the unsurpass'd situation, rivers and bay, sparkling sea-tides, costly and lofty new buildings, façades of marble and iron, of original grandeur and elegance of design, with the masses of gay color, the preponderance of white and blue, the flags flying, the endless ships, the tumultuous streets, Broadway, the heavy, low, musical roar, hardly ever intermitted, even at night; the jobbers' houses, the rich shops, the wharves, the great Central park, and the Brooklyn Park of hills, (as I wander among them this beautiful fall weather, musing, watching, absorbing)—the assemblages of the citizens in their groups, conversations, trades, evening amusements, or along the by-quarters—these, I say, and the like of these, completely satisfy my senses of power, fulness, motion, &c., and give me, through such senses and appetites, and through my esthetic conscience, a continued exaltation and absolute fulfilment. Always and more and more, as I cross the East and North rivers, the ferries, or with the pilots in their pilot-houses, or pass an hour in Wall street, or the gold exchange, I realize, (if we must admit such partialisms,) that not Nature alone is great in her fields of freedom and the open air, in her storms, the shows of night and day, the mountains, forests, seas—but in the artificial, the work of man too is equally great—in this profusion of teeming humanity—in these ingenuities, streets, goods, houses, ships—these hurrying, feverish, electric crowds of men, their complicated business genius, (not least among the geniuses,) and all this mighty, many-threaded wealth and industry concentrated here.

But sternly discarding, shutting our eyes to the glow and grandeur of the general superficial effect, coming down to what is of the only real importance, Personalities, and examining minutely, we question, we ask, Are there, indeed, *men* here worthy the name? Are there athletes? Are there perfect women, to match the generous material luxuriance? Is there a pervading atmosphere of beautiful manners? Are there crops of fine youths, and majestic old persons? Are there arts worthy freedom and a rich people? Is there a great moral and religious civilization—the only justification of a great material one? Confess that to severe eyes, using the moral microscope upon humanity, a sort of dry and flat Sahara appears, these cities, crowded with petty grotesques, malformations, phantoms, playing meaningless antics. Confess that everywhere, in shop, street, church, theatre, barroom, official chair, are pervading flippancy and vulgarity, low cunning, infidelity—everywhere the youth puny, impudent, foppish, prematurely ripe—everywhere an abnormal libidinousness,[13] unhealthy forms, male, female, painted, padded, dyed, chignon'd,[14] muddy complexions, bad blood, the capacity for good motherhood deceasing or deceas'd, shallow notions of beauty, with a range of manners, or rather lack of manners, (considering the advantages enjoy'd,) probably the meanest to be seen in the world.

Of all this, and these lamentable conditions, to breathe into them the breath recuperative of sane and heroic life, I say a new founded literature, not merely to copy and reflect existing surfaces, or pander to what is called taste—not only to amuse, pass away time, celebrate the beautiful, the refined, the past, or exhibit technical, rhythmic, or grammatical dexterity—but a literature underlying life, religious, consistent with science, handling the elements and forces with competent power, teaching and training men—and, as perhaps the most precious of its results, achieving the entire redemption of woman out of these incredible holds and webs of silliness, millinery, and every kind of dyspeptic depletion—and thus insuring to the States a strong and sweet Female Race, a race of perfect Mothers—is what is needed.

And now, in the full conception of these facts and points, and all that they infer, pro and con—with yet unshaken faith in the elements of the American masses, the composites, of both sexes, and even consider'd as individuals—and ever recognizing in them the broadest bases of the best literary esthetic appreciation—I proceed with my speculations, Vistas.

First, let us see what we can make out of a brief, general, sentimental consideration of political democracy, and whence it has arisen, with regard to some of its current features, as an aggregate, and as the basic structure of our future literature and authorship. We shall, it is true, quickly and continually find the origin-idea of the singleness of man, individualism, asserting itself, and cropping forth, even from the opposite ideas. But the mass, or lump character, for imperative reasons, is to be ever carefully weigh'd, borne in mind, and provided for. Only from it, and from its proper regulation and potency, comes the other, comes the chance of individualism. The two are contradictory, but our task is to reconcile them.

We do not, (at any rate I do not,) put it either on the ground that the People, the masses, even the best of them, are, in their latent or exhibited qualities, essentially sensible and good—nor on the ground of their rights; but that good or bad, rights or no rights, the democratic formula is the only safe and preservative one for coming times. We endow the masses with the suffrage for their own sake, no doubt; then, perhaps still more, from another point of view, for community's sake. Leaving the rest to the sentimentalists, we present freedom as sufficient in its scientific aspect, cold as ice, reasoning, deductive, clear and passionless as crystal.

Democracy too is law, and of the strictest, amplest kind. Many suppose, (and often in its own ranks the error,) that it means a throwing aside of law, and running riot. But, briefly, it is the superior law, not alone that of physical force, the body, which, adding to, it supersedes with that of the spirit. Law is the unshakable order of the universe forever; and the law over all, and law of laws, is the law of successions; that of the superior law, in time, gradually supplanting and overwhelming the inferior one. (While, for myself, I would cheerfully

---

[13]Lustfulness.   [14]I.e., with elaborately dressed hair.

agree—first covenanting that the formative tendencies shall be administer'd in favor, or at least not against it, and that this reservation be closely construed—that until the individual or community show due signs, or be so minor and fractional as not to endanger the State, the condition of authoritative tutelage may continue, and self-government must abide its time.) Nor is the esthetic point, always an important one, without fascination for highest aiming souls. The common ambition strains for elevations, to become some privileged exclusive. The master sees greatness and health in being part of the mass; nothing will do as well as common ground. Would you have in yourself the divine, vast, general law? Then merge yourself in it.

And, topping democracy, this most alluring record, that it alone can bind, and ever seeks to bind, all nations, all men, of however various and distant lands, into a brotherhood, a family. It is the old, yet ever-modern dream of earth, out of her eldest and her youngest, her fond philosophers and poets. Not that half only, individualism, which isolates. There is another half, which is adhesiveness or love, that fuses, ties and aggregates, making the races comrades, and fraternizing all. Both are to be vitalized by religion, (sole worthiest elevator of man or State,) breathing into the proud, material tissues, the breath of life. For I say at the core of democracy, finally, is the religious element. All the religions, old and new, are there. Nor may the scheme step forth, clothed in resplendent beauty and command, till these, bearing the best, the latest fruit, the spiritual, shall fully appear.

· · ·

The true gravitation-hold of liberalism in the United States will be a more universal ownership of property, general homesteads, general comfort—a vast, intertwining reticulation of wealth. As the human frame, or, indeed, any object in this manifold universe, is best kept together by the simple miracle of its own cohesion, and the necessity, exercise and profit thereof, so a great and varied nationality, occupying millions of square miles, were firmest held and knit by the principle of the safety and endurance of the aggregate of its middling property owners. So that, from another point of view, ungracious as it may sound, and a paradox after what we have been saying, democracy looks with the suspicious, ill-satisfied eye upon the very poor, the ignorant, and on those out of business. She asks for men and women with occupations, well-off, owners of houses and acres, and with cash in the bank—and with some cravings for literature, too; and must have them, and hastens to make them. Luckily, the seed is already well-sown, and has taken ineradicable root.

· · ·

Then still the thought returns, (like the thread-passage in overtures,)[15] giving the key and echo to these pages. When I pass to and fro, different latitudes, different seasons, beholding the crowds of the great cities, New York, Boston, Philadelphia, Cincinnati, Chicago, St. Louis, San Francisco, New Orleans, Baltimore—when I mix with these interminable swarms of alert, turbulent, good-natured, independent citizens, mechanics, clerks, young persons—at the idea of this mass of men, so fresh and free, so loving and so proud, a singular awe falls upon me. I feel, with dejection and amazement, that among our geniuses and talented writers or speakers, few or none have yet really spoken to this people, created a single image-making work for them, or absorb'd the central spirit and the idiosyncrasies which are theirs—and which, thus, in highest ranges, so far remain entirely uncelebrated, unexpress'd.

[15]A recurring melodic phrase or theme, a musical leitmotif.

Dominion strong is the body's; dominion stronger is the mind's. What has fill'd, and fills to-day our intellect, our fancy, furnishing the standards therein, is yet foreign. The great poems, Shakspere included, are poisonous to the idea of the pride and dignity of the common people, the life-blood of democracy. The models of our literature, as we get it from other lands, ultramarine,[16] have had their birth in courts, and bask'd and grown in castle sunshine; all smells of princes' favors. Of workers of a certain sort, we have, indeed, plenty, contributing after their kind; many elegant, many learn'd, all complacent. But touch'd by the national test, or tried by the standards of democratic personality, they wither to ashes. I say I have not seen a single writer, artist, lecturer, or what not, that has confronted the voiceless but ever erect and active, pervading, underlying will and typic[17] aspiration of the land, in a spirit kindred to itself. Do you call those genteel little creatures American poets? Do you term that perpetual, pistareen,[18] paste-pot work, American art, American drama, taste, verse? I think I hear, echoed as from some mountain-top afar in the west, the scornful laugh of the Genius of these States.

Democracy, in silence, biding its time, ponders its own ideals, not of literature and art only—not of men only, but of women. The idea of the women of America, (extricated from this daze, this fossil and unhealthy air which hangs about the word *lady*,) develop'd, raised to become the robust equals, workers, and, it may be, even practical and political deciders with the men—greater than man, we may admit, through their divine maternity, always their towering, emblematical attribute—but great, at any rate, as man, in all departments; or, rather, capable of being so, soon as they realize it, and can bring themselves to give up toys and fictions, and launch forth, as men do, amid real, independent, stormy life.

Then, as towards our thought's finale, (and, in that, overarching the true scholar's lesson,) we have to say there can be no complete or epical presentation of democracy in the aggregate, or anything like it, at this day, because its doctrines will only be effectually incarnated in any one branch, when, in all, their spirit is at the root and centre. Far, far, indeed, stretch, in distance, our Vistas! How much is still to be disentangled, freed! How long it takes to make this American world see that it is, in itself, the final authority and reliance!

Did you, too, O friend, suppose democracy was only for elections, for politics, and for a party name? I say democracy is only of use there that it may pass on and come to its flower and fruits in manners, in the highest forms of interaction between men, and their beliefs—in religion, literature, colleges, and schools—democracy in all public and private life, and in the army and navy. I have intimated that, as a paramount scheme, it has yet few or no full realizers and believers. I do not see, either, that it owes any serious thanks to noted propagandists or champions, or has been essentially help'd, though often harm'd, by them. It has been and is carried on by all the moral forces, and by trade, finance, machinery, intercommunications, and, in fact, by all the developments of history, and can no more be stopp'd than the tides, or the earth in its orbit. Doubtless, also, it resides, crude and latent, well down in the hearts of the fair average of the American-born people, mainly in the agricultural regions. But it is not yet, there or anywhere, the fully-receiv'd, the fervid, the absolute faith.

I submit, therefore, that the fruition of democracy, on aught like a grand scale, resides altogether in the future. As, under any profound and compre-

[16]Beyond the sea.   [17]Typical.   [18]Of little value.

hensive view of the gorgeous-composite feudal world, we see in it, through the long ages and cycles of ages, the results of a deep, integral, human and divine principle, or fountain, from which issued laws, ecclesia,[19] manners, institutes, costumes, personalities, poems, (hitherto unequall'd,) faithfully partaking of their source, and indeed only arising either to betoken it, or to furnish parts of that varied-flowing display, whose centre was one and absolute—so, long ages hence, shall the due historian or critic make at least an equal retrospect, an equal history for the democratic principle. It too must be adorn'd, credited, with its results—then, when it, with imperial power, through amplest time, has dominated mankind—has been the source and test of all the moral, esthetic, social, political, and religious expressions and institutes of the civilized world—has begotten them in spirit and in form, and has carried them to its own unprecedented heights—has had, (it is possible,) monastics and ascetics, more numerous, more devout than the monks and priests of all previous creeds—has sway'd the ages with a breadth and rectitude tallying Nature's own—has fashion'd, systematized, and triumphantly finish'd and carried out, in its own interest, and with unparallel'd success, a new earth and a new man.

Thus we presume to write, as it were, upon things that exist not, and travel by maps yet unmade, and a blank. But the throes of birth are upon us; and we have something of this advantage in seasons of strong formations, doubts, suspense—for then the afflatus of such themes haply may fall upon us, more or less; and then, hot from surrounding war and revolution, our speech, though without polish'd coherence, and a failure by the standard called criticism, comes forth, real at least as the lightnings.

And may-be we, these days, have, too, our own reward—(for there are yet some, in all lands, worthy to be so encouraged.) Though not for us the joy of entering at the last the conquer'd city—not ours the chance ever to see with our own eyes the peerless power and splendid *eclat* of the democratic principle, arriv'd at meridian, filling the world with effulgence and majesty far beyond those of past history's kings, or all dynastic sway—there is yet, to whoever is eligible among us, the prophetic vision, the joy of being toss'd in the brave turmoil of these times—the promulgation and the path, obedient, lowly reverent to the voice, the gesture of the god, or holy ghost, which others see not, hear not—with the proud consciousness that amid whatever clouds, seductions, or heart-wearying postponements, we have never deserted, never despair'd, never abandon'd the faith.

So much contributed, to be conn'd well, to help prepare and brace our edifice, our plann'd Idea—we still proceed to give it in another of its aspects—perhaps the main, the high façade of all. For to democracy, the leveler, the unyielding principle of the average, is surely join'd another principle, equally unyielding, closely tracking the first, indispensable to it, opposite, (as the sexes are opposite,) and whose existence, confronting and ever modifying the other, often clashing, paradoxical, yet neither of highest avail without the other, plainly supplies to these grand cosmic politics of ours, and to the launch'd forth mortal dangers of republicanism, to-day or any day, the counterpart and offset whereby Nature restrains the deadly original relentlessness of all her first-class laws. This second principle is individuality, the pride and centripetal isolation of a human being in himself—identity—personalism. Whatever the name, its acceptance and thorough infusion through the organization of political commonalty now shooting Aurora-like about the world, are of utmost importance, as the principle itself is

---

[19]Church rules, religious doctrines.

needed for very life's sake. It forms, in a sort, or is to form, the compensating balance-wheel of the successful working machinery of aggregate America.

And, if we think of it, what does civilization itself rest upon—and what object has it, with its religions, arts, schools, &c., but rich, luxuriant, varied personalism? To that, all bends; and it is because toward such result democracy alone, on anything like Nature's scale, breaks up the limitless fallows of humankind, and plants the seed, and gives fair play, that its claims now precede the rest. The literature, songs, esthetics, &c., of a country are of importance principally because they furnish the materials and suggestions of personality for the women and men of that country, and enforce them in a thousand effective ways. As the top-most claim of a strong consolidating of the nationality of these States, is, that only by such powerful compaction can the separate States secure that full and free swing within their spheres, which is becoming to them, each after its kind, so will individuality, with unimpeded branchings, flourish best under imperial republican forms.

To practically enter into politics is an important part of American personalism. To every young man, north and south, earnestly studying these things, I should here, as an offset to what I have said in former pages, now also say, that may-be to views of very largest scope, after all, perhaps the political, (perhaps the literary and sociological,) America goes best about its development its own way— sometimes, to temporary sight, appalling enough. It is the fashion among dil-lettantes and fops (perhaps I myself am not guiltless,) to decry the whole formulation of the active politics of America, as beyond redemption, and to be carefully kept away from. See you that you do not fall into this error. America, it may be, is doing very well upon the whole, notwithstanding these antics of the parties and their leaders, these half-brain'd nominees, the many ignorant ballots, and many elected failures and blatherers. It is the dillettantes, and all who shirk their duty, who are not doing well. As for you, I advise you to enter more strongly yet into politics. I advise every young man to do so. Always inform yourself from parties. They have been useful, and to some extent remain so; but the floating, uncommitted electors, farmers, clerks, mechanics, the masters of parties—watching aloof, inclining victory this side or that side—such are the ones most needed, present and future. For America, if eligible at all to downfall and ruin, is eligible within herself, not without; for I see clearly that the combined foreign world could not beat her down. But these savage, wolfish parties alarm me. Owning no law but their own will, more and more combative, less and less tolerant of the idea of ensemble and of equal brotherhood, the perfect equality of the States, the ever-over-arching American ideas, it behooves you to convey yourself implicitly to no party, nor submit blindly to their dictators, but steadily hold yourself judge and master over all of them.

It must still be reiterated, as, for the purpose of these memoranda, the deep lesson of history and time, that all else in the contributions of a nation or age, through its politics, materials, heroic personalities, military eclat, &c., remains crude, and defers, in any close and thorough-going estimate, until vitalized by national, original archetypes in literature. They only put the nation in form, finally tell anything—prove, complete anything—perpetuate anything. Without doubt, some of the richest and most powerful and populous communities of the antique world, and some of the grandest personalities and events, have, to after and present times, left themselves entirely unbequeath'd. Doubtless, greater than any that have come down to us, were among those lands, heroisms, persons, that have not come down to us at all, even by name, date, or location. Others have arrived safely, as from voyages over wide, century-stretching seas. The little ships, the miracles that have buoy'd them, and by incredible chances safely convey'd them, (or the best of them, their meaning and essence,) over long wastes, darkness, lethargy, ignorance, &c., have been a few inscriptions— a few immortal compositions, small in size, yet compassing what measureless values of reminiscence, contemporary portraitures, manners, idioms, and beliefs, with deepest inference, hint and thought, to tie and touch forever the old, new body, and the old, new soul! These! and still these! bearing the freight so dear—dearer than pride—dearer than love. All the best experience of humanity, folded, saved, freighted to us here. Some of these tiny ships we call Old and New Testament, Homer, Eschylus, Plato, Juvenal, &c., Precious minims![20] I think, if we were forced to choose, rather than have you, and the likes of you, and what belongs to, and has grown of you blotted out and gone, we could better afford, appaling as that would be, to lose all actual ships, this day fasten'd by wharf, or floating on wave, and see them, with all their cargoes, scuttled and sent to the bottom.

Gather'd by geniuses of city, race or age, and put by them in highest of art's forms, namely, the literary form, the peculiar combinations and the outshows of that city, age, or race, its particular modes of the universal attributes and passions, its faiths, heroes, lovers and gods, wars, traditions, struggles, crimes, emotions, joys, (or the subtle spirit of these,) having been pass'd on to us to illumine our own selfhood, and its experiences—what they supply, indispensable and highest, if taken away, nothing else in all the world's boundless storehouses could make up to us, or ever again return.

For us, along the great highways of time, those monuments stand—those forms of majesty and beauty. For us those beacons burn through all the nights. Unknown Egyptians, graving hieroglyphs; Hindus, with hymn and apothegm[21] and endless epic; Hebrew prophet, with spirituality, as in flashes of lightning, conscience like red-hot iron, plaintive songs and screams of vengeance for tyrannies and enslavement; Christ, with bent head, brooding love and peace, like a dove; Greek, creating eternal shapes of physical and esthetic proportion; Roman, lord of satire, the sword, and the codex;[22]—of the figures, some far off and veil'd, others near and visible; Dante, stalking with lean form, nothing but fibre, not a grain of superfluous flesh; Angelo,[23] and the great painters, architects, musicians; rich Shakspere, luxuriant as the sun, artist and singer of feudalism in its sunset, with all the gorgeous colors, owner thereof, and using them at will; and so to such as German Kant and Hegel,[24] where they, though near us, leaping over the ages, sit again, impassive, imperturbable, like the Egyptian gods. Of these, and the like of these, is it too much, indeed, to return to our favorite figure, and view them as orbs and systems of orbs, moving in free paths in the spaces of that other heaven, the kosmic intellect, the soul?

Ye powerful and resplendent ones! ye were, in your atmospheres, grown not for America, but rather for her foes, the feudal and the old—while our genius is democratic and modern. Yet could ye, indeed, but breathe your breath of life into our New World's nostrils—not to enslave us, as now, but, for our needs, to breed a spirit like your own—perhaps, (dare we to say it?) to dominate, even destroy, what you yourselves have left! On your plane, and no less, but even higher and wider, must we mete and measure for to-day and here. I demand

[20]Small things.   [21]Maxim.
[22]Law.   [23]Michelangelo.
[24]Immanuel Kant (1724–1804) and Friedrich Hegel (1770–1831), German philosophers.

races of orbic bards, with unconditional uncompromising sway. Come forth, sweet democratic despots of the west!

By points like these we, in reflection, token what we mean by any land's or people's genuine literature. And thus compared and tested, judging amid the influence of loftiest products only, what do our current copious fields of print, covering in manifold forms, the United States, better, for an analogy, present, than, as in certain regions of the sea, those spreading, undulating masses of squid, through which the whale swimming, with head half out, feeds?

Not but that doubtless our current so-called literature, (like an endless supply of small coin,) performs a certain service, and may-be, too, the service needed for the time, (the preparation-service, as children learn to spell.) Everybody reads, and truly nearly everybody writes, either books, or for the magazines or journals. The matter has magnitude, too, after a sort. But is it really advancing? or, has it advanced for a long while? There is something impressive about the huge editions of the dailies and weeklies, the mountain-stacks of white paper piled in the press-vaults, and the proud, crashing, ten-cylinder presses, which I can stand and watch any time by the half hour. Then, (though the States in the field of imagination present not a single first-class work, not a single great literatus,) the main objects, to amuse, to titilate, to pass away time, to circulate the news, and rumors of news, to rhyme and read rhyme, are yet attain'd, and on a scale of infinity. To-day, in books, in the rivalry of writers, especially novelists, success, (so-call'd,) is for him or her who strikes the mean flat average, the sensational appetite for stimulus, incident, persiflage,[25] &c., and depicts, to the common calibre, sensual, exterior life. To such, or the luckiest of them, as we see, the audiences are limitless and profitable; but they cease presently. While this day, or any day, to workmen portraying interior or spiritual life, the audiences were limited, and often laggard—but they last forever.

Compared with the past, our modern science soars, and our journals serve—but ideal and even ordinary romantic literature, does not, I think, substantially advance. Behold the prolific brood of the contemporary novel, magazine-tale, theatre-play? &c. The same endless thread of tangled and superlative love-story, inherited, apparently from the Amadises and Palmerins[26] of the 13th, 14th, and 15th centuries over there in Europe. The costumes and associations brought down to date, the seasoning hotter and more varied, the dragons and ogres left out—but the *thing*, I should say, has not advanced—is just as sensational, just as strain'd—remains about the same, nor more, nor less.

What is the reason our time, our lands, that we see no fresh local courage, sanity, of our own—the Mississippi, stalwart Western men, real mental and physical facts, Southerners, &c., in the body of our literature? especially the poetic part of it. But always, instead a parcel of dandies and ennuyees, dapper little gentlemen from abroad, who flood us with their thin sentiment of parlors, parasols, piano-songs, tinkling rhymes, the five-hundredth importation—or whimpering and crying about something, chasing one aborted conceit after another, and forever occupied in dyspeptic amours with dyspeptic women. While, current and novel, the grandest events and revolutions, and stormiest passions of history, are crossing to-day with unparallel'd rapidity and magnificence over the stages of our own and all the continents, offering new materials, opening new vistas, with largest needs, inviting the daring launching forth of conceptions in literature, inspired by them, soaring in highest regions, serving art in its highest, (which is only the other name for serving God, and serving

[25]Frivolous talk.   [26]European chivalric romances.

humanity,) where is the man of letters, where is the book, with any nobler aim than to follow in the old track, repeat what has been said before—and, as its utmost triumph, sell well, and be erudite or elegant?

Mark the roads, the processes, through which these States have arrived, standing easy, henceforth ever-equal, ever-compact, in their range to-day. European adventures? the most antique? Asiatic or African? old history—miracles—romances? Rather, our own unquestion'd facts. They hasten, incredible, blazing bright as fire. From the deeds and days of Columbus down to the present, and including the present—and especially the late Secession war[27]—when I con[28] them, I feel, every leaf, like stopping to see if I have not made a mistake, and fall'n on the splendid figments of some dream. But it is no dream. We stand, live, move, in the huge flow of our age's materialism—in its spirituality. We have had founded for us the most positive of lands. The founders have pass'd to other spheres—but what are these terrible duties they have left us?

•   •   •

The old men, I remember as a boy, were always talking of American independence. What is independence? Freedom from all laws or bonds except those of one's own being, control'd by the universal ones. To lands, to man, to woman, what is there at last to each, but the inherent soul, nativity, idiocrasy, free, highest-poised, soaring its own flight, following out itself?

At present, these States, in their theology and social standards, (of greater importance than their political institutions,) are entirely held possession of by foreign lands. We see the sons and daughters of the New World, ignorant of its genius, not yet inaugurating the native, the universal, and the near, still importing the distant, the partial, and the dead. We see London, Paris, Italy—not original, superb, as where they belong—but second-hand here, where they do not belong. We see the shreds of Hebrews, Romans, Greeks; but where, on her own soil, do we see, in any faithful, highest, proud expression, America herself? I sometimes question whether she has a corner in her own house.

Not but that in one sense, and a very grand one, good theology, good art, or good literature, has certain features shared in common. The combination fraternizes, ties the races—is, in many particulars, under laws applicable indifferently to all, irrespective of climate or date, and, from whatever source, appeals to emotions, pride, love, spirituality, common to humankind. Nevertheless, they touch a man closest, (perhaps only actually touch him,) even in these, in their expression, through autochthonic[29] lights and shades, flavors, fondnesses, aversions, specific incidents, illustrations, out of his own nationality, geography, surroundings, antecedents, &c. The spirit and the form are one, and depend far more on association, identity and place, than is supposed. Subtly interwoven with the materiality and personality of a land, a race—Teuton, Turk, Californian, or what not—there is always something—I can hardly tell what it is—history but describes the results of it—it is the same as the untellable look of some human faces. Nature, too, in her stolid forms, is full of it—but to most it is there a secret. This something is rooted in the invisible roots, the profoundest meanings of that place, race, or nationality; and to absorb and again effuse it, uttering words and products as from its midst, and carrying it into highest regions, is the work, or a main part of the work, of any country's true author, poet, historian, lecturer, and perhaps even priest and philosoph. Here, and here only, are the foundations for our really valuable and permanent verse, drama, &c.

---

[27]The American Civil War (1861–1865).   [28]Examine, study.   [29]Indigenous, native.

But at present, (judged by any higher scale than that which finds the chief ends of existence to be to feverishly make money during one-half of it, and by some "amusement," or perhaps foreign travel, flippantly kill time, the other half,) and consider'd with reference to purposes of patriotism, health, a noble personality, religion, and the democratic adjustments, all these swarms of poems, literary magazines, dramatic plays, resultant so far from American intellect, and the formation of our best ideas, are useless and a mockery. They strengthen and nourish no one, express nothing characteristic, give decision and purpose to no one, and suffice only the lowest level of vacant minds.

Of what is called the drama, or dramatic presentation in the United States, as now put forth at the theatres, I should say it deserves to be treated with the same gravity, and on a par with the questions of ornamental confectionery at public dinners, or the arrangement of curtains and hangings in a ball-room—nor more, nor less. Of the other, I will not insult the reader's intelligence, (once really entering into the atmosphere of these Vistas,) by supposing it necessary to show, in detail, why the copious dribble, either of our little or well-known rhymesters, does not fulfil, in any respect, the needs and august occasions of this land. America demands a poetry that is bold, modern, and all-surrounding and kosmical, as she is herself. It must in no respect ignore science or the modern, but inspire itself with science and the modern. It must bend its vision toward the future, more than the past. Like America, it must extricate itself from even the greatest models of the past, and, while courteous to them, must have entire faith in itself, and the products of its own democratic spirit only. Like her, it must place in the van, and hold up at all hazards, the banner of the divine pride of man in himself, (the radical foundation of the new religion.) Long enough have the People been listening to poems in which common humanity, deferential, bends low, humiliated, acknowledging superiors. But America listens to no such poems. Erect, inflated, and fully self-esteeming be the chant; and then America will listen with pleased ears.

Nor may the genuine gold, the gems, when brought to light at last, be probably usher'd forth from any of the quarters currently counted on. To-day, doubtless, the infant genius of American poetic expression, (eluding those highly-refined imported and gilt-edged themes, and sentimental and butterfly flights, pleasant to orthodox publishers—causing tender spasms in the coteries, and warranted not to chafe the sensitive cuticle of the most exquisitely artificial gossamer delicacy,) lies sleeping far away, happily unrecognized and uninjur'd by the coteries, the art-writers, the talkers and critics of the saloons, or the lecturers in the colleges—lies sleeping, aside, unrecking[30] itself, in some western idiom, or native Michigan or Tennessee repartee, or stump-speech—or in Kentucky or Georgia, or the Carolinas—or in some slang or local song or allusion of the Manhattan, Boston, Philadelphia or Baltimore mechanic—or up in the Maine woods—or off in the hut of the California miner, or crossing the Rocky mountains, or along the Pacific railroad—or on the breasts of the young farmers of the northwest, or Canada, or boatmen of the lakes. Rude and coarse nursing-beds, these; but only from such beginnings and stocks, indigenous here, may haply arrive, be grafted, and sprout, in time, flowers of genuine American aroma, and fruits truly and fully our own.

I say it were a standing disgrace to these States—I say it were a disgrace to any nation, distinguish'd above others by the variety and vastness of its territories, its materials, its inventive activity, and the splendid practicality of its people, not

[30]Disregarding.

to rise and soar above others also in its original styles in literature and art, and its own supply of intellectual and esthetic masterpieces, archetypal, and consistent with itself. I know not a land except ours that has not, to some extent, however small, made its title clear. The Scotch have their born ballads, subtly expressing their past and present, and expressing character. The Irish have theirs. England, Italy, France, Spain, theirs. What has America? With exhaustless mines of the richest ore of epic, lyric, tale, tune, picture, &c., in the Four Years' War;[31] with, indeed, I sometimes think, the richest masses of material ever afforded a nation, more variegated, and on a larger scale—the first sign of proportionate, native, imaginative Soul, and first-class works to match, is, (I cannot too often repeat,) so far wanting.

Long ere the second centennial arrives, there will be some forty to fifty great States, among them Canada and Cuba. When the present century closes, our population will be sixty or seventy millions. The Pacific will be ours, and the Atlantic mainly ours. There will be daily electric communication with every part of the globe. What an age! What a land! Where, elsewhere, one so great? The individuality of one nation must, then, as always, lead the world. Can there be any doubt who the leader ought to be? Bear in mind, though, that nothing less than the mightiest original non-subordinated SOUL has ever really, gloriously led, or ever can lead. (This Soul—its other name, in these Vistas is LITERATURE.)

Present literature, while magnificently fulfilling certain popular demands, with plenteous knowledge and verbal smartness, is profoundly sophisticated, insane, and its very joy is morbid. It needs tally and express Nature, and the spirit of Nature, and to know and obey the standards. I say the question of Nature, largely consider'd, involves the question of the esthetic, the emotional, and the religious—and involves happiness. A fitly born and bred race, growing up in right conditions of out-door as much as in-door harmony, activity and development, would probably, from and in those conditions, find it enough merely *to live*—and would, in their relations to the sky, air, water, trees, &c., and to the countless common shows, and in the fact of life itself, discover and achieve happiness—with Being suffused night and day by wholesome extasy, surpassing all the pleasures that wealth, amusement, and even gratified intellect, erudition, or the sense of art, can give.

In the prophetic literature of these States (the reader of my speculations will miss their principal stress unless he allows well for the point that a new Literature, perhaps a new Metaphysics, certainly a new Poetry, are to be, in my opinion, the only sure and worthy supports and expressions of the American Democracy,) Nature, true Nature, and the true idea of Nature, long absent, must, above all, become fully restored, enlarged, and must furnish the pervading atmosphere to poems, and the test of all high literary and esthetic compositions. I do not mean the smooth walks, trimm'd hedges, poseys and nightingales of the English poets, but the whole orb, with its geologic history, the kosmos, carrying fire and snow, that rolls through the illimitable areas, light as a feather, though weighing billions of tons. Furthermore, as by what we now partially call Nature is intended, at most, only what is entertainable by the physical conscience, the sense of matter, and of good animal health—on these it must be distinctly accumulated, incorporated, that man, comprehending these, has in towering superaddition, the moral and spiritual consciences, indicating his destination beyond the ostensible, the mortal.

---

[31]The American Civil War (1861–1865).

To the heights of such estimate of Nature indeed ascending, we proceed to make observations for our Vistas, breathing rarest air. What is I believe called Idealism seems to me to suggest, (guarding against extravagance, and ever modified even by its opposite,) the course of inquiry and desert of favor for our New World metaphysics, their foundation of and in literature, giving hue to all.

The elevating and etherealizing ideas of the unknown and of unreality must be brought forward with authority, as they are the legitimate heirs of the known, and of reality, and at least as great as their parents. Fearless of scoffing, and of the ostent, let us take our stand, our ground, and never desert it, to confront the growing excess and arrogance of realism. To the cry, now victorious—the cry of sense, science, flesh, incomes, farms, merchandise, logic, intellect, demonstrations, solid perpetuities, buildings of brick and iron, or even the facts of the shows of trees, earth, rocks, &c., fear not, my brethren, my sisters, to sound out with equally determin'd voice, that conviction brooding within the recesses of every envision'd soul—illusions! apparitions! figments all! True, we must not condemn the show, neither absolutely deny it, for the indispensability of its meanings; but how clearly we see that, migrate in soul to what we can already conceive of superior and spiritual points of view, and, palpable as it seems under present relations, it all and several might, nay certainly would, fall apart and vanish.

I hail with joy the oceanic, variegated, intense practical energy, the demand for facts, even the business materialism of the current age, our States. But wo to the age or land in which these things, movements, stopping at themselves, do not tend to ideas. As fuel to flame, and flame to the heavens, so must wealth, science, materialism—even this democracy of which we make so much—unerringly feed the highest mind, the soul. Infinitude the flight: fathomless the mystery. Man, so diminutive, dilates beyond the sensible universe, competes with, outcopes space and time, meditating even one great idea. Thus, and thus only, does a human being, his spirit, ascend above, and justify, objective Nature, which, probably nothing in itself, is incredibly and divinely serviceable, indispensable, real, here. And as the purport of objective Nature is doubtless folded, hidden, somewhere here—as somewhere here is what this globe and its manifold forms, and the light of day, and night's darkness, and life itself, with all its experiences, are for—it is here the great literature, especially verse, must get its inspiration and throbbing blood. Then may we attain to a poetry worthy the immortal soul of man, and which, while absorbing materials, and, in their own sense, the shows of Nature, will, above all, have, both directly and indirectly, a freeing, fluidizing, expanding, religious character, exulting with science, fructifying the moral elements, and stimulating aspirations, and meditations on the unknown.

The process, so far, is indirect, and peculiar, and though it may be suggested, cannot be defined. Observing, rapport, and with intuition, the shows and forms presented by Nature, the sensuous luxuriance, the beautiful in living men and women, the actual play of passions, in history and life—and, above all, from those developments either in Nature or human personality in which power, (dearest of all to the sense of the artist,) transacts itself—out of these, and seizing what is in them, the poet, the esthetic worker in any field, by the divine magic of his genius, projects them, their analogies, by curious removes, indirections, in literature and art. (No useless attempt to repeat the material creation, by daguerreotyping the exact likeness by mortal mental means.) This is the image-making faculty, coping with material creation, and rivaling, almost triumphing over it. This alone, when all the other parts of a specimen of literature or art are ready and waiting, can breathe into it the breath of life, and endow it with identity.

"The true question to ask," says the librarian of Congress in a paper read before the Social Science Convention at New York, October, 1869, "The true question to ask respecting a book, is, *has it help'd any human soul?*" This is the hint, statement, not only of the great literatus, his book, but of every great artist. It may be that all works of art are to be first tried by their art qualities, their image-forming talent, and their dramatic, pictorial, plot-constructing, euphonious and other talents. Then, whenever claiming to be first-class works, they are to be strictly and sternly tried by their foundation in, and radiation, in the highest sense, and always indirectly, of the ethic principles, and eligibility to free, arouse, dilate.

As, within the purposes of the Kosmos, and vivifying all meterology, and all the congeries[32] of the mineral, vegetable and animal worlds—all the physical growth and development of man, and all the history of the race in politics, religions, wars, &c., there is a moral purpose, a visible or invisible intention, certainly underlying all—its results and proof needing to be patiently waited for—needing intuition, faith, idiosyncrasy, to its realization, which many, and especially the intellectual, do not have—so in the product, or congeries of the product, of the greatest literatus. This is the last, profoundest measure and test of a first-class literary, or esthetic achievement, and when understood and put in force must fain, I say, lead to works, books, nobler than any hitherto known. Lo! Nature, (the only complete, actual poem,) existing calmly in the divine scheme, containing all, content, careless of the criticisms of a day, or these endless and wordy chatterers. And lo! to the consciousness of the soul, the permanent identity, the thought, the something, before which the magnitude even of democracy, art, literature, &c., dwindles, becomes partial, measurable— something that fully satisfies, (which those do not.) That something is the All, and the idea of All, with the accompanying idea of eternity, and of itself, the soul, buoyant, indestructible, sailing space forever, visiting every region, as a ship the sea. And again lo! the pulsations in all matter, all spirit, throbbing forever—the eternal beats, eternal systole and diastole[33] of life in things— wherefrom I feel and know that death is not the ending, as was thought, but rather the real beginning—and that nothing ever is or can be lost, nor ever die, nor soul, nor matter.

In the future of these States must arise poets immenser far, and make great poems of death. The poems of life are great, but there must be the poems of the purports of life, not only in itself, but beyond itself. I have eulogized Homer, the sacred bards of Jewry, Eschylus, Juvenal, Shakspere, &c., and acknowledged their inestimable value. But, (with perhaps the exception, in some, not all respects, of the second-mention'd,) I say there must, for future and democratic purposes, appear poets, (dare I to say so?) of higher class even than any of those—poets not only possess'd of the religious fire and abandon of Isaiah,[34] luxuriant in the epic talent of Homer, or for proud characters as in Shakspere, but consistent with the Hegelian formulas[35] and consistent with modern science. America needs, and the world needs, a class of bards who will, now and ever, so link and tally the rational physical being of man, with the ensembles of time and space, and with this vast and multiform show, Nature, surrounding him,

[32]Aggregation, collection.

[33]Contraction and expansion, as with the beating of the heart.   [34]Hebrew prophet.

[35]The German philosopher Hegel's dialectical system of thesis, antithesis, and synthesis by which opposites are unified and something new emerges.

ever tantalizing him, equally a part, and yet not a part of him, as to essentially harmonize, satisfy, and put at rest. Faith, very old, now scared away by science, must be restored, brought back by the same power that caused her departure— restored with new sway, deeper, wider, higher than ever. Surely, this universal ennui, this coward fear, this shuddering at death, these low, degrading views, are not always to rule the spirit pervading future society, as it has the past, and does the present. What the Roman Lucretius[36] sought most nobly, yet all too blindly, negatively to do for his age and its successors, must be done positively by some great coming literatus, especially poet, who, while remaining fully poet, will absorb whatever science indicates, with spiritualism, and out of them, and out of his own genius, will compose the great poem of death. Then will man indeed confront Nature, and confront time and space, both with science, and *con amore*,[37] and take his right place, prepared for life, master of fortune and misfortune. And then that which was long wanted will be supplied, and the ship that had it not before in all her voyages, will have an anchor.

Arrived now, definitely, at an apex for these Vistas, I confess that the promulgation and belief in such a class or institution—a new and greater literatus order—its possibility, (nay certainty,) underlies these entire speculations—and that the rest, the other parts, as superstructures, are all founded upon it. It really seems to me the condition, not only of our future national and democratic development, but of our perpetuation. In the highly artificial and materialistic bases of modern civilization, with the corresponding arrangements and methods of living, the force-infusion of intellect alone, the depraving influences of riches just as much as poverty, the absence of all high ideals in character—with the long series of tendencies, shapings, which few are strong enough to resist, and which now seem, with steam-engine speed, to be everywhere turning out the generations of humanity like uniform iron castings—all of which, as compared with the feudal ages, we can yet do nothing better than accept, make the best of, and even welcome, upon the whole, for their oceanic practical grandeur, and their restless wholesale kneading of the masses—I say of all this tremendous and dominant play of solely materialistic bearings upon current life in the United States, with the results as already seen, accumulating, and reaching far into the future, that they must either be confronted and met by at least an equally subtle and tremendous force-infusion for purposes of spiritualization, for the pure conscience, for genuine esthetics, and for absolute and primal manliness and womanliness—or else our modern civilization, with all its improvements, is in vain, and we are on the road to a destiny, a status, equivalent, in its real world, to that of the fabled damned.

Prospecting thus the coming unsped days, and that new order in them— marking the endless train of exercise, development, unwind, in nation as in man, which life is for—we see, fore-indicated, amid these prospects and hopes, new law-forces of spoken and written language—not merely the pedagogue-forms, correct, regular, familiar with precedents, made for matters of outside propriety, fine words, thoughts definitely told out—but a language fann'd by the breath of Nature, which leaps overhead, cares mostly for impetus and effects, and for what it plants and invigorates to grow—tallies life and character, and seldomer tells a thing than suggests or necessitates it. In fact, a new theory of literary composition for imaginative works of the very first class, and especially for highest poems, is the sole course open to these States. Books are to be call'd

[36]Roman poet (first century B.C.). His masterwork, *De Rerum Natura*, was written to counteract the despair and artificiality of his age.   [37]Italian: with love.

for, and supplied, on the assumption that the process of reading is not a half-sleep, but, in highest sense, an exercise, a gymnast's struggle; that the reader is to do something for himself, must be on the alert, must himself or herself construct indeed the poem, argument, history, metaphysical essay—the text furnishing the hints, the clue, the start or frame-work. Not the book needs so much to be the complete thing, but the reader of the book does. That were to make a nation of supple and athletic minds, well-train'd, intuitive, used to depend on themselves, and not on a few coteries of writers.

Investigating here, we see, not that it is a little thing we have, in having the bequeath'd libraries, countless shelves of volumes, records, &c.; yet how serious the danger, depending entirely on them, of the bloodless vein, the nerveless arm, the false application, at second or third hand. We see that the real interest of this people of ours in the theology, history, poetry, politics, and personal models of the past, (the British islands, for instance, and indeed all the past,) is not necessarily to mould ourselves or our literature upon them, but to attain fuller, more definite comparisons, warnings, and the insight to ourselves, our own present, and our own far grander, different, future history, religion, social customs, &c. We see that almost everything that has been written, sung, or stated, of old, with reference to humanity under the feudal and oriental institutes, religions, and for other lands, needs to be re-written, re-sung, re-stated, in terms consistent with the institutions of these States, and to come in range and obedient uniformity with them.

We see, as in the universes of the material kosmos, after meteorological, vegetable, and animal cycles, man at last arises, born through them, to prove them, concentrate them, to turn upon them with wonder and love—to command them, adorn them, and carry them upward into superior realms—so, out of the series of the preceding social and political universes, now arises these States. We see that while many were supposing things established and completed, really the grandest things always remain; and discover that the work of the New World is not ended, but only fairly begun.

We see our land, America, her literature, esthetics, &c., as, substantially, the getting in form, or effusement and statement, of deepest basic elements and loftiest final meanings, of history and man—and the portrayal, (under the eternal laws and conditions of beauty,) of our own physiognomy, the subjective tie and expression of the objective, as from our own combination, continuation, and points of view—and the deposit and record of the national mentality, character, appeals, heroism, wars, and even liberties—where these, and all, culminate in native literary and artistic formulation, to be perpetuated; and not having which native, first-class formulation, she will flounder about, and her other, however imposing, eminent greatness, prove merely a passing gleam; but truly having which, she will understand herself, live nobly, nobly contribute, emanate, and, swinging, poised safely on herself, illumin'd and illuming, become a full-form'd world, and divine Mother not only of material but spiritual worlds, in ceaseless succession through time—the main thing being the average, the bodily, the concrete, the democratic, the popular, on which all the superstructures of the future are to permanently rest.

1867–1870   1871

Emily Dickinson   *1830–1886*

One day in April 1862, Thomas Wentworth Higginson, a poetry critic for The Atlantic
Monthly, *received a letter from Emily Dickinson of Amherst, Massachusetts, asking, "Are
you too deeply occupied to say if my verse is alive?" The four poems she enclosed provoked
an immediate response and began a correspondence that lasted twenty-two years. Although
Emily Dickinson thanked her "preceptor" Higginson for the "surgery" he performed on
her poetry, she wanted his encouragement more than his advice, and she politely ignored
his suggestions for regularizing her rough rhythms and imperfect rhymes and for correcting
her spelling and grammar. Recognizing Emily Dickinson's poetic genius, despite her
violations of poetic convention, Higginson remained her friend and adviser throughout
her life, and after her death he assisted in gathering her poems for publication.*

*Only eight of Emily Dickinson's poems were published while she lived, and it was not
until the appearance of* Poems by Emily Dickinson *(1890), four years after her death,
that her work became available to the general reading public for the first time. The early
critical estimates were mixed. Some reviewers found the poetry "balderdash" suffering
from lack of rhyme, faulty grammar, and incomprehensible metaphors, a "farrago of
illiterate and uneducated sentiment." But other readers found them remarkably pointed
and evocative. As the years passed and as more poems were published, critical estimates
grew more favorable until, with the publication of all her known poetry, in* The Poems
of Emily Dickinson *(1955), the shy, reclusive poet had come to be regarded, with
Whitman and Poe, as one of America's greatest lyric poets.*

*The range of Emily Dickinson's worldly experience was small by any standard. Her
entire life, except for brief visits to nearby Boston and to Washington, D.C., was spent in
and around her birthplace, Amherst. The Dickinsons of Amherst were prominent. Her
grandfather was a founder of Amherst College; for seventy years her father and then her
brother, both lawyers, served as College Treasurer and Trustee. Her mother claimed
Emily's affection, but not her wholehearted respect: "Mother does not care for thought,"
she wrote to Higginson.*

*As Emily Dickinson grew older, she increasingly withdrew from society, seldom leaving
her garden and her large family house. There she wrote poems and letters to her friends
and watched the life of the town from her upstairs bedroom window. Her friends, she said,
were her "estate," and among them were men, other than Higginson, her father, and her
brother, who profoundly affected her creative and emotional life. One of them was her
second "preceptor," the Reverend Charles Wadsworth, whom she met in Philadelphia in
the mid-1850s. The facts of their relationship are obscure, but there is little doubt about
her love for him and for his "kindly spiritual counsel," although they seldom met, and he
was a married man with a family. His departure to California perhaps caused the emotional
crisis she experienced in 1862, provoking a great creative outburst, for in that single year
she wrote the astonishing total of 366 poems.*

*Emily Dickinson lived a more intense and passionate life than was thought by neighbors
and acquaintances who saw her only as an eccentric maiden lady, the "moth" of Amherst,
dressed only in white, who flitted almost ghostlike through her house and garden. Not even
those closest to her knew fully the depth and extent of her emotions or that the nearly 1,800
poems, tied neatly in packets found after her death, would reveal an immensely complex
and passionate sensibility.*

*Her subjects were love, death, nature, immortality, beauty. Written largely in meters
common to Protestant hymn books, her poems employed irregular rhythms, off- or slant-
rhymes, paradox, and a careful balancing of abstract Latinate and concrete Anglo-Saxon
words. Her lines were gnomic and her images kinesthetic, highly concentrated, and intensely
charged with feeling. Her greatest lyrics were on the theme of death, which she typically*

personified as a monarch, a lord, or a kindly but irresistible lover, yet her moods varied widely, from melancholy to exuberance, grief to joy, leaden despair to spiritual intoxication.

Emily Dickinson's poetry at times descended to coyness and sentimentality. She had no firsthand contact with contemporary writers or critics of the highest order. Her favorite authors included Shakespeare, Keats, the Brownings, Ruskin, and Sir Thomas Browne whose uneasy balance of faith and skepticism she shared. Early in life she rebelled against the Calvinism of the Amherst Congregational Church, yet she retained the Calvinist tendency to look inwardly, and she had a Calvinist sense of both the inherent beauty and the frightening coldness of the world. With her fellow New Englanders Jonathan Edwards and Emerson, she perceived beauty in the wholeness and harmonious relationships of nature, and like Edwards and Emerson she has come to stand as a dominant figure in her nation's literary history, a poet whose work reflects a spiritual unrest and a sense of the human predicament that defy all easy categories.

FURTHER READING: *The Complete Poems of Emily Dickinson,* ed. T. Johnson, 1960, 1976; *The Manuscript Books of Emily Dickinson,* ed. R. Franklin, 1981; *The Letters of Emily Dickinson,* 3 vols., ed. T. Johnson, 1958; J. Leyda, *The Years and Hours of Emily Dickinson,* 2 vols., 1960; G. Whicher, *This Was a Poet,* 1938, 1952, 1957; M. Bingham, *Ancestor's Brocades,* 1945, 1967; R. Chase, *Emily Dickinson,* 1951; T. Johnson, *Emily Dickinson,* 1955; T. Ward, *The Capsule of the Mind,* 1961; *The Recognition of Emily Dickinson,* ed. C. Blake and C. Wells, 1964; K. Lubbers, *Emily Dickinson, the Critical Revolution,* 1968; J. Pickard, *Emily Dickinson, an Introduction and Interpretation,* 1967; C. Anderson, *Emily Dickinson's Poetry,* 1960; C. Griffith, *The Long Shadow, Emily Dickinson's Tragic Poetry,* 1964; R. Miller, *The Poetry of Emily Dickinson,* 1968; E. Wylder, *Emily Dickinson's Manuscripts,* 1971; R. Sewall, *The Life of Emily Dickinson,* 1974; R. Weisbuch, *Emily Dickinson's Poetry,* 1975; P. Ferlazzo, *Emily Dickinson,* 1976; S. Cameron, *Lyric Time, Dickinson and the Limits of Genre,* 1979; K. Keller, *The Only Kangaroo Among the Beauty,* 1979; D. Porter, *Dickinson, The Modern Idiom,* 1981; J. Diehl, *Dickinson and the Romantic Imagination,* 1981; *Critical Essays on Emily Dickinson,* ed. P. Ferlazzo, 1984; J. Loving, *Emily Dickinson, The Poet of the Second Story,* 1987; C. Miller, *Emily Dickinson, A Poet's Grammar,* 1987.

TEXT: *The Poems of Emily Dickinson,* 3 vols.; ed. T. Johnson, 1955. Some spelling has been normalized.

49[1]

I never lost as much but twice,
And that was in the sod.
Twice have I stood a beggar
Before the door of God!

Angels—twice descending
Reimbursed my store—
Burglar! Banker—Father!
I am poor once more!
1858?   1890

67

Success is counted sweetest
By those who ne'er succeed.

---

[1]Few of Emily Dickinson's poems were given titles. The numbers used here are from *The Poems of Emily Dickinson,* 3 vols.; ed. T. Johnson, 1955.

To comprehend a nectar
Requires sorest need.

Not one of all the purple Host
Who took the Flag today
Can tell the definition
So clear of Victory

As he defeated—dying—
On whose forbidden ear   10
The distant strains of triumph
Burst agonized and clear!
1859   1878

125

For each ecstatic instant
We must an anguish pay
In keen and quivering ratio
To the ecstacy.

For each beloved hour
Sharp pittances of years—
Bitter contested farthings[1]—
And Coffers heaped with Tears!
1859?   1891

130

These are the days when Birds come back—
A very few—a Bird or two—
To take a backward look.

These are the days when skies resume
The old—old sophistries[1] of June—
A blue and gold mistake.

Oh fraud that cannot cheat the Bee—
Almost the plausibility
Induces my belief.

Till ranks of seeds their witness bear—   10
And softly thro' the altered air
Hurries a timid leaf.

[1]Coins of little value.
[1]Subtle, deceptive reasoning.

Oh Sacrament of summer days,
Oh Last Communion in the Haze—
Permit a child to join.

Thy sacred emblems to partake—
Thy consecrated bread to take
And thine immortal wine!
1859?   1890

165

A *Wounded* Deer—leaps highest—
I've heard the Hunter tell—
'Tis but the Ecstasy of *death*—
And then the Brake is still!

The *Smitten* Rock that gushes!
The *trampled* Steel that springs!
A Cheek is always redder
Just where the Hectic stings!

Mirth is the Mail of Anguish—
In which it Cautious Arm,   10
Lest anybody spy the blood
And "you're hurt" exclaim!
1860?   1890

185

"Faith" is a fine invention
When Gentlemen can *see*—
But *Microscopes* are prudent
In an Emergency.
1860?   1891

210

The thought beneath so slight a film—
Is more distinctly seen—
As laces just reveal the surge—
Or Mists—the Appenine—
1860?   1891

214

I taste a liquor never brewed—
From Tankards scooped in Pearl—
Not all the Frankfort Berries[1]
Yield such an Alcohol!

Inebriate of Air—am I—
And Debauchee of Dew—
Reeling—thro endless summer days—
From inns of Molten Blue—

When "Landlords" turn the drunken Bee
Out of the Foxglove's door—   10
When Butterflies—renounce their "drams"—
I shall but drink the more!

Till Seraphs[2] swing their snowy Hats—
And Saints—to windows run—
To see the little Tippler
From Manzanilla[3] come![4]
1860?   1861, 1890

216

Safe in their Alabaster Chambers—
Untouched by Morning—
And untouched by Noon—
Lie the meek members of the Resurrection—
Rafter of Satin—and Roof of Stone!

Grand go the Years—in the Crescent—above them—
Worlds scoop their Arcs—
And Firmaments—row—
Diadems—drop—and Doges[1]—surrender—
Soundless as dots—on a Disc of Snow—   10
1861   1890

241

I like a look of Agony,
Because I know it's true—

---

[1]Grapes grown in the region of Frankfurt am Main, Germany, and used in making a fine Rhine wine. Another version of this line reads, "Not all the Vats upon the Rhine."
[2]The highest ranking of the nine orders of angels.   [3]A sherry wine exported from Manzanilla, Spain.
[4]Two other versions of the final line exist:
          "Come staggering toward the Sun."
          "Leaning against the—Sun—"
[1]The chief magistrates of Venice (697–1797).

Men do not sham Convulsion,
Nor simulate, a Throe[1]—

The Eyes glaze once—and that is Death—
Impossible to feign
The Beads upon the Forehead
By homely Anguish strung.
1861?   1890

249

Wild Nights—Wild Nights!
Were I with thee
Wild Nights should be
Our luxury!

Futile—the Winds—
To a Heart in port—
Done with the Compass—
Done with the Chart!

Rowing in Eden—
Ah, the Sea!   10
Might I but moor—Tonight—
In Thee!
1861?   1891

258

There's a certain Slant of light,
Winter Afternoons—
That oppresses, like the Heft[1]
Of Cathedral Tunes—

Heavenly Hurt, it gives us—
We can find no scar,
But internal difference,
Where the Meanings, are—

None may teach it—Any—
'Tis the Seal Despair—   10
An imperial affliction
Sent us of the Air—

[1]A spasm.
[1]Weight.

When it comes, the Landscape listens—
Shadows—hold their breath—
When it goes, 'tis like the Distance
On the look of Death—
1861?   1890

280

I felt a Funeral, in my Brain,
And Mourners to and fro
Kept treading—treading—till it seemed
That Sense was breaking through—

And when they all were seated,
A Service, like a Drum—
Kept beating—beating—till I thought
My Mind was going numb—

And then I heard them lift a Box
And creak across my Soul   10
With those same Boots of Lead, again,
Then Space—began to toll,

As all the Heavens were a Bell,
And Being, but an Ear,
And I, and Silence, some strange Race
Wrecked, solitary, here—

And then a Plank in Reason, broke,
And I dropped down, and down—
And hit a World, at every plunge,
And Finished knowing—then—   20
1861?   1896

285

The Robin's my Criterion for Tune—
Because I grow—where Robins do—
But, were I Cuckoo born—
I'd swear by him—
The ode familiar—rules the Noon—
The Buttercup's, my Whim for Bloom—
Because, we're Orchard sprung—
But, were I Britain born,
I'd Daisies spurn—
None but the Nut—October fit—   10
Because, through dropping it,

The Seasons flit—I'm taught—
Without the Snow's Tableau
Winter, were lie—to me—
Because I see—New Englandly—
The Queen, discerns like me—
Provincially—
1861?   1929

287

A Clock stopped—
Not the Mantel's—
Geneva's[1] farthest skill
Can't put the puppet bowing—
That just now dangled still—

An awe came on the Trinket!
The Figures hunched, with pain—
Then quivered out of Decimals—
Into Degreeless Noon—

It will not stir for Doctors—   10
This Pendulum of snow—
This Shopman importunes it—
While cool—concernless No—

Nods from the Gilded pointers—
Nods from the Seconds slim—
Decades of Arrogance between
The Dial life—
And Him—
1861?   1896

301

I reason, Earth is short—
And Anguish—absolute—
And many hurt,
But, what of that?

I reason, we could die—
The best Vitality
Cannot excel Decay,
But, what of that?

I reason, that in Heaven—

[1]Geneva, Switzerland—renowned as a town of clockmakers.

Somehow, it will be even—   10
Some new Equation, given—
But, what of that?
1862?   1890

303

The Soul selects her own Society—
Then—shuts the Door—
To her divine Majority—
Present no more—

Unmoved—she notes the Chariots—pausing—
At her low Gate—
Unmoved—an Emperor be kneeling
Upon her Mat—

I've known her—from an ample nation—
Choose One—   10
Then—close the Valves of her attention—
Like Stone—
1862?   1890

311

It sifts from Leaden Sieves—
It powders all the Wood.
It fills with Alabaster Wool
The Wrinkles of the Road—

It makes an Even Face
Of Mountain, and of Plain—
Unbroken Forehead from the East
Unto the East again—

It reaches to the Fence—
It wraps it Rail by Rail   10
Till it is lost in Fleeces—
It deals Celestial Vail[1]

To Stump, and Stack—and Stem—
A Summer's empty Room—
Acres of Joints, where Harvests were,
Recordless, but for them—

[1]Veil.

It Ruffles Wrists of Posts
As Ankles of a Queen—
Then stills its Artisans—like Ghosts—
Denying they have been—   20
1862?   1891

314

Nature—sometimes sears a Sapling—
Sometimes—scalps a Tree—
Her Green People recollect it
When they do not die—

Fainter Leaves—to Further Seasons—
Dumbly testify—
We—who have the Souls—
Die oftener—Not so vitally—
1862?   1945

324

Some keep the Sabbath going to Church—
I keep it, staying at Home—
With a Bobolink for a Chorister—
And an Orchard, for a Dome—

Some keep the Sabbath in Surplice[1]—
I just wear my Wings—
And instead of tolling the Bell, for Church,
Our little Sexton[2]—sings.

God preaches, a noted Clergyman—
And the sermon is never long   10
So instead of getting to Heaven, at last—
I'm going, all along.
1860?   1864

328

A Bird came down the Walk—
He did not know I saw—

[1] A loose, white robe worn by priests and others who help conduct church services.
[2] A church employee who takes care of church property, rings the church bells, and in some parishes digs graves. Here equated with the bobolink.

He bit an Angleworm in halves
And ate the fellow, raw,

And then he drank a Dew
From a convenient Grass—
And then hopped sidewise to the Wall
To let a Beetle pass—

He glanced with rapid eyes
That hurried all around—
They looked like frightened Beads, I thought—   10
He stirred his Velvet Head

Like one in danger, Cautious,
I offered him a Crumb
And he unrolled his feathers
And rowed him softer home—

Than Oars divide the Ocean,
Too silver for a seam—
Or Butterflies, off Banks of Noon
Leap, plashless[1] as they swim.
1862   1891   20

338

I know that He exists.
Somewhere—in Silence—
He has hid his rare life
From our gross eyes.

'Tis an instant's play.
'Tis a fond Ambush—
Just to make Bliss
Earn her own surprise!

But—should the play
Prove piercing earnest—   10
Should the glee—glaze—
In Death's—stiff—stare—

Would not the fun
Look too expensive!
Would not the jest—
Have crawled too far!
1862   1891

[1]Splashless.

341

After great pain, a formal feeling comes—
The Nerves sit ceremonious, like Tombs—
The stiff Heart questions was it He, that bore,
And Yesterday, or Centuries before?

The Feet, mechanical, go round—
Of Ground, or Air, or Ought—
A Wooden way
Regardless grown,
A Quartz contentment, like a stone—

This is the Hour of Lead—   10
Remembered, if outlived,
As Freezing persons, recollect the Snow—
First—Chill—then Stupor—then the letting go—
1862   1929

401

What Soft—Cherubic Creatures—
These Gentlewomen are—
One would as soon assault a Plush[1]—
Or violate a Star—

Such Dimity[2] Convictions—
A Horror so refined
Of freckled Human Nature—
Of Deity—ashamed[3]—

It's such a common—Glory—
A Fisherman's—Degree—   10
Redemption—Brittle Lady—
Be so—ashamed of Thee—
1862?   1896

414

'Twas like a Maelstrom,[1] with a notch,
That nearer, every Day,
Kept narrowing its boiling Wheel
Until the Agony

[1]Cloth with a long, soft pile.   [2]Cotton fabric, delicate and sheer.
[3]"For whosoever shall be ashamed of me and of my words, of him shall the Son of man be ashamed, when he shall come in his own glory. . . ." Luke 9:26.
[1]A violent whirlpool.

Toyed coolly with the final inch
Of your delirious Hem—
And you dropt, lost,
When something broke—
And let you from a Dream—

As if a Goblin with a Gauge—   10
Kept measuring the Hours—
Until you felt your Second
Weigh, helpless, in his Paws—

And not a Sinew—stirred—could help,
And sense was setting numb—
When God—remembered—and the Fiend
Let go, then, Overcome—

As if your Sentence stood—pronounced—
And you were frozen led
From Dungeon's luxury of Doubt   20
To Gibbets,[2] and the Dead—

And when the Film had stitched your eyes
A Creature gasped "Reprieve"!
Which Anguish was the utterest—then—
To perish, or to live?
1862?   1945

435

Much Madness is divinest Sense—
To a discerning Eye—
Much Sense—the starkest Madness—
'Tis the Majority
In this, as All, prevail—
Assent—and you are sane—
Demur—you're straightway dangerous—
And handled with a Chain—
1862?   1890

441

This is my letter to the World
That never wrote to Me—
The simple News that Nature told—
With tender Majesty

---

[2]Wooden frameworks on which criminals are hanged and left on display as a warning.

Her Message is committed
To Hands I cannot see—
For love of Her—Sweet—countrymen—
Judge tenderly—of Me
1862   1890

448

This was a Poet—It is That
Distills amazing sense
From ordinary Meanings—
And Attar[1] so immense

From the familiar species
That perished by the Door—
We wonder it was not Ourselves
Arrested it—before—

Of Pictures, the Discloser—
The Poet—it is He—   10
Entitles Us—by Contrast—
To ceaseless Poverty—

Of Portion—so unconscious—
The Robbing—could not harm—
Himself—to Him—a Fortune—
Exterior—to Time—
1862?   1929

449

I died for Beauty—but was scarce
Adjusted in the Tomb
When One who died for Truth, was lain
In an adjoining Room—

He questioned softly "Why I failed"?
"For Beauty," I replied—
"And I—for Truth—Themself are One—
We Bretheren, are," He said—

And so, as Kinsmen, met a Night—
We talked between the Rooms—   10
Until the Moss had reached our lips—
And covered up—our names—
1862?   1890

[1]Fragrant oils extracted from flowers.

465

I heard a Fly buzz—when I died—
The Stillness in the Room
Was like the Stillness in the Air—
Between the Heaves of Storm—

The Eyes around—had wrung them dry—
And Breaths were gathering firm
For that last Onset—when the King
Be witnessed—in the Room—

I willed my Keepsakes—Signed away
What portion of me be   10
Assignable—and then it was
There interposed a Fly—

With Blue—uncertain stumbling Buzz—
Between the light—and me—
And then the Windows failed—and then
I could not see to see—
1862?   1896

505

I would not paint—a picture—
I'd rather be the One
Its bright impossibility
To dwell—delicious—on—
And wonder how the fingers feel
Whose rare—celestial—stir—
Evokes so sweet a Torment—
Such sumptuous—Despair—

I would not talk, like Cornets—
I'd rather be the One   10
Raised softly to the Ceilings—
And out, and easy on—
Through Villages of Ether—
Myself endued Balloon
By but a lip of Metal—
The pier to my Pontoon—

Nor would I be a Poet—
It's finer—own the Ear—
Enamored—impotent—content—
The License to revere,   20

A privilege so awful
What would the Dower be,
Had I the Art to stun myself
With Bolts of Melody!
1862   1945

510

It was not Death, for I stood up,
And all the Dead, lie down—
It was not Night, for all the Bells
Put out their Tongues, for Noon.

It was not Frost, for on my Flesh
I felt Siroccos[1]—crawl—
Nor Fire—for just my Marble feet
Could keep a Chancel,[2] cool—

And yet, it tasted, like them all,
The Figures I have seen
Set orderly, for Burial,
Reminded me, of mine—   10

As if my life were shaven,
And fitted to a frame,
And could not breathe without a key,
and 'twas like Midnight, some—

When everything that ticked—has stopped—
And Space stares all around—
Or Grisly frosts—first Autumn morns,
Repeal the Beating Ground—   20

But, most, like Chaos—Stopless—cool—
Without a Chance, or Spar—
Or even a Report of Land—
To justify—Despair.
1862   1891

520

I started Early—Took my Dog—
And visited the Sea—
The Mermaids in the Basement
Came out to look at me—

[1]Hot, Mediterranean winds that originate in the Libyan deserts.
[2]Area of a church where the altar is placed.

And Frigates[1]—in the Upper Floor
Extended Hempen Hands—
Presuming Me to be a Mouse—
Aground—upon the Sands—

But no Man moved Me—till the Tide
Went past my simple Shoe—
And past my Apron—and my Belt
And past my Bodice—too—

And made as He would eat me up—
As wholly as a Dew
Upon a Dandelion's Sleeve—
And then—I started—too—

And He—He followed—close behind—
I felt His Silver Heel
Upon my Ankle—Then my Shoes
Would overflow with Pearl—

Until We met the Solid Town—
No One He seemed to know—
And bowing—with a Mighty look—
At me—The Sea withdrew—
1862?   1891

10

20

528

Mine—by the Right of the White Election!
Mine—by the Royal Seal!
Mine—by the Sign in the Scarlet prison—
Bars—cannot conceal!

Mine—here—in Vision—and in Veto!
Mine—by the Grave's Repeal—
Titled—Confirmed—
Delirious Charter!
Mine—long as Ages steal!
1862?   1890

536

The Heart asks Pleasure—first—
And then—Excuse from Pain—
And then—those little Anodynes[1]

[1]Swift-sailing ships.
[1]Drugs that soothe, relieve pain.

That deaden suffering—

And then—to go to sleep—
And then—if it should be
The will of its Inquisitor
The privilege to die—
1862?   1890

556

The Brain, within its Groove
Runs evenly—and true—
But let a Splinter swerve—
'Twere easier for You—

To put a Current back—
When Floods have slit the Hills—
And scooped a Turnpike for Themselves—
And trodden out the Mills—
1862?   1890

561

I measure every Grief I meet
With narrow, probing, Eyes—
I wonder if It weighs like Mine—
Or has an Easier size.

I wonder if They bore it long—
Or did it just begin—
I could not tell the Date of Mine—
It feels so old a pain—

I wonder if it hurts to live—
And if They have to try—
And whether—could They choose between—   10
It would not be—to die—

I note that Some—gone patient long—
At length, renew their smile—
An imitation of a Light
That has so little Oil—

I wonder if when Years have piled—
Some Thousands—on the Harm—
That hurt them early—such a lapse
Could give them any Balm—   20

Or would they go on aching still
Through Centuries of Nerve—
Enlightened to a large Pain—
In Contrast with the Love—

The Grieved—are many—I am told—
There is the various Cause—
Death—is but one—and comes but once—
And only nails the eyes—

There's Grief of Want—and Grief of Cold—
A sort they call "Despair"—   30
There's Banishment from native Eyes—
In sight of Native Air—

And though I may not guess the kind—
Correctly—yet to me
A piercing Comfort it affords
In passing Calvary[1]—

To note the fashions—of the Cross—
And how they're mostly worn—
Still fascinated to presume
That Some—are like My Own—   40
1862?   1896

585

I like to see it lap the Miles—
And lick the Valleys up—
And stop to feed itself at Tanks
And then—prodigious step

Around a Pile of Mountains—
And supercilious peer
In Shanties—by the sides of Roads—
And then a Quarry pare

To fit its sides
And crawl between   10
Complaining all the while
In horrid—hooting stanza—
Then chase itself down Hill—

And neigh like Boanerges[1]—
Then—prompter than a Star
Stop—docile and omnipotent
At its own stable door—
1862?   1891

[1]The hill, outside Jerusalem, where Jesus was crucified.
[1]Hebrew: Sons of Thunder, a term used to describe loud-voiced preachers and orators.

632

The Brain—is wider than the sky—
For—put them side by side—
The one the other will contain
With ease—and You—beside—

The Brain is deeper than the sea—
For—hold them—Blue to Blue—
The one the other will absorb—
As Sponges—Buckets—do—

The Brain is just the weight of God—
For—Heft them—Pound for Pound—   10
And they will differ—if they do—
As Syllable from Sound—
1862?   1896

640

I cannot live with You—
It would be Life—
And Life is over there—
Behind the Shelf—

The Sexton[1] keeps the Key to—
Putting up
Our Life—His Porcelain—
Like a Cup—

Discarded of the Housewife—
Quaint—or Broke—   10
A newer Sevres[2] pleases—
Old Ones crack—

I could not die—with You—
For One must wait
To shut the Other's Gaze down—
You—could not—

And I—Could I stand by
And see You—freeze—
Without my Right of Frost—
Death's privilege?   20

[1]Church official in charge of a church building and its grounds.
[2]Fine porcelain made in Sèvres, France.

Nor could I rise—with you—
Because Your Face
Would put out Jesus'—
That new Grace

Glow plain—and foreign
On my homesick Eye—
Except that You than He
Shone closer by—

They'd judge Us—How—
For You—served Heaven—You know,   30
Or sought to—
I could not—

Because You saturated Sight—
And I had no more Eyes
For sordid excellence
As Paradise.

And were You lost, I would be—
Though My Name
Rang loudest
On the Heavenly fame—   40

And were You—saved—
And I—condemned to be
Where You were not—
That self—were Hell to Me—

So We must meet apart—
You there—I—here—
With just the Door ajar
That Oceans are—and Prayer—
And that White Sustenance—
Despair—   50
1862?   1890

650

Pain—has an Element of Blank—
It cannot recollect
When it begun—or if there were
A time when it was not—

It has no Future—but itself—
Its Infinite contain
Its Past—enlightened to perceive
New Periods—of Pain.
1862?   1890

657

I dwell in Possibility—
A fairer House than Prose—
More numerous of Windows—
Superior—for Doors—

Of Chambers as the Cedars—
Impregnable of Eye—
And for an Everlasting Roof
The Gambrels[1] of the Sky—

Of Visiters—the fairest—
For Occupation—This—   10
The spreading wide my narrow Hands
To gather Paradise—
1862?
                                                 1929

670

One need not be a Chamber—to be Haunted—
One need not be a House—
The Brain has Corridors—surpassing
Material Place—

Far safer, of a Midnight Meeting
External Ghost
Than its interior Confronting—
That Cooler Host.

Far safer, through an Abbey gallop,
The Stones a'chase[1]—   10
Than Unarmed, one's a'self[2] encounter—
In lonesome Place—

Ourself behind ourself, concealed—
Should startle most—
Assassin hid in our Apartment
Be Horror's least.

The Body—borrows a Revolver—
He bolts the Door—
O'erlooking a superior spectre—
Or More—   20
1863?
                                                 1891

[1]Angled roofs.
[1]I.e., in pursuit.   [2]I.e., own self.

709

Publication—is the Auction
Of the Mind of Man—
Poverty—be justifying
For so foul a thing

Possibly—but We—would rather
From Our Garret go
White—Unto the White Creator—
Than invest—Our Snow—

Thought belong to Him who gave it—
Then—to Him Who bear   10
It's Corporeal illustration—Sell
The Royal Air—

In the Parcel—Be the Merchant
Of the Heavenly Grace—
But reduce no Human Spirit
To Disgrace of Price—
1863?   1929

712

Because I could not stop for Death—
He kindly stopped for me—
The Carriage held but just Ourselves—
And Immortality.

We slowly drove—He knew no haste
And I had put away
My labor and my leisure too,
For His Civility—

We passed the School, where Children strove
At Recess—in the Ring—   10
We passed the Fields of Gazing Grain—
We passed the Setting Sun—

Or rather—He passed Us—
The Dews drew quivering and chill—
For only Gossamer, my Gown—
My Tippet[1]—only Tulle[2]

We paused before a House that seemed
A Swelling of the Ground—
The Roof was scarcely visible—
The Cornice—in the Ground—   20

---

[1] A cape or scarf.   [2] Thin, net fabric.

Since then—'tis Centuries—and yet
Feels shorter than the Day
I first surmised the Horses' Heads
Were toward Eternity—
1863?   1890

745

Renunciation—is a piercing Virtue—
The letting go
A Presence—for an Expectation—
Not now—
The putting out of Eyes—
Just Sunrise—
Lest Day—
Day's Great Progenitor—
Outvie
Renunciation—is the Choosing   10
Against itself—
Itself to justify
Unto itself—
When larger function—
Make that appear—
Smaller—that Covered Vision—Here—
1863?   1929

754

My Life had stood—a Loaded Gun—
In Corners—till a Day
The Owner passed—identified—
And carried Me away—

And now We roam in Sovereign Woods—
And now We hunt the Doe—
And every time I speak for Him—
The Mountains straight reply—

And do I smile, such cordial light
Upon the Valley glow—   10
It is as a Vesuvian[1] face
Had let its pleasure through—

And when at Night—Our good Day done—
I guard My Master's Head—
'Tis better than the Eider-Duck's[2]
Deep Pillow—to have shared—

---

[1] I.e., resembling Mount Vesuvius, a volcano near Naples, Italy.
[2] North American waterfowl highly prized for its soft down.

To foe of His—I'm deadly foe—
None stir the second time—
On whom I lay a Yellow Eye—
Or an emphatic Thumb—   20

Though I than He—may longer live
He longer must—than I—
For I have but the power to kill,
Without—the power to die—
1863?   1929

764

Presentiment—is that long Shadow—on the Lawn—
Indicative that Suns go down—

The Notice to the startled Grass
That Darkness—is about to pass—
1863?   1890

976

Death is a Dialogue between
The Spirit and the Dust.
"Dissolve" says Death—The Spirit "Sir
I have another Trust"—

Death doubts it—Argues from the Ground—
The Spirit turns away
Just laying off for evidence
An Overcoat of Clay.
1864?   1890

986

A narrow Fellow in the Grass
Occasionally rides—
You may have met Him—did you not
His notice sudden is—

The Grass divides as with a Comb—
A spotted shaft is seen—
And then it closes at your feet
And opens further on—

He likes a Boggy Acre
A Floor too cool for corn—
Yet when a Boy, and Barefoot—   10
I more than once at Noon
Have passed, I thought, a Whip lash
Unbraiding in the Sun
When stooping to secure it
It wrinkled, and was gone—

Several of Nature's People
I know, and they know me—
I feel for them a transport
Of cordiality—   20

But never met this Fellow
Attended, or alone
Without a tighter breathing
And Zero at the Bone—
1865   1866, 1891

997

Crumbling is not an instant's Act
A fundamental pause
Delapidation's processes
Are organized Decays.

'Tis first a Cobweb on the Soul
A Cuticle of Dust
A Borer in the Axis
An Elemental Rust—

Ruin is formal—Devils work
Consecutive and slow—   10
Fail in an instant, no man did
Slipping—is Crashe's law.
1865?   1945

1052

I never saw a Moor—
I never saw the Sea—
Yet know I how the Heather looks
And what a Billow be.

I never spoke with God
Nor visited in Heaven—

Yet certain am I of the spot
As if the Checks[1] were given—
1865?   1890

1068

Further in Summer than the Birds
Pathetic from the Grass
A minor Nation celebrates
Its unobtrusive Mass.

No Ordinance[1] be seen
So gradual the Grace
A pensive Custom it becomes
Enlarging Loneliness.

Antiquest felt at Noon
When August burning low   10
Arise this spectral Canticle[2]
Repose to typify

Remit as yet no Grace
No Furrow on the Glow
Yet a Druidic[3] Difference
Enhances Nature now
1866?   1891

1078

The Bustle in a House
The Morning after Death
Is solemnest of industries
Enacted upon Earth—

The Sweeping up the Heart
And putting Love away
We shall not want to use again
Until Eternity.
1866?   1890

1129

Tell all the truth but tell it slant—
Success in Circuit lies

[1]Tokens of verification, tickets.
[1]A church ceremony, such as Communion.
[2]Biblical or ecclesiastical hymn.
[3]I.e., in the manner of pre-Christian, Celtic, nature worshipers.

Too bright for our infirm Delight
The Truth's superb surprise
As Lightning to the Children eased
With explanation kind
The Truth must dazzle gradually
Or every man be blind—
1868?   1945

1207

He preached upon "Breadth" till it argued him narrow—
The Broad are too broad to define
And of "Truth" until it proclaimed him a Liar—
The Truth never flaunted a Sign—

Simplicity fled from his counterfeit presence
As Gold the Pyrites[1] would shun—
What confusion would cover the innocent Jesus
To meet so enabled a Man!
1872?   1891

1463

A Route of Evanescence
With a revolving Wheel—
A Resonance of Emerald—
A Rush of Cochineal[1]—
And every Blossom on the Bush
Adjusts its tumbled Head—
The mail from Tunis,[2] probably,
An easy Morning's Ride—
1879?   1891

1540

As imperceptibly as Grief
The Summer lapsed away—
Too imperceptible at last
To seem like Perfidy—
A Quietness distilled
As Twilight long begun,
Or Nature spending with herself

[1]Iron or copper pyrites, called "fool's gold" because they resemble gold.
[1]A red dye.   [2]City in North Africa.

Sequestered Afternoon—
The Dusk drew earlier in—
The Morning foreign shone—   10
A courteous, yet harrowing Grace,
As Guest, that would be gone—
And thus, without a Wing
Or service of a Keel
Our Summer made her light escape
Into the Beautiful.
1865–1882?   1891

1545

The Bible is an antique Volume—
Written by faded Men
At the suggestion of Holy Spectres—
Subjects—Bethlehem—
Eden—the ancient Homestead—
Satan—the Brigadier—
Judas—the Great Defaulter—
David—the Troubadour—
Sin—a distinguished Precipice
Others must resist—   10
Boys that "believe" are very lonesome—
Other Boys are "lost"—
Had but the Tale a warbling Teller—
All the Boys would come—
Orpheus'[1] Sermon captivated—
It did not condemn—
1879–1882?   1924

1551

Those—dying then,
Knew where they went—
They went to God's Right Hand—
That Hand is amputated now
And God cannot be found—

The abdication of Belief
Makes the Behavior small—
Better an ignis fatuus[1]
Than no illume at all—
1882?   1945

[1]Legendary Greek poet and musician whose music charmed wild beasts, trees, and even rivers.
[1]A misleading light, the will-o'-the-wisp.

1624

Apparently with no surprise
To any happy Flower
The Frost beheads it at its play—
In accidental power—
The blonde Assassin passes on—
That Sun proceeds unmoved
To measure off another Day
For an Approving God.
1884?   1890

1670

In Winter in my Room
I came upon a Worm
Pink lank and warm
But as he was a worm
And worms presume
Not quite with him at home
Secured him by a string
To something neighboring
And went along.

A Trifle afterward   10
A thing occurred
I'd not believe it if I heard
But state with creeping blood
A snake with mottles rare
Surveyed my chamber floor
In feature as the worm before
But ringed with power
The very string with which
I tied him—too
When he was mean and new   20
That string was there—

I shrank—"How fair you are!"
Propitiation's claw—
"Afraid   he hissed
Of me?"
"No cordiality"—
He fathomed me—
Then to a Rhythm *Slim*
Secreted in his Form
As Patterns swim   30
Projected him.

That time I flew
Both eyes his way
Lest he pursue
Nor ever ceased to run
Till in a distant Town
Towns on from mine
I set me down
This was a dream—

                                                          1914

1732

My life closed twice before its close;
It yet remains to see
If immortality unveil
A third event to me,

So huge, so hopeless to conceive
As these that twice befell.
Parting is all we know of heaven,
And all we need of hell.

                                                          1896

1755

To make a prairie it takes a clover and one bee,
One clover, and a bee,
And revery.
The revery alone will do,
If bees are few.

                                                          1896

1760

Elysium[1] is as far as to
The very nearest Room
If in that Room a Friend await
Felicity or Doom—

What fortitude the Soul contains,
That it can so endure
The accent of a coming Foot—
The opening of a Door—
1882?   1890

[1]In classical myth the home of the blessed dead.

Mary E. Wilkins Freeman   *1852–1930*

In the years following the Civil War, decaying villages and abandoned farms marked the landscape of rural New England. Cheap land in the West and the lure of jobs in growing industrial centers to the south drew off the stronger, younger, and more adventuresome. Those who remained behind often lacked the chance or the will to leave. A substantial portion were unmarried women. They were so numerous that the strong-willed New England spinster, the stern old maid, became a public institution, the object of poems, jokes, songs, and newspaper cartoons. It was just such women, waiting tidily in fading New England villages, who became the subjects of Mary Wilkins Freeman's best stories.

Until her marriage in middle age to Dr. Charles Freeman of Metuchen, New Jersey, Mary Eleanor Wilkins lived in Randolph, Massachusetts, and in Brattleboro, Vermont, small towns in decline, with empty stores along the main street and silent mills along the river. She was in frail health as a girl, and in her solitude she turned naturally to reading. As a teenager she wrote and published a number of poems for children, but her decision to make writing her career came when she was in her early twenties and needed a vocation that would help support her family. Her love of books was equaled by a curiosity about the towns of Vermont and Massachusetts. She studied their histories, their distinctive buildings, and the dialect and character of their people.

In 1881 she received ten dollars for a poem published in a children's magazine. Her first book was a collection of children's verse, Decorative Plaques *(1883). Her first success in writing fiction for adults came in 1882 with "A Shadow Story," which won a prize of fifty dollars from a Boston weekly. Two years later, when* Harper's Bazar *accepted "Two Old Lovers" for publication, her career was launched, and her stories were soon in demand by editors of major magazines. She drew the admiration of such literary notables as James Russell Lowell and Henry James. Her stories were republished in England, and from France came requests for permission to translate her stories into French. In all she published thirty-nine volumes. Her best were* A Humble Romance and Other Stories *(1887), and* A New England Nun and Other Stories *(1892), tales of stolid village and farm people in remote New England.*

Mary Wilkins Freeman aimed "to preserve in literature" the "old and probably disappearing ways of New England character." Her stories mix elements of romance, realism, and naturalism. She wrote of strong-minded people whose individualism earns the wrath of friends and village neighbors. She depicted the pinched and stagnating lives of hesitant lovers whose endlessly prolonged courtships are destined never to conclude in marriage. Her work is frequently compared to that of Sarah Orne Jewett. Both wrote as spinster ladies, describing the lives of the men and women of small-town New England. Both have been identified with the local color tradition in American literature—writers whose stories and sketches emphasize the character types, customs, settings, and speech of regions that in nineteenth-century America still preserved their distinct identity.

Yet Mary Freeman's writing was less concerned with locale, more concerned with character. And her writing had a sharp, ironic edge to it that Sarah Orne Jewett seldom attempted. Freeman's stories are written with greater detachment, less sympathetic musing at the dilemmas of her characters. Her view could be sharp, critical, unsparing. Lacking the lenient tenderness that Sarah Orne Jewett exhibited for the people she described, Mary Wilkins Freeman could achieve a realism that to modern eyes more clearly portrays the strength and follies of the people she lived among, a realism that justifiably brought her recognition as "the most truthful recorder in fiction of New England life."

FURTHER READING: *The Best Stories of Mary Wilkins Freeman,* ed. H. Lanier, 1927; *Selected*

Stories of Mary E. Wilkins Freeman, ed. M. Pryse, 1983; *The Infant Sphinx, Collected Letters of Mary E. Wilkins Freeman*, ed. B. Kendrick, 1985; E. Foster, *Mary E. Wilkins Freeman*, 1956; P. Westbrook, *Mary Wilkins Freeman*, 1967.
TEXT: *A New England Nun and Other Stories*, 1891.

A NEW ENGLAND NUN

It was late in the afternoon, and the light was waning. There was a difference in the look of the tree shadows out in the yard. Somewhere in the distance cows were lowing and a little bell was tinkling; now and then a farm-wagon tilted by, and the dust flew; some blue-shirted laborers with shovels over their shoulders plodded past; little swarms of flies were dancing up and down before the people's faces in the soft air. There seemed to be a gentle stir arising over everything for the mere sake of subsidence—a very premonition of rest and hush and night.

This soft diurnal commotion was over Louisa Ellis also. She had been peacefully sewing at her sitting-room window all the afternoon. Now she quilted her needle carefully into her work, which she folded precisely, and laid in a basket with her thimble and thread and scissors. Louisa Ellis could not remember that ever in her life she had mislaid one of these little feminine appurtenances, which had become, from long use and constant association, a very part of her personality.

Louisa tied a green apron round her waist, and got out a flat straw hat with a green ribbon. Then she went into the garden with a little blue crockery bowl, to pick some currants for her tea. After the currants were picked she sat on the back door-step and stemmed them, collecting the stems carefully in her apron, and afterwards throwing them into the hen-coop. She looked sharply at the grass beside the step to see if any had fallen there.

Louisa was slow and still in her movements; it took her a long time to prepare her tea; but when ready it was set forth, with as much grace as if she had been a veritable[1] guest to her own self. The little square table stood exactly in the centre of the kitchen, and was covered with a starched linen cloth whose border pattern of flowers glistened. Louisa had a damask napkin on her tea-tray, where were arranged a cut-glass tumbler full of teaspoons, a silver cream-pitcher, a china sugar-bowl, and one pink china cup and saucer. Louisa used china every day—something which none of her neighbors did. They whispered about it among themselves. Their daily tables were laid with common crockery, their sets of best china stayed in the parlor closet, and Louisa Ellis was no richer nor better bred than they. Still she would use the china. She had for her supper a glass dish full of sugared currants, a plate of little cakes, and one of light white biscuits. Also a leaf or two of lettuce, which she cut up daintily. Louisa was very fond of lettuce, which she raised to perfection in her little garden. She ate quite heartily, though in a delicate, pecking way; it seemed almost surprising that any considerable bulk of the food should vanish.

After tea she filled a plate with nicely baked thin corncakes, and carried them out into the back-yard.

"Cæsar!" she called. "Cæsar! Cæsar!"

There was a little rush, and the clank of a chain, and a large yellow-and-white dog appeared at the door of his tiny hut, which was half hidden among the tall grasses and flowers. Louisa patted him and gave him the corn-cakes. Then she

[1]True.

returned to the house and washed the tea-things, polishing the china carefully. The twilight had deepened; the chorus of the frogs floated in at the open window wonderfully loud and shrill, and once in a while a long sharp drone from a tree-toad pierced it. Louisa took off her green gingham apron, disclosing a shorter one of pink and white print. She lighted her lamp, and sat down again with her sewing.

In about half an hour Joe Dagget came. She heard his heavy step on the walk, and rose and took off her pink-and-white apron. Under that was still another— white linen with a little cambric edging on the bottom; that was Louisa's company apron. She never wore it without her calico sewing apron over it unless she had a guest. She had barely folded the pink and white one with methodical haste and laid it in a table-drawer when the door opened and Joe Dagget entered.

He seemed to fill up the whole room. A little yellow canary that had been asleep in his green cage at the south window woke up and fluttered wildly, beating his little yellow wings against the wires. He always did so when Joe Dagget came into the room.

"Good-evening," said Louisa. She extended her hand with a kind of solemn cordiality.

"Good-evening, Louisa," returned the man, in a loud voice.

She placed a chair for him, and they sat facing each other, with the table between them. He sat bolt-upright, toeing out his heavy feet squarely, glancing with a good-humored uneasiness around the room. She sat gently erect, folding her slender hands in her white-linen lap.

"Been a pleasant day," remarked Dagget.

"Real pleasant," Louisa assented, softly. "Have you been haying?" she asked, after a little while.

"Yes, I've been haying all day, down in the ten-acre lot. Pretty hot work."

"It must be."

"Yes, it's pretty hot work in the sun."

"Is your mother well to-day?"

"Yes, mother's pretty well."

"I suppose Lily Dyer's with her now?"

Dagget colored. "Yes, she's with her," he answered, slowly.

He was not very young, but there was a boyish look about his large face. Louisa was not quite as old as he, her face was fairer and smoother, but she gave people the impression of being older.

"I suppose she's a good deal of help to your mother," she said, further.

"I guess she is; I don't know how mother'd get along without her," said Dagget, with a sort of embarrassed warmth.

"She looks like a real capable girl. She's pretty-looking too," remarked Louisa.

"Yes, she is pretty fair looking."

Presently Dagget began fingering the books on the table. There was a square red autograph album, and a Young Lady's Gift-Book which had belonged to Louisa's mother. He took them up one after the other and opened them; then laid them down again, the album on the Gift-Book.

Louisa kept eying them with mild uneasiness. Finally she rose and changed the position of the books, putting the album underneath. That was the way they had been arranged in the first place.

Dagget gave an awkward little laugh. "Now what difference did it make which book was on top?" said he.

Louisa looked at him with a deprecating smile. "I always keep them that way," murmured she.

"You do beat everything," said Dagget, trying to laugh again. His large face was flushed.

He remained about an hour longer, then rose to take leave. Going out, he stumbled over a rug, and trying to recover himself, hit Louisa's work-basket on the table, and knocked it on the floor.

He looked at Louisa, then at the rolling spools; he ducked himself awkwardly toward them, but she stopped him. "Never mind," said she; "I'll pick them up after you're gone."

She spoke with a mild stiffness. Either she was a little disturbed, or his nervousness affected her, and made her seem constrained in her effort to reassure him.

When Joe Dagget was outside he drew in the sweet evening air with a sigh, and felt much as an innocent and perfectly well-intentioned bear might after his exit from a china shop.

Louisa, on her part, felt much as the kind-hearted, long-suffering owner of the china shop might have done after the exit of the bear.

She tied on the pink, then the green apron, picked up all the scattered treasures and replaced them in her work-basket, and straightened the rug. Then she set the lamp on the floor, and began sharply examining the carpet. She even rubbed her fingers over it, and looked at them.

"He's tracked in a good deal of dust," she murmured. "I thought he must have."

Louisa got a dust-pan and brush, and swept Joe Dagget's track carefully.

If he could have known it, it would have increased his perplexity and uneasiness, although it would not have disturbed his loyalty in the least. He came twice a week to see Louisa Ellis, and every time, sitting there in her delicately sweet room, he felt as if surrounded by a hedge of lace. He was afraid to stir lest he should put a clumsy foot or hand through the fairy web, and he had always the consciousness that Louisa was watching fearfully lest he should.

Still the lace and Louisa commanded perforce his perfect respect and patience and loyalty. They were to be married in a month, after a singular courtship which had lasted for a matter of fifteen years. For fourteen out of the fifteen years the two had not once seen each other, and they had seldom exchanged letters. Joe had been all those years in Australia, where he had gone to make his fortune, and where he had stayed until he made it. He would have stayed fifty years if it had taken so long, and come home feeble and tottering, or never come home at all, to marry Louisa.

But the fortune had been made in the fourteen years, and he had come home now to marry the woman who had been patiently and unquestioningly waiting for him all that time.

Shortly after they were engaged he had announced to Louisa his determination to strike out into new fields, and secure a competency before they should be married. She had listened and assented with the sweet serenity which never failed her, not even when her lover set forth on that long and uncertain journey. Joe, buoyed up as he was by his sturdy determination, broke down a little at the last, but Louisa kissed him with a mild blush, and said good-by.

"It won't be for long," poor Joe had said, huskily; but it was for fourteen years.

In that length of time much had happened. Louisa's mother and brother had died, and she was all alone in the world. But greatest happening of all—a subtle happening which both were too simple to understand—Louisa's feet had turned into a path, smooth maybe under a calm, serene sky, but so straight and unswerving that it could only meet a check at her grave, and so narrow that there was no room for any one at her side.

Louisa's first emotion when Joe Dagget came home (he had not apprised her of his coming) was consternation, although she would not admit it to herself, and he never dreamed of it. Fifteen years ago she had been in love with him—at least she considered herself to be. Just at that time, gently acquiescing with and falling into the natural drift of girlhood, she had seen marriage ahead as a reasonable feature and a probable desirability of life. She had listened with calm docility to her mother's views upon the subject. Her mother was remarkable for her cool sense and sweet, even temperament. She talked wisely to her daughter when Joe Dagget presented himself, and Louisa accepted him with no hesitation. He was the first lover she had ever had.

She had been faithful to him all these years. She had never dreamed of the possibility of marrying any one else. Her life, especially for the last seven years, had been full of a pleasant peace, she had never felt discontented nor impatient over her lover's absence; still she had always looked forward to his return and their marriage as the inevitable conclusion of things. However, she had fallen into a way of placing it so far in the future that it was almost equal to placing it over the boundaries of another life.

When Joe came she had been expecting him, and expecting to be married for fourteen years, but she was much surprised and taken aback as if she had never thought of it.

Joe's consternation came later. He eyed Louisa with an instant confirmation of his old admiration. She had changed but little. She still kept her pretty manner and soft grace, and was, he considered, every whit as attractive as ever. As for himself, his stent[2] was done; he had turned his face away from fortune-seeking, and the old winds of romance whistled as loud and sweet as ever through his ears. All the song which he had been wont to hear in them was Louisa; he had for a long time a loyal belief that he heard it still, but finally it seemed to him that although the winds sang always that one song, it had another name. But for Louisa the wind had never more than murmured; now it had gone down, and everything was still. She listened for a little while with half-wistful attention; then she turned quietly away and went to work on her wedding clothes.

Joe had made some extensive and quite magnificent alterations in his house. It was the old homestead; the newly-married couple would live there, for Joe could not desert his mother, who refused to leave her old home. So Louisa must leave hers. Every morning, rising and going about among her neat maidenly possessions, she felt as one looking her last upon the faces of dear friends. It was true that in a measure she could take them with her, but, robbed of their old environments, they would appear in such new guises that they would almost cease to be themselves. Then there were some peculiar features of her happy solitary life which she would probably be obliged to relinquish altogether. Sterner tasks than these graceful but half-needless ones would probably devolve upon her. There would be a large house to care for; there would be company to entertain; there would be Joe's rigorous and feeble old mother to wait upon; and it would be contrary to all thrifty village traditions for her to keep more than one servant. Louisa had a little still, and she used to occupy herself pleasantly in summer weather with distilling the sweet and aromatic essences from roses and peppermint and spearmint. By-and-by her still must be laid away. Her store

[2]Task.

of essences was already considerable, and there would be no time for her to distil for the mere pleasure of it. Then Joe's mother would think it foolishness; she had already hinted her opinion in the matter. Louisa dearly loved to sew a linen seam, not always for use, but for the simple, mild pleasure which she took in it. She would have been loath to confess how more than once she had ripped a seam for the mere delight of sewing it together again. Sitting at her window during long sweet afternoons, drawing her needle gently through the dainty fabric, she was peace itself. But there was a small chance of such foolish comfort in the future. Joe's mother, domineering, shrewd old matron that she was even in her old age, and very likely even Joe himself, with his honest masculine rudeness, would laugh and frown down all these pretty but senseless old maiden ways.

Louisa had almost the enthusiasm of an artist over the mere order and cleanliness of her solitary home. She had throbs of genuine triumph at the sight of the window-panes which she had polished until they shone like jewels. She gloated gently over her orderly bureau-drawers, with their exquisitely folded contents redolent with lavender and sweet clover and very purity. Could she be sure of the endurance of even this? She had visions, so startling that she half repudiated them as indelicate, of coarse masculine belongings strewn about in endless litter; of dust and disorder arising necessarily from a coarse masculine presence in the midst of all this delicate harmony.

Among her forebodings of disturbance, not the least was with regard to Cæsar. Cæsar was a veritable hermit of a dog. For the greater part of his life he had dwelt in his secluded hut, shut out from the society of his kind and all innocent canine joys. Never had Cæsar since his early youth watched at a woodchuck's hole; never had he known the delights of a stray bone at a neighbor's kitchen door. And it was all on account of a sin committed when hardly out of his puppyhood. No one knew the possible depth of remorse of which this mild-visaged, altogether innocent-looking old dog might be capable; but whether or not he had encountered remorse, he had encountered a full measure of righteous retribution. Old Cæsar seldom lifted up his voice in a growl or a bark; he was fat and sleepy; there were yellow rings which looked like spectacles around his dim old eyes; but there was a neighbor who bore on his hand the imprint of several of Cæsar's sharp white youthful teeth, and for that he had lived at the end of a chain, all alone in a little hut, for fourteen years. The neighbor, who was choleric and smarting with the pain of his wound, had demanded either Cæsar's death or complete ostracism. So Louisa's brother, to whom the dog had belonged, had built him his little kennel and tied him up. It was now fourteen years since, in a flood of youthful spirits, he had inflicted that memorable bite, and with the exception of short excursions, always at the end of the chain, under the strict guardianship of his master or Louisa, the old dog had remained a close prisoner. It is doubtful if, with his limited ambition, he took much pride in the fact, but it is certain that he was possessed of considerable cheap fame. He was regarded by all the children in the village and by many adults as a very monster of ferocity. St. George's dragon could hardly have surpassed in evil repute Louisa Ellis's old yellow dog. Mothers charged their children with solemn emphasis not to go too near to him, and the children listened and believed greedily, with a fascinated appetite for terror, and ran by Louisa's house stealthily, with many sidelong and backward glances at the terrible dog. If perchance he sounded a hoarse bark, there was a panic. Wayfarers chancing into Louisa's yard eyed him with respect, and inquired if the chain were stout. Cæsar at large might have seemed a very ordinary dog, and excited no comment whatever;

chained, his reputation overshadowed him, so that he lost his own proper outlines and looked darkly vague and enormous. Joe Dagget, however, with his good-humored sense and shrewdness, saw him as he was. He strode valiantly up to him and patted him on the head, in spite of Louisa's soft clamor of warning, and even attempted to set him loose. Louisa grew so alarmed that he desisted, but kept announcing his opinion in the matter quite forcibly at intervals. "There ain't a better-natured dog in town," he would say, "and it's down-right cruel to keep him tied up there. Some day I'm going to take him out."

Louisa had very little hope that he would not, one of these days, when their interests and possessions should be more completely fused in one. She pictured to herself Cæsar on the rampage through the quiet and unguarded village. She saw innocent children bleeding in his path. She was herself very fond of the old dog, because he had belonged to her dead brother and he was always very gentle with her; still she had great faith in his ferocity. She always warned people not to go too near him. She fed him on ascetic fare of corn-mush and cakes, and never fired his dangerous temper with heating and sanguinary diet of flesh and bones. Louisa looked at the old dog munching his simple fare, and thought of her approaching marriage and trembled. Still no anticipation of disorder and confusion in lieu of sweet peace and harmony, no forebodings of Cæsar on the rampage, no wild fluttering of her little yellow canary, were sufficient to turn her a hair's-breadth. Joe Dagget had been fond of her and working for her all these years. It was not for her, whatever came to pass, to prove untrue and break his heart. She put the exquisite little stitches into her wedding-garments, and the time went on until it was only a week before her wedding-day. It was a Tuesday evening, and the wedding was to be a week from Wednesday.

There was a full moon that night. About nine o'clock Louisa strolled down the road a little way. There were harvest-fields on either hand, bordered by low stone walls. Luxuriant clumps of bushes grew beside the wall, and trees—wild cherry and old apple-trees—at intervals. Presently Louisa sat down on the wall and looked about her with mildly sorrowful reflectiveness. Tall shrubs of blueberry and meadow-sweet, all woven together and tangled with blackberry vines and horsebriers, shut her in on either side. She had a little clear space between them. Opposite her, on the other side of the road, was a spreading tree; the moon shone between its boughs, and the leaves twinkled like silver. The road was bespread with a beautiful shifting dapple of silver and shadow; the air was full of a mysterious sweetness. "I wonder if it's wild grapes?" murmured Louisa. She sat there some time. She was just thinking of rising, when she heard footsteps and low voices, and remained quiet. It was a lonely place, and she felt a little timid. She thought she would keep still in the shadow and let the persons, whoever they might be, pass her.

But just before they reached her the voices ceased, and the footsteps. She understood that their owners had also found seats upon the stone wall. She was wondering if she could not steal away unobserved, when the voice broke the stillness. It was Joe Dagget's. She sat still and listened.

The voice was announced by a loud sigh, which was familiar as itself. "Well," said Dagget, "you've made up your mind, then, I suppose?"

"Yes," returned another voice; "I'm going day after to-morrow."

"That's Lily Dyer," thought Louisa to herself. The voice embodied itself in her mind. She saw a girl tall and full-figured, with a firm, fair face, looking fairer and firmer in the moonlight, her strong yellow hair braided in a close knot. A girl full of a calm rustic strength and bloom, with a masterful way which might have beseemed a princess. Lily Dyer was a favorite with the village folk;

she had just the qualities to arouse the admiration. She was good and handsome and smart. Louisa had often heard her praises sounded.

"Well," said Joe Dagget, "I ain't got a word to say."

"I don't know what you could say," returned Lily Dyer.

"Not a word to say," repeated Joe, drawing out the words heavily. Then there was a silence. "I ain't sorry," he began at last, "that that happened yesterday—that we kind of let on how we felt to each other. I guess it's just as well we knew. Of course I can't do anything any different. I'm going right on an' get married next week. I ain't going back on a woman that's waited for me fourteen years, an' break her heart."

"If you should jilt her to-morrow, I wouldn't have you," spoke up the girl, with sudden vehemence.

"Well, I ain't going to give you the chance," said he; "but I don't believe you would, either."

"You'd see I wouldn't. Honor's honor, an' right's right. An' I'd never think anything of any man that went against 'em for me or any other girl; you'd find that out, Joe Dagget."

"Well, you'll find out fast enough that I ain't going against 'em for you or any other girl," returned he. Their voices sounded almost as if they were angry with each other. Louisa was listening eagerly.

"I'm sorry you feel as if you must go away," said Joe, "but I don't know but it's best."

"Of course it's best. I hope you and I have got common-sense."

"Well, I suppose you're right." Suddenly Joe's voice got an undertone of tenderness. "Say, Lily," said he, "I'll get along well enough myself, but I can't bear to think—You don't suppose you're going to fret much over it?"

"I guess you'll find out I sha'n't fret much over a married man."

"Well, I hope you won't—I hope you won't, Lily. God knows I do. And—I hope—one of these days—you'll—come across somebody else—"

"I don't see any reason why I shouldn't." Suddenly her tone changed. She spoke in a sweet, clear voice, so loud that she could have been heard across the street. "No, Joe Dagget," said she, "I'll never marry any other man as long as I live. I've got good sense, an' I ain't going to break my heart nor make a fool of myself; but I'm never going to be married, you can be sure of that. I ain't that sort of a girl to feel this way twice."

Louisa heard an exclamation and a soft commotion behind the bushes; then Lily spoke again—the voice sounded as if she had risen. "This must be put a stop to," said she. "We've stayed here long enough. I'm going home."

Louisa sat there in a daze, listening to their retreating steps. After a while she got up and slunk softly home herself. The next day she did her housework methodically; that was as much a matter of course as breathing; but she did not sew on her wedding-clothes. She sat at her window and meditated. In the evening Joe came. Louisa Ellis had never known that she had any diplomacy in her, but when she came to look for it that night she found it, although meek of its kind, among her little feminine weapons. Even now she could hardly believe that she had heard aright, and that she would not do Joe a terrible injury should she break her troth-plight.[3] She wanted to sound him without betraying too soon her own inclinations in the matter. She did it successfully, and they finally came to an understanding; but it was a difficult thing, for he was as afraid of betraying himself as she.

[3]Pledge to marry.

She never mentioned Lily Dyer. She simply said that while she had no cause of complaint against him, she had lived so long in one way that she shrank from making a change.

"Well, I never shrank, Louisa," said Dagget. "I'm going to be honest enough to say that I think maybe it's better this way; but if you'd wanted to keep on, I'd have stuck to you till my dying day. I hope you know that."

"Yes, I do," said she.

That night she and Joe parted more tenderly than they had done for a long time. Standing in the door, holding each other's hands, a last great wave of regretful memory swept over them.

"Well, this ain't the way we've thought it was all going to end, is it, Louisa?" said Joe.

She shook her head. There was a little quiver on her placid face.

"You let me know if there's ever anything I can do for you," said he. "I ain't ever going to forget you, Louisa." Then he kissed her, and went down the path.

Louisa, all alone by herself that night, wept a little, she hardly knew why; but the next morning, on waking, she felt like a queen who, after fearing lest her domain be wrested away from her, sees it firmly insured in her possession.

Now the tall weeds and grasses might cluster around Cæsar's little hermit hut, the snow might fall on its roof year in and year out, but he never would go on a rampage through the unguarded village. Now the little canary might turn itself into a peaceful yellow ball night after night, and have no need to wake and flutter with wild terror against its bars. Louisa could sew linen seams, and distil roses, and dust and polish and fold away in lavender, as long as she listed. That afternoon she sat with her needle-work at the window, and felt fairly steeped in peace. Lily Dyer, tall and erect and blooming, went past; but she felt no qualm. If Louisa Ellis had sold her birthright she did not know it, the taste of the pottage[4] was so delicious, and had been her sole satisfaction for so long. Serenity and placid narrowness had become to her as the birthright itself. She gazed ahead through a long reach of future days strung together like pearls in a rosary, every one like the others, and all smooth and flawless and innocent, and her heart went up in thankfulness. Outside was the fervid summer afternoon; the air was filled with the sounds of the busy harvest of men and birds and bees; there were halloos, metallic clatterings, sweet calls, and long hummings. Louisa sat, prayerfully numbering her days, like an uncloistered nun.

1891

Sarah Orne Jewett   *1849–1909*

Sarah Orne Jewett learned to observe New Englanders as she accompanied her father, a physician, on his daily rounds, visiting patients on farms and in villages near South Berwick, Maine. She was a sickly child, and her formal schooling was irregular. She

---

[4]A thick soup. The reference is to the biblical Esau, who foolishly sold his birthright for a meal of bread and pottage. Genesis 25:29–34.

compensated by reading widely in her father's substantial library: poets; French, Russian, and English novelists; and American writers such as Emerson and Lowell. But later in life she recalled, "The best of my education was received in my father's buggy and the places to which it carried me."

In 1863, after reading a book of regional tales of New England by Harriet Beecher Stowe, Sarah Orne Jewett resolved that she too would become a writer and record permanently and truly the life and the people of Maine that she knew so well. She set out to gather local legends and folk tales. She studied the manners and customs, the peculiarities of speech, and the family histories of farmers and villagers on the mainland and fishermen on the coastal isles. At fourteen she began writing tales and sketches, using pen-names such as Alice Eliot or Sarah Sweet because, as she later explained, she wanted no one to know of her literary ambitions.

When she was eighteen, her first story was published, "Jenny Garrow's Lovers," an amateurish tale filled with melodrama and literary stereotypes. But two years later, in 1869, her writing had so improved that one of her stories was accepted by the illustrious Atlantic Monthly, *America's most respected journal. Over the succeeding years her work continued to appear in the nation's most prestigious magazines, including* The Atlantic Monthly, Scribner's, *and* Harper's. *In 1877 she collected a series of her tales and sketches and published them under the title* Deephaven. *It was the first of more than twenty volumes—short stories, novels, children's books, poems—that she wrote in a career that extended into the twentieth century.*

Although Sarah Orne Jewett traveled widely outside Maine, her best stories and sketches took place in her native state and portrayed the lives of the men and, more often, the women who lived in the villages and on farms of New England following the American Civil War. She rejected the disruptions and grasping values that she saw in nineteenth-century urban life, reaffirming the sturdy goodness of country ways and country people. In such fiction as "A White Heron," her most highly praised short story, she exhibits fundamental themes to which she frequently returned: the virtues of village life and unblemished nature, the tenacious resistance to change exhibited by people living in a rural backwater, and the discord brought by strangers and strange ideas.

Sarah Jewett's stories portray suffering and defeat, yet they celebrate open-hearted innocence, sympathy, kindness, understanding, and sensitivity—the values of the passing age she yearned to honor and labored to record. She was not a literary naturalist, writing of helpless people doomed by fate and harsh environment; still, she emphasized the impact of the natural world upon their lives. The sea, the rocky soil, the fields and forests of Maine, the idyllic summers and the long winters—all shape, for good or ill, the people she describes, binding them to lives they enjoy and endure.

Critics have objected that her stories stress character and scene at the expense of plot and action, that in her fiction she exhibits an extravagant compassion for her characters that frequently borders on sentimentalism. Her writing was purposely muted and pacific, and her range was narrow—Henry James called her work a "beautiful quantum of achievement." Yet the writing in her most notable single volume, The Country of the Pointed Firs *(1896), has brought her praise as the creator of the "best regional fiction to have come out of nineteenth-century America." And her ability to portray the commonplace lives of the men and women she knew—their manners, their beliefs, their New England speech—continues to attract praise and enthusiastic readers more than half a century after her death, long after the world that she described has ceased to be.*

FURTHER READING: *Deephaven and Other Stories*, ed. R. Cary, 1966; *The Uncollected Short Stories of Sarah Orne Jewett*, ed. R. Cary, 1971; *Letters of Sarah Orne Jewett*, ed. A. Fields, 1911; *Sarah Orne Jewett Letters*, ed. R. Cary, 1956, 1967; F. Matthiessen, *Sarah Orne Jewett*,

1929, 1965; J. Frost, *Sarah Orne Jewett*, 1960; R. Cary, *Sarah Orne Jewett*, 1962; M. Thorp, *Sarah Orne Jewett*, 1966; *Appreciation of Sarah Orne Jewett, 29 Interpretive Essays*, ed. E. Cary, 1973; J. Donovan, *Sarah Orne Jewett*, 1980; G. Nagel, *Critical Essays on Sarah Orne Jewett*, 1984; L. Renza, *"A White Heron" and the Question of Minor Literature*, 1984.

TEXT: *A White Heron and Other Stories*, 1886.

A WHITE HERON

1 The woods were already filled with shadows one June evening, just before eight o'clock, though a bright sunset still glimmered faintly among the trunks of the trees. A little girl was driving home her cow, a plodding, dilatory, provoking creature in her behavior, but a valued companion for all that. They were going away from the western light, and striking deep into the dark woods, but their feet were familiar with the path, and it was no matter whether their eyes could see it or not.

There was hardly a night the summer through when the old cow could be found waiting at the pasture bars; on the contrary, it was her greatest pleasure to hide herself away among the high huckleberry bushes, and though she wore a loud bell she had made the discovery that if one stood perfectly still it would not ring. So Sylvia had to hunt for her until she found her, and call Co'! Co'! with never an answering Moo, until her childish patience was quite spent. If the creature had not given good milk and plenty of it, the case would have seemed very different to her owners. Besides, Sylvia had all the time there was, and very little use to make of it. Sometimes in pleasant weather it was a consolation to look upon the cow's pranks as an intelligent attempt to play hide and seek, and as the child had no playmates she lent herself to this amusement with a good deal of zest. Though this chase had been so long that the wary animal herself had given an unusual signal of her whereabouts, Sylvia had only laughed when she came upon Mistress Moolly at the swamp-side, and urged her affectionately homeward with a twig of birch leaves. The old cow was not inclined to wander farther, she even turned in the right direction for once as they left the pasture, and stepped along the road at a good pace. She was quite ready to be milked now, and seldom stopped to browse. Sylvia wondered what her grandmother would say because they were so late. It was a great while since she had left home at half past five o'clock, but everybody knew the difficulty of making this errand a short one. Mrs. Tilley had chased the hornéd torment too many summer evenings herself to blame any one else for lingering, and was only thankful as she waited that she had Sylvia, nowadays, to give such valuable assistance. The good woman suspected that Sylvia loitered occasionally on her own account; there never was such a child for straying about out-of-doors since the world was made! Everybody said that it was a good change for a little maid who had tried to grow for eight years in a crowded manufacturing town, but, as for Sylvia herself, it seemed as if she never had been alive at all before she came to live at the farm. She thought often with wistful compassion of a wretched dry geranium that belonged to a town neighbor.

" 'Afraid of folks,' " old Mrs. Tilley said to herself, with a smile, after she had made the unlikely choice of Sylvia from her daughter's houseful of children, and was returning to the farm. " 'Afraid of folks,' they said! I guess she won't be troubled no great with 'em up to the old place!" When they reached the door of the lonely house and stopped to unlock it, and the cat came to purr loudly, and rub against them, a deserted pussy, indeed, but fat with young robins. Sylvia whispered that this was a beautiful place to live in, and she never should wish to go home.

The companions followed the shady woodroad, the cow taking slow steps, and the child very fast ones. The cow stopped long at the brook to drink, as if the pasture were not half a swamp, and Sylvia stood still and waited, letting her bare feet cool themselves in the shoal water, while the great twilight moths struck softly against her. She waded on through the brook as the cow moved away, and listened to the thrushes with a heart that beat fast with pleasure. There was a stirring in the great boughs overhead. They were full of little birds and beasts that seemed to be wide-awake, and going about their world, or else saying good-night to each other in sleepy twitters. Sylvia herself felt sleepy as she walked along. However, it was not much farther to the house, and the air was soft and sweet. She was not often in the woods so late as this, and it made her feel as if she were a part of the gray shadows and the moving leaves. She was just thinking how long it seemed since she first came to the farm a year ago, and wondering if everything went on in the noisy town just the same as when she was there; the thought of the great red-faced boy who used to chase and frighten her made her hurry along the path to escape from the shadow of the trees.

Suddenly this little woods-girl is horror-stricken to hear a clear whistle not very far away. Not a bird's whistle, which would have a sort of friendliness, but a boy's whistle, determined, and somewhat aggressive. Sylvia left the cow to whatever sad fate might await her, and stepped discreetly aside into the bushes, but she was just too late. The enemy had discovered her, and called out in a very cheerful and persuasive tone, "Halloa, little girl, how far is it to the road? and trembling Sylvia answered almost inaudibly, "A good ways."

She did not dare to look boldly at the tall young man, who carried a gun over his shoulder, but she came out of her bush and again followed the cow, while he walked alongside.

"I have been hunting for some birds," the stranger said kindly, "and I have lost my way, and need a friend very much. Don't be afraid," he added gallantly. "Speak up and tell me what your name is, and whether you think I can spend the night at your house, and go out gunning early in the morning."

Sylvia was more alarmed than before. Would not her grandmother consider her much to blame? But who could have foreseen such an accident as this? It did not appear to be her fault, and she hung her head as if the stem of it were broken, but managed to answer "Sylvy," with much effort when her companion again asked her name.

Mrs. Tilley was standing in the doorway when the trio came into view. The cow gave a loud moo by way of explanation.

"Yes, you'd better speak up for yourself, you old trial! Where'd she tuck herself away this time, Sylvy?" Sylvia kept an awed silence; she knew by instinct that her grandmother did not comprehend the gravity of the situation. She must be mistaking the stranger for one of the farmer-lads of the region.

The young man stood his gun beside the door, and dropped a heavy game-bag beside it; then he bade Mrs. Tilley good-evening, and repeated his wayfarer's story, and asked if he could have a night's lodging.

"Put me anywhere you like," he said. "I must be off early in the morning, before day; but I am very hungry, indeed. You can give me some milk at any rate, that's plain."

"Dear sakes, yes," responded the hostess, whose long slumbering hospitality seemed to be easily awakened. "You might fare better if you went out on the main road a mile or so, but you're welcome to what we've got. I'll milk right off, and you make yourself at home. You can sleep on husks or feathers," she proffered graciously. "I raised them all myself. There's good pasturing for geese just below here towards the ma'sh. Now step round and set a plate for the gentleman, Sylvy!" And Sylvia promptly stepped. She was glad to have something to do, and she was hungry herself.

It was a surprise to find so clean and comfortable a little dwelling in this New England wilderness. The young man had known the horrors of its most primitive housekeeping, and the dreary squalor of that level of society which does not rebel at the companionship of hens. This was the best thrift of an old-fashioned farmstead, though on such a small scale that it seemed like a hermitage. He listened eagerly to the old woman's quaint talk, he watched Sylvia's pale face and shining gray eyes with ever growing enthusiasm, and insisted that this was the best supper he had eaten for a month; then, afterward, the new-made friends sat down in the doorway together while the moon came up.

Soon it would be berry-time, and Sylvia was a great help at picking. The cow was a good milker, though a plaguy thing to keep track of, the hostess gossiped frankly, adding presently that she had buried four children, so that Sylvia's mother, and a son (who might be dead) in California were all the children she had left. "Dan, my boy, was a great hand to go gunning," she explained sadly. "I never wanted for pa'tridges or gray squer'ls while he was to home. He's been a great wand'rer, I expect, and he's no hand to write letters. There, I don't blame him, I'd ha' seen the world myself if it had been so I could.

"Sylvia takes after him," the grandmother continued affectionately, after a minute's pause. "There ain't a foot o' ground she don't know her way over, and the wild creatur's counts her one o' themselves. Squer'ls she'll tame to come an' feed right out o' her hands, and all sorts o' birds. Last winter she got the jay-birds to bangeing[1] here, and I believe she'd a' scanted herself of her own meals to have plenty to throw out amongst 'em, if I hadn't kep' watch. Anything but crows, I tell her, I'm willin' to help support,—though Dan he went an' tamed one o' them that did seem to have reason same as folks. It was round here a good spell after he went away. Dan an' his father they didn't hitch,—but he never held up his head ag'in after Dan had dared him an' gone off."

The guest did not notice this hint of family sorrows in his eager interest in something else.

"So Sylvy knows all about birds, does she?" he exclaimed, as he looked round at the little girl who sat, very demure but increasingly sleepy, in the moonlight. "I am making a collection of birds myself. I have been at it ever since I was a boy." (Mrs. Tilley smiled.) "There are two or three very rare ones I have been hunting for these five years. I mean to get them on my own ground if they can be found."

"Do you cage 'em up?" asked Mrs. Tilley doubtfully, in response to this enthusiastic announcement.

"Oh no, they're stuffed and preserved, dozens and dozens of them," said the ornithologist, "and I have shot or snared every one myself. I caught a glimpse

[1]Gathering.

of a white heron three miles from here on Saturday, and I have followed it in this direction. They have never been found in this district at all. The little white heron, it is," and he turned again to look at Sylvia with the hope of discovering that the rare bird was one of her acquaintances.

But Sylvia was watching a hop-toad in the narrow foot-path.

"You would know the heron if you saw it," the stranger continued eagerly. "A queer tall white bird with soft feathers and long thin legs. And it would have a nest perhaps in the top of a high tree, made of sticks, something like a hawk's nest."

Sylvia's heart gave a wild beat; she knew that strange white bird, and had once stolen softly near where it stood in some bright green swamp grass, away over at the other side of the woods. There was an open place where the sunshine always seemed strangely yellow and hot, where tall, nodding rushes grew, and her grandmother had warned her that she might sink in the soft black mud underneath and never be heard of more. Not far beyond were the salt marshes and beyond those was the sea, the sea which Sylvia wondered and dreamed about, but never had looked upon, though its great voice could often be heard above the noise of the woods on stormy nights.

"I can't think of anything I should like so much as to find that heron's nest," the handsome stranger was saying. "I would give ten dollars to anybody who could show it to me," he added desperately, "and I mean to spend my whole vacation hunting for it if need be. Perhaps it was only migrating, or had been chased out of its own region by some bird of prey."

Mrs. Tilley gave amazed attention to all this, but Sylvia still watched the toad, not divining, as she might have done at some calmer time, that the creature wished to get to its hole under the doorstep, and was much hindered by the unusual spectators at that hour of the evening. No amount of thought, that night, could decide how many wished-for treasures the ten dollars, so lightly spoken of, would buy.

The next day the young sportsman hovered about the woods, and Sylvia kept him company, having lost her first fear of the friendly lad, who proved to be most kind and sympathetic. He told her many things about the birds and what they knew and where they lived and what they did with themselves. And he gave her a jack-knife, which she thought as great a treasure as if she were a desert-islander. All day long he did not once make her troubled or afraid except when he brought down some unsuspecting singing creature from its bough. Sylvia would have liked him vastly better without his gun; she could not understand why he killed the very birds he seemed to like so much. But as the day waned, Sylvia still watched the young man with loving admiration. She had never seen anybody so charming and delightful; the woman's heart, asleep in the child, was vaguely thrilled by a dream of love. Some premonition of that great power stirred and swayed these young foresters who traversed the solemn woodlands with soft-footed silent care. They stopped to listen to a bird's song; they pressed forward again eagerly, parting the branches,—speaking to each other rarely and in whispers; the young man going first and Sylvia following, fascinated, a few steps behind, with her gray eyes dark with excitement.

She grieved because the longed-for white heron was elusive, but she did not lead the guest, she only followed, and there was no such thing as speaking first. The sound of her own unquestioned voice would have terrified her,—it was hard enough to answer yes or no when there was need of that. At last evening began to fall, and they drove the cow home together, and Sylvia smiled with pleasure when they came to the place where she heard the whistle and was afraid only the night before.

2 Half a mile from home, at the farther edge of the woods, where the land was highest, a great pine-tree stood, the last of its generation. Whether it was left for a boundary mark, or for what reason, no one could say; the woodchoppers who had felled its mates were dead and gone long ago, and a whole forest of sturdy trees, pines and oaks and maples, had grown again. But the stately head of this old pine towered above them all and made a landmark for sea and shore miles and miles away. Sylvia knew it well. She had always believed that whoever climbed to the top of it could see the ocean; and the little girl had often laid her hand on the great rough trunk and looked up wistfully at those dark boughs that the wind always stirred, no matter how hot and still the air might be below. Now she thought of the tree with a new excitement, for why, if one climbed it at break of day, could not one see all the world, and easily discover whence the white heron flew, and mark the place, and find the hidden nest?

What a spirit of adventure, what wild ambition! What fancied triumph and delight and glory for the later morning when she could make known the secret! It was almost too real and too great for the childish heart to bear.

All night the door of the little house stood open, and the whippoorwills came and sang upon the very step. The young sportsman and his old hostess were sound asleep, but Sylvia's great design kept her broad awake and watching. She forgot to think of sleep. The short summer night seemed as long as the winter darkness, and at last when the whippoorwills ceased, and she was afraid the morning would after all come too soon, she stole out of the house and followed the pasture path through the woods, hastening toward the open ground beyond, listening with a sense of comfort and companionship to the drowsy twitter of a half-awakened bird, whose perch she had jarred in passing. Alas, if the great wave of human interest which flooded for the first time this dull little life should sweep away the satisfactions of an existence heart to heart with nature and the dumb life of the forest!

There was the huge tree asleep yet in the paling moonlight, and small and hopeful Sylvia began with utmost bravery to mount to the top of it, with tingling, eager blood coursing the channels of her whole frame, with her bare feet and fingers, that pinched and held like bird's claws to the monstrous ladder reaching up, up, almost to the sky itself. First she must mount the white oak tree that grew alongside, where she was almost lost among the dark branches and the green leaves heavy and wet with dew; a bird fluttered off its nest, and a red squirrel ran to and fro and scolded pettishly at the harmless housebreaker. Sylvia felt her way easily. She had often climbed there, and knew that higher still one of the oak's upper branches chafed against the pine trunk, just where its lower boughs were set close together. There, when she made the dangerous pass from one tree to the other, the great enterprise would really begin.

She crept out along the swaying oak limb at last, and took the daring step across into the old pine-tree. The way was harder than she thought; she must reach far and hold fast, the sharp dry twigs caught and held her and scratched her like angry talons, the pitch made her thin little fingers clumsy and stiff as she went round and round the tree's great stem, higher and higher upward. The sparrows and robins in the woods below were beginning to wake and twitter to the dawn, yet it seemed much lighter there aloft in the pine-tree, and the child knew that she must hurry if her project were to be of any use.

The tree seemed to lengthen itself out as she went up, and to reach farther and farther upward. It was like a great main-mast to the voyaging earth; it must truly have been amazed that morning through all its ponderous frame as it felt this determined spark of human spirit creeping and climbing from higher branch to branch. Who knows how steadily the least twigs held themselves to advantage this light, weak creature on her way! The old pine must have loved his new dependent. More than all the hawks, and bats, and moths, and even the sweet-voiced thrushes, was the brave, beating heart of the solitary gray-eyed child. And the tree stood still and held away the winds that June morning while the dawn grew bright in the east.

Sylvia's face was like a pale star, if one had seen it from the ground, when the last thorny bough was past, and she stood trembling and tired but wholly triumphant, high in the tree-top. Yes, there was the sea with the dawning sun making a golden dazzle over it, and toward that glorious east flew two hawks with slow-moving pinions. How low they looked in the air from that height when before one had only seen them far up, and dark against the blue sky. Their gray feathers were as soft as moths; they seemed only a little way from the tree, and Sylvia felt as if she too could go flying away among the clouds. Westward, the woodlands and farms reached miles and miles into the distance; here and there were church steeples, and white villages; truly it was a vast and awesome world.

The birds sang louder and louder. At last the sun came up bewilderingly bright. Sylvia could see the white sails of ships out at sea, and the clouds that were purple and rose-colored and yellow at first began to fade away. Where was the white heron's nest in the sea of green branches, and was this wonderful sight and pageant of the world the only reward for having climbed to such a giddy height? Now look down again, Sylvia, where the green marsh is set among the shining birches and dark hemlocks; there where you saw the white heron once you will see him again; look, look! a white spot of him like a single floating feather comes up from the dead hemlock and grows larger, and rises, and comes close at last, and goes by the landmark pine with steady sweep of wing and outstretched slender neck and crested head. And wait! wait! do not move a foot or a finger, little girl, do not send an arrow of light and consciousness from your two eager eyes, for the heron has perched on a pine bough not far beyond yours, and cries back to his mate on the nest, and plumes his feathers for the new day!

The child gives a long sigh a minute later when a company of shouting cat-birds comes also to the tree, and vexed by their fluttering and lawlessness the solemn heron goes away. She knows his secret now, the wild, light, slender bird that floats and wavers, and goes back like an arrow presently to his home in the green world beneath. Then Sylvia, well satisfied, makes her perilous way down again, not daring to look far below the branch she stands on, ready to cry sometimes because her fingers ache and her lamed feet slip. Wondering over and over again what the stranger would say to her, and what he would think when she told him how to find his way straight to the heron's nest.

"Sylvy, Sylvy!" called the busy old grandmother again and again, but nobody answered, and the small husk bed was empty, and Sylvia had disappeared.

The guest waked from a dream, and remembering his day's pleasure hurried to dress himself that it might sooner begin. He was sure from the way the shy little girl looked once or twice yesterday that she had at least seen the white heron, and now she must really be persuaded to tell. Here she comes now, paler than ever, and her worn old frock is torn and tattered, and smeared with pine pitch. The grandmother and the sportsman stand in the door together and question her, and the splendid moment has come to speak of the dead hemlock-tree by the green marsh.

But Sylvia does not speak after all, though the old grandmother fretfully rebukes her, and the young man's kind appealing eyes are looking straight in her own. He can make them rich with money; he has promised it, and they are poor now. He is so well worth making happy, and he waits to hear the story she can tell.

No, she must keep silence! What is it that suddenly forbids her and makes her dumb? Has she been nine years growing, and now, when the great world for the first time puts out a hand to her, must she thrust it aside for a bird's sake? The murmur of the pine's green branches is in her ears, she remembers how the white heron came flying through the golden air and how they watched the sea and the morning together, and Sylvia cannot speak, she cannot tell the heron's secret and give its life away.

Dear loyalty, that suffered a sharp pang as the guest went away disappointed later in the day, that could have served and followed him and loved him as a dog loves! Many a night Sylvia heard the echo of his whistle haunting the pasture path as she came home with the loitering cow. She forgot even her sorrow at the sharp report of his gun and the piteous sight of thrushes and sparrows dropping silent to the ground, their songs hushed and their pretty feathers stained and wet with blood. Were the birds better friends than their hunter might have been,—who can tell? Whatever treasures were lost to her, woodlands and summer-time, remember! Bring your gifts and graces and tell your secrets to this lonely country child!

1886

Bret Harte   *1836–1902*

Like many other Americans who wrote about the West, Bret Harte was originally an Easterner. Born in Albany, New York, he did not go to California until 1854, following his father's death and his mother's remarriage. His reports of his early life were filled with fantasy and romance. He claimed early genius, to have been reading Shakespeare at the age of six. It is certain that he taught school for a time. He may also have prospected for gold for a short period, and there is evidence that he spent a "brief, delightful hour" in 1857 riding shotgun on a stagecoach for Wells Fargo Express. The job was as dangerous as legend and the movies have represented it: Harte's predecessor as guard was wounded by bandits; his successor was shot and killed.

Harte next became a professional writer, first for a newspaper in northern California. After he imprudently denounced a mob's massacre of sixty Indians, mostly women and children, his life was threatened, and he fled to San Francisco. There, in 1868, he became the first editor of The Overland Monthly, *a magazine that was to be influential and prosperous until he left it. He had published poems and stories prior to his employment on* The Overland Monthly, *but it was while he was its editor that he wrote the works that made him famous: "The Luck of Roaring Camp" appeared in the second issue, soon followed by "The Outcasts of Poker Flat" and his most famous poem, "Plain Language from Truthful James," usually known as "The Heathen Chinee."*

The enormous success of Harte's fiction brought him wide acclaim: Charles Dickens (Harte's favorite author) praised his writing and urged Harte to come to London to work for him; publishers from the East flooded Harte with offers. His career was at its peak; He was a famous writer and editor, he had been appointed Secretary of the U.S. Mint in San Francisco and Professor of Literature at the University of California.

In 1871 Harte accepted an unprecedented contract of ten thousand dollars from The Atlantic Monthly *for twelve "poems and sketches," and he left California for Boston, now so famous that an English newspaper issued daily accounts of his journey from coast to coast. Although he was to live nearly thirty years more, the remainder of his life was disappointment and anticlimax. After California, his writing became self-imitative and repetitious, as he himself admitted late in his life: "I grind out the old tunes on the old organ, and gather up the coppers." Without the immediate inspiration of the West to bring energy to his stories, his sentimentality became more obvious. In his later writings, a dominant theme—moral redemption through sacrifice—was tiresomely repeated. His contract was not renewed by* The Atlantic Monthly, *and, unable to make a living from his writing, he went on a series of lecture tours, served in the diplomatic corps in Germany and Scotland, and spent the last years of his life in England. His last letters are full of his worries over money, self-pitying complaints about his health, and a grieving awareness of a wasted talent.*

In fact, Harte's talent was always minor. Even the best of his stories are overly sentimental; the characters seem deadly similar from tale to poem. Cynical gamblers, gruff but ever-loyal partners, and whores "with hearts of gold" recur again and again. But Harte did imaginatively evoke a vital period in American history—the final settlement of the West. He was the first widely acclaimed, and one of the best, of a score of local color writers who emphasized American regionalism and paved the way for the coming of literary realism. He did, in an age of genteel evasions, frequently treat crucial areas of human experience—sex, love, and death—directly and openly. But perhaps above all, Harte's works and his great, though short-lived, success stand as a notable expression of the world's fascination with life on the American frontier.

FURTHER READING: *The Works of Bret Harte*, 18 vols., 1899, 1981; *Bret Harte, Representative Selections*, ed., J. Harrison, 1941; H. Boynton, *Bret Harte*, 1903, 1973; T. Pemberton, *The Life of Bret Harte*, 1903; G. Stewart, *Bret Harte, Argonaut and Exile*, 1931; R. O'Connor, *Bret Harte*, 1966; M. Duckett, *Mark Twain and Bret Harte*, 1964; P. Morrow, *Bret Harte, Literary Critic*, 1979; L. Barnett, *Bret Harte, A Reference Guide*, 1980.

TEXT: *The Writings of Bret Harte*, 20 vols. 1896–1914.

TENNESSEE'S PARTNER

I do not think that we ever knew his real name. Our ignorance of it certainly never gave us any social inconvenience, for at Sandy Bar in 1854 most men were christened anew. Sometimes these appellatives were derived from some distinctiveness of dress, as in the case of "Dungaree Jack"; or from some peculiarity of habit, as shown in "Saleratus Bill," so called from an undue proportion of that chemical[1] in his daily bread; or from some unlucky slip, as exhibited in "The Iron Pirate," a mild, inoffensive man, who earned that baleful title by his unfortunate mispronunciation of the term "iron pyrites." Perhaps this may have been the beginning of a rude heraldry; but I am constrained to think that it was because a man's real name in that day rested solely upon his own unsupported statement. "Call yourself, Clifford, do you?" said Boston, addressing a timid new-comer with infinite scorn; "hell is full of such Cliffords!" He then introduced the unfortunate man, whose name happened to be really Clifford, as "Jay-bird Charley,"—an unhallowed inspiration of the moment, that clung to him ever after.

But to return to Tennessee's Partner, whom we never knew by any other than this relative title; that he had ever existed as a separate and distinct individuality we only learned later. It seems that in 1853 he left Poker Flat to go to San Francisco, ostensibly to procure a wife. He never got any farther than Stockton. At that place he was attracted by a young person who waited upon the table at the hotel where he took his meals. One morning he said something to her which caused her to smile not unkindly, to somewhat coquettishly break a plate of toast over his upturned, serious simple face, and to retreat to the kitchen. He followed her, and emerged a few moments later, covered with more toast and victory. That day a week they were married by a Justice of the Peace, and returned to Poker Flat. I am aware that something more might be made of this episode, but I prefer to tell it as it was current at Sandy Bar,—in the gulches and barrooms,—where all sentiment was modified by a strong sense of humor.

Of their married felicity but little is known, perhaps for the reason that Tennessee, then living with his partner, one day took occasion to say something to the bride on his own account, at which, it is said, she smiled not unkindly and chastely retreated,—this time as far as Marysville, where Tennessee followed her, and where they went to housekeeping without the aid of a Justice of the Peace. Tennessee's Partner took the loss of his wife simply and seriously, as was his fashion. But to everybody's surprise, when Tennessee one day returned from Marysville, without his partner's wife,—she having smiled and retreated with somebody else,—Tennessee's Partner was the first man to shake his hand and greet him with affection. The boys who had gathered in the cañon to see the shooting were naturally indignant. Their indignation might have found vent in sarcasm but for a certain look in Tennessee's Partner's eye that indicated a lack of humorous appreciation. In fact he was a grave man, with a steady application to practical detail which was unpleasant in a difficulty.

Meanwhile a popular feeling against Tennessee had grown up on the Bar. He was known to be a gambler; he was suspected to be a thief. In these suspicions Tennessee's Partner was equally compromised; his continued intimacy with Tennessee after the affair above quoted could only be accounted for on the hypothesis of a copartnership of crime. At last Tennessee's guilt became flagrant. One day he overtook a stranger on his way to Red Dog. The stranger afterward related that Tennessee beguiled the time with interesting anecdote and reminiscence, but illogically concluded the interview in the following words: "And now, young man, I'll trouble you for your knife, your pistols, and your money. You see your weppings might get you into trouble at Red Dog, and your money's a temptation to the evilly disposed. I think you said your address was San Francisco. I shall endeavor to call." It may be stated here that Tennessee had a fine flow of humor, which no business preoccupation could wholly subdue.

[1]Saleratus, baking soda.

This exploit was his last. Red Dog and Sandy Bar made common cause against the highwayman. Tennessee was hunted in very much the same fashion as his prototype, the grizzly. As the toils[2] closed around him, he made a desperate dash through the Bar, emptying his revolver at the crowd before the Arcade Saloon, and so on up Grizzly Cañon; but at its farther extremity he was stopped by a small man on a gray horse. The men looked at each other a moment in silence. Both were fearless, both self-possessed and independent; and both types of a civilization that in the seventeenth century would have been called heroic, but, in the nineteenth, simply "reckless." "What have you got there?—I call," said Tennessee, quietly. "Two bowers[3] and an ace," said the stranger, as quietly, showing two revolvers and a bowie-knife. "That takes me," returned Tennessee; and with this gamblers' epigram, he threw away his useless pistol, and rode back with his captor.

It was a warm night. The cool breeze which usually sprang up with the going down of the sun behind the *chaparral*-crested mountain was that evening withheld from Sandy Bar. The little cañon was stifling with heated resinous odors, and the decaying drift-wood on the Bar sent forth faint, sickening exhalations. The feverishness of day, and its fierce passions, still filled the camp. Lights moved restlessly along the bank of the river, striking no answering reflection from its tawny current. Against the blackness of the pines the windows of the old loft above the express-office stood out staringly bright; and through their curtainless panes the loungers below could see the forms of those who were even then deciding the fate of Tennessee. And above all this, etched on the dark firmament, rose the Sierra, remote and passionless, crowned with the remoter passionless stars.

The trial of Tennessee was conducted as fairly as was consistent with a judge and jury who felt themselves to some extent obliged to justify, in their verdict, the previous irregularities of arrest and indictment. The law of Sandy Bar was implacable, but not vengeful. The excitement and personal feeling of the chase were over; with Tennessee safe in their hands they were ready to listen patiently to any defence, which they were already satisfied was insufficient. There being no doubt in their own minds, they were willing to give the prisoner the benefit of any that might exist. Secure in the hypothesis that he ought to be hanged, on general principles, they indulged him with more latitude or defence than his reckless hardihood seemed to ask. The Judge appeared to be more anxious than the prisoner, who, otherwise, unconcerned, evidently took a grim pleasure in the responsibility he had created. "I don't take any hand in this yer game," had been his invariable, but good-humored reply to all questions. The Judge— who was also his captor—for a moment vaguely regretted that he had not shot him "on sight," that morning, but presently dismissed this human weakness as unworthy of the judicial mind. Nevertheless, when there was a tap at the door, and it was said that Tennessee's Partner was there on behalf of the prisoner, he was admitted at once without question. Perhaps the younger member of the jury, to whom the proceedings were becoming irksomely thoughtful, hailed him as a relief.

For he was not, certainly, an imposing figure. Short and stout, with a square face, sunburned into a preternatural redness, clad in a loose duck "jumper," and trousers streaked and splashed with red soil, his aspect under any circum-

[2]Snares, traps.   [3]High cards.

stances would have been quaint, and was now even ridiculous. As he stooped to deposit at his feet a heavy carpet-bag he was carrying, it became obvious, from partially developed legends and inscriptions, that the material with which his trousers had been patched had been originally intended for a less ambitious covering. Yet he advanced with great gravity, and after having shaken the hand of each person in the room with labored cordiality, he wiped his serious, perplexed face on a red bandanna handkerchief, a shade lighter than his complexion, laid his powerful hand upon the table to steady himself, and thus addressed the Judge:—

"I was passin' by," he began, by way of apology, "and I thought I'd just step in and see how things was gittin' on with Tennessee thar,—my pardner. It's a hot night. I disremember any sich weather before on the Bar."

He paused a moment, but nobody volunteering any other meteorological recollection, he again had recourse to his pocket-handkerchief, and for some moments mopped his face diligently.

"Have you anything to say in behalf of the prisoner?" said the Judge, finally.

"Thet's it," said Tennessee's Partner, in a tone of relief. "I come yar as Tennessee's pardner,—knowing him nigh on four year, off and on, wet and dry, in luck and out o' luck. His ways ain't allers my ways, but thar ain't any p'ints in that young man, thar ain't any liveliness as he's been up to, as I don't know. And you sez to me, sez you,—confidential-like, and between man and man,—sez you, 'Do you know anything in his behalf?' and I sez to you, sez I,—confidential-like, as between man and man,—'What should a man know of his pardner?'"

"Is this all you have to say?" asked the Judge, impatiently, feeling, perhaps, that a dangerous sympathy of humor was beginning to humanize the Court.

"Thet's so," continued Tennessee's Partner. "It ain't for me to say anything agin' him. And now, what's the case? Here's Tennessee wants money, wants it bad, and does n't like to ask it of his old pardner. Well, what does Tennessee do? He lays for a stranger, and he fetches that stranger. And you lays for *him,* and you fetches *him;* and the honors is easy.[4] And I put it to you, bein' a far-minded man, and to you, gentlemen, all, as far-minded men, ef this is n't so."

"Prisoner," said the Judge, interrupting, "have you any questions to ask this man?"

"No! no!" continued Tennessee's Partner, hastily. "I play this yer hand alone. To come down to the bed-rock, it's just this: Tennessee, thar, has played it pretty rough and expensive-like on a stranger, and on this yer camp. And now, what's the fair thing? Some would say more; some would say less. Here's seventeen hundred dollars in coarse gold and a watch,—it's about all my pile,—and call it square!" And before a hand could be raised to prevent him, he had emptied the contents of the carpet-bag upon the table.

For a moment his life was in jeopardy. One or two men sprang to their feet, several hands groped for hidden weapons, and a suggestion to "throw him from the window" was only overridden by a gesture from the Judge. Tennessee laughed. And apparently oblivious of the excitement, Tennessee's Partner improved the opportunity to mop his face again with his handkerchief.

When order was restored, and the man was made to understand, by the use of forcible figures and rhetoric, that Tennessee's offence could not be condoned by money, his face took a more serious and sanguinary hue, and those who were nearest to him noticed that his rough hand trembled slightly on the table. He

---

[4] I.e., honor cards are equally divided; thus, everything is equal.

hesitated a moment as he slowly returned the gold to the carpet-bag, as if he had not yet entirely caught the elevated sense of justice which swayed the tribunal, and was perplexed with the belief that he had not offered enough. Then he turned to the Judge, and saying, "This yer is a lone hand, played alone, and without my pardner," he bowed to the jury and was about to withdraw, when the Judge called him back. "If you have anything to say to Tennessee, you had better say it now." For the first time that evening the eyes of the prisoner and his stranger advocate met. Tennessee smiled showed his white teeth, and, saying, "Euchred,[5] old man!" held out his hand. Tennessee's Partner took it in his own, and saying, "I just dropped in as I was passin' to see how things was gettin' on," let the hand passively fall, and adding that "it was a warm night," again mopped his face with his handkerchief, and without another word withdrew.

The two men never again met each other alive. For the unparalleled insult of a bribe offered to Judge Lynch—who, whether bigoted, weak, or narrow, was at least incorruptible—firmly fixed in the mind of that mythical personage any wavering determination of Tennessee's fate; and at the break of day he was marched, closely guarded, to meet it at the top of Marley's Hill.

How he met it, how cool he was, how he refused to say anything, how perfect were the arrangements of the committee, were all duly reported, with the addition of a warning moral and example to all future evil-doers, in the Red Dog Clarion, by its editor, who was present, and to whose vigorous English I cheerfully refer the reader. But the beauty of that midsummer morning, the blessed amity of earth and air and sky, the awakened life of the free woods and hills, the joyous renewal and promise of Nature, and above all, the infinite Serenity that thrilled through each, was not reported, as not being a part of the social lesson. And yet, when the weak and foolish deed was done, and a life, with its possibilities and responsibilities, had passed out of the misshapen thing that dangled between earth and sky, the birds sang, the flowers bloomed, the sun shone, as cheerily as before; and possibly the Red Dog Clarion was right.

Tennessee's Partner was not in the group that surrounded the ominous tree. But as they turned to disperse attention was drawn to the singular appearance of a motionless donkey-cart halted at the side of the road. As they approached, they at once recognized the venerable "Jenny" and the two-wheeled cart as the property of Tennessee's Partner,—used by him in carrying dirt from his claim; and a few paces distant the owner of the equipage himself, sitting under a buckeye-tree, wiping the perspiration from his glowing face. In answer to an inquiry, he said he had come for the body of the "diseased," "if it was all the same to the committee." He did n't wish to "hurry anything"; he could "wait." He was not working that day; and when the gentlemen were done with the "diseased," he would take him. "Ef thar is any present," he added, in his simple, serious way, "as would care to jine in the fun'l, they kin come." Perhaps it was from a sense of humor, which I have already intimated was a feature of Sandy Bar,—perhaps it was from something even better than that; but two thirds of the loungers accepted the invitation at once.

It was noon when the body of Tennessee was delivered into the hands of his partner. As the cart drew up to the fatal tree, we noticed that it contained a rough, oblong box,—apparently made from a section of sluicing,[6]—and half filled with bark and the tassels of pine. The cart was further decorated with slips

[5]From the card game euchre, the loser of which is "euchred."
[6]Long boards used in building water channels.

of willow, and made fragrant with buckeye-blossoms. When the body was deposited in the box, Tennessee's Partner drew over it a piece of tarred canvas, and gravely mounting the narrow seat in front, with his feet upon the shafts, urged the little donkey forward. The equipage moved slowly on, at that decorous pace which was habitual with "Jenny" even under less solemn circumstances. The men—half curiously, half jestingly, but all good-humoredly—strolled along beside the cart; some in advance, some a little in the rear of the homely catafalque.[7] But, whether from the narrowing of the road or some present sense of decorum, as the cart passed on, the company fell to the rear in couples, keeping step, and otherwise assuming the external show of a formal procession. Jack Folinsbee, who had at the outset played a funeral march in dumb show[8] upon an imaginary trombone, desisted, from a lack of sympathy and appreciation,—not having, perhaps, your true humorist's capacity to be content with the enjoyment of his own fun.

The way led through Grizzly Cañon,—by this time clothed in funeral drapery and shadows. The redwoods, burying their moccasined feet in the red soil, stood in Indian-file along the track, trailing an uncouth benediction from their bending boughs upon the passing bier. A hare, surprised into helpless inactivity, sat upright and pulsating in the ferns by the roadside, as the *cortège* went by. Squirrels hastened to gain a secure outlook from higher boughs; and the blue-jays, spreading their wings, fluttered before them like outriders, until the outskirts of Sandy Bar were reached, and the solitary cabin of Tennessee's Partner.

Viewed under more favorable circumstances, it would not have been a cheerful place. The unpicturesque site, the rude and unlovely outlines, the unsavory details, which distinguish the nestbuilding of the California miner, were all here, with the dreariness of decay superadded. A few paces from the cabin there was a rough enclosure, which, in the brief days of Tennessee's Partner's matrimonial felicity, had been used as a garden, but was now overgrown with fern. As we approached it we were surprised to find that what we had taken for a recent attempt at cultivation was the broken soil about an open grave.

The cart was halted before the enclosure; and rejecting the offers of assistance with the same air of simple self-reliance he had displayed throughout, Tennessee's Partner lifted the rough coffin on his back, and deposited it, unaided, within the shallow grave. He then nailed down the board which served as a lid; and mounting the little mound of earth beside it, took off his hat, and slowly mopped his face with his handkerchief. This the crowd felt was a preliminary to speech; and they disposed themselves variously on stumps and boulders, and sat expectant.

"When a man," began Tennessee's Partner, slowly, "has been running free all day, what's the natural thing for him to do? Why, to come home. And if he ain't in a condition to go home, what can his best friend do? Why, bring him home! And here's Tennessee has been running free, and we brings him home from his wandering." He paused, and picked up a fragment of quartz, rubbed it thoughtfully on his sleeve, and went on: "It ain't the first time that I've packed him on my back, as you see'd me now. It ain't the first time that I brought him to this yer cabin when he could n't help himself; it ain't the first time that I and 'Jinny' have waited for him on yon hill, and picked him up and so fetched him home, when he could n't speak, and did n't know me. And now that it's the last time, why—" he paused, and rubbed the quartz gently on his sleeve—"you see

[7]Ornamental framework that carries a coffin.　　[8]Silently.

it's sort of rough on his pardner. And now, gentlemen," he added, abruptly, picking up his long-handled shovel, "the fun'l's over; and my thanks, and Tennessee's thanks, to you for your trouble."

Resisting any proffers of assistance, he began to fill in the grave, turning his back upon the crowd, that after a few moments' hesitation gradually withdrew. As they crossed the little ridge that hid Sandy Bar from view, some, looking back, thought they could see Tennessee's Partner, his work done, sitting upon the grave, his shovel between his knees, and his face buried in his red bandanna handkerchief. But it was argued by others that you couldn't tell his face from his handkerchief at that distance; and this point remained undecided.

In the reaction that followed the feverish excitement of that day, Tennessee's Partner was not forgotten. A secret investigation had cleared him of any complicity in Tennessee's guilt, and left only a suspicion of his general sanity. Sandy Bar made a point of calling on him, and proffering various uncouth, but well-meant kindnesses. But from that day his rude health and great strength seemed visibly to decline; and when the rainy season fairly set in, and the tiny grass-blades were beginning to peep from the rocky mound above Tennessee's grave, he took to his bed.

One night, when the pines beside the cabin were swaying in the storm, and trailing their slender fingers over the roof, and the roar and rush of the swollen river were heard below, Tennessee's Partner lifted his head from the pillow, saying, "It is time to go for Tennessee; I must put 'Jinny' in the cart"; and would have risen from his bed but for the restraint. Struggling, he still pursued his singular fancy: "There, now, steady, 'Jinny,'—steady, old girl. How dark it is! Look out for the ruts,—and look out for him, too, old gal. Sometimes, you know, when he's blind drunk, he drops down right in the trail. Keep on straight up to the pine on the top of the hill. Thar—I told you so!—thar he is,—coming this way, too,—all by himself, sober, and his face a-shining. Tennessee! Pardner!"

And so they met.

                                                                                                     1869

George Washington Cable   *1844–1925*

In 1875, the editor of Harper's Magazine *rejected a short story submitted by George Washington Cable. Stories for* Harper's, *the editor explained should be "of a pleasant character," preferably "love tales," whereas Cable had shown "disagreeable aspects of human nature" that left "an unpleasant impression on the mind of the reader." It was not the first time, nor would it be the last, that Cable's writing roused genteel readers to complain of his improprieties. Yet Cable himself had standards of personal behavior so austere, so lofty, that his friend Mark Twain was moved to observe that "when it comes down to moral honesty, limpid innocence, and utterly blameless piety, the Apostles were mere policeman [compared] to Cable." Raised in a strict, religious family, Cable was devoted to daily prayer and Bible reading. In all his lifetime he never smoked or drank, he refused to work or travel on Sunday, and not until he was middle-aged did he permit himself to see a play. Yet he often wrote of violence and death, of racial intermarriage, and of problems of human weakness and desire that to his own age were beyond the bounds of literary decency.*

Cable wrote of a world he knew, of Louisiana and New Orleans, where he was born and raised. His formal education was brief. In 1859 his father died, and fourteen-year-old George quit school and went to work to support his family. He worked as an office boy and then clerked in a store, all the while struggling to educate himself by studying Latin and reading history and literature. During the Civil War he enlisted in the Confederate cavalry and was twice wounded. After the war, Cable worked as a surveyor and then as a bookkeeper for a cotton merchant in New Orleans. Fascinated by New Orleans and its people, Cable began to study the early history of the city and listen to stories of its Negroes and its Creoles (descendants of early Spanish and French settlers). Cable was quick to notice the possibility of using Louisiana as a source for fiction, for he was aware of a growing public interest in local color stories that displayed the speech, the manners, and the character types found in the different regions of the United States.

In 1873 Scribner's Monthly published "Sieur George," the first of many short tales in which Cable described New Orleans, its ancient streets, its decaying buildings, and its colorful inhabitants. In 1879 Cable published Old Creole Days, *a collection of his best stories, including "Sieur George," "Posson Jone," and "Belles Demoiselles Plantation." In 1880 his first and most noteworthy novel appeared,* The Grandissimes, *a story of American "intruders" into the European life of New Orleans early in the 1800s. Having achieved literary success, Cable was at last able to leave business and devote himself fully to writing. Two novels,* Madame Delphine *and* Dr. Sevier, *were published in 1881 and 1884. And he began the lectures and platform readings of his own works that brought him wide recognition throughout the United States.*

At the peak of his fame, Cable turned increasingly from fiction to pamphleteering. He attacked political corruption in the South and spoke out for civil reform and Negro rights. Cable's stories had sometimes stirred resentment among Louisiana's proud Creoles, who were embarrassed by his stories and felt he had held them up to national ridicule. Now the Creoles were joined by others who were indignant at Cable's political attacks and at his vigorous efforts in behalf of racial justice. Cable was charged with stirring social unrest. He was called a turncoat, an "unnatural Southern growth, a bastard sprout" who took advantage of his friends and neighbors for the sake of northern readers and northern dollars. In 1884, faced with growing public hostility and social ostracism, Cable moved his family from New Orleans, eventually settling in Northampton, Massachusetts, where he was to live the rest of his life. He continued his social criticism with The Silent South (1885), *a strong indictment of the treatment given freed slaves. And he wrote* John March, Southerner (1894), *a novel set in the South during the reconstruction years immediately following the Civil War. But Cable could never equal the achievement of his early short stories and novels. His move north had separated him from the people and the scenes he knew best, and his growing willingness to adapt his work to the delicate tastes of magazine and book editors drained his writing of its former power.*

Much of Cable's work now seems melodramatic and burdened with moral teaching. Modern readers often find his dialect transcriptions to be tedious and over-detailed, his plots to be unrealistic and contrived. At its best his fiction was a blend of romance and realism. He depicted the sounds, sights, and characters of an exotic region of America. He was interested in the strange, the colorful, even the grotesque. But unlike many regional writers of his time, Cable described a world of moral complexity devoid of happy endings and certain triumphs. He was the first southern writer to deal seriously with miscegenation, the racial mixing of blacks and whites, in America. He wrote of the rise and decline of social classes and of the burdens that the past imposes on the present—vital themes that reappear in the work of such modern southern writers as Eudora Welty, Flannery O'Connor, Thomas Wolfe, and William Faulkner. Cable was a reformer, a social critic, and a historian. He sacrificed much for the cause of justice and equality in America. But his greatest achievement was his vivid depiction of his native region and its people, especially the Louisiana Creoles who once hated Cable for his descriptions of their life but who now are largely remembered as part of a bygone age that lives only in the stories and tales he wrote.

FURTHER READING: *The Negro Question, A Selection of Writings on Civil Rights in the South* by George W. Cable, ed. A. Turner, 1958; *Creoles and Cajuns, Stories of Old Louisiana*, ed. A. Turner, 1959; L. Biklé, *George W. Cable, His Life and Letters*, 1928; K. Ekström, *George W. Cable, A Study of His Early Life and Work*, 1950; A. Turner, *George W. Cable, A Biography*, 1956; P. Butcher, *George W. Cable, The Northampton Years*, 1959; A. Turner, *Mark Twain and George W. Cable*, 1960; P. Butcher, *George W. Cable*, 1962; L. Rubin, *George W. Cable*, 1969; *Critical Essays on George W. Cable*, ed. A. Turner, 1980.

TEXT: *Old Creole Days*, 1879.

BELLES DEMOISELLES PLANTATION

The original grantee was Count——, assume the name to be De Charleu; the old Creoles[1] never forgive a public mention. He was the French king's commissary. One day, called to France to explain the lucky accident of the commissariat having burned down with his account-books inside, he left his wife, a Choctaw[2] Comptesse, behind.

Arrived at court, his excuses were accepted, and that tract granted him where afterwards stood Belles Demoiselles[3] Plantation. A man cannot remember every thing! In a fit of forgetfulness he married a French gentlewoman, rich and beautiful, and "brought her out."[4] However, "All's well that ends well;" a famine had been in the colony, and the Choctaw Comptesse had starved, leaving nought but a half-caste orphan family lurking on the edge of the settlement, bearing our French gentlewoman's own new name, and being mentioned in Monsieur's will.

And the new Comptesse—she tarried but a twelve month, left Monsieur a lovely son, and departed, led out of this vain world by the swamp-fever.

From this son sprang the proud Creole family of De Charleu. It rose straight up, up, up, generation after generation, tall, branchless, slender, palm-like; and finally, in the time of which I am to tell, flowered with all the rare beauty of a century-plant, in Artemise, Innocente, Felicité, the twins Maria and Martha, Leontine and little Septima; the seven beautiful daughters for whom their home had been fitly named Belles Demoiselles.

The Count's grant had once been a long Pointe,[5] round which the Mississippi used to whirl, and seethe, and foam, that it was horrid to behold. Big whirlpools would open and wheel about in the savage eddies under the low bank, and close up again, and others open, and spin, and disappear. Great circles of muddy surface would boil up from hundreds of feet below, and gloss over, and seem to float away,—sink, come back again under water, and with only a soft hiss surge up again, and again drift off, and vanish. Every few minutes the loamy bank would tip down a great load of earth upon its besieger, and fall back a

[1]Descendants of early Spanish and French settlers.
[2]An Indian tribe living northeast of New Orleans.   [3]French: Beautiful Maidens.
[4]I.e., brought her to America.   [5]A pointed or arrow-shaped plot of land.

foot,—sometimes a yard,—and the writhing river would press after, until at last the Pointe was quite swallowed up, and the great river glided by in a majestic curve, and asked no more; the bank stood fast, the "caving" became a forgotten misfortune, and the diminished grant was a long, sweeping, willowy bend, rustling with miles of sugar-cane.

Coming up the Mississippi in the sailing craft of those early days, about the time one first could descry the white spires of the old St. Louis Cathedral,[6] you would be pretty sure to spy, just over to your right under the levee,[7] Belles Demoiselles Mansion, with its broad veranda and red painted cypress roof, peering over the embankment, like a bird in the nest, half hid by the avenue of willows which one of the departed De Charleus,—he that married a Marot,— had planted on the levee's crown.

The house stood unusually near the river, facing eastward, and standing four-square, with an immense veranda about its sides, and a flight of steps in front spreading broadly downward, as we open arms to a child. From the veranda nine miles of river were seen; and in their compass, near at hand, the shady garden full of rare and beautiful flowers; farther away broad fields of cane and rice, and the distant quarters of the slaves, and on the horizon everywhere a dark belt of cypress forest.

The master was old Colonel De Charleu,—Jean Albert Henri Joseph De Charleu-Marot, and "Colonel" by the grace of the first American governor.[8] Monsieur,—he would not speak to any one who called him "Colonel,"—was a hoary-headed patriarch. His step was firm, his form erect, his intellect strong and clear, his countenance classic, serene, dignified, commanding, his manners courtly, his voice musical,—fascinating. He had had his vices,—all his life; but had borne them, as his race do, with a serenity of conscience and a cleanness of mouth that left no outward blemish on the surface of the gentleman. He had gambled in Royal Street,[9] drank hard in Orleans Street,[10] run his adversary through in the duelling-ground at Slaughter-house Point,[11] and danced and quarrelled at the St. Philippe-street-theatre quadroon balls.[12] Even now, with all his courtesy and bounty, and a hospitality which seemed to be entertaining angels, he was bitter-proud and penurious, and deep down in his hard-finished heart loved nothing but himself, his name, and his motherless children. But these!—their ravishing beauty was all but excuse enough for the unbounded idolatry of their father. Against these seven goddesses he never rebelled. Had they even required him to defraud old De Carlos—

I can hardly say.

Old De Carlos was his extremely distant relative on the Choctaw side. With this single exception, the narrow thread-like line of descent from the Indian wife, diminished to a mere strand by injudicious alliances, and deaths in the gutters of old New Orleans, was extinct. The name, by Spanish contact, had become De Carlos; but this one surviving bearer of it was known to all, and known only, as Injin Charlie.

One thing I never knew a Creole to do. He will not utterly go back on the ties

---

[6]Church (1794) in the center of New Orleans.
[7]Embankment for protection against river floods.
[8]William Claiborne, appointed in March 1806 to administer the new Territory after the United States had acquired it through the Louisiana Purchase.
[9]A street of New Orleans gambling houses.   [10]A street at the center of old New Orleans.
[11]A traditional duelling site, now preserved in a New Orleans city park.
[12]Elegant balls given for young women of one-quarter black ancestry.

of blood, no matter what sort of knots those ties may be. For one reason, he is never ashamed of his or his father's sins; and for another,—he will tell you—he is "all heart!"

So the different heirs of the De Charleu estate had always strictly regarded the rights and interests of the De Carloses, especially their ownership of a block of dilapidated buildings in a part of the city, which had once been very poor property, but was beginning to be valuable. This block had much more than maintained the last De Carlos through a long and lazy lifetime, and, as his household consisted only of himself, and an aged and crippled negress, the inference was irresistible that he "had money." Old Charlie, though by *alias* an "Injin," was plainly a dark white man, about as old as Colonel De Charleu, sunk in the bliss of deep ignorance, shrewd, deaf, and, by repute at least, unmerciful.

The Colonel and he always conversed in English. This rare accomplishment, which the former had learned from his Scotch wife,—the latter from up-river traders,—they found an admirable medium of communication, answering, better than French could, a similar purpose to that of the stick which we fasten to the bit of one horse and breast-gear of another, whereby each keeps his distance. Once in a while, too, by way of jest, English found its way among the ladies of Belles Demoiselles, always signifying that their sire was about to have business with old Charlie.

Now a long-standing wish to buy out Charlie troubled the Colonel. He had no desire to oust him unfairly; he was proud of being always fair; yet he did long to engross the whole estate under one title. Out of his luxurious idleness he had conceived this desire, and thought little of so slight an obstacle as being already somewhat in debt to old Charlie for money borrowed, and for which Belles Demoiselles was, of course, good, ten times over. Lots, buildings, rents, all, might as well be his, he thought, to give, keep, or destroy. "Had he but the old man's heritage. Ah! he might bring that into existence which his *belles demoiselles* had been begging for, 'since many years;' a home,—and such a home,—in the gay city. Here he should tear down this row of cottages, and make his garden wall; there that long rope-walk[13] should give place to vine-covered arbors; the bakery yonder should make way for a costly conservatory; that wine warehouse should come down, and the mansion go up. It should be the finest in the State. Men should never pass it, but they should say—'the palace of the De Charleus; a family of grand descent, a people of elegance and bounty, a line as old as France, a fine old man, and seven daughters as beautiful as happy; whoever dare attempt to marry there must leave his own name behind him!'

"The house should be of stones fitly set, brought down in ships from the land of 'les Yankees,' and it should have an airy belvedere,[14] with a gilded image tiptoeing and shining on its peak, and from it you should see, far across the gleaming folds of the river, the red roof of Belles Demoiselles, the country-seat. At the big stone gate there should be a porter's lodge, and it should be a privilege even to see the ground."

Truly they were a family fine enough, and fancy-free enough to have fine wishes, yet happy enough where they were, to have had no wish but to live there always.

To those, who, by whatever fortune, wandered into the garden of Belles Demoiselles some summer afternoon as the sky was reddening towards evening,

[13] A long room or building where fibers are twisted into rope.
[14] A gallery built on top of a house.

it was lovely to see the family gathered out upon the tiled pavement at the foot of the broad front steps, gayly chatting and jesting, with that ripple of laughter that comes so pleasingly from a bevy of girls. The father would be found seated in their midst, the centre of attention and compliment, witness, arbiter, umpire, critic, by his beautiful children's unanimous appointment, but the single vassal, too, of seven absolute sovereigns.

Now they would draw their chairs near together in eager discussion of some new steps in the dance, or the adjustment of some rich adornment. Now they would start about him with excited comments to see the eldest fix a bunch of violets in his button-hole. Now the twins would move down a walk after some unusual flower, and be greeted on their return with the high-pitched notes of delighted feminine surprise.

As evening came on they would draw more quietly about their paternal centre. Often their chairs were forsaken, and they grouped themselves on the lower steps, one above another, and surrendered themselves to the tender influences of the approaching night. At such an hour the passer on the river, already attracted by the dark figures of the broad-roofed mansion, and its woody garden standing against the glowing sunset, would hear the voices of the hidden group rise from the spot in the soft harmonies of an evening song; swelling clearer and clearer as the thrill of music warmed them into feeling, and presently joined by the deeper tones of the father's voice; then, as the daylight passed quite away, all would be still, and he would know that the beautiful home had gathered its nestlings under its wings.

And yet, for mere vagary, it pleased them not to be pleased.

"Arti!" called one sister to another in the broad hall, one morning,—mock amazement in her distended eyes,—"something is goin' to took place!"

"*Comm-e-n-t?*"[15]—long-drawn perplexity.

"Papa is goin' to town!"

The news passed up stairs.

"Inno!"—one to another meeting in a doorway,—"something is goin' to took place!"

"*Qu'est-ce-que c'est!*"[16]—vain attempt at gruffness.

"Papa is goin' to town!"

The unusual tidings were true. It was afternoon of the same day that the Colonel tossed his horse' bridle to his groom, and stepped up to old Charlie, who was sitting on his bench under a China-tree, his head, as was his fashion, bound in a Madras handkerchief. The "old man" was plainly under the effect of spirits, and smiled a deferential salutation without trusting himself to his feet.

"Eh, well Charlie!"—the colonel raised his voice to suit his kinsman's deafness,—"how is those times with my friend Charlie?"

"Eh?" said Charlie, distractedly.

"Is that goin' well with my friend Charlie?"

"In de house,—call her,"—making a pretence of rising.

"*Non, non!* I don't want,"—the speaker paused to breathe—"ow is collection?"

"Oh!" said Charlie, "every day he make me more poorer!"

"What do you hask for it?" asked the planter indifferently, designating the house by a wave of his whip.

"Ask for w'at?" said Injin Charlie.

"De *house!* What you ask for it?"

---

[15]French: "What?"   [16]French: "What is it?"

"I don't believe," said Charlie.

"What you would *take* for it!" cried the planter.

"Wait for w'at?"

"What you would *take* for the whole block?"

"I don't want to sell him!"

"I'll give you *ten thousand dollah* for it."

"Ten t'ousand dollah for dis house? Oh, no, dat is no price. He is blame good old house,—dat old house." (Old Charlie and the Colonel never swore in presence of each other.) "Forty years dat old house didn't had to be paint! I easy can get fifty t'ousand dollar for dat old house."

"Fifty thousand picayunes;[17] yes," said the Colonel.

"She's a good house. Can make plenty money," pursued the deaf man.

"That's what make you so rich, eh, Charlie?"

"*Non,* I don't make nothing. Too blame clever, me, dat's de troub'. She's a good house,—make money fast like a steamboat,—make a barrel full in a week! Me, I lose money all de days. Too blame clever."

"Charlie!"

"Eh?'

"Tell me what you'll take."

"Make? I don't make *nothing.* Too blame clever."

"What will you *take?*"

"Oh! I got enough already,—half drunk now."

"What will you take for the 'ouse?'

"You want to buy her?'

"I don't know,"—(shrug),—"may*be,*—if you sell it cheap."

"She's a bully old house."

There was a long silence. By and by old Charlie commenced—

"Old Injin Charlie is a low-down dog."

"*C'est vrai, oui!*"[18] retorted the Colonel in an undertone.

"He's got Injin blood in him."

The Colonel nodded assent.

"But he's got some blame good blood, too, ain't it?"

The Colonel nodded impatiently.

"*Bien!*[19] Old Charlie's Injin blood says, 'sell de house, Charlie, you blame old fool!' *Mais,*[20] old Charlie's good blood says, 'Charlie! if you sell dat old house, Charlie, you low-down old dog, Charlie, what de Compte De Charleu make for you grace-gran'-muzzer, de dev' can eat you, Charlie, I don't care.' "

"But you'll sell it anyhow, won't you, old man?"

"No!" And the *no* rumbled off in muttered oaths like thunder out on the Gulf. The incensed old Colonel wheeled and started off.

"Curl!" (Colonel) said Charlie, standing up unsteadily.

The planter turned with an inquiring frown.

"I'll trade with you!" said Charlie.

The Colonel was tempted. " 'Ow'l you trade?" he asked.

"My house for yours!"

The old Colonel turned pale with anger. He walked very quickly back, and came close up to his kinsman.

"Charlie!" he said.

"Injin Charlie,"—with a tipsy nod.

[17]A Spanish coin worth 6¼ American cents.   [18]French: "That's true, yes!"
[19]French: "Right."   [20]French: "But."

But by this time self-control was returning. "Sell Belles Demoiselles to you?" he said in a high key, and then laughed "Ho, ho, ho!" and rode away.

A cloud, but not a dark one, overshadowed the spirits of Belles Demoiselles' plantation. The old master, whose beaming presence had always made him a shining Saturn, spinning and sparkling within the bright circle of his daughters, fell into musing fits, started out of frowning reveries, walked often by himself, and heard business from his overseer fretfully.

No wonder. The daughters knew his closeness in trade, and attributed to it his failure to negotiate for the Old Charlie buildings,—so to call them. They began to depreciate Belles Demoiselles. If a north wind blew, it was too cold to ride. If a shower had fallen, it was too muddy to drive. In the morning the garden was wet. In the evening the grasshopper was a burden. *Ennui*[21] was turned into capital; every headache was interpreted a premonition of ague; and when the native exuberance of a flock of ladies without a want or a care burst out in laughter in the father's face, they spread their French eyes, rolled up their little hands, and with rigid wrists and mock vehemence vowed and vowed again that they only laughed at their misery, and should pine to death unless they could move to the sweet city. "Oh! the theatre! Oh! Orleans Street! Oh! the masquerade! the Place d'Armes! the ball!" and they would call upon Heaven with French irreverence, and fall into each other's arms, and whirl down the hall singing a waltz, end with a grand collision and fall, and, their eyes streaming merriment, lay the blame on the slippery floor, that would some day be the death of the whole seven.

Three times more the fond father, thus goaded, managed, by accident,—business accident,—to see old Charlie and increase his offer; but in vain. He finally went to him formally.

"Eh?" said the deaf and distant relative. "For what you want him, eh? Why you don't stay where you halways be 'appy? Dis is a blame old rat-hole,—good for old Injin Charlie,—da's all. Why you don't stay where you be halways 'appy? Why you don't buy somewheres else?"

"That's none of your business," snapped the planter. Truth was, his reasons were unsatisfactory even to himself.

A sullen silence followed. Then Charlie spoke:

"Well, now, look here; I sell you old Charlie's house."

"*Bien!* and the whole block," said the Colonel.

"Hold on," said Charlie. "I sell you de 'ouse and de block. Den I go and git drunk, and go to sleep; de dev' comes along and says, 'Charlie! old Charlie, you blame low-down old dog, wake up! What you doin' here? Where's de 'ouse what Monsieur le Compte give your grace-gran-muzzer? Don't you see dat fine gentyman, De Charleu, done gone and tore him down and make him over new, you blame old fool, Charlie, you low-down old Injin dog!' "

"I'll give you forty thousand dollars," said the Colonel.

"For de 'ouse?"

"For all."

The deaf man shook his head.

"Forty-five!" said the Colonel.

"What a lie? For what you tell me 'What a lie?' I don't tell you no lie."

"*Non, non!* I give you *forty-five!*" shouted the Colonel.

Charlie shook his head again.

[21]Boredom.

"Fifty!"

He shook it again.

The figures rose and rose to—

"Seventy-five!"

The answer was an invitation to go away and let the owner alone, as he was, in certain specified respects, the vilest of living creatures, and no company for a fine gentyman.

The "fine gentyman" longed to blaspheme,—but before old Charlie!—in the name of pride, how could he? He mounted and started away.

"Tell you what I'll make wid you," said Charlie.

The other, guessing aright, turned back without dismounting, smiling.

"How much Belles Demoiselles hoes me now?" asked the deaf one.

"One hundred and eighty thousand dollars," said the Colonel, firmly.

"Yass," said Charlie. "I don't want Belles Demoiselles."

The old Colonel's quiet laugh intimated it made no difference either way.

"But me," continued Charlie, "me,—I'm got le Compte De Charleu's blood in me, any'ow,—a litt' bit, any'ow, ain't it?"

The Colonel nodded that it was.

"*Bien!* If I go out of dis place and don't go to Belles Demoiselles, de peoples will say,—dey will say, 'Old Charlie he been all doze time tell a blame *lie!* He ain't no kin to his old grace-gran-muzzer, not a blame bit! He don't got nary drop of De Charleu blood to save his blame low-down old Injin soul! No, sare! What I want wid money, den? No, sare! My place for yours!"

He turned to go into the house, just too soon to see the Colonel make an ugly whisk at him with his riding-whip. Then the Colonel, too, moved off.

Two or three times over, as he ambled homeward, laughter broke through his annoyance, as he recalled old Charlie's family pride and the presumption of his offer. Yet each time he could but think better of—not the offer to swap, but the preposterous ancestral loyalty. It was so much better than he could have expected from his "low-down" relative, and not unlike his own whim withal—the proposition which went with it was forgiven.

This last defeat bore so harshly on the master of Belles Demoiselles, that the daughters, reading chagrin in his face, began to repent. They loved their father as daughters can, and when they saw their pretended dejection harassing him seriously they restrained their complaints, displayed more than ordinary tenderness, and heroically and ostentatiously concluded there was no place like Belles Demoiselles. But the new mood touched him more than the old, and only refined his discontent. Here was a man, rich without the care of riches, free from any real trouble, happiness as native to his house as perfume to his garden, deliberately, as it were with premeditated malice, taking joy by the shoulder and bidding her be gone to town, whither he might easily have followed, only that the very same ancestral nonsense that kept Injin Charlie from selling the old place for twice its value prevented him from choosing any other spot for a city home.

But by and by the charm of nature and the merry hearts around him prevailed; the fit of exalted sulks passed off, and after a while the year flared up at Christmas, flickered, and went out.

New Year came and passed, the beautiful garden of Belles Demoiselles put on its spring attire; the seven fair sisters moved from rose to rose; the cloud of discontent had warmed into visible vapor in the rich sunlight of family affection, and on the common memory the only scar of last year's wound was old Charlie's sheer impertinence in crossing the caprice of the De Charleus. The cup of gladness seemed to fill with the filling of the river.

How high that river was! Its tremendous current rolled and tumbled and spun along, hustling the long funeral flotillas of drift,—and how near shore it came! Men were out day and night watching the levee. On windy nights even the old Colonel took part, and grew light-hearted with occupation and excitement, as every minute the river threw a white arm over the levee's top, as though it would vault over. But all held fast, and, as the summer drifted in, the water sunk down into its banks and looked quite incapable of harm.

On a summer afternoon of uncommon mildness, old Colonel Jean Albert Henri Joseph De Charleu-Marot, being in a mood for revery, slipped the custody of his feminine rulers and sought the crown of the levee, where it was his wont to promenade. Presently he sat upon a stone bench,—a favorite seat. Before him lay his broad-spread fields; near by, his lordly mansion; and being still,—perhaps by female contact,—somewhat sentimental, he fell to musing on his past. It was hardly worthy to be proud of. All its morning was reddened with mad frolic, and far toward the meridian it was marred with elegant rioting. Pride had kept him well-nigh useless, and despised the honors won by valor; gaming had dimmed prosperity; death had taken his heavenly wife; voluptuous ease had mortgaged his lands; and yet his house still stood, his sweet-smelling fields were still fruitful, his name was fame enough; and yonder and yonder, among the trees and flowers like angels walking in Eden, were the seven goddesses of his only worship.

Just then a slight sound behind him brought him to this feet. He cast his eyes anxiously to the outer edge of the little strip of bank between the levee's base and the river. There was nothing visible. He paused, with his ear toward the water, his face full of frightened expectation. Ha! There came a single plashing sound, like some great beast slipping into the river, and little waves in a wide semi-circle came out from under the bank and spread over the water!

"My God!"

He plunged down the levee and bounded through the low weeds to the edge of the bank. It was sheer, and the water about four feet below. He did not stand quite on the edge, but fell upon his knees a couple of yards away, wringing his hands, moaning and weeping, and staring through his watery eyes at a fine, long crevice just discernible under the matted grass, and curving outward on either hand toward the river.

"My God!" he sobbed aloud; "my God!" and even while he called, his God answered: the tough Bermuda grass stretched and snapped, the crevice slowly became a gape, and softly, gradually, with no sound but the closing of the water at last, a ton or more of earth settled into the boiling eddy and disappeared.

At the same instant a pulse of the breeze brought from the garden behind, the joyous, thoughtless laughter of the fair mistresses of Belles Demoiselles.

The old Colonel sprang up and clambered over the levee. Then forcing himself to a more composed movement, he hastened into the house and ordered his horse.

"Tell my children to make merry while I am gone," he left word. "I shall be back to-night," and the horse's hoofs clattered down a by-road leading to the city.

"Charlie," said the planter, riding up to a window, from which the old man's nightcap was thrust out, "what you say, Charlie,—my house for yours, eh, Charlie—what you say?"

"Ello!" said Charlie, "from where you come from dis time of to-night?"

"I come from the Exchange[22] in St. Louis Street." (A small fraction of the truth.)

"What you want?" said matter-of-fact Charlie.

"I come to trade."

The low-down relative drew the worsted[23] off his ears. "Oh yass," he said with an uncertain air.

"Well, old man Charlie, what you say: my house for yours,—like you said,—eh, Charlie?"

"I dunno," said Charlie; "it's nearly mine now. Why you don't stay dare youse'f?"

"Because I don't want!" said the Colonel savagely. "Is dat reason enough for you? You better take me in de notion,[24] old man, I tell you,—yes!"

Charlie never winced; but how his answer delighted the Colonel! Quoth Charlie:

"I don't care—I take him!—*mais*, possession give right off."

"Not the whole plantation, Charlie; only"—

"I don't care," said Charlie; "we easy can fix dat. *Mais*, what for you don't want to keep him? I don't want him. You better keep him."

"Don't you try to make no fool of me, old man," cried the planter.

"Oh, no!" said the other. "Oh, no! but you make a fool of yourself, ain't it?"

The dumbfounded Colonel stared; Charlie went on:

"Yass! Belles Demoiselles is more wort' dan tree block like dis one. I pass by dare since two weeks. Oh, pritty Belles Demoiselles! De cane was wave in de wind, de garden smell like a bouquet, de white-cap was jump up and down on de river; seven *belles demoiselles* was ridin' on horses. 'Pritty, pritty, pritty!' says old Charlie. Ah! *Monsieur le père,* 'ow 'appy, 'appy, 'appy!'

"Yass!" he continued—the Colonel still staring—"le Compte De Charleu have two familie. One was low-down Choctaw, one was high up *noblesse*. He gave the low-down Choctaw dis old rat-hole; he give Belles Demoiselles to your granfozzer; and now you don't be *satisfait*. What I'll do wid Belles Demoiselles? She'll break me in two years, yass. And what you'll do wid old Charlie's house, eh? You'll tear her down and make you'se'f a blame old fool. I rather wouldn't trade!"

The planter caught a big breathful of anger, but Charlie went straight on:

"I rather wouldn't, *mais* I will do it for you;—just the same, like Monsieur le Compte would say, 'Charlie, you old fool, I want to shange houses wid you."

So long as the Colonel suspected irony he was angry, but as Charlie seemed, after all, to be certainly in earnest, he began to feel conscience-stricken. He was by no means a tender man, but his lately-discovered misfortune had unhinged him, and this strange, undeserved, disinterested family fealty on the part of Charlie touched his heart. And should he still try to lead him into the pitfall he had dug? He hesitated;—no, he would show him the place by broad daylight, and if he chose to overlook the "caving bank," it would be his own fault;—a trade's a trade.

"Come," said the planter, "come at my house to-night; to-morrow we look at the place before breakfast, and finish the trade."

"For what?" said Charlie.

"Oh, because I got to come in town in the morning."

"I don't want," said Charlie. "How I'm goin' to come dere?"

"I git you a horse at the liberty stable."

---

[22]A saloon.   [23]Wool nightcap.   [24]I.e., "while I'm inclined to trade."

"Well—anyhow—I don't care—I'll go." And they went.

When they had ridden a long time, and were on the road darkened by hedges of Cherokee rose, the Colonel called behind him to the "low-down" scion:

"Keep the road, old man."

"Eh?"

"Keep the road."

"Oh, yes; all right; I keep my word; we don't goin' to play no tricks, eh?"

But the Colonel seemed not to hear. His ungenerous design was beginning to be hateful to him. Not only old Charlie's unprovoked goodness was prevailing; the eulogy on Belles Demoiselles had stirred the depths of an intense love for his beautiful home. True, if he held to it, the caving of the bank, at its present fearful speed, would let the house into the river within three months; but were it not better to lose it so, than sell his birthright? Again,—coming back to the first thought,—to betray his own blood! It was only Injin Charlie; but had not the De Charleu blood just spoken out in him? Unconsciously he groaned.

After a time they struck a path approaching the plantation in the rear, and a little after, passing from behind a clump of live-oaks, they came in sight of the villa. It looked so like a gem, shining through its dark grove, so like a great glow-worm in the dense foliage, so significant of luxury and gayety, that the poor master, from an overflowing heart, groaned again.

"What?" asked Charlie.

The Colonel only drew his rein, and, dismounting mechanically, contemplated the sight before him. The high, arched doors and windows were thrown wide to the summer air, from every opening the bright light of numerous candelabra darted out upon the sparkling foliage of magnolia and bay, and here and there in the spacious verandas a colored lantern swayed in the gentle breeze. A sound of revel fell on the ear, the music of harps; and across one window, brighter than the rest, flitted, once or twice, the shadows of dancers. But oh! the shadows flitting across the heart of the fair mansion's master!

"Old Charlie," said he, gazing fondly at his house, "You and me is both old, eh?"

"Yaas," said the stolid Charlie.

"And we has both been bad enough in our time, eh, Charlie?"

Charlie, surprised at the tender tone, repeated "Yaas."

"And you and me is mighty close?"

"Blame close, yaas."

"But you never know me to cheat, old man!"

"No,"—impassively.

"And do you think I would cheat you now?'

"I dunno," said Charlie. "I don't believe."

"Well, old man, old man,"—his voice began to quiver,—"I sha'nt cheat you now. My God!—old man, I tell you—you better not make the trade!"

"Because for what?" asked Charlie in plain anger; but both looked quickly toward the house! The Colonel tossed his hands wildly in the air, rushed forward a step or two, and giving one fearful scream of agony and fright, fell forward on his face in the path. Old Charlie stood transfixed with horror. Belles Demoiselles, the realm of maiden beauty, the home of merriment, the house of dancing, all in the tremor and glow of pleasure, suddenly sank, with one short, wild wail of terror—sunk, sunk, down, down, down, into the merciless, unfathomable flood of the Mississippi.

Twelve long months were midnight to the mind of the childless father; when they were only half gone, he took his bed; and every day, and every night, old

Charlie, the "low-down," the "fool," watched him tenderly, tended him lovingly, for the sake of his name, his misfortunes, and his broken heart. No woman's step crossed the floor of the sick-chamber, whose western dormer-windows overpeered the dingy architecture of old Charlie's block; Charlie and a skilled physician, the one all interest, the other all gentleness, hope, and patience—these only entered by the door; but by the window came in a sweet-scented evergreen vine, transplanted from the caving bank of Belles Demoiselles. It caught the rays of sunset in its flowery net and let them softly in upon the sick man's bed; gathered the glancing beams of the moon at midnight, and often wakened the sleeper to look, with his mindless eyes, upon their pretty silvery fragments strewn upon the floor.

By and by there seemed—there was—a twinkling dawn of returning reason. Slowly, peacefully, with an increase unseen from day to day, the light of reason came into the eyes, and speech became coherent; but withal there came a failing of the wrecked body, and the doctor said that monsieur was both better and worse.

One evening, as Charlie sat by the vine-clad window with his fireless pipe in his hand, the old Colonel's eyes fell full upon his own, and rested there.

"Charl—," he said with an effort, and his delighted nurse hastened to the bedside and bowed his best ear. There was an unsuccessful effort or two, and then he whispered, smiling with sweet sadness,—

"We didn't trade."

The truth, in this case, was a secondary matter to Charlie; the main point was to give a pleasing answer. So he nodded his head decidedly, as who should say—"Oh yes, we did, it was a bonafide swap!" but when he saw the smile vanish, he tried the other expedient and shook his head with still more vigor, to signify that they had not so much as approached a bargain; and the smile returned.

Charlie wanted to see the vine recognized. He stepped backward to the window with a broad smile, shook the foliage, nodded and looked smart.

"I know," said the Colonel, with beaming eyes,—"many weeks."

The next day—

"Charl—"

The best ear went down.

"Send for a priest."

The priest came, and was alone with him a whole afternoon. When he left, the patient was very haggard and exhausted, but smiled and would not suffer the crucifix to be removed from his breast.

One more morning came. Just before dawn Charlie, lying on a pallet in the room, thought he was called, and came to the bedside.

"Old man," whispered the failing invalid, "is it caving yet?"

Charlie nodded.

It won't pay you out."

"Oh, dat makes not'ing," said Charlie. Two big tears rolled down his brown face. "Dat makes not'in."

The Colonel whispered once more:

"*Mes belles demoiselles!* in paradise;—in the garden—I shall be with them at sunrise;" and so it was.

1874, 1879

Charles Waddell Chesnutt *1858–1932*

Charles Waddell Chesnutt, a black man, was born free in Ohio shortly before the Civil War. He spent much of his early life in North Carolina, first as a teacher, then as a principal of a segregated high school. But Chesnutt disliked the South; he missed "civilization and companionship," and so he moved to New York, in 1883. There he worked as a stenographic reporter and as an accountant, and he began to write poetry and short fiction.

In 1885 and 1886 several of his stories and poems were published in popular magazines, but he seldom received more than five or ten dollars for each. To support his family, he studied law, and he returned to Ohio, where he was admitted to the bar in 1887, scoring the highest mark of all those who took the bar examination. Black lawyers seldom prospered in nineteenth-century America, and Chesnutt was forced to make a living as a legal stenographer. But he continued writing, and recognition came swiftly when the most prestigious magazine in America, The Atlantic Monthly, *published his story "The Goophered Grapevine" in August 1887.*

Many of Chesnutt's stories were folktales in the manner of Joel Chandler Harris, and some were without apparent racial concerns or implications. Other stories dealt with racial matters in ways generally acceptable to the prejudices of the white reading public of his time. Chesnutt's recurring subjects were "passing" (usually portrayed as having disastrous results), humorous intraracial conflicts between mulattoes and full-blooded blacks, and examples of the instinctively wise (but properly subservient) black man fooling the whites. But the stories are often highly ironic, and racial issues were presented in ways that were subtle, forceful, and well ahead of their time.

By 1900, the year of the publication of his first novel, The House Behind the Cedars, *Chesnutt's racial attitudes had become increasingly militant. He condemned and satirized the South and showed that his black heroine's attempt to pass as white was clearly misguided and so led to tragedy. Chesnutt's major criticism was reserved for his novel's protagonist, who did succeed in passing and who thereafter denied his black heritage. In subsequent novels, the* Marrow of Tradition *(1901) and* The Colonel's Dream *(1905), Chesnutt's racial statements became increasingly blunt and candid. His subjects were race riots, racial injustice, and bigotry; he relied less on veiled irony and more on direct statement, and the tone of his novels became more pessimistic. Even William Dean Howells, Chesnutt's patron, criticized the bitterness of* The Marrow of Tradition, *and others said the novel was an attempt to "humiliate the whites."*

Chesnutt had great hopes for the improvement of race relations in the United States, and his novels were conscious attempts to bring such improvement about. Perhaps disillusioned by the failure of his work to lead to any marked change in the relations between blacks and whites, Chesnutt gave up writing after 1905 and retreated to the consolations of family, travel, and work. By today's standards his attitudes seem passive and dated. But his subtlety, irony, and militancy are often unperceived and undervalued, and he remains an important and pivotal figure in the development of black literature in twentieth-century America.

FURTHER READING: H. Chesnutt, *Charles Waddell Chesnutt, Pioneer of the Color Line*, 1952; J. Heermance, *Charles W. Chesnutt*, 1974; *The Short Fiction of Charles W. Chesnutt*, ed. S. Lyons, 1974; F. Keller, *An American Crusade, The Life of Charles Waddell Chesnutt*, 1978; S. Lyons, *Charles W. Chesnutt*, 1980; W. Andrews, *The Literary Career of Charles W. Chesnutt*, 1980; S. Render, *Charles W. Chesnutt*, 1980.

TEXT: "The Goophered Grapevine," *The Conjure Woman*, 1899.

THE GOOPHERED GRAPEVINE

Some years ago my wife was in poor health, and our family doctor, in whose skill and honesty I had implicit confidence, advised a change of climate. I shared, from an unprofessional standpoint, his opinion that the raw winds, the chill rains, and the violent changes of temperature that characterized the winters in the region of the Great Lakes tended to aggravate my wife's difficulty, and would undoubtedly shorten her life if she remained exposed to them. The doctor's advice was that we seek, not a temporary place of sojourn, but a permanent residence, in a warmer and more equable climate. I was engaged at the time in grape-culture in northern Ohio, and, as I liked the business and had given it much study, I decided to look for some other locality suitable for carrying it on. I thought of sunny France, of sleepy Spain, of Southern California, but there were objections to them all. It occurred to me that I might find what I wanted in some one of our own Southern States. It was a sufficient time after the war for conditions in the South to have become somewhat settled; and I was enough of a pioneer to start a new industry, if I could not find a place where grape-culture had been tried. I wrote to a cousin who had gone into the turpentine business in central North Carolina. He assured me, in response to my inquiries, that no better place could be found in the South than the State and neighborhood where he lived; the climate was perfect for health, and, in conjunction with the soil, ideal for grape-culture; labor was cheap, and land could be bought for a mere song. He gave us a cordial invitation to come and visit him while we looked into the matter. We accepted the invitation, and after several days of leisurely travel, the last hundred miles of which were up a river on a sidewheel steamer, we reached our destination, a quaint old town, which I shall call Patesville, because, for one reason, that is not its name. There was a red brick market-house in the public square, with a tall tower, which held a four-faced clock that struck the hours, and from which there pealed out a curfew at nine o'clock. There were two or three hotels, a court-house, a jail, stores, offices, and all the appurtenances of a county seat and a commercial emporium; for while Patesville numbered only four or five thousand inhabitants, of all shades of complexion, it was one of the principal towns in North Carolina, and had a considerable trade in cotton and naval stores.[1] This business activity was not immediately apparent to my unaccustomed eyes. Indeed, when I first saw the town, there brooded over it a calm that seemed almost sabbatic in its restfulness, though I learned later on that underneath its somnolent exterior the deeper currents of life—love and hatred, joy and despair, ambition and avarice, faith and friendship—flowed not less steadily than in livelier latitudes.

We found the weather delightful at that season, the end of summer, and were hospitably entertained. Our host was a man of means and evidently regarded our visit as a pleasure, and we were therefore correspondingly at our ease, and in a position to act with the coolness of judgment desirable in making so radical a change in our lives. My cousin placed a horse and buggy at our disposal, and himself acted as our guide until I became somewhat familiar with the country.

I found that grape-culture, while it had never been carried on to any great extent, was not entirely unknown in the neighborhood. Several planters thereabouts had attempted it on a commercial scale, in former years, with greater or less success; but like most Southern industries, it had felt the blight of war and had fallen into desuetude.

---

[1] Pitch, turpentine, rosin, and other supplies used in maintaining wooden sailing vessels.

I went several times to look at a place that I thought might suit me. It was a plantation of considerable extent, that had formerly belonged to a wealthy man by the name of McAdoo. The estate had been for years involved in litigation between disputing heirs, during which period shiftless cultivation had well-nigh exhausted the soil. There had been a vineyard of some extent on the place, but it had not been attended to since the war, and had lapsed into utter neglect. The vines—here partly supported by decayed and broken-down trellises, there twining themselves among the branches of the slender saplings which had sprung up among them—grew in wild and unpruned luxuriance, and the few scattered grapes they bore were the undisputed prey of the first comer. The site was admirably adapted to grape-raising; the soil, with a little attention, could not have been better; and with the native grape, the luscious scuppernong,[2] as my main reliance in the beginning, I felt sure that I could introduce and cultivate successfully a number of other varieties.

One day I went over with my wife to show her the place. We drove out of the town over a long wooden bridge that spanned a spreading mill-pond, passed the long whitewashed fence surrounding the county fair-ground, and struck into a road so sandy that the horse's feet sank to the fetlocks. Our route lay partly up hill and partly down, for we were in the sand-hill country; we drove past cultivated farms, and then by abandoned fields grown up in scrub-oak and short-leaved pine, and once or twice through the solemn aisles of the virgin forest, where the tall pines, well-nigh meeting over the narrow road, shut out the sun, and wrapped us in cloistral solitude. Once, at a cross-roads, I was in doubt as to the turn to take, and we sat there waiting ten minutes—we had already caught some of the native infection of restfulness—for some human being to come along, who could direct us on our way. At length a little negro girl appeared, walking straight as an arrow, with a piggin[3] full of water on her head. After a little patient investigation, necessary to overcome the child's shyness, we learned what we wished to know, and at the end of about five miles from the town reached our destination.

We drove between a pair of decayed gateposts—the gate itself had long since disappeared—and up a straight sandy lane, between two lines of rotting rail fence, partly concealed by jimson-weeds and briers, to the open space where a dwelling-house had once stood, evidently a spacious mansion, if we might judge from the ruined chimneys that were still standing, and the brick pillars on which the sills rested. The house itself, we had been informed, had fallen a victim to the fortunes of war.

We alighted from the buggy, walked about the yard for a while, and then wandered off into the adjoining vineyard. Upon Annie's complaining of weariness I led the way back to the yard, where a pine log, lying under a spreading elm, afforded a shady though somewhat hard seat. One end of the log was already occupied by a venerable-looking colored man. He held on his knees a hat full of grapes, over which he was smacking his lips with great gusto, and a pile of grapeskins near him indicated that the performance was no new thing. We approached him at an angle from the rear, and were close to him before he perceived us. He respectfully rose as we drew near, and was moving away, when I begged him to keep his seat.

"Don't let us disturb you," I said. "There is plenty of room for us all."

He resumed his seat with somewhat of embarrassment. While he had been standing, I had observed that he was a tall man, and, though slightly bowed by

[2]A muscadine grape.
[3]Wooden pail.

the weight of years, apparently quite vigorous. He was not entirely black, and this fact, together with the quality of his hair, which was about six inches long and very bushy, except on the top of his head, where he was quite bald, suggested a slight strain of other than negro blood. There was a shrewdness in his eyes, too, which was not altogether African, and which, as we afterwards learned from experience, was indicative of a corresponding shrewdness in his character. He went on eating the grapes, but did not seem to enjoy himself quite so well as he had apparently done before he became aware of our presence.

"Do you live around here?" I asked, anxious to put him at his ease.

"Yas, sah. I lives des ober yander, behine de nex' san'-hill, on de Lumberton plank-road."

"Do you know anything about the time when this vineyard was cultivated?"

"Lawd bless you, suh, I knows all about it. Dey ain' na'er a man in dis settlement w'at won' tel you ole Julius McAdoo 'uz bawn en raise' on dis yer same plantation. Is you de Norv'n gemman w'at's gwine ter buy de ole vimya'd?"

"I am looking at it," I replied; "but I don't know that I shall care to buy unless I can be reasonably sure of making something out of it."

"Well, suh, you is a stranger ter me, en I is a stranger ter you, en we is bofe strangers ter one anudder, but 'f I 'uz in yo' place, I wouldn' buy dis vimya'd."

"Why not?" I asked.

"Well, I dunno whe'r you b'lieves in conj'in 'er not,—some er de w'ite folks don't, er says dey don't,—but de truf er de matter is dat dis yer old vimya'd is goophered."

"Is what?" I asked, not grasping the meaning of this unfamiliar word.

"Is goophered,—conju'd, bewitch'. "

He imparted this information with such solemn earnestness, and with such an air of confidential mystery, that I felt somewhat interested, while Annie was evidently much impressed, and drew closer to me.

"How do you know it is bewitched?" I asked.

"I would n' spec' fer you ter b'lieve me 'less you know all 'bout de fac's. But ef you en young miss dere doan' min' lis'nin' ter a ole nigger run on a minute er two w'ile you ere restin', I kin 'splain to you how it all happen'."

We assured him that we would be glad to hear how it all happened, and he began to tell us. At first the current of his memory—or imagination—seemed somewhat sluggish; but as his embarrassment wore off, his language flowed more freely, and the story acquired perspective and coherence. As he became more and more absorbed in the narrative, his eyes assumed a dreamy expression, and he seemed to lose sight of his auditors, and to be living over again in monologue his life on the old plantation.

"Ole Mars Dugal' McAdoo," he began, "bought dis place long many years befo' de wah, en I 'member well w'en he sot out all dis yer part er de plantation in scuppernon's. De vimes growed monst'us fas', en Mars Dugal' made a thousan' gallon er scuppernon' wine eve'y year.

"Now, ef dey's an'thing a nigger lub, nex' ter 'possum, en chick'n, en water-millyums, it's scuppernon's. Dey ain' nuffin dat kin stan' up side'n de scuppernon' fer sweetness; sugar ain't a suckumstance ter scuppernon'. W'en de season is nigh 'bout ober, en de grapes begin ter swivel up des a little wid de wrinkles er ole age,—w'en de skin git sof' en brown,—den de scuppernon' make you smack yo' lip en roll yo' eye en wush fer mo'; so I reckon it ain' very stonishin' dat niggers lub scuppernon'.

"Dey wuz a sight er niggers in de naberhood er de vimya'd. Dere wuz ole Mars Henry Brayboy's niggers, en ole Mars Jeems McLean's niggers, en Mars

Dugal's own niggers; den dey wuz a settlement er free niggers en po' buckrahs[4] down by de Wim'l'ton Road, en Mars Dugal' had de only vimya'd in de naber-hood. I reckon it ain' so much so nowadays, but befo' de wah, in slab'ry times, a nigger did n' mine goin' fi' er ten mile in a night, w'en dey wuz sump'n good ter eat at de yuther een'.

"So atter a w'ile Mars Dugal' begin ter miss his scuppernon's. Co'se he 'cuse' de niggers er it, but dey all 'nied it ter de las'. Mars Dugal's sot spring guns[5] en steel traps, en he en de oberseah sot up nights once't er twice't, tel one night Mars Dugal'—he 'uz a monst'us keerless man—got his leg shot full er cow-peas.[6] But somehow er nudder dey couldn' nebber ketch none er de niggers. I dunner how it happen, but it happen des like I tell you, en de grapes kep' on a-goin' des de same.

"But bimbey ole Mars Dugal' fix' up a plan ter stop it. Dey wuz a conjuh 'oman livin' down 'mongs' de free niggers on de Wim'l'ton Road, en all de darkies fum Rockfish ter Beaver Crick wuz feared er her. She could wuk de mos' powerfulles' kin' er goopher,—could make people hab fits, er rheumatiz, er make 'em des dwinel away en die; en dey say she went out ridin' de niggers at night, fer she wuz a witch 'sides bein' a conjah 'oman. Mars Dugal' hearn 'bout Aun' Peggy's doins, en begun ter 'flect whe'r er no he could n' git her ter he'p him keep de niggers off'n de grapevimes. One day in spring er de year, ole miss pack' up a basket er chick'n en poun'-cake, en a bottle er scuppernon' wine, en Mars Dugal' tuk it in his buggy en driv ober ter Aun' Peggy's cabin. He tuk de basket in, en had a long talk wid Aun' Peggy.

"De nex' day Aun' Peggy come up ter de vimya'd. De niggers seed her slippin' roun', en dey soon foun' out what she 'uz doin' dere. Mars Dugal' had hi'ed her ter goopher de grapevimes. She sa'ntered 'roun' 'mongs' de vimes, en tuk a leaf fum dis one, en a grape-hull fum dat one, en a grape-seed fum anudder one; en den a little twig fum here, en a little pinch er dirt fum dere,—en put it all in a big black bottle, wid a snake's toof en a speckle' hen's gall en some ha'rs fum a black cat's tail, en den fill' de bottle wid scuppernon' wine. W'en she got de goopher all ready en fix', she tuk 'n went out in de woods en buried it under de root uv a red oak tree, en den come back en tole one er de niggers she done goopher de grapevimes, en a'er a nigger w'at eat dem grapes 'ud be sho ter die inside'n twel' mont's.

"Atter dat de niggers let de scuppernon's 'lone, en Mars Dugal' did n' hab no 'casion ter fine no mo' fault; en de season wuz mos' gone, w'en a strange gemman stop at de plantation one night ter see Mars Dugal' on some business; en his coachman, seein' de scuppernon's growin' so nice en sweet, slip 'roun' behine de smoke-house, en et all de scuppernon's he could hole. Nobody did n' notice it at de time, but dat night, on de way home, de gemman's hoss runned away en kill' de coachman. W'en we hearn de noos, Aun' Lucy, de cook, she up'n say she seed de strange nigger eat'n er de scuppernon's behine de smoke-house; en den we knowed de goopher had b'en er wukkin'. Den one er de nigger chilluns runned away fum de quarters one day, en got in de scuppernon's, en died de nex' week. W'ite folks say he die' er de fevuh, but de niggers knowed it wuz de goopher. So you k'n be sho de darkies did n' hab much ter do wid dem scup-pernon' vimes.

"W'en de scuppernon' season 'uz ober fer dat year, Mars Dugal' foun' he had made fifteen hund'ed gallon er wine; en one er de niggers hearn him laffin' wid de oberseah fit ter kill, en sayin' dem fifteen hund'ed gallon er wine wuz monst'us

[4]Whites.   [5]Guns set to fire when a trespasser trips a wire attached to the trigger.
[6]Dried peas used in place of lead buckshot in a shotgun load.

good intrus' on de ten dollars he laid out on de vimya'd. So I 'low ez he paid
Aun' Peggy ten dollars fer to goopher de grapevimes.

"De goopher did n' wuk no mo tel de nex' summer, w'en 'long to'ds de middle
er de season one er de fiel' han's died; en ez dat lef' Mars Dugal' sho't er han's,
he went off ter town fer ter buy anudder. He fotch de noo nigger home wid
'im. He wuz er ole nigger, er de color er a gingy-cake, en ball ez a hoss-apple
on de top er his head. He wuz a peart ole nigger, do', en could do a big day's
wuk.

"Now it happen dat one er de niggers on de nex' plantation, one er ole Mars
Henry Brayboy's niggers, had runned away de day befo', en tuk ter de swamp,
en ole Mars Dugal' en some er de yuther nabor w'ite folks had gone out wid
dere guns en dere dogs fer ter he'p 'em hunt fer de nigger; en de han's on our
own plantation wuz all so flusterated dat we fuhgot ter tell de noo han' 'bout de
goopher on de scuppernon' vimes. Co'se he smell de grapes en see de vimes, an
atter dahk de fus' thing he done wuz ter slip off ter de grapevimes 'dout sayin'
nuffin ter nobody. Nex' mawnin' he tole some er de niggers 'bout de fine bait
er scuppernon' he et de night befo'.

"W'en dey tole 'im 'bout de goopher on de grapevimes, he 'uz dat tarrified
dat he turn pale, en look des like he gwine ter die right in his tracks. De oberseah
come up en axed w'at 'uz de matter; en w'en dey tole 'im Henry be'n eatin' er
de scuppernon's, en got de goopher on 'im, he gin Henry a big drink er w'iskey,
en 'low dat de nex' rainy day he take 'im ober ter Aun't Peggy's, en see ef she
would n' take de goopher off'n him, seein' ez he did n' know nuffin erbout it
tell he done et de grapes.

"Sho nuff, it rain de nex' day, en de oberseah went over ter Aun' Peggy's wid
Henry. En Aun' Peggy say dat bein' ez Henry did n' know 'bout de goopher, en
et de grapes in ign'ance er de conseq'ences, she reckon she mought be able fer
ter take de goopher off'n him. So she fotch out her bottle wid some conjuh
medicine in it, en po'd some out in a go'd fer Henry ter drink. He manage ter
git it down; he say it tas'e like whiskey wid sump'n bitter in it. She 'lowed dat
'ud keep de goopher off'n him tel de spring; but w'en de sap begin ter rise in
de grapevimes he ha' ter come en see her ag'in, en she tell him w'at e's ter do.

"Nex' spring, w'en de sap commence' ter rise in de scuppernon' vime, Henry
tuk a ham one night. What'd de git de ham? *I* doan know; dey wa'n't no hams
on de plantation 'cep'n w'at 'uz in de smoke-house, but *I* never see Henry 'bout
de smoke-house. But ez I wuz a-sayin', he tuk de ham ober ter Aun' Peggy's; en
Aun' Peggy tole 'im dat w'en Mars Dugal' begin ter prune de grapevimes, he
mus' go en take 'n scrape off de sap whar it ooze out'n de cut een's er de vimes,
en 'n'int his ball head wid it; en ef he do dat once't a year de goopher would n'
wuk agin 'im long ez he done it. En bein' ez he fotch her de ham, she fix' it so
he kin eat all de scuppernon' he want.

"So Henry 'n'into his head wid de sap out'n de big grapevime des ha'f way
'twix' de quarters en de big house, en de goopher nebber wuk again him dat
summer. But de beatenes' thing you eber see happen ter Henry. Up ter dat
time he wuz ez ball ez a sweeten' 'tater, but des ez soon ez de young leaves begun
ter come out on de grapevimes, de ha'r begun ter grow out on Henry's head,
en by de middle er de summer he had de bigges' head er ha'r on de plantation.
Befo' dat, Henry had tol'able good ha'r roun' de aidges, but soon ez de young
grapes begun ter come, Henry's ha'r begun to quirl all up in little balls, des like
dis yer reg'lar grapy ha'r, en by de time de grapes got ripe his head look des
like a bunch er grapes. Combin' it did n' do no good; he wuk at it ha'f de night

wid er Jim Crow,[7] en think he git it straighten' out, but in de mawnin' de grapes
'ud be dere des de same. So he gin it up, en tried ter keep de grapes down by
havin' his ha'r cut sho't.

"But dat wa'n't de quares' thing 'bout de goopher. When Henry come ter de
plantation, he wuz gittin' a little ole an stiff in de j'ints. But dat summer he got
des ez spry en libely ez any young nigger on de plantation; fac', he got so biggity
dat Mars Jackson, de oberseah, ha' ter th'eaten ter whip 'im, ef he did n' stop
cuttin' up his didos en behave hisse'f. But de mos' cur'ouses' thing happen' in
de fall, when de sap begin ter go down in de grapevimes. Fus', when de grapes
'uz gethered, de knots begun ter straighten out'n Henry's ha'r; en we'en de
leaves begin ter fall, Henry's ha'r 'mence' ter drap out; en when de vimes 'uz
bar', Henry's head wuz baller 'n it wuz in de spring, en he begin ter git ole en
stiff in de j'ints ag'in, en paid no mo' 'tention ter de gals dyoin' er de whole
winter. En nex' spring, w'en he rub de sap on ag'in, he got young ag'in, en so
soopl en libely dat none er de young niggers on de plantation could n' jump,
ner dance, ner hoe ez much cotton ez Henry. But in de fall er de year his grapes
'mence' ter straighten out, en his j'ints ter git stiff, en his ha'r drap off, en de
rheumatiz begin ter wrastle wid 'im.

"Now, ef you'd 'a' knowed ole Mars Dugal' McAdoo, you'd 'a' knowed dat it
ha' ter be a mighty rainy day when he could n' fine sump'n fer his niggers ter
do, en it ha' ter be a mighty little hole he could n' crawl thoo, en ha' ter be a
monst'us cloudy night when a dollar git by him in de dahkness; en w'en he see
how Henry git young in de spring en ole in defall, he 'lowed ter hisse'f ez how
he could make mo' money out'n Henry dan by wukkin' him in de cotton-fiel'.
'Long de nex' spring, atter de sap 'mence' ter rise, en Henry 'n'int 'is hed en
sta'ted fer ter git young en soopl, Mars Dugal' up 'n tuk Henry ter town, en sole
'im fer fifteen hunder' dollars. Co'se de man w'at bought Henry did n' know
nuffin 'bout de goopher, en Mars Dugal' did n' see no 'casion fer ter till 'im.
Long to'ds de fall, w'en de sap went down, Henry begin ter git ole ag'in same
ez yuzhal, en his noo marster begin ter git skeered les'n he gwine ter lose his
fifteen-hunder'-dollar nigger. He sent fer a mighty fine doctor, but de med'cine
did n' 'pear ter do no good; de goopher had a good holt. Henry tole de doctor
'bout de goopher, but de doctor des laff at 'im.

"One day in de winter Mars Dugal' went ter town, en wuz santerin' 'long de
Main Street, when who should he meet but Henry's noo marster. Dey said
'Hoody,' en Mars Dugal' ax 'im ter hab a seegyar; en atter dey run on awhile
'bout de craps en de weather, Mars Dugal' ax 'im, sorter keerless, like ez ef he
des thought of it,—

" 'How you like de nigger I sole you las' spring?'

"Henry's marster shuck his head en knock de ashes off'n his seegyar.

" 'Spec' I made a bad bahgin when I bought dat nigger. Henry done good
wuk all de summer, but sence de fall set in he 'pears ter be sorter pinin' away.
Dey ain' nuffin pertickler de matter wid 'im—leastways de doctor say so—'cep'n
a tech er de rheumatiz; but his ha'r is all fell out, en ef he don't pick up his
strenk mighty soon, I spec' I'm gwine ter lose 'im.'

"Dey smoked on awhile, en bimeby ole mars say, "Well, a bahgin's a bahgin,
but you en me is good fren's, en I doan wan' ter see you lose all de money you
paid fer dat nigger; en ef w'at you say is so, en I ain't 'sputin' it, he ain't wuf
much now. I 'spec's you wukked him too ha'd dis summer, er e'se de swamps

---

[7]"A small card, resembling a currycomb in construction, and used by negroes in the rural districts
instead of a comb."—Chesnutt's note. Card: a tool with wire teeth, used for carding (combing) fibers.

down here don't agree wid de san'-hill nigger. So you des lemme know, en ef he gits any wusser I'll be willin' ter gib yer five hund'ed dollars fer 'im, en take my chances on his livin'."

"Sho 'nuff, when Henry begun ter draw up wid de rheumatiz en it look like he gwine ter die fer sho, his noo marster sen' fer Mars Dugal', en Mars Dugal' gin him what he promus, en brung Henry home ag'in. He tuk good keer uv 'im dyoin' er de winter,—give 'im w'iskey ter rub his rheumatiz, en terbacker ter smoke, en all he want ter eat,—caze a nigger w'at he could make a thousan' dollars a year off'n did n' grow on eve'y huckleberry bush.

"Nex' spring, w'en de sap ris en Henry's ha'r commence' ter sprout, Mars Dugal' sole 'im ag'in, down in Robeson County dis time; en he kep' dat sellin' business up fer five year er mo'. Henry nebber say nuffin 'bout de goopher ter his noo marsters, 'caze he know he gwine ter be tuk good keer uv de nex' winter, w'en Mars Dugal' buy him back. En Mars Dugal' made 'nuff money off'n Henry ter buy anudder plantation ober on Beaver Crick.

"But 'long 'bout de een' er dat five year dey come a stranger ter stop at de plantation. De fus' day he 'uz dere he went out wid Mars Dugal' en spent all de mawnin' lookin' ober de vimya'd, en atter dinner dey spent all de evenin' playin' kya'ds. De niggers soon 'skiver' dat he wuz a Yankee, en dat he come down ter Norf C'lina fer ter l'arn de w'ite folks how to raise grapes en make wine. He promus Mars Dugal' he c'd make de grapevimes b'ar twice't ez many grapes, en dat de noo winepress he wuz a-sellin' would make mo' d'n twice't ez many gallons er wine. En ole Mars Dugal' des drunk it all in, des 'peared ter be bewitch' wid dat Yankee. W'en de darkies see dat Yankee runnin' 'roun' de vimy'd en diggin' under de grapevimes, dey shuk dere heads, en 'lowed dat dey feared Mars Dugal' losin' his min'. Mars Dugal' had all de dirt dug away fum under de roots er all de scuppernon' vimes, an' let 'em stan' dat away fer a week er mo'. Den dat Yankee made de niggers fix up a mixtry er lime en ashes en manyo,[8] en po' it 'roun' de roots er de grapevimes. Den he 'vise Mars Dugal' fer ter trim de vimes close't, en Mars Dugal' tuck 'n done eve'ything de Yankee tole him ter do. Dyoin' all er dis time, mind yer, dis yer Yankee wuz libbin' off'n de fat er de lan', at de big house, en playin' kya'ds wid Mars Dugal' eve'y night; en dey say Mars Dugal' los' mo'n a thousan' dollars dyoin's er de week dat Yankee wuz a-ruinin' de grapevimes.

"W'en de sap ris nex' spring, ole Henry 'n'inted his head ez yuzhal, en his ha'r 'mence' ter grow des de same ez it done eve'y year. De scuppernon' vimes growed monst'us fas', en de leaves wuz greener en thicker dan dey eber be'n dyoin' my rememb'ance; en Henry's ha'r growed out thicker dan eber, en he 'peared ter git younger 'n younger, en soopler 'n soopler; en seein' ez he wuz sh'ot er han's dat spring, havin' tuk in consid'able noo groun', Mars Dugal' cluded he would n' sell Henry 'tel he git de crap in en de cotton chop'. So he kep' Henry on de plantation.

"But long 'bout time fer de grapes ter come on de scuppernon' vimes, dey 'peared ter come a change ober 'em; de leaves withered en swivel' up, en de young grapes turn' yaller, en bimeby eve'ybody on de plantation could see dat de whole vimya'd wuz dyin'. Mars Dugal' tuk 'n water de vimes en done all he could, but 't wa'n' no use: dat Yankee had done bus' de watermillyum. One time de vimes picked up a bit, en Mars Dugal' 'lowed dey wuz gwine ter come out ag'in; but dat Yankee done dug too close under de roots, en prune de branches

---

[8]The manioc (cassava) or other root crop ground into a meal for use as fertilizer.

too close ter de vime, en all dat lime en ashes done burn' de life out'n de vimes, en dey des kep' a-with'in' en a-swivelin'.

"All dis time de goopher wuz a-wukken'. When de vimes sta'ted ter wither, Henry 'mence' ter complain er his rheumatiz; en when de leaves begin ter dry up, his ha'r 'mence' ter drap out. When de vimes fresh' up a bit, Henry 'd git peart ag'in, en when de vimes wither' ag'in, Henry 'd git ole ag'in, en des kep' gittin' mo' en mo' fitten fer nuffin; he des pined away, en pined away, en fine'ly tuk ter his cabin; en when de big vime whar he got de sap ter 'n'int his head withered en turned yaller en died, Henry died too,—des went out sorter like a cannel. Dey did n't 'pear ter be nuffin de matter wid 'im, 'cep'n' de rheumatiz, but his strenk des dwinnel' away 'tel he did n' hab ernuff lef' ter draw his bref. De goopher had got de under holt, en th'owed Henry dat time fer good en all.

"Mars Dugal' tuk on might'ly 'bout losin' his vimes en his nigger in de same year; en he swo' dat ef he could git holt er dat Yankee he'd wear 'im ter a frazzle, en den chaw up de frazzle; en he'd done it, too, for Mars Dugal' 'uz a monst'us brash man w'en he once git started. He sot de vimya'd out ober ag'in, but it wuz th'ee er fo' year befo' de vimes got ter b'arin' any scuppernon's.

"W'en de wah broke out, Maars Dugal' raise' a comp'ny, en went off ter fight de Yankees. He say he wuz mighty glad dat wah come, en he des want ter kill a Yankee fer eve'y dollar he los' 'long er dat grape-raisin' Yankee. En I 'spec' he would 'a' done it, too, ef de Yankees had n' s'picioned sump'n, en killed him fus'. Atter de s'render ole miss move' ter town, de niggers all scattered 'way fum de plantation, en de vimya'd ain' be'n cultervated sence."

"Is that story true?" asked Annie doubtfully, but seriously, as the old man concluded his narrative.

"It's des ez true ez I'm a-settin' here, miss. Dey's a easy way ter prove it: I kin lead de way right ter Henry's grave ober yander in de plantation buryin'-groun'. En I tell yer w'at, marster, I would n' 'vise you to buy dis yer ole vimya'd, 'caze de goopher's on it yit, en dey ain' no tellin' w'en it's gwine ter crap out."

"But I thought you said all the ole vines died."

Dey did 'pear ter die, but a few un 'em come out ag'in, en is mixed in 'mongs' de yuthers. I ain' skeered ter eat de grapes, 'caze I knows de old vimes fum de noo ones; but wid strangers dey ain' no tellin' w'at mought happen. I would n' 'vise yer ter buy dis vimya'd."

I bought the vineyard, nevertheless, and it has been for a long time in a thriving condition, and is often referred to by the local press as a striking illustration of the opportunities open to Northern capital in the development of Southern industries. The luscious scuppernong holds first rank among our grapes, though we cultivate a great many other varieties, and our income from grapes packed and shipped to the Northern markets is quite considerable. I have not noticed any developments of the goopher in the vineyard, although I have a mild suspicion that our colored assistants do not suffer from want of grapes during the season.

I found, when I bought the vineyard, that Uncle Julius had occupied a cabin on the place for many years, and derived a respectable revenue from the product of the neglected grapevines. This, doubtless, accounted for his advice to me not to buy the vineyard, though whether it inspired the goopher story I am unable to state. I believe, however, that the wages I paid him for his services as coachman, for I gave him employment in that capacity, were more than an equivalent for anything he lost by the sale of the vineyard.

1887

Joel Chandler Harris *1848–1908*

In his Autobiography, *Mark Twain recalled that among the happiest moments of his youth were those at his uncle's farm when he listened raptly while Uncle Dan (later the model for Jim in* Huckleberry Finn*) told the 'immortal tales . . . Uncle Remus Harris was to gather into his books and charm the world with.' The stories of Br'er Fox and Br'er Rabbit had their origins in the folk myths of Europe and Africa, but Harris made them memorable by presenting their humorous and sometimes bitter wisdom through the character and dialect of an old, uneducated former slave, Uncle Remus.*

Written at a time when writers and readers alike were fascinated by local color stories, Harris's tales had much the same appeal as Twain's frontier yarns, Bret Harte's tales of the Sierra miners, and Kate Chopin's portrayals of the Louisiana Creoles. And Harris's tales were object lessons not only for those who, like Br'er Rabbit, paid for their heedlessness and pride but also for all the down-trodden who used their wits to survive and to laugh at their oppressors. Like other regionalist stories, they captured the flavor of a way of life at a single point in time, but like the best of local color fiction, they had a peculiarly human appeal that kept them alive long after the historical and regional peculiarities they described had disappeared.

Harris took most of his stories from Negroes he had known while working as a youth on a Georgia plantation. Later he became a journalist in Macon, New Orleans, and Savannah before serving twenty-four years on the staff of the Atlanta Constitution, *where he published many of the humorous stories of plantation Negroes that made him famous.*

His first volume of collected tales, Uncle Remus, His Songs and Sayings, *appeared in 1880. Numerous other collections followed during the next thirty years, among them* Nights with Uncle Remus *(1883), and* Free Joe and Other Georgian Sketches *(1887), which included "Free Joe and the Rest of the World," the tragic tale of a slave who, granted his freedom, could find no place for himself in the slave-holding South before the Civil War.*

FURTHER READING: *The Complete Tales of Uncle Remus*, ed. R. Chase, 1955; R. Wiggins, *The Life of Joel Chandler Harris*, 1918; J. Harris, *The Life and Letters of Joel Chandler Harris* 1918; A. Harlow, *Joel Chandler Harris*, 1941; S. Brooks, *Joel Chandler Harris, Folklorist*, 1950; P. Cousins, *Joel Chandler Harris, A Biography*, 1968; R. Bickley, *Joel Chandler Harris*, 1978; F. Baer, *Sources and Analogues of the Uncle Remus Tales*, 1980; *Critical Essays on Joel Chandler Harris*, ed. R. Bickley, 1981; B. Bickley, *Joel Chandler Harris*, 1987.
TEXTS: "How Mr. Rabbit Was Too Sharp for Mr. Fox," *Uncle Remus, His Songs and Sayings*, 1880; "Free Joe and the Rest of the World," *Free Joe and Other Georgian Sketches*, 1887.

HOW MR. RABBIT WAS TOO SHARP FOR MR. FOX

"UNCLE REMUS," said the little boy one evening, when he had found the old man with little or nothing to do, "did the Fox kill and eat the Rabbit when he caught him with the Tar-Baby?"

"Law, honey, ain't I tell you 'bout dat?" replied the old darkey, chuckling slyly. "I 'clar ter gracious I ought er tole you dat, but old man Nod[1] wuz ridin'

---

[1] I.e., sleepiness.

on my eyeleds twel[2] a leetle mo'n[3] I'd a dis'member'd my own name, en den on to dat here come yo' mammy hollerin' atter you.

"W'at I tell you w'en I fus' begin? I tole you Brer Rabbit wuz a monstus soon[4] creetur; leas'ways dat's w'at I laid out fer ter tell you. Well, den, honey, don't you go en make no udder calkalashuns, kaze in dem days Brer Rabbit en his fambly wuz at de head er de gang w'en enny racket wuz on han', en dar dey stayed. 'Fo'[5] you begins fer ter wipe yo' eyes 'bout Brer Rabbit, you wait en see whar'bouts Brer Rabbit gwine ter fetch up at. But dat's needer yer ner dar.[6]

"W'en Brer Fox fin' Brer Rabbit mixt up wid de Tar-Baby, he feel mighty good, en he roll on de groun' en laugh. Bimeby he up'n say, sezee:

" 'Well, I speck I got you dis time, Brer Rabbit', sezee; 'maybe I ain't, but I speck I is. You bin runnin' roun' here sassin' atter me a mighty long time, but I speck you done come ter de een' er de row. You bin cuttin' up yo' capers en bouncin' 'roun' in dis neighborhood ontwel[7] you come ter b'lieve yo'se'f de boss er de whole gang. En den you er allers somers[8] whar you got no bizness,' sez Brer Fox, sezee. 'Who ax you fer ter come en strike up a 'quaintance wid dish yer Tar-Baby? En who stuck you up dar whar you iz? Nobody in de roun' worl'. You des tuck en jam yo'se'f on dat Tar-Baby widout waitin' fer enny invite,' sez Brer Fox, sezee, 'en dar you is, en dar you'll stay twel I fixes up a bresh-pile and fiers her up, kaze I'm gwine ter bobbycue you dis day, sho,' sez Brer Fox, sezee.

"Den Brer Rabbit talk mighty 'umble.

" 'I don't keer w'at you do wid me, Brer Fox,' sezee, 'so you don't fling me in dat brier-patch. Roas' me, Brer Fox,' sezee, 'but don't fling me in dat brier-patch,' sezee.

" 'Hit's so much trouble fer ter kindle a fier,' sez Brer Fox, sezee, 'dat I speck I'll hatter hang you,' sezee.

" 'Hang me des ez high as you please, Brer Fox,' sez Brer Rabbit, sezee, 'but do fer de Lord's sake don't fling me in dat brier-patch,' sezee.

" 'I ain't got no string,' sez Brer Fox, sezee, 'en now I speck I'll hatter drown you," sezee.

" 'Drown me des ez deep ez you please, Brer Fox,' sez Brer Rabbit, sezee, 'but don't fling me in dat brier-patch,' sezee.

" 'Dey ain't no water nigh,' sez Brer Fox, sezee, 'en now I speck I'll hatter skin you,' sezee.

" 'Skin me, Brer Fox,' sez Brer Rabbit, sezee, 'snatch out my eyeballs, t'ar out my years[9] by de roots, en cut off my legs,' sezee, 'but do please, Brer Fox, don't fling me in dat brier-patch,' sezee.

"Co'se[10] Brer Fox wanter hurt Brer Rabbit bad ez he kin, so he cotch 'im by de behime legs en slung 'im right in de middle er de brier-patch. Dar wuz a considerabul flutter whar Brer Rabbit struck de bushes, en Brer Fox sorter hang 'roun' fer ter see w'at wuz gwine ter happen. Bimeby he heard somebody call 'im, en way up de hill he see Brer Rabbit settin' cross-legged on a chinkapin[11] log koamin' de pitch out'n his ha'r wid a chip. Den Brer Fox know dat he bin swop off[12] mighty bad. Brer Rabbit wuz bleedzd[13] fer ter fling back some er his sass, en he holler out:

" 'Bred en bawn in a brier-patch, Brer Fox—bred en bawn in a brier-patch!' en wid dat he skip out des ez lively ez a cricket in de embers."

1880

2"Till." 3"More and." 4Quick. 5"Before."
6"Neither here nor there." 7"Until." 8"Somewheres."
9"Ears." 10"Of course." 11Chestnut.
12Tricked. 13Obliged.

FREE JOE AND THE REST OF THE WORLD

The name of Free Joe strikes humorously upon the ear of memory. It is impossible to say why, for he was the humblest, the simplest, and the most serious of all God's living creatures, sadly lacking in all those elements that suggest the humorous. It is certain, moreover, that in 1850 the sober-minded citizens of the little Georgian village of Hillsborough were not inclined to take a humorous view of Free Joe, and neither his name nor his presence provoked a smile. He was a black atom, drifting hither and thither without an owner, blown about by all the winds of circumstance, and given over to shiftlessness.

The problems of one generation are the paradoxes of a succeeding one, particularly if war, or some such incident, intervenes to clarify the atmosphere and strengthen the understanding. Thus, in 1850, Free Joe represented not only a problem of large concern, but, in the watchful eyes of Hillsborough, he was the embodiment of that vague and mysterious danger that seemed to be forever lurking on the outskirts of slavery, ready to sound a shrill and ghostly signal in the impenetrable swamps, and steal forth under the midnight stars to murder, rapine, and pillage—a danger always threatening, and yet never assuming shape; intangible, and yet real; impossible, and yet not improbable. Across the serene and smiling front of safety, the pale outlines of the awful shadow of insurrection sometimes fell. With this invisible panorama as a background, it was natural that the figure of Free Joe, simple and humble as it was, should assume undue proportions. Go where he would, do what he might, he could not escape the finger of observation and the kindling eye of suspicion. His lightest words were noted, his slightest actions marked.

Under all the circumstances it was natural that his peculiar condition should reflect itself in his habits and manners. The slaves laughed loudly day by day, but Free Joe rarely laughed. The slaves sang at their work and danced at their frolics, but no one ever heard Free Joe sing or saw him dance. There was something painfully plaintive and appealing in his attitude, something touching in his anxiety to please. He was of the friendliest nature, and seemed to be delighted when he could amuse the little children who had made a playground of the public square. At times he would please them by making his little dog Dan perform all sorts of curious tricks, or he would tell them quaint stories of the beasts of the field and birds of the air; and frequently he was coaxed into relating the story of his own freedom. That story was brief, but tragical.

In the year of our Lord 1840, when a negro speculator of a sportive turn of mind reached the little village of Hillsborough on his way to the Mississippi region, with a caravan of likely negroes of both sexes, he found much to interest him. In that day and at that time there were a number of young men in the village who had not bound themselves over to repentance for the various misdeeds of the flesh. To these young men the negro speculator (Major Frampton was his name) proceeded to address himself. He was a Virginian, he declared; and, to prove the statement, he referred all the festively inclined young men of Hillsborough to a barrel of peach-brandy in one of his covered wagons. In the minds of these young men there was less doubt in regard to the age and quality of the brandy than there was in regard to the negro trader's birthplace. Major Frampton might or might not have been born in the Old Dominion—that was a matter of consideration and inquiry—but there could be no question as to the mellow pungency of the peach-brandy.

In his own estimation, Major Frampton was one of the most accomplished of men. He had summered at the Virginia Springs; he had been to Philadelphia, to Washington, to Richmond, to Lynchburg, and to Charleston, and had accumulated a great deal of experience which he found useful. Hillsborough was hid in the woods of Middle Georgia, and its general aspect of innocence impressed him. He looked on the young men who had shown their readiness to test his peach-brandy as overgrown country boys who needed to be introduced to some of the arts and sciences he had at his command. Thereupon the major pitched his tents, figuratively speaking, and became, for the time being, a part and parcel of the innocence that characterized Hillsborough. A wiser man would doubtless have made the same mistake.

The little village possessed advantages that seemed to be providentially arranged to fit the various enterprises that Major Frampton had in view. There was the auction block in front of the stuccoed court-house, if he desired to dispose of a few of his negroes; there was a quarter-track, laid out to his hand and in excellent order, if he chose to enjoy the pleasures of horse-racing; there were secluded pine thickets within easy reach, if he desired to indulge in the exciting pastime of cock-fighting; and various lonely and unoccupied rooms in the second story of the tavern, if he cared to challenge the chances of dice or cards.

Major Frampton tried them all with varying luck, until he began his famous game of poker with Judge Alfred Wellington, a stately gentleman with a flowing white beard and mild blue eyes that gave him the appearance of a benevolent patriarch. The history of the game in which Major Frampton and Judge Alfred Wellington took part is something more than a tradition in Hillsborough, for there are still living three or four men who sat around the table and watched its progress. It is said that at various stages of the game Major Frampton would destroy the cards with which they were playing, and send for a new pack, but the result was always the same. The mild blue eyes of Judge Wellington, with few exceptions, continued to overlook "hands" that were invincible—a habit they had acquired during a long and arduous course of training from Saratoga to New Orleans. Major Frampton lost his money, his horses, his wagons, and all his negroes but one, his body-servant. When his misfortune had reached this limit, the major adjourned the game. The sun was shining brightly, and all nature was cheerful. It is said that the major also seemed to be cheerful. However this may be, he visited the court-house, and executed the papers that gave his body-servant his freedom. This being done, Major Frampton sauntered into a convenient pine thicket, and blew out his brains.

The negro thus freed came to be known as Free Joe. Compelled, under the law, to choose a guardian, he chose Judge Wellington, chiefly because his wife Lucinda was among the negroes won from Major Frampton. For several years Free Joe had what may be called a jovial time. His wife Lucinda was well provided for, and he found it a comparatively easy matter to provide for himself; so that, taking all the circumstances into consideration, it is not matter for astonishment that he became somewhat shiftless.

When Judge Wellington died, Free Joe's troubles began. The judge's negroes, including Lucinda, went to his half-brother, a man named Calderwood, who was a hard master and a rough customer generally—a man of many eccentricities of mind and character. His neighbors had a habit of alluding to him as "Old Spite"; and the name seemed to fit him so completely that he was known far and near as "Spite" Calderwood. He probably enjoyed the distinction the name gave him, at any rate he never resented it, and it was not often that he missed an opportunity to show that he deserved it. Calderwood's place was two or three miles from the village of Hillsborough, and Free Joe visited his wife twice a week, Wednesday and Saturday nights.

One Sunday he was sitting in front of Lucinda's cabin, when Calderwood happened to pass that way.

"Howdy, marster," said Free Joe, taking off his hat.

"Who are you?" exclaimed Calderwood abruptly, halting and staring at the negro.

"I'm name' Joe, marster. I'm Lucindy's ole man."

"Who do you belong to?"

"Marse John Evans is my gyardeen, marster."

"Big name—gyardeen. Show your pass."

Free Joe produced that document, and Calderwood read it aloud slowly, as if he found it difficult to get at the meaning:

"To whom it my concern: This is to certify that the boy Joe Frampton has my permission to visit his wife Lucinda."

This was dated at Hillsborough, and signed *"John W. Evans."*

Calderwood read it twice, and then looked at Free Joe, elevating his eyebrows, and showing his discolored teeth.

"Some mighty big words in that there. Evans owns this place, I reckon. When's he comin' down to take hold?"

Free Joe fumbled with his hat. He was badly frightened.

"Lucindy say she speck you wouldn't min' my comin', long ez I behave, marster."

Calderwood tore the pass in pieces and flung it away.

"Don't want no free niggers 'round here," he explained. "There's the big road. It'll carry you to town. Don't let me catch you here no more. Now, mind what I tell you."

Free Joe presented a shabby spectacle as he moved off with his little dog Dan slinking at his heels. It should be said in behalf of Dan, however, that his bristles were up, and that he looked back and growled. It may be that the dog had the advantage of insignificance, but it is difficult to conceive how a dog bold enough to raise his bristles under Calderwood's very eyes could be as insignificant as Free Joe. But both the negro and his little dog seemed to give a new and more dismal aspect to forlornness as they turned into the road and went toward Hillsborough.

After this incident Free Joe appeared to have clearer ideas concerning his peculiar condition. He realized the fact that though he was free he was more helpless than any slave. Having no owner, every man was his master. He knew that he was the object of suspicion, and therefore all his slender resources (ah! how pitifully slender they were!) were devoted to winning, not kindness and appreciation, but toleration; all his efforts were in the direction of mitigating the circumstances that tended to make his condition so much worse than that of the negroes around him—negroes who had friends because they had masters.

So far as his own race was concerned, Free Joe was an exile. If the slaves secretly envied him his freedom (which is to be doubted, considering his miserable condition), they openly despised him, and lost no opportunity to treat him with contumely. Perhaps this was in some measure the result of the attitude which Free Joe chose to maintain toward them. No doubt his instinct taught him that to hold himself aloof from the slaves would be to invite from the whites the toleration which he coveted, and without which even his miserable condition would be rendered more miserable still.

His greatest trouble was the fact that he was not allowed to visit his wife; but he soon found a way out of his difficulty. After he had been ordered away from the Calderwood place, he was in the habit of wandering as far in that direction as prudence would permit. Near the Calderwood place, but not on Calderwood's land, lived an old man named Micajah Staley and his sister Becky Staley. These people were old and very poor. Old Micajah had a palsied arm and hand; but, in spite of this, he managed to earn a precarious living with his turning-lathe.

When he was a slave Free Joe would have scorned these representatives of class known as poor white trash, but now he found them sympathetic and helpful in various ways. From the back door of their cabin he could hear the Calderwood negroes singing at night, and he sometimes fancied he could distinguish Lucinda's shrill treble rising above the other voices. A large poplar grew in the woods some distance from the Staley cabin, and at the foot of this tree Free Joe would sit for hours with his face turned toward Calderwood's. His little dog Dan would curl up in the leaves near by, and the two seemed to be as comfortable as possible.

One Saturday afternoon Free Joe, sitting at the foot of his friendly poplar, fell asleep. How long he slept, he could not tell; but when he awoke little Dan was licking his face, the moon was shining brightly, and Lucinda his wife stood before him laughing. The dog, seeing that Free Joe was asleep, had grown somewhat impatient, and he concluded to make an excursion to the Calderwood place on his own account. Lucinda was inclined to give the incident a twist in the direction of superstition.

"I' uz settn' down front er de fireplace," she said, "cookin' me some meat, w'en all of a sudden I year sumpin at de do'—scratch, scratch. I tuck'n tu'n de meat over, en make out I ain't year it. Bimeby it come dar 'gin—scratch, scratch. I up en open de do', I did, en, bless de Lord! dar wuz little Dan, en it look like ter me dat his ribs done grow terge'er. I gin 'im some bread, en den w'en he start out, I tuck'n foller 'im, kaze, I say ter myse'f, may be my nigger man mought be some's 'roun'. Dat ar little dog got sense, mon."

Free Joe laughed and dropped his hand lightly on Dan's head. For a long time after that he had no difficulty in seeing his wife. He had only to sit by the poplar tree until little Dan could run and fetch her. But after a while the other negroes discovered that Lucinda was meeting Free Joe in the woods, and information of the fact soon reached Calderwood's ears. Calderwood was what is called a man of action. He said nothing; but one day he put Lucinda in his buggy, and carried her to Macon, six miles away. He carried her to Macon, and came back without her; and nobody in or around Hillsborough, or in that section, ever saw her again.

For many a night after that Free Joe sat in the woods and waited. Little Dan would run merrily off and be gone a long time, but he always came back without Lucinda. This happened over and over again. The "willis-whistlers"[1] would call and call, like fantom huntsmen wandering on a far-off shore; the screech-owl would shake and shiver in the depths of the woods: the night-hawks, sweeping by on noiseless wings, would snap their beaks as though they enjoyed the huge joke of which Free Joe and little Dan were the victims; and the whip-poor-wills would cry to each other through the gloom. Each night seemed to be lonelier than the preceding, but Free Joe's patience was proof against loneliness. There came a time, however, when little Dan refused to go after Lucinda. When Free

---

[1]Large shore birds.

Joe motioned him in the direction of the Calderwood place, he would simply move about uneasily and whine; then he would curl up in the leaves and make himself comfortable.

One night, instead of going to the poplar tree to wait for Lucinda, Free Joe went to the Staley cabin, and, in order to make his welcome good, as he expressed it, he carried with him an armful of fat-pine splinters. Miss Becky Staley had a great reputation in those parts as a fortune-teller, and the schoolgirls, as well as older people, often tested her powers in this direction, some in jest and some in earnest. Free Joe placed his humble offering of light-wood in the chimney corner, and then seated himself on the steps, dropping his hat on the ground outside.

"Miss Becky," he said presently, "whar in de name er gracious you reckon Lucindy is?"

"Well, the Lord he'p the nigger!" exclaimed Miss Becky, in a tone that seemed to reproduce, by some curious agreement of sight with sound, her general aspect of peakedness. "Well, the Lord he'p the nigger! hain't you been a-seein' her all this blessed time? She's over at old Spite Calderwood's, if she's anywheres, I reckon."

"No'm, dat I ain't, Miss Becky. I ain't seen Lucindy in now gwine on mighty nigh a mont'."

"Well, it hain't a-gwine to hurt you," said Miss Becky, somewhat sharply. "In my day an' time it wuz allers took to be a bad sign when niggers got to honeyin' 'roun' an' gwine on."

"Yessum," said Free Joe, cheerfully assenting to the proposition—"yessum, dat's so, but me an' my ole 'oman, we 'uz raise terge'er, en dey ain't bin many days w'en we 'uz 'way fum one 'n'er like we is now."

"Maybe she's up an' took up wi' some un else," said Micajah Staley from the corner. "You know what the sayin' is: 'New master, new nigger.'"

"Dat's so, dat's de sayin', but tain't wid my ole 'oman like 'tis wid yuther niggers. Me en her wuz des natally raise up terge'er. Dey's lots likelier niggers dan w'at I is," said Free Joe, viewing his shabbiness with a critical eye, "but I knows Lucindy mos' good ez I does little Dan dar—dat I does."

There was no reply to this, and Free Joe continued:

"Miss Becky, I wish you please, ma'am, take en run yo' kyards en see sump'n n'er 'about Lucindy; kaze ef she sick, I'm gwine dar. Dey ken take en take me up en gimme a stroppin', but I'm gwine dar."

Miss Becky got her cards, but first she picked up a cup, in the bottom of which were some coffee-grounds. These she whirled slowly round and round, ending finally by turning the cup upside down on the hearth and allowing it to remain in that position.

"I'll turn the cup first," said Miss Becky, "and then I'll run the cards and see what they say."

As she shuffled the cards the fire on the hearth burned low, and in its fitful light the gray-haired, thin-featured woman seemed to deserve the weird reputation which rumor and gossip had given her. She shuffled the cards for some moments, gazing intently in the dying fire; then, throwing a piece of pine on the coals, she made three divisions of the pack, disposing them about in her lap. Then she took the first pile, ran the cards slowly through her fingers, and studied them carefully. To the first she added the second pile. The study of these was evidently not satisfactory. She said nothing, but frowned heavily; and the frown deepened as she added the rest of the cards until the entire fifty-two had passed in review before her. Though she frowned, she seemed to be deeply interested. Without changing the relative position of the cards, she ran them all over again. Then she threw a larger piece of pine on the fire, shuffled the cards afresh, divided them into three piles, and subjected them to the same careful and critical examination.

"I can't tell the day when I've seed the cards run this a-way," she said after a while. "What is an' wha ain't, I'll never tell you; but I know what the cards sez."

"W'at does dey say, Miss Becky?" the negro inquired, in a tone the solemnity of which was heightened by its eagerness.

"They er runnin' quare. These here that I'm a-lookin' at," said Miss Becky, "they stan' for the past. Them there, they er the present; and the t'others, they er the future. Here's a bundle"—tapping the ace of clubs with her thumb—"and here's a journey as plain as the nose on a man's face. Here's Lucinda—"

"Whar she, Miss Becky?"

"Here she is—the queen of spades."

Free Joe grinned. The idea seemed to please him immensely.

"Well, well, well!" he exclaimed. "Ef dat don't beat my time! De queen er spades! W'en Lucindy year dat hit'll tickle 'er, sho'!"

Miss Becky continued to run the cards back and forth through her fingers.

"Here's a bundle an' a journey, and here's Lucinda. An' here's ole Spite Calderwood."

She held the cards toward the negro and touched the king of clubs.

"De Lord he'p my soul!" exclaimed Free Joe with a chuckle. "De faver's dar.[2] Yesser, dat's him! W'at de matter 'long wid all un um, Miss Becky?"

The old woman added the second pile of cards to the first, and then the third, still running them through her fingers slowly and critically. By this time the piece of pine in the fireplace had wrapped itself in a mantle of flame, illuminating the cabin and throwing into strange relief the figure of Miss Becky as she sat studying the cards. She frowned ominously at the cards and mumbled a few words to herself. Then she dropped her hands in her lap and gazed once more into the fire. Her shadow danced and capered on the wall and floor behind her, as if, looking over her shoulder into the future, it could behold a rare spectacle. After a while she picked up the cup that had been turned on the hearth. The coffee-grounds, shaken around, presented what seemed to be a most intricate map.

"Here's the journey," said Miss Becky, presently; "here's the big road, here's rivers to cross, here's the bundle to tote." She paused and sighed. "They hain't no names writ here, an' what it all means I'll never tell you. Cajy, I wish you'd be so good as to han' me my pipe."

"I hain't no hand wi' the kyards," said Cajy, as he handed the pipe, "but I reckin I can patch out your misinformation, Becky, bekaze the other day, whiles I was a-finishin' up Mizzers Perdue's rollin'-pin, I hearn a rattlin' in the road. I looked out, an' Spite Calderwood was a-driven' by in his buggy, an' thar sot Lucinda by him. It'd in-about drapt out er my min'."

Free Joe sat on the door-sill and fumbled at his hat, flinging it from one hand to the other.

"You ain't see em gwine back, is you, Mars Cajy?" he asked after a while.

"Ef they went back by this road," said Mr. Staley, with the air of one who is accustomed to weigh well his words, "it must 'a' bin enduring' of the time whiles I was asleep, bekaze I hain't bin no furder from my shop than to yon bed."

"Well, sir!" exclaimed Free Joe in an awed tone, which Mr. Staley seemed to regard as a tribute to his extraordinary powers of statement.

[2] I.e., "the resemblance [favor] is there."

"Ef it's my beliefs you want," continued the old man, "I'll pitch 'em at you fair and free. My beliefs is that Spite Calderwood is gone an' took Lucindy outen the county. Bless your heart and soul! when Spite Calderwood meets the Old Boy[3] in the road they'll be a turrible scuffle. You mark what I tell you."

Free Joe, still fumbling with his hat, rose and leaned against the door-facing. He seemed to be embarrassed. Presently he said:

"I speck I better be gittin' 'long. Nex' time I see Lucindy, I'm gwine tell 'er w'at Miss Becky say 'about de queen er spades—dat I is. Ef dat don't tickle 'er, dey ain't no nigger 'oman never bin tickle'."

He paused a moment, as though waiting for some remark or comment, some confirmation of misfortune, or, at the very least, some endorsement of his suggestion that Lucinda would be greatly pleased to know that she had figured as the queen of spades; but neither Miss Becky nor her brother said anything.

"One minnit ridin' in the buggy 'longside er Mars Spite, en de nex' highfalutin' 'roun' playin' de queen er spades. Mon, deze yer nigger gals gittin' up in de pictur's; dey sholy is."

With a brief "Good night, Miss Becky, Mars Cajy," Free Joe went out into the darkness, followed by little Dan. He made his way to the poplar, where Lucinda had been in the habit of meeting him, and sat down. He sat there a long time; he sat there until little Dan, growing restless, trotted off in the direction of the Calderwood place. Dozing against the poplar, in the gray dawn of the morning, Free Joe heard Spite Calderwood's fox-hounds in full cry a mile away.

"Shoo!" he exclaimed, scratching his head, and laughing to himself, "dem ar dogs is des a-warming' dat old fox up."

But it was Dan the hounds were after, and the little dog came back no more. Free Joe waited and waited, until he grew tired of waiting. He went back the next night and waited, and for many nights thereafter. His waiting was in vain, and yet he never regarded it as in vain. Careless and shabby as he was, Free Joe was thoughtful enough to have his theory. He was convinced that little Dan had found Lucinda, and that some night when the moon was shining brightly through the trees, the dog would rouse him from his dreams as he sat sleeping at the foot of the poplar tree, and he would open his eyes and behold Lucinda standing over him, laughing merrily as of old; and then he thought what fun they would have about the queen of spades.

How many nights Free Joe waited at the foot of the poplar tree for Lucinda and little Dan no one can ever know. He kept no account of them, and they were not recorded by Micajah Staley nor by Miss Becky. The season ran into summer and then into fall. One night he went to the Staley cabin, cut the two old people an armful of wood, and seated himself on the doorsteps, where he rested. He was always thankful—and proud, as it seemed—when Miss Becky gave him a cup of coffee, which she was sometimes thoughtful enough to do. He was especially thankful on this particular night.

"You er still layin' off for to strike up wi' Lucindy out thar in the woods, I reckon," said Micajah Staley, smiling grimly. The situation was not without its humorous aspects.

"Oh, dey er comin', Mars Cajy, dey er comin', sho," Free Joe replied. "I boun' you dey'll come; en w'en dey does come, I'll des take en fetch um yer, whar you kin see um wid you own eyes, you en Miss Becky."

"No," said Mr. Staley, with a quick and emphatic gesture of disapproval. "Don't! don't fetch 'em anywheres. Stay right wi' 'em as long as may be."

---

[3]Satan.

Free Joe chuckled, and slipped away into the night, while the two old people sat gazing in the fire. Finally Micajah spoke.

"Look at that nigger; look at 'im. He's pine-blank as happy now as a killdee[4] by a mill-race. You can't faze 'em. I'd in-about give up my t'other hand ef I could stan' flat-tooted, an' grin at trouble like that there nigger."

"Niggers is niggers," said Miss Becky, smiling grimly, "an' you can't rub it out; yit I lay, I've seed a heap of white people lots meaner'n Free Joe. He grins—an' that's nigger—but I've ketched his under jaw a-tremblin' when Lucindy's name uz brung up. An' I tell you," she went on, bridling up a little, and speaking with almost fierce emphasis, "the Old Boy's done sharpened his claws for Spite Calderwood. You'll see it."

"Me, Rebecca?" said Mr. Staley, hugging his palsied arm; "me? I hope not."

"Well, you'll know it then," said Miss Becky, laughing heartily at her brother's look of alarm.

The next morning Micajah Staley had occasion to go into the woods after a piece of timber. He saw Free Joe sitting at the foot of the poplar, and the sight vexed him somewhat.

"Git up from there," he cried, "an' go an' arn your livin'. A mighty purty pass it's come to, when great big buck niggers can lie a-snorin' in the woods all day, when t'other folks is got to be up an' a-gwine.[5] Git up from there!"

Receiving no response, Mr. Staley went to Free Joe, and shook him by the shoulder; but the negro made no response. He was dead. His hat was off, his head was bent, and a smile was on his face. It was as if he had bowed and smiled when death stood before him, humble to the last. His clothes were ragged; his hands were rough and callous; his shoes were literally tied together with strings; he was shabby in the extreme. A passer-by, glancing at him, could have no idea that such a humble creature had been summoned as a witness before the Lord God of Hosts.

1887

Mark Twain   *1835–1910*

Mark Twain's rise to fame began with the publication in 1865 of "Jim Smiley and His Jumping Frog," a comic western tale (he later called it a "villainous backwoods sketch") that he heard in a mining camp not far from his cabin on Jackass Hill in the California gold country. By the time of his death, forty-five years later, Twain's popularity as an author and lecturer was worldwide, and he had become one of the most celebrated Americans of his day.

"The Notorious Jumping Frog of Calaveras County," as his frog story was later titled, was one of the many tall tales Twain heard in the western mining camps where he had gone in 1861 when he was twenty-five. His adventurous boyhood had been spent in Hannibal, Missouri, on the Mississippi River. At the death of his father, in 1847, Twain

---

[4]A shore bird named after its shrill, two-syllable cry. It feeds at mud flats and shore lines, such as those along a mill-race—the canal that brings water to a mill wheel.

[5]"Going."

had left school to be apprenticed to a printer. A brief but glorious career as a Mississippi River steamboat pilot ended when the river was blockaded at the beginning of the Civil War, and after a short term of soldiering as a Confederate volunteer, Twain went to Nevada, hoping to strike it rich in the silver fields. When his mining schemes failed, he joined the staff of the Virginia City Territorial Enterprise, *exchanged his real name, Samuel L. Clemens, for a pseudonym, "Mark Twain," and began his career as a frontier humorist.*

In 1866, after six years as a miner, newspaper reporter, and lecturer in California, Nevada, and Hawaii, Twain went east, responding, he said, to "a 'call' to literature, of a low order—i.e., humorous." He took with him a reputation as "the wild humorist of the Pacific Slope" and a lively imagination that had led him to turn many of his newspaper "reports" into burlesques and comic sketches.

While in New York, Twain was commissioned by a San Francisco paper to sail on a five-months' voyage with a group of American tourists and to report their confrontations with the cultural and religious shrines of Europe and the Holy Land. Upon his return to America, Twain gathered his irreverent newspaper articles, revised them, and published them as Innocents Abroad *(1869). Next came* Roughing It *(1872), a narrative of his original journey west. His first attempt at novel writing was* The Gilded Age *(1873), on which he collaborated with the journalist and essayist Charles Dudley Warner (1829–1900). The novel was a muddled failure, but it gave its name to the boom times, the post-Civil War age of unbridled individualism and speculation, which it satirized.*

Twain's nostalgic recollections of his early boyhood in Hannibal stirred him to write his "boys' book," Tom Sawyer *(1876) and its sequel,* Huckleberry Finn *(1884). His memories of his three years as a "cub" and master pilot on the Mississippi inspired* Life on the Mississippi *(1883). By the time he came to write* A Connecticut Yankee in King Arthur's Court *(1889), with its angry satire on royalty, religion, and the chivalric ideals of Arthurian England, his work had become more serious and critical. By the 1890s the amused tolerance that had once typified his writing had been displaced by increasingly bitter attacks on the injustices of society and the folly of man. In* Pudd'n-head Wilson *(1894) the humor was slight and the attacks on bigotry furious. By the turn of the century, with the publication of "The Man That Corrupted Hadleyburg" (1900), "To the Person Sitting in Darkness" (1901), and "The Mysterious Stranger" (1916), his obsessive vision of man as a greedy numbskull, oafish, hypocritical, cruel, and predatory, was wholly apparent. By the end of his life, moved by his fears, guilt, and incandescent rages, Twain had come to detest even the readers and audiences who had given him fame and prosperity.*

Although traces of Twain's later pessimism are evident in his earliest works, his change from jovial humorist to despairing determinist has been explained as the result of a series of personal catastrophes. The deaths of his wife and two daughters left him embittered and lonely. The failure of his publishing firm and a series of bad financial investments brought him humiliation and bankruptcy, leading him to travel throughout the world on a lecture series to pay off his debts, a long and exhausting experience he recorded with barely disguised weariness in Following the Equator *(1897). In 1906 he began to record the details of much of the best and the worst of his life, portions of which appeared as his* Autobiography *(1924), published posthumously as was the collection entitled* Letters from the Earth *(1962), which contained the most despairing of his pronouncements and his last raging volleys at the "damned human race."*

Much of Twain's writing was uneven hack work and vastly exaggerated lampoon marred by flippancy and misdirected bitterness. As a satirist he employed his common, lowly characters as vernacular spokesman to deflate the values of the official culture of his day and what he saw as the rattle-brained folly of American politics and imperialism. He was a bitter and withering foe who never forgot insults or flaws, real or imagined, whether from friends or enemies, living or, as in the case of James Fenimore Cooper, dead. Though his best work was weakened by the sound of his fury, by his epic despair, and irrational quirks, he had achieved not only burlesque and bitter comedy but high art. He wrote his masterpiece, Huckleberry Finn, *at a time when the lighthearted qualities of his earlier days were in balance with his later skepticism, and the novel has come to be recognized as one of the great works of American literature. It displayed the major achievements of his art: the carefully controlled point of view with its implicit ironies expressed through the voice of a semiliterate boy, the masterful use of dialects, the felicitous balancing of nostalgic romanticism and realism, humor and pathos, innocence and evil, all united for a journey down the river that serves as the mythic center of the novel. Originally judged to be simply another "boys' book," like* Tom Sawyer, *the story of Huck and Jim and the great river was roundly condemned as too indecent for innocent young eyes, but its inherent appeal— and its scandalous reputation—insured its success, and it has become one of the most popular books of all times, selling over 13,000,000 copies in editions printed throughout the world.*

Through such works as Huckleberry Finn *and* Life on the Mississippi *Twain shaped the world's view of America and had a profound impact on the development of American writing. His presentation of native American material, his use of the vernacular idiom, his departures from the traditions of nineteenth-century gentility, and his sense of alienation influenced numerous American writers of the twentieth century, among them Ernest Hemingway, who acknowledged their common debt by writing, "All modern American literature comes from one book by Mark Twain called* Huckleberry Finn *. . . it's the best book we've had . . . There was nothing before. There has been nothing so good since."*

FURTHER READING: *The Writings of Mark Twain*, 37 Vols., ed. A. Paine, 1922–1925, which will soon be superseded by the following forthcoming editions: *The Mark Twain Papers*, 15 vols. projected, ed. F. Anderson, 1969–, and *The Works of Mark Twain*, 24 vols. projected, ed. J. Gerber, 1972–. A. Paine, *Mark Twain, A Biography*, 3 vols., 1912; V. Brooks, *The Ordeal of Mark Twain*, 1920, 1933; B. DeVoto, *Mark Twain's America*, 1932; E. Wagenknecht, *Mark Twain, The Man and His Work*, 1935, 1961, 1967; E. Branch, *The Literary Apprenticeship of Mark Twain*, 1950; G. Bellamy, *Mark Twain as Literary Artist*, 1950; D. Wecter, *Sam Clemens of Hannibal*, 1952; P. Fatout, *Mark Twain on the Lecture Circuit*, 1960, 1969; W. Blair, *Mark Twain and Huck Finn*, 1960; R. Salomon, *Twain and the Image of History*, 1961; L. Budd, *Mark Twain, Social Philosopher*, 1962; H. Smith, *Mark Twain, The Development of a Writer*, 1962; J. Kaplan, *Mr. Clemens and Mark Twain*, 1966; J. Cox, *M. Twain, The Fate of Humor*, 1966; A. Scott, *Mark Twain at Large*, 1969; M. Geismar, *Mark Twain, An American Prophet*, 1970; J. Seelye, *The True Adventures of Huckleberry Finn*, 1970; H. Hill, *Mark Twain, God's Fool*, 1973, 1975; W. Gibson, *The Art of Mark Twain*, 1976; D. Sloane, *Mark Twain as a Literary Comedian*, 1979; J. Johnson, *Mark Twain and the Limits of Power*, 1982; *Critical Essays on Mark Twain, 1867–1910*, ed. L. Budd, 1983; L. Budd, *Our Mark Twain*, 1983; E. Emerson, *The Authentic Mark Twain*, 1984; E. Long, *The New Mark Twain Handbook*, 1985; J. Wilson, *A Reader's Guide to the Short Stories of Mark Twain*, 1987.

TEXTS: "The Dandy Frightening the Squatter," *Carpet-Bag*, May 1, 1852; "The Notorious Jumping Frog of Calaveras County," "The Story of the Bad Little Boy," and "The Story of the Good Little Boy," *Mark Twain's Sketches, New and Old*, 1875; "Buck Fanshaw's Funeral" and "The Story of the Old Ram," *Roughing It*, 1872; "Whittier Birthday Dinner Speech," *Harvard Library Bulletin*, Spring 1955; "Baker's Bluejay Yarn," *A Tramp Abroad*, 1880; *Adventures of Huckleberry Finn*, 1885; "Fenimore Cooper's Literary Offences," *North American Review*, July 1895; "The Man That Corrupted Hadleyburg," *Harper's*, December 1899; "The War Prayer," *Europe and Elsewhere*, 1923.

THE DANDY FRIGHTENING THE SQUATTER[1]

By S. L. C.

About thirteen years ago, when the now flourishing young city of Hannibal, on the Mississippi River, was but a "wood-yard," surrounded by a few huts, belonging to some hardy *"squatters,"* and such a thing as a steamboat was considered quite a sight, the following incident occurred:

A tall, brawny woodsman stood leaning against a tree which stood upon the bank of the river, gazing at some approaching object, which our readers would easily have discovered to be a steamboat.

About half an hour elapsed, and the boat was moored, and the hands busily engaged in taking on wood.

Now among the many passengers on this boat, both male and female, was a spruce young dandy, with a killing moustache, &c., who seemed bent on making an impression upon the hearts of the young ladies on board, and to do this, he thought he must perform some heroic deed. Observing our squatter friend, he imagined this to be a fine opportunity to bring himself into notice; so, stepping into the cabin,[2] he said:

"Ladies, if you wish to enjoy a good laugh, step out on the guards.[3] I intend to frighten that gentleman into fits who stands on the bank."

The ladies complied with the request, and our dandy drew from his bosom a formidable looking bowie-knife,[4] and thrust it into his belt; then, taking a large horse-pistol[5] in each hand, he seemed satisfied that all was right. Thus equipped, he strode on shore, with an air which seemed to say—"The hopes of a nation depend on me." Marching up to the woodsman, he exclaimed:

"Found you at last, have I? You are the very man I've been looking for these three weeks! Say your prayers!" he continued, presenting his pistols, "you'll make a capital barn door, and I shall drill the key-hole myself!"

The squatter calmly surveyed him a moment, and then, drawing back a step, he planted his huge fist directly between the eyes of his astonished antagonist, who, in a moment, was floundering in the turbid waters of the Mississippi.

Every passenger on the boat had by this time collected on the guards, and the shout that now went up from the crowd speedily restored the crest-fallen hero to his senses, and, as he was sneaking off towards the boat, was thus accosted by his conquerer:

"I say, yeou, next time yeou come around drillin' key-holes, don't forget yer old acquaintances!"

The ladies unanimously voted the knife and pistols to the victor.

1852

---

[1]Published in the Boston *Carpet-Bag*, May 1, 1852, when Twain was sixteen years old. It was his first tale to be published and, with the exception of short contributions he may have made to the Hannibal papers, his first appearance in print.

[2]A large public room for the use of a ship's passengers.

[3]Sections of the deck that extend out from a ship's side.

[4]Hunting knife with a large blade, said to be named after the famous Indian fighter Jim Bowie.

[5]A large pistol usually carried in a holster attached to a horse saddle.

THE NOTORIOUS JUMPING FROG OF CALAVERAS[1] COUNTY

In compliance with the request of a friend of mine, who wrote me from the East, I called on good-natured, garrulous old Simon Wheeler, and inquired after my friend's friend, Leonidas W. Smiley, as requested to do, and I hereunto append the result. I have a lurking suspicion that *Leonidas W.* Smiley is a myth; that my friend never knew such a personage; and that he only conjectured that if I asked old Wheeler about him, it would remind him of his infamous *Jim* Smiley, and he would go to work and bore me to death with some exasperating reminiscence of him as long and as tedious as it should be useless to me. If that was the design, it succeeded.

I found Simon Wheeler dozing comfortably by the bar-room stove of the dilapidated tavern in the decayed mining camp of Angel's,[2] and I noticed that he was fat and bald-headed, and had an expression of winning gentleness and simplicity upon his tranquil countenance. He roused up, and gave me good day. I told him that a friend of mine had commissioned me to make some inquiries about a cherished companion of his boyhood named *Leonidas W.* Smiley—*Rev. Leonidas W.* Smiley, a young minister of the Gospel, who he had heard was at one time a resident of Angel's Camp. I added that if Mr. Wheeler could tell me anything about this Rev. Leonidas W. Smiley, I would feel under many obligations to him.

Simon Wheeler backed me into a corner and blockaded me there with his chair, and then sat down and reeled off the monotonous narrative which follows this paragraph. He never smiled, he never frowned, he never changed his voice from the gentle-flowing key to which he tuned his initial sentence, he never betrayed the slightest suspicion of enthusiasm; but all through the interminable narrative there ran a vein of impressive earnestness and sincerity, which showed me plainly that, so far from his imagining that there was anything ridiculous or funny about his story, he regarded it as a really important matter, and admired its two heroes as men of transcendent genius in *finesse.* I let him go on in his own way, and never interrupted him once.

"Rev. Leonidas W. H'm, Reverend Le—well, there was a feller here once by the name of *Jim* Smiley, in the winter of '49—or maybe it was the spring of '50— I don't recollect exactly, somehow, though what makes me think it was one or the other is because I remember the big flume[3] warn't finished when he first come to the camp; but anyway, he was the curiousest man about always betting on anything that turned up you ever see, if he could get anybody to bet on the other side; and if he couldn't he'd change sides. Any way that suited the other man would suit *him*—any way just so's he got a bet, *he* was satisfied. But still he was lucky, uncommon lucky; he most always come out winner. He was always ready and laying for a chance; there couldn't be no solit'ry thing mentioned but that feller'd offer to bet on it, and take ary side you please, as I was just telling you. If there was a horse-race, you'd find him flush or you'd find him busted at the end of it; if there was a dog-fight, he'd bet on it; if there was a cat-fight, he'd

---

[1] "Pronounced Cal-e-*va*-ras."—Twain's note. First published as "Jim Smiley and His Jumping Frog," in 1865. Later versions were titled "The Celebrated . . ." or, as here, "The Notorious Jumping Frog of Calaveras County."

[2] Angel's Camp, a mining settlement in Calaveras County, California.

[3] An inclined waterway, usually made of wood, through which water is carried for use in hydraulic mining.

bet on it; if there was a chicken-fight, he'd bet on it; why, if there was two birds setting on a fence, he would bet you which one would fly first; or if there was a camp-meeting, he would be there reg'lar to bet on Parson Walker, which he judged to be the best exhorter about here, and so he was too, and a good man. If he even see a straddle-bug[4] start to go anywheres, he would bet you how long it would take him to get to—to wherever he was going to, and if you took him up, he would foller that straddle-bug to Mexico but what he would find out where he was bound for and how long he was on the road. Lots of the boys here has seen that Smiley, and can tell you about him. Why, it never made no difference to *him*—he'd bet on *any* thing—the dangdest feller. Parson Walker's wife laid very sick once for a good while, and it seemed as if they warn't going to save her; but one morning he come in, and Smiley up and asked him how she was, and he said she was considerable better—thank the Lord for his inf'nite mercy—and coming on so smart that with the blessing of Prov'dence she'd get well yet; and Smiley, before he thought, says, 'Well, I'll resk two-and-a-half she don't anyway.'

"Thish-yer Smiley had a mare—the boys called her the fifteen-minute nag, but that was only in fun, you know, because of course she was faster than that— and he used to win money on that horse, for all she was so slow and always had the asthma, or the distemper, or the consumption, or something of that kind. They used to give her two or three hundred yards' start, and then pass her under way; but always at the fag end of the race she'd get excited and desperate like, and come cavorting and straddling up, and scattering her legs around limber, sometimes in the air, and sometimes out to one side among the fences, and kicking up m-o-r-e dust and raising m-o-r-e racket with her coughing and sneezing and blowing her nose—and *always* fetch up at the stand just about a neck ahead, as near as you could cipher it down.

"And he had a little small bull-pup, that to look at him you'd think he warn't worth a cent but to set around and look ornery and lay for a chance to steal something. But as soon as money was up on him he was a different dog; his under-jaw'd begin to stick out like the fo'castle of a steamboat, and his teeth would uncover and shine like the furnaces. And a dog might tackle him and bully-rag him, and bite him, and throw him over his shoulder two or three times, and Andrew Jackson—which was the name of the pup—Andrew Jackson would never let on but what *he* was satisfied, and hadn't expected nothing else—and the bets being doubled and doubled on the other side all the time, till the money was all up; and then all of a sudden he would grab that other dog jest by the j'int of his hind leg and freeze to it—not chaw, you understand, but only just grip and hang on till they throwed up the sponge, if it was a year. Smiley always come out winner on that pup, till he harnessed a dog once that didn't have no hind legs, because they'd been sawed off in a circular saw, and when the thing had gone along far enough, and the money was all up, and he come to make a snatch for his pet holt, he see in a minute how he'd been imposed on, and how the other dog had him in the door, so to speak, and he 'peared surprised, and then he looked sorter discouraged-like, and didn't try no more to win the fight, and so he got shucked out bad. He give Smiley a look, as much as to say his heart was broke, and it was *his* fault, for putting up a dog that hadn't no hind legs for him to take holt of, which was his main dependence in a fight, and then he limped off a piece and laid down and died. It was a good pup, was that Andrew Jackson, and would have made a name for hisself if he'd lived, for the stuff was in him

---

[4]A beetle with long legs, a tumble-bug.

and he had genius—I know it, because he hadn't no opportunities to speak of, and it don't stand to reason that a dog could make such a fight as he could under them circumstances if he hadn't no talent. It always makes me feel sorry when I think of that last fight of his'n, and the way it turned out.

"Well, thish-yer Smiley had rat-tarriers, and chicken cocks, and tomcats and all them kind of things, till you couldn't rest, and you couldn't fetch nothing for him to bet on but he'd match you. He ketched a frog one day, and took him home, and said he cal'lated to educate him; and so he never done nothing for three months but set in his back yard and learn that frog to jump. And you bet you he *did* learn him, too. He'd give him a little punch behind, and the next minute you'd see that frog whirling in the air like a doughnut—see him turn one summerset,[5] or maybe a couple, if he got a good start, and come down flat-footed and all right, like a cat. He got him up so in the matter of ketching flies, and kep' him in practice so constant, that he'd nail a fly every time as fur as he could see him. Smiley said all a frog wanted was education, and he could do 'most anything—and I believe him. Why, I've seen him set Dan'l Webster down here on this floor—Dan'l Webster was the name of the frog—and sing out, 'Flies, Dan'l, flies!" and quicker'n you could wink he'd spring straight up and snake a fly off'n the counter there, and flop down on the floor ag'in as solid as a gob of mud, and fall to scratching the side of his head with his hind foot as indifferent as if he hadn't no idea he'd been doin' any more'n any frog might do. You never see a frog so modest and straightfor'ard as he was, for all he was so gifted. And when it come to fair and square jumping on a dead level, he could get over more ground at one straddle than any animal of his breed you ever see. Jumping on a dead level was his strong suit, you understand; and when it come to that, Smiley would ante up money on him as long as he had a red.[6] Smiley was monstrous proud of his frog, and well he might be, for fellers that had traveled and been everywheres all said he laid over any frog that ever *they* see.

"Well, Smiley kep' the beast in a little lattice box, and he used to fetch him down-town sometimes and lay for a bet. One day a feller—a stranger in the camp, he was—come acrost him with his box, and says:

" 'What might it be that you've got in the box?'

"And Smiley says, sorter indifferent-like, 'It might be a parrot, or it might be a canary, maybe, but it ain't—it's only just a frog.'

"And the feller took it, and looked at it careful, and turned it round this way and that, and says, 'H'm—so 'tis. Well, what's *he* good for?'

" 'Well,' Smiley says, easy and careless, 'he's good enough for *one* thing, I should judge—he can outjump any frog in Calaveras County.'

"The feller took the box again, and took another long, particular look, and give it back to Smiley, and says, very deliberate, 'Well,' he says, 'I don't see no p'ints about that frog that's any better'n any other frog.'

" 'Maybe you don't,' Smiley says. 'Maybe you understand frogs and maybe you don't understand 'em; maybe you've had experience, and maybe you ain't only a amature, as it were. Anyways, I've got *my* opinion, and I'll resk forty dollars that he can outjump any frog in Calaveras County.'

"And the feller studied a minute, and then says, kinder sad-like, 'Well, I'm only a stranger here, and I ain't got no frog; but if I had a frog, I'd bet you.'

"And then Smiley says, 'That's all right—that's all right—if you'll hold my box a minute, I'll go and get you a frog.' And so the feller took the box, and put up his forty dollars along with Smiley's, and set down to wait.

[5]Sommersault. [6]A "red cent," a copper penny.

"So he set there a good while thinking and thinking to himself, and then he got the frog out and prized his mouth open and took a teaspoon and filled him full of quail-shot—filled him pretty near up to his chin—and set him on the floor. Smiley he went to the swamp and slopped around in the mud for a long time, and finally he ketched a frog, and fetched him in, and give him to this feller, and says:

"Now, if you're ready, set him alongside of Dan'l, with his fore paws just even with Dan'l's, and I'll give the word.' Then he says, 'One—two—three—*git!*' and him and the feller touched up the frogs from behind, and the new frog hopped off lively, but Dan'l give a heave, and hysted up his shoulders—so—like a Frenchman, but it warn't no use—he couldn't budge; he was planted as solid as a church, and he couldn't no more stir than if he was anchored out. Smiley was a good deal surprised, and he was disgusted too, but he didn't have no idea what the matter was, of course.

"The feller took the money and started away; and when he was going out at the door, he sorter jerked his thumb over his shoulder—so—at Dan'l, and says again, very deliberate, 'Well,' he says, '*I* don't see no p'ints about that frog that's any better'n any other frog.'

"Smiley he stood scratching his head and looking down at Dan'l a long time, and at last he says, 'I do wonder what in the nation[7] that frog throw'd off for— I wonder if there ain't something the matter with him—he 'pears to look mighty baggy, somehow.' And he ketched Dan'l by the nap of the neck, and hefted him, and says, 'Why blame my cats if he don't weigh five pound!" and turned him upside down and he belched out a double handful of shot. And then he see how it was, and he was the maddest man—he set the frog down and took out after that feller, but he never ketched him. And—"

[Here Simon Wheeler heard his name called from the front yard, and got up to see what was wanted.] And turning to me as he moved away, he said: "Just set where you are, stranger, and rest easy—I ain't going to be gone a second."

But, by your leave, I did not think that a continuation of the history of the enterprising vagabond *Jim* Smiley would be likely to afford me much information concerning the Rev. *Leonidas W.* Smiley, and so I started away.

At the door I met the sociable Wheeler returning, and he button-holed me and recommenced:

"Well, thish-yer Smiley had a yaller one-eyed cow that didn't have no tail, only just a short stump like a bannanner, and—"

However, lacking both time and inclination, I did not wait to hear about the afflicted cow, but took my leave.

1865

THE STORY OF THE BAD LITTLE BOY

Once there was a bad little boy whose name was Jim—though, if you will notice, you will find that bad little boys are nearly always called James in your Sunday-school books. It was strange, but still it was true, that this one was called Jim.

He didn't have any sick mother, either—a sick mother who was pious and had

---

[7]Euphemism for "damnation."

the consumption,[1] and would be glad to lie down in the grave and be at rest but for the strong love she bore her boy, and the anxiety she felt that the world might be harsh and cold toward him when she was gone. Most bad boys in the Sunday-school books are named James, and have sick mothers, who teach them to say, "Now, I lay me down," etc., and sing them to sleep with sweet, plaintive voices, and then kiss them good night, and kneel down by the bedside and weep. But it was different with this fellow. He was named Jim, and there wasn't anything the matter with his mother—no consumption, nor anything of that kind. She was rather stout than otherwise, and she was not pious; moreover, she was not anxious on Jim's account. She said if he were to break his neck it wouldn't be much loss. She always spanked Jim to sleep, and she never kissed him good night; on the contrary, she boxed his ears when she was ready to leave him.

Once this little bad boy stole the key of the pantry, and slipped in there and helped himself to some jam, and filled up the vessel with tar, so that his mother would never know the difference; but all at once a terrible feeling didn't come over him, and something didn't seem to whisper to him, "Is it right to disobey my mother? Isn't it sinful to do this? Where do bad little boys go who gobble up their good kind mother's jam?" and then he didn't kneel down all alone and promise never to be wicked any more, and rise up with a light, happy heart, and go and tell his mother all about it, and beg her forgiveness, and be blessed by her with tears of pride and thankfulness in her eyes. No; that is the way with all other bad boys in the books; but it happened otherwise with this Jim, strangely enough. He ate that jam, and said it was bully, in his sinful, vulgar way; and he put in the tar, and said that was bully also, and laughed, and observed "that the old woman would get up and snort" when she found it out; and when she did find it out, he denied knowing anything about it, and she whipped him severely, and he did the crying himself. Everything about this boy was curious—everything turned out differently with him from the way it does to the bad Jameses in the books.

Once he climbed up in Farmer Acorn's apple tree to steal apples, and the limb didn't break, and he didn't fall and break his arm, and get torn by the farmer's great dog, and then languish on a sick-bed for weeks, and repent and become good. Oh, no; he stole as many apples as he wanted and came down all right; and he was all ready for the dog, too, and knocked him endways with a brick when he came to tear him. It was very strange—nothing like it ever happened in those mild little books with marbled backs,[2] and with pictures in them of men with swallow-tailed coats and bell-crowned hats, and pantaloons that are short in the legs, and women with the waists of their dresses under their arms, and no hoops on.[3] Nothing like it in any of the Sunday-school books.

Once he stole the teacher's penknife, and, when he was afraid it would be found out and he would get whipped, he slipped it into George Wilson's cap—poor Widow Wilson's son, the moral boy, the good little boy of the village, who always obeyed his mother, and never told an untruth, and was fond of his lessons, and infatuated with Sunday-school. And when the knife dropped from the cap, and poor George hung his head and blushed, as if in conscious guilt, and the grieved teacher charged the theft upon him, and was just in the very act of bringing the switch down upon his trembling shoulders, a white-haired, improbable justice of the peace did not suddenly appear in their midst, and

[1]Tuberculosis.
[2]Pretentious books with bindings colored to resemble marble.
[3]Twain describes the "proper" dress of genteel Americans in the mid-nineteenth century.

strike an attitude and say, "Spare this noble boy—there stands the cowering culprit! I was passing the school door at recess, and, unseen myself, I saw the theft committed!" And then Jim didn't get whaled, and the venerable justice didn't read the tearful school a homily, and take George by the hand and say such a boy deserved to be exalted, and then tell him to come and make his home with him, and sweep out the office, and make fires, and run errands, and chop wood, and study law, and help his wife do household labors, and have all the balance of the time to play, and get forty cents a month, and be happy. No; it would have happened that way in the books, but it didn't happen that way to Jim. No meddling old clam of a justice dropped in to make trouble, and so the model boy George got thrashed, and Jim was glad of it because, you know, Jim hated moral boys. Jim said he was "down on them milksops." Such was the coarse language of this bad, neglected boy.

But the strangest thing that ever happened to Jim was the time he went boating on Sunday, and didn't get drowned, and that other time that he got caught out in the storm when he was fishing on Sunday, and didn't get struck by lightning. Why, you might look, and look, all through the Sunday-school books from now till next Christmas, and you would never come across anything like this. Oh, no; you would find that all the bad boys who go boating on Sunday invariably get drowned; and all the bad boys who get caught out in storms when they are fishing on Sunday infallibly get struck by lightning. Boats with bad boys in them always upset on Sunday, and it always storms when bad boys go fishing on the Sabbath. How this Jim ever escaped is a mystery to me.

This Jim bore a charmed life—that must have been the way of it. Nothing could hurt him. He even gave the elephant in the menagerie a plug of tobacco, and the elephant didn't knock the top of his head off with his trunk. He browsed around the cupboard after essence of peppermint, and didn't make a mistake and drink *aqua fortis*.[4] He stole his father's gun and went hunting on the Sabbath, and didn't shoot three or four of his fingers off. He struck his little sister on the temple with his fist when he was angry, and she didn't linger in pain through long summer days, and die with sweet words of forgiveness upon her lips that redoubled the anguish of his breaking heart. No; she got over it. He ran off and went to sea at last, and didn't come back and find himself sad and alone in the world, his loved ones sleeping in the quiet churchyard, and the vine-embowered home of his boyhood tumbled down and gone to decay. Ah, no; he came home as drunk as a piper, and got into the station-house[5] the first thing.

And he grew up and married, and raised a large family, and brained them all with an ax one night, and got wealthy by all manner of cheating and rascality; and now he is the infernalest wickedest scoundrel in his native village, and is universally respected, and belongs to the legislature.

So you see there never was a bad James in the Sunday-school books that had such a streak of luck as this sinful Jim with the charmed life.

1865

THE STORY OF THE GOOD LITTLE BOY[1]

Once there was a good little boy by the name of Jacob Blivens. He always obeyed his parents, no matter how absurd and unreasonable their demands

[4]Nitric acid.   [5]Jail.
[1]"Written about 1865."—Twain's note.

were; and he always learned his book, and never was late at Sabbath-school. He would not play hookey, even when his sober judgment told him it was the most profitable thing he could do. None of the other boys could ever make that boy out, he acted so strangely. He wouldn't lie, no matter how convenient it was. He just said it was wrong to lie, and that was sufficient for him. And he was so honest that he was simply ridiculous. The curious ways that that Jacob had, surpassed everything. He wouldn't play marbles on Sunday, he wouldn't rob birds' nests, he wouldn't give hot pennies to organ-grinders' monkeys; he didn't seem to take any interest in any kind of rational amusement. So the other boys used to try to reason it out and come to an understanding of him, but they couldn't arrive at any satisfactory conclusion. As I said before, they could only figure out a sort of vague idea that he was "afflicted," and so they took him under their protection, and never allowed any harm to come to him.

This good little boy read all the Sunday-school books; they were his greatest delight. This was the whole secret of it. He believed in the good little boys they put in the Sunday-school books; he had every confidence in them. He longed to come across one of them alive once; but he never did. They all died before his time, maybe. Whenever he read about a particularly good one he turned over quickly to the end to see what became of him, because he wanted to travel thousands of miles and gaze on him; but it wasn't any use; that good little boy always died in the last chapter, and there was a picture of the funeral, with all his relations and the Sunday-school children standing around the grave in pantaloons that were too short, and bonnets that were too large, and everybody crying into handkerchiefs that had as much as a yard and a half of stuff in them. He was always headed off in this way. He never could see one of those good little boys on account of his always dying in the last chapter.

Jacob had a noble ambition to be put in a Sunday-school book. He wanted to be put in, with pictures representing him gloriously declining to lie to his mother, and her weeping for joy about it; and pictures representing him standing on the doorstep giving a penny to a poor beggar-woman with six children, and telling her to spend it freely, but not to be extravagant, because extravagance is a sin; and pictures of him magnanimously refusing to tell on the bad boy who always lay in wait for him around the corner as he came from school, and welted him over the head with a lath, and then chased him home, saying "Hi! hi!" as he proceeded. That was the ambition of young Jacob Blivens. He wished to be put in a Sunday-school book. It made him feel a little uncomfortable sometimes when he reflected that the good little boys always died. He loved to live, you know, and this was the most unpleasant feature about being a Sunday-school book boy. He knew it was not healthy to be good. He knew it was more fatal than consumption to be so supernaturally good as the boys in the books were; he knew that none of them had ever been able to stand it long, and it pained him to think that if they put him in a book he wouldn't ever see it, or even if they did get the book out before he died it wouldn't be popular without any picture of his funeral in the back part of it. It couldn't be much of a Sunday-school book that couldn't tell about the advice he gave to the community when he was dying. So at last, of course, he had to make up his mind to do the best he could under the circumstances—to live right, and hang on as long as he could, and have his dying speech all ready when his time came.

But somehow nothing ever went right with this good little boy; nothing ever turned out with him the way it turned out with the good little boys in the books. They always had a good time, and the bad boys had the broken legs; but in his case there was a screw loose somewhere, and it all happened just the other way.

When he found Jim Blake stealing apples, and went under the tree to read to him about the bad little boy who fell out of a neighbor's apple tree and broke his arm, Jim fell out of the tree, too, but he fell on *him* and broke *his* arm, and Jim wasn't hurt at all. Jacob couldn't understand that. There wasn't anything in the books like it.

And once, when some bad boys pushed a blind man over in the mud, and Jacob ran to help him up and receive his blessing, the blind man did not give him any blessing at all, but whacked him over the head with his stick and said he would like to catch him shoving *him* again, and then pretending to help him up. This was not in accordance with any of the books. Jacob looked them all over to see.

One thing that Jacob wanted to do was to find a lame dog that hadn't any place to stay, and was hungry and persecuted, and bring him home and pet him and have that dog's imperishable gratitude. And at last he found one and was happy; and he brought him home and fed him, but when he was going to pet him the dog flew at him and tore all the clothes off him except those that were in front, and made a spectacle of him that was astonishing. He examined authorities, but he could not understand the matter. It was of the same breed of dogs that was in the books, but it acted very differently. Whatever this boy did he got into trouble. The very things the boys in the books got rewarded for turned out to be about the most unprofitable things he could invest in.

Once, when he was on his way to Sunday-school, he saw some bad boys starting off pleasuring in a sailboat. He was filled with consternation, because he knew from his reading that boys who went sailing on Sunday invariably got drowned. So he ran out on a raft to warn them, but a log turned with him and slid him into the river. A man got him out pretty soon, and the doctor pumped the water out of him, and gave him a fresh start with his bellows, but he caught cold and lay sick abed nine weeks. But the most unaccountable thing about it was that the bad boys in the boat had a good time all day, and then reached home alive and well in the most surprising manner. Jacob Blivens said there was nothing like these things in the books. He was perfectly dumbfounded.

When he got well he was a little discouraged, but he resolved to keep on trying anyhow. He knew that so far his experiences wouldn't do to go in a book, but he hadn't yet reached the allotted term of life for good little boys, and he hoped to be able to make a record yet if he could hold on till his time was fully up. If everything else failed he had his dying speech to fall back on.

He examined his authorities, and found that it was now time for him to go to sea as a cabin-boy. He called on a ship captain and made his application, and when the captain asked for his recommendations he proudly drew out a tract and pointed to the words, "To Jacob Blivens, from his affectionate teacher." But the captain was a coarse, vulgar man, and he said, "Oh, that be blowed! *that* wasn't any proof that he knew how to wash dishes or handle a slush-bucket, and he guessed he didn't want him." This was altogether the most extraordinary thing that ever happened to Jacob in all his life. A compliment from a teacher, on a tract, had never failed to move the tenderest emotions of ship captains, and open the way to all offices of honor and profit in their gift—it never had in any book that ever *he* had read. He could hardly believe his senses.

This boy always had a hard time of it. Nothing ever came out according to the authorities with him. At last, one day, when he was around hunting up bad little boys to admonish, he found a lot of them in the old iron foundry fixing up a little joke on fourteen or fifteen dogs, which they had tied together in long procession, and were going to ornament with empty nitro-glycerin cans made fast to their tails. Jacob's heart was touched. He sat down on one of those cans (for he never minded grease when duty was before him), and he took hold of the foremost dog by the collar, and turned his reproving eye upon wicked Tom Jones. But just at that moment Alderman McWelter, full of wrath, stepped in. All the bad boys ran away, but Jacob Blivens rose in conscious innocence and began one of those stately little Sunday-school book speeches which always commence with "Oh, sir!" in dead opposition to the fact that no boy, good or bad, ever starts a remark with "Oh, sir." But the alderman never waited to hear the rest. He took Jacob Blivens by the ear and turned him around, and hit him a whack in the rear with the flat of his hand; and in an instant that good little boy shot out through the roof and soared away toward the sun, with the fragments of those fifteen dogs stringing after him like the tail of a kite. And there wasn't a sign of that alderman or that old iron foundry left on the face of the earth; and, as for young Jacob Blivens, he never got a chance to make his last dying speech after all his trouble fixing it up, unless he made it to the birds; because, although the bulk of him came down all right in a tree-top in an adjoining county, the rest of him was apportioned around among four townships, and so they had to hold five inquests on him to find out whether he was dead or not, and how it occurred. You never saw a boy scattered so.[2]

Thus perished the good little boy who did the best he could, but didn't come out according to the books. Every boy who ever did as he did prospered except him. His case is truly remarkable. It will probably never be accounted for.

1865

from *ROUGHING IT*

Chapter XXXXVII

BUCK FANSHAW'S FUNERAL

Somebody has said that in order to know a community, one must observe the style of its funerals and know what manner of men they bury with most ceremony. I cannot say which class we buried with most éclat[1] in our "flush times," the distinguished public benefactor or the distinguished rough—possibly the two chief grades or grand divisions of society honored their illustrious dead about equally; and hence, no doubt the philosopher I have quoted from would have needed to see two representative funerals in Virgina[2] before forming his estimate of the people.

There was a grand time over Buck Fanshaw when he died. He was a representative citizen. He had "killed his man"—not in his own quarrel, it is true, but in defence of a stranger unfairly beset by numbers. He had kept a sumptuous saloon. He had been the proprietor of a dashing helpmeet whom he could have

[2]"This glycerine catastrophe is borrowed from a floating newspaper item, whose author's name I would give if I knew it."—Twain's note.
[1]French: brilliance, distinction.
[2]Virginia City, Nevada.

discarded without the formality of a divorce. He had held a high position in the fire department and been a very Warwick[3] in politics. When he died there was great lamentation throughout the town, but especially in the vast bottom-stratum of society.

On the inquest it was shown that Buck Fanshaw, in the delirium of a wasting typhoid fever, had taken arsenic, shot himself through the body, cut his throat, and jumped out of a four-story window and broken his neck—and after due deliberation, the jury, sad and tearful, but with intelligence unblinded by its sorrow, brought in a verdict of death "by the visitation of God." What could the world do without juries?

Prodigious preparations were made for the funeral. All the vehicles in town were hired, all the saloons put in mourning, all the municipal and fire-company flags hung at half-mast, and all the firemen ordered to muster in uniform and bring their machines duly draped in black. Now—let us remark in parenthesis— as all the peoples of the earth had representative adventurers in the Silverland, and as each adventurer had brought the slang of his nation or his locality with him, the combination made the slang of Nevada the richest and the most infinitely varied and copious that had ever existed anywhere in the world, perhaps, except in the mines of California in the "early days." Slang was the language of Nevada. It was hard to preach a sermon without it, and be understood. Such phrases as "You bet!" "Oh, no, I reckon not!" "No Irish need apply," and a hundred others, became so common as to fall from the lips of a speaker unconsciously—and very often when they did not touch the subject under discussion and consequently failed to mean anything.

After Buck Fanshaw's inquest, a meeting of the short-haired brotherhood was held, for nothing can be done on the Pacific coast without a public meeting and an expression of sentiment. Regretful resolutions were passed and various committees appointed; among others, a committee of one was deputed to call on the minister, a fragile, gentle, spirituel new fledgling from an Eastern theological seminary, and as yet unacquainted with the ways of the mines. The committeeman, "Scotty" Briggs, made his visit; and in after days it was worth something to hear the minister tell about it. Scotty was a stalwart rough, whose customary suit, when on weighty official business, like committee work, was a fire helmet, flaming red flannel shirt, patent leather belt with spanner[4] and revolver attached, coat hung over arm, and pants stuffed into boot-tops. He formed something of a contrast to the pale theological student. It is fair to say of Scotty, however, in passing, that he had a warm heart, and a strong love for his friends, and never entered into a quarrel when he could reasonably keep out of it. Indeed, it was commonly said that whenever one of Scotty's fights was investigated, it always turned out that it had originally been no affair of his, but that out of native goodheartedness he had dropped in of his own accord to help the man who was getting the worst of it. He and Buck Fanshaw were bosom friends, for years, and had often taken adventurous "potluck" together. On one occasion, they had thrown off their coats and taken the weaker side in a fight among strangers, and after gaining a hard-earned victory, turned and found that the men they were helping had deserted early, and not only that, but had stolen their coats and made off with them! But to return to Scotty's visit to the minister. He was on a sorrowful mission, now, and his face was the picture of woe. Being admitted to the presence he sat down before the clergyman, placed his fire-hat on an unfinished manuscript sermon under the minister's nose, took

[3]Richar Neville (1428–1471), Duke of Warwick, English soldier and statesman.
[4]A wrench made to fit a large bolt or hose coupling.

from it a red silk handkerchief, wiped his brow and heaved a sigh of dismal impressiveness, explanatory of his business. He choked, and even shed tears; but with an effort he mastered his voice and said in lugubrious tones:

"Are you the duck that runs the gospel-mill next door?"

"Am I the—pardon me, I believe I do not understand?"

With another sigh and a half-sob, Scotty rejoined:

"Why you see we are in a bit of trouble, and the boys thought maybe you would give us a lift, if we'd tackle you—that is, if I've got the rights of it and you are the head clerk of the doxology-works[5] next door."

"I am the shepherd in charge of the flock whose fold is next door."

"The which?"

"The spiritual adviser of the little company of believers whose sanctuary adjoins these premises."

Scotty scratched his head, reflected a moment, and then said:

"You ruther hold over me,[6] pard. I reckon I can't call that hand. Ante and pass the buck."

"How? I beg pardon. What did I understand you to say?"

"Well, you've ruther got the bulge[7] on me. Or maybe we've both got the bulge, somehow. You don't smoke[8] me and I don't smoke you. You see, one of the boys has passed in his checks and we want to give him a good send-off, and so the thing I'm on now is to roust out somebody to jerk a little chin-music for us and waltz him through handsome."

"My friend, I seem to grow more and more bewildered. Your observations are wholly incomprehensible to me. Cannot you simplify them in some way? At first I thought perhaps I understood you, but I grope now. Would it not expedite matters if you restricted yourself to categorical statements of fact unencumbered with obstructing accumulations of metaphor and allegory?"

Another pause, and more reflection. Then, said Scotty:

"I'll have to pass, I judge."

"How?"

"You've raised me out, pard."

"I still fail to catch your meaning."

"Why, that last lead of yourn is too many for me—that's the idea. I can't neither trump nor follow suit."

The clergyman sank back in his chair perplexed. Scotty leaned his head on his hand and gave himself up to thought. Presently his face came up, sorrowful but confident.

"I've got it now, so's you can savvy," he said. "What we want is a gospel-sharp. See?"

"A what?"

"Gospel-sharp. Parson."

"Oh! Why did you not say so before? I am a clergyman—a parson."

"Now you talk! You see my blind and straddle it like a man. Put it there!"—extending a brawny paw, which closed over the minister's small hand and gave it a shake indicative of fraternal sympathy and fervent gratification.

"Now we're all right, pard. Let's start fresh. Don't you mind my snuffling a little—becuz we're in a power of trouble. You see, one of the boys has gone up the flume—"

---

[5]A church, where the doxology, a hymn in praise of God, is sung.
[6]I.e., "You hold a better hand." Here and below, Scotty draws terms from card games and billiards.
[7]Advantage.
[8]Understand.

"Gone where?"

"Up the flume—threw up the sponge, you understand."

"Thrown up the sponge?"

"Yes—kicked the bucket—"

"Ah—has departed to that mysterious country from whose bourne no traveler returns."[9]

"Return! I reckon not. Why pard, he's *dead!*"

"Yes, I understand."

"Oh, you do? Well I thought maybe you might be getting tangled some more. Yes, you see he's dead again—"

"*Again?* Why, has he ever been dead before?"

"Dead before? No! Do you reckon a man has got as many lives as a cat? But you bet you he's awful dead now, poor old boy, and I wish I'd never seen this day. I don't want no better friend than Buck Fanshaw. I knowed him by the back; and when I know a man and like him, I freeze to him—you hear *me*. Take him all round, pard, there never was a bullier man in the mines. No man ever knowed Buck Fanshaw to go back on a friend. But it's all up, you know, it's all up. It ain't no use. They've scooped him."

"Scooped him?"

"Yes—death has. Well, well, well, we've got to give him up. Yes indeed. It's a kind of a hard world, after all, *ain't* it? But pard, he was a rustler! You ought to seen him get started once. He was a bully boy with a glass eye! Just spit in his face and give him room according to his strength, and it was just beautiful to see him peel and go in. He was the worst son of a thief that ever drawed breath. Pard, he was *on* it! He was on it bigger than an Injun!"

"On it? On what?"

"On the shoot. On the shoulder. On the fight, you understand. *He* didn't give a continental for *any*body. *Beg* your pardon, friend, for coming so near saying a cuss-word—but you see I'm on an awful strain, in this palaver, on account of having to cramp down and draw everything so mild. But we've got to give him up. There ain't any getting around that, I don't reckon. Now if we can get you to help plant him—"

"Preach the funeral discourse? Assist at the obsequies?"

"Obs'quies is good. Yes. That's it—that's our little game. We are going to get the thing up regardless, you know. He was always nifty himself, and so you bet you his funeral ain't going to be no slouch—solid silver door-plate on his coffin, six plumes on the hearse, and a nigger on the box in a biled shirt and a plug hat[10]—how's that for high? And we'll take care of *you*, pard. We'll fix you all right. There'll be a kerridge for you; and whatever you want, you just 'scape out and we'll 'tend to it. We've got a shebang fixed up for you to stand behind, in No. 1's house, and don't you be afraid. Just go in and toot your horn, if you don't sell a clam. Put Buck through as bully as you can, pard, for anybody that knowed him will tell you that he was one of the whitest men that was ever in the mines. You can't draw it too strong. He never could stand it to see things going wrong. He's done more to make this town quiet and peaceable than any man in it. I've seen him lick four Greasers[11] in eleven minutes, myself. If a thing wanted regulating, *he* warn't a man to go browsing around after somebody to do it, but he would prance in and regulate it himself. He warn't a Catholic. Scasely. He was down on 'em. His word was, 'No Irish need apply!' But it didn't make no

[9]An approximate quotation from *Hamlet*, Act III, Scene 1, lines 79–80.
[10]A top hat.
[11]Slang term of abuse: Mexicans.

difference about that when it came down to what a man's rights was—and so, when some roughs jumped the Catholic bone-yard and started in to stake out town lots in it he *went* for 'em! And he *cleaned* 'em, too! I was there, pard, and I seen it myself."

"That was very well indeed—at least the impulse was—whether the act was strictly defensible or not. Had deceased any religious convictions? That is to say, did he feel a dependence upon, or acknowledge allegiance to a higher power?"

More reflection.

"I reckon you've stumped me again, pard. Could you say it over once more, and say it slow?"

"Well, to simplify it somewhat, was he, or rather had he ever been connected with any organization sequestered from secular concerns and devoted to self-sacrifice in the interests of morality?"

"All down but nine—set 'em up on the other alley, pard."

"What did I understand you to say?"

"Why, you're most too many for me, you know. When you get in with your left I hunt grass every time. Every time you draw, you fill; but I don't seem to have any luck. Let's have a new deal."

"How? Begin again?"

"That's it."

"Very well. Was he a good man, and—"

"There—I see that; don't put up another chip till I look at my hand. A good man, says you? Pard, it ain't no name for it. He was the best man that ever—pard, you would have doted on that man. He could lam any galoot of his inches in America. It was him that put down the riot last election before it got a start; and everybody said he was the only man that could have done it. He waltzed in with a spanner in one hand and a trumpet[12] in the other, and sent fourteen men home on a shutter in less than three minutes. He had that riot all broke up and prevented nice before anybody ever got a chance to strike a blow. He was always for peace, and he would *have* peace—he could not stand disturbances. Pard, he was a great loss to this town. It would please the boys if you could chip in something like that and do him justice. Here once when the Micks[13] got to throwing stones through the Methodis' Sunday-school windows, Buck Fanshaw, all of his notion, shut up his saloon and took a couple of six-shooters and mounted guard over the Sunday school. Says he, 'No Irish need apply!' And they didn't. He was the bulliest man in the mountains, pard! He could run faster, jump higher, hit harder, and hold more tangle-foot whisky without spilling it than any man in seventeen counties. Put that in, pard—it'll please the boys more than anything you could say. And you can say, pard, that he never shook his mother."

"Never shook his mother?"

"That's it—any of the boys will tell you so."

"Well, but why *should* he shake her?"

"That's what *I* say—but some people does."

"Not people of any repute?"

"Well, some that averages pretty so-so."

"In my opinion the man that would offer personal violence to his own mother, ought to—"

"Cheese it, pard; you've banked your ball clean outside the string. What I was a-drivin' at, was, that he never *throwed off* on his mother—don't you see? No

---

[12]A megaphone—for directing the sound of the human voice.
[13]Slang term for Irish Roman Catholics.

indeedy. He give her a house to live in, and town lots, and plenty of money; and he looked after her and took care of her all the time; and when she was down with the small-pox I'm d——d if he didn't set up nights and nuss her himself! *Beg* your pardon for saying it, but it hopped out too quick for yours truly. You've treated me like a gentleman, pard, and I ain't the man to hurt your feelings intentional. I think you're white. I think you're a square man, pard. I like you, and I'll lick any man that don't. I'll lick him till he can't tell himself from a last year's corpse! Put it *there!*" [Another fraternal handshake—and exit.]

The obsequies were all that "the boys" could desire. Such a marvel of funeral pomp had never been seen in Virginia. The plumed hearse, the dirge-breathing brass bands, the closed marts of business, the flags drooping at half mast, the long, plodding procession of uniformed secret societies, military battalions and fire companies, draped engines, carriages of officials, and citizens in vehicles and on foot, attracted multitudes of spectators to the sidewalks, roofs and windows; and for years afterward, the degree of grandeur attained by any civic display in Virginia was determined by comparison with Buck Fanshaw's funeral.

Scotty Briggs, as a pall-bearer and a mourner, occupied a prominent place at the funeral, and when the sermon was finished and the last sentence of the prayer for the dead man's soul ascended, he responded, in a low voice, but with feeling:

"AMEN. No Irish need apply."

As the bulk of the response was without apparent relevancy, it was probably nothing more than a humble tribute to the memory of the friend that was gone; for, as Scotty had once said, it was "his word."

Scotty Briggs, in after days, achieved the distinction of becoming the only convert to religion that was ever gathered from the Virginia roughs; and it transpired that the man who had it in him to espouse the quarrel of the weak out of inborn nobility of spirit was no mean timber whereof to construct a Christian. The making him one did not warp his generosity or diminish his courage; on the contrary it gave intelligent direction to the one and a broader field to the other. If his Sunday-school class progressed faster than the other classes, was it matter for wonder? I think not. He talked to his pioneer small-fry in a language they understood! It was my large privilege, a month before he died, to hear him tell the beautiful story of Joseph and his brethren to his class "without looking at the book." I leave it to the reader to fancy what it was like, as it fell, riddled with slang, from the lips of that grave, earnest teacher, and was listened to by his little learners with a consuming interest that showed that they were as unconscious as he was that any violence was being done to the sacred proprieties!

1872

Chapter LIII

THE STORY OF THE OLD RAM

Every now and then, in these days, the boys used to tell me I ought to get one Jim Blaine to tell me the stirring story of his grandfather's old ram—but they always added that I must not mention the matter unless Jim was drunk at the time—just comfortably and sociably drunk. They kept this up until my curiosity was on the rack to hear the story. I got to haunting Blaine; but it was of no use, the boys always found fault with his condition; he was often moderately but never satisfactorily drunk. I never watched a man's condition with such absorbing interest, and anxious solicitude; I never so pined to see a man uncompromisingly drunk before. At last, one evening I hurried to his cabin, for I learned that this time his situation was such that even the most fastidious could find no fault with it—he was tranquilly, serenely, symmetrically drunk—not a hiccup to mar his voice, not a cloud upon his brain thick enough to obscure his memory. As I entered, he was sitting upon an empty powder-keg, with a clay pipe in one hand and the other raised to command silence. His face was round, red, and very serious; his throat was bare and his hair tumbled; in general appearance and costume he was a stalwart miner of the period. On the pine table stood a candle, and its dim light revealed "the boys" sitting here and there on bunks, candleboxes, powder-kegs, etc. They said:

"Sh—! Don't speak—he's going to commence."

THE STORY OF THE OLD RAM

I found a seat at once, and Blaine said:

"I don't reckon them times will ever come again. There never was a more bullier old ram than what he was. Grandfather fetched him from Illinois—got him of a man by the name of Yates—Bill Yates—maybe you might have heard of him; his father was a deacon—Baptist—and he was a rustler, too; a man had to get up ruther early to get the start of old Thankful Yates; it was him that put the Greens up to j'ining teams with my grandfather when he moved west. Seth Green was prob'ly the pick of the flock; he married a Wilkerson—Sarah Wilkerson—good cretur, she was—one of the likeliest heifers that was ever raised in old Stoddard, everybody said that knowed her. She could heft a bar'l of flour as easy as I can flirt a flapjack. And spin? Don't mention it! Independent? Humph! When Sile Hawkins come a-browsing around her, she let him know that for all his tin he couldn't trot in harness alongside of *her*. You see, Sile Hawkins was—no, it warn't Sile Hawkins, after all—it was a galoot by the name of Filkins—I disremember his first name; but he *was* a stump—come into pra'r-meeting drunk, one night, horraying for Nixon, becuz he thought it was a primary; and old Deacon Ferguson up and scooted him through the window and he lit on old Miss Jefferson's head, poor old filly. She was a good soul—had a glass eye and used to lend it to old Miss Wagner, that hadn't any, to receive company in; it warn't big enough, and when Miss Wagner warn't noticing, it would get twisted around in the socket, and look up, maybe, or out to one side, and every which way, while t'other one was looking as straight ahead as a spyglass. Grown people didn't mind it, but it 'most always made the children cry, it was so sort of scary. She tried packing it in raw cotton, but it wouldn't work, somehow—the cotton would get loose and stick out and look so kind of awful that the children couldn't stand it no way. She was always dropping it out, and turning up her old deadlight on the company empty, and making them oncomfortable, becuz *she* never could tell when it hopped out, being blind on that side, you see. So somebody would have to hunch her and say, 'Your game eye has fetched loose, Miss Wagner, dear'—and then all of them would have to sit and wait till she jammed it in again—wrong side before, as a general thing, and green as a bird's egg, being a bashful cretur and easy sot back before company. But being wrong side before warn't much difference, anyway, becuz her own eye was sky-blue and the glass one was yaller on the front side, so whichever way she turned it it didn't match nohow. Old Miss Wagner was considerable on the borrow, she was. When she had a quilting, or Dorcas S'iety[1] at her house she gen'ally borrowed Miss Higgins's wooden leg to stump around on; it was considerable shorter than her other pin, but much *she* minded that. She said she couldn't abide crutches when she had company, becuz they were so slow; said when she had company and things had to be done, she wanted to get up and hump herself. She was as bald as a jug, and so she used to borrow Miss Jacops's wig—Miss Jacops was the coffin-peddler's wife—a ratty old buzzard, he was, that used to go roosting around where people was sick, waiting for 'em; and there that old rip would sit all day, in the shade, on a coffin that he judged would fit the can'idate; and if it was a slow customer and kind of uncertain, he'd fetch his rations and a blanket along and sleep in the coffin nights. He was anchored out that way, in frosty weather, for about three weeks, once, before old Robbins's place, waiting for him; and after that, for as much as two years, Jacops was not on speaking terms with the old man, on account of his disapp'inting him. He got one of his feet froze, and lost money, too, becuz old Robbins took a favorable turn and got well. The next time Robbins got sick, Jacops tried to make up with him, and varnished up the same old coffin and fetched it along; but old Robbins was too many for him; he had him in, and 'peared to be powerful weak; he bought the coffin for ten dollars and Jacops was to pay it back and twenty-five more besides if Robbins didn't like the coffin after he tried it. And then Robbins died, and at the funeral he bursted off the lid and riz up in his shroud and told the parson to let up on the performances, becuz he could *not* stand such a coffin as that. You see he had been in a trance once before, when he was young, and he took the chances on another, cal'lating that if he made the trip it was money in his pocket, and if he missed fire he couldn't lose a cent. And, by George, he sued Jacops for the rhino[2] and got judgment; and he set up the coffin in his back parlor and said he 'lowed to take his time, now. It was always an aggravation to Jacops, the way that miserable old thing acted. He moved back to Indianny pretty soon—went to Wellsville—Wellsville was the place the Hogadorns was from. Mighty fine family. Old Maryland stock. Old Squire Hogadorn could carry around more mixed licker, and cuss better than 'most any man I ever see. His second wife was the Widder Billings—she that was Becky Martin; her dam was Deacon Dunlop's first wife. Her oldest child, Maria, married a missionary and died in grace—et up by the savages. They et *him,* too, poor feller—biled him. It warn't the custom, so they say, but they explained to friends of his'n that went down there to bring away his things, that they'd tried missionaries every other way and never could get any good out of 'em—and so it annoyed all his relations to find out that that man's life was fooled away just out of a dern'd experiment, so to speak. But mind you, there ain't anything ever really lost; everything that people can't understand and don't see the reason of does good if you only hold on and give it a fair shake; Prov'dence don't fire no blank ca'tridges, boys. That there missionary's substance, unbeknowns to himself, actu'ly converted every last one of them heathens that took a chance at the barbecue. Nothing ever fetched them but that. Don't tell *me* it was an accident that he was biled. There ain't no such a thing as an accident. When my Uncle Lem was leaning up agin a scaffolding once, sick, or drunk, or suthin, an Irishman with a hod full of bricks fell on him out of the third story and broke the old man's back in two places. People said it was an accident. Much

---

[1]A name often adopted by church sewing societies, taken from the biblical Dorcas, a woman "full of good works." Acts 9:36–42.
[2]I.e., money.

accident there was about that. He didn't know what he was there for, but he was there for a good object. If he hadn't been there the Irishman would have been killed. Nobody can ever make me believe anything different from that. Uncle Lem's dog was there. Why didn't the Irishman fall on the dog? Becuz the dog would 'a' seen him a-coming and stood from under. That's the reason the dog warn't app'inted. A dog can't be depended on to carry out a special prov'dence. Mark my words, it was a put-up thing. Accidents don't happen, boys. Uncle Lem's dog—I wish you could 'a' seen that dog. He was a reg'lar shepherd—or ruther he was part bull and part shepherd—splendid animal; belonged to Parson Hagar before Uncle Lem got him. Parson Hagar belonged to the Western Reserve Hagars; prime family; his mother was a Watson; one of his sisters married a Wheeler; they settled in Morgan County, and he got nipped by the machinery in a carpet factory and went through in less than a quarter of a minute; his widder bought the piece of carpet that had his remains wove in, and people come a hundred mile to 'tend the funeral. There was fourteen yards in the piece. She wouldn't let them roll him up, but planted him just so—full length. The church was middling small where they preached the funeral, and they had to let one end of the coffin stick out of the window. They didn't bury him—they planted one end, and let him stand up, same as a monument. And they nailed a sign on it and put—put on—put on it—sacred to—the m-e-m-o-r-y—of four-teen y-a-r-d-s—of three-ply—car---pet—containing all that was—m-o-r-t-a-l—of—of—W-i-l-l-i-a-m—W-h-e-"

Jim Blaine had been growing gradually drowsy and drowsier—his head nod-ded once, twice, three times—dropped peacefully upon his breast, and he fell tranquilly asleep. The tears were running down the boys' cheeks—they were suffocating with suppressed laughter—and had been from the start, though I had never noticed it. I perceived that I was "sold." I learned then that Jim Blaine's peculiarity was that whenever he reached a certain stage of intoxication, no human power could keep him from setting out, with impressive unction, to tell about a wonderful adventure which he had once had with his grandfather's old ram—and the mention of the ram in the first sentence was as far as any man had ever heard him get, concerning it. He always maundered off, interminably, from one thing to another, till his whiskey got the best of him, and he fell asleep. What the thing was that happened to him and his grandfather's old ram is a dark mystery to this day, for nobody has ever yet found out.

1872

WHITTIER BIRTHDAY DINNER SPEECH[1]

Mr. Chairman—This is an occasion peculiarly meet for the digging up of pleasant reminiscences concerning literary folk; therefore I will drop lightly into history myself. Standing here on the shore of the Atlantic & contemplating certain of its biggest literary billows, I am reminded of a thing which happened to me fifteen years ago, when I had just succeeded in stirring up a little Nevadian literary ocean-puddle myself, whose spume-flakes were beginning to blow thinly

[1]On December 17, 1877, Twain spoke at a dinner in Boston commemorating the seventieth birthday of John Greenleaf Whittier. Twain intended his speech to be a triumph of humor. But the effect of his irreverent words on the august audience, which included Longfellow, Emerson, and Holmes, created what Twain later described as "a sort of black frost."

California-wards. I started on an inspection-tramp through the Southern mines of California. I was callow & conceited, & I resolved to try the virtue of my nom de plume. I very soon had an opportunity. I knocked at a miner's lonely log cabin in the foothills of the Sierras just at nightfall. It was snowing at the time. A jaded, melancholy man of fifty, barefooted, opened to me. When he heard my nom de plume, he looked more dejected than before. He let me in—pretty reluctantly, I thought—& after the customary bacon & beans, black coffee & a hot whiskey, I took a pipe. This sorrowful man had not said three words up to this time. Now he spoke up & said in the voice of one who is secretly suffering, "You're the fourth—I'm a-going to move." "The fourth what?" said I. "The fourth littery man that's been here in twenty-four hours—I'm a-going to move." "You don't tell me!" said I; "Who were the others?" "Mr. Longfellow, Mr. Emerson, & Mr. Oliver Wendell Holmes—dad fetch the lot!"

THE MINER'S STORY

You can easily believe I was interested.—I supplicated—three hot whiskies did the rest—& finally the melancholy miner began. Said he—

They came here just at dark yesterday evening, & I let them in, of course. Said they were going to Yo Semite.[2] They were a rough lot—but that's nothing— everybody looks rough that travels afoot. Mr. Emerson was a seedy little bit of a chap—red headed. Mr. Holmes was as fat as a balloon—he weighed as much as three hundred, & had double chins all the way down to his stomach. Mr. Longfellow was built like a prize fighter. His head was cropped & bristly—like as if he had a wig made of hair-brushes. His nose lay straight down his face, like a finger, with the end-joint tilted up. They had been drinking—I could see that.

And what queer talk they used! Mr. Holmes inspected this cabin, then he took me by the button-hole, & says he—

"Through the deep caves of thought
I hear a voice that sings:
Build thee more stately mansions,
O my Soul!"[3]

Says I, "I can't afford it, Mr. Holmes, & moreover I don't want to." Blamed if I liked it pretty well, either, coming from a stranger, that way! However, I started to get out my bacon & beans, when Mr. Emerson came & looked on a while, & then *he* takes me aside by the button-hole & says—

"Give me agates for my meat;
Give me cantharides[4] to eat;
From air & ocean bring me foods,
From all zones & altitudes."[5]

Says I, "Mr. Emerson, if you'll excuse me, this ain't no hotel." You see it sort of riled me—I warn't used to the ways of littery swells. But I went on a-sweating over my work, & next comes Mr. Longfellow & button-holes me, & interrupts me. Says he—

[2]Yosemite Valley, in California.
[3]From "The Chambered Nautilus," by Oliver Wendell Holmes. Twain has altered several of the following quotations for burlesque effect.
[4]An aphrodisiac, commonly called Spanish fly.   [5]Emerson, "Mithridates."

> "Honor be to Mudjekeewis!
> You shall hear how Pau-Puk-Kee-wis—"[6]

But I broke in, & says I, "Begging your pardon, Mr. Longfellow, if you'll be so kind as to hold your yawp for about five minutes, & let me get this grub ready, you'll do me proud." Well, sir, after they'd filled up, I set out the jug. Mr. Holmes looks at it, & then he fires up all of a sudden & yells—

> "Flash out a stream of blood-red wine!—
> For I would drink to other days."[7]

By George, I was getting kind of worked up. I don't deny it, I was getting kind of worked up. I turns to Mr. Holmes, & says I, "Looky-here, my fat friend, I'm a-running this shanty, & if the court knows herself, you'll take whiskey-straight or you'll go dry!" Them's the very words I said to him. Now I didn't want to sass such famous littery people, but you see they kind of forced me. There ain't nothing onreasonable 'bout me; I don't mind a passel of guests a-tread'n on my tail three or four times, but when it comes to *standing* on it, it's different. Well, between drinks they'd swell around the cabin & strike attitudes & spout. Says Mr. Longfellow—

> "This is the forest primeval."[8]

Says Mr. Emerson—

> "Here once the embattled farmers stood,
> And fired the shot heard round the world."[9]

Says I, "O, blackguard the premises as much as you want to—it don't cost you a cent." Well they went on drinking, & pretty soon they got out a greasy old deck & went to playing cut-throat euchre at ten cents a corner—on trust. I begun to notice some pretty suspicious things. Mr. Emerson dealt, looked at his hand, shook his head, says—

> "I am the doubter & the doubt—"

—& calmly bunched the hands & went to shuffling for a new layout. Says he—

> "They reckon ill who leave me out;
> They know not well the subtle ways
> I keep.— — — —I pass, & deal *again!*"[10]

Hang'd if he didn't go ahead & do it, too! O, he was a cool one! Well, in about a minute, things were running pretty tight, but all of a sudden I see by Mr. Emerson's eye that he judged he had 'em. He had already corralled two tricks, & each of the others one. So now he kinds of lifts a little, in his chair, & says—

[6]Longfellow, "Hiawatha."   [7]Holmes, "Mare Rubrum."   [8]Longfellow, "Evangeline."
[9]Emerson, "Concord Hymn."   [10]Emerson, "Brahma."

> "I tire of globes & aces!—
> Too long the game is played!"[11]

—and down he fetches a right bower. Mr. Longfellow smiles as sweet as pie, & says—:

> "Thanks, thanks to thee, my worthy friend,
> For the lesson thou hast taught!"[12]

—and dog my cats if he didn't down with *another* right bower! Well, sir, up jumps Holmes, a war-whooping, as usual, & says—

> "God help them if the tempest swings
> The pine against the palm!"[13]

—and I wish I may go to grass if he didn't swoop down with *another* right bower! Emerson claps his hand on his bowie, Longfellow claps his on his revolver, & I went under a bunk. There was going to be trouble; but that monstrous Holmes rose up, wobbling his double chins, & says he, "Order, gentlemen; the first man that draws, I'll lay down on him & smother him!" All quiet on the Potomac, you bet you! They were pretty how-come-you-so, now, & they begun to blow. Emerson says, "The bulliest thing I ever wrote, was Barbara Frietchie."[14] Says Longfellow, "It don't begin with my Biglow Papers."[15] Says Holmes, "My Thanatopsis[16] lays over 'em both." They mighty near ended in a fight. Then they wished they had some more company—& Mr. Emerson pointed at me & says—

> "Is yonder squalid peasant all
> That this proud nursery could breed?"[17]

He was a-whetting his bowie on his boot—so I let it pass. Well, sir, next they took it into their heads that they would like some music; so they made me stand up & sing "When Johnny Comes Marching Home" till I dropped—at thirteen minutes past four this morning. That's what I've been through, my friend. When I woke at seven, they were leaving, thank goodness, & Mr. Longfellow had my only boots on, & his own under his arm. Says I, "Hold on, there, Evangeline, what you going to do with *them?*"—He says: "Going to make tracks with 'em; because—

> 'Lives of great men all remind us
> We can make our lives sublime;
> And departing, leave behind us
> Footprints on the sands of Time.' "[18]

[As I said, Mr. Twain, you are the fourth in twenty-four hours—and I'm going to move; I ain't suited to a][19] littery atmosphere.

[11]Emerson, "Song of Nature."   [12]Longfellow, "The Village Blacksmith."
[13]Holmes, "A Voice of the Loyal North."   [14]"Barbara Frietchie," by John Greenleaf Whittier.
[15]"The Biglow Papers," by James Russell Lowell.   [16]"Thanatopsis," by William Cullen Bryant.
[17]Emerson, "Monadnoc."   [18]Longfellow, "A Psalm of Life."
[19]A portion of the manuscript is missing here. The bracketed insertion is taken from the version of the speech Twain included in his Autobiographical Dictation.

I said to the miner, "Why my dear sir, *these* were not the gracious singers to whom we & the world pay loving reverence & homage: these were imposters." The miner investigated me with a calm eye for a while, then said he, "Ah— imposters, were they? are *you?*" I did—not pursue the subject; and since then I haven't traveled on my nom de plume enough to hurt. Such is the reminiscence I was moved to contribute, Mr. Chairman. In my enthusiasm I may have exaggerated the details a little, but you will easily forgive me that fault since I believe it is the first time I have ever deflected from perpendicular fact on an occasion like this.

1877

from *A TRAMP ABROAD*

BAKER'S BLUEJAY YARN

Animals talk to each other, of course. There can be no question about that; but I suppose there are very few people who can understand them. I never knew but one man who could. I knew he could, however, because he told me so himself. He was a middle-aged, simple-hearted miner who had lived in a lonely corner of California, among the woods and mountains, a good many years, and had studied the ways of his only neighbors, the beasts and the birds, until he believed he could accurately translate any remark which they made. This was Jim Baker. According to Jim Baker, some animals have only a limited education, and use only very simple words, and scarcely ever a comparison or a flowery figure; whereas, certain other animals have a large vocabulary, a fine command of language and a ready and fluent delivery; consequently these latter talk a great deal; they like it; they are conscious of their talent, and they enjoy "showing off." Baker said, that after long and careful observation, he had come to the conclusion that the bluejays were the best talkers he had found among birds and beast. Said he:—

"There's more *to* a bluejay than any other creature. He has got more moods, and more different kinds of feelings than other creatures; and mind you, whatever a bluejay feels, he can put into language. And no mere commonplace language, either, but rattling, out-and-out book-talk—and bristling with metaphor, too—just bristling! And as for command of language—why *you* never see a bluejay get stuck for a word. No man ever did. They just boil out of him! And another thing: I've noticed a good deal, and there's no bird, or cow, or anything that uses as good grammar as a bluejay. You may say a cat uses good grammar. Well, a cat does—but you let a cat get excited, once; you let a cat get to pulling fur with another cat on a shed, nights, and you'll hear grammar that will give you the lockjaw. Ignorant people think it's the *noise* which fighting cats make that is so aggravating, but it ain't so; it's the sickening grammar they use. Now I've never heard a jay use bad grammar but very seldom; and when they do, they are as ashamed as a human; they shut right down and leave.

"You may call a jay a bird. Well, so he is, in a measure—because he's got feathers on him, and don't belong to no church, perhaps; but otherwise he is just as much a human as you be. And I'll tell you for why. A jay's gifts, and instincts, and feelings, and interests, cover the whole ground. A jay hasn't got any more principle than a Congressman. A jay will lie, a jay will steal, a jay will deceive, a jay will betray; and four times out of five, a jay will go back on his solemnest promise. The sacredness of an obligation is a thing which you can't cram into no bluejay's head. Now on top of all this, there's another thing: a jay can out-swear any gentleman in the mines. You think a cat can swear. Well, a cat can; but you give a bluejay a subject that calls for his reserve-powers, and where is your cat? Don't talk to *me*—I know too much about this thing. And there's yet another thing: in the one little particular of scolding—just good, clean, out-and-out scolding—a bluejay can lay over anything, human or divine. Yes, sir, a jay is everything that a man is. A jay can cry, a jay can laugh, a jay can feel shame, a jay can reason and plan and discuss, a jay likes gossip and scandal, a jay has got a sense of humor, a jay knows when he is an ass just as well as you do—maybe better. If a jay ain't human, he better take in his sign, that's all. Now I'm going to tell you a perfectly true fact about some bluejays.

"When I first begun to understand jay language correctly, there was a little incident happened here. Seven years ago, the last man in this region but me moved away. There stands his house—been empty ever since; a log house, with a plank roof—just one big room, and no more; no ceiling—nothing between the rafters and the floor. Well, one Sunday morning I was sitting out here in front of my cabin, with my cat, taking the sun, and looking at the blue hills, and listening to the leaves rustling so lonely in the trees, and thinking of the home away yonder in the states, that I hadn't heard from in thirteen years, when a bluejay lit on that house, with an acorn in his mouth, and says, 'Hello, I reckon I've struck something.' When he spoke, the acorn dropped out of his mouth and rolled down the roof, of course, but he didn't care; his mind was all on the thing he had struck. It was a knot-hole in the roof. He cocked his head to one side, shut one eye and put the other one to the hole, like a possum looking down a jug; then he glanced up with his bright eyes, gave a wink or two with his wings—which signifies gratification, you understand—and says, 'It looks like a hole, it's located like a hole—blamed if I don't believe it *is* a hole!'

"Then he cocked his head down and took another look; he glances up perfectly joyful, this time; winks his wings and his tail both, and says, 'Oh, no, this ain't no fat thing, I reckon! If I ain't in luck!—why it's a perfectly elegant hole!' So he flew down and got that acorn, and fetched it up and dropped it in, and was just tilting his head back, with the heavenliest smile on his face, when all of a sudden he was paralyzed into a listening attitude and that smile faded gradually out of his countenance like breath off'n a razor, and the queerest look of surprise took its place. Then he says, 'Why, I didn't hear it fall!' He cocked his eye at the hole again, and took a long look; raised up and shook his head; stepped around to the other side of the hole and took another look from that side; shook his head again. He studied a while, then he just went into the *details*—walked round and round the hole and spied into it from every point of the compass. No use. Now he took a thinking attitude on the comb of the roof and scratched the back of his head with his right foot a minute, and finally says, 'Well, it's too many for *me,* that's certain; must be a mighty long hole; however, I ain't got no time to fool around here, I got to 'tend to business; I reckon it's all right—chance it, anyway.'

"So he flew off and fetched another acorn and dropped it in, and tried to flirt his eye to the hole quick enough to see what become of it, but he was too late. He held his eye there as much as a minute; then he raised up and sighed, and says, 'Confound it, I don't seem to understand this thing, no way; however, I'll tackle her again.' He fetched another acorn, and done his level best to see what become of it, but he couldn't. He says, 'Well, *I* never struck no such a hole as this before; I'm of the opinion it's a totally new kind of a hole.' Then he began to get mad. He held in for a spell, walking up and down the comb of the roof and shaking his head and muttering to himself; but his feelings got the upper hand of him, presently, and he broke loose and cussed himself black in the face. I never see a bird take on so about a little thing. When he got through he walks to the hole and looks in again for half a minute; then he says, 'Well, you're a long hole, and a deep hole, and a mighty singular hole altogether—but I've started in to fill you, and I'm d—d if I *don't* fill you, if it takes a hundred years!'

"And with that, away he went. You never see a bird work so since you was born. He laid into his work like a nigger, and the way he hove acorns into that hole for about two hours and a half was one of the most exciting and astonishing spectacles I ever struck. He never stopped to take a look any more—he just hove 'em in and went for more. Well, at last he could hardly flop his wings, he was so tuckered out. He comes a-dropping down, once more, sweating like an ice-pitcher, drops his acorn in and says, '*Now* I guess I've got the bulge on you by this time!' So he bent down for a look. If you'll believe me, when his head come up again he was just pale with rage. He says, 'I've shoveled acorns enough in there to keep the family thirty years, and if I can see a sign of one of 'em I wish I may land in a museum with a belly full of sawdust in two minutes!'

"He just had strength enough to crawl up on to the comb and lean his back agin the chimbly, and then he collected his impressions and begun to free his mind. I see in a second that what I had mistook for profanity in the mines was only just the rudiments, as you may say.

"Another jay was going by, and heard him doing his devotions, and stops to inquire what was up. The sufferer told him the whole circumstance, and says, 'Now yonder's the hole, and if you don't believe me, go and look for yourself.' So this fellow went and looked, and comes back and says, 'How many did you say you put in there?' 'Not any less than two tons,' says the sufferer. The other jay went and looked again. He couldn't seem to make it out, so he raised a yell, and three more jays come. They all examined the hole, they all made the sufferer tell it over again, then they all discussed it, and got off as many leather-headed opinions about it as an average crowd of humans could have done.

"They called in more jays; then more and more till pretty soon this whole region 'peared to have a blue flush about it. There must have been five thousand of them; and such another jawing and disputing and ripping and cussing, you never heard. Every jay in the whole lot put his eye to the hole and delivered a more chuckle-headed opinion about the mystery than the jay that went there before him. They examined the house all over, too. The door was standing half open, and at last one old jay happened to go and light on it and look in. Of course, that knocked the mystery galley-west in a second. There lay the acorns, scattered all over the floor. He flopped his wings and raised a whoop. 'Come here!' he says, 'Come here, everybody; hang'd if this fool hasn't been trying to fill up a house with acorns!' They all came a-swooping down like a blue cloud, and as each fellow lit on the door and took a glance, the whole absurdity of the contract that that first jay had tackled hit him home and he fell over backward suffocating with laughter, and the next jay took his place and done the same.

"Well, sir, they roosted around here on the housetop and the trees for an hour, and guffawed over that thing like human beings. It ain't any use to tell me a bluejay hasn't got a sense of humor, because I know better. And memory, too. They brought jays here from all over the United States to look down that hole, every summer for three years. Other birds, too. And they could all see the point, except an owl that come from Nova Scotia to visit the Yo Semite, and he took this thing in on his way back. He said he couldn't see anything funny in it. But then he was a good deal disappointed about Yo Semite, too."

1880

ADVENTURES OF HUCKLEBERRY FINN[1]

(Tom Sawyer's Comrade)
Scene: The Mississippi
Time: Forty to Fifty Years Ago[2]

NOTICE

PERSONS attempting to find a motive in this narrative will be prosecuted; persons attempting to find a moral in it will be banished; persons attempting to find a plot in it will be shot.

BY ORDER OF THE AUTHOR
PER G.G.,[1] CHIEF OF ORDNANCE.

EXPLANATORY

IN this book a number of dialects are used, to wit: the Missouri negro dialect; the extremest form of the backwoods South-Western dialect; the ordinary "Pike-County"[1] dialect; and four modified varieties of this last. The shadings have not been done in a haphazard fashion, or by guess-work; but painstakingly, and with the trustworthy guidance and support of personal familiarity with these several forms of speech.

I make this explanation for the reason that without it many readers would suppose that all these characters were trying to talk alike and not succeeding.

THE AUTHOR

CHAPTER I

You don't know about me, without you have read a book by the name of "The Adventures of Tom Sawyer,"[1] but that ain't no matter. That book was made by Mr. Mark Twain, and he told the truth, mainly. There was things which he stretched, but mainly he told the truth. That is nothing. I never seen anybody but lied, one time or another, without it was Aunt Polly, or the widow, or maybe Mary.[2] Aunt Polly—Tom's Aunt Polly, she is—and Mary, and the Widow Douglas, is all told about in that book—which is mostly a true book; with some stretchers, as I said before.

Now the way that the book winds up, is this: Tom and me found the money

---

[1]The text is taken from the first American edition (1885). A small number of typographical errors have been silently corrected.

[2]1845–1835.

[1]Twain probably refers to General (and former President) Ulysses S. Grant (1822–1885).

[1]In Missouri.

[1]Published in 1876.   [2]Tom Sawyer's cousin.

that the robbers hid in the cave, and it made us rich. We got six thousand dollars apiece—all gold. It was an awful sight of money when it was piled up. Well, Judge Thatcher, he took it and put it out at interest, and it fetched us a dollar a day apiece, all the year round—more than a body could tell what to do with. The Widow Douglas, she took me for her son, and allowed she would sivilize me; but it was rough living in the house all the time, considering how dismal regular and decent the widow was in all her ways; and so when I couldn't stand it no longer, I lit out. I got into my old rags, and my sugar-hogshead[3] again, and was free and satisfied. But Tom Sawyer, he hunted me up and said he was going to start a band of robbers, and I might join if I would go back to the widow and be respectable. So I went back.

The widow she cried over me, and called me a poor lost lamb, and she called me a lot of other names, too, but she never meant no harm by it. She put me in them new clothes again, and I couldn't do nothing but sweat and sweat, and feel all cramped up. Well, then, the old thing commenced again. The widow rung a bell for supper, and you had to come to time. When you got to the table you couldn't go right to eating, but you had to wait for the widow to tuck down her head and grumble a little over the victuals, though there warn't really anything the matter with them. That is, nothing only everything was cooked by itself. In a barrel of odds and ends it is different; things get mixed up, and the juice kind of swaps around, and the things go better.

After supper she got out her book and learned me about Moses and the Bulrushers;[4] and I was in a sweat to find out all about him; but by-and-by she let it out that Moses had been dead a considerable long time; so then I didn't care no more about him; because I don't take no stock in dead people.

Pretty soon I wanted to smoke, and asked the widow to let me. But she wouldn't. She said it was a mean practice and wasn't clean, and I must try to not do it any more. That is just the way with some people. They get down on a thing when they don't know nothing about it. Here she was a bothering about Moses, which was no kin to her, and no use to anybody, being gone, you see, yet finding a power of fault with me for doing a thing that had some good in it. And she took snuff too; of course that was all right, because she done it herself.

Her sister, Miss Watson, a tolerable slim old maid, with goggles on, had just come to live with her, and took a set at me now, with a spelling-book. She worked me middling hard for about an hour, and then the widow made her ease up. I couldn't stood it much longer. Then for an hour it was deadly dull, and I was fidgety. Miss Watson would say, "Don't put your feet up there, Huckleberry;" and "don't scrunch up like that, Huckleberry—set up straight;" and pretty soon she would say, "Don't gap[5] and stretch like that, Huckleberry—why don't you try to behave?" Then she told me all about the bad place, and I said I wished I was there. She got mad, then, but I didn't mean no harm. All I wanted was to go somewheres; all I wanted was a change, I warn't particular. She said it was wicked to say what I said; said she wouldn't say it for the whole world; *she* was going to live so as to go to the good place. Well, I couldn't see no advantage in going where she was going, so I made up my mind I wouldn't try for it. But I never said so, because it would only make trouble, and wouldn't do no good.

Now she had got a start, and she went on and told me all about the good place. She said all a body would have to do there was to go around all day long with a harp and sing, forever and ever. So I didn't think much of it. But I never

---

[3]A large barrel.
[4]The daughter of Pharaoh found the infant Moses in a basket made of bulrushes. Exodus 2:1–10.
[5]Yawn.

said so. I asked her if she reckoned Tom Sawyer would go there, and, she said, not by a considerable sight. I was glad about that, because I wanted him and me to be together.

Miss Watson she kept pecking at me, and it got tiresome and lonesome. By-and-by they fetched the niggers[6] in and had prayers, and then everybody was off to bed. I went up to my room with a piece of candle and put it on the table. Then I set down in a chair by the window and tried to think of something cheerful, but it warn't no use. I felt so lonesome I most wished I was dead. The stars was shining, and the leaves rustled in the woods ever so mournful; and I heard an owl, away off, who-whooing about somebody that was dead, and a whippowill and a dog crying about somebody that was going to die; and the wind was trying to whisper something to me and I couldn't make out what it was, and so it made the cold shivers run over me. Then away out in the woods I heard that kind of a sound that a ghost makes when it wants to tell about something that's on its mind and can't make itself understood, and so can't rest easy in its grave and has to go about that way every night grieving. I got so down-hearted and scared, I did wish I had some company. Pretty soon a spider went crawling up my shoulder, and I flipped it off and it lit in the candle; and before I could budge it was all shriveled up. I didn't need anybody to tell me that that was an awful bad sign and would fetch me some bad luck, so I was scared and most shook the clothes off of me. I got up and turned around in my tracks three times and crossed my breast every time; and then I tied up a little lock of my hair with a thread to keep witches away. But I hadn't no confidence. You do that when you've lost a horseshoe that you've found, instead of nailing it up over the door, but I hadn't ever heard anybody say it was any way to keep off bad luck when you'd killed a spider.

I set down again, a shaking all over, and got out my pipe for a smoke; for the house was all as still as death, now, and so the widow wouldn't know. Well, after a long time I heard the clock away off in the town go boom—boom—boom—twelve licks—and all still again—stiller than ever. Pretty soon I heard a twig snap, down in the dark amongst the trees—something was a stirring. I set still and listened. Directly I could just barely hear a *"me-yow! me-yow!"* down there. That was good! Says I, *"me-yow! me-yow!"* as soft as I could, and then I put out the light and scrambled out of the window onto the shed. Then I slipped down to the ground and crawled in amongst the trees, and sure enough there was Tom Sawyer waiting for me.

CHAPTER II

We went tip-toeing along a path amongst the trees back towards the end of the widow's garden, stooping down so as the branches wouldn't scrape our heads. When we was passing by the kitchen I fell over a root and made a noise. We scrouched down and laid still. Miss Watson's big nigger, named Jim, was setting in the kitchen door; we could see him pretty clear, because there was a light behind him. He got up and stretched his neck out about a minute, listening. Then he says,

[6]I.e., slaves. "Nigger" (a corruption of "Negro") is considered abusive today. In pre–Civil War America it was widely used merely as a synonym for "slave." The presence of the term throughout the novel is not a sign of intolerance on the part of Twain, as has sometimes been charged, but of his effort to reproduce accurately the common speech of mid-nineteenth-century Americans, both black and white.

"Who dah?"

He listened some more; then he come tip-toeing down and stood right between us; we could a touched him, nearly. Well, likely it was minutes and minutes that there warn't a sound, and we all there so close together. There was a place on my ankle that got to itching; but I dasn't scratch it; and then my ear begun to itch; and next my back, right between my shoulders. Seemed like I'd die if I couldn't scratch. Well, I've noticed that thing plenty of times since. If you are with the quality,[1] or at a funeral, or trying to go to sleep when you ain't sleepy— if you are anywheres where it won't do for you to scratch, why you will itch all over in upwards of a thousand places. Pretty soon Jim says:

"Say—who is you? Whar is you? Dog my cats ef I didn't hear sumf'n. Well, I knows what I's gwyne to do. I's gwyne to set down here and listen tell I hears it agin."

So he set down on the ground betwixt me and Tom. He leaned his back up against a tree, and stretched his legs out till one of them most touched one of mine. My nose begun to itch. It itched till the tears come into my eyes. But I dasn't scratch. Then it begun to itch on the inside. Next I got to itching underneath. I didn't know how I was going to set still. This miserableness went on as much as six or seven minutes; but it seemed a sight longer than that. I was itching in eleven different places now. I reckoned I couldn't stand it more'n a minute longer, but I set my teeth hard and got ready to try. Just then Jim begun to breathe heavy; next he begun to snore—and then I was pretty soon comfortable agin.

Tom he made a sign to me—kind of a little noise with his mouth—and we went creeping away on our hands and knees. When we was ten foot off, Tom whispered to me and wanted to tie Jim to the tree for fun; but I said no; he might wake and make a disturbance, and then they'd find out I warn't in. Then Tom said he hadn't got candles enough, and he would slip in the kitchen and get some more. I didn't want him to try. I said Jim might wake up and come. But Tom wanted to resk it; so we slid in there and got three candles, and Tom laid five cents on the table for pay. Then we got out, and I was in a sweat to get away; but nothing would do Tom but he must crawl to where Jim was, on his hands and knees, and play something on him. I waited, and it seemed a good while, everything was so still and lonesome.

As soon as Tom was back, we cut along the path, around the garden fence, and by-and-by fetched up on the steep top of the hill the other side of the house. Tom said he slipped Jim's hat off of his head and hung it on a limb right over him, and Jim stirred a little, but he didn't wake. Afterwards Jim said the witches bewitched him and put him in a trance, and rode him all over the State, and then set him under the trees again and hung his hat on a limb to show who done it. And next time Jim told it he said they rode him down to New Orleans; and after that, every time he told it he spread it more and more, till by-and-by he said they rode him all over the world, and tired him most to death, and his back was all over saddle-boils. Jim was monstrous proud about it, and he got so he wouldn't hardly notice the other niggers. Niggers would come miles to hear Jim tell about it, and he was more looked up to than any nigger in that country. Strange niggers would stand with their mouths open and look him all over, same as if he was a wonder. Niggers is always talking about witches in the dark by the kitchen fire; but whenever one was talking and letting on to know all about such things, Jim would happen in and say, "H'm! What you know 'bout

---

[1]I.e., quality people, the upper classes.

witches?" and that nigger was corked up and had to take a back seat. Jim always kept that five-center piece around his neck with a string and said it was a charm the devil give to him with his own hands and told him he could cure anybody with it and fetch witches whenever he wanted to, just by saying something to it; but he never told what it was he said to it. Niggers would come from all around there and give Jim anything they had, just for a sight of that five-center piece; but they wouldn't touch it, because the devil had had his hands on it. Jim was most ruined, for a servant, because he got so stuck up on account of having seen the devil and been rode by witches.

Well, when Tom and me got to the edge of the hill-top, we looked away down into the village and could see three or four lights twinkling, where there was sick folks, may be; and the stars over us was sparkling ever so fine; and down by the village was the river, a whole mile broad, and awful still and grand. We went down the hill and found Jo Harper, and Ben Rogers, and two or three more of the boys, hid in the old tanyard. So we unhitched a skiff[2] and pulled down the river two mile and a half, to the big scar on the hillside, and went ashore.

We went to a clump of bushes, and Tom made everybody swear to keep the secret, and then showed them a hole in the hill, right in the thickest part of the bushes. Then we lit the candles and crawled in on our hands and knees. We went about two hundred yards, and then the cave opened up. Tom poked about amongst the passages and pretty soon ducked under a wall where you wouldn't a noticed that there was a hole. We went along a narrow place and got into a kind of room, all damp and sweaty and cold, and there we stopped. Tom says:

"Now we'll start this band of robbers and call it Tom Sawyer's Gang. Everybody that wants to join has got to take an oath, and write his name in blood."

Everybody was willing. So Tom got out a sheet of paper that he had wrote the oath on, and read it. It swore every boy to stick to the band, and never tell any of the secrets; and if anybody done anything to any boy in the band, whichever boy was ordered to kill that person and his family must do it, and he mustn't eat and he mustn't sleep till he had killed them and hacked a cross in their breasts, which was the sign of the band. And nobody that didn't belong to the band could use that mark, and if he did he must be sued; and if he done it again he must be killed. And if anybody that belonged to the band told the secrets, he must have his throat cut, and then have his carcass burnt up and the ashes scattered all around, and his name blotted off the list with blood and never mentioned again by the gang, but have a curse put on it and be forgot, forever.

Everybody said it was a real beautiful oath, and asked Tom if he got it out of his own head. He said, some of it, but the rest was out of pirate books, and robber books, and every gang that was hightoned had it.

Some thought it would be good to kill the *families* of boys that told the secrets. Tom said it was a good idea, so he took a pencil and wrote it in. Then Ben Rogers says:

"Here's Huck Finn, he hain't got no family—what you going to do 'bout him?"

"Well, hain't he got a father?" says Tom Sawyer.

"Yes, he's got a father, but you can't never find him, these days. He used to lay drunk with the hogs in the tanyard, but he hain't been seen in these parts for a year or more."

They talked it over, and they was going to rule me out, because they said every boy must have a family or somebody to kill, or else it wouldn't be fair and

---

[2]A flat-bottomed rowboat.

square for the others. Well, nobody could think of anything to do—everybody was stumped, and set still. I was most ready to cry; but all at once I thought of a way, and so I offered them Miss Watson—they could kill her. Everybody said:

"Oh, she'll do, she'll do. That's all right. Huck can come in."

Then they all stuck a pin in their fingers to get blood to sign with, and I made my mark on the paper.

"Now," says Ben Rogers, "what's the line of business of this Gang?"

"Nothing only robbery and murder," Tom said.

"But who are we going to rob? houses—or cattle—or——"

"Stuff! stealing cattle and such things ain't robbery, it's burglary," says Tom Sawyer. "We ain't burglars. That ain't no sort of style. We are highwaymen. We stop stages and carriages on the road, with masks on, and kill the people and take their watches and money."

"Must we always kill the people?"

"Oh, certainly. It's best. Some authorities think different, but mostly it's considered best to kill them. Except some that you bring to the cave here and keep them till they're ransomed."

"Ransomed? What's that?"

"I don't know. But that's what they do. I've seen it in books; and so of course that's what we've got to do."

"But how can we do it if we don't know what it is?"

"Why blame[3] it all, we've *got* to do it. Don't I tell you it's in the books? Do you want to go to doing different from what's in the books, and get things all muddled up?"

"Oh, that's all very fine to *say,* Tom Sawyer, but how in the nation[4] are these fellows going to be ransomed if we don't know how to do it to them? that's the thing *I* want to get at. Now what do you *reckon* it is?"

"Well, I don't know. But per'aps if we keep them till they're ransomed, it means that we keep them till they're dead."

"Now, that's something *like.* That'll answer. Why couldn't you said that before? We'll keep them till they ransomed to death—and a bothersome lot they'll be, too, eating up everything and always trying to get loose."

"How you talk, Ben Rogers. How can they get loose when there's a guard over them, ready to shoot them down if they move a peg?"

"A guard. Well that *is* good. So somebody's got to set up all night and never get any sleep, just so as to watch them. I think that's foolishness. Why can't a body take a club and ransom them as soon as they get here?"

"Because it ain't in the books so—that's why. Now Ben Rogers, do you want to do things regular, or don't you?—that's the idea. Don't you reckon that the people that made the books knows what's the correct thing to do? Do you reckon *you* can learn 'em anything? Not by a good deal. No, sir, we'll just go on and ransom them in the regular way."

"All right. I don't mind; but I say it's a fool way, anyhow. Say—do we kill the women, too?"

"Well, Ben Rogers, if I was as ignorant as you I wouldn't let on. Kill the women? No—nobody ever saw anything in the books like that. You fetch them to the cave, and you're always as polite as pie to them; and by-and-by they fall in love with you and never want to go home any more."

"Well, if that's the way, I'm agreed, but I don't take no stock in it. Mighty soon we'll have the cave so cluttered up with women, and fellows waiting to be

[3]Euphemism for "damn."   [4]Euphemism for "damnation."

ransomed, that there won't be no place for the robbers. But go ahead, I ain't got nothing to say."

Little Tommy Barnes was asleep, now, and when they waked him up he was scared, and cried, and said he wanted to go home to his ma, and didn't want to be a robber any more.

So they all made fun of him, and called him cry-baby, and that made him mad, and he said he would go straight and tell all the secrets. But Tom give him five cents to keep quiet, and said we would all go home and meet next week and rob somebody and kill some people.

Ben Rogers said he couldn't get out much, only Sundays, and so he wanted to begin next Sunday; but all the boys said it would be wicked to do it on Sunday, and that settled the thing. They agreed to get together and fix a day as soon as they could, and then we elected Tom Sawyer first captain and Jo Harper second captain of the Gang, and so started home.

I clumb up the shed and crept into my window just before day was breaking. My new clothes was all greased up and clayey, and I was dog-tired.

CHAPTER III

Well, I got a good going-over in the morning, from old Miss Watson, on account of my clothes; but the widow she didn't scold, but only cleaned off the grease and clay and looked so sorry that I thought I would behave a while if I could. Then Miss Watson she took me in the closet[1] and prayed, but nothing come of it. She told me to pray every day, and whatever I asked for I would get it. But it warn't so. I tried it. Once I got a fish-line, but no hooks. It warn't any good to me without hooks. I tried for the hooks three or four times, but somehow I couldn't make it work. By-and-by, one day, I asked Miss Watson to try for me, but she said I was a fool. She never told me why, and I couldn't make it out no way.

I set down, one time, back in the woods, and had a long think about it. I says to myself, if a body can get anything they pray for, why don't Deacon Winn get back the money he lost on pork? Why can't the widow get back her silver snuff-box that was stole? Why can't Miss Watson fat up? No, says I to myself, there ain't nothing in it. I went and told the widow about it, and she said the thing a body could get by praying for it was "spiritual gifts." This was too many for me, but she told me what she meant—I must help other people, and do everything I could for other people, and look out for them all the time, and never think about myself. This was including Miss Watson, as I took it. I went out in the woods and turned it over in my mind a long time, but I couldn't see no advantage about it—except for the other people—so at last I reckoned I wouldn't worry about it any more, but just let it go. Sometimes the widow would take me one side and talk about Providence in a way to make a body's mouth water; but maybe next day Miss Watson would take hold and knock it all down again. I judged I could see that there was two Providences, and a poor chap would stand considerable show with the widow's Providence, but if Miss Watson's got him there warn't no help for him any more. I thought it all out, and reckoned I would belong to the widow's, if he wanted me, though I couldn't make out how he was agoing to be any better off then than what he was before, seeing I was so ignorant and so kind of low-down and ornery.

---

[1]"When thou prayest, enter into thy closet. . . ." Matthew 6:6.

Pap he hadn't been seen for more than a year, and that was comfortable for me; I didn't want to see him no more. He used to always whale me when he was sober and could get his hands on me; though I used to take to the woods most of the time when he was around. Well, about this time he was found in the river drowned, about twelve mile above town, so people said. They judged it was him, anyway; said this drowned man was just his size, and was ragged, and had uncommon long hair—which was all like pap—but they couldn't make nothing out of the face, because it had been in the water so long it warn't much like a face at all. They said he was floating on his back in the water. They took him and buried him on the bank. But I warn't comfortable long, because I happened to think of something. I knowed mighty well that a drownded man don't float on his back, but on his face. So I knowed then, that this warn't pap, but a woman dressed up in a man's clothes. So I was uncomfortable again. I judged the old man would turn up again by-and-by, though I wished he wouldn't.

We played robber now and then about a month, and then I resigned. All the boys did. We hadn't robbed nobody, we hadn't killed any people, but only just pretended. We used to hop out of the woods and go charging down on hogdrovers and women in carts taking garden stuff to market, but we never hived[2] any of them. Tom Sawyer called the hogs "ingots," and he called the turnips and stuff "julery" and we would go to the cave and pow-wow[3] over what we had done and how many people we had killed and marked. But I couldn't see no profit in it. One time Tom sent a boy to run about town with a blazing stick, which he called a slogan (which was the sign for the Gang to get together), and then he said he had got secret news by his spies that next day a whole parcel of Spanish merchants and rich A-rabs was going to camp in Cave Hollow with two hundred elephants, and six hundred camels, and over a thousand "sumter" mules,[4] all loaded down with di'monds, and they didn't have only a guard of four hundred soldiers, and so we would lay in ambuscade, as he called it, and kill the lot and scoop the things. He said we must slick up our swords and guns, and get ready. He never could go after even a turnip-cart but he must have the swords and guns all scoured up for it; though they was only lath and broom-sticks, and you might scour at them till you rotted and then they warn't worth a mouthful of ashes more than what they was before. I didn't believe we could lick such a crowd of Spaniards and A-rabs, but I wanted to see the camels and elephants, so I was on hand next day, Saturday, in the ambuscade; and when we got the word, we rushed out of the woods and down the hill. But there warn't no Spaniards and A-rabs, and there warn't no camels nor no elephants. It warn't anything but a Sunday-school picnic, and only a primer-class[5] at that. We busted it up, and chased the children up the hollow; but we never got anything but some doughnuts and jam, though Ben Rogers got a rag doll, and Jo Harper got a hymn-book and a tract; and then the teacher charged in and made us drop everything and cut. I didn't see no di'monds, and I told Tom Sawyer so. He said there was loads of them there, anyway; and he said there was A-rabs there, too, and elephants and things. I said, why couldn't we see them, then? He said if I warn't so ignorant, but had read a book called "Don Quixote,"[6] I would know without asking. He said it was all done by enchantment. He said there was hundreds of soldiers there, and elephants and treasure, and so on, but we had enemies which he called magicians, and they had turned the whole thing into

---

[2]Captured.   [3]Talk.   [4]Pack mules.   [5]First grade.
[6]Cervantes' novel, published in 1605. In the novel, Don Quixote attacks a flock of sheep, later explaining that the sheep were actually an army of knights who had been transformed by a magician.

an infant Sunday School, just out of spite. I said, all right, then the thing for us to do was to go for the magicians. Tom Sawyer said I was a numskull.

"Why," says he, "a magician could call up a lot of genies, and they would hash you up like nothing before you could say Jack Robinson. They are as tall as a tree and as big around as a church."

"Well," I says, "s'pose we got some genies to help *us*—can't we lick the other crowd then?"

"How you going to get them?"

"I don't know. How do *they* get them?"

"Why they rub an old tin lamp or an iron ring, and then the genies come tearing in, with the thunder and lightning a-ripping around and the smoke a-rolling, and everything they're told to do they up and do it. They don't think nothing of pulling a shot tower[7] up by the roots, and belting a Sunday-school superintendent over the head with it—or any other man."

"Who makes them tear around so?"

"Why, whoever rubs the lamp or the ring. They belong to whoever rubs the lamp or the ring, and they've got to do whatever he says. If he tells them to build a palace forty miles long, out of di'monds, and fill it full of chewing gum, or whatever you want, and fetch an emperor's daughter from China for you to marry, they've got to do it—and they've got to do it before sun-up next morning, too. And more—they've got to waltz that palace around over the country wherever you want it, you understand."

"Well," says I, "I think they are a pack of flatheads for not keeping the palace themselves 'stead of fooling them away like that. And what's more—if I was one of them I would see a man in Jericho before I would drop my business and come to him for the rubbing of an old tin lamp."

"How you talk, Huck Finn. Why, you'd *have* to come when he rubbed it, whether you wanted to or not."

"What, and I as high as a tree and as big as a church? All right, then; I *would* come; but I lay I'd make that man climb the highest tree there was in the country."

"Shucks, it ain't no use to talk to you, Huck Finn. You don't seem to know anything, somehow—perfect sap-head."

I thought all this over for two or three days, and then I reckoned I would see if there was anything in it. I got an old tin lamp and an iron ring and went out in the woods and rubbed and rubbed till I sweat like an Injun, calculating to build a palace and sell it; but it warn't no use, none of the genies come. So then I judged that all that stuff was only just one of Tom Sawyer's lies. I reckoned he believed in the A-rabs and the elephants, but as for me I think different. It had all the marks of a Sunday school.

CHAPTER IV

Well, three or four months run along, and it was well into the winter, now. I had been to school most all the time, and could spell, and read, and write just a little, and could say the multiplication table up to six times seven is thirty-five, and I don't reckon I could ever get any further than that if I was to live forever. I don't take no stock in mathematics, anyway.

---

[7]A tower in which pellets are made by pouring molten lead from the top of the tower, through a sieve, into a tank of water.

At first I hated the school, but by-and-by I got so I could stand it. Whenever I got uncommon tired I played hookey, and the hiding I got next day done me good and cheered me up. So the longer I went to school the easier it got to be. I was getting sort of used to the widow's ways, too, and they warn't so raspy on me. Living in a house, and sleeping in a bed, pulled on me pretty tight, mostly, but before the cold weather I used to slide out and sleep in the woods, sometimes, and so that was a rest to me. I liked the old ways best, but I was getting so I liked the new ones, too, a little bit. The widow said I was coming along slow but sure, and doing very satisfactory. She said she warn't ashamed of me.

One morning I happened to turn over the salt-cellar at breakfast. I reached for some of it as quick as I could, to throw over my left shoulder and keep off the bad luck, but Miss Watson was in ahead of me, and crossed me off. She says, "Take your hands away, Huckleberry—what a mess you are always making." The widow put in a good word for me, but that warn't going to keep off the bad luck, I knowed that well enough. I started out, after breakfast, feeling worried and shaky, and wondering where it was going to fall on me, and what it was going to be. There is ways to keep off some kinds of bad luck, but this wasn't one of them kind; so I never tried to do anything, but just poked along low-spirited and on the watchout.

I went down the front garden and clumb over the stile,[1] where you go through the high board fence. There was an inch of new snow on the ground, and I seen somebody's tracks. They had come up from the quarry and stood around the stile a while, and then went on around the garden fence. It was funny they hadn't come in, after standing around so. I couldn't make it out. It was very curious, somehow. I was going to follow around, but I stooped down to look at the tracks first. I didn't notice anything at first, but next I did. There was a cross in the left boot-heel made with big nails, to keep off the devil.

I was up in a second and shinning down the hill. I looked over my shoulder every now and then, but I didn't see nobody. I was at Judge Thatcher's as quick as I could get there. He said:

"Why, my boy, you are all out of breath. Did you come for your interest?"

"No sir," I says; "is there some for me?"

"Oh, yes, a half-yearly is in, last night. Over a hundred and fifty dollars. Quite a fortune for you. You better let me invest it along with your six thousand, because if you take it you'll spend it."

"No, sir," I says, "I don't want to spend it. I don't want it at all—nor the six thousand, nuther. I want you to take it; I want to give it to you—the six thousand and all."

He looked surprised. He couldn't seem to make it out. He says:

"Why, what can you mean, my boy?"

I says, "Don't you ask me no questions about it, please. You'll take it—won't you?"

He says:

"Well I'm puzzled. Is something the matter?"

"Please take it," says I, "and don't ask me nothing—then I won't have to tell no lies."

He studied a while, and then he says:

"Oho-o. I think I see. You want to *sell* all your property to me—not give it. That's the correct idea."

Then he wrote something on a paper and read it over and says:

---

[1] A set of steps up and over a fence.

"There—you see it says 'for a consideration.' That means I have bought it of you and paid you for it. Here's a dollar for you. Now, you sign it."

So I signed it, and left.

Miss Watson's nigger, Jim, had a hair-ball as big as your fist, which had been took out of the fourth stomach of an ox, and he used to do magic with it. He said there was a spirit inside of it, and it knowed everything. So I went to him that night and told him pap was here again, for I found his tracks in the snow. What I wanted to know, was, what he was going to do, and was he going to stay? Jim got out his hair-ball, and said something over it, and then he held it up and dropped it on the floor. It fell pretty solid, and only rolled about an inch. Jim tried it again, and then another time, and it acted just the same. Jim got down on his knees and put his ear against it and listened. But it warn't no use; he said it wouldn't talk. He said sometimes it wouldn't talk without money. I told him I had an old slick counterfeit quarter that warn't no good because the brass showed through the silver a little, and it wouldn't pass nohow, even if the brass didn't show, because it was so slick it felt greasy, and so that would tell on it every time. (I reckoned I wouldn't say nothing about the dollar I got from the judge.) I said it was pretty bad money, but maybe the hair-ball would take it, because maybe it wouldn't know the difference. Jim smelt it, and bit it, and rubbed it, and said he would manage so the hair-ball would think it was good. He said he would split open a raw Irish potato and stick the quarter in between and keep it there all night, and next morning you couldn't see no brass, and it wouldn't feel greasy no more, and so anybody in town would take it in a minute, let alone a hair-ball. Well, I knowed a potato would do that, before, but I had forgot it.

Jim put the quarter under the hair-ball and got down and listened again. This time he said the hair-ball was all right. He said it would tell my whole fortune if I wanted it to. I says, go on. So the hair-ball talked to Jim, and Jim told it to me. He says:

"Yo' ole father doan' know, yit, what he's a-gwyne to do. Sometimes he spec he'll go 'way, en den agin he spec he'll stay. De bes' way is to res' easy en let de ole man take his own way. Dey's two angels hoverin' roun' 'bout him. One uv 'em is white en shiny, en 'tother one is black. De white one gits him to go right, a little while, den de black one sail in en bust it all up. A body can't tell, yit, which one gwyne to fetch him at de las'. But you is all right. You gwyne to have considable trouble in yo' life, en considable joy. Sometimes you gwyne to git hurt, en sometimes you gwyne to git sick; but every time you's gwyne to git well agin. Dey's two gals flying' 'bout you in yo' life. One uv 'em's light en 'tother one is dark. One is rich en 'tother is po'. You's gwyne to marry de po' one fust en de rich one by-en-by. You wants to keep 'way fum de water as much as you kin, en don't run no resk, 'kase it's down in de bills[2] dat you's gwyne to git hung."

When I lit my candle and went up to my room that night, there set pap, his own self!

CHAPTER V

I had shut the door to. Then I turned around, and there he was. I used to be scared of him all the time, he tanned me so much. I reckoned I was scared now,

---

[2]I.e., decreed, predestined.

too; but in a minute I see I was mistaken. That is, after the first jolt, as you may say, when my breath sort of hitched—he being so unexpected; but right away after, I see I warn't scared of him worth bothering about.

He was most fifty, and he looked it. His hair was long and tangled and greasy, and hung down, and you could see his eyes shining through like he was behind vines. It was all black, no gray; so was his long, mixed-up whiskers. There warn't no color in his face, where his face showed; it was white; not like another man's white, but a white to make a body sick, a white to make a body's flesh crawl—a tree-toad white, a fish-belly white. As for his clothes—just rags, that was all. He had one ankle resting on 'tother knee; the boot on that foot was busted, and two of his toes stuck through, and he worked them now and then. His hat was laying on the floor; an old black slouch[1] with the top caved in, like a lid.

I stood a-looking at him; he set there a-looking at me, with his chair tilted back a little. I set the candle down. I noticed the window was up; so he had clumb in by the shed. He kept a-looking me all over. By-and-by he says:

"Starchy clothes—very. You think you're a good deal of a big-bug, *don't* you?"

"Maybe I am, maybe I ain't," I says.

"Don't you give me none o' your lip," says he. "You've put on considerable many frills since I been away. I'll take you down a peg before I get done with you. You're educated, too, they say; can read and write. You think you're better'n your father, now, don't you, because he can't? *I'll* take it out of you. Who told you you might meddle with such hifalut'n foolishness, hey?—who told you you could?"

"The widow. She told me."

"The widow, hey?—and who told the widow she could put in her shovel about a thing that ain't none of her business?"

"Nobody never told her."

"Well, I'll learn her how to meddle. An looky here—you drop that school, you hear? I'll learn people to bring up a boy to put on airs over his own father and let on to be better'n what *he* is. You lemme catch you fooling around that school again, you hear? Your mother couldn't read, and she couldn't write, nuther, before she died. None of the family couldn't, before *they* died. *I* can't; and here you're a-swelling yourself up like this. I ain't the man to stand it—you hear? Say—lemme hear you read."

I took up a book and begun something about General Washington and the wars. When I'd read about a half a minute, he fetched the book a whack with his hand and knocked it across the house. He says:

"It's so. You can do it. I had my doubts when you told me. Now looky here; you stop that putting on frills. I won't have it. I'll lay[2] for you, my smarty; and if I catch you about that school I'll tan you good. First you know you'll get religion, too. I never see such a son."

He took up a little blue and yaller picture of some cows and a boy, and says:

"What's this?"

"It's something they give me for learning my lessons good."

He tore it up, and says—

"I'll give you something better—I'll give you a cowhide."[3]

He set there a-mumbling and a-growling a minute, and then he says—

"*Ain't* you a sweet-scented dandy, though? A bed; and bedclothes; and a look'n glass; and a piece of carpet on the floor—and your own father got to sleep with the hogs in the tanyard. I never see such a son. I bet I'll take some o'these frills

[1]A felt hat with a wide brim.   [2]Lie in wait.   [3]A whipping with a cowhide strap.

out o' you before I'm done with you. Why there ain't no end to your airs—they say you're rich. Hey?—how's that?"

"They lie—that's how."

"Looky here—mind how you talk to me; I'm a-standing about all I can stand, now—so don't gimme no sass. I've been in town two days, and I hain't heard nothing but about you bein' rich. I heard about it away down the river, too. That's why I come. You git me that money to-morrow—I want it."

"I hain't got no money."

"It's a lie. Judge Thatcher's got it. You git it. I want it."

"I hain't got no money, I tell you. You ask Judge Thatcher; he'll tell you the same."

"All right. I'll ask him; and I'll make him pungle,[4] too, or I'll know the reason why. Say—how much you got in your pocket? I want it."

"I hain't got only a dollar, and I want that to—"

"It don't make no difference what you want it for—you just shell it out."

He took it and bit it to see if it was good, and then he said he was going down town to get some whiskey; said he hadn't had a drink all day. When he had got out on the shed, he put his head in again, and cussed me for putting on frills and trying to be better than him; and when I reckoned he was gone, he come back and put his head in again, and told me to mind about that school, because he was going to lay for me and lick me if I didn't drop that.

Next day he was drunk, and he went to Judge Thatcher's and bullyragged[5] him and tried to make him give up the money, but he couldn't, and then he swore he'd make the law force him.

The judge and the widow went to law to get the court to take me away from him and let one of them be my guardian; but it was a new judge that had just come, and he didn't know the old man; so he said courts mustn't interfere and separate families if they could help it; said he'd druther not take a child away from its father. So Judge Thatcher and the widow had to quit on the business.

That pleased the old man till he couldn't rest. He said he'd cowhide me till I was black and blue if I didn't raise some money for him. I borrowed three dollars from Judge Thatcher, and pap took it and got drunk and went a-blowing around and cussing and whooping and carrying on; and he kept it up all over town, with a tin pan, till most midnight; then they jailed him, and next day they had him before court, and jailed him again for a week. But he said *he* was satisfied; said he was boss of his son, and he'd make it warm for *him*.

When he got out the new judge said he was agoing to make a man of him. So he took him to his own house, and dressed him up clean and nice, and had him to breakfast and dinner and supper with the family, and was just old pie to him, so to speak. And after supper he talked to him about temperance and such things till the old man cried, and said he'd been a fool, and fooled away his life; but now he was agoing to turn over a new leaf and be a man nobody wouldn't be ashamed of, and he hoped the judge would help him and not look down on him. The judge said he could hug him for them words; so *he* cried, and his wife she cried again; pap said he'd been a man that had always been misunderstood before, and the judge said he believed it. The old man said that what a man wanted that was down, was sympathy; and the judge said it was so; so they cried again. And when it was bedtime, the old man rose up and held out his hand, and says:

"Look at it gentlemen, and ladies all; take ahold of it; shake it. There's a hand

---

[4]Pay.   [5]Scolded.

that was the hand of a hog; but it ain't so no more; it's the hand of a man that's started in on a new life, and 'll die before he'll go back. You mark them words—don't forget I said them. It's a clean hand now; shake it—don't be afeard."

So they shook it, one after the other, all around, and cried. The judge's wife she kissed it. Then the old man he signed a pledge—made his mark.[6] The judge said it was the holiest time on record, or something like that. Then they tucked the old man into a beautiful room, which was the spare room, and in the night sometime he got powerful thirsty and clumb out onto the porch-roof and slid down a stanchion and traded his new coat for a jug of forty-rod,[7] and clumb back again and had a good old time; and towards daylight he crawled out again, drunk as a fiddler, and rolled off the porch and broke his left arm in two places and was most froze to death when somebody found him after sun-up. And when they come to look at that spare room, they had to take soundings[8] before they could navigate it.

The judge he felt kind of sore. He said he reckoned a body could reform the ole man with a shot-gun, maybe, but he didn't know no other way.

CHAPTER VI

Well, pretty soon the old man was up and around again, and then he went for Judge Thatcher in the courts to make him give up that money, and he went for me, too, for not stopping school. He catched me a couple of times and thrashed me, but I went to school just the same, and dodged him or out-run him most of the time. I didn't want to go to school much, before, but I reckoned I'd go now to spite pap. That law trial was a slow business; appeared like they warn't ever going to get started on it; so every now and then I'd borrow two or three dollars off of the judge for him, to keep from getting a cowhiding. Every time he got money he was drunk; and every time he got drunk he raised Cain around town; and every time he raised Cain he got jailed. He was just suited—this kind of thing was right in his line.

He got to hanging around the widow's too much, and so she told him at last, that if he didn't quit using[1] around there she would make trouble for him. Well, *wasn't* he mad? He said he would show who was Huck Finn's boss. So he watched out for me one day in the spring, and catched me, and took me up the river about three mile, in a skiff, and crossed over to the Illinois shore where it was woody and there warn't no houses but an old log hut in a place where the timber was so thick you couldn't find it if you didn't know where it was.

He kept me with him all the time, and I never got a chance to run off. We lived in that old cabin, and he always locked the door and put the key under his head, nights. He had a gun which he had stole, I reckon, and we fished and hunted, and that was what we lived on. Every little while he locked me in and went down to the store, three miles to the ferry, and traded fish and game for whisky and fetched it home and got drunk and had a good time, and licked me. The widow she found out where I was, by-and-by, and she sent a man over to try to get hold of me, but pap drove him off with the gun, and it warn't long after that till I was used to being where I was, and liked it, all but the cowhide part.

[6]I.e., signed, by making his mark, a written pledge to abstain from alcoholic drink.
[7]Rotgut whiskey judged powerful enough to knock a man 40 rods, 660 feet.
[8]Measure depths, go carefully.
[1]Loitering.

It was kind of lazy and jolly, laying off comfortable all day, smoking and fishing, and no books nor study. Two months or more ran along, and my clothes got to be all rags and dirt, and I didn't see how I'd ever got to like it so well at the widow's, where you had to wash, and eat on a plate, and comb up, and go to bed and get up regular, and be forever bothering over a book and have old Miss Watson pecking at you all the time. I didn't want to go back no more. I had stopped cussing, because the widow didn't like it; but now I took to it again because pap hadn't no objections. It was pretty good times up in the woods there, take it all around.

But by-and-by pap got too handy with his hick'ry, and I couldn't stand it. I was all over welts. He got to going away so much, too, and locking me in. Once he locked me in and was gone three days. It was dreadful lonesome. I judged he had got drowned and I wasn't ever going to get out any more. I was scared. I made up my mind I would fix up some way to leave there. I had tried to get out of that cabin many a time, but I couldn't find no way. There warn't a window to it big enough for a dog to get through. I couldn't get up the chimbly, it was too narrow. The door was thick solid oak slabs. Pap was pretty careful not to leave a knife or anything in the cabin when he was away; I reckon I had hunted the place over as much as a hundred times; well, I was 'most all the time at it, because it was about the only way to put in the time. But this time I found something at last; I found an old rusty wood-saw without any handle; it was laid in between a rafter and the clapboards of the roof. I greased it up and went to work. There was an old horse-blanket nailed against the logs at the far end of the cabin behind the table, to keep the wind from blowing through the chinks and putting the candle out. I got under the table and raised the blanket and went to work to saw a section of the big bottom log out, big enough to let me through. Well, it was a good long job, but I was getting towards the end of it when I heard pap's gun in the woods. I got rid of the signs of my work, and dropped the blanket and hid my saw, and pretty soon pap come in.

Pap warn't in a good humor—so he was his natural self. He said he was down to town, and everything was going wrong. His lawyer said he reckoned he would win his lawsuit and get the money, if they ever got started on the trial; but then there was ways to put it off a long time, and Judge Thatcher knowed how to do it. And he said people allowed there'd be another trial to get me away from him and give me to the widow for my guardian, and they guessed it would win, this time. This shook me up considerable, because I didn't want to go back to the widow's any more and be so cramped up and sivilized, as they called it. Then the old man got to cussing, and cussed everything and everybody he could think of, and then cussed them all over again to make sure he hadn't skipped any, and after that he polished off with a kind of a general cuss all around, including a considerable parcel of people which he didn't know the names of, and so called them what's-his-name, when he got to them, and went right along with his cussing.

He said he would like to see the widow get me. He said he would watch out, and if they tried to come any such game on him he knowed of a place six or seven mile off, to stow me in, where they might hunt till they dropped and they couldn't find me. That made me pretty uneasy again, but only for a minute; I reckoned I wouldn't stay on hand till he got that chance.

The old man made me go to the skiff and fetch the things he had got. There was a fifty-pound sack of corn meal, and a side of bacon, ammunition, and a four-gallon jug of whisky, and an old book and two newspapers for wadding,[2] besides some tow.[3] I toted up a load, and went back and set down on the bow of the skiff to rest. I thought it all over, and I reckoned I would walk off with the gun and some lines, and take to the woods when I run away. I guessed I wouldn't stay in one place, but just tramp right across the country, mostly night times, and hunt and fish to keep alive, and so get so far away that the old man nor the widow couldn't ever find me any more. I judged I would saw out and leave that night if pap got drunk enough, and I reckoned he would. I got so full of it I didn't notice how long I was staying, till the old man hollered and asked me whether I was asleep or drownded.

I got the things all up to the cabin, and then it was about dark. When I was cooking supper the old man took a swig or two and got sort of warmed up, and went to ripping again. He had been drunk over in town, and laid in the gutter all night, and he was a sight to look at. A body would a thought he was Adam, he was just all mud.[4] Whenever his liquor begun to work, he most always went for the govment. This time he says:

"Call this a govment! why, just look at it and see what it's like. Here's the law a-standing ready to take a man's son away from him—a man's own son, which he has had all the trouble and all the anxiety and all the expense of raising. Yes, just as that man has got that son raised at last, and ready to go to work and begin to do suthin' for *him* and give him a rest, the law up and goes for him. And they call *that* govment! That ain't all, nuther. The law backs that old Judge Thatcher up and helps him to keep me out o' my property. Here's what the law does. The law takes a man worth six thousand dollars and upards, and jams him into an old trap of a cabin like this, and lets him go round in clothes that ain't fitten for a hog. They calls that govment! A man can't get his rights in a govment like this. Sometimes I've a mighty notion to just leave the country for good and all. Yes, and I *told* 'em so; I told old Thatcher so to his face. Lots of 'em heard me, and can tell what I said. Says I, for two cents I'd leave the blamed country and never come anear it agin. Them's the very words. I says, look at my hat—if you call it a hat—but the lid raises up and the rest of it goes down till it's below my chin, and then it ain't rightly a hat at all, but more like my head was shoved up through a jint o' stove-pipe. Look at it, says I—such a hat for me to wear—one of the wealthiest men in this town, if I could git my rights.

"Oh, yes, this is a wonderful govment, wonderful. Why, looky here. There was a free nigger there, from Ohio;[5] a mulatter,[6] most as white as a white man. He had the whitest shirt on you ever see, too, and the shiniest hat; and there ain't a man in that town that's got as fine clothes as what he had; and he had a gold watch and chain, and a silver-headed cane—the awfulest old gray-headed nabob[7] in the State. And what do you think? they said he was a p'fessor in a college, and could talk all kinds of languages, and knowed everything. And that ain't the wust. They said he could *vote*, when he was at home. Well, that let me out. Thinks I, what is the country a-coming to? It was 'lection day, and I was just about to go and vote, myself, if I warn't too drunk to get there; but when they told me there was a State in this country where they'd let a nigger vote, I drawed out. I says I'll never vote again. Them's the very words I said; they all

---

[2]The material used to make the plugs inserted to retain the powder charge in a muzzle-loading gun.
[3]Short fibers of flax or hemp.
[4]"And the Lord God formed man of the dust of the ground." Genesis 2:7.
[5]Ohio had no slavery.   [6]Mulatto.   [7]Man of prominence, a "swell."

heard me; and the country may rot for all me—I'll never vote agin as long as I live. And to see the cool way of that nigger—why, he wouldn't a give me the road if I hadn't shoved him out o' the way. I says to the people, why ain't this nigger put up at auction and sold?—that's what I want to know. And what do you reckon they said? Why, they said he couldn't be sold till he's been in the State six months,[8] and he hadn't been there that long yet. There, now—that's a specimen. They call that a govment that can't sell a free nigger till he's been in the State six months. Here's a govment that calls itself a govment, and lets on to be a govment, and thinks it is a govment, and yet's got to set stock-still for six whole months before it can take ahold of a prowling, thieving, infernal, white-shirted free nigger, and—"

Pap was agoing on so, he never noticed where his old limber legs was taking him to, so he went head over heels over the tub of salt pork, and barked both shins, and the rest of his speech was all the hottest kind of language—mostly hove at the nigger and the govment, though he give the tub some, too, all along, here and there. He hopped around the cabin considerable, first on one leg and then on the other, holding first one shin and then the other one, and at last he let out with his left foot all of a sudden and fetched the tub a rattling kick. But it warn't good judgment, because that was the boot that had a couple of his toes leaking out of the front end of it; so now he raised a howl that fairly made a body's hair raise, and down he went in the dirt, and rolled there, and held his toes; and the cussing he done then laid over anything he had ever done previous. He said so his own self, afterwards. He had heard old Sowberry Hagan in his best days, and he said it laid over him, too; but I reckon that was sort of piling it on, maybe.

After supper pap took the jug, and said he had enough whisky there for two drunks and one delirium tremens. That was always his word. I judged he would be blind drunk in about an hour, and then I would steal the key, or saw myself out, one or 'tother. He drank, and drank, and tumbled down on his blankets, by-and-by; but luck didn't run my way. He didn't go sound asleep, but was uneasy. He groaned, and moaned, and thrashed around this way and that, for a long time. At last I got so sleepy I couldn't keep my eyes open, all I could do, and so before I knowed what I was about I was sound asleep, and the candle burning.

I don't know how long I was asleep, but all of a sudden there was an awful scream and I was up. There was pap, looking wild and skipping around every which way and yelling about snakes. He said they was crawling up his leg; and then he would give a jump and scream, and say one had bit him on the cheek— but I couldn't see no snakes. He started and run round and round the cabin, hollering "take him off! take him off! he's biting me on the neck!" I never see a man look so wild in the eyes. Pretty soon he was all fagged out, and fell down panting; then he rolled over and over, wonderful fast, kicking things every which way, and striking and grabbing at the air with his hands, and screaming, and saying there was devils ahold of him. He wore out, by-and-by, and laid still a while, moaning. Then he laid stiller, and didn't make a sound. I could hear the owls and the wolves, away off in the woods, and it seemed terrible still. He was laying over by the corner. By-and-by he raised up, part way, and listened, with his head to one side. He says very low:

"Tramp—tramp—tramp; that's the dead; tramp—tramp—tramp; they're

---

[8]A reference to the fact that in some circumstances a free Negro could be legally re-enslaved.

coming after me; but I won't go—Oh, they're here! don't touch me—don't! hands off!—they're cold; let go—Oh, let a poor devil alone!"

Then he went down on all fours and crawled off begging them to let him alone, and he rolled himself up in his blanket and wallowed in under the old pine table, still a-begging; and then he went to crying. I could hear him through the blanket.

By-and-by he rolled out and jumped up on his feet looking wild, and he see me and went for me. He chased me round and round the place, with a clasp-knife,[9] calling me the Angel of Death and saying he would kill me and then I couldn't come for him no more. I begged, and told him I was only Huck, but he laughed *such* a screechy laugh, and roared and cussed, and kept on chasing me up. Once when I turned short and dodged under his arm he made a grab and got me by the jacket between my shoulders, and I thought I was gone; but I slid out of the jacket quick as lightning, and saved myself. Pretty soon he was all tired out, and dropped down with his back against the door, and said he would rest a minute and then kill me. He put his knife under him, and said he would sleep and get strong, and then he would see who was who.

So he dozed off, pretty soon. By-and-by I got the old split-bottom[10] chair and clumb up, as easy as I could, not to make any noise, and got down the gun. I slipped the ramrod down it to make sure it was loaded, and then I laid it across the turnip barrel, pointing towards pap, and set down behind it to wait for him to stir. And how slow and still the time did drag along.

CHAPTER VII

"Git up! what you 'bout!"

I opened my eyes and looked around, trying to make out where I was. It was after sun-up, and I had been sound asleep. Pap was standing over me, looking sour—and sick, too. He says—

"What you doin' with this gun?"

I judged he didn't know nothing about what he had been doing, so I says:

"Somebody tried to get in, so I was laying for him."

"Why didn't you roust me out?"

"Well, I tried to, but I couldn't; I couldn't budge you."

"Well, all right. Don't stand there palavering[1] all day, but out with you and see if there's a fish on the lines for breakfast. I'll be along in a minute."

He unlocked the door and I cleared out, up the river bank. I noticed some pieces of limbs and such things floating down, and a sprinkling of bark; so I know the river had begun to rise. I reckoned I would have great times, now, if I was over at the town. The June rise used to be always luck for me; because as soon as that rise begins, here comes cord-wood[2] floating down, and pieces of log rafts—sometimes a dozen logs together; so all you have to do is to catch them and sell them to the wood yards and the sawmill.

I went along up the bank with one eye out for pap and 'tother one out for what the rise might fetch along. Well, all at once, here comes a canoe; just a beauty, too, about thirteen or fourteen foot long, riding high like a duck. I shot

[9]A knife with a blade that folds into the clasp (handle).
[10]I.e., with a seat of interwoven wood strips.
[1]Talking idly, jabbering.
[2]Wood cut in four-foot lengths.

head first off of the bank, like a frog, clothes and all on, and struck out for the canoe. I just expected there'd be somebody laying down in it, because people often done that to fool folks, and when a chap had pulled a skiff out most to it they'd raise up and laugh at him. But it warn't so this time. It was a drift-canoe, sure enough, and I clumb in and paddled her ashore. Thinks I the old man will be glad when he sees this—she's worth ten dollars. But when I got to shore pap wasn't in sight yet, and as I was running her into a little creek like a gully, all hung over with vines and willows, I struck another idea; I judged I'd hide her good, and then, stead of taking to the woods when I run off, I'd go down the river about fifty mile and camp in one place for good, and not have such a rough time tramping on foot.

It was pretty close to the shanty, and I thought I heard the old man coming, all the time; but I got her hid; and then I out and looked around a bunch of willows, and there was the old man down the path a piece just drawing a bead on a bird with his gun. So he hadn't seen anything.

When he got along, I was hard at it taking up a "trot" line.[3] He abused me a little for being so slow, but I told him I fell in the river and that was what made me so long. I knowed he would see I was wet, and then he would be asking questions. We got five catfish off the lines and went home.

While we laid off, after breakfast, to sleep up, both of us being about wore out, I got to thinking that if I could fix up some way to keep pap and the widow from trying to follow me, it would be a certainer thing than trusting to luck to get far enough off before they missed me; you see, all kinds of things might happen. Well, I didn't see no way for a while, but by-and-by pap raised up a minute, to drink another barrel of water, and he says:

"Another time a man comes a-prowling round here, you roust me out, you hear? That man warn't here for no good. I'd a shot him. Next time, you roust me out, you hear?"

Then he dropped down and went to sleep again—but what he had been saying give me the very idea I wanted. I says to myself, I can fix it now so nobody won't think of following me.

About twelve o'clock we turned out and went along up the bank. The river was coming up pretty fast, and lots of drift-wood going by on the rise. By-and-by, along comes part of a log raft—nine logs fast together. We went out with the skiff and towed it ashore. Then we had dinner. Anybody but pap would a waited and see the day through, so as to catch more stuff; but that warn't pap's style. Nine logs was enough for one time; he must shove right over to town and sell. So he locked me in and took the skiff and started off towing the raft about half-past three. I judged he wouldn't come back that night. I waited till I reckoned he had got a good start, then I out with my saw and went to work on that log again. Before he was 'tother side of the river I was out of the hole; him and his raft was just a speck on the water away off yonder.

I took the sack of corn meal and took it to where the canoe was hid, and shoved the vines and branches apart and put it in; then I done the same with the side of bacon; then the whisky jug; I took all the coffee and sugar there was, and all the ammunition; I took the wadding; I took the bucket and gourd, I took a dipper and a tin cup, and my old saw and two blankets, and the skillet and the coffee-pot. I took fish-lines and matches and other things—everything that was worth a cent. I cleaned out the place. I wanted an ax, but there wasn't

[3]A long fishing line (usually set in a stream or river) from which hooks are suspended at intervals.

any, only the one out at the wood pile, and I knowed why I was going to leave that. I fetched out the gun, and now I was done.

I had wore the ground a good deal, crawling out of the hole and dragging out so many things. So I fixed that as good as I could from the outside by scattering dust on the place, which covered up the smoothness and the sawdust. Then I fixed the piece of log back into its place, and put two rocks under it and one against it to hold it there,—for it was bent up at that place, and didn't quite touch ground. If you stood four or five foot away and didn't know it was sawed, you wouldn't even notice it; and besides, this was the back of the cabin and it warn't likely anybody would go fooling around there.

It was all grass clear to the canoe; so I hadn't left a track. I followed around to see. I stood on the bank and looked out over the river. All safe. So I took the gun and went up a piece into the woods and was hunting around for some birds, when I see a wild pig; hogs soon went wild in them bottoms after they had got away from the prairie farms. I shot this fellow and took him into camp.

I took the ax and smashed in the door—I beat it and hacked it considerable, a-doing it. I fetched the pig in and took him back nearly to the table and hacked into his throat with the ax, and laid him down on the ground to bleed—I say ground, because it *was* ground—hard packed, and no boards. Well, next I took an old sack and put a lot of big rocks in it,—all I could drag—and I started it from the pig and dragged it to the door and through the woods down to the river and dumped it in, and down it sunk, out of sight. You could easy see that something had been dragged over the ground. I did wish Tom Sawyer was there, I know he would take an interest in this kind of business, and throw in the fancy touches. Nobody could spread himself like Tom Sawyer in such a thing as that.

Well, last I pulled out some of my hair, and bloodied the ax good, and stuck it on the back side, and slung the ax in the corner. Then I took up the pig and held him to my breast with my jacket (so he couldn't drip) till I got a good piece below the house and then dumped him into the river. Now I thought of something else. So I went and got the bag of meal and my old saw out of the canoe and fetched them to the house. I took the bag to where it used to stand, and ripped a hole in the bottom of it with the saw, for there warn't no knives and forks on the place—pap done everything with his clasp-knife, about the cooking. Then I carried the sack about a hundred yards across the grass and through the willows east of the house, to a shallow lake that was five mile wide and full of rushes—and ducks too, you might say, in the season. There was a slough or a creek leading out of it on the other side, that went miles away, I don't know where, but it didn't go to the river. The meal sifted out and made a little track all the way to the lake. I dropped pap's whetstone there too, so as to look like it had been done by accident. Then I tied up the rip in the meal sack with a string, so it wouldn't leak no more, and took it and my saw to the canoe again.

It was about dark, now; so I dropped the canoe down the river under some willows that hung over the bank, and waited for the moon to rise. I made fast to a willow; then I took a bite to eat, and by-and-by laid down in the canoe to smoke a pipe and lay out a plan. I says to myself, they'll follow the track of that sackful of rocks to the shore and then drag the river for me. And they'll follow that meal track to the lake and go browsing down the creek that leads out of it to find the robbers that killed me and took the things. They won't ever hunt the river for anything but my dead carcass. They'll soon get tired of that, and won't bother no more about me. All right; I can stop anywhere I want to. Jackson's

Island is good enough for me; I know that island pretty well, and nobody ever comes there. And then I can paddle over to town, nights, and slink around and pick up things I want. Jackson's Island's the place.

I was pretty tired, and the first thing I knowed, I was asleep. When I woke up I didn't know where I was, for a minute. I set up and looked around, a little scared. Then I remembered. The river looked miles and miles across. The moon was so bright I could a counted the drift logs that went a slipping along, black and still, hundreds of yards out from shore. Everything was dead quiet, and it looked late, and *smelt* late. You know what I mean—I don't know the words to put it in.

I took a good gap and a stretch, and was just going to unhitch and start, when I heard a sound away over the water. I listened. Pretty soon I made it out. It was that dull kind of a regular sound that comes from oars working in rowlocks when it's a still night. I peeped out through the willow branches, and there it was—a skiff, away across the water. I couldn't tell how many was in it. It kept a-coming, and when it was abreast of me I see there warn't but one man in it. Thinks I, maybe it's pap, though I warn't expecting him. He dropped below me, with the current, and by-and-by he come a-swinging up shore in the easy water,[4] and he went by so close I could a reached out the gun and touched him. Well it *was* pap, sure enough—and sober, too, by the way he laid to his oars.

I didn't lose no time. The next minute I was a-spinning down stream soft but quick in the shade of the bank. I made two mile and a half, and then struck out a quarter of a mile or more towards the middle of the river, because pretty soon I would be passing the ferry landing and people might see me and hail me. I got out amongst the drift-wood and then laid down in the bottom of the canoe and let her float. I laid there and had a good rest and a smoke out of my pipe, looking away into the sky, not a cloud in it. The sky looks ever so deep when you lay down on your back in the moonshine; I never knowed it before. And how far a body can hear on the water such nights! I heard people talking at the ferry landing. I heard what they said, too, every word of it. One man said it was getting towards the long days and the short nights, now. 'Tother one said *this* warn't one of the short ones, he reckoned—and then they laughed, and he said it over again and they laughed again; then they waked up another fellow and told him, and laughed, but he didn't laugh; he ripped out something brisk and said let him alone. The first fellow said he 'lowed to tell it to his old woman—she would think it was pretty good; but he said that warn't nothing to some things he had said in his time. I heard one man say it was nearly three o'clock, and he hoped daylight wouldn't wait more than about a week longer. After that, the talk got further and further away, and I couldn't make out the words any more, but I could hear the mumble; and now and then a laugh, too, but it seemed a long ways off.

I was away below the ferry now. I rise up and there was Jackson's Island, about two mile and a half down stream, heavy-timbered and standing up out of the middle of the river, big and dark and solid, like a steamboat without any lights. There warn't any signs of the bar at the head—it was all under water, now.

It didn't take me long to get there. I shot past the head at a ripping rate, the current was so swift, and then I got into the dead water[5] and landed on the side towards the Illinois shore. I run the canoe into a deep dent in the bank that I knowed about; I had to part the willow branches to get in; and when I made fast nobody could a seen the canoe from the outside.

[4]Where the current is slight.
[5]I.e., without current.

I went up and set down on a log at the head of the island and looked out on the big river and the black driftwood, and away over to the town, three mile away, where there was three or four lights twinkling. A monstrous big lumber raft was about a mile up stream, coming along down, with a lantern in the middle of it. I watched it come creeping down, and when it was most abreast of where I stood I heard a man say, "Stern oars, there! heave her head to stab-board!"[6] I heard that just as plain as if the man was by my side.

There was a little gray in the sky, now; so I stepped into the woods and laid down for a nap before breakfast.

CHAPTER VIII

The sun was up so high when I waked, that I judged it was after eight o'clock. I laid there in the grass and the cool shade, thinking about things and feeling rested and ruther comfortable and satisfied. I could see the sun out at one or two holes, but mostly it was big trees all about, and gloomy in there amongst them. There was freckled places on the ground where the light sifted down through the leaves, and the freckled places swapped about a little, showing there was a little breeze up there. A couple of squirrels set on a limb and jabbered at me very friendly.

I was powerful lazy and comfortable—didn't want to get up and cook break-fast. Well, I was dozing off again, when I thinks I hears a deep sound of "boom!" away up the river. I rouses up and rests on my elbow and listens; pretty soon I hears it again. I hopped up and went and looked out at a hole in the leaves, and I see a bunch of smoke laying on the water a long ways up—about abreast the ferry. And there was the ferry-boat full of people, floating along down. I knowed what was the matter, now. "Boom!" I see the white smoke squirt out of the ferry-boat's side. You see, they was firing cannon over the water, trying to make my carcass come to the top.

I was pretty hungry, but it warn't going to do for me to start a fire, because they might see the smoke. So I set there and watched the cannon-smoke and listened to the boom. The river was a mile wide, there, and it always looks pretty on a summer morning—so I was having a good enough time seeing them hunt for my remainders, if I only had a bite to eat. Well, then I happened to think how they always put quicksilver in loaves of bread and float them off because they always go right to the drownded carcass and stop there. So says I, I'll keep a lookout, and if any of them's floating around after me, I'll give them a show. I changed to the Illinois edge of the island to see what luck I could have, and I warn't disappointed. A big double loaf come along, and I most got it, with a long stick, but my foot slipped and she floated out further. Of course I was where the current set in the closest to the shore—I knowed enough for that. But by-and-by along comes another one, and this time I won. I took out the plug and shook out the little dab of quicksilver, and set my teeth in. It was "baker's bread"[1]—what the quality eat—none of your low-down corn-pone.[2]

I got a good place amongst the leaves, and set there on a log, munching the bread and watching the ferry-boat, and very well satisfied. And then something struck me. I says, now I reckon the widow or the parson or somebody prayed that this bread would find me, and here it has gone and done it. So there ain't

---

[6]Starboard, the right-hand side of a ship viewed by an observer looking forward. Larboard, "labboard," the left-hand side.
[1]White bread, made from wheat flour, a luxury.   [2]Corn bread.

no doubt but there is something in that thing. That is, there's something in it when a body like the widow or the parson prays, but it don't work for me, and I reckon it don't work for only just the right kind.

I lit a pipe and had a good long smoke and went on watching. The ferry-boat was floating with the current, and I allowed I'd have a chance to see who was aboard when she come along, because she would come in close, where the bread did. When she'd got pretty well along down towards me, I put out my pipe and went to where I fished out the bread, and laid down behind a log on the bank in a little open place. Where the log forked I could peep through.

By-and-by she come along, and she drifted in so close that they could a run out a plank and walked ashore. Most everybody was on the boat. Pap, and Judge Thatcher, and Bessie Thatcher, and Jo Harper, and Tom Sawyer, and his old Aunt Polly, and Sid and Mary, and plenty more. Everybody was talking about the murder, but the captain broke in and says:

"Look sharp, now; the current sets in the closest here, and maybe he's washed ashore and got tangled amongst the brush at the water's edge. I hope so, anyway."

I didn't hope so. They all crowded up and leaned over the rails, nearly in my face, and kept still, watching with all their might. I could see them first-rate, but they couldn't see me. Then the captain sung out:

'Stand away!" and the cannon let off such a blast right before me that it made me deef with the noise and pretty near blind with the smoke, and I judged I was gone. If they'd a had some bullets in, I reckon they'd a got the corpse they was after. Well, I see I warn't hurt, thanks to goodness. The boat floated on and went out of sight around the shoulder of the island. I could hear the booming, now and then, further and further off, and by-and-by after an hour, I didn't hear it no more. The island was three mile long. I judged they had got to the foot, and was giving it up. But they didn't yet a while. They turned around the foot of the island and started up the channel on the Missouri side, under steam, and booming once in a while as they went. I crossed over to that side and watched them. When they got abreast the head of the island they quit shooting and dropped over to the Missouri shore and went home to the town.

I knowed I was all right now. Nobody else would come a-hunting after me. I got my traps[3] out of the canoe and made me a nice camp in the thick woods. I made a kind of a tent out of my blankets to put my things under so the rain wouldn't get at them. I catched a cat-fish and haggled him open with my saw, and towards sundown I started my camp fire and had supper. Then I set out a line to catch some fish for breakfast.

When it was dark I set by my camp fire smoking, and feeling pretty satisfied; but by-and-by it got sort of lonesome, and so I went and set on the bank and listened to the currents washing along, and counted the stars and drift-logs and rafts that come down, and then went to bed; there ain't no better way to put in time when you are lonesome; you can't stay so, you soon get over it.

And so for three days and nights. No difference—just the same thing. But the next day I went exploring around down through the island. I was boss of it; it all belonged to me, so to say, and I wanted to know all about it; but mainly I wanted to put in the time. I found plenty strawberries, ripe and prime; and green summer-grapes, and green razberries; and the green blackberries was just beginning to show. They would all come handy by-and-by, I judged.

Well, I went fooling along in the deep woods till I judged I warn't far from the foot of the island. I had my gun along, but I hadn't shot nothing; it was for

---

[3]Gear, belongings.

protection; thought I would kill some game nigh home. About this time I mighty near stepped on a good sized snake, and it went sliding off through the grass and flowers, and I after it, trying to get a shot at it. I clipped along, and all of a sudden I bounded right on to the ashes of a camp fire that was still smoking.

My heart jumped up amongst my lungs. I never waited for to look further, but uncocked my gun and went sneaking back on my tiptoes as fast as ever I could. Every now and then I stopped a second, amongst the thick leaves, and listened; but my breath come so hard I couldn't hear nothing else. I slunk along another piece further, then listened again; and so on, and so on; if I see a stump, I took it for a man; if I trod on a stick and broke it, it made me feel like a person had cut one of my breaths in two and I only got half, and the short half, too.

When I got to camp I warn't feeling very brash, there warn't much sand in my craw;[4] but I says, this ain't no time to be fooling around. So I got all my traps into my canoe again so as to have them out of sight, and I put out the fire and scattered the ashes around to look like an old last year's camp, and then clumb a tree.

I reckon I was up in the tree two hours; but I didn't see nothing, I didn't hear nothing—I only *thought* I heard and seen as much as a thousand things. Well, I couldn't stay up there forever; so at last I got down, but I kept in the thick woods and on the lookout all the time. All I could get to eat was berries and what was left over from breakfast.

By the time it was night I was pretty hungry. So when it was good and dark, I slid out from shore before moonrise and paddled over to the Illinois bank—about a quarter of a mile. I went out in the woods and cooked a supper, and I had about made up my mind I would stay there all night, when I hear a *plunkety-plunk, plunkety-plunk*, and says to myself, horses coming; and next I heard people's voices. I got everything into the canoe as quick as I could, and then went creeping through the woods to see what I could find out. I hadn't got far when I hear a man say:

"We better camp here, if we can find a good place; the horses is about beat out. Let's look around."

I didn't wait, but shoved out and paddled away easy. I tied up in the old place, and reckoned I would sleep in the canoe.

I didn't sleep much. I couldn't, somehow, for thinking. And every time I waked up I thought somebody had me by the neck. So the sleep didn't do me no good. By-and-by I says to myself, I can't live this way; I'm agoing to find out who it is that's here on the island with me; I'll find it out or bust. Well, I felt better, right off.

So I took my paddle and slid out from shore just a step or two, and then let the canoe drop along down amongst the shadows. The moon was shining, and outside of the shadows it made it most as light as day. I poked along well onto an hour, everything still as rocks and sound asleep. Well by this time I was most down to the foot of the island. A little ripply, cool breeze begun to blow, and that was as good as saying the night was about done. I give her a turn with the paddle and brung her nose to shore; then I got my gun and slipped out and into the edge of the woods. I set down there on a log and looked out through the leaves. I see the moon go off watch and the darkness begin to blanket the river. But in a little while I see a pale streak over the tree-tops, and knowed the day was coming. So I took my gun and slipped off towards where I had run across that camp fire, stopping every minute or two to listen. But I hadn't no

---

[4]I.e., courage in my heart.

luck, somehow! I couldn't seem to find the place. But by-and-by, sure enough, I catched a glimpse of fire, away through the trees. I went for it, cautious and slow. By-and-by I was close enough to have a look, and there laid a man on the ground. It most give me the fan-tods.[5] He had a blanket around his head, and his head was nearly in the fire. I set there behind a clump of bushes, in about six foot of him, and kept my eyes on him steady. It was getting gray daylight, now. Pretty soon he gapped, and stretched himself, and hove off the blanket, and it was Miss Watson's Jim! I bet I was glad to see him. I says:

"Hello, Jim!" and skipped out.

He bounced up and stared at me wild. Then he drops down on his knees, and puts his hands together and says:

"Doan' hurt me—don't! I hain't ever done no harm to a ghos'. I awluz liked dead people, en done all I could for 'em. You go en git in de river agin, whah you b'longs, en doan' do nuffin to Ole Jim, 'at 'uz awluz yo' fren'."

Well, I warn't long making him understand I warn't dead. I was ever so glad to see Jim. I warn't lonesome now. I told him I warn't afraid of *him* telling the people where I was. I talked along, but he only set there and looked at me; never said nothing. Then I says:

"It's good daylight. Le's get breakfast. Make up your camp fire good."

"What's de use er makin' up de camp fire to cook strawbries en sich truck?[6] But you got a gun, hain't you? Den we kin git sumfn better den strawbries."

"Strawberries and such truck," I says. "Is that what you live on?"

"I couldn' git nuffn else," he says.

"Why, how long you been on the island, Jim?"

"I come heah de night arter you's killed."

"What, all that time?"

"Yes-indeedy."

"And ain't you had nothing but that kind of rubbage to eat?"

"No, sah—nuffn else."

"Well, you must be most starved, ain't you?"

"I reck'n I could eat a hoss. I think I could. How long you ben on de islan'?"

"Since the night I got killed."

"No! W'y, what has you lived on? But you got a gun. Oh, yes, you got a gun. Dat's good. Now you kill sumfn en I'll make up de fire."

So we went over to where the canoe was, and while he built a fire in a grassy open place amongst the trees, I fetched meal and bacon and coffee, and coffee-pot and frying-pan, and sugar and tin cups, and the nigger was set back considerable, because he reckoned it was all done with witchcraft. I catched a good big cat-fish, too, and Jim cleaned him with his knife, and fried him.

When breakfast was ready, we lolled on the grass and eat it smoking hot. Jim laid it in with all his might, for he was most about starved. Then when we had got pretty well stuffed, we laid off and lazied.

By-and-by Jim says:

"But looky here, Huck, who wuz it dat 'uz killed in dat shanty, ef it warn't you?"

Then I told him the whole thing, and he said it was smart. He said Tom Sawyer couldn't get up no better plan than what I had. Then I says:

"How do you come to be here, Jim, and how'd you get here?"

He looked pretty uneasy, and didn't say nothing for a minute. Then he says: "Maybe I better not tell."

[5]Fidgets.   [6]Things, produce.

"Why, Jim?"

"Well, dey's reasons. But you wouldn't tell on me ef I 'uz to tell you, would you, Huck?"

"Blamed if I would, Jim."

"Well, I b'lieve you, Huck. I—I *run off.*"

"Jim!"

"But mind, you said you wouldn't tell—you know you said you wouldn't tell, Huck."

"Well, I did. I said I wouldn't, and I'll stick to it. Honest *injun* I will. People would call me a low down Ab'litionist[7] and despise me for keeping mum—but don't make no difference. I ain't agoing to tell, and I ain't agoing back there anyways. So now, le's know all about it."

"Well, you see, it 'uz dis way. Ole Missus—dat's Miss Watson—she pecks on me all de time, en treats me pooty rough, but she awluz said she wouldn't sell me down to Orleans. But I noticed dey wuz a nigger trader roun' de place considable, lately, en I begin to git oneasy. Well, one night I creeps to de do', pooty late, en de do' warn't quite shet, en I hear ole missus tell de widder she gwyne to sell me down to Orleans[8] but she didn't want to, but she could git eight hund'd dollars for me, en it 'uz sich a big stack o'money she couldn' resis'. De widder she try to git her to say she wouldn' do it, but I never waited to hear de res'. I lit out mighty quick, I tell you.

"I tuck out en shin down de hill en 'spec to steal a skift 'long de sho' som'ers 'bove de town, but dey wuz people a-stirring' yit, so I hid in de ole tumble-down cooper shop[9] on de bank to wait for everybody to go 'way. Well, I wuz dah all night. Dey wuz somebody roun' all de time. 'Long 'about six in de mawnin', skifts begin to go by, en 'bout eight er nine every skift dat went 'long wuz talkin' 'bout how yo' pap come over to de town en say you's killed. Dese las' skifts wuz full o' ladies en genlmen agoin' over for to see de place. Sometimes dey'd pull up at de sho' en take a res' b'fo' dey started acrost, so by de talk I got to know all 'bout de killin'. I 'uz powerful sorry you's killed, Huck, but I ain't no mo', now.

"I laid dah under de shavins all day. I 'uz hungry, but I warn't afeared; bekase I knowed ole missus en de widder wuz goin' to start to de camp-meetn'[10] right arter breakfas' en be gone all day, en dey knows I goes off wid de cattle 'bout daylight, so dey wouldn't 'spec to see me roun' de place, en so dey wouldn' miss me tell arter dark in de evenin'. De yuther servants wouldn' miss me, kase dey'd shin out en take holiday, soon as de ole folks 'uz out'n de way.

"Well, when it come dark I tuck out up de river road, en went 'bout two mile er more to whah dey warn't no houses. I'd made up my mine 'bout what I's agwyne to do. You see ef I kep' on tryin' to git away afoot, de dogs 'ud track me; ef I stole a skift to cross over, dey'd miss dat skift, you see, en dey'd know 'bout whah I'd lan' on de yuther side en whah to pick up my track. So I says, a raff is what I's arter; it doan' *make* no track.

"I see a light a-comin' roun' de p'int, bymeby, so I wade' in en shove' a log ahead o' me, en swum more'n half-way acrost de river, en got in 'mongst de drift-wood, en kep' my head down low, en kinder swum agin de current tell de raff come along. Den I swum to de stern uv it, en tuck aholt. It clouded up en 'uz pooty dark for a little while. So I clumb up en laid down on de planks. De

---

[7]One devoted to the abolition of slavery.

[8]I.e., be "sold down the river" to work as a field hand on a large plantation.

[9]A barrel-maker's shop.

[10]Evangelistic religious meetings held in rural areas and attended by enthusiasts who camp nearby.

men 'uz all 'way yonder in de middle, whah de lantern wuz. De river wuz arisin' en dey wuz a good current; so I reck'n'd 'at by fo' in de mawnin' I'd be twenty-five mile down de river, en den I'd slip in, jis' b'fo' daylight, en swim asho' en take to de woods on de Illinois side.[11]

"But I didn't have no luck. When we 'uz mos' down to de head er de islan', a man begin to come aft wid de lantern. I see it warn't no use fer to wait, so I slid overboad, en struck out fer de islan'. Well, I had a notion I could lan' mos' anywhers, but I couldn't—bank too bluff. I 'uz mos' to de foot er de islan' b'fo' I foun' a good place. I went into de woods en jedged I wouldn' fool wid raffs no mo', long as dey move de lantern roun' so. I had my pipe en a plug er dog-leg,[12] en some matches in my cap, en dey warn't wet, so I 'uz all right."

"And so you ain't had no meat nor bread to eat all this time? Why didn't you get mud-turkles?"

"How you gwyne to git'm? You can't slip up on um en grab um; en how's a body gwyne to hit um wid a rock? How could a body do it in de night? en I warn't gwyne to show myself on de bank in de daytime."

"Well, that's so. You've had to keep in the woods all the time, of course. Did you hear 'em shooting the cannon?"

"Oh, yes. I knowed dey was arter you. I see um go by heah; watched um thoo de bushes."

Some young birds come along, flying a yard or two at a time and lighting. Jim said it was a sign it was going to rain. He said it was a sign when young chickens flew that way, and so he reckoned it was the same way when young birds done it. I was going to catch some of them, but Jim wouldn't let me. He said it was death. He said his father laid mighty sick once, and some of them catched a bird, and his old granny said his father would die, and he did.

And Jim said you musn't count the things you are going to cook for dinner, because that would bring bad luck. The same if you shook the table-cloth after sundown. And he said if a man owned a bee-hive, and that man died, the bees must be told about it before sun-up next morning, or else the bees would all weaken down and quit work and die. Jim said bees wouldn't sting idiots; but I didn't believe that, because I had tried them lots of times myself, and they wouldn't sting me.

I had heard about some of these things before, but not all of them. Jim knowed all kinds of signs. He said he knowed most everything. I said it looked to me like all the signs was about bad luck, and so I asked him if there warn't any good-luck signs. He says:

"Mighty few—an' *dey* ain' no use to a body. What you want to know when good luck's a-comin' for? want to keep it off?" And he said: "Ef you's got hairy arms en a hairy breas', it's a sign dat you's agwyne to be rich. Well, dey's some use in a sign like dat, 'kase it's so fur ahead. You see, maybe you's got to be po' a long time fust, en so you might git discourage' en kill yo'self 'f you didn' know by de sign dat you gwyne to be rich bymeby."

"Have you got hairy arms and hairy breast, Jim?"

"What's de use to ax dat question? don' you see I has?"

"Well, are you rich?"

---

[11]In Illinois, although it was a free state, runaway slaves lacking free papers were subject to arrest and a term of indentured labor. Jim's best chance for escape was to continue down river to the confluence of the Mississippi and Ohio Rivers and thence up the Ohio to a northern state. There proslavery forces were less numerous than in southern Illinois, and Jim could hope to escape to Canada through the Underground Railway.

[12]A plug of cheap leaf tobacco, twisted and bent into the shape of a dog's hind leg.

"No, but I ben rich wunst, and gwyne to be rich agin. Wunst I had foteen dollars, but I tuck to specalat'n', en got busted out."

"What did you speculate in, Jim?"

"Well, fust I tackled stock."

"What kind of stock?"

"Why, live stock. Cattle, you know. I put ten dollars in a cow. But I ain't gwyne to resk no mo' money in stock. De cow up 'n' died on my han's."

"So you lost the ten dollars."

"No, I didn't lose it all. I on'y los' 'bout nine of it. I sole de hide en taller[13] for a dollar en ten cents."

"You had five dollars and ten cents left. Did you speculate any more?"

"Yes. You know dat one-laigged nigger dat b'longs to old Misto Bradish? well, he sot up a bank, en say anybody dat put in a dollar git fo' dollars mo' at de en' er de year. Well, all de niggers went in, but dey didn' have much. I wuz de on'y one dat had much. So I stuck out for mo' dan fo' dollars, en I said 'f I didn' git it I'd start a bank mysef. Well o' course dat nigger want' to keep me out er de business, bekase he say dey warn't business 'nough for two banks, so he say I could put in my five dollars en he pay me thirty-five at de en' er de year."

"So I done it. Den I reck'n'd I'd inves' de thirty-five dollars right off en keep things a-movin'. Dey wuz a nigger name' Bob, dat had ketched a wood-flat,[14] en his marster didn' know it;[15] en I bought it off'n him en told him to take de thirty-five dollars when de en' er de year come; but somebody stole de wood-flat dat night, en nex' day de one-laigged nigger say de bank's busted. So dey didn' none uv us git no money."

"What did you do with the ten cents, Jim?"

"Well, I 'uz gwyne to spen' it, but I had a dream, en de dream tole me to give it to a nigger name' Balum—Balum's Ass[16] dey call him for short, he's one er dem chuckle-heads, you know. But he's lucky, dey say, en I see I warn't lucky. De dream say let Balum inves' de ten cents en he'd make a raise for me. Well, Balum he tuck de money, en when he wuz in church he hear de preacher say dat whoever give to de po' len' to de Lord, en boun' to git his money back a hund'd times. So Balum he tuck en give de ten cents to de po', en laid low to see what wuz gwyne to come of it."

"Well, what did come of it, Jim?"

"Nuffn' never come of it. I couldn' manage to k'leck dat money no way; en Balum he couldn'. I ain' gwyne to len' no mo' money 'dout I see de security. Boun' to git yo' money back a hund'd times, de preacher say! Ef I could git de ten *cents* back, I'd call it squah, en be glad er de chanst."

"Well, it's all right, anyway, Jim, long as you're going to be rich again some time or other."

"Yes—en I's rich now, come to look at it. I owns mysef, en I's wuth eight hund'd dollars. I wisht I had de money, I wouldn' want no mo'."

CHAPTER IX

I wanted to go and look at a place right about the middle of the island, that I'd found when I was exploring; so we started, and soon got to it, because the island was only three miles long and a quarter of a mile wide.

[13]Tallow.   [14]Flat-bottomed boat for carrying wood.

[15]Possessions of a slave were, by law, the property of the slave's owner.

[16]A pun on the Biblical story of Balaam who, blind to the truth, was saved from death by the ass upon which he rode. Numbers 22:21–34.

This place was a tolerable long steep hill or ridge, about forty foot high. We had a rough time getting to the top, the sides were so steep and the bushes so thick. We tramped and clumb around all over it, and by-and-by found a good big cavern in the rock, most up to the top of the side toward Illinois. The cavern was as big as two or three rooms bunched together, and Jim could stand up straight in it. It was cool in there. Jim was for putting our traps in there, right away, but I said we didn't want to be climbing up and down there all the time.

Jim said if we had the canoe hid in a good place, and had all the traps in the cavern, we could rush there if anybody was to come to the island, and they would never find us without dogs. And besides, he said them little birds had said it was going to rain, and did I want the things to get wet?

So we went back and got the canoe and paddled up abreast the cavern, and lugged all the traps up there. Then we hunted up a place close by to hide the canoe in, amongst the thick willows. We took some fish off of the lines and set them again, and begun to get ready for dinner.

The door of the cavern was big enough to roll a hogshead in, and on one side of the door the floor stuck out a little bit and was flat and a good place to build a fire on. So we built it there and cooked dinner.

We spread the blankets inside for a carpet, and eat our dinner in there. We put all the other things handy at the back of the cavern. Pretty soon it darkened up and begun to thunder and lighten; so the birds was right about it. Directly it begun to rain, and it rained like all fury, too, and I never see the wind blow so. It was one of these regular summer storms. It would get so dark that it looked all blue-black outside, and lovely; and the rain would thrash along by so thick that the trees off a little ways looked dim and spider-webby; and here would come a blast of wind that would bend the trees down and turn up the pale underside of the leaves; and then a perfect ripper of a gust would follow along and set the branches to tossing their arms as if they were just wild; and next, when it was just about the bluest and blackest—*fst!* it was as bright as glory and you'd have a little glimpse of tree-tops a-plunging about, away off yonder in the storm, hundreds of yards further than you could see before; dark as sin again in a second, and now you'd hear the thunder let go with an awful crash and then go rumbling, grumbling, tumbling down the sky towards the under side of the world, like rolling empty barrels down stairs, where it's long stairs and they bounce a good deal, you know.

"Jim, this is nice," I says. "I wouldn't want to be nowhere else but here. Pass me along another hunk of fish and some hot corn-bread."

"Well, you wouldn't a ben here, 'f it hadn't a ben for Jim. You'd a ben down dah in de woods widout any dinner, en gittn' mos' drownded, too, dat you would, honey. Chickens knows when it's gwyne to rain, en so do de birds, chile."

The river went on raising and raising for ten or twelve days, till at last it was over the banks. The water was three or four foot deep on the island in the low places and on the Illinois bottom. On that side it was a good many miles wide; but on the Missouri side it was the same old distance across—a half a mile— because the Missouri shore was just a wall of high bluffs.

Daytimes we paddled all over the island in the canoe. It was mighty cool and shady in the deep woods even if the sun was blazing outside. We went winding in and out amongst the trees; and sometimes the vines hung so thick we had to back away and go some other way. Well, on every old broken-down tree, you could see rabbits, and snakes, and such things; and when the island had been overflowed a day or two, they got so tame, on account of being hungry, that you could paddle right up and put your hand on them if you wanted to; but not the snakes and turtles—they would slide off in the water. The ridge our cavern was in, was full of them. We could a had pets enough if we'd wanted them.

One night we catched a little section of a lumber raft—nice pine planks. It was twelve foot wide and about fifteen or sixteen foot long, and the top stood above water six or seven inches, a solid level floor. We could see saw-logs[1] go by in the daylight, sometimes, but we let them go; we didn't show ourselves in daylight.

Another night, when we was up at the head of the island, just before daylight, here comes a frame house down, on the west side. She was a two-story, and tilted over, considerable. We paddled out and got aboard—clumb in at an upstairs window. But it was too dark to see yet, so we made the canoe fast and set in her to wait for daylight.

The light begun to come before we got to the foot of the island. Then we looked in at the window. We could make out a bed, and a table, and two old chairs, and lots of things around about on the floor; and there was clothes hanging against the wall. There was something laying on the floor in the far corner that looked like a man. So Jim says:

"Hello, you!"

But it didn't budge. So I hollered again, and then Jim says:

"De man ain't asleep—he's dead. You hold still—I go en see."

He went and bent down and looked, and says:

"It's a dead man. Yes, indeedy; naked, too. He's ben shot in de back. I reck'n he's ben dead two er three days. Come in, Huck, but doan' look at his face—it's too gashly."

I didn't look at him at all. Jim throwed some old rags over him, but he needn't done it; I didn't want to see him. There was heaps of old greasy cards scattered around over the floor, and old whisky bottles, and a couple of masks made out of black cloth; and all over the walls was the ignorantest kind of words and pictures, made with charcoal. There was two old dirty calico[2] dresses, and a sunbonnet, and some women's under-clothes, hanging against the wall, and some men's clothing, too. We put the lot into the canoe; it might come good. There was a boy's old speckled straw hat on the floor; I took that too. And there was a bottle that had had milk in it; and it had a rag stopper for a baby to suck. We would a took the bottle, but it was broke. There was a seedy old chest, and an old hair trunk[3] with the hinges broke. They stood open, but there warn't nothing left in them that was any account. The way things was scattered about, we reckoned the people left in a hurry and warn't fixed so as to carry off most of their stuff.

We got an old tin lantern, and a butcher knife without any handle, and a bran-new Barlow knife[4] worth two bits in any store, and a lot of tallow candles, and a tin candlestick, and a gourd, and a tin cup, and a ratty old bed-quilt off the bed, and reticule[5] with needles and pins and beeswax and buttons and thread and all such truck in it, and a hatchet and some nails, and a fish-line as thick as my little finger, with some monstrous hooks on it, and a roll of buckskin, and a leather dog-collar, and a horse-shoe, and some vials of medicine that didn't have no label on them; and just as we was leaving I found a tolerable good curry-comb,[6] and Jim he found a ratty old fiddle-bow, and a wooden leg. The straps was broke off of it, but barring that, it was a good enough leg, though it was too

---

[1]Split, in preparation for sawing.   [2]Colorful, printed cotton cloth.
[3]A trunk covered with cowhide from which the hair has not been removed.
[4]A pocketknife.   [5]Small bag, a purse.
[6]Metal comb used for grooming (currying) horses.

long for me and not long enough for Jim, and we couldn't find the other one, though we hunted all around.

And so, take it all around, we made a good haul. When we was ready to shove off, we was a quarter of a mile below the island, and it was pretty broad day; so I made Jim lay down in the canoe and cover up with the quilt, because if he set up, people could tell he was a nigger a good ways off. I paddled over to the Illinois shore, and drifted most a half a mile doing it. I crept up the dead water under the bank, and hadn't no accidents and didn't see nobody. We got home all safe.

CHAPTER X

After breakfast I wanted to talk about the dead man and guess out how he come to be killed, but Jim didn't want to. He said it would fetch bad luck; and besides, he said, he might come and ha'nt us; he said a man that warn't buried was more likely to go a-ha'nting around than one that was planted and comfortable. That sounded pretty reasonable, so I didn't say no more; but I couldn't keep from studying over it and wishing I knowed who shot the man, and what they done it for.

We rummaged the clothes we'd got, and found eight dollars in silver sewed up in the lining of an old blanket overcoat. Jim said he reckoned the people in that house stole the coat, because if they'd a knowed the money was there they wouldn't a left it. I said I reckoned they killed him, too; but Jim didn't want to talk about that. I says:

"Now you think it's bad luck; but what did you say when I fetched in the snake-skin that I found on the top of the ridge day before yesterday? You said it was the worst bad luck in the world to touch a snake-skin with my hands. Well, here's your bad luck! We've raked in all this truck and eight dollars besides. I wish we could have some bad luck like this every day, Jim."

"Never you mind, honey, never you mind. Don't you git too peart.[1] It's a-comin'. Mind I tell you, it's a-comin'."

It did come, too. It was a Tuesday that we had that talk. Well, after dinner Friday, we was laying around in the grass at the upper end of the ridge, and got out of tobacco. I went to the cavern to get some, and found a rattlesnake in there. I killed him, and curled him up on the foot of Jim's blanket, ever so natural, thinking there'd be some fun when Jim found him there. Well, by night I forgot all about the snake, and when Jim flung himself down on the blanket while I struck a light, the snake's mate was there, and bit him.

He jumped up yelling, and the first thing the light showed was the varmint curled up and ready for another spring. I laid him out in a second with a stick, and Jim grabbed pap's whisky jug and begun to pour it down.

He was barefooted, and the snake bit him right on the heel. That all comes of being such a fool as to not remember that wherever you leave a dead snake its mate always comes there and curls around it. Jim told me to chop off the snake's head and throw it away, and then skin the body and roast a piece of it. I done it, and he eat it and said it would help cure him. He made me take off the rattles and tie them around his wrist, too. He said that that would help. Then I slid out quiet and throwed the snakes clear away amongst the bushes; for I warn't going to let Jim find out it was all my fault, not if I could help it.

[1]Smart.

Jim sucked and sucked at the jug, and now and then he got out of his head and pitched around and yelled; but every time he come to himself he went to sucking at the jug again. His foot swelled up pretty big, and so did his leg; but by-an-by the drunk begun to come, and so I judge he was all right; but I'd druther been bit with a snake than pap's whisky.

Jim was laid up for four days and nights. Then the swelling was all gone and he was around again. I made up my mind I wouldn't ever take aholt of a snake-skin again with my hands, now that I see what had come of it. Jim said he reckoned I would believe him next time. And he said that handling a snake-skin was such awful bad luck that maybe we hadn't got to the end of it yet. He said he druther see the new moon over his left shoulder as much as a thousand times than take up a snake-skin in his hand. Well, I was getting to feel that way myself, though I've always reckoned that looking at the new moon over your left shoulder is one of the carelessest and foolishest things a body can do. Old Hank Bunker done it once, and bragged about it; and in less than two years he got drunk and fell off of the shot tower and spread himself out so that he was just a kind of a layer, as you may say; and they slid him edgeways between two barn doors for a coffin, and buried him so, so they say, but I didn't see it. Pap told me. But anyway, it all come of looking at the moon that way, like a fool.

Well, the days went along, and the river went down between its banks again; and about the first thing we done was to bait one of the big hooks with a skinned rabbit and set it and catch a cat-fish that was as big as a man, being six foot two inches long, and weighed over two hundred pounds. We couldn't handle him, of course; he would a flung us into Illinois. We just set there and watched him rip and tear around till he drownded. We found a brass button in his stomach, and a round ball, and lots of rubbage. We split the ball open with the hatchet, and there was a spool in it. Jim said he'd had it there a long time, to coat it over so and make a ball of it. It was as big a fish as was ever catched in the Mississippi, I reckon. Jim said he hadn't ever seen a bigger one. He would a been worth a good deal over at the village. They peddle out such a fish as that by the pound in the market house there; everybody buys some of him; his meat's as white as snow and makes a good fry.

Next morning I said it was getting slow and dull and I wanted to get a stirring up, some way. I said I reckoned I would slip over the river and find out what was going on. Jim liked that notion; but he said I must go in the dark and look sharp. Then he studied it over and said, couldn't I put on some of them old things and dress up like a girl? That was a good notion, too. So we shortened up one of the calico gowns and I turned up my trowser-legs to my knees and got into it. Jim hitched it behind with the hooks, and it was a fair fit. I put on the sun-bonnet and tied it under my chin, and then for a body to look in and see my face was like looking down a joint of stove-pipe. Jim said nobody would know me, even in the daytime hardly. I practiced around all day to get the hang of the things, and by-and-by I could do pretty well in them, only Jim said I didn't walk like a girl; and he said I must quit pulling up my gown to get at my britches pocket. I took notice, and done better.

I started up the Illinois shore in the canoe just after dark.

I started across to the town from a little below the ferry landing, and the drift of the current fetched me in at the bottom of the town. I tied up and started along the bank. There was a light burning in a light shanty that hadn't been lived in for a long time, and I wondered who had took up quarters there. I slipped up and peeped in at the window. There was a woman about forty year old in there, knitting by a candle that was on a pine table. I didn't know her face; she was a stranger, for you couldn't start[2] a face in that town that I didn't know. Now this was lucky, because I was weakening; I was getting afraid I had come; people might know my voice and find me out. But if this woman had been in such a little town two days she could tell me all I wanted to know; so I knocked at the door, and made up my mind I wouldn't forget I was a girl.

CHAPTER XI

"Come in," says the woman, and I did. She says:

"Take a cheer."

I done it. She looked me all over with her little shiny eyes, and says: "What might your name be?"

"Sarah Williams."

"Where 'bouts do you live? In this neighborhood?"

"No'm. In Hookerville, seven mile below. I've walked all the way and I'm all tired out."

"Hungry, too, I reckon. I'll find you something."

"No'm, I ain't hungry. I was so hungry I had to stop two miles below here at a farm; so I ain't hungry no more. It's what makes me so late. My mother's down sick, and out of money and everything, and I come to tell my uncle Abner Moore. He lives at the upper end of the town, she says, I hain't ever been here before. Do you know him?"

"No; but I don't know everybody yet. I haven't lived here quite two weeks. It's a considerable ways to the upper end of the town. You better stay here all night. Take off your bonnet."

"No," I says, "I'll rest a while, I reckon, and go on. I ain't afeard of the dark."

She said she wouldn't let me go by myself, but her husband would be in by-and-by, maybe in a hour and a half, and she'd send him along with me. Then she got to talking about her husband, and about her relations up the river, and her relations down the river, and about how much better off they used to was, and how they didn't know but they'd made a mistake coming to our town, instead of letting well alone—and so on and so on, till I was afeard *I* had made a mistake coming to her to find out what was going on in the town; but by-and-by she dropped onto pap and the murder, and then I was pretty willing to let her clatter right along. She told about me and Tom Sawyer finding the six thousand dollars[1] (only she got it ten) and all about pap and what a hard lot he was, and what a hard lot I was, and at last she got down to where I was murdered. I says:

"Who done it? We've heard considerable about these goings on, down in Hookerville, but we don't know who 'twas that killed Huck Finn."

"Well, I reckon there's a right smart chance[2] of people *here* that'd like to know who killed him. Some thinks old Finn done it himself."

"No—is that so?"

"Most everybody thought it at first. He'll never know how nigh he come to getting lynched. But before night they changed around and judged it was done by a runaway nigger named Jim."

"Why *he*——"

I stopped. I reckoned I better keep still. She run on, and never noticed I had put in at all.

[2]Find, discover.
[1]The sum found by Huck and Tom, as described in *Tom Sawyer*, actually totaled $12,000.
[2]Southern dialect: "a large number."

"The nigger run off the very night Huck Finn was killed. So there's a reward out for him—three hundred dollars. And there's a reward out for old Finn too—two hundred dollars. You see, he come to town the morning after the murder, and told about it, and was out with 'em on the ferry-boat hunt, and right away after he up and left. Before night they wanted to lynch him, but he was gone, you see. Well, next day they found out the nigger was gone; they found out he hadn't ben seen sence ten o'clock the night the murder was done. So then they put it on him, you see, and while they was full of it, next day back comes old Finn and went boo-hooing to Judge Thatcher to get money to hunt for the nigger all over Illinois with. The judge give him some, and that evening he got drunk and was around till after midnight with a couple of mighty hard looking strangers, and then went off with them. Well, he hain't come back sence, and they ain't looking for him back till this thing blows over a little, for people thinks now that he killed his boy and fixed things so folks would think robbers done it, and then he'd get Huck's money without having to bother a long time with a lawsuit. People do say he warn't any too good to do it. Oh, he's sly, I reckon. If he don't come back for a year, he'll be all right. You can't prove anything on him, you know; everything will be quieted down then, and he'll walk into Huck's money as easy as nothing."

"Yes, I reckon so, 'm. I don't see nothing in the way of it. Has everybody quit thinking the nigger done it?"

"Oh, no, not everybody. A good many thinks he done it. But they'll get the nigger pretty soon, now, and maybe they can scare it out of him."

"Why, are they after him yet?"

"Well, you're innocent, ain't you! Does three hundred dollars lay round every day for people to pick up? Some folks thinks the nigger ain't far from here. I'm one of them—but I hain't talked it around. A few days ago I was talking with an old couple that lives next door in the log shanty, and they happened to say hardly anybody ever goes to that island over yonder that they call Jackson's Island. Don't anybody live there? says I. No, nobody, says they. I didn't say any more, but I done some thinking. I was pretty near certain I'd seen smoke over there, about the head of the island, a day or two before that, so I says to myself, like as not that nigger's hiding over there; anyway, says I, it's worth the trouble to give the place a hunt. I hain't seen any smoke sence, so I reckon maybe he's gone, if it was him; but husband's going over to see—him and another man. He was gone up the river; but he got back to-day and I told him as soon as he got here two hours ago."

I had got so uneasy I couldn't set still. I had to do something with my hands; so I took up a needle off of the table and went to threading it. My hands shook, and I was making a bad job of it. When the woman stopped talking, I looked up, and she was looking at me pretty curious, and smiling a little. I put down the needle and thread and let on to be interested—and I was, too—and says:

"Three hundred dollars is a power of money. I wish my mother could get it. Is your husband going over there to-night?"

"Oh, yes. He went up town with the man I was telling you of, to get a boat and see if they could borrow another gun. They'll go over after midnight."

"Couldn't they see better if they was to wait till daytime?"

"Yes. And couldn't the nigger see better, too? After midnight he'll likely be asleep, and they can slip around through the woods and hunt up his camp fire all the better for the dark, if he's got one."

"I didn't think of that."

The woman kept looking at me pretty curious, and I didn't feel a bit comfortable. Pretty soon she says:

"What did you say your name was, honey?"

"M—Mary Williams."

Somehow it didn't seem to me that I said it was Mary before, so I didn't look up; seemed to me I said it was Sarah; so I felt sort of cornered, and was afeared maybe I was looking it, too. I wished the woman would say something more; the longer she set still, the uneasier I was. But now she says:

"Honey, I thought you said it was Sarah when you first come in?"

"Oh, yes'm, I did. Sarah Mary Williams. Sarah's my first name. Some calls me Sarah, some calls me Mary."

"Oh, that's the way of it?"

"Yes'm."

I was feeling better, then, but I wished I was out of there, anyway. I couldn't look up yet.

Well, the woman fell to talking about how hard times was, and how poor they had to live, and how the rats was as free as if they owned the place, and so forth, and so on, and then I got easy again. She was right about the rats. You'd see one stick his nose out of a hole in the corner every little while. She said she had to have things handy to throw at them when she was alone, or they wouldn't give her no peace. She showed me a bar of lead, twisted up into a knot, and said she was a good shot with it generly, but she'd wrenched her arm a day or two ago, and didn't know whether she could throw true, now. But she watched for a chance, and directly she banged away at a rat, but she missed him wide, and said "Ouch!" it hurt her arm so. Then she told me to try for the next one. I wanted to be getting away before the old man got back, but of course I didn't let on. I got the thing, and the first rat that showed his nose I let drive, and if he'd a stayed where he was he'd a been a tolerable sick rat. She said that that was first-rate, and she reckoned I would hive the next one. She went and got the lump of lead and fetched it back and brought along a hank of yarn, which she wanted me to help her with. I held up my two hands and she put the hank over them and went on talking about her and her husband's matters. But she broke off to say:

"Keep your eye on the rats. You better have the lead in your lap, handy."

So she dropped the lump into my lap, just at that moment, and I clapped my legs together on it and she went on talking. But only about a minute. Then she took off the hank and looked me straight in the face, but very pleasant, and says:

"Come, now—what's your real name?"

"Wh-what, mum?"

"What's your real name? Is it Bill, or Tom, or Bob?—or what is it?"

I reckon I shook like a leaf, and I didn't know hardly what to do. But I says:

"Please to don't poke fun at a poor girl like me, mum. If I'm in the way, here, I'll——"

"No, you won't. Set down and stay where you are. I ain't going to hurt you, and I ain't going to tell on you, nuther. You just tell me your secret, and trust me. I'll keep it; and what's more, I'll help you. So'll my old man, if you want him to. You see, you're a runaway 'prentice—that's all. It ain't anything. There ain't any harm in it. You've been treated bad, and you made up your mind to cut. Bless you, child, I wouldn't tell on you. Tell me all about it, now—that's a good boy."

So I said it wouldn't be no use to try to play it any longer, and I would just make a clean breast and tell her everything, but she mustn't go back on her promise. Then I told her my father and mother was dead, and the law had bound me[3] out to a mean old farmer in the country thirty mile back from the river, and he treated me so bad I couldn't stand it no longer; he went away to be gone a couple of days, and so I took my chance and stole some of his daughter's old clothes, and cleared out, and I had been three nights coming the thirty miles; I traveled nights, and hid day-times and slept, and the bag of bread and meat I carried from home lasted me all the way and I had a plenty. I said I believed my uncle Abner Moore would take care of me, and so that was why I struck out for this town of Goshen.

"Goshen, child? This ain't Goshen. This is St. Petersburg.[4] Goshen's ten mile further up the river. Who told you this was Goshen?"

"Why, a man I met at day-break this morning, just as I was going to turn into the woods for my regular sleep. He told me when the roads forked I must take the right hand, and five mile would fetch me to Goshen."

"He was drunk I reckon. He told you just exactly wrong."

"Well, he did act like he was drunk, but it ain't no matter now. I got to be moving along. I'll fetch Goshen before day-light."

"Hold on a minute. I'll put you up a snack to eat. You might want it."

So she put me up a snack, and says:

"Say—when a cow's laying down, which end of her gets up first? Answer up prompt, now—don't stop to study over it. Which end gets up first?"

"The hind end, mum."

"Well, then, a horse?"

"The for'rard end, mum."

"Which side of a tree does the most moss grow on?"

"North side."

"If fifteen cows is browsing on a hillside, how many of them eats with their heads pointed the same direction?"

"The whole fifteen, mum."

"Well, I reckon you *have* lived in the country. I thought maybe you was trying to hocus[5] me again. What's your real name, now?"

"George Peters, mum."

"Well, try to remember it, George. Don't forget and tell me it's Elexander before you go, and then get out by saying it's George-Elexander when I catch you. And don't go about women in that old calico. You do a girl tolerable poor, but you might fool men, maybe. Bless you, child, when you set out to thread a needle, don't hold the thread still and fetch the needle up to it; hold the needle still and poke the thread at it—that's the way a woman most always does; but a man always does t'other way. And when you throw at a rat or anything, hitch yourself up a tip-toe, and fetch your hand up over your head as awkward as you can, and miss your rat about six or seven foot. Throw stiff-armed from the shoulder, like there was a pivot there for it to turn on—like a girl; not from the wrist and elbow, with your arm out to one side, like a boy. And mind you, when a girl tries to catch anything in her lap, she throws her knees apart; she don't clap them together, the way you did when you catched the lump of lead. Why, I spotted you for a boy when you was threading the needle; and I contrived the other things just to make certain. Now trot along to your uncle, Sarah Mary Williams George Elexander Peters, and if you get into trouble you send word

[3]Assigned, as a ward of the court.
[4]Twain's fictional name for Hannibal, Missouri, his boyhood home.   [5]Trick.

to Mrs. Judith Loftus, which is me, and I'll do what I can to get you out of it. Keep the river road, all the way, and next time you tramp, take shoes and socks with you. The river road's a rocky one, and your feet'll be in a condition when you get to Goshen, I reckon."

I went up the bank about fifty yards, and then I doubled on my tracks and slipped back to where my canoe was, a good piece below the house. I jumped in and was off in a hurry. I went up stream far enough to make the head of the island, and then started across. I took off the sun-bonnet, for I didn't want no blinders[6] on, then. When I was about the middle, I hear the clock begin to strike; so I stops and listens; the sound come faint over the water, but clear—eleven. When I struck the head of the island I never waited to blow, though I was most winded, but I shoved right into the timber where my old camp used to be, and started a good fire there on a high-and-dry spot.

Then I jumped in the canoe and dug out for our place a mile and a half below, as hard as I could go. I landed, and slopped through the timber and up the ridge and into the cavern. There Jim laid, sound asleep on the ground. I roused him out and says:

"Git up and hump yourself, Jim! There ain't a minute to lose. They're after us!"

Jim never asked no questions, he never said a word; but the way he worked for the next half an hour showed about how he was scared. By that time everything we had in the world was on our raft and she was ready to be shoved out from the willow cove where she was hid. We put out the camp fire at the cavern the first thing, and didn't show a candle outside after that.

I took the canoe out from shore a little piece and took a look, but if there was a boat around I couldn't see it, for stars and shadows ain't good to see by. Then we got out the raft and slipped along down in the shade, past the foot of the island dead still, never saying a word.

CHAPTER XII

It must a been close onto one o'clock when we got below the island at last, and the raft did seem to go mighty slow. If a boat was to come along, we was going to take to the canoe and break for the Illinois shore; and it was well a boat didn't come, for we hadn't ever thought to put the gun into the canoe, or a fishing-line or anything to eat. We was in ruther too much of a sweat to think of so many things. It warn't good judgment to put *everything* on the raft.

If the men went to the island, I just expect they found the camp fire I built, and watched it all night for Jim to come. Anyways, they stayed away from us, and if my building the fire never fooled them it warn't no fault of mine. I played it as low-down on them as I could.

When the first streak of day begun to show, we tied up to a tow-head in a big bend on the Illinois side, and hacked off cotton-wood branches with the hatchet and covered up the raft with them so she looked like there had been a cave-in in the bank there. A tow-head is a sand-bar that has cotton-woods on it as thick as harrow-teeth.[1]

We had mountains on the Missouri shore and heavy timber on the Illinois side, and the channel was down the Missouri shore at that place, so we warn't

[6]Attachments on a horse's bridle, to restrict vision.
[1]As numerous as teeth on a harrow, a rake.

afraid of anybody running across us. We laid there all day and watched the rafts and steamboats spin down the Missouri shore, and up-bound steamboats[2] fight the big river in the middle. I told Jim all about the time I had jabbering with that woman; and Jim said she was a smart one, and if she was to start after us herself *she* wouldn't set down and watch a camp fire—no, sir, she'd fetch a dog. Well, then, I said, why couldn't she tell her husband to fetch a dog? Jim said he bet she did think of it by the time the men was ready to start, and he believed they must a gone up town to get a dog and so they lost all that time, or else we wouldn't be here on a tow-head sixteen or seventeen mile below the village— no, indeedy, we would be in that same old town again. So I said I didn't care what was the reason they didn't get us, as long as they didn't.

When it was beginning to come on dark, we poked our heads out of the cottonwood thicket and looked up, and down, and across; nothing in sight; so Jim took up some of the top planks of the raft and built a snug wigwam to get under in blazing weather and rainy, and to keep the things dry. Jim made a floor for the wigwam, and raised it a foot or more above the level of the raft, so now the blankets and all the traps was out of the reach of steamboat waves. Right in the middle of the wigwam we made a layer of dirt about five or six inches deep with a frame around it for to hold it to its place; this was to build a fire on in sloppy weather or chilly; the wigwam would keep it from being seen. We made an extra steering oar, too, because one of the others might get broke, on a snag or something. We fixed up a short forked stick to hang the old lantern on; because we must always light the lantern whenever we see a steamboat coming down stream, to keep from getting run over; but we wouldn't have to light it for upstream boats unless we see we was in what they call a "crossing"; for the river was pretty high yet, very low banks being still a little under water; so up-bound boats didn't always run the channel, but hunted easy water.

This second night we run between seven and eight hours, with a current that was making over four miles an hour. We catched fish, and talked, and we took a swim now and then to keep off sleepiness. It was kind of solemn, drifting down the big still river, laying on our backs looking up at the stars, and we didn't ever feel like talking loud, and it warn't often that we laughed, only a little kind of a low chuckle. We had mighty good weather, as a general thing, and nothing ever happened to us at all, that night, nor the next, nor the next.

Every night we passed towns, some of them away up on black hillsides, nothing but just a shiny bed of lights, not a house could you see. The fifth night we passed St. Louis, and it was like the whole world lit up. In St. Petersburg they used to say there was twenty or thirty thousand people in St. Louis, but I never believed it till I see that wonderful spread of lights at two o'clock that still night. There warn't a sound there; everybody was asleep.

Every night, now, I used to slip ashore, towards ten o'clock, at some little village, and buy ten or fifteen cents' worth of meal or bacon or other stuff to eat; and sometimes I lifted a chicken that warn't roosting comfortable, and took him along. Pap always said, take a chicken when you get a chance, because if you don't want him yourself you can easy find somebody that does, and a good deed ain't ever forgot. I never see pap when he didn't want the chicken himself, but that is what he used to say, anyway.

Mornings, before daylight, I slipped into corn fields and borrowed a water-melon, or a mushmelon, or a punkin, or some new corn, or things of that kind. Pap always said it warn't no harm to borrow things, if you was meaning to pay

---

[2]Steamboats going upriver, against the current.

them back, sometime; but the widow said it warn't anything but a soft name for stealing, and no decent body would do it. Jim said he reckoned the widow was partly right and pap was partly right; so the best way would be for us to pick out two or three things from the list and say we wouldn't borrow them any more—then he reckoned it wouldn't be no harm to borrow the others. So we talked it over all one night, drifting along down the river, trying to make up our minds whether to drop the watermelons, or the cantelopes, or the mush-melons, or what. But towards daylight we got it all settled satisfactory, and concluded to drop crabapples and p'simmons. We warn't feeling just right, before that, but it was all comfortable now. I was glad the way it come out, too, because crabapples ain't ever good, and the p'simmons wouldn't be ripe for two or three months yet.

We shot a water-fowl, now and then, that got up too early in the morning or didn't go to bed early enough in the evening. Take it all around, we lived pretty high.

The fifth night below St. Louis we had a big storm after midnight, with a power of thunder and lightning, and the rain poured down in a solid sheet. We stayed in the wigwam and let the raft take care of itself. When the lightning glared out we could see a big straight river ahead, and high rocky bluffs on both sides. By-and-by says I, "Hel-*lo*, Jim, looky younder!" It was a steamboat that had killed herself on a rock. We was drifting straight down for her. The lightning showed her very distinct. She was leaning over, with part of her upper deck above water, and you could see every little chimblyguy[3] clean and clear, and a chair by the big bell, with an old slouch hat hanging on the back of it when the flashes come.

Well, it being away in the night, and stormy, and all so mysterious-like, I felt just the way any other boy would a felt when I see that wreck laying there so mournful and lonesome in the middle of the river. I wanted to get aboard of her and slink around a little, and see what there was there. So I says:

"Le's land on her, Jim."

But Jim was dead against it, at first. He says:

"I doan' want to go fool'n 'long er no wrack. We's doin' blame' well, en we better let blame' well alone, as de good book says. Like as not dey's a watchman on dat wrack."

"Watchman your grandmother," I says; "there ain't nothing to watch but the texas[4] and the pilot-house; and do you reckon anybody's going to resk his life for a texas and a pilot-house such a night as this, when it's likely to break up and wash off down the river any minute?" Jim couldn't say nothing to that, so he didn't try. "And besides," I says, "we might borrow something worth having, out of the captain's stateroom.[5] Seegars, *I* bet you—and cost five cents apiece, solid cash. Steamboat captains is always rich, and get sixty dollars a month, and *they* don't care a cent what a thing costs, you know, long as they want it. Stick a candle in your pocket; I can't rest, Jim, till we give her a rummaging. Do you reckon Tom Sawyer would ever go by this thing? Not for pie, he wouldn't. He'd call it an adventure—that's what he'd call it; and he'd land on that wreck if it was his last act. And wouldn't he throw style into it?—wouldn't he spread himself, nor nothing? Why, you'd think it was Christopher C'lumbus discovering King-dom-Come. I wish Tom Sawyer *was* here."

Jim he grumbled a little, but give in. He said we mustn't talk any more than

[3]Wires that brace (guy) the smoke stacks.
[4]The biggest (hence "texas") cabin on the upper deck of a steamboat.   [5]Sleeping quarters.

we could help, and then talk mighty low. The lightning showed us the wreck again, just in time, and we fetched the starboard derrick,[6] and made fast there.

The deck was high out, here. We went sneaking down the slope of it to labboard,[7] in the dark, towards the texas, feeling our way slow with our feet, and spreading our hands out to fend off the guys, for it was so dark we couldn't see no sign of them. Pretty soon we struck the forward end of the skylight, and clumb onto it; and the next step fetched us in front of the captain's door, which was open, and by Jimminy, away down through the texas-hall we see a light! and all in the same second we seem to hear low voices in yonder!

Jim whispered and said he was feeling powerful sick, and told me to come along. I says, all right; and was going to start for the raft; but just then I heard a voice wail out and say:

"Oh, please don't, boys; I swear I won't ever tell!"

Another voice said, pretty loud:

"It's a lie, Jim Turner. You've acted this way before. You always want more'n your share of the truck, and you've always got it, too, because you've swore 't if you didn't you'd tell. But this time you've said it jest one time too many. You're the meanest, treacherousest hound in this country."

By this time Jim was gone for the raft. I was just a-biling with curiosity; and I says to myself, Tom Sawyer wouldn't back out now, and so I won't either; I'm agoing to see what's going on here. So I dropped on my hands and knees, in the little passage, and crept aft in the dark, till there warn't but about one stateroom betwixt me and the cross-hall of the texas. Then, in there I see a man stretched on the floor and tied hand and foot, and two men standing over him, and one of them had a dim lantern in his hand, and the other one had a pistol. This one kept pointing the pistol at the man's head on the floor and saying—

"I'd *like* to! And I orter, too, a mean skunk!"

The man on the floor would shrivel up, and say: "Oh, please don't, Bill—I hain't ever goin' to tell."

And every time he said that, the man with the lantern would laugh, and say:

" 'Deed you *aint!* You never said no truer thing 'n that, you bet you." And once he said: "Hear him beg! and yit if we hadn't got the best of him and tied him, he'd a killed us both. And what *for?* Jist for noth'n. Jist because we stood on our *rights*—that's what for. But I lay you ain't agoin' to threaten nobody any more, Jim Turner. Put *up* that pistol, Bill."

Bill says:

"I don't want to, Jake Packard. I'm for killin' him—and didn't he kill old Hatfield jist the same way—and don't he deserve it?"

"But I don't *want* him killed, and I've got my reasons for it."

"Bless yo' heart for them words, Jake Packard! I'll never forgit you, long's I live!" says the man on the floor, sort of blubbering.

Packard didn't take no notice of that, but hung up his lantern on a nail, and started towards where I was, there in the dark, and motioned Bill to come. I crawfished[8] as fast as I could, about two yards, but the boat slanted so that I couldn't make very good time; so to keep from getting run over and catched I crawled into a stateroom on the upper side. The man come a-pawing along in the dark, and when Packard got to my stateroom, he says:

"Here—come in here."

And in he come, and Bill after him. But before they got in, I was up in the upper berth, cornered, and sorry I come. Then they stood there, with their

[6]Cargo boom for loading and unloading the ship.   [7]Left (port) side of a ship, looking forward.
[8]Crawled backward.

hands on the ledge of the berth, and talked. I couldn't see them, but I could tell where they was, by the whisky they'd been having. I was glad I didn't drink whisky; but it wouldn't made much difference, anyway, because most of the time they couldn't a treed me because I didn't breathe. I was too scared. And besides, a body *couldn't* breathe, and hear such talk. They talked low and earnest. Bill wanted to kill Turner. He says:

"He's said he'll tell, and he will. If we was to give both our shares to him *now*, it wouldn't make no difference after the row, and the way we've served him. Shore's you're born, he'll turn State's evidence, now you hear *me*. I'm for putting him out of his troubles."

"So'm I," says Packard, very quiet.

"Blame it, I'd sorter begun to think you wasn't. Well, then, that's all right. Les' go and do it."

"Hold on a minute; I hain't had my say yit. You listen to me. Shooting's good, but there's quieter ways if the thing's *got* to be done. But what *I* say, is this; it ain't good sense to go court'n around after a halter,[9] if you git at what you're up to in some way that's jist as good and at the same time don't bring you into no resks. Ain't that so?"

"You bet it is. But how you goin' to manage it this time?"

"Well, my idea is this: we'll rustle around and gether up whatever pickins we've overlooked in the staterooms, and shove for shore and hide the truck. Then we'll wait. Now I say it ain't agoin' to be more 'n two hours befo' this wrack breaks up and washes off down the river. See? He'll be drownded, and won't have nobody to blame for it but his own self. I reckon that's a considerable sight better'n killin' of him. I'm unfavorable to killin' a man as long as you can git around it; it ain't good sense, it ain't good morals. Ain't I right?"

"Yes—I reck'n you are. But s'pose she *don't* break up and wash off?"

"Well, we can wait the two hours, anyway, and see, can't we?"

"All right, then; come along."

So they started, and I lit out, all in a cold sweat, and scrambled forward. It was dark as pitch there; but I said in a kind of a coarse whisper, "Jim!" and he answered up, right at my elbow, with a sort of a moan, and I says:

"Quick, Jim, it ain't no time for fooling around and moaning; there's a gang of murderers in yonder, and if we don't hunt up their boat and set her drifting down the river so these fellows can't get away from the wreck, there's one of 'em going to be in a bad fix. But if we find their boat we can put *all* of 'em in a bad fix—for the Sheriff 'll get 'em. Quick—hurry! I'll hunt the labboard side, you hunt the stabboard. You start at the raft, and—"

"Oh, my lordy, lordy! *Raf'*? Dey ain' no raf' no mo', she done broke loose en gone!—'en here we is!"

CHAPTER XIII

Well, I catched my breath and most fainted. Shut up on a wreck with such a gang as that! But it warn't no time to be sentimentering. We'd *got* to find that boat, now—had to have it for ourselves. So we went a-quaking and shaking down the stabboard side, and slow work it was, too—seemed a week before we got to the stern. No sign of a boat. Jim said he didn't believe he could go any further—so scared he hadn't hardly any strength left, he said. But I said come

[9]Hangman's noose.

on, if we get left on this wreck, we are in a fix, sure. So on we prowled, again. We struck for the stern of the texas, and found it, and then scrabbled along forwards on the skylight, hanging on from shutter to shutter, for the edge of the skylight was in the water. When we got pretty close to the cross-hall door, there was the skiff, sure enough! I could just barely see her. I felt ever so thankful. In another second I would a been aboard of her; but just then the door opened. One of the men stuck his head out, only about a couple of foot from me, and I thought I was gone; but he jerked it in again, and says,

"Heave that blame lantern out o' sight, Bill!"

He flung a bag of something into the boat, and then got in himself, and set down. It was Packard. Then Bill *he* come out and got in. Packard says, in a low voice:

"All ready—shove off!"

I couldn't hardly hang onto the shutters, I was so weak. But Bill says:

"Hold on—'d you go through him?"

"No. Didn't you?"

"No. So he's got his share o' the cash, yet."

"Well, then, come along—no use to take truck and leave money."

"Say—won't he suspicion what we're up to?"

"Maybe he won't. But we got to have it anyway. Come along."

So they got out and went in.

The door slammed to, because it was on the careened side; and in a half second I was in the boat, and Jim come a tumbling after me. I out with my knife and cut the rope, and away we went!

We didn't touch an oar, and we didn't speak nor whisper, nor hardly even breathe. We went gliding swift along, dead silent, past the tip of the paddle-box, and past the stern; then in a second or two more we was a hundred yards below the wreck, and the darkness soaked her up, every last sign of her, and we was safe, and knowed it.

When we was three or four hundred yards down stream, we see the lantern show like a little spark at the texas door, for a second, and we knowed by that that the rascals had missed their boat, and was beginning to understand that they was in just as much trouble, now, as Jim Turner was.

Then Jim manned the oars, and we took out after our raft. Now was the first time that I begun to worry about the men—I reckon I hadn't had time to before. I begun to think how dreadful it was, even for murderers, to be in such a fix. I says to myself, there ain't no telling but I might come to be a murderer myself, yet, and then how would *I* like it? So says I to Jim:

"The first light we see, we'll land a hundred yards below it or above it, in a place where it's a good hiding-place for you and the skiff, and then I'll go and fix up some kind of a yarn, and get somebody to go for that gang and get them out of their scrape, so they can be hung when their time comes."

But that idea was a failure; for pretty soon it begun to storm again, and this time worse than ever. The rain poured down, and never a light showed; everybody in bed, I reckon. We boomed along down the river, watching for lights and watching for our raft. After a long time the rain let up, but the clouds staid, and the lightning kept whimpering, and by-and-by a flash showed us a black thing ahead, floating, and we made for it.

It was the raft, and mighty glad was we to get aboard of it again. We seen a light, now, away down to the right, on shore. So I said I would go for it. The skiff was half full of plunder which that gang had stole, there on the wreck. We hustled it onto the raft in a pile, and I told Jim to float along down, and show a light when he judged he had gone about two mile, and keep it burning till I come; then I manned my oars and shoved for the light. As I got down towards it, three or four more showed—up on a hillside. It was a village. I closed in above the shore-light, and laid on my oars and floated. As I went by, I see it was a lantern hanging on the jackstaff[1] of a double-hull ferry-boat. I skimmed around for the watchman, a-wondering whereabouts he slept; and by-and-by I found him roosting on the bitts,[2] forward, with his head down between his knees. I give his shoulder two or three little shoves, and begun to cry.

He stirred up, in a kind of a startlish way; but when he see it was only me, he took a good gap and stretch, and then he says:

"Hello, what's up? Don't cry, bub. What's the trouble?"

I says:

"Pap, and mam, and sis, and—"

Then I broke down. He says:

"Oh, dang it, now, *don't* take on so, we all has to have our troubles and this'n 'll come out all right. What's the matter with 'em?

"They're—they're—are you the watchman of the boat?"

"Yes," he says, kind of pretty-well-satisfied like. "I'm the captain and the owner, and the mate, and the pilot, and watchman, and head deck-hand; and sometimes I'm the freight and passengers. I ain't as rich as old Jim Hornback, and I can't be so blame' generous and good to Tom, Dick and Harry as what he is, and slam around money the way he does; but I've told him a many a time 't I wouldn't trade places with him; for, says I, a sailor's life's the life for me, and I'm derned if *I'd* live two mile out o' town, where there ain't nothing ever goin' on, not for all his spondulicks[3] and as much more on top of it. Says I——"

I broke in and says:

"They're in an awful peck of trouble, and——"

"*Who* is?"

"Why, pap, and mam, and sis, and Miss Hooker; and if you'd take your ferry-boat and go up there——"

"Up where? Where are they?"

"On the wreck."

"What wreck?"

"Why, there ain't but one."

"What, you don't mean the *Walter Scott?*"

"Yes."

"Good land! what are they doin' *there*, for gracious sakes?"

"Well, they didn't go there a-purpose."

"I bet they didn't! Why, great goodness, there ain't no chance for 'em if they don't git off mighty quick! Why, how in the nation did they ever git into such a scrape?"

"Easy enough. Miss Hooker was a-visiting, up there to the town——"

"Yes, Booth's Landing— go on."

"She was a-visiting, there at Booth's Landing, and just in the edge of the evening she started over with her nigger woman in the horseferry,[4] to stay all night at her friend's house, Miss What-you-may-call-her, I disremember her name, and they lost their steering-oar, and swung around and went a-floating down, stern-first, about two mile, and saddle-baggsed on[5] the wreck, and the ferry man and the nigger woman and the horses was all lost, but Miss Hooker

---

[1]Short pole from which a flag or light can be hung.
[2]Posts fixed on the deck, to which lines can be fastened.
[3]Riches.   [4]Ferry large enough to carry horses.   [5]Wrapped around.

she made a grab and got aboard the wreck. Well, about an hour after dark, we come along down in our trading-scow,[6] and it was so dark we didn't notice the wreck till we was right on it; and so *we* saddlebaggsed; but all of us was saved but Bill Whipple—and oh, he *was* the best cretur!—I most wish't it had been me, I do."

"My George! It's the beatenest thing I ever struck. And *then* what did you all do?"

"Well, we hollered and took on, but it's so wide there, we couldn't make nobody hear. So pap said somebody got to get ashore and get help somehow. I was the only one that could swim, so I made a dash for it, and Miss Hooker she said if I didn't strike help sooner, come here and hunt up her uncle, and he'd fix the thing. I made the land about a mile below, and been fooling along ever since, trying to get people to do something, but they said, 'What, in such a night and such a current? there ain't no sense in it; go for the steam-ferry.' Now if you'll go, and——"

"By Jackson, I'd *like* to, and blame it I don't know but I will; but who in the dingnation's agoin' to *pay* for it? Do you reckon your pap——"

"Why *that's* all right. Miss Hooker she told me, *particular*, that her uncle Hornback——"

"Great guns! is *he* her uncle? Looky here, you break for that light over yonder-way, and turn out west when you git there, and about a quarter of a mile out you'll come to the tavern; tell 'em to dart you out to Jim Hornback's and he'll foot the bill. And don't you fool around any, because he'll want to know the news. Tell him I'll have his niece all safe before he can get to town. Hump yourself, now; I'm agoing up around the corner here, to roust out my engineer."

I struck for the light, but as soon as he turned the corner I went back and got into my skiff and bailed her out and then pulled up shore in the easy water about six hundred yards, and tucked myself in among some woodboats; for I couldn't rest easy till I could see the ferry-boat start. But take it all around, I was feeling rather comfortable on accounts of taking all this trouble for that gang, for not many would a done it. I wished the widow knowed about it. I judged she would be proud of me for helping these rapscallions, because rapscallions and dead beats is the kind the widow and good people takes the most interest in.

Well, before long, here comes the wreck, dim and dusky, sliding along down! A kind of cold shiver went through me, and then I struck out for her. She was very deep, and I see in a minute there warn't much chance for anybody being alive in her. I pulled all around her and hollered a little, but there wasn't any answer; all dead still. I felt a little bit heavy-hearted about the gang, but not much, for I reckoned if they could stand it, I could.

Then here comes the ferry-boat; so I shoved for the middle of the river on a long down-stream slant; and when I judged I was out of eye-reach, I laid on my oars, and looked back and see her go and smell around the wreck for Miss Hooker's remainders, because the captain would know her uncle Hornback would want them; and then pretty soon the ferry-boat give it up and went for shore, and I laid into my work and went a-booming down the river.

It did seem a powerful long time before Jim's light showed up; and when it did show, it looked like it was a thousand mile off. By the time I got there the sky was beginning to get a little gray in the east; so we struck for an island, and hid the raft, and sunk the skiff, and turned in and slept like dead people.

[6]Flat-bottomed cargo boat.

CHAPTER XIV

By-and-by, when we got up, we turned over the truck the gang had stole off of the wreck, and found boots, and blankets, and clothes, and all sorts of other things, and a lot of books, and a spy-glass, and three boxes of seegars. We hadn't ever been this rich before, in neither of our lives. The seegars was prime. We laid off all the afternoon in the woods talking, and me reading the books, and having a general good time. I told Jim all about what happened inside the wreck, and at the ferry-boat; and I said these kinds of things was adventures; but he said he didn't want no more adventures. He said that when I went in the texas and he crawled back to get on the raft and found her gone, he nearly died; because he judged it was all up with *him*, anyway it could be fixed; for if he didn't get saved he would get drownded; and if he did get saved, whoever saved him would send him back home so as to get the reward, and then Miss Watson would see him South, sure. Well, he was right; he was most always right; he had an uncommon level head, for a nigger.

I read considerable to Jim about kings, and dukes, and earls, and such, and how gaudy they dressed, and how much style they put on, and called each other your majesty, and your grace, and your lordship, and so on, 'stead of mister; and Jim's eyes bugged out, and he was interested. He says:

'I didn' know dey was so many un um. I hain't heard 'bout none un um, skasely, but ole King Sollermun, onless you counts dem kings dat's in a pack er k'yards. How much do a king git?"

"Get?" I says; "why, they get a thousand dollars a month if they want it; they can have just as much as they want; everything belongs to them."

"*Ain'* dat gay? En what dey got to do, Huck?"

"*They* don't do nothing! Why how you talk. They just set around."

"No—is dat so?"

"Of course it is. They just set around. Except maybe when there's a war; then they go to the war. But other times they just lazy around; or go hawking—just hawking and sp—Sh!—d' you hear a noise?"

We skipped out and looked; but it warn't nothing but the flutter of a steamboat's wheel, away down coming around the point; so we come back.

"Yes," says I, "and other times, when things is dull, they fuss with the parlyment; and if everybody don't go just so he whacks their heads off. But mostly they hang around the harem."

"Round' de which?"

"Harem."

"What's de harem?"

"The place where he keep his wives. Don't you know about the harem? Solomon had one; he had about a million wives."

"Why, yes, dat's so; I—I'd done forgot it. A harem's a bo'd'n-house, I reck'n. Mos' likely dey has rackety times in de nussery. En I reck'n de wives quarrels considable; en dat 'crease de racket. Yit dey say Sollermun de wises' man dat ever live'. I doan' take no stock in dat. Bekase why: would a wise man want to live in de mids' er sich a blimblammin' all de time? No—'deed he wouldn't. A wise man 'ud take en buil' a biler-factry; en den he could shet *down* de biler-factry when he want to res'."

"Well, but he *was* the wisest man, anyway; because the widow she told me so, her own self."

"I doan k'yer what de widder say, he *warn't* no wise man, nuther. He had some er de dad-fetchedes' ways I ever see. Does you know 'bout dat chile dat he 'uz gwyne to chop in two?"[1]

"Yes, the widow told me all about it."

"*Well*, den! Warn' dat de beatenes' notion in de worl'? You jes' take en look at it a minute. Dah's de stump, dah—dat's one er de women; heah's you—dat's de yuther one; I's Sollermun; en dish-yer dollar bill's de chile. Bofe un you claims it. What does I do? Does I shin aroun' mongs' de neighbors en fine out which un you de bill *do* b'long to, en han' it over to de right one, all safe en soun', de way dat anybody dat had any gumption would? No—I take en whack de bill in *two*, en give half un it to you, en de yuther half to de yuther woman. Dat's de way Sollermun was gwyne to do wid de chile. Now I want to ast you: what's de use er dat half a bill?—can't buy noth'n wid it. En what use is a half a chile? I would'n give a dern for a million un um."

"But hang it, Jim, you've clean missed the point—blame it, you've missed it a thousand mile."

"Who? Me? Go 'long. Doan' talk to *me* 'bout yo' pints. I reck'n I knows sense when I sees it; en dey ain' no sense in sich doin's as dat. De 'spute warn't 'bout a half a chile, de 'spute was 'bout a whole chile; en de man dat think he kin settle a 'spute 'bout a whole chile wid a half a chile, doan' know enough to come in out'n de rain. Doan' talk to me 'bout Sollermun, Huck, I knows him by de back."

"But I tell you you don't get the point."

"Blame de pint! I reck'n I knows what I knows. En mine you, de *real* pint is down furder—it's down deeper. It lays in de way Sollermun was raised. You take a man dat's got on'y one er two chillen; is dat man gwyne to be waseful o' chillen? No, he ain't; he can't 'ford it. *He* know how to value 'em. But you take a man dat's got 'bout five million chillen runnin' roun' de house, en it's diffunt. *He* as soon chop a chile in two as a cat. Dey's plenty mo'. A chile er two, mo'er less, warn't no consekens to Sollermun, dad fetch him!"

I never see such a nigger. If he got a notion in his head once, there warn't no getting it out again. He was the most down on Solomon of any nigger I ever see. So I went to talking about other kings, and let Solomon slide. I told about Louis Sixteenth that got his head cut off in France long time ago; and about his little boy the dolphin,[2] that would a been a king, but they took and shut him up in jail, and some say he died there.

"Po' little chap."

"But some says he got out and got away, and come to America."

"Dat's good! But he'll be pooty lonesome—dey ain' no kings here, is dey, Huck?"

"No."

"Den, he cain't git no situation. What he gwyne to do?"

"Well, I don't know. Some of them gets on the police, and some of them learns people how to talk French."

"Why, Huck, doan' de French people talk de same way we does?"

"*No,* Jim; you couldn't understand a word they said—not a single word."

[1] To halt a dispute about the parentage of a child, Solomon threatened to divide it in two, expecting the real parent to make strenuous objections. I Kings 3:16–28.

[2] The dauphin, eldest then living son of the king of France. Louis Charles (1785–1795?), son of Louis XVI, survived his father's execution during the French Revolution but died in prison. According to legend, he escaped, and numerous imposters thereafter claimed to be the dauphin and thus Louis XVII.

"Well, now, I be ding-busted! How do dat come?"

"*I* don't know; but it's so. I got some of their jabber out of a book. Spose a man was to come to you and say *Polly-voo-franzy*—what would you think?"

"I wouldn' think nuff'n; I'd take en bust him over de head. Dat is, if he warn't white. I wouldn't 'low no nigger to call me dat."

"Shucks, it ain't calling you anything. It's only saying do you know how to talk French."

"Well, den, why couldn't he *say* it?"

"Why, he *is* a-saying it. That's a Frenchman's *way* of saying it."

"Well, it's a blame' ridicklous way, en I doan' want to hear no mo' 'bout it. Dey ain' no sense in it."

"Looky here, Jim; does a cat talk like we do?"

"No, a cat don't."

"Well, does a cow?"

"No, a cow don't, nuther."

"Does a cat talk like a cow, or a cow talk like a cat?"

"No, dey don't."

"It's natural and right for 'em to talk different from each other, ain't it?"

" 'Course."

"And ain't it natural and right for a cat and a cow to talk different from *us?*"

"Why, mos' sholy it is."

"Well, then, why ain't it natural and right for a *Frenchman* to talk different from us? You answer me that."

"Is a cat a man, Huck?"

"No."

"Well, den, dey ain't no sense in a cat talkin' like a man. Is a cow a man?—er is a cow a cat?"

"No, she ain't either of them."

"Well, den, she ain't got no business to talk like either one er the yuther of 'em. Is a Frenchman a man?"

"Yes."

"*Well,* den! Dad blame it, why doan' he *talk* like a man? You answer me *dat!*"

I see it warn't no use wasting words—you can't learn a nigger to argue. So I quit.

CHAPTER XV

We judged that three nights more would fetch us to Cairo,[1] at the bottom of Illinois, where the Ohio River comes in, and that was what we was after. We would sell the raft and get on a steamboat and go way up the Ohio amongst the free States, and then be out of trouble.

Well, the second night a fog begun to come on, and we made for a tow-head to tie to, for it wouldn't do to try to run in fog; but when I paddled ahead in the canoe, with the line, to make fast, there warn't anything but little saplings to tie to. I passed the line around one of them right on the edge of the cut bank,[2] but there was a stiff current, and the raft come booming down so lively she tore it out by the roots and away she went. I see the fog closing down, and it made me so sick and scared I couldn't budge for most a half a minute it seemed to

[1] Pronounced KAY-roh.
[2] Steep bank formed by the cutting force of the river's current.

me—and then there warn't no raft in sight; you couldn't see twenty yards. I jumped into the canoe and run back to the stern and grabbed the paddle and set her back a stroke. But she didn't come. I was in such a hurry I hadn't untied her. I got up and tried to untie her, but I was so excited my hands shook so I couldn't hardly do anything with them.

As soon as I got started I took out after the raft, hot and heavy, right down the tow-head. That was all right as far as it went, but the tow-head warn't sixty yards long, and the minute I flew by the foot of it I shoot out into the solid white fog, and hadn't no more idea which way I was going than a dead man.

Thinks I, it won't do to paddle; first I know I'll run into the bank or a tow-head or something; I got to set still and float, and yet it's mighty fidgety business to have to hold your hands still at such a time. I whooped and listened. Away down there, somewhere, I hears a small whoop, and up comes my spirits. I went tearing after it, listening sharp to hear it again. The next time it come. I see I warn't heading for it but heading away to the right of it. And the next time, I was heading away to the left of it—and not gaining on it much, either, for I was flying around, this way and that and t'other, but it was going straight ahead all the time.

I did wish the fool would think to beat a tin pan, and beat it all the time, but he never did, and it was the still places between the whoops that was making the trouble for me. Well, I fought along, and directly I hears the whoop *behind* me. I was tangled good, now. That was somebody else's whoop, or else I was turned around.

I throwed the paddle down. I heard the whoop again; it was behind me yet, but in a different place; it kept coming, and kept changing its place, and I kept answering, till by-and-by it was in front of me again and I knowed the current had swung the canoe's head down stream and I was all right, if that was Jim and not some other raftsman hollering. I couldn't tell nothing about voices in a fog, for nothing don't look natural nor sound natural in a fog.

The whooping went on, and in about a minute I come a booming down on a cut bank with smoky ghosts of big trees on it, and the current throwed me off to the left and shot by, amongst a lot of snags that fairly roared, the current was tearing by them so swift.

In another second or two it was solid white and still again. I set perfectly still, then, listening to my heart thump, and I reckon I didn't draw a breath while it thumped a hundred.

I just give up, then. I knowed what the matter was. That cut bank was an island, and Jim had gone down t'other side of it. It warn't no tow-head, that you could float by in ten minutes. It had the big timber of a regular island; it might be five or six mile long and more than a half a mile wide.

I kept quiet, with my ears cocked, about fifteen minutes, I reckon. I was floating along, of course, four or five mile an hour; yet you don't ever think of that. No, you *feel* like you are laying dead still on the water; and if a little glimpse of snag slips by, you don't think to yourself how fast *you're* going, but you catch your breath and think, my! how that snag's tearing along. If you think it ain't dismal and lonesome out in a fog that way, by yourself, in the night, you try it once—you'll see.

Next, for about a half an hour, I whoops now and then; at last I hears the answer a long ways off, and tries to follow it, but I couldn't do it, and directly I judged I'd got into a nest of tow-heads, for I had little dim glimpses of them on both sides of me, sometimes just a narrow channel between; and some that I couldn't see, I knowed was there, because I'd hear the wash of the current against the old dead brush and trash that hung over the banks. Well, I warn't long losing the whoops, down amongst the tow-heads; and I only tried to chase them a little while, anyway, because it was worse than chasing a Jack-o-lantern.[3] You never knowed a sound dodge around so, and swap places so quick and so much.

I had to claw away from the bank pretty lively, four or five times, to keep from knocking the islands out of the river; and so I judged the raft must be butting into the bank every now and then, or else it would get further ahead and clear out of hearing—it was floating a little faster than what I was.

Well, I seemed to be in the open river again, by-and-by, but I couldn't hear no sign of a whoop nowheres. I reckoned Jim had fetched up on a snag, maybe, and it was all up with him. I was good and tired, so I laid down in the canoe and said I wouldn't bother no more. I didn't want to go to sleep, of course; but I was so sleepy I couldn't help it; so I thought I would take just one little cat-nap.

But I reckon it was more than a cat-nap, for when I waked up the stars was shining bright, the fog was all gone, and I was spinning down a big bend stern first. First I didn't know where I was; I thought I was dreaming; and when things begun to come back to me, they seemed to come up dim out of last week.

It was a monstrous big river here, with the tallest and the thickest kind of timber on both banks; just a solid wall, as well as I could see, by the stars. I looked away down stream, and seen a black speck on the water. I took out after it, but when I got to it it warn't nothing but a couple of saw-logs made fast together. Then I see another speck, and chased that; then, another, and this time I was right. It was the raft.

When I got to it Jim was setting there with his head down between his knees, asleep, with his right arm hanging over the steering oar. The other oar was smashed off, and the raft was littered up with leaves and branches and dirt. So she'd had a rough time.

I made fast and laid down under Jim's nose on the raft, and begun to gap, and stretch my fists out against Jim, and says:

"Hello, Jim, have I been asleep? Why didn't you stir me up?"

"Goodness gracious, is dat you, Huck? En you ain' dead—you ain' drownded—you's back agin? It's too good for true, honey, it's too good for true. Lemme look at you, chile, lemme feel o' you. No, you ain' dead! you's back agin, 'live en soun', jis de same ole Huck—de same ole Huck, thanks to goodness!"

"What's the matter with you, Jim? You been a drinking?"

"Drinkin'? Has I ben a drinkin'? Has I had a chance to be a drinkin'?"

"Well, then, what makes you talk so wild?"

"How does I talk wild?"

"*How?* why, hain't you been talking about my coming back, and all that stuff, as if I'd been gone away?"

"Huck—Huck Finn, you look me in de eye; look me in de eye. *Hain't* you been gone away?"

"Gone away? Why, what in the nation do you mean? *I* hain't been gone anywheres. Where would I go to?"

"Well, looky here, boss, dey's sumf'n wrong, dey is. Is I *me,* or who *is* I? Is I heah, or whah *is* I? Now dat's what I wants to know."

"Well, I think you're here, plain enough, but I think you're a tangle-headed old fool, Jim."

---

[3]A will-o'-the-wisp, an elusive light.

"I is, is I? Well you answer me dis. Didn't you tote out de line in de canoe, fer to make fas' to de tow-head?"

"No, I didn't. What tow-head? I hain't seen no tow-head."

"You hain't seen no tow-head? Looky here—didn't de line pull loose en de raf' go a hummin' down de river, en leave you en de canoe behine in de fog?"

"What fog?"

"Why *de* fog. De fog dat's ben aroun' all night. En didn't you whoop, en didn't I whoop, tell we got mix' up in de islands en one un us got los' en t'other one was jis' as good as los', 'kase he didn't know whah he wuz? En didn't I bust up agin a lot er dem islands en have a turrible time en mos' git drowned? Now ain' dat so, boss—ain't it so? You answer me dat."

"Well, this is too many for me, Jim. I hain't seen no fog, nor no islands, nor no troubles, nor nothing. I been setting here talking with you all night till you went to sleep about ten minutes ago, and I reckon I done the same. You couldn't a got drunk in that time, so of course you've been dreaming."

"Dad fetch it, how is I gwyne to dream all dat in ten minutes?"

"Well, hang it all, you did dream it, because there didn't any of it happen."

"But Huck, it's all jis' as plain to me as——"

"It don't make no difference how plain it is, there ain't nothing in it. I know, because I've been here all the time."

Jim didn't say nothing for about five minutes, but set there studying over it. Then he says:

"Well, den, I reck'n I did dream it, Huck; but dog my cats ef it ain't de powerfullest dream I ever see. En I hain't ever had no dream b'fo' dat's tired me like dis one."

"Oh, well, that's all right, because a dream does tire a body like everything, sometimes. But this one was a staving[4] dream—tell me all about it, Jim."

So Jim went to work and told me the whole thing right through, just as it happened, only he painted it up considerable. Then he said he must start in and " 'terpret" it, because it was sent for a warning. He said the first tow-head stood for a man that would try to do us some good, but the current was another man that would get us away from him. The whoops was warnings that would come to us every now and then, and if we didn't try hard to make out to understand them they'd just take us into bad luck, 'stead of keeping us out of it. The lot of tow-heads was troubles we was going to get into with quarrelsome people and all kinds of mean folks, but if we minded our business and didn't talk back and aggravate them, we would pull through and get out of the fog and into the big clear river,[5] which was the free States, and wouldn't have no more trouble.

It had clouded up pretty dark just after I got onto the raft, but it was clearing up again, now.

"Oh, well, that's all interpreted well enough, as far as it goes, Jim," I says; "but what does *these* things stand for?"

It was the leaves and rubbish on the raft, and the smashed oar. You could see them first rate, now.

Jim looked at the trash, and then looked at me, and back at the trash again. He had got the dream fixed so strong in his head that he couldn't seem to shake it loose and get the facts back into its place again, right away. But when he did get the thing straightened around, he looked at me steady, without ever smiling, and says:

[4]Smashing.   [5]The Ohio River.

"What do dey stan' for? I's gwyne to tell you. When I got all wore out wid work, en wid de callin' for you, en went to sleep, my heart wuz mos' broke bekase you wuz los', en I didn' k'yer no mo' what become er me en de raf'. En when I wake up en fine you back agin', all safe en soun', de tears come en I could a got down on my knees en kiss' yo' foot I's so thankful. En all you wuz thinkin 'bout wuz how you could make a fool uv ole Jim wid a lie. Dat truck dah is *trash;* en trash is what people is dat puts dirt on de head[6] er dey fren's en makes 'em ashamed."

Then he got up slow, and walked to the wigwam, and went in there, without saying anything but that. But that was enough. It made me feel so mean I could almost kissed *his* foot to get him to take it back.

It was fifteen minutes before I could work myself up to go and humble myself to a nigger—but I done it, and I warn't ever sorry for it afterwards, neither. I didn't do him no more mean tricks, and I wouldn't done that one if I'd a knowed it would make him feel that way.

CHAPTER XVI

We slept most all day, and started out at night, a little ways behind a monstrous long raft that was as long going by as a procession. She had four long sweeps[1] at each end, so we judged she carried as many as thirty men, likely. She had five big wigwams aboard, wide apart, and an open camp fire in the middle, and a tall flag-pole at each end. There was a power of style about her. It *amounted* to something being a raftsman on such a craft as that.

We went drifting down into a big bend, and the night clouded up and got hot. The river was very wide, and was walled with solid timber on both sides; you couldn't see a break in it hardly ever, or a light. We talked about Cairo, and wondered whether we would know it when we got to it. I said likely we wouldn't, because I had heard say there warn't but about a dozen houses there, and if they didn't happen to have them lit up, how was we going to know we was passing a town? Jim said if the two big rivers joined together there, that would show. But I said maybe we might think we was passing the foot of an island and coming into the same old river again. That disturbed Jim—and me too. So the question was, what to do? I said, paddle ashore the first time a light showed, and tell them pap was behind, coming along with a trading-scow, and was a green hand at the business, and wanted to know how far it was to Cairo. Jim thought it was a good idea, so we took a smoke on it and waited.

There warn't nothing to do, now, but to look out sharp for the town, and not pass it without seeing it. He said he'd be mighty sure to see it, because he'd be a free man the minute he seen it, but if he missed it he'd be in the slave country again and no more show[2] for freedom. Every little while he jumps up and says:

"Dah she is!"

But it warn't. It was Jack-o-lanterns, or lightning-bugs; so he set down again, and went to watching, same as before. Jim said it made him all over trembly and feverish to be so close to freedom. Well, I can tell you it made me all over trembly and feverish, too, to hear him, because I begun to get it through my head that he *was* most free—and who was to blame for it? Why, *me.* I couldn't get that out of my conscience, no how nor no way. It got to troubling me so I

[6]A reference to various Old Testament figures who "cast up dust upon their heads" in a gesture of submission and humiliation, as in Ezekiel 27:30.
[1]Long oars used for steering.   [2]Chance.

couldn't rest; I couldn't stay still in one place. It hadn't ever come to me before, what this thing was that I was doing. But now it did; and it staid with me, and scorched me more and more. I tried to make out to myself that *I* warn't to blame, because *I* didn't run Jim off from his rightful owner; but it warn't no use, conscience up and says, every time, "But you knowed he was running for his freedom, and you could a paddled ashore and told somebody." That was so— I couldn't get around that, noway. That was where it pinched. Conscience says to me, "What had poor Miss Watson done to you, that you could see her nigger go off right under your eyes and never say one single word? What did that poor old woman do to you, that you could treat her so mean? Why, she tried to learn you your book, she tried to learn you your manners, she tried to be good to you every way she knowed how. *That's* what she done."

I got to feeling so mean and so miserable I most wished I was dead. I fidgeted up and down the raft, abusing myself to myself, and Jim was fidgeted up and down past me. We neither of us could keep still. Every time he danced around and says, "Dah's Cairo!" it went through me like a shot, and I thought if it *was* Cairo I reckoned I would die of miserableness.

Jim talked out loud all the time while I was talking to myself. He was saying how the first thing he would do when he got to a free State he would go to saving up money and never spend a single cent, and when he got enough he would buy his wife, which was owned on a farm close to where Miss Watson lived; and then they would both work to buy the two children, and if their master wouldn't sell them, they'd get an Ab'litionist to go and steal them.

It most froze me to hear such talk. He wouldn't ever dared to talk such talk in his life before. Just see what a difference it made in him the minute he judged he was about free. It was according to the old saying, "give a nigger an inch and he'll take an ell." Thinks I, this is what comes of my not thinking. Here was this nigger which I had as good as helped to run away, coming right out flat-footed and saying he would steal his children—children that belonged to a man I didn't even know; a man that hadn't ever done me no harm.

I was sorry to hear Jim say that, it was such a lowering of him. My conscience got to stirring me up hotter than ever, until at last I says to it, "Let up on me— it ain't too late, yet—I'll paddle ashore at the first light, and tell." I felt easy, and happy, and light as a feather, right off. All my troubles was gone. I went to looking out sharp for a light, and sort of singing to myself. By-and-by one showed. Jim sings out:

"We's safe. Huck, we's safe! Jump up and crack yo' heels, dat's de good ole Cairo at las', I jis knows it!"

I says:

"I'll take the canoe and go see, Jim. It mightn't be, you know."

He jumped and got the canoe ready, and put his old coat in the bottom for me to set on, and give me the paddle; and as I shoved off, he says:

"Pooty soon I'll be a-shout'n for joy, en I'll say, it's all on accounts o'Huck; I's a free man, en I couldn't ever ben free ef it hadn' ben for Huck; Huck done it. Jim won't ever forgit you, Huck; you's de bes' fren' Jim's ever had; en you's de *only* fren' ole Jim's got now."

I was paddling off, all in a sweat to tell on him; but when he says this, it seemed to kind of take the tuck all out of me. I went along slow then, and I warn't right down certain whether I was glad I started or whether I warn't. When I was fifty yards off, Jim says:

"Dah you goes, de ole true Huck; de on'y white genlman dat ever kep' his promise to ole Jim."

Well, I just felt sick. But I says, I *got* to do it—I can't get *out* of it. Right then, along comes a skiff with two men in it, with guns, and they stopped and I stopped. One of they says:

"What's that, yonder?"

"A piece of a raft," I says.

"Do you belong on it?"

"Yes, sir."

"Any men on it?"

"Only one, sir."

"Well, there's five niggers run off to-night, up yonder above the head of the bend. Is your man white or black?"

I didn't answer up prompt. I tried to, but the words wouldn't come. I tried, for a second or two, to brace up and out with it, but I warn't man enough—hadn't the spunk of a rabbit. I see I was weakening; so I just give up trying, and up and says—

"He's white."

"I reckon we'll go and see for ourselves."

"I wish you would," says I, "because it's pap that's there, and maybe you'd help me tow the raft ashore where the light is. He's sick—and so is mam and Mary Ann."

"Oh, the devil! we're in a hurry, boy. But I s'pose we've got to. Come—buckle to your paddle, and let's get along."

I buckled to my paddle and they laid to their oars. When we had made a stroke or two, I says:

"Pap'll be mighty much obleeged to you, I can tell you. Everybody goes away when I want them to help me tow the raft ashore, and I can't do it by myself."

"Well, that's infernal mean. Odd, too. Say, boy, what's the matter with your father?"

"It's the—a—the—well, it ain't anything, much."

They stopped pulling. It warn't but a mighty little ways to the raft, now. One says:

"Boy, that's a lie. What *is* the matter with your pap? Answer up square, now, and it'll be the better for you."

"I will, sir, I will, honest—but don't leave us, please. It's the—the—gentlemen, if you'll only pull ahead, and let me heave you the head-line,[3] you won't have to come a-near the raft—please do."

"Set her back, John, set her back!" says one. They backed water. "Keep away, boy—keep to looard.[4] Confound it, I just expect the wind has blowed it to us. Your pap's got the small-pox, and you know it precious well. Why didn't you come out and say so? Do you want to spread it all over?"

'Well," says I, a-blubbering, "I've told everybody before, and then they just went away and left us."

"Poor devil, there's something in that. We are right down sorry for you, but we—well, hang it, we don't want the small-pox, you see. Look here, I'll tell you what to do. Don't you try to land by yourself, or you'll smash everything to pieces. You float along down about twenty miles and you'll come to a town on the left-hand side of the river. It will be long after sun-up, then, and when you ask for help, you tell them your folks are all down with chills and fever. Don't be a fool again, and let people guess what is the matter. Now we're trying to do you a kindness; so you just put twenty miles between us, that's a good boy. It

---

[3]Line attached to the prow of a boat.   [4]Leeward, downwind.

wouldn't do any good to land yonder where the light is—it's only a wood-yard.[5] Say—I reckon your father's poor, and I'm bound to say he's in pretty hard luck. Here—I'll put a twenty dollar gold piece on this board, and you get it when it floats by. I feel mighty mean to leave you, but my kingdom! it won't do to fool with small-pox, don't you see?"

"Hold on, Parker," says the other man, "here's a twenty to put on the board for me. Good-bye, boy, you do as Mr. Parker told you, and you'll be all right."

"That's so, my boy—good-bye, good-bye. If you see any runaway niggers, you get help and nab them, and you can make some money by it."

"Good-bye, sir," says I, "I won't let no runaway niggers get by me if I can help it."

They went off, and I got aboard the raft, feeling bad and low, because I knowed very well I had done wrong, and I see it warn't no use for me to try to learn to do right; a body that don't get *started* right when he's little, ain't got no show—when the pinch comes there ain't nothing to back him up and keep him to his work, and so he gets beat. Then I thought a minute, and says to myself, hold on,—spose you'd a done right and give Jim up; would you felt better than what you do now? No, says I, I'd feel bad—I'd feel just the same way I do now. Well, then, says I, what's the use you learning to do right, when it's troublesome to do right and ain't no trouble to do wrong, and the wages is just the same? I was stuck. I couldn't answer that. So I reckoned I wouldn't bother no more about it, but after this always do whichever come handiest at the time.

I went into the wigwam; Jim warn't there. I looked all around; he warn't anywhere. I says:

"Jim!"

"Here I is, Huck, Is dey out o' sight yit? Don't talk loud."

He was in the river, under the stern oar, with just his nose out. I told him they was out of sight, so he come aboard. He says:

"I was a-listenin' to all de talk, en I slips into de river en was gwyne to shove for sho' if dey come aboard. Den I was gwyne to swim to de raf' agin when dey was gone. But lawsy, how you did fool 'em, Huck! Dat *wuz* de smartes' dodge! I tell you, chile, I 'speck it save' ole Jim—old Jim ain't gwyne to forgit you for dat, honey."

Then we talked about the money. It was a pretty good raise, twenty dollars apiece. Jim said we could take deck passage[6] on a steamboat now, and the money would last us as far as we wanted to go in the free States. He said twenty mile more warn't far for the raft to go, but he wished we was already there.

Towards daybreak we tied up, and Jim was mighty particular about hiding the raft good. Then he worked all day fixing things in bundles, and getting all ready to quit rafting.

That night about ten we hove in sight of the lights of a town away down in a left-hand bend.

I went off in the canoe, to ask about it. Pretty soon I found a man out in the river with a skiff, setting a trot-line. I ranged up and says:

"Mister, is that town Cairo?"

"Cairo? no. You must be a blame' fool."

"What town is it, mister?"

"If you want to know, go and find out. If you stay here botherin' around me for about a half a minute longer, you'll get something you won't want."

---

[5]Refueling station for wood-burning steamboats.
[6]Without a private cabin, the cheapest passage.

I paddled to the raft. Jim was awful disappointed, but I said never mind, Cairo would be the next place, I reckoned.

We passed another town before daylight, and I was going out again; but it was high ground, so I didn't go. No high ground about Cairo, Jim said. I had forgot it. We laid up for the day, on a tow-head tolerable close to the left-bank. I begun to suspicion something. So did Jim. I says:

"Maybe we went by Cairo in the fog that night."

He says:

"Doan' less' talk about it, Huck. Po' niggers can't have no luck. I awluz 'spected dat rattle-snake skin warn't done wid its work."

"I wish I'd never seen that snake-skin, Jim—I do wish I'd never laid eyes on it."

"It ain't yo' fault, Huck; you didn' know. Don't you blame yo'self 'bout it."

When it was daylight, here was the clear Ohio water in shore, sure enough, and outside was the old regular Muddy! So it was all up with Cairo.[7]

We talked it all over. It wouldn't do to take to the shore; we couldn't take the raft up the stream, of course. There warn't no way but to wait for dark, and start back in the canoe and take the chances. So we slept all day amongst the cotton-wood thicket, so as to be fresh for the work, and when we went back to the raft about dark the canoe was gone!

We didn't say a word for a good while. There warn't anything to say. We both knowed well enough it was some more work of the rattle-snake skin; so what was the use to talk about it? It would only look like we was finding fault, and that would be bound to fetch more bad luck—and keep on fetching it, too, till we knowed enough to keep still.

By-and-by we talked about what we better do, and found there warn't no way but just to go along down with the raft till we got a chance to buy a canoe to go back in. We warn't going to borrow it when there warn't anybody around, the way pap would do, for that might set people after us.

So we shoved out, after dark, on the raft.

Anybody that don't believe yet, that it's foolishness to handle a snake-skin, after all that that snake-skin done for us, will believe it now, if they read on and see what more it done for us.

The place to buy canoes is off of rafts laying up at shore. But we didn't see no rafts laying up; so we went along during three hours and more. Well, the night got gray, and ruther thick, which is the next meanest thing to fog. You can't tell the shape of the river, and you can't see no distance. It got to be very late and still, and then along comes a steamboat up the river. We lit the lantern, and judged she would see it. Up-stream boats didn't generly come close to us; they go out and follow the bars and hunt for easy water under the reefs; but nights like this they bull right up the channel against the whole river.

We could hear her pounding along, but we didn't see her good till she was close. She aimed right for us. Often they do that and try to see how close they can come without touching; sometimes the wheel bites off a sweep, and then the pilot sticks his head out and laughs, and thinks he's mighty smart. Well, here she comes, and we said she was going to try to shave us; but she didn't seem to be sheering off a bit. She was a big one, and she was coming in a hurry, too, looking like a black cloud with rows of glow-worms around it; but all of a

[7]When Huck sees the clearer waters of the Ohio flowing in the Mississippi, he knows he and Jim have passed beyond the confluence of the two rivers at Cairo, where they had hoped to go up the Ohio River.

sudden she bulged out, big and scary, with a long row of wide-open furnace doors shining like red-hot teeth, and her monstrous bows and guards hanging right over us. There was a yell at us, and a jingling of bells to stop the engines, a pow-wow of cussing, and whistling of steam—and as Jim went overboard on one side and I on the other, she come smashing straight through the raft.

I dived—and I aimed to find the bottom, too, for a thirty-foot wheel had got to go over me, and I wanted it to have plenty of room. I could always stay under water a minute; this time I reckon I staid under water a minute and a half. Then I bounced for the top in a hurry, for I was nearly busting. I popped out to my arm-pits and blowed the water out of my nose, and puffed a bit. Of course there was a booming current; and of course that boat started her engines again ten seconds after she stopped them, for they never cared much for raftsmen; so now she was churning along up the river, out of sight in the thick weather, though I could hear her.

I sung out for Jim, about a dozen times, but I didn't get any answer; so I grabbed a plank that touched me while I was "treading water," and struck out for shore, shoving it ahead of me. But I made out to see that the drift of the current was towards the left-hand shore,[8] which meant that I was in a crossing; so I changed off and went that way.

It was one of these long, slanting, two-mile crossings; so I was a good long time in getting over. I made a safe landing, and clum up the bank. I couldn't see but a little ways, but I went poking along over rough ground for a quarter of a mile or more, and then I run across a big old-fashioned double log house[9] before I noticed it. I was going to rush by and get away, but a lot of dogs jumped out and went to howling and barking at me, and I knowed better than to move another peg.

CHAPTER XVII

In about half a minute somebody spoke out a window, without putting his head out, and says:

"Be done, boys! Who's there?"

I says:

"It's me."

"Who's me?"

"George Jackson, sir."

"What do you want?"

"I don't want nothing, sir. I only want to go along by, but the dogs won't let me."

"What are you prowling around here this time of night, for—hey?"

"I warn't prowling around, sir; I fell overboard off of the steamboat."

"Oh, you did, did you? Strike a light there, somebody. What did you say your name was?"

"George Jackson, sir. I'm only a boy."

"Look here; if you're telling the truth, you needn't be afraid—nobody 'll hurt you. But don't try to budge; stand right where you are. Rouse out Bob and Tom, some of you, and fetch the guns. George Jackson, is there anybody with you?"

"No, sir, nobody."

[8]Kentucky, where the next episode takes place.
[9]A two-room log house, under a single roof and with an open passageway separating the two rooms.

I heard the people stirring around in the house, now, and see a light. The man sung out:

"Snatch that light away, Betsy, you old fool—ain't you got any sense? Put it on the floor behind the front door. Bob, if you and Tom are ready, take your places."

"All ready."

"Now, George Jackson, do you know the Shepherdsons?"

"No, sir—I never heard of them."

"Well, that may be so, and it mayn't. Now, all ready, Step forward, George Jackson. And mind, don't you hurry—come mighty slow. If there's anybody with you, let him keep back—if he shows himself he'll be shot. Come along, now. Come slow; push the door open, yourself—just enough to squeeze in, d' you hear?"

I didn't hurry, I couldn't if I'd a wanted to. I took one slow step at a time, and there warn't a sound, only I thought I could hear my heart. The dogs were as still as the humans, but they followed a little behind me. When I got to the three log door-steps, I heard them unlocking and unbarring and unbolting. I put my hand on the door and pushed it a little and a little more, till somebody said, "There, that's enough—put your head in." I done it, but I judged they would take it off.

The candle was on the floor, and there they all was, looking at me, and me at them, for about a quarter of a minute. Three big men with guns pointed at me, which made me wince, I tell you; the oldest, gray and about sixty, the other two thirty or more—all of them fine and handsome—and the sweetest old gray-headed lady, and back of her two young women which I couldn't see right well. The old gentleman says:

"There—I reckon it's all right. Come in."

As soon as I was in, the old gentleman he locked the door and barred it and bolted it, and told the young men to come in with their guns, and they all went in a big parlor that had a new rag carpet on the floor, and got together in a corner that was out of range of the front windows—there warn't none on the side. They held the candle, and took a good look at me, and all said, "Why *he* ain't a Shepherdson—no, there ain't any Shepherdson about him." Then the old man said he hoped I wouldn't mind being searched for arms, because he didn't mean no harm by it—it was only to make sure. So he didn't pry into my pockets, but only felt outside with his hands, and said it was all right. He told me to make myself easy and at home, and tell all about myself; but the old lady says:

"Why bless you, Saul, the poor thing's as wet as he can be; and don't you reckon it may be he's hungry?"

"True for you, Rachel—I forgot."

So the old lady says:

"Betsy" (this was a nigger woman), "you fly around and get him something to eat, as quick as you can, poor thing; and one of you girls go and wake up Buck and tell him—Oh, here he is himself. Buck, take this little stranger and get the wet clothes off from him and dress him up in some of yours that's dry."

Buck looked about as old as me—thirteen or fourteen[1] or along there, though he was a little bigger than me. He hadn't on anything but a shirt, and he was

---

[1]Elsewhere Twain wrote that Huck was fourteen.

very frowsy-headed. He come in gaping and digging one fist into his eyes, and he was dragging a gun along with the other one. He says:

"Ain't they no Shepherdsons around?"

They said, no, 'twas a false alarm.

"Well," he says, "if they'd a ben some, I reckon I'd a got one."

They all laughed, and Bob says:

"Why, Buck, they might have scalped us all, you've been so slow in coming."

"Well, nobody come after me, and it ain't right. I'm always kep' down; I don't get no show."

"Never mind, Buck, my boy," says the old man, "you'll have show enough, all in good time, don't you fret about that. Go 'long with you now, and do as your mother told you."

When we got up stairs to his room, he got me a coarse shirt and a roundabout[2] and pants of his, and I put them on. While I was at it he asked me what my name was, but before I could tell him, he started to telling me about a blue jay and a young rabbit he had catched in the woods day before yesterday, and he asked me where Moses was when the candle went out. I said I didn't know; I hadn't heard about it before, no way.

"Well, guess," he says.

"How'm I going to guess," says I, "when I never heard tell about it before?"

"But you can guess, can't you? It's just as easy."

"*Which* candle?" I says.

"Why, any candle," he says.

"I don't know where he was," says I; "where was he?"

"Why he was in the *dark!* That's where he was!"

"Well, if you knowed where he was, what did you ask me for?"

"Why, blame it, it's a riddle, don't you see? Say, how long are you going to stay here? You got to stay always. We can just have booming times—they don't have no school now. Do you own a dog? I've got a dog—and he'll go in the river and bring out chips that you throw in. Do you like to comb up, Sundays, and all that kind of foolishness? You bet I don't, but ma she makes me. Confound these ole britches, I reckon I'd better put 'em on, but I'd ruther not, it's so warm. Are you all ready? All right—come along, old hoss."

Cold corn-pone, cold corn-beef, butter and butter-milk—that is what they had for me down there, and there ain't nothing better that ever I've come across yet. Buck and his ma and all of them smoked cob pipes, except the nigger woman, which was gone, and the two young women. They all smoked and talked, and I eat and talked. The young women had quilts around them, and their hair down their backs. They all asked me questions, and I told them how pap and me and all the family was living on a little farm down at the bottom of Arkansaw, and my sister Mary Ann run off and got married and never was heard of no more, and Bill went to hunt them and he warn't heard of no more, and Tom and Mort died, and then there warn't nobody but just me and pap left, and he was just trimmed down to nothing, on account of his troubles; so when he died I took what was left, because the farm didn't belong to us, and started up the river, deck passage, and fell overboard; and that was how I come to be here. So they said I could have a home there as long as I wanted it. Then it was most daylight, and everybody went to bed, and I went to bed with Buck, and when I waked up in the morning, drat it all, I had forgot what my name

---

[2]A jacket.

was. So I laid there about an hour trying to think, and when Buck waked up, I
says:

"Can you spell, Buck?"

"Yes," he says.

"I bet you can't spell my name," says I.

"I bet you what you dare I can," says he.

"All right," says I, "go ahead."

"G-o-r-g-e J-a-x-o-n—there now," he says.

"Well," says I, "you done it, but I didn't think you could. It ain't no slouch of
a name to spell—right off without studying."

I set it down, private, because somebody might want *me* to spell it, next, and
so I wanted to be handy with it and rattle it off like I was used to it.

It was a mighty nice family, and a mighty nice house, too. I hadn't seen no
house out in the country before that was so nice and had so much style. It didn't
have an iron latch on the front door, nor a wooden one with a buckskin string,
but a brass knob to turn, the same as houses in a town. There warn't no bed in
the parlor, not a sign of a bed; but heaps of parlors in towns has beds in them.
There was a big fireplace that was bricked on the bottom, and the bricks was
kept clean and red by pouring water on them and scrubbing them with another
brick; sometimes they washed them over with red water-paint that they call
Spanish-brown, same as they do in town. They had big brass dog-irons[3] that
could hold up a saw-log.[4] There was a clock on the middle of the mantel-piece,
with a picture of a town painted on the bottom half of the glass front, and a
round place in the middle of it for the sun, and you could see the pendulum
swing behind it. It was beautiful to hear that clock tick; and sometimes when
one of these peddlers had been along and scoured her up and got her in good
shape, she would start in and strike a hundred and fifty before she got tuckered
out. They wouldn't took any money for her.

Well, there was a big outlandish parrot on each side of the clock, made out
of something like chalk, and painted up gaudy. By one of the parrots was a cat
made of crockery, and a crockery dog by the other; and when you pressed down
on them they squeaked, but didn't open their mouths nor look different nor
interested. They squeaked through underneath. There was a couple of big wild-
turkey-wing fans spread out behind those things. On a table in the middle of
the room was a kind of a lovely crockery basket that had apples and oranges
and peaches and grapes piled up in it which was much redder and yellower and
prettier than real ones is, but they warn't real because you could see where
pieces had got chipped off and showed the white chalk or whatever it was,
underneath.

This table had a cover made out of beautiful oil-cloth, with a red and blue
spread-eagle painted on it, and a painted border all around. It come all the way
from Philadelphia, they said. There was some books too, piled up perfectly
exact, on each corner of the table. One was a big family Bible, full of pictures.
One was "Pilgrim's Progress,"[5] about a man that left his family, it didn't say why.
I read considerable in it now and then. The statements was interesting, but
tough. Another was "Friendship's Offering,"[6] full of beautiful stuff and poetry;
but I didn't read the poetry. Another was Henry Clay's[7] Speeches, and another

---

[3]Andirons.

[4]A log long and large enough to saw into timbers and beams.

[5]A Christian allegory by the English Puritan John Bunyan (1628–1688).

[6]A gift-book collection of sentimental prose and poetry.

[7]Political leader and orator from Kentucky (1777–1852).

was Dr. Gunn's Family Medicine,[8] which told you all about what to do if a body was sick or dead. There was a Hymn Book, and a lot of other books. And there was nice split-bottom chairs, and perfectly sound, too—not bagged down in the middle and busted, like an old basket.

They had pictures hung on the walls—mainly Washingtons and Lafayettes, and battles, and Highland Marys,[9] and one called "Signing the Declaration." There was some that they called crayons, which one of the daughters which was dead made her own self when she was only fifteen years old. They was different from any pictures I ever see before; blacker, mostly, than is common. One was a woman in a slim black dress, belted small under the arm-pits, with bulges like a cabbage in the middle of the sleeves, and a large black scoop-shovel bonnet with a black veil, and white slim ankles crossed about with black tape, and very wee black slippers, like a chisel, and she was leaning pensive on a tombstone on her right elbow, under a weeping willow, and her other hand hanging down her side holding a white handkerchief and a reticule, and underneath the picture it said "Shall I Never See Thee More Alas." Another one was a young lady with her hair all combed up straight to the top of her head, and knotted there in front of a comb like a chair-back, and she was crying into a handkerchief and had a dead bird laying on its back in her other hand with its heels up, and underneath the picture it said "I Shall Never Hear Thy Sweet Chirrup More Alas." There was one where a young lady was at a window looking up at the moon, and tears running down her cheeks; and she had an open letter in one hand with black sealing-wax showing on one edge of it, and she was mashing a locket with a chain to it against her mouth, and underneath the picture it said "And Art Thou Gone Yes Thou Art Gone Alas." These was all nice pictures, I reckon, but I didn't somehow seem to take to them, because if ever I was down a little, they always give me the fan-tods. Everybody was sorry she died, because she had laid out a lot more of these pictures to do, and a body could see by what she had done what they had lost. But I reckoned, that with her disposition, she was having a better time in the graveyard. She was at work on what they said was her greatest picture when she took sick, and every day and every night it was her prayer to be allowed to live till she got it done, but she never got the chance. It was a picture of a young woman in a long white gown, standing on the rail of a bridge all ready to jump off, with her hair all down her back, and looking up to the moon, with the tears running down her face, and she had two arms folded across her breast, and two arms stretched out in front, and two more reaching up towards the moon—and the idea was, to see which pair would look best and then scratch out all the other arms; but, as I was saying, she died before she got her mind made up, and now they kept this picture over the head of the bed in her room, and every time her birthday come they hung flowers on it. Other times it was hid with a little curtain. The young woman in the picture had a kind of a nice sweet face, but there was so many arms it made her look too spidery, seemed to me.

This young girl kept a scrap-book when she was alive, and used to paste obituaries and accidents and cases of patient suffering in it out of the *Presbyterian Observer*, and write poetry after them out of her own head. It was very good poetry. This is what she wrote about a boy by the name of Stephen Dowling Bots that fell down a well and was drownded:

[8]A medical guide first published in 1830 and still used in 1855.
[9]Mary Campbell, the subject of several elegies by the Scottish poet Robert Burns (1759–1796). She was portrayed in numerous sentimental illustrations.

ODE TO STEPHEN DOWLING BOTS, DEC'D.[10]

And did young Stephen sicken,
  And did young Stephen die?
And did the sad hearts thicken,
  And did the mourners cry?

No; such was not the fate of
  Young Stephen Dowling Bots;
Though sad hearts round him thickened,
  'Twas not from sickness' shots.

No whooping-cough did rack his frame,
  Nor measles drear, with spots;
Not these impaired the sacred name
  Of Stephen Dowling Bots.

Despised love struck not with woe
  That head of curly knots,
Nor stomach troubles laid him low,
  Young Stephen Dowling Bots.

O no. Then list with tearful eye,
  Whilst I his fate do tell.
His soul did from this cold world fly,
  By falling down a well.

They got him out and emptied him;
  Alas it was too late;
His spirit was gone for to sport aloft
  In the realm of the good and great.

If Emmeline Grangerford could make poetry like that before she was fourteen, there ain't no telling what she could a done by-and-by. Buck said she could rattle off poetry like nothing. She didn't ever have to stop to think. He said she would slap down a line, and if she couldn't find anything to rhyme with it she would just scratch it out and slap down another one, and go ahead. She warn't particular, she could write about anything you choose to give her to write about, just so it was sadful. Every time a man died, or a woman died, or a child died, she would be on hand with her "tribute" before he was cold. She called them tributes. The neighbors said it was the doctor first, then Emmeline, then the undertaker— the undertaker never got in ahead of Emmeline but once, and then she hung fire on a rhyme for the dead person's name, which was Whistler. She warn't ever the same, after that; she never complained, but she kind of pined away and did not live long. Poor thing, many's the time I made myself go up to the little room that used to be hers and get out her poor old scrap-book and read in it when her pictures had been aggravating me and I had soured on her a little. I liked all that family, dead ones and all, and warn't going to let anything come between us. Poor Emmeline made poetry about all the dead people when she was alive, and it didn't seem right that there warn't nobody to make some

---

[10]Deceased.

about her, now she was gone; so I tried to sweat out a verse or two myself, but I couldn't seem to make it go, somehow. They kept Emmeline's room trim and nice and all the things fixed in it just the way she liked to have them when she was alive, and nobody ever slept there. The old lady took care of the room herself, though there was plenty of niggers, and she sewed there a good deal and read her Bible there, mostly.

Well, as I was saying about the parlor, there was beautiful curtains on the windows; white, with pictures painted on them, of castles with vines all down the walls, and cattle coming down to drink. There was a little old piano, too, that had tin pans[11] in it, I reckon, and nothing was ever so lovely as to hear the young ladies sing, "The Last Link is Broken"[12] and play "The Battle of Prague"[13] on it. The walls of all the rooms was plastered, and most had carpets on the floors, and the whole house was whitewashed on the outside.

It was a double house, and the big open place betwixt them was roofed and floored, and sometimes the table was there in the middle of the day, and it was a cool, comfortable place. Nothing couldn't be better. And warn't the cooking good, and just bushels of it too!

CHAPTER XVIII

Col. Grangerford was a gentleman, you see. He was a gentleman all over; and so was his family. He was well born, as the saying is, and that's worth as much in a man as it is in a horse, so the Widow Douglas said, and nobody ever denied that she was of the first aristocracy in our town; and pap he always said it, too, though he warn't no more quality than a mud-cat,[1] himself. Col. Grangerford was very tall and very slim, and had a darkish-paly complexion, not a sign of red in it anywheres; he was clean-shaved every morning, all over his thin face, and he had the thinnest kind of lips, and the thinnest kind of nostrils, and a high nose, and heavy eyebrows, and the blackest kind of eyes, sunk so deep back that they seemed like they was looking out of caverns at you, as you may say. His forehead was high, and his hair was black and straight, and hung to his shoulders. His hands was long and thin, and every day of his life he put on a clean shirt and a full suit from head to foot made out of linen so white it hurt your eyes to look at it; and on Sundays he wore a blue tail-coat with brass buttons on it. He carried a mahogany cane with a silver head to it. There warn't no frivolishness about him, not a bit, and he warn't ever loud. He was as kind as he could be—you could feel that, you know, and so you had confidence. Sometimes he smiled, and it was good to see; but when he straightened himself up like a liberty-pole,[2] and the lightning began to flicker out from under his eyebrows you wanted to climb a tree first, and find out what the matter was afterwards. He didn't ever have to tell anybody to mind their manners—everybody was always good mannered where he was. Everybody loved to have him around, too; he was sunshine most always—I mean he made it seem like good weather. When he turned into a cloud-bank it was awful dark for a half minute and that was enough; there wouldn't nothing go wrong again for a week.

[11]Pianos in the nineteenth century were sometimes built with cymbals and bells that could be sounded by striking keys and foot pedals.
[12]A popular, sentimental song published in 1840.
[13]A piece of ranting, bombastic program music (1788) that attempted to recreate the sounds of a military battle.
[1]Catfish.   [2]A tall pole, often topped with a flag, used as a symbol of liberty.

When him and the old lady come down in the morning, all the family got up out of their chairs and give them good-day, and didn't set down again till they had set down. Then Tom and Bob went to the sideboard where the decanters was, and mixed a glass of bitters and handed it to him, and he held it in his hand and waited till Tom's and Bob's was mixed, and then they bowed and said "Our duty to you, sir, madam;" and *they* bowed the least bit in the world and said thank you, and so they drank, all three, and Bob and Tom poured a spoonful of water on the sugar and the mite of whisky or apple brandy in the bottom of their tumblers, and give it to me and Buck, and we drank to the old people too.

Bob was the oldest, and Tom next. Tall, beautiful men with very broad shoulders and brown faces, and long black hair and black eyes. They dressed in white linen from head to foot, like the old gentleman, and wore broad Panama hats.

Then there was Miss Charlotte, she was twenty-five, and tall and proud and grand, but as good as she could be, when she warn't stirred up; but when she was, she had a look that would make you wilt in your tracks, like her father. She was beautiful.

So was her sister, Miss Sophia, but it was a different kind. She was gentle and sweet, like a dove, and she was only twenty.

Each person had their own nigger to wait on them—Buck, too. My nigger had a monstrous easy time, because I warn't used to having anybody do anything for me, but Buck's was on the jump most of the time.

This was all there was of the family, now; but there used to be more—three sons; they got killed; and Emmeline that died.

The old gentleman owned a lot of farms, and over a hundred niggers. Sometimes a stack of people would come there, horseback, from ten to fifteen mile around, and stay five or six days, and have such junketings round about and on the river, and dances and picnics in the woods, day-times, and balls at the house, nights. These people was mostly kin-folks of the family. The men brought their guns with them. It was a handsome lot of quality, I tell you.

There was another clan of aristocracy around there—five or six families—mostly of the name of Shepherdson. They was as high-toned, and well born, and rich and grand, as the tribe of Grangerfords. The Shepherdsons and the Grangerfords used the same steamboat landing, which was about two mile above our house; so sometimes when I went up there with a lot of our folks I used to see a lot of Shepherdsons there, on their fine horses.

One day Buck and me was away out in the woods, hunting, and heard a horse coming. We was crossing the road. Buck says:

"Quick! Jump for the woods!"

We done it, and then peeped down the woods through the leaves. Pretty soon a splendid young man come galloping down the road, setting his horse easy and looking like a soldier. He had his gun across his pommel. I had seen him before. It was young Harney Shepherdson. I heard Buck's gun go off at my ear, and Harney's hat tumbled off from his head. He grabbed his gun and rode straight to the place where we was hid. But we didn't wait. We started through the woods on a run. The woods warn't thick, so I looked over my shoulder, to dodge the bullet, and twice I seen Harney cover Buck with his gun; and then he rode away the way he come—to get his hat, I reckon, but I couldn't see. We never stopped running till we got home. The old gentleman's eyes blazed a minute—'twas pleasure, mainly, I judged—then his face sort of smoothed down, and he says, kind of gentle:

"I don't like that shooting from behind a bush. Why didn't you step into the road, my boy?"

"The Shepherdsons don't, father. They always take advantage."

Miss Charlotte she held her head up like a queen while Buck was telling his tale, and her nostrils spread and her eyes snapped. The two young men looked dark, but never said nothing. Miss Sophia she turned pale, but the color came back when she found the man warn't hurt.

Soon as I could get Buck down by the corn-cribs[3] under the trees by ourselves, I says:

"Did you want to kill him, Buck?"

"Well, I bet I did."

"What did he do to you?"

"Him? He never done nothing to me."

"Well, then, what did you want to kill him for?"

"Why nothing—only it's on account of the feud."

"What's a feud?"

"Why, where was you raised? Don't you know what a feud is?"

"Never heard of it before—tell me about it."

"Well," says Buck, "a feud is this way. A man has a quarrel with another man, and kills him; then that other man's brother kills *him;* then the other brothers on both sides, goes for one another; then the *cousins* chip in—and by-and-by everybody's killed off, and there ain't no more feud. But it's kind of slow, and takes a long time."

"Has this one been going on long, Buck?"

"Well I should *reckon!* it started thirty year ago, or som'ers along there. There was trouble 'bout something and then a lawsuit to settle it; and the suit went agin one of the men, and so he up and shot the man that won the suit—which he would naturally do, of course. Anybody would."

"What was the trouble about, Buck?—land?"

"I reckon maybe—I don't know."

"Well, who done the shooting?—was it a Grangerford or a Shepherdson?"

"Laws, how do *I* know? It was so long ago."

"Don't anybody know?"

"Oh, yes, pa knows, I reckon, and some of the other old folks; but they don't know, now, what the row was about in the first place."

"Has there been many killed, Buck?"

"Yes—right smart chance of funerals. But they don't always kill. Pa's got a few buck-shot in him; but he don't mind it 'cuz he don't weigh much anyway. Bob's been carved up some with a bowie, and Tom's been hurt once or twice."

"Has anybody been killed this year, Buck?"

"Yes, we got one and they got one. 'Bout three months ago, my cousin Bud, fourteen year old, was riding through the woods, on t'other side of the river, and didn't have no weapon with him, which was blame' foolishness, and in a lonesome place he hears a horse a-coming behind him, and see old Baldy Shepherdson a-linkin' after him with his gun in his hand and his white hair a-flying in the wind; and 'stead of jumping off and taking to the brush, Bud 'lowed he could outrun him; so they had it, nip and tuck, for five mile or more, the old man a-gaining all the time; so at last Bud seen it warn't any use, so he stopped

[3]Wooden-frame structures used for drying corn.

and faced around so as to have the bullet holes in front, you know, and the old
man he rode up and shot him down. But he didn't git much chance to enjoy his
luck, for inside of a week, our folks laid *him* out."

"I reckon that old man was a coward, Buck."

"I reckon he *warn't* a coward. Not by a blame' sight. There ain't a coward
amongst them Shepherdsons—not a one. And there ain't no cowards amongst
the Grangerfords, either. Why, that old man kep' up his end in a fight one day,
for a half an hour, against three Grangerfords, and come out winner. They was
all a-horseback; he lit off of his horse and got behind a little wood-pile, and kep'
his horse before him to stop the bullets; but the Grangerfords staid on their
horses and capered around the old man, and peppered away at him, and he
peppered away at them. Him and his horse both went home pretty leady and
crippled, but the Grangerfords had to be *fetched* home—and one of 'em was
dead, and another died the next day. No, sir, if a body's out hunting for cowards,
he don't want to fool away any time amongst them Shepherdsons, becuz they
don't breed any of that *kind*."

Next Sunday we all went to church, about three mile, everybody a-horseback.
The men took their guns along, so did Buck, and kept them between their knees
or stood them handy against the wall. The Shepherdsons done the same. It was
pretty ornery preaching—all about brotherly love, and such-like tiresomeness;
but everybody said it was a good sermon, and they all talked it over going home,
and had such a powerful lot to say about faith, and good works, and free grace,[4]
and preforeordestination,[5] and I don't know what all, that it did seem to me to
be one of the roughest Sundays I had run across yet.

About an hour after dinner everybody was dozing around, some in their
chairs and some in their rooms, and it got to be pretty dull. Buck and a dog was
stretched out on the grass in the sun, sound sleep. I went up to our room, and
judged I would take a nap myself. I found that sweet Miss Sophia standing in
her door, which was next to ours, and she took me in her room and shut the
door very soft, and asked me if I liked her, and I said I did; and she asked me
if I would do something for her and not tell anybody, and I said I would. Then
she said she'd forgot her Testament, and left it in the seat at church, between
two other books and would I slip out quiet and go there and fetch it to her, and
not say nothing to nobody. I said I would. So I slid out and slipped off up the
road, and there warn't anybody at the church, except maybe a hog or two, for
there warn't any lock on the door, and hogs like a puncheon floor[6] in summer-
time because it's cool. If you notice, most folks don't go to church only when
they've got to; but a hog is different.

Says I to myself something's up—it ain't natural for a girl to be in such a sweat
about a Testament; so I give it a shake, and out drops a little piece of paper
with "*Half-past two*" wrote on it with a pencil. I ransacked it, but couldn't find
anything else. I couldn't make anything out of that, so I put the paper in the
book again, and when I got home and up stairs, there was Miss Sophia in her
door waiting for me. She pulled me in and shut the door; then she looked in
the Testament till she found the paper, and as soon as she read it she looked
glad; and before a body could think, she grabbed me and give me a squeeze,
and said I was the best boy in the world, and not to tell anybody. She was mighty
red in the face, for a minute, and her eyes lighted up and it made her powerful
pretty. I was a good deal astonished, but when I got my breath I asked her what

[4]God's grace—election for heaven, given free, without regard for human efforts.
[5]Huck combines the religious doctrines of predestination and foreordination.
[6]A floor of rough, wooden slabs.

the paper was about, and she asked me if I had read it, and I said no, and she asked me if I could read writing, and I told her "no, only coarse-hand,"[7] and then she said the paper warn't anything but a book-mark to keep her place, and I might go and play now.

I went off down to the river, studying over this thing, and pretty soon I noticed that my nigger was following along behind. When we was out of sight of the house, he looked back and around a second, and then comes a-running, and says:

"Mars Jawge, if you'll come down into de swamp, I'll show you a whole stack o' water-moccasins."[8]

Thinks I, that's mighty curious; he said that yesterday. He oughter know a body don't love water-moccasins enough to go around hunting for them. What is he up to anyway? So I says—

"All right, trot ahead."

I followed a half a mile, then he struck out over the swamp and waded ankle deep as much as another half mile. We come to a little flat piece of land which was dry and very thick with trees and bushes and vines, and he says—

"You shove right in dah, jist a few steps, Mars Jawge, dah's whah dey is. I's seed 'm befo', I don't k'yer to see 'em no mo'."

Then he slopped right along and went away, and pretty soon the trees hid him. I poked into the place a-ways, and come to a little open patch as big as a bedroom, all hung around with vines, and found a man laying there asleep—and by jings it was my old Jim!

I waked him up, and I reckoned it was going to be a grand surprise to him to see me again, but it warn't. He nearly cried, he was so glad, but he warn't surprised. Said he swum along behind me, that night, and heard me yell every time, but dasn't answer, because he didn't want nobody to pick *him* up, and take him into slavery again. Says he—

"I got hurt a little, en couldn't swim fas', so I wuz a considable ways behine you, towards de las'; when you landed I reck'ned I could ketch up wid you on de lan' 'dout havin' to shout at you, but when I see dat house I begin to go slow. I 'uz off too far to hear what dey dey say to you—I wuz 'fraid o' de dogs—but when it 'uz all quiet agin, I knowed you's in de house, so I struck out fer de woods to wait for day. Early in de mawnin' some er de niggers come along, gwyne to de fields, en dey tuck me en showed me dis place, whah de dogs can't track me on accounts o' de water, en dey brings me truck to eat every night, en tells me how you's a gitt'n along."

"Why didn't you tell my Jack to fetch me here sooner, Jim?"

"Well, 'twarn't no use to 'sturb you, Huck, tell we could do sumfin—but we's all right, now. I ben a-buyin' pots en pans en vittles, as I got a chanst, en a patchin' up de raf', nights when——"

"*What* raft, Jim?"

"Our ole raf'."

"You mean to say our old raft warn't smashed all to flinders?"

"No, she warn't. She was tore up a good deal—one en' of her was—but dey warn't no great harm done, on'y our traps was mos' all los'. Ef we hadn' dive' so deep en swum so fur under water, en de night hadn' ben so dark, en we warn't so sk'yerd, en ben sich punkin-heads, as de sayin' is, we'd a seed de raf'. But it's jis' as well as we didn't, 'kase now she's all fixed up agin mos' as good as new, en we's got a new lot o' stuff, too, in de place o' what 'uz los'."

---

[7] Large, rough printing by hand.   [8] A species of poisonous snakes.

"Why, how did you get hold of the raft again, Jim—did you catch her?"

"How I gwyne to ketch her, en I out in de woods? No, some er de niggers foun' her ketched on a snag, along heah in de ben', en dey hid her in a crick, 'mongst de willows, en dey wuz so much jawin' 'bout which un 'um she b'long to de mos', dat I come to heah 'bout it pooty soon, so I ups en settles de trouble by tellin' 'um she don't b'long to none uv um, but to you en me; en I ast 'm if dey gwyne to grab a young white genlman's propaty, en git a hid'n for it? Den I gin 'm ten cents apiece, en dey 'uz mighty well satisfied, en wisht some mo' raf's 'ud come along en make 'm rich agin. Dey's mighty good to me, dese niggers is, en whatever I wants 'm to do fur me, I don't have to ast 'm twice, honey. Dat Jack's a good nigger, en pooty smart."

"Yes, he is. He ain't ever told me you was here; told me to come, and he'd show me a lot of water-moccasins. If anything happens, *he* ain't mixed up in it. He can say he never seen us together, and it'll be the truth."

I don't want to talk much about the next day. I reckon I'll cut it pretty short. I waked up about dawn, and was agoing to turn over and go to sleep again, when I noticed how still it was—didn't seem to be anybody stirring. That warn't usual. Next I noticed that Buck was up and gone. Well, I gets up, a-wondering, and goes down stairs—nobody around; everything as still as a mouse. Just the same outside; thinks I, what does it mean? Down by the wood-pile I comes across my Jack, and says:

"What's it all about?"

Says he:

"Don't you know, Mars Jawge?"

"No," says I, "I don't."

"Well, den, Miss Sophia's run off! 'deed she has. She run off in de night, sometime—nobody don't know jis' when—run off to git married to dat young Harney Shepherdson, you know—leastways, so dey 'spec. De fambly foun' it out, 'bout half an hour ago—maybe a little mo'—en' I *tell* you dey warn't no time los. Sich another hurryin' up guns en hosses *you* never see! De women folks has gone for to stir up de relations, en ole Mars Saul en de boys tuck dey guns en rode up de river road for to try to ketch dat young man en kill him 'fo' he kin git acrost de river wid Miss Sophia. I reck'n dey's gwyne to be mighty rough times."

"Buck went off 'thout waking me up."

"Well I reck'n he *did!* Dey warn't gwyne to mix you up in it. Mars Buck he loaded up his gun en 'lowed he's gwyne to fetch home a Shepherdson or bust. Well, dey'll be plenty un 'm dah, I reck'n, en you bet you he'll fetch one ef he gits a chanst."

I took up the river road as hard as I could put. By-and-by I begin to hear guns a good ways off. When I come in sight of the log store and the wood-pile where the steamboat lands, I worked along under the trees and brush till I got to a good place, and then I clumb up into the forks of a cotton-wood that was out of reach, and watched. There was a wood-rank[9] four foot high, a little ways in front of the tree, and first I was going to hide behind that; but maybe it was luckier I didn't.

There was four or five men cavorting around on their horses in the open place before the log store, cussing and yelling, and trying to get at a couple of young chaps that was behind the wood-rank alongside of the steamboat landing—but they couldn't come it. Every time one of them showed himself on the

[9]Stack.

river side of the wood-pile he got shot at. The two boys was squatting back to back behind the pile, so they could watch both ways.

By-and-by the men stopped cavorting around and yelling. They started riding towards the store; then up gets one of the boys, draws a steady bead over the wood-rank, and drops one of them out of his saddle. All the men jumped off of their horses and grabbed the hurt one and started to carry him to the store; and that minute the two boys started on the run. They got half-way to the tree I was in before the men noticed. Then the men see them, and jumped on their horses and took out after them. They gained on the boys, but it didn't do no good, the boys had too good a start; they got to the wood-pile that was in front of my tree, and slipped in behind it, and so they had the bulge[10] on the men again. One of the boys was Buck, and the other was a slim young chap about nineteen years old.

The men ripped around awhile, and then rode away. As soon as they was out of sight, I sung out to Buck and told him. He didn't know what to make of my voice coming out of the tree, at first. He was awful surprised. He told me to watch out sharp and let him know when the men come in sight again; said they was up to some devilment or other—wouldn't be gone long. I wished I was out of that tree, but I dasn't come down. Buck begun to cry and rip, and 'lowed that him and his cousin Joe (that was the other young chap) would make up for this day, yet. He said his father and his two brothers was killed, and two or three of the enemy. Said the Shepherdsons laid for them, in ambush. Buck said his father and brothers ought to waited for their relations—the Shepherdsons was too strong for them. I asked him what was become of young Harney and Miss Sophia. He said they'd got across the river and was safe. I was glad of that; but the way Buck did take on because he didn't manage to kill Harney that day he shot at him—I hain't ever heard anything like it.

All of a sudden, bang! bang! bang! goes three or four guns—the men had slipped around through the woods and come in from behind without their horses! The boys jumped for the river—both of them hurt—and as they swum down the current the men run along the bank shooting at them and singing out, "Kill them, kill them!" It made me so sick I most fell out of the tree. I ain't agoing to tell *all* that happened—it would make me sick again if I was to do that. I wished I hadn't ever come ashore that night, to see such things. I ain't ever going to get shut of them—lots of times I dream about them.

I staid in the tree till it begun to get dark, afraid to come down. Sometimes I heard guns away off in the woods; and twice I seen little gangs of men gallop past the log store with guns; so I reckoned the trouble was still agoing on. I was mighty down-hearted; so I made up my mind I wouldn't ever go anear that house again, because I reckoned I was to blame, somehow. I judged that that piece of paper meant that Miss Sophia was to meet Harney somewheres at half-past two and run off; and I judged I ought to told her father about that paper and the curious way she acted, and then maybe he would a locked her up and this awful mess wouldn't ever happened.

When I got down out of the tree, I crept along down the river bank a piece, and found the two bodies laying in the edge of the water, and tugged at them till I got them ashore; then I covered up their faces, and got away as quick as I could. I cried a little when I was covering up Buck's face, for he was mighty good to me.

It was just dark, now. I never went near the house, but struck through the

[10]Advantage.

woods and made for the swamp. Jim warn't on his island, so I tramped off in a hurry for the crick, and crowded through the willows, red-hot to jump aboard and get out of that awful country—the raft was gone! My souls, but I was scared! I couldn't get my breath for most a minute. Then I raised a yell. A voice not twenty-five foot from me, says—

"Good lan'! is dat you, honey? Doan' make no noise."

It was Jim's voice—nothing ever sounded so good before. I run along the bank a piece and got aboard, and Jim he grabbed me and hugged me, he was so glad to see me. He says—

"Laws bless you, chile, I 'uz right down sho' you'd dead agin. Jack's been heah, he say he reck'n you's ben shot, kase you didn' come home no mo'; so I's jes' dis minute a startin' de raf' down towards de mouf er de crick, so's to be all ready for to shove out en leave soon as Jack comes agin en tells me for certain you *is* dead. Lawsy, I's mighty glad to get you back agin, honey."

I says—

"All right—that's mighty good; they won't find me, and they'll think I've been killed, and floated down the river—there's something up there that'll help them to think so—so don't you lose no time, Jim, but just shove off for the big water[11] as fast as ever you can."

I never felt easy till the raft was two mile below there and out in the middle of the Mississippi. Then we hung up our signal lantern, and judged that we was free and safe once more. I hadn't had a bite to eat since yesterday; so Jim he got out some corn-dodgers[12] and buttermilk, and pork and cabbage, and greens—there ain't nothing in the world so good, when it's cooked right—and whilst I eat my supper we talked, and had a good time. I was powerful glad to get away from the feuds, and so was Jim to get away from the swamp. We said there warn't no home like a raft, after all. Other places do seem so cramped up and smothery, but a raft don't. You feel mighty free and easy and comfortable on a raft.

CHAPTER XIX

Two or three days and nights went by; I reckon I might say they swum by, they slid along so quiet and smooth and lovely. Here is the way we put in the time. It was a monstrous big river down there—sometimes a mile and a half wide; we run nights, and laid up and hid day-times; soon as night was most gone, we stopped navigating and tied up—nearly always in the dead water under a tow-head; and then cut young cotton-woods and willows and hid the raft with them. Then we set out the lines. Next we slid into the river and had a swim, so as to freshen up and cool off; then we set down on the sandy bottom where the water was about knee deep, and watched the daylight come. Not a sound, anywheres—perfectly still—just like the whole world was asleep, only sometimes the bull-frogs a-cluttering, maybe. The first thing to see, looking away over the water, was a kind of dull line—that was the woods on t'other side—you couldn't make nothing else out; then a pale place in the sky; then more paleness, spreading around; then the river softened up away off, and warn't black any more, but gray; you could see little dark spots drifting along, ever so far away—trading scows, and such things; and long black streaks—rafts; sometimes you could hear a sweep screaking; or jumbled up voices, it was so still, and sound come so far;

[11]The main channel of the Mississippi River.   [12]Hard-baked corn-meal cakes.

and by-and-by you could see a streak on the water which you know by the look of the streak that there's a snag there in a swift current which breaks on it and makes that streak look that way; and you see the mist curl up off of the water, and the east reddens up, and the river, and you make out a log cabin in the edge of the woods, away on the bank on t'other side of the river, being a wood-yard, likely, and piled by them cheats so you can throw a dog through it anywheres;[1] then the nice breeze springs up, and comes fanning you from over there, so cool and fresh, and sweet to smell, on account of the woods and the flowers; but sometimes not that way, because they've left dead fish laying around, gars,[2] and such, and they do get pretty rank; and next you've got the full day, and everything smiling in the sun, and the song-birds just going it!

A little smoke couldn't be noticed, now, so we would take some fish off of the lines, and cook up a hot breakfast. And afterwards we would watch the lone-someness of the river, and kind of lazy along, and by-and-by lazy off to sleep. Wake up, by-and-by, and look to see what done it, and maybe see a steamboat, coughing along up stream, so far off towards the other side you couldn't tell nothing about her only whether she was stern-wheel or side-wheel; then for about an hour there wouldn't be nothing to hear nor nothing to see—just solid lonesomeness. Next you'd see a raft sliding by, away off yonder, and maybe a galoot[3] on it chopping, because they're most always doing it on a raft; you'd see the ax flash, and come down—you don't hear nothing; you see that ax go up again, and by the time it's above the man's head, then you hear the *k'chunk!*—it had took all that time to come over the water. So we would put in the day, lazying around, listening to the stillness. Once there was a thick fog, and the rafts and things that went by was beating tin pans so the steamboats wouldn't run over them. A scow or a raft went by so close we could hear them talking and cussing and laughing—heard them plain; but we couldn't see no sign of them; it made you feel crawly, it was like spirits carrying on that way in the air. Jim said he believed it was spirits; but I says:

"No, spirits wouldn't say, 'dern the dern fog.'"

Soon as it was night, out we shoved; when we got her out to about the middle, we let her alone, and let her float wherever the current wanted her to; then we lit the pipes, and dangled our legs in the water and talked about all kinds of things—we was always naked, day and night, whenever the mosquitoes would let us—the new clothes Buck's folks made for me was too good to be comfortable, and besides I didn't go much on clothes, nohow.

Sometimes we'd have that whole river all to ourselves for the longest time. Yonder was the banks and the islands, across the water; and maybe a spark—which was a candle in a cabin window—and sometimes on the water you could see a spark or two—on a raft or a scow, you know; and maybe you could hear a fiddle or a song coming over from one of them crafts. It's lovely to live on a raft. We had the sky, up there, all speckled with stars, and we used to lay on our backs and look up at them, and discuss about whether they was made, or only just happened—Jim he allowed they was made, but I allowed they hap-pened; I judged it would have took too long to *make* so many. Jim said the moon could a *laid* them; well, that looked kind of reasonable, so I didn't say nothing against it, because I've seen a frog lay most as many, so of course it could be done. We used to watch the stars that fell, too, and see them streak down. Jim allowed they'd got spoiled and was hove out of the nest.

---

[1] Woodcutters sold wood by volume to passing steamboats. By stacking their wood loosely, with large gaps, the unscrupulous tried to sell less wood for more money.
[2] A tough, inedible fish, a variety of pike.   [3] Fellow.

Once or twice of a night we would see a steamboat slipping along in the dark, and now and then she would belch a whole world of sparks up out of her chimbleys, and they would rain down in the river and look awful pretty; then she would turn a corner and her lights would wink out and her pow-wow[4] shut off and leave the river still again; and by-and-by her waves would get to us, a long time after she was gone, and joggle the raft a bit, and after that you wouldn't hear nothing for you couldn't tell how long, except maybe frogs or something.

After midnight the people on shore went to bed, and then for two or three hours the shores was black—no more sparks in the cabin windows. These sparks was our clock—the first one that showed again meant morning was coming, so we hunted a place to hide and tie up, right away.

One morning about day-break, I found a canoe and crossed over a chute[5] to the main shore—it was only two hundred yards—and paddled about a mile up a crick amongst the cypress woods, to see if I couldn't get some berries. Just as I was passing a place where a kind of a cow-path crossed the crick, here comes a couple of men tearing up the path as tight as they could foot it. I thought I was a goner, for whenever anybody was after anybody I judged it was *me*—or maybe Jim. I was about to dig out from there in a hurry, but they was pretty close to me then, and sung out and begged me to save their lives—said they hadn't been doing nothing, and was being chased for it—said there was men and dogs a-coming. They wanted to jump right in, but I says—

"Don't you do it. I don't hear the dogs and horses yet; you've got time to crowd through the brush and get up the crick a little ways; then you take to the water and wade down to me and get in—that'll throw the dogs off the scent."

They done it, and soon as they was aboard I lit out for our towhead and in about five or ten minutes we heard the dogs and the men away off, shouting. We heard them come along towards the crick, but couldn't see them; they seemed to stop and fool around a while; then as we got further and further away all the time, we couldn't hardly hear them at all; by the time we had left a mile of woods behind us and struck the river, everything was quiet, and we paddled over to the tow-head and hid in the cotton-woods and was safe.

One of these fellows was about seventy, or upwards, and had a bald head and very gray whiskers. He had an old battered-up slouch hat on, and a greasy blue woolen shirt, and ragged old blue jeans britches stuffed into his boot tops, and home-knit galluses[6]—no, he only had one. He had an old long-tailed blue jeans coat with slick brass buttons, flung over his arm, and both of them had big fat ratty-looking carpet-bags.[7]

The other fellow was about thirty and dressed about as ornery. After breakfast we all laid off and talked, and the first thing that come out was that these chaps didn't know one another.

"What got you into trouble?" says the baldhead to t'other chap.

"Well, I'd been selling an article to take the tartar off the teeth—and it does take it off, too, and generly the enamel along with it—but I staid about one night longer than I ought to, and was just in the act of sliding out when I ran across you on the trail this side of town, and you told me they were coming, and begged me to help you to get off. So I told you I was expecting trouble myself and would scatter out *with* you. That's the whole yarn—what's yourn?"

"Well, I'd ben a-runnin' a little temperance revival thar, 'bout a week, and was the pet of the women-folks, big and little, for I was makin' it mighty warm for the rummies, I *tell* you, and takin' as much as five or six dollars a night—ten

---

[4]Engine noise.   [5]A narrow channel with a swift current.
[6]Suspenders.   [7]Cheap suitcases made out of carpet remnants.

cents a head, children and niggers free—and business a growin' all the time; when somehow or another a little report got around, last night, that I had a way of puttin' in my time with a private jug, on the sly. A nigger rousted me out this mornin', and told me the people was getherin' on the quiet, with their dogs and horses, and they'd be along pretty soon and give me 'bout half an hour's start, and then run me down, if they could; and if they got me they'd tar and feather me and ride me on a rail, sure. I didn't wait for no breakfast—I warn't hungry."

"Old man," says the young one, "I reckon we might double-team[8] it together; what do you think?"

"I ain't undisposed. What's your line—mainly?"

"Jour[9] printer, by trade; do a little in patent medicines; theatre-actor—tragedy, you know; take a turn at mesmerism[10] and phrenology[11] when there's a chance; teach singing-geography school for a change; sling a lecture, sometimes—oh, I do lots of things—most anything that comes handy, so it ain't work. What's your lay?"[12]

"I've done considerble in the doctoring way in my time. Layin' on o' hands[13] is my best holt—for cancer, and paralysis, and sich things; and I k'n tell a fortune pretty good, when I've got somebody along to find out the facts for me. Preachin's my line, too; and workin' camp-meetin's; and missionaryin around."

Nobody never said anything for a while; then the young man hove a sigh and says—

"Alas!"

"What're you alassin' about?" says the baldhead.

"To think I should have lived to be leading such a life, and be degraded down into such company." And he begun to wipe the corner of his eye with a rag.

"Dern your skin, ain't the company good enough for you?" says the baldhead, pretty pert and uppish.

"Yes, it *is* good enough for me; it's as good as I deserve; for who fetched me so low, when I was so high? *I* did myself. I don't blame *you*, gentlemen—far from it; I don't blame anybody. I deserve it all. Let the cold world do its worst; one thing I know—there's a grave somewhere for me. The world may go on just as it's always done, and take everything from me—loved ones, property, everything—but it can't take that. Some day I'll lie down in it and forget it all, and my poor broken heart will be at rest." He went on a-wiping.

"Drot your pore broken heart," says the baldhead; "what are you heaving your pore broken heart at *us* f'r? *We* hain't done nothing."

"No, I know you haven't. I ain't blaming you, gentlemen. I brought myself down—yes, I did it myself. It's right I should suffer—perfectly right—I don't make any moan."

"Brought you down from whar? Whar was you brought down from?"

"Ah, you would not believe me; the world never believes—let it pass—'tis no matter. The secret of my birth——"

"The secret of your birth? Do you mean to say——"

"Gentlemen," says the young man, very solemn, "I will reveal it to you, for I feel I may have confidence in you. By rights I am a duke!"

Jim's eyes bugged out when he heard that; and I reckon mine did, too. Then the baldhead says: "No! you can't mean it?"

[8]Work together, like a team of horses.
[9]Journeyman, i.e., trained.   [10]Hypnotism.
[11]Presuming to read human character from the shape of the head.
[12]Trade, profession.   [13]Faith healing.

"Yes. My great-grandfather, eldest son of the Duke of Bridgewater, fled to this country about the end of the last century, to breathe the pure air of freedom; married here, and died, leaving a son, his own father dying about the same time. The second son of the late duke seized the title and estates—the infant real duke was ignored. I am the lineal descendant of that infant—I am the rightful Duke of Bridgewater; and here am I, forlorn, torn from my high estate, hunted of men, despised by the cold world, ragged, worn, heart-broken, and degraded to the companionship of felons on a raft!"

Jim pitied him ever so much and so did I. We tried to comfort him, but he said it warn't much use, he couldn't be much comforted; said if we was a mind to acknowledge him, that would do him more good than most anything else; so we said we would, if he would tell us how. He said we ought to bow, when we spoke to him, and say "Your Grace," or "My Lord," or "Your Lordship"—and he wouldn't mind it if we called him plain "Bridgewater," which he said was a title, anyway, and not a name; and one of us ought to wait on him at dinner, and do any little thing for him he wanted done.

Well, that was all easy, so we done it. All through dinner Jim stood around and waited on him, and says, "Will yo' Grace have some o' dis, or some o' dat?" and so on, and a body could see it was mighty pleasing to him.

But the old man got pretty silent, by-and-by—didn't have much to say, and didn't look pretty comfortable over all that petting that was going on around that duke. He seemed to have something on his mind. So, along in the afternoon, he says:

"Looky here, Bilgewater," he says, "I'm nation sorry for you, but you ain't the only person that's had troubles like that."

"No?"

"No, you ain't. You ain't the only person that's ben snaked[14] down wrongfully out'n a high place."

"Alas!"

"No, you ain't the only person that's had a secret of his birth." And by jings, *he* begins to cry.

"Hold! What do you mean?"

"Bilgewater, kin I trust you?" says the old man, still sort of sobbing.

"To the bitter death!" He took the old man by the hand and squeezed it, and says, "The secret of your being: speak!"

"Bilgewater, I am the late Dauphin!"

You bet you Jim and me started, this time. Then the duke says:

"You are what?"

"Yes, my friend, it is too true—your eyes is lookin' at this very moment on the pore disappeared Dauphin, Looy the Seventeen, son of Looy the Sixteen and Marry Antonette."

"You! At your age![15] No! You mean you're the late Charlemagne;[16] you must be six or seven hundred years old, at the very least."

"Trouble has done it, Bilgewater, trouble has done it; trouble has brung these gray hairs and this premature balditude. Yes, gentlemen, you see before you, in blue jeans and misery, the wanderin', exiled, trampled-on and sufferin' rightful King of France."

Well, he cried and took on so, that me and Jim didn't know hardly what to do, we was so sorry—and so glad and proud we'd got him with us, too. So we set in, like we done before with the duke, and tried to comfort *him*. But he said

---

[14]Brought, pulled.   [15]Had he lived, the lost dauphin would have been in his fifties.
[16]The Holy Roman Emperor Charles the Great (742–814).

it warn't no use, nothing but to be dead and done with it all could do him any good; though he said it often made him feel easier and better for a while if people treated him according to his rights, and got down on one knee to speak to him, and always called him "Your Majesty," and waited on him first at meals, and didn't set down in his presence till he asked them. So Jim and me set to majestying him, and doing this and that and t'other for him, and standing up till he told us we might set down. This done him heaps of good, and so he got cheerful and comfortable. But the duke kind of soured on him, and didn't look a bit satisfied with the way things was going; still, the king acted real friendly towards him, and said the duke's great-grandfather and all the other Dukes of Bilgewater was a good deal thought of by *his* father and was allowed to come to the palace considerable; but the duke staid huffy a good while, till by-and-by the king says:

"Like as not we got to be together a blamed long time, on this h-yer raft, Bilgewater, and so what's the use o' your bein' sour? It'll only make things oncomfortable. It ain't my fault I warn't born a duke, it ain't your fault you warn't born a king—so what's the use to worry? Make the best o' things the way you find 'em, says I—that's my motto. This ain't no bad thing that we've struck here—plenty grub and an easy life—come, give us your hand, Duke, and less all be friends."

The duke done it, and Jim and me was pretty glad to see it. It took away all the uncomfortableness, and we felt mighty good over it, because it would a been a miserable business to have any unfriendliness on the raft; for what you want, above all things, on a raft, is for everybody to be satisfied, and feel right and kind towards the others.

It didn't take me long to make up my mind that these liars warn't no kings nor dukes, at all, but just low-down humbugs and frauds. But I never said nothing, never let on; kept it to myself; it's the best way; then you don't have no quarrels, and don't get into no trouble. If they wanted us to call them kings and dukes, I hadn't no objections, 'long as it would keep peace in the family; and it warn't no use to tell Jim, so I didn't tell him. If I never learnt nothing else out of pap, I learnt that the best way to get along with his kind of people is to let them have their own way.

CHAPTER XX

They asked us considerable many questions; wanted to know what we covered up the raft that way for, and laid by in the daytime instead of running—was Jim a runaway nigger? Says I—

"Goodness sakes, would a runaway nigger run *south*?"

No, they allowed he wouldn't. I had to account for things some way, so I says:

"My folks was living in Pike County, in Missouri, where I was born, and they all died off but me and pa and my brother Ike. Pa, he 'lowed he'd break up and go down and live with Uncle Ben, who's got a little one-horse place on the river, forty-four mile below Orleans. Pa was pretty poor, and had some debts; so when he'd squared up there warn't nothing left but sixteen dollars and our nigger, Jim. That warn't enough to take us fourteen hundred mile, deck passage nor no other way. Well, when the river rose, pa had a streak of luck one day; he ketched this piece of a raft; so we reckoned we'd go down to Orleans on it. Pa's luck didn't hold out; a steamboat run over the forrard corner of the raft, one night, and we all went overboard and dove under the wheel; Jim and me come up, all right, but pa was drunk, and Ike was only four years old, so they never come up no more. Well, for the next day or two we had considerable trouble, because people was always coming out in skiffs and trying to take Jim away from me, saying they believed he was a runaway nigger. We don't run day-times no more, now; nights they don't bother us."

The duke says—

"Leave me alone to cipher out a way so we can run in the daytime if we want to. I'll think the thing over—I'll invent a plan that'll fix it. We'll let it alone for to-day, because of course we don't want to go by that town yonder in daylight— it mightn't be healthy."

Towards night it begun to darken up and look like rain; the heat lightning was squirting around, low down in the sky, and the leaves was beginning to shiver—it was going to be pretty ugly, it was easy to see that. So the duke and the king went to overhauling our wigwam, to see what the beds was like. My bed was a straw tick[1]—better than Jim's, which was a corn-shuck tick; there's always cobs around about in a shuck tick, and they poke into you and hurt; and when you roll over, the dry shucks sound like you was rolling over in a pile of dead leaves; it makes such a rustling that you wake up. Well, the duke allowed he would take my bed; but the king allowed he wouldn't. He says—

"I should a reckoned the difference in rank would a sejested to you that a corn-shuck bed warn't just fitten for me to sleep on. Your Grace'll take the shuck bed yourself."

Jim and me was in a sweat again, for a minute, being afraid there was going to be some more trouble amongst them; so we was pretty glad when the duke says—

" 'Tis my fate to be always ground into the mire under the iron heel of oppression. Misfortune has broken my once haughty spirit; I yield, I submit; 'tis my fate. I am alone in the world—let me suffer; I can bear it."

We got away as soon as it was good and dark. The king told us to stand well out towards the middle of the river, and not show a light till we got a long ways below the town. We come in sight of the little bunch of lights by-and-by—that was the town, you know—and slid by, about a half a mile out, all right. When we was three-quarters of a mile below, we hoisted up our signal lantern; and about ten o'clock it come on to rain and blow and thunder and lighten like everything; so the king told us to both stay on watch till the weather got better; then him and the duke crawled into the wigwam and turned in for the night. It was my watch below, till twelve, but I wouldn't a turned in, anyway, if I'd had a bed; because a body don't see such a storm as that every day in the week, not by a long sight. My souls, how the wind did scream along! And every second or two there'd come a glare that lit up the white-caps for a half a mile around, and you'd see the islands looking dusty through the rain, and the trees thrashing around in the wind; then comes a *h-wack!*—bum! bum! bumble-umble-um-bum- bum-bum-bum—and the thunder would go rumbling and grumbling away, and quit—and then *rip* comes another flash and another sockdolager.[2] The waves most washed me off the raft, sometimes, but I hadn't any clothes on, and didn't mind. We didn't have no trouble about snags; the lightning was glaring and flittering around so constant that we could see them plenty soon enough to throw her head this way or that and miss them.

I had the middle[3] watch, you know, but I was pretty sleepy by that time, so Jim he said he would stand the first half of it for me; he was always mighty

[1]Mattress.   [2]Tremendous crash.   [3]Midnight to 4 A.M.

good, that way, Jim was. I crawled into the wigwam, but the king and the duke had their legs sprawled around so there warn't no show for me; so I laid outside— I didn't mind the rain, because it was warm, and the waves warn't running so high, now. About two they come up again, though, and Jim was going to call me, but he changed his mind because he reckoned they warn't high enough yet to do any harm; but he was mistaken about that, for pretty soon all of a sudden along comes a regular ripper, and washed me overboard. It most killed Jim a-laughing. He was the easiest nigger to laugh that ever was, anyway.

I took the watch, and Jim he laid down and snored away; and by-and-by the storm let up for good and all; and the first cabin-light that showed, I rousted him out and we slid the raft into hiding-quarters for the day.

The king got out an old ratty deck of cards, after breakfast, and him and the duke played seven-up[4] a while, five cents a game. Then they got tired of it, and allowed they would "lay out a campaign," as they called it. The duke went down into his carpet-bag and fetched up a lot of little printed bills, and read them out loud. One bill said, "The celebrated Dr. Armand de Mantalban of Paris," would "lecture on the Science of Phrenology" at such and such a place, on the blank day of blank, at ten cents admission, and "furnish charts of character at twenty-five cents apiece." The duke said that was *him*. In another bill he was the "world renowned Shakesperean tragedian, Garrick the Younger,[5] of Drury Lane, London." In other bills he had a lot of other names and done other wonderful things, like finding water and gold with a "divining rod,"[6] "dissipating witch-spells," and so on. By-and-by he says—

"But the histrionic muse is the darling. Have you ever trod the boards,[7] Royalty?"

"No," says the king.

"You shall then, before you're three days older, Fallen Grandeur," says the duke. "The first good town we come to, we'll hire a hall and do the sword-fight in Richard III, and the balcony scene in Romeo and Juliet. How does that strike you?"

"I'm in, up to the hub, for anything that will pay, Bilgewater, but you see I don't know nothing about play-actin', and hain't ever seen much of it. I was too small when pap used to have 'em at the palace. Do you reckon you can learn me?"

"Easy!"

"All right. I'm jist a-freezn' for something fresh, anyway. Less commence, right away."

So the duke he told him all about who Romeo was, and who Juliet was, and said he was used to being Romeo, so the king could be Juliet.

"But if Juliet's such a young gal, Duke, my peeled head and my white whiskers is goin' to look oncommon odd on her, maybe."

"No, don't you worry—these country jakes won't ever think of that. Besides, you know, you'll be in costume, and that makes all the difference in the world; Juliet's in a balcony, enjoying the moonlight before she goes to bed, and she's got on her night-gown and her ruffled night-cap. Here are the costumes for the parts."

He got out two or three curtain-calico suits, which he said was meedyevil

[4]A card game in which the winner must score seven points.
[5]David Garrick (1717–1789), British actor, had died the previous century. There was no Garrick the Younger.
[6]A forked rod or stick believed to point magically toward water or buried treasure.
[7]Acted on the stage.

armor for Richard III. and t'other chap,[8] and a long white cotton night-shirt and a ruffled night-cap to match. The king was satisfied; so the duke got out his book and read the parts over in the most splendid spread-eagle[9] way, prancing around and acting at the same time, to show how it had got to be done; then he give the book to the king and told him to get his part by heart.

There was a little one-horse town about three mile down the bend, and after dinner the duke said he had ciphered out his idea about how to run in daylight without it being dangersome for Jim; so he allowed he would go down to the town and fix that thing. The king allowed he would go too, and see if he couldn't strike something. We was out of coffee, so Jim said I better go along with them in the canoe and get some.

When we got there, there warn't nobody stirring; streets empty, and perfectly dead and still, like Sunday. We found a sick nigger sunning himself in a back yard, and he said everybody that warn't too young or too sick or too old, was gone to camp-meeting, about two mile back in the woods. The king got the directions, and allowed he'd go and work that camp-meeting for all it was worth, and I might go, too.

The duke said what he was after was a printing office. We found it; a little bit of a concern, up over a carpenter shop—carpenters and printers all gone to the meeting, and no doors locked. It was a dirty, littered-up place, and had ink marks, and handbills with pictures of horses and runaway niggers on them, all over the walls. The duke shed his coat and said he was all right, now. So me and the king lit out for the camp-meeting.

We got there in about a half an hour, fairly dripping, for it was a most awful hot day. There was as much as a thousand people there, from twenty mile around. The woods was full of teams and wagons, hitched everywheres, feeding out of the wagon troughs and stomping to keep off the flies. There was sheds made out of poles and roofed over with branches, where they had lemonade and gingerbread to sell, and piles of watermelons and green corn and such-like truck.

The preaching was going on under the same kinds of sheds, only they was bigger and held crowds of people. The benches was made out of outside slabs of logs, with holes bored in the round side to drive sticks into for legs. They didn't have no backs. The preachers had high platforms to stand on, at one end of the sheds. The women had on sun-bonnets; and some had linsey-woolsey[10] frocks, some gingham ones, and a few of the young ones had on calico. Some of the young men was barefooted, and some of the children didn't have on any clothes but just a tow-linen[11] shirt. Some of the old women was knitting, and some of the young folks was courting on the sly.

The first shed we come to, the preacher was lining out a hymn.[12] He lined out two lines, everybody sung it, and it was kind of grand to hear it, there was so many of them and they done it in such a rousing way; then he lined out two more for them to sing—and so on. The people woke up more and more, and sung louder and louder; and towards the end, some begun to groan, and some begun to shout. Then the preacher begun to preach; and begun in earnest, too; and went weaving first to one side of the platform and then the other, and then a leaning down over the front of it, with his arms and his body going all the time, and shouting his words out with all his might; and every now and then he would hold up his Bible and spread it open, and kind of pass it around this way

---

[8]The Earl of Richmond.   [9]Ornate, exaggerated.
[10]Coarse cloth of linen, or cotton, and wool.   [11]Rough linen.
[12]Speaking out the words so the congregation, lacking hymnbooks, could follow in song.

and that, shouting, "It's the brazen serpent in the wilderness! Look upon it and live!" And people would shout out, "Glory!—A-a-*men!*" And so he went on, and the people groaning and crying and saying amen:

"Oh, come to the mourners' bench![13] come, black with sin! (*amen!*) come, sick and sore! (*amen!*) come, lame and halt, and blind! (*amen!*) come, pore and needy, sunk in shame! (*a-a-amen!*) come all that's worn, and soiled, and suffering!—come with a broken spirit! come with a contrite heart! come in your rags and sin and dirt! the waters that cleanse is free, the door of heaven stands open—oh, enter in and be at rest! (*a-a-men! glory, glory hallelujah!*)"

And so on. You couldn't make out what the preacher said, any more, on account of the shouting and crying. Folks got up, everywheres in the crowd, and worked their way, just by main strength, to the mourners' bench, with the tears running down their faces; and when all the mourners had got up there to the front benches in a crowd, they sung and shouted, and flung themselves down on the straw, just crazy and wild.

Well, the first I knowed, the king got agoing; and you could hear him over everybody; and next he went a-charging up on the platform and the preacher he begged him to speak to the people, and he done it. He told them he was a pirate—been a pirate for thirty years, out in the Indian Ocean, and his crew was thinned out considerable, last spring, in a fight, and he was home now, to take out some fresh men, and thanks to goodness he'd been robbed last night, and put ashore off a steamboat without a cent, and he was glad of it, it was the blessedest thing that ever happened to him, because he was a changed man now, and happy for the first time in his life; and poor as he was, he was going to start right off and work his way back to the Indian Ocean and put in the rest of his life trying to turn the pirates into the true path; for he could do it better than anybody else, being acquainted with all the pirate crews in that ocean; and though it would take him a long time to get there, without money, he would get there anyway, and every time he convinced a pirate he would say to him, "Don't you thank me, don't you give me no credit, it all belongs to them dear people in Pokeville camp-meeting, natural brothers and benefactors of the race—and that dear preacher there, the truest friend a pirate ever had!"

And then he busted into tears, and so did everybody. Then somebody sings out, "Take up a collection for him, take up a collection!" Well, a half a dozen made a jump to do it, but somebody sings out, "Let *him* pass the hat around!" Then everybody said it, the preacher too.

So the king went all through the crowd with his hat, swabbing his eyes, and blessing the people and praising them and thanking them for being so good to the poor pirates away off there; and every little while the prettiest kind of girls, with the tears running down their cheeks, would up and ask him would he let them kiss him, for to remember him by; and he always done it; and some of them he hugged and kissed as many as five or six times—and he was invited to stay a week; and everybody wanted him to live in their houses, and said they'd think it was an honor; but he said as this was the last day of the camp-meeting he couldn't do no good, and besides he was in a sweat to get to the Indian Ocean right off and go to work on the pirates.

When we got back to the raft and he come to count up, he found he had collected eighty-seven dollars and seventy-five cents. And then he had fetched away a three-gallon jug of whisky, too, that he found under a wagon when we was starting home through the woods. The king said, take it all around, it laid

---

[13]Front seats, near the pulpit, for those who mourn their sins and want to repent.

over any day he'd ever put in the missionarying line. He said it warn't no use talking, heathens don't amount to shucks, alongside of pirates, to work a camp-meeting with.

The duke was thinking *he'd* been doing pretty well, till the king come to show up, but after that he didn't think so so much. He had set up and printed off two little jobs for farmers, in that printing office—horse bills—and took the money, four dollars. And he had got in ten dollars worth of advertisements for the paper, which he said he would put in for four dollars if they would pay in advance—so they done it. The price of the paper was two dollars a year, but he took in three subscriptions for half a dollar apiece on condition of them paying him in advance; they were going to pay in cord-wood and onions, as usual, but he said he had just bought the concern and knocked down the price as low as he could afford it, and was going to run it for cash. He set up a little piece of poetry, which he made, himself, out of his own head—three verses—kind of sweet and saddish—the name of it was, "Yes, crush, cold world, this breaking heart"—and he left that all set up and ready to print in the paper and didn't charge nothing for it. Well, he took in nine dollars and a half, and said he'd done a pretty square day's work for it.

Then he showed us another little job he'd printed and hadn't charged for, because it was for us. It had a picture of a runaway nigger, with a bundle on a stick, over his shoulder, and "$200 reward" under it. The reading was all about Jim, and just described him to a dot. It said he run away from St. Jacques' plantation, forty mile below New Orleans, last winter, and likely went north, and whoever would catch him and send him back, he could have the reward and expenses.

"Now," says duke, "after to-night we can run in the day-time if we want to. Whenever we see anybody coming, we can tie Jim hand and foot with a rope, and lay him in the wigwam and show this handbill and say we captured him up the river, and were too poor to travel on a steamboat, so we got this little raft on credit from our friends and are going down to get the reward. Handcuffs and chains would look better on Jim, but it wouldn't go well with the story of us being so poor. Too much like jewelry. Ropes are the correct thing—we must preserve the unities,[14] as we say on the boards."

We all said the duke was pretty smart, and there couldn't be no trouble about running day-times. We judged we could make miles enough that night to get out of the reach of the pow-wow we reckoned the duke's work in the printing office was going to make in that little town—then we could boom right along, if we wanted to.

We laid low and kept still, and never shoved out till nearly ten o'clock; then we slid by, pretty wide away from the town, and didn't hoist our lantern till we was clear out of sight of it.

When Jim called me to take the watch at four in the morning, he says—

"Huck, does you reck'n we gwyne to run acrost any mo' kings on dis trip?"

"No," I says, "I reckon not."

"Well," says he, "dat's all right, den. I doan' mine one er two kings, but dat's enough. Dis one's powerful drunk, en de duke ain' much better."

I found Jim had been trying to get him to talk French, so he could hear what it was like; but he said he had been in this country so long, and had so much trouble, he'd forgot it.

---

[14]The dramatic unities of time, place, and action of the neoclassic French theater.

CHAPTER XXI

It was after sun-up, now, but we went right on, and didn't tie up. The king and the duke turned out, by-and-by, looking pretty rusty; but after they'd jumped overboard and took a swim, it chippered them up a good deal. After breakfast the king he took a seat on a corner of the raft, and pulled off his boots and rolled up his britches, and let his legs dangle in the water, so as to be comfortable, and lit his pipe, and went to getting his Romeo and Juliet by heart. When he had got it pretty good, him and the duke begun to practice it together. The duke had to learn him over and over again, how to say every speech; and he made him sigh, and put his hand on his heart, and after while he said he done it pretty well; "only," he says, "you mustn't bellow out *Romeo!* that way, like a bull—you must say it soft, and sick, and languishy, so—R-o-o-meo! that is the idea; for Juliet's a dear sweet mere child of a girl, you know, and she don't bray like a jackass."

Well, next they got out a couple of long swords that the duke made out of oak laths, and begun to practice the sword-fight—the duke called himself Richard III.; and the way they laid on, and pranced around the raft was grand to see. But by-and-by the king tripped and fell overboard, and after that they took a rest, and had a talk about all kinds of adventures they'd had in other times along the river.

After dinner, the duke says:

"Well, Capet,[1] we'll want to make this a first-class show, you know, so I guess we'll add a little more to it. We want a little something to answer encores with, anyway."

"What's onkores, Bilgewater?"

The duke told him, and then says:

"I'll answer by doing the Highland fling or the sailor's hornpipe;[2] and you—well, let me see—oh, I've got it—you can do Hamlet's soliloquy."

"Hamlet's which?"

"Hamlet's soliloquy, you know; the most celebrated thing in Shakespeare. Ah, it's sublime, sublime! Always fetches the house. I haven't got it in the book—I've only got one volume—but I reckon I can piece it out from memory. I'll just walk up and down a minute, and see if I can call it back from recollection's vaults."

So he went to marching up and down, thinking, and frowning horrible every now and then; then he would hoist up his eyebrows; next he would squeeze his hand on his forehead and stagger back and kind of moan; next he would sigh, and next he'd let on to drop a tear. It was beautiful to see him. By-and-by he got it. He told us to give attention. Then he strikes a most noble attitude, with one leg shoved forwards, and his arms stretched away up, and his head tilted back, looking up at the sky; and then he begins to rip and rave and grit his teeth; and after that, all through his speech he howled, and spread around, and swelled up his chest, and just knocked the spots out of any acting ever *I* see before. This is the speech—I learned it, easy enough, while he was learning it to the king:

---

[1]Family name of Louis XVI.

[2]Highland fling: a lively Scottish dance. Sailor's hornpipe: a dance in which the performer, accompanied by a hornpipe, acts out the tasks of a sailor.

To be, or not to be; that is the bare bodkin
That makes calamity of so long life;
For who would fardels bear, till Birnam Wood do come
    to Dunsinane,
But that the fear of something after death
Murders the innocent sleep,
Great nature's second course,
And makes us rather sling the arrows of outrageous fortune
Than fly to others that we know not of.
There's the respect must give us pause:
Wake Duncan with thy knocking! I would thou couldst;
For who would bear the whips and scorns of time,
The oppressor's wrong, the proud man's contumely,
The law's delay, and the quietus which his pangs might
    take,
In the dead waste and middle of the night, when church-
    yards yawn
In customary suits of solemn black,
But that the undiscovered country from whose bourne no
    traveler returns,
Breathes forth contagion on the world,
And thus the native hue of resolution, like the poor cat
    i' the adage,
I sicklied o'er with care.
And all the clouds that lowered o'er our housetops,
With this regard their currents turn awry,
And lose the name of action.
'Tis a consummation devoutly to be wished. But soft you,
    the fair Ophelia:
Ope not thy ponderous and marble jaws,
But get thee to a nunnery—go![3]

Well, the old man he liked that speech, and he mighty soon got it so he could do it first rate. It seemed like he was just born for it; and when he had his hand in and was excited, it was perfectly lovely the way he would rip and tear and rair up behind when he was getting it off.

The first chance we got, the duke he had some show bills printed; and after that, for two or three days as we floated along, the raft was a most uncommon lively place, for there warn't nothing but sword-fighting and rehearsing—as the duke called it—going on all the time. One morning, when we was pretty well down the State of Arkansaw, we come in sight of a little one-horse town in a big bend; so we tied up about three-quarters of a mile above it, in the mouth of a crick which was shut in like a tunnel by the cypress trees, and all of us but Jim took the canoe and went down there to see if there was any chance in that place for our show.

We struck it mighty lucky; there was going to be a circus there that afternoon, and the country people was already beginning to come in, in all kinds of old shackly wagons, and on horses. The circus would leave before night, so our show would have a pretty good chance. The duke he hired the court house, and we went around and stuck up our bills. They read like this:

[3]The Duke's soliloquy is a hodgepodge of Shakespeare quotations from *Hamlet, Macbeth,* and *Richard III.*

Shaksperean Revival! ! !
Wonderful Attraction!
For One Night Only!
The world renowned tragedians,
David Garrick, the younger, of Drury Lane Theatre, London,
and
Edmund Kean the elder,[4] of the Royal Haymarket Theatre, White-
chapel, Pudding Lane, Piccadilly, London, and the
Royal Continental Theatres, in their sublime
Shaksperean Spectacle entitled
The Balcony Scene
in
Romeo and Juliet! ! !

Romeo . . . . Mr. Garrick.
Juliet . . . . .Mr. Kean.
Assisted by the whole strength of the company!
New costumes, new scenery, new appointments!
Also:
The thrilling, masterly, and blood-curdling
Broad-sword conflict
In Richard III.! ! !

Richard III . . . . Mr. Garrick.
Richmond. . . . . .Mr. Kean.
also:
(by special request,)
Hamlet's Immortal Soliloquy!
By the Illustrious Kean!
Done by him 300 consecutive nights in Paris!
For One Night Only,
On account of imperative European engagements!
Admission 25 cents; children and servants, 10 cents.

Then we went loafing around the town. The stores and houses was most all old shackly dried-up frame concerns that hadn't even been painted; they was set up three or four foot above ground on stilts, so as to be out of reach of the water when the river was overflowed. The houses had little gardens around them, but they didn't seem to raise hardly anything in them but jimpson weeds, and sunflowers, and ash-piles, and old curled-up boots and shoes, and pieces of bottles, and rags, and played-out tin-ware. The fences was made of different kinds of boards, nailed on at different times; and they leaned every which-way, and had gates that didn't generly have but one hinge—a leather one. Some of the fences had been whitewashed, some time or another, but the duke said it was in Clumbus's time, like enough. There was generly hogs in the garden, and people driving them out.

All the stores was along one street. They had white-domestic[5] awnings in front, and the country people hitched their horses to the awning-posts. There was empty dry-goods boxes under the awnings, and loafers roosting on them all day long, whittling them with their Barlow knives; and chawing tobacco, and gaping and yawning and stretching—a mighty ornery lot. They generly had on yellow straw hats most as wide as an umbrella, but didn't wear no coats nor

[4]British actor (1787?–1833).   [5]Crude canvas.

waistcoats; they called one another Bill, and Buck, and Hank, and Joe, and Andy, and talked lazy and drawly, and used considerable many cuss-words. There was as many as one loafer leaning up against every awning-post, and he most always had his hands in his britches pockets, except when he fetches them out to lend a chaw of tobacco or scratch. What a body was hearing amongst them, all the time was—

"Gimme a chaw'v tobacker, Hank."

"Cain't—I hain't got but one chaw left. Ask Bill."

Maybe Bill he gives him a chaw; maybe he lies and says he ain't got none. Some of them kinds of loafers never has a cent in the world, nor a chaw of tobacco of their own. They get all their chawing by borrowing—they say to a fellow, "I wisht you'd len' me a chaw, Jack, I jist this minute give Ben Thompson the last chaw I had"—which is a lie, pretty much every time; it don't fool nobody but a stranger; but Jack ain't no stranger, so he says—

"*You* give him a chaw, did you? so did your sister's cat's grandmother. You pay me back the chaws you've awready borry'd off'n me, Lafe Buckner, then I'll loan you one or two ton of it, and won't charge you no back intrust, nuther."

"Well, I *did* pay you back some of it wunst."

"Yes, you did—'bout six chaws. You borry'd store tobacker and paid back nigger-head."[6]

Store tobacco is flat black plug, but these fellows mostly chaws the natural leaf twisted. When they borrow a chaw, they don't generly cut it off with a knife, but they set the plug in between their teeth, and gnaw with their teeth and tug at the plug with their hands till they get it in two—then sometimes the one that owns the tobacco looks mournful at it when it's handed back, and says, sarcastic—

"Here, gimme the *chaw,* and you take the *plug.*"

All the streets and lanes was just mud, they warn't nothing else *but* mud— mud as black as tar, and nigh about a foot deep in some places; and two or three inches deep in *all* the places. The hogs loafed and grunted around, everywheres. You'd see a muddy sow and a litter of pigs come lazying along the street and whollop herself right down in the way, where folks had to walk around her, and she'd stretch out, and shut her eyes, and wave her ears, whilst the pigs was milking her, and look as happy as if she was on salary. And pretty soon you'd hear a loafer sing out, "Hi! *so* boy! sick him, Tige!" and away the sow would go, squealing most horrible, with a dog or two swinging to each ear, and three or four dozen more a-coming; and then you would see all the loafers get up and watch the thing out of sight, and laugh at the fun and look grateful for the noise. Then they'd settle back again till there was a dog-fight. There couldn't anything wake them up all over, and make them happy all over, like a dog-fight—unless it might be putting turpentine on a stray dog and setting fire to him, or tying a tin pan to his tail and see him run himself to death.

On the river front some of the houses was sticking out over the bank, and they was bowed and bent, and about ready to tumble in. The people had moved out of them. The bank was caved away under one corner of some others, and that corner was hanging over. People lived in them yet, but it was dangersome, because sometimes a strip of land as wide as a house caves in at a time. Sometimes a belt of land a quarter of a mile deep will start in and cave along and cave along till it all caves into the river in one summer. Such a town as that has to be always moving back, and back, and back, because the river's always gnawing at it.

[6]Cheap, leaf tobacco.

The nearer it got to the noon that day, the thicker and thicker was the wagons and horses in the streets, and more coming all the time. Families fetched their dinners with them, from the country, and eat them in the wagons. There was considerable whisky drinking going on, and I seen three fights. By-and-by somebody sings out—

"Here comes old Boggs!—in from the country for his little old monthly drunk—here he comes, boys!"

All the loafers looked glad—I reckoned they was used to having fun out of Boggs. One of them says—

"Wonder who he's a gwyne to chaw up this time. If he'd a chawed up all the men he's ben a gwyne to chaw up in the last twenty year, he'd have considerble ruputation, now."

Another one says, "I wisht old Boggs 'd threaten me, 'cuz then I'd know I warn't gwyne to die for a thousan' year."

Boggs comes a-tearing along on his horse, whooping and yelling like an Injun, and singing out—

"Cler the track, thar. I'm on the waw-path, and the price uv coffins is a gwyne to raise."

He was drunk, and weaving about in his saddle; he was over fifty year old, and had a very red face. Everybody yelled at him, and laughed at him, and sassed him, and he sassed back, and said he'd attend to them and lay them out in their regular turns, but he couldn't wait now, because he'd come to town to kill old Colonel Sherburn, and his motto was, "meat first, and spoon vittles to top off on."

He see me, and rode up and says—

"Whar'd you come f'm, boy? You prepared to die?"

Then he rode on. I was scared; but a man says—

"He don't mean nothing; he's always a carryin' on like that, when he's drunk. He's the best-naturedest old fool in Arkansaw—never hurt nobody, drunk nor sober."

Boggs rode up before the biggest store in town and bent his head down so he could see under the curtain of the awning, and yells—

"Come out here, Sherburn! Come out and meet the man you've swindled. You're the houn' I'm after, and I'm a gwyne to have you, too!"

And so he went on, calling Sherburn everything he could lay his tongue to, and the whole street packed with people listening and laughing and going on. By-and-by a proud-looking man about fifty-five—and he was a heap the best dressed man in that town, too—steps out of the store, and the crowd drops back on each side to let him come. He says to Boggs, mighty ca'm and slow—he says:

"I'm tired of this; but I'll endure it till one o'clock. Till one o'clock, mind—no longer. If you open your mouth against me only once, after that time, you can't travel so far but I will find you."

Then he turns and goes in. The crowd looked mighty sober; nobody stirred, and there warn't no more laughing. Boggs rode off blackguarding Sherburn as loud as he could yell, all down the street; and pretty soon back he comes and stops before the store, still keeping it up. Some men crowded around him and tried to get him to shut up, but he wouldn't; they told him it would be one o'clock in about fifteen minutes, and so he *must* go home—he must go right away. But it didn't do no good. He cussed away, with all his might, and throwed his hat down in the mud and rode over it, and pretty soon away he went a-raging down the street again, with his gray hair a-flying. Everybody that could get a chance at him tried their best to coax him off of his horse so they could lock him up and get him sober; but it warn't no use—up the street he would tear again, and give Sherburn another cussing. By-and-by somebody says—

"Go for his daughter!—quick, go for his daughter; sometimes he'll listen to her. If anybody can persuade him, she can."

So somebody started on a run. I walked down street a ways, and stopped. In about five or ten minutes, here comes Boggs again—but not on his horse. He was a-reeling across the street towards me, bareheaded, with a friend on both sides of him aholt of his arms and hurrying him along. He was quiet, and looked uneasy; and he warn't hanging back any, but was doing some of the hurrying himself. Somebody sings out—

"Boggs!"

I looked over there to see who said it, and it was that Colonel Sherburn. He was standing perfectly still, in the street, and had a pistol raised in his right hand—not aiming it, but holding it out with the barrel tilted up towards the sky. The same second I see a young girl coming on the run, and two men with her. Boggs and the men turned round, to see who called him, and when they see the pistol the men jumped to one side, and the pistol barrel come down slow and steady to a level—both barrels cocked. Boggs throws up both of his hands, and says, "O Lord, don't shoot!" Bang! goes the first shot, and he staggers back clawing at the air—bang! goes the second one, and he tumbles backwards onto the ground, heavy and solid, with his arms spread out. The young girl screamed out, and comes rushing, and down she throws herself on her father, crying, and saying, "Oh, he's killed him, he's killed him!" The crowd closed up around them, and shouldered and jammed one another, with their necks stretched, trying to see, and people on the inside trying to shove them back, and shouting, "Back, back! give him air, give him air!"

Colonel Sherburn he tossed his pistol onto the ground, and turned around on his heels and walked off.

They took Boggs to a little drug store, the crowd pressing around, just the same, and the whole town following, and I rushed and got a good place at the window, where I was close to him and could see in. They laid him on the floor, and put one large Bible under his head, and opened another one and spread it on his breast—but they tore open his shirt first, and I seen where one of the bullets went in. He made about a dozen long gasps, his breast lifting the Bible up when he drawed in his breath, and letting it down again when he breathed it out—and after that he laid still; he was dead.[7] Then they pulled his daughter away from him, screaming and crying, and took her off. She was about sixteen, and very sweet and gentle-looking, but awful pale and scared.

Well, pretty soon the whole town was there, squirming and scrouging and pushing and shoving to get at the window and have a look, but people that had the places wouldn't give them up, and folks behind them was saying all the time, "Say, now, you've looked enough, you fellows; 'taint right and 'taint fair, for you to stay thar all the time, and never give nobody a chance; other folks has their rights as well as you."

There was considerable jawing back, so I slid out, thinking maybe there was going to be trouble. The streets was full, and everybody was excited. Everybody that seen the shooting was telling how it happened, and there was a big crowd packed around each one of these fellows, stretching their necks and listening. One long lanky man, with long hair and a big white fur stove-pipe hat on the

[7]Twain's description of the death of Boggs closely follows the details of a murder that occurred in Hannibal in 1845. Twain's father served as judge at the subsequent trial. The defendant was acquitted.

back of his head, and a crooked-handled cane, marked out the places on the
ground where Boggs stood, and where Sherburn stood, and the people following
him around from one place to t'other and watching everything he done, and
bobbing their heads to show they understood, and stooping a little and resting
their hands on their thighs to watch him mark the places on the ground with
his cane; and then he stood up straight and stiff where Sherburn had stood,
frowning and having his hat-brim down over his eyes, and sung out, "Boggs!"
and then fetched his cane down slow to a level, and says "Bang!" staggered
backwards, says "Bang!" again, and fell down flat on his back. The people that
had seen the thing said he done it perfect; said it was just exactly the way it all
happened. Then as much as a dozen people got out their bottles and treated
him.

Well, by-and-by somebody said Sherburn ought to be lynched. In about a
minute everybody was saying it; so away they went, mad and yelling, and
snatching down every clothes-line they come to, to do the hanging with.

CHAPTER XXII

They swarmed up the street towards Sherburn's house, a-whooping and
yelling and raging like Injuns, and everything had to clear the way or get run
over and tromped to mush, and it was awful to see. Children was heeling it
ahead of the mob, screaming and trying to get out of the way; and every window
along the road was full of women's heads, and there was nigger boys in every
tree, and bucks and wenches[1] looking over every fence; and as soon as the mob
would get nearly to them they would break and skaddle back out of reach. Lots
of the women and girls was crying and taking on, scared most to death.

They swarmed up in front of Sherburn's palings as thick as they could jam
together, and you couldn't hear yourself think for the noise. It was a little twenty-
foot yard. Some sung out "Tear down the fence! tear down the fence!" Then
there was a racket of ripping and tearing and smashing, and down she goes,
and the front wall of the crowd begins to roll in like a wave.

Just then Sherburn steps out on the roof of his little front porch, with a
double-barrel gun in his hand, and takes his stand, perfectly ca'm and deliberate,
not saying a word. The racket stopped, and the wave sucked back.

Sherburn never said a word—just stood there, looking down. The stillness
was awful creepy and uncomfortable. Sherburn run his eye slow along the
crowd; and wherever it struck, the people tried a little to outgaze him, but they
couldn't; they dropped their eyes and looked sneaky. Then pretty soon Sherburn
sort of laughed; not the pleasant kind, but the kind that makes you feel like
when you are eating bread that's got sand in it.

Then he says, slow and scornful:

"The idea of *you* lynching anybody! It's amusing. The idea of you thinking
you had pluck enough to lynch a *man!* Because you're brave enough to tar and
feather poor friendless cast-out women that come along here, did that make
you think you had grit enough to lay your hands on a *man?* Why a *man's* safe in
the hands of ten thousand of your kind—as long as it's day-time and you're not
behind him.

"Do I know you? I know you clear through. I was born and raised in the
South, and I've lived in the North; so I know the average all around. The average

[1]Young male and female slaves.

man's a coward. In the North he lets anybody walk over him that wants to, and goes home and prays for a humble spirit to bear it. In the South one man, all by himself, has stopped a stage full of men, in the day-time, and robbed the lot. Your newspapers call you a brave people so much that you think you *are* braver than any other people—whereas you're just *as* brave, and no braver. Why don't your juries hang murderers? Because they're afraid the man's friends will shoot them in the back, in the dark—and it's just what they *would* do.

"So they always acquit; and then a *man* goes in the night, with a hundred masked cowards at his back, and lynches the rascal. Your mistake is, that you didn't bring a man with you; that's one mistake, and the other is that you didn't come in the dark, and fetch your masks. You brought *part* of a man—Buck Harkness, there—and if you hadn't had him to start you, you'd a taken it out in blowing.

"You didn't want to come. The average man don't like trouble and danger. *You* don't like trouble and danger. But if only *half* a man—like Buck Harkness, there—shouts 'Lynch him, lynch him!' you're afraid to back down—afraid you'll be found out to be what you are—*cowards*—and so you raise a yell, and hang yourselves onto that half-a-man's coat tail, and come raging up here, swearing what big things you're going to do. The pitifulest thing out is a mob; that's what an army is—a mob; they don't fight with courage that's born in them, but with courage that's borrowed from their mass, and from their officers. But a mob without any *man* at the head of it, is *beneath* pitifulness. Now the thing for *you* to do, is to droop your tails and go home and crawl in a hole. If any real lynching's going to be done, it will be done in the dark, Southern fashion; and when they come they'll bring their masks, and fetch a *man* along. Now *leave*—and take your half-a-man with you"—tossing his gun up across his left arm and cocking it, when he says this.

The crowd washed back sudden, and then broke all apart and went tearing off every which way, and Buck Harkness he heeled it after them, looking tolerable cheap. I could a staid, if I'd a wanted to, but I didn't want to.

I went to the circus, and loafed around the back side till the watchman went by, and then dived in under the tent. I had my twenty-dollar gold piece and some other money, but I reckoned I better save it, because there ain't no telling how soon you are going to need it, away from home and amongst strangers, that way. You can't be too careful. I ain't opposed to spending money on circuses, when there ain't no other way, but there ain't no use in *wasting* it on them.

It was a real bully circus. It was the splendidest sight that ever was, when they all come riding in, two and two, a gentleman and lady, side by side, the men just in their drawers and under-shirts, and no shoes nor stirrups, and resting their hands on their thighs, easy and comfortable—there must a' been twenty of them—and every lady with a lovely complexion, and perfectly beautiful, and looking just like a gang of real sure-enough queens, and dressed in clothes that cost millions of dollars, and just littered with diamonds. It was a powerful fine sight; I never see anything so lovely. And then one by one they got up and stood, and went a-weaving around the ring so gentle and wavy and graceful, the men looking ever so tall and airy and straight, with their heads bobbing and skimming along, away up there under the tent-roof, and every lady's rose-leafy dress flapping soft and silky around her hips, and she looking like the most loveliest parasol.

And then faster and faster they went, all of them dancing, first one foot stuck out in the air and then the other, the horses leaning more and more, and the ring-master going round and round the centre-pole, cracking his whip and shouting "hi!—hi!" and the clown cracking jokes behind him; and by-and-by all hands dropped the reins, and every lady put her knuckles on her hips and every gentleman folded his arms, and then how the horses did lean over and hump themselves! And so, one after the other they all skipped off into the ring, and made the sweetest bow I ever see, and then scampered out, and everybody clapped their hands and went just about wild.

Well, all through the circus they done the most astonishing things; and all the time that clown carried on so it most killed the people. The ring-master couldn't ever say a word to him but he was back at him quick as a wink with the funniest things a body ever said; and how he ever *could* think of so many of them, and so sudden and so pat, was what I couldn't noway understand. Why, I couldn't a thought of them in a year. And by-and-by a drunk man tried to get into the ring—said he wanted to ride; said he could ride as well as anybody that ever was. They argued and tried to keep him out, but he wouldn't listen, and the whole show come to a standstill. Then the people begun to holler at him and make fun of him, and that made him mad, and he begun to rip and tear; so that stirred up the people, and a lot of men begun to pile down off of the benches and swarm towards the ring, saying, "Knock him down! throw him out!" and one or two women begun to scream. So, then, the ringmaster he made a little speech, and said he hoped there wouldn't be no disturbance, and if the man would promise he wouldn't make no more trouble, he would let him ride, if he thought he could stay on the horse. So everybody laughed and said all right, and the man got on. The minute he was on, the horse begun to rip and tear and jump and cavort around, with two circus men hanging onto his bridle trying to hold him, and the drunk man hanging onto his neck, and his heels flying in the air every jump, and the whole crowd of people standing up and shouting and laughing till the tears rolled down. And at last, sure enough, all the circus men could do, the horse broke loose, and away he went like the very nation, round and round the ring, with that sot laying down on him and hanging to his neck, with first one leg hanging most to the ground on one side, and then t'other one on t'other side, and the people just crazy. It warn't funny to me, though; I was all of a tremble to see his danger. But pretty soon he struggled up astraddle and grabbed the bridle, a-reeling this way and that; and the next minute he sprung up and dropped the bridle and stood! and the horse agoing like a house afire too. He just stood up there, a-sailing around as easy and comfortable as if he warn't ever drunk in his life—and then he begun to pull off his clothes and sling them. He shed them so thick they kind of clogged up the air, and altogether he shed seventeen suits. And then, there he was, slim and handsome, and dressed the gaudiest and prettiest you ever saw, and he lit into that horse with his whip and made him fairly hum—and finally skipped off to the dressing-room, and everybody just a-howling with pleasure and astonishment.

Then the ring-master he see how he had been fooled, and he *was* the sickest ring-master you ever see, I reckon. Why, it was one of his own men! He had got up that joke all out of his own head, and never let on to nobody. Well, I felt sheepish enough, to be took in so, but I wouldn't a been in that ring-master's place, not for a thousand dollars. I don't know; there may be bullier circuses than what that one was, but I never struck them yet. Anyways it was plenty good enough for *me;* and wherever I run across it, it can have all of *my* custom, every time.

Well, that night we had *our* show; but there warn't only about twelve people there, just enough to pay expenses. And they laughed all the time, and that made the duke mad; and everybody left, anyway, before the show was over, but one boy which was asleep. So the duke said these Arkansaw lunkheads couldn't come up to Shakspeare; what they wanted was low comedy—and may be something ruther worse than low comedy, he reckoned. He said he could size their style. So next morning he got some big sheets of wrapping-paper and some black paint, and drawed off some handbills and stuck them up all over the village. The bills said:

AT THE COURT HOUSE!
FOR 3 NIGHTS ONLY!
The World-Renowned Tragedians
DAVID GARRICK THE YOUNGER!
AND
EDMUND KEAN THE ELDER!
Of the London and Continental
Theatres,
In their Thrilling Tragedy of
THE KING'S CAMELOPARD[2]
OR
THE ROYAL NONESUCH! ! !
Admission 50 cents.

Then at the bottom was the biggest line of all—which said:

LADIES AND CHILDREN NOT ADMITTED.

"There," says he, "if that line don't fetch them, I don't know Arkansaw!"

CHAPTER XXIII

Well, all day him and the king was hard at it, rigging up a stage, and a curtain, and a row of candles for footlights; and that night the house was jam full of men in no time. When the place couldn't hold no more, the duke he quit tending door and went around the back way and come onto the stage and stood up before the curtain, and made a little speech, and praised up this tragedy, and said it was the most thrillingest one that ever was; and so he went on a-bragging about the tragedy and about Edmund Kean the Elder, which was to play the main principal part in it; and at last when he'd got everybody's expectations up high enough, he rolled up the curtain, and the next minute the king come a-prancing out on all fours, naked; and he was painted all over, ring-streaked-and-striped, all sorts of colors, as splendid as a rainbow. And—but never mind the rest of his outfit, it was just wild, but it was awful funny. The people most killed themselves laughing; and when the king got done capering, and capered off behind the scenes, they roared and clapped and stormed and haw-hawed till he come back and done it over again; and after that, they made him do it another time. Well, it would a made a cow laugh to see the shines that old idiot cut.

Then the duke he lets the curtain down, and bows to the people and says the great tragedy will be performed only two nights more, on accounts of pressing London engagements, where the seats is all sold already for it in Drury Lane;

[2]A giraffe.

and then he makes them another bow, and says if he has succeeded in pleasing them and instructing them, he will be deeply obleeged if they will mention it to their friends and get them to come and see it.

Twenty people sings out:

"What, is it over? Is that *all?*"

The duke says yes. Then there was a fine time. Everybody sings out "sold,"[1] and rose up mad, and was agoing for that stage and them tragedians. But a big fine-looking man jumps up on a bench, and shouts:

"Hold on! Just a word, gentlemen." They stopped to listen. "We are sold— mighty badly sold. But we don't want to be the laughing-stock of this whole town, I reckon, and never hear the last of this thing as long as we live. *No.* What we want, is to go out of here quiet, and talk this show up, and sell the *rest* of the town! Then we'll all be in the same boat. Ain't that sensible?" ("You bet it is!— the jedge is right!" everybody sings out.) "All right, then—not a word about any sell. Go along home, and advise everybody to come and see the tragedy."

Next day you couldn't hear nothing around that town but how splendid that show was. House was jammed again, that night, and we sold this crowd the same way. When me and the king and the duke got home to the raft, we all had a supper; and by-and-by, about midnight, they made Jim and me back her out and float her down the middle of the river and fetch her in and hide her about two mile below town.

The third night the house was crammed again—and they warn't new-comers, this time, but people that was at the show the other two nights. I stood by the duke at the door, and I see that every man that went in had his pockets bulging, or something muffled up under his coat—and I see it warn't no perfumery neither, not by a long sight. I smelt sickly eggs by the barrel, and rotten cabbages, and such things; and if I know the signs of a dead cat being around, and I bet I do, there was sixty-four of them went in. I shoved in there for a minute, but it was too various[2] for me, I couldn't stand it. Well, when the place couldn't hold no more people, the duke he give a fellow a quarter and told him to tend door for him a minute, and then he started around for the stage door, I after him; but the minute we turned the corner and was in the dark, he says:

"Walk fast, now, till you get away from the houses, and then shin for the raft like the dickens was after you!"

I done it, and he done the same. We struck the raft at the same time, and in less than two seconds we was gliding down stream, all dark and still, and edging towards the middle of the river, nobody saying a word. I reckoned the poor king was in for a gaudy time of it with the audience; but nothing of the sort; pretty soon he crawls out from under the wigwam, and says:

"Well, how'd the old thing pan out this time, Duke?"

He hadn't been up town at all.

We never showed a light till we was about ten mile below that village. Then we lit up and had a supper, and the king and the duke fairly laughed their bones loose over the way they'd served them people. The duke says:

"Greenhorns, flatheads! *I* knew the first house would keep mum and let the rest of the town get roped in; and I knew they'd lay for us the third night, and consider it was *their* turn now. Well, it *is* their turn, and I'd give something to know how much they'd take for it. I *would* just like to know how they're putting in their opportunity. They can turn it into a picnic, if they want to—they brought plenty provisions."

[1]"Cheated."   [2]I.e., it was too much.

Them rapscallions took in four hundred and sixty-five dollars in that three nights. I never see money hauled in by the wagon-load like that, before.

By-and-by, when they was asleep and snoring, Jim says:

"Don't it' spise, you, de way dem kings carries on, Huck?"

"No," I says, "it don't."

"Why don't it, Huck?"

"Well, it don't, because it's in the breed. I reckon they're all alike."

"But, Huck, dese kings o' ourn is regular rapscallions; dat's jist what dey is; dey's regular rapscallions."

"Well, that's what I'm a-saying; all kings is mostly rapscallions, as fur as I can make out."

"Is dat so?"

"You read about them once—you'll see. Look at Henry the Eight; this'n 's a Sunday-School Superintendent to *him*. And look at Charles Second, and Louis Fourteen, and Louis Fifteen, and James Second, and Edward Second, and Richard Third, and forty more; beside all them Saxon heptarchies[3] that used to rip around so in old times and raise Cain. My, you ought to seen old Henry the Eight when he was in bloom. He *was* a blossom. He used to marry a new wife every day, and chop off her head next morning. And he would do it just as indifferent as if he was ordering up eggs. 'Fetch up Nell Gwynn,' he says. They fetch her up. Next morning, 'Chop off her head!' And they chop it off. 'Fetch up Jane Shore,' he says; and up she comes. Next morning 'Chop off her head'—and they chop it off. 'Ring up Fair Rosamun.'[4] Fair Rosamun answers the bell. Next morning, 'Chop off her head.' And he made every one of them tell him a tale every night; and he kept that up till he had hogged a thousand and one tales that way, and then he put them all in a book, and called it Domesday Book—which was a good name and stated the case.[5] You don't know kings, Jim, but I know them; and this old rip of ourn is one of the cleanest I've struck in history. Well, Henry he takes a notion he wants to get up some trouble with this country. How does he got at it—give notice?—give the country a show? No. All of a sudden he heaves all the tea in Boston Harbor overboard, and whacks out a declaration of independence, and dares them to come on. That was *his* style— he never give anybody a chance. He had suspicions of his father, the Duke of Wellington. Well, what did he do?—ask him to show up? No—drownded him in a butt of mamsey, like a cat. Spose people left money laying around where he was—what did he do? He collared it. Spose he contracted to do a thing; and you paid him, and didn't set down there and see that he done it—what did he do? he always done the other thing. Spose he opened his mouth—what then? If he didn't shut it up powerful quick, he'd lose a lie, every time. That's the kind of a bug Henry was; and if we'd a had him along 'stead of our kings, he'd a fooled that town a heap worse than ourn done. I don't say that ourn is lambs, because they ain't, when you come right down to the cold facts; but they ain't nothing to *that* old ram, anyway. All I say is, kings is kings, and you got to make allowances. Take them all around, they're a mighty ornery lot. It's the way they're raised."

"But dis one do *smell* so like de nation, Huck."

---

[3]The seven Anglo-Saxon kingdoms of England (Northumbria, Mercia, East Anglia, Essex, Kent, Sussex, and Wessex), and their period of dominance, from the sixth to the ninth century.

[4]Women who were mistresses of English kings of the twelfth, fifteenth, and seventeenth centuries. None was married to King Henry VIII.

[5]Here as elsewhere, Huck mixes the events and characters of history and fiction.

"Well, they all do, Jim. *We* can't help the way a king smells; history don't tell no way."

"Now de duke, he's a tolerble likely man, in some ways."

"Yes, a duke's different. But not very different. This one's a middling hard lot, for a duke. When he's drunk, there ain't no nearsighted man could tell him from a king."

"Well, anyways, I doan' hanker for no mo' un um, Huck. Dese is all I kin stan'."

"It's the way I feel, too, Jim. But we've got them on our hands, and we got to remember what they are, and make allowances. Sometimes I wish we could hear of a country that's out of kings."

What was the use to tell Jim these warn't real kings and dukes? It wouldn't a done no good; and besides, it was just as I said; you couldn't tell them from the real kind.

I went to sleep, and Jim didn't call me when it was my turn. He often done that. When I waked up, just at day-break, he was setting there with his head down betwixt his knees, moaning and mourning to himself. I didn't take notice, nor let on. I knowed what it was about. He was thinking about his wife and his children, away up yonder, and he was low and homesick; because he hadn't ever been away from home before in his life; and I do believe he cared just as much for his people as white folks does for their'n. It don't seem natural, but I reckon it's so. He was often moaning and mourning that way, nights, when he judged I was asleep, and saying, "Po' little 'Lizabeth! po' little Johnny! it's mighty hard; I spec' I ain't ever gwyne to see you no mo', no mo'!" He was a mighty good nigger, Jim was.

But this time I somehow got to talking to him about his wife and young ones; and by-and-by he says:

"What makes me feel so bad dis time, uz bekase I hear sumpn over yonder on de bank like a whack, er a slam, while ago, en it mine me er de time I treat my little 'Lizabeth so ornery. She warn't on'y 'bout fo' year ole, en she tuck de sk'yarlet-fever, an had a powful rough spell; but she got well, en one day she was a-stannin' aroun', en I says to her, I says:

"Shet de do'."

"She never done it; jis' stood dah, kiner smilin' up at me. It make me mad; en I says agin, mighty loud, I says:

" 'Doan' you hear me?—shet de do'!'

"She jis' stood de same way, kiner smilin' up. I was a-bilin'! I says: " 'I lay I *make* you mine!'

"En wid dat I fetch' her a slap side de head dat sont her a-sprawlin'. Den I went into de yuther room, en 'uz gone 'bout ten minutes; en when I come back, dah was dat do' a-stannin' open *yit*, en dat chile stannin' mos' right in it, a-lookin' down and mournin', en de tears runnin' down. My, but I *wuz* mad, I was agwyne for de chile, but jis' den—it was a do' dat open innerds—jis' den, 'long come de wind en slam it to, behind de chile, ker-*blam!*—en my lan', de chile never move'! My breff mos' hop outer me; en I feel so—so—I doan' know *how* I feel, I crope out, all a-tremblin', en crope aroun' en open de do' easy en slow, en poke my head in behine de chile, sof' en still, en all uv a sudden, I says *pow!* jis' as loud as I could yell. *She never budge!* Oh, Huck, I bust out a-crying' en grab her up in my arms, en say, 'Oh, de po' little thing! de Lord God Amighty fogive po' ole Jim, kaze he never gwyne to fogive hisself as long's he live!' Oh, she was plumb deef en dumb, Huck, plumb deef en dumb—en I'd ben a-treat'n her so!"

CHAPTER XXIV

Next day, towards night, we laid up under a little willow towhead out in the middle; where there was a village on each side of the river, and the duke and the king begun to lay out a plan for working them towns. Jim he spoke to the duke, and said he hoped it wouldn't take but a few hours, because it got mighty heavy and tiresome to him when he had to lay all day in the wigwam tied with the rope. You see, when we left him all alone we had to tie him, because if anybody happened on him all by himself and not tied, it wouldn't look much like he was a runaway nigger, you know. So the duke said it *was* kind of hard to have to lay roped all day, and he'd cipher out some way to get around it.

He was uncommon bright, the duke was, and he soon struck it. He dressed Jim up in King Lear's outfit—it was a long curtain-calico gown, and a white horse-hair wig and whiskers; and then he took his theatre-paint and painted Jim's face and hands and ears and neck all over a dead dull solid blue, like a man that's been drownded nine days. Blamed if he warn't the horriblest looking outrage I ever see. Then the duke took and wrote out a sign on a shingle so—

Sick Arab—but harmless when not out of his head.

And he nailed that shingle to a lath, and stood the lath up four or five foot in front of the wigwam. Jim was satisfied. He said it was a sight better than laying tied a couple of years every day and trembling all over every time there was a sound. The duke told him to make himself free and easy, and if anybody ever come meddling around, he must hop out of the wigwam, and carry on a little, and fetch a howl or two like a wild beast, and he reckoned they would light out and leave him alone. Which was sound enough judgment; but you take the average man, and he wouldn't wait for him to howl. Why, he didn't only look like he was dead, he looked considerable more than that.

These rapscallions wanted to try the Nonesuch again, because there was so much money in it, but they judged it wouldn't be safe, because maybe the news might a worked along down by this time. They couldn't hit no project that suited, exactly; so at last the duke said he reckoned he'd lay off and work his brains an hour or two and see if he couldn't put up something on the Arkansaw village; and the king he allowed he would drop over to t'other village, without any plan, but just trust in Providence to lead him the profitable way—meaning the devil, I reckon. We had all bought store clothes where we stopped last; and now the king put his'n on, and he told me to put mine on. I done it, of course. The king's duds was all black, and he did look real swell and starchy. I never knowed how clothes could change a body before. Why, before, he looked like the orneriest old rip that ever was; but now, when he'd take off his new white beaver[1] and make a bow and do a smile, he looked that grand and good and pious that you'd say he had walked right out of the ark, and maybe was old Leviticus[2] himself. Jim cleaned up the canoe, and I got my paddle ready. There was a big steamboat laying at the shore away up under the point, about three mile above town—been there a couple of hours, taking on freight. Says the king:

"Seein' how I'm dressed, I reckon maybe I better arrive down from St. Louis

[1] Hat.
[2] Huck confuses Leviticus, a book of the Old Testament, with Noah, who built the ark and survived the flood.

or Cincinnati, or some other big place. Go for the steamboat, Huckleberry; we'll come down to the village on her."

I didn't have to be ordered twice, to go and take a steamboat ride. I fetched the store a half a mile above the village, and then went scooting along the bluff bank in the easy water. Pretty soon we come to a nice innocent-looking young country jake setting on a log swabbing the sweat off of his face, for it was powerful warm weather; and he had a couple of big carpet-bags by him.

"Run her nose in shore," says the king. I done it. "Wher' you bound for, young man?"

"For the steamboat; going to Orleans."

"Git aboard," says the king. "Hold on a minute, my servant'll he'p you with them bags. Jump out and he'p the gentleman Adolphus"—meaning me, I see.

I done so, and then we all three started on again. The young chap was mighty thankful; said it was tough work toting his baggage such weather. He asked the king where he was going, and the king told him he'd come down the river and landed at the other village this morning, and now he was going up a few miles to see an old friend on a farm up there. The young fellow says:

"When I first see you, I says to myself, 'It's Mr. Wilks, sure, and he come mighty near getting here in time.' But then I says again, 'No, I reckon it ain't him, or else he wouldn't be paddling up the river.' You *ain't* him, are you?"

"No, my name's Blodgett—Elexander Blodgett—*Reverend* Elexander Blodgett, I spose I must say, as I'm one o' the Lord's poor servants. But still I'm jist as able to be sorry for Mr. Wilks for not arriving in time, all the same, if he's missed anything by it—which I hope he hasn't."

"Well, he don't miss any property by it, because he'll get that all right; but he's missed seeing his brother Peter die—which he mayn't mind, nobody can tell as to that—but his brother would a give anything in this world to see *him* before he died; never talked about nothing else all these three weeks; hadn't seen him since they was boys together—and hadn't ever seen his brother William at all—that's the deef and dumb one—William ain't more than thirty or thirty-five. Peter and George was the only ones that come out here; George was the married brother; him and his wife both died last year. Harvey and William's the only ones that's left now; and, as I was saying, they haven't got here in time."

"Did anybody send 'em word?"

"Oh, yes; a month or two ago, when Peter was first took; because Peter said then that he sorter felt like he warn't going to get well this time. You see, he was pretty old, and George's g'yirls was too young to be much company for him, except Mary Jane the redheaded one; and so he was kinder lonesome after George and his wife died, and didn't seem to care much to live. He most desperately wanted to see Harvey—and William too, for that matter—because he was one of them kind that can't bear to make a will. He left a letter behind for Harvey, and said he'd told in it where his money was hid, and how he wanted the rest of the property divided up so George's g'yirls would be all right—for George didn't leave nothing. And that letter was all they could get him to put a pen to."

"Why do you reckon Harvey don't come? Wher' does he live?"

"Oh, he lives in England—Sheffield—preaches there—hasn't ever been in this country. He hasn't had any too much time—and besides he mightn't a got the letter at all, you know."

"Too bad, too bad he couldn't a lived to see his brothers, poor soul. You going to Orleans, you say?"

"Yes, but that ain't only a part of it. I'm going in a ship, next Wednesday, for Ryo Janeero,[3] where my uncle lives."

"It's a pretty long journey. But it'll be lovely; I wisht I was agoing. Is Mary Jane the oldest? How old is the others?"

"Mary Jane's nineteen, Susan's fifteen, and Joann's about fourteen—that's the one that gives herself to good works and has a hare-lip."

"Poor things! to be left alone in the cold world so."

"Well, they could be worse off. Old Peter had friends, and they ain't going to let them come to no harm. There's Hobson, the Babtis' preacher; and Deacon Lot Hovey, and Ben Rucker, and Abner Shackleford, and Levi Bell, the lawyer; and Dr. Robinson, and their wives, and the widow Bartley, and—well, there's a lot of them; but these are the ones that Peter was thickest with, and used to write about sometimes, when he wrote home; so Harvey 'll know where to look for friends when he gets here."

Well, the old man he went on asking questions till he just fairly emptied that young fellow. Blamed if he didn't inquire about everybody and everything in that blessed town, and all about all the Wilkses; and about Peter's business—which was a tanner; and about George's—which was a carpenter; and about Harvey's—which was a dissentering minister; and so on, and so on. Then he says:

"What did you want to walk all the way up to the steamboat for?"

"Because she's a big Orleans boat, and I was afeared she mightn't stop there. When they're deep they won't stop for a hail. A Cincinnati boat will, but this is a St. Louis one."

"Was Peter Wilks well off?"

"Oh, yes, pretty well off. He had houses and land, and it's reckoned he left three or four thousand in cash hid up som'ers."

"When did you say he died?"

"I didn't say, but it was last night."

"Funeral to-morrow, likely?"

"Yes, 'bout the middle of the day."

"Well, it's all terrible sad; but we've all got to go, one time or another. So what we want to do is to be prepared; then we're all right."

"Yes, sir, it's the best way. Ma used to always say that."

When we struck the boat, she was about done loading, and pretty soon she got off. The king never said nothing about going aboard so I lost my ride, after all. When the boat was gone, the king made me paddle up another mile to a lonesome place, and then he got ashore, and says:

"Now, hustle back, right off, and fetch the duke up here, and the new carpetbags. And if he's gone over to t'other side, go over there and git him. And tell him to git himself up regardless. Shove along, now."

I see what *he* was up to; but I never said nothing, of course. When I got back with the duke, we hid the canoe and then they set down on a log, and the king told him everything, just like the young fellow had said it—every last word of it. And all the time he was a doing it, he tried to talk like an Englishman; and he done it pretty well too, for a slouch. I can't imitate him, and so I ain't agoing to try to; but he really done it pretty good. Then he says:

"How are you on the deef and dumb, Bilgewater?"

The duke said, leave him alone for that; said he had played a deef and dumb person on the histrionic boards. So then they waited for a steamboat.

[3]Rio de Janeiro, Brazil.

About the middle of the afternoon a couple of little boats come along, but they didn't come from high enough up the river; but a last there was a big one, and they hailed her. She sent out her yawl, and we went aboard, and she was from Cincinnati; and when they found we only wanted to go four or five mile, they was booming mad, and give us a cussing, and said they wouldn't land us. But the king was ca'm. He says:

"If gentlemen kin afford to pay a dollar a mile apiece, to be took on and put off in a yawl, a steamboat kin afford to carry 'em, can't it?"

So they softened down and said it was all right; and when we got to the village, they yawled us ashore. About two dozen men flocked down, when they see the yawl a coming; and when the king says—

"Kin any of you gentlemen tell me wher' Mr. Peter Wilks lives?" they give a glance at one another, and nodded their heads, as much as to say, "What d' I tell you?" Then one of them says, kind of soft and gentle:

"I'm sorry, sir, but the best we can do is tell you where he *did* live yesterday evening."

Sudden as winking, the ornery old cretur went all to smash, and fell up against the man, and put his chin on his shoulder, and cried down his back, and says:

"Alas, alas, our poor brother—gone, and we never got to see him; oh, it's too, *too* hard!"

Then he turns around, blubbering, and makes a lot of idiotic signs to the duke on his hands, and blamed if *he* didn't drop a carpet-bag and bust out a-crying. If they warn't the beatenest lot, them two frauds, that ever I struck.

Well, the men gethered around, and sympathized with them, and said all sorts of kind things to them, and carried their carpet-bags up the hill for them, and let them lean on them and cry, and told the king all about his brother's last moments, and the king he told it all over again on his hands to the duke, and both of them took on about that dead tanner like they'd lost the twelve disciples. Well, if ever I struck anything like it, I'm a nigger. It was enough to make a body ashamed of the human race.

CHAPTER XXV

The news was all over town in two minutes, and you could see the people tearing down on the run, from every which way, some of them putting on their coats as they come. Pretty soon we was in the middle of a crowd, and the noise of the tramping was like a soldier-march. The windows and door-yards was full; and every minute somebody would say, over a fence:

"Is it *them?*"

And somebody trotting along with the gang would answer back and say, "You bet it is."

When we got to the house, the street in front of it was packed, and the three girls was standing in the door. Mary Jane *was* red-headed, but that don't make no difference, she was most awful beautiful, and her face and her eyes was all lit up like glory, she was so glad her uncles was come. The king he spread his arms, and Mary Jane she jumped for them, and the hare-lip jumped for the duke, and there they *had* it! Everybody most, leastways women, cried for joy to see them meet again at last and have such good times.

Then the king he hunched the duke, private—I see him do it—and then he looked around and see the coffin, over in the corner on two chairs; so then, him and the duke, with a hand across each other's shoulder, and t'other hand to their eyes, walked slow and solemn over there, everybody dropping back to give them room, and all the talk and noise stopping, people saying "Sh!" and all the men taking their hats off and drooping their heads, so you could a heard a pin fall. And when they got there, they bent over and looked in the coffin, and took one sight, and then they bust out a crying so you could a heard them to Orleans, most; and then they put their arms around each other's necks, and hung their chins over each other's shoulders; and then for three minutes, or maybe four, I never see two men leak the way they done. And mind you, everybody was doing the same; and the place was that damp I never see anything like it. Then one of them got on one side of the coffin, and t'other on t'other side, and they kneeled down and rested their foreheads on the coffin, and let on to pray all to theirselves. Well, when it come to that, it worked the crowd like you never see anything like it, and so everybody broke down and went to sobbing right out loud—the poor girls, too; and every woman, nearly, went up to the girls, without saying a word, and kissed them, solemn, on the forehead, and then put their hand on their head, and looked up towards the sky, with the tears running down, and then busted out and went off sobbing and swabbing, and give the next woman a show. I never see anything so disgusting.

Well, by-and-by the king he gets up and comes forward a little, and works himself up and slobbers out a speech, all full of tears and flapdoodle about its being a sore trial for him and his poor brother to lose the diseased and to miss seeing diseased alive, after the long journey of four thousand mile, but it's a trial that's sweetened and sanctified to us by this dear sympathy and these holy tears, and so he thanks them out of his heart and out of his brother's heart, because out of their mouths they can't, words being too weak and cold, and all that kind of rot and slush, till it was just sickening; and then he blubbers out a pious goody-goody Amen, and turns himself loose and goes to crying fit to bust.

And the minute the words was out of his mouth somebody over in the crowd struck up the doxolojer,[1] and everybody joined in with all their might, and it just warmed you up and made you feel as good as church letting out. Music *is* a good thing; and after all that soul-butter and hogwash, I never see it freshen up things so, and sound so honest and bully.

Then the king begins to work his jaws again, and says how him and his nieces would be glad if a few of the main principal friends of the family would take supper here with them this evening, and help set up with the ashes of the diseased; and says if his poor brother laying yonder could speak, he knows who he would name, for they was names that was very dear to him, and mentioned often in his letters; and so he will name the same, to-wit, as follows, vizz:—Rev. Mr. Hobson, and Deacon Lot Hovey, and Mr. Ben Rucker, and Abner Shackleford, and Levi Bell, and Dr. Robinson, and their wives, and the widow Bartley.

Rev. Hobson and Dr. Robinson was down to the end of the town, a-hunting together; that is, I mean the doctor was shipping a sick man to t'other world, and the preacher was pinting him right. Lawyer Bell was away up to Louisville on some business. But the rest was on hand, and so they all come and shook hands with the king and thanked him and talked to him; and then they shook hands with the duke, and didn't say nothing but just kept a-smiling and bobbing their heads like a passel of sapheads whilst he made all sorts of signs with his hands and said "Goo-goo—goo-goo-goo," all the time, like a baby that can't talk.

So the king he blatted along, and managed to inquire about pretty much everybody and dog in town, by his name, and mentioned all sorts of little things

---

[1]Doxology; a hymn in praise of God.

that happened one time or another in the town, or to George's family, or to Peter; and he always let on that Peter wrote him the things, but that was a lie, he got every blessed one of them out of that young flathead that we canoed up to the steamboat.

Then Mary Jane she fetched the letter her father left behind, and the king he read it out loud and cried over it. It give the dwelling-house and three thousand dollars, gold, to the girls; and it give the tanyard (which was doing a good business), along with some other houses and land (worth about seven thousand), and three thousand dollars in gold to Harvey and William, and told where the six thousand cash was hid, down cellar. So these two frauds said they'd go and fetch it up, and have everything square and above-board; and told me to come with a candle. We shut the cellar door behind us, and when they found the bag they spilt it out on the floor, and it was a lovely sight, all of them yaller-boys.[2] My, the way the king's eyes did shine! He slaps the duke on the shoulder, and says:

"Oh, *this* ain't bully, nor noth'n! Oh, no, I reckon not! Why, Biljy, it beats the Nonesuch, *don't* it!"

The duke allowed it did. They pawed the yaller-boys, and sifted them through their fingers and let them jingle down on the floor; and the king says:

"It ain't no use talkin'; bein' brothers to a rich dead man, and representatives of furrin heirs that's got left, is the line for you and me, Bilge. Thish-yer comes of trust'n to Providence. It's the best way, in the long run. I've tried 'em all, and ther' ain't no better way."

Most everybody would a been satisfied with the pile, and took it on trust; but no, they must count it. So they counts it, and it comes out four hundred and fifteen dollars short. Says the King:

"Dern him, I wonder what he done with that four hundred and fifteen dollars?"

They worried over that a while, and ransacked all around for it. Then the duke says:

"Well, he was a pretty sick man, and likely he made a mistake—I reckon that's the way of it. The best way's to let it go, and keep still about it. We can spare it."

"Oh, shucks, yes, we can *spare* it. I don't k'yer noth'n 'bout that—it's the *count* I'm thinkin' about. We want to be awful square and open and above-board, here, you know. We want to lug this h-yer money up stairs and count it before everybody—then ther' ain't noth'n suspicious. But when the dead man says ther's six thous'n dollars, you know, we don't want to——"

"Hold on," says the duke. "Less make up the deffsit"—and he begun to haul out yaller-boys out of his pocket.

"It's a most amaz'n' good idea, duke—you *have* got a rattlin' clever head on you," says the king. "Blest if the old Nonesuch ain't a heppin' us out agin"—and *he* begun to haul out yaller-jackets and stack them up.

It most busted them, but they made up the six thousand clean and clear.

"Say," says the duke, "I got another idea. Le's go up stairs and count this money, and then take and *give it to the girls.*"

"Good land, duke, lemme hug you! It's the most dazzling idea 'at ever a man struck. You have cert'nly got the most astonishin' head I ever see. Oh, this is the boss dodge, ther' ain't no mistake 'bout it. Let 'em fetch along their suspicions now, if they want to—this'll lay 'em out."

When we got up stairs, everybody gethered around the table, and the king

[2]Gold coins.

he counted it and stacked it up, three hundred dollars in a pile—twenty elegant little piles. Everybody looked hungry at it, and licked their chops. Then they raked it into the bag again, and I see the king begin to swell himself up for another speech. He says:

"Friends all, my poor brother that lays yonder, has done generous by them that's left behind in the vale of sorrers. He has done generous by these-yer poor little lambs that he loved and sheltered, and that's left fatherless and motherless. Yes, and we that knowed him, knows that he would a done *more* generous by 'em if he hadn't ben afeard o' woundin' his dear William and me. Now, *wouldn't* he? Ther' ain't no question 'bout it, in *my* mind. Well, then—what kind o' brothers would it be, that 'd stand in his way at sech a time? And what kind o' uncles would it be that'd rob—yes, *rob*—sech poor sweet lambs as these 'at he loved so, at sech a time? If I know William—and I *think* I do—he—well, I'll jest ask him." He turns around and begins to make a lot of signs to the duke with his hands; and the duke he looks at him stupid and leather-headed a while, then all of a sudden he seems to catch his meaning, and jumps for the king, goo-gooing with all his might for joy, and hugs him about fifteen times before he lets up. Then the king says, "I knowed it; I reckon *that*'ll convince anybody the way *he* feels about it. Here, Mary Jane, Susan, Joanner, take the money—take it *all*. It's the gift of him that lays yonder, cold but joyful."

Mary Jane she went for him, Susan and the hare-lip went for the duke, and then such another hugging and kissing I never see yet. And everybody crowded up with the tears in their eyes, and most shook the hands off of them frauds, saying all the time:

"You *dear* good souls!—how *lovely!*—how *could* you!"

Well, then, pretty soon all hands got to talking about the diseased again, and how good he was, and what a loss he was, and all that; and before long a big iron-jawed man worked himself in there from outside, and stood a listening and looking, and not saying anything; and nobody saying anything to him either, because the king was talking and they was all busy listening. The king was saying—in the middle of something he's started in on—

"—they bein' partickler friends o' the diseased. That's why they're invited here this evenin'; but to-morrow we want *all* to come—everybody; for he respected everybody, he liked everybody, and so it's fitten that his funeral orgies sh'd be public."

And so he went a-mooning on and on, liking to hear himself talk, and every little while he fetched in his funeral orgies again, till the duke he couldn't stand it no more; so he writes on a little scrap of paper, "*obsequies,* you old fool," and folds it up and goes to goo-gooing and reaching it over people's heads to him. The king he reads it, and puts it in his pocket, and says:

"Poor William, afflicted as he is, his *heart's* aluz right. Asks me to invite everybody to come to the funeral—wants me to make 'em all welcome. But he needn't a worried—it was jest what I was at."

Then he weaves along again, perfectly ca'm, and goes to dropping in his funeral orgies again every now and then, just like he done before. And when he done it the third time, he says:

"I say orgies, not because it's the common term, because it ain't—obsequies bein' the common term—but because orgies is the right term. Obsequies ain't used in England no more, now—it's gone out. We say orgies now, in England. Orgies is better, because it means the thing you're after, more exact. It's a word that's made up out'n the Greek *orgo,* outside, open, abroad; and the Hebrew *jeesum,* to plant, cover up; hence in*ter.* So, you see, funeral orgies is an open er public funeral."

He was the *worst* I ever struck. Well, the iron-jawed man he laughed right in his face. Everybody was shocked. Everybody says, "Why *doctor!*" and Abner Shackleford says:

"Why, Robinson, hain't you heard the news? This is Harvey Wilks."

The king he smiled eager, and shoved out his flapper, and says:

"*Is* it my poor brother's dear good friend and physician? I——"

"Keep your hands off of me!" says the doctor. "*You* talk like an Englishman—*don't* you? It's the worst imitation I ever heard. *You* Peter Wilks's brother. You're a fraud, that's what you are!"

Well, how they all took on! They crowded around the doctor, and tried to quiet him down, and tried to explain to him, and tell him how Harvey'd showed in forty ways that he *was* Harvey, and knowed everybody by name, and the names of the very dogs, and begged and *begged* him not to hurt Harvey's feelings and the poor girls' feelings, and all that; but it warn't no use, he stormed right along, and said any man that pretended to be an Englishman and couldn't imitate the lingo no better than what he did, was a fraud and a liar. The poor girls was hanging to the king and crying; and all of a sudden the doctor ups and turns on *them.* He says:

"I was your father's friend, and I'm your friend; and I warn you *as* a friend, and an honest one, that wants to protect you and keep you out of harm and trouble, to turn your backs on that scoundrel, and have nothing to do with him, the ignorant tramp, with his idiotic Greek and Hebrew as he calls it. He is the thinnest kind of an imposter—has come here with a lot of empty names and facts which he has picked up somewheres, and you take them for *proofs,* and are helped to fool yourselves by these foolish friends here, who ought to know better. Mary Jane Wilks, you know me for your friend, and for your unselfish friend, too. Now listen to me; turn this pitiful rascal out—I *beg* you to do it. Will you?"

Mary Jane straightened herself up, and my, but she was handsome! she says:

"*Here* is my answer." She hove up the bag of money and put it in the king's hands, and says, "Take this six thousand dollars, and invest it for me and my sisters any way you want to, and don't give us no receipt for it."

Then she put her arm around the king on one side, and Susan and the hare-lip done the same on the other. Everybody clapped their hands and stomped on the floor like a perfect storm, whilst the king held up his head and smiled proud. The doctor says:

"All right, I wash *my* hands of the matter. But I warn you all that a time's coming when you're going to feel sick whenever you think of this day"—and away he went.

"All right, doctor," says the king, kinder mocking him, "we'll try and get 'em to send for you"—which made them all laugh, and they said it was a prime good hit.

CHAPTER XXVI

Well when they was all gone, the king asks Mary Jane how they was off for spare rooms, and she said she had one spare room, which would do for Uncle William, and she'd give her own room to Uncle Harvey, which was a little bigger, and she would turn into the room with her sisters and sleep on a cot; and up garret was a little cubby, with a pallet in it. The king said the cubby would do for his valley—meaning me.

So Mary Jane took us up, and she showed them their rooms, which was plain but nice. She said she'd have her frocks and a lot of other traps took out of her room if they was in Uncle Harvey's way, but he said they warn't. The frocks was hung along the wall, and before them was a curtain made out of calico that hung down to the floor. There was an old hair trunk in one corner, and a guitar box in another, and all sorts of little knick-knacks and jimcracks around, like girls brisken up a room with. The king said it was all the more homely and more pleasanter for these fixings, and so don't disturb them. The duke's room was pretty small, but plenty good enough, and so was my cubby.

That night they had a big supper, and all them men and women was there, and I stood behind the king and the duke's chairs and waited on them, and the niggers waited on the rest. Mary Jane she set at the head of the table with Susan along side of her, and said how bad the biscuits was, and how mean the preserves was, and how ornery and tough the fried chicken was—and all that kind of rot, the way women always do to force out compliments; and the people all knowed everything was tip-top, and said so—said "How *do* you get biscuits to brown so nice?" and "Where, for the land's sake *did* you get these amaz'n pickles?" and all that kind of humbug talky-talk, just the way people always does at a supper, you know.

And when it was all done, me and the hare-lip had supper in the kitchen off of the leavings, whilst the others was helping the niggers clean up the things. The hare-lip she got to pumping me about England, and blest if I didn't think the ice was getting mighty thin, sometimes. She says:

"Did you ever see the king?"

"Who? William Fourth?[1] Well, I bet I have—he goes to our church." I knowed he was dead years ago, but I never let on. So when I says he goes to our church, she says:

"What—regular?"

"Yes—regular. His pew's right over opposite ourn—on 'tother side the pulpit."

"I thought he lived in London?"

"Well, he does. Where *would* he live?"

"But I thought *you* lived in Sheffield?"[2]

I see I was up a stump. I had to let on to get choked with a chicken bone, so as to get time to think how to get down again. Then I says:

"I mean he goes to our church regular when he's in Sheffield. That's only in the summer-time, when he comes there to take the sea baths."

"Why, how you talk—Sheffield ain't on the sea."

"Well, who said it was?"

"Why, you did."

"I *didn't* nuther."

"You did!"

"I didn't."

"You did."

"I never said nothing of the kind."

"Well, what *did* you say, then?"

"Said he come to take the sea *baths*—that's what I said."

"Well, then! how's he going to take the sea baths if it ain't on the sea?"

[1]King of England, 1830–1837.　　[2]English city north of London.

"Looky here," I says; "did you ever see any Congress water?"[3]

"Yes."

"Well, did you have to go to Congress to get it?"

"Why, no."

"Well, neither does William Fourth have to go to the sea to get a sea bath."

How does he get it, then?"

"Gets it the way people down here gets Congress-water—in barrels. There in the palace at Sheffield they've got furnaces, and he wants his water hot. They can't bile that amount of water away off there at the sea. They haven't got no conveniences for it."

"Oh, I see, now. You might a said that in the first place and saved time."

When she said that, I see I was out of the woods again, and so I was comfortable and glad. Next she says:

"Do you go to church, too?"

"Yes—regular."

"Where do you set?"

"Why, in our pew."

"*Whose* pew?"

"Why, *ourn*—your Uncle Harvey's."

"His'n? What does *he* want with a pew?"

"Wants it to set in. What did you *reckon* he wanted with it?"

"Why, I thought he'd be in the pulpit."

Rot him, I forgot he was a preacher. I see I was up a stump again, so I played another chicken bone and got another think. Then I says:

"Blame it, do you suppose there ain't but one preacher to a church?"

"Why, what do they want with more?"

"What!—to preach before a king? I never see such a girl as you. They don't have no less than seventeen."

"Seventeen! My land! Why, I wouldn't set out such a string as that, not if I *never* got to glory. It must take 'em a week."

"Shucks, they don't *all* of 'em preach the same day—only *one* of 'em."

"Well, then, what does the rest of 'em do?"

"Oh, nothing much. Loll around, pass the plate—and one thing or another. But mainly they don't do nothing."

"Well, then, what are they *for?*"

"Why, they're for *style*. Don't you know nothing?"

"Well, I don't *want* to know no such foolishness as that. How is servants treated in England? Do they treat 'em better 'n we treat our niggers?"

"*No!* A servant ain't nobody there. They treat them worse than dogs."

"Don't they give 'em holidays, the way we do, Christmas and New Year's week, and Fourth of July?"

"Oh, just listen! A body could tell *you* hain't ever been to England, by that. Why, Hare-l—why, Joanna, they never see a holiday from year's end to year's end; never go to the circus, nor theatre, nor nigger shows,[4] nor nowheres."

"Nor church?"

"Nor church."

"But *you* always went to church."

Well, I was gone up again. I forgot I was the old man's servant. But next minute I whirled in on a kind of an explanation how a valley was different from a common servant, and *had* to go to church whether he wanted to or not, and

---

[3]Mineral water from the Congress Spring, Saratoga, New York.

[4]Minstrel shows.

set with the family, on account of it's being the law. But I didn't do it pretty good, and when I got done I see she warn't satisfied. She says:

"Honest injun, now, hain't you been telling me a lot of lies?"

"Honest injun," says I.

"None of it at all?"

"None of it at all. Not a lie in it," says I.

"Lay your hand on this book and say it."

I see it warn't nothing but a dictionary, so I laid my hand on it and said it. So then she looked a little better satisfied, and says:

"Well, then, I'll believe some of it; but I hope to gracious if I'll believe the rest."

"What is it you won't believe, Joe?" says Mary Jane, stepping in with Susan behind her. "It ain't right nor kind for you to talk so to him, and him a stranger and so far from his people. How would you like to be treated so?"

"That's always your way, Maim—always sailing in to help somebody before they're hurt. I hain't done nothing to him. He's told some stretchers, I reckon; and I said I wouldn't swallow it all; and that's every bit and grain I *did* say. I reckon he can stand a little thing like that, can't he?"

"I don't care whether 'twas little or whether 'twas big, he's here in our house and a stranger, and it wasn't good of you to say it. If you was in his place, it would make you feel ashamed; and so you oughtn't to say a thing to another person that will make *them* feel ashamed."

"Why, Maim, he said——"

"It don't make no difference what he *said*—that ain't the thing. The thing is for you to treat him *kind,* and not be saying things to make him remember he ain't in his own country and amongst his own folks."

I says to myself, *this* is a girl that I'm letting that old reptile rob her of her money!

Then Susan *she* waltzed in; and if you'll believe me, she did give Hare-lip hark from the tomb![5]

Says I to myself, And this is *another* one that I'm letting him rob her of her money!

Then Mary Jane she took another inning, and went in sweet and lovely again—which was her way—but when she got done there warn't hardly anything left o' poor Hare-lip. So she hollered.

"All right, then," says the other girls, "you just ask his pardon."

She done it, too. And she done it beautiful. She done it so beautiful it was good to hear; and I wished I could tell her a thousand lies, so she could do it again.

I says to myself, this is *another* one that I'm letting him rob her of her money. And when she got through, they all jest laid theirselves out to make me feel at home and know I was amongst friends. I felt so ornery and low down and mean, that I says to myself, My mind's made up; I'll hive[6] that money for them or bust.

So then I lit out—for bed, I said, meaning some time or another. When I got by myself, I went to thinking the thing over. I says to myself, shall I go to that doctor, private, and blow on these frauds? No—that won't do. He might tell who told him; then the king and the duke would make it warm for me. Shall I go, private, and tell Mary Jane? No—I dasn't do it. Her face would give them a hint, sure; they've got the money, and they'd slide right out and get away with it. If she was to fetch in help, I'd get mixed up in the business, before it was

---

[5]A tongue-lashing, scolding, such as to wake the dead.   [6]Secure, capture.

done with, I judge. No, there ain't no good way but one. I got to steal that money, somehow; and I got to steal it some way that they won't suspicion that I done it. They've got a good thing, here; and they ain't agoing to leave till they've played this family and this town for all they're worth, so I'll find a chance time enough. I'll steal, it, and hide it; and by-and-by, when I'm away down the river, I'll write a letter and tell Mary Jane where it's hid. But I better hive it to-night, if I can, because the doctor maybe hasn't let up as much as he lets on he has; he might scare them out of here, yet.

So, thinks I, I'll go and search them rooms. Up stairs the hall was dark, but I found the duke's room, and started to paw around it with my hands; but I recollected it wouldn't be much like the king to let anybody else take care of that money but his own self; so then I went to his room and begun to paw around there. But I see I couldn't do nothing without a candle, and I dasn't light one, of course. So I judged I'd got to do the other thing—lay for them, and eavesdrop. About that time, I hears their footsteps coming, and was going to skip under the bed; I reached for it, but it wasn't where I thought it would be; but I touched the curtain that hid Mary Jane's frocks, so I jumped in behind that and snuggled in amongst the gowns, and stood there perfectly still.

They come in and shut the door; and the first thing the duke done was to get down and look under the bed. Then I was glad I hadn't found the bed when I wanted it. And yet, you know, it's kind of natural to hide under the bed when you are up to anything private. They sets down, then, and the king says:

"Well, what is it? and cut it middlin' short, because it's better for us to be down there a whoopin'-up the mournin' than up here givin' 'em a chance to talk us over."

"Well, this is it, Capet. I ain't easy; I ain't comfortable. That doctor lays on my mind. I wanted to know your plans. I've got a notion, and I think it's a sound one."

"What is it, duke?"

"That we better glide out of this, before three in the morning, and clip it down the river with what we've got. Specially, seeing we got it so easy—*given* back to us, flung at our heads, as you may say, when of course we allowed to have to steal it back. I'm for knocking off and lighting out."

That made me feel pretty bad. About an hour or two ago, it would a been a little different, but now it made me feel bad and disappointed. The king rips out and says:

"What! And not sell out the rest o' the property? March off like a passel o' fools and leave eight or nine thous'n' dollars' worth o' property layin' around jest sufferin' to be scooped in?—and all good salable stuff, too."

The duke he grumbled; said the bag of gold was enough, and he didn't want to go no deeper—didn't want to rob a lot of orphans of *everything* they had.

"Why, how you talk!" says the king. "We shan't rob 'em of nothing at all but jest this money. The people that *buys* the property is the suff'rers; because as soon's it's found out 'at we didn't own it—which won't be long after we've slid—the sale won't be valid, and it'll all go back to the estate. These-yer orphans 'll git their house back agin, and that's enough for *them;* they're young and spry, and k'n easy earn a livin'. *They* ain't agoing to suffer. Why, jest think—there's thous'n's and thous'n's that ain't nigh so well off. Bless you, *they* ain't got noth'n to complain of."

Well, the king he talked him blind; so at last he give in, and said all right, but said he believed it was blame foolishness to stay, and that doctor hanging over them. But the king says:

"Cuss the doctor! What do we k'yer for *him?* Hain't we got all the fools in town on our side? and ain't that a big enough majority in any town?"

So they got ready to go down stairs again. The duke says:

"I don't think we put that money in a good place."

That cheered me up. I'd begun to think I warn't going to get a hint of no kind to help me. The king says:

"Why?"

"Because Mary Jane'll be in mourning from this out; and first you know the nigger that does up the rooms will get an order to box these duds up and put 'em away; and do you reckon a nigger can run across money and not borrow some of it?"

"Your head's level, agin, duke," says the king; and he come a fumbling under the curtain two or three foot from where I was. I stuck tight to the wall, and kept mighty still, though quivery; and I wondered what them fellows would say to me if they catched me; and I tried to think what I'd better do if they did catch me. But the king he got the bag before I could think more than about a half a thought, and he never suspicioned I was around. They took and shoved the bag through a rip in the straw tick that was under the feather bed, and crammed it in a foot or two amongst the straw and said it was all right, now, because a nigger only make up the feather bed, and don't turn over the straw tick only about twice a year, and so it warn't in no danger of getting stole, now.

But I knowed better. I had it out of there before they was half-way down stairs. I groped along up to my cubby, and hid it there till I could get a chance to do better. I judged I better hide it outside of the house somewheres, because if they missed it they would give the house a good ransacking. I knowed that very well. Then I turned in, with my clothes all on; but I couldn't a gone to sleep, if I wanted to, I was in such a sweat to get through with the business. By-and-by I heard the king and the duke come up; so I rolled off of my pallet and laid with my chin at the top of my ladder and waited to see if anything was going to happen. But nothing did.

So I held on till all the late sounds had quit and the early ones hadn't begun, yet; and then I slipped down the ladder.

CHAPTER XXVII

I crept to their doors and listened; they was snoring, so I tip-toed along, and got down stairs all right. There warn't a sound anywheres. I peeped through a crack of the dining-room door, and see the men that was watching the corpse all sound asleep on their chairs. The door was open into the parlor, where the corpse was laying, and there was a candle in both rooms. I passed along, and the parlor door was open; but I see there warn't nobody in there but the remainders of Peter; so I shoved on by; but the front door was locked, and the key wasn't there. Just then I heard somebody coming down the stairs, back behind me. I run in the parlor, and took a swift look around, and the only place I see to hide the bag was in the coffin. The lid was shoved along about a foot, showing the dead man's face down in there, with a wet cloth over it, and his shroud on. I tucked the moneybag in under the lid, just down beyond where his hands was crossed, which made me creep, they was so cold, and then I run back across the room and in behind the door.

The person coming was Mary Jane. She went to the coffin, very soft, and kneeled down and looked in; then she put up her handkerchief and I see she begun to cry, though I couldn't hear her, and her back was to me. I slid out, and as I passed the dining-room I thought I'd make sure them watchers hadn't seen me; so I looked through the crack and everything was all right. They hadn't stirred.

I slipped up to bed, feeling ruther blue, on accounts of the thing playing out that way after I had took so much trouble and run so much resk about it. Says I, if it could stay where it is, all right; because when we get down the river a hundred mile or two, I could write back to Mary Jane, and she could dig him up again and get it; but that ain't the thing that's going to happen; the thing that's going to happen is, the money'll be found when they come to screw on the lid. Then the king 'll get it again, and it 'll be a long day before he gives anybody another chance to smouch[1] it from him. Of course I *wanted* to slide down and get it out of there, but I dasn't try it. Every minute it was getting earlier, now, and pretty soon some of them watchers would begin to stir, and I might get catched—catched with six thousand dollars in my hands that nobody hadn't hired me to take care of. I don't wish to be mixed up in no such business as that, I says to myself.

When I got down stairs in the morning, the parlor was shut up, and the watchers was gone. There warn't nobody around but the family and the widow Bartley and our tribe. I watched their faces to see if anything had been happening, but I couldn't tell.

Towards the middle of the day the undertaker come, with his man, and they set the coffin in the middle of the room on a couple of chairs, and then set all our chairs in rows, and borrowed more from the neighbors till the hall and the parlor and the dining-room was full. I see the coffin lid was the way it was before, but I dasn't go to look in under it, with folks around.

Then the people begun to flock in, and the beats[2] and the girls took seats in the front row at the head of the coffin, and for half an hour the people filed around slow, in single rank, and looked down at the dead man's face a minute, and some dropped in a tear, and it was all very still and solemn, only the girls and the beats holding handkerchiefs to their eyes and keeping their heads bent, and sobbing a little. There warn't no other sound but the scraping of the feet on the floor, and blowing noses—because people always blows them more at a funeral than they do at other places except church.

When the place was packed full, the undertaker he slid around in his black gloves with his softy soothering ways, putting on the last touches, and getting people and things all shipshape and comfortable, and making no more sound than a cat. He never spoke; he moved people around, he squeezed in late ones, he opened up passage-ways, and done it all with nods, and signs with his hands. Then he took his place over against the wall. He was the softest, glidingest, stealthiest man I ever see; and there warn' no more smile to him than there is to a ham.

They had borrowed a melodeum[3]—a sick one; and when everything was ready, a young woman set down and worked it, and it was pretty skreeky and colicky, and everybody joined in and sung, and Peter was the only one that had a good thing, according to my notion. Then the Reverend Hobson opened up, slow and solemn, and begun to talk; and straight off the most outrageous row busted out in the cellar a body ever heard; it was only one dog, but he made a most powerful racket, and he kept it up, right along; the parson he had to stand there, over the coffin, and wait—you couldn't hear yourself think. It was right

---

[1]Steal.   [2]Deadbeats, i.e., the Duke and the Dauphin.   [3]A small, reed organ.

down awkward, and nobody didn't seem to know what to do. But pretty soon they see that long-legged undertaker make a sign to the preacher as much to say, "Don't you worry—just depend on me." Then he stooped down and begun to glide along the wall, just his shoulders showing over the people's heads. So he glided along, and the pow-wow and racket getting more and more outrageous all the time; and at last, when he had gone around two sides of the room, he disappears down cellar. Then, in about two seconds we heard a whack, and the dog he finished up with a most amazing howl or two, and then everything was dead still, and the parson begun his solemn talk where he left off. In a minute or two here comes this undertaker's back and shoulders gliding along the wall again, and so he glided, and glided, around three sides of the room, and then rose up, and shaded his mouth with his hands, and stretched his neck out towards the preacher, over the people's heads, and says, in a kind of a coarse whisper, *"He had a rat!"* Then he drooped down and glided along the wall again to his place. You could see it was a great satisfaction to the people, because naturally they wanted to know. A little thing like that don't cost nothing, and it's just the little things that makes a man to be looked up to and liked. There warn't no more popular man in town than what that undertaker was.

Well, the funeral sermon was very good, but pison long and tiresome; and then the king he shoved in and got off some of his usual rubbage, and at last the job was through, and the undertaker begun to sneak up on the coffin with his screw-driver. I was in a sweat then, and watched him pretty keen. But he never meddled at all; just slid the lid along, as soft as mush, and screwed it down tight and fast. So there I was! I didn't know whether the money was in there, or not. So, says I, spose somebody has hogged that bag on the sly?—now how do *I* know whether to write to Mary Jane or not? 'Spose she dug him up and didn't find nothing—what would she think of me? Blame it, I says, I might get hunted up and jailed; I'd better lay low and keep dark, and not write at all; the thing's awful mixed, now; trying to better it, I've worsened it a hundred times, and I wish to goodness I'd just let it alone, dad fetch the whole business!

They buried him, and we come back home, and I went to watching faces again—I couldn't help it, and I couldn't rest easy. But nothing come of it; the faces didn't tell me nothing.

The king he visited around, in the evening, and sweetened everybody up, and made himself ever so friendly; and he give out the idea that his congregation over in England would be in a sweat about him, so he must hurry and settle up the estate right away, and leave for home. He was very sorry he was so pushed, and so was everybody; they wished he could stay longer, but they said they could see it couldn't be done. And he said of course him and William would take the girls home with him; and that pleased everybody too, because then the girls would be well fixed, and amongst their own relations; and it pleased the girls, too—tickled them so they clean forgot they ever had a trouble in the world; and told him to sell out as quick as he wanted to, they would be ready. Them poor things was that glad and happy it made my heart ache to see them getting fooled and lied to so, but I didn't see no safe way for me to chip in and change the general tune.

Well, blamed if the king didn't bill[4] the house and the niggers and all the property for auction straight off—sale two days after the funeral; but anybody could buy private beforehand if they wanted to.

So the next day after the funeral, along about noontime, the girl's joy got the

[4]Advertise.

first jolt; a couple of nigger traders come along, and the king sold them the niggers reasonable, for three-day drafts[5] as they called it, and away they went, the two sons up the river to Memphis, and their mother down the river to Orleans. I thought them poor girls and them niggers would break their hearts for grief; they cried around each other, and took on so it most made me down sick to see it. The girls said they hadn't ever dreamed of seeing the family separated or sold away from the town. I can't ever get it out of my memory, the sight of them poor miserable girls and niggers hanging around each other's necks and crying; and I reckon I couldn't a stood it all but would a had to bust out and tell on our gang if I hadn't knowed the sale warn't no account and the niggers would be back home in a week or two.

The thing made a big stir in the town, too, and a good many come out flat-footed and said it was scandalous to separate the mother and the children that way. It injured the frauds some; but the old fool he bulled right along, spite of all the duke could say or do, and I tell you the duke was powerful uneasy.

Next day was auction day. About broad-day in the morning, the king and the duke come up in the garret and woke me up, and I see by their look that there was trouble. The king says:

"Was you in my room night before last?"

"No, your majesty"—which was the way I always called him when nobody but our gang warn't around.

"Was you in there yesterday er last night?"

"No, your majesty."

"Honor bright, now—no lies."

"Honor bright, your majesty, I'm telling you the truth. I hain't been near your room since Miss Mary Jane took you and the duke and showed it to you."

The duke says:

"Have you seen anybody else go in there?"

"No, your grace, not as I remember, I believe."

"Stop and think."

I studied a while, and see my chance, then I says:

"Well, I see the niggers go in there several times."

Both of them give a little jump; and looked like they hadn't ever expected it, and then like they *had*. Then the duke says:

"What, *all* of them?"

"No—leastways not all at once. That is, I don't think I ever see them all come *out* at once but just one time."

"Hello—when was that?"

"It was the day we had the funeral. In the morning. It warn't early, because I overslept. I was just starting down the ladder, and I see them."

"Well, go on, *go on*—what did they do? How'd they act?"

"They didn't do nothing. And they didn't act anyway, much, as fur as I see. They tip-toed away; so I seen, easy enough, that they'd shoved in there to do up your majesty's room, or something, sposing you was up; and found you *warn't* up, and so they was hoping to slide out of the way of trouble without waking you up, if they hadn't already waked you up."

"Great guns, *this* is a go!" says the king; and both of them looked pretty sick, and tolerable silly. They stood there a thinking and scratching their heads, a minute, and then the duke he burst into a kind of a little raspy chuckle, and says:

[5]Bank drafts (checks) that can be cashed after three days.

"It does beat all, how neat the niggers played their hand. They let on to be *sorry* they was going out of this region! and I believed they *was* sorry. And so did you, and so did everybody. Don't ever tell *me* any more that a nigger ain't got any histrionic talent. Why, the way they played that thing, it would fool *anybody*. In my opinion, there's a fortune in 'em. If I had capital and a theatre, I wouldn't want a better lay out than that—and here we've gone and sold 'em for a song. Yes, and ain't privileged to sing the song, yet. Say, where *is* that song?—that draft."

"In the bank for to be collected. Where *would* it be?"

"Well, *that's* all right then, thank goodness."

Says I, kind of timid-like:

"Is something gone wrong?"

The king whirls on me and rips out:

"None o' your business! You keep your head shet, and mind y'r own affairs— if you got any. Long as you're in this town, don't you forget *that*, you hear?" Then he says to the duke, "We got to jest swaller it, and say noth'n: mum's the word for *us*."

As they was starting down the ladder, the duke he chuckles again, and says: "Quick sales *and* small profits! It's a good business—yes."

The king snarls around on him and says,

"I was trying to do for the best, in sellin' 'm out so quick. If the profits has turned out to be none, lackin' considable, an none to carry, is it my fault any more'n it's yourn?"

"Well, *they'd* be in this house yet, and we *wouldn't* if I could a got my advice listened to."

The king sassed back, as much as was safe for him, and then swapped around and lit into *me* again. He give me down the banks[6] for not coming and *telling* him I see the niggers come out of his room acting that way—said any fool would a *knowed* something was up. And then waltzed in and cussed *himself* a while; and said it all come of him not laying late and taking his natural rest that morning, and he'd be blamed if he'd ever do it again. So they went off a jawing; and I felt dreadful glad I'd worked it all off onto the niggers and yet hadn't done the niggers no harm by it.

CHAPTER XXVIII

By-and-by it was getting-up time; so I come down the ladder and started for down stairs, but as I come to the girls' room, the door was open, and I see Mary Jane setting by her old hair trunk, which was open and she'd been packing things in it—getting ready to go to England. But she had stopped now, with a folded gown in her lap, and had her face in her hands, crying. I felt awful bad to see it; of course anybody would. I went in there, and says:

"Miss Mary Jane, you can't abear to see people in trouble, and *I* can't—most always. Tell me about it."

So she done it. And it was the niggers—I just expected it. She said the beautiful trip to England was most about spoiled for her; and she didn't know *how* she was ever going to be happy there, knowing the mother and the children warn't ever going to see each other no more—and then busted out bitterer than ever, and flung up her hands, and says:

"Oh, dear, dear, to think they ain't *ever* going to see each other any more!"

[6]A tongue-lashing.

"But they *will*—and inside of two weeks—and I *know* it!" says I.

Laws, it was out before I could think!—and before I could budge, she throws her arms arond my neck, and told me to say it *again*, say it *again*, say it *again!*

I see I had spoke too sudden, and said too much, and was in a close place. I asked her to let me think a minute; and she set there, very impatient and excited, and handsome, but looking kind of happy and eased-up, like a person that's had a tooth pulled out. So I went to studying it out. I says to myself, I reckon a body that ups and tells the truth when he is in a tight place, is taking considerable many resks, though I ain't had no experience, and can't say for certain; but it looks so to me, anyway; and yet here's a case where I'm blest if it don't look to me like the truth is better, and actuly *safer*, than a lie. I must lay it by in my mind, and think it over some time or other, it's so kind of strange and unregular. I never see nothing like it. Well, I says to myself at last, I'm agoing to chance it; I'll up and tell the truth this time, though it does seem most like setting down on a kag of powder and touching it off just to see where you'll go to. Then I says:

"Miss Mary Jane, is there any place out of town a little ways, where you could go and stay three or four days?"

"Yes—Mr. Lothrop's. Why?"

"Never mind why, yet. If I'll tell you how I know the niggers will see each other again—inside of two weeks—here in this house—and *prove* how I know it—will you go to Mr. Lothrop's and stay four days?"

"Four days!" she says; "I'll stay a year!"

"All right," I says, "I don't want nothing more out of *you* than just your word— I druther have it than another man's kiss-the-Bible."[1] She smiled, and reddened up very sweet, and I says, "If you don't mind it, I'll shut the door—and bolt it."

Then I come back and set down again, and says:

"Don't you holler. Just set still, and take it like a man. I got to tell the truth, and you want to brace up. Miss Mary, because it's a bad kind, and going to be hard to take, but there ain't no help for it. These uncles of yourn ain't no uncles at all—they're a couple of frauds—regular dead beats. There, now we're over the worst of it—you can stand the rest middling easy."

It jolted her up like everything, of course; but I was over the shoal water[2] now, so I went right along, her eyes a blazing higher and higher all the time, and told her every blame thing, from where we first struck that young fool going up to the steamboat, clear through to where she flung herself onto the king's breast at the front door and he kissed her sixteen or seventeen times—and then up she jumps, with her face afire like sunset, and says:

"The brute! Come—don't waste a minute—not a *second*—we'll have them tarred and feathered, and flung in the river!"

Says I:

"Cert'nly. But do you mean, *before* you go to Mr. Lothrop's, or——"

"Oh," she says, "what am I *thinking* about!" she says, and set right down again. "Don't mind what I said—please don't—you *won't* now, *will* you?" Laying her silky hand on mine in that kind of a way that I said I would die first. "I never thought, I was so stirred up," she says; "now go on, and I won't do so any more. You tell me what to do, and whatever you say, I'll do it."

"Well," I says, "it's a rough gang, them two frauds, and I'm fixed so I got to travel with them a while longer, whether I want to or not—I druther not tell you why—and if you was to blow on them this town would get me out of their claws, and *I*'d be all right, but there'd be another person that you don't know

[1]Oath sworn on the Bible.
[2]Past the most dangerous water, "over the worst of it."

about who'd be in big trouble. Well, we got to save *him*, hain't we? Of course. Well, then, we won't blow on them."

Saying them words put a good idea in my head. I see how maybe I could get me and Jim rid of the frauds; get them jailed here, and then leave. But I didn't want to run the raft in day-time, without anybody aboard to answer questions but me; so I didn't want the plan to begin working till pretty late to-night. I says:

"Miss Mary Jane, I'll tell you what we'll do—and you won't have to stay at Mr. Lothrop's so long, nuther. How fur is it?"

"A little short of four miles—right out in the country, back here."

"Well, that'll answer. Now you go along out there, and lay low till nine or half-past, to-night, and then get them to fetch you home again—tell them you've thought of something. If you get here before eleven, put a candle in this window, and if I don't turn up, wait *till* eleven, and *then* if I don't turn up it means I'm gone, and out of the way, and safe. Then you come out and spread the news around, and get these beats jailed."

"Good," she says, "I'll do it."

"And if it just happens so that I don't get away, but get took up along with them, you must up and say I told you the whole thing beforehand, and you must stand by me all you can."

"Stand by you, indeed I will. They sha'n't touch a hair of your head!" she says, and I see her nostrils spread and her eyes snap when she said it, too.

"If I get away, I sha'n't be here," I says, "to prove these rapscallions ain't your uncles, and I couldn't do it if I *was* here. I could swear they was beats and bummers, that's all; though that's worth something. Well, there's others can do that better than what I can—and they're people that ain't going to be doubted as quick as I'd be. I'll tell you how to find them. Gimme a pencil and a piece of paper. There—'*Royal Nonesuch, Bricksville.*' Put it away, and don't lose it. When the court wants to find out something about these two, let them send up to Bricksville and say they've got the men that played the Royal Nonesuch, and ask for some witnesses—why, you'll have that entire town down here before you can hardly wink, Miss Mary. And they'll come a-biling, too."

I judged we had got everything fixed about right, now. So I says:

"Just let the auction go right along, and don't worry. Nobody don't have to pay for the things, and they ain't going out of this till they get that money—and the way we've fixed it the sale ain't going to count, and they ain't going to *get* no money. It's just like the way it was with the niggers—it warn't no sale, and the niggers will be back before long. Why, they can't collect the money for the *niggers*, yet—they're in the worst kind of a fix, Miss Mary."

"Well," she says. "I'll run down to breakfast now, and then I'll start straight for Mr. Lothrop's."

" 'Deed, *that* ain't the ticket, Miss Mary Jane." I says, "by no manner of means; go *before* breakfast."

"Why?"

"What did you reckon I wanted you to go at all for, Miss Mary?"

"Well, I never thought—and come to think, I don't know. What was it?"

"Why, it's because you ain't one of these leather-face people. I don't want no better book than what your face is. A body can set down and read it off like coarse print. Do you reckon you can go and face your uncles, when they come to kiss you good-morning, and never—"

"There, there, don't! Yes, I'll go before breakfast—I'll be glad to. And leave my sisters with them?"

"Yes—never mind about them. They've got to stand it yet a while. They might suspicion something if all of you was to go. I don't want you to see them, nor your sisters, nor nobody in this town—if a neighbor was to ask how is your uncles this morning, your face would tell something. No, you go right along, Miss Mary Jane, and I'll fix it with all of them. I'll tell Miss Susan to give your love to your uncles and say you've went away for a few hours for to get a little rest and change, or to see a friend, and you'll be back to-night or early in the morning."

"Gone to see a friend is all right, but I won't have my love given to them."

"Well, then, it sha'n't be." It was well enough to tell *her* so—no harm in it. It was only a little thing to do, and no trouble; and it's the little things that smooths people's roads and most, down here below; it would make Mary Jane comfortable, and it wouldn't cost nothing. Then I says: "There's one more thing—that bag of money."

"Well, they've got that; and it makes me feel pretty silly to think *how* they got it."

"No, you're out, there. They hain't got it."

"Why, who's got it?"

"I wish I knowed, but I don't. I *had* it, because I stole it from them: and I stole it to give to you; and I know where I hid it, but I'm afraid it ain't there no more. I'm awful sorry, Miss Mary Jane, I'm just as sorry as I can be; but I done the best I could; I did, honest. I come nigh getting caught, and I had to shove it into the first place I come to, and run—and it warn't a good place."

"Oh, stop blaming yourself—it's too bad to do it, and I won't allow it—you couldn't help it; it wasn't your fault. Where did you hide it?"

I didn't want to set her to thinking about her troubles again; I couldn't seem to get my mouth to tell her what would make her see that corpse layin' in the coffin with that bag of money on his stomach. So for a minute I didn't say nothing—then I says:

"I'd druther not *tell* you where I put it, Miss Mary Jane, if you don't mind letting me off; but I'll write it for you on a piece of paper, and you can read it along the road to Mr. Lothrop's, if you want to. Do you reckon that'll do?"

"Oh, yes."

So I wrote: "I put it in the coffin. It was in there when you was crying there, away in the night. I was behind the door, and I was mighty sorry for you, Miss Mary Jane."

It made my eyes water a little, to remember her crying there all by herself in the night, and them devils laying there right under her own roof, shaming her and robbing her; and when I folded it up and give it to her, I see the water come into her eyes, too; and she shook me by the hand, hard, and says:

"*Good*-bye—I'm going to do everything just as you've told me; and if I don't ever see you again, I sha'n't ever forget you, and I'll think of you a many and a many a time, and I'll *pray* for you, too!"—and she was gone.

Pray for me! I reckoned if she knowed me she'd take a job that was more nearer her size. But I bet she done it, just the same—she was just that kind. She had the grit to pray for Judas if she took the notion—there warn't no back-down to her, I judge. You may say what you want to, but in my opinion she had more sand[3] in her than any girl I ever see; in my opinion she was just full of sand. It sounds like flattery, but it ain't no flattery. And when it comes to beauty—and goodness too—she lays over them all. I hain't ever seen her since that time

---

[3]Grit, courage.

that I see her go out of that door; no, I hain't ever seen her since, but I reckon I've thought of her a many and a many a million times, and of her saying she would pray for me; and if ever I'd a thought it would do any good for me to pray for *her*, blamed if I wouldn't a done it or bust.

Well, Mary Jane she lit out the back way, I reckon; because nobody see her go. When I struck Susan and the hare-lip, I says:

"What's the name of them people over on t'other side of the river that you all goes to see sometimes?"

They says:

"There's several; but it's the Proctors, mainly."

"That's the name," I says; "I most forgot it. Well, Miss Mary Jane she told me to tell you she's gone over there in a dreadful hurry—one of them's sick."

"Which one?"

"I don't know; leastways I kinder forget; but I think it's——"

"Sakes alive, I hope it ain't *Hanner?*"

"I'm sorry to say it," I says, "but Hanner's the very one."

"My goodness—and she so well only last week! Is she took bad?"

"It ain't no name for it. They set up with her all night, Miss Mary Jane said, and they don't think she'll last many hours."

"Only think of that, now! What's the matter with her!"

I couldn't think of anything reasonable, right off that way, so I says:

"Mumps."

"Mumps your granny! They don't set up with people that's got the mumps."

"They don't, don't they? You better bet they do with *these* mumps. These mumps is different. It's a new kind, Miss Mary Jane said."

"How's it a new kind?"

"Because it's mixed up with other things."

"What other things?"

"Well, measles, and whooping-cough, and erysiplas,[4] and consumption,[5] and yaller jaunders,[6] and brain fever, and I don't know what all."

"My land! And they call it the *mumps?*"

"That's what Miss Mary Jane said."

"Well, what in the nation do they call it the *mumps* for?"

"Why, because it *is* the mumps. That's what it starts with."

"Well, ther' ain't no sense in it. A body might stump his toe, and take pison, and fall down the well, and break his neck, and bust his brains out, and somebody come along and ask what killed him, and some numskull up and say, 'Why, he stumped his *toe.*' Would ther' be any sense in that? No. And ther' ain't no sense in *this,* nuther. Is it ketching?"

"Is it *ketching?* Why, how you talk. Is a *harrow* catching?—in the dark? If you don't hitch onto one tooth, you're bound to on another, ain't you? And you can't get away with that tooth without fetching the whole harrow along, can you? Well, these kind of mumps is a kind of a harrow, as you may say—and it ain't no slouch of a harrow, nuther, you come to get it hitched on good."

"Well, it's awful, I think," says the hare-lip. "I'll go to Uncle Harvey and——"

"Oh, yes," I says, "I *would.* Of *course* I would. I wouldn't lose no time."

"Well, why wouldn't you?"

"Just look at it a minute, and maybe you can see. Hain't your uncles obleeged to get along home to England as fast as they can? And do you reckon they'd be mean enough to go off and leave you to go all that journey by yourselves?

[4]A skin disease.   [5]Tuberculosis.   [6]Yellow jaundice.

You know they'll wait for you. So fur, so good. Your uncle Harvey's a preacher, ain't he? Very well, then; is a *preacher* going to deceive a steamboat clerk? is he going to deceive a *ship clerk?*—so as to get them to let Miss Mary Jane go aboard? Now *you* know he ain't. What *will* he do, then? Why, he'll say, 'It's a great pity, but my church matters has got to get along the best way they can; for my niece has been exposed to the dreadful pluribus-unum[7] mumps, and so it's my bounden duty to set down here and wait the three months it takes to show on her if she's got it.' But never mind, if you think it's best to tell your uncle Harvey——"

"Shucks, and stay fooling around here when we could all be having good times in England whilst we was waiting to find out whether Mary Jane's got it or not? Why, you talk like a muggins."[8]

"Well, anyway, maybe you better tell some of the neighbors."

"Listen at that, now. You do beat all, for natural stupidness. Can't you *see* that *they'd* go and tell? Ther' ain't no way but just to not tell anybody at *all.*"

"Well, maybe you're right—yes, I judge you *are* right."

"But I reckon we ought to tell Uncle Harvey she's gone out a while, anyway, so he won't be uneasy about her."

"Yes, Miss Mary Jane she wanted you to do that. She says, 'Tell them to give Uncle Harvey and William my love and a kiss, and say I've run over the river to see Mr.—Mr.—what *is* the name of that rich family your uncle Peter used to think so much of?—I mean the one that——"

"Why, you must mean the Apthorps, ain't it?"

"Of course; bother them kind of names, a body can't ever seem to remember them, half the time, somehow. Yes, she said, say she has run over for to ask the Apthorps to be sure and come to the auction and buy this house, because she allowed her uncle Peter would rather they had it than anybody else; and she's going to stick to them till they say they'll come, and then, if she ain't too tired, she's coming home; and if she is, she'll be home in the morning anyway. She said, don't say nothing about the Proctors, but only about the Apthorps— which'll be perfectly true, because she *is* going there to speak about their buying the house; I know it, because she told me so, herself."

"All right," she said, and cleared out to lay for her uncles, and give them the love and the kisses, and tell them the message.

Everything was all right now. The girls wouldn't say nothing because they wanted to go to England; and the king and the duke would ruther Mary Jane was off working for the auction than around in reach of Doctor Robinson. I felt very good; I judged I had done it pretty neat—I reckoned Tom Sawyer couldn't a done it no neater himself. Of course he would a throwed more style into it, but I can't do that very handy, not being brung up to it.

Well, they held the auction in the public square, along towards the end of the afternoon, and it strung along, and strung along, and the old man he was on hand and looking his level piousest, up there longside of the auctioneer, and chipping in a little Scripture, now and then, or a little goody-goody saying, of some kind, and the duke he was around goo-gooing for sympathy all he knowed how, and just spreading himself generly.

But by-and-by the thing dragged through, and everything was sold. Everything but a little old trifling lot in the graveyard. So they'd got to work *that* off—I never see such a giraft as the king was for wanting to swallow *everything*.

[7]High-sounding Latin, taken from the United States motto that is stamped on coins: "E Pluribus Unum," One Out of Many.
[8]Fool.

Well, whilst they was at it, a steamboat landed, and in about two minutes up comes a crowd a whooping and yelling and laughing and carrying on, and singing out:

"*Here's* your opposition line! here's your two sets o' heirs to old Peter Wilks—and you pays your money and you takes your choice!"

CHAPTER XXIX

They was fetching a very nice looking old gentleman along, and a nice looking younger one, with his right arm in a sling. And my souls, how the people yelled, and laughed, and kept it up. But I didn't see no joke about it, and I judged it would strain the duke and the king some to see any. I reckoned they'd turn pale. But no, nary a pale did *they* turn. The duke he never let on he suspicioned what was up, but just went a goo-gooing around, happy and satisfied, like a jug that's googling out buttermilk; and as for the king, he just gazed and gazed down sorrowful on them new-comers like it give him the stomach-ache in his very heart to think there could be such frauds and rascals in the world. Oh, he done it admirable. Lots of the principal people gethered around the king, to let him see they was on his side. That old gentleman that had just come looked all puzzled to death. Pretty soon he began to speak, and I see, straight off, he pronounced *like* an Englishman, not the king's way, though the king's *was* pretty good, for an imitation. I can't give the old gent's words, nor I can't imitate him; but he turned around to the crowd, and says, about like this:

"This is a surprise to me which I wasn't looking for; and I'll acknowledge, candid and frank, I ain't very well fixed to meet it and answer it; for my brother and me has had misfortunes, he's broke his arm, and our baggage got put off at a town above here, last night in the night by a mistake. I am Peter Wilks's brother Harvey, and this is his brother William, which can't hear nor speak—and can't even make signs to amount to much, now 't he's only got one hand to work them with. We are who we say we are; and in a day or two, when I get the baggage, I can prove it. But, up till then, I won't say nothing more, but go to the hotel and wait."

So him and the new dummy[1] started off; and the king he laughs, and blethers out:

"Broke his arm—*very* likely *ain't* it?—and very convenient, too, for a fraud that's got to make signs, and hain't learnt how. Lost their baggage! That's *mighty* good!—and mighty ingenious—under the *circumstances!*"

So he laughed again; and so did everybody else, except three or four, or maybe half a dozen. One of these was that doctor; another one was a sharp looking gentleman, with a carpet-bag of the old-fashioned kind made out of carpet-stuff, that had just come off the steamboat and was talking to him in a low voice, and glancing towards the king now and then and nodding their heads—it was Levi Bell, the lawyer that was gone up to Louisville; and another one was a big rough husky that come along and listened to all the old gentleman said, and was listening to the king now. And when the king got done, this husky up and says:

"Say, looky here; if you are Harvey Wilks, when'd you come to this town?"

"The day before the funeral, friend," says the king.

"But what time o' day?"

[1]Deaf mute.

"In the evenin'—'bout an hour er two before sundown."

"*How'd* you come?"

"I come down on the *Susan Powell,* from Cincinnati."

"Well, then, how'd you come to be up the Pint in the *mornin'*—in a canoe?"

"I warn't up at the Pint in the mornin'."

"It's a lie."

Several of them jumped for him and begged him not to talk that way to an old man and preacher.

"Preacher be hanged, he's a fraud and a liar. He was up at the Pint that mornin'. I live up there, don't I? Well, I was up there, and he was up there. I *see* him there. He come in a canoe, along with Tim Collins and a boy."

The doctor he up and says:

"Would you know the boy again if you was to see him, Hines?"

"I reckon I would, but I don't know. Why, yonder he is, now. I know him perfectly easy."

It was me he pointed at. The doctor says:

"Neighbors, I don't know whether the new couple is frauds or not; but if *these* two ain't frauds, I am an idiot, that's all. I think it's our duty to see that they don't get away from here till we've looked into this thing. Come along, Hines; come along, the rest of you. We'll take these fellows to the tavern and affront them with t'other couple, and I reckon we'll find out *something* before we get through."

It was nuts for the crowd, though maybe not for the king's friends; so we all started. It was about sundown. The doctor he led me along by the hand, and was plenty kind enough, but he never let *go* my hand.

We all got in a big room in the hotel, and lit up some candles, and fetched in the new couple. First, the doctor says:

"I don't wish to be too hard on these two men, but *I* think they're frauds, and they may have complices that we don't know nothing about. If they have, won't the complices get away with that bag of gold Peter Wilks left? It ain't unlikely. If these men ain't frauds, they won't object to sending for that money and letting us keep it till they prove they're all right—ain't that so?"

Everybody agreed to that. So I judged they had our gang in a pretty tight place, right at the outstart. But the king he only looked sorrowful, and says:

"Gentlemen, I wish the money was there, for I ain't got no disposition to throw anything in the way of a fair, open, out-and-out investigation o' this misable business; but alas, the money ain't there; you k'n send and see, if you want to."

"Where is it, then?"

"Well, when my niece give it to me to keep for her, I took and hid it inside o' the straw tick o' my bed, not wishin' to bank it for the few days we'd be here, and considerin' the bed a safe place, we not bein' used to niggers, and suppos'n' em honest, like servants in England. The niggers stole it the very next mornin' after I had went down stairs; and when I sold 'em, I hadn't missed the money yit, so they got clean away with it. My servant here k'n tell you 'bout it, gentlemen."

The doctor and several said "Shucks!" and I see nobody didn't altogether believe him. One man asked me if I see the niggers steal it. I said no, but I see them sneaking out of the room and hustling away, and I never thought nothing, only I reckoned they was afraid they had waked up my master and was trying to get away before he made trouble with them. That was all they asked me. Then the doctor whirls on me and says:

"Are *you* English too?"

I says yes; and him and some others laughed, and said, "Stuff!"

Well, then they sailed in on the general investigation, and there we had it, up and down, hour in, hour out, and nobody never said a word about supper, nor ever seemed to think about it—and so they kept it up, and kept it up; and it *was* the worst mixed-up thing you ever see. They made the king tell his yarn, and they made the old gentleman tell his'n; and anybody but a lot of prejudiced chuckleheads would a *seen* that the old gentleman was spinning truth and t'other one lies. And by-and-by they had me up to tell what I knowed. The king he give me a left-handed look out of the corner of his eye, and so I knowed enough to talk on the right side. I begun to tell about Sheffield, and how we lived there, and all about the English Wilkses, and so on; but I didn't get pretty fur till the doctor begun to laugh; and Levi Bell, the lawyer, says:

"Set down, my boy, I wouldn't strain myself, if I was you. I reckon you ain't used to lying, it don't seem to come handy; what you want is practice. You do it pretty awkward."

I didn't care nothing for the compliment, but I was glad to be let off, anyway.

The doctor he started to say something, and turns and says:

"If you'd been in town at first, Levi Bell——"

The king broke in and reached out his hand, and says:

"Why, is this my poor dead brother's old friend that he's wrote so often about?"

The lawyer and him shook hands, and the lawyer smiled and looked pleased, and they talked right along a while, and then got to one side and talked low; and at last the lawyer speaks up and says:

"That'll fix it. I'll take the order and send it, along with your brother's, and then they'll know it's all right."

So they got some paper and a pen, and the king he set down and twisted his head to one side, and chawed his tongue, and scrawled off something; and then they give the pen to the duke—and then for the first time, the duke looked sick. But he took the pen and wrote. So then the lawyer turns to the new old gentleman and says:

"You and your brother please write a line or two and sign your names."

The old gentleman wrote, but nobody couldn't read it. The lawyer looked powerful astonished, and says:

"Well, it beats *me*"—and snaked a lot of old letters out of his pocket, and examined them, and then examined the old man's writing, and then *them* again; and then says: "These old letters is from Harvey Wilks; and here's *these* two's handwritings, and anybody can see *they* didn't write them" (the king and the duke looked sold and foolish, I tell you, to see how the lawyer had took them in), "and here's *this* old gentleman's handwriting, and anybody can tell, easy enough, *he* didn't write them—fact is, the scratches he makes ain't properly *writing,* at all. Now here's some letters from——"

The new old gentleman says:

"If you please, let me explain. Nobody can read my hand but my brother there—so he copies for me. It's *his* hand you've got there, not mine."

"*Well!*" says the lawyer, "this *is* a state of things. I've got some of William's letters too; so if you'll get him to write a line or so we can com——"

"He *can't* write with his left hand," says the old gentleman. "If he could use his right hand, you would see that he wrote his own letters and mine too. Look at both, please—they're by the same hand."

The lawyer done it, and says:

"I believe it's so—and if it ain't so, there's a heap stronger resemblance than I'd noticed before, anyway. Well, well, well! I thought we was right on the track of a solution, but it's gone to grass, partly. But anyway, *one* thing is proved—*these* two ain't either of 'em Wilkses"—and he wagged his head towards the king and the duke.

Well, what do you think?—that muleheaded old fool wouldn't give in *then!* Indeed he wouldn't. Said it warn't no fair test. Said his brother William was the cussedest joker in the world, and hadn't *tried* to write—*he* see William was going to play one of his jokes the minute he put the pen to paper. And so he warmed up and went warbling and warbling right along, till he was actully beginning to believe what he was saying, *himself*—but pretty soon the new old gentleman broke in, and says:

"I've thought of something. Is there anybody here that helped to lay out my br—helped to lay out the late Peter Wilks for burying?"

"Yes," says somebody, "me and Ab Turner done it. We're both here."

Then the old man turns towards the king, and says:

"Peraps this gentleman can tell me what was tatooed on his breast?"

Blamed if the king didn't have to brace up mighty quick, or he'd a squshed down like a bluff bank that the river has cut under, it took him so sudden—and mind you, it was a thing that was calculated to make most *anybody* sqush to get fetched such a solid one as that without any notice—because how was *he* going to know what was tatoed on the man? He whitened a little; he couldn't help it; and it was mighty still in there, and everybody bending a little forwards and gazing at him. Says I to myself, *Now* he'll throw up the sponge—there ain't no more use. Well, did he? A body can't hardly believe it, but he didn't. I reckon he thought he'd keep the thing up till he tired them people out, so they'd thin out, and him and the duke could break loose and get away. Anyway, he set there, and pretty soon he begun to smile, and says:

"Mf! It's a *very* tough question, *ain't* it! Yes, sir, I k'n tell you what's tatooed on his breast. It's jest a small, thin, blue arrow—that's what it is; and if you don't look clost, you can't see it. *Now* what do you say—hey?"

Well, *I* never see anything like that old blister for clean out-and-out cheek.

The new old gentleman turns brisk towards Ab Turner and his pard, and his eye lights up like he judged he'd got the king *this* time, and says:

"There—you've heard what he said! Was there any such mark on Peter Wilks's breast?"

Both of them spoke up and says:

"We didn't see no such mark."

"Good!" says the old gentleman. "Now, what you *did* see on his breast was a small dim P, and a B (which is an initial he dropped when he was young), and a W, with dashes between them, so: P—B—W"—and he marked them that way on a piece of paper. "Come—ain't that what you saw?"

Both of them spoke up again, and says:

"No, we *didn't*. We never seen any marks at all."

Well, everybody *was* in a state of mind, now; and they sings out:

"The whole *bilin'* of 'm's frauds! Le's duck 'em! le's drown 'em! le's ride 'em on a rail!" and everybody was whooping at once, and there was a rattling powwow. But the lawyer he jumps on the table and yells, and says:

"Gentlemen—gentle*men!* Hear me just a word—just a *single* word—if you PLEASE! There's one way yet—let's go and dig up the corpse and look."

That took them.

"Hooray!" they all shouted, and was starting right off; but the lawyer and the doctor sung out:

"Hold on, hold on! Collar all these four men and the boy, and fetch *them* along, too!"

"We'll do it!" they all shouted; "and if we don't find them marks we'll lynch the whole gang!"

I *was* scared, now, I tell you. But there warn't no getting away, you know. They gripped us all, and marched us right along, straight for the graveyard, which was a mile and a half down the river, and the whole town at our heels, for we made noise enough, and it was only nine in the evening.

As we went by our house I wished I hadn't sent Mary Jane out of town; because now if I could tip her the wink, she'd light out and save me, and blow on our dead-beats.

Well, we swarmed along down the river road, just carrying on like wild-cats; and to make it more scary, the sky was darking up, and the lightning beginning to wink and flitter, and the wind to shiver amongst the leaves. This was the most awful trouble and most dangersome I ever was in; and I was kinder stunned; everything was going so different from what I had allowed for; stead of being fixed so I could take my own time, if I wanted to, and see all the fun, and have Mary Jane at my back to save me and set me free when the close-fit come, here was nothing in the world betwixt me and sudden death but just them tatoo-marks. If they didn't find them—

I couldn't bear to think about it; and yet, somehow, I couldn't think about nothing else. It got darker and darker, and it was a beautiful time to give the crowd the slip; but that big husky had me by the wrist—Hines—and a body might as well try to give Goliar[2] the slip. He dragged me right along, he was so excited; and I had to run to keep up.

When they got there they swarmed into the graveyard and washed over it like an overflow. And when they got to the grave, they found they had about a hundred times as many shovels as they wanted, but nobody hadn't thought to fetch a lantern. But they sailed into digging, anyway, by the flicker of the lightning, and sent a man to the nearest house a half a mile off, to borrow one.

So they dug and dug, like everything; and it got awful dark, and the rain started, and the wind swished and swushed along, and the lightning come brisker and brisker, and the thunder boomed; but them people never took no notice of it, they was so full of this business; and one minute you could see everything and every face in that big crowd, and the shovelfuls of dirt sailing up out of the grave, and the next second the dark wiped it all out, and you couldn't see nothing at all.

At last they got out the coffin, and begun to unscrew the lid, and then such another crowding, and shouldering, and shoving as there was, to scrouge in and get a sight, you never see; and in the dark, that way, it was awful. Hines he hurt my wrist dreadful, pulling and tugging so, and I reckon he clean forgot I was in the world, he was so excited and panting.

All of a sudden the lightning let go a perfect sluice of white glare, and somebody sings out:

"By the living jingo, here's the bag of gold on his breast!"

Hines let out a whoop, like everybody else, and dropped my wrist and give a

[2]Goliath.

big surge to burst his way in and get a look, and the way I lit out and shinned for the road in the dark, there ain't nobody can tell.

I had the road all to myself, and I fairly flew—leastways I had it all to myself except the solid dark, and the now-and-then glares, and the buzzing of the rain, and the thrashing of the wind, and the splitting of the thunder; and sure as you are born I did clip it along!

When I struck the town, I see there warn't nobody out in the storm, so I never hunted for no back streets, but humped it straight through the main one; and when I begun to get towards our house I aimed my eye and set it. No light there; the house all dark—which made me feel sorry and disappointed, I didn't know why. But at last, just as I was sailing by, *flash* comes the light in Mary Jane's window! and my heart swelled up sudden, like to burst; and the same second the house and all was behind me in the dark, and wasn't ever going to be before me no more in this world. She *was* the best girl I ever see, and had the most sand.

The minute I was far enough above the town to see I could make the tow-head, I begun to look sharp for a boat to borrow; and the first time the lightning showed me one that wasn't chained, I snatched it and shoved. It was a canoe, and warn't fastened with nothing but a rope. The tow-head was a rattling big distance off, away out there in the middle of the river, but I didn't lose no time; and when I struck the raft at last, I was so fagged I would a just laid down to blow and gasp if I could afforded it. But I didn't. As I sprung aboard I sung out:

"Out with you, Jim, and set her loose! Glory be to goodness, we're shut of them!"

Jim lit out, and was a coming for me with both arms spread, he was so full of joy; but when I glimpsed him in the lightning, my heart shot up in my mouth, and I went overboard backwards; for I forgot he was old King Lear and a drownded A-rab all in one, and it most scared the livers and lights out of me. But Jim fished me out, and was going to hug me and bless me, and so on, he was so glad I was back and we was shut of the king and the duke, but I says:

"Not now—have it for breakfast,[3] have it for breakfast! Cut loose and let her slide!"

So, in two seconds, away we went, a sliding down the river, and it *did* seem so good to be free again and all by ourselves on the big river and nobody to bother us. I had to skip around a bit, and jump up and crack my heels a few times, I couldn't help it; but about the third crack, I noticed a sound that I knowed mighty well—and held my breath and listened and waited—and sure enough, when the next flash busted out over the water, here they come!—and just a laying to their oars and making their skiff hum! It was the king and the duke. So I wilted right down onto the planks, then, and give up; and it was all I could do to keep from crying.

CHAPTER XXX

When they got aboard, the king went for me, and shook me by the collar, and says:

"Tryin' to give us the slip, was ye, you pup! Tired of our company—hey?"

---

[3]Save it for later.

I says:

"No, your majesty, we warn't—*please* don't, your majesty!"

"Quick, then, and tell us what *was* your idea, or I'll shake the insides out o' you!"

"Honest, I'll tell you everything, just as it happened, your majesty. The man that had aholt of me was very good to me, and kept saying he had a boy about as big as me that died last year, and he was sorry to see a boy in such a dangerous fix; and when they was all took by surprise by finding the gold, and made a rush for the coffin, he lets go of me and whispers, 'Heel it, now, or they'll hang ye, sure!' and I lit out. It didn't seem no good for *me* to stay—*I* couldn't do nothing, and I didn't want to be hung if I could get away. So I never stopped running till I found the canoe; and when I got here I told Jim to hurry, or they'd catch me and hang me yet, and said I was afeard you and the duke wasn't alive, now, and I was awful sorry, and so was Jim, and was awful glad when we see you coming, you may ask Jim if I didn't."

Jim said it was so; and the king told him to shut up, and said, "Oh, yes, it's *mighty* likely!" and shook me up again, and said he reckoned he'd drownd me. But the duke says:

"Leggo the boy, you old idiot! Would *you* a done any different? Did you inquire around for *him*, when you got loose? *I* don't remember it."

So the king let go of me, and begun to cuss that town and everybody in it. But the duke says:

"You better a blame sight give *yourself* a good cussing, for you're the one that's entitled to it most. You hain't done a thing, from the start, that had any sense in it, except coming out so cool and cheeky with that imaginary blue-arrow mark. That *was* bright—it was right down bully; and it was the thing that saved us. For if it hadn't been for that, they'd a jailed us till them Englishmen's baggage come—and then—the penitentiary, you bet! But that trick took 'em to the graveyard, and the gold done us a still bigger kindness; for if the excited fools hadn't let go all holts and made that rush to get a look, we'd a slept in our cravats[1] to-night—cravats warranted to *wear*, too—longer than *we'd* need 'em."

They was still a minute—thinking—then the king says, kind of absent-minded like:

"Mf! And we reckoned the *niggers* stole it!"

That made me squirm!

"Yes," says the duke, kinder slow, and deliberate, and sarcastic, "*We* did."

After about a half a minute, the king drawls out:

"Leastways—*I* did."

The duke says, the same way:

"On the contrary—*I* did."

The king kind of ruffles up, and says:

"Looky here, Bilgewater, what'r you referrin' to?"

The duke says, pretty brisk:

"When it comes to that, maybe you'll let me ask, what was *you* referring to?"

"Shucks!" says the king, very sarcastic; "but *I* don't know—maybe you was asleep, and didn't know what you was about."

The duke bristles right up, now, and says:

"Oh, let *up* on this cussed nonsense—do you take me for a blame' fool? Don't you reckon *I* know who hid that money in that coffin?"

"*Yes*, sir! I know you *do* know—because you done it yourself!"

---

[1] I.e., hangman's nooses.

"It's a lie!"—and the duke went for him. The king sings out:

"Take y'r hands off!—leggo my throat!—I take it all back!"

The duke says:

"Well, you just own up, first, that you *did* hide that money there, intending to give me the slip one of these days, and come back and dig it up, and have it all to yourself."

"Wait jest a minute, duke—answer me this one question, honest and fair; if you didn't put the money there, say it, and I'll b'lieve you, and take back everything I said."

"You old scoundrel, I didn't, and you know I didn't. There, now!"

"Well, then, I b'lieve you. But answer me only jest this one more—now *don't* git mad; didn't you have it in your *mind* to hook the money and hide it?"

The duke never said nothing for a little bit; then he says:

"Well—I don't care if I *did*, I didn't *do* it, anyway. But you not only had it in mind to do it, but you *done* it."

"I wisht I may never die if I done it, duke, and that's honest. I won't say I warn't *goin'* to do it, because I *was;* but you—I mean somebody—got in ahead o' me."

"It's a lie! You done it, and you got to *say* you done it, or——"

The king begun to gurgle, and then he gasps out:

" 'Nough!—*I own up!*"

I was very glad to hear him say that, it made me feel much more easier than what I was feeling before. So the duke took his hands off, and says:

"If you ever deny it again, I'll drown you. It's *well* for you to set there and blubber like a baby—it's fitten for you, after the way you've acted. I never see such an old ostrich for wanting to gobble everything—and I a trusting you all the time, like you was my own father. You ought to been ashamed of yourself to stand by and hear it saddled onto a lot of poor niggers and you never say a word for 'em. It makes me feel ridiculous to think I was soft enough to *believe* that rubbage. Cuss you, I can see, now, why you was so anxious to make up the deffersit—you wanted to get what money I'd got out of the Nonesuch and one thing or another, and scoop it *all!*"

The king says, timid, and still a snuffling:

"Why, duke, it was you that said make up the deffersit, it warn't me."

"Dry up! I don't want to hear no more *out* of you!" says the duke. "And *now* you see what you *got* by it. They've got all their own money back, and all of *ourn* but a shekel[2] or two, *besides*. G'long to bed—and don't you deffersit *me* no more deffersits, long 's *you* live!"

So the king sneaked into the wigwam, and took to his bottle for comfort; and before long the duke tackled *his* bottle; and so in about a half an hour they was as thick as thieves again, and the tighter they got, the lovinger they got; and went off a snoring in each other's arms. They both got powerful mellow, but I noticed the king didn't get mellow enough to forget to remember to not deny about hiding the money-bag again. That made me feel easy and satisfied. Of course when they got to snoring, we had a long gabble, and I told Jim everything.

CHAPTER XXXI

We dasn't stop again at any town, for days and days; kept right along down the river. We was down south in the warm weather, now, and a mighty long

[2]An ancient coin of the Near East; here the term is used to mean any coin that does not have high monetary value.

ways from home. We begun to come to trees with Spanish moss on them, hanging down from the limbs like long gray beards. It was the first I ever see it growing, and it made the woods look solemn and dismal. So now the frauds reckoned they was out of danger, and they begun to work the villages again.

First they done a lecture on temperance; but they didn't make enough for them both to get drunk on. Then in another village they started a dancing school; but they didn't know no more how to dance than a kangaroo does; so the first prance they made, the general public jumped in and pranced them out of town. Another time they tried a go at yellocution; but they didn't yellocute long till the audience got up and give them a solid good cussing and made them skip out. They tackled missionarying, and mesmerizering, and doctoring, and telling fortunes, and a little of everything; but they couldn't seem to have no luck. So at last they got just about dead broke, and laid around the raft, as she floated along, thinking, and thinking, and never saying nothing, by the half a day at a time, and dreadful blue and desperate.

And at last they took a change, and begun to lay their heads together in the wigwam and talk low and confidential two or three hours at a time. Jim and me got uneasy. We didn't like the look of it. We judged they was studying up some kind of worse deviltry than ever. We turned it over and over, and at last we made up our minds they was going to break into somebody's house or store, or was going into the counterfeit-money business, or something. So then we was pretty scared, and made up an agreement that we wouldn't have nothing in the world to do with such actions, and if we ever got the least show we would give them the cold shake, and clear out and leave them behind. Well, early one morning we hid the raft in a good safe place about two mile below a little bit of a shabby village, named Pikesville, and the king he went ashore, and told us all to stay hid whilst he went up to town and smelt around to see if anybody had got any wind of the Royal Nonesuch there yet. ("House to rob, you *mean*," says I to myself; "and when you get through robbing it you'll come back here and wonder what's become of me and Jim and the raft—and you'll have to take it out in wondering.") And he said if he warn't back by mid-day, the duke and me would know it was all right, and we was to come along.

So we staid where we was. The duke he fretted and sweated around, and was in a mighty sour way. He scolded us for everything, and we couldn't seem to do nothing right; he found fault with every little thing. Something was a-brewing, sure. I was good and glad when midday come and no king; we could have a change, anyway—and maybe a chance for *the* change, on top of it. So me and the duke went up to the village, and hunted around there for the king, and by-and-by we found him in the back room of a little low doggery,[1] very tight, and a lot of loafers bullyragging him for sport, and he a cussing and threatening with all his might, and so tight he couldn't walk, and couldn't do nothing to them. The duke he begun to abuse him for an old fool, and the king begun to sass back; and the minute they was fairly at it, I lit out, and shook the reefs out of[2] my hind legs, and spun down the river road like a deer—for I see our chance; and I made up my mind that it would be a long day before they ever see me and Jim again. I got down there all out of breath but loaded up with joy, and sung out—

"Set her loose, Jim, we're all right now!"

But there warn't no answer, and nobody come out of the wigwam. Jim was gone! I set up a shout—and then another—and then another one; and run this

[1]Saloon.
[2]Stretched out.

way and that in the woods, whooping and screeching; but it warn't no use—old Jim was gone. Then I set down and cried; I couldn't help it. But I couldn't set still long. Pretty soon I went out on the road, trying to think what I better do, and I run across a boy walking, and asked him if he'd seen a strange nigger, dressed so and so, and he says:

"Yes."

"Whereabouts?" says I.

"Down to Silas Phelps's place, two mile below here. He's a runaway nigger, and they've got him. Was you looking for him?"

"You bet I ain't! I run across him in the woods about an hour or two ago, and he said if I hollered he'd cut my livers out—and told me to lay down and stay where I was; and I done it. Been there ever since; afeard to come out."

"Well," he says, "you needn't be afeard no more, becuz they've got him. He run off f'm down South, som'ers."

"It's a good job they got him."

"Well, I *reckon!* There's two hundred dollars reward on him. It's like picking up money out'n the road."

"Yes, it is—and *I* could a had it if I'd been big enough; I see him *first.* Who nailed him?"

"It was an old fellow—a stranger—and he sold out his chance in him for forty dollars, becuz he's got to go up the river and can't wait. Think o' that, now! You bet *I'd* wait, if it was seven year."

"That's me, every time," says I. "But maybe his chance ain't worth no more than that, if he'll sell it so cheap. Maybe there's something ain't straight about it."

"But it *is*, though—straight as a string. I see the handbill myself. It tells all about him, to a dot—paints him like a picture, and tells the plantation he's frum, below New*r*leans. No-sirree-*bob*, they ain't no trouble 'bout *that* speculation, you bet you. Say, gimme a chaw tobacker, won't ye?"

I didn't have none, so he left. I went to the raft, and set down in the wigwam to think. But I couldn't come to nothing. I thought till I wore my head sore, but I couldn't see no way out of the trouble. After all this long journey, and after all we'd done for them scoundrels, here was it all come to nothing, everything all busted up and ruined, because they could have the heart to serve Jim such a trick as that, and make him a slave again all his life, and amongst strangers, too, for forty dirty dollars.

Once I said to myself it would be a thousand times better for Jim to be a slave at home where his family was, as long as he'd *got* to be a slave, and so I'd better write a letter to Tom Sawyer and tell him to tell Miss Watson where he was. But I soon give up that notion, for two things: she'd be mad and disgusted at his rascality and ungratefulness for leaving her, and so she'd sell him straight down the river again; and if she didn't everybody naturally despises an ungrateful nigger, and they'd make Jim feel it all the time, and so he'd feel ornery and disgraced. And then think of *me!* It would get all around, that Huck Finn helped a nigger to get his freedom; and if I was to ever see anybody from that town again, I'd be ready to get down and lick his boots for shame. That's just the way: a person does a low-down thing, and then he don't want to take no consequences of it. Thinks as long as he can hide it, it ain't no disgrace. That was my fix exactly. The more I studied about this, the more my conscience went to grinding me, and the more wicked and low-down and ornery I got to feeling. And at last, when it hit me all of a sudden that here was the plain hand of Providence slapping me in the face and letting me know my wickedness was being watched all the time from up there in heaven, whilst I was stealing a poor old woman's nigger that hadn't ever done me no harm, and now was showing me there's One that's always on the lookout, and ain't agoing to allow no such miserable doings to go only just so fur and no further, I most dropped in my tracks I was so scared. Well, I tried the best I could to kinder soften it up somehow for myself, by saying I was brung up wicked, and so I warn't so much to blame; but something inside of me kept saying, "There was the Sunday school, you could a gone to it; and if you'd a done it they'd a learnt you, there, that people that acts as I'd been acting about that nigger goes to everlasting fire."

It made me shiver. And I about made up my mind to pray; and see if I couldn't try to quit being the kind of a boy I was, and be better. So I kneeled down. But the words wouldn't come. Why wouldn't they? It warn't no use to try and hide it from Him. Nor from *me,* neither. I knowed very well why they wouldn't come. It was because my heart warn't right; it was because I warn't square; it was because I was playing double. I was letting *on* to give up sin, but away inside of me I was holding to the biggest one of all. I was trying to make my mouth *say* I would do the right thing and the clean thing, and go and write to that nigger's owner and tell where he was; but deep down in me I knowed it was a lie—and He knowed it. You can't pray a lie—I found that out.

So I was full of trouble, full as I could be; and didn't know what to do. At last I had an idea; and I says, I'll go and write the letter—and *then* see if I can pray. Why, it was astonishing, the way I felt as light as a feather, right straight off, and my troubles all gone. So I got a piece of paper and a pencil, all glad and excited, and set down and wrote:

Miss Watson your runaway nigger Jim is down here two mile below Pikesville and Mr. Phelps has got him and he will give him up for the reward if you send.
                                                                HUCK FINN.

I felt good and all washed clean of sin for the first time I had ever felt so in my life, and I knowed I could pray now. But I didn't do it straight off, but laid the paper down and set there thinking—thinking how good it was all this happened so, and how near I come to being lost and going to hell. And went on thinking. And got to thinking over our trip down the river; and I see Jim before me, all the time, in the day, and in the night-time, sometimes moonlight, sometimes storms, and we a floating along, talking, and singing, and laughing. But somehow I couldn't seem to strike no places to harden me against him, but only the other kind. I'd see him standing my watch on top of his'n, stead of calling me, so I could go on sleeping; and see him how glad he was when I come back out of the fog; and when I come to him again in the swamp, up there where the feud was; and such-like times; and would always call me honey, and pet me, and do everything he could think of for me, and how good he always was; and at last I struck the time I saved him by telling the men we had small-pox aboard, and he was so grateful, and said I was the best friend ole Jim ever had in the world, and the *only* one he's got now; and then I happened to look around, and see that paper.

It was a close place. I took it up, and held it in my hand. I was a trembling, because I'd got to decide, forever, betwixt two things, and I knowed it. I studied a minute, sort of holding my breath, and then says to myself:

"All right, then, I'll *go* to hell"—and tore it up.

It was awful thoughts, and awful words, but they was said. And I let them stay said; and never thought no more about reforming. I shoved the whole thing out of my head; and said I would take up wickedness again, which was in my line, being brung up to it, and the other warn't. And for a starter, I would go to work and steal Jim out of slavery again; and if I could think up anything worse, I would do that, too; because as long as I was in, and in for good, I might as well go the whole hog.

Then I set to thinking over how to get at it, and turned over considerable many things in my mind; and at last fixed up a plan that suited me. So then I took the bearings of a woody island that was down the river a piece, and as soon as it was fairly dark I crept out with my raft and went for it, and hid it there, and then turned in. I slept the night through, and got up before it was light, and had my breakfast, and put on my store clothes, and tied up some others and one thing or another in a bundle, and took the canoe and cleared for shore. I landed below where I judged was Phelps's place, and hid my bundle in the woods, and then filled up the canoe with water, and loaded rocks into her and sunk her where I could find her again when I wanted her, about a quarter of a mile below a little steam sawmill that was on the bank.

Then I struck up the road, and when I passed the mill I see a sign on it, "Phelps's Sawmill," and when I come to the farm-houses, two or three hundred yards further along, I kept my eyes peeled, but didn't see nobody around, though it was good daylight, now. But I didn't mind, because I didn't want to see nobody just yet—I only wanted to get the lay of the land. According to my plan, I was going to turn up there from the village, not from below. So I just took a look, and shoved along, straight for town. Well, the very first man I see, when I got there, was the duke. He was sticking up a bill for the Royal Nonesuch—three-night performance—like that other time. *They* had the cheek, them frauds! I was right on him, before I could shirk. He looked astonished, and says:

"Hel-*lo!* Where'd *you* come from?" Then he says, kind of glad and eager, "Where's the raft?—got her in a good place?"

I says:

"Why, that's just what I was agoing to ask your grace."

Then he didn't look so joyful—and says:

"What was your idea for asking *me?*" he says.

"Well," I says, "when I see the king in that doggery yesterday, I says to myself, we can't get him home for hours, till he's soberer; so I went a loafing around town to put in the time, and wait. A man up and offered me ten cents to help him pull a skiff over the river and back to fetch a sheep, and so I went along; but when we was dragging him to the boat, and the man left me aholt of the rope and went behind him to shove him along, he was too strong for me, and jerked loose and run, and we after him. We didn't have no dog, and so we had to chase him all over the country till we tired him out. We never got him till dark, then we fetched him over, and I started down for the raft. When I got there and see it was gone, I says to myself, 'they've got into trouble and had to leave; and they've took my nigger, which is the only nigger I've got in the world, and now I'm in a strange country, and ain't got no property no more, nor nothing, and no way to make my living;' so I set down and cried. I slept in the woods all night. But what *did* become of the raft then?—and Jim, poor Jim!"

"Blamed if *I* know—that is, what's become of the raft. That old fool had made a trade and got forty dollars, and when we found him in the doggery the loafers had matched half dollars with him and got every cent but what he'd spent for whisky; and when I got him home late last night and found the raft gone, we said, 'That little rascal has stole our raft and shook us, and run off down the river.' "

"I wouldn't shake my *nigger,* would I?—the only nigger I had in the world, and the only property."

"We never thought of that. Fact is, I reckon we'd come to consider him *our* nigger; yes, we did consider him so—goodness knows we had trouble enough for him. So when we see the raft was gone, and we flat broke, there warn't anything for it but to try the Royal Nonesuch another shake. And I've pegged along ever since, dry as a powder-horn. Where's that ten cents? Give it here."

I had considerable money, so I give him ten cents, but begged him to spend it for something to eat, and give me some, because it was all the money I had, and I hadn't had nothing to eat since yesterday. He never said nothing. The next minute he whirls on me and says:

"Do you reckon that nigger would blow on us? We'd skin him if he done that!"

"How can he blow? Hain't he run off?"

"No! That old fool sold him, and never divided with me, and the money's gone."

"*Sold* him?" I says, and begun to cry; "why, he was *my* nigger, and that was my money. Where is he?—I want my nigger."

"Well, you can't *get* your nigger, that's all—so dry up your blubbering. Looky here—do you think *you'd* venture to blow on us? Blamed if I think I'd trust you. Why, if you *was* to blow on us——"

He stopped, but I never see the duke look so ugly out of his eyes before. I went on a-whimpering, and says:

"I don't want to blow on nobody; and I ain't got no time to blow, nohow. I got to turn out and find my nigger."

He looked kinder bothered, and stood there with his bills fluttering on his arm, thinking, and wrinkling up his forehead. At last he says:

"I'll tell you something. We got to be here three days. If you'll promise you won't blow, and won't let the nigger blow, I'll tell you where to find him."

So I promised, and he says:

"A farmer by the name of Silas Ph——" and then he stopped. You see he started to tell me the truth; but when he stopped, that way, and begun to study and think again, I reckoned he was changing his mind. And so he was. He wouldn't trust me; he wanted to make sure of having me out of the way the whole three days. So pretty soon he says: "The man that bought him is named Abram Foster—Abram G. Foster—and he lives forty mile back here in the country, on the road to Lafayette."

"All right," I says, "I can walk it in three days. And I'll start this very afternoon."

"No you won't, you'll start *now;* and don't you lose any time about it, neither, nor do any gabbling by the way. Just keep a tight tongue in your head and move right along, and then you won't get into trouble with *us,* d'ye hear?"

That was the order I wanted, and that was the one I played for. I wanted to be left free to work my plans.

"So clear out," he says; "and you can tell Mr. Foster whatever you want to. Maybe you can get him to believe that Jim *is* your nigger—some idiots don't require documents—leastways I've heard there's such down South here. And when you tell him the handbill and the reward's bogus, maybe he'll believe you when you explain to him what the idea was for getting 'em out. Go 'long, now, and tell him anything you want to; but mind you don't work your jaw any *between* here and there."

So I left, and struck for the back country. I didn't look around, but I kinder felt like he was watching me. But I knowed I could tire him out at that. I went straight out in the country as much as a mile, before I stopped; then I doubled back through the woods towards Phelps's. I reckoned I better start in on my plan straight off, without fooling around, because I wanted to stop Jim's mouth till these fellows could get away. I didn't want no trouble with their kind. I'd seen all I wanted to of them, and wanted to get entirely shut of them.

CHAPTER XXXII

When I got there it was still and Sunday-like, and hot and sunshiny—the hands was gone to the fields; and there was them kind of faint dronings of bugs and flies in the air that makes it seem so lonesome and like everybody's dead and gone; and if a breeze fans along and quivers the leaves, it makes you feel mournful, because you feel like it's spirits whispering—spirits that's been dead ever so many years—and you always think they're talking about *you*. As a general thing it makes a body wish *he* was dead, too, and done with it all.

Phelps's was one of these little one-horse cotton plantations; and they all look alike. A rail fence round a two-acre yard; a stile, made out of logs sawed off and up-ended, in steps, like barrels of a different length, to climb over the fence with, and for the women to stand on when they are going to jump onto a horse; some sickly grass-patches in the big yard, but mostly it was bare and smooth, like an old hat with the nap rubbed off; big double log house for the white folks—hewed logs, with the chinks stopped up with mud or mortar, and these mud-stripes been whitewashed some time or another; round-log kitchen, with a big broad, open but roofed passage joining it to the house; log smoke-house back of the kitchen; three little log nigger-cabins in a row t'other side the smoke-house; one little hut all by itself away down against the back fence, and some out-buildings down a piece the other side; ash-hopper,[1] and big kettle to bile soap in, by the little hut; bench by the kitchen door, with bucket of water and a gourd; hound asleep there, in the sun; more hounds asleep, round about; about three shade-trees away off in a corner; some currant bushes and gooseberry bushes in one place by the fence; outside of the fence a garden and a water-melon patch; then the cotton fields begins; and after the fields, the woods.

I went around and clumb over the back stile by the ash-hopper, and started for the kitchen. When I got a little ways, I heard the dim hum of a spinning-wheel wailing along up and sinking along down again; and then I knowed for certain I wished I was dead—for that *is* the lonesomest sound in the whole world.

I went right along, not fixing up any particular plan, but just trusting to Providence to put the right words in my mouth when the time come; for I'd noticed that Providence always did put the right words in my mouth, if I left it alone.

When I got half-way, first one hound and then another got up and went for me, and of course I stopped and faced them, and kept still. And such another pow-wow as they made! In a quarter of a minute I was a kind of a hub of a wheel, as you may say—spokes made out of dogs—circle of fifteen of them packed together around me, with their necks and noses stretched up towards me, a barking and howling; and more a coming; you see them sailing over fences and around corners from everywheres.

[1]A bin for the fireplace ashes from which lye was extracted for use in making soap.

A nigger woman come tearing out of the kitchen with a rolling-pin in her hand, singing out, "Begone! *you* Tige! you Spot! begon sah!" and she fetched first one and then another of them a clip and sent him howling, and then the rest followed; and the next second, half of them come back, wagging their tails around me and making friends with me. There ain't no harm in a hound, nohow.

And behind the woman comes a little nigger girl and two little nigger boys, without anything on but tow-linen shirts, and they hung onto their mother's gown, and peeped out from behind her at me, bashful, the way they always do. And here comes the white woman running from the house, about forty-five or fifty year old, bareheaded, and her spinning-stick in her hand; and behind her comes her little white children, acting the same way the little niggers was doing. She was smiling all over so she could hardly stand—and says:

"It's *you*, at last!—*ain't* it?"

I out with a "Yes'm," before I thought.

She grabbed me and hugged me tight; and then gripped me by both hands and shook and shook; and the tears come in her eyes, and run down over; and she couldn't seem to hug and shake enough, and kept saying, "You don't look as much like your mother as I reckoned you would, but law sakes, I don't care for that, I'm *so* glad to see you! Dear, dear, it does seem like I could eat you up! Children, it's your cousin Tom!—tell him howdy."

But they ducked their heads, and put their fingers in their mouths, and hid behind her. So she run on:

"Lize, hurry up and get him a hot breakfast, right away—or did you get your breakfast on the boat?"

I said I had got it on the boat. So then she started for the house, leading me by the hand, and the children tagging after. When we got there, she set me down in a split-bottomed chair, and set herself down on a little low stool in front of me, holding both of my hands, and says:

"Now I can have a *good* look at you; and laws-a-me, I've been hungry for it a many and a many a time, all these long years, and it's come at last! We been expecting you a couple of days and more. What's kep' you?—boat get aground?"

"Yes'm—she——"

"Don't say yes'm—say Aunt Sally. Where'd she get aground?"

I didn't rightly know what to say, because I didn't know whether the boat would be coming up the river or down. But I go a good deal on instinct; and my instinct said she would be coming up—from down towards Orleans. That didn't help me much, though; for I didn't know the names of bars down that way. I see I'd got to invent a bar, or forget the name of the one we got aground on—or—Now I struck an idea, and fetched it out:

"It warn't the grounding—that didn't keep us back but a little. We blowed out a cylinder-head."

"Good gracious! anybody hurt?"

"No'm. Killed a nigger."

"Well, it's lucky; because sometimes people do get hurt. Two years ago last Christmas, your uncle Silas was coming up from Newrleans on the old *Lally Rook*,[2] and she blowed out a cylinderhead and crippled a man. And I think he died afterwards. He was a Babtist. Your uncle Silas knowed a family in Baton Rouge that knowed his people very well. Yes, I remember, now he *did* die.

---

[2]Named for the beautiful princess in *Lalla Rookh* (1817), a series of oriental tales by the English poet Thomas Moore (1779–1852).

Mortification[3] set in, and they had to amputate him. But it didn't save him. Yes, it was mortification—that was it. He turned blue all over, and died in the hope of a glorious resurrection. They say he was a sight to look at. Your uncle's been up to the town every day to fetch you. And he's gone again, not more'n an hour ago; he'll be back any minute, now. You must a met him on the road, didn't you?—oldish man, with a——"

"No, I didn't see nobody, Aunt Sally. The boat landed just at daylight, and I left my baggage on the wharf-boat[4] and went looking around the town and out a piece in the country, to put in the time and not get here too soon; and so I come down the back way."

"Who'd you give the baggage to?"

"Nobody."

"Why, child, it'll be stole!"

"Not where *I* hid it I reckon it won't," I says.

"How'd you get your breakfast so early on the boat?"

It was kinder thin ice, but I says:

"The captain see me standing around, and told me I better have something to eat before I went ashore; so he took me in the texas to the officers' lunch,[5] and give me all I wanted."

I was getting so uneasy I couldn't listen good. I had my mind on the children all the time; I wanted to get them out to one side, and pump them a little, and find out who I was. But I couldn't get no show, Mrs. Phelps kept it up and run on so. Pretty soon she made the cold chills streak all down my back, because she says:

"But here we're a running on this way, and you hain't told me a word about Sis, nor any of them. Now I'll rest my works a little, and you start up yourn; just tell me *everything*—tell me all about 'm all—every one of 'm; and how they are, and what they're doing, and what they told you to tell me; and every last thing you can think of."

Well, I see I was up a stump—and up it good. Providence had stood by me this fur, all right, but I was hard and tight aground, now. I see it warn't a bit of use to try to go ahead—I'd *got* to throw up my hand. So I says to myself, here's another place where I got to resk the truth. I opened my mouth to begin; but she grabbed me and hustled me in behind the bed, and says:

"Here he comes! stick your head down lower—there, that'll do; you can't be seen, now. Don't you let on you're here. I'll play a joke on him. Children, don't you say a word."

I see I was in a fix, now. But it warn't no use to worry; there warn't nothing to do but just hold still, and try and be ready to stand from under when the lightning struck.

I had just one little glimpse of the old gentleman when he come in, then the bed hid him. Mrs. Phelps she jumps for him and says:

"Has he come?"

"No," says her husband.

"Good-*ness* gracious!" she says, "what in the world *can* have become of him?"

"I can't imagine," says the old gentleman; "and I must say, it makes me dreadful uneasy."

"Uneasy!" she says, "I'm ready to go distracted! He *must* a come; and you've missed him along the road. I *know* it's so—something *tells* me so."

[3]Gangrene.   [4]A floating dock or landing platform.
[5]Mess, eating room.

"Why Sally, I *couldn't* miss him along the road—*you* know that."

"But oh, dear, dear, what *will* Sis say! He must a come! You must a missed him. He——"

"Oh, don't distress me any more'n I'm already distressed. I don't know what in the world to make of it. I'm at my wit's end, and I don't mind acknowledging 't I'm right down scared. But there's no hope that he's come; for he *couldn't* come and me miss him. Sally, it's terrible—just terrible—something's happened to the boat, sure!"

"Why, Silas! Look yonder!—up the road!—ain't that somebody coming?"

He sprung to the window at the head of the bed, and that give Mrs. Phelps the chance she wanted. She stooped down quick, at the foot of the bed, and give me a pull, and out I come; and when he turned back from the window, there she stood, a-beaming and a-smiling like a house afire, and I standing pretty meek and sweaty alongside. The old gentleman stared, and says:

"Why, who's that?"

"Who do you reckon 't is?"

"I hain't no idea. Who *is* it?"

"It's *Tom Sawyer!*"

By jings, I most slumped through the floor. But there warn't no time to swap knives;[6] the old man grabbed me by the hand and shook, and kept on shaking; and all the time, how the woman did dance around and laugh and cry; and then how they both did fire off questions about Sid, Mary, and the rest of the tribe.

But if they was joyful, it warn't nothing to what I was; for it was like being born again, I was so glad to find out who I was. Well, they froze to me for two hours; and at last when my chin was so tired it couldn't hardly go, any more, I had told them more about my family—I mean the Sawyer family—than ever happened to any six Sawyer families. And I explained all about how we blowed out a cylinder-head at the mouth of White River and it took us three days to fix it. Which was all right, and worked first rate; because *they* didn't know but what it would take three days to fix it. If I'd a called it a bolt-head it would a done just as well.

Now I was feeling pretty comfortable all down one side, and pretty uncomfortable all up the other. Being Tom Sawyer was easy and comfortable; and it stayed easy and comfortable till by-and-by I hear a steamboat coughing along down the river—then I says to myself, spose Tom Sawyer come down on that boat?—and spose he steps in here, any minute, and sings out my name before I can throw him a wink to keep quiet? Well, I couldn't *have* it that way—it wouldn't do at all. I must go up the road and waylay him. So I told the folks I reckoned I would go up to the town and fetch down my baggage. The old gentleman was for going along with me, but I said no, I could drive the horse myself, and I druther he wouldn't take no trouble about me.

CHAPTER XXXIII

So I started for town, in the wagon, and when I was half-way I see a wagon coming, and sure enough it was Tom Sawyer, and I stopped and waited till he come along. I says "Hold on!" and it stopped alongside, and his mouth opened up like a trunk, and staid so; and he swallowed two or three times like a person that's got a dry throat, and then says:

[6]I.e., to change plans.

"I hain't ever done you no harm. You know that. So then, what you want to come back and ha'nt *me* for?"

I says:

"I hain't come back—I hain't *gone*."

When he heard my voice, it righted him up some, but he warn't quite satisfied yet. He says:

"Don't you play nothing on me, because I wouldn't on you. Honest injun, now, you ain't a ghost?"

"Honest injun, I ain't," I says.

"Well—I—I—well, that ought to settle it, of course; but I can't somehow seem to understand it, no way. Looky here, warn't you ever murdered at *all?*"

"No. I warn't ever murdered at all—I played it on them. You come in here and feel of me if you don't believe me."

So he done it; and it satisfied him; and he was that glad to see me again, he didn't know what to do. And he wanted to know all about it right off; because it was a grand adventure, and mysterious, and so it hit him where he lived. But I said, leave it alone till by-and-by; and told his driver to wait, and we drove off a little piece, and I told him the kind of a fix I was in, and what did he reckon we better do? He said, let him alone a minute, and don't disturb him. So he thought and thought, and pretty soon he says:

"It's all right, I've got it. Take my trunk in your wagon, and let on it's your'n; and you turn back and fool along slow, so as to get to the house about the time you ought to; and I'll go towards town a piece, and take a fresh start, and get there a quarter or a half an hour after you; and you needn't let on to know me, at first."

I says:

"All right; but wait a minute. There's one more thing—a thing that *nobody* don't know but me. And that is, there's a nigger here that I'm a trying to steal out of slavery—and his name is *Jim*—old Miss Watson's Jim."

He says:

"What! Why Jim is——"

He stopped and went to studying. I says:

"*I* know what you'll say. You'll say it's dirty low-down business; but what if it is?—*I'm* low down; and I'm agoing to steal him, and I want you to keep mum and not let on. Will you?"

His eye lit up, and he says:

"I'll *help* you steal him!"

Well, I let go all holts then, like I was shot. It was the most astonishing speech I ever heard—and I'm bound to say Tom Sawyer fell, considerable, in my estimation. Only I couldn't believe it. Tom Sawyer a *nigger stealer!*

"Oh, shucks," I says, "you're joking."

"I ain't joking, either."

"Well, then," I says, "joking or no joking, if you hear anything said about a runaway nigger, don't forget to remember that *you* don't know nothing about him, and *I* don't know nothing about him."

Then we took the trunk and put it in my wagon, and he drove off his way, and I drove mine. But of course I forgot all about driving slow, on accounts of being glad and full of thinking; so I got home a heap too quick for that length of a trip. The old gentleman was at the door, and he says:

"Why, this is wonderful. Who ever would a thought it was in that mare to do it. I wish we'd a timed her. And she hain't sweated a hair—not a hair. It's wonderful. Why, I wouldn't take a hundred dollars for that horse now; I wouldn't, honest; and yet I'd a sold her for fifteen before, and thought 'twas all she was worth."

That's all he said. He was the innocentest, best old soul I ever see. But it warn't surprising; because he warn't only just a farmer, he was a preacher, too, and had a little one-horse log church down back of the plantation, which he built it himself at his own expense, for a church and school-house, and never charged nothing for his preaching, and it was worth it, too. There was plenty other farmer-preachers like that, and done the same way, down South.

In about half an hour Tom's wagon drove up to the front stile, and Aunt Sally she see it through the window because it was only about fifty yards, and says:

"Why, there's somebody come! I wonder who 'tis? Why, I do believe it's a stranger. Jimmy" (that's one of the children), "run and tell Lize to put on another plate for dinner."

Everybody made a rush for the front door, because, of course, a stranger don't come *every* year, and so he lays over the yaller fever, for interest, when he does come. Tom was over the stile and starting for the house; the wagon was spinning up the road for the village, and we was all bunched in the front door. Tom had his store clothes on, and an audience—and that was always nuts for Tom Sawyer. In them circumstances it warn't no trouble to him to throw in an amount of style that was suitable. He warn't a boy to meeky[1] along up that yard like a sheep; no, he come ca'm and important, like the ram. When he got afront of us, he lifts his hat ever so gracious and dainty, like it was the lid of a box that had butterflies asleep in it and he didn't want to disturb them, and says:

"Mr. Archibald Nichols, I presume?"

"No, my boy," says the old gentleman, "I'm sorry to say't your driver has deceived you; Nichols's place is down a matter of three mile more. Come in, come in."

Tom he took a look back over his shoulder, and says, "Too late—he's out of sight."

"Yes, he's gone, my son, and you must come in and eat your dinner with us; and then we'll hitch up and take you down to Nichols's."

"Oh, I *can't* make you so much trouble; I couldn't think of it. I'll walk—I don't mind the distance."

"But we won't *let* you walk—it wouldn't be Southern hospitality to do it. Come right in."

"Oh, *do*," says Aunt Sally; "it ain't a bit of trouble to us, not a bit in the world. You *must* stay. It's a long, dusty three mile, and we *can't* let you walk. And besides, I've already told 'em to put on another plate, when I see you coming; so you mustn't disappoint us. Come right in, and make yourself at home."

So Tom he thanked them very hearty and handsome, and let himself be persuaded, and come in; and when he was in, he said he was a stranger from Hicksville, Ohio, and his name was William Thompson—and he made another bow.

Well, he run on, and on, and on, making up stuff about Hicksville and everybody in it he could invent, and I getting a little nervous, and wondering how this was going to help me out of my scrape: and at last, still talking along, he reached over and kissed Aunt Sally right on the mouth, and then settled

[1]Come meekly.

back again in his chair, comfortable, and was going on talking; but she jumped up and wiped it off with the back of her hand, and says:

"You owdacious puppy!"

He looked kind of hurt, and says:

"I'm surprised at you, m'am."

"You're s'rp— Why, what do you reckin *I* am? I've a good notion to take and—say, what do you mean by kissing me?"

He looked kind of humble, and says:

"I didn't mean nothing, m'am. I didn't mean no harm. I—I—thought you'd like it."

"Why, you born fool!" She took up the spinning-stick, and it looked like it was all she could do to keep from giving him a crack with it. "What made you think I'd like it?"

"Well, I don't know. Only, they—they—told me you would."

"*They* told you I would. Whoever told you's *another* lunatic. I never heard the beat of it. Who's *they?*"

"Why—everybody. They all said so, m'am."

It was all she could do to hold in; and her eyes snapped, and her fingers worked like she wanted to scratch him; and she says:

"Who's 'everybody?' Out with their names—or ther'll be an idiot short."

He got up and looked distressed, and fumbled his hat, and says:

"I'm sorry, and I warn't expecting it. They told me to. They all told me to. They all said kiss her; and said she'll like it. They all said it—every one of them. But I'm sorry, m'am, and I won't do it no more—I won't, honest."

"You won't, won't you? Well, I sh'd *reckon* you won't!"

"No'm, I'm honest about it; I won't ever do it again. Till you ask me."

"Till I *ask* you! Well, I never see the beat of it in my born days! I lay you'll be the Methusalem-numskull[2] of creation before ever *I* ask you—or the likes of you."

"Well," he says "it does surprise me so. I can't make it out, somehow. They said you would, and I thought you would. But—" He stopped and looked around slow, like he wished he could run across a friendly eye, somewhere's; and fetched up on the old gentleman's, and says, "Didn't *you* think she'd like me to kiss her, sir?"

"Why, no, I—I—well, no, I b'lieve I didn't."

Then he looks on around, the same way, to me—and says:

"Tom, didn't *you* think Aunt Sally 'd open out her arms and say, 'Sid Sawyer——' "

"My land!" she says, breaking in and jumping for him, "you impudent young rascal, to fool a body so—" and was going to hug him, but he fended her off, and says:

"No, not till you've asked me, first."

So she didn't lose no time, but asked him; and hugged him and kissed him, over and over again, and then turned him over to the old man, and he took what was left. And after they got a little quiet again, she says:

"Why, dear me, I never see such a surprise. We warn't looking for *you*, at all, but only Tom. Sis never wrote to me about anybody coming but him."

"It's because it warn't *intended* for any of us to come but Tom," he says; "but I begged and begged, and at the last minute she let me come, too; so coming

[2] I.e., a numbskull as old as Methuselah, the Biblical patriarch said to have lived 969 years. Genesis 5:27.

down the river, me and Tom thought it would be a first-rate surprise for him
to come here to the house first, and for me to by-and-by tag along and drop in
and let on to be a stranger. But it was a mistake, Aunt Sally. This ain't no healthy
place for a stranger to come."

"No—not impudent whelps, Sid. You ought to had your jaws boxed; I hain't
been so put out since I don't know when. But I don't care, I don't mind the
terms—I'd be willing to stand a thousand such jokes to have you here. Well, to
think of that performance! I don't deny it, I was most putrified with astonishment
when you give me that smack."

We had dinner out in that broad open passage betwixt the house and the
kitchen; and there was things enough on that table for seven families—and all
hot, too; none of your flabby tough meat that's laid in a cupboard in a damp
cellar all night and tastes like a hunk of old cold cannibal in the morning.
Uncle Silas he asked a pretty long blessing over it, but it was worth it; and it
didn't cool it a bit, neither, the way I've seen them kind of interruptions do,
lots of times.

There was a considerable good deal of talk, all the afternoon, and me and
Tom was on the lookout all the time, but it warn't no use, they didn't happen
to say nothing about any runaway nigger, and we was afraid to try to work up
to it. But at supper, at night, one of the little boys says:

"Pa, mayn't Tom and Sid and me go to the show?"

"No," says the old man, "I reckon there ain't going to be any; and you couldn't
go if there was; because the runaway nigger told Burton and me all about that
scandalous show, and Burton said he would tell the people; so I reckon they've
drove the owdacious loafers out of town before this time."

So there it was!—but *I* couldn't help it. Tom and me was to sleep in the same
room and bed; so, being tired, we bid good-night and went up to bed, right
after supper, and clumb out of the window and down the lightning-rod, and
shoved for the town; for I didn't believe anybody was going to give the king
and the duke a hint, and so, if I didn't hurry up and give them one they'd get
into trouble sure.

On the road Tom he told me all about how it was reckoned I was murdered,
and how pap disappeared, pretty soon, and didn't come back no more, and
what a stir there was when Jim run away; and I told Tom all about our Royal
Nonesuch rapscallions, and as much of the raft-voyage as I had time to; and as
we struck into the town and up through the middle of it—it was as much as
half-after eight, then—here comes a raging rush of people, with torches, and
an awful whooping and yelling, and banging tin pans and blowing horns; and
we jumped to one side to let them go by; and as they went by, I see they had
the king and the duke astraddle of a rail—that is, I knowed it *was* the king and
the duke, though they was all over tar and feathers, and didn't look like nothing
in the world that was human—just looked like a couple of monstrous big soldier-
plumes.[3] Well, it made me sick to see it; and I was sorry for them poor pitiful
rascals, it seemed like I couldn't ever feel any hardness against them any more
in the world. It was a dreadful thing to see. Human beings *can* be awful cruel
to one another.

We see we was too late—couldn't do no good. We asked some straggler about
it, and they said everybody went to the show looking very innocent; and laid
low and kept dark till the poor old king was in the middle of his cavortings on

---

[3]The decorative feathered crests on military headgear.

the stage; then somebody give a signal, and the house rose up and went for them.

So we poked along back home, and I warn't feeling so brash as I was before, but kind of ornery, and humble, and to blame, somehow—though *I* hadn't done nothing. But that's always the way; it don't make no difference whether you do right or wrong, a person's conscience ain't got no sense, and just goes for him *anyway*. If I had a yaller dog that didn't know no more than a person's conscience does, I would pison him. It takes up more room than all the rest of a person's insides, and yet ain't no good, nohow. Tom Sawyer he says the same.

CHAPTER XXXIV

We stopped talking, and got to thinking. By-and-by Tom says:

"Looky here, Huck, what fools we are, to not think of it before! I bet I know where Jim is."

"No! Where?"

"In that hut down by the ash-hopper. Why, looky here. When we was at dinner, didn't you see a nigger man go in there with some vittles?"

"Yes."

"What did you think the vittles was for?"

"For a dog."

"So'd I. Well, it wasn't for a dog."

"Why?"

"Because part of it was watermelon."

"So it was—I noticed it. Well, it does beat all, that I never thought about a dog not eating watermelon. It shows how a body can see and don't see at the same time."

"Well, the nigger unlocked the padlock when he went in, and he locked it again when he come out. He fetched uncle a key, about the time we got up from table—same key, I bet. Watermelon shows man, lock shows prisoner; and it ain't likely there's two prisoners on such a little plantation, and where the people's all so kind and good. Jim's the prisoner. All right—I'm glad we found it out detective fashion; I wouldn't give shucks for any other way. Now you work your mind and study out a plan to steal Jim, and I will study out one, too; and we'll take the one we like the best."

What a head for just a boy to have! If I had Tom Sawyer's head, I wouldn't trade it off to be a duke, nor mate of a steamboat, nor clown in a circus, nor nothing I can think of. I went to thinking out a plan, but only just to be doing something; I knowed very well where the right plan was going to come from. Pretty soon, Tom says:

"Ready?"

"Yes," I says.

"All right—bring it out."

"My plan is this," I says. "We can easy find out if it's Jim in there. Then get up my canoe to-morrow night, and fetch my raft over from the island. Then the first dark night that comes, steal the key out of the old man's britches, after he goes to bed, and shove off down the river on the raft, with Jim, hiding day-times and running nights, the way me and Jim used to do before. Wouldn't that plan work?"

"*Work?* Why cert'nly, it would work, like rats a fighting. But it's too blame' simple; there ain't nothing *to* it. What's the good of a plan that ain't no more trouble than that? It's as mild as goosemilk. Why, Huck, it wouldn't make no more talk than breaking into a soap factory."

I never said nothing, because I warn't expecting nothing different; but I knowed mighty well that whenever he got *his* plan ready it wouldn't have none of them objections to it.

And it didn't. He told me what it was, and I see in a minute it was worth fifteen of mine, for style, and would make Jim just as free a man as mine would, and maybe get us all killed besides. So I was satisfied, and said we would waltz in on it. I needn't tell what it was, here, because I knowed it wouldn't stay the way it was. I knowed he would be changing it around, every which way, as we went along, and heaving in new bullinesses wherever he got a chance. And that is what he done.

Well, one thing was dead sure; and that was, that Tom Sawyer was in earnest and was actuly going to help steal that nigger out of slavery. That was the thing that was too many for me. Here was a boy that was respectable, and well brung up; and had a character to lose; and folks at home that had characters; and he was bright and not leather-headed; and knowing and not ignorant; and not mean but kind; and yet here he was, without any more pride, or rightness or feeling, than to stoop to this business, and make himself a shame and his family a shame, before everybody. I *couldn't* understand it no way at all. It was outrageous, and I knowed I ought to just up and tell him so; and so be his true friend, and let him quit the thing right where he was, and save himself. And I *did* start to tell him; but he shut me up, and says:

"Don't you reckon I know what I'm about? Don't I generly know what I'm about?"

"Yes."

"Didn't I *say* I was going to help steal the nigger?"

"Yes."

"*Well* then."

That's all he said, and that's all I said. It warn't no use to say any more; because when he said he'd do a thing, he always done it. But *I* couldn't make out how he was willing to go into this thing; so I just let it go, and never bothered no more about it. If he was bound to have it so, *I* couldn't help it.

When we got home, the house was all dark and still; so we went on down to the hut by the ash-hopper, for to examine it. We went through the yard, so as to see what the hounds would do. They knowed us, and didn't make no more noise than country dogs is always doing when anything comes by in the night. When we got to the cabin, we took a look at the front and the two sides; and on the side I warn't acquainted with—which was the north side—we found a square window-hole, up tolerable high, with just one stout board nailed across it. I says:

"Here's the ticket. This hole's big enough for Jim to get through, if we wrench off the board."

Tom says:

"It's as simple as tit-tat-toe, three-in-a-row, and as easy as playing hooky. I should *hope* we can find a way that's a little more complicated than *that*, Huck Finn."

"Well, then," I says, "how'll it do to saw him out, the way I done before I was murdered, that time?"

"That's more *like*," he says. "It's real mysterious, and troublesome, and good," he says; "but I bet we can find a way that's twice as long. There ain't no hurry; le's keep on looking around."

Betwixt the hut and the fence, on the back side, was a lean-to, that joined the hut at the eaves, and was made out of plank. It was as long as the hut, but narrow—only about six foot wide. The door to it was at the south end, and was padlocked. Tom he went to the soap kettle, and searched around and fetched back the iron thing they lift the lid with; so he took it and prized out one of the staples. The chain fell down, and we opened the door and went in, and shut it, and struck a match, and see the shed was only built against the cabin and hadn't no connection with it; and there warn't no floor to the shed, nor nothing in it but some old rusty played-out hoes, and spades, and picks, and a crippled plow. The match went out, and so did we, and shoved in the staple again, and the door was locked as good as ever. Tom was joyful. He says:

"Now we're all right. We'll *dig* him out. It'll take about a week!"

Then we started for the house, and I went in the back door—you only have to pull a buckskin latch-string, they don't fasten the doors—but that warn't romantical enough for Tom Sawyer: no way would do him but he must climb up the lightning-rod. But after he got up half-way about three times, and missed fire and fell every time, and the last time most busted his brains out, he thought he'd got to give it up; but after he was rested, he allowed he would give her one more turn for luck, and this time he made the trip.

In the morning we was up at break of day, and down to the nigger cabins to pet the dogs and make friends with the nigger that fed Jim—if it *was* Jim that was being fed. The niggers was just getting through breakfast and starting for the fields; and Jim's nigger was piling up a tin pan with bread and meat and things; and whilst the others was leaving, the key come from the house.

This nigger had a good-natured, chuckle-headed face, and his wool was all tied up in little bunches with thread. That was to keep witches off. He said the witches was pestering him awful, these nights, and making him see all kinds of strange things, and hear all kinds of strange words and noises, and he didn't believe he was ever witched so long, before, in his life. He got so worked up, and got to running on so about his troubles, he forgot all about what he'd been agoing to do. So Tom says:

"What's the vittles for? Going to feed the dogs?"

The nigger kind of smiled around gradly over his face, like when you heave a brickbat[1] in a mud puddle, and he says:

"Yes, Mars Sid, *a* dog. Cur'us dog, too. Does you want to go en look at 'im?"

"Yes."

I hunched Tom, and whispers:

"You going, right here in the day-break? *That* warn't the plan."

"No, it warn't—but it's the plan *now*."

So, drat him, we went along, but I didn't like it much. When we got in, we couldn't hardly see anything, it was so dark; but Jim was there, sure enough, and could see us; and he sings out:

"Why, *Huck!* En good *lan'!* ain' dat Misto Tom?"

I just knowed how it would be; I just expected it. *I* didn't know nothing to do; and if I had, I couldn't a done it; because that nigger busted in and says:

"Why, de gracious sakes! do he know you genlmen?"

We could see pretty well, now. Tom he looked at the nigger, steady and kind of wondering, and says:

"Does *who* know us?"

"Why, dish-yer runaway nigger."

---

[1] A piece of brick.

"I don't reckon he does; but what put that into your head?"

"What *put* it dar? Didn' he jis' dis minute sing out like he knowed you?"

Tom says, in a puzzle-up kind of way:

"Well, that's mighty curious. *Who* sung out? *When* did he sing out? *What* did he sing out?" And turns to me, perfectly c'am, and says, "Did *you* hear anybody sing out?"

Of course there warn't nothing to be said but the one thing; so I says:

"No; *I* ain't heard nobody say nothing."

Then he turns to Jim, and looks him over like he never see him before; and says:

"Did you sing out?"

"No, sah," says Jim; "*I* hain't said nothing, sah."

"Not a word?"

"No, sah, I hain't said a word."

"Did you ever see us before?"

"No, sah; not as *I* knows on."

So Tom turns to the nigger, which was looking wild and distressed, and says, kind of severe:

"What do you reckon's the matter with you, anyway? What made you think somebody sung out?"

"Oh, it's de dad-blame' witches, sah, en I wisht I was dead, I do. Dey's awluz at it, sah, en dey do mos' kill me, dey sk'yers me so. Please to don't tell nobody 'bout it sah, er ole Mars Silas he'll scole me; 'kase he say dey *ain't* no witches. I jis' wish to goodness he was heah now—*den* what would he say! I jis' bet he couldn't fine no way to git aroun' it *dis* time. But it's awluz jis' so; people dat's *sot,* stays sot; dey won't look into nothn' en fine it out f'r deyselves, en when *you* fine it out en tell um 'bout it, dey doan' b'lieve you."

Tom give him a dime, and said we wouldn't tell nobody; and told him to buy some more thread to tie up his wool with; and then looks at Jim, and says:

"I wonder if Uncle Silas is going to hang this nigger. If I was to catch a nigger that was ungrateful enough to run away, *I* wouldn't give him up, I'd hang him:" And whilst the nigger stepped to the door to look at the dime and bite it to see if it was good, he whispers to Jim, and says:

"Don't ever let on to know us. And if you hear any digging going on nights, it's us: we're going to set you free."

Jim only had time to grab us by the hand and squeeze it, then the nigger come back, and we said we'd come again some time if the nigger wanted us to; and he said he would, more particular if it was dark, because the witches went for him mostly in the dark, and it was good to have folks around then.

CHAPTER XXXV

It would be most an hour yet till breakfast, so we left, and struck down into the wood; because Tom said we got to have *some* light to see how to dig by, and a lantern makes too much, and might get us into trouble; what we must have was a lot of them rotten chunks that's called fox-fire[1] and just makes a soft kind of a glow when you lay them in a dark place. We fetched an armful and hid it in the weeds, and set down to rest, and Tom says, kind of dissatisfied:

"Blame it, this whole thing is just as easy and awkard as it can be. And so it

[1] Luminous glow of fungi on rotting wood.

makes it so rotten difficult to get up a difficult plan. There ain't no watchman to be drugged—now there *ought* to be a watchman. There ain't even a dog to give a sleeping-mixture to. And there's Jim chained by one leg, with a ten-foot chain, to the leg of his bed: why, all you got to do is to lift up the bedstead and slip off the chain. And Uncle Silas he trusts everybody; sends the key to the punkin-headed nigger, and don't send nobody to watch the nigger. Jim could a got out of that window hole before this, only there wouldn't be no use trying to travel with a ten-foot chain on his leg. Why, drat it, Huck, it's the stupidest arrangement I ever see. You got to invent *all* the difficulties. Well, we can't help it, we got to do the best we can with the materials we've got. Anyhow, there's one thing—there's more honor in getting him out through a lot of difficulties and dangers, where there warn't one of them furnished to you by the people who it was their duty to furnish them, and you had to contrive them all out of your own head. Now look at just that one thing of the lantern. When you come down to the cold facts, we simply got to *let on* that a lantern's resky. Why, we could work with a torchlight procession if we wanted to, I believe. Now, whilst I think of it, we got to hunt up something to make a saw out of, the first chance we get."

"What do we want of a saw?"

"What do we *want* of it? Hain't we got to saw the leg of Jim's bed off, so as to get the chain loose?"

"Why, you just said a body cold lift up the bedstead and slip the chain off."

"Well, if that ain't just like you, Huck Finn. You *can* get up the infant-schooliest[2] ways of going at a thing. Why, hain't you ever read any books at all?—Baron Trenck, nor Casanova, nor Benvenuto Chelleeny, nor Henri IV.,[3] nor none of them heroes? Whoever heard of getting a prisoner loose in such an old-maidy way as that? No; the way all the best authorities does, is to saw the bed-leg in two, and leave it just so, and swallow the sawdust, so it can't be found, and put some dirt and grease around the sawed place so the very keenest seneskal[4] can't see no sign of it's being sawed, and thinks the bed-leg is perfectly sound. Then, the night you're ready, fetch the leg a kick, down she goes; slip off your chain, and there you are. Nothing to do but hitch your rope-ladder to the battlements, shin down it, break your leg in the moat—because a ropeladder is nineteen foot too short, you know—and there's your horses and your trusty vassles, and they scoop you up and fling you across a saddle and away you go, to your native Langudoc, or Navarre,[5] or wherever it is. It's gaudy, Huck. I wish there was a moat to this cabin. If we get time, the night of the escape, we'll dig one."

I says:

"What do we want of a moat, when we're going to snake him out from under the cabin?"

But he never heard me. He had forgot me and everything else. He had his chin in his hand, thinking. Pretty soon, he sighs, and shakes his head; then sighs again, and says:

[2]"Nursery-schooliest."

[3]Baron Friedrich von Trenck (1726–1794), Giovanni Giacomo Casanova (1725–1798), Benvenuto Cellini (1500–1571), Henry IV, King of France (1589–1610). All were adventurers who attempted daring escapes.

[4]Seneschal, an official in a medieval household, a steward.

[5]Languedoc, a medieval province of southern France. Navarre, an ancient kingdom in the Pyrenees between France and Spain.

"No, it wouldn't do—there ain't necessity enough for it."

"For what?" I says.

"Why, to saw Jim's leg off," he says.

"Good land!" I says, "why, there ain't *no* necessity for it. And what would you want to saw his leg off for, anyway?"

"Well, some of the best authorities has done it. They couldn't get the chain off, so they just cut their hand off, and shoved. And a leg would be better still. But we got to let that go. There ain't necessity enough in this case; and besides, Jim's a nigger and wouldn't understand the reasons for it, and how it's the custom in Europe; so we'll let it go. But there's one thing—he can have a rope-ladder; we can tear up our sheets and make him a rope-ladder easy enough. And we can send it to him in a pie; it's mostly done that way. And I've et worse pies."

"Why, Tom Sawyer, how you talk," I says; "Jim ain't got no use for a rope-ladder."

"He *has* got use for it. How *you* talk, you better say; you don't know nothing about it. He's *got* to have a rope-ladder; they all do."

"What in the nation can he *do* with it?"

"*Do* with it? He can hide it in his bed, can't he? That's what they all do; and *he's* got to, too. Huck, you don't ever seem to want to do anything that's regular; you want to be starting something fresh all the time. Spose he *don't* do nothing with it? ain't it there in his bed, for a clew, after he's gone? and don't you reckon they'll want clews? Of course they will. And you wouldn't leave them any? That would be a *pretty* howdy-do, *wouldn't* it! I never heard of such a thing."

"Well," I says, "if it's in the regulations, and he's got to have it, all right, let him have it; because I don't wish to go back on no regulations; but there's one thing, Tom Sawyer—if we go to tearing up our sheets to make Jim a rope-ladder, we're going to get into trouble with Aunt Sally, just as sure as you're born. Now, the way I look at it, a hickry-bark ladder don't cost nothing, and don't waste nothing, and is just as good to load up a pie with, and hide in a straw tick, as any rag ladder you can start; and as for Jim, he ain't had no experience, and so *he* don't care what kind of a——"

"Oh, shucks, Huck Finn, if I was as ignorant as you, I'd keep still—that's what *I'd* do. Who ever heard of a state prisoner escaping by a hickry-bark ladder? Why, it's perfectly ridiculous."

"Well, all right, Tom, fix it your own way; but if you'll take my advice, you'll let me borrow a sheet off of the clothes-line."

He said that would do. And that give him another idea, and he says:

"Borrow a shirt, too."

"What do we want of a shirt, Tom?"

"Want it for Jim to keep a journal on."

"Journal your granny—*Jim* can't write."

"Spose he *can't* write—he can make marks on the shirt, can't he, if we make him a pen out of an old pewter spoon or a piece of an old iron barrel-hoop?"

"Why, Tom, we can pull a feather out of a goose and make him a better one; and quicker, too."

"*Prisoners* don't have geese running around the donjon-keep to pull pens out of, you muggins. They *always* make their pens out of the hardest, toughest, troublesome piece of old brass candlestick or something like that they can get their hands on; and it takes them weeks and weeks, and months and months to file it out, too, because they've got to do it by rubbing it on the wall. *They* wouldn't use a goose-quill if they had it. It ain't regular."

"Well, then, what'll we make him the ink out of?"

"Many makes it out of iron-rust and tears; but that's the common sort and women; the best authorities uses their own blood. Jim can do that; and when he wants to send any little common ordinary mysterious message to let the world know where he's captivated, he can write it on the bottom of a tin plate with a fork and throw it out of the window. The Iron Mask[6] always done that, and it's a blame' good way, too."

"Jim ain't got no tin plates. They feed him in a pan."

"That ain't anything; we can get him some."

"Can't nobody *read* his plates."

"That ain't got nothing to *do* with it, Huck Finn. All *he's* got to do is write on the plate and throw it out. You don't *have* to be able to read it. Why, half the time you can't read anything a prisoner writes on a tin plate, or anywhere else."

"Well, then what's the sense in wasting the plates?"

"Why, blame it all, it ain't the *prisoner's* plates."

"But it's *somebody's* plates, ain't it?"

"Well, spos'n it is? What does the *prisoner* care whose——"

He broke off there, because we heard the breakfast-horn blowing. So we cleared out for the house.

Along during the morning I borrowed a sheet and a white shirt off of the clothes-line; and I found an old sack and put them in it, and we went down and got the fox-fire, and put that in too. I called it borrowing, because that was what pap always called it; but Tom said it warn't borrowing, it was stealing. He said we was representing prisoners; and prisoners don't care how they get a thing so they get it, and nobody don't blame them for it, either. It ain't no crime in a prisoner to steal the thing he needs to get away with, Tom said; it's his right; and so, as long as we was representing a prisoner, we had a perfect right to steal anything on this place we had the least use for, to get ourselves out of prison with. He said if we warn't prisoners it would be a very different thing, and nobody but a mean ornery person would steal when he warn't a prisoner. So we allowed we would steal everything there was that come handy. And yet he made a mighty fuss, one day, after that, when I stole a watermelon out of the nigger patch[7] and eat it; and he made me go and give the niggers a dime, without telling them what it was for. Tom said that what he meant was, we could steal anything we *needed*. Well, I says, I needed the watermelon. But he said I didn't need it to get out of prison with, there's where the difference was. He said if I'd a wanted it to hide a knife in, and smuggle it to Jim to kill the seneskal with, it would a been all right. So I let it go at that, though I couldn't see no advantage in my representing a prisoner, if I got to set down and chaw over a lot of gold-leaf[8] distinctions like that, every time I see a chance to hog a watermelon.

Well, as I was saying, we waited that morning till everybody was settled down to business, and nobody in sight around the yard; then Tom he carried the sack into the lean-to whilst I stood off a piece to keep watch. By-and-by he come out, and we went and set down on the wood-pile, to talk. He says:

"Everything's all right, now, except tools; and that's easy fixed."

"Tools?" I says.

"Yes."

---

[6]The legendary masked prisoner in the Bastille who was a character in the romantic novel *Le Vicomte de Bragelonne* (1848–1850), by Alexandre Dumas (1802–1870). Portions of the novel were translated into English in the 1850s.
[7]Slaves' garden.   [8]Thin, superficial.

"Tools for what?"

"Why, to dig with. We ain't agoing to *gnaw* him out, are we?"

"Ain't them old crippled picks and things in there good enough to dig a nigger out with?" I says.

He turns on me looking pitying enough to make a body cry, and says:

"Huck Finn, did you *ever* hear of a prisoner having picks and shovels, and all the modern conveniences in his wardrobe to dig himself out with? Now I want to ask you—if you got any reasonableness in you at all—what kind of a show would *that* give him to be a hero? Why, they might as well lend him the key, and done with it. Picks and shovels—why they wouldn't furnish 'em to a king."

"Well, then," I says, "if we don't want the picks and shovels, what do we want?"

"A couple of case-knives."[9]

"To dig the foundations out from under that cabin with?"

"Yes."

"Confound it, it's foolish, Tom."

"It didn't make no difference how foolish it is, it's the *right* way—and it's the regular way. And there ain't no *other* way, that ever *I* heard of, and I've read all the books that gives any information about these things. They always dig out with a case-knife—and not through dirt, mind you; generly it's through solid rock. And it takes them weeks and weeks and weeks, and for ever and ever. Why, look at one of them prisoners in the bottom dungeon of the Castle Deef,[10] in the harbor of Marseilles, that dug himself out that way; how long was *he* at it, you reckon?"

"I don't know."

"Well, guess."

"I don't know. A month and a half?"

"*Thirty-seven year*—and he come out in China. *That's* the kind. I wish the bottom of *this* fortress was solid rock."

"*Jim* don't know nobody in China."

"What's *that* got to do with it? Neither did that other fellow. But you're always a-wandering off on a side issue. Why can't you stick to the main point?"

"All right—*I* don't care where he comes out, so he *comes* out; and Jim don't, either, I reckon. But there's one thing, anyway—Jim's too old to be dug out with a case-knife. He won't last."

"Yes he will *last,* too. You don't reckon it's going to take thirty-seven years to dig out through a *dirt* foundation, do you?"

"How long will it take, Tom?"

"Well, we can't resk being as long as we ought to, because it mayn't take very long for Uncle Silas to hear from down there by New Orleans. He'll hear Jim ain't from there. Then his next move will be to advertise Jim, or something like that. So we can't resk being as long digging him out as we ought to. By rights I reckon we ought to be a couple of years; but we can't. Things being so uncertain, what I recommend is this: that we really dig right in, as quick as we can; and after that, we can *let on,* to ourselves, that we was at it thirty-seven years. Then we can snatch him out and rush him away the first time there's an alarm. Yes, I reckon that'll be the best way."

"Now, there's *sense* in that," I says. "Letting on don't cost nothing; letting on ain't no trouble; and if it's any object, I don't mind letting on we was at it a

---

[9] Kitchen knives, kept in a case.

[10] The Chateau d'If, a prison in *The Count of Monte Cristo* (1845), by Alexandre Dumas.

hundred and fifty year. It wouldn't strain me none, after I got my hand in. So I'll mosey along now, and smouch[11] a couple of case-knives."

"Smouch three," he says; "we want one to make a saw out of."

"Tom, if it ain't unregular and irreligious to sejest it," I says, "there's an old rusty saw-blade around yonder sticking under the weatherboarding behind the smoke-house."

He looked kind of weary and discouraged-like, and says:

"It ain't no use to try to learn you nothing, Huck. Run along and smouch the knives—three of them." So I done it.

CHAPTER XXXVI

As soon as we reckoned everybody was asleep, that night, we went down the lightning-rod, and shut ourselves up in the lean-to, and got out our pile of fox-fire, and went to work. We cleared everything out of the way, about four or five foot along the middle of the bottom log. Tom said he was right behind Jim's bed now, and we'd dig in under it, and when we got through there couldn't nobody in the cabin ever know there was any hole there, because Jim's counterpin[1] hung down most to the ground, and you'd have to raise it up and look under to see the hole. So we dug and dug, with the case-knives, till most midnight; and then we was dog-tired, and our hands was blistered, and yet you couldn't see we'd done anything, hardly. At last I says:

"This ain't no thirty-seven year job, this is a thirty-eight year job, Tom Sawyer."

He never said nothing. But he sighed, and pretty soon he stopped digging, and then for a good little while I knowed he was thinking. Then he says:

"It ain't no use, Huck, it ain't agoing to work. If we was prisoners it would, because then we'd have as many years as we wanted, and no hurry; and we wouldn't get but a few minutes to dig, every day, while they was changing watches, and so our hands wouldn't get blistered, and we could keep it up right along, year in and year out, and do it right, and the way it ought to be done. But *we* can't fool along, we got to rush; we ain't got no time to spare. If we was to put in another night this way, we'd have to knock off for a week to let our hands get well—couldn't touch a case-knife with them sooner."

"Well, then, what we going to do, Tom?"

"I'll tell you. It ain't right, and it ain't moral, and I wouldn't like it to get out—but there ain't only just the one way; we got to dig him out with the picks, and *let on* it's case-knives."

"*Now* you're *talking!*" I says; "your head gets leveler and leveler all the time, Tom Sawyer," I says. "Picks is the thing, moral or no moral; and as for me, I don't care shucks for the morality of it, nohow. When I start in to steal a nigger, or a watermelon, or a Sunday-school book, I ain't no ways particular how it's done so it's done. What I want is my nigger; or what I want is my watermelon; or what I want is my Sunday-school book; and if a pick's the handiest thing, that's the thing I'm agoing to dig that nigger or that watermelon or that Sunday-school book out with; and I don't give a dead rat what the authorities thinks about it nuther."

"Well," he says, "there's excuse for picks and letting-on in a case like this; if

[11]Steal.
[1]Counterpane; bedspread.

it warn't so, I wouldn't approve of it, nor I wouldn't stand by and see the rules broke—because right is right, and wrong is wrong, and a body ain't got no business doing wrong when he ain't ignorant and knows better. It might answer for *you* to dig Jim out with a pick, *without* any letting-on, because you don't know no better; but it wouldn't for me, because I do know better. Gimme a case-knife."

He had his own by him, but I handed him mine. He flung it down, and says: "Gimme a *case-knife*."

I didn't know just what to do—but then I thought. I scratched around amongst the old tools, and got a pick-ax and give it to him, and he took it and went to work, and never said a word.

He was always just that particular. Full of principle.

So then I got a shovel, and then we picked and shoveled, turn about, and made the fur fly. We stuck to it about a half an hour, which was as long as we could stand up; but we had a good deal of a hole to show for it. When I got up stairs, I looked out at the window and see Tom doing his level best with the lightning-rod, but he couldn't come it, his hands was so sore. At last he says:

"It ain't no use, it can't be done. What you reckon I better do? Can't you think up no way?"

"Yes," I says, "but I reckon it ain't regular. Come up the stairs, and let on it's a lightning-rod."

So he done it.

Next day Tom stole a pewter spoon and a brass candlestick in the house, for to make some pens for Jim out of, and six tallow candles; and I hung around the nigger cabins, and laid for a chance, and stole three tin plates. Tom said it wasn't enough; but I said nobody wouldn't ever see the plates that Jim throwed out, because they'd fall in the dog-fennel and jimpson weeds under the window-hole—then we could tote them back and he could use them over again. So Tom was satisfied. Then he says:

"Now, the thing to study out is, how to get the things to Jim."

"Take them in through the hole," I says, "when we get it done."

He only just looked scornful, and said something about nobody ever heard of such an idiotic idea, and then he went to studying. By-and-by he said he had ciphered out two or three ways, but there warn't no need to decide on any of them yet. Said we'd got to post Jim first.

That night we went down the lightning-rod a little after ten, and took one of the candles along, and listened under the window-hole, and heard Jim snoring; so we pitched it in, and it didn't wake him. Then we whirled in with the pick and shovel, and in about two hours and a half the job was done. We crept in under Jim's bed and into the cabin, and pawed around and found the candle and lit it, and stood over Jim a while, and found him looking hearty and healthy, and then we woke him up gentle and gradual. He was so glad to see us he most cried; and called us honey, and all the pet names he could think of; and was for having us hunt up a cold chisel to cut the chain off of his leg with, right away, and clearing out without losing any time. But Tom he showed him how unregular it would be, and set down and told him all about our plans, and how we could alter them in a minute any time there was an alarm; and not to be the least afraid, because we would see he got away, *sure*. So Jim he said it was all right, and we set there and talked over old times a while, and then Tom asked a lot of questions, and when Jim told him Uncle Silas come in every day or two to pray with him, and Aunt Sally come in to see if he was comfortable and had plenty to eat, and both of them was kind as they could be, Tom says:

"*Now* I know how to fix it. We'll send you some things by them."

I said, "Don't do nothing of the kind; it's one of the most jackass ideas I ever struck;" but he never paid no attention to me; went right on. It was his way when he'd got his plans set.

So he told Jim how we'd have to smuggle in the rope-ladder pie, and other large things, by Nat, the nigger that fed him, and he must be on the lookout, and not be surprised, and not let Nat see him open them; and we would put small things in uncle's coat pockets and he must steal them out; and we would tie things to aunt's apron strings or put them in her apron pocket, if we got a chance; and told him what they would be and what they was for. And told him how to keep a journal on the shirt with his blood, and all that. He told him everything. Jim he couldn't see no sense in the most of it, but he allowed we was white folks and knowed better than him; so he was satisfied, and said he would do it all just as Tom said.

Jim had plenty corn-cob pipes and tobacco; so we had a right down good sociable time; then we crawled out through the hole, and so home to bed, with hands that looked like they'd been chawed. Tom was in high spirits. He said it was the best fun he ever had in his life, and the most intellectural; and said if he could see his way to it we would keep it up all the rest of our lives and leave Jim to our children to get out; for he believed Jim would come to like it better and better the more he got used to it. He said that in that way it could be strung out to as much as eighty year, and would be the best time on record. And he said it would make us all celebrated that had a hand in it.

In the morning we went out to the wood-pile and chopped up the brass candlestick into handy sizes, and Tom put them and the pewter spoon in his pocket. Then we went to the nigger cabins, and while I got Nat's notice off, Tom shoved a piece of candlestick into the middle of a corn-pone that was in Jim's pan, and we went along with Nat to see how it would work, and it just worked noble; when Jim bit into it it most mashed all his teeth out; and there warn't ever anything could a worked better. Tom said so himself. Jim he never let on but what it was only just a piece of rock or something like that that's always getting into bread, you know; but after that he never bit into nothing but what he jabbed his fork into it three or four places, first.

And whilst we was a standing there in the dimmish light, here comes a couple of the hounds bulging in, from under Jim's bed; and they kept on piling in till there was eleven of them, and there warn't hardly room in there to get your breath. By jings, we forgot to fasten that lean-to door. The nigger Nat he only just hollered "witches!" once, and keeled over onto the floor amongst the dogs, and begun to groan like he was dying. Tom jerked the door open and flung out a slab of Jim's meat, and the dogs went for it, and in two seconds he was out himself and back again and shut the door, and I knowed he'd fixed the other door too. Then he went to work on the nigger, coaxing him and petting him, and asking him if he'd been imagining he saw something again. He raised up, and blinked his eyes around, and says:

"Mars Sid, you'll say I's a fool, but if I didn't b'lieve I see most a million dogs, er devils, er some'n, I wisht I may die right heah in dese tracks. I did, mos' sholy. Mars Sid, I *felt* um—I *felt* um, sah; dey was all over me. Dad fetch it, I jis' wisht I could get my han's on one er dem witches jis' wunst—on'y jis' wunst—it's all I'd ast. But mos'ly I wisht dey'd leme 'lone, I does."

Tom says:

"Well, I tell you what *I* think. What makes them come here just at this runaway nigger's breakfast-time? It's because they're hungry; that's the reason. You make them a witch pie; that's the thing for *you* to do."

"But my lan', Mars Sid, how's *I* gwyne to make 'm a witch pie? I doan' know how to make it. I hain't ever hearn er sich a thing b'fo'."

"Well, then, I'll have to make it myself."

"Will you do it, honey?—will you? I'll wusshup de groun' und' yo' foot, I will!"

"All right, I'll do it, seeing it's you, and you've been good to us and showed us the runaway nigger. But you got to be mighty careful. When we come around, you turn your back; and then whatever we've put in the pan, don't you let on you see it at all. And don't you look, when Jim unloads the pan—something might happen, I don't know what. And above all, don't you *handle* the witch-things."

"*Hannel* 'm Mars Sid? What *is* you talkin' 'bout? I wouldn't lay de weight er my fingers on um, not f'r ten hund'd thous'n' billion dollars, I wouldn't."

CHAPTER XXXVII

That was all fixed. So then we went away and went to the rubbage-pile in the back yard where they keep the old boots, and rags, and pieces of bottles, and wore-out tin things, and all such truck, and scratched around and found an old tin washpan and stopped up the holes as well as we could, to bake the pie in, and took it down cellar and stole it full of flour, and started for breakfast and found a couple of shingle-nails that Tom said would be handy for a prisoner to scrabble his name and sorrows on the dungeon walls with, and dropped one of them in Aunt Sally's apron pocket which was hanging on a chair, and t'other we stuck in the band of Uncle Silas's hat, which was on the bureau, because we heard the children say their pa and ma was going to the runaway nigger's house this morning, and then went to breakfast, and Tom dropped the pewter spoon in Uncle Silas's coat pocket, and Aunt Sally wasn't come yet, so we had to wait a little while.

And when she come she was hot, and red, and cross, and couldn't hardly wait for the blessing; and then she went to sluicing out coffee with one hand and cracking the handiest child's head with her thimble with the other, and says:

"I've hunted high, and I've hunted low, and it does beat all, what *has* become of your other shirt."

My heart fell down amongst my lungs and livers and things, and a hard piece of corn-crust started down my throat after it and got met on the road with a cough and was shot across the table and took one of the children in the eye and curled him up like a fishing-worm, and let a cry out of him the size of a war-whoop, and Tom he turned kinder blue around the gills, and it all amounted to a considerable state of things for about a quarter of a minute or as much as that, and I would a sold out for half price if there was a bidder. But after that we was all right again—it was the sudden surprise of it that knocked us so kind of cold. Uncle Silas he says:

"It's most uncommon curious, I can't understand it. I know perfectly well I took it *off*, because——"

"Because you hain't got but one *on*. Just *listen* at the man! *I* know you took it off, and know it by a better way than your wool gethering memory, too, because it was on the clo'es-line yesterday—I see it there myself. But it's gone—that's the long and the short of it, and you'll just have to change to a red flann'l one till I can get time to make a new one. And it'll be the third I've made in two years; it just keep a body on the jump to keep you in shirts; and whatever you do manage to *do* with 'm all, is more'n *I* can make out. A body'd think you *would* learn to take some sort of care of 'em, at your time of life."

"I know it, Sally, and I do try all I can. But it oughtn't to be altogether my fault, because you know I don't see them nor have nothing to do with them except when they're on me; and I don't believe I've ever lost one of them *off* of me."

"Well, it ain't *your* fault if you haven't, Silas—you'd a done it if you could, I reckon. And the shirt ain't all that's gone, nuther. Ther's a spoon gone; and *that* ain't all. There was ten, and now ther's only nine. The calf got the shirt I reckon, but the calf never took the spoon, *that's* certain."

"Why, what else is gone, Sally?"

"Ther's six *candles* gone—that's what. The rats could a got the candles, and I reckon they did; I wonder they don't walk off with the whole place, the way you're always going to stop their holes and don't do it; and if they warn't fools they'd sleep in your hair, Silas—*you'd* never find it out; but you can't lay the *spoon* on the rats, and that I *know*."

"Well, Sally, I'm in fault, and I acknowledge it; I've been remiss; but I won't let to-morrow go by without stopping up them holes."

"Oh, I wouldn't hurry, next year'll do. Matilda Angelina Araminta *Phelps!*"

Whack comes the thimble, and the child snatches her claws out of the sugar-bowl without fooling around any. Just then, the nigger woman steps onto the passage, and says:

"Missus, dey's a sheet gone."

"A *sheet* gone! Well, for the land's sake!"

"I'll stop up them holes *to-day*," says Uncle Silas, looking sorrowful.

"Oh, *do* shet up!—spose the rats took the *sheet? Where's* it gone, Lize?"

"Clah to goodness I hain't no notion, Miss Sally. She wuz on de clo's-line yistiddy, but she doen gone; she ain' dah no mo', now."

"I reckon the world *is* coming to an end. I *never* see the beat of it, in all my born days. A shirt, and a sheet, and a spoon, and six can——"

"Missus," comes a young yaller wench, "dey's a brass cannelstick miss'n."

"Cler out from here, you hussy, er I'll take a skillet to ye!"

Well, she was just a biling. I begun to lay for a chance; I reckoned I would sneak out and go for the woods till the weather moderated. She kept a raging right along, running her insurrection all by herself, and everybody else mighty meek and quiet; and at last Uncle Silas, looking kind of foolish, fishes up that spoon out of his pocket. She stopped, with her mouth open and her hands up; and as for me, I wished I was in Jeruslem or somewheres. But not long; because she says:

"It's *just* as I expected. So you had it in your pocket all the time; and like as not you've got the other things there, too. How'd it get there?"

"I reely don't know, Sally," he says, kind of apologizing, "or you know I would tell. I was a-studying over my text in Acts Seventeen,[1] before breakfast, and I reckon it put it in there not noticing, meaning to put my Testament in, and it must be so, because my Testament ain't in, but I'll go and see, and if the Testament is where I had it, I'll know I didn't put it in, and that will show that I laid the Testament down and took up the spoon, and——"

"Oh, for the land's sake! Give a body a rest! Go 'long now, the hole kit and biling of ye; and don't come nigh me again till I've got back my peace of mind."

---

[1] Acts 17, in the New Testament, which describes the experiences of the Biblical Silas.

I'd a heard her, if she'd a said it to herself, let alone speaking it out; and I'd a got up and obeyed her, if I'd a been dead. As we was passing through the setting-room, the old man he took up his hat, and the shingle-nail fell out on the floor, and he just merely picked it up and laid it on the mantel-shelf, and never said nothing, and went out. Tom see him do it, and remembered about the spoon, and says:

"Well, it ain't no use to send things by *him* no more, he ain't reliable." Then he says: "But he done us a good turn with the spoon, anyway, without knowing it, and so we'll go and do him one without *him* knowing it—stop up his rat-holes."

There was a noble good lot of them, down cellar, and it took us a whole hour, but we done the job tight and good, and ship-shape. Then we heard steps on the stairs, and blowed out our light, and hid; and here comes the old man, with a candle in one hand and a bundle of stuff in t'other, looking as absent-minded as year before last. He went a mooning around, first to one rat-hole and then another, till he'd been to them all. Then he stood about five minutes, picking tallow-drip off of his candle and thinking. Then he turns off slow and dreamy towards the stairs, saying:

"Well, for the life of me I can't remember when I done it. I could show her now that I warn't to blame on account of the rats. But never mind—let it go. I reckon it wouldn't do no good."

And so he went on a mumbling up stairs, and then we left. He was a mighty nice old man. And always is.

Tom was a good deal bothered about what to do for a spoon, but he said we'd got to have it; so he took a think. When he had ciphered it out, he told me how we was to do; then we went and waited around the spoon-basket till we see Aunt Sally coming, and then Tom went to counting the spoons and laying them out to one side, and I slid one of them up my sleeve, and Tom says:

"Why, Aunt Sally, there ain't but nine spoons, *yet*."

She says:

"Go 'long to your play, and don't bother me. I know better, I counted 'm myself."

"Well, I've counted them twice, Aunty, and *I* can't make but nine."

She looked out of all patience, but of course she come to count—anybody would.

"I declare to gracious ther' *ain't* but nine!" she says. "Why, what in the world—plague *take* the things, I'll count 'm again."

So I slipped back the one I had, and when she got done counting, she says:

"Hang the troublesome rubbage, ther's *ten,* now!" and she looked huffy and bothered both. But Tom says:

"Why, Aunty, *I* don't think there's ten."

"You numskull, didn't you see me *count* im?"

"I know, but——"

"Well, I'll count 'm *again*."

So I smouched one, and they come out nine same as the other time. Well, she *was* in a tearing way—just a trembling all over, she was so mad. But she counted and counted, till she got that addled she'd start to count-in the *basket* for a spoon, sometimes; and so, three times they come out right, and three times they come out wrong. Then she grabbed up the basket and slammed it across the house and knocked the cat galley-west;[2] and she said cle'r out and let her have some

---

[2]For a loop.

peace, and if we come bothering around her again betwixt that and dinner, she'd skin us. So we had the odd spoon; and dropped it in her apron pocket whilst she was a giving us our sailing-orders, and Jim got it all right, along with her shingle-nail, before noon. We was very well satisfied with this business, and Tom allowed it was worth twice the trouble it took, because he said *now* she couldn't even count them spoons twice alike again to save her life; and wouldn't believe she'd counted them right, if she *did;* and said that after she'd about counted her head off, for the next three days, he judged she'd give it up and offer to kill anybody that wanted her to ever count them any more.

So we put the sheet back on the line, that night, and stole one out of her closet; and kept on putting it back and stealing it again, for a couple of days, till she didn't know how many sheets she had, any more, and said she didn't *care,* and warn't agoing to bullyrag[3] the rest of her soul out about it, and wouldn't count them again not to save her life, she druther die first.

So we was all right now, as to the shirt and the sheet and the spoon and the candles, by the help of the calf and the rats and the mixed-up counting; and as to the candlestick, it warn't no consequence, it would blow over by-and-by.

But that pie was a job; we had no end of trouble with that pie. We fixed it up away down in the woods, and cooked it there; and we got it done at last, and very satisfactory, too; but not all in one day; and we had to use up three washpans full of flour, before we got through, and we got burnt pretty much all over, in places, and eyes put out with the smoke; because, you see, we didn't want nothing but a crust, and we couldn't prop it up right, and she would always cave in. But of course we thought of the right way at last; which was to cook the ladder, too, in the pie. So then we laid in with Jim, the second night, and tore up the sheet all in little strings, and twisted them together, and long before daylight we had a lovely rope, that you could a hung a person with. We let on it took nine months to make it.

And in the forenoon we took it down to the woods, but it wouldn't go in the pie. Being made of a whole sheet, that way, there was rope enough for forty pies, if we'd a wanted them, and plenty left over for soup, or sausage, or anything you choose. We could a had a whole dinner.

But we didn't need it. All we needed was just enough for the pie, and so we throwed the rest away. We didn't cook none of the pies in the washpan, afraid the solder would melt; but Uncle Silas he had a noble brass warming-pan[4] which he thought considerable of, because it belonged to one of his ancestors with a long wooden handle that come over from England with William the Conqueror in the *Mayflower*[5] or one of them early ships and was hid away up garret with a lot of other old pots and things that was valuable, not on account of being any account because they warn't, but on account of them being relicts, you know, and we snaked her out, private, and took her down there, but she failed on the first pies, because we didn't know how, but she come up smiling on the last one. We took and lined her with dough, and set her in the coals, and loaded her up with rag-rope, and put on a dough roof, and shut down the lid, and put hot embers on top, and stood off five foot, with the long handle, cool and comfortable, and in fifteen minutes she turned out a pie that was a satisfaction to look at. But the person that et it would want to fetch a couple of kags of toothpicks along, for if that rope-ladder wouldn't cramp him down to business, I don't know nothing what I'm talking about, and lay him in enough stomach-ache to last him till next time, too.

---

[3]Mistreat, punish.   [4]Long-handled pan, filled with hot coals and used to warm a bed.
[5]William the Conquerer lived 1027–1087. The *Mayflower* carried the Pilgrims to America in 1620.

Nat didn't look, when we put the witch-pie in Jim's pan; and we put the three tin plates in the bottom of the pan under the vittles; and so Jim got everything all right, and as soon as he was by himself he busted into the pie and hid the rope-ladder inside of his straw-tick, and scratched some marks on a tin plate and throwed it out of the window-hole.

CHAPTER XXXVIII

Making them pens was a distressid-tough job, and so was the saw; and Jim allowed the inscription was going to be the toughest of all. That's the one which the prisoner has to scrabble on the wall. But we had to have it; Tom said we'd *got* to; there warn't no case of a state prisoner not scrabbling his inscription to leave behind, and his coat of arms.

"Look at Lady Jane Grey," he says; "look at Gilford Dudley; look at old Northumberland![1] Why, Huck, spose it *is* considerble trouble?—what you going to do?—how you going to get around it? Jim's *got* to do his inscription and coat of arms. They all do."

Jim says:

"Why, Mars Tom, I hain't got no coat o' arms; I hain't got nuffn but dish-yer ole shirt, en you knows I got to keep de journal on dat."

"Oh, you don't understand, Jim; a coat of arms is very different."

"Well," I says, "Jim's right, anyway, when he says he hain't got no coat of arms, because he hain't."

"I reckon *I* knowed that," Tom says, "but you bet he'll have one before he goes out of this—because he's going out *right,* and there ain't going to be no flaws in his record."

So whilst me and Jim filed away at the pens on a brickbat apiece, Jim a making his'n out of the brass and I making mine out of the spoon, Tom set to work to think out the coat of arms. By-and-by he said he'd struck so many good ones he didn't hardly know which to take, but there was one which he reckoned he'd decide on. He says:

"On the scutcheon[2] we'll have a bend *or* in the dexter base, a saltire *murrey* in the fess, with a dog, couchant, for common charge, and under his foot a chain embattled, for slavery, with a chevron *vert* in a chief engrailed, and three invected lines on a field *azure,* with the nombril points rampant on a dancette indented; crest, a runaway nigger, *sable,* with his bundle over his shoulder on a bar sinister: and a couple of gules for supporters, which is you and me; motto, *Maggiore fretta, minore atto.* Got it out of a book—means, the more haste, the less speed."[3]

"Geewhillikins," I says, "but what does the rest of it mean?"

"We ain't got no time to bother over that," he says, "we got to dig in like all git-out."

"Well, anyway," I says, "what's *some* of it? What's a fess?"

"A fess—a fess is—*you* don't need to know what a fess is. I'll show him how to make it when he gets to it."

---

[1]In 1553, the Duke of Northumberland attempted to make his daughter-in-law, Lady Jane Grey, Queen of England. Subsequently, Northumberland, Lady Jane Grey, and Guilford Dudley, her husband, were first imprisoned and then executed.

[2]An armorial shield. The jumble of technical heraldic terms that follows describes a coat-of-arms made up of a shield decorated with a slanted band of speckled gold, vertical bands of red, a purple cross in the center, a lying dog at the bottom, and a green chevron at the top, all surmounted by the figure of a runaway slave.

[3]Actually, "The more fretting, the less action."

"Shucks, Tom," I says, "I think you might tell a person. What's a bar sinister?"

"Oh, *I* don't know. But he's got to have it. All the nobility does."

That was just his way. If it didn't suit him to explain a thing to you, he wouldn't do it. You might pump at him a week, it wouldn't make no difference.

He'd got all that coat of arms business fixed, so now he started in to finish up the rest of that part of work, which was to plan out a mournful inscription— said Jim got to have one, like they all done. He made up a lot, and wrote them out on a paper, and read them off, so:

1. *Here a captive heart busted.*

2. *Here a poor prisoner, forsook by the world and friends, fretted out his sorrowful life.*

3. *Here a lonely heart broke, and a worn spirit went to its rest, after thirty-seven years of solitary captivity.*

4. *Here, homeless and friendless, after thirty-seven years of bitter captivity, perished a noble stranger, natural son of Louis XIV.*

Tom's voice trembled, whilst he was reading them, and he most broke down. When he got done, he couldn't no way make up his mind which one for Jim to scrabble onto the wall, they was all so good; but at last he allowed he would let him scrabble them all on. Jim said it would take him a year to scrabble such a lot of truck onto the logs with a nail, and he didn't know how to make letters, besides; but Tom said he would block them out for him, and then he wouldn't have nothing to do but just follow the lines. Then pretty soon he says:

"Come to think, the logs ain't agoing to do; they don't have log walls in a dungeon: we got to dig the inscriptions into a rock. We'll fetch a rock."

Jim said the rock was worse than the logs; he said it would take him such a pison long time to dig them into a rock, he wouldn't ever get out. But Tom said he would let me help him do it. Then he took a look to see how me and Jim was getting along with the pens. It was most pesky tedious hard work and slow, and didn't give my hands no show to get well of the sores, and we didn't seem to make no headway, hardly. So Tom says:

"I know how to fix it. We got to have a rock for the coat of arms and mournful inscriptions, and we can kill two birds with that same rock. There's a gaudy big grindstone down at the mill, and we'll smouch it, and carve the things on it, and file out the pens and the saw on it, too."

It warn't no slouch of an idea; and it warn't no slouch of a grindstone nuther; but we allowed we'd tackle it. It warn't quite midnight, yet, so we cleared out for the mill, leaving Jim at work. We smouched the grindstone, and set out to roll her home, but it was a most nation tough job. Sometimes, do what we could, we couldn't keep her from falling over, and she come mighty near mashing us, every time. Tom said she was going to get one of us, sure, before we got through. We got her half way; and then we was plumb played out, and most drownded with sweat. We see it warn't no use, we got to go and fetch Jim, so he raised up his bed and slid the chain off the bed-leg, and wrapt it round and round his neck, and we crawled out through our hole and down there, and Jim and me laid into that grindstone and walked her along like nothing; and Tom super-intended. He could out-superintend any boy I ever see. He knowed how to do everything.

Our hole was pretty big, but it warn't big enough to get the grindstone through; but Jim he took the pick and soon made it big enough. Then Tom marked out them things on it with the nail, and set Jim to work on them, with the nail for a chisel and an iron bolt from the rubbage in the lean-to for a hammer, and told him to work till the rest of his candle quit on him, and then he could go to bed, and hide the grindstone under his straw tick and sleep on it. Then we helped him fix his chain back on the bed-leg, and was ready for bed ourselves. But Tom thought of something, and says:

"You got any spiders in here, Jim?"

"No, sah, thanks to goodness I hain't, Mars Tom."

"All right, we'll get you some."

"But bless you, honey, I doan' *want* none. I's afeard un um. I jis' 's soon have rattlesnakes aroun'."

Tom thought a minute or two, and says:

"It's a good idea. And I reckon it's been done. It *must* a been done; it stands to reason. Yes, it's a prime good idea. Where could you keep it?"

"Keep what, Mars Tom?"

"Why, a rattlesnake."

"De goodness gracious alive, Mars Tom! Why, if dey was a rattlesnake to come in heah, I'd take en bust right out thoo dat log wall, I would, wid my head."

"Why, Jim, you wouldn't be afraid of it, after a little. You could tame it."

"*Tame* it!"

"Yes—easy enough. Every animal is grateful for kindness and petting, and they wouldn't *think* of hurting a person that pets them. Any book will tell you that. You try—that's all I ask; just try for two or three days. Why, you can get him so, in a little while, that he'll love you; and sleep with you; and won't stay away from you a minute; and will let you wrap him round your neck and put his head in your mouth."

"*Please*, Mars Tom—doan' talk so! I can't *stan'* it. He'd *let* me shove his head in my mouf—fer a favor, hain't it? I lay he'd wait a pow'ful long time 'fo' I *ast* him. En mo' en dat, I doan' *want* him to sleep wid me."

"Jim, don't act so foolish. A prisoner's *got* to have some kind of a dumb pet, and if a rattlesnake hain't ever been tried, why, there's more glory to be gained in your being the first to ever try it than any other way you could ever think of to save your life."

"Why, Mars Tom, I doan' *want* no sich glory. Snake take 'n bite Jim's chin off, den *whah* is de glory? No, sah, I doan' want no sich doin's."

"Blame it, can't you *try?* I only want you to try—you needn't keep it up if it don't work."

"But de trouble all *done,* ef de snake bit me while's I's a tryin' him. Mars Tom, I's willin' to tackle mos' anything 'at ain't onreasonable, but ef you en Huck fetches a rattlesnake in heah for me to tame, I's gwyne to *leave,* dat's *shore.*"

"Well, then, let it go, let it go, if you're so bullheaded about it. We can get you some garter-snakes and you can tie some buttons on their tails, and let on they're rattlesnakes, and I reckon that'll have to do."

"I k'n stan' *dem*, Mars Tom, but blame' 'f I couldn't get along widout um, I tell you dat. I never knowed b'fo', 't was so much bother and trouble to be a prisoner."

"Well, it *always* is, when it's done right. You got any rats around here?"

"No, sah, I hain't seed none."

"Well, we'll get you some rats."

"Well, Mars Tom, I doan' *want* no rats. Dey's de dad-blamedest creturs to 'sturb a body, en rustle roun' over 'im, en bite his feet, when he's trying' to sleep, I ever see. No, sah, gimme g'yarter-snakes, 'f I's got to have 'm, but doan' gimme no rats. I ain' got no use f'r um, skasely."

"But Jim, you *got* to have 'em—they all do. So don't make no more fuss about it. Prisoners ain't ever without rats. There ain't no instance of it. And they train them, and pet them, and learn them tricks, and they get to be as sociable as flies. But you got to play music to them. You got anything to play music on?"

"I ain't got nuffn but a coase comb en a piece o' paper, en a juice-harp; but I reck'n dey wouldn' take no stock in a juice-harp."

"Yes they would. *They* don't care what kind of music 'tis. A jews-harp's plenty good enough for a rat. All animals likes music—in a prison they dote on it. Specially, painful music; and you can't get no other kind out of a jews-harp. It always interests them; they come out to see what's the matter with you. Yes, you're all right; you're fixed very well. You want to set on your bed, nights, before you go to sleep, and early in the mornings, and play your jews-harp; play The Last Link Is Broken—that's the thing that'll scoop a rat, quicker'n anything else: and when you've played about two minutes, you'll see all the rats, and the snakes, and spiders, and things begin to feel worried about you, and come. And they'll just fairly swarm over you, and have a noble good time."

"Yes, *dey* will, I reck'n, Mars Tom, but what kine er time is *Jim* havin'? Blest if I kin see de pint. But I'll do it ef I got to. I reck'n I better keep de animals satisfied, en not have no trouble in de house."

Tom waited to think over, and see if there wasn't nothing else; and pretty soon he says:

"Oh—there's one thing I forgot. Could you raise a flower here, do you reckon?"

"I doan' know but maybe I could, Mars Tom; but it's tolable dark in heah, en I ain' got no use f'r no flower, no how, en she'd be a pow'ful sight o' trouble."

"Well, you try it, anyway. Some other prisoners has done it."

"One er dem big cat-tail-lookin' mullen-stalks would grow in heah, Mars Tom, I reck'n, but she wouldn' be wuth half de trouble she'd coss."

"Don't you believe it. We'll fetch you a little one, and you plant it in the corner, over there, and raise it. And don't call it mullen, call it Pitchiola[4]—that's its right name, when it's in a prison. And you want to water it with your tears."

"Why, I got plenty spring water, Mars Tom."

"You don't *want* spring water; you want to water it with your tears. It's the way they do."

"Why, Mars Tom, I lay I kin raise one er dem mullen-stalks twyste wid spring water whiles another man's a *start'n* one wid tears."

"That ain't the idea. You *got* to do it with tears."

"She'll die on my han's, Mars Tom, she sholy will; kase I doan' skasely ever cry."

So Tom was stumped. But he studied it over, and then said Jim would have to worry along the best he could with an onion. He promised he would go to the nigger cabins and drop one, private, in Jim's coffee-pot, in the morning. Jim said he would "jis' 's soon have tobacker in his coffee"; and found so much fault with it, and with the work and bother of raising the mullen, and jews-harping the rats, and petting and flattering up the snakes and spiders and things, on top of all the other work he had to do on pens, and inscriptions, and journals, and things, which made it more trouble and worry and responsibility to be a prisoner than anything he ever undertook, that Tom most lost all patience with him; and said he was just loadened down with more gaudier chances than a prisoner ever had in the world to make a name for himself, and yet he didn't

---

[4]In the romantic novel, *Picciola* (1836), by Joseph Boniface (1798–1865), a prisoner is kept alive by a plant growing in his cell.

know enough to appreciate them, and they was just about wasted on him. So Jim he was sorry, and said he wouldn't behave so no more, and then me and Tom shoved for bed.

CHAPTER XXXIX

In the morning we went up to the village and bought a wire rat trap and fetched it down, and unstopped the best rat hole, and in about an hour we had fifteen of the bulliest kind of ones; and then we took it and put it in a safe place under Aunt Sally's bed. But while we was gone for spiders, little Thomas Franklin Benjamin Jefferson Elexander Phelps found it there, and opened the door of it to see if the rats would come out, and they did; and Aunt Sally she come in, and when we got back she was a standing on top of the bed raising Cain, and the rats was doing what they could to keep off the dull times for her. So she took and dusted us both with the hickry, and we was as much as two hours catching another fifteen or sixteen, drat that meddlesome cub, and they warn't the likeliest, nuther, because the first haul was the pick of the flock. I never see a likelier lot of rats than what that first haul was.

We got a splendid stock of sorted spiders, and bugs, and frogs, and caterpillars, and one thing or another; and we like-to got a hornet's nest, but we didn't. The family was at home. We didn't give it right up, but staid with them as long as we could; because we allowed we'd tire them out or they'd got to tire us out, and they done it. Then we got allycumpain[1] and rubbed on the places, and was pretty near all right again, but couldn't set down convenient. And so we went for the snakes, and grabbed a couple of dozen garters and house-snakes, and put them in a bag, and put it in our room, and by that time it was supper time, and a rattling good honest day's work; and hungry?—oh, no, I reckon not! And there warn't a blessed snake up there, when we went back—we didn't half tie the sack, and they worked out, somehow, and left. But it didn't matter much, because they was still on the premises somewhere. So we judged we could get some of them again. No, there warn't no real scarcity of snakes about the house for a considerable spell. You'd see them dripping from the rafters and places, every now and then; and they generly landed in your plate, or down the back of your neck, and most of the time where you didn't want them. Well, they was handsome, and striped, and there warn't no harm in a million of them; but that never made no difference to Aunt Sally, she despised snakes, be the breed what they might, and she couldn't stand them no way you could fix it; and every time one of them flopped down on her, it didn't make no difference what she was doing, she would just lay that work down and light out. I never see such a woman. And you could hear her whoop to Jericho. You couldn't get her to take aholt of one of them with the tongs. And if she turned over and found one in bed, she would scramble out and lift a howl that you would think the house was afire. She disturbed the old man so, that he said he could most wish there hadn't ever been no snakes created. Why, after every last snake had been gone clear out of the house for as much as a week, Aunt Sally warn't over it yet; she warn't near over it; when she was setting thinking about something, you could touch her on the back of her neck with a feather and she would jump right out of her stockings. It was very curious. But Tom said all women was just so. He said they was made that way; for some reason or other.

[1]Elecampane, a medicinal herb.

We got a licking every time one of our snakes come in her way; and she allowed these lickings warn't nothing to what she would do if we ever loaded up the place again with them. I didn't mind the lickings, because they didn't amount to nothing; but I minded the trouble we had, to lay in another lot. But we got them laid in, and all the other things; and you never see a cabin as blithesome as Jim's was when they'd all swarm out for music and go for him. Jim didn't like the spiders, and the spiders didn't like Jim; and so they'd lay for him and make it mighty warm for him. And he said that between the rats, and the snakes, and the grindstone, there warn't no room in bed for him skasely; and when there was, a body couldn't sleep, it was so lively, and it was always lively, he said, because *they* never all slept at one time, but took turn about, so when the snakes was asleep the rats was on deck, and when the rats turned in the snakes come on watch, so he always had one gang under him, in his way, and t'other gang having a circus over him, and if he got up to hunt a new place, the spiders would take a chance at him as he crossed over. He said if he ever got out, this time, he wouldn't ever be a prisoner again, not for a salary.

Well, by the end of three weeks, everything was in pretty good shape. The shirt was sent in early, in a pie, and every time a rat bit Jim he would get up and write a little in his journal whilst the ink was fresh; the pens was made, the inscriptions and so on was all carved on the grindstone; the bed-leg was sawed in two, and we had et up the sawdust, and it give us a most amazing stomach-ache. We reckoned we was all going to die, but didn't. It was the most undigestible sawdust I ever see; and Tom said the same. But as I was saying, we'd got all the work done, now, at last; and we was all pretty much fagged out, too, but mainly Jim. The old man had wrote a couple of times to the plantation below Orleans to come and get their runaway nigger, but hadn't got no answer, because there warn't no such plantation; so he allowed he would advertise Jim in the St. Louis and New Orleans papers; and when he mentioned the St. Louis ones, it give me the cold shivers, and I see we hadn't no time to lose. So Tom said, now for the nonnamous letters.

"What's them?" I says.

"Warnings to the people that something is up. Sometimes it's done one way, sometimes another. But there's always somebody spying around, that gives notice to the governor of the castle. When Louis XVI was going to light out of the Tooleries, a servant girl done it.[2] It's a very good way, and so is the non-namous letters. We'll use them both. And it's usual for the prisoner's mother to change clothes with him, and she stays in, and he slides out in her clothes. We'll do that too."

"But looky here, Tom, what do we want to *warn* anybody for, that something's up? Let them find it out for themselves—it's their lookout."

"Yes, I know; but you can't depend on them. It's the way they've acted from the very start—left us to do *everything*. They're so confiding and mullet-headed[3] they don't take notice of nothing at all. So if we don't *give* them notice, there won't be nobody nor nothing to interfere with us, and so after all our hard work and trouble this escape 'll go off perfectly flat: won't amount to nothing—won't be nothing *to* it."

"Well, as for me, Tom, that's the way I'd like."

"Shucks," he says, and looked disgusted. So I says:

---

[2]The Tuileries, royal residence in Paris, France (1564–1871). Following the French Revolution, the plans of King Louis XVI to escape his imprisonment were said to have been revealed to the authorities by a chambermaid.

[3]Stupid.

"But I ain't going to make no complaint. Anyway that suits you suits me. What you going to do about the servant-girl?"

"You'll be her. You slide in, in the middle of the night, and hook that yaller girl's frock."

"Why, Tom, that'll make trouble next morning; because of course she prob'bly hain't got any but that one."

"I know; but you don't want it but fifteen minutes, to carry the nonnamous letter and shove it under the front door."

"All right, then, I'll do it; but I could carry it just as handly in my own togs."

"You wouldn't look like a servant-girl *then*, would you?"

"No, but there won't be nobody to see what I look like, *anyway*."

"That ain't got nothing to do with it. The thing for us to do, is just to do our *duty*, and not worry about whether anybody *sees* us do it or not. Hain't you got no principle at all?"

"All right, I ain't saying nothing; I'm the servant-girl. Who's Jim's mother?"

"I'm his mother. I'll hook a gown from Aunt Sally."

"Well, then, you'll have to stay in the cabin when me and Jim leaves."

"Not much. I'll stuff Jim's clothes full of straw and lay it on his bed to represent his mother in disguise, and Jim 'll take the nigger woman's gown[4] off of me and wear it, and we'll all evade together. When a prisoner of style escapes, it's called an evasion. It's always called so when a king escapes, f'rinstance. And the same with a king's son; it don't make no difference whether he's a natural one or an unnatural one."

So Tom he wrote the nonnamous letter, and I smouched the yaller wench's frock, that night, and put it on, and shoved it under the front door, the way Tom told me to. It said:

> *Beware.   Trouble is brewing.   Keep a sharp lookout.*
> Unknown Friend.

Next night we stuck a picture which Tom drawed in blood, of a skull and crossbones, on the front door; and next night another one of a coffin, on the back door. I never see a family in such a sweat. They couldn't been worse scared if the place had a been full of ghosts laying for them behind everything and under the beds and shivering through the air. If a door banged, Aunt Sally she jumped, and said "ouch!" if anything fell, she jumped and said "ouch!" if you happened to touch her, when she warn't noticing, she done the same; she couldn't face noway and be satisfied, because she allowed there was something behind her every time—so she was always a whirling around, sudden, and saying "ouch," and before she'd get two-thirds around, she'd whirl back again, and say it again; and she was afraid to go to bed, but she dasn't set up. So the thing was working very well, Tom said; he said he never see a thing work more satisfactory. He said it showed it was done right.

So he said, now for the grand bulge! So the very next morning at the streak of dawn we got another letter ready, and was wondering what we better do with it, because we heard them say at supper they was going to have a nigger on watch at both doors all night. Tom he went down the lightning-rod to spy around; and the nigger at the back door was asleep, and he stuck it in the back of his neck and come back. This letter said:

---

[4]Some of Twain's editors have considered this an error in consistency and have corrected the text to read "Aunt Sally's gown."

Don't betray me, I wish to be your friend. There is a desprate gang of cutthroats from over in the Ingean Territory[5] *going to steal your runaway nigger to-night, and they have been trying to scare you so as you will stay in the house and not bother them. I am one of the gang, but have got religgion and wish to quit it and lead a honest life again, and will betray the helish design. They will sneak down from northards, along the fence, at midnight exact, with a false key, and go in the nigger's cabin to get him. I am to be off a piece and blow a tin horn if I see any danger; but stead of that, I will* BA *like a sheep soon as they get in and not blow at all; then whilst they are getting his chains loose, you slip there and lock them in, and can kill them at your leisure. Don't do anything but just the way I am telling you, if you do they will suspicion something and raise whoopjamboreehoo. I do not wish any reward but to know I have done the right thing.*

UNKNOWN FRIEND.

CHAPTER XL

We was feeling pretty good, after breakfast, and took my canoe and went over the river a fishing, with a lunch, and had a good time, and took a look at the raft and found her all right, and got home late to supper, and found them in such a sweat and worry they didn't know which end they was standing on, and made us go right off to bed the minute we was done supper, and wouldn't tell us what the trouble was, and never let on a word about the new letter, but didn't need to, because we knowed as much about it as anybody did, and as soon as we was half up stairs and her back was turned, we slid for the cellar cubboard and loaded up a good lunch and took it up to our room and went to bed, and got up about half-past eleven, and Tom put on Aunt Sally's dress that he stole and was going to start with the lunch, but says:

"Where's the butter?"

"I laid out a hunk of it," I says, "on a piece of a corn-pone."

"Well, you *left* it laid out, then—it ain't here."

"We can get along without it," I says.

"We can get along *with* it, too," he says; "just you slide down cellar and fetch it. And then mosey right down the lightning-rod and come along. I'll go and stuff the straw into Jim's clothes to represent his mother in disguise, and be ready to *ba* like a sheep and shove soon as you get there."

So out he went, and down cellar went I. The hunk of butter, big as a person's fist, was where I had left it, so I took up the slab of corn-pone with it on, and blowed out my light, and started up stairs, very stealthy, and got up to the main floor all right, but here comes Aunt Sally with a candle, and I clapped the truck in my hat, and clapped my hat on my head, and the next second she see me; and she says:

"You been down cellar?"

"Yes'm."

"What you been doing down there?"

"Noth'n."

"*Noth'n!*"

"No'm."

"Well, then, what possessed you to go down there, this time of night?"

"I don't know'm."

"You don't *know?* Don't answer me that way, Tom, I want to know what you been *doing* down there?"

"I hain't been doing a single thing, Aunt Sally, I hope to gracious if I have."

[5]From 1834 to 1890, present-day Oklahoma was designated Indian Territory. During those years it was frequently used by outlaws as a refuge from state and federal authorites.

I reckoned she'd let me go, now, and as a generl thing she would; but I spose there was so many strange things going on she was just in a sweat about every little thing that warn't yard-stick straight; so she says, very decided:

"You just march into that setting-room and stay there till I come. You been up to something you no business to, and I lay I'll find out what it is before *I'm* done with you."

So she went away as I opened the door and walked into the setting-room. My, but there was a crowd there! Fifteen farmers, and every one of them had a gun. I was most powerful sick, and slunk to a chair and set down. They was setting around, some of them talking a little, in a low voice, and all of them fidgety and uneasy, but trying to look like they warn't; but I knowed they was, because they was always taking off their hats, and putting them on, and scratching their heads, and changing their seats, and fumbling with their buttons. I warn't easy myself, but I didn't take my hat off, all the same.

I did wish Aunt Sally would come, and get done with me, and lick me, if she wanted to, and let me get away and tell Tom how we'd overdone this thing, and what a thundering hornet's nest we'd got ourselves into, so we could stop fooling around, straight-off, and clear out with Jim before these rips got out of patience and come for us.

At last she come, and begun to ask me questions, but I *couldn't* answer them straight, I didn't know which end of me was up; because these men was in such a fidget now, that some was wanting to start right *now* and lay for them desperadoes, and saying it warn't but a few minutes to midnight; and others was trying to get them to hold on and wait for the sheep-signal; and here was aunty pegging away at the questions, and me a shaking all over and ready to sink down in my tracks I was that scared; and the place getting hotter and hotter, and the butter beginning to melt and run down my neck and behind my ears; and pretty soon, when one of them says, "*I'm* for going and getting in the cabin *first*, and right *now*, and catching them when they come," I most dropped; and a streak of butter come a trickling down my forehead, and Aunt Sally she see it, and turns white as a sheet, and says:

"For the land's sake what *is* the matter with the child!—he's got the brain fever as shore as you're born, and they're oozing out!"

And everybody runs to see, and she snatches off my hat, and out comes the bread, and what was left of the butter, and she grabbed me, and hugged me, and says:

"Oh, what a turn you did give me! and how glad and grateful I am it ain't no worse; for luck's against us, and it never rains but it pours, and when I see that truck I thought we'd lost you, for I knowed by the color and all, it was just like your brains would be if—Dear, dear, whyd'nt you *tell* me that was what you'd been down there for, *I* wouldn't a cared. Now cler out to bed, and don't lemme see no more of you till morning!"

I was up stairs in a second, and down the lightning-rod in another one, and shinning through the dark for the lean-to. I couldn't hardly get my words out, I was so anxious; but I told Tom as quick as I could, we must jump for it, now, and not a minute to lose—the house full of men, yonder, with guns!

His eyes just blazed; and he says:

"No!—is that so? *Ain't* it bully! Why, Huck, if it was to do over again, I bet I could fetch two hundred! If we could put it off till——"

"Hurry! *hurry!*" I says, "Where's Jim?"

"Right at your elbow; if you reach out your arm you can touch him. He's dressed, and everything's ready. Now we'll slide out and give the sheep-signal."

But then we heard the tramp of men coming to the door, and heard them begin to fumble with the padlock; and heard a man say:

"I *told* you we'd be too soon; they haven't come—the door is locked. Here, I'll lock some of you in the cabin and you lay for 'em in the dark and kill 'em when they come; and the rest scatter around a piece, and listen if you can hear 'em coming."

So in they come, but couldn't see us in the dark, and most trod on us whilst we was hustling to get under the bed. But we got under all right, and out through the hole, swift but soft—Jim first, me next, and Tom last, which was according to Tom's orders. Now we was in the lean-to, and heard trampings close by outside. So we crept to the door, and Tom stopped us there and put his eye to the crack, but couldn't make out nothing, it was so dark; and whispered and said he would listen for the steps to get further, and when he nudged us Jim must glide out first, and him last. So he set his ear to the crack and listened, and listened, and listened, and the steps a scraping around, out there, all the time; and at last he nudged us, and we slid out, and stooped down, not breathing, and not making the least noise, and slipped stealthy towards the fence, in Injun file,[1] and got to it, all right, and me and Jim over it; but Tom's britches catched fast on a splinter on the top rail, and then he hear the steps coming, so he had to pull loose, which snapped the splinter and made a noise; and as he dropped in our tracks and started, somebody sings out:

"Who's that? Answer, or I'll shoot!"

But we didn't answer; we just unfurled our heels and shoved. Then there was a rush, and a *bang, bang, bang!* and the bullets fairly whizzed around us! We heard them sing out:

"Here they are! They've broke for the river! after 'em boys! And turn loose the dogs!"

So here they come, full tilt. We could hear them, because they wore boots, and yelled, but we didn't wear no boots, and didn't yell. We was in the path to the mill; and when they got pretty close onto us, we dodged in the bush and let them go by, and then dropped in behind them. They'd had all the dogs shut up, so they wouldn't scare off the robbers; but by this time somebody had let them loose, and here they come, making pow-wow enough for a million; but they was our dogs; so we stopped in our tracks till they catch up; and when they see it warn't nobody but us, and no excitement to offer them, they only just said howdy, and tore right ahead towards the shouting and clattering; and then we up stream again and whizzed along after them till we was nearly to the mill, and then struck up through the bush to where my canoe was tied, and hopped in and pulled for dear life towards the middle of the river, but didn't make no more noise than we was obleeged to. Then we struck out, easy and comfortable, for the island where my raft was; and we could hear them yelling and barking at each other all up and down the bank, till we was so far away the sounds got dim and died out. And when we stepped onto the raft, I says:

"*Now*, old Jim, you're a free man *again*, and I bet you won't ever be a slave nomore."

"En a mighty good job it wuz, too. Huck. It 'uz planned beautiful, en it 'uz *done* beautiful; en dey ain't *nobody* kin git up a plan dat's mo' mixed-up en splendid den what dat one wuz."

We was all as glad as we could be, but Tom was the gladdest of all, because he had a bullet in the calf of his leg.

---

[1]Single file.

When me and Jim heard that, we didn't feel so brash as what we did before. It was hurting him considerable, and bleeding; so we laid him in the wigwam and tore up one of the duke's shirts for to bandage him, but he says:

"Gimme the rags, I can do it myself. Don't stop, now; don't fool around here, and the evasion booming along so handsome; man the sweeps, and set her loose! Boys, we done it elegant—'deed we did. I wish *we'd* a had the handling of Louis XVI., there wouldn't a been no "Son of Saint Louis, ascend to heaven!"[2] wrote down in *his* biography: no, sir, we'd a whooped him over the *border*—that's what we'd a done with *him*—and done it just as slick as nothing at all, too. Man the sweeps—man the sweeps!"

But me and Jim was consulting—and thinking. And after we'd thought a minute, I says:

"Say it, Jim."

So he says:

"Well, den, dis is de way it look to me, Huck. Ef it wuz *him* dat 'uz bein' sot free, en one er de boys wuz to git shot, would he say, 'Go on en save me, nemmine 'bout a doctor f'r to save dis one? Is dat like Mars Tom Sawyer? Would he say dat? You *bet* he wouldn't! *Well,* den, is *Jim* gwyne to say it? No, sah—I doan' budge a step out'n dis place, 'dout a *doctor;* not if it's forty year!"

I knowed he was white inside, and I reckoned he'd say what he did say—so it was all right, now, and I told Tom I was agoing for a doctor. He raised considerble row about it, but me and Jim stuck to it and wouldn't budge; so he was for crawling out and setting the raft loose himself; but we wouldn't let him. Then he give us a piece of his mind—but it didn't do no good.

So when he see me getting the canoe ready, he says:

"Well, then, if you're bound to go, I'll tell you the way to do, when you get to the village. Shut the door, and blindfold the doctor tight and fast, and make him swear to be silent as the grave, and put a purse full of gold in his hand, and then take and lead him all around the back alleys and everywheres, in the dark, and then fetch him here in the canoe, in a roundabout way amongst the islands, and search him and take his chalk away from him, and don't give it back to him till you get him back to the village, or else he will chalk this raft so he can find it again. It's the way they all do."

So I said I would, and left, and Jim was to hide in the woods when he see the doctor coming, till he was gone again.

CHAPTER XLI

The doctor was an old man; a very nice, kind-looking old man, when I got him up. I told him me and my brother was over on Spanish Island hunting, yesterday afternoon, and camped on a piece of a raft we found, and about midnight he must a kicked his gun in his dreams, for it went off and shot him in the leg, and we wanted him to go over there and fix it and not say nothing about it, nor let anybody know, because we wanted to come home this evening, and surprise the folks.

"Who is your folks?" he says.

"The Phelpses, down yonder."

"Oh," he says. And after a minute, he says: "How'd you say he got shot?"

---

[2] A quotation from *The French Revolution* (1837), by the Scottish historian Thomas Carlyle (1795–1881).

"He had a dream," I says, "and it shot him."

"Singular dream," he says.

So he lit up his lantern, and got his saddle-bags, and we started. But when he see the canoe, he didn't like the look of her—said she was big enough for one, but didn't look pretty safe for two. I says:

"Oh, you needn't be afeard, sir, she carried the three of us, easy enough."

"What three?"

"Why, me and Sid, and—and—and *the guns;* that's what I mean."

"Oh," he says.

But he put his foot on the gunnel, and rocked her; and shook his head, and said he reckoned he'd look around for a bigger one. But they was all locked and chained; so he took my canoe, and said for me to wait till he come back, or I could hunt around further, or maybe I better go down home and get them ready for the surprise, if I wanted to. But I said I didn't; so I told him just how to find the raft, and then he started.

I struck an idea, pretty soon. I says to myself, spos'n he can't fix that leg just in three shakes of a sheep's tail, as the saying is? spos'n it takes him three or four days? What are we going to do?—lay around there till he lets the cat out of the bag? No, sir, I know what *I'll* do. I'll wait, and when he comes back, if he says he's got to go any more, I'll get down there, too, if I swim; and we'll take and tie him, and keep him, and shove out down the river; and when Tom's done with him, we'll give him what it's worth, or all we got, and then let him get ashore.

So then I crept into a lumber pile to get some sleep; and next time I waked up the sun was away up over my head! I shot out and went for the doctor's house, but they told me he'd gone away in the night, some time or other, and warn't back yet. Well, thinks I, that looks powerful bad for Tom, and I'll dig out for the island, right off. So away I shoved, and turned the corner, and nearly rammed my head into Uncle Silas's stomach! He says:

"Why, *Tom!* Where you been all this time, you rascal?"

"I hain't been nowheres," I says, "only just hunting for the runaway nigger—me and Sid."

"Why, where ever did you go?" he says. "Your aunt's been mighty uneasy."

"She needn't," I says, "because we was all right. We followed the men and the dogs, but they out-run us, and we lost them; but we thought we heard them on the water, so we got a canoe and took out after them, and crossed over but couldn't find nothing of them; so we cruised along up-shore till we got kind of tired and beat out; and tied up the canoe and went to sleep, and never waked up till about an hour ago, then we paddled over here to hear the news, and Sid's at the post-office to see what he can hear, and I'm branching out to get something to eat for us, and then we're going home."

So then we went to the post-office to get "Sid"; but just as I suspicioned, he warn't there; so the old man he got a letter out of the office, and we waited a while longer but Sid didn't come; so the old man said come along, let Sid foot it home, or canoe-it, when he got done fooling around—but we would ride. I couldn't get him to let me stay and wait for Sid; and he said there warn't no use in it, and I must come along, and let Aunt Sally see we was all right.

When we got home, Aunt Sally was that glad to see me she laughed and cried both, and hugged me, and give me one of them lickings of hern that don't amount to shucks, and said she serve Sid the same when he come.

And the place was plumb full of farmers and farmers' wives, to dinner; and such another clack a body never heard. Old Mrs. Hotchkiss was the worst; her tongue was agoing all the time. She says:

"Well, Sister Phelps, I've ransacked that-air cabin over an' I b'lieve the nigger was crazy. I says so to Sister Damrell—didn't I, Sister Damrell?—s'I, he's crazy, s'I—them's the very words I said. You all hearn me: he's crazy, s'I; everything shows it, s'I. Look as that-air grindstone, s'I; want to tell *me* 't any cretur 'ts in his right mind's 'again' to scrabble all them crazy things onto a grindstone, s'I? Here sich 'n' sich a person busted his heart; 'n' here so 'n' so pegged along for thirty-seven year, 'n' all that—natcherl son o' Louis somebody, 'n' sich everlast'n rubbage. He's plumb crazy, s'I; it's what I says in the fust place, it's what I says in the middle, 'n' it's what I says last 'n' all the time—the nigger's crazy—crazy's Nebokoodneezer,[1] s'I."

"An' look at that air-ladder made out'n rags, Sister Hotchkiss," says old Mrs. Damrell, "what in the name o' goodness *could* he ever want of——"

"The very words I was a-sayin' no longer ago th'n this minute to Sister Utterback, 'n' she'll tell you so herself. Sh-she, look at that-air rag ladder, sh-she; 'n' s'I, yes, *look* at it, s'I—what *could* he a wanted of it, s'I. Sh-she, Sister Hotchkiss, sh-she——"

"But how in the nation'd they ever *git* that grindstone *in* there, *anyway?* 'n' who dug that-air *hole?* 'n' who——"

"My very *words*, Brer Penrod! I was a-sayin'—pass that-air sasser o' m'lasses, won't ye?—I was a-sayin' to Sister Dunlap, jist this minute, how *did* they git that grindstone in there, s'I. Without *help*, mind you—'thout *help! Thar's* wher' 'tis. Don't tell *me*, s'I; there *wuz* help, s'I; 'n' ther' wuz a *plenty* help, too, s'I; ther's ben a *dozen* a-helpin' that nigger, 'n' I lay I'd skin every last nigger on this place, but *I'd* find out who done it, s'I; 'n' moreover, s'I——"

"A *dozen* says you!—*forty* couldn't a done everything that's been done. Look at them case-knife saws and things, how tedious they've been made; look at that bed-leg sawed off with 'm, a week's work for six men; look at that nigger made out'n straw on the bed; and look at——"

"You may *well* say it, Brer Hightower! It's jist as I was a-sayin' to Brer Phelps, his own self. S'e, what do *you* think of it, Sister Hotchkiss, s'e? think o' what, Brer Phelps, s'I? think o' that bed-leg sawed off that a way, s'e? *think* of it, s'I? I lay it never sawed *itself* off, s'I—somebody *sawed* it, s'I; that's my opinion, take it or leave it, it mayn't be no 'count, s'I, but sich as 'tis, it's my opinion, s'I, 'n' if anybody k'n start a better one, s'I, let him *do* it, s'I, that's all. I says to Sister Dunlap, s'I——"

"Why, dog my cats, they must a ben a house-ful o'niggers in there every night for four weeks, to a done all that work, Sister Phelps. Look at that shirt—every last inch of it kivered over with secret African writ'n done with blood! Must a ben a raft uv'm at it right along, all the time, almost. Why, I'd give two dollars to have it read to me; 'n' as for the niggers that wrote it, I 'low I'd take 'n' lash 'm t'll——"

"People to *help* him, Brother Marples! Well, I reckon you'd *think* so, if you'd a been in this house for a while back. Why, they've stole everything they could lay their hands on—and we a watching, all the time, mind you. They stole that shirt right off o' the line! and as for that sheet they made the rag ladder out of ther' ain't no telling how many times they *didn't* steal that; and flour, and candles, and candlesticks, and spoons, and the old warming-pan, and most a thousand things that I disremember, now, and my new calico dress; and me, and Silas,

[1]Nebuchadnezzar, King of Babylon, was deprived of his reason for failure to honor the Lord. Daniel 4:29–37.

and my Sid and Tom on the constant watch day *and* night, as I was'a telling you, and not a one of us could catch hide nor hair, nor sight nor sound of them; and here at the last minute, lo and behold you, they slides right in under our noses, and fools us, and not only fools *us* but the Injun Territory robbers too, and actly gets *away* with that nigger, safe and sound, and that with sixteen men and twenty-two dogs right on their very heels at that very time! I tell you, it just bangs anything I ever *heard* of. Why, *spirits* couldn't a done better, and been no smarter. And I reckon they must a *been* sperits—because, *you* know our dogs, and ther' ain't no better; well, them dogs never even got on the *track* of'm, once! You explain *that* to me, if you can!—*any* of you!"

"Well, it does beat——"

"Laws alive, I never——"

"So help me, I wouldn't a be——"

"*House* thieves as well as——"

"Goodnessgraciousakes, I'd a ben afeard to *live* in sich a——"

"'Fraid to *live!*—why, I was that scared I dasn't hardly go to bed, or get up, or lay down, or *set* down, Sister Ridgeway. Why, they'd steal the very—why, goodness sakes, you can guess what kind of a fluster *I* was in by the time midnight come, last night. I hope to gracious if I warn't afraid they'd steal some o'the family! I was just to that pass, I didn't have no reasoning faculties no more. It looks foolish enough, *now*, in the day-time; but I says to myself, there's my two poor boys asleep, 'way up stairs in that lonesome room, and I declare to goodness I was that uneasy 't I crep' up there and locked 'em in! I *did*. And anybody would. Because, you know, when you get scared, that way, and it keeps running on, and getting worse and worse, all the time, and your wits gets to addling, and you get to doing all sorts o' wild things, and by-and-by you think to yourself, spos'n *I* was a boy, and was away up there, and the door ain't locked, and you—" She stopped, looking kind of wondering, and then she turned her head around slow, and when her eye lit on me—I got up and took a walk.

Says I to myself, I can explain better how we come to not be in that room this morning, if I go out to one side and study over it a little. So I done it. But I dasn't go fur, or she'd a sent for me. And when it was late in the day, the people all went, and then I come in and told her the noise and shooting waked up me and "Sid," and the door was locked, and we wanted to see the fun, so we went down the lightning-rod, and both of us got hurt a little, and we didn't never want to try *that* no more. And then I went on and told her all what I told Uncle Silas before; and then she said she'd forgive us, and maybe it was all right enough anyway, and about what a body might expect of boys, for all boys was a pretty harum-scarum lot, as fur as she could see; and so, as long as no harm hadn't come of it, she judged she better put in her time being grateful we was alive and well and she had us still, stead of fretting over what was past and done. So then she kissed me, and patted me on the head, and dropped into a kind of a brown study; and pretty soon jumps up, and says:

"Why, lawsamercy, it's most night, and Sid not come yet! What *has* become of that boy?"

I see my chance; so I skips and says:

"I'll run right up to town and get him," I says.

"No you won't," she says. "You'll stay right wher' you are; *one's* enough to be lost at a time. If he ain't here to supper, your uncle'll go."

Well, he warn't there to supper; so right after supper uncle went.

He come back about ten, a little bit uneasy; hadn't run across Tom's track. Aunt Sally was a good *deal* uneasy; but Uncle Silas he said there warn't no occasion to be—boys will be boys, he said, and you'll see this one turn up in the morning, all sound and right. So she had to be satisfied. But she said she'd set up for him a while, anyway, and keep a light burning, so he could see it.

And then when I went up to bed she come up with me and fetched her candle, and tucked me in, and mothered me so good I felt mean, and like I couldn't look her in the face; and she sat down on the bed and talked with me a long time, and said what a splendid boy Sid was, and didn't seem to want to ever stop talking about him; and kept asking me every now and then, if I reckoned he could a got lost, or hurt, or maybe drownded, and might be laying at this minute, somewheres, suffering or dead, and she not by him to help him, and so the tears would drip down, silent, and I would tell her that Sid was all right, and would be home in the morning, sure; and she would squeeze my hand, or maybe kiss me, and tell me to say it again, and keep on saying it, because it done her good, and she was in so much trouble. And when she was going away, she looked down in my eyes, so steady and gentle, and says:

"The door ain't going to be locked, Tom; and there's the window and the rod; but you'll be good, *won't* you? And you won't go? For *my* sake."

Laws knows I *wanted* to go, bad enough, to see about Tom, and was all intending to go; but after that, I wouldn't a went, not for kingdoms.

But she was on my mind, and Tom was on my mind; so I slept very restless. And twice I went down the rod, away in the night, and slipped around front, and see her setting there by her candle in the window with her eyes towards the road and the tears in them; and I wished I could do something for her, but I couldn't, only to swear that I wouldn't never do nothing to grieve her any more. And the third time, I waked up at dawn, and slid down, and she was there yet, and her candle was most out, and her old gray head was resting on her hand, and she was asleep.

CHAPTER XLII

The old man was up town again, before breakfast, but couldn't get no track of Tom; and both of them set at the table, thinking, and not saying nothing, and looking mournful, and their coffee getting cold, and not eating anything. And by-and-by the old man says:

"Did I give you the letter?"

"What letter?"

"The one I got yesterday out of the post-office."

"No, you didn't give me no letter."

"Well, I must a forgot it."

So he rummaged his pockets, and then went off somewheres where he had laid it down, and fetched it, and give it to her. She says:

"Why, it's from St. Petersburg—it's from Sis."

I allowed another walk would do me good; but I couldn't stir. But before she could break it open, she dropped and run—for she see something. And so did I. It was Tom Sawyer on a mattress; and that old doctor; and Jim, in *her* calico dress, with his hands tied behind him; and a lot of people. I hid the letter behind the first thing that come handy, and rushed. She flung herself at Tom, crying, and says:

"Oh, he's dead, he's dead, I know he's dead!"

And Tom he turned his head a little, and muttered something or other, which showed he warn't in his right mind; then she flung up her hands, and says:

"He's alive, thank God! And that's enough!" and she snatched a kiss of him, and flew for the house to get the bed ready, and scattering orders right and left at the niggers and everybody else, as fast as her tongue could go, every jump of the way.

I followed the men to see what they was going to do with Jim; and the old doctor and Uncle Silas followed after Tom into the house. The men was very huffy, and some of them wanted to hang Jim, for an example to all the other niggers around there, so they wouldn't be trying to run away, like Jim done, and making such a raft of trouble, and keeping a whole family scared most to death for days and nights. But the others said, don't do it, it wouldn't answer at all, he ain't our nigger, and his owner would turn up and make us pay for him, sure. So that cooled them down a little, because the people that's always the most anxious for to hang a nigger that hain't done just right, is always the very ones that ain't the most anxious to pay for him when they've got their satisfaction out of him.

They cussed Jim considerble, though, and give him a cuff or two, side the head, once in a while, but Jim never said nothing, and he never let on to know me, and they took him to the same cabin, and put his own clothes on him, and chained him again, and not to no bed-leg, this time, but to a big staple drove into the bottom log, and chained his hands, too, and both legs, and said he warn't to have nothing but bread and water to eat, after this, till his owner come or he was sold at auction, because he didn't come in a certain length of time, and filled up our hole, and said a couple of farmers with guns must stand watch around about the cabin every night, and a bull-dog tied to the door in the day-time; and about this time they was through with the job and was tapering off with a kind of generl good-bye cussing, and then the old doctor comes and takes a look, and says:

"Don't be no rougher on him than you're obleeged to, because he ain't a bad nigger. When I got to where I found the boy, I see I couldn't cut the bullet out without some help, and he warn't in no condition for me to leave, to go and get help; and he got a little worse and a little worse, and after a long time he went out of his head, and wouldn't let me come anigh him, any more, and said if I chalked his raft he'd kill me, and no end of wild foolishness like that, and I see I couldn't do anything at all with him; so I says, I got to have *help*, somehow; and the minute I says it, out crawls this nigger from somewheres, and says he'll help, and he done it, too, and done it very well. Of course I judged he must be a runaway nigger, and there I *was!* and there I had to stick, right straight along all the rest of the days, and all night. It was a fix, I tell you! I had a couple of patients with the chills, and of course I'd of liked to run up to town and see them, but I dasn't because the nigger might get away, and then I'd be to blame; and yet never a skiff come close enough for me to hail. So there I had to stick, plumb till daylight this morning' and I never see a nigger that was a better nuss or faithfuller, and yet he was resking his freedom to do it, and was all tired out, too, and I see plain enough he'd been worked main hard, lately. I liked the nigger for that; I tell you, gentlemen, a nigger like that is worth a thousand dollars—and kind treatment, too. I had everything I needed, and the boy was doing as well there as he would a done at home—better, maybe, because it was so quiet; but there I *was*, with both of 'm on my hands; and there I had to stick, till about dawn this morning; then some men in a skiff come by, and as good luck would have it, the nigger was setting by the pallet with his head propped on his knees, sound asleep; so I motioned them in, quiet, and they slipped up on him and grabbed him and tied him before he knowed what he was about, and we never had no trouble. And the boy being in a kind of a flighty sleep, too, we muffled the oars and hitched the raft on, and towed her over very nice and quiet, and the nigger never made the least row nor said a word, from the start. He ain't no bad nigger, gentlemen; that's what I think about him."

Somebody says:

"Well, it sounds very good, doctor, I'm obleeged to say."

Then the others softened up a little, too, and I was mightly thankful to that old doctor for doing Jim that good turn; and I was glad it was according to my judgment of him, too; because I thought he had a good heart in him and was a good man, the first time I see him. Then they all agreed that Jim had acted very well, and was deserving to have some notice took of it, and reward. So every one of them promised, right out and hearty, that they wouldn't cuss him no more.

Then they come out and locked him up. I hoped they was going to say he could have one or two of the chains took off, because they was rotten heavy, or could have meat and greens with his bread and water, but they didn't think of it, and I reckoned it warn't best for me to mix in, but I judged I'd get the doctor's yarn to Aunt Sally, somehow or other, as soon as I'd got through the breakers that was laying just ahead of me. Explanations, I mean, of how I forgot to mention about Sid being shot, when I was telling how him and me put in that dratted night paddling around hunting the runaway nigger.

But I had plenty time. Aunt Sally she stuck to the sick-room all day and all night; and every time I see Uncle Silas mooning around, I dodged him.

Next morning I heard Tom was a good deal better, and they said Aunt Sally was gone to get a nap. So I slips to the sick-room, and if I found him awake I reckoned we could put up a yarn for the family that would wash. But he was sleeping, and sleeping very peaceful, too; and pale, not fire-faced the way he was when he come. So I set down and laid for him to wake. In about a half an hour, Aunt Sally comes gliding in, and there I was, up a stump again! She motioned me to be still, and set down by me, and begun to whisper, and said we could all be joyful now, because all the symptoms was first rate, and he'd been sleeping like that for ever so long, and looking better and peacefuller all the time, and ten to one he'd wake up in his right mind.

So we set there watching, and by-and-by he stirs a bit, and opened his eyes very natural, and takes a look, and says:

"Hello, why I'm at *home!* How's that? Where's the raft?"

"It's all right," I says.

"And *Jim?*"

"The same," I says, but couldn't say it pretty brash. But he never noticed, but says:

"Good! Splendid! *Now* we're all right and safe! Did you tell Aunty?"

I was going to say yes; but she chipped in and says:

"About what, Sid?"

"Why, about the way the whole thing was done."

"What whole thing?"

"Why, *the* whole thing. There ain't but one; how we set the runaway nigger free—me and Tom."

"Good land! Set the run—What *is* the child talking about! Dear, dear, out of his head again!"

"*No,* I ain't out of my HEAD; I know all what I'm talking about. We *did* set him free—me and Tom. We laid out to do it, and we *done* it. And we done it elegant, too." He'd got a start, and she never checked him up, just set and stared and stared, and let him clip along, and I see it warn't no use for *me* to put it. "Why, Aunty, it cost us a power of work—weeks of it—hours and hours, every night, whilst you was all asleep. And we had to steal candles, and the sheet, and the shirt, and your dress, and spoons, and tin plates, and case-knives, and the warming-pan, and the grindstone, and flour, and just no end of things, and you can't think what work it was to make the saws and pens, and inscriptions, and one thing or another, and you can't think *half* the fun it was. And we had to make up the pictures of coffins and things, and nonnamous letters from the robbers, and get up and down the lightning-rod, and dig the hole into the cabin, and make the rope-ladder and send it in cooked up in a pie, and send in spoons and things to work with, in your apron pocket"——

"Mercy sakes!"

——"and load up the cabin with rats and snakes and so on, for company for Jim; and then you kept Tom here so long with the butter in his hat that you come near spilling the whole business, because the men come before we was out of the cabin, and we had to rush, and they heard us and let drive at us, and I got my share, and we dodged out of the path and let them go by, and when the dogs come they warn't interested in us, but went for the most noise, and we got our canoe, and made for the raft, and was all safe, and Jim was a free man, and we done it all by ourselves, and *wasn't* it bully, Aunty!"

"Well, I never heard the likes of it in all my born days! So it was *you*, you little rapscallions, that's been making all this trouble, and turned everybody's wits clean inside out and scared us all most to death. I've as good a notion as ever I had in my life, to take it out o' you this very minute. To think, here I've been, night after night, a—*you* just get well once, you young scamp, and I lay I'll tan the Old Harry[1] out o' both o' ye!"

But Tom, he *was* so proud and joyful, he just *couldn't* hold in, and his tongue just *went* it—she a-chipping in, and spitting fire all along, and both of them going it at once, like a cat-convention; and she says:

"*Well*, you get all the enjoyment you can out of it *now*, for mind I tell you if I catch you meddling with him again——"

"Meddling with *who?*" Tom says, dropping his smile and looking surprised.

"With *who?* Why, the runaway nigger, of course. Who'd you reckon?"

Tom looks at me very grave, and says:

"Tom, didn't you just tell me he was all right? Hasn't he got away?"

"*Him?*" says Aunt Sally; "the runaway nigger? 'Deed he hasn't. They've got him back, safe and sound, and he's in that cabin again, on bread and water, and loaded down with chains, till he's claimed or sold!"

Tom rose square up in bed, with his eye hot, and his nostrils opening and shutting like gills, and sings out to me:

"They hain't no *right* to shut him up! *Shove!*—and don't you lose a minute. Turn him loose! he ain't no slave; he's as free as any cretur that walks this earth!"

"What *does* the child mean?"

"I mean every word I *say*, Aunt Sally, and if somebody don't go, *I'll* go. I've knowed him all his life, and so has Tom, there. Old Miss Watson died two months ago, and she was ashamed she ever was going to sell him down the river, and *said* so; and she set him free in her will."

"Then what on earth did *you* want to set him free for, seeing he was already free?"

[1] The Devil.

"Well, that *is* a question, I must say; and *just* like women! Why, I wanted the *adventure* of it; and I'd a waded neck-deep in blood to—goodness alive, AUNT POLLY!"

If she warn't standing right there, just inside the door, looking as sweet and contented as an angel half-full of pie, I wish I may never!

Aunt Sally jumped for her, and most hugged the head off of her, and cried over her, and I found a good enough place for me under the bed, for it was getting pretty sultry, for *us*, seemed to me. And I peeped out, and in a little while Tom's Aunt Polly shook herself loose and stood there looking across at Tom over her spectacles—kind of grinding him into the earth, you know. And then she says:

"Yes, you *better* turn y'r head away—I would if I was you, Tom."

"Oh, deary me!" says Aunt Sally; "*is* he changed so? Why, that ain't *Tom*, it's Sid; Tom's—Tom's—why, where is Tom? He was here a minute ago."

"You mean where's Huck *Finn*—that's what you mean! I reckon I hain't raised such a scamp as my Tom all these years, not to know him when I *see* him. That *would* be a pretty howdy-do. Come out from under that bed, Huck Finn."

So I done it. But not feeling brash.

Aunt Sally she was one of the mixed-upset looking persons I ever see; except one, and that was Uncle Silas, when he come in, and they told it all to him. It kind of made him drunk, as you may say, and he didn't know nothing at all the rest of the day, and preached a prayer-meeting sermon that night that give him a rattling ruputation, because the oldest man in the world couldn't a understood it. So Tom's Aunt Polly, she told all about who I was, and what; and I had to up and tell how I was in such a tight place that when Mrs. Phelps took me for Tom Sawyer—she chipped in and says, "Oh, go on and call me Aunt Sally, I'm used to it, now, and 'tain't no need to change"——that when Aunt Sally took me for Tom Sawyer, I had to stand it—there warn't no other way, and I knowed he wouldn't mind, because it would be nuts for him, being a mystery, and he'd make an adventure out of it and be perfectly satisfied. And so it turned out, and he let on to be Sid, and made things as soft as he could for me.

And his Aunt Polly she said Tom was right about old Miss Watson setting Jim free in her will; and so, sure enough, Tom Sawyer had gone and took all that trouble and bother to set a free nigger free! and I couldn't ever understand, before, until that minute and that talk, how he *could* help a body set a nigger free, with his bringing-up.

Well, Aunt Polly she said that when Aunt Sally wrote to her that Tom and *Sid* had come, all right and safe, she says to herself:

"Look at that, now! I might have expected it, letting him go off that way without anybody to watch him. So now I got to go and trapse all the way down the river, eleven hundred mile, and find out what the creetur's up to, *this* time; as long as I couldn't seem to get any answer out of you about it."

"Why, I never heard nothing from you," says Aunt Sally.

"Well, I wonder! Why, I wrote to you twice, to ask you what you could mean by Sid being here."

"Well, I never got 'em, Sis."

Aunt Polly, she turns around slow and severe, and says:

"You, Tom!"

"Well—*what?*" he says, kind of pettish.

"Don't you what *me*, you impudent thing—hand out them letters."

"What letters?"

"*Them* letters. I be bound, if I have to take aholt of you I'll——"

"They're in the trunk. There, now. And they're just the same as they was when I got them out of the office. I hain't looked into them, I hain't touched them. But I knowed they'd make trouble, and I thought if you warn't in no hurry, I'd——"

"Well, you *do* need skinning, there ain't no mistake about it. And I wrote another one to tell you I was coming; and I spose he——"

"No, it come yesterday; I hain't read it yet, but *it's* all right, I've got that one."

I wanted to offer to bet two dollars she hadn't, but I reckoned maybe it was just as safe to not to. So, I never said nothing.

CHAPTER THE LAST

The first time I catched Tom, private, I asked him what was his idea, time of the evasion?—what it was he'd planned to do if the evasion worked all right and he managed to set a nigger free that was already free before? And he said, what he had planned in his head, from the start, if we got Jim out all safe, was for us to run him down the river, on the raft, and have adventures plumb to the mouth of the river, and then tell him about his being free, and take him back up home on a steamboat, in style, and pay him for his lost time, and write word ahead and get out all the niggers around, and have them waltz him into town with a torchlight procession and a brass band, and then he would be a hero, and so would we. But I reckoned it was about as well the way it was.

We had Jim out of the chains in no time, and when Aunt Polly and Uncle Silas and Aunt Sally found out how good he helped the doctor nurse Tom, they made a heap of fuss over him, and fixed him up prime, and give him all he wanted to eat, and a good time, and nothing to do. And we had him up to the sick-room; and had a high talk; and Tom give Jim forty dollars for being prisoner for us so patient, and doing it up so good, and Jim was pleased most to death, and busted out, and says:

"*Dah*, now, Huck, what I tell you?—what I tell you up dah on Jackson islan'? I *tole* you I got a hairy breas', en what's de sign un it; en I *tole* you I ben rich wunst, en gwineter to be rich *agin;* en it's come true; en heah she *is! Dah*, now! doan' talk to *me*—signs is *signs*, mine I tell you; en I knowed jis' 's well 'at I 'uz gwineter be rich agin as I's a stannin' heah dis minute!"

And then Tom he talked along, and talked along, and says le's all three slide out of here, one of these nights, and get an outfit, and go for howling adventures amongst the Injuns, over in the Terrority, for a couple of weeks or two; and I says, all right, that suits me, but I ain't got no money for to buy the outfit, and I reckon I couldn't get none from home, because it's likely pap's been back before now, and got it all away from Judge Thatcher and drunk it up.

"No he hain't," Tom says; "it's all there, yet—six thousand dollars and more; and your pap hain't ever been back since. Hadn't when I come away, anyhow."

Jim says, kind of solemn:

"He ain't a comin' back no mo', Huck."

I says:

"Why, Jim?"

"Nemmine why, Huck—but he ain't comin' back no mo'."

But I kept at him; so at last he says:

"Doan' you 'member de house dat was float'n down de river, en dey wuz a man in dah, kivered up, en I went in en unkivered him and didn't let you come in? Well, den, you k'n git yo' money when you wants it; kase dat wuz him."

Tom's most well, now, and got his bullet around his neck on a watch-guard for a watch, and is always seeing what time it is, and so there ain't nothing more to write about, and I am rotten glad of it, because if I'd a knowed what a trouble it was to make a book I wouldn't a tackled it and aint' agoing to no more. But I reckon I got to light out for the Territory ahead of the rest, because Aunt Sally she's going to adopt me and sivilize me and I can't stand it. I been there before.

THE END.   YOURS TRULY, HUCK FINN.

1876–1883   1884, 1885

FENIMORE COOPER'S LITERARY OFFENCES[1]

The *Pathfinder* and *The Deerslayer* stand at the head of Cooper's novels as artistic creations. There are others of his works which contain parts as perfect as are to be found in these, and scenes even more thrilling. Not one can be compared with either of them as a finished whole.

The defects in both of these tales are comparatively slight. They were pure works of art.—*Prof. Lounsbury.*[2]

The five tales reveal an extraordinary fulness of invention.

. . . One of the very greatest characters in fiction, "Natty Bumppo." . . .

The craft of the woodsman, the tricks of the trapper, all the delicate art of the forest, were familiar to Cooper from his youth up.—*Prof. Brander Matthews.*[3]

Cooper is the greatest artist in the domain of romantic fiction yet produced by America.—*Wilkie Collins.*[4]

It seems that it was far from right for the Professor of English Literature in Yale, the Professor of English Literature in Columbia, and Wilkie Collins, to deliver opinions on Cooper's literature without having read some of it. It would have been much more decorous to keep silent and let persons talk who have read Cooper.

Cooper's art has some defects. In one place in *Deerslayer,* and in the restricted space of two-thirds of a page, Cooper has scored 114 offences against literary art out of a possible 115. It breaks the record.

There are nineteen rules governing literary art in the domain of romantic fiction—some say twenty-two. In *Deerslayer* Cooper violated eighteen of them. These eighteen require:

1. That a tale shall accomplish something and arrive somewhere. But the *Deerslayer* tale accomplishes nothing and arrives in the air.

2. They require that the episodes of a tale shall be necessary parts of the tale, and shall help to develop it. But as the *Deerslayer* tale is not a tale, and accomplishes nothing and arrives nowhere, the episodes have no rightful place in the work, since there was nothing for them to develop.

[1]James Fenimore Cooper (1789–1851), American novelist, author of the Leatherstocking Tales: *The Deerslayer* (1841), *The Last of the Mohicans* (1826), *The Pathfinder* (1840), *The Pioneers* (1823), and *The Prairie* (1827). In reporting Cooper's "defects" and attempting his literary destruction, Twain frequently employs gross exaggeration, as a close reading of Cooper's novels will show.

[2]Thomas R. Lounsbury (1838–1915), author of *James Fenimore Cooper* (1882).

[3]Brander Matthews (1852–1929), who had recently written a laudatory essay on the occasion of the centennial of Cooper's birth.

[4]English novelist (1824–1889).

3. They require that the personages in a tale shall be alive, except in the case of corpses, and that always the reader shall be able to tell the corpses from the others. But this detail has often been overlooked in the *Deerslayer* tale.

4. They require that the personages in a tale, both dead and alive, shall exhibit a sufficient excuse for being there. But this detail also has been overlooked in the *Deerslayer* tale.

5. They require that when the personages of a tale deal in conversation, the talk shall sound like human talk, and be talk such as human beings would be likely to talk in the given circumstances, and have a discoverable meaning, also a discoverable purpose, and a show of relevancy, and remain in the neighborhood of the subject in hand, and be interesting to the reader, and help out the tale, and stop when the people cannot think of anything more to say. But this requirement has been ignored from the beginning of the *Deerslayer* tale to the end of it.

6. They require that when the author describes the character of a personage in his tale, the conduct and conversation of that personage shall justify said description. But this law gets little or no attention in the *Deerslayer* tale, as "Natty Bumppo's"[5] case will amply prove.

7. They require that when a personage talks like an illustrated, gilt-edged, tree-calf,[6] hand-tooled, seven-dollar Friendship's Offering[7] in the beginning of a paragraph, he shall not talk like a negro minstrel in the end of it. But this rule is flung down and danced upon in the *Deerslayer* tale.

8. They require that crass stupidities shall not be played upon the reader as "the craft of the woodsman, the delicate art of the forest," by either the author or the people in the tale. But this rule is persistently violated in the *Deerslayer* tale.

9. They require that the personages of a tale shall confine themselves to possibilities and let miracles alone; or, if they venture a miracle, the author must so plausibly set it forth as to make it look possible and reasonable. But these rules are not respected in the *Deerslayer* tale.

10. They require that the author shall make the reader feel a deep interest in the personages of his tale and in their fate; and that he shall make the reader love the good people in the tale and hate the bad ones. But the reader of the *Deerslayer* tale dislikes the good people in it, is indifferent to the others, and wishes they would all get drowned together.

11. They require that the characters in a tale shall be so clearly defined that the reader can tell beforehand what each will do in a given emergency. But in the *Deerslayer* tale this rule is vacated.

In addition to these large rules there are some little ones. These require that the author shall

12. *Say* what he is proposing to say, not merely come near it.
13. Use the right word, not its second cousin.
14. Eschew surplusage.
15. Not omit necessary details.
16. Avoid slovenliness of form.
17. Use good grammar.
18. Employ a simple and straightforward style.

[5] The hero of the Leatherstocking Tales.
[6] Calfskin chemically treated to produce a treelike design and used for elegant bookbinding.
[7] Gift books, typically filled with lofty, sentimental literature and high-toned language.

Even these seven are coldly and persistently violated in the *Deerslayer* tale.

Cooper's gift in the way of invention was not a rich endowment: but such as it was he liked to work it, he was pleased with the effects, and indeed he did some quite sweet things with it. In his little box of stage properties he kept six or eight cunning devices, tricks, artifices for his savages and woodsmen to deceive and circumvent each other with, and he was never so happy as when he was working these innocent things and seeing them go. A favorite one was to make a moccasined person tread in the tracks of the moccasined enemy, and thus hide his own trail. Cooper wore out barrels and barrels of moccasins in working that trick. Another stage-property that he pulled out of his box pretty frequently was his broken twig. He prized his broken twig above all the rest of his effects, and worked it the hardest. It is a restful chapter in any book of his when somebody doesn't step on a dry twig and alarm all the reds and whites for two hundred yards around. Every time a Cooper person is in peril, and absolute silence is worth four dollars a minute, he is sure to step on a dry twig. There may be a hundred handier things to step on, but that wouldn't satisfy Cooper. Cooper requires him to turn out and find a dry twig; and if he can't do it, go and borrow one. In fact the Leather Stocking Series ought to have been called the Broken Twig Series.

I am sorry there is not room to put in a few dozen instances of the delicate art of the forest, as practiced by Natty Bumppo and some of the other Cooperian experts. Perhaps we may venture two or three samples. Cooper was a sailor—a naval officer; yet he gravely tells us how a vessel, driving toward a lee[8] shore in a gale, is steered for a particular spot by her skipper because he knows of an *undertow* there which will hold her back against the gale and save her. For just pure woodcraft, or sailorcraft, or whatever it is, isn't that neat? For several years Cooper was daily in the society of artillery, and he ought to have noticed that when a cannon ball strikes the ground it either buries itself or skips a hundred feet or so; skips again a hundred feet or so—and so on, till it finally gets tired and rolls. Now in one place he loses some "females"—as he always calls women— in the edge of a wood near a plain at night in a fog, on purpose to give Bumppo a chance to show off the delicate art of the forest before the reader. These mislaid people are hunting for a fort. They hear a cannon-blast, and a cannon-ball presently comes rolling into the wood and stops at their feet. To the females this suggests nothing. The case is very different with the admirable Bumppo. I wish I may never know peace again if he doesn't strike out promptly and *follow the track* of that cannon-ball across the plain through the dense fog and find the fort. Isn't it a daisy? If Cooper had any real knowledge of Nature's ways of doing things, he had a most delicate art in concealing the fact. For instances: one of his acute Indian experts, Chingachgook[9] (pronounced Chicago, I think), has lost the trail of a person he is tracking through the forest. Apparently that trail is hopelessly lost. Neither you nor I could ever have guessed out the way to find it. It was very different with Chicago. Chicago was not stumped for long. He turned a running stream out of its course, and there, in the slush in its old bed, were that person's moccasin-tracks. The current did not wash them away, as it would have done in all other like cases—no, even the eternal laws of Nature have to vacate when Cooper wants to put up a delicate job of woodcraft on the reader.

We must be a little wary when Brander Matthews tells us that Cooper's books "reveal an extraordinary fulness of invention." As a rule, I am quite willing to

[8]Protected from the wind.
[9]Natty Bumppo's Indian companion in the Leatherstocking Tales.

accept Brander Matthew's literary judgments and applaud his lucid and graceful phrasing of them; but that particular statement needs to be taken with a few tons of salt. Bless your heart, Cooper hadn't any more invention than a horse; and I don't mean a high class horse, either; I mean a clothes horse. It would be very difficult to find a really clever "situation" in Cooper's books; and still more difficult to find one of any kind which he has failed to render absurd by his handling of it. Look at the episodes of "the caves"; and at the celebrated scuffle between Maqua[10] and those others on the table-land a few days later; and at Hurry Harry's[11] queer water-transit from the castle to the ark; and at Deerslayer's half hour with his first corpse; and at the quarrel between Hurry Harry and Deerslayer later; and at—but choose for yourself; you can't go amiss.

If Cooper had been an observer, his inventive faculty would have worked better, not more interestingly, but more rationally, more plausibly. Cooper's proudest creations in the way of "situations" suffer noticeably from the absence of the observer's protecting gift. Cooper's eye was splendidly inaccurate. Cooper seldom saw anything correctly. He saw nearly all things as through a glass eye, darkly. Of course a man who cannot see the commonest little everyday matters accurately is working at a disadvantage when he is constructing a "situation." In the *Deerslayer* tale Cooper has a stream which is fifty feet wide, where it flows out of a lake; it presently narrows to twenty as it meanders along for no given reason, and yet, when a stream acts like that it ought to be required to explain itself. Fourteen pages later the width of the brook's outlet from the lake has suddenly shrunk thirty feet and become the "narrowest part of the stream." This shrinkage is not accounted for. The stream has bends in it, a sure indication that it has alluvial banks, and cuts them; yet these bends are only thirty and fifty feet long. If Cooper had been a nice and punctilious observer he would have noticed that the bends were oftener nine hundred feet long than short of it.

Cooper made the exit of that stream fifty feet wide in the first place, for no particular reason; in the second place, he narrowed it to less than twenty to accommodate some Indians. He bends a "sapling" to the form of an arch over this narrow passage, and conceals six Indians in its foliage. They are "laying" for a settler's scow or ark which is coming up the stream on its way to the lake; it is being hauled against the stiff current by a rope whose stationary end is anchored in the lake; its rate of progress cannot be more than a mile an hour. Cooper describes the ark, but pretty obscurely. In the matter of dimensions "it was little more than a modern canal boat." Let us guess, then, that it was about 140 feet long. It was of "greater breadth than common." Let us guess, then, that it was about sixteen feet wide. This leviathan had been prowling down bends which were but a third as long as itself, and scraping between banks where it had only two feet of space to spare on each side. We cannot too much admire this miracle. A low-roofed log dwelling occupies "two-thirds of the ark's length"—a dwelling ninety feet long and sixteen feet wide, let us say—a kind of vestibule train. The dwelling has two rooms—each forty-five feet long and sixteen feet wide, let us guess. One of them is the bed-room of the Hutter girls, Judith and Hetty; the other is the parlor, in the day time, at night it is papa's bed chamber. The ark is arriving at the stream's exit, now, whose width has been reduced to less than twenty feet to accommodate the Indians—say to eighteen. There is a foot to spare on each side of the boat. Did the Indians notice that there was going to be a tight squeeze there? Did they notice that they could make money by climbing down out of that arched sapling and just stepping

---

[10]Maqua, a Huron chief in *The Last of the Mohicans*.
[11]Henry March, a white hunter in *The Deerslayer*.

aboard when the ark scraped by? No; other Indians would have noticed these things, but Cooper's Indians never notice anything. Cooper thinks they are marvellous creatures for noticing, but he was almost always in error about his Indians. There was seldom a sane one among them.

The ark is 140 feet long; the dwelling is 90 feet long. The idea of the Indians is to drop softly and secretly from the arched sapling to the dwelling as the ark creeps along under it at the rate of a mile an hour, and butcher the family. It will take the ark a minute and half to pass under. It will take the 90-foot dwelling a minute to pass under. Now, then, what did the six Indians do? It would take you thirty years to guess, and even then you would have to give it up, I believe. Therefore, I will tell you what the Indians did. Their chief, a person of quite extraordinary intellect for a Cooper Indian, warily watched the canal boat as it squeezed along under him, and when he had got his calculations fined down to exactly the right shade, as he judged, he let go and dropped, and *missed the house!* That is actually what he did. He missed the house, and landed in the stern of the scow. It was not much of a fall, yet it knocked him silly. He lay there unconscious. If the house had been 97 feet long, he would have made the trip. The fault was Cooper's, not his. The error lay in the construction of the house. Cooper was no architect.

There still remained in the roost five Indians. The boat has passed under and is now out of their reach. Let me explain what the five did—you would not be able to reason it out for yourself. No. 1 jumped for the boat, but fell in the water astern of it. Then No. 2 jumped for the boat, but fell in the water still further astern of it. Then No. 3 jumped for the boat, and fell a good way astern of it. Then No. 4 jumped for the boat, and fell in the water *away* astern. Then even No. 5 made a jump for the boat—for he was a Cooper Indian. In the matter of intellect, the difference between a Cooper Indian and the Indian that stands in front of the cigar shop is not spacious. The scow episode is really a sublime burst of invention; but it does not thrill, because the inaccuracy of the details throws a sort of air of fictitiousness and general improbability over it. This comes of Cooper's inadequacy as an observer.

The reader will find some examples of Cooper's high talent for inaccurate observation in the account of the shooting match in *The Pathfinder*. "A common wrought nail was driven lightly into the target, its head having been first touched with paint." The color of the paint is not stated—an important omission, but Cooper deals freely in important omissions. No, after all, it was not an important omission; for this nail head is *a hundred yards* from the marksman and could not be seen by them at that distance no matter what its color might be. How far can the best eyes see a common house fly? A hundred yards? It is quite impossible. Very well, eyes that cannot see a house fly that is a hundred yards away cannot see an ordinary nail head at that distance, for the size of the two objects is the same. It takes a keen eye to see a fly or a nail head at fifty yards—one hundred and fifty feet. Can the reader do it?

The nail was lightly driven, its head painted, and game called. Then the Cooper miracles began. The bullet of the first marksman chipped an edge of the nail head; the next man's bullet drove the nail a little way into the target— and removed all the paint. Haven't the miracles gone far enough now? Not to suit Cooper; for the purpose of this whole scheme is to show off his prodigy, Deerslayer-Hawkeye-Long-Rifle-Leather-Stocking-Pathfinder-Bumppo[12] be-fore the ladies.

---

[12]Names given Nathaniel Bumppo in the various Leatherstocking Tales.

"Be all ready to clench it, boys!" cried out Pathfinder, stepping into his friend's tracks the instant they were vacant. "Never mind a new nail; I can see that, though the paint is gone, and what I can see, I can hit at a hundred yards, though it were only a mosquito's eye. Be ready to clench!"

The rifle cracked, the bullet sped its way and the head of the nail was buried in the wood, covered by the piece of flattened lead.

There, you see, is a man who could hunt flies with a rifle, and command a ducal salary in a Wild West show to-day, if we had him back with us.

The recorded feat is certainly surprising, just as it stands; but it is not surprising enough for Cooper. Cooper adds a touch. He had made Pathfinder do this miracle with another man's rifle, and not only that, but Pathfinder did not have even the advantage of loading it himself. He had everything against him, and yet he made that impossible shot, and not only made it, but did it with absolute confidence, saying, "Be ready to clench." Now a person like that would have undertaken that same feat with a brickbat, and with Cooper to help he would have achieved it, too.

Pathfinder showed off handsomely that day before the ladies. His very first feat was a thing which no Wild West show can touch. He was standing with the group of marksmen, observing—a hundred yards from the target, mind: one Jasper raised his rifle and drove the centre of the bull's-eye. Then the quarter-master fired. The target exhibited no result this time. There was a laugh. "It's a dead miss," said Major Lundie. Pathfinder waited an impressive moment or two, then said in that calm, indifferent, know-it-all way of his, "No, Major—he has covered Jasper's bullet, as will be seen if any one will take the trouble to examine the target."

Wasn't it remarkable! How *could* he see that little pellet fly through the air and enter that distant bullet-hole? Yet that is what he did; for nothing is impossible to a Cooper person. Did any of those people have any deep-seated doubts about this thing? No; for that would imply sanity, and these were all Cooper people.

The respect for Pathfinder's skill and for his *quickness and accuracy of sight* (the italics are mine) was so profound and general, that the instant he made this declaration the spectators began to distrust their own opinions, and a dozen rushed to the target in order to ascertain the fact. There, sure enough, it was found that the quartermaster's bullet had gone through the hole made by Jasper's, and that, too, so accurately as to require a minute examination to be certain of the circumstance, which, however, was soon clearly established by discovering one bullet over the other in the stump against which the target was placed.

They made a "minute" examination; but never mind; how could they know that there were two bullets in that hole without digging the latest one out? for neither probe nor eyesight could prove the presence of any more than one bullet. Did they dig? No; as we shall see. It is the Pathfinder's turn now; he steps out before the ladies, takes aim, and fires.

But alas! here is a disappointment; an incredible, an unimaginable disappointment—for the target's aspect is unchanged; there is nothing there but that same old bullet hole!

"If one dared to hint at such a thing," cried major Duncan, "I should say that the Pathfinder has also missed the target."

As nobody had missed it yet, the "also" was not necessary; but never mind about that, for the Pathfinder is going to speak.

"No; no, Major," said he, confidently, "that *would* be a risky declaration. I didn't load the piece, and can't say what was in it, but if it was lead, you will find the bullet driving down those of the Quartermaster and Jasper, else is not my name Pathfinder."

A shout from the target announced the truth of this assertion.

Is the miracle sufficient as it stands? Not for Cooper. The Pathfinder speaks again, as he "now slowly advances towards the stage occupied by the females:"

"That's not all, boys, that's not all; if you find the target touched at all, I'll own to a miss. The Quartermaster cut the wood, but you'll find no wood cut by that last messenger."

The miracle is at last complete. He knew—doubtless *saw*—at the distance of a hundred yards—that his bullet had passed into the hole *without fraying the edges*. There were now three bullets in that one hole—three bullets imbedded processionally in the body of the stump back of the target. Everybody knew this—somehow or other—and yet nobody had dug any of them out to make sure. Cooper is not a close observer, but he is interesting. He is certainly always that, no matter what happens. And he is more interesting when he is not noticing what he is about than when he is. This is a considerable merit.

The conversations in the Cooper books have a curious sound in our modern ears. To believe that such talk really ever came out of people's mouths would be to believe that there was a time when time was of no value to a person who thought he had something to say; when it was the custom to spread a two-minute remark out to ten; when a man's mouth was a rolling-mill,[13] and busied itself all day long in turning four-foot pigs of thought into thirty-foot bars of conversational railroad iron by attenuation; when subjects were seldom faithfully stuck to, but the talk wandered all around and arrived nowhere; when conversations consisted mainly of irrelevancies, with here and there a relevancy, a relevancy with an embarrassed look, as not being able to explain how it got there.

Cooper was certainly not a master in the construction of dialogue. Inaccurate observation defeated him here as it defeated him in so many other enterprises of his. He even failed to notice that the man who talks corrupt English six days in the week must and will talk it on the seventh, and can't help himself. In the *Deerslayer* story he lets Deerslayer talk the showiest kind of book talk sometimes, and at other times the basest of base dialects. For instance, when some one asks him if he has a sweetheart, and if so, where she abides, this is the majestic answer:

"She's in the forest—hanging from the boughs of the trees, in a soft rain—in the dew on the open grass—the clouds that float about in the blue heavens—the birds that sing in the woods—the sweet springs where I slake my thirst—and in all the other glorious gifts that come from God's Providence!"

And he preceded that, a little before, with this:

"It consarns me as all things that touches a fri'nd consarns a fri'nd."

And this is another of his remarks:

"If I was Injin born, now, I might tell of this, or carry in the scalp and boast of the expl'ite afore the whole tribe; or if my inimy had only been a bear"—and so on.

We cannot imagine such a thing as a veteran Scotch Commander-in-Chief

---

[13] A mill where "pigs" (ingots of metal) are shaped into railroad rails.

comporting himself in the field like a windy melodramatic actor, but Cooper could. On one occasion Alice and Cora were being chased by the French through a fog in the neighborhood of their father's fort:[14]

"Point de quartier aux coquins!"[15] cried an eager pursuer, who seemed to direct the operations of the enemy.

"Stand firm and be ready, my gallant 60ths!" suddenly exclaimed a voice above them; "wait to see the enemy; fire low, and sweep the glacis."[16]

"Father! father!" exclaimed a piercing cry out the mist; "it is I! Alice! thy own Elsie! spare, O! save your daughters!"

"Hold!" shouted the former speaker, in the awful tones of parental agony, the sound reaching even to the woods, and rolling back in solemn echo. "'Tis she! God has restored me my children! Throw open the sallyport;[17] to the field, 60ths, to the field; pull not a trigger, lest ye kill my lambs! Drive off these dogs of France with your steel."

Cooper's word-sense was singularly dull. When a person has a poor ear for music he will flat and sharp right along without knowing it. He keeps near the tune, but it is *not* the tune. When a person has a poor ear for words, the result is a literary flatting and sharping; you perceive what he is intending to say, but you also perceive that he doesn't *say* it. This is Cooper. He was not a word-musician. His ear was satisfied with the *approximate* word. I will furnish some circumstantial evidence in support of this charge. My instances are gathered from half a dozen pages of the tale called *Deerslayer*. He uses "verbal," for "oral"; "precision," for "facility"; "phenomena," for "marvels"; "necessary," for "pre-determined"; "unsophisticated," for "primitive"; "preparation," for "expect-ancy"; "rebuked," for "subdued"; "dependent on," for "resulting from"; "fact," for "condition"; "fact," for "conjecture"; "precaution," for "caution"; "explain," for "determine"; "mortified," for "disappointed"; "meretricious," for "facti-tious"; "materially," for "considerably"; "decreasing," for "deepening"; "increas-ing," for "disappearing"; "embedded," for "enclosed"; "treacherous," for "hos-tile"; "stood," for "stooped"; "softened," for "replaced"; "rejoined," for "remarked"; situation," for "condition"; "different," for "differing"; "insensi-ble," for "unsentient"; "brevity," for "celerity"; "distrusted," for "suspicious"; "mental imbecility," for "imbecility"; "eyes," for "sight"; "counteracting," for "opposing"; "funeral obsequies," for "obsequies."

There have been daring people in the world who claimed that Cooper could write English, but they are all dead now—all dead but Lounsbury. I don't remember that Lounsbury makes the claim in so many words, still he makes it, for he says that *Deerslayer* is a "pure work of art." Pure, in that connection, means faultless—faultless in all details—and language is a detail. If Mr. Lounsbury had only compared Cooper's English with the English which he writes himself—but it is plain that he didn't; and so it likely that he imagines until this day that Cooper's is as clean and compact as his own. Now I feel sure, deep down in my heart, that Cooper wrote about the poorest English that exists in our language, and that the English of *Deerslayer* is the very worst that even Cooper ever wrote.

I may be mistaken, but it does seem to me that *Deerslayer* is not a work of art in any sense; it does seem to me that it is destitute of every detail that goes to the making of a work of art; in truth, it seems to me that *Deerslayer* is just simply a literary *delirium tremens*.[18]

[14]In *The Last of the Mohicans.*   [15]French: "Show the rascals no mercy!"
[16]Cleared field that slopes away from a fortress wall.
[17]Small door in a fortress wall, from which troops "sally forth" to battle.
[18]A violent delirium caused by excessive alcohol.

A work of art? It has no invention; it has no order, system, sequence or result; it has no lifelikeness, no thrill, no stir, no seeming of reality; its characters are confusedly drawn, and by their acts and words they prove that they are not the sort of people the author claims that they are; its humor is pathetic; it pathos is funny; its conversations are—oh! indescribable; its love-scenes odious; its English a crime against the language.

Counting these out, what is left is Art. I think we must all admit that.

1895

THE MAN THAT CORRUPTED HADLEYBURG

I

It was many years ago. Hadleyburg was the most honest and upright town in all the region round about. It had kept that reputation unsmirched during three generations, and was prouder of it than of any other of its possessions. It was so proud of it, and so anxious to insure its perpetuation, that it began to teach the principles of honest dealing to its babies in the cradle, and made the like teachings the staple of their culture thenceforward through all the years devoted to their education. Also, throughout the formative years temptations were kept out of the way of the young people, so that their honesty could have every chance to harden and solidify, and become a part of their very bone. The neighboring towns were jealous of this honorable supremacy, and affected to sneer at Hadleyburg's pride in it and call it vanity; but all the same they were obliged to acknowledge that Hadleyburg was in reality an incorruptible town; and if pressed they would also acknowledge that the mere fact that a young man hailed from Hadleyburg was all the recommendation he needed when he went forth from his natal town to seek for responsible employment.

But at last, in the drift of time, Hadleyburg had the ill luck to offend a passing stranger—possibly without knowing it, certainly without caring, for Hadleyburg was sufficient unto itself, and cared not a rap for strangers or their opinions. Still, it would have been well to make an exception in this one's case, for he was a bitter man and revengeful. All through his wanderings during a whole year he kept his injury in mind, and gave all his leisure moments to trying to invent a compensating satisfaction for it. He contrived many plans, and all of them were good, but none of them was quite sweeping enough; the poorest of them would hurt a great many individuals, but what he wanted was a plan which would comprehend the entire town, and not let so much as one person escape unhurt. At last he had a fortunate idea, and when it fell into his brain it lit up his whole head with an evil joy. He began to form a plan at once, saying to himself, "That is the thing to do—I will corrupt the town."

Six months later he went to Hadleyburg, and arrived in a buggy at the house of the old cashier of the bank about ten at night. He got a sack out of the buggy, shouldered it, and staggered with it through the cottage yard, and knocked at the door. A woman's voice said "Come in," and he entered, and set his sack behind the stove in the parlor, saying politely to the old lady who sat reading the *Missionary Herald* by the lamp:

"Pray keep your seat, madam, I will not disturb you. There—now it is pretty well concealed: one would hardly know it was there. Can I see your husband a moment, madam?"

"No, he has gone to Brixton, and might not return before morning."

"Very well, madam, it is no matter. I merely wanted to leave that sack in his care, to be delivered to the rightful owner when he shall be found. I am a stranger; he does not know me; I am merely passing through the town tonight to discharge a matter which has been long in my mind. My errand is now completed, and I go pleased and a little proud, and you will never see me again. There is a paper attached to the sack which will explain everything. Good night, madam."

The old lady was afraid of the mysterious big stranger, and was glad to see him go. But her curiosity was roused, and she went straight to the sack and brought away the paper. It began as follows:

"To be Published; or, the right man sought out by private inquiry—either will answer. This sack contains gold coin weighing a hundred and sixty pounds four ounces—"

"Mercy on us, and the door not locked!"

Mrs. Richards flew to it all in a tremble and locked it, then pulled down the window-shades and stood frightened, worried, and wondering if there was anything else she could do toward making herself and the money more safe. She listened awhile for burglars, then surrendered to curiosity and went back to the lamp and finished reading the paper:

"I am a foreigner, and am presently going back to my own country, to remain there permanently. I am grateful to America for what I have received at her hands during my long stay under her flag; and to one of her citizens—a citizen of Hadleyburg—I am especially grateful for a great kindness done me a year or two ago. Two great kindnesses, in fact. I will explain. I was a gambler. I say I *was*. I was a ruined gambler. I arrived in this village at night, hungry and without a penny. I asked for help—in the dark; I was ashamed to beg in the light. I begged of the right man. He gave me twenty dollars—that is to say, he gave me life, as I considered it. He also gave me fortune; for out of that money I have made myself rich at the gaming-table. And finally, a remark which he made to me has remained with me to this day, and has at last conquered me; and in conquering has saved the remnant of my morals: I shall gamble no more. Now I have no idea who that man was, but I want him found, and I want him to have this money, to give away, throw away, or keep, as he pleases. It is merely my way of testifying my gratitude to him. If I could stay, I would find him myself; but no matter, he will be found. This is an honest town, an incorruptible town, and I know I can trust it without fear. This man can be identified by the remark which he made to me; I feel persuaded that he will remember it.

"And now my plan is this:

If you prefer to conduct the inquiry privately, do so. Tell the contents of this present writing to any one who is likely to be the right man. If he shall answer, "I am the man; the remark I made was so-and-so," apply the test—to wit: open the sack, and in it you will find a sealed envelope containing that remark. If the remark mentioned by the candidate tallies with it, give him the money, ask no further questions, for he is certainly the right man.

"But if you shall prefer a public inquiry, then publish this present writing in the local paper—with these instructions added to wit: Thirty days from now, let the candidate appear at the townhall at eight in the evening (Friday), and hand his remark, in a sealed envelope, to the Rev. Mr. Burgess (if he will be kind enough to act); and let Mr. Burgess there and then destroy the seals of the sack, open it, and see if the remark is correct; if correct, let the money be delivered, with my sincere gratitude, to my benefactor thus identified."

Mrs. Richards sat down, gently quivering with excitement and was soon lost in thinkings—after this pattern: "What a strange thing it is! . . . . And what a fortune for that kind man who set his bread afloat upon the waters! . . . . If it had only been my husband that did it!—for we are so poor, so old and poor! . . . ." Then, with a sigh—"But it was not my Edward; no, it was not he that gave a stranger twenty dollars. It is a pity too; I see it now. . . ." Then, with a shudder— "But it is *gambler's* money! the wages of sin; we couldn't take it; we couldn't touch it. I don't like to be near it; it seems a defilement." She moved to a farther chair. . . . "I wish Edward would come, and take it to the bank; a burglar might come at any moment; it is dreadful to be here all alone with it."

At eleven Mr. Richards arrived, and while his wife was saying, "I am *so* glad you've come!" he was saying, "I'm so tired—tired clear out; it is dreadful to be poor, and have to make these dismal journeys at my time of life. Always at the grind, grind, grind, on a salary—another man's slave, and he sitting at home in his slippers, rich and comfortable."

"I am so sorry for you, Edward, you know that; but be comforted; we have our livelihood; we have our good name—"

"Yes, Mary, and that is everything. Don't mind my talk—it's just a moment's irritation and doesn't mean anything. Kiss me—there, it's all gone now, and I am not complaining any more. What have you been getting? What's in the sack?"

Then his wife told him the great secret. It dazed him for a moment; then he said;

"It weighs a hundred and sixty pounds? Why, Mary, it's for-ty thou-sand dollars—think of it—a whole fortune! Not ten men in this village are worth that much. Give me the paper."

He skimmed through it and said:

"Isn't it an adventure! Why, it's a romance; it's like the impossible things one reads about in books, and never sees in life." He was well stirred up now: cheerful, even gleeful. He tapped his old wife on the cheek, and said, humorously, "Why, we're rich, Mary, rich; all we've got to do is to bury the money and burn the papers. If the gambler ever comes to inquire, we'll merely look coldly upon him and say: 'What is this nonsense you are talking? We have never heard of you and your sack of gold before;' and then he would look foolish, and—"

"And in the mean time, while you are running on with your jokes, the money is still here, and it is fast getting along toward burglar-time."

"True. Very well, what shall we do—make the inquiry private? No, not that, it would spoil the romance. The public method is better. Think what a noise it will make! And it will make all the other towns jealous; for no stranger would trust such a thing to any town but Hadleyburg, and they know it. It's a great card for us. I must get to the printing-office now, or I shall be too late."

"But stop—stop—don't leave me here alone with it, Edward."

But he was gone. For only a little while, however. Not far from his own house he met the editor-proprietor of the paper, and gave him the document, and said, "Here is a good thing for you, Cox—put it in."

"It may be too late, Mr. Richards, but I'll see."

At home again he and his wife sat down to talk the charming mystery over; they were in no condition for sleep. The first question was, Who could the citizen have been who gave the stranger the twenty dollars? It seemed a simple one; both answered it in the same breath—

"Barclay Goodson."

"Yes," said Richards, "he could have done it, and it would have been like him, but there's not another in the town."

"Everybody will grant that, Edward—grant it privately, anyway. For six months, now, the village has been its own proper self once more—honest, narrow, self-righteous, and stingy."

"It was what he always called it, to the day of his death—said it right out publicly, too."

"Yes, and he was hated for it."

"Oh, of course; but he didn't care. I reckon he was the best-hated man among us, except the Reverend Burgess."

"Well, Burgess deserves it—he will never get another congregation here. Mean as the town is, it knows how to estimate *him*. Edward, doesn't it seem odd that the stranger should appoint Burgess to deliver the money?"

"Well, yes—it does. That is—that is—"

"Why so much that-*is*-ing? Would *you* select him?"

"Mary, maybe the stranger knows him better than this village does."

"Much *that* would help Burgess!"

The husband seemed perplexed for an answer; the wife kept a steady eye upon him, and waited. Finally Richards said, with the hesitancy of one who is making a statement which is likely to encounter doubt.

"Mary, Burgess is not a bad man."

His wife was certainly surprised.

"Nonsense!" she exclaimed.

"He is not a bad man. I know. The whole of his unpopularity had its foundation in that one thing—the thing that made so much noise."

"That 'one thing,' indeed! As if that 'one thing' wasn't enough, all by itself."

"Plenty. Plenty. Only he wasn't guilty of it."

"How you talk! Not guilty of it! Everybody knows he *was* guilty."

"Mary, I give you my word—he was innocent."

"I can't believe it, and I don't. How do you know?"

"It is a confession. I am ashamed, but I will make it. I was the only man who knew he was innocent. I could have saved him, and—and—well, you know how the town was wrought up—I hadn't the pluck to do it. It would have turned everybody against me. I felt mean, ever so mean; but I didn't dare; I hadn't the manliness to face that."

Mary look troubled, and for a while was silent. Then she said, stammeringly:

"I—I don't think it would have done for you to—to— One mustn't—er—public opinion—one has to be so careful—so—" it was a difficult road, and she got mired; but after a little she got started again. "It was a great pity, but—Why, we couldn't afford it, Edward—we couldn't indeed. Oh, I wouldn't have had you do it for anything!"

"It would have lost us the good-will of so many people, Mary; and then—and then—"

"What troubles me now is, what *he* thinks of us, Edward."

"He? *He* doesn't suspect I could have saved him."

"Oh, exclaimed the wife, in a tone of relief, "I am glad of that. As long as he doesn't know that you could have saved him, he—he—well, that makes it a great deal better. Why, I might have known he didn't know, because he is always trying to be friendly with us, as little encouragement as we give him. More than once people have twitted me with it. There's the Wilsons, and the Wilcoxes, and the Harknesses, they take a mean pleasure in saying, 'Your friend Burgess,' because they know it pesters me. I wish he wouldn't persist in liking us so; I can't think why he keeps it up."

"I can explain it. It's another confession. When the thing was new and hot, and the town made a plan to ride him on a rail, my conscience hurt me so that I couldn't stand it, and I went privately and gave him notice, and he got out of the town and staid out till it was safe to come back."

"Edward! If the town had found it out—"

"Don't! It scares me yet, to think of it. I repented of it the minute it was done; and I was even afraid to tell you, lest your face might betray it to somebody. I didn't sleep any that night, for worrying. But after a few days I saw that no one was going to suspect me, and after that I got to feeling glad I did it. And I feel glad yet, Mary—glad through and through."

"So do I, now, for it would have been a dreadful way to treat him. Yes, I'm glad; for really you did owe him that, you know. But, Edward, suppose it should come out yet, some day!"

"It won't."

"Why?"

"Because everybody thinks it was Goodson."

"Of course they would!"

"Certainly. And of course *he* didn't care. They persuaded poor old Sawlsberry to go and charge it on him, and he went blustering over there and did it. Goodson looked him over, like as if he was hunting for a place on him that he could despise the most, then he says, 'So you are the Committee of Inquiry, are you?' Sawlsberry said that was about what he was. 'Hm. Do they require particulars, or do you reckon a kind of a *general* answer will do?' 'If they require particulars, I will come back, Mr. Goodson; I will take the general answer first.' 'Very well, then, tell them to go to hell—I reckon that's general enough. And I'll give you some advice, Sawlsberry; when you back for the particulars, fetch a basket to carry the relics of yourself home in.'"

"Just like Goodson; it's got all the marks. He had only one vanity; he thought he could give advice better than any other person."

"It settled the business, and saved us, Mary. The subject was dropped."

"Bless you, I'm not doubting *that*."

Then they took up the gold-sack mystery again, with strong interest. Soon the conversation began to suffer breaks—interruptions caused by absorbed thinkings. The breaks grew more and more frequent. At last Richards lost himself wholly in thought. He sat long, gazing vacantly at the floor, and by-and-by he began to punctuate his thoughts with little nervous movements of his hands that seemed to indicate vexation. Meantime his wife too had relapsed into a thoughtful silence, and her movements were beginning to show a troubled discomfort. Finally Richards got up and strode aimlessly about the room, ploughing his hands through his hair, much as a somnambulist might do who was having a bad dream. Then he seemed to arrive at a definite purpose; and without a word he put on his hat and passed quickly out of the house. His wife sat brooding, with a drawn face, and did not seem to be aware that she was alone. Now and then she murmured, "Lead us not into t. . . .[1] but—but—we are

[1] From The Lord's Prayer: ". . . lead us not into temptation, but deliver us from evil." Matthew 6:13.

so poor, so poor! . . . .Lead us not into. . . . Ah, who would be hurt by it?—and no one would ever know. . . . Lead us. . . ." The voice died out in mumblings. After a little she glanced up and muttered in a half-frightened, half-glad way—

"He is gone! But, oh dear, he may be too late—too late. . . . Maybe not—maybe there is still time." She rose and stood thinking, nervously clasping and unclasping her hands. A slight shudder shook her frame, and she said, out of a dry throat, "God forgive me—it's awful to think such things—but. . . . Lord, how we are made—how strangely we are made!"

She turned the light low, and slipped stealthily over and kneeled down by the sack and felt of its ridgy sides with her hands, and fondled them lovingly; and there was a gloating light in her poor old eyes. She fell into fits of absence; and came half out of them at times to mutter, "If we had only waited!—oh, if we had only waited a little, and not been in such a hurry!"

Meantime Cox had gone home from his office and told his wife all about the strange thing that had happened, and they had talked it over eagerly, and guessed that the late Goodson was the only man in the town who could have helped a suffering stranger with so noble a sum as twenty dollars. Then there was a pause, and the two became thoughtful and silent. And by-and-by nervous and fidgety. At last the wife said, as if to herself,

"Nobody knows this secret but the Richardses . . . and us . . . nobody."

The husband came out of his thinkings with a light start, and gazed wistfully at his wife, whose face was become very pale; then he hestitatingly rose, and glanced furtively at his hat, than at his wife—a sort of mute inquiry. Mrs. Cox swallowed once or twice, with her hand at her throat, then in place of speech she nodded her head. In a moment she was alone, and mumbling to herself.

And now Richards and Cox were hurrying through the deserted streets, from opposite directions. They met, panting, at the foot of the printing-office stairs; by the night-light there they read each other's face. Cox whispered.

"Nobody knows about this but us?"

The whispered answer was,

"Not a soul—on honor, not a soul!"

"If it isn't too late to—"

The men were starting up stairs; at this moment they were overtaken by a boy, and Cox asked,

"Is that you, Johnny?"

"Yes, sir."

"You needn't ship the early mail—nor *any* mail; wait till I tell you."

"It's already gone, sir."

"*Gone?*" It had the sound of an unspeakable disappointment in it.

"Yes, sir. Time-table for Brixton and all the towns beyond changed to-day, sir—had to get the papers in twenty minutes earlier than common. I had to rush; if I had been two minutes later—"

The men turned and walked slowly away, not waiting to hear the rest. Neither of them spoke during ten minutes; then Cox said, in a vexed tone,

"What possessed you to be in such a hurry, I *can't* make out."

The answer was humble enough;

"I see it now, but somehow I never thought, you know, until it was too late. But the next time—"

"Next time be hanged! It won't come in a thousand years."

Then the friends separated without a good-night, and dragged themselves home with the gait of mortally stricken men. At their homes their wives sprang up with an eager "Well?"—then saw the answer with their eyes and sank down sorrowing, without waiting for it to come in words. In both houses a discussion followed of a heated sort—a new thing; there had been discussions before, but not heated ones, not ungentle ones. The discussions tonight were a sort of seeming plagiarisms of each other. Mrs. Richards said,

"If you had only waited, Edward—if you had only stopped to think; but no, you must run straight to the printing-office and spread it all over the world."

"It *said* publish it."

"That is nothing; it also said do it privately, if you liked. There, now—is that true, or not?"

"Why, yes—yes, it is true; but when I thought what a stir it would make, and what a compliment it was to Hadleyburg that a stranger should trust it so—"

"Oh, certainly, I know all that; but if you had only stopped to think, you would have seen that you *couldn't* find the right man, because he is in his grave, and hasn't left chick nor child nor relation behind him; and as long as the money went to somebody that awfully needed it, and nobody would be hurt by it, and—and—"

She broke down, crying. Her husband tried to think of some comforting thing to say, and presently came out with this:

"But after all, Mary, it must be for the best—it *must* be; we know that. And we must remember that it was so ordered—"

"Ordered! Oh, everything's *ordered,* when a person has to find some way out when he has been stupid. Just the same, it was *ordered* that the money should come to us in this special way, and it was you that must take it on yourself to go meddling with the designs of Providence—and who gave you the right? It was wicked, that is what it was—just blasphemous presumption, and no more becoming to a meek and humble professor of—"

"But, Mary, you know how we have been trained all our lives long, like the whole village, till it is absolutely second nature to us to stop not a single moment to think when there's an honest thing to be done—"

"Oh, I know it, I know it—it's been one everlasting training and training and training in honesty—honesty shielded, from the very cradle, against every possible temptation, and so it's *artificial* honesty, and weak as water when temptation comes, as we have seen this night. God knows I never had shade nor shadow of a doubt of my petrified and indestructible honesty until now—and now, under the very first big and real temptation, I—Edward, it is my belief that this town's honesty is as rotten as mine is; as rotten as yours is. It is a mean town, a hard, stingy town, and hasn't a virtue in the world but this honesty it is so celebrated for and so conceited about; and so help me, I do believe that if ever the day comes that its honesty falls under great temptation, its grand reputation will go to ruin like a house of cards. There, now, I've made confession, and I feel better; I am a humbug, and I've been one all my life, without knowing it. Let no man call me honest again—I will not have it."

"I—Well, Mary, I feel a good deal as you do; I certainly do. It seems strange, too, so strange. I never could have believed it—never."

A long silence followed; both were sunk in thought. At last the wife looked up and said,

"I know what you are thinking, Edward."

Richards had the embarrassed look of a person who is caught.

"I am ashamed to confess it, Mary, but—"

"It's no matter, Edward, I was thinking the same question myself."

"I hope so. State it."

"You were thinking, if a body could only guess out *what the remark was* that Goodson made to the stranger."

"It's perfectly true. I feel guilty and ashamed. And you?"

"I'm past it. Let us make a pallet here; we've got to stand watch till the bank vault opens in the morning and admits the sack. . . . Oh, dear, oh, dear—if we hadn't made the mistake!"

The pallet was made, and Mary said:

"The open sesame—what could it have been? I do wonder what that remark could have been? But come; we will get to bed now."

"And sleep?"

"No; think."

"Yes, think."

By this time the Coxes too had completed their spat and their reconciliation, and were turning in—to think, to think, and toss, and fret, and worry over what the remark could possibly have been which Goodson made to the stranded derelict; that golden remark; that remark worth forty thousand dollars, cash.

The reason that the village telegraph-office was open later than usual that night was this: The foreman of Cox's paper was the local representative of the Associated Press. One might say its honorary representative, for it wasn't four times a year that he could furnish thirty words that would be accepted. But this time it was different. His despatch stating what he had caught got an instant answer:

"Send the whole thing—all the details—twelve hundred words."

A colossal order! The foreman filled the bill; and he was the proudest man in the State. By breakfast-time the next morning the name of Hadleyburg the Incorruptible was on every lip in America, from Montreal to the Gulf, from the glaciers of Alaska to the orange groves of Florida; and millions and millions of people were discussing the stranger and his money-sack, and wondering if the right man would be found, and hoping some more news about the matter would come soon—right away.

II

Hadleyburg village woke up world-celebrated—astonished—happy—vain. Vain beyond imagination. Its nineteen principal citizens and their wives went about shaking hands with each other, and beaming, and smiling, and congratulating, and saying *this* thing adds a new word to the dictionary—*Hadleyburg,* synonym for *incorruptible*—destined to live in dictionaries forever! And the minor and unimportant citizens and their wives went around acting in much the same way. Everybody ran to the bank to see the gold-sack; and before noon grieved and envious crowds began to flock in from Brixton and all neighboring towns; and that afternoon and next day reporters began to arrive from everywhere to verify the sack and its history and write the whole thing up anew, and make dashing free-hand pictures of the sack, and of Richard's house, and the bank, and the Presbyterian church, and the Baptist church, and the public square, and the town-hall where the test would be applied and the money delivered; and damnable portraits of the Richardses, and Pinkerton the banker, and Cox, and the foreman, and Reverend Burgess, and the postmaster—and even of Jack Halliday, who was the loafing, good-natured, no-account, irreverent fisherman, hunter, boys' friend, stray-dogs' friend, typical "Sam Lawson"[2] of the town. The little mean, smirking, oily Pinkerton showed the sack to all comers, and rubbed his sleek palms together pleasantly, and enlarged upon the town's fine old reputation for honesty and upon this wonderful endorsement of it, and hoped and believed that the example would now spread far and wide over the American world, and be epoch-making in the matter of moral regeneration. And so on, and so on.

By the end of a week things had quieted down again; the wild intoxication of pride and joy had sobered to a soft, sweet, silent delight—a sort of deep, nameless, unutterable content. All faces bore a look of peaceful, holy happiness.

Then a change came. It was a gradual change: so gradual that its beginnings were hardly noticed; maybe were not noticed at all, except by Jack Halliday, who always noticed everything; and always made fun of it, too, no matter what it was. He began to throw out chaffing remarks about people not looking quite so happy as they did a day or two ago; and next he claimed that the new aspect was deepening to positive sadness; next, that it was taking on a sick look; and finally he said that everybody was become so moody, thoughtful, and absent-minded that he could rob the meanest man in town of a cent out of the bottom of his breeches pocket and not disturb his revery.

At this stage—or at about this stage—a saying like this was dropped at bed-time—with a sigh, usually—by the head of each of the nineteen principal house-holds:

"Ah, what *could* have been the remark that Goodson made!"

And straightway—with a shudder—came this, from the man's wife:

"Oh, *don't!* What horrible thing are you mulling in your mind? Put it away from you, for God's sake!"

But that question was wrung from those men again the next night—and got the same retort. But weaker.

And the third night the men uttered the question yet again—with anguish, and absently. This time—and the following night—the wives fidgeted feebly, and tried to say something. But didn't.

And the night after that they found their tongues and responded—longingly, "Oh, if we *could* only guess!"

Halliday's comments grew daily more and more sparklingly disagreeable and disparaging. He went diligently about, laughing at the town, individually and in mass. But his laugh was the only one left in the village; it fell upon a hollow and mournful vacancy and emptiness. Not even a smile was findable anywhere. Halliday carried a cigar-box around on a tripod, playing that it was a camera, and halted all passers and aimed the thing and said, "Ready!—now look pleasant, please," but not even this capital joke could surprise the dreary faces into any softening.

So three weeks passed—one week was left. It was Saturday evening—after supper. Instead of the aforetime Saturday evening flutter and bustle and shop-ping and larking, the streets were empty and desolate. Richards and his old wife sat apart in their little parlor—miserable and thinking. This was become their evening habit now: the life-long habit which had preceded it, of reading, knitting, and contented chat, or receiving or paying neighborly calls, was dead and gone and forgotten, ages ago—two or three weeks ago; nobody talked now, nobody read, nobody visited—the whole village sat at home, sighing, worrying, silent. Trying to guess out that remark.

[2]The shiftless Yankee humorist in Harriet Beecher Stowe's *Oldtown Folks* (1869) and its sequel *Sam Lawson's Oldtown Fireside Stories* (1872).

The postman left a letter. Richards glanced listlessly at the superscription and the post-mark—unfamiliar, both—and tossed the letter on the table and resumed his might-have-beens and his hopeless dull miseries where he had left them off. Two or three hours later his wife got wearily up and was going away to bed without a good-night—custom now—but she stopped near the letter and eyed it awhile with a dead interest, then broke it open, and began to skim it over. Richards, sitting there with his chair tilted back against the wall and his chin between his knees, heard something fall. It was his wife. He sprang to her side, but she cried out:

"Leave me alone, I am too happy. Read the letter—read it!"

He did. He devoured it, his brain reeling. The letter was from a distant State, and it said:

"I am a stranger to you, but no matter: I have something to tell. I have just arrived home from Mexico, and learned about that episode. Of course you do not know who made that remark, but I know, and I am the only person living who does know. It was *Goodson*. I knew him well, many years ago. I passed through your village that very night, and was his guest till the midnight train came along. I overheard him make that remark to the stranger in the dark—it was in Hale Alley. He and I talked of it the rest of the way home, and while smoking in his house. He mentioned many of your villagers in the course of his talk—most of them in a very uncomplimentary way, but two or three favorably: among these latter yourself. I say 'favorably'—nothing stronger. I remember his saying he did not actually *like* any person in the town—not one; but that you—I *think* he said you—am almost sure—had done him a very great service once, possibly without knowing the full value of it, and he wished he had a fortune, he would leave it to you when he died, and a curse apiece for the rest of the citizens. Now, then, if it was you that did him that service, you are his legitimate heir, and entitled to the sack of gold. I know that I can trust to your honor and honesty, for in a citizen of Hadleyburg these virtues are an unfailing inheritance, and so I am going to reveal to you the remark, well satisfied that if you are not the right man you will seek and find the right one and see that poor Goodson's debt of gratitude for the service referred to is paid. This is the remark: '*You are far from being a bad man; go, and reform.*

HOWARD L. STEPHENSON."

"Oh, Edward, the money is ours, and I am so grateful, *oh*, so grateful—kiss me, dear, it's forever since we kissed—and we needed it so—the money—and now you are free of Pinkerton and his bank, and nobody's slave any more; it seems to me I could fly for joy."

It was a happy half-hour that the couple spent there on the settee caressing each other; it was the old days come again—days that had begun with their courtship and lasted without a break till the stranger brought the deadly money. By-and-by the wife said:

"Oh, Edward, how lucky it was you that did him that grand service, poor Goodson! I never liked him, but I love him now. And it was fine and beautiful of you never to mention it or brag about it." Then, with a touch of reproach, "But you ought to have told *me*, Edward, you ought to have told your wife, you know."

"Well, I—er—well, Mary, you see—"

"Now stop hemming and hawing, and tell me about it, Edward. I always loved you, and now I'm proud of you. Everybody believes there was only one good generous soul in this village, and now it turns out that you—Edward, why don't you tell me?"

"Well—er—er— Why, Mary, I can't!"

"You *can't*? Why can't you?"

"You see, he—well, he—he made me promise I wouldn't."

The wife looked him over, and said, very slowly,

"Made—you—promise? Edward, what do you tell me that for?"

"Mary, do you think I would lie?"

She was troubled and silent for a moment, then she laid her hand within his and said:

"No. . . no. We have wandered far enough from our bearings—God spare us that! In all your life you have never uttered a lie. But now—now that the foundations of things seem to be crumbling from under us, we—we—" She lost her voice for a moment, then said, brokenly, "Lead us not into temptation. . . . I think you made the promise, Edward. Let it rest so. Let us keep away from that ground. Now—that is all gone by; let us be happy again; it is no time for clouds."

Edward found it something of an effort to comply, for his mind kept wandering—trying to remember what the service was that he had done Goodson.

The couple lay awake the most of the night, Mary happy and busy, Edward busy, but not so happy. Mary was planning what she would do with the money. Edward was trying to recall that service. At first his conscience was sore on account of the lie he had told Mary—if it was a lie. After much reflection—suppose it *was* a lie? What then? Was it such a great matter? Aren't we always *acting* lies? Then why not *tell* them? Look at Mary—look what she had done. While he was hurrying off on his honest errand, what was she doing? Lamenting because the papers hadn't been destroyed and the money kept! Is theft better than lying?

That point lost its sting—the lie dropped into the background and left comfort behind it. The next point came to the front: *had* he rendered that service? Well, here was Goodson's own evidence as reported in Stephenson's letter; there could be no better evidence than that—it was even *proof* that he had rendered it. Of course. So that point was settled. . . . No, not quite. He recalled with a wince that this unknown Mr. Stephenson was just a trifle unsure as to whether the performer of it was Richards or some other—and, oh dear, he had put Richards on his honor! He must himself decide whither that money must go—and Mr. Stephenson was not doubting that if he was the wrong man he would go honorably and find the right one. Oh, it was odious to put a man in such a situation—ah, why couldn't Stephenson have left out that doubt! What did he want to intrude that for?

Further reflection. How did it happen that *Richard's* name remained in Stephenson's mind as indicating the right man, and not some other man's name? That looked good. Yes, that looked very good. In fact, it went on looking better and better, straight along—until by-and-by it grew into positive *proof*. And then Richards put the matter at once out of his mind, for he had a private instinct that a proof once established is better left so.

He was feeling reasonably comfortable now, but there was still one other detail that kept pushing itself on his notice: of course he had done that service—that was settled; but what *was* that service? He must recall it—he would not go to sleep till he had recalled it; it would make his peace of mind perfect. And so he thought and thought. He thought of a dozen things—possible services, even probable services—but none of them seemed adequate, none of them seemed large enough, none of them seemed worth the money—worth the fortune Goodson had wished he could leave in his will. And besides, he couldn't remember having done them, anyway. Now, then—now, then—what *kind* of a service would it be that would make a man so inordinately grateful? Ah—the saving of his soul! That must be it. Yes, he could remember, now, how he once set himself the task of converting Goodson, and labored at it as much as he was going to say three months; but upon closer examination it shrunk to a month, then to a week, then to a day, then to nothing. Yes, he remembered, now, and with unwelcome vividness, that, Goodson had told him to go to thunder and mind his own business—*he* wasn't hankering to follow Hadleyburg to heaven!

So that solution was a failure—he hadn't saved Goodson's soul. Richards was discouraged. Then after a little came another idea: had he saved Goodson's property? No, that wouldn't do—he hadn't any. His life? That is it! Of course. Why, he might have thought of it before. This time he was on the right track, sure. His imagination-mill was hard at work in a minute, now.

Thereafter during a stretch of two exhausting hours he was busy saving Goodson's life. He saved it in all kinds of difficult and perilous ways. In every case he got it saved satisfactorily up to a certain point; then, just as he was beginning to get well persuaded that it had really happened, a troublesome detail would turn up which made the whole thing impossible. As in the matter of drowning, for instance. In that case he had swum out and tugged Goodson ashore in an unconscious state with a great crowd looking on and applauding, but when he had got it all thought out and was just beginning to remember all about it a whole swarm of disqualifying details arrived on the ground: the town would have known of the circumstance, Mary would have known of it, it would glare like a limelight in his own memory instead of being an inconspicuous service which he had possibly rendered "without knowing its full value." And at this point he remembered that he couldn't swim, anyway.

Ah—*there* was a point which he had been overlooking from the start: it had to be a service which he had rendered "possibly without knowing the full value of it." Why, really, that ought to be an easy hunt—much easier than those others. And sure enough, by-and-by he found it. Goodson, years and years ago, came near marrying a very sweet and pretty girl, named Nancy Hewitt, but in some way or other the match had been broken off; the girl died, Goodson remained a bachelor, and by-and-by became a soured one and a frank despiser of the human species. Soon after the girl's death the village found out, or thought it had found out, that she carried a spoonful of negro blood in her veins. Richards worked at these details a good while, and in the end he thought he remembered things concerning them which must have gotten mislaid in his memory through long neglect. He seemed to dimly remember that it was *he* that found out about the negro blood; that it was he that told the village; that the village told Goodson where they got it; that he thus saved Goodson from marrying the tainted girl; that he had done him this great service "without knowing the full value of it," in fact without knowing that he *was* doing it; but that Goodson knew the value of it, and what a narrow escape he had had, and so went to his grave grateful to his benefactor and wishing he had a fortune to leave him. It was all clear and simple now, and the more he went over it the more luminous and certain it grew; and at last, when he nestled to sleep satisfied and happy, he remembered the whole thing just as if it had been yesterday. In fact, he dimly remembered Goodson's *telling* him his gratitude once. Meantime Mary had spent six thousand dollars on a new house for herself and a pair of slippers for her pastor, and then had fallen peacefully to rest.

That same Saturday evening the postman had delivered a letter to each of the other principal citizens—nineteen letters in all. No two of the envelopes were alike, and no two of the superscriptions were in the same hand, but the letters inside were just like each other in every detail but one. They were exact copies of the letter received by Richards—handwriting and all—and were all signed by Stephenson, but in place of Richard's name each receiver's own name appeared.

All night long eighteen principal citizens did what their caste-brother Richards was doing at the same time—they put in their energies trying to remember what notable service it was that they had unconsciously done Barclay Goodson. In no case was it a holiday job; still they succeeded.

And while they were at this work which was difficult, their wives put in the night spending the money, which was easy. During that one night the nineteen wives spent an average of seven thousand dollars each out of the forty thousand in the sack—a hundred and thirty-three thousand altogether.

Next day there was a surprise for Jack Halliday. He noticed that the faces of the nineteen chief citizens and their wives bore that expression of peaceful and holy happiness again. He could not understand it, neither was he able to invent any remarks about it that could damage it or disturb it. And so it was his turn to be dissatisfied with life. His private guesses at the reasons for the happiness failed in all instances, upon examination. When he met Mrs. Wilcox and noticed the placid ecstasy in her face, he said to himself, "Her cat has had kittens"—and went and asked the cook; it was not so; the cook had detected the happiness, but did not know the cause. When Halliday found the duplicate ecstasy in the face of "Shadbelly" Billson (village nickname), he was sure some neighbor of Billson's had broken his leg, but inquiry showed that this had not happened. The subdued ecstasy in Gregory Yates's face could mean but one thing—he was a mother-in-law short; it was another mistake. "And Pinkerton—Pinkerton— he has collected ten cents that he thought he was going to lose." And so on, and so on. In some cases the guesses had to remain in doubt, in the others they proved distinct errors. In the end Halliday said to himself, "Anyway it foots up that there's nineteen Hadleyburg families temporarily in heaven; I don't know how it happened; I only know Providence is off duty to-day."

An architect and builder from the next State had lately ventured to set up a small business in this unpromising village, and his sign had now been hanging out a week. Not a customer yet; he was a discouraged man, and sorry he had come. But his weather changed suddenly now. First one and then another chief citizen's wife said to him privately:

"Come to my house Monday week—but say nothing about it for the present. We think of building."

He got eleven invitations that day. That night he wrote his daughter and broke off her match with her student. He said she could marry a mile higher than that.

Pinkerton the banker and two or three other well-to-do men planned country-seats—but waited. That kind don't count their chickens until they are hatched.

The Wilsons devised a grand new thing—a fancy-dress ball. They made no actual promises, but told all their acquaintanceship in confidence that they were thinking the matter over and thought they should give it—"and if we do, you will be invited, of course." People were surprised, and said, one to another, "Why, they are crazy, those poor Wilsons, they can't afford it." Several among the nineteen said privately to their husbands, "It is a good idea; we will keep still till their cheap thing is over, and then *we* will give one that will make it sick."

The days drifted along, and the bill of future squanderings rose higher and higher, wilder and wilder, more and more foolish and reckless. It began to look as if every member of the nineteen would not only spend his whole forty thousand dollars before receiving-day, but be actually in debt by the time he got the money. In some cases light-headed people did not stop with planning to spend, they really spent—on credit. They bought land, mortgages, farms, speculative stocks, fine clothes, horses, and various other things, paid down the bonus, and made themselves liable for the rest—at ten days. Presently the sober second thought came, and Halliday noticed that a ghastly anxiety was beginning to show up in a good many faces. Again he was puzzled, and didn't know what to make of it. "The Wilcox kittens aren't dead, for they weren't born; nobody's broken a leg; there's no shrinkage in mother-in-laws; *nothing* has happened—it is an insolvable mystery."

There was another puzzled man, too—the Rev. Mr. Burgess. For days, wherever he went, people seemed to follow him or to be watching out for him; and if he ever found himself in a retired spot, a member of the nineteen would be sure to appear, thrust an envelope privately into his hand, whisper "To be opened at the town-hall Friday evening," then vanish away like a guilty thing. He was expecting that there might be one claimant for the sack—doubtful, however, Goodson being dead—but it never occurred to him that all this crowd might be claimants. When the great Friday came at last, he found that he had nineteen envelopes.

III

The town-hall had never looked finer. The platform at the end of it was backed by a showy draping of flags; at intervals along the walls were festoons of flags; the gallery fronts were clothed in flags; the supporting columns were swathed in flags; all this was to impress the stranger, for he would be there in considerable force, and in a large degree he would be connected with the press. The house was full. The 412 fixed seats were occupied; also the 68 extra chairs which had been packed into the aisles; the steps of the platform were occupied; some distinguished strangers were given seats on the platform; at the horseshoe of table which fenced the front and sides of the platform sat a strong force of special correspondents who had come from everywhere. It was the best-dressed house the town had ever produced. There were some tolerably expensive toilets there, and in several cases the ladies who wore them had the look of being unfamiliar with that kind of clothes. At least the town thought they had that look, but the notion could have arisen from the town's knowledge of the fact that these ladies had never inhabited such clothes before.

The gold-sack stood on a little table at the front of the platform where all the house could see it. The bulk of the house gazed at it with a burning interest, a mouth-watering interest, a wistful and pathetic interest; a minority of nineteen couples gazed at it tenderly, lovingly, proprietarily, and the male half of this minority kept saying over to themselves the moving little impromptu speeches of thankfulness for the audience's applause and congratulations which they were presently going to get up and deliver. Every now and then one of these got a piece of paper out of his vest pocket and privately glanced at it to refresh his memory.

Of course there was a buzz of conversation going on—there always is; but at last when the Rev. Mr. Burgess rose and laid his hand on the sack he could hear his microbes gnaw, the place was so still. He related the curious history of the sack, then went on to speak in warm terms of Hadleyburg's old and well-earned reputation for spotless honesty, and of the town's just pride in this reputation. He said that this reputation was a treasure of priceless value; that under Providence its value had now become inestimably enhanced, for the recent episode had spread this fame far and wide, and thus had focused the eyes of the American world upon this village, and made its name for all time, as he hoped and believed, a synonym for commercial incorruptibility. [*Applause.*] "And who is to be the guardian of this noble treasure—the community as a whole? No! The responsibility is individual, not communal. From this day forth each and every one of you is in his own person its special guardian, and individually responsible that no harm shall come to it. Do you—does each of you—accept this great trust? [*Tumultuous assent.*] Then all is well. Transmit it to your children and to your children's children. To-day your purity is beyond reproach—see to it that it shall remain so. To-day there is not a person in your community who could be beguiled to touch a penny not his own—see to it that you abide in this grace. [*"We will! we will!"*] This is not the place to make comparisons between ourselves and other communities—some of them ungracious toward us; they have their ways, we have ours; let us be content. [*Applause.*] I am done. Under my hand, my friends, rests a stranger's eloquent recognition of what we are; through him the world will always henceforth know what we are. We do not know who he is, but in your name I utter your gratitude, and ask you to raise your voices in indorsement."

The house rose in a body and made the walls quake with the thunders of its thankfulness for the space of a long minute. Then it sat down, and Mr. Burgess took an envelope out of his pocket. The house held its breath while he slit the envelope open and took from it a slip of paper. He read its contents—slowly and impressively—the audience listening with tranced attention to this magic document, each of whose words stood for an ingot of gold:

" 'The remark which I made to the distressed stranger was this: "You are very far from being a bad man; go, and reform." ' " Then he continued: "We shall know in a moment now whether the remark here quoted corresponds with the one concealed in the sack; and if that shall prove to be so—and it undoubtedly will—this sack of gold belongs to a fellow-citizen who will henceforth stand before the nation as the symbol of the special virtue which has made our own town famous throughout the land—Mr. Billson!"

The house had gotten itself all ready to burst into the proper tornado of applause; but instead of doing it, it seemed stricken with a paralysis; there was a deep hush for a moment or two, then a wave of whispered murmurs swept the place—of about this tenor: "*Billson!* oh, come, this is *too* thin! Twenty dollars to a stranger—or *anybody*—*Billson!* Tell it to the marines!" And now at this point the house caught its breath all of a sudden in a new access of astonishment, for it discovered that whereas in one part of the hall Deacon Billson was standing up with his head meekly bowed, in another part of it Lawyer Wilson was doing the same. There was a wondering silence now for a while. Everybody was puzzled, and nineteen couples were surprised and indignant.

Billson and Wilson turned and stared at each other. Billson asked, bitingly,

"Why do *you* rise, Mr. Wilson?"

"Because I have a right to. Perhaps you will be good enough to explain to the house why *you* rise?"

"With great pleasure. Because I wrote that paper."

"It is an impudent falsity! I wrote it myself."

It was Burgess's turn to be paralyzed. He stood looking vacantly at first one of the men and then the other, and did not seem to know what to do. The house was stupefied. Lawyer Wilson spoke up, now, and said.

"I ask the Chair to read the name signed to that paper."

That brought the Chair to itself, and it read out the name,

" 'John Wharton *Billson*.' "

"There!" shouted Billson, "what have you got to say for yourself, now? And what kind of apology are you going to make to me and to this insulted house for the imposture which you have attempted to play here?"

"No apologies are due, sir; and as for the rest of it, I publicly charge you with pilfering my note from Mr. Burgess and substituting a copy of it signed with your own name. There is no other way by which you could have gotten hold of the test-remark; I alone, of living men, possessed the secret of its wording."

There was likely to be a scandalous state of things if this went on; everybody noticed with distress that the shorthand scribes were scribbling like mad; many people were crying "Chair, Chair! Order! order!" Burgess rapped with his gavel, and said:

"Let us not forget the proprieties due. There has evidently been a mistake somewhere, but surely that is all. If Mr. Wilson gave me an envelope—and I remember now that he did—I still have it."

He took one out of his pocket, opened it, glanced at it, looked surprised and worried, and stood silent a few moments. Then he waved his hand in a wandering and mechanical way, and made an effort or two to say something, then gave it up, despondently. Several voices cried out:

"Read it! read it! What is it?"

So he began in a dazed and sleep-walker fashion:

" '*The remark which I made to the unhappy stranger was this*: "*You are far from being a bad man.* [The house gazed at him, marvelling.] *Go, and reform.*" ' " [*Murmurs:* "Amazing! what can this mean?"] "This one," said the Chair, "is signed Thurlow G. Wilson."

"There!" cried Wilson, "I reckon that settles it! I knew perfectly well my note was purloined."

"Purloined!" retorted Billson. "I'll let you know that neither you nor any man of your kidney must venture to—"

The Chair. "Order gentlemen, order! Take you seats, both of you, please."

They obeyed, shaking their heads and grumbling angrily. The house was profoundly puzzled; it did not know what to do with this curious emergency. Presently Thompson got up. Thompson was the hatter. He would have liked to be a Nineteener; but such was not for him; his stock of hats was not considerable enough for the position. He said:

"Mr. Chairman, if I may be permitted to make a suggestion, can both of these gentlemen be right? I put it to you, sir, can both have happened to say the very same words to the stranger? I seems to me—"

The tanner got up and interrupted him. The tanner was a disgruntled man; he believed himself entitled to be a Nineteener, but he couldn't get recognition. It made him a little unpleasant in his ways and speech. Said he:

"Sho, *that's* not the point! *That* could happen—twice in a hundred years—but not the other thing. *Neither* of them gave the twenty dollars!" (*A ripple of applause.*)

Billson. "*I* did!"

Wilson. "*I* did!"

Then each accused the other of pilfering.

The Chair. "Order! Sit down, if you please—both of you. Neither of the notes has been out of my possession at any moment."

A Voice. "Good—that settles *that!*"

The Tanner. "Mr. Chairman, one thing is now plain: one of these men has been eavesdropping under the other one's bed, and filching family secrets. If it is not unparliamentary to suggest it, I will remark that both are equal to it. [*The*

Chair, "Order! order!"] I withdraw the remark, sir, and will confine myself to suggesting that *if* one of them has overheard the other reveal the test-remark to his wife, we shall catch him now."

A Voice. "How?"

The Tanner. "Easily. The two have not quoted the remark in exactly the same words. You would have noticed that, if there hadn't been a considerable stretch of time and an exciting quarrel inserted between the two readings."

A Voice. "Name the difference."

The Tanner. "The word *very* is in Billson's note, and not in the other."

Many Voices. "That's so—he's right!"

The Tanner. "And so, if the Chair will examine the test-remark in the sack, we shall know which of these two frauds—[*The Chair.* "Order!"]—which of these two adventures—[*The Chair.* "Order! order!"]—which of these two gentlemen—[*laughter and applause*]—is entitled to wear the belt as being the first dishonest blatherskite ever bred in this town—which he has dishonored, and which will be a sultry place for him from now out!" (*Vigorous applause.*)

Many Voices. "Open it!—open the sack!"

Mr. Burgess made a slit in the sack, slid his hand in and brought out an envelope. In it were a couple of folded notes. He said:

"One of these is marked, 'Not to be examined until all written communications which have been addressed to the Chair—if any—shall have been read.' The other is marked 'The Test.' Allow me. It is worded—to wit:

"'I do not require that the first half of the remark which was made to me by my benefactor shall be quoted with exactness, for it was not striking, and could be forgotten; but its closing fifteen words are quite striking, and I think easily rememberable; unless *these* shall be accurately reproduced, let the applicant be regarded as an impostor. My benefactor began by saying he seldom gave advice to any one, but that it always bore the hall-mark[3] of high value when he did give it. Then he said this—and it has never faded from my memory: *"You are far from being a bad man—"*.'"

Fifty Voices. "That settles it—the money's Wilson's! Wilson! Wilson! Speech! Speech!"

People jumped up and crowded around Wilson, wringing his hand and congratulating fervently—meantime the Chair was hammering with the gavel and shouting:

"Order, gentlemen! Order! Order! Let me finish reading, please." When quiet was restored, the reading was resumed—as follows:

"'*"Go, and reform—or, mark my words—some day, for your sins, you will die and go to hell or Hadleyburg—*TRY AND MAKE IT THE FORMER."'"

A ghastly silence followed. First an angry cloud began to settle darkly upon the faces of the citizenship; after a pause the cloud began to rise, and a tickled expression tried to take its place; tried so hard that it was only kept under with great and painful difficulty; the reporters, the Brixtonites, and other strangers bent their heads down and shielded their faces with their hands, and managed to hold in by main strength and heroic courtesy. At this most inopportune time burst upon the stillness the roar of solitary voice—Jack Halliday's:

"*That's* got the hall-mark on it!"

Then the house let go, strangers and all. Even Mr. Burgess's gravity broke down presently, then the audience considered itself officially absolved from all restraint, and it made the most of its privilege. It was a good long laugh, and a

---

[3]I.e., insignia, or stamp.

tempestuously whole-hearted one, but it ceased at last—long enough for Mr. Burgess to try to resume, and for the people to get their eyes partially wiped; then it broke out again; and afterward yet again; then at last Burgess was able to get out these serious words:

"It is useless to try to disguise the fact—we find ourselves in the presence of a matter of grave import. It involves the honor of your town, it strikes at the town's good name. The difference of a single word between the test-remarks offered by Mr. Wilson and Mr. Billson was itself a serious thing, since it indicated that one or the other of these gentlemen had commited a theft—"

The two men were sitting limp, nerveless, crushed; but at these words both were electrified into movement, and started to get up—

"Sit down!" said the Chair, sharply, and they obeyed. "That, as I have said, was a serious thing. And it was—but for only one of them. But the matter has become graver; for the honor of *both* is now in formidable peril. Shall I go even further, and say in inextricable peril? *Both* left out the crucial fifteen words." He paused. During several moments he allowed the pervading stillness to gather and deepen its impressive effects, then added: "There would seem to be but one way whereby this could happen. I ask these gentlemen—Was there *collusion?—agreement?*"

A low murmur sifted through the house; its import was, "He's got them both."

Billson was not used to emergencies; he sat in a helpless collapse. But Wilson was a lawyer. He struggled to his feet, pale and worried, and said:

"I ask the indulgence of the house while I explain this most painful matter. I am sorry to say what I am about to say, since it must inflict irreparable injury upon Mr. Billson, whom I have always esteemed and respected until now, and in whose invulnerability to temptation I entirely believed—as did you all. But for the preservation of my own honor I must speak—and with frankness. I confess with shame—and I now beseech your pardon for it—that I said to the ruined stranger all of the words contained in the test-remark, including the disparaging fifteen. [*Sensation.*] When the late publication was made I recalled them, and I resolved to claim the sack of coin, for by every right I was entitled to it. Now I will ask you to consider this point, and weigh it well: that stranger's gratitude to me that night knew no bounds; he said himself that he could find no words for it that were adequate, and that if he should ever be able he would repay me a thousandfold. Now, then, I ask you this: could I expect—could I believe—could I even remotely imagine—that, feeling as he did, he would do so ungrateful a thing as to add those quite unnecessary fifteen words to his test?—set a trap for me?—expose me as a slanderer of my own town before my own people assembled in a public hall? It was preposterous; it was impossible. His test would contain only the kindly opening clause of my remark. Of that I had no shadow of doubt. You would have thought as I did. You would not have expected a base betrayal from one whom you had befriended and against whom you had committed no offence. And so, with perfect confidence, perfect trust, I wrote on a piece of paper the opening words—ending with "Go, and reform,'—and signed it. When I was about to put it in an envelope I was called into my back office, and without thinking I left the paper lying open on my desk." He stopped, turned his head slowly toward Billson, waited a moment, then added: "I ask you to note this: when I returned, a little later, Mr. Billson was retiring by my street door." (*Sensation.*)

In a moment Billson was on his feet and shouting:

"It's a lie! It's an infamous lie!"

The Chair. "Be seated, sir! Mr. Wilson has the floor."

Billson's friends pulled him into his set and quieted him, and Wilson went on:

"Those are the simple facts. My note was now lying in a different place on the table from where I had left it. I noticed that, but attached no importance to it, thinking a draught had blown it there. That Mr. Billson would read a private paper was a thing which could not occur to me; he was an honorable man, and he would be above that. If you will allow me to say it, I think his extra word '*very*' stands explained; it is attributable to a defect of memory. I was the only man in the world who could furnish here any detail of the test-mark—by *honorable* means. I have finished."

There is nothing in the world like a persuasive speech to fuddle the mental apparatus and upset the convictions and debauch the emotions of an audience not practised in the tricks and delusions of oratory. Wilson sat down victorious. The house submerged him in tides of approving applause; friends swarmed to him and shook him by the hand and congratulated him, and Billson was shouted down and not allowed to say a word. The Chair hammered and hammered with its gavel, and kept shouting,

"But let us proceed, gentlemen, let us proceed!"

At last there was a measurable degree of quiet, and the hatter said,

"But what is there to proceed with, sir, but to deliver the money?"

Voices. "That's it! That's it! Come forward, Wilson!"

The Hatter. "I move three cheers for Mr. Wilson, Symbol of the special virtue which—,"

The cheers burst forth before he could finish; and in the midst of them—and in the midst of the clamor of the gavel also—some enthusiasts mounted Wilson on a big friend's shoulder and were going to fetch him in triumph to the platform. The Chair's voice now rose above the noise—

"Order! To your places! You forget that there is still a document to be read."

When quiet had been restored he took up the document, and was going to read it, but laid it down again saying, "I forgot; this is not be read until all written communications received by me have first been read." He took an envelope out of his pocket, removed its enclosure, glanced at it—seemed astonished—held it out and gazed at it—stared at it.

Twenty or thirty voices cried out:

"What is it? Read it! read it!"

And he did—slowly, and wondering:

" 'The remark which I made to the stranger—[*Voices.* "Hello! how's this?"]—was this: "You are far from being a bad man. [*Voices.* "Great Scott!"] Go, and reform." ' [*Voice.* "Oh, saw my leg off!"] Signed by Mr. Pinkerton the banker."

The pandemonium of delight which turned itself loose now was of a sort to make the judicious weep. Those whose withers were unwrung laughed till the tears ran down; the reporters, in throes of laughter, set down disordered pothooks which would never in the world be decipherable; and a sleeping dog jumped up, scared out of its wits, and barked itself crazy at the turmoil. All manner of cries were scattered through the din: "We're getting rich—*two* Symbols of Incorruptibility!—without counting Billson!" "*Three!*—count Shadbelly in—we can't have too many!" "All right—Billson's elected!" "Alas, poor Wilson—victim of *two* thieves!"

A Powerful Voice. "Silence! The Chair fished up something more out of its pocket."

Voices. "Hurrah! Is it something fresh? Read it! read! read!"

The Chair (reading). " 'The remark which I made,' etc. 'You are far from being a bad man. Go,' etc. Signed, 'Gregory Yates.' "

Tornado of Voices. "Four Symbols!" " 'Rah for Yates!" "Fish again!"

The house was in a roaring humor now, and ready to get all the fun out of the occasion that might be in it. Several Nineteeners, looking pale and distressed, got up and began to work their way toward the aisles, but a score of shouts went up:

"The doors, the doors—close the doors; no Incorruptible shall leave this place! Sit down, everybody!"

Sit down, everybody!"

The mandate was obeyed.

"Fish again! Read! read!"

The Chair fished again, and once more the familiar words began to fall from its lips— " 'You are far from being a bad man—' "

"Name! name! What's his name?"

" 'L. Ingoldsby Sargent.' "

"Five elected! Pile up the Symbols! Go on, go on!"

" 'You are far from being a bad—' "

"Name! name!"

" 'Nicholas Whitworth.' "

"Hooray! hooray! it's a symbolical day!"

Somebody wailed in, and began to sing this rhyme (leaving out "it's") to the lovely *Mikado* tune of "When a man's afraid of a beautiful maid";[4] the audience joined in, with joy; then, just in time, somebody contributed another line—

"And don't you this forget—"

The house roared it out. A third line was at once furnished—

"Corruptibles far from Hadleyburg are—"

The house roared that one too. As the last note died, Jack Halliday's voice rose high and clear, freighted with a final line—

"But the Symbols are here, you bet!"

That was sung, with booming enthusiasm. Then the happy house started in at the beginning and sang the four lines through twice, with immense swing and dash, and finished up with a crashing three-times-three and a tiger for "Hadleyburg the Incorruptible and all Symbols of it which we shall find worthy to receive the hall-mark to-night."

Then the shoutings at the Chair began again, all over the place:

"Go on! go on! Read! read some more! Read all you've got!"

"That's it—go on! We are winning eternal celebrity!"

A dozen men got up now and began to protest. They said that this farce was the work of some abandoned joker, and was an insult to the whole community. Without a doubt these signatures were all forgeries—

"Sit down! sit down! Shut up! You are confessing. We'll find *your* names in the lot."

---

[4]"When a man's afraid,/A beautiful maid/Is a cheering sight to see." W. S. Gilbert, *The Mikado*, Act II (1885).

"Mr. Chairman, how many of those envelopes have you got?"

The Chair counted.

"Together with those that have been already examined, there are nineteen."

A storm of derisive applause broke out.

"Perhaps they all contain the secret. I move that you open them all and read every signature that is attached to a note of that sort—and read also the first eight words of the note."

"Second the motion!"

It was put and carried—uproariously. Then poor old Richards got up, and his wife rose and stood at his side. Her head was bent down, so that none might see that she was crying. Her husband gave her his arm, and so supporting her, he began to speak in a quavering voice:

"My friends, you have known us two—Mary and me—all our lives, and I think you have liked us and respected us—"

The Chair interrupted him:

"Allow me. It is quite true—that which you are saying, Mr. Richards; this town *does* know you two; it *does* like you; it *does* respect you; more—it honors you and *loves* you—"

Halliday's voice rung out:

"That's the hall-marked truth, too! If the Chair is right, let the house speak up and say it. Rise! Now, then—hip! hip! hip!—all together!"

The house rose in mass, faced toward the old couple eagerly, filled the air with a snow-storm of waving handkerchiefs, and delivered the cheers with all its affectionate heart.

The Chair then continued:

"What I was going to say is this: We know your good heart, Mr. Richards, but this is not a time for the exercise of charity toward offenders. [Shouts of "Right! right!"] I see your generous purpose in your face, but I cannot allow you to plead for these men—"

"But I was going to—"

"Please take your seat, Mr. Richards. We must examine the rest of these notes—simple fairness to the men who have already been exposed requires this. As soon as that has been done—I give you my word for this—you shall be heard."

Many Voices. "Right!—the Chair is right—no interruption can be permitted at this stage! Go on!—the names!—the names!—according to the terms of the motion!"

The old couple sat reluctantly down, and the husband whispered to the wife, "It is pitifully hard to have to wait; the shame will be greater than ever when they find we were only going to plead for *ourselves.*"

Straightway the jollity broke loose again with the reading of the names.

" 'You are far from being a bad man—' Signature, 'Robert J. Titmarsh.' "

" 'You are far from being a bad man—' Signature, 'Eliphalet Weeks.' "

" 'You are far from being a bad man—' Signature, 'Oscar B. Wilder.' "

At this point the house lit upon the idea of taking the eight words out of the Chairman's hands. He was not unthankful for that. Thenceforward he held up each note in its turn, and waited. The house droned out the eight words in a massed and measured and musical deep volume of sound (with a daringly close resemblance to a well-known church chant)—" 'You are f-a-r from being a b-a-a-a-d man.' " Then the Chair said, "Signature, 'Archibald Wilcox.' " And so on, and so on, name after name, and everybody had an increasingly and gloriously good time except the wretched Nineteen. Now and then, when a particularly shining name was called, the house made the Chair wait while it chanted the whole of the test-remark from the beginning to the closing words, "And go to hell or Hadleyburg—try and make it the for-or-m-e-r!" and in these special cases they added a grand and agonized and imposing "A-a-a-a-*men!*"

The list dwindled, dwindled, dwindled, poor old Richards keeping tally of the count, wincing when a name resembling his own was pronounced, and waiting in miserable suspense for the time to come when it would be his humiliating privilege to rise with Mary and finish his plea, which he was intending to word thus: ". . . for until now we have never done any wrong thing, but have gone our humble way unreproached. We are very poor, we are old, and have no chick nor child to help us; we were sorely tempted, and we fell. It was my purpose when I got up before to make confession and beg that my name might not be read out in this public place, for it seemed to us that we could not bear it; but I was prevented. It was just; it was our place to suffer with the rest. It has been hard for us. It is the first time we have ever heard our name fall from any one's lips—sullied. Be merciful—for the sake of the better days; make our shame as light to bear as in your charity you can." At this point in his revery Mary nudged him, perceiving that his mind was absent. This house was chanting, "You are f-a-r," etc.

"Be ready," Mary whispered. "Your name comes now; he has read eighteen." The chant ended.

"Next! next! next!" came volleying from all over the house.

Burgess put his hand into his pocket. The old couple, trembling, began to rise. Burgess fumbled a moment, then said,

"I find I have read them all."

Faint with joy and surprise, the couple sank into their seats, and Mary whispered,

"Oh, bless God, we are saved!—he has lost ours—I wouldn't give this for a hundred of those sacks!"

The house burst out with its *Mikado* travesty, and sang it three times with ever-increasing enthusiasm, rising to its feet when it reached for the third time the closing line—

> "But the Symbols are here, you bet!"

and finishing up with cheers and a tiger for "Hadleyburg purity and our eighteen immortal representatives of it."

Then Wingate, the saddler, got up and proposed cheers "for the cleanest man in town, the one solitary important citizen in it who didn't try to steal that money—Edward Richards."

They were given with great and moving heartiness; then somebody proposed that Richards be elected sole Guardian and Symbol of the now Sacred Hadleyburg Tradition, with power and right to stand up and look the whole sarcastic world in the face.

Passed, by acclamation; then they sang the *Mikado* again, and ended it with,

> "And there's *one* Symbol left, you bet!"

There was a pause; then—

A Voice. "Now, then, who's to get the sack?"

The Tanner (with bitter sarcasm). "That's easy. The money has to be divided among the eighteen Incorruptibles. They gave the suffering stranger twenty dollars apiece—and that remark—each in his turn—it took twenty-two minutes for the procession to move past. Staked the stranger—total contribution, $360. All they want is just the loan back—and interest—forty thousand dollars altogether."

Many Voices (derisively). "That's it! Divvy! divvy! Be kind to the poor—don't keep them waiting!"

The Chair. "Order! I now offer the stranger's remaining document. It says: 'If no claimant shall appear [*grand chorus of groans*], I desire that you open the sack and count out the money to the principal citizens of your town, they to take it in trust [*Cries of "Oh! Oh! Oh!"*], and use it in such ways as to them shall seem best for the propagation and preservation of your community's noble reputation for incorruptible honesty [*more cries*]—a reputation to which their names and their efforts will add a new and far-reaching lustre.' [*Enthusiastic outburst of sarcastic applause.*] That seems to be all. No—here is a postscript:

"P.S.—CITIZENS OF HADLEYBURG: There *is* no test-remark—nobody made one. [*Great sensation.*] There wasn't any pauper stranger, nor any twenty-dollar contribution, nor any accompanying benediction and compliment—these are all inventions. [*General buzz and hum of astonishment and delight.*] Allow me to tell my story—it will take but a word or two. I passed through your town at a certain time, and received a deep offence which I had not earned. Any other man would have been content to kill one or two of you and call it square, but to me that would have been a trivial revenge, and inadequate; for the dead do not *suffer*. Besides, I could not kill you all—and, anyway, made as I am, even that would not have satisfied me. I wanted to damage every man in the place, and every woman—and not in their bodies or in their estate, but in their vanity— the place where feeble and foolish people are most vulnerable. So I disguised myself, and came back and studied you. You were easy game. You had an old and lofty reputation for honesty, and naturally you were proud of it—it was your treasure of treasures, the very apple of your eye. As soon as I found out that you carefully and vigilantly kept yourselves and your children *out of temptation,* I knew how to proceed. Why, you simple creatures, the weakest of all weak things is a virtue which has not been tested in the fire. I laid a plan, and gathered a list of names. My project was to corrupt Hadleyburg the Incorruptible. My idea was to make liars and thieves of nearly half a hundred smirchless men and women who had never in their lives uttered a lie or stolen a penny. I was afraid of Goodson. He was neither born nor reared in Hadleyburg. I was afraid that if I started to operate my scheme by getting my letter laid before you, you would say to yourselves, "Goodson is the only man among us who would give away twenty dollars to a poor devil"—and then you might not bite at my bait. But Heaven took Goodson; then I knew I was safe, and I set my trap and baited it. It may be that I shall not catch all the men to whom I mailed the pretended test secret, but I shall catch the most of them, if I know Hadleyburg nature. [*Voices.* "Right—he got every last one of them."] I believe they will even steal ostensible *gamble*-money, rather than miss, poor, tempted, and mistrained fellows. I am hoping to eternally and everlastingly squelch your vanity and give Hadleyburg a new renown—one that will *stick*—and spread far. If I have succeeded, open the sack and summon the Committee on Propagation and Preservation of the Hadleyburg Reputation.' "

A Cyclone of Voices. "Open it! Open it! The Eighteen to the front! Committee on Propagation of the Tradition! Forward—the Incorruptibles!"

The Chair ripped the sack wide, and gathered up a handful of bright, broad, yellow coins, shook them together, then examined them—

"Friends, they are only gilded disks of lead!"

There was a crashing outbreak of delight over this news, and when the noise had subsided, the tanner called out:

"By right of apparent seniority in this business, Mr. Wilson is Chairman of the Committee on Propagation of the Tradition. I suggest that he step forward on behalf of his pals, and receive in trust the money."

A Hundred Voices. "Wilson! Wilson! Wilson! Speech! Speech!"

Wilson (in a voice trembling with anger). "You will allow me to say, and without apologies for my language, *damn* the money!"

A Voice. "Oh, and him a Baptist!"

A Voice. "Seventeen Symbols left! Step up, gentlemen, and assume your trust!"

There was a pause—no response.

The Saddler. "Mr. Chairman, we've got *one* clean man left, anyway, out of the late aristocracy; and he needs money, and deserves it. I move that you appoint Jack Halliday to get up there and auction off that sack of gilt twenty-dollar pieces, and give the result to the right man—the man whom Hadleyburg delights to honor—Edward Richards."

This was received with great enthusiasm, the dog taking a hand again; the saddler started the bids at a dollar, the Brixton folk and Barnum's[5] representative fought hard for it, the people cheered every jump that the bids made, the excitement climbed moment by moment higher and higher, the bidders got on their mettle and grew steadily more and more daring, more and more determined, the jumps went from a dollar up to five, then to ten, then to twenty, then fifty, then to a hundred, then—

At the beginning of the auction Richards whispered in distress to his wife: "Oh, Mary, can we allow it? It—it—you see, it is an honor-reward, a testimonial to purity of character, and—and—can we allow it? Hadn't I better get up and— Oh, Mary, what ought we to do?—what do you think we—" (*Halliday's voice. "Fifteen I'm bid!—fifteen for the sack!—twenty!—ah, thanks!—thirty—thanks again! Thirty, thirty, thirty!—do I hear forty?—forty it is! Keep the ball rolling, gentlemen, keep it rolling!—fifty!—thanks, noble Roman!—going at fifty, fifty, fifty!—seventy!— ninety!—splendid!—a hundred!—pile it up, pile it up!—hundred and twenty—forty!— just in time!—hundred and fifty!—*TWO hundred!—superb! Do I hear two h—thanks!— two hundred and fifty!—")*

"It is another temptation, Edward—I'm all in a tremble—but, oh, we've escaped *one* temptation, and that ought to warn us, to—[*"Six did I hear?—thanks!— six fifty, six f—*SEVEN *hundred!"*] And yet, Edward, when you think—nobody susp—[*"Eight hundred dollars!—hurrah!—make it nine!—Mr. Parson, did I hear you say—thanks!—nine!—this noble sack of virgin lead going at only nine hundred dollars, gilding and all—come! do I hear—a thousand!—gratefully yours!—did some one say eleven?—a sack which is going to be the most celebrated in the whole Uni—"*] Oh, Edward" (beginning to sob), "we are *so* poor!—but—but—do as you think best— do as you think best."

Edward fell—that is, he sat still; sat with a conscience which was not satisfied, but which was overpowered by circumstances.

Meantime a stranger, who looked like an amateur detective gotten up as an impossible English earl, had been watching the evening's proceedings with manifest interest, and with a contented expression in his face; and he had been privately commenting to himself. He was now soliloquizing somewhat like this: "None of the Eighteen are bidding; that is not satisfactory; I must change that— the dramatic unities require it; they must buy the sack they tried to steal; they

---

[5]P. T. Barnum (1810–1891), showman famous for his displays of curiosities and freaks.

must pay a heavy price, too—some of them are rich. And another thing, when I make a mistake in Hadleyburg nature the man that puts that error upon me is entitled to a high honorarium, and some one must pay it. This poor old Richards has brought my judgment to shame; he is an honest man:—I don't understand it, but I acknowledge it. Yes, he saw my deuces-*and* with a straight flush, and by rights the pot is his. And it shall be a jack-pot, too, if I can manage it. He disappointed me, but let that pass."

He was watching the bidding. At a thousand, the market broke; the prices tumbled swiftly. He waited—and still watched. One competitor dropped out; then another, and another. He put in a bid or two, now. When the bids had sunk to ten dollars, he added a five; some one raised him a three; he waited a moment, then flung in a fifty-dollar jump, and the sack was his—at $1282. The house broke out in cheers—then stopped; for he was on his feet, and had lifted his hand. He began to speak.

"I desire to say a word, and ask a favor. I am a speculator in rarities, and I have dealings with persons interested in numismatics all over the world. I can make a profit on this purchase, just as it stands; but there is a way, if I can get your approval, whereby I can make every one of these leaden twenty-dollar pieces worth its face in gold, and perhaps more. Grant me that approval, and I will give part of my gains to your Mr. Richards, whose invulnerable probity you have so justly and so cordially recognized to-night; his share shall be ten thousand dollars, and I will hand him the money to-morrow. [*Great applause from the house.* But the "invulnerable probity" made the Richardses blush prettily; however, it went for modesty, and did no harm.] If you will pass my proposition by a good majority—I would like a two-thirds vote—I will regard that as the town's consent, and that is all I ask. Rarities are always helped by any device which will rouse curiosity and compel remark. Now if I may have your permission to stamp upon the faces of each of these ostensible coins the names of the eighteen gentlemen who—"

Nine-tenths of the audience were on their feet in a moment—dog and all— and the proposition was carried with a whirlwind of approving applause and laughter.

They sat down, and all the Symbols except "Dr." Clay Harkness got up, violently protesting against the proposed outrage, and threatening to—

"I beg you not to threaten me," said the stranger, calmly. "I know my legal rights, and am not accustomed to being frightened at bluster." (*Applause.*) He sat down. "Dr." Harkness saw an opportunity here. He was one of the two very rich men of the place, and Pinkerton was the other. Harkness was proprietor of a mint; that is to say, a popular patent medicine. He was running for the Legislature on one ticket, and Pinkerton on the other. It was a close race and a hot one, and getting hotter every day. Both had strong appetites for money; each had bought a great tract of land, with a purpose: there was going to be a new railway, and each wanted to be in the Legislature and help locate the route to his own advantage; a single vote might make the decision, and with it two or three fortunes. The stake was large, and Harkness was a daring speculator. He was sitting close to the stranger. He leaned over while one or another of the other Symbols was entertaining the house with protests and appeals, and asked, in a whisper,

"What is your price for the sack?"

"Forty thousand dollars."

"I'll give you twenty."

"No."

"Twenty-five."

"No."

"Say thirty."

"The price is forty thousand dollars; not a penny less."

"All right, I'll give it. I will come to the hotel at ten in the morning. I don't want it known; will see you privately."

"Very good." Then the stranger got up and said to the house:

"I find it late. The speeches of these gentlemen are not without merit, not without interest, not without grace; yet if I may be excused I will take my leave. I thank you for the great favor which you have shown me in granting my petition. I ask the Chair to keep the sack for me until to-morrow, and to hand these three five-hundred dollar notes to Mr. Richards." They were passed up to the Chair. "At nine I will call for the sack, and at eleven will deliver the rest of the ten thousand to Mr. Richards in person, at his home. Good-night."

Then he slipped out, and left the audience making a vast noise, which was composed of a mixture of cheers, the *Mikado* song, dog-disapproval, and the chant, "You are f-a-r from being a b-a-a-d man—a-a-a-a-men!"

IV

At home the Richardses had to endure congratulations and compliments until midnight. Then they were left to themselves. They looked a little sad, and they sat silent and thinking. Finally Mary sighed and said,

"Do you think we are to blame, Edward—*much* to blame?" and her eyes wandered to the accusing triplet of big bank-notes lying on the table, where the congratulators had been gloating over them and reverently fingering them. Edward did not answer at once; then he brought out a sigh and said, hesitatingly:

"We—we couldn't help it, Mary. It—well, it was ordered. *All* things are."

Mary glanced up and looked at him steadily, but he didn't return the look. Presently she said:

"I thought congratulations and praises always tasted good. But—it seems to me, now—Edward?"

"Well?"

"Are you going to stay in the bank?"

"N-no."

"Resign?"

"In the morning—by note."

"It does seem best."

Richards bowed his head in his hands and muttered:

"Before, I was not afraid to let oceans of people's money pour through my hands, but—Mary, I am so tired, so tired—"

"We will go to bed."

At nine in the morning the stranger called for the sack and took it to the hotel in a cab. At ten Harkness had a talk with him privately. The stranger asked for and got five checks on a metropolitan bank—drawn to "Bearer."—four for $1500 each, and one for $34,000. He put one of the former in his pocket-book, and the remainder, representing $38,500, he put in an envelope, and with these he added a note, which he wrote after Harkness was gone. At eleven he called at the Richards house and knocked. Mrs. Richards peeped through the shutters, then went and received the envelope, and the stranger disappeared without a word. She came back flushed and a little unsteady on her legs, and gasped out:

"I am sure I recognized him! Last night it seemed to me that maybe I had seen him somewhere before."

"He is the man that brought the sack here?"

"I am almost sure of it."

"Then he is the ostensible Stephenson too, and sold every important citizen in this town with his bogus secret. Now if he has sent checks instead of money, we are sold too, after we thought we had escaped. I was beginning to feel fairly comfortable once more, after my night's rest, but the look of that envelope makes me sick. It isn't fat enough; $8500 in even the largest bank-notes make more bulk than that."

"Edward, why do you object to checks?"

"Checks signed by Stephenson! I am resigned to take the $8500 if it could come in bank-notes—for it does seem that it was so ordered, Mary—but I have never had much courage, and I have not the pluck to try to market a check signed with that disastrous name. It would be a trap. That man tried to catch me; we escaped somehow or other; and now he is trying a new way. If it is checks—"

"Oh, Edward, it is *too* bad!" and she held up the checks and began to cry.

"Put them in the fire! quick! we mustn't be tempted. It is a trick to make the world laugh at *us*, along with the rest, and—Give them to *me*, since you can't do it!" He snatched them and tried to hold his grip till he could get to the stove; but he was human, he was a cashier, and he stopped a moment to make sure of the signature. Then he came near to fainting.

"Fan me, Mary, fan me! They are the same as gold!"

"Oh, how lovely, Edward! Why?"

"Signed by Harkness. What can the mystery of that be, Mary?"

"Edward, do you think—"

"Look here—look at this! Fifteen—fifteen—fifteen—thirty-four. Thirty-eight thousand five hundred! Mary, the sack isn't worth twelve dollars, and Harkness—apparently—has paid about par for it."

"And does it all come to us, do you think—instead of the ten thousand?"

"Why, it looks like it. And the checks are made to 'Bearer,' too."

"Is that good, Edward? What is it for?"

"A hint to collect them at some distant bank, I reckon. Perhaps Harkness doesn't want the matter known. What is that—a note?"

"Yes. It was with the checks."

It was in the "Stephenson" handwriting, but there was no signature. It said:

"I am a disappointed man. Your honesty is beyond the reach of temptation. I had a different idea about it, but I wronged you in that, and I beg pardon, and do it sincerely. I honor you—and that is sincere, too. This town is not worthy to kiss the hem of your garment. Dear sir, I made a square bet with myself that there were nineteen debauchable men in your self-righteous community. I have lost. Take the whole pot, you are entitled to it."

Richards drew a deep sigh, and said:

"It seems written with fire—it burns so. Mary—I am miserable again."

"I, too. Ah, dear, I wish—"

"To think, Mary—he *believes* in me."

"Oh, don't, Edward—I can't bear it."

"If those beautiful words were deserved, Mary—and God knows I believed I deserved them once—I think I could give the forty thousand dollars for them.

And I would put that paper away, as representing more than gold and jewels, and keep it always. But now—We could not live in the shadow of its accusing presence, Mary."

He put it in the fire.

A messenger arrived and delivered an envelope. Richards took from it a note and read it; it was from Burgess.

"You saved me, in a difficult time. I saved you last night. It was at cost of a lie, but I made the sacrifice freely, and out of a grateful heart. None in this village knows so well as I know how brave and good and noble you are. At bottom you cannot respect me, knowing as you do of that matter of which I am accused, and by the general voice condemned; but I beg that you will at least believe that I am a grateful man; it will help me to bear my burden.

[Signed]   BURGESS."

"Saved, once more. And on such terms!" He put the note in the fire. "I—I wish I were dead, Mary, I wish I were out of it all."

"Oh, these are bitter, bitter days, Edward. The stabs, through their very generosity, are so deep—and they come so fast!"

Three days before the election each of two thousand voters suddenly found himself in possession of a prized memento—one of the renowned bogus double-eagles. Around one of its faces was stamped these words:"THE REMARK I MADE TO THE POOR STRANGER WAS—" Around the other face was stamped these: "GO, AND REFORM. (SIGNED) PINKERTON." Thus the entire remaining refuse of the renowned joke was emptied upon a single head, and with calamitous effect. It revived the recent vast laugh and concentrated it upon Pinkerton; and Harkness's election was a walk-over.

Within twenty-four hours after the Richardses had received their checks their consciences were quieting down, discouraged; the old couple were learning to reconcile themselves to the sin which they had committed. But they were to learn, now, that a sin takes on new and real terrors when there seems a chance that it is going to be found out. This gives it a fresh and most substantial and important aspect. At church the morning sermon was of the usual pattern; it was the same old things said in the same old way; they had heard them a thousand times and found them innocuous, next to meaningless, and easy to sleep under; but now it was different: the sermon seemed to bristle with accusations; it seemed aimed straight and specially at people who were concealing deadly sins. After church they got away from the mob of congratulators as soon as they could, and hurried homeward, chilled to the bone at they did not know what—vague, shadowy, indefinite fears. And by chance they caught a glimpse of Mr. Burgess as he turned a corner. He paid no attention to their nod of recognition! He hadn't seen it; but they did not know that. What could his conduct mean? It might mean—it might mean—oh, a dozen dreadful things. Was it possible that he knew that Richards could have cleared him of guilt in that bygone time, and had been silently waiting for a chance to even up accounts? At home, in their distress they got to imagining that their servant might have been in the next room listening when Richards revealed the secret to his wife that he knew of Burgess's innocence; next Richards began to imagine that he had heard the swish of a gown in there at that time; next, he was sure he *had* heard it. They would call Sarah in, on a pretext, and watch her face; if she had been betraying them to Mr. Burgess, it would show in her manner. They asked her some questions—questions which were so random and incoherent and seemingly purposeless that the girl felt sure that the old people's minds had been affected by their sudden good fortune; the sharp and watchful gaze which they bent upon her frightened her, and that completed the business. She blushed, she became nervous and confused, and to the old people these were plain signs of guilt—guilt of some fearful sort or other—without doubt she was a spy and a traitor. When they were alone again they began to piece many unrelated things together and get horrible results out of the combination. When things had got about to the worst, Richards was delivered of a sudden gasp, and his wife asked.

"Oh, what is it?—what is it?"

"The note—Burgess's note! Its language was sarcastic, I see it now." He quoted: "At bottom you cannot respect me, *knowing*, as you do, of *that matter* of which I am accused'—oh, it is perfectly plain, now. God help me! He knows that I know! You see the ingenuity of the phrasing. It was a trap—and like a fool, I walked into it. And Mary—?"

"Oh, it is dreadful—I know what you are going to say—he didn't return your transcript of the pretended test-remark."

"No—kept it to destroy us with. Mary, he has exposed us to some already. I know it—I know it well. I saw it in a dozen faces after church. Ah, he wouldn't answer our nod of recognition—*he* knew what he had been doing!"

In the night the doctor was called. The news went around in the morning that the old couple were rather seriously ill—prostrated by the exhausting excitement growing out of their great windfall, the congratulations, and the late hours, the doctor said. The town was sincerely distressed; for these old people were about all it had left to be proud of, now.

Two days later the news was worse. The old couple were delirious, and were doing strange things. By witness of the nurses, Richards had exhibited checks—for $8,500? No—for an amazing sum—$38,500! What could be the explanation of this gigantic piece of luck?

The following day the nurses had more news—and wonderful. They had concluded to hide the checks, lest harm come to them; but when they searched they were gone from under the patient's pillow—vanished away. The patient said:

"Let the pillow alone; what do you want?"

"We thought it best that the checks—"

"You will never see them again—they are destroyed. They came from Satan. I saw the hell-brand on them, and I knew they were sent to betray me to sin." Then he fell to gabbling strange and dreadful things which were not clearly understandable, and which the doctor admonished them to keep to themselves.

Richards was right; the checks were never seen again.

A nurse must have talked in her sleep, for within two days the forbidden gabblings were the property of the town; and they were of a surprising sort. They seemed to indicate that Richards had been a claimant for the sack himself, and that Burgess had concealed that fact and then maliciously betrayed it.

Burgess was taxed with this and stoutly denied it. And he said it was not fair to attach weight to the chatter of a sick old man who was out of his mind. Still, suspicion was in the air, and there was much talk.

After a day or two it was reported that Mrs. Richards's delirious deliveries were getting to be duplicates of her husband's. Suspicion flamed up into conviction, now, and the town's pride in the purity of its one undiscredited important citizen began to dim down and flicker toward extinction.

Six days passed, then came more news. The old couple were dying. Richards's mind cleared in his latest hour, and he sent for Burgess. Burgess said:

"Let the room be cleared. I think he wishes to say something in privacy."

"No!" said Richards; "I want witnesses. I want you all to hear my confession, so that I may die a man, and not a dog. I was clean—artifically—like the rest; and like the rest I fell when temptation came. I signed a lie, and claimed the miserable sack. Mr. Burgess remembered that I had done him a service and in gratitude (and ignorance) he suppressed my claim and saved me. You know the thing that was charged against Burgess years ago. My testimony, and mine alone, could have cleared him, and I was a coward, and left him to suffer disgrace—"

"No—no—Mr. Richards, you—"

"My servant betrayed my secret to him—"

"No one has betrayed anything to me—"

—"and then he did a natural and justifiable thing; he repented of the saving kindness which he had done me, and he *exposed* me—as I deserved—"

"Never!—I make oath—"

"Out of my heart I forgive him."

Burgess's impassioned protestations fell upon deaf ears; the dying man passed away without knowing that once more he had done poor Burgess a wrong. The old wife died that night.

The last of the sacred Nineteen had fallen a prey to the fiendish sack; the town was stripped of the last rag of its ancient glory. Its mourning was now showy, but it was deep.

By act of the Legislature—upon prayer and petition—Hadleyburg was allowed to change its name to (never mind what—I will not give it away), and leave one word out of the motto that for many generations had graced the town's official seal.

It is an honest town once more, and the man will have to rise early that catches it napping again.

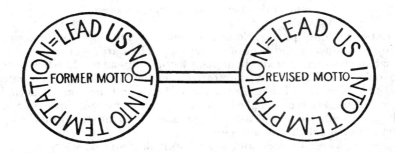

FORMER MOTTO — LEAD US NOT INTO TEMPTATION

REVISED MOTTO — LEAD US INTO TEMPTATION

1899

THE WAR PRAYER[1]

It was a time of great and exalting excitement. The country was up in arms, the war was on, in every breast burned the holy fire of patriotism; the drums were beating, the bands playing, the toy pistols popping, the bunched firecrackers hissing and spluttering; on every hand and far down the receding and fading

---

[1]Dictated by Twain in 1904 or 1905 and first published in 1923.

spread of roofs and balconies a fluttering wilderness of flags flashed in the sun; daily the young volunteers marched down the wide avenue gay and fine in their new uniforms, the proud fathers and mothers and sisters and sweethearts cheering them with voices choked with happy emotion as they swung by; nightly the packed mass meetings listened, panting, to patriot oratory which stirred the deepest deeps of their hearts, and which they interrupted at briefest intervals with cyclones of applause, the tears running down their cheeks the while; in the churches the pastors preached devotion to flag and country, and invoked the God of Battles, beseeching His aid in our good cause in outpouring of fervid eloquence which moved every listener. It was indeed a glad and gracious time, and the half dozen rash spirits that ventured to disapprove of the war and cast a doubt upon its righteousness straightway got such a stern and angry warning that for their personal safety's sake they quickly shrank out of sight and offended no more in that way.

Sunday morning came—next day the battalions would leave for the front; the church was filled; the volunteers were there, their young faces alight with martial dreams—visions of the stern advance, the gathering momentum, the rushing charge, the flashing sabers, the flight of the foe, the tumult, the enveloping smoke, the fierce pursuit, the surrender!—then home from the war, bronzed heroes, welcomed, adored, submerged in golden seas of glory! With the volunteers sat their dear ones, proud, happy, and envied by the neighbors and friends who had no sons and brothers to send forth to the field of honor, there to win for the flag, or failing, die the noblest of noble deaths. The service proceeded; a war chapter from the Old Testament was read; the first prayer was said; it was followed by an organ burst that shook the building, and with one impulse the house rose, with glowing eyes and beating hearts, and poured out that tremendous invocation—

> "God the all-terrible! Thou who ordainest,
> Thunder thy clarion and lightning thy sword!"

Then came the "long" prayer. None could remember the like of it for passionate pleading and moving and beautiful language. The burden of its supplication was, that an ever-merciful and benignant Father of us all would watch over our noble young soldiers, and aid, comfort, and encourage them in their patriotic work; bless them, shield them in the day of battle and the hour of peril, bear them in His mighty hand, make them strong and confident, invincible in the bloody onset; help them to crush the foe, grant to them and to their flag and country imperishable honor and glory—

An aged stranger entered and moved with slow and noiseless step up the main aisle, his eyes fixed upon the minister, his long body clothed in a robe that reached to his feet, his head bare, his white hair descending in a frothy cataract to his shoulders, his seamy face unnaturally pale, pale even to ghastliness. With all eyes following him and wondering, he made his silent way; without pausing, he ascended to the preacher's side and stood there, waiting. With shut lids the preacher, unconscious of his presence, continued his moving prayer, and at last finished it with the words, uttered in fervent appeal, "Bless our arms, grant us the victory, O Lord our God, Father and Protector of our land and flag!"

The stranger touched his arm, motioned him to step aside—which the startled minister did—and took his place. During some moments he surveyed the spellbound audience with solemn eyes, in which burned an uncanny light; then in a deep voice he said:

"I come from the Throne—bearing a message from Almighty God!" The words smote the house with a shock; if the stranger perceived it he gave no attention. "He has heard the prayer of His servant your shepherd, and will grant it if such shall be your desire after I, His messenger, shall have explained to you its import—that is to say, its full import. For it is like unto many of the prayers of men, in that it asks for more than he who utters it is aware of—except he pause and think.

"God's servant and yours has prayed his prayer. Has he paused and taken thought? Is it one prayer? No, it is two—one uttered, the other not. Both have reached the ear of Him Who heareth all supplications, the spoken and the unspoken. Ponder this—keep it in mind. If you would beseech a blessing upon yourself, beware! lest without intent you invoke a curse upon a neighbor at the same time. If you pray for the blessing of rain upon your crop which needs it, by that act you are possibly praying for a curse upon some neighbor's crop which may not need rain and can be injured by it.

"You have heard your servant's prayer—the uttered part of it. I am commissioned of God to put into words the other part of it—that part which the pastor—and also you in your hearts—fervently prayed silently. And ignorantly and unthinkingly? God grant that it was so! You heard these words: 'Grant us the victory, O Lord our God!' That is sufficient. The *whole* of the uttered prayer is compact into those pregnant words. Elaborations were not necessary. When you have prayed for victory you have prayed for many unmentioned results which follow victory—*must* follow it, cannot help but follow it. Upon the listening spirit of God the Father fell also the unspoken part of the prayer. He commandeth me to put it into words. Listen!

"O Lord our Father, our young patriots, idols of our hearts, go forth to battle—be Thou near them! With them—in spirit—we also go forth from the sweet peace of our beloved firesides to smite the foe. O Lord our God, help us to tear their soldiers to bloody shreds with our shells; help us to cover their smiling fields with the pale forms of their patriot dead; help us to drown the thunder of the guns with the shrieks of their wounded, writhing in pain; help us to lay waste their humble homes with a hurricane of fire; help us to wring the hearts of their unoffending widows with unavailing grief; help us to turn them out roofless with their little children to wander unfriended the wastes of their desolated land in rags and hunger and thirst, sports of the sun flames of summer and the icy winds of winter, broken in spirit, worn with travail, imploring Thee for the refuge of the grave and denied it—for our sakes who adore Thee, Lord, blast their hopes, blight their lives, protract their bitter pilgrimage, make heavy their steps, water their way with their tears, stain the white snow with the blood of their wounded feet! We ask it, in the spirit of love, or Him Who is the Source of Love, and Who is the ever-faithful refuge and friend of all that are sore beset and seek His aid with humble and contrite hearts. Amen."

(After a pause.) "Ye have prayed it; if ye still desire it, speak! The messenger of the Most High waits."

It was believed afterward that the man was a lunatic, because there was no sense in what he said.

1904–1905   1923

William Dean Howells   *1837–1920*

As a novelist, critic, and magazine editor, Howells was the leading spokesman of literary realism in nineteenth-century America. In an age of genteel authors, he was one of a new breed, like Twain and Hamlin Garland, raised in humble surroundings in America's midlands. Born in Ohio, the son of a printer, Howells was considered a small-town prodigy. By the age of seven he was setting type in his father's print shop, and though he had little formal education he remained throughout his life an omnivorous reader who could enjoy everything but historical novels, romantic fiction, and detective stories.

At twenty-one he became city editor of the Ohio State Journal *in Columbus. In 1860 he wrote a campaign biography of Lincoln, and after Lincoln was elected President, Howells was rewarded with appointment as American Consul in Venice, Italy. His life in Italy and his reading of Italian literature sharpened his taste for realistic writing and gave him the subject matter for a series of essays on Italian poets, four novels of Americans in Italy, and three travel books, including* Venetian Life *(1866), a collection of sketches that was reissued more than twenty times and became his most profitable book.*

With the end of the Civil War, Howells returned to America and moved to Boston, where he was appointed assistant editor and then editor-in-chief of the nation's most eminent journal, The Atlantic Monthly. *He came to know the literary "gods and half gods and quarter gods of New England," among them Lowell, who was amazed that such a book of "airy elegance" as* Venetian Life *could have been written by a man from "the rough-and-ready West."*

Howells' ten years as editor refined his critical sense while his experiences as an outlander observing the domestic manners of the American middle class gave him the themes and events of his fiction of urban society. In 1872 he published his first novel, Their Wedding Journey, *and in 1881, having written more than a dozen books, six of them novels, Howells left the* Atlantic *and eventually settled in New York where he continued his prolific writing. He wrote over a hundred books—novels, collections of short stories, essays, autobiographies, and verse. His finest novel,* The Rise of Silas Lapham, *was published in 1885. His literary doctrines were partially "summed up" in* Criticism and Fiction *(1891), a selection of essays he had written for his column, "The Editor's Study," which appeared in* Harper's *from 1886 to 1892.*

Howells portrayed the American scene in mansions, summer resorts, railroad cars, and offices. He attempted to make his characters not heroic but "real," with all their virtues and all their "vacancy and tiresomeness." Much of his realism was external, characters and events viewed from without. His works rarely achieved, or sought to achieve, what modern critics think of as psychological depth. He dealt with proprieties. The evils of his characters were slight, their passions restrained, their triumphs few. He avoided the excitements and catastrophes of romanticism just as he avoided sex and sensuality and what he considered to be the sordid excesses of naturalism.

As much as any man he had brought the Age of Realism. His reviews and his personal attention had encouraged the development of Mark Twain, Stephen Crane, Hamlin Garland, and Frank Norris, and he helped introduce to America such famous writers as Ibsen, Dostoyevsky, and Tolstoy. Howells was called the literary symbol of his age; he received honorary degrees from Yale, Columbia, Princeton, and Oxford. Newspaper and magazine writers exalted him, among them Theodore Dreiser, who reported on Howells' climb up "Fame's Ladder." But by the early years of the century his "smiling" realism had been displaced by the naturalism and harsher realisms of the twentieth century; his vogue had passed, and he wrote to Henry James, "I am comparatively a dead cult with my statues cut down and the grass growing over me in the pale moonlight."

FURTHER READING: *The Writings of William Dean Howells*, 6 vols., 1900, now superseded by a new edition in progress: *A Selected Edition of W. D. Howells*, 41 vols. projected, ed. E. Cady, 1968—. *The Complete Plays of W. D. Howells*, ed. W. Meserve, 1960; M. Howells, *Life in Letters of William Dean Howells*, 2 vols., 1928, 1968; J. Woodress, *Howells and Italy*, 1952; E. Carter, *Howells and the Age of Realism*, 1954; E. Cady, *The Road to Realism*, 1956, 1986; E. Cady, *The Realist at War*, 1958, 1986; V. Brooks, *Howells, His Life and World*, 1959; G. Bennett, *William Dean Howells*, 1968; E. Wagenknecht, *William Dean Howells, The Friendly Eye*, 1969; K. Lynn, *William Dean Howells, An American Life*, 1971; G. Bennett, *The Realism of William Dean Howells*, 1973; W. Alexander, *William Dean Howells, The Realist as Humanist*, 1981; K. Eble, *William Dean Howells*, 1982; E. Prioleau, *The Circle of Eros, Sexuality in the Work of William Dean Howells*, 1983; J. Crowley, *The Black Heart's Truth, The Early Career of William Dean Howells*, 1985.

TEXT: "Editha," *Between the Dark and the Daylight*, 1907; *Criticism and Fiction*, 1891.

EDITHA

The air was thick with the war feeling, like the electricity of a storm which has not yet burst. Editha sat looking out into the hot spring afternoon, with her lips parted, and panting with the intensity of the question whether she could let him go. She had decided that she could not let him stay, when she saw him at the end of the still leafless avenue, making slowly up towards the house, with his head down and his figure relaxed. She ran impatiently out on the veranda, to the edge of the steps, and imperatively demanded greater haste of him with her will before she called aloud to him: "George!"

He had quickened his pace in mystical response to her mystical urgence, before he could have heard her; now he looked up and answered, "Well?"

"Oh, how united we are!" she exulted, and then she swooped down the steps to him. "What is it?" she cried.

"It's war," he said, and he pulled her up to him and kissed her.

She kissed him back intensely, but irrelevantly, as to their passion, and uttered from deep in her throat, "How glorious!"

"It's war," he repeated, without consenting to her sense of it; and she did not know just what to think at first. She never knew what to think of him; that made his mystery, his charm. All through their courtship, which was contemporaneous with the growth of the war feeling, she had been puzzled by his want of seriousness about it. He seemed to despise it even more than he abhorred it. She could have understood his abhorring any sort of bloodshed; that would have been a survival of his old life when he thought he would be a minister, and before he changed and took up the law. But making light of a cause so high and noble seemed to show a want of earnestness at the core of his being. Not but that she felt herself able to cope with a congenital defect of that sort, and make his love for her save him from himself. Now perhaps the miracle was already wrought in him. In the presence of the tremendous fact that he announced, all triviality seemed to have gone out of him; she began to feel that. He sank down on the top step, and wiped his forehead with his handkerchief, while she poured out upon him her question of the origin and authenticity of his news.

All the while, in her duplex emotioning, she was aware that now at the very beginning she must put a guard upon herself against urging him, by any word or act, to take the part that her whole soul willed him to take, for the completion of her ideal of him. He was very nearly perfect as he was, and he must be allowed to perfect himself. But he was peculiar, and he might very well be reasoned out of his peculiarity. Before her reasoning went her emotioning: her nature pulling upon his nature, her womanhood upon his manhood, without her knowing the means she was using to the end she was willing. She had always supposed that the man who won her would have done something to win her; she did not know what, but something. George Gearson had simply asked her for her love, on the way home from a concert, and she gave her love to him, without, as it were, thinking. But now, it flashed upon her, if he could do something worthy to *have* won her—be a hero, *her* hero—it would be even better than if he had done it before asking her; it would be grander. Besides, she had believed in the war from the beginning.

"But don't you see, dearest," she said, "that it wouldn't have come to this if it hadn't been in the order of Providence? And I call any war glorious that is for the liberation of people who have been struggling for years against the cruelest oppression. Don't you think so, too?"

"I suppose so," he returned languidly. "But war! Is it glorious to break the peace of the world?"

"That ignoble peace! It was no peace at all, with that crime and shame at our very gates." She was conscious of parroting the current phrases of the newspapers, but it was no time to pick and choose her words. She must sacrifice anything to the high ideal she had for him, and after a good deal of rapid argument she ended with the climax: "But now it doesn't matter about the how or why. Since the war has come, all that is gone. There are no two sides any more. There is nothing now but our country."

He sat with his eyes closed and his head leant back against the veranda, and he remarked, with a vague smile, as if musing aloud, "Our country—right or wrong."[1]

"Yes, right or wrong!" she returned, fervidly. "I'll go and get you some lemonade." She rose rustling, and whisked away; when she came back with two tall glasses of clouded liquid on a tray, and the ice clucking in them, he still sat as she had left him, and she said, as if there had been no interruption: "But there is no question of wrong in this case. I call it a sacred war. A war for liberty and humanity, if ever there was one. And I know you will see it just as I do, yet."

He took half the lemonade at a gulp, and he answered as he set the glass down: "I know you always have the highest ideal. When I differ from you I ought to doubt myself."

A generous sob rose in Editha's throat for the humility of a man, so very nearly perfect, who was willing to put himself below her.

Besides, she felt, more subliminally, that he was never so near slipping through her fingers as when he took that meek way.

"You shall not say that! Only, for once I happen to be right." She seized his hand in her two hands, and poured her soul from her eyes into his. "Don't you think so?" she entreated him.

He released his hand and drank the rest of his lemonade, and she added, "Have mine too," but he shook his head in answering, "I've no business to think so, unless I act so, too."

Her heart stopped a beat before it pulsed on with leaps that she felt in her neck. She had noticed that strange thing in men: they seemed to feel bound to do what they believed, and not think a thing was finished when they said it, as

---

[1]A phrase coined in 1816 by the American naval hero Stephen Decatur (1779–1820).

girls did. She knew what was in his mind, but she pretended not, as she said, "Oh, I am not sure," and then faltered.

He went on as if to himself, without apparently heeding her: "There's only one way of proving one's faith in a thing like this."

She could not say that she understood, but she did understand.

He went on again. "If I believed—if I felt as you do about this war—Do you wish me to feel as you do?"

Now she was really not sure; so she said: "George, I don't know what you mean."

He seemed to muse away from her as before. "There is a sort of fascination in it. I suppose that at the bottom of his heart every man would like at times to have his courage tested, to see how he would act."

"How can you talk in that ghastly way?"

"It *is* rather morbid. Still, that's what it comes to, unless you're swept away by ambition or driven by conviction. I haven't the conviction or the ambition, and the other thing is what it comes to with me. I ought to have been a preacher, after all; then I couldn't have asked it of myself, as I must, now I'm a lawyer. And you believe it's a holy war, Editha?" he suddenly addressed her. "Oh, I know you do! But you wish me to believe so, too?"

She hardly knew whether he was mocking or not, in the ironical way he always had with her plainer mind. But the only thing was to be outspoken with him.

"George, I wish you to believe whatever you think is true, at any and every cost. If I've tried to talk you into anything, I take it all back."

"Oh, I know that, Editha. I know how sincere you are, and how—I wish I had your undoubting spirit! I'll think it over; I'd like to believe as you do. But I don't, now; I don't, indeed. It isn't this war alone; though this seems peculiarly wanton and needless; but it's every war—so stupid; it makes me sick. Why shouldn't this thing have been settled reasonably?"

"Because," she said, very throatily again, "God meant it to be war."

"You think it was God? Yes, I suppose that is what people will say."

"Do you suppose it would have been war if God hadn't meant it?"

"I don't know. Sometimes it seems as if God had put this world into men's keeping to work it as they pleased."

"Now, George, that is blasphemy."

"Well, I won't blaspheme. I'll try to believe in your pocket Providence," he said, and then he rose to go.

"Why don't you stay to dinner?" Dinner at Balcom's Works was at one o'clock.

"I'll come back to supper, if you'll let me. Perhaps I shall bring you a convert."

"Well, you may come back, on that condition."

"All right. If I don't come, you'll understand."

He went away without kissing her, and she felt it a suspension of their engagement. It all interested her intensely; she was undergoing a tremendous experience, and she was being equal to it. While she stood looking after him, her mother came out through one of the long windows onto the veranda, with a catlike softness and vagueness.

"Why didn't he stay to dinner?"

"Because—because—war has been declared," Editha pronounced, without turning.

Her mother said, "Oh, my!" and then said nothing more until she had sat down in one of the large Shaker chairs[2] and rocked herself for some time. Then

[2]Furniture manufactured at Shaker religious communes and characterized by elegant simplicity.

she closed whatever tacit passage of thought there had been in her mind with the spoken words: "Well, I hope *he* won't go."

"And *I* hope he *will*," the girl said, and confronted her mother with a stormy exaltation that would have frightened any creature less unimpressionable than a cat.

Her mother rocked herself again for an interval of cogitation. What she arrived at in speech was: "Well, I guess you've done a wicked thing, Editha Balcom."

The girl said, as she passed indoors through the same window her mother had come out by: "I haven't done anything—yet."

In her room, she put together all her letters and gifts from Gearson, down to the withered petals of the first flower he had offered, with that timidity of his veiled in that irony of his. In the heart of the packet she enshrined her engagement ring which she had restored to the pretty box he had brought it her in. Then she sat down, if not calmly yet strongly, and wrote:

"GEORGE:—I understood when you left me. But I think we had better emphasize your meaning that if we cannot be one in everything we had better be one in nothing. So I am sending these things for your keeping till you have made up your mind.

"I shall always love you, and therefore I shall never marry any one else. But the man I marry must love his country first of all, and be able to say to me,

> " 'I could not love thee, dear, so much,
> Loved I not honor more.'[3]

"There is no honor above America with me. In this great hour there is no other honor.

"Your heart will make my words clear to you. I had never expected to say so much, but it has come upon me that I must say the utmost. EDITHA."

She thought she had worded her letter well, worded it in a way that could not be bettered; all had been implied and nothing expressed.

She had it ready to send with the packet she had tied with red, white, and blue ribbon, when it occurred to her that she was not just to him, that she was not giving him a fair chance. He had said he would go and think it over, and she was not waiting. She was pushing, threatening, compelling. That was not a woman's part. She must leave him free, free, free. She could not accept for her country or herself a forced sacrifice.

In writing her letter she had satisfied the impulse from which it sprang; she could well afford to wait till he had thought it over. She put the packet and the letter by, and rested serene in the consciousness of having done what was laid upon her by her love itself to do, and yet used patience, mercy, justice.

She had her reward. Gearson did not come to tea, but she had given him till morning, when, late at night there came up from the village the sound of a fife and drum, with a tumult of voices, in shouting, singing, and laughing. The noise drew nearer and nearer; it reached the street end of the avenue; there it silenced itself, and one voice, the voice she knew best, rose over the silence. It fell; the air was filled with cheers; the fife and drum struck up, with the shouting, singing, and laughing again, but now retreating; and a single figure came hurrying up the avenue.

She ran down to meet her lover and clung to him. He was very gay, and he put his arm round her with a boisterous laugh. "Well, you must call me Captain

[3]From "To Lucasta, Going to the Wars," by the English poet Richard Lovelace (1618–1658).

now; or Cap, if you prefer; that's what the boys call me. Yes, we've had a meeting at the town-hall, and everybody has volunteered; and they selected me for captain, and I'm going to the war, the big war, the glorious war, the holy war ordained by the pocket Providence that blesses butchery. Come along; let's tell the whole family about it. Call them from their downy beds, father, mother, Aunt Hitty, and all the folks!"

But when they mounted the veranda steps he did not wait for a larger audience; he poured the story out upon Editha alone.

"There was a lot of speaking, and then some of the fools set up a shout for me. It was all going one way, and I thought it would be a good joke to sprinkle a little cold water on them. But you can't do that with a crowd that adores you. The first thing I knew I was sprinkling hell-fire on them. 'Cry havoc, and let slip the dogs of war.'[4] That was the style. Now that it had come to the fight, there were no two parties; there was one country, and the thing was to fight to a finish as quick as possible. I suggested volunteering then and there, and I wrote my name first of all on the roster. Then they elected me—that's all. I wish I had some ice-water."

She left him walking up and down the veranda, while she ran for the ice-pitcher and a goblet, and when she came back he was still walking up and down, shouting the story he had told her to her father and mother, who had come out more sketchily dressed than they commonly were by day. He drank goblet after goblet of the ice-water without noticing who was giving it, and kept on talking, and laughing through his talk wildly. "It's astonishing," he said, "how well the worse reason looks when you try to make it appear the better. Why, I believe I was the first convert to the war in that crowd to-night! I never thought I should like to kill a man; but now I shouldn't care; and the smokeless powder lets you see the man drop that you kill. It's all for the country! What a thing it is to have a country that *can't* be wrong, but if it is, is right, anyway!"

Editha had a great, vital thought, an inspiration. She set down the ice-pitcher on the veranda floor, and ran up-stairs and got the letter she had written him. When at last he noisily bade her father and mother, "Well, good-night. I forgot I woke you up; I sha'n't want any sleep myself," she followed him down the avenue to the gate. There, after the whirling words that seemed to fly away from her thoughts and refuse to serve them, she made a last effort to solemnize the moment that seemed so crazy, and pressed the letter she had written upon him.

"What's this?" he said. "Want me to mail it?"

"No, no. It's for you. I wrote it after you went this morning. Keep it—keep it—and read it sometime—" She thought, and then her inspiration came: "Read it if ever you doubt what you've done, or fear that I regret your having done it. Read it after you've started."

They strained each other in embraces that seemed as ineffective as their words, and he kissed her face with quick, hot breaths that were so unlike him, that made her feel as if she had lost her old lover and found a stranger in his place. The stranger said: "What a gorgeous flower you are, with your red hair, and your blue eyes that look black now, and your face with the color painted out by the white moonshine! Let me hold you under the chin, to see whether I love blood, you tiger-lily!" Then he laughed Gearson's laugh, and released her, scared and giddy. Within her wilfulness she had been frightened by a sense of subtler force in him, and mystically mastered as she had never been before.

---

[4]From Shakespeare's *Julius Caesar*, Act III, Scene i, line 273.

She ran all the way back to the house, and mounted the steps panting. Her mother and father were talking of the great affair. Her mother said: "Wa'n't Mr. Gearson in rather of an excited state of mind? Didn't you think he acted curious?"

"Well, not for a man who'd just been elected captain and had set'em up for the whole of Company A," her father chuckled back.

"What in the world do you mean, Mr. Balcom? Oh! There's Editha!" She offered to follow the girl indoors.

"Don't come, mother!" Editha called, vanishing.

Mrs. Balcom remained to reproach her husband. "I don't see much of anything to laugh at."

"Well, it's catching. Caught it from Gearson. I guess it won't be much of a war, and I guess Gearson don't think so, either. The other fellows will back down as soon as they see we mean it. I wouldn't lose any sleep over it. I'm going back to bed, myself."

Gearson came again next afternoon, looking pale and rather sick, but quite himself, even to his languid irony. "I guess I'd better tell you, Editha, that I consecrated myself to your god of battles last night by pouring too many libations to him down my own throat. But I'm all right now. One has to carry off the excitement, somehow."

"Promise me," she commanded, "that you'll never touch it again!"

"What! Not let the cannikin clink? Not let the soldier drink?[5] Well, I promise."

"You don't belong to yourself now; you don't even belong to *me*. You belong to your country, and you have a sacred charge to keep yourself strong and well for your country's sake. I have been thinking, thinking all night and all day long."

"You look as if you had been crying a little, too," he said, with his queer smile.

"That's all past. I've been thinking, and worshipping *you*. Don't you suppose I know all that you've been through, to come to this? I've followed you every step from your old theories and opinions."

"Well, you've had a long row to hoe."

"And I know you've done this from the highest motives—"

"Oh, there won't be much pettifogging to do till this cruel war is—"

"And you haven't simply done it for my sake. I couldn't respect you if you had."

"Well, then we'll say I haven't. A man that hasn't got his own respect intact wants the respect of all the other people he can corner. But we won't go into that. I'm in for the thing now, and we've got to face our future. My idea is that this isn't going to be a very protracted struggle; we shall just scare the enemy to death before it comes to a fight at all. But we must provide for contingencies, Editha. If anything happens to me—"

"Oh, George!" She clung to him, sobbing.

I don't want you to feel foolishly bound to my memory. I should hate that, wherever I happened to be."

"I am yours, for time and eternity—time and eternity." She liked the words; they satisfied her famine for phrases.

"Well, say eternity; that's all right; but time's another thing; and I'm talking about time. But there is something! My mother! If anything happens—"

She winced, and he laughed. "You're not the bold soldier-girl of yesterday!"

[5]Adapted from Shakespeare's *Othello*, Act II, Scene iii, lines 71–75.

Then he sobered. "If anything happens, I want you to help my mother out. She won't like my doing this thing. She brought me up to think war a fool thing as well as a bad thing. My father was in the Civil War; all through it; lost his arm in it." She thrilled with the sense of the arm round her; what if that should be lost? He laughed as if divining her: "Oh, it doesn't run in the family, as far as I know!" Then he added, gravely: "He came home with misgivings about war, and they grew on him. I guess he and mother agreed between them that I was to be brought up in his final mind about it; but that was before my time. I only knew him from my mother's report of him and his opinions; I don't know whether they were hers first; but they were hers last. This will be a blow to her. I shall have to write and tell her—"

He stopped, and she asked: "Would you like me to write, too, George?"

"I don't believe that would do. No, I'll do the writing. She'll understand a little if I say that I thought the way to minimize it was to make war on the largest possible scale at once—that I felt I must have been helping on the war somehow if I hadn't helped keep it from coming, and I knew I hadn't; when it came, I had no right to stay out of it."

Whether his sophistries satisfied him or not, they satisfied her. She clung to his breast, and whispered, with closed eyes and quivering lips: "Yes, yes, yes!"

"But if anything should happen, you might go to her and see what you could do for her. You know? It's rather far off; she can't leave her chair—"

"Oh, I'll go, if it's the ends of the earth! But nothing will happen! Nothing *can!* I—"

She felt herself lifted with his rising, and Gearson was saying, with his arm still round her, to her father: "Well, we're off at once, Mr. Balcom. We're to be formally accepted at the capital, and then bunched up with the rest somehow, and sent into camp somewhere, and got to the front as soon as possible. We all want to be in the van, of course; we're the first company to report to the Governor. I came to tell Editha, but I hadn't got round to it."

She saw him again for a moment at the capital, in the station, just before the train started southward with his regiment. He looked well, in his uniform, and very soldierly, but somehow girlish, too, with his clean-shaven face and slim figure. The manly eyes and the strong voice satisfied her, and his preoccupation with some unexpected details of duty flattered her. Other girls were weeping and bemoaning themselves, but she felt a sort of noble distinction in the abstraction, the almost unconsciousness, with which they parted. Only at the last moment he said: "Don't forget my mother. It mayn't be such a walk-over as I supposed," and he laughed at the notion.

He waved his hand to her as the train moved off—she knew it among a score of hands that were waved to other girls from the platform of the car, for it held a letter which she knew was hers. Then he went inside the car to read it, doubtless, and she did not see him again. But she felt safe for him through the strength of what she called her love. What she called her God, always speaking the name in a deep voice and with the implication of a mutual understanding, would watch over him and keep him and bring him back to her. If with an empty sleeve, then he should have three arms instead of two, for both of hers should be his for life. She did not see, though, why she should always be thinking of the arm his father had lost.

There were not many letters from him, but they were such as she could have wished, and she put her whole strength into making hers such as she imagined he could have wished, glorifying and supporting him. She wrote to his mother glorifying him as their hero, but the brief answer she got was merely to the effect that Mrs. Gearson was not well enough to write herself, and thanking her for her letter by the hand of some one who called herself "Yrs truly, Mrs. W. J. Andrews."

Editha determined not to be hurt, but to write again quite as if the answer had been all she expected. Before it seemed as if she could have written, there came news of the first skirmish, and in the list of the killed, which was telegraphed as a trifling loss on our side, was Gearson's name. There was a frantic time of trying to make out that it might be, must be, some other Gearson; but the name and the company and the regiment and the State were too definitely given.

Then there was a lapse into depths out of which it seemed as if she never could rise again; then a lift into clouds far above all grief, black clouds, that blotted out the sun, but where she soared with him, with George—George! She had the fever that she expected of herself, but she did not die in it; she was not even delirious, and it did not last long. When she was well enough to leave her bed, her one thought was of George's mother, of his strangely worded wish that she should go to her and see what she could do for her. In the exaltation of the duty laid upon her—it buoyed her up instead of burdening her—she rapidly recovered.

Her father went with her on the long railroad journey from northern New York to western Iowa; he had business out at Davenport, and he said he could just as well go then as any other time; and he went with her to the little country town where George's mother lived in a little house on the edge of the illimitable cornfields, under trees pushed to a top of the rolling prairie. George's father had settled there after the Civil War, as so many other old soldiers had done; but they were Eastern people, and Editha fancied touches of the East in the June rose overhanging the front door, and the garden with early summer flowers stretching from the gate of the paling fence.

It was very low inside the house, and so dim, with the closed blinds, that they could scarcely see one another: Editha tall and black in her crapes which filled the air with smell of their dyes; her father standing decorously apart with his hat on his forearm, as at funerals; a woman rested in a deep arm-chair, and the woman who had let the strangers in stood behind the chair.

The seated woman turned her head round and up, and asked the woman behind her chair: "*Who* did you say?"

Editha, if she had done what she expected of herself, would have gone down on her knees at the feet of the seated figure and said, "I am George's Editha," for answer.

But instead of her own voice she heard that other woman's voice saying: "Well, I don't know as I *did* get the name just right. I guess I'll have to make a little more light in here," and she went and pushed two of the shutters ajar.

Then Editha's father said, in his public will-now-address-a-few-remarks tone: "My name is Balcom, ma'am—Junius H. Balcom, of Balcom's Works. New York; my daughter—"

"Oh!" the seated woman broke in, with a powerful voice, the voice that always surprised Editha from Gearson's slender frame. "Let me see you. Stand round where the light can strike on your face," and Editha dumbly obeyed. "So, you're Editha Balcom," she sighed.

"Yes," Editha said, more like a culprit than a comforter.

"What did you come for?" Mrs. Gearson asked.

Editha's face quivered and her knees shook. "I came—because—because George—" She could go no further.

"Yes," the mother said, "he told me he had asked you to come if he got killed. You didn't expect that, I suppose, when you sent him."

"I would rather have died myself than done it!" Editha said, with more truth in her deep voice than she ordinarily found in it. "I tried to leave him free—"

"Yes, that letter of yours, that came back with his other things, left him free." Editha saw now where George's irony came from.

"It was not to be read before—unless—until—I told him so," she faltered.

"Of course, he wouldn't read a letter of yours, under the circumstances, till he thought you wanted him to. Been sick?" the woman abruptly demanded.

"Very sick," Editha said, with self-pity.

"Daughter's life," her father interposed, "was almost despaired of, at one time."

Mrs. Gearson gave him no heed. "I suppose you would have been glad to die, such a brave person as you! I don't believe *he* was glad to die. He was always a timid boy, that way; he was afraid of a good many things; but if he was afraid he did what he made up his mind to. I suppose he made up his mind to go, but I knew what it cost him by what it cost me when I heard of it. I had been through *one* war before. When you sent him you didn't expect he would get killed."

The voice seemed to compassionate Editha, and it was time. "No," she huskily murmured.

"No, girls don't; women don't when they give their men up to their country. They think they'll come marching back, somehow, just as gay as they went, or if it's an empty sleeve, or even an empty pantaloon, it's all the more glory, and they're so much the prouder of them, poor things!"

The tears began to run down Editha's face; she had not wept till then; but it was now such a relief to be understood that the tears came.

"No, you didn't expect him to get killed," Mrs. Gearson repeated, in a voice which was startlingly like George's again. "You just expected him to kill some one else, some of those foreigners, that weren't there because they had any say about it, but because they had to be there, poor wretches—conscripts, or whatever they call 'em. You thought it would be all right for my George, *your* George, to kill the sons of those miserable mothers and the husbands of those girls that you would never see the faces of." The woman lifted her powerful voice in a psalmlike note. "I thank my God he didn't live to do it! I thank my God they killed him first, and that he ain't livin' with their blood on his hands!" She dropped her eyes, which she had raised with her voice, and glared at Editha. "What you got that black on for?" She lifted herself by her powerful arms so high that her helpless body seemed to hang limp its full length. "Take it off, take it off, before I tear it from your back!"

The lady who was passing the summer near Balcom's Works was sketching Editha's beauty, which lent itself wonderfully to the effects of a colorist. It had come to that confidence which is rather apt to grow between artist and sitter, and Editha had told her everthing.

"To think of your having such a tragedy in your life!" the lady said. She added: "I suppose there are people who feel that way about war. But when you consider the good this war has done—how much it has done for the country! I can't understand such people, for my part. And when you had come all the way out there to console her—got up out of a sick-bed! Well!"

"I think," Editha said, magnanimously, "she wasn't quite in her right mind; and so did papa."

"Yes," the lady said, looking at Editha's lips in nature and then at her lips in art, and giving an empirical touch to them in the picture. "But how dreadful of her! How perfectly—excuse me—how *vulgar!*"

A light broke upon Editha in the darkness which she felt she had been without a gleam of brightness for weeks and months. The mystery that had bewildered her was solved by the word; and from that moment she rose from grovelling in shame and self-pity, and began to live again in the ideal.

1905

from *CRITICISM AND FICTION*[1]

II

"As for those called critics," the author [Edmund Burke] says, "they have generally sought the rule of the arts in the wrong place; they have sought among poems, pictures, engravings, statues, and buildings; but art can never give the rules that make an art. This is, I believe, the reason why artists in general, and poets principally, have been confined in so narrow a circle; they have been rather imitators of one another than of nature. Critics follow them, and therefore can do little as guides. I can judge but poorly of anything while I measure it by no other standard than itself. The true standard of the arts is in every man's power; and an easy observation of the most common, sometimes of the meanest things, in nature will give the truest lights, where the greatest sagacity and industry that slights such observation must leave us in the dark, or, what is worse, amuse and mislead us by false lights."[2]

If this should happen to be true—and it certainly commends itself to acceptance—it might portend an immediate danger to the vested interests of criticism, only that it was written a hundred years ago; and we shall probably have the "sagacity and industry that slights the observation" of nature long enough yet to allow most critics the time to learn some more useful trade than criticism as they pursue it. Nevertheless, I am in hopes that the communistic era in taste foreshadowed by Burke is approaching, and that it will occur within the lives of men now overawed by the foolish old superstition that literature and art are anything but the expression of life, and are to be judged by any other test than that of their fidelity to it. The time is coming, I hope, when each new author, each new artist, will be considered, not in his proportion to any other author or artist, but in his relation to the human nature, known to us all, which it is his privilege, his high duty, to interpret. "The true standard of the artist is in every man's power" already, as Burke says; Michelangelo's[3] "light of the piazza," the glance of the common eye, is and always was the best light on a statue; Goethe's[4] "boys and blackbirds" have in all ages been the real connoisseurs of berries; but hitherto the mass of common men have been afraid to apply their own simplicity, naturalness, and honesty to the appreciation of the beautiful. They have always cast about for the instruction of some one who professed to know better, and

---

[1]A collection of essays selected from those published from 1886 to 1891 in Howells's column, "The Editor's Study," in *Harper's Magazine*.

[2]From *Philosophical Inquiry into the Origins of Our Ideas on the Sublime and Beautiful* (1756), by Edmund Burke (1729–1797), British statesman and orator.

[3]Italian painter and sculptor (1475–1564).

[4]Johann Wolfgang von Goethe (1749–1832), German author.

who browbeat wholesome common-sense into the self-distrust that ends in sophistication. They have fallen generally to the worst of this bad species, and have been "amused[5] and misled" (how pretty that quaint old use of amuse is!) "by the false lights" of critical vanity and self-righteousness. They have been taught to compare what they see and what they read, not with the things that they have observed and known, but with the things that some other artist or writer has done. Especially if they have themselves the artistic impulse in any direction they are taught to form themselves, not upon life, but upon the masters who became masters only by forming themselves upon life. The seeds of death are planted in them, and they can produce only the still-born, the academic. They are not told to take their work into the public square and see if it seems true to the chance passer, but to test it by the work of the very men who refused and decried any other test of their own work. The young writer who attempts to report the phrase and carriage of every-day life, who tries to tell just how he has heard men talk and seen them look, is made to feel guilty of something low and unworthy by the stupid people who would like to have him show how Shakespeare's men talked and looked, or Scott's, or Thackeray's, or Balzac's, or Hawthorne's, or Dickens's;[6] he is instructed to idealize his personages, that is, to take the life-likeness out of them, and put the book-likeness into them. He is approached in the spirit of the wretched pedantry into which learning, much or little, always decays when it withdraws itself and stands apart from experience in an attitude of imagined superiority, and which would say with the same confidence to the scientist: "I see that you are looking at a grasshopper there which you have found in the grass, and I suppose you intend to describe it. Now don't waste your time and sin against culture in that way. I've got a grasshopper here, which has been evolved at considerable pains and expense out of the grasshopper in general; in fact, it's a type. It's made up of wire and cardboard, very prettily painted in a conventional tint, and it's perfectly indestructible. It isn't very much like a real grasshopper, but it's a great deal nicer, and it's served to represent the notion of a grasshopper ever since man emerged from barbarism. You may say that it's artificial. Well, it is artificial; but then it's ideal too; and what you want to do is to cultivate the ideal. You'll find the books full of my kind of grasshopper, and scarcely a trace of yours in any of them. The thing that you are proposing to do is commonplace; but if you say that it isn't commonplace, for the very reason that it hasn't been done before, you'll have to admit that its photographic."

As I said, I hope the time is coming when not only the artist, but the common, average man, who always "has the standard of the arts in his power," will have also the courage to apply it, and will reject the ideal grasshopper wherever he finds it, in science, in literature, in art, because it is not "simple, natural, and honest," because it is not like a real grasshopper. But I will own that I think the time is yet far off, and that the people who have been brought up on the ideal grasshopper, the heroic grasshopper, the impassioned grasshopper, the self-devoted, adventureful, good old romantic cardboard grasshopper, must die out before the simple, honest, and natural grasshopper can have a fair field. I am in no haste to compass the end of these good people, whom I find in the mean time very amusing. It is delightful to meet one of them, either in print or out of it—some sweet elderly lady or excellent gentleman whose youth was pastured

---

[5]In the earlier meaning of "deceived."
[6]Sir Walter Scott (1771–1832), Scottish novelist; William Makepeace Thackeray (1811–1863), English novelist; Honoré de Balzac (1799–1850), French novelist; Charles Dickens (1812–1870), English novelist.

on the literature of thirty or forty years ago—and to witness the confidence with which they preach their favorite authors as all the law and the prophets. They have commonly read little or nothing since, or, if they have, they have judged it by a standard taken from these authors, and never dreamed of judging it by nature; they are destitute of the documents in the case of the later writers; they suppose that Balzac was the beginning of realism, and that Zola[7] is its wicked end; they are quite ignorant, but they are ready to talk you down, if you differ from them, with an assumption of knowledge sufficient for any occasion. The horror, the resentment, with which they receive any question of their literary saints is genuine; you descend at once very far in the moral and social scale, and anything short of offensive personality is too good for you; it is expressed to you that you are one to be avoided, and put down even a little lower than you have naturally fallen.

These worthy persons are not to blame; it is part of their intellectual mission to represent the petrifaction of taste, and to preserve an image of a smaller and cruder and emptier world than we now live in, a world which was feeling its way towards the simple, the natural, the honest, but was a good deal "amused and misled" by lights now no longer mistakable for heavenly luminaries. They belong to a time, just passing away, when certain authors were considered authorities in certain kinds, when they must be accepted entire and not questioned in any particular. Now we are beginning to see and to say that no author is an authority except in those moments when he held his ear close to Nature's lips and caught her very accent. These moments are not continuous with any authors in the past, and they are rare with all. Therefore I am not afraid to say now that the greatest classics are sometimes not at all great, and that we can profit by them only when we hold them, like our meanest contemporaries, to a strict accounting, and verify their work by the standard of the arts which we all have in our power, the simple, the natural, and the honest.

Those good people, those curious and interesting if somewhat musty back-numbers, must always have a hero, an idol of some sort, and it is droll to find Balzac, who suffered from their sort such bitter scorn and hate for his realism while he was alive, now become a fetich in his turn, to be shaken in the faces of those who will not blindly worship him. But it is no new thing in the history of literature: whatever is established is sacred with those who do not think. At the beginning of the century, when romance was making the same fight against effete classicism which realism is making to-day against effete romanticism, the Italian poet Monti[8] declared that "the romantic was the cold grave of the Beautiful," just as the realistic is now supposed to be. The romantic of that day and the real of this are in certain degree the same. Romanticism then sought, as realism seeks now, to widen the bounds of sympathy, to level every barrier against aesthetic freedom, to escape from the paralysis of tradition. It exhausted itself in this impulse; and it remained for realism to assert that fidelity to experience and probability of motive are essential conditions of a great imaginative literature. It is not a new theory, but it has never been universally characterized literary endeavor. When realism becomes false to itself, when it heaps up facts merely, and maps life instead of picturing it, realism will perish too. Every true realist instinctively knows this, and it is perhaps the reason why he is careful of every fact, and feels himself bound to express or to indicate its meaning at the risk of overmoralizing. In life he finds nothing insignificant; all tells for destiny and character; nothing that God has made is contemptible. He

[7]Emile Zola (1840–1902), French naturalistic writer.
[8]Vincenzo Monti (1754–1828), Italian poet.

cannot look upon human life and declare this thing or that thing unworthy of notice, any more than the scientist can declare a fact of the material world beneath the dignity of his inquiry. He feels in every nerve the equality of things and the unity of men; his soul is exalted, not by vain shows and shadows and ideals, but by realities, in which alone the truth lives. In criticism it is his business to break the images of false gods and misshapen heroes, to take away the poor silly toys that many grown people would still like to play with. He cannot keep terms with Jack the Giant-killer or Puss in Boots, under any name or in any place, even when they appear as the convict Vautrec, or the Marquis de Montrivaut, or the Sworn Thirteen Noblemen.[9] He must say to himself that Balzac, when he imagined these monsters, was not Balzac, he was Dumas;[10] he was not realistic, he was romantic.

XVI

"How few materials," says Emerson, "are yet used by our arts! The mass of creatures and of qualities are still hid and expectant," and to break new ground is still one of the uncommonest and most heroic of the virtues. The artists are not alone to blame for the timidity that keeps them in the old furrows of the worn-out fields; most of those whom they live to please, or live by pleasing, prefer to have them remain there; it wants rare virtue to appreciate what is new, as well as to invent it; and the "easy things to understand" are the conventional things. This is why the ordinary English novel, with its hackneyed plot, scenes, and figures, is more comfortable to the ordinary American than an American novel, which deals, at its worst, with comparatively new interests and motives. To adjust one's self to the enjoyment of these costs an intellectual effort, and an intellectual effort is what no ordinary person likes to make. It is only the extraordinary person who can say, with Emerson: "I ask not for the great, the remote, the romantic. . . . I embrace the common; I sit at the feet of the familiar and the low. . . . Man is surprised to find that things near are not less beautiful and wondrous than things remote. . . . The perception of the worth of the vulgar is fruitful in discoveries. . . . The foolish man wonders at the unusual, but the wise man at the usual. . . . To-day always looks mean to the thoughtless; but to-day is a king in disguise. . . . Banks and tariffs, the newspaper and caucus, Methodism and Unitarianism, are flat and dull to dull people, but rest on the same foundations of wonder as the town of Troy and the temple of Delphos."

Perhaps we ought not to deny their town of Troy and their temple of Delphos to the dull people; but if we ought, and if we did, they would still insist upon having them. An English novel, full of titles and rank, is apparently essential to the happiness of such people; their weak and childish imagination is at home in its familiar environment; they know what they are reading; the fact that it is hash many times warmed over reassures them; whereas a story of our own life, honestly studied and faithfully represented, troubles them with varied misgiving. They are not sure that it is literature; they do not feel that it is good society; its characters, so like their own, strike them as commonplace; they say they do not wish to know such people.

Everything in England is appreciable to the literary sense, while the sense of the literary worth of things in America is still faint and weak with most people,

---

[9]Characters in a series of novels, known as La Comédie humaine, by Balzac.

[10]Alexandre Dumas père (1803–1870), French romantic novelist, author of *The Count of Monte Cristo* and *The Three Musketeers*.

with the vast majority who "ask for the great, the remote, the romantic," who cannot "embrace the common," cannot "sit at the feet of the familiar and the low," in the good company of Emerson. We are all, or nearly all, struggling to be distinguished from the mass, and to be set apart in select circles and upper classes like the fine people we have read about. We are really a mixture of the plebian ingredients of the whole world; but that is not bad; our vulgarity consists in trying to ignore "the worth of the vulgar," in believing that the superfine is better.

XVIII

In General Grant's confession of novel-reading there is a sort of inference that he had wasted his time,[1] or else the guilty conscience of the novelist in me imagines such an inference. But however this may be, there is certainly no question concerning the intention of a correspondent who once wrote to me after reading some rather bragging claims I had made for fiction as a mental and moral means. "I have very grave doubts," he said, "as to the whole list of magnificent things that you seem to think novels have done for the race, and can witness in myself many evil things which they have done for me. Whatever in my mental make-up is wild and visionary, whatever is untrue, whatever is injurious, I can trace to the perusal of some work of fiction. Worse than that, they beget such high-strung and supersensitive ideas of life that plain industry and plodding perseverance are despised, and matter-of-fact poverty, or every-day, commonplace distress, meets with no sympathy, if indeed noticed at all, by one who has wept over the impossibly accumulated sufferings of some gaudy hero or heroine."

I am not sure that I had the controversy with this correspondent that he seemed to suppose; but novels are now so fully accepted by every one pretending to cultivated taste—and they really form the whole intellectual life of such immense numbers of people, without question of their influence, good or bad, upon the mind—that it is refreshing to have them frankly denounced, and to be invited to revise one's ideas and feelings in regard to them. A little honesty, or a great deal of honesty, in this quest will do the novel, as we hope yet to have it, and as we have already begun to have it, no harm; and for my own part I will confess that I believe fiction in the past to have been largely injurious, as I believe the stage play to be still almost wholly injurious, through its falsehood, its folly, its wantonness, and its aimlessness. It may be safely assumed that most of the novel-reading which people fancy an intellectual pastime is the emptiest dissipation, hardly more related to thought or the wholesome exercise of the mental faculties than opium-eating; in either case the brain is drugged, and left weaker and crazier for the debauch. If this may be called the negative result of the fiction habit, the positive injury that most novels work is by no means so easily to be measured in the case of young men whose character they help so much to form or deform, and the women of all ages whom they keep so much in ignorance of the world they misrepresent. Grown men have little harm from them, but in the other cases, which are the vast majority, they hurt because they are not true—not because they are malevolent, but because they are idle lies about human nature and the social fabric, which it behooves us to know and to understand, that we may deal justly with ourselves and with one another. One

---

[1] In *The Personal Memoirs of Ulysses S. Grant* (1885–1886).

need not go so far as our correspondent, and trace to the fiction habit "whatever
is wild and visionary, whatever is untrue, whatever is injurious," in one's life;
bad as the fiction habit is it is probably not responsible for the whole sum of evil
in its victims, and I believe that if the reader will use care in choosing from this
fungus-growth with which the fields of literature teem every day, he may nourish
himself as with the true mushroom, at no risk from the poisonous species.

The tests are very plain and simple, and they are perfectly infallible. If a novel
flatters the passions, and exalts them above the principles, it is poisonous; it may
not kill, but it will certainly injure; and this test will alone exclude an entire class
of fiction, of which eminent examples will occur to all. Then the whole spawn
of so-called unmoral romances, which imagine a world where the sins of sense
are unvisited by the penalties following, swift or slow, but inexorably sure, in
the real world, are deadly poison: these do kill. The novels that merely tickle
our prejudices and lull our judgment, or that coddle our sensibilities or pamper
our gross appetite for the marvellous are not so fatal, but they are innutritious,
and clog the soul with unwholesome vapors of all kinds. No doubt they too help
weaken the moral fibre, and make their readers indifferent to "plodding perseverance and plain industry," and to "matter-of-fact poverty and commonplace
distress."

Without taking them too seriously, it still must be owned that the "gaudy hero
and heroine" are to blame for a great deal of harm in the world. That heroine
long taught by example, if not precept, that Love, or the passion or fancy she
mistook for it, was the chief interest of a life, which is really concerned with a
great many other things; that it was lasting in the way she knew it; that it was
worthy of every sacrifice, and was altogether a finer thing than prudence,
obedience, reason; that love alone was glorious and beautiful, and these were
mean and ugly in comparison with it. More lately she has begun to idolize and
illustrate Duty, and she is hardly less mischievous in this new role, opposing
duty, as she did love, to prudence, obedience, and reason. The stock hero,
whom, if we met him, we could not fail to see was a most deplorable person, has
undoubtedly imposed himself upon the victims of the fiction habit as admirable.
With him, too, love was and is the great affair, whether in its old romantic phase
of chivalrous achievement or manifold suffering for love's sake, or its more
recent development of the "virile," the bullying, and the brutal, or its still more
recent agonies of self-sacrifice, as idle and useless as the moral experiences of
the insane asylums. With his vain posturings and his ridiculous splendor he is
really a painted barbarian, the prey of his passions and his delusions, full of
obsolete ideals, and the motives and ethics of a savage, which the guilty author
of his being does his best—or his worst—in spite of his own light and knowledge,
to foist upon the reader as something generous and noble. I am not merely
bringing this charge against that sort of fiction which is beneath literature and
outside of it, "the shoreless lakes of ditch-water," whose miasms fill the air below
the empyrean where the great ones sit; but I am accusing the work of some of
the most famous, who have, in this instance or in that, sinned against the truth,
which can alone exalt and purify men. I do not say that they have constantly
done so, or even commonly done so; but that they have done so at all marks
them as of the past, to be read with the due historical allowance for their epoch
and their conditions. For I believe that, while inferior writers will and must
continue to imitate them in their foibles and their errors, no one hereafter will
be able to achieve greatness who is false to humanity, either in its facts or its
duties. The light of civilization has already broken even upon the novel, and no
conscientious man can now set about painting an image of life without perpetual

question of the verity of his work, and without feeling bound to distinguish so clearly that no reader of his may be misled, between what is right and what is wrong, what is noble and what is base, what is health and what is perdition, in the actions and characters he portrays.

The fiction that aims merely to entertain—the fiction that is to serious fiction as the opera-bouffe,[2] the ballet, and the pantomime are to the true drama—need not feel that burden of this obligation so deeply; but even such fiction will not be gay or trivial to any reader's hurt, and criticism will hold it to account if it passes from painting to teaching folly.

More and more not only the criticism which prints its opinions, but the infinitely vaster and powerfuler criticism which thinks and feels them merely, will make this demand. I confess that I do not care to judge any work of the imagination without first of all applying this test to it. We must ask ourselves before we ask anything else, Is it true?—true to the motives, the impulses, the principles that shape the life of actual men and women? This truth, which necessarily includes the highest morality and the highest artistry—this truth given, the book cannot be wicked and cannot be weak; and without it all graces of style and feats of invention and cunning of construction are so many super-fluities of naughtiness. It is well for the truth to have all these, and shine in them, but for falsehood they are merely meretricious, the bedizenment of the wanton; they atone for nothing, they count for nothing. But in fact they come naturally of truth, and grace it without solicitation; they are added unto it. In the whole range of fiction we know of no true picture of life—that is, of human nature—which is not also a masterpiece of literature, full of divine and natural beauty. It may have no touch or tint of this special civilization or of that; it had better have this local color well ascertained; but the truth is deeper and finer than aspects, and if the book is true to what men and women know of one another's souls it will be true enough, and it will be great and beautiful. It is the conception of literature as something apart from life, superfinely aloof, which makes it really unimportant to the great mass of mankind, without a message or a meaning for them; and it is the notion that a novel may be false in its portrayal of causes and effects that makes literary art contemptible even to those whom it amuses, that forbids them to regard the novelist as a serious or right-minded person. If they do not in some moment of indignation cry out against all novels, as my correspondent does, they remain besotted in the fume of the delusions purveyed to them, with no higher feeling for the author than such maudlin affection as the habitué of an opium-joint perhaps knows for the attendant who fills his pipe with the drug.

Or, as in the case of another correspondent who writes that in his youth he "read a great many novels, but always regarded it as an amusement, like horse-racing and card-playing," for which he had no time when he entered upon the serious business of life, it renders them merely contemptuous. His view of the matter may be commended to the brotherhood and sisterhood of novelists as full of wholesome if bitter suggestion; and we urge them not to dismiss it with high literary scorn as that of some Bœotian[3] dull to the beauty of art. Refuse it as we may, it is still the feeling of the vast majority of people for whom life is earnest, and who find only a distorted and misleading likeness of it in our books. We may fold ourselves in our scholars' gowns, and close the doors of our studies, and affect to despise this rude voice; but we cannot shut it out. It comes to us from wherever men are at work, from wherever they are truly living, and accuses

[2]Comic opera.   [3]Boeotia, in ancient Greece, proverbially the home of dullards.

us of unfaithfulness, of triviality, of mere stage-play; and none of us can escape conviction except he prove himself worthy of his time—a time in which the great masters have brought literature back to life, and filled its ebbing veins with the red tides of reality. We cannot all equal them; we need not copy them; but we can all go to the sources of their inspiration and their power; and to draw from these no one need go far—no one need really go out of himself.

Fifty years ago, Carlyle,[4] in whom the truth was always alive, but in whom it was then unperverted by suffering, by celebrity, and by despair, wrote in his study of Diderot:[5] "Were it not reasonable to prophesy that this exceeding great multitude of novel-writers and such like must, in a new generation, gradually do one of two things: either retire into the nurseries, and work for children, minors, and semi-fatuous persons of both sexes, or else, what were far better, sweep their novel-fabric into the dust-cart, and betake themselves with such faculty as they have to understand and record what is true, of which surely there is, and will forever be, a whole infinitude unknown to us of infinite importance to us? Poetry, it will more and more come to be understood, is nothing but higher knowledge; and the only genuine Romance (for grown persons), Reality."

If, after half a century, fiction still mainly works for "children, minors, and semi-fatuous persons of both sexes," it is nevertheless one of the hopefulest signs of the world's progress that it has begun to work for "grown persons," and if not exactly in the way that Carlyle might have solely intended in urging its writers to compile memoirs instead of building the "novel-fabric," still it has, in the highest and widest sense, already made Reality its Romance. I cannot judge it, I do not even care for it, except as it has done this; and I can hardly conceive of a literary self-respect in these days compatible with the old trade of make-believe, with the production of the kind of fiction which is too much honored by classification with card-playing and horse-racing. But let fiction cease to lie about life; let it portray men and women as they are, actuated by the motives and the passions in the measure we all know; let it leave off painting dolls and working them by springs and wires; let it show the different interests in their true proportions; let it forbear to preach pride and revenge, folly and insanity, egotism and prejudice, but frankly own these for what they are, in whatever figures and occasions they appear; let it not put on fine literary airs; let it speak the dialect, the language, that most Americans know—the language of unaffected people everywhere—and there can be no doubt of an unlimited future, not only of delightfulness but of usefulness, for it.

XXI

It is no doubt such work as Mr. James's that an English essayist (Mr. E. Hughes[1]) has chiefly in mind, in a study of the differences of the English and American novel. He defines the English novel as working from within outwardly, and the American novel as working from without inwardly. The definition is very surprisingly accurate; and the critic's discovery of this fundamental difference is carried into particulars with a distinctness which is as unfailing as the courtesy he has in recognizing the present superiority of American work. He seems to think, however, that the English principle is the better, though why he should think so he does not make so clear. It appears a belated and rather

---

[4]Thomas Carlyle (1795–1881), Scottish essayist and historian.
[5]Denis Diderot (1713–1784), French philosopher.
[1]Eilian Hughes, English literary critic, author of *Some Aspects of Humanity* (1889).

voluntary effect of patriotism, disappointing in a philosopher of his degree; but it does not keep him from very explicit justice to the best characteristics of our fiction. "The American novelist is distinguished for the intellectual grip which he has of his characters. . . . He penetrates below the crust, and he recognizes no necessity of the crust to anticipate what is beneath. . . . He utterly discards heroics; he often even discards anything like a plot. . . . His story proper is often no more than a natural predicament. . . . It is no stage view we have of his characters, but one behind the scenes. . . . We are brought into contact with no strained virtues, illumined by strained light upon strained heights of situation. . . . Whenever he appeals to the emotions it would seem to be with an appeal to the intellect too. . . . because he weaves his story of the finer, less self-evident though common threads of human nature, seldom calling into play the grosser and more powerful strain. . . . Everywhere in his pages we come across acquaintances undisguised. . . . The characters in an American novel are never unapproachable to the reader. . . . The naturalness, with the every-day atmosphere which surrounds it, is one great charm of the American novel. . . . It is throughout examinative, discursory, even more—quizzical. Its characters are undergoing, at the hands of the author, calm, interested observation. . . . He is never caught identifying himself with them; he must preserve impartiality at all costs . . . but . . . the touch of nature is always felt, the feeling of kinship always follows. . . . The strength of the American novel is its optimistic faith. . . . If out of this persistent hopefulness it can evolve for men a new order of trustfulness, a tenet that between man and man there should be less suspicion, more confidence, since human nature sanctions it, its mission will have been more than an æsthetic, it will have been a moral one."

Not all of this will be found true of Mr. James, but all that relates to artistic methods and characteristics will, and the rest is true of American novels generally. For the most part in their range and tendency they are admirable. I will not say they are all good, or that any of them is wholly good; but I find in nearly every one of them a disposition to regard our life without the literary glasses so long thought desirable, and to see character, not as it is in other fiction, but as it abounds outside of all fiction. This disposition sometimes goes with poor enough performance, but in some of our novels it goes with performance that is excellent; and at any rate it is for the present more valuable than evenness of performance. It is what relates American fiction to the only living movement in imaginative literature, and distinguishes by a superior freshness and authenticity any group of American novels from a similarly accidental group of English novels, giving them the same good right to be as the like number of recent Russian novels, French novels, Spanish novels, Italian novels, Norwegian novels.

It is the difference of the American novelist's ideals from those of the English novelist that gives him his advantage, and seems to promise him the future. The love of the passionate and the heroic, as the Englishman has it, is such a crude and unwholesome thing, so deaf and blind to all the most delicate and important facts of art and life, so insensible to the subtle values in either that its presence or absence makes the whole difference, and enables one who is not obsessed by it to thank Heaven that he is not as that other man is.

There can be little question that many refinements of thought and spirit which every American is sensible of in the fiction of this continent, are necessarily lost upon our good kin beyond seas, whose thumb-fingered apprehension requires something gross and palpable for its assurance of reality. This is not their fault, and I am not sure that it is wholly their misfortune: they are made so as not to miss what they do not find, and they are simply content without those subtleties of life and character which it gives us so keen a pleasure to have noted in literature. If they perceive them at all it is as something vague and diaphanous, something that filmily wavers before their sense and teases them, much as the beings of an invisible world might mock one of our material frame by intimations of their presence. It is with reason, therefore, on the part of an Englishman, that Mr. Henley[2] complains of our fiction as a shadow-land, though we find more and more in it the faithful report of our life, its motives and emotions, and all the comparatively etherealized passions and ideals that influence it.

In fact, the American who chooses to enjoy his birthright to the full, lives in a world wholly different from the Englishman's, and speaks (too often through his nose) another language: he breathes a rarefied and nimble air full of shining possibilities and radiant promises which the fog-and-soot-clogged lungs of those less-favored islanders struggle in vain to fill themselves with. But he ought to be modest in his advantage, and patient with the coughing and sputtering of his cousin who complains of finding himself in an exhausted receiver[3] on plunging into one of our novels. To be quite just to the poor fellow, I have had some such experience as that myself in the atmosphere of some of our more attenuated romances.

Yet every now and then I read a book with perfect comfort and much exhilaration, whose scenes the average Englishman would gasp in. Nothing happens; that is, nobody murders or debauches anybody else; there is no arson or pillage of any sort; there is not a ghost, or a ravening beast, or a hair-breadth escape, or a shipwreck, or a monster of self-sacrifice, or a lady five thousand years old in the whole course of the story; "no promenade, no band of music, nossing!" as Mr. Du Maurier's Frenchman said of the meet for a fox-hunt.[4] Yet it is all alive with the keenest interest for those who enjoy the study of individual traits and general conditions as they make themselves known to American experience.

These conditions have been so favorable hitherto (though they are becoming always less so) that they easily account for the optimistic faith of our novel which Mr. Hughes notices. It used to be one of the disadvantages of the practice of romance in America, which Hawthorne more or less whimsically lamented, that there were so few shadows and inequalities in our broad level of prosperity; and it is one of the reflections suggested by Dostoïevsky's[5] novel, The Crime and the Punishment, that whoever struck a note so profoundly tragic in American fiction would do a false and mistaken thing—as false and as mistaken in its way as dealing in American fiction with certain nudities which the Latin peoples seem to find edifying. Whatever their deserts, very few American novelists have been led out to be shot, or finally exiled to the rigors of a winter at Duluth; and in a land where journeymen carpenters and plumbers strike for four dollars a day the sum of hunger and cold is comparatively small, and the wrong from class to class has been almost inappreciable, though all this is changing for the worse. Our novelists, therefore, concern themselves with the more smiling aspects of life, which are the more American, and seek the universal in the individual rather than the social interests. It is worth while, even at the risk of being called commonplace, to be true to our well-to-do actualities; the very passions themselves seem to be softened and

---

[2]William Ernest Henley (1849–1903), English poet and critic.
[3]I.e., in a vacuum, an empty jar.
[4]In *Pictures of English Society* (1884), by George du Maurier (1834–1896), English illustrator and novelist.
[5]Fëdor Dostoyevsky (1821–1881), Russian novelist.

modified by conditions which formerly at least could not be said to wrong any one, to cramp endeavor, or to cross lawful desire. Sin and suffering and shame there must always be in the world, I suppose, but I believe that in this new world of ours it is still mainly from one to another one, and oftener still from one to one's self. We have death too in America, and a great deal of disagreeable and painful disease, which the multiplicity of our patent medicines does not seem to cure; but this is tragedy that comes in the very nature of things, and is not peculiarly American, as the large, cheerful average of health and success and happy life is. It will not do to boast, but it is well to be true to the facts, and to see that, apart from these purely mortal troubles, the race here has enjoyed conditions in which most of the ills that have darkened its annals might be averted by honest work and unselfish behavior.

Fine artists we have among us, and right-minded as far as they go; and we must not forget this at evil moments when it seems as if all the women had taken to writing hysterical improprieties, and some of the men were trying to be at least as hysterical in despair of being as improper. If we kept to the complexion of a certain school—which sadly needs a school-master—we might very well be despondent; but, after all, that school is not representative of our conditions or our intentions. Other traits are much more characteristic of our life and our fiction. In most American novels, vivid and graphic as the best of them are, the people are segregated if not sequestered, and the scene is sparsely populated. The effect may be in instinctive response to the vacancy of our social life, and I shall not make haste to blame it. There are few places, few occasions among us, in which a novelist can get a large number of polite people together, or at least keep them together. Unless he carries a snap-camera his picture of them has no probability; they affect one like the figures perfunctorily associated in such deadly old engravings as that of "Washington Irving and his Friends." Perhaps it is for this reason that we excel in small pieces with three or four figures, or in studies of rustic communities, where there is propinquity if not society. Our grasp of more urbane life is feeble; most attempts to assemble it in our pictures are failures, possibly because it is too transitory, too intangible in its nature with us, to be truthfully represented as really existent.

I am not sure that the Americans have not brought the short story nearer perfection in the all-round sense than almost any other people, and for reasons very simple and near at hand. It might be argued from the national hurry and impatience that it was a literary form peculiarly adapted to the American temperament, but I suspect that its extraordinary development among us is owing much more to more tangible facts. The success of American magazines, which is nothing less than prodigious, is only commensurate with their excellence. Their sort of success is not only from the courage to decide what ought to please, but from the knowledge of what does please; and it is probable that, aside from the pictures, it is the short stories which please the readers of our best magazines. The serial novels they must have, of course; but rather more of course they must have short stories, and by operation of the law of supply and demand, the short stories, abundant in quantity and excellent in quality, are forthcoming because they are wanted. By another operation of the same law, which political economists have more recently taken account of, the demand follows the supply, and short stories are sought for because there is a proven ability to furnish them, and people read them willingly because they are usually very good. The art of writing them is now so disciplined and diffused with us that there is no lack either for the magazines or for the newspaper "syndicates" which deal in them almost to the exclusion of the serials. In other countries the feuilleton[6] of the journals is a novel continued from day to day, but with us the papers, whether daily or weekly, now more rarely print novels, whether they get them at first hand from the writers, as a great many do, or through the syndicates, which purvey a vast variety of literary wares, chiefly for the Sunday editions of the city journals. In the country papers the short story takes place of the chapters of a serial which used to be given.

XXIV

One of the great newspapers the other day invited the prominent American authors to speak their minds upon a point in the theory and practice of fiction which had already vexed some of them. It was the question of how much or how little the American novel ought to deal with certain facts of life which are not usually talked of before young people, and especially young ladies. Of course the question was not decided, and I forgot just how far the balance inclined in favor of a large freedom in the matter. But it certainly inclined that way; one or two writers of the sex which is somehow supposed to have purity in its keeping (as if purity were a thing that did not practically concern the other sex, preoccupied with serious affairs) gave it a rather vigorous tilt to that side. In view of this fact it would not be the part of prudence to make an effort to dress the balance; and indeed I do not know that I was going to make any such effort. But there are some things to say, around and about the subject, which I should like to have some one else say, and which I may myself possibly be safe in suggesting.

One of the first of these is the fact, generally lost sight of by those who censure the Anglo-Saxon novel for its prudishness, that it is really not such a prude after all; and that if it is sometimes apparently anxious to avoid those experiences of life not spoken of before young people, this may be an appearance only. Sometimes a novel which has this shuffling air, this effect of truckling to propriety, might defend itself, if it could speak for itself, by saying that such experiences happened not to come within its scheme, and that, so far from maiming or mutilating itself in ignoring them, it was all the more faithfully representative of the tone of modern life in dealing with love that was chaste, and with passion so honest that it could be openly spoken of before the tenderest society bud at dinner. It might say that the guilty intrigue, the betrayal, the extreme flirtation even, was the exceptional thing in life, and unless the scheme of the story necessarily involved it, that it would be bad art to lug it in, and as bad taste as to introduce such topics in a mixed company. It could say very justly that the novel in our civilization now always addresses a mixed company, and that the vast majority of the company are ladies, and that very many, if not most, of these ladies are young girls. If the novel were written for men and for married women alone, as in continental Europe, it might be altogether different. But the simple fact is that it is not written for them alone among us, and it is a question of writing, under cover of our universal acceptance, things for young girls to read which you would be put out-of-doors for saying to them, or of frankly giving notice of your intention, and so cutting yourself off from the pleasure—and it is a very high and sweet one—of appealing to these vivid,

[6]A literary composition, often a story or chapter of a novel, published in a newspaper.

responsive intelligences, which are none the less brilliant and admirable because they are innocent.

One day a novelist who liked, after the manner of other men, to repine at his hard fate, complained to his friend, a critic, that he was tired of the restriction he had put upon himself in this regard; for it is a mistake, as can be readily shown, to suppose that others impose it. "See how free those French fellows are!" he rebelled. "Shall we always be shut up to our tradition of decency?"

"Do you think it's much worse than being shut up to their tradition of indecency?" said his friend.

Then that novelist began to reflect, and he remembered how sick the invariable motive of the French novel made him. He perceived finally that, convention for convention, ours was not only more tolerable, but on the whole was truer to life, not only to its complexion, but also to its texture. No one will pretend that there is not vicious love beneath the surface of our society; if he did, the fetid explosions of the divorce trials would refute him; but if he pretended that it was in any just sense characteristic of our society, he could be still more easily refuted. Yet it exists, and it is unquestionably the material of tragedy, the stuff from which intense effects are wrought. The question, after owning this fact, is whether these intense effects are not rather cheap effects. I incline to think they are, and I will try to say why I think so, if I may do so without offence. The material itself, the mere mention of it, has an instant fascination; it arrests, it detains, till the last word is said, and while there is anything to be hinted. This is what makes a love intrigue of some sort all but essential to the popularity of any fiction. Without such an intrigue the intellectual equipment of the author must be of the highest, and then he will succeed only with the highest class of readers. But any author who will deal with a guilty love intrigue holds all readers in his hand, the highest with the lowest, as long as he hints the slightest hope of the smallest potential naughtiness. He need not at all be a great author; he may be a very shabby wretch, if he has but the courage or the trick of that sort of thing. The critics will call him "virile" and "passionate"; decent people will be ashamed to have been limed by him; but the low average will only ask another chance of flocking into his net. If he happens to be an able writer, his really fine and costly work will be unheeded, and the lure to the appetite will be chiefly remembered. There may be other qualities which make reputations for other men, but in his case they will count for nothing. He pays this penalty for his success in that kind; and every one pays some such penalty who deals with some such material. It attaches in like manner to the triumphs of the writers who now almost form a school among us, and who may be said to have established themselves in an easy popularity simply by the study of erotic shivers and fervors. They may find their account in the popularity, or they may not; there is no question of the popularity.

But I do not mean to imply that their case covers the whole ground. So far as it goes, though, it ought to stop the mouths of those who complain that fiction is enslaved to propriety among us. It appears that of a certain kind of impropriety it is free to give us all it will, and more. But this is not what serious men and women writing fiction mean when they rebel against the limitations of their art in our civilization. They have no desire to deal with nakedness, as painters and sculptors freely do in the worship of beauty; or with certain facts of life, as the stage does, in the service of sensation. But they ask why, when the conventions of the plastic and histrionic arts liberate their followers to the portrayal of almost any phase of the physical or of the emotional nature, an American novelist may not write a story on the lines of Anna Karenina or Madame Bovary. Sappho[1] they put aside, and from Zola's work they avert their eyes. They do not condemn him or Daudet, necessarily, or accuse their motives; they leave them out of the question; they do not want to do that kind of thing. But they do sometimes wish to do another kind, to touch one of the most serious and sorrowful problems of life in the spirit of Tolstoï and Flaubert, and they ask why they may not. At one time, they remind us, the Anglo-Saxon novelist did deal with such problems—De Foe in his spirit, Richardson in his, Goldsmith[2] in his. At what moment did our fiction lose this privilege? In what fatal hour did the Young Girl arise and seal the lips of Fiction, with a touch of her finger, to some of the most vital interests of life?

Whether I wished to oppose them in their aspiration for greater freedom, or whether I wished to encourage them, I should begin to answer them by saying that the Young Girl had never done anything of the kind. The manners of the novel have been improving with those of its readers; that is all. Gentlemen no longer swear or fall drunk under the table, or abduct young ladies and shut them up in lonely country-houses, or so habitually set about the ruin of their neighbors' wives, as they once did. Generally, people now call a spade an agricultural implement; they have not grown decent without having also grown a little squeamish, but they have grown comparatively decent; there is no doubt about that. They require of a novelist whom they respect unquestionable proof of his seriousness, if he proposes to deal with certain phases of life; they require a sort of scientific decorum. He can no longer expect to be received on the ground of entertainment only; he assumes a higher function, something like that of a physician or a priest, and they expect him to be bound by laws as sacred as those of such professions; they hold him solemnly pledged not to betray them or abuse their confidence. If he will accept the conditions, they give him their confidence, and he may then treat to his greater honor, and not at all to his disadvantage, of such experiences, such relations of men and women as George Eliot[3] treats in Adam Bede, in Daniel Deronda, in Romola, in almost all her books; such as Hawthorne treats in the Scarlet Letter; such as Dickens treats in David Copperfield; such as Thackeray treats in Pendennis, and glances at in every one of his fictions; such as most of the masters of English fiction have at some time treated more or less openly. It is quite false or quite mistaken to suppose that our novels have left untouched these most important realities of life. They have only not made them their stock in trade; they have kept a true perspective in regard to them; they have relegated them in their pictures of life to the space and place they occupy in life itself, as we know it in England and America. They have kept a correct proportion, knowing perfectly well that unless the novel is to be a map, with everything scrupulously laid down in it, a faithful record of life in far the greater extent could be made to the exclusion of guilty love and all its circumstances and consequences.

I justify them in this view not only because I hate what is cheap and meretricious, and hold in peculiar loathing the cant of the critics who require "passion" as something in itself admirable and desirable in a novel, but because I prize

[1]*Anna Karenina* (1875–1876), by Leo Tolstoy (1828–1910), and *Madame Bovary* (1856), by Gustave Flaubert (1821–1880); both dealt with their heroines' love affairs. *Sappho* (1884), by the French naturalistic writer Alphonse Daudet (1840–1897), described a prostitute.

[2]Daniel Defoe (1660?–1731), English author of *Moll Flanders* (1722); Samuel Richardson (1689–1761), English author of *Clarissa Harlow* (1747–1748); and Oliver Goldsmith (1730–1774), English author of *The Vicar of Wakefield* (1766). Each dealt with illicit love.

[3]The pen name of Mary Ann Evans (1819–1880), English novelist.

fidelity in the historian of feeling and character. Most of these critics who demand "passion" would seem to have no conception of any passion but one. Yet there are several other passions: the passion of grief, the passion of avarice, the passion of pity, the passion of ambition, the passion of hate, the passion of envy, the passion of devotion, the passion of friendship; and all these have a greater part in the drama of life than the passion of love, and infinitely greater than the passion of guilty love. Wittingly or unwittingly, English fiction and American fiction have recognized this truth, not fully, not in the measure it merits, but in greater degree than most other fiction.

1891

Henry James   *1843–1916*

Like one of his own characters, Henry James was an artist reconnoitering society, a "passionate pilgrim" in search of experience. His intense perceptions of life undoubtedly owed much to his unusual upbringing. His wealthy father provided his children with tutors and took them back and forth across the Atlantic to give them a European education and expose them to international society. As a youth, James lived in New York, Geneva, London, Paris, and Newport, Rhode Island, where he and his brother William, who later became a distinguished philosopher and psychologist, studied art and enjoyed the society of their American cousins and the children of their wealthy neighbors.

In 1862 James entered the Harvard Law School but soon withdrew and embarked on a literary career. He published his first short story in 1864 at the age of twenty-one. In the next decade, spent alternately in America and Europe, he came under the influence of Flaubert, Turgenev, and Balzac.

In 1871 the Atlantic *serialized James's first novel,* Watch and Ward, *with which he hoped, but failed, to achieve fame. Years later, looking back and finding such early works "hideous," James preferred to declare that his first real novel was* Roderick Hudson *(1875). In 1876, when he was thirty-three, James settled permanently in England and, except for one long visit to the United States, remained in Europe for the rest of his life. The next decade saw the appearance of novels that brought him popular success:* The American *(1877), with its "international" theme of the traditionless American confronting the complexity of European life;* Daisy Miller *(1878), which one American critic described as "an outrage to American girlhood" but which brought James his first international fame; and* The Portrait of a Lady *(1881), the finest example of James's early work.*

The most ambitious novels of James's second period, The Bostonians *(1886),* The Princess Casamassima *(1886), and* The Tragic Muse *(1890), were failures with the public, as were his attempts, in the 1890s, to write for the stage. But James continued to write short stories and novels, and while he never recovered his early popularity, his last novels,* The Wings of the Dove *(1902),* The Ambassadors *(1903), and* The Golden Bowl *(1904), exemplify the mature and formidable style of a third literary period, which critics have come to praise as "The Major Phase."*

In 1915 James, the American expatriate, became a British subject, largely to show his support for the British cause in the First World War. His gesture was his last noteworthy symbolic achievement, for seven months later (February 1916) he died. At the time of his death, James's audience was small. Few of his works remained in print. His writing was no longer in vogue, especially in his native land where he was criticized as anti-American for portraying his fellow Americans as crass and shallow.

Readers in both England and America objected to the narrow emotional and social range of characters drawn from "the hothouse life of the leisured classes." And James was criticized, even parodied, for the obscure and costive style of his final period—a style capable of expressing great subtleties, but a style based on the assumption that the reader was as well-educated, as heedful of implications, and as unhurried as the author himself. James's mannered works were dismissed as "cathedrals of frosted glass," and at the end of his life James himself was forced to acknowledge that his writing had become "insurmountably unsaleable."

But unlike his contemporary Howells, James was to have his greatest influence not on his own age but on the age that followed. And since the 1930s and 1940s, his influence on writers and readers of modern fiction has grown to be immense. His twenty-two novels and over a hundred short stories, and his critical commentaries, are seen as major contributions to the art of fiction itself, helping to free the novel from its alliances with journalism and romantic storytelling. And he has come to be called the "first of the modern psychological novelists" because his novels and stories of men and women confronting complex society are chronicles of the psychological perceptions that James himself defined as the highest form of experience.

FURTHER READING: *The Complete Tales of Henry James*, 12 vols., ed. L. Edel, 1962–1965; *The Tales of Henry James*, 3 vols., ed. M. Aziz, 1973—; *The Complete Plays of Henry James*, ed. L. Edel, 1949; *The Notebooks of Henry James*, ed. F. Matthiessen and K. Murdock, 1947, 1953; *The Letters of Henry James*, 4 vols., ed. L. Edel, 1975–1984; V. Brooks, *The Pilgrimage of Henry James*, 1925; F. Mattheissen, *Henry James, The Major Phase*, 1944; N. Smith, *The Legend of the Master*, 1948; F. Dupee, *Henry James*, 1951, 1956, 1965; L. Edel, *Henry James*, 5 vols., 1953–1972, 2 vols., 1977, 1 vol., 1985; Q. Anderson, *The American Henry James*, 1957; F. Crews, *The Tragedy of Manners, Moral Drama in the Later Novels of Henry James*, 1957; O. Cargill, *Novels of Henry James*, 1961; D. Krook, *The Ordeal of Consciousness in Henry James*, 1962; M. Geismar, *Henry James and the Jacobites*, 1963; D. Jefferson, *Henry James and the Modern Reader*, 1964; S. Putt, *Henry James, A Reader's Guide*, 1966; T. Tanner, *Henry James, Modern Comments*, 1968, 1970; J. Miller, *Theory of Fiction, Henry James*, 1972; L. Auchincloss, *Reading Henry James*, 1975; K. Graham, *Henry James, The Drama of Fulfilment*, 1976; C. Anderson, *Person, Place, and Thing in Henry James's Novels*, 1977; S. Kappeler, *Writing and Reading in Henry James*, 1980; J. Kirschke, *Henry James and Impressionism*, 1981; D. Fogel, *Henry James and the Structure of the Romantic Imagination*, 1981; S. Daugherty, *The Literary Criticism of Henry James*, 1981; R. Norrman, *The Insecure World of Henry James's Fiction*, 1982; M. Jacobson, *Henry James and the Mass Market*, 1983; E. Wagenknecht, *The Novels of Henry James*, 1983; A. Margolis, *Henry James and the Problem of Audience*, 1985; *Critical Essays on Henry James, The Early Novels*, ed. J. Gargano, 1987; *Critical Essays on Henry James, The Late Novels*, ed. J. Gargano, 1987.

TEXTS: *Daisy Miller*, *Cornhill Magazine*, June–July, 1878; "The Real Thing," "The Beast in the Jungle," and "The Jolly Corner," *The Novels and Tales of Henry James*, New York Edition, 26 vols., 1907–1917; *Hawthorne*, 1879; "The Art of Fiction," *Partial Portraits*, 1888.

DAISY MILLER: A STUDY[1]

PART I

At the little town of Vevey, in Switzerland, there is a particularly comfortable hotel. There are, indeed, many hotels; for the entertainment of tourists is the business of the place, which, as many travellers will remember, is seated upon the edge of a remarkably blue lake[2]—a lake that it behoves every tourist to visit. The shore of the lake presents an unbroken array of establishments of this order, of every category, from the "grand hotel" of the newest fashion, with a chalk-white front, a hundred balconies, and a dozen flags flying from its roof, to the little Swiss *pension*[3] of an elder day, with its name inscribed in German-looking lettering upon a pink or yellow wall, and an awkward summerhouse in the angle of the garden. One of the hotels of Vevey, however, is famous, even classical, being distinguished from many of its upstart neighbours by an air both of luxury and of maturity. In this region, in the month of June, American travellers are extremely numerous; it may be said, indeed, that Vevey assumes at this period some of the characteristics of an American watering-place. There are sights and sounds which evoke a vision, an echo, of Newport and Saratoga.[4] There is a flitting hither and thither of "stylish" young girls, a rustling of muslin flounces, a rattle of dance-music in the morning hours, a sound of high-pitched voices at all times. You receive an impression of these things at the excellent inn of the "Trois Couronnes,"[5] and are transported in fancy to the Ocean House or to Congress Hall.[6] But at the "Trois Couronnes," it must be added, there are other features that are much at variance with these suggestions: neat German waiters, who look like secretaries of legation; Russian princesses sitting in the garden; little Polish boys walking about, held by the hand, with their governors; a view of the sunny crest of the Dent du Midi[7] and the Picturesque towers of the Castle of Chillon.[8]

I hardly know whether it was the analogies or the differences that were uppermost in the mind of a young American, who, two or three years ago, sat in the garden of the "Trois Couronnes," looking about him, rather idly, at some of the graceful objects I have mentioned. It was a beautiful summer morning, and in whatever fashion the young American looked at things, they must have seemed to him charming. He had come from Geneva the day before, by the little steamer, to see his aunt, who was staying at the hotel—Geneva having been for a long time his place of residence. But his aunt had a headache—his aunt had almost always a headache—and now she was shut up in her room, smelling camphor, so that he was at liberty to wander about. He was some seven-and-twenty years of age; when his friends spoke of him, they usually said that he was at Geneva, "studying." When his enemies spoke of him they said—but, after all, he had no enemies; he was an extremely amiable fellow, and universally

[1]First published in the *Cornhill Magazine*, June–July 1878 (the text presented here) and later revised by James in 1909 for inclusion in *The Novels and Tales of Henry James*, New York Edition, 26 vols., 1907–1909, 1917.

[2]Lake Geneva.   [3]A residential hotel.

[4]Newport, Rhode Island, and Saratoga Springs, New York, fashionable nineteenth-century American resorts.

[5]French: "Three Crowns."   [6]Hotels at Newport and Saratoga.

[7]Mountain peak in the Swiss Alps, south of Vevey.

[8]Thirteenth-century castle on Lake Geneva, the setting for Byron's poem "The Prisoner of Chillon." (1816).

liked. What I should say is, simply, that when certain persons spoke of him they affirmed the reason of his spending so much time at Geneva was that he was extremely devoted to a lady who lived there—a foreign lady—a person older than himself. Very few Americans—indeed I think none—had ever seen this lady, about whom there were some singular stories. But Winterbourne had an old attachment for the little metropolis of Calvinism;[9] he had been put to school there as a boy, and he had afterwards gone to college there—circumstances which had led to his forming a great many youthful friendships. Many of these he had kept, and they were a source of great satisfaction to him.

After knocking at his aunt's door and learning that she was indisposed, he had taken a walk about the town, and then he had come in to his breakfast. He had now finished his breakfast; but he was drinking a small cup of coffee, which had been served to him on a little table in the garden by one of the waiters who looked like an *attaché*.[10] At last he finished his coffee and lit a cigarette. Presently a small boy came walking along the path—an urchin of nine or ten. The child, who was diminutive for his years, had an aged expression of countenance, a pale complexion, and sharp little features. He was dressed in knickerbockers, with red stockings, which displayed his poor little spindleshanks;[11] he also wore a brilliant red cravat. He carried in his hand a long alpenstock,[12] the sharp point of which he thrust into everything that he approached—the flower-beds, the garden-benches, the trains of the ladies' dresses. In front of Winterbourne he paused, looking at him with a pair of bright, penetrating little eyes.

"Will you give me a lump of sugar?" he asked, in a sharp, hard little voice—a voice immature, and yet, somehow, not young.

Winterbourne glanced at the small table near him, on which his coffee-service rested, and saw that several morsels of sugar remained. "Yes, you may take one," he answered; "but I don't think sugar is good for little boys."

The little boy stepped forward and carefully selected three of the coveted fragments, two of which he buried in the pocket of his knickerbockers, depositing the other as promptly in another place. He poked his alpenstock, lance-fashion, into Winterbourne's bench, and tried to crack the lump of sugar with his teeth.

"Oh, blazes; it's har-r-d!" he exclaimed, pronouncing the adjective in a peculiar manner.

Winterbourne had immediately perceived that he might have the honour of claiming him as a fellow-countryman. "Take care you don't hurt your teeth," he said, paternally.

"I haven't got any teeth to hurt. They have all come out. I have only got seven teeth. My mother counted them last night, and one came out right afterwards. She said she'd slap me if any more came out. I can't help it. It's this old Europe. It's the climate that makes them come out. In America they didn't come out. It's these hotels."

Winterbourne was much amused. "If you eat three lumps of sugar, your mother will certainly slap you," he said.

"She's got to give me some candy, then," rejoined his young interlocutor. "I can't get any candy here—any American candy. American candy's the best candy."

"And are American little boys the best little boys?" asked Winterbourne.

"I don't know. I'm an American boy," said the child.

"I see you are one of the best!" laughed Winterbourne.

[9]The Protestant reformer John Calvin (1509–1564) lived at Geneva (1541–1564).
[10]A minor diplomat, one who is "attached" to an embassy.
[11]Legs.   [12]A long staff with a metal point, used in mountain climbing.

"Are you an American man?" pursued this vivacious infant. And then, on Winterbourne's affirmative reply—"American men are the best," he declared.

His companion thanked him for the compliment; and the child, who had now got astride of his alpenstock, stood looking about him, while he attacked a second lump of sugar. Winterbourne wondered if he himself had been like this in his infancy, for he had been brought to Europe at about this age.

"Here comes my sister!" cried the child, in a moment. "She's an American girl."

Winterbourne looked along the path and saw a beautiful young lady advancing. "American girls are the best girls," he said, cheerfully, to his young companion.

"My sister ain't the best!" the child declared. "She's always blowing[13] at me."

"I imagine that is your fault, not hers," said Winterbourne. The young lady meanwhile had drawn near. She was dressed in white muslin, with a hundred frills and flounces, and knots of pale-coloured ribbon. She was bare-headed; but she balanced in her hand a large parasol, with a deep border of embroidery; and she was strikingly, admirably pretty. "How pretty they are!" thought Winterbourne, straightening himself in his seat, as if he were prepared to rise.

The young lady paused in front of his bench, near the parapet of the garden, which overlooked the lake. The little boy had now converted his alpenstock into a vaulting-pole, by the aid of which he was springing about in the gravel, and kicking it up not a little.

"Randolph," said the young lady, "what *are* you doing?"

"I'm going up the Alps," replied Randolph. "This is the way!" And he gave another little jump, scattering the pebbles about Winterbourne's ears.

"That's the way they come down," said Winterbourne.

"He's an American man!" cried Randolph, in his little hard voice.

The young lady gave no heed to this announcement, but looked straight at her brother. "Well, I guess you had better be quiet," she simply observed.

It seemed to Winterbourne that he had been in a manner presented. He got up and stepped slowly towards the young girl, throwing away his cigarette. "This little boy and I have made acquaintance," he said, with great civility. In Geneva, as he had been perfectly aware, a young man was not at liberty to speak to a young unmarried lady except under certain rarely-occurring conditions; but here at Vevey, what conditions could be better than these?—a pretty American girl coming and standing in front of you in a garden. This pretty American girl, however, on hearing Winterbourne's observation, simply glanced at him; she then turned her head and looked over the parapet, at the lake and the opposite mountains. He wondered whether he had gone too far; but he decided that he must advance farther, rather than retreat. While he was thinking of something else to say, the young lady turned to the little boy again.

"I should like to know where you got that pole," she said.

"I bought it!" responded Randolph.

"You don't mean to say you're going to take it to Italy."

"Yes, I am going to take it to Italy!" the child declared.

The young girl glanced over the front of her dress, and smoothed out a knot or two of ribbon. Then she rested her eyes upon the prospect again. "Well, I guess you had better leave it somewhere," she said, after a moment.

"Are you going to Italy?" Winterbourne inquired, in a tone of great respect.

[13]Yelling.

The young lady glanced at him again. "Yes, sir," she replied. And she said nothing more.

"Are you—a—going over the Simplon?"[14] Winterbourne pursued, a little embarrassed.

"I don't know," she said. "I suppose it's some mountain. Randolph, what mountain are we going over?"

"Going where?" the child demanded.

"To Italy," Winterbourne explained.

"I don't know," said Randolph. "I don't want to go to Italy. I want to go to America."

"Oh, Italy is a beautiful place!" rejoined the young man.

"Can you get candy there?" Randolph loudly inquired.

"I hope not," said his sister. "I guess you have had enough candy, and mother thinks so too."

"I haven't had any for ever so long—for a hundred weeks!" cried the boy, still jumping about.

The young lady inspected her flounces and smoothed her ribbons again; and Winterbourne presently risked an observation upon the beauty of the view. He was ceasing to be embarrassed, for he had begun to perceive that she was not in the least embarrassed herself. There had not been the slightest alteration in her charming complexion; she was evidently neither offended nor fluttered. If she looked another way when he spoke to her, and seemed not particularly to hear him, this was simply her habit, her manner. Yet, as he talked a little more, and pointed out some of the objects of interest in the view, with which she appeared quite unacquainted, she gradually gave him more of the benefit of her glance; and then he saw that this glance was perfectly direct and unshrinking. It was not, however, what would have been called an immodest glance, for the young girl's eyes were singularly honest and fresh. They were wonderfully pretty eyes; and, indeed, Winterbourne had not seen for a long time anything prettier than his fair countrywoman's various features—her complexion, her nose, her ears, her teeth. He had a great relish for feminine beauty; he was addicted to observing and analysing it; and as regards this young lady's face he made several observations. It was not at all insipid, but it was not exactly expressive; and though it was eminently delicate Winterbourne mentally accused it—very forgivingly—of a want of finish. He thought it very possible that Master Randolph's sister was a coquette;[15] he was sure she had a spirit of her own; but in her bright, sweet, superficial little visage there was no mockery, no irony. Before long it became obvious that she was much disposed towards conversation. She told him that they were going to Rome for the winter—she and her mother and Randolph. She asked him if he was a "real American;" she shouldn't have taken him for one; he seemed more like a German—this was said after a little hesitation, especially when he spoke. Winterbourne, laughing, answered that he had met Germans who spoke like Americans; but that he had not, so far as he remembered, met an American who spoke like a German. Then he asked her if she should not be more comfortable in sitting upon the bench which he had just quitted. She answered that she liked standing up and walking about; but she presently sat down. She told him she was from New York State—"if you know where that is." Winterbourne learned more about her by catching hold of her small, slippery brother and making him stand a few minutes by his side.

---

[14]Mountain pass between Switzerland and Italy.   [15]A flirtatious tease.

"Tell me your name, my boy," he said.

"Randolph C. Miller," said the boy, sharply. "And I'll tell you her name;" and he levelled his alpenstock at his sister.

"You had better wait till you are asked!" said this young lady, calmly.

"I should like very much to know your name," said Winterbourne.

"Her name is Daisy Miller!" cried the child. "But that isn't her real name; that isn't her name on her cards."

"It's a pity you haven't got one of my cards!" said Miss Miller.

"Her real name is Annie P. Miller," the boy went on.

"Ask him *his* name," said his sister, indicating Winterbourne.

But on this point Randolph seemed perfectly indifferent; he continued to supply information with regard to his own family. "My father's name is Ezra B. Miller," he announced. "My father ain't in Europe; my father's in a better place than Europe."

Winterbourne imagined for a moment that this was the manner in which the child had been taught to intimate that Mr. Miller had been removed to the sphere of celestial rewards. But Randolph immediately added, "My father's in Schenectady. He's got a big business. My father's rich, you bet."

"Well!" ejaculated Miss Miller, lowering her parasol and looking at the embroidered border. Winterbourne presently released the child, who departed, dragging his alpenstock along the path. "He doesn't like Europe," said the young girl. "He wants to go back."

"To Schenectady, you mean?"

"Yes; he wants to go right home. He hasn't got any boys here. There is one boy here, but he always goes round with a teacher; they won't let him play."

"And your brother hasn't any teacher?" Winterbourne inquired.

"Mother thought of getting him one, to travel round with us. There was a lady told her of a very good teacher; an American lady—perhaps you know her—Mrs. Sanders. I think she came from Boston. She told her of this teacher, and we thought of getting him to travel round with us. But Randolph said he didn't want a teacher travelling round with us. He said he wouldn't have lessons when he was in the cars.[16] And we *are* in the cars about half the time. There was an English lady we met in the cars—I think her name was Miss Featherstone; perhaps you know her. She wanted to know why I didn't give Randolph lessons—give him "instruction," she called it. I guess he could give me more instruction that I could give him. He's very smart."

"Yes," said Winterbourne; "he seems very smart."

"Mother's going to get a teacher for him as soon as we get to Italy. Can you get good teachers in Italy?"

"Very good, I should think," said Winterbourne.

"Or else she's going to find some school. He ought to learn some more. He's only nine. He's going to college." And in this way Miss Miller continued to converse upon the affairs of her family, and upon other topics. She sat there with her extremely pretty hands, ornamented with very brilliant rings, folded in her lap, and with her pretty eyes now resting upon those of Winterbourne, now wandering over the garden, the people who passed by, and the beautiful view. She talked to Winterbourne as if she had known him a long time. He found it very pleasant. It was many years since he had heard a young girl talk so much. It might have been said of this unknown young lady, who had come and sat down beside him upon a bench, that she chattered. She was very quiet;

---

[16]Railroad cars.

she sat in a charming tranquil attitude, but her lips and her eyes were constantly moving. She had a soft, slender, agreeable voice, and her tone was decidedly sociable. She gave Winterbourne a history of her movements and intentions, and those of her mother and brother, in Europe, and enumerated, in particular, the various hotels at which they had stopped. "That English lady, in the cars," she said—"Miss Featherstone—asked me if we didn't all live in hotels in America. I told her I had never been in so many hotels in my life as since I came to Europe. I have never seen so many—it's nothing but hotels." But Miss Miller did not make this remark with a querulous accent; she appeared to be in the best humour with everything. She declared that the hotels were very good, when once you got used to their ways, and that Europe was perfectly sweet. She was not disappointed—not a bit. Perhaps it was because she had heard so much about it before. She had ever so many intimate friends that had been there ever so many times. And then she had had ever so many dresses and things from Paris. Whenever she put on a Paris dress she felt as if she were in Europe.

"It was a kind of a wishing-cap," said Winterbourne.

"Yes," said Miss Miller, without examining this analogy; "it always made me wish I was here. But I needn't have done that for dresses. I am sure they send all the pretty ones to America; you see the most frightful things here. The only thing I don't like," she proceeded, "is the society. There isn't any society; or, if there is, I don't know where it keeps itself. Do you? I suppose there is some society somewhere, but I haven't seen anything of it. I'm very fond of society, and I have always had a great deal of it. I don't mean only in Schenectady, but in New York. I used to go to New York every winter. In New York I had lots of society. Last winter I had seventeen dinners given me; and three of them were by gentlemen," added Daisy Miller. "I have more friends in New York than in Schenectady—more gentleman friends; and more young lady friends too," she resumed in a moment. She paused again for an instant; she was looking at Winterbourne with all her prettiness in her lively eyes and in her light, slightly monotonous smile. "I have always had," she said, "a great deal of gentlemen's society."

Poor Winterbourne was amused, perplexed, and decidedly charmed. He had never yet heard a young girl express herself in just this fashion; never, at least, save in cases where to say such things seemed a kind of demonstrative evidence of a certain laxity of deportment. And yet was he to accuse Miss Daisy Miller of actual or potential *inconduite*,[17] as they said at Geneva? He felt that he had lived at Geneva so long that he had lost a good deal; he had become dishabituated to the American tone. Never, indeed, since he had grown old enough to appreciate things, had he encountered a young American girl of so pronounced a type as this. Certainly she was very charming, but how deucedly sociable! Was she simply a pretty girl from New York State—were they all like that, the pretty girls who had a good deal of gentlemen's society? Or was she also a designing, an audacious, an unscrupulous young person? Winterbourne had lost his instinct in this matter, and his reason could not help him. Miss Daisy Miller looked extremely innocent. Some people had told him that, after all, American girls were exceedingly innocent; and others had told him that, after all, they were not. He was inclined to think Miss Daisy Miller was a flirt—a pretty American flirt. He had never, as yet, had any relations with young ladies of this category. He had known, here in Europe, two or three women—persons older than Miss Daisy Miller, and

[17] French: misconduct.

provided, for respectability's sake, with husbands—who were great coquettes—dangerous, terrible women, with whom one's relations were liable to take a serious turn. But this young girl was not a coquette in that sense; she was very unsophisticated; she was only a pretty American flirt. Winterbourne was almost grateful for having found the formula that applied to Miss Daisy Miller. He leaned back in his seat; he remarked to himself that she had the most charming nose he had ever seen; he wondered what were the regular conditions and limitations of one's intercourse with a pretty American flirt. It presently became apparent that he was on the way to learn.

"Have you been to that old castle?" asked the young girl, pointing with her parasol to the far-gleaming walls of the Château de Chillon.

"Yes, formerly, more than once," said Winterbourne. "You too, I suppose, have seen it?"

"No; we haven't been there. I want to go there dreadfully. Of course I mean to go there. I wouldn't go away from here without having seen that old castle."

"It's a very pretty excursion," said Winterbourne, "and very easy to make. You can drive, you know, or you can go by the little steamer."

"You can go in the cars," said Miss Miller.

"Yes; you can go in the cars," Winterbourne assented.

"Our courier[18] says they take you right up to the castle," the young girl continued. "We were going last week; but my mother gave out. She suffers dreadfully from dyspepsia. She said she couldn't go. Randolph wouldn't go either; he says he doesn't think much of old castles. But I guess we'll go this week, if we can get Randolph."

"Your brother is not interested in ancient monuments?" Winterbourne inquired, smiling.

"He says he don't care much about old castles. He's only nine. He wants to stay at the hotel. Mother's afraid to leave him alone, and the courier won't stay with him; so we haven't been to many places. But it will be too bad if we don't go up there." And Miss Miller pointed again at the Château de Chillon.

"I should think it might be arranged," said Winterbourne. "Couldn't you get some one to stay—for the afternoon—with Randolph?"

Miss Miller looked at him a moment; and then, very placidly—"I wish *you* would stay with him!" she said.

Winterbourne hesitated a moment. "I should much rather go to Chillon with you."

"With me?" asked the young girl, with the same placidity.

She didn't rise, blushing, as a young girl at Geneva would have done; and yet Winterbourne, conscious that he had been very bold, thought it possible she was offended. "With your mother," he answered very respectfully.

But it seemed that both his audacity and his respect were lost upon Miss Daisy Miller. "I guess my mother won't go after all," she said. "She don't like to ride round in the afternoon. But did you really mean what you said just now; that you would like to go up there?"

"Most earnestly," Winterbourne declared.

"Then we may arrange it. If mother will stay with Randolph, I guess Eugenio will."

"Eugenio?" the young man inquired.

"Eugenio's our courier. He doesn't like to stay with Randolph; he's the most

---

[18]A servant who accompanies travelers.

fastidious man I ever saw. But he's a splendid courier. I guess he'll stay at home with Randolph if mother does, and then we can go to the castle."

Winterbourne reflected for an instant as lucidly as possible—"we" could only mean Miss Daisy Miller and himself. This programme seemed almost too agreeable for credence; he felt as if he ought to kiss the young lady's hand. Possibly he would have done so—and quite spoiled the project; but at this moment another person—presumably Eugenio—appeared. A tall, handsome man, with superb whiskers, wearing a velvet morning-coat and a brilliant watch-chain, approached Miss Miller, looking sharply at her companion. "Oh, Eugenio!" said Miss Miller, with the friendliest accent.

Eugenio had looked at Winterbourne from head to foot; he now bowed gravely to the young lady. "I have the honour to inform mademoiselle that luncheon is upon the table."

Miss Miller slowly rose. "See here, Eugenio," she said. "I'm going to that old castle, any way."

"To the Château de Chillon, mademoiselle?" the courier inquired. "Mademoiselle has made arrangements?" he added, in a tone which struck Winterbourne as very impertinent.

Eugenio's tone apparently threw, even to Miss Miller's own apprehension, a slightly ironical light upon the young girl's situation. She turned to Winterbourne, blushing a little—a very little. "You won't back out?" she said.

"I shall not be happy till we go!" he protested.

"And you are staying in this hotel?" she went on. "And you are really an American?"

The courier stood looking at Winterbourne, offensively. The young man, at least, thought his manner of looking an offence to Miss Miller; it conveyed an imputation that she "picked up" acquaintances. "I shall have the honour of presenting to you a person who will tell you all about me," he said smiling, and referring to his aunt.

"Oh, well, we'll go some day," said Miss Miller. And she gave him a smile and turned away. She put up her parasol and walked back to the inn beside Eugenio. Winterbourne stood looking after her; and as she moved away, drawing her muslin furbelows over the gravel, said to himself that she had the *tourmure*[19] of a princess.

He had, however, engaged to do more than proved feasible, in promising to present his aunt, Mrs. Costello, to Miss Daisy Miller. As soon as the former lady had got better of her headache he waited upon her in her apartment; and, after the proper inquiries in regard to her health, he asked her if she had observed, in the hotel, an American family—a mamma, a daughter, and a little boy.

"And a courier?" said Mrs. Costello. "Oh, yes I have observed them. Seen them—heard them—and kept out of their way." Mrs. Costello was a widow with a fortune; a person of much distinction, who frequently intimated that, if she were not so dreadfully liable to sick-headaches, she would probably have left a deeper impress upon her time. She had a long pale face, a high nose, and a great deal of very striking white hair, which she wore in large puffs and *rouleaux*[20] over the top of her head. She had two sons married in New York, and another who was now in Europe. This young man was amusing himself at Hombourg,[21] and, though he was on his travels, was rarely perceived to visit any particular city at the moment selected by his mother for her own appearance there. Her

---

[19]French: appearance.   [20]French: rolls, coils.   [21]A German health resort.

nephew, who had come up to Vevey expressly to see her, was therefore more attentive than those who, as she said, were nearer to her. He had imbibed at Geneva the idea that one must always be attentive to one's aunt. Mrs. Costello had not seen him for many years, and she was greatly pleased with him, manifesting her approbation by initiating him into many of the secrets of that social sway which, as she gave him to understand, she exerted in the American capital.[22] She admitted that she was very exclusive; but, if he were acquainted with New York, he would see that one had to be. And her picture of the minutely hierarchical constitution of the society of that city, which she presented to him in many different lights, was, to Winterbourne's imagination, almost oppressively striking.

He immediately perceived, from her tone, that Miss Daisy Miller's place in the social scale was low. "I am afraid you don't approve of them," he said.

"They are very common," Mrs. Costello declared. "They are the sort of Americans that one does one's duty by not—not accepting."

"Ah, you don't accept them?" said the young man.

"I can't, my dear Frederick. I would if I could, but I can't."

"The young girl is very pretty," said Winterbourne, in a moment.

"Of course she's pretty. But she is very common."

"I see what you mean of course," said Winterbourne, after another pause.

"She has that charming look that they all have," his aunt resumed. "I can't think where they pick it up; and she dressed in perfection—no, you don't know how well she dresses. I can't think where they get their taste."

"But, my dear aunt, she is not, after all, a Comanche savage."

"She is a young lady," said Mrs. Costello, "who has an intimacy with her mamma's courier."

"An intimacy with the courier?" the young man demanded.

"Oh, the mother is just as bad! They treat the courier like a familiar friend—like a gentleman. I shouldn't wonder if he dines with them. Very likely they have never seen a man with such good manners, such fine clothes, so like a gentleman. He probably corresponds to the young lady's idea of a Count. He sits with them in the garden, in the evening. I think he smokes."

Winterbourne listened with interest to these disclosures; they helped him to make up his mind about Miss Daisy. Evidently she was rather wild. "Well," he said, "I am not a courier, and yet she was very charming to me."

"You had better have said at first," said Mrs. Costello with dignity, "that you had made her acquaintance."

"We simply met in the garden and we talked a bit."

"*Tout bonnement!*[23] And pray what did you say?"

"I said I should take the liberty of introducing her to my admirable aunt."

"I am much obliged to you."

"It was to guarantee my respectability," said Winterbourne.

"And pray who is to guarantee hers?"

"Ah, you are cruel!" said the young man. "She's a very nice young girl."

"You don't say that as if you believed it," Mrs. Costello observed.

"She is completely uncultivated," Winterbourne went on. "But she is wonderfully pretty, and, in short, she is very nice. To prove that I believe it, I am going to take her to the Château de Chillon."

"You two are going off there together? I should say it proved just the contrary.

---

[22]America's social capital, New York City.
[23]French: "Is that so!"

How long had you known her, may I ask, when this interesting project was formed? You haven't been twenty-four hours in the house."

"I had known her half an hour!" said Winterbourne, smiling.

"Dear me!" cried Mrs. Costello. "What a dreadful girl!"

Her nephew was silent for some moments. "You really think, then," he began, earnestly, and with a desire for trustworthy information—"you really think that——" But he paused again.

"Think what, sir?" said his aunt.

"That she is the sort of young lady who expects a man—sooner or later—to carry her off?"

"I haven't the least idea what such young ladies expect a man to do. But I really think that you had better not meddle with little American girls that are uncultivated, as you call them. You have lived too long out of the country. You will be sure to make some great mistake. You are too innocent."

"My dear aunt, I am not so innocent," said Winterbourne, smiling and curling his moustache.

"You are too guilty, then!"

Winterbourne continued to curl his moustache, meditatively. "You won't let the poor girl know you then?" he asked at last.

"Is it literally true that she is going to the Château de Chillon with you?"

"I think that she fully intends it."

"Then, my dear Frederick," said Mrs. Costello, "I must decline the honour of her acquaintance. I am an old woman, but I am not too old—thank Heaven—to be shocked!"

"But don't they all do these things—the young girls in America?" Winterbourne inquired.

Mrs. Costello stared a moment. "I should like to see my granddaughters do them!" she declared, grimly.

This seemed to throw some light upon the matter, for Winterbourne remembered to have heard that his pretty cousins in New York were "tremendous flirts." If, therefore, Miss Daisy Miller exceeded the liberal margin allowed to these young ladies, it was probable that anything might be expected of her. Winterbourne was impatient to see her again, and he was vexed with himself that, by instinct, he should not appreciate her justly.

Though he was impatient to see her, he hardly knew what he should say to her about his aunt's refusal to become acquainted with her; but he discovered, promptly enough, that with Miss Daisy Miller there was no great need of walking on tiptoe. He found her that evening in the garden, wandering about in the warm starlight, like an indolent sylph, and swinging to and fro the largest fan he had ever beheld. It was ten o'clock. He had dined with his aunt, had been sitting with her since dinner, and had just taken leave of her till the morrow. Miss Daisy Miller seemed very glad to see him; she declared it was the longest evening she had ever passed.

"Have you been all alone?" he asked.

"I have been walking round with mother. But mother gets tired walking round," she answered.

"Has she gone to bed?"

"No; she doesn't like to go to bed," said the young girl. "She doesn't sleep—not three hours. She says she doesn't know how she lives. She's dreadfully nervous. I guess she sleeps more than she thinks. She's gone somewhere after Randolph; she wants to try to get him to go to bed. He doesn't like to go to bed."

"Let us hope she will persuade him," observed Winterbourne.

"She will talk to him all she can; but he doesn't like her to talk to him," said Miss Daisy, opening her fan. "She's going to try to get Eugenio to talk to him. But he isn't afraid of Eugenio. Eugenio's a splendid courier, but he can't make much impression on Randolph! I don't believe he'll go to bed before eleven." It appears that Randolph's vigil was in fact triumphantly prolonged, for Winterbourne strolled about with the young girl for some time without meeting her mother. "I have been looking round for that lady you want to introduce me to," his companion resumed. "She's your aunt." Then, on Winterbourne's admitting the fact, and expressing some curiosity as to how she learned it, she said she heard all about Mrs. Costello from the chambermaid. She was very quiet and very *comme il faut;*[24] she wore white puffs; she spoke to no one, and she never dined at the *table d'hôte.*[25] Every two days she had a headache. "I think that's a lovely description, headache and all!" said Miss Daisy, chattering along in her thin, gay voice. "I want to know her ever so much. I know just what *your* aunt would be; I know I should like her. She would be very exclusive. I like a lady to be exclusive; I'm dying to be exclusive myself. Well, we *are* exclusive, mother and I. We don't speak to every one—or they don't speak to us. I suppose it's about the same thing. Any way, I shall be ever so glad to know your aunt."

Winterbourne was embarrassed. "She would be most happy," he said; "but I am afraid those headaches will interfere."

The young girl looked at him through the dusk. "But I suppose she doesn't have a headache every day," she said, sympathetically.

Winterbourne was silent a moment. "She tells me she does," he answered at last—not knowing what to say.

Miss Daisy Miller stopped and stood looking at him. Her prettiness was still visible in the darkness; she was opening and closing her enormous fan. "She doesn't want to know me!" she said, suddenly. "Why don't you say so? You needn't be afraid. I'm not afraid!" And she gave a little laugh.

Winterbourne fancied there was a tremor in her voice; he was touched, shocked, mortified by it. "My dear young lady," he protested, "she knows no one. It's her wretched health."

The young girl walked on a few steps, laughing still. "You needn't be afraid," she repeated. "Why should she want to know me?" Then she paused again; she was close to the parapet of the garden, and in front of her was the starlit lake. There was a vague sheen upon its surface, and in the distance were dimly-seen mountain forms. Daisy Miller looked out upon the mysterious prospect, and then she gave another little laugh. "Gracious! she *is* exclusive!" she said. Winterbourne wondered whether she was seriously wounded, and for a moment almost wished that her sense of injury might be such as to make it becoming in him to attempt to reassure and comfort her. He had a pleasant sense that she would be very approachable for consolatory purposes. He felt then, for the instant, quite ready to sacrifice his aunt, conversationally; to admit that she was a proud, rude woman, and to declare that they needn't mind her. But before he had time to commit himself to this perilous mixture of gallantry and impiety, the young lady, resuming her walk, gave an exclamation in quite another tone. "Well; here's mother! I guess she hasn't got Randolph to go to bed." The figure of a lady appeared, at a distance, very indistinct in the darkness, and advancing with a slow and wavering movement. Suddenly it seemed to pause.

"Are you sure it is your mother? Can you distinguish her in this thick dusk?" Winterbourne asked.

---

[24]French: proper.   [25]French: ordinary public dining table.

"Well!" cried Miss Daisy Miller, with a laugh, "I guess I know my own mother. And when she has got on my shawl, too! She is always wearing my things."

The lady in question, ceasing to advance, hovered vaguely about the spot at which she had checked her steps.

"I am afraid your mother doesn't see you," said Winterbourne. "Or perhaps," he added—thinking, with Miss Miller, the joke permissible—"perhaps she feels guilty about your shawl."

"Oh, it's a fearful old thing!" the young girl replied, serenely. "I told her she could wear it. She won't come here, because she sees you."

"Ah, then!" said Winterbourne, "I had better leave you."

"Oh, no; come on!" urged Miss Daisy Miller.

"I'm afraid your mother doesn't approve of my walking with you."

Miss Miller gave him a serious glance. "It isn't for me; it's for you—that is, it's for *her*. Well; I don't know who it's for! But mother doesn't like any of my gentlemen friends. She's right down timid. She always makes a fuss if I introduce a gentleman. But I *do* introduce them—almost always. If I didn't introduce my gentlemen friends to mother," the young girl added, in her little soft, flat monotone, "I shouldn't think I was natural."

"To introduce me," said Winterbourne, "you must know my name." And he proceeded to pronounce it.

"Oh, dear; I can't say all that!" said his companion, with a laugh. But by this time they had come up to Mrs. Miller, who, as they drew near, walked to the parapet of the garden and leaned upon it, looking intently at the lake, and turning her back on them. "Mother!" said the young girl, in a tone of decision. Upon this the elder lady turned round. "Mr. Winterbourne," said Miss Daisy Miller, introducing the young man very frankly and prettily. "Common" she was, as Mrs. Costello had pronounced her; yet it was a wonder to Winterbourne that, with her commonness, she had a singularly delicate grace.

Her mother was a small, spare, light person, with a wandering eye, a very exiguous nose, and a large forehead, decorated with a certain amount of thin, much-frizzled hair. Like her daughter, Mrs. Miller was dressed with extreme elegance; she had enormous diamonds in her ears. So far as Winterbourne could observe, she gave him no greeting—she certainly was not looking at him. Daisy was near her, pulling her shawl straight. "What are you doing, poking round here?" this young lady inquired; but by no means with that harshness of accent which her choice of words may imply.

"I don't know," said her mother, turning towards the lake again.

"I shouldn't think you'd want that shawl!" Daisy exclaimed.

"Well—I do!" her mother answered, with a little laugh.

"Did you get Randolph to go to bed?" asked the young girl.

"No; I couldn't induce him," said Mrs. Miller, very gently. "He wants to talk to the waiter. He likes to talk to that waiter."

"I was telling Mr. Winterbourne," the young girl went on; and to the young man's ear her tone might have indicated that she had been uttering his name all her life.

"Oh, yes!" said Winterbourne; "I have the pleasure of knowing your son."

Randolph's mamma was silent; she turned her attention to the lake. But at last she spoke. "Well, I don't see how he lives!"

"Anyhow, it isn't so bad as it was at Dover," said Daisy Miller.

"And what occurred at Dover?" Winterbourne asked.

"He wouldn't go to bed at all. I guess he sat up all night—in the public parlour. He wasn't in bed at twelve o'clock: I know that."

"It was half-past twelve," declared Mrs. Miller, with mild emphasis.

"Does he sleep much during the day?" Winterbourne demanded.

"I guess he doesn't sleep much," Daisy rejoined.

"I wish he would!" said her mother. "It seems as if he couldn't."

"I think he's real tiresome," Daisy pursued.

Then, for some moments, there was silence. "Well Daisy Miller," said the elder lady, presently, "I shouldn't think you'd want to talk against your own brother!"

"Well, he *is* tiresome, mother," said Daisy, quite without the asperity of a retort.

"He's only nine," urged Mrs. Miller.

"Well, he wouldn't go to that castle," said the young girl. "I'm going there with Mr. Winterbourne."

To this announcement, very placidly made, Daisy's mamma offered no response. Winterbourne took for granted that she deeply disapproved of the projected excursion; but he said to himself that she was a simple, easily-managed person, and that a few deferential protestations would take the edge from her displeasure. "Yes," he began; "Your daughter has kindly allowed me the honour of being her guide."

Mrs. Miller's wandering eyes attached themselves, with a sort of appealing air, to Daisy, who, however, strolled a few steps farther, gently humming to herself. "I presume you will go in the cars," said her mother.

"Yes; or in the boat," said Winterbourne.

"Well, of course, I don't know," Mrs. Miller rejoined. "I have never been to that castle."

"It is a pity you shouldn't go," said Winterbourne, beginning to feel reassured as to her opposition. And yet he was quite prepared to find that, as a matter of course, she meant to accompany her daughter.

"We've been thinking ever so much about going," she pursued; "but it seems as if we couldn't. Of course Daisy—she wants to go round. But there's a lady here—I don't know her name—she says she shouldn't think we'd want to go to see castles *here;* she should think we'd want to wait till we got to Italy. It seems as if there would be so many there," continued Mrs. Miller, with an air of increasing confidence. "Of course, we only want to see the principal ones. We visited several in England," she presently added.

"Ah, yes! in England there are beautiful castles," said Winterbourne. "But Chillon, here, is very well worth seeing."

"Well, if Daisy feels up to it——," said Mrs. Miller, in a tone impregnated with a sense of the magnitude of the enterprise. "It seems as if there was nothing she wouldn't undertake."

"Oh, I think she'll enjoy it!" Winterbourne declared. And he desired more and more to make it a certainty that he was to have the privilege of a *tête-à-tête*[26] with the young lady, who was still strolling along in front of them, softly vocalising. "You are not disposed, madam," he inquired, "to undertake it yourself?"

Daisy's mother looked at him, an instant, askance, and then walked forward in silence. Then—"I guess she had better go alone," she said, simply.

Winterbourne observed to himself that this was a very different type of maternity from that of the vigilant matrons who massed themselves in the forefront of social intercourse in the dark old city at the other end of the lake.

[26]French: private talk.

But his meditations were interrupted by hearing his name very distinctly pronounced by Mrs. Miller's unprotected daughter.

"Mr. Winterbourne!" murmured Daisy.

"Mademoiselle!" said the young man.

"Don't you want to take me out in a boat?"

"At present?" he asked.

"Of course!" said Daisy.

"Well, Annie Miller!" exclaimed her mother.

"I beg you, madam, to let her go," said Winterbourne, ardently; for he had never yet enjoyed the sensation of guiding through the summer starlight a skiff freighted with a fresh and beautiful young girl.

"I shouldn't think she'd want to," said her mother. "I should think she'd rather go indoors."

"I'm sure Mr. Winterbourne wants to take me," Daisy declared. "He's so awfully devoted!"

"I will row you over to Chillon, in the starlight."

"I don't believe it!" said Daisy.

"Well!" ejaculated the elder lady again.

"You haven't spoken to me for half an hour," her daughter went on.

"I have been having some very pleasant conversation with your mother," said Winterbourne.

"Well; I want you to take me out in a boat!" Daisy repeated. They had all stopped, and she had turned round and was looking at Winterbourne. Her face wore a charming smile, her pretty eyes were gleaming, she was swinging her great fan about. No; it's impossible to be prettier than that, thought Winterbourne.

"There are half a dozen boats moored at that landing-place," he said, pointing to certain steps which descended from the garden to the lake. "If you will do me the honour to accept my arm, we will go and select one of them."

Daisy stood there smiling; she threw back her head and gave a little, light laugh. "I like a gentleman to be formal!" she declared.

"I assure you it's a formal offer."

"I was bound I would make you say something," Daisy went on.

"You see it's not very difficult," said Winterbourne. "But I am afraid you are chaffing me."

"I think not, sir," remarked Mrs. Miller, very gently.

"Do, then, let me give you a row," he said to the young girl.

"It's quite lovely, the way you say that!" cried Daisy.

"It will be still more lovely to do it."

"Yes, it would be lovely!" said Daisy. But she made no movement to accompany him; she only stood there laughing.

"I should think you had better find out what time it is," interposed her mother.

"It is eleven o'clock, madam," said a voice, with a foreign accent, out of the neighbouring darkness; and Winterbourne, turning, perceived the florid personage who was in attendance upon the two ladies. He had apparently just approached.

"Oh, Eugenio," said Daisy, "I am going out in a boat!"

Eugenio bowed. "At eleven o'clock, mademoiselle?"

"I am going with Mr. Winterbourne. This very minute."

"Do tell her she can't," said Mrs. Miller to the courier.

"I think you had better not go out in a boat, mademoiselle," Eugenio declared.

Winterbourne wished to Heaven this pretty girl were not so familiar with her courier; but he said nothing.

"I suppose you don't think it's proper!" Daisy exclaimed. "Eugenio doesn't think anything's proper."

"I am at your service," said Winterbourne.

"Does mademoiselle propose to go alone?" asked Eugenio of Mrs. Miller.

"Oh, no; with this gentleman!" answered Daisy's mamma.

The courier looked for a moment at Winterbourne—the latter thought he was smiling—and then, solemnly, with a bow, "As mademoiselle pleases!" he said.

"Oh, I hoped you would make a fuss!" said Daisy. "I don't care to go now."

"I myself shall make a fuss if you don't go," said Winterbourne.

"That's all I want—a little fuss!" And the young girl began to laugh again.

"Mr. Randolph has gone to bed!" the courier announced, frigidly.

"Oh, Daisy; now we can go!" said Mrs. Miller.

Daisy turned away from Winterbourne, looking at him, smiling, and fanning herself. "Good-night," she said; "I hope you are disappointed, or disgusted, or something!"

He looked at her, taking the hand she offered him. "I am puzzled," he answered.

"Well; I hope it won't keep you awake!" she said, very smartly; and, under the escort of the privileged Eugenio, the two ladies passed towards the house.

Winterbourne stood looking after them; he was indeed puzzled. He lingered beside the lake for a quarter of an hour; turning over the mystery of the young girl's sudden familiarities and caprices. But the only very definite conclusion he came to was that he should enjoy deucedly "going off" with her somewhere.

Two days afterwards he went off with her to the Castle of Chillon. He waited for her in the large hall of the hotel, where the couriers, the servants, the foreign tourists were lounging about and staring. It was not the place he should have chosen, but she had appointed it. She came tripping downstairs, buttoning her long gloves, squeezing her folded parasol against her pretty figure, dressed in the perfection of a soberly elegant travelling-costume. Winterbourne was a man of imagination and, as our ancestors used to say, sensibility;[27] as he looked at her dress and, on the great staircase, her little rapid, confiding step, he felt as if there were something romantic going forward. He could have believed he was going to elope with her. He passed out with her among all the idle people that were assembled there; they were all looking at her very hard; she had begun to chatter as soon as she joined him. Winterbourne's preference had been that they should be conveyed to Chillon in a carriage; but she expressed a lively wish to go in the little steamer; she declared that she had a passion for steamboats. There was always such a lovely breeze upon the water, and you saw such lots of people. The sail was not long, but Winterbourne's companion found time to say a great many things. To the young man himself their little excursion was so much of an escapade—an adventure—that, even allowing for her habitual sense of freedom, he had some expectation of seeing her regard it in the same way. But it must be confessed that, in this particular, he was disappointed. Daisy Miller was extremely animated, she was in charming spirits; but she was apparently not at all excited; she was not fluttered; she avoided neither his eyes nor those of any one else; she blushed neither when she looked at him nor when she felt that people were looking at her. People continued to look at her a great

[27]I.e., sensitivity.

deal, and Winterbourne took much satisfaction in his pretty companion's distinguished air. He had been a little afraid that she would talk loud, laugh overmuch, and even, perhaps, desire to move about the boat a good deal. But he quite forgot his fears; he sat smiling, with his eyes upon her face, while, without moving from her place, she delivered herself of a great number of original reflections. It was the most charming garrulity he had ever heard. He had assented to the idea that she was "common;" but was she so, after all, or was he simply getting used to her commonness? Her conversation was chiefly of what metaphysicians term the objective cast; but every now and then it took a subjective turn.

"What on *earth* are you so grave about?" she suddenly demanded, fixing her agreeable eyes upon Winterbourne's.

"Am I grave?" he asked. "I had an idea I was grinning from ear to ear."

"You look as if you were taking me to a funeral. If that's a grin, your ears are very near together."

"Should you like me to dance a hornpipe on the deck?"

"Pray do, and I'll carry round your hat. It will pay the expenses of our journey."

"I never was better pleased in my life," murmured Winterbourne.

She looked at him a moment, and then burst into a little laugh. "I like to make you say those things! You're a queer mixture!"

In the castle, after they had landed, the subjective element decidedly prevailed. Daisy tripped about the vaulted chambers, rustled her skirts in the corkscrew staircases, flirted back with a pretty little cry and a shudder from the edge of the *oubliettes*,[28] and turned a singularly well-shaped ear to everything that Winterbourne told her about the place. But he saw that she cared very little for feudal antiquities, and that the dusky traditions of Chillon made but a slight impression upon her. They had the good fortune to have been able to walk about without other companionship than that of the custodian; and Winterbourne arranged with this functionary that they should not be hurried—that they should linger and pause wherever they chose. The custodian interpreted the bargain generously—Winterbourne, on his side, had been generous—and ended by leaving them quite to themselves. Miss Miller's observations were not remarkable for logical consistency; for anything she wanted to say she was sure to find a pretext. She found a great many pretexts in the rugged embrasures of Chillon for asking Winterbourne sudden questions about himself—his family, his previous history, his tastes, his habits, his intentions—and for supplying information upon corresponding points in her own personality. Of her own tastes, habits, and intentions Miss Miller was prepared to give the most definite, and indeed the most favourable, account.

"Well; I hope you know enough!" she said to her companion, after he had told her the history of the unhappy Bonivard.[29] "I never saw a man that knew so much!" The history of Bonivard had evidently, as they say, gone into one ear and out of the other. But Daisy went on to say that she wished Winterbourne would travel with them and "go round" with them; they might know something, in that case. "Don't you want to come and teach Randolph?" she asked. Winterbourne said that nothing could possibly please him so much; but that he had unfortunately other occupations. "Other occupations? I don't believe it!" said Miss Daisy. "What do you mean? You are not in business." The young man

---

[28]French: oblivions, a term for prison cells sunk below floor level and with openings only at the top.

[29]François de Bonnivard (1496?–1570), Swiss patriot jailed in the Castle of Chillon (1530–1536) and the hero of Byron's *The Prisoner of Chillon*, 1816.

admitted that he was not in business; but he had engagements which, even within a day or two, would force him to go back to Geneva. "Oh, bother!" she said: "I don't believe it!" and she began to talk about something else. But a few moments later, when he was pointing out to her the pretty design of an antique fireplace, she broke out irrelevantly, "You don't mean to say you are going back to Geneva?"

"It is a melancholy fact that I shall have to return to Geneva tomorrow."

"Well, Mr. Winterbourne," said Daisy; "I think you're horrid!"

"Oh, don't say such dreadful things!" said Winterbourne—"just at the last!"

"The last!" cried the young girl; "I call it the first. I have half a mind to leave you here and go straight back to the hotel alone." And for the next ten minutes she did nothing but call him horrid. Poor Winterbourne was fairly bewildered; no young lady had as yet done him the honour to be so agitated by the announcement of his movements. His companion, after this, ceased to pay any attention to the curiosities of Chillon or the beauties of the lake; she opened fire upon the mysterious charmer in Geneva whom she appeared to have instantly taken it for granted that he was hurrying back to see. How did Miss Daisy Miller know that there was a charmer in Geneva? Winterbourne, who denied the existence of such a person, was quite unable to discover; and he was divided between amazement at the rapidity of her induction and amusement at the frankness of her *persiflage.*[30] She seemed to him, in all this, an extraordinary mixture of innocence and crudity. "Does she never allow you more than three days at a time?" asked Daisy, ironically. "Doesn't she give you a vacation in summer? There's no one so hard worked but they can get leave to go off somewhere at this season. I suppose, if you stay another day, she'll come after you in the boat. Do wait over till Friday, and I will go down to the landing to see her arrive!" Winterbourne began to think he had been wrong to feel disappointed in the temper in which the young lady had embarked. If he had missed the personal accent, the personal accent was now making its appearance. It sounded very distinctly, at last, in her telling him she would stop "teasing" him if he would promise her solemnly to come down to Rome in the winter.

"That's not a difficult promise to make," said Winterbourne. "My aunt has taken an apartment in Rome for the winter, and has already asked me to come and see her."

"I don't want you to come for your aunt," said Daisy; "I want you to come for me." And this was the only allusion that the young man was ever to hear her make to his invidious kinswoman. He declared that, at any rate, he would certainly come. After this Daisy stopped teasing. Winterbourne took a carriage, and they drove back to Vevey in the dusk; the young girl was very quiet.

In the evening Winterbourne mentioned to Mrs. Costello that he had spent the afternoon at Chillon, with Miss Daisy Miller.

"The Americans—of the courier?" asked this lady.

"Ah, happily," said Winterbourne, "the courier stayed at home."

"She went with you all alone?"

"All alone."

Mrs. Costello sniffed a little at her smelling-bottle. "And that," she exclaimed, "is the young person whom you wanted me to know!"

---

[30]Banter.

PART II

Winterbourne, who had returned to Geneva the day after his excursion to Chillon, went to Rome towards the end of January. His aunt had been established there for several weeks, and he had received a couple of letters from her. "Those people you were so devoted to last summer at Vevey have turned up here, courier and all," she wrote. "They seem to have made several acquaintances, but the courier continues to be the most *intime*.[1] The young lady, however, is also very intimate with some third-rate Italians, with whom she rackets about in a way that makes much talk. Bring me that pretty novel of Cherbuliez's—'Paule Méré'[2]—and don't come later than the 23rd."

In the natural course of events, Winterbourne, on arriving in Rome, would presently have ascertained Mrs. Miller's address at the American banker's, and have gone to pay his compliments to Miss Daisy. "After what happened at Vevey I think I may certainly call upon them," he said to Mrs. Costello.

"If, after what happens—at Vevey and everywhere—you desire to keep up the acquaintance, you are very welcome. Of course a man may know every one. Men are welcome to the privilege!"

"Pray what is it that happens—here, for instance?" Winterbourne demanded.

"The girl goes about alone with her foreigners. As to what happens further, you must apply elsewhere for information. She has picked up half-a-dozen of the regular Roman fortune-hunters, and she takes them about to people's houses. When she comes to a party she brings with her a gentleman with a good deal of manner and a wonderful moustache."

"And where is the mother?"

"I haven't the least idea. They are very dreadful people."

Winterbourne meditated a moment. "They are very ignorant—very innocent only. Depend upon it they are not bad."

"They are hopelessly vulgar," said Mrs. Costello. "Whether or no being hopelessly vulgar is being 'bad' is a question for the metaphysicians. They are bad enough to dislike, at any rate; and for this short life that is quite enough."

The news that Daisy Miller was surrounded by half-a-dozen wonderful moustaches checked Winterbourne's impulse to go straightway to see her. He had perhaps not definitely flattered himself that he had made an ineffaceable impression upon her heart, but he was annoyed at hearing of a state of affairs so little in harmony with an image that had lately flitted in and out of his own meditations; the image of a very pretty girl looking out of an old Roman window and asking herself urgently when Mr. Winterbourne would arrive. If, however, he determined to wait a little before reminding Miss Miller of his claims to her considerations, he went very soon to call upon two or three other friends. One of these friends was an American lady who had spent several winters at Geneva, where she had placed her children at school. She was a very accomplished woman, and she lived in the Via Gregoriana.[3] Winterbourne found her in a little crimson drawing-room, on a third floor; the room was filled with southern sunshine. He had not been there ten minutes when the servant came in, announcing "Madame Mila!" This announcement was presently followed by the entrance of little Randolph Miller, who stopped in the middle of the room and stood staring at

---

[1]French: "intimate."
[2]Charles Victor Cherbuliez (1829–1899). French novelist, author of *Paule Méré* (1864).
[3]Fashionable street in Rome.

Winterbourne. An instant later his pretty sister crossed the threshold; and then, after a considerable interval, Mrs. Miller slowly advanced.

"I know you!" said Randolph.

"I'm sure you know a great many things," exclaimed Winterbourne, taking him by the hand. "How is your education coming on?"

Daisy was exchanging greetings very prettily with her hostess; but when she heard Winterbourne's voice she quickly turned her head. "Well, I declare!" she said.

"I told you I should come, you know," Winterbourne rejoined, smiling.

"Well—I didn't believe it," said Miss Daisy.

"I am much obliged to you," laughed the young man.

"You might have come to see me!" said Daisy.

"I arrived only yesterday."

"I don't believe that!" the young girl declared.

Winterbourne turned with a protesting smile to her mother; but this lady evaded his glance, and, seating herself, fixed her eyes upon her son. "We've got a bigger place than this," said Randolph. "It's all gold on the walls."

Mrs. Miller turned uneasily in her chair. "I told you if I were to bring you, you would say something!" she murmured.

"I told *you!*" Randolph exclaimed. "I tell *you*, sir!" he added jocosely, giving Winterbourne a thump on the knee. "It *is* bigger, too!"

Daisy had entered upon a lively conversation with her hostess; Winterbourne judged it becoming to address a few words to her mother. "I hope you have been well since we parted at Vevey," he said.

Mrs. Miller now certainly looked at him—at his chin. "Not very well, sir," she answered.

"She's got the dyspepsia," said Randolph. "I've got it too. Father's got it. I've got it most!"

This announcement, instead of embarrassing Mrs. Miller, seemed to relieve her. "I suffer from the liver," she said. "I think it's this climate; it's less bracing than Schenectady, especially in the winter season. I don't know whether you know we reside at Schenectady. I was saying to Daisy that I certainly hadn't found anyone like Dr. Davis, and I didn't believe I should. Oh, at Schenectady, he stands first; they think everything of him. He has so much to do, and yet there was nothing he wouldn't do for me. He said he never saw anything like my dyspepsia, but he was bound to cure it. I'm sure there was nothing he wouldn't try. He was just going to try something new when we came off. Mr. Miller wanted Daisy to see Europe for herself. But I wrote to Mr. Miller that it seems as if I couldn't get on without Dr. Davis. At Schenectady he stands at the very top; and there's a great deal of sickness there, too. It affects my sleep."

Winterbourne had a good deal of pathological gossip with Dr. Davis's patient, during which Daisy chattered unremittingly to her own companion. The young man asked Mrs. Miller how she was pleased with Rome. "Well, I must say I am disappointed," she answered. "We had heard so much about it; I suppose we had heard too much. But we couldn't help that. We had been led to expect something different."

"Ah, wait a little, and you will become very fond of it," said Winterbourne.

"I hate it worse and worse every day!" cried Randolph.

"You are like the infant Hannibal,"[4] said Winterbourne.

---

[4]Carthaginian general (247–183? B.C.) who as a youth swore eternal hatred of Rome.

"No, I ain't!" Randolph declared, at a venture.

"You are not much like an infant," said his mother. "But we have seen places," she resumed, "that I should put a long way before Rome." And in reply to Winterbourne's interrogation, "There's Zurich," she concluded; "I think Zurich is lovely; and we hadn't heard half so much about it."

"The best place we've seen is the City of Richmond!" said Randolph.

"He means the ship," his mother explained. "We crossed in that ship. Randolph had a good time on the City of Richmond."

"It's the best place I've seen," the child repeated. "Only it was turned the wrong way."

"Well, we've got to turn the right way some time," said Mrs. Miller, with a little laugh. Winterbourne expressed the hope that her daughter at least found some gratification in Rome, and she declared that Daisy was quite carried away. "It's on account of the society—the society's splendid. She goes round everywhere; she has made a great number of acquaintances. Of course she goes round more than I do. I must say they have been very sociable; they have taken her right in. And then she knows a great many gentlemen. Oh, she thinks there's nothing like Rome. Of course, it's a great deal pleasanter for a young lady if she knows plenty of gentlemen."

By this time Daisy had turned her attention again to Winterbourne. "I've been telling Mrs. Walker how mean you were!" the young girl announced.

"And what is the evidence you have offered?" asked Winterbourne, rather annoyed at Miss Miller's want of appreciation of the zeal of an admirer who on his way down to Rome had stopped neither at Bologna nor at Florence, simply because of a certain sentimental impatience. He remembered that a cynical compatriot had once told him that American women—the pretty ones, and this gave a largeness to the axiom—were at once the most exacting in the world and the least endowed with a sense of indebtedness.

"Why, you were awfully mean at Vevey," said Daisy. "You wouldn't do anything. You wouldn't stay there when I asked you."

"My dearest young lady," cried Winterbourne, with eloquence, "have I come all the way to Rome to encounter your reproaches?"

"Just hear him say that!" said Daisy to her hostess, giving a twist to a bow on this lady's dress. "Did you ever hear anything so quaint?"

"So quaint, my dear?" murmured Mrs. Walker, in the tone of a partisan of Winterbourne.

"Well, I don't know," said Daisy, fingering Mrs. Walker's ribbons. "Mrs. Walker, I want to tell you something."

"Motherr," interposed Randolph, with his rough ends to his words, "I tell you you've got to go. Eugenio 'll raise something!"

"I'm not afraid of Eugenio," said Daisy, with a toss of her head. "Look here, Mrs. Walker," she went on, "you know I'm coming to your party."

"I am delighted to hear it."

"I've got a lovely dress."

"I am very sure of that."

"But I want to ask a favour—permission to bring a friend."

"I shall be happy to see any of your friends," said Mrs. Walker, turning with a smile to Mrs. Miller.

"Oh, they are not my friends," answered Daisy's mamma, smiling shyly, in her own fashion. "I never spoke to them!"

"It's an intimate friend of mine—Mr. Giovanelli," said Daisy, without a tremor in her clear little voice or a shadow on her brilliant little face.

Mrs. Walker was silent a moment, she gave a rapid glance at Winterbourne. "I shall be glad to see Mr. Giovanelli," she then said.

"He's an Italian," Daisy pursued, with the prettiest serenity. "He's a great friend of mine—he's the handsomest man in the world—except Mr. Winterbourne! He knows plenty of Italians, but he wants to know some Americans. He thinks ever so much of Americans. He's tremendously clever. He's perfectly lovely!"

It was settled that this brilliant personage should be brought to Mrs. Walker's party, and then Mrs. Miller prepared to take her leave. "I guess we'll go back to the hotel," she said.

"You may go back to the hotel, mother, but I'm going to take a walk," said Daisy.

"She's going to walk with Mr. Giovanelli," Randolph proclaimed.

"I am going to the Pincio,"[5] said Daisy, smiling.

"Alone, my dear—at this hour?" Mrs. Walker asked. The afternoon was drawing to a close—it was the hour for the throng of carriages and contemplative pedestrians. "I don't think it's safe, my dear," said Mrs. Walker.

"Neither do I," subjoined Mrs. Miller. "You'll get the fever as sure as you live. Remember what Dr. Davis told you!"

"Give her some medicine before she goes," said Randolph.

The company had risen to its feet; Daisy, still showing her pretty teeth, bent over and kissed her hostess. "Mrs. Walker, you are too perfect," she said. "I'm not going alone; I am going to meet a friend."

"Your friend won't keep you from getting the fever," Mrs. Miller observed.

"Is it Mr. Giovanelli?" asked the hostess.

Winterbourne was watching the young girl; at this question his attention quickened. She stood there smiling and smoothing her bonnet ribbons; she glanced at Winterbourne. Then, while she glanced and smiled, she answered without a shade of hesitation, "Mr. Giovanelli—the beautiful Giovanelli."

"My dear young friend," said Mrs. Walker, taking her hand, pleadingly, "don't walk off to the Pincio at this hour to meet a beautiful Italian."

"Well, he speaks English," said Mrs. Miller.

"Gracious me!" Daisy exclaimed, "I don't want to do anything improper. There's an easy way to settle it." She continued to glance at Winterbourne. "The Pincio is only a hundred yards distant, and if Mr. Winterbourne were as polite as he pretends he would offer to walk with me!"

Winterbourne's politeness hastened to affirm itself, and the young girl gave him gracious leave to accompany her. They passed downstairs before her mother, and at the door Winterbourne perceived Mrs. Miller's carriage drawn up, with the ornamental courier whose acquaintance he had made at Vevey seated within. "Good-by, Eugenio!" cried Daisy, "I'm going to take a walk." The distance from the Via Gregoriana to the beautiful garden at the other end of the Pincian Hill is, in fact, rapidly traversed. As the day was splendid, however, and the concourse of vehicles, walkers, and loungers numerous, the young Americans found this progress much delayed. This fact was highly agreeable to Winterbourne, in spite of his consciousness of his singular situation. The slow-moving, idly-gazing Roman crowd bestowed much attention upon the extremely pretty young foreign lady who was passing through it upon his arm; and he wondered what on earth had been in Daisy's mind when she proposed to expose herself, unattended, to its appre-

---

[5]One of the hills of Rome, with a panoramic view of the city.

ciation. His own mission, to her sense, apparently, was to consign her to the hands of Mr. Giovanelli; but Winterbourne, at once annoyed and gratified, resolved that he would do no such thing.

"Why haven't you been to see me?" asked Daisy. "You can't get out of that."

"I have had the honour of telling you that I have only just stepped out of the train."

"You must have stayed in the train a good while after it stopped!" cried the young girl, with her little laugh. "I suppose you were asleep. You have had time to go to see Mrs. Walker."

"I knew Mrs. Walker—" Winterbourne began to explain.

"I knew where you knew her. You knew her at Geneva. She told me so. Well, you knew me at Vevey. That's just as good. So you ought to have come." She asked him no other question than this; she began to prattle about her own affairs. "We've got splendid rooms at the hotel; Eugenio says they're the best rooms in Rome. We are going to stay all winter—if we don't die of the fever; and I guess we'll stay then. It's a great deal nicer than I thought; I thought it would be fearfully quiet; I was sure it would be awfully poky. I was sure we should be going round all the time with one of those dreadful old men that explain about the pictures and things. But we only had about a week of that, and now I'm enjoying myself. I know ever so many people, and they are all so charming. The society's extremely select. There are all kinds—English, and Germans, and Italians. I think I like the English best. I like their style of conversation. But there are some lovely Americans. I never saw anything so hospitable. There's something or other every day. There's not much dancing; but I must say I never thought dancing was everything. I was always fond of conversation. I guess I shall have plenty at Mrs. Walker's—her rooms are so small." When they had passed the gate of the Pincian Gardens, Miss Miller began to wonder where Mr. Giovanelli might be. "We had better go straight to that place in front," she said, "where you look at the view."

"I certainly shall not help you to find him," Winterbourne declared.

"Then I shall find him without you," said Miss Daisy.

"You certainly won't leave me!" cried Winterbourne.

She burst into her little laugh. "Are you afraid you'll get lost—or run over? But there's Giovanelli, leaning against that tree. He's staring at the woman in the carriages: did you ever see anything so cool?"

Winterbourne perceived at some distance a little man standing with folded arms, nursing his cane. He had a handsome face, an artfully poised hat, a glass in one eye and a nosegay in his buttonhole. Winterbourne looked at him a moment and then said, "Do you mean to speak to that man?"

"Do I mean to speak to him? Why, you don't suppose I mean to communicate by signs?"

"Pray understand, then," said Winterbourne, "that I intend to remain with you."

Daisy stopped and looked at him, without a sign of troubled consciousness in her face; with nothing but the presence of her charming eyes and her happy dimples. "Well, she's a cool one!" thought the young man.

"I don't like the way you say that," said Daisy. "It's too imperious."

"I beg your pardon if I say it wrong. The main point is to give you an idea of my meaning."

The young girl looked at him more gravely, but with eyes that were prettier than ever. "I have never allowed a gentleman to dictate to me, or to interfere with anything I do."

"I think you have made a mistake," said Winterbourne. "You should some-times listen to a gentleman—the right one."

Daisy began to laugh again. "I do nothing but listen to gentlemen!" she exclaimed. "Tell me if Mr. Giovanelli is the right one?"

The gentleman with the nosegay in his bosom had now perceived our two friends, and was approaching the young girl with obsequious rapidity. He bowed to Winterbourne as well as to the latter's companion; he had a brilliant smile, an intelligent eye; Winterbourne thought him not a bad-looking fellow. But he nevertheless said to Daisy—"No, he's not the right one."

Daisy evidently had a natural talent for performing introductions; she men-tioned the name of each of her companions to the other. She strolled along with one of them on each side of her; Mr. Giovanelli, who spoke English very cleverly—Winterbourne afterwards learned that he had practised the idiom upon a great many American heiresses—addressed her a great deal of very polite nonsense; he was extremely urbane, and the young American, who said nothing, reflected upon that profundity of Italian cleverness which enables people to appear more gracious in proportion as they are more acutely disap-pointed. Giovanelli, of course, had counted upon something more intimate; he had not bargained for a party of three. But he kept his temper in a manner which suggested far-stretching intentions. Winterbourne flattered himself that he had taken his measure. "He is not a gentleman," said the young American; "He is only a clever imitation of one. He is a music-master, or a penny-a-liner,[6] or a third-rate artist. Damm his good looks!" Mr. Giovanelli had certainly a very pretty face; but Winterbourne felt a superior indignation at his own lovely fellow-countrywoman's not knowing the difference between a spurious gentle-man and a real one. Giovanelli chattered and jested and made himself wonder-fully agreeable. It was true that if he was an imitation the imitation was brilliant. "Nevertheless," Winterbourne said to himself, "a nice girl ought to know!" And then he came back to the question whether this was in fact a nice girl. Would a nice girl—even allowing for her being a little American flirt—make a rendezvous with a presumably low-lived foreigner? The rendezvous in this case, indeed, had been in broad daylight, and in the most crowded corner of Rome; but was it not impossible to regard the choice of these circumstances as a proof of extreme cynicism? Singular though it may seem, Winterbourne was vexed that the young girl, in joining her *amoroso*,[7] should not appear more impatient of his own company, and he was vexed because of his inclination. It was impossible to regard her as a perfectly well-conducted young lady; she was wanting in a certain indispensable delicacy. It would therefore simplify matters greatly to be able to treat her as the object of one of those sentiments which are called by romancers "lawless passions." That she should seem to wish to get rid of him would help him to think more lightly of her, and to be able to think more lightly of her would make her much less perplexing. But Daisy, on this occasion, continued to present herself as an inscrutable combination of audacity and innocence.

She had been walking some quarter of an hour, attended by her two cavaliers, and responding in a tone of very childish gaiety, as it seemed to Winterbourne, to the pretty speeches of Mr. Giovanelli, when a carriage that had detached itself from the revolving train drew up beside the path. At the same moment Winterbourne perceived that his friend Mrs. Walker—the lady whose house he had lately left—was seated in the vehicle and was beckoning to him. Leaving Miss Miller's side, he hastened to obey her summons. Mrs. Walker was flushed;

[6]A hack writer who works for a penny a line.   [7]Italian: suitor.

she wore an excited air. "It is really too dreadful," she said. "That girl must not do this sort of thing. She must not walk here with you two men. Fifty people have noticed her."

Winterbourne raised his eyebrows. "I think it's a pity to make too much fuss about it."

"It's a pity to let the girl ruin herself!"

"She is very innocent," said Winterbourne.

"She's very crazy!" cried Mrs. Walker. "Did you ever see anything so imbecile as her mother? After you had all left me, just now, I could not sit still for thinking of it. It seemed too pitiful, not even to attempt to save her. I ordered the carriage and put on my bonnet, and came here as quickly as possible. Thank heaven, I have found you!"

"What do you propose to do with us?" asked Winterbourne, smiling.

"To ask her to get in, to drive her about here for half-an-hour, so that the world may see she is not running absolutely wild, and then to take her safely home."

"I don't think it's a very happy thought," said Winterbourne; "but you can try."

Mrs. Walker tried. The young man went in pursuit of Miss Miller, who had simply nodded and smiled at his interlocutor[8] in the carriage, and had gone her way with her companion. Daisy, on learning that Mrs. Walker wished to speak to her, retraced her steps with a perfect good grace and with Mr. Giovanelli at her side. She declared that she was delighted to have a chance to present this gentleman to Mrs. Walker. She immediately achieved the introduction, and declared that she had never in her life seen anything so lovely as Mrs. Walker's carriage-rug.

"I am glad you admire it," said this lady, smiling sweetly. "Will you get in and let me put it over you?"

"Oh, no, thank you," said Daisy. "I shall admire it much more as I see you driving round with it."

"Do get in and drive with me," said Mrs. Walker.

"That would be charming, but it's so enchanting just as I am!" and Daisy gave a brilliant glance at the gentlemen on either side of her.

"It may be enchanting, dear child, but it is not the custom here," urged Mrs. Walker, leaning forward in her victoria[9] with her hands devoutly clasped.

"Well, it ought to be, then!" said Daisy. "If I didn't walk I should expire."

"You should walk with your mother, dear," cried the lady from Geneva, losing patience.

"With my mother, dear!" exclaimed the young girl. Winterbourne saw that she scented interference. "My mother never walked ten steps in her life. And then, you know," she added with a laugh, "I am more than five years old."

"You are old enough to be more reasonable. You are old enough, dear Miss Miller, to be talked about."

Daisy looked at Mrs. Walker, smiling intensely. "Talked about? What do you mean?"

"Come into my carriage and I will tell you."

Daisy turned her quickened glance again from one of the gentlemen beside her to the other. Mr. Giovanelli was bowing to and fro, rubbing down his gloves and laughing very agreeably; Winterbourne thought it a most unpleasant scene.

[8]In later editions James substituted "interlocutrix," a female questioner.
[9]Horse-drawn carriage.

"I don't think I want to know what you mean," said Daisy presently. "I don't think I should like it."

Winterbourne wished that Mrs. Walker would tuck in her carriage-rug and drive away; but this lady did not enjoy being defied, as she afterwards told him. "Should you prefer being thought a very reckless girl?" she demanded.

"Gracious!" exclaimed Daisy. She looked again at Mr. Giovanelli, then she turned to Winterbourne. There was a little pink flush in her cheek; she was tremendously pretty. "Does Mr. Winterbourne think," she asked slowly, smiling, throwing back her head and glancing at him from head to foot, "that—to save my reputation—I ought to get into the carriage?"

Winterbourne coloured; for an instant he hesitated greatly. It seemed so strange to hear her speak that way of her "reputation." But he himself, in fact, must speak in accordance with gallantry. The finest gallantry, here, was simply to tell her the truth; and the truth, for Winterbourne, as the few indications I have been able to give have made him known to the reader, was that Daisy Miller should take Mrs. Walker's advice. He looked at her exquisite prettiness; and then he said very gently, "I think you should get into the carriage."

Daisy gave a violent laugh. "I never heard anything so stiff! If this is improper, Mrs. Walker," she pursued, "then I am all improper, and you must give me up. Good-by; I hope you'll have a lovely ride!" and, with Mr. Giovanelli, who made a triumphantly obsequious salute, she turned away.

Mrs. Walker sat looking after her, and there were tears in Mrs. Walker's eyes. "Get in here, sir," she said to Winterbourne, indicating the place beside her. The young man answered that he felt bound to accompany Miss Miller; whereupon Mrs. Walker declared that if he refused her this favour she would never speak to him again. She was evidently in earnest. Winterbourne overtook Daisy and her companion and, offering the young girl his hand, told her that Mrs. Walker had made an imperious claim upon his society. He expected that in answer she would say something rather free, something to commit herself still further to that "recklessness" from which Mrs. Walker had so charitably endeavoured to dissuade her. But she only shook his hand, hardly looking at him; while Mr. Giovanelli bade him farewell with a too-emphatic flourish of the hat.

Winterbourne was not in the best possible humour as he took his seat in Mrs. Walker's victoria. "That was not clever of you," he said candidly, while the vehicle mingled again with the throng of carriages.

"In such a case," his companion answered, "I don't wish to be clever, I wish to be *earnest!*"

"Well, your earnestness has only offended her and put her off."

"It has happened very well," said Mrs. Walker. "If she is so perfectly determined to compromise herself, the sooner one knows it the better; one can act accordingly."

"I suspect she meant no harm," Winterbourne rejoined.

"So I thought a month ago. But she had been going too far."

"What has she been doing?"

"Everything that is not done here. Flirting with any man she could pick up; sitting in corners with mysterious Italians; dancing all the evening with the same partners; receiving visits at eleven o'clock at night. Her mother goes away when visitors come."

"But her brother," said Winterbourne, laughing, "sits up till midnight."

"He must be edified by what he sees. I'm told that at their hotel every one is talking about her, and that a smile goes round among all the servants when a gentleman comes and asks for Miss Miller."

"The servants be hanged!" said Winterbourne angrily. "The poor girl's fault," he presently added, "is that she is very uncultivated."

"She is naturally indelicate," Mrs. Walker declared. "Take that example this morning. How long had you known her at Vevey?"

"A couple of days."

"Fancy, then, her making it a personal matter that you should have left the place!"

Winterbourne was silent for some moments, then he said, "I suspect, Mrs. Walker, that you and I have lived too long at Geneva!" And he added a request that she should inform him with what particular design she had made him enter her carriage.

"I wished to beg you to cease your relations with Miss Miller—not to flirt with her—to give her no further opportunity to expose herself—to let her alone, in short."

"I'm afraid I can't do that," said Winterbourne. "I like her extremely."

"All the more reason that you shouldn't help her to make a scandal."

"There shall be nothing scandalous in my attentions to her."

"There certainly will be in the way she takes them. But I have said what I had on my conscience," Mrs. Walker pursued. "If you wish to rejoin the young lady I will put you down. Here, by-the-way, you have a chance."

The carriage was traversing that part of the Pincian Garden that overhangs the wall of Rome and overlooks the beautiful Villa Borghese.[10] It is bordered by a large parapet, near which there are several seats. One of the seats, at a distance, was occupied by a gentleman and a lady, towards whom Mrs. Walker gave a toss of her head. At the same moment these persons rose and walked towards the parapet. Winterbourne had asked the coachman to stop; he now descended from the carriage. His companion looked at him a moment in silence; then, while he raised his hat, she drove majestically away. Winterbourne stood there; he had turned his eyes towards Daisy and her cavalier. They evidently saw no one; they were too deeply occupied with each other. When they reached the low gardenwall they stood a moment looking off at the great flat-topped pine-clusters of the Villa Borghese; then Giovanelli seated himself, familiarly, upon the broad ledge of the wall. The western sun in the opposite sky sent out a brilliant shaft through a couple of cloud-bars, whereupon Daisy's companion took her parasol out of her hands and opened it. She came a little nearer and he held the parasol over her; then, still holding it, he let it rest upon her shoulder, so that both of their heads were hidden from Winterbourne. This young man lingered a moment, then he began to walk. But he walked—not towards the couple with the parasol; towards the residence of his aunt, Mrs. Costello.

He flattered himself on the following day that there was no smiling among the servants when he, at least, asked for Mrs. Miller at her hotel. This lady and her daughter, however, were not at home; and on the next day after, repeating his visit, Winterbourne again had the misfortune not to find them. Mrs. Walker's party took place on the evening of the third day, and in spite of the frigidity of his last interview with the hostess Winterbourne was among the guests. Mrs. Walker was one of those American ladies who, while residing abroad, make a point, in their own phrase, of studying European society; and she had on this occasion collected several specimens of her diversely-born fellow-mortals to serve, as it were, as text-books. When Winterbourne arrived Daisy Miller was not there, but in a few moments he saw her mother come in alone, very shyly

[10]Originally the summer palace of the Borghese family, now an art museum and its grounds a public park.

and ruefully. Mrs. Miller's hair above her exposed-looking temples was more frizzled than ever. As she approached Mrs. Walker, Winterbourne also drew near.

"You see I've come all alone," said poor Mrs. Miller. "I'm so frightened; I don't know what to do; it's the first time I've ever been to a party alone— especially in this country. I wanted to bring Randolph or Eugenio, or someone, but Daisy just pushed me off by myself. I ain't used to going round alone."

"And does not your daughter intend to favour us with her society?" demanded Mrs. Walker, impressively.

"Well, Daisy's all dressed," said Mrs. Miller, with that accent of the dispassionate, if not of the philosophic, historian with which she always recorded the current incidents of her daughter's career. "She got dressed on purpose before dinner. But she's got a friend of hers there; that gentleman—the Italian—that she wanted to bring. They've got going at the piano; it seems as if they couldn't leave off. Mr. Giovanelli sings splendidly. But I guess they'll come before very long," concluded Mrs. Miller hopefully.

"I'm sorry she should come—in that way," said Mrs. Walker.

"Well, I told her that there was no use in getting dressed before dinner if she was going to wait three hours," responded Daisy's mamma. "I didn't see the use of her putting on such a dress as that to sit round with Mr. Giovanelli."

"This is most horrible!" said Mrs. Walker, turning away and addressing herself to Winterbourne. *"Elle s'affiche."*[11] It's her revenge for my having ventured to remonstrate with her. When she comes I shall not speak to her."

Daisy came after eleven o'clock, but she was not, on such an occasion, a young lady to wait to be spoken to. She rustled forward in radiant loveliness, smiling and chattering, carrying a large bouquet and attended by Mr. Giovanelli. Everyone stopped talking, and turned and looked at her. She came straight to Mrs. Walker. "I'm afraid you thought I never was coming, so I sent mother off to tell you. I wanted to make Mr. Giovanelli practise some things before he came; you know he sings beautifully, and I want you to ask him to sing. This is Mr. Giovanelli; you know I introduced him to you; he's got the most lovely voice and he knows the most charming set of songs. I made him go over them this evening, on purpose; we had the greatest time at the hotel." Of all this Daisy delivered herself with the sweetest, brightest audibleness, looking now at her hostess and now round the room, while she gave a series of little pats, round her shoulders, to the edges of her dress. "Is there anyone I know?" she asked.

"I think everyone knows you!" said Mrs. Walker pregnantly, and she gave a very cursory greeting to Mr. Giovanelli. This gentleman bore himself gallantly. He smiled and bowed and showed his white teeth, he curled his moustaches and rolled his eyes, and performed all the proper functions of a handsome Italian at an evening party. He sang, very prettily, half-a-dozen songs, though Mrs. Walker afterwards declared that she had been quite unable to find out who asked him. It was apparently not Daisy who had given him his orders. Daisy sat at a distance from the piano, and though she had publicly, as it were, professed a high admiration for his singing, talked, not inaudibly, while it was going on.

"It's a pity these rooms are so small; we can't dance," she said to Winterbourne as if she had seen him five minutes before.

"I am not sorry we can't dance," Winterbourne answered; "I don't dance."

[11]French: "She's making a spectacle of herself."

"Of course you don't dance; you're too stiff," said Miss Daisy. "I hope you enjoyed your drive with Mrs. Walker."

"No, I didn't enjoy it; I preferred walking with you."

"We paired off, that was much better," said Daisy. "But did you ever hear anything so cool as Mrs. Walker's wanting me to get into her carriage and drop poor Mr. Giovanelli, and under the pretext that it was proper? People have different ideas! It would have been most unkind; he had been talking about that walk for ten days."

"He should not have talked about it at all," said Winterbourne; "he would never have proposed to a young lady of this country to walk about the streets with him."

"About the streets?" cried Daisy, with her pretty stare. "Where then would he have proposed to her to walk? The Pincio is not the streets, either; and I, thank goodness, am not a young lady of this country. The young ladies of this country have a dreadfully poky time of it, so far as I can learn; I don't see why I should change my habits for *them*."

"I am afraid your habits are those of a flirt," said Winterbourne gravely.

"Of course they are," she cried, giving him her little smiling stare again. "I'm a fearful, frightful flirt! Did you ever hear of a nice girl that was not? But I suppose you will tell me now that I am not a nice girl."

"You're a very nice girl, but I wish you would flirt with me and me only," said Winterbourne.

"Ah! thank you, thank you very much; you are the last man I should think of flirting with. As I have had the pleasure of informing you, you are too stiff."

"You say that too often," said Winterbourne.

Daisy gave a delighted laugh. "If I could have the sweet hope of making you angry, I should say it again."

"Don't do that; when I am angry I'm stiffer than ever. But if you won't flirt with me, do cease at least to flirt with your friend at the piano; they don't understand that sort of thing here."

"I thought they understood nothing else!" exclaimed Daisy.

"Not in young unmarried women."

"It seems to me much more proper in young unmarried women than in old married ones," Daisy declared.

"Well," said Winterbourne, "when you deal with natives you must go by the custom of the place. Flirting is a purely American custom; it doesn't exist here. So when you show yourself in public with Mr. Giovanelli and without your mother——"

"Gracious! poor mother!" interposed Daisy.

"Though you may be flirting, Mr. Giovanelli is not; he means something else."

"He isn't preaching, at any rate," said Daisy with vivacity. "And if you want very much to know, we are neither of us flirting, we are too good friends for that; we are very intimate friends."

"Ah!" rejoined Winterbourne, "if you are in love with each other it is another affair."

She had allowed him up to this point to talk so frankly that he had no expectation of shocking her by this ejaculation; but she immediately got up, blushing visibly, and leaving him to exclaim mentally that little American flirts were the queerest creatures in the world. "Mr. Giovanelli, at least," she said, giving her interlocutor a single glance, "never says such very disagreeable things to me."

Winterbourne was bewildered; he stood staring. Mr. Giovanelli had finished singing; he left the piano and came over to Daisy. "Won't you come into the other room and have some tea?" he asked, bending before her with his ornamental smile.

Daisy turned to Winterbourne, beginning to smile again. He was still more perplexed, for this inconsequent smile made nothing clear, though it seemed to prove, indeed, that she had a sweetness and softness that reverted instinctively to the pardon of offences. "It has never occurred to Mr. Winterbourne to offer me any tea," she said, with her little tormenting manner.

"I have offered advice," Winterbourne rejoined.

"I prefer weak tea!" cried Daisy, and she went off with the brilliant Giovanelli. She sat with him in the adjoining room, in the embrasure of the window, for the rest of the evening. There was an interesting performance at the piano, but neither of these young people gave heed to it. When Daisy came to take leave of Mrs. Walker, this lady conscientiously repaired the weakness of which she had been guilty at the moment of the young girl's arrival. She turned her back straight upon Miss Miller and left her to depart with what grace she might. Winterbourne was standing near the door; he saw it all. Daisy turned very pale and looked at her mother, but Mrs. Miller was humbly unconscious of any violation of the usual social forms. She appeared, indeed, to have felt an incongruous impulse to draw attention to her own striking observance of them. "Good-night, Mrs. Walker," she said; "we've had a beautiful evening. You see if I let Daisy come to parties without me, I don't want her to go away without me." Daisy turned away, looking with a pale, grave face at the circle near the door; Winterbourne saw that, for the first moment, she was too much shocked and puzzled even for indignation. He on his side was greatly touched.

"That was very cruel," he said to Mrs. Walker.

"She never enters my drawing-room again," replied his hostess.

Since Winterbourne was not to meet her in Mrs. Walker's drawing-room, he went as often as possible to Mrs. Miller's hotel. The ladies were rarely at home, but when he found them the devoted Giovanelli was always present. Very often the brilliant little Roman was in the drawing-room with Daisy alone. Mrs. Miller being apparently constantly of the opinion that discretion is the better part of surveillance. Winterbourne noted, at first with surprise, that Daisy on these occasions was never embarrassed or annoyed by his own entrance; but he very presently began to feel that she had no more surprises for him; the unexpected in her behavior was the only thing to expect. She showed no displeasure at her *tête-à-tête* with Giovanelli being interrupted; she could chatter as freshly and freely with two gentlemen as with one; there was always, in her conversation, the same odd mixture of audacity and puerility. Winterbourne remarked to himself that if she was seriously interested in Giovanelli it was very singular that she should not take more trouble to preserve the sanctity of their interviews, and he liked her the more for her innocent looking indifference and her apparently inexhaustible good humour. He could hardly have said why, but she seemed to him a girl who would never be jealous. At the risk of exciting a somewhat derisive smile on the reader's part, I may affirm that with regard to the women who had hitherto interested him, it very often seemed to Winterbourne among the possibilities that, given certain contingencies, he should be afraid—literally afraid—of these ladies; he had a pleasant sense that he should never be afraid of Daisy Miller. It must be added that this sentiment was not altogether flattering to Daisy; it was part of his conviction, or rather of his apprehension, that she would prove a very light young person.

But she was evidently very much interested in Giovanelli. She looked at him whenever he spoke; she was perpetually telling him to do this and to do that; she was constantly "chaffing" and abusing him. She appeared completely to have forgotten that Winterbourne had said anything to displease her at Mrs. Walker's little party. One Sunday afternoon, having gone to St. Peter's with his aunt, Winterbourne perceived Daisy strolling about the great church in company with the inevitable Giovanelli. Presently he pointed out the young girl and her cavalier to Mrs. Costello. This lady looked at them a moment through her eyeglass, and then she said:

"That's what makes you so pensive in these days, eh?"

"I had not the least idea I was pensive," said the young man.

"You are very much pre-occupied, you are thinking of something."

"And what is it," he asked, "that you accuse me of thinking of?"

"Of that young lady's—Miss Baker's, Miss Chandler's—what's her name? Miss Miller's intrigue with that little barber's block."[12]

"Do you call it an intrigue," Winterbourne asked—"an affair that goes on with such peculiar publicity?"

"That's their folly," said Mrs. Costello, "it's not their merit."

"No," rejoined Winterbourne, with something of that pensiveness to which his aunt had alluded. "I don't believe that there is anything to be called an intrigue."

"I have heard a dozen people speak of it; they say she is quite carried away by him."

"They are certainly very intimate," said Winterbourne.

Mrs. Costello inspected the young couple again with her optical instrument. "He is very handsome. One easily sees how it is. She thinks him the most elegant man in the world, the finest gentleman. She has never seen anything like him; he is better even than the courier. It was the courier probably who introduced him, and if he succeeds in marrying the young lady, the courier will come in for a magnificent commission."

"I don't believe she thinks of marrying him," said Winterbourne, "and I don't believe he hopes to marry her."

"You may be very sure she thinks of nothing. She goes on from day to day, from hour to hour, as they did in the Golden Age. I can imagine nothing more vulgar. And at the same time," added Mrs. Costello, "depend upon it that she may tell you any moment that she is 'engaged.' "

"I think that is more than Giovanelli expects," said Winterbourne.

"Who is Giovanelli?"

"The little Italian. I have asked questions about him and learned something. He is apparently a perfectly respectable little man. I believe he is in a small way a *cavaliere avvocato*.[13] But he doesn't move in what are called the first circles. I think it is really not absolutely impossible that the courier introduced him. He is evidently immensely charmed with Miss Miller. If she thinks him the finest gentleman in the world, he, on his side, has never found himself in personal contact with such splendor, such opulence, such expensiveness, as this young lady's. And then she must seem to him wonderfully pretty and interesting. I rather doubt that he dreams of marrying her. That must appear to him too impossible a piece of luck. He has nothing but his handsome face to offer, and there is a substantial Mr. Miller in that mysterious land of dollars. Giovanelli knows that he hasn't a title to offer. If he were only a count or a *marchese!*[14] He must wonder at his luck at the way they have taken him up."

---

[12]"Dandy."   [13]Italian: "gentleman lawyer."   [14]An Italian rank of nobility, a marquis.

"He accounts for it by his handsome face, and thinks Miss Miller a young lady *qui se passe ses fantaisies!*"[15] said Mrs. Costello.

"It is very true," Winterbourne pursued, "that Daisy and her mamma have not yet risen to that stage of—what shall I call it?—of culture, at which the idea of catching a count or a *marchese* begins. I believe that they are intellectually incapable of that conception."

"Ah! but the *avvocato* can't believe it," said Mrs. Costello.

Of the observation excited by Daisy's "intrigue," Winterbourne gathered that day at St. Peter's sufficient evidence. A dozen of the American colonists in Rome came to talk with Mrs. Costello, who sat on a little portable stool at the base of one of the great pilasters. The vesper service was going forward in splendid chants and organ-tones in the adjacent choir, and meanwhile, between Mrs. Costello and her friends, there was a great deal said about poor little Miss Miller's going really "too far." Winterbourne was not pleased with what he heard; but when, coming out upon the great steps of the church, he saw Daisy, who had emerged before him, get into an open cab with her accomplice and roll away through the cynical streets of Rome, he could not deny to himself that she was going very far indeed. He felt very sorry for her—not exactly that he believed that she had completely lost her head, but because it was painful to hear so much that was pretty, and undefended, and natural, assigned to a vulgar place among the categories of disorder. He made an attempt after this to give a hint to Mrs. Miller. He met one day in the Corso[16] a friend—a tourist like himself—who had just come out of the Doria Palace,[17] where he had been walking through the beautiful gallery. His friend talked for a moment about the superb portrait of Innocent X, by Velasquez,[18] which hangs in one of the cabinets of the palace, and then said, "And in the same cabinet, by-the-way, I had the pleasure of contemplating a picture of a different kind—that pretty American girl who you pointed out to me last week." In answer to Winterbourne's inquiries, his friend narrated that the pretty American girl—prettier than ever—was seated with a companion in the secluded nook in which the great papal protrait was enshrined.

"Who was her companion?" asked Winterbourne.

"A little Italian with a bouquet in his button hole. The girl is delightfully pretty, but I thought I understood from you the other day that she was a young lady *du meilleur monde.*"[19]

"So she is!" answered Winterbourne; and having assured himself that his informant had seen Daisy and her companion but five minutes before, he jumped into a cab and went to call on Mrs. Miller. She was at home; but she apologised to him for receiving him in Daisy's absence.

"She's gone out somewhere with Mr. Giovanelli," said Mrs. Miller. "She's always going round with Mr. Giovanelli."

"I have noticed that they are very intimate," Winterbourne observed.

"Oh! it seems as if they couldn't live without each other!" said Mrs. Miller. "Well, he's a real gentleman anyhow. I keep telling Daisy she's engaged!"

"And what does Daisy say?"

"Oh, she says she isn't engaged. But she might as well be!" this impartial parent resumed. "She goes on as if she was. But I've made Mr. Giovanelli promise to tell me, if *she* doesn't. I should want to write to Mr. Miller about it—shouldn't you?"

---

[15]French: "who gives in to her own whims."   [16]Roman street.   [17]Roman baroque palace.
[18]Diego Rodríguez de Silva y Velásquez (1599–1660), Spanish painter whose portrait of Pope Innocent X (1649) is in the Doria Gallery in Rome.
[19]French: "of the better society."

Winterbourne replied that he certainly should; and the state of mind of Daisy's mamma struck him as so unprecedented in the annals of parental vigilance that he gave up as utterly irrelevant the attempt to place her upon her guard.

After this Daisy was never at home, and Winterbourne ceased to meet her at the houses of their common acquaintance because, as he perceived, these shrewd people had quite made up their minds that she was going too far. They ceased to invite her, and they intimated that they desired to express to observant Europeans the great truth that, though Miss Daisy Miller was a young American lady, her behaviour was not representative—was regarded by her compatriots as abnormal. Winterbourne wondered how she felt about all the cold shoulders that were turned towards her, and sometimes it annoyed him to suspect that she did not feel at all. He said to himself that she was too light and childish, too uncultivated and unreasoning, too provincial, to have reflected upon her ostracism or even to have perceived it. Then at other moments he believed that she carried about in her elegant and irresponsible little organism a defiant, passionate, perfectly observant consciousness of the impression she produced. He asked himself whether Daisy's defiance came from the consciousness of innocence or from her being, essentially, a young person of the reckless class. It must be admitted that holding oneself to a belief in Daisy's "innocence" came to seem to Winterbourne more and more a matter of fine-spun gallantry. As I have already had occasion to relate, he was angry at finding himself reduced to chopping logic about this young lady; he was vexed at his want of instinctive certitude as to how far her eccentricities were generic, national, and how far they were personal. From either view of them he had somehow missed her, and now it was too late. She was "carried away" by Mr. Giovanelli.

A few days after his brief interview with her mother, he encountered her in that beautiful abode of flowering desolation known as the Palace of the Cæsars.[20] The early Roman spring had filled the air with bloom and perfume, and the rugged surface of the Palatine was muffled with tender verdure. Daisy was strolling along the top of one of those great mounds of ruin that are embanked with mossy marble and paved with monumental inscriptions. It seemed to him that Rome had never been so lovely as just then. He stood looking off at the enchanting harmony of line and colour that remotely encircles the city, inhaling the softly humid odours and feeling the freshness of the year and the antiquity of the place reaffirm themselves in mysterious interfusion. It seemed to him also that Daisy had never looked so pretty; but this had been an observation of his whenever he met her. Giovanelli was at her side, and Giovanelli, too, wore an aspect of even unwonted brilliancy.

"Well," said Daisy, "I should think you would be lonesome!"

"Lonesome?" asked Winterbourne.

"You are always going round by yourself. Can't you get anyone to walk with you?"

"I am not so fortunate," said Winterbourne, "as your companion."

Giovanelli, from the first, had treated Winterbourne with distinguished politeness; he listened with a deferential air to his remarks; he laughed, punctiliously, at his pleasantries; he seemed disposed to testify to his belief that Winterbourne was a superior young man. He carried himself in no degree like a jealous wooer; he had obviously a great deal of tact; he had no objection to your expecting a little humility of him. It even seemed to Winterbourne at times that Giovanelli would find a certain mental relief in being able to have a private

[20]Ruins of palaces erected by the Caesars on the Palatine Hill, in Rome.

understanding with him—to say to him, as an intelligent man, that, bless you, *he* knew how extraordinary was this young lady, and didn't flatter himself with delusive—or at least *too* delusive—hopes of matrimony and dollars. On this occasion he strolled away from his companion to pluck a sprig of almond blossom, which he carefully arranged in his button hole.

"I know why you say that," said Daisy, watching Giovanelli. "Because you think I go round too much with *him!*" And she nodded at her attendant.

"Every one thinks so—if you care to know," said Winterbourne.

"Of course I care to know!" Daisy exclaimed seriously. "But I don't believe it. They are only pretending to be shocked. They don't really care a straw what I do. Besides, I don't go round so much."

"I think you will find they do care. They will show it—disagreeably."

Daisy looked at him a moment. "How—disagreeably?"

"Haven't you noticed anything?" Winterbourne asked.

"I have noticed you. But I noticed you were as stiff as an umbrella the first time I saw you."

"You will find I am not so stiff as several others," said Winterbourne, smiling.

"How shall I find it?"

"By going to see the others."

"What will they do to me?"

"They will give you the cold shoulder. Do you know what that means?"

Daisy was looking at him intently; she began to colour. "Do you mean as Mrs. Walker did the other night?"

"Exactly!" said Winterbourne.

She looked away at Giovanelli, who was decorating himself with his almond-blossom. Then looking back at Winterbourne—"I shouldn't think you would let people be so unkind!" she said.

"How can I help it?" he asked.

"I should think you would say something."

"I do say something," and he paused a moment. "I say that your mother tells me she believes you are engaged."

"Well, she does," said Daisy very simply.

Winterbourne began to laugh. "And does Randolph believe it?" he asked.

"I guess Randolph doesn't believe anything," said Daisy. Randolph's scepticism excited Winterbourne to further hilarity, and he observed that Giovanelli was coming back to them. Daisy, observing it too, addressed herself again to her countryman. "Since you have mentioned it," she said, "I *am* engaged." . . . Winterbourne looked at her; he had stopped laughing. "You don't believe it!" she added.

He was silent a moment; and then, "Yes, I believe it!" he said.

"Oh, no, you don't," she answered. "Well, then—I am not!"

The young girl and her cicerone[21] were on their way to the gate of the enclosure, so that Winterbourne, who had but lately entered, presently took leave of them. A week afterwards he went to dine at a beautiful villa on the Cælian Hill,[22] and, on arriving, dismissed his hired vehicle. The evening was charming, and he promised himself the satisfaction of walking home beneath the Arch of Constantine[23] and past the vaguely-lighted monuments of the Forum.[24] There was a waning moon in the sky, and her radiance was not brilliant, but she was veiled in a thin cloud-curtain which seemed to diffuse and equalise

[21]Guide.   [22]One of the hills of Rome.
[23]Memorial arch built to celebrate a Roman military victory in A.D. 312.
[24]Administrative and business center of ancient Rome.

it. When, on his return from the villa (it was eleven o'clock), Winterbourne approached the dusky circle of the Colosseum, it recurred to him, as a lover of the picturesque, that the interior, in the pale moonshine, would be well worth a glance. He turned aside and walked to one of the empty arches, near which, as he observed, an open carriage—one of the little Roman streetcabs—was stationed. Then he passed in, among the cavernous shadows of the great structure, and emerged upon the clear and silent arena. The place had never seemed to him more impressive. One-half of the gigantic circus[25] was in deep shade; the other was sleeping in the luminous dusk. As he stood there he began to murmur Byron's famous lines, out of "Manfred;"[26] but before he had finished his quotation he remembered that if nocturnal meditations in the Colosseum are recommended by the poets, they are deprecated by the doctors. The historic atmosphere was there, certainly; but the historic atmosphere, scientifically considered, was no better than a villainous miasma. Winterbourne walked to the middle of the arena, to take a more general glance, intending thereafter to make a hasty retreat. The great cross in the centre was covered with shadow; it was only as he drew near it that he made it out distinctly. Then he saw that two persons were stationed upon the low steps which formed its base. One of these was a woman, seated; her companion was standing in front of her.

Presently the sound of the woman's voice came to him distinctly in the warm night-air. "Well, he looks at us as one of the old lions or tigers may have looked at the Christian martyrs!" These were the words he heard, in the familiar accent of Miss Daisy Miller.

"Let us hope he is not very hungry," responded the ingenious Giovanelli. "He will have to take me first; you will serve for dessert!"

Winterbourne stopped, with a sort of horror; and, it must be added, with a sort of relief. It was as if a sudden illumination had been flashed upon the ambiguity of Daisy's behaviour and the riddle had become easy to read. She was a young lady whom a gentleman need no longer be at pains to respect. He stood there looking at her—looking at her companion, and not reflecting that though he saw them vaguely, he himself must have been more brightly visible. He felt angry with himself that he had bothered so much about the right way of regarding Miss Daisy Miller. Then, as he was going to advance again, he checked himself; not from the fear that he was doing her injustice, but from a sense of the danger of appearing unbecomingly exhilarated by this sudden revulsion from cautious criticism. He turned away towards the entrance of the place; but as he did so he heard Daisy speak again.

"Why, it was Mr. Winterbourne! He saw me—and he cuts me!"

What a clever little reprobate she was, and how smartly she played at injured innocence! But he wouldn't cut her. Winterbourne came forward again, and went towards the great cross. Daisy had got up; Giovanelli lifted his hat. Winterbourne had not begun to think simply of the craziness, from a sanitary point of view, of a delicate young girl lounging away the evening in this nest of malaria. What if she *were* a clever little reprobate? that was no reason for her dying of the *perniciosa*.[27] "How long have you been here?" he asked, almost brutally.

Daisy, lovely in the flattering moonlight, looked at him a moment. Then— "All the evening," she answered gently. . . . "I never saw anything so pretty."

---

[25]Arena.

[26]"I do remember me, that in my youth,/When I was wandering,—upon such a night—/I stood within the Coliseum's wall,/Midst the chief relics of almighty Rome." From Byron's verse drama "Manfred" (1817), Act III, Scene iv, lines 8–11.

[27]Italian: malaria, the Roman fever.

"I am afraid," said Winterbourne, "that you will not think Roman fever very pretty. This is the way people catch it. I wonder," he added, turning to Giovanelli, "that you, a native Roman, should countenance such a terrible indiscretion."

"Ah," said the handsome native, "for myself, I am not afraid,"

"Neither am I—for you! I am speaking for this young lady."

Giovanelli lifted his well-shaped eyebrows and showed his brilliant teeth. But he took Winterbourne's rebuke with docility. "I told the Signorina it was a grave indiscretion; but when was the Signorina ever prudent?"

"I never was sick, and I don't mean to be!" The Signorina declared. "I don't look like much, but I'm healthy! I was bound to see the Colosseum by moonlight; I shouldn't have wanted to go home without that; and we have had the most beautiful time, haven't we, Mr. Giovanelli? If there has been any danger, Eugenio can give me some pills. He has got some splendid pills."

"I should advise you," said Winterbourne, "to drive home as fast as possible and take one!"

"What you say is very wise," Giovanelli rejoined. "I will go and make sure the carriage is at hand." And he went forward rapidly.

Daisy followed with Winterbourne. He kept looking at her; she seemed not in the least embarrassed. Winterbourne said nothing; Daisy chattered about the beauty of the place. "Well, I *have* seen the Colosseum by moonlight!" she exclaimed. "That's one good thing." Then, noticing Winterbourne's silence, she asked him why he didn't speak. He made no answer; he only began to laugh. They passed under one of the dark archways; Giovanelli was in front with the carriage. Here Daisy stopped a moment, looking at the young American. "*Did* you believe I was engaged the other day?" she asked.

"It doesn't matter what I believed the other day," said Winterbourne, still laughing.

"Well, what do you believe now?"

"I believe that it makes very little difference whether you are engaged or not!"

He felt the young girl's pretty eyes fixed upon him through the thick gloom of the archway; she was apparently going to answer. But Giovanelli hurried her forward. "Quick, quick," he said; "if we get in by midnight we are quite safe."

Daisy took her seat in the carriage, and the fortunate Italian placed himself beside her. "Don't forget Eugenio's pills!" said Winterbourne, as he lifted his hat.

"I don't care," said Daisy, in a little strange tone, "Whether I have Roman fever or not!" Upon this the cab-driver cracked his whip, and they rolled away over the desultory patches of the antique pavement.

Winterbourne—to do him justice, as it were—mentioned to no one that he had encountered Miss Miller, at midnight, in the Colosseum with a gentleman; but nevertheless, a couple of days later, the fact of her having been there under these circumstances was known to every member of the little American circle, and commented accordingly. Winterbourne reflected that they had of course known it at the hotel, and that, after Daisy's return, there had been an exchange of remarks between the porter and the cab-driver. But the young man was conscious at the same moment that it had ceased to be a matter of serious regret to him that the little American flirt should be "talked about" by low-minded menials. These people, a day or two later, had serious information to give: the little American flirt was alarmingly ill. Winterbourne, when the rumor came to him, immediately went to the hotel for more news. He found that two or three charitable friends had preceded him, and that they were being entertained in Mrs. Miller's salon by Randolph.

"It's going round at night," said Randolph—"that's what made her sick. She's always going round at night. I shouldn't think she'd want to—it's so plaguey dark. You can't see anything here at night, except when there's a moon. In America there's always a moon!" Mrs. Miller was invisible; she was now, at least, giving her daughter the advantage of her society. It was evident that Daisy was dangerously ill.

Winterbourne went often to ask for news of her, and once he saw Mrs. Miller, who, though deeply alarmed, was—rather to his surprise—perfectly composed, and, as it appeared, a most efficient and judicious nurse. She talked a good deal about Dr. Davis, but Winterbourne paid her the compliment of saying to himself that she was not, after all, such a monstrous goose. "Daisy spoke of you the other day," she said to him. "Half the time she doesn't know what she's saying, but that time I think she did. She gave me a message; she told me to tell you. She told me to tell you that she never was engaged to that handsome Italian. I am sure I am very glad; Mr. Giovanelli hasn't been near us since she was taken ill. I thought he was so much a gentleman; but I don't call that very polite! A lady told me that he was afraid I was angry with him for taking Daisy round at night. Well, so I am; but I suppose he knows I'm a lady. I would scorn to scold him. Any way, she says, she's not engaged. I don't know why she wanted you to know; but she said to me three times—"Mind you tell Mr. Winterbourne.' And then she told me to ask if you remembered the time you went to that castle, in Switzerland. But I said I wouldn't give any such messages as that. Only, if she is not engaged, I'm sure I'm glad to know it."

But, as Winterbourne has said, it mattered very little. A week after this the poor girl died; it had been a terrible case of the fever. Daisy's grave was in the little Protestant cemetery, in an angle of the wall of imperial Rome, beneath the cypresses and the thick spring-flowers. Winterbourne stood there beside it, with a number of other mourners; a number larger than the scandal excited by the young lady's career would have led you to expect. Near him stood Giovanelli, who came nearer still before Winterbourne turned away. Giovanelli was very pale; on this occasion he had no flower in his button-hole; he seemed to wish to say something. At last he said, "She was the most beautiful young lady I ever saw, and the most amiable." And then he added in a moment, "And she was the most innocent."

Winterbourne looked at him, and presently repeated his words, "And the most innocent?"

"The most innocent!"

Winterbourne felt sore and angry. "Why the devil," he asked, "did you take her to that fatal place?"

Mr. Giovanelli's urbanity was apparently imperturbable. He looked on the ground a moment, and then he said, "For myself, I had no fear; and she wanted to go."

"That was no reason!" Winterbourne declared.

The subtle Roman again dropped his eyes. "If she had lived, I should have got nothing. She would never have married me, I am sure."

"She would never have married you?"

"For a moment I hoped so. But no. I am sure."

Winterbourne listened to him; he stood staring at the raw protuberance among the April daisies. When he turned away again Mr. Giovanelli, with his light slow step, had retired.

Winterbourne almost immediately left Rome; but the following summer he again met his aunt, Mrs. Costello, at Vevey. Mrs. Costello was fond of Vevey.

In the interval Winterbourne had often thought of Daisy Miller and her mystifying manners. One day he spoke of her to his aunt—said it was on his conscience he had done her injustice.

"I am sure I don't know," said Mrs. Costello. "How did your injustice affect her?"

"She sent me a message before her death which I didn't understand at the time. But I have understood it since. She would have appreciated one's esteem."

"Is that a modest way," asked Mrs. Costello, "of saying that she would have reciprocated one's affection?"

Winterbourne offered no answer to this question; but he presently said, "You were right in that remark that you made last summer. I was booked to make a mistake. I have lived too long in foreign parts."

Nevertheless, he went back to live at Geneva, whence there continue to come the most contradictory accounts of his motives of sojourn: a report that he is "studying" hard—an intimation that he is much interested in a very clever foreign lady.

1878   1878

THE REAL THING

I

When the porter's wife, who used to answer the house-bell, announced "A gentleman and a lady, sir," I had, as I often had in those days—the wish being father to the thought—an immediate vision of sitters. Sitters my visitors in this case proved to be; but not in the sense I should have preferred. There was nothing at first however to indicate that they might n't have come for a portrait. The gentleman, a man of fifty, very high and very straight, with a moustache slightly grizzled and a dark grey walking-coat admirably fitted, both of which I noted professionally—I don't mean as a barber or yet as a tailor—would have struck me as a celebrity if celebrities often were striking. It was a truth of which I had for some time been conscious that a figure with a good deal of frontage[1] was, as one might say, almost never a public institution. A glance at the lady helped to remind me of this paradoxical law: she also looked too distinguished to be a "personality." Moreover one would scarcely come across two variations together.

Neither of the pair immediately spoke—they only prolonged the preliminary gaze suggesting that each wished to give the other a chance. They were visibly shy; they stood there letting me take them in—which, as I afterwards perceived, was the most practical thing they could have done. In this way their embarrassment served their cause. I had seen people painfully reluctant to mention that they desired anything so gross as to be represented on canvas; but the scruples of my new friends appeared almost insurmountable. Yet the gentleman might have said "I should like a portrait of my wife," and the lady might have said "I should like a portrait of my husband." Perhaps they were n't husband and wife—this naturally would make the matter more delicate. Perhaps they wished to be done together—in which case they ought to have brought a third person to break the news.

[1] I.e., imposing appearance.

"We come from Mr. Rivet," the lady finally said with a dim smile that had the effect of a moist sponge passed over a "sunk"[2] piece of painting, as well as of a vague allusion to vanished beauty. She was as tall and straight, in her degree, as her companion, and with ten years less to carry. She looked as sad as a woman could look whose face was not charged with expression; that is her tinted oval mask showed waste as an exposed surface shows friction. The hand of time had played over her freely, but to an effect of elimination. She was slim and stiff, and so well-dressed, in dark blue cloth, with lappets[3] and pockets and buttons, that it was clear she employed the same tailor as her husband. The couple had an indefinable air of prosperous thrift—they evidently got a good deal of luxury for their money. If I was to be one of their luxuries it would behove me to consider my terms.

"Ah Claude Rivet recommended me?" I echoed; and I added that it was very kind of him, though I could reflect that, as he only painted landscape, this was n't a sacrifice.

The lady looked very hard at the gentleman, and the gentleman looked round the room. Then staring at the floor a moment and stroking his moustache, he rested his pleasant eyes on me with the remark: "He said you were the right one."

"I try to be, when people want to sit."

"Yes, we should like to," said the lady anxiously.

"Do you mean together?"

My visitors exchanged a glance. "If you could do anything with *me* I suppose it would be double," the gentleman stammered.

"Oh yes, there's naturally a higher charge for two figures than for one."

We should like to make it pay," the husband confessed.

"That's very good of you," I returned, appreciating so unwonted a sympathy— for I supposed he meant pay the artist.

A sense of strangeness seemed to dawn on the lady. "We mean for the illustrations—Mr. Rivet said you might put one in."

"Put in—an illustration?" I was equally confused.

"Sketch her off, you know," said the gentleman, colouring.

It was only then that I understood the service Claude Rivet had rendered me; he had told them how I worked in black-and-white, for magazines, for story-books, for sketches of contemporary life, and consequently had copious employment for models. These things were true, but it was not less true—I may confess it now; whether because the aspiration was to lead to everything or to nothing I leave the reader to guess—that I could n't get the honours, to say nothing of the emoluments, of a great painter of portraits out of my head. My "illustrations" were my pot-boilers; I looked to a different branch of art—far and away the most interesting it had always seemed to me—to perpetuate my fame. There was no shame in looking to it also to make my fortune; but that fortune was by so much further from being made from the moment my visitors wished to be "done" for nothing. I was disappointed; for in the pictorial sense I had immediately *seen* them. I had seized their type—I had already settled what I would do with it. Something that would n't absolutely have pleased them, I afterwards reflected.

"Ah you're—you're—a—?" I began as soon as I had mastered my surprise. I could n't bring out the dingy word "models": it seemed so little to fit the case.

"We have n't had much practice," said the lady.

[2]Faded.   [3]Folds, or flaps.

"We've got to *do* something, and we've thought that an artist in your line might perhaps make something of us," he husband threw off. He further mentioned that they did n't know many artists and that they had gone first, on the off-chance—he painted views of course, but sometimes put in figures; perhaps I remembered—to Mr. Rivet, whom they had met a few years before at a place in Norfolk where he was sketching.

"We used to sketch a little ourselves," the lady hinted.

"It's very awkward, but we absolutely *must* do something," her husband went on.

"Of course we're not so *very* young," she admitted with a wan smile.

With the remark that I might as well know something more about them the husband had handed me a card extracted from a neat new pocket-book—their appurtenances were all of the freshest—and inscribed with the words "Major Monarch." Impressive as these words were they did n't carry my knowledge much further; but my visitor presently added: "I've left the army and we've had the misfortune to lose our money. In fact our means are dreadfully small."

"It's awfully trying—a regular strain," said Mrs. Monarch.

They evidently wished to be discreet—to take care not to swagger because they were gentlefolk. I felt them willing to recognise this as something of a drawback, at the same time that I guessed at an underlying sense—their consolation in adversity—that they *had* their points. They certainly had; but these advantages struck me as preponderantly social; such for instance as would help to make a drawing-room look well. However, a drawing-room was always, or ought to be, a picture.

In consequence of his wife's allusion to their age Major Monarch observed: "Naturally it's more for the figure that we thought of going in. We can still hold ourselves up." On the instant I saw that the figure was indeed their strong point. His "naturally" did n't sound vain, but it lighted up the question. "*She* has the best one," he continued, nodding at his wife with a pleasant after-dinner absence of circumlocution. I could only reply, as if we were in fact sitting over our wine, that this did n't prevent his own from being very good; which led him in turn to make answer: "We thought that if you ever have to do people like us we might be something like it. *She* particularly—for a lady in a book, you know."

I was so amused by them that, to get more of it, I did my best to take their point of view; and though it was an embarrassment to find myself appraising physically, as if they were animals on hire or useful blacks, a pair of whom I should have expected to meet only in one of the relations in which criticism is tacit, I looked at Mrs. Monarch judicially enough to be able to exclaim after a moment with conviction: "Oh yes, a lady in a book!" She was singularly like a bad illustration.

"We'll stand up, if you like," said the Major; and he raised himself before me with a really grand air.

I could take his measure at a glance—he was six feet two and a perfect gentleman. It would have paid any club in process of formation and in want of a stamp to engage him at a salary to stand in the principal window. What struck me at once was that in coming to me they had rather missed their vocation; they could surely have been turned to better account for advertising purposes. I could n't of course see the thing in detail, but I could see them make somebody's fortune—I don't mean their own. There was something in them for a waistcoat-maker, an hotel-keeper or a soap-vendor. I could imagine "We always use it" pinned on their bosoms with the greatest effect; I had a vision of the brilliancy with which they would launch a table d'hôte.[4]

Mrs. Monarch sat still, not from pride but from shyness, and presently her husband said to her: "Get up, my dear, and show how smart you are." She obeyed, but she had no need to get up to show it. She walked to the end of the studio and then came back blushing, her fluttered eyes on the partner of her appeal. I was reminded of an incident I had accidentally had a glimpse of in Paris—being with a friend there, a dramatist about to produce a play, when an actress came to him to ask to be entrusted with a part. She went through her paces before him, walked up and down as Mrs. Monarch was doing. Mrs. Monarch did it quite as well, but I abstained from applauding. It was very odd to see such people apply for such poor pay. She looked as if she had ten thousand a year. Her husband had used the word that described her: she was in the London current jargon essentially and typically "smart." Her figure was, in the same order of ideas, conspicuously and irreproachably "good." For a woman of her age her waist was surprisingly small; her elbow moreover had the orthodox crook. She held her head at the conventional angle, but why did she come to *me*? She ought to have tried on jackets at a big shop. I feared my visitors were not only destitute but "artistic"—which would be a great complication. When she sat down again I thanked her, observing that what a draughtsman most valued in his model was the faculty of keeping quiet.

"Oh *she* can keep quiet," said Major Monarch. Then he added jocosely: "I've always kept her quiet."

"I'm not a nasty fidget, am I?" It was going to wring tears from me, I felt, the way she hid her head, ostrich-like, in the other broad bosom.

The owner of this expanse addressed his answer to me. "Perhaps it is n't out of place to mention—because we ought to be quite business-like, ought n't we?—that when I married her she was known as the Beautiful Statue."

"Oh dear!" said Mrs. Monarch ruefully.

"Of course I should want a certain amount of expression," I rejoined.

"Of *course*!"—and I had never heard such unanimity.

"And then I suppose you know that you'll get awfully tired."

"Oh, we *never* get tired!" they eagerly cried.

"Have you had any kind of practice?"

They hesitated—they looked at each other. "We've been photographed— *immensely*," said Mrs. Monarch.

"She means the fellows have asked us themselves," added the Major.

"I see—because you're so good-looking."

"I don't know what they thought, but they were always after us."

"We always got our photographs for nothing," smiled Mrs. Monarch.

"We might have brought some, my dear," her husband remarked.

"I'm not sure we have any left. We've given quantities away," she explained to me.

"With our autographs and that sort of thing," said the Major.

"Are they to be got in the shops?" I enquired as a harmless pleasantry.

"Oh yes, *hers*—they used to be."

"Not now," said Mrs. Monarch with her eyes on the floor.

---

[4]I.e., a restaurant.

II

I could fancy the "sort of thing" they put on the presentation copies of their photographs, and I was sure they wrote a beautiful hand. It was odd how quickly I was sure of everything that concerned them. If they were now so poor as to have to earn shillings and pence they could never have had much of a margin. Their good looks had been their capital, and they had good-humouredly made the most of the career that this resource marked out for them. It was in their faces, the blankness, the deep intellectual repose of the twenty years of country-house visiting that had given them pleasant intonations. I could see the sunny drawing-rooms, sprinkled with periodicals she did n't read, in which Mrs. Monarch had continuously sat; I could see the wet shrubberies in which she had walked, equipped to admiration for either exercise. I could see the rich covers[1] the Major had helped to shoot and the wonderful garments in which, late at night, he repaired to the smoking-room to talk about them. I could imagine their leggings and waterproofs, their knowing tweeds and rugs, their rolls of sticks and cases of tackle and neat umbrellas; and I could evoke the exact appearance of their servants and the compact variety of their luggage on the platforms of country stations.

They gave small tips, but they were liked; they did n't do anything themselves, but they were welcome. They looked so well everywhere; they gratified the general relish for stature, complexion and "form." They knew it without fatuity or vulgarity, and they respected themselves in consequence. They were n't superficial; they were thorough and kept themselves up—it had been their line. People with such a taste for activity had to have some line. I could feel how even in a dull house they could have been counted on for the joy of life. At present something had happened—it didn't matter what, their little income had grown less, it had grown least—and they had to do something for pocket-money. Their friends could like them, I made out, without liking to support them. There was something about them that represented credit—their clothes, their manners, their type; but if credit is a large empty pocket in which an occasional chink reverberates, the chink at least must be audible. What they wanted of me was to help to make it so. Fortunately they had no children—I soon divined that. They would also perhaps wish our relations to be kept secret: this was why it was "for the figure"—the reproduction of the face would betray them.

I liked them—I felt, quite as their friends must have done—they were so simple; and I had no objection to them if they would suit. But somehow with all their perfections I did n't easily believe in them. After all they were amateurs, and the ruling passion of my life was the detestation of the amateur. Combined with this was another perversity—an innate preference for the represented subject over the real one: the defect of the real one was so apt to be a lack of representation. I liked things that appeared; then one was sure. Whether they *were* or not was a subordinate and almost always a profitless question. There were other considerations, the first of which was that I already had two or three recruits in use, notably a young person with big feet, in alpaca, from Kilburn, who for a couple of years had come to me regularly for my illustrations and with whom I was still—perhaps ignobly—satisfied. I frankly explained to my visitors how the case stood, but they had taken more precautions than I supposed. They had reasoned out their opportunity, for Claude Rivet had told them of the projected *édition de luxe* of one of the writers of our day—the rarest of the

[1]Woods and thickets from which game is driven for hunters.

novelists—who, long neglected by the multitudinous vulgar and dearly prized by the attentive (need I mention Philip Vincent?) had had the happy fortune of seeing, late in life, the dawn and then the full light of a higher criticism; an estimate in which on the part of the public there was something really of expiation. The edition preparing, planned by a publisher of taste, was practically an act of high reparation; the wood-cuts with which it was to be enriched were the homage of English art to one of the most independent representatives of English letters. Major and Mrs. Monarch confessed to me they had hoped I might be able to work *them* into my branch of the enterprise. They knew I was to do the first of the books, "Rutland Ramsay," but I had to make clear to them that my participation in the rest of the affair—this first book was to be a test— must depend on the satisfaction I should give. If this should be limited my employers would drop me with scarce common forms. It was therefore a crisis for me, and naturally I was making special preparations, looking about for new people, should they be necessary, and securing the best types. I admitted however that I should like to settle down to two or three good models who would do for everything.

"Should we have often to—a—put on special clothes?" Mrs. Monarch timidly demanded.

"Dear yes—that's half the business."

"And should we be expected to supply our own costumes?"

"Oh no; I've got a lot of things. A painter's models put on—or put off— anything he likes."

"And you mean—a—the same?"

"The same?"

Mrs. Monarch looked at her husband again.

"Oh she was just wondering," he explained, "if the costumes are in *general* use." I had to confess that they were, and I mentioned further that some of them—I had a lot of genuine greasy last-century things—had served their time, a hundred years ago, on living world-stained men and women; on figures not perhaps so far removed, in that vanished world, from *their* type, the Monarchs', *quoi!*[2] of a breeched and bewigged age. "We'll put on anything that *fits*," said the Major.

"Oh I arrange that—they fit in the pictures."

"I'm afraid I should do better for the modern books. I'd come as you like," said Mrs. Monarch.

"She has got a lot of clothes at home: they might do for contemporary life," her husband continued.

"Oh I can fancy scenes in which you'd be quite natural." And indeed I could see the slipshod rearrangements of stale properties—the stories I tried to produce pictures for without the exasperation of reading them—whose sandy tracts the good lady might help to people. But I had to return to the fact that for this sort of work—the daily mechanical grind—I was already equipped: the people I was working with were fully adequate.

"We only thought we might be more like *some* characters," said Mrs. Monarch mildly, getting up.

Her husband also rose; he stood looking at me with a dim wistfulness that was touching in so fine a man. "Would n't it be rather a pull sometimes to have— a—to have—?" He hung fire; he wanted me to help him by phrasing what he meant. But I could n't—I did n't know. So he brought it out awkwardly: "The

[2]French: what!

real thing; a gentleman, you know, or a lady." I was quite ready to give a general assent—I admitted that there was a great deal in that. This encouraged Major Monarch to say, following up his appeal with an unacted gulp: "It's awfully hard—we've tried everything." The gulp was communicative; it proved too much for his wife. Before I knew it Mrs. Monarch had dropped again upon a divan and burst into tears. Her husband sat down beside her, holding one of her hands; whereupon she quickly dried her eyes with the other, while I felt embarrassed as she looked up at me. "There is n't a confounded job I have n't applied for—waited for—prayed for. You can fancy we'd be pretty bad first. Secretaryships and that sort of thing? You might as well ask for a peerage. I'd be *anything*—I'm strong; a messenger or a coalheaver. I'd put on a gold-laced cap and open carriage-doors in front of the haberdasher's; I'd hang about a station to carry portmanteaux;[3] I'd be a postman. But they won't *look* at you; there are thousands as good as yourself already on the ground. *Gentlemen,* poor beggars, who've drunk their wine, who've kept their hunters!"

I was as reassuring as I knew how to be, and my visitors were presently on their feet again while, for the experiment, we agreed on an hour. We were discussing it when the door opened and Miss Churm came in with a wet umbrella. Miss Churm had to take the omnibus to Maida Vale and then walk half a mile. She looked a trifle blowsy and slightly splashed. I scarcely ever saw her come in without thinking afresh how odd it was that, being so little in herself, she should yet be so much in others. She was a meagre little Miss Churm, but was such an ample heroine of romance. She was only a freckled cockney,[4] but she could represent everything, from a fine lady to a shepherdess; she had the faculty as she might have had a fine voice or long hair. She could n't spell and she loved beer, but she had two or three "points," and practice, and a knack, and mother-wit, and a whimsical sensibility, and love of the theatre, and seven sisters, and not an ounce of respect, especially for the *h*. The first thing my visitors saw was that her umbrella was wet, and in their spotless perfection they visibly winced at it. The rain had come on since their arrival.

"I'm all in a soak; there *was* a mess of people in the 'bus. I wish you lived near a stytion," said Miss Churm. I requested her to get ready as quickly as possible, and she passed into the room in which she always changed her dress. But before going out she asked me what she was to get into this time.

"It's the Russian princess, don't you know?" I answered; "the one with the 'golden eyes,' in black velvet, for the long thing in the *Cheapside*."[5]

"Golden eyes? I *say!*" cried Miss Churm, while my companions watched her with intensity as she withdrew. She always arranged herself, when she was late, before I could turn round; andI kept my visitors a little on purpose, so that they might get an idea, from seeing her, what would be expected of themselves. I mentioned that she was quite my notion of an excellent model—she was really very clever.

"Do you think she looks like a Russian princess?" Major Monarch asked with lurking alarm.

"When I make her, yes."

"Oh if you have to *make* her—!" he reasoned, not without point.

"That's the most you can ask. There are so many who are not makeable."

"Well now, *here's* a lady"—and with a persuasive smile he passed his arm into his wife's—"who's already made!"

---

[3]Large suitcases.

[4]A slum dweller in London's East End, hence a member of the lower class.

[5]A magazine named for a commercial street in London.

"Oh I'm not a Russian princess," Mrs. Monarch protested a little coldly. I could see she had known some and did n't like them. There at once was a complication of a kind I never had to fear with Miss Churm.

This young lady came back in black velvet—the gown was rather rusty and very low on her lean shoulders—and with a Japanese fan in her red hands. I reminded her that in the scene I was doing she had to look over some one's head. "I forget whose it is; but it does n't matter. Just look over a head."

"I'd rather look over a stove," said Miss Churm; and she took her station near the fire. She fell into position, settled herself into a tall attitude, gave a certain backward inclination to her head and a certain forward droop to her fan, and looked, at least to my prejudiced sense, distinguished and charming, foreign and dangerous. We left her looking so while I went downstairs with Major and Mrs. Monarch.

"I believe I could come about as near as that," said Mrs. Monarch.

"Oh you think she's shabby, but you must allow for the alchemy of art."

However, they went off with an evident increase of comfort founded on their demonstrable advantage in being the real thing. I could fancy them shuddering over Miss Churm. She was very droll about them when I went back, for I told her what they wanted.

"Well, if *she* can sit I'll tyke to bookkeeping," said my model.

"She's very ladylike," I replied as an innocent form of aggravation.

"So much the worse for *you*. That means she can't turn round."

"She'll do for the fashionable novels."

"Oh yes, she'll *do* for them!" my model humorously declared. "Ain't they bad enough without her?" I had often sociably denounced them to Miss Churm.

III

It was for the elucidation of a mystery in one of these works that I first tried Mrs. Monarch. Her husband came with her, to be useful if necessary—it was sufficiently clear that as a general thing he would prefer to come with her. At first I wondered if this were for "propriety's" sake—if he were going to be jealous and meddling. The idea was too tiresome, and if it had been confirmed it would speedily have brought our acquaintance to a close. But I soon saw there was nothing in it and that if he accompanied Mrs. Monarch it was—in addition to the chance of being wanted—simply because he had nothing else to do. When they were separate his occupation was gone and they never *had* been separate. I judged rightly that in their awkward situation their close union was their main comfort and that this union had no weak spot. It was a real marriage, an encouragement to the hesitating, a nut for pessimists to crack. Their address was humble—I remember afterwards thinking it had been the only thing about them that was really professional—and I could fancy the lamentable lodgings in which the Major would have been left alone. He could sit there more or less grimly with his wife—he could n't sit there anyhow without her.

He had too much tact to try and make himself agreeable when he could n't be useful; so when I was too absorbed in my work to talk he simply sat and waited. But I liked to hear him talk—it made my work, when not interrupting it, less mechanical, less special. To listen to him was to combine the excitement of going out with the economy of staying at home. There was only one hindrance—that I seemed not to know any of the people this brilliant couple had known. I think he wondered extremely, during the term of our intercourse, whom the deuce I *did* know. He had n't a stray sixpence of an idea to fumble for, so we did n't spin it very fine; we confined ourselves to questions of leather and even of liquor—saddlers and breeches-makers and how to get excellent claret cheap—and matters like "good trains" and the habits of small game. His lore on these last subjects was astonishing—he managed to interweave the stationmaster with the ornithologist. When he could n't talk about greater things he could talk cheerfully about smaller, and since I could n't accompany him into reminiscences of the fashionable world he could lower the conversation without a visible effort to my level.

So earnest a desire to please was touching in a man who could so easily have knocked one down. He looked after the fire and had an opinion on the draught of the stove without my asking him, and I could see that he thought many of my arrangements not half knowing. I remember telling him that if I were only rich I'd offer him a salary to come and teach me how to live. Sometimes he gave a random sigh of which the essence might have been: "Give me even such a bare old barrack as *this,* and I'd do something with it!" When I wanted to use him he came alone; which was an illustration of the superior courage of women. His wife could bear her solitary second floor, and she was in general more discreet; showing by various small reserves that she was alive to the propriety of keeping our relations markedly professional—not letting them slide into sociability. She wished it to remain clear that she and the Major were employed, not cultivated, and if she approved of me as a superior, who could be kept in his place, she never thought me quite good enough for an equal.

She sat with great intensity, giving the whole of her mind to it, and was capable of remaining for an hour almost as motionless as before a photographer's lens. I could see she had been photographed often, but somehow the very habit that made her good for that purpose unfitted her for mine. At first I was extremely pleased with her ladylike air, and it was a satisfaction, on coming to follow her lines, to see how good they were and how far they could lead the pencil. But after a little skirmishing I began to find her too insurmountably stiff; do what I would with it my drawing looked like a photograph or a copy of a photograph. Her figure had no variety of expression—she herself had no sense of variety. You may say that this was my business and was only a question of placing her. Yet I placed her in every conceivable position and she managed to obliterate their differences. She was always a lady certainly, and into the bargain was always the same lady. She was the real thing, but always the same thing. There were moments when I rather writhed under the serenity of her confidence that she *was* the real thing. All her dealings with me and all her husband's were an implication that this was lucky for *me.* Meanwhile I found myself trying to invent types that approached her own, instead of making her own transform itself— in the clever way that was not impossible for instance to poor Miss Churm. Arrange as I would and take the precautions I would, she always came out, in my pictures, too tall—landing me in the dilemma of having represented a fascinating woman as seven feet high, which (out of respect perhaps to my own very much scantier inches) was far from my idea of such a personage.

The case was worse with the Major—nothing I could do would keep *him* down, so that he became useful only for the representation of brawny giants. I adored variety and range, I cherished human accidents, the illustrative note; I wanted to characterise closely, and the thing in the world I most hated was the danger of being ridden by a type. I had quarrelled with some of my friends about it; I had parted company with them for maintaining that one *had* to be, and that if the type was beautiful—witness Raphael and Leonardo[1]—the servitude was only a gain. I was neither Leonardo nor Raphael—I might only be a presumptuous young modern searcher; but I held that everything was to be sacrificed sooner than character. When they claimed that the obsessional form could easily *be* character I retorted, perhaps superficially, "Whose?" It could n't be everybody's—it might end in being nobody's.

After I had drawn Mrs. Monarch a dozen times I felt surer even than before that the value of such a model as Miss Churm resided precisely in the fact that she had no positive stamp, combined of course with the other fact that what she did have was a curious and inexplicable talent for imitation. Her usual appearance was like a curtain which she could draw up at request for a capital performance. This performance was simply suggestive; but it was a word to the wise—it was vivid and pretty. Sometimes even I thought it, though she was plain herself, too insipidly pretty; I made it a reproach to her that the figures drawn from her were monotonously (*bêtement,*[2] as we used to say) graceful. Nothing made her more angry: it was so much her pride to feel she could sit for characters that had nothing in common with each other. She would accuse me at such moments of taking away her "reputytion."

It suffered a certain shrinkage, this queer quantity, from the repeated visits of my new friends. Miss Churm was greatly in demand, never in want of employment, so I had no scruple in putting her off occasionally, to try them more at my ease. It was certainly amusing at first to do the real thing—it was amusing to do Major Monarch's trousers. They *were* the real thing, even if he did come out colossal. It was amusing to do his wife's back hair—it was so mathematically neat—and the particular "smart" tension of her tight stays. She lent herself especially to positions in which the face was somewhat averted or blurred; she abounded in ladylike back views and *profils perdus.*[3] When she stood erect she took naturally one of the attitudes in which court-painters represent queens and princesses; so that I found myself wondering whether, to draw out this accomplishment, I could n't get the editor of the *Cheapside* to publish a really royal romance, "A Tale of Buckingham Palace." Sometimes however the real thing and the make-believe came into contact; by which I mean that Miss Churm, keeping an appointment or coming to make one on days when I had much work in hand, encountered her invidious rivals. The encounter was not on their part, for they noticed her no more than if she had been the housemaid; not from intentional loftiness, but simply because as yet, professionally, they did n't know how to fraternise, as I could imagine they would have liked—or at least that the Major would. They could n't talk about the omnibus[4]—they always walked; and they did n't know what else to try—she was n't interested in good trains or cheap claret. Besides, they must have felt—in the air—that she was amused at them, secretly derisive of their ever knowing how. She wasn't a person to conceal the limits of her faith if she had had a chance to show them. On the other hand Mrs. Monarch did n't think her tidy; for why else did she take pains to say to me—it was going out of the way, for Mrs. Monarch—that she did n't like dirty women?

One day when my young lady happened to be present with my other sitters— she even dropped in, when it was convenient, for a chat—I asked her to be so

[1]Raphael Sanzio (1483–1520) and Leonardo da Vinci (1452–1519), Italian painters.
[2]French: stupidly.
[3]French: lost profiles, poses that show the back of the head more than the profile.
[4]Bus.

good as to lend a hand in getting tea, a service with which she was familiar and which was one of a class that, living as I did in a small way, with slender domestic resources, I often appealed to my models to render. They liked to lay hands on my property, to break the sitting, and sometimes the china—it made them feel Bohemian. The next time I saw Miss Churm after this incident she surprised me greatly by making a scene about it—she accused me of having wished to humiliate her. She had n't resented the outrage at the time, but had seemed obliging and amused, enjoying the comedy of asking Mrs. Monarch, who sat vague and silent, whether she would have cream and sugar, and putting an exaggerated simper into the question. She had tried intonations—as if she too wished to pass for the real thing—till I was afraid my other visitors would take offence.

   Oh they were determined not to do this, and their touching patience was the measure of their great need. They would sit by the hour, uncomplaining, till I was ready to use them; they would come back on the chance of being wanted and would walk away cheerfully if it failed. I used to go to the door with them to see in what magnificent order they retreated. I tried to find other employment for them—I introduced them to several artists. But they didn't "take," for reasons I could appreciate, and I became rather anxiously aware that after such disappointments they fell back upon me with a heavier weight. They did me the honour to think me most *their* form. They were n't romantic enough for the painters, and in those days there were few serious workers in black-and-white. Besides, they had an eye to the great job I had mentioned to them—they had secretly set their hearts on supplying the right essence for my pictorial vindication of our fine novelist. They knew that for this undertaking I should want no costume-effects, none of the frippery of past ages—that it was a case in which everything would be contemporary and satirical and presumably genteel. If I could work them into it their future would be assured, for the labour would of course be long and the occupation steady.

   One day Mrs. Monarch came without her husband—she explained his absence by his having had to go to the City.[5] While she sat there in her usual relaxed majesty there came at the door a knock which I immediately recognised as the subdued appeal of a model out of work. It was followed by the entrance of a young man whom I at once saw to be a foreigner and who proved in fact an Italian acquainted with no English word but my name, which he uttered in a way that made it seem to include all others. I had n't then visited his country, nor was I proficient in his tongue; but as he was not so meanly constituted— what Italian is?—as to depend only on that member of expression he conveyed to me, in familiar but graceful mimicry, that he was in search of exactly the employment in which the lady before me was engaged. I was not struck with him at first, and while I continued to draw I dropped few signs of interest or encouragement. He stood his ground however—not importunately, but with a dumb dog-like fidelity in his eyes that amounted to innocent impudence, the manner of a devoted servant—he might have been in the house for years— unjustly suspected. Suddenly it struck me that this very attitude and expression made a picture; whereupon I told him to sit down and wait till I should be free. There was another picture in the way he obeyed me, and I observed as I worked that there were others still in the way he looked wonderingly, with his head thrown back, about the high studio. He might have been crossing himself in

[5]London's financial and commercial center.

Saint Peter's. Before I finished I said to myself "The fellow's a bankrupt orange-monger, but a treasure."

When Mrs. Monarch withdrew he passed across the room like a flash to open the door for her, standing there with the rapt pure gaze of the young Dante spellbound by the young Beatrice.[6] As I never insisted, in such situations, on the blankness of the British domestic, I reflected that he had the making of a servant—and I needed one, but could n't pay him to be only that—as well as of a model; in short I resolved to adopt my bright adventurer if he would agree to officiate in the double capacity. He jumped at my offer, and in the event my rashness—for I had really known nothing about him—wasn't brought home to me. He proved a sympathetic though a desultory ministrant, and had in a wonderful degree the *sentiment de la pose*.[7] It was uncultivated, instinctive, a part of the happy instinct that had guided him to my door and helped him to spell out my name on the card nailed to it. He had had no other introduction to me than a guess, from the shape of my high north window, seen outside, that my place was a studio and that as a studio it would contain an artist. He had wandered to England in search of fortune, like other itinerants, and had embarked, with a partner and a small green hand-cart, on the sale of penny ices. The ices had melted away and the partner had dissolved in their train. My young man wore tight yellow trousers with reddish stripes and his name was Oronte. He was sallow but fair, and when I put him into some old clothes of my own he looked like an Englishman. He was as good as Miss Churm, who could look, when requested, like an Italian.

IV

I thought Mrs. Monarch's face slightly convulsed when, on her coming back with her husband, she found Oronte installed. It was strange to have to recognise in a scrap of a lazzarone[1] a competitor to her magnificent Major. It was she who scented danger first, for the Major was anecdotically unconscious. But Oronte gave us tea, with a hundred eager confusions—he had never been concerned in so queer a process—and I think she thought better of me for having at last an "establishment." They saw a couple of drawings that I had made of the establishment, and Mrs. Monarch hinted that it never would have struck her he had sat for them. "Now the drawings you make from *us,* they look exactly like us," she reminded me, smiling in triumph; and I recognised that this was indeed just their defect. When I drew the Monarchs I could n't anyhow get away from them—get into the character I wanted to represent; and I hadn't the least desire my model should be discoverable in my picture. Miss Churm never was, and Mrs. Monarch thought I hid her, very properly, because she was vulgar; whereas if she was lost it was only as the dead who go to heaven are lost—in the gain of an angel the more.

By this time I had got a certain start with "Rutland Ramsay," the first novel in the great projected series; that is I had produced a dozen drawings, several with the help of the Major and his wife, and I had sent them in for approval. My understanding with the publishers, as I have already hinted, had been that

---

[6]Beatrice Portinari (1266–1290), Florentine woman said to be the ideal and the inspiration of the poet Dante, who first saw her when he was nine.

[7]French: instinct for posing.

[1]Italian: beggar.

I was to be left to do my work, in this particular case, as I liked, with the whole book committed to me; but my connexion with the rest of the series was only contingent. There were moments when, frankly, it *was* a comfort to have the real thing under one's hand; for there were characters in "Rutland Ramsay" that were very much like it. There were people presumably as erect as the Major and women of as good a fashion as Mrs. Monarch. There was a great deal of countryhouse life—treated, it is true, in a fine fanciful ironical generalised way—and there was a considerable implication of knickerbockers[2] and kilts. There were certain things I had to settle at the outset; such things for instance as the exact appearance of the hero and the particular bloom and figure of the heroine. The author of course gave me a lead, but there was a margin for interpretation. I took the Monarchs into my confidence, I told them frankly what I was about, I mentioned my embarrassments and alternatives. "Oh take *him!*" Mrs. Monarch murmured sweetly, looking at her husband; and "What could you want better than my wife?" the Major enquired with the comfortable candour that now prevailed between us.

I was n't obliged to answer these remarks—I was only obliged to place my sitters. I was n't easy in mind, and I postponed a little timidly perhaps the solving of my question. The book was a large canvas, the other figures were numerous, and I worked off at first some of the episodes in which the hero and the heroine were not concerned. When once I had set *them* up I should have to stick to them—I could n't make my young man seven feet high in one place and five feet nine in another. I inclined on the whole to the latter measurement, though the Major more than once reminded me that *he* looked about as young as any one. It was indeed quite possible to arrange him, for the figure, so that it would have been difficult to detect his age. After the spontaneous Oronte had been with me a month, and after I had given him to understand several times over that his native exuberance would presently constitute an insurmountable barrier to our further intercourse, I waked to a sense of his heroic capacity. He was only five feet seven, but the remaining inches were latent. I tried him almost secretly at first, for I was really rather afraid of the judgment my other models would pass on such a choice. If they regarded Miss Churm as little better than a snare what would they think of the representation by a person so little the real thing as an Italian street-vendor of a protagonist formed by a public school?

If I went a little in fear of them it was n't because they bullied me, because they had got an oppressive foothold, but because in their really pathetic decorum and mysteriously permanent newness they counted on me so intensely. I was therefore very glad when Jack Hawley came home: he was always of such good counsel. He painted badly himself, but there was no one like him for putting his finger on the place. He had been absent from England for a year; he had been somewhere—I don't remember where—to get a fresh eye. I was in a good deal of dread of any such organ, but we were old friends; he had been away for months and a sense of emptiness was creeping into my life. I had n't dodged a missile for a year.

He came back with a fresh eye, but with the same old black velvet blouse, and the first evening he spent in my studio we smoked cigarettes till the small hours. He had done no work himself, he had only got the eye; so the field was clear for the production of my little things. He wanted to see what I had produced for the *Cheapside,* but he was disappointed in the exhibition. That at least seemed the meaning of two or three comprehensive groans which, as he lounged on my

[2]Trousers gathered at the knee, knickers.

big divan, his leg folded under him, looking at my latest drawings, issued from
his lips with the smoke of the cigarette.

"What's the matter with you?" I asked.

"What's the matter with *you?*"

"Nothing save that I'm mystified."

"You are indeed. You're quite off the hinge. What's the meaning of this new
fad?" And he tossed me, with visible irreverence, a drawing in which I happened
to have depicted both my elegant models. I asked if he did n't think it good,
and he replied that it struck him as execrable, given the sort of thing I had
always represented myself to him as wishing to arrive at; but I let that pass—I
was so anxious to see exactly what he meant. The two figures in the picture
looked colossal, but I supposed this was *not* what he meant, inasmuch as, for
aught he knew to the contrary, I might have been trying for some such effect.
I maintained that I was working exactly in the same way as when he last had
done me the honour to tell me I might do something some day. "Well, there's
a screw loose somewhere," he answered; "wait a bit and I'll discover it." I
depended upon him to do so: where else was the fresh eye? But he produced
at last nothing more luminous than "I don't know—I don't like your types."
This was lame for a critic who had never consented to discuss with me anything
but the question of execution, the direction of strokes and the mystery of values.

"In the drawings you've been looking at I think my types are very handsome."

"Oh, they won't do!"

"I've been working with new models."

"I see you have. *They* won't do."

"Are you very sure of that?"

"Absolutely—they're stupid."

"You mean *I* am—for I ought to get around that."

"You *can't*—with such people. Who are they?"

I told him, so far as was necessary, and he concluded heartlessly: *"Ce sont des
gens qu'il faut mettre à la porte."*[3]

"You've never seen them; they're awfully good"—I flew to their defence.

"Not seen them? Why all this recent work of yours drops to pieces with them.
It's all I want to see of them."

"No one else has said anything against it—the *Cheapside* people are pleased."

"Every one else is an ass, and the *Cheapside* people the biggest asses of all.
Come, don't pretend at this time of day to have pretty illusions about the public,
especially about publishers and editors. It's not for *such* animals you work—it's
for those who know, *coloro che sanno,*[4] so keep straight for *me* if you can't keep
straight for yourself. There was a certain sort of thing you used to try for—and
a very good thing is was. But this twaddle is n't *in* it." When I talked with Hawley
later about "Rutland Ramsay" and its possible successors he declared that I must
get back into my boat again or I should go to the bottom. His voice in short was
the voice of warning.

I noted the warning, but I did n't turn my friends out of doors. They bored
me a good deal; but the very fact that they bored me admonished me not to
sacrifice them—if there was anything to be done with them—simply to irritation.
As I look back at this phase they seem to me to have pervaded my life not a
little. I have a vision of them as most of the time in my studio, seated against
the wall on an old velvet bench to be out of the way, and resembling the while
a pair of patient courtiers in a royal ante-chamber. I'm convinced that during

---

[3]French: "They are people one must show to the door," i.e., get rid of.

[4]Italian: "those who know," a quotation from Dante's *Inferno*, Canto IV, line 131.

the coldest weeks of the winter they held their ground because it saved them fire. Their newness was losing its gloss, and it was impossible not to feel them objects of charity. Whenever Miss Churm arrived they went away, and after I was fairly launched in "Rutland Ramsay" Miss Churm arrived pretty often. They managed to express to me tacitly that they supposed I wanted her for the low life of the book, and I let them suppose it, since they had attempted to study the work—it was lying about the studio—without discovering that it dealt only with the highest circles. They had dipped into the most brilliant of our novelists without deciphering many passages. I still took an hour from them, now and again, in spite of Jack Hawley's warning; it would be time enough to dismiss them, if dismissal should be necessary, when the rigour of the season was over. Hawley had made their acquaintance—he had met them at my fireside—and thought them a ridiculous pair. Learning that he was a painter they tried to approach him, to show him too that they were the real thing; but he looked at them, across the big room, as if they were miles away; they were a compendium of everything he most objected to in the social system of his country. Such people as that, all convention and patent-leather, with ejaculations that stopped conversation, had no business in a studio. A studio was a place to learn to see, and how could you see through a pair of feather-beds?

The main inconvenience I suffered at their hands was that at first I was shy of letting it break upon them that my artful little servant had begun to sit to me for "Rutland Ramsay." They knew I had been odd enough—they were prepared by this time to allow oddity to artist—to pick a foreign vagabond out of the streets when I might have had a person with whiskers and credentials; but it was some time before they learned how high I rated his accomplishments. They found him in an attitude more than once, but they never doubted I was doing him as an organ-grinder. There were several things they never guessed, and one of them was that for a striking scene in the novel, in which a footman briefly figured, it occurred to me to make use of Major Monarch as the menial. I kept putting this off, I did n't like to ask him to don the livery—beside the difficulty of finding a livery to fit him. At last, one day late in the winter, when I was at work on the despised Oronte, who caught one's idea on the wing, and was in the glow of feeling myself go very straight, they came in, the Major and his wife, with their society laugh about nothing (there was less and less to laugh at); came in like country-callers—they always reminded me of that—who have walked across the park after church and are presently persuaded to stay to luncheon. Luncheon was over, but they could stay to tea—I knew they wanted it. The fit was on me, however, and I could n't let my ardour cool and my work wait, with the fading daylight, while my model prepared it. So I asked Mrs. Monarch is she would mind laying it out—a request which for an instant brought all the blood to her face. Her eyes were on her husband's for a second, and some mute telegraphy passed between them. Their folly was over the next instant; his cheerful shrewdness put an end to it. So far from pitying their wounded pride, I must add, I was moved to give it as complete a lesson as I could. They bustled about together and got out the cups and saucers and made the kettle boil. I know they felt as if they were waiting on my servant, and when the tea was prepared I said: "He'll have a cup, please—he's tired." Mrs. Monarch brought him one where he stood, and he took it from her as if he had been a gentleman at a party squeezing a crush-hat with an elbow.

Then it came over me that she had made a great effort for me—made it with a kind of nobleness—and that I owed her a compensation. Each time I saw her after this I wondered what the compensation could be. I could n't go on doing the wrong thing to oblige them. Oh it *was* the wrong thing, the stamp of the work for which they sat—Hawley was not the only person to say it now. I sent in a large number of the drawings I had made for "Rutland Ramsay," and I received a warning that was more to the point than Hawley's. The artistic adviser of the house for which I was working was of opinion that many of my illustrations were not what had been looked for. Most of these illustrations were the subjects in which the Monarchs had figured. Without giving into the question of what *had* been looked for, I had to face the fact that at this rate I should n't get the other books to do. I hurled myself in despair on Miss Churm—I put her through all her paces. I not only adopted Oronte publicly as my hero, but one morning when the Major looked in to see if I did n't require him to finish a *Cheapside* figure for which he had begun to sit the week before, I told him I had changed my mind—I'd do the drawing from my man. At this my visitor turned pale and stood looking at me. "Is *he* your idea of an English gentleman?" he asked.

I was disappointed, I was nervous, I wanted to get on with my work; so I replied with irritation: "Oh my dear Major—I can't be ruined for *you!*"

It was a horrid speech, but he stood another moment—after which, without a word, he quitted the studio. I drew a long breath, for I said to myself that I should n't see him again. I had n't told him definitely that I was in danger of having my work rejected, but I was vexed at his not having felt the catastrophe in the air, read with me the moral of our fruitless collaboration, the lesson that in the deceptive atmosphere of art even the highest respectability may fail of being plastic.

I did n't owe my friends money, but I did see them again. They reappeared together three days later, and, given all the other facts, there was something tragic in that one. It was a clear proof they could find nothing else in life to do. They had threshed the matter out in a dismal conference—they had digested the bad news that they were not in for the series. If they were n't useful to me even for the *Cheapside* their function seemed difficult to determine, and I could only judge at first that they had come, forgivingly, decorously, to take a last leave. This made me rejoice in secret that I had little leisure for a scene; for I had placed both my other models in position together and I was pegging away at a drawing from which I hoped to derive glory. It had been suggested by the passage in which Rutland Ramsay, drawing up a chair to Artemisia's piano-stool, says extraordinary things to her while she ostensibly fingers out a difficult piece of music. I had done Miss Churm at the piano before—it was an attitude in which she knew how to take on an absolutely poetic grace. I wished the two figures to "compose" together with intensity, and my little Italian had entered perfectly into my conception. The pair were vividly before me, the piano had been pulled out; it was a charming show of blended youth and murmured love, which I had only to catch and keep. My visitors stood and looked at it, and I was friendly to them over my shoulder.

They made no response, but I was used to silent company and went on with my work, only a little disconcerted—even though exhilarated by the sense that *this* was at least the ideal thing—at not having got rid of them after all. Presently I heard Mrs. Monarch's sweet voice beside or rather above me: "I wish her hair were a little better done." I looked up and she was staring with a strange fixedness at Miss Churm, whose back was turned to her. "Do you mind my just touching it?" she went on—a question which made me spring up for an instant as with the instinctive fear that she might do the young lady a harm. But she quieted me with a glance I shall never forget—I confess I should like to have been able to paint *that*—and went for a moment to my model. She spoke to her softly, laying a hand on her shoulder and bending over her; and as the girl, understanding, gratefully assented, she disposed her rough curls, with a few quick passes, in such a way as to make Miss Churm's head twice as charming. It was one of the most heroic personal services I've ever seen rendered. Then Mrs. Monarch turned away with a low sigh and, looking about her as if for something to do, stooped to the floor with a noble humility and picked up a dirty rag that had dropped out of my paint-box.

The Major meanwhile had also been looking for something to do, and, wandering to the other end of the studio, saw before him my breakfast-things neglected, unremoved. "I say, can't I be useful here?" he called out to me with an irrepressible quaver. I assented with a laugh that I fear was awkward, and for the next ten minutes, while I worked, I hear the light clatter of china and the tinkle of spoons and glass. Mrs. Monarch assisted her husband—they washed up my crockery, they put it away. They wandered off into my little scullery, and I afterwards found that they had cleaned my knives and that my slender stock of plate had an unprecedented surface. When it came over me, the latent eloquence of what they were doing, I confess that my drawing was blurred for a moment—the picture swam. They had accepted their failure, but they could n't accept their fate. They had bowed their heads in bewilderment to the perverse and cruel law in virtue of which the real thing could be so much less precious than the unreal; but they did n't want to starve. If my servants were my models, then my models might be my servants. They would reverse the parts—the others would sit for the ladies and gentlemen and *they* would do the work. They would still be in the studio—it was an intense dumb appeal to me not to turn them out. "Take us on," they wanted to say—"we'll do *anything*."

My pencil dropped from my hand; my sitting was spoiled and I got rid of my sitters, who were also evidently rather mystified and awestruck. Then, alone with the Major and his wife I had a most uncomfortable moment. He put their prayer into a single sentence: "I say, you know—just let *us* do for you, can't you?" I could n't—it was dreadful to see them emptying my slops, but I pretended I could, to oblige them, for about a week. Then I gave them a sum of money to go away, and I never saw them again. I obtained the remaining books, but my friend Hawley repeats that Major and Mrs. Monarch did me a permanent harm, got me into false ways. If it be true I'm content to have paid the price—for the memory.

1892, 1909

THE BEAST IN THE JUNGLE

I

What determined the speech that startled him in the course of their encounter scarcely matters, being probably but some words spoken by himself quite without intention—spoken as they lingered and slowly moved together after their renewal of acquaintance. He had been conveyed by friends an hour or two before to the house at which she was staying; the party of visitors at the other house, of whom he was one, and thanks to whom it was his theory, as always, that he was lost in the crowd, had been invited over to luncheon. There had been after

luncheon much dispersal, all in the interest of the original motive, a view of
Weatherend itself and the fine things, intrinsic features, pictures, heirlooms,
treasures of all the arts, that made the place almost famous; and the great rooms
were so numerous that guests could wander at their will, hang back from the
principal group and in cases where they took such matters with the last seriousness give themselves up to mysterious appreciations and measurements.
There were persons to be observed, singly or in couples, bending toward objects
in out-of-the-way corners with their hands on their knees and their heads
nodding quite as with the emphasis of an excited sense of smell. When they
were two they either mingled their sounds of ecstasy or melted into silences of
even deeper import, so that there were aspects of the occasion that gave it for
Marcher much the air of the "look round," previous to a sale highly advertised,
that excites or quenches, as may be, the dream of acquisition. The dream of
acquisition at Weatherend would have had to be wild indeed, and John Marcher
found himself, among such suggestions, disconcerted almost equally by the
presence of those who knew too much and by that of those who knew nothing.
The great rooms caused so much poetry and history to press upon him that he
needed some straying apart to feel in a proper relation with them, though this
impulse was not, as happened, like the gloating of some of his companions, to
be compared to the movements of a dog sniffing a cupboard. It had an issue
promptly enough in a direction that was not to have been calculated.

It led, briefly, in the course of the October afternoon, to his closer meeting
with May Bartram, whose face, a reminder, yet not quite a remembrance, as
they sat much separated at a very long table, had begun merely by troubling
him rather pleasantly. It affected him as the sequel of something of which he
had lost the beginning. He knew it, and for the time quite welcomed it, as a
continuation, but did n't know what it continued, which was an interest or an
amusement the greater as he was also somehow aware—yet without a direct sign
from her—that the young woman herself had n't lost the thread. She had n't
lost it, but she would n't give it back to him, he saw, without some putting forth
of his hand for it; and he not only saw that, but saw several things more, things
odd enough in the light of the fact that at the moment some accident of grouping
brought them face to face he was still merely fumbling with the idea that any
contact between them in the past would have had no importance. If it had had
no importance he scarcely knew why his actual impression of her should so seem
to have so much; the answer to which, however, was that in such a life as they
all appeared to be leading for the moment one could but take things as they
came. He was satisfied, without in the least being able to say why, that this young
lady might roughly have ranked in the house as a poor relation; satisfied also
that she was not there on a brief visit, but was more or less a part of the
establishment—almost a working, a remunerated part. Did n't she enjoy at
periods a protection that she paid for by helping, among other services, to show
the place and explain it, deal with the tiresome people, answer questions about
the dates of the building, the styles of the furniture, the authorship of the
pictures, the favourite haunts of the ghost? It was n't that she looked as if you
could have given her shillings—it was impossible to look less so. Yet when she
finally drifted toward him, distinctly handsome, though ever so much older—
older than when he had seen her before—it might have been as an effect of her
guessing that he had, within the couple of hours, devoted more imagination to
her than to all the others put together, and had thereby penetrated to a kind of
truth that the others were too stupid for. She *was* there on harder terms than

any one; she was there as a consequence of things suffered, one way and another, in the interval of years; and she remembered him very much as she was remembered—only a good deal better.

By the time they at last thus came to speech they were alone in one of the rooms—remarkable for a fine portrait over the chimneyplace—out of which their friends had passed, and the charm of it was that even before they had spoken they had practically arranged with each other to stay behind for talk. The charm, happily, was in other things too—partly in there being scarce a spot at Weatherend without something to stay behind for. It was in the way the autumn day looked into the high windows as it waned; the way the red light, breaking at the close from under a low sombre sky, reached out in a long shaft and played over old wainscots, old tapestry, old gold, old colour. It was most of all perhaps in the way she came to him as if, since she had been turned on to deal with the simpler sort, he might, should he choose to keep the whole thing down, just take her mild attention for a part of her general business. As soon as he heard her voice, however, the gap was filled up and the missing link supplied; the slight irony he divined in her attitude lost its advantage. He almost jumped at it to get there before her. "I met you years and years ago in Rome. I remember all about it." She confessed to disappointment—she had been so sure he did n't; and to prove how well he did he began to pour the particular recollections that popped up as he called for them. Her face and her voice, all at his service now, worked the miracle—the impression operating like the torch of a lamplighter who touches into flame, one by one, a long row of gas-jets. Marcher flattered himself the illumination was brilliant, yet he was really still more pleased on her showing him, with amusement, that in his haste to make everything right he had got most things rather wrong. It had n't been at Rome— it had been at Naples; and it had n't been eight years before—it had been more nearly ten. She had n't been, either, with her uncle and aunt, but with her mother and her brother; in addition to which it was not with the Pembles *he* had been, but with the Boyers, coming down in their company from Rome—a point on which she insisted, a little to his confusion, and as to which she had her evidence in hand. The Boyers she had known, but did n't know the Pembles, though she had heard of them, and it was the people he was with who had made them acquainted. The incident of the thunderstorm that had raged round them with such violence as to drive them for refuge into an excavation—this incident had not occurred at the Palace of the Cæsars, but at Pompeii,[1] on an occasion when they had been present there at an important find.

He accepted her amendments, he enjoyed her corrections, though the moral of them was, she pointed out, that he *really* did n't remember the least thing about her; and he only felt it as a drawback that when all was made strictly historic there did n't appear much of anything left. They lingered together still, she neglecting her office—for from the moment he was so clever she had no proper right to him—and both neglecting the house, just waiting as to see if a memory or two more would n't again breathe on them. It had n't taken them many minutes, after all, to put down on the table, like the cards of a pack, those that constituted their respective hands; only what came out was that the pack was unfortunately not perfect—that the past, invoked, invited, encouraged, could give them, naturally, no more than it had. It had made them anciently meet—her at twenty, him at twenty-five; but nothing was so strange, they seemed to say to each other, as that, while so occupied, it had n't done a little more for

[1] Not at Rome, the site of the Palace of the Caesars, but near Naples—at the ruined city of Pompeii, where archaeological excavations were being made.

them. They looked at each other as with the feeling of an occasion missed; the present would have been so much better if the other, in the far distance, in the foreign land, had n't been so stupidly meagre. There were n't apparently, all counted, more than a dozen little old things that had succeeded in coming to pass between them; trivialities of youth, simplicities of freshness, stupidities of ignorance, small possible germs, but too deeply buried—too deeply (did n't it seem?) to sprout after so many years. Marcher could only feel he ought to have rendered her some service—saved her from a capsized boat in the Bay or at least recovered her dressing-bag, filched from her cab in the streets of Naples by a lazzarone with a stiletto. Or it would have been nice if he could have been taken with fever all alone at his hotel, and she could have come to look after him, to write to his people, to drive him out in convalescence. *Then* they would be in possession of the something or other that their actual show seemed to lack. It yet somehow presented itself, this show, as too good to be spoiled; so that they were reduced for a few minutes more to wondering a little helplessly why— since they seemed to know a certain number of the same people—their reunion had been so long averted. They did n't use that name for it, but their delay from minute to minute to join the others was a kind of confession that they did n't quite want it to be a failure. Their attempted supposition of reasons for their not having met but showed how little they knew of each other. There came in fact a moment when Marcher felt a positive pang. It was vain to pretend she was an old friend, for all the communities were wanting, in spite of which it was as an old friend that he saw she would have suited him. He had new ones enough—was surrounded with them for instance on the stage of the other house; as a new one he probably would n't have so much as noticed her. He would have liked to invent something, get her to make-believe with him that some passage of a romantic or critical kind *had* originally occurred. He was really almost reaching out in imagination—as against time—for something that would do, and saying to himself that if it did n't come this sketch of a fresh start would show for quite awkwardly bungled. They would separate, and now for no second or no third chance. They would have tried and not succeeded. Then it was, just at the turn, as he afterwards made it out to himself, that, everything else failing, she herself decided to take up the case and, as it were, save the situation. He felt as soon as she spoke that she had been consciously keeping back what she said and hoping to get on without it; a scruple in her that immensely touched him when, by the end of three or four minutes more, he was able to measure it. What she brought out, at any rate, quite cleared the air and supplied the link—the link it was so odd he should frivolously have managed to lose.

"You know you told me something I've never forgotten and that again and again has made me think of you since; it was that tremendously hot day when we went to Sorrento,[2] across the bay, for the breeze. What I allude to was what you said to me, on the way back, as we sat under the awning of the boat enjoying the cool. Have you forgotten?

He had forgotten and was even more surprised than ashamed. But the great thing was that he saw in this no vulgar reminder of any "sweet" speech. The vanity of women had long memories, but she was making no claim on him of a compliment or a mistake. With another woman, a totally different one, he might have feared the recall possibly even of some imbecile "offer." So, in having to say that he had indeed forgotten, he was conscious rather of a loss than of a

---

[2]A resort town on the Bay of Naples.

gain; he already saw an interest in the manner of her mention. "I try to think—but I give it up. Yet I remember the Sorrento day."

"I'm not very sure you do," May Bartram after a moment said; "and I'm not very sure I ought to want you to. It's dreadful to bring a person back at any time to what he was ten years before. If you've lived away from it," she smiled, "so much the better."

"Ah, if *you* have n't why should I?" he asked.

"Lived away, you mean, from what I myself was?"

"From what *I* was. I was of course an ass," Marcher went on; "but I would rather know from you just the sort of ass I was than—from the moment you have something in your mind—not know anything."

Still, however, she hesitated. "But if you've completely ceased to be that sort—?"

"Why I can then all the more bear to know. Besides, perhaps I have n't."

"Perhaps. Yet if you have n't," she added, "I should suppose you'd remember. Not indeed that *I* in the least connect with my impression the invidious name you use. If I had only thought you foolish," she explained, "the thing I speak of would n't so have remained with me. It was about yourself." She waited as if it might come to him; but as, only meeting her eyes in wonder, he gave no sign, she burnt her ships. "Has it ever happened?"

Then it was that, while he continued to stare, a light broke for him and the blood slowly came to his face, which began to burn with recognition. "Do you mean I told you—?" But he faltered, lest what came to him should n't be right, lest he should only give himself away.

"It was something about yourself that it was natural one should n't forget—that is if one remembered you at all. That's why I ask you," she smiled, "if the thing you then spoke of has ever come to pass?"

Oh then he saw, but he was lost in wonder and found himself embarrassed. This, he also saw, made her sorry for him, as if her allusion had been a mistake. It took him but a moment, however, to feel it had n't been, much as it had been a surprise. After the first little shock of it her knowledge on the contrary began, even if rather strangely, to taste sweet to him. She was the only other person in the world then who would have it, and she had had it all these years, while the fact of his having so breathed his secret had unaccountably faded from him. No wonder they could n't have met as if nothing had happened. "I judge," he finally said, "that I know what you mean. Only I had strangely enough lost any sense of having taken you so far into my confidence."

"Is it because you've taken so many others as well?"

"I've taken nobody. Not a creature since then."

"So that I'm the only person who knows?"

"The only person in the world."

"Well," she quickly replied, "I myself have never spoken. I've never, never repeated of you what you told me." She looked at him so that he perfectly believed her. Their eyes met over it in such a way that he was without a doubt. "And I never will."

She spoke with an earnestness that, as if almost excessive, put him at ease about her possible derision. Somehow the whole question was a new luxury to him—that is from the moment she was in possession. If she did n't take the sarcastic view she clearly took the sympathetic, and that was what he had had, in all the long time, from no one whomsoever. What he felt was that he could n't at present have begun to tell her, and yet could profit perhaps exquisitely by the accident of having done so of old. "Please don't then. We're just right as it is."

"Oh I am," she laughed, "if you are!" To which she added: "Then you do still feel in the same way?"

It was impossible he should n't take to himself that she was really interested, though it all kept coming as perfect surprise. He had thought of himself so long as abominably alone, and lo he was n't alone a bit. He had n't been, it appeared, for an hour—since those moments on the Sorrento boat. It was *she* who had been, he seemed to see as he looked at her—she who had been made so by the graceless fact of his lapse of fidelity. To tell her what he had told her—what had it been but to ask something of her? something that she had given, in her charity, without his having, by a remembrance, by a return of the spirit, failing another encounter, so much as thanked her. What he had asked of her had been simply at first not to laugh at him. She had beautifully not done so for ten years, and she was not doing so now. So he had endless gratitude to make up. Only for that he must see just how he had figured to her. "What, exactly, was the account I gave?"

"Of the way you did feel? Well, it was very simple. You said you had had from your earliest time, as the deepest thing within you, the sense of being kept for something rare and strange, possibly prodigious and terrible, that was soon or later to happen to you, that you had in your bones the foreboding and the conviction of, and that would perhaps overwhelm you."

"Do you call that very simple?" John Marcher asked.

She thought a moment. "It was perhaps because I seemed, as you spoke, to understand it."

"You do understand it?" he eagerly asked.

Again she kept her kind eyes on him. "You still have the belief?"

"Oh!" he exclaimed helplessly. There was too much to say.

"Whatever it's to be," she clearly made out, "it has n't yet come."

He shook his head in complete surrender now. "It has n't yet come. Only, you know, it is n't anything I'm to *do,* to achieve in the world, to be distinguished or admired for. I'm not such an ass as *that.* It would be much better, no doubt, if I were."

"It's to be something you're merely to suffer?"

"Well, say to wait for—to have to meet, to face, to see suddenly break out in my life; possibly destroying all further consciousness, possibly annihilating me; possibly, on the other hand, only altering everything, striking at the root of all my world and leaving me to the consequences, however they shape themselves."

She took this in, but the light in her eye continued for him not to be that of mockery. "Is n't what you describe perhaps but the expectation—or at any rate the sense of danger, familiar to so many people—of falling in love?"

John Marcher wondered. "Did you ask me that before?"

"No—I was n't so free-and-easy then. But it's what strikes me now."

"Of course," he said after a moment, "it strikes you. Of course it strikes *me.* Of course what's in store for me may be no more than that. The only thing is," he went on, "that I think if it had been that I should by this time know."

"Do you mean because you've *been* in love?" And then as he but looked at her in silence: "You've been in love, and it has n't meant such a cataclysm, has n't proved the great affair?"

"Here I am, you see. It has n't been overwhelming."

"Then it has n't been love," said May Bartram.

"Well, I at least thought it was. I took it for that—I've taken it till now. It was agreeable, it was delightful, it was miserable," he explained. "But it was n't strange. It was n't what *my* affair's to be."

"You want something all to yourself—something that nobody else knows or *has* known?"

"It is n't a question of what I 'want'—God knows I don't want anything. It's only a question of the apprehension that haunts me—that I live with day by day."

He said this so lucidly and consistently that he could see it further impose itself. If she had n't been interested before she'd have been interested now. "Is it a sense of coming violence?"

Evidently now too again he liked to talk of it. "I don't think of it as—when it does come—necessarily violent. I only think of it as natural and as of course above all unmistakeable. I think of it simply as *the* thing. *The* thing will of itself appear natural."

"Then how will it appear strange?"

Marcher bethought himself. "It won't—to *me*."

"To whom then?"

"Well," he replied, smiling at last, "say to you."

"Oh then I'm to be present?"

"Why, you *are* present—since you know."

"I see." She turned it over. "But I mean at the catastrophe."[3]

At this, for a minute, their lightness gave way to their gravity; it was as if the long look they exchanged held them together. "It will only depend on yourself—if you'll watch with me."

"Are you afraid?" she asked.

"Don't leave me *now*," he went on.

"Are you afraid?" she repeated.

"Do you think me simply out of my mind?" he pursued instead of answering. "Do I merely strike you as a harmless lunatic?"

"No," said May Bartram. "I understand you. I believe you."

"You mean you feel how my obsession—poor old thing!—may correspond to some possible reality?"

"To some possible reality."

"Then you *will* watch with me?"

She hesitated, then for the third time put her question. "Are you afraid?"

"Did I tell you I was—at Naples?"

"No, you said nothing about it."

"Then I don't know. And I should *like* to know," said John Marcher. "You'll tell me yourself whether you think so. If you'll watch with me you'll see."

"Very good then." They had been moving by this time across the room, and at the door, before passing out, they paused as for the full wind-up of their understanding. "I'll watch with you," said May Bartram.

II

The fact that she "knew"—knew and yet neither chaffed him nor betrayed him—had in a short time begun to constitute between them a goodly bond, which became more marked when, within the year that followed their afternoon

---

[3]The final dramatic event in a play.

at Weatherend, the opportunities for meeting multiplied. The event that thus promoted these occasions was the death of the ancient lady her great-aunt, under whose wing, since losing her mother, she had to such an extent found shelter, and who, though but the widowed mother of the new successor to the property, had succeeded—thanks to a high tone and a high temper—in not forfeiting the supreme position at the great house. The deposition of this personage arrived but with her death, which, followed by many changes, made in particular a difference for the young woman in whom Marcher's expert attention had recognised from the first a dependent with a pride that might ache though it did n't bristle. Nothing for a long time had made him easier than the thought that the aching must have been much soothed by Miss Bartram's now finding herself able to set up a small home in London. She had acquired property, to an amount that made that luxury just possible, under her aunt's extremely complicated will, and when the whole matter began to be straightened out, which indeed took time, she let him know that the happy issue was at last in view. He had seen her again before that day, both because she had more than once accompanied the ancient lady to town and because he had paid another visit to the friends who so conveniently made of Weatherend one of the charms of their own hospitality. These friends had taken him back there; he had achieved there again with Miss Bartram some quiet detachment; and he had in London succeeded in persuading her to more than one brief absence from her aunt. They went together, on these latter occasions, to the National Gallery and the South Kensington Museum, where, among vivid reminders, they talked of Italy at large—not now attempting to recover, as at first, the taste of their youth and their ignorance. That recovery, the first day at Weatherend, had served its purpose well, had given them quite enough; so that they were, to Marcher's sense, no longer hovering about the headwaters of their stream, but had felt their boat pushed sharply off and down the current.

They were literally afloat together; for our gentleman this was marked, quite as marked as that the fortunate cause of it was just the buried treasure of her knowledge. He had with his own hands dug up this little hoard, brought to light—that is to within reach of the dim day constituted by their discretions and privacies—the object of value the hiding-place of which he had, after putting it into the ground himself, so strangely, so long forgotten. The rare luck of his having again just stumbled on the spot made him indifferent to any other question; he would doubtless have devoted more time to the odd accident of his lapse of memory if he had n't been moved to devote so much to the sweetness, the comfort, as he felt, for the future, that this accident itself had helped to keep fresh. It had never entered into his plan that any one should "know," and mainly for the reason that it was n't in him to tell any one. That would have been impossible, for nothing but the amusement of a cold world would have waited on it. Since, however, a mysterious fate had opened his mouth betimes, in spite of him, he would count that a compensation and profit by it to the utmost. That the right person *should* know tempered the asperity of his secret more even than his shyness had permitted him to imagine; and May Bartram was clearly right, because—well, because there she was. Her knowledge simply settled it; he would have been sure enough by this time had she been wrong. There was that in his situation, no doubt, that disposed him too much to see her as a mere confidant, taking all her light for him from the fact—the fact only—of her interest in his predicament; from her mercy, sympathy, seriousness, her consent not to regard him as the funniest of the funny. Aware, in fine, that her price for him was just in her giving him this constant sense of his being admirably spared, he was careful to remember that she had also a life of her own, with things that might happen to *her*, things that in friendship one should likewise take account of. Something fairly remarkable came to pass with him, for that matter, in this connexion—something represented by a certain passage of his consciousness, in the suddenest way, from one extreme to the other.

He had thought himself, so long as nobody knew, the most disinterested person in the world, carrying his concentrated burden, his perpetual suspense, ever so quietly, holding his tongue about it, giving others no glimpse of it nor of its effect upon his life, asking of them no allowance and only making on his side all those that were asked. He had n't disturbed people with the queerness of their having to know a haunted man, though he had had moments of rather special temptation on hearing them say they were forsooth "unsettled." If they were as unsettled as he was—he who had never been settled for an hour in his life—they would know what it meant. Yet it was n't, all the same, for him to make them, and he listened to them civilly enough. This was why he had such good—though possibly such rather colourless—manners; this was why, above all, he could regard himself, in a greedy world, as decently—as in fact perhaps even a little sublimely—unselfish. Our point is accordingly that he valued this character quite sufficiently to measure his present danger of letting it lapse, against which he promised himself to be much on his guard. He was quite ready, none the less, to be selfish just a little, since surely no more charming occasion for it had come to him. "Just a little," in a word, was just as much as Miss Bartram, taking one day with another, would let him. He never would be in the least coercive, and would keep well before him the lines on which consideration for her—the very highest—ought to proceed. He would thoroughly establish the heads under which her affairs, her requirements, her peculiarities—he went so far as to give them the latitude of that name—would come into their intercourse. All this naturally was a sign of how much he took the intercourse itself for granted. There was nothing more to be done about *that*. It simply existed; had sprung into being with her first penetrating question to him in the autumn light there at Weatherend. The real form it should have taken on the basis that stood out large was the form of their marrying. But the devil in this was that the very basis itself put marrying out of the question. His conviction, his apprehension, his obsession, in short, was n't a privilege he could invite a woman to share; and that consequence of it was precisely what was the matter with him. Something or other lay in wait for him, amid the twists and the turns of the months and the years, like a crouching beast in the jungle. It signified little whether the crouching beast were destined to slay him or to be slain. The definite point was the inevitable spring of the creature; and the definite lesson from that was that a man of feeling did n't cause himself to be accompanied by a lady on a tiger-hunt. Such was the image under which he had ended by figuring his life.

They had at first, none the less, in the scattered hours spent together, made no allusion to that view of it; which was a sign he was handsomely alert to give that he did n't expect, that he in fact did n't care, always to be talking about it. Such a feature in one's outlook was really like a hump on one's back. The difference it made every minute of the day existed quite independently of discussion. One discussed of course *like* a hunchback, for there was always, if nothing else, the hunchback face. That remained, and she was watching him; but people watched best, as a general thing, in silence, so that such would be predominantly the manner of their vigil. Yet he did n't want, at the same time, to be tense and solemn; tense and solemn was what he imagined he too much showed for with other people. The thing to be, with the one person who knew, was easy and natural—to make the reference rather than be seeming to avoid it, to avoid it rather than be seeming to make it, and to keep it, in any case, familiar, facetious even, rather than pedantic and portentous. Some such consideration as the latter was doubtless in his mind for instance when he wrote pleasantly to Miss Bartram that perhaps the great thing he had so long felt as in the lap of the gods was no more than this circumstance, which touched him so nearly, of her acquiring a house in London. It was the first allusion they had yet again made, needing any other hitherto so little; but when she replied, after having given him the news, that she was by no means satisfied with such a trifle as the climax to so special a suspense, she almost set him wondering if she had n't even a larger conception of singularity for him than he had for himself. He was at all events destined to become aware little by little, as time went by, that she was all the while looking at his life, judging it, measuring it, in the light of the thing she knew, which grew to be at last, with the consecration of the years, never mentioned between them save as "the real truth" about him. That had always been his own form of reference to it, but she adopted the form so quietly that, looking back at the end of a period, he knew there was no moment at which it was traceable that she had, as he might say, got inside his idea, or exchanged the attitude of beautifully indulging for that of still more beautifully believing him.

It was always open to him to accuse her of seeing him but as the most harmless of maniacs, and this, in the long run—since it covered so much ground—was his easiest description of their friendship. He had a screw loose for her, but she liked him in spite of it and was practically, against the rest of the world, his kind wise keeper, unremunerated but fairly amused and, in the absence of other near ties, not disreputably occupied. The rest of the world of course thought him queer, but she, she only, knew how, and above all why, queer; which was precisely what enabled her to dispose the concealing veil in the right folds. She took his gaiety from him—since it had to pass with them for gaiety—as she took everything else; but she certainly so far justified by her unerring touch his finer sense of the degree to which he had ended by convincing her. *She* at least never spoke of the secret of his life except as "the real truth about you," and she had in fact a wonderful way of making it seem, as such, the secret of her own life too. That was in fine how he so constantly felt her as allowing for him; he could n't on the whole call it anything else. He allowed for himself, but she, exactly, allowed still more; partly because, better placed for a sight of the matter, she traced his unhappy perversion through reaches of its course into which he could scarce follow it. He knew how he felt, but, besides knowing that, she knew how he *looked* as well; he knew each of the things of importance he was insidiously kept from doing, but she could add up the amount they made, understand how much, with a lighter weight on his spirit, he might have done, and thereby establish how, clever as he was, he fell short. Above all she was in the secret of the difference between the forms he went through—those of his little office under Government, those of caring for his modest patrimony, for his library, for his garden in the country, for the people in London whose invitations he accepted and repaid—and the detachment that reigned beneath them and that made of all behaviour, all that could in the least be called behaviour, a long act of dissimulation. What it had come to was that he wore a mask painted with the social simper, out of the eyeholes of which there looked eyes of an expression not in the least matching the other features. This the stupid world, even after years, had never more than half-discovered. It was only May Bartram who had, and she achieved, by an art indescribable, the feat of at once—or perhaps it was only alternately—meeting the eyes from in front and mingling her own vision, as from over his shoulder, with their peep through the apertures.

So while they grew older together she did watch with him, and so she let this association give shape and colour to her own existence. Beneath *her* forms as well detachment had learned to sit, and behaviour had become for her, in the social sense, a false account of herself. There was but one account of her that would have been true all the while and that she could give straight to nobody, least of all to John Marcher. Her whole attitude was a virtual statement, but the perception of that only seemed called to take its place for him as one of the many things necessarily crowded out of his consciousness. If she had moreover, like himself, to make sacrifices to their real truth, it was to be granted that her compensation might have affected her as more prompt and more natural. They had long periods, in this London time, during which, when they were together, a stranger might have listened to them without in the least pricking up his ears; on the other hand the real truth was equally liable at any moment to rise to the surface, and the auditor would then have wondered indeed what they were talking about. They had from an early hour made up their mind that society was, luckily, unintelligent, and the margin allowed them by this had fairly become one of their commonplaces. Yet there were still moments when the situation turned almost fresh—usually under the effect of some expression drawn from herself. Her expressions doubtless repeated themselves, but her intervals were generous. "What saves us, you know, is that we answer so completely to so usual an appearance: that of the man and woman whose friendship has become such a daily habit—or almost—as to be at last indispensable." That for instance was a remark she had frequently enough had occasion to make, though she had given it at different times different developments. What we are especially concerned with is the turn it happened to take from her one afternoon when he had come to see her in honour of her birthday. This anniversary had fallen on a Sunday, at a season of thick fog and general outward gloom; but he had brought her his customary offering, having known her now long enough to have established a hundred small traditions. It was one of his proofs to himself, the present he made her on her birthday, that he hadn't sunk into real selfishness. It was mostly nothing more than a small trinket, but it was always fine of its kind, and he was regularly careful to pay for it more than he thought he could afford. "Our habit saves you at least, don't you see? because it makes you, after all, for the vulgar, indistinguishable from other men. What's the most inveterate mark of men in general? Why the capacity to spend endless time with dull women—to spend it I won't say without being bored, but without minding that they are, without being driven off at a tangent by it; which comes to the same thing. I'm your dull woman, a part of the daily bread for which you pray at church. That covers your tracks more than anything."

"And what covers yours?" asked Marcher, whom his dull woman could mostly to this extent amuse. "I see of course what you mean by your saving me, in this way and that, so far as other people are concerned—I've seen it all along. Only what is it that saves *you*? I often think, you know, of that."

She looked as if she sometimes thought of that, too, but rather in a different way. "Where other people, you mean, are concerned?"

"Well, you're really so in with me, you know—as a sort of result of my being so in with yourself. I mean of my having such an immense regard for you, being so tremendously mindful of all you've done for me. I sometimes ask myself if it's quite fair. Fair I mean to have so involved and—since one may say it—interested you. I almost feel as if you hadn't really had time to do anything else."

"Anything else but be interested?" she asked. "Ah, what else does one ever want to be? If I've been 'watching' with you, as we long ago agreed I was to do, watching's always in itself an absorption."

"Oh certainly," John Marcher said, "if you had n't had your curiosity—! Only does n't it sometimes come to you as time goes on that your curiosity is n't being particularly repaid?"

May Bartram had a pause. "Do you ask that, by any chance, because you feel at all that yours is n't? I mean because you have to wait so long."

Oh he understood what she meant! "For the thing to happen that never does happen? For the beast to jump out? No, I'm just where I was about it. It is n't a matter as to which I can *choose*, I can decide for a change. It is n't one as to which there *can* be a change. It's in the lap of the gods. One 's in the hands of one's law—there one is. As to the form the law will take, the way it will operate, that's its own affair."

"Yes," Miss Bartram replied; "of course one's fate's coming, of course it *has* come in its own form and its own way, all the while. Only, you know, the form and the way in your case were to have been—well, something so exceptional and, as one may say, so particularly *your* own."

Something in this made him look at her with suspicion. "You say 'were to *have* been,' as if in your heart you had begun to doubt."

"Oh!" she vaguely protested.

"As if you believed," he went on, "that nothing will now take place."

She shook her head slowly but rather inscrutably. "You're far from my thought."

He continued to look at her. "What then is the matter with you?"

"Well," she said after another wait, "the matter with me is simply that I'm more sure than ever my curiosity, as you call it, will be but too well repaid."

They were frankly grave now; he had got up from his seat, had turned once more about the little drawing-room to which, year after year, he brought his inevitable topic; in which he had, as he might have said, tasted their intimate community with every sauce, where every object was as familiar to him as the things of his own house and the very carpets were worn with his fitful walk very much as the desks in old counting-houses are worn by the elbows of generations of clerks. The generations of his nervous moods had been at work there, and the place was the written history of his whole middle life. Under the impression of what his friend had just said he knew himself, for some reason, more aware of these things; which made him, after a moment, stop again before her. "Is it possibly that you've grown afraid?"

"Afraid?" He thought, as she repeated the word, that his question had made her, a little, change colour; so that, lest he should have touched on a truth, he explained very kindly: "You remember that that was what you asked *me* long ago—that first day at Weatherend."

"Oh yes, and you told me you did n't know—that I was to see for myself. We've said little about it since, even in so long a time."

"Precisely," Marcher interposed—"quite as if it were too delicate a matter for us to make free with. Quite as if we might find, on pressure, that I *am* afraid. For then," he said, "we should n't, should we? quite know what to do."

She had for the time no answer to this question. "There have been days when I thought you were. Only, of course," she added, "there have been days when we have thought almost anything."

"Everything. Oh!" Marcher softly groaned as with a gasp, half-spent, at the face, more uncovered just then than it had been for a long while, of the imagination always with them. It had always had its incalculable moments of glaring out, quite as with the very eyes of the very Beast, and used as he was to them, they could still draw from him the tribute of a sigh that rose from the depths of his being. All they had thought, first and last, rolled over him; the past seemed to have been reduced to mere barren speculation. This in fact was what the place had just struck him as so full of—the simplification of everything but the state of suspense. That remained only by seeming to hang in the void surrounding it. Even his original fear, if fear it had been, had lost itself in the desert. "I judge, however," he continued, "that you see I'm not afraid now."

"What I see, as I make it out, is that you've achieved something almost unprecedented in the way of getting used to danger. Living with it so long and so closely you've lost your sense of it; you know it's there, but you're indifferent, and you cease even, as of old, to have to whistle in the dark. Considering what the danger is," May Bartram wound up, "I'm bound to say I don't think your attitude could well be surpassed."

John Marcher faintly smiled. "It's heroic?"

"Certainly—call it that."

It was what he would have liked indeed to call it. "I *am* then a man of courage?"

"That's what you were to show me."

He still, however, wondered. "But does n't the man of courage know what he's afraid of—or *not* afraid of? I don't know *that,* you see. I don't focus it. I can't name it. I only know I'm exposed."

"Yes, but exposed—how shall I say?—so directly. So intimately. That's surely enough."

"Enough to make you feel then—as what we may call the end and the upshot of our watch—that I'm not afraid?"

"You're not afraid. But it is n't," she said, "the end of our watch. That is it is n't the end of yours. You've everything still to see."

"Then why have n't *you?*" he asked. He had had, all along, today, the sense of her keeping something back, and he still had it. As this was his first impression of that it quite made a date. The case was the more marked as she did n't at first answer; which in turn made him go on. "You know something I don't." Then his voice, for that of a man of courage, trembled a little. "You know what's to happen." Her silence, with the face she showed, was almost a confession—it made him sure. "You know, and you're afraid to tell me. It's so bad that you're afraid I'll find out."

All this might be true, for she did look as if, unexpectedly to her, he had crossed some mystic line that she had secretly drawn round her. Yet she might, after all, not have worried; and the real climax was that he himself, at all events, need n't. "You'll never find out."

III

It was all to have made, none the less, as I have said, a date; which came out in the fact that again and again, even after long intervals, other things that passed between them wore in relation to this hour but the character of recalls and results. Its immediate effect had been indeed rather to lighten insistence—almost to provoke a reaction; as if their topic had dropped by its own weight and as if moreover, for that matter, Marcher had been visited by one of his occasional warnings against egotism. He had kept up, he felt, and very decently on the whole, his consciousness of the importance of not being selfish, and it was true that he had never sinned in that direction without promptly enough trying to press the scales the other way. He often repaired his fault, the season permitting, by inviting his friend to accompany him to the opera; and it not infrequently thus happened that, to show he did n't wish her to have but one sort of food for her mind, he was the cause of her appearing there with him a dozen nights in the month. It even happened that, seeing her home at such times, he occasionally went in with her to finish, as he called it, the evening, and, the better to make his point, sat down to the frugal but always careful little supper that awaited his pleasure. His point was made, he thought, by his not eternally insisting with her on himself; made for instance, at such hours, when it befell that, her piano at hand and each of them familiar with it, they went over passages of the opera together. It chanced to be on one of these occasions, however, that he reminded her of her not having answered a certain question he had put to her during the talk that had taken place between them on her last birthday. "What is it that saves *you?*"—saved her, he meant, from that appearance of variation from the usual human type. If he had practically escaped remark, as she pretended, by doing, in the most important particular, what most men do—find the answer to life in patching up in alliance of a sort with a woman no better than himself—how had she escaped it, and how could the alliance, such as it was, since they must suppose it had been more or less noticed, have failed to make her rather positively talked about?

"I never said," May Bartram replied, "that it had n't made me a good deal talked about."

"Ah well then you're not 'saved.'"

"It has n't been a question for me. If you've had your woman I've had," she said, "my man."

"And you mean that makes you all right?"

Oh it was always as if there were so much to say! "I don't know why it should n't make me—humanly, which is what we're speaking of—as right as it makes you."

"I see," Marcher returned. "'Humanly,' no doubt, as showing that you're living for something. Not, that is, just for me and my secret."

May Bartram smiled. "I don't pretend it exactly shows that I'm not living for you. It's my intimacy with you that's in question."

He laughed as he saw what she meant. "Yes, but since, as you say, I'm only, so far as people make out, ordinary, you're—are n't you?—no more than ordinary either. You help me to pass for a man like another. So if I *am*, as I understand you, you're not compromised. Is that it?"

She had another of her waits, but she spoke clearly enough. "That's it. It's all that concerns me—to help you to pass for a man like another."

He was careful to acknowledge the remark handsomely. "How kind, how beautiful, you are to me! How shall I ever repay you?"

She had her last grave pause, as if there might be a choice of ways. But she chose. "By going on as you are."

It was into this going on as he was that they relapsed, and really for so long a time that the day inevitably came for a further sounding of their depths. These depths, constantly bridged over by a structure firm enough in spite of its lightness and of its occasional oscillation in the somewhat vertiginous air, invited on occasion, in the interest of their nerves, a dropping of the plummet and a measurement of the abyss. A difference had been made moreover, once for all, by the fact that she had all the while not appeared to feel the need of rebutting his charge of an idea within her that she did n't dare to express—a charge uttered just before one of the fullest of their later discussions ended. It had come up for him then that she "knew" something and that what she knew was bad—too bad to tell him. When he had spoken of it as visibly so bad that she was afraid he might find it out, her reply had left the matter too equivocal to be let alone and yet, for Marcher's special sensibility, almost too formidable again to touch. He circled about it at a distance that alternately narrowed and widened and that still was n't much affected by the consciousness in him that there was nothing she could "know," after all, any better than he did. She had no source of knowledge he had n't equally—except of course that she might have finer nerves. That was what women had where they were interested; they made out things, where people were concerned, that the people often could n't have made out for themselves. Their nerves, their sensibility, their imagination, were conductors and revealers, and the beauty of May Bartram was in particular that she had given herself so to his case. He felt in these days what, oddly enough, he had never felt before, the growth of a dread of losing her by some catastrophe—some catastrophe that yet would n't all be *the* catastrophe: partly because she had almost of a sudden begun to strike him as more useful to him than ever yet, and partly by reason of an appearance of uncertainty in her health, coincident and equally new. It was characteristic of the inner detachment he had hitherto so successfully cultivated and to which our whole account of him is a reference, it was characteristic that his complications, such as they were, had never yet seemed so as at this crisis to thicken about him, even to the point of making him ask himself if he were, by any chance, of a truth, within sight or sound, within touch or reach, within the immediate jurisdiction, of the thing that waited.

When the day came, as come it had to, that his friend confessed to him her fear of a deep disorder in her blood, he felt somehow the shadow of a change and the chill of a shock. He immediately began to imagine aggravations and disasters, and above all to think of her peril as the direct menace for himself of personal privation. This indeed gave him one of those partial recoveries of equanimity that were agreeable to him—it showed him that what was still first in his mind was the loss she herself might suffer. "What if she should have to die before knowing, before seeing—?" It would have been brutal, in the early stages of her trouble, to put that question to her; but it had immediately sounded for him to his own concern, and the possibility was what most made him sorry for her. If she did "know," moreover, in the sense of her having had some—what should he think?—mystical irresistible light, this would make the matter not better, but worse, inasmuch as her original adoption of his own curiosity had quite become the basis of her life. She had been living to see what would *be* to be seen, and it would quite lacerate her to have to give up before the accomplishment of the vision. These reflexions, as I say, quickened his generosity; yet, make them as he might, he saw himself, with the lapse of the period, more and more disconcerted. It lapsed for him with a strange steady sweep, and the oddest oddity was that it gave him, independently of the threat of much inconvenience, almost the only positive suprise his career, if career it could be called, had yet offered him. She kept the house as she had never done; he had to go to her to see her—she could meet him nowhere now, though there was scarce a corner of their loved old London in which she had n't in the past, at one time or another, done so; and he found her always seated by her fire in the deep old-fashioned chair she was less and less able to leave. He had been struck one day, after an absence exceeding his usual measure, with her suddenly looking much older to him than he had ever thought of her being; then he recognized that the suddenness was all on his side—he had just simply and suddenly noticed. She looked older because inevitably, after so many years, she *was* old, or almost; which was of course true in still greater measure of her companion. If she was old, or almost, John Marcher assuredly was, and yet it was her showing of the lesson, not his own, that brought the truth home to him. His surprises began here; when once they had begun they multiplied; they came rather with a rush; it was as if, in the oddest way in the world, they had all been kept back, sown in a thick cluster, for the late afternoon of life, the time at which for people in general the unexpected has died out.

One of them was that he should have caught himself—for he *had* so done— *really* wondering if the great accident would take form now as nothing more than his being condemned to see this charming woman, this admirable friend, pass away from him. He had never so unreservedly qualified her as while confronted in thought with such a possibility; in spite of which there was small doubt for him that as an answer to his long riddle the mere effacement of even so fine a feature of his situation would be an abject anticlimax. It would represent, as connected with his past attitude, a drop of dignity under the shadow of which his existence could only become the most grotesque of failures. He had been far from holding it a failure—long as he had waited for the appearance that was to make it a success. He had waited for quite another thing, not for such a thing as that. The breath of his good faith came short, however, as he recognised how long he had waited, or how long at least his companion had. That she, at all events, might be recorded as having waited in vain—this affected him sharply, and all the more because of his at first having done little more than amuse himself with the idea. It grew more grave as the gravity of her condition grew, and the state of mind it produced in him, which he himself ended by watching as if it had been some definite disfigurement of his outer person, may pass for another of his surprises. This conjoined itself still with another, the really stupefying consciousness of a question that he would have allowed to shape itself had he dared. What did everything mean—what, that is, did *she* mean, she and her vain waiting and her probable death and the soundless admonition of it all—unless that, at this time of day, it was simply, it was overwhelmingly too late? He had never at any stage of his queer consciousness admitted the whisper of such a correction; he had never till within these last few months been so false to his conviction as not to hold that what was to come to him had time, whether *he* struck himself as having it or not. That at last, at last, he certainly had n't it, to speak of, or had it but in the scantiest measure—such, soon enough, as things went with him, became the inference with which his old obsession had to reckon: and this it was not helped to do by the more and more confirmed appearance that the great vagueness casting the long shadow in which he had lived had, to attest itself, almost no margin left. Since it was in Time that he was to have met his fate, so it was in Time that his fate was to have acted; and as he waked up to the sense of no longer being young, which was exactly the sense of being stale, just as that, in turn, was the sense of being weak, he waked up to another matter beside. It all hung together; they were subject, he and the great vagueness, to an equal and indivisible law. When the possibilities themselves had accordingly turned stale, when the secret of the gods had grown faint, had perhaps even quite evaporated, that, and that only, was failure. It would n't have been failure to be bankrupt, dishonoured, pilloried, hanged; it was failure not to be anything. And so, in the dark valley into which his path had taken its unlooked-for twist, he wondered not a little as he groped. He did n't care what awful crash might

overtake him, with what ignominy or what monstrosity he might yet be associated—since he was n't after all too utterly old to suffer—if it would only be
decently proportionate to the posture he had kept, all his life, in the threatened
presence of it. He had but one desire left—that he should n't have been "sold."

IV

Then it was that, one afternoon, while the spring of the year was young and
new she met all in her own way his frankest betrayal of these alarms. He had
gone in late to see her, but evening had n't settled and she was presented to him
in that long fresh light of waning April days which affects us often with a sadness
sharper than the greyest hours of autumn. The week had been warm, the spring
was supposed to have begun early, and May Bartram sat, for the first time in
the year, without a fire; a fact that, to Marcher's sense, gave the scene of which
she formed part a smooth and ultimate look, an air of knowing, in its immaculate
order and cold meaningless cheer, that it would never see a fire again. Her own
aspect—he could scarce have said why—intensified this note. Almost as white
as wax, with the marks and signs in her face as numerous and as fine as if they
had been etched by a needle, with soft white draperies relieved by a faded green
scarf on the delicate tone of which the years had further refined, she was the
picture of a serene and exquisite but impenetrable sphinx, whose head, or
indeed all whose person, might have been powdered with silver. She was a
sphinx, yet with her white petals and green fronds she might have been a lily
too—only an artificial lily, wonderfully imitated and constantly kept, without
dust or stain, though not exempt from a slight droop and a complexity of faint
creases, under some clear glass bell. The perfection of household care, of high
polish and finish, always reigned in her rooms, but they now looked most as if
everything had been wound up, tucked in, put away, so that she might sit with
folded hands and with nothing more to do. She was "out of it," to Marcher's
vision; her work was over; she communicated with him as across some gulf or
from some island of rest that she had already reached, and it made him feel
strangely abandoned. Was it—or rather was n't it—that if for so long she had
been watching with him the answer to their question must have swum into her
ken and taken on its name, so that her occupation was verily gone? He had as
much as charged her with this in saying to her, many months before, that she
even then knew something she was keeping from him. It was a point he had
never since ventured to press, vaguely fearing as he did that it might become a
difference, perhaps a disagreement, between them. He had in this later time
turned nervous, which was what he in all the other years had never been; and
the oddity was that his nervousness should have waited till he had begun to
doubt, should have held off so long as he was sure. There was something, it
seemed to him, that the wrong word would bring down on his head, something
that would so at least ease off his tension. But he wanted not to speak the wrong
word; that would make everything ugly. He wanted the knowledge he lacked
to drop on him, if drop it could, by its own august weight. If she was to forsake
him it was surely for her to take leave. This was why he did n't directly ask her
again what she knew; but it was also why, approaching the matter from another
side, he said to her in the course of his visit: "What do you regard as the very
worst that at this time of day *can* happen to me?"

He had asked her that in the past often enough; they had, with the odd
irregular rhythm of their intensities and avoidances, exchanged ideas about it

and then had seen the ideas washed away by cool intervals, washed like figures traced in sea-sand. It had ever been the mark of their talk that the oldest allusions in it required but a little dismissal and reaction to come out again, sounding for the hour as new. She could thus at present meet his enquiry quite freshly and patiently. "Oh yes, I've repeatedly thought, only it always seemed to me of old that I could n't quite make up my mind. I thought of dreadful things, between which it was difficult to choose; and so must you have done."

"Rather! I feel now as if I had scarce done anything else. I appear to myself to have spent my life in thinking of nothing *but* dreadful things. A great many of them I've at different times named to you, but there were others I could n't name."

"They were too, too dreadful?"

"Too, too dreadful—some of them."

She looked at him a minute, and there came to him as he met it an inconsequent sense that her eyes, when one got their full clearness, were still as beautiful as they had been in youth, only beautiful with a strange cold light—a light that somehow was a part of the effect, if it was n't rather a part of the cause, of the pale hard sweetness of the season and the hour. "And yet," she said at last, "there are horrors we've mentioned."

It deepened the strangeness to see her, as such a figure in such a picture, talk of "horrors," but she was to do in a few minutes something stranger yet—though even of this he was to take the full measure but afterwards—and the note of it already trembled. It was, for the matter of that, one of the signs that her eyes were having again the high flicker of their prime. He had to admit, however, what she said. "Oh yes, there were times when we did go far." He caught himself in the act of speaking as if it all were over. Well, he wished it were; and the consummation depended for him clearly more and more on his friend.

But she had now a soft smile. "Oh far—!"

It was oddly ironic. "Do you mean you're prepared to go further?"

She was frail and ancient and charming as she continued to look at him, yet it was rather as if she had lost the thread. "Do you consider that we went far?"

"Why I thought it the point you were just making—that we *had* looked most things in the face."

"Including each other?" She still smiled. "But you're quite right. We've had together great imaginations, often great fears; but some of them have been unspoken."

"Then the worst—we have n't faced that. I *could* face it, I believe, if I knew what you think it. I feel," he explained, "as if I had lost my power to conceive such things." And he wondered if he looked as blank as he sounded. "It's spent."

"Then why do you assume," she asked, "that mine is n't?"

"Because you've given me signs to the contrary. It is n't a question for you of conceiving, imagining, comparing. It is n't a question now of choosing." At last he came out with it." "You know something I don't. You've shown me that before."

These last words had affected her, he made out in a moment, exceedingly, and she spoke with firmness. "I've shown you, my dear, nothing."

He shook his head. "You can't hide it."

"Oh, oh!" May Bartram sounded over what she could n't hide. It was almost a smothered groan.

"You admitted it months ago, when I spoke of it to you as of something you were afraid I should find out. Your answer was that I could n't, that I would n't, and I don't pretend I have. But you had something therefore in mind, and

I now see how it must have been, how it still is, the possibility that, of all possibilities, has settled itself for you as the worst. This," he went on, "is why I appeal to you. I'm only afraid of ignorance to-day—I'm not afraid of knowledge." And then as for a while she said nothing: "What makes me sure is that I see in your face and feel here, in the air and amid these appearances, that you're out of it. You've done. You've had your experience. You leave me to my fate."

Well, she listened, motionless and white in her chair, as on a decision to be made, so that her manner was fairly an avowal, though still, with a small fine inner stiffness, an imperfect surrender. "It *would* be the worst," she finally let herself say. "I mean the thing I've never said."

It hushed him a moment. "More monstrous than all the monstrosities we've named?"

"More monstrous. Is n't that what you sufficiently express," she asked, "in calling it the worst?"

Marcher thought. "Assuredly—if you mean, as I do, something that includes all the loss and all the shame that are thinkable."

"It would if it *should* happen," said May Bartram. "What we're speaking of, remember, is only my idea."

"It's your belief," Marcher returned. "That's enough for me. I feel your beliefs are right. Therefore if, having this one, you give me no more light on it, you abandon me."

"No, no!" she repeated. "I'm with you—don't you see?—still." And as to make it more vivid to him she rose from her chair—a movement she seldom risked in these days—and showed herself, all draped and all soft, in her fairness and slimness. "I have n't forsaken you."

It was really, in its effort against weakness, a generous assurance, and had the success of the impulse not, happily, been great, it would have touched him to pain more than to pleasure. But the cold charm in her eyes had spread, as she hovered before him, to all the rest of her person, so that it was for the minute almost a recovery of youth. He could n't pity her for that; he could only take her as she showed—as capable even yet of helping him. It was as if, at the same time, her light might at any instant go out; wherefore he must make the most of it. There passed before him with intensity the three or four things he wanted most to know; but the question that came of itself to his lips really covered the others. "Then tell me if I shall consciously suffer."

She promptly shook her head. "Never!"

It confirmed the authority he imputed to her, and it produced on him an extraordinary effect. "Well, what's better than that? Do you call that the worst?"

"You think nothing is better?" she asked.

She seemed to mean something so special that he again sharply wondered, though still with the dawn of a prospect of relief. "Why not, if one does n't *know*?" After which, as their eyes, over his question, met in a silence, the dawn deepened and something to his purpose came prodigiously out of her very face. His own, as he took it in, suddenly flushed to the forehead, and he gasped with the force of a perception to which, on the instant, everything fitted. The sound of his gasp filled the air; then he became articulate. "I see—if I don't suffer!"

In her own look, however, was doubt. "You see what?"

"Why what you mean—what you've always meant."

She again shook her head. "What I mean is n't what I've always meant. It's different."

"It's something new?"

She hung back from it a little. "Something new. It's not what you think. I see what you think."

His divination drew breath then; only her correction might be wrong. "It is n't that I *am* a blockhead?" he asked between faintness and grimness. "It is n't that it's all a mistake?"

"A mistake?" she pityingly echoed. *That* possibility, for her, he saw, would be monstrous; and if she guaranteed him the immunity from pain it would accordingly not be what she had in mind. "Oh no," she declared; "It's nothing of that sort. You've been right."

Yet he could n't help asking himself if she were n't, thus pressed, speaking but to save him. It seemed to him he should be most in a hole if his history should prove all a platitude. "Are you telling me the truth, so that I shan't have been a bigger idiot that I can bear to know? I *have n't* lived with a vain imagination, in the most besotted illusion? I have n't waited but to see the door shut in my face?"

She shook her head again. "However the case stands *that* is n't the truth. Whatever the reality, it *is* a reality. The door is n't shut. The door's open," said May Bartram.

"Then something's to come?"

She waited once again, always with her cold sweet eyes on him. "It's never too late." She had, with her gliding step, diminished the distance between them, and she stood nearer to him, close to him, a minute, as if still charged with the unspoken. Her movement might have been for some finer emphasis of what she was at once hesitating and deciding to say. He had been standing by the chimney-piece, fireless and sparely adorned, a small perfect old French clock and two morsels of rosy Dresden constituting all its furniture; and her hand grasped the shelf while she kept him waiting, grasped it a little as for support and encouragement. She only kept him waiting, however; that is he only waited. It had become suddenly, from her movement and attitude, beautiful and vivid to him that she had something more to give him; her wasted face delicately shone with it—it glittered almost as with the white lustre of silver in her expression. She was right, incontestably, for what he saw in her face was the truth, and strangely, without consequence, while their talk of it as dreadful was still in the air, she appeared to present it as inordinately soft. This, prompting bewilderment, made him but gape the more gratefully for her revelation, so that they continued for some minutes silent, her face shining at him, her contact imponderably pressing, and his stare all kind but all expectant. The end, none the less, was that what he had expected failed to come to him. Something else took place instead, which seemed to consist at first in the mere closing of her eyes. She gave way at the same instant to a slow fine shudder, and though he remained staring—though he stared in fact but the harder—turned off and regained her chair. It was the end of what she had been intending, but it left him thinking only of that.

"Well, you don't say—?"

She had touched in her passage a bell near the chimney and had sunk back strangely pale. "I'm afraid I'm too ill."

"Too ill to tell me?" It sprang up sharp to him, and almost to his lips, the fear she might die without giving him light. He checked himself in time from so expressing his question, but she answered as if she had heard the words.

"Don't you know—now?"

" 'Now'—?" She had spoken as if some difference had been made within the moment. But her maid, quickly obedient to her bell, was already with them. "I know nothing." And he was afterwards to say to himself that he must have spoken with odious impatience, such an impatience as to show that, supremely disconcerted, he washed his hands of the whole question.

"Oh!" said May Bartram.

"Are you in pain?" he asked as the woman went to her.

"No," said May Bartram.

Her maid, who had put an arm round her as if to take her to her room, fixed on him eyes that appealingly contradicted her; in spite of which, however, he showed once more his mystification. "What then has happened?"

She was once more, with her companion's help, on her feet, and, feeling withdrawal imposed on him, he had blankly found his hat and gloves and had reached the door. Yet he waited for her answer. "What *was* to," she said.

V

He came back the next day, but she was then unable to see him, and as it was literally the first time this had occurred in the long stretch of their acquaintance he turned away, defeated and sore, almost angry—or feeling at least that such a break in their custom was really the beginning of the end—and wandered alone with his thoughts, especially with the one he was least able to keep down. She was dying and he would lose her; she was dying and his life would end. He stopped in the Park, into which he had passed, and stared before him at his recurrent doubt. Away from her the doubt pressed again; in her presence he had believed her, but as he felt his forlornness he threw himself into the explanation that, nearest at hand, had most of a miserable warmth for him and least of a cold torment. She had deceived him to save him—to put him off with something in which he should be able to rest. What could the thing that was to happen to him be, after all, but just this thing that had begun to happen? Her dying, her death, his consequent solitude—*that* was what he had figured as the Beast in the Jungle, that was what had been in the lap of the gods. He had had her word for it as he left her—what else on earth could she have meant? It was n't a thing of a monstrous order; not a fate rare and distinguished; not a stroke of fortune that overwhelmed and immortalised; it had only the stamp of the common doom. But poor Marcher at this hour judged the common doom sufficient. It would serve his turn, and even as the consummation of infinite waiting he would bend his pride to accept it. He sat down on a bench in the twilight. He had n't been a fool. Something had *been*, as she had said, to come. Before he rose indeed it had quite struck him that the final fact really matched with the long avenue through which he had had to reach it. As sharing his suspense and as giving herself all, giving her life, to bring it to an end, she had come with him every step of the way. He had lived by her aid, and to leave her behind would be cruelly, damnably to miss her. What could be more overwhelming than that?

Well, he was to know within the week, for though she kept him a while at bay, left him restless and wretched during a series of days on each of which he asked about her only again to have to turn away, she ended his trial by receiving him where she had always received him. Yet she had been brought out at some hazard into the presence of so many of the things that were, consciously, vainly, half their past, and there was scant service left in the gentleness of her mere desire, all too visible, to check his obsession and wind up his long trouble. That was clearly what she wanted, the one thing more for her own peace while she could still put out her hand. He was so affected by her state that, once seated by her chair, he was moved to let everything go; it was she herself therefore who brought him back, took up again, before she dismissed him, her last word of the other time. She showed how she wished to leave their business in order. "I'm not sure you understood. You've nothing to wait for more. It *has* come."

Oh how he looked at her! "Really?"

"Really."

"The thing that, as you said, *was* to?"

"The thing that we began in our youth to watch for."

Face to face with her once more he believed her; it was a claim to which he had so abjectly little to oppose. "You mean that it has come as a positive definite occurrence, with a name and a date?"

"Positive. Definite. I don't know about the 'name,' but oh with a date!"

He found himself again too helplessly at sea. "But come in the night—come and passed me by?"

May Bartram had her strange faint smile. "Oh no, it has n't passed you by!"

"But if I have n't been aware of it and it has n't touched me—?"

"Ah your not being aware of it"—and she seemed to hesitate an instant to deal with this—"your not being aware of it is the strangeness *in* the strangeness. It's the wonder *of* the wonder." She spoke as with the softness almost of a sick child, yet now at last, at the end of all, with the perfect straightness of a sibyl. She visibly knew that she knew, and the effect on him was of something coordinate, in its high character, with the law that had ruled him. It was the true voice of the law; so on her lips would the law itself have sounded. "It *has* touched you," she went on. "It has done its office. It has made you all its own."

"So utterly without my knowing it?"

"So utterly without your knowing it." His hand, as he leaned to her, was on the arm of her chair, and, dimly smiling always now, she placed her own on it. "It's enough if *I* know it."

"Oh!" he confusedly breathed, as she herself of late so often had done.

"What I long ago said is true. You'll never know now, and I think you ought to be content. You've *had* it," said May Bartram.

"But had what?"

"Why what was to have marked you out. The proof of your law. It has acted. I'm too glad," she then bravely added, "to have been able to see what it's *not.*"

He continued to attach his eyes to her, and with the sense that it was all beyond him, and that *she* was too, he would still have sharply challenged her had n't he so felt it an abuse of her weakness to do more than take devoutly what she gave him, take it hushed as to a revelation. If he did speak, it was out of the foreknowledge of his loneliness to come. "If you're glad of what it's 'not' it might then have been worse?"

She turned her eyes away, she looked straight before her; with which after a moment: "Well, you know our fears."

He wondered. "It's something then we never feared?"

On this slowly she turned to him. "Did we ever dream, with all our dreams, that we should sit and talk of it thus?"

He tried for a little to make out that they had; but it was as if their dreams, numberless enough, were in solution in some thick cold mist through which thought lost itself. "It might have been that we could n't talk?"

"Well"—she did her best for him—"not from this side. This, you see," she said, "is the *other* side."

"I think," poor Marcher returned, "that all sides are the same to me." Then, however, as she gently shook her head in correction: "We might n't, as it were, have got across—?"

"To where we are—no. We're *here*"—she made her weak emphasis.

"And much good does it do us!" was her friend's frank comment.

"It does us the good it can. It does us the good that *it* is n't here. It's past. It's behind," said May Bartram. "Before—" but her voice dropped.

He had got up, not to tire her, but it was hard to combat his yearning. She after all told him nothing but that his light had failed—which he knew well enough without her. "Before—?" he blankly echoed.

"Before, you see, it was always to *come*. That kept it present."

"Oh I don't care what comes now! Besides," Marcher added, "it seems to me I liked it better present, as you say, than I can like it absent with *your* absence."

"Oh mine!"—and her pale hands made light of it.

"With the absence of everything." He had a dreadful sense of standing there before her for—so far as anything but this proved, this bottomless drop was concerned—the last time of their life. It rested on him with a weight he felt he could scarce bear, and this weight it apparently was that still pressed out what remained in him of speakable protest. "I believe you; but I can't begin to pretend I understand. *Nothing,* for me, is past; nothing *will* pass till I pass myself, which I pray my stars may be as soon as possible. Say, however," he added, "that I've eaten my cake, as you contend, to the last crumb—how can the thing I've never felt at all be the thing I was marked out to feel?"

She met him perhaps less directly, but she met him unperturbed. "You take your 'feelings' for granted. You were to suffer your fate. That was not necessarily to know it."

"How in the world—when what is such knowledge but suffering?"

She looked up at him a while in silence. "No—you don't understand."

"I suffer," said John Marcher.

"Don't, don't!"

"How can I help at least *that?*"

"*Don't!*" May Bartram repeated.

She spoke it in a tone so special, in spite of her weakness, that he stared an instant—stared as if some light, hitherto hidden, had shimmered across his vision. Darkness again closed over it, but the gleam had already become for him an idea. "Because I have n't the right—?"

"Don't *know*—when you need n't," she mercifully urged. "You need n't—for we should n't."

"Should n't?" If he could but know what she meant!

"No—it's too much."

"Too much?" he still asked but, with a mystification that was the next moment of a sudden to give way. Her words, if they meant something, affected him in this light—the light also of her wasted face—as meaning *all,* and the sense of what knowledge had been for herself came over him with a rush which broke through into a question. "Is it of that then you're dying?"

She but watched him, gravely at first, as to see, with this, where he was, and she might have seen something or feared something that moved her sympathy. "I would live for you still—if I could." Her eyes closed a little, as if, withdrawn into herself, she were for a last time trying. "But I can't!" she said as she raised them again to take leave of him.

She could n't indeed, as but too promptly and sharply appeared, and he had no vision of her after this that was anything but darkness and doom. They had parted for ever in that strange talk; access to her chamber of pain, rigidly guarded, was almost wholly forbidden him; he was feeling now moreover, in the face of doctors, nurses, the two or three relatives attracted doubtless by the presumption of what she had to "leave," how few were the rights, as they were called in such cases, that he had to put forward, and how odd it might even seem that their intimacy should n't have given him more of them. The stupidest fourth cousin had more, even though she had been nothing in such a person's life. She had been a feature of features in *his,* for what else was it to have been so indispensable? Strange beyond saying were the ways of existence, baffling for him the anomaly of his lack, as he felt it to be, of producible claim. A woman might have been, as it were, everything to him, and it might yet present him in no connexion that any one seemed held to recognise. If this was the case in these closing weeks it was the case more sharply on the occasion of the last offices rendered, in the great grey London cemetery, to what had been mortal, to what had been precious, in his friend. The concourse at her grave was not numerous, but he saw himself treated as scarce more nearly concerned with it than if there had been a thousand others. He was in short from this moment face to face with the fact that he was to profit extraordinarily little by the interest May Bartram had taken in him. He could n't quite have said what he expected, but he had n't surely expected this approach to a double privation. Not only had her interest failed him, but he seemed to feel himself unattended—and for a reason he could n't seize—by the distinction, the dignity, the propriety, if nothing else, of the man markedly bereaved. It was as if in the view of society he had not *been* markedly bereaved, as if there still failed some sign or proof of it, and as if none the less his character could never be affirmed nor the deficiency ever made up. There were moments as the weeks went by when he would have liked, by some almost aggressive act, to take his stand on the intimacy of his loss, in order that it *might* be questioned and his retort, to the relief of his spirit, so recorded; but the moments of an irritation more helpless followed fast on these, the moments during which, turning things over with a good conscience but with a bare horizon, he found himself wondering if he ought n't to have begun, so to speak, further back.

He found himself wondering indeed at many things, and this last speculation had others to keep it company. What could he have done, after all, in her lifetime, without giving them both, as it were, away? He could n't have made known she was watching him, for that would have published the superstition of the Beast. This was what closed his mouth now—now that the Jungle had been threshed to vacancy and that the Beast had stolen away. It sounded too foolish and too flat; the difference for him in this particular, the extinction in his life of the element of suspense, was such as in fact to surprise him. He could scarce have said what the effect resembled; the abrupt cessation, the positive prohibition, of music perhaps, more than anything else, in some place all adjusted and all accustomed to sonority and to attention. If he could at any rate have conceived lifting the veil from his image at some moment of the past (what had he done, after all, if not lift it to *her?*) so to do this to-day to talk to people at large of the Jungle cleared and confide to them that he now felt it as safe, would have been not only to see them listen as to a goodwife's tale, but really to hear himself tell one. What it presently came to in truth was that poor Marcher waded through his beaten grass, where no life stirred, where no breath sounded, where no evil eye seemed to gleam from a possible lair, very much as if vaguely looking for the Beast, and still more as if acutely missing it. He walked about in existence that had grown strangely more spacious, and, stopping fitfully in places where the undergrowth of life struck him as closer, asked himself yearningly, wondered secretly and sorely, if it would have lurked here or there. It would have at all events *sprung;* what was at least complete was his belief in the truth itself of the assurance given him. The change from his old sense to his new was absolute and final: what was to happen *had* so absolutely and finally happened that he was as little able to know a fear for his future as to know a hope; so absent in short was any question of anything still to come. He was to live entirely with the other question, that of his unidentified past, that of his having to see his fortune impenetrably muffled and masked.

The torment of this vision then his occupation; he could n't perhaps have consented to live but for the possibility of guessing. She had told him, his friend, not to guess; she had forbidden him, so far as he might, to know, and she had even in a sort denied the power in him to learn: which were so many things, precisely, to deprive him of rest. It was n't that he wanted, he argued for fairness, that anything past and done should repeat itself; it was only that he should n't as an anticlimax, have been taken sleeping so sound as not to be able to win back by an effort of thought the lost stuff of consciousness. He declared to himself at moments that he would either win it back or have done with consciousness for ever; he made this idea his one motive in fine, made it so much his passion that none other, to compare with it, seemed ever to have touched him. The lost stuff of consciousness became thus for him as a strayed or stolen child to an unappeasable father; he hunted it up and down very much as if he were knocking at doors and enquiring of the police. This was the spirit in which, inevitably, he set himself to travel; he started on a journey that was to be as long as he could make it; it danced before him that, as the other side of the globe could n't possibly have less to say to him, it might, by a possibility of suggestion, have more. Before he quitted London, however, he made a pilgrimage to May Bartram's grave, took his way to it through the endless avenues of the grim suburban metropolis, sought it out in the wilderness of tombs, and, though he had come but for the renewal of the act of farewell, found himself, when he had at last stood by it, beguiled into long intensities. He stood for an hour, powerless to turn away and yet powerless to penetrate the darkness of death; fixing with his eyes her inscribed name and date, beating his forehead against the fact of the secret they kept, drawing his breath, while he waited, as if some sense would in pity of him rise from the stones. He kneeled on the stones, however, in vain; they kept what they concealed; and if the face of the tomb did become a face for him it was because her two names became a pair of eyes that did n't know him. He gave them a last long look, but no palest light broke.

VI

He stayed away, after this, for a year; he visited the depths of Asia, spending himself on scenes of romantic interest, of superlative sanctity; but what was present to him everywhere was that for a man who had known what *he* had known the world was vulgar and vain. The state of mind in which he had lived for so many years shone out to him, in reflexion, as a light that coloured and refined, a light beside which the glow of the East was garish, cheap and thin. The terrible truth was that he had lost—with everything else—a distinction as well; the things he saw could n't help being common when he had become common to look at them. He was simply now one of them himself—he was in the dust, without a peg for the sense of difference; and there were hours when, before the temples of gods and the sepulchres of kings, his spirit turned for nobleness of association to the barely discriminated slab in the London suburb. That had become for him, and more intensely with time and distance, his one witness of a past glory. It was all that was left to him for proof or pride, yet the past glories of Pharaohs were nothing to him as he thought of it. Small wonder then that he came back to it on the morrow of his return. He was drawn there this time as irresistibly as the other, yet with a confidence, almost, that was doubtless the effect of the many months that had elapsed. He had lived, in spite of himself, into his change of feeling, and in wandering over the earth had wandered, as might be said, from the circumference to the centre of his desert. He had settled to his safety and accepted perforce his extinction; figuring to himself, with some colour, in the likeness of certain little old men he remembered to have seen, of whom, all meagre and wizened as they might look, it was related that they had in their time fought twenty duels or been loved by ten princesses. They indeed had been wondrous for others while he was but wondrous for himself; which, however, was exactly the cause of his haste to renew the wonder by getting back, as he might put it, into his own presence. That had quickened his steps and checked his delay. If his visit was prompt it was because he had been separated so long from the part of himself that alone he now valued.

It's accordingly not false to say that he reached his goal with a certain elation and stood there again with a certain assurance. The creature beneath the sod *knew* of his rare experience, so that, strangely now, the place had lost for him its mere blankness of expression. It met him in mildness—not, as before, in mockery; it wore for him the air of conscious greeting that we find, after absence, in things that have closely belonged to us and which seem to confess of themselves to the connexion. The plot of ground, the graven tablet, the tended flowers affected him so as belonging to him that he resembled for the hour a contented landlord reviewing a piece of property. Whatever had happened—well, had happened. He had not come back this time with the vanity of that question, his former worrying. "What, *what?*" now practically so spent. Yet he would none the less never again so cut himself off from the spot; he would come back to it every month, for if he did nothing else by its aid he at least held up his head. It thus grew for him, in the oddest way, a positive resource; he carried out his idea of periodical returns, which took their place at last among the most inveterate of his habits. What it all amounted to, oddly enough, was that in his finally so simplified world this garden of death gave him the few square feet of earth on which he could still most live. It was as if, being nothing anywhere else for any one, nothing even for himself, he were just everything here, and if not for a crowd of witnesses or indeed for any witness but John Marcher, then by clear right of the register that he could scan like an open page. The open page was the tomb of his friend, and *there* were the facts of the past, there the truth of his life, there the backward reaches in which he could lose himself. He did this from time to time with such effect that he seemed to wander through the old years with his hand in the arm of a companion who was, in the most extraordinary manner, his other, his younger self; and to wander, which was more extraordinary yet, round and round a third presence—not wandering she, but stationary, still whose eyes, turning with his revolution, never ceased to follow him, and whose seat was his point, so to speak, of orientation. Thus in short he settled to live—feeding all on the sense that he once *had* lived, and dependent on it not alone for a support but for an identity.

It sufficed him in its way for months and the year elapsed; it would doubtless even have carried him further but for an accident, superficially slight, which moved him, quite in another direction, with a force beyond any of his impressions of Egypt or of India. It was a thing of the merest chance—the turn, as he afterwards felt, of a hair, though he was indeed to live to believe that if light had n't come to him in this particular fashion it would still have come in another. He was to live to believe this, I say, though he was not to live, I may not less definitely mention, to do much else. We allow him at any rate the benefit of the conviction, struggling up for him at the end, that, whatever might have happened or not happened, he would have come round of himself to the light. The incident of an autumn day had put the match to the train laid from of old by his misery. With the light before him he knew that even of late his ache had only been smothered. It was strangely drugged, but it throbbed; at the touch it began to bleed. And the touch, in the event, was the face of a fellow mortal. This face, one grey afternoon when the leaves were thick in the alleys, looked into Marcher's own, at the cemetery, with an expression like the cut of a blade. He felt it, that is, so deep down that he winced at the steady thrust. The person who so mutely assaulted him was a figure he had noticed, on reaching his own goal, absorbed by a grave a short distance away, a grave apparently fresh, so that the emotion of the visitor would probably match it for frankness. This fact alone forbade further attention, though during the time he stayed he remained vaguely conscious of his neighbour, a middle-aged man apparently, in mourning whose bowed back, among the clustered monuments and mortuary yews, was constantly presented. Marcher's theory that these were elements in contact with which he himself revived, had suffered, on this occasion, it may be granted, a marked, an excessive check. The autumn day was dire for him as none had recently been, and he rested with a heaviness he had not yet known on the low stone table that bore May Bartram's name. He rested without power to move, as if some spring in him, some spell vouchsafed, had suddenly been broken for ever. If he could have done that moment as he wanted he would simply have stretched himself on the slab that was ready to take him, treating it as a place prepared to receive his last sleep. What in all the wide world had he now to keep awake for? He stared before him with the question, and it was then that, as one of the cemetery walks passed near him, he caught the shock of the face.

His neighbour at the other grave had withdrawn, as he himself, with force enough in him, would have done by now, and was advancing along the path on his way to one of the gates. This brought him close, and his pace was slow, so that—and all the more as there was a kind of hunger in his look—the two men were for a minute directly confronted. Marcher knew him at once for one of the deeply stricken—a perception so sharp that nothing else in the picture comparatively lived, neither his dress, his age, nor his presumable character and class; nothing lived but the deep ravage of the features he showed. He *showed* them—that was the point; he was moved, as he passed, by some impulse that was either a signal for sympathy or, more possibly, a challenge to an opposed sorrow. He might already have been aware of our friend, might at some previous hour have noticed in him the smooth habit of the scene, with which the state of his own senses so scantly consorted, and might thereby have been stirred as by an overt discord. What Marcher was at all events conscious of was in the first place that the image of scarred passion presented to him was conscious too—of something that profaned the air; and in the second that, roused, startled, shocked, he was yet the next moment looking after it, as it went, with envy. The most extraordinary thing that had happened to him—though he had given that name to other matters as well—took place, after his immediate vague stare, as a consequence of this impression. The stranger passed, but the raw glare of his grief remained, making our friend wonder in pity what wrong, what wound it expressed, that injury not to be healed. What had the man *had*, to make him by the loss of it so bleed and yet live?

Something—and this reached him with a pang—that *he*, John Marcher, had n't; the proof of which was precisely John Marcher's arid end. No passion had ever touched him, for this was what passion meant; he had survived and maundered and pined, but where had been *his* deep ravage? The extraordinary thing we speak of was the sudden rush of the result of this question. The sight that had just met his eyes named to him, as in letters of quick flame, something he had utterly, insanely missed, and what he had missed made these things a train of fire, made them mark themselves in an anguish of inward throbs. He had seen *outside* of his life, not learned it within, the way a woman was mourned when she had been loved for herself: such was the force of his conviction of the meaning of the stranger's face, which still flared for him as a smoky torch. It had n't come to him, the knowledge, on the wings of experience; it had brushed him, jostled him, upset him, with the disrespect of chance, the insolence of accident. Now that the illumination had begun, however, it blazed to the zenith, and what he presently stood there gazing at was the sounded void of his life. He gazed, he drew breath, in pain; he turned in his dismay, and, turning, he had before him in sharper incision than ever the open page of his story. The name on the table smote him as the passage of his neighbour had done, and what it said to him, full in the face, was the *she* was what he had missed. This was the awful thought, the answer to all the past, the vision at the dread clearness of which he grew as cold as the stone beneath him. Everything fell together, confessed, explained, overwhelmed; leaving him most of all stupefied at the blindness he had cherished. The fate he had been marked for he had met with a vengeance—he had emptied the cup to the lees; he had been the man of his time, *the* man, to whom nothing on earth was to have happened. That was the rare stroke—that was his visitation. So he saw it, as we say, in pale horror, while the pieces fitted and fitted. So *she* had seen it while he didn't, and so she served at this hour to drive the truth home. It was the truth, vivid and monstrous, that all the while he had waited the wait was itself his portion. This the companion of his vigil had at a given moment made out, and she had then offered him the chance to baffle his doom. One's doom, however, was never baffled, and on the day she told him his own had come down she had seen him but stupidly stare at the escape she offered him.

The escape would have been to love her; then, *then* he would have lived. *She* had lived—who could say now with what passion?—since she had loved him for himself; whereas he had never thought of her (ah how it hugely glared at him!) but in the chill of his egotism and the light of her use. Her spoken words came back to him—the chain stretched and stretched. The Beast had lurked indeed, and the Beast, at its hour, had sprung; it had sprung in that twilight of the cold April when, pale, ill, wasted, but all beautiful, and perhaps even then recoverable, she had risen from her chair to stand before him, and let him imaginably guess. It had sprung as he did n't guess; it had sprung as she hopelessly turned from him, and the mark, by the time he left her, had fallen where it *was* to fall. He had justified his fear and achieved his fate; he had failed, with the last exactitude, of all he was to fail of; and a moan now rose to his lips as he remembered she had prayed he might n't know. This horror of waking—*this* was knowledge, knowledge under the breath of which the very tears in his eyes seemed to freeze. Through them, none the less, he tried to fix it and hold it; he kept it there before him so that he might feel the pain. That at least, belated and bitter, had something of the taste of life. But the bitterness suddenly sickened him, and it was as if, horribly, he saw, in the truth, in the cruelty of his image, what had been appointed and done. He saw the Jungle of his life and saw the lurking Beast; then, while he looked, perceived it, as by a stir of the air, rise, huge and hideous, for the leap that was to settle him. His eyes darkened—it was close; and, instinctively turning, in his hallucination, to avoid it, he flung himself, face down, on the tomb.

1902   1903, 1909

THE JOLLY CORNER

I

"Every one asks me what I 'think' of everything," said Spencer Brydon; "and I make answer as I can—begging or dodging the question, putting them off with any nonsense. It would n't matter to any of them really," he went on, "for, even were it possible to meet in that stand-and-deliver[1] way so silly a demand on so big a subject, my 'thoughts' would still be almost altogether about something that concerns only myself." He was talking to Miss Staverton, with whom for a couple of months now he had availed himself of every possible occasion to talk; this disposition and this resource, this comfort and support, as the situation in fact presented itself, having promptly enough taken the first place in the considerable array of rather unattenuated surprises attending his so strangely belated return to America. Everything was somehow a surprise; and that might be natural when one had so long and so consistently neglected everything, taken pains to give surprises so much margin for play. He had given them more than thirty years—thirty-three, to be exact; and they now seemed to him to have organised their performance quite on the scale of that licence. He had been twenty-three on leaving New York—he was fifty-six to-day: unless indeed he were to reckon as he had sometimes, since his repatriation, found himself feeling; in which case he would have lived longer than is often allotted to man. It would have taken a century, he repeatedly said to himself, and said also to Alice Staverton, it would have taken a longer absence and a more averted mind than those even of which he had been guilty, to pile up the differences, the newnesses, the queernesses, above all the bignesses, for the better or the worse, that at present assaulted his vision wherever he looked.

The great fact all the while however had been the incalculability; since he *had* supposed himself, from decade to decade, to be allowing, and in the most liberal and intelligent manner, for brilliancy of change. He actually saw that he had allowed for nothing; he missed what he would have been sure of finding, he found what he would never have imagined. Proportions and values were upside-down; the ugly things he had expected, the ugly things of his faraway youth, when he had too promptly waked up to a sense of the ugly—these uncanny phenomena place him rather, as it happened, under the charm; whereas the "swagger" things, the modern, the monstrous, the famous things, those he had more particularly, like thousands of ingenuous enquirers every year, come over to see, were exactly his sources of dismay. They were as so many set traps for

[1] Boldly defiant.

displeasure, above all for reaction, of which his restless tread was constantly pressing the spring. It was interesting, doubtless, the whole show, but it would have been too disconcerting had n't a certain finer truth saved the situation. He had distinctly not, in this steadier light, come over *all* for the monstrosities; he had come, not only in the last analysis but quite on the face of the act, under an impulse with which they had nothing to do. He had come—putting the thing pompously—to look at his "property," which he had thus for a third of a century not been within four thousand miles of; or, expressing it less sordidly, he had yielded to the humour of seeing again his house on the jolly corner, as he usually, and quite fondly, described it—the one in which he had first seen the light, in which various members of his family had lived and had died, in which the holidays of his overschooled boyhood had been passed and the few social flowers of his chilled adolescence gathered, and which, alienated then for so long a period, had, through the successive deaths of his two brothers and the termination of old arrangements, come wholly into his hands. He was the owner of another, not quite so "good"—the jolly corner having been, from far back, superlatively extended and consecrated; and the value of the pair represented his main capital, with an income consisting, in these later years, of their respective rents which (thanks precisely to their original excellent type) had never been depressingly low. He could live in "Europe," as he had been in the habit of living, on the product of these flourishing New York leases, and all the better since, that of the second structure, the mere number in its long row, having within a twelvemonth fallen in,[2] renovation at a high advance[3] had proved beautifully possible.

These were items of property indeed, but he had found himself since his arrival distinguishing more than ever between them. The house within the street, two bristling blocks westward, was already in course of reconstruction as a tall mass of flats; he had acceded, some time before, to overtures for this conversion—in which, now that it was going forward, it had been not the least of his astonishments to find himself able, on the spot, and though without a previous ounce of such experience, to participate with a certain intelligence, almost with a certain authority. He had lived his life with his back so turned to such concerns and his face addressed to those of so different an order that he scarce knew what to make of this lively stir, in a compartment of his mind never yet penetrated, of a capacity for business and a sense for construction. These virtues, so common all round him now, had been dormant in his own organism—where it might be said of them perhaps that they had slept the sleep of the just. At present, in the splendid autumn weather—the autumn at least was a pure boon in the terrible place—he loafed about his "work" undeterred, secretly agitated; not in the least "minding" that the whole proposition, as they said, was vulgar and sordid, and ready to climb ladders, to walk the plank, to handle materials and look wise about them, to ask questions, in fine, and challenge explanations and really "go into" figures.

It amused, it verily quite charmed him; and, by the same stroke, it amused, and even more, Alice Staverton, though perhaps charming her perceptibly less. She was n't however, going to be better-off for it, as *he* was—and so astonishingly much: nothing was now likely, he knew, ever to make her better-off than she found herself, in the afternoon of life, as the delicately frugal possessor and tenant of the small house in Irving Place[4] to which she had subtly managed to cling through her almost unbroken New York career. If he

[2]Expired.   [3]Rent increase.
[4]A fashionable street in New York City.

knew the way to it now better than to any other address among the dreadful multiplied numberings which seemed to him to reduce the whole place to some vast ledger-page, overgrown, fantastic, of ruled and criss-crossed lines and figures—if he had formed, for his consolation, that habit, it was really not a little because of the charm of his having encountered and recognised, in the vast wilderness of the wholesale, breaking through the mere gross generalis-ation of wealth and force and success, a small still scene where items and shades, all delicate things, kept the sharpness of the notes of a high voice perfectly trained, and where economy hung about like the scent of a garden. His old friend lived with one maid and herself dusted her relics and trimmed her lamps and polished her silver; she stood off, in the awful modern crush, when she could, but she sallied forth and did battle when the challenge was really to "spirit," the spirit she after all confessed to, proudly and a little shyly, as to that of the better time, that of *their* common, their quite far-away and antediluvian social period and order. She made use of the street-cars when need be, the terrible things that people scrambled for as the panic-stricken at sea scramble for the boats; she affronted, inscrutably, under stress, all the public concussions and ordeals; and yet, with that slim mystifying grace of her appearance, which defied you to say if she were a fair young woman who looked older through trouble, or a fine smooth older one who looked young through successful indifference; with her precious reference, above all, to memories and histories into which he could enter, she was as exquisite for him as some pale pressed flower (a rarity to begin with), and, failing other sweet-ness, she was a sufficient reward of his effort. They had communities of knowl-edge, "their" knowledge (this discriminating possessive was always on her lips) of presences of the other age, presences all overlaid, in his case, by the expe-rience of a man and the freedom of a wanderer, overlaid by pleasure, by infidelity, by passages of life that were strange and dim to her, just by "Europe" in short, but still unobscured, still exposed and cherished, under the pious visitation of the spirit from which she had never been diverted.

She had come with him one day to see how his "apartment-house" was rising; he had helped her over gaps and explained to her plans, and while they were there had happened to have, before her, a brief but lively discussion with the man in charge, the representative of the building-firm that had undertaken his work. He had found himself quite "standing-up" to this personage over a failure on the latter's part to observe some detail of one of the noted conditions, and had so lucidly argued his case that, besides ever so prettily flushing, at the time, for sympathy in his triumph, she had afterwards said to him (though to a slightly greater effort of irony) that he had clearly for too many years neglected a real gift. If he had but stayed at home he would have anticipated the inventor of the sky-scraper. If he had but stayed at home he would have discovered his genius in time really to start some new variety of awful architectural hare and run it till it burrowed in a gold-mine. He was to remember these words, while the weeks elapsed, for the small silver ring they had sounded over the queerest and deepest of his own lately most disguised and most muffled vibrations.

It had begun to be present to him after the first fortnight, it had broken out with the oddest abruptness, this particular wanton wonderment: it met him there—and this was the image under which he himself judged the matter, or at least, not a little, thrilled and flushed with it—very much as he might have been met by some strange figure, some unexpected occupant, at a turn of one of the dim passages of an empty house. The quaint analogy quite hauntingly remained with him, when he did n't indeed rather improve it by a still intenser form: that of his opening a door behind which he would have made sure of finding nothing, a door into a room shuttered and void, and yet so coming, with a great suppressed start, on some quite erect confronting presence, something planted in the middle of the place and facing him through the dusk. After that visit to the house in construction he walked with his companion to see the other and always so much the better one, which in the eastward direction formed one of the corners, the "jolly" one precisely, of the street now so generally dishonoured and disfigured in its westward reaches, and of the comparatively conservative Avenue. The Avenue still had pretensions, as Miss Staverton said, to decency; the old people had mostly gone, the old names were unknown, and here and there an old association seemed to stray, all vaguely, like some very aged person, out too late, whom you might meet and feel the impulse to watch or follow, in kindness, for safe restoration to shelter.

They went in together, our friends; he admitted himself with his key, as he kept no one there, he explained, preferring, for his reasons, to leave the place empty, under a simple arrangement with a good woman living in the neighbourhood and who came for a daily hour to open windows and dust and sweep. Spencer Brydon had his reasons and was growingly aware of them; they seemed to him better each time he was there, though he did n't name them all to his companion, any more than he told her as yet how often, how quite absurdly often, he himself came. He only let her see for the present, while they walked through the great blank rooms, that absolute vacancy reigned and that, from top to bottom, there was nothing but Mrs. Muldoon's broomstick, in a corner, to tempt the burglar. Mrs. Muldoon was then on the premises, and she loquaciously attended the visitors, preceding them from room to room and pushing back shutters and throwing up sashes—all to show them, as she remarked, how little there was to see. There was little indeed to see in the great gaunt shell where the main dispositions and the general apportionment of space, the style of an age of ampler allowances, had nevertheless for its master their honest pleading message, affecting him as some good old servant's, some lifelong retainer's appeal for a character,[5] or even for a retiring-pension; yet it was also a remark of Mrs. Muldoon's that, glad as she was to oblige him by her noonday round, there was a request she greatly hoped he would never make of her. If he should wish her for any reason to come in after dark she would just tell him, if he "plased," that he must ask it of somebody else.

The fact that there was nothing to see did n't militate for the worthy woman against what one *might* see, and she put it frankly to Miss Staverton that no lady could be expected to like, could she? "craping up to thim top storeys in the ayvil hours." The gas and the electric light were off the house, and she fairly evoked a gruesome vision of her march through the great grey rooms—so many of them as there were too!—with her glimmering taper. Miss Staverton met her honest glare with a smile and the profession that she herself certainly would recoil from such an adventure. Spencer Brydon meanwhile held his peace—for the moment; the question of the "evil" hours in his old home had already become too grave for him. He had begun some time since to "crape," and he knew just why a packet of candles addressed to that pursuit had been stowed by his own hand, three weeks before, at the back of a drawer of the fine old sideboard that occupied, as a "fixture," the deep recess in the dining-room. Just now he laughed at his companions—quickly however changing the subject; for the reason that, in the first place, his laugh struck him even at that moment as starting the odd

[5] A letter of recommendation, a character reference.

echo, the conscious human resonance (he scarce knew how to qualify it) that sounds made while he was there alone sent back to his ear or his fancy; and that, in the second, he imagined Alice Staverton for the instant on the point of asking him, with a divination, if he ever so prowled. There were divinations he was unprepared for, and he had at all events averted enquiry by the time Mrs. Muldoon had left them, passing on to other parts.

There was happily enough to say, on so consecrated a spot, that could be said freely and fairly; so that a whole train of declarations was precipitated by his friend's having herself broken out, after a yearning look round: "But I hope you don't mean they want you to pull *this* to pieces!" His answer came, promptly, with his reawakened wrath; it was of course exactly what they wanted, and what they were "at" him for, daily, with the iteration of people who could n't for their life understand a man's liability to decent feelings. He had found the place, just as it stood and beyond what he could express, an interest and a joy. There were values other than the beastly rent-values, and in short, in short—! But it was thus Miss Staverton took him up. "In short you're to make so good a thing of your sky-scraper that, living in luxury on *those* ill-gotten gains, you can afford for a while to be sentimental here!" Her smile had for him, with the words, the particular mild irony with which he found half her talk suffused; an irony without bitterness and that came, exactly, from her having so much imagination—not, like the cheap sarcasms with which one heard most people, about the world of "society," bid for the reputation of cleverness, from nobody's really having any. It was agreeable to him at this very moment to be sure that when he had answered, after a brief demur, "Well yes; so, precisely, you may put it!" her imagination would still do him justice. He explained that even if never a dollar were to come to him from the other house he would nevertheless cherish this one; and he dwelt, further, while they lingered and wandered, on the fact of the stupefaction he was already exciting, the positive mystification he felt himself create.

He spoke of the value of all he read into it, into the mere sight of the walls, mere shapes of the old rooms, mere sound of the floors, mere feel, in his hand, of the old silver-plated knobs of the several mahogany doors, which suggested the pressure of the palms of the dead; the seventy years of the past in fine that these things represented, the annals of nearly three generations, counting his grandfather's, the one that had ended there, and the impalpable ashes of his long-extinct youth, afloat in the very air like microscopic motes. She listened to everything; she was a woman who answered intimately but who utterly did n't chatter. She scattered abroad therefore no cloud of words; she could assent, she could agree, above all she could encourage, without doing that. Only at the last she went a little further than he had done himself. "And then how do you know? You may still, after all, want to live here." It rather indeed pulled him up, for it was n't what he had been thinking, at least in her sense of the words. "You mean I may decide to stay on for the sake of it?"

"Well, *with* such a home—!" But, quite beautifully, she had too much tact to dot so monstrous an *i*, and it was precisely an illustration of the way she did n't rattle. How could any one—of any wit—insist on any one else's "wanting" to live in New York?

"Oh," he said, "I *might* have lived here (since I had my opportunity early in life); I might have put in here all these years. Then everything would have been different enough—and, I dare say, 'funny' enough. But that's another matter. And then the beauty of it—I mean of my perversity, of my refusal to agree to a 'deal'—is just in the total absence of a reason. Don't you see that if I had a reason about the matter at all it would *have* to be the other way, and would then be inevitably a reason of dollars? There are no reasons here *but* of dollars. Let us therefore have none whatever—not the ghost of one."

They were back in the hall then for departure, but from where they stood the vista was large, through an open door, into the great square main saloon, with its almost antique felicity of brave spaces between windows. Her eyes came back from that reach and met his own a moment. "Are you very sure the 'ghost' of one does n't, much rather, serve—?"

He had a positive sense of turning pale. But it was as near as they were then to come. For he made answer, he believed, between a glare and a grin; "Oh ghosts—of course the place must swarm with them! I should be ashamed of it if it did n't. Poor Mrs. Muldoon's right, and it's why I have n't asked her to do more than look in."

Miss Staverton's gaze again lost itself, and things she did n't utter, it was clear, came and went in her mind. She might even for the minute, off there in the fine room, have imagined some element dimly gathering. Simplified like the deathmask of a handsome face, it perhaps produced for her just then an effect akin to the stir of an expression in the "set" commemorative plaster. Yet whatever her impression may have been she produced instead a vague platitude. "Well, if it were only furnished and lived in—!"

She appeared to imply that in case of its being still furnished he might have been a little less opposed to the idea of a return. But she passed straight into the vestibule, as if to leave her words behind her, and the next moment he had opened the house-door and was standing with her on the steps. He closed the door and, while he re-pocketed his key, looking up and down, they took in the comparatively harsh actuality of the Avenue, which reminded him of the assault of the outer light of the Desert on the traveller emerging from an Egyptian tomb. But he risked before they stepped into the street his gathered answer to her speech. "For me it *is* lived in. For me it *is* furnished." At which it was easy for her to sigh "Ah yes—!" all vaguely and discreetly; since his parents and his favourite sister, to say nothing of other kin, in numbers, had run their course and met their end there. That represented, within the walls, ineffaceable life.

It was a few days after this that, during an hour passed with her again, he had expressed his impatience of the too flattering curiosity—among the people he met—about his appreciation of New York. He had arrived at none at all that was socially producible, and as for that matter of his "thinking" (thinking the better or the worse of anything there) he was wholly taken up with one subject of thought. It was mere vain egoism, and it was moreover, if she liked, a morbid obsession. He found all things come back to the question of what he personally might have been, how he might have led his life and "turned out," if he had not so, at the outset, given it up. And confessing for the first time to the intensity within him of this absurd speculation—which but proved also, no doubt, the habit of too selfishly thinking—he affirmed the impotence there of any other source of interest, any other native appeal. "What would it have made of me, what would it have made of me? I keep for ever wondering, all idiotically; as if I could possibly know! I see what it has made of dozens of others, those I meet, and it positively aches within me, to the point of exasperation, that it would have made something of me as well. Only I can't make out *what*, and the worry of it, the small rage of curiosity never to be satisfied, brings back what I remember to have felt, once or twice, after judging best, for reasons, to burn some important letter unopened. I've been sorry, I've hated it—I've never known what was in the letter. You may of course say it's a trifle—!"

"I don't say it's a trifle," Miss Staverton gravely interrupted.

She was seated by her fire, and before her, on his feet and restless, he turned to and fro between this intensity of his idea and a fitful and unseeing inspection, through his single eye-glass, of the dear little old objects on her chimney-piece. Her interruption made him for an instant look at her harder. "I should n't care if you did!" he laughed, however; "and it's only a figure, at any rate, for the way I now feel. *Not* to have followed my perverse young course—and almost in the teeth of my father's curse, as I may say; not to have kept it up, so, 'over there,' from that day to this, without a doubt or a pang; not, above all, to have liked it, to have loved it, so much, loved it, no doubt, with such an abysmal conceit of my own preference: some variation from *that,* I say, must have produced some different effect for my life and for my 'form.' I should have stuck here—if it had been possible; and I was too young, at twenty-three, to judge, *pour deux sous,*[6] whether it *were* possible. If I had waited I might have seen it was, and then I might have been, by staying here, something nearer to one of these types who have been hammered so hard and made so keen by their conditions. It is n't that I admire them so much—the question of any charm in them, or of any charm, beyond that of the rank money-passion, exerted by their conditions *for* them, has nothing to do with the matter: it's only a question of what fantastic, yet perfectly possible, development of my own nature I may n't have missed. It comes over me that I had then a strange *alter ego* deep down somewhere within me, as the full-blown flower is the small tight bud, and that I just took the course, I just transferred him to the climate, that blighted him for once and for ever."

"And you wonder about the flower," Miss Staverton said. "So do I, if you want to know; and so I've been wondering these several weeks. I believe in the flower," she continued, "I feel it would have been quite splendid, quite huge and monstrous."

"Monstrous above all!" her visitor echoed; "and I imagine, by the same stroke, quite hideous and offensive."

"You don't believe that," she returned; "if you did you would n't wonder. You'd know, and that would be enough for you. What you feel—and what I feel *for* you—is that you'd have had power."

"You'd have liked me that way?" he asked.

She barely hung fire. "How should I not have liked you?"

"I see. You'd have liked me, have preferred me, a billionaire!"

"How should I not have liked you?" she simply again asked.

He stood before her still—her question kept him motionless. He took it in, so much there was of it; and indeed his not otherwise meeting it testified to that. "I know at least what I am," he simply went on; "the other side of the medal's clear enough. I've not been edifying—I believe I'm thought in a hundred quarters to have been barely decent. I've followed strange paths and worshipped strange gods; it must have come to you again and again—in fact you've admitted to me as much—that I was leading, at any time these thirty years, a selfish frivolous scandalous life. And you see what it has made of me."

She just waited, smiling at him. "You see what it has made of *me.*"

"Oh you're a person whom nothing can have altered. You were born to be what you are, anywhere, anyway: you've the perfection nothing else could have blighted. And don't you see how, without my exile, I should n't have been waiting till now—?" But he pulled up for the strange pang.

"The great thing to see," she presently said, "seems to me to be that it has

[6]French: "two-cents worth."

spoiled nothing. It has n't spoiled your being here at last. It has n't spoiled this.
It has n't spoiled your speaking—" She also however faltered.

He wondered at everything her controlled emotion might mean. "Do you
believe then—too dreadfully!—that I *am* as good as I might ever have been?"

"Oh no! Far from it!" With which she got up from her chair and was nearer
to him. "But I don't care," she smiled.

"You mean I'm good enough?"

She considered a little. "Will you believe it if I say so? I mean will you let that
settle your question for you?" And then as if making out in his face that he drew
back from this, that he had some idea which, however absurd, he could n't yet
bargain away: "Oh you don't care either—but very differently: you don't care
for anything but yourself."

Spencer Brydon recognised it—it was in fact what he had absolutely professed.
Yet he importantly qualified. "*He* is n't myself. He's the just so totally other
person. But I do want to see him," he added. "And I can. And I shall."

Their eyes met for a minute while he guessed from something in hers that
she divined his strange sense. But neither of them otherwise expressed it, and
her apparent understanding, with no protesting shock, no easy derision, touched
him more deeply than anything yet, constituting for his stifled perversity, on
the spot, an element that was like breathable air. What she said however was
unexpected. "Well, *I've* seen him."

"You—?"

"I've seen him in a dream."

"Oh, a 'dream'—!" It let him down.

"But twice over," she continued. "I saw him as I see you now."

"You've dreamed the same dream—?"

"Twice over," she repeated. "The very same."

This did somehow a little speak to him, as it also gratified him. "You dream
about me at that rate?"

"Ah about *him!*" she smiled.

His eyes again sounded her. "Then you know all about him." And as she said
nothing more: "What's the wretch like?"

She hesitated, and it was as if he were pressing her so hard that, resisting for
reasons of her own, she had to turn away. "I'll tell you some other time!"

II

It was after this that there was most of a virtue for him, most of a cultivated
charm, most of a preposterous secret thrill, in the particular form of surrender
to his obsession and of address to what he more and more believed to be his
privilege. It was what in these weeks he was living for—since he really felt life
to begin but after Mrs. Muldoon had retired from the scene and, visiting the
ample house from attic to cellar, making sure he was alone, he knew himself in
a safe possession and, as he tacitly expressed it, let himself go. He sometimes
came twice in the twenty-four hours; the moments he liked best were those of
gathering dusk, of the short autumn twilight; this was the time of which, again
and again, he found himself hoping most. Then he could, as seemed to him,
most intimately wander and wait, linger and listen, feel his fine attention, never
in his life before so fine, on the pulse of the great vague place: he preferred the
lampless hour and only wished he might have prolonged each day the deep
crepuscular spell. Later—rarely much before midnight, but then for a consid-

erable vigil—he watched with his glimmering light; moving slowly, holding it high, playing it far, rejoicing above all, as much as he might, in open vistas, reaches of communication between rooms and by passages; the long straight chance or show, as he would have called it, for the revelation he pretended to invite. It was a practice he found he could perfectly "work" without exciting remark; no one was in the least the wiser for it; even Alice Staverton, who was moreover a well of discretion, did n't quite fully imagine.

He let himself in and let himself out with the assurance of calm proprietorship; and accident so far favoured him that, if a fat Avenue "Officer"[1] had happened on occasion to see him entering at eleven-thirty, he had never yet, to the best of his belief, been noticed as emerging at two. He walked there on the crisp November nights, arrived regularly at the evening's end; it was as easy to do this after dining out as to take his way to a club or to his hotel. When he left his club, if he had n't been dining out, it was ostensibly to go to his hotel; and when he left his hotel, if he had spent a part of the evening there, it was ostensibly to go to his club. Everything was easy in fine; everything conspired and promoted: there was truly even in the strain of his experience something that glossed over, something that salved and simplified, all the rest of consciousness. He circulated, talked, renewed, loosely and pleasantly, old relations—met indeed, so far as he could, new expectations and seemed to make out on the whole that in spite of the career, of such different contacts, which he had spoken of to Miss Staverton as ministering so little, for those who might have watched it, to edification, he was positively rather liked than not. He was a dim secondary social success— and all with people who had truly not an idea of him. It was all mere surface sound, this murmur of their welcome, this popping of their corks—just as his gestures of response were the extravagant shadows, emphatic in proportion as they meant little, of some game of *ombres chinoises*.[2] He projected himself all day, in thought, straight over the bristling line of hard unconscious heads and into the other, the real, the waiting life; the life that, as soon as he had heard behind him the click of his great house-door, began for him, on the jolly corner, as beguilingly as the slow opening bars of some rich music follows the tap of the conductor's wand.

He always caught the first effect of the steel point of his stick on the old marble of the hall pavement, large black-and-white squares that he remembered as the admiration of his childhood and that had then made in him, as he now saw, for the growth of an early conception of style. This effect was the dim reverberating tinkle as of some far-off bell hung who should say where?—in the depths of the house, of the past, of that mystical other world that might have flourished for him had he not, for weal or woe, abandoned it. On this impression he did ever the same thing; he put his stick noiselessly away in a corner—feeling the place once more in the likeness of some great glass bowl, all precious concave crystal, set delicately humming by the play of a moist finger round its edge. The concave crystal held, as it were, this mystical other world, and the indescribably fine murmur of its rim was the sigh there, the scarce audible pathetic wail to his strained ear, of all the old baffled forsworn possibilities. What he did therefore by this appeal of his hushed presence was to wake them into such measure of ghostly life as they might still enjoy. They were shy, all but unappeasably shy, but they were n't really sinister; as least they were n't as he had hitherto felt them—before they had taken the Form he so yearned to make them take, the

---

[1]Policeman.

[2]French: Chinese shadows; a play or show in which the actors' shadows are projected onto a screen before an audience.

Form he at moments saw himself in the light of fairly hunting on tiptoe, the points of his evening-shoes, from room to room and from storey to storey.

That was the essence of his vision—which was all rank folly, if one would, while he was out of the house and otherwise occupied, but which took on the last verisimilitude as soon as he was placed and posted. He knew what he meant and what he wanted; it was as clear as the figure on a cheque presented in demand for cash. His *alter ego* "walked"—that was the note of his image of him, while his image of his motive for his own odd pastime was the desire to waylay him and meet him. He roamed, slowly, warily, but all restlessly, he himself did— Mrs. Muldoon had been right, absolutely, with her figure of their "craping"; and the presence he watched for would roam restlessly too. But it would be as cautious and as shifty; the conviction of its probable, it fact its already quite sensible, quite audible evasion of pursuit grew for him from night to night, laying on him finally a rigour to which nothing in his life had been comparable. It had been the theory of many superficially-judging persons, he knew, that he was wasting that life in a surrender to sensations, but he had tasted of no pleasure so fine as his actual tension, had been introduced to no sport that demanded at once the patience and the nerve of this stalking of a creature more subtle, yet at bay perhaps more formidable, than any beast of the forest. The terms, the comparisons, the very practices of the chase positively came again into play; there were even moments when passages of his occasional experience as a sportsman, stirred memories, from his younger time, of moor and mountain and desert, revived for him—and to the increase of his keenness—by the tremendous force of analogy. He found himself at moments—once he had placed his single light on some mantleshelf or in some recess—stepping back into shelter or shade, effacing himself behind a door or in an embrasure, as he had sought of old the vantage of rock and tree; he found himself holding his breath and living in the joy of the instant, the supreme suspense created by big game alone.

He was n't afraid (though putting himself the question as he believed gentlemen on Bengal tiger-shoots or in close quarters with the great bear of the Rockies had been known to confess to having put it); and this indeed—since here at least he might be frank!—because of the impression, so intimate and so strange, that he himself produced as yet a dread, produced certainly a strain, beyond the liveliest he was likely to feel. They fell for him into categories, they fairly became familiar, the signs, for his own perception, of the alarm his presence and his viligance created; though leaving him always to remark, portentously, on his probably having formed a relation, his probably enjoying a consciousness, unique in the experience of man. People enough, first and last, had been in terror of apparitions, but who had ever before so turned the tables and become himself, in the apparitional world, an incalculable terror? He might have found this sublime had he quite dared to think of it; but he did n't too much insist, truly, on that side of his privilege. With habit and repetition he gained to an extraordinary degree the power to penetrate the dusk of distances and the darkness of corners, to resolve back into their innocence the treacheries of uncertain light, the evil-looking forms taken in the gloom by mere shadows, by accidents of the air, by shifting effects of perspective; putting down his dim luminary he could still wander on without it, pass into other rooms and, only knowing it was there behind him in case of need, see his way about, visually project for his purpose a comparative clearness. It made him feel, this acquired faculty, like some monstrous stealthy cat; he wondered if he would have glared at these moments with large shining yellow eyes, and what it might n't verily be, for the poor hardpressed *alter ego,* to be confronted with such a type.

He liked however the open shutters; he opened everywhere those Mrs. Muldoon had closed, closing them as carefully afterwards, so that she should n't notice; he liked—oh this he did like, and above all in the upper rooms!—the sense of the hard silver of the autumn stars through the window-panes, and scarcely less the flare of the street-lamps below, the white electric lustre which it would have taken curtains to keep out. This was human actual social; this was of the world he had lived in and he was more at his ease certainly for the countenance, coldly general and impersonal, that all the while and in spite of his detachment it seemed to give him. He had support of course mostly in the rooms at the wide front and the prolonged side; it failed him considerably in the central shades and the parts at the back. But if he sometimes, on his rounds, was glad of his optical reach, so none the less often the rear of the house affected him as the very jungle of his prey. The place was there more subdivided; a large "extension" in particular, where small rooms for servants had been multiplied, abounded in nooks and corners, in closets and passages, in the ramifications especially of an ample back staircase over which he leaned, many a time, to look far down—not deterred from his gravity even while aware that he might, for a spectator, have figured some solemn simpleton playing at hide-and-seek. Outside in fact he might himself make that ironic *rapprochement;*[3] but within the walls, and in spite of the clear windows, his consistency was proof against the cynical light of New York.

It had belonged to that idea of the exasperating consciousness of his victim to become a real test for him; since he had quite put it to himself from the first that, oh distinctly! he could "cultivate" his whole perception. He had felt it as above all open to cultivation—which indeed was but another name for his manner of spending his time. He was bringing it on, bringing it to perfection, by practice; in consequence of which it had grown so fine that he was now aware of impressions, attestations of his general postulate, that could n't have broken upon him at once. This was the case more specifically with a phenomenon at last quite frequent for him in the upper rooms, the recognition—absolutely unmistakeable, and by a turn dating from a particular hour, his resumption of his campaign after a diplomatic drop, a calculated absence of three nights—of his being definitely followed, tracked at a distance carefully taken and to the express end that he should the less confidently, less arrogantly, appear to himself merely to pursue. It worried, it finally quite broke him up, for it proved, of all the conceivable impressions, the one least suited to his book. He was kept in sight while remaining himself—as regards the essence of his position—sightless, and his only recourse then was in abrupt turns, rapid recoveries of ground. He wheeled about, retracing his steps, as if he might so catch in his face at least the stirred air of some other quick revolution. It was indeed true that his fully dislocalised thought of these manœuvres recalled to him Pantaloon, at the Christmas farce, buffeted and tricked from behind by ubiquitous Harlequin;[4] but it left intact the influence of the conditions themselves each time he was re-exposed to them, so that in fact this association, had he suffered it to become constant, would on a certain side have but ministered to his intenser gravity. He had made, as I have said, to create on the premises the baseless sense of a reprieve, his three absences; and the result of the third was to confirm the after-effect of the second.

On his return, that night—the night succeeding his last intermission—he

---

[3]Integration, correlation.

[4]The aged buffoon, Pantaloon, and his trickster servant, Harlequin, are traditional masked characters in European pantomime comedies.

stood in the hall and looked up the staircase with a certainty more intimate than any he had yet known. "He's *there*, at the top, and waiting—not, as in general, falling back for disappearance. He's holding his ground, and it's the first time—which is a proof, is n't it? that something has happened for him." So Brydon argued with his hand on the banister and his foot on the lowest stair; in which position he felt as never before the air chilled by his logic. He himself turned cold in it, for he seemed of a sudden to know what now was involved. "Harder pressed?—yes, he takes it in, with its thus making clear to him that I've come, as they say, 'to stay.' He finally does n't like and can't bear it, in the sense, I mean, that his wrath, his menaced interest, now balances with his dread. I've hunted him till he has 'turned': that, up there, is what has happened—he's the fanged or the antlered animal brought at last to bay." There came to him, as I say—but determined by an influence beyond my notation!—the acuteness of this certainty; under which however the next moment he had broken into a sweat that he would as little have consented to attribute to fear as he would have dared immediately to act upon it for enterprise. It marked none the less a prodigious thrill, a thrill that represented sudden dismay, no doubt, but also represented, and with the self-same throb, the strangest, the most joyous, possibly the next minute almost the proudest, duplication of consciousness.

"He has been dodging, retreating, hiding, but now, worked up to anger, he'll fight!"—this intense impression made a single mouthful, as it were, of terror and applause. But what was wondrous was that the applause, for the felt fact, was so eager, since, if it was his other self he was running to earth, this ineffable identity was thus in the last resort not unworthy of him. It bristled there—somewhere near at hand, however unseen still—as the hunted thing, even as the trodden worm of the adage *must* at last bristle; and Brydon at this instant tasted probably of a sensation more complex than had ever before found itself consistent with sanity. It was as if it would have shamed him that a character so associated with his own should triumphantly succeed in just skulking, should to the end not risk the open; so that the drop of this danger was, on the spot, a great lift of the whole situation. Yet with another rare shift of the same subtlety he was already trying to measure by how much more he himself might now be in peril of fear; so rejoicing that he could, in another form, actively inspire that fear, and simultaneously quaking for the form in which he might passively know it.

The apprehension of knowing it must after a little have grown in him, and the strangest moment of his adventure perhaps, the most memorable or really most interesting, afterwards, of his crisis, was the lapse of certain instants of concentrated conscious *combat*, the sense of a need to hold on to something, even after the manner of a man slipping and slipping on some awful incline; the vivid impulse, above all, to move, to act, to charge, somehow and upon something—to show himself, in a word, that he was n't afraid. The state of "holding-on" was thus the state to which he was momentarily reduced; if there had been anything, in the great vacancy, to seize, he would presently have been aware of having clutched it as he might under a shock at home have clutched the nearest chair-back. He had been surprised at any rate—of this he *was* aware—into something unprecedented since his original appropriation of the place; he had closed his eyes, held them tight, for a long minute, as with the instinct of dismay and that terror of vision. When he opened them the room, the other contiguous rooms, extraordinarily, seemed lighter—so light, almost, that at first he took the change for day. He stood firm, however that might be, just where he had paused; his resistance had helped him—it was as if there were something he had tided over. He knew after a little what this was—it had been in the imminent danger of flight. He had stiffened his will against going; without this he would have made for the stairs, and it seemed to him that, still with his eyes closed, he would have descended them, would have known how, straight and swiftly, to the bottom.

Well, as he had held out, here he was—still at the top, among the more intricate upper rooms and with the gauntlet of the others, of all the rest of the house, still to run when it should be his time to go. He would go at his time—only at his time: did n't he go every night very much at the same hour? He took out his watch—there was light for that: it was scarcely a quarter past one, and he had never withdrawn so soon. He reached his lodgings for the most part at two—with his walk of a quarter of an hour. He would wait for the last quarter—he would n't stir till then; and he kept his watch there with his eyes on it, reflecting while he held it that this deliberate wait, a wait with an effort, which he recognised, would serve perfectly for the attestation he desired to make. It would prove his courage—unless indeed the latter might most be proved by his budging at last from his place. What he mainly felt now was that, since he had n't originally scuttled, he had his dignities—which had never in his life seemed so many—all to preserve and to carry aloft. This was before him in truth as a physical image, an image almost worthy of an age of greater romance. That remark indeed glimmered for him only to glow the next instant with a finer light; since what age of romance, after all, could have matched either the state of his mind, or "objectively," as they said, the wonder of his situation? The only difference would have been that, brandishing his dignities over his head as in a parchment scroll, he might then—that is in the heroic time—have proceeded downstairs with a drawn sword in his other grasp.

At present, really, the light he had set down on the mantel of the next room would have to figure his sword; which utensil, in the course of a minute, he had taken the requisite number of steps to possess himself of. The door between the rooms was open, and from the second another door opened to a third. These rooms, as he remembered, gave all three upon a common corridor as well, but there was a fourth, beyond them, without issue save through the preceding. To have moved, to have heard his step again, was appreciably a help; though even in recognising this he lingered once more a little by the chimney-piece on which his light had rested. When he next moved, just hesitating where to turn, he found himself considering a circumstance that, after his first and comparatively vague apprehension of it, produced in him the start that often attends some pang of recollection, the violent shock of having ceased happily to forget. He had come into sight of the door in which the brief chain of communication ended and which he now surveyed from the nearer threshold, the one not directly facing it. Placed at some distance to the left of this point, it would have admitted him to the last room of the four, the room without other approach or egress, had it not, to his intimate conviction, been closed *since* his former visitation, the matter probably of a quarter of an hour before. He stared with all his eyes at the wonder of the fact, arrested again where he stood and again holding his breath while he sounded its sense. Surely it had been *subsequently* closed—that is it had been on his previous passage indubitably open!

He took it full in the face that something had happened between—that he couldn n't not have noticed before (by which he meant on his original tour of all the rooms that evening) that such a barrier had exceptionally presented itself. He had indeed since that moment undergone an agitation so extraordinary that it might have muddled for him any earlier view; and he tried to convince himself that he might perhaps then have gone into the room and, inadvertently, automatically, on coming out, have drawn the door after him. The difficulty was that this exactly was what he never did; it was against his whole policy, as he might have said, the essence of which was to keep vistas clear. He had them from the first, as he was well aware, quite on the brain: the strange apparition, at the far end of one of them, of his baffled "prey" (which had become by so sharp an irony so little the term now to apply!) was the form of success his imagination had most cherished, projecting into it always a refinement of beauty. He had known fifty times the start of perception that had afterwards dropped; had fifty times gasped to himself "There!" under some fond brief hallucination. The house, as the case stood, admirably lent itself; he might wonder at the taste, the native architecture of the particular time, which could rejoice so in the multiplication of doors—the opposite extreme to the modern, the actual almost complete proscription of them; but it had fairly contributed to provoke this obsession of the presence encountered telescopically, as he might say, focussed and studied in diminishing perspective and as by a rest for the elbow.

It was with these considerations that his present attention was charged—they perfectly availed to make what he saw portentous. He *could n't*, by any lapse, have blocked that aperture; and if he had n't, if it was unthinkable, why what else was clear but that there had been another agent? Another agent?—he had been catching, as he felt, a moment back, the very breath of him; but when had he been so close as in this simple, this logical, this completely personal act? It was so logical, that is, that one might have *taken* it for personal; yet for what did Brydon take it, he asked himself, while, softly panting, he felt his eyes almost leave their sockets. Ah this time at last they *were*, the two, the opposed projections of him, in presence; and this time, as much as one would, the question of danger loomed. With it rose, as not before, the question of courage—for what he knew the blank face of the door to say to him was "Show us how much you have!" It stared, it glared back at him with that challenge; it put to him the two alternatives: should he just push it open or not? Oh to have this consciousness was to *think*— and to think, Brydon knew, as he stood there, was, with the lapsing moments, not to have acted! Not to have acted—that was the misery and the pang—was even still not to act; was in fact *all* to feel the thing in another, in a new and terrible way. How long did he pause and how long did he debate? There was presently nothing to measure it; for his vibration had already changed—as just by the effect of its intensity. Shut up there, at bay, defiant, and with the prodigy of the thing palpably proveably *done,* thus giving notice like some stark sign-board—under that accession of accent the situation itself had turned; and Brydon at last remarkably made up his mind on what it had turned to.

It had turned altogether to a different admonition; to a supreme hint, for him, of the value of Discretion! This slowly dawned, no doubt—for it could take its time; so perfectly, on his threshold, had he been stayed, so little as yet had he either advanced or retreated. It was the strangest of all things that now when, by his taking ten steps and applying his hand to a latch, or even his shoulder and his knee, if necessary, to a panel, all the hunger of his prime need might have been met, his high curiosity crowned, his unrest assuaged—it was amazing, but it was also exquisite and rare, that insistence should have, at a touch, quite dropped from him. Discretion—he jumped at that; and yet, not verily, at such a pitch, because it saved his nerves or his skin, but because, much more valuably it saved the situation. When I say he "jumped" at it I feel the consonance of this term with the fact that—at the end indeed of I know not how long—he did move again, he crossed straight to the door. He would n't touch it—it seemed now that he might *if* he would: he would only just wait there a little, to show, to prove, that he would n't. He had thus another station, close to the thin partition by which revelation was denied him; but with his eyes bent and his hands held off in a mere intensity of stillness. He listened as if there had been something to hear, but this attitude, while it lasted, was his own communication. "If you won't then—good: I spare you and I give up. You affect me as by the appeal positively for pity: you convince me that for reasons rigid and sublime—what do I know?—we both of us should have suffered. I respect them then, and, though moved and privileged as, I believe, it has never been given to man, I retire, I renounce—never, on my honour, to try again. So rest for ever—and let *me!*"

That, for Brydon was the deep sense of this last demonstration—solemn, measured, directed, as he felt it to be. He brought it to a close, he turned away; and now verily he knew how deeply he had been stirred. He retraced his steps, taking up his candle, burnt, he observed, well-nigh to the socket, and marking again, lighten it as he would, the distinctness of his footfall; after which, in a moment, he knew himself at the other side of the house. He did here what he had not yet done at these hours—he opened half a casement, one of those in the front, and let in the air of the night; a thing he would have taken at any time previous for a sharp rupture of his spell. His spell was broken now, and it did n't matter—broken by his concession and his surrender, which made it idle henceforth that he should ever come back. The empty street—its other life so marked even by the great lamplit vacancy—was within call, within touch; he stayed there as to be in it again, high above it though he was still perched; he watched as for some comforting common fact, some vulgar human note, the passage of a scavenger or a thief, some night-bird however base. He would have blessed that sign of life; he would have welcomed positively the slow approach of his friend the policeman, whom he had hitherto only sought to avoid, and was not sure that if the patrol had come into sight he might n't have felt the impulse to get into relation with it, to hail it, on some pretext, from his fourth floor.

The pretext that would n't have been too silly or too compromising, the explanation that would have saved his dignity and kept his name, in such a case, out of the papers, was not definite to him: he was so occupied with the thought of recording his Discretion—as an effect of the vow he had just uttered to his intimate adversary—that the importance of this loomed large and something had overtaken all ironically his sense of proportion. If there had been a ladder applied to the front of the house, even one of the vertiginous perpendiculars employed by painters and roofers and sometimes left standing overnight, he would have managed somehow, astride of the window-sill, to compass by out-stretched leg and arm that mode of descent. If there had been some such uncanny thing as he had found in his room at hotels, a workable fire-escape in the form of notched cable or a canvas shoot, he would have availed himself of it as a proof—well, of his present delicacy. He nursed that sentiment, as the question stood, a little in vain, and even—at the end of he scarce knew, once more, how long—found it, as by the action on his mind of the failure of response of the outer world, sinking back to vague anguish. It seemed to him he had waited an age for some stir of the great grim hush; the life of the town was itself under a spell—so unnaturally, up and down the whole prospect of known and rather ugly objects, the blankness and the silence lasted. Had they ever, he asked himself, the hard-faced houses, which had begun to look livid in the dim dawn, had they ever spoken so little to any need of his spirit? Great builded voids, great crowded stillnesses put on, often, in the heart of cities, for the small hours, a sort of sinister mask, and it was of this large collective negation that Brydon presently became conscious—all the more that the break of day was, almost incredibly, now at hand, proving to him what a night he had made of it.

He looked again at his watch, saw what had become of his time-values (he had taken hours for minutes—not, as in other tense situations, minutes for hours) and the strange air of the streets was but the weak, the sullen flush of a dawn in which everything was still locked up. His choked appeal from his own open window had been the sole note of life, and he could but break off at last as for a worse despair. Yet while so deeply demoralised he was capable again of an impulse denoting—at least by his present measure—extraordinary resolution; of retracing his steps to the spot where he had turned cold with the extinction of his last pulse of doubt as to there being in the place another presence than his own. This required an effort strong enough to sicken him; but he had his reason, which overmastered for the moment everything else. There was the whole of the rest of the house to traverse, and how should he screw himself to that if the door he had seen closed were at present open? He could hold to the idea that the closing had practically been for him an act of mercy, a chance offered him to descend, depart, get off the ground and never again profane it. This conception held together, it worked; but what it meant for him depended now clearly on the amount of forbearance his recent action, or rather his recent inaction, had engendered. The image of the "presence," whatever it was, waiting there for him to go—this image had not yet been so concrete for his nerves as when he stopped short of the point at which certainty would have come to him. For, with all his resolution, or more exactly with all his dread, he did stop short— he hung back from really seeing. The risk was too great and his fear too definite: it took at this moment an awful specific form.

He knew—yes, as he had never known anything—that, *should* he see the door open, it would all too abjectly be the end of him. It would mean that the agent of his shame—for his shame was the deep abjection—was once more at large and in general possession; and what glared him thus in the face was the act that this would determine for him. It would send him straight about to the window he had left open, and by that window, be long ladder and dangling rope as absent as they would, he saw himself uncontrollably insanely fatally take his way to the street. The hideous chance of this he at least could avert; but he could only avert it by recoiling in time from assurance. He had the whole house to deal with, this fact was still there; only he now knew that uncertainty alone could start him. He stole back from where he had checked himself—merely to do so was suddenly like safety—and, making blindly for the greater staircase, left gaping rooms and sounding passages behind. Here was the top of the stairs, with a fine large dim descent and three spacious landings to mark off. His instinct was all for mildness, but his feet were harsh on the floors, and, strangely, when he had in a couple of minutes become aware of this, it counted somehow for help. He could n't have spoken, the tone of his voice would have scared him, and the common conceit or resource of "whistling in the dark" (whether literally or figuratively) have appeared basely vulgar; yet he liked none the less to hear himself go, and when he had reached his first landing—taking it all with no rush, but quite steadily—that stage of success drew from him a gasp of relief.

The house, withal, seemed immense, the scale of space again inordinate; the open rooms, to no one of which his eyes deflected, gloomed in their shuttered state like mouths of caverns; only the high skylight that formed the crown of the deep well created for him a medium in which he could advance, but which might have been, for queerness of colour, some watery under-world. He tried to think of something noble, as that his property was really grand, a splendid possession; but his nobleness took the form too of the clear delight with which he was finally to sacrifice it. They might come in now, the builders, the destroyers—they might come as soon as they would. At the end of two flights he had dropped to another zone, and from the middle of the third, with only one more left, he recognised the influence of the lower windows, of half-drawn blinds, of the occasional gleam of street-lamps, of the glazed spaces of the vestibule. This was the bottom of the sea, which showed an illumination of its own and which he even saw paved—when at a given moment he drew up to sink a long look over the banisters—with the marble squares of his childhood. By that time indubitably he felt, as he might have said in a commoner cause, better; it had allowed him to stop and draw breath, and the ease increased with the sight of the old black-and-white slabs. But what he most felt was that now surely, with the element of impunity pulling him as by hard firm hands, the case was settled for what he might have seen above had he dared that last look. The closed door, blessedly remote now, was still closed—and he had only in short to reach that of the house.

He came down further, he crossed the passage forming the access to the last flight; and if here again he stopped an instant it was almost for the sharpness of the thrill of assured escape. It made him shut his eyes—which opened again to the straight slope of the remainder of the stairs. Here was impunity still, but impunity almost excessive; inasmuch as the sidelights and the higher fan-tracery of the entrance were glimmering straight into the hall; an appearance produced, he the next instant saw, by the fact that the vestibule gaped wide, that the hinged halves of the inner door had been thrown far back. Out of that again the *question* sprang at him, making his eyes as he felt, half-start from his head, as they had done, at the top of the house, before the sign of the other door. If he had left that one open, had n't he left this one closed, and was n't he now in *most* immediate presence of some inconceivable occult activity? It was as sharp, the question, as a knife in his side, but the answer hung fire still and seemed to lose itself in the vague darkness to which the thin admitted dawn, glimmering archwise over the whole outer door, made a semicircular margin, a cold silvery nimbus that seemed to play a little as he looked—to shift and expand and contract.

It was as if there had been something within it, protected by indistinctness and corresponding in extent with the opaque surface behind, the painted panels of the last barrier to his escape, of which the key was in his pocket. The indistinctness mocked him even while he stared, affected him as somehow shrouding or challenging certitude, so that after faltering an instant on his step he let himself go with the sense that here *was* at last something to meet, to touch, to take, to know—something all unnatural and dreadful, but to advance upon which was the condition for him either of liberation or of supreme defeat. The penumbra, dense and dark, was the virtual screen of a figure which stood in it as still as some image erect in a niche or as some black-vizored sentinel guarding a treasure. Brydon was to know afterwards, was to recall and make out, the particular thing he had believed during the rest of his descent. He saw, in its great grey glimmering margin, the central vagueness diminish, and he felt it to be taking the very form toward which, for so many days, the passion of his curiosity had yearned. It gloomed, it loomed, it was something, it was somebody, the prodigy of a personal presence.

Rigid and conscious, spectral yet human, a man of his own substance and stature waited there to measure himself with his power to dismay. This only could it be—this only till he recognised, with his advance, that what made the face dim was the pair of raised hands that covered it and in which, so far from being offered in defiance, it was buried as for dark deprecation. So Brydon, before him, took him in; with every fact of him now, in the higher light, hard and acute—his planted stillness, his vivid truth, his grizzled bent head and white masking hands, his queer actuality of evening-dress, of dangling double eye-glass, of gleaming silk lappet and white linen, of pearl button and gold watch-guard and polished shoe. No portrait by a great modern master could have presented him with more intensity, thrust him out of his frame with more art, as if there had been "treatment," of the consummate sort, in his every shade and salience. The revulsion, for our friend, had become, before he knew it, immense—this drop, in the act of apprehension, to the sense of his adversary's inscrutable manœuvre. That meaning at least, while he gaped, it offered him; for he could but gape at his other self in this other anguish, gape as a proof that *he,* standing there for the achieved, the enjoyed, the triumphant life, could n't be faced in his triumph. Was n't the proof in the splendid covering hands, strong and completely spread?—so spread and so intentional that, in spite of a special verity that surpassed every other, the fact that one of these hands had lost two fingers, which were reduced to stumps, as if accidentally shot away, the face was effectually guarded and saved.

"Saved," though, *would* it be?—Brydon breathed his wonder till the very impunity of his attitude and the very insistence of his eyes produced, as he felt, a sudden stir which showed the next instant as a deeper portent, while the head raised itself, the betrayal of a braver purpose. The hands, as he looked, began to move, to open; then, as if deciding in a flash, dropped from the face and left it uncovered and presented. Horror, with the sight, had leaped into Brydon's throat, gasping there in a sound he could n't utter; for the bared identity was too hideous as *his,* and his glare was the passion of his protest. The face, *that* face, Spencer Brydon's?—he searched it still, but looking away from it in dismay and denial, falling straight from his height of sublimity. It was unknown, incon-ceivable, awful, disconnected from any possibility—! He had been "sold," he inwardly moaned, stalking such game as this: the presence before him was a presence, the horror within him a horror, but the waste of his nights had been only grotesque and the success of his adventure an irony. Such an identity fitted his at *no* point, made its alternative monstrous. A thousand times yes, as it came upon him nearer now—the face was the face of a stranger. It came upon him nearer now, quite as one of those expanding fantastic images projected by the magic lantern of childhood; for the stranger, whoever he might be, evil, odious, blatant, vulgar, had advanced as for aggression, and he knew himself give ground. Then harder pressed still, sick with the force of his shock, and falling back as under the hot breath and the roused passion of a life larger than his own, a rage of personality before which his own collapsed, he felt the whole vision turn to darkness and his very feet give way. His head went round; he was going; he had gone.

III

What had next brought him back, clearly—though after how long?—was Mrs. Muldoon's voice, coming to him from quite near, from so near that he seemed presently to see her as kneeling on the ground before him while he lay looking up at her; himself not wholly on the ground, but half-raised and upheld—

conscious, yes of tenderness of support and, more particularly, of a head pillowed in extraordinary softness and faintly refreshing fragrance. He considered, he wondered, his wit but half at his service; then another face intervened, bending more directly over him, and he finally knew that Alice Staverton had made her lap an ample and perfect cushion to him, and that she had to this end seated herself on the lowest degree of the staircase, the rest of his long person remaining stretched on his old black-and-white slabs. They were cold, these marble squares of his youth; but *he* somehow was not, in this rich return to consciousness—the most wonderful hour, little by little, that he had ever known, leaving him, as it did, so gratefully, so abysmally passive, and yet as with a treasure of intelligence waiting all round him for quiet appropriation; dissolved, he might call it, in the air of the place and producing the golden glow of a late autumn afternoon. He had come back, yes—come back from further away than any man but himself had ever travelled; but it was strange how with this sense what he had come back *to* seemed really the great thing, and as if his prodigious journey had been all for the sake of it. Slowly but surely this consciousness grew, his vision of his state thus completing itself: he had been miraculously *carried* back—lifted and carefully borne as from where he had been picked up, the uttermost end of an interminable grey passage. Even with this he was suffered to rest, and what had now brought him to knowledge was the break in the long mild motion.

It had brought him to knowledge, to knowledge—yes, this was the beauty of his state; which came to resemble more and more that of a man who has gone to sleep on some news of a great inheritance, and then, after dreaming it away, after profaning it with matters strange to it, has waked up again to serenity of certitude and has only to lie and watch it grow. This was the drift of his patience—that he had only to let it shine on him. He must moreover, with intermissions, still have been lifted and borne; since why and how else should he have known himself, later on, with the afternoon glow intenser, no longer at the foot of his stairs—situated as these now seemed at that dark other end of his tunnel—but on a deep window-bench of his high saloon, over which had been spread, couch-fashion, a mantle of soft stuff lined with grey fur that was familiar to his eyes and that one of his hands kept fondly feeling as for its pledge of truth. Mrs. Muldoon's face had gone, but the other, the second he had recognised, hung over him in a way that showed how he was still propped and pillowed. He took it all in, and the more he took it the more it seemed to suffice: he was as much at peace as if he had had food and drink. It was the two women who had found him, on Mrs. Muldoon's having plied, at her usual hour, her latch-key—and on her having above all arrived while Miss Staverton still lingered near the house. She had been turning away, all anxiety, from worrying the vain bell-handle—her calculation having been of the hour of the good woman's visit; but the latter, blessedly, had come up while she was still there, and they had entered together. He had then lain, beyond the vestibule, very much as he was lying now—quite, that is, as he appeared to have fallen, but all so wondrously without bruise or gash; only in a depth of stupor. What he most took in, however, at present, with the steadier clearance, was that Alice Staverton had for a long unspeakable moment not doubted he was dead.

"It must have been that I *was*." He made it out as she held him. "Yes—I can only have died. You brought me literally to life. Only," he wondered, his eyes rising to her, "only, in the name of all the benedictions, how?"

It took her but an instant to bend her face and kiss him, and something in the manner of it, and in the way her hands clasped and locked his head while he felt the cool charity and virtue of her lips, something in all this beatitude somehow answered everything. "And now I keep you," she said.

"Oh keep me, keep me!" he pleaded while her face still hung over him: in response to which it dropped again and stayed close, clingingly close. It was the seal of their situation—of which he tasted the impress for a long blissful moment in silence. But he came back. "Yet how did you know—?"

"I was uneasy. You were to have come, you remember—and you had sent no word."

"Yes, I remember—I was to have gone to you at one to-day." It caught on to their "old" life and relation—which were so near and so far. "I was still out there in my strange darkness—where was it, what was it? I must have stayed there so long." He could but wonder at the depth and the duration of his swoon.

"Since last night?" she asked with a shade of fear for her possible indiscretion.

"Since this morning—it must have been: the cold dim dawn of to-day. Where have I been," he vaguely wailed, "where have I been?" He felt her hold him close, and it was as if this helped him now to make in all security his mild moan. "What a long dark day!"

All in her tenderness she had waited a moment. "In the cold dim dawn?" she quavered.

But he had already gone on piecing together the parts of the whole prodigy. "As I did n't turn up you came straight—?"

She barely cast about. "I went first to your hotel—where they told me of your absence. You had dined out last evening and had n't been back since. But they appeared to know you had been at your club."

"So you had the idea of *this*—?"

"Of what?" she asked in a moment.

"Well—of what has happened."

"I believed at least you'd have been here. I've known, all along," she said, "that you've been coming."

"Known' it—?"

"Well, I've believed it. I said nothing to you after that talk we had a month ago—but I felt sure. I knew you *would*," she declared.

"That I'd persist, you mean?"

"That you'd see him."

"Ah but I did n't!" cried Brydon with his long wail. "There's somebody—an awful beast; whom I brought, too horribly, to bay. But it's not me."

At this she bent over him again, and her eyes were in his eyes. "No—it's not you." And it was as if, while her face hovered, he might have made out in it, had n't it been so near, some particular meaning blurred by a smile. "No, thank heaven," she repeated—"it's not you! Of course it was n't to have been."

"Ah but it *was*," he gently insisted. And he stared before him now as he had been staring for so many weeks. "I was to have known myself."

"You could n't!" she returned consolingly. And then reverting, and as if to account further for what she had herself done, "But it was n't only *that*, that you had n't been at home," she went on. "I waited till the hour at which we had found Mrs. Muldoon that day of my going with you; and she arrived, as I've told you, while, failing to bring any one to the door, I lingered in my despair on the steps. After a while, if she had n't come, by such a mercy, I should have found means to hunt her up. But she was n't," said Alice Staverton, as if once more with her fine intention—"it was n't only that."

His eyes, as he lay, turned back to her. "What more then?"

She met it, the wonder she had stirred. "In the cold dim dawn, you say? Well, in the cold dim dawn of this morning I too saw you."

"Saw *me*—?"

"Saw *him*," said Alice Staverton. "It must have been at the same moment."

He lay an instant taking it in—as if he wished to be quite reasonable. "At the same moment?"

"Yes—in my dream again, the same one I've named to you. He came back to me. Then I knew it for a sign. He had come to you."

At this Brydon raised himself; he had to see her better. She helped him when she understood his movement, and he sat up, steadying himself beside her there on the window-bench and with his right hand grasping her left. "*He* did n't come to me."

"You came to yourself," she beautifully smiled.

"Ah I've come to myself now—thanks to you, dearest. But this brute, with his awful face—this brute's a black stranger. He's none of *me*, even as I *might* have been," Brydon sturdily declared.

But she kept the clearness that was like the breath of infallibility. "Is n't the whole point that you'd have been different?"

He almost scowled for it. "As different as *that*—?"

Her look again was more beautiful to him than the things of this world. "Have n't you exactly wanted to know *how* different? So this morning," she said, "you appeared to me."

"Like *him*?"

"A black stranger!"

"Then how did you know it was I?"

"Because, as I told you weeks ago, my mind, my imagination, had worked so over what you might, what you might n't have been—to show you, you see, how I've thought of you. In the midst of that you came to me—that my wonder might be answered. So I knew," she went on; "and believed that, since the question held you too so fast, as you told me that day, you too would see for yourself. And when this morning I again saw I knew it would be because you had—and also then, from the first moment, because you somehow wanted me. *He* seemed to tell me of that. So why," she strangely smiled, "should n't I like him?"

It brought Spencer Brydon to his feet. "You 'like' that horror—?"

"I *could* have liked him. And to me," she said, "he was no horror. I had accepted him."

" 'Accepted'—?" Brydon oddly sounded.

"Before, for the interest of his difference—yes. And as *I* did n't disown him, as *I* knew him—which you at last, confronted with him in his difference, so cruelly did n't, my dear—well, he must have been, you see, less dreadful to me. And it may have pleased him that I pitied him."

She was beside him on her feet, but still holding his hand—still with her arm supporting him. But though it all brought for him thus a dim light, "You 'pitied' him?" he grudgingly, resentfully asked.

"He has been unhappy, he has been ravaged," she said.

"And have n't I been unhappy? Am not I—you've only to look at me!—ravaged?"

"Ah I don't say I like him *better*," she granted after a thought. "But he's grim, he's worn—and things have happened to him. He does n't make shift, for sight, with your charming monocle."

"No"—it struck Brydon: "I could n't have sported mine 'downtown.' They'd have guyed[1] me there."

"His great convex pince-nez—I saw it, I recognised the kind—is for his poor ruined sight. And his poor right hand—!"

"Ah!" Brydon winced—whether for his proved identity or for his lost fingers. Then, "He has a million a year," he lucidly added. "But he has n't you."

"And he is n't—no, he is n't—*you!*" she murmured as he drew her to his breast.

1906   1908, 1909

from *HAWTHORNE*[1]

In quiet provincial Salem, Nathaniel Hawthorne passed the greater part of his boyhood, as well as many years of his later life. Mr. Lathrop[2] has much to say about the ancient picturesqueness of the place, and about the mystic influences it would project upon such a mind and character as Hawthorne's. These things are always relative, and in appreciating them everything depends upon the point of view. Mr. Lathrop writes for American readers, who in such a matter as this are very easy to please. Americans have, as a general thing, a hungry passion for the picturesque, and they are so fond of local colour that they contrive to perceive it in localities in which the amateurs of other countries would detect only the most neutral tints. History, as yet, has left in the United States but so thin and impalpable a deposit that we very soon touch the hard substratum of nature; and nature herself, in the Western World, has the peculiarity of seeming rather crude and immature. The very air looks new and young; the light of the sun seems fresh and innocent, as if it knew as yet but few of the secrets of the world and none of the weariness of shining; the vegetation has the appearance of not having reached its majority. A large juvenility is stamped upon the face of things, and in the vividness of the present, the past, which died so young and had time to produce so little, attracts but scanty attention. I doubt whether English observers would discover any very striking trace of it in the ancient town of Salem. Still, with all respect to a York and a Shrewsbury, to a Toledo and a Verona,[3] Salem has a physiognomy in which the past plays a more important part than the present. It is of course a very recent past; but one must remember that the dead of yesterday are not more alive than those of a century ago. I know not of what picturesqueness Hawthorne was conscious in his respectable birthplace; I suspect his perception of it was less keen than his biographer assumes it to have been; but he must have felt at least that, of whatever complexity of earlier life there had been in the country, the elm-shadowed streets of Salem were a recognisable memento. He has made considerable mention of the place, here and there, in his tales; but he has nowhere dilated upon it very lovingly, and it is noteworthy that in *The House of the Seven Gables,* the only one of his novels of which the scene is laid in it, he has by no means availed himself of the opportunity to give a description

[1]Ridiculed.

[1]Published in England in 1879, as one of the volumes in The English Men of Letters series, James's *Hawthorne* has been called "the first extended study ever made of an American writer."

[2]Hawthorne's son-in-law George Parsons Lathrop (1851–1898), who had published a biography of Hawthorne in 1876.

[3]York and Shrewsbury in England, Toledo in Spain, and Verona in Italy.

of it. He had of course a filial fondness for it—a deep-seated sense of connection with it; but he must have spent some very dreary years there, and the two feelings, the mingled tenderness and rancour, are visible in the Introduction to *The Scarlet Letter*.

"The old town of Salem," he writes—"my native place, though I have dwelt much away from it, both in boyhood and in maturer years—possesses, or did possess, a hold on my affections, the force of which I have never realized during my seasons of actual residence here. Indeed, so far as the physical aspect is concerned, with its flat unvaried surface, covered chiefly with wooden houses, few or none of which pretend to architectural beauty; its irregularity, which is neither picturesque nor quaint, but only tame; its long and lazy street, lounging wearisomely through the whole extent of the peninsula, with Gallows Hill and New Guinea at one end, and a view of the almshouse at the other—such being the features of my native town, it would be quite as reasonable to form a sentimental attachment to a disarranged chequer-board."

But he goes on to say that he has never divested himself of the sense of intensely belonging to it—that the spell of the continuity of his life with that of his predecessors has never been broken. "It is no matter that the place is joyless for him; that he is weary of the old wooden houses, the mud and the dust, the dead level of site and sentiment, the chill east wind, and the chilliest of social atmosphere;—all these, and whatever faults besides he may see or imagine, are nothing to the purpose. The spell survives, and just as powerfully as if the natal spot were an earthly paradise." There is a very American quality in this perpetual consciousness of a spell on Hawthorne's part; it is only in a country where newness and change and brevity of tenure are the common substance of life, that the fact of one's ancestors having lived for a hundred and seventy years in a single spot would become an element of one's morality. It is only an imaginative American that would feel urged to keep reverting to this circumstance, to keep analysing and cunningly considering it.

. . . To English eyes the oldest and most honourable of the smaller American towns must seem in a manner primitive and rustic; the shabby, straggling, village-quality appears marked in them, and their social tone is not unnaturally inferred to bear the village stamp. Village-like they are, and it would be no gross incivility to describe them as large, respectable, prosperous, democratic villages. But even a village, in a great and vigorous democracy, where there are no overshadowing squires, where the "county" has no social existence, where the villagers are conscious of no superincumbent strata of gentility, piled upwards into vague regions of privilege—even a village is not an institution to accept of more or less graceful patronage; it thinks extremely well of itself, and is absolute in its own regard. . . . When we think of what the conditions of intellectual life, of taste, must have been in a small New England town fifty years ago;[4] and when we think of a young man of beautiful genius, with a love of literature and romance, of the picturesque, of style and form and colour, trying to make a career for himself in the midst of them, compassion for the young man becomes our dominant sentiment, and we see the large, dry, village-picture in perhaps almost too hard a light. It seems to me, then, that it was possibly a blessing for Hawthorne that he was not expansive and inquisitive, that he lived much to himself, and asked but little of his *milieu*. If he had been exacting and ambitious, if his appetite had been large and his knowledge various, he would probably have found the bounds of Salem intolerably narrow. But his culture had been of a simple sort—

---

[4]In 1829, when Hawthorne was twenty-five.

there was little of any other sort to be obtained in America in those days—and though he was doubtless haunted by visions of more suggestive opportunities, we may safely assume that he was not, to his own perception, the object of compassion that he appears to a critic who judges him after half a century's civilisation has filtered into the twilight of that earlier time. If New England was socially a very small place in those days, Salem was a still smaller one; and if the American tone at large was intensely provincial, that of New England was not greatly helped by having the best of it. The state of things was extremely natural, and there could be now no greater mistake than to speak of it with a redundancy of irony. American life had begun to constitute itself from the foundations; it had begun to *be,* simply; it was at an immeasureable distance from having begun to enjoy. I imagine there was no appreciable group of people in New England at that time proposing to itself to enjoy life; this was not an undertaking for which any provision had been made, or to which any encouragement was offered. Hawthorne must have vaguely entertained some such design upon destiny; but he must have felt that his success would have to depend wholly upon his own ingenuity. I say he must have proposed to himself to enjoy, simply because he proposed to be an artist, and because this enters inevitably into the artist's scheme. There are a thousand ways of enjoying life, and that of the artist is one of the most innocent. But for all that, it connects itself with the idea of pleasure. He proposes to give pleasure, and to give it he must first get it. Where he gets it will depend upon circumstances, and circumstances were not encouraging to Hawthorne.

⋅ ⋅ ⋅

I know not at what age he began to keep a diary; the first entries in the American volumes are of the summer of 1835. There is a phrase in the preface to his novel of *Transformation,*[5] which must have lingered in the minds of many Americans who have tried to write novels, and to lay the scene of them in the Western world. "No author, without a trial, can conceive of the difficulty of writing a romance about a country where there is no shadow, no antiquity, no mystery, no picturesque and gloomy wrong, nor anything but a commonplace prosperity, in broad and simple daylight, as is happily the case with my dear native land." The perusal of Hawthorne's American Note-Books operates as a practical commentary upon this somewhat ominous text. It does so at least to my own mind; it would be too much, perhaps, to say that the effect would be the same for the usual English reader. An American reads between the lines— he completes the suggestions—he constructs a picture. I think I am not guilty of any gross injustice in saying that the picture he constructs from Hawthorne's American diaries, though by no means without charms of its own, is not, on the whole, an interesting one. It is characterised by an extraordinary blankness—a curious paleness of colour and paucity of detail. Hawthorne, as I have said, has a large and healthy appetite for detail, and one is, therefore, the more struck with the lightness of the diet to which his observation was condemned. For myself, as I turn the pages of his journals, I seem to see the image of the crude and simple society in which he lived. I use these epithets, of course, not invidiously, but descriptively: if one desire to enter as closely as possible into Hawthorne's situation, one must endeavour to reproduce his circumstances. We are struck with the large number of elements that were absent from them, and the coldness, the thinness, the blankness, to repeat my epithet, present themselves so vividly that our foremost feeling is that of compassion for a romancer looking

---

[5]The title of the English edition of *The Marble Faun* (1860).

for subjects in such a field. It takes so many things, as Hawthorne must have felt later in life, when he made the acquaintance of the denser, richer, warmer European spectacle—it takes such an accumulation of history and custom, such a complexity of manners and types, to form a fund of suggestion for a novelist. If Hawthorne had been a young Englishman, or a young Frenchman of the same degree of genius, the same cast of mind, the same habits, his consciousness of the world around him would have been a very different affair; however obscure, however reserved, his own personal life, his sense of the life of his fellow-mortals would have been almost infinitely more various. The negative side of the spectacle on which Hawthorne looked out, in his contemplative saunterings and reveries, might, indeed, with a little ingenuity, be made almost ludicrous; one might enumerate the items of high civilisation, as it exists in other countries, which are absent from the texture of American life, until it should become a wonder to know what was left. No State, in the European sense of the word, and indeed barely a specific national name. No sovereign, no court, no personal loyalty, no aristocracy, no church, no clergy, no army, no diplomatic service, no country gentlemen, no palaces, no castles, nor manors, nor old country-houses, nor parsonages, nor thatched cottages, nor ivied ruins; no cathedrals, nor abbeys, nor little Norman churches: no great Universities nor public schools—no Oxford, nor Eton, nor Harrow;[6] no literature, no novels, no museums, no pictures, no political society, no sporting class—no Epsom nor Ascot![7] Some such list as that might be drawn up of the absent things in American life—especially in the American life of forty years ago, the effect of which, upon an English or a French imagination, would probably, as a general thing, be appalling. The natural remark, in the almost lurid light of such an indictment, would be that if these things are left out, everything is left out. The American knows that a good deal remains; what it is that remains—that is his secret, his joke, as one may say. It would be cruel, in this terrible denudation, to deny him the consolation of his natural gift, that "American humour" of which of late years we have heard so much.

1879   1879

THE ART OF FICTION

I should not have affixed so comprehensive a title to these few remarks, necessarily wanting in any completeness upon a subject the full consideration of which would carry us far, did I not seem to discover a pretext for my temerity in the interesting pamphlet lately published under this name by Mr. Walter Besant.[1] Mr. Besant's lecture at the Royal Institution[2]—the original form of his pamphlet—appears to indicate that many persons are interested in the art of fiction, and are not indifferent to such remarks, as those who practise it may attempt to make about it. I am therefore anxious not to lose the benefit of this favourable association, and to edge in a few words under cover of the attention which Mr. Besant is sure to have excited. There is something very encouraging in his having put into form certain of his ideas on the mystery of story-telling.

[6]Ancient English schools for the sons of the upper class.
[7]Fashionable English racetracks.
[1]Sir Walter Besant (1836–1901), English novelist, historian, and literary critic.
[2]In London.

It is a proof of life and curiosity—curiosity on the part of the brotherhood of novelists as well as on the part of their readers. Only a short time ago it might have been supposed that the English novel was not what the French call *discutable*.[3] It had no air of having a theory, a conviction, a consciousness of itself behind it—of being the expression of an artistic faith, the result of choice and comparison. I do not say it was necessarily the worse for that: it would take much more courage than I possess to intimate that the form of the novel as Dickens and Thackeray (for instance) saw it had any taint of incompleteness. It was, however, *naïf*[4] (if I may help myself out with another French word); and evidently if it be destined to suffer in any way for having lost its *naïveté* it has now an idea of making sure of the corresponding advantages. During the period I have alluded to there was a comfortable, good-humoured feeling abroad that a novel is a novel, as a pudding is a pudding, and that our only business with it could be to swallow it. But within a year or two, for some reason or other, there have been signs of returning animation—the era of discussion would appear to have been to a certain extent opened. Art lives upon discussion, upon experiment, upon curiosity, upon variety of attempt, upon the exchange of views and the comparison of standpoint; and there is a presumption that those times when no one has anything particular to say about it, and has no reason to give for practice or preference, though they may be times of honour, are not times of development—are times, possibly even, a little of dulness. The successful application of any art is a delightful spectacle, but the theory too is interesting; and though there is a great deal of the latter without the former I suspect there has never been a genuine success that has not had a latent core of conviction. Discussion, suggestion, formulation, these things are fertilising when they are frank and sincere. Mr. Besant has set an excellent example in saying what he thinks, for his part, about the way in which fiction should be written, as well as about the way in which it should be published; for his view of the "art," carried on into an appendix, covers that too. Other labourers in the same field will doubtless take up the argument, they will give it the light of their experience, and the effect will surely be to make our interest in the novel a little more what it had for some time threatened to fail to be—a serious, active, inquiring interest, under protection of which this delightful study may, in moments of confidence, venture to say a little more what it thinks of itself.

It must take itself seriously for the public to take it so. The old superstition about fiction being "wicked" has doubtless died out in England; but the spirit of it lingers in a certain oblique regard directed toward any story which does not more or less admit that it is only a joke. Even the most jocular novel feels in some degree the weight of the proscription that was formerly directed against literary levity: the jocularity does not always succeed in passing for orthodoxy. It is still expected, though perhaps people are ashamed to say it, that a production which is after all only a "make-believe" (for what else is a "story"?) shall be in some degree apologetic—shall renounce the pretension of attempting really to represent life. This, of course, any sensible, wide-awake story declines to do, for it quickly perceives that the tolerance granted to it on such a condition is only an attempt to stifle it disguised in the form of generosity. The old evangelical hostility to the novel, which was as explicit as it was narrow, and which regarded it as little less favourable to our immortal part than a stage-play, was in reality far less insulting. The only reason for the existence of a novel is that it does attempt to represent life. When it relinquishes this attempt, the same attempt

---

[3]French: debatable, discussable.   [4]French: naive.

that we see on the canvas of the painter, it will have arrived at a very strange pass. It is not expected of the picture that it will make itself humble in order to be forgiven; and the analogy between the art of the painter and the art of the novelist is, so far as I am able to see, complete. Their inspiration is the same, their process (allowing for the different quality of the vehicle), is the same, their success is the same. They may learn from each other, they may explain and sustain each other. Their cause is the same, and the honour of one is the honour of another. The Mahometans think a picture an unholy thing, but it is a long time since any Christian did,[5] and it is therefore the more odd that in the Christian mind the traces (dissimulated though they may be) of a suspicion of the sister art should linger to this day. The only effectual way to lay it to rest is to emphasise the analogy to which I just alluded—to insist on the fact that as the picture is reality, so the novel is history. That is the only general description (which does it justice) that we may give of the novel. But history also is allowed to represent life; it is not, any more than painting, expected to apologise. The subject-matter of fiction is stored up likewise in documents and records, and if it will not give itself away, as they say in California, it must speak with assurance, with the tone of the historian. Certain accomplished novelists have a habit of giving themselves away which must often bring tears to the eyes of people who take their fiction seriously. I was lately struck, in reading over many pages of Anthony Trollope,[6] with his want of discretion in this particular. In a digression, a parenthesis or an aside, he concedes to the reader that he and this trusting friend are only "making believe." He admits that the events he narrates have not really happened, and that he can give his narrative any turn the reader may like best. Such a betrayal of a sacred office seems to me, I confess, a terrible crime; it is what I mean by the attitude of apology, and it shocks me every whit as much in Trollope as it would have shocked me in Gibbon or Macaulay.[7] It implies that the novelist is less occupied in looking for the truth (the truth, of course I mean, that he assumes, the premises that we must grant him, whatever they may be), than the historian, and in doing so it deprives him at a stroke of all his standing-room. To represent and illustrate the past, the actions of men, is the task of either writer, and the only difference that I can see is, in proportion as he succeeds, to the honour of the novelist, consisting as it does in his having more difficulty in collecting his evidence, which is so far from being purely literary. It seems to me to give him a great character, the fact that he has at once so much in common with the philosopher and the painter; this double analogy is a magnificent heritage.

It is of all this evidently that Mr. Besant is full when he insists upon the fact that fiction is one of the *fine* arts, deserving in its turn of all the honours and emoluments that have hitherto been reserved for the successful profession of music, poetry, painting, architecture. It is impossible to insist too much on so important a truth, and the place that Mr. Besant demands for the work of the novelist may be represented, a trifle less abstractly, by saying that he demands not only that it shall be reputed artistic, but that it shall be reputed very artistic indeed. It is excellent that he should have struck this note, for his doing so indicates that there was need of it, that his proposition may be to many people a novelty. One rubs one's eyes at the thought; but the rest of Mr. Besant's essay

---

[5]Figural representation was forbidden in early Islam, a tradition that remains in many Islamic countries. Similarly, the early Christian church opposed the making and worship of religious portraits (icons) as a form of idolatry.

[6]Anthony Trollope (1815–1882), English novelist.

[7]Edward Gibbon (1737–1794) and Thomas Babington Macaulay (1800–1859), English historians.

confirms the relation. I suspect in truth that it would be possible to confirm it still further, and that one would not be far wrong in saying that in addition to the people to whom it has never occured that a novel ought to be artistic, there are a great many others who, if this principle were urged upon them, would be filled with an indefinable mistrust. They would find it difficult to explain their repugnance, but it would operate strongly to put them on their guard. "Art," in our Protestant communities, where so many things have got so strangely twisted about, is supposed in certain circles to have some vaguely injurious effect upon those who make it an important consideration, who let it weigh in the balance. It is assumed to be opposed in some mysterious manner to morality, to amusement, to instruction. When it is embodied in the work of the painter (the sculptor is another affair!) you know what it is: it stands there before you, in the honesty of pink and green and a gilt frame; you can see the worst of it at a glance, and you can be on your guard. But when it is introduced into literature it becomes more insidious—there is danger of its hurting you before you know it. Literature should be either instructive or amusing, and there is in many minds an impression that these artistic preoccupations, the search for form, contribute to neither end, interfere indeed with both. They are too frivolous to be edifying, and too serious to be diverting; and they are moreover priggish and paradoxical and superfluous. That, I think, represents the manner in which the latent thought of many people who read novels as an exercise in skipping would explain itself if it were to become articulate. They would argue, of course, that a novel ought to be "good," but they would interpret this term in a fashion of their own, which indeed would considerably vary from one critic to another. One would say that being good means representing virtuous and aspiring characters, placed in prominent positions; another would say that it depends on a "happy ending," on a distribution at the last of prizes, pensions, husbands, wives, babies, millions, appended paragraphs, and cheerful remarks. Another still would say that it means being full of incident and movement, so that we shall wish to jump ahead, to see who was the mysterious stranger, and if the stolen will was ever found, and shall not be distracted from this pleasure by any tiresome analysis or "description." But they would all agree that the "artistic" idea would spoil some of their fun. One would hold it accountable for all the description, another would see it revealed in the absence of sympathy. Its hostility to a happy ending would be evident, and it might even in some cases render any ending at all impossible. The "ending" of a novel is, for many persons, like that of a good dinner, a course of dessert and ices, and the artist in fiction is regarded as a sort of meddlesome doctor who forbids agreeable aftertastes. It is therefore true that this conception of Mr. Besant's of the novel as a superior form encounters not only a negative but a positive indifference. It matters little that as a work of art it should really be as little or as much of its essence to supply happy endings, sympathetic characters, and an objective tone, as if it were a work of mechanics: the association of ideas, however incongruous, might easily be too much for it if an eloquent voice were not sometimes raised to call attention to the fact that it is at once as free and as serious a branch of literature as any other.

Certainly this might sometimes be doubted in presence of the enormous number of works of fiction that appeal to the credulity of our generation, for it might easily seem that there could be no great character in a commodity so quickly and easily produced. It must be admitted that good novels are much compromised by bad ones, and that the field at large suffers discredit from overcrowding. I think, however, that this injury is only superficial, and that the superabundance of written fiction proves nothing against the principle itself. It has been vulgarised, like all other kinds of literature, like everything else to-day, and it has proved more than some kinds accessible to vulgarisation. But there is as much difference as there ever was between a good novel and a bad one: the bad is swept with all the daubed canvases and spoiled marble into some unvisited limbo, or infinite rubbish-yard beneath the back-windows of the world, and the good subsists and emits its light and stimulates our desire for perfection. As I shall take the liberty of making but a single criticism of Mr. Besant, whose tone is so full of the love of his art, I may as well have done with it at once. He seems to me to mistake in attempting to say so definitely before hand what sort of an affair the good novel will be. To indicate the danger of such an error as that has been the purpose of these few pages; to suggest that certain traditions on the subject, applied *á priori,* have already had much to answer for, and that the good health of an art which undertakes so immediately to reproduce life must demand that it be perfectly free. It lives upon exercise, and the very meaning of exercise is freedom. The only obligation to which in advance we may hold a novel, without incurring the accusation of being arbitrary, is that it be interesting. That general responsibility rests upon it, but it is the only one I can think of. The ways in which it is at liberty to accomplish this result (of interesting us) strike me as innumerable, and such as can only suffer from being marked out or fenced in by prescription. They are as various as the temperament of man, and they are successful in proportion as they reveal a particular mind, different from others. A novel is in its broadest definition a personal, a direct impression of life; that, to begin with, constitutes its value, which is greater or less according to the intensity of the impression. But there will be no intensity at all, and therefore no value, unless there is freedom to feel and say. The tracing of a line to be followed, of a tone to be taken, of a form to be filled out, is a limitation of that freedom and a suppression of the very thing that we are most curious about. The form, it seems to me, is to be appreciated after the fact; then the author's choice has been made, his standard has been indicated; then we can follow lines and directions and compare tones and resemblances. Then in a word we can enjoy one of the most charming of pleasures, we can estimate quality, we can apply the test of execution. The execution belongs to the author alone; it is what is most personal to him, and we measure him by that. The advantage, the luxury, as well as the torment and responsibility of the novelist, is that there is no limit to what he may attempt as an executant—no limit to his possible experiments, efforts, discoveries, successes. Here it is especially that he works, step by step, like his brother of the brush, of whom we may always say that he has painted his picture in a manner best known to himself. His manner is his secret, not necessarily a jealous one. He cannot disclose it as a general thing if he would; he would be at a loss to teach it to others. I say this with a due recollection of having insisted on the community of method of the artist who paints a picture and the artist who writes a novel. The painter *is* able to teach the rudiments of his practice, and it is possible, from the study of good work (granted the aptitude), both to learn how to paint and to learn how to write. Yet it remains true, without injury to the *rapprochement,*[8] that the literary artist would be obliged to say to his pupil much more than the other, "Ah, well, you must do it as you can!" It is a question of degree, a matter of delicacy. If there are exact sciences, there are also exact arts, and the grammar of painting is so much more definite that it makes the difference.

---

[8]French: comparison.

I ought to add, however, that if Mr. Besant says at the beginning of his essay that the "laws of fiction may be laid down and taught with as much precision and exactness as the laws of harmony, perspective, and proportion," he mitigates what might appear to be extravagance by applying his remark to "general" laws, and by expressing most of these rules in a manner with which it would certainly be unaccommodating to disagree. That the novelist must write from his experience, that his "characters must be real and such as might be met with in actual life;" that "a young lady brought up in a quiet country village should avoid descriptions of garrison life," and "a writer whose friends and personal experiences belong to the lower middle-class should carefully avoid introducing his characters into society;" that one should enter one's notes in a common-place book; that one's figures should be clear in outline; that making them clear by some trick of speech or of carriage is a bad method, and "describing them at length" is a worse one; that English Fiction should have a "conscious moral purpose;" that "it is almost impossible to estimate too highly the value of careful workmanship—that, is, of style;" that "the most important point of all is the story," that "the story is everything": these are principles with most of which it is surely impossible not to sympathise. That remark about the lower middle-class writer and his knowing his place is perhaps rather chilling; but for the rest I should find it difficult to dissent from any one of these recommendations. At the same time, I should find it difficult positively to assent to them, with the exception, perhaps, of the injunction as to entering one's notes in a common-place book. They scarcely seem to me to have the quality that Mr. Besant attributes to the rules of the novelist—the "precision and exactness" of "the laws of harmony, perspective, and proportion." They are suggestive, they are even inspiring, but they are not exact, though they are doubtless as much so as the case admits of: which is proof of that liberty of interpretation for which I just contended. For the value of these different injunctions—so beautiful and so vague—is wholly in the meaning one attaches to them. The characters, the situation, which strike one as real will be those that touch and interest one most, but the measure of reality is very difficult to fix. The reality of Don Quixote or of Mr. Micawber[9] is a very delicate shade; it is a reality so coloured by the author's vision that, vivid as it may be, one would hesitate to propose it as a model: one would expose one's self to some very embarrassing questions on the part of a pupil. It goes without saying that you will not write a good novel unless you possess the sense of reality; but it will be difficult to give you a recipe for calling that sense into being. Humanity is immense, and reality has a myriad forms; the most one can affirm is that some of the flowers of fiction have the odour of it, and others have not; as for telling you in advance how your nosegay should be composed, that is another affair. It is equally excellent and inconclusive to say that one must write from experience; to our supposititious aspirant such a declaration might savour of mockery. What kind of experience is intended, and where does it begin and end? Experience is never limited, and it is never complete; it is an immense sensibility, a kind of huge spiderweb of the finest silken threads suspended in the chamber of consciousness, and catching every airborne particle in its tissue. It is the very atmosphere of the mind; and when the mind is imaginative—much more when it happens to be that of a man of genius—it takes to itself the faintest hints of life, it converts the very pulses of the air into revelations. The young lady living in a village has only to be a damsel upon whom nothing is lost to make it quite unfair (as it seems to me) to declare

[9]The hero of Cervantes's *Don Quixote* (written 1605–1615) and a character in Dickens's *David Copperfield* (written 1849–1850), respectively.

to her that she shall have nothing to say about the military. Greater miracles have been seen than that, imagination assisting, she should speak the truth about some of these gentlemen. I remember an English novelist, a woman of genius, telling me that she was much commended for the impression she had managed to give in one of her tales of the nature and way of life of the French Protestant youth. She had been asked where she learned so much about this recondite being, she had been congratulated on her peculiar opportunities. These opportunities consisted in her having once, in Paris, as she ascended a staircase, passed an open door where, in the household of a *pasteur*,[10] some of the young Protestants were seated at table round a finished meal. The glimpse made a picture; it lasted only a moment, but that moment was experience. She had got her direct personal impression, and she turned out her type. She knew what youth was, and what Protestantism; she also had the advantage of having seen what it was to be French, so that she converted these ideas into a concrete image and produced a reality. Above all, however, she was blessed with the faculty which when you give it an inch takes an ell, and which for the artist is a much greater source of strength than any accident of residence or of place in the social scale. The power to guess the unseen from the seen, to trace the implication of things, to judge the whole piece by the pattern, the condition of feeling life in general so completely that you are well on your way to knowing any particular corner of it—this cluster of gifts may almost be said to constitute experience, and they occur in country and in town, and in the most differing stages of education. If experience consists of impressions, it may be said that impressions *are* experience, just as (have we not seen it?) they are the very air we breathe. Therefore, if I should certainly say to a novice, "Write from experience and experience only," I should feel that this was rather a tantalising monition if I were not careful immediately to add, "Try to be one of the people on whom nothing is lost!"

I am far from intending by this to minimise the importance of exactness—of truth of detail. One can speak best from one's own taste, and I may therefore venture to say that the air of reality (solidity of specification) seems to me to be the supreme virtue of a novel—the merit on which all its other merits (including that conscious moral purpose of which Mr. Besant speaks) helplessly and submissively depend. If it be not there they are all as nothing, and if these be there, they owe their effect to the success with which the author has produced the illusion of life. The cultivation of this success, the study of this exquisite process, form, to my taste, the beginning and the end of the art of the novelist. They are his inspiration, his despair, his reward, his torment, his delight. It is here in very truth that he competes with life; it is here that he competes with his brother the painter in *his* attempt to render the look of things, the look that conveys their meaning, to catch the colour, the relief, the expression, the surface, the substance of the human spectacle. It is in regard to this that Mr. Besant is well inspired when he bids him take notes. He cannot possibly take too many. He cannot possibly take enough. All life solicits him, and to "render" the simplest surface, to produce the most momentary illusion, is a very complicated business. His case would be easier, and the rule would be more exact, if Mr. Besant had been able to tell him what notes to take. But this, I fear, he can never learn in any manual; it is the business of his life. He has to take a great many in order to select a few, he has to work them up as he can, and even the guides and philosophers who might have most to say to him must leave him alone when it

---

[10]French: pastor.

comes to the application of precepts, as we leave the painter in communion with his palette. That his characters "must be clear in outline," as Mr. Besant says— he feels that down to his boots; but how he shall make them so is a secret between his good angel and himself. It would be absurdly simple if he could be taught that a great deal of "description" would make them so, or that on the contrary the absence of description and the cultivation of dialogue, or the absence of dialogue and the multiplication of "incident," would rescue him from his diffi- culties. Nothing, for instance, is more possible than that he be of a turn of mind for which this odd, literal opposition of description and dialogue, incident and description, has little meaning and light. People often talk of these things as if they had a kind of internecine distinctness, instead of melting into each other at every breath, and being intimately associated parts of one general effort of expression. I cannot imagine composition existing in a series of blocks, nor conceive, in any novel worth discussing at all, of a passage of description that is not in its intention narrative, a passage of dialogue that is not in its intention descriptive, a touch of truth of any sort that does not partake of the nature of the incident, or an incident that derives its interest from any other source than the general and only source of the success of a work of art—that of being illustrative. A novel is a living thing, all one and continuous, like any other organism, and in proportion as it lives will it be found, I think, that in each of the parts there is something of each of the other parts. The critic who over the close texture of a finished work shall pretend to trace a geography of items will mark some frontiers as artificial, I fear, as any that have been known to history. There is an old-fashioned distinction between the novel of character and the novel of incident which must have cost many a smile to the intending fabulist who was keen about his work. It appears to me as little to the point as the equally celebrated distinction between the novel and the romance—to answer as little to any reality. There are bad novels and good novels, as there are bad pictures and good pictures; but that is the only distinction in which I see any meaning, and I can as little imagine speaking of a novel of character as I can imagine speaking of a picture of character. When one says picture one says of character, when one says novel one says of incident, and the terms may be transposed at will. What is character but the determination of incident? What is incident but the illustration of character? What is either a picture or a novel that is *not* of character? What else do we seek in it and find in it? It is an incident for a woman to stand up with her hand resting on a table and look out at you in a certain way; or if it be not an incident I think it will be hard to say what it is. At the same time is an expression of character. If you say you don't see it (character in *that—allons donc!*),[11] this is exactly what the artist who has reasons of his own for thinking he *does* see it undertakes to show you. When a young man makes up his mind that he had not faith enough after all to enter the church as he intended, that is an incident, though you may not hurry to the end of the chapter to see whether perhaps he doesn't change once more. I do not say that these are extraordinary or startling incidents. I do not pretend to estimate the degree of interest proceeding from them, for this will depend upon the skill of the painter. It sounds almost puerile to say that some incidents are intrinsically much more important than others, and I need not take this precaution after having professed my sympathy for the major ones in remarking that the only classification of the novel that I can understand is into that which has life and that which has it not.

[11]French: nonsense!

The novel and the romance, the novel of incident and that of character—these clumsy separations appear to me to have been made by critics and readers for their own convenience, and to help them out of some of their occasional queer predicaments, but to have little reality or interest for the producer, from whose point of view it is of course that we are attempting to consider the art of fiction. The case is the same with another shadowy category which Mr. Besant apparently is disposed to set up—that of the "modern English novel"; unless indeed it be that in this matter he has fallen into an accidental confusion of standpoints. It is not quite clear whether he intends the remarks in which he alludes to it to be didactic or historical. It is as difficult to suppose a person intending to write a modern English as to suppose him writing an ancient English novel: that is a label which begs the question. One writes the novel, one paints the picture, of one's language and of one's time, and calling it modern English will not, alas! make the difficult task any easier. No more, unfortunately, will calling this or that work of one's fellow-artist a romance—unless it be, of course, simply for the pleasantness of the thing, as for instance when Hawthorne gave this heading to his story of *Blithedale*.[12] The French, who have brought the theory of fiction to remarkable completeness, have but one name for the novel, and have not attempted smaller things in it, that I can see, for that. I can think of no obligation to which the "romancer" would not be held equally with the novelist; the standard of execution is equally high for each. Of course it is of execution that we are talking—that being the only point of a novel that is open to contention. This is perhaps too often lost sight of, only to produce interminable confusions and cross-purposes. We must grant the artist his subject, his idea, his *donnée*:[13] our criticism is applied only to what he makes of it. Naturally I do not mean that we are bound to like it or find it interesting: in case we do not our course is perfectly simple—to let it alone. We may believe that of a certain idea even the most sincere novelist can make nothing at all, and the event may perfectly justify our belief; but the failure will have been a failure to execute, and it is in the execution that the fatal weakness is recorded. If we pretend to respect the artist at all, we must allow him his freedom of choice, in the face, in particular cases, of innumerable presumptions that the choice will not fructify. Art derives a considerable part of its beneficial exercise from flying in the face of presumptions, and some of the most interesting experiments of which it is capable are hidden in the bosom of common things. Gustave Flaubert has written a story about the devotion of a servant-girl to a parrot,[14] and the production, highly finished as it is, cannot on the whole be called a success. We are perfectly free to find it flat, but I think it might have been interesting; and I, for my part, am extremely glad he should have written it; it is a contribution to our knowledge of what can be done—or what cannot. Ivan Turgénieff has written a tale about a deaf and dumb serf and a lap-dog[15] and the thing is touching, loving, a little masterpiece. He struck the note of life where Gustave Flaubert missed it—he flew in the face of a presumption and achieved a victory.

Nothing, of course, will ever take the place of the good old fashion of "liking" a work of art or not liking it: the most improved criticism will not abolish that primitive, that ultimate test. I mention this to guard myself from the accusation of intimating that the idea, the subject, of a novel or a picture, does not matter. It matters, to my sense, in the highest degree, and if I might put up a prayer it

---

[12]*The Blithedale Romance* (1852).   [13]French: fundamental idea, theme.
[14]"Un Coeur simple" (1877), by the French novelist Gustave Flaubert (1821–1880).
[15]"Mumu" (1856), by the Russian novelist Ivan Turgenev (1818–1883).

would be that artists should select none but the richest. Some, as I have already hastened to admit, are much more remunerative than others, and it would be a world happily arranged in which persons intending to treat them should be exempt from confusions and mistakes. This fortunate condition will arrive only, I fear, on the same day that critics become purged from error. Meanwhile, I repeat, we do not judge the artist with fairness unless we say to him, "Oh, I grant you your starting-point, because if I did not I should seem to prescribe to you, and heaven forbid I should take that responsibility. If I pretend to tell you what you must not take, you will call upon me to tell you then what you must take; in which case I shall be prettily caught. Moreover, it isn't till I have accepted your data that I can begin to measure you. I have the standard, the pitch; I have no right to tamper with your flute and then criticise your music. Of course I may not care for your idea at all; I may think it silly, or stale, or unclean; in which case I wash my hands of you altogether. I may content myself with believing that you will not have succeeded in being interesting, but I shall, of course, not attempt to demonstrate it, and you will be as indifferent to me as I am to you. I needn't remind you that there are all sorts of tastes: who can know it better? Some people, for excellent reasons, don't like to read about carpenters; others, for reasons even better, don't like to read about courtesans. Many object to Americans. Others (I believe they are mainly editors and publishers) won't look at Italians. Some readers don't like quiet subjects; others don't like bustling ones. Some enjoy a complete illusion, others the consciousness of large concessions. They choose their novels accordingly, and if they don't care about your idea they won't, *a fortiori*,[16] care about your treatment."

So that it comes back very quickly, as I have said, to the liking: in spite of M. Zola,[17] who reasons less powerfully than he represents,[18] and who will not reconcile himself to this absoluteness of taste, thinking that there are certain things that people ought to like, and that they can be made to like. I am quite at a loss to imagine anything (at any rate in this matter of fiction) that people *ought* to like or dislike. Selection will be sure to take care of itself, for it has a constant motive behind it. That motive is simply experience. As people feel life, so they will feel the art that is most closely related to it. This closeness of relation is what we should never forget in talking of the effort of the novel. Many people speak of it as a factitious, artificial form, a product of ingenuity, the business of which is to alter and arrange the things that surround us, to translate them into conventional, traditional moulds. This, however, is a view of the matter which carries us but a very short way, condemns the art to an eternal repetition of a few familiar *clichés*, cuts short its development, and leads us straight up to a dead wall. Catching the very note and trick, the strange irregular rhythm of life, that is the attempt whose strenuous force keeps Fiction upon her feet. In proportion as in what she offers us we see life *without* rearrangement do we feel that we are touching the truth; in proportion as we see it *with* rearrangement do we feel that we are being put off with a substitute, a compromise and convention. It is not uncommon to hear an extraordinary assurance of remark in regard to this matter of rearranging, which is often spoken of as if it were the last word of art. Mr. Besant seems to me in danger of falling into the great error with his rather unguarded talk about "selection." Art is essentially selection, but it is a selection whose main care is to be typical, to be inclusive. For many people art means rose-coloured window-panes, and selection means picking a bouquet for Mrs.

[16]Latin: with greater reason.   [17]Émile Zola (1840–1902), French novelist and critic.
[18]I.e., his critical arguments are less powerful than his fiction.

Grundy.[19] They will tell you glibly that artistic considerations have nothing to do with the disagreeable, with the ugly; they will rattle off shallow commonplaces about the province of art and the limits of art till you are moved to some wonder in return as to the province and the limits of ignorance. It appears to me that no one can ever have made a seriously artistic attempt without becoming conscious of an immense increase—a kind of revelation—of freedom. One perceives in that case—by the light of a heavenly ray—that the province of art is all life, all feeling, all observation, all vision. As Mr. Besant so justly intimates, it is all experience. That is a sufficient answer to those who maintain that it must not touch the sad things of life, who stick into its divine unconscious bosom little prohibitory inscriptions on the end of sticks, such as we see in public gardens— "It is forbidden to walk on the grass; it is forbidden to touch the flowers; it is not allowed to introduce dogs or to remain after dark; it is requested to keep to the right." The young aspirant in the line of fiction whom we continue to imagine will do nothing without taste, for in that case his freedom would be of little use to him; but the first advantage of his taste will be to reveal to him the absurdity of the little sticks and tickets. If he have taste, I must add, of course he will have ingenuity, and my disrespectful reference to that quality just now was not meant to imply that it is useless in fiction. But it is only a secondary aid; the first is a capacity for receiving straight impressions.

Mr. Besant has some remarks on the question of "the story" which I shall not attempt to criticise, though they seem to me to contain a singular ambiguity, because I do not think I understand them. I cannot see what is meant by talking as if there were a part of a novel which is the story and part of it which for mystical reasons is not—unless indeed the distinction be made in a sense in which it is difficult to suppose that any one should attempt to convey anything. "The story," if it represents anything, represents the subject; the idea, the *donnée* of the novel; and there is surely no "school"—Mr. Besant speaks of a school— which urges that a novel should be all treatment and no subject. There must assuredly be something to treat; every school is intimately conscious of that. This sense of the story being the idea, the starting-point, of the novel, is the only one that I see in which it can be spoken of as something different from its organic whole; and since in proportion as the work is successful the idea permeates and penetrates it, informs and animates it, so that every word and every punctuation-point contribute directly to the expression, in that proportion do we lose our sense of the story being a blade which may be drawn more or less out of its sheath. The story and the novel, the idea and the form, are the needle and thread, and I never heard of a guild of tailors who recommend the use of the thread without the needle, or the needle without the thread. Mr. Besant is not the only critic who may be observed to have spoken as if there were certain things in life which constitute stories, and certain others which do not. I find the same odd implication in an entertaining article in the *Pall Mall Gazette,* devoted, as it happens, to Mr. Besant's lecture. "The story is the thing!" says this graceful writer, as if with a tone of opposition to some other idea. I should think it was, as every painter who, as the time for "sending in"[20] his picture looms in the distance, finds himself still in quest of a subject—as every belated artist not fixed about his theme will heartily agree. There are some subjects which speak to us and others which do not, but he would be a clever man who

---

[19]I.e., submitting to convention and prudish taste. Mrs. Grundy, a character in *Speed the Plow* (1798), a play by Thomas Morton (1764–1838), has come to stand as a symbol of those interested only in the "safe" aspects of life and art.
[20]Submitting for exhibition.

should undertake to give a rule—an index expurgatorius[21]—by which the story and the no-story should be known apart. It is impossible (to me at least) to imagine any such rule which shall not be altogether arbitrary. The writer in the *Pall Mall* opposes the delightful (as I suppose) novel of *Margot la Balafrée*[22] to certain tales in which "Bostonian nymphs" appear to have "rejected English dukes for psychological reasons." I am not acquainted with the romance just designated, and can scarcely forgive the *Pall Mall* critic for not mentioning the name of the author, but the title appears to refer to a lady who may have received a scar in some heroic adventure. I am inconsolable at not being acquainted with this episode, but am utterly at a loss to see why it is a story when the rejection (or acceptance) of a duke is not, and why a reason, psychological or other, is not a subject when a cicatrix[23] is. They are all particles of the multitudinous life with which the novel deals, and surely no dogma which pretends to make it lawful to touch the one and unlawful to touch the other will stand for a moment on its feet. It is the special picture that must stand or fall, according as it seem to possess truth or to lack it. Mr. Besant does not, to my sense, light up the subject by intimating that a story must, under penalty of not being a story, consist of "adventures." Why of adventures more than of green spectacles? He mentions a category of impossible things, and among them he places "fiction without adventure." Why without adventure, more than without matrimony, or celibacy, or parturition,[24] or cholera, or hydropathy,[25] or Jansenism?[26] This seems to me to bring the novel back to the hapless little *rôle* of being an artificial, ingenious thing—bring it down from its large, free character of an immense and exquisite correspondence with life. And what *is* adventure, when it comes to that, and by what sign is the listening pupil to recognise it? It is an adventure—an immense one—for me to write this little article; and for a Bostonian nymph to reject an English duke is an adventure only less stirring, I should say, than for an English duke to be rejected by a Bostonian nymph. I see dramas within dramas in that, and innumerable points of view. A psychological reason is, to my imagination, an object adorably pictorial; to catch the tint of its complexion—I feel as if that idea might inspire one to Titianesque[27] efforts. There are few things more exciting to me, in short, than a psychological reason, and yet, I protest, the novel seems to me the most magnificent form of art. I have just been reading, at the same time, the delightful story of *Treasure Island,* by Mr. Robert Louis Stevenson[28] and, in a manner less consecutive, the last tale from M. Edmond de Goncourt, which is entitled *Chérie.*[29] One of these works treats of murders, mysteries, islands of dreadful renown, hairbreadth escapes, miraculous coincidences and buried doubloons. The other treats of a little French girl who lived in a fine house in Paris, and died of wounded sensibility because no one would marry her. I call *Treasure Island* delightful, because it appears to me to have succeeded wonderfully in what it attempts; and I venture to bestow no epithet upon *Chérie,* which strikes me as having failed deplorably in what it attempts—

---

[21]Latin: expurgatory index; here used to mean a standard by which to judge.

[22]A novel (1884) by Fortuné du Boisgobey (1821–1891), French romantic novelist. "Balafrée" means "the scar-faced woman."

[23]Scar. [24]Childbirth.

[25]The use of water to treat disease.

[26]Doctrines of Bishop Cornelis Jansen (1585–1638), Dutch theologian who taught an extreme form of predestination and emphasized the saving power of divine grace.

[27]In the manner of the Venetian painter Titian (1487?–1576), who was renowned for his realism and rich coloring.

[28]English writer (1850–1894), author of *Treasure Island* (1883).

[29]Novel (1884) by Edmond Huot de Goncourt (1822–1896).

that is in tracing the development of the moral consciousness of a child. But one of these productions strikes me as exactly as much of a novel as the other, and as having a "story" quite as much. The moral consciousness of a child is as much a part of life as the islands of the Spanish Main, and the one sort of geography seems to me to have those "surprises" of which Mr. Besant speaks quite as much as the other. For myself (since it comes back in the last resort, as I say, to the preference of the individual), the picture of the child's experience has the advantage that I can at successive steps (an immense luxury, near to the "sensual pleasure" of which Mr. Besant's critic in the *Pall Mall* speaks) say Yes or No, as it may be, to what the artist puts before me. I have been a child in fact, but I have been on a quest for a buried treasure only in supposition, and it is a simple accident that with M. de Goncourt I should have for the most part to say No. With George Eliot,[30] when she painted that country with a far other intelligence, I always said Yes.

The most interesting part of Mr. Besant's lecture is unfortunately the briefest passage—his very cursory allusion to the "conscious moral purpose" of the novel. Here again it is not very clear whether he be recording a fact or laying down a principle; it is a great pity that in the latter case he should not have developed his idea. This branch of the subject is of immense importance, and Mr. Besant's few words point to considerations of the widest reach, not to be lightly disposed of. He will have treated the art of fiction but superficially who is not prepared to go every inch of the way that these considerations will carry him. It is for this reason that at the beginning of these remarks I was careful to notify the reader that my reflections on so large a theme have no pretension to be exhaustive. Like Mr. Besant, I have left the question of the morality of the novel till the last, and at the last I find I have used up my space. It is a question surrounded with difficulties, as witness the very first that meets us, in the form of a definite question, on the threshold. Vagueness, in such a discussion, is fatal, and what is the meaning of your morality and your conscious moral purpose? Will you not define your terms and explain how (a novel being a picture) a picture can be either moral or immoral? You wish to paint a moral picture or carve a moral statue: will you not tell us how you would set about it? We are discussing the Art of Fiction; questions of art are questions (in the widest sense) of execution; questions of morality are quite another affair, and will you not let us see how it is that you find it so easy to mix them up? These things are so clear to Mr. Besant that he has deduced from them a law which he sees embodied in English Fiction, and which is "a truly admirable thing and a great cause for congratulation." It is a great cause for congratulation indeed when such thorny problems become as smooth as silk. I may add that in so far as Mr. Besant perceives that in point of fact English Fiction has addressed itself preponderantly to these delicate questions he will appear to many people to have made a vain discovery. They will have been positively struck, on the contrary, with the moral timidity of the usual English novelist; with his (or with her) aversion to face the difficulties with which on every side the treatment of reality bristles. He is apt to be extremely shy (whereas the picture that Mr. Besant draws is a picture of boldness), and the sign of his work, for the most part, is a cautious silence on certain subjects. In the English novel (by which of course I mean the American as well), more than in any other, there is a traditional difference between that which people know and that which they agree to admit that they know, that which they see and that which they speak of, that which they feel to be a part of life and that

[30]George Eliot (Mary Ann Evans), English novelist (1819–1880). James refers to her novel *Silas Marner* (1861).

which they allow to enter into literature. There is the great difference, in short, between what they talk of in conversation and what they talk of in print. The essence of moral energy is to survey the whole field, and I should directly reverse Mr. Besant's remark and say not that the English novel has a purpose, but that it has a diffidence. To what degree a purpose in a work of art is a source of corruption I shall not attempt to inquire; the one that seems to me least dangerous is the purpose of making a perfect work. As for our novel, I may say lastly on this score that as we find it in England to-day it strikes me as addressed in a large degree to "young people," and that this in itself constitutes a presumption that it will be rather shy. There are certain things which it is generally agreed not to discuss, not even to mention, before young people. That is very well, but the absence of discussion is not a symptom of the moral passion. The purpose of the English novel—"a truly admirable thing, and a great cause for congratulation"—strikes me therefore as rather negative.

There is one point at which the moral sense and the artistic sense lie very near together; that is in the light of the very obvious truth that the deepest quality of a work of art will always be the quality of the mind of the producer. In proportion as that intelligence is fine will the novel, the picture, the statue partake of the substance of beauty and truth. To be constituted of such elements is, to my vision, to have purpose enough. No good novel will ever proceed from a superficial mind; that seems to me an axiom which, for the artist in fiction, will cover all needful moral ground: if the youthful aspirant take it to heart it will illuminate for him many of the mysteries of "purpose." There are many other useful things that might be said to him, but I have come to the end of my article, and can only touch them as I pass. The critic in the *Pall Mall Gazette*, whom I have already quoted, draws attention to the danger, in speaking of the art of fiction, of generalising. The danger that he has in mind is rather, I imagine, that of particularising, for there are some comprehensive remarks which, in addition to those embodied in Mr. Besant's suggestive lecture, might without fear of misleading him be addressed to the ingenuous student. I should remind him first of the magnificence of the form that is open to him, which offers to sight so few restrictions and such innumerable opportunities. The other arts, in comparison, appear confined and hampered; the various conditions under which they are exercised are so rigid and definite. But the only condition that I can think of attaching to the composition of the novel is, as I have already said, that it be sincere. This freedom is a splendid privilege, and the first lesson of the young novelist is to learn to be worthy of it. "Enjoy it as it deserves," I should say to him; "take possession of it, explore it to its utmost extent, publish it, rejoice in it. All life belongs to you, and do not listen either to those who would shut you up into corners of it and tell you that it is only here and there that art inhabits, or to those who would persuade you that this heavenly messenger wings her way outside of life altogether, breathing a superfine air, and turning away her head from the truth of things. There is no impression of life, no manner of seeing it and feeling it, to which the plan of the novelist may not offer a place; you have only to remember that talents so dissimilar as those of Alexandre Dumas and Jane Austen, Charles Dickens and Gustave Flaubert have worked in this field with equal glory. Do not think too much about optimism and pessimism; try and catch the colour of life itself. In France to-day we see a prodigious effort (that of Emile Zola, to whose solid and serious work no explorer of the capacity of the novel can allude without respect) we see an extraordinary effort vitiated by a spirit of pessimism on a narrow basis. M. Zola is magnificent, but he strikes an English reader as ignorant; he has an air of working in the dark; if he had as much light as energy, his results would be of the highest value. As for the aberrations of a shallow optimism, the ground (of English fiction especially) is strewn with their brittle particles as with broken glass. If you must indulge in conclusions, let them have the taste of a wide knowledge. Remember that your first duty is to be as complete as possible—to make as perfect a work. Be generous and delicate and pursue the prize."

                                                                                                    1884, 1888

Ambrose Bierce   *1842–1914*

In 1914, when he was seventy-one, Ambrose Bierce left the United States to report on the Mexican Revolution as an observer with the rebel army of Pancho Villa. One month after he arrived he wrote to a friend, "Pray for me—real hard." Shortly afterward Bierce disappeared, never to be seen again, and his mysterious fate has fascinated his biographers and his readers almost as much as the details of his misanthropic life. Bierce was born the child of poor farmers at Horse Cave Creek, Meigs County, in southeast Ohio. When he was four his family moved to a farm in Indiana, where he went to school. His parents' religious fervor left him with a lifelong hatred of faith and piety; his unhappy childhood is partially reflected in his stories filled with deaths, maimings, and the separations of parents, children, and families.

When Bierce was fifteen he went to work as a printer's devil on an antislavery newspaper in Indiana. Later he attended the Kentucky Military Institute for a year. And in 1861, with the outbreak of the Civil War, he enlisted in the Union Army. Bierce served with distinction throughout the war, rising from the rank of private to lieutenant and finally to the rank of brevet major. He re-enlisted twice and fought in some of the greatest and bloodiest battles of the war: Shiloh, Chickamauga, Lookout Mountain, Missionary Ridge.

Following the war, Bierce went west, first working in the San Francisco Mint but gradually establishing a career as a journalist, polemicist, and writer of fiction. He spent the years from 1872 to 1876 in London, where his slashing brand of journalism won him fame and the title "Bitter Bierce." But he returned to California to write for William Randolph Hearst's San Francisco Examiner. *Bierce's writing, especially his fiction, was sardonic and obsessed with death. It has been said that "Death" was perhaps "his only character." In fact, the idea of death was not only central to Bierce's writing, it dominated his life. His early and crucial experiences in the Civil War had brought him face to face with a horrible and futile slaughter that had destroyed his youthful, romantic optimism. And in his later life Bierce was tortured by personal and professional disasters: friends and relatives fought bitterly with him, became estranged, committed suicide, died tragically. He grew increasingly cynical and malevolent, his writing vitriolic, filled with invective.*

Excerpts from his popular Devil's Dictionary *appeared from 1881 to 1906; it was a collection of waspish, witty epigrams and definitions that reflected the tone and flavor of much of his work. He defined "Bride" as "A woman with a fine prospect of happiness behind her"; "Christian" as "One who believes that the New Testament is a divinely inspired book admirably suited to the spiritual needs of his neighbor"; "Birth" as "The first and direst of all disasters." From 1867 until his disappearance, Bierce was a major figure in the development of American literary realism. He wrote essays, short stories, and major journalistic pieces. He was called a "West Coast Samuel Johnson," and his cynical and scathing newspaper articles were enormously popular. But his finest achievement is found in his short stories, tales about men trapped in the labyrinths of endless struggle, blinded by folly and romantic hope, abandoned to a cold and brutal providence.*

FURTHER READING: *Collected Works of Ambrose Bierce*, 12 vols., ed. W. Neale, 1909–1912; *Ambrose Bierce, Skepticism and Dissent*, ed. L. Berkove, 1980; *The Letters of Ambrose Bierce*, ed. B. Pope, 1922, 1967; V. Starrett, *Ambrose Bierce*, 1920; C. Grattan, *Bitter Bierce*, 1929; C. McWilliams, *Ambrose Bierce, A Biography*, 1929, 1967; P. Fatout, *Ambrose Bierce, The Devil's Lexicographer*, 1951; P. Fatout, *Ambrose Bierce and the Black Hills*, 1956; R. O'Conner, *Ambrose Bierce, A Biography*, 1967; M. Grenander, *Ambrose Bierce*, 1971; S. Woodruff, *The Short Stories of Ambrose Bierce*, 1964; *Critical Essays on Ambrose Bierce*, ed. C. Davidson, 1982; L. Berkove, *Ambrose Bierce, A Braver Man than Anybody Knew*, 1983; C. Davidson, *The Experimental Fictions of Ambrose Bierce*, 1984.

TEXT: *Tales of Soldiers and Civilians*, 1892.

AN OCCURRENCE AT OWL CREEK BRIDGE

I

A man stood upon a railroad bridge in northern Alabama, looking down into the swift water twenty feet below. The man's hands were behind his back, the wrists bound with a cord. A rope loosely encircled his neck. It was attached to a stout cross-timber above his head, and the slack fell to the level of his knees. Some loose boards laid upon the sleepers[1] supporting the metals of the railway supplied a footing for him and his executioners—two private soldiers of the Federal army, directed by a sergeant, who in civil life may have been a deputy sheriff. At a short remove upon the same temporary platform was an officer in the uniform of his rank, armed. He was a captain. A sentinel at each end of the bridge stood with his rifle in the position known as "support," that is to say, vertical in front of the left shoulder, the hammer resting on the forearm thrown straight across the chest—a formal and unnatural position, enforcing an erect carriage of the body. It did not appear to be the duty of these two men to know what was occurring at the center of the bridge; they merely blockaded the two ends of the foot plank which traversed it.

Beyond one of the sentinels, nobody was in sight; the railroad ran straight away into a forest for a hundred yards, then, curving, was lost to view. Doubtless there was an outpost farther along. The other bank of the stream was open ground—a gentle acclivity crowned with a stockade of vertical tree trunks, loopholed for rifles, with a single embrasure through which protruded the muzzle of a brass cannon commanding the bridge. Midway of the slope between bridge and fort were the spectators—a single company of infantry in line, at "parade rest," the butts of the rifles on the ground, the barrels inclining slightly backward against the right shoulder, the hands crossed upon the stock. A lieutenant stood at the right of the line, the point of his sword upon the ground, his left hand resting upon his right. Excepting the group of four at the center of the bridge, not a man moved. The company faced the bridge, staring stonily, motionless. The sentinels, facing the banks of the stream, might have been statues to adorn the bridge. The captain stood with folded arms, silent, observing the work of his subordinates, but making no sign. Death is a dignitary who when

---

[1]Ties, wooden beams to which railroad tracks are attached.

he comes announced is to be received with formal manifestations of respect, even by those most familiar with him. In the code of military etiquette silence and fixity are forms of deference.

The man who was engaged in being hanged was apparently about thirty-five years of age. He was a civilian, if one might judge from his dress, which was that of a planter. His features were good—a straight nose, firm mouth, broad forehead, from which his long, dark hair was combed straight back, falling behind his ears to the collar of his well-fitting frock coat. He wore a mustache and pointed beard, but no whiskers; his eyes were large and dark gray, and had a kindly expression which one would hardly have expected in one whose neck was in the hemp. Evidently this was no vulgar assassin. The liberal military code makes provision for hanging many kinds of people, and gentlemen are not excluded.

The preparations being complete, the two private soldiers stepped aside and each drew away the plank upon which he had been standing. The sergeant turned to the captain, saluted, and placed himself immediately behind that officer, who in turn moved apart one pace. These movements left the condemned man and the sergeant standing on the two ends of the same plank, which spanned three of the crossties of the bridge. The end upon which the civilian stood almost, but not quite reached a fourth. This plank had been held in place by the weight of the captain; it was now held by that of the sergeant. At a signal from the former, the latter would step aside, the plank would tilt, and the condemned man go down between two ties. The arrangement commended itself to his judgment as simple and effective. His face had not been covered nor his eyes bandaged. He looked a moment at his "unsteadfast footing," then let his gaze wander to the swirling water of the stream racing madly beneath his feet. A piece of dancing driftwood caught his attention and his eyes followed it down the current. How slowly it appeared to move! What a sluggish stream!

He closed his eyes in order to fix his last thoughts upon his wife and children. The water, touched to gold by the early sun, the brooding mists under the banks at some distance down the stream, the fort, the soldiers, the piece of drift—all had distracted him. And now he became conscious of a new disturbance. Striking through the thought of his dear ones was a sound which he could neither ignore nor understand, a sharp, distinct, metallic percussion like the stroke of a blacksmith's hammer upon the anvil; it had the same ringing quality. He wondered what it was, and whether immeasurably distant or near by—it seemed both. Its recurrence was regular, but as slow as the tolling of a death knell. He awaited each stroke with impatience and—he knew not why—apprehension. The intervals of silence grew progressively longer; the delays became maddening. With their greater infrequency the sounds increased in strength and sharpness. They hurt his ear like the thrust of a knife; he feared he would shriek. What he heard was the ticking of his watch.

He unclosed his eyes and saw again the water below him. "If I could free my hands," he thought, "I might throw off the noose and spring into the stream. By diving I could evade the bullets, and, swimming vigorously, reach the bank, take to the woods, and get away home. My home, thank God, is as yet outside their lines; my wife and little ones are still beyond the invader's farthest advance."

As these thoughts, which have here to be set down in words, were flashed into the doomed man's brain rather than evolved from it, the captain nodded to the sergeant. The sergeant stepped aside.

II

Peyton Farquhar was a well-to-do planter of an old and highly respected Alabama family. Being a slave owner and like other slave owners a politician, he was naturally an original secessionist and ardently devoted to the Southern cause. Circumstances of an imperious nature, which it is unnecessary to relate here, had prevented him from taking service with the gallant army which had fought the disastrous campaigns ending with the fall of Corinth,[1] and he chafed under the inglorious restraint, longing for the release of his energies, the larger life of the soldier, the opportunity for distinction. That opportunity, he felt, would come, as it comes to all in war time. Meanwhile he did what he could. No service was too humble for him to perform in aid of the South, no adventure too perilous for him to undertake if consistent with the character of a civilian who was at heart a soldier, and who in good faith and without too much qualification assented to at least a part of the frankly villainous dictum that all is fair in love and war.

One evening while Farquhar and his wife were sitting on a rustic bench near the entrance to his grounds, a gray-clad[2] soldier rode up to the gate and asked for a drink of water. Mrs. Farquhar was only too happy to serve him with her own white hands. While she was gone to fetch the water, her husband approached the dusty horseman and inquired eagerly for news from the front.

"The Yanks are repairing the railroads," said the man, "and are getting ready for another advance. They have reached the Owl Creek bridge, put it in order, and built a stockade on the north bank. The commandant has issued an order, which is posted everywhere, declaring that any civilian caught interfering with the railroad, its bridges, tunnels, or trains will be summarily hanged. I saw the order."

"How far is it to the Owl Creek bridge?" Farquhar asked.

"About thirty miles."

"Is there no force on this side the creek?"

"Only a picket post half a mile out, on the railroad, and a single sentinel at this end of the bridge."

"Suppose a man—a civilian and student of hanging—should elude the picket post and perhaps get the better of the sentinel," said Farquhar, smiling, "what could he accomplish?"

The soldier reflected. "I was there a month ago," he replied. "I observed that the flood of last winter had lodged a great quantity of driftwood against the wooden pier at this end of the bridge. It is now dry and would burn like tow."

The lady had now brought the water, which the soldier drank. He thanked her ceremoniously, bowed to her husband, and rode away. An hour later, after nightfall, he repassed the plantation, going northward in the direction from which he had come. He was a Federal scout.

III

As Peyton Farquhar fell straight downward through the bridge he lost consciousness and was as one already dead. From this state he was awakened—ages later, it seemed to him—by the pain of a sharp pressure upon his throat, followed

---

[1]Corinth, Mississippi, occupied by Union forces in May, 1862.
[2]I.e., dressed in the gray uniform of a Confederate soldier.

by a sense of suffocation. Keen, poignant agonies seemed to shoot from his neck downward through every fiber of his body and limbs. These pains appeared to flash along well-defined lines of ramification and to beat with an inconceivably rapid periodicity. They seemed like streams of pulsating fire heating him to an intolerable temperature. As to his head, he was conscious of nothing but a feeling of fullness—of congestion. These sensations were unaccompanied by thought. The intellectual part of his nature was already effaced; he had power only to feel, and feeling was torment. He was conscious of motion. Encompassed in a luminous cloud, of which he was now merely the fiery heart, without material substance, he swung through unthinkable arcs of oscillation, like a vast pendulum. Then all at once, with terrible suddenness, the light about him shot upward with the noise of a loud plash; a frightful roaring was in his ears, and all was cold and dark. The power of thought was restored; he knew that the rope had broken and he had fallen into the stream. There was no additional strangulation; the noose about his neck was already suffocating him and kept the water from his lungs. To die of hanging at the bottom of a river!—the idea seemed to him ludicrous. He opened his eyes in the darkness and saw above him a gleam of light, but how distant, how inaccessible! He was still sinking, for the light became fainter and fainter until it was a mere glimmer. Then it began to grow and brighten, and he knew that he was rising toward the surface—knew it with reluctance, for he was now very comfortable. "To be hanged and drowned," he thought, "that is not so bad; but I do not wish to be shot." No, I will not be shot, that is not fair."

He was not conscious of an effort, but a sharp pain in his wrist apprised him that he was trying to free his hands. He gave the struggle his attention, as an idler might observe the feat of a juggler, without interest in the outcome. What splendid effort!—what magnificent, what super-human strength! Ah, that was a fine endeavor! Bravo! The cord fell away; his arms parted and floated upward, the hands dimly seen on each side in the growing light. He watched them with a new interest as first one and then the other pounced upon the noose at his neck. They tore it away and thrust it fiercely aside, its undulations resembling those of a water snake. "Put it back, put it back!" He thought he shouted these words to his hands, for the undoing of the noose had been succeeded by the direst pang that he had yet experienced. His neck ached horribly; his brain was on fire; his heart, which had been fluttering faintly, gave a great leap, trying to force itself out at his mouth. His whole body was racked and wrenched with an insupportable anguish! But his disobedient hands gave no heed to the command. They beat the water vigorously with quick, downward strokes, forcing him to the surface. He felt his head emerge; his eyes were blinded by the sunlight; his chest expanded convulsively, and with a supreme and crowning agony his lungs engulfed a great draught of air, which instantly he expelled in a shriek!

He was now in full possession of his physical senses. They were, indeed, preternaturally keen and alert. Something in the awful disturbance of his organic system had so exalted and refined them that they made record of things never before perceived. He felt the ripples upon his face and heard their separate sounds as they struck. He looked at the forest on the bank of the stream, saw the individual trees, the leaves and the veining of each leaf—saw the very insects upon them: the locusts, the brilliant-bodied flies, the gray spiders stretching their webs from twig to twig. He noted the prismatic colors in all the dewdrops upon a million blades of grass. The humming of the gnats that danced above the eddies of the stream, the beating of the dragonflies' wings, the strokes of the water spiders' legs, like oars which had lifted their boat—all these made audible music. A fish slid along beneath his eyes and he heard the rush of its body parting the water.

He had come to the surface facing down the stream; in a moment the visible world seemed to wheel slowly round, himself the pivotal point, and he saw the bridge, the fort, the soldiers upon the bridge, the captain, the sergeant, the two privates, his executioners. They were in silhouette against the blue sky. They shouted and gesticulated, pointing at him. The captain had drawn his pistol, but did not fire; the others were unarmed. Their movements were grotesque and horrible, their forms gigantic.

Suddenly he heard a sharp report and something struck the water smartly within a few inches of his head, spattering his face with spray. He heard the second report, and saw one of the sentinels with his rifle at his shoulder, a light cloud of blue smoke rising from the muzzle. The man in the water saw the eye of the man on the bridge gazing into his own through the sights of the rifle. He observed that it was a gray eye and remembered having read that gray eyes were keenest, and that all famous marksmen had them. Nevertheless, this one had missed.

A counterswirl had caught Farquhar and turned him half round; he was again looking into the forest on the bank opposite the fort. The sound of a clear, high voice in a monotonous singsong now rang out behind him and came across the water with distinctness that pierced and subdued all other sounds, even the beating of the ripples in his ears. Although no soldier, he had frequented camps enough to know the dread significance of that deliberate, drawling, aspirated chant; the lieutenant on shore was taking part in the morning's work. How coldly and pitilessly—with what an even, calm intonation, presaging and enforcing tranquillity in the men—with what accurately measured intervals fell those cruel words:

"Attention, company! . . . Shoulder arms! . . . Ready! . . . Aim! . . . Fire!"

Farquhar dived—dived as deeply as he could. The water roared in his ears like the voice of Niagara, yet he heard the dulled thunder of the volley and, rising again toward the surface, met shining bits of metal, singularly flattened, oscillating slowly downward. Some of them touched him on the face and hands, then fell away, continuing their descent. One lodged between his collar and his neck; it was uncomfortably warm and he snatched it out.

As he rose to the surface, gasping for breath, he saw that he had been a long time under water; he was perceptibly farther downstream—nearer to safety. The soldiers had almost finished reloading; the metal ramrods flashed all at once in the sunshine as they were drawn from the barrels, turned in the air, and thrust into their sockets. The two sentinels fired again, independently and ineffectually.

The hunted man saw all this over his shoulder; he was now swimming vigorously with the current. His brain was as energetic as his arms and legs; he thought with the rapidity of lightning.

"The officer," he reasoned, "will not make that martinet's error a second time. It is as easy to dodge a volley as a single shot. He has probably already given the command to fire at will. God help me, I cannot dodge them all!"

An appalling plash within two yards of him was followed by a loud, rushing sound, *diminuendo,*[3] which seemed to travel back through the air to the fort and died in an explosion which stirred the very river to its deeps! A rising sheet of water, which curved over him, fell down upon him, blinded him, strangled him!

[3]Italian: diminishing in volume.

The cannon had taken a hand in the game. As he shook his head free from the commotion of the smitten water, he heard the deflected shot humming through the air ahead, and in an instant it was cracking and smashing the branches in the forest beyond.

"They will not do that again," he thought; "the next time they will use a charge of grape.[4] I must keep my eye upon the gun; the smoke will apprise me—the report arrives too late; it lags behind the missile. That is a good gun."

Suddenly he felt himself whirled round and round—spinning like a top. The water, the banks, the forests, the now distant bridge, fort, and men—all were commingled and blurred. Objects were represented by their colors only; circular horizontal streaks of color—that was all he saw. He had been caught in a vortex and was being whirled on with a velocity of advance and gyration which made him giddy and sick. In a few moments he was flung upon the gravel at the foot of the left bank of the stream—the southern bank—and behind a projecting point which concealed him from his enemies. The sudden arrest of his motion, the abrasion of one of his hands on the gravel, restored him, and he wept with delight. He dug his fingers into the sand, threw it over himself in handfuls, and audibly blessed it. It looked like gold, like diamonds, rubies, emeralds; he could think of nothing beautiful which it did not resemble. The trees upon the bank were giant garden plants; he noted a definite order in their arrangement, inhaled the fragrance of their blooms. A strange, roseate light shone through the spaces among their trunks and the wind made in their branches the music of aeolian harps.[5] He had no wish to perfect his escape—was content to remain in that enchanting spot until retaken.

A whiz and rattle of grapeshot among the branches high above his head roused him from his dream. The baffled cannoneer had fired him a random farewell. He sprang to his feet, rushed up the sloping bank, and plunged into the forest.

All that day he traveled, laying his course by the rounding sun. The forest seemed interminable; nowhere did he discover a break in it, not even a wood-man's road. He had not known that he lived in so wild a region. There was something uncanny in the revelation.

By nightfall he was fatigued, footsore, famishing. The thought of his wife and children urged him on. At last he found a road which led him in what he knew to be the right direction. It was wide and straight as a city street, yet it seemed untraveled. No fields bordered it, no dwelling anywhere. Not so much as the barking of a dog suggested human habitation. The black bodies of the great trees formed a straight wall on both sides, terminating on the horizon in a point, like a diagram in a lesson in perspective. Overhead, as he looked up through this rift in the wood, shone great golden stars looking unfamiliar and grouped in strange constellations. He was sure they were arranged in some order which had a secret and malign significance. The wood on either side was full of singular noises, among which—once, twice, and again—he distinctly heard whispers in an unknown tongue.

His neck was in pain and lifting his hand to it he found it horribly swollen. He knew that it had a circle of black where the rope had bruised it. His eyes felt congested; he could no longer close them. His tongue was swollen with thirst; he relieved its fever by thrusting it forward from between his teeth into the cool air. How softly the turf had carpeted the untraveled avenue—he could no longer feel the roadway beneath his feet!

[4]Grapeshot, a cluster of iron balls fired from a cannon.
[5]Stringed instruments that sound when exposed to the wind.

Doubtless, despite his suffering, he had fallen asleep while walking, for now he sees another scene—perhaps he has merely recovered from a delirium. He stands at the gate of his own home. All is as he left it, and all bright and beautiful in the morning sunshine. He must have traveled the entire night. As he pushes open the gate and passes up the wide white walk, he sees a flutter of female garments; his wife, looking fresh and cool and sweet, steps down from the veranda to meet him. At the bottom of the steps she stands waiting, with a smile of ineffable joy, an attitude of matchless grace and dignity. Ah, how beautiful she is! He springs forward with extended arms. As he is about to clasp her, he feels a stunning blow upon the back of the neck; a blinding white light blazes all about him with a sound like the shock of a cannon—then all is darkness and silence!

Peyton Farquhar was dead; his body, with a broken neck, swung gently from side to side beneath the timbers of the Owl Creek bridge.

1890, 1891

Hamlin Garland   *1860–1940*

Hamlin Garland's descriptions of Middle Western farm life were the first realistic literary portrayals of America's nineteenth-century agricultural frontier. Like the other "Prairie Realists," who wrote of the trials of the native Americans and the foreigners, all immigrants in a new world, Garland countered the prevailing romantic views of America's midland by describing it not as a "New Eden," but as a land of hardship and bitter disappointment.

Garland's parents had emigrated from Maine to a farm near West Salem, Wisconsin, where Hamlin Garland was born shortly before the Civil War. The family then moved from Wisconsin to Iowa and then to the Dakota Territory in a fruitless search for success and plenty. In 1884 Garland left the "middle border" to return to the East, the struggles of his parents having convinced him that the rural Midwest was a land not of promise but of poverty and oppressive toil. Settling in Boston, Garland began to educate himself by spending long hours in the Boston Public Library, studying history, European literature, and Darwinian theories of evolution. He studied and taught in the Boston School of Oratory, lectured on literature, and began writing sketches of the midland prairies he had left behind.

Garland's first collection of stories was published as Main-Travelled Roads *(1891), a book described by William Dean Howells as "full of the bitter and burning dust, the foul and trampled slush of the common avenues of life." The novels, short stories, and auto- biographies that followed were a blend of grimly realistic details and optimistic romantic attitudes, a form of modified naturalism that Garland called "Veritism" and described, in* Crumbling Idols *(1894), as a literature that moved beyond naturalism and examined the harsh and ugly realities of life, not merely to record, but also to interpret and improve the life of the common man.*

Garland's later writings grew increasingly romantic and sentimental, partly because success had mellowed him and partly because of a desire to meet the demands of the literary marketplace. His greatest achievement remained his early literary effort to come to terms with American experience, to show one aspect of the frontier as it actually was, not as it had been conceived by nostalgic city-dwellers and by readers of popular fiction. "I have lived the life," Garland wrote in A Son of the Middle Border *(1917), "and I know that farming is not entirely made up of berrying, tossing the new-mown hay, and singing 'The Old Oaken Bucket' on the porch by moonlight."*

FURTHER READING: *The Works of Hamlin Garland,* 44 volumes projected, ed. D. Pizer, is now in progress; *A Son of the Middle Border,* 1917; *Roadside Meetings,* 1930; *Hamlin Garland's Diary,* ed. D. Pizer, 1969; D. Pizer, *Hamlin Garland's Early Work and Career,* 1960; J. Holloway, *Hamlin Garland,* 1960; J. McCullough, *Hamlin Garland,* 1978; J. Nagel, *Critical Essays on Hamlin Garland,* 1982; C. Silet and R. Welch, *The Critical Reception of Hamlin Garland, 1891–1978,* 1983.
TEXT: *Main-Travelled Roads,* 1891.

THE RETURN OF A PRIVATE

I

The nearer the train drew toward La Crosse,[1] the soberer the little group of "vets" became. On the long way from New Orleans, they had beguiled tedium with jokes and friendly chaff; or with planning with elaborate detail what they were going to do now, after the war. A long journey, slowly, irregularly, yet persistently pushing northward. When they entered on Wisconsin territory they gave a cheer, and another when they reached Madison, but after that they sank into a dumb expectancy. Comrades dropped off at one or two points beyond, until there were only four or five left who were bound for La Crosse County.

Three of them were gaunt and brown, the fourth was gaunt and pale, with signs of fever and ague upon him. One had a great scar down his temple, one limped, and they all had unnaturally large, bright eyes, showing emaciation. There were no bands greeting them at the station, no banks of gayly dressed ladies waving handkerchiefs and shouting "Bravo!" as they came in on the caboose of a freight train into the towns that had cheered and blared at them on their way to war. As they looked out or stepped upon the platform for a moment, while the train stood at the station, the loafers looked at them indifferently. Their blue coats, dusty and grimy, were too familiar now to excite notice, much less a friendly word. They were the last of the army to return, and the loafers were surfeited with such sights.

The train jogged forward so slowly that it seemed likely to be midnight before they should reach La Crosse. The little squad grumbled and swore, but it was no use; the train would not hurry, and, as a matter of fact, it was nearly two o'clock when the engine whistled "down brakes."

All of the group were farmers, living in districts several miles out of the town, and all were poor.

"Now, boys," said Private Smith, he of the fever and ague, "we are landed in La Crosse in the night. We've got to stay somewhere till mornin'. Now I ain't got no two dollars to waste on a hotel. I've got a wife and children, so I'm goin' to roost on a bench and take the cost of a bed out of my hide."

"Same here," put in one of the other men. "Hide'll grow on again, dollars'll come hard. It's goin' to be mighty hot skirmishin' to find a dollar these days."

"Don't think they'll be a deputation of citizens waitin' to 'scort us to a hotel, eh?" said another. His sarcasm was too obvious to require an answer.

[1]In western Wisconsin.

Smith went on. "Then at daybreak we'll start for home—at least, I will."

"Well, I'll be dummed if I'll take two dollars out o' *my* hide," one of the younger men said. "I'm goin' to a hotel, ef I don't never lay up a cent."

"That'll do f'r you," said Smith; "but if you had a wife an' three young uns dependin' on yeh—"

"Which I ain't, thank the Lord! and don't intend havin' while the court knows itself."

The station was deserted, chill, and dark, as they came into it at exactly a quarter to two in the morning. Lit by the oil lamps that flared a dull red light over the dingy benches, the waiting room was not an inviting place. The younger man went off to look up a hotel, while the rest remained and prepared to camp down on the floor and benches. Smith was attended to tenderly by the other men, who spread their blankets on the bench for him, and, by robbing themselves, made quite a comfortable bed, though the narrowness of the bench made his sleeping precarious.

It was chill, though August, and the two men, sitting with bowed heads, grew stiff with cold and weariness, and were forced to rise now and again and walk about to warm their stiffened limbs. It did not occur to them, probably, to contrast their coming home with their going forth, or with the coming home of the generals, colonels, or even captains—but to Private Smith, at any rate, there came a sickness at heart almost deadly as he lay there on his hard bed and went over his situation.

In the deep of the night, lying on a board in the town where he had enlisted three years ago, all elation and enthusiasm gone out of him, he faced the fact that with the joy of home-coming was already mingled the bitter juice of care. He saw himself sick, worn out, taking up the work on his half-cleared farm, the inevitable mortgage standing ready with open jaw to swallow half his earnings. He had given three years of his life for a mere pittance of pay, and now!—

Morning dawned at last, slowly, with a pale yellow dome of light rising silently above the bluffs, which stand like some huge storm-devastated castle, just east of the city. Out to the left the great river swept on its massive yet silent way to the south. Bluejays called across the water from hillside to hillside through the clear, beautiful air, and hawks began to skim the tops of the hills. The older men were astir early, but Private Smith had fallen at last into a sleep, and they went out without waking him. He lay on his knapsack, his gaunt face turned toward the ceiling, his hands clasped on his breast, with a curious pathetic effect of weakness and appeal.

An engine switching near woke him at last, and he slowly sat up and stared about. He looked out of the window and saw that the sun was lightening the hills across the river. He rose and brushed his hair as well as he could, folded his blankets up, and went out to find his companions. They stood gazing silently at the river and at the hills.

"Looks natcher'l, don't it?" they said, as he came out.

"That's what it does," he replied. "An it looks good. D'yeh see that peak?" He pointed at a beautiful symmetrical peak, rising like a slightly truncated cone, so high that it seemed the very highest of them all. It was touched by the morning sun and it glowed like a beacon, and a light scarf of gray morning fog was rolling up its shadowed side.

"My farm's just beyond that. Now, if I can only ketch a ride, we'll be home by dinner-time."

"I'm talkin' about breakfast," said one of the others.

"I guess it's one more meal o' hardtack f'r me," said Smith.

They foraged around, and finally found a restaurant with a sleepy old German behind the counter, and procured some coffee, which they drank to wash down their hardtack.

"Time'll come," said Smith, holding up a piece by the corner, "when this'll be a curiosity."

"I hope to God it will! I bet I've chawed hardtack enough to shingle every house in the coolly.[2] I've chawed it when my lampers[3] was down, and when they wasn't. I've took it dry, soaked, and mashed. I've had it wormy, musty, sour, and blue-mouldy. I've had it in little bits and big bits; 'fore coffee an' after coffee. I'm ready f'r a change. I'd like t' git holt jest about now o' some of the hot biscuits my wife c'n make when she lays herself out f'r company."

"Well, if you set there gabblin', you'll never *see* yer wife."

"Come on," said Private Smith. "Wait a moment, boys; less take suthin'. It's on me." He led them to the rusty tin dipper which hung on a nail beside the wooden water-pail, and they grinned and drank. Then shouldering their blankets and muskets, which they were "takin' home to the boys," they struck out on their last march.

"They called that coffee Jayvy,"[4] grumbled one of them, "but it never went by the road where government Jayvy resides. I reckon I know coffee from peas."[5]

They kept together on the road along the turnpike, and up the winding road by the river, which they followed for some miles. The river was very lovely, curving down along its sandy beds, pausing now and then under broad basswood trees, or running in dark, swift, silent currents under tangles of wild grapevines, and drooping alders, and haw trees. At one of these lovely spots the three vets sat down on the thick green sward to rest, "on Smith's account." The leaves of the trees were as fresh and green as in June, the jays called cheery greetings to them, and kingfishers darted to and fro with swooping, noiseless flight.

"I tell yeh, boys, this knocks the swamps of Loueesiana into kingdom come."

"You bet. All they c'n raise down there is snakes, niggers, and p'rticler hell."

"An' fightin' men," put in the older man.

"An' fightin' men. If I had a good hook an' line I'd sneak a pick'rel out o' that pond. Say, remember that time I shot that alligator—"

"I guess we'd better be crawlin' along," interrupted Smith, rising and shouldering his knapsack, with considerable effort, which he tried to hide.

"Say, Smith, lemme give you a lift on that."

"I guess I c'n manage," said Smith, grimly.

"Course. But, yo' see, I may not have a chance right off to pay yeh back for the times you've carried my gun and hull caboodle. Say, now, gimme that gun, anyway."

"All right, if yeh feel like it, Jim," Smith replied, and they trudged along doggedly in the sun, which was getting higher and hotter each half-mile.

"Ain't it queer there ain't no teams coming' along," said Smith, after a long silence.

"Well, no, seein' it's Sunday."

"By jinks, that's a fact. It *is* Sunday. I'll get home in time f'r dinner, sure!" he exulted. "She don't hev dinner usially till about *one* on Sundays." And he fell into a muse, in which he smiled.

---

[2]Coulee, a valley or ravine.
[3]Lampas, an ailment of horses, characterized by pain and swelling in the roof of the mouth.
[4]Java. From the name of the Indonesian island from which coffee was imported.
[5]I.e., "coffee" made from roasted peas.

"Well, I'll git home jest about six o'clock, jest about when the boys are milkin' the cows," said old Jim Cranby. "I'll step into the barn, an' then I'll say: *'Heah!* why ain't this milkin' done before this time o' day?' An' then won't they yell!" he added, slapping his thigh in great glee.

Smith went on. "I'll jest go up the path. Old Rover'll come down the road to meet me. He won't bark; he'll know me, an' he'll come down waggin' his tail an' showin' his teeth. That's his way of laughin'. An' so I'll walk up to the kitchen door, an' I'll say, *'Dinner,* f'r a hungry man!' An' then she'll jump up, an'—"

He couldn't go on. His voice choked at the thought of it. Saunders, the third man, hardly uttered a word, but walked silently behind the others. He had lost his wife the first year he was in the army. She died of pneumonia, caught in the autumn rains while working in the fields in his place.

They plodded along till at last they came to parting of the ways. To the right the road continued up the main valley; to the left it went over the big ridge.

"Well, boys," began Smith as they grounded their muskets and looked away up the valley, "here's where we shake hands. We've marched together a good many miles, an' now I s'pose we're done."

"Yes, I don't think we'll do any more of it f'r a while. I don't want to, I know."

"I hope I'll see yeh once in a while, boys, to talk over old times."

"Of course," said Saunders, whose voice trembled a little, too. "It ain't *exactly* like dyin'." They all found it hard to look at each other.

"But we'd ought'r go home with you," said Cranby. "You'll never climb that ridge with all them things on yer back."

"Oh, I'm all right! Don't worry about me. Every step takes me nearer home, yeh see. Well, good-by, boys."

They shook hands. "Good-by. Good luck!"

"Same to you. Lemme know how you find things at home."

"Good-by."

"Good-by."

He turned once before they passed out of sight, and waved his cap, and they did the same, and all yelled. Then all marched away with their long, steady, loping, veteran step. The solitary climber in blue walked on for a time, with his mind filled with the kindness of his comrades, and musing upon the many wonderful days they had had together in camp and field.

He thought of his chum, Billy Tripp. Poor Billy! A "minie" ball[6] fell into his breast one day, fell wailing like a cat, and tore a great ragged hole in his heart. He looked forward to a sad scene with Billy's mother and sweetheart. They would want to know all about it. He tried to recall all that Billy had said, and the particulars of it, and there was little to remember, just that wild wailing sound high in the air, a dull slap, a short, quick, expulsive groan, and the boy lay with his face in the dirt in the ploughed field they were marching across.

That was all. But all the scenes he had since been through had not dimmed the horror, the terror of that moment, when his boy comrade fell, with only a breath between a laugh and a death-groan. Poor handsome Billy! Worth millions of dollars was his young life.

These sombre recollections gave way at length to more cheerful feelings as he began to approach his home coolly. The fields and houses grew familiar, and in one or two he was greeted by people seated in the doorways. But he was in no mood to talk, and pushed on steadily, though he stopped and accepted a drink of milk once at the well-side of a neighbor.

[6]A rifle bullet named after its inventor, Claude Etienne Minie (1814–1879).

The sun was burning hot on that slope, and his step grew slower, in spite of his iron resolution. He sat down several times to rest. Slowly he crawled up the rough, reddish-brown road, which wound along the hillside, under great trees, through dense groves of jack oaks, with tree-tops far below him on his left hand, and the hills far above him on his right. He crawled along like some minute, wingless variety of fly.

He ate some hardtack, sauced with wild berries, when he reached the summit of the ridge, and sat there for some time, looking down into his home coolly.

Sombre, pathetic figure! His wide, round, gray eyes gazing down into the beautiful valley, seeing and not seeing, the splendid cloud-shadows sweeping over the western hills and across the green and yellow wheat far below. His head drooped forward on his palm, his shoulders took on a tired stoop, his cheekbones showed painfully. An observer might have said, "He is looking down upon his own grave."

II

Sunday comes in Western wheat harvest with such sweet and sudden relaxation to man and beast that it would be holy for that reason, if for no other, and Sundays are usually fair in harvest-time. As one goes out into the field in the hot morning sunshine, with no sound abroad save the crickets and the indescribably pleasant silken rustling of the riped grain, the reaper and the very sheaves in the stubble seem to be resting, dreaming.

Around the house, in the shade of the trees, the men sit, smoking, dozing, or reading the papers, while the women, never resting, move about at the housework. The men eat on Sundays, about the same as on other days, and breakfast is no sooner over and out of the way than dinner begins.

But at the Smith farm there were no men dozing or reading. Mrs. Smith was alone with her three children, Mary, nine, Tommy, six, and little Ted, just past four. Her farm, rented to a neighbor, lay at the head of a coolly or narrow gully, made at some far-off post-glacial period by the vast and angry floods of water which gullied these tremendous furrows in the level prairie—furrows so deep that undisturbed portions of the original level rose like hills on either side, rose to quite considerable mountains.

The chickens wakened her as usual that Sabbath morning from dreams of her absent husband, from whom she had not heard for weeks. The shadows drifted over the hills, down the slopes, across the wheat, and up the opposite wall in a leisurely way, as if, being Sunday, they could take it easy also. The fowls clustered about the housewife as she went out into the yard. Fuzzy little chickens swarmed out from the coops, where their clucking and perpetually disgruntled mothers tramped about, petulantly, thrusting their heads through the spaces between the slats.

A cow called in a deep, musical bass, and a calf answered from a little pen near by, and a pig scurried guiltily out of the cabbages. Seeing all this, seeing the pig in the cabbages, the tangle of grass in the garden, the broken fence which she had mended again and again—the little woman, hardly more than a girl, sat down and cried. The bright Sabbath morning was only a mockery without him!

A few years ago they had bought this farm, paying part, mortgaging the rest in the usual way. Edward Smith was a man of terrible energy. He worked "nights and Sundays," as the saying goes, to clear the farm of its brush and of its insatiate mortgage! In the midst of his Herculean struggle came the call for volunteers, and with the grim and unselfish devotion to this country which made the Eagle Brigade able to "whip its weight in wildcats," he threw down his scythe and a grub-axe,[1] turned his cattle loose, and became a blue-coated cog in a vast machine for killing men, and not thistles. While the millionaire sent his money to England for safe-keeping, this man, with his girl-wife and three babies, left them on a mortgaged farm, and went away to fight for an idea. It was foolish, but it was sublime for all that.

That was three years before, and the young wife, sitting on the well-curb[2] on this bright Sabbath harvest morning, was righteously rebellious. It seemed to her that she had borne her share of the country's sorrow. Two brothers had been killed, the renter in whose hands her husband had left the farm had proved a villain; one year the farm had been without crops, and now the overripe grain was waiting the tardy hand of the neighbor who had rented it, and who was cutting his own grain first.

About six weeks before, she had received a letter saying, "We'll be discharged in a little while." But no other word had come from him. She had seen by the papers that his army was being discharged, and from day to day other soldiers slowly percolated in blue streams back into the State and county, but still *her* hero did not return.

Each week she had told the children that he was coming, and she had watched the road so long that it had become unconscious; and as she stood at the well, or by the kitchen door, her eyes were fixed unthinkingly on the road that wound down the coolly.

Nothing wears on the human soul like waiting. If the stranded mariner, searching the sun-bright seas, could once give up hope of a ship, that horrible grinding on his brain would cease. It was this waiting, hoping, on the edge of despair, that gave Emma Smith no rest.

Neighbors said, with kind intentions: "He's sick, maybe, an' can't start north just yet. He'll come along one o' these days."

"Why don't he write?" was her question, which silenced them all. This Sunday morning it seemed to her as if she could not stand it longer. The house seemed intolerably lonely. So she dressed the little ones in their best calico dresses and home-made jackets, and closing up the house, set off down the coolly to old Mother Gray's.

"Old Widder Gray" lived at the "mouth of the coolly." She was a widow woman with a large family of stalwart boys and laughing girls. She was the visible incarnation of hospitality and optimistic poverty. With Western open-heartedness she fed every mouth that asked food of her, and worked herself to death as cheerfully as her girls danced in the neighborhood harvest dances.

She waddled down the path to meet Mrs. Smith with a broad smile on her face.

"Oh, you little dears! Come right to your granny. Gimme a kiss! Come right in, Mis' Smith. How are yeh, anyway? Nice mornin', ain't it? Come in an' set down. Everything's in a clutter, but that won't scare you any."

She led the way into the best room, a sunny, square-room, carpeted with a faded and patched rag carpet, and papered with white-and-green-striped wall-paper, where a few faded effigies of dead members of the family hung in various sized oval walnut frames. The house resounded with singing, laughter, whistling, tramping of heavy boots, and riotous scufflings. Half-grown boys came to the

---

[1] A mattock used for digging, a grubbinghoe.   [2] The frame enclosing the mouth of a well.

door and crooked their fingers at the children, who ran out, and were soon heard in the midst of the fun.

"Don't s'pose you've heard from Ed?" Mrs. Smith shook her head. "He'll turn up some day, when you ain't lookin' for 'm." The good old soul had said that so many times that poor Mrs. Smith derived no comfort from it any longer.

"Liz heard from Al the other day. He's comin' some day this week. Anyhow, they expect him."

"Did he say anything of—"

"No, he didn't." Mrs. Gray admitted. "But then it was only a short letter, anyhow. Al ain't much for writin', anyhow.—But come out and see my new cheese. I tell yeh, I don't believe I ever had better luck in my life. If Ed should come, I want you should take him up a piece of this cheese."

It was beyond human nature to resist the influence of that noisy, hearty, loving household, and in the midst of the singing and laughing the wife forgot her anxiety, for the time at least, and laughed and sang with the rest.

About eleven o'clock a wagon-load more drove up to the door, and Bill Gray, the widow's oldest son, and his whole family, from Sand Lake Coolly, piled out amid a good-natured uproar. Every one talked at once, except Bill, who sat in the wagon with his wrists on his knees, a straw in his mouth, and an amused twinkle in his blue eyes.

"Ain't heard nothin' o' Ed, I s'pose?" he asked in a kind of bellow. Mrs. Smith shook her head. Bill, with a delicacy very striking in such a great giant, rolled his quid in his mouth, and said:

"Didn't know but you had. I hear two or three of the Sand Lake boys are comin'. Left New Orleenes some time this week. Didn't write nothin' about Ed, but no news is good news in such cases, mother always says."

"Well, go put out yer team," said Mrs. Gray, "an' go 'n bring me in some taters, an', Sim, you go see if you c'n find some corn. Sadie, you put on the water to bile. Come now, hustle yer boots, all o' yeh. If I feed this yer crowd, we've got to have some raw materials. If y' think 'm goin' to feed yeh on pie—you're jest mightily mistaken."

The children went off into the fields, the girls put dinner on to boil, and then went to change their dresses and fix their hair. "Somebody might come," they said.

"Land sakes, I *hope* not! I don't know where in time I'd set 'em, 'less they'd eat at the second table," Mrs. Gray laughed, in pretended dismay.

The two older boys, who had served their time in the army, lay out on the grass before the house, and whittled and talked desultorily about the war and the crops, and planned buying a threshing-machine. The older girls and Mrs. Smith helped enlarge the table and put on the dishes, talking all the time in that cheery, incoherent, and meaningful way a group of such women have,—a conversation to be taken for its spirit rather than for its letter, though Mrs. Gray at last got the ear of them all and dissertated at length on girls.

"Girls in love ain't no use in the whole blessed week," she said. "Sundays they're a lookin' down the road, expectin' he'll *come*. Sunday afternoons they can't think o' nothin' else, 'cause he's *here*. Monday mornin' they're sleepy and kind o' dreamy and slimpsy, and good f'r nothin' on Tuesday and Wednesday. Thursday they git absent-minded, an' begin to look off toward Sundays agin, an' mope aroun' and let the dishwater git cold, right under their noses. Friday they break dishes, an' go off in the best room an' snivel, an' look out o' the winder. Saturdays they have queer spurts o' workin' like all p'ssessed, an' spurts o' frizzin' their hair. An' Sunday they begin it all over agin."

The girls giggled and blushed, all through this tirade from their mother, their broad faces and powerful frames anything but suggestive of lackadaisical sentiment. But Mrs. Smith said:

"Now, Mrs. Gray, I hadn't ought to stay to dinner. You've got—"

"Now you set right down! If any of them girls' beaus comes, they'll have to take what's left, that's all. They ain't s'posed to have much appetite, nohow. No, you're goin' to stay if they starve, an' they ain't no danger o' that."

At one o'clock the long table was piled with boiled potatoes, cords of boiled corn on the cob, squash and pumpkin pies, hot biscuit, sweet pickles, bread and butter, and honey. Then one of the girls took down a conch-shell from a nail, and going to the door, blew a long, fine, free blast, that showed there was no weakness of lungs in her ample chest.

Then the children came out of the forest of corn, out of the creek, out of the loft of the barn, and out of the garden.

"They come to their feed f'r all the world jest like the pigs when y' holler 'poo-ee!' See 'em scoot!" laughed Mrs. Gray, every wrinkle on her face shining with delight.

The men shut up their jack-knives, and surrounded the horse-trough to souse their faces in the cold, hard water, and in a few moments the table was filled with a merry crowd, and a row of wistful-eyed youngsters circled the kitchen wall, where they stood first on one leg and then on the other, in impatient hunger.

"Now pitch in, Mrs. Smith," said Mrs. Gray presiding over the table. "You know these men critters. They'll eat every grain of it, if yeh give 'em a chance. I swan, they're made o' India-rubber, their stomachs is, I know it."

"Haf to eat to work," said Bill, gnawing a cob with a swift, circular motion that rivalled a corn-sheller in results.

"More like workin' to eat," put in one of the girls, with a giggle. "More eat 'n work with you."

"*You* needn't say anything, Net. Any one that'll eat seven ears—"

"I didn't, no such thing. You piled your cobs on my plate."

"That'll do to tell Ed Varney. It won't go down here where we know yeh."

"Good land! Eat all yeh want! There's plenty more in the fiel's, but I can't afford to give you young uns tea. The tea is for us women-folks, and 'specially f'r Miss' Smith an' Bill's wife. We're a-goin' to tell fortunes by it."

One by one the men filled up and shoved back, and one by one the children slipped into their places, and by two o'clock the women alone remained around the debris-covered table, sipping their tea and telling fortunes.

As they got well down to the grounds in the cup, they shook them with a circular motion in the hand, and then turned them bottom-side-up quickly in the saucer, then twirled them three or four times one way, and three or four times the other, during a breathless pause. Then Mrs. Gray lifted the cup, and gazing into it with profound gravity, pronounced the impending fate.

It must be admitted that, to a critical observer, she had abundant preparation for hitting close to the mark, as when she told the girls that "somebody was comin'." "It's a man," she went on gravely. "He is cross-eyed—"

"Oh, you hush!" cried Nettie.

"He has red hair, and is death on b'iled corn and hot biscuit."

The others shrieked with delight.

"But he's goin' to get the mitten, that red-headed feller is, for I see another feller comin' up behind him."

"Oh, lemme see, lemme see!" cried Nettie.

"Keep off," said the priestess, with a lofty gesture. "His hair is black. He don't eat so much, and he works more."

The girls exploded in a shriek of laughter, and pounded their sister on the back.

At last came Mrs. Smith's turn, and she was trembling with excitement as Mrs. Gray again composed her jolly face to what she considered a proper solemnity of expression.

"Somebody is comin' to *you*," she said, after a long pause. "He's got a musket on his back. He's a soldier. He's almost here. See?"

She pointed at two little tea-stems, which really formed a faint suggestion of a man with a musket on his back. He had climbed nearly to the edge of the cup. Mrs. Smith grew pale with excitement. She trembled so she could hardly hold the cup in her hand as she gazed into it.

"It's Ed," cried the old woman. "He's on the way home. Heavens an' earth! There he is now!" She turned and waved her hand out toward the road. They rushed to the door to look where she pointed.

A man in a blue coat, with a musket on his back, was toiling slowly up the hill on the sun-bright, dusty road, toiling slowly, with bent head half hidden by a heavy knapsack. So tired it seemed that walking was indeed a process of falling. So eager to get home he would not stop, would not look aside, but plodded on, amid the cries of the locusts, the welcome of the crickets, and the rustle of the yellow wheat. Getting back to God's country, and his wife and babies!

Laughing, crying, trying to call him and the children at the same time, the little wife, almost hysterical, snatched her hat and ran out into the yard. But the soldier had disappeared over the hill into the hollow beyond, and, by the time she had found the children, he was too far away for her voice to reach him. And, besides, she was not sure it was her husband, for he had not turned his head at their shouts. This seemed so strange. Why didn't he stop to rest at his old neighbor's house? Tortured by hope and doubt, she hurried up the coolly as fast as she could push the baby wagon, the blue-coated figure just ahead pushing steadily, silently forward up the coolly.

When the excited, panting little group came in sight of the gate they saw the blue-coated figure standing, leaning upon the rough rail fence, his chin on his palms, gazing at the empty house. His knapsack, canteen, blankets, and musket lay upon the dusty grass at his feet.

He was like a man lost in a dream. His wide, hungry eyes devoured the scene. The rough lawn, the little unpainted house, the field of clear yellow wheat behind it, down across which streamed the sun, now almost ready to touch the high hill to the west, the crickets crying merrily, a cat on the fence near by, dreaming, unmindful of the stranger in blue—

How peaceful it all was. O God! How far removed from all camps, hospitals, battle lines. A little cabin in a Wisconsin coolly, but it was majestic in its peace. How did he ever leave it for those years of tramping, thirsting, killing?

Trembling, weak with emotion, her eyes on the silent figure, Mrs. Smith hurried up to the fence. Her feet made no noise in the dust and grass, and they were close upon him before he knew of them. The oldest boy ran a little ahead. He will never forget that figure, that face. It will always remain as something epic, that return of the private. He fixed his eyes on the pale face covered with a ragged beard.

"Who *are* you, sir?" asked the wife, or, rather, started to ask, for he turned, stood a moment, and then cried:

"Emma!"

"Edward!"

The children stood in a curious row to see their mother kiss this bearded, strange man, the elder girl sobbing sympathetically with her mother. Illness had left the soldier partly deaf, and this added to the strangeness of his manner.

But the youngest child stood away, even after the girl had recognized her father and kissed him. The man turned then to the baby, and said in a curiously unpaternal tone:

"Come here, my little man; don't you know me?" But the baby backed away under the fence and stood peering at him critically.

"My little man!" What meaning in those words! This baby seemed like some other woman's child, and not the infant he had left in his wife's arms. The war had come between him and his baby—he was only a strange man to him, with big eyes; a soldier, with mother hanging to his arm, and talking in a loud voice.

"And this is Tom," the private said, drawing the oldest boy to him. "*He'll* come and see me. *He* knows his poor old pap when he comes home from the war."

The mother heard the pain and reproach in his voice and hastened to apologize.

"You've changed so, Ed. He can't know yeh. This is papa, Teddy; come and kiss him—Tom and Mary do. Come, won't you?" But Teddy still peered through the fence with solemn eyes, well out of reach. He resembled a half-wild kitten that hesitates, studying the tones of one's voice.

"I'll fix him," said the soldier, and sat down to undo his knapsack, out of which he drew three enormous and very red apples. After giving one to each of the older children, he said:

"*Now* I guess he'll come. Eh, my little man? Now come see your pap."

Teddy crept slowly under the fence, assisted by the overzealous Tommy, and a moment later was kicking and squalling in his father's arms. Then they entered the house, into the sitting room, poor, bare, art-forsaken little room, too, with its rag carpet, its square clock, and its two or three chromos[3] and pictures from *Harper's Weekly* pinned about.

"Emma, I'm all tired out," said Private Smith, as he flung himself down on the carpet as he used to do, while his wife brought a pillow to put under his head, and the children stood about munching their apples.

"Tommy, you run and get me a pan of chips, and Mary, you get the tea-kettle on, and I'll go and make some biscuit."

And the soldier talked. Question after question he poured forth about the crops, the cattle, the renter, the neighbors. He slipped his heavy government brogan shoes off his poor, tired, blistered feet, and lay out with utter, sweet relaxation. He was a free man again, no longer a soldier under command. At supper he stopped once, listened and smiled. "That's old Spot. I know her voice. I s'pose that's her calf out there in the pen. I can't milk her to-night, though. I'm too tired. But I tell you, I'd like a drink o' her milk. What's become of old Rove?"

"He died last winter. Poisoned, I guess." There was a moment of sadness for them all. It was some time before the husband spoke again, in a voice that trembled a little.

"Poor old feller! He'd 'a' known me half a mile away. I expected him to come down the hill to meet me. It 'ud 'a' been more like comin' home if I could 'a'

[3]Colored illustrations.

seen him comin' down the road an' waggin' his tail, an' laughin' that way he has. I tell yeh, it kind o' took hold o' me to see the blinds down an' the house shut up."

"But, yeh see, we—we expected you'd write again 'fore you started. And then we thought we'd see you if you *did* come," she hastened to explain.

"Well, I ain't worth a cent on writin'. Besides, it's just as well yeh didn't know when I was comin'. I tell you, it sounds good to hear them chickens out there, an' turkeys, an' the crickets. Do you know they don't have just the same kind o' crickets down South? Who's Sam hired t' help cut yer grain?"

"The Ramsey boys."

"Looks like a good crop; but I'm afraid I won't do much gettin' it cut. This cussed fever an' ague has got me down pretty low. I don't know when I'll get rid of it. I'll bet I've took twenty-five pounds of quinine if I've taken a bit. Gimme another biscuit, I tell yeh, they taste good, Emma. I ain't had anything like it— Say, if you'd 'a' hear'd me braggin' to th' boys about your butter 'n' biscuits I'll bet your ears 'ud 'a' burnt."

The private's wife colored with pleasure. "Oh, you're always a-braggin' about your things. Everybody makes good butter."

"Yes; old lady Snyder, for instance."

"Oh, well, she ain't to be mentioned. She's Dutch."

"Or old Mis' Snively. One more cup o' tea, Mary. That's my girl! I'm feeling better already. I just b'lieve the matter with me is I'm *starved*."

This was a delicious hour, one long to be remembered. They were like lovers again. But their tenderness, like that of a typical American family, found utterance in tones, rather than in words. He was praising her when praising her biscuit, and she knew it. They grew soberer when he showed where he had been struck, one ball burning the back of his hand, one cutting away a lock of hair from his temple, and one passing through the calf of his leg. The wife shuddered to think how near she had come to being a soldier's widow. Her waiting no longer seemed hard. This sweet, glorious hour effaced it all.

Then they rose, and all went out into the garden and down to the barn. He stood beside her while she milked old Spot. They began to plan fields and crops for next year.

His farm was weedy and encumbered, a rascally renter had run away with his machinery (departing between two days), his children needed clothing, the years were coming upon him, he was sick and emaciated, but his heroic soul did not quail. With the same courage with which he had faced his Southern march he entered upon a still more hazardous future.

Oh, that mystic hour! The pale man with big eyes standing there by the well, with his young wife by his side. The vast moon swinging above the eastern peaks, the cattle winding down the pasture slopes with jangling bells, the crickets singing, the stars blooming out sweet and far and serene; the katydids rhythmically calling, the little turkeys crying querulously, as they settled to roost in the poplar tree near the open gate. The voices at the well drop lower, the little ones nestle in their father's arms at last, and Teddy falls asleep there.

The common soldier of the American volunteer army had returned. His war with the South was over, and his fight, his daily running fight with nature and against the injustice of his fellowmen, was begun again.

1890

Charlotte Perkins Gilman   *1860–1935*

Like the heroine of her finest short story, "The Yellow Wallpaper," Charlotte Perkins Gilman saw the world as a place where individual lives are often smothered by the power of convention and authority. Her own life was marred by an unhappy childhood, an ill-fated first marriage, recurring mental breakdowns, and public rejection of the social reforms for which she wrote and spoke. Yet, in the last half of the twentieth century, many of the ideals to which she devoted her life have become a part of the nation's fabric of beliefs, and she is now recognized as a vital force in the history of reform in the United States.

She was born Charlotte Perkins in Hartford, Connecticut. Among her ancestors were the renowned New England preacher Henry Ward Beecher and the most famous woman of nineteenth-century America, Harriet Beecher Stowe, the author of Uncle Tom's Cabin. *Charlotte Perkins seemed destined for a genteel and congenial New England upbringing, but shortly after her birth, her father abandoned his family, leaving his wife and children to lives strained by poverty and emotional deprivation.*

As a result, Charlotte Perkins received little formal education. But, she was an avid reader of history and literature, and she had a natural talent for art. After a brief period of study at the Rhode Island School of Design, in Providence, she got a job designing greeting cards. Later she worked as a children's tutor. And she began to write.

Her first publication, a short article in the Providence Journal, *appeared in 1883. In the following year she married a fellow art student, Charles Stetson, but the marriage was a failure almost from the start. Charlotte Perkins Stetson rejected the submissive role deemed proper for nineteenth-century married women. She refused to subside into a life solely devoted to the wifely duties of housekeeping, childrearing, and obedience to her husband. Instead, she focused her energies on painting and on writing poems, essays, and short stories.*

In 1884, the year of her marriage, her first poem was published. Entitled "In Duty Bound," it began, significantly enough, "In duty bound, a life hemmed in . . . ." And for the rest of her life, her writing reflected the belief that the patriarchal culture surrounding her was one that denigrated women, hemmed them in, thwarted their natural desires for intellectual growth and expression.

Oppressed by her unhappy marriage, she suffered periodic sieges of mental depression, and she was taken to the celebrated physician S. Weir Mitchell, a neurologist known for his "rest-cure" for nervous disorders. The "rest-cure" prescribed for Charlotte Stetson required her isolation from just those modes of self-expression and intellectual growth that had sustained her sense of independence. She was told never again to write, never to paint, never to read for more than two hours a day.

It was the most advanced medical treatment of the age, and its ideal of the tranquilized mental patient anticipated much psychiatric therapy of the late twentieth century. But Charlotte Perkins Stetson saw that her sanity lay not in submission to her physician or her husband but in her freedom and independence. In 1887, to escape her "rest-cure" and her marriage, she moved to California, where she divorced her husband and supported herself by running a boarding house.

Free of the restraints of marriage, she began to speak out boldly on political and social issues. She wrote and lectured on women's rights and argued for a utopian socialism that would end social injustice. Soon women's clubs and church groups began to seek her out as a lecturer. More and more magazines and newspapers published her essays and articles.

In 1900 she married George Gilman. It was a successful marriage—her new husband shared many of her social and political views—and she now wrote as Charlotte Perkins Gilman, but she continued her crusade for women's rights. From 1889 to 1891 she had served as editor of the Pacific Monthly, *a journal of social and political commentary published in Los Angeles. Later she edited* The Impress, *a journal of the Pacific Coast Women's Association, and from 1909 to 1916 she published and edited* The Forerunner, *a monthly magazine for which she wrote almost the entire contents—editorials, stories, articles, book reviews, poems, even the advertisements.*

For five years in the 1890s Charlotte Perkins Gilman toured America as a lecturer, arguing that women were dominated by their fathers and husbands, that women were entrapped by their innocence and their upbringing. She insisted that home was more often a prison than a shelter, and she encouraged women to assert their rights and free themselves from unthinking devotion to cooking, cleaning, church, and children.

Censorious critics said that she "despised the home" more than any other American. They denounced her as a "man-hater" and argued that her feminism and her assaults on masculinity were revenge against the father who had abandoned her as a child. Later critics have pointed out that her sympathies were primarily for middle-class women and that she showed little concern for the destitute, for minorities, or for the millions of immigrants struggling to survive in late nineteenth-century America.

In part the criticism came because Charlotte Perkins Gilman was so effective and so untiring a worker for reform. In recent years she has been called one of the "ancestral mothers" of the modern feminist movement, but she wrote prolifically on a wide variety of political, social, and economic topics: poverty, health care, civil justice, the rights of labor. She published more than a thousand articles in addition to short stories, novels, and hundreds of poems. Her most significant book, Women and Economics (1893), *is a lengthy study of the ways in which male dominance was reinforced by the economic system of her society. A popular success, and widely influential in the 1890s, the book's arguments remain cogent today, nearly a century after its publication.*

Charlotte Perkins Gilman said that she wrote not to create literature but to improve the world, and she was most effective as an ideologue and a polemicist. Much of her writing was hasty—a quick response to the questions of the day. Her fiction was often stereotyped, repetitious stories of women who take charge of their lives, break the restraints imposed by a "masculinist" society, and are thereby destined to live happily ever after.

But in "The Yellow Wallpaper" she created a story of complex literary artistry. It has been called one of the best horror stories of the nineteenth century, and it has many of the elements of Gothic horror tales: the female in distress, the isolated mansion, the locked room, the threat of masculine torment.

In writing the story, Charlotte Perkins Gilman had drawn on her experience with mental illness. "The Yellow Wallpaper" was, in part, her retaliation for the suffering she had experienced. Her own explanation was that she wrote the story to expose the mistakes made by medical science in treating the insane. But "The Yellow Wallpaper" is more than a frightening tale, more than an effort to redress a grievance or correct therapeutic errors. It anticipates the psychological fiction of the twentieth century in its portrayal of alienation and of misunderstood suffering in a complacent society. It foreshadows the modern world's preoccupation with psychosis, distorted perceptions, receding distinctions between reality and hallucination. It is a surrealist picture of a tormented, isolated individual, and it is a call for understanding of a woman lost in a world without comprehension or memory, writhing in the tangles of madness and dead hope.

FURTHER READING: *The Charlotte Perkins Gilman Reader,* ed. A. Lane, 1980; *The Living of Charlotte Perkins Gilman, An Autobiography,* 1935; M. Hill, *Charlotte Perkins Gilman, The Making of a Radical Feminist,* 1980; B. Winkler, *Victorian Daughters,* 1980.

TEXT: "The Yellow Wallpaper," *New England Magazine,* January 1892.

THE YELLOW WALLPAPER

It is very seldom that mere ordinary people like John and myself secure ancestral halls for the summer.

A Colonial mansion, a hereditary estate, I would say a haunted house and reach the height of romantic felicity—but that would be asking too much of fate!

Still I will proudly declare that there is something queer about it.

Else, why should it be let so cheaply? And why have stood so long untenanted?

John laughs at me, of course, but one expects that.

John is practical in the extreme. He has no patience with faith, an intense horror of superstition, and he scoffs openly at any talk of things not to be felt and seen and put down in figures.

John is a physician, and *perhaps*—(I would not say it to a living soul, of course, but this is dead paper and a great relief to my mind)—*perhaps* that is one reason I do not get well faster.

You see, he does not believe I am sick! And what can one do?

If a physician of high standing, and one's own husband, assures friends and relatives that there is really nothing the matter with one but temporary nervous depression—a slight hysterical tendency—what is one to do?

My brother is also a physician, and also of high standing, and he says the same thing.

So I take phosphates or phosphites[1]—whichever it is—and tonics, and air and exercise, and journeys, and am absolutely forbidden to "work" until I am well again.

Personally, I disagree with their ideas.

Personally, I believe that congenial work, with excitement and change, would do me good.

But what is one to do?

I did write for a while in spite of them; but it *does* exhaust me a good deal—having to be so sly about it, or else meet with heavy opposition.

I sometimes fancy that in my condition, if I had less opposition and more society and stimulus—but John says the very worst thing I can do is to think about my condition, and I confess it always makes me feel bad.

So I will let it alone and talk about the house.

The most beautiful place! It is quite alone, standing well back from the road, quite three miles from the village. It makes me think of English places that you read about, for there are hedges and walls and gates that lock, and lots of separate little houses for the gardeners and people.

There is a *delicious* garden! I never saw such a garden—large and shady, full of box-bordered[2] paths, and lined with long grape-covered arbors with seats under them.

There were greenhouses, but they are all broken now.

There was some legal trouble, I believe, something about the heirs and co-heirs; anyhow, the place has been empty for years.

That spoils my ghostliness, I am afraid, but I don't care—there is something strange about the house—I can feel it.

I even said so to John one moonlight evening, but he said what I felt was a draught, and shut the window.

[1]Carbonated water and acid phosphate, flavored with fruit syrup.
[2]I.e., with borders of box, an evergreen shrub.

I get unreasonably angry with John sometimes. I'm sure I never used to be so sensitive. I think it is due to this nervous condition.

But John says if I feel so I shall neglect proper self-control; so I take pains to control myself—before him, at least, and that makes me very tired.

I don't like our room a bit. I wanted one downstairs that opened onto the piazza and had roses all over the window, and such pretty old-fashioned chintz hangings! But John would not hear of it.

He said there was only one window and not room for two beds, and no near room for him if he took another.

He is very careful and loving, and hardly lets me stir without special direction.

I have a schedule prescription for each hour in the day; he takes all care from me, and so I feel basely ungrateful not to value it more.

He said he came here solely on my account, that I was to have perfect rest and all the air I could get. "Your exercise depends on your strength, my dear," said he, "and your food somewhat on your appetite; but air you can absorb all the time." So we took the nursery at the top of the house.

It is a big, airy room, the whole floor nearly, with windows that look all ways, and air and sunshine galore. It was nursery first, and then playroom and gymnasium, I should judge, for the windows are barred for little children, and there are rings and things in the walls.

The paint and paper look as if a boy's school had used it. It is stripped off— the paper—in great patches all around the head of my bed, about as far as I can reach, and in a great place on the other side of the room low down. I never saw a worse paper in my life. One of the those sprawling, flamboyant patterns committing every artistic sin.

It is dull enough to confuse the eye in following, pronounced enough constantly to irritate and provoke study, and when you follow the lame uncertain curves for a little distance they suddenly commit suicide—plunge off at outrageous angles, destroy themselves in unheard-of contradictions.

The color is repellent, almost revolting: a smouldering unclean yellow, strangely faded by the slow-turning sunlight. It is a dull yet lurid orange in some places, a sickly sulphur tint in others.

No wonder the children hated it! I should hate it myself if I had to live in this room long.

There comes John, and I must put this away—he hates to have me write a word.

* * * * *

We have been here two weeks, and I haven't felt like writing before, since that first day.

I am sitting by the window now, up in this atrocious nursery, and there is nothing to hinder my writing as much as I please, save lack of strength.

John is away all day, and even some nights when his cases are serious.

I am glad my case is not serious!

But these nervous troubles are dreadfully depressing.

John does not know how much I really suffer. He knows there is no reason to suffer, and that satisfies him.

Of course it is only nervousness. It does weigh on me so not to do my duty in any way!

I meant to be such a help to John, such a real rest and comfort, and here I am a comparative burden already!

Nobody would believe what an effort it is to do what little I am able—to dress and entertain, and order things.

It is fortunate Mary is so good with the baby. Such a dear baby!

And yet I *cannot* be with him, it makes me so nervous.

I suppose John never was nervous in his life. He laughs at me so about this wallpaper!

At first he meant to repaper the room, but afterward he said that I was letting it get the better of me, and that nothing was worse for a nervous patient than to give way to such fancies.

He said that after the wallpaper was changed it would be the heavy bedstead, and then the barred windows, and then that gate at the head of the stairs, and so on.

"You know the place is doing you good," he said, "and really, dear, I don't care to renovate the house just for a three months' rental."

"Then do let us go downstairs," I said. "There are such pretty rooms there."

Then he took me in his arms and called me a blessed little goose, and said he would go down cellar, if I wished, and have it whitewashed into the bargain.

But he is right enough about the beds and windows and things.

It is as airy and comfortable a room as anyone need wish, and, of course, I would not be so silly as to make him uncomfortable just for a whim.

I'm really getting quite fond of the big room, all but that horrid paper.

Out of one window I can see the garden—those mysterious deep-shaded arbors, the riotous old-fashioned flowers, and bushes and gnarly trees.

Out of another I get a lovely view of the bay and a little private wharf belonging to the estate. There is a beautiful shaded lane that runs down there from the house. I always fancy I see people walking in these numerous paths and arbors, but John has cautioned me not to give way to fancy in the least. He says that with my imaginative power and habit of story-making, a nervous weakness like mine is sure to lead to all manner of excited fancies, and that I ought to use my will and good sense to check the tendency. So I try.

I think sometimes that if I were only well enough to write a little it would relieve the press of ideas and rest me.

But I find I get pretty tired when I try.

It is so discouraging not to have any advice and companionship about my work. When I get really well, John says we will ask Cousin Henry and Julia down for a long visit; but he says he would as soon put fireworks in my pillow-case as to let me have those stimulating people about now.

I wish I could get well faster.

But I must not think about that. This paper looks to me as if it *knew* what a vicious influence it had!

There is a recurrent spot where the pattern lolls like a broken neck and two bulbous eyes stare at you upside down.

I get positively angry with the impertinence of it and the everlastingness. Up and down and sideways they crawl, and those absurd unblinking eyes are everywhere. There is one place where two breadths didn't match, and the eyes go all up and down the line, one a little higher than the other.

I never saw so much expression in an inanimate thing before, and we all know how much expression they have! I used to lie awake as a child and get more entertainment and terror out of blank walls and plain furiture than most children could find in a toy-store.

I remember what a kindly wink the knobs of our big old bureau used to have, and there was one chair that always seemed like a strong friend.

I used to feel that if any of the other things looked too fierce I could always hop into that chair and be safe.

The furniture in this room is no worse than inharmonious, however, for we had to bring it all from downstairs. I suppose when this was used as a playroom they had to take the nursery things out, and no wonder! I never saw such ravages as the children have made here.

The wallpaper, as I said before, is torn off in spots, and it sticketh closer than a brother[3]—they must have had perseverance as well as hatred.

Then the floor is scratched and gouged and splintered, the plaster itself is dug out here and there, and this great heavy bed, which is all we found in the room, looks as if it had been through the wars.

But I don't mind it a bit—only the paper.

There comes John's sister. Such a dear girl as she is, and so careful of me! I must not let her find me writing.

She is a perfect and enthusiastic housekeeper, and hopes for no better profession. I verily believe she thinks it is the writing which made me sick!

But I can write when she is out, and see her a long way off from these windows.

There is one that commands the road, a lovely shaded winding road, and one that just looks off over the country. A lovely country, too, full of great elms and velvet meadows.

This wallpaper has a kind of sub-pattern in a different shade, a particularly irritating one, for you can only see it in certain lights, and not clearly then.

But in the places where it isn't faded and where the sun is just so—I can see a strange, provoking, formless sort of figure that seems to skulk about behind that silly and conspicuous front design.

There's sister on the stairs!

Well, the Fourth of July is over! The people are all gone, and I am tired out. John thought it might do me good to see a little company, so we just had Mother and Nellie and the children down for a week.

Of course I didn't do a thing. Jennie sees to everything now.

But it tired me all the same.

John says if I don't pick up faster he shall send me to Weir Mitchell[4] in the fall.

But I don't want to go there at all. I had a friend who was in his hands once, and she says he is just like John and my brother, only more so!

Besides, it is such an undertaking to go so far.

I don't feel as if it was worthwhile to turn my hand over for anything, and I'm getting dreadfully fretful and querulous.

I cry at nothing, and cry most of the time.

Of course I don't when John is here, or anybody else, but when I am alone.

And I am alone a good deal just now. John is kept in town very often by serious cases, and Jennie is good and lets me alone when I want her to.

So I walk a little in the garden or down that lovely lane, sit on the porch under the roses, and lie down up here a good deal.

I'm getting really fond of the room in spite of the wallpaper. Perhaps *because* of the wallpaper.

It dwells in my mind so!

I lie here on this great immovable bed—it is nailed down, I believe—and follow that pattern about by the hour. It is as good as gymnastics, I assure you. I start, we'll say, at the bottom, down in the corner over there where it has not

---

[3]"There is a friend that sticketh closer than a brother." Proverbs 18:24.

[4]Silas Weir Mitchell (1829–1914), American physician known for his "rest-cure" treatment of "nervous disorders."

been touched, and I determine for the thousandth time that I *will* follow that pointless pattern to some sort of a conclusion.

I know a little of the principle of design, and I know this thing was not arranged on any laws of radiation, or alternation, or repetition, or symmetry, or anything else that I ever heard of.

It is repeated, of course, by the breadths, but not otherwise.

Looked at in one way, each breadth stands alone; the bloated curves and flourishes—a kind of "debased Romanesque" with delirium tremens—go waddling up and down in isolated columns of fatuity.

But, on the other hand, they connect diagonally, and the sprawling outlines run off in great slanting waves of optic horror, like a lot of wallowing sea-weeds in full chase.

The whole thing goes horizontally, too, at least it seems so, and I exhaust myself trying to distinguish the order of its going in that direction.

They have used a horizontal breadth for a frieze, and that adds wonderfully to the confusion.

There is one end of the room where it is almost intact, and there, when the crosslights fade and the low sun shines directly upon it, I can almost fancy radiation after all—the interminable grotesque seems to form around a common center and rush off in headlong plunges of equal distraction.

It makes me tired to follow it. I will take a nap, I guess.

I don't know why I should write this.

I don't want to.

I don't feel able.

And I know John would think it absurd. But I *must* say what I feel and think in some way—it is such a relief!

But the effort is getting to be greater than the relief.

Half the time now I am awfully lazy, and lie down ever so much. John says I mustn't lose my strength, and has me take cod liver oil and lots of tonics and things, to say nothing of ale and wine and rare meat.

Dear John! He loves me very dearly, and hates to have me sick. I tried to have a real earnest reasonable talk with him the other day, and tell him how I wish he would let me go and make a visit to Cousin Henry and Julia.

But he said I wasn't able to go, nor able to stand it after I got there; and I did not make out a very good case for myself, for I was crying before I had finished.

It is getting to be a great effort for me to think straight. Just this nervous weakness, I suppose.

And dear John gathered me up in his arms, and just carried me upstairs and laid me on the bed, and sat by me and read to me till it tired my head.

He said I was his darling and his comfort and all he had, and that I must take care of myself for his sake, and keep well.

He says no one but myself can help me out of it, that I must use my will and self-control and not let any silly fancies run away with me.

There's one comfort—the baby is well and happy, and does not have to occupy this nursery with the horrid wallpaper.

If we had not used it, that blessed child would have! What a fortunate escape! Why, I wouldn't have a child of mine, an impressionable little thing, live in such a room for worlds.

I never thought of it before, but it is lucky that John kept me here after all; I can stand it so much easier than a baby, you see.

Of course I never mention it to them any more—I am too wise—but I keep watch for it all the same.

There are things in that wallpaper that nobody knows about but me, or ever will.

Behind that outside pattern the dim shapes get clearer every day.

It is always the same shape, only very numerous.

And it is like a woman stooping down and creeping about behind that pattern. I don't like it a bit. I wonder—I begin to think—I wish John would take me away from here!

It is so hard to talk with John about my case, because he is so wise, and because he loves me so.

But I tried it last night.

It was moonlight. The moon shines in all around just as the sun does.

I hate to see it sometimes, it creeps so slowly, and always comes in by one window or another.

John was asleep and I hated to waken him, so I kept still and watched the moonlight on that undulating wallpaper till I felt creepy.

The faint figure behind seemed to shake the pattern, just as if she wanted to get out.

I got up softly and went to feel and see if the paper *did* move, and when I came back John was awake.

"What is it, litle girl?" he said. "Don't go walking about like that—you'll get cold."

I thought it was a good time to talk, so I told him that I really was not gaining here, and that I wished he would take me away.

"Why, darling!" said he. "Our lease will be up in three weeks, and I can't see how to leave before.

"The repairs are not done at home, and I cannot possibly leave town just now. Of course, if you were in any danger, I could and would, but you really are better, dear, whether you can see it or not. I am a doctor, dear, and I know. You are gaining flesh and color, your appetite is better, I feel really much easier about you."

"I don't weigh a bit more," said I, "nor as much; and my appetite may be better in the evening when you are here but it is worse in the morning when you are away!"

"Bless her little heart!" said he with a big hug. "She shall be as sick as she pleases! But now let's improve the shining hours by going to sleep, and talk about it in the morning!"

"And you won't go away?" I asked gloomily.

"Why, how can I, dear? It is only three weeks more and then we will take a nice little trip of a few days while Jennie is getting the house ready. Really, dear, you are better!"

"Better in body perhaps—" I began, and stopped short, for he sat up straight and looked at me with such a stern, reproachful look that I could not say another word.

"My darling," said he, "I beg of you, for my sake and for our child's sake, as well as for your own, that you will never for one instant let that idea enter your mind! There is nothing so dangerous, so fascinating, to a temperament like yours. It is a false and foolish fancy. Can you not trust me as a physician when I tell you so?"

So of course I said no more on that score, and we went to sleep before long. He thought I was asleep first, but I wasn't, and lay there for hours trying to decide whether that front pattern and the back pattern really did move together or separately.

On a pattern like this, by daylight, there is a lack of sequence, a defiance of law, that is a constant irritant to a normal mind.

The color is hideous enough, and unreliable enough, and infuriating enough, but the pattern is torturing.

You think you have mastered it, but just as you get well under way in following, it turns a back-somersault and there you are. It slaps you in the face, knocks you down, and tramples upon you. It is like a bad dream.

The outside pattern is a florid arabesque, reminding one of a fungus. If you can imagine a toadstool in joints, an interminable string of toadstools, budding and sprouting in endless convolutions—why, that is something like it.

That is, sometimes!

There is one marked peculiarity about this paper, a thing nobody seems to notice but myself, and that is that it changes as the light changes.

When the sun shoots in through the east window—I always watch for that first long, straight ray—it changes so quickly that I never can quite believe it.

That is why I watch it always.

By moonlight—the moon shines in all night when there is a moon—I wouldn't know it was the same paper.

At night in any kind of light, in twilight, candlelight, lamplight, and worst of all by moonlight, it becomes bars! The outside pattern, I mean, and the woman behind it is as plain as can be.

I didn't realize for a long time what the thing was that showed behind, that dim sub-pattern, but now I am quite sure it is a woman.

By daylight she is subdued, quiet. I fancy it is the pattern that keeps her so still. It is so puzzling. It keeps me quiet by the hour.

I lie down ever so much now. John says it is good for me, and to sleep all I can.

Indeed he started the habit by making me lie down for an hour after each meal.

It is a very bad habit, I am convinced, for you see, I don't sleep.

And that cultivates deceit, for I don't tell them I'm awake—oh, no!

The fact is I am getting a little afraid of John.

He seems very queer sometimes, and even Jennie has an inexplicable look.

It strikes me occasionally, just as a scientific hypothesis, that perhaps it is the paper!

I have watched John when he did not know I was looking, and come into the room suddenly on the most innocent excuses, and I've caught him several times *looking at the paper!* And Jennie too. I caught Jennie with her hand on it once.

She didn't know I was in the room, and when I asked her in a quiet, a very quiet voice, with the most restrained manner possible, what she was doing with the paper, she turned around as if she had been caught stealing, and looked quite angry—asked me why I should frighten her so!

Then she said that the paper stained everything it touched, that she had found yellow smooches[5] on all my clothes and John's and she wished we would be more careful!

Did not that sound innocent? But I know she was studying that pattern, and I am determined that nobody shall find it out but myself!

Life is very much more exciting now than it used to be. You see, I have something

---

[5]Smudges, smears.

more to expect, to look forward to, to watch. I really do eat better, and am more quiet than I was.

John is so pleased to see me improve! He laughed a little the other day, and said I seemed to be flourishing in spite of my wallpaper.

I turned it off with a laugh. I had no intention of telling him it was *because* of the wallpaper—he would make fun of me. He might even want to take me away.

I don't want to leave now until I have found it out. There is a week more, and I think that will be enough.

I'm feeling so much better!

I don't sleep much at night, for it is so interesting to watch developments; but I sleep a good deal during the daytime.

In the daytime it is tiresome and perplexing.

There are always new shoots on the fungus, and new shades of yellow all over it. I cannot keep count of them, though I have tried conscientiously.

It is the strangest yellow, that wallpaper! It makes me think of all the yellow things I ever saw—not beautiful ones like buttercups, but old, foul, bad yellow things.

But there is something else about that paper—the smell! I noticed it the moment we came into the room, but with so much air and sun it was not bad. Now we have had a week of fog and rain, and whether the windows are open or not, the smell is here.

It creeps all over the house.

I find it hovering in the dining-room, skulking in the parlor, hiding in the hall, lying in wait for me on the stairs.

It gets into my hair.

Even when I go to ride, if I turn my head suddenly and surprise it—there is that smell!

Such a peculiar odor, too! I have spent hours in trying to analyze it, to find what it smelled like.

It is not bad—at first—and very gentle, but quite the subtlest, most enduring odor I ever met.

In this damp weather it is awful. I wake up in the night and find it hanging over me.

It used to disturb me at first. I thought seriously of burning the house—to reach the smell.

But now I am used to it. The only thing I can think of that it is like is the *color* of the paper! A yellow smell.

There is a very funny mark on this wall, low down, near the mopboard. A streak that runs round the room. It goes behind every piece of furniture, except the bed, a long, straight, even *smooch*, as if it had been rubbed over and over.

I wonder how it was done and who did it, and what they did it for. Round and round and round—round and round and round—it makes me dizzy!

I really have discovered something at last.

Through watching so much at night, when it changes so, I have finally found out.

The front pattern *does* move—and no wonder! The woman behind shakes it!

Sometimes I think there are a great many women behind, and sometimes only one, and she crawls around fast, and her crawling shakes it all over.

Then in the very bright spots she keeps still, and in the very shady spots she just takes hold of the bars and shakes them hard.

And she is all the time trying to climb through. But nobody could climb through that pattern—it strangles so; I think that is why it has so many heads.

They get through, and then the pattern strangles them off and turns them upside down, and makes their eyes white!

If those heads were covered or taken off it would not be half so bad.

I think that woman gets out in the daytime!

And I'll tell you why—privately—I've seen her!

I can see her out of every one of my windows!

It is the same woman, I know, for she is always creeping, and most women do not creep by daylight.

I see her in that long shaded lane, creeping up and down. I see her in those dark grape arbors, creeping all around the garden.

I see her on that long road under the trees, creeping along, and when a carriage comes she hides under the blackberry vines.

I don't blame her a bit. It must be very humiliating to be caught creeping by daylight!

I always lock the door when I creep by daylight. I can't do it at night, for I know John would suspect something at once.

And John is so queer now that I don't want to irritate him. I wish he would take another room! Besides, I don't want anybody to get that woman out at night but myself.

I often wonder if I could see her out of all the windows at once.

But, turn as fast as I can, I can only see out of one at one time.

And though I always see her, she *may* be able to creep faster than I can turn! I have watched her sometimes away off in the open country, creeping as fast as a cloud shadow in a wind.

If only that top pattern could be gotten off from the under one! I mean to try it, little by little.

I have found out another funny thing, but I shan't tell it this time! It does not do to trust people too much.

There are only two more days to get this paper off, and I believe John is beginning to notice. I don't like the look in his eyes.

And I heard him ask Jennie a lot of professional questions about me. She had a very good report to give.

She said I slept a good deal in the daytime.

John knows I don't sleep very well at night, for all I'm so quiet!

He asked me all sorts of questions, too, and pretended to be very loving and kind.

As if I couldn't see through him!

Still, I don't wonder he acts so, sleeping under this paper for three months.

It only interests me, but I feel sure John and Jennie are affected by it.

* * * * *

Hurrah! This is the last day, but it is enough. John is to stay in town over night, and won't be out until this evening.

Jennie wanted to sleep with me—the sly thing; but I told her I should undoubtedly rest better for a night all alone.

That was clever, for really I wasn't alone a bit! As soon as it was moonlight and that poor thing began to crawl and shake the pattern, I got up and ran to help her.

I pulled and she shook. I shook and she pulled, and before morning we had peeled off yards of that paper.

A strip about as high as my head and half around the room.

And then when the sun came and that awful pattern began to laugh at me, I declared I would finish it today!

We go away tomorrow, and they are moving all my furniture down again to leave things as they were before.

Jennie looked at the wall in amazement, but I told her merrily that I did it out of pure spite at the vicious thing.

She laughed and said she wouldn't mind doing it herself, but I must not get tired.

How she betrayed herself that time!

But I am here, and no person touches this paper but Me—not *alive*!

She tried to get me out of the room—it was too patent! But I said it was so quiet and empty and clean now that I believed I would lie down again and sleep all I could, and not to wake me even for dinner—I would call when I woke.

So now she is gone, and the servants are gone, and the things are gone, and there is nothing left but that great bedstead nailed down, with the canvas mattress we found on it.

We shall sleep downstairs tonight, and take the boat home tomorrow.

I quite enjoy the room, now it is bare again.

How those children did tear about here!

This bedstead is fairly gnawed!

But I must get to work.

I have locked the door and thrown the key down into the front path.

I don't want to go out, and I don't want to have anybody come in, till John comes.

I want to astonish him.

I've got a rope up here that even Jennie did not find. If that woman does get out, and tries to get away, I can tie her!

But I forgot I could not reach far without anything to stand on!

This bed will *not* move!

I tried to lift and push it until I was lame, and then I got so angry I bit off a little piece at one corner—but it hurt my teeth.

Then I peeled off all the paper I could reach standing on the floor. It sticks horribly and the pattern just enjoys it! All those strangled heads and bulbous eyes and waddling fungus growths just shriek with derision!

I'm getting angry enough to do something desperate. To jump out of the window would be admirable exercise, but the bars are too strong even to try.

Besides I wouldn't do it. Of course not. I know well enough that a step like that is improper and might be misconstrued.

I don't like to *look* out of the windows even—there are so many of those creeping women, and they creep so fast.

I wonder if they all come out of that wallpaper as I did?

But I am securely fastened now by my well-hidden rope—you don't get *me* out in the road there!

I suppose I shall have to get back behind the pattern when it comes night, and that is hard!

It is so pleasant to be out in this great room and creep around as I please!

I don't want to go outside. I won't, even if Jennie asks me to.

For outside you have to creep on the ground, and everything is green instead of yellow.

But here I can creep smoothly on the floor, and my shoulder just fits in that long smooch around the wall, so I cannot lose my way.

Why, there's John at the door!

It is no use, young man, you can't open it!

How he does call and pound!

Now he's crying to Jennie for an axe.

It would be a shame to break down that beautiful door!

"John, dear!" said I in the gentlest voice. "The key is down by the front steps, under a plantain leaf!"

That silenced him for a few moments.

Then he said, very quietly indeed, "Open the door, my darling!"

"I can't," said I. "The key is down by the front door under a plantain leaf!" And then I said it again, several times, very gently and slowly, and said it so often that he had to go and see, and he got it of course, and came in. He stopped short by the door.

"What is the matter?" he cried. "For God's sake, what are you doing!"

I kept on creeping just the same, but I looked at him over my shoulder.

"I've got out at last," said I, "in spite of you and Jane. And I've pulled off most of the paper, so you can't put me back!"

Now why should that man have fainted? But he did, and right across my path by the wall, so that I had to creep over him every time!

1892

Kate Chopin 1851–1904

Although she became famous for her Louisiana dialect stories, Kate Chopin had been born and lived most of her life in St. Louis, Missouri. As the daughter of Thomas O'Flaherty, an Irish immigrant who had become a rich merchant in St. Louis, she was educated in a Roman Catholic convent school, learned fluent French, and became "one of the acknowledged belles" of society. At the age of nineteen she married Oscar Chopin (the name was pronounced in the French manner), who took his new bride to live in New Orleans, the picturesque and cosmopolitan city dominated by French Creole culture.

In 1879, after a decade in New Orleans, Oscar Chopin's business failed, and he moved his family to central Louisiana, where he managed plantations and ran a village store. In 1883 he died of swamp fever, and the next year Kate Chopin returned with her six children to St. Louis. Financially independent, bored with life as a society matron, she began to write poetry, sketches, and fiction dealing with Louisiana Creoles (descendants of early French and Spanish colonists), Cajuns (whose French ancestors had been exiled to Louisiana from Acadia in Canada in the eighteenth century), and the Negroes and half-breed Indians of the cities and back country.

In 1889 she began a novel, At Fault (1890), a conventional, sentimental story set in a Louisiana plantation. The novel was a failure, but soon Kate Chopin had begun to sell her local color stories to newspapers and such national magazines as the Century and Vogue. By 1898 she had written three novels (one of which she left unpublished and later destroyed) and nearly a hundred stories. Collections of her local color tales of Creoles and Cajuns had been published in Bayou Folk (1894) and A Night in Acadie (1897).

In 1899 she published her third novel, The Awakening, later described as the story of "a sensuous woman who follows her inclinations." It was her masterpiece, but its theme of infidelity and the passions of its heroine brought condemnation from critics. The Awakening was judged "too strong drink for moral babes," a book that "should be labeled poison." It was banned from libraries, and its author was shunned by St. Louis society. Five years later Kate Chopin died. Her shocking novel fell into obscurity; she was remembered only as one of the local-color writers who exploited the idioms and idiosyncrasies of the exotic provinces of America. Not until the 1950s did critical reevaluation begin to emphasize her subtle power to go beyond the conventions of popular "ladies fiction" and to portray the problems of race and show the anguish of men and women stripped of illusions, bereft of complacency and love.

FURTHER READING: *The Complete Works of Kate Chopin*, 2 vols., ed. P. Seyersted, 1969; D. Rankin, *Kate Chopin, and Her Creole Stories*, 1932; P. Seyersted, *Kate Chopin*, 1969, 1980; P. Skaggs, *Kate Chopin*, 1985.

TEXT: *The Awakening*, 1899.

THE AWAKENING

I

A green and yellow parrot, which hung in a cage outside the door, kept repeating over and over:

"*Allez vous-en! Allez vous-en! Sapristi!*[1] That's all right!"

He could speak a little Spanish, and also a language which nobody understood, unless it was the mocking-bird that hung on the other side of the door, whistling his fluty notes out upon the breeze with maddening persistence.

Mr. Pontellier, unable to read his newspaper with any degree of comfort, arose with an expression and an exclamation of disgust. He walked down the gallery and across the narrow "bridges" which connected the Lebrun cottages one with the other. He had been seated before the door of the main house. The parrot and the mocking-bird were the property of Madame Lebrun, and they had the right to make all the noise they wished. Mr. Pontellier had the privilege of quitting their society when they ceased to be entertaining.

He stopped before the door of his own cottage, which was the fourth one from the main building and next to the last. Seating himself in a wicker rocker which was there, he once more applied himself to the task of reading the newspaper. The day was Sunday; the paper was a day old. The Sunday papers had not yet reached Grand Isle.[2] He was already acquainted with the market reports, and he glanced restlessly over the editorials and bits of news which he had not had time to read before quitting New Orleans the day before.

Mr. Pontellier wore eye-glasses. He was a man of forty, of medium height and rather slender build; he stooped a little. His hair was brown and straight, parted on one side. His beard was neatly and closely trimmed.

Once in a while he withdrew his glance from the newspaper and looked about him. There was more noise than ever over at the house. The main building was called "the house," to distinguish it from the cottages. The chattering and whistling birds were still at it. Two young girls, the Farival twins, were playing a duet from "Zampa"[3] upon the piano. Madame Lebrun was bustling in and out, giving orders in a high key to a yard-boy whenever she got inside the house, and directions in an equally high voice to a dining-room servant whenever she got outside. She was a fresh, pretty woman, clad always in white with elbow sleeves. Her starched skirts crinkled as she came and went. Farther down, before

---

[1]French: "Go away! Go away! For God's sake!"
[2]An island in the Gulf of Mexico, south of New Orleans.
[3]A romantic opera (1831) by the French composer Louis Hérold (1791–1833).

one of the cottages, a lady in black was walking demurely up and down, telling her beads.[4] A good many persons of the *pension*[5] had gone over to the *Chênière Caminada*[6] in Beaudelet's lugger[7] to hear mass. Some young people were out under the water-oaks playing croquet. Mr. Pontellier's two children were there— sturdy little fellows of four and five. A quadroon[8] nurse followed them about with a far-away, meditative air.

Mr. Pontellier finally lit a cigar and began to smoke, letting the paper drag idly from his hand. He fixed his gaze upon a white sunshade[9] that was advancing at snail's pace from the beach. He could see it plainly between the gaunt trunks of the water-oaks and across the stretch of yellow camomile. The gulf looked far away, melting hazily into the blue of the horizon. The sunshade continued to approach slowly. Beneath its pink-lined shelter were his wife, Mrs. Pontellier, and young Robert Lebrun. When they reached the cottage, the two seated themselves with some appearance of fatigue upon the upper step of the porch, facing each other, each leaning against a supporting post.

"What folly! to bathe at such an hour in such heat!" exclaimed Mr. Pontellier. He himself had taken a plunge at daylight. That was why the morning seemed long to him.

"You are burnt beyond recognition," he added, looking at his wife as one looks at a valuable piece of personal property which has suffered some damage. She held up her hands, strong, shapely hands, and surveyed them critically, drawing up her lawn[10] sleeves above the wrists. Looking at them reminded her of her rings, which she had given to her husband before leaving for the beach. She silently reached out to him, and he, understanding, took the rings from his vest pocket and dropped them into her open palm. She slipped them upon her fingers; then clasping her knees, she looked across at Robert and began to laugh. The rings sparkled upon her fingers. He sent back an answering smile.

"What is it?" asked Pontellier, looking lazily and amused from one to the other. It was some utter nonsense; some adventure out there in the water, and they both tried to relate it at once. It did not seem half so amusing when told. They realized this, and so did Mr. Pontellier. He yawned and stretched himself. Then he got up, saying he had half a mind to go over to Klein's hotel and play a game of billiards.

"Come go along, Lebrun," he proposed to Robert. But Robert admitted quite frankly that he preferred to stay where he was and talk to Mrs. Pontellier.

"Well, send him about his business when he bores you, Edna," instructed her husband as he prepared to leave.

"Here, take the umbrella," she exclaimed, holding it out to him. He accepted the sunshade, and lifting it over his head descended the steps and walked away.

"Coming back to dinner?" his wife called after him. He halted a moment and shrugged his shoulders. He felt in his vest pocket; there was a ten-dollar bill there. He did not know; perhaps he would return for the early dinner and perhaps he would not. It all depended upon the company which he found over at Klein's and the size of "the game." He did not say this, but she understood it, and laughed, nodding good-by to him.

Both children wanted to follow their father when they saw him starting out. He kissed them and promised to bring them back bonbons and peanuts.

[4]I.e., using a string of beads to count prayers, such as those of the Rosary.
[5]French: boarding house.   [6]An island in the Gulf of Mexico, near Grand Isle.
[7]Small vessel with a four-sided sail that hangs obliquely on the mast.
[8]A person with one-quarter Negro ancestry.   [9]Parasol.
[10]Fine linen or cotton cloth.

II

Mrs. Pontellier's eyes were quick and bright; they were a yellowish brown, about the color of her hair. She had a way of turning them swiftly upon an object and holding them there as if lost in some inward maze of contemplation or thought.

Her eyebrows were a shade darker than her hair. They were thick and almost horizontal, emphasizing the depth of her eyes. She was rather handsome than beautiful. Her face was captivating by reason of a certain frankness of expression and a contradictory subtle play of features. Her manner was engaging.

Robert rolled a cigarette. He smoked cigarettes because he could not afford cigars, he said. He had a cigar in his pocket which Mr. Pontellier had presented him with, and he was saving it for his after-dinner smoke.

This seemed quite proper and natural on his part. In coloring he was not unlike his companion. A clean-shaved face made the resemblance more pronounced than it would otherwise have been. There rested no shadow of care upon his open countenance. His eyes gathered in and reflected the light and languor of the summer day.

Mrs. Pontellier reached over for a palm-leaf fan that lay on the porch and began to fan herself, while Robert sent between his lip light puffs from his cigarette. They chatted incessantly: about the things around them; their amusing adventure out in the water—it had again assumed its entertaining aspect; about the wind, the trees, the people who had gone to the *Chênière;* about the children playing croquet under the oaks, and the Farival twins, who were now performing the overture to "The Poet and the Peasant."[1]

Robert talked a good deal about himself. He was very young, and did not know any better. Mrs. Pontellier talked a little about herself for the same reason. Each was interested in what the other said. Robert spoke of his intention to go to Mexico in the autumn, where fortune awaited him. He was always intending to go to Mexico, but some way never got there. Meanwhile he held on to his modest position in a mercantile house in New Orleans, where an equal familiarity with English, French and Spanish gave him no small value as a clerk and correspondent.

He was spending his summer vacation, as he always did, with his mother at Grand Isle. In former times, before Robert could remember, "the house" had been a summer luxury of the Lebruns. Now, flanked by its dozen or more cottages, which were always filled with exclusive visitors from the "*Quartier Français,*"[2] it enabled Madame Lebrun to maintain the easy and comfortable existence which appeared to be her birthright.

Mrs. Pontellier talked about her father's Mississippi plantation and her girl-hood home in the old Kentucky blue-grass country. She was an American woman, with a small infusion of French which seemed to have been lost in dilution. She read a letter from her sister, who was away in the East, and who had engaged herself to be married. Robert was interested, and wanted to know what manner of girls the sisters were, what the father was like, and how long the mother had been dead.

When Mrs. Pontellier folded the letter it was time for her to dress for the early dinner.

"I see Léonce isn't coming back," she said, with a glance in the direction

---

[1]A light opera (1846) by the Austrian composer Franz von Suppé (1819–1895).
[2]French: "French Quarter," the oldest part of New Orleans, where descendants of early French settlers lived in the nineteenth century.

whence her husband had disappeared. Robert supposed he was not, as there were a good many New Orleans club men over at Klein's.

When Mrs. Pontellier left him to enter her room, the young man descended the steps and strolled over toward the croquet players, where, during the half-hour before dinner, he amused himself with the little Pontellier children, who were very fond of him.

III

It was eleven o'clock that night when Mr. Pontellier returned from Klein's hotel. He was in an excellent humor, in high spirits, and very talkative. His entrance awoke his wife, who was in bed and fast asleep when he came in. He talked to her while he undressed, telling her anecdotes and bits of news and gossip that he had gathered during the day. From his trousers pockets he took a fistful of crumpled bank notes and a good deal of silver coin, which he piled on the bureau indiscriminately with keys, knife, handkerchief, and whatever else happened to be in his pockets. She was overcome with sleep, and answered him with little half utterances.

He thought it very discouraging that his wife, who was the sole object of his existence, evinced so little interest in things which concerned him, and valued so little his conversation.

Mr. Pontellier had forgotten the bonbons and peanuts for the boys. Notwith-standing he loved them very much, and went into the adjoining room where they slept to take a look at them and make sure that they were resting comfort-ably. The result of his investigation was far from satisfactory. He turned and shifted the youngsters about in bed. One of them began to kick and talk about a basket full of crabs.

Mr. Pontellier returned to his wife with the information that Raoul had a high fever and needed looking after. Then he lit a cigar and went and sat near the open door to smoke it.

Mrs. Pontellier was quite sure Raoul had no fever. He had gone to bed perfectly well, she said, and nothing had ailed him all day. Mr. Pontellier was too well acquainted with fever symptoms to be mistaken. He assured her the child was consuming[1] at that moment in the next room.

He reproached his wife with her inattention, her habitual neglect of the children. If it was not a mother's place to look after children, whose on earth was it? He himself had his hands full with his brokerage business. He could not be in two places at once; making a living for his family on the street, and staying at home to see that no harm befell them. He talked in a monotonous, insistent way.

Mrs. Pontellier sprang out of bed and went into the next room. She soon came back and sat on the edge of the bed, leaning her head down on the pillow. She said nothing, and refused to answer her husband when he questioned her. When his cigar was smoked out he went to bed, and in half a minute he was fast asleep.

Mrs. Pontellier was by that time thoroughly awake. She began to cry a little, and wiped her eyes on the sleeve of her *peignoir*.[2] Blowing out the candle, which her husband had left burning, she slipped her bare feet into a pair of satin

---

[1] Running a temperature.   [2] A loose dressing gown, a negligee.

mules[3] at the foot of the bed and went out on the porch, where she sat down in the wicker chair and began to rock gently to and fro.

It was then past midnight. The cottages were all dark. A single faint light gleamed out from the hallway of the house. There was no sound abroad except the hooting of an old owl in the top of a water-oak, and the everlasting voice of the sea, that was not uplifted at that soft hour. It broke like a mournful lullaby upon the night.

The tears came so fast to Mrs. Pontellier's eyes that the damp sleeve of her *peignoir* no longer served to dry them. She was holding the back of her chair with one hand; her loose sleeve had slipped almost to the shoulder of her uplifted arm. Turning, she thrust her face, steaming and wet, into the bend of her arm, and she went on crying there, not caring any longer to dry her face, her eyes, her arms. She could not have told why she was crying. Such experiences as the foregoing were not uncommon in her married life. They seemed never before to have weighed much against the abundance of her husband's kindness and a uniform devotion which had come to be tacit and self-understood.

An indescribable oppression, which seemed to generate in some unfamiliar part of her consciousness, filled her whole being with a vague anguish. It was like a shadow, like a mist passing across her soul's summer day. It was strange and unfamiliar; it was a mood. She did not sit there inwardly upbraiding her husband, lamenting at Fate, which had directed her footsteps to the path which they had taken. She was just having a good cry to herself. The mosquitoes made merry over her, biting her firm, round arms and nipping at her bare insteps.

The little stinging, buzzing imps succeeded in dispelling a mood which might have held her there in the darkness half a night longer.

The following morning Mr. Pontellier was up in good time to take the rockaway[4] which was to convey him to the steamer at the wharf. He was returning to the city to his business, and they would not see him again at the Island till the coming Saturday. He had regained his composure, which seemed to have been somewhat impaired the night before. He was eager to be gone, as he looked forward to a lively week in Carondelet Street.[5]

Mr. Pontellier gave his wife half of the money which he had brought away from Klein's hotel the evening before. She liked money as well as most women, and accepted it with no little satisfaction.

"It will buy a handsome wedding present for Sister Janet!" she exclaimed, smoothing out the bills as she counted them one by one.

"Oh! we'll treat Sister Janet better than that, my dear," he laughed, as he prepared to kiss her good-by.

The boys were tumbling about, clinging to his legs, imploring that numerous things be brought back to them. Mr. Pontellier was a great favorite, and ladies, men, children, even nurses, were always on hand to say good-by to him. His wife stood smiling and waving, the boys shouting, as he disappeared in the old rockaway down the sandy road.

A few days later a box arrived for Mrs. Pontellier from New Orleans. It was from her husband. It was filled with *friandises*,[6] with luscious and toothsome bits—the finest of fruits, *patés*,[7] a rare bottle or two, delicious syrups, and bonbons in abundance.

Mrs. Pontellier was always very generous with the contents of such a box; she was quite used to receiving them when away from home. The *patés*, and fruit

---

[3]Slippers.   [4]A light four-wheeled carriage, manufactured in Rockaway, New Jersey.
[5]Financial and commercial center of New Orleans.   [6]French: delicacies.
[7]French: rich meat pastes.

were brought to the dining-room; the bonbons were passed around. And the ladies, selecting with dainty and discriminating fingers and a little greedily, all declared that Mr. Pontellier was the best husband in the world. Mrs. Pontellier was forced to admit that she knew of none better.

IV

It would have been a difficult matter for Mr. Pontellier to define to his own satisfaction or any one else's wherein his wife failed in her duty toward their children. It was something which he felt rather than perceived, and he never voiced the feeling without subsequent regret and ample atonement.

If one of the little Pontellier boys took a tumble whilst at play, he was not apt to rush crying to his mother's arms for comfort; he would more likely pick himself up, wipe the water out of his eyes and the sand out of his mouth, and go on playing. Tots as they were, they pulled together and stood their ground in childish battles with doubled fists and uplifted voices, which usually prevailed against the other brother-tots. The quadroon nurse was looked upon as a huge encumbrance, only good to button up waists and panties and to brush and part hair; since it seemed to be a law of society that hair must be parted and brushed.

In short, Mrs. Pontellier was not a mother-woman. The mother-women seemed to prevail that summer at Grand Isle. It was easy to know them, fluttering about with extended, protecing wings when any harm, real or imaginary, threatened their precious brood. They were women who idolized their children, worshiped their husbands, and esteemed it a holy privilege to efface themselves as individuals and grow wings as ministering angels.

Many of them were delicious in the rôle; one of them was the embodiment of every womanly grace and charm. If her husband did not adore her, he was a brute, deserving of death by slow torture. Her name was Adèle Ratignolle. There are no words to describe her save the old ones that have served so often to picture the bygone heroine of romance and the fair lady of our dreams. There was nothing subtle or hidden about her charms; her beauty was all there, flaming and apparent: the spungold hair that comb nor confining pin could restrain; the blue eyes that were like nothing but sapphires; two lips that pouted, that were so red one could only think of cherries or some other delicious crimson fruit in looking at them. She was growing a little stout, but it did not seem to detract an iota from the grace of every step, pose, gesture. One would not have wanted her white neck[1] a mite less full or her beautiful arms more slender. Never were hands more exquisite than hers, and it was a joy to look at them when she threaded her needle or adjusted her gold thimble to her taper[2] middle finger as she sewed away on the little night-drawers or fashioned a bodice or a bib.

Madame Ratignolle was very fond of Mrs. Pontellier, and often she took her sewing and went over to sit with her in the afternoons. She was sitting there the afternoon of the day the box arrived from New Orleans. She had possession of the rocker, and she was busily engaged in sewing upon a diminutive pair of night-drawers.

She had brought the pattern of the drawers for Mrs. Pontellier to cut out—a marvel of construction, fashioned to enclose a baby's body so effectually that

[1]A term used in the nineteenth century as a genteel synonym for "bosom" or "breast."
[2]Tapered.

only two small eyes might look out from the garment, like an Eskimo's. They were designed for winter wear, when treacherous drafts came down chimneys and insidious currents of deadly cold found their way through key-holes.

Mrs. Pontellier's mind was quite at rest concerning the present material needs of her children, and she could not see the use of anticipating and making winter night garments the subject of her summer meditations. But she did not want to appear unamiable and uninterested, so she had brought forth newspapers, which she spread upon the floor of the gallery, and under Madame Ratignolle's directions she had cut a pattern of the impervious garment.

Robert was there, seated as he had been the Sunday before, and Mrs. Pontellier also occupied her former position on the upper step, leaning listlessly against the post. Beside her was a box of bonbons, which she held out at intervals to Madame Ratignolle.

That lady seemed at a loss to make a selection, but finally settled upon a stick of nougat, wondering if it were not too rich; whether it could possibly hurt her. Madame Ratignolle had been married seven years. About every two years she had a baby. At that time she had three babies, and was beginning to think of a fourth one. She was always talking about her "condition." Her "condition" was in no way apparent, and no one would have known a thing about it but for her persistence in making it the subject of conversation.

Robert started to reassure her, asserting that he had known a lady who had subsisted upon nougat during the entire—but seeing the color mount into Mrs. Pontellier's face he checked himself and changed the subject.

Mrs. Pontellier, though she had married a Creole,[3] was not thoroughly at home in the society of Creoles; never before had she been thrown so intimately among them. There were only Creoles that summer at Lebrun's. They all knew each other, and felt like one large family, among whom existed the most amicable relations. A characteristic which distinguished them and which impressed Mrs. Pontellier most forcibly was their entire absence of prudery. Their freedom of expression was at first incomprehensible to her, though she had no difficulty in reconciling it with a lofty chastity which in the Creole woman seems to be inborn and unmistakable.

Never would Edna Pontellier forget the shock with which she heard Madame Ratignolle relating to old Monsieur Farival the harrowing story of one of her *accouchements*,[4] withholding no intimate detail. She was growing accustomed to like shocks, but she could not keep the mounting color back from her cheeks. Oftener than once her coming had interrupted the droll story with which Robert was entertaining some amused group of married women.

A book had gone the rounds of the *pension*. When it came her turn to read it, she did so with profound astonishment. She felt moved to read the book in secret and solitude, though none of the others had done so—to hide it from view at the sound of approaching footsteps. It was openly criticized and freely discussed at table. Mrs. Pontellier gave over being astonished, and concluded that wonders would never cease.

V

They formed a congenial group sitting there that summer afternoon—Madame Ratignolle sewing away, often stopping to relate a story or incident with

[3]A term meaning "native," used in Louisiana to describe native-born descendants of early French and Spanish settlers.   [4]French: childbirths.

much expressive gesture of her perfect hands; Robert and Mrs. Pontellier sitting idle, exchanging occasional words, glances or smiles which indicated a certain advanced stage of intimacy and *camaraderie.*

He had lived in her shadow during the past month. No one thought anything of it. Many had predicted that Robert would devote himself to Mrs. Pontellier when he arrived. Since the age of fifteen, which was eleven years before, Robert each summer at Grand Isle had constituted himself the devoted attendant of some fair dame or damsel. Sometimes it was a young girl, again a widow; but as often as not it was some interesting married woman.

For two consecutive seasons he lived in the sunlight of Mademoiselle Duvigné's presence. But she died between summers; then Robert posed as an inconsolable; prostrating himself at the feet of Madame Ratignolle for whatever crumbs of sympathy and comfort she might be pleased to vouchsafe.

Mrs. Pontellier liked to sit and gaze at her fair companion as she might look upon a faultless Madonna.

"Could any one fathom the cruelty beneath that fair exterior?" murmured Robert. "She knew that I adored her once, and she let me adore her. It was 'Robert, come; go; stand up; sit down; do this; do that; see if the baby sleeps; my thimble, please, that I left God knows where. Come and read Daudet[1] to me while I sew.'"

"*Par exemple!*[2] I never had to ask. You were always there under my feet, like a troublesome cat."

"You mean like an adoring dog. And just as soon as Ratignolle appeared on the scene, then it *was* like a dog. '*Passez! Adieu! Allez vous-en!*'"[3]

"Perhaps I feared to make Alphonse jealous," she interjoined, with excessive naïveté. That made them all laugh. The right hand jealous of the left! The heart jealous of the soul! But for that matter, the Creole husband is never jealous; with him the gangrene passion is one which has become dwarfed by disuse.

Meanwhile Robert, addressing Mrs. Pontellier, continued to tell of his one time hopeless passion for Madame Ratignolle; of sleepless nights, of consuming flames till the very sea sizzled when he took his daily plunge. While the lady at the needle kept up a little running, contemptuous comment:

"*Blaguer—farceur—gros bête, va!*"[4]

He never assumed this serio-comic tone when alone with Mrs. Pontellier. She never knew precisely what to make of it; at that moment it was impossible for her to guess how much of it was jest and what proportion was earnest. It was understood that he had often spoken words of love to Madame Ratignolle, without any thought of being taken seriously. Mrs. Pontellier was glad he had not assumed a similar rôle toward herself. It would have been unacceptable and annoying.

Mrs. Pontellier had brought her sketching materials, which she sometimes dabbled with in an unprofessional way. She liked the dabbling. She felt in it satisfaction of a kind which no other employment afforded her.

She had long wished to try herself on Madame Ratignolle. Never had that lady seemed a more tempting subject than at that moment, seated there like some sensuous Madonna, with the gleam of the fading day enriching her splendid color.

Robert crossed over and seated himself upon the step below Mrs. Pontellier, that he might watch her work. She handled her brushes with a certain ease and freedom which came, not from long and close acquaintance with them, but from

[1]Alphonse Daudet (1840–1897), popular French novelist.   [2]French: "For heaven's sake!"
[3]French: "Go on! Good-bye! Go away!"   [4]French: "Joker—trickster—big fool, go!"

a natural aptitude. Robert followed her work with close attention, giving forth little ejaculatory expressions of appreciation in French, which he addressed to Madame Ratignolle.

"Mais ce n'est pas mal! Elle s'y connaît, elle a de la force, oui."[5]

During his oblivious attention he once quietly rested his head against Mrs. Pontellier's arm. As gently she repulsed him. Once again he repeated the offense. She could not but believe it to be thoughtlessness on his part; yet that was no reason she should submit to it. She did not remonstrate, except again to repulse him quietly but firmly. He offered no apology.

The picture completed bore no resemblance to Madame Ratignolle. She was greatly disappointed to find that it did not look like her. But it was a fair enough piece of work, and in many respects satisfying.

Mrs. Pontellier evidently did not think so. After surveying the sketch critically she drew a broad smudge of paint across its surface, and crumpled the paper between her hands.

The youngsters came tumbling up the steps, the quadroon following at the respectful distance which they required her to observe. Mrs. Pontellier made them carry her paints and things into the house. She sought to detain them for a little talk and some pleasantry. But they were greatly in earnest. They had only come to investigate the contents of the bonbon box. They accepted without murmuring what she chose to give them, each holding out two chubby hands scoop-like, in the vain hope that they might be filled; and then away they went.

The sun was low in the west, and the breeze soft and languorous that came up from the south, charged with the seductive odor of the sea. Children, freshly befurbelowed,[6] were gathering for their games under the oaks. Their voices were high and penetrating.

Madame Ratignolle folded her sewing, placing thimble, scissors and thread all neatly together in the roll, which she pinned securely. She complained of faintness. Mrs. Pontellier flew for the cologne water and a fan. She bathed Madame Ratignolle's face with cologne, while Robert plied the fan with unnecessary vigor.

The spell was soon over, and Mrs. Pontellier could not help wondering if there were not a little imagination responsible for its origin, for the rose tint had never faded from her friend's face.

She stood watching the fair woman walk down the long line of galleries with the grace and majesty which queens are sometimes supposed to possess. Her little ones ran to meet her. Two of them clung about her white skirts, the third she took from its nurse and with a thousand endearments bore it along in her own fond, encircling arms. Though, as everybody well knew, the doctor had forbidden her to lift so much as a pin!

"Are you going bathing?" asked Robert of Mrs. Pontellier. It was not so much a question as a reminder.

"Oh, no," she answered, with a tone of indecision. "I'm tired; I think not." Her glance wandered from his face away toward the Gulf, whose sonorous murmur reached her like a loving but imperative entreaty.

"Oh, come!" he insisted. "You mustn't miss your bath. Come on. The water must be delicious; it will not hurt you. Come."

He reached up for her big, rough straw hat that hung on a peg outside the

---

[5]French: "Not bad at all! She knows what she's doing, she has ability, yes."
[6]I.e., dressed in fussy, elaborate clothes.

door, and put it on her head. They descended the steps, and walked away together toward the beach. The sun was low in the west and the breeze was soft and warm.

VI

Edna Pontellier could not have told why, wishing to go to the beach with Robert, she should in the first place have declined, and in the second place have followed in obedience to one of the two contradictory impulses which impelled her.

A certain light was beginning to dawn dimly within her,—the light which, showing the way, forbids it.

At that early period it served but to bewilder her. It moved her to dreams, to thoughtfulness, to the shadowy anguish which had overcome her the midnight when she had abandoned herself to tears.

In short, Mrs. Pontellier was beginning to realize her position in the universe as a human being, and to recognize her relations as an individual to the world within and about her. This may seem like a ponderous weight of wisdom to descend upon the soul of a young woman of twenty-eight—perhaps more wisdom than the Holy Ghost is usually pleased to vouchsafe to any woman.

But the beginning of things, of a world especially, is necessarily vague, tangled, chaotic, and exceedingly disturbing. How few of us ever emerge from such beginning! How many souls perish in its tumult!

The voice of the sea is seductive; never ceasing, whispering, clamoring, murmuring, inviting the soul to wander for a spell in abysses of solitude; to lose itself in mazes of inward contemplation.

The voice of the sea speaks to the soul. The touch of the sea is sensuous, enfolding the body in its soft, close embrace.

VII

Mrs. Pontellier was not a woman given to confidences, a characteristic hitherto contrary to her nature. Even as a child she had lived her own small life all within herself. At a very early period she had apprehended instinctively the dual life— that outward existence which conforms, the inward life which questions.

That summer at Grand Isle she began to loosen a little the mantle of reserve that had always enveloped her. There may have been—there must have been— influences, both subtle and apparent, working in their several ways to induce her to do this; but the most obvious was the influence of Adèle Ratignolle. The excessive physical charm of the Creole had first attracted her, for Edna had a sensuous susceptibility to beauty. Then the candor of the woman's whole existence, which every one might read, and which formed so striking a contrast to her own habitual reserve—this might have furnished a link. Who can tell what metals the gods use in forging the subtle bond which we call sympathy, which we might as well call love.

The two women went away one morning to the beach together, arm in arm, under the huge white sunshade. Edna had prevailed upon Madame Ratignolle to leave the children behind, though she could not induce her to relinquish a diminutive roll of needlework, which Adèle begged to be allowed to slip into the depths of her pocket. In some unaccountable way they had escaped from Robert.

The walk to the beach was no inconsiderable one, consisting as it did of a long, sandy path, upon which a sporadic and tangled growth that bordered it on either side made frequent and unexpected inroads. There were acres of yellow camomile[1] reaching out on either hand. Further away still, vegetable gardens abounded, with frequent small plantations of orange or lemon trees intervening. The dark green clusters glistened from afar in the sun.

The women were both of goodly height, Madame Ratignolle possessing the more feminine and matronly figure. The charm of Edna Pontellier's physique stole insensibly upon you. The lines of her body were long, clean and symmetrical; it was a body which occasionally fell into splendid poses; there was no suggestion of the trim, stereotyped fashion-plate about it. A casual and indiscriminating observer, in passing, might not cast a second glance upon the figure. But with more feeling and discernment he would have recognized the noble beauty of its modeling, and the graceful severity of poise and movement, which made Edna Pontellier different from the crowd.

She wore a cool muslin that morning—white, with a waving vertical line of brown running through it; also a white linen collar and the big straw hat which she had taken from the peg outside the door. The hat rested any way on her yellow-brown hair, that waved a little, was heavy, and clung close to her head.

Madame Ratignolle, more careful of her complexion, had twined a gauze veil about her head. She wore dogskin[2] gloves, with gauntlets that protected her wrists. She was dressed in pure white, with a fluffiness of ruffles that became her. The draperies and fluttering things which she wore suited her rich, luxuriant beauty as a greater severity of line could not have done.

There were a number of bath-houses along the beach, of rough but solid construction, built with small, protecting galleries facing the water. Each house consisted of two compartments, and each family at Lebrun's possessed a compartment for itself, fitted out with all the essential paraphernalia of the bath and whatever other conveniences the owners might desire. The two women had no intention of bathing; they had just strolled down to the beach for a walk and to be alone and near the water. The Pontellier and Ratignolle compartments adjoined one another under the same roof.

Mrs. Pontellier had brought down her key through force of habit. Unlocking the door of her bath-room she went inside, and soon emerged, bringing a rug, which she spread upon the floor of the gallery, and two huge hair pillows covered with crash,[3] which she placed against the front of the building.

The two seated themselves there in the shade of the porch, side by side, with their backs against the pillows and their feet extended. Madame Ratignolle removed her veil, wiped her face with a rather delicate handkerchief, and fanned herself with the fan which she always carried suspended somewhere about her person by a long, narrow ribbon. Edna removed her collar and opened her dress at the throat. She took the fan from Madame Ratignolle and began to fan both herself and her companion. It was very warm, and for a while they did nothing but exchange remarks about the heat, the sun, the glare. But there was a breeze blowing, a choppy, stiff wind that whipped the water into froth. It fluttered the skirts of the two women and kept them for a while engaged in adjusting, readjusting, tucking in, securing hair-pins and hat-pins. A few persons were

[1] A strong-scented flower, a variety of aster.
[2] Thick leather gloves made from the skins of dogs and sheep.   [3] Coarse, heavy linen cloth.

sporting some distance away in the water. The beach was very still of human sound at that hour. The lady in black was reading her morning devotions on the porch of a neighboring bath-house. Two young lovers were exchanging their hearts' yearnings beneath the children's tent, which they had found unoccupied.

Edna Pontellier, casting her eyes about, had finally kept them at rest upon the sea. The day was clear and carried the gaze out as far as the blue sky went; there were a few white clouds suspended idly over the horizon. A lateen sail[4] was visible in the direction of Cat Island, and others to the south seemed almost motionless in the far distance.

"Of whom—of what are you thinking?" asked Adèle of her companion, whose countenance she had been watching with a little amused attention, arrested by the absorbed expression which seemed to have seized and fixed every feature into a statuesque repose.

"Nothing," returned Mrs. Pontellier, with a start, adding at once: "How stupid! But it seems to me it is the reply we make instinctively to such a question. Let me see," she went on, throwing back her head and narrowing her fine eyes till they shone like two vivid points of light. "Let me see. I was really not conscious of thinking of anything; but perhaps I can retrace my thoughts."

"Oh! never mind!" laughed Madame Ratignolle. "I am not quite so exacting. I will let you off this time. It is really too hot to think, especially to think about thinking."

"But for the fun of it," persisted Edna. "First of all, the sight of the water stretching so far away, those motionless sails against the blue sky, made a delicious picture that I just wanted to sit and look at. The hot wind beating in my face made me think—without any connection that I can trace—of a summer day in Kentucky, of a meadow that seemed as big as the ocean to the very little girl walking through the grass, which was higher than her waist. She threw out her arms as if swimming when she walked, beating the tall grass as one strikes out in the water. Oh, I see the connection now!"

"Where were you going that day in Kentucky, walking through the grass?"

"I don't remember now. I was just walking diagonally across a big field. My sun-bonnet obstructed the view. I could see only the stretch of green before me, and I felt as if I must walk on forever, without coming to the end of it. I don't remember whether I was frightened or pleased. I must have been entertained."

"Likely as not it was Sunday," she laughed; "and I was running away from prayers, from the Presbyterian service, read in a spirit of gloom by my father that chills me yet to think of."

"And have you been running away from prayers ever since, *ma chère?*"[5] asked Madame Ratignolle, amused.

"No! oh, no!" Edna hastened to say. "I was a little unthinking child in those days, just following a misleading impulse without question. On the contrary, during one period of my life religion took a firm hold upon me; after I was twelve and until—until—why, I suppose until now, though I never thought much about it—just driven along by habit. But do you know," she broke off, turning her quick eyes upon Madame Ratignolle and leaning forward a little so as to bring her face quite close to that of her companion, "sometimes I feel this summer as if I were walking through the green meadow again; idly, aimlessly, unthinking and unguided."

Madame Ratignolle laid her hand over that of Mrs. Pontellier, which was near

[4]The oblique-hanging sail characteristic of a lugger.   [5]French: "My dear."

her. Seeing that the hand was not withdrawn, she clasped it firmly and warmly. She even stroked it a little, fondly, with the other hand, murmuring in an undertone, *"Pauvre chèrie."*[6]

The action was at first a little confusing to Edna, but she soon lent herself readily to the Creole's gentle caress. She was not accustomed to an outward and spoken expression of affection, either in herself or in others. She and her younger sister, Janet, had quarreled a good deal through force of unfortunate habit. Her older sister, Margaret, was matronly and dignified, probably from having assumed matronly and housewifely responsibilities too early in life, their mother having died when they were quite young. Margaret was not effusive: she was practical. Edna had had an occasional girl friend, but whether accidentally or not, they seemed to have been all of one type—the self-contained. She never realized that the reserve of her own character had much, perhaps everything, to do with this. Her most intimate friend at school had been one of rather exceptional intellectual gifts, who wrote fine-sounding essays, which Edna admired and strove to imitate; and with her she talked and glowed over the English classics, and sometimes held religious and political controversies.

Edna often wondered at one propensity which sometimes had inwardly disturbed her without causing any outward show or manifestation on her part. At a very early age—perhaps it was when she traversed the ocean of waving grass—she remembered that she had been passionately enamored of a dignified and sad-eyed cavalry officer who visited her father in Kentucky. She could not leave his presence when he was there, nor remove her eyes from his face, which was something like Napoleon's, with a lock of black hair falling across the forehead. But the cavalry officer melted imperceptibly out of her existence.

At another time her affections were deeply engaged by a young gentleman who visited a lady on a neighboring plantation. It was after they went to Mississippi to live. The young man was engaged to be married to the young lady, and they sometimes called upon Margaret, driving over of afternoons in a buggy. Edna was a little miss, just merging into her teens; and the realization that she herself was nothing, nothing, nothing to the engaged young man was a bitter affliction to her. But he, too, went the way of dreams.

She was a grown young woman when she was overtaken by what she supposed to be the climax of her fate. It was when the face and figure of a great tragedian began to haunt her imagination and stir her senses. The persistence of the infatuation lent it an aspect of genuineness. The hopelessness of it colored it with the lofty tunes of a great passion.

The picture of the tragedian stood enframed upon her desk. Any one may possess the portrait of a tragedian without exciting suspicion or comment. (This was a sinister reflection which she cherished.) In the presence of others she expressed admiration for his exalted gifts, as she handed the photograph around and dwelt upon the fidelity of the likeness. When alone she sometimes picked it up and kissed the cold glass passionately.

Her marriage to Léonce Pontellier was purely an accident, in this respect resembling many other marriages which masquerade as the decrees of Fate. It was in the midst of her secret great passion that she met him. He fell in love, as men are in the habit of doing, and pressed his suit with an earnestness and an ardor which left nothing to be desired. He pleased her; his absolute devotion flattered her. She fancied there was a sympathy of thought and taste between them, in which fancy she was mistaken. Add to this the violent opposition of

---

[6]French: "Poor darling."

her father and her sister Margaret to her marriage with a Catholic, and we need seek no further for the motives which led her to accept Monsieur Pontellier for her husband.

The acme of bliss, which would have been a marriage with the tragedian, was not for her in this world. As the devoted wife of a man who worshipped her, she felt she would take her place with a certain dignity in the world of reality, closing the portals forever behind her upon the realm of romance and dreams.

But it was not long before the tragedian had gone to join the cavalry officer and the engaged young man and a few others; and Edna found herself face to face with the realities. She grew fond of her husband, realizing with some unaccountable satisfaction that no trace of passion or excessive and fictitious warmth colored her affection, thereby threatening its dissolution.

She was fond of her children in an uneven, impulsive way. She would sometimes gather them passionately to her heart; she would sometimes forget them. The year before they had spent part of the summer with their grandmother Pontellier in Iberville. Feeling secure regarding their happiness and welfare, she did not miss them except with an occasional intense longing. Their absence was a sort of relief, though she did not admit this, even to herself. It seemed to free her of a responsibility which she had blindly assumed and for which Fate had not fitted her.

Edna did not reveal so much as all this to Madame Ratignolle that summer day when they sat with faces turned to the sea. But a good part of it escaped her. She had put her head down on Madame Ratignolle's shoulder. She was flushed and felt intoxicated with the sound of her own voice and the unaccustomed taste of candor. It muddled her like wine, or like a first breath of freedom.

There was the sound of approaching voices. It was Robert, surrounded by a troop of children, searching for them. The two little Pontelliers were with him, and he carried Madame Ratignolle's little girl in his arms. There were other children beside, and two nurse-maids followed, looking disagreeable and resigned.

The women at once rose and began to shake out their draperies and relax their muscles. Mrs. Pontellier threw the cushions and rug into the bath-house. The children all scampered off to the awning, and they stood there in a line, gazing upon the intruding lovers, still exchanging their vows and sighs. The lovers got up, with only a silent protest, and walked slowly away somewhere else.

The children possessed themselves of the tent, and Mrs. Pontellier went over to join them.

Madame Ratignolle begged Robert to accompany her to the house; she complained of cramp in her limbs and stiffness of the joints. She leaned draggingly upon his arm as they walked.

VIII

"Do me a favor, Robert," spoke the pretty woman at his side, almost as soon as she and Robert had started on their slow, homeward way. She looked up in his face, leaning on his arm beneath the encircling shadow of the umbrella which he had lifted.

"Granted; as many as you like," he returned, glancing down into her eyes that were full of thoughtfulness and some speculation.

"I only ask for one; let Mrs. Pontellier alone."

"*Tiens!*" he exclaimed, with a sudden, boyish laugh. "*Voilà que Madame Ratig-nolle est jalouse!*"[1]

"Nonsense! I'm in earnest; I mean what I say. Let Mrs. Pontellier alone."

"Why?" he asked; himself growing serious at his companion's solicitation.

"She is not one of us; she is not like us. She might make the unfortunate blunder of taking you seriously."

His face flushed with annoyance, and taking off his soft hat he began to beat it impatiently against his leg as he walked. "Why shouldn't she take me seriously?" he demanded sharply. "Am I a comedian, a clown, a jack-in-the-box? Why shouldn't she? You Creoles! I have no patience with you! Am I always to be regarded as a feature of an amusing programme? I hope Mrs. Pontellier does take me seriously. I hope she had discernment enough to find in me something besides the *blagueur*. If I thought there was any doubt—"

"Oh, enough, Robert!" she broke into his heated outburst. "You are not thinking of what you are saying. You speak with about as little reflection as we might expect from one of those children down there playing in the sand. If your attentions to any married women here were ever offered with any intention of being convincing, you would not be the gentleman we all know you to be, and you would be unfit to associate with the wives and daughters of the people who trust you."

Madame Ratignolle had spoken what she believed to be the law and the gospel. The young man shrugged his shoulders impatiently.

"Oh! well! That isn't it," slamming his hat down vehemently upon his head. "You ought to feel that such things are not flattering to say to a fellow."

"Should our whole intercourse consist of an exchange of compliments? *Ma foi!*"[2]

"It isn't pleasant to have a woman tell you—" he went on, unheedingly, but breaking off suddenly: "Now if I were like Arobin—you remember Alcée Arobin and that story of the consul's wife at Biloxi?"[3] And he related the story of Alcée Arobin and the consul's wife; and another about the tenor of the French Opera,[4] who received letters which should never have been written; and still other stories, grave and gay, till Mrs. Pontellier and her possible propensity for taking young men seriously was apparently forgotten.

Madame Ratignolle, when they had regained her cottage, went in to take the hour's rest which she considered helpful. Before leaving her, Robert begged her pardon for the impatience—he called it rudeness—with which he had received her well-meant caution.

"You made one mistake, Adèle," he said, with a light smile; "there is no earthly possibility of Mrs. Pontellier ever taking me seriously. You should have warned me against taking myself seriously. Your advice might then have carried some weight and given me subject for some reflection. *Au revoir.*[5] But you look tired," he added, solicitously. "Would you like a cup of bouillon? Shall I stir you a toddy?[6] Let me mix you a toddy with a drop of Angostura."

She acceded to the suggestion of bouillon, which was grateful and acceptable. He went himself to the kitchen, which was a building apart from the cottages and lying to the rear of the house. And he himself brought her the golden-

[1]French: "Look! . . . . Behold that Madame Ratignolle is jealous!"
[2]French: "Really!"   [3]A resort town on the Gulf coast of Mississippi.
[4]An opera company in nineteenth-century New Orleans.   [5]French: "Good-bye."
[6]A sweetened drink of spirits and hot water.

brown bouillon, in a dainty Sèvres cup,[7] with a flaky cracker or two on the saucer.

She thrust a bare, white arm from the curtain which shielded her open door, and received the cup from his hands. She told him he was a *bon garçon*,[8] and she meant it. Robert thanked her and turned away toward "the house."

The lovers were just entering the grounds of the *pension*. They were leaning toward each other as the water-oaks bent from the sea. There was not a particle of earth beneath their feet. Their heads might have been turned upside-down, so absolutely did they tread upon blue ether. The lady in black, creeping behind them, looked a trifle paler and more jaded than usual. There was no sign of Mrs. Pontellier and the children. Robert scanned the distance for any such apparition. They would doubtless remain away till the dinner hour. The young man ascended to his mother's room. It was situated at the top of the house, made up of odd angles and a queer, sloping ceiling. Two broad dormer windows looked out toward the Gulf, and as far across it as a man's eye might reach. The furnishings of the room were light, cool, and practical.

Madame Lebrun was busily engaged at the sewing-machine. A little black girl sat on the floor, and with her hands worked the treadle of the machine. The Creole woman does not take any chances which may be avoided of imperiling her health.

Robert went over and seated himself on the broad sill of one of the dormer windows. He took a book from his pocket and began energetically to read it, judging by the precision and frequency with which he turned the leaves. The sewing-machine made a resounding clatter in the room; it was of a ponderous, by-gone make. In the lulls, Robert and his mother exchanged bits of desultory conversation.

"Where is Mrs. Pontellier?"

"Down at the beach with the children."

"I promised to lend her the Goncourt.[9] Don't forget to take it down when you go; it's there on the bookshelf over the small table." Clatter, clatter, clatter, bang! for the next five or eight minutes.

"Where is Victor going with the rockaway?"

"The rockaway? Victor?"

"Yes; down there in front. He seems to be getting ready to drive away somewhere."

"Call him." Clatter, clatter!

Robert uttered a shrill, piercing whistle which might have been heard back at the wharf.

"He won't look up."

Madame Lebrun flew to the window. She called "Victor!" She waved a handkerchief and called again. The young fellow below got into the vehicle and started the horse off at a gallop.

Madame Lebrun went back to the machine, crimson with annoyance. Victor was the younger son and brother—a *tête montée*,[10] with a temper which invited violence and a will which no ax could break.

"Whenever you say the word I'm ready to thrash any amount of reason into him that he's able to hold."

"If your father had only lived!" Clatter, clatter, clatter, clatter, bang! It was a

[7]A costly porcelain cup made in Sèvres, France.   [8]French: good boy.
[9]A novel by the French writers Edmond (1822–1896) and Jules (1839–1870) Goncourt.
[10]French: headstrong person.

fixed belief with Madame Lebrun that the conduct of the universe and all things pertaining thereto would have been manifestly of a more intelligent and higher order had not Monsieur Lebrun been removed to other spheres during the early years of their married life.

"What do you hear from Montel?" Montel was a middle-aged gentleman whose vain ambition and desire for the past twenty years had been to fill the void which Monsieur Lebrun's taking off had left in the Lebrun household. Clatter, clatter, bang, clatter!

"I have a letter somewhere," looking in the machine drawer and finding the letter in the bottom of the work-basket. "He says to tell you he will be in Vera Cruz[11] the beginning of next month"—clatter, clatter!—"and if you still have the intention of joining him"—bang! clatter, clatter, bang!

"Why didn't you tell me so before, mother? You know I wanted—" Clatter, clatter, clatter!

"Do you see Mrs. Pontellier starting back with the children? She will be in late to luncheon again. She never starts to get ready for luncheon till the last minute." Clatter, clatter! "Where are you going?"

"Where did you say the Goncourt was?"

IX

Every light in the hall was ablaze; every lamp turned as high as it could be without smoking the chimney or threatening explosion. The lamps were fixed at intervals against the wall, encircling the whole room. Some one had gathered orange and lemon branches, and with these fashioned graceful festoons between. The dark green of the branches stood out and glistened against the white muslin curtains which draped the windows, and which puffed, floated, and flapped at the capricious will of a stiff breeze that swept up from the Gulf.

It was Saturday night a few weeks after the intimate conversation held between Robert and Madame Ratignolle on their way from the beach. An unusual number of husbands, fathers, and friends had come down to stay over Sunday; and they were being suitably entertained by their families, with the material help of Madame Lebrun. The dining tables had all been removed to one end of the hall, and the chairs ranged about in rows and in clusters. Each little family group had had its say and exchanged its domestic gossip earlier in the evening. There was now an apparent disposition to relax; to widen the circle of confidences and give a more general tone to the conversation.

Many of the children had been permitted to sit up beyond their usual bedtime. A small band of them were lying on their stomachs on the floor looking at the colored sheets of the comic papers which Mr. Pontellier had brought down. The little Pontellier boys were permitting them to do so, and making their authority felt.

Music, dancing, and a recitation or two were the entertainments furnished, or rather, offered. But there was nothing systematic about the programme, no appearance of prearrangement nor even premeditation.

At an early hour in the evening the Farival twins were prevailed upon to play the piano. They were girls of fourteen, always clad in the Virgin's colors, blue and white, having been dedicated to the Blessed Virgin at their baptism. They played a duet from "Zampa," and at the earnest solicitation of every one present followed it with the overture to "The Poet and the Peasant."

[11]Mexican city on the Gulf of Mexico.

"*Allez vous-en! Sapristi!*" shrieked the parrot outside the door. He was the only being present who possessed sufficient candor to admit that he was not listening to these gracious performances for the first time that summer. Old Monsieur Farival, grandfather of the twins, grew indignant over the interruption, and insisted upon having the bird removed and consigned to regions of darkness. Victor Lebrun objected; and his decrees were as immutable as those of Fate. The parrot fortunately offered no further interruption to the entertainment, the whole venom of his nature apparently having been cherished up and hurled against the twins in that one impetuous outburst.

Later a young brother and sister gave recitations, which every one present had heard many times at winter evening entertainments in the city.

A little girl performed a skirt dance in the center of the floor. The mother played her accompaniments and at the same time watched her daughter with greedy admiration and nervous apprehension. She need have had no apprehension. The child was mistress of the situation. She had been properly dressed for the occasion in black tulle[1] and black silk tights. Her little neck and arms were bare, and her hair, artifically crimped, stood out like fluffy black plumes over her head. Her poses were full of grace, and her little black-shod toes twinkled as they shot out and upward with a rapidity and suddenness which were bewildering.

But there was no reason why every one should not dance. Madame Ratignolle could not, so it was she who gaily consented to play for the others. She played very well, keeping excellent waltz time and infusing an expression into the strains which was indeed inspiring. She was keeping up her music on account of the children, she said; because she and her husband both considered it a means of brightening the home and making it attractive.

Almost every one danced but the twins, who could not be induced to separate during the brief period when one or the other should be whirling around the room in the arms of a man. They might have danced together, but they did not think of it.

The children were sent to bed. Some went submissively; others with shrieks and protests as they were dragged away. They had been permitted to sit up till after the ice-cream, which naturally marked the limit of human indulgence.

The ice-cream was passed around with cake—gold and silver cake arranged on platters in alternate slices; it had been made and frozen during the afternoon back of the kitchen by two black women, under the supervision of Victor. It was pronounced a great success—excellent if it had only contained a little less vanilla or a little more sugar, if it had been frozen a degree harder, and if the salt might have been kept out of portions of it. Victor was proud of his achievement, and went about recommending it and urging every one to partake of it to excess.

After Mrs. Pontellier had danced twice with her husband, once with Robert, and once with Monsieur Ratignolle, who was thin and tall and swayed like a reed in the wind when he danced, she went out on the gallery and seated herself on the low window-sill, where she commanded a view of all that went on in the hall and could look out toward the Gulf. There was a soft effulgence in the east. The moon was coming up, and its mystic shimmer was casting a million lights across the distant, restless water.

"Would you like to hear Mademoiselle Reisz play?" asked Robert, coming out on the porch where she was. Of course Edna would like to hear Mademoiselle Reisz play; but she feared it would be useless to entreat her.

[1]Thin, fine netting, usually of silk, used for veils and dresses.

"I'll ask her," he said. "I'll tell her that you want to hear her. She likes you. She will come." He turned and hurried away to one of the far cottages, where Mademoiselle Reisz was shuffling away. She was dragging a chair in and out of her room, and at intervals objecting to the crying of a baby, which a nurse in the adjoining cottage was endeavoring to put to sleep. She was a disagreeable little woman, no longer young, who had quarreled with almost every one, owing to a temper which was self-assertive and a disposition to trample upon the rights of others. Robert prevailed upon her without any too great difficulty.

She entered the hall with him during a lull in the dance. She made an awkward, imperious little bow as she went in. She was a homely woman, with small weazened[2] face and body and eyes that glowed. She had absolutely no taste in dress, and wore a batch of rusty black lace with a bunch of artificial violets pinned to the side of her hair.

"Ask Mrs. Pontellier what she would like to hear me play," she requested of Robert. She sat perfectly still before the piano, not touching the keys, while Robert carried her message to Edna at the window. A general air of surprise and genuine satisfaction fell upon every one as they saw the pianist enter. There was a settling down, and a prevailing air of expectancy everywhere. Edna was a trifle embarrassed at being thus signaled out for the imperious little woman's favor. She would not dare to choose, and begged that Mademoiselle Reisz would please herself in her selections.

Edna was what she herself called very fond of music. Musical strains, well rendered, had a way of evoking pictures in her mind. She sometimes liked to sit in the room of mornings when Madame Ratignolle played or practiced. One piece which that lady played Edna had entitled "Solitude." It was a short, plaintive, minor strain. The name of the piece was something else, but she called it "Solitude." When she heard it there came before her imagination the figure of a man standing beside a desolate rock on the seashore. He was naked. His attitude was one of hopeless resignation as he looked toward a distant bird winging its flight away from him.

Another piece called to her mind a dainty young woman clad in an Empire gown,[3] taking mincing dancing steps as she came down a long avenue between tall hedges. Again, another reminded her of children at play, and still another of nothing on earth but a demure lady stroking a cat.

The very first chords which Mademoiselle Reisz struck upon the piano sent a keen tremor down Mrs. Pontellier's spinal column. It was not the first time she had heard an artist at the piano. Perhaps it was the first time she was ready, perhaps the first time her being was tempered to take an impress of the abiding truth.

She waited for the material pictures which she thought would gather and blaze before her imagination. She waited in vain. She saw no pictures of solitude, of hope, of longing, or of despair. But the very passions themselves were aroused within her soul, swaying it, lashing it, as the waves daily beat upon her splendid body. She trembled, she was choking, and the tears blinded her.

Mademoiselle had finished. She arose, and bowing her stiff, lofty bow, she went away, stopping for neither thanks nor applause. As she passed along the gallery she patted Edna upon the shoulder.

"Well, how did you like my music?" she asked. The young woman was unable to answer; she pressed the hand of the pianist convulsively. Mademoiselle Reisz

---

[2]Wizened: aged, wrinkled.
[3]A long gown with a high waist, fashionable during the Napoleonic era.

perceived her agitation and even her tears. She patted her again upon the shoulder as she said:

"You are the only one worth playing for. Those others? Bah!" and she went shuffling and sidling on down the gallery toward her room.

But she was mistaken about "those others." Her playing had aroused a fever of enthusiasm. "What passion!" "What an artist!" "I have always said no one could play Chopin[4] like Mademoiselle Reisz!" "That last prelude! Bon Dieu![5] It shakes a man!"

It was growing late, and there was a general disposition to disband. But some one, perhaps it was Robert, thought of a bath[6] at that mystic hour and under that mystic moon.

X

At all events Robert proposed it, and there was not a dissenting voice. There was not one but was ready to follow when he led the way. He did not lead the way, however, he directed the way; and he himself loitered behind with the lovers, who had betrayed a dispostion to linger and hold themselves apart. He walked between them, whether with malicious or mischievous intent was not wholly clear, even to himself.

The Pontelliers and Ratignolles walked ahead; the women leaning upon the arms of their husbands. Edna could hear Robert's voice behind them, and could sometimes hear what he said. She wondered why he did not join them. It was unlike him not to. Of late he had sometimes held away from her for an entire day, redoubling his devotion upon the next and the next, as though to make up for hours that had been lost. She missed him the days when some pretext served to take him away from her, just as one misses the sun on a cloudy day without having thought much about the sun when it was shining.

The people walked in little groups toward the beach. They talked and laughed; some of them sang. There was a band playing down at Klein's hotel, and the strains reached them faintly, tempered by the distance. There were strange, rare odors abroad—a tangle of the sea smell and of weeds and damp, new-plowed earth, mingled with the heavy perfume of a field of white blossoms somewhere near. But the night sat lightly upon the sea and the land. There was no weight of darkness; there were no shadows. The white light of the moon had fallen upon the world like the mystery and the softness of sleep.

Most of them walked into the water as though into a native element. The sea was quiet now, and swelled lazily in broad billows that melted into one another and did not break except upon the beach in little foamy crests that coiled back like slow, white serpents.

Edna had attempted all summer to learn to swim. She had received instructions from both the men and women; in some instances from the children. Robert had pursued a system of lessons almost daily; and he was nearly at the point of discouragement in realizing the futility of his efforts. A certain ungovernable dread hung about her when in the water, unless there was a hand near by that might reach out and reassure her.

But that night she was like the little tottering, stumbling, clutching child, who of a sudden realizes its powers, and walks for the first time alone, boldly and

[4]Frederic Chopin (1810–1849), Polish composer and pianist.   [5]French: "Good God!"
[6]A swim.

with over-confidence. She could have shouted for joy. She did shout for joy, as with a sweeping stroke or two she lifted her body to the surface of the water.

A feeling of exultation overtook her, as if some power of significant import had been given her to control the working of her body and her soul. She grew daring and reckless, overestimating her strength. She wanted to swim far out, where no woman had swum before.

Her unlooked-for achievement was the subject of wonder, applause, and admiration. Each one congratulated himself that his special teachings had accomplished this desired end.

"How easy it is!" she thought. "It is nothing," she said aloud; "why did I not discover before that it was nothing. Think of the time I have lost splashing about like a baby!" She would not join the groups in their sports and bouts, but intoxicated with her newly conquered power, she swam out alone.

She turned her face seaward to gather in an impression of space and solitude, which the vast expanse of water, meeting and melting with the moonlit sky, conveyed to her excited fancy. As she swam she seemed to be reaching out for the unlimited in which to lose herself.

Once she turned and looked toward the shore, toward the people she had left there. She had not gone any great distance—that is, what would have been a great distance for an experienced swimmer. But to her unaccustomed vision the stretch of water behind her assumed the aspect of a barrier which her unaided strength would never be able to overcome.

A quick vision of death smote her soul, and for a second of time appalled and enfeebled her senses. But by an effort she rallied her staggering faculties and managed to regain the land.

She made no mention of her encounter with death and her flash of terror, except to say to her husband, "I thought I should have perished out there alone."

"You were not so very far, my dear; I was watching you," he told her.

Edna went at once to the bath-house, and she had put on her dry clothes and was ready to return home before the others had left the water. She started to walk away alone. They all called to her and shouted to her. She waved a dissenting hand, and went on, paying no further heed to their renewed cries which sought to detain her.

"Sometimes I am tempted to think that Mrs. Pontellier is capricious," said Madame Lebrun, who was amusing herself immensely and feared that Edna's abrupt departure might put an end to the pleasure.

"I know she is," assented Mr. Pontellier; "sometimes, not often."

Edna had not traversed a quarter of the distance on her way home before she was overtaken by Robert.

"Did you think I was afraid?" she asked him, without a shade of annoyance.

"No; I knew you weren't afraid."

"Then why did you come? Why didn't you stay out there with the others?"

"I never thought of it."

"Thought of what?"

"Of anything. What difference does it make?"

"I'm very tired," she uttered, complainingly.

"I know you are."

"You don't know anything about it. Why should you know? I never was so exhausted in my life. But it isn't unpleasant. A thousand emotions have swept through me to-night. I don't comprehend half of them. Don't mind what I'm saying; I am just thinking aloud. I wonder if I shall ever be stirred again as Mademoiselle Reisz's playing moved me to-night. I wonder if any night on earth will ever again be like this one. It is like a night in a dream. The people about me are like some uncanny, half-human beings. There must be spirits abroad tonight."

"There are," whispered Robert. "Didn't you know this was the twenty-eighth of August?"

"The twenty-eighth of August?"

"Yes. On the twenty-eighth of August, at the hour of midnight, and if the moon is shining—the moon must be shining—a spirit that has haunted these shores for ages rises up from the Gulf. With its own penetrating vision the spirit seeks some one mortal worthy to hold him company, worthy of being exalted for a few hours into realms of the semi-celestials. His search has always hitherto been fruitless, and he has sunk back, disheartened, into the sea. But to-night he found Mrs. Pontellier. Perhaps he will never wholly release her from the spell. Perhaps she will never again suffer a poor, unworthy earthling to walk in the shadow of her divine presence."

"Don't banter me," she said, wounded at what appeared to be his flippancy. He did not mind the entreaty, but the tone with its delicate note of pathos was like a reproach. He could not explain; he could not tell her that he had penetrated her mood and understood. He said nothing except to offer her his arm, for, by her own admission, she was exhausted. She had been walking alone with her arms hanging limp, letting her white skirts trail along the dewy path. She took his arm, but she did not lean upon it. She let her hand lie listlessly, as though her thoughts were elsewhere—somewhere in advance of her body, and she was striving to overtake them.

Robert assisted her into the hammock which swung from the post before her door out to the trunk of a tree.

"Will you stay out here and wait for Mr. Pontellier?" he asked.

"I'll stay out here. Good-night."

"Shall I get you a pillow?"

"There's one here," she said, feeling about, for they were in the shadow.

"It must be soiled; the children have been tumbling it about."

"No matter." And having discovered the pillow, she adjusted it beneath her head. She extended herself in the hammock with a deep breath of relief. She was not a supercilious or an over-dainty woman. She was not much given to reclining in the hammock, and when she did so it was with no cat-like suggestion of voluptous ease, but with a beneficent repose which seemed to invade her whole body.

"Shall I stay with you till Mr. Pontellier comes?" asked Robert, seating himself on the outer edge of one of the steps and taking hold of the hammock rope which was fastened to the post.

"If you wish. Don't swing the hammock. Will you get my white shawl which I left on the window-sill over at the house?"

"Are you chilly?"

"No; but I shall be presently."

"Presently?" he laughed. "Do you know what time it is? How long are you going to stay out here?"

"I don't know. Will you get the shawl?"

"Of course I will," he said, rising. He went over to the house, walking along the grass. She watched his figure pass in and out of the strips of moonlight. It was past midnight. It was very quiet.

When he returned with the shawl she took it and kept it in her hand. She did not put it around her.

"Did you say I should stay till Mr. Pontellier came back?"

"I said you might if you wished to."

He seated himself again and rolled a cigarette, which he smoked in silence. Neither did Mrs. Pontellier speak. No multitude of words could have been more significant than those moments of silence, or more pregnant with the first-felt throbbings of desire.

When the voices of the bathers were heard approaching, Robert said goodnight. She did not answer him. He thought she was asleep. Again she watched his figure pass in and out of the strips of moonlight as he walked away.

XI

"What are you doing out here, Edna? I thought I should find you in bed," said her husband, when he discovered her lying there. He had walked up with Madame Lebrun and left her at the house. His wife did not reply.

"Are you asleep?" he asked, bending down close to look at her.

"No." Her eyes gleamed bright and intense, with no sleepy shadows, as they looked into his.

"Do you know it is past one o'clock? Come on," and he mounted the steps and went into their room.

"Edna!" called Mr. Pontellier from within, after a few moments had gone by.

"Don't wait for me," she answered. He thrust his head through the door.

"You will take cold out there," he said, irritably. "What folly is this? Why don't you come in?"

"It isn't cold; I have my shawl."

"The mosquitoes will devour you."

"There are no mosquitoes."

She heard him moving about the room; every sound indicating impatience and irritation. Another time she would have gone in at his request. She would, through habit, have yielded to his desire; not with any sense of submission or obedience to his compelling wishes, but unthinkingly, as we walk, move, sit, stand, go through the daily treadmill of the life which has been portioned out to us.

"Edna, dear, are you not coming in soon?" he asked again, this time fondly, with a note of entreaty.

"No; I am going to stay out here."

"This is more than folly," he blurted out. "I can't permit you to stay out there all night. You must come in the house instantly."

With a writhing motion she settled herself more securely in the hammock. She perceived that her will had blazed up, stubborn and resistant. She could not at that moment have done other than denied and resisted. She wondered if her husband had ever spoken to her like that before, and if she had submitted to his command. Of course she had; she remembered that she had. But she could not realize why or how she should have yielded, feeling as she then did.

"Léonce, go to bed," she said. "I mean to stay out here. I don't wish to go in, and I don't intend to. Don't speak to me like that again; I shall not answer you."

Mr. Pontellier had prepared for bed, but he slipped on an extra garment. He opened a bottle of wine, of which he kept a small and select supply in a buffet of his own. He drank a glass of the wine and went out on the gallery and offered a glass to his wife. She did not wish any. He drew up the rocker, hoisted his slippered feet on the rail, and proceeded to smoke a cigar. He smoked two cigars; then he went inside and drank another glass of wine. Mrs. Pontellier again declined to accept a glass when it was offered to her. Mr. Pontellier once more seated himself with elevated feet, and after a reasonable interval of time smoked some more cigars.

Edna began to feel like one who awakens gradually out of a dream, a delicious, grotesque, impossible dream, to feel again the realities pressing into her soul. The physical need for sleep began to overtake her; the exuberance which had sustained and exalted her spirit left her helpless and yielding to the conditions which crowded her in.

The stillest hour of the night had come, the hour before dawn, when the world seems to hold its breath. The moon hung low, and had turned from silver to copper in the sleeping sky. The old owl no longer hooted, and the water-oaks had ceased to moan as they bent their heads.

Edna arose, cramped from lying so long and still in the hammock. She tottered up the steps, clutching feebly at the post before passing into the house.

"Are you coming in, Léonce?" she asked, turning her face toward her husband.

"Yes, dear," he answered, with a glance following a misty puff of smoke. "Just as soon as I have finished my cigar."

XII

She slept but a few hours. They were troubled and feverish hours, disturbed with dreams that were intangible, that eluded her, leaving only an impression upon her half-awakened senses of something unattainable. She was up and dressed in the cool of the early morning. The air was invigorating and steadied somewhat her faculties. However, she was not seeking refreshment or help from any source, either external or from within. She was blindly following whatever impulse moved her, as if she had placed herself in alien hands for direction, and freed her soul of responsibility.

Most of the people at that early hour were still in bed and asleep. A few, who intended to go over to the *Chênière* for mass, were moving about. The lovers, who had laid their plans the night before, were already strolling toward the wharf. The lady in black, with her Sunday prayer-book, velvet and gold-clasped, and her Sunday silver beads, was following them at no great distance. Old Monsieur Farival was up, and was more than half inclined to do anything that suggested itself. He put on his big straw hat, and taking his umbrella from the stand in the hall, followed the lady in black, never overtaking her.

The little negro girl who worked Madame Lebrun's sewing-machine was sweeping the galleries with long, absent-minded strokes of the broom. Edna sent her up into the house to awaken Robert.

"Tell him I am going to the *Chênière*. The boat is ready; tell him to hurry."

He had soon joined her. She had never sent for him before. She had never asked for him. She had never seemed to want him before. She did not appear conscious that she had done anything unusual in commanding his presence. He was apparently equally unconscious of anything extraordinary in the situation. But his face was suffused with a quiet glow when he met her.

They went together back to the kitchen to drink coffee. There was no time to wait for any nicety of service. They stood outside the window and the cook passed them their coffee and a roll, which they drank and ate from the window-sill. Edna said it tasted good. She had not thought of coffee nor of anything. He told her he had often noticed that she lacked forethought.

"Wasn't it enough to think of going to the *Chênière* and waking you up?" she laughed. "Do I have to think of everything?—as Léonce says when he's in a bad humor. I don't blame him; he'd never be in a bad humor if it weren't for me."

They took a short cut across the sands. At a distance they could see the curious procession moving toward the wharf—the lovers, shoulder to shoulder, creeping; the lady in black, gaining steadily upon them; old Monsieur Farival, losing ground inch by inch, and a young barefooted Spanish girl, with a red kerchief on her head and a basket on her arm, bringing up the rear.

Robert knew the girl, and he talked to her a little in the boat. No one present understood what they said. Her name was Mariequita. She had a round, sly, piquant face and pretty black eyes. Her hands were small, and she kept them folded over the handle of her basket. Her feet were broad and coarse. She did not strive to hide them. Edna looked at her feet, and noticed the sand and slime between her brown toes.

Beaudelet grumbled because Mariequita was there, taking up so much room. In reality he was annoyed at having old Monsieur Farival, who considered himself the better sailor of the two. But he would not quarrel with so old a man as Monsieur Farival, so he quarreled with Mariequita. The girl was deprecatory at one moment, appealing to Robert. She was saucy the next, moving her head up and down, making "eyes" at Robert and making "mouths" at Beaudelet.

The lovers were all alone. They saw nothing, they heard nothing. The lady in black was counting her beads for the third time. Old Monsieur Farival talked incessantly of what he knew about handling a boat, and of what Beaudelet did not know on the same subject.

Edna liked it all. She looked Mariequita up and down, from her ugly brown toes to her pretty black eyes, and back again.

"Why does she look at me like that?" inquired the girl of Robert.

"Maybe she thinks you are pretty. Shall I ask her?"

"No. Is she your sweetheart?"

"She's a married lady, and has two children."

"Oh! well! Francisco ran away with Sylvano's wife, who had four children. They took all his money and one of the children and stole his boat."

"Shut up!"

"Does she understand?"

"Oh, hush!"

"Are those two married over there—leaning on each other?"

"Of course not," laughed Robert.

"Of course not," echoed Mariequita, with a serious, confirmatory bob of the head.

The sun was high up and beginning to bite. The swift breeze seemed to Edna to bury the sting of it into the pores of her face and hands. Robert held his umbrella over her.

As they went cutting sidewise through the water, the sails bellied taut, with the wind filling and overflowing them. Old Monsieur Farival laughed sardonically at something as he looked at the sails, and Beaudelet swore at the old man under his breath.

Sailing across the bay to the *Chênière Caminada*, Edna felt as if she were being borne away from some anchorage which had held her fast, whose chains had been loosening—had snapped the night before when the mystic spirit was abroad, leaving her free to drift withersoever she chose to set her sails. Robert spoke to her incessantly; he no longer noticed Mariequita. The girl had shrimps in her bamboo basket. They were covered with Spanish moss. She beat the moss down impatiently, and muttered to herself sullenly.

"Let us go to Grande Terre[1] to-morrow," said Robert in a low voice.

"What shall we do there?"

"Climb up the hill to the old fort and look at the little wriggling gold snakes, and watch the lizards sun themselves."

She gazed away toward Grande Terre and thought she would like to be alone there with Robert, in the sun, listening to the ocean's roar and watching the slimy lizards writhe in and out among the ruins of the old fort.

"And the next day or the next we can sail to the Bayou Brulow,"[2] he went on.

"What shall we do there?"

"Anything—cast bait for fish."

"No; we'll go back to Grande Terre. Let the fish alone."

"We'll go wherever you like," he said. "I'll have Tonie come over and help me patch and trim my boat. We shall not need Beaudelet nor any one. Are you afraid of the pirogue?"[3]

"Oh, no."

"Then I'll take you some night in the pirogue when the moon shines. Maybe your Gulf spirit will whisper to you in which of these islands the treasures are hidden—direct you to the very spot, perhaps."

"And in a day we should be rich!" she laughed. "I'd give it all to you, the pirate gold and every bit of treasure we could dig up. I think you would know how to spend it. Pirate gold isn't a thing to be hoarded or utilized. It is something to squander and throw to the four winds, for the fun of seeing the golden specks fly."

"We'd share it, and scatter it together," he said. His face flushed.

They all went together up to the quaint little Gothic church of Our Lady of Lourdes, gleaming all brown and yellow with paint in the sun's glare.

Only Beaudelet remained behind, tinkering at his boat, and Mariequita walked away with her basket of shrimps, casting a look of childish ill-humor and reproach at Robert from the corner of her eye.

XIII

A feeling of oppression and drowsiness overcame Edna during the service. Her head began to ache, and the lights on the altar swayed before her eyes. Another time she might have made an effort to regain her composure; but her one thought was to quit the stifling atmosphere of the church and reach the open air. She arose, climbing over Robert's feet with a muttered apology. Old Monsieur Farival, flurried, curious, stood up, but upon seeing that Robert had followed Mrs. Pontellier, he sank back into his seat. He whispered an anxious inquiry of the lady in black, who did not notice him or reply, but kept her eyes fastened upon the pages of her velvet prayer-book.

"I felt giddy and almost overcome," Edna said, lifting her hands instinctively to her head and pushing her straw hat up from her forehead. "I couldn't have stayed through the service." They were outside in the shadow of the church. Robert was full of solicitude.

---

[1]An island near Grand Isle, in the Gulf of Mexico.
[2]A village, built on raised platforms, in the marshlands of the Gulf Coast.   [3]Dugout canoe.

"It was folly to have thought of going in the first place, let alone staying. Come over to Madame Antoine's; you can rest there." He took her arm and led her away, looking anxiously and continuously down into her face.

How still it was, with only the voice of the sea whispering through the reeds that grew in the salt-water pools! The long line of little gray, weather-beaten houses nestled peacefully among the orange trees. It must always have been God's day on that low, drowsy island, Edna thought. They stopped, leaning over a jagged fence made of sea-drift, to ask for water. A youth, a mild-faced Acadian,[1] was drawing water from the cistern, which was nothing more than a rusty buoy, with an opening on one side, sunk in the ground. The water which the youth handed to them in a tin pail was not cold to taste, but it was cool to her heated face, and it greatly revived and refreshed her.

Madame Antoine's cot[2] was at the far end of the village. She welcomed them with all the native hospitality, as she would have opened her door to let the sunlight in. She was fat, and walked heavily and clumsily across the floor. She could speak no English, but when Robert made her understand that the lady who accompanied him was ill and desired to rest, she was all eagerness to make Edna feel at home and to dispose of her comfortably.

The whole place was immaculately clean, and the big, four-poster bed, snow-white, invited one to repose. It stood in a small side room which looked out across a narrow grass plot toward the shed, where there was a disabled boat lying keel upward.

Madame Antoine had not gone to mass. Her son Tonie had, but she supposed he would soon be back, and she invited Robert to be seated and wait for him. But he went and sat outside the door and smoked. Madame Antoine busied herself in the large front room preparing dinner. She was boiling mullets[3] over a few red coals in the huge fireplace.

Edna, left alone in the little side room, loosened her clothes, removing the greater part of them. She bathed her face, her neck and arms in the basin that stood between the windows. She took off her shoes and stockings and stretched herself in the very center of the high, white bed. How luxurious it felt to rest thus in a strange, quaint bed, with its sweet country odor of laurel lingering about the sheets and mattress! She stretched her strong limbs that ached a little. She ran her fingers through her loosened hair for a while. She looked at her round arms as she held them straight up and rubbed them one after the other, observing closely, as if it were something she saw for the first time, the fine, firm quality and texture of her flesh. She clasped her hands easily above her head, and it was thus she fell asleep.

She slept lightly at first, half awake and drowsily attentive to the things about her. She could hear Madame Antoine's heavy, scraping tread as she walked back and forth on the sanded floor. Some chickens were clucking outside the windows, scratching for bits of gravel in the grass. Later she half heard the voices of Robert and Tonie talking under the shed. She did not stir. Even her eyelids rested numb and heavily over her sleepy eyes. The voices went on—Tonie's slow, Acadian drawl, Robert's quick, soft, smooth French. She understood French imperfectly unless directly addressed, and the voices were only part of the other drowsy, muffled sounds lulling her senses.

When Edna awoke it was with the conviction that she had slept long and soundly. The voices were hushed under the shed. Madame Antoine's step was no longer to be heard in the adjoining room. Even the chickens had gone

[1]A descendant of the French Canadians who were expelled in 1755 from Acadia (Nova Scotia) and migrated to the Louisiana Gulf Coast.   [2]Cottage.   [3]Fish.

elsewhere to scratch and cluck. The mosquito bar was drawn over her; the old woman had come in while she slept and let down the bar. Edna arose quietly from the bed, and looking between the curtains of the window, she saw by the slanting rays of the sun that the afternoon was far advanced. Robert was out there under the shed, reclining in the shade against the sloping keel of the overturned boat. He was reading from a book. Tonie was no longer with him. She wondered what had become of the rest of the party. She peeped out at him two or three times as she stood washing herself in the little basin between the windows.

Madame Antoine had laid some coarse, clean towels upon a chair, and had placed a box of *poudre de riz*[4] within easy reach. Edna dabbed the powder upon her nose and cheeks as she looked her herself closely in the little distorted mirror which hung on the wall above the basin. Her eye were bright and wide awake and her face glowed.

When she had completed her toilet she walked into the adjoining room. She was very hungry. No one was there. But there was a cloth spread upon the table that stood against the wall, and a cover was laid for one, with a crusty brown loaf and a bottle of wine beside the plate. Edna bit a piece from the brown loaf, tearing it with her strong, white teeth. She poured some of the wine into the glass and drank it down. Then she went softly out of doors, and plucking an orange from the low-hanging bough of a tree, threw it at Robert, who did not know she was awake and up.

An illumination broke over his whole face when he saw her and joined her under the orange tree.

"How many years have I slept?" she inquired. "The whole island seems changed. A new race of beings must have sprung up, leaving only you and me as past relics. How many ages ago did Madame Antoine and Tonie die? and when did our people from Grand Isle disappear from the earth?"

He familiarly adjusted a ruffle upon her shoulder.

"You have slept precisely one hundred years. I was left here to guard your slumbers; and for one hundred years I have been out under the shed reading a book. The only evil I couldn't prevent was to keep a broiled fowl from drying up."

"If it has turned to stone, still will I eat it," said Edna, moving with him into the house. "But really, what has become of Monsieur Farival and the others?"

"Gone hours ago. When they found that you were sleeping they thought it best not to awake you. Any way, I wouldn't have let them. What was I here for?"

"I wonder if Léonce will be uneasy!" she speculated, as she seated herself at table.

"Of course not; he knows you are with me," Robert replied, as he busied himself among sundry pans and covered dishes which had been left standing on the hearth.

"Where are Madame Antoine and her son?" asked Edna.

"Gone to Vespers,[5] and to visit some friends, I believe. I am to take you back in Tonie's boat whenever you are ready to go."

He stirred the smoldering ashes till the broiled fowl began to sizzle afresh. He served her with no mean repast, dripping[6] the coffee anew and sharing it with her. Madame Antoine had cooked little else than the mullets, but while Edna slept Robert had foraged the island. He was childishly gratified to discover

---

[4]French: face-powder.   [5]Evening church service.   [6]Brewing.

her appetite, and to see the relish with which she ate the food which he had procured for her.

"Shall we go right away?" she asked, after draining her glass and brushing together the crumbs of the crusty loaf.

"The sun isn't as low as it will be in two hours," he answered.

"The sun will be gone in two hours."

"Well, let it go; who cares!"

They waited a good while under the orange trees, till Madame Antoine came back, panting, waddling, with a thousand apologies to explain her absence. Tonie did not dare to return. He was shy, and would not willingly face any woman except his mother.

It was very pleasant to stay there under the orange trees, while the sun dipped lower and lower, turning the western sky to flaming copper and gold. The shadows lengthened and crept out like stealthy, grotesque monsters across the grass.

Edna and Robert both sat upon the ground—that is, he lay upon the ground beside her, occasionally picking at the hem of her muslin gown.

Madame Antoine seated her fat body, broad and squat, upon a bench beside the door. She had been talking all the afternoon, and had wound herself up to the story-telling pitch.

And what stories she told them! But twice in her life she had left the *Chênière Caminada,* and then for the briefest span. All her years she had squatted and waddled there upon the island, gathering legends of the Baratarians[7] and the sea. The night came on, with the moon to lighten it. Edna could hear the whispering voices of dead men and the click of muffled gold.

When she and Robert stepped into Tonie's boat, with the red lateen sail, misty spirit forms were prowling in the shadows and among the reeds, and upon the water were phantom ships, speeding to cover.

XIV

The youngest boy, Etienne, had been very naughty, Madame Ratignolle said, as she delivered him into the hands of his mother. He had been unwilling to go to bed and had made a scene; whereupon she had taken charge of him and pacified him as well as she could. Raoul had been in bed and asleep for two hours.

The youngster was in his long white nightgown, that kept tripping him up as Madame Ratignolle led him along by the hand. With the other chubby fist he rubbed his eyes, which were heavy with sleep and ill humor. Edna took him in her arms, and seating herself in the rocker, began to coddle and caress him, calling him all manner of tender names, soothing him to sleep.

It was not more than nine o'clock. No one had yet gone to bed but the children.

Léonce had been very uneasy at first, Madame Ratignolle said, and had wanted to start at once for the *Chênière.* But Monsieur Farival had assured him that his wife was only overcome with sleep and fatigue, that Tonie would bring her safely back later in the day; and he had thus been dissuaded from crossing the bay. He had gone over to Klein's, looking up some cotton broker whom he wished to see in regard to securities, exchanges, stocks, bonds, or something of

---

[7]Those who lived on Barataria Bay, an inlet of the Gulf of Mexico near the mouth of the Mississippi. In earlier days, it was a refuge for smugglers and pirates.

the sort, Madame Ratignolle did not remember what. He said he would not remain away late. She herself was suffering from heat and oppression, she said. She carried a bottle of salts and a large fan. She would not consent to remain with Edna, for Monsieur Ratignolle was alone, and he detested above all things to be left alone.

When Etienne had fallen asleep Edna bore him into the back room, and Robert went and lifted the mosquito bar that she might lay the child comfortably in his bed. The quadroon had vanished. When they emerged from the cottage Robert bade Edna good-night.

"Do you know we have been together the whole livelong day, Robert—since early this morning?" she said at parting.

"All but the hundred years when you were sleeping. Good-night."

He pressed her hand and went away in the direction of the beach. He did not join any of the others, but walked alone toward the Gulf.

Edna stayed outside, awaiting her husband's return. She had no desire to sleep or to retire; nor did she feel like going over to sit with the Ratignolles, or to join Madame Lebrun and a group whose animated voices reached here as they sat in conversation before the house. She let her mind wander back over her stay at Grand Isle; and she tried to discover wherein this summer had been different from any and every other summer of her life. She could only realize that she herself—her present self—was in some way different from the other self. That she was seeing with different eyes and making the acquaintance of new conditions in herself that colored and changed her environment, she did not yet suspect.

She wondered why Robert had gone away and left her. It did not occur to her to think he might have grown tired of being with her the livelong day. She was not tired, and she felt that he was not. She regretted that he had gone. It was so much more natural to have him stay when he was not absolutely required to leave her.

As Edna waited for her husband she sang low a little song that Robert had sung as they crossed the bay. It began with "Ah! *Si tu savais*,"[1] and every verse ended with "*si tu savais*."[8]

Robert's voice was not pretentious. It was musical and true. The voice, the notes, the whole refrain haunted her memory.

XV

When Edna entered the dining-room one evening a little late, as was her habit, an unusually animated conversation seemed to be going on. Several persons were talking at once, and Victor's voice was predominating, even over that of his mother. Edna had returned late from her bath, had dressed in some haste, and her face was flushed. Her head, set off by her dainty white gown, suggested a rich, rare blossom. She took her seat at table between old Monsieur Farival and Madame Ratignolle.

As she seated herself and was about to begin to eat her soup, which had been served when she entered the room, several persons informed her simultaneously that Robert was going to Mexico. She laid her spoon down and looked about her bewildered. He had been with her, reading to her all the morning, and had

[8]French: "Couldst thou but know," the title of a song by the Irish composer Michael Balfe (1808–1870).

never even mentioned such a place as Mexico. She had not seen him during the afternoon; she had heard some one say he was at the house, upstairs with his mother. This she had thought nothing of, though she was surprised when he did not join her later in the afternoon, when she went down to the beach.

She looked across at him, where he sat beside Madame Lebrun, who presided. Edna's face was a blank picture of bewilderment, which she never thought of disguising. He lifted his eyebrows with the pretext of a smile as he returned her glance. He looked embarrassed and uneasy.

"When is he going?" she asked of everybody in general, as if Robert were not there to answer for himself.

"To-night!" "This very evening!" "Did you ever!" "What possesses him!" were some of the replies she gathered, uttered simultaneously in French and English.

"Impossible!" she exclaimed. "How can a person start off from Grand Isle to Mexico at a moment's notice, as if he were going over to Klein's or to the wharf or down to the beach?"

"I said all along I was going to Mexico; I've been saying so for years!" cried Robert, in an excited and irritable tone, with the air of a man defending himself against a swarm of stinging insects.

Madame Lebrun knocked on the table with her knife handle.

"Please let Robert explain why he is going, and why he is going to-night," she called out. "Really, this table is getting to be more and more like Bedlam[1] every day, with everybody talking at once. Sometimes—I hope God will forgive me—but positively, sometimes I wish Victor would lose the power of speech."

Victor laughed sardonically as he thanked his mother for her holy wish, of which he failed to see the benefit to anybody, except that it might afford her a more ample opportunity and license to talk herself.

Monsieur Farival thought that Victor should have been taken out in midocean in his earliest youth and drowned. Victor thought there would be more logic in thus disposing of old people with an established claim for making themselves universally obnoxious. Madame Lebrun grew a trifle hysterical; Robert called his brother some sharp, hard names.

"There's nothing much to explain, mother," he said; though he explained, nevertheless—looking chiefly at Edna—that he could only meet the gentleman whom he intended to join at Vera Cruz by taking such and such a steamer, which left New Orleans on such a day; that Beaudelet was going out with his lugger-load of vegetables that night, which gave him an opportunity of reaching the city and making his vessel in time.

"But when did you make up your mind to all this?" demanded Monsieur Farival.

"This afternoon," returned Robert, with a shade of annoyance.

"At what time this afternoon?" persisted the old gentleman, with nagging determination, as if he were cross-questioning a criminal in a court of justice.

"At four o'clock this afternoon, Monsieur Farival," Robert replied, in a high voice and with a lofty air, which reminded Edna of some gentleman on the stage.

She had forced herself to eat most of her soup, and now she was picking the flaky bits of a *court bouillon*[2] with her fork.

The lovers were profiting by the general conversation on Mexico to speak in whispers of matters which they rightly considered were interesting to no one but themselves. The lady in black had once received a pair of prayer-beads of

---

[1]A lunatic asylum.   [2]Fish cooked in a highly seasoned sauce.

curious workmanship from Mexico, with very special indulgence[3] attached to them, but she had never been able to ascertain whether the indulgence extended outside the Mexican border. Father Fochel of the Cathedral had attempted to explain it; but he had not done so to her satisfaction. And she begged that Robert would interest himself, and discover, if possible, whether she was entitled to the indulgence accompanying the remarkably curious Mexican prayer-beads.

Madame Ratignolle hoped that Robert would exercise extreme caution in dealing with the Mexicans, who, she considered, were a treacherous people, unscrupulous and revengeful. She trusted she did them no injustice in thus condemning them as a race. She had known personally but one Mexican, who made and sold excellent tamales, and whom she would have trusted implicitly, so soft-spoken was he. One day he was arrested for stabbing his wife. She never knew whether he had been hanged or not.

Victor had grown hilarious, and was attempting to tell an anecdote about a Mexican girl who served chocolate one winter in a restaurant in Dauphine Street. No one would listen to him but old Monsieur Farival, who went into convulsions over the droll story.

Edna wondered if they had all gone mad, to be talking and clamoring at that rate. She herself could think of nothing to say about Mexico or the Mexicans.

"At what time do you leave?" she asked Robert.

"At ten," he told her. "Beaudelet wants to wait for the moon."

"Are you all ready to go?"

"Quite ready. I shall only take a hand-bag, and shall pack my trunk in the city."

He turned to answer some question put to him by his mother, and Edna, having finished her black coffee, left the table.

She went directly to her room. The little cottage was close and stuffy after leaving the outer air. But she did not mind; there appeared to be a hundred different things demanding her attention indoors. She began to set the toilet-stand to rights, grumbling at the negligence of the quadroon, who was in the adjoining room putting the children to bed. She gathered together stray garments that were hanging on the backs of chairs, and put each where it belonged in closet or bureau drawer. She changed her gown for a more comfortable and commodious wrapper. She rearranged her hair, combing and brushing it with unusual energy. Then she went in and assisted the quadroon in getting the boys to bed.

They were very playful and inclined to talk—to do anything but lie quiet and go to sleep. Edna sent the quadroon away to her supper and told her she need not return. Then she sat and told the children a story. Instead of soothing it excited them, and added to their wakefulness. She left them in heated argument, speculating about the conclusion of the tale which their mother promised to finish the following night.

The little black girl came in to say that Madame Lebrun would like to have Mrs. Pontellier go and sit with them over at the house till Mr. Robert went away. Edna returned answer that she had already undressed, that she did not feel quite well, but perhaps she would go over to the house later. She started to dress again, and got as far advanced as to remove her *peignoir*. But changing her mind once more she resumed the *peignoir*, and went outside and sat down before her door. She was over-heated and irritable, and fanned herself energetically for a while. Madame Ratignolle came down to discover what was the matter.

[3]Power to release one from the punishments due for sins.

"All that noise and confusion at the table must have upset me," replied Edna, "and moreover, I hate shocks and surprises. The idea of Robert starting off in such a ridiculously sudden and dramatic way! As if it were a matter of life and death! Never saying a word about it all morning when he was with me."

"Yes," agreed Madame Ratignolle. "I think it was showing us all—you especially—very little consideration. It wouldn't have surprised me in any of the others; those Lebruns are all given to heroics. But I must say I should never have expected such a thing from Robert. Are you not coming down? Come on, dear; it doesn't look friendly."

"No," said Edna, a little sullenly. "I can't go to the trouble of dressing again; I don't feel like it."

"You needn't dress; you look all right; fasten a belt around your waist. Just look at me!"

"No," persisted Edna; "but you go on. Madame Lebrun might be offended if we both stayed away."

Madame Ratignolle kissed Edna good-night, and went away, being in truth rather desirous of joining in the general and animated conversation which was still in progress concerning Mexico and the Mexicans.

Somewhat later Robert came up, carrying his hand-bag.

"Aren't you feeling well?" he asked.

"Oh, well enough. Are you going right away?"

He lit a match and looked at his watch. "In twenty minutes," he said. The sudden and brief flare of the match emphasized the darkness for a while. He sat down upon a stool which the children had left out on the porch.

"Get a chair," said Edna.

"This will do," he replied. He put on his soft hat and nervously took it off again, and wiping his face with his handerchief, complained of the heat.

"Take the fan," said Edna, offering it to him.

"Oh, no! Thank you. It does no good; you have to stop fanning some time, and feel all the more uncomfortable afterward."

"That's one of the ridiculous things which men always say. I have never known one to speak otherwise of fanning. How long will you be gone?"

"Forever, perhaps. I don't know. It depends upon a good many things."

"Well, in case it shouldn't be forever, how long will it be?"

"I don't know."

"This seems to me perfectly preposterous and uncalled for. I don't like it. I don't understand your motive for silence and mystery, never saying a word to me about it this morning." He remained silent, not offering to defend himself. He only said, after a moment:

"Don't part from me in an ill-humor. I never knew you to be out of patience with me before."

"I don't want to part in any ill-humor," she said. "But can't you understand? I've grown used to seeing you, to having you with me all the time, and your action seems unfriendly, even unkind. You don't even offer an excuse for it. Why, I was planning to be together, thinking of how pleasant it would be to see you in the city next winter."

"So was I," he blurted. "Perhaps that's the—" He stood up suddenly and held out his hand. "Good-by, my dear Mrs. Pontellier; good-by. You won't—I hope you won't completely forget me." She clung to his hand, striving to detain him.

"Write to me when you get there, won't you, Robert?" she entreated.

"I will, thank you. Good-by."

How unlike Robert! The merest acquaintance would have said something more emphatic than "I will, thank you; good-by," to such a request.

He had evidently already taken leave of the people over at the house, for he descended the steps and went to join Beaudelet, who was out there with an oar across his shoulder waiting for Robert. They walked away in the darkness. She could only hear Beaudelet's voice; Robert had apparently not even spoken a word of greeting to his companion.

Edna bit her handkerchief convulsively, striving to hold back and to hide, even from herself as she would have hidden from another, the emotion which was troubling—tearing—her. Her eyes were brimming with tears.

For the first time she recognized anew the symptoms of infatuation which she had felt incipiently as a child, as a girl in her earliest teens, and later as a young woman. The recognition did not lessen the reality, the poignancy of the revelation by any suggestion or promise of instability. The past was nothing to her; offered no lesson which she was willing to heed. The future was a mystery which she never attempted to penetrate. The present alone was significant; was hers, to torture her as it was doing then with the biting conviction that she had lost that which she had held, that she had been denied that which her impassioned, newly awakened being demanded.

XVI

"Do you miss your friend greatly?" asked Mademoiselle Reisz one morning as she came creeping up behind Edna, who had just left her cottage on her way to the beach. She spent much of her time in the water since she had acquired finally the art of swimming. As their stay at Grand Isle drew near its close, she felt that she could not give too much time to a diversion which afforded her the only real pleasurable moments that she knew. When Mademoiselle Reisz came and touched her upon the shoulder and spoke to her, the woman seemed to echo the thought which was ever in Edna's mind; or better, the feeling which constantly possessed her.

Robert's going had some way taken the brightness, the color, the meaning out of everything. The conditions of her life were in no way changed, but her whole existence was dulled, like a faded garment which seems to be no longer worth wearing. She sought him everywhere—in others whom she induced to talk about him. She went up in the mornings to Madame Lebrun's room, braving the clatter of the old sewing-machine. She sat there and chatted at intervals as Robert had done. She gazed around the room at the pictures and photographs hanging upon the wall, and discovered in some corner an old family album, which she examined with the keenest interest, appealing to Madame Lebrun for enlightenment concerning the many figures and faces which she discovered between its pages.

There was a picture of Madame Lebrun with Robert as a baby, seated in her lap, a round-faced infant with a fist in his mouth. The eyes alone in the baby suggested the man. And that was he also in kilts, at the age of five, wearing long curls and holding a whip in his hand. It made Edna laugh, and she laughed, too, at the portrait in his first long trousers; while another interested her, taken when he left for college, looking thin, long-faced, with eyes full of fire, ambition and great intentions. But there was no recent picture, none which suggested the Robert who had gone away five days ago, leaving a void and wilderness behind him.

"Oh, Robert stopped having his pictures taken when he had to pay for them himself! He found wiser use for his money, he says," explained Madame Lebrun. She had a letter from him, written before he left New Orleans. Edna wished to see the letter, and Madame Lebrun told her to look for it either on the table or the dresser, or perhaps it was on the mantelpiece.

The letter was on the bookshelf. It possessed the greatest interest and attraction for Edna; the envelope, its size and shape, the post-mark, the handwriting. She examined every detail of the outside before opening it. There were only a few lines, setting forth that he would leave the city that afternoon, that he had packed his trunk in good shape, that he was well, and sent her his love and begged to be affectionately remembered to all. There was no special message to Edna except a postscript saying that if Mrs. Pontellier desired to finish the book which he had been reading to her, his mother would find it in his room, among other books there on the table. Edna experienced a pang of jealousy because he had written to his mother rather than to her.

Every one seemed to take for granted that she missed him. Even her husband, when he came down the Saturday following Robert's departure, expressed regret that he had gone.

"How do you get on without him, Edna?" he asked.

"It's very dull without him," she admitted. Mr. Pontellier had seen Robert in the city, and Edna asked him a dozen questions or more. Where had they met? On Carondelet Street, in the morning. They had gone "in" and had a drink and a cigar together. What had they talked about? Chiefly about his prospects in Mexico, which Mr. Pontellier thought were promising. How did he look? How did he seem—grave, or gay, or how? Quite cheerful, and wholly taken up with the idea of his trip, which Mr. Pontellier found altogether natural in a young fellow about to seek fortune and adventure in a strange, queer country.

Edna tapped her foot impatiently, and wondered why the children persisted in playing in the sun when they might be under the trees. She went down and led them out of the sun, scolding the quadroon for not being more attentive.

It did not strike her as in the least grotesque that she should be making of Robert the object of conversation and leading her husband to speak of him. The sentiment which she entertained for Robert in no way resembled that which she felt for her husband, or had ever felt, or ever expected to feel. She had all her life long been accustomed to harbor thoughts and emotions which never voiced themselves. They had never taken the form of struggles. They belonged to her and were her own, and she entertained the conviction that she had a right to them and that they concerned no one but herself. Edna had once told Madame Ratignolle that she would never sacrifice herself for her children, or for any one. Then had followed a rather heated argument; the two women did not appear to understand each other or to be talking the same language. Edna tried to appease her friend, to explain.

"I would give up the unessential; I would give my money, I would give my life for my children; but I wouldn't give myself. I can't make it more clear; it's only something which I am beginning to comprehend, which is revealing itself to me."

"I don't know what you would call the essential, or what you mean by the unessential," said Madame Ratignolle, cheerfully; "but a woman who would give her life for her children could do no more than that—your Bible tells you so. I'm sure I couldn't do more than that."

"Oh, yes you could!" laughed Edna.

She was not surprised at Mademoiselle Reisz's question the morning that lady, following her to the beach, tapped her on the shoulder and asked if she did not greatly miss her young friend.

"Oh, good morning, Mademoiselle; is it you? Why, of course I miss Robert. Are you going down to bathe?"

"Why should I go down to bathe at the very end of the season when I haven't been in the surf all summer," replied the woman, disagreeably.

"I beg your pardon," offered Edna, in some embarrassment, for she should have remembered that Mademoiselle Reisz's avoidance of the water had furnished a theme for much pleasantry. Some among them thought it was on account of her false hair, or the dread of getting the violets wet, while others attributed it to the natural aversion for water sometimes believed to accompany the artistic temperament. Mademoiselle offered Edna some chocolates in a paper bag, which she took from her pocket, by way of showing that she bore no ill feeling. She habitually ate chocolates for their sustaining quality; they contained much nutriment in small compass, she said. They saved her from starvation, as Madame Lebrun's table was utterly impossible; and no one save so impertinent a woman as Madame Lebrun could think of offering such food to people and requiring them to pay for it.

"She must feel very lonely without her son," said Edna, desiring to change the subject. "Her favorite son, too. It must have been quite hard to let him go."

Mademoiselle laughed maliciously.

"Her favorite son! Oh, dear! Who could have been imposing such a tale upon you? Aline Lebrun lives for Victor, and for Victor alone. She has spoiled him into the worthless creature he is. She worships him and the ground he walks on. Robert is very well in a way, to give up all the money he can earn to the family, and keep the barest pittance for himself. Favorite son, indeed! I miss the poor fellow myself, my dear. I liked to see him and to hear him about the place—the only Lebrun who is worth a pinch of salt. He comes to see me often in the city. I like to play to him. That Victor! hanging would be too good for him. It's a wonder Robert hasn't beaten him to death long ago."

"I thought he had great patience with his brother," offered Edna, glad to be talking about Robert, no matter what was said.

"Oh! he thrashed him well enough a year or two ago," said Mademoiselle. "It was about a Spanish girl whom Victor considered that he had some sort of claim upon. He met Robert one day talking to the girl, or walking with her, or bathing with her, or carrying her basket—I don't remember what;—and he became so insulting and abusive that Robert gave him a thrashing on the spot that has kept him comparatively in order for a good while. It's about time he was getting another."

"Was her name Mariequita?" asked Edna.

"Mariequita—yes, that was it; Mariequita. I had forgotten. Oh, she's a sly one, and a bad one, that Mariequita!"

Edna looked down at Mademoiselle Reisz and wondered how she could have listened to her venom so long. For some reason she felt depressed, almost unhappy. She had not intended to go into the water; but she donned her bathing suit, and left Mademoiselle alone, seated under the shade of the children's tent. The water was growing cooler as the season advanced. Edna plunged and swam about with an abandon that thrilled and invigorated her. She remained a long time in the water, half hoping that Mademoiselle Reisz would not wait for her.

But Mademoiselle waited. She was very amiable during the walk back, and raved much over Edna's appearance in her bathing suit. She talked about music. She hoped that Edna would go to see her in the city, and wrote her address with the stub of a pencil on a piece of card which she found in her pocket.

"When do you leave?" asked Edna.

"Next Monday; and you?"

"The following week," answered Edna, adding, "It has been a pleasant summer, hasn't it, Mademoiselle?"

"Well," agreed Mademoiselle Reisz, with a shrug, "rather pleasant, if it hadn't been for the mosquitoes and the Farival twins."

XVII

The Pontelliers possessed a very charming home on Esplanade Street[1] in New Orleans. It was a large, double cottage, with a broad front veranda, whose round, fluted columns supported the sloping roof. The house was painted a dazzling white; the outside shutters, or jalousies, were green. In the yard, which was kept scrupulously neat, were flowers and plants of every description which flourish in South Louisiana. Within doors the appointments were perfect after the conventional type. The softest carpets and rugs covered the floors; rich and tasteful draperies hung at doors and windows. There were paintings, selected with judgment and discrimination, upon the walls. The cut glass, the silver, the heavy damask which daily appeared upon the table were the envy of many women whose husbands were less generous than Mr. Pontellier.

Mr. Pontellier was very fond of walking about his house examining its various appointments and details, to see that nothing was amiss. He greatly valued his possessions, chiefly because they were his, and derived genuine pleasure from contemplating a painting, a statuette, a rare lace curtain—no matter what— after he had bought it and placed it among his household goods.

On Tuesday afternoons—Tuesday being Mrs. Pontellier's reception day[2]— there was a constant stream of callers—women who came in carriages or in the street cars, or walked when the air was soft and distance permitted. A light-colored mulatto boy, in dress coat and bearing a diminutive silver tray for the reception of cards, admitted them. A maid, in white fluted cap, offered the callers liqueur, coffee, or chocolate, as they might desire. Mrs. Pontellier, attired in a handsome reception gown, remained in the drawing-room the entire afternoon receiving her visitors. Men sometimes called in the evening with their wives.

This had been the programme which Mrs. Pontellier had religiously followed since her marriage, six years before. Certain evenings during the week she and her husband attended the opera or sometimes the play.

Mr. Pontellier left his home in the mornings between nine and ten o'clock, and rarely returned before half-past six or seven in the evening—dinner being served at half-past seven.

He and his wife seated themselves at table one Tuesday evening, a few weeks after their return from Grand Isle. They were alone together. The boys were being put to bed; the patter of their bare, escaping feet could be heard occasionally, as well as the pursuing voice of the quadroon, lifted in mild protest and entreaty. Mrs. Pontellier did not wear her usual Tuesday reception gown;

[1] A fashionable street, lined with the elegant homes of the rich and socially prominent.

[2] That day, each week, when an upper-class woman received visitors in her home. To be "out" to a visitor calling on "reception day" was a great insult.

she was in ordinary house dress. Mr. Pontellier, who was observant about such things, noticed it, as he served the soup and handled it to the boy in waiting.

"Tired out, Edna? Whom did you have? Many callers?" he asked. He tasted his soup and began to season it with pepper, salt, vinegar, mustard—everything within reach.

"There were a good many," replied Edna, who was eating her soup with evident satisfaction. "I found their cards when I got home; I was out."

"Out!" exclaimed her husband, with something like genuine consternation in his voice as he laid down the vinegar cruet and looked at her through his glasses. "Why, what could have taken you out on Tuesday? What did you have to do?"

"Nothing. I simply felt like going out, and I went out."

"Well, I hope you left some suitable excuse," said her husband, somewhat appeased, as he added a dash of cayenne pepper to the soup.

"No, I left no excuse. I told Joe to say I was out, that was all."

"Why, my dear, I should think you'd understand by this time that people don't do such things; we've got to observe *les convenances*[3] if we ever expect to get on and keep up with the procession. If you felt that you had to leave home this afternoon, you should have left some suitable explanation for your absence.

"This soup is really impossible; it's strange that woman hasn't learned yet to make a decent soup. Any free-lunch stand in town serves a better one. Was Mrs. Belthrop here?"

"Bring the tray with the cards, Joe. I don't remember who was here."

The boy retired and returned after a moment, bringing the tiny silver tray, which was covered with ladies' visiting cards. He handed it to Mrs. Pontellier.

"Give it to Mr. Pontellier," she said.

Joe offered the tray to Mr. Pontellier, and removed the soup.

Mr. Pontellier scanned the names of his wife's callers, reading some of them aloud, with comments as he read.

" 'The Misses Delasidas.' I worked a big deal in futures[4] for their father this morning; nice girls; it's time they were getting married. 'Mrs. Belthrop.' I tell you what it is, Edna; you can't afford to snub Mrs. Belthrop. Why, Belthrop could buy and sell us ten times over. His business is worth a good, round sum to me. You'd better write her a note. 'Mrs. James Highcamp.' Hugh! the less you have to do with Mrs. Highcamp, the better. 'Madame Laforcé.' Came all the way from Carrolton,[5] too, poor old soul. 'Miss Wiggs.' 'Mrs. Eleanor Boltons.' " He pushed the cards aside.

"Mercy!" exclaimed Edna, who had been fuming. "Why are you taking the thing so seriously and making such a fuss over it?"

"I'm not making any fuss over it. But it's just such seeming trifles that we've got to take seriously; such things count."

The fish was scorched. Mr. Pontellier would not touch it. Edna said she did not mind a little scorched taste. The roast was in some way not to his fancy, and he did not like the manner in which the vegetables were served.

"It seems to me," he said, "we spend money enough in this house to procure at least one meal a day which a man could eat and retain his self-respect."

"You used to think the cook was a treasure," returned Edna, indifferently.

"Perhaps she was when she first came; but cooks are only human. They need looking after, like any other class of persons that you employ. Suppose I didn't

[3]French: "the social conventions."
[4]Speculative purchase of stocks or other commodities, bought now for future delivery when, it is hoped, their value will have risen.
[5]A western section of New Orleans. Formerly a separate village, it was absorbed by the city in 1874.

look after the clerks in my office, just let them run things their own way; they'd soon make a nice mess of me and my business."

"Where are you going?" asked Edna, seeing that her husband arose from table without having eaten a morsel except a taste of the highly-seasoned soup.

"I'm going to get my dinner at the club. Good night." He went into the hall, took his hat and stick from the stand, and left the house.

She was somewhat familiar with such scenes. They had often made her very unhappy. On a few previous occasions she had been completely deprived of any desire to finish her dinner. Sometimes she had gone into the kitchen to administer a tardy rebuke to the cook. Once she went to her room and studied the cookbook during an entire evening, finally writing out a menu for the week, which left her harassed with a feeling that, after all, she had accomplished no good that was worth the name.

But that evening Edna finished her dinner alone, with forced deliberation. Her face was flushed and her eyes flamed with some inward fire that lighted them. After finishing her dinner she went to her room, having instructed the boy to tell any other callers that she was indisposed.

It was a large, beautiful room, rich and picturesque in the soft, dim light which the maid had turned low. She went and stood at an open window and looked out upon the deep tangle of the garden below. All the mystery and witchery of the night seemed to have gathered there amid the perfumes and the dusky and tortuous outlines of flowers and foliage. She was seeking herself and finding herself in just such sweet, half-darkness which met her moods. But the voices were not soothing that came to her from the darkness and the sky above and the stars. They jeered and sounded mournful notes without promise, devoid even of hope. She turned back into the room and began to walk to and fro down its whole length, without stopping, without resting. She carried in her hands a thin handkerchief, which she tore into ribbons, rolled into a ball, and flung from her. Once she stopped, and taking off her wedding ring, flung it upon the carpet. When she saw it lying there, she stamped her heel upon it, striving to crush it. But her small boot heel did not make an indenture, not a mark upon the little glittering circlet.

In a sweeping passion she seized a glass vase from the table and flung it upon the tiles of the hearth. She wanted to destroy something. The crash and clatter were what she wanted to hear.

A maid, alarmed at the din of breaking glass, entered the room to discover what was the matter.

"A vase fell upon the hearth," said Edna. "Never mind; leave it till morning."

"Oh! you might get some of the glass in your feet, ma'am," insisted the young woman, picking up bits of the broken vase that were scattered upon the carpet. "And here's your ring, ma'am, under the chair."

Edna held out her hand, and taking the ring, slipped it upon her finger.

XVIII

The following morning Mr. Pontellier, upon leaving for his office, asked Edna if she would not meet him in town in order to look at some new fixtures for the library.

"I hardly think we need new fixtures, Léonce. Don't let us get anything new; you are too extravagant. I don't believe you ever think of saving or putting by."

"The way to become rich is to make money, my dear Edna, not to save it," he said. He regretted that she did not feel inclined to go with him and select new fixtures. He kissed her good-by, and told her she was not looking well and must take care of herself. She was unusually pale and very quiet.

She stood on the front veranda as he quitted the house, and absently picked a few sprays of jessamine[1] that grew upon a trellis near by. She inhaled the odor of the blossoms and thrust them into the bosom of her white morning gown. The boys were dragging along the banquette[2] a small "express wagon," which they had filled with blocks and sticks. The quadroon was following them with little quick steps, having assumed a fictitious animation and alacrity for the occasion. A fruit vender was crying his wares in the street.

Edna looked straight before her with a self-absorbed expression upon her face. She felt no interest in anything about her. The street, the children, the fruit vender, the flowers growing there under her eyes, were all part and parcel of an alien world which had suddenly become antagonistic.

She went back into the house. She had thought of speaking to the cook concerning her blunders of the previous night; but Mr. Pontellier had saved her that disagreeable mission, for which she was so poorly fitted. Mr. Pontellier's arguments were usually convincing with those whom he employed. He left home feeling quite sure that he and Edna would sit down that evening, and possibly a few subsequent evenings, to a dinner deserving of the name.

Edna spent an hour or two in looking over some of her old sketches. She could see their shortcomings and defects, which were glaring in her eyes. She tried to work a little, but found she was not in the humor. Finally she gathered together a few of the sketches—those which she considered the least discreditable; and she carried them with her when, a little later, she dressed and left the house. She looked handsome and distinguished in her street gown. The tan of the seashore had left her face, and her forehead was smooth, white, and polished beneath her heavy, yellow-brown hair. There were a few freckles on her face, and a small dark mole near the under lip and one on the temple, half-hidden in her hair.

As Edna walked along the street she was thinking of Robert. She was still under the spell of her infatuation. She had tried to forget him, realizing the inutility of remembering. But the thought of him was like an obsession, ever pressing itself upon her. It was not that she dwelt upon details of their acquaintance, or recalled in any special or peculiar way his personality; it was his being, his existence, which dominated her thought, fading sometimes as if it would melt into the mist of the forgotten, reviving again with an intensity which filled her with an incomprehensible longing.

Edna was on her way to Madame Ratignolle's. Their intimacy, begun at Grand Isle, had not declined, and they had seen each other with some frequency since their return to the city. The Ratignolles lived at no great distance from Edna's home, on the corner of a side street, where Monsieur Ratignolle owned and conducted a drug store which enjoyed a steady and prosperous trade. His father had been in the business before him, and Monsieur Ratignolle stood well in the community and bore an enviable reputation for integrity and clear-headedness. His family lived in commodious apartments over the store, having an entrance on the side within the *porte cochère*.[3] There was something which Edna thought very French, very foreign, about their whole manner of living. In the large and pleasant salon which extended across the width of the house, the Ratignolles

---

[1]Jasmine.   [2]Sidewalk.
[3]A carriage entrance with a porch roof to protect passengers from the weather.

entertained their friends once a fortnight with a *soirée musicale*,[4] sometimes diversified by card-playing. There was a friend who played upon the 'cello. One brought his flute and another his violin, while there were some who sang and a number who performed upon the piano with various degrees of taste and agility. The Ratignolles' *soirées musicales* were widely known, and it was considered a privilege to be invited to them.

Edna found her friend engaged in assorting the clothes which had returned that morning from the laundry. She at once abandoned her occupation upon seeing Edna, who had been ushered without ceremony into her presence.

" 'Cité can do it as well as I; it is really her business," she explained to Edna, who apologized for interrupting her. And she summoned a young black woman, whom she instructed, in French, to be very careful in checking off the list which she handed her. She told her to notice particularly if a fine linen handkerchief of Monsieur Ratignolle's, which was missing last week, had been returned; and to be sure to set to one side such pieces as required mending and darning.

Then placing an arm around Edna's waist, she led her to the front of the house, to the salon, where it was cool and sweet with the odor of great roses that stood upon the hearth in jars.

Madame Ratignolle looked more beautiful than ever there at home, in a negligé which left her arms almost wholly bare and exposed the rich, melting curves of her white throat.

"Perhaps I shall be able to paint your picture some day," said Edna with a smile when they were seated. She produced the roll of sketches and started to unfold them. "I believe I ought to work again. I feel as if I wanted to be doing something. What do you think of them? Do you think it worth while to take it up again and study some more? I might study for a while with Laidpore."

She knew that Madame Ratignolle's opinion in such a matter would be next to valueless, that she herself had not alone decided, but determined; but she sought the words of praise and encouragement that would help her to put heart into her venture.

"Your talent is immense, dear!"

"Nonsense!" protested Edna, well pleased.

"Immense, I tell you," persisted Madame Ratignolle, surveying the sketches one by one, at close range, then holding them at arm's length, narrowing her eyes, and dropping her head on one side. "Surely, this Bavarian peasant is worthy of framing; and this basket of apples! never have I seen anything more lifelike. One might almost be tempted to reach out a hand and take one."

Edna could not control a feeling which bordered upon complacency at her friend's praise, even realizing, as she did, its true worth. She retained a few of the sketches, and gave all the rest to Madame Ratignolle, who appreciated the gift far beyond its value and proudly exhibited the pictures to her husband when he came up from the store a little later for his midday dinner.

Mr. Ratignolle was one of those men who are called the salt of the earth. His cheerfulness was unbounded, and it was matched by his goodness of heart, his broad charity, and common sense. He and his wife spoke English with an accent which was only discernible through its un-English emphasis and a certain carefulness and deliberation. Edna's husband spoke English with no accent whatever. The Ratignolles understood each other perfectly. If ever the fusion of two

[4]An evening musical party.

human beings into one has been accomplished on this sphere it was surely in their union.

As Edna seated herself at table with them she thought, "Better a dinner of herbs,"[5] though it did not take her long to discover that [it] was no dinner of herbs, but a delicious repast, simple, choice, and in every way satisfying.

Monsieur Ratignolle was delighted to see her, though he found her looking not so well as at Grand Isle, and he advised a tonic. He talked a good deal on various topics, a little politics, some city news and neighborhood gossip. He spoke with an animation and earnestness that gave an exaggerated importance to every syllable he uttered. His wife was keenly interested in everything he said, laying down her fork the better to listen, chiming in, taking the words out of his mouth.

Edna felt depressed rather than soothed after leaving them. The little glimpse of domestic harmony which had been offered her, gave her no regret, no longing. It was not a condition of life which fitted her, and she could see in it but an appalling and hopeless ennui. She was moved by a kind of commiseration for Madame Ratignolle,—a pity for that colorless existence which never uplifted its possessor beyond the region of blind contentment, in which no moment of anguish ever visited her soul, in which she would never have the taste of life's delirium. Edna vaguely wondered what she meant by "life's delirium." It had crossed her thought like some unsought extraneous impression.

XIX

Edna could not help but think that it was very foolish, very childish, to have stamped upon her wedding ring and smashed the crystal vase upon the tiles. She was visited by no more outbursts, moving her to such futile expedients. She began to do as she liked and to feel as she liked. She completely abandoned her Tuesdays at home, and did not return the visits of those who had called upon her. She made no ineffectual efforts to conduct her household *en bonne ménagère*,[1] going and coming as it suited her fancy, and, so far as she was able, lending herself to any passing caprice.

Mr. Pontellier had been a rather courteous husband so long as he met a certain tacit submissiveness in his wife. But her new and unexpected line of conduct completely bewildered him. It shocked him. Then her absolute disregard for her duties as a wife angered him. When Mr. Pontellier became rude, Edna grew insolent. She had resolved never to take another step backward.

"It seems to me the utmost folly for a woman at the head of a household, and the mother of children, to spend in an atelier[2] days which would be better employed contriving for the comfort of her family."

"I feel like painting," answered Edna. "Perhaps I shan't always feel like it."

"Then in God's name paint! but don't let the family go to the devil. There's Madame Ratignolle; because she keeps up her music, she doesn't let everything else go to chaos. And she's more of a musician than you are a painter."

"She isn't a musician, and I'm not a painter. It isn't on account of painting that I let things go."

"On account of what, then?"

---

[5]"Better is a dinner of herbs where love is, than a stalled ox and hatred therewith." Proverbs 15:17.
[1]French: as a good housekeeper.   [2]Art studio.

"Oh! I don't know. Let me alone; you bother me."

It sometimes entered Mr. Pontellier's mind to wonder if his wife were not growing a little unbalanced mentally. He could see plainly that she was not herself. That is, he could not see that she was becoming herself and daily casting aside that fictitious self which we assume like a garment with which to appear before the world.

Her husband let her alone as she requested, and went away to his office. Edna went up to her atelier—a bright room in the top of the house. She was working with great energy and interst, without accomplishing anything, however, which satisfied her even in the smallest degree. For a time she had the whole household enrolled in the service of art. The boys posed for her. They thought it amusing at first, but the occupation soon lost its attractiveness when they discovered that it was not a game arranged especially for their entertainment. The quadroon sat for hours before Edna's palette, patient as a savage, while the house-maid took charge of the children, and the drawing-room went undusted. But the housemaid, too, served her term as model when Edna perceived that the young woman's back and shoulders were molded on classic lines, and that her hair, loosened from its confining cap, became an inspiration. While Edna worked she sometimes sang low the little air, "*Ah! si tu savais!*"

It moved her with recollections. She could hear again the ripple of the water, the flapping sail. She could see the glint of the moon upon the bay, and could feel the soft, gusty beating of the hot south wind. A subtle current of desire passed through her body, weakening her hold upon the brushes and making her eyes burn.

There were days when she was very happy without knowing why. She was happy to be alive and breathing, when her whole being seemed to be one with the sunlight, the color, the odors, the luxuriant warmth of some perfect Southern day. She liked then to wander alone in the strange and unfamiliar places. She discovered many a sunny, sleepy corner, fashioned to dream in. And she found it good to dream and to be alone and unmolested.

There were days when she was unhappy, she did not know why,—when it did not seem worth while to be glad or sorry, to be alive or dead; when life appeared to her like a grotesque pandemonium and humanity like worms struggling blindly toward inevitable annihilation. She would not work on such a day, nor weave fancies to stir her pulses and warm her blood.

XX

It was during such a mood that Edna hunted up Mademoiselle Reisz. She had not forgotten the rather disagreeable impression left upon her by their last interview; but she nevertheless felt a desire to see her—above all, to listen while she played upon the piano. Quite early in the afternoon she started upon her quest for the pianist. Unfortunately she had mislaid or lost Mademoiselle Reisz's card, and looking up her address in the city directory, she found that the woman lived on Bienville Street, some distance away. The directory which fell into her hands was a year or more old, however, and upon reaching the number indicated, Edna discovered that the house was occupied by a respectable family of mulattoes who had *chambres garnies*[1] to let. They had been living there for six months, and knew absolutely nothing of a Mademoiselle Reisz. In fact, they

---

[1]French: furnished rooms.

knew nothing of any of their neighbors; their lodgers were all people of the highest distinction, they assured Edna. She did not linger to discuss class distinctions with Madame Pouponne, but hastened to a neighboring grocery store, feeling sure that Mademoiselle would have left her address with the proprietor.

He knew Mademoiselle Reisz a good deal better than he wanted to know her, he informed his questioner. In truth, he did not want to know her at all, or anything concerning her—the most disagreeable and unpopular woman who ever lived in Bienville Street. He thanked heaven she had left the neighborhood, and was equally thankful that he did not know where she had gone.

Edna's desire to see Mademoiselle Reisz had increased tenfold since these unlooked-for obstacles had arisen to thwart it. She was wondering who could give her the information she sought, when it suddenly occurred to her that Madame Lebrun would be the one most likely to do so. She knew it was useless to ask Madame Ratignolle, who was on the most distant terms with the musician, and preferred to know nothing concerning her. She had once been almost as emphatic in expressing herself upon the subject as the corner grocer.

Edna knew that Madame Lebrun had returned to the city, for it was the middle of November. And she also knew where the Lebruns lived, on Chartres Street.

Their home from the outside looked like a prison, with iron bars before the door and lower windows. The iron bars were a relic of the old *régime*,[2] and no one had ever thought of dislodging them. At the side was a high fence enclosing the garden. A gate or door opening upon the street was locked. Edna rang the bell at this side garden gate, and stood upon the banquette, waiting to be admitted.

It was Victor who opened the gate for her. A black woman, wiping her hands upon her apron, was close at his heels. Before she saw them Edna could hear them in altercation, the woman—plainly an anomaly—claiming the right to be allowed to perform her duties, one of which was to answer the bell.

Victor was surprised and delighted to see Mrs. Pontellier, and he made no attempt to conceal either his astonishment or his delight. He was a dark-browed, good-looking youngster of nineteen, greatly resembling his mother, but with ten times her impetuosity. He instructed the black woman to go at once and inform Madame Lebrun that Mrs. Pontellier desired to see her. The woman grumbled a refusal to do part of her duty when she had not been permitted to do it all, and started back to her interrupted task of weeding the garden. Whereupon Victor administered a rebuke in the form of a volley of abuse, which, owing to its rapidity and incoherence, was all but incomprehensible to Edna. Whatever it was, the rebuke was convincing, for the woman dropped her hoe and went mumbling into the house.

Edna did not wish to enter. It was very pleasant there on the side porch, where there were chairs, a wicker lounge, and a small table. She seated herself, for she was tired from her long tramp; and she began to rock gently and smooth out the folds of her silk parasol. Victor drew up his chair beside her. He at once explained that the black woman's offensive conduct was all due to imperfect training, as he was not there to take her in hand. He had only come up from the island the morning before, and expected to return next day. He stayed all winter at the island; he lived there, and kept the place in order and got things ready for the summer visitors.

But a man needed occasional relaxation, he informed Mrs. Pontellier, and

[2]A term used to describe the period (1766–1803) when New Orleans was ruled by Spanish governors.

every now and again he drummed up a pretext to bring him to the city. My! but he had had a time of it the evening before! He wouldn't want his mother to know, and he began to talk in a whisper. He was scintillant with recollections. Of course, he couldn't think of telling Mrs. Pontellier all about it, she being a woman and not comprehending such things. But it all began with a girl peeping and smiling at him through the shutters as he passed by. Oh! but she was a beauty! Certainly he smiled back, and went up and talked to her. Mrs. Pontellier did not know him if she supposed he was one to let an opportunity like that escape him. Despite herself, the youngster amused her. She must have betrayed in her look some degree of interest or entertainment. The boy grew more daring, and Mrs. Pontellier might have found herself, in a little while, listening to a highly colored story but for the timely appearance of Madame Lebrun.

That lady was still clad in white, according to her custom of the summer. Her eyes beamed an effusive welcome. Would not Mrs. Pontellier go inside? Would she partake of some refreshment? Why had she not been there before? How was that dear Mr. Pontellier and how were those sweet children? Had Mrs. Pontellier ever known such a warm November?

Victor went and reclined on the wicker lounge behind his mother's chair, where he commanded a view of Edna's face. He had taken her parasol from her hands while he spoke to her, and he now lifted it and twirled it above him as he lay on his back. When Madame Lebrun complained that it was *so* dull coming back to the city; that she saw *so* few people now; that even Victor, when he came up from the island for a day or two, had *so* much to occupy him and engage his time; then it was that the youth went into contortions on the lounge and winked mischievously at Edna. She somehow felt like a confederate in crime, and tried to look severe and disapproving.

There had been but two letters from Robert, with little in them, they told her. Victor said it was really not worth while to go inside for the letters, when his mother entreated him to go in search of them. He remembered the contents, which in truth he rattled off very glibly when put to the test.

One letter was written from Vera Cruz and the other from the City of Mexico. He had met Montel, who was doing everything toward his advancement. So far, the financial situation was no improvement over the one he had left in New Orleans, but of course the prospects were vastly better. He wrote of the City of Mexico, the buildings, the people and their habits, the conditions of life which he found there. He sent his love to the family. He inclosed a check to his mother, and hoped she would affectionately remember him to all his friends. That was about the substance of the two letters. Edna felt that if there had been a message for her, she would have received it. The despondent frame of mind in which she had left home began again to overtake her, and she remembered that she wished to find Mademoiselle Reisz.

Madame Lebrun knew where Mademoiselle Reisz lived. She gave Edna the address, regretting that she would not consent to stay and spend the remainder of the afternoon, and pay a visit to Mademoiselle Reisz some other day. The afternoon was already well advanced.

Victor escorted her out upon the banquette, lifted her parasol, and held it over her while he walked to the car[3] with her. He entreated her to bear in mind that the disclosures of the afternoon were strictly confidential. She laughed and bantered him a little, remembering too late that she should have been dignified and reserved.

---

[3]Streetcar.

"How handsome Mrs. Pontellier looked!" said Madame Lebrun to her son.

"Ravishing!" he admitted. "The city atmosphere has improved her. Some way she doesn't seem like the same woman."

XXI

Some people contended that the reason Mademoiselle Reisz always chose apartments up under the roof was to discourage the approach of beggars, peddlars and callers. There were plenty of windows in her little front room. They were for the most part dingy, but as they were nearly always open it did not make so much difference. They often admitted into the room a good deal of smoke and soot; but at the same time all the light and air that there was came through them. From her windows could be seen the crescent of the river, the masts of ships and the big chimneys of the Mississippi steamers. A magnificent piano crowded the apartment. In the next room she slept, and in the third and last she harbored a gasoline stove on which she cooked her meals when disinclined to descend to the neighboring restaurant. It was there also that she ate, keeping her belongings in a rare old buffet, dingy and battered from a hundred years of use.

When Edna knocked at Mademoiselle Reisz's front room door and entered, she discovered that person standing beside the window, engaged in mending or patching an old prunella gaiter.[1] The little musician laughed all over when she saw Edna. Her laugh consisted of a contortion of the face and all the muscles of the body. She seemed strikingly homely, standing there in the afternoon light. She still wore the shabby lace and the artificial bunch of violets on the side of her head.

"So you remembered me at last," said Mademoiselle. "I had said to myself, 'Ah, bah! she will never come.'"

"Did you want me to come?" asked Edna with a smile.

"I had not thought much about it," answered Mademoiselle. The two had seated themselves on a little bumpy sofa which stood against the wall. "I am glad, however, that you came. I have the water boiling back there, and was just about to make some coffee. You will drink a cup with me. And how is *la belle dame?*[2] Always handsome! always healthy! always contented!" She took Edna's hand between her strong wiry fingers, holding it loosely without warmth, and executing a sort of double theme upon the back and palm.

"Yes," she went on; "I sometimes thought: 'She will never come. She promised as those women in society always do, without meaning it. She will not come.' For I really don't believe you like me, Mrs. Pontellier."

"I don't know whether I like you or not," replied Edna, gazing down at the little woman with a quizzical look.

The candor of Mrs. Pontellier's admission greatly pleased Mademoiselle Reisz. She expressed her gratification by repairing forthwith to the region of the gasoline stove and rewarding her guest with the promised cup of coffee. The coffee and the biscuit accompanying it proved very acceptable to Edna, who had declined refreshment at Madame Lebrun's and was now beginning to feel hungry. Mademoiselle set the tray which she brought in upon a small table near at hand, and seated herself once again on the lumpy sofa.

[1]A high-button shoe with a cloth upper that covers the ankle.
[2]French: "the beautiful lady."

"I have had a letter from your friend," she remarked, as she poured a little cream into Edna's cup and handed it to her.

"My friend?"

"Yes, your friend Robert. He wrote to me from the City of Mexico."

"Wrote to *you?*" repeated Edna in amazement, stirring her coffee absently.

"Yes, to me. Why not? Don't stir all the warmth out of your coffee; drink it. Though the letter might as well have been sent to you; it was nothing but Mrs. Pontellier from beginning to end."

"Let me see it," requested the young woman, entreatingly.

"No; a letter concerns no one but the person who writes it and the one to whom it is written."

"Haven't you just said it concerned me from beginning to end?"

"It was written about you, not to you. 'Have you seen Mrs. Pontellier? How is she looking?' he asked. 'As Mrs. Pontellier says,' or 'as Mrs. Pontellier once said.' 'If Mrs. Pontellier should call upon you, play for her that Impromptu of Chopin's,[3] my favorite. I heard it here a day or two ago, but not as you play it. I should like to know how it affects her,' and so on, as if he supposed we were constantly in each other's society."

"Let me see the letter."

"Oh, no."

"Have you answered it?"

"No."

"Let me see the letter."

"No, and again, no."

"Then play the Impromptu for me."

"It is growing late; what time do you have to be home?"

"Time doesn't concern me. Your question seems a little rude. Play the Impromptu."

"But you have told me nothing of yourself. What are you doing?"

"Painting!" laughed Edna. "I am becoming an artist. Think of it!"

"Ah! an artist! You have pretensions, Madame."

"Why pretensions? Do you think I could not become an artist?"

"I do not know you well enough to say. I do not know your talent or your temperament. To be an artist includes much; one must possess many gifts—absolute gifts—which have not been acquired by one's own effort. And, moreover, to succeed, the artist must possess the courageous soul."

"What do you mean by the courageous soul?"

"Courageous, *ma foi!*[4] The brave soul. The soul that dares and defies."

"Show me the letter and play for me the Impromptu. You see that I have persistence. Does that quality count for anything in art?"

"It counts with a foolish old woman whom you have captivated," replied Mademoiselle, with her wriggling laugh.

The letter was right there at hand in the drawer of the little table upon which Edna had just placed her coffee cup. Mademoiselle opened the drawer and drew forth the letter, the topmost one. She placed it in Edna's hands, and without further comment arose and went to the piano.

Mademoiselle played a soft interlude. It was an improvisation. She sat low at the instrument, and the lines of her body settled into ungraceful curves and angles that gave it an appearance of deformity. Gradually and imperceptibly

---

[3]"Fantaisie-Impromptu in C-Sharp Minor," better known today in America as "I'm Always Chasing Rainbows."   [4]French: "to be sure!"

the interlude melted into the soft opening minor chords of the Chopin Impromptu.

Edna did not know when the Impromptu began or ended. She sat in the sofa corner reading Robert's letter by the fading light. Mademoiselle had glided from the Chopin into the quivering love-notes of Isolde's song,[5] and back again to the Impromptu with its soulful and poignant longing.

The shadows deepened in the little room. The music grew strange and fantastic—turbulent, insistent, plaintive and soft with entreaty. The shadows grew deeper. The music filled the room. It floated out upon the night, over the housetops, the crescent of the river, losing itself in the silence of the upper air.

Edna was sobbing, just as she had wept one midnight at Grand Isle when strange, new voices awoke in her. She arose in some agitation to take her departure. "May I come again, Mademoiselle?" she asked at the threshold.

"Come whenever you feel like it. Be careful; the stairs and landings are dark; don't stumble."

Mademoiselle reëntered and lit a candle. Robert's letter was on the floor. She stooped and picked it up. It was crumpled and damp with tears. Mademoiselle smoothed the letter out, restored it to the envelope, and replaced it in the table drawer.

XXII

One morning on his way into town Mr. Pontellier stopped at the house of his old friend and family physician, Doctor Mandelet. The Doctor was a semi-retired physician, resting, as the saying is, upon his laurels. He bore a reputation for wisdom rather than skill—leaving the active practice of medicine to his assistants and younger contemporaries—and was much sought for in matters of consultation. A few families, united to him by bonds of friendship, he still attended when they required the services of a physician. The Pontelliers were among these.

Mr. Pontellier found the Doctor reading at the open window of his study. His house stood rather far back from the street, in the center of a delightful garden, so that it was quiet and peaceful at the old gentleman's study window. He was a great reader. He stared up disapprovingly over his eye-glasses as Mr. Pontellier entered, wondering who had the temerity to disturb him at that hour of the morning.

"Ah, Pontellier! Not sick, I hope. Come and have a seat. What news do you bring this morning?" He was quite portly, with a profusion of gray hair, and small blue eyes which age had robbed of much of their brightness but none of their penetration.

"Oh! I'm never sick, Doctor. You know that I come of tough fiber—of that old Creole race of Pontelliers that dry up and finally blow away. I came to consult—no, not precisely to consult—to talk to you about Edna. I don't know what ails her."

"Madame Pontellier not well?" marveled the Doctor. "Why, I saw her—I think it was a week ago—walking along Canal Street, the picture of health, it seemed to me."

[5]A song sung by Isolde to her dead lover, Tristan, before she herself dies of grief, in the opera *Tristan and Isolde* (1857–1859), by Richard Wagner (1813–1883).

"Yes, yes; she seems quite well," said Mr. Pontellier, leaning forward and whirling his stick between his two hands; "but she doesn't act well. She's odd, she's not like herself. I can't make her out, and I though perhaps you'd help me."

"How does she act?" inquired the doctor.

"Well, it isn't easy to explain," said Mr. Pontellier, throwing himself back in his chair. "She lets the housekeeping go to the dickens."

"Well, well; women are not all alike, my dear Pontellier. We've got to consider—"

"I know that; I told you I couldn't explain. Her whole attitude—toward me and everybody and everything—has changed. You know I have a quick temper, but I don't want to quarrel or be rude to a woman, especially my wife; yet I'm driven to it, and feel like ten thousand devils after I've made a fool of myself. She's making it devilishly uncomfortable for me," he went on nervously. "She's got some sort of notion in her head concerning the eternal rights of women; and—you understand—we meet in the morning at the breakfast table."

The old gentleman lifted his shaggy eyebrows, protruded his thick nether lip, and tapped the arms of his chair with his cushioned fingertips.

What have you been doing to her, Pontellier?"

"Doing! *Parbleu!*"[1]

"Has she," asked the Doctor, with a smile, "has she been associating of late with a circle of pseudo-intellectual women—super-spiritual superior beings? My wife has been telling me about them."

"That's the trouble," broke in Mr. Pontellier, "she hasn't been associating with any one. She has abandoned her Tuesdays at home, has thrown over all her acquaintances, and goes tramping about by herself, moping in the street-cars, getting in after dark. I tell you she's peculiar. I don't like it; I feel a little worried over it."

This was a new aspect for the Doctor. "Nothing hereditary?" he asked, seriously. "Nothing peculiar about her family antecedents, is there?"

"Oh, no, indeed! She comes of sound old Presbyterian Kentucky stock. The old gentleman, her father, I have heard, used to atone for his weekday sins with his Sunday devotions. I know for a fact, that his race horses literally ran away with the prettiest bit of Kentucky farming land I ever laid eyes upon. Margaret— you know Margaret—she has all the Presbyterianism undiluted. And the youngest is something of a vixen. By the way, she gets married in a couple of weeks from now."

"Send your wife up to the wedding," exclaimed the Doctor, foreseeing a happy solution. "Let her stay among her own people for a while; it will do her good."

"That's what I want her to do. She won't go to the marriage. She says a wedding is one of the most lamentable spectacles on earth. Nice thing for a woman to say to her husband!" exclaimed Mr. Pontellier, fuming anew at the recollection.

"Pontellier," said the Doctor, after a moment's reflection, "let your wife alone for a while. Don't bother her, and don't let her bother you. Woman, my dear friend, is a very peculiar and delicate organism—a sensitive and highly organized woman, such as I know Mrs. Pontellier to be, is especially peculiar. It would require an inspired psychologist to deal successfully with them. And when ordinary fellows like you and me attempt to cope with their idiosyncrasies the

[1]French: "Good heavens!"

result is bungling. Most women are moody and whimsical. This is some passing whim of your wife, due to some cause or causes which you and I needn't try to fathom. But it will pass happily over, especially if you let her alone. Send her around to see me."

"Oh! I couldn't do that; there'd be no reason for it," objected Mr. Pontellier.

"Then I'll go around and see her," said the Doctor. "I'll drop in to dinner some evening *en bon ami.*"[2]

"Do! by all means," urged Mr. Pontellier. "What evening will you come? Say Thurdsay. Will you come Thursday?" he asked, rising to take his leave.

"Very well; Thursday. My wife may possibly have some engagement for me Thursday. In case she has, I shall let you know. Otherwise, you may expect me."

"I am going to New York on business very soon. I have a big scheme on hand, and want to be on the field proper to pull the ropes and handle the ribbons.[3] We'll let you in on the inside if you say so, Doctor," he laughed.

"No, I thank you, my dear sir," returned the Doctor. "I leave such ventures to you younger men with the fever of life still in your blood."

"What I wanted to say," continued Mr. Pontellier, with his hand on the knob; "I may have to be absent a good while. Would you advise me to take Edna along?"

"By all means, if she wishes to go. If not, leave her here. Don't contradict her. The mood will pass, I assure you. It may take a month, two, three months— possibly longer, but it will pass; have patience."

"Well, good-by, *à jeudi,*"[4] said Mr. Pontellier, as he let himself out.

The doctor would have liked during the course of conversation to ask, "Is there any man in the case?" but he knew his Creole too well to make such a blunder as that.

He did not resume his book immediately, but sat for a while meditatively looking out into the garden.

XXIII

Edna's father was in the city, and had been with them several days. She was not very warmly or deeply attached to him, but they had certain tastes in common, and when together they were companionable. His coming was in the nature of a welcome disturbance; it seemed to furnish a new direction for her emotions.

He had come to purchase a wedding gift for his daughter, Janet, and an outfit for himself in which he might make a creditable appearance at her marriage. Mr. Pontellier had selected the bridal gift, as every one immediately connected with him always deferred to his taste in such matters. And his suggestions on the question of dress—which too often assumes the nature of a problem—were of inestimable value to his father-in-law. But for the past few days the old gentleman had been upon Edna's hands, and in his society she was becoming acquainted with a new set of sensations. He had been a colonel in the Confederate army, and still maintained, with the title, the military bearing which had always accompanied it. His hair and mustache were white and silky, emphasizing the rugged bronze of his face. He was tall and thin, and wore his coats padded, which gave a fictitious breadth and depth to his shoulders and chest. Edna and her father looked very distinguished together, and excited a good deal of notice

[2]French: "as a good friend."   [3]Reins, i.e., to be in control.   [4]French: "until Thursday."

during their perambulations. Upon his arrival she began by introducing him to her atelier and making a sketch of him. He took the whole matter very seriously. If her talent had been ten-fold greater than it was, it would not have surprised him, convinced as he was that he had bequeathed to all of his daughters the germs of a masterful capability, which only depended upon their own efforts to be directed toward successful achievement.

Before her pencil he sat rigid and unflinching, as he had faced the cannon's mouth in days gone by. He resented the intrusion of the children, who gaped with wondering eyes at him, sitting so stiff up there in their mother's bright atelier. When they drew near he motioned them away with an expressive action of the foot, loath to disturb the fixed lines of his countenance, his arms, or his rigid shoulders.

Edna, anxious to entertain him, invited Mademoiselle Reisz to meet him, having promised him a treat in her piano playing; but Mademoiselle declined the invitation. So together they attended a *soirée musicale* at the Ratignolle's. Monsieur and Madame Ratignolle made much of the Colonel, installing him as the guest of honor and engaging him at once to dine with them the following Sunday, or any day which he might select. Madame coquetted with him in the most captivating and naïve manner, with eyes, gestures, and a profusion of compliments, till the Colonel's head felt thirty years younger on his padded shoulders. Edna marveled, not comprehending. She herself was almost devoid of coquetry.

There were one or two men whom she observed at the *soirée musicale;* but she would never have felt moved to any kittenish display to attract their notice—to any feline or feminine wiles to express herself toward them. Their personality attracted her in an agreeable way. Her fancy selected them, and she was glad when a lull in the music gave them an opportunity to meet her and talk with her. Often on the street the glance of strange eyes had lingered in her memory, and sometimes had disturbed her.

Mr. Pontellier did not attend these *soirées musicales.* He considered them *bourgeois,*[1] and found more diversion at the club. To Madame Ratignolle he said the music dispensed at her *soirées* was too "heavy," too far beyond his untrained comprehension. His excuse flattered her. But she disapproved of Mr. Pontellier's club, and she was frank enough to tell Edna so.

"It's a pity Mr. Pontellier doesn't stay home more in the evenings. I think you would be more—well, if you don't mind my saying it— more united, if he did."

"Oh! dear no!" said Edna, with a blank look in her eyes. "What should I do if he stayed home? We wouldn't have anything to say to each other."

She had not much of anything to say to her father, for that matter; but he did not antagonize her. She discovered that he interested her, though she realized that he might not interest her long; and for the first time in her life she felt as if she were thoroughly acquainted with him. He kept her busy serving him and ministering to his wants. It amused her to do so. She would not permit a servant or one of the children to do anything for him which she might do herself. Her husband noticed, and thought it was the expression of a deep filial attachment which he had never suspected.

The Colonel drank numerous "toddies" during the course of the day, which left him, however, imperturbed. He was an expert at concocting strong drinks. He had even invented some, to which he had given fantastic names, and for

---

[1]French: middle-class.

whose manufacture he required diverse ingredients that it devolved upon Edna to procure for him.

When Doctor Mandelet dined with the Pontelliers on Thursday he could discern in Mrs. Pontellier no trace of that morbid condition which her husband had reported to him. She was excited and in a manner radiant. She and her father had been to the race course, and their thoughts when they seated themselves at the table were still occupied with the events of the afternoon, and their talk was still of the track. The Doctor had not kept pace with turf affairs. He had certain recollections of racing in what he called "the good old times" when the Lecompte stables flourished, and he drew upon his fund of memories so that he might not be left out and seem wholly devoid of the modern spirit. But he failed to impose upon the Colonel, and was even far from impressing him with this trumped up knowledge of bygone days. Edna had staked her father on his last venture, with the most gratifying results to both of them. Besides, they had met some very charming people, according to the Colonel's impressions. Mrs. Mortimer Merriman and Mrs. James Highcamp, who were there with Alcée Arobin, had joined them and had enlivened the hours in a fashion that warmed him to think of.

Mr. Pontellier himself had no particular leaning toward horse-racing, and was even rather inclined to discourage it as a pastime, especially when he considered the fate of that blue-grass farm in Kentucky. He endeavored in a general way, to express a particular disapproval, and only succeeded in arousing the ire and opposition of his father-in-law. A pretty dispute followed, in which Edna warmly espoused her father's cause and the Doctor remained neutral.

He observed his hostess attentively from under his shaggy brows, and noted a subtle change which had transformed her from the listless woman he had known into a being who, for the moment, seemed palpitant with the forces of life. Her speech was warm and energetic. There was no repression in her glance or gesture. She reminded him of some beautiful, sleek animal waking up in the sun.

The dinner was excellent. The claret was warm and the champagne was cold, and under their beneficent influence the threatened unpleasantness melted and vanished with the fumes of the wine.

Mr. Pontellier warmed up and grew reminiscent. He told some amusing plantation experiences, recollections of old Iberville and his youth, when he hunted 'possum in company with some friendly darky; thrashed the pecan trees, shot the grosbec,[2] and roamed the woods and fields in mischievous idleness.

The Colonel, with little sense of humor and the fitness of things, related a somber episode of those dark and bitter days, in which he had acted a conspicuous part and always formed a central figure. Nor was the Doctor happier in his selection, when he told the old, ever new and curious story of the waning of a woman's love, seeking strange, new channels, only to return to its legitimate source after days of fierce unrest. It was one of the many little human documents which had been unfolded to him during his long career as a physician. The story did not seem especially to impress Edna. She had one of her own to tell, of a woman who paddled away with her lover one night in a pirogue and never came back. They were lost amid the Baratarian Islands, and no one ever heard of them or found trace of them from that day to this. It was a pure invention. She said that Madame Antoine had related it to her. That, also, was an invention.

[2]French: gross beak, the night heron, a game-bird with a large bill.

Perhaps it was a dream she had had. But every glowing word seemed real to those who listened. They could feel the hot breath of the Southern night; they could hear the long sweep of the pirogue through the glistening moonlit water, the beating of birds' wings, rising startled from among the reeds in the salt-water pools; they could see the faces of the lovers, pale, close together, rapt in oblivious forgetfulness, drifting into the unknown.

The champagne was cold, and its subtle fumes played fantastic tricks with Edna's memory that night.

Outside, away from the glow of the fire and the soft lamplight, the night was chill and murky. The Doctor doubled his old-fashioned cloak across his breast as he strode home through the darkness. He knew his fellow-creatures better than most men; knew that inner life which so seldom unfolds itself to unanointed eyes. He was sorry he had accepted Pontellier's invitation. He was growing old, and beginning to need rest and an imperturbed spirit. He did not want the secrets of other lives thrust upon him.

"I hope it isn't Arobin," he muttered to himself as he walked. "I hope to heaven it isn't Alcée Arobin."

XXIV

Edna and her father had a warm, and almost violent dispute upon the subject of her refusal to attend her sister's wedding. Mr. Pontellier declined to interfere, to interpose either his influence or his authority. He was following Doctor Mandelet's advice, and letting her do as she liked. The Colonel reproached his daughter for her lack of filial kindness and respect, her want of sisterly affection and womanly consideration. His arguments were labored and unconvincing. He doubted if Janet would accept any excuse—forgetting that Edna had offered none. He doubted if Janet would ever speak to her again, and he was sure Margaret would not.

Edna was glad to be rid of her father when he finally took himself off with his wedding garments and his bridal gifts, with his padded shoulders, his Bible reading, his "toddies" and ponderous oaths.

Mr. Pontellier followed him closely. He meant to stop at the wedding on his way to New York and endeavor by every means which money and love could devise to atone somewhat for Edna's incomprehensible action.

"You are too lenient, too lenient by far, Léonce," asserted the Colonel. "Authority, coercion are what is needed. Put your foot down good and hard; the only way to manage a wife. Take my word for it."

The Colonel was perhaps unaware that he had coerced his own wife into her grave. Mr. Pontellier had a vague suspicion of it which he thought it needless to mention at that late day.

Edna was not so consciously gratified at her husband's leaving home as she had been over the departure of her father. As the day approached when he was to leave her for a comparatively long stay, she grew melting and affectionate, remembering his many acts of consideration and his repeated expressions of an ardent attachment. She was solicitous about his health and his welfare. She bustled around, looking after his clothing, thinking about heavy underwear, quite as Madame Ratignolle would have done under similar circumstances. She cried when he went away, calling him her dear, good friend, and she was quite certain she would grow lonely before very long and go to join him in New York.

But after all, a radiant peace settled upon her when she at last found herself alone. Even the children were gone. Old Madame Pontellier had come herself and carried them off to Iberville with their quadroon. The old madame did not venture to say she was afraid they would be neglected during Léonce's absence; she hardly ventured to think so. She was hungry for them—even a little fierce in her attachment. She did not want them to be wholly "children of the pavement," she always said when begging to have them for a space. She wished them to know the country, with its streams, its fields, its woods, its freedom, so delicious to the young. She wished them to taste something of the life their father had lived and known and loved when he, too, was a little child.

When Edna was at last alone, she breathed a big, genuine sigh of relief. A feeling that was unfamiliar but very delicious came over her. She walked all through the house, from one room to another, as if inspecting it for the first time. She tried the various chairs and lounges, as if she had never sat and reclined upon them before. And she perambulated around the outside of the house, investigating, looking to see if windows and shutters were secure and in order. The flowers were like new acquaintances; she approached them in a familiar spirit, and made herself at home among them. The garden walks were damp, and Edna called to the maid to bring out her rubber sandals. And there she stayed, and stooped, digging around the plants, trimming, picking dead, dry leaves. The children's little dog came out, interfering, getting in her way. She scolded him, laughed at him, played with him. The garden smelled so good and looked so pretty in the afternoon sunlight. Edna plucked all the bright flowers she could find, and went into the house with them, she and the little dog.

Even the kitchen assumed a sudden interesting character which she had never before perceived. She went in to give directions to the cook, to say that the butcher would have to bring much less meat, that they would require only half their usual quantity of bread, of milk and groceries. She told the cook that she herself would be greatly occupied during Mr. Pontellier's absence, and she begged her to take all thought and responsibility of the larder upon her own shoulders.

That night Edna dined alone. The candelabra, with a few candles in the center of the table, gave all the light she needed. Outside the circle of light in which she sat, the large dining-room looked solemn and shadowy. The cook, placed upon her mettle, served a delicious repast—a luscious tenderloin broiled *à point*.[1] The wine tasted good; the *marron glacé*[2] seemed to be just what she wanted. It was so pleasant, too, to dine in a comfortable *peignoir*.

She thought a little sentimentally about Léonce and the children, and wondered what they were doing. As she gave a dainty scrap or two to the doggie, she talked intimately to him about Etienne and Raoul. He was beside himself with astonishment and delight over these companionable advances, and showed his appreciation by his little quick, snappy barks and a lively agitation.

Then Edna sat in the library after dinner and read Emerson[3] until she grew sleepy. She realized that she had neglected her reading, and determined to start anew upon a course of improving studies, now that her time was completely her own to do with as she liked.

After a refreshing bath, Edna went to bed. And as she snuggled comfortably beneath the eiderdown a sense of restfulness invaded her, such as she had not known before.

[1]French: to perfection.   [2]French: candied chestnuts.
[3]Ralph Waldo Emerson (1803–1882), whose essays emphasize the virtues of independence and individualism.

XXV

When the weather was dark and cloudy Edna could not work. She needed the sun to mellow and temper her mood to the sticking point. She had reached a stage when she seemed to be no longer feeling her way, working, when in the humor, with sureness and ease. And being devoid of ambition, and striving not toward accomplishment, she drew satisfaction from the work in itself.

On rainy or melancholy days Edna went out and sought the society of the friends she had made at Grand Isle. Or else she stayed indoors and nursed a mood with which she was becoming too familiar for her own comfort and peace of mind. It was not despair; but it seemed to her as if life were passing by, leaving its promise broken and unfulfilled. Yet there were other days when she listened, was led on and deceived by fresh promises which her youth held out to her.

She went again to the races, and again. Alcée Arobin and Mrs. Highcamp called for her one bright afternoon in Arobin's drag.[1] Mrs. Highcamp was a wordly but unaffected, intelligent, slim, tall blonde woman in the forties, with an indifferent manner and blue eyes that stared. She had a daughter who served her as a pretext for cultivating the society of young men of fashion. Alcée Arobin was one of them. He was a familiar figure at the race course, the opera, the fashionable clubs. There was a perpetual smile in his eyes, which seldom failed to awaken a corresponding cheerfulness in any one who looked into them and listened to his good-humored voice. His manner was quiet, and at times a little insolent. He possessed a good figure, a pleasing face, not overburdened with depth of thought or feeling; and his dress was that of the conventional man of fashion.

He admired Edna extravagantly, after meeting her at the races with her father. He had met her before on other occasions, but she had seemed to him unapproachable until that day. It was at his instigation that Mrs. Highcamp called to ask her to go with them to the Jockey Club[2] to witness the turf event of the season.

There were possibly a few track men out there who knew the race horse as well as Edna, but there was certainly none who knew it better. She sat between her two companions as one having authority to speak. She laughed at Arobin's pretensions, and deplored Mrs. Highcamp's ignorance. The race horse was a friend and intimate associate of her childhood. The atmosphere of the stables and the breath of the blue grass paddock revived in her memory and lingered in her nostrils. She did not perceive that she was talking like her father as the sleek geldings ambled in review before them. She played for very high stakes, and fortune favored her. The fever of the game flamed in her cheeks and eyes, and it got into her blood and into her brain like an intoxicant. People turned their heads to look at her, and more than one lent an attentive ear to her utterances, hoping thereby to secure the elusive but everdesired "tip." Arobin caught the contagion of excitement which drew him to Edna like a magnet. Mrs. Highcamp remained, as usual, unmoved, with her indifferent stare and uplifted eyebrows.

Edna stayed and dined with Mrs. Highcamp upon being urged to do so. Arobin also remained and sent away his drag.

The dinner was quiet and uninteresting, save for the cheerful efforts of Arobin to enliven things. Mrs. Highcamp deplored the absence of her daughter from the races, and tried to convey to her what she had missed by going to the "Dante

---

[1]A large coach with seats inside and on the roof.
[2]A social club for the rich and prominent.

reading"[3] instead of joining them. The girl held a geranium leaf up to her nose and said nothing, but looked knowing and noncommittal. Mr. Highcamp was a plain, bald-headed man, who only talked under compulsion. He was unresponsive. Mrs. Highcamp was full of delicate courtesy and consideration toward her husband. She addressed most of her conversation to him at table. They sat in the library after dinner and read the evening papers together under the droplight;[4] while the younger people went into the drawing-room near by and talked. Miss Highcamp played some selections from Grieg[5] upon the piano. She seemed to have apprehended all of the composer's coldness and none of his poetry. While Edna listened she could not help wondering if she had lost her taste for music.

When the time came for her to go home, Mr. Highcamp grunted a lame offer to escort her, looking down at his slippered feet with tactless concern. It was Arobin who took her home. The car ride was long, and it was late when they reached Esplanade Street. Arobin asked permission to enter for a second to light his cigarette—his match safe[6] was empty. He filled his match safe, but did not light his cigarette until he left her, after she had expressed her willingness to go to the races with him again.

Edna was neither tired nor sleepy. She was hungry again, for the Highcamp dinner, though of excellent quality, had lacked abundance. She rummaged in the larder and brought forth a slice of Gruyère[7] and some crackers. She opened a bottle of beer which she found in the icebox. Edna felt extremely restless and excited. She vacantly hummed a fantastic tune as she poked at the wood embers on the hearth and munched a cracker.

She wanted something to happen—something, anything; she did not know what. She regretted that she had not made Arobin stay a half hour to talk over the horses with her. She counted the money she had won. But there was nothing else to do, so she went to bed, and tossed there for hours in a sort of monotonous agitation.

In the middle of the night she remembered that she had forgotten to write her regular letter to her husband; and she decided to do so next day and tell him about her afternoon at the Jockey Club. She lay wide awake composing a letter which was nothing like the one which she wrote next day. When the maid awoke her in the morning Edna was dreaming of Mr. Highcamp playing the piano at the entrance of a music store on Canal Street, while his wife was saying to Alcée Arobin, as they boarded an Esplanade Street car:

"What a pity that so much talent has been neglected! but I must go."

When, a few days later, Alcée Arobin again called for Edna in his drag, Mrs. Highcamp was not with him. He said they would pick her up. But as that lady had not been apprised of his intention of picking her up, she was not at home. The daughter was just leaving the house to attend the meeting of a branch Folk Lore Society, and regretted that she could not accompany them. Arobin appeared nonplused, and asked Edna if there were any one else she cared to ask.

She did not deem it worth while to go in search of any of the fashionable acquaintances from whom she had withdrawn herself. She thought of Madame Ratignolle, but knew that her fair friend did not leave the house, except to take a languid walk around the block with her husband after nightfall. Mademoiselle Reisz would have laughed at such a request from Edna. Madame Lebrun might

---

[3] A group reading of works by Dante Alighieri (1265–1321), Italian author of *The Divine Comedy*.
[4] A lamp that can be lowered or raised to control the light.
[5] Edvard Grieg (1843–1907), Norwegian composer.
[6] Fireproof container for matches.   [7] Cheese from Gruyère, Switzerland.

have enjoyed the outing, but for some reason Edna did not want her. So they went alone, she and Arobin.

The afternoon was intensely interesting to her. The excitement came back upon her like a remittent fever. Her talk grew familiar and confidential. It was no labor to become intimate with Arobin. His manner invited easy confidence. The preliminary stage of becoming acquainted was one which he always endeavored to ignore when a pretty and engaging woman was concerned.

He stayed and dined with Edna. He stayed and sat beside the wood fire. They laughed and talked; and before it was time to go he was telling her how different life might have been if he had known her years before. With ingenuous frankness he spoke of what a wicked, ill-disciplined boy he had been, and impulsively drew up his cuff to exhibit upon his wrist the scar from a saber cut which he had received in a duel outside of Paris when he was nineteen. She touched his hand as she scanned the red cicatrice[8] on the inside of his white wrist. A quick impulse that was somewhat spasmodic impelled her fingers to close in a sort of clutch upon his hand. He felt the pressure of her pointed nails in the flesh of his palm.

She arose hastily and walked toward the mantel.

"The sight of a wound or scar always agitates and sickens me," she said. "I shouldn't have looked at it."

"I beg your pardon," he entreated, following her; "it never occurred to me that it might be repulsive."

He stood close to her, and the effrontery in his eyes repelled the old, vanishing self in her, yet drew all her awakening sensuousness. He saw enough in her face to impel him to take her hand and hold it while he said his lingering good night.

"Will you go to the races again?" he asked.

"No," she said. "I've had enough of the races. I don't want to lose all the money I've won, and I've got to work when the weather is bright, instead of—"

"Yes; work; to be sure. You promised to show me your work. What morning may I come up to your atelier? To-morrow?"

"No!"

"Day after?"

"No, no."

"Oh, please don't refuse me! I know something of such things. I might help you with a stray suggestion or two."

"No, Good night. Why don't you go after you have said good night? I don't like you," she went on in a high, excited pitch, attempting to draw away her hand. She felt that her words lacked dignity and sincerity, and she knew that he felt it.

"I'm sorry you don't like me. I'm sorry I offended you. How have I offended you? What have I done? Can't you forgive me?" And he bent and pressed his lips upon her hand as if he wished never more to withdraw them.

"Mr. Arobin," she complained, "I'm greatly upset by the excitement of the afternoon; I'm not myself. My manner must have misled you in some way. I wish you to go, please." She spoke in a monotonous, dull tone. He took his hat from the table, and stood with eyes turned from her, looking into the dying fire. For a moment or two he kept an impressive silence.

"Your manner has not misled me, Mrs. Pontellier," he said finally. "My own emotions have done that. I couldn't help it. When I'm near you, how could I help it? Don't think anything of it, don't bother, please. You see, I go when you

_____
[8]Scar.

command me. If you wish me to stay away, I shall do so. If you let me come back, I—oh! you will let me come back?"

He cast one appealing glance at her, to which she made no response. Alcée Arobin's manner was so genuine that it often deceived even himself.

Edna did not care or think whether it were genuine or not. When she was alone she looked mechanically at the back of her hand which he had kissed so warmly. Then she leaned her head down on the mantelpiece. She felt somewhat like a woman who in a moment of passion is betrayed into an act of infidelity, and realizes the significance of the act without being wholly awakened from its glamour. The thought was passing vaguely through her mind, "What would he think?"

She did not mean her husband; she was thinking of Robert Lebrun. Her husband seemed to her now like a person whom she had married without love as an excuse.

She lit a candle and went up to her room. Alcée Arobin was absolutely nothing to her. Yet his presence, his manners, the warmth of his glances, and above all the touch of his lips upon her hand had acted like a narcotic upon her.

She slept a languorous sleep, interwoven with vanishing dreams.

XXVI

Alcée Arobin wrote Edna an elaborate note of apology, palpitant with sincerity. It embarrassed her; for in a cooler, quieter moment it appeared to her absurd that she should have taken his action so seriously, so dramatically. She felt sure that the significance of the whole occurrence had lain in her own self-consciousness. If she ignored his note it would give undue importance to a trivial affair. If she replied to it in a serious spirit it would still leave in his mind the impression that she had in a susceptible moment yielded to his influence. After all, it was no great matter to have one's hand kissed. She was provoked at his having written the apology. She answered in as light and bantering a spirit as she fancied it deserved, and she said would be glad to have him look in upon her at work whenever he felt the inclination and his business gave him the opportunity.

He responded at once by presenting himself at her home with all his disarming naïveté. And then there was scarcely a day which followed that she did not see him or was not reminded of him. He was prolific in pretexts. His attitude became one of good-humored subservience and tacit adoration. He was ready at all times to submit to her moods, which were as often kind as they were cold. She grew accustomed to him. They became intimate and friendly by imperceptible degrees, and then by leaps. He sometimes talked in a way that astonished her at first and brought the crimson into her face; in a way that pleased her at last, appealing to the animalism that stirred impatiently within her.

There was nothing which so quieted the turmoil of Edna's senses as a visit to Mademoiselle Reisz. It was then, in the presence of that personality which was offensive to her, that the woman, by her divine art, seemed to reach Edna's spirit and set it free.

It was misty, with heavy, lowering atmosphere, one afternoon, when Edna climbed the stairs to the pianist's apartments under the roof. Her clothes were dripping with moisture. She felt chilled and pinched as she entered the room. Mademoiselle was poking at a rusty stove that smoked a little and warmed the room indifferently. She was endeavoring to heat a pot of chocolate on the stove.

The room looked cheerless and dingy to Edna as she entered. A bust of Beethoven, covered with a hood of dust, scowled at her from the mantelpiece.

"Ah! here comes the sunlight!" exclaimed Mademoiselle, rising from her knees before the stove. "Now it will be warm and bright enough; I can let the fire alone."

She closed the stove door with a bang, and approaching, assisted in removing Edna's dripping mackintosh.

"You are cold; you look miserable. The chocolate will soon be hot. But would you rather have a taste of brandy? I have scarcely touched the bottle which you brought me for my cold." A piece of red flannel was wrapped around Mademoiselle's throat; a stiff neck compelled her to hold her head on one side.

"I will take some brandy," said Edna, shivering as she removed her gloves and overshoes. She drank the liquor from the glass as a man would have done. Then flinging herself upon the uncomfortable sofa she said, "Mademoiselle, I am going to move away from my house on Esplanade Street."

"Ah!" ejaculated the musician, neither surprised nor especially interested. Nothing ever seemed to astonish her very much. She was endeavoring to adjust the bunch of violets which had become loose from its fastening in her hair. Edna drew her down upon the sofa, and taking a pin from her own hair, secured the shabby artificial flowers in their accustomed place.

"Aren't you astonished?"

"Passably. Where are you going? to New York? to Iberville? to your father in Mississippi? where?"

"Just two steps away," laughed Edna, "in a little four-room house around the corner. It looks so cozy, so inviting and restful, whenever I pass by; and it's for rent. I'm tired looking after that big house. It never seemed like mine, anyway— like home. It's too much trouble. I have to keep too many servants. I am tired bothering with them."

"That is not your true reason, *ma belle*.[1] There is no use in telling me lies. I don't know your reason, but you have not told me the truth." Edna did not protest or endeavor to justify herself.

"The house, the money that provides for it, are not mine. Isn't that enough reason?"

"They are your husband's," returned Mademoiselle, with a shrug and a malicious elevation of the eyebrows.

"Oh! I see there is no deceiving you. Then let me tell you: It is a caprice. I have a little money of my own from my mother's estate, which my father sends me by driblets. I won a large sum this winter on the races, and I am beginning to sell my sketches. Laidpore is more and more pleased with my work; he says it grows in force and individuality. I cannot judge that myself, but I feel that I have gained in ease and confidence. However, as I said, I have sold a good many through Laidpore. I can live in the tiny house for little or nothing, with one servant. Old Celestine, who works occasionally for me, says she will come stay with me and do my work. I know I shall like it, like the feeling of freedom and independence."

"What does your husband say?"

"I have not told him yet. I only thought of it this morning. He will think I am demented, no doubt. Perhaps you think so."

Mademoiselle shook her head slowly. "Your reason is not yet clear to me," she said.

---

[1] French: "my beauty."

Neither was it quite clear to Edna herself; but it unfolded itself as she sat for a while in silence. Instinct had prompted her to put away her husband's bounty in casting off her allegiance. She did not know how it would be when he returned. There would have to be an understanding, an explanation. Conditions would some way adjust themselves, she felt; but whatever came, she had resolved never again to belong to another than herself.

"I shall give a grand dinner before I leave the old house!" Edna exclaimed. "You will have to come to it, Mademoiselle. I will give you everything that you like to eat and drink. We shall sing and laugh and be merry for once." And she uttered a sigh that came from the very depths of her being.

If Mademoiselle happened to have received a letter from Robert during the interval of Edna's visits, she would give her the letter unsolicited. And she would seat herself at the piano and play as her humor prompted her while the young woman read the letter.

The little stove was roaring; it was red-hot, and the chocolate in the tin sizzled and sputtered. Edna went forward and opened the stove door, and Mademoiselle rising, took a letter from under the bust of Beethoven and handed it to Edna.

"Another! so soon!" she exclaimed, her eyes filled with delight. "Tell me, Mademoiselle, does he know that I see his letters?"

"Never in the world! He would be angry and would never write to me again if he thought so. Does he write to you? Never a line. Does he send you a message? Never a word. It is because he loves you, poor fool, and is trying to forget you, since you are not free to listen to him or to belong to him."

"Why do you show me his letters, then?"

"Haven't you begged for them? Can I refuse you anything? Oh! you cannot deceive me," and Mademoiselle approached her beloved instrument and began to play. Edna did not at once read the letter. She sat holding it in her hand, while the music penetrated her whole being like an effulgence, warming and frightening the dark places of her soul. It prepared her for joy and exultation.

"Oh!" she exclaimed, letting the letter fall to the floor. "Why did you not tell me?" She went and grasped Mademoiselle's hands up from the keys. "Oh! unkind! malicious! Why did you not tell me?"

"That he was coming back? No great news, *ma foi*.[2] I wonder he did not come long ago." "But when, when?" cried Edna, impatiently. "He does not say when."

"He says 'very soon.' You know as much about it as I do; it is all in the letter."

"But why? Why is he coming? Oh, if I thought—" and she snatched the letter from the floor and turned the pages this way and that way, looking for the reason, which was left untold.

"If I were young and in love with a man," said Mademoiselle, turning on the stool and pressing her wiry hands between her knees as she looked down at Edna, who sat on the floor holding the letter, "it seems to me he would have to be some *grand espirit*;[3] a man with lofty aims and ability to reach them; one who stood high enough to attract the notice of his fellow-men. It seems to me if I were young and in love I should never deem a man of ordinary caliber worthy of my devotion."

"Now it is you who are telling lies and seeking to deceive me, Mademoiselle; or else you have never been in love, and know nothing about it. Why," went on Edna, clasping her knees and looking up into Mademoiselle's twisted face, "do you suppose a woman knows why she loves? Does she select? Does she say to herself: 'Go to! Here is a distinguised statesman with presidential possibilities;

[2]French: "to be sure."   [3]French: "great soul."

I shall proceed to fall in love with him.' Or, 'I shall set my heart upon this musician, whose fame is on every tongue?' Or, 'This financier, who controls the world's money markets?' "

"You are purposely misunderstanding me, *ma reine*.[4] Are you in love with Robert?"

"Yes," said Edna. It was the first time she had admitted it, and a glow overspread her face, blotching it with red spots.

"Why?" asked her companion, "Why do you love him when you ought not to?"

Edna, with a motion or two, dragged herself on her knees before Madomoiselle Reisz, who took the glowing face between her two hands.

"Why? Because his hair is brown and grows away from his temples; because he opens and shuts his eyes, and his nose is a little out of drawing; because he has two lips and a square chin, and a little finger which he can't straighten from having played baseball too energetically in his youth. Because—"

"Because you do, in short," laughed Mademoiselle. "What will you do when he comes back?" she asked.

"Do? Nothing, except feel glad and happy to be alive."

She was already glad and happy to be alive at the mere thought of his return. The murky, lowering sky, which had depressed her a few hours before, seemed bracing and invigorating as she splashed through the streets on her way home.

She stopped at a confectioner's and ordered a huge box of bonbons for the children in Iberville. She slipped a card in the box, on which she scribbled a tender message and sent an abundance of kisses.

Before dinner in the evening Edna wrote a charming letter to her husband, telling him of her intention to move for a while into the little house around the block, and to give a farewell dinner before leaving, regretting that he was not there to share it, to help her out with the menu and assist her in entertaining the guests. Her letter was brilliant and brimming with cheerfulness.

XXVII

"What is the matter with you?" asked Arobin that evening. "I never found you in such a happy mood." Edna was tired by that time, and was reclining on the lounge before the fire.

"Don't you know the weather prophet has told us we shall see the sun pretty soon?"

"Well, that ought to be reason enough," he acquiesced. "You wouldn't give me another if I sat here all night imploring you." He sat close to her on a low tabouret,[1] and as he spoke his fingers lightly touched the hair that fell a little over her forehead. She liked the touch of his fingers through her hair, and closed her eyes sensitively.

"One of these days," she said, "I'm going to pull myself together for a while and think—try to determine what character of a woman I am; for, candidly, I don't know. By all the codes which I am acquainted with, I am a devilishly wicked specimen of the sex.[2] But some way I can't convince myself that I am. I must think about it."

"Don't. What's the use? Why should you bother thinking about it when I can

[4]French: "my dear."
[1]A seat without arms or back.   [2]I.e., the female sex.

tell you what manner of woman you are." His fingers strayed occasionally down to her warm, smooth cheeks and firm chin, which was growing a little full and double.

"Oh, yes! You will tell me that I am adorable; everything that is captivating. Spare yourself the effort."

"No; I shan't tell you anything of the sort, though I shouldn't be lying if I did."

"Do you know Mademoiselle Reisz?" she asked irrelevantly.

"The pianist? I know her by sight. I've heard her play."

"She says queer things sometimes in a bantering way that you don't notice at the time and you find yourself thinking about afterward."

"For instance?"

"Well, for instance, when I left her to-day, she put her arms around me and felt my shoulder blades, to see if my wings were strong, she said. 'The bird that would soar above the level plain of tradition and prejudice must have strong wings. It is a sad spectacle to see the weaklings bruised, exhausted, fluttering back to earth.' "

"Whither would you soar?"

"I'm not thinking of any extraordinary flights. I only half comprehend her."

"I've heard she's partially demented," said Arobin.

"She seems to me wonderfully sane," Edna replied.

"I'm told she's extremely disagreeable and unpleasant. Why have you introduced her at a moment when I desired to talk of you?"

"Oh! talk of me if you like," cried Edna, clasping her hands beneath her head; "but let me think of something else while you do."

"I'm jealous of your thoughts to-night. They're making you a little kinder than usual; but some way I feel as if they were wandering, as if they were not here with me." She only looked at him and smiled. His eyes were very near. He leaned upon the lounge with an arm extended across her, while the other hand still rested upon her hair. They continued silently to look into each other's eyes. When he leaned forward and kissed her, she clasped his head, holding his lips to hers.

It was the first kiss of her life to which her nature had really responded. It was a flaming torch that kindled desire.

XXVIII

Edna cried a little that night after Arobin left her. It was only one phase of the multitudinous emotions which had assailed her. There was with her an overwhelming feeling of irresponsibility. There was the shock of the unexpected and the unaccustomed. There was her husband's reproach looking at her from the external things around her which he had provided for her external existence. There was Robert's reproach making itself felt by a quicker, fiercer, more overpowering love, which had awakened within her toward him. Above all, there was understanding. She felt as if a mist had been lifted from her eyes, enabling her to look upon and comprehend the significance of life, that monster made up of beauty and brutality. But among the conflicting sensations which assailed her, there was neither shame nor remorse. There was a dull pang of regret because it was not the kiss of love which had inflamed her, because it was not love which had held this cup of life to her lips.

XXIX

Without even waiting for an answer from her husband regarding his opinion or wishes in the matter, Edna hastened her preparations for quitting her home on Esplanade Street and moving into the little house around the block. A feverish anxiety attended her every action in that direction. There was no moment of deliberation, no interval of repose between the thought and its fulfillment. Early upon the morning following those hours passed in Arobin's society, Edna set about securing her new abode and hurrying her arrangements for occupying it. Within the precincts of her home she felt like one who has entered and lingered within the portals of some forbidden temple in which a thousand muffled voices bade her begone.

Whatever was her own in this house, everything which she had acquired aside from her husband's bounty, she caused to be transported to the other house, supplying simple and meager deficiences from her own resources.

Arobin found her with rolled sleeves, working in company with the housemaid when he looked in during the afternoon. She was splendid and robust, and had never appeared handsomer than in the old blue gown, with a red silk handker-chief knotted at random around her head to protect her hair from the dust. She was mounted upon a high step-ladder, unhooking a picture from the wall when he entered. He had found the front door open, and had followed his ring by walking in unceremoniously.

"Come down!" he said. "Do you want to kill yourself?" She greeted him with affected carelessness, and appeared absorbed in her occupation.

If he had expected to find her languishing, reproachful, or indulging in sentimental tears, he must have been greatly surprised.

He was no doubt prepared for any emergency, ready for any one of the foregoing attitudes, just as he bent himself easily and naturally to the situation which confronted him.

"No," she answered; "Ellen is afraid to mount the ladder. Joe is working over at the 'pigeon house'—that's the name Ellen gives it, because it's so small and looks like a pigeon house—and some one has to do this."

Arobin pulled off his coat, and expressed himself ready and willing to tempt fate in her place. Ellen brought him one of her dust-caps, and went into contortions of mirth, which she found it impossible to control, when she saw him put it on before the mirror as grotesquely as he could. Edna herself could not refrain from smiling when she fastened it at his request. So it was he who in turn mounted the ladder, unhooking pictures and curtains, and dislodging ornaments as Edna directed. When he had finished he took off his dust-cap and went out to wash his hands.

Edna was sitting on the tabouret, idly brushing the tips of a feather duster along the carpet when he came in again.

"Is there anything more you will let me do?" he asked.

"That is all," she answered. "Ellen can manage the rest." She kept the young woman occupied in the drawing-room, unwilling to be left alone with Arobin.

"What about the dinner?" he asked; "the grand event, the *coup d'état?*"[1]

"It will be day after to-morrow. Why do you call it the *'coup d'état?'* Oh! it will be very fine; all my best of everything—crystal, silver and gold, Sèvres, flowers, music, and champagne to swim in. I'll let Léonce pay the bills. I wonder what he'll say when he sees the bills."

---

[1] French: "a sudden, decisive effort," "a masterstroke."

"And you ask me why I call it a *coup d'état?*" Arobin had put on his coat, and he stood before her and asked if his cravat was plumb. She told him it was, looking no higher than the tip of his collar.

"When do you go to the 'pigeon house?'—with all due acknowledgement to Ellen."

"Day after to-morrow, after the dinner. I shall sleep there."

"Ellen, will you very kindly get me a glass of water?" asked Arobin. "The dust in the curtains, if you will pardon me for hinting such a thing, has parched my throat to a crisp."

"While Ellen gets the water," said Edna, rising, "I will say good-by and let you go. I must get rid of this grime, and I have a million things to do and think of."

"When shall I see you?" asked Arobin, seeking to detain her, the maid having left the room.

"At the dinner, of course. You are invited."

"Not before?—not to-night or to-morrow morning or to-morrow noon or night? Or the day after morning or noon? Can't you see yourself, without my telling you, what an eternity it is?"

He had followed her into the hall and to the foot of the stairway, looking up at her as she mounted with her face half turned to him.

"Not an instant sooner," she said. But she laughed and looked at him with eyes that at once gave him courage to wait and made it torture to wait.

XXX

Though Edna had spoken of the dinner as a very grand affair, it was in truth a very small affair and very select, in so much as the guests invited were few and were selected with discrimination. She had counted upon an even dozen seating themselves at her round mahogany board, forgetting for the moment that Madame Ratignolle was to the last degree *souffrante*[1] and unpresentable, and not foreseeing that Madame Lebrun would send a thousand regrets at the last moment. So there were only ten, after all, which made a cozy, comfortable number.

There were Mr. and Mrs. Merriman, a pretty, vivacious little woman in the thirties; her husband, a jovial fellow, something of a shallow-pate, who laughed a good deal at other people's witticisms, and had thereby made himself extremely popular. Mrs. Highcamp had accompanied them. Of course, there was Alcée Arobin; and Mademoiselle Reisz had consented to come. Edna had sent her a fresh bunch of violets with black lace trimmings for her hair. Monsieur Ratignolle brought himself and his wife's excuses. Victor Lebrun, who happened to be in the city, bent upon relaxation, had accepted with alacrity. There was a Miss Mayblunt, no longer in her teens, who looked at the world through lorgnettes and with the keenest interest. It was thought and said that she was intellectual; it was suspected of her that she wrote under a *nom de guerre*.[2] She had come with a gentleman by the name of Gouvernail, connected with one of the daily papers, of whom nothing special could be said, except that he was observant and seemed quiet and inoffensive. Edna herself made the tenth, and at half-past eight they seated themselves at table, Arobin and Monsieur Ratignolle on either side of their hostess.

[1]French: ill.   [2]French: fictitious name.

Mrs. Highcamp sat between Arobin and Victor Lebrun. Then came Mrs. Merriman, Mr. Gouvernail, Miss Mayblunt, Mr. Merriman, and Mademoiselle Reisz next to Monsieur Ratignolle.

There was something extremely gorgeous about the appearance of the table, an effect of splendor conveyed by a cover of pale yellow satin under strips of lace-work. There were wax candles in massive brass candelabra, burning softly under yellow silk shades; full, fragrant roses, yellow and red, abounded. There were silver and gold, as she had said there would be, and crystal which glittered like the gems which the women wore.

The ordinary stiff dining chairs had been discarded for the occasion and replaced by the most commodious and luxurious which could be collected throughout the house. Mademoiselle Reisz, being exceedingly diminutive, was elevated upon cushions, as small children are sometimes hoisted at table upon bulky volumes.

"Something new, Edna?" exclaimed Miss Mayblunt, with lorgnette directed toward a magnificent cluster of diamonds that sparkled, that almost sputtered, in Edna's hair, just over the center of her forehead.

"Quite new; 'brand' new, in fact; a present from my husband. It arrived this morning from New York. I may as well admit that this is my birthday, and that I am twenty-nine. In good time I expect you to drink my health. Meanwhile, I shall ask you to begin with this cocktail, composed—would you say 'composed?' " with an appeal to Miss Mayblunt—"composed by my father in honor of Sister Janet's wedding."

Before each guest stood a tiny glass that looked and sparkled like a garnet gem.

"Then, all things considered," spoke Arobin, "it might not be amiss to start out by drinking the Colonel's health in the cocktail which he composed, on the birthday of the most charming of women—the daughter whom he invented."

Mr. Merriman's laugh at this sally was such a genuine outburst and so contagious that it started the dinner with an agreeable swing that never slackened.

Miss Mayblunt begged to be allowed to keep her cocktail untouched before her, just to look at. The color was marvelous! She could compare it to nothing she had ever seen, and the garnet lights which it emitted were unspeakably rare. She pronounced the Colonel an artist, and stuck to it.

Monsieur Ratignolle was prepared to take things seriously: the *mets*, the *entre-mets*,[3] the service, the decorations, even the people. He looked up from his pompano[4] and inquired of Arobin if he were related to the gentleman of that name who formed one of the firm of Laitner and Arobin, lawyers. The young man admitted that Laitner was a warm personal friend, who permitted Arobin's name to decorate the firm's letterheads and to appear upon a shingle that graced Perdido Street.

"There are so many inquisitive people and institutions abounding," said Arobin, "that one is really forced as a matter of convenience these days to assume the virtue of an occupation if he has it not."

Monsieur Ratignolle stared a little, and turned to ask Mademoiselle Reisz if she considered the symphony concerts up to the standard which had been set the previous winter. Mademoiselle Reisz answered Monsieur Ratignolle in French, which Edna thought a little rude, under the circumstances, but characteristic. Mademoiselle had only disagreeable things to say of the symphony concerts, and insulting remarks to make of all the musicians of New Orleans,

[3]French: the main dish, the side dishes.
[4]A variety of fish found in the Gulf of Mexico, one of the most delicious of all food fishes.

singly and collectively. All her interest seemed to be centered upon the delicacies placed before her.

Mr. Merriman said that Mr. Arobin's remark about inquisitive people reminded him of a man from Waco[5] the other day at the St. Charles Hotel—but as Mr. Merriman's stories were always lame and lacking point, his wife seldom permitted him to complete them. She interrupted him to ask if he remembered the name of the author whose book she had bought the week before to send to a friend in Geneva. She was talking "books" with Mr. Gouvernail and trying to draw from him his opinion upon current literary topics. Her husband told the story of the Waco man privately to Miss Mayblunt, who pretended to be greatly amused and to think it extremely clever.

Mrs. Highcamp hung with languid but unaffected interest upon the warm and impetuous volubility of her left-hand neighbor, Victor Lebrun. Her attention was never for a moment withdrawn from him after seating herself at table; and when he turned to Mrs. Merriman, who was prettier and more vivacious than Mrs. Highcamp, she waited with easy indifference for an opportunity to reclaim his attention. There was the occasional sound of music, of mandolins, sufficiently removed to be an agreeable accompaniment rather than an interruption to the conversation. Outside the soft, monotonous splash of a fountain could be heard; the sound penetrated into the room with the heavy odor of jessamine that came through the open windows.

The golden shimmer of Edna's satin gown spread in rich folds on either side of her. There was a soft fall of lace encircling her shoulders. It was the color of her skin, without the glow, the myriad living tints that one may sometimes discover in vibrant flesh. There was something in her attitude, in her whole appearance when she leaned her head against the high-backed chair and spread her arms, which suggested the regal woman, the one who rules, who looks on, who stands alone.

But as she sat there amid her guests, she felt the old ennui overtaking her; the hopelessness which so often assailed her, which came upon her like an obsession, like something extraneous, independent of volition. It was something which announced itself; a chill breath that seemed to issue from some vast cavern wherein discords wailed. There came over her the acute longing which always summoned into her spiritual vision the presence of the beloved one, overpowering her at once with a sense of the unattainable.

The moments glided on, while a feeling of good fellowship passed around the circle like a mystic cord, holding and binding these people together with jest and laughter. Monsieur Ratignolle was the first to break the pleasant charm. At ten o'clock he excused himself. Madame Ratignolle was waiting for him at home. She was *bien souffrante*,[6] and she was filled with vague dread, which only her husband's presence could allay.

Mademoiselle Reisz arose with Monsieur Ratignolle, who offered to escort her to the car. She had eaten well; she had tasted the good, rich wines, and they must have turned her head, for she bowed pleasantly to all as she withdrew from table. She kissed Edna upon the shoulder, and whispered: *"Bonne nuit, ma reine; soyez sage."*[7] She had been a little bewildered upon rising, or rather, descending from her cushions, and Monsieur Ratignolle gallantly took her arm and led her away.

Mrs. Highcamp was weaving a garland of roses, yellow and red. When she had finished the garland, she laid it lightly upon Victor's black curls. He was

[5]Waco, Texas.   [6]French: quite ill.   [7]French: "Good night, my dear; be good."

reclining far back in the luxurious chair, holding a glass of champagne to the light.

As if a magician's wand had touched him, the garland of roses transformed him into a vision of Oriental beauty. His cheeks were the color of crushed grapes, and his dusky eyes glowed with a languishing fire.

"*Sapristi!*" exclaimed Arobin.

But Mrs. Highcamp had one more touch to add to the picture. She took from the back of her chair a white silken scarf, with which she had covered her shoulders in the early part of the evening. She draped it across the boy in graceful folds, and in a way to conceal his black, conventional evening dress. He did not seem to mind what she did to him, only smiled showing a faint gleam of white teeth, while he continued to gaze with narrowing eyes at the light through his glass of champagne.

"Oh! to be able to paint in color rather than in words!" exclaimed Miss Mayblunt, losing herself in a rhapsodic dream as she looked at him.

> " 'There was a graven image of Desire
> Painted with red blood on a ground of gold.' "[8]

murmured Gouvernail, under his breath.

The effect of the wine upon Victor was to change his accustomed volubility into silence. He seemed to have abandoned himself to a reverie, and to be seeing pleasing visions in the amber bead.

"Sing," entreated Mrs. Highcamp. "Won't you sing to us?"

"Let him alone," said Arobin.

"He's posing," offered Mr. Merriman; "let him have it out."

"I believe he's paralyzed," laughed Mrs. Merriman. And leaning over the youth's chair, she took the glass from his hand and held it to his lips. He sipped the wine slowly, and when he had drained the glass she laid it upon the table and wiped his lips with her little filmy handkerchief.

"Yes, I'll sing for you," he said, turning in his chair toward Mrs. Highcamp. He clasped his hands behind his head, and looking up at the ceiling began to hum a little, trying his voice like a musician tuning an instrument. Then, looking at Edna, he began to sing:

> "Ah! si tu savais!"

"Stop!" she cried, "don't sing that. I don't want you to sing it," and she laid her glass so impetuously and blindly upon the table as to shatter it against a caraffee. The wine spilled over Arobin's legs and some of it trickled down upon Mrs. Highcamp's black gauze gown. Victor had lost all idea of courtesy, or else he thought his hostess was not in earnest, for he laughed and went on:

> "Ah! si tu savais
> Ce que tes yeux me disent"—[9]

"Oh! you mustn't! you mustn't," exclaimed Edna, and pushing back her chair she got up, and going behind him placed her hand over his mouth. He kissed the soft palm that pressed upon his lips.

"No, no, I won't, Mrs. Pontellier. I didn't know you meant it," looking up at

---

[8]From the sonnet "A Cameo," by Algernon Charles Swinburne (1837–1909).
[9]French: "Ah! Couldst thou but know/What thine eyes tell me"—

her with caressing eyes. The touch of his lips was like a pleasing sting to her hand. She lifted the garland of roses from his head and flung it across the room.

"Come, Victor; you've posed long enough. Give Mrs. Highcamp her scarf."

Mrs. Highcamp undraped the scarf from about him with her own hands. Miss Mayblunt and Mr. Gouvernail suddenly conceived the notion that it was time to say good night. And Mr. and Mrs. Merriman wondered how it could be so late.

Before parting from Victor, Mrs. Highcamp invited him to call upon her daughter, who she knew would be charmed to meet him and talk French and sing French songs with him. Victor expressed his desire and intention to call upon Miss Highcamp at the first opportunity which presented itself. He asked if Arobin were going his way. Arobin was not.

The mandolin players had long since stolen away. A profound stillness had fallen upon the broad, beautiful street. The voices of Edna's disbanding guests jarred like a discordant note upon the quiet harmony of the night.

XXXI

"Well?" questioned Arobin, who had remained with Edna after the others had departed.

"Well," she reiterated, and stood up, stretching her arms, and feeling the need to relax her muscles after having been so long seated.

"What next?" he asked.

"The servants are all gone. They left when the musicians did. I have dismissed them. The house has to be closed and locked, and I shall trot around to the pigeon house, and shall send Celestine over in the morning to straighten things up."

He looked around, and began to turn out some of the lights.

"What about upstairs?" he inquired.

"I think it is all right; but there may be a window or two unlatched. We had better look; you might take a candle and see. And bring me my wrap and hat on the foot of the bed in the middle room."

He went up with the light, and Edna began closing doors and windows. She hated to shut in the smoke and the fumes of the wine. Arobin found her cape and hat, which he brought down and helped her to put on.

When everything was secured and the lights put out, they left through the front door, Arobin locking it and taking the key, which he carried for Edna. He helped her down the steps.

"Will you have a spray of jessamine?" he asked, breaking off a few blossoms as he passed.

"No; I don't want anything."

She seemed disheartened, and had nothing to say. She took his arm, which he offered her, holding up the weight of her satin train with the other hand. She looked down, noticing the black line of his leg moving in and out so close to her against the yellow shimmer of her gown. There was the whistle of a railway train somewhere in the distance, and the midnight bells were ringing. They met no one in their short walk.

The "pigeon-house" stood behind a locked gate, and a shallow *parterre*[1] that had been somewhat neglected. There was a small front porch, upon which a

[1]French: garden.

long window and the front door opened. The door opened directly into the parlor; there was no side entry. Back in the yard was a room for servants, in which old Celestine had been ensconced.

Edna had left a lamp burning low upon the table. She had succeeded in making the room look habitable and homelike. There were some books on the table and a lounge near at hand. On the floor was a fresh matting, covered with a rug or two; and on the walls hung a few tasteful pictures. But the room was filled with flowers. These were a surprise to her. Arobin had sent them, and had had Celestine distribute then during Edna's absence. Her bedroom was adjoining, and across a small passage were the dining-room and kitchen.

Edna seated herself with every appearance of discomfort.

"Are you tired?" he asked.

"Yes, and chilled, and miserable. I feel as if I had been wound up to a certain pitch—too tight—and something inside of me had snapped."

She rested her head against the table upon her bare arm.

"You want to rest," he said, "and to be quiet. I'll go; I'll leave you and let you rest."

"Yes," she replied.

He stood up beside her and smoothed her hair with his soft, magnetic hand. His touch conveyed to her a certain physical comfort. She could have fallen quietly asleep there if he had continued to pass his hand over her hair. He brushed the hair upward from the nape of her neck.

"I hope you will feel better and happier in the morning," he said. "You have tried to do too much in the past few days. The dinner was the last straw; you might have dispensed with it."

"Yes," she admitted; "it was stupid."

"No, it was delightful; but it has worn you out." His hand strayed to her beautiful shoulders, and he could feel the response of her flesh to his touch. He seated himself beside her and kissed her lightly upon the shoulder.

"I thought you were going away," she said, in an uneven voice.

"I am, after I have said good night."

"Good night," she murmured.

He did not answer, except to continue to caress her. He did not say good night until she had become supple to his gentle, seductive entreaties.

XXXII

When Mr. Pontellier learned of his wife's intention to abandon her home and take up her residence elsewhere he immediately wrote her a letter of unqualified disapproval and remonstrance. She had given reasons which he was unwilling to acknowledge as adequate. He hoped she had not acted upon her rash impulse; and he begged her to consider first, foremost, and above all else, what people would say. He was not dreaming of scandal when he uttered this warning; that was a thing which would never have entered into his mind to consider in connection with his wife's name or his own. He was simply thinking of his financial integrity. It might get noised about that the Pontelliers had met with reverses, and were forced to conduct their *ménage*[1] on a humbler scale than heretofore. It might do incalculable mischief to his business prospects.

But remembering Edna's whimsical turn of mind of late, and foreseeing that

[1]French: household.

she had immediately acted upon her impetuous determination, he grasped the situation with his usual promptness and handled it with his well-known business tact and cleverness.

The same mail which brought to Edna his letter of disapproval carried instructions—the most minute instructions—to a well-known architect concerning the remodeling of his home, changes which he had long contemplated, and which he desired carried forward during his temporary absence.

Expert and reliable packers and movers were engaged to convey the furniture, carpets, pictures—everything movable, in short—to places of security. And in an incredibly short time the Pontellier house was turned over to the artisans. There was to be an addition—a small snuggery; there was to be frescoing, and hardwood flooring was to be put into such rooms as had not yet been subjected to this improvement.

Furthermore, in one of the daily papers appeared a brief notice to the effect that Mr. and Mrs. Pontellier were contemplating a summer sojourn abroad, and that their handsome residence on Esplanade Street was undergoing sumptuous alterations, and would not be ready for occupancy until their return. Mr. Pontellier had saved appearances!

Edna admired the skill of his maneuver, and avoided any occasion to balk his intentions. When the situation as set forth by Mr. Pontellier was accepted and taken for granted, she was apparently satisfied that it should be so.

The pigeon-house pleased her. It at once assumed the intimate character of a home, while she herself invested it with a charm which it reflected like a warm glow. There was with her a feeling of having descended in the social scale, with a corresponding sense of having risen in the spiritual. Every step which she took toward relieving herself from obligations added to her strength and expansion as an individual. She began to look with her own eyes; to see and to apprehend the deeper undercurrents of life. No longer was she content to "feed upon opinion" when her own soul had invited her.

After a little while, a few days, in fact, Edna went up and spent a week with her children in Iberville. They were delicious February days, with all the summer's promise hovering in the air.

How glad she was to see the children! She wept for very pleasure when she felt their little arms clasping her; their hard, ruddy cheeks pressed against her own glowing cheeks. She looked into their faces with hungry eyes that could not be satisfied with looking. And what stories they had to tell their mother! About the pigs, the cows, the mules! About riding to the mill behind Gluglu; fishing back in the lake with their Uncle Jasper; picking pecans with Lidie's little black brood, and hauling chips in their express wagon. It was a thousand times more fun to haul real chips for old lame Susie's real fire than to drag painted blocks along the banquette on Esplanade Street!

She went with them herself to see the pigs and the cows, to look at the darkies laying the cane, to thrash the pecan trees, and catch fish in the back lake. She lived with them a whole week long, giving them all of herself, and gathering and filling herself with their young existence. They listened, breathless, when she told them the house in Esplanade Street was crowded with workmen, hammering, nailing, sawing, and filling the place with clatter. They wanted to know where their bed was; what had been done with their rocking-horse; and where did Joe sleep, and where had Ellen gone, and the cook? But, above all, they were fired with a desire to see the little house around the block. Was there any place to play? Were there any boys next door? Raoul, with pessimistic foreboding, was convinced that there were only girls next door. Where would they sleep, and where would papa sleep? She told them the fairies would fix it all right.

The old Madame was charmed with Edna's visit, and showered all manner of delicate attentions upon her. She was delighted to know that the Esplanade Street house was in a dismantled condition. It gave her the promise and pretext to keep the children indefinitely.

It was with a wrench and a pang that Edna left her children. She carried away with her the sound of their voices and the touch of their cheeks. All along the journey homeward their presence lingered with her like the memory of a delicious song. But by the time she had regained the city the song no longer echoed in her soul. She was again alone.

XXXIII

It happened sometimes when Edna went to see Mademoiselle Reisz that the little musician was absent, giving a lesson or making some small necessary household purchase. The key was always left in a secret hiding-place in the entry, which Edna knew. If Mademoiselle happened to be away, Edna would usually enter and wait for her return.

When she knocked at Mademoiselle Reisz's door one afternoon there was no response; so unlocking the door, as usual, she entered and found the apartment deserted; as she had expected. Her day had been quite filled up, and it was for a rest, for a refuge, and to talk about Robert, that she sought out her friend.

She had worked at her canvas—a young Italian character study—all the morning, completing the work without the model; but there had been many interruptions, some incident to her modest housekeeping, and others of a social nature.

Madame Ratignolle had dragged herself over, avoiding the too public thoroughfares, she said. She complained that Edna had neglected her much of late. Besides, she was consumed with curiosity to see the little house and the manner in which it was conducted. She wanted to hear all about the dinner party; Monsieur Ratignolle had left *so* early. What had happened after she left? The champagne and grapes which Edna sent over were *too* delicious. She had so little appetite; they had refreshed and toned her stomach. Where on earth was she going to put Mr. Pontellier in that little house, and the boys? And then she made Edna promise to go to her when her hour of trial overtook her.

"At any time—any time of the day or night, dear," Edna assured her.

Before leaving Madame Ratignolle said:

"In some way you seem to me like a child, Edna. You seem to act without a certain amount of reflection which is necessary in this life. That is the reason I want to say you mustn't mind if I advise you to be a little careful while you are living alone. Why don't you have some one come and stay with you? Wouldn't Mademoiselle Reisz come?"

"No; she wouldn't wish to come, and I shouldn't want her always with me."

"Well, the reason—you know how evil-minded the world is—some one was talking of Alcée Arobin visiting you. Of course, it wouldn't matter if Mr. Arobin had not such a dreadful reputation. Monsieur Ratignolle was telling me that his attentions alone are considered enough to ruin a woman's name."

"Does he boast of his successes?" asked Edna, indifferently, squinting at her picture.

"No, I think not. I believe he is a decent fellow as far as that goes. But his character is so well known among the men. I shan't be able to come back and see you; it was very, very imprudent to-day."

"Mind the step!" cried Edna.

"Don't neglect me," entreated Madame Ratignolle; "and you don't mind what I said about Arobin, or having some one to stay with you."

"Of course not," Edna laughed. "You may say anything you like to me." They kissed each other good-by. Madame Ratignolle had not far to go, and Edna stood on the porch a while watching her walk down the street.

Then in the afternoon Mrs. Merriman and Mrs. Highcamp had made their "party call." Edna felt that they might have dispensed with the formality. They had also come to invite her to play *vingt-et-un*[1] one evening at Mrs. Merriman's. She was asked to go early, to dinner, and Mr. Merriman or Mr. Arobin would take her home. Edna accepted in a half-hearted way. She sometimes felt very tired of Mrs. Highcamp and Mrs. Merriman.

Late in the afternoon she sought refuge with Mademoiselle Reisz, and stayed there alone, waiting for her, feeling a kind of repose invade her with the very atmosphere of the shabby, unpretentious little room.

Edna sat at the window, which looked out over the house-tops and across the river. The window frame was filled with pots of flowers, and she sat and picked the dry leaves from a rose geranium. The day was warm, and the breeze which blew from the river was very pleasant. She removed her hat and laid it on the piano. She went on picking the leaves and digging around the plants with her hat pin. Once she thought she heard Mademoiselle Reisz approaching. But it was a young black girl, who came in, bringing a small bundle of laundry, which she deposited in the adjoining room, and went away.

Edna seated herself at the piano, and softly picked out with one hand the bars of a piece of music which lay open before her. A half-hour went by. There was the occasional sound of people going and coming in the lower hall. She was growing interested in her occupation of picking out the aria, when there was a second rap at the door. She vaguely wondered what these people did when they found Mademoiselle's door locked.

"Come in," she called, turning her face toward the door. And this time it was Robert Lebrun who presented himself. She attempted to rise; she could not have done so without betraying the agitation which mastered her at sight of him, so she fell back upon the stool, only exclaiming, "Why, Robert!"

He came and clasped her hand, seemingly without knowing what he was saying or doing.

"Mrs. Pontellier! How do you happen—oh! how well you look! Is Mademoiselle Reisz not here? I never expected to see you."

"When did you come back?" asked Edna in an unsteady voice, wiping her face with her handkerchief. She seemed ill at ease on the piano stool, and he begged her to take the chair by the window. She did so, mechanically, while he seated himself on the stool.

"I returned day before yesterday," he answered, while he leaned his arm on the keys, bringing forth a crash of discordant sound.

"Day before yesterday!" she repeated, aloud; and went on thinking to herself, "day before yesterday," in a sort of an uncomprehending way. She had pictured him seeking her at the very first hour, and he had lived under the same sky since day before yesterday; while only by accident had he stumbled upon her. Mademoiselle must have lied when she said, "Poor fool, he loves you."

[1]French: twenty-one, a card game.

"Day before yesterday," she repeated, breaking off a spray of Mademoiselle's geranium; "then if you had not met me here to-day you wouldn't—when—that is, didn't you mean to come and see me?"

"Of course, I should have gone to see you. There have been so many things—" he turned the leaves of Mademoiselle's music nervously. "I started in at once yesterday with the old firm. After all there is as much chance for me here as there was there—that is, I might find it profitable some day. The Mexicans were not very congenial."

So he had come back because the Mexicans were not congenial; because business was as profitable here as there; because of reason, and not because he cared to be near her. She remembered the day she sat on the floor, turning the pages of his letter, seeking the reason which was left untold.

She had not noticed how he looked—only feeling his presence; but she turned deliberately and observed him. After all, he had been absent but a few months, and was not changed. His hair—the color of hers—waved back from his temples in the same way as before. His skin was not more burned than it had been at Grand Isle. She found in his eyes, when he looked at her for one silent moment, the same tender caress, with an added warmth and entreaty which had not been there before—the same glance which had penetrated to the sleeping places of her soul and awakened them.

A hundred times Edna had pictured Robert's return, and imagined their first meeting. It was usually at her home, whither he had sought her out at once. She always fancied him expressing or betraying in some way his love for her. And here, the reality was that they sat ten feet apart, she at the window, crushing geranium leaves in her hand and smelling them, he twirling around on the piano stool, saying:

"I was very much surprised to hear of Mr. Pontellier's absence; it's a wonder Mademoiselle Reisz did not tell me; and your moving—mother told me yesterday. I should think you would have gone to New York with him, or to Iberville with the children, rather than be bothered here with housekeeping. And you are going abroad, too, I hear. We shan't have you at Grand Isle next summer; it won't seem—do you see much of Mademoiselle Reisz? She often spoke of you in the few letters she wrote."

"Do you remember that you promised to write to me when you went away?" A flush overspread his whole face.

"I couldn't believe that my letters would be of any interest to you."

"That is an excuse; it isn't the truth." Edna reached for her hat on the piano. She adjusted it, sticking the hat pin through the heavy coil of hair with some deliberation.

"Are you not going to wait for Mademoiselle Reisz?" asked Robert.

"No; I have found when she is absent this long, she is liable not to come back till late." She drew on her gloves, and Robert picked up his hat.

"Won't you wait for her?" asked Edna.

"Not if you think she will not be back till late," adding, as if suddenly aware of some discourtesy in his speech, "and I should miss the pleasure of walking home with you." Edna locked the door and put the key back in its hiding-place.

They went together, picking their way across muddy streets and side-walks encumbered with the cheap display of small tradesmen. Part of the distance they rode in the car, and after disembarking, passed the Pontellier mansion, which looked broken and half torn asunder. Robert had never known the house, and looked at it with interest.

"I never knew you in your home," he remarked.

"I am glad you did not."

"Why?" She did not answer. They went on around the corner, and it seemed as if her dreams were coming true after all, when he followed her into the little house.

"You must stay and dine with me, Robert. You see I am all alone, and it is so long since I have seen you. There is so much I want to ask you."

She took off her hat and gloves. He stood irresolute, making some excuse about his mother who expected him; he even muttered something about an engagement. She struck a match and lit the lamp on the table; it was growing dusk. When he saw her face in the lamp-light, looking pained, with all the soft lines gone out of it, he threw his hat aside and seated himself.

"Oh! you know I want to stay if you will let me!" he exclaimed. All the softness came back. She laughed, and went and put her hand on his shoulder.

"This is the first moment you have seemed like the old Robert. I'll go tell Celestine." She hurried away to tell Celestine to set an extra place. She even sent her off in search of some added delicacy which she had not thought of for herself. And she recommended great care in dripping the coffee and having the omelet done to a proper turn.

When she reëntered, Robert was turning over magazines, sketches, and things that lay upon the table in great disorder. He picked up a photograph, and exclaimed:

"Alcée Arobin! What on earth is his picture doing here?"

"I tried to make a sketch of his head one day," answered Edna, "and he thought the photograph might help me. It was at the other house. I thought it had been left there. I must have packed it up with my drawing materials."

"I should think you would give it back to him if you have finished with it."

"Oh! I have a great many such photographs. I never think of returning them. They don't amount to anything." Robert kept on looking at the picture.

"It seems to me—do you think his head worth drawing? Is he a friend of Mr. Pontellier's? You never said you knew him."

"He isn't a friend of Mr. Pontellier's; he's a friend of mine. I always knew him—that is, it is only of late that I know him pretty well. But I'd rather talk about you, and know what you have been seeing and doing and feeling out there in Mexico." Robert threw aside the picture.

"I've been seeing the waves and the white beach of Grand Isle; the quiet, grassy street of the *Chênière;* the old fort at Grand Terre. I've been working like a machine, and feeling like a lost soul. There was nothing interesting."

She leaned her head upon her hand to shade her eyes from the light.

"And what have you been seeing and doing and feeling all these days?" he asked.

"I've been seeing the waves and the white beach of Grand Isle; the quiet, grassy street of the *Chênière Caminada;* the old sunny fort at Grande Terre. I've been working with a little more comprehension than a machine, and still feeling like a lost soul. There was nothing interesting."

"Mrs. Pontellier, you are cruel," he said, with feeling, closing his eyes and resting his head back in his chair. They remained in silence till old Celestine announced dinner.

XXXIV

The dining-room was very small. Edna's round mahogany would have almost filled it. As it was there was but a step or two from the little table to the kitchen, to the mantel, the small buffet, and the side door that opened out on the narrow brick-paved yard.

A certain degree of ceremony settled upon them with the announcement of dinner. There was no return to personalities. Robert related incidents of his sojourn in Mexico, and Edna talked of events likely to interest him, which had occurred during his absence. The dinner was of ordinary quality, except for the few delicacies which she had sent out to purchase. Old Celestine, with a bandana *tignon*[1] twisted about her head, hobbled in and out, taking a personal interest in everything; and she lingered occasionally to talk patois[2] with Robert, whom she had known as a boy.

He went out to a neighboring cigar stand to purchase cigarette papers, and when he came back he found that Celestine had served the black coffee in the parlor.

"Perhaps I shouldn't have come back," he said. "When you are tired of me, tell me to go."

"You never tire me. You must have forgotten the hours and hours at Grand Isle in which we grew accustomed to each other and used to being together."

"I have forgotten nothing at Grand Isle," he said, not looking at her, but rolling a cigarette. His tobacco pouch, which he laid upon the table, was a fantastic embroidered silk affair, evidently the handiwork of a woman.

"You used to carry your tobacco in a rubber pouch," said Edna, picking up the pouch and examining the needle work.

"Yes; it was lost."

"Where did you buy this one? In Mexico?"

"It was given to me by a Vera Cruz girl; they are very generous," he replied, striking a match and lighting his cigarette.

"They are very handsome, I suppose, those Mexican women; very picturesque, with their black eyes and their lace scarfs."

"Some are; others are hideous. Just as you find women everywhere."

"What was she like—the one who gave you the pouch? You must have known her very well."

"She was very ordinary. She wasn't of the slightest importance. I knew her well enough."

"Did you visit at her house? Was it interesting? I should like to know and hear about the people you met, and the impressions they made on you."

"There are some people who leave impressions not so lasting as the imprint of an oar upon the water."

"Was she such a one?"

"It would be ungenerous for me to admit that she was of that order and kind." He thrust the pouch back in his pocket, as if to put away the subject with the trifle which had brought it up.

Arobin dropped in with a message from Mrs. Merriman, to say that the card party was postponed on account of the illness of one of her children.

"How do you do, Arobin?" said Robert, rising from the obscurity.

"Oh! Lebrun. To be sure! I heard yesterday you were back. How did they treat you down in Mexique?"

"Fairly well."

"But not well enough to keep you there. Stunning girls, though, in Mexico. I

[1] A turban made with a bright colored kerchief.
[2] A local dialect of French, mixed with words from English, Spanish, etc.

thought I should never get away from Vera Cruz when I was down there a couple of years ago."

"Did they embroider slippers and tobacco pouches and hat-bands and things for you?" asked Edna.

"Oh! my! no! I didn't get so deep in their regard. I fear they made more impression on me than I made on them."

"You were less fortunate than Robert, then."

"I am always less fortunate than Robert. Has he been imparting tender confidences?"

"I've been imposing myself long enough," said Robert, rising, and shaking hands with Edna. "Please convey my regards to Mr. Pontellier when you write."

He shook hands with Arobin and went away.

"Fine fellow, that Lebrun," said Arobin when Robert had gone. "I never heard you speak of him."

"I knew him last summer at Grand Isle," she replied. "Here is that photograph of yours. Don't you want it?"

"What do I want with it? Throw it away." She threw it back on the table.

"I'm not going to Mrs. Merriman's," she said. "If you see her, tell her so. But perhaps I had better write. I think I shall write now, and say that I am sorry her child is sick, and tell her not to count on me."

"It would be a good scheme," acquiesced Arobin. "I don't blame you; stupid lot!"

Edna opened the blotter, and having procured paper and pen, began to write the note. Arobin lit a cigar and read the evening paper, which he had in his pocket.

"What is the date?" she asked. He told her.

"Will you mail this for me when you go out?"

"Certainly." He read to her little bits out of the newspaper, while she straightened things on the table.

"What do you want to do?" he asked, throwing aside the paper. "Do you want to go out for a walk or a drive or anything? It would be a fine night to drive."

"No; I don't want to do anything but just be quiet. You go away and amuse yourself. Don't stay."

"I'll go away if I must; but I shan't amuse myself. You know that I only live when I am near you."

He stood up to bid her good night.

"Is that one of the things you always say to women?"

"I have said it before, but I don't think I ever came so near meaning it," he answered with a smile. There were no warm lights in her eyes; only a dreamy, absent look.

"Good night. I adore you. Sleep well," he said, and he kissed her hand and went away.

She stayed alone in a kind of reverie—a sort of stupor. Step by step she lived over every instant of the time she had been with Robert after he had entered Mademoiselle Reisz's door. She recalled his words, his looks. How few and meager they had been for her hungry heart! A vision—a transcendently seductive vision of a Mexican girl arose before her. She writhed with a jealous pang. She wondered when he would come back. He had not said he would come back. She had been with him, had heard his voice and touched his hand. But some way he had seemed nearer to her off there in Mexico.

XXXV

The morning was full of sunlight and hope. Edna could see before her no denial—only the promise of excessive joy. She lay in bed awake, with bright eyes full of speculation. "He loves you, poor fool." If she could but get that conviction firmly fixed in her mind, what mattered about the rest? She felt she had been childish and unwise the night before in giving herself over to despondency. She recapitulated the motives which no doubt explained Robert's reserve. They were not insurmountable; they would not hold if he really loved her; they could not hold against her own passion, which he must come to realize in time. She pictured him going to his business that morning. She even saw how he was dressed; how he walked down one street, and turned the corner of another; saw him bending over his desk, talking to people who entered the office, going to his lunch, and perhaps watching for her on the street. He would come to her in the afternoon or evening, sit and roll his cigarette, talk a little, and go away as he had done the night before. But how delicious it would be to have him there with her! She would have no regrets, nor seek to penetrate his reserve if he still chose to wear it.

Edna ate her breakfast only half dressed. The maid brought her a delicious printed scrawl from Raoul, expressing his love, asking her to send him some bonbons, and telling her they had found that morning ten tiny white pigs all lying in a row beside Lidie's big white pig.

A letter also came from her husband, saying he hoped to be back early in March, and then they would get ready for that journey abroad which he had promised her so long, which he felt now fully able to afford; he felt able to travel as people should, without any thought of small economies—thanks to his recent speculations in Wall Street.

Much to her surprise she received a note from Arobin, written at midnight from the club. It was to say good morning to her, to hope she had slept well, to assure her of his devotion, which he trusted she in some faintest manner returned.

All these letters were pleasing to her. She answered the children in a cheerful frame of mind, promising them bonbons, and congratulating them upon their happy find of the little pigs.

She answered her husband with friendly evasiveness,—not with any fixed design to mislead him, only because all sense of reality had gone out of her life; she had abandoned herself to Fate, and awaited the consequences with indifference.

To Arobin's note she made no reply. She put it under Celestine's stove-lid.

Edna worked several hours with much spirit. She saw no one but a picture dealer, who asked her if it were true that she was going abroad to study in Paris.

She said possibly she might, and he negotiated with her for some Parisian studies to reach him in time for the holiday trade in December.

Robert did not come that day. She was keenly disappointed. He did not come the following day, nor the next. Each morning she awoke with hope, and each night she was a prey to despondency. She was tempted to seek him out. But far from yielding to the impulse, she avoided any occasion which might throw her in his way. She did not go to Mademoiselle Reisz's nor pass by Madame Lebrun's, as she might have done if he had still been in Mexico.

When Arobin, one night, urged her to drive with him, she went—out to the lake, on the Shell Road. His horses were full of mettle, and even a little unmanageable. She liked the rapid gait at which they spun along, and the quick, sharp sound of the horses' hoofs on the hard road. They did not stop anywhere to eat or to drink. Arobin was not needlessly imprudent. But they ate and they drank when they regained Edna's little dining-room—which was comparatively early in the evening.

It was late when he left her. It was getting to be more than a passing whim with Arobin to see her and be with her. He had detected the latent sensuality, which unfolded under his delicate sense of her nature's requirements like a torpid, torrid, sensitive blossom.

There was no despondency when she fell asleep that night; nor was there hope when she awoke in the morning.

XXXVI

There was a garden out in the suburbs; a small, leafy corner, with a few green tables under the orange trees. An old cat slept all day on the stone step in the sun, and an old *mulatresse*[1] slept her idle hours away in her chair at the open window, till some one happened to knock on one of the green tables. She had milk and cream cheese to sell, and bread and butter. There was no one who could make such excellent coffee or fry a chicken so golden brown as she.

The place was too modest to attract the attention of people of fashion, and so quiet as to have escaped the notice of those in search of pleasure and dissipation. Edna had discovered it accidentally one day when the high-board gate stood ajar. She caught sight of a little green table, blotched with the checkered sunlight that filtered through the quivering leaves overhead. Within she had found the slumbering *mulatresse,* the drowsy cat, and a glass of milk which reminded her of the milk she had tasted in Iberville.

She often stopped there during her perambulations; sometimes taking a book with her, and sitting an hour or two under the trees when she found the place deserted. Once or twice she took a quiet dinner there alone, having instructed Celestine beforehand to prepare no dinner at home. It was the last place in the city where she would have expected to meet any one she knew.

Still she was not astonished when, as she was partaking of a modest dinner late in the afternoon, looking into an open book, stroking the cat, which had made friends with her—she was not greatly astonished to see Robert come in at the tall garden gate.

"I am destined to see you only by accident," she said, shoving the cat off the chair beside her. He was surprised, ill at ease, almost embarrassed at meeting her thus so unexpectedly.

"Do you come here often?" he asked.

"I almost live here,' she said.

"I used to drop in very often for a cup of Catiche's good coffee. This is the first time since I came back."

"She'll bring you a plate, and you will share my dinner. There's always enough for two—even three." Edna had intended to be indifferent and as reserved as he when she meet him; she had reached the determination by a laborious train of reasoning, incident to one of her despondent moods. But her resolve melted when she saw him before her, seated there beside her in the little garden, as if a designing Providence had led him into her path.

"Why have you kept away from me, Robert?" she asked, closing the book that lay open upon the table.

[1]French: mulatto woman, one of mixed black and white ancestry.

"Why are you so personal, Mrs. Pontellier? Why do you force me to idiotic subterfuges?" he exclaimed with sudden·warmth. "I suppose there's no use telling you I've been very busy, or that I've been sick, or that I've been to see you and not found you at home. Please let me off with any one of these excuses."

"You are the embodiment of selfishness," she said. "You save yourself something—I don't know what—but there is some selfish motive, and in sparing yourself you never consider for a moment what I think, or how I feel your neglect and indifference. I suppose this is what you would call unwomanly; but I have got into a habit of expressing myself. It doesn't matter to me, and you may think me unwomanly if you like."

"No; I only think you cruel, as I said the other day. Maybe not intentionally cruel; but you seem to be forcing me into disclosures which can result in nothing; as if you would have me bare a wound for the pleasure of looking at it, without the intention or power of healing it."

"I'm spoiling your dinner, Robert; never mind what I say. You haven't eaten a morsel."

"I only came in for a cup of coffee." His sensitive face was all disfigured with excitement.

"Isn't this a delightful place?" she remarked. "I am so glad it has never actually been discovered. It is so quiet, so sweet, here. Do you notice there is scarcely a sound to be heard? It's so out of the way; and a good walk from the car. However, I don't mind walking. I always feel so sorry for women who don't like to walk; they miss so much—so many rare little glimpses of life; and we women learn so little of life on the whole.

"Catiche's coffee is always hot. I don't know how she manages it, here in open air. Celestine's coffee gets cold bringing it from the kitchen to the dining-room. Three lumps! How can you drink it so sweet? Take some of the cress with your chop; it's so biting and crisp. Then there's the advantage of being able to smoke with your coffee out here. Now, in the city—aren't you going to smoke?"

"After a while," he said, laying a cigar on the table.

"Who gave it to you?" she laughed.

"I bought it. I suppose I'm getting reckless; I bought a whole box." She was determined not to be personal again and make him uncomfortable.

The cat made friends with him, and climbed into his lap when he smoked his cigar. He stroked her silky fur, and talked a little about her. He looked at Edna's book, which he had read; and he told her the end, to save her the trouble of wading through it, he said.

Again he accompanied her back to her home; and it was after dusk when they reached the little "pigeon-house." She did not ask him to remain, which he was grateful for, as it permitted him to stay without the discomfort of blundering through an excuse which he had no intention of considering. He helped her to light the lamp; then she went into her room to take off her hat and to bathe her face and hands.

When she came back Robert was not examining the pictures and magazines as before; he sat off in the shadow, leaning his head back on the chair as if in a reverie. Edna lingered a moment beside the table, arranging the books there. Then she went across the room to where he sat. She bent over the arm of his chair and called his name.

"Robert," she said, "are you asleep?"

"No," he answered, looking up at her.

She leaned over and kissed him—a soft, cool, delicate kiss, whose voluptuous sting penetrated his whole being—then she moved away from him. He followed, and took her in his arms, just holding her close to him. She put her hand up to his face and pressed his cheek against her own. The action was full of love and tenderness. He sought her lips again. Then he drew her down upon the sofa beside him and held her hand in both of his.

"Now you know," he said, "now you know what I have been fighting against since last summer at Grand Isle; what drove me away and drove me back again."

"Why have you been fighting against it?" she asked. Her face glowed with soft lights.

"Why? Because you were not free; you were Léonce Pontellier's wife. I couldn't help loving you if you were ten times his wife; but so long as I went away from you and kept away I could help telling you so." She put her free hand up to his shoulder, and then against his cheek, rubbing it softly. He kissed her again. His face was warm and flushed.

"There in Mexico I was thinking of you all the time, and longing for you."

"But not writing to me," she interrupted.

"Something put into my head that you cared for me; and I lost my senses. I forgot everything but a wild dream of your some way becoming my wife."

"Your wife!"

"Religion, loyalty, everything would give way if only you cared."

"Then you must have forgotten that I was Léonce Pontellier's wife."

"Oh! I was demented, dreaming of wild, impossible things, recalling men who had set their wives free, we have heard of such things."

"Yes, we have heard of such things."

"I came back full of vague, mad intentions. And when I got here—"

"When you got here you never came near me!" She was still caressing his cheek.

"I realized what a cur I was to dream of such a thing, even if you had been willing."

She took his face between her hands and looked into it as if she would never withdraw her eyes more. She kissed him on the forehead, the eyes, the cheeks, and the lips.

"You have been a very, very foolish boy, wasting your time dreaming of impossible things when you speak of Mr. Pontellier setting me free! I am no longer one of Mr. Pontellier's possessions to dispose of or not. I give myself where I choose. If he were to say, 'Here, Robert, take her and be happy; she is yours,' I should laugh at you both."

His face grew a little white. "What do you mean?" he asked.

There was a knock at the door. Old Celestine came in to say that Madame Ratignolle's servant had come around the back way with a message that Madame had been taken sick and begged Mrs. Pontellier to go to her immediately.

"Yes, yes," said Edna, rising; "I promised. Tell her yes—to wait for me. I'll go back with her."

"Let me walk over with you," offered Robert.

"No," she said; "I will go with the servant." She went into her room to put on her hat, and when she came in again she sat once more upon the sofa beside him. He had not stirred. She put her arms about his neck.

"Good-by, my sweet Robert. Tell me good-by." He kissed her with a degree of passion which had not before entered into his caress, and strained her to him.

"I love you," she whispered, "only you; no one but you. It was you who woke me last summer out of life-long, stupid dream. Oh! you have made me so unhappy with your indifference. Oh! I have suffered, suffered! Now you are here we shall love each other, my Robert. We shall be everything to each other. Nothing else in the world is of any consequence. I must go to my friend; but you will wait for me? No matter how late; you will wait for me, Robert?"

"Don't go; don't go! Oh! Edna, stay with me," he pleaded. "Why should you go? Stay with me, stay with me."

"I shall come back as soon as I can; I shall find you here." She buried her face in his neck, and said good-by again. Her seductive voice, together with his great love for her, had enthralled his senses, had deprived him of every impulse but the longing to hold her and keep her.

<h1 style="text-align:center">XXXVII</h1>

Edna looked in at the drug store. Monsieur Ratignolle was putting up a mixture himself, very carefully, dropping a red liquid into a tiny glass. He was grateful to Edna for having come; her presence would be a comfort to his wife. Madame Ratignolle's sister, who had always been with her at such trying times, had not been able to come up from the plantation, and Adèle had been inconsolable until Mrs. Pontellier so kindly promised to come to her. The nurse had been with them at night for the past week, as she lived a great distance away. And Dr. Mandelet had been coming and going all the afternoon. They were then looking for him any moment.

Edna hastened upstairs by a private stairway that led from the rear of the store to the apartments above. The children were all sleeping in a back room. Madame Ratignolle was in the salon, whither she had strayed in her suffering impatience. She sat on the sofa, clad in an ample white *peignoir,* holding a handkerchief tight in her hand with a nervous clutch. Her face was drawn and pinched, her sweet blue eyes haggard and unnatural. All her beautiful hair had been drawn back and plaited. It lay in a long braid on the sofa pillow, coiled like a golden serpent. The nurse, a comfortable looking *Griffe*[1] woman in white apron and cap, was urging her to return to her bedroom.

"There is no use, there is no use," she said at once to Edna. "We must get rid of Mandelet; he is getting too old and careless. he said he would be here at half-past seven; now it must be eight. See what time it is, Joséphine."

The woman was possessed of a cheerful nature, and refused to take any situation too seriously, especially a situation with which she was so familiar. She urged Madame to have courage and patience. But Madame only set her teeth hard into her under lip, and Edna saw the sweat gather in beads on her white forehead. After a moment or two she uttered a profound sigh and wiped her face with the handkerchief rolled in a ball. She appeared exhausted. The nurse gave her a fresh handkerchief, sprinkled with cologne water.

"This is too much!" she cried. "Mandelet ought to be killed! Where is Alphonse? Is it possible I am to be abandoned like this—neglected by every one?'"

"Neglected, indeed!" exclaimed the nurse. Wasn't she there? And here was Mrs. Pontellier leaving, no doubt, a pleasant evening at home to devote to her? And wasn't Monsieur Ratignolle coming that very instant through the hall? And Joséphine was quite sure she had heard Doctor Mandelet's coupé. Yes, there is was, down at the door.

Adèle consented to go back to her room. She sat on the edge of a little low couch next to her bed.

---

[1]French: the child of a mulatto and a Negro.

Doctor Mandelet paid no attention to Madame Ratignolle's upbraidings. He was accustomed to them at such times, and was too well convinced of her loyalty to doubt it.

He was glad to see Edna, and wanted her to go with him into the salon and entertain him. But Madame Ratignolle would not consent that Edna should leave her for an instant. Between agonizing moments, she chatted a little, and said it took her mind off her sufferings.

Edna began to feel uneasy. She was seized with a vague dread. Her own like experiences seemed far away, unreal, and only half remembered. She recalled faintly an ecstasy of pain, the heavy odor of chloroform, a stupor which had deadened sensation, and an awakening to find a little new life to which she had given being, added to the great unnumbered multitude of souls that come and go.

She began to wish she had not come; her presence was not necessary. She might have invented a pretext for staying away; she might even invent a pretext now for going. But Edna did not go. With an inward agony, with a flaming outspoken revolt against the ways of Nature, she witnessed the scene [of] torture.

She was still stunned and speechless with emotion when later she leaned over her friend to kiss her and softly say good-by. Adèle, pressing her cheek, whispered in an exhausted voice: "Think of the children, Edna. Oh think of the children! Remember them!"

XXXVIII

Edna still felt dazed when she got outside in the open air. The Doctor's coupé had returned for him and stood before the *porte cochère*. She did not wish to enter the coupé, and told Doctor Mandelet she would walk; she was not afraid, and would go alone. He directed his carriage to meet him at Mrs. Pontellier's, and he started to walk home with her.

Up—away up, over the narrow street between the tall houses, the stars were blazing. The air was mild and caressing, but cool with the breath of spring and the night. They walked slowly, the Doctor with a heavy, measured tread and his hands behind him; Edna, in an absent-minded way, as she had walked one night at Grand Isle, as if her thoughts had gone ahead of her and she was striving to overtake them.

"You shouldn't have been there, Mrs. Pontellier," he said. "That was no place for you. Adèle is full of whims at such times. There were a dozen women she might have had with her, unimpressionable women. I felt that it was cruel, cruel. You shouldn't have gone."

"Oh, well!" she answered, indifferently. "I don't know that it matters after all. One has to think of the children some time or other; the sooner the better."

"When is Léonce coming back?"

"Quite soon. Some time in March."

"And you are going abroad?"

"Perhaps—no, I am not going. I'm not going to be forced into doing things. I don't want to go abroad. I want to be let alone. Nobody has any right—except children, perhaps—and even then, it seems to me—or it did seem—" She felt that her speech was voicing the incoherency of her thoughts, and stopped abruptly.

"The trouble is," sighed the Doctor, grasping her meaning intuitively, "that youth is given up to illusions. It seems to be a provision of Nature; a decoy to secure mothers for the race. And Nature takes no account of moral consequences, or arbitrary conditions which we create, and which we feel obliged to maintain at any cost."

"Yes," she said. "The years that are gone seem like dreams—if one might go on sleeping and dreaming—but to wake up and find—oh! well! perhaps it is better to wake up after all, even to suffer, rather than to remain a dupe to illusions all one's life."

"It seems to me, my dear child," said the Doctor at parting, holding her hand, "you seem to me to be in trouble. I am not going to ask for your confidence. I will only say that if ever you feel moved to give it to me, perhaps I might help you. I know I would understand, and I tell you there are not many who would— not many, my dear."

"Some way I don't feel moved to speak of things that trouble me. Don't think I am ungrateful or that I don't appreciate your sympathy. There are periods of despondency and suffering which take possession of me. But I don't want anything but my own way. That is wanting a good deal, of course, when you have to trample upon the lives, the hearts, the prejudices of others—but no matter—still, I shouldn't want to trample upon the little lives. Oh! I don't know what I'm saying, Doctor. Good night. Don't blame me for anything."

"Yes, I will blame you if you don't come and see me soon. We will talk of things you never have dreamt of talking about before. It will do us both good. I don't want you to blame yourself, whatever comes. Good night, my child."

She let herself in at the gate, but instead of entering she sat upon the step of the porch. The night was quiet and soothing. All the tearing emotion of the last few hours seemed to fall away from her like a somber, uncomfortable garment, which she had but to loosen to be rid of. She went back to that hour before Adèle had sent for her; and her senses kindled afresh in thinking of Robert's words, the pressure of his arms, and the feeling of his lips upon her own. She could picture at the moment no greater bliss on earth than possession of the beloved one. His expression of love had already given him to her in part. When she thought that he was there at hand, waiting for her, she grew numb with the intoxication of expectancy. It was so late; he would be asleep perhaps. She would awaken him with a kiss. She hoped he would be asleep that she might arouse him with her caresses.

Still, she remembered Adèle's voice whispering, "Think of the children; think of them." She meant to think of them; that determination had driven into her soul like a death wound—but not to-night. To-morrow would be time to think of everything.

Robert was not waiting for her in the little parlor. He was nowhere at hand. The house was empty. But he had scrawled on a piece of paper that lay in the lamplight:

"I love you. Good-by—because I love you."

Edna grew faint when she read the words. She went and sat on the sofa. Then she stretched herself out there, never uttering a sound. She did not sleep. She did not go to bed. The lamp sputtered and went out. She was still awake in the morning, when Celestine unlocked the kitchen door and came in to light the fire.

XXXIX

Victor, with hammer and nails and scraps of scantling,[1] was patching a corner of one of the galleries. Mariequita sat near by, dangling her legs, watching him work, and handing him nails from the tool-box. The sun was beating down upon them. The girl covered her head with her apron folded into a square pad. They had been talking for an hour or more. She was never tired of hearing Victor describe the dinner at Mrs. Pontellier's. He exaggerated every detail, making it appear a veritable Lucullean feast.[2] The flowers were in tubs, he said. The champagne was quaffed from huge golden goblets. Venus rising from the foam[3] could have presented no more entrancing a spectacle than Mrs. Pontellier, blazing with beauty and diamonds at the head of the board, while the other women were all of them youthful houris,[4] possessed of incomparable charms.

She got it into her head that Victor was in love with Mrs. Pontellier, and he gave her evasive answers, framed so as to confirm her belief. She grew sullen and cried a little, threatening to go off and leave him to his fine ladies. There were a dozen men crazy about her at the *Chênière;* and since it was the fashion to be in love with married people, why, she could run away any time she liked to New Orleans with Célina's husband.

Célina's husband was a fool, a coward, and a pig, and to prove it to her, Victor intended to hammer his head into a jelly the next time he encountered him. This assurance was very consoling to Mariequita. She dried her eyes, and grew cheerful at the prospect.

They were still talking of the dinner and the allurements of city life when Mrs. Pontellier herself slipped around the corner of the house. The two youngsters stayed dumb with amazement before what they considered to be an apparition. But it was really she in flesh and blood, looking tired and a little travel-stained.

"I walked up from the wharf," she said, "and heard the hammering. I supposed it was you, mending the porch. It's a good thing. I was always tripping over those loose planks last summer. How dreary and deserted everything looks!"

It took Victor some time to comprehend that she had come in Beaudelet's lugger, that she had come alone, and for no purpose but to rest.

"There's nothing fixed up yet, you see. I'll give you my room; it's the only place."

"Any corner will do," she assured him.

"And if you can stand Philomel's cooking," he went on, "though I might try to get her mother while you are here. Do you think she would come?" turning to Mariequita.

Mariequita thought that perhaps Philomel's mother might come for a few days, and money enough.

Beholding Mrs. Pontellier make her appearance, the girl had at once suspected a lovers' rendezvous. But Victor's astonishment was so genuine, and Mrs. Pontellier's indifference so apparent, that the disturbing notion did not lodge long in her brain. She contemplated with the greatest interest this woman who gave the most sumptuous dinners in America, and who had all the men in New Orleans at her feet.

[1] Timber.
[2] I.e., like those of Licinius Lucullus, a rich Roman who was famous for his banquets.
[3] In Roman myth, Venus, the goddess of love and beauty, was created out of sea foam.
[4] Beautiful nymphs who dwell in the Moslem paradise.

"What time will you have dinner?" asked Edna. "I'm very hungry; but don't get anything extra."

"I'll have it ready in little or no time," he said, bustling and packing away his tools. "You may go to my room to brush up and rest yourself. Mariequita will show you."

"Thank you," said Edna. "But, do you know, I have a notion to go down to the beach and take a good wash and even a little swim, before dinner?"

"The water is too cold!" they both exclaimed. "Don't think of it."

"Well, I might go down and try—dip my toes in. Why, it seems to me the sun is hot enough to have warmed the very depths of the ocean. Could you get me a couple of towels? I'd better go right away, so as to be back in time. It would be a little too chilly if I waited till this afternoon."

Mariequita ran over to Victor's room, and returned with some towels, which she gave to Edna.

"I hope you have fish for dinner," said Edna, as she started to walk away; "but don't do anything extra if you haven't."

"Run and find Philomel's mother," Victor instructed the girl. "I'll go to the kitchen and see what I can do. By Gimminy! Women have no consideration! She might have sent me word."

Edna walked on down to the beach rather mechanically, not noticing anything special except that the sun was hot. She was not dwelling upon any particular train of thought. She had done all the thinking which was necessary after Robert went away, when she lay awake upon the sofa till morning.

She had said over and over to herself: "To-day it is Arobin; to-morrow it will be some one else. It makes no difference to me, it doesn't matter about Léonce Pontellier—but Raoul and Etienne!" She understood now clearly what she had meant long ago when she said to Adèle Ratignolle that she would give up the unessential, but she would never sacrifice herself for her children.

Despondency had come upon her there in the wakeful night, and had never lifted. There was no one thing in the world that she desired. There was no human being whom she wanted near her except Robert; and she even realized that the day would come when he, too, and the thought of him would melt out of her existence, leaving her alone. The children appeared before her like antagonists who had overcome her; who had overpowered and sought to drag her into the soul's slavery for the rest of her days. But she knew a way to elude them. She was not thinking of these things when she walked down to the beach.

The water of the Gulf stretched out before her, gleaming with the million lights of the sun. The voice of the sea is seductive, never ceasing, whispering, clamoring, murmuring, inviting the soul to wander in abysses of solitude. All along the white beach, up and down, there was no living thing in sight. A bird with a broken wing was beating the air above, reeling, fluttering, circling disabled down, down to the water.

Edna had found her old bathing suit still hanging, faded, upon its accustomed peg.

She put it on, leaving her clothing in the bath-house. But when she was there beside the sea, absolutely alone, she cast the unpleasant, pricking garments from her, and for the first time in her life she stood naked in the open air, at the mercy of the sun, the breeze that beat upon her, and the waves that invited her.

How strange and awful it seemed to stand naked under the sky! how delicious! She felt like some new-born creature, opening its eyes in a familiar world that it had never known.

The foamy wavelets curled up to her white feet, and coiled like serpents about her ankles. She walked out. The water was chill, but she walked on. The water was deep, but she lifted her white body and reached out with a long, sweeping stroke. The touch of the sea is sensuous, enfolding the body in its soft, close embrace.

She went on and on. She remembered the night she swam far out, and recalled the terror that seized her at the fear of being unable to regain the shore. She did not look back now, but went on and on, thinking of the blue-grass meadow that she had traversed when a little child, believing that it had no beginning and no end.

Her arms and legs were growing tired.

She thought of Léonce and the children. They were a part of her life. But they need not have thought that they could possess her, body and soul. How Mademoiselle Reisz would have laughed, perhaps sneered, if she knew! "And you call yourself an artist! What pretensions, Madame! The artist must possess the courageous soul that dares and defies."

Exhaustion was pressing upon and overpowering her.

"Good-by—because I love you." He did not know; he did not understand. He would never understand. Perhaps Doctor Mandelet would have understood if she had seen him—but it was too late; the shore was far behind her, and her strength was gone.

She looked into the distance, and the old terror flamed up for an instant, then sank again. Edna heard her father's voice and her sister Margaret's. She heard the barking of an old dog that was chained to the sycamore tree. The spurs of the cavalry officer clanged as he walked across the porch. There was the hum of bees, and the musky odor of pinks filled the air.

1897–1898   1899

Stephen Crane *1871–1900*

Stephen Crane's father was a Methodist preacher in Newark, New Jersey, Crane's birth-place. His mother was a social leader and temperance crusader. Both parents exhibited a characteristic nineteenth-century faith in the benevolence of God, in the existence of free will, and in the significance of man in the universe—ideas that their son, in the course of his short and tempestuous life, would attack with humor and savage irony.

Crane had originally hoped to be a soldier, but in 1890, after two and a half years at a military prep school in New York, he entered Lafayette College to study mining-engineering. After one term he left Lafayette and transferred to Syracuse University. There he devoted most of his efforts to playing varsity baseball, working as a local correspondent for the New York Tribune, and writing his first short stories. After less than a year at Syracuse, Crane withdrew and moved to New York City. There he mingled with Bohemian art students living in tenements, and he struggled to earn his way as a free-lance journalist contributing items to New York newspapers.

Crane's observation of life on New York's Bowery and his reading of exposés of New York slum life provided him with much of the background material for his first novel, Maggie, A Girl of the Streets *(1893). It was the first naturalistic novel written by an American, and its stark description of squalor and immorality was so shocking for its time* that Crane, unable to find an interested publisher, was obliged to publish the novel at his own expense. In 1895 he published his first book of poems, **The Black Riders**, short, caustic, free-verse parables of the absurdity of the human condition. In the same year **The Red Badge of Courage** was published in book form, bringing Crane international acclaim.

His travels as a reporter for a newspaper syndicate took him through the American West, to Mexico, and to Florida where he joined in the unsuccessful gun-running expedition to Cuba that led to his most famous short story, "The Open Boat." In 1897 Crane settled in England, became friends with Joseph Conrad and Henry James, and labored mightily at writing fiction and doing editorial hackwork in an effort to pay for his extravagant style of living. The next year, in spite of ill health, Crane went to Cuba as a war correspondent reporting on the Spanish-American War for the New York World. When he returned to England early in 1899 he was suffering from tuberculosis, and in June 1900, after traveling to a German sanitorium to seek a cure, Crane died. He was twenty-eight.

His early writing had been burlesques and satires, expressions of the same ironic detachment that is evident in his slum novel **Maggie**. Crane had announced that his ambition as a writer was to achieve personal honesty. His aim was to deflate romantic idealism and portray men battered and alone in a hostile world. He has been viewed as an uncompromising determinist, a literary naturalist who saw human beings as wholly controlled by their environment and their heredity. At the same time he has been seen as a Christian symbolist expressing faith in the ultimate understanding and redemption of man. Crane was a pioneer of a new literary realism that was impressionistic in its vivid imagery, in its characterizations, and in its narrative style. And he was a master of irony, scrutinizing the persistent illusions of men and the disparity between their buoyant expectations and their doom.

FURTHER READING: *The Works of Stephen Crane*, 12 vols., ed. W. Follett. 1925–1927, 1963, now superseded by *The Works of Stephen Crane*, 10 vols., ed. F. Bowers, 1969–1975; *Stephen Crane, Letters*, ed. R. Stallman and L. Gilkes, 1960; T. Beer, *Stephen Crane*, 1923; J. Berryman, *Stephen Crane*, 1950, 1962, 1980; E. Cady, *Stephen Crane*, 1962, 1980; J. Colvert, *Stephen Crane*, 1984; D. Hoffman, *The Poetry of Stephen Crane*, 1957; E. Solomon, *Stephen Crane, From Parody to Realism*, 1966; R. Stallman, *Stephen Crane*, 1968; D. Gibson, *The Fiction of Stephen Crane*, 1968; M. LaFrance, *A Reading of Stephen Crane*, 1971; *Stephen Crane in Transition, Centenary Essays*, ed. J. Katz, 1972; *Stephen Crane's Career*, ed. T. Gullason, 1973; F. Bergon, *Stephen Crane's Artistry*, 1975; J. Nagel, *Stephen Crane and Literary Impressionism*, 1980; C. Wolford, *The Anger of Stephen Crane*, 1983; M. Fried, *Realism, Writing, Disfiguration*, 1987.

TEXTS: *The Poems of Stephen Crane*, ed. J. Katz, 1966; "The Open Boat," *The Works of Stephen Crane*, Vol. V, *Tales of Adventure*, ed. F. Bowers, intr. J. Levenson, 1970; *Maggie, A Girl of the Streets*, 1893; *The Red Badge of Courage*, 1895.

BLACK RIDERS CAME FROM THE SEA[1]

Black riders came from the sea.
There was clang and clang of spear and shield,
And clash and clash of hoof and heel,
Wild shouts and the wave of hair

[1]Crane's poems were published without titles. The titles used here were supplied by the editor.

In the rush upon the wind:
Thus the ride of Sin.
1894   1895

IN THE DESERT

In the desert
I saw a creature, naked, bestial,
Who, squatting upon the ground,
Held his heart in his hands,
And ate of it.
I said: "Is it good, friend?"
"It is bitter—bitter," he answered;
"But I like it
Because it is bitter,
And because it is my heart."
1894   1895

A GOD IN WRATH

A god in wrath
Was beating a man;
He cuffed him loudly
With thunderous blows
That rang and rolled over the earth.
All people came running.
The man screamed and struggled,
And bit madly at the feet of the god.
The people cried:
"Ah, what a wicked man!"
And—
"Ah, what a redoubtable god!"
1894   1895

I SAW A MAN PURSUING THE HORIZON

I saw a man pursuing the horizon;
Round and round they sped.
I was disturbed at this;
I accosted the man.
"It is futile," I said,
"You can never—"

"You lie," he cried,
And ran on.
1894   1895

SUPPOSING THAT I SHOULD HAVE THE COURAGE

Supposing that I should have the courage
To let a red sword of virtue
Plunge into my heart,
Letting to the weeds of the ground
My sinful blood,
What can you offer me?
A gardened castle?
A flowery kingdom?

What? A hope?
Then hence with your red sword of virtue.
1894   1895

ON THE HORIZON THE PEAKS ASSEMBLED

On the horizon the peaks assembled;
And as I looked,
The march of the mountains began.
As they marched, they sang:
"Aye! We come! We come!"
1894   1895

A MAN FEARED THAT HE MIGHT FIND AN ASSASSIN

A man feared that he might find an assassin;
Another that he might find a victim.
One was more wise than the other.
1894   1895

DO NOT WEEP, MAIDEN, FOR WAR IS KIND

Do not weep, maiden, for war is kind.
Because your lover threw wild hands toward the sky
And the affrighted steed ran on alone,
Do not weep.
War is kind.

Hoarse, booming drums of the regiment,
Little souls who thirst for fight,
These men were born to drill and die.
The unexplained glory flies above them,

Great is the Battle-God, great, and his Kingdom—   10
A field where a thousand corpses lie.

Do not weep, babe, for war is kind.
Because your father tumbled in the yellow trenches,
Raged at his breast, gulped and died,
Do not weep.
War is kind.

Swift blazing flag of the regiment,
Eagle with crest of red and gold,
These men were born to drill and die.
Point for them the virtue of slaughter,
Make plain to them the excellence of killing   20
And a field where a thousand corpses lie.

Mother whose heart hung humble as a button
On the bright splendid shroud of your son,
Do not weep.
War is kind.
1895   1896, 1899

A MAN SAID TO THE UNIVERSE

A man said to the universe:
"Sir, I exist!"
"However," replied the universe,
"The fact has not created in me
A sense of obligation."
1894   1899

A MAN ADRIFT ON A SLIM SPAR

A man adrift on a slim spar
A horizon smaller than the rim of a bottle
Tented waves rearing lashy dark points
The near whine of froth in circles.
            God is cold.   10

The incessant raise and swing of the sea
And growl after growl of crest
The sinkings, green, seething, endless
The upheaval half-completed.
            God is cold.

The seas are in the hollow of The Hand;
Oceans may be turned to a spray
Raining down through the stars
Because of a gesture of pity toward a babe.
Oceans may become grey ashes,
Die with a long moan and a roar
Amid the tumult of the fishes
And the cries of the ships,
Because The Hand beckons the mice.

A horizon smaller than a doomed assassin's cap,   20
Inky, surging tumults
A reeling, drunken sky and no sky
A pale hand sliding from a polished spar.
                    God is cold.

The puff of a coat imprisoning air.
A face kissing the water-death
A weary slow sway of a lost hand
And the sea, the moving sea, the sea.
                    God is cold.

1897   1929

MAGGIE
A GIRL OF THE STREETS

A STORY OF NEW YORK

CHAPTER I

A very little boy stood upon a heap of gravel for the honor of Rum Alley. He was throwing stones at howling urchins from Devil's Row who were circling madly about the heap and pelting at him.

His infantile countenance was livid with fury. His small body was writhing in the delivery of great, crimson oaths.

"Run, Jimmie, run! Dey'll get yehs," screamed a retreating Rum Alley child.

"Naw," responded Jimmie with a valiant roar, "dese micks[1] can't make me run."

Howls of renewed wrath went up from Devil's Row throats. Tattered gamins[2] on the right made a furious assault on the gravel heap. On their small, convulsed faces there shone the grins of true assassins. As they charged, they threw stones and cursed in shrill chorus.

The little champion of Rum Alley stumbled precipitately down the other side. His coat had been torn to shreds in a scuffle, and his hat was gone. He had bruises on twenty parts of his body, and blood was dripping from a cut in his head. His wan features wore a look of a tiny, insane demon.

On the ground, children from Devil's Row closed in on their antagonist. He

---

[1]"Irish."   [2]Street children, urchins.

crooked his left arm defensively about his head and fought with cursing fury. The little boys ran to and fro, dodging, hurling stones and swearing in barbaric trebles.

From a window of an apartment house that upreared its form from amid squat, ignorant stables, there leaned a curious woman. Some laborers, unloading a scow at a dock at the river,[3] paused for a moment and regarded the fight. The engineer of a passive tugboat hung lazily to a railing and watched. Over on the Island,[4] a worm of yellow convicts came from the shadow of a grey ominous building and crawled slowly along the river's bank.

A stone had smashed into Jimmie's mouth. Blood was bubbling over his chin and down upon his ragged shirt. Tears made furrows on his dirt-stained cheeks. His thin legs had begun to tremble and turn weak, causing his small body to reel. His roaring curses of the first part of the fight had changed to a blasphemous chatter.

In the yells of the whirling mob of Devil's Row children there were notes of joy like songs of triumphant savagery. The little boys seemed to leer gloatingly at the blood upon the other child's face.

Down the avenue came boastfully sauntering a lad of sixteen years, although the chronic sneer of an ideal manhood already sat upon his lips. His hat was tipped with an air of challenge over his eye. Between his teeth, a cigar stump was tilted at the angle of defiance. He walked with a certain swing of the shoulders which appalled the timid. He glanced over into the vacant lot in which the little raving boys from Devil's Row seethed about the shrieking and tearful child from Rum Alley.

"Gee!" he murmured with interest. "A scrap. Gee!"

He strode over to the cursing circle, swinging his shoulders in a manner which denoted that he held victory in his fists. He approached at the back of one of the most deeply engaged of the Devil's Row children.

"Ah, what deh hell," he said, and smote the deeply engaged one on the back of the head. The little boy fell to the ground and gave a hoarse, tremendous howl. He scrambled to his feet, and perceiving, evidently, the size of his assailant, ran quickly off, shouting alarms. The entire Devil's Row party followed him. They came to a stand a short distance away and yelled taunting oaths at the boy with the chronic sneer. The latter, momentarily, paid no attention to them.

"What deh hell, Jimmie?" he asked of the small champion.

Jimmie wiped his blood-wet features with his sleeve.

"Well, it was dis way, Pete, see! I was goin' teh lick dat Riley kid and dey all pitched on me."

Some Rum Alley children now came forward. The party stood for a moment exchanging vainglorious remarks with Devil's Row. A few stones were thrown at long distances, and words of challenge passed between small warriors. Then the Rum Alley contingent turned slowly in the direction of their home street. They began to give, each to each, distorted versions of the fight. Causes of retreat in particular cases were magnified. Blows dealt in the fight were enlarged to catapultian power, and stones thrown were alleged to have hurtled with infinite accuracy. Valor grew strong again, and the little boys began to swear with great spirit.

"Ah, we blokies[5] kin lick deh hull damn Row," said a child, swaggering.

[3]New York City's East River, separating Brooklyn from Manhattan.
[4]Blackwell's Island (present-day Roosevelt Island) in the East River. It was the site of city poorhouses, hospitals, and prisons.
[5]"Fellows."

Little Jimmie was striving to stanch the flow of blood from his cut lips. Scowling, he turned upon the speaker.

"Ah, where deh hell was yeh when I was doin' all deh fightin'?" he demanded. "Youse kids makes me tired."

"Ah, go ahn," replied the other argumentatively.

Jimmie replied with heavy contempt. "Ah, youse can't fight, Blue Billie! I kin lick yeh wid one han'."

"Ah, go ahn," replied Billie again.

"Ah," said Jimmie threateningly.

"Ah," said the other in the same tone.

They struck at each other, clinched, and rolled over on the cobble stones.

"Smash'im, Jimmie, kick deh damn guts out of 'im," yelled Pete, the lad with the chronic sneer, in tones of delight.

The small combatants pounded and kicked, scratched and tore. They began to weep and their curses struggled in their throats with sobs. The other little boys clasped their hands and wriggled their legs in excitement. They formed a bobbing circle about the pair.

A tiny spectator was suddenly agitated.

"Cheese it, Jimmie, cheese it! Here comes yer fader," he yelled.

The circle of little boys instantly parted. They drew away and waited in ecstatic awe for that which was about to happen. The two little boys fighting in the modes of four thousand years ago, did not hear the warning.

Up the avenue there plodded slowly a man with sullen eyes. He was carrying a dinner pail and smoking an apple-wood pipe.

As he neared the spot where the little boys strove, he regarded them listlessly. But suddenly he roared an oath and advanced upon the rolling fighters.

"Here, you Jim, git up, now, while I belt yer life out, you damned disorderly brat."

He began to kick into the chaotic mass on the ground. The boy Billie felt a heavy boot strike his head. He made a furious effort and disentangled himself from Jimmie. He tottered away, damning.

Jimmie arose painfully from the ground and confronting his father, began to curse him. His parent kicked him. "Come home, now," he cried, "an' stop yer jawin', er I'll lam[6] the everlasting head off yehs."

They departed. The man paced placidly along with the apple-wood emblem of serenity between his teeth. The boy followed a dozen feet in the rear. He swore luridly, for he felt that it was degradation for one who aimed to be some vague soldier, or a man of blood with a sort of sublime license, to be taken home by a father.

CHAPTER II

Eventually they entered into a dark region where, from a careening building, a dozen gruesome doorways gave up loads of babies to the street and the gutter. A wind of early autumn raised yellow dust from cobbles and swirled it against an hundred windows. Long streamers of garments fluttered from fire-escapes. In all unhandy places there were buckets, brooms, rags and bottles. In the street infants played or fought with other infants or sat stupidly in the way of vehicles.

[6]"Beat."

Formidable women, with uncombed hair and disordered dress, gossiped while leaning on railings, or screamed in frantic quarrels. Withered persons, in curious postures of submission to something, sat smoking pipes in obscure corners. A thousand odors of cooking food came forth to the street. The building quivered and creaked from the weight of humanity stamping about in its bowels.

A small ragged girl dragged a red, bawling infant along the crowded ways. He was hanging back, baby-like, bracing his wrinkled, bare legs.

The little girl cried out: "Ah, Tommie, come ahn. Dere's Jimmie and fader. Don't be a-pullin' me back."

She jerked the baby's arm impatiently. He fell on his face, roaring. With a second jerk she pulled him to his feet, and they went on. With the obstinacy of his order, he protested against being dragged in a chosen direction. He made heroic endeavors to keep on his legs, denounce his sister and consume a bit of orange peeling which he chewed between the times of his infantile orations.

As the sullen-eyed man, followed by the blood-covered boy, drew near, the little girl burst into reproachful cries, "Ah, Jimmie, youse bin fightin' agin."

The urchin swelled disdainfully.

"Ah, what deh hell, Mag. See?"

The little girl upbraided him. "Youse allus fightin', Jimmie, an' yeh knows it puts mudder out when yehs come home half dead, an' it's like we'll all get a poundin'."

She began to weep. The babe threw back his head and roared at his prospects.

"Ah, what deh hell!" cried Jimmie. "Shut up er I'll smack yer mout'. See?"

As his sister continued her lamentations, he suddenly swore and struck her. The little girl reeled and, recovering herself, burst into tears and quaveringly cursed him. As she slowly retreated her brother advanced dealing her cuffs. The father heard and turned about.

"Stop that, Jim, d'yeh hear? Leave yer sister alone on the street. It's like I can never beat any sense into yer damned wooden head."

The urchin raised his voice in defiance to his parent and continued his attacks. The babe bawled tremendously, protesting with great violence. During his sister's hasty manœuvres, he was dragged by the arm.

Finally the procession plunged into one of the gruesome doorways. They crawled up dark stairways and along cold, gloomy halls. At last the father pushed open a door and they entered a lighted room in which a large woman was rampant.

She stopped in a career from a seething stove to a pan-covered table. As the father and children filed in she peered at them.

"Eh, what? Been fightin' agin, by Gawd!" She threw herself upon Jimmie. The urchin tried to dart behind the others and in the scuffle the babe, Tommie, was knocked down. He protested with his usual vehemence, because they had bruised his tender shins against a table leg.

The mother's massive shoulders heaved with anger. Grasping the urchin by the neck and shoulder she shook him until he rattled. She dragged him to an unholy sink, and, soaking a rag in water, began to scrub his lacerated face with it. Jimmie screamed in pain and tried to twist his shoulders out of the clasp of the huge arms.

The babe sat on the floor watching the scene, his face in contortions like that of a woman at a tragedy. The father, with a newly-ladened pipe in his mouth, crouched on a backless chair near the stove. Jimmie's cries annoyed him. He turned about and bellowed at his wife:

"Let the damned kid alone for a minute, will yeh, Mary? Yer allus poundin' 'im. When I come nights I can't git no rest 'cause yer allus poundin' a kid. Let up, d'yeh hear? Don't be allus poundin' a kid."

The woman's operations on the urchin instantly increased in violence. At last she tossed him to a corner where he limply lay cursing and weeping.

The wife put her immense hands on her hips and with a chieftain-like stride approached her husband.

"Ho," she said, with a great grunt of contempt. "An' what in the devil are you stickin' your nose for?"

The babe crawled under the table and, turning, peered out cautiously. The ragged girl retreated and the urchin in the corner drew his legs carefully beneath him.

The man puffed his pipe calmly and put his great mudded boots on the back part of the stove.

"Go teh hell," he murmured, tranquilly.

The woman screamed and shook her fists before her husband's eyes. The rough yellow of her face and neck flared suddenly crimson. She began to howl.

He puffed imperturbably at his pipe for a time, but finally arose and began to look out at the window into the darkening chaos of back yards.

"You've been drinkin', Mary," he said. "You'd better let up on the bot', ol' woman, or you'll git done."

"You're a liar. I ain't had a drop," she roared in reply.

They had a lurid altercation, in which they damned each other's souls with frequence.

The babe was staring out from under the table, his small face working in his excitement.

The ragged girl went stealthily over to the corner where the urchin lay.

"Are yehs hurted much, Jimmie?" she whispered timidly.

"Not a damn bit! See?" growled the little boy.

"Will I wash deh blood?"

"Naw!"

"Will I—"

"When I catch dat Riley kid I'll break 'is face! Dat's right! See?"

He turned his face to the wall as if resolved to grimly bide his time.

In the quarrel between husband and wife, the woman was victor. The man grabbed his hat and rushed from the room, apparently determined upon a vengeful drunk. She followed to the door and thundered at him as he made his way down-stairs.

She returned and stirred up the room until her children were bobbing about like bubbles.

"Git outa deh way," she persistently bawled, waving feet with their dishevelled shoes near the heads of her children. She shrouded herself, puffing and snorting, in a cloud of steam at the stove, and eventually extracted a frying-pan full of potatoes that hissed.

She flourished it. "Come teh yer suppers, now," she cried with sudden exasperation. "Hurry up, now, er I'll help yeh!"

The children scrambled hastily. With prodigious clatter they arranged themselves at table. The babe sat with his feet dangling high from a precarious infant chair and gorged his small stomach. Jimmie forced, with feverish rapidity, the grease-enveloped pieces between his wounded lips. Maggie, with side glances of fear of interruption, ate like a small pursued tigress.

The mother sat blinking at them. She delivered reproaches, swallowed potatoes and drank from a yellow-brown bottle. After a time her mood changed and she wept as she carried little Tommie into another room and laid him to sleep with his fists doubled in an old quilt of faded red and green grandeur. Then she came and moaned by the stove. She rocked to and fro upon a chair, shedding tears and crooning miserably to the two children about their "poor mother" and "yer fader, damn 'is soul."

The little girl plodded between the table and the chair with a dish-pan on it. She tottered on her small legs beneath burdens of dishes.

Jimmie sat nursing his various wounds. He cast furtive glances at his mother. His practised eye perceived her gradually emerge from a muddled mist of sentiment until her brain burned in drunken heat. He sat breathless.

Maggie broke a plate.

The mother started to her feet as if propelled.

"Good Gawd," she howled. Her eyes glittered on her child with sudden hatred. The fervent red of her face turned almost to purple. The little boy ran to the halls, shrieking like a monk in an earthquake.

He floundered about in darkness until he found the stairs. He stumbled, panic-striken, to the next floor. An old woman opened a door. A light behind her threw a flare on the urchin's quivering face.

"Eh, Gawd, child, what is it dis time? Is yer fader beatin' yer mudder, or yer mudder beatin' yer fader?"

CHAPTER III

Jimmie and the old woman listened long in the hall. Above the muffled roar of conversation, the dismal wailings of babies at night, the thumping of feet in unseen corridors and rooms, mingled with the sound of varied hoarse shoutings in the street and the rattling of wheels over cobbles, they heard the screams of the child and the roars of the mother die away to a feeble moaning and a subdued bass muttering.

The old woman was a gnarled and leathery personage who could don, at will, an expression of great virtue. She possessed a small music box capable of one tune, and a collection of "God bless yehs" pitched in assorted keys of fervency. Each day she took a position upon the stones of Fifth Avenue,[1] where she crooked her legs under her and crouched immovable and hideous, like an idol. She received daily a small sum in pennies. It was contributed, for the most part, by persons who did not make their homes in that vicinity.

Once, when a lady had dropped her purse on the sidewalk, the gnarled woman had grabbed it and smuggled it with great dexterity beneath her cloak. When she was arrested she had cursed the lady into a partial swoon, and with her aged limbs, twisted from rheumatism, had almost kicked the stomach out of a huge policeman whose conduct upon that occasion she referred to when she said: "The police, damn 'em."

"Eh, Jimmie, it's cursed shame," she said. "Go, now, like a dear an' buy me a can,[2] an' if yer mudder raises 'ell all night yehs can sleep here."

Jimmie took a tendered tin-pail and seven pennies and departed. He passed into the side door of a saloon and went to the bar. Straining up on his toes he raised the pail and pennies as high as his arms would let him. He saw two hands

[1] Fashionable street in New York City.
[2] I.e., a pail (canister) of beer. In the 1880s and 1890s the conventional tin beer pail held about two quarts.

thrust down and take them. Directly the same hands let down the filled pail and he left.

In front of the gruesome doorway he met a lurching figure. It was his father, swaying about on uncertain legs.

"Give me deh can. See?" said the man, threateningly.

"Ah, come off! I got dis can fer dat ol' woman an' it 'ud be dirt teh swipe it. See?" cried Jimmie.

The father wrenched the pail from the urchin. He grasped it in both hands and lifted it to his mouth. He glued his lips to the under edge and tilted his head. His hairy throat swelled until it seemed to grow near his chin. There was a tremendous gulping movement and the beer was gone.

The man caught his breath and laughed. He hit his son on the head with the empty pail. As it rolled clanging into the street, Jimmie began to scream and kicked repeatedly at his father's shins.

"Look at deh dirt what yeh done me," he yelled. "Deh ol' woman 'ill be raisin' hell."

He retreated to the middle of the street, but the man did not pursue. He staggered toward the door.

"I'll club hell outa yeh when I ketch yeh," he shouted, and disappeared.

During the evening he had been standing against a bar drinking whiskies and declaring to all comers, confidentially: "My home reg'lar livin' hell! Damndes' place! Reg'lar hell! Why do I come an' drink' whisk' here thish way? 'Cause home reg'lar livin' hell!"

Jimmie waited a long time in the street and then crept warily up through the building. He passed with great caution the door of the gnarled woman, and finally stopped outside his home and listened.

He could hear his mother moving heavily about among the furniture of the room. She was chanting in a mournful voice, occasionally interjecting bursts of volcanic wrath at the father, who, Jimmie judged, had sunk down on the floor or in a corner.

"Why deh blazes don' chere try teh keep Jim from fightin'? I'll break yer jaw," she suddenly bellowed.

The man mumbled with drunken indifference. "Ah, wha' deh hell. W'a's odds? Wha' makes kick?"

"Because he tears 'is clothes, yeh damn fool," cried the woman in supreme wrath.

The husband seemed to become aroused. "Go teh hell," he thundered fiercely in reply. There was a crash against the door and something broke into clattering fragments. Jimmie partially suppressed a howl and darted down the stairway. Below he paused and listened. He heard howls and curses, groans and shrieks, confusingly in chorus as if a battle were raging. With all was the crash of splintering furniture. The eyes of the urchin glared in fear that one of them would discover him.

Curious faces appeared in doorways, and whispered comments passed to and fro. "Ol' Johnson's raisin' hell again."

Jimmie stood until the noises ceased and the other inhabitants of the tenement had all yawned and shut their doors. Then he crawled up-stairs with the caution of an invader of a panther den. Sounds of labored breathing came through the broken door-panels. He pushed the door open and entered, quaking.

A glow from the fire threw red hues over the bare floor, the cracked and soiled plastering, and the overturned and broken furniture.

In the middle of the floor lay his mother asleep. In one corner of the room his father's limp body hung across the seat of a chair.

The urchin stole forward. He began to shiver in dread of awakening his parents. His mother's great chest was heaving painfully. Jimmie paused and looked down at her. Her face was inflamed and swollen from drinking. Her yellow brows shaded eye-lids that had grown blue. Her tangled hair tossed in waves over her forehead. Her mouth was set in the same lines of vindictive hatred that it had, perhaps, borne during the fight. Her bare, red arms were thrown out above her head in positions of exhaustion, something, mayhap, like those of a sated villain.

The urchin bended over his mother. He was fearful lest she should open her eyes, and the dread within him was so strong, that he could not forbear to stare, but hung as if fascinated over the woman's grim face.

Suddenly her eyes opened. The urchin found himself looking straight into that expression, which, it would seem, had the power to change his blood to salt. He howled piercingly and fell backward.

The woman floundered for a moment, tossed her arms about her head as if in combat, and again began to snore.

Jimmie crawled back in the shadows and waited. A noise in the next room had followed his cry at the discovery that his mother was awake. He grovelled in the gloom, the eyes from out his drawn face riveted upon the intervening door.

He heard it creak, and then the sound of a small voice came to him. "Jimmie! Jimmie! Are yehs dere?" it whispered. The urchin started. The thin, white face of his sister looked at him from the doorway of the other room. She crept to him across the floor.

The father had not moved, but lay in the same death-like sleep. The mother writhed in uneasy slumber, her chest wheezing as if she were in the agonies of strangulation. Out at the window a florid moon was peering over dark roofs, and in the distance the waters of a river glimmered pallidly.

The small frame of the ragged girl was quivering. Her featurers were haggard from weeping, and her eyes gleamed from fear. She grasped the urchin's arm in her little trembling hands and they huddled in a corner. The eyes of both were drawn, by some force, to stare at the woman's face, for they thought she need only to awake and all fiends would come from below.

They crouched until the ghost-mists of dawn appeared at the window, drawing close to the panes, and looking in at the prostrate, heaving body of the mother.

CHAPTER IV

The babe, Tommie, died. He went away in a white, insignificant coffin, his small waxen hand clutching a flower that the girl, Maggie, had stolen from an Italian.

She and Jimmie lived.

The inexperienced fibres of the boy's eyes were hardened at an early age. He became a young man of leather. He lived some red years without laboring. During that time his sneer became chronic. He studied human nature in the gutter, and found it no worse than he thought he had reason to believe it. He never conceived a respect for the world, because he had begun with no idols that it had smashed.

He clad his soul in armor by means of happening hilariously in at a mission church where a man composed his sermons of "yous." While they got warm at the stove, he told his hearers just where he calculated they stood with the Lord. Many of the sinners were impatient over the pictured depths of their degradation. They were waiting for soup-tickets.

A reader of words of wind-demons might have been able to see the portions of a dialogue pass to and fro between the exhorter and his hearers.

"You are damned," said the preacher. And the reader of sounds might have seen the reply go forth from the ragged people: "Where's our soup?"

Jimmie and a companion sat in a rear seat and commented upon the things that didn't concern them, with all the freedom of English gentlemen. When they grew thirsty and went out their minds confused the speaker with Christ.

Momentarily, Jimmie was sullen with thoughts of a hopeless altitude where grew fruit. His companion said that if he should ever meet God he would ask for a million dollars and a bottle of beer.

Jimmie's occupation for a long time was to stand on street-corners and watch the world go by, dreaming blood-red dreams at the passing of pretty women. He menaced mankind at the intersections of streets.

On the corners he was in life and of life. The world was going on and he was there to perceive it.

He maintained a belligerent attitude toward all well-dressed men. To him fine raiment was allied to weakness, and all good coats covered faint hearts. He and his order were kings, to a certain extent, over the men of untarnished clothes, because these latter dreaded, perhaps, to be either killed or laughed at.

Above all things he despised obvious Christians and ciphers with the chrysanthemums of aristocracy in their button-holes. He considered himself above both of these classes. He was afraid of neither the devil nor the leader of society.

When he had a dollar in his pocket his satisfaction with existence was the greatest thing in the world. So, eventually, he felt obliged to work. His father died and his mother's years were divided up into periods of thirty days.

He became a truck driver. He was given the charge of a pains-taking pair of horses and a large rattling truck. He invaded the turmoil and tumble of the down-town streets and learned to breathe maledictory defiance at the police who occasionally used to climb up, drag him from his perch and beat him.

In the lower part of the city he daily involved himself in hideous tangles. If he and his team chanced to be in the rear he preserved a demeanor of serenity, crossing his legs and bursting forth into yells when foot-passengers took dangerous dives beneath the noses of his champing horses. He smoked his pipe calmly for he knew that his pay was marching on.

If in the front and the key-truck of chaos, he entered terrifically into the quarrel that was raging to and fro among the drivers on their high seats, and sometimes roared oaths and violently got himself arrested.

After a time his sneer grew so that it turned its glare upon all things. He became so sharp that he believed in nothing. To him the police were always actuated by malignant impulses and the rest of the world was composed, for the most part, of despicable creatures who were all trying to take advantage of him and with whom, in defense, he was obliged to quarrel on all possible occasions. He himself occupied a down-trodden position that had a private but distinct element of grandeur in its isolation.

The most complete cases of aggravated idiocy were, to his mind, rampant upon the front platforms of all of the street cars. At first his tongue strove with these beings, but he eventually was superior. He became immured like an African cow. In him grew a majestic contempt for those strings of street cars that followed him like intent bugs.

He fell into the habit, when starting on a long journey, of fixing his eye on a high and distant object, commanding his horses to begin, and then going into a sort of a trance of observation. Multitudes of drivers might howl in his rear, and passengers might load him with opprobrium, he would not awaken until some blue policeman turned red and began to frenziedly tear bridles and beat the soft noses of the responsible horses.

When he paused to contemplate the attitude of the police toward himself and his fellows, he believed that they were the only men in the city who had no rights. When driving about, he felt that he was held liable by the police for anything that might occur in the streets, and was the common prey of all energetic officials. In revenge, he resolved never to move out of the way of anything, until formidable circumstances, or a much larger man than himself forced him to it.

Foot-passengers were mere pestering flies with an insane disregard for their legs and his convenience. He could not conceive their maniacal desires to cross the streets. Their madness smote him with eternal amazement. He was continually storming at them from his throne. He sat aloft and denounced their frantic leaps, plunges, dives and straddles.

When they would thrust at, or parry, the noses of his champing horses, making them swing their heads and move their feet, disturbing a solid dreamy repose, he swore at the men as fools, for he himself could perceive that Providence had caused it clearly to be written, that he and his team had the unalienable right to stand in the proper path of the sun chariot, and if they so minded, obstruct its mission or take a wheel off.

And, perhaps, if the god-driver had an ungovernable desire to step down, put up his flame-colored fists and manfully dispute the right of way, he would have probably been immediately opposed by a scowling mortal with two sets of very hard knuckles.

It is possible, perhaps, that this young man would have derided, in an axle-wide alley, the approach of a flying ferry boat. Yet he achieved a respect for a fire engine. As one charged toward his truck, he would drive fearfully upon a sidewalk, threatening untold people with annihilation. When an engine would strike a mass of blocked trucks, splitting it into fragments, as a blow annihilates a cake of ice, Jimmie's team could usually be observed high and safe, with whole wheels, on the sidewalk. The fearful coming of the engine could break up the most intricate muddle of heavy vehicles at which the police had been swearing for the half of an hour.

A fire engine was enshrined in his heart as an appalling thing that he loved with a distant dog-like devotion. They had been known to overturn streetcars. Those leaping horses, striking sparks from the cobbles in their forward lunge, were creatures to be ineffably admired. The clang of the gong pierced his breast like a noise of remembered war.

When Jimmie was a little boy, he began to be arrested. Before he reached a great age, he had a fair record.

He developed too great a tendency to climb down from his truck and fight with other drivers. He had been in quite a number of miscellaneous fights, and in some general bar-room rows that had become known to the police. Once he had been arrested for assaulting a Chinaman. Two women in different parts of the city, and entirely unknown to each other, caused him considerable annoyance by breaking forth, simultaneously, at fateful intervals, into wailings about marriage and support and infants.

Nevertheless, he had, on a certain star-lit evening, said wonderingly and quite reverently: "Deh moon looks like hell, don't it?"

CHAPTER V

The girl, Maggie, blossomed in a mud puddle. She grew to be a most rare and wonderful production of a tenement district, a pretty girl.

None of the dirt of Rum Alley seemed to be in her veins. The philosophers up-stairs, down-stairs and on the same floor puzzled over it.

When a child, playing and fighting with gamins in the street, dirt disguised her. Attired in tatters and grime, she went unseen.

There came a time, however, when the young men of the vicinity said: "Dat Johnson goil is a puty good looker." About this period her brother remarked to her: "Mag, I'll tell yeh dis! See? Yeh've edder got teh go teh hell or go teh work!" Whereupon she went to work, having the feminine aversion of going to hell.

By a chance, she got a position in an establishment where they made collars and cuffs. She received a stool and a machine in a room where sat twenty girls of various shades of yellow discontent. She perched on the stool and treadled at her machine all day, turning out collars, the name of whose brand could be noted for its irrelevancy to anything in connection with collars. At night she returned home to her mother.

Jimmie grew large enough to take the vague position of head of the family. As incumbent of that office, he stumbled up-stairs late at night, as his father had done before him. He reeled about the room, swearing at his relations, or went to sleep on the floor.

The mother had gradually arisen to that degree of fame that she could bandy words with her acquaintances among the police-justices. Court-officials called her by her first name. When she appeared they pursued a course which had been theirs for months. They invariably grinned and cried out: "Hello, Mary, you here again?" Her gray head wagged in many a court. She always besieged the bench with voluble excuses, explanations, apologies and prayers. Her flaming face and rolling eyes were a sort of familiar sight on the Island.[1] She measured time by means of sprees, and was eternally swollen and dishevelled.

One day the young man, Pete, who as a lad had smitten the Devil's Row urchin in the back of the head and put to flight the antagonists of his friend, Jimmie, strutted upon the scene. He met Jimmie one day on the street, promised to take him to a boxing match in Williamsburg,[2] and called for him in the evening.

Maggie observed Pete.

He sat on a table in the Johnson home and dangled his checked legs with an enticing nonchalance. His hair was curled down over his forehead in an oiled bang. His rather pugged nose seemed to revolt from contact with a bristling moustache of short, wire-like hairs. His blue double-breasted coat, edged with black braid, buttoned close to a red puff tie, and his patent-leather shoes looked like murder-fitted weapons.

[1] I.e., in the city's prison on Blackwell's Island in the East River.
[2] A section of Brooklyn, across the East River from Manhattan.

His mannerisms stamped him as a man who had a correct sense of his personal superiority. There was valor and contempt for circumstances in the glance of his eye. He waved his hands like a man of the world, who dismisses religion and philosophy, and says "Fudge." He had certainly seen everything and with each curl of his lip, he declared that it amounted to nothing. Maggie thought he must be a very elegant and graceful bartender.

He was telling tales to Jimmie.

Maggie watched him furtively, with half-closed eyes, lit with a vague interest.

"Hully gee! Dey makes me tired," he said. "Mos' e'ry day some farmer[3] comes in an' tries teh run deh shop. See? But dey gits t'rowed right out! I jolt dem right out in deh street before dey knows where dey is! See?"

"Sure," said Jimmie.

"Dere was a mug come in deh place deh odder day wid an idear he wus goin' teh own deh place! Hully gee, he wus goin' teh own deh place! I see he had a still[4] on an' I didn' wanna giv'im no stuff, so I says: 'Git deh hell outa here an' don' make no trouble,' I says like dat! See? 'Git deh hell outa here an' don' make no trouble'; like dat. 'Git deh hell outa here,' I says. See?"

Jimmie nodded understandingly. Over his features played an eager desire to state the amount of his valor in a similar crisis, but the narrator proceeded.

"Well, deh blokie he says: 'T'hell wid it! I ain' lookin' for no scrap,' he says (See?) 'but' he says, 'I'm 'spectable cit'zen an' I wanna drink an' purtydamnsoon, too.' See? 'Deh hell,' I says. Like dat! 'Deh hell,' I says. See? 'Don' make no trouble,' I says. Like dat. 'Don' make no trouble.' See? Den deh mug he squared off an' said he was fine as silk wid his dukes (See?) an' he wanned a drink damnquick. Dat's what he said. See?"

"Sure," repeated Jimmie.

Pete continued. "Say, I jes' jumped deh bar an' deh way I plunked[5] dat blokie was great. See? Dat's right! In deh jaw! See? Hully gee, he t'rowed a spittoon true deh front windee. Say, I taut I'd drop dead. But deh boss, he comes in after an' he says, 'Pete, yehs done jes' right! Yeh've gota keep order an' it's all right.' See? 'It's all right,' he says. Dat's what he said."

The two held a technical discussion.

"Dat bloke was a dandy," said Pete, in conclusion, "but he hadn' oughta made no trouble. Dat's what I says teh dem: 'Don' come in here an' make no trouble,' I says, like dat. 'Don' make no trouble.' See?"

As Jimmie and his friend exchanged tales descriptive of their prowess, Maggie leaned back in the shadow. Her eyes dwelt wonderingly and rather wistfully upon Pete's face. The broken furniture, grimy walls, and general disorder and dirt of her home of a sudden appeared before her and began to take a potential aspect. Pete's aristocratic person looked as if it might soil. She looked keenly at him, occasionally, wondering if he was feeling contempt. But Pete seemed to be enveloped in reminiscence.

"Hully gee," said he, "dose mugs can't faze me. Dey knows I kin wipe up deh street wid any t'ree of dem."

When he said, "Ah, what deh hell," his voice was burdened with disdain for the inevitable and contempt for anything that fate might compel him to endure.

Maggie perceived that here was the beau ideal of a man. Her dim thoughts were often searching for far away lands where, as God says, the little hills sing together[6] in the morning. Under the trees of her dream-gardens there had always walked a lover.

---

[3]"Yokel," "dolt."   [4]"Drunk."   [5]"Hit."
[6]"The little hills rejoice on every side." Psalm 65:12.

CHAPTER VI

Pete took note of Maggie.

"Say, Mag, I'm stuck on yer shape. It's outa sight," he said, parenthetically, with an affable grin.

As he became aware that she was listening closely, he grew still more eloquent in his descriptions of various happenings in his career. It appeared that he was invincible in fights.

"Why," he said, referring to a man with whom he had had a misunderstanding, "dat mug scrapped like a damn dago.[1] Dat's right. He was dead easy. See? He taut he was a scrapper! But he foun' out diff'ent ! Hully gee."

He walked to and fro in the small room, which seemed then to grow even smaller and unfit to hold his dignity, the attribute of a supreme warrior. That swing of the shoulders that had frozen the timid when he was but a lad had increased with his growth and education at the ratio of ten to one. It, combined with the sneer upon his mouth, told mankind that there was nothing in space which could appall him. Maggie marvelled at him and surrounded him with greatness. She vaguely tried to calculate the altitude of the pinnacle from which he must have looked down upon her.

"I met a chump deh odder day way up in deh city," he said. "I was goin' teh see a frien' of mine. When I was a-crossin' deh street deh chump runned plump inteh me, an' den he turns aroun' an' says, 'Yer insolen' ruffin,' he says, like dat. 'Oh, gee,' I says, 'oh, gee, go teh hell and git off deh eart',' I says, like dat. See? 'Go teh hell an' git off deh eart',' like dat. Den deh blokie he got wild. He says I was a contempt'ble scoun'el, er some'ting like dat, an' he says I was doom' teh everlastin' pe'dition an' all like dat. 'Gee,' I says, 'gee! Deh hell I am,' I says. 'Deh hell I am,' like dat. An' den I slugged 'im. See?"

With Jimmie in his company, Pete departed in a sort of a blaze of glory from the Johnson home. Maggie, leaning from the window, watched him as he walked down the street.

Here was a formidable man who disdained the strength of a world full of fists. Here was one who had contempt for brass-clothed power; one whose knuckles could defiantly ring against the granite of law. He was a knight.

The two men went from under the glimmering street-lamp and passed into shadows.

Turning, Maggie contemplated the dark, dust-stained walls, and the scant and crude furniture of her home. A clock, in a splintered and battered oblong box of varnished wood, she suddenly regarded as an abomination. She noted that it ticked raspingly. The almost vanished flowers in the carpet-pattern, she conceived to be newly hideous. Some faint attempts she had made with blue ribbon, to freshen the appearance of a dingy curtain, she now saw to be piteous.

She wondered what Pete dined on.

She reflected upon the collar and cuff factory. It began to appear to her mind as a dreary place of endless grinding. Pete's elegant occupation brought him, no doubt, into contact with people who had money and manners. It was probable that he had a large acquaintance of pretty girls. He must have great sums of money to spend.

To her the earth was composed of hardships and insults. She felt instant admiration for a man who openly defied it. She thought that if the grim angel

---

[1] "Italian."

of death should clutch his heart, Pete would shrug his shoulders and say: "Oh, ev'ryt'ing goes."

She anticipated that he would come again shortly. She spent some of her week's pay in the purchase of flowered cretonne[2] for a lambrequin.[3] She made it with infinite care and hung it to the slightly-careening mantel, over the stove, in the kitchen. She studied it with painful anxiety from different points in the room. She wanted it to look well on Sunday night when, perhaps, Jimmie's friend would come. On Sunday night, however, Pete did not appear.

Afterward the girl looked at it with a sense of humiliation. She was now convinced that Pete was superior to admiration for lambrequins.

A few evenings later Pete entered with fascinating innovations in his apparel. As she had seen him twice and he had different suits on each time, Maggie had a dim impression that his wardrobe was prodigiously extensive.

"Say, Mag," he said, "put on yer bes' duds Friday night an' I'll take yehs teh deh show. See?"

He spent a few moments in flourishing his clothes and then vanished, without having glanced at the lambrequin.

Over the eternal collars and cuffs in the factory Maggie spent the most of three days in making imaginary sketches of Pete and his daily environment. She imagined some half dozen women in love with him and thought he must lean dangerously toward an indefinite one, whom she pictured with great charms of person, but with an altogether contemptible disposition.

She thought he must live in a blare of pleasure. He had friends, and people who were afraid of him.

She saw the golden glitter of the place where Pete was to take her. An entertainment of many hues and many melodies where she was afraid she might appear small and mouse-colored.

Her mother drank whiskey all Friday morning. With lurid face and tossing hair she cursed and destroyed furniture all Friday afternoon. When Maggie came home at half-past six her mother lay asleep amidst the wreck of chairs and a table. Fragments of various household utensils were scattered about the floor. She had vented some phase of drunken fury upon the lambrequin. It lay in a bedraggled heap in the corner.

"Hah," she snorted, sitting up suddenly, "where deh hell yeh been? Why deh hell don' yeh come earlier? Been loafin' round deh streets. Yer gettin' teh be a reg'lar devil."

When Pete arrived Maggie, in a worn black dress, was waiting for him in the midst of a floor strewn with wreckage. The curtain at the window had been pulled by a heavy hand and hung by one tack, dangling to and fro in the draft through the cracks at the sash. The knots of blue ribbons appeared like violated flowers. The fire in the stove had gone out. The displaced lids and open doors showed heaps of sullen gray ashes. The remnants of a meal, ghastly, like dead flesh, lay in a corner. Maggie's red mother, stretched on the floor, blasphemed and gave her daughter a bad name.

CHAPTER VII

An orchestra of yellow silk women and bald-headed men on an elevated stage near the centre of a great green-hued hall, played a popular waltz. The place

[2]Heavy fabric used for curtains and upholstery.
[3]Decorative drape, a valance.

was crowded with people grouped about little tables. A battalion of waiters slid among the throng, carrying trays of beer glasses and making change from the inexhaustible vaults of their trousers pockets. Little boys, in the costumes of French chefs, paraded up and down the irregular aisles vending fancy cakes. There was a low rumble of conversation and a subdued clinking of glasses. Clouds of tobacco smoke rolled and wavered high in air about the dull gilt of the chandeliers.

The vast crowd had an air throughout of having just quitted labor. Men with calloused hands and attired in garments that showed the wear of an endless trudge[1] for a living, smoked their pipes contentedly and spent five, ten, or perhaps fifteen cents for beer. There was a mere sprinkling of kid-gloved men who smoked cigars purchased elsewhere. The great body of the crowd was composed of people who showed that all day they strove with their hands. Quiet Germans, with maybe their wives and two or three children, sat listening to the music, with the expressions of happy cows. An occasional party of sailors from a war-ship, their faces pictures of sturdy health, spent the earlier hours of the evening at the small round tables. Very infrequent tipsy men, swollen with the value of their opinions, engaged their companions in earnest and confidential conversation. In the balcony, and here and there below, shone the impassive faces of women. The nationalities of the Bowery[2] beamed upon the stage from all directions.

Pete aggressively walked up a side aisle and took seats with Maggie at a table beneath the balcony.

"Two beehs!"

Leaning back he regarded with eyes of superiority the scene before them. This attitude affected Maggie strongly. A man who could regard such a sight with indifference must be accustomed to very great things.

It was obvious that Pete had been to this place many times before, and was very familiar with it. A knowledge of this fact made Maggie feel little and new.

He was extremely gracious and attentive. He displayed the consideration of a cultured gentleman who knew what was due.

"Say, what deh hell? Bring deh lady a big glass! What deh hell use is dat pony?"[3]

"Don't be fresh, now," said the waiter, with some warmth, as he departed.

"Ah, git off deh eart'," said Pete, after the other's retreating form.

Maggie perceived that Pete brought forth all his elegance and all his knowledge of high-class customs for her benefit. Her heart warmed as she reflected upon his condescension.

The orchestra of yellow silk women and bald-headed men gave vent to a few bars of anticipatory music and a girl, in a pink dress with short skirts, galloped upon the stage. She smiled upon the throng as if in acknowledgment of a warm welcome, and began to walk to and fro, making profuse gesticulations and singing, in brazen soprano tones, a song, the words of which were inaudible. When she broke into the swift rattling measures of a chorus some half-tipsy men near the stage joined in the rollicking refrain and glasses were pounded rhythmically upon the tables. People leaned forward to watch her and to try to catch the words of the song. When she vanished there were long rollings of applause.

Obedient to more anticipatory bars, she reappeared amidst the half-sup-

[1]Struggle.   [2]Slum area on Manhattan's Lower East Side.
[3]A small drinking glass that holds about five ounces.

pressed cheering of the tipsy men. The orchestra plunged into dance music and the laces of the dancer fluttered and flew in the glare of gas jets. She divulged the fact that she was attired in some half dozen skirts. It was patent that any one of them would have proved adequate for the purpose for which skirts are intended. An occasional man bent forward, intent upon the pink stockings. Maggie wondered at the splendor of the costume and lost herself in calculations of the cost of the silks and laces.

The dancer's smile of stereotyped enthusiasm was turned for ten minutes upon the faces of her audience. In the finale she fell into some of those grotesque attitudes which were at the time popular among the dancers in the theatres uptown, giving to the Bowery public the phantasies of the aristocratic theatre-going public, at reduced rates.

"Say, Pete," said Maggie, leaning forward, "dis is great."

"Sure," said Pete, with proper complacence.

A ventriloquist followed the dancer. He held two fantastic dolls on his knees. He made them sing mournful ditties and say funny things about geography and Ireland.

"Do dose little men talk?" asked Maggie.

"Naw," said Pete, "it's some damn fake. See?"

Two girls, on the bills[4] as sisters, came forth and sang a duet that is heard occasionally at concerts given under church auspices. They supplemented it with a dance which of course can never be seen at concerts given under church auspices.

After the duettists had retired, a woman of debatable age sang a negro melody. The chorus necessitated some grotesque waddlings supposed to be an imitation of a plantation darkey, under the influence, probably, of music and the moon. The audience was just enthusiastic enough over it to have her return and sing a sorrowful lay,[5] whose lines told of a mother's love and a sweetheart who waited and a young man who was lost at sea under the most harrowing circumstances. From the faces of a score or so in the crowd, the self-contained look faded. Many heads were bent forward with eagerness and sympathy. As the last distressing sentiment of the piece was brought forth, it was greeted by that kind of applause which rings as sincere.

As a final effort, the singer rendered some verses which described a vision of Britain being annihilated by America, and Ireland bursting her bonds. A carefully prepared crisis was reached in the last line of the last verse, where the singer threw out her arms and cried, "The star-spangled banner." Instantly a great cheer swelled from the throats of the assemblage of the masses. There was a heavy rumble of booted feet thumping the floor. Eyes gleamed with sudden fire, and calloused hands waved frantically in the air.

After a few moments' rest, the orchestra played crashingly, and a small fat man burst out upon the stage. He began to roar a song and stamp back and forth before the footlights, wildly waving a glossy silk hat and throwing leers, or smiles, broadcast. He made his face into fantastic grimaces until he looked like a pictured devil on a Japanese kite. The crowd laughed gleefully. His short, fat legs were never still a moment. He shouted and roared and bobbed his shock of red wig until the audience broke out in excited applause.

Pete did not pay much attention to the progress of events upon the stage. He was drinking beer and watching Maggie.

---

[4]Posters, advertisements. [5]Ballad.

Her cheeks were blushing with excitement and her eyes were glistening. She drew deep breaths of pleasure. No thoughts of the atmosphere of the collar and cuff factory came to her.

When the orchestra crashed finally, they jostled their way to the sidewalk with the crowd. Pete took Maggie's arm and pushed a way for her, offering to fight with a man or two.

They reached Maggie's home at a late hour and stood for a moment in front of the gruesome doorway.

"Say, Mag," said Pete, "give us a kiss for takin' yeh teh deh show, will yer?"

Maggie laughed, as if startled, and drew away from him.

"Naw, Pete," she said, "dat wasn't in it."

"Ah, what deh hell?" urged Pete.

The girl retreated nervously.

"Ah, what deh hell?" repeated he.

Maggie darted into the hall, and up the stairs. She turned and smiled at him, then disappeared.

Pete walked slowly down the street. He had something of an astonished expression upon his features. He paused under a lamppost and breathed a low breath of surprise.

"Gawd," he said, "I wonner if I've been played fer a duffer."[6]

CHAPTER VIII

As thoughts of Pete came to Maggie's mind, she began to have an intense dislike for all of her dresses.

"What deh hell ails yeh? What makes yeh be allus fixin' and fussin'? Good Gawd," her mother would frequently roar at her.

She began to note, with more interest, the well-dressed women she met on the avenues. She envied elegance and soft palms. She craved those adornments of person which she saw every day on the street, conceiving them to be allies of vast importance to women.

Studying faces, she thought many of the women and girls she chanced to meet, smiled with serenity as though forever cherished and watched over by those they loved.

The air in the collar and cuff establishment strangled her. She knew she was gradually and surely shrivelling in the hot, stuffy room. The begrimed windows rattled incessantly from the passing of elevated trains. The place was filled with a whirl of noises and odors.

She wondered as she regarded some of the grizzled women in the room, mere mechanical contrivances sewing seams and grinding out, with heads bended over their work, tales of imagined or real girl-hood happiness, past drunks, the baby at home, and unpaid wages. She speculated how long her youth would endure. She began to see the bloom upon her cheeks as valuable.

She imagined herself, in an exasperating future, as a scrawny woman with an eternal grievance. Too, she thought Pete to be a very fastidious person concerning the appearance of women.

She felt she would love to see somebody entangle their fingers in the oily beard of the fat foreigner who owned the establishment. He was a detestable creature. He wore white socks with low shoes.[1]

[6]"Fool."

[1]High-topped shoes were standard male dress until the 1920s when low-cut oxfords became fashionable.

He sat all day delivering orations, in the depths of a cushioned chair. His pocketbook deprived them of the power of retort.

"What een hell do you sink I pie fife dolla' a week for? Play? No, py damn!"

Maggie was anxious for a friend to whom she could talk about Pete. She would have liked to discuss his admirable mannerisms with a reliable mutual friend. At home, she found her mother often drunk and always raving.

It seems that the world had treated this woman very badly, and she took a deep revenge upon such portions of it as came within her reach. She broke furniture as if she were at last getting her rights. She swelled with virtuous indignation as she carried the lighter articles of household use, one by one under the shadows of the three gilt balls,[2] where Hebrews chained them with chains of interest.

Jimmie came when he was obliged to by circumstances over which he had no control. His well-trained legs brought him staggering home and put him to bed some nights when he would rather have gone elsewhere.

Swaggering Pete loomed like a golden sun to Maggie. He took her to a dime museum where rows of meek freaks astonished her. She contemplated their deformities with awe and thought them a sort of chosen tribe.

Pete, racking his brains for amusement, discovered the Central Park Menagerie[3] and the Museum of Arts.[4] Sunday afternoons would sometimes find them at these places. Pete did not appear to be particularly interested in what he saw. He stood around looking heavy, while Maggie giggled in glee.

Once at the Menagerie he went into a trance of admiration before the spectacle of a very small monkey threatening to thrash a cageful because one of them had pulled his tail and he had not wheeled about quickly enough to discover who did it. Ever after Pete knew that monkey by sight and winked at him, trying to induce him to fight with other and larger monkeys.

At the Museum, Maggie said, "Dis is outa sight."

"Oh hell," said Pete, "wait till next summer an' I'll take yehs to a picnic."

While the girl wandered in the vaulted rooms, Pete occupied himself in returning stony stare for stony stare, the appalling scrutiny of the watch-dogs of the treasures. Occasionally he would remark in loud tones: "Dat jay[5] has got glass eyes," and sentences of the sort. When he tired of this amusement he would go to the mummies and moralize over them.

Usually he submitted with silent dignity to all which he had to go through, but, at times, he was goaded into comment.

"What deh hell," he demanded once.

"Look at all dese little jugs! Hundred jugs in a row! Ten rows in a case an' 'bout a t'ousand cases! What deh blazes use is dem?"

Evenings during the week he took her to see plays in which the brain-clutching heroine was rescued from the palatial home of her guardian, who is cruelly after her bonds,[6] by the hero with the beautiful sentiments. The latter spent most of his time out at soak[7] in pale-green snow storms, busy with a nickel-plated revolver, rescuing aged strangers from villains.

Maggie lost herself in sympathy with the wanderers swooning in snow storms beneath happy-hued church windows. And a choir within singing "Joy to the World." To Maggie and the rest of the audience this was transcendental realism. Joy always within, and they, like the actor, inevitably without. Viewing it, they hugged themselves in ecstatic pity of their imagined or real condition.

The girl thought the arrogance and granite-heartedness of the magnate of

[2]Traditional symbol for a pawnshop.   [3]Zoo.   [4]Metropolitan Museum of Art.
[5]"Dope," "jerk."   [6]Interest-bearing certificates; i.e., her riches.   [7]In the wet.

the play was very accurately drawn. She echoed the maledictions that the occupants of the gallery showered on this individual when his lines compelled him to expose his extreme selfishness.

Shady persons in the audience revolted from the pictured villainy of the drama. With untiring zeal they hissed vice and applauded virtue. Unmistakably bad men evinced an apparently sincere admiration for virtue.

The loud gallery was overwhelmingly with the unfortunate and the oppressed. They encouraged the struggling hero with cries, and jeered the villain, hooting and calling attention to his whiskers. When anybody died in the pale-green snow storms, the gallery mourned. They sought out the painted misery and hugged it as akin.

In the hero's erratic march from poverty in the first act, to wealth and triumph in the final one, in which he forgives all the enemies that he has left, he was assisted by the gallery, which applauded his generous and noble sentiments and confounded the speeches of his opponents by making irrelevant but very sharp remarks. Those actors who were cursed with villainy parts were confronted at every turn by the gallery. If one of them rendered lines containing the most subtle distinctions between right and wrong, the gallery was immediately aware if the actor meant wickedness, and denounced him accordingly.

The last act was a triumph for the hero, poor and of the masses, the representative of the audience, over the villain and the rich man, his pockets stuffed with bonds, his heart packed with tyrannical purposes, imperturbable amid suffering.

Maggie always departed with raised spirits from the showing places of the melodrama. She rejoiced at the way in which the poor and virtuous eventually surmounted the wealthy and wicked. The theatre made her think. She wondered if the culture and refinement she had seen imitated, perhaps grotesquely, by the heroine on the stage, could be acquired by a girl who lived in a tenement house and worked in a shirt factory.

CHAPTER IX

A group of urchins were intent upon the side door of a saloon. Expectancy gleamed from their eyes. They were twisting their fingers in excitement.

"Here she comes," yelled one of them suddenly.

The group of urchins burst instantly asunder and its individual fragments were spread in a wide, respectable half-circle about the point of interest. The saloon door opened with a crash, and the figure of a woman appeared upon the threshold. Her grey hair fell in knotted masses about her shoulders. Her face was crimsoned and wet with perspiration. Her eyes had a rolling glare.

"Not a damn cent more of me money will yehs ever get, not a damn cent. I spent me money here fer t'ree years an' now yehs tells me yeh'll sell me no more stuff! T'hell wid yeh, Johnnie Murckre! 'Disturbance'? Disturbance be damned! T'hell wid yeh, Johnnie—"

The door received a kick of exasperation from within and the woman lurched heavily out on the sidewalk.

The gamins in the half-circle became violently agitated. They began to dance about and hoot and yell and jeer. Wide dirty grins spread over each face.

The woman made a furious dash at a particularly outrageous cluster of little boys. They laughed delightedly and scampered off a short distance, calling out over their shoulders to her. She stood tottering on the curbstone and thundered at them.

"Yeh devil's kids," she howled, shaking red fists. The little boys whooped in glee. As she started up the street they fell in behind and marched uproariously. Occasionally she wheeled about and made charges on them. They ran nimbly out of reach and taunted her.

In the frame of a gruesome doorway she stood for a moment cursing them. Her hair straggled, giving her crimson features a look of insanity. Her great fists quivered as she shook them madly in the air.

The urchins made terrific noises until she turned and disappeared. Then they filed quietly in the way they had come.

The woman floundered about in the lower hall of the tenement house and finally stumbled up the stairs. On an upper hall a door was opened and a collection of heads peered curiously out, watching her. With a wrathful snort the woman confronted the door, but it was slammed hastily in her face and the key was turned.

She stood for a few minutes, delivering a frenzied challenge at the panels.

"Come out in deh hall, Mary Murphy, damn yeh, if yehs want a row.[1] Come ahn, yeh overgrown terrier, come ahn."

She began to kick the door with her great feet. She shrilly defied the universe to appear and do battle. Her cursing trebles brought heads from all doors save the one she threatened. Her eyes glared in every direction. The air was full of her tossing fists.

"Come ahn, deh hull damn gang of yehs, come ahn," she roared at the spectators. An oath or two, cat-calls, jeers and bits of facetious advice were given in reply. Missiles clattered about her feet.

"What deh hell's deh matter wid yeh?" said a voice in the gathered gloom, and Jimmie came forward. He carried a tin dinner-pail in his hand and under his arm a brown truckman's apron done in a bundle. "What deh hell's wrong?" he demanded.

"Come out, all of yehs, come out," his mother was howling. "Come ahn an' I'll stamp yer damn brains under me feet."

"Shet yer face, an' come home, yeh damned old fool," roared Jimmie at her. She strided up to him and twirled her fingers in his face. Her eyes were darting flames of unreasoning rage and her frame trembled with eagerness for a fight.

"T'hell wid yehs! An' who deh hell are yehs? I ain't given' a snap of me fingers fer yehs," she bawled at him. She turned her huge back in tremendous disdain and climbed the stairs to the next floor.

Jimmie followed, cursing blackly. At the top of the flight he seized his mother's arm and started to drag her toward the door of their room.

"Come home, damn yeh," he gritted between his teeth.

"Take yer hands off me! Take yer hands off me," shrieked his mother.

She raised her arm and whirled her great fist at her son's face. Jimmie dodged his head and the blow struck him in the back of the neck. "Damn yeh," gritted he again. He threw out his left hand and writhed his fingers about her middle arm. The mother and the son began to sway and struggle like gladiators.

"Whoop!" said the Rum Alley tenement house. The hall filled with interested spectators.

"Hi, ol' lady, dat was a dandy!"

"T'ree to one on deh red!"

---

[1] Squabble, argument.

"Ah, stop yer damn scrappin'!"

The door of the Johnson home opened and Maggie looked out. Jimmie made a supreme cursing effort and hurled his mother into the room. He quickly followed and closed the door. The Rum Alley tenement swore disappointedly and retired.

The mother slowly gathered herself up from the floor. Her eyes glittered menacingly upon her children.

"Here, now," said Jimmie, "we've had enough of dis. Sit down, an' don' make no trouble."

He grasped her arm, and twisting it, forced her into a creaking chair.

"Keep yer hands off me," roared his mother again.

"Damn yer ol' hide," yelled Jimmie, madly. Maggie shrieked and ran into the other room. To her there came the sound of a storm of crashes and curses. There was a great final thump and Jimmie's voice cried: "Dere damn yeh, stay still," Maggie opened the door now, and went warily out. "Oh, Jimmie."

He was leaning against the wall and swearing. Blood stood upon bruises on his knotty fore-arms where they had scraped against the floor or the walls in the scuffle. The mother lay screeching on the floor, the tears running down her furrowed face.

Maggie, standing in the middle of the room, gazed about her. The usual upheaval of the tables and chairs had taken place. Crockery was strewn broadcast in fragments. The stove had been disturbed on its legs, and now leaned idiotically to one side. A pail had been upset and water spread in all directions.

The door opened and Pete appeared. He shrugged his shoulders. "Oh, Gawd," he observed.

He walked over to Maggie and whispered in her ear. "Ah, what deh hell, Mag? Come ahn and we'll have a hell of a time."

The mother in the corner upreared her head and shook her tangled locks.

"Teh hell wid him and you," she said, glowering at her daughter in the gloom. Her eyes seemed to burn balefully. "Yeh've gone teh deh devil, Mag Johnson, yehs knows yehs have gone teh deh devil. Yer a disgrace teh yer people, damn yeh. An' now, git out an' go ahn wid dat doe-faced jude[2] of yours. Go teh hell wid him, damn yeh, an' a good riddance. Go teh hell an' see how yeh likes it."

Maggie gazed long at her mother.

"Go teh hell now, an' see how yeh likes it. Git out. I won't have sech as yehs in me house! Get out, d'yeh hear! Damn yeh, git out!"

The girl began to tremble.

At this instant Pete came forward. "Oh, what deh hell, Mag, see," whispered he softly in her ear. "Dis all blows over. See? Deh ol' woman 'ill be right in deh mornin'. Come ahn out wid me! We'll have a hell of a time."

The woman on the floor cursed. Jimmie was intent upon his bruised fore-arms. The girl cast a glance about the room filled with a chaotic mass of debris, and at the red, writhing body of her mother.

"Go teh hell an' good riddance."

She went.

---

[2]"Dude," "dandy."

CHAPTER X

Jimmie had an idea it wasn't common courtesy for a friend to come to one's home and ruin one's sister. But he was not sure how much Pete knew about the rules of politeness.

The following night he returned home from work at rather a late hour in the evening. In passing through the halls he came upon the gnarled and leathery old woman who possessed the music box. She was grinning in the dim light that drifted through dust-stained panes. She beckoned to him with a smudged forefinger.

"Ah, Jimmie, what do yehs t'ink I got onto las' night. It was deh funnies' t'ing I ever saw," she cried, coming close to him and leering. She was trembling with eagerness to tell her tale. "I was by me door las' night when yer sister and her jude feller came in late, oh, very late. An' she, the dear, she was a-cryin' as if her heart would break, she was. It was deh funnies' t'ing I ever saw. An' right out here by me door she asked him did he love her, did he. An' she was a-cryin' as if her heart would break, poor t'ing. An' him, I could see by deh way what he said it dat she had been askin' orften, he says: 'Oh, hell, yes,' he says, says he, 'Oh, hell, yes.'"

Storm-clouds swept over Jimmie's face, but he turned from the leathery old woman and plodded on up-stairs.

"Oh, hell, yes," called she after him. She laughed a laugh that was like a prophetic croak. "'Oh, hell, yes,' he says, says he, 'Oh, hell, yes.'"

There was no one in at home. The rooms showed that attempts had been made at tidying them. Parts of the wreckage of the day before had been repaired by an unskilful hand. A chair or two and the table, stood uncertainly upon legs. The floor had been newly swept. Too, the blue ribbons had been restored to the curtains, and the lambrequin, with its immense sheaves of yellow wheat and red roses of equal size, had been returned, in a worn and sorry state to its position at the mantel. Maggie's jacket and hat were gone from the nail behind the door.

Jimmie walked to the window and began to look through the blurred glass. It occurred to him to vaguely wonder, for an instant, if some of the women of his acquaintance had brothers.

Suddenly, however, he began to swear.

"But he was me frien'! I brought 'im here! Dat's deh hell of it!"

He fumed about the room, his anger gradually rising to the furious pitch.

"I'll kill deh jay! Dat's what I'll do! I'll kill deh jay!"

He clutched his hat and sprang toward the door. But it opened and his mother's great form blocked the passage.

"What deh hell's deh matter wid yeh?" exclaimed she, coming into the rooms.

Jimmie gave vent to a sardonic curse and then laughed heavily.

"Well, Maggie's gone teh deh devil! Dat's what! See?"

"Eh?" said his mother.

"Maggie's gone teh deh devil! Are yehs deaf?" roared Jimmie, impatiently.

"Deh hell she has," murmured the mother, astounded.

Jimmie grunted, and then began to stare out at the window. His mother sat down in a chair, but a moment later sprang erect and delivered a maddened whirl of oaths. Her son turned to look at her as she reeled and swayed in the middle of the room, her fierce face convulsed with passion, her blotched arms raised high in imprecation.

"May Gawd curse her forever," she shrieked. "May she eat nothin' but stones and deh dirt in deh street. May she sleep in deh gutter an' never see deh sun shine agin. Deh damn—"

"Here, now," said her son. "Take a drop on yourself."

The mother raised lamenting eyes to the ceiling.

"She's deh devil's own chil', Jimmie," she whispered. "Ah, who would t'ink such a bad girl could grow up in our fambly, Jimmie, me son. Many deh hour I've spent in talk wid dat girl an' tol' her if she ever went on deh streets I'd see her damned. An' after all her bringing' up an' what I tol' her and talked wid her, she goes teh deh bad, like a duck teh water."

The tears rolled down her furrowed face. Her hands trembled.

"An' den when dat Sadie MacMallister next door to us was sent teh deh devil by dat feller what worked in deh soap-factory; didn't I tell our Mag dat if she—"

"Ah, dat's anudder story," interrupted the brother. "Of course, dat Sadie was nice an' all dat—but—see—it ain't dessame as if—well, Maggie was diff'ent— see—she was diff'ent."

He was trying to formulate a theory that he had always unconsciously held, that all sisters, excepting his own, could advisedly be ruined.

He suddenly broke out again. "I'll go t'ump hell outa deh mug what did her deh harm. I'll kill 'im! He t'inks he kin scrap, but when he gits me a-chasin' 'im he'll fin' out where he's wrong, deh damned duffer. I'll wipe up deh street wid 'im."

In a fury he plunged out of the doorway. As he vanished the mother raised her head and lifted both hands, entreating.

"May Gawd curse her forever," she cried.

In the darkness of the hallway Jimmie discerned a knot of women talking volubly. When he strode by they paid no attention to him.

"She allus was a bold thing," he heard one of them cry in an eager voice. "Dere wasn't a feller come teh deh house but she'd try teh mash[1] 'im. My Annie says deh shameless t'ing tried teh ketch her feller, her own feller, what we useter know his fader."

"I could a' tol' yehs dis two years ago," said a woman, in a key of triumph. "Yessir, it was over two years ago dat I says teh my ol' man, I says, 'Dat Johnson girl ain't straight,' I says. 'Oh, hell,' he says. 'Oh, hell.' 'Dat's all right,' I says, 'but I know what I knows,' I says, 'an' it 'ill come out later. You wait an' see,' I says, 'you see.'"

"Anybody what had eyes could see dat dere was somethin' wrong wid dat girl. I didn't like her actions."

On the street Jimmie met a friend. "What deh hell?" asked the latter.

Jimmie explained. "An' I'll t'ump 'im till he can't stand."

"Oh, what deh hell," said the friend. "What's deh use! Yeh'll git pulled in![2] Everybody 'ill be onto it! An' ten plunks![3] Gee!"

Jimmie was determined. "He t'inks he kin scrap, but he'll fin' out diff'ent."

"Gee," remonstrated the friend. "What deh hell?"

CHAPTER XI

On a corner a glass-fronted building shed a yellow glare upon the pavements. The open mouth of a saloon called seductively to passengers to enter and annihilate sorrow or create rage.

[1]"Ogle," "flirt with."   [2]"Arrested."   [3]"Dollars."

The interior of the place was papered in olive and bronze tints of imitation leather. A shining bar of counterfeit massiveness extended down the side of the room. Behind it a great mahogany-appearing sideboard reached the ceiling. Upon its shelves rested pyramids of shimmering glasses that were never disturbed. Mirrors set in the face of the sideboard multiplied them. Lemons, oranges and paper napkins, arranged with mathematical precision, sat among the glasses. Many-hued decanters of liquor perched at regular intervals on the lower shelves. A nickel-plated cash register occupied a position in the exact centre of the general effect. The elementary senses of it all seemed to be opulence and geometrical accuracy.

Across from the bar a smaller counter held a collection of plates upon which swarmed frayed fragments of crackers, slices of boiled ham, dishevelled bits of cheese, and pickles swimming in vinegar. An odor of grasping, begrimed hands and munching mouths pervaded.

Pete, in a white jacket, was behind the bar bending expectantly toward a quiet stranger. "A beeh," said the man. Pete drew a foam-topped glassful and set it dripping upon the bar.

At this moment the light bamboo doors at the entrance swung open and crashed against the siding. Jimmie and a companion entered. They swaggered unsteadily but belligerently toward the bar and looked at Pete with bleared and blinking eyes.

"Gin," said Jimmie.

"Gin," said the companion.

Pete slid a bottle and two glasses along the bar. He bended his head sideways as he assiduously polished away with a napkin at the gleaming wood. He had a look of watchfulness upon his features.

Jimmie and his companion kept their eyes upon the bartender and conversed loudly in tones of contempt.

"He's a dindy masher, ain't he, by Gawd?" laughed Jimmie.

"Oh, hell, yes," said the companion, sneering widely. "He's great, he is. Git onto deh mug on deh blokie. Dat's enough to make a feller turn hand-springs in 'is sleep."

The quiet stranger moved himself and his glass a trifle further away and maintained an attitude of oblivion.

"Gee! ain't he hot stuff!"

"Git onto his shape! Great Gawd!"

"Hey," cried Jimmie, in tones of command. Pete came along, with a sullen dropping of the under lip.

"Well," he growled, "what's eatin' yehs?"

"Gin," said Jimmie.

"Gin," said the companion.

As Pete confronted them with the bottle and the glasses, they laughed in his face. Jimmie's companion, evidently overcome with merriment, pointed a grimy forefinger in Pete's direction.

"Say, Jimmie," demanded he, "what deh hell is dat behind deh bar?"

"Damned if I knows," replied Jimmie. They laughed loudly. Pete put down a bottle with a bang and turned a formidable face toward them. He disclosed his teeth and his shoulders heaved restlessly.

"You fellers can't guy[1] me," he said. "Drink yer stuff an' git out an' don' make no trouble."

[1]"Ridicule."

Instantly the laughter faded from the faces of the two men and expressions of offended dignity immediately came.

"Who deh hell has said anyt'ing teh you," cried they in the same breath.

The quiet stranger looked at the door calculatingly.

"Ah, come off," said Pete to the two men. "Don't pick me up for no jay. Drink yer rum an' git out an' don' make no trouble."

"Oh, deh hell," airily cried Jimmie.

"Oh, deh hell," airily repeated his companion.

"We goes when we git ready! See!" continued Jimmie.

"Well," said Pete in a threatening voice, "don' make no trouble."

Jimmie suddenly leaned forward with his head on one side. He snarled like a wild animal.

"Well, what if we does? See?" said he.

Dark blood flushed into Pete's face, and he shot a lurid glance at Jimmie.

"Well, den we'll see whose deh bes' man, you or me," he said.

The quiet stranger moved modestly toward the door.

Jimmie began to swell with valor.

"Don' pick me up fer no tenderfoot. When yeh tackles me yeh tackles one of deh bes' men in deh city. See? I'm a scrapper, I am. Ain't dat right, Billie?"

"Sure, Mike," responded his companion in tones of conviction.

"Oh, hell," said Pete, easily. "Go fall on yerself."

The two men again began to laugh.

"What deh hell is dat talking'?" cried the companion.

"Damned if I knows," replied Jimmie with exaggerated contempt.

Pete made a furious gesture. "Git outa here now, an' don' make no trouble. See? Youse fellers er lookin' fer a scrap an' it's damn likely yeh'll fin' one if yeh keeps on shootin' off yer mout's. I know yehs! See? I kin lick better men dan yehs ever saw in yer lives. Dat's right! See? Don' pick me up fer no stuff er yeh might be jolted out in deh street before yeh knows where yeh is. When I comes from behind dis bar, I t'rows yehs bote inteh deh street. See?"

"Oh, hell," cried the two men in chorus.

The glare of a panther came into Pete's eyes. "Dat's what I said! Unnerstan'?"

He came through a passage at the end of the bar and swelled down upon the two men. They stepped promptly forward and crowded close to him.

They bristled like three roosters. They moved their heads pugnaciously and kept their shoulders braced. The nervous muscles about each mouth twitched with a forced smile of mockery.

"Well, what deh hell yer goin' teh do?" gritted Jimmie.

Pete stepped warily back, waving his hands before him to keep the men from coming too near.

"Well, what deh hell yer goin' teh do?" repeated Jimmie's ally. They kept close to him, taunting and leering. They strove to make him attempt the initial blow.

"Keep back, now! Don' crowd me," ominously said Pete.

Again they chorused in contempt. "Oh, hell!"

In a small, tossing group, the three men edged for positions like frigates contemplating battle.

"Well, why deh hell don' yeh try teh t'row us out?" cried Jimmie and his ally with copious sneers.

The bravery of bull-dogs sat upon the faces of the men. Their clenched fists moved like eager weapons.

The allied two jostled the bartender's elbows, glaring at him with feverish eyes and forcing him toward the wall.

Suddenly Pete swore redly. The flash of action gleamed from his eyes. He threw back his arm and aimed a tremendous, lightning-like blow at Jimmie's face. His foot swung a step forward and the weight of his body was behind his fist. Jimmie ducked his head, Bowery-like, with the quickness of a cat. The fierce, answering blows of him and his ally crushed on Pete's bowed head.

The quiet stranger vanished.

The arms of the combatants whirled in the air like flails. The faces of the men, at first flushed to flame-colored anger, now began to fade to the pallor of warriors in the blood and heat of a battle. Their lips curled back and stretched tightly over the gums in ghoul-like grins. Through their white, gripped teeth struggled hoarse whisperings of oaths. Their eyes glittered with murderous fire.

Each head was huddled between its owner's shoulders, and arms were swinging with marvelous rapidity. Feet scraped to and fro with a loud scratching sound upon the sanded floor. Blows left crimson blotches upon pale skin. The curses of the first quarter minute of the fight died away. The breaths of the fighters came wheezingly from their lips and the three chests were straining and heaving. Pete at intervals gave vent to low, labored hisses, that sounded like a desire to kill. Jimmie's ally gibbered at times like a wounded maniac. Jimmie was silent, fighting with the face of a sacrificial priest. The rage of fear shone in all their eyes and their blood-colored fists swirled.

At a tottering moment a blow from Pete's hand struck the ally and he crashed to the floor. He wriggled instantly to his feet and grasping the quiet stranger's beer glass from the bar, hurled it at Pete's head.

High on the wall it burst like a bomb, shivering fragments flying in all directions. Then missiles came to every man's hand. The place had heretofore appeared free of things to throw, but suddenly glass and bottles went singing through the air. They were thrown point blank at bobbing heads. The pyramid of shimmering glasses, that had never been disturbed, changed to cascades as heavy bottles were flung into them. Mirrors splintered to nothing.

The three frothing creatures on the floor buried themselves in a frenzy for blood. There followed in the wake of missiles and fists some unknown prayers, perhaps for death.

The quiet stranger had sprawled very pyrotechnically out on the sidewalk. A laugh ran up and down the avenue for the half of a block.

"Dey've t'rowed a bloke inteh deh street."

People heard the sound of breaking glass and shuffling feet within the saloon and came running. A small group, bending down to look under the bamboo doors, watching the fall of glass, and three pairs of violent legs, changed in a moment to a crowd.

A policeman came charging down the sidewalk and bounced through the doors into the saloon. The crowd bended and surged in absorbing anxiety to see.

Jimmie caught first sight of the on-coming interruption. On his feet he had the same regard for a policeman that, when on his truck, he had for a fire engine. He howled and ran for the side door.

The officer made a terrific advance, club in hand. One comprehensive sweep of the long night stick threw the ally to the floor and forced Pete to a corner. With his disengaged hand he made a furious effort at Jimmie's coattails. Then he regained his balance and paused.

"Well, well, you are a pair of pictures. What in hell yeh been up to?"

Jimmie, with his face drenched in blood, escaped up a side street, pursued a short distance by some of the more law-loving, or excited individuals of the crowd.

Later, from a corner safely dark, he saw the policeman, the ally and the bartender emerge from the saloon. Pete locked the doors and then followed up the avenue in the rear of the crowd-encompassed policeman and his charge.

On first thoughts Jimmie, with his heart throbbing at battle heat, started to go desperately to the rescue of his friend, but he halted.

"Ah, what deh hell?" he demanded of himself.

CHAPTER XII

In a hall of irregular shape sat Pete and Maggie drinking beer. A submissive orchestra dictated to by a spectacled man with frowsy hair and a dress suit, industriously followed the bobs of his head and the waves of his baton. A ballad singer, in a dress of flaming scarlet, sang in the inevitable voice of brass. When she vanished, men seated at the tables near the front applauded loudly, pounding the polished wood with their beer glasses. She returned attired in less gown, and sang again. She received another enthusiastic encore. She reappeared in still less gown and danced. The deafening rumble of glasses and clapping of hands that followed her exit indicated an overwhelming desire to have her come on for the fourth time, but the curiosity of the audience was not gratified.

Maggie was pale. From her eyes had been plucked all look of self-reliance. She leaned with a dependent air toward her companion. She was timid, as if fearing his anger or displeasure. She seemed to beseech tenderness of him.

Pete's air of distinguished valor had grown upon him until it threatened stupendous dimensions. He was infinitely gracious to the girl. It was apparent to her that his condescension was a marvel.

He could appear to strut even while sitting still and he showed that he was a lion of lordly characteristics by the air with which he spat.

With Maggie gazing at him wonderingly, he took pride in commanding the waiters who were, however, indifferent or deaf.

"Hi, you, git a russle[1] on yehs! What deh hell yehs lookin' at? Two more beehs, d'yeh hear?"

He leaned back and critically regarded the person of a girl with a straw-colored wig who upon the stage was flinging her heels in somewhat awkward imitation of a well-known danseuse.[2]

At times Maggie told Pete long confidential tales of her former home life, dwelling upon the escapades of the other members of the family and the difficulties she had to combat in order to obtain a degree of comfort. He responded in tones of philanthropy. He pressed her arm with an air of reassuring proprietorship.

"Dey was damn jays," he said, denouncing the mother and brother.

The sound of the music which, by the efforts of the frowsy-headed leader, drifted to her ears through the smoke-filled atmosphere, made the girl dream. She thought of her former Rum Alley environment and turned to regard Pete's strong protecting fists. She thought of the collar and cuff manufactory and the eternal moan of the proprietor: "What een hell do you sink I pie fife dolla a

---

[1]"Move."   [2]Female ballet dancer.

week for? Play? No, py damn." She contemplated Pete's man-subduing eyes and noted that wealth and prosperity was indicated by his clothes. She imagined a future, rose-tinted, because of its distance from all that she previously had experienced.

As to the present she perceived only vague reasons to be miserable. Her life was Pete's and she considered him worthy of the charge. She would be disturbed by no particular apprehensions, so long as Pete adored her as he now said he did. She did not feel like a bad woman. To her knowledge she had never seen any better.

At times men at other tables regarded the girl furtively. Pete, aware of it, nodded at her and grinned. He felt proud.

"Mag, yer a bloomin' good-looker," he remarked, studying her face through the haze. The men made Maggie fear, but she blushed at Pete's words as it became apparent to her that she was the apple of his eye.

Grey-bearded men, wonderfully pathetic in their dissipation, stared at her through clouds. Smooth-cheeked boys, some of them with faces of stone and mouths of sin, not nearly so pathetic as the grey heads, tried to find the girl's eyes in the smoke wreaths. Maggie considered she was not what they thought her. She confined her glances to Pete and the stage.

The orchestra played negro melodies and a versatile drummer pounded, whacked, clattered and scratched on a dozen machines to make noise.

Those glances of the men, shot at Maggie from under half-closed lids, made her tremble. She thought them all to be worse men than Pete.

"Come, let's go," she said.

As they went out Maggie perceived two women seated at a table with some men. They were painted and their cheeks had lost their roundness. As she passed them the girl, with a shrinking movement, drew back her skirts.

CHAPTER XIII

Jimmie did not return home for a number of days after the fight with Pete in the saloon. When he did, he approached with extreme caution.

He found his mother raving. Maggie had not returned home. The parent continually wondered how her daughter could come to such a pass. She had never considered Maggie as a pearl dropped unstained into Rum Alley from Heaven, but she could not conceive how it was possible for her daughter to fall so low as to bring disgrace upon her family. She was terrific in denunciation of the girl's wickedness.

The fact that the neighbors talked of it, maddened her. When women came in, and in the course of their conversation casually asked, "Where's Maggie dese days?" the mother shook her fuzzy head at them and appalled them with curses. Cunning hints inviting confidence she rebuffed with violence.

"An' wid all deh bringin' up she had, how could she?" moaningly she asked of her son. "Wid all deh talkin' wid her I did an' deh t'ings I tol' her to remember? When a girl is bringed up deh way I bringed up Maggie, how kin she go teh deh devil?"

Jimmie was transfixed by these questions. He could not conceive how under the circumstances his mother's daughter and his sister could have been so wicked.

His mother took a drink from a squdgy[1] bottle that sat on the table. She continued her lament.

[1]Dirty.

"She had a bad heart, dat girl did, Jimmie. She was wicked teh deh heart an' we never knowed it."

Jimmie nodded, admitting the fact.

"We lived in deh same house wid her an' I brought her up an' we never knowed how bad she was."

Jimmie nodded again.

"Wid a home like dis an' a mudder like me, she went teh deh bad," cried the mother, raising her eyes.

One day, Jimmie came home, sat down in a chair and began to wriggle about with a new and strange nervousness. At last he spoke shamefacedly.

"Well, look-a-here, dis t'ing queers us! See? We're queered! An' maybe it 'ud be better if I—well, I t'ink I kin look 'er up an'—maybe it 'ud be better if I fetched her home an—"

The mother started from her chair and broke forth into a storm of passionate anger.

"What! Let 'er come an' sleep under deh same roof wid her mudder agin! Oh, yes, I will, won't I? Sure? Shame on yehs, Jimmie Johnson, fer sayin' such a t'ing teh yer own mudder—teh yer own mudder! Little did I t'ink when yehs was a babby playin' about me feet dat ye'd grow up teh say sech a t'ing teh yer mudder—yer own mudder. I never taut—"

Sobs choked her and interrupted her reproaches.

"Dere ain't nottin' teh raise sech hell about," said Jimmie. "I on'y says it 'ud be better if we keep dis t'ing dark, see? It queers us! See?"

His mother laughed a laugh that seemed to ring through the city and be echoed and reechoed by countless other laughs. "Oh, yes, I will, won't I? Sure!

"Well, yeh must take me fer a damn fool," said Jimmie, indignant at his mother for mocking him. "I didn't say we'd make 'er inteh a little tin angel, ner nottin', but deh way it is now she can queer us! Don' che see?"

"Aye, she'll git tired of deh life atter a while an' den she'll wanna be a-comin' home, won' she, deh beast! I'll let 'er in den, won' I?"

"Well, I didn' mean none of dis prod'gal bus'ness anyway," explained Jimmie.

"It wasn't no prod'gal dauter, yeh damn fool," said the mother. "It was prod'gal son,[2] anyhow."

"I know dat," said Jimmie.

For a time they sat in silence. The mother's eyes gloated on a scene her imagination could call before her. Her lips were set in a vindictive smile.

"Aye, she'll cry, won' she, an' carry on, an' tell how Pete, or some odder feller, beats 'er an' she'll say she's sorry an' all dat an' she ain't happy, she ain't, an' she wants to come home agin, she does."

With grim humor, the mother imitated the possible wailing notes of the daughter's voice.

"Den I'll take 'er in, won't I, deh beast. She kin cry 'er two eyes out on deh stones of deh street before I'll dirty deh place wid her. She abused an' ill-treated her own mudder—her own mudder what loved her an' she'll never git anodder chance dis side of hell."

Jimmie thought he had a great idea of women's frailty, but he could not understand why any of his kin should be victims.

"Damn her," he fervidly said.

Again he wondered vaguely if some of the women of his acquaintance had brothers. Nevertheless, his mind did not for an instant confuse himself with

[2]The parable of the sinful son who was welcomed home by his father is told in Luke 15:11–32.

those brothers nor his sister with theirs. After the mother had, with great difficulty, suppressed the neighbors, she went among them and proclaimed her grief. "May Gawd forgive dat girl," was her continual cry. To attentive ears she recited the whole length and breadth of her woes.

"I bringed 'er up deh way a dauter oughta be bringed up an' dis is how she served me! She went teh deh devil deh first chance she got! May Gawd forgive her."

When arrested for drunkenness she used the story of her daughter's downfall with telling effect upon the police-justices. Finally one of them said to her, peering down over his spectacles: "Mary, the records of this and other courts show that you are the mother of forty-two daughters who have been ruined. The case is unparalleled in the annals of this court, and this court thinks—"

The mother went through life shedding large tears of sorrow. Her red face was a picture of agony.

Of course Jimmie publicly damned his sister that he might appear on a higher social plane. But, arguing with himself, stumbling about in ways that he knew not, he, once, almost came to a conclusion that his sister would have been more firmly good had she better known why. However, he felt that he could not hold such a view. He threw it hastily aside.

CHAPTER XIV

In a hilarious hall there were twenty-eight tables and twenty-eight women and a crowd of smoking men. Valiant noise was made on a stage at the end of the hall by an orchestra composed of men who looked as if they had just happened in. Soiled waiters ran to and fro, swooping down like hawks on the unwary in the throng; clattering along the aisles with trays covered with glasses; stumbling over women's skirts and charging two prices for everything but beer, all with a swiftness that blurred the view of the cocoanut palms and dusty monstrosities painted upon the walls of the room. A bouncer, with an immense load of business upon his hands, plunged about in the crowd, dragging bashful strangers to prominent chairs, ordering waiters here and there and quarreling furiously with men who wanted to sing with the orchestra.

The usual smoke cloud was present, but so dense that heads and arms seemed entangled in it. The rumble of conversation was replaced by a roar. Plenteous oaths heaved through the air. The room rang with the shrill voices of women bubbling o'er with drink-laughter. The chief element in the music of the orchestra was speed. The musicians played in intent fury. A woman was singing and smiling upon the stage, but no one took notice of her. The rate at which the piano, cornet and violins were going, seemed to impart wildness to the half-drunken crowd. Beer glasses were emptied at a gulp and conversation became a rapid chatter. The smoke eddied and swirled like a shadowy river hurrying toward some unseen falls. Pete and Maggie entered the hall and took chairs at a table near the door. The woman who was seated there made an attempt to occupy Pete's attention and, failing, went away.

Three weeks had passed since the girl had left home. The air of spaniel-like dependence had been magnified and showed its direct effect in the peculiar off-handedness and ease of Pete's ways toward her.

She followed Pete's eyes with hers, anticipating with smiles gracious looks from him.

A woman of brilliance and audacity, accompanied by a mere boy, came into the place and took seats near them.

At once Pete sprang to his feet, his face beaming with glad surprise.

"By Gawd, there's Nellie," he cried.

He went over to the table and held out an eager hand to the woman.

"Why, hello, Pete, me boy, how are you," said she, giving him her fingers.

Maggie took instant note of the woman. She perceived that her black dress fitted her to perfection. Her linen collar and cuffs were spotless. Tan gloves were stretched over her well-shaped hands. A hat of a prevailing fashion perched jauntily upon her dark hair. She wore no jewelry and was painted with no apparent paint. She looked clear-eyed through the stares of the men.

"Sit down, and call your lady-friend over," she said cordially to Pete. At his beckoning Maggie came and sat between Pete and the mere boy.

"I thought yeh were gone away fer good," began Pete, at once. "When did yeh git back? How did dat Buff'lo bus'ness turn out?"

The woman shrugged her shoulders. "Well, he didn't have as many stamps[1] as he tried to make out, so I shook him, that's all."

"Well, I'm glad teh see yehs back in deh city," said Pete, with awkward gallantry.

He and the woman entered into a long conversation, exchanging reminiscences of days together. Maggie sat still, unable to formulate an intelligent sentence upon the conversation and painfully aware of it.

She saw Pete's eyes sparkle as he gazed upon the handsome stranger. He listened smilingly to all she said. The woman was familiar with all his affairs, asked him about mutual friends, and knew the amount of his salary.

She paid no attention to Maggie, looking toward her once or twice and apparently seeing the wall beyond.

The mere boy was sulky. In the beginning he had welcomed with acclamations the additions.

"Let's all have a drink! What'll you take, Nell? And you, Miss what's-your-name. Have a drink, Mr.———, you, I mean."

He had shown a sprightly desire to do the talking for the company and tell all about his family. In a loud voice he declaimed on various topics. He assumed a patronizing air toward Pete. As Maggie was silent, he paid no attention to her. He made a great show of lavishing wealth upon the woman of brilliance and audacity.

"Do keep still, Freddie! You gibber like an ape, dear," said the woman to him. She turned away and devoted her attention to Pete.

"We'll have many a good time together again, eh?"

"Sure, Mike," said Pete, enthusiastic at once.

"Say," whispered she, leaning forward, "let's go over to Billie's and have a heluva time."

"Well, it's dis way! See?" said Pete. "I got dis lady frien' here."

"Oh, t'hell with her," argued the woman.

Pete appeared disturbed.

"All right," said she, nodding her head at him. "All right for you! We'll see the next time you ask me to go anywheres with you."

Pete squirmed.

"Say," he said, beseechingly, "come wid me a minit an' I'll tell yer why."

The woman waved her hand.

---

[1]Paper dollars.

"Oh, that's all right, you needn't explain, you know. You wouldn't come merely because you wouldn't come, that's all there is of it."

To Pete's visible distress she turned to the mere boy, bringing him speedily from a terrific rage. He had been debating whether it would be the part of a man to pick a quarrel with Pete, or would he be justified in striking him savagely with his beer glass without warning. But he recovered himself when the woman turned to renew her smilings. He beamed upon her with an expression that was somewhat tipsy and inexpressibly tender.

"Say, shake that Bowery jay," requested he, in a loud whisper.

"Freddie, you are so droll," she replied.

Pete reached forward and touched the woman on the arm.

"Come out a minit while I tells yeh why I can't go wid yer. Yer doin' me dirt, Nell! I never taut ye'd do me dirt, Nell. Come on, will yer?" He spoke in tones of injury.

"Why, I don't see why I should be interested in your explanations," said the woman, with a coldness that seemed to reduce Pete to a pulp.

His eyes pleaded with her. "Come out a minit while I tells yeh."

The woman nodded slightly at Maggie and the mere boy, " 'Scuse me."

The mere boy interrupted his loving smile and turned a shrivelling glare upon Pete. His boyish countenance flushed and he spoke, in a whine, to the woman:

"Oh, I say, Nellie, this ain't a square deal, you know. You aren't goin' to leave me and go off with that duffer, are you? I should think—"

"Why, you dear boy, of course I'm not," cried the woman, affectionately. She bended over and whispered in his ear. He smiled again and settled in his chair as if resolved to wait patiently.

As the woman walked down between the rows of tables, Pete was at her shoulder talking earnestly, apparently in explanation. The woman waved her hands with studied airs of indifference. The doors swung behind them, leaving Maggie and the mere boy seated at the table.

Maggie was dazed. She could dimly perceive that something stupendous had happened. She wondered why Pete saw fit to remonstrate with the woman, pleading for forgiveness with his eyes. She thought she noted an air of submission about her leonine Pete. She was astounded.

The mere boy occupied himself with cock-tails and a cigar. He was tranquilly silent for half an hour. Then he bestirred himself and spoke.

"Well," he said, sighing, "I knew this was the way it would be." There was another stillness. The mere boy seemed to be musing.

"She was pulling m'leg. That's the whole amount of it," he said suddenly. "It's a bloomin' shame the way that girl does. Why, I've spent over two dollars in drinks to-night. And she goes off with that plug-ugly who looks as if he had been hit in the face with a coin-die.[2] I call it rocky treatment for a fellah like me. Here, waiter, bring me a cock-tail and make it damned strong."

Maggie made no reply. She was watching the doors. "It's a mean piece of business," complained the mere boy. He explained to her how amazing it was that anybody should treat him in such a manner. "But I'll get square with her, you bet. She won't get far ahead of yours truly, you know," he added, winking. "I'll tell her plainly that it was bloomin' mean business. And she won't come it over me with any of her 'now-Freddie-dears.' She thinks my name is Freddie,

[2]A heavy, metal tool used for imprinting coins.

you know, but of course it ain't. I always tell these people some name like that, because if they got onto your right name they might use it sometime. Understand? Oh, they don't fool me much."

Maggie was paying no attention, being intent upon the doors. The mere boy relapsed into a period of gloom, during which he exterminated a number of cock-tails with a determined air, as if replying defiantly to fate. He occasionally broke forth into sentences composed of invectives joined together in a long string.

The girl was still staring at the doors. After a time the mere boy began to see cobwebs just in front of his nose. He spurred himself into being agreeable and insisted upon her having a charlotte-russe[3] and a glass of beer.

"They's gone," he remarked, "they's gone." He looked at her through the smoke wreaths. "Shay, lil' girl, we mightish well make bes' of it. You ain't such bad-lookin' girl, y'know. Not half bad. Can't come up to Nell, though. No, can't do it! Well, I should shay not! Nell fine-lookin' girl! F—i—n—ine. You look damn bad longsider her, but by y'self ain't so bad. Have to do anyhow. Nell gone. On'y you left. Not half bad, though."

Maggie stood up.

"I'm going home," she said.

The mere boy started.

"Eh? What? Home," he cried, struck with amazement. "I beg pardon, did hear say home?"

"I'm going home," she repeated.

"Great Gawd, what hava struck," demanded the mere boy of himself, stupefied.

In a semi-comatose state he conducted her on board an up-town car, ostentatiously paid her fare, leered kindly at her through the rear window and fell off the steps.

CHAPTER XV

A forlorn woman went along a lighted avenue. The street was filled with people desperately bound on missions. An endless crowd darted at the elevated station stairs and the horse cars were thronged with owners of bundles.

The pace of the forlorn woman was slow. She was apparently searching for some one. She loitered near the doors of saloons and watched men emerge from them. She scanned furtively the faces in the rushing stream of pedestrians. Hurrying men, bent on catching some boat or train, jostled her elbows, failing to notice her, their thoughts fixed on distant dinners.

The forlorn woman had a peculiar face. Her smile was no smile. But when in repose her features had a shadowy look that was like a sardonic grin, as if some one had sketched with cruel forefinger indelible lines about her mouth.

Jimmie came strolling up the avenue. The woman encountered him with an aggrieved air.

"Oh, Jimmie, I've been lookin' all over fer yehs—," she began.

Jimmie made an impatient gesture and quickened his pace.

"Ah, don't bodder me! Good Gawd!" he said, with the savageness of a man whose life is pestered.

The woman followed him along the sidewalk in somewhat the manner of a suppliant.

[3]Dessert cake filled with whipped cream or custard.

"But, Jimmie," she said, "yehs told me ye'd—"

Jimmie turned upon her fiercely as if resolved to make a last stand for comfort and peace.

"Say, fer Gawd's sake, Hattie, don' foller me from one end of deh city teh deh odder. Let up, will yehs! Give me a minute's res', can't yehs? Yehs makes me tired, allus taggin' me. See? Ain' yehs got no sense? Do yehs want people teh get onto me? Go chase yerself, fer Gawd's sake."

The woman stepped closer and laid her fingers on his arm. "But, look-a-here—"

Jimmie snarled. "Oh, go teh hell."

He darted into the front door of a convenient saloon and a moment later came out into the shadows that surrounded the side door. On the brilliantly lighted avenue he perceived the forlorn woman dodging about like a scout. Jimmie laughed with an air of relief and went away.

When he arrived home he found his mother clamoring. Maggie had returned. She stood shivering beneath the torrent of her mother's wrath.

"Well, I'm damned," said Jimmie in greeting.

His mother, tottering about the room, pointed a quivering forefinger.

"Lookut her, Jimmie, lookut her. Dere's yer sister, boy. Dere's yer sister. Lookut her! Lookut her!"

She screamed in scoffing laughter.

The girl stood in the middle of the room. She edged about as if unable to find a place on the floor to put her feet.

"Ha, ha, ha," bellowed the mother. "Dere she stands! Ain' she purty? Lookut her! Ain' she sweet, deh beast? Lookut her! Ha, ha, lookut her!"

She lurched forward and put her red and seamed hands upon her daughter's face. She bent down and peered keenly up into the eyes of the girl.

"Oh, she's jes' dessame as she ever was, ain' she? She's her mudder's purty darlin' yit, ain' she? Lookut her, Jimmie! Come here, fer Gawd's sake, and lookut her."

The loud, tremendous sneering of the mother brought the denizens of the Rum Alley tenement to their doors. Women came in the hallways. Children scurried to and fro.

"What's up? Dat Johnson party on anudder tear?"

"Naw! Young Mag's come home!"

"Deh hell yeh say?"

Through the open doors curious eyes stared in at Maggie. Children ventured into the room and ogled her, as if they formed the front row at a theatre. Women, without, bended toward each other and whispered, nodding their heads with airs of profound philosophy. A baby, overcome with curiosity concerning this object at which all were looking, sidled forward and touched her dress, cautiously, as if investigating a red-hot stove. Its mother's voice rang out like a warning trumpet. She rushed forward and grabbed her child, casting a terrible look of indignation at the girl.

Maggie's mother paced to and fro, addressing the doorful of eyes, expounding like a glib showman at a museum. Her voice rang through the building.

"Dere she stands," she cried, wheeling suddenly and pointing with dramatic finger. "Dere she stands! Lookut her! Ain' she a dindy? An' she was so good as to come home teh her mudder, she was! Ain' she a beaut'? Ain' she a dindy? Fer Gawd's sake!"

The jeering cries ended in another burst of shrill laughter.

The girl seemed to awaken. "Jimmie—"

He drew hastily back from her.

"Well, now, yer a hell of a t'ing, ain' yeh?" he said, his lips curling in scorn. Radiant virtue sat upon his brow and his repelling hands expressed horror of contamination.

Maggie turned and went.

The crowd at the door fell back precipitately. A baby falling down in front of the door, wrenched a scream like a wounded animal from its mother. Another woman sprang forward and picked it up, with a chivalrous air, as if rescuing a human being from an oncoming express train.

As the girl passed down through the hall, she went before open doors framing more eyes strangely microscopic, and sending broad beams of inquisitive light into the darkness of her path. On the second floor she met the gnarled old woman who possessed the music box.

"So," she cried, " 'ere yehs are back again, are yehs? An' dey've kicked yehs out? Well, come in an' stay wid me teh-night. I ain' got no moral standin.' "

From above came an unceasing babble of tongues, over all of which rang the mother's derisive laughter.

CHAPTER XVI

Pete did not consider that he had ruined Maggie. If he had thought that her soul could never smile again, he would have believed the mother and brother, who were pyrotechnic[1] over the affair, to be responsible for it.

Besides, in his world, souls did not insist upon being able to smile. "What deh hell?"

He felt a trifle entangled. It distressed him. Revelations and scenes might bring upon him the wrath of the owner of the saloon, who insisted upon respectability of an advanced type.

"What deh hell do dey wanna raise such a smoke[2] about it fer?" demanded he of himself, disgusted with the attitude of the family. He saw no necessity for anyone's losing their equilibrium merely because their sister or their daughter had stayed away from home.

Searching about in his mind for possible reasons for their conduct, he came upon the conclusion that Maggie's motives were correct, but that the two others wished to snare him. He felt pursued.

The woman of brilliance and audacity whom he had met in the hilarious hall showed a disposition to ridicule him.

"A little pale thing with no spirit," she said. "Did you note the expression of her eyes? There was something in them about pumpkin pie and virtue. That is a peculiar way the left corner of her mouth has of twitching, isn't it? Dear, dear, my cloud-compelling Pete, what are you coming to?"

Pete asserted at once that he never was very much interested in the girl. The woman interrupted him, laughing.

"Oh, it's not of the slightest consequence to me, my dear young man. You needn't draw maps for my benefit. Why should I be concerned about it?"

But Pete continued with his explanations. If he was laughed at for his tastes in women, he felt obliged to say that they were only temporary or indifferent ones.

[1]Explosive, like fireworks.
[2]Fuss.

The morning after Maggie had departed from home, Pete stood behind the bar. He was immaculate in white jacket and apron and his hair was plastered over his brow with infinite correctness. No customers were in the place. Pete was twisting his napkined fist slowly in a beer glass, softly whistling to himself and occasionally holding the object of his attention between his eyes and a few weak beams of sunlight that had found their way over the thick screens and into the shaded room.

With lingering thoughts of the woman of brilliance and audacity, the bartender raised his head and stared through the varying cracks between the swaying bamboo doors. Suddenly the whistling pucker faded from his lips. He saw Maggie walking slowly past. He gave a great start, fearing for the previously mentioned eminent respectability of the place.

He threw a swift, nervous glance about him, all at once feeling guilty. No one was in the room.

He went hastily over to the side door. Opening it and looking out, he perceived Maggie standing, as if undecided, on the corner. She was searching the place with her eyes.

As she turned her face toward him Pete beckoned to her hurriedly, intent upon returning with speed to a position behind the bar and to the atmosphere of respectability upon which the proprietor insisted.

Maggie came to him, the anxious look disappearing from her face and a smile wreathing her lips.

"Oh, Pete—," she began brightly.

The bartender made a violent gesture of impatience.

"Oh, my Gawd," cried he, vehemently. "What deh hell do yeh wanna hang aroun' here fer? Do yeh wanna git me inteh trouble?" he demanded with an air of injury.

Astonishment swept over the girl's features. "Why, Pete! yeh tol' me—"

Pete glanced profound irritation. His countenance reddened with the anger of a man whose respectability is being threatened.

"Say, yehs makes me tired. See? What deh hell deh yeh wanna tag aroun' atter me fer? Yeh'll git me inteh trouble wid deh ol' man an' dey'll be hell teh pay! If he sees a woman roun' here he'll go crazy an' I'll lose me job! See? Ain' yehs got no sense? Don't be allus bodderin' me. See? Yer brudder come in here an' raised hell an' deh ol' man hada put up fer it! An' now I'm done! See? I'm done."

The girl's eyes stared into his face. "Pete, don' yeh remem—"

"Oh, hell," interrupted Pete, anticipating.

The girl seemed to have a struggle with herself. She was apparently bewildered and could not find speech. Finally she asked in a low voice: "But where kin I go?"

The question exasperated Pete beyond the powers of endurance. It was a direct attempt to give him some responsibility in a matter that did not concern him. In his indignation he volunteered information.

"Oh, go teh hell," cried he. He slammed the door furiously and returned, with an air of relief, to his respectability.

Maggie went away.

She wandered aimlessly for several blocks. She stopped once and asked aloud a question of herself: "Who?"

A man who was passing near her shoulder, humorously took the questioning word as intended for him.

"Eh? What? Who? Nobody! I didn't say anything," he laughingly said, and continued his way.

Soon the girl discovered that if she walked with such apparent aimlessness, some men looked at her with calculating eyes. She quickened her step, frightened. As a protection, she adopted a demeanor of intentness as if going somewhere.

After a time she left rattling avenues and passed between rows of houses with sternness and stolidity stamped upon their features. She hung her head for she felt their eyes grimly upon her.

Suddenly she came upon a stout gentleman in a silk hat and a chaste black coat, whose decorous row of buttons reached from his chin to his knees.[3] The girl had heard of the Grace of God and she decided to approach this man.

His beaming, chubby face was a picture of benevolence and kind-heartedness. His eyes shone good-will.

But as the girl timidly accosted him, he gave a convulsive movement and saved his respectability by a vigorous side-step. He did not risk it to save a soul. For how was he to know that there was a soul before him that needed saving?

CHAPTER XVII

Upon a wet evening, several months after the last chapter, two interminable rows of cars, pulled by slipping horses, jangled along a prominent side-street. A dozen cabs, with coat-enshrouded drivers, clattered to and fro. Electric lights, whirring softly, shed a blurred radiance. A flower dealer, his feet tapping impatiently, his nose and his wares glistening with rain-drops, stood behind an array of roses and chrysanthemums. Two or three theatres emptied a crowd upon the storm-swept pavements. Men pulled their hats over their eyebrows and raised their collars to their ears. Women shrugged impatient shoulders in their warm cloaks and stopped to arrange their skirts for a walk through the storm. People having been comparatively silent for two hours burst into a roar of conversation, their hearts still kindling from the glowings of the stage.

The pavements became tossing seas of umbrellas. Men stepped forth to hail cabs or cars, raising their fingers in varied forms of polite request or imperative demand. An endless procession wended toward elevated stations. An atmosphere of pleasure and prosperity seemed to hang over the throng, born, perhaps, of good clothes and of having just emerged from a place of forgetfulness.

In the mingled light and gloom of an adjacent park, a handful of wet wanderers, in attitudes of chronic dejection, was scattered among the benches.

A girl of the painted cohorts of the city went along the street. She threw changing glances at men who passed her, giving smiling invitations to men of rural or untaught pattern and usually seeming sedately unconscious of the men with a metropolitan seal upon their faces.

Crossing glittering avenues, she went into the throng emerging from the places of forgetfulness. She hurried forward through the crowd as if intent upon reaching a distant home, bending forward in her handsome cloak, daintily lifting her skirts and picking for her well-shod feet the dryer spots upon the pavements.

The restless doors of saloons, clashing to and fro, disclosed animated rows of men before bars and hurrying barkeepers.

[3]A soutane, a cassock (with buttons down the front) worn by clergymen.

A concert hall gave to the street faint sounds of swift, machine-like music, as if a group of phantom musicians were hastening.

A tall young man, smoking a cigarette with a sublime air, strolled near the girl. He had on evening dress, a moustache, a chrysanthemum, and a look of ennui, all of which he kept carefully under his eye. Seeing the girl walk on as if such a young man as he was not in existence, he looked back transfixed with interest. He stared glassily for a moment, but gave a slight convulsive start when he discerned that she was neither new, Parisian, nor theatrical. He wheeled about hastily and turned his stare into the air, like a sailor with a search-light.

A stout gentleman, with pompous and philanthropic whiskers, went stolidly by, the broad of his back sneering at the girl.

A belated man in business clothes, and in haste to catch a car, bounced against her shoulder. "Hi, there, Mary, I beg your pardon! Brace up, old girl." He grasped her arm to steady her, and then was away running down the middle of the street.

The girl walked on out of the realm of restaurants and saloons. She passed more glittering avenues and went into darker blocks than those where the crowd travelled.

A young man in light overcoat and derby hat received a glance shot keenly from the eyes of the girl. He stopped and looked at her, thrusting his hands in his pockets and making a mocking smile curl his lips. "Come, now, old lady," he said, "you don't mean to tell me that you sized me up for a farmer?"

A laboring man marched along with bundles under his arms. To her remarks, he replied: "It's a fine evenin', ain't it?"

She smiled squarely into the face of a boy who was hurrying by with his hands buried in his overcoat, his blonde locks bobbing on his youthful temples, and a cheery smile of unconcern upon his lips. He turned his head and smiled back at her, waving his hands.

"Not this eve—some other eve!"

A drunken man, reeling in her pathway, began to roar at her. "I ain' ga' no money, dammit," he shouted, in a dismal voice. He lurched on up the street, wailing to himself, "Dammit, I ain' ga' no money. Damn ba' luck. Ain' ga' no more money."

The girl went into gloomy districts near the river, where the tall black factories shut in the street and only occasional broad beams of light fell across the pavements from saloons. In front of one of these places, from whence came the sound of a violin vigorously scraped, the patter of feet on boards and the ring of loud laughter, there stood a man with blotched features.

"Ah, there," said the girl.

"I've got a date," said the man.

Further on in the darkness she met a ragged being with shifting, blood-shot eyes and grimy hands. "Ah, what deh hell? T'ink I'm a millionaire?"

She went into the blackness of the final block. The shutters of the tall buildings were closed like grim lips. The structures seemed to have eyes that looked over her, beyond her, at other things. Afar off the lights of the avenues glittered as if from an impossible distance. Street car bells jingled with a sound of merriment.

When almost to the river the girl saw a great figure. On going forward she perceived it to be a huge fat man in torn and greasy garments. His grey hair straggled down over his forehead. His small, bleared eyes, sparkling from amidst great rolls of red fat, swept eagerly over the girl's upturned face. He laughed, his brown, disordered teeth gleaming under a grey, grizzled moustache from which beer-drops dripped. His whole body gently quivered and shook like that of a dead jelly fish. Chuckling and leering, he followed the girl of the crimson legions.

At their feet the river appeared a deathly black hue. Some hidden factory sent up a yellow glare, that lit for a moment the waters lapping oilily against timbers. The varied sounds of life, made joyous by distance and seeming unapproachableness, came faintly and died away to a silence.

CHAPTER XVIII

In a partitioned-off section of a saloon sat a man with a half dozen women, gleefully laughing, hovering about him. The man had arrived at that stage of drunkenness where affection is felt for the universe.

"I'm good f'ler, girls," he said, convincingly. "I'm damn good f'ler. An'body treats me right, I allus trea's zem right! See?"

The women nodded their heads approvingly. "To be sure," they cried in hearty chorus. "You're the kind of a man we like, Pete. You're outa sight! What yeh goin' to buy this time, dear?"

"An'thin' yehs wants, damn it," said the man in an abandonment of good will. His countenance shone with the true spirit of benevolence. He was in the proper mode of missionaries. He would have fraternized with obscure Hottentots.[1] And above all, he was overwhelmed in tenderness for his friends, who were all illustrious.

"An'thin' yehs wants, damn it," repeated he, waving his hands with beneficent recklessness. "I'm good f'ler, girls, an' if an'body treats me right I—here," called he through an open door to a waiter, "bring girls drinks, damn it. What 'ill yehs have, girls? An'thin' yehs wants, damn it!"

The waiter glanced in with the disgusted look of the man who serves intoxicants for the man who takes too much of them. He nodded his head shortly at the order from each individual, and went.

"Damn it," said the man, "we're havin' heluva time. I like you girls! Damn'd if I don't! Yer right sort! See?"

He spoke at length and with feeling, concerning the excellencies of his assembled friends.

"Don' try pull man's leg, but have a heluva time! Das right! Das way teh do! Now, if I sawght yehs tryin' work me fer drinks, wouldn' buy damn t'ing! But yer right sort, damn it! Yehs know how ter treat a f'ler, an' I stays by yehs 'til spen' las' cent! Das right! I'm good f'ler an' I knows when an'body treats me right!"

Between the times of the arrival and departure of the waiter, the man discoursed to the women on the tender regard he felt for all living things. He laid stress upon the purity of his motives in all dealings with men in the world and spoke of the fervor of his friendship for those who were amiable. Tears welled slowly from his eyes. His voice quavered when he spoke to them.

Once when the waiter was about to depart with an empty tray, the man drew a coin from his pocket and held it forth.

"Here," said he, quite magnificently," "here's quar'."

The waiter kept his hands on his tray.

"I don' want yer money," he said.

[1]South African tribesmen.

The other put forth the coin with tearful insistence.

"Here, damn it," cried he, "tak't! Yer damn goo' f'ler an' I wan' yehs tak't!"

"Come, come, now," said the waiter, with the sullen air of a man who is forced into giving advice. "Put yer mon in yer pocket! Yer loaded an' yehs on'y makes a damn fool of yerself."

As the latter passed out of the door the man turned pathetically to the women.

"He don' know I'm damn goo' f'ler," cried he, dismally.

"Never you mind, Pete, dear," said a woman of brilliance and audacity, laying her hand with great affection upon his arm. "Never you mind, old boy! We'll stay by you, dear!"

"Das ri'," cried the man, his face lighting up at the soothing tones of the woman's voice. "Das ri, I'm damn goo' f'ler an' w'en anyone trea's me ri', I treats zem ri'! Shee!"

"Sure!" cried the women. "And we're not goin' back on you, old man."

The man turned appealing eyes to the woman of brilliance and audacity. He felt that if he could be convicted of a contemptible action he would die.

"Shay, Nell, damn it, I allus trea's yehs shquare, didn' I? I allus been goo' f'ler wi' yehs, ain't I, Nell?"

"Sure you have, Pete," assented the woman. She delivered an oration to her companions. "Yessir, that's a fact. Pete's a square fellah, he is. He never goes back on a friend. He's the right kind an' we stay by him, don't we, girls?"

"Sure," they exclaimed. Looking lovingly at him they raised their glasses and drank his health.

"Girlsh," said the man, beseechingly, "I allus trea's yehs ri', didn' I? I'm goo' f'ler, ain' I, girlsh?"

"Sure," again they chorused.

"Well," said he finally, "le's have nozzer drink, zen."

"That's right," hailed a woman, "that's right. Yer no bloomin' jay! Yer spends yer money like a man. Dat's right."

The man pounded the table with his quivering fists.

"Yessir," he cried, with deep earnestness, as if someone disputed him. "I'm damn goo' f'ler, an' w'en anyone trea's me ri', I allus trea's—le's have nozzer drink."

He began to beat the wood with his glass.

"Shay," howled he, growing suddenly impatient. As the waiter did not then come, the man swelled with wrath.

"Shay," howled he again.

The waiter appeared at the door.

"Bringsh drinksh," said the man.

The waiter disappeared with the orders.

"Zat f'ler damn fool," cried the man. "He insul' me! I'm ge'man! Can' stan' be insul'! I'm goin' lickim when comes!"

"No, no," cried the women, crowding about and trying to subdue him. "He's all right! He didn't mean anything! Let it go! He's a good fellah!"

"Din' he insul' me?" asked the man earnestly.

"No," said they. "Of course he didn't! He's all right!"

"Sure he didn' insul' me?" demanded the man, with deep anxiety in his voice.

"No, no! We know him! He's a good fellah. He didn't mean anything."

"Well, zen," said the man, resolutely. "I'm go' 'pol'gize!"

When the waiter came, the man struggled to the middle of the floor.

"Girlsh shed you insul' me! I shay damn lie! I 'pol'gize!"

"All right," said the waiter.

The man sat down. He felt a sleepy but strong desire to straighten things out and have a perfect understanding with everybody.

"Nell, I allus trea's yeh shquare, din' I? Yeh likes me, don' yehs, Nell? I'm goo' f'ler?"

"Sure," said the woman of brilliance and audacity.

"Yeh knows I'm stuck on yehs, don' yehs, Nell?

"Sure," she repeated, carelessly.

Overwhelmed by a spasm of drunken adoration, he drew two or three bills from his pocket, and, with the trembling fingers of an offering priest, laid them on the table before the woman.

"Yehs knows, damn it, yehs kin have all got, 'cause I'm stuck on yehs, Nell, damn't, I—I'm stuck on yehs, Nell—buy drinksh—damn't—we're havin' heluva time—w'en anyone trea's me ri'—I—damn't, Nell—we're havin' heluva—time."

Shortly he went to sleep with his swollen face fallen forward on his chest.

The women drank and laughed, not heeding the slumbering man in the corner. Finally he lurched forward and fell groaning to the floor.

The women screamed in disgust and drew back their skirts.

"Come ahn," cried one, starting up angrily, "let's get out of here."

The woman of brilliance and audacity stayed behind, taking up the bills and stuffing them into a deep, irregularly-shaped pocket. A guttural snore from the recumbent man caused her to turn and look down at him.

She laughed. "What a damn fool," she said, and went.

The smoke from the lamps settled heavily down in the little compartment, obscuring the way out. The smell of oil, stifling in its intensity, pervaded the air. The wine from an overturned glass dripped softly down upon the blotches on the man's neck.

CHAPTER XIX

In a room a woman sat at a table eating like a fat monk in a picture.

A soiled, unshaven man pushed open the door and entered.

"Well," said he, "Mag's dead."

"What?" said the woman, her mouth filled with bread.

"Mag's dead," repeated the man.

"Deh hell she is," said the woman. She continued her meal. When she finished her coffee she began to weep.

"I kin remember when her two feet was no bigger dan yer t'umb, and she weared worsted boots," moaned she.

"Well, whata dat?" said the man.

"I kin remember when she weared worsted boots," she cried.

The neighbors began to gather in the hall, staring in at the weeping woman as if watching the contortions of a dying dog. A dozen women entered and lamented with her. Under their busy hands the rooms took on that appalling appearance of neatness and order with which death is greeted.

Suddenly the door opened and a woman in a black gown rushed in with outstretched arms. "Ah, poor Mary," she cried, and tenderly embraced the moaning one.

"Ah, what ter'ble affliction is dis,' ' continued she. Her vocabulary was derived from mission churches. "Me poor Mary, how I feel fer yehs! Ah, what a ter'ble affliction is a disobed'ent chil'."

Her good, motherly face was wet with tears. She trembled in eagerness to express her sympathy. The mourner sat with bowed head, rocking her body heavily to and fro, and crying out in a high, strained voice that sounded like a dirge[1] on some forlorn pipe.

"I kin remember when she weared worsted boots an' her two feets was no bigger dan yer t'umb an' she weared worsted boots. Miss Smith," she cried, raising her streaming eyes.

"Ah, me poor Mary," sobbed the woman in black. With low, coddling cries, she sank on her knees by the mourner's chair, and put her arms about her. The other women began to groan in different keys.

"Yer poor misguided chil' is gone now, Mary, an' let us hope it's fer deh bes'. Yeh'll fergive her now, Mary, won't yehs, dear, all her disobed'ence? All her t'ankless behavior to her mudder an' all her badness? She's gone where her ter'ble sins will be judged."

The woman in black raised her face and paused. The inevitable sunlight came streaming in at the windows and shed a ghastly cheerfulness upon the faded hues of the room. Two or three of the spectators were sniffling, and one was loudly weeping. The mourner arose and staggered into the other room. In a moment she emerged with a pair of faded baby shoes held in the hollow of her hand.

"I kin remember when she used to wear dem," cried she. The women burst anew into cries as if they had all been stabbed. The mourner turned to the soiled and unshaven man.

"Jimmie, boy, go git yer sister! Go git yer sister an' we'll put deh boots on her feets!"

"Dey won't fit her now, yeh damn fool," said the man.

"Got git yer sister, Jimmie," shrieked the woman, confronting him fiercely.

The man swore sullenly. He went over to a corner and slowly began to put on his coat. He took his hat and went out, with a dragging, reluctant step.

The woman in black came forward and again besought the mourner.

"Yeh'll fergive her, Mary! Yeh'll fergive yer bad, bad chil'! Her life was a curse an' her days were black an' yeh'll fergive yer bad girl? She's gone where her sins will be judged."

"She's gone where her sins will be judged," cried the other women, like a choir at a funeral.

"Deh Lord gives and deh Lord takes away," said the woman in black, raising her eyes to the sunbeams.

"Deh Lord gives and deh Lord takes away," responded the others.

"Yeh'll fergive her, Mary!" pleaded the woman in black. The mourner essayed to speak but her voice gave way. She shook her great shoulders frantically, in an agony of grief. Hot tears seemed to scald her quivering face. Finally her voice came and arose like a scream of pain.

"Oh, yes, I'll fergive her! I'll fergive her!"

1891–1893   1893, 1896

---

[1]Song of mourning.

THE RED BADGE OF COURAGE

AN EPISODE OF THE AMERICAN CIVIL WAR[1]

CHAPTER I

The cold passed reluctantly from the earth, and the retiring fogs revealed an army stretched out on the hills, resting. As the landscape changed from brown to green, the army awakened, and began to tremble with eagerness at the noise of rumors. It cast its eyes upon the roads, which were growing from long troughs of liquid mud to proper thoroughfares. A river, amber-tinted in the shadow of its banks, purled at the army's feet; and at night, when the stream had become of a sorrowful blackness, one could see across it the red, eyelike gleam of hostile campfires set in the low brows of distant hills.

Once a certain tall soldier developed virtues and went resolutely to wash a shirt. He came flying back from a brook waving his garment bannerlike. He was swelled with a tale he had heard from a reliable friend, who had heard it from a truthful cavalryman, who had heard it from his trustworthy brother, one of the orderlies at division headquarters. He adopted the important air of a herald in red and gold.

"We're goin' t' move t' morrah—sure," he said pompously to a group in the company street. "We're goin' 'way up the river, cut across, an' come around in behint 'em."

To his attentive audience he drew a loud and elaborate plan of a very brilliant campaign. When he had finished, the blue-clothed men scattered into small arguing groups between the rows of squat brown huts. A negro teamster who had been dancing upon a cracker box with the hilarious encouragement of twoscore soldiers was deserted. He sat mournfully down. Smoke drifted lazily from a multitude of quaint chimneys.

"It's a lie! that's all it is—a thunderin' lie!" said another private loudly. His smooth face was flushed, and his hands were thrust sulkily into his trousers' pockets. He took the matter as an affront to him. "I don't believe the derned old army's ever going to move. We're set. I've got ready to move eight times in the last two weeks, and we ain't moved yet."

The tall soldier felt called upon to defend the truth of a rumor he himself had introduced. He and the loud one came near to fighting over it.

A corporal began to swear before the assemblage. He had just put a costly board floor in his house, he said. During the early spring he had refrained from adding extensively to the comfort of his environment because he had felt that the army might start on the march at any moment. Of late, however, he had been impressed that they were in a sort of eternal camp.

Many of the men engaged in a spirited debate. One outlined in a peculiarly lucid manner all the plans of the commanding general. He was opposed by men who advocated that there were other plans of campaign. They clamored at each other, numbers making futile bids for the popular attention. Meanwhile, the soldier who had fetched the rumor bustled about with much importance. He was continually assailed by questions.

"What's up, Jim?"

"Th' army's goin' t' move."

[1]Although the battle described in the novel is unidentified, the details of the action most nearly resemble those of the Battle of Chancellorsville, fought in Virginia in May 1863.

"Ah, what yeh talkin' about? How yeh know it is?"

"Well, yeh kin b'lieve me er not, just as yeh like. I don't care a hang."

There was much food for thought in the manner in which he replied. He came near to convincing them by disdaining to produce proofs. They grew much excited over it.

There was a youthful private who listened with eager ears to the words of the tall soldier and to the varied comments of his comrades. After receiving a fill of discussions concerning marches and attacks, he went to his hut and crawled through an intricate hole that served it as a door. He wished to be alone with some new thoughts that had lately come to him.

He lay down on a wide bunk that stretched across the end of the room. In the other end, cracker boxes were made to serve as furniture. They were grouped about the fireplace. A picture from an illustrated weekly was upon the log walls, and three rifles were paralleled on pegs. Equipments hung on handy projections, and some tin dishes lay upon a small pile of firewood. A folded tent was serving as a roof. The sunlight, without, beating upon it, made it glow a light yellow shade. A small window shot an oblique square of whiter light upon the cluttered floor. The smoke from the fire at times neglected the clay chimney and wreathed into the room, and this flimsy chimney of clay and sticks made endless threats to set ablaze the whole establishment.

The youth was in a little trance of astonishment. So they were at last going to fight. On the morrow, perhaps, there would be a battle, and he would be in it. For a time he was obliged to labor to make himself believe. He could not accept with assurance an omen that he was about to mingle in one of those great affairs of the earth.

He had, of course, dreamed of battles all his life—of vague and bloody conflicts that had thrilled him with their sweep and fire. In visions he had seen himself in many struggles. He had imagined peoples secure in the shadow of his eagle-eyed prowess. But awake he had regarded battles as crimson blotches on the pages of the past. He had put them as things of the bygone with his thought-images of heavy crowns and high castles. There was a portion of the world's history which he had regarded as the time of wars, but it, he thought, had been long gone over the horizon and had disappeared forever.

From his home his youthful eyes had looked upon the war in his own country with distrust. It must be some sort of a play affair. He had long despaired of witnessing a Greeklike struggle. Such would be no more, he had said. Men were better, or more timid. Secular and religious education had effaced the throat-grappling instinct, or else firm finance held in check the passions.

He had burned several times to enlist. Tales of great movements shook the land. They might not be distinctly Homeric, but there seemed to be much glory in them. He had read of marches, sieges, conflicts, and he had longed to see it all. His busy mind had drawn for him large pictures extravagant in color, lurid with breathless deeds.

But his mother had discouraged him. She had affected to look with some contempt upon the quality of his war ardor and patriotism. She could calmly seat herself and with no apparent difficulty give him many hundreds of reasons why he was of vastly more importance on the farm than on the field of battle. She had had certain ways of expression that told him that her statements on the subject came from a deep conviction. Moroever, on her side, was his belief that her ethical motive in the argument was impregnable.

At last, however, he had made firm rebellion against this yellow light thrown upon the color of his ambitions. The newspapers, the gossip of the village, his own picturings, had aroused him to an uncheckable degree. They were in truth fighting finely down there. Almost every day the newspapers printed accounts of a decisive victory.

One night, as he lay in bed, the winds had carried to him the clangoring of the church bell as some enthusiast jerked the rope frantically to tell the twisted news of a great battle. This voice of the people rejoicing in the night had made him shiver in a prolonged ecstasy of excitement. Later, he had gone down to his mother's room and had spoken thus: "Ma, I'm going to enlist."

"Henry, don't you be a fool," his mother had replied. She had then covered her face with the quilt. There was an end to the matter for that night.

Nevertheless, the next morning he had gone to a town that was near his mother's farm and had enlisted in a company that was forming[2] there. When he had returned home his mother was milking the brindle[3] cow. Four others stood waiting. "Ma, I've enlisted," he had said to her diffidently. There was a short silence. "The Lord's will be done, Henry," she had finally replied, and had then continued to milk the brindle cow.

When he had stood in the doorway with his soldier's clothes on his back, and with the light of excitement and expectancy in his eyes almost defeating the glow of regret for the home bonds, he had seen two tears leaving their trails on his mother's scarred cheeks.

Still, she had disappointed him by saying nothing whatever about returning with his shield or on it.[4] He had privately primed himself for a beautiful scene. He had prepared certain sentences which he thought could be used with touching effect. But her words destroyed his plans. She had doggedly peeled potatoes and addressed him as follows: "You watch out, Henry, an' take good care of yerself in this here fighting business—you watch out, an' take good care of yerself. Don't go a-thinkin' you can lick the hull rebel army at the start, because yeh can't. Yer jest one little feller amongst a hull lot of others, and yeh've got to keep quiet an' do what they tell yeh. I know how you are, Henry.

"I've knet yeh eight pair of socks, Henry, and I've put in all yer best shirts, because I want my boy to be jest as warm and comf'able as anybody in the army. Whenever they got holes in 'em, I want yeh to send 'em right-away back to me, so's I kin dern 'em.

"An' allus be careful an' choose yer comp'ny. There's lots of bad men in the army, Henry. The army makes 'em wild, and they like nothing better than the job of leading off a young feller like you, as ain't never been away from home much and has allus had a mother, an' a-learning 'em to drink and swear. Keep clear of them folks, Henry. I don't want yeh to ever do anything, Henry, that yeh would be 'shamed to let me know about. Jest think as if I was a-watchin' yeh. If yeh keep that in yer mind allus, I guess yeh'll come out about right.

"Yeh must allus remember yer father, too, child, an' remember he never drunk a drop of licker in his life, and seldom swore a cross oath.

"I don't know what else to tell yeh, Henry, excepting that yeh must never do no shirking, child, on my account. If so be a time comes when yeh have to be

[2]In spite of a conscription law, passed in 1863, the North relied primarily on volunteers who enlisted for a period of three years. Most companies in the Union army were raised by local citizens and then were joined to state militia regiments and sent into battle.

[3]Gray or brown with dark streaks.

[4]According to Plutarch, Spartan warriors went off to war bidden by their mothers to return "with your shield or upon it," i.e., return either undefeated or dead, not having cast aside the shield to flee.

kilt or do a mean thing, why, Henry, don't think of anything 'cept what's right, because there's many a woman has to bear up 'ginst sech things these times, and the Lord'll take keer of us all.

"Don't forget about the socks and the shirts, child; and I've put a cup of blackberry jam with yer bundle, because I know yeh like it above all things. Good-by, Henry. Watch out, and be a good boy."

He had, of course, been impatient under the ordeal of this speech. It had not been quite what he expected, and he had borne it with an air of irritation. He departed feeling vague relief.

Still, when he had looked back from the gate, he had seen his mother kneeling among the potato parings. Her brown face, upraised, was stained with tears, and her spare form was quivering. He bowed his head and went on, feeling suddenly ashamed of his purposes.

From his home he had gone to the seminary[5] to bid adieu to many schoolmates. They had thronged about him with wonder and admiration. He had felt the gulf now between them and had swelled with calm pride. He and some of his fellows who had donned blue were quite overwhelmed with privileges for all of one afternoon, and it had been a very delicious thing. They had strutted.

A certain light-haired girl had made vivacious fun at his martial spirit, but there was another and darker girl whom he had gazed at steadfastly, and he thought she grew demure and sad at sight of his blue and brass. As he had walked down the path between the rows of oaks, he had turned his head and detected her at a window watching his departure. As he perceived her, she had immediately begun to stare up through the high tree branches at the sky. He had seen a good deal of flurry and haste in her movement as she changed her attitude. He often thought of it.

On the way to Washington[6] his spirit had soared. The regiment was fed and caressed at station after station until the youth had believed that he must be a hero. There was a lavish expenditure of bread and cold meats, coffee, and pickles and cheese. As he basked in the smiles of the girls and was patted and complimented by the old men, he had felt growing within him the strength to do mighty deeds of arms.

After complicated journeyings with many pauses, there had come months of monotonous life in a camp. He had had the belief that real war was a series of death struggles with small time in between for sleep and meals; but since his regiment had come to the field the army had done little but sit still and try to keep warm.

He was brought then gradually back to his old ideas. Greeklike struggles would be no more. Men were better, or more timid. Secular and religious education had effaced the throat-grappling instinct, or else firm finance held in check the passions.

He had grown to regard himself merely as a part of a vast blue demonstration. His province was to look out, as far as he could, for his personal comfort. For recreation he could twiddle his thumbs and speculate on the thoughts which must agitate the minds of the generals. Also, he was drilled and drilled and reviewed, and drilled and drilled and reviewed.

The only foes he had seen were some pickets[7] along the river bank. They were a sun-tanned, philosophical lot, who sometimes shot reflectively at the

---

[5]A high school.
[6]Northern troops to be used in the Virginia campaigns were first sent to Washington, D.C., before proceeding south into Virginia.   [7]Sentries.

blue[8] pickets. When reproached for this afterward, they usually expressed sorrow, and swore by their gods that the guns had exploded without their permission. The youth, on guard duty one night, conversed across the stream with one of them. He was a slightly ragged man, who spat skillfully between his shoes and possessed a great fund of bland and infantile assurance. The youth liked him personally.

"Yank," the other had informed him, "yer a right dum[9] good feller." This sentiment, floating to him upon the still air, had made him temporarily regret war.

Various veterans had told him tales. Some talked of gray, bewhiskered hordes who were advancing with relentless curses and chewing tobacco with unspeakable valor; tremendous bodies of fierce soldiery who were sweeping along like the Huns.[10] Others spoke of tattered and eternally hungry men who fired despondent powders. "They'll charge through hell's fire an' brimstone t' git a holt on a haversack, an' sech stomachs ain't a-lastin' long," he was told. From the stories, the youth imagined the red, live bones sticking out through slits in the faded uniforms.

Still, he could not put a whole faith in veterans' tales, for recruits were their prey. They talked much of smoke, fire, and blood, but he could not tell how much might be lies. They persistently yelled "Fresh fish!"[11] at him, and were in no wise to be trusted.

However, he perceived now that it did not greatly matter what kind of soldiers he was going to fight, so long as they fought, which fact no one disputed. There was a more serious problem. He lay in his bunk pondering upon it. He tried to mathematically prove to himself that he would not run from a battle.

Previously he had never felt obligated to wrestle too seriously with this question. In his life he had taken certain things for granted, never challenging his belief in ultimate success, and bothering little about means and roads. But here he was confronted with a thing of moment. It had suddenly appeared to him that perhaps in a battle he might run. He was forced to admit that as far as war was concerned he knew nothing of himself.

A sufficient time before he would have allowed the problem to kick its heels at the outer portals of his mind, but now he felt compelled to give serious attention to it.

A little panic-fear grew in his mind. As his imagination went forward to a fight, he saw hideous possibilities. He contemplated the lurking menaces of the future, and failed in an effort to see himself standing stoutly in the midst of them. He recalled his visions of broken-bladed glory, but in the shadow of the impending tumult he suspected them to be impossible pictures.

He sprang from the bunk and began to pace nervously to and fro. "Good Lord, what's th' matter with me?" he said aloud.

He felt that in this crisis his laws of life were useless. Whatever he had learned of himself was here to no avail. He was an unknown quantity. He saw that he would again be obliged to experiment as he had in early youth. He must accumulate information of himself, and meanwhile he resolved to remain close upon his guard lest those qualities of which he knew nothing should everlastingly disgrace him. "Good Lord!" he repeated in dismay.

After a time the tall soldier slid dexterously through the hole. The loud private followed. They were wrangling.

[8]Union troops were dressed in blue.   [9]Damn.
[10]Nomadic tribesmen from Asia who had invaded and pillaged Europe around A.D. 450.
[11]I.e., "Rookie!"

"That's all right," said the tall soldier as he entered. He waved his hand expressively. "You can believe me or not, jest as you like. All you got to do is to sit down and wait as quiet as you can. Then pretty soon you'll find out I was right."

His comrade grunted stubbornly. For a moment he seemed to be searching for a formidable reply. Finally he said: "Well, you don't know everything in the world, do you?"

"Didn't say I knew everything in the world," retorted the other sharply. He began to stow various articles snugly into his knapsack.

The youth, pausing in his nervous walk, looked down at the busy figure. "Going to be a battle, sure, is there, Jim?" he asked.

"Of course there is," replied the tall soldier. "Of course there is. You jest wait 'till to-morrow, and you'll see one of the biggest battles ever was. You jest wait."

"Thunder!" said the youth.

"Oh, you'll see fighting this time, my boy, what'll be regular out-and-out fighting," added the tall soldier, with the air of a man who is about to exhibit a battle for the benefit of his friends.

"Huh!" said the loud one from a corner.

"Well," remarked the youth, "like as not this story'll turn out jest like them others did."

"Not much it won't," replied the tall soldier, exasperated. "Not much it won't. Didn't the cavalry all start this morning?" He glared about him. No one denied his statement. "The cavalry started this morning," he continued. "They say there ain't hardly any cavalry left in camp. They're going to Richmond, or some place, while we fight all the Johnnies.[12] It's some dodge like that. The regiment's got orders, too. A feller what seen 'em go to headquarters told me a little while ago. And they're raising blazes all over camp—anybody can see that."

"Shucks!" said the loud one.

The youth remained silent for a time. At last he spoke to the tall soldier. "Jim!"

"What?"

"How do you think the reg'ment 'll do?"

"Oh, they'll fight all right, I guess, after they once get into it," said the other with cold judgment. He made a fine use of the third person. "There's been heaps of fun poked at 'em because they're new, of course, and all that; but they'll fight all right, I guess."

"Think any of the boys 'll run?" persisted the youth.

"Oh, there may be a few of 'em run, but there's them kind in every regiment, 'specially when they first goes under fire," said the other in a tolerant way. "Of course it might happen that the hull kit-and-boodle might start and run, if some big fighting came first-off, and then again they might stay and fight like fun. But you can't bet on nothing. Of course they ain't never been under fire yet, and it ain't likely they'll lick the hull rebel army all-to-oncet the first time; but I think they'll fight better than some, if worse than others. That's the way I figger. They call the reg'ment 'Fresh fish' and everything; but the boys come of good stock, and most of 'em 'll fight like sin after they oncet git shootin'," he added, with a mighty emphasis on the last four words.

"Oh, you think you know——" began the loud soldier with scorn.

The other turned savagely upon him. They had a rapid altercation, in which they fastened upon each other various strange epithets.

[12]The Confederate soldier was nicknamed Johnny Reb; the Union soldier, Billy Yank.

The youth at last interrupted them. "Did you ever think you might run yourself, Jim?" he asked. On concluding the sentence he laughed as if he had meant to aim a joke. The loud soldier also giggled.

The tall private waved his hand. "Well," said he profoundly, "I've thought it might get too hot for Jim Conklin in some of them scrimmages, and if a whole lot of boys started and run, why, I s'pose I'd start and run. And if I once started to run, I'd run like the devil, and no mistake. But if everybody was a-standing and a-fighting, why, I'd stand and fight. Be jiminey, I would. I'll bet on it."

"Huh!" said the loud one.

The youth of this tale felt gratitude for these words of his comrade. He had feared that all of the untried men possessed a great and correct confidence. He now was in a measure reassured.

CHAPTER II

The next morning the youth discovered that his tall comrade had been the fast-flying messenger of a mistake. There was much scoffing at the latter by those who had yesterday been firm adherents of his views, and there was even a little sneering by men who had never believed the rumor. The tall one fought with a man from Chatfield Corners[1] and beat him severely.

The youth felt, however, that his problem was in no wise lifted from him. There was, on the contrary, an irritating prolongation. The tale had created in him a great concern for himself. Now, with the newborn question in his mind, he was compelled to sink back into his old place as part of a blue demonstration.

For days he made ceaseless calculations, but they were all wonderously unsatisfactory. He found that he could establish nothing. He finally concluded that the only way to prove himself was to go into the blaze, and then figuratively to watch his legs to discover their merits and faults. He reluctantly admitted that he could not sit still and with a mental slate and pencil derive an answer. To gain it, he must have blaze, blood, and danger, even as a chemist requires this, that, and the other. So he fretted for an opportunity.

Meanwhile he continually tried to measure himself by his comrades. The tall soldier, for one, gave him some assurance. This man's serene unconcern dealt him a measure of confidence, for he had known him since childhood, and from his intimate knowledge he did not see how he could be capable of anything that was beyond him, the youth. Still, he thought that his comrade might be mistaken about himself. Or, on the other hand, he might be a man heretofore doomed to peace and obscurity, but, in reality, made to shine in war.

The youth would have liked to have discovered another who suspected himself. A sympathetic comparison of mental notes would have been a joy to him.

He occasionally tried to fathom a comrade with seductive sentences. He looked about to find men in the proper mood. All attempts failed to bring forth any statement which looked in any way like a confession to those doubts which he privately acknowledged in himself. He was afraid to make an open declaration of his concern, because he dreaded to place some unscrupulous confidant upon the high plane of the unconfessed from which elevation he could be derided.

In regard to his companions his mind wavered between two opinions, according to his mood. Sometimes he inclined to believing them all heroes. In

[1]Here and elsewhere, Crane indicates that Henry Fleming's fictitious unit was from New York State.

fact, he usually admitted in secret the superior development of the higher qualities in others. He could conceive of men going very insignificantly about the world bearing a load of courage unseen, and although he had known many of his comrades through boyhood, he began to fear that his judgment of them had been blind. Then, in other moments, he flouted these theories, and assured himself that his fellows were all privately wondering and quaking.

His emotions made him feel strange in the presence of men who talked excitedly of a prospective battle as of a drama they were about to witness, with nothing but eagerness and curiosity apparent in their faces. It was often that he suspected them to be liars.

He did not pass such thoughts without severe condemnation of himself. He dinned reproaches at times. He was convicted by himself of many shameful crimes against the gods of traditions.

In his great anxiety his heart was continually clamoring at what he considered the intolerable slowness of the generals. They seemed content to perch tranquilly on the river bank, and leave him bowed down by the weight of a great problem. He wanted it settled forthwith. He could not long bear such a load, he said. Sometimes his anger at the commanders reached an acute stage, and he grumbled about the camp like a veteran.

One morning, however, he found himself in the ranks of his prepared regiment. The men were whispering speculations and recounting the old rumors. In the gloom before the break of the day their uniform glowed a deep purple hue. From across the river the red eyes[2] were still peering. In the eastern sky there was a yellow patch like a rug laid for the feet of the coming sun; and against it, black and patternlike, loomed the gigantic figure of the colonel on a gigantic horse.

From off in the darkness came the trampling of feet. The youth could occasionally see dark shadows that moved like monsters. The regiment stood at rest for what seemed a long time. The youth grew impatient. It was unendurable the way these affairs were managed. He wondered how long they were to be kept waiting.

As he looked all about him and pondered upon the mystic gloom, he began to believe that at any moment the ominous distance might be aflare, and the rolling crashes of an engagement come to his ears. Staring once at the red eyes across the river, he conceived them to be growing larger, as the orbs of a row of dragons advancing. He turned toward the colonel and saw him left his gigantic arm and calmly stroke his mustache.

At last he heard from along the road at the foot of the hill the clatter of a horse's galloping hoofs. It must be the coming of orders. He bent forward, scarce breathing. The exciting clickety-click, as it grew louder and louder, seemed to be beating upon his soul. Presently a horseman with jangling equipment drew rein before the colonel of the regiment. The two held a short, sharp-worded conversation. The men in the foremost ranks craned their necks.

As the horseman wheeled his animal and galloped away he turned to shout over his shoulder, "Don't forget that box of cigars!" The colonel mumbled in reply. The youth wondered what a box of cigars had to do with war.

A moment later the regiment went swinging off into the darkness. It was now like one of those moving monsters wending with many feet. The air was heavy, and cold with dew. A mass of wet grass, marched upon, rustled like silk.

There was an occasional flash and glimmer of steel from the backs of all these

[2]Enemy campfires.

huge crawling reptiles. From the road came creakings and grumblings as some surly guns were dragged away.

The men stumbled along still muttering speculations. There was a subdued debate. Once a man fell down, and as he reached for his rifle a comrade, unseeing, trod upon his hand. He of the injured fingers swore bitterly and aloud. A low, tittering laugh went among his fellows.

Presently they passed into a roadway and marched forward with easy strides. A dark regiment moved before them, and from behind also came the tinkle of equipments on the bodies of marching men.

The rushing yellow of the developing day went on behind their backs. When the sun rays at last struck full and mellowingly upon the earth, the youth saw that the landscape was streaked with two long, thin, black columns which disappeared on the brow of a hill in front and rearward vanished in a wood. They were like two serpents crawling from the cavern of the night.

The river was not in view. The tall soldier burst into praises of what he thought to be his powers of perception.

Some of the tall one's companions cried with emphasis that they, too, had evolved the same thing, and they congratulated themselves upon it. But there were others who said that the tall one's plan was not the true one at all. They persisted with other theories. There was a vigorous discussion.

The youth took no part in them. As he walked along in careless line he was engaged with his own eternal debate. He could not hinder himself from dwelling upon it. He was despondent and sullen, and threw shifting glances about him. He looked ahead, often expecting to hear from the advance the rattle of firing.

But the long serpents crawled slowly from hill to hill without bluster of smoke. A dun-colored cloud of dust floated away to the right. The sky overhead was of a fairy blue.

The youth studied the faces of his companions, ever on the watch to detect kindred emotions. He suffered disappointment. Some ardor of the air which was causing the veteran commands to move with glee—almost with song—had infected the new regiment. The men began to speak of victory as of a thing they knew. Also, the tall soldier received his vindication. They were certainly going to come around in behind the enemy. They expressed commiseration for that part of the army which had been left upon the river bank, felicitating themselves upon being a part of a blasting host.

The youth, considering himself as separated from the others, was saddened by the blithe and merry speeches that went from rank to rank. The company wags all made their best endeavors. The regiment tramped to the tune of laughter.

The blatant soldier often convulsed whole files by his biting sarcasms aimed at the tall one.

And it was not long before all the men seemed to forget their mission. Whole brigades grinned in unison, and regiments laughed.

A rather fat soldier attempted to pilfer a horse from a dooryard. He planned to load his knapsack upon it. He was escaping with his prize when a young girl rushed from the house and grabbed the animal's mane. There followed a wrangle. The young girl, with pink cheeks and shining eyes, stood like a dauntless statue.

The observant regiment, standing at rest in the roadway, whooped at once, and entered whole-souled upon the side of the maiden. The men became so engrossed in this affair that they entirely ceased to remember their own large war. They jeered the piratical private, and called attention to various defects in his personal appearance; and they were wildly enthusiastic in support of the young girl.

To her, from some distance, came bold advice. "Hit him with a stick."

There were crows and catcalls showered upon him when he retreated without the horse. The regiment rejoiced at his downfall. Loud and vociferous congratulations were showered upon the maiden, who stood panting and regarding the troops with defiance.

At nightfall the column broke into regimental pieces, and the fragments went into the fields to camp. Tents sprang up like strange plants. Camp fires, like red, peculiar blossoms, dotted the night.

The youth kept from intercourse with his companions as much as circumstances would allow him. In the evening he wandered a few paces into the gloom. From this little distance the many fires, with the black forms of men passing to and fro before the crimson rays, made weird and satanic effects.

He lay down in the grass. The blades pressed tenderly against his cheek. The moon had been lighted and was hung in a treetop. The liquid stillness of the night enveloping him made him feel vast pity for himself. There was a caress in the soft winds; and the whole mood of the darkness, he thought, was one of sympathy for himself in his distress.

He wished, without reserve, that he was at home again making the endless rounds from the house to the barn, from the barn to the fields, from the fields to the barn, from the barn to the house. He remembered he had often cursed the brindle cow and her mates, and had sometimes flung milking stools. But, from his present point of view, there was a halo of happiness about each of their heads, and he would have sacrificed all the brass buttons on the continent to have been enabled to return to them. He told himself that he was not formed for a soldier. And he mused seriously upon the radical differences between himself and those men who were dodging implike around the fires.

As he mused thus he heard the rustle of grass, and upon turning his head, discovered the loud soldier. He called out, "Oh, Wilson!"

The latter approached and looked down. "Why, hello, Henry; is it you? What you doing here?"

"Oh, thinking," said the youth.

The other sat down and carefully lighted his pipe. "You're getting blue, my boy. You're looking thundering peeked. What the dickens is wrong with you?"

"Oh, nothing," said the youth.

The loud soldier launched then into the subject of the anticipated fight. "Oh, we've got 'em now!" As he spoke his boyish face was wreathed in a gleeful smile, and his voice had an exultant ring. "We've got 'em now. At last, by the eternal thunders, we'll lick 'em good!"

"If the truth was known," he added, more soberly, "*they've* licked *us* about every clip up to now; but this time—this time—we'll lick 'em good!"

"I thought you was objecting to this march a little while ago," said the youth coldly.

"Oh, it wasn't that," explained the other. "I don't mind marching, if there's going to be fighting at the end of it. What I hate is this getting moved here and moved there, with no good coming of it, as far as I can see, excepting sore feet and damned short rations."

"Well, Jim Conklin says we'll get a plenty of fighting this time."

"He's right for once, I guess, though I can't see how it come. This time we're in for a big battle, and we've got the best end of it, certain sure. Gee rod! how we will thump 'em!"

He arose and began to pace to and fro excitedly. The thrill of his enthusiasm made him walk with an elastic step. He was sprightly, vigorous, fiery in his belief in success. He looked into the future with clear, proud eye, and he swore with the air of an old soldier.

The youth watched him for a moment in silence. When he finally spoke his voice was as bitter as dregs. "Oh, you're going to do great things, I s'pose!"

The loud soldier blew a thoughtful cloud of smoke from his pipe. "Oh, I don't know," he remarked with dignity; "I don't know. I s'pose I'll do as well as the rest. I'm going to try like thunder." He evidently complimented himself upon the modesty of this statement.

"How do you know you won't run when the time comes?" asked the youth.

"Run?" said the loud one; "run?—of course not!" He laughed.

"Well," continued the youth, "lots of good-a-'nough men have thought they was going to do great things before the fight, but when the time come they skedaddled."

"Oh, that's all true, I s'pose," replied the other; "but I'm not going to skedaddle. The man that bets on my running will lose his money, that's all." He nodded confidently.

"Oh, shucks!" said the youth. "You ain't the bravest man in the world, are you?"

"No, I ain't," exclaimed the loud soldier indignantly; "and I didn't say I was the bravest man in the world, neither. I said I was going to do my share of fighting—that's what I said. And I am, too. Who are you, anyhow? You talk as if you thought you was Napoleon Bonaparte." He glared at the youth for a moment, and then strode away.

The youth called in a savage voice after his comrade: "Well, you needn't git mad about it!" But the other continued on his way and made no reply.

He felt alone in space when his injured comrade had disappeared. His failure to discover any mite of resemblance in their view points made him more miserable than before. No one seemed to be wrestling with such a terrific personal problem. He was a mental outcast.

He went slowly to his tent and stretched himself on a blanket by the side of the snoring tall soldier. In the darkness he saw visions of a thousand-tongued fear that would babble at his back and cause him to flee, while others were going coolly about their country's business. He admitted that he would not be able to cope with this monster. He felt that every nerve in his body would be an ear to hear the voices, while other men would remain stolid and deaf.

And as he sweated with the pain of these thoughts, he could hear low, serene sentences. "I'll bid five." "Make it six." "Seven." "Seven goes."

He stared at the red, shivering reflection of a fire on the white wall of his tent until, exhausted and ill from the monotony of his suffering, he fell asleep.

CHAPTER III

When another night came the columns, changed to purple streaks, filed across two pontoon bridges.[1] A glaring fire wine-tinted the waters of the river. Its rays, shining upon the moving masses of troops, brought forth here and there sudden gleams of silver or gold. Upon the other shore a dark and mysterious range of hills was curved against the sky. The insect voices of the night sang solemnly.

---

[1]Temporary bridges with roadways supported by boats or pontoons.

After this crossing the youth assured himself that at any moment they might be suddenly and fearfully assaulted from the caves of the lowering woods. He kept his eyes watchfully upon the darkness.

But his regiment went unmolested to a camping place, and its soldiers slept the brave sleep of wearied men. In the morning they were routed out with early energy, and hustled along a narrow road that led deep into the forest.

It was during this rapid march that the regiment lost many of the marks of a new command.

The men had begun to count the miles upon their fingers, and they grew tired. "Sore feet an' damned short rations, that's all," said the loud soldier. There was perspiration and grumblings. After a time they began to shed their knapsacks. Some tossed them unconcernedly down; others hid them carefully, asserting their plans to return for them at some convenient time. Men extricated themselves from thick shirts. Presently few carried anything but their necessary clothing, blankets, haversacks, canteens, and arms and ammunition. "You can now eat and shoot," said the tall soldier to the youth. "That's all you want to do."

There was sudden change from the ponderous infantry of theory to the light and speedy infantry of practice. The regiment, relieved of a burden, received a new impetus. But there was much loss of valuable knapsacks, and, on the whole, very good shirts.

But the regiment was not yet veteranlike in appearance. Veteran regiments in the army were likely to be very small aggregations of men. Once, when the command had first come to the field, some perambulating veterans, noting the length of their columns, had accosted them thus: "Hey, fellers, what brigade is that?" And when the men had replied that they formed a regiment and not a brigade, the older soldiers had laughed,[2] and said, "O Gawd!"

Also, there was too great a similarity in the hats. The hats of a regiment should properly represent the history of headgear for a period of years. And, moreover, there were no letters of faded gold speaking from the colors. They were new and beautiful, and the color bearer habitually oiled the pole.

Presently the army again sat down to think. The odor of the peaceful pines was in the men's nostrils. The sound of monotonous axe blows rang through the forest, and the insects, nodding upon their perches, crooned like old women. The youth returned to his theory of a blue demonstration.

One gray dawn, however, he was kicked in the leg by the tall soldier, and then, before he was entirely awake, he found himself running down a wood road in the midst of men who were panting from the first effects of speed. His canteen banged rhythmically upon his thigh, and his haversack bobbed softly. His musket bounced a trifle from his shoulder at each stride and made his cap feel uncertain upon his head.

He could hear the men whisper jerky sentences: "Say—what's all this—about?" "What th' thunder—we—skedaddlin' this way fer?" "Billie—keep off m' feet. Yeh run—like a cow." And the loud soldier's shrill voice could be heard: "What th' devil they in sich a hurry for?"

The youth thought the damp fog of early morning moved from the rush of a great body of troops. From the distance came a sudden spatter of firing.

He was bewildered. As he ran with his comrades he strenuously tried to think, but all he knew was that if he fell down those coming behind would tread upon

---

[2]A brigade was composed of two or more regiments. After severe losses a veteran brigade and its regiments were sometimes reduced to half strength or less. By being at full strength, Henry's regiment revealed itself as untested in battle and therefore worthy of the veteran soldiers' scorn.

him. All his faculties seemed to be needed to guide him over and past obstructions. He felt carried along by a mob.

The sun spread disclosing rays, and, one by one, regiments burst into view
like armed men just born of the earth. The youth perceived that the time had
come. He was about to be measured. For a moment he felt in the face of his
great trial like a babe, and the flesh over his heart seemed very thin. He seized
time to look about him calculatingly.

But he instantly saw that it would be impossible for him to escape from the
regiment. It inclosed him. And there were iron laws of tradition and law on
four sides. He was in a moving box.

As he perceived this fact it occurred to him that he had never wished to come
to the war. He had not enlisted of his free will. He had been dragged by the
merciless government. And now they were taking him out to be slaughtered.

The regiment slid down a bank and wallowed across a little stream. The
mournful current moved slowly on, and from the water, shaded black, some
white bubble eyes looked at the men.

As they climbed the hill on the farther side artillery began to boom. Here
the youth forgot many things as he felt a sudden impulse of curiosity. He
scrambled up the bank with a speed that could not be exceeded by a blood-
thirsty man.

He expected a battle scene.

There were some little fields girted and squeezed by a forest. Spread over the
grass and in among the tree trunks, he could see knots and waving lines of
skirmishers who were running hither and thither and firing at the landscape.
A dark battle line lay upon a sunstruck clearing that gleamed orange color. A
flag fluttered.

Other regiments floundered up the bank. The brigade was formed in line of
battle, and after a pause started slowly through the woods in the rear of the
receding skirmishers, who were continually melting into the scene to appear
again farther on. They were always busy as bees, deeply absorbed in their little
combats.

The youth tried to observe everything. He did not use care to avoid trees and
branches, and his forgotten feet were constantly knocking against stones or
getting entangled in briers. He was aware that these battalions with their commotions were woven red and startling into the gentle fabric of softened greens
and browns. It looked to be a wrong place for a battlefield.

The skirmishers in advance fascinated him. Their shots into thickets and at
distant and prominent trees spoke to him of tragedies—hidden, mysterious,
solemn.

Once the line encountered the body of a dead soldier. He lay upon his back
staring at the sky. He was dressed in an awkward suit of yellowish brown. The
youth could see that the soles of his shoes had been worn to the thinness of
writing paper, and from a great rent in one the dead foot projected piteously.
And it was as if fate had betrayed the soldier. In death it exposed to his enemies
that poverty which in life he had perhaps concealed from his friends.

The ranks opened covertly to avoid the corpse. The invulnerable dead man
forced a way for himself. The youth looked keenly at the ashen face. The wind
raised the tawny beard. It moved as if a hand were stroking it. He vaguely
desired to walk around and around the body and stare; the impulse of the living
to try to read in dead eyes the answer to the Question.

During the march the ardor which the youth had acquired when out of view
of the field rapidly faded to nothing. His curiosity was quite easily satisfied. If

an intense scene had caught him with its wild swing as he came to the top of the bank, he might have gone roaring on. This advance upon Nature was too calm. He had opportunity to reflect. He had time in which to wonder about himself and to attempt to probe his sensations.

Absurd ideas took hold upon him. He thought that he did not relish the landscape. It threatened him. A coldness swept over his back, and it is true that his trousers felt to him that they were no fit for his legs at all.

A house standing placidly in the distant fields had to him an ominous look. The shadows of the woods were formidable. He was certain that in this vista there lurked fierce-eyed hosts. The swift thought came to him that the generals did not know what they were about. It was all a trap. Suddenly those close forests would bristle with rifle barrels. Ironlike brigades would appear in the rear. They were all going to be sacrificed. The generals were stupid. The enemy would presently swallow the whole command. He glared about him, expecting to see the stealthy approach of his death.

He thought that he must break from the ranks and harangue his comrades. They must not all be killed like pigs; and he was sure it would come to pass unless they were informed of these dangers. The generals were idiots to send them marching into a regular pen. There was but one pair of eyes in the corps. He would step forth and make a speech. Shrill and passionate words came to his lips.

The line, broken into moving fragments by the ground, went calmly on through fields and woods. The youth looked at the men nearest him, and saw, for the most part, expressions of deep interest, as if they were investigating something that had fascinated them. One or two stepped with overvaliant airs as if they were already plunged into war. Others walked as upon thin ice. The greater part of the untested men appeared quiet and absorbed. They were going to look at war, the red animal—war, the blood-swollen god. And they were deeply engrossed in this march.

As he looked the youth gripped his outcry at his throat. He saw that even if the men were tottering with fear they would laugh at his warning. They would jeer him, and, if practicable, pelt him with missiles. Admitting that he might be wrong, a frenzied declamation of the kind would turn him into a worm.

He assumed, then, the demeanor of one who knows that he is doomed alone to unwritten responsibilities. He lagged, with tragic glances at the sky.

He was surprised presently by the young lieutenant of his company, who began heartily to beat him with a sword, calling out in a loud and insolent voice: "Come, young man, get up into ranks there. No skulking 'll do here." He mended his pace with suitable haste. And he hated the lieutenant, who had no appreciation of fine minds. He was a mere brute.

After a time the brigade was halted in the cathedral light of a forest. The busy skirmishers were still popping. Through the aisles of the wood could be seen the floating smoke from their rifles. Sometimes it went up in little balls, white and compact.

During this halt many men in the regiment began erecting tiny hills in front of them. They used stones, sticks, earth, and anything they thought might turn a bullet. Some built comparatively large ones, while others seemed content with little ones.

This procedure caused a discussion among the men. Some wished to fight like duelists, believing it to be correct to stand erect and be, from their feet to their foreheads, a mark. They said they scorned the devices of the cautious. But the others scoffed in reply, and pointed to the veterans on the flanks who were digging at the ground like terriers. In a short time there was quite a barricade along the regimental fronts. Directly, however, they were ordered to withdraw from that place.

This astounded the youth. He forgot his stewing over the advance movement. "Well, then, what did they march us out here for?" he demanded of the tall soldier. The latter with calm faith began a heavy explanation, although he had been compelled to leave a little protection of stones and dirt to which he had devoted much care and skill.

When the regiment was aligned in another position each man's regard for his safety caused another line of small intrenchments. They ate their noon meal behind a third one. They were moved from this one also. They were marched from place to place with apparent aimlessness.

The youth had been taught that a man became another thing in a battle. He saw his salvation in such a change. Hence this waiting was an ordeal to him. He was in a fever of impatience. He considered that there was denoted a lack of purpose on the part of the generals. He began to complain to the tall soldier. "I can't stand this much longer," he cried. "I don't see what good it does to make us wear out our legs for nothin'." He wished to return to camp, knowing that this affair was a blue demonstration; or else to go into a battle and discover that he had been a fool in his doubts, and was, in truth, a man of traditional courage. The strain of present circumstances he felt to be intolerable.

He philosophical tall soldier measured a sandwich of cracker and pork and swallowed it in a nonchalant manner. "Oh, I suppose we must go reconnoitering around the country jest to keep 'em from getting too close, or to develop[3] 'em, or something."

"Huh!" said the loud soldier.

"Well," cried the youth, still fidgeting, "I'd rather do anything 'most than go tramping 'round the country all day doing no good to nobody and jest tiring ourselves out."

"So would I," said the loud soldier. "It ain't right. I tell you if anybody with any sense was a-running' this army it——"

"Oh, shut up!" roared the tall private: "You little fool. You little damn' cuss. You ain't had that there coat and them pants on for six months, and yet you talk as if——"

"Well, I wanta do some fighting anyway," interrupted the other. "I didn't come here to walk. I could 'ave walked to home—'round an' 'round the barn, if I jest wanted to walk."

The tall one, red-faced, swallowed another sandwich as if taking poison in despair.

But gradually, as he chewed, his face became again quiet and contented. He could not rage in fierce argument in the presence of such sandwiches. During his meals he always wore an air of blissful contemplation of the food he had swallowed. His spirit seemed then to be communing with the viands.

He accepted new environment and circumstance with great coolness, eating from his haversack at every opportunity. On the march he went along with the stride of a hunter, objecting to neither gait nor distance. And he had not raised his voice when he had been ordered away from three little protective piles of earth and stone, each of which had been an engineering feat worthy of being made sacred to the name of his grandmother.

In the afternoon the regiment went out over the same ground it had taken

[3]"Scout."

in the morning. The landscape then ceased to threaten the youth. He had been close to it and become familiar with it.

When, however, they began to pass into a new region, his old fears of stupidity and incompetence reassailed him, but this time he doggedly let them babble. He was occupied with his problem, and in his desperation he concluded that the stupidity did not greatly matter.

Once he thought he had concluded that it would be better to get killed directly and end his troubles. Regarding death thus out of the corner of his eye, he conceived it to be nothing but rest, and he was filled with a momentary astonishment that he should have made an extraordinary commotion over the mere matter of getting killed. He would die; he would go to some place where he would be understood. It was useless to expect appreciation of his profound and fine senses from such men as the lieutenant. He must look to the grave for comprehension.

The skirmish fire increased to a long clattering sound. With it was mingled far-away cheering. A battery spoke.

Directly the youth would see the skirmishers running. They were pursued by the sound of musketry fire. After a time the hot, dangerous flashes of the rifles were visible. Smoke clouds went slowly and insolently across the fields like observant phantoms. The din became crescendo, like the roar of an oncoming train.

A brigade ahead of them and on the right went into action with a rending roar. It was as if it had exploded. And thereafter it lay stretched in the distance behind a long gray wall, that one was obliged to look twice at to make sure that it was smoke.

The youth, forgetting his neat plan of getting killed, gazed spellbound. His eyes grew wide and busy with the action of the scene. His mouth was a little ways open.

Of a sudden he felt a heavy and sad hand laid upon his shoulder. Awakening from his trance of observation he turned and beheld the loud soldier.

"It's my first and last battle, old boy," said the latter, with intense gloom. He was quite pale and his girlish lip was trembling.

"Eh?" murmured the youth in great astonishment.

"It's my first and last battle, old boy," continued the loud soldier. "Something tells me——"

"What?"

"I'm a gone coon this first time and—and I w-want you to take these here things—to—my—folks." He ended in a quavering sob of pity for himself. He handed the youth a little packet done up in a yellow envelope.

"Why, what the devil——" began the youth again.

But the other gave him a glance as from the depths of a tomb, and raised his limp hand in a prophetic manner and turned away.

CHAPTER IV

The brigade was halted in the fringe of a grove. The men crouched among the trees and pointed their restless guns out at the fields. They tried to look beyond the smoke.

Out of this haze they could see running men. Some shouted information and gestured as they hurried.

The men of the new regiment watched and listened eagerly, while their tongues ran on in gossip of the battle. They mouthed rumors that had flown like birds out of the unknown.

"They say Perry has been driven in with big loss."

"Yes, Carrott went t' th' hospital. He said he was sick. That smart lieutenant is commanding 'G' Company. Th' boys say they won't be under Carrott no more if they all have t' desert. They allus knew he was a——"

"Hannises' batt'ry is took."

"It ain't either. I saw Hannises' batt'ry off on th' left not more'n fifteen minutes ago."

"Well——"

"Th' general, he ses he is goin' t' take th' hull cammand of th' 304th when we go inteh action, an' then he ses we'll do sech fightin' as never another one reg'ment done."

"They say we're catchin' it over on th' left. They say th' enemy driv' our line inteh a devil of a swamp an' took Hannises' batt'ry."

"No sech thing. Hannises' batt'ry was 'long here 'bout a minute ago."

"That young Hasbrouck, he makes a good off'cer. He ain't afraid 'a nothin'."

"I met one of th' 148th Maine boys an' he ses his brigade fit th' hull rebel army fer four hours over on th' turnpike road an' killed about five thousand of 'em. He ses one more sech fight as that an' th' war'll be over."

"Bill wasn't scared either. No, sir! It wasn't that. Bill ain't a-gittin' scared easy. He was jest mad, that's what he was. When that feller trod on his hand, he up an' sed that he was willin' t' give his hand t' his country, but he be dumbed if he was goin' t' have every dumb bushwhacker[1] in th' kentry walkin' 'round on it. So he went t' th' hospital disregardless of th' fight. Three fingers was crunched. Th' dern doctor wanted t' amputate 'm, an' Bill, he raised a heluva row, I hear. He's a funny feller."

The din in front swelled to a tremendous chorus. The youth and his fellows were frozen to silence. They could see a flag that tossed in the smoke angrily. Near it were the blurred and agitated forms of troops. There came a turbulent stream of men across the fields. A battery changing position at a frantic gallop scattered the stragglers right and left.

A shell screaming like a storm banshee[2] went over the huddled heads of the reserves. It landed in the grove, and exploding redly flung the brown earth. There was a little shower of pine needles.

Bullets began to whistle among the branches and nip at the trees. Twigs and leaves came sailing down. It was as if a thousand axes, wee and invisible, were being wielded. Many of the men were constantly dodging and ducking their heads.

The lieutenant of the youth's company was shot in the hand. He began to swear so wondrously that a nervous laugh went along the regimental line. The officer's profanity sounded conventional. It relieved the tightened senses of the new men. It was as if he had hit his fingers with a tack hammer at home.

He held the wounded member carefully away from his side so that the blood would not drip upon his trousers.

The captain of the company, tucking his sword under his arm, produced a handkerchief and began to bind with it the lieutenant's wound. And they disputed as to how the binding should be done.

The battle flag in the distance jerked about madly. It seemed to be struggling

---

[1]Guerrilla, irregular soldier.
[2]A spirit, in Gaelic folklore, whose loud wailing foretells an approaching death.

to free itself from an agony. The billowing smoke was filled with horizontal flashes.

Men running swiftly emerged from it. They grew in numbers until it was seen that the whole command was fleeing. The flag suddenly sank down as if dying. Its motion as it fell was a gesture of despair.

Wild yells came from behind the walls of smoke. A sketch in gray and red dissolved into a moblike body of men who galloped like wild horses.

The veteran regiments on the right and left of the 304th immediately began to jeer. With the passionate song of the bullets and the banshee shrieks of shells were mingled loud catcalls and bits of facetious advice concerning places of safety.

But the new regiment was breathless with horror. "Gawd! Saunders's got crushed!" whispered the man at the youth's elbow. They shrank back and crouched as if compelled to await a flood.

The youth shot a swift glance along the blue ranks of the regiment. The profiles were motionless, carven; and afterward he remembered that the color sergeant[3] was standing with his legs apart, as if he expected to be pushed to the ground.

The following throng went whirling around the flank. Here and there were officers carried along on the stream like exasperated chips. They were striking about them with their swords and with their left fists, punching every head they could reach. They cursed like highwaymen.

A mounted officer displayed the furious anger of a spoiled child. He raged with his head, his arms, and his legs.

Another, the commander of the brigade, was galloping about bawling. His hat was gone and his clothes were awry. He resembled a man who has come from bed to go to a fire. The hoofs of his horse often threatened the heads of the running men, but they scampered with singular fortune. In this rush they were apparently all deaf and blind. They heeded not the largest and longest of the oaths that were thrown at them from all directions.

Frequently over this tumult could be heard the grim jokes of the critical veterans; but the retreating men apparently were not even conscious of the presence of an audience.

The battle reflection that shone for an instant in the faces on the mad current made the youth feel that forceful hands from heaven would not have been able to have held him in place if he could have got intelligent control of his legs.

There was an appalling imprint upon these faces. The struggle in the smoke had pictured an exaggeration of itself on the bleached cheeks and in the eyes wild with one desire.

The sight of this stampede exerted a floodlike force that seemed able to drag sticks and stones and men from the ground. They of the reserves had to hold on. They grew pale and firm, and red and quaking.

The youth achieved one little thought in the midst of this chaos. The composite monster which had caused the other troops to flee had not then appeared. He resolved to get a view of it, and then, he thought he might very likely run better than the best of them.

CHAPTER V

There were moments of waiting. The youth thought of the village street at home before the arrival of the circus parade on a day in the spring. He remem-

[3]Flagbearer.

bered how he had stood, a small, thrillful boy, prepared to follow the dingy lady upon the white horse, or the band in its faded chariot. He saw the yellow road, the lines of expectant people, and the sober houses. He particularly remembered an old fellow who used to sit upon a cracker box in front of the store and feign to despise such exhibitions. A thousand details of color and form surged in his mind. The old fellow upon the cracker box appeared in middle prominence. Some one cried, "Here they come!"

There was rustling and muttering among the men. They displayed a feverish desire to have every possible cartridge ready to their hands. The boxes[1] were pulled around into various positions, and adjusted with great care. It was as if seven hundred new bonnets were being tried on.

The tall soldier, having prepared his rifle, produced a red handkerchief of some kind. He was engaged in knotting it about his throat with exquisite attention to its position, when the cry was repeated up and down the line in a muffled roar of sound.

"Here they come! Here they come!" Gun locks clicked.

Across the smoke-infested fields came a brown swarm of running men who were giving shrill yells. They came on, stooping and swinging their rifles at all angles. A flag, tilted forward, sped near the front.

As he caught sight of them the youth was momentarily startled by a thought that perhaps his gun was not loaded. He stood trying to rally his faltering intellect so that he might recollect the moment when he had loaded, but he could not.

A hatless general pulled his dripping horse to a stand near the colonel of the 304th. He shook his fist in the other's face. "You've got to hold 'em back!" he shouted, savagely; "you've got to hold 'em back!"

In his agitation the colonel began to stammer. "A-all r-right, General, all right, by Gawd!" We-we 'll do our—we-we 'll d-d-do—do our best, General." The general made a passionate gesture and galloped away. The colonel, perchance to relieve his feelings, began to scold like a wet parrot. The youth, turning swiftly to make sure that the rear was unmolested, saw the commander regarding his men in a highly resentful manner, as if he regretted above everything his association with them.

The man at the youth's elbow was mumbling, as if to himself: "Oh, we 're in for it now! oh, we 're in for it now!"

The captain of the company had been pacing excitedly to and fro in the rear. He coaxed in schoolmistress fashion, as to a congregation of boys with primers. His talk was an endless repetition. "Reserve your fire, boys—don't shoot till I tell you—save your fire—wait till they get close up—don't be damned fools——"

Perspiration streamed down the youth's face, which was soiled like that of a weeping urchin. He frequently, with a nervous movement, wiped his eyes with his coat sleeve. His mouth was still a little ways open.

He got the one glance at the foe-swarming field in front of him, and instantly ceased to debate the question of his piece being loaded. Before he was ready to begin—before he had announced to himself that he was about to fight—he threw the obedient, well-balanced rifle into position and fired a first wild shot. Directly he was working at his weapon like an automatic affair.

He suddenly lost concern for himself, and forgot to look at a menacing fate. He became not a man but a member. He felt that something of which he was a part—a regiment, an army, a cause, or a country—was in a crisis. He was welded

---

[1]Leather boxes attached to the belt and holding a supply of paper cartridges, each containing a powder charge.

into a common personality which was dominated by a single desire. For some moments he could not flee, no more than a little finger can commit a revolution from a hand.

If he had thought the regiment was about to be annihilated perhaps he could have amputated himself from it. But its noise gave him assurance. The regiment was like a firework that, once ignited, proceeds superior to circumstances until its blazing vitality fades. It wheezed and banged with a mighty power. He pictured the ground before it as strewn with the discomfited.

There was a consciousness always of the presence of his comrades about him. He felt the subtle battle brotherhood more potent even than the cause for which they were fighting. It was a mysterious fraternity born of the smoke and danger of death.

He was at a task. He was like a carpenter who has made many boxes, making still another box, only there was furious haste in his movements. He, in his thought, was careering off in other places, even as the carpenter who as he works whistles and thinks of his friend or his enemy, his home or a saloon. And these jolted dreams were never perfect to him afterward, but remained a mass of blurred shapes.

Presently he began to feel the effects of the war atmosphere—a blistering sweat, a sensation that his eyeballs were about to crack like hot stones. A burning roar filled his ears.

Following this came a red rage. He developed the acute exasperation of a pestered animal, a well-meaning cow worried by dogs. He had a mad feeling against his rifle, which could only be used against one life at a time. He wished to rush forward and strangle with his fingers. He craved a power that would enable him to make a world-sweeping gesture and brush all back. His impotency appeared to him, and made his rage into that of a driven beast.

Buried in the smoke of many rifles his anger was directed not so much against the men who he knew were rushing toward him as against the swirling battle phantoms which were choking him, stuffing their smoke robes down his parched throat. He fought frantically for respite for his senses, for air, as a babe being smothered attacks the deadly blankets.

There was a blare of heated rage mingled with a certain expression of intentness on all faces. Many of the men were making low-toned noises with their mouths, and these subdued cheers, snarls, imprecations, prayers, made a wild, barbaric song that went as an undercurrent of sound, strange and chantlike with the resounding chords of the war march. The man at the youth's elbow was babbling. In it there was something soft and tender like the monologue of a babe. The tall soldier was swearing in a loud voice. From his lips came a black procession of curious oaths. Of a sudden another broke out in a querulous way like a man who has mislaid his hat. "Well, why don't they support us? Why don't they send supports? Do they think——"

The youth in his battle sleep heard this as one who dozes hears.

There was a singular absence of heroic poses. The men bending and surging in their haste and rage were in every impossible attitude. The steel ramrods[2] clanked and clanged with incessant din as the men pounded them furiously into

[2]Early in the war both Northern and Southern troops were armed with smooth-bore, muzzle-loading muskets. As the war continued, muzzle-loading guns with rifled bores and firing conical "minie balls" were introduced, extending the range of effective fire from about 200 yards to half a mile. Muzzle-loading muskets and rifles were loaded by ramming a bullet home on top of a paper cartridge. The fall of the hammer detonated a percussion cap that ignited the main powder charge in the cartridge, propelling the lead bullet, or "ball."

the hot rifle barrels. The flaps of the cartridge boxes were all unfastened, and bobbed idiotically with each movement. The rifles, once loaded, were jerked to the shoulder and fired without apparent aim into the smoke or at one of the blurred and shifting forms which upon the field before the regiment had been growing larger and larger like puppets under a magician's hand.

The officers, at their intervals, rearward, neglected to stand in picturesque attitudes. They were bobbing to and fro roaring directions and encouragements. The dimensions of their howls were extraordinary. They expended their lungs with prodigal wills. And often they nearly stood upon their heads in their anxiety to observe the enemy on the other side of the tumbling smoke.

The lieutenant of the youth's company had encountered a soldier who had fled screaming at the first volley of his comrades. Behind the lines these two were acting a little isolated scene. The man was blubbering and staring with sheeplike eyes at the lieutenant, who had seized him by the collar and was pommeling him. He drove him back into the ranks with many blows. The soldier went mechanically, dully, with his animal-like eyes upon the officer. Perhaps there was to him a divinity expressed in the voice of the other—stern, hard, with no reflection of fear in it. He tried to reload his gun, but his shaking hands prevented. The lieutenant was obliged to assist him.

The men dropped here and there like bundles. The captain of the youth's company had been killed in an early part of the action. His body lay stretched out in the position of a tired man resting, but upon his face there was an astonished and sorrowful look, as if he thought some friend had done him an ill turn. The babbling man was grazed by a shot that made the blood stream widely down his face. He clapped both hands to his head. "Oh!" he said, and ran. Another grunted suddenly as if he had been struck by a club in the stomach. He sat down and gazed ruefully. In his eyes there was mute, indefinite reproach. Farther up the line a man, standing behind a tree, had had his knee joint splintered by a ball. Immediately he had dropped his rifle and gripped the tree with both arms. And there he remained, clinging desperately and crying for assistance that he might withdraw his hold upon the tree.

At last an exultant yell went along the quivering line. The firing dwindled from an uproar to a last vindictive popping. As the smoke slowly eddied away, the youth saw that the charge had been repulsed. The enemy were scattered into reluctant groups. He saw a man climb to the top of the fence, straddle the rail, and fire a parting shot. The waves had receded, leaving bits of dark *débris* upon the ground.

Some in the regiment began to whoop frenziedly. Many were silent. Apparently they were trying to contemplate themselves.

After the fever had left his veins, the youth thought that at last he was going to suffocate. He became aware of the foul atmosphere in which he had been struggling. He was grimy and dripping like a laborer in a foundry. He grasped his canteen and took a long swallow of the warmed water.

A sentence with variations went up and down the line. "Well, we 've helt 'em back. We've helt 'em back; derned if we haven't." The men said it blissfully, leering at each other with dirty smiles.

The youth turned to look behind him and off to the right and off to the left. He experienced the joy of a man who at last finds leisure in which to look about him.

Under foot there were a few ghastly forms motionless. They lay twisted in fantastic contortions. Arms were bent and heads were turned in incredible ways.

It seemed that the dead men must have fallen from some great height to get into such positions. They looked to be dumped out upon the ground from the sky.

From a position in the rear of the grove a battery was throwing shells over it. The flash of the guns startled the youth at first. He thought they were aimed directly at him. Through the trees he watched the black figures of the gunners as they worked swiftly and intently. Their labor seemed a complicated thing. He wondered how they could remember its formula in the midst of confusion.

The guns squatted in a row like savage chiefs. They argued with abrupt violence. It was a grim pow-wow. Their busy servants ran hither and thither.

A small procession of wounded men were going drearily toward the rear. It was a flow of blood from the torn body of the brigade.

To the right and to the left were the dark lines of other troops. Far in front he thought he could see lighter masses protruding in points from the forest. They were suggestive of unnumbered thousands.

Once he saw a tiny battery go dashing along the line of the horizon. The tiny riders were beating the tiny horses.

From a sloping hill came the sound of cheerings and clashes. Smoke welled slowly through the leaves.

Batteries were speaking with thunderous oratorical effort. Here and there were flags, the red in the stripes dominating. They splashed bits of warm color upon the dark lines of troops.

The youth felt the old thrill at the sight of the emblem. They were like beautiful birds strangely undaunted in a storm.

As he listened to the din from the hillside, to a deep pulsating thunder that came from afar to the left, and to the lesser clamors which came from many directions, it occurred to him that they were fighting, too, over there, and over there, and over there. Heretofore he had supposed that all the battle was directly under his nose.

As he gazed around him the youth felt a flash of astonishment at the blue, pure sky and the sun gleaming on the trees and fields. It was surprising that Nature had gone tranquilly on with her golden process in the midst of so much devilment.

CHAPTER VI

The youth awakened slowly. He came gradually back to a position from which he could regard himself. For moments he had been scrutinizing his person in a dazed way as if he had never before seen himself. Then he picked up his cap from the ground. He wriggled in his jacket to make a more comfortable fit, and kneeling relaced his shoe. He thoughtfully mopped his reeking features.

So it was all over at last! The supreme trial had been passed. The red, formidable difficulties of war had been vanquished.

He went into an ecstasy of self-satisfaction. He had the most delightful sensations of his life. Standing as if apart from himself, he viewed that last scene. He perceived that the man who had fought thus was magnificent.

He felt that he was a fine fellow. He saw himself even with those ideals which he had considered as far beyond him. He smiled in deep gratification.

Upon his fellows he beamed tenderness and good will. "Gee! ain't it hot, hey?"

he said affably to a man who was polishing his streaming face with his coat sleeves.

"You bet!" said the other, grinning sociably. "I never seen sech dumb hotness." He sprawled out luxuriously on the ground. "Gee, yes! An' I hope we don't have no more fightin' till a week from Monday."

There was some handshakings and deep speeches with men whose features were familiar, but with whom the youth now felt the bonds of tied hearts. He helped a cursing comrade to bind up a wound of the shin.

But, of a sudden, cries of amazement broke out along the ranks of the new regiment. "Here they come ag'in! Here they come ag'in!" The man who had sprawled upon the ground started up and said, "Gosh!"

The youth turned quick eyes upon the field. He discerned forms begin to swell in masses out of a distant wood. He again saw the tilted flag speeding forward.

The shells, which had ceased to trouble the regiment for a time, came swirling again, and exploded in the grass or among the leaves of the trees. They looked to be strange war flowers bursting into fierce bloom.

The men groaned. The luster faded from their eyes. Their smudged countenances now expressed a profound dejection. They moved their stiffened bodies slowly, and watched in sullen mood the frantic approach of the enemy. The slaves toiling in the temple of this god began to feel rebellion at his harsh tasks.

They fretted and complained each to each. "Oh, say, this is too much of a good thing! Why can't somebody send us supports?"

"We ain't never goin' to stand this second banging. I didn't come here to fight the hull damn' rebel army."

There was one who raised a doleful cry. "I wish Bill Smithers had trod on my hand, insteader me treddin' on his'n." The sore joints of the regiment creaked as it painfully floundered into position to repulse.

The youth stared. Surely, he thought, this impossible thing was not about to happen. He waited as if he expected the enemy to suddenly stop, apologize, and retire bowing. It was all a mistake.

But the firing began somewhere on the regimental line and ripped along in both directions. The level sheets of flame developed great clouds of smoke that tumbled and tossed in the mild wind near the ground for a moment, and then rolled through the ranks as through a grate. The clouds were tinged an earthlike yellow in the sunrays and in the shadow were a sorry blue. The flag was sometimes eaten and lost in this mass of vapor, but more often it projected, sun-touched, resplendent.

Into the youth's eyes there came a look that one can see in the orbs of a jaded horse. His neck was quivering with nervous weakness and the muscles of his arms felt numb and bloodless. His hands, too, seemed large and awkward as if he was wearing invisible mittens. And there was a great uncertainty about his knee joints.

The words that comrades had uttered previous to the firing began to recur to him. "Oh, say, this is too much of a good thing! What do they take us for— why don't they sent supports? I didn't come here to fight the hull damned rebel army."

He began to exaggerate the endurance, the skill, and the valor of those who were coming. Himself reeling from exhaustion, he was astonished beyond measure at such persistency. They must be machines of steel. It was very gloomy struggling against such affairs, wound up perhaps to fight until sundown.

He slowly lifted his rifle and catching a glimpse of the thickspread field he blazed at a cantering cluster. He stopped then and began to peer as best he could through the smoke. He caught changing views of the ground covered with men who were all running like pursued imps, and yelling.

To the youth it was an onslaught of redoubtable dragons. He became like the man who lost his legs at the approach of the red and green monster. He waited in a sort of a horrified, listening attitude. He seemed to shut his eyes and wait to be gobbled.

A man near him who up to this time had been working feverishly at his rifle suddenly stopped and ran with howls. A lad whose face had borne an expression of exalted courage, the majesty of him who dares give his life, was, at an instant, smitten abject. He blanched like one who has come to the edge of a cliff at midnight and is suddenly made aware. There was a revelation. He, too, threw down his gun and fled. There was no shame in his face. He ran like a rabbit.

Others began to scamper away through the smoke. The youth turned his head, shaken from his trance by this movement as if the regiment was leaving him behind. He saw the few fleeting forms.

He yelled then with fright and swung about. For a moment, in the great clamor, he was like a proverbial chicken. He lost the direction of safety. Destruction threatened him from all points.

Directly he began to speed toward the rear in great leaps. His rifle and cap were gone. His unbuttoned coat bulged in the wind. The flap of his cartridge box bobbed wildly, and his canteen, by its slender cord, swung out behind. On his face was all the horror of those things which he imagined.

The lieutenant sprang forward bawling. The youth saw his features wrathfully red, and saw him make a dab with his sword. His one thought of the incident was that the lieutenant was a peculiar creature to feel interested in such matters upon this occasion.

He ran like a blind man. Two or three times he fell down. Once he knocked his shoulder so heavily against a tree that he went headlong.

Since he had turned his back upon the fight his fears had been wondrously magnified. Death about to thrust him between the shoulder blades was far more dreadful than death about to smite him between the eyes. When he thought of it later, he conceived the impression that it is better to view the appalling than to be merely within hearing. The noises of the battle were like stones; he believed himself liable to be crushed.

As he ran on he mingled with others. He dimly saw men on his right and on his left, and he heard footsteps behind him. He thought that all the regiment was fleeing, pursued by these ominous crashes.

In his flight the sound of these following footsteps gave him his one meager relief. He felt vaguely that death must make a first choice of the men who were nearest; the initial morsels for the dragons would be then those who were following him. So he displayed the zeal of an insane sprinter in his purpose to keep them in the rear. There was a race.

As he, leading, went across a little field, he found himself in a region of shells. They hurtled over his head with long wild screams. As he listened he imagined them to have rows of cruel teeth that grinned at him. Once one lit before him and the livid lighting of the explosion effectually barred the way in his chosen direction. He groveled on the ground and then springing up went careering off through some bushes.

He experienced a thrill of amazement when he came within view of a battery in action. The men there seemed to be in conventional moods, altogether unaware of the impending annihilation. The battery was disputing with a distant antagonist and the gunners were wrapped in admiration of their shooting. They were continually bending in coaxing postures over the guns. They seemed to be patting them on the back and encouraging them with words. The guns, stolid and undaunted, spoke with dogged valor.

The precise gunners were coolly enthusiastic. They lifted their eyes every chance to the smoke-wreathed hillock from whence the hostile battery addressed them. The youth pitied them as he ran. Methodical idiots! Machine-like fools! The refined joy of planting shells in the midst of the other battery's formation would appear a little thing when the infantry came swooping out of the woods.

The face of a youthful rider, who was jerking his frantic horse with an abandon of temper he might display in a placid barnyard, was impressed deeply upon his mind. He knew that he looked upon a man who would presently be dead.

Too, he felt a pity for the guns, standing, six good comrades, in a bold row.

He saw a brigade going to the relief of its pestered fellows. He scrambled upon a wee hill and watched it sweeping finely, keeping formation in difficult places. The blue of the line was crusted with steel color, and the brilliant flags projected. Officers were shouting.

This sight also filled him with wonder. The brigade was hurrying briskly to be gulped into the infernal mouths of the war god. What manner of men were they, anyhow? Ah, it was some wondrous breed! Or else they didn't comprehend—the fools.

A furious order caused commotion in the artillery. An officer on a bounding horse made maniacal motions with his arms. The teams went swinging up from the rear, the guns were whirled about, and the battery scampered away. The cannon with their noses poked slantingly at the ground grunted and grumbled like stout men, brave but with objections to hurry.

The youth went on, moderating his pace since he had left the place of noises.

Later he came upon a general of division seated upon a horse that pricked its ears in an interested way at the battle. There was a great gleaming of yellow and patent leather about the saddle and bridle. The quiet man astride looked mouse-colored upon such a splendid charger.

A jingling staff was galloping hither and thither. Sometimes the general was surrounded by horsemen and at other times he was quite alone. He looked to be much harassed. He had the appearance of a business man whose market is swinging up and down.

The youth went slinking around this spot. He went as near as he dared trying to overhear words. Perhaps the general, unable to comprehend chaos, might call upon him for information. And he could tell him. He knew all concerning it. Of a surety the force was in a fix, and any fool could see that if they did not retreat while they had opportunity—why——

He felt that he would like to thrash the general, or at least approach and tell him in plain words exactly what he thought him to be. It was criminal to stay calmly in one spot and make no effort to stay destruction. He loitered in a fever of eagerness for the division commander to apply to him.

As he warily moved about, he heard the general call out irritably: "Tompkins, go over an' see Taylor, an' tell him not t' be in such an all-fired hurry; tell him t' halt his brigade in th' edge of th' woods; tell him t' detach a reg'ment—say I think th' center 'll break if we don't help it out some; tell him t' hurry up."

A slim youth on a fine chestnut horse caught these swift words from the mouth of his superior. He made his horse bound into a gallop almost from a walk in his haste to go upon his mission. There was a cloud of dust.

A moment later the youth saw the general bounce excitedly in his saddle.

"Yes, by heavens, they have!" The officer leaned forward. His face was aflame with excitement. "Yes, by heavens, they 've held 'im! They 've held 'im!"

He began to blithely roar at his staff: "We'll wallop 'im now. We'll wallop 'im now. We've got 'em sure." He turned suddenly upon an aid: "Here—you—Jones—quick—ride after Tompkins—see Taylor—tell him t' go in—everlastingly—like blazes—anything."

As another officer sped his horse after the first messenger, the general beamed upon the earth like a sun. In his eyes was a desire to chant a pæan.[1] He kept repeating, "They 've held 'em, by heavens!"

His excitement made his horse plunge, and he merrily kicked and swore at it. He held a little carnival of joy on horseback.

CHAPTER VII

The youth cringed as if discovered in a crime. By heavens, they had won after all! The imbecile line had remained and become victors. He could hear cheering.

He lifted himself upon his toes and looked in the direction of the fight. A yellow fog lay wallowing on the treetops. From beneath it came the clatter of musketry. Hoarse cries told of an advance.

He turned away amazed and angry. He felt that he had been wronged.

He had fled, he told himself, because annihilation approached. He had done a good part in saving himself, who was a little piece of the army. He had considered the time, he said, to be one in which it was the duty of every little piece to rescue itself if possible. Later the officers could fit the little pieces together again, and make a battle front. If none of the little pieces were wise enough to save themselves from the flurry of death at such a time, why, then, where would be the army? It was all plain that he had proceeded according to very correct and commendable rules. His actions had been sagacious things. They had been full of strategy. They were the work of a master's legs.

Thoughts of his comrades came to him. The brittle blue line had withstood the blows and won. He grew bitter over it. It seemed that the blind ignorance and stupidity of those little pieces had betrayed him. He had been overturned and crushed by their lack of sense in holding the position, when intelligent deliberation would have convinced them that it was impossible. He, the enlightened man who looks afar in the dark, had fled because of his superior perceptions and knowledge. He felt a great anger against his comrades. He knew it could be proved that they had been fools.

He wondered what they would remark when later he appeared in camp. His mind heard howls of derision. Their density would not enable them to understand his sharper point of view.

He began to pity himself acutely. He was ill used. He was trodden beneath the feet of an iron injustice. He had proceeded with wisdom and from the most righteous motives under heaven's blue only to be frustrated by hateful circumstances.

A dull, animal-like rebellion against his fellows, war in the abstract, and fate grew within him. He shambled along with bowed head, his brain in a tumult of agony and despair. When he looked loweringly up, quivering at each sound, his eyes had the expression of those of a criminal who thinks his guilt little and his punishment great, and knows that he can find no words.

[1] A song of triumph.

He went from the fields into a thick woods, as if resolved to bury himself. He wished to get out of hearing of the crackling shots which were to him like voices.

The ground was cluttered with vines and bushes, and the trees grew close and spread out like bouquets. He was obliged to force his way with much noise. The creepers, catching against his legs, cried out harshly as their sprays were torn from the barks of trees. The swishing saplings tried to make known his presence to the world. He could not conciliate the forest. As he made his way, it was always calling out protestations. When he separated embraces of trees and vines the disturbed foliages waved their arms and turned their face leaves toward him. He dreaded lest these noisy motions and cries should bring men to look at him. So he went far, seeking dark and intricate places.

After a time the sound of musketry grew faint and the cannon boomed in the distance. The sun, suddenly apparent, blazed among the trees. The insects were making rhythmical noises. They seemed to be grinding their teeth in unison. A woodpecker stuck his impudent head around the side of a tree. A bird flew on lighthearted wing.

Off was the rumble of death. It seemed now that Nature had no ears.

This landscape gave him assurance. A fair field holding life. It was the religion of peace. It would die if its timid eyes were compelled to see blood. He conceived Nature to be a woman with a deep aversion to tragedy.

He threw a pine cone at a jovial squirrel, and he ran with chattering fear. High in a treetop he stopped, and, poking his head cautiously from behind a branch, looked down with an air of trepidation.

The youth felt triumphant at this exhibition. There was the law, he said. Nature had given him a sign. The squirrel, immediately upon recognizing danger, had taken to his legs without ado. He did not stand stolidly baring his furry belly to the missile, and die with an upward glance at the sympathetic heavens. On the contrary, he had fled as fast as his legs could carry him; and he was but an ordinary squirrel, too—doubtless no philosopher of his race. The youth wended, feeling that Nature was of his mind. She re-enforced his argument with proofs that lived where the sun shone.

Once he found himself almost into a swamp. He was obliged to walk upon bog tufts and watch his feet to keep from the oily mire. Pausing at one time to look about him he saw, out at some black water, a small animal pounce in and emerge directly with a gleaming fish.

The youth went again into the deep thickets. The brushed branches made a noise that drowned the sounds of cannon. He walked on, going from obscurity into promises of a great obscurity.

At length he reached a place where the high, arching boughs made a chapel. He softly pushed the green doors aside and entered. Pine needles were a gentle brown carpet. There was a religious half light.

Near the threshold he stopped, horror-stricken at the sight of a thing.

He was being looked at by a dead man who was seated with his back against a columnlike tree. The corpse was dressed in a uniform that once had been blue, but was now faded to a melancholy shade of green. The eyes, staring at the youth, had changed to the dull hue to be seen on the side of a dead fish. The mouth was open. Its red had changed to an appalling yellow. Over the gray skin of the face ran little ants. One was trundling some sort of a bundle along the upper lip.

The youth gave a shriek as he confronted the thing. He was for moments turned to stone before it. He remained staring into the liquid-looking eyes. The dead man and the living man exchanged a long look. Then the youth cautiously put one hand behind him and brought it against a tree. Leaning upon this he retreated, step by step, with his face still toward the thing. He feared that if he turned his back the body might spring up and stealthily pursue him.

The branches, pushing against him, threatened to throw him over upon it. His unguided feet, too, caught aggravatingly in brambles; and with it all he received a subtle suggestion to touch the corpse. As he thought of his hand upon it he shuddered profoundly.

At last he burst the bonds which had fastened him to the spot and fled, unheeding the underbrush. He was pursued by a sight of the black ants swarming greedily upon the gray face and venturing horribly near to the eyes.

After a time he paused, and, breathless and panting, listened. He imagined some strange voice would come from the dead throat and squawk after him in horrible menaces.

The trees about the portal of the chapel moved soughingly in a soft wind. A sad silence was upon the little guarding edifice.

CHAPTER VIII

The trees began softly to sing a hymn of twilight. The sun sank until slanted bronze rays struck the forest. There was a lull in the noises of insects as if they had bowed their beaks and were making a devotional pause. There was silence save for the chanted chorus of the trees.

Then, upon this stillness, there suddenly broke a tremendous clangor of sounds. A crimson roar came from the distance.

The youth stopped. He was transfixed by this terrific medley of all noises. It was as if worlds were being rended. There was the ripping sound of musketry and the breaking crash of the artillery.

His mind flew in all directions. He conceived the two armies to be at each other panther fashion. He listened for a time. Then he began to run in the direction of the battle. He saw that it was an ironical thing for him to be running thus toward that which he had been at such pains to avoid. But he said, in substance, to himself that if the earth and the moon were about to clash, many persons would doubtless plan to get upon the roofs to witness the collision.

As he ran, he became aware that the forest had stopped its music, as if at last becoming capable of hearing the foreign sounds. The trees hushed and stood motionless. Everything seemed to be listening to the crackle and clatter and ear-shaking thunder. The chorus pealed over the still earth.

It suddenly occurred to the youth that the fight in which he had been was, after all, but perfunctory popping. In the hearing of this present din he was doubtful if he had seen real battle scenes. This uproar explained a celestial battle; it was tumbling hordes a-struggle in the air.

Reflecting, he saw a sort of a humor in the point of view of himself and his fellows during the late encounter. They had taken themselves and the enemy very seriously and had imagined that they were deciding the war. Individuals must have supposed that they were cutting the letters of their names deep into everlasting tablets of brass, or enshrining their reputations forever in the hearts of their countrymen, while, as to fact, the affair would appear in printed reports under a meek and immaterial title. But he saw that it was good, else, he said, in battle every one would surely run save forlorn hopes and their ilk.

He went rapidly on. He wished to come to the edge of the forest that he might peer out.

As he hastened, there passed through his mind pictures of stupendous conflicts. His accumulated thought upon such subjects was used to form scenes. The noise was as the voice of an eloquent being, describing.

Sometimes the brambles formed chains and tried to hold him back. Trees, confronting him, stretched out their arms and forbade him to pass. After its previous hostility this new resistance of the forest filled him with a fine bitterness. It seemed that Nature could not be quite ready to kill him.

But he obstinately took roundabout ways, and presently he was where he could see long gray walls of vapor where lay battle lines. The voices of cannon shook him. The musketry sounded in long irregular surges that played havoc with his ears. He stood regardant for a moment. His eyes had an awestruck expression. He gawked in the direction of the fight.

Presently he proceeded again on his forward way. The battle was like the grinding of an immense and terrible machine to him. Its complexities and powers, its grim processes, fascinated him. He must go close and see it produce corpses.

He came to a fence and clambered over it. On the far side, the ground was littered with clothes and guns. A newspaper, folded up, lay in the dirt. A dead soldier was stretched with his face hidden in his arm. Farther off there was a group of four or five corpses keeping mournful company. A hot sun had blazed upon the spot.

In this place the youth felt that he was an invader. This forgotten part of the battle ground was owned by the dead men, and he hurried, in the vague apprehension that one of the swollen forms would rise and tell him to begone.

He came finally to a road from which he could see in the distance dark and agitated bodies of troops, smoke-fringed. In the lane was a blood-stained crowd streaming to the rear. The wounded men were cursing, groaning, and wailing. In the air, always, was a mighty swell of sound that it seemed could sway the earth. With the courageous words of the artillery and the spiteful sentences of the musketry mingled red cheers. And from this region of noises came the steady current of the maimed.

One of the wounded men had a shoeful of blood. He hopped like a schoolboy in a game. He was laughing hysterically.

One was swearing that he had been shot in the arm through the commanding general's mismanagement of the army. One was marching with an air imitative of some sublime drum major. Upon his features was an unholy mixture of merriment and agony. As he marched he sang a bit of doggerel in a high and quavering voice:

> "Sing a song 'a vic'try,
> A pocketful 'a bullets,
> Five an' twenty dead men
> Baked in a—pie."

Parts of the procession limped and staggered to this tune.

Another had the gray seal of death already upon his face. His lips were curled in hard lines and his teeth were clinched. His hands were bloody from where he had pressed them upon his wound. He seemed to be awaiting the moment when he should pitch headlong. He stalked like the specter of a soldier, his eyes burning with the power of a stare into the unknown.

There were some who proceeded sullenly, full of anger at their wounds, and ready to turn upon anything as an obscure cause.

An officer was carried along by two privates. He was peevish. "Don't joggle so, Johnson, yeh fool," he cried. "Think m' leg is made of iron? If yeh can't carry me decent, put me down an' let some one else do it."

He bellowed at the tottering crowd who blocked the quick march of his bearers. "Say, make way there, can't yeh? Make way, dickens take it all."

They sulkily parted and went to the roadsides. As he was carried past they made pert remarks to him. When he raged in reply and threatened them, they told him to be damned.

The shoulder of one of the tramping bearers knocked heavily against the spectral soldier who was staring into the unknown.

The youth joined this crowd and marched along with it. The torn bodies expressed the awful machinery in which the men had been entangled.

Orderlies and couriers occasionally broke through the throng in the roadway, scattering wounded men right and left, galloping on followed by howls. The melancholy march was continually disturbed by the messengers, and sometimes by bustling batteries that came swinging and thumping down upon them, the officers shouting orders to clear the way.

There was a tattered man, fouled with dust, blood and powder stain from hair to shoes, who trudged quietly at the youth's side. He was listening with eagerness and much humility to the lurid descriptions of a bearded sergeant. His lean features wore an expression of awe and admiration. He was like a listener in a country store to wondrous tales told among the sugar barrels. He eyed the story-teller with unspeakable wonder. His mouth was agape in yokel fashion.

The sergeant, taking note of this, gave pause to his elaborate history while he administered a sardonic comment. "Be keerful, honey, you'll be a-ketchin' flies," he said.

The tattered man shrank back abashed.

After a time he began to sidle near to the youth, and in a diffident way try to make him a friend. His voice was gentle as a girl's voice and his eyes were pleading. The youth saw with surprise that the soldier had two wounds, one in the head, bound with a bloodsoaked rag, and the other in the arm, making that member dangle like a broken bough.

After they had walked together for some time the tattered man mustered sufficient courage to speak. "Was pretty good fight, wa'n't it?" he timidly said. The youth, deep in thought, glanced up at the bloody and grim figure with its lamblike eyes. "What?"

"Was pretty good fight, wa'n't it?"

"Yes," said the youth shortly. He quickened his pace.

But the other hobbled industriously after him. There was an air of apology in his manner, but he evidently thought that he needed only to talk for a time, and the youth would perceive that he was a good fellow.

"Was pretty good fight, wa'n't it?" he began in a small voice, and then he achieved the fortitude to continue. "Dern me if I ever see fellers fight so. Laws, how they did fight! I knowed th' boys 'd like it when they onct got square at it. Th' boys ain't had no fair chanct up t' now, but this time they showed what they was. I knowed it 'd turn out this way. Yeh can't lick them boys. No, sir! They're fighters, they be."

He breathed a deep breath of humble admiration. He had looked at the youth for encouragement several times. He received none, but gradually he seemed to get absorbed in his subject.

"I was talkin' 'cross pickets with a boy from Georgie, onct, an' that boy, he ses,

'Your fellers 'll all run like hell when they onct hearn a gun,' he ses. 'Mebbe they will,' I ses, 'but I don't b'lieve none of it,' I ses; 'an' b'jiminey,' I ses back t' 'um, 'mebbe your fellers 'll run like hell when they onct hearn a gun,' I ses. He larfed. Well, they didn't run t' day, did they, hey? No sir! They fit, an' fit, an' fit."

His homely face was suffused with a light of love for the army which was to him all things beautiful and powerful.

After a time he turned to the youth. "Where yeh hit, ol' boy?" he asked in a brotherly tone.

The youth felt instant panic at this question, although at first its full import was not borne in upon him.

"What?" he asked.

"Where yeh hit?" repeated the tattered man.

"Why," began the youth, "I—I—that is—why—I——"

He turned away suddenly and slid through the crowd. His brow was heavily flushed, and his fingers were picking nervously at one of his buttons. He bent his head and fastened his eyes studiously upon the button as if it were a little problem.

The tattered man looked after him in astonishment.

CHAPTER IX

The youth fell back in the procession until the tattered soldier was not in sight. Then he started to walk on with the others.

But he was amid wounds. The mob of men was bleeding. Because of the tattered soldier's question he now felt that his shame could be viewed. He was continually casting sidelong glances to see if the men were contemplating the letters of guilt he felt burned into his brow.

At times he regarded the wounded soldiers in an envious way. He conceived persons with torn bodies to be peculiarly happy. He wished that he, too, had a wound, a red badge of courage.

The spectral soldier was at his side like a stalking reproach. The man's eyes were still fixed in a stare into the unknown. His gray, appalling face had attracted attention in the crowd, and men, slowing to his dreary pace, were walking with him. They were discussing his plight, questioning him and giving him advice. In a dogged way he repelled them, signing to them to go on and leave him alone. The shadows of his face were deepening and his tight lips seemed holding in check the moan of great despair. There could be seen a certain stiffness in the movements of his body, as if he were taking infinite care not to arouse the passion of his wounds. As he went on, he seemed always looking for a place, like one who goes to choose a grave.

Something in the gesture of the man as he waved the bloody and pitying soldiers away made the youth start as if bitten. He yelled in horror. Tottering forward he laid a quivering hand upon the man's arm. As the latter slowly turned his waxlike features toward him, the youth screamed:

"Gawd! Jim Conklin!"

The tall soldier made a little commonplace smile. "Hello, Henry," he said.

The youth swayed on his legs and glared strangely. He stuttered and stammered. "Oh, Jim—oh, Jim—oh, Jim——"

The tall soldier held out his gory hand. There was a curious red and black combination of new blood and old blood upon it. "Where yeh been, Henry?"

he asked. He continued in a monotonous voice, "I thought mebee yeh got keeled over. There 's been thunder t' pay t'-day. I was worryin' about it a good deal."

The youth still lamented. "Oh, Jim—oh, Jim—oh, Jim——"

"Yeh know," said the tall soldier, "I was out there." He made a careful gesture. "An', Lord what a circus! An', b'jiminey, I got shot—I got shot. Yes, b'jiminey, I got shot." He reiterated this fact in a bewildered way, as if he did not know how it came about.

The youth put forth anxious arms to assist him, but the tall soldier went firmly on as if propelled. Since the youth's arrival as a guardian for his friend, the other wounded men had ceased to display much interest. They occupied themselves again in dragging their own tragedies toward the rear.

Suddenly, as the two friends marched on, the tall soldier seemed to be overcome by a terror. His face turned to a semblance of gray paste. He clutched the youth's arm and looked all about him, as if dreading to be overheard. Then he began to speak in a shaking whisper:

"I tell yeh what I'm 'fraid of, Henry—I 'll tell yeh what I 'm 'fraid of. I 'm 'fraid I'll fall down—an' then yeh know—them damned artillery wagons—they like as not 'll run over me. That's what I'm 'fraid of——"

The youth cried out to him hysterically: "I 'll take care of yeh, Jim! I'll take care of yeh! I swear t' Gawd I will!"

"Sure—will yeh, Henry?" the tall soldier beseeched.

"Yes—yes—I tell yeh—I'll take care of yeh, Jim!" protested the youth. He could not speak accurately because of the gulpings in his throat.

But the tall soldier continued to beg in a lowly way. He now hung babelike to the youth's arm. His eyes rolled in the wildness of his terror. "I was allus a good friend t' yeh, wa'n't I, Henry? I 've allus been a pretty good feller, ain't I? An' it ain't much t' ask, is it? Jest t' pull me along outer th' road? I 'd do it fer you, wouldn't I, Henry?"

He paused in piteous anxiety to await his friend's reply.

The youth had reached an anguish where the sobs scorched him. He strove to express his loyalty, but he could only make fantastic gestures.

However, the tall soldier seemed suddenly to forget all those fears. He became again the grim, stalking specter of a soldier. He went stonily forward. The youth wished his friend to lean upon him, but the other always shook his head and strangely protested. "No—no—no—leave me be—leave me be——"

His look was fixed again upon the unknown. He moved with mysterious purpose, and all of the youth's offers he brushed aside. "No—no—leave me be—leave me be——"

The youth had to follow.

Presently the latter heard a voice talking softly near his shoulders. Turning he saw that it belonged to the tattered soldier. "Ye 'd better take 'im outa th' road, pardner. There 's a batt'ry comin' helitywhoop down th' road an' he 'll git runned over. He's a goner anyhow in about five minutes—yeh kin see that. Ye 'd better take 'im outa th' road. Where th' blazes does he git his stren'th from?"

"Lord knows!" cried the youth. He was shaking his hands helplessly.

He ran forward presently and grasped the tall soldier by the arm. "Jim! Jim!" he coaxed, "come with me."

The tall soldier weakly tried to wrench himself free. "Huh," he said vacantly. He stared at the youth for a moment. At last he spoke as if dimly comprehending. "Oh! Inteh th' fields? Oh!"

He started blindly through the grass.

The youth turned once to look at the lashing riders and jouncing guns of the battery. He was startled from this view by a shrill outcry from the tattered man.
"Gawd! He's runnin'!"

Turning his head swiftly, the youth saw his friend running in a staggering and stumbling way toward a little clump of bushes. His heart seemed to wrench itself almost free from his body at this sight. He made a noise of pain. He and the tattered man began a pursuit. There was a singular race.

When he overtook the tall soldier he began to plead with all the words he could find. "Jim—Jim—what are you doing—what makes you do this way— you 'll hurt yerself."

The same purpose was in the tall soldier's face. He protested in a dulled way, keeping his eyes fastened on the mystic place of his intentions. "No—no—don't tech me—leave me be—leave me be——"

The youth, aghast and filled with wonder at the tall soldier, began quaveringly to question him. "Where yeh goin', Jim? What you thinking about? Where you going? Tell me, won't you, Jim?"

The tall soldier faced about as upon relentless pursuers. In his eyes there was a great appeal. "Leave me be, can't yeh? Leave me be fer a minnit."

The youth recoiled. "Why, Jim," he said, in a dazed way, "what's the matter with you?"

The tall soldier turned and, lurching dangerously, went on. The youth and the tattered soldier followed, sneaking as if whipped, feeling unable to face the stricken man if he should again confront them. They began to have thoughts of a solemn ceremony. There was something ritelike in these movements of the doomed soldier. And there was a resemblance in him to a devotee of a mad religion, blood-sucking, muscle-wrenching, bone-crushing. They were awed and afraid. They hung back lest he have at command a dreadful weapon.

At last, they saw him stop and stand motionless. Hastening up, they perceived that his face wore an expression telling that he had at last found the place for which he had struggled. His spare figure was erect; his bloody hands were quietly at his side. He was waiting with patience for something that he had come to meet. He was at the rendezvous. They paused and stood, expectant.

There was a silence.

Finally, the chest of the doomed soldier began to heave with a strained motion. It increased in violence until it was as if an animal was within and was kicking and tumbling furiously to be free.

This spectacle of gradual strangulation made the youth writhe, and once as his friend rolled his eyes, he saw something in them that made him sink wailing to the ground. He raised his voice in a last supreme call.

"Jim—Jim—Jim——"

The tall soldier opened his lips and spoke. He made a gesture. "Leave me be—don't tech me—leave me be——"

There was another silence while he waited.

Suddenly, his form stiffened and straightened. Then it was shaken by a prolonged ague. He stared into space. To the two watchers there was a curious and profound dignity in the firm lines of his awful face.

He was invaded by a creeping strangeness that slowly enveloped him. For a moment the tremor of his legs caused him to dance a sort of hideous hornpipe. His arms beat wildly about his head in expression of implike enthusiasm.

His tall figure stretched itself to its full height. There was a slight rending sound. Then it began to swing forward, slow and straight, in the manner of a falling tree. A swift muscular contortion made the left shoulder strike the ground first.

The body seemed to bounce a little way from the earth. "God!" said the tattered soldier.

The youth had watched, spellbound, this ceremony at the place of meeting. His face had been twisted into an expression of every agony he had imagined for his friend.

He now sprang to his feet and, going closer, gazed upon the pastelike face. The mouth was open and the teeth showed in a laugh.

As the flap of the blue jacket fell away from the body, he could see that the side looked as if it had been chewed by wolves.

The youth turned, with sudden, livid rage, toward the battlefield. He shook his fist. He seemed about to deliver a philippic.[1]

"Hell——"

The red sun was pasted in the sky like a wafer.

CHAPTER X

The tattered man stood musing.

"Well, he was reg'lar jim-dandy fer nerve, wa'n't he," said he finally in a little awestruck voice. "A reg'lar jim-dandy." He thoughtfully poked one of the docile hands with his foot. "I wonner where he got 'is stren'th from? I never seen a man do like that before. It was a funny thing. Well, he was a reg'lar jim-dandy."

The youth desired to screech out his grief. He was stabbed, but his tongue lay dead in the tomb of his mouth. He threw himself again upon the ground and began to brood.

The tattered man stood musing.

"Look-a-here, pardner," he said, after a time. He regarded the corpse as he spoke. "He's up an' gone, ain't 'e, an' we might as well begin t' look out fer ol' number one. This here thing is all over. He 's up an' gone, ain't 'e? An' he 's all right here. Nobody won't bother 'im. An' I must say I ain't enjoying any great health m'self these days."

The youth, awakened by the tattered soldier's tone, looked quickly up. He saw that he was swinging uncertainly on his legs and that his face had turned to a shade of blue.

"Good Lord!" he cried, "you ain't goin' t'—not you, too."

The tattered man waved his hand. "Nary die," he said. "All I want is some pea soup an' a good bed. Some pea soup," he repeated dreamfully.

The youth arose from the ground. "I wonder where he came from. I left him over there." He pointed. "And now I find 'im here. And he was coming from over there, too." He indicated a new direction. They both turned toward the body as if to ask of it a question.

"Well," at length spoke the tattered man, "there ain't no use in our stayin' here an' trying' t' ask him anything."

The youth nodded an assent wearily. They both turned to gaze for a moment at the corpse.

---

[1]A speech of insult or invective—resembling the speeches by the Athenian statesman Demosthenes (385?–322 B.C.) against Philip of Macedon (382–336 B.C.).

The youth murmured something.

"Well, he was a jim-dandy, wa'n't 'e?" said the tattered man as if in response.

They turned their backs upon it and started away. For a time they stole softly, treading with their toes. It remained laughing there in the grass.

"I'm commencin' t' feel pretty bad," said the tattered man, suddenly breaking one of his little silences. "I'm commencin' t' feel pretty damn' bad."

The youth groaned. "O Lord!" He wondered if he was to be the tortured witness of another grim encounter.

But his companion waved his hand reassuringly. "Oh, I'm not goin' t' die yit! There too much dependin' on me fer me t' die yit. No, sir! Nary die! I *can't!* Ye'd oughta see th' swad[1] a chil'ren I've got, an' all like that."

The youth glancing at his companion could see by the shadow of a smile that he was making some kind of fun.

As they plodded on the tattered soldier continued to talk. "Besides, if I died, I wouldn't die th' way that feller did. That was th' funniest thing. I'd jest flop down, I would. I never seen a feller die th' way that feller did.

"Yeh know Tom Jamison, he lives next door t' me up home. He's a nice feller, he is, an' we was allus good friends. Smart, too. Smart as a steel trap. Well, when we was a-fightin' this afternoon, all-of-a-sudden he begin t' rip up an' cuss an' beller at me. 'Yer shot, yeh blamed infernal!'—he swear horrible—he ses t' me. I put up m' hand t' m' head an' when I looked at m' fingers, I seen, sure 'nough, I was shot. I give a holler an' begin t' run, but b'fore I could git away another one hit me in th' arm an' whirl' me clean 'round. I got skeared when they was all a-shooting' b'hind me an' I run t' beat all, but I cotch it pretty bad. I've an idee I'd a' been fightin' yit, if t'was n't fer Tom Jamison."

Then he made a calm announcement: "There's two of 'em—little ones—but they 're beginnin' t' have fun with me now. I don't be'lieve I kin walk much furder."

They went slowly on in silence. "Yeh look pretty peek-ed yerself," said the tattered man at last. "I bet yeh 've got a worser one than yeh think. Ye'd better take keer of yer hurt. It don't do t' let sech things go. It might be inside mostly, an' them plays thunder. Where is it located?" But he continued his harangue without waiting for a reply. "I see' a feller git hit plum in th' head when my reg'ment was a-standin' at ease onct. An' everybody yelled out to 'im: Hurt, John? Are yeh hurt much? 'No," ses he. He looked kinder surprised, an' he went on tellin' 'em how he felt. He sed he didn't feel nothing'. But, by dad, th' first thing that feller knowed he was dead. Yes, he was dead—stone dead. So, yeh wanta watch out. Yeh might have some queer kind 'a hurt yerself. Yeh can't never tell. Where is your'n located?"

The youth had been wriggling since the introduction of this topic. He now gave a cry of exasperation and made a furious motion with his hand. "Oh, don't bother me!" he said. He was enraged against the tattered man, and could have strangled him. His companions seemed ever to play intolerable parts. They were ever upraising the ghost of shame on the stick of their curiosity. He turned toward the tattered man as one at bay. "Now, don't bother me," he repeated with desperate menace.

"Well, Lord knows I don't wanta bother anybody," said the other. There was a little accent of despair in his voice as he replied, "Lord knows I 've gota 'nough m' own t' tend to."

The youth, who had been holding a bitter debate with himself and casting

[1]Slang, "crowd."

glances of hatred and contempt at the tattered man, here spoke in a hard voice. "Good-by," he said.

The tattered man looked at him in gaping amazement. "Why—why, pardner, where yeh goin'?" he asked unsteadily. The youth looking at him, could see that he, too, like that other one, was beginning to act dumb and animal-like. His thoughts seemed to be floundering about in his head. "Now—now—look—a— here, you Tom Jamison—now—I won't have this—this here won't do. Where— where yeh goin'?"

The youth pointed vaguely. "Over there," he replied.

"Well, now look—a—here—now," said the tattered man, rambling on in idiot fashion. His head was hanging forward and his words were slurred. "This thing won't do, now, Tom Jamison. It won't do. I know yeh, yeh pig-headed devil. Yeh wanta go trompin' off with a bad hurt. It ain't right—now—Tom Jamison— it ain't. Yeh wanta leave me take keer of yeh, Tom Jamison. It ain't—right—it ain't—fer yeh t' go—trompin' off—with a bad hurt—it ain't—ain't—ain't right— it ain't."

In reply the youth climbed a fence and started away. He could hear the tattered man bleating plaintively.

Once he faced about angrily. "What?"

"Look—a—here, now, Tom Jamison—now—it ain't——"

The youth went on. Turning at a distance he saw the tattered man wandering about helplessly in the field.

He now thought that he wished he was dead. He believed that he envied those men whose bodies lay strewn over the grass of the fields and on the fallen leaves of the forest.

The simple questions of the tattered man had been knife thrusts to him. They asserted a society that probes pitilessly at secrets until all is apparent. His late companion's chance persistency made him feel that he could not keep his crime concealed in his bosom. It was sure to be brought plain by one of those arrows which cloud the air and are constantly pricking, discovering, proclaiming those things which are willed to be forever hidden. He admitted that he could not defend himself against this agency. It was not within the power of vigilance.

CHAPTER XI

He became aware that the furnace roar of the battle was growing louder. Great brown clouds had floated to the still heights of air before him. The noise, too, was approaching. The woods filtered men and the fields became dotted.

As he rounded a hillock, he perceived that the roadway was now a crying mass of wagons, teams, and men. From the heaving tangle issued exhortations, commands, imprecations. Fear was sweeping it along. The cracking whips bit and horses plunged and tugged. The white-topped wagons strained and stumbled in their exertions like fat sheep.

The youth felt comforted in a measure by this sight. They were all retreating. Perhaps, then, he was not so bad after all. He seated himself and watched the terror-stricken wagons. They fled like soft, ungainly animals. All the roarers and lashers served to help him to magnify the dangers and horrors of the engagement that he might try to prove to himself that the thing with which men could charge him was in truth a symmetrical[1] act. There was an amount of pleasure to him in watching the wild march of this vindication.

[1] Balanced, appropriate.

Presently the calm head of a forward-going column of infantry appeared in the road. It came swiftly on. Avoiding the obstructions gave it the sinuous movement of a serpent. The men at the head butted mules with their musket stocks. They prodded teamsters indifferent to all howls. The men forced their way through parts of the dense mass by strength. The blunt head of the column pushed. The raving teamsters swore many strange oaths.

The commands to make way had the ring of a great importance in them. The men were going forward to the heart of the din. They were to confront the eager rush of the enemy. They felt the pride of their onward movement when the remainder of the army seemed trying to dribble down this road. They tumbled teams about with a fine feeling that it was no matter so long as their column got to the front in time. This importance made their faces grave and stern. And the backs of the officers were very rigid.

As the youth looked at them the black weight of his woe returned to him. He felt that he was regarding a procession of chosen beings. The separation was as great to him as if they had marched with weapons of flame and banners of sunlight. He could never be like them. He could have wept in his longings.

He searched about in his mind for an adequate malediction for the indefinite cause, the thing upon which men turn the words of final blame. It—whatever it was—was responsible for him, he said. There lay the fault.

The haste of the column to reach the battle seemed to the forlorn young man to be something much finer than stout fighting. Heroes, he thought, could find excuses in that long seething lane. They could retire with perfect self-respect and make excuses to the stars.

He wondered what those men had eaten that they could be in such haste to force their way to grim chances of death. As he watched his envy grew until he thought that he wished to change lives with one of them. He would have liked to have used a tremendous force, he said, throw off himself and become a better. Swift pictures of himself, apart, yet in himself, came to him—a blue desperate figure leading lurid charges with one knee forward and a broken blade high— a blue, determined figure standing before a crimson and steel assault, getting calmly killed on a high place before the eye of all. He thought of the magnificent pathos of his dead body.

These thoughts uplifted him. He felt the quiver of war desire. In his ears, he heard the ring of victory. He knew the frenzy of a rapid successful charge. The music of the trampling feet, the sharp voices, the clanking arms of the column near him made him soar on the red wings of war. For a few moments he was sublime.

He thought that he was about to start for the front. Indeed, he saw a picture of himself, dust-stained, haggard, panting, flying to the front at the proper moment to seize and throttle the dark, leering witch of calamity.

Then the difficulties of the thing began to drag at him. He hesitated, balancing awkwardly on one foot.

He had no rifle; he could not fight with his hands, said he resentfully to his plan. Well, rifles could be had for the picking. They were extraordinarily profuse.

Also, he continued, it would be a miracle if he found his regiment. Well, he could fight with any regiment.

He started forward slowly. He stepped as if he expected to tread upon some explosive thing. Doubts and he were struggling.

He would truly be a worm if any of his comrades should see him returning thus, the marks of his flight upon him. There was a reply that the intent fighters did not care for what happened rearward saving that no hostile bayonets appeared there. In the battle-blur his face would, in a way, be hidden, like the face of a cowled man.

But then he said that his tireless fate would bring forth, when the strife lulled for a moment, a man to ask of him an explanation. In imagination he felt the scrutiny of his companions as he painfully labored through some lies.

Eventually, his courage expended itself upon these objections. The debates drained him of his fire.

He was not cast down by this defeat of his plan, for, upon studying the affair carefully, he could not but admit that the objections were very formidable.

Furthermore, various ailments had begun to cry out. In their presence he could not persist in flying high with the wings of war; they rendered it almost impossible for him to see himself in a heroic light. He tumbled headlong.

He discovered that he had a scorching thirst. His face was so dry and grimy that he thought he could feel his skin crackle. Each bone of his body had an ache in it, and seemingly threatened to break with each movement. His feet were like two sores. Also, his body was calling for food. It was more powerful than a direct hunger. There was a dull, weightlike feeling in his stomach, and, when he tried to walk, his head swayed and he tottered. He could not see with distinctness. Small patches of green mist floated before his vision.

While he had been tossed by many emotions, he had not been aware of ailments. Now they beset him and made clamor. As he was at last compelled to pay attention to them, his capacity for self-hate was multiplied. In despair, he declared that he was not like those others. He now conceded it to be impossible that he should ever become a hero. He was a craven loon. Those pictures of glory were piteous things. He groaned from his heart and went staggering off.

A certain mothlike quality within him kept him in the vicinity of the battle. He had a great desire to see, and to get news. He wished to know who was winning.

He told himself that, despite his unprecedented suffering, he had never lost his greed for a victory, yet, he said in a half-apologetic manner to his conscience, he could not but know that a defeat for the army this time might mean many favorable things for him. The blows of the enemy would splinter regiments into fragments. Thus, many men of courage, he considered, would be obliged to desert the colors and scurry like chickens. He would appear as one of them. They would be sullen brothers in distress, and he could then easily believe he had not run any farther or faster than they. And if he himself could believe in his virtuous perfection, he conceived that there would be small trouble in convincing all others.

He said, as if in excuse for this hope, that previously the army had encountered great defeats and in a few months had shaken off all blood and tradition of them, emerging as bright and valiant as a new one; thrusting out of sight the memory of disaster, and appearing with the valor and confidence of unconquered legions. The shrilling voices of the people at home would pipe dismally for a time, but various generals were usually compelled to listen to these ditties. He of course felt no compunctions for proposing a general as a sacrifice. He could not tell who the chosen for the barbs might be, so he could center no direct sympathy upon him. The people were afar and he did not conceive public opinion to be accurate at long range. It was quite probable they would hit the wrong man who, after he had recovered from his amazement, would perhaps spend the rest of his days in writing replies to the songs of his alleged failure. It would be very fortunate, no doubt, but in this case a general was of no consequence to the youth.

In a defeat there would be a roundabout vindication of himself. He thought it would prove, in a manner, that he had fled early because of his superior powers of perception. A serious prophet upon predicting a flood should be the first man to climb a tree. This would demonstrate that he was indeed a seer.

A moral vindication was regarded by the youth as a very important thing. Without salve, he could not, he thought, wear the sore badge of his dishonor through life. With his heart continually assuring him that he was despicable, he could not exist without making it, through his actions, apparent to all men.

If the army had gone gloriously on he would be lost. If the din meant that now his army's flags were tilted forward he was a condemned wretch. He would be compelled to doom himself to isolation. If the men were advancing, their indifferent feet were tramping upon his chances for a successful life.

As these thoughts went rapidly through his mind, he turned upon them and tried to thrust them away. He denounced himself as a villain. He said that he was the most unutterably selfish man in existence. His mind pictured the soldiers who would place their defiant bodies before the spear of the yelling battle fiend, and as he saw their dripping corpses on an imagined field, he said that he was their murderer.

Again he thought that he wished he was dead. He believed that he envied a corpse. Thinking of the slain, he achieved a great contempt for some of them, as if they were guilty for thus becoming lifeless. They might have been killed by lucky chances, he said, before they had had opportunities to flee or before they had been really tested. Yet they would receive laurels from tradition. He cried out bitterly that their crowns were stolen and their robes of glorious memories were shams. However, he still said that it was a great pity he was not as they.

A defeat of the army had suggested itself to him as a means of escape from the consequences of his fall. He considered, now, however, that it was useless to think of such a possibility. His education had been that success for that mighty blue machine was certain; that it would make victories as a contrivance turns out buttons. He presently discarded all his speculations in the other direction. He returned to the creed of soldiers.

When he perceived again that it was not possible for the army to be defeated, he tried to bethink him of a fine tale which he could take back to his regiment, and with it turn the expected shafts of derision.

But, as he mortally feared these shafts, it became impossible for him to invent a tale he felt he could trust. He experimented with many schemes, but threw them aside one by one as flimsy. He was quick to see vulnerable places in them all.

Furthermore, he was much afraid that some arrow of scorn might lay him mentally low before he could raise his protecting tale.

He imagined the whole regiment saying: "Where's Henry Fleming? He run, didn't 'e? Oh, my!" He recalled various persons who would be quite sure to leave him no peace about it. They would doubtless question him with sneers, and laugh at his stammering hesitation. In the next engagement they would try to keep watch of him to discover when he would run.

Wherever he went in camp, he would encounter insolent and lingeringly cruel stares. As he imagined himself passing near a crowd of comrades, he could hear some one say, "There he goes!"

Then, as if the heads were moved by one muscle, all the faces were turned toward him with wide, derisive grins. He seemed to hear some one make a humorous remark in a low tone. At it the others all crowed and cackled. He was a slang phrase.

CHAPTER XII

The column that had butted stoutly at the obstacles in the roadway was barely out of the youth's sight before he saw dark waves of men come sweeping out of the woods and down through the fields. He knew at once that the steel fibers had been washed from their hearts. They were bursting from their coats and their equipments as from entanglements. They charged down upon him like terrified buffaloes.

Behind them blue smoke curled and clouded above the treetops, and through the thickets he could sometimes see a distinct pink glare. The voices of the cannon were clamoring in interminable chorus.

The youth was horror-stricken. He stared in agony and amazement. He forgot that he was engaged in combating the universe. He threw aside his mental pamphlets on the philosophy of the retreated and rules for the guidance of the damned.

The fight was lost. The dragons were coming with invincible strides. The army, helpless in the matted thickets and blinded by the overhanging night, was going to be swallowed. War, the red animal, war, the blood-swollen god, would have bloated fill.

Within him something bade to cry out. He had the impulse to make a rallying speech, to sing a battle hymn, but he could only get his tongue to call into the air: "Why—why—what—what's th' matter?"

Soon he was in the midst of them. They were leaping and scampering all about him. Their blanched faces shone in the dusk. They seemed, for the most part, to be very burly men. The youth turned from one to another of them as they galloped along. His incoherent questions were lost. They were heedless of his appeals. They did not seem to see him.

They sometimes gabbled insanely. One huge man was asking of the sky: "Say, where de plank road? Where de plank road!" It was as if he had lost a child. He wept in his pain and dismay.

Presently, men were running hither and thither in all ways. The artillery booming, forward, rearward, and on the flanks made jumble of ideas of direction. Landmarks had vanished into the gathered gloom. The youth began to imagine that he had got into the center of the tremendous quarrel, and he could perceive no way out of it. From the mouths of the fleeing men came a thousand wild questions, but no one made answers.

The youth, after rushing about and throwing interrogations at the heedless bands of retreating infantry, finally clutched a man by the arm. They swung around face to face.

"Why—why——" stammered the youth struggling with his balking tongue.

The man screamed: "Let go me! Let go me!" His face was livid and his eyes were rolling uncontrolled. He was heaving and panting. He still grasped his rifle, perhaps having forgotten to release his hold upon it. He tugged frantically, and the youth being compelled to lean forward was dragged several paces.

"Let go me! Let go me!"

"Why—why——" stuttered the youth.

"Well, then!" bawled the man in a lurid rage. He adroitly and fiercely swung his rifle. It crushed upon the youth's head. The man ran on.

The youth's fingers had turned to paste upon the other's arm. The energy was smitten from his muscles. He saw the flaming wings of lightning flash before his vision. There was a deafening rumble of thunder within his head.

Suddenly his legs seemed to die. He sank writhing to the ground. He tried to arise. In his efforts against the numbing pain he was like a man wrestling with a creature of the air.

There was a sinister struggle.

Sometimes he would achieve a position half erect, battle with the air for a moment, and then fall again, grabbing at the grass. His face was of a clammy pallor. Deep groans were wrenched from him.

At last, with a twisting movement, he got upon his hands and knees, and from thence, like a babe trying to walk, to his feet. Pressing his hands to his temples he went lurching over the grass.

He fought an intense battle with his body. His dulled senses wished him to swoon and he opposed them stubbornly, his mind portraying unknown dangers and mutilations if he should fall upon the field. He went tall soldier fashion. He imagined secluded spots where he could fall and be unmolested. To search for one he strove against the tide of his pain.

Once he put his hand to the top of his head and timidly touched the wound. The scratching pain of the contact made him draw a long breath through his clinched teeth. His fingers were dabbled with blood. He regarded them with a fixed stare.

Around him he could hear the grumble of jolted cannon as the scurrying horses were lashed toward the front. Once, a young officer on a besplashed charger nearly ran him down. He turned and watched the mass of guns, men, and horses sweeping in a wide curve toward a gap in a fence. The officer was making excited motions with a gauntleted hand. The guns followed the teams with an air of unwillingness, of being dragged by the heels.

Some officers of the scattered infantry were cursing and railing like fishwives. Their scolding voices could be heard above the din. Into the unspeakable jumble in the roadway rode a squadron of cavalry. The faded yellow of their facings[1] shone bravely. There was a mighty altercation.

The artillery were assembling as if for a conference.

The blue haze of evening was upon the field. The lines of forest were long purple shadows. One cloud lay along the western sky partly smothering the red.

As the youth left the scene behind him, he heard the guns suddenly roar out. He imagined them shaking in black rage. They belched and howled like brass devils guarding a gate. The soft air was filled with the tremendous remonstrance. With it came the shattering peal of opposing infantry. Turning to look behind him, he could see sheets of orange light illumine the shadowy distance. There were subtle and sudden lightnings in the far air. At times he thought he could see heaving masses of men.

He hurried on in the dusk. The day had faded until he could barely distinguish place for his feet. The purple darkness was filled with men who lectured and jabbered. Sometimes he could see them gesticulating against the blue and somber sky. There seemed to be a great ruck of men and munitions spread about in the forest and in the fields.

---

[1]Ornamental trimming on their uniforms. Yellow traditionally is used to signify cavalry.

The little narrow roadway now lay lifeless. There were overturned wagons like sun-dried boulders. The bed of the former torrent was choked with the bodies of horses and splintered parts of war machines.

It had come to pass that his wound pained him but little. He was afraid to move rapidly, however, for a dread of disturbing it. He held his head very still and took many precautions against stumbling. He was filled with anxiety, and his face was pinched and drawn in anticipation of the pain of any sudden mistake of his feet in the gloom.

His thoughts, as he walked, fixed intently upon his hurt. There was a cool, liquid feeling about it and he imagined blood moving slowly down under his hair. His head seemed swollen to a size that made him think his neck to be inadequate.

The new silence of his wound made much worriment. The little blistering voices of pain that had called out from his scalp were, he thought, definite in their expression of danger. By them he believed that he could measure his plight. But when they remained ominously silent he became frightened and imagined terrible fingers that clutched into his brain.

Amid it he began to reflect upon various incidents and conditions of the past. He bethought him of certain meals his mother had cooked at home, in which those dishes of which he was particularly fond had occupied prominent positions. He saw the spread table. The pine walls of the kitchen were glowing in the warm light from the stove. Too, he remembered how he and his companions used to go from the schoolhouse to the bank of a shaded pool. He saw his clothes in disorderly array upon the grass of the bank. He felt the swash of the fragrant water upon his body. The leaves of the overhanging maple rustled with melody in the wind of youthful summer.

He was overcome presently by a dragging weariness. His head hung forward and his shoulders were stooped as if he were bearing a great bundle. His feet shuffled along the ground.

He held continuous arguments as to whether he should lie down and sleep at some near spot, or force himself on until he reached a certain haven. He often tried to dismiss the question, but his body persisted in rebellion and his senses nagged at him like pampered babies.

At last he heard a cheery voice near his shoulder: "Yeh seem t' be in a pretty bad way, boy."

The youth did not look up, but he assented with thick tongue. "Uh!"

The owner of the cheery voice took him firmly by the arm. "Well," he said, with a round laugh, "I'm goin' your way. Th' hull gang is goin' your way. An' I guess I kin give yeh a lift." They began to walk like a drunken man and his friend.

As they went along, the man questioned the youth and assisted him with the replies like one manipulating the mind of a child. Sometimes he interjected anecdotes. "What reg'ment do yeh b'long teh? Eh? What's that? Th' 304th N' York? Why, what corps is that in? Oh, it is? Why, I thought they wasn't engaged t'-day—they 're 'way over in the' center. Oh, they was, eh? Well, pretty nearly everybody got their share 'a fightin' t'-day. By dad, I give myself up fer dead any number 'a times. There was shootin' here an' shootin' there, an' hollerin' here an' hollerin' there, in th' damn' darkness, until I couldn't tell t' save m' soul which side I was on. Sometimes I thought I was sure 'nough from Ohier, an' other times I could 'a swore I was from th' bitter end of Florida. It was th' most mixed up dern thing I ever see. An' these here hull woods is a reg'lar mess. It'll be a miracle if we find our reg'ments t'-night. Pretty soon, though, we 'll meet a'plenty of guards an' provost-guards,[2] an' one thing an' another. Ho! there they go with an off'cer, I guess. Look at his hand a-draggin'. He 's got all th' war he wants, I bet. He won't be talkin' so big about his reputation an' all when they go t' sawin' off his leg. Poor feller! My brother's got whiskers jest like that. How did yeh git 'way over here, anyhow? Your reg'ment is a long way from here, ain't it? Well, I guess we can find it. Yeh know there was a boy killed in my comp'ny t'-day that I thought th' world an' all of. Jack was a nice feller. By ginger, it hurt like thunder t' see ol' Jack jest git knocked flat. We was a-standin' purty peaceable fer a spell, 'though there was men runnin' ev'ry way all 'round us, an' while we was a-standin' like that, 'long come a big fat feller. He began t' peck at Jack's elbow, an' he ses: 'Say, where's th' road t' th' river?' An' Jack, he never paid no attention, an th' feller kept on a-peckin' at his elbow an' sayin': 'Say, where 's th' road t' th' river?' Jack was a-lookin' ahead all th' time tryin' t' see th' Johnnies comin' through th' woods, an' he never paid no attention t' this big fat feller fer a long time, but at last he turned 'round an' he ses: 'Ah, go t' hell an' find th' road t' th' river!' An' jest then a shot slapped him bang on th' side th' head. He was a sergeant, too. Them was his last words. Thunder, I wish we was sure 'a findin' our reg'ments t'-night. It's goin' t' be long huntin'. But I guess we kin do it."

In the search which followed, the man of the cheery voice seemed to the youth to possess a wand of a magic kind. He threaded the mazes of the tangled forest with a strange fortune. In encounters with guards and patrols he displayed the keenness of a detective and the valor of a gamin.[3] Obstacles fell before him and became of assistance. The youth, with his chin still on his breast, stood woodenly by while his companion beat ways and means out of sullen things.

The forest seemed a vast hive of men buzzing about in frantic circles, but the cheery man conducted the youth without mistakes, until at last he began to chuckle with glee and self-satisfaction. "Ah, there yeh are! See that fire?"

The youth nodded stupidly.

"Well, there's where your reg'ment is. An' now, good-by, ol' boy, good luck t' yeh."

A warm and strong hand clasped the youth's languid fingers for an instant, and then he heard a cheerful and audacious whistling as the man strode away. As he who had so befriended him was thus passing out of his life, it suddenly occurred to the youth that he had not once seen his face.

CHAPTER XIII

The youth went slowly toward the fire indicated by his departed friend. As he reeled, he bethought him of the welcome his comrades would give him. He had a conviction that he would soon feel in his sore heart the barbed missiles of ridicule. He had no strength to invent a tale; he would be a soft target.

He made vague plans to go off into the deeper darkness and hide, but they were all destroyed by the voices of exhaustion and pain from his body. His ailments, clamoring, forced him to seek the place of food and rest, at whatever cost.

He swung unsteadily toward the fire. He could see the forms of men throwing black shadows in the red light, and as he went nearer it became known to him in some way that the ground was strewn with sleeping men.

[2]Military police.   [3]A bold, streetwise boy.

Of a sudden he confronted a black and monstrous figure. A rifle barrel caught some glinting beams. "Halt! halt!" He was dismayed for a moment, but he presently thought that he recognized the nervous voice. As he stood tottering before the rifle barrel, he called out: "Why, hello, Wilson, you—you here?"

The rifle was lowered to a position of caution and the loud soldier came slowly forward. He peered into the youth's face. "That you, Henry?"

"Yes, it's—it's me."

"Well, well, ol' boy," said the other, "by ginger, I'm glad t' see yeh! I give yeh up fer a goner. I thought yeh was dead sure enough." There was husky emotion in his voice.

The youth found that now he could barely stand upon his feet. There was a sudden sinking of his forces. He thought he must hasten to produce his tale to protect him from the missiles already at the lips of his redoubtable comrades. So, staggering before the loud soldier, he began: "Yes, yes. I've—I've had an awful time. I've been all over. Way over on th' right. Ter'ble fightin' over there. I had an awful time. I got separated from th' reg'ment. Over on th' right, I got shot. In th' head. I never see sech fightin'. Awful time. I don't see how I could a' got separated from th' reg'ment. I got shot, too."

His friend had stepped forward quickly. "What? Got shot? Why didn't yeh say so first? Poor ol' boy, we must—hol' on a minnit; what am I doin'. I'll call Simpson."

Another figure at that moment loomed in the gloom. They could see that it was the corporal. "Who yeh talkin' to, Wilson?" he demanded. His voice was anger-toned. "Who yeh talkin' to? Yeh th' derndest sentinel—why—hello, Henry, you here? Why, I thought you was dead four hours ago! Great Jerusalem, they keep turnin' up every ten minutes or so! We thought we'd lost forty-two men by straight count, but if they keep on a-comin' this way, we'll git th' comp'ny all back by mornin' yit. Where was yeh?"

"Over on th' right. I got separated"—began the youth with considerable glibness.

But his friend had interrupted hastily. "Yes, an' he got shot in th' head an' he's in a fix, an' we must see t' him right away." He rested his rifle in the hollow of his left arm and his right around the youth's shoulder.

"Gee, it must hurt like thunder!" he said.

The youth leaned heavily upon his friend. "Yes, it hurts—hurts a good deal," he replied. There was a faltering in his voice.

"Oh," said the corporal. He linked his arm in the youth's and drew him forward. "Come on, Henry. I'll take keer 'a yeh."

As they went on together the loud private called out after them: "Put 'im t' sleep in my blanket, Simpson. An'—hol' on a minnit—here's my canteen. It's full 'a coffee. Look at his head by th' fire an' see how it looks. Maybe it's a pretty bad un. When I git relieved in a couple 'a minnits, I'll be over an' see t' him."

The youth's senses were so deadened that his friend's voice sounded from afar and he could scarcely feel the pressure of the corporal's arm. He submitted passively to the latter's directly strength. His head was in the old manner hanging forward upon his breast. His knees wobbled.

The corporal led him into the glare of the fire. "Now, Henry," he said, "let's have look at yer ol' head."

The youth sat down obediently and the corporal, laying aside his rifle, began to fumble in the bushy hair of his comrade. He was obliged to turn the other's head so that the full flush of the fire light would beam upon it. He puckered his mouth with a critical air. He drew back his lips and whistled through his teeth when his fingers came in contact with the splashed blood and the rare wound.

"Ah, here we are!" he said. He awkwardly made further investigations. "Jest as I thought," he added, presently. "Yeh've been grazed by a ball. It's raised a queer lump jest as if some feller had lammed yeh on th' head with a club. It stopped a-bleedin' long time ago. Th' most about it is that in th' mornin' yeh'll feel that a number ten hat wouldn't fit yeh. An' your head'll be all het up an' feel as dry as burnt pork. An' yeh may git a lot 'a other sicknesses, too, by mornin'. Yeh can't never tell. Still, I don't much think so. It's jest a damn' good belt on th' head, an' nothin' more. Now, you jest sit here an' don't move, while I go rout out th' relief. Then I'll send Wilson t' take keer 'a yeh."

The corporal went away. The youth remained on the ground like a parcel. He stared with a vacant look into the fire.

After a time he aroused, for some part, and the things about him began to take form. He saw that the ground in the deep shadows was cluttered with men, sprawling in every conceivable posture. Glancing narrowly into the more distant darkness, he caught occasional glimpses of visages that loomed pallid and ghostly, lit with a phosphorescent glow. These faces expressed in their lines the deep stupor of the tired soldiers. They made them appear like men drunk with wine. This bit of forest might have appeared to an ethereal wanderer as a scene of the result of some frightful debauch.

On the other side of the fire the youth observed an officer asleep, seated bolt upright, with his back against a tree. There was something perilous in his position. Badgered by dreams, perhaps, he swayed with little bounces and starts, like an old, toddy-stricken grandfather in a chimney corner. Dust and stains were upon his face. His lower jaw hung down as if lacking strength to assume its normal position. He was the picture of an exhausted soldier after a feast of war.

He had evidently gone to sleep with his sword in his arms. These two had slumbered in an embrace, but the weapon had been allowed in time to fall unheeded to the ground. The brass-mounted hilt lay in contact with some parts of the fire.

Within the gleam of rose and orange light from the burning sticks were other soldiers, snoring and heaving, or lying deathlike in slumber. A few pairs of legs were stuck forth, rigid and straight. The shoes displayed the mud or dust of marches and bits of rounded trousers, protruding from the blankets, showed rents and tears from hurried pitchings through the dense brambles.

The fire crackled musically. From its swelled light smoke. Overhead the foliage moved softly. The leaves, with their faces turned toward the blaze, were colored shifting hues of silver, often edged with red. Far off to the right, through a window in the forest could be seen a handful of stars lying, like glittering pebbles, on the black level of the night.

Occasionally, in this low-arched hall, a soldier would arouse and turn his body to a new position, the experience of his sleep having taught him of uneven and objectionable places upon the ground under him. Or, perhaps, he would lift himself to a sitting posture, blink at the fire for an unintelligent moment, throw a swift glance at his prostrate companion, and then cuddle down again with a grunt of sleepy content.

The youth sat in a forlorn heap until his friend the loud young soldier came, swinging two canteens by their light strings, "Well, now, Henry, ol' boy," said the latter, "we'll have yeh fixed up in jest about a minnit."

He had the bustling ways of an amateur nurse. He fussed around the fire and stirred the sticks to brilliant exertions. He made his patient drink largely from the canteen that contained the coffee. It was to the youth a delicious draught. He tilted his head afar back and held the canteen long to his lips. The cool mixture went caressingly down his blistered throat. Having finished, he sighed with comfortable delight.

The loud young soldier watched his comrade with an air of satisfaction. He later produced an extensive handkerchief from his pocket. He folded it into a manner of bandage and soused water from the other canteen upon the middle of it. This crude arrangement he bound over the youth's head, tying the ends in a queer knot at the back of the neck.

"There," he said, moving off and surveying his deed, "yeh look like th' devil, but I bet yeh feel better."

The youth contemplated his friend with grateful eyes. Upon his aching and swelling head the cold cloth was like a tender woman's hand.

"Yeh don't holler ner say nothin'," remarked his friend approvingly. "I know I'm a blacksmith at takin' keer 'a sick folks, an' yeh never squeaked. Yer a good un, Henry. Most 'a men would a' been in th' hospital long ago. A shot in th' head ain't foolin' business."

The youth made no reply, but began to fumble with the buttons of his jacket.

"Well, come, now," continued his friend, "come on. I must put yeh t' bed an' see that yeh git a good night's rest."

The other got carefully erect, and the loud young soldier led him among the sleeping forms lying in groups and rows. Presently he stooped and picked up his blankets. He spread the rubber one upon the ground and placed the woolen one about the youth's shoulders.

"There now," he said, "lie down an' git some sleep."

The youth, with his manner of doglike obedience, got carefully down like a crone stooping. He stretched out with a murmur of relief and comfort. The ground felt like the softest couch.

But of a sudden he ejaculated: "Hol' on a minnit! Where you goin' t' sleep?"

His friend waved his hand impatiently. "Right down there by yeh."

"Well, but hol' on a minnit," continued the youth. "What yeh goin' t' sleep in? I've got your——"

The loud young soldier snarled: "Shet up an' go on t' sleep. Don't be makin' a damn' fool 'a yerself," he said severely.

After the reproof the youth said no more. An exquisite drowsiness had spread through him. The warm comfort of the blanket enveloped him and made a gentle languor. His head fell forward on his crooked arm and his weighted lids went softly down over his eyes. Hearing a splatter of musketry from the distance, he wondered indifferently if those men sometimes slept. He gave a long sigh, snuggled down into his blanket, and in a moment was like his comrades.

CHAPTER XIV

When the youth awoke it seemed to him that he had been asleep for a thousand years, and he felt sure that he opened his eyes upon an unexpected world. Gray mists were slowly shifting before the first efforts of the sun rays. An impending splendor could be seen in the eastern sky. An icy dew had chilled his face, and immediately upon arousing he curled farther down into his blanket. He stared for a while at the leaves overhead, moving in a heraldic wind of the day.

The distance was splintering and blaring with the noise of fighting. There was in the sound an expression of a deadly persistency, as if it had not begun and was not to cease.

About him were the rows and groups of men that he had dimly seen the previous night. They were getting a last draught of sleep before the awakening. The gaunt, careworn features and dusty figures were made plain by this quaint light at the dawning, but it dressed the skin of the men in corpselike hues and made the tangled limbs appear pulseless and dead. The youth started up with a little cry when his eyes first swept over this motionless mass of men, thickspread upon the ground, pallid, and in strange postures. His disordered mind interpreted the hall of the forest as a charnel place.[1] He believed for an instant that he was in the house of the dead, and he did not dare to move lest these corpses start up, squalling and squawking. In a second, however, he achieved his proper mind. He swore a complicated oath at himself. He saw that this somber picture was not a fact of the present, but a mere prophecy.

He heard then the noise of a fire crackling briskly in the cold air, and, turning his head, he saw his friend pottering busily about a small blaze. A few other figures moved in the fog, and he heard the hard cracking of axe blows.

Suddenly there was a hollow rumble of drums. A distant bugle sang faintly. Similar sounds, varying in strength, came from near and far over the forest. The bugles called to each other like brazen gamecocks. The near thunder of the regimental drums rolled.

The body of men in the woods rustled. There was a general uplifting of heads. A murmuring of voices broke upon the air. In it there was much bass of grumbling oaths. Strange gods were addressed in condemnation of the early hours necessary to correct war. An officer's peremptory tenor rang out and quickened the stiffened movement of the men. The tangled limbs unraveled. The corpse-hued faces were hidden behind fists that twisted slowly in the eye sockets.

The youth sat up and gave vent to an enormous yawn. "Thunder!" he remarked petulantly. He rubbed his eyes, and then putting up his hand felt carefully of the bandage over his wound. His friend, perceiving him to be awake, came from the fire. "Well Henry, ol' man, how do yeh feel this mornin'?" he demanded.

The youth yawned again. Then he puckered his mouth to a little pucker. His head, in truth, felt precisely like a melon, and there was an unpleasant sensation at his stomach.

"Oh, Lord, I feel pretty bad," he said.

"Thunder!" exclaimed the other. "I hoped ye'd feel all right this mornin'. Let's see th'; bandage—I guess it's slipped." He began to tinker at the wound in rather a clumsy way until the youth exploded.

"Gosh-dern it!" he said in sharp irritation; "you're the hangdest man I ever saw! You wear muffs on your hands. Why in good thunderation can't you be more easy? I'd rather you'd stand off an' throw guns at it. Now, go slow, an' don't act as if you was nailing down carpet."

He glared with insolent command at his friend, but the latter answered soothingly. "Well, well, come now, an' git some grub," he said. "Then, maybe, yeh'll feel better."

At the fireside the loud young soldier watched over his comrade's wants with tenderness and care. He was very busy marshaling the little black vagabonds of tin cups and pouring into them the streaming, iron colored mixture from a

---

[1]A building in which dead bodies or the bones of the dead are deposited.

small and sooty tin pail. He had some fresh meat, which he roasted hurriedly upon a stick. He sat down then and contemplated the youth's appetite with glee.

The youth took note of a remarkable change in his comrade since those days of camp life upon the river bank. He seemed no more to be continually regarding the proportions of his personal prowess. He was not furious at small words that pricked his conceits. He was no more a loud young soldier. There was about him now a fine reliance. He showed a quiet belief in his purposes and his abilities. And this inward confidence evidently enabled him to be indifferent to little words of other men aimed at him.

The youth reflected. He had been used to regarding his comrade as a blatant child with an audacity grown from his experience, thoughtless, headstrong, jealous, and filled with a tinsel courage. A swaggering babe accustomed to strut in his own dooryard. The youth wondered where had been born these new eyes; when his comrade had made the great discovery that there were many men who would refuse to be subjected by him. Apparently, the other had now climbed a peak of wisdom from which he could perceive himself as a very wee thing. And the youth saw that ever after it would be easier to live in his friend's neighborhood.

His comrade balanced his ebony coffee-cup on his knee. "Well, Henry," he said, "what d'yeh think th' chances are? D'yeh think we'll wallop'em?"

The youth considered for a moment. "Day-b'fore-yesterday," he finally replied, with boldness, "you would'a' bet you'd lick the hull kit-an'-boodle all by yourself."

His friend looked a trifle amazed. "Would I?" he asked. He pondered. "Well, perhaps I would," he decided at last. He stared humbly at the fire.

The youth was quite disconcerted at this surprising reception of his remarks. "Oh, no, you wouldn't either," he said, hastily trying to retrace.

But the other made a deprecating gesture. "Oh, yeh needn't mind, Henry," he said. "I believe I was a pretty big fool in those days." He spoke as after a lapse of years.

There was a little pause.

"All th' officers say we've got th' rebs in a pretty tight box," said the friend, clearing his throat in a commonplace way. "They all seem t' think we've got 'em jest where we want 'em."

"I don't know about that," the youth replied. "What I seen over on th' right makes me think it was th' other way about. From where I was, it looked as if we was gettin' a good poundin' yestirday."

"D'yeh think so?" inquired the friend. "I thought we handled 'em pretty rough yestirday."

"Not a bit," said the youth. "Why, lord, man, you didn't see nothing of the fight. Why!" Then a sudden thought came to him. "Oh! Jim Conklin's dead."

His friend started. "What? Is he? Jim Conklin?"

The youth spoke slowly. "Yes. He's dead. Shot in th' side."

"Yeh don't say so. Jim Conklin. . . . poor cuss!"

All about them were other small fires surrounded by men with their little black utensils. From one of these near came sudden sharp voices in a row. It appeared that two light-footed soldiers had been teasing a huge, bearded man, causing him to spill coffee upon his blue knees. The man had gone into a rage and had sworn comprehensively. Stung by his language, his tormentors had immediately bristled at him with a great show of resenting unjust oaths. Possibly there was going to be a fight.

The friend arose and went over to them, making pacific motions with his arms. "Oh, here, now, boys, what's th' use?" he said. "We'll be at th' rebs in less'n an hour. What's th' good fightin' 'mong ourselves?"

One of the light-footed soldiers turned upon him red-faced and violent. "Yeh needn't come around here with yer preachin.' I s'pose yeh don't approve 'a fightin' since Charley Morgan licked yeh; but I don't see what business this here is 'a yours or anybody else."

"Well, it ain't," said the friend mildly. "Still I hate t' see——"

There was a tangled argument.

"Well, he—," said the two, indicating their opponent with accusative forefingers.

The huge soldier was quite purple with rage. He pointed at the two soldiers with his great hand, extended clawlike. "Well, they——"

But during this argumentative time the desire to deal blows seemed to pass, although they said much to each other. Finally the friend returned to his old seat. In a short while the three antagonists could be seen together in an amiable bunch.

"Jimmie Rogers ses I'll have t' fight him after th' battle t'-day," announced the friend as he again seated himself. "He ses he don't allow no interferin' in his business. I hate t' see th' boys fightin' 'mong themselves."

The youth laughed. "Yer changed a good bit. Yeh ain't at all like yeh was. I remember when you an' that Irish feller——" He stopped and laughed again.

"No, I didn't use t' be that way," said his friend thoughtfully. "That's true 'nough."

"Well, I didn't mean——" began the youth.

The friend made another deprecatory gesture. "Oh, yeh needn't mind, Henry."

There was another little pause.

"Th' reg'ment lost over half th' men yestirday," remarked the friend eventually. "I thought a course they was all dead, but, laws, they kep' a-comin' back last night until it seems, after all, we didn't lose but a few. They'd been scattered all over, wanderin' around in th' woods, fightin' with other reg'ments, an' everything. Jest like you done."

"So?" said the youth.

CHAPTER XV

The regiment was standing at order arms at the side of a lane, waiting for the command to march, when suddenly the youth remembered the little packet enwrapped in a faded yellow envelope which the loud young soldier with lugubrious words had intrusted to him. It made him start. He uttered an exclamation and turned toward his comrade.

"Wilson!"

"What?"

His friend, at his side in the ranks, was thoughtfully staring down the road. From some cause his expression was at that moment very meek. The youth, regarding him with sidelong glances, felt impelled to change his purpose. "Oh, nothing," he said.

His friend turned his head in some surprise, "Why, what was yeh goin' t' say?"

"Oh, nothing," repeated the youth.

He resolved not to deal the little blow. It was sufficient that the fact made him glad. It was not necessary to knock his friend on the head with the misguided packet.

He had been possessed of much fear of his friend, for he saw how easily questionings could make holes in his feelings. Lately, he had assured himself that the altered comrade would not tantalize him with a persistent curiosity, but he felt certain that during the first period of leisure his friend would ask him to relate his adventures of the previous day.

He now rejoiced in the possession of a small weapon with which he could prostrate his comrade at the first signs of a cross-examination. He was master. It would now be he who could laugh and shoot the shafts of derision.

The friend had, in a weak hour, spoken with sobs of his own death. He had delivered a melancholy oration previous to his funeral, and had doubtless in the packet of letters, presented various keepsakes to relatives. But he had not died, and thus he had delivered himself into the hands of the youth.

The latter felt immensely superior to his friend, but he inclined to condescension. He adopted toward him an air of patronizing good humor.

His self-pride was now entirely restored. In the shade of its flourishing growth he stood with braced and self-confident legs, and since nothing could now be discovered he did not shrink from an encounter with the eyes of judges, and allowed no thought of his own to keep him from an attitude of manfulness. He had performed his mistakes in the dark, so he was still a man.

Indeed, when he remembered his fortunes of yesterday, and looked at them from a distance he began to see something fine there. He had license to be pompous and veteranlike.

His panting agonies of the past he put out of his sight.

In the present, he declared to himself that it was only the doomed and the damned who roared with sincerity at circumstance. Few but they ever did it. A man with a full stomach and the respect of his fellows had no business to scold about anything that he might think to be wrong in the ways of the universe, or even with the ways of society. Let the unfortunates rail; the others may play marbles.

He did not give a great deal of thought to these battles that lay directly before him. It was not essential that he should plan his ways in regard to them. He had been taught that many obligations of a life were easily avoided. The lessons of yesterday had been that retribution was a laggard and blind. With these facts before him he did not deem it necessary that he should become feverish over the possibilities of the ensuing twenty-four hours. He could leave much to chance. Besides, a faith in himself had secretly blossomed. There was a little flower of confidence growing within him. He was now a man of experience. He had been out among the dragons, he said, and he assured himself that they were not so hideous as he had imagined them. Also, they were inaccurate; they did not sting with precision. A stout heart often defied, and defying, escaped.

And, furthermore, how could they kill him who was the chosen of gods and doomed to greatness?

He remembered how some of the men had run from the battle. As he recalled their terror-struck faces he felt a scorn for them. They had surely been more fleet and more wild than was absolutely necessary. They were weak mortals. As for himself, he had fled with discretion and dignity.

He was aroused from this reverie by his friend, who, having hitched about nervously and blinked at the trees for a time, suddenly coughed in an introductory way, and spoke.

"Fleming!"

"What?"

The friend put his hand up to his mouth and coughed again. He fidgeted in his jacket.

"Well," he gulped, at last, "I guess yeh might as well give me back them letters."
Dark, prickling blood had flushed into his cheeks and brow.

"All right, Wilson," said the youth. He loosened two buttons of his coat, thrust
in his hand, and brought forth the packet. As he extended it to his friend the
latter's face was turned from him.

He had been slow in the act of producing the packet because during it he had
been trying to invent a remarkable comment upon the affair. He could conjure
nothing of sufficient point. He was compelled to allow his friend to escape
unmolested with his packet. And for this he took unto himself considerable
credit. It was a generous thing.

His friend at his side seemed suffering great shame. As he contemplated him,
the youth felt his heart grow more strong and stout. He had never been compelled to blush in such manner for his acts; he was an individual of extraordinary
virtues.

He reflected, with condescending pity: "Too bad! Too bad! The poor devil,
it makes him feel tough!"

After this incident, and as he reviewed the battle pictures he had seen, he felt
quite competent to return home and make the hearts of the people glow with
stories of war. He could see himself in a room of warm tints telling tales to
listeners. He could exhibit laurels. They were insignificant; still, in a district
where laurels were infrequent, they might shine.

He saw his gaping audience picturing him as the central figure in blazing
scenes. And he imagined the consternation and the ejaculations of his mother
and the young lady at the seminary as they drank his recitals. Their vague
feminine formula for beloved ones doing brave deeds on the field of battle
without risk of life would be destroyed.

CHAPTER XVI

A sputtering of musketry was always to be heard. Later, the cannon had
entered the dispute. In the fog-filled air their voices made a thudding sound.
The reverberations were continual. This part of the world led a strange, battleful
existence.

The youth's regiment was marched to relieve a command that had lain long
in some damp trenches. The men took positions behind a curving line of rifle
pits that had been turned up, like a large furrow, along the line of woods. Before
them was a level stretch, peopled with short, deformed stumps. From the woods
beyond came the dull popping of the skirmishers and pickets, firing in the fog.
From the right came the noise of a terrific fracas.

The men cuddled behind the small embankment and sat in easy attitudes
awaiting their turn. Many had their backs to the firing. The youth's friend lay
down, buried his face in his arms, and almost instantly, it seemed, he was in a
deep sleep.

The youth leaned his breast against the brown dirt and peered over at the
woods and up and down the line. Curtains of trees interfered with his ways of
vision. He could see the low line of trenches but for a short distance. A few idle
flags were perched on the dirt hills. Behind them were rows of dark bodies with
a few heads sticking curiously over the top.

Always the noise of skirmishers came from the woods on the front and left,
and the din on the right had grown to frightful proportions. The guns were
roaring without an instant's pause for breath. It seemed that the cannon had

come from all parts and were engaged in a stupendous wrangle. It became impossible to make a sentence heard.

The youth wished to launch a joke—a quotation from newspapers. He desired to say, "All quiet on the Rappahannock,"[1] but the guns refused to permit even a comment upon their uproar. He never successfully concluded the sentence. But at last the guns stopped, and among the men in the rifle pits rumors again flew, like birds, but they were now for the most part black creatures who flapped their wings drearily near to the ground and refused to rise on any wings of hope. The men's faces grew doleful from the interpreting of omens. Tales of hesitation and uncertainty on the part of those high in place and responsibility came to their ears. Stories of disaster were borne into their minds with many proofs. This din of musketry on the right, growing like a released genie of sound, expressed and emphasized the army's plight.

The men were disheartened and began to mutter. They made gestures expressive of the sentence: "Ah, what more can we do?" And it could always be seen that they were bewildered by the alleged news and could not fully comprehend a defeat.

Before the gray mists had been totally obliterated by the sun rays, the regiment was marching in a spread column that was retiring carefully through the woods. The disordered hurrying lines of the enemy could sometimes be seen down through the groves and little fields. They were yelling, shrill and exultant.

At this sight the youth forgot many personal matters and became greatly enraged. He exploded in loud sentences. "B'jiminey, we're generaled by a lot 'a lunkheads."

"More than one feller has said that t'-day," observed a man.

His friend, recently aroused, was still very drowsy. He looked behind him until his mind took in the meaning of the movement. Then he sighed. "Oh, well, I s'pose we got licked," he remarked sadly.

The youth had a thought it would not be handsome for him to freely condemn other men. He made an attempt to restrain himself, but the words upon his tongue were too bitter. He presently began a long and intricate denunciation of the commander of the forces.

"Mebbe, it wa'n't all his fault—not all together. He did th' best he knowed. It's our luck t' git licked often," said his friend in a weary tone. He was trudging along with stooped shoulders and shifting eyes like a man who has been caned and kicked.

"Well, don't we fight like the devil? Don't we do all that men can?" demanded the youth loudly.

He was secretly dumfounded at this sentiment when it came from his lips. For a moment his face lost its valor and he looked guiltily about him. But no one questioned his right to deal in such words, and presently he recovered his air of courage. He went on to repeat a statement he had heard going from group to group at the camp that morning. "The brigadier said he never saw a new reg'ment fight the way we fought yestirday, didn't he? And we didn't do better than many another reg'ment, did we? Well, then, you can't say it's th' army's fault, can you?"

In his reply, the friend's voice was stern. "A course not," he said. "No man dare say we don't fight like th' devil. No man will ever dare say it. Th' boys fight like hell-roosters. But still—still, we don't have no luck."

[1]Said in ironic contrast to the wartime announcement "All quiet along the Potomac," often quoted by Northern newspapers in reporting the lack of fighting by the Union army in Virginia.

"Well, then, if we fight like the devil an' don't ever whip, it must be the general's fault," said the youth grandly and decisively. "And I don't see any sense in fighting and fighting and fighting, yet always losing through some derned old lunkhead of a general."

A sarcastic man who was tramping at the youth's side, then spoke lazily. "Mebbee yeh think yeh fit th' hull battle yestirday, Fleming," he remarked.

The speech pierced the youth. Inwardly he was reduced to an abject pulp by these chance words. His legs quaked privately. He cast a frightened glance at the sarcastic man.

"Why, no," he hastened to say in a conciliating voice, "I don't think I fought the whole battle yesterday."

But the other seemed innocent of any deeper meaning. Apparently, he had no information. It was merely his habit. "Oh!" he replied in the same tone of calm derision.

The youth, nevertheless, felt a threat. His mind shrank from going near to the danger, and thereafter he was silent. The significance of the sarcastic man's words took from him all loud moods that would make him appear prominent. He became suddenly a modest person.

There was low-toned talk among the troops. The officers were impatient and snappy, their countenances clouded with the tales of misfortune. The troops, sifting through the forest, were sullen. In the youth's company once a man's laugh rang out. A dozen soldiers turned their faces quickly toward him and frowned with vague displeasure.

The noise of firing dogged their footsteps. Sometimes, it seemed to be driven a little way, but it always returned again with increased insolence. The men muttered and cursed, throwing black looks in its direction.

In a clear space the troops were at last halted. Regiments and brigades, broken and detached through their encounters with thickets, grew together again and lines were faced toward the pursuing bark of the enemy's infantry.

This noise, following like the yelpings of eager, metallic hounds, increased to a loud and joyous burst, and then, as the sun went serenely up the sky, throwing illuminating rays into the gloomy thickets, it broke forth into prolonged pealings. The woods began to crackle as if afire.

"Whoop-a-dadee," said a man, "here we are! Everybody fightin'. Blood an' destruction."

"I was willin' t' bet they'd attack as soon as th' sun got fairly up," savagely asserted the lieutenant who commanded the youth's company. He jerked without mercy at his little mustache. He strode to and fro with dark dignity in the rear of his men, who were lying down behind whatever protection they had collected.

A battery had trundled into position in the rear and was thoughtfully shelling the distance. The regiment, unmolested as yet, awaited the moment when the gray shadows of the woods before them should be slashed by the lines of flame. There was much growling and swearing.

"Good Gawd," the youth grumbled, "we're always being chased around like rats! It makes me sick. Nobody seems to know where we go or why we go. We just get fired around them pillar to post and get licked here and get licked there, and nobody knows what it's done for. It makes a man feel like a damn' kitten in a bag. Now, I'd like to know what the eternal thunders we was marched into these woods for anyhow, unless it was to give the rebs a regular pot shot at us. We came in here and got our legs all tangled up in these cussed briers, and then we begin to fight and the rebs had an easy time of it. Don't tell me it's just luck! I know better. It's this derned old——"

The friend seemed jaded, but he interrupted his comrade with a voice of calm confidence. "It'll turn out all right in th' end," he said.

"Oh, the devil it will! You always talk like a dog-hanged parson. Don't tell me! I know——"

At this time there was an interposition by the savage-minded lieutenant, who was obliged to vent some of his inward dissatisfaction upon his men. "You boys shut right up! There no need 'a your wastin' your breath in long-winded arguments about this an' that an' th' other. You've been jawin' like a lot 'a old hens. All you've got t' do is to fight, an' you'll get plenty 'a that t' do in about ten minutes. Less talkin' an' more fightin' is what's best for you boys. I never saw sech gabbling jackasses."

He paused, ready to pounce upon any man who might have the temerity to reply. No words being said, he resumed his dignified pacing.

"There's too much chin music an' too little fightin' in this war, anyhow," he said to them, turning his head for a final remark.

The day had grown more white, until the sun shed his full radiance upon the thronged forest. A sort of a gust of battle came sweeping toward that part of the line where lay the youth's regiment. The front shifted a trifle to meet it squarely. There was a wait. In this part of the field there passed slowly the intense moments that precede the tempest.

A single rifle flashed in a thicket before the regiment. In an instant it was joined by many others. There was a mighty song of clashes and crashes that went sweeping through the woods. The guns in the rear, aroused and enraged by shells that had been thrown burrlike at them, suddenly involved themselves in a hideous altercation with another band of guns. The battle roar settled to a rolling thunder, which was a single, long explosion.

In the regiment there was a peculiar kind of hesitation denoted in the attitudes of the men. They were worn, exhausted, having slept but little and labored much. They rolled their eyes toward the advancing battle as they stood awaiting the shock. Some shrank and flinched. They stood as men tied to stakes.

CHAPTER XVII

This advance of the enemy had seemed to the youth like a ruthless hunting. He began to fume with rage and exasperation. He beat his foot upon the ground, and scowled with hate at the swirling smoke that was approaching like a phantom flood. There was a maddening quality in this seeming resolution of the foe to give him no rest, to give him no time to sit down and think. Yesterday he had fought and had fled rapidly. There had been many adventures. For to-day he felt that he had earned opportunities for contemplative repose. He could have enjoyed portraying to uninitiated listeners various scenes at which he had been a witness or ably discussing the processes of war with the other proved men. Too it was important that he should have time for physical recuperation. He was sore and stiff from his experiences. He had received his fill of all exertions, and he wished to rest.

But those other men seemed never to grow weary; they were fighting with their old speed. He had a wild hate for the relentless foe. Yesterday, when he had imagined the universe to be against him, he had hated it, little gods and big gods; to-day he hated the army of the foe with the same great hatred. He was not going to be badgered of his life, like a kitten chased by boys, he said. It was not well to drive men into final corners; at those moments they could all develop teeth and claws.

He leaned and spoke into his friend's ear. He menaced the woods with a gesture. "If they keep on chasing us, by Gawd, they'd better watch out. Can't stand *too* much."

The friend twisted his head and made a calm reply. "If they keep on a-chasin' us they'll drive us all inteh th' river."

The youth cried out savagely at this statement. He crouched behind a little tree, with his eyes burning hatefully and his teeth set in a curlike snarl. The awkward bandage was still about his head, and upon it, over his wound, there was a spot of dry blood. His hair was wondrously tousled, and some straggling, moving locks hung over the cloth of the bandage down toward his forehead. His jacket and shirt were open at the throat, and exposed his young bronzed neck. There could be seen spasmodic gulpings at his throat.

His fingers twined nervously about his rifle. He wished that it was an engine of annihilating power. He felt that he and his companions were being taunted and derided from sincere convictions that they were poor and puny. His knowledge of his inability to take vengeance for it made his rage into a dark and stormy specter, that possessed him and made him dream of abominable cruelties. The tormentors were flies sucking insolently at his blood, and he thought that he would have given his life for a revenge of seeing their faces in pitiful plights.

The winds of battle had swept all about the regiment, until the one rifle, instantly followed by others, flashed in its front. A moment later the regiment roared forth its sudden and valiant retort. A dense wall of smoke settled slowly down. It was furiously slit and slashed by the knifelike fire from the rifles.

To the youth the fighters resembled animals tossed for a death struggle into a dark pit. There was a sensation that he and his fellows, at bay, were pushing back, always pushing fierce onslaughts of creatures who were slippery. Their beams of crimson seemed to get no purchase upon the bodies of their foes; the latter seemed to evade them with ease, and come through, between, around, and about with unopposed skill.

When, in a dream, it occurred to the youth that his rifle was an impotent stick, he lost sense of everything but his hate, his desire to smash into pulp the glittering smile of victory which he could feel upon the faces of his enemies.

The blue smoke-swallowed line curled and writhed like a snake stepped upon. It swung its ends to and fro in an agony of fear and rage.

The youth was not conscious that he was erect upon his feet. He did not know the direction of the ground. Indeed, once he even lost the habit of balance and fell heavily. He was up again immediately. One thought went through the chaos of his brain at the time. He wondered if he had fallen because he had been shot. But the suspicion flew away at once. He did not think more of it.

He had taken up a first position behind the little tree, with a direct determination to hold it against the world. He had not deemed it possible that his army could that day succeed, and from this felt the ability to fight harder. But the throng had surged in all ways, until he lost directions and locations, save that he knew where lay the enemy.

The flames bit him, and the hot smoke broiled his skin. His rifle barrel grew so hot that ordinarily he could not have borne it upon his palms; but he kept on stuffing cartridges into it, and pounding them with his clanking, bending ramrod. If he aimed at some changing form through the smoke, he pulled his trigger with a fierce grunt, as if he were dealing a blow of the fist with all his strength.

When the enemy seemed falling back before him and his fellows, he went instantly forward, like a dog who, seeing his foes lagging, turns and insists upon being pursued. And when he was compelled to retire again, he did it slowly, sullenly, taking steps of wrathful despair.

Once he, in his intent hate, was almost alone, and was firing, when all those near him had ceased. He was so engrossed in his occupation that he was not aware of a lull.

He was recalled by a hoarse laugh and a sentence that came to his ears in a voice of contempt and amazement. "Yeh infernal fool, don't yeh know enough t' quit when there ain't anything t' shoot at? Good Gawd!"

He turned then and, pausing with his rifle thrown half into position, looked at the blue line of his comrades. During this moment of leisure they seemed all to be engaged in staring with astonishment at him. They had become spectators. Turning to the front again he saw, under the lifted smoke, a deserted ground.

He looked bewildered for a moment. Then there appeared upon the glazed vacancy of his eyes a diamond point of intelligence. "Oh," he said, comprehending.

He returned to his comrades and threw himself upon the ground. He sprawled like a man who had been thrashed. His flesh seemed strangely on fire, and the sounds of the battle continued in his ears. He groped blindly for his canteen.

The lieutenant was crowing. He seemed drunk with fighting. He called out to the youth: "By heavens, if I had ten thousand wild cats like you I could tear th' stomach outa this war in less'n a week!" He puffed out his chest with large dignity as he said it.

Some of the men muttered and looked at the youth in awestruck ways. It was plain that as he had gone on loading and firing and cursing without the proper intermission, they had found time to regard him. And they now looked upon him as a war devil.

The friend came staggering to him. There was some fright and dismay in his voice. "Are yeh all right, Fleming? Do yeh feel all right? There ain't nothin' th' matter with yeh, Henry, is there?"

"No," said the youth with difficulty. His throat seemed full of knobs and burrs.

These incidents made the youth ponder. It was revealed to him that he had been a barbarian, a beast. He had fought like a pagan who defends his religion. Regarding it, he saw that it was fine, wild, and, in some ways, easy. He had been a tremendous figure, no doubt. By this struggle he had overcome obstacles which he had admitted to be mountains. They had fallen like paper peaks, and he was now what he called a hero. And he had not been aware of the process. He had slept and, awakening, found himself a knight.

He lay and basked in the occasional stares of his comrades. Their faces were varied in degrees of blackness from the burned powder. Some were utterly smudged. They were reeking with perspiration, and their breaths came hard and wheezing. And from these soiled expanses they peered at him.

"Hot work! Hot work!" cried the lieutenant deliriously. He walked up and down, restless and eager. Sometimes his voice could be heard in a wild, incomprehensible laugh.

When he had a particularly profound thought upon the science of war he always unconsciously addressed himself to the youth.

There was some grim rejoicing by the men. "By thunder, I bet this army'll never see another new reg'ment like us!"

"You bet!"

> "A dog, a woman, an' a walnut tree,
> Th' more yeh beat 'em, th' better they be!

That's like us."

"Lost a piler men, they did. If an ol' woman swep' up th' woods she'd git a dustpanful."

"Yes, an' if she'll come around ag'in in 'bout an hour she'll git a pile more."

The forest still bore its burden of clamor. From off under the trees came the rolling clatter of the musketry. Each distant thicket seemed a strange porcupine with quills of flame. A cloud of dark smoke, as from smoldering ruins, went up toward the sun now bright and gay in the blue, enameled sky.

CHAPTER XVIII

The ragged line had respite for some minutes, but during its pause the struggle in the forest became magnified until the trees seemed to quiver from the firing and the ground to shake from the rushing of the men. The voices of the cannon were mingled in a long and interminable row. It seemed difficult to live in such an atmosphere. The chests of the men strained for a bit of freshness, and their throats craved water.

There was one shot through the body, who raised a cry of bitter lamentation when came this lull. Perhaps he had been calling out during the fighting also, but at that time no one had heard him. But now the men turned at the woeful complaints of him upon the ground.

"Who is it? Who is it?"

"It's Jimmie Rogers. Jimmie Rogers."

When their eyes first encountered him there was a sudden halt, as if they feared to go near. He was thrashing about in the grass, twisting his shuddering body into many strange postures. He was screaming loudly. This instant's hesitation seemed to fill him with a tremendous, fantastic contempt, and he damned them in shrieked sentences.

The youth's friend had a geographical illusion concerning a stream, and he obtained permission to go for some water. Immediately canteens were showered upon him. "Fill mine, will yeh?" "Bring me some, too." "And me, too." He departed, laden. The youth went with his friend, feeling a desire to throw his heated body into the stream and, soaking there, drink quarts.

They made a hurried search for the supposed stream, but did not find it. "No water here," said the youth. They turned without delay and began to retrace their steps.

From their position as they again faced toward the place of the fighting, they could of course comprehend a greater amount of the battle than when their visions had been blurred by the hurling smoke of the line. They could see dark stretches winding along the land, and on one cleared space there was a row of guns making gray clouds, which were filled with large flashes of orange-colored flame. Over some foliage they could see the roof of a house. One window, glowing a deep murder red, shone squarely through the leaves. From the edifice a tall leaning tower of smoke went far into the sky.

Looking over their own troops, they saw mixed masses slowly getting into regular form. The sunlight made twinkling points of the bright steel. To the rear there was a glimpse of a distant roadway as it curved over a slope. It was crowded with retreating infantry. From all the interwoven forest arose the smoke and bluster of the battle. The air was always occupied by a blaring.

Near where they stood shells were flip-flapping and hooting. Occasional bullets buzzed in the air and spanged into tree trunks. Wounded men and other stragglers were slinking through the woods.

Looking down an aisle of the grove, the youth and his companion saw a jangling general and his staff almost ride upon a wounded man, who was crawling on his hands and knees. The general reined strongly at his charger's opened and foamy mouth and guided it with dexterous horsemanship past the man. The latter scrambled in wild and torturing haste. His strength evidently failed him as he reached a place of safety. One of his arms suddenly weakened, and he fell, sliding over upon his back. He lay stretched out, breathing gently.

A moment later the small, creaking cavalcade was directly in front of the two soldiers. Another officer, riding with the skillful abandon of a cowboy, galloped his horse to a position directly before the general. The two unnoticed foot soldiers made a little show of going on, but they lingered near in the desire to overhear the conversation. Perhaps, they thought, some great inner historical things would be said.

The general, whom the boys knew as the commander of their division, looked at the other officer and spoke coolly, as if he were criticising his clothes. "Th' enemy's formin' over there for another charge," he said. "It'll be directed against Whiterside, an' I fear they'll break through there unless we work like thunder t' stop them."

The other swore at his restive horse, and then cleared his throat. He made a gesture toward his cap. "It'll be hell t' pay stoppin' them," he said shortly.

"I presume so," remarked the general. Then he began to talk rapidly and in a lower tone. He frequently illustrated his words with a pointing finger. The two infantrymen could hear nothing until finally he asked: "What troops can you spare?"

The officer who rode like a cowboy reflected for an instant. "Well," he said, "I had to order in th' 12th to help th' 76th, an' I haven't really got any. But there's th' 304th. They fight like a lot 'a mule drivers. I can spare them best of any."

The youth and his friend exchanged glances of astonishment.

The general spoke sharply. "Get 'em ready, then. I'll watch developments from here, an' send you word when t' start them. It'll happen in five minutes."

As the other officer tossed his fingers toward his cap and wheeling his horse, started away, the general called out to him in a sober voice: "I don't believe many of your mule drivers will get back."

The other shouted something in reply. He smiled.

With scared faces, the youth and his companion hurried back to the line.

These happenings had occupied an incredibly short time, yet the youth felt that in them he had been made aged. New eyes were given to him. And the most startling thing was to learn suddenly that he was very insignificant. The officer spoke of the regiment as if he referred to a broom. Some part of the woods needed sweeping, perhaps, and he merely indicated a broom in a tone properly indifferent to its fate. It was war, no doubt, but it appeared strange.

As the two boys approached the line, the lieutenant perceived them and swelled with wrath. "Fleming—Wilson—how long does it take yeh to git water, anyhow—where yeh been to?"

But his oration ceased as he saw their eyes, which were large with great tales.

"We're goin' t' charge—we're goin' t' charge!" cried the youth's friend, hastening with his news.

"Charge?" said the lieutenant. "Charge? Well, b'Gawd! Now, this is real fightin'." Over his soiled countenance there went a boastful smile. "Charge? Well, b'Gawd!"

A little group of soldiers surrounded the two youths. "Are we, sure 'nough? Well, I'll be derned! Charge? What fer? What at? Wilson, you're lyin'."

"I hope to die," said the youth, pitching his tones to the key of angry remonstrance. "Sure as shooting, I tell you."

And his friend spoke in re-enforcement. "Not by a blame sight, he ain't lyin'. We heard 'em talkin'."

They caught sight of two mounted figures a short distance from them. One was the colonel of the regiment and the other was the officer who had received orders from the commander of the division. They were gesticulating at each other. The soldier, pointing at them, interpreted the scene.

One man had a final objection: "How could yeh hear 'em talkin'?" But the men, for a large part, nodded, admitting that previously the two friends had spoken truth.

They settled back into reposeful attitudes with airs of having accepted the matter. And they mused upon it, with a hundred varieties of expression. It was an engrossing thing to think about. Many tightened their belts carefully and hitched at their trousers.

A moment later the officers began to bustle among the men, pushing them into a more compact mass and into a better alignment. They chased those that straggled and fumed at a few men who seemed to show by their attitudes that they had decided to remain at that spot. They were like critical shepherds struggling with sheep.

Presently, the regiment seemed to draw itself up and heave a deep breath. None of the men's faces were mirrors of large thoughts. The soldiers were bended and stooped like sprinters before a signal. Many pairs of glinting eyes peered from the grimy faces toward the curtains of the deeper woods. They seemed to be engaged in deep calculations of time and distance.

They were surrounded by the noises of the monstrous altercation between the two armies. The world was fully interested in other matters. Apparently, the regiment had its small affair to itself.

The youth, turning, shot a quick, inquiring glance at his friend. The latter returned to him the same manner of look. They were the only ones who possessed an inner knowledge. "Mule drivers—hell t' pay—don't believe many will get back." It was an ironical secret. Still, they saw no hesitation in each other's faces, and they nodded a mute and unprotesing assent when a shaggy man near them said in a meek voice: "We'll git swallowed."

CHAPTER XIX

The youth stared at the land in front of him. Its foliages now seemed to veil powers and horrors. He was unaware of the machinery of orders that started the charge, although from the corners of his eyes he saw an officer, who looked like a boy a-horseback, come galloping, waving his hat. Suddenly he felt a straining and heaving among the men. The line fell slowly forward like a toppling wall, and, with a convulsive gasp that was intended for a cheer, the regiment began its journey. The youth was pushed and jostled for a moment before he understood the movement at all, but directly he lunged ahead and began to run.

He fixed his eye upon a distant and prominent clump of trees where he had concluded the enemy were to be met, and he ran toward it as toward a goal. He had believed throughout that it was a mere question of getting over an unpleasant matter as quickly as possible, and he ran desperately, as if pursued for a murder. His face was drawn hard and tight with the stress of his endeavor. His eyes were fixed in a lurid glare. And with his soiled and disordered dress, his red and inflamed features surmounted by the dingy rag with its spot of blood, his wildly swinging rifle and banging accouterments, he looked to be an insane soldier.

As the regiment swung from its position out into a cleared space the woods and thickets before it awakened. Yellow flames leaped toward it from many directions. The forest made a tremendous objection.

The line lurched straight for a moment. Then the right wing swung forward; it in turn was surpassed by the left. Afterward the center careered to the front until the regiment was a wedge-shaped mass, but an instant later the opposition of the bushes, trees, and uneven places on the ground split the command and scattered it into detached clusters.

The youth, light-footed, was unconsciously in advance. His eyes still kept note of the clump of trees. From all places near it the clannish yell of the enemy could be heard. The little flames of rifles leaped from it. The song of the bullets was in the air and shells snarled among the treetops. One tumbled directly into the middle of a hurrying group and exploded in crimson fury. There was an instant's spectacle of a man, almost over it, throwing up his hands to shield his eyes.

Other men, punched by bullets, fell in grotesque agonies. The regiment left a coherent trail of bodies.

They had passed into a clearer atmosphere. There was an effect like a revelation in the new appearance of the landscape. Some men working madly at a battery were plain to them, and the opposing infantry's lines were defined by the gray walls and fringes of smoke.

It seemed to the youth that he saw everything. Each blade of green grass was bold and clear. He thought that he was aware of every change in the thin, transparent vapor that floated idly in sheets. The brown or gray trunks of the trees showed each roughness of their surfaces. And the men of the regiment, with their starting eyes and sweating faces, running madly, or falling, as if thrown headlong, to queer, heaped-up corpses—all were comprehended. His mind took a mechanical but firm impression, so that afterward everything was pictured and explained to him, save why he himself was there.

But there was a frenzy made from this furious rush. The men, pitching forward insanely, had burst into cheerings, moblike and barbaric, but tuned in strange keys that can arouse the dullard and the stoic. It made a mad enthusiasm that, it seemed, would be incapable of checking itself before granite and brass. There was the delirium that encounters despair and death, and is heedless and blind to the odds. It is a temporary but sublime absence of selfishness. And because it was of this order was the reason, perhaps, why the youth wondered, afterward, what reasons he could have had for being there.

Presently the straining pace ate up the energies of the men. As if by agreement, the leaders began to slacken their speed. The volleys directed against them had had a seeming windlike effect. The regiment snorted and blew. Among some stolid trees it began to falter and hesitate. The men, staring intently, began to wait for some of the distant walls of smoke to move and disclose to them the scene. Since much of their strength and their breath had vanished, they returned to caution. They were become men again.

The youth had a vague belief that he had run miles, and he thought, in a way, that he was now in some new and unknown land.

The moment the regiment ceased its advance the protesting splutter of musketry became a steadied roar. Long and accurate fringes of smoke spread out. From the top of a small hill came level belchings of yellow flame that caused an inhuman whistling in the air.

The men, halted, had opportunity to see some of their comrades dropping with moans and shrieks. A few lay under foot, still or wailing. And now for an instant the men stood, their rifles slack in their hands, and watched the regiment dwindle. They appeared dazed and stupid. This spectacle seemed to paralyze them, overcome them with a fatal fascination. They stared woodenly at the sights, and, lowering their eyes, looked from face to face. It was a strange pause, and a strange silence.

Then, above the sounds of the outside commotion, arose the roar of the lieutenant. He strode suddenly forth, his infantile features black with rage.

"Come on, yeh fools!" he bellowed. "Come on! Yeh can't stay here. Yeh must come on." He said more, but much of it could not be understood.

He started rapidly forward, with his head turned toward the men. "Come on," he was shouting. The men stared with blank and yokel-like eyes at him. He was obliged to halt and retrace his steps. He stood then with his back to the enemy and delivered gigantic curses into the faces of the men. His body vibrated from the weight and force of his imprecations. And he could string oaths with the facility of a maiden who strings beads.

The friend of the youth aroused. Lurching suddenly forward and dropping to his knees, he fired an angry shot at the persistent woods. This action awakened the men. They huddled no more like sheep. They seemed suddenly to bethink them of their weapons, and at once commenced firing. Belabored by their officers, they began to move forward. The regiment, involved like a cart involved in mud and muddle, started unevenly with many jolts and jerks. The men stopped now every few paces to fire and load, and in this manner moved slowly on from trees to trees.

The flaming opposition in their front grew with their advance until it seemed that all forward ways were barred by the thin leaping tongues, and off to the right an ominous demonstration could sometimes be dimly discerned. The smoke lately generated was in confusing clouds that made it difficult for the regiment to proceed with intelligence. As he passed through each curling mass the youth wondered what would confront him on the farther side.

The command went painfully forward until an open space interposed between them and the lurid lines. Here, crouching and cowering behind some trees, the men clung with desperation, as if threatened by a wave. They looked wild-eyed, and as if amazed at this furious disturbance they had stirred. In the storm there was an ironical expression of their importance. The faces of the men, too, showed a lack of a certain feeling of responsibility for being there. It was as if they had been driven. It was the dominant animal failing to remember in the supreme moments the forceful causes of various superficial qualities. The whole affair seemed incomprehensible to many of them.

As they halted thus the lieutenant again began to bellow profanely. Regardless of the vindictive threats of the bullets, he went about coaxing, berating, and bedamning. His lips, that were habitually in a soft and childlike curve, were now writhed into unholy contortions. He swore by all possible deities.

Once he grabbed the youth by the arm. "Come on, yeh lunkhead!" he roared. "Come on! We'll all git killed if we stay here. We've on'y got t' go across that lot. An' then"—the remainder of his idea disappeared in a blue haze of curses.

The youth stretched forth his arm. "Cross there?" His mouth was puckered in doubt and awe.

"Certainly, Jest 'cross th' lot! We can't stay here," screamed the lieutenant. He poked his face close to the youth and waved his bandaged hand. "Come on!" Presently he grappled with him as if for a wrestling bout. It was as if he planned to drag the youth by the ear on to the assault.

The private felt a sudden unspeakable indignation against his officer. He wrenched fiercely and shook him off.

"Come on yerself, then," he yelled. There was a bitter challenge in his voice.

They galloped together down the regimental front. The friend scrambled after them. In front of the colors the three men began to bawl: "Come on! come on!" They danced and gyrated like tortured savages.

The flag, obedient to these appeals, bended its glittering form and swept toward them. The men wavered in indecision for a moment, and then with a long, wailful cry the dilapidated regiment surged forward and began its new journey.

Over the field went the scurrying mass. It was a handful of men splattered into the faces of the enemy. Toward it instantly sprang the yellow tongues. A vast quantity of blue smoke hung before them. A mighty banging made ears valueless.

The youth ran like a madman to reach the woods before a bullet could discover him. He ducked his head low, like a football player. In his haste his eyes almost closed, and the scene was a wild blur. Pulsating saliva stood at the corners of his mouth.

Within him, as he hurled himself forward, was born a love, a despairing fondness for this flag which was near him. It was a creation of beauty and invulnerability. It was a goddess, radiant, that bended its form with an imperious gesture to him. It was a woman, red and white, hating and loving, that called him with the voice of his hopes. Because no harm could come to it he endowed it with power. He kept near, as if it could be a saver of lives, and an imploring cry went from his mind.

In the mad scramble he was aware that the color sergeant flinched suddenly, as if struck by a bludgeon. He faltered, and then became motionless, save for his quivering knees.

He made a spring and a clutch at the pole. At the same instant his friend grabbed it from the other side. They jerked at it, stout and furious, but the color sergeant was dead, and the corpse would not relinquish its trust. For a moment there was a grim encounter. The dead man, swinging with bended back, seemed to be obstinately tugging, in ludicrous and awful ways, for the possession of the flag.

It was past in an instant of time. They wrenched the flag furiously from the dead man, and, as they turned again, the corpse swayed forward with bowed head. One arm swung high, and the curved hand fell with heavy protest on the friend's unheeding shoulder.

CHAPTER XX

When the two youths turned with the flag they saw that much of the regiment had crumbled away, and the dejected remnant was coming slowly back. The men, having hurled themselves in projectile fashion, had presently expended their forces. They slowly retreated, with their faces still toward the spluttering woods, and their hot rifles still replying to the din. Several officers were giving orders, their voices keyed to screams.

"Where in hell yeh goin'?" the lieutenant was asking in a sarcastic howl. And a red-bearded officer, whose voice of triple brass could plainly be heard, was commanding: "Shoot into 'em! Shoot into 'em, Gawd damn their souls!" There was a *mêlée* of screeches, in which the men were ordered to do conflicting and impossible things.

The youth and his friend had a small scuffle over the flag. "Give it t' me!" "No, let me keep it!" Each felt satisfied with the other's possession of it, but each felt bound to declare, by an offer to carry the emblem, his willingness to further risk himself. The youth roughly pushed his friend away.

The regiment fell back to the stolid trees. There it halted for a moment to blaze at some dark forms that had begun to steal upon its track. Presently it resumed its march again, curving among the tree trunks. By the time the depleted regiment had again reached the first open space they were receiving a fast and merciless fire. There seemed to be mobs all about them.

The greater part of the men, discouraged, their spirits worn by the turmoil, acted as if stunned. They accepted the pelting of the bullets with bowed and weary heads. It was of no purpose to strive against walls. It was of no use of batter themselves against granite. And from this consciousness that they had attempted to conquer an unconquerable thing there seemed to arise a feeling that they had been betrayed. They glowered with bent brows, but dangerously, upon some of the officers, more particularly upon the red-bearded one with the voice of triple brass.

However, the rear of the regiment was fringed with men, who continued to shoot irritably at the advancing foes. They seemed resolved to make every trouble. The youthful lieutenant was perhaps the last man in the disordered mass. His forgotten back was toward the enemy. He had been shot in the arm. It hung straight and rigid. Occasionally he would cease to remember it, and be about to emphasize an oath with a sweeping gesture. The multiplied pain caused him to swear with incredible power.

The youth went along with slipping, uncertain feet. He kept watchful eyes rearward. A scowl of mortification and rage was upon his face. He had thought of a fine revenge upon the officer who had referred to him and his fellows as mule drivers. But he saw that it could not come to pass. His dreams had collapsed when the mule drivers, dwindling rapidly, had wavered and hesitated on the little clearing, and then had recoiled. And now the retreat of the mule drivers was a march of shame to him.

A dagger-pointed gaze from without his blackened face was held toward the enemy, but his greater hatred was riveted upon the man, who, not knowing him, had called him a mule driver.

When he knew that he and his comrades had failed to do anything in successful ways that might bring the little pangs of a kind of remorse upon the officer, the youth allowed the rage of the baffled to possess him. This cold officer upon a monument, who dropped epithets unconcernedly down, would be finer as a dead man, he thought. So grievous did he think it that he could never possess the secret right to taunt truly in answer.

He had pictured red letters of curious revenge. "We *are* mule drivers, are we?" and now he was compelled to throw them away.

He presently wrapped his heart in the cloak of his pride and kept the flag erect. He harangued his fellows, pushing against their chests with his free hand. To those he knew well he made frantic appeals, beseeching them by name. Between him and the lieutenant, scolding and near to losing his mind with rage, there was felt a subtle fellowship and equality. They supported each other in all manner of hoarse, howling protests.

But the regiment was a machine run down. The two men babbled at a forceless thing. The soldiers who had heart to go slowly were continually shaken in their resolves by a knowledge that comrades were slipping with speed back to the lines. It was difficult to think of reputation when others were thinking of skins. Wounded men were left crying on this black journey.

The smoke fringes and flames blustered always. The youth, peering once through a sudden rift in a cloud, saw a brown mass of troops, interwoven and magnified until they appeared to be thousands. A fierce-hued flag flashed before his vision.

Immediately, as if the uplifting of the smoke had been prearranged, the discovered troops burst into a rasping yell, and a hundred flames jetted toward the retreating band. A rolling gray cloud again interposed as the regiment doggedly replied. The youth had to depend again upon his misused ears, which were trembling and buzzing from the *mêlée* of musketry and yells.

The way seemed eternal. In the clouded haze men became panic-stricken with the thought that the regiment had lost its path, and was proceeding in a perilous direction. Once the men who headed the wild procession turned and came pushing back against their comrades, screaming that they were being fired upon from points which they had considered to be toward their own lines. At this cry a hysterical fear and dismay beset the troops. A soldier, who heretofore had been ambitious to make the regiment into a wise little band that would proceed calmly amid the huge-appearing difficulties, suddenly sank down and buried his face in his arms with an air of bowing to a doom. From another a shrill lamentation rang out filled with profane allusions to a general. Men ran hither and thither, seeking with their eyes roads of escape. With serene regularity, as if controlled by a schedule, bullets buffed into men.

The youth walked stolidly into the midst of the mob, and with his flag in his hands took a stand as if he expected an attempt to push him to the ground. He unconsciously assumed the attitude of the color bearer in the fight of the preceding day. He passed over his brow a hand that trembled. His breath did not come freely. He was choking during this small wait for the crisis.

His friend came to him. "Well, Henry, I guess this is good-by—John."[1]

"Oh, shut up, you damned fool!" replied the youth, and he would not look at the other.

The officers labored like politicians to beat the mass into a proper circle to face the menaces. The ground was uneven and torn. The men curled into depressions and fitted themselves snugly behind whatever would frustrate a bullet.

The youth noted with vague surprise that the lieutenant was standing mutely with his legs far apart and his sword held in the manner of a cane. The youth wondered what had happened to his vocal organs that he no more cursed.

There was something curious in this little intent pause of the lieutenant. He was like a babe which, having wept its fill, raises its eyes and fixed upon a distant toy. He was engrossed in this contemplation, and the soft under lip quivered from self-whispered words.

---

[1] I.e., "good-by for sure," "this is the end."

Some lazy and ignorant smoke curled slowly. The men, hiding from the bullets, waited anxiously for it to lift and disclose the plight of the regiment.

The silent ranks were suddenly thrilled by the eager voice of the youthful lieutenant bawling out: "Here they come! Right onto us, b'Gawd!" His further words were lost in a roar of wicked thunder from the men's rifles.

The youth's eyes had instantly turned in the direction indicated by the awakened and agitated lieutenant, and he had seen the haze of treachery disclosing a body of soldiers of the enemy. They were so near that he could see their features. There was a recognition as he looked at the types of faces. Also he perceived with dim amazement that their uniforms were rather gay in effect, being light gray, accented with a brilliant-hued facing. Too, the clothes seemed new.

These troops had apparently been going forward with caution, their rifles held in readiness, when the youthful lieutenant had discovered them and their movement had been interrupted by the volley from the blue regiment. From the moment's glimpse, it was derived that they had been unaware of the proximity of their dark-suited foes or had mistaken the direction. Almost instantly they were shut utterly from the youth's sight by the smoke from the energetic rifles of his companions. He strained his vision to learn the accomplishment of the volley, but the smoke hung before him.

The two bodies of troops exchanged blows in the manner of a pair of boxers. The fast angry firing went back and forth. The men in blue were intent with the despair of their circumstances and they seized upon the revenge to be had at close range. Their thunder swelled loud and valiant. Their curving front bristled with flashes and the place resounded with the clangor of their ramrods. The youth ducked and dodged for a time and achieved a few unsatisfactory views of the enemy. There appeared to be many of them and they were replying swiftly. They seemed moving toward the blue regiment step by step. He seated himself gloomily on the ground with his flag between his knees.

As he noted the vicious, wolflike temper of his comrades he had a sweet thought that if the enemy was about to swallow the regimental broom as a large prisoner, it could at least have the consolation of going down with bristles forward.

But the blows of the antagonist began to grow more weak. Fewer bullets ripped the air, and finally, when the men slackened to learn of the fight, they could see only dark, floating smoke. The regiment lay still and gazed. Presently some chance whim came to the pestering blur, and it began to coil heavily away. The men saw a ground vacant of fighters. It would have been an empty stage if it were not for a few corpses that lay thrown and twisted into fantastic shapes upon the sward.

At sight of this tableau, many of the men in blue sprang from behind their covers and made an ungainly dance of joy. Their eyes burned and a hoarse cheer of elation broke from their dry lips.

It had begun to seem to them that events were trying to prove that they were impotent. These little battles had evidently endeavored to demonstrate that the men could not fight well. When on the verge of submission to these opinions, the small duel had showed them that the proportions were not impossible, and by it they had revenged themselves upon their misgivings and upon the foe.

The impetus of enthusiasm was theirs again. They gazed about them with looks of uplifted pride, feeling new trust in the grim, always confident weapons in their hands. And they were men.

CHAPTER XXI

Presently they knew that no firing threatened them. All ways seemed once more opened to them. The dusty blue lines of their friends were disclosed a short distance away. In the distance there were many colossal noises, but in all this part of the field there was a sudden stillness.

They perceived that they were free. The depleted band drew a long breath of relief and gathered itself into a bunch to complete its trip.

In this last length of journey the men began to show strange emotions. They hurried with nervous fear. Some who had been dark and unfaltering in the grimmest moments now could not conceal an anxiety that made them frantic. It was perhaps that they dreaded to be killed in insignificant ways after the times for proper military deaths had passed. Or, perhaps, they thought it would be too ironical to get killed at the portals of safety. With backward looks of perturbation, they hastened.

As they approached their own lines there was some sarcasm exhibited on the part of a gaunt and bronzed regiment that lay resting in the shade of trees. Questions were wafted to them.

"Where th' hell yeh been?"

"What yeh comin' back fer?"

"Why didn't yeh stay there?"

"Was it warm out there, sonny?"

"Goin' home now, boys?"

One shouted in taunting mimicry: "Oh, mother, come quick an' look at th' sojers!"

There was no reply from the bruised and battered regiment, save that one man made broadcast challenges to fist fights and the red-bearded officer walked rather near and glared in great swashbuckler style at a tall captain in the other regiment. But the lieutenant suppressed the man who wished to fist fight, and the tall captain, flushing at the little fanfare of the red-bearded one, was obliged to look intently at some trees.

The youth's tender flesh was deeply stung by these remarks. From under his creased brows he glowered with hate at the mockers. He meditated upon a few revenges. Still, many in the regiment hung their heads in criminal fashion, so that it came to pass that the men trudged with sudden heaviness, as if they bore upon their bended shoulders the coffin of their honor. And the youthful lieutenant, recollecting himself, began to mutter softly in black curses.

They turned when they arrived at their old position to regard the ground over which they had charged.

The youth in this contemplation was smitten with a large astonishment. He discovered that the distances, as compared with the brilliant measurings of his mind, were trivial and ridiculous. The stolid trees, where much had taken place, seemed incredibly near. The time, too, now that he reflected, he saw to have been short. He wondered at the number of emotions and events that had been crowded into such little spaces. Elfin thoughts must have exaggerated and enlarged everything, he said.

It seemed, then, that there was bitter justice in the speeches of the gaunt and bronzed veterans. He veiled a glance of disdain at his fellows who strewed the ground, choking with dust, red from perspiration, misty-eyed, disheveled.

They were gulping at their canteens, fierce to wring every mite of water from them, and they polished at their swollen and watery features with coat sleeves and bunches of grass.

However, to the youth there was a considerable joy in musing upon his performances during the charge. He had had very little time previously in which to appreciate himself, so that there was now much satisfaction in quietly thinking of his actions. He recalled bits of color that in the flurry had stamped themselves unawares upon his engaged senses.

As the regiment lay heaving from its hot exertions the officer who had named them as mule drivers came galloping along the line. He had lost his cap. His tousled hair streamed wildly, and his face was dark with vexation and wrath. His temper was displayed with more clearness by the way in which he managed his horse. He jerked and wrenched savagely at his bridle, stopping the hard-breathing animal with a furious pull near the colonel of the regiment. He immediately exploded in reproaches which came unbidden to the ears of the men. They were suddenly alert, being always curious about black words between officers.

"Oh, thunder, MacChesney, what an awful bull you made of this thing!" began the officer. He attempted low tones, but his indignation caused certain of the men to learn the sense of his words. "What an awful mess you made! Good Lord, man, you stopped about a hundred feet this side of a very pretty success! If your men had gone a hundred feet farther you would have made a great charge, but as it is—what a lot of mud diggers you've got anyway!"

The men, listening with bated breath, now turned their curious eyes upon the colonel. They had a ragamuffin interest in this affair.

The colonel was seen to straighten his form and put one hand forth in oratorical fashion. He wore an injured air; it was as if a deacon had been accused of stealing. The men were wiggling in an ecstasy of excitement.

But of a sudden the colonel's manner changed from that of a deacon to that of a Frenchman. He shrugged his shoulders. "Oh, well, general, we went as far as we could," he said calmly.

"As far as you could? Did you, b'Gawd?" snorted the other. "Well, that wasn't very far, was it?" he added, with a glance of cold contempt into the other's eyes. "Not very far, I think. You were intended to make a diversion in favor of Whiterside. How well you succeeded your own ears can now tell you." He wheeled his horse and rode stiffly away.

The colonel, bidden to hear the jarring noises of an engagement in the woods to the left, broke out in vague damnations.

The lieutenant, who had listened with an air of impotent rage to the interview, spoke suddenly in firm and undaunted tones. "I don't care what a man is— whether he is a general or what—if he says th' boys didn't put up a good fight out there he's a damned fool."

"Lieutenant," began the colonel, severely, "this is my own affair, and I'll trouble you——"

The lieutenant made an obedient gesture. "All right, colonel, all right," he said. He sat down with an air of being content with himself.

The news that the regiment had been reproached went along the line. For a time the men were bewildered by it. "Good thunder!" they ejaculated, staring at the vanishing form of the general. They conceived it to be a huge mistake.

Presently, however, they began to believe that in truth their efforts had been called light. The youth could see his conviction weigh upon the entire regiment until the men were like cuffed and cursed animals, but withal rebellious.

The friend, with a grievance in his eye, went to the youth. "I wonder what he does want," he said. "He must think we went out there an' played marbles! I never see sech a man!"

The youth developed a tranquil philosophy for these moments of irritation. "Oh, well," he rejoined, "he probably didn't see nothing of it at all and got mad as blazes, and concluded we were a lot of sheep, just because we didn't do what he wanted done. It's a pity old Grandpa Henderson got killed yesterday—he'd have known that we did our best and fought good. It's just our awful luck, that's what."

"I should say so," replied the friend. He seemed to be deeply wounded at an injustice. "I should say we did have awful luck! There's no fun in fightin' fer people when everything yeh do—no matter what—ain't done right. I have a notion t' stay behind next time an' let 'em take their ol' charge an' go t' th' devil with it."

The youth spoke soothingly to his comrade. "Well, we both did good. I'd like to see the fool what'd say we both didn't do as good as we could!"

"Of course we did," declared the friend stoutly. "An' I'd break th' feller's neck if he was as big as a church. But we're all right, anyhow, for I heard one feller say that we two fit th' best in th' reg'ment, an' they had a great argument 'bout it. Another feller, 'a course, he had t' up an' say it was a lie—he seen all what was goin' on an' he never seen us from th' beginnin' t' th' end. An' a lot more struck in an' ses it wasn't a lie—we did fight like thunder, an' they give us quite a send-off. But this is what I can't stand—these everlastin' ol' soldiers, titterin' an' laughin', an' then that general, he's crazy."

The youth exclaimed with sudden exasperation: "He's a lunkhead! He makes me mad. I wish he'd come along next time. We'd show 'im what——"

He ceased because several men had come hurrying up. Their faces expressed a bringing of great news.

"O Flem, yeh jest oughta heard!" cried one, eagerly.

"Heard what?" said the youth.

"Yeh jest oughta heard!" repeated the other, and he arranged himself to tell his tidings. The others made an excited circle. "Well, sir, th' colonel met your lieutenant right by us—it was damnedest thing I ever heard—an' he ses: 'Ahem! ahem!' he ses. 'Mr. Hasbrouck!' he ses, 'by th' way, who was that lad what carried th' flag?' he ses. There, Flemin', what d' yeh think 'a that? 'Who was th' lad what carried th' flag?' he ses, an' th' lieutenant, he speaks up right away: 'That's Flemin', an' he's a jimhickey,' he ses, right away. What? I say he did. 'A jimhickey,' he ses—those 'r his words. He did too. I say he did. If you kin tell this story better than I kin, go ahead an' tell it. Well, then, keep yer mouth shet. Th' lieutenant, he ses: 'He's a jimhickey,' an' th' colonel, he ses: 'Ahem! ahem! he is, indeed, a very good man t' have, ahem! He kep' th' flag 'way t' th' front. I saw 'im. He's a good un,' ses th' colonel. 'You bet,' ses th' lieutenant, 'he an' a feller named Wilson was at th' head 'a th' charge, an' howlin' like Indians all th' time,' he ses. 'Head 'a th' charge all th' time,' he ses. 'A feller named Wilson,' he ses. There, Wilson, m'boy, put that in a letter an' send it hum t' yer mother, hay? 'A feller named Wilson,' he ses. An' th' colonel, he ses: 'Were they indeed? Ahem! ahem! My sakes!' he ses. 'At th' head 'a th' reg'ment?' he ses. 'They were,' ses th' lieutenant. 'My sakes!' ses th' colonel. He ses: 'Well, well, well,' he ses, 'those two babies?' 'They were,' ses th' lieutenant. 'Well, well,' ses th' colonel, 'they deserve t' be major-generals,' he ses. 'That deserve t' be major-generals.' "

The youth and his friend had said: "Huh!" "Yer lyin', Thompson." "Oh, go t' blazes!" "He never sed it." "Oh, what a lie!" "Huh!" But despite these youthful scoffings and embarrassments, they knew that their faces were deeply flushing from thrills of pleasure. They exchanged a secret glance of joy and congratulation.

They speedily forgot many things. The past held no pictures of error and disappointment. They were very happy, and their hearts swelled with grateful affection for the colonel and the youthful lieutenant.

CHAPTER XXII

When the woods again began to pour forth the dark-hued masses of the enemy the youth felt serene self-confidence. He smiled briefly when he saw men dodge and duck at the long screechings of shells that were thrown in giant handfuls over them. He stood, erect and tranquil, watching the attack begin against a part of the line that made a blue curve along the side of an adjacent hill. His vision being unmolested by smoke from the rifles of his companions, he had opportunities to see parts of the hard fight. It was a relief to perceive at last from whence came some of these noises which had been roared into his ears.

Off a short way he saw two regiments fighting a little separate battle with two other regiments. It was in a cleared space, wearing a set-apart look. They were blazing as if upon a wager, giving and taking tremendous blows. The firings were incredibly fierce and rapid. These intent regiments apparently were oblivious of all larger purposes of war, and were slugging each other as if at a matched game.

In another direction he saw a magnificent brigade going with the evident intention of driving the enemy from a wood. They passed in out of sight and presently there was a most awe-inspiring racket in the wood. The noise was unspeakable. Having stirred this prodigious uproar, and, apparently, finding it too prodigious, the brigade, after a little time, came marching airily out again with its fine formation in nowise disturbed. There were no traces of speed in its movements. The brigade was jaunty and seemed to point a proud thumb at the yelling wood.

On a slope to the left there was a long row of guns, gruff and maddened, denouncing the enemy, who, down through the woods, were forming for another attack in the pitiless monotony of conflicts. The round red discharges from the guns made a crimson flare and a high, thick smoke. Occasional glimpses could be caught of groups of the toiling artillerymen. In the rear of this row of guns stood a house, calm and white, amid bursting shells. A congregation of horses, tied to a long railing, were tugging frenziedly at their bridles. Men were running hither and thither.

The detached battle between the four regiments lasted for some time. There chanced to be no interference, and they settled their dispute by themselves. They struck savagely and powerfully at each other for a period of minutes, and then the lighter-hued regiments faltered and drew back, leaving the dark-blue lines shouting. The youth could see the two flags shaking with laughter amid the smoke remnants.

Presently there was a stillness, pregnant with meaning. The blue lines shifted and changed a trifle and stared expectantly at the silent woods and fields before them. The hush was solemn and churchlike, save for a distant battery that, evidently unable to remain quiet, sent a faint rolling thunder over the ground. It irritated, like the noises of unrepressed boys. The men imagined that it would prevent their perched ears from hearing the first words of the new battle.

Of a sudden the guns on the slope roared out a message of warning. A spluttering sound had begun in the woods. It swelled with amazing speed to a profound clamor that involved the earth in noises. The splitting crashes swept along the lines until an interminable roar was developed. To those in the midst of it, it became a din fitted to the universe. It was the whirring and thumping of gigantic machinery, complications among the smaller stars. The youth's ears were filled up. They were incapable of hearing more.

On an incline over which a road wound he saw wild and desperate rushes of men perpetually backward and forward in riotous surges. These parts of the opposing armies were two long waves that pitched upon each other madly at dictated points. To and fro they swelled. Sometimes, one side by its yells and cheers would proclaim decisive blows, but a moment later the other side would be all yells and cheers. Once the youth saw a spray of light forms go in houndlike leaps toward the waving blue lines. There was much howling, and presently it went away with a vast mouthful of prisoners. Again, he saw a blue wave dash with such thunderous force against a gray obstruction that it seemed to clear the earth of it and leave nothing but trampled sod. And always in their swift and deadly rushes to and fro the men screamed and yelled like maniacs.

Particular pieces of fence or secure positions behind collections of trees were wrangled over, as gold thrones or pearl bedsteads. There were desperate lunges at these chosen spots seemingly every instant, and most of them were bandied like light toys between the contending forces. The youth could not tell from the battle flags flying like crimson foam in many directions which color of cloth was winning.

His emaciated regiment bustled forth with undiminished fierceness when its time came. When assaulted again by bullets, the men burst out in a barbaric cry of rage and pain. They bent their heads in aims of intent hatred behind the projected hammers of their guns. Their ramrods clanged loud with fury as their eager arms pounded the cartridges into the rifle barrels. The front of the regiment was a smoke-wall penetrated by the flashing points of yellow and red.

Wallowing in the fight, they were in an astonishingly short time re-smudged. They surpassed in stain and dirt all their previous appearances. Moving to and fro with strained exertion, jabbering the while, they were, with their swaying bodies, black faces, and glowing eyes, like strange and ugly fiends jigging heavily in the smoke.

The lieutenant, returning from a tour after a bandage, produced from a hidden receptacle of his mind new and portentous oaths suited to the emergency. Strings of expletives he swung lashlike over the backs of his men, and it was evident that his previous efforts had in nowise impaired his resources.

The youth, still the bearer of colors, did not feel his idleness. He was deeply absorbed as a spectator. The crash and swing of the great drama made him lean forward, intent-eyed, his face working in small contortions. Sometimes he prattled, words coming unconsciously from him in grotesque exclamations. He did not know that he breathed; that the flag hung silently over him, so absorbed was he.

A formidable line of the enemy came within dangerous range. They could be seen plainly—tall, gaunt men with excited faces running with long strides toward a wandering fence.

At sight of this danger the men suddenly ceased their cursing monotone. There was an instant of strained silence before they threw up their rifles and fired a plumping volley at the foes. There had been no order given; the men, upon recognizing the menace, had immediately let drive their flock of bullets without waiting for word of command.

But the enemy were quick to gain the protection of the wandering line of fence. They slid down behind it with remarkable celerity, and from this position they began briskly to slice up the blue men.

These latter braced their energies for a great struggle. Often, white clinched teeth shone from the dusky faces. Many heads surged to and fro, floating upon a pale sea of smoke. Those behind the fence frequently shouted and yelped in taunts and gibelike cries, but the regiment maintained a stressed silence. Perhaps, at this new assault the men recalled the fact that they had been named mud diggers, and it made their situation thrice bitter. They were breathlessly intent upon keeping the ground and thrusting away the rejoicing body of the enemy. They fought swiftly and with a despairing savageness denoted in their expressions.

The youth had resolved not to budge whatever should happen. Some arrows of scorn that had buried themselves in his heart had generated strange and unspeakable hatred. It was clear to him that his final and absolute revenge was to be achieved by his dead body lying, torn and guttering, upon the field. This was to be a poignant retaliation upon the officer who had said "mule drivers," and later "mud diggers," for in all the wild graspings of his mind for a unit responsible for his sufferings and commotions he always seized upon the man who had dubbed him wrongly. And it was his idea, vaguely formulated, that his corpse would be for those eyes a great and salt reproach.

The regiment bled extravagantly. Grunting bundles of blue began to drop. The orderly sergeant of the youth's company was shot through the cheeks. Its supports being injured, his jaw hung afar down, disclosing in the wide cavern of his mouth a pulsing mass of blood and teeth. And with it all he made attempts to cry out. In his endeavor there was a dreadful earnestness, as if he conceived that one great shriek would make him well.

The youth saw him presently go rearward. His strength seemed in nowise impaired. He ran swiftly, casting wild glances for succor.

Others fell down about the feet of their companions. Some of the wounded crawled out and away, but many lay still, their bodies twisted into impossible shapes.

The youth looked once for his friend. He saw a vehement young man, powder-smeared and frowzled, whom he knew to be him. The lieutenant, also, was unscathed in his position at the rear. He had continued to curse, but it was now with the air of a man who was using his last box of oaths.

For the fire of the regiment had begun to wane and drip. The robust voice, that had come strangely from the thin ranks, was growing rapidly weak.

CHAPTER XXIII

The colonel came running along back of the line. There were other officers following him. "We must charge'm!" they shouted. "We must charge'm!" they cried with resentful voices, as if anticipating a rebellion against this plan by the men.

The youth, upon hearing the shouts, began to study the distance between him and the enemy. He made vague calculations. He saw that to be firm soldiers they must go forward. It would be death to stay in the present place, and with all the circumstances to go backward would exalt too many others. Their hope was to push the galling foes away from the fence.

He expected that his companions, weary and stiffened, would have to be driven to this assault, but as he turned toward them he perceived with a certain surprise that they were giving quick and unqualified expressions of assent. There was an ominous, clanging overture to the charge when the shafts of the bayonets rattled upon the rifle barrels. At the yelled words of command the soldiers sprang forward in eager leaps. There was new and unexpected force in the movement of the regiment. A knowledge of its faded and jaded condition made the charge appear like a paroxysm, a display of the strength that comes before a final feebleness. The men scampered in insane fever of haste, racing as if to achieve a sudden success before an exhilarating fluid should leave them. It was a blind and despairing rush by the collection of men in dusty and tattered blue, over a green sward and under a sapphire sky, toward a fence, dimly outlined in smoke, from behind which spluttered the fierce rifles of enemies.

The youth kept the bright colors to the front. He was waving his free arm in furious circles, the while shrieking mad calls and appeals, urging on those that did not need to be urged, for it seemed that the mob of blue men hurling themselves on the dangerous group of rifles were again grown suddenly wild with an enthusiasm of unselfishness. From the many firings starting toward them, it looked as if they would merely succeed in making a great sprinkling of corpses on the grass between their former position and the fence. But they were in a state of frenzy, perhaps because of forgotten vanities, and it made an exhibition of sublime recklessness. There was no obvious questioning, nor figurings, nor diagrams. There were, apparently, no considered loopholes. It appeared that the swift wings of their desires would have shattered against the iron gates of the impossible.

He himself felt the daring spirit of a savage, religion-mad. He was capable of profound sacrifices, a tremendous death. He had no time for dissections, but he knew that he thought of the bullets only as things that could prevent him from reaching the place of his endeavor. There were subtle flashings of joy within him that thus should be his mind.

He strained all his strength. His eyesight was shaken and dazzled by the tension of thought and muscle. He did not see anything excepting the mist of smoke gashed by the little knives of fire, but he knew that in it lay the aged fence of a vanished farmer protecting the snuggled bodies of the gray men.

As he ran a thought of the shock of contact gleamed in his mind. He expected a great concussion when the two bodies of troops crashed together. This became a part of his wild battle madness. He could feel the onward swing of the regiment about him and he conceived of a thunderous, crushing blow that would prostrate the resistance and spread consternation and amazement for miles. The flying regiment was going to have a catapultian effect. This dream made him run faster among his comrades, who were giving vent to hoarse and frantic cheers.

But presently he could see that many of the men in gray did not intend to abide the blow. The smoke, rolling, disclosed men who ran, their faces still turned. These grew to a crowd, who retired stubbornly. Individuals wheeled frequently to send a bullet at the blue wave.

But at one part of the line there was a grim and obdurate group that made no movement. They were settled firmly down behind posts and rails. A flag, ruffled and fierce, waved over them and their rifles dinned fiercely.

The blue whirl of men got very near, until it seemed that in truth there would be a close and frightful scuffle. There was an expressed disdain in the opposition of the little group, that changed the meaning of the cheers of the men in blue. They became yells of wrath, directed, personal. The cries of the two parties were now in sound an interchange of scathing insults.

They in blue showed their teeth; their eyes shone all white. They launched themselves as at the throats of those who stood resisting. The space between dwindled to an insignificant distance.

The youth had centered the gaze of his soul upon that other flag. Its possession would be high pride. It would express bloody minglings, near blows. He had a gigantic hatred for those who made great difficulties and complications. They cause it to be as a craved treasure of mythology, hung amid tasks and contrivances of danger.

He plunged like a mad horse at it. He was resolved it should not escape if wild blows and darings of blows could seize it. His own emblem, quivering and aflare, was winging toward the other. It seemed there would shortly be an encounter of strange beaks and claws, as of eagles.

The swirling body of blue men came to a sudden halt at close and disastrous range and roared a swift volley. The group in gray was split and broken by this fire, but its riddled body still fought. The men in blue yelled again and rushed in upon it.

The youth, in his leapings, saw, as through a mist, a picture of four or five men stretched upon the ground or writhing upon their knees with bowed heads as if they had been stricken by bolts from the sky. Tottering among them was the rival color bearer, who the youth saw had been bitten vitally by the bullets of the last formidable volley. He perceived this man fighting a last struggle, the struggle of one whose legs are grasped by demons. It was a ghastly battle. Over his face was the bleach of death, but set upon it were the dark and hard lines of desperate purpose. With this terrible grin of resolution he hugged his precious flag to him and was stumbling and staggering in his design to go the way that led to safety for it.

But his wounds always made it seem that his feet were retarded, held, and he fought a grim fight, as with invisible ghouls fastened greedily upon his limbs. Those in advance of the scampering blue men, howling cheers, leaped at the fence. The despair of the lost was in his eyes as he glanced back at them.

The youth's friend went over the obstruction in a tumbling heap and sprang at the flag as a panther at prey. He pulled at it and, wrenching it free, swung up its red brilliancy with a mad cry of exultation even as the color bearer, gasping, lurched over in a final throe and, stiffening convulsively, turned his dead face to the ground. There was much blood upon the grass blades.

At the place of success there began more wild clamorings of cheers. The men gesticulated and bellowed in an ecstasy. When they spoke it was as if they considered their listener to be a mile away. What hats and caps were left to them they often slung high in the air.

At one part of the line four men had been swooped upon, and they now sat as prisoners. Some blue men were about them in an eager and curious circle. The soldiers had trapped strange birds, and there was an examination. A flurry of fast questions was in the air.

One of the prisoners was nursing a superficial wound in the foot. He cuddled it baby-wise, but he looked up from it often to curse with an astonishing utter abandon straight at the noses of his captors. He consigned them to red regions; he called upon the pestilential wrath of strange gods. And with it all he was singularly free from recognition of the finer points of the conduct of prisoners of war. It was as if a clumsy clod had trod upon his toe and he conceived it to be his privilege, his duty, to use deep, resentful oaths.

Another, who was a boy in years, took his plight with great calmness and apparent good nature. He conversed with the men in blue, studying their faces with his bright and keen eyes. They spoke of battles and conditions. There was an acute interest in all their faces during this exchange of view points. It seemed a great satisfaction to hear voices from where all had been darkness and speculation.

The third captive sat with a morose countenance. He preserved a stoical and cold attitude. To all advances he made one reply without variation. "Ah, go t' hell!"

The last of the four was always silent and, for the most part, kept his face turned in unmolested directions. From the views the youth received he seemed to be in a state of absolute dejection. Shame was upon him, and with it profound regret that he was, perhaps, no more to be counted in the ranks of his fellows. The youth could detect no expression that would allow him to believe that the other was giving a thought to his narrowed future, the pictured dungeons, perhaps, and starvations and brutalities, liable to the imagination. All to be seen was shame for captivity and regret for the right to antagonize.

After the men had celebrated sufficiently they settled down behind the old rail fence, on the opposite side to the one from which their foes had been driven. A few shot perfunctorily at distant marks.

There was some long grass. The youth nestled in it and rested, making a convenient rail support the flag. His friend, jubilant and glorified, holding his treasure with vanity, came to him there. They sat side by side and congratulated each other.

CHAPTER XXIV

The roarings that had stretched in a long line of sound across the face of the forest began to grow intermittent and weaker. The stentorian speeches of the artillery continued in some distant encounter, but the crashes of the musketry had almost ceased. The youth and his friend of a sudden looked up, feeling a deadened form of distress at the waning of these noises, which had become a part of life. They could see changes going on among the troops. There were marchings this way and that way. A battery wheeled leisurely. On the crest of a small hill was the thick gleam of many departing muskets.

The youth arose. "Well, what now, I wonder?" he said. By his tone he seemed to be preparing to resent some new monstrosity in the way of dins and smashes. he shaded his eyes with his grimy hand and gazed over the field.

His friend also arose and stared. "I bet we're goin' t' git along out of this an' back over th' river," said he.

"Well, I swan!" said the youth.

They waited, watching. Within a little while the regiment received orders to retrace its way. The men got up grunting from the grass, regretting the soft repose. They jerked their stiffened legs, and stretched their arms over their heads. One man swore as he rubbed his eyes. They all groaned "O Lord!" They had as many objections to this change as they would have had to a proposal for a new battle.

They trampled slowly back over the field across which they had run in a mad scamper.

The regiment marched until it had joined its fellows. The reformed brigade, in column, aimed through a wood at the road. Directly they were in a mass of dust-covered troops, and were trudging along in a way parallel to the enemy's lines as these had been defined by the previous turmoil.

They passed within view of a stolid white house, and saw in front of it groups of their comrades lying in wait behind a neat breastwork. A row of guns were booming at a distant enemy. Shells thrown in reply were raising clouds of dust and splinters. Horsemen dashed along the line of entrenchments.

At this point of its march the division curved away from the field and went winding off in the direction of the river. When the significance of this movement had impressed itself upon the youth he turned his head and looked over his shoulder toward the trampled and *débris*-strewed ground. He breathed a breath of new satisfaction. He finally nudged his friend. "Well, it's all over," he said to him.

His friend gazed backward. "B'Gawd, it is," he assented. They mused.

For a time the youth was obliged to reflect in a puzzled and uncertain way. His mind was undergoing a subtle change. It took moments for it to cast off its battleful ways and resume its accustomed course of thought. Gradually his brain emerged from the clogged clouds, and at last he was enabled to more closely comprehend himself and circumstance.

He understood then that the existence of shot and counter-shot was in the past. He had dwelt in a land of strange, squalling upheavals and had come forth. He had been where there was red of blood and black of passion, and he was escaped. His first thoughts were given to rejoicings at this fact.

Later he began to study his deeds, his failures, and his achievements. Thus, fresh from scenes where many of his usual machines of reflection had been idle, from where he had proceeded sheeplike, he struggled to marshal all his acts.

At last they marched before him clearly. From this present view point he was enabled to look upon them in spectator fashion and to criticise them with some correctness, for his new condition had already defeated certain sympathies.

Regarding his procession of memory he felt gleeful and unregretting, for in it his public deeds were paraded in great and shining prominence. Those performances which had been witnessed by his fellows marched now in wide purple and gold, having various deflections. They went gayly with music. It was pleasure to watch these things. He spent delightful minutes viewing the gilded images of memory.

He saw that he was good. He recalled with a thrill of joy the respectful comments of his fellows upon his conduct.

Nevertheless, the ghost of his flight from the first engagement appeared to him and danced. There were small shoutings in his brain about these matters. For a moment he blushed, and the light of his soul flickered with shame.

A specter of reproach came to him. There loomed the dogging memory of the tattered soldier—he who, gored by bullets and faint for blood, had fretted concerning an imagined wound in another; he who had loaned his last of strength and intellect for the tall soldier; he who, blind with weariness and pain, had been deserted in the field.

For an instant a wretched chill of sweat was upon him at the thought that he might be detected in the thing. As he stood persistently before his vision, he gave vent to a cry of sharp irritation and agony.

His friend turned. "What's the matter, Henry?" he demanded. The youth's reply was an outburst of crimson oaths.

As he marched along the little branch-hung roadway among his prattling companions this vision of cruelty brooded over him. It clung near him always and darkened his view of these deeds in purple and gold. Whichever way his thoughts turned they were followed by the somber phantom of the desertion in the fields. He looked stealthily at his companions, feeling sure that they must discern in his face evidences of this pursuit. But they were plodding in ragged array, discussing with quick tongues the accomplishments of the late battle.

"Oh, if a man should come up an' ask me, I'd say we got a dum good lickin'."

"Lickin'—in yer eye! We ain't licked, sonny. We're goin' down here aways, swing aroun', and' come in behint 'em."

"Oh, hush, with your comin' in behint 'em. I've seen all 'a that I wanta. Don't tell me about comin' in behint——"

"Bill Smithers, he ses he'd rather been in ten hundred battles than been in that heluva hospital. He ses they got shootin' in th' night-time, an' shells dropped plum among 'em in th' hospital. He ses sech hollerin' he never see."

"Hasbrouck? He's th' best off'cer in this here reg'ment. He's a whale."

"Didn't I tell yeh we'd come aroun' in behint 'em? Didn't I tell yeh so? We——"

"Oh, shet yeh mouth!"

For a time this pursuing recollection of the tattered man took all elation from the youth's veins. He saw his vivid error, and he was afraid that it would stand before him all his life. He took no share in the chatter of his comrades, nor did he look at them or know them, save when he felt sudden suspicion that they were seeing his thoughts and scrutinizing each detail of the scene with the tattered soldier.

Yet gradually he mustered force to put the sin at a distance. And at last his eyes seemed to open to some new ways. He found that he could look back upon the brass and bombast of his earlier gospels and see them truly. He was gleeful when he discovered that he now despised them.

With this conviction came a store of assurance. He felt a quiet manhood, nonassertive but of sturdy and strong blood. He knew that he would no more quail before his guides wherever they should point. He had been to touch the great death, and found that, after all, it was but the great death. He was a man.

So it came to pass that as he trudged from the place of blood and wrath his soul changed. He came from hot plowshares[1] to prospects of clover tranquilly, and it was as if hot plowshares were not. Scars faded as flowers.

It rained. The procession of weary soldiers became a bedraggled train, despondent and muttering, marching with churning effort in a trough of liquid brown mud under a low, wretched sky. Yet the youth smiled, for he saw that the world was a world for him, though many discovered it to be made of oaths and walking sticks. He had rid himself of the red sickness of battle. The sultry nightmare was in the past. He had been an animal blistered and sweating in the heat and pain of war. He turned now with a lover's thirst to images of tranquil skies, fresh meadows, cool brooks—an existence of soft and eternal peace.

Over the river a golden ray of sun came through the hosts of leaden rain clouds.

1894, 1895

---

[1]Possibly a reference to Isaiah 2:4, "they shall beat their swords into plowshares," or a reference to the medieval "ordeal by fire," in which the person to be tested was required to grasp hot iron or to walk with bare feet over a row of heated plowshares.

THE OPEN BOAT

A Tale Intended to Be After the Fact.
Being the Experience of Four Men
from the Sunk Steamer Commodore[1]

I

None of them knew the color of the sky. Their eyes glanced level, and were fastened upon the waves that swept toward them. These waves were of the hue of slate, save for the tops, which were of foaming white, and all of the men knew the colors of the sea. The horizon narrowed and widened, and dipped and rose, and at all times its edge was jagged with waves that seemed thrust up in points like rocks.

Many a man ought to ha .e a bath-tub larger than the boat which here rode upon the sea. These waves were most wrongfully and barbarously abrupt and tall, and each froth-top was a problem in small boat navigation.

The cook squatted in the bottom and looked with both eyes at the six inches of gunwale[2] which separated him from the ocean. His sleeves were rolled over his fat forearms, and the two flaps of his unbuttoned vest dangled as he bent to bail out the boat. Often he said: "gawd! That was a narrow clip." As he remarked it he invariably gazed eastward over the broken sea.

The oiler,[3] steering with one of the two oars in the boat, sometimes raised himself suddenly to keep clear of water that swirled in over the stern. It was a thin little oar and it seemed often ready to snap.

The correspondent, pulling at the other oar, watched the waves and wondered why he was there.

The injured captain, lying in the bow, was at this time buried in that profound dejection and indifference which comes, temporarily at least, to even the bravest and most enduring when, willy nilly, the firm fails, the army loses, the ship goes down. The mind of the master of a vessel is rooted deep in the timbers of her, though he command for a day or a decade, and this captain had on him the stern impression of a scene in the grays of dawn of seven turned faces, and later a stump of a top-mast with a white ball on it that slashed to and fro at the waves, went low and lower, and down. Thereafter there was something strange in his voice. Although steady, it was deep with mourning, and of a quality beyond oration or tears.

"Keep 'er a little more south, Billie," said he.

" 'A little more south,' sir," said the oiler in the stern.

A seat in this boat was not unlike a seat upon a bucking broncho, and, by the same token, a broncho is not much smaller. The craft pranced and reared, and plunged like an animal. As each wave came, and she rose for it, she seemed like a horse making at a fence outrageously high. The manner of her scramble over these walls of water is a mystic thing, and, moreover, at the top of them were ordinarily these problems in white water, the foam racing down from the summit

---

[1]Crane, on his way to report the Cuban Revolution, was aboard the tug *Commodore*, bound for Cuba with a cargo of arms for the revolutionaries, when it sank off the coast of Florida, January 2, 1897. After almost thirty hours at sea in a small dingey, Crane landed at Daytona, Florida. Soon thereafter he shaped the details of his experience into a short story.

[2]The upper sides of a boat.

[3]A crewman of a ship's engine-room who oils machinery.

of each wave, requiring a new leap, and a leap from the air. Then, after scornfully bumping a crest, she would slide, and race, and splash down a long incline and arrive bobbing and nodding in front of the next menace.

A singular disadvantage of the sea lies in the fact that after successfully surmounting one wave you discover that there is another behind it just as important and just as nervously anxious to do something effective in the way of swamping boats. In a ten-foot dingey one can get an idea of the resources of the sea in the line of waves that is not probable to the average experience, which is never at sea in a dingey. As each salty wall of water approached, it shut all else from the view of the men in the boat, and it was the final outburst of the ocean, the last effort of the grim water. There was a terrible grace in the move of the waves, and they came in silence, save for the snarling of the crests.

In the wan light, the faces of the men must have been gray. Their eyes must have glinted in strange ways as they gazed steadily astern. Viewed from a balcony, the whole thing would doubtlessly have been weirdly picturesque. But the men in the boat had no time to see it, and if they had had leisure there were other things to occupy their minds. The sun swung steadily up the sky, and they knew it was broad day because the color of the sea changed from slate to emerald-green, streaked with amber lights, and the foam was like tumbling snow. The process of the breaking day was unknown to them. They were aware only of this effect upon the color of the waves that rolled toward them.

In disjointed sentences the cook and the correspondent argued as to the difference between a life-saving station and a house of refuge. The cook had said: "There's a house of refuge just north of the Mosquito Inlet Light, and as soon as they see us, they'll come off in their boat and pick us up."

"As soon as who see us?" said the correspondent.

"The crew," said the cook.

"Houses of refuge don't have crews," said the correspondent. "As I understand them, they are only places where clothes and grub are stored for the benefit of shipwrecked people. They don't carry crews."

"Oh, yes, they do," said the cook.

"No, they don't," said the correspondent.

"Well, we're not there yet, anyhow," said the oiler, in the stern.

"Well," said the cook, "perhaps it's not a house of refuge that I'm thinking of as being near Mosquito Inlet Light. Perhaps it's a life-saving station."

"We're not there yet," said the oiler, in the stern.

II

As the boat bounced from the top of each wave, the wind tore through the hair of the hatless men, and as the craft plopped her stern down again the spray slashed past them. The crest of each of these waves was a hill, from the top of which the men surveyed, for a moment, a broad tumultuous expanse, shining and wind-riven. It was probably splendid. It was probably glorious, this play of the free sea, wild with lights of emerald and white and amber.

"Bully good thing it's an on-shore wind," said the cook. "If not, where would we be? Wouldn't have a show."

"That's right," said the correspondent.

The busy oiler nodded his assent.

Then the captain, in the bow, chuckled in a way that expressed humor, contempt, tragedy, all in one. "Do you think we've got much of a show, now, boys?" said he.

Whereupon the three were silent, save for a trifle of hemming and hawing. To express any particular optimism at this time they felt to be childish and stupid, but they all doubtless possessed this sense of the situation in their mind. A young man thinks doggedly at such times. On the other hand, the ethics of their condition was decidedly against any open suggestion of hopelessness. So they were silent.

"Oh, well," said the captain, soothing his children, "we'll get ashore all right."

But there was that in his tone which made them think, so the oiler quoth: "Yes! If this wind holds!"

The cook was bailing. "Yes! If we don't catch hell in the surf."

Canton flannel[1] gulls flew near and far. Sometimes they sat down on the sea, near patches of brown sea-weed that rolled over the waves with a movement like carpets on a line in a gale. The birds sat comfortably in groups, and they were envied by some in the dingey, for the wrath of the sea was no more to them than it was to a covey of prairie chickens a thousand miles inland. Often they came very close and stared at the men with black bead-like eyes. At these times they were uncanny and sinister in their unblinking scrutiny, and the men hooted angrily at them, telling them to be gone. One came, and evidently decided to alight on the top of the captain's head. The bird flew parallel to the boat and did not circle, but made short sidelong jumps in the air in chicken-fashion. His black eyes were wistfully fixed upon the captain's head. "Ugly brute," said the oiler to the bird. "You look as if you were made with a jack-knife." The cook and the correspondent swore darkly at the creature. The captain naturally wished to knock it away with the end of the heavy painter,[2] but he did not dare do it, because anything resembling an emphatic gesture would have capsized this freighted boat, and so with his open hand, the captain gently and carefully waved the gull away. After it had been discouraged from the pursuit the captain breathed easier on account of his hair, and others breathed easier because the bird struck their minds at this time as being somehow gruesome and ominous.

In the meantime the oiler and the correspondent rowed. And also they rowed.

They sat together in the same seat, and each rowed an oar. Then the oiler took both oars; then the correspondent took both oars; then the oiler; then the correspondent. They rowed and they rowed. The very ticklish part of the business was when the time came for the reclining one in the stern to take his turn at the oars. By the very last star of truth, it is easier to steal eggs from under a hen than it was to change seats in the dingey. First the man in the stern slid his hand along the thwart[3] and moved with care, as if he were of Sèvres.[4] Then the man in the rowing seat slid his hand along the other thwart. It was all done with the most extraordinary care. As the two sidled past each other, the whole party kept watchful eyes on the coming wave, and the captain cried: "Look out now! Steady there!"

The brown mats of sea-weed that appeared from time to time were like islands, bits of earth. They were travelling, apparently, neither one way nor the other. They were, to all intents, stationary. They informed the men in the boat that it was making progress slowly toward the land.

The captain, rearing cautiously in the bow, after the dingey soared on a great swell, said that he had seen the light-house at Mosquito Inlet. Presently the cook

---

[1]Cotton flannel.   [2]Rope for tying the boat to a wharf.
[3]A rower's seat built into the boat crosswise (athwart) to the keel.
[4]Delicate china made in Sèvres, France.

remarked that he had seen it. The correspondent was at the oars, then, and for some reason he too wished to look at the light-house, but his back was toward the far shore and the waves were important, and for some time he could not seize an opportunity to turn his head. But at last there came a wave more gentle than the others, and when at the crest of it he swiftly scoured the western horizon.

"See it?" said the captain.

"No," said the correspondent, slowly, "I didn't see anything."

"Look again," said the captain. He pointed. "It's exactly in that direction."

At the top of another wave, the correspondent did as he was bid, and this time his eyes chanced on a small still thing on the edge of the swaying horizon. It was precisely like the point of a pin. It took an anxious eye to find a light-house so tiny.

"Think we'll make it, Captain?"

"If this wind holds and the boat don't swamp, we can't do much else," said the captain.

The little boat, lifted by each towering sea, and splashed viciously by the crests, made progress that in the absence of sea-weed was not apparent to those in her. She seemed just a wee thing wallowing, miraculously, top-up, at the mercy of five oceans. Occasionally, a great spread of water, like white flames, swarmed into her.

"Bail her, cook," said the captain, serenely.

"All right, Captain," said the cheerful cook.

III

It would be difficult to describe the subtle brotherhood of men that was here established on the seas. No one said that it was so. No one mentioned it, but it dwelt in the boat, and each man felt it warm him. They were a captain, an oiler, a cook, and a correspondent, and they were friends, friends in a more curiously ironbound degree than may be common. The hurt captain, lying against the water-jar in the bow, spoke always in a low voice and calmly but he could never command a more ready and swiftly obedient crew than the motley three of the dingey. It was more than a mere recognition of what was best for the common safety. There was surely in it a quality that was personal and heartfelt. And after this devotion to the commander of the boat there was this comradeship that the correspondent, for instance, who had been taught to be cynical of men, knew even at the time was the best experience of his life. But no one said that it was so. No one mentioned it.

"I wish we had a sail," remarked the captain. "We might try my overcoat on the end of an oar and give you two boys a chance to rest." So the cook and the correspondent held the mast and spread wide the overcoat, the oiler steered, and the little boat made good way with her new rig. Sometimes the oiler had to scull sharply to keep a sea from breaking into the boat, but otherwise sailing was a success.

Meanwhile the light-house had been growing slowly larger. It had now almost assumed color, and appeared like a little gray shadow on the sky. The man at the oars could not be prevented from turning his head rather often to try for a glimpse of this little gray shadow.

At last, from the top of each wave the men in the tossing boat could see land. Even as the light-house was an upright shadow on the sky, this land seemed but a long black shadow on the sea. It certainly was thinner than paper. "We must be about opposite New Smyrna," said the cook, who had coasted this shore often in schooners. "Captain, by the way, I believe they abandoned that life-saving station there about a year ago."

"Did they?" said the captain.

The wind slowly died away. The cook and the correspondent were not now obliged to slave in order to hold high the oar. But the waves continued their old impetuous swooping at the dingey, and the little craft, no longer under way, struggled woundily over them. The oiler or the correspondent took the oars again.

Shipwrecks are *apropos* of nothing. If men could only train for them and have them occur when the men had reached pink condition, there would be less drowning at sea. Of the four in the dingey none had slept any time worth mentioning for two days and two nights previous to embarking in the dingey, and in the excitement of clambering about the deck of a foundering ship they had also forgotten to eat heartily.

For these reasons, and for others, neither the oiler nor the correspondent was fond of rowing at this time. The correspondent wondered ingenuously how in the name of all that was sane could there be people who thought it amusing to row a boat. It was not an amusement; it was a diabolical punishment, and even a genius of mental aberrations could never conclude that it was anything but a horror to the muscles and a crime against the back. He mentioned to the boat in general how the amusement of rowing struck him, and the weary-faced oiler smiled in full sympathy. Previously to the foundering, by the way, the oiler had worked double-watch in the engine-room of the ship.

"Take her easy, now, boys," said the captain. "Don't spend yourselves. If we have to run a surf you'll need all your strength, because we'll sure have to swim for it. Take your time."

Slowly the land arose from the sea. From a black line it became a line of black and a line of white—trees and sand. Finally, the captain said that he could make out a house on the shore. "That's the house of refuge, sure," said the cook. "They'll see us before long, and come out after us."

The distant light-house reared high. "The keeper ought to be able to make us out now, if he's looking through a glass," said the captain. "He'll notify the life-saving people."

"None of those other boats could have got ashore to give word of the wreck," said the oiler, in a low voice. "Else the life-boat would be out hunting us."

Slowly and beautifully the land loomed out of the sea. The wind came again. It had veered from the northeast to the southeast. Finally, a new sound struck the ears of the men in the boat. It was the low thunder of the surf on the shore. "We'll never be able to make the light-house now," said the captain. "Swing her head a little more north, Billie."

" 'A little more north,' sir," said the oiler.

Whereupon the little boat turned her nose once more down the wind, and all but the oarsman watched the shore grow. Under the influence of this expansion doubt and direful apprehension were leaving the minds of the men. The management of the boat was still most absorbing, but it could not prevent a quiet cheerfulness. In an hour, perhaps, they would be ashore.

Their back-bones had become thoroughly used to balancing in the boat and they now rode this wild colt of a dingey like circus men. The correspondent thought that he had been drenched to the skin, but happening to feel in the top pocket of his coat, he found therein eight cigars. Four of them were soaked with seawater; four were perfectly scatheless. After a search, somebody produced three dry matches, and thereupon the four waifs rode impudently in their little boat, and with an assurance of an impending rescue shining in their eyes, puffed at the big cigars and judged well and ill of all men. Everybody took a drink of water.

IV

"Cook," remarked the captain, "there don't seem to be any signs of life about your house of refuge."

"No," replied the cook. "Funny they don't see us!"

A broad stretch of lowly coast lay before the eyes of the men. It was dunes topped with dark vegetation. The roar of the surf was plain, and sometimes they could see the white lip of a wave as it spun up the beach. A tiny house was blocked out black upon the sky. Southward, the slim light-house lifted its little gray length.

Tide, wind, and waves were swinging the dingey northward. "Funny they don't see us," said the men.

The surf's roar was here dulled, but its tone was, nevertheless, thunderous and mighty. As the boat swam over the great rollers, the men sat listening to this roar. "We'll swamp sure," said everybody.

It is fair to say here that there was not a life-saving station within twenty miles in either direction, but the men did not know this fact and in consequence they made dark and opprobrious remarks concerning the eyesight of the nation's life-savers. For scowling men sat in the dingey and surpassed records in the invention of epithets.

"Funny they don't see us."

The light-heartedness of a former time had completely faded. To their sharpened minds it was easy to conjure pictures of all kinds of incompetency and blindness and indeed, cowardice. There was the shore of the populous land, and it was bitter and bitter to them that from it came no sign.

"Well," said the captain, ultimately, "I suppose we'll have to make a try for ourselves. If we stay out here too long, we'll none of us have strength left to swim after the boat swamps."

And so the oiler, who was at the oars, turned the boat straight for the shore. There was a sudden tightening of muscles. There was some thinking.

"If we don't all get ashore—" said the captain. "If we don't all get ashore, I suppose you fellows know where to send news of my finish?"

They then briefly exchanged some addresses and admonitions. As for the reflections of the men, there was a great deal of rage in them. Perchance they might be formulated thus: "If I am going to be drowned—if I am going to be drowned—if I am going to be drowned, why, in the name of the seven mad gods who rule the sea, was I allowed to come thus far and contemplate sand and trees? Was I brought here merely to have my nose dragged away as I was about to nibble the sacred cheese of life? It is preposterous. If this old ninny-woman, Fate, cannot do better than this, she should be deprived of the management of men's fortunes. She is an old hen who knows not her intention. If she has decided to drown me, why did she not do it in the beginning and save me all this trouble. The whole affair is absurd. . . . But, no, she cannot mean to drown me. She dare not drown me.

She cannot drown me. Not after all this work." Afterward the man might have had an impulse to shake his fist at the clouds. "Just you drown me, now, and then hear what I call you!"

The billows that came at this time were more formidable. They seemed always just about to break and roll over the little boat in a turmoil of foam. There was a preparatory and long growl in the speech of them. No mind unused to the sea would have concluded that the dingey could ascend these sheer heights in time. The shore was still afar. The oiler was a wily surfman. "Boys," he said, swiftly, "she won't live three minutes more and we're too far out to swim. Shall I take her to sea again, Captain?"

"Yes! Go ahead!" said the captain.

This oiler, by a series of quick miracles, and fast and steady oarsmanship, turned the boat in the middle of the surf and took her safely to sea again.

There was a considerable silence as the boat bumped over the furrowed sea to deeper water. Then somebody in gloom spoke. "Well, anyhow, they must have seen us from the shore by now."

The gulls went in slanting flight up the wind toward the gray desolate east. A squall, marked by dingy clouds, and clouds brick-red, like smoke from a burning building, appeared from the southeast.

"What do you think of those life-saving people? Ain't they peaches?"

"Funny they haven't seen us."

"Maybe they think we're out here for sport! Maybe they think we're fishin'. Maybe they think we're damned fools."

It was a long afternoon. A changed tide tried to force them southward, but wind and wave said northward. Far ahead, where coastline, sea, and sky formed their mighty angle, there were little dots which seemed to indicate a city on the shore.

"St. Augustine?"

The captain shook his head. "Too near Mosquito Inlet."

And the oiler rowed, and then the correspondent rowed. Then the oiler rowed. It was a weary business. The human back can become the seat of more aches and pains than are registered in books for the composite anatomy of a regiment. It is a limited area, but it can become the theatre of innumerable muscular conflicts, tangles, wrenches, knots, and other comforts.

"Did you ever like to row, Billie?" asked the correspondent.

"No," said the oiler. "Hang it."

When one exchanged the rowing-seat for a place in the bottom of the boat, he suffered a bodily depression that caused him to be careless of everything save an obligation to wiggle one finger. There was cold sea-water swashing to and fro in the boat, and he lay in it. His head, pillowed on a thwart, was within an inch of the swirl of a wave crest, and sometimes a particularly obstreperous sea came in-board and drenched him once more. But these matters did not annoy him. It is almost certain that if the boat had capsized he would have tumbled comfortably out upon the ocean as if he felt sure that it was a great soft mattress.

"Look! There's a man on the shore!"

"Where?"

"There! See 'im? See 'im?"

"Yes, sure! He's walking along."

"Now he's stopping. Look! He's facing us!"

"He's waving at us!"

"So he is! By thunder!"

"Ah, now, we're all right! Now we're all right! There'll be a boat out here for us in half an hour."

"He's going on. He's running. He's going up to that house there."

The remote beach seemed lower than the sea, and it required a searching glance to discern the little black figure. The captain saw a floating stick and they rowed to it. A bath-towel was by some weird chance in the boat, and, tying this on the stick, the captain waved it. The oarsman did not dare turn his head, so he was obliged to ask questions.

"What's he doing now?"

"He's standing still again. He's looking, I think. . . . There he goes again. Toward the house. . . . Now he's stopped again."

"Is he waving at us?"

"No, not now; he was, though."

"Look! There comes another man!"

"He's running."

"Look at him go, would you."

"Why, he's on a bicycle. Now he's met the other man. They're both waving at us. Look!"

"There comes something up the beach."

"What the devil is that thing?"

"Why, it looks like a boat."

"Why, certainly it's a boat."

"No, it's on wheels."

"Yes, so it is. Well, that must be the life-boat. They drag them along shore on a wagon."

"That's the life-boat, sure."

"No, by———, it's—it's an omnibus."

"I tell you it's a life-boat."

"It is not! It's an omnibus. I can see it plain. See? One of those big hotel omnibuses."

"By thunder, you're right. It's an omnibus, sure as fate. What do you suppose they are doing with an omnibus? Maybe they are going around collecting the life-crew, hey?"

"That's it, likely. Look! There's a fellow waving a little black flag. He's standing on the steps of the omnibus. There come those other two fellows. Now they're all talking together. Look at the fellow with the flag. Maybe he ain't waving it!"

"That ain't a flag, is it? That's his coat. Why, certainly, that's his coat."

"So it is. It's his coat. He's taken it off and is waving it around his head. But would you look at him swing it!"

"Oh, say, there isn't any life-saving station here. That's just a winter resort hotel omnibus that has brought over some of the boarders to see us drown."

"What's that idiot with the coat mean? What's he signaling, anyhow?"

"It looks as if he were trying to tell us to go north. There must be a life-saving station up there."

"No! He thinks we're fishing. Just giving us a merry hand. See? Ah, there, Willie."

"Well, I wish I could make something out of those signals. What do you suppose he means?"

"He don't mean anything. He's just playing."

"Well, if he'd just signal us to try the surf again, or to go to sea and wait, or go north, or go south, or go to hell—there would be some reason in it. But look at him. He just stands there and keeps his coat revolving like a wheel. The ass!"

"There come more people."

"Now there's quite a mob. Look! Isn't that a boat?"

"Where? Oh, I see where you mean. No, that's no boat."

"That fellow is still waving his coat."

"He must think we like to see him do that. Why don't he quit it. It don't mean anything."

"I don't know. I think he is trying to make us go north. It must be that there's a life-saving station there somewhere."

"Say, he ain't tired yet. Look at 'im wave."

"Wonder how long he can keep that up. He's been revolving his coat ever since he caught sight of us. He's an idiot. Why aren't they getting men to bring a boat out. A fishing boat—one of those big yawls—could come out here all right. Why don't he do something?"

"Oh, it's all right, now."

"They'll have a boat out here for us in less than no time, now that they've seen us."

A faint yellow tone came into the sky over the low land. The shadows on the sea slowly deepened. The wind bore coldness with it, and the men began to shiver.

"Holy smoke!" said one, allowing his voice to express his impious mood, "if we keep on monkeying out here! If we've got to flounder out here all night!"

"Oh, we'll never have to stay here all night! don't you worry. They've seen us now, and it won't be long before they'll come chasing out after us."

The shore grew dusky. The man waving a coat blended gradually into the gloom, and it swallowed in the same manner the omnibus and the group of people. The spray, when it dashed uproariously over the side, made the voyagers shrink and swear like men who were being branded.

"I'd like to catch the chump who waved the coat. I feel like soaking him one, just for luck."

"Why? What did he do?"

"Oh, nothing, but then he seemed so damned cheerful."

In the meantime the oiler rowed, and then the correspondent rowed, and then the oiler rowed. Gray-faced and bowed forward, they mechanically, turn by turn, plied the leaden oars. The form of the light-house had vanished from the southern horizon, but finally a pale star appeared, just lifting from the sea. The streaked saffron in the west passed before the all-merging darkness, and the sea to the east was black. The land had vanished, and was expressed only by the low and drear thunder of the surf.

"If I am going to be drowned—if I am going to be drowned—if I am going to be drowned, why, in the name of the seven mad gods who rule the sea, was I allowed to come thus far and contemplate sand and trees? Was I brought here merely to have my nose dragged away as I was about to nibble the sacred cheese of life?"

The patient captain, drooped over the water-jar, was sometimes obliged to speak to the oarsman.

"Keep her head up! Keep her head up!"

" 'Keep her head up,' sir." The voices were weary and low.

This was surely a quiet evening. All save the oarsman lay heavily and listlessly in the boat's bottom. As for him, his eyes were just capable of noting the tall black waves that swept forward in a most sinister silence, save for an occasional subdued growl of a crest.

The cook's head was on a thwart, and he looked without interest at the water under his nose. He was deep in other scenes. Finally he spoke. "Billie," he murmured, dreamfully, "what kind of pie do you like best?"

V

"Pie," said the oiler and the correspondent, agitatedly. "Don't talk about those things, blast you!"

"Well," said the cook, "I was just thinking about ham sandwiches, and—"

A night on the sea in an open boat is a long night. As darkness settled finally, the shine of the light, lifting from the sea in the south, changed to full gold. On the northern horizon a new light appeared, a small bluish gleam on the edge of the waters. These two lights were the furniture of the world. Otherwise there was nothing but waves.

Two men huddled in the stern, and distances were so magnificent in the dingey that the rower was enabled to keep his feet partly warmed by thrusting them under his companions. Their legs indeed extended far under the rowing-seat until they touched the feet of the captain forward. Sometimes, despite the efforts of the tired oarsman, a wave came piling into the boat, an icy wave of the night, and the chilling water soaked them anew. They would twist their bodies for a moment and groan, and sleep the dead sleep once more, while the water in the boat gurgled about them as the craft rocked.

The plan of the oiler and the correspondent was for one to row until he lost the ability, and then arouse the other from his sea-water couch in the bottom of the boat.

The oiler plied the oars until his head drooped forward, and the overpowering sleep blinded him. And he rowed yet afterward. Then he touched a man in the bottom of the boat, and called his name. "Will you spell for me a little while?" he said, meekly.

"Sure, Billie," said the correspondent, awakening and dragging himself to a sitting position. They exchanged places carefully, and the oiler, cuddling down in the sea-water at the cook's side, seemed to go to sleep instantly.

The particular violence of the sea had ceased. The waves came without snarling. The obligation of the man at the oars was to keep the boat headed so that the tilt of the rollers would not capsize her, and to preserve her from filling when the crests rushed past. The black waves were silent and hard to be seen in the darkness. Often one was almost upon the boat before the oarsman was aware.

In a low voice the correspondent addressed the captain. He was not sure that the captain was awake, although this iron man seemed to be always awake. "Captain, shall I keep her making for that light north, sir?"

The same steady voice answered him. "Yes. Keep it about two points off the port bow."

The cook had tied a life-belt around himself in order to get even the warmth which this clumsy cork contrivance could donate, and he seemed almost stove-like when a rower, whose teeth invariably chattered wildly as soon as he ceased his labor, drooped down to sleep.

The correspondent, as he rowed, looked down at the two men sleeping under foot. The cook's arm was around the oiler's shoulders, and, with their fragmentary clothing and haggard faces, they were the babes of the sea, a grotesque rendering of the old babes in the wood.

Later he must have grown stupid at his work, for suddenly there was a growling of water, and a crest came with a roar and a swash into the boat, and it was a wonder that it did not set the cook afloat in his life-belt. The cook continued to sleep, but the oiler sat up, blinking his eyes and shaking with the new cold.

"Oh, I'm awful sorry, Billie," said the correspondent, contritely.

"That's all right, old boy," said the oiler, and lay down again and was asleep.

Presently it seemed that even the captain dozed, and the correspondent thought that he was the one man afloat on all the oceans. The wind had a voice as it came over the waves, and it was sadder than the end.

There was a long, loud swishing astern of the boat, and a gleaming trail of phosphorescence, like blue flame, was furrowed on the black waters. It might have been made by a monstrous knife.

Then there came a stillness, while the correspondent breathed with the open mouth and looked at the sea.

Suddenly there was another swish and another long flash of bluish light, and this time it was alongside the boat, and might almost have been reached with an oar. The correspondent saw an enormous fin speed like a shadow through the water, hurling the crystalline spray and leaving the long glowing trail.

The correspondent looked over his shoulder at the captain. His face was hidden, and he seemed to be asleep. He looked at the babes of the sea. They certainly were asleep. So, being bereft of sympathy, he leaned a little way to one side and swore softly into the sea.

But the thing did not then leave the vicinity of the boat. Ahead or astern, on one side or the other, at intervals long or short, fled the long sparkling streak, and there was to be heard the whiroo of the dark fin. The speed and power of the thing was greatly to be admired. It cut the water like a gigantic and keen projectile.

The presence of this biding thing did not affect the man with the same horror that it would if he had been a picknicker. He simply looked at the sea dully and swore in an undertone.

Nevertheless, it is true that he did not wish to be alone with the thing. He wished one of his companions to awaken by chance and keep him company with it. But the captain hung motionless over the water-jar and the oiler and the cook in the bottom of the boat were plunged in slumber.

VI

"If I am going to be drowned—if I am going to be drowned—if I am going to be drowned, why, in the name of the seven mad gods who rule the sea, was I allowed to come thus far and contemplate sand and trees?"

During this dismal night, it may be remarked that a man would conclude that it was really the intention of the seven mad gods to drown him, despite the abominable injustice of it. For it was certainly an abominable injustice to drown a man who had worked so hard, so hard. The man felt it would be a crime most unnatural. Other people had drowned at sea since galleys swarmed with painted sails, but still——

When it occurs to a man that nature does not regard him as important, and that she feels she would not maim the universe by disposing of him, he at first wishes to throw bricks at the temple, and he hates deeply the fact that there are no bricks and no temples. Any visible expression of nature would surely be pelleted with his jeers.

Then, if there be no tangible thing to hoot, he feels, perhaps, the desire to confront a personification and indulge in pleas, bowed to one knee, and with hands supplicant, saying: "Yes, but I love myself."

A high cold star on a winter's night is the word he feels that she says to him. Thereafter he knows the pathos of his situation.

The men in the dingey had not discussed these matters, but each had, no doubt, reflected upon them in silence and according to his mind. There was seldom any expression upon their faces save the general one of complete weariness. Speech was devoted to the business of the boat.

To chime the notes of his emotion, a verse mysteriously entered the correspondent's head. He had even forgotten that he had forgotten this verse, but it suddenly was in his mind.

> A soldier of the Legion lay dying in Algiers,
> There was lack of woman's nursing, there was dearth
>   of woman's tears;
> But a comrade stood beside him, and he took that
>   comrade's hand,
> And he said: "I never more shall see my own, my
>   native land."[1]

In his childhood, the correspondent had been made acquainted with the fact that a soldier of the legion lay dying in Algiers, but he had never regarded it as important. Myriads of his school-fellows had informed him of the soldier's plight, but the dinning had naturally ended by making him perfectly indifferent. He had never considered it his affair that a soldier of the Legion lay dying in Algiers, nor had it appeared to him as a matter for sorrow. It was less to him than the breaking of a pencil's point.

Now, however, it quaintly came to him as a human, living thing. It was no longer merely a picture of a few throes in the breast of a poet, meanwhile drinking tea and warming his feet at the grate; it was an actuality—stern, mournful, and fine.

The correspondent plainly saw the soldier. He lay on the sand with his feet out straight and still. While his pale left hand was upon his chest in an attempt to thwart the going of his life, the blood came between his fingers. In the far Algerian distance, a city of low square forms was set against a sky that was faint with the last sunset hues. The correspondent, plying the oars and dreaming of the slow and slower movements of the soldier, was moved by a profound and perfectly impersonal comprehension. He was sorry for the soldier of the Legion who lay dying in Algiers.

The thing which had followed the boat and waited had evidently grown bored at the delay. There was no longer to be heard the slash of the cut-water, and there was no longer the flame of the long trail. The light in the north still glimmered, but it was apparently no nearer to the boat. Sometimes the boom of the surf rang in the correspondent's ears, and he turned the craft seaward then and rowed harder. Southward, some one had evidently built a watch-fire on the beach. It was too low and too far to be seen, but it made a shimmering,

[1]A condensed version of the sentimental poem "Bingen on the Rhine" (1883), by Caroline E. S. Norton (1808–1877).

roseate reflection upon the bluff back of it, and this could be discerned from the boat. The wind came stronger, and sometimes a wave suddenly raged out like a mountain-cat and there was to be seen the sheen and sparkle of a broken crest.

The captain, in the bow, moved on his water-jar and sat erect. "Pretty long night," he observed to the correspondent. He looked at the shore. "Those life-saving people take their time."

"Did you see that shark playing around?"

"Yes, I saw him. He was a big fellow, all right."

"Wish I had known you were awake."

Later the correspondent spoke into the bottom of the boat.

"Billie!" There was a slow and gradual disentanglement. "Billie, will you spell me?"

"Sure," said the oiler.

As soon as the correspondent touched the cold comfortable seawater in the bottom of the boat, and had huddled close to the cook's life-belt he was deep in sleep, despite the fact that his teeth played all the popular airs. This sleep was so good to him that it was but a moment before he heard a voice call his name in a tone that demonstrated the last stages of exhaustion. "Will you spell me?"

"Sure, Billie."

The light in the north had mysteriously vanished, but the correspondent took his course from the wide-awake captain.

Later in the night they took the boat farther out to sea, and the captain directed the cook to take one oar at the stern and keep the boat facing the seas. He was to call out if he should hear the thunder of the surf. This plan enabled the oiler and the correspondent to get respite together. "We'll give those boys a chance to get into shape again," said the captain. They curled down and, after a few preliminary chatterings and trembles, slept once more the dead sleep. Neither knew they had bequeathed to the cook the company of another shark, or perhaps the same shark.

As the boat caroused on the waves, spray occasionally bumped over the side and gave them a fresh soaking, but this had no power to break their repose. The ominous slash of the wind and the water affected them as it would have affected mummies.

"Boys," said the cook, with the notes of every reluctance in his voice, "she's drifted in pretty close. I guess one of you had better take her to sea again." The correspondent, aroused, heard the crash of the toppled crests.

As he was rowing, the captain gave him some whiskey and water, and this steadied the chills out of him. "If I ever get ashore and anybody shows me even a photograph of an oar——"

At last there was a short conversation.

"Billie. . . . Billie, will you spell me?"

"Sure," said the oiler.

VII

When the correspondent again opened his eyes, the sea and the sky were each of the gray hue of the dawning. Later, carmine and gold was painted upon the waters. The morning appeared finally, in its splendor, with a sky of pure blue, and the sunlight flamed on the tips of the waves.

On the distant dunes were set many little black cottages, and a tall white wind-mill reared above them. No man, nor dog, nor bicycle appeared on the beach. The cottages might have formed a deserted village.

The voyagers scanned the shore. A conference was held in the boat. "Well," said the captain, "if no help is coming, we might better try a run through the surf right away. If we stay out here much longer we will be too weak to do anything for ourselves at all." The others silently acquiesced in this reasoning. The boat was headed for the beach. The correspondent wondered if none ever ascended the tall wind-tower, and if then they never looked seaward. This tower was a giant, standing with its back to the plight of the ants. It represented in a degree, to the correspondent, the serenity of nature amid the struggles of the individual—nature in the wind, and nature in the vision of men. She did not seem cruel to him then, nor beneficent, nor treacherous, nor wise. But she was indifferent, flatly indifferent. It is, perhaps, plausible that a man in this situation, impressed with the unconcern of the universe, should see the innumerable flaws of his life and have them taste wickedly in his mind and wish for another chance. A distinction between right and wrong seems absurdly clear to him, then, in this new ignorance of the grave-edge, and he understands that if he were given another opportunity he would mend his conduct and his words, and be better and brighter during an introduction, or a tea.

"Now, boys," said the captain, "she is going to swamp sure. All we can do is to work her in as far as possible, and then when she swamps, pile out and scramble for the beach. Keep cool now, and don't jump until she swamps sure."

The oiler took the oars. Over his shoulders he scanned the surf. "Captain," he said, "I think I'd better bring her about, and keep her head-on to the seas and back her in."

"All right Billie," said the captain. "Back her in." The oiler swung the boat then and, seated in the stern, the cook and the correspondent were obliged to look over their shoulders to contemplate the lonely and indifferent shore.

The monstrous inshore rollers heaved the boat high until the men were again enabled to see the white sheets of water scudding up the slanted beach. "We won't get in very close," said the captain. Each time a man could wrest his attention from the rollers, he turned his glance toward the shore, and in the expression of the eyes during this contemplation there was a singular quality. The correspondent, observing the others, knew that they were not afraid, but the full meaning of their glances was shrouded.

As for himself, he was too tired to grapple fundamentally with the fact. He tried to coerce his mind into thinking of it, but the mind was dominated at this time by the muscles, and the muscles said they did not care. It merely occurred to him that if he should drown it would be a shame.

There were no hurried words, no pallor, no plain agitation. The men simply looked at the shore. "Now, remember to get well clear of the boat when you jump," said the captain.

Seaward the crest of a roller suddenly fell with a thunderous crash, and the long white comber came roaring down upon the boat.

"Steady now," said the captain. The men were silent. They turned their eyes from the shore to the comber and waited. The boat slid up the incline, leaped at the furious top, bounced over it, and swung down the long back of the wave. Some water had been shipped and the cook bailed it out.

But the next crest crashed also. The tumbling boiling flood of white water caught the boat and whirled it almost perpendicular. Water swarmed in from all sides. The correspondent had his hands on the gunwale at this time, and when the water entered at that place he swiftly withdrew his fingers, as if he objected to wetting them.

The little boat, drunken with this weight of water, reeled and snuggled deeper into the sea.

"Bail her out, cook! Bail her out," said the captain.

"All right, Captain," said the cook.

"Now, boys, the next one will do for us, sure," said the oiler. "Mind to jump clear of the boat."

The third wave moved forward, huge, furious, implacable. It fairly swallowed the dingey, and almost simultaneously the men tumbled into the sea. A piece of life-belt had lain in the bottom of the boat, and as the correspondent went overboard he held this to his chest with his left hand.

The January water was icy, and he reflected immediately that it was colder than he had expected to find it off the coast of Florida. This appeared to his dazed mind as a fact important enough to be noted at the time. The coldness of the water was sad; it was tragic. This fact was somehow so mixed and confused with his opinion of his own situation that it seemed almost a proper reason for tears. The water was cold.

When he came to the surface he was conscious of little but the noisy water. Afterward he saw his companions in the sea. The oiler was ahead in the race. He was swimming strongly and rapidly. Off to the correspondent's left, the cook's great white and corked back bulged out of the water, and in the rear the captain was hanging with his one good hand to the keel of the overturned dingey.

There was a certain immovable quality to a shore, and the correspondent wondered at it amid the confusion of the sea.

It seemed also very attractive, but the correspondent knew that it was a long journey, and he paddled leisurely. The piece of life-preserver lay under him, and sometimes he whirled down the incline of a wave as if he were on a hand-sled.

But finally he arrived at a place in the sea where travel was beset with difficulty. He did not pause swimming to inquire what matter of current had caught him, but there his progress ceased. The shore was set before him like a bit of scenery on a stage, and he looked at it and understood with his eyes each detail of it.

As the cook passed, much farther to the left, the captain was calling to him. "Turn over on your back, cook! Turn over on your back and use the oar."

"All right, sir." The cook turned on his back, and, paddling with an oar, went ahead as if he were a canoe.

Presently the boat also passed to the left of the correspondent with the captain clinging with one hand to the keel. He would have appeared like a man raising himself to look over a board fence, if it were not for the extraordinary gymnastics of the boat. The correspondent marvelled that the captain could still hold to it.

They passed on, nearer to shore—the oiler, the cook, the captain—and following them went the water-jar, bouncing gayly over the seas.

The correspondent remained in the grip of this strange new enemy—a current. The shore, with its white slope of sand and its green bluff, topped with little silent cottages, was spread like a picture before him. It was very near to him then, but he was impressed as one who in a gallery looks at a scene from Brittany or Holland.

He thought: "Am I going to drown? Can it be possible? Can it be possible?

Can it be possible?" Perhaps an individual must consider his own death to be the final phenomenon of nature.

But later a wave perhaps whirled him out of this small deadly current, for he found suddenly that he could again make progress toward the shore. Later still, he was aware that the captain, clinging with one hand to the keel of the dingey, had his face turned away from the shore and toward him, and was calling his name. "Come to the boat! Come to the boat!"

In his struggle to reach the captain and the boat, he reflected that when one gets properly wearied, drowning must really be a comfortable arrangement, a cessation of hostilities accompanied by a large degree of relief, and he was glad of it, for the main thing in his mind for some moments had been horror of the temporary agony. He did not wish to be hurt.

Presently he saw a man running along the shore. He was undressing with most remarkable speed. Coat, trousers, shirt, everything flew magically off him.

"Come to the boat," called the captain.

"All right, Captain." As the correspondent paddled, he saw the captain let himself down to bottom and leave the boat. Then the correspondent performed his one little marvel of the voyage. A large wave caught him and flung him with ease and supreme speed completely over the boat and far beyond it. It struck him even then as an event in gymnastics, and a true miracle of the sea. An overturned boat in the surf is not a plaything to a swimming man.

The correspondent arrived in water that reached only to his waist, but his condition did not enable him to stand for more than a moment. Each wave knocked him into a heap, and the under-tow pulled at him.

Then he saw the man who had been running and undressing, and undressing and running, come bounding into the water. He dragged ashore the cook, and then waded toward the captain, but the captain waved him away, and sent him to the correspondent. He was naked, naked as a tree in winter, but a halo was about his head, and he shone like a saint. He gave a strong pull, and a long drag, and a bully heave at the correspondent's hand. The correspondent, schooled in the minor formulae, said: "Thanks, old man." But suddenly the man cried: "What's that?" He pointed a swift finger. The correspondent said: "Go."

In the shallows, face downward, lay the oiler. His forehead touched sand that was periodically, between each wave, clear of the sea.

The correspondent did not know all that transpired afterward.

When he achieved safe ground he fell, striking the sand with each particular part of his body. It was as if he had dropped from a roof, but the thud was grateful to him.

It seems that instantly the beach was populated with men with blankets, clothes, and flasks, and women with coffee-pots and all the remedies sacred to their minds. The welcome of the land to the men from the sea was warm and generous, but a still and dripping shape was carried slowly up the beach, and the land's welcome for it could only be the different and sinister hospitality of the grave.

When it came night, the white waves paced to and fro in the moonlight, and the wind brought the sound of the great sea's voice to the men on shore, and they felt that they could then be interpreters.

1897   1897

Frank Norris   *1870–1902*

*Perhaps as much as any other writer, Frank Norris, in his life and works, revealed the
contradictions and paradoxes of America at the turn of the century. He was a confirmed
realist who rejected the conventions of popular sentimental fiction, but like one of his own
characters, he was sometimes drawn to search for "True Romance," to "see everything
through a rose-coloured mist—a mist that dulled all harsh outlines, all crude and violent
colors." The principal influences on his ideas and writing came from Harvard College
and from the French literary world, yet he felt that the "big American novel is going to
come out of the West." His first published work,* Yvernele, A Tale of Feudal France
*(1891), was a lengthy romantic poem on a medieval theme, but in the work that followed
he became the foremost exponent of literary naturalism in nineteenth-century America.*

*Norris was born in Chicago and moved to San Francisco with his parents when he was
fourteen. After prep school he studied art in London and Paris and attended the University
of California, where he first read the work of Zola. He spent a year at Harvard, and there
he began work on his novels* McTeague *(1899) and* Vandover and the Brute *(1914).
From Harvard, Norris went to South Africa to write travel sketches, but he got involved
in the politics of the Boer War and was expelled from the country. Returning to San
Francisco, he went to work for a magazine which published a number of his short stories,
including "A Deal in Wheat," and serialized his first novel,* Moran of the Lady Letty
(1898), a wild tale of pirate adventure.

*In 1898 Norris went to Cuba to report the Spanish-Ameican War for McClure's
Magazine. He became an editor for the publishing firm of Doubleday, and in 1899 his
novel,* McTeague, *was published, creating a literary scandal because of its sensational
treatment of greed and degeneracy. In the same year Norris conceived his most ambitious
work, three novels on the American West and the growth and distribution of wheat. The
first book,* The Octopus, *dealing with the strangling greed of railroad owners and the
growing of wheat, appeared in 1901 and was immediately successful. The second,* The
Pit *(1903), dealt with the marketing of wheat. The third novel, which was to be named*
The Wolf *and portray the consumption of the wheat in Europe, was never written. Norris
had just completed the second volume of the trilogy when he died from a ruptured appendix
in October 1902.*

*Norris is often criticized for excessive sentiment in his realistic fiction, for his romantic
reliance on the regenerative power of love, and for his philosophical inconsistencies. He
was, in fact, less interested in literary or social theories than in achieving dramatic power
in stories of individuals moved by forces of heredity and forces of history that they could
not control and rarely understood. Norris believed that fiction can express the truth of life
better than any other art, "better than painting, better than poetry, better than music." It
was for him a means of getting at truth, of cutting through the "tissues and wrappings of
flesh, down deep into the red, living heart of things."*

FURTHER READING: *The Complete Edition of Frank Norris,* 10 vols., 1928 [1929]; *The Literary
Criticism of Frank Norris,* ed. D. Pizer, 1962; *The Letters of Frank Norris,* ed. F. Walker, 1956;
F. Walker, *Frank Norris, A Biography,* 1932; E. Marchand, *Frank Norris, A Study,* 1942; W.
French, *Frank Norris,* 1962; D. Pizer, *The Novels of Frank Norris,* 1966; W. Dillingham,
Frank Norris, Instinct and Art, 1969; D. Graham, *The Fiction of Frank Norris,* 1978; *Critical
Essays on Frank Norris,* ed. D. Graham, 1980; *Frank Norris, The Critical Reception,* ed. J.
McElrath, 1981.

TEXT: *The Complete Works of Frank Norris,* 7 vols., 1903.

A DEAL IN WHEAT

I

THE BEAR[1]—WHEAT AT SIXTY-TWO

As Sam Lewiston backed the horse into the shafts of his buckboard and began hitching the tugs to the whiffletree,[2] his wife came out from the kitchen door of the house and drew near, and stood for some time at the horse's head, her arms folded and her apron rolled around them. For a long moment neither spoke. They had talked over the situation so long and so comprehensively the night before that there seemed to be nothing more to say.

The time was late in the summer, the place a ranch in southwestern Kansas, and Lewiston and his wife were two of a vast population of farmers, wheat growers, who at that moment were passing through a crisis—a crisis that at any moment might culminate in tragedy. Wheat was down to sixty-six.

At length Emma Lewiston spoke.

"Well," she hazarded, looking vaguely out across the ranch toward the horizon, leagues distant; "well, Sam, there's always that offer of brother Joe's. We can quit—and go to Chicago—if the worst comes."

"And give up!" exclaimed Lewiston, running the lines through the torets.[3] "Leave the ranch! Give up! After all these years!"

His wife made no reply for the moment. Lewiston climbed into the buckboard and gathered up the lines. "Well, here goes for the last try, Emmie," he said. "Good-by, girl. Maybe things will look better in town to-day."

"Maybe," she said gravely. She kissed her husband good-by and stood for some time looking after the buckboard traveling toward the town in a moving pillar of dust.

"I don't know," she murmured at length; "I don't know just how we're going to make out."

When he reached town, Lewiston tied the horse to the iron railing in front of the Odd Fellows' Hall, the ground floor of which was occupied by the post-office, and went across the street and up the stairway of a building of brick and granite—quite the most pretentious structure of the town—and knocked at a door upon the first landing. The door was furnished with a pane of frosted glass, on which in gold letters, was inscribed "Bridges & Co., Grain Dealers."

Bridges himself, a middle-aged man who wore a velvet skullcap and who was smoking a Pittsburg stogie, met the farmer at the counter and the two exchanged perfunctory greetings.

"Well," said Lewiston, tentatively, after a while.

"Well, Lewiston," said the other, "I can't take that wheat of yours at any better than sixty-two."

"Sixty-*two*."

"It's the Chicago price that does it, Lewiston. Truslow is bearing the stuff for all he's worth. It's Truslow and the bear clique that stick the knife to us. The price broke again this morning. We've just got a wire."

"Good heavens," murmured Lewiston, looking vaguely from side to side.

---

[1]In the jargon of stock exchanges, "bears" are traders who profit from a falling ("bear") market; "bulls" profit from a rising ("bull") market.

[2]Pivoted bar to which harness lines (tugs) are fastened.

[3]Harness rings.

"That—that ruins me. I *can't* carry my grain any longer—what with storage charges and—and— Bridges, I don't see just how I'm going to make out. Sixty-two cents a bushel! Why, man, what with this and with that it's cost me nearly a dollar a bushel to raise that wheat, and now Truslow——"

He turned away abruptly with a quick gesture of infinite discouragement.

He went down the stairs, and making his way to where his buckboard was hitched, got in, and, with eyes vacant, the reins slipping and sliding in his limp, half-open hands, drove slowly back to the ranch. His wife had seen him coming, and met him as he drew up before the barn.

"Well?" she demanded.

"Emmie," he said as he got out of the buckboard, laying his arm across her shoulder, "Emmie, I guess we'll take up with Joe's offer. We'll go to Chicago. We're cleaned out!"

II

THE BULL—WHEAT AT A DOLLAR-TEN

. . . —— and said Party of the Second Part further covenants and agrees to merchandise such wheat in foreign ports, it being understood and agreed between the Party of the First Part and the Party of the Second Part that the wheat hereinbefore mentioned is released and sold to the Party of the Second Part for export purposes only, and not for consumption or distribution within the boundaries of the United States of America or of Canada.

"Now, Mr. Gates, if you will sign for Mr. Truslow, I guess that'll be all," remarked Hornung when he had finished reading.

Hornung affixed his signature to the two documents and passed them over to Gates, who signed for his principal client. Truslow—or, as he had been called ever since he had gone into the fight against Hornung's corner—the Great Bear. Hornung's secretary was called in and witnessed the signatures, and Gates thrust the contract into his Gladstone bag[1] and stood up, smoothing his hat.

"You will deliver the warehouse receipts for the grain," began Gates.

"I'll send a messenger to Truslow's office before noon," interrupted Hornung. "You can pay by certified check through the Illinois Trust people."

When the other had taken himself off, Hornung sat for some moments gazing abstractedly toward his office windows, thinking over the whole matter. He had just agreed to release to Truslow, at the rate of one dollar and ten cents per bushel, one hundred thousand out of the two million and odd bushels of wheat that he, Hornung, controlled, or actually owned. And for the moment he was wondering if, after all, he had done wisely in not goring the Great Bear to actual financial death. He had made him pay one hundred thousand dollars. Truslow was good for this amount. Would it not have been better to have put a prohibitive figure on the grain and forced the Bear into bankruptcy? True, Hornung would then be without his enemy's money, but Truslow would have been eliminated from the situation, and that—so Hornung told himself—was always a consummation most devoutly, strenuously and diligently to be striven for. Truslow once dead was dead, but the Bear was never more dangerous than when desperate.

"But so long as he can't get *wheat*," muttered Hornung at the end of his reflections, "he can't hurt me. And he can't get it. That I *know*."

[1]A traveling bag with a rigid frame and flexible sides, named for William Gladstone (1809–1898), British statesman.

For Hornung controlled the situation. So far back as the February of that year an "unknown bull" had been making his presence felt on the floor of the Board of Trade. By the middle of March the commercial reports of the daily press had begun to speak of "the powerful bull clique"; a few weeks later that legendary condition of affairs implied and epitomized in the magic words "Dollar Wheat" had been attained, and by the first of April, when the price had been boosted to one dollar and ten cents a bushel, Hornung had disclosed his hand, and in place of mere rumors, the definite and authoritative news that May wheat had been cornered in the Chicago Pit[2] went flashing around the world from Liverpool to Odessa and from Duluth to Buenos Ayres.

It was—as the veteran operators were persuaded—Truslow himself who had made Hornung's corner possible. The Great Bear had for once overreached himself, and, believing himself all-powerful, had hammered the price just the fatal fraction too far down. Wheat had gone to sixty-two—for the time, and under the circumstances, an abnormal price. When the reaction came it was tremendous. Hornung saw his chance, seized it, and in a few months had turned the tables, had cornered the product, and virtually driven the bear clique out of the pit.

On the same day that the delivery of the hundred thousand bushels was made to Truslow, Hornung met his broker at his lunch club.

"Well," said the latter, "I see you let go that line of stuff to Truslow."

Hornung nodded; but the broker added:

"Remember, I was against it from the very beginning. I know we've cleared up over a hundred thou'. I would have fifty times preferred to have lost twice that and *smashed Truslow dead*. Bet you what you like he makes us pay for it somehow."

"Huh!" grunted his principal. "How about insurance and warehouse charges, and carrying expenses on that lot? Guess we'd have had to pay those, too, if we'd held on."

But the other put up his chin, unwilling to be persuaded. "I won't sleep easy," he declared, "till Truslow is busted."

III

THE PIT

Just as Going mounted the steps on the edge of the pit the great gong struck, a roar of a hundred voices developed with the swiftness of successive explosions, the rush of a hundred men surging downward to the centre of the pit filled the air with the stamp and grind of feet, a hundred hands in eager strenuous gestures tossed upward from out the brown of the crowd, the official reporter in his cage on the margin of the pit leaned far forward with straining ear to catch the opening bid, and another day of battle was begun.

Since the sale of the hundred thousand bushels of wheat to Truslow the "Hornung crowd" had steadily shouldered the price higher until on this particular morning it stood at one dollar and a half. That was Hornung's price. No one else had any grain to sell.

But not ten minutes after the opening, Going was surprised out of all countenance to hear shouted from the other side of the pit these words:

[2]Area in the exchange where actual trading is done. A speculator has "cornered" the market when the speculator owns enough of a commodity to control the selling price.

"Sell May at one-fifty."

Going was for the moment touching elbows with Kimbark on one side and with Merriam on the other, all three belonging to the "Hornung crowd." Their answering challenge of *"Sold"* was as the voice of one man. They did not pause to reflect upon the strangeness of the circumstance. (That was for afterward.) Their response to the offer was as unconscious as reflex action and almost as rapid, and before the pit was well aware of what had happened the transaction of one thousand bushels was down upon Going's trading-card and fifteen hundred dollars had changed hands. But here was a marvel—the whole available supply of wheat cornered, Hornung master of the situation, invincible, unassailable; yet behold a man willing to sell, a Bear bold enough to raise his head.

"That was Kennedy, wasn't it, who made that offer?" asked Kimbark, as Going noted down the trade—"Kennedy, that new man?"

"Yes; who do you suppose he's selling for; who's willing to go short at this stage of the game?"

"Maybe he ain't short."

"Short! Great heavens, man; where'd he get the stuff?"

"Blamed if I know. We can account for every handful of May. Steady! Oh, there he goes again."

"Sell a thousand May at one-fifty," vociferated the bear-broker, throwing out his hand, one finger raised to indicate the number of "contracts" offered. This time it was evident that he was attacking the Hornung crowd deliberately, for, ignoring the jam of traders that swept toward him, he looked across the pit to where Going and Kimbark were shouting *"Sold! Sold!"* and nodded his head.

A second time Going made memoranda of the trade, and either the Hornung holdings were increased by two thousand bushels of May wheat or the Hornung bank account swelled by at least three thousand dollars of some unknown short's money.

Of late—so sure was the bull crowd of its position—no one had even thought of glancing at the inspection sheet on the bulletin board. But now one of Going's messengers hurried up to him with the announcement that this sheet showed receipts at Chicago for that morning of twenty-five thousand bushels, and not credited to Hornung. Some one had got hold of a line of wheat overlooked by the "clique" and was dumping it upon them.

"Wire the Chief," said Going over his shoulder to Merriam. This one struggled out of the crowd, and on a telegraph blank scribbled:

"Strong bear movement—New man—Kennedy—Selling in lots of five contracts—Chicago receipts twenty-five thousand."

The message was despatched, and in a few moments the answer came back, laconic, of military terseness.

"Support the market."

And Going obeyed, Merriam and Kimbark following, the new broker fairly throwing the wheat at them in thousand-bushel lots.

"Sell May at 'fifty; sell May; sell May." A moment's indecision, an instant's hesitation, the first faint suggestion of weakness, and the market would have broken under them. But for the better part of four hours they stood their ground, taking all that was offered, in constant communication with the Chief, and from time to time stimulated and steadied by his brief, unvarying command:

"Support the market."

At the close of the session they had bought in the twenty-five thousand bushels of May. Hornung's position was as stable as a rock, and the price closed even with the opening figure—one dollar and a half.

But the morning's work was the talk of all La Salle Street.[1] Who was back of the raid? What was the meaning of this unexpected selling? For weeks the Pit trading had been merely nominal. Truslow, the Great Bear, from whom the most serious attack might have been expected, had gone to his country seat at Geneva Lake, in Wisconsin, declaring himself to be out of the market entirely. He went bass fishing every day.

IV

THE BELT LINE

On a certain day toward the middle of the month, at a time when the mysterious Bear had unloaded some eighty thousand bushels upon Hornung, a conference was held in the library of Hornung's home. His broker attended it, and also a clean-faced, bright-eyed individual whose name of Cyrus Ryder might have been found upon the pay-roll of a rather well-known detective agency. For upward of half an hour after the conference began the detective spoke, the other two listening attentively, gravely.

"Then, last of all," concluded Ryder, "I made out I was a hobo, and began stealing rides on the Belt Line Railroad. Know the road? It just circles Chicago. Truslow owns it. Yes? Well, then I began to catch on. I noticed that cars of certain numbers—thirty-one naught thirty-four, thirty-two one ninety—well, the numbers don't matter, but anyhow, these cars were always switched on to the sidings by Mr. Truslow's main elevator D soon as they came in. The wheat was shunted in, and they were pulled out again. Well, I spotted one car and stole a ride on her. Say, look here, *that car went right around the city on the Belt, and came back to D again, and the same wheat in her all the time.* The grain was reinspected—it was raw, I tell you—and the warehouse receipts made out just as though the stuff had come in from Kansas or Iowa."

"The same wheat all the time!" interrupted Hornung.

"The same wheat—your wheat, that you sold to Truslow."

"Great snakes!" ejaculated Hornung's broker. "Truslow never took it abroad at all."

"Took it abroad! Say, he's just been running it around Chicago, like the supers in 'Shenandoah,'[1] round an' round, so you'd think it was a new lot, an' selling it back to you again."

"No wonder we couldn't account for so much wheat."

"Bought it from us at one-ten, and made us buy it back—our own wheat—at one-fifty."

Hornung and his broker looked at each other in silence for a moment. Then all at once Hornung struck the arm of his chair with his fist and exploded in a roar of laughter. The broker stared for one bewildered moment, then followed his example.

[1]Location of the Chicago Board of Trade.
[1]The supernumeraries, or "extras," in the cast of the Civil War play *Shenandoah* (1888) marched in a continuous circle across and behind the stage to give the impression of a vast army.

"Sold! Sold!" shouted Hornung almost gleefully. "Upon my soul it's as good as a Gilbert and Sullivan show. And we— Oh, Lord! Billy, shake on it, and hats off to my distinguished friend, Truslow. He'll be President some day. Hey! What? Prosecute him? Not I."

"He's done us out of a neat hatful of dollars for all that," observed the broker, suddenly grave.

"Billy, it's worth the price."

"We've got to make it up somehow."

"Well, tell you what. We were going to boost the price to one seventy-five next week, and make that our settlement figure."

"Can't do it now. Can't afford it."

"No. Here; we'll let out a big link; we'll put wheat at two dollars, and let it go at that."

"Two it is, then," said the broker.

V

THE BREAD LINE

The street was very dark and absolutely deserted. It was a district on the "South Side," not far from the Chicago River, given up largely to wholesale stores, and after nightfall was empty of all life. The echoes slept but lightly hereabouts, and the slightest footfall, the faintest noise, woke them upon the instant and sent them clamoring up and down the length of the pavement between the iron-shuttered fronts. The only light visible came from the side door of a certain "Vienna" bakery, where at one o'clock in the morning loaves of bread were given away to any who should ask. Every evening about nine o'clock the outcasts began to gather about the side door. The stragglers came in rapidly, and the line—the "bread line," as it was called—began to form. By midnight it was usually some hundred yards in length, stretching almost the entire length of the block.

Toward ten in the evening, his coat collar turned up against the fine drizzle that pervaded the air, his hands in his pockets, his elbows gripping his sides, Sam Lewiston came up and silently took his place at the end of the line.

Unable to conduct his farm upon a paying basis at the time when Truslow, the "Great Bear," had sent the price of grain down to sixty-two cents a bushel, Lewiston had turned over his entire property to his creditors, and, leaving Kansas for good, had abandoned farming, and had left his wife at her sister's boarding-house in Topeka with the understanding that she was to join him in Chicago so soon as he had found a steady job. Then he had come to Chicago and had turned workman. His brother Joe conducted a small hat factory on Archer Avenue, and for a time he found there a meagre employment. But difficulties had occurred, times were bad, the hat factory was involved in debts, the repealing of a certain import duty on manufactured felt overcrowded the home market with cheap Belgian and French products, and in the end his brother had assigned[1] and gone to Milwaukee.

Thrown out of work, Lewiston drifted aimlessly about Chicago, from pillar to post, working a little, earning here a dollar, there a dime, but always sinking, sinking, till at last the ooze of the lowest bottom dragged at his feet and the rush

[1] Turned over his remaining property to his creditors.

of the great ebb went over him and engulfed him and shut him out from the light, and a park bench became his home and the "bread line" his chief make-shift of subsistence.

He stood now in the infolding drizzle, sodden, stupefied with fatigue. Before and behind stretched the line. There was no talking. There was no sound. The street was empty. It was so still that the passing of a cable-car in the adjoining thoroughfare grated like prolonged rolling explosions, beginning and ending at immeasurable distances. The drizzle descended incessantly. After a long time midnight struck.

There was something ominous and gravely impressive in this interminable line of dark figures, close-pressed, soundless; a crowd, yet absolutely still; a close-packed, silent file, waiting, waiting in the vast deserted night-ridden street; waiting without a word, without a movement, there under the night and under the slow-moving mists of rain.

Few in the crowd were professional beggars. Most of them were workmen, long since out of work, forced into idleness by long-continued "hard times," by ill luck, by sickness. To them the "bread line" was a godsend. At least they could not starve. Between jobs here in the end was something to hold them up—a small platform, as it were, above the sweep of black water, where for a moment they might pause and take breath before the plunge.

The period of waiting on this night of rain seemed endless to those silent, hungry men; but at length there was a stir. The line moved. The side door opened. Ah, at last! They were going to hand out the bread.

But instead of the usual white-aproned under-cook with his crowded hampers there now appeared in the doorway a new man—a young fellow who looked like a bookkeeper's assistant. He bore in his hand a placard, which he tacked to the outside of the door. Then he disappeared within the bakery, locking the door after him.

A shudder of poignant despair, an unformed, inarticulate sense of calamity, seemed to run from end to end of the line. What had happened? Those in the rear, unable to read the placard, surged forward, a sense of bitter disappointment clutching at their hearts.

The line broke up, disintegrated into a shapeless throng—a throng that crowded forward and collected in front of the shut door whereon the placard was affixed. Lewiston, with the others, pushed forward. On the placard he read these words:

"Owing to the fact that the price of grain has been increased to two dollars a bushel, there will be no distribution of bread from this bakery until further notice."

Lewiston turned away, dumb, bewildered. Till morning he walked the streets, going on without purpose, without direction. But now at last his luck had turned. Overnight the wheel of his fortunes had creaked and swung upon its axis, and before noon he had found a job in the street-cleaning brigade. In the course of time he rose to be first shift-boss, then deputy inspector, then inspector, promoted to the dignity of driving a red wagon with rubber tires and drawing a salary instead of mere wages. The wife was sent for and a new start made.

But Lewiston never forgot. Dimly he began to see the significance of things. Caught once in the cogs and wheels of a great and terrible engine, he had seen—none better—its workings. Of all the men who had vainly stood in the "bread line" on that rainy night in early summer, he, perhaps, had been the only one who had struggled up to the surface again. How many others had gone down in the great ebb? Grim question; he dared not think how many.

He had seen the two ends of a great wheat operation—a battle between Bear and Bull. The stories (subsequently published in the city's press) of Truslow's counter move in selling Hornung his own wheat, supplied the unseen section. The farmer—he who raised the wheat—was ruined upon one hand; the working-man—he who consumed it—was ruined upon the other. But between the two, the great operators, who never saw the wheat they traded in, bought and sold the world's food, gambled in the nourishment of entire nations, practiced their tricks, their chicanery and oblique shifty "deals," were reconciled in their differences, and went on through their appointed way, jovial, contented, enthroned, and unassailable.

1902

A PLEA FOR ROMANTIC FICTION

Let us at the start make a distinction. Observe that one speaks of romanticism and not sentimentalism. One claims that the latter is as distinct from the former as is that other form of art which is called Realism. Romance has been often put upon and overburdened by being forced to bear the onus of abuse that by right should fall to sentiment; but the two should be kept very distinct, for a very high and illustrious place will be claimed for romance, while sentiment will be handed down the scullery[1] stairs.

Many people to-day are composing mere sentimentalism, and calling it and causing it to be called Romance; so with those who are too busy to think much upon these subjects, but who none the less love honest literature, Romance, too, has fallen into disrepute. Consider now the cut-and-thrust[2] stories. They are all labeled Romances, and it is very easy to get the impression that Romance must be an affair of cloaks and daggers, or moonlight and golden hair. But this is not so at all. The true Romance is a more serious business than this. It is not merely a conjurer's trick-box full of flimsy quackeries, tinsel and claptraps, meant only to amuse, and relying upon deception to do even that. Is it not something better than this? Can we not see in it an instrument, keen, finely tempered, flawless—an instrument with which we may go straight through the clothes and tissues and wrappings of flesh down deep into the red, living heart of things?

Is all this too subtle, too merely speculative and intrinsic, too *précieuse*[3] and nice and "literary"? Devoutly one hopes the contrary. So much is made of so-called Romanticism in present-day fiction that the subject seems worthy of discussion, and a protest against the misuse of a really noble and honest formula of literature appears to be timely—misuse, that is, in the sense of limited use. Let us suppose for the moment that a romance can be made out of a cut-and-thrust business. Good Heavens, are there no other things that are romantic, even in this—falsely, falsely called—humdrum world of to-day? Why should it be that so soon as the novelist addresses himself—seriously—to the consideration of contemporary life he must abandon Romance and take up the harsh, loveless, colorless, blunt tool called Realism?

Now, let us understand at once what is meant by Romance and what by

[1] Room where dirty kitchen-work is done.   [2] Sword-play, swashbuckling.
[3] French: artificial, affected.

Realism. Romance, I take it, is the kind of fiction that takes cognizance of variations from the type of normal life. Realism is the kind of fiction that confines itself to the type of normal life. According to this definition, then, Romance may even treat of the sordid, the unlovely—as, for instance, the novels of M. Zola.[4] (Zola has been dubbed a Realist, but he is, on the contrary, the very head of the Romanticists.) Also, Realism, used as it sometimes is as a term of reproach, need not be in the remotest sense or degree offensive, but on the other hand respectable as a church and proper as a deacon—as, for instance, the novels of Mr. Howells.

The reason why one claims so much for Romance, and quarrels so pointedly with Realism, is that Realism stultifies itself. It notes only the surface of things. For it, Beauty is not even skin deep, but only a geometrical plane, without dimensions and depth, a mere outside. Realism is very excellent so far as it goes, but it goes no further than the Realist himself can actually see, or actually hear. Realism is minute; it is the drama of a broken teacup, the tragedy of a walk down the block, the excitement of an afternoon call, the adventure of an invitation to dinner. It is the visit to my neighbor's house, a formal visit, from which I may draw no conclusions. I see my neighbor and his friends—very, oh, such very! probable people—and that is all. Realism bows upon the doormat and goes away and says to me, as we link arms on the sidewalk: "That is life." And I say it is not. It is not, as you would very well see if you took Romance with you to call upon your neighbor.

Lately you have been taking Romance a weary journey across the water—ages and the flood of years—and haling her into the fuzzy, musty, worm-eaten, moth-riddled, rust-corroded "Grandes Salles"[5] of the Middle Ages and the Renaissance, and she has found the drama of a bygone age for you there. But would you take her across the street to your neighbor's front parlor (with the bisque[6] fisher-boy on the mantel and the photograph of Niagara Falls on glass hanging in the front window); would you introduce her there? Not you. Would you take a walk with her on Fifth Avenue, or Beacon Street, or Michigan Avenue?[7] No, indeed. Would you choose her for a companion of a morning spent in Wall Street,[8] or an afternoon in the Waldorf-Astoria?[9] You just guess you would not.

She would be out of place, you say—inappropriate. She might be awkward in my neighbor's front parlor, and knock over the little bisque fisher-boy. Well, she might. If she did, you might find underneath the base of the statuette, hidden away, tucked away—what? God knows. But something that would be a complete revelation of my neighbor's secretest life.

So you think Romance would stop in the front parlor and discuss medicated flannels and mineral waters with the ladies! Not for more than five minutes. She would be off upstairs with you, prying, peeping, peering into the closets of the bedroom, into the nursery, into the sitting-room; yes, and into that little iron box screwed to the lower shelf of the closet in the library; and into those compartments and pigeon-holes of the *secretaire*[10] in the study. She would find a heartache (maybe) between the pillows of the mistress's bed, and a memory carefully secreted in the master's deed-box. She would come upon a great hope amid the books and papers of the study-table of the young man's room, and—perhaps—who knows?—an affair, or, great Heavens, an intrigue, in the scented ribbons and gloves and hairpins of the young lady's bureau. And she would pick here a little and there a little, making up a bag of hopes and fears and a

[4]Emile Zola (1840–1902): French naturalistic novelist.   [5]French: "Great Halls."
[6]Pottery.   [7]Fashionable streets in New York City, Boston, and Chicago.
[8]New York City financial district.   [9]Elegant New York City hotel.   [10]Writing desk.

package of joys and sorrows—great ones, mind you—and then come down to the front door, and, stepping out into the street, hand you the bag and package and say to you—"That is Life!"

Romance does very well in the castles of the Middle Ages and the Renaissance chateaux, and she has the *entrée* there and is very well received. That is all well and good. But let us protest against limiting her to such places and such times. You will find her, I grant you, in the chatelaine's[11] chamber and the dungeon of the man-at-arms; but if you choose to look for her, you will find her equally at home in the brownstone house on the corner and in the office building downtown. And this very day, in this very hour, she is sitting among the rags and wretchedness, the dirt and despair of the tenements of the East Side of New York.

"What?" I hear you say, "look for Romance—the lady of the silken robes and golden crown, our beautiful, chaste maiden of soft voice and gentle eyes—look for her among the vicious ruffians, male and female, of Allen Street and Mulberry Bend?"[12] I tell you she is there, and to your shame be it said you will not know her in those surroundings. You, the aristocrats, who demand the fine linen and the purple in your fiction; you, the sensitive, the delicate, who will associate with your Romance only so long as she wears a silken gown. You will not follow her to the slums, for you believe that Romance should only amuse and entertain you, singing you sweet songs and touching the harp of silver strings with rosy-tipped fingers. If haply she should call to you from the squalor of a dive, or the awful degradation of a disorderly house, crying: "Look! listen! This, too, is life. These, too, are my children! Look at them, know them and, knowing, help!" Should she call thus you would stop your ears; you would avert your eyes and you would answer, "Come from there, Romance. Your place is not there!" And you would make of her a harlequin, a tumbler, a sword-dancer, when, as a matter of fact, she should be by right divine a teacher sent from God.

She will not often wear the robe of silk, the golden crown, the jeweled shoon;[13] will not always sweep the silver harp. An iron note is hers if so she choose, and coarse garments, and stained hands; and, meeting her thus, it is for you to know her as she passes—know her for the same young queen of the blue mantle and lilies. She can teach you if you will be humble to learn—teach you by showing. God help you if at last you take from Romance her mission of teaching; if you do not believe that she has a purpose—a nobler purpose and a mightier than mere amusement, mere entertainment. Let Realism do the entertainment with its meticulous presentation of teacups, rag carpets, wall-paper and haircloth sofas, stopping with these, going no deeper than it sees, choosing the ordinary, the untroubled, the commonplace.

But to Romance belongs the wide world for range, and the unplumbed depths of the human heart, and the mystery of sex, and the problems of life, and the black, unsearched penetralia of the soul of man. You, the indolent, must not always be amused. What matter the silken clothes, what matter the prince's houses? Romance, too, is a teacher, and if—throwing aside the purple—she wears the camel's-hair and feeds upon the locusts, it is to cry aloud unto the people, "Prepare ye the way of the Lord; make straight his path."[14]

1901

---

[11]Mistress of a castle or manor house.
[12]Streets in New York City's slum district.   [13]Shoes.
[14]The raiment, food, and words of John the Baptist. Matthew 3:3.

Jack London *1876–1916*

Jack London was the illegitimate son of a father who was a wandering astrologer and a mother who was a spiritualist and medium. Born in San Francisco, London was raised in Oakland, where he roamed the waterfront and attended school only occasionally, but, as he reported in his autobiographical novel, Martin Eden *(1909), he read constantly, as much as nineteen hours a day. He "rode the rods" over the Sierras to the East, was jailed for vagrancy in Buffalo at eighteen, worked as an "oyster pirate" in San Francisco Bay, stealing from the oyster beds belonging to other fishermen. He sailed as a seaman on a sealing trip to Japan and in 1896 joined the gold rush to the Klondike, where he found no gold but gathered ample material for the brutal, vigorous life he portrayed in* The Call of the Wild *(1903) and* White Fang *(1906), novels of man and beast struggling against the tremendous forces of nature.*

From 1900 to 1916 London wrote more than fifty books, earning a million dollars, which he spent (as quickly as he earned it) in a frantic search for contentment. But London found gratification neither in his writing nor in his personal life, and his last years were marked by struggles with alcoholism and mental disintegration. He died, probably by his own hand, when he was forty.

From Social Darwinism London had absorbed the idea that to survive, man must adapt to irresistible natural forces and to "the stress and strain of life, its fevers and sweats and wild indulgences." Although his writing is often categorized simply as literary naturalism, the sources of his ideas were complex. London was most deeply influenced by the seemingly irreconcilable opposites of Nietzsche and Marx. From Nietzsche he borrowed the idea of the super human beings, evident in its most destructive form in Wolf Larsen, the predatory hero of London's The Sea Wolf *(1904). From Marx he took the idea of the need for social reform and of the power of economic determinism, concepts he embodied in his socialistic treatises,* The War of the Classes *(1905) and* The Human Drift *(1907), and in his terrifying vision of the coming of totalitarianism,* The Iron Heel *(1907).*

London was a storyteller of great emotional power and excitement, a master of tempo and pace whose adventure stories continue to fascinate a large reading public. He was, as a writer, bold, sensational, tragic and, like his characters, a champion and a victim of the "wild indulgences" of life and nature.

FURTHER READING: *Letters from Jack London*, ed. K. Hendricks and I. Shepard, 1965; C. London, *The Book of Jack London*, 2 vols., 1921; J. London, *Jack London and His Times*, 1939, 1968; I. Stone, *Sailor on Horseback, The Biography of Jack London*, 1938; P. Foner, *Jack London, American Rebel*, 1947; R. O'Connor, *Jack London, A Biography*, 1964; F. Walker, *Jack London and the Klondike*, 1966; E. Labor, *Jack London*, 1974; J. McClintock, *White Logic, Jack London's Short Stories*, 1975; A. Sinclair, *Jack, A Biography of Jack London*, 1977, 1983; R. Kingman, *A Pictorial Life of Jack London*, 1981; J. Perry, *Jack London, An American Myth*, 1981; J. Hedrick, *Solitary Comrade, Jack London and His Work*, 1982; C. Watson, *The Novels of Jack London*, 1983; *Critical Essays on Jack London*, ed. J. Tavernier-Courbin, 1983; J. Lundquist, *Jack London*, 1987.

TEXT: *Children of the Frost*, 1902.

THE LAW OF LIFE

Old Koskoosh listened greedily. Though his sight had long since faded, his hearing was still acute, and the slightest sound penetrated to the glimmering intelligence which yet abode behind the withered forehead, but which no longer gazed forth upon the things of the world. Ah! That was Sit-cum-to-ha, shrilly anathematizing the dogs as she cuffed and beat them into the harnesses. Sit-cum-to-ha was his daughter's daughter, but she was too busy to waste a thought upon her broken grandfather, sitting alone there in the snow, forlorn and helpless. Camp must be broken. The long trail waited while the short day refused to linger. Life called her, and the duties of life, not death. And he was very close to death now.

The thought made the old man panicky for the moment, and he stretched forth a palsied hand which wandered tremblingly over the small heap of dry wood beside him. Reassured that it was indeed there, his hand returned to the shelter of his mangy furs, and he again fell to listening. The sulky crackling of half-frozen hides told him that the chief's moose-skin lodge had been struck, and even then was being rammed and jammed into portable compass. The chief was his son, stalwart and strong, headman of the tribesmen, and a mighty hunter. As the women toiled with the camp luggage, his voice rose, chiding them for their slowness. Old Koskoosh strained his ears. It was the last time he would hear that voice. There went Geehow's lodge! And Tusken's! Seven, eight, nine, only the shaman's[1] could be still standing. There! They were at work upon it now. He could hear the shaman grunt as he piled it on the sled. A child whimpered, and a woman soothed it with soft, crooning gutturals. Little Koo-tee, the old man thought, a fretful child, and not overstrong. It would die soon, perhaps, and they would burn a hole through the frozen tundra and pile rocks above to keep the wolverines away. Well, what did it matter? A few years at best, and as many an empty belly as a full one. And in the end, Death waited, ever-hungry and hungriest of them all.

What was that? Oh, the men lashing the sleds and drawing tight the thongs. He listened, who would listen no more. The whiplashes snarled and bit among the dogs. Hear them whine! How they hated the work and the trail! They were off! Sled after sled churned slowly away into the silence. They were gone. They had passed out of his life, and he faced the last bitter hour alone. No. The snow crunched beneath a moccasin; a man stood beside him; upon his head a hand rested gently. His son was good to do this thing. He remembered other old men whose sons had not waited after the tribe. But his son had. He wandered away into the past, till the young man's voice brought him back.

"It is well with you?" he asked.

And the old man answered, "It is well."

"There be wood beside you," the younger man continued, "and the fire burns bright. The morning is gray, and the cold has broken. It will snow presently. Even now it is snowing."

"Aye, even now it is snowing."

"The tribesmen hurry. Their bales are heavy and their bellies flat with lack of feasting. The trail is long and they travel fast. I go now. It is well?"

"It is well. I am as a last year's leaf, clinging lightly to the stem. The first breath that blows, and I fall. My voice is become like an old woman's. My eyes no longer show me the way of my feet, and my feet are heavy, and I am tired. It is well."

He bowed his head in content till the last noise of the complaining snow had died away, and he knew his son was beyond recall. Then his hand crept out in haste to the wood. It alone stood between him and the eternity that yawned in upon him. At last the measure of his life was a handful of faggots. One by one

[1]Medicine man's.

they would go to feed the fire, and just so, step by step, death would creep upon him. When the last stick had surrendered up its heat, the frost would begin to gather strength. First his feet would yield, then his hands; and the numbness would travel, slowly, from the extremities to the body. His head would fall forward upon his knees, and he would rest. It was easy. All men must die.

He did not complain. It was the way of life, and it was just. He had been born close to the earth, close to the earth he had lived, and the law thereof was not new to him. It was the law of all flesh. Nature was not kindly to the flesh. She had no concern for that concrete thing called the individual. Her interest lay in the species, the race. This was the deepest abstraction old Koskoosh's barbaric mind was capable of, but he grasped it firmly. He saw it exemplified in all life. The rise of the sap, the bursting greenness of the willow bud, the fall of the yellow leaf—in this alone was told the whole history. But one task did Nature set the individual. Did he not perform it, he died. Did he perform it, it was all the same, he died. Nature did not care; there were plenty who were obedient, and it was only the obedience in this matter, not the obedient, which lived and lived always. The tribe of Koskoosh was very old. The old men he had known when a boy had known old men before them. Therefore it was true that the tribe lived, that it stood for the obedience of all its members, way down into the forgotten past, whose very resting places were unremembered. They did not count; they were episodes. They had passed away like clouds from a summer sky. He also was an episode and would pass away. Nature did not care. To life she set one task, gave one law. To perpetuate was the task of life, its law was death. A maiden was a good creature to look upon, full-breasted and strong, with spring to her step and light in her eyes. But her task was yet before her. The light in her eyes brightened, her step quickened, she was now bold with the young men, now timid, and she gave them of her own unrest. And ever she grew fairer and yet fairer to look upon, till some hunter, able no longer to withhold himself, took her to his lodge to cook and toil for him and to become the mother of his children. And with the coming of her offspring her looks left her. Her limbs dragged and shuffled, her eyes dimmed and bleared, and only the little children found joy against the withered cheek of the old squaw by the fire. Her task was done. But a little while, on the first pinch of famine or the first long trail, and she would be left, even as he had been left, in the snow, with a little pile of wood. Such was the law.

He placed a stick carefully upon the fire and resumed his meditations. It was the same everywhere, with all things. The mosquitoes vanished with the first frost. The little tree squirrel crawled away to die. When age settled upon the rabbit it became slow and heavy and could no longer outfoot its enemies. Even the big bald-face grew clumsy and blind and quarrelsome, in the end to be dragged down by a handful of yelping huskies. He remembered how he had abandoned his own father on an upper reach of the Klondike one winter, the winter before the missionary came with his talk books and his box of medicines. Many a time had Koskoosh smacked his lips over the recollection of that box, though now his mouth refused to moisten. The "painkiller" had been especially good. But the missionary was a bother after all, for he brought no meat into the camp, and he ate heartily, and the hunters grumbled. But he chilled his lungs on the divide by the Mayo, and the dogs afterward nosed the stones away and fought over his bones.

Koskoosh placed another stick on the fire and harked back deeper into the past. There was the time of the great famine, when the old men crouched empty-bellied to the fire, and let fall from their lips dim traditions of the ancient day when the Yukon ran wide open for three winters, and then lay frozen for three summers. He had lost his mother in that famine. In the summer the salmon run had failed, and the tribe looked forward to the winter and the coming of the caribou. Then the winter came, but with it there were no caribou. Never had the like been known, not even in the lives of the old men. But the caribou did not come, and it was the seventh year, and the rabbits had not replenished, and the dogs were naught but bundles of bones. And through the long darkness the children wailed and died, and the women, and the old men; and not one in ten of the tribe lived to meet the sun when it came back in the spring. That *was* a famine!

But he had seen times of plenty, too, when the meat spoiled on their hands, and the dogs were fat and worthless with overeating—times when they let the game go unkilled, and the women were fertile, and the lodges were cluttered with sprawling men-children and women-children. Then it was the men became high-stomached, and revived ancient quarrels, and crossed the divides to the south to kill the Pellys, and to the west that they might sit by the dead fires of the Tananas. He remembered, when a boy, during a time of plenty, when he saw a moose pulled down by the wolves. Zing-ha lay with him in the snow and watched—Zing-ha, who later became the craftiest of hunters, and who, in the end, fell through an air hole on the Yukon. They found him, a month afterward, just as he had crawled halfway out and frozen stiff to the ice.

But the moose. Zing-ha and he had gone out that day to play at hunting after the manner of their fathers. On the bed of the creek they struck the fresh track of a moose, and with it the tracks of many wolves. "An old one," Zing-ha, who was quicker at reading the sign, said, "an old one who cannot keep up with the herd. The wolves have cut him out from his brothers, and they will never leave him." And it was so. It was their way. By day and by night, never resting, snarling on his heels, snapping at his nose, they would stay by him to the end. How Zing-ha and he felt the blood lust quicken! The finish would be a sight to see!

Eager-footed, they took the trail, and even he, Koskoosh, slow of sight and an unversed tracker, could have followed it blind, it was so wide. Hot were they on the heels of the chase, reading the grim tragedy, fresh-written, at every step. Now they came to where the moose had made a stand. Thrice the length of a grown man's body, in every direction, had the snow been stamped about and uptossed. In the midst were the deep impressions of the splay-hoofed game, and all about, everywhere, were the lighter footmarks of the wolves. Some, while their brothers harried the kill, had lain to one side and rested. The full-stretched impress of their bodies in the snow was as perfect as though made the moment before. One wolf had been caught in a wild lunge of the maddened victim and trampled to death. A few bones, well picked, bore witness.

Again, they ceased the uplift of their snowshoes at a second stand. Here the great animal had fought desperately. Twice had he been dragged down, as the snow attested, and twice had he shaken his assailants clear and gained footing once more. He had done his task long since, but none the less was life dear to him. Zing-ha said it was a strange thing, a moose once down to get free again; but this one certainly had. The shaman would see signs and wonders in this when they told him.

And yet again, they came to where the moose had made to mount the bank and gain the timber. But his foes had laid on from behind, till he reared and fell back upon them, crushing two deep into the snow. It was plain the kill was at hand, for their brothers had left them untouched. Two more stands were hurried past, brief in time length and very close together. The trail was red now, and the clean stride of the great beast had grown short and slovenly. Then they heard the first sounds of the battle—not the full-throated chorus of the chase, but the short, snappy bark which spoke of close quarters and teeth to flesh. Crawling up the wind, Zing-ha bellied it through the snow, and with him crept he, Koskoosh, who was to be chief of the tribesmen in the years to come. Together they shoved aside the underbranches of a young spruce and peered forth. It was the end they saw.

The picture, like all of youth's impressions, was still strong with him, and his dim eyes watched the end played out as vividly as in that far-off time. Koskoosh marveled at this, for in the days which followed, when he was a leader of men and a head of councilors, he had done great deeds and made his name a curse in the mouths of the Pellys, to say naught of the strange white man he had killed, knife to knife, in open fight.

For long he pondered on the days of his youth, till the fire died down and the frost bit deeper. He replenished it with two sticks this time, and gauged his grip on life by what remained. If Sit-cum-to-ha had only remembered her grandfather, and gathered a larger armful, his hours would have been longer. It would have been easy. But she was ever a careless child, and honored not her ancestors from the time the Beaver, son of the son of Zing-ha, first cast eyes upon her. Well, what mattered it? Had he not done likewise in his own quick youth? For a while he listened to the silence. Perhaps the heart of his son might soften, and he would come back with the dogs to take his old father on with the tribe to where the caribou ran thick and the fat hung heavy upon them.

He strained his ears, his restless brain for the moment stilled. Not a stir, nothing. He alone took breath in the midst of the great silence. It was very lonely. Hark! What was that? A chill passed over his body. The familiar, long-drawn howl broke the void, and it was close at hand. Then on his darkened eyes was projected the vision of the moose—the old bull moose—the torn flanks and bloody sides, the riddled mane, and the great branching horns, down low and tossing to the last. He saw the flashing forms of gray, the gleaming eyes, the lolling tongues, the slavered fangs. And he saw the inexorable circle close in till it became a dark point in the midst of the stamped snow.

A cold muzzle thrust against his cheek, and at its touch his soul leaped back to the present. His hand shot into the fire and dragged out a burning faggot. Overcome for the nonce by his hereditary fear of men, the brute retreated, raising a prolonged call to his brothers; and greedily they answered, till a ring of crouching, jaw-slobbering gray was stretched round about. The old man listened to the drawing in of this circle. He waved his hand wildly, and sniffs turned to snarls; but the panting brutes refused to scatter. Now one wormed his chest forward, dragging his haunches after, now a second, now a third; but never a one drew back. Why should he cling to life? he asked, and dropped the blazing stick into the snow. It sizzled and went out. The circle grunted uneasily but held its own. Again he saw the last stand of the old bull moose, and Koskoosh dropped his head wearily upon his knees. What did it matter after all? Was it not the law of life?

1901, 1902

Edith Wharton 1862–1937

Henry James, the close friend of her later years, called Edith Wharton "an angel of devastation"; a more respectful public has come to regard her as the grande dame *of American letters. She was, like Henry James, born into a wealthy and privileged society whose character she unflinchingly recorded in her fiction. The daughter of one of New York's oldest families, she was christened Edith Newbold Jones, and educated as befit her elevated class. She was tutored at home and taken for extended tours abroad, where she acquired her lifelong admiration for European art and culture. In 1885, after her formal "coming out," she married Edward Wharton, a wealthy Bostonian some years her senior. The marriage was unfortunate: the two had little in common besides a desire for amiable companionship, and some years later Edward Wharton developed a mental disorder that eventually left him insane.*

Gradually, and perhaps out of boredom with the stultifying life of a society matron, Edith Wharton began writing short fiction. After collaborating on a popular treatise on interior decorating, she published her first collection of stories, The Greater Inclination *(1889). The book's unexpected success, as she later said, "broke the chains that had held me so long in a kind of torpor," and thereafter she worked increasingly toward the discipline and craftsmanship of a serious author. Two novels and more stories followed, and in 1905* The House of Mirth *established her reputation as a writer. It also revealed her major strengths—an intimate knowledge of New York society and an ability to dramatize the plight of individuals trapped by its rigid conventions and code of manners.*

With her husband's final mental breakdown, Edith Wharton gained a divorce and settled permanently in Paris. Out of this troubled time came her best-known short novel, Ethan Frome *(1911), a tragedy of spiritual isolation and despair in a rural New England setting.* The Reef, *one of her "Jamesian" novels, appeared in 1912, followed by* The Custom of the Country *(1913),* Summer *(1917), and the novel for which she received the Pulitzer Prize,* The Age of Innocence *(1920).*

The Age of Innocence, *her finest work, is in many ways her most characteristic. Its setting is the world she knew best: upper-class New York in the decade of the seventies. The novel's theme was the conflict between social conformity and personal fulfillment. Primarily a novel of manners, it probed beneath external codes of conduct—especially those surrounding marriage and divorce—to examine the underlying moral values that help to shape human behavior.*

The quality and the significance of Edith Wharton's fiction declined with the passing of the genteel era that she understood so well, and as a result, the best-known of her last works were nonfiction: a discussion of the principles of her craft entitled The Writing of Fiction *(1925) and her autobiographical* A Backward Glance *(1934). The upheavals of the First World War had brought changes in American life that she could not admire and to which she would not adjust. The America of the 1920s and 1930s seemed crass and evermore materialistic, and in her final years Edith Wharton remained away from the United States, living in Europe where she could preserve an older way of life and where she could castigate American vulgarity from afar.*

FURTHER READING: *The Collected Short Stories of Edith Wharton,* 2 vols., ed. R. Lewis, 1968; *The Letters of Edith Wharton,* eds. R. Lewis and N. Lewis, 1988; B. Nevius, *Edith Wharton, A Study of Her Fiction,* 1953; M. Lyde, *Edith Wharton,* 1959; O. Coolidge, *Edith Wharton, 1862–1937,* 1964; G. Kellogg, *The Two Lives of Edith Wharton,* 1965; M. Bell, *Edith Wharton and Henry James,* 1965; *Edith Wharton, A Collection of Critical Essays,* ed. I. Howe, 1962; G. Walton, *Edith Wharton, A Critical Interpretation,* 1970, 1983; G. Lindberg, *Edith Wharton and the Novel of Manners,* 1975; R. Lewis, *Edith Wharton,* 1975; M. McDowell, *Edith Wharton,*

1975; C. Wolff, *A Feast of Words, The Triumph of Edith Wharton*, 1977; E. Ammons, *Edith Wharton's Argument with America*, 1980; C. Rae, *Edith Wharton's New York Quartet*, 1984; J. Fryer, *The Imaginative Structures of Edith Wharton and Willa Cather*, 1986; *Edith Wharton*, ed. H. Bloom, 1986.

TEXT: *The Descent of Man*, 1904.

THE OTHER TWO

I

Waythorn, on the drawing-room hearth, waited for his wife to come down to dinner.

It was their first night under his own roof, and he was surprised at his thrill of boyish agitation. He was not so old, to be sure—his glass[1] gave him little more than the five-and-thirty years to which his wife confessed—but he had fancied himself already in the temperate zone; yet here he was listening for her step with a tender sense of all it symbolised, with some old trail of verse about the garlanded nuptial door-posts floating through his enjoyment of the pleasant room and the good dinner just beyond it.

They had been hastily recalled from their honeymoon by the illness of Lily Haskett, the child of Mrs. Waythorn's first marriage. The little girl, at Waythorn's desire, had been transferred to his house on the day of her mother's wedding, and the doctor, on their arrival, broke the news that she was ill with typhoid, but declared that all the symptoms were favourable. Lily could show twelve years of unblemished health, and the case promised to be a light one. The nurse spoke as reassuringly, and after a moment of alarm Mrs. Waythorn had adjusted herself to the situation. She was very fond of Lily—her affection for the child had perhaps been her decisive charm in Waythorn's eyes—but she had the perfectly balanced nerves which her little girl had inherited, and no woman ever wasted less tissue in unproductive worry. Waythorn was therefore quite prepared to see her come in presently, a little late because of a last look at Lily, but as serene and well-appointed as if her good-night kiss had been laid on the brow of health. Her composure was restful to him; it acted as ballast to his somewhat unstable sensibilities. As he pictured her bending over the child's bed he thought how soothing her presence must be in illness: her very step would prognosticate recovery.

His own life had been a gray one, from temperament rather than circumstance, and he had been drawn to her by the unperturbed gaiety which kept her fresh and elastic at an age when most women's activities are growing either slack or febrile. He knew what was said about her; for, popular as she was, there had always been a faint undercurrent of detraction. When she had appeared in New York, nine or ten years earlier, as the pretty Mrs. Haskett whom Gus Varick had unearthed somewhere—was it in Pittsburg or Utica?—society, while promptly accepting her, had reserved the right to cast a doubt on its own indiscrimination. Enquiry, however, established her undoubted connection with a socially reigning family, and explained her recent divorce as the natural result of a runaway match at seventeen; and as nothing was known of Mr. Haskett it was easy to believe the worst of him.

Alice Haskett's remarriage with Gus Varick was a passport to the set whose recognition she coveted, and for a few years the Varicks were the most popular

[1] Mirror.

couple in town. Unfortunately the alliance was brief and stormy, and this time the husband had his champions. Still, even Varick's staunchest supporters admitted that he was not meant for matrimony, and Mrs. Varick's grievances were of a nature to bear the inspection of the New York courts. A New York divorce is in itself a diploma of virtue,[2] and in the semiwidowhood of this second separation Mrs. Varick took on an air of sanctity, and was allowed to confide her wrongs to some of the most scrupulous ears in town. But when it was known that she was to marry Waythorn there was a momentary reaction. Her best friends would have preferred to see her remain in the rôle of the injured wife, which was as becoming to her as crape to a rosy complexion. True, a decent time had elapsed, and it was not even suggested that Waythorn had supplanted his predecessor. People shook their heads over him, however, and one grudging friend, to whom he affirmed that he took the step with his eyes open, replied oracularly: "Yes—and with your ears shut."

Waythorn could afford to smile at these innuendoes. In the Wall Street phrase, he had "discounted" them. He knew that society has not yet adapted itself to the consequences of divorce, and that till the adaptation takes place every woman who uses the freedom the law accords her must be her own social justification. Waythorn had an amused confidence in his wife's ability to justify herself. His expectations were fulfilled, and before the wedding took place Alice Varick's group had rallied openly to her support. She took it all imperturbably: she had a way of surmounting obstacles without seeming to be aware of them, and Waythorn looked back with wonder at the trivialities over which he had worn his nerves thin. He had the sense of having found refuge in a richer, warmer nature than his own, and his satisfaction, at the moment, was humourously summed up in the thought that his wife, when she had done all she could for Lily, would not be ashamed to come down and enjoy a good dinner.

The anticipation of such enjoyment was not, however, the sentiment expressed by Mrs. Waythorn's charming face when she presently joined him. Though she had put on her most engaging teagown she had neglected to assume the smile that went with it, and Waythorn thought he had never seen her look so nearly worried.

"What is it?" he asked. "Is anything wrong with Lily?"

"No; I've just been in and she's still sleeping." Mrs. Waythorn hesitated. "But something tiresome has happened."

He had taken her two hands, and now perceived that he was crushing a paper between them.

"This letter?"

"Yes—Mr. Haskett has written—I mean his lawyer has written."

Waythorn felt himself flush uncomfortably. He dropped his wife's hands. "What about?"

"About seeing Lily. You know the courts——"

"Yes, yes," he interrupted nervously.

Nothing was known about Haskett in New York. He was vaguely supposed to have remained in the outer darkness from which his wife had been rescued, and Waythorn was one of the few who were aware that he had given up his business in Utica and followed her to New York in order to be near his little girl. In the days of his wooing, Waythorn had often met Lily on the doorstep, rosy and smiling, on her way "to see papa."

"I am so sorry," Mrs. Waythorn murmured.

[2]In the early 1900s in New York State, adultery was the only legal justification for divorce.

He roused himself. "What does he want?"

"He wants to see her. You know she goes to him once a week."

"Well—he doesn't expect her to go to him now, does he?"

"No—he has heard of her illness; but he expects to come here."

"Here?"

Mrs. Waythorn reddened under his gaze. They looked away from each other.

"I'm afraid he has the right. . . . You'll see. . . ." She made a proffer of the letter.

Waythorn moved away with a gesture of refusal. He stood staring about the softly lighted room, which a moment before had seemed so full of bridal intimacy.

"I'm so sorry," she repeated. "If Lily could have been moved——"

"That's out of the question," he returned impatiently.

"I suppose so."

Her lip was beginning to tremble, and he felt himself a brute.

"He must come, of course," he said. "What is—his day?"

"I'm afraid—to-morrow."

"Very well. Send a note in the morning."

The butler entered to announce dinner.

Waythorn turned to his wife. "Come—you must be tired. It's beastly, but try to forget about it," he said, drawing her hand through his arm.

"You're so good, dear. I'll try," she whispered back.

Her face cleared at once, and as she looked at him across the flowers, between the rosy candle-shades, he saw her lips waver back into a smile.

"How pretty everything is!" she sighed luxuriously.

He turned to the butler. "The champagne at once, please. Mrs. Waythorn is tired."

In a moment or two their eyes met above the sparkling glasses. Her own were quite clear and untroubled: he saw that she had obeyed his injunction and forgotten.

II

Waythorn, the next morning, went down town earlier than usual. Haskett was not likely to come till the afternoon, but the instinct of flight drove him forth. He meant to stay away all day—he had thoughts of dining at his club. As his door closed behind him he reflected that before he opened it again it would have admitted another man who had as much right to enter it as himself, and the thought filled him with a physical repugnance.

He caught the "elevated" at the employés' hour, and found himself crushed between two layers of pendulous humanity. At Eighth Street the man facing him wriggled out, and another took his place. Waythorn glanced up and saw that it was Gus Varick. The men were so close together that it was impossible to ignore the smile of recognition on Varick's handsome overblown face. And after all—why not? They had always been on good terms, and Varick had been divorced before Waythorn's attentions to his wife began. The two exchanged a word on the perennial grievance of the congested trains, and when a seat at their side was miraculously left empty the instinct of self-preservation made Waythorn slip into it after Varick.

The latter drew the stout man's breath of relief. "Lord—I was beginning to feel like a pressed flower." He leaned back, looking unconcernedly at Waythorn. "Sorry to hear that Sellers is knocked out again."

"Sellers?" echoed Waythorn, starting at his partner's name.

Varick looked surprised. "You didn't know he was laid up with the gout?"

"No. I've been away—I only got back last night." Waythorn felt himself reddening in anticipation of the other's smile.

"Ah—yes; to be sure. And Sellers's attack came on two days ago. I'm afraid he's pretty bad. Very awkward for me, as it happens, because he was just putting through a rather important thing for me."

"Ah?" Waythorn wondered vaguely since when Varick had been dealing in "important things." Hitherto he had dabbled only in the shallow pools of speculation, with which Waythorn's office did not usually concern itself.

It occurred to him that Varick might be talking at random, to relieve the strain of their propinquity. That strain was becoming momentarily more apparent to Waythorn, and when, at Cortlandt Street, he caught sight of an acquaintance and had a sudden vision of the picture he and Varick must present to an initiated eye, he jumped up with a muttered excuse.

"I hope you'll find Sellers better," said Varick civilly, and he stammered back: "If I can be of any use to you——" and let the departing crowd sweep him to the platform.

At his office he heard that Sellers was in fact ill with the gout, and would probably not be able to leave the house for some weeks.

"I'm sorry it should have happened so, Mr. Waythorn," the senior clerk said with affable significance. "Mr. Sellers was very much upset at the idea of giving you such a lot of extra work just now."

"Oh, that's no matter," said Waythorn hastily. He secretly welcomed the pressure of additional business, and was glad to think that, when the day's work was over, he would have to call at his partner's on the way home.

He was late for luncheon, and turned in at the nearest restaurant instead of going to his club. The place was full, and the waiter hurried him to the back of the room to capture the only vacant table. In the cloud of cigar-smoke Waythorn did not at once distinguish his neighbours: but presently, looking about him, he saw Varick seated a few feet off. This time, luckily, they were too far apart for conversation, and Varick, who faced another way, had probably not even seen him; but there was an irony in their renewed nearness.

Varick was said to be fond of good living, and as Waythorn sat despatching his hurried luncheon he looked across half enviously at the other's leisurely degustation of his meal. When Waythorn first saw him he had been helping himself with critical deliberation to a bit of Camembert at the ideal point of liquefaction, and now, the cheese removed, he was just pouring his *café double* from its little two-storied earthen pot. He poured slowly, his ruddy profile bent above the task, and one beringed white hand steadying the lid of the coffee-pot; then he stretched his other hand to the decanter of cognac at his elbow, filled a liqueur-glass, took a tentative sip, and poured the brandy into his coffee-cup.

Waythorn watched him in a kind of fascination. What was he thinking of—only of the flavour of the coffee and the liqueur? Had the morning's meeting left no more trace in his thoughts than on his face? Had his wife so completely passed out of his life that even this odd encounter with her present husband, within a week after her remarriage, was no more than an incident in his day? And as Waythorn mused, another idea struck him: had Haskett ever met Varick as Varick and he had just met? The recollection of Haskett perturbed him, and he rose and left the restaurant, taking a circuitous way out to escape the placid irony of Varick's nod.

It was after seven when Waythorn reached home. He thought the footman who opened the door looked at him oddly.

"How is Miss Lily?" he asked in haste.

"Doing very well, sir. A gentleman——"

"Tell Barlow to put off dinner for half an hour," Waythorn cut him off, hurrying upstairs.

He went straight to his room and dressed without seeing his wife. When he reached the drawing-room she was there, fresh and radiant. Lily's day had been good; the doctor was not coming back that evening.

At dinner Waythorn told her of Sellers's illness and of the resulting complications. She listened sympathetically, adjuring him not to let himself be overworked, and asking vague feminine questions about the routine of the office. Then she gave him the chronicle of Lily's day; quoted the nurse and doctor, and told him who had called to inquire. He had never seen her more serene and unruffled. It struck him, with a curious pang, that she was very happy in being with him, so happy that she found a childish pleasure in rehearsing the trivial incidents of her day.

After dinner they went to the library, and the servant put the coffee and liqueurs on a low table before her and left the room. She looked singularly soft and girlish in her rosy pale dress, against the dark leather of one of his bachelor armchairs. A day earlier the contrast would have charmed him.

He turned away now, choosing a cigar with affected deliberation.

"Did Haskett come?" he asked, with his back to her.

"Oh yes—he came."

"You didn't see him, of course?"

She hesitated a moment. "I let the nurse see him."

That was all. There was nothing more to ask. He swung round toward her, applying a match to his cigar. Well, the thing was over for a week, at any rate. He would try not to think of it. She looked up at him, a trifle rosier than usual, with a smile in her eyes.

"Ready for your coffee, dear?"

He leaned against the mantelpiece, watching her as she lifted the coffee-pot. The lamplight struck a gleam from her bracelets and tipped her soft hair with brightness. How light and slender she was, and how each gesture flowed into the next! She seemed a creature all compact of harmonies. As the thought of Haskett receded, Waythorn felt himself yielding again to the joy of possessorship. They were his, those white hands with their flitting motions, his the light haze of hair, the lips and eyes. . . .

She set down the coffee-pot, and reached for the decanter of cognac, measured off a liqueur-glass and poured it into his cup.

Waythorn uttered a sudden exclamation.

"What is the matter?" she said, startled.

"Nothing; only—I don't take cognac in my coffee."

"Oh, how stupid of me," she cried.

Their eyes met, and she blushed a sudden agonised red.

III

Ten days later, Mr. Sellers, still house-bound, asked Waythorn to call on his way down town.

The senior partner, with his swaddled foot propped up by the fire, greeted his associate with an air of embarrassment.

"I'm sorry, my dear fellow; I've got to ask you to do an awkward thing for me."

Waythorn waited, and the other went on, after a pause apparently given to the arrangement of his phrases: "The fact is, when I was knocked out I had just gone into a rather complicated piece of business for—Gus Varick."

"Well?" said Waythorn, with an attempt to put him at his ease.

"Well—it's this way; Varick came to me the day before my attack. He had evidently had an inside tip from somebody, and had made about a hundred thousand. He came to me for advice, and I suggested his going in with Vanderlyn."

"Oh, the deuce!" Waythorn exclaimed. He saw in a flash what had happened. The investment was an alluring one, but required negotiation. He listened quietly while Sellers put the case before him, and, the statement ended, he said: "You think I ought to see Varick?"

"I'm afraid I can't as yet. The doctor is obdurate. And this thing can't wait. I hate to ask you, but no one else in the office knows the ins and outs of it."

Waythorn stood silent. He did not care a farthing for the success of Varick's venture, but the honour of the office was to be considered, and he could hardly refuse to oblige his partner.

"Very well," he said, "I'll do it."

That afternoon, apprised by telephone, Varick called at the office. Waythorn, waiting in his private room, wondered what the others thought of it. The newspapers, at the time of Mrs. Waythorn's marriage, had acquainted their readers with every detail of her previous matrimonial ventures, and Waythorn could fancy the clerks smiling behind Varick's back as he was ushered in.

Varick bore himself admirably. He was easy without being undignified, and Waythorn was conscious of cutting a much less impressive figure. Varick had no experience of business, and the talk prolonged itself for nearly an hour while Waythorn set forth with scrupulous precision the details of the proposed transaction.

"I'm awfully obliged to you," Varick said as he rose. "The fact is I'm not used to having much money to look after, and I don't want to make an ass of myself—" He smiled, and Waythorn could not help noticing that there was something pleasant about his smile. "It feels uncommonly queer to have enough cash to pay one's bills. I'd have sold my soul for it a few years ago!"

Waythorn winced at the illusion. He had heard it rumoured that a lack of funds had been one of the determining causes of the Varick separation, but it did not occur to him that Varick's words were intentional. It seemed more likely that the desire to keep clear of embarrassing topics had fatally drawn him into one. Waythorn did not wish to be outdone in civility.

"We'll do the best we can for you," he said. "I think this is a good thing you're in."

"Oh, I'm sure it's immense. It's awfully good of you——" Varick broke off, embarrassed. "I suppose the thing's settled now—but if——"

"If anything happens before Sellers is about, I'll see you again," said Waythorn quietly. He was glad, in the end, to appear the more self-possessed of the two.

·   ·   ·   ·   ·   ·   ·   ·

The course of Lily's illness ran smooth, and as the days passed Waythorn grew used to the idea of Haskett's weekly visit. The first time the day came round, he stayed out late, and questioned his wife as to the visit on his return.

She replied at once that Haskett had merely seen the nurse downstairs, as the doctor did not wish any one in the child's sick-room till after the crisis.

The following week Waythorn was again conscious of the recurrence of the day, but had forgotten it by the time he came home to dinner. The crisis of the disease came a few days later, with a rapid decline of fever, and the little girl was pronounced out of danger. In the rejoicing which ensued the thought of Haskett passed out of Waythorn's mind, and one afternoon, letting himself into the house with a latch-key, he went straight to his library without noticing a shabby hat and umbrella in the hall.

In the library he found a small effaced-looking man with a thinnish gray beard sitting on the edge of a chair. The stranger might have been a piano-tuner, or one of those mysteriously efficient persons who are summoned in emergencies to adjust some detail of the domestic machinery. He blinked at Waythorn through a pair of gold-rimmed spectacles and said mildly: "Mr. Waythorn, I presume? I am Lily's father."

Waythorn flushed. "Oh——" he stammered uncomfortably. He broke off, disliking to appear rude. Inwardly he was trying to adjust the actual Haskett to the image of him projected by his wife's reminiscences. Waythorn had been allowed to infer that Alice's first husband was a brute.

"I am sorry to intrude," said Haskett, with his over-the-counter politeness.

"Don't mention it," returned Waythorn, collecting himself. "I suppose the nurse has been told?"

"I presume so. I can wait," said Haskett. He had a resigned way of speaking, as though life had worn down his natural powers of resistance.

Waythorn stood on the threshold, nervously pulling off his gloves.

"I'm sorry you've been detained. I will send for the nurse," he said; and as he opened the door he added with an effort: "I'm glad we can give you a good report of Lily." He winced as the *we* slipped out, but Haskett seemed not to notice it.

"Thank you, Mr. Waythorn. It's been an anxious time for me."

"Ah, well, that's past. Soon she'll be able to go to you." Waythorn nodded and passed out. In his own room he flung himself down with a groan. He hated the womanish sensibility which made him suffer so acutely from the grotesque chances of life. He had known when he married that his wife's former husbands were both living, and that amid the multiplied contacts of modern existence there were a thousand chances to one that he would run against one or the other, yet he found himself as much disturbed by his brief encounter with Haskett as though the law had not obligingly removed all difficulties in the way of their meeting.

Waythorn sprang up and began to pace the room nervously. He had not suffered half as much from his two meetings with Varick. It was Haskett's presence in his own house that made the situation so intolerable. He stood still, hearing steps in the passage.

"This way, please," he heard the nurse say. Haskett was being taken upstairs, then: not a corner of the house but was open to him. Waythorn dropped into another chair, staring vaguely ahead of him. On his dressing-table stood a photograph of Alice, taken when he had first known her. She was Alice Varick then—how fine and exquisite he had thought her! Those were Varick's pearls about her neck. At Waythorn's instance they had been returned before her marriage. Had Haskett ever given her any trinkets—and what had become of them, Waythorn wondered? He realised suddenly that he knew very little of Haskett's past or present situation; but from the man's appearance and manner of speech he could reconstruct with curious precision the surroundings of Alice's first marriage. And it startled him to think that she had, in the background of her life, a phase of existence so different from anything with which he had connected her. Varick, whatever his faults, was a gentleman, in the conventional, traditional sense of the term: the sense which at that moment seemed, oddly enough, to have most meaning to Waythorn. He and Varick had the same social habits, spoke the same language, understood the same allusions. But this other man . . . it was grotesquely uppermost in Waythorn's mind that Haskett had worn a made-up tie attached with an elastic. Why should that ridiculous detail symbolise the whole man? Waythorn was exasperated by his own paltriness, but the fact of the tie expanded, forced itself on him, became as it were the key to Alice's past. He could see her, as Mrs. Haskett, sitting in a "front parlour" furnished in plush, with a pianola, and a copy of "Ben Hur" on the centre-table. He could see her going to the theatre with Haskett—or perhaps even to a "Church Sociable"—she in a "picture hat" and Haskett in a black frock-coat, a little creased, with the made-up tie on an elastic. On the way home they would stop and look at the illuminated shop-windows, lingering over the photographs of New York actresses. On Sunday afternoons Haskett would take her for a walk, pushing Lily ahead of them in a white enamelled perambulator, and Waythorn had a vision of the people they would stop and talk to. He could fancy how pretty Alice must have looked, in a dress adroitly constructed from the hints of a New York fashion-paper, and how she must have looked down on the other women, chafing at her life, and secretly feeling that she belonged in a bigger place.

For the moment his foremost thought was one of wonder at the way in which she had shed the phase of existence which her marriage with Haskett implied. It was as if her whole aspect, every gesture, every inflection, every allusion, were a studied negation of that period of her life. If she had denied being married to Haskett she could hardly have stood more convicted of duplicity than in this obliteration of the self which had been his wife.

Waythorn started up, checking himself in the analysis of her motives. What right had he to create a fantastic effigy of her and then pass judgment on it? She had spoken vaguely of her first marriage as unhappy, had hinted, with becoming reticence, that Haskett had wrought havoc among her young illusions. . . . It was a pity for Waythorn's peace of mind that Haskett's very inoffensiveness shed a new light on the nature of those illusions. A man would rather think that his wife has been brutalised by her first husband than that the process has been reversed.

IV

"Mr. Waythorn, I don't like that French governess of Lily's."

Haskett, subdued and apologetic, stood before Waythorn in the library, revolving his shabby hat in his hand.

Waythorn, surprised in his armchair over the evening paper, stared back perplexedly at his visitor.

"You'll excuse my asking to see you," Haskett continued. "But this is my last visit, and I thought if I could have a word with you it would be a better way than writing to Mrs. Waythorn's lawyer."

Waythorn rose uneasily. He did not like the French governess either; but that was irrelevant.

"I am not so sure of that," he returned stiffly; "but since you wish it I will give your message to—my wife." He always hesitated over the possessive pronoun in addressing Haskett.

The latter sighed. "I don't know as that will help much. She didn't like it when I spoke to her."

Waythorn turned red. "When did you see her?" he asked.

"Not since the first day I came to see Lily—right after she was taken sick. I remarked to her then that I didn't like the governess."

Waythorn made no answer. He remembered distinctly that, after that first visit, he had asked his wife if she had seen Haskett. She had lied to him then, but she had respected his wishes since; and the incident cast a curious light on her character. He was sure she would not have seen Haskett that first day if she had divined that Waythorn would object, and the fact that she did not divine it was almost as disagreeable to the latter as the discovery that she had lied to him.

"I don't like the woman," Haskett was repeating with mild persistency. "She ain't straight, Mr. Waythorn—she'll teach the child to be underhand. I've noticed a change in Lily—she's too anxious to please—and she don't always tell the truth. She used to be the straightest child, Mr. Waythorn——" He broke off, his voice a little thick. "Not but what I want her to have a stylish education," he ended.

Waythorn was touched. "I'm sorry, Mr. Haskett; but frankly, I don't quite see what I can do."

Haskett hesitated. Then he laid his hat on the table, and advanced to the hearth-rug, on which Waythorn was standing. There was nothing aggressive in his manner, but he had the solemnity of a timid man resolved on a decisive measure.

"There's just one thing you can do, Mr. Waythorn," he said. "You can remind Mrs. Waythorn that, by the decree of the courts, I am entitled to have a voice in Lily's bringing up." He paused, and went on more deprecatingly: "I'm not the kind to talk about enforcing my rights, Mr. Waythorn. I don't know as I think a man is entitled to rights he hasn't known how to hold on to; but this business of the child is different. I've never let go there—and I never mean to."

. . . .

The scene left Waythorn deeply shaken. Shamefacedly, in indirect ways, he had been finding out about Haskett; and all that he had learned was favourable. The little man, in order to be near his daughter, had sold out his share in a profitable business in Utica, and accepted a modest clerkship in a New York manufacturing house. He boarded in a shabby street and had few acquaintances. His passion for Lily filled his life. Waythorn felt that this exploration of Haskett was like groping about with a dark-lantern in his wife's past; but he saw now that there were recesses his lantern had not explored. He had never enquired into the exact circumstances of his wife's first matrimonial rupture. On the surface all had been fair. It was she who had obtained the divorce, and the court had given her the child. But Waythorn knew how many ambiguities such a verdict might cover. The mere fact that Haskett retained a right over his daughter implied an unsuspected compromise. Waythorn was an idealist. He always refused to recognise unpleasant contingencies till he found himself confronted with them, and then he saw them followed by a special train of consequences. His next days were thus haunted, and he determined to try to lay the ghosts by conjuring them up in his wife's presence.

When he repeated Haskett's request a flame of anger passed over her face; but she subdued it instantly and spoke with a slight quiver of outraged motherhood.

"It is very ungentlemanly of him," she said.

The word grated on Waythorn. "That is neither here nor there. It's a bare question of rights."

She murmured: "It is not as if he could ever be a help to Lily——"

Waythorn flushed. This was even less to his taste. "The question is," he repeated, "what authority has he over her?"

She looked downward, twisting herself a little in her seat. "I am willing to see him—I thought you objected," she faltered.

In a flash he understood that she knew the extent of Haskett's claims. Perhaps it was not the first time she had resisted them.

"My objecting has nothing to do with it," he said coldly; "if Haskett has a right to be consulted you must consult him."

She burst into tears, and he saw that she expected him to regard her as a victim.

Haskett did not abuse his rights. Waythorn had felt miserably sure that he would not. But the governess was dismissed, and from time to time the little man demanded an interview with Alice. After the first outburst she accepted the situation with her usual adaptability. Haskett had once reminded Waythorn of the piano-tuner, and Mrs. Waythorn, after a month or two, appeared to class him with that domestic familiar. Waythorn could not but respect the father's tenacity. At first he had tried to cultivate the suspicion that Haskett might be "up to" something, that he had an object in securing a foothold in the house. But in his heart Waythorn was sure of Haskett's single-mindedness; he even guessed in the latter a mild contempt for such advantages as his relation with the Waythorns might offer. Haskett's sincerity of purpose made him invulnerable, and his successor had to accept him as a lien on the property.

. . . .

Mr. Sellers was sent to Europe to recover from his gout, and Varick's affairs hung on Waythorn's hands. The negotiations were prolonged and complicated; they necessitated frequent conferences between the two men, and the interests of the firm forbade Waythorn's suggesting that his client should transfer his business to another office.

Varick appeared well in the transaction. In moments of relaxation his coarse streak appeared, and Waythorn dreaded his geniality; but in the office he was concise and clear-headed, with a flattering deference to Waythorn's judgment. Their business relations being so affably established, it would have been absurd for the two men to ignore each other in society. The first time they met in a drawing-room, Varick took up their intercourse in the same easy key, and his hostess's grateful glance obliged Waythorn to respond to it. After that they ran across each other frequently, and one evening at a ball Waythorn, wandering through the remoter rooms, came upon Varick seated beside his wife. She coloured a little, and faltered in what she was saying; but Varick nodded to Waythorn without rising, and the latter strolled on.

In the carriage, on the way home, he broke out nervously: "I didn't know you spoke to Varick."

Her voice trembled a little. "It's the first time—he happened to be standing near me; I didn't know what to do. It's so awkward, meeting everywhere—and he said you had been very kind about some business."

"That's different," said Waythorn.

She paused a moment. "I'll do just as you wish," she returned pliantly. "I thought it would be less awkward to speak to him when we meet."

Her pliancy was beginning to sicken him. Had she really no will of her own—

no theory about her relation to these men? She had accepted Haskett—did she mean to accept Varick? It was "less awkward," as she had said, and her instinct was to evade difficulties or to circumvent them. With sudden vividness Waythorn saw how the instinct had developed. She was "as easy as an old shoe"—a shoe that too many feet had worn. Her elasticity was the result of tension in too many different directions. Alice Haskett—Alice Varick—Alice Waythorn—she had been each in turn, and had left hanging to each name a little of her privacy, a little of her personality, a little of the inmost self where the unknown god abides.

"Yes—it's better to speak to Varick," said Waythorn wearily.

V

The winter wore on, and society took advantage of the Waythorns' acceptance of Varick. Harassed hostesses were grateful to them for bridging over a social difficulty, and Mrs. Waythorn was held up as a miracle of good taste. Some experimental spirits could not resist the diversion of throwing Varick and his former wife together, and there were those who thought he found a zest in the propinquity. But Mrs. Waythorn's conduct remained irreproachable. She neither avoided Varick nor sought him out. Even Waythorn could not but admit that she had discovered the solution of the newest social problem.

He had married her without giving much thought to that problem. He had fancied that a woman can shed her past like a man. But now he saw that Alice was bound to hers both by the circumstances which forced her into continued relation with it, and by the traces it had left on her nature. With grim irony Waythorn compared himself to a member of a syndicate. He held so many shares in his wife's personality and his predecessors were his partners in the business. If there had been any element of passion in the transaction he would have felt less deteriorated by it. The fact that Alice took her change of husbands like a change of weather reduced the situation to mediocrity. He could have forgiven her for blunders, for excesses; for resisting Haskett, for yielding to Varick; for anything but her acquiescence and her tact. She reminded him of a juggler tossing knives; but the knives were blunt and he knew they would never cut her.

And then, gradually, habit formed a protecting surface for his sensibilities. If he paid for each day's comfort with the small change of his illusions, he grew daily to value the comfort more and set less store upon the coin. He had drifted into a dulling propinquity with Haskett and Varick and he took refuge in the cheap revenge of satirising the situation. He even began to reckon up the advantages which accrued from it, to ask himself if it were not better to own a third of a wife who knew how to make a man happy than a whole one who had lacked opportunity to acquire the art. For it *was* an art, and made up, like all others, of concessions, eliminations and embellishments; of lights judiciously thrown and shadows skilfully softened. His wife knew exactly how to manage the lights, and he knew exactly to what training she owed her skill. He even tried to trace the source of his obligations, to discriminate between the influences which had combined to produce his domestic happiness: he perceived that Haskett's commonness had made Alice worship good breeding, while Varick's liberal construction of the marriage bond had taught her to value the conjugal virtues; so that he was directly indebted to his predecessors for the devotion which made his life easy if not inspiring.

From this phase he passed into that of complete acceptance. He ceased to satirise himself because time dulled the irony of the situation and the joke lost its humour with its sting. Even the sight of Haskett's hat on the hall table had ceased to touch the springs of epigram. The hat was often seen there now, for it had been decided that it was better for Lily's father to visit her than for the little girl to go to his boarding-house. Waythorn, having acquiesced in this arrangement, had been surprised to find how little difference it made. Haskett was never obtrusive, and the few visitors who met him on the stairs were unaware of his identity. Waythorn did not know how often he saw Alice, but with himself Haskett was seldom in contact.

One afternoon, however, he learned on entering that Lily's father was waiting to see him. In the library he found Haskett occupying a chair in his usual provisional way. Waythorn always felt grateful to him for not leaning back.

"I hope you'll excuse me, Mr. Waythorn," he said rising. "I wanted to see Mrs. Waythorn about Lily, and your man asked me to wait here till she came in."

"Of course," said Waythorn, remembering that a sudden leak had that morning given over the drawing-room to the plumbers.

He opened his cigar-case and held it out to his visitor, and Haskett's acceptance seemed to mark a fresh stage in their intercourse. The spring evening was chilly, and Waythorn invited his guest to draw up his chair to the fire. He meant to find an excuse to leave Haskett in a moment; but he was tired and cold, and after all the little man no longer jarred on him.

The two were enclosed in the intimacy of their blended cigar-smoke when the door opened and Varick walked into the room. Waythorn rose abruptly. It was the first time that Varick had come to the house, and the surprise of seeing him, combined with the singular inopportuneness of his arrival, gave a new edge to Waythorn's blunted sensibilities. He stared at his visitor without speaking.

Varick seemed too preoccupied to notice his host's embarrassment.

"My dear fellow," he exclaimed in his most expansive tone, "I must apologise for tumbling in on you in this way, but I was too late to catch you down town, and so I thought——"

He stopped short, catching sight of Haskett, and his sanguine colour deepened to a flush which spread vividly under his scant blond hair. But in a moment he recovered himself and nodded slightly. Haskett returned the bow in silence, and Waythorn was still groping for speech when the footman came in carrying a tea-table.

The intrusion offered a welcome vent to Waythorn's nerves. "What the deuce are you bringing this here for?" he said sharply.

"I beg your pardon, sir, but the plumbers are still in the drawing-room, and Mrs. Waythorn said she would have tea in the library." The footman's perfectly respectful tone implied a reflection on Waythorn's reasonableness.

"Oh, very well," said the latter resignedly, and the footman proceeded to open the folding tea-table and set out its complicated appointments. While this interminable process continued the three men stood motionless, watching it with a fascinated stare, till Waythorn, to break the silence, said to Varick: "Won't you have a cigar?"

He held out the case he had just tendered to Haskett, and Varick helped himself with a smile. Waythorn looked about for a match, and finding none, proffered a light from his own cigar. Haskett, in the background, held his ground mildly, examining his cigar-tip now and then, and stepping forward at the right moment to knock its ashes into the fire.

The footman at last withdrew, and Varick immediately began: "If I could just say half a word to you about this business——"

"Certainly," stammered Waythorn; "in the dining-room——"

But as he placed his hand on the door it opened from without, and his wife appeared on the threshold.

She came in fresh and smiling, in her street dress and hat, shedding a fragrance from the boa[1] which she loosened in advancing.

"Shall we have tea in here, dear?" she began; and then she caught sight of Varick. Her smile deepened, veiling a slight tremor of surprise.

"Why, how do you do?" she said with a distinct note of pleasure.

As she shook hands with Varick she saw Haskett standing behind him. Her smile faded for a moment, but she recalled it quickly, with a scarcely perceptible side-glance at Waythorn.

"How do you do, Mr. Haskett?" she said, and shook hands with him a shade less cordially.

The three men stood awkwardly before her, till Varick, always the most self-possessed, dashed into an explanatory phrase.

"We—I had to see Waythorn a moment on business," he stammered, brick-red from chin to nape.

Haskett stepped forward with his air of mild obstinacy. "I am sorry to intrude; but you appointed five o'clock—" he directed his resigned glance to the timepiece on the mantel.

She swept aside their embarrassment with a charming gesture of hospitality.

"I'm so sorry—I'm always late; but the afternoon was so lovely." She stood drawing off her gloves, propitiatory and graceful, diffusing about her a sense of ease and familiarity in which the situation lost its grotesqueness. "But before talking business," she added brightly, "I'm sure every one wants a cup of tea."

She dropped into her low chair by the tea-table, and the two visitors, as if drawn by her smile, advanced to receive the cups she held out.

She glanced about for Waythorn, and he took the third cup with a laugh.

1904

Theodore Dreiser *1871–1945*

Theodore Dreiser was America's greatest literary naturalist. One of thirteen children, he was raised in Terre Haute, Indiana, in misery and bruising poverty. His penniless German immigrant father was fiercely pious, obsessed by religion. His mother was gentle, helpless, and illiterate—Dreiser himself taught her to read and write. His wandering and shiftless brothers and sisters, with their public drunkenness, illegitimate babies, and jail terms brought him despair and constant humiliation.

At fifteen Dreiser fled from home and went to Chicago, where he washed dishes in a cheap restaurant, clerked in a store, and painted advertising signs. He read constantly and, like one of his own helpless characters, he dreamt of wealth and social success in the great metropolis. When he was eighteen, a sympathetic teacher helped him enter the University of Indiana, but Dreiser quit after a year and returned to Chicago, where he

[1] A long, fluffy scarf.

embarked on another series of menial jobs and wandered the city streets at night, storing up impressions of drunks, thieves, prostitutes, and beggars.

Finally he got a job on a newspaper and began a career that took him to St. Louis, Cleveland, Pittsburgh, and eventually New York City, where he became a free-lance journalist and a magazine editor. He read widely the evolutionary theorizing of such philosophers as Thomas Huxley and Herbert Spencer, and as the last remnants of Dreiser's religious faith drained away he was left with the deterministic belief that man is merely a mechanism moved by chemical and physical forces beyond his control.

In 1899 he began writing Sister Carrie. *When he submitted the manuscript to a publisher it was rejected because it was thought likely to offend "the feminine readers who control the destinies of so many novels. . . ." In 1900, when the novel was finally accepted and published, only 456 copies were sold, and Dreiser earned so little in royalties ($68.40) that he came to believe the novel had been "suppressed" by censorious prudes. Not until 1907, when it was reissued, did* Sister Carrie *finally reach a sizable reading public and begin to shape the development of American literature.*

In 1911 Dreiser published Jennie Gerhardt, *whose heroine, misled and victimized by fate, was modeled after Dreiser's own sisters. In 1912 he published* The Financier, *the first of a trilogy on the ruthlessness of American capitalism that included* The Titan *(1914) and* The Stoic *(published posthumously in 1947). In 1925* An American Tragedy *appeared, Dreiser's greatest work and a critical and financial success.*

Dreiser's works, like the man himself, are ponderous and sprawling. His prose is fumbling, inexact, cliché-ridden; yet its piling up of details can produce striking portrayals of human experience. Dreiser's powerful frankness widened the social and sexual range possible for literature in America. He struck at the American myth that success and fame are to be achieved by work and virtue. He was seized by a dark, chaotic view of life, yet his determinism was softened by a romantic sensibility and by a powerful sympathy for people at radical odds with society, characters Dreiser saw as "haunted by poverty," filled with "gallant dreams," but "helpless in the clutch of relentless fate."

FURTHER READING: *Letters of Theodore Dreiser,* 3 vols., R. Elias, 1959; D. Dudley, *Dreiser and the Land of the Free,* 1932, 1946; R. Elias, *Theodore Dreiser, Apostle of Nature, 1949;* F. Matthiessen, *Theodore Dreiser,* 1951; *The Stature of Theodore Dreiser,* ed. A. Kazin and C. Shapiro, 1955; P. Gerber, *Theodore Dreiser,* 1964; W. Swanberg, *Dreiser,* 1965; C. Shapiro, *Theodore Dreiser, Our Bitter Patriot,* 1962; Y. Hakutani, *Young Dreiser,* 1980; R. Lingeman, *Theodore Dreiser,* 1986; J. McAleer, *Theodore Dreiser, An Introduction and Interpretation,* 1968; R. Lehan, *Theodore Dreiser, His World and His Novels,* 1969; E. Moers, *Two Dreisers, The Man and the Novelist,* 1970; R. Warren, *Homage to Theodore Dreiser, 1971;* D. Pizer, *The Novels of Theodore Dreiser,* 1976; *Critical Essays on Theodore Dreiser,* ed. D. Pizer, 1981; L. Hussman, *Dreiser and His Fiction,* 1983; J. Griffin, *The Small Canvas, An Introduction to Dreiser's Short Fiction,* 1985.

TEXT: *Free and Other Stories,* 1918.

NIGGER JEFF

The city editor was waiting for one of his best reporters, Elmer Davies by name, a vain and rather self-sufficient youth who was inclined to be of that turn of mind which sees in life only a fixed and ordered process of rewards and punishments. If one did not do exactly right, one did not get along well. On the contrary, if one did, one did. Only the so-called evil were really punished, only the good truly rewarded—or Mr. Davies had heard this so long in his youth that he had come nearly to believe it. Presently he appeared. He was dressed in a new spring suit, a new hat and new shoes. In the lapel of his coat was a small bunch of violets. It was one o'clock of a sunny spring afternoon, and he was feeling exceedingly well and good-natured—quite fit, indeed. The world was going unusually well with him. It seemed worth singing about.

"Read that, Davies," said the city editor, handing him the clipping. "I'll tell you afterward what I want you to do."

The reporter stood by the editorial chair and read:

Pleasant Valley, Ko.,[1] April 16.

"A most dastardly crime has just been reported here. Jeff Ingalls, a negro, this morning assaulted Ada Whitaker, the nineteen-year-old daughter of Morgan Whitaker, a well-to-do farmer, whose home is four miles south of this place. A posse, headed by Sheriff Mathews, has started in pursuit. If he is caught, it is thought he will be lynched."

The reporter raised his eyes as he finished. What a terrible crime! What evil people there were in the world! No doubt such a creature ought to be lynched, and that quickly.

"You had better go out there Davies," said the city editor. "It looks as if something might come of that. A lynching up here would be a big thing. There's never been one in this state."

Davies smiled. He was always pleased to be sent out of town. It was a mark of appreciation. The city editor rarely sent any of the other men on these big stories. What a nice ride he would have!

As he went along, however, a few minutes later he began to meditate on this. Perhaps, as the city editor had suggested, he might be compelled to witness an actual lynching. That was by no means so pleasant in itself. In his fixed code of rewards and punishments he had no particular place for lynchings, even for crimes of the nature described, especially if he had to witness the lynching. It was too horrible a kind of reward or punishment. Once, in line of duty, he had been compelled to witness a hanging, and that had made him sick—deathly so— even though carried out as a part of the due process of law of his day and place. Now, as he looked at this fine day and his excellent clothes, he was not so sure that this was a worthwhile assignment. Why should he always be selected for such things—just because he could write? There were others—lots of men on the staff. He began to hope as he went along that nothing really serious would come of it, that they would catch the man before he got there and put him in jail—or, if the worst had to be—painful thought!—that it would be all over by the time he got there. Let's see—the telegram had been filed at nine A.M. It was now one-thirty and would be three by the time he got out there, all of that. That would give them time enough, and then, if all were well, or ill, as it were, he could just gather the details of the crime and the—aftermath—and return. The mere thought of an approaching lynching troubled him greatly, and the farther he went the less he liked it.

He found the village of Pleasant Valley a very small affair indeed, just a few dozen houses nestling between green slopes of low hills, with one small business corner and a rambling array of lanes. One or two merchants of K——, the city from which he had just arrived, lived out here, but otherwise it was very rural. He took notes of the whiteness of the little houses, the shimmering beauty of the small stream one had to cross in going from the depot. At the one main corner a few men were gathered about a typical village barroom. Davies headed for this as being the most likely source of information.

[1]When the story was first published (1901) Dreiser used "Mo.," indicating "Missouri," rather than the fictional "Ko."

In mingling with this company at first he said nothing about his being a newspaper man, being very doubtful as to its effect upon them, their freedom of speech and manner.

The whole company was apparently tense with interest in the crime which still remained unpunished, seemingly craving excitement and desirous of seeing something done about it. No such opportunity to work up wrath and vent their stored-up animal propensities had probably occurred here in years. He took this occasion to inquire into the exact details of the attack, where it had occurred, where the Whitakers lived. Then, seeing that mere talk prevailed here, he went away thinking that he had best find out for himself how the victim was. As yet she had not been described, and it was necessary to know a little something about her. Accordingly, he sought an old man who kept a stable in the village, and procured a horse. No carriage was to be had, Davies was not an excellent rider, but he made a shift of it. The Whitaker home was not so very far away—about four miles out—and before long he was knocking at its front door, set back a hundred feet from the rough country road.

"I'm from the *Times*," he said to the tall, raw-boned woman who opened the door, with an attempt at being impressive. His position as reporter in this matter was a little dubious; he might be welcome, and he might not. Then he asked if this were Mrs. Whitaker, and how Miss Whitaker was by now.

"She's doing very well," answered the woman, who seemed decidedly stern, if repressed and nervous, a Spartan type. "Won't you come in? She's rather feverish, but the doctor says she'll probably be all right later on." She said no more.

Davies acknowledged the invitation by entering. He was very anxious to see the girl, but she was sleeping under the influence of an opiate, and he did not care to press the matter at once.

"When did this happen?" he asked.

"About eight o'clock this morning," said the woman. "She started to go over to our next door neighbor here, Mr. Edmonds, and this negro met her. We didn't know anything about it until she came crying through the gate and dropped down in here."

"Were you the first one to meet her?" asked Davies.

"Yes, I was the only one," said Mrs. Whitaker. "The men had all gone to the fields."

Davies listened to more of the details, the type and history of the man, and then rose to go. Before doing so he was allowed to have a look at the girl, who was still sleeping. She was young and rather pretty. In the yard he met a country man who was just coming to get home news. The latter imparted more information.

"They're lookin' all around south of here," he said, speaking of a crowd which was supposed to be searching. "I expect they'll make short work of him if they get him. He can't get away very well, for he's on foot, wherever he is. The sheriff's after him too, with a deputy or two. I believe. He'll be tryin' to save him an' take him over to Clayton, but I don't believe he'll be able to do it, not if the crowd catches him first."

So, thought Davies, he would probably have to witness a lynching after all. The prospect was most unhappy.

"Does any one know where this negro lived?" he asked heavily, a growing sense of his duty weighing upon him.

"Oh, right down here a little way," replied the farmer. "Jeff Ingalls was his name. We all know him around here. He worked for one and another of the farmers hereabouts, and don't appear to have had such a bad record, either, except for drinkin' a little now and then. Miss Ada recognized him, all right. You follow this road to the next crossing and turn to the right. It's a little log house that sets back off the road—something like that one you see down the lane there, only it's got lots o' chips scattered about."

Davies decided to go there first, but changed his mind. It was growing late, and he thought he had better return to the village. Perhaps by now developments in connection with the sheriff or the posse were to be learned.

Accordingly, he rode back and put the horse in the hands of its owner, hoping that all had been concluded and that he might learn of it here. At the principal corner much the same company was still present, arguing, fomenting, gesticulating. They seemed parts of different companies that earlier in the day had been out searching. He wondered what they had been doing since, and then decided to ingratiate himself by telling them he had just come from the Whitakers and what he had learned there of the present condition of the girl and the movements of the sheriff.

Just then a young farmer came galloping up. He was coatless, hatless, breathless.

"They've got him!" he shouted excitedly. "They've got him!"

A chorus of "whos," "wheres" and "whens" greeted this information as the crowd gathered about the rider.

"Why, Mathews caught him up here at his own house!" exclaimed the latter, pulling out a handkerchief and wiping his face. "He must 'a' gone back there for something. Mathews's takin' him over to Clayton, so they think, but they don't project he'll ever get there. They're after him now, but Mathews says he'll shoot the first man that tries to take him away."

"Which way'd he go?" exclaimed the men in chorus, stirring as if to make an attack.

"'Cross Sellers' Lane," said the rider. "The boys think he's goin' by way of Baldwin."

"Whoopee!" yelled one of the listeners. "We'll get him away from him, all right! Are you goin', Sam?"

"You bet! said the latter. "Wait'll I get my horse!"

"Lord!" thought Davies. "To think of being (perforce) one of a lynching party—a hired spectator!"

He delayed no longer, however, but hastened to secure his horse again. He saw that the crowd would be off in a minute to catch up with the sheriff. There would be information in that quarter, drama very likely.

"What's doin'?" inquired the liveryman as he noted Davies' excited appearance.

"They're after him," replied the latter nervously. "The sheriff's caught him. They're going now to try to take him away from him, or that's what they say. The sheriff is taking him over to Clayton, by way of Baldwin. I want to get over there if I can. Give me the horse again, and I'll give you a couple of dollars more."

The liveryman led the horse out, but not without many provisionary cautions as to the care which was to be taken of him, the damages which would ensue if it were not. He was not to be ridden beyond midnight. If one were wanted for longer than that Davies must get him elsewhere or come and get another, to all of which Davies promptly agreed. He then mounted and rode away.

When he reached the corner again several of the men who had gone for their horses were already there, ready to start. The young man who had brought the news had long since dashed off to other parts.

Davies waited to see which road this new company would take. Then through as pleasant a country as one would wish to see, up hill and down dale, with charming vistas breaking upon the gaze at every turn, he did the riding of his life. So disturbed was the reporter by the grim turn things had taken that he scarcely noted the beauty that was stretched before him, save to note that it was so. Death! Death! The proximity of involuntary and enforced death was what weighed upon him now.

In about an hour the company had come in sight of the sheriff, who, with two other men, was driving a wagon he had borrowed along a lone country road. The latter was sitting at the back, a revolver in each hand, his face toward the group, which at sight of him trailed after at a respectful distance. Excited as every one was, there was no disposition, for the time being at least, to halt the progress of the law.

"He's in that wagon," Davies heard one man say. "Don't you see they've got him in there tied and laid down?"

Davies looked.

"That's right," said another. "I see him now."

"What we ought to do," said a third, who was riding near the front, "is to take him away and hang him. That's just what he deserves, and that's what he'll get before we're through to-day."

"Yes!" called the sheriff, who seemed to have heard this. "You're not goin' to do any hangin' this day, so you just might as well go on back." He did not appear to be much troubled by the appearance of the crowd.

"Where's old man Whitaker?" asked one of the men who seemed to feel that they needed a leader. "He'd get him quick enough!"

"He's with the other crowd, down below Olney," was the reply.

"Somebody ought to go an' tell him."

"Clark's gone," assured another, who hoped for the worst.

Davies rode among the company a prey to mingled and singular feelings. He was very much excited and yet depressed by the character of the crowd which, in so far as he could see, was largely impelled to its jaunt by curiosity and yet also able under sufficient motivation on the part of some one—any one, really— to kill too. There was not so much daring as a desire to gain daring from others, an unconscious wish or impulse to organize the total strength or will of those present into one strength or one will, sufficient to overcome the sheriff and inflict death upon his charge. It was strange—almost intellectually incomprehensible—and yet so it was. The men were plainly afraid of the determined sheriff. They thought something ought to be done, but they did not feel like getting into trouble.

Mathews, a large, solemn, sage, brown man in worn clothes and a faded brown hat, contemplated the recent addition to his trailers with apparent indifference. Seemingly he was determined to protect his man and avoid mob justice, come what may. A mob should not have him if he had to shoot, and if he shot it would be to kill. Finally, since the company thus added to did not dash upon him, he seemingly decided to scare them off. Apparently he thought he could do this, since they trailed like calves.

"Stop a minute!" he called to his driver.

The latter pulled up. So did the crowd behind. Then the sheriff stood over the prostrate body of the negro, who lay in the jolting wagon beneath him, and called back:

"Go 'way from here, you people! Go on, now! I won't have you follerin' after me!"

"Give us the nigger!" yelled one in a half-bantering, half-derisive tone of voice.

"I'll give ye just two minutes to go on back out o' this road," returned the sheriff grimly, pulling out his watch and looking at it. They were about a hundred feet apart. "If you don't, I'll clear you out!"

"Give us the nigger!"

"I know you, Scott," answered Mathews, recognizing the voice, "I'll arrest every last one of ye to-morrow. Mark my word!"

The company listened in silence, the horses champing and twisting.

"We've got a right to foller," answered one of the men.

"I give ye fair warning," said the sheriff, jumping from his wagon and leveling his pistols as he approached. "When I count five I'll begin to shoot!"

He was a serious and stalwart figure as he approached, and the crowd fell back a little.

"Git out o' this now!" he yelled. "One—Two——"

The company turned completely and retreated, Davies among them.

"We'll foller him when he gits further on," said one of the men in explanation.

"He's got to do it," said another. "Let him git a little ways ahead."

The sheriff returned to his wagon and drove on. He seemed, however, to realize that he would not be obeyed and that safety lay in haste alone. His wagon was traveling fast. If only he could lose them or get a good start he might possibly get to Clayton and the strong county jail by morning. His followers, however, trailed him swiftly as might be, determined not to be left behind.

"He's goin' to Baldwin," said one of the company of which Davies was a member.

"Where's that?" asked Davies.

"Over west o' here, about four miles."

"Why is he going there?"

"That's where he lives. I guess he thinks if he kin git 'im over there he kin purtect 'im till he kin git more help from Clayton. I cal'late he'll try an' take 'im over yet to-night, or early in the mornin' shore."

Davies smiled at the man's English. This country-side lingo always fascinated him.

Yet the men lagged, hesitating as to what to do. They did not want to lose sight of Mathews, and yet cowardice controlled them. They did not want to get into direct altercation with the law. It wasn't their place to hang the man, although plainly they felt that he ought to be hanged, and that it would be a stirring and exciting thing if he were. Consequently they desired to watch and be on hand— to get old Whitaker and his son Jake, if they could, who were out looking elsewhere. They wanted to see what the father and brother would do.

The quandary was solved by one of the men, who suggested that they could get to Baldwin by going back to Pleasant Valley and taking the Sand River pike, and that in the meantime they might come upon Whitaker and his son en route, or leave word at his house. It was a shorter cut than this the sheriff was taking, although he would get there first now. Possibly they could beat him at least to Clayton, if he attempted to go on. The Clayton road was back via Pleasant Valley, or near it, and easily intercepted. Therefore, while one or two remained to trail the sheriff and give the alarm in case he did attempt to go on to Clayton, the rest, followed by Davies, set off at a gallop to Pleasant Valley. It was nearly dusk now when they arrived and stopped at the corner store—supper time. The fires of evening meals were marked by upcurling smoke from chimneys. Here, somehow, the zest to follow seemed to depart. Evidently the sheriff had worsted them for the night. Morg Whitaker, the father, had not been found; neither had Jake. Perhaps they had better eat. Two or three had already secretly fallen away.

They were telling the news of what had occurred so far to one of the two storekeepers who kept the place, when suddenly Jake Whitaker, the girl's brother, and several companions came riding up. They had been scouring the territory to the north of the town, and were hot and tired. Plainly they were unaware of the developments of which the crowd had been a part.

"The sheriff's got 'im!" exclaimed one of the company, with that blatance which always accompanies the telling of great news in small rural companies. "He taken him over to Baldwin in a wagon a coupla hours ago."

"Which way did he go?" asked the son, whose hardy figure, worn, hand-me-down clothes and rakish hat showed up picturesquely as he turned here and there on his horse.

"'Cross Seller' Lane. You won't git 'em that-a-way, though, Jake. He's already over there by now. Better take the short cut."

A babble of voices now made the scene more interesting. One told how the negro had been caught, another that the sheriff was defiant, a third that men were still tracking him or over there watching, until all the chief points of the drama had been spoken if not heard.

Instantly suppers were forgotten. The whole customary order of the evening was overturned once more. The company started off on another excited jaunt, up hill and down dale, through the lovely country that lay between Baldwin and Pleasant Valley.

By now Davies was very weary of this procedure and of his saddle. He wondered when, if ever, this story was to culminate, let alone he write it. Tragic as it might prove, he could not nevertheless spend an indefinite period trailing a possibility, and yet, so great was the potentiality of the present situation, he dared not leave. By contrast with the horror impending, as he now noted, the night was so beautiful that it was all but poignant. Stars were already beginning to shine. Distant lamps twinkled like yellow eyes from the cottages in the alleys and on the hillsides. The air was fresh and tender. Some pea-fowls were crying afar off, and the east promised a golden moon.

Silently the assembled company trotted on—no more than a score in all. In the dusk, and with Jake ahead, it seemed too grim a pilgrimage for joking. Young Jake, riding silently toward the front, looked as if tragedy were all he craved. His friends seemed considerately to withdraw from him, seeing that he was the aggrieved.

After an hour's riding Baldwin came into view, lying in a sheltering cup of low hills. Already its lights were twinkling softly and there was still an air of honest firesides and cheery suppers about it which appealed to Davies in his hungry state. Still, he had no thought now of anything save this pursuit.

Once in the village, the company was greeted by calls of recognition. Everybody seemed to know what they had come for. The sheriff and his charge were still there, so a dozen citizens volunteered. The local storekeepers and loungers followed the cavalcade up the street to the sheriff's house, for the riders had now fallen into a solemn walk.

"You won't get him though, boys," said one whom Davies later learned was

Seavey, the village postmaster and telegraph operator, a rather youthful person of between twenty-five and thirty, as they passed his door. "He's got two deputies in there with him, or did have, and they say he's going to take him over to Clayton."

At the first street corner they were joined by the several men who had followed the sheriff.

"He tried to give us the slip," they volunteered excitedly, "but he's got the nigger in the house, there, down in the cellar. The deputies ain't with him. They've gone somewhere for help—Clayton, maybe."

"How do you know?"

"We saw 'em go out that back way. We think we did, anyhow."

A hundred feet from the sheriff's little white cottage, which backed up against a sloping field, the men parleyed. Then Jake announced that he proposed to go boldly up to the sheriff's door and demand the negro.

"If he don't turn him out I'll break in the door an' take him!" he said.

"That's right! We'll stand by you, Whitaker," commented several.

By now the throng of unmounted natives had gathered. The whole village was up and about, its one street alive and running with people. Heads appeared at doors and windows. Riders pranced up and down, hallooing. A few revolver shots were heard. Presently the mob gathered even closer to the sheriff's gate, and Jake stepped forward as leader. Instead, however, of going boldly up to the door as at first it appeared he would, he stopped at the gate, calling to the sheriff.

"Hello, Mathews!"

"Eh, eh, eh!" bellowed the crowd.

The call was repeated. Still no answer. Apparently to the sheriff delay appeared to be his one best weapon.

Their coming, however, was not as unexpected as some might have thought. The figure of the sheriff was plainly to be seen close to one of the front windows. He appeared to be holding a double-barreled shotgun. The negro, as it developed later, was cowering and chattering in the darkest corner of the cellar, hearkening no doubt to the voices and firing of the revolvers outside.

Suddenly, and just as Jake was about to go forward, the front door of the house flew open, and in the glow of a single lamp inside appeared first the double-barreled end of the gun, followed immediately by the form of Mathews, who held the weapon poised ready for a quick throw to the shoulder. All except Jake fell back.

"Mr. Mathews," he called deliberately, "we want that nigger!"

"Well, you can't git 'im!" replied the sheriff. "He's not here."

"Then what you got that gun fer?" yelled a voice.

Mathews made no answer.

"Better give him up, Mathews," called another, who was safe in the crowd, "or we'll come in an' take him!"

"No you won't," said the sheriff defiantly. "I said the man wasn't here. I say it ag'in. You couldn't have him if he was, an' you can't come in my house! Now if you people don't want trouble you'd better go on away."

"He's down in the cellar!" yelled another.

"Why don't you let us see?" asked another.

Mathews waved his gun slightly.

"You'd better go away from here now," cautioned the sheriff. "I'm tellin' ye! I'll have warrants out for the lot o' ye, if ye don't mind!"

The crowd continued to simmer and stew, while Jake stood as before. He was very pale and tense, but lacked initiative.

"He won't shoot," called some one at the back of the crowd. "Why don't you go in, Jake, an' git him?"

"Sure! Rush in. That's it!" observed a second.

"He won't, eh?" replied the sheriff softly. Then he added in a lower tone, "The first man that comes inside that gate takes the consequences."

No one ventured inside the gate; many even fell back. It seemed as if the planned assault had come to nothing.

"Why not go around the back way?" called some one else.

"Try it!" replied the sheriff. "See what you find on that side! I told you you couldn't come inside. You'd better go away from here now before ye git into trouble," he repeated. "You can't come in, an' it'll only mean bloodshed."

There was more chattering and jesting while the sheriff stood on guard. He, however, said no more. Nor did he allow the banter, turmoil and lust for tragedy to disturb him. Only, he kept his eye on Jake, on whose movements the crowd seemed to hang.

Time passed, and still nothing was done. The truth was that young Jake, put to the test, was not sufficiently courageous himself, for all his daring, and felt the weakness of the crowd behind him. To all intents and purposes he was alone, for he did not inspire confidence. He finally fell back a little, observing, "I'll git 'im before mornin', all right," and now the crowd itself began to disperse, returning to its stores and homes or standing about the postoffice and the one village drugstore. Finally, Davies smiled and came away. He was sure he had the story of a defeated mob. The sheriff was to be his great hero. He proposed to interview him later. For the present, he meant to seek out Seavey, the telegraph operator, and arrange to file a message, then see if something to eat was not to be had somewhere.

After a time he found the operator and told him what he wanted—to write and file a story as he wrote it. The latter indicated a table in the little postoffice and telegraph station which he could use. He became very much interested in the reporter when he learned he was from the *Times,* and when Davies asked where he could get something to eat said he would run across the street and tell the proprietor of the only boarding house to fix him something which he could consume as he wrote. He appeared to be interested in how a newspaper man would go about telling a story of this kind over a wire.

"You start your story," he said, "and I'll come back and see if I can get the *Times* on the wire,"

Davies sat down and began his account. He was intent on describing things to date, the uncertainty and turmoil, and apparent victory of the sheriff. Plainly the courage of the latter had won, and it was all so picturesque. "A foiled lynching," he began, and as he wrote the obliging postmaster, who had by now returned, picked up the pages and carefully deciphered them for himself.

"That's all right. I'll see if I can get the *Times* now," he commented.

"Very obliging postmaster," thought Davies as he wrote, but he had so often encountered pleasant and obliging people on his rounds that he soon dropped that thought.

The food was brought, and still Davies wrote on, munching as he did so. In a little while the *Times* answered an often-repeated call.

"Davies at Baldwin," ticked the postmaster, "get ready for quite a story!"

"Let 'er go!" answered the operator at the *Times,* who had been expecting this dispatch.

As the events of the day formulated themselves in his mind, Davies wrote and turned over page after page. Between whiles he looked out through the small window before him where afar off he could see a lonely light twinkling against a hillside. Not infrequently he stopped his work to see if anything new was happening, whether the situation was in any danger of changing, but apparently it was not. He then proposed to remain until all possibility of a tragedy, this night anyhow, was eliminated. The operator also wandered about, waiting for an accumulation of pages upon which he could work but making sure to keep up with the writer. The two became quite friendly.

Finally, his dispatch nearly finished, he asked the postmaster to caution the night editor at K—— to the effect, that if anything more happened before one in the morning he would file it, but not to expect anything more as nothing might happen. The reply came that he was to remain and await developments. Then he and the postmaster sat down to talk.

About eleven o'clock, when both had about convinced themselves that all was over for this night anyhow, and the lights in the village had all but vanished, a stillness of the purest, summery-est, country-est quality having settled down, a faint beating of hoofs, which seemed to suggest the approach of a large cavalcade, could be heard out on the Sand River pike as Davies by now had come to learn it was, back or northwest of the postoffice. At the sound the postmaster got up, as did Davies, both stepping outside and listening. On it came, and as the volume increased, the former said, "Might be help for the sheriff, but I doubt it. I telegraphed Clayton six times to-day. They wouldn't come that way, though. It's the wrong road." Now, thought Davies nervously, after all there might be something to add to his story, and he had so wished that it was all over! Lynchings, as he now felt, were horrible things. He wished people wouldn't do such things— take the law, which now more than ever he respected, into their own hands. It was too brutal, cruel. That negro cowering there in the dark probably, and the sheriff all taut and tense, worrying over his charge and his duty, were not happy things to contemplate in the face of such a thing as this. It was true that the crime which had been committed was dreadful, but still why couldn't people allow the law to take its course? It was so much better. The law was powerful enough to deal with cases of this kind.

"They're comin' back, all right," said the postmaster solemnly, as he and Davies stared in the direction of the sound which grew louder from moment to moment.

"It's not any help from Clayton, I'm afraid."

"By George, I think you're right!" answered the reporter, something telling him that more trouble was at hand. "Here they come!"

As he spoke there was a clattering of hoofs and crunching of saddle girths as a large company of men dashed up the road and turned into the narrow street of the village, the figure of Jake Whitaker and an older bearded man in a wide black hat riding side by side in front.

"There's Jake," said the postmaster, "and that's his father riding beside him there. The old man's a terror when he gets his dander up. Sompin's sure to happen now."

Davies realized that in his absence writing a new turn had been given to things. Evidently the son had returned to Pleasant Valley and organized a new posse or gone out to meet his father.

Instantly the place was astir again. Lights appeared in doorways and windows, and both were thrown open. People were leaning or gazing out to see what new movement was afoot. Davies noted at once that there was none of the brash enthusiasm about this company such as had characterized the previous descent. There was grimness everywhere, and he now began to feel that this was the beginning of the end. After the cavalcade had passed down the street toward the sheriff's house, which was quite dark now, he ran after it, arriving a few moments after the former which was already in part dismounted. The townspeople followed. The sheriff, as it now developed, had not relaxed any of his vigilance, however; he was not sleeping, and as the crowd reappeared the light inside reappeared.

By the light of the moon, which was almost overhead, Davies was able to make out several of his companions of the afternoon, and Jake, the son. There were many more, though, now, whom he did not know, and foremost among them this old man.

The latter was strong, iron-gray, and wore a full beard. He looked very much like a blacksmith.

"Keep your eye on the old man," advised the postmaster, who had by now come up and was standing by.

While they were still looking, the old man went boldly forward to the little front porch of the house and knocked at the door. Some one lifted a curtain at the window and peeped out.

"Hello, in there!" cried the old man, knocking again.

"What do you want?" asked a voice.

"I want that nigger!"

"Well, you can't have him! I've told you people that once."

"Bring him out or I'll break down the door!" said the old man.

"If you do it's at your own risk. I know you, Whitaker, an' you know me. I'll give ye two minutes to get off that porch!"

"I want that nigger, I tell ye!"

"If ye don't git off that porch I'll fire through the door," said the voice solemnly. "One—Two——"

The old man backed cautiously away.

"Come out, Mathews!" yelled the crowd. "You've got to give up this time. We ain't goin' back without him."

Slowly the door opened, as if the individual within were very well satisfied as to his power to handle the mob. He had done it once before this night, why not again? It revealed his tall form, armed with his shotgun. He looked around very stolidly, and then addressed the old man as one would a friend.

"Ye can't have him, Morgan," he said. "It's ag'in' the law. You know that as well as I do."

"Law or no law," said the old man, "I want that nigger!"

"I tell you I can't let you have him, Morgan. It's ag'in' the law. You know you oughtn't to be comin' around here at this time o'night actin' so."

"Well, I'll take him then," said the old man, making a move.

"Stand back!" shouted the sheriff, leveling his gun on the instant. "I'll blow ye into kingdom come, sure as hell!"

A noticeable movement on the part of the crowd ceased. The sheriff lowered his weapon as if he thought the danger were once more over.

"You-all ought to be ashamed of yerselves," he went on, his voice sinking to a gentle neighborly reproof, "tryin' to upset the law this way."

"The nigger didn't upset no law, did he?" asked one derisively.

"Well, the law's goin' to take care of the nigger now," Mathews made answer.

"Give us that scoundrel, Mathews; you'd better do it," said the old man. "It'll save a heap o' trouble."

"I'll not argue with ye, Morgan. I said ye couldn't have him, an' ye can't. If ye want bloodshed, all right. But don't blame me. I'll kill the first man that tries to make a move this way."

He shifted his gun handily and waited. The crowd stood outside his little fence murmuring.

Presently the old man retired and spoke to several others. There was more murmuring, and then he came back to the dead line.

"We don't want to cause trouble, Mathews," he began explanatively, moving his hand oratorically, "but we think you ought to see that it won't do any good to stand out. We think that ——"

Davies and the postmaster were watching young Jake, whose peculiar attitude attracted their attention. The latter was standing poised at the edge of the crowd, evidently seeking to remain unobserved. His eyes were on the sheriff, who was hearkening to the old man. Suddenly, as the father talked and when the sheriff seemed for a moment mollified and unsuspecting, he made a quick run for the porch. There was an intense movement all along the line as the life and death of the deed became apparent. Quickly the sheriff drew his gun to his shoulder. Both triggers were pressed at the same time, and the gun spoke, but not before Jake was in and under him. The latter had been in sufficient time to knock the gun barrel upward and fall upon his man. Both shots blazed harmlessly over the heads of the crowd in red puffs, and then followed a general onslaught. Men leaped the fence by tens and crowded upon the little cottage. They swarmed about every side of the house and crowded upon the porch, where four men were scuffling with the sheriff. The latter soon gave up, vowing vengeance and the law. Torches were brought, and a rope. A wagon drove up and was backed into the yard. Then began the calls for the negro.

As Davies contemplated all this he could not help thinking of the negro who during all this turmoil must have been crouching in his corner in the cellar, trembling for his fate. Now indeed he must realize that his end was near. He could not have dozed or lost consciousness during the intervening hours, but must have been cowering there, wondering and praying. All the while he must have been terrified lest the sheriff might not get him away in time. Now, at the sound of horses' feet and the new murmurs of contention, how must his body quake and his teeth chatter!

"I'd hate to be that nigger," commented the postmaster grimly, "but you can't do anything with 'em. The county oughta sent help."

"It's horrible, horrible!" was all Davies could say.

He moved closer to the house, with the crowd, eager to observe every detail of the procedure. Now it was that a number of the men, as eager in their search as bloodhounds, appeared at a low cellar entryway at the side of the house carrying a rope. Others followed with torches. Headed by father and son they began to descend into the dark hole. With impressive daring, Davies, who was by no means sure that he would be allowed but who was also determined if possible to see, followed.

Suddenly, in the farthest corner, he espied Ingalls. The latter in his fear and agony had worked himself into a crouching position, as if he were about to spring. His nails were apparently forced into the earth. His eyes were rolling, his mouth foaming.

"Oh, my Lawd, boss," he moaned, gazing almost as one blind, at the lights, "oh, my Lawd, boss, don't kill me! I won't do it no mo'. I didn't go to do it. I didn't mean to dis time. I was just drunk, boss. Oh, my Lawd! My Lawd!" His teeth chattered the while his mouth seemed to gape open. He was no longer sane really, but kept repeating monotonously, "Oh, my Lawd!"

"Here he is boys! Pull him out," cried the father.

The negro now gave one yell of terror and collapsed, falling prone. He quite bounded as he did so, coming down with a dead chug on the earthen floor. Reason had forsaken him. He was by now a groveling, foaming brute. The last gleam of intelligence was that which notified him of the set eyes of his pursuers.

Davies, who by now had retreated to the grass outside before this sight, was standing but ten feet back when they began to reappear after seizing and binding him. Although shaken to the roots of his being, he still had all the cool observing powers of the trained and relentless reporter. Even now he noted the color values of the scene, the red, smoky heads of the torches, the disheveled appearance of the men, the scuffling and pulling. Then all at once he clapped his hands over his mouth, almost unconscious of what he was doing.

"Oh, my God!" he whispered, his voice losing power.

The sickening sight was that of the negro, foaming at the mouth, bloodshot as to his eyes, his hands working convulsively, being dragged up the cellar steps feet foremost. They had tied a rope about his waist and feet, and so had hauled him out, leaving his head to hang and drag. The black face was distorted beyond all human semblance.

"Oh, my God!" said Davies again, biting his fingers unconsciously.

The crowd gathered about now more closely than ever, more horror-stricken than gleeful at their own work. None apparently had either the courage or the charity to gainsay what was being done. With a kind of mechanical deftness now the negro was rudely lifted and like a sack of wheat thrown into the wagon. Father and son now mounted in front to drive and the crowd took to their horses, content to clatter, a silent cavalcade, behind. As Davies afterwards concluded, they were not so much hardened lynchers perhaps as curious spectators, the majority of them, eager for any variation—any excuse for one—to the dreary commonplaces of their existences. The task to most—all indeed—was entirely new. Wide-eyed and nerve-racked, Davies ran for his own horse and mounting followed. He was so excited he scarcely knew what he was doing.

Slowly the silent company now took its way up the Sand River pike whence it had come. The moon was still high, pouring down a wash of silvery light. As Davies rode he wondered how he was to complete his telegram, but decided that he could not. When this was over there would be no time. How long would it be before they would really hang him? And would they? The whole procedure seemed so unreal, so barbaric that he could scarcely believe it—that he was a part of it. Still they rode on.

"Are they really going to hang him?" he asked of one who rode beside him, a total stranger who seemed however not to resent his presence.

"That's what they got 'im for," answered the stranger.

And think, he thought to himself, to-morrow night he would be resting in his own good bed back in K——!

Davies dropped behind again and into silence and tried to recover his nerves. He could scarcely realize that he, ordinarily accustomed to the routine of the city, its humdrum and at least outward social regularity, was a part of this. The night was so soft, the air so refreshing. The shadowy trees were stirring with a cool night wind. Why should any one have to die this way? Why couldn't the people of Baldwin or elsewhere have bestirred themselves on the side of the law before this, just let it take its course? Both father and son now seemed brutal, the injury to the daughter and sister not so vital as all this. Still, also, custom seemed to require death in this way for this. It was like some axiomatic, mathematic law—hard, but custom. The silent company, an articulated, mechanical and therefore terrible thing, moved on. It also was axiomatic, mathematic. After a time he drew near to the wagon and looked at the negro again.

The latter, as Davies was glad to note, seemed still out of his sense. He was breathing heavily and groaning, but probably not with any conscious pain. His eyes were fixed and staring, his face and hands bleeding as if they had been scratched or trampled upon. He was crumpled limply.

But Davies could stand it no longer now. He fell back, sick at heart, content to see no more. It seemed a ghastly, murderous thing to do. Still the company moved on and he followed, past fields lit white by the moon, under dark, silent groups of trees, through which the moonlight fell in patches, up low hills and down into valleys, until at last a little stream came into view, the same little stream, as it proved, which he had seen earlier to-day and for a bridge over which they were heading. Here it ran now, sparkling like electricity in the night. After a time the road drew closer to the water and then crossed directly over the bridge, which could be seen a little way ahead.

Up to this the company now rode and then halted. The wagon was driven up on the bridge, and father and son got out. All the riders, including Davies, dismounted, and a full score of them gathered about the wagon from which the negro was lifted, quite as one might a bag. Fortunately, as Davies now told himself, he was still unconscious, an accidental mercy. Nevertheless he decided now that he could not witness the end, and went down by the waterside slightly above the bridge. He was not, after all, the utterly relentless reporter. From where he stood, however, he could see long beams of iron projecting out over the water, where the bridge was braced, and some of the men fastening a rope to a beam, and then he could see that they were fixing the other end around the negro's neck.

Finally the curious company stood back, and he turned his face away.

"Have you anything to say?" a voice demanded.

There was no answer. The negro was probably lolling and groaning, quite as unconscious as he was before.

Then came the concerted action of a dozen men, the lifting of the black mass into the air, and then Davies saw the limp form plunge down and pull up with a creaking sound of rope. In the weak moonlight it seemed as if the body were struggling, but he could not tell. He watched, wide-mouthed and silent, and then the body ceased moving. Then after a time he heard the company making ready to depart, and finally it did so, leaving him quite indifferently to himself and his thoughts. Only the black mass swaying in the pale light over the glimmering water seemed human and alive, his sole companion.

He sat down upon the bank and gazed in silence. Now the horror was gone. The suffering was ended. He was no longer afraid. Everything was summery and beautiful. The whole cavalcade had disappeared; the moon finally sank. His horse, tethered to a sapling beyond the bridge, waited patiently. Still he sat. He might now have hurried back to the small postoffice in Baldwin and attempted to file additional details of this story, providing he could find Seavey, but it would have done no good. It was quite too late, and anyhow what did it matter? No other reporter had been present, and he could write a fuller, sadder, more colorful story on the morrow. He wondered idly what had become of Seavey? Why had he not followed? Life seemed so sad, so strange, so mysterious, so inexplicable.

As he still sat there the light of morning broke, a tender lavender and gray in the east. Then came the roseate hues of dawn, all the wondrous coloring of celestial halls, to which the waters of the stream responded. The white pebbles shone pinkily at the bottom, the grass and sedges first black now gleamed a translucent green. Still the body hung there black and limp against the sky, and now a light breeze sprang up and stirred it visibly. At last he arose, mounted his horse and made his way back to Pleasant Valley, too full of the late tragedy to be much interested in anything else. Rousing his liveryman, he adjusted his difficulties with him by telling him the whole story, assuring him of his horse's care and handing him a five-dollar bill. Then he left, to walk and think again.

Since there was no train before noon and his duty plainly called him to a portion of another day's work here, he decided to make a day of it, idling about and getting additional details as to what further might be done. Who would cut the body down? What about arresting the lynchers—the father and son, for instance? What about the sheriff now? Would he act as he threatened? If he telegraphed the main fact of the lynching his city editor would not mind, he knew, his coming late, and the day here was so beautiful. He proceeded to talk with citizens and officials, rode out to the injured girl's home, rode to Baldwin to see the sheriff. There was a singular silence and placidity in that corner. The latter assured him that he knew nearly all of those who had taken part, and proposed to swear out warrants for them, but just the same Davies noted that he took his defeat as he did his danger, philosophically. There was no real activity in that corner later. He wished to remain a popular sheriff, no doubt.

It was sundown again before he remembered that he had not discovered whether the body had been removed. Nor had he heard why the negro came back, nor exactly how he was caught. A nine o'clock evening train to the city giving him a little more time for investigation, he decided to avail himself of it. The negro's cabin was two miles out along a pine-shaded road, but so pleasant was the evening that he decided to walk. En route, the last rays of the sinking sun stretched long shadows of budding trees across his path. It was not long before he came upon the cabin, a one-story affair set well back from the road and surrounded with a few scattered trees. By now it was quite dark. The ground between the cabin and the road was open, and strewn with the chips of a woodpile. The roof was sagged, and the windows patched in places, but for all that it had the glow of a home. Through the front door, which stood open, the blaze of a wood-fire might be seen, its yellow light filling the interior with a golden glow.

Hesitating before the door, Davies finally knocked. Receiving no answer he looked in on the battered cane chairs and aged furniture with considerable interest. It was a typical negro cabin, poor beyond the need of description. After a time a door in the rear of the room opened and a little negro girl entered carrying a battered tin lamp without any chimney. She had not heard his knock and started perceptibly at the sight of his figure in the doorway. Then she raised her smoking lamp above her head in order to see better, and approached.

There was something ridiculous about her unformed figure and loose gingham dress, as he noted. Her feet and hands were so large. Her black head was strongly emphasized by little pigtails of hair done up in white twine, which stood out all over her head. Her dark skin was made apparently more so by constrast with her white teeth and the whites of her eyes.

Davies looked at her for a moment but little moved now by the oddity which ordinarily would have amused him, and asked, "Is this where Ingalls lived?"

The girl nodded her head. She was exceedingly subdued, and looked as if she might have been crying.

"Has the body been brought here?"

"Yes, suh," she answered, with a soft negro accent.

"When did they bring it?"

"Dis moanin'."

"Are you his sister?"

"Yes, suh."

"Well, can you tell me how they caught him? When did he come back, and what for?" He was feeling slightly ashamed to intrude thus.

"In de afternoon, about two."

"And what for?" repeated Davies.

"To see us," answered the girl. "To see my motha'."

"Well, did he want anything? He didn't come just to see her, did he?"

"Yes, suh," said the girl, "he come to say good-by. We doan know when dey caught him." Her voice wavered.

"Well, didn't he know he might get caught?" asked Davies sympathetically, seeing that the girl was so moved.

"Yes suh, I think he did."

She still stood very quietly holding the poor battered lamp up, and looking down.

"Well, what did he have to say?" asked Davies.

"He didn' have nothin' much to say, suh. He said he wanted to see motha'. He was a-goin' away."

The girl seemed to regard Davies as an official of some sort, and he knew it.

"Can I have a look at the body?" he asked.

The girl did not answer, but started as if to lead the way.

"When is the funeral?" he asked.

"Tomorra'."

The girl then led him through several bare sheds of room strung in a row to the furthermost one of the line. This last seemed a sort of storage shed for odds and ends. It had several windows, but they were quite bare of glass and open to the moonlight save for a few wooden boards nailed across from the outside. Davies had been wondering all the while where the body was and at the lonely and forsaken air of the place. No one but this little pig-tailed girl seemed about. If they had any colored neighbors they were probably afraid to be seen here.

Now, as he stepped into this cool, dark, exposed outer room, the desolation seemed quite complete. It was very bare, a mere shed or wash-room. There was the body in the middle of the room, stretched upon an ironing board which rested on a box and a chair, and covered with a white sheet. All the corners of the room were quite dark. Only its middle was brightened by splotches of silvery light.

Davies came forward, the while the girl left him, still carrying her lamp. Evidently she thought the moon lighted up the room sufficiently, and she did not feel equal to remaining. He lifted the sheet quite boldly, for he could see well enough, and looked at the still, black form. The face was extremely distorted, even in death, and he could see where the rope had tightened. A bar of cool moonlight lay just across the face and breast. He was still looking, thinking soon to restore the covering, when a sound, half sigh, half groan, reached his ears.

At it he started as if a ghost had made it. It was so eerie and unexpected in this dark place. His muscles tightened. Instantly his heart went hammering like mad. His first impression was that it must have come from the dead.

"Oo-o-ohh!" came the sound again, this time whimpering, as if some one were crying.

Instantly he turned, for now it seemed to come from a corner of the room, the extreme corner to his right, back of him. Greatly disturbed, he approached, and then as his eyes strained he seemed to catch the shadow of something, the figure of a woman, perhaps, crouching against the walls, huddled up, dark, almost indistinguishable.

"Oh, oh, oh!" the sound now repeated itself, even more plaintively than before.

Davies began to understand. He approached slowly, then more swiftly desired to withdraw, for he was in the presence of an old black mammy, doubled up and weeping. She was in the very niche of the two walls, her head sunk on her knees, her body quite still. "Oh, oh, oh!" she repeated, as he stood there near her.

Davies drew silently back. Before such grief his intrusion seemed cold and unwarranted. The guiltlessness of the mother—her love—how could one balance that against the other? The sensation of tears came to his eyes. He instantly covered the dead and withdrew.

Out in the moonlight he struck a brisk pace, but soon stopped and looked back. The whole dreary cabin, with its one golden eye, the door, seemed such a pitiful thing. The weeping mammy, alone in her corner—and he had come back to say "Good-by!" Davies swelled with feeling. The night, the tragedy, the grief, he saw it all. But also with the cruel instinct of the budding artist that he already was, he was beginning to meditate on the character of story it would make—the color, the pathos. The knowledge now that it was not always exact justice that was meted out to all and that it was not so much the business of the writer to indict as to interpret was borne in on him with distinctness by the cruel sorrow of the mother, whose blame, if any, was infinitesimal.

"I'll get it all in!" he exclaimed feelingly, if triumphantly at last. "I'll get it all in!"

1901, 1918

Henry Adams   *1838–1918*

Henry Adams was born into the most distinguished family in America. His great-grandfather (John Adams) and grandfather (John Quincy Adams) were Presidents of the United States; his father, Charles Francis Adams, was a congressman, diplomat, and public servant of great talent and merit. Henry Adams himself was educated at Harvard; he traveled and studied abroad, and he enjoyed the company and friendship of America's greatest politicians, artists, and intellectuals. He was a novelist, a professor at Harvard, a historian of great stature and significance. He was rich, worldly, cultivated. And he was also a self-professed "failure."

After graduating from Harvard, Adams first tried law, studying briefly at the University of Berlin; but he soon abandoned his studies to serve as his father's secretary, first in Washington, after his father had been elected to Congress, and then in London, after Lincoln appointed Henry's father Minister to Great Britain during the Civil War. After the war, Adams drifted into journalism, writing about politics for the Nation *and the* North American Review.

In 1870 he was appointed assistant professor of medieval history at Harvard, and he was made editor of the North American Review. *Adams quickly became an important and influential teacher, but teaching limited the time he could devote to writing, and after seven years he left Harvard and moved to Washington, D.C., to be at the center of the nation's politics and history. In 1879 he began work on his great undertaking, the nine-volume* History of the United States of America During the Administrations of Thomas Jefferson and James Madison *(1889–1891); and he wrote two novels,* Democracy *(1880) and* Esther *(1884).*

Following the death of his wife in 1885, Adams began to travel throughout the world. His journeys lasted nearly fifteen years. He visited the South Seas, Australia, Japan, Russia, and Scandinavia. He lived much of the time in Paris, where he began to study extensively the Middle Ages. In 1895, while traveling in the north of France, he became fascinated by the cathedrals of Normandy. He saw them as symbols of unity in a chaotic, meaningless world, and he wrote of them in one of his most important books, Mont-Saint-Michel and Chartres *(1904).*

Adams had lived into an alien world of ceaseless change. He believed it was a distempered world that honored not thought but energy, not service to mankind but material success. And as the twentieth century unfolded, he grew more and more pessimistic about American civilization and his own achievements. Yet his sense of the decline of culture and his sense of personal failure inspired his greatest work, The Education of Henry Adams *(1907, 1918).*

The Education *followed in the autobiographical tradition established by Benjamin Franklin, John Woolman, and Frederick Douglass. It was a memoir in which Adams, describing himself in the third person, presented his background, his schooling, his experiences in life—the things that shaped his mind. He recorded his efforts to extract reason and purpose from the discordant experience of America. His "education" was his eventual discovery that all mankind's science and knowledge had not resolved the basic mysteries of life or revealed whether the universe is controlled by divine unity or by the movement of chaotic force. Adams wanted to believe that life is rational and predictable. He found instead that life is filled with ironic change, that life is, ultimately, an elusive mystery.*

FURTHER READING: *The Education of Henry Adams,* ed. E. Samuels, 1974; *The Selected Letters of Henry Adams,* ed. N. Arvin, 1951; *The Letters of Henry Adams,* Vols. I–III, ed. J. C. Levenson et al., 1982; E. Samuels, *The Young Henry Adams,* 1948; E. Samuels, *Henry Adams, The Middle Years,* 1958; E. Samuels, *Henry Adams, The Major Phase,* 1964; H. Jordy, *Henry Adams, Scientific Historian,* 1952, 1963; E. Stevenson, *Henry Adams,* 1956; 1961; E. Chalfant, *Both Sides of the Ocean, A Biography of Henry Adams, His first Life, 1838–1862,* 1982; J. Levenson, *The Mind and Art of Henry Adams,* 1957, 1968; G. Hochfield, *Henry Adams, An Introduction and Interpretation,* 1962; V. Wagner, *The Suspension of Henry Adams,* 1969; M. Lyon, *Symbol and Idea in Henry Adams,* 1969; J. Conder, *A Formula of His Own, Henry Adams' Literary Experiment,* 1970; R. Mane, *Henry Adams on the Road to Chartres,* 1971; J. Murray, *Henry Adams,* 1974; J. Rowe, *Henry Adams and Henry James,* 1976; E. Harbert, *The Force So Much Closer Home, Henry Adams and the Adams Family,* 1977; F. Bishop, *Henry Adams,* 1979; W. Dusinberre, *Henry Adams, The Myth of Failure,* 1980; D. Contosta, *Henry Adams and The American Experience,* 1980; *Critical Essays on Henry Adams,* ed. E. Harbert, 1981; H. Kaplan, *Henry Adams and the Naturalist Tradition in American Fiction,* 1981; W. Wasserstrum, *The Ironies of Progress, Henry Adams and the American Dream,* 1984.

TEXT: *The Education of Henry Adams,* 1918.

from *THE EDUCATION OF HENRY ADAMS*

CHAPTER I

QUINCY[1] (1838–1848)

Under the shadow of Boston State House,[2] turning its back on the house of John Hancock,[3] the little passage called Hancock Avenue runs, or ran, from Beacon Street, skirting the State House grounds, to Mount Vernon Street, on the summit of Beacon Hill; and there, in the third house below Mount Vernon Place, February 16, 1838, a child was born, and christened later by his uncle, the minister of the First Church after the tenets of Boston Unitarianism, as Henry Brooks Adams.

Had he been born in Jerusalem under the shadow of the Temple and circumcised in the Synagogue by his uncle the high priest, under the name of Israel Cohen, he would scarcely have been more distinctly branded, and not much more heavily handicapped in the races of the coming century, in running for such stakes as the century was to offer; but, on the other hand, the ordinary traveller, who does not enter the field of racing, finds advantage in being, so to speak, ticketed through life, with the safeguards of an old, established traffic. Safeguards are often irksome, but sometimes convenient, and if one needs them at all, one is apt to need them badly. A hundred years earlier, such safeguards as his would have secured any young man's success; and although in 1838 their value was not very great compared with what they would have had in 1738, yet the mere accident of starting a twentieth-century career from a nest of associations so colonial—so troglodytic[4]—as the First Church, the Boston State House, Beacon Hill, John Hancock and John Adams,[5] Mount Vernon Street and Quincy, all crowding on ten pounds of unconscious babyhood, was so queer as to offer a subject of curious speculation to the baby long after he had witnessed the solution. What could become of such a child of the seventeenth and eighteenth centuries, when he should wake up to find himself required to play the game of the twentieth? Had he been consulted, would he have cared to play the game at all, holding such cards as he held, and suspecting that the game was to be one of which neither he nor any one else back to the beginning of time knew the rules or the risks or the stakes? He was not consulted and was not responsible, but had he been taken into the confidence of his parents, he would certainly have told them to change nothing as far as concerned him. He would have been astounded by his own luck. Probably no child, born in the year, held better cards than he. Whether life was an honest game of chance, or whether the cards were marked and forced, he could not refuse to play his excellent hand. He could never make the usual plea of irresponsibility. He accepted the situation as though he had been a party to it, and under the same circumstances would do it again, the more readily for knowing the exact values. To his life as a whole he was a consenting, contracting party and partner from the moment he was born to the moment he died. Only with that understanding—as a consciously assenting

---

[1]Quincy, Massachusetts (near Boston), the ancestral home of the Adams family.
[2]The Massachusetts state capitol building, on Beacon Hill, in the center of old Boston.
[3]American political leader (1737–1793) whose signature was written first (and largest) on the Declaration of Independence. He was the first governor of the state of Massachusetts.
[4]Primitive.
[5]The second President of the United States and Henry Adams's great grandfather.

member in full partnership with the society of his age—had his education an interest to himself or to others.

As it happened, he never got to the point of playing the game at all; he lost himself in the study of it, watching the errors of the players; but this is the only interest in the story, which otherwise has no moral and little incident. A story of education—seventy years of it—the practical value remains to the end in doubt, like other values about which men have disputed since the birth of Cain and Abel; but the practical value of the universe has never been stated in dollars. Although every one cannot be a Gargantua-Napoleon-Bismarck[6] and walk off with the great bells of Notre Dame, every one must bear his own universe, and most persons are moderately interested in learning how their neighbors have managed to carry theirs.

This problem of education, started in 1838, went on for three years, while the baby grew, like other babies, unconsciously, as a vegetable, the outside world working as it never had worked before, to get his new universe ready for him. Often in old age he puzzled over the question whether, on the doctrine of chances, he was at liberty to accept himself or his world as an accident. No such accident had ever happened before in human experience. For him, alone, the old universe was thrown into the ash-heap and a new one created. He and his eighteenth-century, troglodytic Boston were suddenly cut apart—separated for-ever—in act if not in sentiment, by the opening of the Boston and Albany Railroad;[7] the appearance of the first Cunard steamers in the bay;[8] and the telegraphic messages which carried from Baltimore to Washington the news that Henry Clay and James K. Polk were nominated for the Presidency. This was in May, 1844; he was six years old; his new world was ready for use and only fragments of the old met his eyes.

Of all this that was being done to complicate his education, he knew only the color of yellow. He first found himself sitting on a yellow kitchen floor in strong sunlight. He was three years old when he took this earliest step in education; a lesson of color. The second followed soon; a lesson of taste. On December 3, 1841, he developed scarlet fever. For several days he was as good as dead, reviving only under the careful nursing of his family. When he began to recover strength, about January 1, 1842, his hunger must have been stronger than any other pleasure or pain, for while in after life he retained not the faintest recollection of his illness, he remembered quite clearly his aunt entering the sick-room bearing in her hand a saucer with a baked apple.

The order of impressions retained by memory might naturally be that of color and taste, although one would rather suppose that the sense of pain would be first to educate. In fact, the third recollection of the child was that of discomfort. The moment he could be removed, he was bundled up in blankets and carried from the little house in Hancock Avenue to a larger one which his parents were to occupy for the rest of their lives in the neighboring Mount Vernon Street. The season was midwinter, January 10, 1842, and he never forgot his acute distress for want of air under his blankets, or the noises of moving furniture.

As a means of variation from a normal type, sickness in childhood ought to

---

[6]In the fictional *Life of Gargantua and Pantagruel* (1552), by Francois Rebelais (1494?–1553), the giant Gargantua accomplished prodigious feats, which Adams compares to the achievements of Napoleon Bonaparte (1769–1821), Emperor of France, and of Otto von Bismarck (1815–1898), Chancellor of Germany.

[7]The railroad, connecting Boston, Massachusetts and Albany, New York, was opened in 1841.

[8]Regular transatlantic steamship service, by the Cunard Company, between Boston and Europe began in 1840.

have a certain value not to be classed under any fitness or unfitness of natural selection; and especially scarlet fever affected boys seriously, both physically and in character, though they might through life puzzle themselves to decide whether it had fitted or unfitted them for success; but this fever of Henry Adams took greater and greater importance in his eyes, from the point of view of education, the longer he lived. At first, the effect was physical. He fell behind his brothers[9] two or three inches in height, and proportionally in bone and weight. His character and processes of mind seemed to share in this fining-down process of scale. He was not good in a fight, and his nerves were more delicate than boys' nerves ought to be. He exaggerated these weaknesses as he grew older. The habit of doubt; of distrusting his own judgment and of totally rejecting the judgment of the world; the tendency to regard every question as open; the hesitation to act except as a choice of evils; the shirking of responsibility; the love of line, form, quality; the horror of ennui; the passion for companionship and the antipathy to society—all these are well-known qualities of New England character in no way peculiar to individuals but in this instance they seemed to be stimulated by the fever, and Henry Adams could never make up his mind whether, on the whole, the change of character was morbid or healthy, good or bad for his purpose. His brothers were the type; he was the variation.

As far as the boy knew, the sickness did not affect him at all, and he grew up in excellent health, bodily and mental, taking life as it was given; accepting its local standards without a difficulty, and enjoying much of it as keenly as any other boy of his age. He seemed to himself quite normal, and his companions seemed always to think him so. Whatever was peculiar about him was education, not character, and came to him, directly and indirectly, as the result of that eighteenth-century inheritance which he took with his name.

The atmosphere of education in which he lived was colonial, revolutionary, almost Cromwellian,[10] as though he were steeped, from his greatest grandmother's birth, in the odor of political crime. Resistance to something was the law of New England nature; the boy looked out on the world with the instinct of resistance; for numberless generations his predecessors had viewed the world chiefly as a thing to be reformed, filled with evil forces to be abolished, and they saw no reason to suppose that they had wholly succeeded in the abolition; the duty was unchanged. That duty implied not only resistance to evil, but hatred of it. Boys naturally look on all force as an enemy, and generally find it so, but the New Englander, whether boy or man, in his long struggle with a stingy or hostile universe, had learned also to love the pleasure of hating; his joys were few.

Politics, as a practice, whatever its professions, had always been the systematic organization of hatreds, and Massachusetts politics had been as harsh as the climate. The chief charm of New England was harshness of contrasts and extremes of sensibility—a cold that froze the blood, and a heat that boiled it—so that the pleasure of hating—one's self if no better victim offered—was not its rarest amusement; but the charm was a true and natural child of the soil, not a cultivated weed of the ancients. The violence of the contrast was real and made the strongest motive of education. The double exterior nature gave life its relative values. Winter and summer, cold and heat, town and country, force

---

[9]Henry Adams had three brothers: John Quincy Adams II (1833–1894), Charles Francis Adams, Jr. (1835–1915), and Brooks Adams (1848–1927).

[10]Oliver Cromwell (1599–1658), Puritan revolutionary and Lord Protector of England (1653–1658).

and freedom, marked two modes of life and thought, balanced like lobes of the brain. Town was winter confinement, school, rule, discipline; straight gloomy streets, piled with six feet of snow in the middle; frosts that made the snow sing under wheels or runners; thaws when the streets became dangerous to cross; society of uncles, aunts, and cousins who expected children to behave themselves, and who were not always gratified; above all else, winter represented the desire to escape and go free. Town was restraint, law, unity. Country, only seven miles away, was liberty, diversity, outlawry, the endless delight of mere sense impressions given by nature for nothing, and breathed by boys without knowing it.

Boys are wild animals, rich in the treasures of sense, but the New England boy had a wider range of emotions than boys of more equable climates. He felt his nature crudely, as it was meant. To the boy Henry Adams summer was drunken. Among senses, smell was the strongest—smell of hot-woods and sweet-fern in the scorching summer noon; of new-mown hay; of ploughed earth; of box hedges; of peaches, lilacs, syringas; of stables, barns, cow-yards; of salt water and low tide on the marshes; nothing came amiss. Next to smell came taste, and the children knew the taste of everything they saw or touched; from pennyroyal and flagroot to the shell of a pignut and the letters of a spelling-book—the taste of A-B, AB, suddenly revived on the boy's tongue sixty years afterwards. Light, line, and color as sensual pleasures, came later and were as crude as the rest. The New England light is glare, and the atmosphere harshens color. The boy was a full man before he ever knew what was meant by atmosphere; his idea of pleasure in light was the blaze of a New England sun. His idea of color was a peony, with the dew of early morning on its petals. The intense blue of the sea, as he saw it a mile or two away, from the Quincy hills; the cumuli in a June afternoon sky; the strong reds and greens and purples of colored prints and children's picture-books, as the American colors then ran; these were ideals. The opposites, or antipathies, were the cold grays of November evenings, and the thick, muddy thaws of Boston winter. With such standards, the Bostonian could not but develop a double nature. Life was a double thing. After a January blizzard, the boy who could look with pleasure into the violent snow-glare of the cold white sunshine, with its intense light and shade, scarcely knew what was meant by tone. He could reach it only by education.

Winter and summer, then, were two hostile lives, and bred two separate natures. Winter was always the effort to live; summer was tropical license. Whether the children rolled in the grass, or waded in the brook, or swam in the salt ocean, or sailed in the bay, or fished for smelts in the creeks, or netted minnows in the salt-marshes, or took to the pine-woods and the granite quarries, or chased muskrats and hunted snapping-turtles in the swamps, or mushrooms or nuts on the autumn hills, summer and country were always sensual living, while winter was always compulsory learning. Summer was the multiplicity of nature; winter was school.

The bearing of the two seasons on the education of Henry Adams was no fancy; it was the most decisive force he ever knew; it ran through life, and made the division between its perplexing, warring, irreconcilable problems, irreducible opposites, with growing emphasis to the last year of study. From earliest childhood the boy was accustomed to feel that, for him, life was double. Winter and summer, town and country, law and liberty, were hostile, and the man who pretended they were not, was in his eyes a schoolmaster—that is, a man employed to tell lies to little boys. Though Quincy was but two hours' walk from Beacon Hill, it belonged in a different world. For two hundred years, every Adams, from father to son, had lived within sight of State Street,[11] and sometimes had lived in it, yet none had ever taken kindly to the town, or been taken kindly by it. The boy inherited his double nature. He knew as yet nothing about his great-grandfather, who had died a dozen years before his own birth: he took for granted that any great-grandfather of his must have always been good, and his enemies wicked; but he divined his great-grandfather's character from his own. Never for a moment did he connect the two ideas of Boston and John Adams; they were separate and antagonistic; the idea of John Adams went with Quincy. He knew his grandfather John Quincy Adams[12] only as an old man of seventy-five or eighty who was friendly and gentle with him, but except that he heard his grandfather always called "the President," and his grandmother "the Madam," he had no reason to suppose that his Adams grandfather differed in character from his Brooks grandfather[13] who was equally kind and benevolent. He liked the Adams side best, but for no other reason than that it reminded him of the country, the summer, and the absence of restraint. Yet he felt also that Quincy was in a way inferior to Boston, and that socially Boston looked down on Quincy. The reason was clear enough even to a five-year old child. Quincy had no Boston style. Little enough style had either; a simpler manner of life and thought could hardly exist, short of cave-dwelling. The flint-and-steel with which his grandfather Adams used to light his own fires in the early morning was still on the mantel-piece of his study. The idea of a livery or even a dress for servants, or of an evening toilette, was next to blasphemy. Bathrooms, water-supplies, lighting, heating, and the whole array of domestic comforts, were unknown at Quincy. Boston had already a bathroom, water-supply, a furnace, and gas. The superiority of Boston was evident, but a child liked it no better for that.

The magnificence of his grandfather Brooks's house in Pearl Street or South Street has long ago disappeared, but perhaps his country house at Medford may still remain to show what impressed the mind of a boy in 1845 with the idea of city splendor. The President's place at Quincy was the larger and older and far the more interesting of the two; but a boy felt at once its inferiority in fashion. It showed plainly enough its want of wealth. It smacked of colonial age, but not of Boston style or plush curtains. To the end of his life he never quite overcame the prejudice thus drawn in with his childish breath. He never could compel himself to care for nineteenth-century style. He was never able to adopt it, any more than his father or grandfather or great-grandfather had done. Not that he felt it as particularly hostile, for he reconciled himself to much that was worse; but because, for some remote reason, he was born an eighteenth-century child. The old house at Quincy was eighteenth century. What style it had was in its Queen Anne mahogany panels and its Louise Seize chairs and sofas.[14] The panels belonged to an old colonial Vassall[15] who built the house; the furniture had been brought back from Paris in 1789 or 1801 or 1817, along with porcelain and books and much else of old diplomatic remnants; and neither of the two eighteenth-century styles—neither English Queen Anne nor French Louis Seize—was comfortable for a boy, or for any one else. The dark mahogany had

[11]Boston financial and commercial district.

[12]Sixth President of the United States (1825–1829).

[13]Peter Chardon Brooks (1767–1849), Henry Adams's maternal grandfather and reputedly the richest man in Boston.

[14]Architecture and furniture of the styles prevailing during the reign of Queen Anne of England (1702–1714) and the reign of Louis XVI, King of France (1774–1793).

[15]John Adams bought the house from Leonard Vassall in 1787. It had been built by Vassall's grandfather in 1731.

been painted white to suit daily life in winter gloom. Nothing seemed to favor, for a child's objects, the older forms. On the contrary, most boys, as well as grown-up people, preferred the new, with good reason, and the child felt himself distinctly at a disadvantage for the taste.

Nor had personal preference any share in his bias. The Brooks grandfather was as amiable and as sympathetic as the Adams grandfather. Both were born in 1767, and both died in 1848. Both were kind to children, and both belonged rather to the eighteenth than to the nineteenth centuries. The child knew no difference between them except that one was associated with winter and the other with summer; one with Boston, the other with Quincy. Even with Medford, the association was hardly easier. Once as a very young boy he was taken to pass a few days with his grandfather Brooks under charge of his aunt, but became so violently homesick that within twenty-four hours he was brought back in disgrace. Yet he could not remember ever being seriously homesick again.

The attachment to Quincy was not altogether sentimental or wholly sympathetic. Quincy was not a bed of thornless roses. Even there the curse of Cain set its mark.[16] There as elsewhere a cruel universe combined to crush a child. As though three or four vigorous brothers and sisters, with the best will, were not enough to crush any child, every one else conspired towards an education which he hated. From cradle to grave this problem of running order through chaos, direction through space, discipline through freedom, unity through multiplicity, has always been, and must always be, the task of education, as it is the moral of religion, philosophy, science, art, politics, and economy; but a boy's will is his life, and he dies when it is broken, as the colt dies in harness, taking a new nature in becoming tame. Rarely has the boy felt kindly towards his tamers. Between him and his master has always been war. Henry Adams never knew a boy of his generation to like a master, and the task of remaining on friendly terms with one's own family, in such a relation, was never easy.

All the more singular it seemed afterwards to him that his first serious contact with the President should have been a struggle of will, in which the old man almost necessarily defeated the boy, but instead of leaving, as usual in such defeats, a lifelong sting, left rather an impression of as fair treatment as could be expected from a natural enemy. The boy met seldom with such restraint. He could not have been much more than six years old at the time—seven at the utmost—and his mother had taken him to Quincy for a long stay with the President during the summer. What became of the rest of the family he quite forgot; but he distinctly remembered standing at the house door one summer morning in a passionate outburst of rebellion against going to school. Naturally his mother was the immediate victim of his rage; that is what mothers are for, and boys also; but in this case the boy had his mother at unfair disadvantage, for she was a guest, and had no means of enforcing obedience. Henry showed a certain tactical ability by refusing to start, and he met all efforts at compulsion by successful, though too vehement protest. He was in fair way to win, and was holding his own, with sufficient energy, at the bottom of the long staircase which led up to the door of the President's library, when the door opened, and the old man slowly came down. Putting on his hat, he took the boy's hand without a word, and walked with him, paralyzed by awe, up the road to the town. After the first moments of consternation at this interference in a domestic dispute, the boy reflected that an old gentleman close on eighty would never trouble himself to walk near a mile on a hot summer morning over a shadeless road to

---

[16]The Lord cursed and marked Cain after Cain slew his brother Abel. Genesis 4:15.

take a boy to school, and that it would be strange if a lad imbued with the passion of freedom could not find a corner to dodge around, somewhere before reaching the school door. Then and always, the boy insisted that this reasoning justified his apparent submission; but the old man did not stop, and the boy saw all his strategical points turned, one after another, until he found himself seated inside the school, and obviously the centre of curious if not malevolent criticism. Not till then did the President release his hand and depart.

The point was that this act, contrary to the inalienable rights of boys, and nullifying the social compact, ought to have made him dislike his grandfather for life. He could not recall that it had this effect even for a moment. With a certain maturity of mind, the child must have recognized that the President, though a tool of tyranny, had done his disreputable work with a certain intelligence. He had shown no temper, no irritation, no personal feeling, and had made no display of force. Above all, he had held his tongue. During their long walk he had said nothing; he had uttered no syllable of revolting cant about the duty of obedience and the wickedness of resistance to law; he had shown no concern in the matter; hardly even a consciousness of the boy's existence. Probably his mind at that moment was actually troubling itself little about his grandson's iniquities and much about the iniquities of President Polk,[17] but the boy could scarcely at that age feel the whole satisfaction of thinking that President Polk was to be the vicarious victim of his own sins, and he gave his grandfather credit for intelligent silence. For this forbearance he felt instinctive respect. He admitted force as a form of right; he admitted even temper, under protest; but the seeds of a moral education would at that moment have fallen on the stoniest soil in Quincy, which is, as every one knows, the stoniest glacial and tidal drift known in any Puritan land.

Neither party to this momentary disagreement can have felt rancor, for during these three or four summers the old President's relations with the boy were friendly and almost intimate. Whether his older brothers and sisters were still more favored he failed to remember, but he was himself admitted to a sort of familiarity which, when in his turn he had reached old age, rather shocked him, for it must have sometimes tried the President's patience. He hung about the library; handled the books; deranged the papers; ransacked the drawers; searched the old purses and pocket-books for foreign coins; drew the swordcane; snapped the travelling-pistols; upset everything in the corners, and penetrated the President's dressing-closet where a row of tumblers, inverted on the shelf, covered caterpillars which were supposed to become moths or butterflies, but never did. The Madam bore with fortitude the loss of the tumblers which her husband purloined for these hatcheries; but she made protest when he carried off her best cut-glass bowls to plant with acorns or peachstones that he might see the roots grow, but which, she said, he commonly forgot like the caterpillars.

At that time the President rode the hobby of tree-culture, and some fine old trees should still remain to witness it, unless they have been improved off the ground; but his was a restless mind, and although he took his hobbies seriously and would have been annoyed had his grandchild asked whether he was bored like an English duke, he probably cared more for the processes than for the results, so that his grandson was saddened by the sight and smell of peaches and pears, the best of their kind, which he brought up from the garden to rot on his shelves for seed. With the inherited virtues of his Puritan ancestors, the

[17]James K. Polk (1795–1849), eleventh President of the United States. Many New Englanders objected to what they believed to be his pro-slavery sentiments.

little boy Henry conscientiously brought up to him in his study the finest peaches he found in the garden, and ate only the less perfect. Naturally he ate more by way of compensation, but the act showed that he bore no grudge. As for his grandfather, it is even possible that he may have felt a certain self-reproach for his temporary role of schoolmaster—seeing that his own career did not offer proof of the worldly advantages of docile obedience—for there still exists somewhere a little volume of critically edited Nursery Rhymes with the boy's name in full written in the President's trembling hand on the fly-leaf. Of course there was also the Bible, given to each child at birth, with the proper inscription in the President's hand on the fly-leaf; while their grandfather Brooks supplied the silver mugs.

So many Bibles and silver mugs had to be supplied, that a new house, or cottage, was built to hold them. It was "on the hill," five minutes' walk above "the old house," with a far view eastward over Quincy Bay, and northward over Boston. Till his twelfth year, the child passed his summers there, and his pleasures of childhood mostly centered in it. Of education he had as yet little to complain. Country schools were not very serious. Nothing stuck to the mind except home impressions, and the sharpest were those of kindred children; but as influences that warped a mind, none compared with the mere effect of the back of the President's bald head, as he sat in his pew on Sundays, in line with that of President Quincy,[18] who, though some ten years younger, seemed to children about the same age. Before railways entered the New England town, every parish church showed half-a-dozen of these leading citizens, with gray hair, who sat on the main aisle in the best pews, and had sat there, or in some equivalent dignity, since the time of St. Augustine,[19] if not since the glacial epoch. It was unusual for boys to sit behind a President grandfather, and to read over his head the tablet in memory of a President great-grandfather, who had "pledged his life, his fortune, and his sacred honor" to secure the independence of his country and so forth; but boys naturally supposed, without much reasoning, that other boys had the equivalent of President grandfathers, and that churches would always go on, with the bald-headed leading citizens on the main aisle, and Presidents or their equivalents on the walls. The Irish gardener once said to the child: "You'll be thinkin' you'll be President too!" The casuality[20] of the remark made so strong an impression on his mind that he never forgot it. He could not remember ever to have thought on the subject; to him, that there should be a doubt of his being President was a new idea. What had been would continue to be. He doubted neither about Presidents nor about Churches, and no one suggested at that time a doubt whether a system of society which had lasted since Adam would outlast one Adams more.

The Madam was a little more remote than the President, but more decorative. She stayed much in her own room with the Dutch tiles, looking out on her garden with the box walks, and seemed a fragile creature to a boy who sometimes brought her a note or a message, and took distinct pleasure in looking at her delicate face under what seemed to him very becoming caps. He liked her refined figure; her gentle voice and manner; her vague effect of not belonging there, but to Washington or to Europe, like her furniture, and writing-desk with little glass doors above and little eighteenth-century volumes in old binding,

[18]Josiah Quincy (1772–1864), president of Harvard College (1829–1845). He was actually only five years younger than John Quincy Adams.
[19]A.D. 354–430.   [20]Uncertainty.

labelled "Peregrine Pickle" or "Tom Jones" or "Hannah More."[21] Try as she might, the Madam could never be Bostonian, and it was her cross in life, but to the boy it was her charm. Even at that age, he felt drawn to it. The Madam's life had been in truth far from Boston. She was born in London in 1775, daughter of Joshua Johnson, an American merchant, brother of Governor Thomas Johnson of Maryland; and Catherine Nuth, of an English family in London. Driven from England by the Revolutionary War, Joshua Johnson took his family to Nantes,[22] where they remained till the peace. The girl Louisa Catherine was nearly ten years old when brought back to London, and her sense of nationality must have been confused; but the influence of the Johnsons and the services of Joshua obtained for him from President Washington the appointment of Consul in London on the organization of the Government in 1790. In 1794 President Washington appointed John Quincy Adams Minister to The Hague.[23] He was twenty-seven years old when he returned to London, and found the Consul's house a very agreeable haunt. Louisa was then twenty.

At that time, and long afterwards, the Consul's house, far more than the Minister's, was the centre of contact for travelling Americans, either official or other. The Legation was a shifting point, between 1785 and 1815; but the Consulate, far down in the City,[24] near the Tower,[25] was convenient and inviting; so inviting that it proved fatal to young Adams. Louisa was charming, like a Romney[26] portrait, but among her many charms that of being a New England woman was not one. The defect was serious. Her future mother-in-law, Abigail,[27] a famous New England woman whose authority over her turbulent husband, the second President, was hardly so great as that which she exercised over her son, the sixth to be, was troubled by the fear that Louisa might not be made of stuff stern enough, or brought up in conditions severe enough, to suit a New England climate, or to make an efficient wife for her paragon son, and Abigail was right on that point, as on most others where sound judgment was involved; but sound judgment is sometimes a source of weakness rather than of force, and John Quincy already had reason to think that his mother held sound judgments on the subject of daughters-in-law which human nature, since the fall of Eve, made Adams helpless to realize. Being three thousand miles away from his mother, and equally far in love, he married Louisa in London, July 26, 1797, and took her to Berlin to be the head of the United States Legation. During three or four exciting years, the young bride lived in Berlin; whether she was happy or not, whether she was content or not, whether she was socially successful or not, her descendants did not surely know; but in any case she could by no chance have become educated there for a life in Quincy or Boston. In 1801 the overthrow of the Federalist Party[28] drove her and her husband to America, and she became at last a member of the Quincy household, but by that time her children needed all her attention, and she remained there with occasional winters in Boston and Washington, till 1809. Her husband was made

[21]*The Adventures of Peregrine Pickle* (1751) and *Tom Jones* (1749), English novels by Tobias Smollett (1721–1771) and Henry Fielding (1707–1754), respectively. Hannah More (1745–1833) was an English religious writer.
[22]City in France.   [23]The capital of the Netherlands.
[24]The financial center of London.   [25]The Tower of London.
[26]George Romney (1734–1802), English painter, famous for his graceful portraits of women.
[27]Abigail Smith Adams (1744–1818), wife of the second President of the United States, John Adams (1735–1826), and mother of John Quincy Adams.
[28]In the presidential election of 1800, Thomas Jefferson of the Republican Party defeated the incumbent John Adams of the Federalist Party. After Jefferson assumed office (March 1801) numerous Federalist appointees, including John Quincy Adams, were removed from office.

Senator in 1803, and in 1809 was appointed Minister to Russia. She went with him to St. Petersburg, taking her baby, Charles Francis, born in 1807; but broken-hearted at having to leave her two older boys behind. The life at St. Petersburg was hardly gay for her; they were far too poor to shine in that extravagant society; but she survived it, though her little girl baby did not, and in the winter of 1814–15, alone with the boy of seven years old, crossed Europe from St. Petersburg to Paris, in her travelling-carriage, passing through the armies, and reaching Paris in the *Cent Jours*[29] after Napoleon's return from Elba. Her husband next went to England as Minister, and she was for two years at the Court of the Regent.[30] In 1817 her husband came home to be Secretary of State, and she lived for eight years in F Street,[31] doing her work of entertainer for President Monroe's administration. Next she lived four miserable years in the White House. When that chapter was closed in 1829, she had earned the right to be tired and delicate, but she still had fifteen years to serve as wife of a Member of the House, after her husband went back to Congress in 1833.[32] Then it was that the little Henry, her grandson, first remembered her, from 1843 to 1848, sitting in her panelled room, at breakfast, with her heavy silver teapot and sugar-bowl and cream-jug, which still exist somewhere as an heirloom of the modern safety-vault. By that time she was seventy years old or more, and thoroughly weary of being beaten about a stormy world. To the boy she seemed singularly peaceful, a vision of silver gray, presiding over her old President and her Queen Anne mahogany; an exotic, like her Sèvres china; an object of deference to every one, and of great affection to her son Charles; but hardly more Bostonian than she had been fifty years before, on her wedding-day, in the shadow of the Tower of London.

Such a figure was even less fitted than that of her old husband, the President, to impress on a boy's mind, the standards of the coming century. She was Louis Seize, like the furniture. The boy knew nothing of her interior life, which had been, as the venerable Abigail, long since at peace, foresaw, one of severe stress and little pure satisfaction. He never dreamed that from her might come some of those doubts and self-questionings, those hesitations, those rebellions against law and discipline, which marked more than one of her descendants; but he might even then have felt some vague instinctive suspicion that he was to inherit from her the seeds of the primal sin,[33] the fall from grace, the curse of Abel, that he was not of pure New England stock, but half exotic. As a child of Quincy he was not a true Bostonian, but even as a child of Quincy he inherited a quarter taint of Maryland blood. Charles Francis, half Marylander by birth, had hardly seen Boston till he was ten years old, when his parents left him there at school in 1817, and he never forgot the experience. He was to be nearly as old as his mother had been in 1845, before he quite accepted Boston, or Boston quite accepted him.

A boy who began his education in these surroundings, with physical strength inferior to that of his brothers, and with a certain delicacy of mind and bone, ought rightly to have felt at home in the eighteenth century and should, in

---

[29]French: "Hundred Days," the name given to the period, from March to June 1815, when Napoleon escaped from Elba, regained power in France, and was finally defeated at Waterloo.

[30]The Prince of Wales, later George IV, ruled as Regent of England (1811–1820) during the period that his father, George III (1738–1820), was disabled by insanity.

[31]In Washington, D.C.

[32]Following his presidency (1825–1829), John Quincy Adams served as a member of the House of Representatives from Massachusetts (1831–1848).

[33]The sin of Adam and Eve, which led to their expulsion from Eden. The curse laid upon them was inherited by all their descendants, beginning with Cain and Abel.

proper self-respect, have rebelled against the standards of the nineteenth. The atmosphere of his first ten years must have been very like that of his grandfather at the same age, from 1767 till 1776, barring the battle of Bunker Hill, and even as late as 1846, the battle of Bunker Hill remained actual. The tone of Boston society was colonial. The true Bostonian always knelt in self-abasement before the majesty of English standards; far from concealing it as a weakness, he was proud of it as his strength. The eighteenth century ruled society long after 1850. Perhaps the boy began to shake it off rather earlier than most of his mates.

Indeed this prehistoric stage of education ended rather abruptly with his tenth year. One winter morning he was conscious of a certain confusion in the house in Mount Vernon Street, and gathered, from such words as he could catch, that the President, who happened to be then staying there, on his way to Washington, had fallen and hurt himself. Then he heard the word paralysis. After that day he came to associate the word with the figure of his grandfather, in a tall-backed, invalid armchair, on one side of the spare bedroom fireplace, and one of his old friends, Dr. Parkman or P. P. F. Degrand,[34] on the othe side, both dozing.

The end of this first, or ancestral and Revolutionary, chapter came on February 21, 1848—and the month of February brought life and death as a family habit—when the eighteenth century, as an actual and living companion, vanished. If the scene on the floor of the House, when the old President fell,[35] struck the still simple-minded American public with a sensation unusually dramatic, its effect on a ten-year-old boy, whose boy-life was fading away with the life of his grandfather, could not be slight. One had to pay for Revolutionary patriots; grandfathers and grandmothers; Presidents; diplomats; Queen Anne mahogany and Louis Seize chairs, as well as for Stuart[36] portraits. Such things warp young life. Americans commonly believed that they ruined it, and perhaps the practical common-sense of the American mind judged right. Many a boy might be ruined by much less than the emotions of the funeral service in the Quincy church, with its surroundings of national respect and family pride. By another dramatic chance it happened that the clergyman of the parish, Dr. Lunt,[37] was an unusual pulpit orator, the ideal of a somewhat austere intellectual type, such as the school of Buckminster and Channing[38] inherited from the old Congregational clergy. His extraordinarily refined appearance, his dignity of manner, his deeply cadenced voice, his remarkable English and his fine appreciation, gave to the funeral service a character that left an overwhelming impression on the boy's mind. He was to see many great functions—funerals and festivals—in after life, till his only thought was to see no more, but he never again witnessed anything nearly so impressive to him as the last services at Quincy over the body of one President and the ashes of another.

The effect of the Quincy service was deepened by the official ceremony which afterwards took place in Faneuil Hall,[39] when the boy was taken to hear his

---

[34]George Parkman (1790–1849), a Boston physician; Peter P. F. Degrand, a banker and politician.
[35]John Quincy Adams suffered a stroke on February 21, 1848 while standing on the floor of the House of Representatives. He died two days later.
[36]Gilbert Charles Stuart (1755–1826), American portrait painter.
[37]The Reverend William Parsons Lunt (1805–1857).
[38]Joseph Buckminster (1784–1812) and William Ellery Channing (1780–1842), Unitarian clergymen.
[39]Boston meeting hall, built in 1740, famous as a landmark of the American Revolution.

uncle, Edward Everett,[40] deliver a Eulogy. Like all Mr. Everett's orations, it was an admirable piece of oratory, such as only an admirable orator and scholar could create; too good for a ten-year-old boy to appreciate at its value; but already the boy knew that the dead President could not be in it, and had even learned why he would have been out of place there; for knowledge was beginning to come fast. The shadow of the War of 1812 still hung over State Street; the shadow of the Civil War to come had already begun to darken Faneuil Hall. No rhetoric could have reconciled Mr. Everett's audience to his subject. How could he say there, to an assemblage of Bostonians in the heart of mercantile Boston, that the only distinctive mark of all the Adamses since old Sam Adams's father[41] a hundred and fifty years before, had been their inherited quarrel with State Street,[42] which had again and again broken out into riot, bloodshed, personal feuds, foreign and civil war, wholesale banishments and confiscations, until the history of Florence was hardly more turbulent[43] than that of Boston? How could he whisper the word Hartford Convention[44] before the men who had made it? What would have been said had he suggested the chance of Secession and Civil War?

Thus already, at ten years old, the boy found himself standing face to face with a dilemma that might have puzzled an early Christian. What was he?— where was he going? Even then he felt that something was wrong, but he concluded that it must be Boston. Quincy had always been right, for Quincy represented a moral principle—the principle of resistance to Boston. His Adams ancestors must have been right, since they were always hostile to State Street. If State Street was wrong, Quincy must be right! Turn the dilemma as he pleased, he still came back on the eighteenth century and the law of Resistance; of Truth; of Duty, and of Freedom. He was a ten-year-old priest and politician. He could under no circumstances have guessed what the next fifty years had in store, and no one could teach him; but sometimes, in his old age, he wondered—and could never decide—whether the most clear and certain knowledge would have helped him. Supposing he had seen a New York stock-list of 1900, and had studied the statistics of railways, telegraphs, coal, and steel—would he have quitted his eighteenth-century, his ancestral prejudices, his abstract ideals, his semi-clerical training, and the rest, in order to perform an expiatory pilgrimage to State Street, and ask for the fatted calf of his grandfather Brooks and a clerkship in the Suffolk Bank?[45]

Sixty years afterwards he was still unable to make up his mind. Each course had its advantages, but the material advantages, looking back, seemed to lie wholly in State Street.

---

[40]Unitarian clergyman, orator, and statesman (1794–1865). He was president of Harvard College from 1846 to 1849.

[41]Samuel Adams (1689–1748) was a colonial Massachusetts politician and legislator. His son, Sam Adams (1722–1803), was a leader in the movement for the American Revolution and a second cousin of President John Adams.

[42]The Adams family had traditionally stood against slavery and against the commercial expansionism advocated by the financial and mercantile interests of Boston's State Street.

[43]A reference to the political upheavals in Florence, Italy in the fifteenth and sixteenth centuries.

[44]A secret political meeting in Hartford, Connecticut (1814), to organize New England opposition to continuance of the War of 1812. A declaration of New England's secession from the Union was considered but not made.

[45]I.e., to turn from his previous principles and adopt principles symbolized by his wealthy grandfather and by the Suffolk Bank, a rich and powerful Boston bank chartered in 1818.

CHAPTER IV

HARVARD COLLEGE (1854–1858)

One day in June, 1854, young Adams walked for the last time down the steps of Mr. Dixwell's school in Boylston Place, and felt no sensation but one of unqualified joy that this experience was ended. Never before or afterwards in his life did he close a period so long as four years without some sensation of loss—some sentiment of habit—but school was what in after life he commonly heard his friends denounce as an intolerable bore. He was born too old for it. The same thing could be said of most New England boys. Mentally they were never boys. Their education as men should have begun at ten years old. They were fully five years more mature than the English or European boy for whom schools were made. For the purposes of future advancement, as afterwards appeared, these first six years of a possible education were wasted in doing imperfectly what might have been done perfectly in one, and in any case would have had small value. The next regular step was Harvard College. He was more than glad to go. For generation after generation, Adamses and Brookses and Boylstons and Gorhams had gone to Harvard College, and although none of them, as far as known, had ever done any good there, or thought himself the better for it, custom, social ties, convenience, and, above all, economy, kept each generation in the track. Any other education would have required a serious effort, but no one took Harvard College seriously. All went there because their friends went there, and the College was their ideal of social self-respect.

Harvard College, as far as it educated at all, was a mild and liberal school, which sent young men into the world with all they needed to make respectable citizens, and something of what they wanted to make useful ones. Leaders of men it never tried to make. Its ideals were altogether different. The Unitarian clergy had given to the College a character of moderation, balance, judgment, restraint, what the French called *mesure;* excellent traits, which the College attained with singular success, so that its graduates could commonly be recognized by the stamp, but such a type of character rarely lent itself to autobiography. In effect, the school created a type but not a will. Four years of Harvard College, if successful, resulted in an autobiographical blank, a mind on which only a water-mark had been stamped.

The stamp, as such things went, was a good one. The chief wonder of education is that it does not ruin everybody concerned in it, teachers and taught. Sometimes in after life, Adams debated whether in fact it had not ruined him and most of his companions, but, disappointment apart, Harvard College was probably less hurtful than any other university then in existence. It taught little, and that little ill, but it left the mind open, free from bias, ignorant of facts, but docile. The graduate had few strong prejudices. He knew little, but his mind remained supple, ready to receive knowledge.

What caused the boy most disappointment was the little he got from his mates. Speaking exactly, he got less than nothing, a result common enough in education. Yet the College Catalogue for the years 1854 to 1861 shows a list of names rather distinguished in their time. Alexander Agassiz and Phillips Brooks led it; H. H. Richardson and O. W. Holmes[1] helped to close it. As a rule the most

---

[1]Alexander Agassiz (1835–1910), geologist and mining engineer; Phillips Brooks (1835–1893), rector of Trinity Church, Boston; Henry Richardson (1838–1886), American architect; Oliver Wendell Holmes, Jr. (1841–1935), son of the Brahmin poet and Justice of the U.S. Supreme Court (1902–1925).

promising of all die early, and never get their names into a Dictionary of Contemporaries, which seems to be the only popular standard of success. Many died in the war. Adams knew them all, more or less; he felt as much regard, and quite as much respect for them then, as he did after they won great names and were objects of a vastly wider respect; but, as help towards education, he got nothing whatever from them or they from him until long after they had left college. Possibly the fault was his, but one would like to know how many others shared it. Accident counts for much in companionship as in marriage. Life offers perhaps only a score of possible companions, and it is mere chance whether they meet as early as school or college, but it is more than a chance that boys brought up together under like conditions have nothing to give each other. The Class of 1858, to which Henry Adams belonged, was a typical collection of young New Englanders, quietly penetrating and aggressively commonplace; free from meanness, jealousies, intrigues, enthusiasms, and passions; not exceptionally quick; not consciously sceptical; singularly indifferent to display, artifice, florid expression, but not hostile to it when it amused them; distrustful of themselves, but little disposed to trust any one else; with not much humor of their own, but full of readiness to enjoy the humor of others; negative to a degree that in the long run became positive and triumphant. Not harsh in manners or judgment, rather liberal and open-minded, they were still as a body the most formidable critics one would care to meet, in a long life exposed to criticism. They never flattered, seldom praised; free from vanity, they were not intolerant of it; but they were objectiveness itself; their attitude was a law of nature; their judgment beyond appeal, not an act either of intellect or emotion or of will, but a sort of gravitation.

This was Harvard College incarnate, but even for Harvard College, the Class of 1858 was somewhat extreme. Of unity this band of nearly one hundred young men had no keen sense, but they had equally little energy of repulsion. They were pleasant to live with, and above the average of students—German, French, English, or what not—but chiefly because each individual appeared satisfied to stand alone. It seemed a sign of force; yet to stand alone is quite natural when one has no passions; still easier when one has no pains.

Into this unusually dissolvent medium, chance insisted on enlarging Henry Adams's education by tossing a trio of Virginians as little fitted for it as Sioux Indians to a treadmill. By some further affinity, these three outsiders fell into relations with the Bostonians among whom Adams as a schoolboy belonged, and in the end with Adams himself, although they and he knew well how thin an edge of friendship separated them in 1856 from mortal enmity. One of the Virginians[2] was the son of Colonel Robert E. Lee, of the Second United States Cavalry; the two others who seemed instinctively to form a staff for Lee, were town-Virginians from Petersburg. A fourth outsider came from Cincinnati and was half Kentuckian, N. L. Anderson,[3] Longworth on the mother's side. For the first time Adams's education brought him in contact with new types and taught him their values. He saw the New England type measure itself with another, and he was part of the process.

Lee, known through life as "Roony," was a Virginian of the eighteenth century, much as Henry Adams was a Bostonian of the same age. Roony Lee had changed little from the type of his grandfather, Light Horse Harry.[4] Tall, largely built,

---

[2]William Henry Fitzhugh Lee (1837–1891). His father was Commanding General of the Army of Northern Virginia during the American Civil War.

[3]Nicholas Longworth Anderson (1838–1892), a Union general during the American Civil War.

[4]Henry Lee (1756–1818), American Revolutionary War hero.

handsome, genial, with liberal Virginian openness towards all he liked, he had also the Virginian habit of command and took leadership as his natural habit. No one cared to contest it. None of the New Englanders wanted command. For a year, at least, Lee was the most popular and prominent young man in his class, but then seemed to drop into the background. The habit of command was not enough, and the Virginian had little else. He was simple beyond analysis; so simple that even the simple New England student could not realize him. No one knew enough to know how ignorant he was; how childlike; how helpless before the relative complexity of a school. As an animal, the Southerner seemed to have every advantage, but even as an animal he steadily lost ground.

The lesson in education was vital to these young men, who, within ten years, killed each other by scores in the act of testing their college conclusions. Strictly, the Southerner had no mind; he had temperament. He was not a scholar; he had no intellectual training; he could not analyze an idea, and he could not even conceive of admitting two; but in life one could get along very well without ideas, if one had only the social instinct. Dozens of eminent statesmen were men of Lee's type, and maintained themselves well enough in the legislature, but college was a sharper test. The Virginian was weak in vice itself, though the Bostonian was hardly a master of crime. The habits of neither were good; both were apt to drink hard and to live low lives; but the Bostonian suffered less than the Virginian. Commonly the Bostonian would take some care of himself even in his worst stages, while the Virginian became quarrelsome and dangerous. When a Virginian had brooded a few days over an imaginary grief and sub-stantial whiskey, none of his Northern friends could be sure that he might not be waiting, round the corner, with a knife or pistol, to revenge insult by the dry light of *delirium tremens;* and when things reached this condition, Lee had to exhaust his authority over his own staff. Lee was a gentleman of the old school, and, as every one knows, gentlemen of the old school drank almost as much as gentlemen of the new school; but this was not his trouble. He was sober even in the excessive violence of political feeling in those years; he kept his temper and his friends under control.

Adams liked the Virginians. No one was more obnoxious to them, by name and prejudice; yet their friendship was unbroken and even warm. At a moment when the immediate future posed no problem in education so vital as the relative energy and endurance of North and South, this momentary contact with South-ern character was a sort of education for its own sake; but this was not all. No doubt the self-esteem of the Yankee, which tended naturally to self-distrust, was flattered by gaining the slow conviction that the Southerner, with his slave-owning limitations, was as little fit to succeed in the struggle of modern life as though he were still a maker of stone axes, living in caves, and hunting the *bos primigenius*,[5] and that every quality in which he was strong, made him weaker; but Adams had begun to fear that even in this respect one eighteenth-century type might not differ deeply from another. Roony Lee had changed little from the Virginian of a century before; but Adams was himself a good deal nearer the type of his great-grandfather than to that of a railway superintendent. He was little more fit than the Virginians to deal with a future America which showed no fancy for the past. Already Northern society betrayed a preference for economists over diplomats or soldiers—one might even call it a jealousy—against which two eighteenth-century types had little chance to live, and which they had in common to fear.

[5]Latin: original ox.

Nothing short of this curious sympathy could have brought into close relations two young men so hostile as Roony Lee and Henry Adams, but the chief difference between them as collegians consisted only in their difference of scholarship: Lee was a total failure; Adams a partial one. Both failed, but Lee felt his failure more sensibly, so that he gladly seized the chance of escape by accepting a commission offered him by General Winfield Scott in the force then being organized against the Mormons.[6] He asked Adams to write his letter of acceptance, which flattered Adams's vanity more than any Northern compliment could do, because, in days of violent political bitterness, it showed a certain amount of good temper. The diplomat felt his profession.

If the student got little from his mates, he got little more from his masters. The four years passed at college were, for his purposes, wasted. Harvard College was a good school, but at bottom what the boy disliked most was any school at all. He did not want to be one in a hundred—one per cent of an education. He regarded himself as the only person for whom his education had value, and he wanted the whole of it. He got barely half of an average. Long afterwards, when the devious path of life led him back to teach in his turn what no student naturally cared or needed to know, he diverted some dreary hours of faculty-meetings by looking up his record in the class-lists, and found himself graded precisely in the middle. In the one branch he most needed—mathematics— barring the few first scholars, failure was so nearly universal that no attempt at grading could have had value, and whether he stood fortieth or ninetieth must have been an accident or the personal favor of the professor. Here his education failed lamentably. At best he could never have been a mathematician; at worst he would never have cared to be one; but he needed to read mathematics, like any other universal language, and he never reached the alphabet.

Beyond two or three Greek plays, the student got nothing from the ancient languages. Beyond some incoherent theories of free-trade and protection, he got little from Political Economy. He could not afterwards remember to have heard the name of Karl Marx mentioned, or the title of "Capital."[7] He was equally ignorant of Auguste Comte.[8] These were the two writers of his time who most influenced its thought. The bit of practical teaching he afterwards reviewed with most curiosity was the course in Chemistry, which taught him a number of theories that befogged his mind for a lifetime. The only teaching that appealed to his imagination was a course of lectures by Louis Agassiz[9] on the Glacial Period and Palæontology, which had more influence on his curiosity than the rest of the college instruction altogether. The entire work of the four years could have been easily put into the work of any four months in after life.

Harvard College was a negative force, and negative forces have value. Slowly it weakened the violent political bias of childhood, not by putting interests in its place, but by mental habits which had no bias at all. It would also have weakened the literary bias, if Adams had been capable of finding other amusement, but the climate kept him steady to desultory and useless reading, till he had run through libraries of volumes which he forgot even to their title-pages. Rather by instinct than by guidance, he turned to writing, and his professors or tutors

---

[6]Winfield Scott (1786–1866), appointed General in Chief of the U.S. Army in 1841. In the late 1850s, the clashes between federal authorities and Mormons had led to the sending of army troops to Utah Territory to suppress rebellion.

[7]*Das Kapital*, by Karl Marx (1818–1883), was not published until 1867, nine years after Adams had left Harvard.

[8]French philosopher (1798–1857).

[9]Swiss-born American naturalist (1807–1873).

occasionally gave his English composition a hesitating approval; but in that branch, as in all the rest, even when he made a long struggle for recognition, he never convinced his teachers that his abilities, at their best, warranted placing him on the rank-list, among the first third of his class. Instructors generally reach a fairly accurate gauge of their scholars' powers. Henry Adams himself held the opinion that his instructors were very nearly right, and when he became a professor in his turn, and made mortifying mistakes in ranking his scholars, he still obstinately insisted that on the whole, he was not far wrong. Student or professor, he accepted the negative standard because it was the standard of the school.

He never knew what other students thought of it, or what they thought they gained from it; nor would their opinion have much affected his. From the first, he wanted to be done with it, and stood watching vaguely for a path and a direction. The world outside seemed large, but the paths that led into it were not many and lay mostly through Boston, where he did not want to go. As it happened, by pure chance, the first door of escape that seemed to offer a hope led into Germany, and James Russell Lowell opened it.

Lowell, on succeeding Longfellow as Professor of Belles-Lettres, had duly gone to Germany, and had brought back whatever he found to bring. The literary world then agreed that truth survived in Germany alone, and Carlyle, Matthew Arnold, Renan, Emerson,[10] with scores of popular followers, taught the German faith. The literary world had revolted against the yoke of coming capitalism—its money-lenders, its bank directors, and its railway magnates. Thackeray and Dickens followed Balzac in scratching and biting the unfortunate middle class with savage ill-temper, much as the middle class had scratched and bitten the Church and Court for a hundred years before. The middle class had the power, and held its coal and iron well in hand, but the satirists and idealists seized the press, and as they were agreed that the Second Empire[11] was a disgrace to France and a danger to England, they turned to Germany because at that moment Germany was neither economical nor military, and a hundred years behind western Europe in the simplicity of its standards. German thought, method, honesty, and even taste, became the standards of scholarship. Goethe was raised to the rank of Shakespeare—Kant ranked as a law-giver above Plato. All serious scholars were obliged to become German, for German thought was revolutionizing criticism. Lowell had followed the rest, not very enthusiastically, but with sufficient conviction, and invited his scholars to join him. Adams was glad to accept the invitation, rather for the sake of cultivating Lowell than Germany, but still in perfect good faith. It was the first serious attempt he had made to direct his own education, and he was sure of getting some education out of it; not perhaps anything that he expected, but at least a path.

Singularly circuitous and excessively wasteful of energy the path proved to be, but the student could never see what other was open to him. He could have done no better had he foreseen every stage of his coming life, and he would probably have done worse. The preliminary step was pure gain. James Russell Lowell had brought back from Germany the only new and valuable part of its universities, the habit of allowing students to read with him privately in his study. Adams asked the privilege, and used it to read a little, and to talk a great deal, for the personal contact pleased and flattered him, as that of older men

---

[10]The English writers Thomas Carlyle (1795–1881) and Matthew Arnold (1822–1888), the French historian Joseph Ernest Renan (1823–1892), and the American essayist and poet Ralph Waldo Emerson (1803–1882) were much influenced by German culture and philosophy.

[11]The French Empire (1852–1870) under Napoleon III.

ought to flatter and please the young even when they altogether exaggerate its value. Lowell was a new element in the boy's life. As practical a New Englander as any, he leaned towards the Concord faith rather than towards Boston[12] where he properly belonged; for Concord, in the dark days of 1856, glowed with pure light. Adams approached it in much the same spirit as he would have entered a Gothic Cathedral, for he well knew that the priests regarded him as only a worm. To the Concord Church all Adamses were minds of dust and emptiness, devoid of feeling, poetry or imagination; little higher than the common scourings of State Street; politicians of doubtful honesty; natures of narrow scope; and already, at eighteen years old, Henry had begun to feel uncertainty about so many matters more important than Adamses that his mind rebelled against no discipline merely personal, and he was ready to admit his unworthiness if only he might penetrate the shrine. The influence of Harvard College was beginning to have its effect. He was slipping away from fixed principles; from Mount Vernon Street; from Quincy; from the eighteenth century; and his first steps led toward Concord.

He never reached Concord, and to Concord Church he, like the rest of mankind who accepted a material universe, remained always an insect, or something much lower—a man. It was surely no fault of his that the universe seemed to him real; perhaps—as Mr. Emerson justly said—it was so; in spite of the long-continued effort of a lifetime, he perpetually fell back into the heresy that if anything universal was unreal, it was himself and not the appearances; it was the poet and not the banker; it was his own thought, not the thing that moved it. He did not lack the wish to be transcendental. Concord seemed to him, at one time, more real than Quincy; yet in truth Russell Lowell was as little transcendental as Beacon Street. From him the boy got no revolutionary thought whatever—objective or subjective as they used to call it—but he got good-humored encouragement to do what amused him, which consisted in passing two years in Europe after finishing the four years of Cambridge.

The result seemed small in proportion to the effort, but it was the only positive result he could ever trace to the influence of Harvard College, and he had grave doubts whether Harvard College influenced even that. Negative results in plenty he could trace, but he tended towards negation on his own account, as one side of the New England mind had always done, and even there he could never feel sure that Harvard College had more than reflected a weakness. In his opinion the education was not serious, but in truth hardly any Boston student took it seriously, and none of them seemed sure that President Walker himself, or President Felton[13] after him, took it more seriously than the students. For them all, the college offered chiefly advantages vulgarly called social, rather than mental.

Unluckily for this particular boy, social advantages were his only capital in life. Of money he had not much, of mind not more, but he could be quite certain that, barring his own faults, his social position would never be questioned. What he needed was a career in which social position had value. Never in his life would he have to explain who he was; never would he have need of acquaintance to strengthen his social standing; but he needed greatly some one to show him how to use the acquaintance he cared to make. He made no acquaintance in college which proved to have the smallest use in after life. All his Boston friends

---

[12]I.e., leaned toward the transcendentalism of Concord rather than the conventional Unitarianism of Boston.

[13]James Walker (1794–1874), president of Harvard College (1853–1860). Cornelius Felton (1807–1862), president of Harvard College (1860–1862).

he knew before, or would have known in any case, and contact of Bostonian with Bostonian was the last education these young men needed. Cordial and intimate as their college relations were, they all flew off in different directions the moment they took their degrees. Harvard College remained a tie, indeed, but a tie little stronger than Beacon Street and not so strong as State Street. Strangers might perhaps gain something from the college if they were hard pressed for social connections. A student like H. H. Richardson, who came from far away New Orleans, and had his career before him to chase rather than to guide, might make valuable friendships at college. Certainly Adams made no acquaintance there that he valued in after life so much as Richardson, but still more certainly the college relation had little to do with the later friendship. Life is a narrow valley, and the roads run close together. Adams would have attached himself to Richardson in any case, as he attached himself to John LaFarge or Augustus St. Gaudens or Clarence King or John Hay,[14] none of whom were at Harvard College. The valley of life grew more and more narrow with years, and certain men with common tastes were bound to come together. Adams knew only that he would have felt himself on a more equal footing with them had he been less ignorant, and had he not thrown away ten years of early life in acquiring what he might have acquired in one.

Socially or intellectually, the college was for him negative and in some ways mischievous. The most tolerant man of the world could not see good in the lower habits of the students, but the vices were less harmful than the virtues. The habit of drinking—though the mere recollection of it made him doubt his own veracity, so fantastic it seemed in later life—may have done no great or permanent harm; but the habit of looking at life as a social relation—an affair of society—did no good. It cultivated a weakness which needed no cultivation. If it had helped to make men of the world, or give the manners and instincts of any profession—such as temper, patience, courtesy, or a faculty of profiting by the social defects of opponents—it would have been education better worth having than mathematics or languages; but so far as it helped to make anything, it helped only to make the college standard permanent through life. The Bostonian educated at Harvard College remained a collegian, if he stuck only to what the college gave him. If parents went on, generation after generation, sending their children to Harvard College for the sake of its social advantages, they perpetuated an inferior social type, quite as ill-fitted as the Oxford[15] type for success in the next generation.

Luckily the old social standard of the college, as President Walker or James Russell Lowell still showed it, was admirable, and if it had little practical value or personal influence on the mass of students, at least it preserved the tradition for those who liked it. The Harvard graduate was neither American nor European, nor even wholly Yankee; his admirers were few, and his critics many; perhaps his worst weakness was his self-criticism and self-consciousness; but his ambitions, social or intellectual, were not necessarily cheap even though they might be negative. Afraid of serious risks, and still more afraid of personal ridicule, he seldom made a great failure of life, and nearly always led a life more or less worth living. So Henry Adams, well aware that he could not succeed as a scholar, and finding his social position beyond improvement or need of effort, betook himself to the single ambition which otherwise would scarcely have seemed a true outcome of the college, though it was the last remnant of the old Unitarian supremacy. He took to the pen. He wrote.

[14]Noted Americans of Adams's generation.
[15]I.e., Oxford University in England.

The College Magazine printed his work, and the College Societies listened to his addresses. Lavish of praise the readers were not; the audiences, too, listened in silence; but this was all the encouragement any Harvard collegian had a reasonable hope to receive; grave silence was a form of patience that meant possible future acceptance; and Henry Adams went on writing. No one cared enough to criticize, except himself who soon began to suffer from reaching his own limits. He found that he could not be this—or that—or the other; always precisely the things he wanted to be. He had not wit or scope or force. Judges always ranked him beneath a rival, if he had any; and he believed the judges were right. His work seemed to him thin, commonplace, feeble. At times he felt his own weakness so fatally that he could not go on; when he had nothing to say, he could not say it, and he found that he had very little to say at best. Much that he then wrote must be still in existence in print or manuscript, though he never cared to see it again, for he felt no doubt that it was in reality just what he thought it. At best it showed only a feeling for form; an instinct of exclusion. Nothing shocked—not even its weakness.

Inevitably an effort leads to an ambition—creates it—and at that time the ambition of the literary student, which almost took place of the regular prizes of scholarship, was that of being chosen as the representative of his class—the Class Orator—at the close of their course. This was political as well as literary success, and precisely the sort of eighteenth-century combination that fascinated an eighteenth-century boy. The ideal lurked in his mind, at first as a dream, in no way serious or even possible, for he stood outside the number of what were known as popular men. Year by year, his position seemed to improve, or perhaps his rivals disappeared, until at last, to his own great astonishment, he found himself a candidate. The habits of the college permitted no active candidacy; he and his rivals had not a word to say for or against themselves, and he was never even consulted on the subject; he was not present at any of the proceedings, and how it happened he never could quite divine, but it did happen, that one evening on returning from Boston he received notice of his election, after a very close contest, as Class Orator over the head of the first scholar, who was undoubtedly a better orator and a more popular man. In politics the success of the poorer candidate is common enough, and Henry Adams was a fairly trained politician, but he never understood how he managed to defeat not only a more capable but a more popular rival.

To him the election seemed a miracle. This was no mock-modesty; his head was as clear as ever it was in an indifferent canvass, and he knew his rivals and their following as well as he knew himself. What he did not know, even after four years of education, was Harvard College. What he could never measure was the bewildering impersonality of the men, who, at twenty years old, seemed to set no value either on official or personal standards. Here were nearly a hundred young men who had lived together intimately during four of the most impressionable years of life, and who, not only once but again and again, in different ways, deliberately, seriously, dispassionately, chose as their representatives precisely those of their companions who seemed least to represent them. As far as these Orators and Marshals had any position at all in a collegiate sense, it was that of indifference to the college. Henry Adams never professed the smallest faith in universities of any kind, either as boy or man, nor had he the faintest admiration for the university graduate, either in Europe or in America; as a collegian he was only known apart from his fellows by his habit of standing outside the college; and yet the singular fact remained that this commonplace body of young men chose him repeatedly to express his and their commonplaces. Secretly, of course, the successful candidate flattered himself—and them—with the hope that they might perhaps not be so commonplace as they thought themselves; but this was only another proof that all were identical. They saw in him a representative—the kind of representative they wanted—and he saw in them the most formidable array of judges he could ever meet, like so many mirrors of himself, an infinite reflection of his own shortcomings.

All the same, the choice was flattering; so flattering that it actually shocked his vanity; and would have shocked it more, if possible, had he known that it was to be the only flattery of the sort he was ever to receive. The function of Class Day was, in the eyes of nine-tenths of the students, altogether the most important of the college, and the figure of the Orator was the most conspicuous in the function. Unlike the Orators at regular Commencements, the Class Day Orator stood alone, or had only the Poet for rival. Crowded into the large church, the students, their families, friends, aunts, uncles and chaperones, attended all the girls of sixteen or twenty who wanted to show their summer dresses or fresh complexions, and there, for an hour or two, in a heat that might have melted bronze, they listened to an Orator and a Poet in clergyman's gowns, reciting such platitudes as their own experience and their mild censors permitted them to utter. What Henry Adams said in his Class Oration of 1858 he soon forgot to the last word, nor had it the least value for education; but he naturally remembered what was said of it. He remembered especially one of his eminent uncles or relations remarking that, as the work of so young a man, the oration was singularly wanting in enthusiasm. The young man—always in search of education—asked himself whether, setting rhetoric aside, this absence of enthusiasm was a defect or a merit, since, in either case, it was all that Harvard College taught, and all that the hundred young men, whom he was trying to represent, expressed. Another comment threw more light on the effect of the college education. One of the elderly gentlemen noticed the orator's "perfect self-possession." Self-possession indeed! If Harvard College gave nothing else, it gave calm. For four years each student had been obliged to figure daily before dozens of young men who knew each other to the last fibre. One had done little but read papers to Societies, or act comedy in the Hasty Pudding,[16] not to speak of all sorts of regular exercises, and no audience in future life would ever be so intimately and terribly intelligent as these. Three-fourths of the graduates would rather have addressed the Council of Trent[17] or the British Parliament than have acted Sir Anthony Absolute or Dr. Ollapod[18] before a gala audience of the Hasty Pudding. Self-possession was the strongest part of Harvard College, which certainly taught men to stand alone, so that nothing seemed stranger to its graduates than the paroxysms of terror before the public which often overcame the graduates of European universities. Whether this was, or was not, education, Henry Adams never knew. He was ready to stand up before any audience in America or Europe, with nerves rather steadier for the excitement, but whether he should ever have anything to say, remained to be proved. As yet he knew nothing. Education had not begun.

[16]A student drama club at Harvard.
[17]Roman Catholic council that met in 1563 to deal with the problems created for the Church of Rome by the Protestant Reformation.
[18]Characters in Richard Brinsley Sheridan's *The Rivals* (1775) and in George Colman's *Poor Gentleman* (1801) respectively. Adams, as a member of Hasty Pudding, had acted in both plays.

CHAPTER XXV

THE DYNAMO AND THE VIRGIN[1] (1900)

Until the Great Exposition of 1900[2] closed its doors in November, Adams haunted it, aching to absorb knowledge, and helpless to find it. He would have liked to know how much of it could have been grasped by the best-informed man in the world. While he was thus meditating chaos, Langley[3] came by, and showed it to him. At Langley's behest, the Exhibition dropped its superfluous rags and stripped itself to the skin, for Langley knew what to study, and why, and how; while Adams might as well have stood outside in the night, staring at the Milky Way. Yet Langley said nothing new, and taught nothing that one might not have learned from Lord Bacon,[4] three hundred years before; but though one should have known the "Advancement of Science" as well as one knew the "Comedy of Errors,"[5] the literary knowledge counted for nothing until some teacher should show how to apply it. Bacon took a vast deal of trouble in teaching King James I[6] and his subjects, American or other, towards the year 1620, that true science was the development or economy of forces; yet an elderly American in 1900 knew neither the formula nor the forces; or even so much as to say to himself that his historical business in the Exposition concerned only the economies or developments of force since 1893, when he began the study at Chicago.[7]

Nothing in education is so astonishing as the amount of ignorance it accumulates in the form of inert facts. Adams had looked at most of the accumulations of art in the storehouses called Art Museums; yet he did not know how to look at the art exhibits of 1900. He had studied Karl Marx and his doctrines of history[8] with profound attention, yet he could not apply them at Paris. Langley, with the ease of a great master of experiment, threw out of the field every exhibit that did not reveal a new application of force, and naturally threw out, to begin with, almost the whole art exhibit. Equally, he ignored almost the whole industrial exhibit. He led his pupil directly to the forces. His chief interest was in new motors to make his airship feasible, and he taught Adams the astonishing complexities of the new Daimler motor,[9] and of the automobile, which, since 1893, had become a nightmare at a hundred kilometres an hour, almost as destructive as the electric tram which was only ten years older; and threatening to become as terrible as the locomotive steam-engine itself, which was almost exactly Adams's own age.

Then he showed his scholar the great hall of dynamos, and explained how little he knew about electricity or force of any kind, even of his own special sun, which spouted heat in inconceivable volume, but which, as far as he knew, might spout less or more, at any time, for all the certainty he felt in it. To him, the dynamo itself was but an ingenious channel for conveying somewhere the heat

[1]Michael Faraday (1791–1867) developed the first dynamo (electrical generator) in 1831. For Adams the dynamo came to represent the vast, impersonal forces of an emerging industrial society. Here Adams compares the dynamo, the symbol of modern technology, to the Virgin Mary, the symbol of medieval Christianity.

[2]The Paris Exposition of April–November 1900. Among its exhibits were the world's largest dynamos, transformers, and electric motors.

[3]Samuel Langley (1834–1906), American scientist.

[4]Francis Bacon (1561–1626), English philosopher and scientist, author of *The Advancement of Learning* (1605).

[5]Shakespeare's play, 1594.   [6]King of England (1603–1625).

[7]Adams saw similar technological exhibits at the Columbian Exposition in Chicago in 1893.

[8]Karl Marx (1818–1883) set forth his theories of history in *Das Kapital* (1867).

[9]Gottlieb Daimler (1834–1900), German developer of the internal-combustion engine.

latent in a few tons of poor coal hidden in a dirty engine-house carefully kept out of sight; but to Adams the dynamo became a symbol of infinity. As he grew accustomed to the great gallery of machines, he began to feel the forty-foot dynamos as a moral force, much as the early Christians felt the Cross. The planet itself seemed less impressive, in its old-fashioned, deliberate, annual or daily revolution, than this huge wheel, revolving within arm's-length at some vertiginous speed, and barely murmuring—scarcely humming an audible warning to stand a hair's-breadth further for respect of power—while it would not wake the baby lying close against its frame. Before the end, one began to pray to it; inherited instinct taught the natural expression of man before silent and infinite force. Among the thousand symbols of ultimate energy, the dynamo was not so human as some, but it was the most expressive.

Yet the dynamo, next to the steam-engine, was the most familiar of exhibits. For Adams's objects its value lay chiefly in its occult mechanism. Between the dynamo in the gallery of machines and the engine-house outside, the break of continuity amounted to abysmal fracture for a historian's objects. No more relation could he discover between the steam and the electric current than between the Cross and the cathedral. The forces were interchangeable if not reversible, but he could see only an absolute *fiat* in electricity as in faith. Langley could not help him. Indeed, Langley seemed to be worried by the same trouble, for he constantly repeated that the new forces were anarchical, and specially that he was not responsible for the new rays, that were little short of parricidal in their wicked spirit towards science. His own rays, with which he had doubled the solar spectrum, were altogether harmless and beneficent; but Radium denied its God—or, what was to Langley the same thing, denied the truths of his Science. The force was wholly new.[10]

A historian who asked only to learn enough to be as futile as Langley or Kelvin,[11] made rapid progress under this teaching, and mixed himself up in the tangle of ideas until he achieved a sort of Paradise of ignorance vastly consoling to his fatigued senses. He wrapped himself in vibrations and rays which were new, and he would have hugged Marconi and Branly[12] had he met them, as he hugged the dynamo; while he lost his arithmetic in trying to figure out the equation between the discoveries and the economies of force. The economies, like the discoveries, were absolute, supersensual, occult; incapable of expression in horse-power. What mathematical equivalent could he suggest as the value of a Branly coherer? Frozen air, or the electric furnace, had some scale or measurement, no doubt, if somebody could invent a thermometer adequate to the purpose; but X-rays[13] had played no part whatever in man's consciousness, and the atom itself had figured only as a fiction of thought. In these seven years man had translated himself into a new universe which had no common scale of measurement with the old. He had entered a supersensual world, in which he could measure nothing except by chance collisions of movements imperceptible to his senses, perhaps even imperceptible to his instruments, but perceptible to each other, and so to some known ray at the end of the scale. Langley seemed

[10]In 1881 Langley had measured the sun's radiation and demonstrated that the solar spectrum is far greater than had previously been thought. The subsequent discovery of radium revealed a different kind of radiation, caused by the disintegration of the atom, the further study of which led to revolutionary discoveries in atomic and nuclear physics.

[11]William Thomson, Lord Kelvin (1824–1907), British scientist.

[12]Guglielmo Marconi (1874–1937), Italian inventor of the radio telegraph. Edouard Branly (1846–1940), French inventor of a coherer (detector) of radio waves.

[13]Discovered in 1895 by William Roentgen (1845–1923).

prepared for anything, even for an indeterminable number of universes inter-fused—physics stark mad in metaphysics.

Historians undertake to arrange sequences,—called stories, or histories—assuming in silence a relation of cause and effect. These assumptions, hidden in the depths of dusty libraries, have been astounding, but commonly unconscious and childlike; so much so, that if any captious critic were to drag them to light, historians would probably reply, with one voice, that they had never supposed themselves required to know what they were talking about. Adams, for one, had toiled in vain to find out what he meant. He had even published a dozen volumes of American history for no other purpose than to satisfy himself whether, by the severest process of stating, with the least possible comment, such facts as seemed sure, in such order as seemed rigorously consequent, he could fix for a familiar moment a necessary sequence of human movement. The result had satisfied him as little as at Harvard College. Where he saw sequence, other men saw something quite different, and no one saw the same unit of measure. He cared little about his experiments and less about his statesmen, who seemed to him quite as ignorant as himself and, as a rule, no more honest; but he insisted on a relation of sequence, and if he could not reach it by one method, he would try as many methods as science knew. Satisfied that the sequence of men led to nothing and that the sequence of their society could lead no further, while the mere sequence of time was artificial, and the sequence of thought was chaos, he turned at last to the sequence of force; and thus it happened that, after ten years' pursuit, he found himself lying in the Gallery of Machines at the Great Exposition of 1900, his historical neck broken by the sudden irruption of forces totally new.

Since no one else showed much concern, an elderly person without other cares had no need to betray alarm. The year 1900 was not the first to upset schoolmasters. Copernicus and Galileo[14] had broken many professsorial necks about 1600; Columbus had stood the world on its head towards 1500; but the nearest approach to the revolution of 1900 was that of 310, when Constantine set up the Cross.[15] The rays that Langley disowned, as well as those which he fathered, were occult, supersensual, irrational; they were a revelation of mysterious energy like that of the Cross; they were what, in terms of mediæval science, were called immediate modes of the divine substance.

The historian was thus reduced to his last resources. Clearly if he was bound to reduce all these forces to a common value, this common value could have no measure but that of their attraction on his own mind. He must treat them as they had been felt; as convertible, reversible, interchangeable attractions on thought. He made up his mind to venture it; he would risk translating rays into faith. Such a reversible process would vastly amuse a chemist, but the chemist could not deny that he, or some of his fellow physicists, could feel the force of both. When Adams was a boy in Boston, the best chemist[16] in the place had probably never heard of Venus except by way of scandal,[17] or of the Virgin except as idolatry;[18] neither had he heard of dynamos or automobiles or radium;

---

[14]Copernicus (1473–1543) asserted and Galileo (1564–1642) affirmed that the earth moves around the sun.

[15]The Emperor Constantine I (288?–337) legalized Christianity in the Roman Empire in 313.

[16]A pharmacist, druggist.

[17]I.e., druggists knew of Venus (Roman goddess of love) only because they dispensed medicines for the disease of Venus—venereal disease.

[18]Protestants reject the worship of the Virgin Mary as a form of idolatry or false worship.

yet his mind was ready to feel the force of all, though the rays were unborn and the women were dead.

Here opened another totally new education, which promised to be by far the most hazardous of all. The knife-edge along which he must crawl, like Sir Lancelot in the twelfth century,[19] divided two kingdoms of force which had nothing in common but attraction. They were as different as a magnet is from gravitation, supposing one knew what a magnet was, or gravitation, or love. The force of the Virgin was still felt at Lourdes,[20] and seemed to be as potent as X-rays; but in America neither Venus nor Virgin ever had value as force—at most as sentiment. No American had ever been truly afraid of either.

This problem in dynamics gravely perplexed an American historian. The Woman had once been supreme; in France she still seemed potent, not merely as a sentiment, but as a force. Why was she unknown in America? For evidently America was ashamed of her, and she was ashamed of herself, otherwise they would not have strewn fig-leaves[21] so profusely all over her. When she was a true force, she was ignorant of fig-leaves, but the monthly-magazine-made American female had not a feature that would have been recognized by Adam. The trait was notorious, and often humorous, but any one brought up among Puritans knew that sex was sin. In any previous age, sex was strength. Neither art nor beauty was needed. Every one, even among Puritans, knew that neither Diana of the Ephesians[22] nor any of the Oriental goddesses was worshipped for her beauty. She was goddess because of her force; she was the animated dynamo; she was reproduction—the greatest and most mysterious of all energies; all she needed was to be fecund. Singularly enough, not one of Adams's many schools of education had ever drawn his attention to the opening lines of Lucretius, though they were perhaps the finest in all Latin literature, where the poet invoked Venus exactly as Dante invoked the Virgin:—

"Quae quoniam rerum naturam *sola* gubernas."[23]

The Venus of Epicurean philosophy survived in the Virgin of the Schools:[24]—

"Donna, sei tanto grande, e tanto vali,
Che qual vuol grazia, e a te non ricorre,
Sua disianza vuol volar senz' ali."[25]

All this was to American thought as though it had never existed. The true American knew something of the facts, but nothing of the feelings; he read the letter, but he never felt the law. Before this historical chasm, a mind like that of Adams felt itself helpless; he turned from the Virgin to the Dynamo as though he were a Branly coherer. On one side, at the Louvre and at Chartres, as he knew by the record of work actually done and still before his eyes, was the

[19]A reference to a test of valor undergone by Sir Lancelot in a medieval chivalric story.
[20]French shrine dedicated to the Virgin Mary.
[21]Used to cover the sexual organs of human figures in paintings and statues.
[22]Fertility goddess of the ancient Near East.
[23]Latin: "Since thou alone dost govern the nature of things." From *De Rerum Natura* ("On the Nature of Things"), I, 21, by the Roman poet Lucretius (99?–55? B.C.).
[24]I.e., the Virgin as described by scholastic philosophers of the middle ages.
[25]Italian: "Lady [Virgin Mary], thou art so great and so much worth,/That he who wishes grace and seeks not thee,/Would have his wish fly upward without wings." Dante, *Paradiso*, Canto XXXIII, lines 13–15.

highest energy ever known to man, the creator of four-fifths of his noblest art, exercising vastly more attraction over the human mind than all the steam-engines and dynamos ever dreamed of; and yet this energy was unknown to the American mind. An American Virgin would never dare command; an American Venus would never dare exist.

The question, which to any plain American of the nineteenth century seemed as remote as it did to Adams, drew him almost violently to study, once it was posed; and on this point Langleys were as useless as though they were Herbert Spencers[26] or dynamos. The idea survived only as art. There one turned as naturally as though the artist were himself a woman. Adams began to ponder, asking himself whether he knew of any American artist who had ever insisted on the power of sex, as every classic had always done; but he could think only of Walt Whitman; Bret Harte, as far as the magazines would let him venture; and one or two painters, for the flesh-tones. All the rest had used sex for sentiment, never for force; to them, Eve was a tender flower, and Herodias[27] an unfeminine horror. American art, like the American language and American education, was as far as possible sexless. Society regarded this victory over sex as its greatest triumph, and the historian readily admitted it, since the moral issue, for the moment, did not concern one who was studying the relations of unmoral force. He cared nothing for the sex of the dynamo until he could measure its energy.

Vaguely seeking a clue, he wandered through the art exhibit, and, in his stroll, stopped almost every day before St. Gaudens's General Sherman,[28] which had been given the central post of honor. St. Gaudens himself was in Paris, putting on the work his usual interminable last touches, and listening to the usual contradictory suggestions of brother sculptors. Of all the American artists who gave to American art whatever life it breathed in the seventies, St. Gaudens was perhaps the most sympathetic, but certainly the most inarticulate. General Grant or Don Cameron[29] had scarcely less instinct of rhetoric than he. All the others— the Hunts, Richardson, John La Farge, Stanford White[30]—were exuberant; only St. Gaudens could never discuss or dilate on an emotion, or suggest artistic arguments for giving to his work the forms that he felt. He never laid down the law, or affected the despot, or became brutalized like Whistler[31] by the brutalities of his world. He required no incense; he was no egoist; his simplicity of thought was excessive; he could not imitate, or give any form but his own to the creations of his hand. No one felt more strongly than he the strength of other men, but the idea that they could affect him never stirred an image in his mind.

This summer his health was poor and his spirits were low. For such a temper, Adams was not the best companion, since his own gaiety was not *folle*;[32] but he risked going now and then to the studio on Mont Parnasse[33] to draw him out

[26]English philosopher and Social Darwinist (1820–1903).

[27]Wife of King Herod. She caused the death of John the Baptist. Mark 6:17–28.

[28]Statue of American Civil War General William T. Sherman by Augustus Saint-Gaudens (1848–1907), Irish-American sculptor. Then on display in Paris, the statue is now in Central Park in New York City.

[29]James Donald Cameron (1833–1918), Senator from Pennsylvania, Secretary of War under President Ulysses S. Grant, and a friend of Adams. Both Grant and Cameron were known to be spare with words.

[30]William Morris Hunt (1824–1879), painter; Richard Morris Hunt (1828–1895), architect; Henry Richardson (1838–1886), architect; John La Farge (1835–1910), artist; Stanford White (1853–1906), architect.

[31]James McNeill Whistler (1834–1903), acid-tongued American painter.

[32]French: extravagant, excessive.   [33]Artists' quarter in Paris.

for a stroll in the Bois de Boulogne,[34] or dinner as pleased his moods, and in return St. Gaudens sometimes let Adams go about in his company.

Once St. Gaudens took him down to Amiens,[35] with a party of Frenchmen, to see the cathedral. Not until they found themselves actually studying the sculpture of the western portal, did it dawn on Adams's mind that, for his purposes, St. Gaudens on that spot had more interest to him than the cathedral itself. Great men before great monuments express great truths, provided they are not taken too solemnly. Adams never tired of quoting the supreme phrase of his idol Gibbon,[36] before the Gothic cathedrals: "I darted a contemptuous look on the stately monuments of superstition." Even in the footnotes of his history, Gibbon had never inserted a bit of humor more human than this, and one would have paid largely for a photograph of the fat little historian, on the background of Notre Dame of Amiens, trying to persuade his readers—perhaps himself—that he was darting a contemptuous look on the stately monument, for which he felt in fact the respect which every man of his vast study and active mind always feels before objects worthy of it; but besides the humor, one felt also the relation. Gibbon ignored the Virgin, because in 1789 religious monuments were out of fashion. In 1900 his remark sounded fresh and simple as the green fields to ears that had heard a hundred years of other remarks, mostly no more fresh and certainly less simple. Without malice, one might find it more instructive than a whole lecture of Ruskin.[37] One sees what one brings, and at that moment Gibbon brought the French Revolution. Ruskin brought reaction against the Revolution. St. Gaudens had passed beyond all. He liked the stately monuments much more than he liked Gibbon or Ruskin; he loved their dignity; their unity; their scale; their lines; their lights and shadows; their decorative sculpture; but he was even less conscious than they of the force that created it all—the Virgin, the Woman—by whose genius "the stately monuments of superstition" were built, through which she was expressed. He would have seen more meaning in Isis with the cow's horns, at Edfoo,[38] who expressed the same thought. The art remained, but the energy was lost even upon the artist.

Yet in mind and person St. Gaudens was a survival of the 1500s; he bore the stamp of the Renaissance, and should have carried an image of the Virgin round his neck, or stuck in his hat, like Louis XI.[39] In mere time he was a lost soul that had strayed by chance into the twentieth century, and forgotten where it came from. He writhed and cursed at his ignorance, much as Adams did at his own, but in the opposite sense. St. Gaudens was a child of Benvenuto Cellini,[40] smothered in an American cradle. Adams was a quintessence of Boston, devoured by curiosity to think like Benvenuto. St. Gaudens's art was starved from birth, and Adams's instinct was blighted from babyhood. Each had but half of a nature, and when they came together before the Virgin of Amiens they ought both to have felt in her the force that made them one; but it was not so. To Adams she became more than ever a channel of force; to St. Gaudens she remained as before a channel of taste.

[34]Park in Paris.

[35]City north of Paris. Its Gothic cathedral, dedicated to the Virgin Mary, is the largest in France.

[36]Edward Gibbon (1737–1794), English author of *The Decline and Fall of the Roman Empire* (1776–1788). Here Adams paraphrases an entry from Gibbon's *French Journal* for February 21, 1763.

[37]John Ruskin (1819–1900), English critic of art and architecture.

[38]Egyptian fertility goddess whose statue Adams had seen at Edfu on the Nile River. She was often portrayed with a cow's horns.

[39]King of France (1423–1483). Extremely pious, he traditionally wore religious emblems on his clothing.

[40]Italian goldsmith and sculptor (1500–1571).

For a symbol of power, St. Gaudens instinctively preferred the horse, as was plain in his horse and Victory of the Sherman monument. Doubtless Sherman also felt it so. The attitude was so American that, for at least forty years, Adams had never realized that any other could be in sound taste. How many years had he taken to admit a notion of what Michael Angelo and Rubens[41] were driving at? He could not say; but he knew that only since 1895 had he begun to feel the Virgin or Venus as force, and not everywhere even so. At Chartres—perhaps at Lourdes—possibly at Cnidos[42] if one could still find there the divinely naked Aphrodite of Praxiteles[43]—but otherwise one must look for force to the goddesses of Indian mythology. The idea died out long ago in the German and English stock. St. Gaudens at Amiens was hardly less sensitive to the force of the female energy than Matthew Arnold at the Grande Chartreuse.[44] Neither of them felt goddesses as power—only as reflected emotion, human expression, beauty, purity, taste, scarcely even as sympathy. They felt a railway train as power; yet they, and all other artists, constantly complained that the power embodied in a railway train could never be embodied in art. All the steam in the world could not, like the Virgin, build Chartres.

Yet in mechanics, whatever the mechanicians might think, both energies acted as interchangeable forces on man, and by action on man all known force may be measured. Indeed, few men of science measured force in any other way. After once admitting that a straight line was the shortest distance between two points, no serious mathematician cared to deny anything that suited his convenience, and rejected no symbol, unproved or unproveable, that helped him to accomplish work. The symbol was force, as a compass-needle or a triangle was force, as the mechanist might prove by losing it, and nothing could be gained by ignoring their value. Symbol or energy, the Virgin had acted as the greatest force the Western world ever felt, and had drawn man's activities to herself more strongly than any other power, natural or supernatural, had ever done; the historian's business was to follow the track of the energy; to find where it came from and where it went to; its complex source and shifting channels; its values, equivalents, conversions. It could scarcely be more complex than radium; it could hardly be deflected, diverted, polarized, absorbed more perplexingly than other radiant matter. Adams knew nothing about any of them, but as a mathematical problem of influence on human progress, though all were occult, all reacted on his mind, and he rather inclined to think the Virgin easiest to handle.

The pursuit turned out to be long and tortuous, leading at last into the vast forest of scholastic science. From Zeno to Descartes, hand in hand with Thomas Aquinas, Montaigne, and Pascal,[45] one stumbled as stupidly as though one were still a German student of 1860.[46] Only with the instinct of despair could one force one's self into this old thicket of ignorance after having been repulsed at

---

[41]Michelangelo (1475–1564), Italian artist; Peter Paul Rubens (1577–1640), Flemish painter.

[42]Ancient Greek city in Asia Minor (present-day Turkey), site of the "Aphrodite" of the sculptor Praxiteles, one of the most famous statues of the ancient world.

[43]Greek sculptor (4th century B.C.)

[44]In "Stanzas from the Grande Chartreuse" (1855), the English poet Matthew Arnold (1822–1888) laments the loss of the faith that inspired earlier Christians.

[45]Zeno of Citium (334?–262? B.C.), Greek philosopher; René Descartes (1596–1650), French philosopher and mathematician; St. Thomas Aquinas (1225?–1274), Roman Catholic philosopher; Michel Eyquem de Montaigne (1533–1592), French essayist; Blaise Pascal (1623–1662), French mathematician and moralist.

[46]After his graduation from Harvard, Henry Adams continued his studies, in Germany (1858–1860).

a score of entrances more promising and more popular. Thus far, no path had led anywhere, unless perhaps to an exceedingly modest living. Forty-five years of study had proved to be quite futile for the pursuit of power; one controlled no more force in 1900 than in 1850, although the amount of force controlled by society had enormously increased. The secret of education still hid itself somewhere behind ignorance, and one fumbled over it as feebly as ever. In such labyrinths, the staff is a force almost more necessary than the legs; the pen becomes a sort of blind-man's dog, to keep him from falling into the gutters. The pen works for itself, and acts like a hand, modelling the plastic material over and over again to the form that suits it best. The form is never arbitrary, but is a sort of growth like crystallization, as any artist knows too well; for often the pencil or pen runs into side-paths and shapelessness, loses its relations, stops or is bogged. Then it has to return on its trail, and recover, if it can, its line of force. The result of a year's work depends more on what is struck out than on what is left in; on the sequence of the main lines of thought, than on their play or variety. Compelled once more to lean heavily on this support, Adams covered more thousands of pages with figures as formal as though they were algebra, laboriously striking out, altering, burning, experimenting, until the year had expired, the Exposition had long been closed, and winter drawing to its end, before he sailed from Cherbourg, on January 19, 1901, for home.

CHAPTER XXXIII

A Dynamic Theory of History (1904)

A dynamic theory, like most theories, begins by begging the question: it defines Progress as the development and economy of Forces. Further, it defines force as anything that does, or helps to do work. Man is a force; so is the sun; so is a mathematical point, though without dimensions or known existence.

Man commonly begs the question again by taking for granted that he captures the forces. A dynamic theory, assigning attractive force to opposing bodies in proportion to the law of mass, takes for granted that the forces of nature capture man. The sum of force attracts; the feeble atom or molecule called man is attracted; he suffers education or growth; he is the sum of the forces that attract him; his body and his thought are alike their product; the movement of the forces controls the progress of his mind, since he can know nothing but the motions which impinge on his senses, whose sum makes education.

For convenience as an image, the theory may liken man to a spider in its web, watching for chance prey. Forces of nature dance like flies before the net, and the spider pounces on them when it can; but it makes many fatal mistakes, though its theory of force is sound. The spider-mind acquires a faculty of memory, and, with it, a singular skill of analysis and synthesis, taking apart and putting together in different relations the meshes of its trap. Man had in the beginning no power of analysis or synthesis approaching that of the spider, or even of the honey-bee; but he had acute sensibility to the higher forces. Fire taught him secrets that no other animal could learn; running water probably taught him even more, especially in his first lessons of mechanics; the animals helped to educate him, thrusting themselves into his hands merely for the sake of their food, and carrying his burdens or supplying his clothing; the grasses and grains were academies of study. With little or no effort on his part, all these forces formed his thought, induced his action, and even shaped his figure.

Long before history began, his education was complete, for the record could not have been started until he had been taught to record. The universe that had formed him took shape in his mind as a reflection of his own unity, containing all forces except himself. Either separately, or in groups, or as a whole, these forces never ceased to act on him, enlarging his mind as they enlarged the surface foliage of a vegetable, and the mind needed only to respond, as the forests did, to these attractions. Susceptibility to the highest forces is the highest genius; selection between them is the highest science; their mass is the highest educator. Man always made, and still makes, grotesque blunders in selecting and measuring forces, taken at random from the heap, but he never made a mistake in the value he set on the whole, which he symbolized as unity and worshipped as God. To this day, his attitude towards it had never changed, though science can no longer give to force a name.

Man's function as a force of nature was to assimilate other forces as he assimilated food. He called it the love of power. He felt his own feebleness, and he sought for an ass or a camel, a bow or a sling, to widen his range of power, as he sought a fetish or a planet in the world beyond. He cared little to know its immediate use, he could afford to throw nothing away which he could conceive to have possible value in this or any other existence. He waited for the object to teach him its use, or want of use, and the process was slow. He may have gone on for hundreds of thousands of years, waiting for Nature to tell him her secrets; and, to his rivals among the monkeys, Nature has taught no more than at their start; but certain lines of force were capable of acting on individual apes, and mechanically selecting types of race or sources of variation. The individual that responded or reacted to lines of new force then was possibly the same individual that reacts on it now, and his conception of the unity seems never to have changed in spite of the increasing diversity of forces; but the theory of variation is an affair of other science than history, and matters nothing to dynamics. The individual or the race would be educated on the same lines of illusion, which, according to Arthur Balfour,[1] had not essentially varied down to the year 1900.

To the highest attractive energy, man gave the name of divine, and for its control he invented the science called Religion, a word which meant, and still means, cultivation of occult force whether in detail or mass. Unable to define Force as unity, man symbolized it and pursued it, both in himself, and in the infinite, as philosophy and theology; the mind is itself the subtlest of all known forces, and its self-introspection necessarily created a science which had the singular value of lifting his education, at the start, to the finest, subtlest, and broadest training both in analysis and synthesis, so that, if language is a test, he must have reached his highest powers early in his history; while the mere motive remained as simple an appetite for power as the tribal greed which led him to trap an elephant. Hunger, whether for food or for the infinite, sets in motion multiplicity and infinity of thought, and the sure hope of gaining a share of infinite power in eternal life would lift most minds to effort.

He had reached this completeness five thousand years ago, and added nothing to his stock of known forces for a very long time. The mass of nature exercised on him so feeble an attraction that one can scarcely account for his apparent motion. Only a historian of very exceptional knowledge would venture to say at what date between 3000 B.C. and 1000 A.D., the momentum of Europe was

---

[1] Arthur Balfour (1848–1930), British scientist and statesman. In a speech, "Reflections Suggested by the New Theory of Matter," given August 1904, Balfour observed that until recently, mankind lacked accurate scientific knowledge of the material world, and therefore "down to, say, five years ago, our race has, without exception, lived and died in a world of illusions."

greatest; but such progress as the world made consisted in economies of energy rather than in its development; it was proved in mathematics, measured by names like Archimedes, Aristarchus, Ptolemy, and Euclid;[2] or in Civil Law, measured by a number of names which Adams had begun life by failing to learn; or in coinage, which was most beautiful near its beginning, and most barbarous at its close; or it was shown in roads, or the size of ships, or harbors; or by the use of metals, instruments, and writing; all of them economies of force, sometimes more forceful than the forces they helped; but the roads were still travelled by the horse, the ass, the camel, or the slave; the ships were still propelled by sails or oars; the lever, the spring, and the screw bounded the region of applied mechanics. Even the metals were old.

Much the same thing could be said of religious or supernatural forces. Down to the year 300[3] of the Christian era they were little changed, and in spite of Plato[4] and the sceptics were more apparently chaotic than ever. The experience of three thousand years had educated society to feel the vastness of Nature, and the infinity of her resources of power, but even this increase of attraction had not yet caused economies in its methods of pursuit.

There the Western world stood till the year A.D. 305, when the Emperor Diocletian[5] abdicated; and there it was that Adams broke down on the steps of Ara Cœli,[6] his path blocked by the scandalous failure of civilization at the moment it had achieved complete success. In the year 305 the empire had solved the problems of Europe more completely than they have ever been solved since. The Pax Romana,[7] the Civil Law, and Free Trade should, in four hundred years, have put Europe far in advance of the point reached by modern society in the four hundred years since 1500, when conditions were less simple.

The efforts to explain, or explain away, this scandal had been incessant, but none suited Adams unless it were the economic theory of adverse exchanges and exhaustion of minerals; but nations are not ruined beyond a certain point by adverse exchanges, and Rome had by no means exhausted her resources. On the contrary, the empire developed resources and energies quite astounding. No other four hundred years of history before A.D. 1800 knew anything like it; and although some of these developments, like the Civil Law, the roads, aqueducts, and harbors, were rather economies than force, yet in northwestern Europe alone the empire had developed three energies—France, England, and Germany—competent to master the world. The trouble seemed rather to be that the empire developed too much energy, and too fast.

A dynamic law requires that two masters—nature and man—must go on, reacting upon each other, without stop, as the sun and a comet react on each

---

[2]Archimedes (287?–212 B.C.), Greek mathematician; Aristarchus (3rd century B.C.), Greek astronomer, the first to assert that the earth revolves around the sun; Claudius Ptolemaeus (2nd century A.D.), Greek-Egyptian astronomer; Euclid (3rd century B.C.), Greek geometer.

[3]Adams refers to the emergence of Christianity as a powerful spiritual and political force in the Roman Empire early in the fourth century A.D.

[4]Greek philosopher (427?–347 B.C.) who asserted that the universe is ultimately harmonious. Like the later skeptic philosophers, he believed that the best method of inquiry is constantly to question assumptions. Both Plato and the later skeptics questioned whether man can penetrate surface appearances and perceive reality and the truth.

[5]Roman emperor (284–305). He resisted the spread of Christianity and persecuted Christians. Following his abdication in 305, his successor, Constantine I (288?–337), decreed the Edict of Milan (313) that Christianity was to be tolerated as a legal religion in the Roman Empire.

[6]Latin: Altar of Heaven, the name of a Franciscan church (1348) on the Capitoline Hill in Rome.

[7]Latin: Roman Peace, the peace and stability imposed by force of arms throughout the Roman Empire.

other, and that any appearance of stoppage is illusive. The theory seems to exact excess, rather than deficiency, of action and reaction to account for the dissolution of the Roman Empire, which should, as a problem of mechanics, have been torn to pieces by acceleration. If the student means to try the experiment of framing a dynamic law, he must assign values to the forces of attraction that caused the trouble; and in this case he has them in plain evidence. With the relentless logic that stamped Roman thought, the empire, which had established unity on earth, could not help establishing unity in heaven. It was induced by its dynamic necessities to economize the gods.

The Church has never ceased to protest against the charge that Christianity ruined the empire,[8] and, with its usual force, has pointed out that its reforms alone saved the State. Any dynamic theory gladly admits it. All it asks is to find and follow the force that attracts. The Church points out this force in the Cross, and history needs only to follow it. The empire loudly asserted its motive. Good taste forbids saying that Constantine the Great speculated as audaciously as a modern stock-broker on values of which he knew at the utmost only the volume; or that he merged all uncertain forces into a single trust, which he enormously overcapitalized, and forced on the market; but this is the substance of what Constantine himself said in his Edict of Milan in the year 313, which admitted Christianity into the Trust of State Religions. Regarded as an Act of Congress, it runs: "We have resolved to grant to Christians as well as all others the liberty to practise the religion they prefer, in order that whatever exists of divinity or celestial power may help and favor us and all who are under our government." The empire pursued power—not merely spiritual but physical—in the sense in which Constantine issued his army order the year before, at the battle of the Milvian Bridge: *In hoc signo vinces!*[9] using the Cross as a train of artillery, which, to his mind, it was. Society accepted it in the same character. Eighty years afterwards, Theodosius marched against his rival Eugene[10] with the Cross for physical champion; and Eugene raised the image of Hercules[11] to fight for the pagans; while society on both sides looked on, as though it were a boxing-match, to decide a final test of force between the divine powers. The Church was powerless to raise the ideal. What is now known as religion affected the mind of old society but little. The laity, the people, the million, almost to a man, bet on the gods as they bet on a horse.

No doubt the Church did all it could to purify the process, but society was almost wholly pagan in its point of view, and was drawn to the Cross because, in its system of physics, the Cross had absorbed all the old occult or fetish-power. The symbol represented the sum of nature—the Energy of modern science— and society believed it to be as real as X-rays; perhaps it was! The emperors used it like gunpowder in politics; the physicians used it like rays in medicine; the dying clung to it as the quintessence of force, to protect them from the forces of evil on their road to the next life.

Throughout these four centuries the empire knew that religion disturbed economy, for even the cost of heathen incense affected the exchanges; but no one could afford to buy or construct a costly and complicated machine when he could hire an occult force at trifling expense. Fetish-power was cheap and

---

[8]A charge made by various historians, among them Edward Gibbon in his *Decline and Fall of the Roman Empire* (1776–1788).

[9]Latin: "Under this sign you shall conquer!"

[10]In 394 Theodosius (346?–395), the Christian Roman Emperor of the East, defeated Eugenius, the pagan Roman Emperor of the West.

[11]Hero of classical myth.

satisfactory, down to a certain point. Turgot and Auguste Comte[12] long ago fixed this stage of economy as a necessary phase of social education, and historians seem now to accept it as the only gain yet made towards scientific history. Great numbers of educated people—perhaps a majority— cling to the method still, and practise it more or less strictly; but, until quite recently, no other was known. The only occult power at man's disposal was fetish. Against it, no mechanical force could compete except within narrow limits.

Outside of occult or fetish-power, the Roman world was incredibly poor. It knew but one productive energy resembling a modern machine—the slave. No artificial force of serious value was applied to production or transportation, and when society developed itself so rapidly in political and social lines, it had no other means of keeping its economy on the same level than to extend its slave-system and its fetish-system to the utmost.

The result might have been stated in a mathematical formula as early as the time of Archimedes,[13] six hundred years before Rome fell. The economic needs of a violently centralizing society forced the empire to enlarge its slave-system until the slave-system consumed itself and the empire too, leaving society no resource but further enlargement of its religious system in order to compensate for the losses and horrors of the failure. For a vicious circle, its mathematical completeness approached perfection. The dynamic law of attraction and reaction needed only a Newton[14] to fix it in algebraic form.

At last, in 410, Alaric[15] sacked Rome, and the slave-ridden, agricultural, uncommercial Western Empire—the poorer and less Christianized half— went to pieces. Society, though terribly shocked by the horrors of Alaric's storm, felt still more deeply the disappointment in its new power, the Cross, which had failed to protect its Church. The outcry against the Cross became so loud among Christians that its literary champion, Bishop Augustine[16] of Hippo—a town between Algiers and Tunis—was led to write a famous treatise in defence of the Cross, familiar still to every scholar, in which he defended feebly the mechanical value of the symbol—arguing only that pagan symbols equally failed—but insisted on its spiritual value in the *Civitas Dei* which had taken the place of the *Civitas Romae* in human interest. "Granted that we have lost all we had! Have we lost faith? Have we lost piety? Have we lost the wealth of the inner man who is rich before God? These are the wealth of Christians!" The *Civitas Dei*, in its turn, became the sum of attraction for the Western world, though it also showed the same weakness in mechanics that had wrecked the *Civitas Romae*. St. Augustine and his people perished at Hippo towards 430, leaving society in appearance dull to new attraction.

Yet the attraction remained constant. The delight of experimenting on occult force of every kind is such as to absorb all the free thought of the human race. The gods did their work; history has no quarrel with them; they led, educated, enlarged the mind; taught knowledge; betrayed ignorance, stimulated effort. So little is known about the mind—whether social, racial, sexual or heritable; whether material or spiritual; whether animal, vegetable or mineral—that history is inclined to avoid it altogether; but nothing forbids one to admit, for

[12]Anne Robert Jacques Turgot (1727–1781), French economist; Auguste Comte (1798–1857), French philosopher.

[13]Archimedes (287?–212 B.C.), Greek mathematician and inventor.

[14]Isaac Newton (1642–1727), English mathematician, physicist, astronomer.

[15]Alaric (370?–410), King of the Visigoths. His army sacked the city of Rome in 410 A.D.

[16]Bishop of Hippo in Roman Africa and author of *Civitas Dei* (*The City of God*), a defense of Christianity.

convenience, that it may assimilate food like the body, storing new force and growing, like a forest, with the storage. The brain has not yet revealed its mysterious mechanism of gray matter. Never has Nature offered it so violent a stimulant as when she opened to it the possibility of sharing infinite power in eternal life, and it might well need a thousand years of prolonged and intense experiment to prove the value of the motive. During these so-called Middle Ages, the Western mind reacted in many forms, on many sides, expressing its motives in modes, such as Romanesque and Gothic architecture, glass windows and mosaic walls, sculpture and poetry, war and love, which still affect some people as the noblest work of man, so that, even to-day, great masses of idle and ignorant tourists travel from far countries to look at Ravenna and San Marco, Palermo and Pisa, Assisi, Cordova, Chartres,[17] with vague notions about the force that created them, but with a certain surprise that a social mind of such singular energy and unity should still lurk in their shadows.

The tourist more rarely visits Constantinople or studies the architecture of Sancta Sofia,[18] but when he does, he is distinctly conscious of forces not quite the same. Justinian has not the simplicity of Charlemagne.[19] The Eastern Empire showed an activity and variety of forces that classical Europe had never possessed. The navy of Nicephoras Phocas[20] in the tenth century would have annihilated in half an hour any navy that Carthage or Athens or Rome ever set afloat. The dynamic scheme began by asserting rather recklessly that between the Pyramids (B.C. 3000), and the Cross (A.D. 300), no new force affected Western progress, and antiquarians may easily dispute the fact; but in any case the motive influence, old or new, which raised both Pyramids and Cross was the same attraction of power in a future life that raised the dome of Sancta Sofia and the Cathedral at Amiens, however much it was altered, enlarged, or removed to distance in space. Therefore, no single event has more puzzled historians than the sudden, unexplained appearance of at least two new natural forces of the highest educational value in mechanics, for the first time within record of history. Literally, these two forces seemed to drop from the sky at the precise moment when the Cross on one side and the Crescent[21] on the other, proclaimed the complete triumph of the *Civitas Dei*. Had the Manichean doctrine[22] of Good and Evil as rival deities been orthodox, it would alone have accounted for this simultaneous victory of hostile powers.

Of the compass, as a step towards demonstration of the dynamic law, one may confidently say that it provided, better than any other force, the widening scope of the mind, since it widened immensely the range of contact between nature and thought. The compass educated. This must prove itself as needing no proof.

Of Greek fire[23] and gunpowder, the same thing cannot certainly be said, for they have the air of accidents due to the attraction of religious motives. They belong to the spiritual world; or to the doubtful ground of Magic which lay between Good and Evil. They were chemical forces, mostly explosive, which

[17]Cities in Italy, Sicily, Spain, and France; sites of famous Christian churches and shrines.

[18]Cathedral of Saint Sophia (Hagia Sophia) the masterpiece of Byzantine architecture in Constantinople (modern Istanbul), built in the sixth century by Justinian, the Emperor of Byzantium. It was converted into a mosque in 1453 after Constantinople fell to the Moslem Turks.

[19]Charlemagne (742?–814), Holy Roman Emperor (800–814).

[20]Emperor of the Eastern Roman Empire from 963 to 969.

[21]The symbol of Islam.

[22]Of the third-century Persian philosopher Mani, who taught that the world is ruled by two divine forces: darkness (evil) and light (good).

[23]Incendiary compounds used, in ancient battle, like napalm.

acted and still act as the most violent educators ever known to man, but they were justly feared as diabolic, and whatever insolence man may have risked towards the milder teachers of his infancy, he was an abject pupil towards explosives. The Sieur de Joinville[24] left a record of the energy with which the relatively harmless Greek fire educated and enlarged the French mind in a single night in the year 1249, when the crusaders were trying to advance on Cairo.[25] The good king St. Louis and all his staff dropped on their knees at every fiery flame that flew, praying—"God have pity on us!" and never had man more reason to call on his gods than they, for the battle of religion between Christian and Saracen was trifling compared with that of education between gunpowder and the Cross.

The fiction that society educated itself, or aimed at a conscious purpose, was upset by the compass and gunpowder which dragged and drove Europe at will through frightful bogs of learning. At first, the apparent lag for want of volume in the new energies lasted one or two centuries, which closed the great epochs of emotion by the Gothic cathedrals and scholastic theology. The moment has Greek beauty and more than Greek unity, but it was brief; and for another century or two, Western society seemed to float in space without apparent motion. Yet the attractive mass of nature's energy continued to attract, and education became more rapid than ever before. Society began to resist, but the individual showed greater and greater insistence, without realizing what he was doing. When the Crescent drove the Cross in ignominy from Constantinople in 1453,[26] Gutenberg and Fust[27] were printing their first Bible at Mainz under the impression that they were helping the Cross. When Columbus discovered the West Indies in 1492, the Church looked on it as a victory of the Cross. When Luther and Calvin[28] upset Europe half a century later, they were trying, like St. Augustine, to substitute the *Civitas Dei* for the *Civitas Romae*. When the Puritans set out for New England in 1620,[29] they too were looking to found a *Civitas Dei* in State Street;[30] and when Bunyan made his Pilgrimage in 1678, he repeated St. Jerome.[31] Even when, after centuries of license, the Church reformed its discipline, and, to prove it, burned Giordano Bruno in 1600, besides condemning Galileo in 1630[32]—as science goes on repeating to us every day—it condemned anarchists, not atheists. None of the astronomers were irreligious men; all of them made a point of magnifying God through his works; a form of science which did their religion no credit. Neither Galileo nor Kepler, neither Spinoza nor Descartes, neither Leibnitz[33] nor Newton, any more than Constan-

---

[24]Sire Jean de Joinville (1224?–1317), French historian.

[25]During the Seventh Crusade (1248–1254), the Christian armies under Louis IX (1214–1270), King of France, failed in their attempt to take the city of Cairo, Egypt.

[26]In 1453, the Christian city of Constantinople (present-day Istanbul) was conquered by the Moslem Turks whose symbol was the crescent.

[27]Johann Gutenberg (1397?–1468), German printer often said to have been the first European to use movable type. Johann Fust (1400?–1466?), German printer and Gutenberg's partner.

[28]Protestant reformers of the sixteenth century.

[29]Adams confuses the Pilgrim Separatists, who settled in Plymouth in 1620, with the Puritans who established Boston in 1630.

[30]I.e., to set up a theocracy in Boston.

[31]The Puritan writer John Bunyan (1628–1688) published his *Pilgrim's Progress* in 1678. St. Jerome (347?–420) produced the Vulgate (Latin) translation of the Bible.

[32]Giordano Bruno (1548?–1600), Italian philosopher, executed for heresy. Galileo (1564–1642), Italian astronomer, escaped execution by renouncing his belief that the earth moves around the sun.

[33]Johannes Kepler (1571–1630), German astronomer; Baruch Spinoza (1632–1677), Dutch philosopher; Gottfried Wilhelm von Leibnitz (1646–1716), German philosopher.

tine the Great—if so much— doubted Unity. The utmost range of their heresies reached only its personality.

This persistence of thought-inertia is the leading idea of modern history. Except as reflected in himself, man has no reason for assuming unity in the universe, or an ultimate substance, or a prime-motor. The *a priori* insistence on this unity ended by fatiguing the more active—or reactive—minds; and Lord Bacon tried to stop it. He urged society to lay aside the idea of evolving the universe from a thought, and to try evolving thought from the universe. The mind should observe and register forces—take them apart and put them together—without assuming unity at all. "Nature, to be commanded, must be obeyed." "The imagination must be given not wings but weights." As Galileo reversed the action of earth and sun, Bacon[34] reversed the relation of thought to force. The mind was thenceforth to follow the movement of matter, and unity must be left to shift for itself.

The revolution in attitude seemed voluntary, but in fact was as mechanical as the fall of a feather. Man created nothing. After 1500, the speed of progress so rapidly surpassed man's gait as to alarm every one, as though it were the acceleration of a falling body which the dynamic theory takes it to be. Lord Bacon was as much astonished by it as the Church was, and with reason. Suddenly society felt itself dragged into situations altogether new and anarchic—situations which it could not affect, but which painfully affected it. Instinct taught it that the universe in its thought must be in danger when its reflection lost itself in space. The danger was all the greater because men of science covered it with "larger synthesis," and poets called the undevout astronomer mad. Society knew better. Yet the telescope held it rigidly standing on its head; the microscope revealed a universe that defied the senses; gunpowder killed whole races that lagged behind; the compass coerced the most imbruted mariner to act on the impossible idea that the earth was round; the press drenched Europe with anarchism. Europe saw itself, violently resisting, wrenched into false positions, drawn along new lines as a fish that is caught on a hook; but unable to understand by what force it was controlled. The resistance was often bloody, sometimes humorous, always constant. Its contortions in the eighteenth century are best studied in the wit of Voltaire, but all history and all philosophy from Montaigne and Pascal to Schopenhauer and Nietzsche[35] deal with nothing else; and still, throughout it all, the Baconian law held good; thought did not evolve nature, but nature evolved thought. No one considerable man of science dared face the stream of thought; and the whole number of those who acted, like Franklin, as electric conductors of the new forces from nature to man, down to the year 1800, did not exceed a few score, confined to a few towns in Western Europe. Asia refused to be touched by the stream, and America, except for Franklin, stood outside.

Very slowly the accretion of these new forces, chemical and mechanical, grew in volume until they acquired sufficient mass to take the place of the old religious science, substituting their attraction for the attractions of the *Civitas Dei,* but the process remained the same. Nature, not mind, did the work that the sun does on the planets. Man depended more and more absolutely on forces other than his own, and on instruments which superseded his senses. Bacon foretold it:

[34]Sir Francis Bacon (1561–1626), English scientist and statesman.
[35]Voltaire (1694–1778), French philosopher; Blaise Pascal (1623–1662), French mathematician and moralist; Arthur Schopenhauer (1778–1860) and Friedrich Nietzsche (1844–1900), German philosophers.

"Neither the naked hand nor the understanding, left to itself, can effect much. It is by instruments and helps that the work is done." Once done, the mind resumed its illusion, and society forgot its impotence; but no one better than Bacon knew its tricks, and for his true followers science always meant self-restraint, obedience, sensitivities to impulse from without. "Non fingendum aut excogitandum sed inveniendum quid Natura faciat aut ferat."[36]

The success of this method staggers belief, and even to-day can be treated by history only as a miracle of growth, like the sports of nature. Evidently a new variety of mind had appeared. Certain men merely held out their hands—like Newton, watched an apple; like Franklin, flew a kite; like Watt, played with a tea-kettle[37]—and great forces of nature stuck to them as though she were playing ball. Governments did almost nothing but resist. Even gunpowder and ordnance, the great weapon of government, showed little development between 1400 and 1800. Society was hostile or indifferent, as Priestley and Jenner, and even Fulton,[38] with reason complained in the most advanced societies in the world, while its resistance became acute wherever the Church held control; until all mankind seemed to draw itself out in a long series of groups, dragged on by an attractive power in advance, which even the leaders obeyed without understanding, as the planets obeyed gravity, or the trees obeyed heat and light.

The influx of new force was nearly spontaneous. The reaction of mind on the mass of nature seemed not greater than that of a comet on the sun; and had the spontaneous influx of force stopped in Europe, society must have stood still, or gone backward, as in Asia or Africa. Then only economies of process would have counted as new force, and society would have been better pleased; for the idea that a new force must be in itself a good is only an animal or vegetable instinct. As Nature developed her hidden energies, they tended to become destructive. Thought itself became tortured, suffering reluctantly, impatiently, painfully, the coercion of new method. Easy thought had always been movement of inertia, and mostly mere sentiment; but even the processes of mathematics measured feebly the needs of force.

The stupendous acceleration after 1800 ended with the appearance of the new class of supersensual forces, before which the man of science stood at first as bewildered and helpless, as in the fourth century, a priest of Isis[39] before the Cross of Christ.

This, then, or something like this, would be a dynamic formula of history. Any schoolboy knows enough to object at once that it is the oldest and most universal of all theories. Church and State, theology and philosophy, have always preached it, differing only in the allotment of energy between nature and man. Whether the attractive energy has been called God or Nature, the mechanism has been always the same, and history is not obliged to decide whether the Ultimate tends to a purpose or not, or whether ultimate energy is one or many. Every one admits that the will is a free force, habitually decided by motives. No one denies that motives exist adequate to decide the will; even though it may not always be conscious of them. Science has proved that forces, sensible and

[36]Latin: "One must not merely theorize about what nature does or produces; one must investigate." From Bacon's *De augmentis scientarium* (1623).

[37]James Watt (1736–1819), Scottish inventor of the first practical steam engine; according to legend, he got his idea from watching a boiling teakettle.

[38]Joseph Priestley (1733–1804), English philosopher and scientist; Edward Jenner (1749–1823), English physician, developed inoculation against smallpox; Robert Fulton (1765–1815), American developer of the steamboat. All three were attacked for their discoveries and inventions.

[39]Pagan Egyptian goddess.

occult, physical and metaphysical, simple and complex, surround, traverse, vibrate, rotate, repel, attract, without stop; that man's senses are conscious of few, and only in a partial degree; but that, from the beginning of organic existence his consciousness has been induced, expanded, trained in the lines of his sensitiveness; and that the rise of his faculties from a lower power to a higher, or from a narrower to a wider field, may be due to the function of assimilating and storing outside force or forces. There is nothing unscientific in the idea that, beyond the lines of force felt by the senses, the universe may be—as it has always been—either a supersensuous chaos or a divine unity, which irresistibly attracts, and is either life or death to penetrate. Thus far, religion, philosophy, and science seem to go hand in hand. The schools begin their vital battle only there. In the earlier stages of progress, the forces to be assimilated were simple and easy to absorb, but, as the mind of man enlarged its range, it enlarged the field of complexity, and must continue to do so, even into chaos, until the reservoirs of sensuous or supersensuous energies are exhausted, or cease to affect him, or until he succumbs to their excess.

For past history, this way of grouping its sequences may answer for a chart of relations, although any serious student would need to invent another, to compare or correct its errors; but past history is only a value of relation to the future, and this value is wholly one of convenience, which can be tested only by experiment. Any law of movement must include, to make it a convenience, some mechanical formula of acceleration.

1907, 1918

Twentieth-Century Literature

T HE United States began the twentieth century with a population of less than 76,000,000, almost two thirds of it living on farms and in rural villages. The dominant symbol of mobility and industrialism that would soon transform American life had just begun to appear: in all the land there were only 8,000 horseless carriages and a mere 150 miles of paved country roads.

By 1989 the population had more than tripled, rising to 268,000,000. The vast majority of Americans now lived in large urban centers. They owned nearly 200,000,000 motor vehicles, enough to hold the entire population of Europe in the front seats. They traveled on 3,000,000 miles of roads and streets; more land in the United States was paved than remained in virgin wilderness. The nation's wealth and its technological achievements on earth and in space had astonished the world.

In 1900 the American arts were poised on the brink of a turbulent modernity. In little more than two decades American painters, architects, composers, and writers would adopt a variety of avant-garde doctrines so revolutionary as to exhaust the traditional vocabulary of the arts and require the creation of new descriptive terms: futurism, expressionism, post-impressionism, dadaism, imagism, and surrealism.

The coming changes could be seen in the visual arts early in the century. The first exhibit of modern European art in the United States took place in 1908. Five years later a vast art show, held in a National Guard armory in New York City, marked a turning point in American cultural history and introduced large numbers of Americans to modern art for the first time. Of the 1,600 works in the Armory Show, many departed radically from past tradition: urban slums and human derelicts were portrayed with harsh realism by American artists of what the newspapers derisively called the "Ash Can School"; paintings by European artists were filled with the swirling lines of neo-impressionism or with the geometric fragments and shifting viewpoints of the new cubism that seemed to defy all logic. Such "artistic anarchism" stunned the public and made the Armory Show an enormous *succès de scandale*. Bewildered critics scoffed at the show's "freak art"; students of traditional art hanged the new, radical artists in effigy; former President Theodore Roosevelt dismissed the startling paintings and sculpture as work of "the lunatic fringe." But the Armory Show of 1913 signaled the rise of artistic ideals that would dominate American art throughout the twentieth century.

In the years preceding World War I, nineteenth-century realism and naturalism remained vital forces in American literature. Henry James, now living in England, published two of his greatest novels, *The Ambassadors* (1903) and *The Golden Bowl* (1904). The literary naturalists Stephen Crane and Frank Norris died in the first years of the century, but Theodore Dreiser's *Sister Carrie*, a commercial and critical failure when first published in 1900, was reissued in 1907 and won high praise for its grim, naturalistic portrayal of American society.

Early in the century Ezra Pound and T. S. Eliot published works that would change the nature of American poetry. But the impact of modernist writers on the general reading public was only slight. The genteel tradition and popular romanticism still dominated the nation's literary tastes.

In 1900 the best-selling novel in the United States was *To Have and To Hold*, a now forgotten historical romance by Mary Johnston. In 1902, the best seller was Owen Wister's *The Virginian*, a western that established a pattern for hundreds of cowboy adventure stories and movies that have since been produced (it was revived as a television serial in the 1960s). Yet the most popular single work of fiction published in the entire period (by the 1980s its sales far exceeded 5,000,000 copies) was a juvenile fantasy, *The Wonderful Wizard of Oz* (1900).

The growth of mass-circulation periodicals created a rich marketplace for popular writers. By the 1920s, general-audience magazines that had circulations in the millions were paying as much as six thousand dollars for a short story and sixty thousand dollars for a serial (the equivalent of almost three hundred thousand dollars in modern purchasing power). During the depression years of the 1930s, the profitable mass market for literature temporarily declined, but after World War II it expanded enormously with the growth of the population, the increase of wealth and education, the expansion of mass-distribution book clubs, and the technological advances in printing that made possible the publishing of vast numbers of inexpensive paperbacks.

In the early 1900s, a rising number of "little magazines" brought numerous avant-garde writers to the attention of a limited but sophisticated audience. The most influential was *Poetry: A Magazine of Verse*, founded in Chicago by Harriet Monroe in 1912. Its first issue contained two poems by Ezra Pound. In 1915 it printed T. S. Eliot's "The Love Song of J. Alfred Prufrock." Within a few years it had published works by Edwin Arlington Robinson, Carl Sandburg, and Robert Frost, followed soon after by Robinson Jeffers, Wallace Stevens, and Hart Crane. Their works forced changes in the traditional relationships between poets and their audiences, requiring learned and sophisticated readers armed with modernist sympathies.

Although the form and direction of modern American literature had clearly begun to emerge in the first decades of the century, the First World War (1914–1918) stands as the great dividing line between the nineteenth century and contemporary America. World War I had its origins in the political turmoil of the early 1900s and in the vain rivalries of European imperial powers that had once seemed to be the glory of the age. For the United States the war began as a crusade for purity and democracy, and at its end, President Woodrow Wilson proclaimed that Americans had gained everything for which they had fought. But out of the war's catastrophes and appalling waste came little more than a sense of the failure of political leaders and a belief in the futility of hope. No abiding solutions to the world's problems had been found, and the years following the war saw the resurgence of nationalism and the rise of a new totalitarianism that would bring on World War II in less than a quarter of a century.

Writers of the first postwar era self-consciously declared that they were a "Lost Generation," devoid of faith and alienated from a civilization that was "botched," as Ezra Pound described it, "an old bitch gone in the teeth." Yet in the decade of the 1920s American literature achieved a new diversity and reached its greatest heights. The publication in 1922 of T. S. Eliot's *The Wasteland,* the most significant American poem of the twentieth century, helped to establish a modern tradition of literature rich with learning and symbolism. In 1920, Sinclair Lewis published his memorable denunciation of American small-town provincialism in *Main Street,* and in the same year Theodore Dreiser began writing his masterpiece of naturalism, *An American Tragedy* (1925). F. Scott Fitzgerald summarized the experiences and attitudes of the decade in his short stories and in his novel *The Great Gatsby* (1926). Ernest Hemingway wrote *The Sun Also Rises* (1926), and *A Farewell to Arms* (1929), and William Faulkner published one of the most influential American novels of the age, *The Sound and the Fury* (1929).

After the First World War a group of new American dramatists emerged, and the American theater ceased to be wholly dependent on the dramatic traditions of Europe. Experimental playwrights, hostile to outworn and timid theatrical convention, created works of tragedy, stark realism, and social protest. In the "new American theater" plots, dialogue, staging, and acting differed radically from the bland dramatic fare of an earlier day. Plays by "advanced" dramatists won large audiences and drew widespread critical acclaim. Early in the 1920s the most prominent of the new American playwrights, Eugene O'Neill, established an international reputation with such plays as *The Emperor Jones* (1920), *Anna Christie* (1921) and *The Hairy Ape* (1922).

The years between the two world wars were a time of new directions and new achievements in all the arts. Numerous museums and galleries were established—New York's Museum of Modern Art was founded in 1929. The term *modern art* had been used as early as the 1890s to describe the works of artists who deliberately chose to depart from the traditional forms, techniques, and subjects of familiar European art history. By the 1920s, words such as *modernism* and *modernistic* were part of the everyday vocabulary of millions of Americans who confronted the experimentalism of twentieth-century painting and sculpture. New theories of art sprouted, justifying flat abstractions or surrealism with nightmarish representations of the unconscious. Art came to be accepted as diverse, unusual, indecipherable. Artists attempted to present meanings without depicting conventional forms or familiar things, just as modernist literature often seemed to consist of poetry and prose that was incoherent, inexplicable.

It was also an age of artistic grandiloquence. The American skyscraper became the preeminent achievement of twentieth-century architecture. The American motion picture industry rose to world dominance. And with the establishment of such music schools as Eastman and Julliard after World War I, American-trained musicians at last began to challenge successfully the graduates of famous European music conservatories. The jazz music of American blacks—the most influential art form ever to originate in the United States—spread throughout the world, and in 1938, when Benny Goodman led a racially mixed jazz orchestra in a concert at prestigious Carnegie Hall in New York City, it was clear that jazz had at last been accepted by even the most cultured and rarified audiences.

With the slow disintegration of old prejudices came the *Harlem Renaissance,* a burst of literary achievement in the 1920s by black playwrights, novelists, and poets, like Countee Cullen, who presented new insights into the American experience and prepared the way for the emergence of numerous black writers after mid-century.

In 1929 the stock market crashed, and the Great Depression of the 1930s began, cataclysmic events that shattered public complacency and transformed American society. The abrupt end of what had seemed to be permanent prosperity weakened the nation's confidence in its government and in its political leaders. American artists of all kinds began to produce works of political and social criticism. Painters created harsh visions of American life on farms and in cities. Photographers recorded the miseries of poverty and want. John Steinbeck and other writers described the sweat-drenched lives of factory workers and migrant farmers in journalistic reports, in short stories, and in such memorable novels as *Of Mice and Men* (1937) and *The Grapes of Wrath* (1939).

The social upheavals and the artistic declarations of the Great Depression years changed with the prosperity and turmoil brought by the Second World War (1939–1945). And after the war a new generation of American authors appeared, writing in the skeptical, ironic tradition of the earlier realists and naturalists. The writers of the 1950s used a prose style modeled on the works of Ernest Hemingway and F. Scott Fitzgerald, narrative techniques derived from William Faulkner, and psychological insights taken from the writing of Sigmund Freud and his followers. But in the 1960s and 1970s America's prose writers turned increasingly to experimental techniques, to absurd humor, and to mocking examination of the irrational and the disordered.

Among the most prominent post-World War II American writers is Norman Mailer. His best-selling novel, *The Naked and the Dead* (1948), portrayed the war as a meaningless sacrifice directed by ruthless martinets and filled with physical and spiritual obscenities. In the following decades, Mailer remained conspicuous by writing journalistic narratives that recorded his experiences as an observer and participant in the most visible calamities of the age. Southern short story writers and novelists, among them Eudora Welty and Flannery O'Connor, were inspired by Faulkner and the regional traditions in literature to write of the grotesque humor and the menacing violence of life in small-town and rural America. Saul Bellow, Bernard Malamud, and Philip Roth portrayed the dilemmas of misfit heroes yearning for meaningful lives and moral regeneration. The anti-hero, alternately a victim, a rebel, or a bumbling failure, became a commonplace in American fiction. Innovative writers, such as Donald Barthelme, began writing short, sardonic stories about worlds where words and ideas lose validity and complacent hope is often absurd.

The theater in America, beset by rising costs and competition from television, lost momentum after World War II. Its former vitality survived primarily in productions *off Broadway* and in experimental presentations in regional theaters and on college campuses. The works of the most notable American dramatists of the period range from familiar American realism to obscure psychological surrealism. The realistic plays of Arthur Miller reflect the struggles of individuals in society and the failure of the American ideal of success. From Tennessee Williams came gothic dramas of oversensitive souls stifled by fate and their own genteel illusions. Williams's plays are rich with symbols, as are those of Edward Albee, whose work is further distinguished by its searing dialogue and ambiguous intent.

Since World War II, more poetry has been published and read in America than in any earlier period of its history. As new poets emerged and as new audiences were created, critical values changed. Such poetic monuments of the

964

past as T. S. Eliot and Robert Frost went temporarily out of fashion. New schools of poets, seeking guidance and inspiration, turned instead to Walt Whitman, William Carlos Williams, Wallace Stevens, and Ezra Pound. One of the most visible poets of the age, Allen Ginsberg, emerged out of the phenomenon of the postwar "Beat Generation," and in such poems as "Howl" and in his wide-ranging public appearances he offered Whitmanesque recitations of the glories and the vulgarities of America, amazing and shocking audiences who were used to the learned obscurities of Pound and Eliot or who were comfortable with the seemingly benign and rustic wisdom of Robert Frost.

Theodore Roethke, though tormented by doubt, exuberantly celebrated the mysteries of life. And Robert Lowell recorded his dilemmas and suffering in a confessional mode of poetry that is intensely private and that often focuses on the catastrophes of modern existence. A growing number of women writers appeared, novelists and short story writers such as Joyce Carol Oates, Anne Beattie, and Alice Walker, poets such as Sylvia Plath, Anne Sexton, Adrienne Rich, and Amy Clampitt, who brought a new force and a new perspective to American literature.

From the 1960s to the end of the 1980s, American writers confronted a world of ferocious change and accelerating technology. Electronic computers (1946), transistors (1947), and lasers (1958) were part of a space-age technology that achieved unprecedented mastery of nature when the Apollo Eleven landed men on the moon in 1969. American technical and material abundance meant that for the first time in history, the vast majority of Americans ceased to worry about the prospect of suffering primary want.

But as the United States became the world's preeminent Republic of Technology, it seemed also to become a land without yesterdays, a land of instant obsolescence and constant need to recycle and replenish. Differences and distinctions seemed to merge. Individualism seemed diluted. Americans often seemed to think alike, dress alike, and eat alike in a kingdom of bland mediocrity created and sustained by the all-powerful and inescapable force of television.

By the end of the 1980s, more than 98 percent of all households in the United States had at least one television set. The nation's most popular magazine, *TV Guide*, had a weekly circulation of 17,000,000 copies, greater than any other publication in the history of the world. The average American watched television more than thirty hours a week; the average high school graduating senior, who had spent 11,000 hours in the classroom, had spent 15,000 hours watching television. The national addiction to TV was growing so vast, critics argued, that Americans were in danger of becoming homogenized simpletons, with goals dictated by TV commercials, with values drawn from the sentimental platitudes revered in TV sitcoms.

But in spite of such threatening changes, the United States remains the nation of greatest political and social diversity and opportunity in the world, a land where more than 20,000,000 foreign-born men and women now live, where immigrants arrive at the rate of 600,000 a year, where more than 300 languages and dialects are spoken, where 250 different religious denominations coexist. And within that pluralistic society American poets, playwrights, novelists, and essayists, influenced by the contraries and the varieties they perceive, continue to explore their own lives and their own visions of the land and its people, confronting the great questions of American civilization and forming their experiences into timeless myth, just as their colonial American forebears did three centuries before.

Edwin Arlington Robinson   *1869–1935*

The first major poet of twentieth-century America, E. A. Robinson fitted the romantic stereotype of the poet as a lonely, struggling genius. Through much of his life he experienced personal tragedy, poverty, and public disregard—all of which were reflected in his somber, often stoical poetry. He was the third son of a small-town Maine businessman and of a mother whose New England ancestors included the early colonial poet Anne Bradstreet. Except for some juvenile poems, Robinson showed little aptitude as a youth. He was an indifferent student, and after his graduation from high school his father refused the expense of his further education. Eventually, when he was almost twenty-two, Robinson managed to enroll as a special student at Harvard, but after two years he left Harvard and returned home to Gardiner, Maine.

During the next few years he completed two books of poetry, the first of which, The Torrent and the Night Before *(1896), he published at his own expense. With the appearance of his second book,* The Children of the Night *(1897), he left home and moved to New York. Gardiner, Maine, which appeared as Tilbury Town in Robinson's poems, provided him with a colorful array of New England character types—drunkards, dreamers, and misfits with names like Richard Cory, Bewick Finzer, and Eben Flood. They embodied the spiritual drought and moral failure that Robinson made the thematic center of much of his work.*

In New York, Robinson tried his hand at journalism and later worked as a timekeeper on the construction of the New York subway. Following the publication in 1902 of Captain Craig, *he received, with the help of President Theodore Roosevelt, a job at the New York Customs House, and in 1910 he published his fourth book of poems,* The Town Down the River. *The following year Robinson spent his first summer at the MacDowell Colony for artists in the New Hampshire countryside, where he was to return every summer for the rest of his life. There, with freedom to concentrate on his writing, Robinson began his most productive years. The appearance of* The Man Against the Sky *(1916) marked the beginning of his reputation. The next decade saw the publication of* The Three Taverns *(1920),* Avon's Harvest *(1921), and* Dionysus in Doubt *(1925). His* Collected Poems *(1921) brought him the first of three Pulitzer Prizes, and his long narrative poem* Tristram *(1927) became a best seller.*

Robinson was a transitional figure between the nineteenth and twentieth centuries. His life spanned the waning years of the genteel era and the rebellious period of disillusionment that followed World War I. An older generation found his poetry dangerously radical, marred by formlessness; the modernists found it tamely conservative. His deepest roots were in the Puritan ethic of his forebears. His fascination with the interior drama of human defeat earned him a reputation for pessimism, but it was a pessimism qualified by the positive values of a New England conscience—endurance, moral courage, and the conviction that, as he once put it, "There's a good deal to live for, but a man has to go through hell really to find it out."

FURTHER READING: *Selected Poems of Edwin Arlington Robinson,* ed. M. Zabel, 1965, 1966; *Uncollected Poems and Prose of Edwin Arlington Robinson,* ed. R. Cary, 1975; *Selected Letters of Edwin Arlington Robinson,* ed. R. Torrence, 1940; M. Van Doren, *Edwin Arlington Robinson,* 1927; H. Hagedorn, *Edwin Arlington Robinson, A Biography,* 1938; E. Kaplan, *Philosophy in the Poetry of Edwin Arlington Robinson,* 1940; Y. Winters, *Edwin Arlington Robinson,* 1946; E. Neff, *Edwin Arlington Robinson,* 1948; E. Barnard, *Edwin Arlington Robinson, A Critical Study,* 1952; E. Fussell, *Edwin Arlington Robinson, The Literary Background of a Traditional Poet,* 1954; W. Anderson, *Edwin Arlington Robinson,* 1967; W. Robinson, *Edwin Arlington Robinson, A Poetry of the Act,* 1967; H. Franchere, *Edwin Arlington Robinson,*

1968; L. Coxe, *Edwin Arlington Robinson, The Life of Poetry*, 1968; *Edwin Arlington Robinson, Centenary Essays*, ed. E. Barnard, 1973; R. Cary, *Early Reception of Edwin Arlington Robinson*, 1974; C. Joyner, *Edwin Arlington Robinson, A Reference Guide*, 1978.
  TEXT: *Collected Poems of Edwin Arlington Robinson*, 1937.

LUKE HAVERGAL

Go to the western gate, Luke Havergal,
There where the vines cling crimson on the wall,
And in the twilight wait for what will come.
The leaves will whisper there of her, and some,
Like flying words, will strike you as they fall;
But go, and if you listen she will call.
Go to the western gate, Luke Havergal—
Luke Havergal.

No, there is not a dawn in eastern skies
To rift the fiery night that's in your eyes;   10
But there, where western glooms are gathering,
The dark will end the dark, if anything:
God slays Himself with every leaf that flies,
And hell is more than half of paradise.
No, there is not a dawn in eastern skies—
In eastern skies.

Out of a grave I come to tell you this,
Out of a grave I come to quench the kiss
That flames upon your forehead with a glow
That blinds you to the way that you must go.   20
Yes, there is yet one way to where she is,
Bitter, but one that faith may never miss.
Out of a grave I come to tell you this—
To tell you this.

There is the western gate, Luke Havergal,
There are the crimson leaves upon the wall.
Go, for the winds are tearing them away,—
Nor think to riddle[1] the dead words they say,
Nor any more to feel them as they fall;
But go, and if you trust her she will call.   30
There is the western gate, Luke Havergal—
Luke Havergal.

                                                                    1896

ZOLA

Because he puts the compromising chart
Of hell before your eyes, you are afraid;

[1]Interpret.

Because he counts the price that you have paid
For innocence, and counts it from the start,
You loathe him. But he sees the human heart
Of God meanwhile, and in His hand was weighed
Your squeamish and emasculate crusade
Against the grim dominion of his art.

Never until we conquer the uncouth
Connivings of our shamed indifference   10
(We call it Christian faith) are we to scan
The racked and shrieking hideousness of Truth
To find, in hate's polluted self-defence
Throbbing, the pulse, the divine heart of man.

                                                              1896

RICHARD CORY

Whenever Richard Cory went down town,
We people on the pavement looked at him:
He was a gentleman from sole to crown,
Clean favored, and imperially slim.

And he was always quietly arrayed,
And he was always human when he talked;
But still he fluttered pulses when he said
"Good-morning," and he glittered when he walked.

And he was rich—yes, richer than a king—
And admirably schooled in every grace: 10
In fine, we thought that he was everything
To make us wish that we were in his place.

So on we worked, and waited for the light,
And went without the meat, and cursed the bread;
And Richard Cory, one calm summer night,
Went home and put a bullet through his head.

                                                              1897

CLIFF KLINGENHAGEN

Cliff Klingenhagen had me in to dine
With him one day; and after soup and meat,
And all the other things there were to eat,
Cliff took two glasses and filled one with wine
And one with wormwood.[1] Then without a sign
For me to choose at all, he took the draught
Of bitterness himself, and lightly quaffed
It off, and said the other one was mine.

[1]The bitter oil extracted from the wormwood plant.

And when I asked him what the deuce he meant
By doing that, he only looked at me   10
And smiled, and said it was a way of his.
And though I know the fellow, I have spent
Long time a-wondering when I shall be
As happy as Cliff Klingenhagen is.

1897

MINIVER CHEEVY

Miniver Cheevy, child of scorn,
    Grew lean while he assailed the seasons;
He wept that he was ever born,
    And he had reasons.

Miniver loved the days of old
    When swords were bright and steeds were prancing;
The vision of a warrior bold
    Would set him dancing.

Miniver sighed for what was not,
    And dreamed, and rested from his labors;   10
He dreamed of Thebes and Camelot,[1]
    And Priam's[2] neighbors.

Miniver mourned the ripe renown
    That made so many a name so fragrant;
He mourned Romance, now on the town,
    And Art, a vagrant.

Miniver loved the Medici,[3]
    Albeit he had never seen one;
He would have sinned incessantly
    Could he have been one.   20

Miniver cursed the commonplace
    And eyed a khaki suit with loathing;
He missed the mediæval grace
    Of iron clothing.

Miniver scorned the gold he sought,
    But sore annoyed was he without it;
Miniver thought, and thought, and thought,
    And thought about it.

Miniver Cheevy, born too late,
    Scratched his head and kept on thinking;   30
Miniver coughed, and called it fate,
    And kept on drinking.

1907

[1]Thebes: name of cities in ancient Egypt and Greece; Camelot: legendary site of King Arthur's palace.
[2]Mythological King of Troy during the Trojan War.
[3]Powerful family of Renaissance Florence, Italy, with a reputation for predatory ruthlessness and sinfulness.

FOR A DEAD LADY

No more with overflowing light
Shall fill the eyes that now are faded,
Nor shall another's fringe with night
Their woman-hidden world as they did.
No more shall quiver down the days
The flowing wonder of her ways,
Whereof no language may requite
The shifting and the many-shaded.

The grace, divine, definitive,
Clings only as a faint forestalling;   10
The laugh that love could not forgive
Is hushed, and answers to no calling;
The forehead and the little ears
Have gone where Saturn keeps the years;
The breast where roses could not live
Has done with rising and with falling.

The beauty, shattered by the laws
That have creation in their keeping,
No longer trembles at applause,
Or over children that are sleeping;   20
And we who delve in beauty's lore
Know all that we have known before
Of what inexorable cause
Makes Time so vicious in his reaping.

                                            1909

HOW ANNANDALE WENT OUT

"THEY called it Annandale—and I was there
To flourish, to find words, and to attend:
Liar, physician, hypocrite, and friend,
I watched him; and the sight was not so fair
As one or two that I have seen elsewhere:
An apparatus not for me to mend—
A wreck, with hell between him and the end,
Remained of Annandale; and I was there.

"I knew the ruin as I knew the man;
So put the two together, if you can,   10
Remembering the worst you know of me.
Now view yourself as I was, on the spot—
With a slight kind of engine. Do you see?
Like this . . . You wouldn't hang me? I thought not."

                                            1910

EROS TURANNOS[1]

She fears him, and will always ask
   What fated her to choose him;
She meets in his engaging mask
   All reasons to refuse him;
But what she meets and what she fears
Are less than are the downward years;
Drawn slowly to the foamless weirs[2]
   Of age, were she to lose him.

Between a blurred sagacity
   That once had power to sound him,   10
And Love, that will not let him be
   The Judas[3] that she found him,
Her pride assuages her almost,
And if it were alone the cost.—
He sees that he will not be lost,
   And waits and looks around him.

A sense of ocean and old trees
   Envelops and allures him;
Tradition, touching all he sees,
   Beguiles and reassures him;   20
And all her doubts of what he says
Are dimmed with what she knows of days—
Till even prejudice delays
   And fades, and she secures him.

The falling leaf inaugurates
   The reign of her confusion;
The pounding wave reverberates
   The dirge of her illusion;
And home, where passion lived and died,
Becomes a place where she can hide.   30
While all the town and harbor side
   Vibrate with her seclusion.

We tell you, tapping on our brows,
   The story as it should be,—
As if the story of a house
   Were told, or ever could be;
We'll have no kindly veil between
Her visions and those we have seen—
As if we guessed what hers have been,
   Or what they are or would be.   40

[1]Greek: Love, the Tyrant.
[2]A trap of fencing or stakes set in a stream to catch fish.
[3]Christ's disciple who betrayed Him.

Meanwhile we do no harm; for they
   That with a god have striven,
Not hearing much of what we say,
   Take what the god has given;
Though like waves breaking it may be
Or like a changed familiar tree,
Or like a stairway to the sea
   Where down the blind are driven.

1914

BEWICK FINZER

Time was when his half million drew
   The breath of six per cent;
But soon the worm of what-was-not
   Fed hard on his content;
And something crumbled in his brain
   When his half million went.

Time passed, and filled along with his
   The place of many more;
Time came, and hardly one of us
   Had credence to restore,   10
From what appeared one day, the man
   Whom we had known before.

The broken voice, the withered neck,
   The coat worn out with care,
The cleanliness of indigence,
   The brilliance of despair,
The fond imponderable dreams
   Of affluence,—all were there.

Poor Finzer, with his dreams and schemes,
   Fares hard now in the race,   20
With heart and eye that have a task
   When he looks in the face
Of one who might so easily
   Have been in Finzer's place.

He comes unfailing for the loan
   We give and then forget;
He comes, and probably for years
   Will he be coming yet,—
   Familiar as an old mistake,
   And futile as regret.   30

1916

THE MAN AGAINST THE SKY

Between me and the sunset, like a dome
Against the glory of a world on fire,
Now burned a sudden hill,
Bleak, round, and high, by flame-lit height made higher,
With nothing on it for the flame to kill
Save one who moved and was alone up there
To loom before the chaos and the glare
As if he were the last god going home
Unto his last desire.

Dark, marvelous, and inscrutable he moved on   10
Till down the fiery distance he was gone,
Like one of those eternal, remote things
That range across a man's imaginings
When a sure music fills him and he knows
What he may say thereafter to few men,—
The touch of ages having wrought
An echo and a glimpse of what he thought
A phantom or a legend until then;
For whether lighted over ways that save,
Or lured from all repose,   20
If he go on too far to find a grave,
Mostly alone he goes.

Even he, who stood where I had found him,
On high with fire all round him,
Who moved along the molten west,
And over the round hill's crest
That seemed half ready with him to go down,
Flame bitten and flame-cleft,
As if there were to be no last thing left
Of a nameless unimaginable town,—   30
Even he who climbed and vanished may have taken
Down to the perils of a depth not known,
From death defended though by men forsaken,
The bread that every man must eat alone;
He may have walked while others hardly dared
Look on to see him stand where many fell;
And upward out of that, as out of hell,
He may have sung and striven
To mount where more of him shall yet be given,
Bereft of all retreat,   40
To sevenfold heat,—
As on a day when three in Dura shared
The furnace,[1] and were spared

[1]Three Jews, Shadrach, Meshach, and Abednego, refused to worship the golden idol set up at Dura in Babylon by Nebuchadnezzar. Although thrown into a fiery furnace, they were protected by the Lord and emerged unharmed. Daniel 2:1–27.

For glory by that King of Babylon
Who made himself so great that God, who heard,
Covered him with long feathers, like a bird.[2]

Again, he may have gone down easily,
By comfortable altitudes, and found,
As always, underneath him solid ground
Whereon to be sufficient and to stand   50
Possessed already of the promised land,
Far stretched and fair to see:
A good sight, verily,
And one to make the eyes of her who bore him
Shine glad, with hidden tears.
Why question of his ease of who before him,
In one place or another where they left
Their names as far behind them as their bones,
And yet by dint of slaughter toil and theft,
And shrewdly sharpened stones,   60
Carved hard the way for his ascendency
Through deserts of lost years?
Why trouble him now who sees and hears
No more than what his innocence requires,
And therefore to no other height aspires
Than one at which he neither quails nor tires?
He may do more by seeing what he sees
Than others eager for iniquities;
He may, by seeing all things for the best,
Incite futurity to do the rest.   70

Or with an even likelihood,
He may have met with atrabilious[3] eyes
The fires of time on equal terms and passed
Indifferently down, until at last
His only kind of grandeur would have been,
Apparently, in being seen.
He may have had for evil or for good
No argument; he may have had no care
For what without himself went anywhere
To failure or to glory, and least of all   80
For such a stale, flamboyant miracle;
He may have been the prophet of an art
Immovable to old idolatries;
He may have been a player without a part,
Annoyed that even the sun should have the skies
For such a flaming way to advertise;
He may have been a painter sick at heart
With Nature's toiling for a new surprise;
He may have been a cynic, who now, for all

[2]For his arrogance Nebuchadnezzar was "driven from men" and his hairs were grown like eagles' feathers, and his nails like birds' claws." Daniel 4:33.
[3]Gloomy, peevish.

Of anything divine that his effete   90
Negation may have tasted,
Saw truth in his own image, rather small,
Forebore to fever the ephemeral,
Found any barren height a good retreat
From any swarming street,
And in the sun saw power superbly wasted;
And when the primitive old-fashioned stars
Came out again to shine on joys and wars
More primitive, and all arrayed for doom,
He may have proved a world a sorry thing   100
In his imagining,
And life a lighted highway to the tomb.

Or, mounting with infirm unsearching tread,
His hopes to chaos led,
He may have stumbled up there from the past,
And with an aching strangeness viewed the last
Abysmal conflagration of his dreams,—
A flame where nothing seems
To burn but flame itself, by nothing fed;
And while it all went out,   110
Not even the faint anodyne of doubt
May then have eased a painful going down
From pictured heights of power and lost renown,
Revealed at length to his outlived endeavor
Remote and unapproachable forever;
And at his heart there may have gnawed
Sick memories of a dead faith foiled and flawed
And long dishonored by the living death
Assigned alike by chance
To brutes and hierophants;[4]   120
And anguish fallen on those he loved around him
May once have dealt the last blow to confound him,
And so have left him as death leaves a child,
Who sees it all too near;
And he who knows no young way to forget
May struggle to the tomb unreconciled.
Whatever suns may rise or set
There may be nothing kinder for him here
Than shafts and agonies;
And under these   130
He may cry out and stay on horribly;
Or, seeing in death too small a thing to fear,
He may go forward like a stoic Roman
Where pangs and terrors in his pathway lie,—
Or, seizing the swift logic of a woman,
Curse God and die.[5]

---

[4]Those who explain sacred (religious) mysteries, priests.
[5]Advice given the devout but despairing Job by his wife. Job. 2:9.

Or maybe there, like many another one
Who might have stood aloft and looked ahead,
Black-drawn against wild red,
He may have built, unawed by fiery gules[6]   140
That in him no commotion stirred,
A living reason out of molecules
Why molecules occurred,
And one for smiling when he might have sighed
Had he seen far enough,
And in the same inevitable stuff
Discovered an odd reason too for pride
In being what he must have been by laws
Infrangible and for no kind of cause.
Deterred by no confusion or surprise.   150
He may have seen with his mechanic eyes
A world without a meaning, and had room,
Alone amid magnificence and doom,
To build himself an airy monument
That should, or fail him in his vague intent,
Outlast an accidental universe—
To call it nothing worse—
Or, by the borrowing guile
Of Time disintegrated and effaced,
Like once-remembered mighty trees go down   160
To ruin, of which by man may now be traced
No part sufficient even to be rotten,
And in the book of things that are forgotten
Is entered as a thing not quite worth while.
He may have been so great
That satraps[7] would have shivered at his frown,
And all he prized alive may rule a state
No larger than a grave that holds a clown;
He may have been a master of his fate,
And of his atoms,—ready as another   170
In his emergence to exonerate
His father and his mother;
He may have been a captain of a host,
Self-eloquent and ripe for prodigies,
Doomed here to swell by dangerous degrees,
And then give up the ghost.
Nahum's great grasshoppers[8] were such as these,
Sun-scattered and soon lost.

Whatever the dark road he may have taken,
This man who stood on high   180
And faced alone the sky,
Whatever drove or lured or guided him,—
A vision answering a faith unshaken,
An easy trust assured of easy trials,

---

[6]Heraldic term for "red."   [7]Subordinates, underlings.
[8]The old Testament prophet Nahum condemned the evil city of Nineveh and compared its leaders to "grasshoppers" who flee when the sun rises. Nahum 3:17.

A sick negation born of weak denials,
A crazed abhorrence of an old condition,
A blind attendance on a brief ambition,—
Whatever stayed him or derided him,
His way was even as ours;
And we, with all our wounds and all our powers,   190
Must each await alone at his own height
Another darkness or another light;
And there, of our poor self dominion reft,
If inference and reason shun
Hell, Heaven, and Oblivion,
May thwarted will (perforce precarious,
But for our conservation better thus)
Have no misgiving left
Of doing yet what here we leave undone;
Or if unto the last of these we cleave,   200
Believing or protesting we believe
In such an idle and ephemeral
Florescence of the diabolical,—
If, robbed of two fond old enormities,
Our being had no onward auguries,
What then were this great love of ours to say
For launching other lives to voyage again
A little farther into time and pain,
A little faster in a futile chase
For a kingdom and a power and a Race   210
That would have still in sight
A manifest end of ashes and eternal night?
Is this the music of the toys we shake
So loud,—as if there might be no mistake
Somewhere in our indomitable will?
Are we no greater than the noise we make
Along one blind atomic pilgrimage
Whereon by crass chance billeted we go
Because our brains and bones and cartilage
Will have it so?   220
If this we say, then let us all be still
About our share in it, and live and die
More quietly thereby.

Where was he going, this man against the sky?
You know not, nor do I.
But this we know, if we know anything:
That we may laugh and fight and sing
And of our transience here make offering
To an orient Word[9] that will not be erased,
Or, save in incommunicable gleams   230
Too permanent for dreams,
Be found or known.
No tonic and ambitious irritant

[9]"In the beginning was the Word, and the Word was with God, and the Word was God." John I:I.

Of increase or of want
Has made an otherwise insensate waste
Of ages overthrown
A ruthless, veiled, implacable foretaste
Of other ages that are still to be
Depleted and rewarded variously
Because a few, by fate's economy,   240
Shall seem to move the world the way it goes;
No soft evangel of equality,
Safe-cradled in a communal repose
That huddles into death and may at last
Be covered well with equatorial snows—
And all for what, the devil only knows—
Will aggregate an inkling to confirm
The credit of a sage or of a worm,
Or tell us why one man in five
Should have a care to stay alive   250
While in his heart he feels no violence
Laid on his humor and intelligence
When infant Science makes a pleasant face
And waves again that hollow toy, the Race;
No planetary trap where souls are wrought
For nothing but the sake of being caught
And sent again to nothing will attune
Itself to any key of any reason
Why man should hunger through another season
To find out why 'twere better late than soon   260
To go away and let the sun and moon
And all the silly stars illuminate
A place for creeping things,
And those that root and trumpet and have wings,
And herd and ruminate,
Or dive and flash and poise in rivers and seas,
Or by their loyal tails in lofty trees
Hang screeching lewd victorious derision
Of man's immortal vision.

Shall we, because Eternity records   270
Too vast an answer for the time-born words
We spell, whereof so many are dead that once
In our capricious lexicons
Were so alive and final, hear no more
The Word itself, the living word
That none alive has ever heard
Or ever spelt,
And few have ever felt
Without the fears and old surrenderings
And terrors that began   280
When Death let fall a feather from his wings
And humbled the first man?
Because the weight of our humility,
Wherefrom we gain

A little wisdom and much pain,
Falls here too sore and there too tedious,
Are we in anguish or complacency,
Not looking far enough ahead
To see by what mad couriers we are led
Along the roads of the ridiculous,   290
To pity ourselves and laugh at faith
And while we curse life bear it?
And if we see the soul's dead end in death,
Are we to fear it?
What folly is here that has not yet a name
Unless we say outright that we are liars?
What have we seen beyond our sunset fires
That lights again the way by which we came?
Why pay we such a price, and one we give
So clamoringly, for each racked empty day   300
That leads one more last human hope away,
As quiet fiends would lead past our crazed eyes
Our children to an unseen sacrifice?
If after all that we have lived and thought,
All comes to Nought,—
If there be nothing after Now,
And we be nothing anyhow,
And we know that,—why live?
'Twere sure but weaklings' vain distress
To suffer dungeons where so many doors   310
Will open on the cold eternal shores
That look sheer down
To the dark tideless floods of Nothingness
Where all who know may drown.

                                                1916

MR. FLOOD'S PARTY

Old Eben Flood, climbing alone one night
Over the hill between the town below
And the forsaken upland hermitage
That held as much as he should ever know
On earth again of home, paused warily.
The road was his with not a native near;
And Eben, having leisure, said aloud,
For no man else in Tilbury Town to hear:

"Well, Mr. Flood, we have the harvest moon
Again, and we may not have many more;   10
The bird is on the wing,[1] the poet says,

---

[1] An allusion to a quatrain in Edward FitzGerald's *The Rubáiyát of Omar Khayyám* (1859): "Come, fill the Cup, and in the fire of Spring / Your Winter-garment of Repentance fling: / The Bird of Time has but a little way / To flutter—and the Bird is on the Wing."

And you and I have said it here before.
Drink to the bird." He raised up to the light
The jug that he had gone so far to fill,
And answered huskily: "Well, Mr. Flood,
Since you propose it, I believe I will."

Alone, as if enduring to the end
A valiant armor of scarred hopes outworn,
He stood there in the middle of the road
Like Roland's ghost winding a silent horn.[2]   20
Below him, in the town among the trees,
Where friends of other days had honored him,
A phantom salutation of the dead
Rang thinly till old Eben's eyes were dim.

Then, as a mother lays her sleeping child
Down tenderly, fearing it may awake,
He set the jug down slowly at his feet
With trembling care, knowing that most things break;
And only when assured that on firm earth
It stood, as the uncertain lives of men   30
Assuredly did not, he paced away,
And with his hand extended paused again:

"Well, Mr. Flood, we have not met like this
In a long time; and many a change has come
To both of us, I fear, since last it was
We had a drop together. Welcome home!"
Convivially returning with himself,
Again he raised the jug up to the light;
And with an acquiescent quaver said:
"Well, Mr. Flood, if you insist, I might.   40

"Only a very little, Mr. Flood—
For auld lang syne. No more, sir; that will do."
So, for the time, apparently it did,
And Eben evidently thought so too;
For soon amid the silver loneliness
Of night he lifted up his voice and sang,
Secure, with only two moons listening,
Until the whole harmonious landscape rang—

"For auld lang syne." The weary throat gave out,
The last word wavered, and the song was done.   50
He raised again the jug regretfully
And shook his head, and was again alone.

---

[2]Roland, the embattled hero of the medieval French romance *Chanson de Roland,* proudly waited
until he was overwhelmed before sounding his horn to summon help.

There was not much that was ahead of him,
And there was nothing in the town below—
Where strangers would have shut the many doors
That many friends had opened long ago.

1920

Robert Frost   *1874–1963*

To his rural New England neighbors, Robert Frost was an unlikely farmer who wrote poetry into the late hours and milked his cows at midnight. To much of the American public, he was a white-thatched, rustic sage, a poet of rural simplicity and public virtue. To intimate friends, he was a man frequently driven by a cantankerous desire to carry on what he called his "lover's quarrel with the world."

Although he came to be known as a poet of New England, Frost was born in San Francisco and spent his early childhood in the Far West. At the death of his father, when Frost was eleven, the family moved to Salem, New Hampshire. After graduating from high school as valedictorian and class poet in 1892, Frost entered Dartmouth College but soon left to work at odd jobs and to write poetry. In 1897 he tried college again—Harvard—but he left at the end of two years, having acquired an enduring dislike for academic convention.

For the next twelve years Frost eked out a minimal living by teaching and farming while continuing to write his poems. In 1912 he decided to venture everything on a literary career. Leaving New Hampshire, he sailed for England, where he hoped "to write poetry without furthur scandal to friends or family." In London, he soon found a publisher, and his first book, A Boy's Will *(1913), brought him to the attention of influential critics, among them the American expatriate Ezra Pound, who praised Frost as an authentic poet, "vurry Amur'k'n."*

Following the publication of a second volume of poems, North of Boston *(1914), Frost returned home, determined to win recognition in his native land. To support himself he taught in colleges and gave poetry readings throughout much of the United States. His fame grew with the appearance of a succession of books:* Mountain Interval *(1916),* New Hampshire *(1923),* West-Running Brook *(1928),* A Further Range *(1936),* A Witness Tree *(1942),* Steeple Bush *(1947)* In the Clearing *(1962). By the end of his life he had become a national bard; he received honorary degrees from forty-four colleges and universities and won four Pulitzer Prizes; the United States Senate passed resolutions honoring his birthdays, and when he was eighty-seven he read his poetry at the inauguration of President John F. Kennedy.*

Frost had rejected the revolutionary poetic principles of his contemporaries, choosing instead "the old-fashioned way to be new." He employed the plain speech of rural New Englanders and preferred the short, traditional forms of lyric and narrative. As a poet of nature he had obvious affinities with romantic writers, notably Wordsworth and Emerson. He saw nature as a storehouse of analogy and symbol, announcing, "I'm always saying something that's just the edge of something more," but he had little faith in religious dogma or speculative thought. His concern with nature reflected deep moral uncertainties, and his poetry, for all its apparent simplicity, often probes mysteries of darkness and irrationality in the bleak and chaotic landscapes of an indifferent universe where men and women stand alone, bereft, unaided, and perplexed.

FURTHER READING: *Selected Prose of Robert Frost*, ed. H. Cox and E. Lathem, 1966; *Selected Letters of Robert Frost*, ed. L. Thompson, 1964; S. Cox, *A Swinger of Birches*, 1957; L. Thompson, *Robert Frost, The Early Years*, 1966; L. Thompson, *Robert Frost, The Years of Triumph*, 1970; L. Thompson, R. Winnick, *Robert Frost, The Later Years*, 1976; W. Pritchard, *Frost, A Literary Life Reconsidered*, 1984; S. Burnshaw, *Robert Frost Himself*, 1986; L. Thompson, *Fire and Ice, The Art and Thought of Robert Frost*, 1942; R. Cook, *The Dimensions of Robert Frost*, 1959; J. Lynen, *The Pastoral Art of Robert Frost*, 1960; R. Squires, *The Major Themes of Robert Frost*, 1963; P. Gerber, *Robert Frost*, 1966, 1982; *Robert Frost, Centennial Essays*, 3 vols., ed. J. Thorpe, 1974–1978; R. Brower, *The Poetry of Robert Frost*, 1963; F. Lentricchia, *Robert Frost, Modern Poetics and the Landscape of Self*, 1975; R. Poirier, *Robert Frost, The Work of Knowing*, 1977; K. Harris, *Robert Frost, Studies of the Poetry*, 1979; J. Kemp, *Robert Frost and New England*, 1979; J. Potter, *Robert Frost Handbook*, 1980; T. Sharma, *Robert Frost's Poetic Style*, 1981; P. Gerber, *Critical Essays on Robert Frost*, 1984; *Robert Frost*, ed. H. Bloom, 1986.

TEXT: *The Poetry of Robert Frost*, ed. E. Lathem, 1969.

THE TUFT OF FLOWERS

I went to turn the grass once after one
Who mowed it in the dew before the sun.

The dew was gone that made his blade so keen
Before I came to view the leveled scene.

I looked for him behind an isle of trees;
I listened for his whetstone on the breeze.

But he had gone his way, the grass all mown,
And I must be, as he had been—alone,

"As all must be," I said within my heart,
"Whether they work together or apart."   10

But as I said it, swift there passed me by
On noiseless wings a bewildered butterfly,

Seeking with memories grown dim o'er night
Some resting flower of yesterday's delight.

And once I marked his flight go round and round,
As where some flower lay withering on the ground.

And then he flew as far as eye could see,
And then on tremulous wing came back to me.

I thought of questions that have no reply,
And would have turned to toss the grass to dry;   20

But he turned first, and led my eye to look
At a tall tuft of flowers beside a brook,

A leaping tongue of bloom the scythe had spared
Beside a reedy brook the scythe had bared.

The mower in the dew had loved them thus,
By leaving them to flourish, not for us,

Nor yet to draw one thought of ours to him,
But from sheer morning gladness at the brim.

The butterfly and I had lit upon,
Nevertheless, a message from the dawn,   30

That made me hear the wakening birds around,
And hear his long scythe whispering to the ground,

And feel a spirit kindred to my own;
So that henceforth I worked no more alone;

But glad with him, I worked as with his aid,
And weary, sought at noon with him the shade;

And dreaming, as it were, held brotherly speech
With one whose thought I had not hoped to reach.

"Men work together," I told him from the heart,
"Whether they work together or apart."   40
                                          1906, 1913

MENDING WALL

Something there is that doesn't love a wall,
That sends the frozen-ground-swell under it
And spills the upper boulders in the sun,
And makes gaps even two can pass abreast.
The work of hunters is another thing:
I have come after them and made repair
Where they have left not one stone on a stone,
But they would have the rabbit out of hiding,
To please the yelping dogs. The gaps I mean,
No one has seen them made or heard them made,   10
But at spring mending-time we find them there.
I let my neighbor know beyond the hill;
And on a day we meet to walk the line
And set the wall between us once again.
We keep the wall between us as we go.
To each the boulders that have fallen to each.
And some are loaves and some so nearly balls
We have to use a spell to make them balance:
"Stay where you are until our backs are turned!"

We wear our fingers rough with handling them.   20
Oh, just another kind of outdoor game,
One on a side. It comes to little more:
There where it is we do not need the wall:
He is all pine and I am apple orchard.
My apple trees will never get across
And eat the cones under his pines, I tell him.
He only says,"Good fences make good neighbors."
Spring is the mischief in me, and I wonder
If I could put a notion in his head:
"*Why* do they make good neighbors? Isn't it   30
Where there are cows? But here there are no cows.
Before I built a wall I'd ask to know
What I was walling in or walling out,
And to whom I was like to give offense.
Something there is that doesn't love a wall,
That wants it down." I could say "Elves" to him,
But it's not elves exactly, and I'd rather
He said it for himself. I see him there,
Bringing a stone grasped firmly by the top
In each hand, like an old-stone savage armed.   40
He moves in darkness as it seems to me,
Not of woods only and the shade of trees.
He will not go behind his father's saying,
And he likes having thought of it so well
He says again, "Good fences make good neighbors."

                                                            1914

HOME BURIAL

He saw her from the bottom of the stairs
Before she saw him. She was starting down,
Looking back over her shoulder at some fear.
She took a doubtful step and then undid it
To raise herself and look again. He spoke
Advancing toward her: "What is it you see
From up there always?—for I want to know."
She turned and sank upon her skirts at that,
And her face changed from terrified to dull.
He said to gain time: "What is it you see?"   10
Mounting until she cowered under him.
"I will find out now—you must tell me, dear."
She, in her place, refused him any help,
With the least stiffening of her neck and silence.
She let him look, sure that he couldn't see,
Blind creature; and awhile he didn't see.
But at last he murmured, "Oh," and again, "Oh."

"What is it—what?" she said.

> "Just that I see."

"You don't," she challenged. "Tell me what it is."

"The wonder is I didn't see at once.   20
I never noticed it from here before.
I must be wonted[1] to it—that's the reason.
The little graveyard where my people are!
So small the window frames the whole of it.
Not so much larger than a bedroom, is it?
There are three stones of slate and one of marble,
Broad-shouldered little slabs there in the sunlight
On the sidehill. We haven't to mind *those*.
But I understand: it is not the stones,
But the child's mound——"

> "Don't, don't, don't,
don't," she cried.   30

She withdrew, shrinking from beneath his arm
That rested on the banister, and slid downstairs;
And turned on him with such a daunting look,
He said twice over before he knew himself:
"Can't a man speak of his own child he's lost?"

"Not you!—Oh, where's my hat? Oh, I don't need it!
I must get out of here. I must get air.—
I don't know rightly whether any man can."

"Amy! Don't go to someone else this time.
Listen to me. I won't come down the stairs."   40
He sat and fixed his chin between his fists.
"There's something I should like to ask you, dear."

"You don't know how to ask it."

> "Help me, then."

Her fingers moved the latch for all reply.

"My words are nearly always an offense.
I don't know how to speak of anything
So as to please you. But I might be taught,
I should suppose. I can't say I see how.
A man must partly give up being a man
With womenfolk. We could have some arrangement   50
By which I'd bind myself to keep hands off
Anything special you're a-mind to name.
Though I don't like such things 'twixt those that love.

---

[1]Accustomed.

Two that don't love can't live together without them,
But two that do can't live together with them."
She moved the latch a little. "Don't—don't go.
Don't carry it to someone else this time.
Tell me about it if it's something human.
Let me into your grief. I'm not so much
Unlike other folks as your standing there   60
Apart would make me out. Give me my chance.
I do think, though, you overdo it a little.
What was it brought you up to think it the thing
To take your mother-loss of a first child
So inconsolably—in the face of love.
You'd think his memory might be satisfied——"

"There you go sneering now!"

                              "I'm not, I'm not!
You make me angry. I'll come down to you.
God, what a woman! And it's come to this,
A man can't speak of his own child that's dead."   70

"You can't because you don't know how to speak.
If you had any feelings, you that dug
With your own hand—how could you?—his little grave;
I saw you from that very window there,
Making the gravel leap and leap in air,
Leap up, like that, like that, and land so lightly
And roll back down the mound beside the hole.
I thought, Who is that man? I didn't know you.
And I crept down the stairs and up the stairs
To look again, and still your spade kept lifting.   80
Then you came in. I heard your rumbling voice
Out in the kitchen, and I don't know why,
But I went near to see with my own eyes.
You could sit there with the stains on your shoes
Of the fresh earth from your own baby's grave
And talk about your everyday concerns.
You had stood the spade up against the wall
Outside there in the entry, for I saw it."

"I shall laugh the worst laugh I ever laughed.
I'm cursed. God, if I don't believe I'm cursed."   90

"I can repeat the very words you were saying:
'Three foggy mornings and one rainy day
Will rot the best birch fence a man can build.'
Think of it, talk like that at such a time!
What had how long it takes a birch to rot
To do with what was in the darkened parlor?
You *couldn't* care! The nearest friends can go
With anyone to death, comes so far short
They might as well not try to go at all.

No, from the time when one is sick to death,   100
One is alone, and he dies more alone.
Friends make pretense of following to the grave,
But before one is in it, their minds are turned
And making the best of their way back to life
And living people, and things they understand.
But the world's evil. I won't have grief so
If I can change it. Oh, I won't, I won't!"

"There, you have said it all and you feel better.
You won't go now. You're crying. Close the door.
The heart's gone out of it: why keep it up?   110
Amy! There's someone coming down the road!"

"*You*—oh, you think the talk is all. I must go—
Somewhere out of this house, How can I make you——"

"If—you—do!" She was opening the door wider.
"Where do you mean to go? First tell me that.
I'll follow and bring you back by force. I *will!*——"

                                                    1914

AFTER APPLE-PICKING

My long two-pointed ladder's sticking through a tree
Toward heaven still,
And there's a barrel that I didn't fill
Beside it, and there may be two or three
Apples I didn't pick upon some bough.
But I am done with apple-picking now.
Essence of winter sleep is on the night,
The scent of apples: I am drowsing off.
I cannot rub the strangeness from my sight
I got from looking through a pane of glass   10
I skimmed this morning from the drinking trough
And held against the world of hoary grass.
It melted, and I let it fall and break.
But I was well
Upon my way to sleep before it fell,
And I could tell
What form my dreaming was about to take.
Magnified apples appear and disappear,
Stem end and blossom end,
And every fleck of russet showing clear.   20
My instep arch not only keeps the ache,
It keeps the pressure of a ladder-round.
I feel the ladder sway as the boughs bend
And I keep hearing from the cellar bin
The rumbling sound

Of load on load of apples coming in.
For I have had too much
Of apple-picking: I am overtired
Of the great harvest I myself desired.
There were ten thousand thousand fruit to touch,   30
Cherish in hand, lift down, and not let fall.
For all
That struck the earth,
No matter if not bruised or spiked with stubble,
Went surely to the cider-apple heap
As of no worth.
One can see what will trouble
This sleep of mine, whatever sleep it is.
Were he not gone,
The woodchuck could say whether it's like his   40
Long sleep, as I describe its coming on,
Or just some human sleep.

1914

THE WOOD-PILE

Out walking in the frozen swamp one gray day,
I paused and said, "I will turn back from here.
No, I will go on farther—and we shall see."
The hard snow held me, save where now and then
One foot went through. The view was all in lines
Straight up and down of tall slim trees
Too much alike to mark or name a place by
So as to say for certain I was here
Or somewhere else: I was just far from home.
A small bird flew before me. He was careful   10
To put a tree between us when he lighted,
And say no word to tell me who he was
Who was so foolish as to think what *he* thought.
He thought that I was after him for a feather—
The white one in his tail; like one who takes
Everything said as personal to himself.
One flight out sideways would have undeceived him.
And then there was a pile of wood for which
I forgot him and let his little fear
Carry him off the way I might have gone,   20
Without so much as wishing him good-night.
He went behind it to make his last stand.
It was a cord of maple, cut and split
And piled—and measured, four by four by eight.
And not another like it could I see.
No runner tracks in this year's snow looped near it.
And it was older sure than this year's cutting
Or even last year's or the year's before.
The wood was gray and the bark warping off it

And the pile somewhat sunken. Clematis[1]　　　　　　　　30
Had wound string round and round it like a bundle.
What held it, though, on one side was a tree
Still growing, and on one a stake and prop,
These latter about to fall. I thought that only
Someone who lived in turning to fresh tasks
Could so forget his handiwork on which
He spent himself, the labor of his ax,
And leave it there far from a useful fireplace
To warm the frozen swamp as best it could
With the slow smokeless burning of decay.　　　　　　40

　　　　　　　　　　　　　　　　　　　1914

THE ROAD NOT TAKEN

Two roads diverged in a yellow wood,
And sorry I could not travel both
And be one traveler, long I stood
And looked down one as far as I could
To where it bent in the undergrowth;

Then took the other, as just as fair,
And having perhaps the better claim,
Because it was grassy and wanted wear;
Though as for that, the passing there
Had worn them really about the same,　　　　　　10

And both that morning equally lay
In leaves no step had trodden black.
Oh, I kept the first for another day!
Yet knowing how way leads on to way,
I doubted if I should ever come back.

I shall be telling this with a sigh
Somewhere ages and ages hence:
Two roads diverged in a wood, and I—
I took the one less traveled by,
And that has made all the difference.　　　　　　20
1914–1915　　　　　　　　　　　1915, 1916

AN OLD MAN'S WINTER NIGHT

All out-of-doors looked darkly in at him
Through the thin frost, almost in separate stars,
That gathers on the pane in empty rooms.

[1] A flowering vine.

What kept his eyes from giving back the gaze
Was the lamp tilted near them in his hand.
What kept him from remembering what it was
That brought him to that creaking room was age.
He stood with barrels round him—at a loss.
And having scared the cellar under him
In clomping here, he scared it once again   10
In clomping off—and scared the outer night,
Which has its sounds, familiar, like the roar
Of trees and crack of branches, common things,
But nothing so like beating on a box.
A light he was to no one but himself
Where now he sat, concerned with he knew what,
A quiet light, and then not even that.
He consigned to the moon—such as she was,
So late-arising—to the broken moon,
As better than the sun in any case   20
For such a charge, his snow upon the roof,
His icicles along the wall to keep;
And slept. The log that shifted with a jolt
Once in the stove, disturbed him and he shifted,
And eased his heavy breathing, but still slept.
One aged man—one man—can't keep a house,
A farm, a countryside, or if he can,
It's thus he does it of a winter night.
1906   1916

BIRCHES

When I see birches bend to left and right
Across the lines of straighter darker trees,
I like to think some boy's been swinging them.
But swinging doesn't bend them down to stay
As ice storms do. Often you must have seen them.
Loaded with ice a sunny winter morning
After a rain. They click upon themselves
As the breeze rises, and turn many-colored
As the stir cracks and crazes their enamel.
Soon the sun's warmth makes them shed crystal shells   10
Shattering and avalanching on the snow crust—
Such heaps of broken glass to sweep away
You'd think the inner dome of heaven had fallen.
They are dragged to the withered bracken by the load,
And they seem not to break; though once they are bowed
So low for long, they never right themselves:
You may see their trunks arching in the woods
Years afterwards, trailing their leaves on the ground
Like girls on hands and knees that throw their hair
Before them over their heads to dry in the sun.   20
But I was going to say when Truth broke in

With all her matter of fact about the ice storm,
I should prefer to have some boy bend them
As he went out and in to fetch the cows—
Some boy too far from town to learn baseball,
Whose only play was what he found himself,
Summer or winter, and could play alone.
One by one he subdued his father's trees
By riding them down over and over again
Until he took the stiffness out of them,   30
And not one but hung limp, not one was left
For him to conquer. He learned all there was
To learn about not launching out too soon
And so not carrying the tree away
Clear to the ground. He always kept his poise
To the top branches, climbing carefully
With the same pains you use to fill a cup
Up to the brim, and even above the brim.
Then he flung outward, feet first, with a swish,
Kicking his way down through the air to the ground.   40
So was I once myself a swinger of birches.
And so I dream of going back to be.
It's when I'm weary of considerations,
And life is too much like a pathless wood
Where your face burns and tickles with the cobwebs
Broken across it, and one eye is weeping
From a twig's having lashed across it open.
I'd like to get away from earth awhile
And then come back to it and begin over.
May no fate willfully misunderstand me   50
And half grant what I wish and snatch me away
Not to return. Earth's the right place for love:
I don't know where it's likely to go better.
I'd like to go by climbing a birch tree,
And climb black branches up a snow-white trunk
Toward heaven, till the tree could bear no more,
But dipped its top and set me down again.
That would be good both going and coming back.
One could do worse than be a swinger of birches.
1913–1914   1915

THE OVEN BIRD[1]

There is a singer everyone has heard,
Loud, a mid-summer and a mid-wood bird,
Who makes the solid tree trunks sound again.
He says that leaves are old and that for flowers
Mid-summer is to spring as one to ten.
He says the early petal-fall is past,

[1]An American warbler that builds a dome-shaped nest.

When pear and cherry bloom went down in showers
On sunny days a moment overcast;
And comes that other fall we name the fall.
He says the highway dust is over all.   10
The bird would cease and be as other birds
But that he knows in singing not to sing.
The question that he frames in all but words
Is what to make of a diminished thing.
1906–07   1916

PUTTING IN THE SEED

You come to fetch me from my work tonight
When supper's on the table, and we'll see
If I can leave off burying the white
Soft petals fallen from the apple tree
(Soft petals, yes, but not so barren quite,
Mingled with these, smooth bean and wrinkled pea),
And go along with you ere you lose sight
Of what you came for and become like me,
Slave to a springtime passion for the earth.
How Love burns through the Putting in the Seed   10
On through the watching for that early birth
When, just as the soil tarnishes with weed,
The sturdy seedling with arched body comes
Shouldering its way and shedding the earth crumbs.
1906–1907   1914, 1916

THE WITCH OF COÖS[1]

I stayed the night for shelter at a farm
Behind the mountain, with a mother and son,
Two old-believers.[2] They did all the talking.

MOTHER. Folks think a witch who has familiar spirits
She could call up to pass a winter evening,
But won't, should be burned at the stake or something.
Summoning spirits isn't "Button, button,
Who's got the button," I would have them know.

SON. Mother can make a common table rear
And kick with two legs like an army mule.   10

---

[1]A county in New Hampshire.   [2]I.e., believers in superstitions and folklore.

MOTHER.   And when I've done it, what good have I done?
Rather than tip a table for you, let me
Tell you what Ralle the Sioux Control[3] once told me.
He said the dead had souls, but when I asked him
How could that be—I thought the dead were souls—
He broke my trance. Don't that make you suspicious
That there's something the dead are keeping back?
Yes, there's something the dead are keeping back.

SON.   You wouldn't want to tell him what we have
Up attic, mother?

MOTHER.   Bones—a skeleton.   20

SON.   But the headboard of mother's bed is pushed
Against the attic door: the door is nailed.
It's harmless. Mother hears it in the night,
Halting perplexed behind the barrier
Of door and headboard. Where it wants to get
Is back into the cellar where it came from.

MOTHER.   We'll never let them, will we, son? We'll never!

SON.   It left the cellar forty years ago
And carried itself like a pile of dishes
Up one flight from the cellar to the kitchen,   30
Another from the kitchen to the bedroom,
Another from the bedroom to the attic,
Right past both father and mother, and neither stopped it.
Father had gone upstairs; mother was downstairs.
I was a baby: I don't know where I was.

MOTHER.   The only fault my husband found with me—
I went to sleep before I went to bed,
Especially in winter when the bed
Might just as well be ice and the clothes snow.
The night the bones came up the cellar stairs   40
Toffile had gone to bed alone and left me,
But left an open door to cool the room off
So as to sort of turn me out of it.
I was just coming to myself enough
To wonder where the cold was coming from,
When I heard Toffile upstairs in the bedroom
And thought I heard him downstairs in the cellar.
The board we had laid down to walk dry-shod on
When there was water in the cellar in spring
Struck the hard cellar bottom. And then someone   50
Began the stairs, two footsteps for each step,
The way a man with one leg and a crutch,
Or a little child, comes up. It wasn't Toffile:

[3]The spirit, in this case an Indian, believed to control the remarks of a medium during a séance.

It wasn't anyone who could be there.
The bulkhead double doors were double-locked
And swollen tight and buried under snow.
The cellar windows were banked up with sawdust
And swollen tight and buried under snow.
It was the bones. I knew them—and good reason.
My first impulse was to get to the knob   60
And hold the door. But the bones didn't try
The door; they halted helpless on the landing,
Waiting for things to happen in their favor.
The faintest restless rustling ran all through them.
I never could have done the thing I did
If the wish hadn't been too strong in me
To see how they were mounted for this walk.
I had a vision of them put together
Not like a man, but like a chandelier.
So suddenly I flung the door wide on him.   70
A moment he stood balancing with emotion,
And all but lost himself. (A tongue of fire
Flashed out and licked along his upper teeth.
Smoke rolled inside the sockets of his eyes.)
Then he came at me with one hand outstretched,
The way he did in life once; but this time
I struck the hand off brittle on the floor,
And fell back from him on the floor myself.
The finger-pieces slid in all directions.
(Where did I see one of those pieces lately?   80
Hand me my button box—it must be there.)
I sat up on the floor and shouted, "Toffile,
It's coming up to you." It had its choice
Of the door to the cellar or the hall.
It took the hall door for the novelty,
And set off briskly for so slow a thing,
Still going every which way in the joints, though,
So that it looked like lightning or a scribble,
From the slap I had just now given its hand.
I listened till it almost climbed the stairs   90
From the hall to the only finished bedroom,
Before I got up to do anything;
Then ran and shouted, "Shut the bedroom door,
Toffile, for my sake!" "Company?" he said,
"Don't make me get up; I'm too warm in bed."
So lying forward weakly on the handrail
I pushed myself upstairs, and in the light
(The kitchen had been dark) I had to own
I could see nothing. "Toffile, I don't see it.
It's with us in the room, though. It's the bones."   100
"What bones?" "The cellar bones—out of the grave."
That made him throw his bare legs out of bed
And sit up by me and take hold of me.
I wanted to put out the light and see
If I could see it, or else mow the room,

With our arms at the level of our knees,
And bring the chalk-pile down. "I'll tell you what—
It's looking for another door to try.
The uncommonly deep snow has made him think
Of his old song, "The Wild Colonial Boy,"   110
He always used to sing along the tote road.[4]
He's after an open door to get outdoors.
Let's trap him with an open door up attic."
Toffile agreed to that, and sure enough,
Almost the moment he was given an opening,
The steps began to climb the attic stairs.
I heard them. Toffile didn't seem to hear them.
"Quick!" I slammed to the door and held the knob.
"Toffile, get nails." I made him nail the door shut
And push the headboard of the bed against it.   120
Then we asked was there anything
Up attic that we'd ever want again.
The attic was less to us than the cellar.
If the bones liked the attic, let them have it.
Let them stay in the attic. When they sometimes
Come down the stairs at night and stand perplexed
Behind the door and headboard of the bed,
Brushing their chalky skull with chalky fingers,
With sounds like the dry rattling of a shutter,
That's what I sit up in the dark to say—   130
To no one anymore since Toffile died.
Let them stay in the attic since they went there.
I promised Toffile to be cruel to them
For helping them be cruel once to him.

SON.   We think they had a grave down in the cellar.

MOTHER.   We know they had a grave down in the cellar.

SON.   We never could find out whose bones they were.

MOTHER.   Yes, we could too, son. Tell the truth for once.
They were a man's his father killed for me.
I mean a man he killed instead of me.   140
The least I could do was help dig their grave.
We were about it one night in the cellar.
Son knows the story: but 'twas not for him
To tell the truth, suppose the time had come.
Son looks surprised to see me end a lie
We'd kept up all these years between ourselves
So as to have it ready for outsiders.
But tonight I don't care enough to lie—
I don't remember why I ever cared.
Toffile, if he were here, I don't believe   150
Could tell you why he ever cared himself. . . .

[4]A road used for hauling goods.

She hadn't found the finger-bone she wanted
Among the buttons poured out in her lap.
I verified the name next morning: Toffile.
The rural letter box said Toffile Lajway.

                                                    1922, 1923

FOR ONCE, THEN, SOMETHING

Others taunt me with having knelt at well-curbs
Always wrong to the light, so never seeing
Deeper down in the well than where the water
Gives me back in a shining surface picture
Me myself in the summer heaven, godlike,
Looking out of a wreath of fern and cloud puffs.
Once, when trying with chin against a well-curb,
I discerned, as I thought, beyond the picture,
Through the picture, a something white, uncertain,
Something more of the depths—and then I lost it.   10
Water came to rebuke the too clear water.
One drop fell from a fern, and lo, a ripple
Shook whatever it was lay there at bottom,
Blurred it, blotted it out. What was that whiteness?
Truth? A pebble of quartz? For once, then, something.

                                                    1920

FIRE AND ICE

Some say the world will end in fire,
Some say in ice.
From what I've tasted of desire
I hold with those who favor fire.
But if it had to perish twice,
I think I know enough of hate
To say that for destruction ice
Is also great
And would suffice.

                                                    1920

DUST OF SNOW

The way a crow
Shook down on me
The dust of snow
From a hemlock tree

Has given my heart
A change of mood
And saved some part
Of a day I had rued.

1920

DESIGN

I found a dimpled spider, fat and white,
On a white heal-all,[1] holding up a moth
Like a white piece of rigid satin cloth—
Assorted characters of death and blight
Mixed ready to begin the morning right,
Like the ingredients of a witches' broth—
A snow-drop spider, a flower like a froth,
And dead wings carried like a paper kite.

What had that flower to do with being white,
The wayside blue and innocent heal-all?   10
What brought the kindred spider to that height,
Then steered the white moth thither in the night?
What but design of darkness to appall?—
If design govern in a thing so small.

1922

NOTHING GOLD CAN STAY

Nature's first green is gold,
Her hardest hue to hold.
Her early leaf's a flower;
But only so an hour.
Then leaf subsides to leaf.
So Eden sank to grief,
So dawn goes down to day.
Nothing gold can stay.

1923

STOPPING BY WOODS
ON A SNOWY EVENING

Whose woods these are I think I know.
His house is in the village, though;
He will not see me stopping here
To watch his woods fill up with snow.

[1]A plant, normally with blue blossoms, reputed to have healing powers.

My little horse must think it queer
To stop without a farmhouse near
Between the woods and frozen lake
The darkest evening of the year.

He gives his harness bells a shake
To ask if there is some mistake.   10
The only other sound's the sweep
Of easy wind and downy flake.

The woods are lovely, dark and deep,
But I have promises to keep,
And miles to go before I sleep,
And miles to go before I sleep.

                                                        1923

ONCE BY THE PACIFIC

The shattered water made a misty din.
Great waves looked over others coming in,
And thought of doing something to the shore
That water never did to land before.
The clouds were low and hairy in the skies,
Like locks blown forward in the gleam of eyes.
You could not tell, and yet it looked as if
The shore was lucky in being backed by cliff,
The cliff in being backed by continent;
It looked as if a night of dark intent   10
Was coming, and not only a night, an age
Someone had better be prepared for rage.
There would be more than ocean-water broken
Before God's last *Put out the Light* was spoken.

                                                        1926

ACQUAINTED WITH THE NIGHT

I have been one acquainted with the night.
I have walked out in rain—and back in rain.
I have outwalked the furthest city light.

I have looked down the saddest city lane.
I have passed by the watchman on his beat
And dropped my eyes, unwilling to explain.

I have stood still and stopped the sound of feet
When far away an interrupted cry
Came over houses from another street,

But not to call me back or say good-by;   10
And further still at an unearthly height
One luminary clock against the sky

Proclaimed the time was neither wrong nor right.
I have been one acquainted with the night.

                                            1928

WEST-RUNNING BROOK

"Fred, where is north?"

                        "North? North is there, my love.
The brook runs west."

                        "West-Running Brook then call it."
(West-Running Brook men call it to this day.)
"What does it think it's doing running west
When all the other country brooks flow east
To reach the ocean? It must be the brook
Can trust itself to go by contraries
The way I can with you—and you with me—
Because we're—we're—I don't know what we are.
What are we?"

                "Young or new?"

                                "We must be something   10
We've said we two. Let's change that to we three.
As you and I are married to each other,
We'll both be married to the brook. We'll build
Our bridge across it, and the bridge shall be
Our arm thrown over it asleep beside it.
Look, look, it's waving to us with a wave
To let us know it hears me."

                                "Why, my dear,
That wave's been standing off this jut of shore—
(The black stream, catching on a sunken rock,
Flung backward on itself in one white wave,   20
And the white water rode the black forever,
Not gaining but not losing, like a bird
White feathers from the struggle of whose breast
Flecked the dark stream and flecked the darker pool
Below the point, and were at last driven wrinkled
In a white scarf against the far-shore alders.)
"That wave's been standing off this jut of shore
Ever since rivers, I was going to say,
Were made in heaven. It wasn't waved to us."

"It wasn't, yet it was. If not to you,   30
It was to me—in an annunciation."[1]

"Oh, if you take it off to lady-land,
As't were the country of the Amazons[2]
We men must see you to the confines of
And leave you there, ourselves forbid to enter—
It is your brook! I have no more to say."

"Yes, you have, too. Go on. You thought of something."

"Speaking of contraries, see how the brook
In that white wave runs counter to itself.
It is from that in water we were from   40
Long, long before we were from any creature.
Here we, in our impatience of the steps,
Get back to the beginning of beginnings,
The stream of everything that runs away.
Some say existence like a Pirouot
And Pirouette,[3] forever in one place,
Stands still and dances, but it runs away;
It seriously, sadly, runs away
To fill the abyss's void with emptiness.
It flows beside us in this water brook,   50
But it flows over us. It flows between us
To separate us for a panic moment.
It flows between us, over us, and *with* us.
And it is time, strength, tone, light, life, and love—
And even substance lapsing unsubstantial;
The universal cataract of death
That spends to nothingness—and unresisted,
Save by some strange resistance in itself,
Not just a swerving, but a throwing back,
As if regret were in it and were sacred.   60
It has this throwing backward on itself
So that the fall of most of it is always
Raising a little, sending up a little.
Our life runs down in sending up the clock.
The brook runs down in sending up our life.
The sun runs down in sending up the brook.
And there is something sending up the sun.
It is this backward motion toward the source,
Against the stream, that most we see ourselves in,
The tribute of the current to the source.   70
It is from this in nature we are from.
It is most us."

"Today will be the day

---

[1]An important announcement, such as the annunciation (revelation) to the Virgin Mary that she was to be the mother of Christ.
[2]In classical myth the tribe of female warriors who lived in Asia Minor in a society where women dominated and men were subjugated.
[3]Frost refers to traditional characters in French pantomime.

You said so."

"No, today will be the day
You said the brook was called West-Running Brook."

"Today will be the day of what we both said."

1928

DESERT PLACES

Snow falling and night falling fast, oh, fast
In a field I looked into going past,
And the ground almost covered smooth in snow,
But a few weeds and stubble showing last.

The woods around it have it—it is theirs.
All animals are smothered in their lairs.
I am too absent-spirited to count;
The loneliness includes me unawares.

And lonely as it is, that loneliness
Will be more lonely ere it will be less—   10
A blanker whiteness of benighted[1] snow
With no expression, nothing to express.

They cannot scare me with their empty spaces
Between stars—on stars where no human race is.
I have it in me so much nearer home
To scare myself with my own desert places.

1934

NEITHER OUT FAR NOR IN DEEP

The people along the sand
All turn and look one way.
They turn their back on the land.
They look at the sea all day.

As long as it takes to pass
A ship keeps raising its hull;
The wetter ground like glass
Reflects a standing gull.

The land may vary more;
But wherever the truth may be—   10

[1]Overtaken by night or darkness.

The water comes ashore,
And the people look at the sea.

They cannot look out far.
They cannot look in deep.
But when was that ever a bar
To any watch they keep?

                                          1934

PROVIDE, PROVIDE

The witch that came (the withered hag)
To wash the steps with pail and rag
Was once the beauty Abishag,[1]

The picture pride of Hollywood.
Too many fall from great and good
For you to doubt the likelihood.

Die early and avoid the fate.
Or if predestined to die late,
Make up your mind to die in state.

Make the whole stock exchange your own!   10
If need be occupy a throne,
Where nobody can call *you* crone.

Some have relied on what they knew,
Others on being simply true.
What worked for them might work for
    you.

No memory of having starred
Atones for later disregard
Or keeps the end from being hard.

Better to go down dignified
With boughten friendship at your side   20
Than none at all. Provide, provide!

                                          1934

THE SILKEN TENT

She is as in a field a silken tent
At midday when a sunny summer breeze

[1]Beautiful young virgin who cared for King David in his old age. I Kings 1:2-4.

Has dried the dew and all its ropes relent,
So that in guys[1] it gently sways at ease,
And its supporting central cedar pole,
That is its pinnacle to heavenward
And signifies the sureness of the soul,
Seems to owe naught to any single cord,
But strictly held by none, is loosely bound
By countless silken ties of love and thought   10
To everything on earth the compass round,
And only by one's going slightly taut
In the capriciousness of summer air
Is of the slightest bondage made aware.

1939, 1942

THE MOST OF IT

He thought he kept the universe alone;
For all the voice in answer he could wake
Was but the mocking echo of his own
From some tree-hidden cliff across the lake.
Some morning from the boulder-broken beach
He would cry out on life, that what it wants
Is not its own love back in copy speech,
But counter-love, original response.
And nothing ever came of what he cried
Unless it was the embodiment that crashed   10
In the cliff's talus[1] on the other side,
And then in the far-distant water splashed,
But after a time allowed for it to swim,
Instead of proving human when it neared
And someone else additional to him,
As a great buck it powerfully appeared,
Pushing the crumpled water up ahead,
And landed pouring like a waterfall,
And stumbled through the rocks with horny tread,
And forced the underbrush—and that was all.   20

1946

THE GIFT OUTRIGHT[1]

The land was ours before we were the land's.
She was our land more than a hundred years
Before we were her people. She was ours
In Massachusetts, in Virginia,

[1]Supporting ropes.
[1]Rock debris at the foot of a cliff.
[1]Recited by Frost at the inauguration of President John F. Kennedy, January 1961.

But we were England's, still colonials,
Possessing what we still were unpossessed by,
Possessed by what we now no more possessed.
Something we were withholding made us weak
Until we found out that it was ourselves
We were withholding from our land of living,   10
And forthwith found salvation in surrender.
Such as we were we gave ourselves outright
(The deed of gift was many deeds of war)
To the land vaguely realizing westward,
But still unstoried, artless, unenhanced,
Such as she was, such as she would become.

                                                        1942

DIRECTIVE

Back out of all this now too much for us,
Back in a time made simple by the loss
Of detail, burned, dissolved, and broken off
Like graveyard marble sculpture in the weather,
There is a house that is no more a house
Upon a farm that is no more a farm
And in a town that is no more a town.
The road there, if you'll let a guide direct you
Who only has at heart your getting lost,
May seem as if it should have been a quarry—   10
Great monolithic knees the former town
Long since gave up pretense of keeping covered.
And there's a story in a book about it:
Besides the wear of iron wagon wheels
The ledges show lines ruled southeast-northwest,
The chisel work of an enormous Glacier
That braced his feet against the Arctic Pole.
You must not mind a certain coolness from him
Still said to haunt this side of Panther Mountain.
Nor need you mind the serial ordeal   20
Of being watched from forty cellar holes
As if by eye pairs out of forty firkins.[1]
As for the woods' excitement over you
That sends light rustle rushes to their leaves,
Charge that to upstart inexperience.
Where were they all not twenty years ago?
They think too much of having shaded out
A few old pecker-fretted[2] apple trees.
Make yourself up a cheering song of how
Someone's road home from work this once was,   30

¹Small barrels.
²I.e., marked by woodpeckers.

Who may be just ahead of you on foot
Or creaking with a buggy load of grain.
The height of the adventure is the height
Of country where two village cultures faded
Into each other. Both of them are lost.
And if you're lost enough to find yourself
By now, pull in your ladder road behind you
And put a sign up CLOSED to all but me.
Then make yourself at home. The only field
Now left's no bigger than a harness gall.[3]   40
First there's the children's house of make-believe,
Some shattered dishes underneath a pine,
The playthings in the playhouse of the children.
Weep for what little things could make them glad.
Then for the house that is no more a house,
But only a belilaced cellar hole,
Now slowly closing like a dent in dough.
This was no playhouse but a house in earnest.
Your destination and your destiny's
A brook that was the water of the house,   50
Cold as a spring as yet so near its source,
Too lofty and original to rage.
(We know the valley streams that when aroused
Will leave their tatters hung on barb and thorn.)
I have kept hidden in the instep arch
Of an old cedar at the waterside
A broken drinking goblet like the Grail[4]
Under a spell so the wrong ones can't find it,
So can't get saved, as Saint Mark says they mustn't[5]
(I stole the goblet from the children's playhouse.)   60
Here are your waters and your watering place.
Drink and be whole again beyond confusion.
1946   1946, 1947

FORGIVE, O LORD

Forgive, O Lord, my little jokes on Thee
And I'll forgive Thy great big one on me.
1959

IN WINTER IN THE WOODS ALONE[1]

In winter in the woods alone
Against the trees I go.

---

[3]A sore, caused by a chafing harness.
[4]The Holy Grail, the cup said to have been used by Jesus at the Last Supper.
[5]"And he said unto them, unto you it is given to know the mystery of the kingdom of God; but unto them that are without, all these things are done in parables: That seeing they may see, and not perceive; and hearing they may hear, and not understand; lest at any time they should be converted and their sins should be forgiven them." Mark 4:11–12.
[1]Frost left the poem untitled. The present title has been supplied by the editor.

I mark a maple for my own
And lay the maple low.

At four o'clock I shoulder ax,
And in the afterglow
I link a line of shadowy tracks
Across the tinted snow.

I see for Nature no defeat
In one tree's overthrow   10
Or for myself in my retreat
For yet another blow.

1963

Carl Sandburg   *1878–1967*

Like his contemporary, Robert Frost, Carl Sandburg lived to enjoy enormous popular acclaim; by the end of his life he had become a familiar figure to national television audiences who listened to him read his poems, sing folk ballads, and tell anecdotes about Abraham Lincoln. But unlike Frost, Sandburg never gained the broad approval of the literary establishment, the critics whom Sandburg in turn accused of taking snobbish pride in the fact that "the average truck driver . . . can't understand them."

Sandburg longed, as had his literary forebear Walt Whitman, to be a poet of the people, to be read by "farmers, thieves, and deacons—and not by little cliques." His poetic exaltation of the ordinary man and the commonplace world was largely the result of a deeply imbedded Populism, absorbed during his youth. Born in Illinois, the son of Swedish immigrants, he left public school when he was thirteen, took on odd jobs, and became a housepainter's apprentice. Although he later attended college, his formal education had less impact on him than did the people he came to know while he wandered throughout America, working as a milkman, porter, stagehand, brickmaker, dishwasher, housepainter, carpenter, salesman, and newspaper reporter.

In 1912 Sandburg moved to Chicago, where he eventually joined the staff of the Chicago Daily News. *His colloquial poetry, with its apparently spontaneous free-verse unorthodoxies, appeared in such volumes as* Chicago Poems *(1916),* Cornhuskers *(1918),* Smoke and Steel *(1920),* Slabs of the Sunburnt West *(1922), and in* The People, Yes *(1936). Sandburg's poems reflected the folklore and history of the land and his faith in a vital America of the masses. In Abraham Lincoln, Sandburg saw the supreme justification for a faith in the wisdom of the common man, and it was a mythic Lincoln, the hero of the people, who emerged from the six-volume Lincoln biography,* The Prairie Years *and* The War Years *(1926–1939), that earned Sandburg a Pulitzer Prize for history, in 1940.*

Sandburg's writing is an expression of Whitmanian optimism and democratic sentiment shaped by the rhythms of midwestern speech. His poetry ranges from the abbreviated imagism of "Fog" to such free-verse effusions as "Chicago" and The People, Yes, *unrestrained portrayals of America's rich diversity, descriptions of the virtues of the ordinary people, the mob, that Sandburg saw as the vindication of democratic life.*

FURTHER READING: *The Letters of Carl Sandburg,* ed. H. Mitgang, 1968; B. Weirick, *From Whitman to Sandburg,* 1924; K. Detzer, *Carl Sandburg,* 1941; R. Crowder, *Carl Sandburg,* 1964; H. Durnell, *The America of Carl Sandburg,* 1965; J. Haas, *Carl Sandburg,* 1967; N. Callahan, *Carl Sandburg, Lincoln of Our Literature,* 1969; G. Allen, *Carl Sandburg,* 1972; N. Callahan, *Carl Sandburg, His Life and Works,* 1988.

TEXT: *The Complete Poems of Carl Sandburg,* 1970.

CHICAGO

Hog Butcher for the World,
Tool Maker, Stacker of Wheat,
Player with Railroads and the Nation's Freight Handler;
Stormy, husky, brawling,
City of the Big Shoulders:

They tell me you are wicked and I believe them, for I have seen your
    painted women under the gas lamps luring the farm boys.
And they tell me you are crooked and I answer: Yes, it is true I have
    seen the gunman kill and go free to kill again.
And they tell me you are brutal and my reply is: On the faces of
    women and children I have seen the marks of wanton hunger.
And having answered so I turn once more to those who sneer at this
    my city, and I give them back the sneer and say to them:
Come and show me another city with lifted head singing so proud to
    be alive and coarse and strong and cunning.   10
Flinging magnetic curses amid the toil of piling job on job, here is a
    tall bold slugger set vivid against the little soft cities;
Fierce as a dog with tongue lapping for action, cunning as a savage
    pitted against the wilderness,
      Bareheaded,
      Shoveling,
      Wrecking,
      Planning,
      Building, breaking, rebuilding,
Under the smoke, dust all over his mouth, laughing with white
    teeth,
Under the terrible burden of destiny laughing as a young man
    laughs,
Laughing even as an ignorant fighter laughs who has never lost a
    battle,   20
Bragging and laughing that under his wrist is the pulse, and under
    his ribs the heart of the people,
                Laughing!
Laughing the stormy, husky, brawling laughter of Youth, half-naked,
    sweating, proud to be Hog Butcher, Tool Maker, Stacker of Wheat,
    Player with Railroads and Freight Handler to the Nation.

1914

THE HARBOR

Passing through huddled and ugly walls
By doorways where women
Looked from their hunger-deep eyes,
Haunted with shadows of hunger-hands,
Out from the huddled and ugly walls,
I came sudden, at the city's edge,
On a blue burst of lake,
Long lake waves breaking under the sun
On a spray-flung curve of shore;
And a fluttering storm of gulls,   10
Masses of great gray wings
And flying white bellies
Veering and wheeling free in the open.

1916

HAPPINESS

I asked professors who teach the meaning of life to tell me what is
    happiness.
And I went to famous executives who boss the work of thousands of
    men.
They all shook their heads and gave me a smile as though I was try-
    ing to fool with them.
And then one Sunday afternoon I wandered out along the Desplaines
    river.
And I saw a crowd of Hungarians under the trees with their women
    and children and a keg of beer and an accordion.

1916

GRACELAND

Tomb of a millionaire,
A multi-millionaire, ladies and gentlemen,
Place of the dead where they spend every year
The usury of twenty-five thousand dollars
For upkeep and flowers
To keep fresh the memory of the dead.
The merchant prince gone to dust
Commanded in his written will
Over the signed name of his last testament
Twenty-five thousand dollars be set aside   10
For roses, lilacs, hydrangeas, tulips,
For perfume and color, sweetness of remembrance
Around his last long home.

(A hundred cash girls want nickels to go to the movies tonight.
In the back stalls of a hundred saloons, women are at tables
Drinking with men or waiting for men jingling loose silver dollars
  in their pockets.
In a hundred furnished rooms is a girl who sells silk or dress goods
  or leather stuff for six dollars a week wages
And when she pulls on her stockings in the morning she is reckless
  about God and the newspapers and the police, the talk of her
  home town or the name people call her.)

                                                             1916

FOG

       The fog comes
       on little cat feet.

       It sits looking
       over harbor and city
       on silent haunches
       and then moves on.
                   1916

COOL TOMBS

When Abraham Lincoln was shoveled into the tombs, he forgot the
  copperheads[1] and the assassin[2] . . . in the dust, in the cool tombs.

And Ulysses Grant lost all thought of con men and Wall Street, cash
  and collateral turned ashes . . . in the dust, in the cool tombs.

Pocahontas' body, lovely as a poplar, sweet as a red haw[3] in November or a pawpaw[4] in May, did she wonder? Does she remember? . . . in the dust, in the cool tombs?

Take any streetful of people buying clothes and groceries, cheering
  a hero or throwing confetti and blowing tin horns . . . tell me
  if the lovers are losers . . . tell me if any get more than the
  lovers . . . in the dust . . . in the cool tombs.

                                                             1918

GRASS

       Pile the bodies high at Austerlitz and Waterloo.[1]
       Shovel them under and let me work—

[1]Northerners who supported the Confederacy during the Civil War.
[2]John Wilkes Booth (1838–1865).
[3]Hawthorn berry.   [4]The fruit of the papaw tree.
[1]Battlefields of the Napoleonic Wars. Battlefields cited below are of the American Civil War
(Gettysburg) and World War I (Ypres and Verdun).

I am the grass; I cover all.

And pile them high at Gettysburg
And pile them high at Ypres and Verdun.
Shovel them under and let me work.
Two years, ten years, and passengers ask the conductor:

What place is this?
Where are we now?

I am the grass.
Let me work.

1918

from *THE PEOPLE, YES*

The people will live on.
The learning and blundering people will live on.
They will be tricked and sold and again sold
And go back to the nourishing earth for rootholds.
The people so peculiar in renewal and comeback,
You can't laugh off their capacity to take it.
The mammoth rests between his cyclonic dramas.

The people so often sleepy, weary, enigmatic,
is a vast huddle with many units saying:

"I earn my living.   10
I make enough to get by
and it takes all my time.
If I had more time
I could do more for myself
and maybe for others.
I could read and study
and talk things over
and find out about things.
It takes time.
I wish I had the time."   20

The people is a tragic and comic two-face:
hero and hoodlum: phantom and gorilla twisting to moan with a gargoyle mouth: "They
buy me and sell me . . . it's a game . . .
sometime I'll break loose . . ."

Once having marched
Over the margins of animal necessity,
Over the grim line of sheer subsistence
   Then man came
To the deeper rituals of his bones,
To the lights lighter than any bones,
To the time for thinking things over,
To the dance, the song, the story,
Or the hours given over to dreaming,   30
   Once having so marched.

Between the finite limitations of the five senses
and the endless yearnings of man for the beyond
the people hold to the humdrum bidding of work and food
while reaching out when it comes their way
for lights beyond the prisms of the five senses,
for keepsakes lasting beyond any hunger or death.
   This reaching is alive.
The panderers and liars have violated and smutted it.
   Yet this reaching is alive yet   40
   for lights and keepsakes.

       The people know the salt of the sea
       and the strength of the winds
       lashing the corners of the earth.
       The people take the earth
       as a tomb of rest and a cradle of hope.
       Who else speaks for the Family of Man?
       They are in tune and step
       with constellations of universal law.

       The people is a polychrome,   50
       a spectrum and a prism
       held in a moving monolith,
       a console organ of changing themes,
       a clavilux[1] of color poems
       wherein the sea offers fog
       and the fog moves off in rain
       and the Labrador sunset shortens
       to a nocturne of clear stars
       serene over the shot spray
       of northern lights.   60

   The steel mill sky is alive.
   The fire breaks white and zigzag
   shot on a gun-metal gloaming.
   Man is a long time coming.
   Man will yet win.
   Brother may yet line up with brother:

[1]An instrument designed to throw patterns of light on a screen, often accompanied by music. A
color organ.

This old anvil laughs at many broken hammers.
There are men who can't be bought.
The fireborn are at home in fire.
The stars make no noise.   70
You can't hinder the wind from blowing.
Time is a great teacher.
Who can live without hope?

In the darkness with a great bundle of grief
    the people march.
In the night, and overhead a shovel of stars for
    keeps, the people march:
                            "Where to? what next?"

                                                    1936

Willa Cather   *1873–1947*

In 1883, when she was nine, Willa Cather's family migrated westward from her birthplace in Virginia to the prairie lands of Nebraska. There she grew up among the pioneering European immigrants whose qualities of courage, sensitivity, and perseverance she was later to portray in her novels and short stories of rural and small-town America.

After graduating from the University of Nebraska in 1895, she returned east, to Pennsylvania, where she worked on a Pittsburgh newspaper and taught English in a high school. In 1900 she began publishing poems and short stories. Her first book, a collection of poems, April Twilights, *appeared in 1903. Following the publication of a collection of her short stories,* The Troll Garden *(1905), she moved to New York City, where she worked for six years on the editorial staff of* McClure's Magazine.

Her first novel, Alexander's Bridge *(1912), was set in England, but she soon returned to the frontier world of the prairies with* O Pioneers! *(1913). Next came* The Song of the Lark *(1915),* My Ántonia *(1918), and collections of short stories:* Youth and the Bright Medusa *(1920) and* Obscure Destinies *(1932). In her later years she came to perceive the sprawling cities of the East and the joyless materialism of the twentieth century as symbolic expressions of a decline in order and meaning, and she turned to depictions of the more distant past. She wrote of the struggles of early Roman Catholic missionaries among the Indians of New Mexico in* Death Comes for the Archbishop *(1927) and of the lives of settlers in seventeenth-century Quebec in* Shadows on the Rock *(1931). Yet, like the prairie realists and the local colorists of the nineteenth century, her greatest achievement remained her portrayals, with fine simplicity and what she called "the gift of sympathy," of ordinary men and women who struggled to find meaningful lives in the midst of adversity and who stood for the noble ideals of an age that had passed.*

FURTHER READING: *The Novels and Stories of Willa Cather,* 13 vols., 1937–1941; *Willa Cather's Collected Short Fiction,* ed. V. Faulkner, 1965, 1970; R. Rapin, *Willa Cather,* 1930; M. Bennett, *The World of Willa Cather,* 1951, 1961; D. Daiches, *Willa Cather, A Critical Introduction,* 1951; E. Brown and L. Edel, *Willa Cather, A Critical Biography,* 1953; E. Sergeant, *Willa Cather, A Memoir,* 1953, 1963; E. Lewis, *Willa Cather Living,* 1953; P.

Gerber, *Willa Cather*, 1975; P. Robinson, *Willa, The Life of Willa Cather*, 1983; J. Woodress, *Willa Cather, A Literary Life*, 1987; J. Randall, *The Landscape and the Looking Glass, Willa Cather's Search for Value*, 1960; E. and L. Bloom, *Willa Cather's Gift of Sympathy*, 1962; *Willa Cather and Her Critics*, ed. J. Schroeter, 1967; J. Woodress, *Willa Cather, Her Life and Art*, 1970, 1982; D. McFarland, *Willa Cather*, 1972; *The Art of Willa Cather*, ed. B. Slote, V. Faulkner, 1974; D. Stouck, *Willa Cather's Imagination*, 1975; M. Arnold, *Willa Cather's Short Fiction*, 1984; *Critical Essays on Willa Cather*, ed. J. Murphy, 1984; *Willa Cather*, ed. H. Bloom, 1986.

TEXT: *Obscure Destinies*, 1932.

NEIGHBOUR ROSICKY

I

When Doctor Burleigh told neighbour Rosicky he had a bad heart, Rosicky protested.

"So? No, I guess my heart was always pretty good. I got a little asthma, maybe. Just a awful short breath when I was pitchin' hay last summer, dat's all."

"Well now, Rosicky, if you know more about it than I do, what did you come to me for? It's your heart that makes you short of breath, I tell you. You're sixty-five years old, and you've always worked hard, and your heart's tired. You've got to be careful from now on, and you can't do heavy work any more. You've got five boys at home to do it for you."

The old farmer looked up at the Doctor with a gleam of amusement in his queer triangular-shaped eyes. His eyes were large and lively, but the lids were caught up in the middle in a curious way, so that they formed a triangle. He did not look like a sick man. His brown face was creased but not wrinkled, he had a ruddy colour in his smooth-shaven cheeks and in his lips, under his long brown moustache. His hair was thin and ragged around his ears, but very little grey. His forehead, naturally high and crossed by deep parallel lines, now ran all the way up to his pointed crown. Rosicky's face had the habit of looking interested,—suggested a contented disposition and a reflective quality that was gay rather than grave. This gave him a certain detachment, the easy manner of an onlooker and observer.

"Well, I guess you ain't got no pills fur a bad heart, Doctor Ed. I guess the only thing is fur me to git me a new one."

Doctor Burleigh swung round in his desk-chair and frowned at the old farmer. "I think if I were you I'd take a little care of the old one, Rosicky."

Rosicky shrugged. "Maybe I don't know how. I expect you mean fur me not to drink my coffee no more."

"I wouldn't, in your place. But you'll do as you choose about that. I've never yet been able to separate a Bohemian[1] from his coffee or his pipe. I've quit trying. But the sure thing is you've got to cut out farm work. You can feed the stock and do chores about the barn, but you can't do anything in the fields that makes you short of breath."

"How about shelling corn?"

"Of course not!"

Rosicky considered with puckered brows.

"I can't make my heart go no longer'n it wants to, can I, Doctor Ed?"

"I think it's good for five or six years yet, maybe more, if you'll take the strain

---

[1] A native of Bohemia, in Czechoslovakia.

off it. Sit around the house and help Mary. If I had a good wife like yours, I'd want to stay around the house."

His patient chuckled. "It ain't no place fur a man. I don't like no old man hanging round the kitchen too much. An' my wife, she's a awful hard worker her own self."

"That's it; you can help her a little. My Lord, Rosicky, you are one of the few men I know who has a family he can get some comfort out of; happy dispositions, never quarrel among themselves, and they treat you right. I want to see you live a few years and enjoy them."

"Oh, they're good kids, all right," Rosicky assented.

The Doctor wrote him a prescription and asked him how his oldest son, Rudolph, who had married in the spring, was getting on. Rudolph had struck out for himself, on rented land. "And how's Polly? I was afraid Mary mightn't like an American daughter-in-law, but it seems to be working out all right."

"Yes, she's a fine girl. Dat widder woman bring her daughters up very nice. Polly got lots of spunk, an' she got some style, too. Da's nice, for young folks to have some style." Rosicky inclined his head gallantly. His voice and his twinkly smile were an affectionate compliment to his daughter-in-law.

"It looks like a storm, and you'd better be getting home before it comes. In town in the car?" Doctor Burleigh rose.

"No, I'm in de wagon. When you got five boys, you ain't got much chance to ride round in de Ford. I ain't much for cars, noway."

"Well, it's a good road out to your place; but I don't want you bumping around in a wagon much. And never again on a hay-rake, remember!"

Rosicky placed the Doctor's fee delicately behind the desk-telephone, looking the other way, as if this were an absent-minded gesture. He put on his plush cap and his corduroy jacket with a sheepskin collar, and went out.

The Doctor picked up his stethoscope and frowned at it as if he were seriously annoyed with the instrument. He wished it had been telling tales about some other man's heart, some old man who didn't look the Doctor in the eye so knowingly, or hold out such a warm brown hand when he said good-bye. Doctor Burleigh had been a poor boy in the country before he went away to medical school; he had known Rosicky almost ever since he could remember, and he had a deep affection for Mrs. Rosicky.

Only last winter he had had such a good breakfast at Rosicky's, and that when he needed it. He had been out all night on a long, hard confinement case at Tom Marshall's,—a big rich farm where there was plenty of stock and plenty of feed and a great deal of expensive farm machinery of the newest model, and no comfort whatever. The woman had too many children and too much work, and she was no manager. When the baby was born at last, and handed over to the assisting neighbour woman, and the mother was properly attended to, Burleigh refused any breakfast in that slovenly house, and drove his buggy— the snow was too deep for a car—eight miles to Anton Rosicky's place. He didn't know another farm-house where a man could get such a warm welcome, and such good strong coffee with rich cream. No wonder the old chap didn't want to give up his coffee!

He had driven in just when the boys had come back from the barn and were washing up for breakfast. The long table, covered with a bright oilcloth, was set out with dishes waiting for them, and the warm kitchen was full of the smell of coffee and hot biscuit and sausage. Five big handsome boys, running from twenty to twelve, all with what Burleigh called natural good manners,—they hadn't a bit of the painful self-consciousness he himself had to struggle with when he was a lad. One ran to put his horse away, another helped him off with his fur coat and hung it up, and Josephine, the youngest child and the only daughter, quickly set another place under her mother's direction.

With Mary, to feed creatures was the natural expression of affection,—her chickens, the calves, her big hungry boys. It was a rare pleasure to feed a young man whom she seldom saw and of whom she was as proud as if he belonged to her. Some country housekeepers would have stopped to spread a white cloth over the oilcloth, to change the thick cups and plates for their best china, and the wooden-handled knives for plated ones. But not Mary.

"You must take us as you find us, Doctor Ed. I'd be glad to put out my good things for you if you was expected, but I'm glad to get you any way at all."

He knew she was glad,—she threw back her head and spoke out as if she were announcing him to the whole prairie. Rosicky hadn't said anything at all; he merely smiled his twinkling smile, put some more coal on the fire, and went into his own room to pour the Doctor a little drink in a medicine glass. When they were all seated, he watched his wife's face from his end of the table and spoke to her in Czech. Then, with the instinct of politeness which seldom failed him, he turned to the Doctor and said shyly; "I was just tellin' her not to ask you no questions about Mrs. Marshall till you eat some breakfast. My wife, she's terrible fur to ask questions."

The boys laughed, and so did Mary. She watched the Doctor devour her biscuit and sausage, too much excited to eat anything herself. She drank her coffee and sat taking in everything about her visitor. She had known him when he was a poor country boy, and was boastfully proud of his success, always saying: "What do people go to Omaha for, to see a doctor, when we got the best one in the State right here?" If Mary liked people at all, she felt physical pleasure in the sight of them, personal exultation in any good fortune that came to them. Burleigh didn't know many women like that, but he knew she was like that.

When his hunger was satisfied, he did, of course, have to tell them about Mrs. Marshall and he noticed what a friendly interest the boys took in the matter.

Rudolph, the oldest one (he was still living at home then), said: "The last time I was over there, she was lifting them big heavy milkcans, and I knew she oughtn't to be doing it."

"Yes, Rudolph told me about that when he come home, and I said it wasn't right," Mary put in warmly. "It was all right for me to do them things up to the last, for I was terrible strong, but that woman's weakly. And do you think she'll be able to nurse it, Ed?" She sometimes forgot to give him the title she was so proud of. "And to think of your being up all night and then not able to get a decent breakfast! I don't know what's the matter with such people."

"Why, Mother," said one of the boys, "if Doctor Ed had got breakfast there, we wouldn't have him here. So you ought to be glad."

"He knows I'm glad to have him, John, any time. But I'm sorry for that poor woman, how bad she'll feel the Doctor had to go away in the cold without his breakfast."

"I wish I'd been in practice when these were getting born." The doctor looked down the row of close-clipped heads. "I missed some good breakfasts by not being."

The boys began to laugh at their mother because she flushed so red, but she stood her ground and threw up her head. "I don't care, you wouldn't have got away from this house without breakfast. No doctor ever did. I'd have had something ready fixed that Anton could warm up for you."

The boys laughed harder than ever, and exclaimed at her: "I'll bet you would!" "She would, that!"

"Father, did you get breakfast for the doctor when we were born?"

"Yes, and he used to bring me my breakfast, too, mighty nice. I was always awful hungry!" Mary admitted with a guilty laugh.

While the boys were getting the Doctor's horse, he went to the window to examine the house plants. "What do you do to your geraniums to keep them blooming all winter, Mary? I never pass this house that from the road I don't see your windows full of flowers."

She snapped off a dark red one, and a ruffled new green leaf, and put them in his buttonhole. "There, that looks better. You look too solemn for a young man, Ed. Why don't you git married? I'm worried about you. Settin' at breakfast, I looked at you real hard, and I seen you've got some grey hairs already."

"Oh, yes! They're coming. Maybe they'd come faster if I married."

"Don't talk so. You'll ruin your health eating at the hotel. I could send your wife a nice loaf of nut bread, if you only had one. I don't like to see a young man getting grey. I'll tell you something, Ed; you make some strong black tea and keep it handy in a bowl, and every morning just brush it into your hair, an' it'll keep the grey from showin' much. That's the way I do!"

Sometimes the Doctor heard the gossipers in the drug-store wondering why Rosicky didn't get on faster. He was industrious, and so were his boys, but they were rather free and easy, weren't pushers, and they didn't always show good judgment. They were comfortable, they were out of debt, but they didn't get much ahead. Maybe, Doctor Burleigh reflected, people as generous and warm-hearted and affectionate as the Rosickys never got ahead much; maybe you couldn't enjoy your life and put it into the bank, too.

II

When Rosicky left Doctor Burleigh's office he went into the farm-implement store to light his pipe and put on his glasses and read over the list Mary had given him. Then he went into the general merchandise place next door and stood about until the pretty girl with the plucked eyebrows, who always waited on him, was free. Those eyebrows, two thin India-ink strokes, amused him, because he remembered how they used to be. Rosicky always prolonged his shopping by a little joking; the girl knew the old fellow admired her, and she liked to chaff with him.

"Seems to me about every other week you buy ticking, Mr. Rosicky, and always the best quality," she remarked as she measured off the heavy bolt with red stripes.

"You see, my wife is always makin' goose-fedder pillows, an' de thin stuff don't hold in dem little down-fedders."

"You must have lots of pillows at your house."

"Sure. She makes quilts of dem, too. We sleeps easy. Now she's makin' a fedder quilt for my son's wife. You know Polly, that married my Rudolph. How much my bill, Miss Pearl?"

"Eight eighty-five."

"Chust make it nine, and put in some candy fur de women."

"As usual. I never did see a man buy so much candy for his wife. First thing you know, she'll be getting too fat."

"I'd like dat. I ain't much fur all dem slim women like what de style is now."

"That's one for me, I suppose, Mr. Bohunk!" Pearl sniffed and elevated her India-ink strokes.

When Rosicky went out to his wagon, it was beginning to snow,—the first snow of the season, and he was glad to see it. He rattled out of town and along the highway through a wonderfully rich stretch of country, the finest farms in the county. He admired this High Prairie, as it was called, and always liked to drive through it. His own place lay in a rougher territory, where there was some clay in the soil and it was not so productive. When he bought his land, he hadn't the money to buy on High Prairie; so he told his boys, when they grumbled, that if their land hadn't some clay in it, they wouldn't own it at all. All the same, he enjoyed looking at these fine farms, as he enjoyed looking at a prize bull.

After he had gone eight miles, he came to the graveyard, which lay just at the edge of his own hay-land. There he stopped his horses and sat still on his wagon seat, looking about at the snowfall. Over yonder on the hill he could see his own house, crouching low, with the clump of orchard behind and the windmill before, and all down the gentle hill-slope the rows of pale gold cornstalks stood out against the white field. The snow was falling over the cornfield and the pasture and the hay-land, steadily, with very little wind,—a nice dry snow. The graveyard had only a light wire fence about it and was all overgrown with long red grass. The fine snow, settling into this red grass and upon the few little evergreens and the headstones, looked very pretty.

It was a nice graveyard, Rosicky reflected, sort of snug and homelike, not cramped or mournful,—a big sweep all round it. A man could lie down in the long grass and see the complete arch of the sky over him, hear the wagons go by; in summer the mowing-machine rattled right up to the wire fence. And it was so near home. Over there across the cornstalks his own roof and windmill looked so good to him that he promised himself to mind the Doctor and take care of himself. He was awful fond of his place, he admitted. He wasn't anxious to leave it. And it was a comfort to think that he would never have to go farther than the edge of his own hayfield. The snow, falling over his barnyard and the graveyard, seemed to draw things together like. And they were all old neighbours in the graveyard, most of them friends; there was nothing to feel awkward or embarrassed about. Embarrassment was the most disagreeable feeling Rosicky knew. He didn't often have it,—only with certain people whom he didn't understand at all.

Well, it was a nice snowstorm; a fine sight to see the snow falling so quietly and graciously over so much open country. On his cap and shoulders, on the horses' backs and manes, light, delicate, mysterious it fell; and with it a dry cool fragrance was released into the air. It meant rest for vegetation and men and beasts, for the ground itself; a season of long nights for sleep, leisurely breakfasts, peace by the fire. This and much more went through Rosicky's mind, but he merely told himself that winter was coming, clucked to his horses, and drove on.

When he reached home, John, the youngest boy, ran out to put away his team for him, and he met Mary coming up from the outside cellar with her apron full of carrots. They went into the house together. On the table, covered with oilcloth figured with clusters of blue grapes, a place was set, and he smelled hot coffee-cake of some kind. Anton never lunched in town; he thought that extravagant, and anyhow he didn't like the food. So Mary always had something ready for him when he got home.

After he was settled in his chair, stirring his coffee in a big cup, Mary took out of the oven a pan of *kolache* stuffed with apricots, examined them anxiously to see whether they had got too dry, put them beside his plate, and then sat down opposite him.

Rosicky asked her in Czech if she wasn't going to have any coffee.

She replied in English, as being somehow the right language for transacting business: "Now what did Doctor Ed say, Anton? You tell me just what."

"He said I was to tell you some compliments, but I forgot 'em." Rosicky's eyes twinkled.

"About you, I mean. What did he say about your asthma?"

"He says I ain't got no asthma." Rosicky took one of the little rolls in his broad brown fingers. The thickened nail of his right thumb told the story of his past.

"Well, what is the matter? And don't try to put me off."

"He don't say nothing much, only I'm a little older, and my heart ain't so good like it used to be."

Mary started and brushed her hair back from her temples with both hands as if she were a little out of her mind. From the way she glared, she might have been in a rage with him.

"He says there's something the matter with your heart? Doctor Ed says so?"

"Now don't yell at me like I was a hog in de garden, Mary. You know I always did like to hear a woman talk soft. He didn't say anything de matter wid my heart, only it ain't so young like it used to be, an' he tell me not to pitch hay or run de corn-sheller."

Mary wanted to jump up, but she sat still. She admired the way he never under any circumstances raised his voice or spoke roughly. He was city-bred, and she was country-bred; she often said she wanted her boys to have their papa's nice ways.

"You never have no pain there, do you? It's your breathing and your stomach that's been wrong. I wouldn't believe nobody but Doctor Ed about it. I guess I'll go see him myself. Didn't he give you no advice?"

"Chust to take it easy like, an' stay round de house dis winter. I guess you got some carpenter work for me to do. I kin make some new shelves for you, and I want dis long time to build a closet in de boys' room and make dem two little fellers keep dere clo'es hung up."

Rosicky drank his coffee from time to time, while he considered. His moustache was of the soft long variety and came down over his mouth like the teeth of a buggy-rake over a bundle of hay. Each time he put down his cup, he ran his blue handkerchief over his lips. When he took a drink of water, he managed very neatly with the back of his hand.

Mary sat watching him intently, trying to find any change in his face. It is hard to see anyone who has become like your own body to you. Yes, his hair had got thin, and his high forehead had deep lines running from left to right. But his neck, always clean shaved except in the busiest seasons, was not loose or baggy. It was burned a dark reddish brown, and there were deep creases in it, but it looked firm and full of blood. His cheeks had a good colour. On either side of his mouth there was a half-moon down the length of his cheek, not wrinkles, but two lines that had come there from his habitual expression. He was shorter and broader than when she married him; his back had grown broad and curved, a good deal like the shell of an old turtle, and his arms and legs were short.

He was fifteen years older than Mary, but she had hardly ever thought about it before. He was her man, and the kind of man she liked. She was rough, and he was gentle,—city-bred, as she always said. They had been shipmates on a rough voyage and had stood by each other in trying times. Life had gone well with them because, at bottom, they had the same ideas about life. They agreed, without discussion, as to what was most important and what was secondary. They didn't often exchange opinions, even in Czech,—it was as if they had thought the same thought together. A good deal had to be sacrificed and thrown overboard in a hard life like theirs, and they had never disagreed as to the things that could go. It had been a hard life, and a soft life, too. There wasn't anything brutal in the short, broad-backed man with the three-cornered eyes and the forehead that went on to the top of his skull. He was a city man, a gentle man, and though he had married a rough farm girl, he had never touched her without gentleness.

They had been at one accord not to hurry through life, not to be always skimping and saving. They saw their neighbours buy more land and feed more stock than they did, without discontent. Once when the creamery agent came to the Rosickys to persuade them to sell him their cream, he told them how much money the Fasslers, their nearest neighbours, had made on their cream last year.

"Yes," said Mary, "and look at them Fassler children! Pale, pinched little things, they look like skimmed milk. I'd rather put some colour into my children's faces than put money into the bank."

The agent shrugged and turned to Anton.

"I guess we'll do like she says," said Rosicky.

III

Mary very soon got into town to see Doctor Ed, and then she had a talk with her boys and set a guard over Rosicky. Even John, the youngest, had his father on his mind. If Rosicky went to throw hay down from the loft, one of the boys ran up the ladder and took the fork from him. He sometimes complained that though he was getting to be an old man, he wasn't an old woman yet.

That winter he stayed in the house in the afternoons and carpentered, or sat in the chair between the window full of plants and the wooden bench where the two pails of drinking-water stood. This spot was called "Father's corner," though it was not a corner at all. He had a shelf there, where he kept his Bohemian papers and his pipes and tobacco, and his shears and needles and thread and tailor's thimble. Having been a tailor in his youth, he couldn't bear to see a woman patching at his clothes, or at the boys'. He liked tailoring, and always patched all the overalls and jackets and work shirts. Occasionally he made over a pair of pants one of the older boys had outgrown, for the little fellow.

While he sewed, he let his mind run back over his life. He had a good deal to remember, really; life in three countries. The only part of his youth he didn't like to remember was the two years he had spent in London, in Cheapside, working for a German tailor who was wretchedly poor. Those days, when he was nearly always hungry, when his clothes were dropping off him for dirt, and the sound of a strange language kept him in continual bewilderment, had left a sore spot in his mind that wouldn't bear touching.

He was twenty when he landed at Castle Garden in New York, and he had a protector who got him work in a tailor shop in Vesey Street, down near the Washington Market. He looked upon that part of his life as very happy. He became a good workman, he was industrious, and his wages were increased from time to time. He minded his own business and envied nobody's good fortune. He went to night school and learned to read English. He often did overtime work and was well paid for it, but somehow he never saved anything. He couldn't refuse a loan to a friend, and he was self-indulgent. He liked a good dinner, and a little went for beer, a little for tobacco; a good deal went to the girls. He often stood through an opera on Saturday nights; he could get standing-room for a dollar. Those were the great days of opera in New York, and it gave a fellow something to think about for the rest of the week. Rosicky had a quick ear, and a childish love of all the stage splendour; the scenery, the costumes, the ballet. He usually went with a chum, and after the performance they had beer and maybe some oysters somewhere. It was a fine life; for the first five years or so it satisfied him completely. He was never hungry or cold or dirty, and everything amused him; a fire, a dog fight, a parade, a storm, a ferry ride. He thought New York the finest, richest, friendliest city in the world.

Moreover, he had what he called a happy home life. Very near the tailor shop was a small furniture-factory, where an old Austrian, Loeffler, employed a few skilled men and made unusual furniture, most of it to order, for the rich German housewives up-town. The top floor of Loeffler's five-storey factory was a loft, where he kept his choice lumber and stored the odd pieces of furniture left on his hands. One of the young workmen he employed was a Czech, and he and Rosicky became fast friends. They persuaded Loeffler to let them have a sleeping-room in one corner of the loft. They bought good beds and bedding and had their pick of the furniture kept up there. The loft was low-pitched, but light and airy, full of windows, and good-smelling by reason of the fine lumber put up there to season. Old Loeffler used to go down to the docks and buy wood from South America and the East from the sea captains. The young men were as foolish about their house as a bridal pair. Zichec, the young cabinet-maker, devised every sort of convenience, and Rosicky kept their clothes in order. At night and on Sundays, when the quiver of machinery underneath was still, it was the quietest place in the world, and on summer nights all the sea winds blew in. Zichec often practised on his flute in the evening. They were both fond of music and went to the opera together. Rosicky thought he wanted to live like that for ever.

But as the years passed, all alike, he began to get a little restless. When spring came round, he would begin to feel fretted, and he got to drinking. He was likely to drink too much of a Saturday night. On Sunday he was languid and heavy, getting over his spree. On Monday he plunged into work again. So he never had time to figure out what ailed him, though he knew something did. When the grass turned green in Park Place, and the lilac hedge at the back of Trinity churchyard put out its blossoms, he was tormented by a longing to run away. That was why he drank too much; to get a temporary illusion of freedom and wide horizons.

Rosicky, the old Rosicky, could remember as if it were yesterday the day when the young Rosicky found out what was the matter with him. It was on a Fourth of July afternoon, and he was sitting in Park Place in the sun. The lower part of New York was empty. Wall Street, Liberty Street, Broadway, all empty. So much stone and asphalt with nothing going on, so many empty windows. The emptiness was intense, like the stillness in a great factory when the machinery stops and the belts and bands cease running. It was too great a change, it took all the strength out of one. Those blank buildings, without the stream of life pouring through them, were like empty jails. It struck young Rosicky that this was the trouble with big cities; they built you in from the earth itself, cemented you away from any contact with the ground. You lived in an unnatural world, like the fish in an aquarium, who were probably much more comfortable than they ever were in the sea.

On that very day he began to think seriously about the articles he had read in the Bohemian papers, describing prosperous Czech farming communities in the West. He believed he would like to go out there as a farm hand; it was hardly possible that he could ever have land of his own. His people had always been workmen; his father and grandfather had worked in shops. His mother's parents had lived in the country, but they rented their farm and had a hard time to get along. Nobody in his family had ever owned any land,—that belonged to a different station of life altogether. Anton's mother died when he was little, and he was sent into the country to her parents. He stayed with them until he was twelve, and formed those ties with the earth and the farm animals and growing things which are never made at all unless they are made early. After his grand-father died, he went back to live with his father and stepmother, but she was very hard on him, and his father helped him to get passage to London.

After that Fourth of July day in Park Place, the desire to return to the country never left him. To work on another man's farm would be all he asked; to see the sun rise and set and to plant things and watch them grow. He was a very simple man. He was like a tree that has not many roots, but one tap-root that goes down deep. He subscribed for a Bohemian paper printed in Chicago, then for one printed in Omaha. His mind got farther and farther west. He began to save a little money to buy his liberty. When he was thirty-five, there was a great meeting in New York of Bohemian athletic societies, and Rosicky left the tailor shop and went home with the Omaha delegates to try his fortune in another part of the world.

IV

Perhaps the fact that his own youth was well over before he began to have a family was one reason why Rosicky was so fond of his boys. He had almost a grandfather's indulgence for them. He had never had to worry about any of them—except, just now, a little about Rudolph.

On Saturday night the boys always piled into the Ford, took little Josephine, and went to town to the moving-picture show. One Saturday morning they were talking at the breakfast table about starting early that evening, so that they would have an hour or so to see the Christmas things in the stores before the show began. Rosicky looked down the table.

"I hope you boys ain't disappointed, but I want you to let me have de car tonight. Maybe some of you can go in with de neighbours."

Their faces fell. They worked hard all week, and they were still like children. A new jack-knife or a box of candy pleased the older ones as much as the little fellow.

"If you and Mother are going to town," Frank said, "maybe you could take a couple of us along with you, anyway."

"No, I want to take de car down to Rudolph's, and let him an' Polly go in to de show. She don't git into town enough, an' I'm afraid she's gettin' lonesome, an' he can't afford no car yet."

That settled it. The boys were a good deal dashed. Their father took another piece of apple-cake and went on: "Maybe next Saturday night de two little fellers can go along wid dem."

"Oh, is Rudolph going to have the car every Saturday night?" Rosicky did not reply at once; then he began to speak seriously:

"Listen, boys; Polly ain't lookin' so good. I don't like to see nobody lookin' sad. It comes hard fur a town girl to be a farmer's wife. I don't want no trouble to start in Rudolph's family. When it starts, it ain't so easy to stop. An American girl don't git used to our ways all at once. I like to tell Polly she and Rudolph can have the car every Saturday night till after New Year's, if it's all right with you boys."

"Sure it's all right, Papa," Mary cut in. "And it's good you thought about that. Town girls is used to more than country girls. I lay awake nights, scared she'll make Rudolph discontented with the farm."

The boys put as good a face on it as they could. They surely looked forward to their Saturday nights in town. That evening Rosicky drove the car the half-mile down to Rudolph's new, bare little house.

Polly was in a short-sleeved gingham dress, clearing away the supper dishes. She was a trim, slim little thing, with blue eyes and shingled yellow hair, and her eyebrows were reduced to a mere brush-stroke, like Miss Pearl's.

"Good evening, Mr. Rosicky. Rudolph's at the barn, I guess." She never called him father, or Mary mother. She was sensitive about having married a foreigner. She never in the world would have done it if Rudolph hadn't been such a handsome, persuasive fellow and such a gallant lover. He had graduated in her class in the high school in town, and their friendship began in the ninth grade. Rosicky went in, though he wasn't exactly asked. "My boys ain't goin' to town tonight, an' I brought de car over fur you two to go in to de picture show."

Polly, carrying dishes to the sink, looked over her shoulder at him. "Thank you. But I'm late with my work tonight, and pretty tired. Maybe Rudolph would like to go in with you."

"Oh, I don't go to de shows! I'm too old-fashioned. You won't feel so tired after you ride in de air a ways. It's a nice clear night, an' it ain't cold. You go an' fix yourself up, Polly, an' I'll wash de dishes an' leave everything nice fur you."

Polly blushed and tossed her bob. "I couldn't let you do that, Mr. Rosicky. I wouldn't think of it."

Rosicky said nothing. He found a bib apron on a nail behind the kitchen door. He slipped it over his head and then took Polly by her two elbows and pushed her gently toward the door of her own room. "I washed up de kitchen many times for my wife, when de babies was sick or somethin'. You go an' make yourself look nice. I like you to look prettier'n any of dem town girls when you go in. De young folks must have some fun, an' I'm goin to look out fur you, Polly."

That kind, reassuring grip on her elbows, the old man's funny bright eyes, made Polly want to drop her head on his shoulder for a second. She restrained herself, but she lingered in his grasp at the door of her room, murmuring tearfully: "You always lived in the city when you were young, didn't you? Don't you ever get lonesome out here?"

As she turned round to him, her hand fell naturally into his, and he stood holding it and smiling into her face with his peculiar, knowing, indulgent smile without a shadow of reproach in it. "Dem big cities is all right fur de rich, but dey is terrible hard fur de poor."

"I don't know. Sometimes I think I'd like to take a chance. You lived in New York, didn't you?"

"An' London. Da's bigger still. I learned my trade dere. Here's Rudolph comin', you better hurry."

"Will you tell me about London some time?"

"Maybe. Only I ain't no talker, Polly. Run an' dress yourself up."

The bedroom door closed behind her, and Rudolph came in from the outside, looking anxious. He had seen the car and was sorry any of his family should come just then. Supper hadn't been a very pleasant occasion. Halting in the doorway, he saw his father in a kitchen apron, carrying dishes to the sink. He flushed crimson and something flashed in his eye. Rosicky held up a warning finger.

"I brought de car over fur you an' Polly to go to de picture show, an' I made her let me finish here so you won't be late. You go put on a clean shirt, quick!"

"But don't the boys want the car, Father?"

"Not tonight dey don't." Rosicky fumbled under his apron and found his pants pocket. He took out a silver dollar and said in a hurried whisper: "You go an' buy dat girl some ice cream an' candy tonight, like you was courtin'. She's awful good friends wid me."

Rudolph was very short of cash, but he took the money as if it hurt him. There had been a crop failure all over the country. He had more than once been sorry he'd married this year.

In a few minutes the young people came out, looking clean and a little stiff. Rosicky hurried them off, and then he took his own time with the dishes. He scoured the pots and pans and put away the milk and swept the kitchen. He put some coal in the stove and shut off the draughts, so the place would be warm for them when they got home late at night. Then he sat down and had a pipe and listened to the clock tick.

Generally speaking, marrying an American girl was certainly a risk. A Czech should marry a Czech. It was lucky that Polly was the daughter of a poor widow woman; Rudolph was proud, and if she had a prosperous family to throw up at him, they could never make it go. Polly was one of four sisters, and they all worked; one was book-keeper in the bank, one taught music, and Polly and her younger sister had been clerks, like Miss Pearl. All four of them were musical, had pretty voices, and sang in the Methodist choir, which the eldest sister directed.

Polly missed the sociability of a store position. She missed the choir, and the company of her sisters. She didn't dislike housework, but she disliked so much of it. Rosicky was a little anxious about this pair. He was afraid Polly would grow so discontented that Rudy would quit the farm and take a factory job in Omaha. He had worked for a winter up there, two years ago, to get money to marry on. He had done very well, and they would always take him back at the stockyards. But to Rosicky that meant the end of everything for his son. To be a landless man was to be a wage-earner, a slave, all your life; to have nothing, to be nothing.

Rosicky thought he would come over and do a little carpentering for Polly after the New Year. He guessed she needed jollying. Rudolph was a serious sort of chap, serious in love and serious about his work.

Rosicky shook out his pipe and walked home across the fields. Ahead of him the lamplight shone from his kitchen windows. Suppose he were still in a tailor shop on Vesey Street, with a bunch of pale, narrow-chested sons working on machines, all coming home tired and sullen to eat supper in a kitchen that was a parlour also; with another crowded, angry family quarrelling just across the dumbwaiter shaft, and squeaking pulleys at the windows where dirty washings hung on dirty lines above a court full of old brooms and mops and ash-cans. . . .

He stopped by the windmill to look up at the frosty winter stars and draw a long breath before he went inside. That kitchen with the shining windows was dear to him; but the sleeping fields and bright stars and the noble darkness were dearer still.

V

On the day before Christmas the weather set in very cold; no snow, but a bitter, biting wind that whistled and sang over the flat land and lashed one's face like fine wires. There was baking going on in the Rosicky kitchen all day, and Rosicky sat inside, making over a coat that Albert had outgrown into an overcoat for John. Mary had a big red geranium in bloom for Christmas, and a row of Jerusalem cherry trees, full of berries. It was the first year she had ever grown these; Doctor Ed brought her the seeds from Omaha when he went to some medical convention. They reminded Rosicky of plants he had seen in England; and all afternoon, as he stitched, he sat thinking about those two years in London, which his mind usually shrank from even after all this while.

He was a lad of eighteen when he dropped down into London, with no money and no connexions except the address of a cousin who was supposed to be working at a confectioner's. When he went to the pastry shop, however, he found that the cousin had gone to America. Anton tramped the streets for several days, sleeping in doorways and on the Embankment, until he was in utter despair. He knew no English, and the sound of the strange language all about him confused him. By chance he met a poor German tailor who had learned his trade in Vienna, and could speak a little Czech. This tailor, Lifschnitz, kept a repair shop in a Cheapside basement, underneath a cobbler. He didn't much need an apprentice, but he was sorry for the boy and took him in for no wages but his keep and what he could pick up. The pickings were supposed to be coppers given you when you took work home to a customer. But most of the customers called for their clothes themselves, and the coppers that came Anton's way were very few. He had, however, a place to sleep. The tailor's family lived upstairs in three rooms; a kitchen, a bedroom, where Lifschnitz and his wife and five children slept, and a living-room. Two corners of this living-room were curtained off for lodgers; in one Rosicky slept on an old horsehair sofa, with a feather quilt to wrap himself in. The other corner was rented to a wretched, dirty boy, who was studying the violin. He actually practised there. Rosicky was dirty, too. There was no way to be anything else. Mrs. Lifschnitz got the water she cooked and washed with from a pump in a brick court, four flights down. There were bugs in the place, and multitudes of fleas, though the poor woman did the best she could. Rosicky knew she often went empty to give another potato or a spoonful of dripping to the two hungry, sad-eyed boys who lodged with her. He used to think he would never get out of there, never get a clean shirt on his back again. What would he do, he wondered, when his clothes actually dropped to pieces and the worn cloth wouldn't hold patches any longer?

It was still early when the old farmer put aside his sewing and his recollections. The sky had been a dark grey all day, with not a gleam of sun, and the light failed at four o'clock. He went to shave and change his shirt while the turkey was roasting. Rudolph and Polly were coming over for supper.

After supper they sat around in the kitchen, and the younger boys were saying how sorry they were it hadn't snowed. Everybody was sorry. They wanted a deep snow that would lie long and keep the wheat warm, and leave the ground soaked when it melted.

"Yes, sir!" Rudolph broke out fiercely; "if we have another dry year like last year, there's going to be hard times in this country."

Rosicky filled his pipe. "You boys don't know what hard times is. You don't owe nobody, you got plenty to eat an' keep warm, an' plenty water to keep clean. When you got them, you can't have it very hard."

Rudolph frowned, opened and shut his big right hand, and dropped it clenched upon his knee. "I've got to have a good deal more than that, Father, or I'll quit this farming gamble. I can always make good wages railroading, or at the packing house, and be sure of my money."

"Maybe so," his father answered dryly.

Mary, who had just come in from the pantry and was wiping her hands on the roller towel, thought Rudy and his father were getting too serious. She brought her darning-basket and sat down in the middle of the group.

"I ain't much afraid of hard times, Rudy," she said heartily. "We've had a plenty, but we've always come through. Your father wouldn't never take nothing very hard, not even hard times. I got a mind to tell you a story on him. Maybe you boys can't hardly remember the year we had that terrible hot wind, that burned everything up on the Fourth of July? All the corn an' the gardens. An' that was in the days when we didn't have alfalfa yet,—I guess it wasn't invented.

"Well, that very day your father was out cultivatin' corn, and I was here in the kitchen makin' plum preserves. We had bushels of plums that year. I noticed it was terrible hot, but it's always hot in the kitchen when you're preservin', an' I was too busy with my plums to mind. Anton come in from the field about three o'clock, an' I asked him what was the matter.

" 'Nothin',' he says, 'but it's pretty hot, an' I think I won't work no more today.' He stood round for a few minutes, an' then he says: 'Ain't you near through? I want you should git up a nice supper for us tonight. It's Fourth of July.'

"I told him to git along, that I was right in the middle of preservin', but the plums would taste good on hot biscuit. 'I'm goin' to have fried chicken, too,' he says, and he went off an' killed a couple. You three oldest boys was little fellers, playin' round outside, real hot an' sweaty, an' your father took you to the horse tank down by the windmill an' took off your clothes an' put you in. Them two box-elder trees was little then, but they made shade over the tank. Then he took off all his own clothes, an' got in with you. While he was playin' in the water with you, the Methodist preacher drove into our place to say how all the neighbours was goin' to meet at the schoolhouse that night, to pray for rain. He drove right to the windmill, of course, and there was your father and you three with no clothes on. I was in the kitchen door, an' I had to laugh, for the preacher acted like he ain't never seen a naked man before. He surely was embarrassed, an' your father couldn't git to his clothes; they was all hangin' up on the windmill to let the sweat dry out of 'em. So he laid in the tank where he was, an' put one of you boys on top of him to cover him up a little, an' talked to the preacher.

"When you got through playin' in the water, he put clean clothes on you and a clean shirt on himself, an' by that time I'd begun to get supper. He says: 'It's too hot in here to eat comfortable. Let's have a picnic in the orchard. We'll eat our supper behind the mulberry hedge, under them linden trees.'

"So he carried our supper down, an' a bottle of my wild-grape wine, an' everything tasted good, I can tell you. The wind got cooler as the sun was goin' down, and it turned out pleasant, only I noticed how the leaves was curled up on the linden trees. That made me think, an' I asked your father if that hot wind all day hadn' been terrible hard on the gardens an' the corn.

" 'Corn,' he says, 'there ain't no corn.'

" 'What you talkin' about?' I said. 'Ain't we got forty acres?'

" 'We ain't got an ear,' he says, 'nor nobody else ain' got none. All the corn in this country was cooked by three o'clock today, like you'd roasted it in an oven.'

" 'You mean you won't get no crop at all?' I asked him. I couldn't believe it, after he'd worked so hard.

" 'No crop this year,' he says. 'That's why we're havin' a picnic. We might as well enjoy what we got.'

"An' that's how your father behaved, when all the neighbours was so discouraged they couldn't look you in the face. An' we enjoyed ourselves that year, poor as we was, an' our neighbours wasn't a bit better off for bein' miserable. Some of 'em grieved till they got poor digestions and couldn't relish what they did have."

The younger boys said they thought their father had the best of it. But Rudolph was thinking that, all the same, the neighbours had managed to get ahead more, in the fifteen years since that time. There must be something wrong about his father's way of doing things. He wished he knew what was going on in the back of Polly's mind. He knew she liked his father, but he knew, too, that she was afraid of something. When his mother sent over coffee-cake, or prune tarts or a loaf of fresh bread, Polly seemed to regard them with a certain suspicion. When she observed to him that his brothers had nice manners, her tone implied that it was remarkable they should have. With his mother she was stiff and on her guard. Mary's hearty frankness and gusts of good humour irritated her. Polly was afraid of being unusual or conspicuous in any way, of being "ordinary," as she said!

When Mary had finished her story, Rosicky laid aside his pipe.

"You boys like me to tell you about some of dem hard times I been through in London?" Warmly encouraged, he sat rubbing his forehead along the deep creases. It was bothersome to tell a long story in English (he nearly always talked to the boys in Czech), but he wanted Polly to hear this one.

"Well, you know about dat tailor shop I worked in in London? I had one Christmas dere I ain't never forgot. Times was awful bad before Christmas; de boss ain't got much work, an' have it awful hard to pay his rent. It ain't so much fun, bein' poor in a big city like London, I'll say! All de windows is full of good t'ings to eat, an' all de pushcarts in de streets is full, an' you smell 'em all de time, an' you ain't got no money,—not a damn bit. I didn't mind de cold so much, though I didn't have no overcoat, chust a short jacket I'd outgrowed so it wouldn't meet on me, an' my hands was chapped raw. But I always had a good appetite, like you all know, an' de sight of dem pork pies in de windows was awful fur me!

"Day before Christmas was terrible foggy dat year, an' dat fog gits into your bones and makes you all damp like. Mrs. Lifschnitz didn't give us nothin' but a little bread an' drippin' for supper, because she was savin' to try for to give us a good dinner on Christmas Day. After supper de boss say I can go an' enjoy myself, so I went into de streets to listen to de Christmas singers. Dey sing old songs an' make very nice music, an' I run round after dem a good ways, till I got awful hungry. I t'ink maybe if I go home, I can sleep till morning an' forgit my belly.

"I went into my corner real quiet, and roll up in my fedder quilt. But I ain't got my head down, till I smell somet'ing good. Seem like it git stronger an' stronger, an' I can't git to sleep noway. I can't understand dat smell. Dere was a gas light in a hall across de court, dat always shine in at my window a little. I got up an' look round. I got a little wooden box in my corner fur a stool, 'cause I ain't got no chair. I picks up dat box, and under it dere is a roast goose on a platter! I can't believe my eyes. I carry it to de window where de light comes in, an' touch it and smell it to find out, an' den I taste it to be sure. I say, I will eat chust one little bite of dat goose, so I can go to sleep, and tomorrow I won't eat none at all. But I tell you, boys, when I stop, one half of dat goose was gone!"

The narrator bowed his head, and the boys shouted. But little Josephine slipped behind his chair and kissed him on the neck beneath his ear.

"Poor little Papa, I don't want him to be hungry!"

"Da's long ago, child. I ain't never been hungry since I had your mudder to cook fur me."

"Go on and tell us the rest, please," said Polly.

"Well, when I come to realize what I done, of course, I felt terrible. I felt better in de stomach, but very bad in de heart. I set on my bed wid dat platter on my knees, an' it all come to me; how hard dat poor woman save to buy dat goose, and how she get some neighbour to cook it dat got more fire, an' how she put it in my corner to keep it away from dem hungry children. Dey was a old carpet hung up to shut my corner off, an' de children wasn't allowed to go in dere. An' I know she put it in my corner because she trust me more'n she did de violin boy. I can't stand it to face her after I spoil de Christmas. So I put on my shoes and go out into de city. I tell myself I better throw myself in de river; but I guess I ain't dat kind of a boy.

"It was after twelve o'clock, an' terrible cold, an' I start out to walk about London all night. I walk along de river awhile, but dey was lots of drunks all along; men, and women too. I chust move along to keep away from de police. I git onto de Strand, an' den over to New Oxford Street, where dere was a big German restaurant on de ground floor, wid big windows all fixed up fine, an' I could see de people havin' parties inside. While I was lookin' in, two men and two ladies come out, laughin' and talkin' and feelin' happy about all dey been eatin' and drinkin', and dey was speakin' Czech,—not like de Austrians, but like de home folks talk it.

"I guess I went crazy, an' I done what I ain't never done before nor since. I went right to dem gay people an' begun to beg dem: 'Fellow-countrymen, for God's sake give me money enough to buy a goose!'

"Dey laugh, of course, but de ladies speak awful kind to me, an' dey take me back into de restaurant and give me hot coffee and cakes, an' make me tell all about how I happened to come to London, an' what I was doin' dere. Dey take my name and where I work down on paper, an' both of dem ladies give me ten shillings.

"De big market at Covent Garden[1] ain't very far away, an' by dat time it was open. I go dere an' buy a big goose an' some pork pies, an' potatoes and onions, an' cakes an' oranges fur de children,—all I could carry! When I git home, everybody is still asleep. I pile all I bought on de kitchen table, an' go in an' lay down on my bed, an' I ain't waken up till I hear dat woman scream when she come out into her kitchen. My goodness, but she was surprise! She laugh an' cry at de same time, an' hug me and waken all de children. She ain't stop fur no breakfast; she git de Christmas dinner ready dat morning, and we all sit

[1] London wholesale market for vegetables, fruit, and flowers.

down an' eat all we can hold. I ain't never seen dat violin boy have all he can hold before.

"Two three days after dat, de two men come to hunt me up, an' dey ask my boss, and he give me a good report an' tell dem I was a steady boy all right. One of dem Bohemians was very smart an' run a Bohemian newspaper in New York, an' de odder was a rich man, in de importing business, an' dey been travelling togedder. Dey told me how t'ings was easier in New York, an' offered to pay my passage when dey was goin' home soon on a boat. My boss say to me: 'You go. You ain't got no chance here, an' I like to see you git ahead, fur you always been a good boy to my woman, and fur dat fine Christmas dinner you give us all,' An' da's how I got to New York."

That night when Rudolph and Polly, arm in arm, were running home across the fields with the bitter wind at their backs, his heart leaped for joy when she said she thought they might have his family come over for supper on New Year's Eve. "Let's get up a nice supper, and not let your mother help at all; make her be company for once."

"That would be lovely of you, Polly," he said humbly. He was a very simple, modest boy, and he, too, felt vaguely that Polly and her sisters were more experienced and worldly than his people.

VI

The winter turned out badly for farmers. It was bitterly cold, and after the first light snows before Christmas there was no snow at all,—and no rain. March was as bitter as February. On those days when the wind fairly punished the country, Rosicky sat by his window. In the fall he and the boys had put in a big wheat planting, and now the seed had frozen in the ground. All that land would have to be ploughed up and planted over again, planted in corn. It had happened before, but he was younger then, and he never worried about what had to be. He was sure of himself and of Mary; he knew they could bear what they had to bear, that they would always pull through somehow. But he was not so sure about the young ones, and he felt troubled because Rudolph and Polly were having such a hard start.

Sitting beside his flowering window while the panes rattled and the wind blew in under the door, Rosicky gave himself to reflection as he had not done since those Sundays in the loft of the furniture-factory in New York, long ago. Then he was trying to find what he wanted in life for himself; now he was trying to find what he wanted for his boys, and why it was he so hungered to feel sure they would be here, working this very land, after he was gone.

They would have to work hard on the farm, and probably they would never do much more than make a living. But if he could think of them as staying here on the land, he wouldn't have to fear any great unkindness for them. Hardships, certainly; it was a hardship to have the wheat freeze in the ground when seed was so high; and to have to sell your stock because you had no feed. But there would be other years when everything came along right, and you caught up. And what you had was your own. You didn't have to choose between bosses and strikers, and go wrong either way. You didn't have to do with dishonest and cruel people. They were the only things in his experience he had found terrifying and horrible; the look in the eyes of a dishonest and crafty man, of a scheming and rapacious woman.

In the country, if you had a mean neighbour, you could keep off his land and make him keep off yours. But in the city, all the foulness and misery and brutality of your neighbours was part of your life. The worst things he had come upon in his journey through the world were human,—depraved and poisonous specimens of man. To this day he could recall certain terrible faces in the London streets. There were mean people everywhere, to be sure, even in their own country town here. But they weren't tempered, hardened, sharpened, like the treacherous people in cities who live by grinding or cheating or poisoning their fellow-men. He had helped to bury two of his fellow-workmen in the tailoring trade, and he was distrustful of the organized industries that see one out of the world in big cities. Here, if you were sick, you had Doctor Ed to look after you; and if you died, fat Mr. Haycock, the kindest man in the world, buried you.

It seemed to Rosicky that for good, honest boys like his, the worst they could do on the farm was better than the best they would be likely to do in the city. If he'd had a mean boy, now, one who was crooked and sharp and tried to put anything over on his brothers, then town would be the place for him. But he had no such boy. As for Rudolph, the discontented one, he would give the shirt off his back to anyone who touched his heart. What Rosicky really hoped for his boys was that they could get through the world without ever knowing much about the cruelty of human beings. "Their mother and me ain't prepared them for that," he sometimes said to himself.

These thoughts brought him back to a grateful consideration of his own case. What an escape he had had, to be sure! He, too, in his time, had had to take money for repair work from the hand of a hungry child who let it go so wistfully; because it was money due his boss. And now, in all these years, he had never had to take a cent from anyone in bitter need,—never had to look at the face of a woman become like a wolf's from struggle and famine. When he thought of these things, Rosicky would put on his cap and jacket and slip down to the barn and give his work-horses a little extra oats, letting them eat it out of his hand in their slobbery fashion. It was his way of expressing what he felt, and made him chuckle with pleasure.

The spring came warm, with blue skies,—but dry, dry as a bone. The boys began ploughing up the wheat-fields to plant them over in corn. Rosicky would stand at the fence corner and watch them, and the earth was so dry it blew up in clouds of brown dust that hid the horses and the sulky plough and the driver. It was a bad outlook.

The big alfalfa-field that lay between the home place and Rudolph's came up green, but Rosicky was worried because during that open windy winter a great many Russian thistle plants had blown in there and lodged. He kept asking the boys to rake them out; he was afraid their seed would root and "take the alfalfa." Rudolph said that was nonsense. The boys were working so hard planting corn, their father felt he couldn't insist about the thistles, but he set great store by that big alfalfa field. It was a feed you could depend on,—and there was some deeper reason, vague, but strong. The peculiar green of that clover woke early memories in old Rosicky, went back to something in his childhood in the old world. When he was a little boy, he had played in fields of that strong blue-green colour.

One morning, when Rudolph had gone to town in the car, leaving a work-team idle in his barn, Rosicky went over to his son's place, put the horses to the buggy-rake, and set about quietly raking up those thistles. He behaved with guilty caution, and rather enjoyed stealing a march on Doctor Ed, who was just then taking his first vacation in seven years of practice and was attending a clinic in Chicago. Rosicky got the thistles raked up, but did not stop to burn them.

That would take some time, and his breath was pretty short, so he thought he had better get the horses back to the barn.

He got them into the barn and to their stalls, but the pain had come on so sharp in his chest that he didn't try to take the harness off. He started for the house, bending lower with every step. The cramp in his chest was shutting him up like a jack-knife. When he reached the windmill, he swayed and caught at the ladder. He saw Polly coming down the hill, running with the swiftness of a slim greyhound. In a flash she had her shoulder under his armpit.

"Lean on me, Father, hard! Don't be afraid. We can get to the house all right."

Somehow they did, though Rosicky became blind with pain; he could keep on his legs, but he couldn't steer his course. The next thing he was conscious of was lying on Polly's bed, and Polly bending over him wringing out bath towels in hot water and putting them on his chest. She stopped only to throw coal into the stove, and she kept the tea-kettle and the black pot going. She put these hot applications on him for nearly an hour, she told him afterwards, and all that time he was drawn up stiff and blue, with the sweat pouring off him.

As the pain gradually loosed its grip, the stiffness went out of his jaws, the black circles round his eyes disappeared, and a little of his natural colour came back. When his daughter-in-law buttoned his shirt over his chest at last, he sighed.

"Da's fine, de way I feel now, Polly. It was a awful bad spell, an' I was so sorry it all come on you like it did."

Polly was flushed and excited. "Is the pain really gone? Can I leave you long enough to telephone over to your place?"

Rosicky's eyelids fluttered. "Don't telephone, Polly. It ain't no use to scare my wife. It's nice and quiet here, an' if I ain't too much trouble to you, just let me lay still till I feel like myself. I ain't got no pain now. It's nice here."

Polly bent over him and wiped the moisture from his face. "Oh, I'm so glad it's over!" she broke out impulsively. "It just broke my heart to see you suffer so, Father."

Rosicky motioned her to sit down on the chair where the teakettle had been, and looked up at her with that lively affectionate gleam in his eyes. "You was awful good to me, I won't never forget dat. I hate it to be sick on you like dis. Down at de barn I say to myself, dat young girl ain't had much experience in sickness, I don't want to scare her, an' maybe she's got a baby comin' or somet'ing.

Polly took his hand. He was looking at her so intently and affectionately and confidingly; his eyes seemed to caress her face, to regard it with pleasure. She frowned with her funny streaks of eyebrows, and then smiled back at him.

"I guess maybe there is something of that kind going to happen. But I haven't told anyone yet, not my mother or Rudolph. You'll be the first to know."

His hand pressed hers. She noticed that it was warm again. The twinkle in his yellow-brown eyes seemed to come nearer.

"I like mighty well to see dat little child, Polly," was all he said. Then he closed his eyes and lay half-smiling. But Polly sat still, thinking hard. She had a sudden feeling that nobody in the world, not her mother, not Rudolph, or anyone, really loved her as much as old Rosicky did. It perplexed her. She sat frowning and trying to puzzle it out. It was as if Rosicky had a special gift for loving people, something that was like an ear for music or an eye for colour. It was quiet, unobtrusive; it was merely there. You saw it in his eyes,—perhaps that was why they were merry. You felt it in his hands, too. After he dropped off to sleep, she sat holding his warm, broad, flexible brown hand. She had never seen another in the least like it. She wondered if it wasn't a kind of gypsy hand, it was so alive and quick and light in its communications,—very strange in a farmer. Nearly all the farmers she knew had huge lumps of fists, like mauls, or they were knotty and bony and uncomfortable-looking, with stiff fingers. But Rosicky's was like quicksilver, flexible, muscular, about the colour of a pale cigar, with deep, deep creases across the palm. It wasn't nervous, it wasn't a stupid lump; it was a warm brown human hand, with some cleverness in it, a great deal of generosity, and something else which Polly could only call "gypsy-like,"— something nimble and lively and sure, in the way that animals are.

Polly remembered that hour long afterwards; it had been like an awakening to her. It seemed to her that she had never learned so much about life from anything as from old Rosicky's hand. It brought her to herself; it communicated some direct and untranslatable message.

When she heard Rudolph coming in the car, she ran out to meet him.

"Oh, Rudy, your father's been awful sick! He raked up those thistles he's been worrying about, and afterwards he could hardly get to the house. He suffered so I was afraid he was going to die."

Rudolph jumped to the ground. "Where is he now?"

"On the bed. He's asleep. I was terribly scared, because, you know, I'm so fond of your father." She slipped her arm through his and they went into the house. That afternoon they took Rosicky home and put him to bed, though he protested that he was quite well again.

The next morning he got up and dressed and sat down to breakfast, with his family. He told Mary that his coffee tasted better than usual to him, and he warned the boys not to bear any tales to Doctor Ed when he got home. After breakfast he sat down by his window to do some patching and asked Mary to thread several needles for him before she went to feed her chickens,—her eyes were better than his, and her hands steadier. He lit his pipe and took up John's overalls. Mary had been watching him anxiously all morning, and as she went out of the door with her bucket of scraps, she saw that he was smiling. He was thinking, indeed, about Polly, and how he might never have known what a tender heart she had if he hadn't got sick over there. Girls nowadays didn't wear their heart on their sleeve. But now he knew Polly would make a fine woman after the foolishness wore off. Either a woman had that sweetness at her heart or she hadn't. You couldn't always tell by the look of them; but if they had that, everything came out right in the end.

After he had taken a few stitches, the cramp began in his chest, like yesterday. He put his pipe cautiously down on the window-sill and bent over to ease the pull. No use,—he had better try to get to his bed if he could. He rose and groped his way across the familiar floor, which was rising and falling like the deck of a ship. At the door he fell. When Mary came in, she found him lying there, and the moment she touched him she knew that he was gone.

Doctor Ed was away when Rosicky died, and for the first few weeks after he got home he was hard driven. Every day he said to himself that he must get out to see that family that had lost their father. One soft, warm moonlight night in early summer he started for the farm. His mind was on other things, and not until his road ran by the graveyard did he realize that Rosicky wasn't over there on the hill where the red lamplight shone, but here, in the moonlight. He stopped his car, shut off the engine, and sat there for a while.

A sudden hush had fallen on his soul. Everything here seemed strangely moving and significant, though signifying what, he did not know. Close by the wire fence stood Rosicky's mowing-machine, where one of the boys had been cutting hay that afternoon; his own work-horses had been going up and down there. The new-cut hay perfumed all the night air. The moonlight silvered the long, billowy grass that grew over the graves and hid the fence; the few little evergreens stood out black in it, like shadows in a pool. The sky was very blue and soft, the stars rather faint because the moon was full.

For the first time it struck Doctor Ed that this was really a beautiful graveyard. He thought of city cemeteries; acres of shrubbery and heavy stone, so arranged and lonely and unlike anything in the living world. Cities of the dead, indeed; cities of the forgotten, of the "put away." But this was open and free, this little square of long grass which the wind for ever stirred. Nothing but the sky overhead, and the many-coloured fields running on until they met that sky. The horses worked here in summer; the neighbours passed on their way to town; and over yonder, in the cornfield, Rosicky's own cattle would be eating fodder as winter came on. Nothing could be more undeathlike than this place; nothing could be more right for a man who had helped to do the work of great cities and had always longed for the open country and had got to it at last. Rosicky's life seemed to him complete and beautiful.

1928   1930, 1932

Gertrude Stein   *1874–1946*

To the world at large, Gertrude Stein and the life she led have always been more fascinating than the books she wrote or the literary theories she devised. She lived most of her life in France, where she was the confidante of celebrated artists and writers. She was the patron of Pablo Picasso and the subject of one of his most famous paintings. Writers such as Thornton Wilder, Sherwood Anderson, F. Scott Fitzgerald, and Ernest Hemingway came to her apartment in Paris to listen to her ideas on modern literature.

By the 1930s, her association with avant-garde art and her own eccentric literary works had made her a familiar symbol of modernism. Those who had never read her books could quote her famous line "A rose is a rose is a rose is a rose" or identify her as the author of:

> *Pigeons on the grass alas.*
> *Pigeons on the grass alas.*
> *Shorter longer grass short longer longer shorter yellow grass pigeons large*
>   *pigeons on the shorter longer yellow grass alas pigeons on the grass.*

She was born in Allegheny, Pennsylvania, and for much of her childhood she lived in Oakland, California. Her family was well-to-do and she enjoyed a privileged life, indulged by servants, governesses, and tutors. At eighteen she entered Radcliffe College in Cambridge, Massachusetts, and there she developed her interest in writing. Later critics and biographers would find it significant that her professor of composition praised her "unusual power of abstract thought" but complained, "Your vehemence runs away with your syntax" and gave her a C.

She also attended the classes of the famous psychologist William James, a Harvard professor and the brother of the novelist Henry James. In 1897, with James's encouragement, she entered Johns Hopkins University to study medicine and prepare for research in the pyschology of perception and understanding. But she found medical school to be tedious, constricting. She was bored by her teachers and her fellow students. They, in turn, had little patience with her imperious self-assurance. In 1901, in her last term, she made little effort to study, failed most of her courses, and left the university without an M.D. degree.

She then decided to move to Europe, where she could live comfortably on the inheritance she had received with the death of her father. In 1904 she settled in Paris, and with her brother Leo, a student of modern art, she began to collect the paintings of Cézanne, Renoir, Matisse, and Picasso. Soon the Stein apartment became a gathering place, a salon, for avant-garde artists and writers from Europe and America. One of the regular visitors was Pablo Picasso, whom Gertrude Stein admired both for the vitality of his painting and for the entertaining and venomous remarks he made about his fellow artists.

In 1905 Picasso began to paint his famous portrait of Gertrude Stein, and in the same year she began writing her first book, Three Lives *(1909), stories of three women, one of them "The Gentle Lena," who submit to their fate in a world they cannot control.* Three Lives *has been called a masterpiece of realism, and it remains one of her most successful and least obscure works. Her next important book,* Tender Buttons *(1914), a collection of observations on objects and forms, departed radically from convention, stressing "the value of the individual word" so that the reader might see actual objects rather than the mere printed text that described them.*

In 1922 she published Geography and Plays, *a collection of poems, plays, and descriptions of people and places that is rich with puns, rhythmic phrases, and the word repetitions that had become characteristic of her style.* The Making of Americans, *her long and sprawling novel of an American family, was, she believed, her literary masterwork. It appeared in 1925, and that same year she was invited to lecture on her literary theories at Cambridge and Oxford Universities in England.*

Her theories of literary language, grammar, vocabulary, and prose form were published six years later in How to Write *(1931). One of her most obscure and difficult works, it had a narrow audience; but she soon began work on a book that would bring her, for the first time, to the attention of a large reading public. It was* The Autobiography of Alice B. Toklas *(1933). Supposedly written by her longtime companion Alice B. Toklas, it was in fact Gertrude Stein's own memoirs. Her descriptions of life in Paris and the famous people she had known made the book widely popular in Europe and in the United States, where it became a book club selection and was later published as a paperback.*

The following year her opera Four Saints in Three Acts *was produced on Broadway. Set to music by the American composer Virgil Thomson,* Four Saints in Three Acts *battered operatic conventions with an exuberant vigor that left audiences noisily cheering or stunned into puzzled silence. Capitalizing on her new fame, and notoriety, Gertrude Stein returned to America in 1934 for a lecture tour. She became a national celebrity, pictured in newspapers and quoted on the radio. American editors and book publishers who had once rejected her writing as too obscure, too exotic for their readers, now urged her to send them her essay and book manuscripts.*

She was at the peak of her fame, and in the remaining years of the 1930s and in the 1940s more than twenty volumes of her works were published. In all she wrote more than fifty books and was renowned both as a famous writer and as "The Matron Saint of Paris Art," "The Sibyl of Montparnasse." When she died in 1946, it seemed as though a cultural monument in Paris had fallen.

The renown that Gertrude Stein had achieved was, she believed, fully warranted. A self-proclaimed genius, she equated herself with Homer, and to a friend she once remarked, "Besides Shakespeare and me, who do you think there is?" She had profound confidence in her judgments about life as well as art. She drove her car only in forward gear and refused to use road maps lest they restrict her freedom. She imperiously expected her readers to adopt her literary standards and accept her patterns of discourse. And she was unfor-giving of those who disagreed with her—among them Ernest Hemingway, whom she at first admired but later criticized as "yellow," an insult he repaid with pitiless malice in A Moveable Feast *(1964).*

In her writing she often departed from conventional word order and coherence. She submerged her meaning in cryptic language and puzzling abstractions in an attempt to go beneath the surface of language to essential reality. She believed that repetition of words and phrases could erase their superficial meaning and reveal their true sense. William Carlos Williams said she was "smashing every connotation that words have ever had, in order to get them back clean."

Her psychological studies had taught her that experience in life is jumbled, disorganized, and she insisted that literature should recreate that jumbled experience. Therefore tradi-tional fiction, with clearly understandable characters and with events organized in se-quential time, was false because it presented an artificial world that had never existed.

Her theories have significantly influenced critical inquiry into art and literature. Yet Gertrude Stein remains important not only as a theorist but as a literary stylist who recorded the movement of her own mind as she confronted her world and the world of women like "Gentle Lena." It was a world of profound social, cultural, and intellectual change, a world marked by economic upheavals, artistic and social revolutions, and world wars. She also knew it to be a paradoxical world of unattainable answers and unknown questions. In her final words, spoken as she lay dying in a Paris hospital, she asked, "What is the answer?" And when no one responded, she demanded, "In that case, what is the question?"

FURTHER READING: J. Mellow, *Charmed Circle, Gertrude Stein and Company*, 1974; D. Sutherland, *Gertrude Stein, A Biography of Her Work*, 1951; B. Reid, *Art by Subtraction, A Dissenting Opinion on Gertrude Stein*, 1958; J. Brinnin, *The Third Rose, Gertrude Stein and Her World*, 1959; R. Bridgman, *Gertrude Stein in Pieces*, 1970; R. Dubnick, *The Structure of Obscurity*, 1984; J. Walker, *The Making of a Modernist*, 1984; *Critical Essays on Gertrude Stein*, ed. M. Hoffman, 1986; *Gertrude Stein*, ed. H. Bloom, 1986.
TEXTS: "The Gentle Lena," *Three Lives*, 1909.

from *THREE LIVES*

THE GENTLE LENA

Lena was patient, gentle, sweet and german. She had been a servant for four years and had liked it very well.

Lena had been brought from Germany to Bridgepoint by a cousin and had been in the same place there for four years.

This place Lena had found very good. There was a pleasant, unexacting mistress and her children, and they all liked Lena very well.

There was a cook there who scolded Lena a great deal but Lena's german patience held no suffering and the good incessant woman really only scolded so for Lena's good.

Lena's german voice when she knocked and called the family in the morning was as awakening, as soothing, and as appealing, as a delicate soft breeze in midday, summer. She stood in the hallway every morning a long time in her unexpectant and unsuffering german patience calling to the young ones to get up. She would call and wait a long time and then call again, always even, gentle, patient, while the young ones fell back often into that precious, tense, last bit of sleeping that gives a strength of joyous vigor in the young, over them that have come to the readiness of middle age, in their awakening.

Lena had good hard work all morning, and on the pleasant, sunny afternoons she was sent out into the park to sit and watch the little two year old girl baby of the family.

The other girls, all them that make the pleasant, lazy crowd, that watch the children in the sunny afternoons out in the park, all liked the simple, gentle, german Lena very well. They all, too, liked very well to tease her, for it was so easy to make her mixed and troubled, and all helpless, for she could never learn to know just what the other quicker girls meant by the queer things they said.

The two or three of these girls, the ones that Lena always sat with, always worked together to confuse her. Still it was pleasant, all this life for Lena.

The little girl fell down sometimes and cried, and then Lena had to soothe her. When the little girl would drop her hat, Lena had to pick it up and hold it. When the little girl was bad and threw away her playthings, Lena told her she could not have them and took them from her to hold until the little girl should need them.

It was all a peaceful life for Lena, almost as peaceful as a pleasant leisure. The other girls, of course, did tease her, but then that only made a gentle stir within her.

Lena was a brown and pleasant creature, brown as blonde races often have them brown, brown, not with the yellow or the red or the chocolate brown of sun burned countries, but brown with the clear color laid flat on the light toned skin beneath, the plain, spare brown that makes it right to have been made with hazel eyes, and not too abundant straight, brown hair, hair that only later deepens itself into brown from the straw yellow of a german childhood.

Lena had the flat chest, straight back and forward falling shoulders of the patient and enduring working woman, though her body was now still in its milder girlhood and work had not yet made these lines too clear.

The rarer feeling that there was with Lena, showed in all the even quiet of her body movements, but in all it was the strongest in the patient, old-world ignorance, and earth made pureness of her brown, flat, soft featured face. Lena had eyebrows that were a wondrous thickness. They were black, and spread, and very cool, with their dark color and their beauty, and beneath them were her hazel eyes, simple and human, with the earth patience of the working, gentle, german woman.

Yes it was all a peaceful life for Lena. The other girls, of course, did tease her, but then that only made a gentle stir within her.

"What you got on your finger Lena," Mary, one of the girls she always sat with, one day asked her. Mary was good natured, quick, intelligent and Irish.

Lena had just picked up the fancy paper made accordion that the little girl had dropped beside her, and was making it squeak sadly as she pulled it with her brown, strong, awkward finger.

"Why, what is it, Mary, paint?" said Lena, putting her finger to her mouth to taste the dirt spot.

"That's awful poison Lena, don't you know?" said Mary, "that green paint that you just tasted."

Lena had sucked a good deal of the green paint from her finger. She stopped and looked hard at the finger. She did not know just how much Mary meant by what she said.

"Ain't it poison, Nellie, that green paint, that Lena sucked just now," said Mary. "Sure it is Lena, its real poison, I ain't foolin' this time anyhow."

Lena was a little troubled. She looked hard at her finger where the paint was, and she wondered if she had really sucked it.

It was still a little wet on the edges and she rubbed it off a long time on the inside of her dress, and in between she wondered and looked at the finger and thought, was it really poison that she had just tasted.

"Ain't it too bad, Nellie, Lena should have sucked that," Mary said.

Nellie smiled and did not answer. Nellie was dark and thin, and looked Italian. She had a big mass of black hair that she wore high up on her head, and that made her face look very fine.

Nellie always smiled and did not say much, and then she would look at Lena to perplex her.

And so they all three sat with their little charges in the pleasant sunshine a long time. And Lena would often look at her finger and wonder if it was really poison that she had just tasted and then she would rub her finger on her dress a little harder.

Mary laughed at her and teased her and Nellie smiled a little and looked queerly at her.

Then it came time, for it was growing cooler, for them to drag together the little ones, who had begun to wander, and to take each one back to its own mother. And Lena never knew for certain whether it was really poison, that green stuff that she had tasted.

During these four years of service, Lena always spent her Sundays out at the house of her aunt, who had brought her four years before to Bridgepoint.

This aunt, who had brought Lena, four years before, to Bridgepoint, was a hard, ambitious, well meaning, german woman. Her husband was a grocer in the town, and they were very well to do. Mrs. Haydon, Lena's aunt, had two daughters who were just beginning as young ladies, and she had a little boy who was not honest and who was very hard to manage.

Mrs. Haydon was a short, stout, hard built, german woman. She always hit the ground very firmly and compactly as she walked. Mrs. Haydon was all a compact and well hardened mass, even to her face, reddish and darkened from its early blonde, with its hearty, shiny, cheeks, and doubled chin well covered over with the uproll from her short, square neck.

The two daughters, who were fourteen and fifteen, looked like unkneaded, unformed mounds of flesh beside her.

The elder girl, Mathilda, was blonde, and slow, and simple, and quite fat. The younger, Bertha, who was almost as tall as her sister, was dark, and quicker, and she was heavy, too, but not really fat.

These two girls the mother had brought up very firmly. They were well taught for their position. They were always both well dressed, in the same kinds of hats and dresses, as is becoming in two german sisters. The mother liked to have them dressed in red. Their best clothes were red dresses, made of good heavy cloth, and strongly trimmed with braid of a glistening black. They had stiff, red felt hats, trimmed with black velvet ribbon, and a bird. The mother dressed matronly, in a bonnet and in black, always sat between her two big daughters, firm, directing, and repressed.

The only weak spot in this good woman's conduct was the way she spoiled her boy, who was not honest and who was very hard to manage.

The father of this family was a decent, quiet, heavy, and uninterfering german man. He tried to cure the boy of his bad ways, and make him honest, but the mother could not make herself let the father manage, and so the boy was brought up very badly.

Mrs. Haydon's girls were now only just beginning as young ladies, and so to get her niece, Lena, married, was just then the most important thing that Mrs. Haydon had to do.

Mrs. Haydon had four years before gone to Germany to see her parents, and had taken the girls with her. This visit had been for Mrs. Haydon most successful, though her children had not liked it very well.

Mrs. Haydon was a good and generous woman, and she patronized her parents grandly, and all the cousins who came from all about to see her. Mrs. Haydon's people were of the middling class of farmers. They were not peasants, and they lived in a town of some pretension, but it all seemed very poor and smelly to Mrs. Haydon's american born daughters.

Mrs. Haydon liked it all. It was familiar, and then here she was so wealthy and important. She listened and decided, and advised all of her relations how to do things better. She arranged their present and their future for them, and showed them how in the past they had been wrong in all their methods.

Mrs. Haydon's only trouble was with her two daughters, whom she could not make behave well to her parents. The two girls were very nasty to all their numerous relations. Their mother could hardly make them kiss their grand-parents, and every day the girls would get a scolding. But then Mrs. Haydon was so very busy that she did not have time to really manage her stubborn daughters.

These hard working, earth-rough german cousins were to these american born children, ugly and dirty and as far below them as were italian or negro workmen, and they could not see how their mother could ever bear to touch them, and then all the women dressed so funny, and were worked all rough and different.

The two girls stuck up their noses at them all, and always talked in English to each other about how they hated all these people and how they wished their mother would not do so. The girls could talk some German, but they never chose to use it.

It was her eldest brother's family that most interested Mrs. Haydon. Here there were eight children, and out of the eight, five of them were girls.

Mrs. Haydon thought it would be a fine thing to take one of these girls back with her to Bridgepoint and get her well started. Everybody liked that she should do so, and they were all willing that it should be Lena.

Lena was the second girl in her large family. She was at this time just seventeen years old. Lena was not an important daughter in the family. She was always sort of dreamy and not there. She worked hard and went very regularly at it, but even good work never seemed to bring her near.

Lena's age just suited Mrs. Haydon's purpose. Lena could first go out to service, and learn how to do things, and then, when she was a little older, Mrs. Haydon could get her a good husband. And then Lena was so still and docile, she would never want to do things her own way. And then, too, Mrs. Haydon, with all her hardness had wisdom, and she could feel the rarer strain there was in Lena.

Lena was willing to go with Mrs. Haydon. Lena did not like her german life very well. It was not the hard work but the roughness that disturbed her. The people were not gentle, and the men when they were glad were very boisterous, and would lay hold of her and roughly tease her. They were good people enough around her, but it was all harsh and dreary for her.

Lena did not really know that she did not like it. She did not know that she was always dreamy and not there. She did not think whether it would be different for her away off there in Bridgepoint. Mrs. Haydon took her and got her different kinds of dresses, and then took her with them to the steamer. Lena did not really know what it was that had happened to her.

Mrs. Haydon, and her daughters, and Lena traveled second class on the steamer. Mrs. Haydon's daughters hated that their mother should take Lena. They hated to have a cousin, who was to them, little better than a nigger, and then everybody on the steamer there would see her. Mrs. Haydon's daughters said things like this to their mother, but she never stopped to hear them, and the girls did not dare to make their meaning very clear. And so they could only go on hating Lena hard, together. They could not stop her from going back with them to Bridgepoint.

Lena was very sick on the voyage. She thought, surely before it was over that she would die. She was so sick she could not even wish that she had not started. She could not eat, she could not moan, she was just blank and scared, and sure that every minute she would die. She could not hold herself in, nor help herself in her trouble. She just staid where she had been put, pale, and scared, and weak, and sick, and sure that she was going to die.

Mathilda and Bertha Haydon had no trouble from having Lena for a cousin on the voyage, until the last day that they were on the ship, and by that time they had made their friends and could explain.

Mrs. Haydon went down every day to Lena, gave her things to make her better, held her head when it was needful, and generally was good and did her duty by her.

Poor Lena had no power to be strong in such trouble. She did not know how to yield to her sickness nor endure. She lost all her little sense of being in her suffering. She was so scared, and then at her best, Lena, who was patient, sweet and quiet, had not self-control, nor any active courage.

Poor Lena was so scared and weak, and every minute she was sure that she would die.

After Lena was on land again a little while, she forgot all her bad suffering. Mrs. Haydon got her the good place, with the pleasant unexacting mistress, and her children, and Lena began to learn some English and soon was very happy and content.

All her Sundays out Lena spent at Mrs. Haydon's house. Lena would have liked much better to spend her Sundays with the girls she always sat with, and who often asked her, and who teased her and made a gentle stir within her, but it never came to Lena's unexpectant and unsuffering german nature to do something different from what was expected of her, just because she would like it that way better. Mrs. Haydon had said that Lena was to come to her house every other Sunday, and so Lena always went there.

Mrs. Haydon was the only one of her family who took any interest in Lena. Mr. Haydon did not think much of her. She was his wife's cousin and he was good to her, but she was for him stupid, and a little simple, and very dull, and sure some day to need help and to be in trouble. All young poor relations, who were brought from Germany to Bridgepoint were sure, before long, to need help and to be in trouble.

The little Haydon boy was always very nasty to her. He was a hard child for any one to manage, and his mother spoiled him very badly. Mrs. Haydon's daughters as they grew older did not learn to like Lena any better. Lena never knew that she did not like them either. She did not know that she was only happy with the other quicker girls, she always sat with in the park, and who laughed at her and always teased her.

Mathilda Haydon, the simple, fat, blonde, older daughter felt very badly that she had to say that this was her cousin Lena, this Lena who was little better for her than a nigger. Mathilda was an overgrown, slow, flabby, blonde, stupid, fat girl, just beginning as a woman; thick in her speech and dull and simple in her mind, and very jealous of all her family and of other girls, and proud that she could have good dresses and new hats and learn music, and hating very badly to have a cousin who was a common servant. And then Mathilda remembered very strongly that dirty nasty place that Lena came from and that Mathilda had so turned up her nose at, and where she had been made so angry because her mother scolded her and liked all those rough cow-smelly people.

Then, too, Mathilda would get very mad when her mother had Lena at their parties, and when she talked about how good Lena was, to certain german mothers in whose sons, perhaps, Mrs. Haydon might find Lena a good husband. All this would make the dull, blonde, fat Mathilda very angry. Sometimes she would get so angry that she would, in her thick, slow way, and with jealous anger blazing in her light blue eyes, tell her mother that she did not see how she could like that nasty Lena; and then her mother would scold Mathilda, and tell her that she knew her cousin Lena was poor and Mathilda must be good to poor people.

Mathilda Haydon did not like relations to be poor. She told all her girl friends what she thought of Lena, and so the girls would never talk to Lena at Mrs. Haydon's parties. But Lena in her unsuffering and unexpectant patience never really knew that she was slighted. When Mathilda was with her girls in the street or in the park and would see Lena, she always turned up her nose and barely nodded to her, and then she would tell her friends how funny her mother was to take care of people like that Lena, and how, back in Germany, all Lena's people lived just like pigs.

The younger daughter, the dark, large, but not fat, Bertha Haydon, who was very quick in her mind, and in her ways, and who was the favorite with her father, did not like Lena, either. She did not like her because for her Lena was a fool and so stupid, and she would let those Irish and Italian girls laugh at her and tease her, and everybody always made fun of Lena, and Lena never got mad, or even had sense enough to know that they were all making an awful fool of her.

Bertha Haydon hated people to be fools. Her father, too, thought Lena was a fool, and so neither the father nor the daughter ever paid any attention to Lena, although she came to their house every other Sunday.

Lena did not know how all the Haydons felt. She came to her aunt's house all her Sunday afternoons that she had out, because Mrs. Haydon had told her she must do so. In the same way Lena always saved all of her wages. She never thought of any way to spend it. The german cook, the good woman who always scolded Lena, helped her to put it in the bank each month, as soon as she got it. Sometimes before it got into the bank to be taken care of, somebody would ask Lena for it. The little Haydon boy sometimes asked and would get it, and sometimes some of the girls, the ones Lena always sat with, needed some more money; but the german cook, who always scolded Lena, saw to it that this did not happen very often. When it did happen she would scold Lena very sharply, and for the next few months she would not let Lena touch her wages, but put it in the bank for her on the same day that Lena got it.

So Lena always saved her wages, for she never thought to spend them, and she always went to her aunt's house for her Sundays because she did not know that she could do anything different.

Mrs. Haydon felt more and more every year that she had done right to bring Lena back with her, for it was all coming out just as she had expected. Lena was good and never wanted her own way, she was learning English, and saving all her wages, and soon Mrs. Haydon would get her a good husband.

All these four years Mrs. Haydon was busy looking around among all the german people that she knew for the right man to be Lena's husband, and now at last she was quite decided.

The man Mrs. Haydon wanted for Lena was a young german-american tailor, who worked with his father. He was good and all the family were very saving, and Mrs. Haydon was sure that this would be just right for Lena, and then too, this young tailor always did whatever his father and his mother wanted.

This old german tailor and his wife, the father and the mother of Herman Kreder, who was to marry Lena Mainz, were very thrifty, careful people. Herman was the only child they had left with them, and he always did everything they wanted. Herman was now twenty-eight years old, but he had never stopped being scolded and directed by his father and his mother. And now they wanted to see him married.

Herman Kreder did not care much to get married. He was a gentle soul and a little fearful. He had a sullen temper, too. He was obedient to his father and his mother. He always did his work well. He often went out on Saturday nights and on Sundays, with other men. He liked it with them but he never became really joyous. He liked to be with men and he hated to have women with them. He was obedient to his mother, but he did not care much to get married.

Mrs. Haydon and the elder Kreders had often talked the marriage over. They all three liked it very well. Lena would do anything that Mrs. Haydon wanted, and Herman was always obedient in everything to his father and his mother. Both Lena and Herman were saving and good workers and neither of them ever wanted their own way.

The elder Kreders, everybody knew, had saved up all their money, and they were hard, good german people, and Mrs. Haydon was sure that with these people Lena would never be in any trouble. Mr. Haydon would not say anything about it. He knew old Kreder had a lot of money and owned some good houses, and he did not care what his wife did with that simple, stupid Lena, so long as she would be sure never to need help or to be in trouble.

Lena did not care much to get married. She liked her life very well where she was working. She did not think much about Herman Kreder. She thought he was a good man and she always found him very quiet. Neither of them ever spoke much to the other. Lena did not care much just then about getting married.

Mrs. Haydon spoke to Lena about it very often. Lena never answered anything at all. Mrs. Haydon thought, perhaps Lena did not like Herman Kreder. Mrs. Haydon could not believe that any girl not even Lena, really had no feeling about getting married.

Mrs. Haydon spoke to Lena very often about Herman. Mrs. Haydon sometimes got very angry with Lena. She was afraid that Lena, for once, was going to be stubborn, now when it was all fixed right for her to be married.

"Why you stand there so stupid, why don't you answer," said Mrs. Haydon one Sunday, at the end of a long talking that she was giving Lena about Herman Kreder, and about Lena's getting married to him.

"Yes ma'am," said Lena, and then Mrs. Haydon was furious with this stupid Lena. "Why don't you answer with some sense, Lena, when I ask you if you don't like Herman Kreder. You stand there so stupid and don't answer just like you ain't heard a word what I been saying to you. I never see anybody like you, Lena. If you going to burst out at all, why don't you burst out sudden instead of standing there so silly and don't answer. And here I am so good to you, and find you a good husband so you can have a place to live in all your own. Answer me, Lena, don't you like Herman Kreder? He is a fine young fellow, almost too good for you, Lena, when you stand there so stupid and don't make no answer. There ain't many poor girls that get the chance you got now to get married."

"Why, I do anything you say, Aunt Mathilda. Yes, I like him. He don't say much to me, but I guess he is a good man, and I do anything you say for me to do."

"Well then Lena, why you stand there so silly all the time and not answer when I asked you."

"I didn't hear you say you wanted I should say anything to you. I didn't know you wanted me to say nothing. I do whatever you tell me it's right for me to do. I marry Herman Kreder, if you want me."

And so for Lena Mainz the match was made.

Old Mrs. Kreder did not discuss the matter with her Herman. She never thought that she needed to talk such things over with him. She just told him about getting married to Lena Mainz who was a good worker and very saving and never wanted her own way, and Herman made his usual little grunt in answer to her.

Mrs. Kreder and Mrs. Haydon fixed the day and made all the arrangements for the wedding and invited everybody who ought to be there to see them married.

In three months Lena Mainz and Herman Kreder were to be married.

Mrs. Haydon attended to Lena's getting all the things that she needed. Lena had to help a good deal with the sewing. Lena did not sew very well. Mrs. Haydon scolded because Lena did not do it better, but then she was very good to Lena, and she hired a girl to come and help her. Lena still stayed on with her pleasant mistress, but she spent all her evenings and her Sundays with her aunt and all the sewing.

Mrs. Haydon got Lena some nice dresses. Lena liked that very well. Lena liked having new hats even better, and Mrs. Haydon had some made for her by a real milliner who made them very pretty.

Lena was nervous these days, but she did not think much about getting married. She did not know really what it was, that, which was always coming nearer.

Lena liked the place where she was with the pleasant mistress and the good cook, who always scolded, and she liked the girls she always sat with. She did not ask if she would like being married any better. She always did whatever her aunt said and expected, but she was always nervous when she saw the Kreders with their Herman. She was excited and she liked her new hats, and everybody teased her and every day her marrying was coming nearer, and yet she did not really know what it was, this that was about to happen to her.

Herman Kreder knew more what it meant to be married and he did not like it very well. He did not like to see girls and he did not want to have to have one always near him. Herman always did everything that his father and his mother wanted and now they wanted that he should be married.

Herman had a sullen temper; he was gentle and he never said much. He liked to go out with other men, but he never wanted that there should be any women with them. The men all teased him about getting married. Herman did not mind the teasing but he did not like very well the getting married and having a girl always with him.

Three days before the wedding day, Herman went away to the country to be gone over Sunday. He and Lena were to be married Tuesday afternoon. When the day came Herman had not been seen or heard from.

The old Kreder couple had not worried much about it. Herman always did everything they wanted and he would surely come back in time to get married. But when Monday night came, and there was no Herman, they went to Mrs. Haydon to tell her what had happened.

Mrs. Haydon got very much excited. It was hard enough to work so as to get everything all ready, and then to have that silly Herman go off that way, so no one could tell what was going to happen. Here was Lena and everything all ready, and now they would have to make the wedding later so that they would know that Herman would be sure to be there.

Mrs. Haydon was very much excited, and then she could not say much to the old Kreder couple. She did not want to make them angry, for she wanted very badly now that Lena should be married to their Herman.

At last it was decided that the wedding should be put off a week longer. Old Mr. Kreder would go to New York to find Herman, for it was very likely that Herman had gone there to his married sister.

Mrs. Haydon sent word around, about waiting until a week from that Tuesday, to everybody that had been invited, and then Tuesday morning she sent for Lena to come down to see her.

Mrs. Haydon was very angry with poor Lena when she saw her. She scolded her hard because she was so foolish, and now Herman had gone off and nobody could tell where he had gone to, and all because Lena always was so dumb and silly. And Mrs. Haydon was just like a mother to her, and Lena always stood there so stupid and did not answer what anybody asked her, and Herman was so silly too, and now his father had to go and find him. Mrs. Haydon did not think that any old people should be good to their children. Their children always were so thankless, and never paid any attention, and older people were always doing things for their good. Did Lena think it gave Mrs. Haydon any pleasure, to work so hard to make Lena happy, and get her a good husband, and then Lena was so thankless and never did anything that anybody wanted. It was a lesson to poor Mrs. Haydon not to do things any more for anybody. Let everybody take care of themselves and never come to her with any troubles; she knew better now than to meddle to make other people happy. It just made trouble for her and her husband did not like it. He always said she was too good, and nobody ever thanked her for it, and there Lena was always standing stupid and not answering anything anybody wanted. Lena could always talk enough to those silly girls she liked so much, and always sat with, but who never did anything for her except to take away her money, and here was her aunt who tried so hard and was so good to her and treated her just like one of her own children and Lena stood there, and never made any answer and never tried to please her aunt, or to do anything that her aunt wanted. "No, it ain't no use your standin' there and cryin', now, Lena. Its too late now to care about that Herman. You should have cared some before, and then you wouldn't have to stand and cry now, and be a disappointment to me, and then I get scolded by my husband for taking care of everybody, and nobody ever thankful. I am glad you got the sense to feel sorry now, Lena, anyway, and I try to do what I can to help you out in your trouble, only you don't deserve to have anybody take any trouble for you. But perhaps you know better next time. You go home now and take care you don't spoil your clothes and that new hat, you had no business to be wearin' that this morning, but you ain't got no sense at all, Lena. I never in my life see anybody be so stupid."

Mrs. Haydon stopped and poor Lena stood there in her hat, all trimmed with pretty flowers, and the tears coming out of her eyes, and Lena did not know what it was that she had done, only she was not going to be married and it was a disgrace for a girl to be left by a man on the very day she was to be married.

Lena went home all alone, and cried in the street car.

Poor Lena cried very hard all alone in the street car. She almost spoiled her new hat with her hitting it against the window in her crying. Then she remembered that she must not do so.

The conductor was a kind man and he was very sorry when he saw her crying. "Don't feel so bad, you get another feller, you are such a nice girl," he said to make her cheerful. "But Aunt Mathilda said now, I never get married," poor Lena sobbed out for her answer. "Why you really got trouble like that," said the conductor, "I just said that now to josh you. I didn't ever think you really was left by a feller. He must be a stupid feller. But don't you worry, he wasn't much good if he could go away and leave you, lookin' to be such a nice girl. You just tell all your trouble to me, and I help you." The car was empty and the conductor sat down beside her to put his arm around her, and to be a comfort to her. Lena suddenly remembered where she was, and if she did things like that her aunt would scold her. She moved away from the man into the corner. He laughed, "Don't be scared," he said, "I wasn't going to hurt you. But you just keep up your spirit. You are a real nice girl, and you'll be sure to get a real good husband. Don't you let nobody fool you. You're all right and I don't want to scare you."

The conductor went back to his platform to help a passenger get on the car. All the time Lena stayed in the street car, he would come in every little while and reassure her, about her not to feel so bad about a man who hadn't no more sense than to go away and leave her. She'd be sure yet to get a good man, she needn't be so worried, he frequently assured her.

He chatted with the other passenger who had just come in, a very well dressed old man, and then with another who came in later, a good sort of a working man, and then another who came in, a nice lady, and he told them all about Lena's having trouble, and it was too bad there were men who treated a poor girl so badly. And everybody in the car was sorry for poor Lena and the workman tried to cheer her, and the old man looked sharply at her, and said she looked like a good girl, but she ought to be more careful and not to be so careless, and things like that would not happen to her, and the nice lady went and sat beside her and Lena liked it, though she shrank away from being near her.

So Lena was feeling a little better when she got off the car, and the conductor helped her, and he called out to her, "You be sure you keep up a good heart now. He wasn't no good that feller and you were lucky for to lose him. You'll get a real man yet, one that will be better for you. Don't you be worried, you're a real nice girl as I ever see in such trouble," and the conductor shook his head and went back into his car to talk it over with the other passengers he had there.

The german cook, who always scolded Lena, was very angry when she heard the story. She never did think Mrs. Haydon would do so much for Lena, though she was always talking so grand about what she could do for everybody. The good german cook always had been a little distrustful of her. People who always thought they were so much never did really do things right for anybody. Not that Mrs. Haydon wasn't a good woman. Mrs. Haydon was a real, good, german woman, and she did really mean to do well by her niece Lena. The cook knew that very well, and she had always said so, and she always had liked and respected Mrs. Haydon, who always acted very proper to her, and Lena was so backward, when there was a man to talk to, Mrs. Haydon did have hard work when she tried to marry Lena. Mrs. Haydon was a good woman, only she did talk sometimes too grand. Perhaps this trouble would make her see it wasn't always so easy to do, to make everybody do everything just like she wanted. The cook was very sorry now for Mrs. Haydon. All this must be such a disappointment, and such a worry to her, and she really had always been very good to Lena. But Lena had better go and put on her other clothes and stop with all that crying. That wouldn't do nothing now to help her, and if Lena would be a good girl, and just be real patient, her aunt would make it all come out right yet for her. "I just tell Mrs. Aldrich, Lena, you stay here yet a little longer. You know she is always so good to you, Lena, and I know she let you, and I tell her all about that stupid Herman Kreder. I got no patience, Lena, with anybody who can be so stupid. You just stop now with your crying, Lena, and take off them good clothes and put them away so you don't spoil them when you need them, and you can help me with the dishes and everything will come off better for you. You see if I ain't right by what I tell you. You just stop crying now Lena quick, or else I scold you."

Lena still choked a little and was very miserable inside her but she did everything just as the cook told her.

The girls Lena always sat with were very sorry to see her look so sad with her trouble. Mary the Irish girl sometimes got very angry with her. Mary was always very hot when she talked of Lena's aunt Mathilda, who thought she was so grand, and had such stupid, stuck up daughters. Mary wouldn't be a fat fool like that ugly tempered Mathilda Haydon, not for anything anybody could ever give her. How Lena could keep on going there so much when they all always acted as if she was just dirt to them, Mary never could see. But Lena never had any sense of how she should make people stand round for her, and that was always all the trouble with her. And poor Lena, she was so stupid to be sorry for losing that gawky fool who didn't ever know what he wanted and just said "ja" to his mamma and his papa, like a baby, and was scared to look at a girl straight, and then sneaked away the last day like as if somebody was going to do something to him. Disgrace, Lena talking about disgrace! It was a disgrace for a girl to be seen with the likes of him, let alone to be married to him. But that poor Lena, she never did know how to show herself off for what she was really. Disgrace to have him go away and leave her. Mary would just like to get a chance to show him. If Lena wasn't worth fifteen like Herman Kreder, Mary would just eat her own head all up. It was a good riddance Lena had of that Herman Kreder and his stingy, dirty parents, and if Lena didn't stop crying about it,—Mary would just naturally despise her.

Poor Lena, she knew very well how Mary meant it all, this she was always saying to her. But Lena was very miserable inside her. She felt the disgrace it was for a decent german girl that a man should go away and leave her. Lena knew very well that her aunt was right when she said the way Herman had acted to her was a disgrace to everyone that knew her. Mary and Nellie and the other girls she always sat with were always very good to Lena but that did not make her trouble any better. It was a disgrace the way Lena had been left, to any decent family, and that could never be made any different to her.

And so the slow days wore on, and Lena never saw her Aunt Mathilda. At last on Sunday she got word by a boy to go and see her aunt Mathilda. Lena's heart beat quick for she was very nervous now with all this that had happened to her. She went just as quickly as she could to see her Aunt Mathilda.

Mrs. Haydon quick, as soon as she saw Lena, began to scold her for keeping her aunt waiting so long for her, and for not coming in all the week to see her, to see if her aunt should need her, and so her aunt had to send a boy to tell her. But it was easy, even for Lena, to see that her aunt was not really angry with her. It wasn't Lena's fault, went on Mrs. Haydon, that everything was going to happen all right for her. Mrs. Haydon was very tired taking all this trouble for her, and when Lena couldn't even take trouble to come and see her aunt, to see if she needed anything to tell her. But Mrs. Haydon really never minded things like that when she could do things for anybody. She was tired now, all the trouble she had been taking to make things right for Lena, but perhaps now Lena heard it she would learn a little to be thankful to her. "You get all ready to be married Tuesday. Lena, you hear me." said Mrs. Haydon to her. "You come here Tuesday morning and I have everything all ready for you. You wear your new dress I got you, and your hat with all them flowers on it, and you be very careful coming you don't get your things all dirty, you so careless all the time, Lena, and not thinking, and you act sometimes you never got no head at all on you. You go home now, and you tell your Mrs. Aldrich that you leave her Tuesday. Don't you go forgetting now, Lena, anything I ever told you what you should do to be careful. You be a good girl, now Lena. You get married Tuesday to Herman Kreder." And that was all Lena ever knew of what had happened all this week to Herman Kreder. Lena forgot there was anything to know about it. She was really to be married Tuesday, and her Aunt Mathilda said she was a good girl, and now there was no disgrace left upon her.

Lena now fell back into the way she always had of being always dreamy and not here, the way she always had been, except for the few days she was so excited, because she had been left by a man the very day she was to have been married. Lena was a little nervous all these last days, but she did not think much about what it meant for her to be married.

Herman Kreder was not so content about it. He was quiet and was sullen and he knew he could not help it. He knew now he just had to let himself get married. It was not that Herman did not like Lena Mainz. She was as good as any other girl could be for him. She was a little better perhaps than other girls he saw, she was so very quiet, but Herman did not like to always have to have a girl around him. Herman had always done everything that his mother and his father wanted. His father had found him in New York, where Herman had gone to be with his married sister.

Herman's father when he had found him coaxed Herman a long time and went on whole days with his complaining to him, always troubled but gentle and quite patient with him, and always he was worrying to Herman about what was the right way his boy Herman should always do, always whatever it was his mother ever wanted from him, and always Herman never made him any answer.

Old Mr. Kreder kept on saying to him, he did not see how Herman could think now, it could be any different. When you make a bargain you just got to stick right to it, that was the only way old Mr. Kreder could ever see it, and saying you would get married to a girl and she got everything all ready, that was a bargain just like one you make in business and Herman he had made it, and now Herman he would just have to do it, old Mr. Kreder didn't see there was any other way a good boy like his Herman had, to do it. And then too that Lena Mainz was such a nice girl and Herman hadn't ought to really give his father so much trouble and make him pay out all that money, to come all the way to New York just to find him, and they both lose all that time from their working, when all Herman had to do was just to stand up, for an hour, and then he would be all right married, and it would be all over for him, and then everything at home would never be any different to him.

And his father went on; there was his poor mother saying always how her Herman always did everything before she ever wanted, and now just because he got notions in him, and wanted to show people how he could be stubborn, he was making all this trouble for her, and making them pay all that money just to run around and find him. "You got no idea Herman, how bad mama is feeling about the way you been acting Herman," said old Mr. Kreder to him. "She says she never can understand how you can be so thankless Herman. It hurts her very much you been so stubborn, and she find you such a nice girl for you, like Lena Mainz who is always just so quiet and always saves up all her wages, and she never wanting her own way at all like some girls are always all the time to have it, and your mama trying so hard, just so you could be comfortable Herman to be married, and then you act so stubborn Herman. You like all young people Herman, you think only about yourself, and what you are just wanting, and your mama she is thinking only what is good for you to have, for you in the future. Do you think your mama wants to have a girl around to be a bother, for herself, Herman. Its just for you Herman she is always thinking, and she talks always about how happy she will be, when she sees her Herman married to a nice girl, and then when she fixed it all up so good for you, so it never would be any bother to you, just the way she wanted you should like it, and you say yes all right, I do it, and then you go away like this and act stubborn, and make all this trouble everybody to take for you, and we spend money, and I got to travel all round to find you. You come home now with me Herman and get married, and I tell your mama she better not say anything to you about how much it cost me to come all the way to look for you—Hey Herman," said his father coaxing, "Hey, you come home now and get married. All you got to do Herman is just to stand up for an hour Herman, and then you don't never to have any more bother to it—Hey Herman!—you come home with me to-morrow and get married. Hey Herman."

Herman's married sister liked her brother Herman, and she had always tried to help him, when there was anything she knew he wanted. She liked it that he was so good and always did everything that their father and their mother wanted, but still she wished it could be that he could have more his own way, if there was anything he ever wanted.

But now she thought Herman with his girl was very funny. She wanted that Herman should be married. She thought it would do him lots of good to get married. She laughed at Herman when she heard the story. Until his father came to find him, she did not know why it was Herman had come just then to New York to see her. When she heard the story she laughed a good deal at her brother Herman and teased him a good deal about his running away, because he didn't want to have a girl to be all the time around him.

Herman's married sister liked her brother Herman, and she did not want him not to like to be with women. He was good, her brother Herman, and it would surely do him good to get married. It would make him stand up for himself stronger. Herman's sister always laughed at him and always she would try to reassure him. "Such a nice man as my brother Herman acting like as if he was afraid of women. Why the girls all like a man like you Herman, if you didn't always run away when you saw them. It do you good really Herman to get married, and then you got somebody you can boss around when you want to. It do you good Herman to get married, you see if you don't like it, when you really done it. You go along home now with papa, Herman and get married to that Lena. You don't know how nice you like it Herman when you try once how you can do it. You just don't be afraid of nothing, Herman. You good enough for any girl to marry, Herman. Any girl be glad to have a man like you to be always with them Herman. You just go along home with papa and try it what I say, Herman. Oh you so funny Herman, when you sit there, and then run away and leave your girl behind you. I know she is crying like anything Herman for to lose you. Don't be bad to her Herman. You go along home with papa now and get married Herman. I'd be awful ashamed Herman, to really have a brother didn't have spirit enough to get married, when a girl is just dying for to have him. You always like me to be with you Herman. I don't see why you say you don't want a girl to be all the time around you. You always been good to me Herman, and I know you always be good to that Lena, and you soon feel just like as if she had always been there with you. Don't act like as if you wasn't a nice strong man, Herman. Really I laugh at you Herman, but you know I like awful well to see you real happy. You go home and get married to that Lena, Herman. She is a real pretty girl and real nice and good and quiet and she make my brother Herman very happy. You just stop your fussing now with Herman, papa. He go with you to-morrow papa, and you see he like it so much to be married, he make everybody laugh just to see him be so happy. Really truly, that's the way it will be with you Herman. You just listen to me what I tell you Herman." And so his sister laughed at him and reassured him, and his father kept on telling what the mother always said about her Herman, and he coaxed him and Herman never said anything in answer, and his sister packed his things up and was very cheerful with him, and she kissed him, and then she laughed and then she kissed him, and his father went and bought the tickets for the train, and at last late on Sunday he brought Herman back to Bridgepoint with him.

It was always very hard to keep Mrs. Kreder from saying what she thought, to her Herman, but her daughter had written her a letter, so as to warn her not to say anything about what he had been doing, to him, and her husband came in with Herman and said, "Here we are come home mama, Herman and me, and we are very tired it was so crowded coming," and then he whispered to her. "You be good to Herman, mama, he didn't mean to make us so much trouble," and so old Mrs. Kreder, held in what she felt was so strong in her to say to her Herman. She just said very stiffly to him, "I'm glad to see you come home to-day, Herman." Then she went to arrange it all with Mrs. Haydon.

Herman was now again just like he always had been, sullen and very good, and very quiet, and always ready to do whatever his mother and his father wanted. Tuesday morning came, Herman got his new clothes on and went with his father and his mother to stand up for an hour and get married. Lena was there in her new dress, and her hat with all the pretty flowers, and she was very nervous for now she knew she was really very soon to be married. Mrs. Haydon had everything all ready. Everybody was there just as they should be and very soon Herman Kreder and Lena Mainz were married.

When everything was really over, they went back to the Kreder house together. They were all now to live together, Lena and Herman and the old father and the old mother, in the house where Mr. Kreder had worked so many years as a tailor, with his son Herman always there to help him.

Irish Mary had often said to Lena she never did see how Lena could ever want to have anything to do with Herman Kreder and his dirty stingy parents. The old Kreders were to an Irish nature, a stingy, dirty couple. They had not the free-hearted, thoughtless, fighting, mud bespattered, ragged, peat-smoked cabin dirt that irish Mary knew and could forgive and love. Theirs was the german dirt of saving, of being dowdy and loose and foul in your clothes so as to save them and yourself in washing, having your hair greasy to save it in the soap and drying, having your clothes dirty, not in freedom, but because so it was cheaper, keeping the house close and smelly because so it cost less to get it heated, living so poorly not only so as to save money but so they should never even know themselves that they had it, working all the time not only because from their nature they just had to and because it made them money but also that they never could be put in any way to make them spend their money.

This was the place Lena now had for her home and to her it was very different than it could be for an irish Mary. She too was german and was thrifty, though she was always so dreamy and not there. Lena was always careful with things and she always saved her money, for that was the only way she knew how to do it. She never had taken care of her own money and she never had thought how to use it.

Lena Mainz had been, before she was Mrs. Herman Kreder, always clean and decent in her clothes and in her person, but it was not because she ever thought about it or really needed so to have it, it was the way her people did in the german country where she came from, and her Aunt Mathilda and the good german cook who always scolded, had kept her on and made her, with their scoldings, always more careful to keep clean and to wash real often. But there was no deep need in all this for Lena and so, though Lena did not like the old Kreders, though she really did not know that, she did not think about their being stingy dirty people.

Herman Kreder was cleaner than the old people, just because it was his nature to keep cleaner, but he was used to his mother and his father, and he never thought that they should keep things cleaner. And Herman too always saved all his money, except for that little beer he drank when he went out with other men of an evening the way he always liked to do it, and he never thought of any other way to spend it. His father had always kept all the money for them and he always was doing business with it. And then too Herman really had no money, for he always had worked for his father, and his father had never thought to pay him.

And so they began all four to live in the Kreder house together, and Lena began soon with it to look careless and a little dirty, and to be more lifeless with it, and nobody ever noticed much what Lena wanted, and she never really knew herself what she needed.

The only real trouble that came to Lena with their living all four there together, was the way old Mrs. Kreder scolded. Lena had always been used to being scolded, but this scolding of old Mrs. Kreder was very different from the way she ever before had had to endure it.

Herman, now he was married to her, really liked Lena very well. He did not care very much about her but she never was a bother to him being there around him, only when his mother worried and was nasty to them because Lena was so careless, and did not know how to save things right for them with their eating, and all the other ways with money, that the old woman had to save it,

Herman Kreder had always done everything his mother and his father wanted but he did not really love his parents very deeply. With Herman it was always only that he hated to have any struggle. It was all always all right with him when he could just go along and do the same thing over every day with his working, and not to hear things, and not to have people make him listen to their anger. And now his marriage, and he just knew it would, was making trouble for him. It made him hear more what his mother was always saying, with her scolding. He had to really hear it now because Lena was there, and she was so scared and dull always when she heard it. Herman knew very well with his mother, it was all right if one ate very little and worked hard all day and did not hear her when she scolded, the way Herman always had done before they were so foolish about his getting married and having a girl there to be all the time around him, and now he had to help her so the girl could learn too, not to hear it when his mother scolded, and not to look so scared, and not to eat much, and always to be sure to save it.

Herman really did not know very well what he could do to help Lena to understand it. He could never answer his mother back to help Lena, that never would make things any better for her, and he never could feel in himself any way to comfort Lena, to make her strong not to hear his mother, in all the awful ways she always scolded. It just worried Herman to have it like that all the time around him. Herman did not know much about how a man could make a struggle with a mother, to do much to keep her quiet, and indeed Herman never knew much how to make a struggle against anyone who really wanted to have anything very badly. Herman all his life never wanted anything so badly, that he would really make a struggle against any one to get it. Herman all his life only wanted to live regular and quiet, and not talk much and to do the same way every day like every other with his working. And now his mother had made him get married to this Lena and now with his mother making all that scolding, he had all this trouble and this worry always on him.

Mrs. Haydon did not see Lena now very often. She had not lost her interest in her niece Lena, but Lena could not come much to her house to see her, it would not be right, now Lena was a married woman. And then too Mrs. Haydon had her hands full just then with her two daughters, for she was getting them ready to find them good husbands, and then too her own husband now worried her very often about her always spoiling that boy of hers, so he would be sure to turn out no good and be a disgrace to a german family, and all because his mother always spoiled him. All these things were very worrying now to Mrs. Haydon, but still she wanted to be good to Lena, though she could not see her very often. She only saw her when Mrs. Haydon went to call on Mrs. Kreder or when Mrs. Kreder came to see Mrs. Haydon, and that never could be very often. Then too these days Mrs. Haydon could not scold Lena, Mrs. Kreder was always there with her, and it would not be right to scold Lena when Mrs. Kreder was there, who had now the real right to do it. And so her aunt always said nice things now to Lena, and though Mrs. Haydon sometimes was a little worried when she saw Lena looking sad and not careful, she did not have time just then to really worry much about it.

Lena now never any more saw the girls she always used to sit with. She had no way now to see them and it was not in Lena's nature to search out ways to see them, nor did she now ever think much of the days when she had been used to see them. They never any of them had come to the Kreder house to see her. Not even Irish Mary had ever thought to come to see her. Lena had been soon forgotten by them. They had soon passed away from Lena and now Lena never thought any more that she had ever known them.

The only one of her old friends who tried to know what Lena liked and what she needed, and who always made Lena come to see her, was the good german cook who had always scolded. She now scolded Lena hard for letting herself go so, and going out when she was looking so untidy. "I know you going to have a baby Lena, but that's no way for you to be looking. I am ashamed most to see you come and sit here in my kitchen, looking so sloppy and like you never used to Lena. I never see anybody like you Lena. Herman is very good to you, you always say so, and he don't treat you bad ever though you don't deserve to have anybody good to you, you so careless all the time, Lena, letting yourself go like you never had anybody tell you what was the right way you should know how to be looking. No, Lena, I don't see no reason you should let yourself go so and look so untidy Lena, so I am ashamed to see you sit there looking so ugly, Lena. No Lena that ain't no way ever I see a woman make things come out better, letting herself go so every way and crying all the time like as if you had real trouble. I never wanted to see you marry Herman Kreder, Lena, I knew what you got to stand with that old woman always, and that old man, he is so stingy too and he don't say things out but he ain't any better in his heart than his wife with her bad ways, I know that Lena, I know they don't hardly give you enough to eat, Lena, I am real sorry for you, Lena, you know that Lena, but that ain't any way to be going round so untidy Lena, even if you have got all that trouble. You never see me do like that Lena, though sometimes I got a headache so I can't see to stand to be working hardly, and nothing comes right with all my cooking, but I always see Lena, I look decent. That's the only way a german girl can make things come out right Lena. You hear me what I am saying to you Lena. Now you eat something nice Lena, I got it all ready for you, and you wash up and be careful Lena and the baby will come all right to you, and then I make your Aunt Mathilda see that you live in a house soon all alone with Herman and your baby, and then everything go better for you. You hear me what I say to you Lena. Now don't let me ever see you come looking like this any more Lena, and you just stop with that always crying. You ain't got no reason to be sitting there now with all that crying, I never see anybody have trouble it did them any good to do the way you are doing, Lena. You hear me Lena. You go home now and you be good the way I tell you Lena, and I see what I can do. I make your Aunt Mathilda make old Mrs. Kreder let you be till you get your baby all right. Now don't you be scared and so silly Lena. I don't like to see you act so silly Lena when really you got a nice man and so many things really any girl should be grateful to be having. Now you go home Lena to-day and you do the way I say, to you, and I see what I can do to help you."

"Yes Mrs. Aldrich" said the good german woman to her mistress later, "Yes Mrs. Aldrich that's the way it is with them girls when they want so to get married. They dont know when they got it good Mrs. Aldrich. They never know what it is they're really wanting when they got it, Mrs. Aldrich. There's that poor Lena, she just been here crying and looking so careless so I scold her, but that was no good that marrying for that poor Lena, Mrs. Aldrich. She do look so pale and sad now Mrs. Aldrich, it just break my heart to see her. She was a good girl was Lena, Mrs. Aldrich, and I never had no trouble with her like I got with so many young girls nowadays, Mrs. Aldrich, and I never see any girl any better to work right than our Lena, and now she got to stand it all the time with that old woman Mrs. Kreder. My! Mrs. Aldrich, she is a bad old woman to her. I never see Mrs. Aldrich how old people can be so bad to young girls and not have no kind of patience with them. If Lena could only live with her Herman, he ain't so bad the way men are, Mrs. Aldrich, but he is just the way always his mother wants him, he ain't got no spirit in him, and so I don't really see no help for that poor Lena. I know her aunt, Mrs. Haydon, meant it all right for her Mrs. Aldrich, but poor Lena, it would be better for her if her Herman had stayed there in New York that time he went away to leave her. I don't like it the way Lena is looking now, Mrs. Aldrich. She looks like as if she don't have no life left in her hardly, Mrs. Aldrich, she just drags around and looks so dirty and after all the pains I always took to teach her and to keep her nice in her ways and looking. It don't do no good to them, for them girls to get married Mrs. Aldrich, they are much better when they only know it, to stay in a good place when they got it, and keep on regular with their working. I don't like it the way Lena looks now Mrs. Aldrich. I wish I knew some way to help that poor Lena, Mrs. Aldrich, but she she is a bad old woman, that old Mrs. Kreder, Herman's mother. I speak to Mrs. Haydon real soon, Mrs. Aldrich, I see what we can do now to help that poor Lena."

These were really bad days for poor Lena. Herman always was real good to her and now he even sometimes tried to stop his mother from scolding Lena. "She ain't well now mama, you let her be now you hear me. You tell me what it is you want she should be doing, I tell her. I see she does it right just the way you want it mama. You let be, I say now mama, with that always scolding Lena. You let be, I say now, you wait till she is feeling better." Herman was getting really strong to struggle, for he could see that Lena with that baby working hard inside her, really could not stand it any longer with his mother and the awful ways she always scolded.

It was a new feeling Herman now had inside him that made him feel he was strong to make a struggle. It was new for Herman Kreder really to be wanting something, but Herman wanted strongly now to be a father, and he wanted badly that his baby should be a boy and healthy. Herman never had cared really very much about his father and his mother, though always, all his life, he had done everything just as they wanted, and he had never really cared much about his wife, Lena, though he always had been very good to her, and had always tried to keep his mother off her, with the awful way she always scolded, but to be really a father of a little baby, that feeling took hold of Herman very deeply. He was almost ready, so as to save his baby from all trouble, to really make a strong struggle with his mother and with his father, too, if he would not help him to control his mother.

Sometimes Herman even went to Mrs. Haydon to talk all this trouble over. They decided then together, it was better to wait there all four together for the baby, and Herman could make Mrs. Kreder stop a little with her scolding, and then when Lena was a little stronger, Herman should have his own house for her, next door to his father, so he could always be there to help him in his working, but so they could eat and sleep in a house where the old woman could not control them and they could not hear her awful scolding.

And so things went on, the same way, a little longer. Poor Lena was not feeling any joy to have a baby. She was scared the way she had been when she was so sick on the water. She was scared now every time when anything would hurt her. She was scared and still and lifeless, and sure that every minute she would die. Lena had no power to be strong in this kind of trouble, she could only sit still and be scared, and dull, and lifeless, and sure that every minute she would die.

Before very long, Lena had her baby. He was a good, healthy little boy, the baby. Herman cared very much to have the baby. When Lena was a little stronger he took a house next door to the old couple, so he and his own family could eat and sleep and do the way they wanted. This did not seem to make much change now for Lena. She was just the same as when she was waiting with her baby. She just dragged around and was careless with her clothes and all lifeless, and she acted always and lived on just as if she had no feeling. She always did everything regular with the work, the way she always had had to do it, but she never got back any spirit in her. Herman was always good and kind, and always helped her with her working. He did everything he knew to help her. He always did all the active new things in the house and for the baby. Lena did what she had to do the way she always had been taught it. She always just kept going now with her working, and she was always careless, and dirty, and a little dazed, and lifeless. Lena never got any better in herself of this way of being that she had had ever since she had been married.

Mrs. Haydon never saw any more of her niece, Lena. Mrs. Haydon had now so much trouble with her own house, and her daughters getting married, and her boy, who was growing up, and who always was getting so much worse to manage. She knew she had done right by Lena. Herman Kreder was a good man, she would be glad to get one so good, sometimes, for her own daughters, and now they had a home to live in together, separate from the old people, who had made their trouble for them. Mrs. Haydon felt she had done very well by her niece, Lena, and she never thought now she needed any more to go and see her. Lena would do very well now without her aunt to trouble herself any more about her.

The good german cook who had always scolded, still tried to do her duty like a mother to poor Lena. It was very hard now to do right by Lena. Lena never seemed to hear now what anyone was saying to her. Herman was always doing everything he could to help her. Herman always, when he was home, took good care of the baby. Herman loved to take care of his baby. Lena never thought to take him out or to do anything she didn't have to.

The good cook sometimes made Lena come to see her. Lena would come with her baby and sit there in the kitchen, and watch the good woman cooking, and listen to her sometimes a little, the way she used to, while the good german woman scolded her for going around looking so careless when now she had no trouble, and sitting there so dull, and always being just so thankless. Sometimes Lena would wake up a little and get back into her face her old, gentle, patient, and unsuffering sweetness, but mostly Lena did not seem to hear much when the good german woman scolded. Lena always liked it when Mrs. Aldrich her good mistress spoke to her kindly, and then Lena would seem to go back and feel herself to be like she was when she had been in service. But mostly Lena just lived along and was careless in her clothes, and dull, and lifeless.

By and by Lena had two more little babies. Lena was not so much scared now when she had the babies. She did not seem to notice very much when they hurt her, and she never seemed to feel very much now about anything that happened to her.

They were very nice babies, all these three that Lena had, and Herman took good care of them always. Herman never really cared much about his wife, Lena. The only things Herman ever really cared for were his babies. Herman always was very good to his children. He always had a gentle, tender way when he held them. He learned to be very handy with them. He spent all the time he was not working, with them. By and by he began to work all day in his own home so that he could have his children always in the same room with him.

Lena always was more and more lifeless and Herman now mostly never thought about her. He more and more took all the care of their three children. He saw to their eating right and their washing, and he dressed them every morning, and he taught them the right way to do things, and he put them to their sleeping, and he was now always every minute with them. Then there was to come to them, a fourth baby. Lena went to the hospital near by to have the baby. Lena seemed to be going to have much trouble with it. When the baby was come out at last, it was like its mother lifeless. While it was coming, Lena had grown very pale and sicker. When it was all over Lena had died, too, and nobody knew just how it had happened to her.

The good german cook who had always scolded Lena, and had always to the last day tried to help her, was the only one who ever missed her. She remembered how nice Lena had looked all the time she was in service with her, and how her voice had been so gentle and sweet-sounding, and how she always was a good girl, and how she never had to have any trouble with her, the way she always had with all the other girls who had been taken into the house to help her. The good cook sometimes spoke so of Lena when she had time to have a talk with Mrs. Aldrich, and this was all the remembering there now ever was of Lena.

Herman Kreder now always lived very happy, very gentle, very quiet, very well content alone with his three children. He never had a woman any more to be all the time around him. He always did all his own work in his house, when he was through every day with the work he was always doing for his father. Herman always was alone, and he always worked alone, until his little ones were big enough to help him. Herman Kreder was very well content now and he always lived very regular and peaceful, and with every day just like the next one, always alone now with his three good, gentle children.

1909

Sherwood Anderson   *1876–1941*

In his stories of rural and small-town life, Sherwood Anderson sought to portray what he called "the ugliness of life, the strange beauty of life. . . ." His sketches and tales drew upon his own experiences in the American Midwest at the end of the nineteenth century. He had grown up in the small town of Clyde, Ohio, the original of the fictional Winesburg, Ohio, that was the setting of his most notable work. When he was twenty he left home, drawn to the metropolis of Chicago, where he took a job as a laborer. When the Spanish-American War (1898) gave him the chance to escape the dull routine of day-labor, he enlisted, serving in the army for a year. After the war he returned to Chicago, where he worked as an advertising salesman and began to write his first tales and sketches. In 1907 he moved to Elyria, Ohio, to establish a paint firm, but his literary ambitions soon came into conflict with his duties as a small-town businessman, and in 1913 he abandoned his business, returned once again to Chicago, and at the age of thirty-seven began his life as a writer, asserting, "I will be a servant to words alone."

He wrote Windy McPherson's Son *(1916)* and Marching Men *(1917), novels about successful men who abandoned their own selfish aims to become Populist heroes, helping the "little people." In 1919 he published* Winesburg, Ohio, *his masterpiece, a collection of tales of the "grotesque" characters he had known during his youth in Ohio. Anderson's successful volumes of short stories,* The Triumph of the Egg *(1921),* Horses and Men *(1923), and* Death in the Woods *(1933), contained work of great merit, but his later novels, among them* Many Marriages *(1923),* Dark Laughter *(1925), and* Kit Brandon *(1936), were failures and showed only flashes of the finer qualities of his earlier writing.*

Anderson was preoccupied by a desire to describe the agonies and the failures of the unsuccessful, the deprived, and the inarticulate. His range was narrow, and his idealized perceptions of innocence were sometimes shallow. Yet his sensitive depictions of poverty and eccentricity and his deceptively simple style, with its matter-of-fact midwestern sentences, opened new perspectives for twentieth-century literature. He influenced a wide range of American writers: Hart Crane, Steinbeck, Thomas Wolfe, Hemingway, and William Faulkner who, in 1956, acknowledged Anderson as "the father of my generation of American writers and the tradition of American writing which our successors will carry on."

FURTHER READING: *Letters of Sherwood Anderson,* ed. H. Jones and W. Rideout, 1953; *Sherwood Anderson, Collected Letters,* ed. C. Modlin, 1983; *Sherwood Anderson's Memoirs,* ed. R. White, 1969; J. Schevill, *Sherwood Anderson, His Life and Work,* 1951; I. Howe, *Sherwood Anderson,* 1951, 1966; R. Burbank, *Sherwood Anderson,* 1964; *The Achievement of Sherwood Anderson, Essays in Criticism,* ed. R. White, 1966; D. Anderson, *Sherwood Anderson, An Introduction and Interpretation,* 1967; *Sherwood Anderson, A Collection of Critical Essays,* ed. W. Rideout, 1974; *Critical Essays on Sherwood Anderson,* ed. D. Anderson, 1981.

TEXT: *Death in the Woods and Other Stories,* 1933.

DEATH IN THE WOODS

I

She was an old woman and lived on a farm near the town in which I lived. All country and small-town people have seen such old women, but no one knows much about them. Such an old woman comes into town driving an old worn-out horse or she comes afoot carrying a basket. She may own a few hens and have eggs to sell. She brings them in a basket and takes them to a grocer. There she trades them in. She gets some salt pork and some beans. Then she gets a pound or two of sugar and some flour.

Afterwards she goes to the butcher's and asks for some dog-meat. She may spend ten or fifteen cents, but when she does she asks for something. Formerly the butchers gave liver to any one who wanted to carry it away. In our family we were always having it. Once one of my brothers got a whole cow's liver at the slaughter-house near the fair-grounds in our town. We had it until we were sick of it. It never cost a cent. I have hated the thought of it ever since.

The old farm woman got some liver and a soupbone. She never visited with any one, and as soon as she got what she wanted she lit out for home. It made quite a load for such an old body. No one gave her a lift. People drive right down a road and never notice an old woman like that.

There was such an old woman who used to come into town past our house one Summer and Fall when I was a young boy and was sick with what was called inflammatory rheumatism. She went home later carrying a heavy pack on her back. Two or three large gaunt-looking dogs followed at her heels.

The old woman was nothing special. She was one of the nameless ones that hardly any one knows, but she got into my thoughts. I have just suddenly now, after all these years, remembered her and what happened. It is a story. Her name was Grimes, and she lived with her husband and son in a small unpainted house on the bank of a small creek four miles from town.

The husband and son were a tough lot. Although the son was but twenty-one, he had already served a term in jail. It was whispered about that the woman's husband stole horses and ran them off to some other county. Now and then, when a horse turned up missing, the man had also disappeared. No one ever caught him. Once, when I was loafing at Tom Whitehead's livery-barn, the man came there and sat on the bench in front. Two or three other men were there, but no one spoke to him. He sat for a few minutes and then got up and went away. When he was leaving he turned around and stared at the men. There was a look of defiance in his eyes. "Well, I have tried to be friendly. You don't want to talk to me. It has been so wherever I have gone in this town. If, some day, one of your fine horses turns up missing, well, then what?" He did not say anything actually. "I'd like to bust one of you on the jaw," was about what his eyes said. I remember how the look in his eyes made me shiver.

The old man belonged to a family that had had money once. His name was Jake Grimes. It all comes back clearly now. His father, John Grimes, had owned a sawmill when the country was new, and had made money. Then he got to drinking and running after women. When he died there wasn't much left.

Jake blew in the rest. Pretty soon there wasn't any more lumber to cut and his land was nearly all gone.

He got his wife off a German farmer, for whom he went to work one June day in the wheat harvest. She was a young thing then and scared to death. You see, the farmer was up to something with the girl—she was, I think, a bound girl and his wife had her suspicions. She took it out on the girl when the man wasn't around. Then, when the wife had to go off to town for supplies, the farmer got after her. She told young Jake that nothing really ever happened, but he didn't know whether to believe it or not.

He got her pretty easy himself, the first time he was out with her. He wouldn't have married her if the German farmer hadn't tried to tell him where to get off. He got her to go riding with him in his buggy one night when he was threshing on the place, and then he came for her the next Sunday night.

She managed to get out of the house without her employer's seeing, but when she was getting into the buggy he showed up. It was almost dark, and he just popped up suddenly at the horse's head. He grabbed the horse by the bridle and Jake got out his buggy-whip.

They had it out all right! The German was a tough one. Maybe he didn't care whether his wife knew or not. Jake hit him over the face and shoulders with the buggy-whip, but the horse got to acting up and he had to get out.

Then the two men went for it. The girl didn't see it. The horse started to run away and went nearly a mile down the road before the girl got him stopped. Then she managed to tie him to a tree beside the road. (I wonder how I know all this. It must have stuck in my mind from small-town tales when I was a boy.) Jake found her there after he got through with the German. She was huddled up in the buggy seat, crying, scared to death. She told Jake a lot of stuff, how the German had tried to get her, how he chased her once into the barn, how another time, when they happened to be alone in the house together, he tore her dress open clear down the front. The German, she said, might have got her that time if he hadn't heard his old woman drive in at the gate. She had been off to town for supplies. Well, she would be putting the horse in the barn. The German managed to sneak off to the fields without his wife seeing. He told the girl he would kill her if she told. What could she do? She told a lie about ripping her dress in the barn when she was feeding the stock. I remember now that she was a bound girl and did not know where her father and mother were. Maybe she did not have any father. You know what I mean.

Such bound children were often enough cruelly treated. They were children who had no parents, slaves really. There were very few orphan homes then. They were legally bound into some home. It was a matter of pure luck how it came out.

II

She married Jake and had a son and daughter, but the daughter died.

Then she settled down to feed stock. That was her job. At the German's place she had cooked the food for the German and his wife. The wife was a strong woman with big hips and worked most of the time in the fields with her husband. She fed them and fed the cows in the barn, fed the pigs, the horses and the chickens. Every moment of every day, as a young girl, was spent feeding something.

Then she married Jake Grimes and he had to be fed. She was a slight thing, and when she had been married for three or four years, and after the two children were born, her slender shoulders became stooped.

Jake always had a lot of big dogs around the house, that stood near the unused sawmill near the creek. He was always trading horses when he wasn't stealing something and had a lot of poor bony ones about. Also he kept three or four pigs and a cow. They were all pastured in the few acres left of the Grimes place and Jake did little enough work.

He went into debt for a threshing outfit and ran it for several years, but it did not pay. People did not trust him. They were afraid he would steal the grain at night. He had to go a long way off to get work and it cost too much to get there. In the Winter he hunted and cut a little firewood, to be sold in some nearby town. When the son grew up he was just like the father. They got drunk together. If there wasn't anything to eat in the house when they came home the old man gave his old woman a cut over the head. She had a few chickens of her own and had to kill one of them in a hurry. When they were all killed she wouldn't have any eggs to sell when she went to town, and then what would she do?

She had to scheme all her life about getting things fed, getting the pigs fed so they would grow fat and could be butchered in the Fall. When they were butchered her husband took most of the meat off to town and sold it. If he did not do it first the boy did. They fought sometimes and when they fought the old woman stood aside trembling.

She had got the habit of silence anyway—that was fixed. Sometimes, when she began to look old—she wasn't forty yet—and when the husband and son were both off, trading horses or drinking or hunting or stealing, she went around the house and the barnyard muttering to herself.

How was she going to get everything fed?—that was her problem. The dogs had to be fed. There wasn't enough hay in the barn for the horses and the cow. If she didn't feed the chickens how could they lay eggs? Without eggs to sell how could she get things in town, things she had to have to keep the life of the farm going? Thank heaven, she did not have to feed her husband—in a certain way. That hadn't lasted long after their marriage and after the babies came. Where he went on his long trips she did not know. Sometimes he was gone from home for weeks, and after the boy grew up they went off together.

They left everything at home for her to manage and she had no money. She

knew no one. No one ever talked to her in town. When it was Winter she had
to gather sticks of wood for her fire, had to try to keep the stock fed with very
little grain.

The stock in the barn cried to her hungrily, the dogs followed her about. In
the Winter the hens laid few enough eggs. They huddled in the corners of the
barn and she kept watching them. If a hen lays an egg in the barn in the Winter
and you do not find it, it freezes and breaks.

One day in Winter the old woman went off to town with a few eggs and the
dogs followed her. She did not get started until nearly three o'clock and the
snow was heavy. She hadn't been feeling very well for several days and so she
went muttering along scantily clad, her shoulders stooped. She had an old grain
bag in which she carried her eggs, tucked away down in the bottom. There
weren't many of them, but in Winter the price of eggs is up. She would get a
little meat in exchange for the eggs, some salt pork, a little sugar, and some
coffee perhaps. It might be the butcher would give her a piece of liver.

When she had got to town and was trading in her eggs the dogs lay by the
door outside. She did pretty well, got the things she needed, more than she had
hoped. Then she went to the butcher and he gave her some liver and some dog-
meat.

It was the first time any one had spoken to her in a friendly way for a long
time. The butcher was alone in his shop when she came in and was annoyed by
the thought of such a sick-looking old woman out on such a day. It was bitter
cold and the snow, that had let up during the afternoon, was falling again. The
butcher said something about her husband and her son, swore at them, and the
old woman stared at him, a look of mild surprise in her eyes as he talked. He
said that if either the husband or the son were going to get any of the liver or
the heavy bones with scraps of meat hanging to them that he had put into the
grain bag, he'd see him starve first.

Starve, eh? Well, things had to be fed. Men had to be fed, and the horses that
weren't any good but maybe could be traded off, and the poor thin cow that
hadn't given any milk for three months.

Horses, cows, pigs, dogs, men.

III

The old woman had to get back before darkness came if she could. The dogs
followed at her heels, sniffing at the heavy grain bag she had fastened on her
back. When she got to the edge of town she stopped by a fence and tied the bag
on her back with a piece of rope she had carried in her dress-pocket for just
that purpose. That was an easier way to carry it. Her arms ached. It was hard
when she had to crawl over fences and once she fell over and landed in the
snow. The dogs went frisking about. She had to struggle to get to her feet again,
but she made it. The point of climbing over the fences was that there was a short
cut over a hill and through a woods. She might have gone around by the road,
but it was a mile farther that way. She was afraid she couldn't make it. And then,
besides, the stock had to be fed. There was a little hay left and a little corn.
Perhaps her husband and son would bring some home when they came. They
had driven off in the only buggy the Grimes family had, a rickety thing, a rickety
horse hitched to the buggy, two other rickety horses led by halters. They were
going to trade horses, get a little money if they could. They might come home
drunk. It would be well to have something in the house when they came back.

The son had an affair on with a woman at the county seat, fifteen miles away. She was a rough enough woman, a tough one. Once, in the Summer, the son had brought her to the house. Both she and the son had been drinking. Jake Grimes was away and the son and his woman ordered the old woman about like a servant. She didn't mind much; she was used to it. Whatever happened she never said anything. That was her way of getting along. She had managed that way when she was a young girl at the German's and ever since she had married Jake. That time her son brought his woman to the house they stayed all night, sleeping together just as though they were married. It hadn't shocked the old woman, not much. She had got past being shocked early in life.

With the pack on her back she went painfully along across an open field, wading in the deep snow, and got into the woods.

There was a path, but it was hard to follow. Just beyond the top of the hill, where the woods was thickest, there was a small clearing. Had some one once thought of building a house there? The clearing was as large as a building lot in town, large enough for a house and a garden. The path ran along the side of the clearing, and when she got there the old woman sat down to rest at the foot of a tree.

It was a foolish thing to do. When she got herself placed, the pack against the tree's trunk, it was nice, but what about getting up again? She worried about that for a moment and then quietly closed her eyes.

She must have slept for a time. When you are about so cold you can't get any colder. The afternoon grew a little warmer and the snow came thicker than ever. Then after a time the weather cleared. The moon even came out.

There were four Grimes dogs that had followed Mrs. Grimes into town, all tall gaunt fellows. Such men as Jake Grimes and his son always kept just such dogs. They kick and abuse them, but they stay. The Grimes dogs, in order to keep from starving, had to do a lot of foraging for themselves, and they had been at it while the old woman slept with her back to the tree at the side of the clearing. They had been chasing rabbits in the woods and in adjoining fields and in their ranging had picked up three other farm dogs.

After a time all the dogs came back to the clearing. They were excited about something. Such nights, cold and clear and with a moon, do things to dogs. It may be that some old instinct, come down from the time when they were wolves and ranged the woods in packs on Winter nights, comes back into them.

The dogs in the clearing, before the old woman, had caught two or three rabbits and their immediate hunger had been satisfied. They began to play, running in circles in the clearing. Round and round they ran, each dog's nose at the tail of the next dog. In the clearing, under the snow-laden trees and under the wintry moon they made a strange picture, running thus silently, in a circle their running had beaten in the soft snow. The dogs made no sound. They ran around and around in the circle.

It may have been that the old woman saw them doing that before she died. She may have awakened once or twice and looked at the strange sight with dim old eyes.

She wouldn't be very cold now, just drowsy. Life hangs on a long time. Perhaps the old woman was out of her head. She may have dreamed of her girlhood, at the German's, and before that, when she was a child and before her mother lit out and left her.

Her dreams couldn't have been very pleasant. Not many pleasant things had happened to her. Now and then one of the Grimes dogs left the running circle and came to stand before her. The dog thrust his face close to her face. His red tongue was hanging out.

The running of the dogs may have been a kind of death ceremony. It may have been that the primitive instinct of the wolf, having been aroused in the dogs by the night and the running, made them somehow afraid.

"Now we are no longer wolves. We are dogs, the servants of men. Keep alive, man! When man dies we become wolves again."

When one of the dogs came to where the old woman sat with her back against the tree and thrust his nose close to her face he seemed satisfied and went back to run with the pack. All the Grimes dogs did it at some time during the evening, before she died. I knew all about it afterward, when I grew to be a man, because once in a woods in Illinois, on another Winter night, I saw a pack of dogs act just like that. The dogs were waiting for me to die as they had waited for the old woman that night when I was a child, but when it happened to me I was a young man and had no intention whatever of dying.

The old woman died softly and quietly. When she was dead and when one of the Grimes dogs had come to her and had found her dead all the dogs stopped running.

They gathered about her.

Well, she was dead now. She had fed the Grimes dogs when she was alive, what about now?

There was the pack on her back, the grain bag containing the piece of salt pork, the liver the butcher had given her, the dog-meat, the soup bones. The butcher in town, having been suddenly overcome with a feeling of pity, had loaded her grain bag heavily. It had been a big haul for the old woman.

It was a big haul for the dogs now.

IV

One of the Grimes dogs sprang suddenly out from among the others and began worrying the pack on the old woman's back. Had the dogs really been wolves that one would have been the leader of the pack. What he did, all the others did.

All of them sank their teeth into the grain bag the old woman had fastened with ropes to her back.

They dragged the old woman's body out into the open clearing. The worn-out dress was quickly torn from her shoulders. When she was found, a day or two later, the dress had been torn from her body clear to the hips, but the dogs had not touched her body. They had got the meat out of the grain bag, that was all. Her body was frozen stiff when it was found, and the shoulders were so narrow and the body so slight that in death it looked like the body of some charming young girl.

Such things happened in towns of the Middle West, on farms near town, when I was a boy. A hunter out after rabbits found the old woman's body and did not touch it. Something, the beaten round path in the little snow-covered clearing, the silence of the place, the place where the dogs had worried the body trying to pull the grain bag away or tear it open—something startled the man and he hurried off to town.

I was in Main street with one of my brothers who was town newsboy and who was taking the afternoon papers to the stores. It was almost night.

The hunter came into a grocery and told his story. Then he went to a hardware-shop and into a drugstore. Men began to gather on the sidewalks. Then they started out along the road to the place in the woods.

My brother should have gone on about his business of distributing papers but he didn't. Every one was going to the woods. The undertaker went and the town marshal. Several men got on a dray and rode out to where the path left the road and went into the woods, but the horses weren't very sharply shod and slid about on the slippery roads. They made no better time than those of us who walked.

The town marshal was a large man whose leg had been injured in the Civil War. He carried a heavy cane and limped rapidly along the road. My brother and I followed at his heels, and as we went other men and boys joined the crowd.

It had grown dark by the time we got to where the old woman had left the road but the moon had come out. The marshal was thinking there might have been a murder. He kept asking the hunter questions. The hunter went along with his gun across his shoulders, a dog following at his heels. It isn't often a rabbit hunter has a chance to be so conspicuous. He was taking full advantage of it, leading the procession, with the town marshal. "I didn't see any wounds. She was a beautiful young girl. Her face was buried in the snow. No I didn't know her." As a matter of fact, the hunter had not looked closely at the body. He had been frightened. She might have been murdered and some one might spring out from behind a tree and murder him. In a woods, in the late afternoon, when the trees are all bare and there is white snow on the ground, when all is silent, something creepy steals over the mind and body. If something strange or uncanny has happened in the neighborhood all you think about is getting away from there as fast as you can.

The crowd of men and boys had got to where the old woman had crossed the field and went, following the marshal and the hunter, up the slight incline and into the woods.

My brother and I were silent. He had his bundle of papers in a bag slung across his shoulder. When he got back to town he would have to go on distributing his papers before he went home to supper. If I went along, as he had no doubt already determined I should, we would both be late. Either mother or our older sister would have to warm our supper.

Well, we would have something to tell. A boy did not get such a chance very often. It was lucky we just happened to go into the grocery when the hunter came in. The hunter was a country fellow. Neither of us had ever seen him before.

Now the crowd of men and boys had got to the clearing. Darkness comes quickly on such Winter nights, but the full moon made everything clear. My brother and I stood near the tree, beneath which the old woman had died.

She did not look old, lying there in that light, frozen and still. One of the men turned her over in the snow and I saw everything. My body trembled with some strange mystical feeling and so did my brother's. It might have been the cold.

Neither of us had ever seen a woman's body before. It may have been the snow, clinging to the frozen flesh, that made it look so white and lovely, so like marble. No woman had come with the party from town; but one of the men, he was the town blacksmith, took off his overcoat and spread it over her. Then he gathered her into his arms and started off to town, all the others following silently. At that time no one knew who she was.

V

I had seen everything, had seen the oval in the snow, like a miniature racetrack, where the dogs had run, had seen how the men were mystified, had seen the white bare young-looking shoulders, had heard the whispered comments of the men.

The men were simply mystified. They took the body to the undertaker's, and when the blacksmith, the hunter, the marshal and several others had got inside they closed the door. If father had been there perhaps he could have got in, but we boys couldn't.

I went with my brother to distribute the rest of his papers and when we got home it was my brother who told the story.

I kept silent and went to bed early. It may have been I was not satisfied with the way he told it.

Later, in the town, I must have heard other fragments of the old woman's story. She was recognized the next day and there was an investigation.

The husband and son were found somewhere and brought to town and there was an attempt to connect them with the woman's death, but it did not work. They had perfect enough alibis.

However, the town was against them. They had to get out. Where they went I never heard.

I remember only the picture there in the forest, the men standing about, the naked girlish-looking figure, face down in the snow, the tracks made by the running dogs and the clear cold Winter sky above. White fragments of clouds were drifting across the sky. They went racing across the little open space among the trees.

The scene in the forest had become for me, without my knowing it, the foundation for the real story I am now trying to tell. The fragments, you see, had to be picked up slowly, long afterwards.

Things happened. When I was a young man I worked on the farm of a German. The hired-girl was afraid of her employer. The farmer's wife hated her.

I saw things at that place. Once later, I had a half uncanny, mystical adventure with dogs in an Illinois forest on a clear, moonlit Winter night. When I was a schoolboy, and on a Summer day, I went with a boy friend out along a creek some miles from town and came to the house where the old woman had lived. No one had lived in the house since her death. The doors were broken from the hinges; the window lights were all broken. As the boy and I stood in the road outside, two dogs, just roving farm dogs no doubt, came running around the corner of the house. The dogs were tall, gaunt fellows and came down to the fence and glared through at us, standing in the road.

The whole thing, the story of the old woman's death, was to me as I grew older like music heard from far off. The notes had to be picked up slowly one at a time. Something had to be understood.

The woman who died was one destined to feed animal life. Anyway, that is all she ever did. She was feeding animal life before she was born, as a child, as a young woman working on the farm of the German, after she married, when she grew old and when she died. She fed animal life in cows, in chickens, in pigs, in horses, in dogs, in men. Her daughter had died in childhood and with her one son she had no articulate relations. On the night when she died she was hurrying homeward, bearing on her body food for animal life.

She died in the clearing in the woods and even after her death continued feeding animal life.

You see it is likely that, when my brother told the story, that night when we got home and my mother and sister sat listening, I did not think he got the point. He was too young and so was I. A thing so complete has its own beauty.

I shall not try to emphasize the point. I am only explaining why I was dissatisfied then and have been ever since. I speak of that only that you may understand why I have been impelled to try to tell the simple story over again.

1926, 1933

John Dos Passos   *1896–1970*

In 1917, John Dos Passos called himself "red, radical and revolutionary." Over the next decades he wrote novels, plays, and news stories that attacked capitalism, big business, and big government. Editors of popular journals considered his work too radical to be published in their magazines. He wrote instead for the communist journal New Masses—*but he did so, he later said, not to support communism but because he wanted to give voice to his own "pacifist radical tendency."*

Dos Passos consistently spoke out for the underdog, for the laboring men and women of America, the oppressed, the impoverished. He saw the United States as divided into two nations: those who are well-to-do and those who do without. But by the early 1930s Dos Passos's political views had begun to shift. By 1937 he could write that the Communist Party was "fundamentally opposed to our democracy" and that Marxism was a "reactionary force and an impediment to progress."

As the years passed, Dos Passos seemed to move ever more to the right. He became a contributor to publications in the United States that espoused the conservative cause. His former hatred of business turned to admiration; his defense of organized labor changed to sharp attack. In his last years he supported the American involvement in Vietnam and spoke out against the "hysteria" of those who objected to the war. Dos Passos seemed to be a classic example of the young radical who becomes more and more conservative as he grows older and richer. But from another perspective his entire career may be seen not as a shift from political left to right but as an obstinate defense of the individual against whatever giant impersonal system Dos Passos believed at the time to be most threatening.

Few American writers have attempted to create such a broad picture of the social and political nature of the United States. Dos Passos depicts the nation in its passage through extraordinary events: wars, depressions, political upheavals. And through these events he maintains the same focus: that of a man with a deep concern for his native land. Dos Passos was born in Chicago in 1896, the grandson of an impoverished Portuguese immigrant. His father, a successful corporation lawyer, could provide his son with European travel, send him to fashionable prep schools and then to Harvard. In 1916, after graduating from college, Dos Passos went to Spain to study art and architecture. The next year he left his studies to serve as a volunteer ambulance driver for the Red Cross in France and Italy during the First World War.

When the war ended Dos Passos set out to make his way as a journalist. He became deeply involved with the crucial political and social issues of the day: he reported on the Sacco and Vanzetti case and the Great Depression of the 1930s; he wrote articles on the suffering of exploited peasants in Mexico and described labor battles between large corporations and striking coalminers in Kentucky. For fifty years, from 1920 to 1970, Dos Passos continually wrote on the social and political events that profoundly shaped modern-day America. He was the author of histories, travel books, essays, and a dozen noteworthy novels, beginning with One Man's Initiation *(1917),* Three Soldiers *(1921), and* Manhattan Transfer *(1925).*

His greatest achievement was writing the three novels that make up the trilogy U.S.A.: The 42nd Parallel *(1930),* 1919 *(1932), and* The Big Money *(1936). They were a penetrating depiction of the disillusionment that followed the First World War. Called "collective novels" because they showed men and women in the mass, they presented a vast panorama of American society. Dos Passos portrayed the rapidly shifting scenes and the endless variety of life in America. He used new narrative techniques derived from impressionistic art, from experimental cinema, and from "stream of consciousness" novels that presented the flow of thought in the human mind. He interrupted the narratives with insertions of capsule biographies, "Camera Eyes," and "Newsreels," using "quick-flash" techniques—blending pieces of news stories, song lyrics, and newspaper headlines.*

From his writing a central image emerges: the individual dwarfed by the size and power of society—the common man, the solitary figure battling against what Dos Passos called "the Leviathan State." Dos Passos defined himself as an observer. He attempted to report accurately what he saw, not what ought to be. His view of life was harsh, unsentimental, and critics have called his writing a "fiction of despair." He created a portrait of the nation by describing its ordinary citizens, but he did not assume an inevitable triumph for the common man. He believed that in a world of materialism and conflict no final triumph is possible, that at best a tolerable equilibrium might be maintained, but only with unceasing resistance to all ideas and all powers that would promise to improve the lot of men and women at the cost of their liberties.

FURTHER READING: J. Wrenn, *John Dos Passos*, 1961; R. Davis, *John Dos Passos*, 1962; J. Brantley, *The Fiction of John Dos Passos*, 1968; *Dos Passos, The Critics, and the Writer's Intention*, ed. A. Belkind, 1971; M. Landsberg, *Dos Passos' Path to U.S.A., A Political Biography 1912–1936*, 1972; *Dos Passos, A Collection of Critical Essays*, ed. A Hook, 1974; G. Becker, *John Dos Passos*, 1974; I. Colley, *Dos Passos and the Fiction of Despair*, 1978; L. Wagner, *Dos Passos, Artist as American*, 1979; T. Ludington, *John Dos Passos, A Twentieth-Century Odyssey*, 1980; R. Rosen, *John Dos Passos, Politics and the Writer*, 1981; V. Carr, *Dos Passos, A Life*, 1984; M. Clark, *Dos Passos's Early Fiction*, 1987.

TEXT: *U.S.A.*, 1938.

from *U.S.A.*

PREFACE[1]

The young man walks fast by himself through the crowd that thins into the night streets; feet are tired from hours of walking; eyes greedy for warm curve of faces, answering flicker of eyes, the set of a head, the lift of a shoulder, the way hands spread and clench; blood tingles with wants; mind is a beehive of hopes buzzing and stinging; muscles ache for the knowledge of jobs, for the roadmender's pick and shovel work, the fisherman's knack with a hook when

[1]Published in 1938 as a preface to the three novels, *The 42nd Parallel*, *1919*, and *The Big Money*, collected in the trilogy *U.S.A.*

he hauls on the slithery net from the rail of the lurching trawler, the swing of the bridgeman's arm as he slings down the whitehot rivet, the engineer's slow grip wise on the throttle, the dirtfarmer's use of his whole body when, whoaing the mules, he yanks the plow from the furrow. The young man walks by himself searching through the crowd with greedy eyes, greedy ears taut to hear, by himself, alone.

The streets are empty. People have packed into subways, climbed into street-cars and buses; in the stations they've scampered for suburban trains; they've filtered into lodgings and tenements, gone up in elevators into apartmenthouses. In a showwindow two sallow windowdressers in their shirtsleeves are bringing out a dummy girl in a red evening dress, at a corner welders in masks lean into sheets of blue flame repairing a cartrack, a few drunk bums shamble along, a sad streetwalker fidgets under an arclight. From the river comes the deep rumbling whistle of a steamboat leaving dock. A tug hoots far away.

The young man walks by himself, fast but not fast enough, far but not far enough (faces slide out of sight, talk trails into tattered scraps, footsteps tap fainter in alleys); he must catch the last subway, the streetcar, the bus, run up the gangplanks of all the steamboats, register at all the hotels, work in the cities, answer the wantads, learn the trades, take up the jobs, live in all the boarding-houses, sleep in all the beds. One bed is not enough, one job is not enough, one life is not enough. At night, head swimming with wants, he walks by himself alone.

No job, no woman, no house, no city.

Only the ears busy to catch the speech are not alone; the ears are caught tight, linked tight by the tendrils of phrased words, the turn of a joke, the singsong fade of a story, the gruff fall of a sentence; linking tendrils of speech twine through the city blocks, spread over pavements, grow out along broad parked avenues, speed with the trucks leaving on their long night runs over roaring highways, whisper down sandy byroads past wornout farms, joining up cities and fillingstations, roundhouses, steamboats, planes groping along airways; words call out on mountain pastures, drift slow down rivers widening to the sea and the hushed beaches.

It was not in the long walks through jostling crowds at night that he was less alone, or in the training camp at Allentown, or in the day on the docks at Seattle, or in the empty reek of Washington City hot boyhood summer nights, or in the meal on Market Street,[2] or in the swim off the red rocks at San Diego, or in the bed full of fleas in New Orleans, or in the cold razorwind off the lake, or in the gray faces trembling in the grind of gears in the street under Michigan Avenue,[3] or in the smokers of limited expresstrains, or walking across country, or riding up the dry mountain canyons, or the night without a sleepingbag among frozen beartracks in the Yellowstone, or canoeing Sundays in the Quinnipiac;[4]

but in his mother's words telling about longago, in his father's telling about when I was a boy, in the kidding stories of uncles, in the lies the kids told at school, the hired man's yarns, the tall tales the doughboys told after taps;

it was the speech that clung to the ears, the link that tingled in the blood; U.S.A.

U.S.A. is the slice of a continent. U.S.A. is a group of holding companies, some aggregations of trade unions, a set of laws bound in calf, a radio network, a chain of moving picture theatres, a column of stock-quotations rubbed out and written in by a Western Union boy on a blackboard, a publiclibrary full of

---

[2]In San Francisco.   [3]In Chicago.   [4]River in Connecticut.

old newspapers and dogeared historybooks with protests scrawled on the margins in pencil. U.S.A. is the world's greatest rivervalley fringed with mountains and hills, U.S.A. is a set of bigmouthed officials with too many bankaccounts. U.S.A. is a lot of men buried in their uniforms in Arlington Cemetery.[5] U.S.A. is the letters at the end of an address when you are away from home. But mostly U.S.A. is the speech of the people.

1938

from *THE 42ND PARALLEL*

PROTEUS[1]

Steinmetz[2] was a hunchback,
son of a hunchback lithographer.
   He was born in Breslau in eighteen sixtyfive, graduated with highest honors at seventeen from the Breslau Gymnasium,[3] went to the University of Breslau to study mathematics;
   mathematics to Steinmetz was muscular strength and long walks over the hills and the kiss of a girl in love and big evenings spent swilling beer with your friends;
   on his broken back he felt the topheavy weight of society the way workingmen felt it on their straight backs, the way poor students felt it, was a member of a socialist club, editor of a paper called *The People's Voice.*

   Bismarck[4] was sitting in Berlin like a big paper-weight to keep the new Germany feudal, to hold down the empire for his bosses the Hohenzollerns.[5]
   Steinmetz had to run off to Zurich[6] for fear of going to jail; at Zurich his mathematics woke up all the professors at the Polytechnic;
   but Europe in the eighties was no place for a penniless German student with a broken back and a big head filled with symbolic calculus and wonder about electricity that is mathematics made power and a socialist at that.

   With a Danish friend he sailed for America steerage on an old French line boat *La Champagne,*
   lived in Brooklyn at first and commuted to Yonkers[7] where he had a twelvedollar a week job with Rudolph Eichemeyer[8] who was a German exile from fortyeight an inventor and electrician and owner of a factory where he made hatmaking machinery and electrical generators.
   In Yonkers he [Steinmetz] worked out the theory of the Third Harmonics

---

[5]The National Cemetery, Arlington, Virginia.
[1]In Greek myth, Proteus, an old man of the sea, could alter his shape at will, to escape his enemies.
[2]Karl August Steinmetz (1865–1923), a German engineer and inventor. Forced to flee Germany because of his political views, he came to the United States in 1889 and changed his name to Charles Proteus Steinmetz.
[3]A secondary school that prepares students for entrance into a university.
[4]Otto von Bismarck (1815–1898), German statesman known as the "Iron Chancellor." From 1871 to 1890 he served as the first Chancellor of the newly united Germany.
[5]The royal family that ruled Germany from 1871 to 1918.
[6]In Switzerland.   [7]Near New York City.
[8]Rudolf Eickemeyer (1831–1895), German inventor who came to the United States in 1850, after the failure of the liberal revolution of 1848 in Germany.

and the law of hysteresis which states in a formula the hundredfold relations between the metallic heat, density, frequency when the poles change places in the core of a magnet under an alternating current.

It is Steinmetz's law of hysteresis that makes possible all the transformers that crouch in little boxes and gableroofed houses in all the hightension lines all over everywhere. The mathematical symbols of Steinmetz's law are the patterns of all transformers everywhere.

In eighteen ninetytwo when Eichemeyer sold out to the corporation that was to form General Electric, Steinmetz was entered in the contract along with other valuable apparatus. All his life Steinmetz was a piece of apparatus belonging to General Electric.

First his laboratory was at Lynn, then it was moved and the little hunchback with it to Schenectady, the electric city.

General Electric humored him, let him be a socialist, let him keep a greenhouseful of cactuses lit up by mercury lights, let him have alligators, talking crows and a gila monster for pets and the publicity department talked up the wizard, the medicine man who knew the symbols that opened up the doors of Ali Baba's cave.[9]

Steinmetz jotted a formula on his cuff and next morning a thousand new powerplants had sprung up and the dynamos sang dollars and the silence of the transformers was all dollars,

and the publicity department poured oily stories into the ears of the American public every Sunday and Steinmetz became the little parlor magician,

who made a toy thunderstorm in his laboratory and made all the toy trains run on time and the meat stay cold in the icebox and the lamp in the parlor and the great lighthouses and the searchlights and the revolving beams of light that guide airplanes at night towards Chicago, New York, St. Louis, Los Angeles,

and they let him be a socialist and believe that human society could be improved the way you can improve a dynamo and they let him be pro-German and write a letter offering his services to Lenin[10] because mathematicians are so impractical who make up formulas by which you can build powerplants, factories, subway systems, light, heat, air, sunshine but not human relations that affect the stockholders' money and the directors' salaries.

Steinmetz was a famous magician and he talked to Edison[11] tapping with the Morse code on Edison's knee.
> because Edison was so very deaf
> and he went out West
> to make speeches that nobody understood
> and he talked to Bryan[12] about God on a railroad train
> and all the reporters stood round while he and Einstein
> met face to face,
> but they couldn't catch what they said

---

[9] Ali Baba, in the *Arabian Nights,* used the magic words "open sesame" to open the doors to the treasure cave of the Forty Thieves.

[10] Vladimir Ilych Lenin (1870–1924), Russian revolutionary and founder of Bolshevism.

[11] Thomas Alva Edison (1847–1931), American inventor.

[12] William Jennings Bryan (1860–1925), American political leader and defender of religious fundamentalism.

and Steinmetz was the most valuable piece of apparatus General Electric had

until he wore out and died.

1930

from *1919*

NEWSREEL XLIII

the placards borne by the radicals were taken away from them, their clothing torn and eyes blackened before the service and ex-service men had finished with them

34 Die After Drinking Wood Alcohol   Trains in France May Soon Stop Gerard Throws His Hat into the Ring[1]

SUPREME COURT DASHES LAST HOPE OF MOIST MOUTH[2]

LIFE BOAT CALLED BY ROCKET SIGNALS SEARCHES IN VAIN FOR SIXTEEN HOURS

America I love you
You're like a sweetheart of mine

LES GENS SAGES FUIENT LES REUNIONS POLITIQUES[3]

WALLSTREET CLOSES WEAK: FEARS TIGHT MONEY

From ocean to ocean
For you my devotion
Is touching each boundary line

LITTLE CARUSO EXPECTED[4]

his mother, Mrs. W. D. McGillicudy, said: "My first husband was killed while crossing tracks in front of a train, my second husband was killed in the same way and now it is my son

Just like a little baby
Climbing its mother's knee

[1]James Watson Gerard (1867–1951), American lawyer and Ambassador to Germany, 1913–1917. In 1919 Gerard declared his intention to seek nomination as the Democratic presidential candidate in the national elections of 1920. The Democratic convention chose instead James M. Cox, who was in turn defeated by the Republican candidate, Warren G. Harding.
[2]A reference to the United States Supreme Court decision that upheld the legality of the Volstead Act and the Eighteenth Amendment establishing Prohibition in the United States.
[3]French: Wise people shun political gatherings.
[4]A reference to Gloria Caruso (born December 18, 1919), daughter of Enrico Caruso (1873–1921), Italian operatic tenor.

MACHINEGUNS MOW DOWN MOBS IN KNOXVILLE[5]

America I love you

Aviators Lived for Six Days on Shellfish
    the police compelled the demonstrators to lower these flags and ordered the convention not to exhibit any red emblems save the red in the starry banner of the United States; it may not be indiscreet to state, however, in any case it cannot dim his glory, that General Pershing was confined to his stateroom through seasickness when the message arrived. Old Fellow of 89 Treasures Chewinggum as Precious Souvenir Couldn't Maintain His Serenity In Closing League Debates

And there's a hundred million others like me

1932

THE BODY OF AN AMERICAN[1]

Whereas   theCongressoftheunitedstates   byaconcurrentresolutionadoptedon the4thdayofmarch lastauthorizedthe Secretaryofwar to cause to be brought to theunitedstatesthe body of an Americanwhowasamemberoftheamericanexpedition-aryforcesineurope   wholosthislifeduringtheworldwarandwhoseidentityhas notbeenestablished for burial inthememorialamphitheatreofthe nationalcemeteryat arlingtonvirginia

In the tarpaper morgue at Chalons-sur-Marne[2] in the reek of chloride of lime[3] and the dead, they picked out the pine box that held all that was left of
    enie menie minie moe plenty other pine boxes stacked up there containing what they'd scraped up of Richard Roe
    and other person or persons unknown. Only one can go. How did they pick John Doe?
    Make sure he ain't a dinge,[4] boys,
    make sure he ain't a guinea or a kike,[5]
    how can you tell a guy's a hundredpercent when all you've got's a gunnysack full of bones, bronze buttons stamped with the screaming eagle and a pair of roll puttees?
    . . . and the gagging chloride and the puky dirt-stench of the yearold dead . . .

    The day withal was too meaningful and tragic for applause. Silence, tears, songs and

[5]A reference to the suppression of race riots that occurred in Knoxville, Tennessee, August 31–September 1, 1919.
[1]On March 4, 1921, the United States Congress authorized the burial, in the Arlington National Cemetery, of an unknown American soldier killed in France in the First World War. The burial ceremony took place on Armistice Day, November 11, 1921.
[2]In October, 1921, the bodies of four unknown American soldiers were exhumed from a military cemetery in France and taken to Chalons-sur-Marne, a village east of Paris. There one of the four bodies was selected for burial at Arlington National Cemetary as the Unknown Soldier.
[3]A disinfectant powder.   [4]Slang for "Negro."   [5]Slang for "an Italian or a Jew."

prayer, muffled drums and soft music were the instrumentalities today of national approbation.

John Doe was born (thudding din of blood in love into the shuddering soar of a man and a woman alone indeed together lurching into

and ninemonths sick drowse waking into scared agony and the pain and blood and mess of birth). John Doe was born

and raised in Brooklyn, in Memphis, near the lakefront in Cleveland, Ohio, in the stench of the stockyards in Chi, on Beacon Hill, in an old brick house in Alexandria Virginia, on Telegraph Hill, in a halftimbered Tudor cottage in Portland the city of roses,

in the Lying-In Hospital old Morgan endowed[6] on Stuyvesant Square,

across the railroad tracks, out near the country club, in a shack cabin tenement apartmenthouse exclusive residential suburb;

scion of one of the best families in the social register, won first prize in the baby parade at Coronado Beach, was marbles champion of the Little Rock grammarschools, crack basketball player at the Booneville High, quarterback at the State Reformatory, having saved the sheriff's kid from drowning in the Little Missouri River was invited to Washington to be photographed shaking hands with the President on the White House steps;—

though this was a time of mourning, such an assemblage necessarily has about it a touch of color. In the boxes are seen the court uniforms of foreign diplomats, the gold braid of our own and foreign fleets and armies, the black of the conventional morning dress of American statesmen, the varicolored furs and outdoor wrapping garments of mothers and sisters come to mourn, the drab and blue of soldiers and sailors, the glitter of musical instruments and the white and black of a vested choir

—busboy harveststiff hogcaller boyscout champeen cornshucker of Western Kansas bellhop at the United States Hotel at Saratoga Springs office boy callboy fruiter telephone lineman longshoreman lumberjack plumber's helper,

worked for an exterminating company in Union City, filled pipes in an opium joint in Trenton, N.J.

Y.M.C.A. secretary, express agent, truckdriver, fordmechanic, sold books in Denver Colorado: Madam would you be willing to help a young man work his way through college?

President Harding,[7] with a reverence seemingly more significant because of his high temporal station, concluded his speech:

We are met today to pay the impersonal tribute;
the name of him whose body lies before us took flight with his imperishable soul . . .
as a typical soldier of this representative democracy he fought and died believing in the indisputable justice of his country's cause . . .

by raising his right hand and asking the thousands within the sound of his voice to join in the prayer:

Our Father which art in heaven hallowed be thy name . . .

Naked he went into the army;

[6]In 1897 John Pierpont Morgan (1837–1913), American banking magnate, donated $1,000,000 for the building of a lying-in (maternity) hospital in New York City.
[7]Warren Gamaliel Harding (1865–1923), 29th President of the United States. He spoke at the services for the Unknown Soldier held at Arlington Cemetery, November 11, 1921.

they weighed you, measured you, looked for flat feet, squeezed your penis
to see if you had clap, looked up your anus to see if you had piles, counted your
teeth, made you cough, listened to your heart and lungs, made you read the
letters on the card, charted your urine and your intelligence,
    gave you a service record for a future (imperishable soul)
    and an identification tag stamped with your serial number to hang around
your neck, issued O D[8] regulation equipment, a condiment can and a copy of
the articles of war.
    Atten'SHUN suck in your gut you c——r wipe that smile off your face eyes
right wattja tink dis is a choirch-social? For-war-D'ARCH.
    John Doe.
    and Richard Roe and other person or persons unknown
    drilled hiked, manual of arms, ate slum,[9] learned to salute, to soldier, to
loaf in the latrines, forbidden to smoke on deck, overseas guard duty, forty men
and eight horses,[10] shortarm inspection[11] and the ping of shrapnel and the shrill
bullets combing the air and the sorehead woodpeckers the machineguns mud
cooties[12] gasmasks and the itch.
    Say feller tell me how I can get back to my outfit.

John Doe had a head
for twentyodd years intensely the nerves of the eyes the ears the palate the
tongue the fingers the toes the armpits, the nerves warmfeeling under the skin
charged the coiled brain with hurt sweet warm cold mine must dont sayings
print headlines:
    Thou shalt not the multiplication table long division, Now is the time for
all good men knocks but once at a young man's door, It's a great life if Ish
gebibbel,[13] The first five year'll be the Safety First, Suppose a hun tried to rape
you my country right or wrong, Catch 'em young, What he dont know wont
treat 'em rough, Tell 'em nothing, He got what was coming to him he got his,
This is a white man's country, Kick the bucket, Gone west, If you dont like it
you can croaked him
    Say buddy cant you tell me how I can get back to my outfit?

    Cant help jumpin when them things go off, give me the trots them things
do. I lost my identification tag swimmin in the Marne, roughhousin with a guy
while we was waitin to be deloused, in bed with a girl named Jeanne (Love
moving picture wet French postcard dream began with saltpeter[14] in the coffee
and ended at the propho station[15]);—
    Say soldier for chrissake cant you tell me how I can get back to my outfit?
    John Doe's
heart pumped blood:
alive thudding silence of blood in your ears
    down in the clearing in the Oregon forest where the punkins were punkin-
color pouring into the blood through the eyes and the fallcolored trees and the

---

[8]Olive drab, the color used for military uniforms and equipment.
[9]"Slumgullion," a slang term for "stew."
[10]To show carrying capacity, French railway cars used for transporting troops in World War I were marked "40 hommes, 8 chevaux"—40 men, 8 horses.
[11]Slang term for inspection of genitals for signs of venereal disease.
[12]Lice.   [13]Yiddish: I don't worry.
[14]Potassium nitrate, thought to be capable of depressing sexual appetite.
[15]Short for "prophylactic station," a medical dispensary for treatment and prevention of venereal disease.

bronze hoopers were hopping through the dry grass, where tiny striped snails hung on the underside of the blades and the flies hummed, wasps droned, bumblebees buzzed, and the woods smelt of wine and mushrooms and apples, homey smell of fall pouring into the blood,

and I dropped the tin hat[16] and the sweaty pack and lay flat with the dogday sun licking my throat and adamsapple and the tight skin over the breastbone.

The shell had his number on it.

The blood ran into the ground.

The service record dropped out of the filing cabinet when the quartermaster sergeant got blotto that time they had to pack up and leave the billets in a hurry.
The identification tag was in the bottom of the Marne.

The blood ran into the ground, the brains oozed out of the cracked skull and were licked up by the trenchrats, the belly swelled and raised a generation of bluebottle flies,
and the incorruptible skeleton,
and the scraps of dried viscera and skin bundled in khaki

they took to Chalons-sur-Marne
and laid it out in a pine coffin
and took it home to God's Country on a battleship
and buried it in a sarcophagus in the Memorial Amphitheatre in the Arlington National Cemetery
and draped the Old Glory over it
and the bugler played taps
and Mr. Harding prayed to God and the diplomats and the generals and the admirals and the brasshats and the politicians and the handsomely dressed ladies out of the society column of the *Washington Post* stood up solemn
and thought how beautiful sad Old Glory God's Country it was to have the bugler play taps and the three volleys made their ears ring.

Where his chest ought to have been they pinned
the Congressional Medal, the D.S.C.,[17] the Medaille Militaire, the Belgian Croix de Guerre, the Italian gold medal, the Vitutea Militara sent by Queen Marie of Rumania, the Czechoslovak war cross, the Virtuti Militari of the Poles, a wreath sent by Hamilton Fish, Jr., of New York,[18] and a little wampum presented by a deputation of Arizona redskins in warpaint and feathers. All the Washingtonians brought flowers.

Woodrow Wilson brought a bouquet of poppies.[19]

1932

[16]Military steel helmet.
[17]The Congressional Medal of Honor and the Distinguished Service Cross, American military awards for valor.
[18]Hamilton Fish (b. 1888), United States Congressman and author of the Congressional resolution that established the memorial to the Unknown Soldier.
[19]Woodrow Wilson (1856–1924), 28th President of the United States. In ill health, Wilson rode in a carriage for only a short distance in the funeral procession. In honor of the American war dead, he wore an American Legion memorial poppy in his lapel. He did not attend the ceremonies at Arlington Cemetery.

from *THE BIG MONEY*

NEWSREEL LXVI[1]

HOLMES DENIES STAY[2]

A better world's in birth[3]

Tiny Wasps Imported From Korea In Battle To Death With Asiatic Beetle

BOY CARRIED MILE DOWN SEWER; SHOT OUT ALIVE

CHICAGO BARS MEETINGS[4]

For justice thunders condemnation

Washington Keeps Eye On Radicals

Arise rejected of the earth

PARIS BRUSSELS MOSCOW GENEVA ADD THEIR VOICES

It is the final conflict
Let each stand in his place

Geologist Lost In Cave Six Days

The International Party

SACCO AND VANZETTI MUST DIE

Shall be the human race.

Much I thought of you when I was lying in the death house—the singing, the kind tender voices of the children from the playground where there was all the life and the joy of liberty—just one step from the wall that contains the buried agony of three buried souls.[5] *It would remind me so often of you and of your sister and I wish I could see you every*

[1]"Newsreel LXVI" and "The Camera Eye (50)" refer to the celebrated trial and execution of Nicola Sacco and Bartolomeo Vanzetti, who had been charged with a murder committed in Massachusetts in 1920. Liberal supporters of Sacco and Vanzetti insisted that the two men were innocent of the crime and had been convicted solely because of their unpopular, radical political views.

[2]On August 20, 1927, three days before the execution of Sacco and Vanzetti, Justice Oliver Wendell Holmes of the United States Supreme Court refused to order a "stay" or "halt" to the scheduled execution.

[3]This quotation and the six italicized lines interspersed below are from "The Internationale," the revolutionary song of Communism.

[4]As the execution date approached, protest meetings were held throughout the United States and Europe.

[5]Imprisoned with Sacco and Vanzetti and also awaiting execution was Celestino F. Madeiros, a convicted murderer.

moment, but I feel better that you will not come to the death house so that you could not see the horrible picture of three living in agony waiting to be electrocuted.[6]

1936

THE CAMERA EYE (50)[1]

they have clubbed us off the streets   they are stronger   they are rich   they hire and fire the politicians the newspapereditors the old judges the small men with reputations the collegepresidents the wardheelers (listen businessmen collegepresidents judges   America will not forget her betrayers) they hire the men with guns   the uniforms the policecars the patrolwagons

all right you have won   you will kill the brave men our friends tonight

there is nothing left to do   we are beaten   we the beaten crowd together in these old dingy schoolrooms on Salem Street shuffle up and down the gritty creaking stairs sit hunched with bowed heads on benches and hear the old words of the haters of oppression   made new in sweat and agony tonight

our work is over   the scribbled phrases   the nights typing releases the smell of the printshop the sharp reek of newprinted leaflets the rush for Western Union stringing words into wires the search for stinging words to make you feel who are your oppressors America

America our nation has been beaten by strangers who have turned our language inside out who have taken the clean words our fathers spoke and made them slimy and foul

their hired men sit on the judge's bench they sit back with their feet on the tables under the dome of the State House they are ignorant of our beliefs they have the dollars the guns the armed forces the powerplants

they have built the electricchair and hired the executioner to throw the switch

all right we are two nations

America our nation has been beaten by strangers who have bought the laws and fenced off the meadows and cut down the woods for pulp and turned our pleasant cities into slums and sweated the wealth out of our people and when they want to they hire the executioner to throw the switch

but do they know that the old words of the immigrants are being renewed in blood and agony tonight do they know that the old American speech of the haters of oppression is new tonight in the mouth of an old woman from Pittsburgh of a husky boilermaker from Frisco who hopped freights clear from the Coast to come here in the mouth of a Back Bay[2] socialworker in the mouth of an Italian printer of a hobo from Arkansas   the language of the beaten nation is not forgotten in our ears tonight

the men in the deathhouse made the old words new before they died

If it had not been for these things, I might have lived out my life talking at streetcorners to scorning men. I might have died unknown, unmarked, a failure. This is our career and our triumph. Never in our full life can we hope to do such work for tolerance, for justice, for man's understanding of man as now we do by an accident.[3]

---

[6]A passage taken from a letter written by Nicola Sacco to his son, Dante, August 18, 1927.

[1]In the following passages Dos Passos draws upon his experiences while working for the Sacco and Vanzetti Defense Committee in Boston during the 1920s.

[2]A fashionable residential section of Boston.

[3]A passage from a statement made by Vanzetti after he was sentenced, April 9, 1927.

now their work is over   the immigrants haters of oppression lie quiet in black suits in the little undertaking parlor in the North End the city is quiet   the men of the conquering nation are not to be seen on the streets

they have won why are they scared to be seen on the streets? on the streets you see only the downcast faces of the beaten   the streets belong to the beaten nation   all the way to the cemetery where the bodies of the immigrants are to be burned   we line the curbs in the drizzling rain we crowd the wet sidewalks elbow to elbow silent pale looking with scared eyes at the coffins

we stand defeated America

1936

NEWSREEL LXVIII

WALL STREET STUNNED

This is not Thirty-eight but it's old Ninety-seven
You must put her in Center on time[1]

MARKET SURE TO RECOVER FROM SLUMP

Decline in Contracts

POLICE TURN MACHINE GUNS ON COLORADO MINE STRIKERS
KILL 5 WOUND 40

sympathizers appeared on the scene just as thousands of office workers were pouring out of the buildings at the lunch hour. As they raised their placard high and started an indefinite march from one side to the other, they were jeered and hooted not only by the office workers but also by workmen on a building under construction

NEW METHODS OF SELLING SEEN

Rescue Crews Try To Upend Ill-fated Craft While Waiting for Pontoons

He looked 'round an' said to his black greasy fireman
Jus' shovel in a little more coal
And when we cross that White Oak Mountain
You can watch your Ninety-seven roll

I find your column interesting and need advice. I have saved four thousand dollars which I want to invest for a better income. Do you think I might buy stocks?

[1] Here, and below, Dos Passos inserts verses from a folk song, "The Wreck of the Old 97," about a spectacular train crash in 1903.

POLICE KILLER FLICKS CIGARETTE AS HE
GOES TREMBLING TO DOOM

PLAY AGENCIES IN RING OF SLAVE GIRL MARTS

Maker of Love Disbarred as Lawyer

Oh the right wing clothesmakers[2]
And the Socialist fakers
They make by the workers . . .
Double cross

They preach Social-ism
But practice Fasc-ism
To keep capitalism
By the boss

MOSCOW CONGRESS OUSTS OPPOSITION[3]

It's a mighty rough road from Lynchburg to Danville
An' a line on a three mile grade
It was on that grade he lost his average
An' you see what a jump he made

MILL THUGS IN MURDER RAID

    here is the most dangerous example of how at the decisive moment the bourgeois ideology liquidates class solidarity and turns a friend of the working-class of yesterday into a most miserable propagandist for imperialism today

RED PICKETS FINED FOR PROTEST HERE

We leave our home in the morning
We kiss our children goodby

OFFICIALS STILL HOPE FOR RESCUE OF MEN

He was goin' downgrade makin' ninety miles an hour
When his whistle broke into a scream
He was found in the wreck with his hand on the throttle
An' was scalded to death with the steam

RADICALS FIGHT WITH CHAIRS AT UNITY MEETING

[2]Here, and below, Dos Passos inserts verses from a workers' protest song.
[3]On December 18, 1927, at the Fifteenth Congress of the Communist Party, held in Moscow, the "Oppositionist" faction of the party was expelled from membership. The move firmly established Joseph Stalin's complete control over Soviet Russia and the Communist Party.

PATROLMEN PROTECT REDS

U.S. CHAMBER OF COMMERCE URGES CONFIDENCE

REAL VALUES UNHARMED

While we slave for the bosses
Our children scream an' cry
But when we draw our money
Our grocery bills to pay

PRESIDENT SEES PROSPERITY NEAR

Not a cent to spend for clothing
Not a cent to lay away

STEAMROLLER IN ACTION AGAINST MILITANTS

MINERS BATTLE SCABS

But we cannot buy for our children
Our wages are too low
Now listen to me you workers
Both you women and men
Let us win for them the victory
I'm sure it ain't no sin

CARILLON PEALS IN SINGING TOWER[4]

the President declared it was impossible to view the increased advantages for the many without smiling at those who a short time ago expressed so much fear lest our country might come under the control of a few individuals of great wealth

HAPPY CROWDS THRONG CEREMONY

on a tiny island nestling like a green jewel in the lake that mirrors the singing tower, the President today participated in the dedication of a bird sanctuary and its pealing carillon, fulfilling the dream of an immigrant boy.

VAG[1]

The young man waits at the edge of the concrete, with one hand he grips a rubbed suitcase of phony leather, the other hand almost making a fist, thumb up

---

[4]A bell tower built in a Florida wildlife sanctuary by the Dutch-born American philanthropist Edward Bok (1863–1930). President Calvin Coolidge spoke at the dedication ceremonies, February 1, 1929.
[1]Slang for "vagrant," "vagabond." This section is the conclusion of *U.S.A.*

that moves in ever so slight an arc when a car slithers past, a truck roars clatters; the wind of cars passing ruffles his hair, slaps grit in his face.

Head swims, hunger has twisted the belly tight,

he has skinned a heel through the torn sock, feet ache in the broken shoes, under the threadbare suit carefully brushed off with the hand, the torn drawers have a crummy feel, the feel of having slept in your clothes; in the nostrils lingers the staleness of discouraged carcasses crowded into a transient camp, the carbolic stench of the jail, on the taut cheeks the shamed flush from the boring eyes of cops and deputies, railroadbulls (they eat three squares a day, they are buttoned into wellmade clothes, they have wives to sleep with, kids to play with after supper, they work for the big men who buy their way, they stick their chests out with the sureness of power behind their backs). Git the hell out, scram. Know what's good for you, you'll make yourself scarce. Gittin' tough, eh? Think you kin take it, eh?

The punch in the jaw, the slam on the head with the nightstick, the wrist grabbed and twisted behind the back, the big knee brought up sharp into the crotch,

the walk out of town with sore feet to stand and wait at the edge of the hissing speeding string of cars where the reek of ether and lead and gas melts into the silent grassy smell of the earth.

Eyes black with want seek out the eyes of the drivers, a hitch, a hundred miles down the road.

Overhead in the blue a plane drones. Eyes follow the silver Douglas that flashes once in the sun and bores its smooth way out of sight into the blue.

(The transcontinental passengers sit pretty, big men with bankaccounts, highlypaid jobs, who are saluted by doormen; telephonegirls say goodmorning to them. Last night after a fine dinner, drinks with friends, they left Newark. Roar of climbing motors slanting up into the inky haze. Lights drop away. An hour staring along a silvery wing at a big lonesome moon hurrying west through curdling scum. Beacons flash in a line across Ohio.

At Cleveland the plane drops banking in a smooth spiral, the string of lights along the lake swings in a circle. Climbing roar of the motors again; slumped in the soft seat drowsing through the flat moonlight night.

Chi. A glimpse of the dipper. Another spiral swoop from cool into hot air thick with dust and the reek of burnt prairies.

Beyond the Mississippi dawn creeps up behind through the murk over the great plains. Puddles of mist go white in the Iowa hills, farms, fences, silos, steel glint from a river. The blinking eyes of the beacons reddening into day. Watercourses vein the eroded hills.

Omaha. Great cumulus clouds, from coppery churning to creamy to silvery white, trail brown skirts of rain over the hot plains. Red and yellow badlands, tiny horned shapes of cattle.

Cheyenne. The cool high air smells of sweetgrass.

The tightbaled clouds to westward burst and scatter in tatters over the strawcolored hills. Indigo mountains jut rimrock. The plane breasts a huge crumbling cloudbank and toboggans over bumpy air across green and crimson slopes into the sunny dazzle of Salt Lake.

The transcontinental passenger thinks contracts, profits, vacationtrips, mighty continent between Atlantic and Pacific, power, wires humming dollars, cities jammed, hills empty, the indiantrail leading into the wagonroad, the macadamed pike, the concrete skyway; trains, planes; history the billiondollar speedup,

and in the bumpy air over the desert ranges towards Las Vegas sickens and vomits into the carton container the steak and mushrooms he ate in New York. No matter, silver in the pocket, greenbacks in the wallet, drafts, certified checks, plenty restaurants in L.A.)

The young man waits on the side of the road; the plane has gone; thumb moves in a small arc when a car tears hissing past. Eyes seek the driver's eyes. A hundred miles down the road. Head swims, belly tightens, wants crawl over his skin like ants:

went to school, books said opportunity, ads promised speed, own your home, shine bigger than your neighbor, the radiocrooner whispered girls, ghosts of platinum girls coaxed from the screen, millions in winnings were chalked up on the boards in the offices, paychecks were for hands willing to work, the cleared desk of an executive with three telephones on it;

waits with swimming head, needs knot the belly, idle hands numb, beside the speeding traffic.

A hundred miles down the road.

1936, 1938

Ring Lardner *1885–1933*

Like Mark Twain, Ring Lardner belongs to that group of American writers who came to literature by way of journalism. And like Twain, he often used comedy and humor to present a scathing view of Americans and American life. Lardner was born Ringgold Wilmer Lardner in Niles, Michigan. His father was rich, the town's leading citizen; his lively, talented mother wrote plays, stories, and poems. The ninth and youngest child in the family, Ring Lardner was indulged and protected in his childhood. Born with a deformed foot (later corrected by surgery), he wore a leg brace until he was eleven, and for the first twelve years of his life he was schooled at home by his mother and a tutor. Later in life he acknowledged that after he finally entered public school he did most of his "studying" at the billiard table.

Lardner graduated from high school at sixteen, but he had little interest in going to college. After a misspent year training to become a mechanical engineer, he worked at odd jobs or "rested" from the exertion of his engineering studies. In 1905 he got a job as a reporter for the South Bend, Indiana, Times *and began to see a world that was rarely as benign and comforting as his own childhood had been. Within three years he became a sports writer for the Chicago* Examiner *and eventually a sports columnist for the Chicago* Tribune.

Working for a big-city newspaper brought Lardner into contact with the professional athletes and with the vernacular American speech he later presented in the stories that first earned him nationwide popularity. In 1914 he published a series of six stories in the Saturday Evening Post *describing the life and attitudes of a bush-league baseball player. Two years later the stories were issued in a single volume under the title* You Know Me, Al *(1916). It was the first of many collections of Lardner's short fiction that would be published over the next twenty years. But in spite of his successes, Lardner disparaged his reputation as a literary artist and called himself a journalist. Yet his work covered a far wider range than just journalism. In addition to newspaper articles and short stories he wrote song lyrics, movie scenarios, verse, and essays. In 1917 he served briefly as a war* correspondent in France for Collier's *magazine. He wrote skits for Broadway shows and a self-mocking autobiography,* The Story of a Wonder Man *(1927). Eventually he wrote more than twenty volumes, but most notable were two collections of his short stories,* How to Write Short Stories *(1924) and* The Love Nest *(1926).*

It has been said that Lardner's mordant short stories picture a world populated only by "mental sadists, four-flushers, intolerable gossipers, meal-ticket females, interfering morons, brainless flirts, liars, brutes, spiteful snobs, vulgar climbers; dishonest jockeys, selfish children" and worse. His characters frequently inhabit a drab and commonplace world; they seldom learn, often suffer, and rarely see themselves for what they are. Lardner so well portrayed shallow-brained men and women, meddling in each other's lives, and the squabbling of couples amid their ruined marriages that one critic named him "the epic recorder of the Great American Bicker."

Lardner has also earned praise for his ability to portray the vernacular speech of Americans. Unlike the local color writers who preceded him, Lardner described the speech not of America's geographical regions but of America's character types: business men, housewives, professional athletes, predatory females seeking the dubious joys of marriage, self-deluded young men—all of whom unwittingly reveal themselves in the words they speak and the letters they write.

Lardner's writing brought him fame and money, but he never escaped from the cynicism and the fundamental distrust of humankind that was a basis for his satiric power. He was a persistent misanthrope whose social criticism rose from disgust at the false values he perceived in modern life. His writing lacked the epic quality, the breadth and power of the work of Melville or Twain, but like them he gave clear expression to a deep pessimism about the fate of mankind, and he had a distinctly American perception of the ugliness beneath the surface of life, the gloom behind the laughter, the failure that seems always to overhaul success.

FURTHER READING: *Ring Around Max: The Correspondence of Ring Lardner and Max Perkins,* 1973; *Letters from Ring,* ed. C. Caruthers, 1979; R. Lardner, Jr., *The Lardners, My Family Remembered,* 1977; D. Elder, *Ring Lardner, A Biography,* 1956; O. Friedrich, *Ring Lardner,* 1965; W. Patrick, *Ring Lardner,* 1963; M. Geismar, *Ring Lardner and the Portrait of Folly,* 1972; J. Yardley, *Ring, A Biography of Ring Lardner,* 1977; E. Evans, *Ring Lardner,* 1979.
TEXT: *How to Write Short Stories,* 1924.

SOME LIKE THEM COLD

N.Y., Aug. 3.

DEAR MISS GILLESPIE: How about our bet now as you bet me I would forget all about you the minute I hit the big town and would never write you a letter. Well girlie it looks like you lose so pay me. Seriously we will call all bets off as I am not the kind that bet on a sure thing and it sure was a sure thing that I would not forget a girlie like you and all that is worrying me is whether it may not be the other way round and you are wondering who this fresh guy is that is writeing you this letter. I bet you are so will try and refreshen your memory.

Well girlie I am the handsome young man that was wondering round the Lasalle st. station[1] Monday and "happened" to sit down beside of a mighty pretty girlie who was waiting to meet her sister from Toledo and the train was late and I am glad of it because if it had not of been that little girlie and I would never

---

[1]Railroad station in Chicago, Illinois.

of met. So for once I was a lucky guy but still I guess it was time I had some luck as it was certainly tough luck for you and I to both be liveing in Chi all that time and never get together till a half hour before I was leaveing town for good.

Still "better late than never" you know and maybe we can make up for lost time though it looks like we would have to do our makeing up at long distants unless you make good on your threat and come to N.Y. I wish you would do that little thing girlie as it looks like that was the only way we would get a chance to play round together as it looks like they was little or no chance of me comeing back to Chi as my whole future is in the big town. N.Y. is the only spot and specially for a man that expects to make my liveing in the song writeing game as her is the Mecca for that line of work and no matter how good a man may be they don't get no recognition unless they live in N.Y.

Well girlie you asked me to tell you all about my trip. Well I remember you saying that you would give anything to be makeing it yourself but as far as the trip itself was conserned you ought to be thankful you did not have to make it as you would of sweat your head off. I know I did specially wile going through Ind. Monday P.M. but Monday night was the worst of all trying to sleep and finely I give it up and just layed there with the prespiration rolling off me though I was laying on top of the covers and nothing on but my underwear.

Yesterday was not so bad as it rained most of the A.M. comeing through N.Y. state and in the P.M. we road along side of the Hudson all P.M. Some river girlie and just looking at it makes a man forget all about the heat and everything else except a certain girlie who I seen for the first time Monday and then only for a half hour but she is the kind of a girlie that a man don't need to see her only once and they would be no danger of forgetting her. There I guess I better lay off that subject or you will think I am a "fresh guy."

Well that is about all to tell you about the trip only they was one amuseing incidence that come off yesterday which I will tell you. Well they was a dame got on the train at Toledo Monday and had the birth opp. mine but I did not see nothing of her that night as I was out smoking till late and she hit the hay early but yesterday A.M. she come in the dinner and sit at the same table with me and tried to make me and it was so raw that the dinge waiter seen it and give me the wink and of course I paid no tension and I waited till she got through so as they would be no danger of her folling me out but she stopped on the way out to get a tooth pick and when I come out she was out on the platform with it so I tried to brush right by but she spoke up and asked me what time it was and I told her and she said she guessed her watch was slow so I said maybe it just seemed slow on acct. of the company it was in.

I don't know if she got what I was driveing at or not but any way she give up trying to make me and got off at Albany. She was a good looker but I have no time for gals that tries to make strangers on a train.

Well if I don't quit you will think I am writeing a book but will expect a long letter in answer to this letter and we will see if you can keep your promise like I have kept mine. Don't disapoint me girlie as I am all alone in a large city and hearing from you will keep me from getting home sick for old Chi though I never thought so much of the old town till I found out you lived there. Don't think that is kidding girlie as I mean it.

You can address me at this hotel as it looks like I will be here right along as it is on 47th st. right off of old Broadway and handy to everything and am only paying $21 per wk, for my rm. and could of got one for $16 but without bath but am glad to pay the differents as am lost without my bath in the A.M. and sometimes at night too.

Tomorrow I expect to commence fighting the "battle of Broadway" and will let you know how I come out that is if you answer this letter. In the mean wile girlie au reservoir and don't do nothing I would not do.

Your new friend (?)

CHAS. F. LEWIS.

Chicago, Ill., Aug. 6

MY DEAR MR. LEWIS: Well, that certainly was a "surprise party" getting your letter and you are certainly a "wonder man" to keep your word as I am afraid most men of your sex are gay deceivers but maybe you are "different." Any way it sure was a surprise and will gladly pay the bet if you will just tell me what it was we bet. Hope it was not money as I am a "working girl" but if it was not more than a dollar or two will try to dig it up even if I have to "beg, borrow or steal."

Suppose you will think me a "case" to make a bet and then forget what it was, but you must remember, Mr. Man, that I had just met you and was "dazzled." Joking aside I was rather "fussed" and will tell you why. Well, Mr. Lewis, I suppose you see lots of girls like the one you told me about that you saw on the train who tried to "get acquainted" but I want to assure you that I am not one of those kind and sincerely hope you will believe me when I tell you that you was the first man I ever spoke to meeting them like that and my friends and the people who know me would simply faint if they knew I ever spoke to a man without a "proper introduction."

Believe me, Mr. Lewis, I am not that kind and I don't know now why I did it only that you was so "different" looking if you know what I mean and not at all like the kind of men that usually try to force their attentions on every pretty girl they see. Lots of times I act on impulse and let my feelings run away from me and sometimes I do things on the impulse of the moment which I regret them later on, and that is what I did this time, but hope you won't give me cause to regret it and I know you won't as I know you are not that kind of a man a specially after what you told me about the girl on the train. But any way as I say, I was in a "daze" so can't remember what it was we bet, but will try and pay it if it does not "break" me.

Sis's train got in about ten minutes after yours had gone and when she saw me what do you think was the first thing she said? Well, Mr. Lewis, she said: "Why Mibs (That is a pet name some of my friends have given me) what has happened to you? I never seen you have as much color." So I passed it off with some remark about the heat and changed the subject as I certainly was not going to tell her that I had just been talking to a man who I had never met or she would of dropped dead from the shock. Either that or she would not of believed me as it would be hard for a person who knows me well to imagine me doing a thing like that as I have quite a reputation for "squelching" men who try to act fresh. I don't mean anything personal by that, Mr. Lewis, as am a good judge of character and could tell without you telling me that you are not that kind.

Well, Sis and I have been on the "go" ever since she arrived as I took yesterday and today off so I could show her the "sights" though she says she would be perfectly satisfied to just sit in the apartment and listen to me "rattle on." Am afraid I am a great talker, Mr. Lewis, but Sis says it is as good as a show to hear me talk as I tell things in such a different way as I cannot help from seeing the humorous side of everything and she says she never gets tired of listening to me, but of course she is my sister and thinks the world of me, but she really does laugh like she enjoyed my craziness.

Maybe I told you that I have a tiny little apartment which a girl friend of mine and I have together and it is hardly big enough to turn round in, but still it is "home" and I am a great home girl and hardly ever care to go out evenings except occasionally to the theatre or dance. But even if our "nest" is small we are proud of it and Sis complimented us on how cozy it is and how "homey" it looks and she said she did not see how we could afford to have everything so nice and Edith (my girl friend) said: "Mibs deserves all the credit for that. I never knew a girl who could make a little money go a long ways like she can." Well, of course she is my best friend and always saying nice things about me, but I do try and I hope I get results. Have always said that good taste and being careful is a whole lot more important than lots of money though it is nice to have it.

You must write and tell me how you are getting along in the "battle of Broadway" (I laughed when I read that) and whether the publishers like your songs though I know they will. Am crazy to hear them and hear you play the piano as I love good jazz music even better than classical, though I suppose it is terrible to say such a thing. But I usually say just what I think though sometimes I wish afterwards I had not of. But still I believe it is better for a girl to be her own self and natural instead of always acting. But am afraid I will never have a chance to hear you play unless you come back to Chi and pay us a visit as my "threat" to come to New York was just a "threat" and I don't see any hope of ever getting there unless some rich New Yorker should fall in love with me and take me there to live. Fine chance for poor little me, eh Mr. Lewis?

Well, I guess I have "rattled on" long enough and you will think I am writing a book unless I quit and besides, Sis has asked me as a special favor to make her a pie for dinner. Maybe you don't know it, Mr. Man, but I am quite famous for my pie and pastry, but I don't suppose a "genius" is interested in common things like that.

Well, be sure and write soon and tell me what N.Y. is like and all about it and don't forget the little girlie who was "bad" and spoke to a strange man in the station and have been blushing over it ever since.

Your friend(?)

MAYBELLE GILLESPIE.

N.Y., Aug. 10.

DEAR GIRLIE: I bet you will think I am a fresh guy commenceing that way but Miss Gillespie is too cold and a man can not do nothing cold in this kind of weather specially in this man's town which is the hottest place I ever been in and I guess maybe the reason why New Yorkers is so bad is because they think they are all ready in H—— and can not go no worse place no matter how they behave themselves. Honest girlie I certainly envy you being where there is a breeze off the old Lake and Chi may be dirty but I never heard of nobody dying because they was dirty but four people died here yesterday on acct. of the heat and I seen two different women flop right on Broadway and had to be taken away in the ambulance and it could not of been because they was dressed too warm because it would be impossible for the women here to leave off any more cloths.

Well have not had much luck yet in the battle of Broadway as all the heads of the big music publishers is out of town on their vacation and the big boys is the only ones I will do business with as it would be silly for a man with the stuff I have got to waste my time on somebody that is just on the staff and have not got the final say. But I did play a couple of my numbers for the people up to

Levy's and Goebel's and they went crazy over them in both places. So it looks like all I have to do is wait for the big boys to get back and then play my numbers for them and I will be all set. What I want is to get taken on the staff of one of the big firms as that gives a man the inside and they will plug your numbers more if you are on the staff. In the mean wile have not got nothing to worry me but am just seeing the sights of the big town as have saved up enough money to play round for a wile and any way a man that can play piano like I can don't never have to worry about starveing. Can certainly make the old music box talk girlie and am always good for a $75 or $100 job.

Well have been here a week now and on the go every minute and I thought I would be lonesome down here but no chance of that as I have been treated fine by the people I have met and have sure met a bunch of them. One of the boys living in the hotel is a vaudeville actor and he is a member of the Friars club[2] and took me over there to dinner the other night and some way another the bunch got wise that I could play piano so of course I had to sit down and give them some of my numbers and everybody went crazy over them. One of the boys I met there was Paul Sears the song writer but he just writes the lyrics and has wrote a bunch of hits and when he heard some of my melodies he called me over to one side and said he would like to work with me on some numbers. How is that girlie as he is one of the biggest hit writers in N.Y.

N.Y. has got some mighty pretty girlies and I guess it would not be hard to get acquainted with them and in fact several of them has tried to make me since I been here but I always figure that a girl must be something wrong with her if she tries to make a man that she don't know nothing about so I pass them all up. But I did meet a couple of pips that a man here in the hotel went up on Riverside Drive to see them and insisted on me going along and they got on some way that I could make a piano talk so they was nothing but I must play for them so I sit down and played some of my own stuff and they went crazy over it.

One of the girls wanted I should come up and see her again, and I said I might but I think I better keep away as she acted like she wanted to vamp[3] me and I am not the kind that likes to play round with a gal just for their company and dance with them etc. but when I see the right gal that will be a different thing and she won't have to beg me to come and see her as I will camp right on her trail till she says yes. And it won't be none of these N.Y. fly by nights neither. They are all right to look at but a man would be a sucker to get serious with them as they might take you up and next thing you know you would have a wife on your hands that don't know a dish rag from a waffle iron.

Well girlie will quit and call it a day as it is too hot to write any more and I guess I will turn on the cold water and lay in the tub a wile and then turn in. Don't forget to write to

Your friend,

CHAS. F. LEWIS.

Chicago, Ill., Aug. 13

DEAR MR. MAN: Hope you won't think me a "silly Billy" for starting my letter that way but "Mr. Lewis" is so formal and "Charles" is too much the other way and any way I would not dare call a man by their first name after only knowing them only two weeks. Though I may as well confess that Charles is my favorite

---

[2] A social club for members of the theatrical profession.
[3] Tempt, seduce.

name for a man and have always been crazy about it as it was my father's name. Poor old dad, he died of cancer three years ago, but left enough insurance so that mother and we girls were well provided for and do not have to do anything to support ourselves though I have been earning my own living for two years to make things easier for mother and also because I simply can't bear to be doing nothing as I feel like a "drone." So I flew away from the "home nest" though mother felt bad about it as I was her favorite and she always said I was such a comfort to her as when I was in the house she never had to worry about how things would go.

But there I go gossiping about my domestic affairs just like you would be interested in them though I don't see how you could be though personaly I always like to know all about my friends, but I know men are different so will try and not bore you any longer. Poor Man, I certainly feel sorry for you if New York is as hot as all that. I guess it has been very hot in Chi, too, at least everybody has been complaining about how terrible it is. Suppose you will wonder why I say "I guess" and you will think I ought to know if it is hot. Well, sir, the reason I say "I guess" is because I don't feel the heat like others do or at least I don't let myself feel it. That sounds crazy I know, but don't you think there is a good deal in mental suggestion and not letting yourself feel things? I believe that if a person simply won't allow themselves to be affected by disagreeable things, why such things won't bother them near as much. I know it works with me and that is the reason why I am never cross when things go wrong and "keep smiling" no matter what happens and as far as the heat is concerned, why I just don't let myself feel it and my friends say I don't even look hot no matter if the weather is boiling and Edith, my girl friend, often says that I am like a breeze and it cools her off just to have me come in the room. Poor Edie suffers terribly during the hot weather and says it almost makes her mad at me to see how cool and unruffled I look when everybody else is perspiring and have red faces etc.

I laughed when I read what you said about New York being so hot that people thought it was the "other place." I can appreciate a joke, Mr. Man, and that one did not go "over my head." Am still laughing at some of the things you said in the station though they probably struck me funnier than they would most girls as I always see the funny side and sometimes something is said and I laugh and the others wonder what I am laughing at as they cannot see anything in it themselves, but it is just the way I look at things so of course I cannot explain to them why I laughed and they think I am crazy. But I had rather part with almost anything rather than my sense of humour as it helps me over a great many rough spots.

Sis has gone back home though I would of liked to of kept her here much longer, but she had to go though she said she would of liked nothing better than to stay with me and just listen to me "rattle on." She always says it is just like a show to hear me talk as I always put things in such a funny way and for weeks after she has been visiting me she thinks of some of the things I said and laughs over them. Since she left Edith and I have been pretty quiet though poor Edie wants to be on the "go" all the time and tries to make me go out with her every evening to the pictures and scolds me when I say I had rather stay home and read and calls me a "book worm." Well, it is true that I had rather stay home with a good book than go to some crazy old picture and the last two nights I have been reading myself to sleep with Robert W. Service's poems.[4] Don't you love Service or don't you care for "highbrow" writings?

[4]Canadian versifier (1874–1958). His most famous work was "The Shooting of Dan McGrew."

Personly there is nothing I love more than to just sit and read a good book or sit and listen to somebody play the piano, I mean if they can really play and I really believe I like popular music better than the classical though I suppose that is a terrible thing to confess, but I love all kinds of music but a specially the piano when it is played by somebody who can really play.

Am glad you have not "fallen" for the "ladies" who have tried to make your acquaintance in New York. You are right in thinking there must be something wrong with girls who try to "pick up" strange men as no girl with self respect would do such a thing and when I say that, Mr. Man, I know you will think it is a funny thing for me to say on account of the way our friendship started, but I mean it and I assure you that was the first time I ever done such a thing in my life and would never of thought of doing it had I not known you were the right kind of a man as I flatter myself that I am a good judge of character and can tell pretty well what a person is like by just looking at them and I assure you I had made up my mind what kind of a man you were before I allowed myself to answer your opening remark. Otherwise I am the last girl in the world that would allow myself to speak to a person without being introduced to them.

When you write again you must tell me all about the girl on Riverside Drive and what she looks like and if you went to see her again and all about her. Suppose you will think I am a little old "curiosity shop" for asking all those questions and will wonder why I want to know. Well, sir, I won't tell you why, so there, but I insist on you answering all questions and will scold you if you don't. Maybe you will think that the reason why I am so curious is because I am "jealous" of the lady in question. Well, sir, I won't tell you whether I am or not, but will keep you "guessing." Now, don't you wish you knew?

Must close or you will think I am going to "rattle on" forever or maybe you have all ready become disgusted and torn my letter up. If so all I can say is poor little me—she was a nice little girl and meant well, but the man did not appreciate her.

There! Will stop or you will think I am crazy if you do not all ready.

Yours (?)

MAYBELLE.

N.Y., Aug. 20.

DEAR GIRLIE: Well girlie I suppose you thought I was never going to answer your letter but have been busier than a one armed paper hanger the last week as have been working on a number with Paul Sears who is one of the best lyric writers in N.Y. and has turned out as many hits as Berlin or Davis[5] or any of them. And believe me girlie he has turned out another hit this time that is he and I have done it together. It is all done now and we are just waiting for the best chance to place it but will not place it nowheres unless we get the right kind of a deal but maybe will publish it ourselves.

The song is bound to go over big as Sears has wrote a great lyric and I have give it a great tune or at least every body that has heard it goes crazy over it and it looks like it would go over bigger than any song since Mammy[6] and would not be surprised to see it come out the hit of the year. If it is handled right we will make a bbl. of money and Sears says it is a cinch we will clean up as much as $25000 apiece which is pretty fair for one song but this one is not like the most of them but has got a great lyric and I have wrote a melody that will knock

---

[5]Irving Berlin (b. 1888) and Benny Davis (b. 1895), American popular song writers.
[6]"My Mammy," popular song of the 1920s.

them out of their seats. I only wish you could hear it girlie and hear it the way I play it. I had to play it over and over about 50 times at the Friars last night.

I will copy down the lyric of the chorus so you can see what it is like and get the idea of the song though of course you can't tell much about it unless you hear it played and sang. The title of the song is When They're Like You and here is the chorus:

> "Some like them hot, some like them cold.
> Some like them when they're not too darn old.
> Some like them fat, some like them lean.
> Some like them only at sweet sixteen.
> Some like them dark, some like them light.
> Some like them in the park, late at night.
> Some like them fickle, some like them true,
> But the time I like them is when they're like you."

How is that for a lyric and I only wish I could play my melody for you as you would go nuts over it but will send you a copy as soon as the song is published and you can get some of your friends to play it over for you and I know you will like it though it is a different melody when I play it or when somebody else plays it.

Well girlie you will see how busy I have been and am libel to keep right on being busy as we are not going to let the grass grow under our feet but as soon as we have got this number placed we will get busy on another one as a couple like that will put me on Easy st. even if they don't go as big as we expect but even 25 grand is a big bunch of money and if a man could only turn out one hit a year and make that much out of it I would be on Easy st. and no more hammering on the old music box in some cabaret.

Who ever we take the song to we will make them come across with one grand for advance royaltys and that will keep me going till I can turn out another one. So the future looks bright and rosey to yours truly and I am certainly glad I come to the big town though sorry I did not do it a whole lot quicker.

This is a great old town girlie and when you have lived her a wile you wonder how you ever stood for a burg like Chi which is just a hick town along side of this besides being dirty etc. and a man is a sucker to stay there all their life specially a man in my line of work as N.Y. is the Mecca for a man that has got the musical gift. I figure that all the time I spent in Chi I was just wasteing my time and never really started to live till I come down here and I have to laugh when I think of the boys out there that is trying to make a liveing in the song writeing game and most of them starve to death all their life and the first week I am down here I meet a man like Sears and the next thing you know we have turned out a song that will make us a fortune.

Well girlie you asked me to tell you about the girlie up on the Drive that tried to make me and asked me to come and see her again. Well I can assure you you have no reasons to be jealous in that quarter as I have not been back to see her as I figure it is wasteing my time to play round with a dame like she that wants to go out somewheres every night and if you married her she would want a house on 5th ave. with a dozen servants so I have passed her up as that is not my idea of home.

What I want when I get married is a real home where a man can stay home and work and maybe have a few of his friends in once in a wile and entertain them or go to a good musical show once in a wile and have a wife that is in sympathy with you and not nag at you all the wile but be a real help mate. The girlie up on the Drive would run me ragged and have me in the poor house inside of a year even if I was makeing 25 grand out of one song. Besides she wears a make up that you would have to blast to find out what her face looks like. So I have not been back there and don't intend to see her again so what is the use of me telling you about her. And the only other girlie I have met is a sister of Paul Sears who I met up to his house wile we was working on the song but she don't hardly count as she has not got no use for the boys but treats them like dirt and Pauls says she is the coldest proposition he ever seen.

Well I don't know no more to write and besides have got a date to go out to Paul's place for dinner and play some of my stuff for him so as he can see if he wants to set words to some more of my melodies. Well don't do nothing I would not do and have as good a time as you can in old Chi and will let you know how we come along with the song.

CHAS. F. LEWIS

Chicago, Ill., Aug. 23.

DEAR MR. MAN: I am thrilled to death over the song and think the words awfully pretty and am crazy to hear the music which I know must be great. It must be wonderful to have the gift of writing songs and then hear people play and sing them and just think of making $25,000 in such a short time. My, how rich you will be and I certainly congratulate you though am afraid when you are rich and famous you will have no time for insignificant little me or will you be an exception and remember your "old" friends even when you are up in the world? I sincerely hope so.

Will look forward to receiving a copy of the song and will you be sure and put your name on it? I am all ready very conceited just to think that I know a man that writes songs and makes all that money.

Seriously I wish you success with your next song and I laughed when I read your remark about being busier than a one armed paper hanger. I don't see how you think up all those comparisons and crazy things to say. The next time one of the girls asks me to go out with them I am going to tell them I can't go because I am busier than a one armed paper hanger and then they will think I made it up and say: "The girl is clever."

Seriously I am glad you did not go back to see the girl on the Drive and am also glad you don't like girls who make themselves up so much as I think it is disgusting and would rather go round looking like a ghost than put artificial color on my face. Fortunately I have a complexion that does not need "fixing" but even if my coloring was not what it is I would never think of lowering myself to "fix" it. But I must tell you a joke that happened just the other day when Edith and I were out at lunch and there was another girl in the restaurant whom Edie knew and she introduced her to me and I noticed how this girl kept staring at me and finally she begged my pardon and asked if she could ask me a personal question and I said yes and she asked me if my complexion was really "mine." I assured her it was and she said: "Well, I thought so because I did not think anybody could put it on so artistically. I certainly envy you." Edie and I both laughed.

Well, if that girl envies me my complexion, why I envy you living in New York. Chicago is rather dirty though I don't let that part of it bother me as I bathe and change my clothing so often that the dirt does not have time to "settle." Edie often says she cannot see how I always keep so clean looking and says I always look like I had just stepped out of a band box. She also calls me a fish (jokingly) because I spend so much time in the water. But seriously I do love to bathe and never feel so happy as when I have just "cleaned up" and put on fresh clothing.

Edie has just gone out to see a picture and was cross at me because I would not go with her. I told her I was going to write a letter and she wanted to know to whom and I told her and she said: "You write to him so often that a person would almost think you was in love with him." I just laughed and turned it off, but she does say the most embarrassing things and I would be angry if it was anybody but she that said them.

Seriously I had much rather sit here and write letters or read or just sit and dream than go out to some crazy old picture show except once in a while I do like to go the the theater and see a good play and a specially a musical play if the music is catchy. But as a rule I am contented to just stay home and feel cozy and lots of evenings Edie and I sit here without saying hardly a word to each other though she would love to talk but she knows I had rather be quiet and she often says it is just like living with a deaf and dumb mute to live with me because I make so little noise round the apartment. I guess I was born to be a home body as I so seldom care to go "gadding."

Though I do love to have company once in awhile, just a few congenial friends whom I can talk to and feel at home with and play cards or have some music. My friends love to drop in here, too, as they say Edie and I always give them such nice things to eat. Though poor Edie has not much to do with it, I am afraid, as she hates anything connected with cooking which is one of the things I love best of anything and I often say that when I begin keeping house in my own home I will insist on doing most of my own work as I would take so much more interest in it than a servant, though I would want somebody to help me a little if I could afford it as I often think a woman that does all her own work is liable to get so tired that she loses interest in the bigger things of life like books and music. Though after all what bigger thing is there than home making a specially for a woman?

I am sitting in the dearest old chair that I bought yesterday at a little store on the North Side. That is my one extravagance, buying furniture and things for the house, but I always say it is economy in the long run as I will always have them and have use for them and when I can pick them up at a bargain I would be silly not to. Though heavens knows I will never be "poor" in regards to furniture and rugs and things like that as mother's house in Toledo is full of lovely things which she says she is going to give to Sis and myself as soon as we have real homes of our own. She is going to give me the first choice as I am her favorite. She has the loveliest old things that you could not buy now for love or money including lovely old rugs and a piano which Sis wanted to have a player attachment put on it but I said it would be an insult to the piano so we did not get one. I am funny about things like that, a specially old furniture and feel towards them like people whom I love.

Poor mother, I am afraid she won't live much longer to enjoy her lovely old things as she has been suffering for years from stomach trouble and the doctor says it has been worse lately instead of better and her heart is weak besides. I am going home to see her a few days this fall as it may be the last time. She is very cheerful and always says she is ready to go now as she has had enough joy out of life and all she would like would be to see her girls settled down in their own homes before she goes.

There I go, talking about my domestic affairs again and I will bet you are bored to death though personly I am never bored when my friends tell me about themselves. But I won't "rattle on" any longer, but will say good night and don't forget to write and tell me how you come out with the song and thanks for sending me the words to it. Will you write a song about me some time? I would be thrilled to death! But I am afraid I am not the kind of girl that inspires men to write songs about them, but am just a quiet "mouse" that loves home and am not giddy enough to be the heroine of a song.

Well, Mr. Man, good night and don't wait so long before writing again to

Yours (?)

MAYBELLE.

N.Y., Sept. 8.

DEAR GIRLIE: Well girlie have not got your last letter with me so cannot answer what was in it as I have forgotten if there was anything I was supposed to answer and besides have only a little time to write as I have a date to go out on a party with the Sears. We are going to the Georgie White[7] show and afterwards somewheres for supper. Sears is the boy who wrote the lyric to my song and it is him and his sister I am going to the party with. The sister is a cold fish that has no use for men but she is show crazy and insists on Paul takeing her to 3 or 4 of them a week.

Paul wants me to give up my room here and come and live with them as they have plenty of room and I am running a little low on money but don't know if I will do it or not as am afraid I would freeze to death in the same house with a girl like the sister as she is ice cold but she don't hang round the house much as she is always takeing trips or going to shows or somewheres.

So far we have not had no luck with the song. All the publishers we have showed it to has went crazy over it but they won't make the right kind of a deal with us and if they don't loosen up and give us a decent royalty rate we are libel to put the song out ourselves and show them up. The man up to Goebel's told us the song was O.K. and he liked it but it was more of a production number than anything else and ought to go in a show like the Follies[8] but they won't be in N.Y. much longer and what we ought to do is hold it till next spring.

Mean wile I am working on some new numbers and also have taken a position with the orchestra at the Wilton and am going to work there starting next week. They pay good money $60 and it will keep me going.

Well girlie that is about all the news. I believe you said your father was sick and hope he is better and also hope you are getting along O.K. and take care of yourself. When you have nothing else to do write to your friend,

CHAS. F. LEWIS.

Chicago, Ill., Sept. 11.

DEAR MR. LEWIS: Your short note reached me yesterday and must say I was puzzled when I read it. It sounded like you was mad at me though I cannot think of any reason why you should be. If there was something I said in my last letter that offended you I wish you would tell me what it was and I will ask your pardon though I cannot remember anything I could of said that you could take offense at. But if there was something, why I assure you, Mr. Lewis, that I did not mean anything by it. I certainly did not intend to offend you in any way.

Perhaps it is nothing I wrote you, but you are worried on account of the

[7]George White (1890–1968), producer of musical reviews.
[8]Annual musical revue staged (1907–1931) by Florenz Ziegfield (1869–1932).

publishers not treating you fair in regards to your song and that is why your letter sounded so distant. If that is the case I hope that by this time matters have rectified themselves and the future looks brighter. But any way, Mr. Lewis, don't allow yourself to worry over business cares as they will all come right in the end and I always think it is silly for people to worry themselves sick over temporary troubles, but the best way is to "keep smiling" and look for the "silver lining" in the cloud. That is the way I always do and no matter what happens, I manage to smile and my girl friend, Edie, calls me Sunny because I always look on the bright side.

Remember also, Mr. Lewis, that $60 is a salary that a great many men would like to be getting and are living on less than that and supporting a wife and family on it. I always say that a person can get along on whatever amount they make if they manage things in the right way.

So if it is business troubles, Mr. Lewis, I say don't worry, but look on the bright side. But if it is something I wrote in my last letter that offended you I wish you would tell me what it was so I can apologize as I assure you I meant nothing and would not say anything to hurt you for the world.

Please let me hear from you soon as I will not feel comfortable until I know I am not to blame for the sudden change.

Sincerely,

MAYBELLE GILLESPIE.

N.Y., Sept. 24.

DEAR MISS GILLESPIE: Just a few lines to tell you the big news or at least it is big news to me. I am engaged to be married to Paul Sears' sister and we are going to be married early next month and live in Atlantic City where the orchestra I have been playing with has got an engagement in one of the big cabarets.

I know this will be a surprise to you as it was even a surprise to me as I did not think I would ever have the nerve to ask the girlie the big question as she was always so cold and acted like I was just in the way. But she said she supposed she would have to marry somebody some time and she did not dislike me as much as most of the other men her brother brought round and she would marry me with the understanding that she would not have to be a slave and work round the house and also I would have to take her to a show or somewheres every night and if I could not take her myself she would "run wild" alone. Atlantic City will be O.K. for that as a lot of new shows opens down there and she will be able to see them before they get to the big town. As for her being a slave, I would hate to think of marrying a girl and then have them spend their lives in druggery round the house. We are going to live in a hotel till we find something better but will be in no hurry to start house keeping as we will have to buy all new furniture.

Betsy is some doll when she is all fixed up and believe me she knows how to fix herself up. I don't know what she uses but it is weather proof as I have been out in a rain storm with her and we both got drowned but her face stayed on. I would almost think it was real only she tells me different.

Well girlie I may write to you again once in a wile as Betsy says she don't give a dam if I write to all the girls in the world just so I don't make her read the answers but that is all I can think of to say now except good bye and good luck and may the right man come along soon and he will be a lucky man getting a girl that is such a good cook and got all that furniture etc.

But just let me give you a word of advice before I close and that is don't never speak to strange men who you don't know nothing about as they may get you wrong and think you are trying to make them. It just happened that I knew better so you was lucky in my case but the luck might not last.

Your friend,

CHAS. F. LEWIS.

MY DEAR MR. LEWIS: Thanks for your advice and also thank your fiance for her generosity in allowing you to continue your correspondence with her "rivals," but personly I have no desire to take advantage of that generosity as I have something better to do than read letters from a man like you, a specially as I have a man friend who is not so generous as Miss Sears and would strongly object to my continuing a correspondence with another man. It is at his request that I am writing this note to tell you not to expect to hear from me again.

Allow me to congratulate you on your engagement to Miss Sears and I am sure she is to be congratulated too, though if I met the lady I would be tempted to ask her to tell me her secret, namely how she is going to "run wild" on $60.

Sincerely,

MABELLE GILLESPIE.
1921, 1924

Eugene O'Neill *1888–1953*

Eugene O'Neill was born in a Broadway hotel and raised in the world of the American theater. His father was a famous actor, and in early childhood Eugene O'Neill toured with his parents in theatrical road companies traveling throughout the United States. At the age of eighteen he entered Princeton, but at the end of his freshman year he was expelled for a drunken prank and "general hell-raising." He went to New York City, where he took a secretarial job in a business firm. When he was twenty he sailed to Central America to prospect for gold and then signed as an ordinary seaman on ships sailing to South America, Africa, and Europe.

After three years of wandering he returned to New York, where he supported himself with odd jobs and lived in water-front dives among human outcasts like those he later depicted in his plays. When he was twenty-four an attack of tuberculosis, worsened by his own rebellious dissipations, sent him to a sanitarium. During his illness he decided to become a playwright, and after his convalescence he enrolled at Harvard to study the drama. In 1914 he published Thirst and Other One-Act Plays. *Two years later* Bound East for Cardiff *was staged, followed in 1917 by* The Long Voyage Home.

During the 1920s and early thirties O'Neill achieved a series of theatrical triumphs with the production of such plays as Beyond the Horizon *(1920)—for which he was awarded the first of four Pulitzer Prizes—*The Emperor Jones *(1920),* Anna Christie *(1921),* The Hairy Ape *(1922),* Desire Under the Elms *(1924), and* Strange Interlude *(1928). In 1931 his* Mourning Becomes Electra *was widely proclaimed a dramatic masterpiece, and in 1936 he became the second American, after Sinclair Lewis, to win a Nobel Prize for Literature. O'Neill had won wealth and international renown,* *but in the late 1930s he withdrew into retirement and seclusion; his critical reputation declined, and his works vanished from the popular stage. In 1946 he returned to the theater with* The Iceman Cometh, *a long and notable tragedy portraying a haunted man struggling to break free of his illusions. But not until the production of* Long Day's Journey into Night *in 1956, three years after O'Neill's death, was there a lasting revival of interest in his works.*

O'Neill was a restless theatrical experimenter. His writing was shaped by European expressionistic drama and by literary naturalists such as Jack London, who showed man caught by overwhelming forces in a world indifferent to suffering and hope. O'Neill's plays were frequently autobiographical, pessimistic expressions of the agonies of his own life and of the degeneration he saw around him. He viewed humanity as caged, like the hero of The Hairy Ape, *living in disharmony with nature and dehumanized by a materialistic society.*

O'Neill's plays are sometimes disparaged for their social pleading, their nihilism, and their occasional lapses into "overheated rhetoric." Yet his psychological probing of alienation and his depiction of the suffering of ordinary mortals made him America's most influential playwright. In little more than a single decade he transformed the American theater, changing it "utterly," in the words of Sinclair Lewis, "from a false world of neat and competent trickery into a world of splendor and fear and greatness."

FURTHER READING: S. Winther, *Eugene O'Neill, A Critical Study*, 1934, 1961; R. Skinner, *Eugene O'Neill, A Poet's Quest*, 1935, 1964; E. Engel, *The Haunted Heroes of Eugene O'Neill*, 1953; D. Falk, *Eugene O'Neill and the Tragic Tension*, 1958; *O'Neill and His Plays*, ed. O. Cargill, N. Fagin, and W. Fischer, 1961; D. Alexander, *The Tempering of Eugene O'Neill*, 1962; J. Miller, *Eugene O'Neill and the American Critic*, 1962; A. and B. Gelb, *O'Neill*, 1962, 1973; F. Carpenter, *Eugene O'Neill*, 1964, 1979; J. Raleigh, *The Plays of Eugene O'Neill*, 1965; L. Schaeffer, *O'Neill, Son and Playwright*, 1968; T. Bogard, *Contour in Time, The Plays of Eugene O'Neill*, 1972; L. Chabrowe, *Ritual and Pathos, The Theater of O'Neill*, 1976; *Eugene O'Neill, A Collection of Criticism*, ed. E. Griffin, 1976; J. Chothia, *Forging a Language, A Study of the Plays of Eugene O'Neill*, 1980; V. Floyd, *Eugene O'Neill, A World View*, 1980; C. Sinha, *Eugene O'Neill's Tragic Vision*, 1981; N. Berlin, *Eugene O'Neill*, 1982; *Eugene O'Neill's Critics*, ed. H. Frenz and S. Tuck, 1984; *Critical Essays on Eugene O'Neill*, ed. J. Martine, 1984; M. Renald, *The Eugene O'Neill Companion*, 1984; J. Barlow, *Final Acts*, 1985; *Critical Approaches to O'Neill*, ed. J. Stoupe, 1987.

TEXT: *The Plays of Eugene O'Neill*, 3 vols., 1951.

THE HAIRY APE

CHARACTERS

ROBERT SMITH, "YANK"
PADDY
LONG
MILDRED DOUGLAS
HER AUNT
SECOND ENGINEER
A GUARD
A SECRETARY OF AN ORGANIZATION
Stokers, Ladies, Gentlemen, etc.

SCENES

Scene I: The firemen's forecastle of an ocean liner—an hour after sailing from New York.

SCENE ONE

The firemen's forecastle of a transatlantic liner an hour after sailing from New York for the voyage across. Tiers of narrow, steel bunks, three deep, on all sides. An entrance in rear. Benches on the floor before the bunks. The room is crowded with men, shouting, cursing, laughing, singing—a confused, inchoate uproar swelling into a sort of unity, a meaning—the bewildered, furious, baffled defiance of a beast in a cage. Nearly all of the men are drunk. Many bottles are passed from hand to hand. All are dressed in dungaree pants, heavy ugly shoes. Some wear singlets, but the majority are stripped to the waist.

The treatment of this scene, or any other scene in the play, should by no means be naturalistic. The effect sought after is a cramped space in the bowels of a ship, imprisoned by white steel. The lines of bunks, the uprights supporting them, cross each other like the steel framework of a cage. The ceiling crushes down upon the men's heads. They cannot stand upright. This accentuates the natural stooping posture which shoveling coal and the resultant overdevelopment of back and shoulder muscles have given them. The men themselves should resemble those pictures in which the appearance of Neanderthal Man is guessed at. All are hairy-chested, with long arms of tremendous power, and low, receding brows above their small, fierce, resentful eyes. All the civilized white races are represented, but except for the slight differentiation in color of hair, skin, eyes, all these men are alike.

The curtain rises on a tumult of sound. YANK *is seated in the foreground. He seems broader, fiercer, more truculent, more powerful, more sure of himself than the rest. They respect his superior strength—the grudging respect of fear. Then, too, he represents to them a self-expression, the very last word in what they are, their most highly developed individual.*

VOICES. Gif me trink dere, you!
    'Ave a wet!
    Salute!
    Gesundheit!
    Skoal!
    Drunk as a lord, God stiffen you!
    Here's how!
    Luck!
    Pass back that bottle, damn you!
    Pourin' it down his neck!
    Ho, Froggy! Where the devil have you been?
    La Touraine.[1]
    I hit him smash in yaw, py Gott!
    Jenkins—the First—he's a rotten swine—
    And the coppers nabbed him—and I run—
    I like peer better. It don't pig head gif you.

[1] A French ocean liner.

A slut, I'm saying'! She robbed me aslape—
To hell with 'em all!
You're a bloody liar!
Say dot again! (*Commotion. Two men about to fight are pulled apart.*)
No scrappin' now!
Tonight—
See who's the best man!
Bloody Dutchman!
Tonight on the for'ard square.
I'll bet on Dutchy.
He packa da wallop, I tella you!
Shut up, Wop!
No fightin', maties. We're all chums, ain't we?
(*A voice starts bawling a song.*)
   "Beer, beer, glorious beer!
   Fill yourselves right up to here."

 YANK. (*for the first time seeming to take notice of the uproar about him, turns around threateningly—in a tone of contemptuous authority*) Choke off dat noise! Where d'yuh get dat beer stuff? Beer, hell! Beer's for goils—and Dutchmen. Me for somep'n with a kick to it. Gimmie a drink, one of youse guys. (*Several bottles are eagerly offered. He takes a tremendous gulp at one of them; then, keeping the bottle in his hand, glares belligerently at the owner, who hastens to acquiesce in this robbery by saying*) All righto, Yank. Keep it and have another. (YANK *contemptuously turns his back on the crowd again. For a second there is an embarrassed silence. Then—*)

 VOICES. We must be passing the Hook.[2]
  She's beginning to roll to it.
  Six days in hell—and then Southampton.[3]
  Py Yesus, I vish somepody take my first vatch for me!
  Gittin' seasick, Square-head?
  Drink up and forget it!
  What's in your bottle?
  Gin.
  Dot's nigger trink.
  Absinthe? It's doped. You'll go off your chump, Froggy!
  Cochon![4]
  Whisky, that's the ticket!
  Where's Paddy?
  Going asleep.
  Sing up that whisky song, Paddy. (*They all turn to an old, wizened Irishman who is dozing, very drunk, on the benches forward. His face is extremely monkey-like with all the sad, patient pathos of that aminal in his small eyes.*)
  Singa da song, Caruso Pat!
  He's gettin' old. The drink is too much for him.
  He's too drunk.

 PADDY. (*blinking about him, starts to his feet resentfully, swaying, holding on to the edge of a bunk*) I'm never too drunk to sing. 'Tis only when I'm dead to the world I'd be wishful to sing at all. (*With a sort of sad contempt*) "Whisky Johnny," ye want? A chanty, ye want? Now that's a queer wish from the ugly like of you, God help you. But no matther. (*He starts to sing in a thin, nasal doleful tone:*)

[2]Sandy Hook, a peninsula at the mouth of New York Bay. [3]In England.
[4]French: "Pig!"

> *"Oh, whisky is the life of man!*
>   *Whisky! O Johnny!* (They all join in on this.)
> *Oh, whisky is the life of man!*
>   *Whisky for my Johnny!* (Again chorus.)
> *"Oh, whisky drove my old man mad!*
>   *Whisky! O Johnny!*
> *Oh, whisky drove my old man mad!*
>   *Whisky for my Johnny!"*

YANK. (*again turning around scornfully*) Aw hell! Nix on dat old sailing ship stuff! All dat bull's dead, see? And you're dead, too, yuh damned old Harp,[5] on'y yuh don't know it. Take it easy, see. Give us a rest. Nix on de loud noise. (*With a cynical grin*) Can't youse see I'm tryin' to t'ink?

ALL. (*repeating the word after him as one with the same cynical amused mockery*) Think! (*The chorused word has a brazen metallic quality as if their throats were phonograph horns. It is followed by a general uproar of hard, barking laughter.*)

VOICES. Don't be cracking your head wit ut, Yank.
  You gat headache, py yingo!
  One thing about it—it rhymes with drink!
  Ha, ha, ha!
  Drink, don't think!
  Drink, don't think!
  Drink, don't think! (*A whole chorus of voices has taken up this refrain, stamping on the floor, pounding on the benches with fists.*)

YANK. (*taking a gulp from his bottle—good-naturedly*) Aw right. Can de noise. I got yuh de foist time. (*The uproar subsides. A very drunken sentimental tenor begins to sing*):

> *"Far away in Canada,*
>   *Far across the sea,*
> *There's a lass who fondly waits*
>   *Making a home for me—"*

YANK. (*fiercely contemptuous*) Shut up, yuh lousy boob! Where d'yuh get dat tripe? Home? Home, hell! I'll make a home for yuh! I'll knock yuh dead. Home! T'hell wit home! Where d'yu get dat tripe? Dis is home, see? What d'yuh want with home? (*Proudly*) I runned away from mine when I was a kid. On'y too glad to beat it, dat was me. Home was lickings for me, dat's all. But yuh can bet your shoit no one ain't never licked me since! Wanter try it, any of youse? Huh! I guess not. (*In a more placated but still contemptuous tone*) Goils waitin' for yuh, huh? Aw, hell! Dat's all tripe. Dey don't wait for no one. Dey'd double-cross yuh for a nickel. Dey're all tarts, get me? Treat 'em rough, dat's me. To hell wit 'em. Tarts, dat's what, de whole bunch of 'em.

LONG. (*very drunk, jumps on a bench excitedly, gesticulating with a bottle in his hand*) Listen 'ere, Comrade! Yank 'ere is right. 'E says this 'ere stinkin' ship is our 'ome. And 'e says as 'ome is 'ell. And 'e's right! This is 'ell. We lives in 'ell, Comrades— and right enough we'll die in it. (*Raging*) and who's ter blame, I arsk yer? We ain't. We wasn't born this rotten way. All men is born free and ekal. That's in the bleedin' Bible, maties. But what d'they care for the Bible—them lazy, bloated swine what travels first cabin? Them's the ones. They dragged us down 'til we're

---

[5]Slang term for "Irishman."

on'y wage slaves in the bowels of a bloody ship, sweatin, burnin' up, eatin' coal dust! Hit's them's ter blame—the damned Capitalist class! (*There had been a gradual murmur of contemptuous resentment rising among the men until now he is interrupted by a storm of catcalls, hisses, boos, hard laughter.*)

VOICES. Turn it off!
        Shut up!
        Sit down!
        Closa da face!
        Tamn fool! (*Etc.*)

YANK. (*standing up and glaring at* LONG) Sit down before I knock yuh down! (LONG *makes haste to efface himself.* YANK *goes on contemptuously*) De Bible, huh? De Cap'tlist class, huh? Aw nix on dat Salvation Army-Socialist bull, Git a soapbox! Hire a hall! Come and be saved, huh? Jerk us to Jesus, huh? Aw g'wan! I've listened to lots of guys like you, see. Yuh're all wrong. Wanter know what I t'ink? Yuh ain't no good for no one. Yuh're de bunk. Yuh ain't got no noive, get me? Yuh're yellow, dat's what. Yellow, dat's you. Say! What's dem slobs in de foist cabin got to do wit us? We're better men dan dey are, ain't we? Sure! One of us guys could clean up de whole mob with one mit. Put one of 'em down here for one watch in de stokehole, what'd happen? Dey'd carry him off on a stretcher. Dem boids don't amount to nothin'. Dey're just baggage. Who makes dis old tub run? Ain't it us guys? Well den, we belong, don't we? We belong and dey don't. Dat's all. (*A loud chorus of approval.* YANK *goes on*) As for dis bein' hell— aw, nuts! Yuh lost your noive, dat's what. Dis is a man's job, get me? It belongs. It runs dis tub. No stiffs need apply. But yuh're a stiff, see? Yuh're yellow, dat's you.

VOICES. (*with a great hard pride in them*)
        Righto!
        A man's job!
        Talk is cheap, Long.
        He never could hold up his end.
        Divil take him!
        Yank's right. We make it go.
        Py Gott, Yank say right ting!
        We don't need no one cryin' over us.
        Makin' speeches.
        Throw him out!
        Yellow!
        Chuck him overboard!
        I'll break his jaw for him!
        (*They crowd around* LONG *threateningly.*)

YANK. (*half good-natured again—contemptuously*) Aw, take it easy. Leave him alone. He ain't woith a punch. Drink up. Here's how, whoever owns dis. (*He takes a long swallow from his bottle. All drink with him. In a flash all is hilarious amiability again, back-slapping, loud talk, etc.*)

PADDY. (*who has been sitting in a blinking, melancholy daze—suddenly cries out in a voice full of sorrow*) We belong to this, you're saying? We make the ship to go, you're saying? Yerra[6] then, that Almighty God have pity on us! (*His voice runs into the wail of a keen,[7] he rocks back and forth on his bench. The men stare at him, startled and impressed in spite of themselves*) Oh, to be back in the fine days of my youth, ochone![8] Oh, there was fine beautiful ships them days—clippers wid tall

---

[6]Irish: "Truly."   [7]A lamentation for the dead.   [8]Irish: "alas!"

masts touching the sky—fine strong men in them—men that was sons of the sea as if 'twas the mother that bore them. Oh, the clean skins of them, and the clear eyes, the straight backs and full chests of them! Brave men they was, and bold men surely! We'd be sailing out, bound down round the Horn[9] maybe. We'd be making sail in the dawn, with a fair breeze, singing a chanty song wid no care to it. And astern the land would be sinking low and dying out, but we'd give it no heed but a laugh, and never a look behind. For the day that was, was enough, for we was free men—and I'm thinking 'tis only slaves do be giving heed to the day that's gone or the day to come—until they're old like me. (*With a sort of religious exaltation*) Oh, to be scudding south again wid the power of the Trade Wind driving her on steady through the nights and the days! Full sail on her! Nights and days! Nights when the foam of the wake would be flaming wid fire, when the sky'd be blazing and winking wid stars. Or the full of the moon maybe. Then you'd see her driving through the gray night, her sails stretching aloft all silver and white, not a sound on the deck, the lot of us dreaming dreams, till you'd believe 'twas no real ship at all you was on but a ghost ship like the *Flying Dutchman* they say does be roaming the seas forevermore widout touching a port. And there was the days, too. A warm sun on the clean decks. Sun warming the blood of you, and wind over the miles of shiny green ocean like strong drink to your lungs. Work—aye, hard work—but who'd mind that at all? Sure, you worked under the sky and 'twas work wid skill and daring to it. And wid the day done, in the dog watch, smoking me pipe at ease, the lookout would be raising land maybe, and we'd see the mountains of South Americy wid the red fire of the setting sun painting their white tops and clouds floating by them! (*His tone of exaltation ceases. He goes on mournfully*) Yerra, what's the use of talking? 'Tis a dead man's whisper. (*To* YANK *resentfully*) 'Twas them days men belonged to ships, not now. 'Twas them days a ship was part of the sea, and a man was part of a ship, and the sea joined all together and made it one. (*Scornfully*) Is it one wid this you'd be, Yank—black smoke from the funnels smudging the sea, smudging the decks—the bloody engines pounding and throbbing and shaking—wid divil a sight of sun or a breath of clean air—choking our lungs wid coal dust—breaking our backs and hearts in the hell of the stokehole—feeding the bloody furnace—feeding our lives along wid the coal, I'm thinking—caged in by steel from a sight of the sky like bloody apes in the Zoo!(*With a harsh laugh*) Ho-ho, divil mend you! Is it to belong to that you're wishing? Is it a flesh and blood wheel of the engines you'd be?

YANK. (*who has been listening with a contemptuous sneer, barks out the answer*) Sure ting! Dat's me. What about it?

PADDY. (*as if to himself—with great sorrow*) Me time is past due. That a great wave wid sun in the heart of it may sweep me over the side sometime I'd be dreaming of the days that's gone![10]

YANK. Aw, yuh crazy Mick![10] (*He springs to his feet and advances on* PADDY *threateningly—then stops, fighting some queer struggle within himself—lets his hands fall to his sides—contemptuously*) Aw, take it easy. Yuh're aw right, at dat. Yuh're bugs, dat's all—nutty as a cuckoo. All dat tripe yuh been pullin'—Aw, dat's all right. On'y it's dead, get me? Yuh don't belong no more, see. Yuh don't get de stuff. Yuh're too old. (*Disgustedly*) But aw say, come up for air oncet in a while, can't yuh? See what's happened since yuh croaked. (*He suddenly bursts forth vehemently, growing more and more excited*) Say! Sure! Sure I meant it! What de hell—Say, lemme talk! Hey! Hey, you old Harp! Hey, youse guys! Say, listen to me—wait

[9]Cape Horn, at the southern tip of South America.
[10]Slang term for "Irishman."

a moment—I gotter talk, see. I belong and he don't. He's dead but I'm livin'. Listen to me! Sure I'm part of de engines! Why de hell not! Dey move, don't dey? Dey're speed, ain't dey? Dey smash trou, don't dey? Twenty-five knots a hour! Dat's goin' some! Dat's new stuff! Dat belongs! But him, he's too old. He gets dizzy. Say, listen. All dat crazy tripe about suns and winds, fresh air and de rest of it—Aw hell, dat's all a dope dream! Hittin' de pipe of de past, dat's what he's doin'. He's old and don't belong no more. But me, I'm young! I'm in de pink! I move wit it. It, get me! I mean de ting dat's de guts of all dis. It ploughs trou all de tripe he's been sayin'. It blows dat up! It knocks dat dead! It slams dat offen de face of de oith! It, get me! De engines and de coal and de smoke and all de rest of it! He can't breathe and swallow coal dust, but I kin, see? Dat's fresh air for me! Dat's food for me! I'm new, get me? Hell in de stokehole? Sure! It takes a man to work in hell. Hell, sure, dat's my fav'rite climate. I eat it up! I git fat on it! It's me makes it hot! It's me makes it roar! It's me makes it move! Sure, on'y for me everything stops. It all goes dead, get me? De noise and smoke and all de engines movin' de woild, dey stop. Dere ain't nothin' no more! Dat's what I'm sayin'. Everything else dat makes de woild move, somep'n makes it move. It can't move witout somep'n else, see? Den yuh get down to me. I'm at de bottom, get me! Dere ain't nothin' foither. I'm de end! I'm de start! I start somep'n and de woild moves! It—dat's me!—de new dat's moiderin' de old! I'm de ting in coal dat makes it boin; I'm steam and oil for de engines; I'm de ting in noise dat makes yuh hear it; I'm smoke and express trains and steamers and factory whistles; I'm de ting in gold dat makes it money! And I'm what makes iron into steel! Steel, dat stands for de whole ting! And I'm steel—steel—steel! I'm de muscles in steel, de punch behind it! (*As he says this he pounds with his fist against the steel bunks. All the men, roused to a pitch of frenzied self-glorification by his speech, do likewise. There is a deafening metallic roar, through which* YANK'S *voice can be heard bellowing*) Slaves, hell! We run de whole woiks. All de rich guys dat tink dey're somep'n, dey ain't nothin'! Dey don't belong. But us guys, we're in de move, we're at de bottom, de whole ting is us! (PADDY *from the start of* YANK'S *speech has been taking one gulp after another from his bottle, at first frightenedly, as if he were afraid to listen, then desperately, as if to drown his senses, but finally has achieved complete indifferent, even amused, drunkenness.* YANK *sees his lips moving. He quells the uproar with a shout*) Hey, youse guys, take it easy! Wait a moment! De nutty Harp is sayin' somep'n.

   PADDY. (*is heard now—throws his head back with a mocking burst of laughter*) Ho-ho-ho-ho-ho—

   YANK. (*drawing back his fist, with a snarl*) Aw! Look out who yuh're givin' the bark!

   PADDY. (*begins to sing the "Miller of Dee' with enormous good nature*)

> "I care for nobody, no, not I,
> And nobody cares for me."

   YANK. (*good-natured himself in a flash, interrupts* PADDY *with a slap on the bare back like a report*) Dat's de stuff! Now you're gettin' wise to somep'n. Care for nobody, dat's de dope! To hell with 'em all! And nix on nobody else carin'. I kin care for myself, get me! (*Eight bells sound, muffled, vibrating through the steel walls as if some enormous brazen gong were imbedded in the heart of the ship. All the men jump up mechanically, file through the door silently close upon each other's heels in what is very like a prisoner's lockstep.* YANK *slaps* PADDY *on the back*) Our watch, yuh old Harp!

(*Mockingly*) Come on down in hell. Eat up de coal dust. Drink in de heat. It's it, see! Act like yuh liked it, yuh better—or croak yuhself.

PADDY. (*with jovial defiance*) To the divil wid it; I'll not report this watch. Let thim log[11] me and be damned. I'm no slave the like of you. I'll be sittin' here at me ease, and drinking, and thinking, and dreaming dreams.

YANK. (*contemptuously*) Tinkin' and dreamin', what'll that get yuh? What's tinkin' got to do wit it? We move, don't we? Speed, ain't it? Fog, dat's all you stand for. But we drive trou dat, don't we? We split dat up and smash trou—twenty-five knots an hour! (*Turns his back on* PADDY *scornfully*) Aw, yuh make me sick! Yuh don't belong! (*He strides out the door in rear.* PADDY *hums to himself, blinking drowsily.*)

CURTAIN

SCENE TWO

Two days out. A section of the promenade deck. MILDRED DOUGLAS *and her aunt are discovered reclining in deck chairs. The former is a girl of twenty, slender, delicate, with a pale, pretty face marred by a self-conscious expression of disdainful superiority. She looks fretful, nervous and discontented, bored by her own anemia. Her aunt is a pompous and proud—and fat—old lady. She is a type even to the point of a double chin and lorgnettes.[1] She is dressed pretentiously, as if afraid her face alone would never indicate her position in life.* MILDRED *is dressed all in white.*

The impression to be conveyed by this scene is one of the beautiful, vivid life of the sea all about—sunshine on the deck in a great flood, the fresh sea wind blowing across it. In the midst of this, these two incongruous, artificial figures, inert and disharmonious, the elder like a gray lump of dough touched up with rouge, the younger looking as if the vitality of her stock had been sapped before she was conceived, so that she is the expression not of its life energy but merely of the artificialities that energy had won for itself in the spending.

MILDRED. (*looking up with affected dreaminess*) How the black smoke swirls back against the sky! Is it not beautiful?

AUNT. (*without looking up*) I dislike smoke of any kind.

MILDRED. My great-grandmother smoked a pipe—a clay pipe.

AUNT. (*ruffling*) Vulgar!

MILDRED. She was too distant a relative to be vulgar. Time mellows pipes.

AUNT. (*pretending boredom but irritated*) Did the sociology you took up at college teach you that—to play the ghoul on every possible occasion, excavating old bones? Why not let your great-grandmother rest in her grave?

MILDRED. (*dreamily*) With her pipe beside her—puffing in Paradise.

AUNT. (*with spite*) Yes, you are a natural born ghoul. You are even getting to look like one, my dear.

MILDRED. (*in a passionless tone*) I detest you, Aunt. (*Looking at her critically*) Do you know what you remind me of? Of a cold pork pudding against a background of linoleum tablecloth in the kitchen of a—but the possibilities are wearisome. (*She closes her eyes.*)

AUNT. (*with a bitter laugh*) *Merci*[2] for your candor. But since I am and must be

---

[11]Enter charges of disobedience into the ship's log (record).
[1]Eyeglasses with a handle.
[2]French: "Thanks."

your chaperon—in appearance, at least—let us patch up some sort of armed truce. For my part you are quite free to indulge any pose of eccentricity that beguiles you—as long as you observe the amenities—

MILDRED. (*drawling*) The inanities?

AUNT. (*going on as if she hadn't heard*) After exhausting the morbid thrills of social service work on New York's East Side[3]—how they must have hated you, by the way, the poor that you made so much poorer in their own eyes!—you are now bent on making your slumming international. Well, I hope Whitechapel will provide the needed nerve tonic. Do not ask me to chaperon you there, however. I told your father I would not. I loathe deformity. We will hire an army of detectives and you may investigate everything—they allow you to see.

MILDRED. (*protesting with a trace of genuine earnestness*) Please do not mock my attempts to discover how the other half lives. Give me credit for some sort of groping sincerity in that at least. I would like to help them. I would like to be some use in the world. Is it my fault I don't know how? I would like to be sincere, to touch life somewhere. (*With weary bitterness*) But I'm afraid I have neither the vitality nor integrity. All that was burnt out in our stock before I was born. Grandfather's blast furnaces, flaming to the sky, melting steel, making millions—then father keeping those home fires burning, making more millions—and little me at the tail-end of it all. I'm a waste product in the Bessemer process[4]—like the millions. Or rather, I inherit the acquired trait of the by-product, wealth, but none of the energy, none of the strength of the steel that made it. I am sired by gold and damned by it, as they say at the race track—damned in more ways than one. (*She laughs mirthlessly.*)

AUNT. (*unimpressed—superciliously*) You seem to be going in for sincerity today. It isn't becoming to you, really—except as an obvious pose. Be as artificial as you are, I advise. There's a sort of sincerity in that, you know. And, after all, you must confess you like that better.

MILDRED. (*again affected and bored*) Yes, I suppose I do. Pardon me for my outburst. When a leopard complains of its spots, it must sound rather grotesque. (*In a mocking tone*) Purr, little Leopard. Purr, scratch, tear, kill, gorge yourself and be happy—only stay in the jungle where your spots are camouflaged. In a cage they make you conspicuous.

AUNT. I don't know what you are talking about.

MILDRED. It would be rude to talk about anything to you. Let's just talk. (*She looks at her wrist watch*) Well, thank goodness, it's about time for them to come for me. That ought to give me a new thrill, Aunt.

AUNT. (*affectedly troubled*) You don't mean to say you're really going? The dirt—the heat must be frightful—

MILDRED. Grandfather started as a puddler.[5] I should have inherited an immunity to heat that would make a salamander[6] shiver. It will be fun to put it to the test.

AUNT. But don't you have to have the captain's—or someone's— permission to visit the stokehole?

MILDRED. (*with a triumphant smile*) I have it—both his and the chief engineer's. Oh, they didn't want to at first, in spite of my social service credentials. They didn't seem a bit anxious that I should investigate how the other half lives and works on a ship. So I had to tell them that my father, the president of Nazareth

---

[3]A district of tenements and slums, as is London's Whitechapel, below.
[4]A process for making steel.
[5]A steelworker.   [6]Mythical animal thought to endure fire without harm.

Steel, chairman of the board of directors of this line, had told me it would be all right.

AUNT. He didn't.

MILDRED. How naïve age makes one! But I said he did, Aunt. I even said he had given me a letter to them—which I had lost. And they were afraid to take the chance that I might be lying. (*Excitedly*) So it's ho! for the stokehole. The second engineer is to escort me. (*Looking at her watch again*) It's time. And here he comes, I think. (*The* SECOND ENGINEER *enters. He is a husky, fine-looking man of thirty-five or so. He stops before the two and tips his cap, visibly embarrassed and ill-at-ease.*)

SECOND ENGINEER. Miss Douglas?

MILDRED. (*Throwing off her rugs and getting to her feet*) Are we all ready to start?

SECOND ENGINEER. In just a second, ma'am. I'm waiting for the Fourth.[7] He's coming along.

MILDRED. (*with a scornful smile*) You don't care to shoulder this responsibility alone, is that it?

SECOND ENGINEER. (*forcing a smile*) Two are better than one. (*Disturbed by her eyes, glances out to sea—blurts out*) A fine day we're having.

MILDRED. Is it?

SECOND ENGINEER. A nice warm breeze—

MILDRED. It feels cold to me.

SECOND ENGINEER. But it's hot enough in the sun—

MILDRED. Not hot enough for me. I don't like Nature. I was never athletic.

SECOND ENGINEER. (*forcing a smile*) Well you'll find it hot enough where you're going.

MILDRED. Do you mean hell?

SECOND ENGINEER. (*flabbergasted, decides to laugh*) Ho-ho! No, I mean the stokehole.

MILDRED. My grandfather was a puddler. He played with boiling steel.

SECOND ENGINEER. (*all at sea—uneasy*) Is that so? Hum, you'll excuse me, ma'am, but are you intending to wear that dress?

MILDRED. Why not?

SECOND ENGINEER. You'll likely rub against oil and dirt. It can't be helped.

MILDRED. It doesn't matter. I have lots of white dresses.

SECOND ENGINEER. I have an old coat you might throw over—

MILDRED. I have fifty dresses like this. I will throw this one into the sea when I come back. That ought to wash it clean, don't you think?

SECOND ENGINEER. (*doggedly*) There's ladders to climb down that are none too clean—and dark alleyways—

MILDRED. I will wear this very dress and none other.

SECOND ENGINEER. No offense meant. It's none of my business. I was only warning you—

MILDRED. Warning? That sounds thrilling.

SECOND ENGINEER. (*looking down the deck—with a sigh of relief*) There's the Fourth now. He's waiting for us. If you'll come—

MILDRED. Go on. I'll follow you. (*He goes.* MILDRED *turns a mocking smile on her aunt*) An oaf—but a handsome, virile oaf.

AUNT. (*scornfully*) Poser!

MILDRED. Take care. He said there were dark alleyways—

AUNT. (*in the same tone*) Poser!

---

[7]I.e., the fourth-ranking Engineering Officer.

MILDRED. (*biting her lips angrily*) You are right. But would that my millions were not so anemically chaste!

AUNT. Yes, for a fresh pose I have no doubt you would drag the name of Douglas in the gutter!

MILDRED. From which it sprang. Good-by, Aunt. Don't pray to hard that I may fall into the fiery furnace.

AUNT. Poser!

MILDRED. (*viciously*) Old hag! (*She slaps her aunt insultingly across the face and walks off, laughing gaily.*)

AUNT. (*screams after her*) I said poser!

CURTAIN

SCENE THREE

The stokehole. In the rear, the dimly-outlined bulks of the furnaces and boilers. High overhead one hanging electric bulb sheds just enough light through the murky air laden with coal dust to pile up masses of shadows everywhere. A line of men, stripped to the waist, is before the furnace doors. They bend over, looking neither to right nor left, handling their shovels as if they were part of their bodies, with a strange, awkward, swinging rhythm. They use the shovels to throw open the furnace doors. Then from these fiery round holes in the black a flood of terrific light and heat pours full upon the men who are outlined in silhouette in the crouching, inhuman attitudes of chained gorillas. The men shovel with a rhythmic motion, swinging as on a pivot from the coal which lies in heaps on the floor behind to hurl it into the flaming mouths before them. There is a tumult of noise—the brazen clang of the furnace doors as they are flung open or slammed shut, the grating, teeth-gritting grind of steel against steel, of crunching coal. This clash of sounds stuns one's ears with its rending dissonance. But there is order in it, rhythm, a mechanical regulated recurrence, a tempo. And rising above all, making the air hum with the quiver of liberated energy, the roar of leaping flames in the furnaces, the monotonous throbbing beat of the engines.

As the curtain rises, the furnace doors are shut. The men are taking a breathing spell. One or two are arranging the coal behind them, pulling it into more accessible heaps. The others can be dimly made out leaning on their shovels in relaxed attitudes of exhaustion.

PADDY. (*from somewhere in the line—plaintively*) Yerra, will this divil's own watch nivir end? Me back is broke. I'm destroyed entirely.

YANK. (*from the center of the line—with exuberant scorn*) Aw, yuh make me sick! Lie down and croak, why don't yuh? Always beefin', dat's you! Say, dis is a cinch! Dis was made for me! It's my meat, get me! (*A whistle is blown—a thin, shrill note from somewhere overhead in the darkness.* YANK *curses without resentment*) Dere's de damn engineer crackin' de whip. He tinks we're loafin'.

PADDY. (*vindictively*) God stiffen him!

YANK. (*in an exultant tone of command*) Come on, youse guys! Git into de game! She's gittin' hungry! Pile some grub in her. Trow it into her belly! Come on now, all of youse! Open her up! (*At this last all the men, who have followed his movements of getting into position, throw open their furnace doors with a deafening clang. The fiery light floods over their shoulders as they bend round for the coal. Rivulets of sooty sweat have traced maps on their backs. The enlarged muscles form bunches of high light and shadow.*)

YANK. (*chatting a count as he shovels without seeming effort*) One—two—tree—(*His voice rising exultantly in the joy of battle*) Dat's de stuff! Let her have it! All togedder now! Sling it into her! Let her ride! Shoot de piece now! Call de toin on her! Drive her into it! Feel her move! Watch her smoke! Speed, dat's her middle name! Give her coal, youse guys! Coal, dat's her booze! Drink it up, baby! Let's see yuh sprint! Dig in and gain a lap! Dere she go-o-es. (*This last in the chanting formula of the gallery gods at the six-day bike race. He slams his furnace door shut. The others do likewise with as much unison as their wearied bodies will permit. The effect is one of one fiery eye after another being blotted out with a series of accompanying bangs.*)

PADDY. (*groaning*) Me back is broke. I'm bate out—bate—(*There is a pause. Then the inexorable whistle sounds again from the dim regions above the electric light. There is a growl of cursing rage from all sides.*)

YANK. (*shaking his fist upward—contemptuously*) Take it easy dere, you! Who d'yuh tink's runnin' dis game, me or you? When I get ready, we move. Not before! When I get ready, get me!

VOICES. (*approvingly*)   That's the stuff!
                         Yank tal him, py golly!
                         Yank ain't affeerd.
                         Goot poy, Yank!
                         Give him hell!
                         Tell 'im 'e's a bloody swine!
                         Bloody slave-driver!

YANK. (*contemptuously*) He ain't got no noive. He's yellow, get me? All de engineers is yellow. Dey got streaks a mile wide. Aw, to hell wit him! Let's move, youse guys. We had a rest. Come on, she needs it! Give her pep! It ain't for him. Him and his whistle, dey don't belong. But we belong, see! We gotter feed de baby! Come on! (*He turns and flings his furnace door open. They all follow his lead. At this instant the SECOND and FOURTH ENGINEERS enter from darkness on the left with MILDRED between them. She starts, turns paler, her pose is crumbling, she shivers with fright in spite of the blazing heat, but forces herself to leave the ENGINEERS and take a few steps nearer the men. She is right behind YANK. All this happens quickly while the men have their backs turned.*)

YANK. Come on, youse guys! (*He is turning to get coal when the whistle sounds again in a peremptory, irritating note. This drives YANK into a sudden fury. While the other men have turned full around and stopped dumbfoundedly by the spectacle of MILDRED standing there in her white dress, YANK does not turn far enough to see her. Besides, his head is thrown back, he blinks upward through the murk trying to find the owner of the whistle, he brandishes his shovel murderously over his head in one hand, pounding on his chest, gorilla-like, with the other, shouting*) Toin off dat whistle! Come down outa dere, yuh yellow, brass-buttoned, Belfast bum, yuh! Come down and I'll knock yer brains out! Yuh lousy, stinkin', yellow mut of a Catholic-moiderin' bastard! Come down and I'll moider yuh! Pullin dat whistle on me, huh? I'll show yuh! I'll crash yer skull in! I'll drive yer teet-down yer troat! I'll slam yer nose trou de back of yer head! I'll cut yer guts out for a nickel, yuh lousy boob, yuh dirty, crummy, muck-eatin' son of a— (*Suddenly he becomes conscious of all the other men staring at something directly behind his back. He whirls defensively with a snarling, murderous growl, crouching to spring, his lips drawn back over his teeth, his small eyes gleaming ferociously. He sees MILDRED, like a white apparition in the full light from the open furnace doors. He glares into her eyes, turned to stone. As for her, during his speech she has listened, paralyzed with horror, terror, her whole personality crushed, beaten in, collapsed, by the terrific impact of this unknown, abysmal brutality, naked and shameless. As she looks at his gorilla face, as his eyes bore into hers, she utters a low, choking cry and shrinks away from him, putting both hands up before her eyes to shut out the sight of his face, to protect her own. This startles* YANK *to a reaction. His mouth falls open, his eyes grow bewildered.)*

MILDRED. *(about to faint—to the* ENGINEERS, *who now have her one by each arm— whimperingly)* Take me away! Oh, the filthy beast! *(She faints. They carry her quickly back, disappearing in the darkness at the left, rear. An iron door clangs shut. Rage and bewildered fury rush back on* YANK. *He feels himself insulted in some unknown fashion in the very heart of his pride. He roars "God damn yuh!" and hurls his shovel after them at the door which has just closed. It hits the steel bulkhead with a clang and falls clattering on the steel floor. From overhead the whistle sounds again in a long, angry, insistent command.)*

CURTAIN

SCENE FOUR

The firemen's forecastle. YANK'S *watch has just come off duty and had dinner. Their faces and bodies shine from a soap-and-water scrubbing but around their eyes, where a hasty dousing does not touch, the coal dust sticks like black make-up, giving them a queer, sinister expression.* YANK *has not washed either face or body. He stands out in contrast to them, a blackened, brooding figure. He is seated forward on a bench in the exact attitude of Rodin's "The Thinker."[1] The others, most of them smoking pipes, are staring at* YANK *half-apprehensively, as if fearing an outburst; half-amusedly, as if they saw a joke somewhere that tickled them.*

VOICES. He ain't ate nothin'.
         Py golly, a fallar gat to gat grub in him.
         Divil a lie.
         Yank feeda da fire, no feeda da face.
         Ha-ha.
         He ain't even washed hisself.
         He's forgot.
         Hey, Yank, you forgot to wash.
YANK. *(sullenly)* Forgot nothin'! To hell with washin'.
VOICES. It'll stick to you.
         It'll get under your skin.
         Give yer the bleedin' itch, that's wot.
VOICES. It'll stick to you.
         It makes spots on you—like a leopard.
         Like a piebald nigger, you mean.
         Better wash up, Yank.
         You sleep better.
         Wash up, Yank!
         Wash up! Wash up!
YANK. *(resentfully)* Aw say, youse guys. Lemme alone. Can't youse see I'm tryin' to tink?
ALL. *(repeating the word after him as one with cynical mockery)* Think! *(The word has a brazen, metallic quality as if their throats were phonograph horns. It is followed by a chorus of hard, barking laughter.)*
YANK. *(springing to his feet and glaring at them belligerently)* Yes, tink! Tink, dat's

[1]Statue by Auguste Rodin (1840–1917), French sculptor.

what I said! What about it? (*They are silent, puzzled by his sudden resentment at what used to be one of his jokes.* YANK *sits down again in the same attitude of "The Thinker."*)

VOICES. Leave him alone.

He's got a grouch on.

Why wouldn't he?

PADDY. (*with a wink at the others*) Sure I know what's the matther. 'Tis aisy to see. He's fallen in love. I'm telling you.

ALL. (*repeating the word after him as one with cynical mockery*) Love! (*The word has a brazen, metallic quality as if their throats were phonograph horns. It is followed by a chorus of hard, barking laughter.*)

YANK. (*with a contemptuous snort*) Love, Hell! Hate, dat's what. I've fallen in hate, get me?

PADDY. (*philosophically*) 'Twould take a wise man to tell one from the other. (*With a bitter, ironical scorn, increasing as he goes on*) But I'm telling you it's love that's in it. Sure what else but love for us poor bastes in the stokehole would be bringing a fine lady, dressed like a white quane, down a mile of ladders and steps to be havin' a look at us (*A growl of anger goes up from all sides.*)

LONG. (*jumping on a bench—hectically*) Hinsultin' us! Hinsultin' us, the bloody cow! And them bloody engineers! What right 'as they got to be exhibitin' us 's if we was bleedin' monkeys in a menagerie? Did we sign for hinsults to our dignity as 'onest workers? Is that in the ship's articles?[2] You kin bloody well bet it ain't! But I knows why they done it. I arsked a deck steward 'o she was and 'e told me. 'Er old man's a bleedin' millionaire, a bloody Capitalist! 'E's got enuf bloody gold to sink this bleedin' ship! 'E makes arf the bloody steel in the world! 'E owns this bloody boat! And you and me, Comrades, we're 'is slaves! and the skipper and mates and engineers, they're 'is slaves! And she's 'is bloody daughter and we're all 'er slaves, too! And she gives 'er orders as 'ow she wants to see the bloody animals below decks and down they takes 'er! (*There is a roar of rage from all sides.*)

YANK. (*blinking at him bewilderedly*) Say! Wait a moment! Is all dat straight goods?

LONG. Straight as string! The bleedin' steward as waits on 'em, 'e told me about 'er. And what're we goin' ter do, I arsks yer? 'Ave we got ter swaller 'er hinsults like dogs? It ain't in the ship's articles. I tell yer we got a case. We kin go to law—

YANK. (*with abysmal contempt*) Hell! Law!

ALL. (*repeating the word after him as one with cynical mockery*) Law! (*The word has a brazen metallic quality as if their throats were phonograph horns. It is followed by a chorus of hard, barking laughter.*)

LONG. (*feeling the ground slipping from under his feet—desperately*) As voters and citizens we kin force the bloody governments—

YANK. (*with abysmal contempt*) Hell! Governments!

ALL. (*repeating the word after him as one with cynical mockery*) Governments! (*The word has a brazen metallic quality as if their throats were phonograph horns. It is followed by a chorus of hard, barking laughter.*)

LONG. (*hysterically*) We're free and equal in the sight of God—

YANK. (*with abysmal contempt*) Hell! God!

ALL. (*repeating the word after him as one with cynical mockery.*) God! (*The word has a brazen, metallic quality as if their throats were phonograph horns. It is followed by a chorus of hard, barking laughter.*)

---

[2]Employment contract.

YANK. (*witheringly*) Aw, join de Salvation Army!

ALL. Sit down! Shut up! Damn fool! Sea-lawyer![3] (LONG *slinks back out of sight.*)

PADDY. (*continuing the trend of his thoughts as if he had never been interrupted—bitterly*) And there she was standing behind us, and the Second pointing at us like a man you'd hear in a circus would be saying: In this cage is a queerer kind of baboon than ever you'd find in darkest Africa. We roast them in their own sweat—and be damned if you won't hear some of them saying they like it! (*He glances scornfully at* YANK.)

YANK. (*with a bewildered uncertain growl*) Aw!

PADDY. And there was Yank roarin' curses and turning round wid his shovel to brain her—and she looked at him, and him at her—

YANK. (*slowly*) She was all white. I tought she was a ghost. Sure.

PADDY. (*with heavy, biting sarcasm*) 'Twas love at first sight, divil a doubt of it! If you'd seen the endearin' look on her pale mug when she shriveled away with her hands over her eyes to shut out the sight of him! Sure, 'twas as if she'd seen a great hairy ape escaped from the Zoo!

YANK. (*stung—with a growl of rage*) Aw!

PADDY. And the loving way Yank heaved his shovel at the skull of her, only she was out the door! (*A grin breaking over his face*) 'Twas touching, I'm telling you! It put the touch of home, swate home in the stokehole. (*There is a roar of laughter from all.*)

YANK. (*glaring at* PADDY *menacingly*) Aw, choke dat off, see!

PADDY. (*not heeding him—to the others*) And her grabbin' at the Second's arm for protection. (*With a grotesque imitation of a woman's voice*) Kiss me, Engineer dear, for it's dark down here and me old man's in Wall Street making money! Hug me tight, darlin', for I'm afeered in the dark and me mother's on deck makin' eyes at the skipper! (*Another roar of laughter.*)

YANK. (*threateningly*) Say! What yuh tryin' to do, kid me, yuh old Harp!

PADDY. Divil a bit! Ain't I wishin' myself you'd brained her?

YANK. (*fiercely*) I'll brain her! I'll brain her yet, wait 'n' see! (*Coming over to* PADDY—*slowly*) Say, is dat what she called me—a hairy ape?

PADDY. She looked it at you if she didn't say the word itself.

YANK. (*grinning horribly*) Hairy ape, huh? Sure! Dat's de way she looked at me aw right. Hairy ape! So dat's me, huh? (*Bursting into rage—as if she were still in front of him*) Yuh skinny tart! Yuh white-faced bum, yuh! I'll show you who's a ape! (*Turning to the others, bewilderment seizing him again*) Say, youse guys. I was bawlin' him out for pullin' de whistle on us. You heard me. And den I seen youse lookin' at somep'n and I tought he'd sneaked down to come up in back of me, and I hopped round to knock him dead wit de shovel. And dere she was wit de light on her! Christ, yuh coulda pushed me over with a finger! I was scared, get me? Sure I tought she was a ghost, see? She was all in white like dey wrap around stiffs. You seen her. Kin yuh blame me? She didn't belong, dat's what. And den when I come to and seen it was a real skoit and seen de way she was lookin' at me—like Paddy said—Christ, I was sore, get me? I don't stand for dat stuff from nobody. And I flung de shovel—on'y she'd beat it. (*Furiously*) I wished it'd banged her! I wished it'd knocked her block off!

LONG. And be 'anged for murder or 'lectrocuted? She ain't bleedin' well worth it.

YANK. I don't give a damn what! I'd be square wit her, wouldn't I? Tink I

---

[3]A complainer, trouble-maker.

wanter let her put somep'n over on me? Tink I'm goin' to let her git away wit
dat stuff? Yuh don't know me! No one ain't never put nothin' over on me and
got away wit it, see!—not dat kind of stuff—no guy and no skoit neither! I'll fix
her! Maybe she'll come down again—

VOICE. No chance, Yank. You scared her out of a year's growth.

YANK. I scared her? Why de hell should I scare her? Who de hell is she? Ain't
she de same as me? Hairy ape, huh? (*With his old confident bravado*) I'll show her
I'm better'n her, if she on'y knew it. I belong and she don't, see! I move and
she's dead! Twenty-five knots a hour, dat's me! Dat carries her but I make dat.
She's on'y baggage. Sure! (*Again bewilderedly*) But, Christ, she was funny lookin'!
Did yuh pipe her hands? White and skinny. Yuh could see de bones through
'em. And her mush, dat was dead white, too. And her eyes, dey was like dey'd
seen a ghost. Me, dat was! Sure! Hairy ape! Ghost, huh? Look at dat arm! (*He
extends his right arm, swelling out of the great muscles*) I coulda took her wit dat, wit
just my little finger even, and broke her in two. (*Again bewilderedly*) Say, who is
dat skoit, huh? What is she? What's she come from? Who made her? Who give
her de noive to look at me like dat? Dis ting's got my goat right. I don't get her.
She's new to me. What does a skoit like her mean, huh? She don't belong, get
me! I can't see her. (*With growing anger*) But one ting I'm wise to, aw right, aw
right! Youse all kin bet your shoits I'll git even wit her. I'll show her if she tinks
she—She grinds de organ and I'm on de string, huh? I'll fix her! Let her come
down again and I'll fling her in de furnace! She'll move den! She won't shiver
at nothin', den! Speed, dat'll be her! She'll belong den! (*He grins horribly*)

PADDY. She'll never come. She's had her belly-full, I'm telling you. She'll be
in bed now, I'm thinking, wid ten doctors and nurses feedin' her salts[4] to clean
the fear out of her.

YANK. (*enraged*) Yuh think I made her sick, too, do yuh? Just lookin' at me,
huh? Hairy ape, huh? (*In a frenzy of rage*) I'll fix her! I'll tell her where to git off!
She'll git down on her knees and take it back or I'll bust de face offen her!
(*Shaking one fist upward and beating on his chest with the other*) I'll find yuh! I'm
comin', d'yuh hear? I'll fix yuh, God damn yuh! (*He makes a rush for the door.*)

VOICES. Stop him!
         He'll get shot!
         He'll murder her!
         Trip him up!
         Hold him!
         Gott, he's strong!
         Hold him down!
         Look out for a kick!
         Pin his arms!

(*They have all piled on him and, after a fierce struggle, by sheer weight of numbers
have borne him to the floor just inside the door.*)

PADDY. (*who has remained detached*) Kape him down till he's cooled off. (*Scornfully*) Yerra, Yank, you're a great fool. Is it payin' attention at all you are to the
like of that skinny sow widout one drop of rale blood in her?

YANK. (*frenziedly, from the bottom of the heap*) She done me doit! She done me
doit, didn't she? I'll git square wit her! I'll get her some way! Git offen me, youse
guys! Lemme up! I'll show her who's a ape!

CURTAIN

[4]A laxative, such as Epsom salts.

SCENE FIVE

Three weeks later. A corner of Fifth Avenue in the Fifties on a fine Sunday morning. A general atmosphere of clean, well-tidied, wide street; a flood of mellow, tempered sunshine; gentle, genteel breezes. In the rear, the show windows of two shops, a jewelry establishment on the corner, a furrier's next to it. Here the adornments of extreme wealth are tantalizingly displayed. The jeweler's window is gaudy with glittering diamonds, emeralds, rubies, pearls, etc., fashioned in ornate tiaras, crowns, necklaces, collars, etc. From each piece hangs an enormous tag from which a dollar sign and numerals in intermittent electric lights wink out the incredible prices. The same in the furrier's. Rich furs of all varieties hang there bathed in a downpour of artificial light. The general effect is of a background of magnificence cheapened and made grotesque by commercialism, a background in tawdry disharmony with the clear light and sunshine on the street itself.

Up the side street YANK *and* LONG *come swaggering.* LONG *is dressed in shore clothes, wears a black Windsor tie, cloth cap.* YANK *is in his dirty dungarees. A fireman's cap with black peak is cocked defiantly on the side of his head. He has not shaved for days and around his fierce, resentful eyes—as around those of* LONG *to a lesser degree—the black smudge of coal dust still sticks like make-up. They hesitate and stand together at the corner, swaggering, looking around them with a forced, defiant contempt.*

LONG. (*indicating it all with an oratorical gesture*) Well, 'ere we are. Fif' Avenoo. This 'ere's their bleedin' private lane, as yer might say. (*Bitterly*) We're trespassers 'ere. Proletarians keep orf the grass!

YANK. (*dully*) I don't see no grass, yuh boob. (*Staring at the sidewalk*) Clean, ain't it? Yuh could eat a fried egg offen it. The white wings[1] got some job sweepin' dis up. (*Looking up and down the avenue—surlily*) Where's all de white-collar stiffs yuh said was here—and de skoits—*her* kind?

LONG. In church, blarst 'em! Arskin' Jesus to give 'em more money.

YANK. Choich, huh? I useter go to church onct—sure—when I was a kid. Me old man and woman, dey made me. Dey never went demselves, dough. Always got too big a head on Sunday mornin', dat was dem. (*With a grin*) Dey was scrappers for fair, bot' of dem. On Satiday nights when dey bot' got a skinful dey could put up a bout oughter been staged at de Garden.[2] When dey got trough dere wasn't a chair or table with a leg under it. Or else dey bot' jumped on me for somep'n. Dat was where I loined to take punishment. (*Wit a grin and a swagger*) I'm a chip offen de old block, get me?

LONG. Did yer old man follow the sea?

YANK. Naw. Worked along shore. I runned away when me old lady croaked wit de tremens.[3] I helped at truckin' and in de market. Den I shipped in de stokehole. Sure. Dat belongs. De rest was nothin'. (*Looking around him*) I ain't never seen dis before. De Brooklyn waterfront, dat was where I was dragged up. (*Taking a deep breath*) Dis ain't so bad at dat, huh?

LONG. Not bad? Well, we pays for it wiv our bloody sweat, if yer wants to know!

YANK. (*with sudden angry disgust*) Aw, hell! I don't see no one, see—like her. All dis gives me a pain. It don't belong. Say, ain't dere a back room around dis

---

[1]White-uniformed street cleaners.
[2]Madison Square Garden in New York City, an arena sometimes used for boxing matches.
[3]Delirium tremens, a violent delirium caused by alcoholism.

dump? Let's go shoot a ball.[4] All dis is too clean and quiet and dolled-up, get me! It gives me a pain.

LONG. Wait and yer'll bloody well see—

YANK. I don't wait for no one. I keep on de move. Say, what yuh drag me up here for, anyway? Tryin' to kid me, yuh simp, yuh?

LONG. Yer wants to get back at 'er, don't yer? That's what yer been sayin' every bloomin' hour since she hinsulted yer.

YANK. (*vehemently*) Sure ting I do! Didn't I try to get even wit her in Southampton? Didn't I sneak on de dock and wait for her by de gangplank? I was goin' to spit in her pale mug. Sure, right in her pop-eyes! Dat woulda made me even, see? But no chanct. Dere was a whole army of plainclothes bulls around. Dey spotted me and gimme de bum's rush. I never seen her. But I'll git square wit her yet, you watch. (*Furiously*) De lousy tart! She tinks she kin get away wit moider—but not wit me! I'll fix her! I'll tink of a way!

LONG. (*as disgusted as he dares to be*) Ain't that why I brought yer up 'ere—to show yer? Yer been lookin' at this 'ere 'ole affair wrong. Yer been actin' an' talkin' 's if it was all a bleedin' personal matter between yer and that bloody cow. I wants to convince yer she was on'y a representative of 'er clarss. I wants to awaken yer bloody clarss consciousness. Then yer'll see it's 'er clarss yer've got to fight, not 'er alone. There's a ole mob of 'em like 'er, Gawd blind 'em!

YANK. (*spitting on his hands—belligerently*) De more de merrier when I gits started. Bring on de gang!

LONG. Yer'll see 'em in arf a mo', when that church lets out. (*He turns and sees the window display in the two stores for the first time*) Blimey![5] Look at that, will yer? (*They both walk back and stand looking in the jeweler's.* LONG *flies into a fury*) Just look at this 'ere bloomin' mess! Just look at it! Look at the bleedin' prices on 'em— more'n our 'ole bloody stokehole makes in ten voyages sweatin' in 'ell! And they—'er and 'er bloody clarss—buys 'em for toys to dangle on 'em! One of these 'ere would buy scoff[6] for a starvin' family for a year!

YANK. Aw, cut de sob stuff! T' hell wit de starvin' family! Yuh'll be passin' de hat to me next. (*With naïve admiration*) Say, dem tings is pretty huh? Bet yuh dey'd hock for a piece of change aw right. (*Then turning away, bored*) But, aw hell, what good are dey? Let her have 'em. Dey don't belong no more'n she does. (*With a gesture of sweeping the jewelers into oblivion*) All dat don't count, get me?

LONG. (*who hs moved to the furrier's—indignantly*) And I s'pose this 'ere don't count neither—skins of poor, 'armless animals slaughtered so as 'er and 'ers can keep their bleedin' noses warm!

YANK. (*who has been staring at something inside—with queer excitement*) Take a slant at dat! Git it de once-over! Monkey fur—two t'ousand bucks! (*Bewilderedly*) Is dat straight goods—monkey fur! What de hell—?

LONG. (*bitterly*) It's straight enuf. (*With grim humor*) They wouldn't bloody well pay that for a 'airy ape's skin—no, nor for the 'ole livin' ape with all 'is 'ead, and a body, and soul thrown in!

YANK. (*clenching his fists, his face growing pale with rage as if the skin in the window were a personal insult*) Trowin' it up in my face! Christ! I'll fix her!

LONG. (*excitedly*) Church is out. 'Ere they come, the bleedin' swine. (*After a glance at* YANK's *lowering face—uneasily*) Easy goes, Comrade. Keep yer bloomin' temper. Remember force defeats itself. It ain't our weapon. We must impress

---

[4]I.e., shoot pool.
[5]A slang contraction of "God blind me!"   [6]Slang: "food."

our demands through peaceful means—the votes of the on-marching proletarians of the bloody world!

YANK. (*with abysmal contempt*) Votes, hell! votes is a joke, see. Votes for women! Let dem do it!

LONG. (*still more uneasily*) Calm, now. Treat 'em wiv the proper contempt. Observe the bleedin' parasites but 'old yer 'orses.

YANK. (*angrily*) Git away from me! Yuh're yellow, dat's what. Force, dat's me! De punch, dat's me every time, see! (*The crowd from church enter from the right, sauntering slowly and affectedly, their heads held stiffly up, looking neither to right nor left, talking in toneless, simpering voices. The women are rouged, calcimined, dyed, overdressed to the nth degree. The men are in Prince Alberts,[7] high hats, spats, canes, etc. A procession of gaudy marionettes, yet with something of the relentless horror of Frankensteins in their detached, mechanical unawareness.*)

VOICES. Dear Doctor Caiphas! He is so sincere!
What was the sermon?
I dozed off.
About the radicals, my dear—and the false doctrines that are being
   preached.
We must organize a hundred per cent American bazaar.
And let everyone contribute one one-hundredth per cent of their
   income tax.
What an original idea!
We can devote the proceeds to rehabilitating the veil of the temple.[8]
But that has been done so many times.

YANK. (*glaring from one to the other of them—with an insulting snort of scorn*) Huh! Huh! (*Without seeming to see him, they make wide detours to avoid the spot where he stands in the middle of the sidewalk.*)

LONG. (*frightenedly*) Keep yer bloomin' mouth shut, I tells yer.

YANK. (*viciously*) G'wan! Tell it to Sweeney! (*He swaggers away and deliberately lurches into a top-hatted gentleman, then glares at him pugnaciously*) Say, who d'yuh tink yuh're bumpin'? Tink yuh own de oith?

GENTLEMAN. (*coldly and affectedly*) I beg your pardon. (*He has not looked at* YANK *and passes on without a glance, leaving him bewildered.*)

LONG. (*rushing up and grabbing* YANK'S *arm*) 'Ere! Come away! This wasn't what I meant. Yer'll 'ave the bloody coppers down on us.

YANK. (*savagely—giving him a push that sends him sprawling*) G'wan!

LONG. (*picks himself up—hysterically*) I'll pop orf then. This ain't what I meant. And whatever 'appens, yer can't blame me. (*He slinks off left.*)

YANK. T' hell wit youse! (*He approaches a lady—with a vicious grin and a smirking wink*) Hello, Kiddo. How's every little ting? Got anything on for tonight? I know an old boiler down to de docks we kin crawl into. (*The lady stalks by without a look, without a change of pace.* YANK *turns to others—insultingly*) Holy smokes, what a mug! Go hide yuhself before de horses shy at yuh. Gee, pipe de heine[9] on dat one! Say, youse, yuh look like de stoin[10] of a ferryboat. Paint and powder! All dolled up to kill! Yuh look like stiffs laid out for de boneyard! Aw, g'wan, de lot of youse! Yuh give me an eyeache. Yuh don't belong, get me! Look at me, why don't youse dare? I belong, dat's me! (*Pointing to skyscraper across the street which is in process of construction—with bravado*) See dat building goin' up dere? See de steel work? Steel, dat's me! Youse guys live on it and tink yuh're somep'n.

---

[7]Elegant, long-tailed suit coats.
[8]The curtain hung before a church sanctuary, usually during Lent.
[9]I.e., "look at the rump."   [10]The stern, the rear end.

But I'm *in* it, see! I'm de hoistin' engine dat makes it go up! I'm it—de inside and bottom of it! Sure! I'm steel and steam and smoke and de rest of it! It moves—speed—twenty-five stories up—and me at de top and bottom—movin'! Youse simps don't move. Yuh're on'y dolls I winds up to see 'm spin. Yuh're de garbage, get me—de leavin's—de ashes we dump over de side! Now, what 'a' yuh gotta say? (*But as they seem neither to see nor hear him, he flies into a fury*) Bums! Pigs! Tarts! Bitches! (*He turns in a rage on the men, bumping viciously into them but not jarring them the least bit. Rather it is he who recoils after each collision. He keeps growling*) Git off de oith! G'wan, yuh bum! Look where yuh're goin', can't yuh? Git out here! Fight, why don't yuh? Put up yer mits! Don't be a dog! Fight or I'll knock yuh dead!(*but, without seeming to see him, they all answer with mechanical affected politeness* "I beg your pardon." *Then at a cry from one of the women they all scurry to the furrier's window.*)

THE WOMAN. (*ecstatically, with a gasp of delight*) Monkey fur! (*The whole crowd of men and women chorus after her in the same tone of affected delight.* "Monkey fur!")

YANK. (*with a jerk of his head back on his shoulders, as if he had received a punch full in the face—raging*) I see yuh, all in white! I see yuh, yuh white-faced tart, yuh! Hairy ape, huh? I'll hairy ape yuh! (*He bends down and grips at the street curbing as if to pluck it out and hurl it. Foiled in this, snarling with passion, he leaps to the lamppost on the corner and tries to pull it up for a club. Just at that moment a bus is heard rumbling up. A fat, high-hatted, spatted gentleman runs out from the side street. He calls out plaintively* "Bus! Bus! Stop here!" *and runs full tilt into the bending, straining* YANK, *who is bowled off his balance.*)

YANK. (*seeing a fight—with a roar of joy as he springs to his feet*) At last! Bus, huh? I'll bust yuh! (*He lets drive a terrific swing, his fist landing full on the fat gentleman's face. But the gentleman stands unmoved as if nothing had happened.*)

GENTLEMAN. I beg your pardon. (*Then irritably*) You have made me lose my bus. (*He claps his hands and begins to scream*) Officer! officer! (*Many police whistles shrill out on the instant and a whole platoon of policemen rush in on* YANK *from all sides. He tries to fight but is clubbed to the pavement and fallen upon. The crowd at the window have not moved or noticed this disturbance. The clanging gong of the patrol wagon approaches with a clamoring din.*)

CURTAIN

SCENE SIX

Night of the following day. A row of cells in the prison on Blackwell's Island.[1] *The cells extend back diagonally from right front to left rear. They do not stop, but disappear in the dark background as if they ran on, numberless, into infinity. One electric bulb from the low ceiling of the narrow corridor sheds its light through the heavy steel bars of the cell at the extreme front and reveals part of the interior.* YANK *can be seen within, crouched on the edge of his cot in the attitude of Rodin's "The Thinker." His face is spotted with black and blue bruises. A blood-stained bandage is wrapped around his head.*

YANK. (*suddenly starting as if awakening from a dream, reaches out and shakes the bars—aloud to himself, wonderingly*) Steel. Dis is de Zoo, huh? (*A burst of hard, barking laughter comes from the unseen occupants of the cells, runs back down the tier, and abruptly ceases.*)

---

[1]Island in the East River in New York City, now called Roosevelt Island.

VOICES. (*mockingly*) The Zoo? That's a new name for this coop—a damn good
  name!
  Steel, eh? You said a mouthful. This is the old iron house.
  Who is that boob talkin'?
  He's the bloke they brung in out of his head. The bulls had beat him
  up fierce.
YANK. (*dully*) I musta been dreamin'. I thought I was in a cage at de Zoo—but
de apes don't talk, do dey?
VOICES. (*with mocking laughter*) You're in a cage aw right.
  A coop!
  A pen!
  A sty!
  A kennel! (*Hard laughter—a pause.*)
  Say, guy! Who are you? No, never mind lying. What are you?
  Yes, tell us your sad story. What's your game?
  What did they jug yuh for?
YANK. (*dully*) I was a fireman—stokin' on de liners.(*Then with sudden rage,
rattling his cell bars*) I'm a hairy ape, get me? And I'll bust youse all in de jaw if
yuh don't lay off kiddin' me.
VOICES. Huh! You're a hard boiled duck, ain't you!
  When you spit, it bounces! (*Laughter.*)
  Aw, can it. He's a regular guy. Ain't you?
  What did he say he was—a ape?
YANK. (*defiantly*) Sure ting! Ain't dat what youse all are—apes? (*A silence. Then
a furious rattling of bars down the corridor*).
A VOICE. (*thick with rage*) I'll show yuh who's a ape, yuh bum!
VOICES. Ssshh! Nix!
  Can de noise!
  Piano!
  You'll have the guard down on us!
YANK. (*scornfully*) De guard? Yuh mean de keeper, don't yuh? (*Angry excla-
mations from all the cells.*)
VOICE. (*placatingly*) Aw, don't pay no attention to him. He's off his nut from
the beatin'-up he got. Say, you guy! We're waitin' to hear what they landed you
for—or ain't yuh tellin'?
YANK. Sure, I'll tell youse. Sure! Why de hell not? On'y—youse won't get me.
Nobody gets me but me, see? I started to tell de Judge and all he says was: "Toity
days to tink it over."—Tink it over! Christ, dat's all I been doin' for weeks! (*After
a pause*) I was trying' to git even wit someone, see?—someone dat done me doit.
VOICES. (*cynically*) De old stuff, I bet. Your goil, huh?
  Give yuh the double-cross, huh?
  That's them ever time!
  Did yuh beat up de odder guy?
YANK. (*disgustedly*) Aw, yuh're all wrong! Sure dere was a skoit in it—but not
what youse mean, not dat old tripe. Dis was a new kind of skoit. She was dolled
up all in white—in de stokehole. I tought she was a ghost. Sure. (*A pause.*)
VOICES. (*whispering*) Gee, he's still nutty.
  Let him rave. It's fun listenin'.
YANK. (*unheeding—groping in his thoughts*) Her hands—dey was skinny and
white like dey wasn't real but painted on somep'n. Dere was a million miles from
me to her—twenty-five knots a hour. She was like some dead ting de cat brung
in. Sure, dat's what. She didn't belong. She belonged in de window of a toy

store, or on de top of a garbage can, see! Sure! (*He breaks out angrily*) But would yuh believe it, she had de noive to do me doit. She lamped[2] me like she was seein' somep'n broke loose from de menagerie. Christ, yuh'd oughter seen her eyes! (*He rattles the bars of his cell furiously*) But I'll get back at her yet, you watch! And if I can't find her I'll take it out on de gang she runs wit. I'm wise to where dey hangs out now. I'll show her who belongs! I'll show her who's in de move and who ain't. You watch my smoke!

VOICES. (*serious and joking*) Dat's de talkin'!

　　Take her for all she's got!

　　What was this dame, anyway? Who was she, eh?

YANK. I dunno. First cabin stiff. Her old man's a millionaire, dey says—name of Douglas.

VOICES. Douglas? That's the president of the Steel Trust, I bet.

　　Sure. I seen his mug in de papers.

　　He's filthy with dough.

VOICE. Hey, feller, take a tip from me. If you want to get back at that dame, you better join the Wobblies. You'll get some action then.

YANK. Wobblies? What de hell's dat?

VOICE. Ain't you ever heard of the I. W. W.?[3]

YANK. Naw. What is it?

VOICE. A gang of blokes—a tough gang. I been readin' about 'em today in the paper. The guard give me the *Sunday Times*. There's a long spiel about 'em. It's from a speech made in the Senate by a guy named Senator Queen. (*He is in the cell next to* YANK'S. *There is a rustling of paper*) Wait'll I see if I got light enough and I'll read you. Listen (*He reads*) "There is a menace existing in this country today which threatens the vitals of our fair Republic—as foul a menace against the very life-blood of the American Eagle as was the foul conspiracy of Catiline[4] against the eagles of ancient Rome!"

VOICE. (*disgustedly*) Aw, hell! Tell him to salt de tail of dat eagle!

VOICE. (*reading*) "I refer to that devil's brew of rascals, jailbirds, murderers, and cutthroats who libel all honest working men by calling themselves the Industrial Workers of the World; but in the light of their nefarious plots, I call them the Industrial *Wreckers* of the World!"

YANK. (*with vengeful satisfaction*) Wreckers, dat's right dope! Dat belongs! Me for dem!

VOICE. Ssshh! (*Reading*) "This fiendish organization is a foul ulcer on the fair body of our Democracy—"

VOICE. Democracy, hell! Give him the boid, fellers—the raspberry! (*They do.*)

VOICE. Ssshh! (*Reading*) "Like Cato[5] I say to this Senate, the I. W. W. must be destroyed! For they represent an ever-present dagger pointed at the heart of the greatest nation the world has ever known, where all men are born free and equal, with equal opportunities to all, where the Founding Fathers have guaranteed to each one happiness, where Truth, Honor, Liberty, Justice, and the Brotherhood of Man are a religion absorbed with one's mother's milk, taught at our father's knee, sealed, signed, and stamped upon the glorious Constitution of these United States!" (*A perfect storm of hisses, catcalls, boos, and hard laughter.*)

VOICES. (*scornfully*) Hurrah for de Fort' of July!

---

[2] I.e., "looked at."

[3] Industrial Workers of the World, a radical labor organization founded in 1905. Its members were nicknamed "Wobblies."

[4] Lucius Sergius Catilina (108?–62 B.C.), Roman revolutionary conspirator.

[5] Marcus Porcius Cato (234–149 B.C.), Roman Senator who urged the destruction of Carthage.

Pass de hat!
Liberty!
Justice!
Honor!
Opportunity!
Brotherhood!

ALL. (*with abysmal scorn*) Aw, hell!

VOICE. Give that Queen Senator guy the bark! All togedder now—one—two—tree—(*A terrific chorus of barking and yapping.*)

GUARD. (*from a distance*) Quiet there, youse—or I'll git the hose. (*The noise subsides.*)

YANK. (*with growling rage*) I'd like to catch dat senator guy alone for a second. I'd loin him some trute!

VOICE. Ssshh! Here's where he gits down to cases on the Wobblies. (*Reads*) "They plot with fire in one hand and dynamite in the other. They stop not before murder to gain their ends, nor at the outraging of defenseless womanhood. They would tear down society, put the lowest scum in the seats of the mighty, turn Almighty God's revealed plan for the world topsy-turvy, and make of our sweet and lovely civilization a shambles, a desolation where man, God's masterpiece, would soon degenerate back to the ape!"

VOICE. (*to* YANK) Hey, you guy. There's your ape stuff again.

YANK. (*with a growl of fury*) I got him. So dey blow up tings, do dey? Dey turn tings around, do dey? Hey, lend me dat paper, will yuh?

VOICE. Sure. Give it to him. On'y keep it to yourself, see. We don't wanter listen to no more of that slop.

VOICE. Here you are. Hide it under your mattress.

YANK. (*reaching out*) Tanks. I can't read much but I kin manage. (*He sits, the paper in the hand at his side, in the attitude of Rodin's "The Thinker." A pause. Several snores from down the corridor. Suddenly* YANK *jumps to his feet with a furious groan as if some appalling thought had crashed on him—bewilderedly*) Sure—her old man—president of de Steel Trust—makes half de steel in de world—steel—where I tought I belonged—drivin' trou—movin'—in dat—to make *her*—and cage me in for her to spit on! Christ! (*He shakes the bars of his cell door till the whole tier trembles. Irritated, protesting exclamations from those awakened or trying to get to sleep*) He made dis—dis cage! Steel! *It* don't belong, dat's what! Cages, cells, locks, bolts, bars—dat's what it means!—holdin' me down with him at de top! But I'll drive trou! Fire, dat melts it! I'll be fire—under de heap—fire dat never goes out—hot as hell—breakin' out in de night—(*While he has been saying this last he has shaken his cell door to a clanging accompaniment. As he comes to the "breakin' out" he seizes one bar with both hands and, putting his two feet up against the others so that his position is parallel to the floor like a monkey's, he gives a great wrench backwards. The bar bends like a licorice stick under his tremendous strength. Just at this moment the* PRISON GUARD *rushes in, dragging a hose behind him.*)

GUARD. (*angrily*) I'll loin youse bums to wake me up! (*Sees* YANK) Hello, it's you, huh? Got the D. T.'s[6] hey? Well, I'll cure 'em. I'll drown your snakes for yuh! (*Noticing the bar*) Hell, look at dat bar bended! On'y a bug is strong enough for dat!

YANK. (*glaring at him*) Or a hairy ape, yuh big yellow bum! Look out! Here I come! (*He grabs another bar.*)

GUARD. (*scared now—yelling off left*) Toin de hose on, Ben!—full pressure! And

---

[6]Delirium tremens.

call de others—and a straitjacket! (*The curtain is falling. As it hides* YANK *from view, there is a splattering smash as the stream of water hits the steel of* YANK'S *cell.*)

CURTAIN

SCENE SEVEN

Nearly a month later. An I. W. W. local near the waterfront, showing the interior of a front room on the ground floor, and the street outside. Moonlight on the narrow street, buildings massed in black shadow. The interior of the room, which is general assembly room, office, and reading room, resembles some dingy settlement boys' club. A desk and high stool are in one corner. A table with papers, stacks of pamphlets, chairs about it, is at center. The whole is decidedly cheap, banal, commonplace and unmysterious as a room could be. The SECRETARY *is perched on the stool making entries in a large ledger. An eye shade casts his face into shadows. Eight or ten men, longshoremen, iron workers, and the like, are grouped about the table. Two are playing checkers. One is writing a letter. Most of them are smoking pipes. A big signboard is on the wall at the rear, "Industrial Workers of the World—Local No. 57."*

YANK *comes down the street outside. He is dressed as in Scene Five. He moves cautiously, mysteriously. He comes to a point opposite the door; tiptoes softly up to it, listens, is impressed by the silence within, knocks carefully, as if he were guessing at the password to some secret rite. Listens. No answer. Knocks again a bit louder. No answer, Knocks impatiently, much louder.*

SECRETARY. (*turning around on his stool*) What the hell is that—someone knocking? (*Shouts*) Come in, why don't you? (*All the men in the room look up.* YANK *opens the door slowly, gingerly, as if afraid of an ambush. He looks around for secret doors, mystery, is taken aback by the commonplaceness of the room and the men in it, thinks he may have gotten in the wrong place, then sees the signboard on the wall and is reassured.*)

YANK. (*blurts out*) Hello.

MEN. (*reservedly*) Hello.

YANK. (*more easily*) I thought I'd bumped into de wrong dump.

SECRETARY. (*scrutinizing him carefully*) Maybe you have. Are you a member?

YANK. Naw, not yet. Dat's what I come for—to join.

SECRETARY. That's easy. What's your job—longshore?

YANK. Naw, Fireman—stoker on de liners.

SECRETARY. (*with satisfaction*) Welcome to our city. Glad to know you people are waking up at last. We haven't got many members in your line.

YANK. Naw. Dey're all dead to de woild.

SECRETARY. Well, you can help to wake 'em. What's your name? I'll make out your card.

YANK. (*confused*) Name? Lemme tink.

SECRETARY. (*sharply*) Don't you know your own name?

YANK. Sure; but I been just Yank for so long—Bob, dat's it—Bob Smith.

SECRETARY. (*writing*) Robert Smith. (*Fills out the rest of the card*) Here you are. Cost you half a dollar.

YANK. Is dat all—four bits? Dat's easy. (*Gives the* SECRETARY *the money.*)

SECRETARY. (*throwing it in drawer*) Thanks. Well, make yourself at home. No introductions needed. There's literature on the table. Take some of those pamphlets with you to distribute aboard ship. They may bring results. Sow the seed, only go about it right. Don't get caught and fired. We got plenty out of work.

What we need is men who can hold their jobs—and work for us at the same time.

YANK. Sure. (*But he still stands, embarrassed and uneasy.*)

SECRETARY. (*looking at him—curiously*) What did you knock for? Think we had a coon in uniform to open doors?

YANK. Naw. I tought it was locked—and dat yuh'd wanter give me the once-over trou a peep-hole or somep'n to see if I was right.

SECRETARY. (*alert and suspicious but with an easy laugh*) Think we were running a crap game? That door is never locked. What put that in your nut?

YANK. (*with a knowing grin, convinced that this is all camouflage, a part of the secrecy*) Dis burg is full of bulls, ain't it?

SECRETARY. (*sharply*) What have the cops got to do with us? We're breaking no laws.

YANK. (*with a knowing wink*) Sure. Youse wouldn't for woilds. Sure. I'm wise to dat.

SECRETARY. You seem to be wise to a lot of stuff none of us knows about.

YANK. (*with another wink*) Aw, dat's aw right, see. (*Then made a bit resentful by the suspicious glances from all sides*) Aw, can it! Youse needn't put me trou de toid degree. Can't youse see I belong? Sure! I'm reg'lar. I'll stick, get me? I'll shoot de woiks for youse. Dat's why I wanted to join in.

SECRETARY. (*breezily, feeling him out*) That's the right spirit. Only are you sure you understand what you've joined? It's all plain and above board; still, some guys get a wrong slant on us. (*Sharply*) What's your notion of the purpose of the I. W. W.?

YANK. Aw, I know all about it.

SECRETARY. (*sarcastically*) Well, give us some of your valuable information.

YANK. (*cunningly*) I know enough not to speak outa my toin. (*Then resentfully again*) Aw, say! I'm reg'lar. I'm wise to de game. I know yuh got to watch your step with a stranger. For all youse know, I might be a plain-clothes dick, or somep'n, dat's what yuh're tinkin', huh? Aw, forget it! I belong, see? Ask any guy down to de docks if I don't.

SECRETARY. Who said you didn't?

YANK. After I'm 'nitiated, I'll show yuh.

SECRETARY. (*astounded*) Initiated? There's no initiation.

YANK. (*disappointed*) Ain't there no password—no grip or nothin'?

SECRETARY. What'd you think this is—the Elks—or the Black Hand?[1]

YANK. De Elks, hell! De Black Hand, dey're a lot of yellow back-stickin' Ginees.[2] Dis is a man's gang, ain't it?

SECRETARY. You said it! That's why we stand on our two feet in the open. We got no secrets.

YANK. (*surprised but admiringly*) Yuh mean to say yuh always run wide open—like dis?

SECRETARY. Exactly.

YANK. Den yuh sure got your noive wit youse!

SECRETARY. (*sharply*) Just what was it made you want to join us? Come out with that straight.

YANK. Yuh call me? Well, I got noive, too! Here's my hand. Yuh wanter blow tings up, don't yuh? Well, dat's me! I belong!

---

[1]Elks: an American fraternal organization. Black Hand: Italian underworld organization of the mid-nineteenth century.
[2]"Guineas," slang term for "Italians."

SECRETARY. (*with pretended carelessness*) You mean change the unequal conditions of society by legitimate direct action—or with dynamite?

YANK. Dynamite! Blow it offen de oith—steel—all de cages—all de factories, steamers, buildings, jails—de Steel Trust and all dat makes it go.

SECRETARY. So—that's your idea, eh? And did you have any special job in that line you wanted to propose to us? (*He makes a sign to the men, who get up cautiously one by one and group behind* YANK.)

YANK. (*boldly*) Sure, I'll come out wit it. I'll show youse I'm one of de gang. Dere's dat millionaire guy, Douglas—

SECRETARY. President of the Steel Trust, you mean? Do you want to assassinate him?

YANK. Naw, dat don't get yuh nothin'. I mean blow up de factory, de woiks, where he makes de steel. Dat's what I'm after—to blow up de steel, knock all de steel in de woild up to de moon. Dat'll fix tings! (*Eagerly, with a touch of bravado*) I'll do it by me lonesome! I'll show yuh! Tell me where his woiks is, how to git there, all de dope. Gimme de stuff, de old butter—and watch me do de rest! Watch de smoke and see it move! I don't give a damn if dey nab me—long as it's done! I'll soive life for it—and give 'em de laugh! (*Half to himself*) And I'll write her a letter and tell her de hairy ape done it. Dat'll square tings.

SECRETARY. (*stepping away from* YANK) Very interesting. (*He gives a signal. The men, huskies all, throw themselves on* YANK *and before he knows it they have his legs and arms pinioned. But he is too flabbergasted to make a struggle, anyway. They feel him over for weapons.*)

MAN. No gat, no knife. Shall we give him what's what and put the boots to him?

SECRETARY. No. He isn't worth the trouble we'd get into. He's too stupid. (*He comes closer and laughs mockingly in* YANK'S *face*) Ho-ho! By God, this is the biggest joke they've put up on us yet. Hey, you Joke! Who sent you—Burns or Pinkerton?[3] No, by God, you're such a bonehead I'll bet you're in the Secret Service! Well, you dirty spy, you rotten agent provocator, you can go back and tell whatever skunk is paying you blood-money for betraying your brothers that he's wasting his coin. You couldn't catch a cold. And tell him that all he'll ever get on us, or ever has got, is just his own sneaking plots that he's framed up to put us in jail. We are what our manifesto says we are, neither more nor less— and we'll give him a copy of that any time he calls. And as for you—(*He glares scornfully at* YANK, *who is sunk in an oblivious stupor*) Oh, hell, what's the use of talking? You're a brainless ape.

YANK. (*aroused by the word to fierce but futile struggles*) What's dat, you Sheeny[4] bum, yuh!

SECRETARY. Throw him out, boys. (*In spite of his struggles, this is done with gusto and éclat. Propelled by several parting kicks,* YANK *lands sprawling in the middle of the narrow cobbled street. With a growl he starts to get up and storm the closed door, but stops bewildered by the confusion in his brain, pathetically impotent. He sits there, brooding, in as near the attitude of Rodin's "The Thinker" as he can get in his position.*)

YANK. (*bitterly*) So dem boids don't tink I belong, neider. Aw, to hell wit 'em! Dey're in de wrong pew—de same old bull—soap-boxes and Salvation Army— no guts! Cut out an hour offen de job a day and make me happy! Gimme a dollar more a day and make me happy! Tree square a day, and cauliflowers in de front yard—ekal rights—a woman and kids—a lousy vote—and I'm all fixed for Jesus, huh? Aw, hell! What does dat get yuh? Dis ting's in your inside, but

---

[3]Detective agencies.   [4]Slang term for "Jewish."

it ain't your belly. Feedin' your face—sinkers and coffee—dat don't touch it. It's way down—at de bottom. Yuh can't grab it, and yuh can't stop it. It moves, and everything moves. It stops and de whole woild stops. Dat's me now—I don't tick, see?—I'm a busted Ingersoll,[5] dat's what. Steel was me, and I owned de woild. Now I ain't steel, and de woild owns me. Aw, hell! I can't see—it's all dark, get me? It's all wrong! (*He turns a bitter mocking face up like an ape gibbering at the moon*) Say, youse up dere, Man in de Moon, yuh look so wise, gimme de answer, huh? Slip me de inside dope, de information right from de stable— where do I get off at, huh?

A POLICEMAN. (*who has come up the street in time to hear this last—with grim humor*) You'll get off at the station, you boob, if you don't get up out of that and keep movin'.

YANK. (*looking up at him—with a hard, bitter laugh*) Sure! Lock me up! Put me in a cage! Dat's de on'y answer yuh know. G'wan lock me up!

POLICEMAN. What you been doin'?

YANK. Enuf to gimme life for! I was born, see? Sure, dat's de charge. Write it in de blotter. I was born, get me!

POLICEMAN. (*jocosely*) God pity your old woman! (*Then matter-of-factly*) But I've no time for kidding. You're soused. I'd run you in but it's too long a walk to the station. Come on now, get up, or I'll fan your ears with this club. Beat it now! (*He hauls* YANK *to his feet.*)

YANK. (*in a vague mocking tone*) Say, where do I go from here?

POLICEMAN. (*giving him a push—with a grin, indifferently*) Go to hell.

CURTAIN

SCENE EIGHT

Twilight of the next day. The monkey house at the Zoo. One spot of clear gray light falls on the front of one cage so that the interior can be seen. The other cages are vague, shrouded in shadow from which chatterings pitched in a conversational tone can be heard. On the one cage a sign from which the word "gorilla" stands out. The gigantic animal himself is seen squatting on his haunches on a bench in much the same attitude of Rodin's "The Thinker." YANK *enters from the left. Immediately a chorus of angry chattering and screeching breaks out. The gorilla turns his eyes but makes no sound or move.*

YANK. (*with a hard, bitter laugh*) Welcome to your city, huh? Hail, hail, de gang's all here! (*At the sound of his voice the chattering dies away into an attentive silence.* YANK *walks up to the gorilla's cage and, leaning over the railing, stares in at its occupant, who stares back at him, silent and motionless. There is a pause of dead stillness. Then* YANK *begins to talk in a friendly confidential tone, half mockingly, but with a deep undercurrent of sympathy*) Say, yuh're some hard-lookin' guy, ain't yuh? I seen lots of tough nuts dat de gang called gorillas, but yuh're de foist real one I ever seen. Some chest yuh got, and shoulders, and dem arms and mits! I bet yuh got a punch in eider fist dat'd knock 'em all silly! (*This with genuine admiration. The gorilla, as if he understood, stands upright, swelling out his chest and pounding on it with his fist.* YANK *grins sympathetically*) Sure, I get yuh. Yuh challenge de whole woild, huh? Yuh got what I was sayin' even if yuh muffed de woids (*Then bitterness creeping in*) And why wouldn't yuh get me? Ain't we both members of de same club—de Hairy Apes? (*They stare at each other—a pause—then* YANK *goes on slowly*

[5]An brand of inexpensive watch.

and bitterly) So yuh're what she seen when she looked at me, de white-faced tart!
I was you to her, get me? On'y outa de cage—broke out—free to moider her,
see? Sure! Dat's what she tought. She wasn't wise dat I was in a cage, too—
worser'n yours—sure—a damn sight—'cause you got some chanct to bust loose—
but me— (*He grows confused*) Aw, hell! It's all wrong, ain't it? (*A pause*) I s'pose
yuh wanter know what I'm doin' here, huh? I been warmin' a bench down to
de Battery[1]—ever since last night. Sure. I seen de sun come up. Dat was pretty,
too—all red and pink and green. I was lookin' at de skyscrapers—steel—and all
de ships comin' in, sailin' out, all over de oith—and dey was steel, too. De sun
was warm, dey wasn't no clouds, and dere was a breeze blowin'. Sure, it was
great stuff. I got it aw right—what Paddy said about dat bein' de right dope—
on'y I couldn't get *in* it, see? I couldn't belong in dat. It was over my head. And
I kept tinkin'—and den I beat it up here to see what youse was like. And I waited
till dey was all gone to git yuh alone. Say, how d'yuh feel sittin' in dat pen all de
time, havin' to stand for 'em comin' and starin' at yuh—de white-faced, skinny
tarts and de boobs what marry 'em—makin' fun of yuh, laughin' at yuh, gittin'
scared of yuh—damn 'em! (*He pounds on the rail with is fist. The gorilla rattles the
bars of his cage and snarls. All the other monkeys set up an angry chattering in the
darkness.* YANK *goes on excitedly*) Sure! Dat's de way it hits me, too. On'y yuh're
lucky, see? You don't belong wit 'em and yuh know it. But me, I belong wit
'em—but I don't, see? Dey don't belong wit me, dat's what. Get me? Tinkin' is
hard—(*He passes one hand across his forehead with a painful gesture. The gorilla growls
impatiently.* YANK *goes on gropingly*) It's dis way, what I'm drivin' at. Youse can sit
and dope dream in de past, green woods, de jungle and de rest of it. Den yuh
belong and dey don't. Den yuh kin laugh at 'em, see? Yuh're de champ of de
world. But me—I ain't got no past to tink in, nor nothin' dat's comin', on'y what's
now—and dat don't belong. Sure, you're de best off! You can't tink, can yuh?
Yuh can't talk neider. But I kin make a bluff at talkin' and tinkin'— a'most git
away wit it—a'most!—and dat's where de joker comes in. (*He laughs*) I ain't on
oith and I ain't in heaven, get me? I'm in de middle tryin' to separate 'em, takin'
all de woist punches from bot' of 'em. Maybe dat's what dey call hell, huh? But
you, yuh're at de bottom. You belong? Sure! Yuh're de on'y one in de woild dat
does, yuh lucky stiff! (*The gorilla growls proudly*) And dat's why dey gotter put
yuh in a cage, see? (*The gorilla roars angrily*) Sure! Yuh get me. It beats it when
you try to tink it or talk it—it's way down—deep—behind—you 'n' me we feel
it. Sure! Bot' members of dis club! (*He laughs—then in a savage tone*) What de
hell! T' hell wit it! A little action, dat's our meat! Dat belongs! Knock 'em down
and keep bustin' 'em till dey croaks yuh with a gat—wit a steel! Sure! are yuh
game? Dey've looked at youse, ain't dey—in a cage? Wanter get even? Wanter
wind up like a sport 'stead of croaken' slow in dere? (*The gorilla roars an emphatic
affirmative.* YANK *goes on with a sort of furious exaltation*) Sure! Yuh're reg'lar! Yuh'll
stick to de finish! Me 'n' you, huh?—bot' members of dis club! We'll put up one
last star bout dat'll knock 'em offen deir seats! Dey'll have to make de cages
stronger after we're trou! (*The gorilla is straining at his bars, growling, hopping from
one foot to the other.* YANK *takes a jimmy from under his coat and forces the lock on the
cage door. He throws this open*) Pardon from de governor! Step out and shake
hands. I'll take yuh for a walk down 'Fif' Avenoo. We'll knock 'em offen de oith
and croak with de band playin'. Come on, Brother. (*The gorilla scrambles gingerly
out of his cage. Goes to* YANK *and stands looking at him.* YANK *keeps his mocking tone—
holds out his hand*) Shake—de secret grip of our order. (*Something, the tone of*

[1]A park at the southern end of Manhattan Island.

mockery, perhaps, suddenly enrages the animal. With a spring he wraps his huge arms around YANK *in a murderous hug. There is a cracking snap of crushed ribs—a gasping cry, still mocking, from* YANK) Hey, I didn't say kiss me! (*The gorilla lets the crushed body slip to the floor; stands over it uncertainly, considering; then picks it up, throws it in the cage, shuts the door, and shuffles off menacingly into the darkness at left. A great uproar of frightened chattering and whimpering comes from the other cages. Then* YANK *moves, groaning, opening his eyes, and there is silence. He mutters painfully*) Say—dey oughter match him—with Zybszko.[2] He got me, aw right. I'm trou. Even him didn't tink I belonged. (*Then, with sudden passionate despair*) Christ, where do I get off at? Where do I fit in? (*Checking himself as suddenly*) Aw, what de hell! No squawkin', see! No quittin', get me! Croak wit your boots on! (*He grabs hold of the bars of the cage and hauls himself painfully to his feet—looks around him bewilderedly— forces a mocking laugh*) In de cage, huh? (*In the strident tones of a circus barker*) Ladies and gents, step forward and take a slant at de one and only—(*His voice weakening*) one and original—Hairy Ape from de wilds of—(*He slips in a heap on the floor and dies. The monkeys set up a chattering, whimpering wail. And, perhaps, the Hairy Ape at last belongs.*

CURTAIN   1922

Ezra Pound   *1885–1972*

"E.P."—for two generations the mere initials have identified the father of modernism, the first and the last of a band of revolutionists who changed the course of twentieth-century poetry. Those whose lives he affected comprise a roster of some of the most distinguished writers of his time. Yeats, Eliot, D. H. Lawrence, Joyce, Frost, and Williams are only a few of those who acknowledged their debt. He survived them all, and not until his death at the age of eighty-seven in Venice did it seem that a remarkable literary era had finally ended.

Pound was born in Hailey, Idaho, and raised in Pennsylvania. At fifteen he entered college, already proficient in Latin and resolved that by the age of thirty he "would know more about poetry than any man living." He attended Hamilton College and the University of Pennsylvania, where he majored in romance philology while reading his way through a large portion of classical and European literatures. At Pennsylvania, from which he received his M.A. in 1906, he associated with two other young poets—and future imagists— William Carlos Williams and Hilda Doolittle. An academic teaching career lasted four months: he was fired from his first job, at Wabash College, for having a woman in his room. The following year he sailed as a deckhand on a cattle boat for Europe and remained there for most of his life.

From Venice, where he published (and then reviewed) a first book of poems, A Lume Spento *(1908), Pound settled in London and with characteristic aplomb set about to reform English letters and "To resuscitate the dead art / of poetry." The London years, between 1908 and 1920, were those in which his dictum "Make it new!" became the rallying cry of modernism, and, as London became the center of literary activity, Pound*

---

[2]Stanislaus Zbyszko, a famous wrestler of the 1920s.

became the center of the center—discovering, coaching, promoting, and serving as a tireless gadfly to whatever new talent came his way.

With T. E. Hulme, he started imagism, the writing of short, free-verse poems presenting a single image; with Wyndham Lewis, he promoted vorticism, a literary version of cubism that argued for a poetry of "vigorous impact" with a single image at its "vortex." He published translations of Chinese poetry and Japanese Noh drama, initiating the orientalist techniques that became a modernist vogue. As overseas editor for Harriet Monroe's Poetry Magazine *he used its pages, along with those of other little magazines, to explain his principles of reform and to introduce such poets as Eliot and Frost to American audiences. During these years he was also writing some of his best poetry.* Personae, *his most important collection, first appeared in 1909 and was repeatedly reprinted with additions from subsequent major books—*Ripostes *(1912) and* Lustra *(1916). At the same time he was at work on the early sections of the* Cantos, *the projected epic poem that was to be his life's work.*

After World War I, Pound summarized his disillusionment with the war and with England in Hugh Selwyn Mauberley *(1920). He then moved to Paris, for the next four years, as a lesser but still potent force, moving among the British and American expatriates of the "Lost Generation."*

The turning point came in 1924 when Pound moved on to Italy. Under Mussolini's spell, he became preoccupied with economic theory, issuing increasingly violent diatribes against American capitalism, usury, and the Jews. His views are reflected in the Cantos *and in such prose works as* Jefferson and/or Mussolini *(1935). With the outbreak of World War II, he began broadcasting pro-Fascist propaganda to England and America. When the war ended, he was arrested, charged with treason, and held in an outdoor cage at an American prison camp near Pisa, Italy. He was returned to the United States for trial, but, after psychiatric examination, he was declared insane and interned at St. Elizabeths Hospital, a mental institution near Washington, D.C. In 1948 the* Pisan Cantos, *written by Pound during his imprisonment near Pisa, Italy, was awarded the Bollingen Prize by a group of distinguished literary judges. The furor that resulted from the awarding of a prize to a "traitor" divided the literary world. Eventually, through the intervention of Frost, Eliot, Hemingway, and others, Pound was released and allowed to return to Italy. The* Cantos, *now numbering over a hundred, ended in 1960, and Pound retired to silence.*

Although the controversy that began with the Pisan Cantos *has continued to spur partisan assessments of Pound's achievement, his importance during the second and third decades of the century is beyond question. His best poems, like all his poetry, represent a wide diversity of forms. Among them, certainly, are some of the early, finely wrought, imagist pieces, his translations from the Chinese and from the Anglo-Saxon "Seafarer," and* Mauberley. *In the* Cantos *his innovative techniques often failed him, yet some individual passages contain his greatest work. At the end of his life Pound acknowledged his failure as a social theorist and as a poet. He had become the lost leader for the poetry of a departed age. Few literary figures had stirred such hatred, fewer still had labored so prodigiously for poetry and aroused such gratitude and admiration.*

FURTHER READING: *The Letters of Ezra Pound, 1907–1941*, ed. D. Paige, 1950; C. Norman, *Ezra Pound*, 1960; J. Cornell, *The Trial of Ezra Pound*, 1966; N. Stock, *The Life of Ezra Pound*, 1970, 1982; J. Tyell, *Ezra Pound*, 1987; H. Kenner, *The Poetry of Ezra Pound*, 1951, 1968; G. Dekker, *The Cantos of Ezra Pound*, 1963; N. de Nagy, *Ezra Pound's Poetics*, 1966; K. Goodwin, *The Influence of Ezra Pound*, 1966; N. Stock, *Reading the Cantos*, 1967; T. Jackson, *The Early Poetry of Ezra Pound*, 1968; K. Ruthven, *A Guide to Ezra Pound's "Personae" (1926)*, 1969; H. Witemeyer, *The Poetry of Ezra Pound*, ed. E. Hesse, 1969; D. Pearlman, *The Barb of Time*, 1970; C. Brooke-Rose, *A ZBC Ezra Pound*, 1971; E. Homberger, *Ezra Pound, The Critical Heritage*, 1972; H. Kenner, *The Pound Era*, 1972; D. Davie, *Ezra Pound*,

1976; C. Heymann, *Ezra Pound, the Last Rower,* 1976; R. Bush, *The Genesis of Pound's Cantos,* 1976; J. Wilhelm, *The Later Cantos of Ezra Pound,* 1977; C. Terrell, *A Companion to the Cantos of Ezra Pound,* 2 vols., 1980, 1984; W. Flory, *Ezra Pound and the Cantos,* 1980; P. Ackroyd, *Ezra Pound and His World,* 1981; P. Nichols, *Ezra Pound, Politics, Economics, and Writing,* 1984; J. Wilhelm, *The American Roots of Ezra Pound,* 1985; *Ezra Pound,* ed. H. Bloom, 1987; K. Lindberg, *Reading Pound Reading,* 1987.

TEXTS: *Personae,* 1949; *The Cantos of Ezra Pound,* 1970; *Literary Essays of Ezra Pound,* ed. T. S. Eliot, 1954.

MR. HOUSMAN'S[1] MESSAGE

O woe, woe,
People are born and die,
We also shall be dead pretty soon
Therefore let us act as if we were
         dead already.

The bird sits on the hawthorn tree
But he dies also, presently.
Some lads get hung, and some get shot.
Woeful is this human lot.
    Woe! woe, etcetera. . . .[2]   10

London is a woeful place,
Shropshire is much pleasanter.
Then let us smile a little space
Upon fond nature's morbid grace.
    Oh, Woe, woe, woe, etcetera. . . .
                 1911, 1926

PORTRAIT D'UNE FEMME[1]

Your mind and you are our Sargasso Sea,[2]
London has swept about you this score[3] years
And bright ships left you this or that in fee:[4]
Ideas, old gossip, oddments of all things,
Strange spars of knowledge and dimmed wares of price.
Great minds have sought you—lacking someone else.
You have been second always. Tragical?
No. You preferred it to the usual thing:
One dull man, dulling and uxorious,[5]
One average mind—with one thought less, each year.   10
Oh, you are patient, I have seen you sit

[1]Alfred Edward Housman (1859–1936), English lyric poet, author of *A Shropshire Lad* (1896).
[2]Marks of ellipsis in poetry, here and below, are Pounds.
[1]French: Portrait of a Lady.
[2]An area of the North Atlantic Ocean, known for its entangling, floating seaweed.
[3]Twenty.   [4]Payment.   [5]Submissive to one's wife.

Hours, where something might have floated up.
And now you pay one. Yes, you richly pay.
You are a person of some interest, one comes to you
And takes strange gain away:
Trophies fished up; some curious suggestion;
Fact that leads nowhere; and a tale or two,
Pregnant with mandrakes,[6] or with something else
That might prove useful and yet never proves,
That never fits a corner or shows use,   20
Or finds its hour upon the loom of days:
The tarnished, gaudy, wonderful old work;
Idols and ambergris[7] and rare inlays,
These are your riches, your great store; and yet
For all this sea-hoard of deciduous[8] things,
Strange woods half sodden, and new brighter stuff:
In the slow float of differing light and deep,
No! there is nothing! In the whole and all,
Nothing that's quite your own.
            Yet this is you.   30

               1912, 1926

THE SEAFARER[1]

From the Anglo-Saxon

May I for my own self song's truth reckon,
Journey's jargon, how I in harsh days
Hardship endured oft.
Bitter breast-cares have I abided,
Known on my keel many a care's hold,
And dire sea-surge, and there I oft spent
Narrow nightwatch nigh the ship's head
While she tossed close to cliffs. Coldly afflicted,
My feet were by frost benumbed.
Chill its chains are; chafing sighs   10
Hew my heart round and hunger begot
Mere-weary[2] mood. Lest man know not
That he on dry land loveliest liveth,
List how I, care-wretched, on ice-cold sea,
Weathered the winter, wretched outcast
Deprived of my kinsmen;
Hung with hard ice-flakes, where hail-scur[3] flew,
There I heard naught save the harsh sea
And ice-cold wave, at whiles the swan cries,

[6]An herb. Its roots were thought to have magical properties, among them the power to promote conception in women.
[7]Waxy substance, from whales, used in making perfume.
[8]Passing, impermanent.
[1]Pound's "translation" of an Old English poem whose author is unknown.   [2]Sea-weary.
[3]I.e., hailstones.

Did for my games the gannet's[4] clamour,   20
Sea-fowls' loudness was for me laughter,
The mews'[5] singing all my mead-drink.[6]
Storms, on the stone-cliffs beaten, fell on the stern
In icy feathers; full oft the eagle screamed
With spray on his pinion.[7]
               Not any protector
May make merry man faring needy.
This he little believes, who aye in winsome life
Abides 'mid burghers some heavy business,
Wealthy and wine-flushed, how I weary oft   30
Must bide above brine.
Neareth nightshade, snoweth from north,
Frost froze the land, hail fell on earth then,
Corn of the coldest. Nathless[8] there knocketh now
The heart's thought that I on high streams
The salt-wavy tumult traverse alone.
Moaneth alway my mind's lust
That I fare forth, that I afar hence
Seek out a foreign fastness.
For this there's no mood-lofty man over earth's midst,   40
Not though he be given his good, but will have in his youth greed;
Nor his deed to the daring, nor his king to the faithful
But shall have his sorrow for sea-fare
Whatever his lord will.
He hath not heart for harping, nor in ring-having
Nor winsomeness to wife, nor world's delight
Nor any whit else save the wave's slash,
Yet longing comes upon him to fare forth on the water.
Bosque[9] taketh blossom, cometh beauty of berries,
Fields to fairness, land fares brisker,   50
All this admonisheth man eager of mood,
The heart turns to travel so that he then thinks
On flood-ways to be far departing.
Cuckoo calleth with gloomy crying,
He singeth summerward, bodeth sorrow,
The bitter heart's blood. Burgher knows not—
He the prosperous man—what some perform
Where wandering them widest draweth.
So that but now my heart burst from my breastlock,
My mood 'mid the mere-flood,[10]   60
Over the whale's acre, would wander wide.
On earth's shelter cometh oft to me,
Eager and ready, the crying lone-flyer,
Whets for the whale-path the heart irresistibly,
O'er tracks of ocean; seeing that anyhow
My lord deems to me this dead life
On loan[11] and on land, I believe not
That any earth-weal[12] eternal standeth

---

[4]A large seabird.   [5]Gulls.   [6]An alcoholic drink made of fermented honey, malt, and yeast.
[7]Feathers.   [8]Nevertheless.   [9]Woods.   [10]Sea-flood, tide.   [11]Temporarily.
[12]Earthly prosperity, well-being.   [13]Praise.   [14]Brave.

Save there be somewhat calamitous
That, ere a man's tide go, turn it to twain. 70
Disease or oldness or sword-hate
Beats out the breath from doom-gripped body.
And for this, every earl whatever, for those speaking after—
Laud[13] of the living, boasteth some last word,
That he will work ere he pass onward,
Frame on the fair earth 'gainst foes his malice,
Daring ado, . . .
So that all men shall honour him after
And his laud beyond them remain 'mid the English,
Aye, for ever, a lasting life's-blast, 80
Delight 'mid the doughty.[14]
                    Days little durable,
And all arrogance of earthen riches,
There come now no kings nor Cæsars
Nor gold-giving lords like those gone.
Howe'er in mirth most magnified,
Whoe'er lived in life most lordliest,
Drear[15] all this excellence, delights undurable!
Waneth the watch, but the world holdeth.
Tomb hideth trouble. The blade is layed low.
Earthly glory ageth and seareth. 90
No man at all going the earth's gait,
But age fares against him, his face paleth,
Grey-haired he groaneth, knows gone companions,
Lordly men, are to earth o'ergiven,
Nor may he then the flesh-cover, whose life ceaseth,
Nor eat the sweet nor feel the sorry,[16]
Nor stir hand nor think in mid heart,
And though he strew the grave with gold,
His born brothers, their buried bodies
Be an unlikely treasure hoard. 100

1912

A VIRGINAL[1]

No, no! Go from me. I have left her lately.
I will not spoil my sheath with lesser brightness,
For my surrounding air hath a new lightness;
Slight are her arms, yet they have bound me straitly
And left me cloaked as with a gauze of æther;[2]
As with sweet leaves; as with subtle clearness.
Oh, I have picked up magic in her nearness
To sheathe me half in half the things that sheathe her.

---

[15]Dreary.   [16]Pain, sorrow.
[1]A spinet, a small musical instrument like a harpsichord, popular in the 17th century. The name was derived from its being played by young girls, virgins.
[2]Celestial, heavenly air.

No, no! Go from me. I have still the flavour,
Soft as spring wind that's come from birchen bowers.   10
Green come the shoots, aye April in the branches,
As winter's wound with her sleight hand she staunches,
Hath of the trees a likeness of the savour:
As white their bark, so white this lady's hours.

                                                            1912

THE RETURN

See, they return; ah, see the tentative
Movements, and the slow feet,
The trouble in the pace and the uncertain
Wavering!

See, they return, one, and by one,
With fear, as half-awakened;
As if the snow should hesitate
And murmur in the wind,
                and half turn back;
These were the "Wing'd-with-Awe,"
                Inviolable.   10

Gods of the wingèd shoe!
With them the silver hounds,
                sniffing the trace of air!

Haie! Haie!
        These were the swift to harry;
These the keen-scented;
These were the souls of blood.

Slow on the leash,
                pallid the leash-men!

                                                            1912

SALUTATION

O generation of the thoroughly smug
        and thoroughly uncomfortable,
I have seen fishermen picnicking in the sun,
I have seen them with untidy families,
I have seen their smiles full of teeth
        and heard ungainly laughter.
And I am happier than you are,
And they were happier than I am;

And the fish swim in the lake
and do not even own clothing.

1913, 1916

THE REST

O helpless few in my country,
O remnant enslaved!

Artists broken against her,
A-stray, lost in the villages,
Mistrusted, spoken-against,

Lovers of beauty, starved,
Thwarted with systems,
Helpless against the control;

You who can not wear yourselves out
By persisting to successes,   10
You who can only speak,
Who can not steel yourselves into reiteration;

You of the finer sense,
Broken against false knowledge,
You who can know at first hand,
Hated, shut in, mistrusted:

Take thought:
I have weathered the storm,
I have beaten out my exile.

1913, 1916

A PACT

I make a pact with you, Walt Whitman—
I have detested you long enough.
I come to you as a grown child
Who has had a pig-headed father;
I am old enough now to make friends
It was you that broke the new wood,
Now is a time for carving.

We have one sap and one root—
Let there be commerce between us.
1913, 1916

IN A STATION OF THE METRO[1]

The apparition of these faces in the crowd;
Petals on a wet, black bough.
1913, 1916

THE RIVER-MERCHANT'S WIFE:
A LETTER

While my hair was still cut straight across my forehead
I played about the front gate, pulling flowers.
You came by on bamboo stilts, playing horse,
You walked about my seat, playing with blue plums.
And we went on living in the village of Chokan:
Two small people, without dislike or suspicion.

At fourteen I married My Lord you.
I never laughed, being bashful.
Lowering my head, I looked at the wall.
Called to, a thousand times, I never looked back.   10

At fifteen I stopped scowling,
I desired my dust to be mingled with yours
Forever and forever and forever.
Why should I climb the look out?

At sixteen you departed,
You went into far Ku-to-yen, by the river of swirling
    eddies,
And you have been gone five months.
The monkeys make sorrowful noise overhead.

You dragged your feet when you went out.
By the gate now, the moss is grown, the different
    mosses,   20
Too deep to clear them away!
The leaves fall early this autumn, in wind.
The paired butterflies are already yellow with August
Over the grass in the West garden;
They hurt me. I grow older.

[1]The Paris subway.

If you are coming down through the narrows of the
    river Kiang,
Please let me know beforehand,
And I will come out to meet you
    As far as Cho-fu-Sa.

        By Rihaku[1]
        1915

from *HUGH SELWYN MAUBERLEY*

(LIFE AND CONTACTS)

I

E. P. ODE POUR L'ELECTION DE SON
SEPULCHRE[1]

For three years, out of key with his time,
He strove to resuscitate the dead art
Of poetry; to maintain "the sublime"
In the old sense. Wrong from the start—

No, hardly, but seeing he had been born
In a half savage country, out of date;
Bent resolutely on wringing lilies from the acorn;
Capaneus;[2] trout for factitious bait;

Ἴδμεν γάρ τοι πάνθ᾽, ὅσ᾽ ἐνὶ Τροίῃ[3]
Caught in the unstopped ear;   10
Giving the rocks small lee-way
The chopped seas held him, therefore, that year.

His true Penelope[4] was Flaubert,[5]
He fished by obstinate isles;
Observed the elegance of Circe's[6] hair
Rather than the mottoes on sun-dials.[7]

Unaffected by "the march of events,"
He passed from men's memory in *l'an trentiesme*
De son eage;[8] the case presents
No adjunct to the Muses' diadem.   20

[1]Japanese name for the Chinese poet Li Po (701–762) whose poem Pound translates and adapts.
[1]French? "E. P. [Ezra Pound] Ode on the Choice of His Tomb." The title is taken from "De l'élection de son sépulchre," an ode by the French poet Pierre de Ronsard (1524–1585).
[2]One of seven heroes who attacked Thebes. For his defiance of Zeus he was struck dead by a thunderbolt.
[3]Greek: "For we know everything that is in Troy," from the alluring song of the Sirens (*Odyssey*, Book XII, line 189). Odysseus ordered his sailors' ears to be sealed with wax so they would not hear the Sirens' song and destroy themselves, while he had himself tied to the ship's mast so that he might listen safely with "unstopped ear."
[4]Odysseus's wife.   [5]Gustave Flaubert (1821–1880), French novelist.
[6]The enchantress who turned Odysseus's crew into swine.   [7]Common place sayings, often "Time Flies."
[8]French: "the thirtieth year of his life," a quotation adapted from *Le Testament* by the French poet François Villon (1431–1463?).

II

The age demanded an image
Of its accelerated grimace,
Something for the modern stage,
Not, at any rate, an Attic[1] grace;

Not, not certainly, the obscure reveries
Of the inward gaze;
Better mendacities
Than the classics in paraphrase!

The "age demanded" chiefly a mould in plaster,
Made with no loss of time,   30
A prose kinema,[2] not, not assuredly, alabaster
Or the "sculpture" of rhyme.

III

The tea-rose tea-gown, etc.
Supplants the mousseline of Cos,[1]
The pianola[2] "replaces"
Sappho's barbitos.[3]

Christ follows Dionysus,[4]
Phallic and ambrosial
Made way for macerations;[5]
Caliban casts out Ariel.[6]

All things are a flowing,
Sage Heracleitus[7] says;   40
But a tawdry cheapness
Shall outlast our days.

Even the Christian beauty
Defects—after Samothrace;[8]
We see τò καλòυ[9]
Decreed in the market place.

Faun's flesh is not to us,
Nor the saint's vision.
We have the press for wafer;[10]
Franchise for circumcision.   50

[1]Characteristic of ancient Attica or Athens, hence elegant.
[2]Greek: motion, whence "cinema" for "moving picture."
[1]Fine cloth from the Greek island of Cos.   [2]Player piano.
[3]Sappho: sixth-century B.C. Greek poetess; barbitos: a lyre.
[4]Greek god of fertility and of wine.   [5]Religious fasts.
[6]Two characters in Shakespeare's *The Tempest*—Caliban: gross and bestial; Ariel: beautiful and ethereal.
[7]Greek philosopher (sixth century B.C.) who emphasized the principle of change.
[8]Greek island where the statue "Winged Victory" was found, and the home of a religious cult.
[9]Greek: the beautiful.   [10]Of the Christian communion service.

All men, in law, are equals.
Free of Pisistratus,[11]
We choose a knave or an eunuch
To rule over us.

O bright Apollo,
τίν' ἄνδρα, τίν' ἥρωα, τίνα Θεὸν,[12]
What god, man, or hero
Shall I place a tin wreath upon!   60

                                        IV
These fought in any case,
and some believing,
          pro domo,[1] in any case . . .

Some quick to arm,
some for adventure,
some from fear of weakness,
some from fear of censure,
some for love of slaughter, in imagination,
learning later . . .
some in fear, learning love of slaughter;   70

Died some, pro patria,
          non "dulce" non "et decor"[2]. . .
walked eye-deep in hell
believing in old men's lies, then unbelieving
came home, home to a lie,
home to many deceits,
home to old lies and new infamy;
usury age-old and age-thick
and liars in public places.

Daring as never before, wastage as never before.   80
Young blood and high blood,
fair cheeks, and fine bodies;

fortitude as never before

frankness as never before,
disillusions as never told in the old days,
hysterias, trench confessions,
laughter out of dead bellies.

[11]Athenian tyrant (sixth century B.C.).
[12]Greek: "what man, what hero, what god," Pound's adaptation from one of the *Olympian Odes*
by the Greek lyric poet Pindar (c. 522–442 B.C.).
[1]Latin: for home, Pound's adaptation from *De Domo Sua* by the Roman statesman and orator
Cicero (106–43 B.C.).
[2]Latin: "for country, neither 'sweet' nor 'fitting'." Pound ironically adapts Horace's "Dulce et
decorum est pro patria mori," "It is sweet and fitting to die for one's country." (*Odes*, Book III, Ode
ii, line 13).

V

There died a myriad,
And of the best, among them,
For an old bitch gone in the teeth,   90
For a botched civilization,

Charm, smiling at the good mouth,
Quick eyes gone under earth's lid,

For two gross of broken statues,
For a few thousand battered books.

YEUX GLAUQUES[1]
Gladstone[2] was still respected,
When John Ruskin[3] produced
"Kings' Treasuries"; Swinburne
And Rossetti[4] still abused.

Fœtid Buchanan[5] lifted up his voice   100
When that faun's head of hers[6]
Became a pastime for
Painters and adulterers.

The Burne-Jones cartons[7]
Have preserved her eyes;
Still, at the Tate, they teach
Cophetua to rhapsodize;

Thin like brook-water,
With a vacant gaze.
The English Rubaiyat[8] was still-born   110
In those days.

The thin, clear gaze, the same
Still darts out faun-like from the half-ruin'd face,
Questing and passive. . . .
"Ah, poor Jenny's case"[9]. . .

[1]French: Glaucous [sea-green] Eyes.
[2]William Gladstone (1809–1898), four times Prime Minister of England (1868–1894).
[3]John Ruskin (1819–1900), English essayist whose "Of Kings' Treasuries" (1865) attacked the philistinism of England.
[4]Algernon Charles Swinburne (1837–1909), English poet and critic; Dante Gabriel Rossetti (1828–1882), English poet and painter.
[5]Robert Buchanan (1841–1901). English critic who attacked Rossetti, Swinburne, and others of "The Fleshly School of Poetry" for their sensuality.
[6]Elizabeth Siddal, a painters' model and later Rossetti's wife. She had sea-green eyes.
[7]Sir Edward Burne-Jones (1833–1898), English painter. Cartons, or cartoons, are preliminary sketches for a painting. Burne-Jones used Elizabeth Siddal as a model in his painting *King Cophetua and the Begger Maid*, which now hangs in the Tate Gallery in London.
[8]*The Rubáiyát of Omar Khayyám* (1859), translated by Edward FitzGerald (1809–1883), was at first ignored by the public.
[9]"Jenny," a poem by Rossetti describing a prostitute, attacked by Buchanan.

Bewildered that a world
Shows no surprise
At her last maquero's[10]
Adulteries.

"SIENA MI FE'; DISFECEMI
MAREMMA"[1]

Among the pickled fœtuses and bottled bones,   120
Engaged in perfecting the catalogue,
I found the last scion of the
Senatorial families of Strasbourg, Monsieur Verog.[2]

For two hours he talked of Gallifet;[3]
Of Dowson; of the Rhymers' Club;[4]
Told me how Johnson (Lionel)[5] died
By falling from a high stool in a pub . . .

But showed no trace of alcohol
At the autopsy, privately performed—
Tissue preserved—the pure mind   130
Arose toward Newman[6] as the whiskey warmed.

Dowson found harlots cheaper than hotels;
Headlam[7] for uplift; Image[8] impartially imbued
With raptures for Bacchus, Terpsichore and the Church.
So spoke the author of "The Dorian Mood,"

M. Verog, out of step with the decade,
Detached from his contemporaries,
Neglected by the young,
Because of these reveries.

BRENNBAUM

The sky-like limpid eyes,   140
The circular infant's face,
The stiffness from spats to collar
Never relaxing into grace;

[10]Pimp's—from French "maquereau."

[1]Italian: "Siena bore me; Maremma undid me," from Dante's *Purgatorio* (Canto V, line 135), spoken by a Sienese woman who had been murdered (for her infidelity) in Maremma in Tuscany.

[2]Pound's name for Victor Gustave Plarr (1863–1929), the biographer of Ernest Dowson (1867–1900). Plarr was the author of a volume of poems, *In the Dorian Mood* (1896). He was born in Strasbourg.

[3]Gaston Alexandre August, Marquis de Galliffet (1830–1909), French general.

[4]Literary club founded in 1891 by a group of English "Decadent" poets.

[5]English poet and critic (1867–1902), member of the Rhymers' Club and an ardent Roman Catholic.

[6]John Henry Cardinal Newman (1801–1890), who converted numerous English intellectuals to Roman Catholicism.

[7]The Rev. Stewart Headlam (1847–1924), an associate of the "Decadent" poets.

[8]Selwyn Image (1849–1930), editor of a literary magazine of the 1890s.

The heavy memories of Horeb, Sinai and the forty
      years,[1]
Showed only when the daylight fell
Level across the face
Of Brennbaum "The Impeccable."

MR. NIXON[1]

In the cream gilded cabin of his steam yacht
Mr. Nixon advised me kindly, to advance with fewer   150
Dangers of delay. "Consider
      "Carefully the reviewer.

"I was as poor as you are;
"When I began I got, of course,
"Advance on royalties, fifty at first," said Mr.
      Nixon,
"Follow me, and take a column,
"Even if you have to work free.

"Butter reviewers. From fifty to three hundred
"I rose in eighteen months;
"The hardest nut I had to crack
"Was Dr. Dundas.[2]   160

"I never mentioned a man but with the view
"Of selling my own works.
"The tip's a good one, as for literature
"It gives no man a sinecure.

"And no one knows, at sight, a masterpiece.
"And give up verse, my boy,
"There's nothing in it."

   .   .   .   .

Likewise a friend of Bloughram's[3] once advised me:
Don't kick against the pricks.
Accept opinion. The "Nineties" tried your game   170
And died, there's nothing in it.

X

Beneath the sagging roof
The stylist[1] has taken shelter,
Unpaid, uncelebrated,
At last from the world's welter

[1]Moses saw the burning bush and heard the Lord at Horeb, received the laws of the Lord at Sinai, and for forty years led the Israelites as they wandered in the desert.
[1]According to Pound, "a fictitious name for a real person," probably the successful English novelist Arnold Bennett (1867–1931).
[2]A literary critic and editor, as yet unidentified.
[3]A reference to the title character, a compromiser, in "Bishop Blougram's Apology" (1855) by Robert Browning (1812–1889). Pound added the *h* to "Blougram."
[1]Possibly a reference to the English novelist Ford Madox Ford (1873–1939).

Nature receives him;
With a placid and uneducated mistress
He exercises his talents
And the soil meets his distress.

The haven from sophistications and contentions   180
Leaks through its thatch;
He offers succulent cooking;
The door has a creaking latch.

XI

"Conservatrix of Milésien"[1]
Habits of mind and feeling,
Possibly. But in Ealing[2]
With the most bank-clerkly of Englishmen?   190

No, "Milésian" is an exaggeration.
No instinct has survived in her
Older than those her grandmother
Told her would fit her station.

XII

"Daphne[1] with her thighs in bark
Stretched toward me her leavy hands,"—
Subjectively. In the stuffed-satin drawing-room
I await The Lady Valentine's commands,

Knowing my coat has never been
Of precisely the fashion
To stimulate, in her,
A durable passion;

Doubtful, somewhat, of the value   200
Of well-gowned approbation
Of literary effort,
But never of The Lady Valentine's vocation:

Poetry, her border of ideas,
The edge, uncertain, but a means of blending
With other strata
Where the lower and higher have ending;

A hook to catch the Lady Jane's attention,
A modulation toward the theatre,
Also, in the case of revolution,   210
A possible friend and comforter.

[1]I.e., "Woman conservator of the cultural traditions of the ancient Greek city of Miletus." The quotation is adapted from a phrase by the French writer Remy de Gourmont (1858–1915) and also alludes to the erotic *Milesian Tales* by Aristides of Miletus (second century B.C.).
[2]A suburb of London.
[1]The nymph Daphne was transformed into a laurel tree to save her from her pursuer, Apollo. The two-line quotation is from *Le Château du souvenir*, by Theophile Gautier (1811–1872).

. . . .

Conduct, on the other hand, the soul
"Which the highest cultures have nourished"
To Fleet St.[2] where
Dr. Johnson flourished;

Beside this thoroughfare
The sale of half-hose has
Long since superseded the cultivation
Of Pierian roses.[3]

Envoi (1919)[1]

Go, dumb-born book,   220
Tell her that sang me once that the song of Lawes:[2]
Hadst thou but song
As thou hast subjects known,
Then were there cause in thee that should condone
Even my faults that heavy upon me lie,
And build her glories their longevity.

Tell her that sheds
Such treasure in the air,
Recking naught else but that her graces give
Life to the moment,
I would bid them live   230
As roses might, in magic amber laid,
Red overwrought with orange and all made
One substance and one colour
Braving time.

Tell her that goes
With songs upon her lips
But sings not out the song, nor knows
The maker of it, some other mouth,
May be as fair as hers,   240
Might, in new ages, gain her worshippers,
When our two dusts with Waller's shall be laid,
Siftings on siftings in oblivion,
Till change hath broken down
All things save Beauty alone.   1920, 1926, 1949

[2]A London literary center in the time of Dr. Samuel Johnson (1709–1784).
[3]From Pieria, in Thessaly, Greece, the birthplace of the Muses.
[1]The "Envoi," or "concluding remarks," is based on the poem "Go, Lovely Rose," by the English
poet Edmund Waller (1606–1687).
[2]Henry Lawes (1596–1662), English musician who set "Go, Lovely Rose" to music.

from *THE CANTOS*

I[1]

And then went down to the ship,
Set keel to breakers, forth on the godly sea, and
We[2] set up mast and sail on that swart ship,
Bore sheep aboard her, and our bodies also
Heavy with weeping, and winds from sternward
Bore us out onward with bellying canvas,
Circe's[3] this craft, the trim-coifed goddess,
Then sat we amidships, wind jamming the tiller,
Thus with stretched sail, we went over sea till day's end.
Sun to his slumber, shadows o'er all the ocean,   10
Came we then to the bounds of deepest water,
To the Kimmerian lands,[4] and peopled cities
Covered with close-webbed mist, unpierced ever
With glitter of sun-rays
Nor with stars stretched, nor looking back from heaven
Swartest night stretched over wretched men there,
The ocean flowing backward, came we then to the place
Aforesaid by Circe.
Here did they rites, Perimedes and Eurylochus,[5]
And drawing sword from my hip   20
I dug the ell-square pitkin;[6]
Poured we libations unto each the dead,
First mead and then sweet wine, water mixed with white flour.
Then prayed I many a prayer to the sickly death's-heads;
As set in Ithaca, sterile bulls of the best
For sacrifice, heaping the pyre with goods,
A sheep to Tiresias only, black and a bell-sheep.[7]
Dark blood flowed in the fosse,[8]
Souls out of Erebus,[9] cadaverous dead, of brides
Of youths and of the old who had borne much;   30
Souls stained with recent tears, girls tender,
Men many, mauled with bronze lance heads,
Battle spoil, bearing yet dreory[10] arms,
These many crowded about me; with shouting,
Pallor upon me, cried to my men for more beasts;
Slaughtered the herds, sheep slain of bronze;

[1]Canto I is based on Homer's *Odyssey* (Book XI) and describes the visit of Odysseus to Hades (the underworld).
[2]Odysseus and his companions.
[3]The enchantress Circe instructed Odysseus how to sail to Hades, where he could learn from Theban prophet Tiresias how to return home to Ithaca.
[4]Cimmeria, a mist-shrouded land at the edge of the world, near the entrance to Hades, where Odysseus met the spirits of the dead.
[5]Two of Odysseus's companions.   [6]A small pit, an arm's-length (one ell) square.
[7]The sheep, wearing a bell, that leads the flock.   [8]Ditch.
[9]Place of darkness where the souls of the dead passed on their way to Hades.
[10]Anglo-Saxon: bloody.

Poured ointment, cried to the gods,
To Pluto[11] the strong, and praised Proserpine;
Unsheathed the narrow sword,
I sat to keep off the impetuous impotent dead,   40
Till I should hear Tiresias.
But first Elpenor[12] came, our friend Elpenor,
Unburied, cast on the wide earth,
Limbs that we left in the house of Circe,
Unwept, unwrapped in sepulchre, since toils urged other.
Pitiful spirit. And I cried in hurried speech:
"Elpenor, how art thou come to this dark coast?
"Cam'st thou afoot, outstripping seamen?"
            And he in heavy speech:
"Ill fate and abundant wine. I slept in Circe's ingle.[13]   50
"Going down the long ladder unguarded,
"I fell against the buttress,
"Shattered the nape-nerve,[14] the soul sought Avernus.[15]
"But thou, O King, I bid remember me, unwept, unburied,
"Heap up mine arms, be tomb by sea-bord, and inscribed:
"*A man of no fortune, and with a name to come.*
"And set my oar up, that I swung mid fellows."

And Anticlea[16] came, whom I beat off, and then Tiresias Theban,
Holding his golden wand, knew me, and spoke first:
"A second time?[17] why? man of ill star,
"Facing the sunless dead and this joyless region?
"Stand from the fosse, leave me my bloody bever[18]
"For soothsay,"[19]
            And I stepped back,
And he strong with the blood, said then: "Odysseus
"Shalt return through spiteful Neptune,[20] over dark seas,
"Lose all companions." And then Anticlea came.
Lie quiet Divus. I mean, that is Andreas Divus,[21]
In officina Wecheli, 1538,[22] out of Homer.
And he[23] sailed, by Sirens and thence outward and away   70
And unto Circe.
            Venerandam,[24]
In the Cretan's[25] phrase, with the golden crown, Aphrodite,

[11]Greek god who ruled the underworld with his queen Persephone (Proserpine).
[12]One of Odysseus's companions who had died. His spirit speaks, below.
[13]Chimney-corner, hence house.   [14]Neck-nerve.
[15]Italian lake that is, according to Virgil, the entrance to the underworld.
[16]The mother of Odysseus. She had died during his absence from Ithaca. Odysseus had been instructed by Circe to spurn his mother's spirit until Tiresias had spoken.
[17]This was their second meeting.   [18]Drink.
[19]Before prophesying, Tiresias had to drink of the sacrificial blood.
[20]Roman god of the sea.
[21]Pound intrudes to address Andreas Divus, author of a Latin translation of the *Odyssey*, published in Paris in 1538, a copy of which Pound owned.
[22]Latin: "at the workshop of Wechel," a phrase taken from the imprint in Pound's copy of Divus.
[23]Odysseus.
[24]Latin: Compelling admiration, a reference to Aphrodite, Greek goddess of love.
[25]The Cretan, Georgius Dartona, whose Latin translations of the Homeric hymns (including a hymn to Aphrodite) were included in the book by Divus.

Cypri munimenta sortita est,[26] mirthful, oricalchi,[27] with golden
Girdles and breast bands, thou with dark eyelids
Bearing the golden bough of Argicida.[28] So that:

1917, 1919, 1925

II

Hang it all, Robert Browning,[1]
there can be but the one "Sordello."
But Sordello, and my Sordello?
Lo Sordels si fo di Mantovana.[2]
So-shu[3] churned in the sea.
Seal sports in the spray-whited circles of cliff-wash,
Sleek head, daughter of Lir,[4]
  eyes of Picasso[5]
Under black fur-hood, lithe daughter of Ocean;
And the wave runs in the beach-groove: 10
"Eleanor, ἑλέναυς and ἑλέπτολις!"[6]
  And poor old Homer blind, blind as a bat,
Ear, ear for the sea-surge, murmur of old men's voices:
"Let her go back to the ships,[7]
Back among Grecian faces, lest evil come on our own,
Evil and further evil, and a curse cursed on our children,
Moves, yes she moves like a goddess
And has the face of a god
  and the voice of Schoeney's[8] daughters,
And doom goes with her in walking,   20
Let her go back to the ships,
  back among Grecian voices."

[26]Latin: "The fortifications of Cyprus were her chosen realm." A quotation from Dartona's hymn to Aphrodite. According to legend Aphrodite first appeared in Cyprus.

[27]Pound's spelling of Latin *orichalci*, "of copper." Dartona described Aphrodite wearing copper earrings.

[28]Latin: slayer of Argos. In classical myth, Hermes slew the 100-eyed Argos. One of the 12 Olympian gods, Hermes carried a golden staff with which he conducted the souls of the dead to Hades.

[1]English poet (1812–1889), author of the poem *Sordello* (1840). Here, Sordello refers to the title character of Browning's poem and to an actual man, a thirteenth-century Italian poet, who appeared in Dante's *Purgatorio* (VI).

[2]Provençal: Sordello was from the region around Mantua.

[3]The Japanese name for the Chinese philosopher Chuang Tzu. "Churned in the sea" is perhaps meant to echo a Chinese pronunciation of "Chuang Tzu" and to suggest "churned in the sea of experience."

[4]Celtic sea god.

[5]Pablo Picasso (1881–1973), Spanish Cubist painter. Pound suggests that the eyes of the figures in Picasso's paintings are dark, like those of the seal described here.

[6]Greek: "ship-destroying" and "town-destroying." An adaptation of a quotation from the *Agamemnon* (lines 689–690), by Aeschylus, which describes Helen of Troy as "ship-destroying, man-destroying, and town-destroying." Pound substitutes "Eleanor" for "man-destroying" (Greek "elandros"), and thereby alludes both to Helen of Troy and to Eleanor of Aquitaine (1122?–1204), who likewise brought discord among men.

[7]The quotation beginning here is from *The Iliad* (Book III, lines 158–160). The old men of Troy speak of Helen as they see Menelaus and Paris fight.

[8]Atlanta, the daughter of Schoeneus, challenged her suitors to a footrace. Those she defeated were put to death.

And by the beach-run, Tyro,[9]
    Twisted arms of the sea-god,
Lithe sinews of water, gripping her, cross-hold,
And the blue-gray glass of the wave tents them,
Glare azure of water, cold-welter, close cover,
Quiet sun-tawny sand-stretch,
The gulls broad out their wings,
    nipping between the splay feathers;   30
Snipe come for their bath,
    bend out their wing-joints,
Spread wet wings to the sun-film,
And by Scios,[10]
    to left of the Naxos[11] passage,
Naviform[12] rock overgrown,
    algae cling to its edge,
There is a wine-red glow in the shallows,
    a tin flash in the sun-dazzle.

The ship landed in Scios,   40
    men wanting spring-water,
And by the rock-pool a young boy loggy with vine-must,[13]
    "To Naxos? Yes, we'll take you to Naxos,
Cum' along lad." "Not that way!"
"Aye that way is Naxos."
    And I said: "It's a straight ship."
And an ex-convict out of Italy[14]
    knocked me into the fore-stays,
(He was wanted for manslaughter in Tuscany)
    And the whole twenty against me,   50
Mad for a little slave money.
    And they took her out of Scios
And off her course . . .
    And the boy came to, again, with the racket,
And looked out over the bows,
    and to eastward, and to the Naxos passage.
God-sleight then, god-sleight:
    Ship stock fast in sea-swirl,
Ivy upon the oars, King Pentheus,[15]
    grapes with no seed but sea-foam,   60
Ivy in scupper-hole.

[9]A mortal raped by the sea-god Poseidon, who caused a great wave to curl over them for concealment.
[10]Chios, Greek island near Naxos, in the Aegean Sea.
[11]Greek island known for its wine and as a center for the worship of Dionysus (Bacchus).
[12]Having the shape of a ship.
[13]Fermenting grape juice. The boy is Dionysus to whom the grape wine and ivy are sacred.
[14]In Greek myth, Dionysus, hoping to go to Naxos, took passage on a ship manned by Italian pirates. Only one member of the crew, the steersman, recognized him as a god. The others resolved to change course to Asia where they could sell their passenger as a slave. Dionysus then caused the ship to halt; ivy entangled the masts and sails, wine flowed over the deck, and wild beasts appeared to guard him. The pirates, frightened by the magic, the "god-sleight," leaped into the sea and were changed into dolphins. Only the steersman was spared.
[15]The steersman, Acoetes, is reciting the story to Pentheus of Thebes to warn him of the power of Dionysus.

Aye, I, Accœtes, stood there,
       and the god stood by me,
Water cutting under the keel,
Sea-break from stern forrards,
       wake running off from the bow,
And where was gunwale, there now was vine-trunk,
And tenthril were cordage had been,
       grape-leaves on the rowlocks,
Heavy vine on the oarshafts,   70
And, out of nothing, a breathing,
       hot breath on my ankles,
Beasts like shadows in glass,
       a furred tail upon nothingness.
Lynx-purr, and heathery smell of beasts,
       where tar smell had been,
Sniff and pad-foot of beasts,
       eye-glitter out of black air.
The sky overshot, dry, with no tempest,
Sniff and pad-foot of beasts,   80
       fur brushing my knee-skin,
Rustle of airy sheaths,
       dry forms in the *œther.*[16]
And the ship like a keel in ship-yard,
       slung like an ox in smith's sling,
Ribs stuck fast in the ways,
       grape-cluster over pin-rack,
       void air taking pelt.
Lifeless air become sinewed,
       feline leisure of panthers,   90
Leopards sniffing the grape shoots by scupper-hole,
Crouched panthers by fore-hatch,
And the sea blue-deep about us,
       green-ruddy in shadows,
And Lyæus:[17] "From now, Accœtes, my altars,
Fearing no bondage,
       fearing no cat of the wood,
Safe with my lynxes,
       feeding grapes to my leopards,
Olibanum[18] is my incense,   100
       the vines grow in my homage."

The back-swell now smooth in the rudder-chains,
Black snout of a porpoise
       where Lycabs[19] had been,
Fish-scales on the oarsmen.
       And I worship.
I have seen what I have seen.
       When they brought the boy I said:
"He has a god in him,
       though I do not know which god."   110

[16]Latin: air.   [17]Another name for Dionysus.
[18]Frankincense.   [19]One of the sailors who had tried to abduct Dionysus.

And they kicked me into the fore-stays.
I have seen what I have seen:
  Medon's[20] face like the face of a dory,[21]
Arms shrunk into fins. And you, Pentheus,
Had as well listen to Tiresias, and to Cadmus,[22]
  or your luck will go out of you.
Fish-scales over groin muscles,
  lynx-purr amid sea. . .
And of a later year,
  pale in the wine-red algæ,   120
If you will lean over the rock,
  the coral face under wave-tinge,
Rose-paleness under water-shift,
  Ileuthyeria,[23] fair Dafne[24] of sea-bords,
The swimmer's arms turned to branches,
Who will say in what year,
  fleeing what band of tritons,
The smooth brows, seen, and half seen,
  now ivory stillness.

And So-shu churned in the sea, So-shu also,   130
  using the long moon for a churn-stick. . .
Lithe turning of water,
  sinews of Poseidon,
Black azure and hyaline,[25]
  glass wave over Tyro,
Close cover, unstillness,
  bright welter of wave-cords,
Then quiet water,
  quiet in the buff sands,
Sea-fowl stretching wing-joints,   140
  splashing in rock-hollows and sand-hollows
In the wave-runs by the half-dune;
Glass-glint of wave in the tide-rips against sunlight,
  pallor of Hesperus,[26]
Grey peak of the wave,
  wave, colour of grape's pulp,

Olive grey in the near,
  far, smoke grey of the rock-slide,
Salmon-pink wings of the fish-hawk
  cast grey shadows in water,
The tower like a one-eyed great goose   150
  cranes up out of the olive-grove,

[20]Another sailor. [21]A fish.
[22]Grandfather of Pentheus and founder of Thebes. With Tiresias he had urged Pentheus not to forbid the worship of Dionysus.
[23]A nymph.
[24]Daphne, the nymph who was turned into a tree to save her from her pursuer, Apollo.
[25]Clear, transparent. [26]The evening star (the planet Venus).

And we have heard the fauns chiding Proteus[27]
     in the smell of hay under the olive-trees,
And the frogs singing against the fauns
     in the half-light.
And. . .

                       1917, 1925

XLV

With *Usura*[1]
With usura hath no man a house of good stone
each block cut smooth and well fitting
that design might cover their face,
with usura
hath no man a painted paradise on his church wall
harpes et luz[2]
or where virgin receiveth message
and halo projects from incision,
with usura   10
seeth no man Gonzaga[3] his heirs and his concubines
no picture is made to endure nor to live with
but it is made to sell and sell quickly
with usura, sin against nature,
is thy bread ever more of stale rags
is thy bread dry as paper,
with no moutain wheat, no strong flour
with usura the line grows thick
with usura is no clear demarcation
and no man can find site for his dwelling.   20
Stone cutter is kept from his stone
weaver is kept from his loom
WITH USURA
wool comes not to market
sheep bringeth no gain with usura
Usura is a murrain,[4] usura
blunteth the needle in the maid's hand
and stoppeth the spinner's cunning. Pietro Lombardo[5]
came not by usura
Duccio[6] came not by usura   30
nor Pier della Francesca; Zuan Bellin'[7] not by usura

---

[27]Greek sea god who could assume different shapes.
 [1]Latin: usury, interest paid for money borrowed. Pound uses the term to refer generally to greed for money.
 [2]French: harps and lutes.
 [3]Probably an allusion to the Italian Luigi Gonzaga (1267–1360), who established the princely house that ruled Mantua between the fourteenth and eighteenth centuries.
 [4]Plague.   [5]Italian sculptor (1435–1515).
 [6]Duccio di Buoninsegna (1260?–1318?), the first great Sienese painter.
 [7]Piero della Francesca (1420?–1492) and Giovanni Bellini (1430?–1516), Italian painters.

nor was 'La Calunnia'[8] painted.
Came not by usura Angelico; came not Ambrogio
      Praedis,[9]
Came no church of cut stone signed: *Adamo me fecit.*[10]
Not by usura St Trophime[11]
Not by usura Saint Hilaire,[12]
Usura rusteth the chisel
It rusteth the craft and the craftsman
It gnaweth the thread in the loom
None learneth to weave gold in her pattern;   40
Azure hath a canker by usura; cramoisi[13] is unbroidered
Emerald findeth no Memling[14]
Usura slayeth the child in the womb
It stayeth the young man's courting
It hath brought palsey to bed, lyeth
between the young bride and her bridegroom
                    CONTRA NATURAM[15]
They have brought whores for Eleusis[16]
Corpses are set to banquet
at behest of usura.   50

                                                    1936, 1937

LXXXI

Zeus lies in Ceres' bosom[1]
Taishan[2] is attended of loves
            under Cythera,[3] before sunrise
and he said: "Hay aqui mucho catolicismo—(sounded catoli*th*ismo)
      y muy poco reliHion"[4]
and he said: "Yo creo que los reyes desaparecen"[5]
(Kings will, I think, disappear)
That was Padre José Elizondo[6]
            in 1906 and in 1917
or about 1917   10
      and Dolores[7] said: "Come pan, niño," eat bread, me lad

[8]A painting by the Italian Sandro Botticelli (1445?–1510).
[9]Fra Angelico (1387?–1455) and Ambrogio de Predis (1455?–1506?), Italian painters.
[10]Latin: "Adam made me," the signature of the architect of the Church of San Zeno Maggiore in Verona, Italy.
[11]Church in Arles, France.   [12]Church in Poitiers, France.   [13]French: crimson cloth.
[14]Hans Memling (1430?–1495), Flemish painter.
[15]Latin: contrary to nature.   [16]Ancient religious sanctuary near Athens.
[1]Zeus, ruler of the Greek gods. Ceres, Roman goddess of agriculture and fertility.
[2]Sacred mountain in China. Pound associates it with a mountain peak he could see from his prison near Pisa, Italy.
[3]I.e., under the moon. Pound identifies Aphrodite (Cythera), the Greek goddess of love and fertility, with the moon.
[4]Spanish: "There is much Catholicism here and very little religion."
[5]Translated in the next line.
[6]Spanish priest who helped Pound obtain copies of a manuscript pertaining to Guido Cavalcanti (fl. 1250–1300), an Italian poet whose work Pound translated.
[7]The subject of a painting by the American artist John Singer Sargent (1856–1925).

Sargent had painted her
      before he descended[8]
(i.e. if he descended
      but in those days he did thumb sketches,
impressions of the Velázquez in the Museo del Prado[9]
and books cost a peseta,[10]
      brass candlesticks in proportion,
hot wind came from the marshes
      and death-chill from the mountains.   20
And later Bowers[11] wrote: "but such hatred,
      I have never conceived such"
and the London reds wouldn't show up his friends
      (i.e. friends of Franco[12]
working in London) and in Alcázar[13]
forty years gone, they said: go back to the station to eat
you can sleep here for a peseta"
      goat bells tinkled all night
      and the hostess grinned: Eso es luto, *haw!*
mi marido es muerto[14]   30
      (it is mourning, my husband is dead)
when she gave me paper to write on
with a black border half an inch or more deep,
      say 5/8ths, of the locanda[15]
"We call *all* foreigners frenchies"
and the egg broke in Cabranez' pocket,
      thus making history. Basil[16] says
they beat drums for three days
till all the drumheads were busted
      (simple village fiesta)
and as for his life in the Canaries . . .   40
Possum[17] observed that the local portagoose[18] folk dance
was danced by the same dancers in divers localities
      in political welcome . . .
the technique of demonstration
      Cole studied that (not G.D.H., Horace)[19]
"You will find" said old André Spire,[20]
that every man on that board (Crédit Agricole)
has a brother-in-law

[8]I.e., declined in ability.
[9]Picture gallery in Madrid, Spain. There Sargent studied and copied paintings by Diego Rodríguez de Silva y Velasquez (1599–1660), Spanish painter.
[10]Small Spanish coin.
[11]Claude G. Bowers (1878–1958), American historian and United States Ambassador to Spain during the Spanish Civil War (1936–1939).
[12]Francisco Franco (1892–1975), victorious fascist general in the Spanish Civil War and dictator of Spain (1939–1972).
[13]Town in central Spain.   [14]Translated in next line.   [15]Italian: inn.
[16]Basil Bunting (b. 1900), English poet and a friend of Pound. From 1933 to 1936 Bunting lived in the Canary Islands off the coast of Africa.
[17]A nickname for T. S. Eliot.   [18]Slang for "Portuguese."
[19]G. D. H. Cole (1880–1859), English economist. Horace Cole (b. 1874), English businessman and magazine writer.
[20]French writer (1868–1966). Pound quotes his cynical appraisal of the directors of the French Agricultural Bank (Crédit Agricole).

"You the one, I the few"
                said John Adams   50
speaking of fears in the abstract
            to his volatile friend Mr Jefferson.[21]
(To break the pentameter, that was the first heave)[22]
or as Jo Bard[23] says: they never speak to each other,
if it is baker and concierge[24] visibly
            it is La Rouchefoucauld and de Maintenon[25] audibly.
"Te cavero le budella"
                "La corato a te"[26]
In less than a geological epoch
                said Henry Mencken[27]   60
"Some cook, some do not cook[28]
            some things cannot be altered"
'Ινγξ. . . . .'εμὸν ποτί δῶμα τὸν ἄνδρα[29]
What counts is the cultural level,
            thank Benin for this table ex packing box[30]
"doan yu tell no one I made it"
            from a mask fine as any in Frankfurt
"It'll get you offn th' groun"
            Light as the branch of Kuanon[31]
And at first disappointed with shoddy   70
the bare ram-shackle quais, but then saw the
high buggy wheels
                and was reconciled,
George Santayana arriving in the port of Boston
and kept to the end of his life that faint *thethear*[32]
of the Spaniard
                as a grace quasi imperceptible
            as did Muss[33] the *v* for *u* of Romagna

[21]In his famous correspondence with Thomas Jefferson, John Adams observed that Jefferson most feared the power of a single man, such as a president, to destroy democracy. Adams, on the other hand, most feared the oligarchy, the rich and powerful upper class.

[22]I.e., To break the tradition of using pentameter verse, that was the first task. Pound believed it was the duty of English poets to cease using iambic pentameter because it is, he argued, artificial.

[23]Joseph Bard (b. 1892), English essayist and critic.

[24]French: doorkeeper.

[25]François, Duc de La Rochefoucauld (1613–1680) and Françoise, Marquise de Maintenon (1635–1719), French writers. Pound suggests their courtly and elegant prose is as artificial as iambic pentameter English verse.

[26]Italian: "I'll cut your guts out." "I'll cut out yours."

[27]In March 1937, H. L. Mencken wrote to Pound, "I believe that all schemes of monetary reform collide inevitably with the nature of man in the mass. He can't be convinced in anything less than a geological epoch."

[28]Pound's wife refused to serve as family cook.

[29]Greek: "Little wheel [return that] man to my house." A quotation from the second *Idyll* of Theocritus, in which a girl uses a magic charm-wheel to summon her lover.

[30]A Negro, imprisoned with Pound at Pisa, made him a table to write on. Pound calls him Benin because he resembles the bronze masks made by the Benin people of Nigeria. Pound had seen a collection of the masks in an anthropological institute in Frankfurt, Germany.

[31]Chinese goddess of mercy.

[32]American philosopher (1863–1952). Born in Spain, he preserved the Castilian Spanish pronunciation of *th* for *c* in such words as "cecear," Spanish: "to lisp." Lines 70 to 80 refer to his arrival in America—described in his *Persons and Places*, 1944.

[33]Benito Mussolini (1883–1945), fascist dictator of Italy (1922–1945), was from the district of Romagna in northern Italy.

and said the grief was a full act
      repeated for each new condoleress   80
working up to a climax.
and George Horace said he wd/ "get Beveridge" (Senator)[34]
Beveridge wouldn't talk and he wouldn't write for the papers
but George got him by campin' in his hotel
and assailin' him at lunch breakfast an' dinner
      three articles
and my ole man went on hoein' corn
      while George was a-tellin' him,
come across a vacant lot
      where you'd occasionally see a wild rabbit   90
or mebbe only a loose one
      AOI![35]
    a leaf in the current
      at my grates no Althea[36]
LIBRETTO[37] Yet
Ere the season died a-cold
Borne upon a zephyr's shoulder
I rose through the aureate sky
    Lawes and Jenkyns guard thy rest
    Dolmetsch ever be thy guest,[38]   100
Has he tempered the viol's wood
To enforce   both the grave   and the acute?[39]
Has he curved us the bowl of the lute?
    Lawes and Jenkyns guard thy rest
    Dolmetsch ever be thy guest
Hast 'ou fashioned so airy a mood
    To draw up leaf from the root
Hast 'ou found   a cloud   so light
    As seemed neither mist nor shade?

    Then resolve me, tell me aright   110
    If Waller sang or Dowland[40] played.

    Your eyen two wol sleye me sodenly
    I may the beauté of hem nat susteyne[41]

And for 180 years almost nothing.

[34]George Horace Lorimer (1868–1937), editor of the *Saturday Evening Post;* Albert J. Beveridge (1862–1927), United States Senator from Indiana (1899–1911). In 1899, at Lorimer's insistence, Beveridge agreed to write a series of articles for the *Saturday Evening Post.* Lorimer, a neighbor of the Pounds in suburban Philadelphia, sometimes spoke with Pound's father while he worked in his backyard garden.

[35]A cry of anguish.

[36]In "To Althea from Prison" (1649), by the English poet Richard Lovelace (1618–1657), the imprisoned lover believes his divine Althea comes "to whisper at the grates" of his cell window.

[37]The words or text set to music in an opera or other dramatic musical work. Here it indicates the beginning of a song sung to Pound by Aphrodite.

[38]Henry Lawes (1596–1662) and John Jenkins (1592–1678), English musicians and composers. Arnold Dolmetsch (1858–1940), French musician, instrument maker, and relative of distinguished American scholars.

[39]Renaissance musical terms used to describe lower (grave) and higher (acute) notes.

[40]Edmund Waller, English poet (1606–1687); John Dowland (1563–1626), English composer.

[41]A quotation from *Merciless Beauty,* a love poem attributed to Chaucer.

Ed ascoltando al leggier mormorio[42]
  there came new subtlety of eyes into my tent,
whether of spirit or hypostasis,[43]
  but what the blindfold hides
or at carneval
       nor any pair showed anger   120
  Saw but the eyes and stance between the eyes,
colour, diastasis,[44]
  careless or unaware it had not the
 whole tent's room
nor was place for the full Eιδώζ[45]
interpass, penetrate
  casting but shade beyond the other lights
   sky's clear
   night's sea
   green of the mountain pool   130
   shone from the unmasked eyes in half-mask's space.
What thou lovest well remains,
     the rest is dross
What thou lov'st well shall not be reft from thee
What thou lov'st well is thy true heritage
Whose world, or mine or theirs
    or is it of none?
First came the seen, then thus the palpable
  Elysium,[46] though it were in the halls of hell,
What thou lovest well is thy true heritage   140
What thou lovest well shall not be reft from thee.

The ant's a centaur in his dragon world.
Pull down thy vanity, it is not man
Made courage, or made order, or made grace,
  Pull down thy vanity, I say pull down.
Learn of the green world what can be thy place
In scaled invention or true artistry,
Pull down thy vanity,
      Paquin[47] pull down!
The green casque has outdone your elegance.[48]

"Master thyself, then others shall thee beare"[49]   150
  Pull down thy vanity,
Thou art a beaten dog beneath the hail,
A swollen magpie in a fitful sun,
Half black half white
Nor knowst'ou wing from tail
Pull down thy vanity
   How mean thy hates
Fostered in falsity,

[42]Italian: And listening to the light murmur.
[43]Divine substance, i.e., Aphrodite.
[44]Interval. [45]Greek: knowing. [46]Paradise.
[47]A Parisian dress designer.
[48]I.e., the green forms of insects outdo the artificial designs of Paquin.
[49]A paraphrase of Chaucer's *Ballade of Good Counsel*, line 13.

> Pull down thy vanity,
> Rathe[50] to destroy, niggard[51] in charity,   160
> Pull down thy vanity,
> > I say pull down.
>
> But to have done instead of not doing
> > this is not vanity
> To have, with decency, knocked
> That a Blunt should open[52]
> > To have gathered from the air a live tradition
> or from a fine old eye the unconquered flame
> This is not vanity.
> > Here error is all in the not done,   170
> all in the diffidence that faltered . . .[53]

1947, 1948

A RETROSPECT

There has been so much scribbling about a new fashion in poetry, that I may perhaps be pardoned this brief recapitulation and retrospect.

In the spring or early summer of 1912, 'H.D.', Richard Aldington[1] and myself decided that we were agreed upon the three principles following:

1. Direct treatment of the 'thing' whether subjective or objective.

2. To use absolutely no word that does not contribute to the presentation.

3. As regarding rhythm: to compose in the sequence of the musical phrase, not in sequence of a metronome.

Upon many points of taste and predilection we differed, but agreeing upon these three positions we thought we had as much right to a group name, at least as much right, as a number of French 'schools' proclaimed by Mr. Flint in the August number of Harold Monro's magazine for 1911.[2]

This school has since been 'joined' or 'followed' by numerous people who, whatever their merits, do not show any signs of agreeing with the second specification. Indeed *vers libre*[3] has become as prolix and as verbose as any of the flaccid varieties that preceded it. It has brought faults of its own. The actual language and phrasing is often as bad as that of our elders without even the excuse that the words are shovelled in to fill a metric pattern or to complete the noise of a rhyme-sound. Whether or no the phrases followed by the followers are musical must be left to the reader's decision. At times I can find a marked metre in 'vers libres,' as stale and hackneyed as any pseudo-Swinburnian,[4] at times the writers seem to follow no musical structure whatever. But it is, on the

---

[50]Early, quick.   [51]Stingy.

[52]A reference to Matthew 7:7, "knock, and it shall be opened unto you." Wilfred Blunt (1840–1922), English poet and political essayist whose independent ways were much admired by Pound.

[53]Pound's ellipses.

[1]'H. D.,' Hilda Doolittle (1886–1961), American poet; Richard Aldington (1892–1962), English-American poet and novelist; with Pound, H. D., and Amy Lowell, Aldington was one of the founders of Imagism.

[2]Frank Stewart Flint (b. 1885), English poet and translator whose essay "Imagisme" appeared in *Poetry Review*, published by Harold Monro (1879–1932).

[3]Free verse that follows no regular rhythmic, stanzaic, or rhyme pattern.

[4]Modeled after the melodic poetry of Algernon Charles Swinburne.

whole, good that the field should be ploughed. Perhaps a few good poems have come from the new method, and if so it is justified.

Criticism is not a circumscription or a set of prohibitions. It provides fixed points of departure. It may startle a dull reader into alertness. That little of it which is good is mostly in stray phrases; or if it be an older artist helping a younger it is in great measure but rules of thumb, cautions gained by experience.

I set together a few phrases on practical working about the time the first remarks on imagisme were published. The first use of the word 'Imagiste' was in my note to T. E. Hulme's[5] five poems, printed at the end of my 'Ripostes' in the autumn of 1912. I reprint my cautions from *Poetry*[6] for March, 1913.

A FEW DON'TS

An 'Image' is that which presents an intellectual and emotional complex in an instant of time. I use the term 'complex' rather in the technical sense employed by the newer psychologists, such as Hart,[7] though we might not agree absolutely in our application.

It is the presentation of such a 'complex' instantaneously which gives that sense of sudden liberation; that sense of freedom from time limits and space limits; that sense of sudden growth, which we experience in the presence of the greatest works of art.

It is better to present one Image in a lifetime than to produce voluminous works.

All this, however, some may consider open to debate. The immediate necessity is to tabulate A LIST OF DON'TS for those beginning to write verses. I can not put all of them into Mosaic negative.

To begin with, consider the three propositions (demanding direct treatment, economy of words, and the sequence of the musical phrase), not as dogma—never consider anything as dogma—but as the result of long contemplation, which, even if it is some one else's contemplation, may be worth consideration.

Pay no attention to the criticism of men who have never themselves written a notable work. Consider the discrepancies between the actual writing of the Greek poets and dramatists, and the theories of the Graeco-Roman grammarians, concocted to explain their metres.

LANGUAGE

Use no superfluous word, no adjective which does not reveal something.

Don't use such an expression as 'dim lands *of peace*'. It dulls the image. It mixes an abstraction with the concrete. It comes from the writer's not realizing that the natural object is always the adequate symbol.

Go in fear of abstractions. Do not retell in mediocre verse what has already been done in good prose. Don't think any intelligent person is going to be deceived when you try to shirk all the difficulties of the unspeakably difficult art of good prose by chopping your composition into line lengths.

What the expert is tired of today the public will be tired of tomorrow.

---

[5]English writer (1883–1917), called the "father of imagism."
[6]A "Magazine of Verse" founded in Chicago in 1912 by Harriet Monroe (1861–1936).
[7]Bernard Hart (1879–1966), English psychiatrist.

Don't imagine that the art of poetry is any simpler than the art of music, or that you can please the expert before you have spent at least as much effort on the art of verse as the average piano teacher spends on the art of music.

Be influenced by as many great artists as you can, but have the decency either to acknowledge the debt outright, or to try to conceal it.

Don't allow 'influence' to mean merely that you mop up the particular decorative vocabulary of some one or two poets whom you happen to admire. A Turkish war correspondent was recently caught red-handed babbling in his despatches of 'dove-grey' hills, or else it was 'pearl-pale', I can not remember. Use either no ornament or good ornament.

RHYTHM AND RHYME

Let the candidate fill his mind with the finest cadences he can discover, preferably in a foreign language,[8] so that the meaning of the words may be less likely to divert his attention from the movement; e.g. Saxon charms, Hebridean Folk Songs, the verse of Dante, and the lyrics of Shakespeare—if he can dissociate the vocabulary from the cadence. Let him dissect the lyrics of Goethe coldly into their component sound values, syllables long and short, stressed and unstressed, into vowels and consonants.

It is not necessary that a poem should rely on its music, but if it does rely on its music that music must be such as will delight the expert.

Let the neophyte know assonance and alliteration, rhyme immediate and delayed, simple and polyphonic, as a musician would expect to know harmony and counterpoint and all the minutiae of his craft. No time is too great to give to these matters or to any one of them, even if the artist seldom have need of them.

Don't imagine that a thing will 'go' in verse just because it's too dull to go in prose.

Don't be 'viewy'—leave that to the writers of pretty little philosophic essays. Don't be descriptive; remember that the painter can describe a landscape much better than you can, and that he has to know a deal more about it.

When Shakespeare talks of the 'Dawn in russet mantle clad' he presents something which the painter does not present. There is in this line of his nothing that one can call description; he presents.

Consider the way of the scientists rather than the way of an advertising agent for a new soap.

The scientist does not expect to be acclaimed as a great scientist until he has *discovered* something. He begins by learning what has been discovered already. He goes from that point onward. He does not bank on being a charming fellow personally. He does not expect his friends to applaud the results of his freshman class work. Freshmen in poetry are unfortunately not confined to a definite and recognizable class room. They are 'all over the shop'. Is it any wonder 'the public is indifferent to poetry?'

Don't chop your stuff into separate *iambs*. Don't make each line stop dead at the end, and then begin every next line with a heave. Let the beginning of the next line catch the rise of the rhythm wave, unless you want a definite longish pause.

In short, behave as a musician, a good musician, when dealing with that phase

[8]"This is for rhythm, his vocabulary must of course be found in his native tongue."—Pound's note.

of your art which has exact parallels in music. The same laws govern, and you are bound by no others.

Naturally, your rhythmic structure should not destroy the shape of your words, or their natural sound, or their meaning. It is improbable that, at the start, you will be able to get a rhythm-structure strong enough to affect them very much, though you may fall a victim to all sorts of false stopping due to line ends and cæsurae.

The Musician can rely on pitch and the volume of the orchestra. You can not. The term harmony is misapplied in poetry; it refers to simultaneous sounds of different pitch. There is, however, in the best verse a sort of residue of sound which remains in the ear of the hearer and acts more or less as an organ-base.

A rhyme must have in it some slight element of surprise if it is to give pleasure; it need not be bizarre or curious, but it must be well used if used at all.

Vide further Vildrac and Duhamel's[9] notes on rhyme in *'Technique Poétique'*.

That part of your poetry which strikes upon the imaginative *eye* of the reader will lose nothing by translation into a foreign tongue; that which appeals to the ear can reach only those who take it in the original.

Consider the definiteness of Dante's presentation, as compared with Milton's rhetoric. Read as much of Wordsworth as does not seem too unutterably dull.

If you want the gist of the matter go to Sappho, Catullus, Villon, Heine[10] when he is in the vein, Gautier when he is not too frigid; or, if you have not the tongues, seek out the leisurely Chaucer. Good prose will do you no harm, and there is good discipline to be had by trying to write it.

Translation is likewise good training, if you find that your original matter 'wobbles' when you try to rewrite it. The meaning of the poem to be translated can not 'wobble'.

If you are using a symmetrical form, don't put in what you want to say and then fill up the remaining vacuums with slush.

Don't mess up the perception of one sense by trying to define it in terms of another. This is usually only the result of being too lazy to find the exact word. To this clause there are possibly exceptions.

The first three simple prescriptions will throw out nine-tenths of all the bad poetry now accepted as standard and classic; and will prevent you from many a crime of production.

'. . . *Mais d'abord il faut être un poète'*,[11] as MM. Duhamel and Vildrac have said at the end of their little book, *'Notes sur la Technique Poétique.'*

CREDO

Rhythm.—I believe in an 'absolute rhythm', a rhythm, that is, in poetry which corresponds exactly to the emotion or shade of emotion to be expressed. A man's rhythm must be interpretative, it will be, therefore, in the end, his own, uncounterfeiting, uncounterfeitable.

Symbols.—I believe that the proper and perfect symbol is the natural object, that if a man use 'symbols' he must so use them that their symbolic function does not obtrude; so that *a* sense, and the poetic quality of the passage, is not

[9]Charles Vildrac (1882–1971) and Georges Duhamel (1884–1966), French poets, authors of *Notes sur la Technique Poétique*, 1925.

[10]Sappho, Greek poetess (sixth century B.C.); Catullus (84?–54? B.C.), Roman poet; François Villon (1431–1463), French poet; Heinrich Heine (1797–1856), German poet.

[11]French: "But, to begin with, one must be a poet."

lost to those who do not understand the symbol as such, to whom, for instance, a hawk is a hawk.

Technique.—I believe in technique as the test of a man's sincerity; in law when it is ascertainable; in the trampling down of every convention that impedes or obscures the determination of the law, or the precise rendering of the impulse.

Form.—I think there is a 'fluid' as well as a 'solid' content, that some poems may have form as a tree has form, some as water poured into a vase. That most symmetrical forms have certain uses. That a vast number of subjects cannot be precisely, and therefore not properly rendered in symmetrical forms.

'Thinking that alone worthy wherein the whole art is employed'.[12] I think the artist should master all known forms and systems of metric, and I have with some persistence set about doing this, searching particularly into those periods wherein the systems came to birth or attained their maturity. It has been complained, with some justice, that I dump my note-books on the public. I think that only after a long struggle will poetry attain such a degree of development, or, if you will, modernity, that it will vitally concern people who are accustomed, in prose, to Henry James and Anatole France, in music to Debussy.[13] I am constantly contending that it took two centuries of Provence and one of Tuscany to develop the media of Dante's masterwork, that it took the latinists of the Renaissance, and the Pleiade,[14] and his own age of painted speech to prepare Shakespeare his tools. It is tremendously important that great poetry be written, it makes no jot of difference who writes it. The experimental demonstrations of one man may save the time of many—hence my furore over Arnaut Daniel[15]— if a man's experiments try out one new rime, or dispense conclusively with one iota of currently accepted nonsense, he is merely playing fair with his colleagues when he chalks up his result.

No man ever writes very much poetry that 'matters'. In bulk, that is, no one produces much that is final, and when a man is not doing this highest thing, thus saying the thing once for all and perfectly; when he is not matching Ποικιλόθρον᾽, ἀθάνατ᾽ Ἀφρόδιτα,[16] or 'Hist—said Kate the Queen', he had much better be making the sorts of experiment which may be of use to him in his later work, or to his successors.

'The lyf so short, the craft so long to lerne.' It is a foolish thing for a man to begin his work on a too narrow foundation, it is a disgraceful thing for a man's work not to show steady growth and increasing fineness from first to last.

As for 'adaptations'; one finds that all the old masters of painting recommend to their pupils that they begin by copying masterwork, and proceed to their own composition.

As for 'Every man his own poet', the more every man knows about poetry the better. I believe in every one writing poetry who wants to; most do. I believe in every man knowing enough of music to play 'God bless our home' on the harmonium, but I do not believe in every man giving concerts and printing his sin.

The mastery of any art is the work of a lifetime. I should not discriminate

---

[12]"Dante, *De Volgari Eloquio*,"—Pound's note.

[13]François Anatole Thibault (1844–1924), French writer; Claude Achille Debussy (1862–1918), French composer.

[14]A group of sixteenth-century French poets who celebrated the writers of antiquity. Their name came from the legendary Pleiades, daughters of Atlas, who were transformed into stars.

[15]Provençal troubador (twelfth century). In Dante's *Purgatorio* (XXVI, line 117), he is described as the "miglior fabbro," the "better craftsman." He invented the sestina form (six six-line stanzas) used by Dante and Petrarch.

[16]Greek: "Shimmering-throned, immortal Aphrodite," a quotation from Sappho.

between the 'amateur' and the 'professional'. Or rather I should discriminate quite often in favour of the amateur, but I should discriminate between the amateur and the expert. It is certain that the present chaos will endure until the Art of poetry has been preached down the amateur gullet, until there is such a general understanding of the fact that poetry is an art and not a pastime; such a knowledge of technique; of technique of surface and technique of content, that the amateurs will cease to try to drown out the masters.

If a certain thing was said once for all in Atlantis or Arcadia, in 450 Before Christ or in 1290 after, it is not for us moderns to go saying it over, or to go obscuring the memory of the dead by saying the same thing with less skill and less conviction.

My pawing over the ancients and semi-ancients has been one struggle to find out what has been done, once for all, better than it can ever be done again, and to find out what remains for us to do, and plenty does remain, for if we still feel the same emotions as those which launched the thousand ships, it is quite certain that we come on these feelings differently, through different nuances, by different intellectual gradations. Each age has its own abounding gifts yet only some ages transmute them into matter of duration. No good poetry is ever written in a manner twenty years old, for to write in such a manner shows conclusively that the writer thinks from books, convention and *cliché*, and not from life, yet a man feeling the divorce of life and his art may naturally try to resurrect a forgotten mode if he finds in that mode some leaven, or if he think he sees in it some element lacking in contemporary art which might unite that art again to its sustenance, life.

In the art of Daniel and Cavalcanti,[17] I have seen that precision which I miss in the Victorians, that explicit rendering, be it of external nature, or of emotion. Their testimony is of the eyewitness, their symptoms are first hand.

As for the nineteenth century, with all respect to its achievements, I think we shall look back upon it as a rather blurry, messy sort of period, a rather sentimentalistic, mannerish sort of a period. I say this without any self-righteousness, with no self-satisfaction.

As for there being a 'movement' or my being of it, the conception of poetry as a 'pure art' in the sense in which I use the term, revived with Swinburne. From the puritanical revolt to Swinburne, poetry had been merely the vehicle—yes, definitely, Arthur Symons'[18] scruples and feelings about the word not withholding—the ox-cart and post-chaise for transmitting thoughts poetic or otherwise. And perhaps the 'great Victorians', though it is doubtful, and assuredly the 'nineties' continued the development of the art, confining their improvements, however, chiefly to sound and to refinements of manner.

Mr Yeats[19] has once and for all stripped English poetry of its perdamnable rhetoric. He has boiled away all that is not poetic—and a good deal that is. He has become a classic in his own lifetime and *nel mezzo del cammin*.[20] He has made our poetic idiom a thing pliable, a speech without inversions.

Robert Bridges, Maurice Hewlett and Frederic Manning are[21] in their different ways seriously concerned with overhauling the metric, in testing the language

[17]Guido Cavalcanti (1255?–1300), Italian lyric poet.
[18]Arthur Symons (1865–1945), English poet and critic.
[19]William Butler Yeats (1865–1939), Anglo-Irish poet.
[20]"Midway in the journey," a quotation from the first line of Dante's *Inferno*.
[21]"(Dec. 1911)."—Pound's note. He cites Robert Bridges (1844–1930), Poet Laureate of England (1913–1930); Maurice Hewlett (1861–1923), English novelist and poet; Frederic Manning (1887–1935), Australian poet who lived in England.

and its adaptability to certain modes. Ford Hueffer[22] is making some sort of experiments in modernity. The Provost of Oriel[23] continues his translation of the *Divina Commedia*.

As to Twentieth century poetry, and the poetry which I expect to see written during the next decade or so, it will, I think, move against poppy-cock, it will be harder and saner, it will be what Mr Hewlett calls 'nearer the bone'. It will be as much like granite as it can be, its force will lie in its truth, its interpretative power (of course, poetic force does always rest there); I mean it will not try to seem forcible by rhetorical din, and luxurious riot. We will have fewer painted adjectives impeding the shock and stroke of it. At least for myself, I want it so, austere, direct, free from emotional slither.

What is there now, in 1917, to be added?

. . . . .

1918

T. S. Eliot *1888–1965*

In the period between the two world wars, poetry and criticism were largely dominated by a single figure, T. S. Eliot. Even more than Ezra Pound, he shaped the tastes and the critical vocabulary of a generation. The Waste Land, *the most startling and innovative of Eliot's poems, had the effect, as William Carlos Williams remarked, of "an atom bomb"; and in the decades that followed, Eliot became the major poet writing in English and the authoritative voice of modern criticism—esteemed, imitated, and quoted on both sides of the Atlantic.*

Eliot was a descendant of a prominent New England family dating from the seventeenth century. He was born in St. Louis, Missouri. In his youth he attended a Boston preparatory school and then entered Harvard, where he studied literature and philosophy. He served as editor of the Harvard Advocate, *and he developed, from reading the poetry of the French symbolists, his early poetic style. From Harvard, Eliot went to Europe to complete a doctoral dissertation on F. H. Bradley, an English philosopher from whom Eliot derived one of his pervasive themes, the "isolated consciousness."*

When World War I began, Eliot settled in London, where he worked as a bank clerk. In 1917, in the wake of a fateful meeting with Ezra Pound, Eliot published his first book of poems, Prufrock and Other Observations. *He became an editor of the* Egoist *and then founding editor of the* Criterion, *for which he wrote some of his early reviews and criticism. Then in 1922,* The Waste Land *(dedicated to its editor, Pound) became the poem that set the tone of the postwar era. Emphasizing the decay of Western culture, Eliot's poem was heralded as the major document of modern despair. Its ranging meters and fragmented style—an interweaving of reminiscences, vignettes, literary allusions, and anthropological lore—became models of modernist techniques.*

[22]Ford Madox Ford (1873–1939), English novelist.
[23]Charles Lancelot Shadwell (1840–1919), Provost of Oriel College, Oxford (1905–1914), whose translations of Dante had begun to appear in the 1880s.

Loosely patterned upon medieval Grail legend, The Waste Land *reflects the theme and direction of Eliot's own life: the quest for salvation. In the years that followed, Eliot's writing expressed a deepening conservatism in religion and politics. In 1927 he startled many admirers by announcing his adoption of British citizenship and his conversion to the Church of England. The change was paralleled by the movement of his poetry from the secular to the ascetic—from the pessimism of "Gerontion" (1919), to the religious faith of "Ash Wednesday" (1930), the "conversion" poem drawn from the Anglican service and the disciplines of Christian asceticism. Eliot's poetry culminated in the religious meditations of* Four Quartets *(1936–1943), in which the theme of spiritual quest becomes both personal and universal, presenting man's effort to transcend the force of time and to achieve the "still moment" of the eternal.*

In his later years Eliot devoted himself mainly to verse drama, a genre he had long wanted to restore to the modern stage. His first play, based upon the martyrdom of Saint Thomas á Becket, Murder in the Cathedral *(1935), met with some success. The later plays, in contemporary settings, include* The Family Reunion *(1939),* The Cocktail Party *(1950),* The Confidential Clerk *(1954), and* The Elder Statesman *(1958). Although Eliot's plays are often impressive in their poetry, in general, their sophisticated moral and religious issues has kept them from achieving wide popular appreciation.*

The antiromantic tendency of Eliot's literary criticism was evident with his first book of essays, The Sacred Wood *(1920). His focus upon the English writers of the sixteenth and seventeenth centuries led to a general reassessment of poetic tradition. Most notable was his "discovery" of the Metaphysical poets, in an essay that made John Donne and his followers a contemporary vogue. In 1948 Eliot's achievements were recognized by awards of the British Order of Merit and the Nobel Prize for literature. In the years that followed, Eliot's reputation declined, yet he continued to the end to exercise authority in the world of letters, just as his masterpiece,* The Waste Land, *has remained one of the most influential poems of the twentieth century.*

FURTHER READINGS: *Collected Plays*, 1962; *The Waste Land, A Facsimile and Transcript of the Original Drafts*, ed. Valerie Eliot, 1971; H. Howarth, *Notes of Some Figures Behind T. S. Eliot*, 1964; R. Sencourt, *T. S. Eliot, A Memoir*, 1971; R. Kirk, *Eliot and His Age*, 1972; S. Spender, *T. S. Eliot*, 1976; L. Gordon, *Eliot's Early Years*, 1977; P. Ackroyd, *T. S. Eliot, A Life*, 1984; F. Matthiessen, *The Achievement of T. S. Eliot*, 1935, 1947; *T. S. Eliot, A Selected Critique*, ed. L. Unger, 1948; H. Gardner, *The Art of T. S. Eliot*, 1949; D. Maxwell, *The Poetry of T. S. Eliot*, 1952; G. Williamson, *A Reader's Guide to T. S. Eliot*, 1953; H. Kenner, *The Invisible Poet, T. S. Eliot*, 1959; D. Jones, *The Plays of T. S. Eliot*, 1960; K. Smidt, *Poetry and Belief in the Work of T. S. Eliot*, 1961; A. George, *T. S. Eliot, His Mind and Art*, 1962; P. Headings, *T. S. Eliot*, 1964, 1982; L. Unger, *T. S. Eliot, Monuments and Patterns*, 1966; H. Blamires, *Word Unheard, A Guide Through Eliot's Four Quartets*, 1969; M. Desmond, *The Poetry of T. S. Eliot*, 1970; G. Patterson, *T. S. Eliot, Poems in the Making*, 1971; B. Bergonzi, *T. S. Eliot*, 1971; A. Austin, *T. S. Eliot, The Literary and Social Criticism*, 1971; D. Traversi, *T. S. Eliot, The Longer Poems*, 1976; H. Gardner, *The Composition of the "Four Quartets,"* 1977; A. Moody, *Thomas Stearns Eliot, Poet*, 1979; C. Behr, *T. S. Eliot, A Chronology of His Life and Works*, 1982; G. Smith, *The Waste Land*, 1983; *T. S. Eliot*, ed. H. Bloom, 1985; M. Ellmann, *The Poetics of Immortality*, 1987.

TEXT: *Collected Poems, 1909–1962*, 1963, with corrections supplied by the editor; *Selected Essays*, 1960.

THE LOVE SONG OF J. ALFRED PRUFROCK

S'io credessi che mia risposta fosse
a persona che mai tornasse al mondo,
questa fiamma staria senza più scosse.

Ma per ciò che giammai di questo fondo
non tornò vivo alcun, s'i'odo il vero,
senza tema d'infamia ti rispondo.[1]

Let us go then, you and I,
When the evening is spread out against the sky
Like a patient etherised upon a table;
Let us go through certain half-deserted streets,
The muttering retreats
Of restless nights in one-night cheap hotels
And sawdust restaurants with oyster-shells:
Streets that follow like a tedious argument
Of insidious intent
To lead you to an overwhelming question. . .[2]   10
Oh, do not ask, "What is it?"
Let us go and make our visit.

In the room the women come and go
Talking of Michelangelo.

The yellow fog that rubs its back upon the window-panes,
The yellow smoke that rubs its muzzle on the window-panes,
Licked its tongue into the corners of the evening,
Lingered upon the pools that stand in drains,
Let fall upon its back the soot that falls from chimneys,
Slipped by the terrace, made a sudden leap,   20
And seeing that it was a soft October night,
Curled once about the house, and fell asleep.

And indeed there will be time
For the yellow smoke that slides along the street
Rubbing its back upon the window-panes;
There will be time, there will be time
To prepare a face to meet the faces that you meet;
There will be time to murder and create,
And time for all the works and days[3] of hands
That lift and drop a question on your plate;   30
Time for you and time for me,
And time yet for a hundred indecisions,
And for a hundred visions and revisions,
Before the taking of a toast and tea.

In the room the women come and go
Talking of Michelangelo.

[1]"If I thought my reply were to one who could ever return to the world, this flame would shake no more; but since, if what I hear is true, none ever did return alive from this depth, I answer you without fear of infamy." The flame (or spirit) of Guido de Montefeltro, suffering in Hades for his sins, confesses to the poet Dante (*Inferno*, Canto XXVII, lines 61–66).

[2]Here, and throughout, the ellipsis points are Eliot's and do not indicate omissions by the editor.

[3]A reference to *Works and Days*, a poem, by the ancient Greek poet Hesiod, on the rural life and labors of a peasant.

And indeed there will be time
To wonder, "Do I dare?" and, "Do I dare?"
Time to turn back and descend the stair,
With a bald spot in the middle of my hair—   40
(They will say: "How his hair is growing thin!")
My morning coat, my collar mounting firmly to the chin,
My necktie rich and modest, but asserted by a simple pin—
(They will say: "But how his arms and legs are thin!")
Do I dare
Disturb the universe?
In a minute there is time
For decisions and revisions which a minute will reverse.

For I have known them all already, known them all—
Have known the evenings, mornings, afternoons,   50
I have measured out my life with coffee spoons;
I know the voices dying with a dying fall
Beneath the music from a farther room.
    So how should I presume?

And I have known the eyes already, known them all—
The eyes that fix you in a formulated phrase,
And when I am formulated, sprawling on a pin,
When I am pinned and wriggling on the wall,
Then how should I begin
To spit out all the butt-ends of my days and ways?   60
    And how should I presume?

And I have known the arms already, known them all—
Arms that are braceleted and white and bare
(But in the lamplight, downed with light brown hair!)
Is it perfume from a dress
That makes me so digress?
Arms that lie along a table, or wrap about a shawl.
    And should I then presume?
    And how should I begin?
          .   .   .   .   .

Shall I say, I have gone at dusk through narrow streets   70
And watched the smoke that rises from the pipes
Of lonely men in shirt-sleeves, leaning out of windows? . . .

I should have been a pair of ragged claws
Scuttling across the floors of silent seas.
          .   .   .   .   .

And the afternoon, the evening, sleeps so peacefully!
Smoothed by long fingers,
Asleep . . . tired . . . or it malingers,
Stretched on the floor, here beside you and me.
Should I, after tea and cakes and ices,
Have the strength to force the moment to its crisis?   80

But though I have wept and fasted, wept and prayed,
Though I have seen my head (grown slightly bald) brought in upon a
    platter,[4]
I am no prophet—and here's no great matter;
I have seen the moment of my greatness flicker,
And I have seen the eternal Footman hold my coat, and snicker,
And in short, I was afraid.

And would it have been worth it, after all,
After the cups, the marmalade, the tea,
Among the porcelain, among some talk of you and me,
Would it have been worth while,   90
To have bitten off the matter with a smile,
To have squeezed the universe into a ball
To roll it towards some overwhelming question,
To say: "I am Lazarus, come from the dead,[5]
Come back to tell you all, I shall tell you all"—
If one, settling a pillow by her head,
    Should say: "That is not what I meant at all.
    That is not it, at all."

And would it have been worth it, after all,
Would it have been worth while,   100
After the sunsets and the dooryards and the sprinkled streets,
After the novels, after the teacups, after the skirts that trail along
    the floor—
And this, and so much more?—
It is impossible to say just what I mean!
But as if a magic lantern threw the nerves in patterns on a screen:
Would it have been worth while
If one, settling a pillow or throwing off a shawl,
And turning toward the window, should say:
    "That is not it at all,
    That is not what I meant, at all."   110
    . . . . .

No! I am not Prince Hamlet, nor was meant to be;
Am an attendant lord, one that will do
To swell a progress,[6] start a scene or two,
Advise the prince: no doubt, an easy tool,
Deferential, glad to be of use,
Politic, cautious, and meticulous;
Full of high sentence,[7] but a bit obtuse;
At times, indeed, almost ridiculous—
Almost, at times, the Fool.

I grow old . . . I grow old . . .   120
I shall wear the bottoms of my trousers rolled.[8]

[4]The prophet John the Baptist was beheaded and his head brought on a platter to Salome, the
daughter of Herodias. Matthew 14:1–11.
[5]Jesus raised Lazarus from the dead. John 11:1–44.
[6]To be part of a royal procession.   [7]Judgment, pronouncement.
[8]To form fashionable cuffs.

Shall I part my hair behind? Do I dare to eat a peach?
I shall wear white flannel trousers, and walk upon the beach.
I have heard the mermaids[9] singing, each to each.

I do not think that they will sing to me.

I have seen them riding seaward on the waves
Combing the white hair of the waves blown back
When the wind blows the water white and black.

We have lingered in the chambers of the sea
By sea-girls wreathed with seaweed red and brown   130
Till human voices wake us, and we drown.
1910–1911   1915, 1917

PRELUDES

I

The winter evening settles down
With smell of steaks in passageways.
Six o'clock.
The burnt-out ends of smoky days.
And now a gusty shower wraps
The grimy scraps
Of withered leaves about your feet
And newspapers from vacant lots;
The showers beat
On broken blinds and chimney-pots,   10
And at the corner of the street
A lonely cab-horse steams and stamps.
And then the lighting of the lamps.

II

The morning comes to consciousness
Of faint stale smells of beer
From the sawdust-trampled street
With all its muddy feet that press
To early coffee-stands.

With the other masquerades
That times resumes,
One thinks of all the hands
That are raising dingy shades
In a thousand furnished rooms.   10

III

You tossed a blanket from the bed,
You lay upon your back, and waited;
You dozed, and watched the night revealing

[9]Mythical alluring creatures, half woman and half fish.

The thousand sordid images
Of which your soul was constituted;
They flickered against the ceiling.
And when all the world came back
And the light crept up between the shutters
And you heard the sparrows in the gutters,
You had such a vision of the street   10
As the street hardly understands;
Sitting along the bed's edge, where
You curled the papers from your hair,
Or clasped the yellow soles of feet
In the palms of both soiled hands.

IV

His soul stretched tight across the skies
That fade behind a city block,
Or trampled by insistent feet
At four and five and six o'clock;
And short square fingers stuffing pipes,
And evening newspapers, and eyes
Assured of certain certainties,
The conscience of a blackened street
Impatient to assume the world.

I am moved by fancies that are curled   10
Around these images, and cling:
The notion of some infinitely gentle
Infinitely suffering thing.

Wipe your hand across your mouth, and
    laugh;
The worlds revolve like ancient women
Gathering fuel in vacant lots.
1910–1911   1915, 1917

THE HIPPOPOTAMUS

*Similiter et omnes revereantur Diaconos, ut mandatum Jesu Christi; et Episcopum,
ut Jesum Christum, existentem filium Patris; Presbyteros autem, ut concilium Dei et
conjunctionem Apostolorum. Sine his Ecclesia non vocatur; de quibus suadeo vos sic
habeo.*   S. IGNATII AD TRALLIANOS.[1]

*And when this epistle is read among you, cause that it be read also in the church of
the Laodiceans.*[2]

[1]Latin: "In like manner, let all reverence the Deacons as Jesus Christ, and the Bishop as the Father,
and the Presbyters as the council of God, and the assembly of the Apostles. Without these there is
no Church. Concerning all which I am persuaded that ye think after the same manner." From a
letter defending church hierarchy, sent by St. Ignatius (first century), Bishop of Antioch, to the
congregation at Tralles in Asia Minor.
[2]From Colossians 4:16, St. Paul's letter to the congregation at Colossae, near Laodicea, in Asia
Minor, arguing against false teachings and asserting the supreme power of Christ.

The broad-backed hippopotamus
Rests on his belly in the mud;
Although he seems so firm to us
He is merely flesh and blood.

Flesh and blood is weak and frail,
Susceptible to nervous shock;
While the True Church can never fail
For it is based upon a rock.

The hippo's feeble steps may err
In compassing material ends,   10
While the True Church need never stir
To gather in its dividends.

The 'potamus can never reach
The mango on the mango-tree;
But fruits of pomegranate and peach
Refresh the Church from over sea.

At mating time the hippo's voice
Betrays inflexions hoarse and odd,
But every week we hear rejoice
The Church, at being one with God.   20

The hippopotamus's day
Is passed in sleep; at night he hunts;
God works in a mysterious way—
The Church can sleep and feed at once.

I saw the 'potamus take wing
Ascending from the damp savannas,
And quiring angels round him sing
The praise of God, in loud hosannas.

Blood of the Lamb shall wash him clean
And him shall heavenly arms enfold,   30
Among the saints he shall be seen
Performing on a harp of gold

He shall be washed as white as snow,
By all the martyr'd virgins kist,
While the True Church remains below
Wrapt in the old miasmal mist.

                                            1917, 1919

SWEENEY AMONG THE NIGHTINGALES

ὤμοι, πέπληγμαι καιρίαν υληγὴν ἔσω.[1]

[1]Greek: "Alas! I am struck deep with a deadly blow." (Aeschylus, *Agamemnon*, line 1343).

Apeneck Sweeney spreads his knees
Letting his arms hang down to laugh,
The zebra stripes along his jaw
Swelling to maculate[2] giraffe.

The circles of the stormy moon
Slide westward toward the River Plate,[3]
Death and the Raven[4] drift above
And Sweeney guards the hornèd gate.[5]

Gloomy Orion and the Dog[6]
Are veiled; and hushed the shrunken seas;   10
The person in the Spanish cape
Tries to sit on Sweeney's knees

Slips and pulls the table cloth
Overturns a coffee-cup,
Reorganised upon the floor
She yawns and draws a stocking up;

The silent man in mocha brown
Sprawls at the window-sill and gapes;
The waiter brings in oranges
Bananas figs and hothouse grapes;   20

The silent vertebrate in brown
Contracts and concentrates, withdraws;
Rachel *née* Rabinovitch
Tears at the grapes with murderous paws;

She and the lady in the cape
Are suspect, thought to be in league;
Therefore the man with heavy eyes
Declines the gambit, shows fatigue,

Leaves the room and reappears
Outside the window, leaning in,   30
Branches of wistaria
Circumscribe a golden grin;

The host with someone indistinct
Converses at the door apart,
The nightingales are singing near
The Convent of the Sacred Heart,

And sang within the bloody wood
When Agamemnon[7] cried aloud,

---

[2]Spotted.   [3]Rio de la Plata, estuary in South America.
[4]The constellation Corvus, the Crow.
[5]In classical myth, one of the two gates to the land of the dead. From the gate of ivory issue dreams that are false. From the gate of horn issue dreams that come true.
[6]The constellations Orion and Canis Major.
[7]Leader of the Greeks besieging Troy. Upon returning home he was murdered by his wife, Clytemnestra.

And let their liquid siftings fall
To stain the stiff dishonoured shroud.   40
                              1918, 1919

GERONTION[1]

Thou has nor youth nor age
But as it were an after-dinner's sleep
Dreaming on both.[2]

Here I am, an old man in a dry month
Being read to by a boy, waiting for rain.
I was neither at the hot gates[3]
Nor fought in the warm rain
Nor knee deep in the salt marsh, heaving a cutlass,
Bitten by flies, fought.
My house is a decayed house,
And the Jew squats on the window sill, the owner,
Spawned in some estaminet[4] of Antwerp,
Blistered in Brussels, patched and peeled in London.   10
The goat coughs at night in the field overhead;
Rocks, moss, stonecrop,[5] iron, merds.[6]
The woman keeps the kitchen, makes tea,
Sneezes at evening, poking the peevish gutter.
                              I an old man,
A dull head among windy spaces.

Signs are taken for wonders. "We would see a sign!"[7]
The word within a word,[8] unable to speak a word,
Swaddled with darkness. In the juvescence[9] of the year
Came Christ the tiger   20

In depraved May, dogwood and chestnut, flowering judas,[10]
To be eaten, to be divided, to be drunk
Among whispers; by Mr. Silvero[11]
With caressing hands, at Limoges[12]
Who walked all night in the next room;

[1]A name derived from Greek "geron," "an old man."
[2]Shakespeare, *Measure for Measure* (Act III, Scene i, lines 32–34).
[3]At Thermopylae (Greek: "hot gates") the Greeks battled the Persian invaders under Xerxes (480 B.C.).
[4]A cheap café.   [5]A scrubby plant.   [6]French: excrement.
[7]Jesus rebuked the doubting Pharisees when they said, "Master we would see a sign from thee." Matthew 12:38–39.
[8]"In the beginning was the Word, and the Word was with God, and the Word was God." John 1:1.
[9]Juvenescence, youth.
[10]The tree on which Judas was said to have hanged himself.
[11]An acquaintance (like Hakagawa, below) recalled by the aged Gerontion.
[12]French city noted for fine porcelain.

By Hakagawa, bowing among the Titans;[13]
By Madame de Tornquist, in the dark room
Shifting the candles; Fräulein von Kulp
Who turned in the hall, one hand on the door.
    Vacant shuttles   30
Weave the wind. I have no ghosts,
An old man in a draughty house
Under a windy knob.

After such knowledge, what forgiveness? Think now
History has many cunning passages, contrived corridors
And issues; deceives with whispering ambitions,
Guides us by vanities. Think now
She gives when our attention is distracted,
And what she gives, gives with such supple confusions
That the giving famishes the craving. Gives too late   40
What's not believed in, or if still believed,
In memory only, reconsidered passion. Gives too soon
Into weak hands, what's thought can be dispensed with
Till the refusal propagates a fear. Think
Neither fear nor courage saves us. Unnatural-vices
Are fathered by our heroism. Virtues
Are forced upon us by our impudent crimes.
These tears are shaken from the wrath-bearing tree.[14]

The tiger springs in the new year. Us he devours. Think at last
We have not reached conclusion, when I   50
Stiffen in a rented house. Think at last
I have not made this show purposelessly
And it is not by any concitation[15]
Of the backward devils.
I would meet you upon this honestly.
I that was near your heart was removed therefrom
To lose beauty in terror, terror in inquisition.
I have lost my passion: why should I need to keep it
Since what is kept must be adulterated?
I have lost my sight, smell, hearing, taste and touch: 60
How should I use them for your closer contact?

These with a thousand small deliberations
Protract the profit of their chilled delirium,
Excite the membrane, when the sense has cooled,
With pungent sauces, multiply variety
In a wilderness of mirrors. What will the spider do,
Suspend its operations, will the weevil
Delay? De Bailhache, Fresca, Mrs. Cammel,[16] whirled
Beyond the circuit of the shuddering Bear[17]
In fractured atoms. Gull against the wind, in the windy straits   70

[13]Paintings by the Italian artist Titian (1477–1576).
[14]The tree from which Adam and Eve ate the forbidden fruit. Genesis 2:16–17; 3:16–19.
[15]Agitation, excitement.
[16]Other names recollected by Gerontion.
[17]One of constellations Ursa, the Big or Little Dipper.

Of Belle Isle,[18] or running on the Horn.[19]
White feathers in the snow, the Gulf claims,
And an old man driven by the Trades[20]
To a sleepy corner.
                                        Tenants of the house.
Thoughts of a dry brain in a dry season.
1919   1920

THE WASTE LAND[1]

*"Nam Sibyllam quidem Cumis ego ipse oculis meis vidi in ampulla pendere, et cum
illi pueri dicerent: Σίβυλλα τί θέλεις; respondebat illa: ἀποθανεῖν θέλω."[2]*

For Ezra Pound
il miglior fabbro.[3]

I. THE BURIAL OF THE DEAD[4]

April is the cruellest month, breeding
Lilacs out of the dead land, mixing
Memory and desire, stirring
Dull roots with spring rain.
Winter kept us warm, covering
Earth in forgetful snow, feeding
A little life with dried tubers.
Summer surprised us, coming over the Starnbergersee[5]
With a shower of rain; we stopped in the colonnade,
And went on in sunlight, into the Hofgarten,[6]   10
And drank coffee, and talked for an hour.
Bin gar keine Russin, stamm' aus Litauen, echt deutsch.[7]
And when we were children, staying at the archduke's,
My cousin's, he took me out on a sled,
And I was frightened. He said, Marie,
Marie, hold on tight. And down we went.
In the mountains, there you feel free.
I read, much of the night, and go south in the winter.

[18]Straits between Labrador and Newfoundland, Canada.
[19]Cape Horn, at the southern tip of South America.   [20]Trade winds.
    [1]Footnotes to this poem and to Eliot's "Notes on 'The Waste Land' " (pages 1177–1181) are supplied
by the editor.
    [2]"For I myself saw with my own eyes the Sibyl of Cumae [in Italy] hanging in a bottle; and when
the boys cried to her, 'Sibyl, what do you want?' she used to reply, 'I want to die.' " (Petronius,
Satyricon, Chapter XLVIII). The Sibyl, a prophetess, had been given long life by Apollo, but she
had failed to ask for eternal youth and health.
    [3]"The better craftsman," a quotation from Dante's *Purgatorio* (Canto XXVI, line 117). Pound had
assisted Eliot in writing "The Waste Land."
    [4]The title of the services for the dead in *The Book of Common Prayer* of the Church of England.
    [5]Lake near Munich, Germany.   [6]Public park in Munich.
    [7]German: I'm not Russian; I come from Lithuania, pure German.

What are the roots that clutch, what branches grow
Out of this stony rubbish? Son of man,   20
You cannot say, or guess, for you know only
A heap of broken images, where the sun beats,
And the dead tree gives no shelter, the cricket no relief,
And the dry stone no sound of water. Only
There is shadow under this red rock,
(Come in under the shadow of this red rock),
And I will show you something different from either
Your shadow at morning striding behind you
Or your shadow at evening rising to meet you;
I will show you fear in a handful of dust.   30
　　　　Frisch weht der Wind
　　　　Der Heimat zu.
　　　　Mein Irisch Kind,
　　　　Wo weilest du?[8]
"You gave me hyacinths[9] first a year ago;
"They called me the hyacinth girl."
—Yet when we came back, late, from the hyacinth garden,
Your arms full, and your hair wet, I could not
Speak, and my eyes failed, I was neither
Living nor dead, and I knew nothing,   40
Looking into the heart of light, the silence.
Oed' und leer das Meer.[10]

Madame Sosostris, famous clairvoyante,
Had a bad cold, nevertheless
Is known to be the wisest woman in Europe,
With a wicked pack of cards.[11] Here, said she,
Is your card, the drowned Phoenician Sailor,
(Those are pearls that were his eyes.[12] Look!)
Here is Belladonna, the Lady of the Rocks,
The lady of situations.   50
Here is the man with three staves, and here the Wheel,
And here is the one-eyed merchant, and this card,
Which is blank, is something he carries on his back,
Which I am forbidden to see. I do not find
The Hanged Man. Fear death by water.
I see crowds of people, walking round in a ring.
Thank you. If you see dear Mrs. Equitone,
Tell her I bring the horoscope myself:
One must be so careful these days.

Unreal City,   60
Under the brown fog of a winter dawn,

---

[8]"Fresh blows the wind / To the homeland / My Irish child; / Where are you waiting?" See Eliot's note, I, line 31 (page 1178).
[9]A flower named for Hyacinthus, ancient Greek fertility god. The Hyacinthia, a resurrection festival in his honor, was celebrated in July to commemorate the seasonal rebirth and growth of vegetation.
[10]"Desolate and empty the sea." See Eliot's note, I, line 42.
[11]Tarot cards, used in fortune-telling. See Eliot's note, I, line 46.
[12]From Shakespeare's *The Tempest* (Act I, Scene ii, line 398).

A crowd flowed over London Bridge, so many,
I had not thought death had undone so many.[13]
Sighs, short and infrequent, were exhaled,
And each man fixed his eyes before his feet.
Flowed up the hill and down King William Street,
To where Saint Mary Woolnoth[14] kept the hours
With a dead sound on the final stroke of nine.
There I saw one I knew, and stopped him, crying: "Stetson!
"You who were with me in the ships at Mylae![15]   70
"That corpse you planted last year in your garden,
"Has it begun to sprout? Will it bloom this year?
"Or has the sudden frost disturbed its bed?
"O keep the Dog far hence, that's friend to men,
"Or with his nails he'll dig it up again![16]
"You! hypocrite lecteur!—mon semblable,—mon frère!"[17]

II. A GAME OF CHESS

The Chair she sat in, like a burnished throne,
Glowed on the marble,[18] where the glass
Held up by standards wrought with fruited vines
From which a golden Cupidon[19] peeped out   80
(Another hid his eyes behind his wing)
Doubled the flames of sevenbranched candelabra
Reflecting light upon the table as
The glitter of her jewels rose to meet it,
From satin cases poured in rich profusion.
In vials of ivory and coloured glass
Unstoppered, lurked her strange synthetic perfumes,
Unguent, powdered, or liquid—troubled, confused
And drowned the sense in odours; stirred by the air
That freshened from the window, these ascended   90
In fattening the prolonged candle-flames,
Flung their smoke into the laquearia,[20]
Stirring the pattern on the coffered ceiling.
Huge sea-wood fed with copper
Burned green and orange, framed by the coloured stone,
In which sad light a carvèd dolphin swam.
Above the antique mantel was displayed
As though a window gave upon the sylvan scene[21]

[13]A quotation from Dante's *Inferno*. See Eliot's note, I, line 63.
[14]London church.
[15]Site of a Roman naval victory over the Carthaginians (260 B.C.).
[16]An adaptation from John Webster's *The White Devil* (1612): "But keep the wolf far thence, that's foe to men, / For with his nails he'll dig them up again." (Act V, Scene iv, lines 97–98).
[17]French: "hypocrite reader!—my likeness,—my brother!" See Eliot's note, I, line 76.
[18]An adaptation of the description of Cleopatra's barge in Shakespeare's *Antony and Cleopatra:* "The barge she sat in, like a burnish'd throne, / Burn'd on the water." (Act II, Scene ii, lines 196–197).
[19]A statue of Cupid, Roman god of love.
[20]Fretted ceiling. See Eliot's note, II, line 92.
[21]A reference to *Paradise Lost* (Book IV, line 140) where Milton describes the Garden of Eden.

The change of Philomel,[22] by the barbarous king
So rudely forced; yet there the nightingale   100
Filled all the desert with inviolable voice
And still she cries, and still the world pursues,
"Jug Jug"[23] to dirty ears.
And other withered stumps of time
Were told upon the walls; staring forms
Leaned out, leaning, hushing the room enclosed.
Footsteps shuffled on the stair.
Under the firelight, under the brush, her hair
Spread out in fiery points
Glowed into words, then would be savagely still.   110

"My nerves are bad to-night. Yes, bad. Stay with me.
"Speak to me. Why do you never speak? Speak.
"What are you thinking of? What thinking? What?
"I never know what you are thinking. Think."

I think we are in rats' alley
Where the dead men lost their bones.

"What is that noise?"
                      The wind under the door.
"What is that noise now? What is the wind doing?"
                      Nothing again nothing.   120
                                              "Do

     "You know nothing? Do you see nothing? Do you remember
Nothing?"

     I remember
Those are pearls that were his eyes.
"Are you alive, or not? Is there nothing in your head?"
                                              But

O O O O that Shakespeherian Rag—
It's so elegant
So intelligent[24]   130

"What shall I do now? What shall I do?
"I shall rush out as I am, and walk the street
"With my hair down, so. What shall we do tomorrow?
"What shall we ever do?"
                      The hot water at ten.
And if it rains, a closed car at four.
And we shall play a game of chess,
Pressing lidless eyes and waiting for a knock upon the door.

[22]In classical legend Philomel was raped by Tereus, King of Thrace. The gods then turned her
into a nightingale. The story is told in Ovid's *Metamorphoses*. See Eliot's note, II, line 99.
[23]Words traditionally used in English poetry to represent the song of the nightingale.
[24]Lines adapted from the lyrics of *That Shakesperian Rag*, a popular song of 1912.

When Lil's husband got demobbed,[25] I said—
I didn't mince my words, I said to her myself,   140
HURRY UP PLEASE IT'S TIME[26]
Now Albert's coming back, make yourself a bit smart.
He'll want to know what you done with that money he gave you
To get yourself some teeth. He did, I was there.
You have them all out, Lil, and get a nice set,
He said, I swear, I can't bear to look at you.
And no more can't I, I said, and think of poor Albert,
He's been in the army four years, he wants a good time,
And if you don't give it him, there's others will, I said.
Oh is there, she said. Something o' that, I said.   150
Then I'll know who to thank, she said, and give me a straight look.
HURRY UP PLEASE IT'S TIME
If you don't like it you can get on with it, I said,
Others can pick and choose if you can't.
But if Albert makes off, it won't be for lack of telling.
You ought to be ashamed, I said, to look so antique.
(And her only thirty-one.)
I can't help it, she said, pulling a long face,
It's them pills I took, to bring it off, she said
(She's had five already, and nearly died of young George.)   160
The chemist[27] said it would be all right, but I've never been the same.
You *are* a proper fool, I said.
Well, if Albert won't leave you alone, there it is, I said,
What you get married for if you don't want children?
HURRY UP PLEASE IT'S TIME
Well, that Sunday Albert was home, they had a hot gammon,[28]
And they asked me in to dinner, to get the beauty of it hot—
HURRY UP PLEASE IT'S TIME
HURRY UP PLEASE IT'S TIME
Goonight Bill. Goonight Lou. Goonight May. Goonight.   170
Ta ta. Goonight. Goonight.
Good night, ladies, good night, sweet ladies, good night, good night.[29]

III. THE FIRE SERMON

The river's tent is broken; the last fingers of leaf
Clutch and sink into the wet bank. The wind
Crosses the brown land, unheard. The nymphs are departed.
Sweet Thames, run softly, till I end my song.[30]
The river bears no empty bottles, sandwich papers,
Silk handkerchiefs, cardboard boxes, cigarette ends
Or other testimony of summer nights. The nymphs are departed.

[25]Demobilized from the army.
[26]English pubkeeper's call to announce closing time.
[27]English "pharmacist."   [28]Smoked ham.
[29]From the speech by Ophelia, after she has gone mad. Shakespeare, *Hamlet* (Act IV, Scene v, lines 72–74).
[30]A quotation from Edmund Spenser's "Prothalamion" (1596), which describes an elegant procession of nymphs down the river Thames.

And their friends, the loitering heirs of City directors;[31]　　　　180
Departed, have left no addresses.
By the waters of Leman I sat down and wept[32] . . .
Sweet Thames, run softly till I end my song,
Sweet Thames, run softly, for I speak not loud or long.
But at my back in a cold blast I hear[33]
The rattle of the bones, and chuckle spread from ear to ear.
A rat crept softly through the vegetation
Dragging its slimy belly on the bank
While I was fishing in the dull canal
On a winter evening round behind the gashouse　　　　190
Musing upon the king my brother's wreck
And on the king my father's death before him.[34]
White bodies naked on the low damp ground
And bones cast in a little low garret,
Rattled by the rat's foot only, year to year.
But at my back from time to time I hear
The sound of horns and motors, which shall bring
Sweeney to Mrs. Porter[35] in the spring.
O the moon shone bright on Mrs. Porter
And on her daughter　　　　200
They wash their feet in soda water
Et, O ces voix d'enfants chantant dans la coupole.[36]

Twit twit twit
Jug jug jug jug jug jug
So rudely forc'd.
Tereu[37]

Unreal City
Under the brown fog of a winter noon
Mr. Eugenides,[38] the Smyrna[39] merchant
Unshaven, with a pocket full of currants　　　　210
C.i.f. London: documents at sight,[40]
Asked me in demotic[41] French
To luncheon at the Cannon Street Hotel
Followed by a weekend at the Metropole.

[31]Directors of business firms in the City, the financial district of London.
[32]From the lamentations of the Jews exiled from Palestine: "By the rivers of Babylon, there we sat down, yea, we wept, when we remembered Zion." Psalm 137. Eliot substitutes "Leman," the French name for Lake Geneva, Switzerland.
[33]Adapted from "To His Coy Mistress," by Andrew Marvell (1621–1678): "But at my back I always hear / Time's wingéd chariot hurrying near" (lines 21–22).
[34]Adapted from the words of Ferdinand, son of the King of Naples, in Shakespeare's *The Tempest* (Act I, Scene ii, lines 389–391): "Sitting on a bank, / Weeping against the King my father's wreck, / This music crept by me upon the waters."
[35]Here, as elsewhere in Eliot's poetry, Sweeney represents crude humankind. Mrs. Porter and her daughter were whores described in a bawdy song popular with British troops in World War I. See Eliot's note, III, line 199.
[36]French: "And, O those voices of children [choirboys] singing in the dome." From "Parsifal," a sonnet by Paul Verlaine (1844–1896).
[37]A conventional representation, with "jug, jug," of the nightingale's song and an allusion to King Tereus, the despoiler of Philomela.
[38]Greek for *wellborn*.　　[39]Seaport in Turkey.
[40]Business terms used in the buying and selling of commodities. See Eliot's note, III, line 210.
[41]Vulgar.

At the violet hour, when eyes and back
Turn upward from the desk, when the human engine waits
Like a taxi throbbing waiting
I Tiresias, though blind, throbbing between two lives,[42]
Old man with wrinkled female breasts, can see
At the violet hour, the evening hour that strives   220
Homeward, and brings the sailor home from sea,[43]
The typist home at teatime, clears her breakfast, lights
Her stove, and lays out food in tins.
Out of the window perilously spread
Her drying combinations[44] touched by the sun's last rays,
On the divan are piled (at night her bed)
Stockings, slippers, camisoles, and stays.[45]
I Tiresias, old man with wrinkled dugs[46]
Perceived the scene, and foretold the rest—
I too awaited the expected guest.   230
He, the young man carbuncular,[47] arrives,
A small house agent's clerk, with one bold stare,
One of the low on whom assurance sits
As a silk hat on a Bradford millionaire.[48]
The time is now propitious, as he guesses,
The meal is ended, she is bored and tired,
Endeavours to engage her in caresses
Which still are unreproved, if undesired.
Flushed and decided, he assaults at once;
Exploring hands encounter no defence;   240
His vanity requires no response,
And makes a welcome of indifference.
(And I Tiresias have foresuffered all
Enacted on this same divan or bed;
I who have sat by Thebes below the wall
And walked among the lowest of the dead.)[49]
Bestows one final patronising kiss,
And gropes his way, finding the stairs unlit . . .

She turns and looks a moment in the glass,
Hardly aware of her departed lover;   250
Her brain allows one half-formed thought to pass:
"Well now that's done: and I'm glad it's over."
When lovely woman stoops to folly and
Paces about her room again, alone,
She smoothes her hair with automatic hand,

[42]Tiresias, a blind prophet in Greek myth, had been transformed into a woman for seven years. See Eliot's note, III, line 218.
[43]Eliot refers (see his note) to "Sappho's lines," probably a reference to her poem to Hesperus, the Evening Star that brings "home all things the bright morning dispersed." Eliot may also have had in mind the lines from "Requiem" by Robert Louis Stevenson (1850–1894): "Home is the sailor, home from the sea."
[44]One-piece underwear.
[45]Camisoles: short, sleeveless underwear. Stays: corset with bone stiffeners.
[46]Breasts.   [47]Afflicted with carbuncles, boils.
[48]One of the newly rich from the English industrial city of Bradford.
[49]Tiresias made his prophecies in Thebes, where he lived, and in Hades, the underworld, after his death.

And puts a record on the gramophone.[50]

"This music crept by me upon the waters"[51]
And along the Strand,[52] up Queen Victoria Street.
O City, City, I can sometimes hear
Beside a public bar in Lower Thames Street,   260
The pleasant whining of a mandoline
And a clatter and a chatter from within
Where fishmen lounge at noon: where the walls
Of Magnus Martyr[53] hold
Inexplicable splendour of Ionian white and gold.

       The river sweats
       Oil and tar
       The barges drift
       With the turning tide
       Red sails   270
       Wide
       To leeward, swing on the heavy spar.
       The barges wash
       Drifting logs
       Down Greenwich Reach[54]
       Past the Isle of Dogs.[55]
              Weialala leia
              Wallala leialala[56]
       Elizabeth and Leicester[57]
       Beating oars   280
       The stern was formed
       A gilded shell
       Red and gold
       The brisk swell
       Rippled both shores
       Southwest wind
       Carried down stream
       The peal of bells
       White towers
              Weialala leia   290
              Wallala leialala

       "Trams[58] and dusty trees.
       Highbury bore me. Richmond and Kew

[50]An ironic adaptation from Oliver Goldsmith's *The Vicar of Wakefield* (Chapter 29): "When lovely woman stoops to folly, / And finds too late that men betray; / What charm can soothe her melancholy? / What art can wash her guilt away?"

[51]From *The Tempest.* See footnote 34 above.   [52]A London street.

[53]A London church built by Sir Christopher Wren (1632–1723). See Eliot's note, III, line 264.

[54]The Thames River at Greenwich.   [55]A peninsula in the Thames.

[56]The refrain in the song of the Rhine-maidens from the opera *Die Götterdämmerung,* by Richard Wagner (1813–1883)

[57]Queen Elizabeth I of England and Robert Dudley, the Earl of Leicester. Their boat-ride on the Thames (see Eliot's note, III, line 279) is contrasted to the three sordid love affairs that follow (lines 292–308).

[58]Streetcars.

Undid me.[59] By Richmond I raised my knees
Supine on the floor of a narrow canoe."

"My feet are at Moorgate,[60] and my heart
Under my feet. After the event
He wept. He promised 'a new start.'
I made no comment. What should I resent?

"On Margate Sands.[61]   300
I can connect
Nothing with nothing.
The broken fingernails of dirty hands.
My people humble people who expect
Nothing."
        la la

To Carthage then I came[62]

Burning burning burning burning[63]
O Lord Thou pluckest me out[64]
O Lord Thou pluckest   310

burning

IV. DEATH BY WATER

Phlebas the Phoenician, a fortnight dead,
Forgot the cry of gulls, and the deep sea swell
And the profit and loss.
        A current under sea
Picked his bones in whispers. As he rose and fell
He passed the stages of his age and youth
Entering the whirlpool.
        Gentile or jew
O you who turn the wheel[65] and look to windward,   320
Consider Phlebas, who was once handsome and tall as you.

V. WHAT THE THUNDER SAID[66]

After the torchlight red on sweaty faces
After the frosty silence in the gardens

[59]Highbury: London suburb; Richmond and Kew: park and resort areas near London. Eliot echoes the lines from Dante, "Siena bore me; Maremma undid me," used also by Ezra Pound in one of his "Hugh Selwyn Mauberley" poems.

[60]Slum area of London.   [61]A seaside resort on the Thames.

[62]From St. Augustine's *Confessions* (Book III, Chapter i). See Eliot's note, III, line 307.

[63]From the Fire Sermon of Buddha, which calls for a life free of fiery passion. See Eliot's note, III, line 308.

[64]In his *Confessions*, St. Augustine thanks the Lord for plucking him from his broiling, unholy loves. See Eliot's note, III, line 309.

[65]The wheel of fortune or (more likely) a ship's steersman's wheel.

[66]In the Indian *Upanishads*, the Lord speaks through the thunder.

After the agony in stony places
The shouting and the crying
Prison and palace and reverberation
Of thunder of spring over distant mountains
He who was living is now dead[67]
We who were living are now dying
With a little patience 330

Here is no water but only rock
Rock and no water and the sandy road
The road winding above among the mountains
Which are mountains of rock without water
If there were water we should stop and drink
Amongst the rock one cannot stop or think
Sweat is dry and feet are in the sand
If there were only water amongst the rock
Dead mountain mouth of carious[68] teeth that cannot spit
Here one can neither stand nor lie nor sit 340
There is not even silence in the mountains
But dry sterile thunder without rain
There is not even solitude in the mountains
But red sullen faces sneer and snarl
From doors of mudcracked houses
            If there were water

   And no rock
   If there were rock
   And also water
   And water 350
   A spring
   A pool among the rock
   If there were the sound of water only
   Not the cicada
   And dry grass singing
   But sound of water over a rock
   Where the hermit-thrush sings in the pine trees
   Drip drop drip drop drop drop drop
   But there is no water

Who is the third, who walks always beside you?[69] 360
When I count, there are only you and I together
But when I look ahead up the white road
There is always another one walking beside you
Gliding wrapt in a brown mantle, hooded
I do not know whether a man or a woman
—But who is that on the other side of you?

[67]Lines 322–328 refer to Christ's ordeal after The Last Supper and His martyrdom.
[68]Decayed.
[69]After His crucifixion, Christ appeared before two travelers to Emmaus. Luke 24:13–31. See also Eliot's note, V, line 360.

What is that sound high in the air[70]
Murmur of maternal lamentation
Who are those hooded hordes swarming
Over endless plains, stumbling in cracked earth   370
Ringed by the flat horizon only
What is the city over the mountains
Cracks and reforms and bursts in the violet air
Falling towers
Jerusalem Athens Alexandria
Vienna London
Unreal

A woman drew her long black hair out tight
And fiddled whisper music on those strings
And bats with baby faces in the violet light   380
Whistled, and beat their wings
And crawled head downward down a blackened wall
And upside down in air were towers
Tolling reminiscent bells, that kept the hours
And voices singing out of empty cisterns and exhausted wells.

In this decayed hole among the mountains
In the faint moonlight, the grass is singing
Over the tumbled graves, about the chapel
There is the empty chapel,[71] only the wind's home.
It has no windows, and the door swings,
Dry bones can harm no one.   390
Only a cock stood on the rooftree
Co co rico co co rico
In a flash of lightning. Then a damp gust
Bringing rain

Ganga[72] was sunken, and the limp leaves
Waited for rain, while the black clouds
Gathered far distant, over Himavant.[73]
The jungle crouched, humped in silence.
Then spoke the thunder   400
DA
Datta:[74] what have we given?
My friend, blood shaking my heart
The awful daring of a moment's surrender
Which an age of prudence can never retract
By this, and this only, we have existed
Which is not to be found in our obituaries
Or in memories draped by the beneficent spider
Or under seals broken by the lean solicitor
In our empty rooms   410

[70]Lines 367–377 allude to the upheavals resulting from the Russian Revolution that threatened the centers of civilization: Jerusalem, Athens, Alexandria, etc. See Eliot's note, V, lines 366–77.
[71]The Chapel Perilous wherein the knight was prepared for his quest for the Holy Grail.
[72]The Ganges River.   [73]The Himalaya Mountains.
[74]Sanskrit: "Give." From the words of the thunder in the *Upanishads.*

DA
Dayadhvam:[75] I have heard the key
Turn in the door once and turn once only
We think of the key, each in his prison
Thinking of the key, each confirms a prison
Only at nightfall, aethereal rumours
Revive for a moment a broken Coriolanus[76]
DA
Damyata:[77] The boat responded
Gaily, to the hand expert with sail and oar 420
The sea was calm, your heart would have responded
Gaily, when invited, beating obedient
To controlling hands

                         I sat upon the shore
Fishing,[78] with the arid plain behind me
Shall I at least set my lands in order?[79]
London Bridge is falling down falling down falling down
Poi s'ascose nel foco che gli affina[80]
Quando fiam uti chelidon[81]—O swallow swallow
Le Prince d'Aquitaine á la tour abolie[82] 430
These fragments I have shored against my ruins
Why then Ile fit you.[83] Hieronymo's mad againe.[84]
Datta. Dayadhvam. Damyata.

                Shantih   shantih   shantih[85]
1914?–1922   1922

NOTES ON "THE WASTE LAND"[1]

Not only the title, but the plan and a good deal of the incidental symbolism of the poem were suggested by Miss Jessie L. Weston's book on the Grail legend:

[75]Sanskrit: "Sympathize."
[76]Roman general and title character of Shakespeare's *Coriolanus.* He was ruined by his pride and the ingratitude of the masses.
[77]Sanskrit: "Control yourselves."
[78]The Fisher King, to whom Eliot alludes, is, like Christ, a symbol of resurrection. See Eliot's note, V, line 425.
[79]"Thus saith the Lord, Set thine house inorder: for thou shalt die, and not live." Isaiah 38:1.
[80]Italian: Then he hid himself in the flame that purifies them," i.e., the flame that destroys lust. Dante, *Purgatorio* (Canto XXVI, *line* 148).
[81]"When shall I be like the swallow?" From the anonymous Latin poem (fourth century?) "Pervigilium Veneris" ("The Vigil of Venus"), celebrating love and the return of spring. See Eliot's note, V, line 429.
[82]French: "The Prince of Aquitaine at the ruined tower." From the sonnet "El Desdichado" by Gérard de Nerval (1808–1855).
[83]From *The Spanish Tragedy* by Thomas Kyd (1557?–1595?). The words are spoken by Hieronymo, who seeks revenge for the murder of his son.
[84]The subtitle of *The Spanish Tragedy.*
[85]Sanskrit: "The Peace which passeth understanding." See Eliot's note, V, line 434.
[1]In *The Frontiers of Criticism* (1956) Eliot wrote, "When it came to print *The Waste Land* as a little book [1922]—for the poem on its first appearance in *The Dial* [1922] and in *The Criterion* [1922] had no notes whatever—it was discovered that the poem was inconveniently short, so I set to work to expand the notes, in order to provide a few more pages of printed matter. . . ."

From Ritual to Romance (Cambridge). Indeed, so deeply am I indebted, Miss Weston's book will elucidate the difficulties of the poem much better than my notes can do; and I recommend it (apart from the great interest of the book itself) to any who think such elucidation of the poem worth the trouble. To another work of anthropology I am indebted in general, one which has influenced our generation profoundly; I mean *The Golden Bough*;[2] I have used especially the two volumes *Adonis, Attis, Osiris*. Anyone who is acquainted with these works will immediately recognise in the poem certain references to vegetation ceremonies.

I. THE BURIAL OF THE DEAD

Line 20. Cf. Ezekiel II, i.

23. Cf. Ecclesiastes XII, v.

31. V. *Tristan und Isolde*, I, verses 5–8.

42. Id. III, verse 24.

46. I am not familiar with the exact constitution of the Tarot pack of cards, from which I have obviously departed to suit my own convenience. The Hanged Man, a member of the traditional pack, fits my purpose in two ways: because he is associated in my mind with the Hanged God of Frazer, and because I associate him with the hooded figure in the passage of the disciples to Emmaus in Part V. The Phoenician Sailor and the Merchant appear later; also the "crowds of people," and Death by Water is executed in Part IV. The Man with Three Staves (an authentic member of the Tarot pack) I associate, quite arbitrarily, with the Fisher King himself.

60. Cf. Baudelaire:

"Fourmillante cité, cité pleine de rêves,
Où le spectre en plein jour raccroche le passant."[3]

63. Cf. *Inferno*, III, 55–57:

"si lunga tratta
di gente, ch'io non avrei mai creduto
che morte tanta n'avesse disfatta."[4]

64. Cf. *Inferno*, IV, 25–27:

"Quivi, secondo che per ascoltare,
"non avea pianto, ma' che di sospiri,
"che l'aura eterna facevan tremare."[5]

68. A phenomenon which I have often noticed.

74. Cf. the Dirge in Webster's *White Devil*.

76. V. Baudelaire, Preface to *Fleurs du mal*.

II. A GAME OF CHESS

77. Cf. *Antony and Cleopatra*, II, ii, l. 190.

92. Laquearia. V. *Aeneid*, I, 726:

dependent lychni laquearibus aureis incensi, et noctem flammis funalia vincunt.[6]

98. Sylvan scene. V. Milton, *Paradise Lost*, IV, 140.

[2]Anthropological study (1890) of myth and religion, by Sir James Frazer (1854–1941).

[3]"Swarming city, city full of dreams, / Where the ghost in broad daylight accosts the passerby." From the opening lines of the poem "Les Sept Vieillards" ("The Seven Old Men"), by the French poet Charles Baudelaire (1821–1867).

[4]"So long a train of people, I should never have believed death had undone so many."

[5]"Here was no complaint, that could be heard, except of sighs, which caused the eternal air to tremble."

[6]"Lighted lamps hang from the gold, fretted ceiling, and flaming torches drive out the night."

99. V. Ovid, *Metamorphoses*, VI, Philomela.
100. Cf. Part III, l. 204.
115. Cf. Part III, l. 195.
118. Cf. Webster: "Is the wind in that door still?"[7]
126. Cf. Part I, l. 37, 48.
138. Cf. the game of chess in Middleton's *Women Beware Women.*[8]

III. THE FIRE SERMON

176. V. Spenser, *Prothalamion.*
192. Cf. *The Tempest,* I, ii.
196. Cf. Marvell, *To His Coy Mistress.*
197. Cf. Day, *Parliament of Bees:*
   "When of the sudden, listening, you shall hear,
   "A noise of horns and hunting, which shall bring
   "Actaeon to Diana in the spring,
   "Where all shall see her naked skin[9] . . ."
199. I do not know the origin of the ballad from which these lines are taken: it was reported to me from Sydney, Australia.
202. V. Verlaine, *Parsifal.*
210. The currants were quoted at a price "cost insurance and freight to London"; and the Bill of Lading, etc., were to be handed to the buyer upon payment of the sight draft.
218. Tiresias, although a mere spectator and not indeed a "character," is yet the most important personage in the poem, uniting all the rest. Just as the one-eyed merchant, seller of currants, melts into the Phoenician Sailor, and the latter is not wholly distinct from Ferdinand Prince of Naples,[10] so all the women are one woman, and the two sexes meet in Tiresias. What Tiresias *sees,* in fact, is the substance of the poem. The whole passage from Ovid is of great anthropological interest:
   ". . . Cum Iunone iocos et maior vestra profecto est
   Quam, quae contingit maribus," dixisse, "voluptas."
   Illa negat; placuit quae sit sententia docti
   Quaerere Tiresiae: venus huic erat utraque nota.
   Nam duo magnorum viridi coeuntia silva
   Corpora serpentum baculi violaverat ictu
   Deque viro factus, mirabile, femina septem
   Egerat autumnos; octavo rursus eosdem
   Vidit et "est vestrae si tanta potentia plagae,"
   Dixit "ut auctoris sortem in contraria mutet,
   Nunc quoque vos feriam!" percussis anguibus isdem
   Forma prior rediit genetivaque venit imago.
   Arbiter hic igitur sumptus de lite iocosa
   Dicta Iovis firmat; gravius Saturnia iusto
   Nec pro materia fertur doluisse suique
   Iudicis aeterna damnavit lumina nocte,
   At pater omnipotens (neque enim licet inrita cuiquam
   Facta dei fecisse deo) pro lumine adempto

---

[7]I.e., "Is he breathing still?" Spoken of a dying man in John Webster's *The Devil's Law-Case* (1623).
[8]In Thomas Middleton's play (1657) a young wife is seduced while her guardian is occupied with a game of chess.
[9]From "Character 3" of John Day's Elizabethan verse dialogues, *The Parliament of Bees* (1641).
[10]In Shakespeare's *The Tempest.*

Scire futura dedit poenamque levavit honore.[11]

221. This may not appear as exact as Sappho's lines, but I had in mind the "longshore" or "dory" fisherman, who returns at nightfall.

253. V. Goldsmith, the song in *The Vicar of Wakefield*.

257. V. *The Tempest*, as above.

264. The interior of St. Magnus Martyr is to my mind one of the finest among Wren's interiors. See *The Proposed Demolition of Nineteen City Churches:* (P.S. King & Son, Ltd.).

266. The Song of the (three) Thames-daughters begins here. From line 292 to 306 inclusive they speak in turn. V. *Götterdämmerung*, III, i: the Rhine-daughters.[12]

279. V. Froude, *Elizabeth*, Vol. I, ch. iv, letter of De Quadra to Philip of Spain: "In the afternoon we were in a barge, watching the games on the river. (The queen) was alone with Lord Robert and myself on the poop, when they began to talk nonsense, and went so far that Lord Robert at last said, as I was on the spot there was no reason why they should not be married if the queen pleased."[13]

293. Cf. *Purgatorio*, V. 133:
"Ricorditi di me, che son la Pia;
"Siena mi fe', disfecemi Maremma."[14]

307. V. St. Augustine's *Confessions:* "to Carthage then I came, where a cauldron of unholy loves sang all about mine ears."

308. The complete text of the Buddha's Fire Sermon (which corresponds in importance to the Sermon on the Mount) from which these words are taken, will be found translated in the late Henry Clarke Warren's *Buddhism in Translation* (Harvard Oriental Series). Mr. Warren was one of the great pioneers of Buddhist studies in the Occident.

309. From St. Augustine's *Confessions* again. The collocation of these two representatives of eastern and western asceticism, as the culmination of this part of the poem, is not an accident.

V. WHAT THE THUNDER SAID

In the first part of Part V three themes are employed: the journey to Emmaus, the approach to the Chapel Perilous (see Miss Weston's book) and the present decay of eastern Europe.

357. This is *Turdus aonalaschkae pallasii*, the hermit-thrush which I have heard in Quebec Province. Chapman says *(Handbook of Birds of Eastern North America)* "it is most at home in secluded woodland and thickety retreats. . . . Its notes are not remarkable for variety or volume, but in purity and sweetness of tone and

[11]The Latin quotation, from Ovid's *Metamorphoses* (Book III, lines 320–338), may be summarized as: "Jove and Juno once argued whether women or men received more pleasure in love-making. To settle the argument they agreed to ask Tiresias, who had once been transformed into a woman. Tiresias, agreeing with Jove, said that women received more pleasure. The answer so angered Juno that she blinded Tiresias. Whereupon, as compensation, Jove gave the blind Tiresias the power to know the future."

[12]Eliot compares the three modern daughters of the Thames with the three legendary Rhinemaidens in *Die Götterdämmerung*, one of the four operas in Richard Wagner's *Der Ring des Nibelungen* (1853–1870).

[13]The quotation, taken from a letter from the Spanish Ambassador (Bishop de Quadra) to his king, appeared in a biography of Queen Elizabeth I by the English historian James Anthony Froude (1818–1894).

[14]Italian: "Remember me, who am La Pia; Siena bore me, Maremma undid me.' Spoken by a Sienese woman, La Pia, who was killed in Maremma.

exquisite modulation they are unequalled." Its "water-dripping song" is justly celebrated.

360. The following lines were stimulated by the account of one of the Antarctic expeditions (I forget which, but I think one of Shackleton's): it was related that the party of explorers, at the extremity of their strength, had the constant delusion that there was *one more member* than could actually be counted.

366–77. Cf. Hermann Hesse, *Blick ins Chaos:* "Schon ist halb Europa, schon ist zumindest der halbe Osten Europas auf dem Wege zum Chaos, fährt betrunken im heiligen Wahn am Abgrund entlang und singt dazu, singt betrunken und hymnisch wie Dmitri Karamasoff sang. Ueber diese Lieder lacht der Bürger beleidigt, der Heilige und Seher hört sie mit Tränen."[15]

402. "Datta, dayadhvam, damyata" (Give, sympathise, control). The fable of the meaning of the Thunder is found in the *Brihadaranyaka—Upanishad,* 5, 1. A translation is found in Deussen's *Sechzig Upanishads des Veda,* p. 489.

408. Cf. Webster, *The White Devil,* V, vi:
". . . they'll remarry
Ere the worm pierce your winding-sheet, ere the spider
Make a thin curtain for your epithaphs."

412. Cf. *Inferno,* XXXIII, 46:
"ed io sentii chiavar l'uscio di sotto
all'orrible torre."[16]

Also F. H. Bradley, *Appearance and Reality,* p. 346.
"My external sensations are no less private to myself than are my thoughts or my feelings. In either case my experience falls within my own circle, a circle closed on the outside; and, with all its elements alike, every sphere is opaque to the others which surround it. . . . In brief, regarded as an existence which appears in a soul, the whole world for each is peculiar and private to that soul."

425. V. Weston: *From Ritual to Romance;* chapter on the Fisher King.

428. V. *Purgatorio,* XXVI, 48.
" 'Ara vos prec er aquella valor
'que vos condus al som de l'escalina,
'sovegna vos a temps de ma dolor.'
Poi s'ascose nel foco che gli affina."[17]

429. V. *Pervigilium Veneris.* Cf. Philomela in Parts II and III.

430. V. Gerard de Nerval, Sonnet *El Desdichado.*

432. V. Kyd's *Spanish Tragedy.*

434. Shantih. Repeated as here, a formal ending to an Upanishad. "The Peace which passeth understanding" is our equivalent to this word.

---

[15]"Already half of Europe, already at least half of Eastern Europe, is on the way to chaos, going drunk, in spiritual madness, along the edge of the abyss, while singing drunkenly and rapturously, as did Dimitri Karamazov [in Dostoyevsky's *The Brothers Karamazov*]. The shocked bourgeois laughs at these songs; the saint and the prophet hear them with tears." From *A Glimpse into Chaos* by Herman Hesse (1877–1962), German poet and novelist.

[16]"And below I heard the door of the horrible tower being locked."

[17]"Now I pray you, by the goodness that guides you to the top of this stairway [i.e., to paradise], be mindful in due season of my pain.' Then he hid himself in the flame that purifies." The words are spoken to Dante by the poet Arnaut Daniel, who is suffering for his sins of lust.

JOURNEY OF THE MAGI[1]

'A cold coming we had of it,
Just the worst time of the year
For a journey, and such a long journey:
The ways deep and the weather sharp,
The very dead of winter.'[2]
And the camels galled,[3] sore-footed, refractory,
Lying down in the melting snow.
There were times we regretted
The summer palaces on slopes, the terraces,
And the silken girls bringing sherbet.   10
Then the camel men cursing and grumbling
And running away, and wanting their liquor and women,
And the night-fires going out, and the lack of shelters,
And the cities hostile and the towns unfriendly
And the villages dirty and charging high prices:
A hard time we had of it.
At the end we preferred to travel all night,
Sleeping in snatches,
With the voices singing in our ears, saying
That this was all folly.   20

Then at dawn we came down to a temperate valley,
Wet, below the snow line, smelling of vegetation,
With a running stream and a water-mill beating the
    darkness,
And three trees on the low sky.[4]
And an old white horse[5] galloped away in the meadow.
Then we came to a tavern with vine-leaves over the lintel,[6]
Six hands at an open door dicing for pieces of silver,[7]
And feet kicking the empty wine-skins.
But there was no information, and so we continued
And arrived at evening, not a moment too soon   30
Finding the place; it was (you may say) satisfactory.

All this was a long time ago, I remember,
And I would do it again, but set down
This set down
This: were we led all that way for

---

[1]One of a series of lyrics, the "Ariel Poems," on the theme of death and rebirth. The speaker is one of the three wise men whose journey to Bethlehem, to the birth of Christ, is described in Matthew 2:1–11.

[2]The first five lines are taken from a nativity sermon by Lancelot Andrewes (1555–1626), Bishop of Winchester.

[3]Rubbed raw by their harness.

[4]A suggestion of the three crosses on Calvary and the "darkness over all the land." Matthew 27:38, 45.

[5]"Behold a white horse; and he that sat upon him was Faithful and True." Revelation 19:11.

[6]The Israelites marked their door lintels with sacrificial blood so that the Lord would pass over them when he smote the Egyptians. Exodus 12:7–13. Here, the vine leaves on the tavern door suggest instead the vegetation sacred to such pagan fertility gods as Dionysus, god of wine.

[7]A suggestion of the silver paid Judas for the betrayal of Christ.

Birth or Death? There was a Birth, certainly,
We had evidence and no doubt. I had seen birth and death,
But had thought they were different; this Birth was
Hard and bitter agony for us, like Death, our death.
We returned to our places, these Kingdoms,   40
But no longer at ease here, in the old dispensation,
With an alien people clutching their gods.
I should be glad of another death.

                                                              1927

BURNT NORTON[1]

τοῦ λόγον δ'ἐόντος ξυνοῦ ζώονσιν οἱ πολλοί
ὡ6 ἰδίαν ἔχοντες ψρόνησιν.
            I. p. 77. Fr. 2.
ὁδὸ6 ἄνω κάτω μία καὶ ὠντή.
            I. p. 89. Fr. 60.
Diels: *Die Fragmente der Vorsokratiker* (Herakleitos).[2]

                                I

Time present and time past
Are both perhaps present in time future,
And time future contained in time past.
If all time is eternally present
All time is unredeemable.
What might have been is an abstraction
Remaining a perpetual possibility
Only in a world of speculation.
What might have been and what has been
Point to one end, which is always present.   10
Footfalls echo in the memory
Down to the passage which we did not take
Towards the door we never opened
Into the rose-garden.[3] My words echo
Thus, in your mind.
                    But to what purpose
Disturbing the dust on a bowl of rose-leaves
I do not know.
            Other echoes

[1]One of Eliot's "Four Quartets," poems (including "East Coker," "The Dry Salvages," and "Little Gidding") on the doctrines of Christianity and on the concepts of time and consciousness. The title, "Burnt Norton," was taken from the name of a country house in Gloucestershire, England, that Eliot had visited in 1934.

[2]The epigraphs are from Hermann Diel's edition (1909) of the writings of Heraclitus, Greek philosopher (sixth century B.C.), who taught that the world is in a constant process of change. The epigraphs read: "Although the Word, the Logos, is universal, most people live as if they had their own special rules." "The way up and the way down are one and the same." To Greek philosophers the Word, or Logos, represented the principle of reason and universal order. To Christians it became the will and thought of God as in John 1:1: "In the beginning was the Word . . . and the Word was God."

[3]The rose, a conventional symbol of human love and passion, is used by Eliot to suggest a mystical union of body and spirit.

Inhabit the garden. Shall we follow?   20
Quick, said the bird, find them, find them,
Round the corner. Through the first gate,
Into our first world, shall we follow
The deception of the thrush? Into our first world.
There they were, dignified, invisible,
Moving without pressure, over the dead leaves,
In the autumn heat, through the vibrant air,
And the bird called, in response to
The unheard music hidden in the shrubbery,
And the unseen eyebeam crossed, for the roses   30
Had the look of flowers that are looked at.
There they were as our guests, accepted and accepting.
So we moved, and they, in a formal pattern,
Along the empty alley, into the box circle,
To look down into the drained pool.
Dry the pool, dry concrete, brown edged,
And the pool was filled with water out of sunlight,
And the lotos rose, quietly, quietly,
The surface glittered out of heart of light,
And they were behind us, reflected in the pool.   40
Then a cloud passed, and the pool was empty.
Go, said the bird, for the leaves were full of children,
Hidden excitedly, containing laughter.
Go, go, go, said the bird: human kind
Cannot bear very much reality.
Time past and time future
What might have been and what has been
Point to one end, which is always present.

                                   II
Garlic and sapphires in the mud
Clot the bedded axle-tree.   50
The trilling wire in the blood
Sings below inveterate scars
Appeasing long forgotten wars.
The dance along the artery
The circulation of the lymph
Are figured in the drift of stars
Ascend to summer in the tree
We move above the moving tree
In light upon the figured leaf
And hear upon the sodden floor   60
Below, the boarhound and the boar
Pursue their pattern as before
But reconciled among the stars.

At the still point of the turning world. Neither flesh nor fleshless;
Neither from nor towards; at the still point, there the dance is,
But neither arrest nor movement. And do not call it fixity,
Where past and future are gathered. Neither movement from
     nor towards,

Neither ascent nor decline. Except for the point, the still point,
There would be no dance, and there is only the dance.
I can only say, *there* we have been: but I cannot say where.   70
And I cannot say, how long, for that is to place it in time.

The inner freedom from the practical desire,
The release from action and suffering, release from the inner
And the outer compulsion, yet surrounded
By a grace of sense, a white light still and moving,
Erhebung[4] without motion, concentration
Without elimination, both a new world
And the old made explicit, understood
In the completion of its partial ecstasy,
The resolution of its partial horror.   80
Yet the enchainment of past and future
Woven in the weakness of the changing body,
Protects mankind from heaven and damnation
Which flesh cannot endure.
                    Time past and time future
Allow but a little consciousness.
To be conscious is not to be in time
But only in time can the moment in the rose-garden,
The moment in the arbour where the rain beat,
The moment in the draughty church at smokefall   90
Be remembered; involved with past and future.
Only through time time is conquered.

                         III
Here is a place of disaffection
Time before and time after
In a dim light: neither daylight
Investing form with lucid stillness
Turning shadow into transient beauty
With slow rotation suggesting permanence
Nor darkness to purify the soul
Emptying the sensual with deprivation   100
Cleansing affection from the temporal.
Neither plenitude nor vacancy. Only a flicker
Over the strained time-ridden faces
Distracted from distraction by distraction
Filled with fancies and empty of meaning
Tumid apathy with no concentration
Men and bits of paper, whirled by the cold wind
That blows before and after time,
Wind in and out of unwholesome lungs
Time before and time after.   110
Eructation[5] of unhealthy souls
Into the faded air, the torpid
Driven on the wind that sweeps the gloomy hills of London,

[4]German: Exaltation.
[5]Belching.

Hampstead and Clerkenwell, Campden and Putney,
Highgate, Primrose and Ludgate. Not here
Not here the darkness, in this twittering world.

Descend lower, descend only
Into the world of perpetual solitude,
World not world, but that which is not world,
Internal darkness, deprivation   120
And destitution of all property,
Desiccation of the world of sense,
Evacuation of the world of fancy,
Inoperancy of the world of spirit;
This is the one way, and the other
Is the same, not in movement
But abstention from movement; while the world moves
In appetency, on its metalled ways
Of time past and time future.

                              IV
Time and the bell have buried the day,   130
The black cloud carries the sun away.
Will the sunflower turn to us, will the clematis
Stray down, bend to us; tendril and spray
Clutch and cling?
Chill
Fingers of yew be curled
Down on us? After the kingfisher's wing
Has answered light to light, and is silent, the light is still
At the still point of the turning world.

                              V
Words move, music moves   140
Only in time; but that which is only living
Can only die. Words, after speech, reach
Into the silence. Only by the form, the pattern,
Can words or music reach
The stillness, as a Chinese jar still
Moves perpetually in its stillness.
Not the stillness of the violin, while the note lasts,
Not that only, but the co-existence,
Or say that the end precedes the beginning,
And the end and the beginning were always there   150
Before the beginning and after the end.
And all is always now. Words strain,
Crack and sometimes break, under the burden,
Under the tension, slip, slide, perish,
Decay with imprecision, will not stay in place,
Will not stay still. Shrieking voices
Scolding, mocking, or merely chattering,
Always assail them. The Word in the desert
Is mostly attacked by voices of temptation,[6]

---

[6]A reference to Christ's temptation by the devil, in the wilderness. Luke 4:1–12.

The crying shadow in the funeral dance,   160
The loud lament of the disconsolate chimera.

    The detail of the pattern is movement,
    As in the figure of the ten stairs.[7]
    Desire itself is movement
    Not in itself desirable;
    Love is itself unmoving,
    Only the cause and end of movement,
    Timeless, and undesiring
    Except in the aspect of time
    Caught in the form of limitation   170
    Between un-being and being.
    Sudden in a shaft of sunlight
    Even while the dust moves
    There rises the hidden laughter
    Of children in the foliage
    Quick now, here, now, always—
Ridiculous the waste sad time
Stretching before and after.
1934–1935   1936

TRADITION AND
THE INDIVIDUAL TALENT

I

In English writing we seldom speak of tradition, though we occasionally apply its name in deploring its absence. We cannot refer to "the tradition" or to "a tradition"; at most, we employ the adjective in saying that the poetry of So-and-so is "traditional" or even "too traditional." Seldom, perhaps, does the word appear except in a phrase of censure. If otherwise, it is vaguely approbative, with the implication, as to the work approved, of some pleasing archaeological reconstruction. You can hardly make the word agreeable to English ears without this comfortable reference to the reassuring science of archaeology.

Certainly the word is not likely to appear in our appreciations of living or dead writers. Every nation, every race, has not only its own creative, but its own critical turn of mind; and is even more oblivious of the shortcomings and limitations of its critical habits than of those of its creative genius. We know, or think we know, from the enormous mass of critical writing that has appeared in the French language the critical method or habit of the French; we only conclude (we are such unconscious people) that the French are "more critical" than we, and sometimes even plume ourselves a little with the fact, as if the French were the less spontaneous. Perhaps they are; but we might remind ourselves that criticism is as inevitable as breathing, and that we should be none the worse for articulating what passes in our minds when we read a book and feel an emotion about it, for criticizing our own minds in their work of criticism. One of the facts that might come to light in this process is our tendency to insist,

[7]Symbolic steps leading the soul upward to union with God.

when we praise a poet, upon those aspects of his work in which he least resembles any one else. In these aspects or parts of his work we pretend to find what is individual, what is the peculiar essence of the man. We dwell with satisfaction upon the poet's difference from his predecessors, especially his immediate predecessors; we endeavour to find something that can be isolated in order to be enjoyed. Whereas if we approach a poet without this prejudice we shall often find that not only the best, but the most individual parts of his work may be those in which the dead poets, his ancestors, assert their immortality most vigorously. And I do not mean the impressionable period of adolescence, but the period of full maturity.

Yet if the only form of tradition, of handing down, consisted in following the ways of the immediate generation before us in a blind or timid adherence to its successes, "tradition" should positively be discouraged. We have seen many such simple currents soon lost in the sand; and novelty is better than repetition. Tradition is a matter of much wider significance. It cannot be inherited, and if you want it you must obtain it by great labour. It involves, in the first place, the historical sense, which we may call nearly indispensable to any one who would continue to be a poet beyond his twenty-fifth year; and the historical sense involves a perception, not only of the pastness of the past, but of its presence; the historical sense compels a man to write not merely with his own generation in his bones, but with a feeling that the whole of the literature of Europe from Homer and within it the whole of the literature of his own country has a simultaneous existence and composes a simultaneous order. This historical sense, which is a sense of the timeless as well as of the temporal and of the timeless and of the temporal together, is what makes a writer traditional. And it is at the same time what makes a writer most acutely conscious of his place in time, of his own contemporaneity.

No poet, no artist of any art, has his complete meaning alone. His significance, his appreciation is the appreciation of his relation to the dead poets and artists. You cannot value him alone; you must set him, for contrast and comparison, among the dead. I mean this as a principle of aesthetic, not merely historical, criticism. The necessity that he shall conform, that he shall cohere, is not onesided; what happens when a new work of art is created is something that happens simultaneously to all the works of art which preceded it. The existing monuments form an ideal order among themselves, which is modified by the introduction of the new (the really new) work of art among them. The existing order is complete before the new work arrives; for order to persist after the supervention of novelty, the whole *existing* order must be, if ever so slightly, altered; and so the relations, proportions, values of each work of art toward the whole are readjusted; and this is conformity between the old and the new. Whoever has approved this idea of order, of the form of European, of English literature will not find it preposterous that the past should be altered by the present as much as the present is directed by the past. And the poet who is aware of this will be aware of great difficulties and responsibilities.

In a peculiar sense he will be aware also that he must inevitably be judged by the standards of the past. I say judged, not amputated, by them; not judged to be as good as, or worse or better than, the dead; and certainly not judged by the canons of dead critics. It is a judgment, a comparison, in which two things are measured by each other. To conform merely would be for the new work not really to conform at all; it would not be new, and would therefore not be a work of art. And we do not quite say that the new is more valuable because it fits in; but its fitting in is a test of its value—a test, it is true, which can only be slowly and cautiously applied, for we are none of us infallible judges of conformity. We say: it appears to conform, and is perhaps individual, or it appears individual, and may conform; but we are hardly likely to find that it is one and not the other.

To proceed to a more intelligible exposition of the relation of the poet to the past: he can neither take the past as a lump, an indiscriminate bolus,[1] nor can he form himself wholly on one or two private admirations, nor can he form himself wholly upon one preferred period. The first course is inadmissible, the second is an important experience of youth, and the third is a pleasant and highly desirable supplement. The poet must be very conscious of the main current, which does not at all flow invariably through the most distinguished reputations. He must be quite aware of the obvious fact that art never improves, but that the material of art is never quite the same. He must be aware that the mind of Europe—the mind of his own country—a mind which he learns in time to be much more important than his own private mind—is a mind which changes, and that this change is a development which abandons nothing *en route,* which does not superannuate either Shakespeare, or Homer, or the rock drawing of the Magdalenian[2]—draughtsmen. That this development, refinement perhaps, complication certainly, is not, from the point of view of the artist, any improvement. Perhaps not even an improvement from the point of view of the psychologist or not to the extent which we imagine; perhaps only in the end based upon a complication in economics and machinery. But the difference between the present and the past is that the conscious present is an awareness of the past in a way and to an extent which the past's awareness of itself cannot show.

Some one said: "The dead writers are remote from us because we *know* so much more than they did." Precisely, and they are that which we know.

I am alive to a usual objection to what is clearly part of my programme for the *métier*[3] of poetry. The objection is that the doctrine requires a ridiculous amount of erudition (pedantry), a claim which can be rejected by appeal to the lives of poets in any pantheon. It will even be affirmed that much learning deadens or perverts poetic sensibility. While, however, we persist in believing that a poet ought to know as much as will not encroach upon his necessary receptivity and necessary laziness, it is not desirable to confine knowledge to whatever can be put into a useful shape for examinations, drawing-rooms, or the still more pretentious modes of publicity. Some can absorb knowledge, the more tardy must sweat for it. Shakespeare acquired more essential history from Plutarch[4] than most men could from the whole British Museum. What is to be insisted upon is that the poet must develop or procure the consciousness of the past and that he should continue to develop this consciousness throughout his career.

What happens is a continual surrender of himself as he is at the moment to something which is more valuable. The progress of an artist is a continual self-sacrifice, a continual extinction of personality.

There remains to define this process of depersonalization and its relation to the sense of tradition. It is in this depersonalization that art may be said to approach the condition of science. I, therefore, invite you to consider, as a suggestive analogy, the action which takes place when a bit of finely filiated platinum is introduced into a chamber containing oxygen and sulphur dioxide.

[1]A large pill.   [2]Paleolithic.   [3]French: craft.
[4]Greek biographer and philosopher. (A.D. 46?–120?). An English translation of his *Parallel Lives* (biographies of notable Greeks and Romans) provided much of the material used by Shakespeare in writing his Roman plays.

II

Honest criticism and sensitive appreciation are directed not upon the poet but upon the poetry. If we attend to the confused cries of the newspaper critics and the *susurrus*[5] of popular repetition that follows, we shall hear the names of poets in great numbers; if we seek not Blue-book[6] knowledge but the enjoyment of poetry, and ask for a poem, we shall seldom find it. I have tried to point out the importance of the relation of the poem to other poems by other authors, and suggested the conception of poetry as a living whole of all the poetry that has been written. The other aspect of this Impersonal theory of poetry is the relation of the poem to its author. And I hinted, by an analogy, that the mind of the mature poet differs from that of the immature one not precisely in any valuation of "personality," not being necessarily more interesting, or having "more to say," but rather by being a more finely perfected medium in which special, or very varied, feelings are at liberty to enter into new combinations.

The analogy was that of the catalyst. When the two gases previously mentioned are mixed in the presence of a filament of platinum, they form sulphurous acid. This combination takes place only if the platinum is present; nevertheless the newly formed acid contains no trace of platinum, and the platinum itself is apparently unaffected; has remained inert, neutral, and unchanged. The mind of the poet is the shred of platinum. It may partly or exclusively operate upon the experience of the man himself; but, the more perfect the artist, the more completely separate in him will be the man who suffers and the mind which creates; the more perfectly will the mind digest and transmute the passions which are its material.

The experience, you will notice, the elements which enter the presence of the transforming catalyst, are of two kinds: emotions and feelings. The effect of a work of art upon the person who enjoys it is an experience different in kind from any experience not of art. It may be formed out of one emotion, or may be a combination of several; and various feelings, inhering for the writer in particular words or phrases or images, may be added to compose the final result. Or great poetry may be made without the direct use of any emotion whatever: composed out of feelings solely. Canto XV of the *Inferno* (Brunetto Latini)[7] is a working up of the emotion evident in the situation; but the effect, though single as that of any work of art, is obtained by considerable complexity of detail. The last quatrain gives an image, a feeling attaching to an image, which "came," which did not develop simply out of what precedes, but which was probably in suspension in the poet's mind until the proper combination arrived for it to add itself to. The poet's mind is in fact a receptacle for seizing and storing up numberless feelings, phrases, images, which remain there until all the particles which can unite to form a new compound are present together.

If you compare several representative passages of the greatest poetry you see how great is the variety of types of combination, and also how completely any semi-ethical criterion of "sublimity" misses the mark. For it is not the "greatness," the intensity, of the emotions, the components, but the intensity of the artistic process, the pressure, so to speak, under which the fusion takes place, that

[5]Latin: whispering, murmuring.

[6]An official publication of the British government, named for its blue cover.

[7]Italian philosopher (1212–1294) whose works and teachings influenced Dante. In Canto XV of the *Inferno* Dante portrays Latini as tormented in Hell for having scoffed at God. The last quatrain of the canto suggests that Latini is triumphant because of his worldly wisdom and his art even though he must suffer in Hell because of his worldly sins.

counts. The episode of Paolo and Francesca[8] employs a definite emotion, but the intensity of the poetry is something quite different from whatever intensity in the supposed experience it may give the impression of. It is no more intense, furthermore, than Canto XXVI, the voyage of Ulysses,[9] which has not the direct dependence upon an emotion. Great variety is possible in the process of transmutation of motion: the murder of Agamemnon,[10] or the agony of Othello,[11] gives an artistic effect apparently closer to a possible original than the scenes from Dante. In the *Agamemnon,* the artistic emotion approximates to the emotion of an actual spectator; in *Othello* to the emotion of the protagonist himself. But the difference between art and the event is always absolute; the combination which is the murder of Agamemnon is probably as complex as that which is the voyage of Ulysses. In either case there has been a fusion of elements. The ode of Keats[12] contains a number of feelings which have nothing particular to do with the nightingale, but which the nightingale, partly, perhaps, because of its attractive name, and partly because of its reputation, served to bring together.

The point of view which I am struggling to attack is perhaps related to the metaphysical theory of the substantial unity of the soul: for my meaning is, that the poet has, not a "personality" to express, but a particular medium, which is only a medium and not a personality, in which impressions and experiences combine in peculiar and unexpected ways. Impressions and experiences which are important for the man may take no place in the poetry, and those which become important in the poetry may play quite a negligible part in the man, the personality.

I will quote a passage which is unfamiliar enough to be regarded with fresh attention in the light—or darkness—of these observations:

> *And now methinks I could e'en chide myself*
> *For doating on her beauty, though her death*
> *Shall be revenged after no common action.*
> *Does the silkworm expend her yellow labours*
> *For thee? For thee does she undo herself?*
> *Are lordships sold to maintain ladyships*
> *For the poor benefit of a bewildering minute?*
> *Why does yon fellow falsify highways,*
> *And put his life between the judge's lips,*
> *To refine such a thing—keeps horse and men*
> *To beat their valours for her? . . .*[13]

In this passage (as is evident if it is taken in its context) there is a combination of positive and negative emotions: an intensely strong attraction toward beauty and an equally intense fascination by the ugliness which is contrasted with it and which destroys it. This balance of contrasted emotion is in the dramatic situation to which the speech is pertinent, but that situation alone is inadequate to it. This

[8]Illicit lovers whose torments are described by Dante in the *Inferno,* Canto V.

[9]In Canto XXVI of the *Inferno,* Ulysses, who is portrayed as confined to Hell for giving "false counseling," speaks of his last voyage.

[10]The murder of Agamemnon by his wife, Clytemnestra, and her lover, Aegisthus, is portrayed in the *Agamemnon,* by the Greek dramatist Aeschylus (525–456 B.C.).

[11]Othello's agony, after he has murdered his wife for infidelity only to discover that she was innocent, is portrayed in Shakespeare's *Othello* (1607).

[12]"Ode to a Nightingale" (1819) by the English poet John Keats (1795–1821).

[13]From *The Revenger's Tragedy* (Act III, Scene v, lines 68–78) by Cyril Tourneur (1575?–1626?), English dramatist.

is, so to speak, the structural emotion, provided by the drama. But the whole effect, the dominant tone, is due to the fact that a number of floating feelings, having an affinity to this emotion by no means superficially evident, have combined with it to give us a new art emotion.

It is not in his personal emotions, the emotions provoked by particular events in his life, that the poet is in any way remarkable or interesting. His particular emotions may be simple, or crude, or flat. The emotion in his poetry will be a very complex thing, but not with the complexity of the emotions of people who have very complex or unusual emotions in life. One error, in fact, of eccentricity in poetry is to seek for new human emotions to express; and in this search for novelty in the wrong place it discovers the perverse. The business of the poet is not to find new emotions, but to use the ordinary ones and, in working them up into poetry, to express feelings which are not in actual emotions at all. And emotions which he has never experienced will serve his turn as well as those familiar to him. Consequently, we must believe that "emotion recollected in tranquillity"[14] is an inexact formula. For it is neither emotion, nor recollection, nor, without distortion of meaning, tranquillity. It is a concentration, and a new thing resulting from the concentration, of a very great number of experiences which to the practical and active person would not seem to be experiences at all; it is a concentration which does not happen consciously or of deliberation. These experiences are not "recollected," and they finally unite in an atmosphere which is "tranquil" only in that it is a passive attending upon the event. Of course this is not quite the whole story. There is a great deal, in the writing of poetry, which must be conscious and deliberate. In fact, the bad poet is usually unconscious where he ought to be conscious, and conscious where he ought to be unconscious. Both errors tend to make him "personal." Poetry is not a turning loose of emotion, but an escape from emotion; it is not the expression of personality, but an escape from personality. But, of course, only those who have personality and emotions know what it means to want to escape from these things.

III

ὁ δὲ νοῦς ἴσως θειότερόν τι χαί ἀπθές ἐστιν.[15]

This essay proposes to halt at the frontier of metaphysics or mysticism, and confine itself to such practical conclusions as can be applied by the responsible person interested in poetry. To divert interest from the poet to the poetry is a laudable aim; for it would conduce to a juster estimation of actual poetry, good and bad. There are many people who appreciate the expression of sincere emotion in verse, and there is a smaller number of people who can appreciate technical excellence. But very few know when there is an expression of *significant* emotion, emotion which has its life in the poem and not in the history of the poet. The emotion of art is impersonal. And the poet cannot reach this impersonality without surrendering himself wholly to the work to be done. And he is not likely to know what is to be done unless he lives in what is not merely the

---

[14]From the "Preface" to William Wordsworth's *Lyrical Ballads* (1800). In the "Preface" Wordsworth asserts that poetry arises out of "emotion recollected in tranquillity."

[15]A quotation from *De Anima* (Book I, Chapter iv, 408 b 29), in which Aristotle asserts that the intellect (as part of the soul) is indestructible: Memory, loving, and hating all die with the body, "while the intellect is doubtless a thing more divine and is unaffected."

present, but the present moment of the past, unless he is conscious, not of what is dead, but of what is already living.

1919, 1920

Hilda Doolittle (H. D.)   *1886–1961*

Hilda Doolittle first met Ezra Pound at a Halloween party when she was fifteen. The meeting and their friendship profoundly influenced the course of her life and her writing. He was sixteen and a precocious student at the University of Pennsylvania. Later he introduced her to his fellow student William Carlos Williams, and the three became close friends, sharing a lifetime interest in literature and writing poetry. Pound had written his first poem at the age of eleven, and he took it upon himself to instruct his friends. He tutored Hilda Doolittle in Latin and Greek poetry, and later in life she wrote that she had seen him as "immensely sophisticated, immensely superior."

In 1904, Hilda Doolittle entered Bryn Mawr College, near her home in Philadelphia, where one of her classmates was the future poet Marianne Moore. But after two years because of poor health, Hilda Doolittle withdrew from Bryn Mawr, and for the next five years she lived at home with her family and worked at becoming a writer.

In 1908 Pound moved to England. In 1911 Hilda Doolittle followed, beginning an expatriate life (supported initially by her father) that was to continue until her death in Switzerland in 1961. In London, Pound introduced her to other writers and helped get her work published in the recently established American magazine Poetry, *to which Pound had been appointed "foreign correspondent."*

She joined with Pound, and others, including the Englishman Richard Aldington, whom she later married, to form a group opposed to the decorative and sentimental poetry of the nineteenth century. They identified themselves as Imagists and called for poems that were brief, incisive, and direct. The poems had the vocabulary and the rhythms of spoken prose, and presented fresh images of concrete objects rather than vague abstractions.

Three of Hilda Doolittle's poems appeared in the fourth issue of Poetry, *their author identified, at Pound's suggestion, only as "H. D., Imagiste." They were the first poems to be labeled "Imagist," and Pound described them as "Objective—no slither; direct—no excessive use of adjectives, no metaphors that won't permit examination." In 1914, Pound published* Des Imagistes: An Anthology *and in it included work by the Americans William Carlos Williams, Amy Lowell, himself, and six poems by "H. D." Two years later her first book was published,* Sea Garden, *a collection of poems that showed the influence of Imagism and her interest in classical poetry.*

During the war years of 1915, 1916, and 1917, at the peak of the Imagist movement, H. D.'s poems were prominent in the editions of the Imagist anthology Some Imagist Poets. *But the years of the First World War also brought her a series of personal calamities. Her brother was killed in the fighting in France; her home was bombed during one of the German Zeppelin raids on London, and her marriage to Richard Aldington began to break up. In 1919 she and Aldington separated.*

The end of her marriage brought H. D. acute emotional and psychological distress, but she was rescued by Winifred Ellerman, a wealthy English women she had met in 1918. Ellerman, who used the pen name Bryher and later won fame as a writer of historical novels, had much admired H. D.'s poetry, and after H. D.'s separation from Aldington, the two women went on a tour of Greece and America. They finally settled in Switzerland where H. D., supported by her benefactor, continued her literary work.

In 1921 H. D.'s second volume of poetry, Hymen, appeared. Three years later Heliodora and Other Poems *was published, and in 1925 H. D.'s three books of poetry were combined and published as* Collected Poems of H. D. *They contained her most notable poems, and although she eventually published a total of thirteen volumes of poems, plays, essays, and novels, she never surpassed the achievement of her early writing in the Imagist tradition.*

Her last work, Helen in Egypt *(1961), a book-length poem, retold the story of the abduction of Helen by Paris, the resulting Trojan War, and its aftermath. It was written not from the point of view of the male heroes, as poets had traditionally done, but from the point of view of Helen. The* Poem *was H. D.'s most ambitious work, and its feminist viewpoint is in part responsible for the revival of interest in her works that has occurred in the 1980s.*

Helen in Egypt *also shows how far H. D. had developed beyond the severe limits of Imagism, a departure that was inevitable for most Imagist poets and about which she remarked, "I don't know that labels matter very much. One writes the kind of poetry one likes. Other people put labels on it. Imagism was something that was important for poets learning their craft early in this century. But after learning his craft, the poet will find his true direction."*

FURTHER READING R. Aldington, *Life for Life's Sake,* 1941; T. Swann, *The Classical World of H. D.,* 1962; V. Quinn, *Hilda Doolittle,* 1967; S. Friedman, *Psyche Reborn, The Emergence of H. D.,* 1981; J. Robinson, *H. D., The Life and Work of an American Poet,* 1982; B. Guest, *Herself Defined, The Poet H. D. and Her World,* 1984.

TEXT: *H. D., Collected Poems,* ed. L. Martz, 1983.

MID-DAY

The light beats upon me.
I am startled—
a split leaf crackles on the paved floor—
I am anguished—defeated.

A slight wind shakes the seed-pods—
my thoughts are spent
as the black seeds.
My thoughts tear me,
I dread their fever.
I am scattered in its whirl.   10
I am scattered like
the hot shrivelled seeds.

The shrivelled seeds
are split on the path—
the grass bends with dust,
the grape slips
under its crackled leaf:
yet far beyond the spent seed-pods,
and the blackened stalks of mint,
the poplar is bright on the hill,   20

the poplar spreads out,
deep-rooted among trees.

O poplar, you are great
among the hill-stones,
while I perish on the path
among the crevices of the rocks.

1916

GARDEN

I

You are clear
O rose, cut in rock,
hard as the descent of hail.

I could scrape the colour
from the petals
like spilt dye from a rock.

If I could break you
I could break a tree.

If I could stir
I could break a tree—   10
I could break you.

II

O wind, rend open the heat,
cut apart the heat,
rend it to tatters.

Fruit cannot drop
through this thick air—
fruit cannot fall into heat
that presses up and blunts
the point of pears   10
and rounds the grapes.

Cut the heat—
plough through it,
turning it on either side
of your path.

1916

OREAD[1]

Whirl up, sea—
whirl your pointed pines,
splash your great pines

[1]In classical myth, a nymph of hills and mountains.

on our rocks,
hurl your green over us,
cover us with your pools of fir.

                    1914, 1924

LEDA[1]

Where the slow river
meets the tide,
a red swan lifts red wings
and darker beak,
and underneath the purple down
of his soft breast
uncurls his coral feet.

Through the deep purple
of the dying heat
of sun and mist,   10
the level ray of sun-beam
has caressed
the lily with dark breast,
and flecked with richer gold
its golden crest.

Where the slow lifting
of the tide,
floats into the river
and slowly drifts
among the reeds,   20
and lifts the yellow flags,
he floats
where tide and river meet.

Ah kingly kiss—
no more regret
nor old deep memories
to mar the bliss;
where the low sedge is thick,
the gold day-lily
outspreads and rests   30
beneath soft fluttering
of red swan wings
and the warm quivering
of the red swan's breast.

                    1919, 1921

[1]In Greek myth, Leda was raped by Zeus, who had assumed the form of a swan.

HELIODORA[1]

He and I sought together,
over the spattered table,
rhymes and flowers,
gifts for a name.

He said, among others,
I will bring
(and the phrase was just and good,
but not as good as mine,)
"the narcissus that loves the rain."

We strove for a name,   10
while the light of the lamps burnt thin
and the outer dawn came in,
a ghost, the last at the feast
or the first,
to sit within
with the two that remained
to quibble in flowers and verse
over a girl's name.

He said, "the rain, loving,"
I said, "the narcissus, drunk,   20
drunk with the rain."

Yet I had lost
for he said,
"the rose, the lover's gift,
is loved of love,"
he said it,
"loved of love;"
I waited, even as he spoke,
to see the room filled with a light,
as when in winter   30
the embers catch in a wind
when a room is dank;
so it would be filled, I thought,
our room with a light
when he said
(and he said it first,)
"the rose, the lover's delight,
is loved of love,"
but the light was the same.

Then he caught,   40
seeing the fire in my eyes,

[1]A beautiful woman, subject of epigrams written by the ancient Greek poet Meleager, whose words are quoted, in italics, in the poem.

my fire, my fever, perhaps
for he leaned
with the purple wine
stained on his sleeve,
and said this:
"did you ever think
a girl's mouth
caught in a kiss,
is a lily that laughs?"   50

I had not.
I saw it now
as men must see it forever afterwards;
no poet could write again,
"the red-lily,
a girl's laugh caught in a kiss;"
it was his to pour in the vat
from which all poets dip and quaff,
for poets are brothers in this.

So I saw the fire in his eyes,   60
it was almost my fire,
(he was younger,)
I saw the face so white,
my heart beat,
it was almost my phrase;
I said, "surprise the muses,
take them by surprise;
it is late,
rather it is dawn-rise,
those ladies sleep, the nine,[2]   70
our own king's mistresses."

A name to rhyme,
flowers to bring to a name,
what was one girl faint and shy,
with eyes like the myrtle,
(I said: "her underlids
are rather like myrtle,")
to vie with the nine?

Let him take the name,
he had the rhymes,   80
"the rose, loved of love,
the lily, a mouth that laughs,"
he had the gift,
"the scented crocus,
the purple hyacinth,"
what was one girl to the nine?

---

[2]The nine muses of the arts, in classical myth.

He said:
"I will make her a wreath;"
he said:
"I will write it thus: 90

I will bring you the lily that laughs,
I will twine
with soft narcissus, the myrtle,
sweet crocus, white violet,
the purple hyacinth, and last,
the rose, loved-of-love,
that these may drip on your hair
the less soft flowers,
may mingle sweet with the sweet
of Heliodoras's locks,   100
myrrh[3]*-curled.*"
(He wrote myrrh-curled,
I think, the first.)

I said:
"they sleep, the nine,"
when he shouted swift and
    passionate:
"*that* for the nine!
above the hills
the sun is about to wake,
and to-day white violets   110
shine beside white lilies
adrift on the mountain side;
to-day the narcissus opens
that loves the rain."

I watched him to the door,
catching his robe
as the wine-bowl crashed to the floor,
spilling a few wet lees,[4]
(ah, his purple hyacinth!)
I saw him out of the door,   120
I thought:
there will never be a poet
in all the centuries after this,
who will dare write,
after my friend's verse,
"a girl's mouth
is a lily kissed."

HELEN[1]

All Greece hates
the still eyes in the white face,

---

[3]An aromatic resin, from Arabia, hence: perfumed.   [4]Wine sediment.
[1]Greek myth, the daughter of Leda and Zeus and the wife of Agamemnon. Helen's abduction by
Paris was the cause of the Trojan War.

the lustre as of olives
where she stands,
and the white hands.

All Greece reviles
the wan face when she smiles,
hating it deeper still
when it grows wan and white,
remembering past enchantments   10
and past ills.

Greece sees unmoved,
God's daughter, born of love,
the beauty of cool feet
and slenderest knees,
could love indeed the maid,
only if she were laid,
white ash amid funereal
     cypresses.

                                              1924

LETHE[1]

Nor skin nor hide nor fleece
     Shall cover you,
Nor curtain of crimson nor fine
Shelter of cedar-wood be over you,
     Nor the fir-tree
     Nor the pine.

Nor sight of whin nor gorse[2]
     Nor river-yew,
Nor fragrance of flowering bush,
Nor wailing of reed-bird to waken you,   10
     Nor of linnet,
     Nor of thrush.

Nor word nor touch nor sight
     Of lover, you
Shall long through the night but for this:
The roll of the full tide to cover you
     Without question,
     Without kiss.

                                              1924

Epitaph

So I may say,
"I died of living,
having lived one hour";

---

[1] A river in Hades in classical myth. To drink its water brings forgetfulness.
[2] Shrubs.

so they may say,
"she died soliciting
illicit fervour";

so you may say,
"Greek flower; Greek ecstasy
reclaims for ever

one who died   10
following
intricate songs' lost measure."
1931

E. E. Cummings   *1894–1962*

From the time he left college in 1916 until his death in 1962, E. E. Cummings held only one formal job: for three months he answered letters for a mail-order firm. Later he compared those three months to his time spent in a French concentration camp during the First World War. For Cummings, life was too important to spend in pursuit of the material success desired by "most people." Instead he chose to be a dedicated, full-time artist: a painter, a novelist, a playwright, an "nonlecturer"—but most of all a poet.

Edward Estlin Cummings was born in Cambridge, Massachusetts. His father was a Harvard professor who later served as a Unitarian minister in Boston. Cummings went to Harvard, and at his graduation gave the commencement address, speaking on "The New Art." In 1917, after taking his M.A. at Harvard and suffering his brief ordeal as a mail-order letter writer, Cummings went to France to serve as a volunteer ambulance driver with the Red Cross in World War I.

Shortly after arriving in France, Cummings was imprisoned for three months in a concentration camp, partly because of the stupidity of the French military authorities and partly because of Cummings's own stubbornness (he refused to say he hated the Germans; he would only admit that he loved the French). After influential friends secured his release, Cummings was encouraged to write about his experiences. The result was The Enormous Room *(1922), a novel that was the first significant statement of his lifelong dedication to individual freedom and his opposition to the dehumanizing forces he saw in the modern world.*

After World War I, Cummings returned to Europe to study painting. He joined the artistic expatriates who flourished in Paris in the 1920s, and whose experimentation in the visual arts profoundly influenced Cummings's literary development. In 1923 Cummings's first volume of poetry, Tulips and Chimneys, *was published. The following year he returned to America, and in 1925 he published* XLI Poems. *During the remainder of his life he traveled widely and wrote expansively: plays, a book describing a journey to Russia,* Eimi *(1933), and the poems that made him famous.*

Cummings's poetry was noted for its eccentric and playful style: its unusual typography, odd spellings, and deliberate grammatical tricks. But beneath the surface of trickery and apparent formlessness, his poetry is curiously conventional. He was a love poet in the romantic tradition; he celebrated families, parents, children, fun, and the old-fashioned virtues. He admired youth, spring, and all things natural. He hated automatic patriotism and intellectualism, the rationality that, he believed, stifles man's ability to feel deeply. He fiercely condemned the inhumanity of science and technology, writing, "Never will mankind become human . . . until it rises up and smashes its machines." He found modern conveniences contemptible; he shunned electricity in his home, hated radio and television, and called packaged food "Battle Creek seaweed." Above all he loved poetry. Reading to an indifferent audience in 1950, he finally grew angry and stormed out, shouting at his apathetic listeners, "Well, write poetry, for God's sake; it's the only thing that matters."

FURTHER READING: *Selected Letters of E. E. Cummings*, ed. F. Dupee and G. Stade, 1969; C. Norman, *The Magic Maker, E. E. Cummings*, 1958, 1964; R. Kennedy, *Dreams in the Mirror, A Biography of E. E. Cummings*, 1980; N. Friedman, *E. E. Cummings, The Art of His Poetry*, 1960; B. Marks, *E. E. Cummings*, 1964; N. Friedman, *E. E. Cummings, The Growth of a Writer*, 1964, 1980; R. Wegner, *The Poetry and Prose of E. E. Cummings*, 1965; E. Triem, *E. E. Cummings*, 1969; B. Dumas, *A Remembrance of Miracles*, 1974; G. Lane, *I Am, A Study of E. E. Cummings' Poems*, 1976; *E. E. Cummings, The Critical Reception*, ed. L. Dendinger, 1979; R. Kidder, *E. E. Cummings, An Introduction to the Poetry*, 1979; *Critical Essays on E. E. Cummings*, ed. G. Rotella, 1984.

TEXT: *The Complete Poems, 1913–1962*, 1972.

[All in green went my love riding][1]

All in green went my love riding
On a great horse of gold
into the silver dawn.

four lean hounds crouched low and smiling
the merry deer ran before.

Fleeter be they than dappled dreams
the swift sweet deer
the red rare deer.

Four red roebuck at a white water
the cruel bugle sang before.   10

Horn at hip went my love riding
riding the echo down
into the silver dawn.

four lean hounds crouched low and smiling
the level meadows ran before.

Softer be they than slippered sleep
the lean lithe deer
the fleet flown deer.

Four fleet does at a gold valley
the famished arrow sang before.   20

[1]Titles in brackets are supplied by the editor.

Bow at belt went my love riding
riding the mountain down
into the silver dawn.

four lean hounds crouched low and smiling
the sheer peaks ran before.

Paler be they than daunting death
the sleek slim deer
the tall tense deer.

Four tall stags at a green mountain
the lucky hunter sang before.   30

All in green went my love riding
on a great horse of gold
into the silver dawn.

four lean hounds crouched low and smiling
my heart fell dead before.

                              1916, 1923

[when god lets my body be]

when god lets my body be

From each brave eye shall sprout a tree
fruit that dangles therefrom

the purpled world will dance upon
Between my lips which did sing

a rose shall beget the spring
that maidens whom passion wastes

will lay between their little breasts
My strong fingers beneath the snow

Into strenuous birds shall go   10
my love walking in the grass

their wings will touch with her face
and all the while shall my heart be

With the bugle and nuzzle of the sea

                              1920, 1923

[in Just—]

in Just—
spring   when the world is mud-
luscious the little
lame balloonman

whistles   far   and wee

and eddieandbill come
running from marbles and
piracies and it's
spring

when the world is puddle-wonderful   10

the queer
old balloonman whistles
far   and   wee
and bettyandisbel come dancing

from hopscotch and jump-rope and

it's
spring
and
        the

            goat-footed   20

balloonMan   whistles
far
and
wee

                        1920, 1923

[O sweet spontaneous]

O sweet spontaneous
earth how often have
the
doting

        fingers of
prurient philosophers pinched
and
poked

thee
, has the naughty thumb   10

　　of science prodded
　　thy

　　　　beauty　　. how
　　often have religions taken
　　thee upon their scraggy knees
　　squeezing and

　　buffeting thee that thou mightest conceive
　　gods
　　　　(but
　true　　　　　　　　　　　　　　　　　　　　　　　20

　　to the incomparable
　　couch of death thy
　　rhythmic
　　lover
　　　　thou answerest

　　them only with

　　　　　spring)
　　　　　　　　　　　　　1920, 1923

[Buffalo Bill's[1] defunct]

Buffalo Bill's
defunct
　　who used to
　　ride a watersmooth-silver
　　　　　　　　stallion
and break onetwothreefourfive pigeonsjustlikethat
　　　　　　　　　　　　　　　Jesus

he was a handsome man
　　　　　　　　　　and what i want to know is
how do you like your blueeyed boy　　　　　　　　10
Mister Death
　　　　　　　　　　　1920, 1923

[the Cambridge ladies who live in furnished souls]

　　the Cambridge ladies who live in furnished souls
　　are unbeautiful and have comfortable minds
　　(also, with the church's protestant blessings

[1]William F. Cody (1846–1917), American frontiersman and later a star performer in "Buffalo Bill's Wild West Show," which toured America and Europe in the 1880s and 1890s.

daughters, unscented shapeless spirited)
they believe in Christ and Longfellow, both dead,
are invariably interested in so many things—
at the present writing one still finds
delighted fingers knitting for the is it Poles?
perhaps. While permanent faces coyly bandy
scandal of Mrs. N and Professor D   10
.... the Cambridge ladies do not care, above
Cambridge if sometimes in its box of
sky lavender and cornerless, the
moon rattles like a fragment of angry candy

                                    1922, 1923

[nobody loses all the time]

nobody loses all the time

i had an uncle named
Sol who was a born failure and
nearly everybody said he should have gone
into vaudeville perhaps because my Uncle Sol could
sing McCann He Was A Diver on Xmas Eve like Hell Itself which
may or may not account for the fact that my Uncle

Sol indulged in that possibly most inexcusable
of all to use a highfalootin phrase
luxuries that is or to   10
wit farming and be
it needlessly
added

my Uncle Sol's farm
failed because the chickens
ate the vegetables so
my Uncle Sol had a
chicken farm till the
skunks ate the chickens when

my Uncle Sol   20
had a skunk farm but
the skunks caught cold and
died and so
my Uncle Sol imitated the
skunks in a subtle manner

or by drowning himself in the watertank
but somebody who'd given my Uncle Sol a Victor
Victrola and records while he lived presented to
him upon the auspicious occasion of his decease a
scrumptious not to mention splendiferous funeral with   30
tall boys in black gloves and flowers and everything and

i remember we all cried like the Missouri
when my Uncle Sol's coffin lurched because
somebody pressed a button
(and down went
my Uncle
Sol

and started a worm farm)

                                                      1923, 1926

["next to of course god america i"]

"next to of course god america i
love you land of the pilgrims' and so forth oh
say can you see by the dawn's early my
country 'tis of centuries come and go
and are no more what of it we should worry
in every language even deafanddumb
thy sons acclaim your glorious name by gorry
by jingo by gee by gosh by gum
why talk of beauty what could be more beauti-
ful than these heroic happy dead   10
who rushed like lions to the roaring slaughter
they did not stop to think they died instead
then shall the voice of liberty be mute?"

He spoke. And drank rapidly a glass of water
                                                      1925, 1926

[my sweet old etcetera]

my sweet old etcetera
aunt lucy during the recent

war could and what
is more did tell you just
what everybody was fighting

for,
my sister

isabel created hundreds
(and
hundreds)of socks not to   10
mention shirts fleaproof earwarmers

etcetera wristers etcetera, my
mother hoped that

i would die etcetera
bravely of course my father used
to become hoarse talking about how it was
a privilege and if only he
could meanwhile my

self etcetera lay quietly
in the deep mud et   20

cetera
(dreaming,
et
    cetera, of
Your smile
eyes knees and of your Etcetera)

                                                    1926

[i sing of Olaf glad and big]

i sing of Olaf glad and big
whose warmest heart recoiled at war:
a conscientious object-or

his wellbelovéd colonel(trig
westpointer most succinctly bred)
took erring Olaf soon in hand;
but—though an host of overjoyed
noncoms(first knocking on the head
him)do through icy waters roll
that helplessness which others stroke   10
with brushes recently employed
anent this muddy toiletbowl,
while kindred intellects evoke
allegiance per blunt instruments—
Olaf(being to all intents
a corpse and wanting any rag
upon what God unto him gave)
responds, without getting annoyed
"I will not kiss your fucking flag"

straightway the silver bird looked grave   20
(departing hurriedly to shave)

but—though all kinds of officers
(a yearning nation's blueeyed pride)
their passive prey did kick and curse
until for wear their clarion
voices and boots were much the worse,
and egged the firstclassprivates on

his rectum wickedly to tease
by means of skilfully applied
bayonets roasted hot with heat—   30
Olaf(upon what were once knees)
does almost ceaselessly repeat
"there is some shit I will not eat"

our president,being of which
assertions duly notified
threw the yellowsonofabitch
into a dungeon,where he died

Christ(of His mercy infinite)
i pray to see;and Olaf, too

preponderatingly because   40
unless statistics lie he was
more brave than me:more blond than you.
                              1931

[somewhere i have never travelled,gladly beyond]

somewhere i have never travelled,gladly beyond
any experience,your eyes have their silence:
in your most frail gesture are things which enclose me,
or which i cannot touch because they are too near

your slightest look easily will unclose me
though i have closed myself as fingers,
you open always petal by petal myself as Spring opens
(touching skillfully,mysteriously)her first rose

or if your wish be to close me,i and
my life will shut very beautifully,suddenly,   10
as when the heart of this flower imagines
the snow carefully everywhere descending;

nothing which we are to perceive in this world equals
the power of your intense fragility:whose texture
compels me with the colour of its countries,
rendering death and forever with each breathing

(i do not know what it is about you that closes
and opens;only something in me understands
the voice of your eyes is deeper than all roses)
nobody,not even the rain,has such small hands   20
                              1931

[r–p–o–p–h–e–s–s–a–g–r]

                    r–p–o–p–h–e–s–s–a–g–r
            who
a)s w(e loo)k
upnowgath
            PPEGORHRASS
                                eringint(o–
aThe):l
        eA
          !p:
S   a   10
                        (r
    rIvInG   .gRrEaPsPhOs)
                                        to
rea(be)rran(com)gi(e)ngly
,grasshopper;
                                        1932, 1935

[this little bride & groom are]

        this little bride & groom are
        standing)in a kind
        of crown he dressed
        in black candy she

        veiled with candy white
        carrying a bouquet of
        pretend flowers this
        candy crown with this candy

        little bride & little
        groom in it kind of stands on
        a thin ring which stands on a much
        less thin very much more

        big & kinder of ring & which
        kinder of stands on a
        much more than very much
        biggest & thickest & kindest

        of ring & all one two three rings
        are cake & everything is protected by
        cellophane against anything(because
        nothing really exists
                                        1938

[anyone lived in a pretty how town]

anyone lived in a pretty how town
(with up so floating many bells down)
spring summer autumn winter
he sang his didn't he danced his did.

Women and men(both little and small)
cared for anyone not at all
they sowed their isn't they reaped their same
sun moon stars rain

children guessed(but only a few
and down they forgot as up they grew   10
autumn winter spring summer)
that noone loved him more by more

when by now and tree by leaf
she laughed his joy she cried his grief
bird by snow and stir by still
anyone's any was all to her

someones married their everyones
laughed their cryings and did their dance
(sleep wake hope and then)they
said their nevers they slept their dream   20

stars rain sun moon
(and only the snow can begin to explain
how children are apt to forget to remember
with up so floating many bells down)

one day anyone died i guess
(and noone stooped to kiss his face)
busy folk buried them side by side
little by little and was by was

all by all and deep by deep
and more by more they dream their sleep   30
noone and anyone earth by april
wish by spirit and if by yes.

Women and men(both dong and ding)
summer autumn winter spring
reaped their sowing and went their came
sun moon stars rain

1940

[my father moved through dooms of love]

my father moved through dooms of love
through sames of am through haves of give,
singing each morning out of each night
my father moved through depths of height

this motionless forgetful where
turned at his glance to shining here;
that if(so timid air is firm)
under his eyes would stir and squirm

newly as from unburied which
floats the first who,his april touch   10
drove sleeping selves to swarm their fates
woke dreamers to their ghostly roots

and should some why completely weep
my father's fingers brought her sleep:
vainly no smallest voice might cry
for he could feel the mountains grow.

Lifting the valleys of the sea
my father moved through griefs of joy;
praising a forehead called the moon
singing desire into begin   20

joy was his song and joy so pure
a heart of star by him could steer
and pure so now and now so yes
the wrists of twilight would rejoice

keen as midsummer's keen beyond
conceiving mind of sun will stand,
so strictly(over utmost him
so hugely)stood my father's dream

his flesh was flesh his blood was blood:
no hungry man but wished him food;   30
no cripple wouldn't creep one mile
uphill to only see him smile.

Scorning the pomp of must and shall
my father moved through dooms of feel;
his anger was as right as rain
his pity was as green as grain

septembering arms of year extend
less humbly wealth to foe and friend
than he to foolish and to wise
offered immeasurable is   40

proudly and(by octobering flame
beckoned)as earth will downward climb,
so naked for immortal work
his shoulders marched against the dark

his sorrow was as true as bread:
no liar looked him in the head;
if every friend became his foe
he'd laugh and build a world with snow.

My father moved through theys of we,
singing each new leaf out of each tree   50
(and every child was sure that spring
danced when she heard my father sing)

then let men kill which cannot share,
let blood and flesh be mud and mire,
scheming imagine,passion willed,
freedom a drug that's bought and sold

giving to steal and cruel kind,
a heart to fear,to doubt a mind,
to differ a disease of same,
conform the pinnacle of am   60

though dull were all we taste as bright,
bitter all utterly things sweet,
maggoty minus and dumb death
all we inherit,all bequeath

and nothing quite so least as truth
—i say though hate were why men breathe—
because my father lived his soul
love is the whole and more than all

                                              1940

[a salesmen is an it that stinks Excuse]

a salesmen is an it that stinks Excuse

Me whether it's president of the you were say
or a jennelman name misder finger isn't
important whether it's millions of other punks
or just a handful absolutely doesn't
matter and whether it's in lonjewray

or shrouds is immaterial it stinks

a salesman is an it that stinks to please

but whether to please itself or someone else
makes no more difference than if it sells   10
hate condoms education snakeoil vac
uumcleaners terror strawberries democ
ra(caveat emptor[1])cy superfluous hair

or Think We've Met subhuman rights Before
                                            1943, 1944

[pity this busy monster,manunkind,]

pity this busy monster,manunkind,

not. Progress is a comfortable disease:
your victim(death and life safely beyond)

plays with the bigness of his littleness
—electrons deify one razorblade
into a mountainrange;lenses extend

unwish through curving wherewhen till unwish
returns on its unself.
                        A world of made
is not a world of born—pity poor flesh   10

and trees,poor stars and stones,but never this
fine specimen of hypermagical

ultraomnipotence. We doctors know

a hopeless case if—listen:there's a hell
of a good universe next door;let's go
                                            1943, 1944

[what if a much of a which of a wind]

what if a much of a which of a wind
gives the truth to summer's lie;
bloodies with dizzying leaves the sun
and yanks immortal stars awry?
Blow king to beggar and queen to seem
(blow friend to fiend:blow space to time)
—when skies are hanged and oceans drowned,
the single secret will still be man

[1]Latin: let the buyer beware.

what if a keen of a lean wind flays
screaming hills with sleet and snow: 10
strangles valleys by ropes of thing
and stifles forests in white ago?
Blow hope to terror; blow seeing to blind
(blow pity to envy and soul to mind)
—whose hearts are mountains, roots are trees,
it's they shall cry hello to the spring

what if a dawn of a doom of a dream
bites this universe in two,
peels forever out of his grave
and sprinkles nowhere with me and you?   20
Blow soon to never and never to twice
(blow life to isn't:blow death to was)
—all nothing's only our hugest home;
the most who die,the more we live

1943, 1944

[so many selves(so many fiends and gods]

so many selves(so many fiends and gods
each greedier than every)is a man
(so easily one in another hides;
yet man can,being all,escape from none)

so huge a tumult is the simplest wish:
so pitiless a massacre the hope
most innocent(so deep's the mind of flesh
and so awake that waking calls asleep)

so never is most lonely man alone
(his briefest breathing lives some planet's year,   10
his longest life's a heartbeat of some sun;
his least unmotion roams the youngest star)

—how should a fool that calls him "I" presume
to comprehend not numerable whom?

1948, 1950

[when serpents bargain for the right to squirm]

when serpents bargain for the right to squirm
and the sun strikes to gain a living wage—
when thorns regard their roses with alarm
and rainbows are insured against old age

when every thrush may sing no new moon in
if all screech-owls have not okayed his voice
—and any wave signs on the dotted line
or else an ocean is compelled to close

when the oak begs permission of the birch
to make an acorn—valleys accuse their   10
mountains of having altitude—and march
denounces april as a saboteur

then we'll believe in that incredible
unanimal mankind(and not until)

                                                        1948, 1950

[l(a]

l(a

le
af
fa

ll

s)
one
l

iness
                                                        1958

Hart Crane   *1899–1932*

Although the quantity of his work was small (he published only two volumes of poetry in his lifetime), Hart Crane has achieved a position in the first rank of American poets. His fame rests primarily on his extraordinary and controversial poems, yet his life was so turbulent, so much the model for popular, exaggerated notions of the poet, that it, too, has been partly responsible for his renown.

Crane was a neurotic, self-destructive alcoholic and an avowed homosexual whose life was a chaotic jumble of emotional confusion and despair. Born in Ohio in 1899, he spent much of his early life with his grandparents in refuge from the fierce wrangling of his strong-willed mother and father. Crane's father, a successful manufacturer of candy (he invented Life Savers), tried unsuccessfully to make his son into a businessman; Crane's mother, a domineering woman of artistic pretensions, imposed her religious enthusiasms on her son's consciousness.

Crane began to write poetry as a schoolboy. He published his first poem when he was seventeen, and in the same year he dropped out of school to begin a life of wandering and frantic excess, interrupted by periods of intense creativity. In his early twenties, Crane finally managed to break with his family, an event that coincided with the writing of his first major poems. He then left Ohio for New York City, where he unknowingly moved into a room once occupied by Washington Roebling, the builder of the Brooklyn Bridge. There Crane began work on the loosely unified series of poems out of which he eventually created The Bridge.

In 1926 his first volume of poetry, White Buildings, *was published. But the book received mixed reviews, and Crane's life turned sour once more. After a final, bitter argument with his mother, he fled to Europe. Seven months later he returned to New York, and there, late in 1929, he finished his masterpiece,* The Bridge. *In 1930 he went to Mexico, where he planned to write an epic poem on Mexican history and where he sought to create a stable emotional life, but in April 1932, while returning from Mexico to New York by sea, Crane walked to the stern of his ship, leaped into the sea, and drowned. He was thirty-two.*

The Bridge *was Crane's endeavor to write a national epic, a "mythical synthesis of America" such as Walt Whitman had attempted in* Leaves of Grass. *Written partly in refutation of T. S. Eliot's* The Waste Land, *which Crane felt was too pessimistic and ignored "spiritual events and possibilities,"* The Bridge *reflected Crane's desire to find unity in an age of disharmony and disbelief. He wanted to unite, literally and figuratively, the old and the new, east and west, man and God. That he failed is conceded by many; he achieved poetic intensity at the expense of clarity and reason; his poetry is flawed by vague meanings and jumbled images and symbols. Nevertheless, the force of his poetic imagination and his extraordinary power to portray the human quest for unity, love, and beauty have brought him recognition as one of the finest poets of twentieth-century America, despite his tormented, brief life and the ravaging emotions that led to his destruction.*

FURTHER READING: *The Letters of Hart Crane, 1916–1932,* ed. B. Weber, 1952, 1965; B. Weber, *Hart Crane, A Biographical and Critical Study,* 1948, 1970; J. Unterecker, *Voyager, A Life of Hart Crane,* 1969; V. Quinn, *Hart Crane,* 1963; R. Lewis, *The Poetry of Hart Crane,* 1967; H. Liebowitz, *Hart Crane,* 1968; R. Butterfield, *The Broken Arc, A Study of Hart Crane,* 1969; M. Uroff, *Hart Crane, The Patterns of His Poetry,* 1974; R. Sugg, *Hart Crane's The Bridge,* 1976; S. Hazo, *Smithereened Apart, A Critique of Hart Crane,* 1977; *Critical Essays on Hart Crane,* ed. D. Clark, 1982; *Hart Crane, A Reference Guide,* ed. J. Schwartz, 1983; E. Brunner, *Splendid Failure, Hart Crane and the Making of The Bridge,* 1985.

TEXT: *The Complete Poems and Selected Letters and Prose of Hart Crane,* ed. B. Weber, 1966.

BLACK TAMBOURINE

The interests of a black man in a cellar
Mark tardy judgment on the world's closed door.
Gnats toss in the shadow of a bottle,
And a roach spans a crevice in the floor.

Æsop,[1] driven to pondering, found

---

[1]Legendary ancient Greek, author of fables.

Heaven with the tortoise and the hare;
Fox brush and sow ear top his grave
And mingling incantations on the air.

The black man, forlorn in the cellar,
Wanders in some mid-kingdom, dark, that lies,   10
Between his tambourine, stuck on the wall,
And, in Africa, a carcass quick with flies.

                                        1926

CHAPLINESQUE[1]

We make our meek adjustments,
Contented with such random consolations
As the wind deposits
In slithered and too ample pockets.

For we can still love the world, who find
A famished kitten on the step, and know
Recesses for it from the fury of the street,
Or warm torn elbow coverts.

We will sidestep, and to the final smirk
Dally the doom of that inevitable thumb   10
That slowly chafes its puckered index toward us,
Facing the dull squint with what innocence
And what surprise!

And yet these fine collapses are not lies
More than the pirouettes of any pliant cane;
Our obsequies are, in a way, no enterprise.
We can evade you, and all else but the heart:
What blame to us if the heart live on.

The game enforces smirks; but we have seen
The moon in lonely alleys make   20
A grail of laughter of an empty ash can,
And through all sound of gaiety and quest
Have heard a kitten in the wilderness.

                                        1921, 1926

AT MELVILLE'S[1] TOMB

Often beneath the wave, wide from this ledge
The dice of drowned men's bones he saw bequeath

---

[1]Inspired by the comedian Charles Chaplin, whom Crane saw in the movie *The Kid,* in 1921.
[1]Herman Melville (1819–1891). He is buried at Woodlawn Cemetery in New York City.

An embassy. Their numbers as he watched,
Beat on the dusty shore and were obscured.

And wrecks passed without sound of bells,
The calyx[2] of death's bounty giving back
A scattered chapter, livid hieroglyph,
The portent wound in corridors of shells.

Then in the circuit calm of one vast coil,
Its lashings charmed and malice reconciled,   10
Frosted eyes there were that lifted altars;
And silent answers crept across the stars.

Compass, quadrant and sextant contrive
No farther tides . . .[3] High in the azure steeps
Monody shall not wake the mariner.
This fabulous shadow only the sea keeps.

                                                         1926

VOYAGES

I

Above the fresh ruffles of the surf
Bright striped urchins flay each other with sand.
They have contrived a conquest for shell shucks,
And their fingers crumble fragments of baked weed
Gaily digging and scattering.

And in answer to their treble interjections
The sun beats lightning on the waves,
The waves fold thunder on the sand;
And could they hear me I would tell them:

O brilliant kids, frisk with your dog,   10
Fondle your shells and sticks, bleached
By time and the elements; but there is a line
You must not cross nor ever trust beyond it
Spry cordage of your bodies to caresses
To lichen-faithful from too wide a breast.
The bottom of the sea is cruel.
1921–1923   1923, 1926

II

—And yet this great wink of eternity,
Of rimless floods, unfettered leewardings,

---

[2]"This calyx refers in a double ironic sense both to cornucopia and vortex made by a sinking vessel."—Crane.
[3]Here, and throughout, the ellipsis points are Crane's and do not indicate omissions by the editor.

Samite[1] sheeted and processioned where
Her undinal[2] vast belly moonward bends,
Laughing the wrapt inflections of our love;

Take this Sea, whose diapason[3] knells
On scrolls of silver snowy sentences,
The sceptred terror of whose sessions rends
As her demeanors motion well or ill,
All but the pieties of lovers' hands.   10

And onward, as bells of San Salvador[4]
Salute the crocus lustres of the stars,
In these poinsettia meadows of her tides,—
Adagios of islands, O my Prodigal,
Complete the dark confessions her veins spell.

Mark how her turning shoulders wind the hours,
And hasten while her penniless rich palms
Pass superscription of bent foam and wave,—
Hasten, while they are true,—sleep, death, desire,
Close round one instant in one floating flower.   20

Bind us in time, O Seasons clear, and awe.
O minstrel galleons of Carib fire,
Bequeath us to no earthly shore until
Is answered in the vortex of our grave
The seal's wide spindrift[5] gaze toward paradise.
1924   1926

                                III

Infinite consanguinity[1] it bears—
This tendered theme of you that light
Retrieves from sea plains where the sky
Resigns a breast that every wave enthrones;
While ribboned water lanes I wind
Are laved and scattered with no stroke
Wide from your side, whereto this hour
The sea lifts, also, reliquary hands.

And so, admitted through black swollen gates
That must arrest all distance otherwise,—   10
Past whirling pillars and lithe pediments,
Light wrestling there incessantly with light,
Star kissing star through wave on wave unto

[1]Heavy silk, threaded with silver and gold, used in medieval ecclesiastical robes.
[2]From Undine, a water goddess—hence, "oceanic."
[3]Musical notes or harmony.
[4]A reference to the legendary tolling bells of a sunken city off San Salvador.
[5]Sea foam.
[1]Blood relationship.

Your body rocking!
                 and where death, if shed,
Presumes no carnage, but this single change,—
Upon the steep floor flung from dawn to dawn
The silken skilled transmemberment of song;

Permit me voyage, love, into your hands . . .
1924   1926

from *THE BRIDGE*

TO BROOKLYN BRIDGE

How many dawns, chill from his rippling rest
The seagull's wings shall dip and pivot him,
Shedding white rings of tumult, building high
Over the chained bay waters Liberty—

Then, with inviolate curve, forsake our eyes
As apparitional as sails that cross
Some page of figures to be filed away;
—Till elevators drop us from our day . . .

I think of cinemas, panoramic sleights
With multitudes bent toward some flashing scene   10
Never disclosed, but hastened to again,
Foretold to other eyes on the same screen;

And Thee,[1] across the harbor, silver-paced
As though the sun took step of thee, yet left
Some motion ever unspent in thy stride,—
Implicitly thy freedom staying thee!

Out of some subway scuttle, cell or loft
A bedlamite[2] speeds to thy parapets,
Tilting there momently, shrill shirt ballooning,
A jest falls from the speechless caravan.   20

Down Wall,[3] from girder into street noon leaks,
A rip-tooth of the sky's acetylene;
All afternoon the cloud-flown derricks turn . . .
Thy cables breathe the North Atlantic still.

And obscure as that heaven of the Jews,
Thy guerdon[4] . . . Accolade thou dost bestow
Of anonymity time cannot raise:
Vibrant reprieve and pardon thou dost show.

[1]I.e., Brooklyn Bridge.   [2]Madman.
[3]Wall Street in New York City.   [4]Reward.

O harp and altar, of the fury fused,
(How could mere toil align thy choiring strings!)   30
Terrific threshold of the prophet's pledge,
Prayer of pariah, and the lover's cry,—

Again the traffic lights that skim thy swift
Unfractioned idiom, immaculate sigh of stars,
Beading thy path—condense eternity:
And we have seen night lifted in thine arms.

Under thy shadow by the piers I waited;
Only in darkness is thy shadow clear.
The City's fiery parcels all undone,
Already snow submerges an iron year . . .   40

O Sleepless as the river under thee,
Vaulting the sea, the prairies' dreaming sod,
Unto us lowliest sometime sweep, descend
And of the curveship lend a myth to God.
1926   1927, 1930

POWHATAN'S DAUGHTER

"—Pocahuntus, a well-featured but wanton yong girle . . . of the age of eleven or twelve years, get the boyes forth with her into the market place, and make them wheele, falling on their hands, turning their heels upwards, whom she would followe, and wheele so herself, naked as she was, all the fort over."[1]

THE HARBOR DAWN

400 years and more . . . or is it from the soundless shore of sleep that time

Insistently through sleep—a tide of voices—
They meet you listening midway in your dream,
The long, tired sounds, fog-insulated noises:
Gongs in white surplices, beshrouded wails,
Far strum of fog horns . . . signals dispersed in veils.

And then a truck will lumber past the wharves
As winch engines begin throbbing on some deck;
Or a drunken stevedore's howl and thud below
Comes echoing alley-upward through dim snow.

And if they take your sleep away sometimes   10
They give it back again. Soft sleeves of sound
Attend the darkling harbor, the pillowed bay;
Somewhere out there in blankness steam

[1]From William Strachey, *Historie of Travell into Virginia Britania*, written 1609–1612, first published 1849.

Spills into steam, and wanders, washed away
—Flurried by keen fifings, eddied
Among distant chiming buoys—adrift. The sky,
Cool feathery fold, suspends, distills
This wavering slumber. . . . Slowly—
Immemorially the window, the half-covered chair
Ask nothing but this sheath of pallid air.   20

recalls you to your   And you beside me, blessèd now while sirens
love, there in a   Sing to us, stealthily weave us into day—
waking dream to   Serenely now, before day claims our eyes
merge your seed   Your cool arms murmurously about me lay.

While myriad snowy hands are clustering at the
    panes—

      your hands within my hands are deeds;
      my tongue upon your throat—singing
      arms close; eyes wide, undoubtful
            dark
                        drink the dawn—
      a forest shudders in your hair!   30

—with whom?   The window goes blond slowly. Frostily clears.
From Cyclopean[1] towers across Manhattan waters
—Two—three bright window-eyes aglitter, disk
The sun, released—aloft with cold gulls hither.

Who is the woman   The fog leans one last moment on the sill.
with us in the   Under the mistletoe of dreams, a star—
dawn? . . . whose   As though to join us at some distant hill—
is the flesh our feet   Turns in the waking west and goes to sleep.
have moved upon
1926   1927, 1930

VAN WINKLE

Streets spread past   Macadam, gun-grey as the tunny's[1] belt,
store and   Leaps from Far Rockaway to Golden Gate:[2]
factory—sped by   Listen! the miles a hurdy-gurdy grinds—
sunlight and her   Down gold arpeggios mile on mile unwinds.
smile. . .

Times earlier, when you hurried off to school,
—It is the same hour though a later day—
You walked with Pizarro in a copybook,
And Cortes rode up, reining tautly in—
Firmly as coffee grips the taste,—and away!

[1]Gigantic—as though built by giants.
[1]A tuna.
[2]I.e., from the Atlantic to the Pacific.

Like Memory, she
is time's truant,
shall take you by
the hand. . .

There was Priscilla's[3] cheek close in the wind.   10
And Captain Smith,[4] all beard and certainty,
And Rip Van Winkle bowing by the way,—
"Is this Sleepy Hollow,[5] friend—?" And he—

> *And Rip forgot the office hours,*
>   *and he forgot the pay;*
>   *Van Winkle sweeps a tenement*
>   *way down on Avenue A,—*

The grind-organ says . . . Remember, remember
The cinder pile at the end of the backyard
Where we stoned the family of young   20
Garter snakes under . . . And the monoplanes
We launched—with paper wings and twisted
Rubber bands . . . Recall—recall

                                        the rapid tongues
That flittered from under the ash heap day
After day whenever your stick discovered
Some sunning inch of unsuspecting fibre—
It flashed back at your thrust, as clean as fire.

> *And Rip was slowly made aware*
>   *that he, Van Winkle, was not here*   30
>   *nor there. He woke and swore he'd seen Broadway*
>   *a Catskill daisy chain in May—*

So memory, that strikes a rhyme out of a box,
Or splits a random smell of flowers through glass—
Is it the whip stripped from the lilac tree
One day in spring my father took to me,
Or is it the Sabbatical, unconscious smile
My mother almost brought me once from church
And once only, as I recall—?

It flickered through the snow screen, blindly   40
It forsook her at the doorway, it was gone
Before I had left the window. It
Did not return with the kiss in the hall.

Macadam, gun-grey as the tunny's belt,
Leaps from Far Rockaway to Golden Gate. . . .
Keep hold of that nickel for car-change, Rip,—
Have you got your *"Times"*[6]—?
And hurry along, Van Winkle—it's getting late!

                                                1927, 1930

---

[3]Priscilla Alden of the Pilgrim Colony at Plymouth.
[4]John Smith, English explorer said to have been rescued by Pocahontas.
[5]The setting of "The Legend of Sleepy Hollow" (1819), by Washington Irving.
[6]The *New York Times*.

THE RIVER

. . . and past the
din and slogans of
the year—

Stick your patent name on a signboard
brother—all over—going west—young man
Tintex—Japalac—Certain-teed Overalls[1] ads
and lands sakes! under the new playbill ripped
in the guaranteed corner—see Bert Williams[2] what?
Minstrels when you steal a chicken just
save me the wing for if it isn't
Erie it ain't for miles around a
Mazda—and the telegraphic night coming on Thomas

a Ediford[3]—and whistling down the tracks   10
a headlight rushing with the sound—can you
imagine—while an EXPRESS makes time like
SCIENCE—COMMERCE and the HOLYGHOST
RADIO ROARS IN EVERY HOME WE HAVE THE NORTHPOLE
WALLSTREET AND VIRGINBIRTH WITHOUT STONES OR
WIRES OR EVEN RUNning brooks connecting ears
and no more sermons windows flashing roar
breathtaking—as you like it . . . eh?

              So the 20th Century—so
whizzed the Limited—roared by and left   20
three men, still hungry on the tracks, ploddingly
watching the tail lights wizen and converge, slipping
gimleted and neatly out of sight

                    *   *   *

The last bear, shot drinking in the Dakotas
Loped under wires[4] that span the mountain stream.
Keen instruments, strung to a vast precision

to those whose
addresses are never
near

Bind town to town and dream to ticking dream.
But some men take their liquor slow—and count
—Though they'll confess no rosary nor clue—
The river's minute by the far brook's year.   30
Under a world of whistles, wires and steam
Caboose-like they go ruminating through
Ohio, Indiana—blind baggage—
To Cheyenne tagging . . . Maybe Kalamazoo.

Time's rendings, time's blendings they construe
As final reckonings of fire and snow;
Strange bird-wit, like the elemental gist
Of unwalled winds they offer, singing low
My Old Kentucky Home and *Casey Jones,*

[1]Brands of cloth dye, shellac, and men's overalls.
[2]Negro vaudeville comedian (1877–1922).
[3]A pun that combines the names of the inventor Thomas A. Edison (1847–1931), the auto-maker Henry Ford (1863–1947), and the Archbishop of Canterbury and saint, Thomas à Becket (1118?–1170).
[4]Telegraph and telephone wires.

Some Sunny Day. I heard a road-gang chanting so.   40
And afterwards, who had a colt's eyes—one said,
"Jesus! Oh I remember watermelon days!" And sped
High in a cloud of merriment, recalled
"—And when my Aunt Sally Simpson smiled," he
        drawled—
"It was almost Louisiana, long ago."
"There's no place like Booneville though, Buddy,"
One said, excising a last burr from his vest,
"—For early trouting." Then peering in the can,
"—But I kept on the tracks." Possessed, resigned.
He trod the fire down pensively and grinned,   50
Spreading dry shingles of a beard. . . .

                                    Behind
My father's cannery works I used to see
Rail-squatters ranged in nomad raillery,
The ancient men—wifeless or runaway
Hobo-trekkers that forever search
An empire wilderness of freight and rails.
Each seemed a child, like me, on a loose perch,
Holding to childhood like some termless play.
John, Jake or Charley, hopping the slow freight   60
—Memphis to Tallahassee—riding the rods,
Blind fists of nothing, humpty-dumpty clods.

Yet they touch something like a key perhaps.
From pole to pole across the hills, the states
but who have   —They know a body under the wide rain;
touched her,   Youngsters with eyes like fjords, old reprobates
knowing her   With racetrack jargon,—dotting immensity
without name   They lurk across her, knowing her yonder breast
Snow-silvered, sumac-stained or smoky blue—
Is past the valley-sleepers, south or west.   70
—As I have trod the rumorous midnights, too,

And past the circuit of the lamp's thin flame
(O Nights that brought me to her body bare!)
Have dreamed beyond the print that bound her name.
Trains sounding the long blizzards out—I heard
Wail into distances I knew were hers.
Papooses crying on the wind's long mane
Screamed redskin dynasties that fled the brain,
—Dead echoes! But I knew her body there,
Time like a serpent down her shoulder, dark,   80
And space, an eaglet's wing, laid on her hair.

Under the Ozarks, domed by Iron Mountain,[5]
The old gods of the rain lie wrapped in pools
Where eyeless fish curvet a sunken fountain

[5]In southeast Missouri.

nor the myths of
her fathers . . .

And re-descend with corn from querulous crows.
Such pilferings make up their timeless eatage,
Propitiate them for their timber torn
By iron, iron—always the iron dealt cleavage!
They doze, now, below axe and powder horn.

And Pullman breakfasters glide glistening steel.   90
From tunnel into field—iron strides the dew—
Straddles the hill, a dance of wheel on wheel.
You have a half-hour's wait at Siskiyou,[6]
Or stay the night and take the next train through.
Southward, near Cairo[7] passing, you can see

The Ohio merging,—borne down Tennessee;
And if it's summer and the sun's in dusk
Maybe the breeze will lift the River's musk
—As though the waters breathed that you might know
Memphis Johnny, Steamboat Bill, Missouri Joe.   100
Oh, lean from the window, if the train slows down,
As though you touched hands with some ancient clown,
—A little while gaze absently below
And hum *Deep River* with them while they go.

Yes, turn again and sniff once more—look see,
O Sheriff, Brakeman and Authority—
Hitch up your pants and crunch another quid,[8]
For you, too, feed the River timelessly.
And few evade full measure of their fate;
Always they smile out eerily what they seem.   110
I could believe he joked at heaven's gate—
Dan Midland[9]—jolted from the cold brake-beam.

Down, down—born pioneers in time's despite,
Grimed tributaries to an ancient flow—
They win no frontier by their wayward plight,
But drift in stillness, as from Jordan's brow.[10]

You will not hear it as the sea; even stone
Is not more hushed by gravity . . . But slow,
As loth to take more tribute—sliding prone
Like one whose eyes were buried long ago   120

The River, spreading, flows—and spends your dream.
What are you, lost within this tideless spell?
You are your father's father, and the stream—
A liquid theme that floating niggers swell.

Damp tonnage and alluvial march of days—
Nights turbid, vascular with silted shale
And roots surrendered down of moraine clays:
The Mississippi drinks the farthest dale.

[6]In northern California.   [7]In southern Illinois.   [8]Wad of chewing tobacco.
[9]A legendary hobo killed while "riding the rods."
[10]The bank of the Jordan river in Palestine.

O quarrying passion, undertowed sunlight!
The basalt surface drags a jungle grace   130
Ochreous and lynx-barred in lengthening might;
Patience! and you shall reach the biding place!

Over De Soto's bones[11] the freighted floors
Throb past the City storied of three thrones.[12]
Down two more turns the Mississippi pours
(Anon tall ironsides up from salt lagoons)

And flows within itself, heaps itself free.
All fades but one thin skyline 'round . . . Ahead
No embrace opens but the stinging sea;
The River lifts itself from its long bed,   140

Poised wholly on its dream, a mustard glow
Tortured with history, its one will—flow!
—The Passion spreads in wide tongues, choked and
      slow,
Meeting the Gulf, hosannas silently below.
1926   1928, 1930

THE DANCE

Then you shall see
her truly—your
blood remembering
its first invasion of
her secrecy, its first
encounters with her
kin, her chieftain
lover . . . his shade
that haunts the
lakes and hills

The swift red flesh, a winter king—
Who squired the glacier woman down the sky?
She ran the neighing canyons all the spring;
She sprouted arms; she rose with maize—to die.

And in the autumn drouth, whose burnished hands
With mineral wariness found out the stone
Where prayers, forgotten, streamed the mesa sands?
He holds the twilight's dim, perpetual throne.

Mythical brows we saw retiring—loth,
Disturbed and destined, into denser green.   10
Greeting they sped us, on the arrow's oath:
Now lie incorrigibly what years between . . .

There was a bed of leaves, and broken play;
There was a veil upon you, Pocahontas, bride—
O Princess whose brown lap was virgin May;
And bridal flanks and eyes hid tawny pride.

I left the village for dogwood. By the canoe
Tugging below the mill-race, I could see
Your hair's keen crescent running, and the blue
First moth of evening take wing stealthily.   20

[11]The Spanish explorer Hernando de Soto (1500–1542) was buried in the Mississippi River near
present-day New Orleans.
[12]New Orleans was governed alternately by the monarchies of France, Spain, and England.

What laughing chains the water wove and threw!
I learned to catch the trout's moon whisper; I
Drifted how many hours I never knew,
But, watching, saw that fleet young crescent die,—

And one star, swinging, take its place, alone,
Cupped in the larches of the mountain pass—
Until, immortally, it bled into the dawn.
I left my sleek boat nibbling margin grass . . .

I took the portage climb, then chose
A further valley-shed; I could not stop.   30
Feet nozzled wat'ry webs of upper flows;
One white veil gusted from the very top.

O Appalachian Spring! I gained the ledge;
Steep, inaccessible smile that eastward bends
And northward reaches in that violet wedge
Of Adirondacks!—wisped of azure wands,

Over how many bluffs, tarns, streams I sped!
—And knew myself within some boding shade:—
Grey tepees tufting the blue knolls ahead,
Smoke swirling through the yellow chestnut
      glade . . .   40

A distant cloud, a thunder-bud—it grew,
That blanket of the skies: the padded foot
Within,—I heard it; 'til its rhythm drew,
—Siphoned the black pool from the heart's hot root!

A cyclone threshes in the turbine crest,
Swooping in eagle feathers down your back;
Know, Maquokeeta, greeting; know death's best;
—Fall, Sachem,[1] strictly as the tamarack!

A birch kneels. All her whistling fingers fly.
The oak grove circles in a crash of leaves;   50
The long moan of a dance is in the sky.
Dance, Maquokeeta: Pocahontas grieves . . .

And every tendon scurries toward the twangs
Of lightning deltaed down your saber hair.
Now snaps the flint in every tooth; red fangs
And splay tongues thinly busy the blue air . . .

Dance, Maquokeeta! snake that lives before,
That casts his pelt, and lives beyond! Sprout, horn!
Spark, tooth! Medicine-man, relent, restore—   60
Lie to us,—dance us back the tribal morn!

[1]Chief.

Spears and assemblies: black drums thrusting on—
O yelling battlements,—I, too, was liege
To rainbows currying each pulsant bone:
Surpassed the circumstance, danced out the siege!

And buzzard-circleted,screamed from the stake;
I could not pick the arrows from my side.
Wrapped in that fire, I saw more escorts wake—
Flickering, sprint up the hill groins like a tide.

I heard the hush of lava wrestling your arms,
And stag teeth foam about the raven throat;   70
Flame cataracts of heaven in seething swarms
Fed down your anklets to the sunset's moat.

O, like the lizard in the furious noon,
That drops his legs and colors in the sun,
—And laughs, pure serpent, Time itself, and moon
Of his own fate, I saw thy change begun!

And saw thee dive to kiss that destiny
Like one white meteor, sacrosanct and blent
At last with all that's consummate and free
There, where the first and last gods keep thy tent.   80

                    *   *   *

Thewed of the levin,[2] thunder-shod and lean,
Lo, through what infinite seasons dost thou gaze—
Across what bivouacs of thine angered slain,
And see'st thy bride immortal in the maize!

Totem and fire-gall, slumbering pyramid—
Though other calendars now stack the sky,
Thy freedom is her largesse, Prince, and hid
On paths thou knewest best to claim her by.

High unto Labrador the sun strikes free
Her speechless dream of snow, and stirred again,   90
She is the torrent and the singing tree;
And she is virgin to the last of men . . .

West, west and south! winds over Cumberland
And winds across the Llano[3] grass resume
Her hair's warm sibilance. Her breasts are fanned
O stream by slope and vineyard—into bloom!

And when the caribou slant down for salt
Do arrows thirst and leap? Do antlers shine
Alert, star-triggered in the listening vault
Of dusk?—And are her perfect brows to thine?   100

[2] I.e., muscled by the lightning.   [3] Prairie.

We danced, O Brave, we danced beyond their farms,
In cobalt desert closures made our vows . . .
Now is the strong prayer folded in thine arms,
The serpent with the eagle in the boughs.

1927, 1930

INDIANA

. . . and read her
in a mother's
farewell gaze.

The morning glory, climbing the morning long
    Over the lintel on its wiry vine,
Closes before the dusk, furls in its song
    As I close mine . . .

And bison thunder rends my dreams no more
    As once my womb was torn, my boy, when you
Yielded your first cry at the prairie's door . . .
    Your father knew

Then, though we'd buried him behind us, far
    Back on the gold trail—then his lost bones stirred . . .   10
But you who drop the scythe to grasp the oar
    Knew not, nor heard.

How we, too, Prodigal, once rode off, too—
    Waved Seminary Hill a gay good-bye . . .
We found God lavish there in Colorado
    But passing sly.

The pebbles sang, the firecat slunk away
    And glistening through the sluggard freshets came
In golden syllables loosed from the clay
    His gleaming name.   20

A dream called Eldorado[1] was his town,
    It rose up shambling in the nuggets' wake,
It had no charter but a promised crown
    Of claims to stake.

But we,—too late, too early, howsoever—
    Won nothing out of fifty-nine[2]—those years—
But gilded promise, yielded to us never,
    And barren tears . . .

The long trail back! I huddled in the shade
    Of wagon-tenting looked out once and saw   30
Bent westward, passing on a stumbling jade[3]
    A homeless squaw—

[1]Legendary city of gold.
[2]1859—the year of the gold rush to Colorado.
[3]A broken-down horse.

Perhaps a halfbreed. On her slender back
   She cradled a babe's body, riding without rein.
Her eyes, strange for an Indian's, were not black
   But sharp with pain

And like twin stars. They seemed to shun the gaze
   Of all our silent men—the long team line—
Until she saw me—when their violet haze
   Lit with love shine . . .   40

I held you up—I suddenly the bolder,
   Knew that mere words could not have brought us nearer.
She nodded—and that smile across her shoulder
   Will still endear her

As long as Jim, your father's memory, is warm.
   Yes, Larry, now you're going to sea, remember
You were the first—before Ned and his farm,—
   First-born, remember—

And since then—all that's left to me of Jim
   Whose folks, like mine, came out of Arrowhead.   50
And you're the only one with eyes like him—
   Kentucky bred!

I'm standing still, I'm old, I'm half of stone!
   Oh, hold me in those eyes' engaging blue;
There's where the stubborn years gleam and atone,—
   Where gold is true!

Down the dim turnpike to the river's edge—
   Perhaps I'll hear the mare's hoofs to the ford . . .
Write me from Rio[4] . . . and you'll keep your pledge;
   I know your word!   60

Come back to Indiana—not too late!
   (Or will you be a ranger to the end?)
Good-bye . . . Good-bye . . . oh, I shall always wait
   You, Larry, traveller—
               stranger,
                    son,
                      —my friend—

1929   1930

THE TUNNEL

To Find the
Western path
Right thro' the
Gates of Wrath.
   BLAKE[1]

---

[4]Rio de Janeiro, Brazil.
[1]From "Morning" (lines 1–2), by William Blake (1757–1827), English poet.

Performances, assortments, résumés—
Up Times Square to Columbus Circle[2] lights
Channel the congresses, nightly sessions,
Refractions of the thousand theatres, faces—
Mysterious kitchens. . . . You shall search them all.
Someday by heart you'll learn each famous sight
And watch the curtain lift in hell's despite;
You'll find the garden in the third act dead,
Finger your knees—and wish yourself in bed
With tabloid crime-sheets perched in easy sight. 10

      Then let you reach your hat
      and go.
      As usual, let you—also
      walking down—exclaim
      to twelve upward leaving
      a subscription praise
      for what time slays.

Or can't you quite make up your mind to ride;
A walk is better underneath the L[3] a brisk
Ten blocks or so before? But you find yourself 20
Preparing penguin flexions of the arms,—
As usual you will meet the scuttle yawn:
The subway yawns the quickest promise home.

Be minimum, then, to swim the hiving swarms
Out of the Square, the Circle burning bright—
Avoid the glass doors gyring[4] at your right,
Where boxed alone a second, eyes take fright
—Quite unprepared rush naked back to light:
And down beside the turnstile press the coin
Into the slot. The gongs already rattle. 30

      And so
      of cities you bespeak
      subways, rivered under streets
      and rivers. . . . In the car
      the overtone of motion
      underground, the monotone
      of motion is the sound
      of other faces, also underground—

      "Let's have a pencil Jimmy—living now
      at Floral Park 40

---

[2]Along Broadway, in New York City.
[3]The elevated railway.   [4]Spinning.

Flatbush[5]—on the fourth of July—
like a pigeon's muddy dream—potatoes
to dig in the field—travlin the town—too—
night after night—the Culver line[6]—the
girls all shaping up—it used to be—"

Our tongues recant like beaten weather vanes.
This answer lives like verdigris,[7] like hair
Beyond extinction, surcease of the bone;
And repetition freezes—"What

"what do you want? getting weak on the links?   50
fandaddle daddy don't ask for change—IS THIS
FOURTEENTH? it's half past six she said—if
you don't like my gate why did you
swing on it, why *didja*
swing on it
anyhow—"

          And somehow anyhow swing—

The phonographs of hades in the brain
Are tunnels that re-wind themselves, and love
A burnt match skating in a urinal—   60
Somewhere above Fourteenth TAKE THE EXPRESS
To brush some new presentiment of pain—

"But I want service in this office SERVICE
I said—after
the show she cried a little afterwards but—"

Whose head is swinging from the swollen strap?
Whose body smokes along the bitten rails,
Bursts from a smoldering bundle far behind
In back forks of the chasms of the brain,—
Puffs from a river stump far out behind   70
In interborough fissures of the mind . . . ?

And why do I often meet your visage[8] here,
Your eyes like agate lanterns—on and on
Below the toothpaste and the dandruff ads?
—And did their riding eyes right through your side,
And did their eyes like unwashed platters ride?
And Death, aloft,—gigantically down
Probing through you—toward me, O evermore!
And when they dragged your retching flesh,
Your trembling hands that night through Baltimore—   80

---

[5]Section of New York City in the borough of Brooklyn.
[6]A former branch of the Brooklyn Rapid Transit system; originally elevated, later converted to a subway.
[7]A greenish-blue substance.
[8]The poet addresses Edgar Allan Poe.

That last night on the ballot rounds,[9] did you
Shaking, did you deny the ticket, Poe?

For Gravesend Manor change at Chambers Street.[10]
The platform hurries along to a dead stop.

The intent escalator lifts a serenade
Stilly
Of shoes, umbrellas, each eye attending its shoe, then
Bolting outright somewhere above where streets
Burst suddenly in rain. . . . The gongs recur:
Elbows and levers, guard and hissing door.   90
Thunder is galvothermic[11] here below. . . . The car
Wheels off. The train rounds, bending to a scream,
Taking the final level for the dive
Under the river—
And somewhat emptier than before,
Demented, for a hitching second, humps; then
Lets go. . . . Toward corners of the floor
Newspapers wing, revolve and wing.
Blank windows gargle signals through the roar.

And does the Dæmon take you home, also,   100
Wop washerwoman, with the bandaged hair?
After the corridors are swept, the cuspidors—
The gaunt sky-barracks cleanly now, and bare,
O Genoese,[12] do you bring mother eyes and hands
Back home to children and to golden hair?

Dæmon, demurring and eventful yawn!
Whose hideous laughter is a bellows mirth
—Or the muffled slaughter of a day in birth—
O cruelly to inoculate the brinking dawn
With antennæ toward worlds that glow and sink;—   110
To spoon us out more liquid than the dim
Locution of the eldest star, and pack
The conscience navelled in the plunging wind,
Umbilical to call—and straightway die!

O caught like pennies beneath soot and steam,
Kiss of our agony thou gatherest;
Condensed, thou takest all—shrill ganglia
Impassioned with some song we fail to keep.
And yet, like Lazarus,[13] to feel the slope,
The sod and billow breaking,—lifting ground,   120

[9]A reference to the death of Poe in Baltimore, on Election Day, October 7, 1849.
[10]Near the southern tip of Manhattan Island.
[11]Galvanothermic; i.e., produces heat by electricity.
[12]Christopher Columbus.
[13]Jesus raised Lazarus from the dead, John 11:43–44.

—A sound of waters bending astride the sky
Unceasing with some Word that will not die. . . !

* * *

A tugboat, wheezing wreaths of steam,
Lunged past, with one galvanic blare stove up the
   River.
I counted the echoes assembling, one after one,
Searching, thumbing and midnight on the piers.
Lights, coasting, left the oily tympanum of waters;
The blackness somewhere gouged glass on a sky.
And this thy harbor, O my City, I have driven under,
Tossed from the coil of ticking towers. . . . Tomorrow,   130
And to be. . . . Here by the River that is East—
Here at the waters' edge the hands drop memory;
Shadowless in that abyss they unaccounting lie.
How far away the star has pooled the sea—
Or shall the hands be drawn away, to die?

Kiss of our agony Thou gatherest,
      O Hand of Fire
          gatherest—
1926   1927, 1930

ATLANTIS

Music is then the knowledge of that which relates to love in harmony and system.
                                          PLATO[1]

Through the bound cable strands, the arching path
Upward, veering with light, the flight of strings—
Taut miles of shuttling moonlight syncopate
The whispered rush, telepathy of wires.
Up the index of night, granite and steel—
Transparent meshes—fleckless and gleaming staves—
Sibylline voices[2] flicker, waveringly stream
As though a god were issue of the strings. . . .

And through that cordage, threading with its call
One are synoptic of all tides below—   10
Their labyrinthine mouths of history
Pouring reply as though all ships at sea
Complighted in one vibrant breath made cry,—
"Make thy love sure—to weave whose song we ply!"
—From black embankments, moveless soundings hailed,
So seven oceans answer from their dream.

[1]From the *Symposium*, III, 403.
[2]Voices of the Sibyls, female oracles and prophets of the ancient world.

And on, obliquely up bright carrier bars
New octaves trestle the twin monoliths
Beyond whose frosted capes the moon bequeaths
Two worlds of sleep (O arching strands of song!)—   20
Onward and up the crystal-flooded aisle
White tempest nets file upward, upward ring
With silver terraces the humming spars,
The loft of vision, palladium helm of stars.

Sheerly the eyes, like seagulls stung with rime[3]—
Slit and propelled by glistening fins of light—
Pick biting way up towering looms that press
Sidelong with flight of blade on tendon blade
—Tomorrows into yesteryear—and link
What cipher-script of time no traveller reads   30
But who, through smoking pyres of love and death,
Searches the timeless laugh of mythic spears.

Like hails, farewells—up planet-sequined heights
Some trillion whispering hammers glimmer Tyre:[4]
Serenely, sharply up the long anvil cry
Of inchling æons silence rivets Troy.[5]
And you, aloft there—Jason![6] hesting[7] shout!
Still wrapping harness to the swarming air!
Silvery the rushing wake, surpassing call,
Beams yelling Æolus![8] splintered in the straights!   40

From gulfs unfolding, terrible of drums,
Tall Vision-of-the-Voyage, tensely spare—
Bridge, lifting night to cycloramic crest
Of deepest day—O Choir, translating time
Into what multitudinous Verb the suns
And synergy of waters ever fuse, recast
In myriad syllables,—Psalm of Cathay![9]
O Love, thy white, pervasive Paradigm . . . !

We left the haven hanging in the night—
Sheened harbor lanterns backward fled the keel.   50
Pacific here at time's end, bearing corn,—
Eyes stammer through the pangs of dust and steel.
And still the circular, indubitable frieze
Of heaven's meditations, yoking wave
To kneeling wave, one song devoutly binds—
The vernal strophe chimes from deathless strings!

[3]White frost.
[4]Ancient Phoenician city.
[5]Scene of the Trojan war described by Homer.
[6]Greek leader in the quest for the Golden Fleece.
[7]Commanding.
[8]Keeper of the winds in classical myth.
[9]Ancient name for China.

O Thou steeled Cognizance whose leap commits
The agile precincts of the lark's return;
Within whose lariat sweep encinctured sing
In single chrysalis the many twain,   60
Of stars Thou art the stitch and stallion glow
And like an organ, Thou, with sound of doom—
Sight, sound and flesh Thou leadest from time's realm
As love strikes clear direction for the helm.

Swift peal of secular light, intrinsic Myth
Whose fell unshadow is death's utter wound,—
O River-throated—iridescently upborne
Through the bright drench and fabric of our veins;
With white escarpments swinging into light,
Sustained in tears the cities are endowed   70
And justified conclamant with ripe fields
Revolving through their harvests in sweet torment.

Forever Deity's glittering Pledge, O Thou
Whose canticle fresh chemistry assigns
To wrapt inception and beatitude,—
Always through blinding cables, to our joy,
Of thy white seizure springs the prophecy:
Always through spiring cordage, pyramids
Of silver sequel, Deity's young name
Kinetic of white choiring wings . . . ascends.   80

Migrations that must needs void memory,
Inventions that cobblestone the heart,—
Unspeakable Thou Bridge to Thee, O Love.
Thy pardon for this history, whitest Flower,
O Answerer of all,—Anemone,—
Now while thy petals spend the suns about us, hold—
(O Thou whose radiance doth inherit me)
Atlantis,—hold thy floating singer late!

So to thine Everpresence, beyond time,
Like spears ensanguined[10] of one tolling star   90
That bleeds infinity—the orphic[11] strings,
Sidereal phalanxes, leap and converge:
—One Song, one Bridge of Fire! Is it Cathay,
Now pity steeps the grass and rainbows ring
The serpent with the eagle in the leaves . . . ?
Whispers antiphonal[12] in azure swing.
1926   1930

THE BROKEN TOWER

The bell-rope that gathers God at dawn
Dispatches me as though I dropped down the knell

---

[10]Made bloody.
[11]Mystic, oracular. In Greek myth the musician Orpheus could charm animals and even the gods.
[12]Like a psalm or an anthem sung in response during church service.

Of a spent day—to wander the cathedral lawn
From pit to crucifix, feet chill on steps from hell.

Have you not heard, have you not seen that corps
Of shadows in the tower, whose shoulders sway
Antiphonal carillons launched before
The stars are caught and hived in the sun's ray?

The bells, I say, the bells break down their tower;
And swing I know not where. Their tongues engrave   10
Membrane through marrow, my long-scattered score
Of broken intervals . . . And I, their sexton slave!

Oval encyclicals in canyons heaping
The impasse high with choir. Banked voices slain!
Pagodas, campaniles with reveilles outleaping—
O terraced echoes prostrate on the plain! . . .

And so it was I entered the broken world
To trace the visionary company of love, its voice
An instant in the wind (I know not whither hurled)
But not for long to hold each desperate choice.   20

My word I poured. But was it cognate, scored
Of that tribunal monarch of the air
Whose thigh embronzes earth, strikes crystal Word
In wounds pledged once to hope—cleft to despair?

The steep encroachments of my blood left me
No answer (could blood hold such a lofty tower
As flings the question true?)—or is it she
Whose sweet mortality stirs latent power?—

And through whose pulse I hear, counting the strokes
My veins recall and add, revived and sure   30
The angelus of wars my chest evokes:
What I hold healed, original now, and pure . . .

And builds, within, a tower that is not stone
(Not stone can jacket heaven)—but slip
Of pebbles,—visible wings of silence sown
In azure circles, widening as they dip

The matrix of the heart, lift down the eye
That shrines the quiet lake and swells a tower . . .
The commodious, tall decorum of that sky
Unseals her earth, and lifts love in its shower.   40

1932

Wallace Stevens   *1879–1955*

Wallace Stevens—are we for him?
Brother, he's our father!

Theodore Roethke was speaking for the next generation when he thus paid tribute to the man who, in his final years, became one of the most noted of American poets. A reticent man who placed unusual value upon his privacy, Stevens remained during his lifetime something of a mystery. He successfully pursued two seemingly incompatible careers: business and art. His business, he said, was "insurance," and unlike his most distinguished contemporaries, Pound, Eliot, and Williams, he was rarely comfortable in the role of professional poet. He lived a quiet, secluded life; he disliked giving public readings; and in his last years he refused a Harvard lectureship on the grounds that acceptance would force his retirement from "the office." Yet for over forty years he was deeply dedicated to poetry, and many younger poets would have agreed with Roethke's assertion that they had been influenced by a master.

Stevens spent his boyhood in his birthplace, Reading, Pennsylvania. His father was a prosperous attorney. Stevens's earliest ambition was to be a writer, and after three years at Harvard, where he published poems in the Harvard Advocate, *he went to New York in 1900 for a try at journalism. But the following year, on his father's advice, he entered the New York Law School. Admitted to the bar in 1904, he worked for several law firms before marrying and moving to Connecticut, where he eventually rose to the position of vice-president of the Hartford Accident and Indemnity Company.*

During his years in New York, with the modernist movement gaining momentum, Stevens became acquainted with a number of young writers in New York City, among them the poets William Carlos Williams and Marianne Moore. Stevens also began submitting his own poems to the little magazines and, for a time, tried writing for the experimental theater. It was not until 1923, however, that Stevens, at the age of 44, was finally persuaded to publish a book of poems, Harmonium. *The book's poor reception (fewer than one hundred copies were sold) and its author's growing business responsibilities almost led him to abandon poetry. For over a decade he published little, but with the reprinting of* Harmonium *(1931) and with the resulting increase in critical attention, Stevens began his years of steady publication.*

In 1935 he published Ideas of Order. *Then followed* The Man with the Blue Guitar *(1937),* Parts of a World *(1942),* Transport to Summer *(1947), and* The Auroras of Autumn *(1950). These, along with a collection of his occasional lectures on poetry,* The Necessary Angel *(1951), established him as a major American poet. For the publication of his* Collected Poems *(1954) he received the National Book Award and the Pulitzer Prize. After his death, his previously uncollected work appeared in* Opus Posthumous *(1957), and his* Letters *were published in 1966.*

From the beginning it was evident that Harmonium *was part of a revolution in American poetry. Although some of its best poems, including "Sunday Morning," are relatively traditional in form, the book baffled even the most sophisticated. Stevens had rebelled against the "stale intelligence" of the past. Setting out "to make a new intelligence prevail," he invoked the comic, the strange, the bizarre. He adopted a variety of experimental styles, created poetic surfaces of frenchified elegance, exotic imagery, odd sounds, curious analogies, and inscrutable titles.*

For many readers it seemed that Stevens had carried originality to the point of mere eccentricity, and he was called a "dandy," a "virtuoso of the inane," a writer of "near nonsense." But beneath his gaudiest surfaces, Stevens's abiding concerns were clearly present. He confronted the contemporary abandonment of traditional values and sought to come to terms with the confusions of his time. The problem of the relation between the ideal and the real became a constant theme in his later poetry, and he elaborated a series of oppositions between inner and outer worlds—between subject and object, perceiver and perceived, fiction and fact, or as he most often phrased it, between "imagination and reality." These contraries meet ultimately in his concept of a "supreme fiction," a modern mythology he offered as a replacement for the mythologies of the past, a new vision with "which men could propose to themselves a fulfilment." Although he constantly dealt with the nature of poetry, Stevens became in his later work increasingly meditative and philosophical, an intellectual elitist, at times difficult and obscure, who wrote, as he admitted, "for a gallery of one's own."

FURTHER READINGS: S. Morse, *Wallace Stevens, Poetry as Life*, 1970; H. Stevens, *Souvenirs and Prophecies, The Young Wallace Stevens*, 1977; P. Brazeau, *Parts of a World, Wallace Stevens Remembered*, 1983; J. Richardson, *Wallace Stevens, The Early Years*, 1986; F. Kermode, *Wallace Stevens*, 1961; *The Achievement of Wallace Stevens*, ed. A. Brown and R. Haller, 1962; J. Benziger, *Images of Eternity*, 1962; D. Fuchs, *The Comic Spirit of Wallace Stevens*, 1962; J. Enck, *Wallace Stevens, Images and Judgments*, 1964; H. Wells, *Introduction to Wallace Stevens*, 1964; J. Riddel, *The Clairvoyant Eye*, 1965; E. Nasser, *Wallace Stevens, An Anatomy of Figuration*, 1965; H. Stern, *Wallace Stevens, Art of Uncertainty*, 1966; F. Doggett, *Stevens' Poetry of Thought*, 1966; R. Sukenick, *Wallace Stevens, Musing the Obscure*, 1967; J. Baird, *The Dome and the Rock, Structure in the Poetry of Wallace Stevens*, 1968; W. Burney, *Wallace Stevens*, 1968; H. Vendler, *On Extended Wings, Wallace Stevens' Longer Poems*, 1969; R. Blessing, *Wallace Stevens's "Whole Harmonium,"* 1970; M. Benamou, *Wallace Stevens and the Symbolist Imagination*, 1972; W. Litz, *Introspective Voyage, The Poetic Development of Wallace Stevens*, 1972; S. Weston, *Wallace Stevens, An Introduction*, 1977; *Wallace Stevens, A Celebration*, ed. F. Doggett, 1980; H. Vendler, *Wallace Stevens, Words Chosen out of Desire*, 1984; M. Bates, *Wallace Stevens, A Mythology of Self*, 1985.

TEXT: "The Course of a Particular" is from *Opus Posthumous*, 1957; all other poems are from *The Collected Poems of Wallace Stevens*, 1954.

PETER QUINCE AT THE CLAVIER[1]

I

Just as my fingers on these keys
Make music, so the selfsame sounds
On my spirit make a music, too.

Music is feeling, then, not sound;
And thus it is that what I feel,
Here in this room, desiring you,

Thinking of your blue-shadowed silk,
Is music. It is like the strain
Waked in the elders by Susanna.[2]

---

[1] The keyboard of a musical instrument.
[2] A reference to the story of Daniel and Susanna in the Apocrypha of the Bible. Two elders were obsessed with lust for Susanna. When rejected by her they falsely charged her with fornication. When they were questioned by Daniel their lies were exposed, and they were put to death.

Of a green evening, clear and warm,   10
She bathed in her still garden, while
The red-eyed elders watching, felt

The basses of their beings throb
In witching chords, and their thin blood
Pulse pizzicati[3] of Hosanna.[4]

                                        II
In the green water, clear and warm,
Susanna lay.
She searched
The touch of springs,
And found   20
Concealed imaginings.
She sighed,
For so much melody.

Upon the bank, she stood
In the cool
Of spent emotions.
She felt, among the leaves,
The dew
Of old devotions.

She walked upon the grass,   30
Still quavering.
The winds were like her maids,
On timid feet,
Fetching her woven scarves,
Yet wavering.

A breath upon her hand
Muted the night.
She turned—
A cymbal crashed,
And roaring horns.   40

                                        III
Soon, with a noise like tambourines,
Came her attendant Byzantines.[5]

They wondered why Susanna cried
Against the elders by her side;

And as they whispered, the refrain
Was like a willow swept by rain.

[3]Musical notes made by plucking a stringed instrument.
[4]A cry of adoration or praise.
[5]Natives of the ancient city of Byzantium (present-day Istanbul, Turkey).

Anon, their lamps' uplifted flame
Revealed Susanna and her shame.

And then, the simpering Byzantines
Fled, with a noise like tambourines.   50

IV

Beauty is momentary in the mind—
The fitful tracing of a portal;
But in the flesh it is immortal.
The body dies; the body's beauty lives.
So evenings die, in their green going,
A wave, interminably flowing.
So gardens die, their meek breath scenting
The cowl of winter, done repenting.
So maidens die, to the auroral
Celebration of a maiden's choral.   60
Susanna's music touched the bawdy strings
Of those white elders; but, escaping,
Left only Death's ironic scraping.
Now, in its immortality, it plays
On the clear viol of her memory,
And makes a constant sacrament of praise.

                                          1915, 1923

DISILLUSIONMENT OF TEN O'CLOCK

The houses are haunted
By white night-gowns.
None are green,
Or purple with green rings,
Or green with yellow rings,
Or yellow with blue rings.
None of them are strange,
With socks of lace
And beaded ceintures.[1]
People are not going   10
To dream of baboons and periwinkles.[2]
Only, here and there, an old sailor,
Drunk and asleep in his boots,
Catches tigers
In red weather.

                                          1915, 1923

SUNDAY MORNING

I

Complacencies of the peignoir,[1] and late
Coffee and oranges in a sunny chair,

---

[1]Belts, sashes.   [2]A plant with blue and white flowers.
[1]A woman's negligee, a dressing gown.

And the green freedom of a cockatoo
Upon a rug mingle to dissipate
The holy hush of ancient sacrifice.
She dreams a little, and she feels the dark
Encroachment of that old catastrophe,
As a calm darkens among water-lights.
The pungent oranges and bright, green wings
Seem things in some procession of the dead,   10
Winding across wide water, without sound.
The day is like wide water, without sound,
Stilled for the passing of her dreaming feet
Over the seas, to silent Palestine,
Dominion of the blood and sepulchre.

II

Why should she give her bounty to the dead?
What is divinity if it can come
Only in silent shadows and in dreams?
Shall she not find in comforts of the sun,
In pungent fruit and bright, green wings, or else   20
In any balm or beauty of the earth,
Things to be cherished like the thought of heaven?
Divinity must live within herself:
Passions of rain, or moods in falling snow;
Grievings in loneliness, or unsubdued
Elations when the forest blooms; gusty
Emotions on wet roads on autumn nights;
All pleasures and all pains, remembering
The bough of summer and the winter branch.
These are the measures destined for her soul.   30

III

Jove[2] in the clouds had his inhuman birth.
No mother suckled him, no sweet land gave
Large-mannered motions to his mythy mind.
He moved among us, as a muttering king,
Magnificent, would move among his hinds,[3]
Until our blood, commingling, virginal,
With heaven, brought such requital to desire
The very hinds discerned it, in a star.
Shall our blood fail? Or shall it come to be
The blood of paradise? And shall the earth   40
Seem all of paradise that we shall know?
The sky will be much friendlier then than now,
A part of labor and a part of pain,
And next in glory to enduring love,
Not this dividing and indifferent blue.

[2]Jupiter, god of the sky and chief Roman deity.
[3]Servants, farm hands.

IV

She says, "I am content when wakened birds,
Before they fly, test the reality
Of misty fields, by their sweet questionings;
But when the birds are gone, and their warm fields
Return no more, where, then, is paradise?"   50
There is not any haunt of prophecy,
Nor any old chimera[4] of the grave,
Neither the golden underground, nor isle
Melodious, where spirits gat them home,
Nor visionary south, nor cloudy palm
Remote on heaven's hill, that has endured
As April's green endures; or will endure
Like her remembrance of awakened birds,
Or her desire for June and evening, tipped
By the consummation of the swallow's wings.   60

V

She says, "But in contentment I still feel
The need of some imperishable bliss."
Death is the mother of beauty; hence from her,
Alone, shall come fulfilment to our dreams
And our desires. Although she strews the leaves
Of sure obliteration on our paths,
The path sick sorrow took, the many paths
Where triumph rang its brassy phrase, or love
Whispered a little out of tenderness,
She makes the willow shiver in the sun   70
For maidens who were wont to sit and gaze
Upon the grass, relinquished to their feet.
She causes boys to pile new plums and pears
On disregarded plate. The maidens taste
And stray impassioned in the littering leaves.

VI

Is there no change of death in paradise?
Does ripe fruit never fall? Or do the boughs
Hang always heavy in that perfect sky,
Unchanging, yet so like our perishing earth,
With rivers like our own that seek for seas   80
They never find, the same receding shores
That never touch with inarticulate pang?
Why set the pear upon those river-banks
Or spice the shores with odors of the plum?
Alas, that they should wear our colors there,
The silken weavings of our afternoons,
And pick the strings of our insipid lutes!
Death is the mother of beauty, mystical,
Within whose burning bosom we devise
Our earthly mothers waiting, sleeplessly.   90

[4]A terrifying monster in Greek myth.

VII

Supple and turbulent, a ring of men
Shall chant in orgy on a summer morn
Their boisterous devotion to the sun,
Not as a god, but as a god might be,
Naked among them, like a savage source.
Their chant shall be a chant of paradise,
Out of their blood, returning to the sky;
And in their chant shall enter, voice by voice,
The windy lake wherein their lord delights,
The trees, like serafin,[5] and echoing hills,   100
That choir among themselves long afterward.
They shall know well the heavenly fellowship
Of men that perish and of summer morn.
And whence they came and whither they shall go
The dew upon their feet shall manifest.

VIII

She hears, upon that water without sound,
A voice that cries, "The tomb in Palestine
Is not the porch of spirits lingering.
It is the grave of Jesus, where he lay."
We live in an old chaos of the sun,   110
Or old dependency of day and night,
Or island solitude, unsponsored, free,
Of that wide water, inescapable.
Deer walk upon our mountains, and the quail
Whistle about us their spontaneous cries;
Sweet berries ripen in the wilderness;
And, in the isolation of the sky,
At evening, casual flocks of pigeons make
Ambiguous undulations as they sink,
Downward to darkness, on extended wings.   120

                              1915, 1923

DOMINATION OF BLACK

At night, by the fire,
The colors of the bushes
And of the fallen leaves,
Repeating themselves,
Turned in the room,
Like the leaves themselves
Turning in the wind.
Yes: but the color of the heavy hemlocks
Came striding.
And I remembered the cry of the peacocks.   10

[5]Seraphim, heavenly beings.

The colors of their tails
Were like the leaves themselves
Turning in the wind,
In the twilight wind.
They swept over the room,
Just as they flew from the boughs of the
    hemlocks
Down to the ground.
I heard them cry—the peacocks.
Was it a cry against the twilight
Or against the leaves themselves
Turning in the wind,
Turning as the flames
Turned in the fire,
Turning as the tails of the peacocks
Turned in the loud fire,
Loud as the hemlocks
Full of the cry of the peacocks?
Or was it a cry against the hemlocks?

Out of the window,
I saw how the planets gathered
Like the leaves themselves
Turning in the wind.
I saw how the night came,
Came striding like the color of the heavy
    hemlocks.
I felt afraid.
And I remembered the cry of the peacocks.
1916, 1923

THE PLOT AGAINST THE GIANT

FIRST GIRL

When this yokel comes maundering,
Whetting his hacker,
I shall run before him,
Diffusing the civilest odors
Out of geraniums and unsmelled flowers.
It will check him.

SECOND GIRL

I shall run before him,
Arching cloths besprinkled with colors
As small as fish-eggs.
The threads
Will abash him.

THIRD GIRL

Oh, la . . .[1] le pauvre![2]
I shall run before him,
With a curious puffing.
He will bend his ear then.
I shall whisper
Heavenly labials in a world of gutturals.   20
It will undo him.

                                              1917, 1923

THE DEATH OF A SOLDIER

Life contracts and death is expected,
As in a season of autumn.
The soldier falls.

He does not become a three-days personage,
Imposing his separation,
Calling for pomp.

Death is absolute and without memorial,
As in a season of autumn,
When the wind stops,

When the wind stops and, over the heavens,   10
The clouds go, nevertheless,
In their direction.

                                              1918, 1931

ANECDOTE OF THE JAR

I placed a jar in Tennessee,
And round it was, upon a hill.
It made the slovenly wilderness
Surround that hill.

The wilderness rose up to it,
And sprawled around, no longer wild.
The jar was round upon the ground
And tall and of a port in air.

It took dominion everywhere.
The jar was gray and bare.   10
It did not give of bird or bush,
Like nothing else in Tennessee.

                                              1919, 1923

[1]Here, and throughout, the ellipsis points are Stevens's.
[2]French: the poor thing!

THE SNOW MAN

One must have a mind of winter
To regard the frost and the boughs
Of the pine-trees crusted with snow;

And have been cold a long time
To behold the junipers shagged with ice,
The spruces rough in the distant glitter

Of the January sun; and not to think
Of any misery in the sound of the wind,
In the sound of a few leaves,

Which is the sound of the land   10
Full of the same wind
That is blowing in the same bare place

For the listener, who listens in the snow,
And, nothing himself, beholds
Nothing that is not there and the nothing that is.

                                    1921, 1923

A HIGH-TONED OLD CHRISTIAN WOMAN

Poetry is the supreme fiction, madame.
Take the moral law and make a nave[1] of it
And from the nave build haunted heaven. Thus,
The conscience is converted into palms,
Like windy citherns[2] hankering for hymns.
We agree in principle. That's clear. But take
The opposing law and make a peristyle,[3]
And from the peristyle project a masque[4]
Beyond the planets. Thus, our bawdiness,
Unpurged by epitaph, indulged at last,   10
Is equally converted into palms,
Squiggling like saxophones. And palm for palm,
Madame, we are where we began. Allow,
Therefore, that in the planetary scene
Your disaffected flagellants,[5] well-stuffed,
Smacking their muzzy[6] bellies in parade,
Proud of such novelties of the sublime,

[1] The main body of a rectangular church building.
[2] A medieval musical instrument of the guitar family, a zither.
[3] A series of columns around a building or a courtyard.
[4] A festive dance or drama in which the actors wore masks.
[5] Those who flagellate, or whip, themselves in religious ceremonies. Hence those who undergo self-punishment.
[6] Dull-spirited, or befuddled by drink.

Such tink and tank and tunk-a-tunk-tunk,
May, merely may, madame, whip from themselves
A jovial hullabaloo among the spheres.   20
This will make widows wince. But fictive things
Wink as they will. Wink most when widows wince.

                                              1922, 1923

THE EMPEROR OF ICE-CREAM

Call the roller of big cigars,
The muscular one, and bid him whip
In kitchen cups concupiscent curds.
Let the wenches dawdle in such dress
As they are used to wear, and let the boys
Bring flowers in last month's newspapers.
Let be be finale of seem.
The only emperor is the emperor of ice-cream.

Take from the dresser of deal,[1]
Lacking the three glass knobs, that sheet   10
On which she embroidered fantails[2] once
And spread it so as to cover her face.
If her horny feet protrude, they come
To show how cold she is, and dumb.
Let the lamp affix its beam.
The only emperor is the emperor of ice-cream.

                                              1922, 1923

THE IDEA OF ORDER AT KEY WEST

She sang beyond the genius of the sea.
The water never formed to mind or voice,
Like a body wholly body, fluttering
Its empty sleeves; and yet its mimic motion
Made constant cry, caused constantly a cry,
That was not ours although we understood,
Inhuman, of the veritable ocean.

The sea was not a mask. No more was she.
The song and water were not medleyed sound
Even if what she sang was what she heard,   10
Since what she sang was uttered word by word.
It may be that in all her phrases stirred
The grinding water and the gasping wind;
But it was she and not the sea we heard.

---

[1]Made of cheap pine or fir planks.
[2]Fan-shaped designs, like the tails of birds.

For she was the maker of the song she sang.
The ever-hooded, tragic-gestured sea
Was merely a place by which she walked to sing.
Whose spirit is this? we said, because we knew
It was the spirit that we sought and knew
That we should ask this often as she sang.   20

If it was only the dark voice of the sea
That rose, or even colored by many waves;
If it was only the outer voice of sky
And cloud, of the sunken coral water-walled,
However clear, it would have been deep air,
The heaving speech of air, a summer sound
Repeated in a summer without end
And sound alone. But it was more than that,
More even than her voice, and ours, among
The meaningless plungings of water and the wind,   30
Theatrical distances, bronze shadows heaped
On high horizons, mountainous atmospheres
Of sky and sea.
                    It was her voice that made
The sky acutest at its vanishing.
She measured to the hour its solitude.
She was the single artificer of the world
In which she sang. And when she sang, the sea,
Whatever self it had, became the self
That was her song, for she was the maker. Then we,   40
As we beheld her striding there alone,
Knew that there never was a world for her
Except the one she sang and, singing, made.

Ramon Fernandez,[1] tell me, if you know,
Why, when the singing ended and we turned
Toward the town, tell why the glassy lights,
The lights in the fishing boats at anchor there,
As the night descended, tilting the air,
Master the night and portioned out the sea,
Fixing emblazoned zones and fiery poles,   50
Arranging, deepening, enchanting night.

Oh! Blessed rage for order, pale Ramon,
The maker's rage to order words of the sea,
Words of the fragrant portals, dimly-starred,
And of ourselves and of our origins,
In ghostlier demarcations, keener sounds.

                                    1934, 1935

[1]Stevens reported that he chose this name at random: "Ramon Fernandez was not intended to
be anyone at all."

DRY LOAF

It is equal to living in a tragic land
To live in a tragic time.
Regard now the sloping, mountainous rocks
And the river that batters its way over stones,
Regard the hovels of those that live in this land.

That was what I painted behind the loaf,
The rocks not even touched by snow,
The pines along the river and the dry men blown
Brown as the bread, thinking of birds
Flying from burning countries and brown sand shores,   10

Birds that came like dirty water in waves
Flowing above the rocks, flowing over the sky,
As if the sky was a current that bore them along,
Spreading them as waves spread flat on the shore,
One after another washing the mountains bare.

It was the battering of drums I heard,
It was hunger, it was the hungry that cried
And the waves, the waves were soldiers moving,
Marching and marching in a tragic time
Below me, on the asphalt, under the trees.   20

It was soldiers went marching over the rocks
And still the birds came, came in watery flocks,
Because it was spring and the birds had to come.
No doubt that soldiers had to be marching
And the drums had to be rolling, rolling, rolling.

                                                1938, 1942

THE BLUE BUILDINGS IN THE SUMMER AIR

I

Cotton Mather[1] died when I was a boy. The books
He read, all day, all night and all the nights,
Had got him nowhere. There was always the doubt,
That made him preach the louder, long for a church
In which his voice would roll its cadences,
After the sermon, to quiet that mouse in the wall.

II

Over a wooden Boston, the sparkling Byzantine
Was everything that Cotton Mather was
And more. Yet the eminent thunder from the mouse,

[1] American Puritan preacher (1663–1728).

The grinding in the arches of the church,   10
The plaster dropping, even dripping, down,
The mouse, the moss, the woman on the shore . . .

                    III
If the mouse should swallow the steeple, in its time . . .
It was a theologian's needle, much
Too sharp for that. The shore, the sea, the sun,
Their brilliance through the lattices, crippled
The chandeliers, their morning glazes spread
In opal blobs along the walls and floor.

                    IV
Look down now, Cotton Mather, from the blank.
Was heaven where you thought? It must be there.   20
It must be where you think it is, in the light
On bed-clothes, in an apple on a plate.
It is the honey-comb of the seeing man.
It is the leaf the bird brings back to the boat.

                    V
Go, mouse, go nibble at Lenin in his tomb.[2]
Are you not le plus pur,[3] you ancient one?
Cut summer down to find the honey-comb.
You are one . . . Go hunt for honey in his hair.
You are one of the not-numberable mice
Searching all day, all night, for the honey-comb.   30
                                        1938, 1942

OF MODERN POETRY

The poem of the mind in the act of finding
What will suffice. It has not always had
To find: the scene was set; it repeated what
Was in the script.
                    Then the theatre was changed
To something else. Its past was a souvenir.
It has to be living, to learn the speech of the place.
It has to face the men of the time and to meet
The women of the time. It has to think about war
And it has to find what will suffice. It has   10
To construct a new stage. It has to be on that stage
And, like an insatiable actor, slowly and
With meditation, speak words that in the ear,
In the delicatest ear of the mind, repeat,
Exactly, that which it wants to hear, at the sound

[2]Vladimir Ilyich Ulyanov (1870–1924), Russian Communist leader. His tomb, containing his embalmed body, is in Red Square in Moscow.
[3]French: the most pure.

Of which, an invisible audience listens,
Not to the play, but to itself, expressed
In an emotion as of two people, as of two
Emotions becoming one. The actor is
A metaphysician in the dark, twanging   20
An instrument, twanging a wiry string that gives
Sounds passing through sudden rightnesses, wholly
Containing the mind, below which it cannot descend,
Beyond which it has no will to rise.
                                        It must
Be the finding of a satisfaction, and may
Be a man of skating, a woman dancing, a woman
Combing. The poem of the act of the mind.

                                                        1940, 1942

NO POSSUM, NO SOP, NO TATERS

He is not here, the old sun,
As absent as if we were asleep.

The field is frozen. The leaves are dry.
Bad is final in this light.

In this bleak air the broken stalks
Have arms without hands. They have trunks

Without legs or, for that, without heads.
They have heads in which a captive cry

Is merely the moving of a tongue.
Snow sparkles like eyesight falling to earth,   10

Like seeing fallen brightly away.
The leaves hop, scraping on the ground.

It is deep January. The sky is hard.
The stalks are firmly rooted in ice.

It is in this solitude, a syllable,
Out of these gawky flitterings,

Intones its single emptiness,
The savagest hollow of winter-sound.

It is here, in this bad, that we reach
The last purity of the knowledge of good.   20

The crow looks rusty as he rises up.
Bright is the malice in his eye . . .

One joins him there for company,
But at a distance, in another tree.

1943, 1947

THE COURSE OF A PARTICULAR

Today the leaves cry, hanging on branches swept by wind,
Yet the nothingness of winter becomes a little less.
It is still full of icy shades and shapen snow.

The leaves cry . . . One holds off and merely hears the cry.
It is a busy cry, concerning someone else.
And though one says that one is part of everything.

There is a conflict, there is a resistance involved;
And being part is an exertion that declines:
One feels the life of that which gives life as it is.

The leaves cry. It is not a cry of divine attention,   10
Nor the smoke-drift of puffed-out heroes, nor human cry.
It is the cry of leaves that do not transcend themselves,

In the absence of fantasia, without meaning more
Than they are in the final finding of the ear, in the thing
Itself, until, at last, the cry concerns no one at all.

1951, 1957

FINAL SOLILOQUY OF THE
INTERIOR PARAMOUR

Light the first light of evening, as in a room
In which we rest and, for small reason, think
The world imagined is the ultimate good.

This is, therefore, the intensest rendezvous.
It is in that thought that we collect ourselves,
Out of all the indifferences, into one thing:

Within a single thing, a single shawl
Wrapped tightly round us, since we are poor, a
      warmth,
A light, a power, the miraculous influence.

Here, now, we forget each other and ourselves.   10

We feel the obscurity of an order, a whole,
A knowledge, that which arranged the rendezvous.

Within its vital boundary, in the mind.
We say God and the imagination are one . . .
How high that highest candle lights the dark.

Out of this same light, out of the central mind,
We make a dwelling in the evening air,
In which being there together is enough.

                                                         1951, 1953

THE PLAIN SENSE OF THINGS

After the leaves have fallen, we return
To a plain sense of things. It is as if
We had come to an end of the imagination,
Inanimate in an inert savoir.

It is difficult even to choose the adjective
For this blank cold, this sadness without cause.
The great structure has become a minor house.
No turban walks across the lessened floors.

The greenhouse never so badly needed paint.
The chimney is fifty years old and slants to one side.   10
A fantastic effort has failed, a repetition
In a repetitiousness of men and flies.

Yet the absence of the imagination had
Itself to be imagined. The great pond,
The plain sense of it, without reflections, leaves,
Mud, water like dirty glass, expressing silence

Of a sort, silence of a rat come out to see,
The great pond and its waste of the lilies, all this
Had to be imagined as an inevitable knowledge,
Required, as a necessity requires.   20

                                                         1952, 1954

William Carlos Williams *1883–1963*

William Carlos Williams aimed at reproducing immediate experience. He professed a doctrine of "No ideas but in things." Like Ezra Pound, Williams wanted to "ruffle the skirts of prudes"; he wanted to break away from poetic convention and to repudiate what he considered to be the learned rhetoric of such literary patricians as T. S. Eliot and Wallace Stevens.

Williams was a physician. He studied medicine at the University of Pennsylvania, where he met Ezra Pound. Following a postgraduate year in Germany studying pediatrics, Williams returned to his birthplace, Rutherford, New Jersey, and there he practiced medicine for the next forty years, until his retirement in 1951. He published his first volume of poetry, Poems *(1909), at his own expense (at a cost of fifty dollars). It was a thin volume of imitative verse that sold only "about four copies" at thirty-five cents each, but it was the first of the more than forty volumes of stories, novels, plays, essays, and poetry that were to come.*

In 1913 he published a second volume of verse, The Tempers, *followed by* Al Que Quiere! *(1917),* Kora in Hell *(1920),* Sour Grapes *(1921). In 1923 he published* Spring and All, *which contained his most famous poem, "The Red Wheelbarrow." Collected editions of his poems appeared in 1934 and 1938. His most ambitious work,* Paterson, *was a long, epic poem, a montage of images and themes mixed with the details of American history, published in installments, the first book in 1946, the sixth, posthumously, in 1963.*

Williams's revolutionary ideas led him to write poetry that was simple, direct, and apparently formless. He seemed to be a "nonliterary" writer, yet his poetry, for all its freshness and apparent spontaneity, was the result of constant rewriting and refinement. Like Whitman he used commonplace American scenes and speech to portray contemporary urban America. And like Whitman he was a significant force in the freeing of poetry from the restraints and predictive regularity of traditional rhythms and meters. His range was small; and he has since been criticized as an "aw shucks," "gee willikins" innocent who made the fatal assumption that the chief literary and human value is "openness." Yet he was a prime literary innovator, just as he was the poet of the twentieth century most sensitive to the sumptuous squalor of modern America.

Until the last decade of his life Williams saw himself as the great neglected American poet. Common readers had shunned him and erudite critics had scorned him. But in his last years, Williams was elevated in the public mind to the role of the good, gray poet, just as Whitman had been before him. Having once been a literary revolutionary, he became, at last, domesticated, a popular favorite, the benign poet-physician, best known as the creator of that imagistic red wheelbarrow, glistening in the rain.

FURTHER READING: *The Collected Poems of William Carlos Williams,* 2 vols., ed. A. Litz and C. MacGowan, 1986, 1988; *The Autobiography of William Carlos Williams,* 1951; *The Selected Letters of William Carlos Williams,* ed. J. Thirwall, 1957; V. Koch, *William Carlos Williams,* 1950; R. Whittemore, *William Carlos Williams, Poet from Jersey,* 1975; P. Mariani, *William Carlos Williams, A New World Naked,* 1981; L. Wagner, *The Poems of William Carlos Williams,* 1964; A. Ostrom, *The Poetic World of William Carlos Williams,* 1966; T. Whitaker, *William Carlos Williams,* 1968; J. Guimond, *The Art of William Carlos Williams,* 1968; L. Wagner, *The Prose of William Carlos Williams,* 1970; J. Breslin, *William Carlos Williams, An American Artist,* 1970; M. Weaver, *William Carlos Williams, The American Background,* 1971; J. Mazzaro, *William Carlos Williams, The Later Poems,* 1973; R. Coles, *William Carlos Williams, The Knack of Survival in America,* 1975; R. Doyle, *William Carlos Williams and the American Poem,* 1982; H. Sayre, *The Visual Art of William Carlos Williams,* 1983; S. Cushman, *William Carlos Williams and the Meanings of Measure,* 1985.

TEXTS: *The Collected Earlier Poems of William Carlos Williams*, 1951; *The Desert Music*, 1954; *The Collected Later Poems of William Carlos Williams*, 1963; *Journey to Love*, 1955; *Pictures from Brueghel*, 1962; *The Farmers' Daughters, The Collected Stories of William Carlos Williams*, 1961.

HIC JACET[1]

The coroner's merry little children
    Have such twinkling brown eyes.
Their father is not of gay men
    And their mother jocular in no wise,
Yet the coroner's merry little children
    Laugh so easily.

They laugh because they prosper.
    Fruit for them is upon all branches.
Lo! how they jibe at loss, for
    Kind heaven fills their little paunches!   10
It's the coroner's merry, merry children
    Who laugh so easily.

          1912, 1913

CON BRIO[1]

Miserly, is the best description of that poor fool
Who holds Lancelot to have been a morose fellow,
Dolefully brooding over the events which had naturally to follow
The high time of his deed with Guinevere.[2]
He has a sick historical sight, if I judge rightly,
To believe any such thing as that ever occurred.
But, by the god of blood, what else is it that has deterred
Us all from an out and out defiance of fear
But this same perdamnable miserliness,
Which cries about our necks how we shall have less and less   10
Than we have now if we spend too wantonly?
Bah, this sort of slither is below contempt!
In the same vein we should have apple trees exempt
From bearing anything but pink blossoms all the year,
Fixed permanent lest their bellies wax unseemly, and the dear
Innocent days of them be wasted quite.
How can we have less? Have we not the deed?
Lancelot thought little, spent his gold and rode to fight
Mounted, if God was willing, on a good steed.

          1913

[1]Latin: Here Lieth.
[1]Italian: With Vigor.
[2]The wife of King Arthur; she committed adultery with Sir Lancelot.

THE YOUNG HOUSEWIFE

At ten A.M. the young housewife
moves about in negligee behind
the wooden walls of her husband's house.
I pass solitary in my car.

Then again she comes to the curb
to call the ice-man, fish-man, and stands
shy, uncorseted, tucking in
stray ends of hair, and I compare her
to a fallen leaf.

The noiseless wheels of my car   10
rush with a crackling sound over
dried leaves as I bow and pass smiling.

                              1916

PASTORAL

When I was younger
it was plain to me
I must make something of myself.
Older now
I walk back streets
admiring the houses
of the very poor:
roof out of line with sides
the yards cluttered
with old chicken wire, ashes,   10
furniture gone wrong;
the fences and outhouses
built of barrel-staves
and parts of boxes, all,
if I am fortunate,
smeared a bluish green
that properly weathered
pleases me best
of all colors.

            No one   20
will believe this
of vast import to the nation.

                    1917

TRACT

I will teach you my townspeople
how to perform a funeral

for you have it over a troop
of artists—
unless one should scour the world—
you have the ground sense necessary.

See! the hearse leads.
I begin with a design for a hearse.
For Christ's sake not black—
nor white either—and not polished!   10
Let it be weathered—like a farm wagon—
with gilt wheels (this could be
applied fresh at small expense)
or no wheels at all:
a rough dray[1] to drag over the ground.

Knock the glass out!
My God—glass, my townspeople!
For what purpose? Is it for the dead
to look out or for us to see
how well he is housed or to see   20
the flowers or the lack of them—
or what?
To keep the rain and snow from him?
He will have a heavier rain soon:
pebbles and dirt and what not.
Let there be no glass—
and no upholstery, phew!
and no little brass rollers
and small easy wheels on the bottom—
my townspeople what are you thinking of?   30

A rough plain hearse then
with gilt wheels and no top at all.
On this the coffin lies
by its own weight.

        No wreaths please—
especially no hot house flowers.
Some common memento is better,
something he prized and is known by:
his old clothes—a few books perhaps—
God knows what! You realize   40
how we are about these things
my townspeople—
something will be found—anything
even flowers if he had come to that.
So much for the hearse.

[1]A low cart, without sides.

For heaven's sake though see to the driver!
Take off the silk hat; In fact
that's no place at all for him—
up there unceremoniously
dragging our friend out to his own dignity!   50
Bring him down—bring him down!
Low and inconspicuous! I'd not have him ride
on the wagon at all—damn him—
the undertaker's understrapper!
Let him hold the reins
and walk at the side
and inconspicuously too!

Then briefly as to yourselves:
Walk behind—as they do in France,
seventh class, or if you ride   60
Hell take curtains! Go with some show
of inconvenience; sit openly—
to the weather as to grief.
Or do you think you can shut grief in?
What—from us? We who have perhaps
nothing to lose? Share with us
share with us—it will be money
in your pockets.
                    Go now
I think you are ready.   70
                                        1916, 1917

DANSE RUSSE

If when my wife is sleeping
and the baby and Kathleen
are sleeping
and the sun is a flame-white disc
in silken mists
above shining trees,—
if I in my north room
dance naked, grotesquely
before my mirror
waving my shirt round my head   10
and singing softly to myself:
"I am lonely, lonely.
I was born to be lonely,
I am best so!"
If I admire my arms, my face,
my shoulders, flanks, buttocks
against the yellow drawn shades,—

Who shall say I am not
the happy genius of my household?
                    1916, 1917

EPITAPH

An old willow with hollow branches
slowly swayed his few high bright tendrils
and sang:

Love is a young green willow
shimmering at the bare wood's edge.

                                        1919, 1921

TO WAKEN AN OLD LADY

Old age is
a flight of small
cheeping birds
skimming
bare trees
above a snow glaze.
Gaining and failing
they are buffeted
by a dark wind—
But what?   10
On harsh weedstalks
the flock has rested,
the snow
is covered with broken
seedhusks
and the wind tempered
by a shrill
piping of plenty.

                                        1920, 1921

QUEEN-ANN'S-LACE[1]

Her body is not so white as
anemone petals nor so smooth—nor
so remote a thing. It is a field
of the wild carrot taking
the field by force; the grass
does not raise above it.
Here is no question of whiteness,
white as can be, with a purple mole
at the center of each flower.
Each flower is a hand's span   10
of her whiteness. Wherever

---

[1]A wild carrot, which has clusters of white flowers often with a purple blossom in the center.

his hand has lain there is
a tiny purple blemish. Each part
is a blossom under his touch
to which the fibres of her being
stem one by one, each to its end,
until the whole field is a
white desire, empty, a single stem,
a cluster, flower by flower,
a pious wish to whiteness gone over—   20
or nothing.

                                        1921

SPRING AND ALL

By the road to the contagious hospital
under the surge of the blue
mottled clouds driven from the
northeast—a cold wind. Beyond, the
waste of broad, muddy fields
brown with dried weeds, standing and fallen

patches of standing water
the scattering of tall trees

All along the road the reddish
purplish, forked, upstanding, twiggy   10
stuff of bushes and small trees
with dead, brown leaves under them
leafless vines—

Lifeless in appearance, sluggish
dazed spring approaches—

They enter the new world naked,
cold, uncertain of all
save that they enter. All about them
the cold, familiar wind—

Now the grass, tomorrow   20
the stiff curl of wildcarrot leaf

One by one objects are defined—
It quickens: clarity, outline of leaf

But now the stark dignity of
entrance—Still, the profound change
has come upon them: rooted, they
grip down and begin to awaken

                                        1923

TO ELSIE

The pure products of America
go crazy—
mountain folk from Kentucky

or the ribbed north end of
Jersey
with its isolate lakes and

valleys, its deaf-mutes, thieves
old names
and promiscuity between

devil-may-care men who have taken   10
to railroading
out of sheer lust of adventure—

and young slatterns, bathed
in filth
from Monday to Saturday

to be tricked out that night
with gauds
from imaginations which have no

peasant traditions to give them
character   20
but flutter and flaunt

sheer rags—succumbing without
emotion
save numbed terror

under some hedge of choke-cherry
or viburnum—
which they cannot express—

Unless it be that marriage
perhaps
with a dash of Indian blood   30

will throw up a girl so desolate
so hemmed round
with disease or murder

that she'll be rescued by an
agent—
reared by the state and

sent out at fifteen to work in
some hard-pressed
house in the suburbs—

some doctor's family, some Elsie— 40
voluptuous water
expressing with broken

brain the truth about us—
her great
ungainly hips and flopping breasts

addressed to cheap
jewelry
and rich young men with fine eyes

as if the earth under our feet
were 50
an excrement of some sky

and we degraded prisoners
destined
to hunger until we eat filth

while the imagination strains
after deer
going by fields of goldenrod in

the stifling heat of September
Somehow
it seems to destroy us 60

It is only in isolate flecks that
something
is given off

No one
to witness
and adjust, no one to drive the car
1923

THE RED WHEELBARROW

so much depends
upon

a red wheel
barrow

glazed with rain
water

beside the white
chickens.
1923

AT THE BALL GAME

The crowd at the ball game
is moved uniformly

by a spirit of uselessness
which delights them—

all the exciting detail
of the chase

and the escape, the error
the flash of genius—

all to no end save beauty
the eternal—   10

So in detail they, the crowd,
are beautiful

for this
to be warned against

saluted and defied—
It is alive, venomous

it smiles grimly
its words cut—

The flashy female with her
mother, gets it—   20

The Jew gets it straight—it
is deadly, terrifying—

It is the Inquisition, the
Revolution

It is beauty itself
that lives

day by day in them
idly—

This is
the power of their faces   30

It is summer, it is the solstice
the crowd is

cheering, the crowd is laughing
in detail

permanently, seriously
without thought
                                        1923

THE ROSE

The rose is obsolete
but each petal ends in
an edge, the double facet
cementing the grooved
columns of air—The edge
cuts without cutting
meets—nothing—renews
itself in metal or porcelain—

whither? It ends—

But if it ends   10
the start is begun
so that to engage roses
becomes a geometry—

Sharper, neater, more cutting
figured in majolica[1]—
the broken plate
glazed with a rose

Somewhere the sense
makes copper roses
steel roses—   20

The rose carried weight of love
but love is at an end—of roses

It is at the edge of the
petal that love waits

Crisp, worked to defeat
laboredness—fragile
plucked, moist, half-raised
cold, precise, touching

What

The place between the petal's   30
edge and the

[1]Earthenware pottery covered with a decorative glaze.

From the petal's edge a line starts
that being of steel
infinitely fine, infinitely
rigid penetrates
the Milky Way
without contact—lifting
from it—neither hanging
nor pushing—

The fragility of the flower   40
unbruised
penetrates space.

                                        1923

BETWEEN WALLS

the back wings
of the

hospital where
nothing

will grow lie
cinders

in which shine
the broken

pieces of a green
bottle   10

                        1934

THIS IS JUST TO SAY

I have eaten
the plums
that were in
the icebox

and which
you were probably
saving
for breakfast

Forgive me
they were delicious   10
so sweet
and so cold
¹1934

THE YACHTS

contend in a sea which the land partly encloses
shielding them from the too-heavy blows
of an ungoverned ocean which when it chooses

tortures the biggest hulls, the best man knows
to pit against its beatings, and sinks them pitilessly.
Mothlike in mists, scintillant in the minute

brilliance of cloudless days, with broad bellying sails
they glide to the wind tossing green water
from their sharp prows while over them the crew crawls

ant-like, solicitously grooming them, releasing,   10
making fast as they turn, lean far over and having
caught the wind again, side by side, head for the mark.

In a well guarded arena of open water surrounded by
lesser and greater craft which, sycophant, lumbering
and flittering follow them, they appear youthful, rare

as the light of a happy eye, live with the grace
of all that in the mind is fleckless, free and
naturally to be desired. Now the sea which holds them

is moody, lapping their glossy sides, as if feeling
for some slightest flaw but fails completely.   20
Today no race. Then the wind comes again. The yachts

move, jockeying for a start, the signal is set and they
are off. Now the waves strike at them but they are too
well made, they slip through, though they take in canvas.

Arms with hands grasping seek to clutch at the prows.
Bodies thrown recklessly in the way are cut aside.
It is a sea of faces about them in agony, in despair

until the horror of the race dawns staggering the mind,
the whole sea become an entanglement of watery bodies
lost to the world bearing what they cannot hold. Broken, 30

beaten, desolate, reaching from the dead to be taken up
they cry out, failing, failing! their cries rising
in waves still as the skillful yachts pass over.

¹1935

THESE

are the desolate, dark weeks
when nature in its barrenness
equals the stupidity of man.

The year plunges into night
and the heart plunges
lower than night

to an empty, windswept place
without sun, stars or moon
but a peculiar light as of thought

that spins a dark fire—   10
whirling upon itself until,
in the cold, it kindles

to make a man aware of nothing
that he knows, not loneliness
itself—Not a ghost but

would be embraced—emptiness,
despair—(They
whine and whistle) among

the flashes and booms of war;
houses of whose rooms   20
the cold is greater than can be thought,

the people gone that we loved,
the beds lying empty, the couches
damp, the chairs unused—

Hide it away somewhere
out of the mind, let it get roots
and grow, unrelated to jealous

ears and eyes—for itself
In this mine they come to dig—all.
Is this the counterfoil to sweetest   30

music? The source of poetry that
seeing the clock stopped, says,
The clock has stopped

that ticked yesterday so well?
and hears the sound of lakewater
splashing—that is now stone.

1938

RALEIGH WAS RIGHT[1]

We cannot go to the country
for the country will bring us no peace
What can the small violets tell us
that grow on furry stems in
the long grass among lance shaped leaves?

Though you praise us
and call to mind the poets
who sung of our loveliness
it was long ago!
long ago! when country people   10
would plow and sow with
flowering minds and pockets at ease—
if ever this were true.

Not now, Love itself a flower
with roots in a parched ground.
Empty pockets make empty heads.
Cure it if you can but
do not believe that we can live
today in the country
for the country will bring us no peace.   20

                              1940, 1941

SEAFARER

The sea will wash in
but the rocks—jagged ribs
riding the cloth of foam
or a knob or pinnacles
        with gannets[1]—
are the stubborn man.

He invites the storm, he
lives by it! instinct
with fears that are not fears
but prickles of ecstasy,   10

---

[1]Christopher Marlowe's famous lyric on the idyllic glories of love, "The Passionate Shepherd to His Love" (1599), inspired many responses of which "The Nymph's Reply to the Shepherd," by Sir Walter Raleigh (1552–1618), was the best and the most skeptical.
[1]Large seabirds.

           a secret liquor, a fire
           that inflames his blood to
           coldness so that the rocks
           seem rather to leap
           at the sea than the sea
           to envelop them. They strain
           forward to grasp ships
           or even the sky itself that
           bends down to be torn
           upon them. To which he says,   20
           It is I! who am the rocks!
           Without me nothing laughs.
                              1948, 1950

THE DESCENT

The descent beckons
             as the ascent beckoned.
                          Memory is a kind
of accomplishment,
             a sort of renewal
                          even
an imitation, since the spaces it opens are new places
             inhabited by hordes
                          heretofore unrealized,
of new kinds   —   10
             since their movements
                          are toward new objectives
(even though formerly they were abandoned).

No defeat is made up entirely of defeat—since
the world it opens is always a place
             formerly
                          unsuspected. A
world lost,
             a world unsuspected,
                          beckons to new places   20
and no whiteness (lost) is so white as the memory
of whiteness   .

With evening, love wakens
             though its shadows
                          which are alive by reason
of the sun shining—
             grow sleepy now and drop away
                          from desire   .

Love without shadows stirs now
             beginning to awaken   30
                          as night
advances.

The descent
       made up of despairs
           and without accomplishment
realizes a new awakening:
         which is a reversal
of despair.
      For what we cannot accomplish, what
is denied to love,   40
       what we have lost in the anticipation—
         a descent follows,
endless and indestructible   .

                            1948, 1954

from *PATERSON*

SUNDAY IN THE PARK[1]

I.

Outside
        outside myself
               there is a world,
he rumbled, subject to my incursions
—a world
        (to me) at rest,
           which I approach
concretely—

       The scene's the Park
       upon the rock,
       female to the city   10

—upon whose body Paterson[2] instructs his thoughts
(concretely)
        —late spring,
     a Sunday afternoon!

—and goes by the footpath to the cliff (counting:
the proof)
        himself among the others,
—treads there the same stones
on which their feet slip as they climb,   20
paced by their dogs!

    laughing, calling to each other—

[1]Garret Mountain Park, which overlooks the city of Paterson, New Jersey.
[2]The male personification (also "Dr. P.") of the city of Paterson. The park itself is personified as a woman.

Wait for me!

.   .   the ugly legs of the young girls,
pistons too powerful for delicacy!
the men's arms, red, used to heat and cold,
to toss quartered beeves[3] and   .

Yah! Yah! Yah! Yah!

—over-riding
the risks: 30
pouring down!
For the flower of a day!

Arrived breathless, after a hard climb he,
looks back (beautiful but expensive!) to
the pearl-grey towers! Re-turns
and starts, possessive, through the trees,

— that love,
that is not, is not in those terms
to which I'm still the positive
in spite of all;   40
the ground dry, — passive-possessive

Walking —

Thickets gather about groups of squat sand-pine,
all but from bare rock   .   .

—a scattering of man-high cedars (sharp cones),
antlered sumac   .

—roots, for the most part, writhing
upon the surface
(so close are we to ruin every
day!)   50
searching the punk-dry rot

Walking —

The body is tilted slightly forward from the basic standing
position and the weight thrown on the ball of the foot,
while the other thigh is lifted and the leg and opposite
arm are swung forward (fig. 6B). Various muscles, aided[4]

Despite my having said that I'd never write to you again, I do so now

[3]Archaic plural of "beef."
[4]A technical description of walking, taken from a text on physiology—the first of several prose
interpolations drawn from newspapers, history books, and from letters such as that immediately
following.

because I find, with the passing of time, that the outcome of my failure with you has been the complete damming up of all my creative capacities in a particularly disastrous manner such as I have never before experienced. 60

For a great many weeks now (whenever I've tried to write poetry) every thought I've had, even every feeling, has been struck off some surface crust of myself which began gathering when I first sensed that you were ignoring the real contents of my last letters to you, and which finally congealed into some impenetrable substance when you asked me to quit corresponding with you altogether without even an explanation.

That kind of blockage, exiling one's self from one's self—have you ever experienced it? I dare say you have, at moments; and if so, you can well understand what a serious psychological injury it amounts to when turned 70 into a permanent day-to-day condition.[5]

How do I love you?[6] These!

(He hears! Voices . indeterminate! Sees them
moving, in groups, by twos and fours — filtering
off by way of the many bypaths.)

I asked him, What do you do?

He smiled patiently, The typical American question.
In Europe they would ask, What are you doing? Or,
What are you doing now?

What do I do? I listen, to the water falling. (No 80
sound of it here but with the wind!) This is my entire
occupation.

No fairer day ever dawned anywhere than May 2, 1880, when the German Singing Societies of Paterson met on Garret Mountain, as they did many years before on the first Sunday in May.

However the meeting of 1880 proved a fatal day, when William Dalzell, who owned a piece of property near the scene of the festivities, shot John Joseph Van Houten. Dalzell claimed that the visitors had in previous years walked over his garden and was determined that this year he would stop them from crossing any part of his grounds.

Immediately after the shot the quiet group of singers was turned into 90 an infuriated mob who would take Dalzell into their own hands. The mob then proceeded to burn the barn into which Dalzell had retreated from the angry group.

Dalzell fired at the approaching mob from a window in the barn and one of the bullets struck a little girl in the cheek. . . . Some of the Paterson Police rushed Dalzell out of the barn [to] the house of John Ferguson some half furlong away.

The crowd now numbered some ten thousand,

[5]Here and below Williams quotes from letters he received in the 1940s from Marcia Nardi, an aspiring poet.

[6]A paraphrase of the first line of one of the "Sonnets from the Portuguese" (XLIII) by the English poet Elizabeth Barrett Browning (1806–1861).

"a great beast!"[7]

for many had come from the city to join the conflict. The   100
case looked serious, for the Police were greatly outnumbered. The crowd
then tried to burn the Ferguson house and Dalzell went to the house of
John McGuckin. While in this house it was that Sergeant John McBride
suggested that it might be well to send for William McNulty, Dean of Saint
Joseph's Catholic Church.

In a moment the Dean set on a plan. He proceeded to the scene in a
hack. Taking Dalzell by the arm, in full view of the infuriated mob, he led
the man to the hack and seating himself by his side, ordered the driver to
proceed. The crowd hesitated, bewildered between the bravery of the
Dean and   110

Signs everywhere of birds nesting, while
in the air, slow, a crow zigzags
with heavy wings before the wasp-thrusts
of smaller birds circling about him
that dive from above stabbing for his eyes

Walking —

he leaves the path, finds hard going
across-field, stubble and matted brambles
seeming a pasture—but no pasture   .
—old furrows, to say labor sweated or   120
had sweated here   .
                                        a flame,
spent.

        The file-sharp grass   .
When! from before his feet, half-tripping,
picking a way, there starts
                a flight of empurpled wings!
—invisibly created (their
jackets dust-grey) from the dust kindled
to sudden ardor!   130

                They fly away, churring! until
their strength spent they plunge
to the coarse cover again and disappear
—but leave, livening the mind, a flashing
of wings and a churring song   .

AND a grasshopper of red basalt, boot-long,[8]
tumbles from the core of his mind,
a rubble-bank disintegrating beneath a
tropic downpour

[7]A quotation drawn from the assertion, often attributed to Alexander Hamilton, that "the people
is a great beast."

[8]Williams alludes to a thirteen-inch, Aztec, carved-stone grasshopper discovered in the nineteenth
century on Chapultepec (Aztecan: Grasshopper Hill) in Mexico City. It is on display in the National
Anthropological Museum of Mexico.

Chapultepec! grasshopper hill!   140
—a matt[9] stone solicitously instructed
to bear away some rumor
of the living presence that has preceded
it, out-precedented its breath   .

These wings do not unfold for flight—
no need!
the weight (to the hand) finding
a counter-weight or counter buoyancy
by the mind's wings   .

He is afraid! What then?   150

Before his feet, at each step, the flight
is renewed. A burst of wings, a quick
churring sound   :

            courriers to the ceremonial of love!

    —aflame in flight!
                —aflame only in flight!

                No flesh but the caress!

        He is led forward by their announcing wings.

If that situation with you (your ignoring those particular letters and then
your final note) had belonged to the inevitable lacrimae rerum[10] (as did,   160
for instance, my experience with Z.) its result could not have been (as it
has been) to destroy the validity for me myself *of* myself, because in that
case nothing to do with my sense of personal identity would have been
maimed—the cause of one's frustrations in such instances being not *in*
one's self nor in the other person but merely in the sorry scheme of things.
But since your ignoring those letters was not "natural" in that sense (or
rather since to regard it as unnatural I am forced, psychologically, to feel
that what I wrote you about, was sufficiently trivial and unimportant and
absurd to merit your evasion) it could not but follow that that whole side
of life connected with those letters should in consequence take on for my   170
own self that same kind of unreality and inaccessibility which the inner
lives of other people often have for us.

        —his mind a red stone carved to be
        endless flight   .
        Love that is a stone endlessly in flight,
        so long as stone shall last bearing
        the chisel's stroke   .

            .   .   and is lost and covered
        with ash, falls from an undermined bank

[9]Unpolished, dull.
[10]From the *Aeneid*, Book I, line 462, "Sunt lacrimae rerum" ("There are tears for misfortune"),
by the Roman poet Virgil (70–19 B.C.).

and — begins churring!   180
AND DOES, the stone after the life!

The stone lives, the flesh dies
—we know nothing of death.

—boot long
window-eyes that front the whole head,
                   Red stone! as if
a light still clung in them   .

Love

           combating sleep
        —————————————
          the sleep   190
piecemeal

    Shortly after midnight, August 20, 1878, special officer Goodridge,
when, in front of the Franklin House, heard a strange squealing noise
down towards Ellison Street. Running to see what was the matter, he found
a cat at bay under the water table at Clark's hardware store on the corner,
confronting a strange black animal too small to be a cat and entirely too
large for a rat. The officer ran up to the spot and the animal got in under
the grating of the cellar window, from which it frequently poked its head
with a lightning rapidity. Mr. Goodridge made several strikes at it with his
club but was unable to hit it. Then officer Keyes came along and as soon   200
as he saw it, he said it was a mink, which confirmed the theory that Mr.
Goodridge had already formed. Both tried for a while to hit it with their
clubs but were unable to do so, when finally officer Goodridge drew his
pistol and fired a shot at the animal. The shot evidently missed its mark,
but the noise and powder so frightened the little joker that it jumped out
into the street, and made down into Ellison Street at a wonderful gait,
closely followed by the two officers. The mink finally disappeared down a
cellar window under the grocery store below Spangermacher's lager beer
saloon, and that was the last seen of it. The cellar was examined again in
the morning, but nothing further could be discovered of the little critter   210
that had caused so much fun.

Without invention nothing is well spaced,
unless the mind change, unless
the stars are new measured, according
to their relative positions, the
line will not change, the necessity
will not matriculate: unless there is
a new mind there cannot be a new
line,[11] the old will go on
repeating itself with recurring
deadliness: without invention   220

———————
[11] I.e., poetic line.

nothing lies under the witch-hazel
bush, the alder does not grow from among
the hummocks margining the all
but spent channel of the old swale,[12]
the small foot-prints
of the mice under the overhanging
tufts of the bunch-grass will not
appear: without invention the line
will never again take on its ancient
divisions when the word, a supple word,   230
lived in it, crumbled now to chalk.

Under the bush they lie protected
from the offending sun—

11 o'clock
          They seem to talk

—a park, devoted to pleasure : devoted to   .   grasshoppers!

3 colored girls, of age! stroll by
—their color flagrant,
                their voice vagrant   240
their laughter wild, flagillant,[13] dissociated
from the fixed scene   .

But the white girl, her head
upon an arm, a butt between her fingers
lies under the bush   .   .

Semi-naked, facing her, a sunshade
over his eyes,
he talks with her

—the jalopy half hid
behind them in the trees—   250
I bought a new bathing suit, just

pants and a brassier   :
the breasts and
the pudenda covered—beneath

the sun in frank vulgarity.
Minds beaten thin
by waste—among

the working classes SOME sort
of breakdown
has occurred. Semi-roused   260

[12]Low-lying, marshy ground.
[13]I.e., laughter that lashes, whips.

they lie upon their blanket
face to face,
mottled by the shadows of the leaves

upon them, unannoyed,
at least here unchallenged.
Not undignified.   .

talking, flagrant beyond all talk
in perfect domesticity—
And having bathed

and having eaten (a few   270
sandwiches)
their pitiful thoughts do meet

in the flesh—surrounded
by churring loves! Gay wings
to bear them (in sleep)

—their thoughts alight,
away
.   .   among the grass

Walking —

across the old swale—a dry wave in the ground   280
tho' marked still by the line of Indian alders
.   .   they (the Indians) would weave
in and out, unseen, among them along the stream

.   come out whooping between the log
house and men working the field, cut them
off! they having left their arms in the block-
house, and—without defense—carry them away
into captivity. One old man   .

            Forget it! for God's sake, Cut
            out that stuff   .   290

Walking   —

he rejoins the path and sees, on a treeless
knoll—the red path choking it—
a stone wall, a sort of circular
redoubt against the sky, barren and
unoccupied. Mount. Why not?

                        A chipmunk,
with tail erect, scampers among the stones.

(Thus the mind grows, up flinty pinnacles)

but as he leans, in his stride,   300
at sight of a flint arrow-head
        (it is not)
             —there
in the distance, to the north, appear
to him the chronic hills   .

               Well, so they are.

                   He stops short:
Who's here?

     To a stone bench, to which she's leashed, within the
wall a man in tweeds—a pipe hooked in his jaw—is combing out a new-   310
washed Collie bitch. The deliberate comb-strokes part the long hair—even
her face he combs though her legs tremble slightly—until it lies, as he
designs, like ripples in white sand giving off its clean-dog odor. The floor,
stone slabs, she stands patiently before his caresses in that bare "sea chamber"

         .   to the right
from this vantage, the observation tower
in the middle distance stands up prominently
from its pubic grove

DEAR B. Please excuse me for not having told you this when I was over to
your house. I had no courage to answer your questions so I'll write it.   320
Your dog *is* going to have puppies although I prayed she would be okey.
It wasn't that she was left alone as she never was but I used to let her out
at dinner time while I hung up my clothes. At the time, it was on a
Thursday, my mother-in-law had some sheets and table cloths out on the
end of the line. I figured the dogs wouldn't come as long as I was there
and none came thru my yard or near the apartment. He must have come
between your hedge and the house. *Every few* seconds I would run to the
end of the line or peek under the sheets to see if Musty was alright. She
was until I looked a minute too late. I took sticks and stones after the dog
but he wouldn't beat it. George gave me plenty of hell and I started praying   330
that I had frightened the other dog so much that nothing had happened.
I know you'll be cursing like a son-of-a-gun and probably won't ever speak
to me again for not having told you. Don't think I haven't been worrying
about Musty. She's occupied my mind every day since that awful event.
You won't think so highly of me now and feel like protecting me. Instead
I'll bet you could kill . . .

     And still the picnickers come on, now
early afternoon, and scatter through the
trees over the fenced-in acres   .

                  Voices!   340
multiple and inarticulate   .   voices
clattering loudly to the sun, to
the clouds. Voices!
assaulting the air gaily from all sides.

—among which the ear strains to catch
the movement of one voice among the rest
—a reed-like voice
                    of peculiar accent

Thus she finds what peace there is, reclines,   350
before his approach, stroked
by their clambering feet—for pleasure

                    It is all for
pleasure   .   their feet   .   aimlessly
            wandering

The "great beast" come to sun himself
                            as he may
.   .   their dreams mingling,
aloof

Let us be reasonable!

                    Sunday in the park,   360
limited by the escarpment, eastward; to
the west abutting on the old road: recreation
with a view! the binoculars chained
to anchored stanchions along the east wall—
            beyond which, a hawk
                            soars!

—a trumpet sounds fitfully.

Stand at the rampart (use a metronome
if your ear is deficient, one made in Hungary
if you prefer)   370
and look away north by east where the church
spires still spend their wits against
the sky   .   to the ball-park
in the hollow with its minute figures running
—beyond the gap where the river
plunges into the narrow gorge, unseen

—and the imagination soars, as a voice
beckons, a thundrous voice, endless
—as sleep: the voice
that has ineluctably called them—   380
                    that unmoving roar!
churches and factories
                    (at a price)
together, summoned them from the pit   .

—his voice, one among many (unheard)
moving under all.

                         The mountain quivers.
Time! Count! Sever and mark time!

So during the early afternoon, from place
to place he moves,   390
his voice mingling with other voices
—the voice in his voice
opening his old throat, blowing out his lips,
kindling his mind (more
than his mind will kindle)

                    —following the hikers.

At last he comes to the idlers' favorite
haunts, the picturesque summit, where
the blue-stone (rust-red where exposed)
has been faulted at various levels   400
              (ferns rife among the stones)
into rough terraces and partly closed in
dens of sweet grass, the ground gently sloping.

Loiterers in groups straggle
over the bare rock-table—scratched by their
boot-nails more than the glacier scratched
them—walking indifferent through
each other's privacy   .

                    —in any case,
the center of movement, the core of gaiety.   410

Here a young man, perhaps sixteen,
is sitting with his back to the rock among
some ferns playing a guitar, dead pan   .
The rest are eating and drinking.

                         The big guy
in the black hat is too full to move   .

                         but Mary
is up!
         Come on! Wassa ma'? You got
broken leg?   420

              It is this air!
                    the air of the Midi[14]
and the old cultures intoxicates them:
present!

              —lifts one arm holding the cymbals
of her thoughts, cocks her old head
and dances! raising her skirts:

[14]The south of France.

La la la la!

What a bunch of bums! Afraid somebody see
you?   430
          Blah!
                    Excrementi!
                         —she spits.
Look a' me, Grandma! Everybody too damn
lazy.

This is the old, the very old, old upon old,
the undying: even to the minute gestures,
the hand holding the cup, the wine
spilling, the arm stained by it:
                                        Remember   440

the peon[15] in the lost
Eisenstein film[16] drinking

from a wine-skin with the abandon
of a horse drinking

so that it slopped down his chin?
down his neck, dribbling

over his shirt-front and down
onto his pants—laughing, toothless?

                              Heavenly man!

—the leg raised, verisimilitude   .   450
even to the coarse contours of the leg, the
bovine touch! The leer, the cave of it,
the female of it facing the male, the satyr—
               (Priapus!)[17]
with that lonely implication, goatherd
and goat, fertility, the attack, drunk,
cleansed   .

               Rejected. Even the film
suppressed   :   but   .   persistent

The picnickers laugh on the rocks celebrating   460
the varied Sunday of their loves with
its declining light—

[15]Spanish: peasant.
[16]*Que Viva Mexico*, an unfinished film about peasant life, by the Russian film director Sergei
Eisenstein (1898–1948).
[17]Greek god of masculine fertility.

Walking —

> look down (from a ledge) into this grassy
> den
>> (somewhat removed from the traffic)
>>> above whose brows
> a moon! where she lies sweating at his side:

>>> She stirs, distraught,
> against him—wounded (drunk), moves   470
> against him (a lump) desiring,
> against him, bored   .

> flagrantly bored and sleeping, a
> beer bottle still grasped spear-like
> in his hand   :

> while the small, sleepless boys, who
> have climbed the columnar rocks
> overhanging the pair (where they lie
> overt upon the grass, besieged—

> careless in their narrow cell under   480
> the crowd's feet) stare down,
>>> from history!
> at them, puzzled and in the sexless
> light (of childhood) bored equally,
> go charging off   .

>>> There where
> the movement throbs openly
> and you can hear the Evangelist shouting!
>>> —moving nearer
>> she—lean as a goat—leans   490
>> her lean belly to the man's backside
>> toying with the clips of his
>> suspenders   .

> —to which he adds his useless voice:
> until there moves in his sleep
> a music that is whole, unequivocal (in
> his sleep, sweating in his sleep—laboring
> against sleep, agasp!)
>>> —and does not waken.

> Sees, alive (asleep)   500
>> —the fall's roar entering
> his sleep (to be fulfilled)
>>> reborn
> in his sleep—scattered over the mountain
> severally   .

>> —by which he woos her, severally.

And the amnesic crowd (the scattered),
called about — strains
to catch the movement of one voice   .

                                  hears,   510
           Pleasure! Pleasure!

                                —feels,
half dismayed, the afternoon of complex
voices its own—
              and is relieved
                     (relived)

         A cop is directing traffic
         across the main road up
         a little wooded slope toward
         the conveniences:[18]   520

                           oaks, choke-cherry,
dogwoods, white and green, iron-wood   :
humped roots matted into the shallow soil
—mostly gone: rock out-croppings
polished by the feet of the picnickers:
sweetbarked sassafras   .

leaning from the rancid grease:
                         deformity—

—to be deciphered (a horn, a trumpet!)
an elucidation by multiplicity,   530
a corrosion, a parasitic curd, a clarion
for belief, to be good dogs   :

NO DOGS ALLOWED AT LARGE IN THIS PARK

1946–1948   1948

COME ON!

     A different kind of thought
         blander
                  and more desperate
    like that of
         Sergeant So-and-So
             at the road
   in Belleau Wood:[1]

[18]Public toilets.

[1]At the Battle of Belleau Wood (1918), in France, during the First World War, an unknown U.S. Marine sergeant was reported to have led an American attack on the German lines with the cry, "Come on, you sons-of-bitches! Do you want to live forever?"

               Come on!
                         Do you want to live
            forever?—
                    That
                              is the essence
            of poetry.
                    But it does not
                              always
               take the same form.
                    For the most part
                              it consists
               in listening
                         to the nightingale
                              or fools.
                                        1955

LANDSCAPE WITH THE FALL OF ICARUS

            According to Brueghel[1]
            when Icarus fell
            it was spring

            a farmer was ploughing
            his field
            the whole pageantry

            of the year was
            awake tingling
            near

            the edge of the sea   10
            concerned
            with itself

            sweating in the sun
            that melted
            the wings' wax

            unsignificantly
            off the coast
            there was

            a splash quite unnoticed
            this was   20
            Icarus drowning
                    1960, 1962

[1]Pieter Brueghel (1525?–1569), Flemish artist whose painting "Landscape with the Fall of Icarus" (1555?) displays just such a pastoral scene as Williams describes.

THE KNIFE OF THE TIMES

As the years passed the girls who had been such intimates as children still remained true to one another.

Ethel by now had married. Maura had married; the one having removed to Harrisburg, the other to New York City. And both began to bring up families. Ethel especially went in for children. Within a very brief period, comparatively speaking, she had three of them, then four, then five and finally six. And through it all, she kept in constant touch with her girlhood friend, dark-eyed Maura, by writing long intimate letters.

At first these had been news chit chat, ending always however in continued protestations of that love which the women had enjoyed during their childhood. Maura showed them to her husband and both enjoyed their full newsy quality dealing as they did with people and scenes with which both were familiar.

But after several years, as these letters continued to flow, there came a change in them. First the personal note grew more confidential. Ethel told about her children, how she had had one after the other—to divert her mind, to distract her thoughts from their constant brooding. Each child would raise her hopes of relief, each anticipated delivery brought only renewed disappointment. She confided more and more in Maura. She loved her husband; it was not that. In fact, she didn't know what it was save that she, Ethel, could never get her old friend Maura out of her mind.

Until at last the secret was out. It is you, Maura, that I want. Nothing but you. Nobody but you can appease my grief. Forgive me if I distress you with this confession. It is the last thing in this world that I desire. But I cannot contain myself longer.

Thicker and faster came the letters. Full love missives they were now without the least restraint.

Ethel wrote letters now such as Maura wished she might at some time in her life have received from a man. She was told that all these years she had been dreamed of, passionately, without rival, without relief. Now, surely, Maura did not dare show the letters to her husband. He would not understand.

They affected her strangely, they frightened her, but they caused a shrewd look to come into her dark eyes and she packed them carefully away where none should ever come upon them. She herself was occupied otherwise but she felt tenderly toward Ethel, loved her in an old remembered manner—but that was all. She was disturbed by the turn Ethel's mind had taken and thanked providence her friend and she lived far enough apart to keep them from embarrassing encounters.

But, in spite of the lack of adequate response to her advances, Ethel never wavered, never altered in her passionate appeals. She begged her friend to visit her, to come to her, to live with her. She spoke of her longings, to touch the velvet flesh of her darling's breasts, her thighs. She longed to kiss her to sleep, to hold her in her arms. Franker and franker became her outspoken lusts. For which she begged indulgence.

Once she implored Maura to wear a silk chemise which she was sending, to wear it for a week and to return it to her, to Ethel, unwashed, that she might wear it in her turn constantly upon her.

Then, after twenty years, one day Maura received a letter from Ethel asking her to meet her—and her mother, in New York. They were expecting a sister back from Europe on the *Mauretania* and they wanted Maura to be there—for old times' sake.

Maura consented. With strange feelings of curiosity and not a little fear, she stood at the gate of the Pennsylvania station waiting for her friend to come out at the wicket on the arrival of the Harrisburg express. Would she be alone? Would her mother be with her really? Was it a hoax? Was the woman crazy, after all? And, finally, would she recognize her?

There she was and her mother along with her. After the first stare, the greetings on all sides were quiet, courteous and friendly. The mother dominated the moment. Her keen eyes looked Maura up and down once, then she asked the time, when would the steamer dock, how far was the pier and had they time for lunch first?

There was plenty of time. Yes, let's lunch. But first Ethel had a small need to satisfy and asked Maura if she would show her the way. Maura led her friend to the Pay Toilets and there, after inserting the coin, Ethel opened the door and, before Maura could find the voice to protest, drew her in with herself and closed the door after her.

What a meeting! What a release! Ethel took her friend into her arms and between tears and kisses, tried in some way, as best she could, to tell her of her happiness. She fondled her old playmate, hugged her, lifted her off her feet in the eager impressment of her desire, whispering into her ear, stroking her hair, her face, touching her lips, her eyes; holding her, holding her about as if she could never again release her.

No one could remain cold to such an appeal, as pathetic to Maura as it was understandable and sincere, she tried her best to modify its fury, to abate it, to control. But, failing that, she did what she could to appease her old friend. She loved Ethel, truly, but all this show was beyond her. She did not understand it, she did not know how to return it. But she was not angry, she found herself in fact in tears, her heart touched, her lips willing.

Time was slipping by and they had to go.

At lunch Ethel kept her foot upon the toe of Maura's slipper. It was a delirious meal for Maura with thinking of old times, watching the heroic beauty of the old lady and, while keeping up a chatter of small conversation, intermixed with recollections, to respond secretly as best she could to Ethel's insistent pressures.

At the pier there was a long line waiting to be admitted to the enclosure. It was no use—Ethel from behind constantly pressed her body against her embarrassed friend, embarrassed not from lack of understanding or sympathy, but for fear lest one of the officers and Customs inspectors who were constantly watching them should detect something out of the ordinary.

But the steamer was met, the sister saluted; the day came to an end and the hour of parting found Ethel still keeping close, close to the object of her lifelong adoration.

What shall I do? thought Maura afterward on her way home, on the train alone. Ethel had begged her to visit her, to go to her, to spend a week at least with her, to sleep with her. Why not?

1932

THE USE OF FORCE

They were new patients to me, all I had was the name, Olson. Please come down as soon as you can, my daughter is very sick.

When I arrived I was met by the mother, a big startled looking woman, very clean and apologetic who merely said, Is this the doctor? and let me in. In the back, she added. You must excuse us, doctor, we have her in the kitchen where it is warm. It is very damp here sometimes.

The child was fully dressed and sitting on her father's lap near the kitchen table. He tried to get up, but I motioned for him not to bother, took off my overcoat and started to look things over. I could see that they were all very nervous, eyeing me up and down distrustfully. As often, in such cases, they weren't telling me more than they had to, it was up to me to tell them; that's why they were spending three dollars on me.

The child was fairly eating me up with her cold, steady eyes, and no expression to her face whatever. She did not move and seemed, inwardly, quiet; an unusually attractive little thing, and as strong as a heifer in appearance. But her face was flushed, she was breathing rapidly, and I realized that she had a high fever. She had magnificent blonde hair, in profusion. One of those picture children often reproduced in advertising leaflets and the photogravure sections of the Sunday papers.

She's had a fever for three days, began the father and we don't know what it comes from. My wife has given her things, you know, like people do, but it don't do no good. And there's been a lot of sickness around. So we tho't you'd better look her over and tell us what is the matter.

As doctors often do I took a trial shot at it as a point of departure. Has she had a sore throat?

Both parents answered me together, No . . . No, she says her throat don't hurt her.

Does your throat hurt you? added the mother to the child. But the little girl's expression didn't change nor did she move her eyes from my face.

Have you looked?

I tried to, said the mother, but I couldn't see.

As it happens we have been having a number of cases of diphtheria in the school to which this child went during that month and we were all, quite apparently, thinking of that, though no one had as yet spoken of the thing.

Well, I said, suppose we take a look at the throat first. I smiled in my best professional manner and asking for the child's first name I said, come on, Mathilda, open your mouth and let's take a look at your throat.

Nothing doing.

Aw, come on, I coaxed, just open your mouth wide and let me take a look. Look, I said opening both hands wide, I haven't anything in my hands. Just open up and let me see.

Such a nice man, put in the mother. Look how kind he is to you. Come on, do what he tells you to. He won't hurt you.

At that I ground my teeth in disgust. If only they wouldn't use the word "hurt" I might be able to get somewhere. But I did not allow myself to be hurried or disturbed but speaking quietly and slowly I approached the child again.

As I moved my chair a little nearer suddenly with one catlike movement both her hands clawed instinctively for my eyes and she almost reached them too. In fact she knocked my glasses flying and they fell, though unbroken, several feet away from me on the kitchen floor.

Both the mother and father almost turned themselves inside out in embarrassment and apology. You bad girl, said the mother, taking her and shaking her by one arm. Look what you've done. The nice man . . .

For heaven's sake, I broke in. Don't call me a nice man to her. I'm here to look at her throat on the chance that she might have diphtheria and possibly die of it. But that's nothing to her. Look here, I said to the child, we're going to look at your throat. You're old enough to understand what I'm saying. Will you open it now by yourself or shall we have to open it for you?

Not a move. Even her expression hadn't changed. Her breaths however were coming faster and faster. Then the battle began. I had to do it. I had to have a throat culture for her own protection. But first I told the parents that it was entirely up to them. I explained the danger but said that I would not insist on a throat examination so long as they would take the responsibility.

If you don't do what the doctor says you'll have to go to the hospital, the mother admonished her severely.

Oh yeah? I had to smile to myself. After all, I had already fallen in love with the savage brat, the parents were contemptible to me. In the ensuing struggle they grew more and more abject, crushed, exhausted while she surely rose to magnificent heights of insane fury of effort bred of her terror of me.

The father tried his best, and he was a big man but the fact that she was his daughter, his shame at her behavior and his dread of hurting her made him release her just at the critical moment several times when I had almost achieved success, till I wanted to kill him. But his dread also that she might have diphtheria made him tell me to go on, go on though he himself was almost fainting, while the mother moved back and forth behind us raising and lowering her hands in an agony of apprehension.

Put her in front of you on your lap, I ordered, and hold both her wrists.

But as soon as he did the child let out a scream. Don't, you're hurting me. Let go of my hands. Let them go I tell you. Then she shrieked terrifyingly, hysterically. Stop it! Stop it! You're killing me!

Do you think she can stand it, doctor! said the mother.

You get out, said the husband to his wife. Do you want her to die of diphtheria? Come on now, hold her, I said.

Then I grasped the child's head with my left hand and tried to get the wooden tongue depressor between her teeth. She fought, with clenched teeth, desperately! But now I also had grown furious—at a child. I tried to hold myself down but I couldn't. I know how to expose a throat for inspection. And I did my best. When finally I got the wooden spatula behind the last teeth and just the point of it into the mouth cavity, she opened up for an instant but before I could see anything she came down again and gripping the wooden blade between her molars she reduced it to splinters before I could get it out again.

Aren't you ashamed, the mother yelled at her. Aren't you ashamed to act like that in front of the doctor?

Get me a smooth-handled spoon of some sort, I told the mother. We're going through with this. The child's mouth was already bleeding. Her tongue was cut and she was screaming in wild hysterical shrieks. Perhaps I should have desisted and come back in an hour or more. No doubt it would have been better. But I have seen at least two children lying dead in bed of neglect in such cases, and feeling that I must get a diagnosis now or never I went at it again. But the worst of it was that I too had got beyond reason. I could have torn the child apart in my own fury and enjoyed it. It was a pleasure to attack her. My face was burning with it.

The damned little brat must be protected against her own idiocy, one says to one's self at such times. Others must be protected against her. It is a social necessity. And all these things are true. But a blind fury, a feeling of adult shame, bred of a longing for muscular release are the operatives. One goes on to the end.

In a final unreasoning assault I overpowered the child's neck and jaws. I forced the heavy silver spoon back of her teeth and down her throat till she gagged. And there it was—both tonsils covered with membrane. She had fought valiantly to keep me from knowing her secret. She had been hiding that sore throat for three days at least and lying to her parents in order to escape just such an outcome as this.

Now truly she *was* furious. She had been on the defensive before but now she attacked. Tried to get off her father's lap and fly at me while tears of defeat blinded her eyes.

1933, 1938

Robinson Jeffers *1887–1962*

Robinson Jeffers's disturbing narrations of the decay of modern culture have marked him as one of the misanthropes of American literature, a "poet of inhumanism." He saw mankind as fatally detached from nature and morbidly pursuing material goods and sensual pleasure. Little in Jeffers's early life foreshadowed his pessimistic vision of man and society. He was born to a comfortably prosperous family in Pittsburgh, Pennsylvania. His father, a Presbyterian preacher and theologian, tutored him in languages, the classics, and the Bible and sent him to school in Switzerland and Germany. After his graduation from college, Jeffers briefly studied for an M.A. in literature, attended medical school for three years, and then studied forestry and the law. When a modest inheritance freed him from the necessity of earning a living he settled near Monterey, California, on what he called the "future-ridden coast," a land "pregnant with dreams." There he built a stone house and tower overlooking the Pacific and withdrew from the world to write poetry.

Jeffers's early work, Flagons and Apples *(1912) and* Californians *(1916), was conventional and undistinguished. In 1924 he published* Tamar, and Other Poems, *a volume whose desolate reflections on the futility of man's aspirations brought Jeffers his first recognition. In volumes that soon followed,* The Woman at Point Sur *(1927),* Cawdor *(1928),* Dear Judas *(1929), and through such later works as* The Double Axe *(1948),* Hungerfield *(1952), and* The Beginning of the End *(1963), he reiterated his denunciation of modern life.*

The long, melodic lines of his free-verse and blank-verse poems were Whitmanesque, yet Jeffers's poetic aim was not "to open up new fields for poetry, but only to reclaim old freedom." His ideas where formed by the tragic vision of life he had absorbed from classical literature and by the deterministic doctrines of late nineteenth-century science. Ultimately he came to foresee with pleasure the eventual destruction of humankind, a species that, to Jeffers, had long since cast off its divinity and had become merely "the animals Christ was rumored to have died for."

FURTHER READING: *The Selected Letters of Robinson Jeffers, 1897–1962,* ed. A. Ridgeway, 1968; L. Powell, *Robinson Jeffers, The Man and His Work,* 1932, 1934, 1940; R. Gilbert, *Shine, Perishing Republic, Robinson Jeffers and the Tragic Sense in Modern Poetry,* 1936;

R. Squires, *The Loyalties of Robinson Jeffers,* 1956, 1963; M. Monjian, *Robinson Jeffers, A Study in Inhumanism,* 1958; F. Carpenter, *Robinson Jeffers,* 1962; M. Bennet, *The Stone Mason of Tor House,* 1966; Brother Antoninus (W. Everson), *Robinson Jeffers, Fragments of an Older Fury,* 1968; A. Coffin, *Robinson Jeffers, Poet of Inhumanism,* 1970; R. Brophy, *Robinson Jeffers, Myth, Ritual, and Symbol in His Narrative Poems,* 1973; J. Shebl, *In This Wild Water,* 1976; W. Nolte, *Rock and Hawk, Robinson Jeffers and the Romantic Agony,* 1978; R. Zaller, *The Cliffs of Solitude, A Reading of Robinson Jeffers,* 1983; J. Karman, *Robinson Jeffers, Poet of California,* 1987.

TEXTS: *The Selected Poetry of Robinson Jeffers,* 1959.

BOATS IN A FOG

Sports and gallantries, the stage, the arts, the antics of dancers,
The exuberant voices of music,
Have charm for children but lack nobility; it is bitter earnestness
That makes beauty; the mind
Knows, grown adult.
          A sudden fog-drift muffled the ocean,
A throbbing of engines moved in it,
At length, a stone's throw out, between the rocks and the vapor,
One by one moved shadows
Out of the mystery, shadows, fishing-boats, trailing each other   10
Following the cliff for guidance,
Holding a difficult path between the peril of the sea-fog
And the foam on the shore granite.
One by one, trailing their leader, six crept by me,
Out of the vapor and into it,
The throb of their engines subdued by the fog, patient and
    cautious,
Coasting all round the peninsula
Back to the buoys in Monterey[1] harbor. A flight of pelicans
Is nothing lovelier to look at;
The flight of the planets is nothing nobler; all the arts lose virtue   20
Against the essential reality
Of creatures going about their business among the equally
Earnest elements of nature.

                      1925

HURT HAWKS

I

The broken pillar of the wing jags from the clotted shoulder,
The wing trails like a banner in defeat,
No more to use the sky forever but live with famine
And pain a few days: cat nor coyote
Will shorten the week of waiting for death, there is game with-
    out talons.

[1] In California.

He stands under the oak-bush and waits
The lame feet of salvation; at night he remembers freedom
And flies in a dream, the dawns ruin it.
He is strong and pain is worse to the strong, incapacity is worse.
The curs of the day come and torment him   10
At distance, no one but death the redeemer will humble that
     head,
The intrepid readiness, the terrible eyes.
The wild God of the world is sometimes merciful to those
That ask mercy, not often to the arrogant.
You do not know him, you communal people, or you have forgotten
     him;
Intemperate and savage, the hawk remembers him;
Beautiful and wild, the hawks, and men that are dying, remember
     him.

                                   II
I'd sooner, except the penalties, kill a man than a hawk; but the
     great redtail
Had nothing left but unable misery
From the bone too shattered for mending, the wing that trailed
     under his talons when he moved.   20
We had fed him six weeks, I gave him freedom,
He wandered over the foreland hill and returned in the evening,
     asking for death,
Not like a beggar, still eyed with the old
Implacable arrogance. I gave him the lead gift in the twilight.
     What fell was relaxed,
Owl-downy, soft feminine feathers; but what
Soared: the fierce rush: the night-herons by the flooded river
     cried fear at its rising
Before it was quite unsheathed from reality.

                                                                    1928

SHINE, PERISHING REPUBLIC

While this America settles in the mould of its vulgarity, heavily
     thickening to empire,
And protest, only a bubble in the molten mass, pops and sighs out,
     and the mass hardens,

I sadly smiling remember that the flower fades to make fruit, the
     fruit rots to make earth
Out of the mother; and through the spring exultances, ripeness
     and decadence; and home to the mother.

You making haste haste on decay: not blameworthy; life is good,
     be it stubbornly long or suddenly

A mortal splendor: meteors are not needed less than mountains:
    shine, perishing republic.

But for my children, I would have them keep their distance from
    the thickening center; corruption
Never has been compulsory, when the cities lie at the monster's
    feet there are left the mountains.

And boys, be in nothing so moderate as in love of man, a clever
    servant, insufferable master.
There is the trap that catches noblest spirits, that caught—they
    say—God, when he walked on earth.   10

                                                              1930

THE PURSE-SEINE[1]

Our sardine fishermen work at night in the dark of the moon;
    daylight or moonlight
They could not tell where to spread the net, unable to see the
    phosphorescence of the shoals[2] of fish.
They work northward from Monterey, coasting Santa Cruz; off
    New Year's Point or off Pigeon Point[3]
The look-out man will see some lakes of milk-color light on the
    sea's night-purple; he points, and the helmsman
Turns the dark prow, the motorboat circles the gleaming shoal
    and drifts out her seine-net. They close the circle
And purse the bottom of the net, then with great labor haul it in.

                                              I cannot tell you
How beautiful the scene is, and a little terrible, then, when the
    crowded fish
Know they are caught, and wildly beat from one wall to the
    other of their closing destiny the phosphorescent.
Water to a pool of flame, each beautiful slender body sheeted
    with flame, like a live rocket   10
A comet's tail wake of clear yellow flame; while outside the
    narrowing
Floats and cordage of the net great sea-lions come up to watch,
    sighing in the dark; the vast walls of night
Stand erect to the stars.

                        Lately I was looking from a night mountain-top
On a wide city, the colored splendor, galaxies of light: how could
    I help but recall the seine-net
Gathering the luminous fish? I cannot tell you how beautiful
    the city appeared, and a little terrible.

[1]A fishing net that closes like a purse.
[2]Schools, swarms.
[3]Points on the Pacific coast, near Monterey, California.

I thought, We have geared the machines and locked all together
    into interdependence; we have built the great cities; now
There is no escape. We have gathered vast populations incapable
    of free survival, insulated
From the strong earth, each person in himself helpless, on all
    dependent. The circle is closed, and the net
Is being hauled in. They hardly feel the cords drawing, yet they
    shine already. The inevitable mass-disasters   20
Will not come in our time nor in our children's, but we and our
    children
Must watch the net draw narrower, government take all powers
    —or revolution, and the new government
Take more than all, add to kept bodies kept souls—or anarchy,
    the mass-disasters.

                  These things are Progress;
Do you marvel our verse is troubled or frowning, while it keeps
    its reason? Or it lets go, lets the mood flow
In the manner of the recent young men into mere hysteria, splin-
    tered gleams, crackled laughter. But they are quite wrong.
There is no reason for amazement: surely one always knew that
    cultures decay, and life's end is death.

                                        1937

Marianne Moore *1887–1972*

By the end of her life Marianne Moore was well known as one of America's most devoted baseball fans and as one of its premier poets. Her devotion to baseball won her the honor of throwing out the first ball at the opening of the 1968 season at Yankee Stadium in New York. Her poetic descriptions of exotic animals and plants, and things as varied as steam rollers and quartz crystal clocks, won her numerous awards and the distinction of being described as "The World's Greatest Living Observer."

    She spent her childhood near St. Louis, Missouri, and in Carlisle, Pennsylvania. After her graduation from Bryn Mawr College in 1909, she returned to Carlisle, where she taught for four years in a U.S. Government school for Indians. In 1916, having already begun to distinguish herself as one of the nation's innovative "new poets," she moved east, eventually settling in New York City. She worked in the New York Public Library and then became editor of a literary magazine, The Dial, *all the while developing her meticulous and subtle poetic craft. Her first book,* Poems *(1921), was published in England by her friends and without her knowledge. In 1924 her prize-winning volume* Observations *appeared, followed by* The Pangolin *(1936),* What Are Years *(1941), and* Nevertheless *(1944). Her* Collected Poems *were published in 1951, and in a single year (1952), she received a Bollingen Prize, a Pulitzer Prize, and a National Book Award for Poetry.*

    Marianne Moore was a book reviewer, translator, and essayist, as well as poet, and her sprightly and eccentric ways were, to many, as engaging as her fresh and compact writing.

She had an acute eye for detail, and her poetry is marked by movements from "imagistic" portrayals of visible objects to metaphysical reflections. She sprinkled her poetry with quotations, which she compared to "collections of flies in amber." She used near or approximate rhyme and light rhyme—in which the rhyming syllables of words are unaccented. Much of her verse was syllabic, relying on the number of syllables in a poetic line, rather than on a conventional pattern of stress accents, to produce a subdued metrical cadence. As a result, some of her poems display the rhetorical qualities of succinct prose, yet with their carefully controlled forms, their glittering surfaces, and their intellectual complexities they are expressions of an authentic poetic imagination and "lit with piercing glances into the life of things."

FURTHER READING: *A Marianne Moore Reader*, 1961; *The Complete Prose of Marianne Moore*, ed. P. Willis, 1986; B. Engel, *Marianne Moore*, 1964; J. Garrigue, *Marianne Moore*, 1965; A. Weatherhead, *The Edge of the Image*, 1967; G. Nitchie, *Marianne Moore, An Introduction to the Poetry*, 1969; *Marianne Moore, A Collection of Critical Essays*, ed. C. Tomlinson, 1969; D. Hall, *Marianne Moore, The Cage and the Animal*, 1970; L. Stapleton, *Marianne Moore, The Poet's Advance*, 1978; B. Costello, *Marianne Moore, Imaginary Possessions*, 1981; E. Phillips, *Marianne Moore*, 1982; T. Martin, *Marianne Moore, Subversive Modernist*, 1986; J. Slatin, *The Savage's Romance, The Poetry of Marianne Moore*, 1986; G. Schulman, *Marianne Moore, The Poetry of Engagement*, 1987.

TEXT: The text of "Poetry" is from *Collected Poems*, 1951; all other poems are from *The Complete Poems of Marianne Moore*, 1980.

TO A STEAM ROLLER

The illustration
is nothing to you without the application.
    You lack half wit. You crush all the particles down
        into close conformity, and then walk back and forth on them.

Sparkling chips of rock
are crushed down to the level of the parent block.
    Were not "impersonal judgment in aesthetic
        matters, a metaphysical impossibility," you

might fairly achieve
it. As for butterflies, I can hardly conceive   10
    of one's attending upon you, but to question
        the congruence of the complement is vain, if it exists.

                                 1915, 1921

THE MONKEYS

winked too much and were afraid of snakes. The zebras,
                              supreme in
their abnormality; the elephants with their fog-colored skin
    and strictly practical appendages
        were there, the small cats; and the parakeet—

trivial and humdrum on examination, destroying
bark and portions of the food it could not eat.

I recall their magnificence, now not more magnificent
that it is dim. It is difficult to recall the ornament,

  speech, and precise manner of what one might
    call the minor acquaintances twenty   10
      years back; but I shall not forget him—that Gilgamesh[1]
                                      among
        the hairy carnivora—that cat with the

wedge-shaped, slate-gray marks on its forelegs and the resolute
                                      tail,
  astringently remarking, "They have imposed on us with their pale
    half-fledged protestations, trembling about
      in inarticulate frenzy, saying
        it is not for us to understand art; finding it
        all so difficult, examining the thing

as if it were inconceivably arcanic, as symmet-
rically frigid as if it had been carved out of chrysoprase[2]   20
  or marble—strict with tension, malignant
    in its power over us and deeper
      than the sea when it proffers flattery in exchange for
                                      hemp,
        rye, flax, horses, platinum, timber, and fur."
                                      1917, 1921, 1935

THE FISH

        wade
        through black jade.
          Of the crow-blue mussel shells, one keeps
          adjusting the ash heaps;
            opening and shutting itself like

        an
        injured fan.
          The barnacles which encrust the side
          of the wave, cannot hide
            there for the submerged shafts of the   10

        sun,
        split like spun
          glass, move themselves with spotlight switfness
          into the crevices—
            in and out, illuminating

[1]Legendary Babylonian hero.   [2]Green-colored quartz.

the
turquoise sea
   of bodies. The water drives a wedge
   of iron through the iron edge
      of the cliff; whereupon the stars,   20

pink
rice-grains, ink-
   bespattered jellyfish, crabs like green
   lilies, and submarine
      toadstools, slide each on the other.

All
external
   marks of abuse are present on this
   defiant edifice—
      all the physical features of   30

ac-
cident—lack
   of cornice, dynamite grooves, burns, and
   hatchet strokes, these things stand
      out on it; the chasm side is

dead.
Repeated
   evidence has proved that it can live
   on what can not revive
      its youth. The sea grows old in it.   40
                 1918, 1921

POETRY[1]

I, too, dislike it: there are things that are important beyond
     all this fiddle.
Reading it, however, with a perfect contempt for it, one
     discovers in
it after all, a place for the genuine.
     Hands that can grasp, eyes
     that can dilate, hair that can rise
        if it must, these things are important not because a

high-sounding interpretation can be put upon them but be-
     cause they are
useful. When they become so derivative as to become
     unintelligible,

<hr>

[1]The text reprinted here is from *Collected Poems* (1951). In a revised version, published in *The Complete Poems* (1967), the poem was reduced to three lines: "I, too, dislike it. / Reading it, however, with a perfect contempt for it, one discovers in / it, after all, a place for the genuine."

the same thing may be said for all of us, that we
    do not admire what   10
      we cannot understand: the bat
        holding on upside down or in quest of something to

eat, elephants pushing, a wild horse taking a roll, a tireless
      wolf under
    a tree, the immovable critic twitching his skin like a horse
      that feels a flea, the base-
    ball fan, the statistician—
      nor is it valid
        to discriminate against "business documents and

school-books";[2] all these phenomena are important. One
      must make a distinction
    however: when dragged into prominence by half poets,
      the result is not poetry,
    nor till the poets among us can be   20
      "literalists of
      the imagination"[3]—above
        insolence and triviality and can present

for inspection, "imaginary gardens with real toads in them,"
      shall we have
    it. In the meantime, if you demand on the one hand,
    the raw material of poetry in
      all its rawness and
      that which is on the other hand
        genuine, you are interested in poetry.

                                   1919, 1935

THE STEEPLE-JACK[1]

Dürer[2] would have seen a reason for living
    in a town like this, with eight stranded whales
to look at; with the sweet sea air coming into your house
    on a fine day, from water etched
      with waves as formal as the scales
      on a fish.

  [2]"Diary of Tolstoy, p. 84: 'Where the boundary between prose and poetry lies, I shall never be able to understand. The question is raised in manuals of style, yet the answer to it lies beyond me. Poetry is verse: prose is not verse. Or else poetry is everything with the exception of business documents and school books.' "—Moore's note. The quotation is from *The Diaries of Leo Tolstoy* (1917).

  [3]"Yeats, *Ideas of Good and Evil* (A. H. Bullen, 1903), p. 182. 'The limitation of his view was from the very intensity of his vision; he was a too literal realist of imagination, as others are of nature; and because he believed that the figures seen by the mind's eye, when exalted by inspiration, were "eternal existences," symbols of divine essences, he hated every grace of style that might obscure their lineaments' "—Moore's note. The quotation is from an essay, "William Blake and His Illustrations to the *Divine Comedy*," by William Butler Yeats.

  [1]First published in 1932, and repeatedly revised. The version presented here is from the 1967 *Complete Poems.*

  [2]Albrecht Dürer (1471–1528), German painter and engraver who, like Marianne Moore, found metaphysical significance in everyday things.

One by one in two's and three's, the seagulls keep
    flying back and forth over the town clock,
or sailing around the lighthouse without moving their wings—
rising steadily with a slight
    quiver of the body—or flock   10
mewing where

a sea the purple of the peacock's neck is
    paled to greenish azure as Dürer changed
the pine green of the Tyrol[3] to peacock blue and guinea
gray. You can see a twenty-five-
    pound lobster; and fish nets arranged
to dry. The

whirlwind fife-and-drum of the storm bends the salt
    marsh grass, disturbs stars in the sky and the   20
star on the steeple; it is a privilege to see so
much confusion. Disguised by what
    might seem the opposite, the sea-
side flowers and

trees are favored by the fog so that you have
    the tropics at first hand: the trumpet vine,
foxglove, giant snapdragon, a salpiglossis[4] that has
spots and stripes; morning-glories, gourds,
    or moon-vines trained on fishing twine
at the back door: 30

cattails, flags, blueberries and spiderwort,
    striped grass, lichens, sunflowers, asters, daisies—
yellow and crab-claw ragged sailors[5] with green bracts[6]—toad-
    plant,
petunias, ferns; pink lilies, blue
    ones, tigers; poppies; black sweet-peas.
The climate

is not right for the banyan, frangipani, or
    jack-fruit trees; or for exotic serpent
life. Ring lizard and snakeskin for the foot, if you see fit;
but here they've cats, not cobras, to   40
    keep down the rats. The diffident
little newt

with white pin-dots on black horizontal spaced-
    out bands lives here; yet there is nothing that
ambition can buy or take away. The college student
named Ambrose sits on the hillside
    with his not-native books and hat
and sees boats

[3]Alpine region of Austria and northern Italy.
[4]South American herb.
[5]The bluebottle or cornflower.   [6]Leaves.

at sea progress white and rigid as if in
　　a groove. Liking an elegance of which   50
the source is not bravado, he knows by heart the antique
sugar-bowl shaped summerhouse of
　　　　interlacing slats, and the pitch
of the church

spire, not true, from which a man in scarlet lets
　　　　down a rope as a spider spins a thread;
he might be part of a novel, but on the sidewalk a
sign says C. J. Poole, Steeple Jack,
　　　　in black and white; and one in red
and white says   60

Danger. The church portico has four fluted
　　　　columns, each a single piece of stone, made
modester by whitewash. This would be a fit haven for
waifs, children, animals, prisoners,
　　　　and presidents who have repaid
sin-driven

senators by not thinking about them. The
　　　　place has a schoolhouse, a post-office in a
store, fish-houses, hen-houses, a three-masted schooner on
the stocks. The hero, the student,   70
　　　　the steeple jack, each in his way,
is at home.

It could not be dangerous to be living
　　　　in a town like this, of simple people,
who have a steeple-jack placing danger signs by the church
while he is gilding the solid-
　　　　pointed star, which on a steeple
stands for hope.

　　　　　　　　　　　　　　　　　　　　　1932, 1935, 1961, 1967

NO SWAN SO FINE

"No water so still as the
　　　　dead fountains of Versailles,"[1] No swan,
with swart blind look askance
and gondoliering legs, so fine
　　　　as the chintz china one with fawn-
brown eyes and toothed gold
collar on to show whose bird it was.

Lodged in the Louis Fifteenth

[1] "'There is no water so still as in the dead fountains of Versailles.' Percy Phillip, *New York Times Magazine*, May 10, 1931."—Moore's note.

candelabrum[2]-tree of cockscomb-
tinted buttons, dahlias,   10
sea urchins, and everlastings,
    it perches on the branching foam
of polished sculptured
flowers—at ease and tall. The king is dead.
                          1932, 1935

THE STUDENT

"In America," began
the lecturer, "everyone must have a
degree. The French do not think that
all can have it, they don't say everyone
must go to college."[1] We
incline to feel, here,
that although it may be unnecessary

to know fifteen languages,
one degree is not too much. With us, a
school—like the singing tree of which   10
the leaves were mouths that sang in concert[2]—
is both a tree of knowledge
and of liberty,—
seen in the unanimity of college

mottoes, *lux et veritas,*
Christo et ecclesiae, sapiet
felici.[3] It may be that we have not knowledge, just opinions, that
    we are undergraduates,
not students; we know we have been told with smiles, by
    expatriates   20

of whom we had asked "When will
your experiment be finished?" "Science
is never finished."[4] Secluded
from domestic strife, Jack Bookworm led a college life, says
    Goldsmith;[5]
and here also as in France or Oxford, study is beset with

[2]"A pair of Louis XV candelabra with Dresden figures of swans belonging to Lord Balfour."—
Moore's note. The age of Louis XV, King of France (1715–1774), was one of ornate and delicate
art.
[1]" '*Les Ideals de l'Éducation Française,*' lecture, December 3, 1931, by M. Auguste Desclos, Director-
adjoint, Office National des Universités et Écoles Françaises de Paris."—Moore's note.
[2]" 'Each leaf was a mouth, and every leaf joined in concert.' *Arabian Nights.*"—Moore's note.
[3]Latin: "lux et veritas" ("Light and truth"), the motto of Yale University; "Christo et ecclesiae"
("For Christ and church"), words carried on the seals of Harvard University from 1693 to 1935;
sapie[n]t[es] felici (the wise are fortunate).
[4]"Albert Einstein to an American student, *New York Times.*"—Moore's note.
[5]In the poem "The Double Transformation: A Tale" (1760), by the British writer Oliver Goldsmith
(1730?–1770), Jack Bookworm led a life "Secluded from domestic strife"—until he married.

dangers—with bookworms, mildews,
and complaisancies. But someone in New
England has known enough to say
that the student is patience personified, a variety   30
of hero, "patient of neglect and of reproach,"—who can "hold by

himself."[6] You can't beat hens to
make them lay. Wolf's wool is the best of wool
but it cannot be sheared, because
the wolf will not comply.[7] With knowledge as with wolves'
      surliness,
the student studies voluntarily, refusing to be less

than individual. He
"gives his opinion and then rests upon it";[8]
he renders service when there is   40
no reward, and is too reclusive for some things to seem to touch
him; not because he has no feeling but because he has so much.

                                             1932, 1942, 1967

THE PANGOLIN[1]

Another armored animal—scale
      lapping scale with spruce-cone regularity until they
form the uninterrupted central
      tail-row! This near artichoke with head and legs and
                                    grit-equipped gizzard,
      the night miniature artist engineer is,
            yes, Leonardo da Vinci's replica—
            impressive animal and toiler of whom we seldom hear.
            Armor seems extra. But for him,
                  the closing ear-ridge[2]—
                  or bare ear lacking even this small   10
                  eminence and similarly safe

contracting nose and eye apertures
      impenetrably closable, are not; a true ant-eater,
not cockroach-eater, who endures
      exhausting solitary trips through unfamiliar ground at night,

---

[6]"Emerson in *The American Scholar:* 'There can be no scholar without the heroic mind'; 'let him hold by himself; . . . patient of neglect, patient of reproach.' "—Moore's note.

[7]"Edmund Burke, November 1781, in reply to Fox: 'There is excellent wool on the back of a wolf and therefore he must be sheared . . . . But will he comply?"—Moore's note. Edmund Burke (1729–1797) and Charles James Fox (1749–1806), British statesmen and orators, members of Parliament.

[8]"Henry McBride, *New York Sun*, December 12, 1931: 'Dr. Valentiner . . . has the typical reserve of the student. He does not enjoy the active battle of opinion that invariably rages when a decision is announced that can be weighed in great sums of money. He gives his opinion firmly and rests upon that.' "—Moore's note.

[1]A scaly anteater.

[2]"The 'closing ear-ridge,' and certain other detail, from 'Pangolins' by Robert T. Hatt; *Natural History*, December, 1935."—Moore's note.

returning home before sunrise; stepping in the moonlight,
   on the moonlight peculiarly,[3] that the outside
     edges of his hands may bear the weight and save the
                   claws
   for digging. Serpentined about
     the tree, he draws   20
       away from danger unpugnaciously,
       with no sound but a harmless hiss; keeping

the fragile grace of the Thomas-
   of-Leighton Buzzard Westminster Abbey wrought-iron
                   vine,[4] or
rolls himself into a ball that has
   power to defy all effort to unroll it; strongly untailed, neat
head for core, on neck not breaking off, with curled-in feet.
   Nevertheless he has sting-proof scales; and nest
     of rocks closed with earth from inside, which he can
                 thus darken.
   Sun and moon and day and night and man and beast   30
     each with a splendor
       which man in all his vileness cannot
       set aside; each with an excellence!

"Fearful yet to be feared," the armored
   ant-eater met by the driver-ant does not turn back, but
engulfs what he can, the flattened sword-
   edged leafpoints on the tail and artichoke set leg- and
                   body-plates
   quivering violently when it retaliates
     and swarms on him. Compact like the furled fringed frill
       on the hat-brim of Gargallo's[5] hollow iron head of a   40
   matador, he will drop and will
     then walk away
       unhurt, although if unintruded on,
       he cautiously works down the tree, helped

by his tail. The giant-pangolin-
   tail, graceful tool, as prop or hand or broom or ax, tipped like
an elephant's trunk with special skin,
   is not lost on this ant- and stone-swallowing uninjurable
   artichoke which simpletons thought a living fable
     whom the stones had nourished, whereas ants had done   50
       so. Pangolins are not aggressive animals; between
     dusk and day they have the not unchain-like machine-like
       form and frictionless creep of a thing
       made graceful by adversities, con-

versities. To explain grace requires
   a curious hand. If that which is at all were not forever,

---

[3] "'Stepping . . . peculiarly,' See Lyddeker's *Royal Natural History*."—Moore's note.
[4] "Thomas of Leighton Buzzard's vine: a fragment of ironwork in Westminster Abbey."—Moore's note.
[5] Pablo Gargallo (1881–1934), Spanish sculptor.

why would those who graced the spires
with animals and gathered there to rest, on cold luxurious
low stone seats—a monk and monk and monk—between the
        thus   60
  ingenious roof supports, have slaved to confuse
  grace with a kindly manner, time in which to pay a
        debt
  the cure for sins, a graceful use
    of what are yet
      approved stone mullions[6] branching out across
    the perpendiculars? A sailboat
was the first machine.[7] Pangolins, made
  for moving quietly also, are models of exactness,
on four legs; on hind feet plantigrade,[8]
with certain postures of a man. Beneath sun and moon,
        man slaving
to make his life more sweet, leaves half the flowers worth
      having,   70
    needing to choose wisely how to use his strength;
    a paper-maker like the wasp; a tractor of foodstuffs,
like the ant; spidering a length
    of web from bluffs
      above a stream; in fighting, mechanicked
    like the pangolin; capsizing in

disheartenment. Bedizened or stark
  naked, man, the self, the being we call human, writing-
master to this world, griffons a dark
  "Like does not like like that is obnoxious"; and writes error
      with four   80
r's. Among animals, *one* has a sense of humor.
  Humor saves a few steps, it saves years. Unignorant,
  modest and unemotional, and all emotion,
  he has everlasting vigor,
    power to grow,
      though there are few creatures who can make one
    breathe faster and make one erecter.

Not afraid of anything is he,
  and then goes cowering forth, tread paced to meet an obstacle
at every step. Consistent with the   90
  formula—warm blood, no gills, two pairs of hands and a few
      hairs—that
  is a mammal; there he sits in his own habitat,
    serge-clad, strong-shod. The prey of fear, he, always
    curtailed, extinguished, thwarted by the dusk, work
        partly done,
    says to the alternating blaze,
    "Again the sun!

[6] A slender bar dividing the lights (or panes) of windows.
[7] "See F. L. Morse, *Power: Its Application from the 17th Dynasty to the 20th Century*."—Moore's note.
[8] Walking with heels and soles touching the ground, like a human.

anew each day; and new and new and new,
that comes into and steadies my soul."

1936

THE MIND IS AN ENCHANTING THING

is an enchanted thing
    like the glaze on a
katydid-wing
        subdivided by sun
        till the nettings are legion.
Like Gieseking playing Scarlatti;[1]

like the apteryx-awl[2]
    as a beak, or the
kiwi's rain shawl
        of haired feathers, the mind   10
        feeling its way as though blind,
walks along with its eyes on the ground.

It has memory's ear
    that can hear without
having to hear.
        Like the gyroscope's fall,
        truly unequivocal
because trued by regnant certainty,

it is a power of
    strong enchantment. It   20
is like the dove-
        neck animated by
        sun; it is memory's eye;
it's conscientious inconsistency.

It tears off the veil; tears
    the temptation, the
mist the heart wears,
        from its eyes—if the heart
        has a face; it takes apart
dejection. It's fire in the dove-neck's   30

iridescence; in the
    inconsistencies

[1]Walter Gieseking (1895–1956), German pianist: Alessandro Scarlatti (1659–1725), Italian composer.
[2]A flightless bird with a long bill like an awl and hairlike plumage, a kiwi.

of Scarlatti.
>   Unconfusion submits
>   its confusion to proof; it's
>   not a Herod's oath[3] that cannot change.

>   1943, 1944

APPARITION OF SPLENDOR

Partaking of the miraculous
>   since never known literally,
Dürer's rhinoceros[1]
>   might have startled us equally
>   if black-and-white-spined elaborately.

Like another porcupine, or fern,
>   the mouth in an arching egret
was too black to discern
>   till exposed as a silhouette;
>   but the double-embattled thistle of jet—   10

disadvantageous supposedly—
>   has never shot a quill. Was it
some joyous fantasy,
>   plain eider-eared exhibit
>   of spines rooted in the sooty moss,

or "train supported by porcupines—
>   a fairy's eleven yards long"?[2] . . .
as when the lightning shines
>   on thistlefine spears, among
>   prongs in lanes above lanes of a shorter prong,   20

"with the forest for nurse,"[3] also dark
>   at the base—where needle-debris
springs and shows no footmark;
>   the setting for a symmetry
>   you must not touch unless you are a fairy.

Maine should be pleased that its animal
>   is not a waverer, and rather
than fight, lets the primed quill fall.
>   Shallow oppressor, intruder,
>   insister, you have found a resister.   30

>   1952, 1956

[3]King Herod, delighted with Salome's dance, swore to grant her any reward. When she asked for the head of John the Baptist, Herod, out of regard for his oath, had John beheaded. Matthew 14:3–11.
[1]A reference to Albrecht Dürer's famous woodcut of a rhinoceros.
[2]"Oliver Goldsmith in one of his essays refers to a 'blue fairy with a train eleven yards long, supported by porcupines.' "—Moore's note.
[3]" 'All over spines, with the forest for nurse.' 'The Hedgehog, the Fox, and the Flies,' Book Twelve, Fable XIII, *The Fables of La Fontaine*. . . . "—Moore's note.

Countée Cullen   *1903–1946*

He was born Countée Porter and raised in Baltimore and in New York City. When he was fifteen he was adopted by the Reverend Frederick Cullen, a Methodist minister in Harlem, who took his foster son on a tour of the Holy Land and to the literary shrines of Europe and strongly encouraged his academic interests. Cullen went to New York University, where he was elected to Phi Beta Kappa and won awards for his poetry. In 1925, Color, *his first book of poems, was published. By the time he was twenty-six, he had published three more volumes:* Copper Sun *(1927),* The Ballad of the Brown Girl *(1927), and* The Black Christ *(1929). He wrote a Harlem novel,* One Way to Heaven *(1932), translated Euripides's* Medea *(1935), and served as an editor for two important Negro magazines of the day:* Opportunity, Journal of Negro Life, *and* The Crisis, *an official periodical of the NAACP. But after his early, prolific years, Cullen's productivity declined, and he supported himself mainly by teaching French in the New York public schools, although he continued to write verse and in 1946 collaborated in writing a Broadway musical,* St. Louis Woman. *In 1947 his collected poems were published posthumously under the title* On These I Stand.*

Cullen, a conscientious, dedicated craftsman, was one of the most notable writers of the Harlem Renaissance, a period of remarkable literary achievement by black writers in New York City during the 1920s. Cullen's techniques were conventional; his models were the romantic poets, not black poets, and he often insisted that his poems in particular and poetry in general should be free from political or racial matters. At other times he could not escape the fact of his race. His finest poem, "Heritage," is an assertion of the black American's relationship with Africa, and he came to acknowledge that "in spite of myself, I find that I am actuated by a strong sense of race consciousness. This grows upon me." Cullen was caught between his conflicting allegiances to his art, his country, and his race, but, like other black writers after him, he managed to create a body of memorable writing out of disparate loyalties and ideologies and out of his struggles in a world that made "a poet black, and bid him sing."

FURTHER READING: B. Ferguson, *Countée Cullen and the Negro Renaissance*, 1966; M. Perry, *A Bio-Biography of Countée Cullen, 1903–1946*, 1971; A. Shucard, *Countee Cullen*, 1984.

TEXTS: *On These I Stand*, 1947.

YET DO I MARVEL

I doubt not God is good, well-meaning, kind,
And did He stoop to quibble could tell why
The little buried mole continues blind,
Why flesh that mirrors Him must some day die,
Make plain the reason tortured Tantalus[1]
Is baited by the fickle fruit, declare
If merely brute caprice dooms Sisyphus[2]

---

[1]In Greek myth, Tantalus, for his defiance of the gods, was condemned forever to stand, "tantalized," with food and drink just beyond his grasp.
[2]A crafty deceiver in Greek myth who was condemned eternally to push a huge stone up the slope of a hill.

To struggle up a never-ending stair.
Inscrutable His ways are, and immune
To catechism by a mind too strewn   10
With petty cares to slightly understand
What awful brain compels His awful hand.
Yet do I marvel at this curious thing:
To make a poet black, and bid him sing!

                                                        1924, 1925

A SONG OF PRAISE

(For one who praised his lady's being fair.)

You have not heard my love's dark throat,
    Slow-fluting like a reed,
Release the perfect golden note
    She caged there for my need.

Her walk is like the replica
    Of some barbaric dance
Wherein the soul of Africa
    Is winged with arrogance.

And yet so light she steps across
    The ways her sure feet pass,   10
She does not dent the smoothest moss
    Or bend the thinnest grass.

My love is dark as yours is fair,
    Yet lovelier I hold her
Than listless maids with pallid hair,
    And blood that's thin and colder.

You-proud-and-to-be-pitied one,
    Gaze on her and despair;
Then seal your lips until the sun
    Discovers one as fair.   20

                                                        1924, 1925

FOR A LADY I KNOW

She even thinks that up in heaven
    Her class lies late and snores,
While poor black cherubs rise at seven
    To do celestial chores.

                                                        1924, 1925

INCIDENT

(For Eric Walrond)

Once riding in old Baltimore,
     Heart-filled, head-filled with glee,
I saw a Baltimorean
     Keep looking straight at me.

Now I was eight and very small,
     And he was no whit bigger,
And so I smiled, but he poked out
     His tongue, and called me, "Nigger."

I saw the whole of Baltimore
     From May until December;
Of all the things the happened there
     That's all that I remember.
                         1924, 1924

FROM THE DARK TOWER

(To Charles S. Johnson)

We shall not always plant while others reap
The golden increment of bursting fruit,
Not always countenance, abject and mute,
That lesser men should hold their brothers cheap;
Not everlastingly while others sleep
Shall we beguile their limbs with mellow flute,
Not always bend to some more subtle brute;
We were not made eternally to weep.

The night whose sable breast relieves the stark
White stars is no less lovely being dark   10
And there are buds that cannot bloom at all
In light, but crumple, piteous, and fall;
So in the dark we hide the heart that bleeds,
And wait, and tend our agonizing seeds.
                         1924, 1927

A BROWN GIRL DEAD

With two white roses on her breasts,
     White candles at head and feet,
Dark Madonna of the grave she rests;
     Lord Death has found her sweet.

Her mother pawned her wedding ring
  To lay her out in white;
She'd be so proud she'd dance and sing
  To see herself tonight.

                                                1925

HERITAGE

(For Harold Jackman)

What is Africa to me:
Copper sun or scarlet sea,
Jungle star or jungle track,
Strong bronzed me, or regal black
Women from whose loins I sprang
When the birds of Eden sang?
One three centuries removed
From the scenes his fathers loved,
Spicy grove, cinnamon tree,
What is Africa to me?   10

So I lie, who all day long
Want no sound except the song
Sung by wild barbaric birds
Goading massive jungle herds,
Juggernauts of flesh that pass
Trampling tall defiant grass
Where young forest lovers lie,
Plighting troth beneath the sky.
So I lie, who always hear,
Though I cram against my ear   20
Both my thumbs, and keep them there,
Great drums throbbing through the
    air.
So I die, whose fount of pride,
Dear distress, and joy allied,
Is my somber flesh and skin,
With the dark blood dammed within
Like great pulsing tides of wine
That, I fear, must burst the fine
Channels of the chafing net
Where they surge and foam and fret.   30

Africa? A book one thumbs
Listlessly, till slumber comes.
Unremembered are her bats
Circling through the night, her cats

Crouching in the river reeds,
Stalking gentle flesh that feeds
By the river brink; no more
Does the bugle-throated roar
Cry that monarch claws have leapt
From the scabbards where they slept.   40
Silver snakes that once a year
Doff the lovely coats you wear,
Seek no covert in your fear
Lest a mortal eye should see;
What's your nakedness to me?
Here no leprous flowers rear
Fierce corollas[1] in the air;
Here no bodies sleek and wet,
Dripping mingled rain and sweat,
Tread the savage measures of
Jungle boys and girls in love.   50
What is last year's snow to me,
Last year's anything? The tree
Budding yearly must forget
How its past arose or set—
Bough and blossom, flower, fruit,
Even what shy bird with mute
Wonder at her travail there,
Meekly labored in its hair.
One three centuries removed   60
From the scenes his fathers loved,
Spicy grove, cinnamon tree,
What is Africa to me?

So I lie, who finds no peace
Night or day, no slight release
From the unremittant beat
Made by cruel padded feet
Walking through my body's street.
Up and down they go, and back,
Treading out a jungle track.   70
So I lie, who never quite
Safely sleep from rain at night—
I can never rest at all
When the rain begins to fall;
Like a soul gone mad with pain
I must match its weird refrain;
Ever must I twist and squirm,
Writhing like a baited worm,
While its primal measures drip
Through my body, crying, "Strip!   80
Doff this new exuberance.
Come and dance the Lover's Dance!"
In an old remembered way
Rain works on me night and day.

[1]Petals.

Quaint, outlandish heathen gods
Black men fashion out of rods,
Clay, and brittle bits of stone,
In a likeness like their own
My conversion came high-priced;
I belong to Jesus Christ,   90
Preacher of humility;
Heathen gods are naught to me.

Father, Son, and Holy Ghost,
So I make an idle boast;
Jesus of the twice-turned cheek,[2]
Lamb of God, although I speak
With my mouth thus, in my heart
Do I play a double part.
Ever at Thy glowing altar
Must my heart grow sick and falter,   110
Wishing He I served were black,
Thinking then it would not lack
Precedent of pain to guide it,
Let who would or might deride it;
Surely then this flesh would know
Yours had borne a kindred woe.
Lord, I fashion dark gods, too,
Daring even to give You
Dark despairing features where,
Crowned with dark rebellious hair,   110
Patience wavers just so much as
Mortal grief compels, while touches
Quick and hot, of anger, rise
To smitten cheek and weary eyes.
Lord, forgive me if my need
Sometimes shapes all human creed.
All day long and all night through,
One thing only must I do:
Quench my pride and cool my blood,
Lest I perish in the flood.   120
Lest a hidden ember set
Timber that I thought was wet
Burning like the dryest flax,
Melting like the merest wax,
Lest the grave restore its dead.
Not yet has my heart or head
In the least way realized
They and I are civilized.

                                      1925

---

[2]". . . whosoever shall smite thee on thy right cheek, turn to him the other also." Matthew 5:39.

SCOTTSBORO[1], TOO, IS WORTH ITS SONG

(A poem to American poets)

I said:
Now will the poets sing,—
Their cries go thundering
Like blood and tears
Into the nation's ears,
Like lightning dart
Into the nation's heart.
Against disease and death and all things fell,
And war,
Their strophes rise and swell   10
To jar
The foe smug in his citadel.

Remembering their sharp and pretty
Tunes for Sacco and Vanzetti,[2]
I said:
Here too's a cause divinely spun
For those whose eyes are on the sun,
Here in epitome
Is all disgrace
And epic wrong,
Like wine to brace
The minstrel heart, and blare it into song.

Surely, I said,
Now will the poets sing.
But they have raised no cry.
I wonder why.

1934, 1940

John Crowe Ransom   *1888–1974*

A first-rate poet himself, John Crowe Ransom was also an eminent teacher of poets and poetry and a leader in two of the most influential critical movements of the twentieth century. A native of Tennessee, Ransom received his undergraduate degree from

[1]In 1931, nine black youths were indicted at Scottsboro, Alabama, for the rape of two white girls. The procedures followed at the subsequent trials and the dubious testimony of the accusers provoked numerous protests by those who believed the defendants were innocent victims of antiblack bigotry.

[2]In 1920, Nicola Sacco and Bartolomeo Vanzetti were arrested in Massachusetts for robbery and murder. Their case stirred worldwide demonstrations by those supporters who charged that their arrest, conviction, and subsequent execution (1927) occurred only because the two men were foreigners and had unpopular, radical political views.

Vanderbilt University in 1909. After studying in England as a Rhodes Scholar at Oxford University, he returned to Vanderbilt, where he joined the English Department in 1914 and became a founder of "The Fugitive" group (named after the periodical The Fugitive, *which he edited). Along with Allen Tate, Robert Penn Warren, and others, Ransom argued against the dominance of modern industrialism, science, and urbanism and stood for the virtues of the agrarian life, tradition, and literature. Ransom contributed key essays to the two volumes which present the group's ideas,* I'll Take My Stand *(1930) and* Who Owns America? *(1936).*

In 1937 Ransom left Vanderbilt to become professor of Poetry at Kenyon College in Ohio. At Kenyon he founded another important literary magazine, The Kenyon Review, *and became a leading exponent of the "New Criticism," which advocated the close study of literary texts isolated as much as possible from social, historical, and biographical considerations. Collections of Ransom's essays include* God without Thunder *(1930), which attacks modern secularism;* The World's Body *(1938), in which he asserts the superiority of literature over science; and* The New Criticism *(1941), which contains his major statements about literary criticism.*

Most of Ransom's verse was written in the 1920s. The majority of it appeared in three volumes: Poems about God *(1919);* Chills and Fever *(1924);* Two Gentlemen in Bonds *(1927). His poetry reveals many of the same characteristics as his criticism. To Ransom, poetry, like religion, shows man his true limitations and thus leads to humility and self-knowledge, while science leads men to pride and arrogant power. Ransom's recurring themes are traditional and classic: love, death, and mutability. His poetry is tightly constructed, his versification is formal, and his diction is frequently archaic. Ransom's most notable quality is his irony, which often portrays the dualism of humans attracted to opposites: childhood and age, science and faith, platonic and carnal love, mind and body. The result is unsentimental, verbally precise poetry whose quality far exceeds its quantity.*

FURTHER READING: *Selected Essays of John Crowe Ransom,* ed. T. Young and J. Hindle, 1984; *Selected Letters of John Crowe Ransom,* ed. G. Core and T. Young, 1985; J. Stewart, *John Crowe Ransom,* 1962; T. Young, *Gentleman in a Dustcoat, A Biography of John Crowe Ransom,* 1977; K. Knight, *The Poetry of John Crowe Ransom,* 1964; R. Buffington, *The Equilibrist, A Study of John Crowe Ransom's Poems, 1916–1963,* 1967; *John Crowe Ransom, Essays and a Bibliography,* ed. T. Young, 1968; T. Parsons, *John Crowe Ransom,* 1969; J. Magner, *John Crowe Ransom, Critical Principles and Preoccupations,* 1971; T. Young, *John Crowe Ransom,* 1971; M. Williams, *The Poetry of John Crowe Ransom,* 1972.

TEXT: *Selected Poems,* 1963.

HERE LIES A LADY

Here lies a lady of beauty and high degree.
Of chills and fever she died, of fever and chills,
The delight of her husband, her aunt, an infant of three,
And of medicos marveling sweetly on her ills.

For either she burned, and her confident eyes would blaze,
And her fingers fly in a manner to puzzle their heads—
What was she making? Why, nothing; she sat in a maze
Of old scraps of laces, snipped into curious shreds—

Or this would pass, and the light of her fire decline

Till she lay discouraged and cold, like a thin stalk white
    and blown,   10
And would not open her eyes, to kisses, to wine;
The sixth of these states was her last; the cold settled down.

Sweet ladies, long may ye bloom, and toughly I hope
    ye may thole,[1]
But was she not lucky? In flowers and lace and mourning,
In love and great honor we bade God rest her soul
After six little spaces of chill, and six of burning.

                            1923

BELLS FOR JOHN WHITESIDE'S DAUGHTER

There was such speed in her little body,
And such lightness in her footfall,
It is no wonder her brown study[1]
Astonishes us all.

Her wars were bruited[2] in our high window.
We looked among orchard trees and beyond
Where she took arms against her shadow,
Or harried unto the pond

The lazy geese, like a snow cloud
Dripping their snow on the green grass,   10
Tricking and stopping, sleepy and proud,
Who cried in goose, Alas,

For the tireless heart within the little
Lady with rod that made them rise
From their noon apple-dreams and scuttle
Goose-fashion under the skies!

But now go the bells, and we are ready,
In one house we are sternly stopped
To say we are vexed at her brown study,
Lying so primly propped.   20

CAPTAIN CARPENTER

Captain Carpenter rose up in his prime
Put on his pistols and went riding out
But he got wellnigh nowhere at that time

[1]Endure.
[1]Somber meditation.   [2]Reported.

Till he fell in with ladies in a rout.[1]

It was a pretty lady and all her train[2]
That played with him so sweetly but before
An hour she'd taken a sword with all her main
And twined[3] him of his nose for evermore.

Captain Carpenter mounted up one day
And rode straightway into a stranger rogue   10
That looked unchristian but be that as may
The Captain did not wait upon prologue.

But drew upon him out of his great heart
The other swung against him with a club
And cracked his two legs at the shinny part
And let him roll and stick like any tub.

Captain Carpenter rode many a time
From male and female took he sundry harms
He met the wife of Satan crying "I'm
The she-wolf bids you shall bear no more arms."   20

Their strokes and counters whistled in the wind
I wish he had delivered half his blows
But where she should have made off like a hind
The bitch bit off his arms at the elbows.

And Captain Carpenter parted with his ears
To a black devil that used him in this wise
O Jesus ere his threescore and ten years
Another had plucked out his sweet blue eyes.

Captain Carpenter got up on his roan
And sallied from the gate in hell's despite   30
I heard him asking in the grimmest tone
If any enemy yet there was to fight?

"To any adversary it is fame
If he risk to be wounded by my tongue
Or burnt in two beneath my red heart's flame
Such are the perils he is cast among.

"But if he can he has a pretty choice
From an anatomy with little to lose
Whether he cut my tongue and take my voice
Or whether it be my round red heart he choose."   40

It was the neatest knave that ever was seen
Stepping in perfume from his lady's bower
Who at this word put in his merry mien
And fell on Captain Carpenter like a tower.

[1]A fashionable assembly, or party.   [2]Followers, attendants.
[3]Severed, deprived.

I would not knock old fellows in the dust
But there lay Captain Carpenter on his back
His weapons were the old heart in his bust
And a blade shook between rotten teeth alack.

The rogue in scarlet and grey soon knew his mind   50
He wished to get his trophy and depart
With gentle apology and touch refined
He pierced him and produced the Captain's heart.

God's mercy rest on Captain Carpenter now
I thought him Sirs an honest gentleman
Citizen husband soldier and scholar enow[4]
Let jangling kites[5] eat of him if they can.

But God's deep curses follow after those
That shore him of his goodly nose and ears
His legs and strong arms at the two elbows
And eyes that had not watered seventy years.   60

The curse of hell upon the sleek upstart
That got the Captain finally on his back
And took the red red vitals of his heart
And made the kites to whet their beaks clack
    clack.

                                                    1924

BLUE GIRLS

Twirling your blue skirts, travelling the sward
Under the towers of your seminary,
Go listen to your teachers old and contrary
Without believing a word.

Tie the white fillets then about your hair
And think no more of what will come to pass
Than bluebirds that go walking on the grass
And chattering on the air.

Practise your beauty, blue girls, before it fail;
And I will cry with my loud lips and publish   10
Beauty which all our power shall never establish,
It is so frail.

For I could tell you a story which is true;
I know a lady with a terrible tongue,
Blear eyes fallen from blue,
All her perfections tarnished—yet it is not long
Since she was lovelier than any of you.

                                                    1924

[4]Enough.   [5]Predatory birds.

PIAZZA PIECE

—I am a gentleman in a dustcoat trying
To make you hear. Your ears are soft and small
And listen to an old man not at all,
They want the young men's whispering and sighing.
But see the roses on your trellis dying
And hear the spectral singing of the moon;
For I must have my lovely lady soon,
I am a gentleman in a dustcoat trying.

—I am a lady young in beauty waiting
Until my truelove comes, and then we kiss.   10
But what grey man among the vines is this
Whose words are dry and faint as in a dream?
Back from my trellis, Sir, Before I scream!
I am a lady young in beauty waiting.

                                                     1925

THE EQUILIBRISTS[1]

Full of her long white arms and milky skin
He had a thousand times remembered sin.
Alone in the press of people traveled he,
Minding her jacinth, and myrrh, and ivory.

Mouth he remembered: the quaint orifice
From which came heat that flamed upon the kiss,
Till cold words came down spiral from the head.
Grey doves from the officious tower illsped.

Body: it was a white field ready for love,
On her body's field, with the gaunt tower above,   10
The lilies grew, beseeching him to take,
If he would pluck and wear them, bruise and break.

Eyes talking: Never mind the cruel words,
Embrace my flowers, but not embrace the swords.
But what they said, the doves came straightway flying
And unsaid: Honor, Honor, they came crying.

Importunate her doves. Too pure, too wise,
Clambering on his shoulder, saying, Arise,
Leave me now, and never let us meet,
Eternal distance now command thy feet.   20

[1]Those who balance themselves, such as acrobats or tightrope performers.

Predicament indeed, which thus discovers
Honor among thieves, Honor between lovers.
O such a little word is Honor, they feel!
But the grey word is between them cold as steel.

At length I saw these lovers fully were come
Into their torture of equilibrium;
Dreadfully had forsworn each other, and yet
They were bound each to each, and they did not forget.

And rigid as two painful stars, and twirled
About the clustered night their prison world,   30
They burned with fierce love always to come near,
But honor beat them back and kept them clear.

Ah, the strict lovers, they are ruined now!
I cried in anger. But with puddled brow
Devising for those gibbeted and brave
Came I descanting: Man, what would you have?

For spin your period out, and draw your breath,
A kinder saeculum[2] begins with Death.
Would you ascend to Heaven and bodiless dwell?
Or take your bodies honorless to Hell?   40

In Heaven you have heard no marriage is,[3]
No white flesh tinder to your lecheries,
Your male and female tissue sweetly shaped
Sublimed away, and furious blood escaped.

Great lovers lie in Hell, the stubborn ones
Infatuate of the flesh upon the bones;
Stuprate,[4] they rend each other when they kiss,
The pieces kiss again, no end to this.

But still I watched them spinning, orbited nice.
Their flames were not more radiant than their ice.   50
I dug in the quiet earth and wrought the tomb.
And made these lines to memorize their doom:—

EPITAPH

Equilibrists lie here; stranger, tread light;
Close, but untouching in each other's sight;
Mouldered the lips and ashy the tall skull.
Let them lie perilous and beautiful.

1925

[2]Latin: age, period of time.
[3]Jesus explained that in heaven, the blessed "neither marry, nor are given in marriage." Matthew 22:30.
[4]Latin: defiled.

Jean Toomer *1894–1967*

From beginning to end, Jean Toomer's life vacillated between the white and black worlds. His father deserted his family after a year of marriage, and Toomer grew up unhappily in the home of his maternal grandfather, who had once been Acting Governor of Louisiana during the Reconstruction period after the Civil War. Following high school, Toomer restlessly shifted from one city and from one college to another. He studied agriculture at the University of Wisconsin and in Massachusetts; he entered a physical training program in Chicago; he studied sociology and history at colleges in New York City, sold cars in Chicago, taught physical education in Milwaukee, worked in a shipyard in New Jersey.

After several years of wandering, Toomer returned to his grandfather's home in Washington, D.C. There he began to write and quickly succeeded, placing poems in several avant-garde magazines. In 1921, still restless, he went to Georgia, as superintendent of a rural black school. Although he was there but four months, his stay deeply influenced him, and provided him with the material for his novel Cane *(1923).*

The book, with its mixture of poems, quasi-dramas, and short fiction, was widely acclaimed as a notable contribution to the experimental fiction of the time and as a major work in the history of black literature. Toomer became one of the leaders, along with Langston Hughes and Countée Cullen, of the Harlem Literary Renaissance of the 1920s. Following the publication of Cane, *Toomer went to France, and there he fell under the influence of Georges Gurdjieff, a Russian philosopher whose mystical system, "Unitism," helped turn Toomer away from the world of daily experience and into a private world of introspection. For a time Toomer continued to write, but his work became increasingly abstract, and he published little. In his last years he became a Quaker and lectured occasionally at Quaker meetings. By the end of his life he had retreated almost completely into literary obscurity, yet in* Cane *he had created a literary monument, a testament to his perception of the uprooted lives of black men and women living in white America.*

FURTHER READING: *The Wayward and the Seeking, A Collection of the Writings of Jean Toomer,* ed. D. Turner, 1981; *The Collected Poems of Jean Toomer,* eds. R. Jones and M. Latimer, 1988; *Anger and Beyond, The Negro Writer in the United States,* ed. H. Hill, 1966; *Studies in Cane,* ed. F. Durham, 1971; B. Benson and M. Dillard, *Jean Toomer,* 1980; N. McKay, *Jean Toomer, A Study of His Literary Life and Work,* 1984.

TEXT: *Cane,* 1923.

BLOOD-BURNING MOON

I

Up from the skeleton stone walls, up from the rotting floor boards and the solid hand-hewn beams of oak of the pre-war cotton factory, dusk came. Up from the dusk the full moon came. Glowing like a fired pine-knot, it illumined the great door and soft showered the Negro shanties aligned along the single street of factory town. The full moon in the great door was an omen. Negro women improvised songs against its spell.

Louisa sang as she came over the crest of the hill from the white folks' kitchen. Her skin was the color of oak leaves on young trees in fall. Her breasts, firm and up-pointed like ripe acorns. And her singing had the low murmur of winds in fig trees. Bob Stone, younger son of the people she worked for, loved her.

By the way the world reckons things, he had won her. By measure of that warm glow which came into her mind at thought of him, he had won her. Tom Burwell, whom the whole town called Big Boy, also loved her. But working in the fields all day, and far away from her, gave him no chance to show it. Though often enough of evenings he had tried to. Somehow, he never got along. Strong as he was with hands upon the ax or plow, he found it difficult to hold her. Or so he thought. But the fact was that he held her to factory town more firmly than he thought for. His black balanced, and pulled against, the white of Stone, when he thought of them. And her mind was vaguely upon them as she came over the crest of the hill, coming from the white folks' kitchen. As she sang softly at the evil face of the full moon.

A strange stir was in her. Indolently, she tried to fix upon Bob or Tom as the cause of it. To meet Bob in the canebrake, as she was going to do an hour or so later, was nothing new. And Tom's proposal which she felt on its way to her could be indefinitely put off. Separately, there was no unusual significance to either one. But for some reason, they jumbled when her eyes gazed vacantly at the rising moon. And from the jumble came the stir that was strangely within her. Her lips trembled. The slow rhythm of her song grew agitant and restless. Rusty black and tan spotted hounds, lying in the dark corners of porches or prowling around back yards, put their noses in the air and caught its tremor. They began plaintively to yelp and howl. Chickens woke up and cackled. Intermittently, all over the countryside dogs barked and roosters crowed as if heralding a weird dawn or some ungodly awakening. The women sang lustily. Their songs were cotton-wads to stop their ears. Louisa came down into factory town and sank wearily upon the step before her home. The moon was rising towards a thick cloud-bank which soon would hide it.

> Red nigger moon. Sinner!
> Blood-burning moon. Sinner!
> Come out that fact'ry door.

II

Up from the deep dusk of a cleared spot on the edge of the forest a mellow glow arose and spread fan-wise into the low-hanging heavens. And all around the air was heavy with the scent of boiling cane. A large pile of cane-stalks lay like ribboned shadows upon the ground. A mule, harnessed to a pole, trudged lazily round and round the pivot of the grinder. Beneath a swaying oil lamp, a Negro alternately whipped out at the mule, and fed cane-stalks to the grinder. A fat boy waddled pails of fresh ground juice between the grinder and the boiling stove. Steam came from the copper boiling pan. The scent of cane came from the copper pan and drenched the forest and the hill that sloped to factory town, beneath its fragrance. It drenched the men in circle seated around the stove. Some of them chewed at the white pulp of stalks, but there was no need for them to, if all they wanted was to taste the cane. One tasted it in factory town. And from factory town one could see the soft haze thrown by the glowing stove upon the low-hanging heavens.

Old David Georgia stirred the thickening syrup with a long ladle, and every so often drew it off. Old David Georgia tended his stove and told tales about the white folk, about moonshining and cotton picking, and about sweet nigger gals, to the men who sat there about his stove to listen to him. Tom Burwell chewed cane-stalk and laughed with the others till someone mentioned Louisa. Till some one said something about Louisa and Bob Stone, about the silk stockings she must have gotten from him. Blood ran up Tom's neck hotter than the glow that flooded from the stove. He sprang up. Glared at the men and said, "She's my gal." Will Manning laughed. Tom strode over to him. Yanked him up and knocked him to the ground. Several of Manning's friends got up to fight for him. Tom whipped out a long knife and would have cut them to shreds if they hadnt ducked into the woods. Tom had had enough. He nodded to Old David Georgia and swung down the path to factory town. Just then, the dogs started barking and the roosters began to crow. Tom felt funny. Away from the fight, away from the stove, chill got to him. He shivered. He shuddered when he saw the full moon rising towards the cloud-bank. He who didnt give a godam for the fears of old women. He forced his mind to fasten on Louisa. Bob Stone. Better not be. He turned into the street and saw Louisa sitting before her home. He went towards her, ambling, touched the brim of a marvelously shaped, spotted, felt hat, said he wanted to say something to her, and then found that he didnt know what he had to say, or if he did, that he couldnt say it. He shoved his big fists in his overalls, grinned, and started to move off.

"Youall want me, Tom?"

"Thats what us wants, sho, Louisa."

"Well, here I am—"

"An here I is, but that aint ahelpin none, all th same."

"You wanted to say something? . . ."

"I did that, sho. But words is like th spots on dice: no matter how y fumbles em, there's times when they jes wont come. I dunno why. Seems like th love I feels fo yo done stole m tongue. I got it now. Whee! Louisa, honey, I oughtnt tell y, I feel I oughtnt cause yo is young and goes t church an I has had other gals, but Louisa I sho do love y. Lil gal, Ise watched y from them first days when youall sat right here befo yo door befo th well an sang sometimes in a way that like t broke m heart. Ise carried y with me into th fields, day after day, an after that, an I sho can plow when yo is there, an I can pick cotton. Yassur! Come near beatin Barlo yesterday. I sho did. Yassur! An next year if old Stone'll trust me, I'll have a farm. My own. My bales will buy you what y gets from white folks now. Silk stockings an purple dresses—course I dont believe what some folks been whisperin as t how y gets them things now. White folks always did do for niggers what they likes. An they jes cant help alikin yo, Louisa. Bob Stone likes y. Course he does. But not th way folks is awhisperin. Does he, hon?"

"I dont know what you mean, Tom"

"Course y dont. Ise already cut two niggers. Had t hon, t tell em so. Niggers always tryin t make somethin out a nothin. And then besides, white folks aint up t them tricks so much nowadays. Godam better not be. Leastawise not with yo. Cause I wouldn't stand f it. Nassur."

"What would you do, Tom?"

"Cut him jes like I cut a nigger."

"No, Tom—"

"I said I would an there aint no mo to it. But that aint th talk f now. Sing, honey Louisa, an while I'm listenin t y I'll be makin love."

Tom took her hand in his. Against the tough thickness of his own, hers felt soft and small. His huge body slipped down to the step beside her. The full moon sank upward into the deep purple of the cloud-bank. An old woman brought a lighted lamp and hung it on the common well whose bulky shadow squatted in the middle of the road, opposite Tom and Louisa. The old woman lifted the well-lid, took hold the chain, and began drawing up the heavy bucket. As she did so, she sang. Figures shifted, restless-like, between lamp and window in the front rooms of the shanties. Shadows of the figures fought each other on the gray dust of the road. Figures raised the windows and joined the old woman in song. Louisa and Tom, the whole street, singing:

> Red nigger moon. Sinner!
> Blood-burning moon. Sinner!
> Come out that fact'ry door.

III

Bob Stone sauntered from his veranda out into the gloom of fir trees and magnolias. The clear white of his skin paled, and the flush of his cheeks turned purple. As if to balance this outer change, his mind became consciously a white man's. He passed the house with its huge open hearth which, in the days of slavery, was the plantation cookery. He saw Louisa bent over that hearth. He went in as a master should and took her. Direct, honest, bold. None of this sneaking that he had to go through now. The contrast was repulsive to him. His family had lost ground. Hell no, his family still owned the niggers, practically. Damned if they did, or he wouldnt have to duck around so. What would they think if they knew? His mother? His sister? He shouldnt mention them, shouldnt think of them in this connection. There in the dusk he blushed at doing so. Fellows about town were all right, but how about his friends up North? He could see them incredible, repulsed. They didnt know. The thought first made him laugh. Then, with their eyes still upon him, he began to feel embarrassed. He felt the need of explaining things to them. Explain hell. They wouldnt understand, and moreover, who ever heard of a Southerner getting on his knees to any Yankee, or anyone. No sir. He was going to see Louisa to-night, and love her. She was lovely—in her way. Nigger way. What way was that? Damned if he knew. Must know. He'd known her long enough to know. Was there something about niggers that you couldnt know? Listening to them at church didnt tell you anything. Looking at them didnt tell you anything. Talking to them didnt tell you anything—unless it was gossip, unless they wanted to talk. Of course, about farming, and licker, and craps—but those werent nigger. Nigger was something more. How much more? Something to be afraid of, more? Hell no. Who ever heard of being afraid of a nigger? Tom Burwell. Cartwell had told him that Tom went with Louisa after she reached home. No sir. No nigger had ever been with his girl. He'd like to see one try. Some position for him to be in. Him, Bob Stone, of the old Stone family, in a scrap with a nigger over a nigger girl. In the good old days . . . Ha! Those were the days. His family had lost ground. Not so much, though. Enough for him to have cut through old Lemon's canefield by way of the woods, that he might meet her. She was worth it. Beautiful nigger gal. Why nigger? Why not, just gal? No, it was because she was a nigger that he went to her. Sweet. . . The scent of boiling cane came to him. Then he saw the rich glow of the stove. He heard the voices of the men circled around it. He was about to skirt the clearing when he heard his own name mentioned. He stopped. Quivering. Leaning against a tree, he listened.

"Bad nigger. Yassur, he sho is one bad nigger when he gets started."

"Tom Burwell's been on th gang[1] three times fo cuttin men."

---

[1] I.e., sentenced to a prison chain gang.

"What y think he's agwine t do t Bob Stone?"

"Dunno yet. He aint found out. When he does—Baby!"

"Aint no tellin."

"Young Stone aint no quitter an I ken tell y that. Blood of th old uns in his veins."

"Thats right. He'll scrap, sho."

"Be gettin too hot f niggers round this away."

"Shut up, nigger. Y dont know what y talkin bout."

Bob Stone's ears burned as though he had been holding them over the stove. Sizzling heat welled up within him. His feet felt as if they rested on red-hot coals. They stung him to quick movement. He circled the fringe of the glowing. Not a twig cracked beneath his feet. He reached the path that led to factory town. Plunged furiously down it. Halfway along, a blindness within him veered him aside. He crashed into the bordering canebrake. Cane leaves cut his face and lips. He tasted blood. He threw himself down and dug his fingers in the ground. The earth was cool. Cane-roots took the fever from his hands. After a long while, or so it seemed to him, the thought came to him that it must be time to see Louisa. He got to his feet and walked calmly to their meeting place. No Louisa. Tom Burwell had her. Veins in his forehead bulged and distended. Saliva moistened the dried blood on his lips. He bit down on his lips. He tasted blood. Not his own blood; Tom Burwell's blood. Bob drove through the cane and out again upon the road. A hound swung down the path before him towards factory town. Bob couldnt see it. The dog loped aside to let him pass. Bob's blind rushing made him stumble over it. He fell with a thud that dazed him. The hound yelped. Answering yelps came from all over the countryside. Chickens cackled. Roosters crowed, heralding the bloodshot eyes of southern awakening. Singers in the town were silenced. They shut their windows down. Palpitant between the rooster crows, a chill hush settled upon the huddled forms of Tom and Louisa. A figure rushed from the shadow and stood before them. Tom popped to his feet.

"Whats y want?"

"I'm Bob Stone."

"Yassur—an I'm Tom Burwell. Whats y want?"

Bob lunged at him. Tom side-stepped, caught him by the shoulder, and flung him to the ground. Straddled him.

"Let me up."

"Yassur—but watch yo doins, Bob Stone."

A few dark figures, drawn by the sound of scuffle, stood about them. Bob sprang to his feet.

"Fight like a man, Tom Burwell, an I'll lick y."

Again he lunged. Tom side-stepped and flung him to the ground. Straddled him.

"Get off me, you godam nigger you."

"Yo sho has started somethin now. Get up."

Tom yanked him up and began hammering at him. Each blow sounded as if it smashed into a precious, irreplaceable soft something. Beneath them, Bob staggered back. He reached in his pocket and whipped out a knife.

"Thats my game, sho."

Blue flash, a steel blade slashed across Bob Stone's throat. He had a sweetish sick feeling. Blood began to flow. Then he felt a sharp twitch of pain. He let his knife drop. He slapped one hand against his neck. He pressed the other on top of his head as if to hold it down. He groaned. He turned, and staggered towards the crest of the hill in the direction of white town. Negroes who had seen the fight slunk into their homes and blew the lamps out. Louisa, dazed, hysterical, refused to go indoors. She slipped, crumbled, her body loosely propped against the woodwork of the well. Tom Burwell leaned against it. He seemed rooted there.

Bob reached Broad Street. White men rushed up to him. He collapsed in their arms.

"Tom Burwell. . . ."

White men like ants upon a forage rushed about. Except for the taut hum of their moving, all was silent. Shotguns, revolvers, rope, kerosene, torches. Two high-powered cars with glaring search-lights. They came together. The taut hum rose to a low roar. Then nothing could be heard but the flop of their feet in the thick dust of the road. The moving body of their silence preceded over the crest of the hill into factory town. It flattened the Negroes beneath it. It rolled to the wall of the factory, where it stopped. Tom knew that they were coming. He couldn't move. And then he saw the search-lights of the two cars glaring down on him. A quick shot went through him. He stiffened. He started to run. A yell went up from the mob. Tom wheeled about and faced them. They poured down on him. They swarmed. A large man with dead-white face and flabby cheeks came to him and almost jabbed a gun-barrel through his guts.

"Hands behind y, nigger."

Tom's wrists were bound. The big man shoved him to the well. Burn him over it, and when the woodwork caved in, his body would drop to the bottom. Two deaths for a godam nigger. Louisa was driven back. The mob pushed in. Its pressure, its momentum was too great. Drag him to the factory. Wood and stakes already there. Tom moved in the direction indicated. But they had to drag him. They reached the great door. Too many to get in there. The mob divided and flowed around the walls to either sides. The big man shoved him through the door. The mob pressed in from the sides. Taut humming. No words. A stake was sunk into the ground. Rotting floor boards piled around it. Kerosene poured on the rotting floor boards. Tom bound to the stake. His breast was bare. Nail scratches let little lines of blood trickle down and mat into the hair. His face, his eyes were wet and stony. Except for irregular breathing, one would have thought him already dead. Torches were flung onto the pile. A great flare muffled in black smoke shot upward. The mob yelled. The mob was silent. Now Tom could be seen within the flames. Only his head, erect, lean, like a blackened stone. Stench of burning flesh soaked the air. Tom's eyes popped. His head settled downward. The mob yelled. Its yell echoed against the skeleton stone walls and sounded like a hundred yells. Like a hundred mobs yelling. Its yell thudded against the thick front wall and fell back. Ghost of a yell slipped through the flames and out the great door of the factory. It fluttered like a dying thing down the single street of factory town. Louisa, upon the step before her home, did not hear it, but her eyes opened slowly. They saw the full moon glowing in the great door. The full moon, an evil thing, an omen, soft showering the homes of folks she knew. Where were they, these people? She'd sing, and perhaps they'd come out and join her. Perhaps Tom Burwell would come. At any rate, the full moon in the great door was an omen which she must sing to:

> Red nigger moon. Sinner!
> Blood-burning moon. Sinner!
> Come out that fact'ry door.

1923

Zora Neale Hurston *1901?–1960*

Zora Neale Hurston was born in Eatonville, Florida, about 1901. Eatonville was one of the few completely black towns in the United States, and her early childhood was free of the racism experienced by most black children growing up in mixed black and white communities. Her father was a carpenter and Baptist preacher, a man of consequence in the community. But it was her mother who most influenced her life. She had been a schoolteacher before her marriage, and she encouraged her daughter to reach out in life, to "jump at the sun."

Zora's mother died when Zora was still a child, and she was sent away to school where she confronted for the first time the agonies of growing up black among whites. When her father encountered financial troubles, Zora was removed from school, returned home, and left to care for herself. She worked as a maid, and as a receptionist. Later she ran off to work as a wardrobe girl with a theatrical group touring Florida and the South. For a time she lived in Baltimore where she got a job as a waitress and took high school classes. In 1918 she moved to Washington, D.C., and entered Howard University hoping to prepare herself to be a writer. She enrolled in literature classes, joined the campus literary club, and published her first short story in the club's literary journal.

When one of her stories was published in a New York magazine, she left Washington, D.C. and moved to New York. She was a woman of high spirits, a born storyteller, and she immediately found a wide circle of friends. With their help she got a job as secretary to the liberal, best-selling novelist Fannie Hurst. And with help from friends Zora Neale Hurston received a scholarship to Barnard College, graduating with a bachelor's degree in 1928.

Her class papers had attracted the attention of her anthropology professor, and after graduation she was awarded a fellowship to return to the South to collect folklore. When she returned to New York, she tried writing stage sketches, based on the material she had collected. In 1932 she produced her own stage review, The Great Day. *The show was a critical success, but it earned too little money to pay its way.*

In 1934 her first novel, Jonah's Gourd Vine, *was published. The novel, also based on the folklore material she had collected, won positive reviews and was selected as one of the offerings of the Book-of-the-Month Club. The success of* Jonah's Gourd Vine *encouraged her publishers to bring out* Mules and Men *the following year. A collection of her writings, it reprinted her finest short story "The Gilded Six-Bits," which had appeared in 1933 in* Story Magazine.

In 1936, she received a fellowship from the Guggenheim Foundation to support further research. She went to the Caribbean to collect more black folklore, and while she was there she wrote her second novel, Their Eyes Were Watching God *(1937). The novel, set in Eatonville, told of a young black woman determined to find self-realization and love. It was Zora Neale Hurston's finest novel and a critical success.*

At the urging of her publishers, she began work on an autobiography. When Dust Tracks on a Road *appeared in 1942 it was an award-winning popular success, but activist black critics charged that she had failed to deal realistically with black life in white America, that she had neglected the burning issues of racism. Her response was that she wanted only to write about human beings, "My interest lies in what makes a man or woman do such-and-so regardless of his color."*

For a brief time during World War II she taught at a black college in Florida. She wrote another novel, but it was rejected by her publishers. She then changed publishers and submitted the manuscript of a different novel which was accepted and published as Seraph on the Suwanee *(1948). It received favorable reviews, but to the surprise of Zora Neale Hurston's readers, it was not about blacks but about whites.*

Her best work had appeared in the 1930s. Her career now began its decline. Her manuscripts were increasingly rejected by publishers, and her personal life was shattered when she became the victim of charges (later disproven) that she had molested children. Her "crime" was widely reported in lurid newspaper stories, and Zora Neale Hurston, feeling betrayed by her friends and by the system of legal justice, disappeared, later to be discovered working as a housemaid in Florida.

She continued to write magazine articles on the life of black men and women in America, and over the years she worked on a novel of the Jews and the Biblical Herod, but the manuscript was rejected by every publishing house she sent it to. In her last years she supported herself by working as a librarian, by school teaching, and by writing articles for a local weekly newspaper. In 1960 she died, penniless, in a welfare home in Florida.

Zora Neale Hurston's career had been remarkable. She had published more books than any other American black woman. Her critics charged that she presented a "whitewashed" picture of American blacks, and it is true that she lacked the vision or the power to portray the extent and the bitterness of the struggle of black men and women in the United States. Yet her desire was not to create political change but to portray the black culture and the black experience that she had known. In recording the people and events of a time and place that are gone, in presenting the dialects and customs of people she knew so well, she helped to preserve a part of the black tradition in America, and she had been a major force in preparing the way for her literary descendants, black men and women whose prose and poetry have become so important a part of modern life and art in America.

FURTHER READING: D. Turner, *In a Minor Chord*, 1971; R. Hemenway, *Zora Neale Hurston, A Literary Biography*, 1977; L. Howard, *Zora Neale Hurston*, 1980; K. Holloway, *The Character of the Word, The Texts of Zora Neale Hurston*, 1987.

TEXT: "The Gilded Six-Bits," *Story Magazine*, August 1933.

THE GILDED SIX-BITS

It was a Negro yard around a Negro house in a Negro settlement that looked to the payroll of the G and G Fertilizer works for its support.

But there was something happy about the place. The front yard was parted in the middle by a sidewalk from gate to door-step, a sidewalk edged on either side by quart bottles driven neck down into the ground on a slant. A mess of homey flowers planted without a plan but blooming cheerily from their helter-skelter places. The fence and house were whitewashed. The porch and steps scrubbed white.

The front door stood open to the sunshine so that the floor of the front room could finish drying after its weekly scouring. It was Saturday. Everything clean from the front gate to the privy house. Yard raked so that the strokes of the rake would make a pattern. Fresh newspaper cut in fancy edge on the kitchen shelves.

Missie May was bathing herself in the galvanized washtub in the bedroom. Her dark-brown skin glistened under the soapsuds that skittered down from her wash rag. Her stiff young breasts thrust forward aggressively like broad-based cones with the tips lacquered in black.

She heard men's voices in the distance and glanced at the dollar clock on the dresser.

"Humph! Ah'm way behind time t'day! Joe gointer be heah 'fore Ah git mah clothes on if Ah don't make haste."

She grabbed the clean meal sack at hand and dried herself hurriedly and began to dress. But before she could tie her slippers, there came the ring of singing metal on wood. Nine times.

Missie May grinned with delight. She had not seen the big tall man come stealing in the gate and creep up the walk grinning happily at the joyful mischief he was about to commit. But she knew that it was her husband throwing silver dollars in the door for her to pick up and pile beside her plate at dinner. It was this way every Saturday afternoon. The nine dollars hurled into the open door, he scurried to a hiding place behind the cape jasmine bush and waited.

Missie May promptly appeared at the door in mock alarm.

"Who dat chunkin' money in mah do'way?" She demanded. No answer from the yard. She leaped off the porch and began to search the shrubbery. She peeped under the porch and hung over the gate to look up and down the road. While she did this, the man behind the jasmine darted to the china berry tree. She spied him and gave chase.

"Nobody ain't gointer be chunkin' money at me and Ah not do 'em nothin'," she shouted in mock anger. He ran around the house with Missie May at his heels. She overtook him at the kitchen door. He ran inside but could not close it after him before she crowded in and locked with him in a rough and tumble. For several minutes the two were a furious mass of male and female energy. Shouting, laughing, twisting, turning, tussling, tickling each other in the ribs; Missie May clutching onto Joe and Joe trying, but not too hard, to get away.

"Missie May, take yo' hand out mah pocket!" Joe shouted out between laughs.

"Ah ain't, Joe, not lessen you gwine gimme whateve' it is good you got in yo' pocket. Turn it go, Joe, do Ah'll tear yo' clothes."

"Go on tear 'em. You de one dat pushes de needles round heah. Move yo' hand Missie May."

"Lemme git dat paper sack out yo' pocket. Ah bet its candy kisses."

"Tain't. Move yo' hand. Woman ain't go no business in a man's clothes nohow. Go way."

Missie May gouged way down and gave an upward jerk and triumphed.

"Unhhunh! Ah got it. It 'tis so candy kisses. Ah knowed you had somethin' for me in yo' clothes. Now Ah got to see whut's in every pocket you got."

Joe smiled indulgently and let his wife go through all of his pockets and take out the things that he had hidden there for her to find. She bore off the chewing gum, the cake of sweet soap, the pocket handkerchief as if she had wrested them from him, as if they had not been bought for the sake of this friendly battle.

"Whew! dat play-fight done got me all warmed up." Joe exclaimed. "Got me some water in de kittle?"

"Yo' water is on de fire and yo' clean things is cross de bed. Hurry up and wash yo'self and git changed so we kin eat. Ah'm hongry." As Missie said this, she bore the steaming kettle into the bedroom.

"You ain't hongry, sugar," Joe contradicted her. "Youse jes' a little empty. Ah'm de one whut's hongry. Ah could eat up camp meetin', back off 'ssociation, and drink Jurdan dry. Have it on de table when Ah git out de tub."

"Don't you mess wid mah business, man. You git in yo' clothes. Ah'm a real wife, not no dress and breath. Ah might not look lak one, but if you burn me, you won't git a thing but wife ashes."

Joe splashed in the bedroom and Missie May fanned around in the kitchen. A fresh red and white checked cloth on the table. Big pitcher of buttermilk beaded with pale drops of butter from the churn. Hot fried mullet, crackling bread, ham hock atop a mound of string beans and new potatoes, and perched on the window-sill a pone of spicy potato pudding.

Very little talk during the meal but that little consisted of banter that pretended to deny affection but in reality flaunted it. Like when Missie May reached for a second helping of the tater pone. Joe snatched it out of her reach.

After Missie May had made two or three unsuccessful grabs at the pan, she begged, "Aw, Joe gimme some mo' dat tater pone."

"Nope, sweetenin' is for us men-folks. Y'all pritty lil frail eels don't need nothin' lak dis. You too sweet already."

"Please, Joe."

"Naw, naw. Ah don't want you to git no sweeter than whut you is already. We goin' down de road a lil piece t'night so you go put on yo' Sunday-go-to-meetin' things."

Missie May looked at her husband to see if he was playing some prank. "Sho nuff, Joe?"

"Yeah. We goin' to de ice cream parlor."

"Where de ice cream parlor at, Joe?"

"A new man done come heah from Chicago and he done got a place and took and opened it up for a ice cream parlor, and bein' as it's real swell, Ah wants you to be one de first ladies to walk in dere and have some set down."

"Do Jesus, Ah ain't knowed nothin' 'bout it. Who de man done it?"

"Mister Otis D. Slemmons, of spots and places—Memphis, Chicago, Jacksonville, Philadelphia and so on."

"Dat heavy-set man wid his mouth full of gold teethes?"

"Yeah, Where did you see 'im at?"

"Ah went down to de sto' tuh git a box of lye and Ah seen 'im standin' on de corner talkin' to some of de mens, and Ah come on back and went to scrubbin' de floor, and he passed and tipped his hat whilst Ah was scourin' de steps. Ah thought Ah never seen *him* befo'."

Joe smiled pleasantly. "Yeah, he's up to date. He got de finest clothes Ah ever seen on a colored man's back."

"Aw, he don't look no better in his clothes than you do in yourn. He got a puzzlegut on 'im and he so chuckle-headed, he got a pone behind his neck."

Joe looked down at his own abdomen and said wistfully, "Wisht Ah had a build on me lak he got. He ain't puzzle-gutted, honey. He jes' got a corperation. Dat make 'im look lak a rich white man. All rich mens is got some belly on 'em."

"Ah seen de pitchers of Henry Ford and he's a spare-built man and Rockefeller look lak he ain't got but one gut. But Ford and Rockefeller and dis Slemmons and all de rest kin be as many-gutted as dey please, Ah'm satisfied wid you jes' lak you is, baby. God took pattern after a pine tree and built you noble. Youse a pritty man, and if Ah knowed any way to make you mo' pritty still Ah'd take and do it."

Joe reached over gently and toyed with Missie May's ear. "You jes' say dat cause you love me, but Ah know Ah can't hold no light to Otis D. Slemmons. Ah ain't never been nowhere and Ah ain't got nothin' but you."

Missie May got on his lap and kissed him and he kissed back in kind. Then he went on. "All de womens is crazy 'bout 'im everywhere he go."

"How you know dat, Joe?"

"He tole us so hisself."

"Dat don't make it so. His mouf is cut cross-ways, ain't it? Well, he kin lie jes' lak anybody else."

"Good Lawd, Missie! You womens sho is hard to sense into things. He's got a five-dollar gold piece for a stick-pin and he got a ten-dollar gold piece on his watch chain and his mouf is jes' crammed full of gold teethes. Sho wisht it wuz mine. And whut make it so cool, he got money 'cumulated. And womens give it all to 'im."

"Ah don't see whut de womens see on 'im. Ah wouldn't give 'im a wink if de sheriff wuz after 'im."

"Well, he tole us how de white womens in Chicago give 'im all dat gold money. So he don't 'low nobody to touch it at all. Not even put dey finger on it. Dey tole 'im not to. You kin make 'miration at it, but don't tetch it."

"Whyn't he stay up dere where dey so crazy 'bout 'im?"

"Ah reckon dey done made 'im vast-rich and he wants to travel some. He say dey wouldn't leave 'im hit a lick of work. He got mo' lady people crazy 'bout him than he kin shake a stick at."

"Joe, Ah hates to see you so dumb. Dat stray nigger jes' tell y'all anything and y'all b'lieve it."

"Go 'head on now, honey and put on yo' clothes. He talkin' 'bout his pritty womens—Ah want 'im to see *mine*."

Missie May went off to dress and Joe spent the time trying to make his stomach punch out like Slemmons' middle. He tried the rolling swagger of the stranger, but found that his tall bone-and-muscle stride fitted ill with it. He just had time to drop back into his seat before Missie May came in dressed to go.

On the way home that night Joe was exultant. "Didn't Ah say ole Otis was swell? Can't he talk Chicago talk? Wuzn't dat funny whut he said when great big fat ole Ida Armstrong come in? He asted me, "Who is dat broad wid de forte shake?' Dat's a new word. Us always thought forty was a set of figgers but he showed us where it means a whole heap of things. Sometimes he don't say forty, he jes' say thirty-eight and two and dat mean de same thing. Know whut he tole me when Ah wuz payin' for our ice cream? He say, "Ah have to hand it to you, Joe. Dat wife of yours is jes' thirty-eight and two. Yessuh, she's forte!' Ain't he killin'?"

"He'll do in case of a rush. But he sho is got uh heap uh gold on 'im. Dat's de first time Ah ever seed gold money. It lookted good on him sho nuff, but it'd look a whole heap better on you."

"Who, me? Missie May youse crazy! Where would a po' man lak me git gold money from?"

Missie May was silent for a minute, then she said, "Us might find some goin' long de road some time. Us could."

"Who would be losin' gold money round heah? We ain't even seen none dese white folks wearin' no gold money on dey watch chain. You must be figgerin' Mister Packard or Mister Cadillac goin' pass through heah."

"You don't know whut been lost 'round heah. Maybe somebody way back in memorial times lost they gold money and went on off and it ain't never been found. And then if we wuz to find it, you could wear some 'thout havin' no gang of womens lak dat Slemmons say he got."

Joe laughed and hugged her. "Don't be so wishful 'bout me. Ah'm satisifed de way Ah is. So long as Ah be yo' husband, Ah don't keer 'bout nothin' else. Ah'd ruther all de other womens in de world to be dead than for you to have de toothache. Less we go to bed and git our night rest."

It was Saturday night once more before Joe could parade his wife in Slemmons' ice cream parlor again. He worked the night shift and Saturday was his only night off. Every other evening around six o'clock he left home, and dying dawn saw him hustling home around the lake where the challenging sun flung a flaming sword from east to west across the trembling water.

That was the best part of life—going home to Missie May. Their whitewashed house, the mock battle on Saturday, the dinner and ice cream parlor afterwards, church on Sunday nights when Missie outdressed any woman in town—all, everything was right.

One night around eleven the acid ran out at the G. and G. The foreman knocked off the crew and let the steam die down. As Joe rounded the lake on his way home, a lean moon rode the lake in a silver boat. If anybody had asked Joe about the moon on the lake, he would have said he hadn't paid it any attention. But he saw it with his feelings. It made him yearn painfully for Missie, Creation obsessed him. He thought about children. They had been married for more than a year now. They had money put away. They ought to be making little feet for shoes. A little boy child would be about right.

He saw a dim light in the bedroom and decided to come in through the kitchen door. He could wash the fertilizer dust off himself before presenting himself to Missie May. It would be nice for her not to know that he was there until he slipped into his place in bed and hugged her back. She always liked that.

He eased the kitchen door open slowly and silently, but when he went to set his dinner bucket on the table he bumped it into a pile of dishes, and something crashed to the floor. He heard his wife gasp in fright and hurried to reassure her.

"Iss me, honey. Don't get skeered."

There was a quick, large movement in the bedroom. A rustle, a thud, and a stealthy silence. The light went out.

What? Robbers? Murderers? Some varmint attacking his helpless wife, perhaps. He struck a match, threw himself on guard and stepped over the door-sill into the bedroom.

The great belt on the wheel of Time slipped and eternity stood still. By the match light he could see the man's legs fighting with his breeches in his frantic desire to get them on. He had both chance and time to kill the intruder in his helpless condition—half in and half out of his pants—but he was too weak to take action. The shapeless enemies of humanity that live in the hours of Time had waylaid Joe. He was assaulted in his weakness. Like Samson awakening after his haircut. So he just opened his mouth and laughed.

The match went out and he struck another and lit the lamp. A howling wind raced across his heart, but underneath its fury he heard his wife sobbing and Slemmons pleading for his life. Offering to buy it with all that he had. "Please, suh, don't kill me. Sixty-two dollars at de sto'. Gold money."

Joe just stood. Slemmons looked at the window, but it was screened. Joe stood out like a rough-backed mountain between him and the door. Barring him from escape, from sunrise, from life.

He considered a surprise attack upon the big clown that stood there laughing like a chessy cat. But before his fist could travel an inch, Joe's own rushed out to crush him like a battering ram. Then Joe stood over him.

"Git into yo' damn rags, Slemmons, and dat quick."

Slemmons scrambled to his feet and into his vest and coat. As he grabbed his hat, Joe's fury overrode his intentions and he grabbed at Slemmons with his left hand and struck at him with his right. The right landed. The left grazed the front of his vest. Slemmons was knocked a somersault into the kitchen and fled through the open door. Joe found himself alone with Missie May, with the golden watch charm clutched in his left fist. A short bit of broken chain dangled between his fingers.

Missie May was sobbing. Wails of weeping without words. Joe stood, and after awhile he found out that he had something in his hand. And then he stood and felt without thinking and without seeing with his natural eyes. Missie May kept on crying and Joe kept on feeling so much and not knowing what to do with all his feelings, he put Slemmons' watch charm in his pants pocket and took a good laugh and went to bed.

"Missie May, whut you cryin' for?"

"Cause Ah love you so hard and Ah know you don't love *me* no mo'."

Joe sank his face into the pillow for a spell then he said huskily, "You don't know de feelings of dat yet, Missie May."

"Oh Joe, honey, he said he wuz gointer give me dat gold money and he jes' kept on after me—"

Joe was very still and silent for a long time. Then he said, "Well, don't cry no mo', Missie May. Ah got yo' gold piece for you."

The hours went past on their rusty ankles. Joe still and quiet on one bed-rail and Missie May wrung dry of sobs on the other. Finally the sun's tide crept upon the shore of night and drowned all its hours. Missie May with her face stiff and streaked towards the window saw the dawn come into her yard. It was day. Nothing more. Joe wouldn't be coming home as usual. No need to fling open the front door and sweep off the porch, making it nice for Joe. Never no more breakfast to cook; no more washing and starching of Joe's jumper-jackets and pants. No more nothing. So why get up?

With this strange man in her bed, she felt embarrassed to get up and dress. She decided to wait till he had dressed and gone. Then she would get up, dress quickly and be gone forever beyond reach of Joe's looks and laughs. But he never moved. Red light turned to yellow, then white.

From beyond the no-man's land between them came a voice. A strange voice that yesterday had been Joe's.

"Missie May, ain't you gonna fix me no breakfus'?"

She sprang out of bed. "Yeah, Joe. Ah didn't reckon you wuz hongry."

No need to die today. Joe needed her for a few more minutes anyhow.

Soon there was a roaring fire in the cook stove. Water bucket full and two chickens killed. Joe loved fried chicken and rice. She didn't deserve a thing and good Joe was letting her cook him some breakfast. She rushed hot biscuits to the table as Joe took his seat.

He ate with his eyes in his plate. No laughter, no banter.

"Missie May, you ain't eatin' yo' breakfus'."

"Ah don't choose none, Ah thank yuh."

His coffee cup was empty. She sprang to refill it. When she turned from the stove and bent to set the cup beside Joe's plate, she saw the yellow coin on the table between them.

She slumped into her seat and wept into her arms.

Presently Joe said calmly, "Missie May, you cry too much. Don't look back lak Lot's wife and turn to salt."

The sun, the hero of every day, the impersonal old man that beams as brightly on death as on birth, came up every morning and raced across the blue dome and dipped into the sea of fire every evening. Water ran down hill and birds nested.

Missie knew why she didn't leave Joe. She couldn't. She loved him too much, but she could not understand why Joe didn't leave her. He was polite, even kind at times, but aloof.

There were no more Saturday romps. No ringing silver dollars to stack beside her plate. No pockets to rifle. In fact the yellow coin in his trousers was like a monster hiding in the cave of his pockets to destroy her.

She often wondered if he still had it, but nothing could have induced her to ask nor yet to explore his pockets to see for herself. Its shadow was in the house whether or no.

One night Joe came home around midnight and complained of pains in the back. He asked Missie to rub him down with liniment. It had been three months since Missie had touched his body and it all seemed strange. But she rubbed him. Grateful for the chance. Before morning, youth triumphed and Missie exulted. But the next day, as she joyfully made up their bed, beneath her pillow she found the piece of money with the bit of chain attached.

Alone to herself, she looked at the thing with loathing, but look she must. She took it into her hands with trembling and saw first thing that it was no gold piece. It was a gilded half dollar. Then she knew why Slemmons had forbidden anyone to touch his gold. He trusted village eyes at a distance not to recognize his stick-pin as a gilded quarter, and his watch charm as a four-bit piece.

She was glad at first that Joe had left it there. Perhaps he was through with her punishment. They were man and wife again. Then another thought came clawing at her. He had come home to buy from her as if she were any woman in the long house. Fifty cents for her love. As if to say that he could pay as well as Slemmons. She slid the coin into his Sunday pants pocket and dressed herself and left his house.

Halfway between her house and the quarters she met her husband's mother, and after a short talk she turned and went back home. Never would she admit defeat to that woman who prayed for it nightly. If she had not the substance of marriage she had the outside show. Joe must leave *her*. She let him see she didn't want his old gold four-bits too.

She saw no more of the coin for some time though she knew that Joe could not help finding it in his pocket. But his health kept poor, and he came home at least every ten days to be rubbed.

The sun swept around the horizon, trailing its robes of weeks and days. One morning as Joe came in from work, he found Missie May chopping wood. Without a word he took the ax and chopped a huge pile before he stopped.

"You ain' got no business choppin' wood, and you know it."

"How come? Ah been choppin' it for de last longest."

"Ah ain't blind. You makin' feet for shoes."

"Won't you be glad to have a lil baby chile, Joe?"

"You know dat 'thout astin' me."

"Iss gointer be a boy chile and de very spit of you."

"You reckon, Missie May?"

"Who else could it look lak?"

Joe said nothing, but he thrust his hand deep into his pocket and fingered something there.

It was almost six months later Missie May took to bed and Joe went and got his mother to come wait on the house.

Missie May delivered a fine boy. Her travail was over when Joe came in from work one morning. His mother and the old women were drinking great bowls of coffee around the fire in the kitchen.

The minute Joe came into the room his mother called him aside.

"How did Missie May make out?" he asked quickly.

"Who, dat gal? She strong as a ox. She gointer have plenty mo'. We done fixed her wid de sugar and lard to sweeten her for de nex' one."

Joe stood silent awhile.

"You ain't ast 'bout de baby, Joe. You oughter be mighty proud cause he sho is de spittin' image of yuh, son. Dat's yourn all right, if you never git another one, dat un is yourn. And you know Ah'm mighty proud too, son, cause Ah never thought well of you marryin' Missie May cause her ma used tuh fan her foot round right smart and Ah been mighty skeered dat Missie May wuz gointer git misput on her road."

Joe said nothing. He fooled around the house till late in the day then just before he went to work, he went and stood at the foot of the bed and asked his wife how she felt. He did this every day during the week.

On Saturday he went to Orlando to make his market. It had been a long time since he had done that.

Meat and lard, meal and flour, soap and starch. Cans of corn and tomatoes. All the staples. He fooled around town for awhile and bought bananas and apples. Way after while he went around to the candy store.

"Hellow, Joe," the clerk greeted him. "Ain't seen you in a long time."

"Nope, Ah ain't been heah. Been round in spots and places."

"Want some of them molasses kisses you always buy?"

"Yessuh." He threw the gilded half dollar on the counter. "Will dat spend?"

"Whut is it, Joe? Well, I'll be doggone! A gold-plated four-bit piece. Where'd you git it, Joe?"

"Offen a stray nigger dat come through Eatonville. He had it on his watch chain for a charm—goin' round making out iss gold money. Ha ha! He had a quarter on his tie pin and it wuz all golded up too. Tryin' to fool people. Makin' out he so rich and everything. Ha! Ha! Tryin' to tole off folkses wives from home."

"How did you git it, Joe? Did he fool you, too?"

"Who, me? Naw suh! He ain't fooled me none. Know whut Ah done? He come round me wid his smart talk. Ah hauled off and knocked 'im down and took his old four-bits way from 'im. Gointer buy my wife some good ole lasses kisses wid it. Gimme fifty cents worth of dem candy kisses."

"Fifty cents buys a mightly lot of candy kisses, Joe. Why don't you split it up and take some chocolate bars, too. They eat good, too."

'Yessuh, dey do, but Ah wants all dat in kisses. Ah got a lil boy chile home now. Tain't a week old yet, but he kin suck a sugar tit and maybe eat one them kisses hisself."

Joe got his candy and left the store. The clerk turned to the next customer. "Wisht I could be like these darkies. Laughin' all the time. Nothin' worries 'em."

Back in Eatonville, Joe reached his own front door. There was the ring of singing metal on wood. Fifteen times. Missie May couldn't run to the door, but she crept there as quickly as she could.

"Joe Banks, Ah hear you chunkin' money in mah do'way. You wait till Ah got mah strength back and Ah'm gointer fix you for dat."

1933

Thomas Wolfe   *1900–1938*

Thomas Wolfe was born in the mountain town of Asheville, North Carolina, the youngest of eight children. His father was a stonecutter, fond of Shakespeare and rhetoric, and he saw to it that his precocious son, Tom, unlike the other poor children of that rural region, was educated in a private school, where his writing talent was first recognized and encouraged. Thomas Wolfe went on to the University of North Carolina and, after graduation, to Harvard, where he developed his literary talents by studying playwriting, and after two years at Harvard, received an M.A. degree.

From Harvard, Wolfe moved to New York, where he taught at New York University. But a trip to Europe begun in the fall of 1924, interrupted his teaching career and led to crucial events in his development as a writer: after a memorable year in Europe, he met on the return voyage Aline Bernstein, a married woman eighteen years older than Wolfe. She became Wolfe's confidante, editor, and inspiration. With her emotional and financial support he completed Look Homeward, Angel, *his first novel. It was submitted to Scribner's in 1929, where it was read by Maxwell Perkins, who was also the editor of Fitzgerald and Hemingway. Working closely with Perkins, Wolfe revised the manuscript, and it was published in October 1929.*

The novel, which corresponds closely to the experiences of Wolfe's first twenty years, was a critical success, and it was singled out for particular praise in 1930 by Sinclair Lewis in his Nobel Prize acceptance speech. The only people who did not like the book, it seemed, were the inhabitants of Wolfe's home town who felt insulted by their portraits in a novel drawn so clearly from Wolfe's own background. In 1935, again with substantial help from Perkins, Wolfe published what is in effect a sequel to his first book, Of Time and the River. *It continued the story of Eugene Gant, Wolfe's own fictional equivalent. But the book met with less critical favor than* Look Homeward, Angel. *Reviewers objected to the biographical basis and formlessness of the novel. Barnard De Voto, a noted critic of American literature, was concise: Wolfe may be a genius, but "genius is not enough." Perhaps more significant for Wolfe than the mixed reviews was the fact that he broke with his editor, Perkins—and his publisher, Scribner's.*

Fortunately for Wolfe, he soon established a similar relationship with Edward Aswell, an editor at Harper and Brothers, and in 1938, Wolfe delivered an enormous manuscript of nearly a million words. While Aswell was working on the manuscript, Wolfe went on a tour of the western United States. There he contracted pneumonia. Subsequently it was discovered that he was suffering from tuberculosis of the brain. He returned to the East, to Baltimore, where he died on September 15, 1938. He was thirty-seven.

From the mass of material Wolfe had left behind, his editor fashioned three posthumously published books: the novels The Web and the Rock *(1939) and* You Can't Go Home Again *(1940), and a compilation of sketches, fiction, and drama,* The Hills Beyond *(1941). Like the earlier novels they reveal Wolfe's strengths and weaknesses: his creative energy made his writing rich with vitality and human sensations; at the same time, this energy was so uncontrolled and excessive as to overwhelm his novels with undigested experiences and ill-defined ideas. In places his work shines with passion, excitement, the joys of life. In others it is dulled by insistent emotional pleading, by intensity without respite.*

He attempted a great task: he wished to discover "an entire universe" and "a complete language"; he wanted to portray the wide range of the American experience, and to that end he planned an elaborate, structured, myth-laden series of works spanning the history of America. But death came too soon, and today Thomas Wolfe is best remembered as the author of a few formless but powerful novels. Yet his work also includes essays plays, and short stories, and it is paradoxical that in such shorter works, where the limitations of space and time impose a need for restraint and control, Wolfe achieves some of his best work, marked by vitality and power, and with clear insight into the turbulence and the breadth of American life.

FURTHER READING: *The Letters of Thomas Wolfe*, ed. E. Nowell, 1956; *The Letters of Thomas Wolfe to His Mother*, ed. C. Holman and S. Ross, 1968; *The Notebooks of Thomas Wolfe*, 2 vols., ed. R. Kennedy and P. Reeves, 1970; E. Nowell, *Thomas Wolfe, A Biography*, 1960; R. Kennedy, *The Window of Memory, The Literary Career of Thomas Wolfe*, 1962; A. Turnbull, *Thomas Wolfe*, 1968; H. Muller, *Thomas Wolfe*, 1947; *The World of Thomas Wolfe*, ed. C. Holman, 1962; P. Johnson, *The Art of Thomas Wolfe*, 1963; B. McElderry, *Thomas Wolfe*, 1964; *Thomas Wolfe, Three Decades of Criticism*, ed. L. Field, 1968; *Thomas Wolfe, The Critical Reception*, ed. P. Reeves, 1974; *The Loneliness at the Core, Studies in Thomas Wolfe*, ed. C. Holman, 1975; L. Gurko, *Thomas Wolfe, Beyond the Romantic Ego*, 1975; E. Evans, *Thomas Wolfe*, 1984; *Critical Essays on Thomas Wolfe*, ed. S. Phillipson, 1985.

TEXT: *From Death to Morning*, 1935.

ONLY THE DEAD KNOW BROOKLYN

Dere's no guy livin' dat known Brooklyn t'roo an' t'roo, because it'd take a guy a lifetime just to find his way aroun' duh f—— town.

So like I say, I'm waitin' for my train t' come when I sees dis big guy standin' deh—dis is duh foist I eveh see of him. Well, he's lookin' wild, y'know, an' I can see dat he's had plenty, but still he's holdin' it; he talks good an' is walkin' straight enough. So den, dis big guy steps up to a little guy dat's standin' deh, an' says, "How d'yuh get t' eighteent' Avenoo an' Sixty-sevent' Street?" he says.

"Jesus! Yuh got me, chief," duh little guy says to him. "I ain't been heah long myself. Where is duh place?" he says. "Out in duh Flatbush section somewhere?"

"Nah," duh big guy says. "It's out in Bensonhoist. But I was neveh deh befoeh. How d'yuh get deh?"

"Jesus," duh little guy says, scratchin' his head, y'know—yuh could see duh little guy didn't know his way about—"yuh got me, chief. I neveh hoid of it. Do any of youse guys know where it is?" he says to me.

"Sure, I says. "It's out in Bensonhoist. Yuh take duh Fourt' Avenoo express, get off at Fifty-nint' Street, change to a Sea Beach local deh, get off at Eighteent' Avenoo an' Sixty-toid, an' den walk down foeh blocks. Dat's all yuh got to do," I says.

"G'wan!" some wise guy dat I neveh seen befoeh pipes up. "Whatcha talkin' about?" he says—oh, he was wise, y'know. "Duh guy is crazy! I tell yuh what yuh do," he says to duh big guy. "Yuh change to duh West End line at Toity-sixt'," he tells him. "Get off at Noo Utrecht an' Sixteent' Avenoo," he says. "Walk two blocks oveh, foeh blocks up," he says, "an' you'll be right deh." Oh, a *wise* guy, y'know.

"Oh, yeah?" I says. "Who told *you* so much?" He got me sore because he was so wise about it. "How long you been livin' heah?" I says.

"All my life," he says. "I was bawn in Williamsboig," he says. "An' I can tell you t'ings about dis town you neveh hoid of," he says.

"Yeah?" I says.

"Yeah," he says.

"Well, den, you can tell me t'ings about dis town dat nobody else has eveh hoid of, either. Maybe you make it all up yoehself at night," I says, "befoeh you go to sleep—like cuttin' out papeh dolls, or somp'n."

"Oh, yeah?" he says. "You're pretty wise, ain't yuh?"

"Oh, I don't know," I says. "Duh boids ain't usin my head for Lincoln's statue yet," I says. "But I'm wise enough to know a phony when I see one."

"Yeah?" he says. "A wise guy, huh? Well, you're so wise dat some one's goin' t'bust yuh one right on duh snoot some day," he says. "Dat's how wise *you* are."

Well, my train was comin', or I'da smacked him den and dere, but when I seen duh train was comin', all I said was, "All right, mugg! I'm sorry I can't stay to take keh of you, but I'll be seein' yuh sometime, I hope, out in duh cemetery." So den I says to duh big guy, who'd been standin' deh all duh time, "You come wit me," I says. So when we gets onto duh train I says to him, "Where yuh goin' out in Bensonhoist?" I says. "What numbeh are yuh lookin' for?" I says. *You* know—I t'ought if he told me duh address I might be able to help him out.

"Oh," he says, "I'm not lookin' for no one. I don't know no one out deh."

"Then whatcha goin' out deh for?" I says.

"Oh," duh guy says, "I'm just goin' out to see duh place," he says. "I like duh sound of duh name—Bensonhoist, y'know—so I t'ought I'd go out an' have a look at it."

"Whatcha tryin' t'hand me?" I says. "Whatcha tryin' t'do—kid me?" *You* know, I t'ought duh guy was bein' wise wit me.

"No," he says, "I'm tellin' yuh duh troot. I like to go out an' take a look at places wit nice names like dat. I like to go out an' look at all kinds of places," he says.

"How'd yuh know deh was such a place," I says, "if yuh neveh been deh befoeh?"

"Oh," he says, "I got a map."

"A *map?*" I says.

"Sure," he says, "I got a map dat ells me about all dese places. I take it wit me every time I come out heah," he says.

And Jesus! Wit dat, he pulls it out of his pocket, an' so help me, but he's *got* it—he's tellin' duh troot—a big map of duh whole f—— place with all duh different pahts mahked out. You know—Canarsie an' East Noo Yawk an' Flatbush, Bensonhoist, Sout' Brooklyn, duh Heights, Bay Ridge, Greenpernt—duh whole goddam layout, he's got it right deh on duh map.

"You been to any of dose places?" I says.

"Sure," he says, "I been to most of 'em. I was down in Red Hook just last night," he says.

"Jesus! Red Hook!" I says. "Whatcha do down deh?"

"Oh," he says, "nuttin' much. I just walked aroun'. I went into a coupla places an' had a drink," he says, "but most of the time I just walked aroun'."

"Just walked aroun'?" I says.

"Sure," he says, "just lookin' at t'ings, y'know."

"Oh," he says, "I don't know duh name of duh place, but I could find it on my map," he says. "One time I was walkin' across some big fields where deh ain't no houses," he says, "but I could see ships oveh deh all lighted up. Dey was loadin'. So I walks across duh fields," he says, "to where duh ships are."

"Sure," I says, "I know where you was. You was down to duh Erie Basin."

"Yeah," he says, "I guess dat was it. Dey had some of dose big elevators an' cranes an' dey was loadin' ships, an' I could see some ships in drydock all lighted up, so I walks across duh fields to where dey are," he says.

"Den what did yuh do?" I says.

"Oh," he says, "nuttin' much. I came on back across duh fields after a while an' went into a coupla places an' had a drink."

"Didn't nuttin' happen while yuh was in dere?" I says.

"No," he says. "Nuttin' much. A coupla guys was drunk in one of duh places an' started a fight, but dey bounced 'em out," he says, "an' den one of duh guys stahted to come back again, but duh bartender gets his baseball bat out from under duh counteh, so duh guy goes on."

"Jesus!" I said, "Red Hook!"

"Sure," he says. "Dat's where it was, all right."

"Well, you keep outa deh," I says. "You stay away from deh."

"Why?" he says. "What's wrong wit it?"

"Oh," I says, "it's a good place to stay away from, dat's all. It's a good place to keep out of."

"Why?" he says. "Why is it?"

Jesus! Whatcha gonna do wit a guy as dumb as dat? I saw it wasn't no use to try to tell him nuttin', he wouldn't know what I was talkin' about, so I just says to him, "Oh, nuttin'. Yuh might get lost down deh, dat's all."

"Lost?" he says. "No, *I* wouldn't get lost. I got a map," he says.

A map! Red Hook! Jesus!

So den duh guy begins to ast me all kinds of nutty questions: how big was Brooklyn an' could I find my way aroun' in it, an' how long would it take a guy to know duh place.

"Listen!" I says. "You get dat idea outa yoeh head right now," I says. "You ain't neveh gonna get to know Brooklyn," I says. "Not in a hunderd yeahs. I been livin' heah all my life," I says, "an' I don't even know all deh is to know about it, so how do you expect to know duh town," I says, "when you don't even live heah?"

"Yes," he says, "but I got a map to help me find my way about."

"Map or no map," I says, "yuh ain't gonna get to know Brooklyn wit no map," I says.

"Can you swim?" he says, just like dat. Jesus! By dat time, y'know, I begun to see dat guy was some kind of nut. He'd had plenty to drink, of course, but he had dat crazy look in his eye I didn't like. "Can you swim?" he says.

"Sure," I says. "Can't you?"

"No," he says. "Not more'n a stroke or two. I neveh loined good."

"Well, it's easy," I says. "All yuh need is a little confidence. Duh way I loined, me older bruddeh pitched me off duh dock one day when I was eight yeahs old, cloes an' all. 'You'll swim,' he says. 'You'll swim all right—or drown.' An', believe me, I *swam!* When yuh know yuh got to, you'll do it. Duh only t'ing yuh need is confidence. An' once you've loined," I says, "you've got nuttin' else to worry about. You'll neveh forget it. It's somp'n dat stays wit yuh as long as yuh live."

"Can you swim good?" he says.

"Like a fish," I tells him. "I'm a regulah fish in duh wateh," I says. "I loined to swim right off duh docks wit all duh oddeh kids," I says.

"What would you do if yuh saw a man drownin'?" duh guy says.

"Do? Why, I'd jump in an' pull him out," I says. "Dat's what I'd do."

"Did yuh eveh see a man drown?" he says.

"Sure," I says. "I see two guys—bot' times at Coney Island. Dey got out too far, an' neider one could swim. Dey drowned befoeh any one could get to 'em."

"What becomes of people after dey've drowned out heah?" he says.

"Drowned out where?" I says.

"Out heah in Brooklyn."

"I don't know whatcha mean," I says. "Neveh hoid of no one drownin' heah
in Brooklyn, unless you mean a swimmin' pool. Yuh can't drown in Brooklyn,"
I says. "Yuh gotta drown somewhere else—in duh ocean, where dere's wateh."

"Drownin'," duh guy says, lookin' at his map. "Drownin'." Jesus! I could see
by den he was some kind of nut, he had dat crazy expression in his eyes when
he looked at you, an' I didn't know what he might do. So we was comin' to a
station, an' it wasn't my stop, but I got off anyway, an' waited for duh next train.

"Drownin'," duh guy says, lookin' at his map. "Drownin'."

Jesus! I've t'ought about dat guy a t'ousand times since den an' wondered
what eveh happened to 'm goin' out to look at Bensonhoist because he liked
duh name! Walkin' aroun' t'roo Red Hook by himself at night an' lookin' at his
map! How many people did I see get drowned out heah in Brooklyn! How long
would it take a guy with a good map to know all deh was to know about Brooklyn!

Jesus! What a nut *he* was! I wondeh what eveh happened to 'im, anyway! I
wondeh if some one knocked him on duh head, or if he's still wanderin' aroun'
in duh subway in duh middle of duh night wit his little map! Duh poor guy!
Say, I've got to laugh, at dat, when I t'ink about him! Maybe he's found out by
now dat he'll neveh live long enough to know duh whole of Brooklyn. It'd take
a guy a lifetime to know Brooklyn t'roo an' t'roo. An' even den, yuh wouldn't
know it all.

1935

THE FAR AND THE NEAR

On the outskirts of a little town upon a rise of land that swept back from the
railway there was a tidy little cottage of white boards, trimmed vividly with green
blinds. To one side of the house there was a garden neatly patterned with plots
of growing vegetables, and an arbor for the grapes which ripened late in August.
Before the house there were three mighty oaks which sheltered it in their clean
and massive shade in summer, and to the other side there was a border of gay
flowers. the whole place had an air of tidiness, thrift, and modest comfort.

Every day, a few minutes after two o'clock in the afternoon, the limited express
between two cities passed this spot. At that moment the great train, having halted
for a breathing-space at the town near by, was beginning to lengthen evenly
into its stroke, but it had not yet reached the full drive of its terrific speed. It
swung into view deliberately, swept past with a powerful swaying motion of the
engine, a low smooth rumble of its heavy cars upon pressed steel, and then it
vanished in the cut. For a moment the progress of the engine could be marked
by heavy bellowing puffs of smoke that burst at spaced intervals above the edges
of the meadow grass, and finally nothing could be heard but the solid clacking
tempo of the wheels receding into the drowsy stillness of the afternoon.

Every day for more than twenty years, as the train had approached this house,
the engineer had blown on the whistle, and every day, as soon as she heard this
signal, a woman had appeared on the back porch of the little house and waved
to him. At first she had a small child clinging to her skirts, and now this child
had grown to full womanhood, and every day she, too, came with her mother
to the porch and waved.

The engineer had grown old and gray in service. He had driven his great
train, loaded with its weight of lives, across the land ten thousand times. His
own children had grown up and married, and four times he had seen before

him on the tracks the ghastly dot of tragedy converging like a cannon ball to its eclipse of horror at the boiler head—a light spring wagon filled with children, with its clustered row of small stunned faces; a cheap automobile stalled upon the tracks, set with wooden figures of people paralyzed with fear; a battered hobo walking by the rail, too deaf to hear the whistle's warning; and a form flung past his window with a scream—all this the man had seen and known. He had known all the grief, the joy, the peril and the labor such a man could know; he had grown seamed and weathered in his loyal service, and now, schooled by the qualities of faith and courage and humbleness that attended his labor, he had grown old, and had the grandeur and the wisdom these men have.

But no matter what peril or tragedy he had known, the vision of the little house and the women waving to him with a brave free motion of the arm had become fixed in the mind of the engineer as something beautiful and enduring, something beyond all change and ruin, and something that would always be the same, no matter what mishap, grief or error might break the iron schedule of his days.

The sight of the little house and of these two women gave him the most extraordinary happiness he had ever known. He had seen them in a thousand lights, a hundred weathers. He had seen them through the harsh bare light of wintry gray across the brown and frosted stubble of earth, and he had seen them again in the green luring sorcery of April.

He felt for them and for the little house in which they lived such tenderness as a man might feel for his own children, and at length the picture of their lives was carved so sharply in his heart that he felt that he knew their lives completely, to every hour and moment of the day, and he resolved that one day, when his years of service should be ended, he would go and find these people and speak at last with them whose lives had been so wrought into his own.

That day came. At last the engineer stepped from a train onto the station platform of the town where these two women lived. His years upon the rail had ended. He was a pensioned servant of his company, with no more work to do. The engineer walked slowly through the station and out into the streets of the town. Everything was as strange to him as if he had never seen this town before. As he walked on, his sense of bewilderment and confusion grew. Could this be the town he had passed ten thousand times? Were these the same houses he had seen so often from the high windows of his cab? It was all as unfamiliar, as disquieting as a city in a dream, and the perplexity of his spirit increased as he went on.

Presently the houses thinned into the straggling outposts of the town, and the street faded into a country road—the one on which the women lived. And the man plodded on slowly in the heat and dust. At length he stood before the house he sought. He knew at once that he had found the proper place. He saw the lordly oaks before the house, the flower beds, the garden and the arbor, and farther off, the glint of rails.

Yes, this was the house he sought, the place he had passed so many times, the destination he had longed for with such happiness. But now that he had found it, now that he was here, why did his hand falter on the gate; why had the town, the road, the earth, the very entrance to this place he loved turned unfamiliar as the landscape of some ugly dream? Why did he now feel this sense of confusion, doubt and hopelessness?

At length he entered the gate, walked slowly up the path and in a moment more had mounted three short steps that led up to the porch, and was knocking at the door. Presently he heard steps in the hall, the door was opened, and a woman stood facing him.

And instantly, with a sense of bitter loss and grief, he was sorry he had come. He knew at once that the woman who stood there looking at him with a mistrustful eye was the same woman who had waved to him so many thousand times. But her face was harsh and pinched and meager; the flesh sagged wearily in sallow folds, and the small eyes peered at him with timid suspicion and uneasy doubt. All the brave freedom, the warmth and the affection that he had read into her gesture, vanished in the moment that he saw her and heard her unfriendly tongue.

And now his own voice sounded unreal and ghastly to him as he tried to explain his presence, to tell her who he was and the reason he had come. But he faltered on, fighting stubbornly against the horror of regret, confusion, disbelief that surged up in his spirit, drowning all his former joy and making his act of hope and tenderness seem shameful to him.

At length the woman invited him almost unwillingly into the house, and called her daughter in a harsh shrill voice. Then, for a brief agony of time, the man sat in an ugly little parlor, and he tried to talk while the two women stared at him with a dull, bewildered hostility, a sullen, timorous restraint.

And finally, stammering a crude farewell, he departed. He walked away down the path and then along the road toward town, and suddenly he knew that he was an old man. His heart, which had been brave and confident when it looked along the familiar vista of the rails, was now sick with doubt and horror as it saw the strange and unsuspected visage of an earth which had always been within a stone's throw of him, and which he had never seen or known. And he knew that all the magic of that bright lost way, the vista off that shining line, the imagined corner of that small good universe of hope's desire, was gone forever, could never be got back again.

1935

F. Scott Fitzgerald *1896–1940*

In 1925 T. S. Eliot described The Great Gatsby, *written by F. Scott Fitzgerald, as "the first step that American fiction has taken since Henry James." Fitzgerald seemed destined for almost unlimited success as one of America's great writers, but only a few years later, John Dos Passos began a letter to him by calling him a "poor miserable bastard" who was spilling his talent out "in little pieces." In the early 1920s Fitzgerald was the embodiment as well as the chronicler of the Jazz Age (a term for which he was largely responsible). He was handsome, uninhibited, and successful. He not only wrote some the the best prose, he drank the best wines, knew the best people, went to the best parties, and lived as though the money would never stop. Even in 1931, two years after the stock market crash and well into the Great Depression, Fitzgerald's writing earned nearly forty thousand dollars. But the money stopped. And the acclaim. In 1939 his royalties totaled only thirty-three dollars; by the following year not a single one of his books was in print. His life, which had represented the fulfillment of the American dream of wealth and achievement, seemed to end in a nightmare of squandered talent and despair.*

He was born Francis Scott Key Fitzgerald (among his forebears was the author of The Star Spangled Banner). In his hometown of St. Paul, Minnesota, his family was considered socially prominent and genteelly poor. With the financial aid of relatives he was sent to prep school and to Princeton. In college he compiled a record of social triumphs and academic failures, and in 1917, in his senior year, he left Princeton to serve in World War I. In Alabama, where he was sent for military training, he fell hopelessly in love with Zelda Sayre. She was an embodiment of all his romantic notions of a Southern Belle, and when Fitzgerald was discharged from the army in 1919, he was determined to win success, fame, and Zelda. He took a job with an advertising agency and worked on short stories and a novel at night. Eventually his first novel, This Side of Paradise, was accepted for publication. The book appeared in March 1920. A week later Fitzgerald and Zelda were married.

This Side of Paradise, with its portrayal of the casual dissipations of "flaming youth," was an immediate commercial success, and Zelda and Scott Fitzgerald attempted to live up to—or even beyond—his fictional portraits of scandalous young men and women. They swam in public fountains in New York, rode to parties on the hoods of taxis, fought with waiters, and danced on dining tables. Life had become a long cocktail party, yet Fitzgerald managed somehow to continue writing. In 1922 he published his second novel, The Beautiful and Damned, and a collection of short stories, Tales of the Jazz Age. In 1923 he wrote a satirical play, The Vegetable, Or from Postman to President. It was a critical and financial failure, and to maintain his extravagant life-style, Fitzgerald ground out short stories rapidly for money, which he squandered just as rapidly. In 1925 Fitzgerald managed to complete The Great Gatsby. It was a critical success but a commercial disappointment; it sold only about half as many copies as either of his first two novels, and it earned little more than enough to repay his debts to his publishers.

Over the next two years Fitzgerald wrote little; it was, in his own words, a time of "1000 parties and no work." In desperation he went to Hollywood, in 1927, for his first period of screen writing, an occupation that was to sustain him for much of his remaining life. In 1934 Tender is the Night was published. The year of its publication, it sold only 13,000 copies, and although it is a precise indictment of irresponsible social values of the 1930s the critics harshly accused Fitzgerald of ignoring the Depression while writing a frivolous novel about neurotic Americans who preferred Europe over their native land.

Battered by the illness of his wife (in the 1930s Zelda began to suffer a series of mental breakdowns), by his own alcoholism, and by the failures of his writing, Fitzgerald now worked mainly in Hollywood. He continued to engage in periodic drinking bouts and grew seriously ill. In November 1940 he suffered a heart attack and a second one a month later. On December 21, 1940 he died. He was forty-four. His last novel, The Last Tycoon, remained unfinished.

At the time of his death Fitzgerald was considered (when considered at all) as a failed literary hope, a writer victimized by his own indulgences. But since the 1940s his literary reputation has steadily risen. Today he is judged to be one of the major American prose writers of this century. In a number of his short stories, and in his finest novels, The Great Gatsby and Tender is the Night, Fitzgerald had revealed, as no other American writer had, the stridency of an age of glittering innocence. In vivid and graceful prose he had, at the same time, portrayed the hollowness of the American worship of riches and the unending American dreams of love, splendor, and gratified desire.

FURTHER READING: *The Stories of F. Scott Fitzgerald*, ed. M. Cowley, 1951; *The Fitzgerald Reader*, ed. A. Mizener, 1963; *The Price Was High, The Uncollected Stories of F. Scott Fitzgerald*, ed. M. Bruccoli, 1979; *The Notebooks of F. Scott Fitzgerald*, ed. M. Bruccoli, 1980; *The Letters of F. Scott Fitzgerald*, ed. A. Turnbull, 1963; *Correspondence of F. Scott Fitzgerald*, ed. M. Bruccoli and M. Duggan, 1980; *The Crack-Up*, ed., E. Wilson, 1945; A. Mizener, *The Far*

Side of Paradise, A Biography, 1951, 1967; S. Graham and G. Frank, *Beloved Infidel,* 1958; A. Turnbull, *Scott Fitzgerald*, 1962; R. Sklar, *F. Scott Fitzgerald, The Last Laocoön*, 1967; A. Latham, *Crazy Sundays, F. Scott Fitzgerald in Hollywood*, 1971; S Mayfield, *Exiles from Paradise, Zelda and Scott Fitzgerald*, 1972; M. Bruccoli, *Some Sort of Epic Grandeur, The Life of F. Scott Fitzgerald*, 1983; A. LeVot, *F. Scott Fitzgerald*, 1983; J. Mellow, *Invented Lives*, 1984; K. Eble, *F. Scott Fitzgerald*, 1963, 1977; J. Miller, *F. Scott Fitzgerald, His Art and His Technique*, 1964; S. Perosa, *The Art of F. Scott Fitzgerald*, 1965; R. Lehan, *F. Scott Fitzgerald and the Craft of Fiction*, 1966; J. Bryer, *The Critical Reputation of F. Scott Fitzgerald*, 1967; M. Hindus, *F. Scott Fitzgerald, An Introduction and Interpretation*, 1968; M. Stern, *The Golden Moment, The Novels of F. Scott Fitzgerald*, 1970; *The Romantic Egoists*, ed. M. Bruccoli, *et al*, 1974; B. Way, *F. Scott Fitzgerald and the Art of Social Fiction*, 1980; *The Short Stories of F. Scott Fitzgerald*, ed. J. Bryer, 1982; S. Donaldson, *Fool for Love, F. Scott Fitzgerald*, 1983; *Critical Essays on F. Scott Fitzgerald's The Great Gatsby*, ed. S. Donaldson, 1984; *New Essays on The Great Gatsby*, ed. M. Bruccoli, 1985.

TEXT: *The Great Gatsby*, 1925. Typographical corrections and textual changes have been made by the editor.

THE GREAT GATSBY

> *Then wear the gold hat, if that will move her;*
> *If you can bounce high, bounce for her too,*
> *Till she cry "Lover, gold-hatted, high-bouncing lover,*
> *I must have you!"*
> —THOMAS PARKE D'INVILLIERS.[1]

ONCE AGAIN
TO
ZELDA

CHAPTER I

In my younger and more vulnerable years my father gave me some advice that I've been turning over in my mind ever since.

"Whenever you feel like criticizing any one," he told me, "just remember that all the people in this world haven't had the advantages that you've had."

He didn't say any more, but we've always been unusually communicative in a reserved way, and I understood that he meant a great deal more than that. In consequence, I'm inclined to reserve all judgments, a habit that has opened up many curious natures to me and also made me the victim of not a few veteran bores. The abnormal mind is quick to detect and attach itself to this quality when it appears in a normal person, and so it came about that in college I was unjustly accused of being a politician, because I was privy to the secret griefs of wild, unknown men. Most of the confidences were unsought—frequently I have feigned sleep, preoccupations, or a hostile levity when I realized by some unmistakable sign that an intimate revelation was quivering on the horizon; for the intimate revelations of young men, or at least the terms in which they express them, are usually plagiaristic and marred by obvious suppressions. Reserving

[1]The epigraph is by Fitzgerald. D'Invilliers is a character in Fitzgerald's novel *This Side of Paradise* (1920).

judgments is a matter of infinite hope. I am still a little afraid of missing something if I forget that, as my father snobbishly suggested, and I snobbishly repeat, a sense of the fundamental decencies is parcelled out unequally at birth.

And, after boasting this way of my tolerance, I come to the admission that it has a limit. Conduct may be founded on the hard rock or the wet marshes, but after a certain point I don't care what it's founded on. When I came back from the East last autumn I felt that I wanted the world to be in uniform and at a sort of moral attention forever; I wanted no more riotous excursions with privileged glimpses into the human heart. Only Gatsby, the man who gives his name to this book, was exempt from my reaction—Gatsby, who represented everything for which I have an unaffected scorn. If personality is an unbroken series of successful gestures, then there was something gorgeous about him, some heightened sensitivity to the promises of life, as if he were related to one of those intricate machines that register earthquakes ten thousand miles away. This responsiveness had nothing to do with that flabby impressionability which is dignified under the name of the "creative temperament"—it was an extraordinary gift for hope, a romantic readiness such as I have never found in any other person and which it is not likely I shall ever find again. No—Gatsby turned out all right at the end; it is what preyed on Gatsby, what foul dust floated in the wake of his dreams that temporarily closed out my interest in the abortive sorrows and short-winded elations of men.

My family have been prominent, well-to-do people in this Middle Western city for three generations. The Carraways are something of a clan, and we have a tradition that we're descended from the Dukes of Buccleuch,[1] but the actual founder of my line was my grandfather's brother, who came here in fifty-one, sent a substitute to the Civil War,[2] and started the wholesale hardware business that my father carries on today.

I never saw this great-uncle, but I'm supposed to look like him—with special reference to the rather hard-boiled painting that hangs in father's office. I graduated from New Haven[3] in 1915, just a quarter of a century after my father, and a little later I participated in that delayed Teutonic migration known as the Great War.[4] I enjoyed the counterraid so thoroughly that I came back restless. Instead of being the warm center of the world, the Middle West now seemed like the ragged edge of the universe—so I decided to go East and learn the bond business. Everybody I knew was in the bond business, so I supposed it could support one more single man. All my aunts and uncles talked it over as if they were choosing a prep school for me, and finally said, "Why—ye-es," with very grave, hesitant faces. Father agreed to finance me for a year, and after various delays I came East, permanently, I thought, in the spring of twenty-two.

The practical thing was to find rooms in the city, but it was a warm season, and I had just left a country of wide lawns and friendly trees, so when a young man at the office suggested that we take a house together in a commuting town, it sounded like a great idea. He found the house, a weather-beaten cardboard bungalow at eighty a month, but at the last minute the firm ordered him to Washington, and I went out to the country alone. I had a dog—at least I had

---

[1]Scottish dukedom originating in the seventeenth century. Pronounced "buhk*loo*."
[2]During the American Civil War (1861–1865), conscription laws allowed a man to gain permanent exemption from service in the Union army by hiring a substitute to enlist in his place.
[3]I.e., Yale University in New Haven, Connecticut.
[4]World War I (1914–1918). The invasion of Belgium and France by the German armies in 1914 was often compared to the migratory invasion of Western Europe by Germanic (Teutonic) tribes in the fourth and fifth centuries A.D.

him for a few days until he ran away—and an old Dodge and a Finnish woman, who made my bed and cooked breakfast and muttered Finnish wisdom to herself over the electric stove.

It was lonely for a day or so until one morning some man, more recently arrived than I, stopped me on the road.

"How do you get to West Egg village?"[5] he asked helplessly.

I told him. And as I walked on I was lonely no longer. I was a guide, a pathfinder, an original settler. He had casually conferred on me the freedom of the neighborhood.[6]

And so with the sunshine and the great bursts of leaves growing on the trees, just as things grow in fast movies, I had that familiar conviction that life was beginning over again with the summer.

There was so much to read, for one thing, and so much fine health to be pulled down out of the young breath-giving air. I bought a dozen volumes on banking and credit and investment securities, and they stood on my shelf in red and gold like new money from the mint, promising to unfold the shining secrets that only Midas and Morgan and Mæcenas[7] knew. And I had the high intention of reading many other books besides. I was rather literary in college—one year I wrote a series of very solemn and obvious editorials for the *Yale News*[8]—and now I was going to bring back all such things into my life and become again that most limited of all specialists, the "well-rounded man." This isn't just an epigram—life is much more successfully looked at from a single window, after all.

It was a matter of chance that I should have rented a house in one of the strangest communities in North America. It was on that slender riotous island which extends itself due east of New York—and where there are, among other natural curiosities, two unusual formations of land. Twenty miles from the city a pair of enormous eggs, identical in contour and separated only by a courtesy bay, jut out into the most domesticated body of salt water in the western hemisphere, the great wet barnyard of Long Island Sound.[9] They are not perfect ovals—like the egg in the Columbus story, they are both crushed flat at the contact end[10]—but their physical resemblance must be a source of perpetual confusion to the gulls that fly overhead. To the wingless a more arresting phenomenon is their dissimilarity in every particular except shape and size.

I lived at West Egg, the—well, the less fashionable of the two, though this is a most superficial tag to express the bizarre and not a little sinister contrast between them. My house was at the very tip of the egg, only fifty yards from the Sound, and squeezed between two huge places that rented for twelve or fifteen thousand a season. The one on my right was a colossal affair by any standard—it was a factual imitation of some Hôtel de Ville in Normandy,[11] with a tower on one side, spanking new under a thin beard of raw ivy, and a marble

---

[5]The events of the novel take place on Long Island and the island of Manhattan (a borough of New York City). Most place names in the novel are real, but West Egg, East Egg, Port Roosevelt, the "valley of ashes," Gad's Hill, and other names are fictitious.

[6]A reference to the ancient custom by which English towns granted to visitors the rights of citizenship (the "freedom of the town"), an honor usually given only to the rich and powerful.

[7]Midas: in Greek legend, a mythical king whose touch turned everything to gold. Morgan: John Pierpont Morgan (1837–1913), a wealthy American banker. Maecenas: Caius Maecenas (74?–8 B.C.), a wealthy Roman statesman and a patron of the arts.

[8]Yale University newspaper.

[9]Inlet of the Atlantic Ocean that separates Long Island from Connecticut.

[10]According to legend, Christopher Columbus, challenged to stand an egg upright on a table, did so by crushing one end flat. When his solution was derided as obvious, Columbus replied that it was obvious only after it had been discovered.

[11]I.e., in the style of a city hall (French: hôtel de ville) in Normandy, France.

swimming pool, and more than forty acres of lawn and garden. It was Gatsby's mansion. Or, rather, as I didn't know Mr. Gatsby, it was a mansion inhabited by a gentleman of that name. My own house was an eyesore, but it was a small eyesore, and it had been overlooked, so I had a view of the water, a partial view of my neighbor's lawn, and the consoling proximity of millionaires—all for eighty dollars a month.

Across the courtesy bay the white palaces of fashionable East Egg glittered along the water, and the history of the summer really begins on the evening I drove over there to have dinner with the Tom Buchanans. Daisy was my second cousin once removed, and I'd known Tom in college. And just after the war I spent two days with them in Chicago.

Her husband, among various physical accomplishments, had been one of the most powerful ends that ever played football at New Haven—a national figure in a way, one of those men who reach such an acute limited excellence at twenty-one that everything afterward savors of anticlimax. His family were enormously wealthy—even in college his freedom with money was a matter for reproach—but now he'd left Chicago and come East in a fashion that rather took your breath away; for instance, he'd brought down a string of polo ponies from Lake Forest.[12] It was hard to realize that a man in my own generation was wealthy enough to do that.

Why they came East I don't know. They had spent a year in France for no particular reason, and then drifted here and there unrestfully wherever people played polo and were rich together. This was a permanent move, said Daisy over the telephone, but I didn't believe it—I had no sight into Daisy's heart, but I felt that Tom would drift on forever seeking, a little wistfully, for the dramatic turbulence of some irrecoverable football game.

And so it happened that on a warm windy evening I drove over to East Egg to see two old friends whom I scarcely knew at all. Their house was even more elaborate than I expected, a cheerful red-and-white Georgian Colonial mansion,[13] overlooking the bay. The lawn started at the beach and ran toward the front door for a quarter of a mile, jumping over sun-dials and brick walls and burning[14] gardens—finally when it reached the house drifting up the side in bright vines as though from the momentum of its run. The front was broken by a line of French windows,[15] glowing now with reflected gold and wide open to the warm windy afternoon, and Tom Buchanan in riding clothes was standing with his legs apart on the front porch.

He had changed since his New Haven years. Now he was a sturdy straw-haired man of thirty with a rather hard mouth and a supercilious manner. Two shining arrogant eyes had established dominance over his face and gave him the appearance of always leaning aggressively forward. Not even the effeminate swank of his riding clothes could hide the enormous power of that body—he seemed to fill those glistening boots until he strained the top lacing, and you could see a great pack of muscle shifting when his shoulder moved under his thin coat. It was a body capable of enormous leverage—a cruel body.

His speaking voice, a gruff husky tenor, added to the impression of fractious-

[12] An affluent suburb of Chicago.

[13] An architectural style developed during the reigns of George I, George II, and George III of England (1714–1820), and based on classical Greek and Roman designs. In America, the term "Georgian" is commonly applied to buildings of classical design made of red brick with white-stone trim and white-painted woodwork.

[14] Bright, glowing.

[15] Full-length doors with rectangular glass panes from top to bottom.

ness he conveyed. There was a touch of paternal contempt in it, even toward people he liked—and there were men at New Haven who had hated his guts.

"Now, don't think my opinion on these matters is final," he seemed to say, "just because I'm stronger and more of a man than you are." We were in the same senior society,[16] and while we were never intimate I always had the impression that he approved of me and wanted me to like him with some harsh, defiant wistfulness of his own.

We talked for a few minutes on the sunny porch.

"I've got a nice place here," he said, his eyes flashing about restlessly.

Turning me around by one arm, he moved a broad flat hand along the front vista, including in its sweep a sunken Italian garden,[17] a half acre of deep, pungent roses, and a snub-nosed motor-boat that bumped the tide offshore.

"It belonged to Demaine, the oil man." He turned me around again, politely and abruptly. "We'll go inside."

We walked through a high hallway into a bright rosy-colored space, fragilely bound into the house by French windows at either end. The windows were ajar and gleaming white against the fresh grass outside that seemed to grow a little way into the house. A breeze blew through the room, blew curtains in at one end and out the other like pale flags, twisting them up toward the frosted wedding-cake of the ceiling, and then rippled over the wine-colored rug, making a shadow on it as wind does on the sea.

The only completely stationary object in the room was an enormous couch on which two young women were buoyed up as though upon an anchored balloon. They were both in white, and their dresses were rippling and fluttering as if they had just been blown back in after a short flight around the house. I must have stood for a few moments listening to the whip and snap of the curtains and the groan of a picture on the wall. Then there was a boom as Tom Buchanan shut the rear windows and the caught wind died out about the room, and the curtains and the rugs and the two young women ballooned slowly to the floor.

The younger of the two was a stranger to me. She was extended full length at her end of the divan, completely motionless, and with her chin raised a little, as if she were balancing something on it which was quite likely to fall. If she saw me out of the corner of her eyes she gave no hint of it—indeed, I was almost surprised into murmuring an apology for having disturbed her by coming in.

The other girl, Daisy, made an attempt to rise—she leaned slightly forward with a conscientious expression—then she laughed, an absurd, charming little laugh, and I laughed too and came forward into the room.

"I'm p-paralyzed with happiness."

She laughed again, as if she said something very witty, and held my hand for a moment, looking up into my face, promising that there was no one in the world she so much wanted to see. That was a way she had. She hinted in a murmur that the surname of the balancing girl was Baker. (I've heard it said that Daisy's murmur was only to make people lean toward her; an irrelevant criticism that made it no less charming.)

At any rate, Miss Baker's lips fluttered, she nodded at me almost imperceptibly, and then quickly tipped her head back again—the object she was balancing had obviously tottered a little and given her something of a fright. Again a sort of apology arose to my lips. Almost any exhibition of complete self-sufficiency draws a stunned tribute from me.

---

[16]One of six secret societies for seniors at Yale. Election to membership was considered a high social distinction.

[17]Formal gardens of elaborate geometric design, often adorned with fountains and pavilions.

I looked back at my cousin, who began to ask me questions in her low, thrilling voice. It was the kind of voice that the ear follows up and down, as if each speech is an arrangement of notes that will never be played again. Her face was sad and lovely with bright things in it, bright eyes and a bright passionate mouth, but there was an excitement in her voice that men who had cared for her found difficult to forget: a singing compulsion, a whispered "Listen," a promise that she had done gay, exciting things just a while since and that there were gay, exciting things hovering in the next hour.

I told her how I had stopped off in Chicago for a day on my way East, and how a dozen people had sent their love through me.

"Do they miss me?"she cried ecstatically.

"The whole town is desolate. All the cars have the left rear wheel painted black as a mourning wreath, and there's a persistent wail all night along the north shore."

"How gorgeous! Let's go back, Tom. Tomorrow!" Then she added irrelevantly: "You ought to see the baby."

"I'd like to."

"She's asleep. She's three years old. Haven't you ever seen her?"

"Never."

"Well, you ought to see her. She's——"

Tom Buchanan, who had been hovering restlessly about the room, stopped and rested his hand on my shoulder.

"What you doing, Nick?"

"I'm a bond man."

"Who with?"

I told him.

"Never heard of them," he remarked decisively.

This annoyed me.

"You will," I answered shortly. "You will if you stay in the East."

"Oh, I'll stay in the East, don't you worry," he said, glancing at Daisy and then back at me, as if he were alert for something more. "I'd be a God damned fool to live anywhere else."

At this point Miss Baker said: "Absolutely!" with such suddenness that I started—it was the first word she had uttered since I came into the room. Evidently it surprised her as much as it did me, for she yawned and with a series of rapid, deft movements stood up into the room.

"I'm stiff," she complained, "I've been lying on that sofa for as long as I can remember."

"Don't look at me," Daisy retorted, "I've been trying to get you to New York all afternoon."

"No, thanks," said Miss Baker to the four cocktails just in from the pantry, "I'm absolutely in training."

Her host looked at her incredulously.

"You are!" He took down his drink as if it were a drop in the bottom of a glass. "How you ever get anything done is beyond me."

I looked at Miss Baker, wondering what it was she "got done." I enjoyed looking at her. She was a slender, small-breasted girl, with an erect carriage, which she accentuated by throwing her body backward at the shoulders like a young cadet. Her gray sun-strained eyes looked back at me with polite reciprocal curiosity out of a wan, charming, discontented face. It occurred to me now that I had seen her, or a picture of her, somewhere before.

"You live in West Egg," she remarked contemptuously. "I know somebody there."

"I don't know a single——"

"You must know Gatsby."

"Gatsby?" demanded Daisy. "What Gatsby?"

Before I could reply that he was my neighbor dinner was announced; wedging his tense arm imperatively under mine, Tom Buchanan compelled me from the room as though he were moving a checker to another square.

Slenderly, languidly, their hands set lightly on their hips, the two young women preceded us out onto a rosy-colored porch, open toward the sunset, where four candles flickered on the table in the diminished wind.

"Why *candles?*" objected Daisy, frowning. She snapped them out with her fingers. "In two weeks it'll be the longest day in the year."[18] She looked at us all radiantly. "Do you always watch for the longest day of the year and then miss it? I always watch for the longest day in the year and then miss it."

"We ought to plan something," yawned Miss Baker, sitting down at the table as if she were getting into bed.

"All right," said Daisy. "What'll we plan?" She turned to me helplessly: "What do people plan?"

Before I could answer her eyes fastened with an awed expression on her little finger.

"Look!" she complained; "I hurt it."

We all looked—the knuckle was black and blue.

"You did it, Tom," she said accusingly. "I know you didn't mean to, but you *did* do it. That's what I get for marrying a brute of a man, a great, big, hulking physical specimen of a——"

"I hate that word hulking," objected Tom crossly, "even in kidding."

"Hulking," insisted Daisy.

Sometimes she and Miss Baker talked at once, unobtrusively and with a bantering inconsequence that was never quite chatter, that was as cool as their white dresses and their impersonal eyes in the absence of all desire. They were here, and they accepted Tom and me, making only a polite pleasant effort to entertain or to be entertained. They knew that presently dinner would be over and a little later the evening too would be over and casually put away. It was sharply different from the West, where an evening was hurried from phase to phase toward its close, in a continually disappointed anticipation or else in sheer nervous dread of the moment itself.

"You make me feel uncivilized, Daisy," I confessed on my second glass of corky[19] but rather impressive claret. "Can't you talk about crops or something?"

I meant nothing in particular by this remark, but it was taken up in an unexpected way.

"Civilization's going to pieces," broke out Tom violently. "I've gotten to be a terrible pessimist about things. Have you read *The Rise of the Colored Empires* by this man Goddard?"[20]

"Why, no," I answered, rather surprised by his tone.

"Well, it's a fine book, and everybody ought to read it. The idea is if we don't

---

[18]June 21.

[19]Corky: marred by the scent of a tainted cork. Claret: dry, red wine from Bordeaux in France.

[20]Probably an allusion to *The Rising Tide of Color* by Lothrop Stoddard (1920). Stoddard forecast a fatal decline of civilization, because the proportion of white Northern Europeans in the world's population was falling.

look out the white race will be—will be utterly submerged. It's all scientific stuff; it's been proved."

"Tom's getting very profound," said Daisy, with an expression of unthoughtful sadness. "He reads deep books with long words in them. What was that word we——"

"Well, these books are all scientific," insisted Tom, glancing at her impatiently. "This fellow has worked out the whole thing. It's up to us, who are the dominant race, to watch out or these other races will have control of things."

"We've got to beat them down," whispered Daisy, winking ferociously toward the fervent sun.

"You ought to live in California——" began Miss Baker, but Tom interrupted her by shifting heavily in his chair.

"This idea is that we're Nordics. I am, and you are, and you are, and——" After an infinitesimal hesitation he included Daisy with a slight nod, and she winked at me again. "——And we've produced all the things that go to make civilization—oh, science and art, and all that. Do you see?"

There was something pathetic in his concentration, as if his complacency, more acute than of old, was not enough to him any more. When, almost immediately, the telephone rang inside and the butler left the porch Daisy seized upon the momentary interruption and leaned toward me.

"I'll tell you a family secret," she whispered enthusiastically. "It's about the butler's nose. Do you want to hear about the butler's nose?"

"That's why I came over tonight."

"Well, he wasn't always a butler; he used to be the silver polisher for some people in New York that had a silver service for two hundred people. He had to polish it from morning till night, until finally it began to affect his nose——"

"Things went from bad to worse," suggested Miss Baker.

"Yes. Things went from bad to worse, until finally he had to give up his position."

For a moment the last sunshine fell with romantic affection upon her glowing face; her voice compelled me forward breathlessly as I listened—then the glow faded, each light deserting her with lingering regret, like children leaving a pleasant street at dusk.

The butler came back and murmured something close to Tom's ear, whereupon Tom frowned, pushed back his chair, and without a word went inside. As if his absence quickened something within her, Daisy leaned forward again, her voice glowing and singing.

"I love to see you at my table, Nick. You remind me of a—of a rose, an absolute rose. Doesn't he?" She turned to Miss Baker for confirmation: "An absolute rose?"

This was untrue. I am not even faintly like a rose. She was only extemporizing, but a stirring warmth flowed from her, as if her heart was trying to come out to you concealed in one of those breathless, thrilling words. Then suddenly she threw her napkin on the table and excused herself and went into the house.

Miss Baker and I exchanged a short glance consciously devoid of meaning. I was about to speak when she sat up alertly and said "Sh!" in a warning voice. A subdued impassioned murmur was audible in the room beyond, and Miss Baker leaned forward unashamed, trying to hear. The murmur trembled on the verge of coherence, sank down, mounted excitedly, and then ceased altogether.

"This Mr. Gatsby you spoke of is my neighbor——" I said.

"Don't talk. I want to hear what happens."

"Is something happening?" I inquired innocently.

"You mean to say you don't know?" said Miss Baker, honestly surprised. "I thought everybody knew."

"I don't."

"Why——" she said hesitantly, "Tom's got some woman in New York."

"Got some woman?" I repeated blankly.

Miss Baker nodded.

"She might have the decency not to telephone him at dinner time. Don't you think?"

Almost before I had grasped her meaning there was the flutter of a dress and the crunch of leather boots, and Tom and Daisy were back at the table.

"It couldn't be helped!" cried Daisy with tense gayety.

She sat down, glanced searchingly at Miss Baker and then at me, and continued: "I looked outdoors for a minute, and it's very romantic outdoors. There's a bird on the lawn that I think must be a nightingale come over on the Cunard or White Star Line.[21] He's singing away——" Her voice sang: "It's romantic, isn't it, Tom?"

"Very romantic," he said, and then miserably to me: "If it's light enough after dinner, I want to take you down to the stables."

The telephone rang inside, startlingly, and as Daisy shook her head decisively at Tom the subject of the stables, in fact all subjects, vanished into air. Among the broken fragments of the last five minutes at table I remember the candles being lit again, pointlessly, and I was conscious of wanting to look squarely at every one, and yet to avoid all eyes. I couldn't guess what Daisy and Tom were thinking, but I doubt if even Miss Baker, who seemed to have mastered a certain hardy scepticism, was able utterly to put this fifth guest's shrill metallic urgency out of mind. To a certain temperament the situation might have seemed intriguing—my own instinct was to telephone immediately for the police.

The horses, needless to say, were not mentioned again. Tom and Miss Baker, with several feet of twilight between them, strolled back into the library, as if to a vigil beside a perfectly tangible body, while, trying to look pleasantly interested and a little deaf, I followed Daisy around a chain of connecting verandas to the porch in front. In its deep gloom we sat down side by side on a wicker settee.

Daisy took her face in her hands as if feeling its lovely shape, and her eyes moved gradually out into the velvet dusk. I saw that turbulent emotions possessed her, so I asked what I thought would be some sedative questions about her little girl.

"We don't know each other very well, Nick," she said suddenly. "Even if we are cousins. You didn't come to my wedding."

"I wasn't back from the war."

"That's true." She hesitated. "Well, I've had a very bad time, Nick, and I'm pretty cynical about everything."

Evidently she had reason to be. I waited but she didn't say any more, and after a moment I returned rather feebly to the subject of her daughter.

"I suppose she talks, and—eats, and everything."

"Oh, yes." She looked at me absently. "Listen, Nick; let me tell you what I said when she was born. Would you like to hear?"

"Very much."

"It'll show you how I've gotten to feel about—things. Well, she was less than

---

[21]English passenger-ship lines the vessels of which traveled between America and Great Britain. The nightingale, a songbird native to the Old World, has often been identified with English Romantic poetry.

an hour old and Tom was God knows where. I woke up out of the ether with an utterly abandoned feeling, and asked the nurse right away if it was a boy or a girl. She told me it was a girl, and so I turned my head away and wept. 'All right,' I said, 'I'm glad it's a girl. And I hope she'll be a fool—that's the best thing a girl can be in this world, a beautiful little fool.'

"You see I think everything's terrible anyhow," she went on in a convinced way. "Everybody thinks so—the most advanced people. And I *know*. I've been everywhere and seen everything and done everything." Her eyes flashed around her in a defiant way, rather like Tom's, and she laughed with thrilling scorn. "Sophisticated—God, I'm sophisticated!"

The instant her voice broke off, ceasing to compel my attention, my belief, I felt the basic insincerity of what she had said. It made me uneasy, as though the whole evening had been a trick of some sort to exact a contributory emotion from me. I waited, and sure enough, in a moment she looked at me with an absolute smirk on her lovely face, as if she had asserted her membership in a rather distinguished secret society to which she and Tom belonged.

Inside, the crimson room bloomed with light. Tom and Miss Baker sat at either end of the long couch and she read aloud to him from the *Saturday Evening Post*[22]—the words, murmurous and uninflected, running together in a soothing tune. The lamp-light, bright on his boots and dull on the autumn-leaf yellow of her hair, glinted along the paper as she turned a page with a flutter of slender muscles in her arms.

When we came in she held us silent for a moment with a lifted hand.

"To be continued," she said, tossing the magazine on the table, "in our very next issue."

Her body asserted itself with a restless movement of her knee, and she stood up.

"Ten o'clock," she remarked, apparently finding the time on the ceiling. "Time for this good girl to go to bed."

"Jordan's going to play in the tournament tomorrow," explained Daisy, "over at Westchester."[23]

"Oh—you're *Jor*dan Baker."

I knew now why her face was familiar—its pleasing contemptuous expression had looked out at me from many rotogravure[24] pictures of the sporting life at Asheville and Hot Springs and Palm Beach.[25] I had heard some story of her too, a critical unpleasant story, but what it was I had forgotten long ago.

"Good night," she said softly. "Wake me at eight, won't you?"

"If you'll get up."

"I will. Good night, Mr. Carraway. See you anon."

"Of course you will," confirmed Daisy. "In fact I think I'll arrange a marriage. Come over often, Nick, and I'll sort of—oh—fling you together. You know—lock you up accidentally in linen closets and push you out to sea in a boat, and all that sort of thing——"

"Good night," called Miss Baker from the stairs. "I haven't heard a word."

"She's a nice girl," said Tom after a moment. "They oughtn't to let her run around the country this way."

---

[22] A general magazine widely popular in the United States from the 1920s to the 1960s.
[23] An affluent suburban county north of New York City.
[24] A newspaper section devoted to pictures, named for the rotogravure process for printing photographs on a rotary press.
[25] Fashionable resorts in North Carolina, Virginia, and Florida.

"Who oughtn't to?" inquired Daisy coldly.

"Her family."

"Her family is one aunt about a thousand years old. Besides, Nick's going to look after her, aren't you, Nick? She's going to spend lots of week-ends out here this summer. I think the home influence will be very good for her."

Daisy and Tom looked at each other for a moment in silence.

"Is she from New York?" I asked quickly.

"From Louisville. Our white girlhood was passed together there. Our beautiful white——"

"Did you give Nick a little heart-to-heart talk on the veranda?" demanded Tom suddenly.

"Did I?" She looked at me. "I can't seem to remember, but I think we talked about the Nordic race. Yes, I'm sure we did. It sort of crept upon us and first thing you know——"

"Don't believe everything you hear, Nick," he advised me.

I said lightly that I had heard nothing at all, and a few minutes later I got up to go home. They came to the door with me and stood side by side in a cheerful square of light. As I started my motor Daisy peremptorily called: "Wait!

"I forgot to ask you something, and it's important. We heard you were engaged to a girl out West."

"That's right," corroborated Tom kindly. "We heard that you were engaged."

"It's a libel. I'm too poor."

"But we heard it," insisted Daisy, surprising me by opening up again in a flower-like way. "We heard it from three people, so it must be true."

Of course I knew what they were referring to, but I wasn't even vaguely engaged. The fact that gossip had published the banns[26] was one of the reasons I had come East. You can't stop going with an old friend on account of rumors, and on the other hand I had no intention of being rumored into marriage.

Their interest rather touched me and made them less remotely rich—nevertheless, I was confused and a little disgusted as I drove away. It seemed to me that the thing for Daisy to do was to rush out of the house, child in arms—but apparently there were no such intentions in her head. As for Tom, the fact that he "had some woman in New York" was really less surprising than that he had been depressed by a book. Something was making him nibble at the edge of stale ideas as if his sturdy physical egotism no longer nourished his peremptory heart.

Already it was deep summer on roadhouse roofs and in front of wayside garages, where new red gas-pumps sat out in pools of light, and when I reached my estate at West Egg I ran the car under its shed and sat for a while on an abandoned grass roller in the yard. The wind had blown off, leaving a loud, bright night, with wings beating in the trees and a persistent organ sound as the full bellows of the earth blew the frogs full of life. The silhouette of a moving cat wavered across the moonlight, and turning my head to watch it, I saw that I was not alone—fifty feet away a figure had emerged from the shadow of my neighbor's mansion and was standing with his hands in his pockets regarding the silver pepper of the stars. Something in his leisurely movements and the secure position of his feet upon the lawn suggested that it was Mr. Gatsby himself, come out to determine what share was his of our local heavens.

I decided to call to him. Miss Baker had mentioned him at dinner, and that would do for an introduction. But I didn't call to him, for he gave a sudden

[26]A public announcement of a forthcoming marriage.

intimation that he was content to be alone—he stretched out his arms toward the dark water in a curious way, and, far as I was from him, I could have sworn he was trembling. Involuntarily I glanced seaward—and distinguished nothing except a single green light, minute and far away, that might have been the end of a dock. When I looked once more for Gatsby he had vanished, and I was alone again in the unquiet darkness.

CHAPTER II

ABOUT half way between West Egg and New York the motor road hastily joins the railroad and runs beside it for a quarter of a mile, so as to shrink away from a certain desolate area of land. This is a valley of ashes—a fantastic farm where ashes grow like wheat into ridges and hills and grotesque gardens; where ashes take the forms of houses and chimneys and rising smoke and, finally, with a transcendent effort, of men, who move dimly and already crumbling through the powdery air. Occasionally a line of gray cars crawls along an invisible track, gives out a ghastly creak, and comes to rest, and immediately the ash-gray men swarm up with leaden spades and stir up an impenetrable cloud, which screens their obscure operations from your sight.

But above the gray land and the spasms of bleak dust which drift endlessly over it, you perceive, after a moment, the eyes of Doctor T. J. Eckleburg. The eyes of Doctor T. J. Eckleburg are blue and gigantic—their retinas[1] are one yard high. They look out of no face, but, instead, from a pair of enormous yellow spectacles which pass over a nonexistent nose. Evidently some wild wag of an oculist set them there to fatten his practice in the borough of Queens,[2] and then sank down himself into eternal blindness, or forgot them and moved away. But his eyes, dimmed a little by many paintless days under sun and rain, brood on over the solemn dumping ground.

The valley of ashes is bounded on one side by a small foul river, and, when the drawbridge is up to let barges through, the passengers on waiting trains can stare at the dismal scene for as long as half an hour. There is always a halt there of at least a minute, and it was because of this that I first met Tom Buchanan's mistress.

The fact that he had one was insisted upon wherever he was known. His acquaintances resented the fact that he turned up in popular restaurants with her and, leaving her at a table, sauntered about, chatting with whomsoever he knew. Though I was curious to see her, I had no desire to meet her—but I did. I went up to New York with Tom on the train one afternoon, and when we stopped by the ashheaps he jumped to his feet and, taking hold of my elbow, literally forced me from the car.

"We're getting off," he insisted. "I want you to meet my girl."

I think he'd tanked up a good deal at luncheon, and his determination to have my company bordered on violence. The supercilious assumption was that on Sunday afternoon I had nothing better to do.

I followed him over a low whitewashed railroad fence, and we walked back a hundred yards along the road under Doctor Eckleburg's persistent stare. The only building in sight was a small block of yellow brick sitting on the edge of the waste land, a sort of compact Main Street ministering to it, and contiguous to

---

[1]Retinas, at the backs of the eyeballs, are not visible. Perhaps Fitzgerald meant "irises" or "pupils."
[2]One of the five boroughs (political subdivisions) of New York City.

absolutely nothing. One of the three shops it contained was for rent and another was an all-night restaurant, approached by a trail of ashes; the third was a garage—*Repairs.* GEORGE B. WILSON. *Cars bought and sold.*—and I followed Tom inside.

The interior was unprosperous and bare; the only car visible was the dust-covered wreck of a Ford which crouched in a dim corner. It had occurred to me that this shadow of a garage must be a blind, and that sumptuous and romantic apartments were concealed overhead, when the proprietor himself appeared in the door of an office, wiping his hands on a piece of waste. He was a blond, spiritless man, anæmic, and faintly handsome. When he saw us a damp gleam of hope sprang into his light blue eyes.

"Hello, Wilson, old man," said Tom, slapping him jovially on the shoulder. "How's business?"

"I can't complain," answered Wilson unconvincingly. "When are you going to sell me that car?"

"Next week; I've got my man working on it now."

"Works pretty slow, don't he?"

"No, he doesn't," said Tom coldly. "And if you feel that way about it, maybe I'd better sell it somewhere else after all."

"I don't mean that," explained Wilson quickly. "I just meant——"

His voice faded off and Tom glanced impatiently around the garage. Then I heard footsteps on a stairs, and in a moment the thickish figure of a woman blocked out the light from the office door. She was in the middle thirties, and faintly stout, but she carried her surplus flesh sensuously as some women can. Her face, above a spotted dress of dark blue crêpe-de-chine,[3] contained no facet or gleam of beauty, but there was an immediately perceptible vitality about her as if the nerves of her body were continually smouldering. She smiled slowly and, walking through her husband as if he were a ghost, shook hands with Tom, looking him flush in the eye. Then she wet her lips, and without turning around spoke to her husband in a soft, coarse voice:

"Get some chairs, why don't you, so somebody can sit down."

"Oh, sure," agreed Wilson hurriedly, and went toward the little office, mingling immediately with the cement color of the walls. A white ashen dust veiled his dark suit and his pale hair as it veiled everything in the vicinity—except his wife, who moved close to Tom.

"I want to see you," said Tom intently. "Get on the next train."

"All right."

"I'll meet you by the news-stand on the lower level."

She nodded and moved away from him just as George Wilson emerged with two chairs from his office door.

We waited for her down the road and out of sight. It was a few days before the Fourth of July, and a gray, scrawny Italian child was setting torpedoes[4] in a row along the railroad track.

"Terrible place, isn't it," said Tom, exchanging a frown with Doctor Eckleburg.

"Awful."

"It does her good to get away."

"Doesn't her husband object?"

"Wilson? He thinks she goes to see her sister in New York. He's so dumb he doesn't know he's alive."

---

[3]A soft, crinkled fabric used in fine clothing.
[4]Small fireworks that explode when crushed or thrown against a hard surface.

So Tom Buchanan and his girl and I went up together to New York—or not quite together, for Mrs. Wilson sat discreetly in another car. Tom deferred that much to the sensibilities of those East Eggers who might be on the train.

She had changed her dress to a brown figured muslin, which stretched tight over her rather wide hips as Tom helped her to the platform in New York. At the news-stand she bought a copy of *Town Tattle*[5] and a moving-picture magazine, and in the station drug-store some cold cream and a small flask of perfume. Upstairs, in the solemn echoing drive she let four taxicabs drive away before she selected a new one, lavender-colored with gray upholstery, and in this we slid out from the mass of the station into the flowing sunshine. But immediately she turned sharply from the window and, leaning forward, tapped on the front glass.

"I want to get one of those dogs," she said earnestly. "I want to get one for the apartment. They're nice to have—a dog."

We backed up to a gray old man who bore an absurd resemblance to John D. Rockefeller.[6] In a basket swung from his neck cowered a dozen very recent puppies of an indeterminate breed.

"What kind are they?" asked Mrs. Wilson eagerly, as he came to the taxi-window.

"All kinds. What kind do you want, lady?"

"I'd like to get one of those police dogs; I don't suppose you got that kind?

The man peered doubtfully into the basket, plunged in his hand and drew one up, wriggling, by the back of the neck.

"That's no police dog," said Tom.

"No, it's not exactly a po*lice* dog," said the man with disappointment in his voice. "It's more of an Airedale." He passed his hand over the brown washrag of a back. "Look at that coat. Some coat. That's a dog that'll never bother you with catching cold."

"I think it's cute," said Mrs. Wilson enthusiastically. "How much is it?"

"That dog?" He looked at it admiringly. "That dog will cost you ten dollars."

The Airedale—undoubtedly there was an Airedale concerned in it somewhere, though its feet were startlingly white—changed hands and settled down into Mrs. Wilson's lap, where she fondled the weatherproof coat with rapture.

"Is it a boy or a girl?" she asked delicately.

"That dog? That dog's a boy."

"It's a bitch," said Tom decisively. "Here's your money. Go and buy ten more dogs with it."

We drove over to Fifth Avenue,[7] so warm and soft, almost pastoral, on the summer Sunday afternoon that I wouldn't have been surprised to see a great flock of white sheep turn the corner.

"Hold on," I said, "I have to leave you here."

"No, you don't," interposed Tom quickly.

"Myrtle'll be hurt if you don't come up to the apartment. Won't you, Myrtle?"

"Come on," she urged. "I'll telephone my sister Catherine. She's said to be very beautiful by people who ought to know."

"Well, I'd like to, but——"

We went on, cutting back again over the Park[8] toward the West Hundreds. At 158th Street the cab stopped at one slice in a long white cake of apartment-

[5]A society gossip magazine.
[6]John D. Rockefeller (1839–1937), American oil tycoon.
[7]Street of elegant shops in New York City.
[8]Central Park on the island of Manhattan, New York City.

houses. Throwing a regal homecoming glance around the neighborhood, Mrs. Wilson gathered up her dog and her other purchases, and went haughtily in.

"I'm going to have the McKees come up," she announced as we rose in the elevator. "And, of course, I got to call up my sister, too."

The apartment was on the top floor—a small living-room, a small dining-room, a small bedroom, and a bath. The living-room was crowded to the doors with a set of tapestried furniture entirely too large for it, so that to move about was to stumble continually over scenes of ladies swinging in the gardens of Versailles.[9] The only picture was an over-enlarged photograph, apparently a hen sitting on a blurred rock. Looked at from a distance, however, the hen resolved itself into a bonnet, and the countenance of a stout old lady beamed down into the room. Several old copies of *Town Tattle* lay on the table together with a copy of *Simon Called Peter*[10] and some of the small scandal magazines of Broadway. Mrs. Wilson was first concerned with the dog. A reluctant elevator-boy went for a box full of straw and some milk, to which he added on his own initiative a tin of large, hard dog-biscuits—one of which decomposed apathetically in the saucer of milk all afternoon. Meanwhile Tom brought out a bottle of whiskey from a locked bureau door.

I have been drunk just twice in my life, and the second time was that afternoon; so everything that happened has a dim, hazy cast over it, although until after eight o'clock the apartment was full of cheerful sun. Sitting on Tom's lap Mrs. Wilson called up several people on the telephone; then there were no cigarettes, and I went out to buy some at the drugstore on the corner. When I came back they had disappeared, so I sat down discreetly in the living-room and read a chapter of *Simon Called Peter*—either it was terrible stuff or the whiskey distorted things, because it didn't make any sense to me.

Just as Tom and Myrtle (after the first drink Mrs. Wilson and I called each other by our first names) reappeared, company commenced to arrive at the apartment-door.

The sister, Catherine, was a slender, worldly girl of about thirty, with a solid, sticky bob[11] of red hair, and a complexion powdered milky white. Her eyebrows had been plucked and then drawn on again at a more rakish angle, but the efforts of nature toward the restortion of the old alignment gave a blurred air to her face. When she moved about there was an incessant clicking as innumerable pottery bracelets jingled up and down upon her arms. She came in with such a proprietary haste, and looked around so possessively at the furniture that I wondered if she lived here. But when I asked her she laughed immoderately, repeated my question aloud, and told me she lived with a girl friend at a hotel.

Mr. McKee was a pale, feminine man from the flat below. He had just shaved, for there was a white spot of lather on his cheekbone, and he was most respectful in his greeting to every one in the room. He informed me that he was in the "artistic game," and I gathered later that he was a photographer and had made the dim enlargement of Mrs. Wilson's mother which hovered like an ectoplasm[12] on the wall. His wife was shrill, languid, handsome, and horrible. She told me

[9]I.e., upholstered with needlepoint copies of tapestries showing eighteenth century scenes of amusement at the Royal Palace at Versailles, near Paris, France.

[10]1921 novel based on the life of Saint Peter, by the English writer and popularizer of religious topics, Robert Keable (1887–1927).

[11]A style of short hair. Newly fashionable in the early 1920s, bobbed hair for women was often taken as a sign of carefree disregard for tradition and feminine propriety.

[12]Misty substance into which spirits of the dead are said to materialize when summoned by spiritualists.

with pride that her husband had photographed her a hundred and twenty-seven times since they had been married.

Mrs. Wilson had changed her costume some time before, and now was attired in an elaborate afternoon dress of cream-colored chiffon, which gave out a continual rustle as she swept about the room. With the influence of the dress her personality had also undergone a change. The intense vitality that had been so remarkable in the garage was converted into impressive hauteur.[13] Her laughter, her gestures, her assertions became more violently affected moment by moment, and as she expanded the room grew smaller around her, until she seemed to be revolving on a noisy, creaking pivot through the smoky air.

"My dear," she told her sister in a high, mincing shout, "most of these fellas will cheat you every time. All they think of is money. I had a woman up here last week to look at my feet, and when she gave me the bill you'd of thought she had my appendicitis[14] out."

"What was the name of the woman?" asked Mrs. McKee.

"Mrs. Eberhardt. She goes around looking at people's feet in their own homes."

"I like your dress," remarked Mrs. McKee, "I think it's adorable."

Mrs. Wilson rejected the compliment by raising her eyebrow in disdain.

"It's just a crazy old thing," she said. "I just slip it on sometimes when I don't care what I look like."

"But it looks wonderful on you, if you know what I mean," pursued Mrs. McKee. "If Chester could only get you in that pose I think he could make something of it."

We all looked in silence at Mrs. Wilson, who removed a strand of hair from over her eyes and looked back at us with a brilliant smile. Mr. McKee regarded her intently with his head on one side, and then moved his hand back and forth slowly in front of his face.

"I should change the light," he said after a moment. "I'd like to bring out the modelling of the features. And I'd try to get hold of all the back hair."

"I wouldn't think of changing the light," cried Mrs. McKee. "I think it's——"

Her husband said "*Sh!*" and we all looked at the subject again, whereupon Tom Buchanan yawned audibly and got to his feet.

"You McKees have something to drink," he said. "Get some more ice and mineral water, Myrtle, before everybody goes to sleep."

"I told that boy about the ice." Myrtle raised her eyebrows in despair at the shiftlessness of the lower orders. "These people! You have to keep after them all the time."

She looked at me and laughed pointlessly. Then she flounced over to the dog, kissed it with ecstasy, and swept into the kitchen, implying that a dozen chefs awaited her orders there.

"I've done some nice things out on Long Island," asserted Mr. McKee.

Tom looked at him blankly.

"Two of them we have framed downstairs."

"Two what?" demanded Tom.

[13]Haughtiness, arrogance.

[14]Spelled "appendicitus" in Fitzgerald's manuscript and in the first edition of the novel, perhaps to suggest Myrtle's uneducated speech. In later editions of the novel, Fitzgerald's publishers changed the spelling to "appendicitis."

"Two studies. One of them I call *Montauk Point*[15]—*The Gulls*, and the other I call *Montauk Point—The Sea*."

The sister Catherine sat down beside me on the couch.

"Do you live down on Long Island, too?" she inquired.

"I live at West Egg."

"Really? I was down there at a party about a month ago. At a man named Gatsby's. Do you know him?"

"I live next door to him."

"Well, they say he's a nephew or a cousin of Kaiser Wilhelm's.[16] That's where all his money comes from."

"Really?"

She nodded.

"I'm scared of him. I'd hate to have him get anything on me."

This absorbing information about my neighbor was interrupted by Mrs. McKee's pointing suddenly at Catherine:

"Chester, I think you could do something with *her*," she broke out, but Mr. McKee only nodded in a bored way, and turned his attention to Tom.

"I'd like to do more work on Long Island, if I could get the entry. All I ask is that they should give me a start."

"Ask Myrtle," said Tom, breaking into a short shout of laughter as Mrs. Wilson entered with a tray. "She'll give you a letter of introduction, won't you, Myrtle?"

"Do what?" she asked, startled.

"You'll give McKee a letter of introduction to your husband, so he can do some studies of him." His lips moved silently for a moment as he invented. "*George B. Wilson at the Gasoline Pump*, or something like that."

Catherine leaned close to me and whispered in my ear:

"Neither of them can stand the person they're married to."

"Can't they?"

"Can't *stand* them." She looked at Myrtle and then at Tom. "What I say is, why go on living with them if they can't stand them? If I was them I'd get a divorce and get married to each other right away."

"Doesn't she like Wilson either?"

The answer to this was unexpected. It came from Myrtle, who had overheard the question, and it was violent and obscene.

"You see," cried Catherine triumphantly. She lowered her voice again. "It's really his wife that's keeping them apart. She's a Catholic, and they don't believe in divorce."

Daisy was not a Catholic, and I was a little shocked at the elaborateness of the lie.

"When they do get married," continued Catherine, "they're going West to live for a while until it blows over."

"It'd be more discreet to go to Europe."

"Oh, do you like Europe?" she exclaimed surprisingly. "I just got back from Monte Carlo."[17]

"Really."

"Just last year. I went over there with another girl."

"Stay long?"

---

[15]The easternmost tip of Long Island, on the Atlantic Ocean.

[16]Wilhelm II (1859–1941), German emperor (1888–1918).

[17]Town in the principality of Monaco, on the French Mediterranean coast, famous for its gambling casino.

"No, we just went to Monte Carlo and back. We went by way of Marseilles. We had over twelve hundred dollars when we started, but we got gypped out of it all in two days in the private rooms. We had an awful time getting back, I can tell you. God, how I hated that town!"

The late afternoon sky bloomed in the window for a moment like the blue honey of the Mediterranean—then the shrill voice of Mrs. McKee called me back into the room.

"I almost made a mistake, too," she declared vigorously. "I almost married a little kike[18] who'd been after me for years. I knew he was below me. Everybody kept saying to me: 'Lucille, that man's 'way below you!' but if I hadn't met Chester, he'd of got me sure."

"Yes, but listen," said Myrtle Wilson, nodding her head up and down, "at least you didn't marry him."

"I know I didn't."

"Well, I married him," said Myrtle, ambiguously. "And that's the difference between your case and mine."

"Why did you, Myrtle?" demanded Catherine. "Nobody forced you to."

Myrtle considered.

"I married him because I thought he was a gentleman," she said finally. "I thought he knew something about breeding, but he wasn't fit to lick my shoe."

"You were crazy about him for a while," said Catherine.

"Crazy about him!" cried Myrtle incredulously. "Who said I was crazy about him? I never was any more crazy about him than I was about that man there."

She pointed suddenly at me, and every one looked at me accusingly. I tried to show by my expression that I had played no part in her past.

"The only *crazy* I was was when I married him. I knew right away I made a mistake. He borrowed somebody's best suit to get married in, and never even told me about it, and the man came after it one day when he was out." She looked around to see who was listening. " 'Oh, is that your suit?' I said. 'This is the first I ever heard about it.' But I gave it to him and then I lay down and cried to beat the band all afternoon."

"She really ought to get away from him," resumed Catherine to me. "They've been living over that garage for eleven years. And Tom's the first sweetie she ever had."

The bottle of whiskey—a second one—was now in constant demand by all present, excepting Catherine, who "felt just as good on nothing at all." Tom rang for the janitor and sent him for some celebrated sandwiches, which were a complete supper in themselves. I wanted to get out and walk eastward toward the park[19] through the soft twilight, but each time I tried to go I became entangled in some wild, strident argument which pulled me back, as if with ropes, into my chair. Yet high over the city our line of yellow windows must have contributed their share of human secrecy to the casual watcher in the darkening streets, and I was him too, looking up and wondering. I was within and without, simultaneously enchanted and repelled by the inexhaustible variety of life.

Myrtle pulled her chair close to mine, and suddenly her warm breath poured over me the story of her first meeting with Tom.

"It was on the two little seats facing each other that are always the last ones left on the train. I was going up to New York to see my sister and spend the night. He had on a dress suit and patent leather shoes, and I couldn't keep my eyes off

---

[18]Contemptuous slang meaning Jew.

[19]Nick's walk eastward would actually carry him parallel to the northern end of Central Park.

him, but every time he looked at me I had to pretend to be looking at the advertisement over his head. When we came into the station he was next to me, and his white shirt-front pressed against my arm, and so I told him I'd have to call a policeman, but he knew I lied. I was so excited that when I got into a taxi with him I didn't hardly know I wasn't getting into a subway train. All I kept thinking about, over and over, was 'You can't live forever; you can't live forever.' "

She turned to Mrs. McKee and the room rang full of her artificial laughter.

"My dear," she cried, "I'm going to give you this dress as soon as I'm through with it. I've got to get another one tomorrow. I'm going to make a list of all the things I've got to get. A massage and a wave, and a collar for the dog, and one of those cute little ash-trays where you touch a spring, and a wreath with a black silk bow for mother's grave that'll last all summer. I got to write down a list so I won't forget all the things I got to do."

It was nine o'clock—almost immediately afterward I looked at my watch and found it was ten. Mr. McKee was asleep on a chair with his fists clenched in his lap, like a photograph of a man of action. Taking out my handkerchief I wiped from his cheek the remains of the spot of dried lather that had worried me all the afternoon.

The little dog was sitting on the table looking with blind eyes through the smoke, and from time to time groaning faintly. People disappeared, reappeared, made plans to go somewhere, and then lost each other, searched for each other, found each other a few feet away. Some time toward midnight Tom Buchanan and Mrs. Wilson stood face to face, discussing, in impassioned voices, whether Mrs. Wilson had any right to mention Daisy's name.

"Daisy! Daisy! Daisy!" shouted Mrs. Wilson. "I'll say it whenever I want to! Daisy! Dai——"

Making a short deft movement, Tom Buchanan broke her nose with his open hand.

Then there were bloody towels upon the bathroom floor, and women's voices scolding, and high over the confusion a long broken wail of pain. Mr. McKee awoke from his doze and started in a daze toward the door. When he had gone half way he turned around and stared at the scene—his wife and Catherine scolding and consoling as they stumbled here and there among the crowded furniture with articles of aid, and the despairing figure on the couch, bleeding fluently, and trying to spread a copy of *Town Tattle* over the tapestry scenes of Versailles. Then Mr. McKee turned and continued on out the door. Taking my hat from the chandelier, I followed.

"Come to lunch some day," he suggested, as we groaned down in the elevator.

"Where?"

"Anywhere."

"Keep your hands off the lever," snapped the elevator boy.

"I beg your pardon," said Mr. McKee with dignity, "I didn't know I was touching it."

"All right," I agreed, "I'll be glad to."

. . . I was standing beside his bed and he was sitting up between the sheets, clad in his underwear, with a great portfolio in his hands.

"Beauty and the Beast . . . Loneliness . . . Old Grocery Horse . . . Brook'n Bridge. . . ."

Then I was lying half asleep in the cold lower level of the Pennsylvania Station, staring at the morning *Tribune*,[20] and waiting for the four o'clock train.

---

[20]The *New York Tribune*, a New York City daily newspaper. It ceased publication in the 1960s.

CHAPTER III

THERE was music from my neighbor's house through the summer nights. In his blue gardens men and girls came and went like moths among the whisperings and the champagne and the stars. At high tide in the afternoon I watched his guests diving from the tower of his raft, or taking the sun on the hot sand of his beach while his two motor-boats slit the waters of the Sound, drawing aquaplanes[1] over cataracts of foam. On week-ends his Rolls-Royce became an omnibus, bearing parties to and from the city between nine in the morning and long past midnight, while his station wagon scampered like a brisk yellow bug to meet all trains. And on Mondays eight servants, including an extra gardener, toiled all day with mops and scrubbing-brushes and hammers and garden-shears, repairing the ravages of the night before.

Every Friday five crates of oranges and lemons arrived from a fruiterer in New York—every Monday these same oranges and lemons left his back door in a pyramid of pulpless halves. There was a machine in the kitchen which could extract the juice of two hundred oranges in half an hour if a little button was pressed two hundred times by a butler's thumb.

At least once a fortnight a corps of caterers came down with several hundred feet of canvas and enough colored lights to make a Christmas tree of Gatsby's enormous garden. On buffet tables, garnished with glistening hors-d'œuvre, spiced baked hams crowded against salads of harlequin designs and pastry pigs and turkeys bewitched to a dark gold. In the main hall a bar with a real brass rail was set up, and stocked with gins and liquors and with cordials so long forgotten that most of his female guests were too young to know one from another.

By seven o'clock the orchestra has arrived, no thin five-piece affair, but a whole pitful of oboes and trombones and saxophones and viols and cornets and piccolos, and low and high drums. The last swimmers have come in from the beach now and are dressing upstairs; the cars from New York are parked five deep in the drive, and already the halls and salons and verandas are gaudy with primary colors, and hair shorn in strange new ways, and shawls beyond the dreams of Castile.[2] The bar is in full swing, and floating rounds of cocktails permeate the garden outside, until the air is alive with chatter and laughter, and casual innuendo and introductions forgotten on the spot, and enthusiastic meetings between women who never knew each other's names.

The lights grow brighter as the earth lurches away from the sun, and now the orchestra is playing yellow cocktail music, and the opera of voices pitches a key higher. Laughter is easier minute by minute, spilled with prodigality, tipped out at a cheerful word. The groups change more swiftly, swell with new arrivals, dissolve and form in the same breath; already there are wanderers, confident girls who weave here and there among the stouter and more stable, become for a sharp, joyous moment the center of a group, and then, excited with triumph, glide on through the sea-change of faces and voices and color under the constantly changing light.

Suddenly one of these gypsies, in trembling opal, seizes a cocktail out of the air, dumps it down for courage and, moving her hands like Frisco,[3] dances out

[1] A small platform on which a standing rider is towed by a speedboat—the forerunner of modern water skis.

[2] Elegant and expensive lace shawls (mantillas) from Spain (Castile), worn on the head and shoulders.

[3] Joe Frisco, nightclub comedian of the 1920s through the 1940s, noted for his fluttering hand movements.

alone on the canvas platform. A momentary hush; the orchestra leader varies his rhythm obligingly for her, and there is a burst of chatter as the erroneous news goes around that she is Gilda Gray's[4] understudy from the *Follies*. The party has begun.

I believe that on the first night I went to Gatsby's house I was one of the few guests who had actually been invited. People were not invited—they went there. They got into automobiles which bore them out to Long Island, and somehow they ended up at Gatsby's door. Once there they were introduced by somebody who knew Gatsby, and after that they conducted themselves according to the rules of behavior associated with amusement parks. Sometimes they came and went without having met Gatsby at all, came for the party with a simplicity of heart that was its own ticket of admission.

I had been actually invited. A chauffeur in a uniform of robin's-egg blue crossed my lawn early that Saturday morning with a surprisingly formal note from his employer: the honor would be entirely Gatsby's, it said, if I would attend his "little party" that night. He had seen me several times, and had intended to call on me long before, but a peculiar combination of circumstances had prevented it—signed Jay Gatsby, in a majestic hand.

Dressed up in white flannels[5] I went over to his lawn a little after seven, and wandered around rather ill at ease among swirls and eddies of people I didn't know—though here and there was a face I had noticed on the commuting train. I was immediately struck by the number of young Englishmen dotted about; all well dressed, all looking a little hungry, and all talking in low, earnest voices to solid and prosperous Americans. I was sure that they were selling something: bonds or insurance or automobiles. They were at least agonizingly aware of the easy money in the vicinity and convinced that it was theirs for a few words in the right key.

As soon as I arrived I made an attempt to find my host, but the two or three people of whom I asked his whereabouts stared at me in such an amazed way, and denied so vehemently any knowledge of his movements, that I slunk off in the direction of the cocktail table—the only place in the garden where a single man could linger without looking purposeless and alone.

I was on my way to get roaring drunk from sheer embarrassment when Jordan Baker came out of the house and stood at the head of the marble steps, leaning a little backward and looking with contemptuous interest down into the garden.

Welcome or not, I found it necessary to attach myself to someone before I should begin to address cordial remarks to the passers-by.

"Hello!" I roared, advancing toward her. My voice seemed unnaturally loud across the garden.

"I thought you might be here," she responded absently as I came up. "I remembered you lived next door to——"

She held my hand impersonally, as a promise that she'd take care of me in a minute, and gave ear to two girls in twin yellow dresses, who stopped at the foot of the steps.

"Hello!" they cried together. "Sorry you didn't win."

That was for the golf tournament. She had lost in the finals the week before.

"You don't know who we are," said one of the girls in yellow, "but we met you here about a month ago."

[4]An American dancer (1899–1959), "Queen of the Shimmy," star of *The Ziegfeld Follies* and nightclubs in the 1920s and 1930s.
[5]Trousers of white wool flannel, traditional summer dress of fashionable men in the first decades of the twentieth century.

"You've dyed your hair since then," remarked Jordan, and I started, but the girls had moved casually on and her remark was addressed to the premature moon, produced like the supper, no doubt, out of a caterer's basket. With Jordan's slender golden arm resting in mine, we descended the steps and sauntered about the garden. A tray of cocktails floated at us through the twilight, and we sat down at a table with the two girls in yellow and three men, each one introduced to us as Mr. Mumble.

"Do you come to these parties often?" inquired Jordan of the girl beside her.

"The last one was the one I met you at," answered the girl, in an alert confident voice. She turned to her companion: "Wasn't it for you, Lucille?"

It was for Lucille, too.

"I like to come," Lucille said. "I never care what I do, so I always have a good time. When I was here last I tore my gown on a chair, and he asked me my name and address—inside of a week I got a package from Croirier's with a new evening gown in it."

"Did you keep it?" asked Jordan.

"Sure I did. I was going to wear it tonight, but it was too big in the bust and had to be altered. It was gas blue with lavender beads. Two hundred and sixty-five dollars."

"There's something funny about a fellow that'll do a thing like that," said the other girl eagerly. "He doesn't want any trouble with *anybody*."

"Who doesn't?" I inquired.

"Gatsby. Somebody told me——"

The two girls and Jordan leaned together confidentially.

"Somebody told me they thought he killed a man once."

A thrill passed over all of us. The three Mr. Mumbles bent forward and listened eagerly.

"I don't think it's so much *that*," argued Lucille sceptically; "it's more that he was a German spy during the war."

One of the men nodded in confirmation.

"I heard that from a man who knew all about him, grew up with him in Germany," he assured us positively.

"Oh, no," said the first girl, "it couldn't be that, because he was in the American army during the war." As our credulity switched back to her she leaned forward with enthusiasm. "You look at him sometimes when he thinks nobody's looking at him. I'll bet he killed a man."

She narrowed her eyes and shivered. Lucille shivered. We all turned and looked around for Gatsby. It was testimony to the romantic speculation he inspired that there were whispers about him from those who had found little that it was necessary to whisper about in this world.

The first supper—there would be another one after midnight—was now being served, and Jordan invited me to join her own party, who were spread around a table on the other side of the garden. There were three married couples and Jordan's escort, a persistent undergraduate given to violent innuendo, and obviously under the impression that sooner or later Jordan was going to yield him up her person to a greater or lesser degree. Instead of rambling, this party had preserved a dignified homogeneity, and assumed to itself the function of representing the staid nobility of the country-side—East Egg condescending to West Egg, and carefully on guard against its spectroscopic gayety.

"Let's get out," whispered Jordan, after a somehow wasteful and inappropriate half-hour; "this is much too polite for me."

We got up, and she explained that we were going to find the host: I had never met him, she said, and it was making me uneasy. The undergraduate nodded in a cynical, melancholy way.

The bar, where we glanced first, was crowded, but Gatsby was not there. She couldn't find him from the top of the steps, and he wasn't on the veranda. On a chance we tried an important-looking door, and walked into a high Gothic library,[6] panelled with carved English oak, and probably transported complete from some ruin overseas.

A stout, middle-aged man, with enormous owl-eyed spectacles, was sitting somewhat drunk on the edge of a great table, staring with unsteady concentration at the shelves of books. As we entered he wheeled excitedly around and examined Jordan from head to foot.

"What do you think?" he demanded impetuously.

"About what?"

He waved his hand toward the book-shelves.

"About that. As a matter of fact you needn't bother to ascertain. I ascertained. They're real."

"The books?"

He nodded.

"Absolutely real—have pages and everything. I thought they'd be a nice durable cardboard. Matter of fact, they're absolutely real. Pages and—Here! Lemme show you."

Taking our scepticism for granted, he rushed to the bookcases and returned with Volume One of the Stoddard *Lectures*.[7]

"See!" he cried triumphantly. "It's a bona-fide piece of printed matter. It fooled me. This fella's a regular Belasco.[8] It's a triumph. What thoroughness! What realism! Knew when to stop, too—didn't cut the pages.[9] But what do you want? What do you expect?"

He snatched the book from me and replaced it hastily on its shelf, muttering that if one brick was removed the whole library was liable to collapse.

"Who brought you?" he demanded. "Or did you just come? I was brought. Most people were brought."

Jordan looked at him alertly, cheerfully, without answering.

"I was brought by a woman named Roosevelt," he continued. "Mrs. Claud Roosevelt. Do you know her? I met her somewhere last night. I've been drunk for about a week now, and I thought it might sober me up to sit in a library."

"Has it?"

"A little bit, I think. I can't tell yet. I've only been here an hour. Did I tell you about the books? They're real. They're——"

"You told us."

We shook hands with him gravely and went back outdoors.

There was dancing now on the canvas in the garden; old men pushing young girls backward in eternal graceless circles, superior couples holding each other tortuously, fashionably, and keeping in the corners—and a great number of single girls dancing individualistically or relieving the orchestra for a moment of the burden of the banjo or the traps. By midnight the hilarity had increased.

---

[6]A room with a ribbed, arched ceiling resembling the design of fourteenth- and fifteenth-century Gothic churches.

[7]Travel books, first published in 1897, compiled from the lectures of John Lawson Stoddard (1850–1930), whose talks on "the world's famous places and people" were popular in the first decades of the twentieth century.

[8]David Belasco (1853–1931), an American theatrical producer famous for his detailed and realistic stage settings.

[9]Book pages that remain joined at their edges, and therefore unopened and unread.

A celebrated tenor had sung in Italian, and a notorious contralto had sung in jazz, and between the numbers people were doing "stunts" all over the garden, while happy, vacuous bursts of laughter rose toward the summer sky. A pair of stage twins, who turned out to be the girls in yellow, did a baby act in costume, and champagne was served in glasses bigger than finger-bowls. The moon had risen higher, and floating in the Sound was a triangle of silver scales, trembling a little to the stiff, tinny drip of the banjoes on the lawn.

I was still with Jordan Baker. We were sitting at a table with a man of about my age and a rowdy little girl, who gave way upon the slightest provocation to uncontrollable laughter. I was enjoying myself now. I had taken two finger-bowls of champagne, and the scene had changed before my eyes into something significant, elemental, and profound.

At a lull in the entertainment the man looked at me and smiled.

"Your face is familiar," he said, politely. "Weren't you in the Third Division[10] during the war?"

"Why, yes. I was in the Ninth Machine-Gun Battalion."[11]

"I was in the Seventh Infantry[12] until June nineteen-eighteen. I knew I'd seen you somewhere before."

We talked for a moment about some wet, gray little villages in France. Evidently he lived in this vicinity, for he told me that he had just bought a hydro-plane,[13] and was going to try it out in the morning.

"Want to go with me, old sport? Just near the shore along the Sound."

"What time?"

"Any time that suits you best."

It was on the tip of my tongue to ask his name when Jordan looked around and smiled.

"Having a gay time now?" she inquired.

"Much better." I turned again to my new acquaintance. "This is an unusual party for me. I haven't even seen the host. I live over there——" I waved my hand at the invisible hedge in the distance, "and this man Gatsby sent over his chauffeur with an invitation."

For a moment he looked at me as if he failed to understand.

"I'm Gatsby," he said suddenly.

"What!" I exclaimed. "Oh, I beg your pardon."

"I thought you knew, old sport. I'm afraid I'm not a very good host."

He smiled understandingly—much more than understandingly. It was one of those rare smiles with a quality of external reassurance in it, that you may come across four or five times in life. It faced—or seemed to face—the whole eternal world for an instant, and then concentrated on *you* with an irresistible prejudice in your favor. It understood you just so far as you wanted to be understood, believed in you as you would like to believe in yourself, and assured you that it had precisely the impression of you that, at your best, you hoped to convey. Precisely at that point it vanished—and I was looking at an elegant young roughneck, a year or two over thirty, whose elaborate formality of speech just missed being absurd. Some time before he introduced himself I'd got a strong impression that he was picking his words with care.

Almost at the moment when Mr. Gatsby identified himself, a butler hurried

[10]The Third Infantry Division of the U.S. Army.

[11]In the U.S. Army during World War I, machine guns were not distributed throughout an infantry division but were concentrated in specially trained machine-gun units.

[12]The Seventh Infantry Regiment, one of the regiments of the Third Division.

[13]A seaplane.

toward him with the information that Chicago was calling him on the wire. He excused himself with a small bow that included each of us in turn.

"If you want anything just ask for it, old sport," he urged me. "Excuse me. I will rejoin you later."

When he was gone I turned immediately to Jordan—constrained to assure her of my surprise. I had expected that Mr. Gatsby would be a florid and corpulent person in his middle years.

"Who is he?" I demanded. "Do you know?"

"He's just a man named Gatsby."

"Where is he from, I mean? And what does he do?"

"Now *you're* started on the subject," she answered with a wan smile. "Well, he told me once he was an Oxford man."

A dim background started to take shape behind him, but at her next remark it faded away.

"However, I don't believe it."

"Why not?"

"I don't know," she insisted, "I just don't think he went there."

Something in her tone reminded me of the other girl's "I think he killed a man," and had the effect of stimulating my curiosity. I would have accepted without question the information that Gatsby sprang from the swamps of Louisiana or from the lower East Side of New York.[14] That was comprehensible. But young men didn't—at least in my provincial inexperience I believed they didn't—drift coolly out of nowhere and buy a palace on Long Island Sound.

"Anyhow, he gives large parties," said Jordan, changing the subject with an urbane distaste for the concrete. "And I like large parties. They're so intimate. At small parties there isn't any privacy."

There was the boom of a bass drum, and the voice of the orchestra leader rang out suddenly above the echolalia of the garden.

"Ladies and gentlemen," he cried. "At the request of Mr. Gatsby we are going to play for you Mr. Vladimir Tostoff's[15] latest work, which attracted so much attention at Carnegie Hall[16] last May. If you read the papers, you know there was a big sensation." He smiled with jovial condescension, and added: "Some sensation!" Whereupon everybody laughed.

"The piece is known," he concluded lustily, "as *Vladimir Tostoff's Jazz History of the World*."

The nature of Mr. Tostoff's composition eluded me, because just as it began my eyes fell on Gatsby, standing alone on the marble steps and looking from one group to another with approving eyes. His tanned skin was drawn attractively tight on his face and his short hair looked as though it were trimmed every day. I could see nothing sinister about him. I wondered if the fact that he was not drinking helped to set him off from his guests, for it seemed to me that he grew more correct as the fraternal hilarity increased. When the *Jazz History of the World* was over, girls were putting their heads on men's shoulders in a puppyish, convivial way, girls were swooning backward playfully into men's arms, even into groups, knowing that someone would arrest their falls—but no one swooned backward on Gatsby, and no French bob touched Gatsby's shoulder, and no singing quartets were formed with Gatsby's head for one link.

"I beg your pardon."

Gatsby's butler was suddenly standing beside us.

[14]An area of slums in Manhattan.
[15]A fictitious name that puns on "tossed off," frivolous.
[16]A concert hall in New York City.

"Miss Baker?" he inquired. "I beg your pardon, but Mr. Gatsby would like to speak to you alone."

"With me?" she exclaimed in surprise.

"Yes, madame."

She got up slowly, raising her eyebrows at me in astonishment, and followed the butler toward the house. I noticed that she wore her evening-dress, all her dresses, like sports clothes—there was a jauntiness about her movements as if she had first learned to walk upon golf courses on clean, crisp mornings.

I was alone and it was almost two. For some time confused and intriguing sounds had issued from a long, many-windowed room which overhung the terrace. Eluding Jordan's undergraduate, who was now engaged in an obstetrical conversation with two chorus girls, and who implored me to join him, I went inside.

The large room was full of people. One of the girls in yellow was playing the piano, and beside her stood a tall, red-haired young lady from a famous chorus, engaged in song. She had drunk a quantity of champagne, and during the course of her song she had decided, ineptly, that everything was very, very sad—she was not only singing, she was weeping too. Whenever there was a pause in the song she filled it with gasping, broken sobs, and then took up the lyric again in a quavering soprano. The tears coursed down her cheeks—not freely, however, for when they came into contact with her heavily beaded eyelashes they assumed an inky color, and pursued the rest of their way in slow black rivulets. A humorous suggestion was made that she sing the notes on her face, whereupon she threw up her hands, sank into a chair, and went off into a deep vinous sleep.

"She had a fight with a man who says he's her husband," explained a girl at my elbow.

I looked around. Most of the remaining women were now having fights with men said to be their husbands. Even Jordan's party, the quartet from East Egg, were rent asunder by dissension. One of the men was talking with curious intensity to a young actress, and his wife, after attempting to laugh at the situation in a dignified and indifferent way, broke down entirely and resorted to flank attacks—at intervals she appeared suddenly at his side like an angry diamond, and hissed: "You promised!" into his ear.

The reluctance to go home was not confined to wayward men. The hall was at present occupied by two deplorably sober men and their highly indignant wives. The wives were sympathizing with each other in slightly raised voices.

"Whenever he sees I'm having a good time he wants to go home."

"Never heard anything so selfish in my life."

"We're always the first ones to leave."

"So are we."

"Well, we're almost the last tonight," said one of the men sheepishly. "The orchestra left half an hour ago."

In spite of the wives' agreement that such malevolence was beyond credibility, the dispute ended in a short struggle, and both wives were lifted, kicking, into the night.

As I waited for my hat in the hall the door of the library opened and Jordan Baker and Gatsby came out together. He was saying some last word to her, but the eagerness in his manner tightened abruptly into formality as several people approached him to say good-by.

Jordan's party were calling impatiently to her from the porch, but she lingered for a moment to shake hands.

"I've just heard the most amazing thing," she whispered. "How long were we in there?"

"Why, about an hour."

"It was . . . simply amazing," she repeated abstractedly. "But I swore I wouldn't tell it and here I am tantalizing you." She yawned gracefully in my face. "Please come and see me. . . . Phone book. . . . Under the name of Mrs. Sigourney Howard. . . . My aunt. . . ." She was hurrying off as she talked—her brown hand waved a jaunty salute as she melted into her party at the door.

Rather ashamed that on my first appearance I had stayed so late, I joined the last of Gatsby's guests, who were clustered around him. I wanted to explain that I'd hunted for him early in the evening and to apologize for not having known him in the garden.

"Don't mention it," he enjoined me eagerly. "Don't give it another thought, old sport." The familiar expression held no more familiarity than the hand which reassuringly brushed my shoulder. "And don't forget we're going up in the hydroplane tomorrow morning, at nine o'clock."

Then the butler, behind his shoulder:

"Philadelphia wants you on the 'phone, sir."

"All right, in a minute. Tell them I'll be right there. . . . Good night."

"Good night."

"Good night." He smiled—and suddenly there seemed to be a pleasant significance in having been among the last to go, as if he had desired it all the time. "Good night, old sport. . . . Good night."

But as I walked down the steps I saw that the evening was not quite over. Fifty feet from the door a dozen headlights illuminated a bizarre and tumultuous scene. In the ditch beside the road, right side up, but violently shorn of one wheel, rested a new coupé which had left Gatsby's drive not two minutes before. The sharp jut of a wall accounted for the detachment of the wheel, which was now getting considerable attention from half a dozen curious chauffeurs. However, as they had left their cars blocking the road, a harsh, discordant din from those in the rear had been audible for some time, and added to the already violent confusion of the scene.

A man in a long duster[17] had dismounted from the wreck and now stood in the middle of the road, looking from the car to the tire and from the tire to the observers in a pleasant, puzzled way.

"See!" he explained. "It went in the ditch."

The fact was infinitely astonishing to him, and I recognized first the unusual quality of wonder, and then the man—it was the late patron of Gatsby's library.

"How'd it happen?"

He shrugged his shoulders.

"I know nothing whatever about mechanics," he said decisively.

"But how did it happen? Did you run into the wall?"

"Don't ask me," said Owl Eyes, washing his hands of the whole matter. "I know very little about driving—next to nothing. It happened, and that's all I know."

"Well, if you're a poor driver you oughtn't to try driving at night."

"But I wasn't even trying," he explained indignantly. "I wasn't even trying."

An awed hush fell upon the bystanders.

"Do you want to commit suicide?"

---

[17]A long, lightweight coat, worn in open cars to protect clothes against road dust.

"You're lucky it was just a wheel! A bad driver and not even *try*ing!"

"You don't understand," explained the criminal. "I wasn't driving. There's another man in the car."

The shock that followed this declaration found voice in a sustained "Ah-h-h!" as the door of the coupé swung slowly open. The crowd—it was now a crowd—stepped back involuntarily, and when the door had opened wide there was a ghostly pause. Then, very gradually, part by part, a pale, dangling individual stepped out of the wreck, pawing tentatively at the ground with a large uncertain dancing shoe.

Blinded by the glare of the headlights and confused by the incessant groaning of the horns, the apparition stood swaying for a moment before he perceived the man in the duster.

"Wha's matter?" he inquired calmly. "Did we run outa gas?"

"Look!"

Half a dozen fingers pointed at the amputated wheel—he stared at it for a moment, and then looked upward as though he suspected that it had dropped from the sky.

"It came off," someone explained.

He nodded.

"At first I din' notice we'd stopped."

A pause. Then, taking a long breath and straightening his shoulders, he remarked in a determined voice:

"Wonder'ff tell me where there's a gas'line station?"

At least a dozen men, some of them little better off than he was, explained to him that wheel and car were no longer joined by any physical bond.

"Back out," he suggested after a moment. "Put her in reverse."

"But the *wheel's* off!"

He hesitated.

"No harm in trying," he said.

The caterwauling horns had reached a crescendo and I turned away and cut across the lawn toward home. I glanced back once. A wafer of a moon was shining over Gatsby's house, making the night fine as before, and surviving the laughter and the sound of his still glowing garden. A sudden emptiness seemed to flow now from the windows and the great doors, endowing with complete isolation the figure of the host, who stood on the porch, his hand up in a formal gesture of farewell.

Reading over what I have written so far, I see I have given the impression that the events of three nights several weeks apart were all that absorbed me. On the contrary, they were merely casual events in a crowded summer, and, until much later, they absorbed me infinitely less than my personal affairs.

Most of the time I worked. In the early morning the sun threw my shadow westward as I hurried down the white chasms of lower New York to the Probity Trust. I knew the other clerks and young bond-salesmen by their first names, and lunched with them in dark, crowded restaurants on little pig sausages and mashed potatoes and coffee. I even had a short affair with a girl who lived in Jersey City and worked in the accounting department, but her brother began throwing mean looks in my direction, so when she went on her vacation in July I let it blow quietly away.

I took dinner usually at the Yale Club[18]—for some reason it was the gloom-

[18]A club in New York City for alumni of Yale University.

iest event of my day—and then I went upstairs to the library and studied investments and securities for a conscientious hour. There were generally a few rioters around, but they never came into the library, so it was a good place to work. After that, if the night was mellow, I strolled down Madison Avenue past the old Murray Hill Hotel, and over 33d Street to the Pennsylvania Station.[19]

I began to like New York, the racy, adventurous feel of it at night, and the satisfaction that the constant flicker of men and women and machines gives to the restless eye. I liked to walk up Fifth Avenue and pick out romantic women from the crowd and imagine that in a few minutes I was going to enter into their lives, and no one would ever know or disapprove. Sometimes, in my mind, I followed them to their apartments on the corners of hidden streets, and they turned and smiled back at me before they faded through a door into warm darkness. At the enchanted metropolitan twilight I felt a haunting loneliness sometimes, and felt it in others—poor young clerks who loitered in front of windows waiting until it was time for a solitary restaurant dinner—young clerks in the dusk, wasting the most poignant moments of night and life.

Again at eight o'clock, when the dark lanes of the Forties were five deep with throbbing taxicabs, bound for the theater district,[20] I felt a sinking in my heart. Forms leaned together in the taxis as they waited, and voices sang, and there was laughter from unheard jokes, and lighted cigarettes outlined unintelligible gestures inside. Imagining that I, too, was hurrying toward gayety and sharing their intimate excitement, I wished them well.

For a while I lost sight of Jordan Baker, and then in midsummer I found her again. At first I was flattered to go places with her, because she was a golf champion, and every one knew her name. Then it was something more. I wasn't actually in love, but I felt a sort of tender curiosity. The bored haughty face that she turned to the world concealed something—most affectations conceal something eventually, even though they don't in the beginning—and one day I found what it was. When we were on a house party together up in Warwick,[21] she left a borrowed car out in the rain with the top down, and then lied about it—and suddenly I remembered the story about her that had eluded me that night at Daisy's. At her first big golf tournament there was a row that nearly reached the newspapers—a suggestion that she had moved her ball from a bad lie in the semi-final round. The thing approached the proportions of a scandal—then died away. A caddy retracted his statement, and the only other witness admitted that he might have been mistaken. The incident and the name had remained together in my mind.

Jordan Baker instinctively avoided clever, shrewd men, and now I saw that this was because she felt safer on a plane where any divergence from a code would be thought impossible. She was incurably dishonest. She wasn't able to endure being at a disadvantage and, given this unwillingness, I suppose she had begun dealing in subterfuges when she was very young in order to keep that cool, insolent smile turned to the world and yet satisfy the demands of her hard, jaunty body.

It made no difference to me. Dishonesty in a woman is a thing you never blame deeply—I was casually sorry, and then I forgot. It was on that same house party that we had a curious conversation about driving a car. It started because

[19]A New York City railroad station; the terminal for trains to and from Long Island.

[20]The theater district of New York City—then centered on 42nd Street—where performances traditionally began at 8:30 p.m.

[21]A suburb fifty miles northwest of New York City.

she passed so close to some workmen that our fender flicked a button on one man's coat.

"You're a rotten driver," I protested. "Either you ought to be more careful, or you oughtn't to drive at all."

"I am careful."

"No, you're not."

"Well, other people are," she said lightly.

"What's that got to do with it?"

"They'll keep out of my way," she insisted. "It takes two to make an accident."

"Suppose you met somebody just as careless as yourself."

"I hope I never will," she answered. "I hate careless people. That's why I like you."

Her gray, sun-strained eyes stared straight ahead, but she had deliberately shifted our relations, and for a moment I thought I loved her. But I am slow-thinking and full of interior rules that act as brakes on my desires, and I knew that first I had to get myself definitely out of that tangle back home. I'd been writing letters once a week and signing them: "Love, Nick," and all I could think of was how, when that certain girl played tennis, a faint mustache of perspiration appeared on her upper lip. Nevertheless there was a vague understanding that had to be tactfully broken off before I was free.

Every one suspects himself of at least one of the cardinal virtues, and this is mine: I am one of the few honest people that I have ever known.

CHAPTER IV

On Sunday morning while church bells rang in the villages alongshore, the world and its mistress returned to Gatsby's house and twinkled hilariously on his lawn.

"He's a bootlegger," said the young ladies, moving somewhere between his cocktails and his flowers. "One time he killed a man who had found out that he was nephew to Von Hindenburg[1] and second cousin to the devil. Reach me a rose, honey, and pour me a last drop into that there crystal glass."

Once I wrote down on the empty spaces of a time-table the names of those who came to Gatsby's house that summer. It is an old time-table now, disintegrating at its folds, and headed "This schedule in effect July 5th, 1922." But I can still read the gray names, and they will give you a better impression than my generalities of those who accepted Gatsby's hospitality and paid him the subtle tribute of knowing nothing whatever about him.

From East Egg, then, came the Chester Beckers and the Leeches, and a man named Bunsen, whom I knew at Yale, and Doctor Webster Civet, who was drowned last summer up in Maine. And the Hornbeams and the Willie Voltaires, and a whole clan named Blackbuck, who always gathered in a corner and flipped up their noses like goats at whosoever came near. And the Ismays and the Chrysties (or rather Hubert Auerbach and Mr. Chrystie's wife), and Edgar Beaver, whose hair, they say, turned cotton-white one winter afternoon for no good reason at all.

Clarence Endive was from East Egg, as I remember. He came only once, in

---

[1]Paul Von Hindenburg (1847–1934), German field marshal in World War I, later president of Germany (1925–1934).

white knickerbockers,[2] and had a fight with a bum named Etty in the garden. From farther out on the Island came the Cheadles and the O. R. P. Schraeders, and the Stonewall Jackson Abrams of Georgia, and the Fishguards and the Ripley Snells. Snell was there three days before he went to the penitentiary, so drunk out on the gravel drive that Mrs. Ulysses Swett's automobile ran over his right hand. The Dancies came, too, and S. B. Whitebait, who was well over sixty, and Maurice A. Flink, and the Hammerheads, and Beluga the tobacco importer, and Beluga's girls.

From West Egg came the Poles and the Mulreadys and Cecil Roebuck and Cecil Schoen and Gulick the state senator and Newton Orchid, who controlled Films Par Excellence, and Eckhaust and Clyde Cohen and Don S. Schwartze (the son) and Arthur McCarty, all connected with the movies in one way or another. And the Catlips and the Bembergs and G. Earl Muldoon, brother to that Muldoon who afterward strangled his wife. Da Fontano the promoter came there, and Ed Legros and James B. ("Rot-Gut") Ferret and the De Jongs and Ernest Lilly—they came to gamble, and when Ferret wandered into the garden it meant he was cleaned out and Associated Traction would have to fluctuate profitably next day.[3]

A man named Klipspringer was there so often and so long that he became known as "the boarder"—I doubt if he had any other home. Of theatrical people there were Gus Waize and Horace O'Donavan and Lester Myer and George Duckweed and Francis Bull. Also from New York were the Chromes and the Backhyssons and the Dennickers and Russel Betty and the Corrigans and the Kellehers and the Dewars and the Scullys and S. W. Belcher and the Smirkes and the young Quinns, divorced now, and Henry L. Palmetto, who killed himself by jumping in front of a subway train in Times Square.

Benny McClenahan arrived always with four girls. They were never quite the same ones in physical person, but they were so identical one with another that it inevitably seemed they had been there before. I have forgotten their names— Jaqueline, I think, or else Consuela, or Gloria or Judy or June, and their last names were either the melodious names of flowers and months or the sterner ones of the great American capitalists whose cousins, if pressed, they would confess themselves to be.

In addition to all these I can remember that Faustina O'Brien came there at least once and the Baedeker girls and young Brewer, who had his nose shot off in the war, and Mr. Albrucksburger and Miss Haag, his fiancée, and Ardita Fitz-Peters and Mr. P. Jewett, once head of the American Legion, and Miss Claudia Hip, with a man reputed to be her chauffeur, and a prince of something, whom we called Duke, and whose name, if I ever knew it, I have forgotten.

All these people came to Gatsby's house in the summer.

At nine o'clock, one morning late in July, Gatsby's gorgeous car lurched up the rocky drive to my door and gave out a burst of melody from its three-noted horn. It was the first time he had called on me, though I had gone to two of his parties, mounted in his hydroplane, and, at his urgent invitation, made frequent use of his beach.

"Good morning, old sport. You're having lunch with me today and I thought we'd ride up together."

He was balancing himself on the dashboard of his car with that resourcefulness

---

[2]Knickers. Men's short trousers, gathered at the knees.
[3]I.e., that the price of the stock for Associated Traction would be manipulated on the New York Stock Exchange so that insiders could make a profit.

of movement that is so peculiarly American—that comes, I suppose, with the absence of lifting work or rigid sitting in youth and, even more, with the formless grace of our nervous, sporadic games. This quality was continually breaking through his punctilious manner in the shape of restlessness. He was never quite still; there was always a tapping foot somewhere or the impatient opening and closing of a hand.

He saw me looking with admiration at his car.

"It's pretty, isn't it, old sport?" He jumped off to give me a better view. "Haven't you ever seen it before?"

I'd seen it. Everybody had seen it. It was a rich cream color, bright with nickel, swollen here and there in its monstrous length with triumphant hat-boxes and supper-boxes and tool-boxes, and terraced with a labyrinth of wind-shields that mirrored a dozen suns. Sitting down behind many layers of glass in a sort of green leather conservatory, we started to town.

I had talked with him perhaps half a dozen times in the past month and found, to my disappointment, that he had little to say. So my first impression, that he was a person of some undefined consequence, had gradually faded and he had become simply the proprietor of an elaborate road-house next door.

And then came that disconcerting ride. We hadn't reached West Egg village before Gatsby began leaving his elegant sentences unfinished and slapping himself indecisively on the knee of his caramel-colored suit.

"Look here, old sport," he broke out surprisingly. "What's your opinion of me, anyhow?"

A little overwhelmed, I began the generalized evasions which that question deserves.

"Well, I'm going to tell you something about my life," he interrupted. "I don't want you to get a wrong idea of me from all these stories you hear."

So he was aware of the bizarre accusations that flavored conversation in his halls.

"I'll tell you God's truth." His right hand suddenly ordered divine retribution to stand by. "I am the son of some wealthy people in the Middle West—all dead now. I was brought up in America but educated at Oxford, because all my ancestors have been educated there for many years. It is a family tradition."

He looked at me sideways—and I knew why Jordan Baker had believed he was lying. He hurried the phrase "educated at Oxford," or swallowed it, or choked on it, as though it had bothered him before. And with this doubt, his whole statement fell to pieces, and I wondered if there wasn't something a little sinister about him, after all.

"What part of the Middle West?" I inquired casually.

"San Francisco."

"I see."

"My family all died and I came into a good deal of money."

His voice was solemn, as if the memory of that sudden extinction of a clan still haunted him. For a moment I suspected that he was pulling my leg, but a glance at him convinced me otherwise.

"After that I lived like a young rajah in all the capitals of Europe—Paris, Venice, Rome—collecting jewels, chiefly rubies, hunting big game, painting a little, things for myself only, and trying to forget something very sad that had happened to me long ago."

With an effort I managed to restrain my incredulous laughter. The very phrases were worn so threadbare that they evoked no image except that of a turbaned "character" leaking sawdust at every pore as he pursued a tiger through the Bois de Boulogne.[4]

"Then came the war, old sport. It was a great relief, and I tried very hard to die, but I seemed to bear an enchanted life. I accepted a commission as first lieutenant when it began. In the Argonne Forest[5] I took the remains of my two machine-gun detachments so far forward that there was a half-mile gap on either side of us where the infantry couldn't advance. We stayed there two days and two nights, a hundred and thirty men with sixteen Lewis guns,[6] and when the infantry came up at last they found the insignia of three German divisions among the piles of dead. I was promoted to be a major, and every Allied government gave me a decoration—even Montenegro,[7] little Montenegro down on the Adriatic Sea!"

Little Montenegro! He lifted up the words and nodded at them—with his smile. The smile comprehended Montenegro's troubled history and sympathized with the brave struggles of the Montenegrin people. It appreciated fully the chain of national circumstances which had elicited this tribute from Montenegro's warm little heart. My incredulity was submerged in fascination now; it was like skimming hastily through a dozen magazines.

He reached in his pocket, and a piece of metal, slung on a ribbon, fell into my palm.

"That's the one from Montenegro."

To my astonishment, the thing had an authentic look. "Orderi di Danilo," ran the circular legend, "Montenegro, Nicolas Rex."

"Turn it."

"Major Jay Gatsby," I read, "For Valour Extraordinary."

"Here's another thing I always carry. A souvenir of Oxford days. It was taken in Trinity Quad[8]—the man on my left is now the Earl of Doncaster."

It was a photograph of half a dozen young men in blazers loafing in an archway through which were visible a host of spires. There was Gatsby, looking a little, not much, younger—with a cricket bat in his hand.

Then it was all true. I saw the skins of tigers flaming in his palace on the Grand Canal;[9] I saw him opening a chest of rubies to ease, with their crimson-lighted depths, the gnawings of his broken heart.

"I'm going to make a big request of you today," he said, pocketing his souvenirs with satisfaction, "so I thought you ought to know something about me. I didn't want you to think I was just some nobody. You see, I usually find myself among strangers because I drift here and there trying to forget the sad thing that happened to me." He hesitated. "You'll hear about it this afternoon."

"At lunch?"

"No, this afternoon. I happened to find out that you're taking Miss Baker to tea."

"Do you mean you're in love with Miss Baker?"

"No, old sport, I'm not. But Miss Baker has kindly consented to speak to you about this matter."

[4]Park on the Seine River in Paris, France.
[5]The battlefield in France where American troops engaged in bitter fighting against the Germans in the final months (September–November, 1918) of World War I.
[6]Light machine guns, named for their American developer, Isaac Lewis.
[7]Now a part of Yugoslavia, Montenegro was an independent nation in 1914 and fought with the Allies against Germany and Austria in World War I.
[8]The Quadrangle (courtyard) of Trinity College, Oxford University.
[9]The main waterway of Venice, Italy, lined with the palatial homes of the rich.

I hadn't the faintest idea what "this matter" was, but I was more annoyed than interested. I hadn't asked Jordan to tea in order to discuss Mr. Jay Gatsby. I was sure the request would be something utterly fantastic, and for a moment I was sorry I'd ever set foot upon his overpopulated lawn.

He wouldn't say another word. His correctness grew on him as we neared the city. We passed Port Roosevelt, where there was a glimpse of red-belted ocean-going ships, and sped along a cobbled slum lined with the dark, undeserted saloons of the faded-gilt nineteen-hundreds. Then the valley of ashes opened out on both sides of us, and I had a glimpse of Mrs. Wilson straining at the garage pump with panting vitality as we went by.

With fenders spread like wings we scattered light through half Astoria[10]—only half, for as we twisted among the pillars of the elevated I heard the familiar "jug-jug-*spat*!" of a motorcycle, and a frantic policeman rode alongside.

"All right, old sport," called Gatsby. We slowed down. Taking a white card from his wallet, he waved it before the man's eyes.

"Right you are," agreed the policeman, tipping his cap. "Know you next time, Mr. Gatsby. Excuse *me*!"

"What was that?" I inquired. "The picture of Oxford?"

"I was able to do the commissioner a favor once, and he sends me a Christmas card every year."

Over the great bridge, with the sunlight through the girders making a constant flicker upon the moving cars, with the city rising up across the river in white heaps and sugar lumps all built with a wish out of non-olfactory[11] money. The city seen from the Queensboro[12] Bridge is always the city seen for the first time, in its first wild promise of all the mystery and the beauty in the world.

A dead man passed us in a hearse heaped with blooms, followed by two carriages for friends. The friends looked out at us with the tragic eyes and short upper lips of southeastern Europe, and I was glad that the sight of Gatsby's splendid car was included in their somber holiday. As we crossed Blackwell's Island[13] a limousine passed us, driven by a white chauffeur, in which sat three modish negroes, two bucks and a girl. I laughed aloud as the yolks of their eyeballs rolled toward us in haughty rivalry.

"Anything can happen now that we've slid over this bridge," I thought; "anything at all. . . ."

Even Gatsby could happen, without any particular wonder.

Roaring noon. In a well-fanned Forty-second Street cellar I met Gatsby for lunch. Blinking away the brightness of the street outside, my eyes picked him out obscurely in the anteroom, talking with another man.

"Mr. Carraway, this is my friend Mr. Wolfsheim."[14]

A small, flat-nosed Jew raised his large head and regarded me with two fine growths of hair which luxuriated in either nostril. After a moment I discovered his tiny eyes in the half-darkness.

"—So I took one look at him," said Mr. Wolfsheim, shaking my hand earnestly, "and what do you think I did?"

---

[10]A neighborhood in Queens (on Long Island).
[11]Odorless, hence untainted.
[12]A bridge connecting the island of Manhattan with Queens.
[13]Island in the East River, between Manhattan and Queens, now called Roosevelt Island.
[14]In his manuscript and in the first edition of the novel Fitzgerald spelled the name "Wolfshiem." In later editions of the novel, Fitzgerald's publishers changed the spelling to the more conventional "Wolfsheim."

"What?" I inquired politely.

But evidently he was not addressing me, for he dropped my hand and covered Gatsby with his expressive nose.

"I handed the money to Katspaugh and I sid: 'All right, Katspaugh, don't pay him a penny till he shuts his mouth.' He shut it then and there."

Gatsby took an arm of each of us and moved forward into the restaurant, whereupon Mr. Wolfsheim swallowed a new sentence he was starting and lapsed into a somnambulatory abstraction.

"Highballs?" asked the head waiter.

"This is a nice restaurant here," said Mr. Wolfsheim, looking at the Presbyterian nymphs on the ceiling. "But I like across the street better!"

"Yes, highballs," agreed Gatsby, and then to Mr. Wolfsheim: "It's too hot over there."

"Hot and small—yes," said Mr. Wolfsheim, "but full of memories."

"What place is that?" I asked.

"The old Metropole."

"The old Metropole," brooded Mr. Wolfsheim gloomily. "Filled with faces dead and gone. Filled with friends gone now forever. I can't forget so long as I live the night they shot Rosy Rosenthal there.[15] It was six of us at the table, and Rosy had eat and drunk a lot all evening. When it was almost morning the waiter came up to him with a funny look and says somebody wants to speak to him outside. 'All right,' says Rosy, and begins to get up, and I pulled him down in his chair.

" 'Let the bastards come in here if they want you, Rosy, but don't you, so help me, move outside this room.'

"It was four o'clock in the morning then, and if we'd of raised the blinds we'd of seen daylight."

"Did he go?" I asked innocently.

"Sure he went." Mr. Wolfsheim's nose flashed at me indignantly. "He turned around at the door and says: 'Don't let that waiter take away my coffee!' Then he went out on the sidewalk, and they shot him three times in his full belly and drove away."

"Four of them were electrocuted," I said, remembering.

"Five, with Becker." His nostrils turned to me in an interested way. "I understand you're looking for a business gonnegtion."

The juxtaposition of these two remarks was startling. Gatsby answered for me:

"Oh, no," he exclaimed, "this isn't the man."

"No?" Mr. Wolfsheim seemed disappointed.

"This is just a friend. I told you we'd talk about that some other time."

"I beg your pardon," said Mr. Wolfsheim, "I had a wrong man."

A succulent hash arrived, and Mr. Wolfsheim, forgetting the more sentimental atmosphere of the old Metropole, began to eat with ferocious delicacy. His eyes, meanwhile, roved very slowly all around the room—he completed the arc by turning to inspect the people directly behind. I think that, except for my presence, he would have taken one short glance beneath our own table.

"Look here, old sport," said Gatsby, leaning toward me, "I'm afraid I made you a little angry this morning in the car."

There was the smile again, but this time I held out against it.

[15]On July 16, 1912, Herman "Rosy" Rosenthal was murdered by four men outside the Hotel Metropole in New York City. The four murderers and Charles Becker, a New York City policeman implicated in the crime, were later executed.

"I don't like mysteries," I answered, "and I don't understand why you won't come out frankly and tell me what you want. Why has it all got to come through Miss Baker?"

"Oh, it's nothing underhand," he assured me. "Miss Baker's a great sportswoman, you know, and she'd never do anything that wasn't all right."

Suddenly he looked at his watch, jumped up, and hurried from the room leaving me with Mr. Wolfsheim at the table.

"He has to telephone," said Mr. Wolfsheim, following him with his eyes. "Fine fellow, isn't he? Handsome to look at and a perfect gentleman."

"Yes."

"He's an Oggsford man."

"Oh!"

"He went to Oggsford College in England. You know Oggsford College?"

"I've heard of it."

"It's one of the most famous colleges in the world."

"Have you known Gatsby for a long time?" I inquired.

"Several years," he answered in a gratified way. "I made the pleasure of his acquaintance just after the war. But I knew I had discovered a man of fine breeding after I talked with him an hour. I said to myself: 'There's the kind of man you'd like to take home and introduce to your mother and sister.' " He paused. "I see you're looking at my cuff buttons."

I hadn't been looking at them, but I did now. They were composed of oddly familiar pieces of ivory.

"Finest specimens of human molars," he informed me.

"Well!" I inspected them. "That's a very interesting idea."

"Yeah." He flipped his sleeves up under his coat. "Yeah, Gatsby's very careful about women. He would never so much as look at a friend's wife."

When the subject of this instinctive trust returned to the table and sat down Mr. Wolfsheim drank his coffee with a jerk and got to his feet.

"I have enjoyed my lunch," he said, "and I'm going to run off from you two young men before I outstay my welcome."

"Don't hurry, Meyer," said Gatsby, without enthusiasm. Mr. Wolfsheim raised his hand in a sort of benediction.

"You're very polite, but I belong to another generation," he announced solemnly. "You sit here and discuss your sports and your young ladies and your——" He supplied his imaginary noun with another wave of his hand. "As for me, I am fifty years old, and I won't impose myself on you any longer."

As he shook hands and turned away his tragic nose was trembling. I wondered if I had said anything to offend him.

"He becomes very sentimental sometimes," explained Gatsby. "This is one of his sentimental days. He's quite a character around New York—a denizen of Broadway."

"Who is he, anyhow, an actor?"

"No."

"A dentist?"

"Meyer Wolfsheim? No, he's a gambler." Gatsby hesitated, then added coolly: "He's the man who fixed the World Series back in 1919."[16]

---

[16]In 1919 eight members of the Chicago White Sox baseball team conspired to lose the World Series against the Cincinnati Reds. The resulting investigation of the "Black Sox" scandal revealed that the players had been bribed with $100,000 by a syndicate of New York gamblers, several of whom were never brought to trial.

"Fixed the World Series?" I repeated.

The idea staggered me. I remembered, of course, that the World's Series had been fixed in 1919, but if I had thought of it at all I would have thought of it as a thing that merely *happened*, the end of some inevitable chain. It never occurred to me that one man could start to play with the faith of fifty million people—with the single-mindedness of a burglar blowing a safe.

"How did he happen to do that?" I asked after a minute.

"He just saw the opportunity."

"Why isn't he in jail?"

"They can't get him, old sport. He's a smart man."

I insisted on paying the check. As the waiter brought my change I caught sight of Tom Buchanan across the crowded room.

"Come along with me for a minute," I said; "I've got to say hello to someone."

When he saw us Tom jumped up and took half a dozen steps in our direction.

"Where've you been?" he demanded eagerly. "Daisy's furious because you haven't called up."

"This is Mr. Gatsby, Mr. Buchanan."

They shook hands briefly, and a strained, unfamiliar look of embarrassment came over Gatsby's face.

"How've you been, anyhow?" demanded Tom of me. "How'd you happen to come up this far to eat?"

"I've been having lunch with Mr. Gatsby."

I turned toward Mr. Gatsby, but he was no longer there.

One October day in nineteen-seventeen——

(said Jordan Baker that afternoon, sitting up very straight on a straight chair in the tea-garden at the Plaza Hotel)[17]

——I was walking along from one place to another, half on the sidewalks and half on the lawns. I was happier on the lawns because I had on shoes from England with rubber nobs on the soles that bit into the soft ground. I had on a new plaid skirt also that blew a little in the wind, and whenever this happened the red, white, and blue banners in front of all the houses stretched out stiff and said *tut-tut-tut-tut*, in a disapproving way.

The largest of the banners and the largest of the lawns belonged to Daisy Fay's house. She was just eighteen, two years older than me, and by far the most popular of all the young girls in Louisville. She dressed all in white, and had a little white roadster, and all day long the telephone rang in her house and excited young officers from Camp Taylor[18] demanded the privilege of monopolizing her that night. "Anyways, for an hour!"

When I came opposite her house that morning her white roadster was beside the curb, and she was sitting in it with a lieutenant I had never seen before. They were so engrossed in each other that she didn't see me until I was five feet away.

"Hello, Jordan," she called unexpectedly. "Please come here."

I was flattered that she wanted to speak to me, because of all the older girls I admired her most. She asked me if I was going to the Red Cross and make bandages. I was. Well, then, would I tell them that she couldn't come that day? The officer looked at Daisy while she was speaking, in a way that every young girl wants to be looked at sometime, and because it seemed romantic to me I

---

[17]Expensive hotel at the southern end of Central Park. The Plaza's indoor tea-garden restaurant was (and remains today) a fashionable place to take afternoon tea.

[18]U.S. Army training camp near Louisville, Kentucky.

have remembered the incident ever since. His name was Jay Gatsby, and I didn't lay eyes on him again for over four years—even after I'd met him on Long Island I didn't realize it was the same man.

That was nineteen-seventeen. By the next year I had a few beaux myself, and I began to play in tournaments, so I didn't see Daisy very often. She went with a slightly older crowd—when she went with anyone at all. Wild rumors were circulating about her—how her mother had found her packing her bag one winter night to go to New York and say good-by to a soldier who was going overseas. She was effactually prevented, but she wasn't on speaking terms with her family for several weeks. After that she didn't play around with the soldiers any more, but only with a few flat-footed, short-sighted young men in town, who couldn't get into the army at all.

By the next autumn she was gay again, gay as ever. She had a début after the Armistice, and in February she was presumably engaged to a man from New Orleans. In June she married Tom Buchanan of Chicago, with more pomp and circumstance than Louisville ever knew before. He came down with a hundred people in four private cars,[19] and hired a whole floor of the Seelbach Hotel, and the day before the wedding he gave her a string of pearls valued at three hundred and fifty thousand dollars.

I was a bridesmaid. I came into her room half an hour before the bridal dinner, and found her lying on her bed as lovely as the June night in her flowered dress—and as drunk as a monkey. She had a bottle of Sauterne[20] in one hand and a letter in the other.

" 'Gratulate me," she muttered. "Never had a drink before, but oh how I do enjoy it."

"What's the matter, Daisy?"

I was scared, I can tell you; I'd never seen a girl like that before.

"Here, deares'." She groped around in a wastebasket she had with her on the bed and pulled out the string of pearls. "Take 'em downstairs and give 'em back to whoever they belong to. Tell 'em all Daisy's change' her mine. Say: 'Daisy's change' her mine!' "

She began to cry—she cried and cried. I rushed out and found her mother's maid, and we locked the door and got her into a cold bath. She wouldn't let go of the letter. She took it into the tub with her and squeezed it up into a wet ball, and only let me leave it in the soap-dish when she saw that it was coming to pieces like snow.

But she didn't say another word. We gave her spirits of ammonia and put ice on her forehead and hooked her back into her dress, and half an hour later, when we walked out of the room, the pearls were around her neck and the incident was over. Next day at five o'clock she married Tom Buchanan without so much as a shiver, and started off on a three months' trip to the South Seas.

I saw them in Santa Barbara when they came back, and I thought I'd never seen a girl so mad about her husband. If he left the room for a minute she'd look around uneasily, and say: "Where's Tom gone?" and wear the most abstracted expression until she saw him coming in the door. She used to sit on the sand with his head in her lap by the hour, rubbing her fingers over his eyes and looking at him with unfathomable delight. It was touching to see them together— it made you laugh in a hushed, fascinated way. That was in August. A week after I left Santa Barbara Tom ran into a wagon on the Ventura road[21] one

---

[19]Private railroad cars.

[20]A semi-sweet white wine from the Sauterne region of France.

[21]The road south from Santa Barbara, California, to the city of Ventura, near Los Angeles.

night, and ripped a front wheel off his car. The girl who was with him got into the papers, too, because her arm was broken—she was one of the chambermaids in the Santa Barbara Hotel.

The next April Daisy had her little girl, and they went to France for a year. I saw them one spring in Cannes, and later in Deauville,[22] and then they came back to Chicago to settle down. Daisy was popular in Chicago, as you know. They moved with a fast crowd, all of them young and rich and wild, but she came out with an absolutely perfect reputation. Perhaps because she doesn't drink. It's a great advantage not to drink among hard-drinking people. You can hold your tongue, and, moreover, you can time any little irregularity of your own so that everybody else is so blind that they don't see or care. Perhaps Daisy never went in for amour at all—and yet there's something in that voice of hers. . . .

Well, about six weeks ago, she heard the name Gatsby for the first time in years. It was when I asked you—do you remember?—if you knew Gatsby in West Egg. After you had gone home she came into my room and woke me up, and said: "What Gatsby?" and when I described him—I was half asleep—she said in the strangest voice that it must be the man she used to know. It wasn't until then that I connected this Gatsby with the officer in her white car.

When Jordan Baker had finished telling all this we had left the Plaza for half an hour and were driving in a victoria[23] through Central Park. The sun had gone down behind the tall apartments of the movie stars in the West Fifties, and the clear voices of little girls, already gathered like crickets on the grass, rose through the hot twilight:

> "I'm the Sheik of Araby.
> Your love belongs to me.
> At night when you're asleep
> Into your tent I'll creep——"[24]

"It was a strange coincidence," I said.

"But it wasn't a coincidence at all."

"Why not?"

"Gatsby bought that house so that Daisy would be just across the bay."

Then it had not been merely the stars to which he had aspired on that June night. He came alive to me, delivered suddenly from the womb of his purposeless splendor.

"He wants to know," continued Jordan, "if you'll invite Daisy to your house some afternoon and then let him come over."

The modesty of the demand shook me. He had waited five years and bought a mansion where he dispensed starlight to casual moths—so that he could "come over" some afternoon to a stranger's garden.

"Did I have to know all this before he could ask such a little thing?"

"He's afraid, he's waited so long. He thought you might be offended. You see, he's a regular tough underneath it all."

Something worried me.

---

[22]Cannes: seaside resort in southern France, on the Mediterranean. Deauville: seaside resort in northern France, on the English Channel.

[23]An open, horse-drawn carriage, named for Victoria, queen of Great Britain and Ireland (1837–1901).

[24]A popular song published in 1921.

"Why didn't he ask you to arrange a meeting?"

"He wants her to see his house," she explained. "And your house is right next door."

"Oh!"

"I think he half expected her to wander into one of his parties, some night," went on Jordan, "but she never did. Then he began asking people casually if they knew her, and I was the first one he found. It was that night he sent for me at his dance, and you should have heard the elaborate way he worked up to it. Of course, I immediately suggested a luncheon in New York—and I thought he'd go mad:

" 'I don't want to do anything out of the way!' he kept saying. 'I want to see her right next door.'

"When I said you were a particular friend of Tom's, he started to abandon the whole idea. He doesn't know very much about Tom, though he says he's read a Chicago paper for years just on the chance of catching a glimpse of Daisy's name."

It was dark now, and as we dipped under a little bridge I put my arm around Jordan's golden shoulder and drew her toward me and asked her to dinner. Suddenly I wasn't thinking of Daisy and Gatsby any more, but of this clean, hard, limited person, who dealt in universal scepticism, and who leaned back jauntily just within the circle of my arm. A phrase began to beat in my ears with a sort of heady excitement: "There are only the pursued, the pursuing, the busy, and the tired."

"And Daisy ought to have something in her life," murmured Jordan to me.

"Does she want to see Gatsby?"

"She's not to know about it. Gatsby doesn't want her to know. You're just supposed to invite her to tea."

We passed a barrier of dark trees, and then the façade of Fifty-ninth Street, a block of delicate pale light, beamed down into the park. Unlike Gatsby and Tom Buchanan, I had no girl whose disembodied face floated along the dark cornices and blinding signs, and so I drew up the girl beside me, tightening my arms. Her wan, scornful mouth smiled, and so I drew her up again closer, this time to my face.

CHAPTER V

WHEN I came home to West Egg that night I was afraid for a moment that my house was on fire. Two o'clock and the whole corner of the peninsula was blazing with light, which fell unreal on the shrubbery and made thin elongating glints upon the roadside wires. Turning a corner, I saw that it was Gatsby's house, lit from tower to cellar.

At first I thought it was another party, a wild rout that had resolved itself into "hide-and-go-seek" or "sardines-in-the-box" with all the house thrown open to the game. But there wasn't a sound. Only wind in the trees, which blew the wires and made the lights go off and on again as if the house had winked into the darkness. As my taxi groaned away I saw Gatsby walking toward me across his lawn.

"Your place looks like the World's Fair,"[1] I said.

[1]Beginning with the Chicago Columbian Exhibition of 1893, world's fairs were noted for lavish use of electric lights.

"Does it?" He turned his eyes toward it absently. "I have been glancing into some of the rooms. Let's go to Coney Island,[2] old sport. In my car."

"It's too late."

"Well, suppose we take a plunge in the swimming-pool? I haven't made use of it all summer."

"I've got to go to bed."

"All right."

He waited, looking at me with suppressed eagerness.

"I talked with Miss Baker," I said after a moment. "I'm going to call up Daisy tomorrow and invite her over here to tea."

"Oh, that's all right," he said carelessly. "I don't want to put you to any trouble."

"What day would suit you?"

"What day would suit *you?*" he corrected me quickly. "I don't want to put you to any trouble, you see."

"How about the day after tomorrow?"

He considered for a moment. Then, with reluctance:

"I want to get the grass cut," he said.

We both looked at the grass—there was a sharp line where my ragged lawn ended and the darker, well-kept expanse of his began. I suspected that he meant my grass.

"There's another little thing," he said uncertainly, and hesitated.

"Would you rather put it off for a few days?" I asked.

"Oh, it isn't about that. At least——" He fumbled with a series of beginnings. "Why, I thought—why, look here, old sport, you don't make much money, do you?"

"Not very much."

This seemed to reassure him and he continued more confidently.

"I thought you didn't, if you'll pardon my—You see, I carry on a little business on the side, a sort of side line, you understand. And I thought that if you don't make very much—You're selling bonds, aren't you, old sport?"

"Trying to."

"Well, this would interest you. It wouldn't take up much of your time and you might pick up a nice bit of money. It happens to be a rather confidential sort of thing."

I realize now that under different circumstances that conversation might have been one of the crises of my life. But, because the offer was obviously and tactlessly for a service to be rendered, I had no choice except to cut him off there.

"I've got my hands full," I said. "I'm much obliged but I couldn't take on any more work."

"You wouldn't have to do any business with Wolfsheim." Evidently he thought that I was shying away from the "gonnegtion" mentioned at lunch, but I assured him he was wrong. He waited a moment longer, hoping I'd begin a conversation, but I was too absorbed to be responsive, so he went unwillingly home.

The evening had made me light-headed and happy; I think I walked into a deep sleep as I entered my front door. So I don't know whether or not Gatsby went to Coney Island, or for how many hours he "glanced into rooms" while his house blazed gaudily on. I called up Daisy from the office next morning, and invited her to come to tea.

"Don't bring Tom," I warned her.

---

[2]A beach resort and amusement park in Brooklyn, New York, on the Atlantic shore.

"What?"

"Don't bring Tom."

"Who is 'Tom'?" she asked innocently.

The day agreed upon was pouring rain. At eleven o'clock a man in a raincoat, dragging a lawn-mower, tapped at my front door and said that Mr. Gatsby had sent him over to cut my grass. This reminded me that I had forgotten to tell my Finn to come back, so I drove into West Egg village to search for her among soggy, whitewashed alleys and to buy some cups and lemons and flowers.

The flowers were unnecessary, for at two o'clock a greenhouse arrived from Gatsby's, with innumerable receptacles to contain it. An hour later the front door opened nervously, and Gatsby, in a white flannel suit, silver shirt, and gold-colored tie, hurried in. He was pale, and there were dark signs of sleeplessness beneath his eyes.

"Is everything all right?" he asked immediately.

"The grass looks fine, if that's what you mean."

"What grass?" he inquired blankly. "Oh, the grass in the yard." He looked out the window at it, but, judging from his expression, I don't believe he saw a thing.

"Looks very good," he remarked vaguely. "One of the papers said they thought the rain would stop about four. I think it was *The Journal*.[3] Have you got everything you need in the shape of—of tea?"

I took him into the pantry, where he looked a little reproachfully at the Finn. Together we scrutinized the twelve lemon cakes from the delicatessen shop.

"Will they do?" I asked.

"Of course, of course! They're fine!" and he added hollowly, " . . . old sport."

The rain cooled about half-past three to a damp mist, through which occasional thin drops swam like dew. Gatsby looked with vacant eyes through a copy of Clay's *Economics*,[4] starting at the Finnish tread that shook the kitchen floor, and peering toward the bleared windows from time to time as if a series of invisible but alarming happenings were taking place outside. Finally he got up and informed me, in an uncertain voice, that he was going home.

"Why's that?"

"Nobody's coming to tea. It's too late!" He looked at his watch as if there was some pressing demand on his time elsewhere. "I can't wait all day."

"Don't be silly; it's just two minutes to four."

He sat down miserably, as if I had pushed him, and simultaneously there was the sound of a motor turning into my lane. We both jumped up, and, a little harrowed myself, I went out into the yard.

Under the dripping bare lilac-trees a large open car was coming up the drive. It stopped. Daisy's face, tipped sideways beneath a three-cornered lavender hat, looked out at me with a bright ecstatic smile.

"Is this absolutely where you live, my dearest one?"

The exhilarating ripple of her voice was a wild tonic in the rain. I had to follow the sound of it for a moment, up and down, with my ear alone, before any words came through. A damp streak of hair lay like a dash of blue paint across her cheek, and her hand was wet with glistening drops as I took it to help her from the car.

"Are you in love with me," she said low in my ear, "or why did I have to come alone?"

[3] A New York City daily newspaper.

[4] *Economics, An Introduction for the General Reader*, Henry Clay, 1918.

"That's the secret of Castle Rackrent.[5] Tell your chauffeur to go far away and spend an hour."

"Come back in an hour, Ferdie." Then in a grave murmur: "His name is Ferdie."

"Does the gasoline affect his nose?"

"I don't think so," she said innocently. "Why?"

We went in. To my overwhelming surprise the living-room was deserted.

"Well, that's funny," I exclaimed.

"What's funny?"

She turned her head as there was a light dignified knocking at the front door. I went out and opened it. Gatsby, pale as death, with his hands plunged like weights in his coat pockets, was standing in a puddle of water glaring tragically into my eyes.

With his hands still in his coat pockets he stalked by me into the hall, turned sharply as if he were on a wire, and disappeared into the living-room. It wasn't a bit funny. Aware of the loud beating of my own heart I pulled the door to against the increasing rain.

For half a minute there wasn't a sound. Then from the living-room I heard a sort of choking murmur and part of a laugh, followed by Daisy's voice on a clear artificial note:

"I certainly am awfully glad to see you again."

A pause; it endured horribly. I had nothing to do in the hall, so I went into the room.

Gatsby, his hands still in his pockets, was reclining against the mantelpiece in a strained counterfeit of perfect ease, even of boredom. His head leaned back so far that it rested against the face of a defunct mantelpiece clock, and from this position his distraught eyes stared down at Daisy, who was sitting, frightened but graceful, on the edge of a stiff chair.

"We've met before," muttered Gatsby. His eyes glanced momentarily at me, and his lips parted with an abortive attempt at a laugh. Luckily the clock took this moment to tilt dangerously at the pressure of his head, whereupon he turned and caught it with trembling fingers, and set it back in place. Then he sat down, rigidly, his elbow on the arm of the sofa and his chin in his hand.

"I'm sorry about the clock," he said.

My own face had now assumed a deep tropical burn. I couldn't muster up a single commonplace out of the thousand in my head.

"It's an old clock," I told them idiotically.

I think we all believed for a moment that it had smashed in pieces on the floor.

"We haven't met for many years," said Daisy, her voice as matter-of-fact as it could ever be.

"Five years next November."

The automatic quality of Gatsby's answer set us all back at least another minute. I had them both on their feet with the desperate suggestion that they help me make tea in the kitchen when the demoniac Finn brought it in on a tray.

Amid the welcome confusion of cups and cakes a certain physical decency established itself. Gatsby got himself into a shadow and, while Daisy and I talked, looked conscientiously from one to the other of us with tense, unhappy eyes. However, as calmness wasn't an end in itself, I made an excuse at the first possible moment, and got to my feet.

[5]The home of the Rackrent family, described in the novel *Castle Rackrent* (1800) by the Irish writer Maria Edgeworth (1767–1849).

"Where are you going?" demanded Gatsby in immediate alarm.

"I'll be back."

"I've got to speak to you about something before you go."

He followed me wildly into the kitchen, closed the door, and whispered: "Oh, God!" in a miserable way.

"What's the matter?"

"This is a terrible mistake," he said, shaking his head from side to side, "a terrible, terrible mistake."

"You're just embarrassed, that's all," and luckily I added: "Daisy's embarrassed too."

"She's embarrassed?" he repeated incredulously.

"Just as much as you are."

"Don't talk so loud."

"You're acting like a little boy," I broke out impatiently. "Not only that, but you're rude. Daisy's sitting in there all alone."

He raised his hand to stop my words, looked at me with unforgettable reproach, and, opening the door cautiously, went back into the other room.

I walked out the back way—just as Gatsby had when he had made his nervous circuit of the house half an hour before—and ran for a huge black knotted tree, whose massed leaves made a fabric against the rain. Once more it was pouring, and my irregular lawn, well-shaved by Gatsby's gardener, abounded in small, muddy swamps and prehistoric marshes. There was nothing to look at from under the tree except Gatsby's enormous house, so I stared at it, like Kant at his church steeple,[6] for half an hour. A brewer had built it early in the "period" craze, a decade before, and there was a story that he'd agreed to pay five years' taxes on all the neighboring cottages if the owners would have their roofs thatched with straw. Perhaps their refusal took the heart out of his plan to Found a Family—he went into an immediate decline. His children sold his house with the black wreath still on the door. Americans, while occasionally willing to be serfs, have always been obstinate about being peasantry.

After half an hour, the sun shone again, and the grocer's automobile rounded Gatsby's drive with the raw material for his servants' dinner—I felt sure he wouldn't eat a spoonful. A maid began opening the upper windows of his house, appeared momentarily in each, and, leaning from a large central bay, spat meditatively into the garden. It was time I went back. While the rain continued it had seemed like the murmur of their voices, rising and swelling a little now and then with gusts of emotion. But in the new silence I felt that silence had fallen within the house too.

I went in—after making every possible noise in the kitchen, short of pushing over the stove—but I don't believe they heard a sound. They were sitting at either end of the couch, looking at each other as if some question had been asked, or was in the air, and every vestige of embarrassment was gone. Daisy's face was smeared with tears, and when I came in she jumped up and began wiping at it with her handkerchief before a mirror. But there was a change in Gatsby that was simply confounding. He literally glowed; without a word or a gesture of exultation a new well-being radiated from him and filled the little room.

"Oh, hello, old sport," he said, as if he hadn't seen me for years. I thought for a moment he was going to shake hands.

"It's stopped raining."

"Has it?" When he realized what I was talking about, that there were twinkle-

[6]At the close of day, the German philosopher Immanuel Kant (1724–1804) habitually sat by the stove in his house, pondering philosophical questions while gazing at the steeple of a nearby church.

bells of sunshine in the room, he smiled like a weather man, like an ecstatic patron of recurrent light, and repeated the news to Daisy. "What do you think of that? It's stopped raining."

"I'm glad, Jay." Her throat, full of aching, grieving beauty, told only of her unexpected joy.

"I want you and Daisy to come over to my house," he said, "I'd like to show her around."

"You're sure you want me to come?"

"Absolutely, old sport."

Daisy went upstairs to wash her face—too late I thought with humiliation of my towels—while Gatsby and I waited on the lawn.

"My house looks well, doesn't it?" he demanded. "See how the whole front of it catches the light."

I agreed that it was splendid.

"Yes." His eyes went over it, every arched door and square tower. "It took me just three years to earn the money that bought it."

"I thought you inherited your money."

"I did, old sport," he said automatically, "but I lost most of it in the big panic—the panic of the war."

I think he hardly knew what he was saying, for when I asked him what business he was in he answered: "That's my affair," before he realized that it wasn't an appropriate reply.

"Oh, I've been in several things," he corrected himself. "I was in the drug business and then I was in the oil business. But I'm not in either one now." He looked at me with more attention. "Do you mean you've been thinking over what I proposed the other night?"

Before I could answer, Daisy came out of the house and two rows of brass buttons on her dress gleamed in the sunlight.

"That huge place *there*?" she cried pointing.

"Do you like it?"

"I love it, but I don't see how you live there all alone."

"I keep it always full of interesting people, night and day. People who do interesting things. Celebrated people."

Instead of taking the short cut along the Sound we went down to the road and entered by the big postern.[7] With enchanting murmurs Daisy admired this aspect or that of the feudal silhouette against the sky, admired the gardens, the sparkling odor of jonquils and the frothy odor of hawthorn and plum blossoms and the pale gold odor of kiss-me-at-the-gate. It was strange to reach the marble steps and find no stir of bright dresses in and out the door, and hear no sound but bird voices in the trees.

And inside, as we wandered through Marie Antoinette music-rooms and Restoration salons,[8] I felt that there were guests concealed behind every couch and table, under orders to be breathlessly silent until we had passed through. As Gatsby closed the door of "the Merton College Library"[9] I could have sworn I heard the owl-eyed man break into ghostly laughter.

---

[7]A rear gate.

[8]I.e., rooms decorated in the stately neoclassical French styles of the eighteenth and nineteenth centuries—named for Marie Antoinette (1755–1793), queen of France (1744–1793), and for the Restoration period in French history (1814–1830), when the Bourbon kings were briefly restored to the throne of France.

[9]The medieval library of Merton College at Oxford University. Established in the fourteenth century, the library is renowned as the oldest in England.

We went upstairs, through period bedrooms swathed in rose and lavender silk and vivid with new flowers, through dressing-rooms and poolrooms, and bathrooms, with sunken baths—intruding into one chamber where a dishevelled man in pajamas was doing liver exercises on the floor. It was Mr. Klipspringer, the "boarder." I had seen him wandering hungrily about the beach that morning. Finally we came to Gatsby's own apartment, a bedroom and a bath, and an Adam study,[10] where we sat down and drank a glass of some Chartreuse[11] he took from a cupboard in the wall.

He hadn't once ceased looking at Daisy, and I think he revalued everything in his house according to the measure of response it drew from her well loved eyes. Sometimes, too, he stared around at his possessions in a dazed way, as though in her actual and astounding presence none of it was any longer real. Once he nearly toppled down a flight of stairs.

His bedroom was the simplest room of all—except where the dresser was garnished with a toilet set of pure dull gold. Daisy took the brush with delight, and smoothed her hair, whereupon Gatsby sat down and shaded his eyes and began to laugh.

"It's the funniest thing, old sport," he said hilariously. "I can't—When I try to——"

He had passed visibly through two states and was entering upon a third. After his embarrassment and his unreasoning joy he was consumed with wonder at her presence. He had been full of the idea so long, dreamed it right through to the end, waited with his teeth set, so to speak, at an inconceivable pitch of intensity. Now, in the reaction, he was running down like an overwound clock.[12]

Recovering himself in a minute he opened for us two hulking patent cabinets[13] which held his massed suits and dressing-gowns and ties, and his shirts, piled like bricks in stacks a dozen high.

"I've got a man in England who buys me clothes. He sends over a selection of things at the beginning of each season, spring and fall."

He took out a pile of shirts and began throwing them, one by one, before us, shirts of sheer linen and thick silk and fine flannel, which lost their folds as they fell and covered the table in many-colored disarray. While we admired he brought more and the soft rich heap mounted higher—shirts with stripes and scrolls and plaids in coral and apple-green and lavender and faint orange, with monograms of Indian blue. Suddenly, with a strained sound, Daisy bent her head into the shirts and began to cry stormily.

"They're such beautiful shirts," she sobbed, her voice muffled in the thick folds. "It makes me sad because I've never seen such—such beautiful shirts before."

After the house, we were to see the grounds and the swimming-pool, and the hydroplane and the mid-summer flowers—but outside Gatsby's window it began to rain again, so we stood in a row looking at the corrugated surface of the Sound.

[10]A room decorated in the ornamented eighteenth-century neoclassical style of Robert Adam (1728–1792) and his brother, James Adam (1730–1794), Scottish architects and designers.

[11]Liqueur produced in France at La Grande Chartreuse, the chief monastery of the Carthusian religious order.

[12]I.e., speedily, like a clock with escapement controls broken through overwinding.

[13]Large wardrobe cabinets with numerous shelves and drawers and with space for hanging clothes. Popular in the last of the 19th century, such specially designed (hence "patented") cabinets were, by the early years of the twentieth century, looked upon by the well-to-do as outdated novelties and no longer stylish.

"If it wasn't for the mist we could see your home across the bay," said Gatsby. "You always have a green light that burns all night at the end of your dock."

Daisy put her arm through his abruptly, but he seemed absorbed in what he had just said. Possibly it had occurred to him that the colossal significance of that light had now vanished forever. Compared to the great distance that had separated him from Daisy it had seemed very near to her, almost touching her. It had seemed as close as a star to the moon. Now it was again a green light on a dock. His count of enchanted objects had diminished by one.

I began to walk about the room, examining various indefinite objects in the half darkness. A large photograph of an elderly man in yachting costume attracted me, hung on the wall over his desk.

"Who's this?"

"That? That's Mr. Dan Cody, old sport."

The name sounded faintly familiar.

"He's dead now. He used to be my best friend years ago."

There was a small picture of Gatsby, also in yachting costume, on the bureau—Gatsby with his head thrown back defiantly—taken apparently when he was about eighteen.

"I adore it," exclaimed Daisy. "The pompadour! You never told me you had a pompadour—or a yacht."

"Look at this," said Gatsby quickly. "Here's a lot of clippings—about you."

They stood side by side examining it. I was going to ask to see the rubies when the phone rang, and Gatsby took up the receiver.

"Yes. . . . Well, I can't talk now. . . . I can't talk now, old sport. . . . I said a *small* town. . . . He must know what a small town is. . . . Well, he's no use to us if Detroit is his idea of a small town. . . . "

He rang off.

"Come here *quick*!" cried Daisy at the window.

The rain was still falling, but the darkness had parted in the west, and there was a pink and golden billow of foamy clouds above the sea.

"Look at that," she whispered, and then after a moment: "I'd like to just get one of those pink clouds and put you in it and push you around."

I tried to go then, but they wouldn't hear of it; perhaps my presence made them feel more satisfactorily alone.

"I know what we'll do," said Gatsby, "we'll have Klipspringer play the piano."

He went out of the room calling "Ewing!" and returned in a few minutes accompanied by an embarrassed, slightly worn young man, with shell-rimmed glasses and scanty blond hair. He was now decently clothed in a sport shirt, open at the neck, sneakers, and duck trousers of a nebulous hue.

"Did we interrupt your exercises?" inquired Daisy politely.

"I was asleep," cried Mr. Klipspringer, in a spasm of embarrassment. "That is, I'd *been* asleep. Then I got up. . . ."

"Klipspringer plays the piano," said Gatsby, cutting him off. "Don't you, Ewing, old sport?"

"I don't play well. I don't—I hardly play at all. I'm all out of prac——"

"We'll go downstairs," interrupted Gatsby. He flipped a switch. The gray windows disappeared as the house glowed full of light.

In the music-room Gatsby turned on a solitary lamp beside the piano. He lit Daisy's cigarette from a trembling match, and sat down with her on a couch far across the room, where there was no light save what the gleaming floor bounced in from the hall.

When Klipspringer had played "The Love Nest"[14] he turned around on the bench and searched unhappily for Gatsby in the gloom.

"I'm all out of practice, you see. I told you I couldn't play. I'm all out of prac——"

"Don't talk so much, old sport," commanded Gatsby. "Play!"

> "In the morning,
> In the evening,
> Ain't we got fun——"[15]

Outside the wind was loud and there was a faint flow of thunder along the Sound. All the lights were going on in West Egg now; the electric trains, men-carrying, were plunging home through the rain from New York. It was the hour of a profound human change, and excitement was generating on the air.

> "One thing's sure and nothing's surer
> The rich get richer and the poor get—children.
> In the meantime,
> In between time——"

As I went over to say good-by I saw that the expression of bewilderment had come back into Gatsby's face, as though a faint doubt had occurred to him as to the quality of his present happiness. Almost five years! There must have been moments even that afternoon when Daisy tumbled short of his dreams—not through her own fault, but because of the colossal vitality of his illusion. It had gone beyond her, beyond everything. He had thrown himself into it with a creative passion, adding to it all the time, decking it out with every bright feather that drifted his way. No amount of fire or freshness can challenge what a man will store up in his ghostly heart.

As I watched him he adjusted himself a little, visibly. His hand took hold of hers, and as she said something low in his ear he turned toward her with a rush of emotion. I think that voice held him most, with its fluctuating, feverish warmth, because it couldn't be over-dreamed—that voice was a deathless song.

They had forgotten me, but Daisy glanced up and held out her hand; Gatsby didn't know me now at all. I looked once more at them and they looked back at me, remotely, possessed by intense life. Then I went out of the room and down the marble steps into the rain, leaving them there together.

CHAPTER VI

ABOUT this time an ambitious young reporter from New York arrived one morning at Gatsby's door and asked him if he had anything to say.

"Anything to say about what?" inquired Gatsby politely.

"Why—any statement to give out."

It transpired after a confused five minutes that the man had heard Gatsby's name around his office in a connection which he either wouldn't reveal or didn't fully understand. This was his day off and with laudable initiative he had hurried out "to see."

[14]A popular song, first presented in the musical show *Mary* (1920).
[15]Lyrics from "Ain't We Got Fun," a popular vaudeville song published in 1921.

It was a random shot, and yet the reporter's instinct was right. Gatsby's notoriety, spread about by the hundreds who had accepted his hospitality and so become authorities upon his past, had increased all summer until he fell just short of being news. Contemporary legends such as the "underground pipe-line to Canada"[1] attached themselves to him, and there was one persistent story that he didn't live in a house at all, but in a boat that looked like a house and was moved secretly up and down the Long Island shore. Just why these inventions were a source of satisfaction to James Gatz of North Dakota isn't easy to say.

James Gatz—that was really, or at least legally, his name. He had changed it at the age of seventeen and at the specific moment that witnessed the beginning of his career—when he saw Dan Cody's yacht drop anchor over the most insidious flat on Lake Superior. It was James Gatz who had been loafing along the beach that afternoon in a torn green jersey and a pair of canvas pants, but it was already Jay Gatsby who borrowed a rowboat, pulled out to the *Tuolumne*, and informed Cody that a wind might catch him and break him up in half an hour.

I suppose he'd had the name ready for a long time, even then. His parents were shiftless and unsuccessful farm people—his imagination had never really accepted them as his parents at all. The truth was that Jay Gatsby of West Egg, Long Island, sprang from his Platonic[2] conception of himself. He was a son of God—a phrase which, if it means anything, means just that—and he must be about His Father's business, the service of a vast, vulgar, and meretricious beauty. So he invented just the sort of Jay Gatsby that a seventeen-year-old boy would be likely to invent, and to this conception he was faithful to the end.

For over a year he had been beating his way along the south shore of Lake Superior as a clam-digger and a salmon-fisher or in any other capacity that brought him food and bed. His brown, hardening body lived naturally through the half-fierce, half-lazy work of the bracing days. He knew women early, and since they spoiled him he became contemptuous of them, of young virgins because they were ignorant, of the others because they were hysterical about things which in his overwhelming self-absorbtion he took for granted.

But his heart was in a constant, turbulent riot. The most grotesque and fantastic conceits haunted him in his bed at night. A universe of ineffable gaudiness spun itself out in his brain while the clock ticked on the wash-stand and the moon soaked with wet light his tangled clothes upon the floor. Each night he added to the pattern of his fancies until drowsiness closed down upon some vivid scene with an oblivious embrace. For a while these reveries provided an outlet for his imagination; they were a satisfactory hint of the unreality of reality, a promise that the rock of the world was founded securely on a fairy's wing.

An instinct toward his future glory had led him, some months before, to the small Lutheran college of St. Olaf in southern Minnesota. He stayed there two weeks, dismayed at its ferocious indifference to the drums of his destiny, to destiny itself, and despising the janitor's work with which he was to pay his way through. Then he drifted back to Lake Superior, and he was still searching for

---

[1]During Prohibition (1919–1933), illegal alcoholic beverages were so abundantly available that many people came to believe a secret underground pipeline must exist, extending across the border from nonprohibition Canada to the United States.

[2]Idealized. The Greek philosopher Plato (427?–347 B.C.) taught that only ideas are real and that they provide the patterns from which the human senses extract meaning.

something to do on the day that Dan Cody's yacht dropped anchor in the shallows alongshore.

Cody was fifty years old then, a product of the Nevada silver fields, of the Yukon, of every rush for metal since seventy-five.[3] The transactions in Montana copper that made him many times a millionaire found him physically robust but on the verge of soft-mindedness, and, suspecting this, an infinite number of women tried to separate him from his money. The none too savory ramifications by which Ella Kaye, the newspaper woman, played Madame de Maintenon[4] to his weakness and sent him to sea in a yacht, were common knowledge to the turgid sub-journalism of 1902. He had been coasting along all too hospitable shores for five years when he turned up as James Gatz's destiny in Little Girl Bay.

To young Gatz, resting on his oars and looking up at the railed deck, that yacht represented all the beauty and glamour in the world. I suppose he smiled at Cody—he had probably discovered that people liked him when he smiled. At any rate Cody asked him a few questions (one of them elicited the brand new name) and found that he was quick and extravagantly ambitious. A few days later he took him to Duluth and bought him a blue coat, six pair of white duck[5] trousers, and a yachting cap. And when the *Tuolumne* left for the West Indies and the Barbary Coast[6] Gatsby left too.

He was employed in a vague personal capacity—while he remained with Cody he was in turn steward, mate, skipper, secretary, and even jailor, for Dan Cody sober knew what lavish doings Dan Cody drunk might soon be about, and he provided for such contingencies by reposing more and more trust in Gatsby. The arrangement lasted five years, during which the boat went three times around the Continent. He might have lasted indefinitely except for the fact that Ella Kaye came on board one night in Boston and a week later Dan Cody inhospitably died.

I remember the portrait of him up in Gatsby's bedroom, a gray, florid man with a hard, empty face—the pioneer debauchee, who during one phase of American life brought back to the Eastern seaboard the savage violence of the frontier brothel and saloon. It was indirectly due to Cody that Gatsby drank so little. Sometimes in the course of gay parties women used to rub champagne into his hair; for himself he formed the habit of letting liquor alone.

And it was from Cody that he inherited money—a legacy of twenty-five thousand dollars. He didn't get it. He never understood the legal device that was used against him, but what remained of the millions went intact to Ella Kaye. He was left with his singularly appropriate education; the vague contour of Jay Gatsby had filled out to the substantiality of a man.

He told me all this very much later, but I've put it down here with the idea of exploding those first wild rumors about his antecedents, which weren't even faintly true. Moreover he told it to me at a time of confusion, when I had reached the point of believing everything and nothing about him. So I take advantage

---

[3]I.e., he had taken part in every rush to find precious metals since 1875—when gold was discovered in Deadwood Gulch, South Dakota.

[4]Françoise d'Aubigné (1635–1719), Marquise de Maintenon, second wife of the French king Louis XIV and a dominating influence in his life.

[5]Heavy cotton cloth.

[6]Waterfront area of San Francisco, a district of saloons and brothels, named after the pirate coast of North Africa.

of this short halt, while Gatsby, so to speak, caught his breath, to clear this set of misconceptions away.

It was a halt, too, in my association with his affairs. For several weeks I didn't see him or hear his voice on the phone—mostly I was in New York, trotting around with Jordan and trying to ingratiate myself with her senile aunt—but finally I went over to his house one Sunday afternoon. I hadn't been there two minutes when somebody brought Tom Buchanan in for a drink. I was startled, naturally, but the really surprising thing was that it hadn't happened before.

They were a party of three on horseback—Tom and a man named Sloane and a pretty woman in a brown riding-habit, who had been there previously.

"I'm delighted to see you," said Gatsby, standing on his porch. "I'm delighted that you dropped in."

As though they cared!

"Sit right down. Have a cigarette or a cigar." He walked around the room quickly, ringing bells. "I'll have something to drink for you in just a minute."

He was profoundly affected by the fact that Tom was there. But he would be uneasy anyhow until he had given them something, realizing in a vague way that was all they came for. Mr. Sloane wanted nothing. A lemonade? No, thanks. A little champagne? Nothing at all, thanks. . . . I'm sorry——

"Did you have a nice ride?"

"Very good roads around here."

"I suppose the automobiles——"

"Yeah."

Moved by an irresistible impulse, Gatsby turned to Tom, who had accepted the introduction as a stranger.

"I believe we've met somewhere before, Mr. Buchanan."

"Oh, yes," Tom, gruffly polite, but obviously not remembering. "So we did. I remember very well."

"About two weeks ago."

"That's right. You were with Nick here."

"I know your wife," continued Gatsby, almost aggressively.

"That so?"

Tom turned to me.

"You live near here, Nick?"

"Next door."

"That so?"

Mr. Sloane didn't enter into the conversation but lounged back haughtily in his chair; the woman said nothing either—until unexpectedly, after two high-balls, she became cordial.

"We'll all come over to your next party, Mr. Gatsby," she suggested. "What do you say?"

"Certainly; I'd be delighted to have you."

"Be ver' nice," said Mr. Sloane, without gratitude. "Well—think ought to be starting home."

"Please don't hurry," Gatsby urged them. He had control of himself now, and he wanted to see more of Tom. "Why don't you—why don't you stay for supper? I wouldn't be surprised if some other people dropped in from New York."

"You come to supper with *me*," said the lady enthusiastically. "Both of you."

This included me. Mr. Sloane got to his feet.

"Come along," he said—but to her only.

"I mean it," she insisted. "I'd love to have you. Lots of room."

Gatsby looked at me questioningly. He wanted to go, and he didn't see that Mr. Sloane had determined he shouldn't.

"I'm afraid I won't be able to," I said.

"Well, you come," she urged, concentrating on Gatsby.

Mr. Sloane murmured something close to her ear.

"We won't be late if we start now," she insisted aloud.

"I haven't got a horse," said Gatsby. "I used to ride in the army, but I've never bought a horse. I'll have to follow you in my car. Excuse me for just a minute."

The rest of us walked out on the porch, where Sloane and the lady began an impassioned conversation aside.

"My God, I believe the man's coming," said Tom. "Doesn't he know she doesn't want him?"

"She says she does want him."

"She has a big dinner party and he won't know a soul there." He frowned. "I wonder where in the devil he met Daisy. By God, I may be old-fashioned in my ideas, but women run around too much these days to suit me. They meet all kinds of crazy fish."

Suddenly Mr. Sloane and the lady walked down the steps and mounted their horses.

"Come on," said Mr. Sloane to Tom, "we're late. We've got to go." And then to me: "Tell him we couldn't wait, will you?"

Tom and I shook hands, the rest of us exchanged a cool nod, and they trotted quickly down the drive, disappearing under the foliage just as Gatsby, with hat and light overcoat in hand, came out the front door.

Tom was evidently perturbed at Daisy's running around alone, for on the following Saturday night he came with her to Gatsby's party. Perhaps his presence gave the evening its peculiar quality of oppressiveness—it stands out in my memory from Gatsby's other parties that summer. There were the same people, or at least the same sort of people, the same profusion of champagne, the same many-colored, many-keyed commotion, but I felt an unpleasantness in the air, a pervading harshness that hadn't been there before. Or perhaps I had merely grown used to it, grown to accept West Egg as a world complete in itself, with its own standards and its own figures, second to nothing because it had no consciousness of being so, and now I was looking at it again, through Daisy's eyes. It is invariably saddening to look through new eyes at things upon which you have expended your own powers of adjustment.

They arrived at twilight, and, as we strolled out among the sparkling hundreds, Daisy's voice was playing murmurous tricks in her throat.

"These things excite me *so*," she whispered. "If you want to kiss me any time during the evening, Nick, just let me know and I'll be glad to arrange it for you. Just mention my name. Or present a green card. I'm giving out green——"

"Look around," suggested Gatsby.

"I'm looking around. I'm having a marvelous——"

"You must see the faces of many people you've heard about."

Tom's arrogant eyes roamed the crowd.

"We don't go around very much," he said; "in fact, I was just thinking I don't know a soul here."

"Perhaps you know that lady." Gatsby indicated a gorgeous, scarcely human orchid of a woman who sat in state under a white-plum tree. Tom and Daisy stared, with that peculiarly unreal feeling that accompanies the recognition of a hitherto ghostly celebrity of the movies.

"She's lovely," said Daisy.

"The man bending over her is her director."

He took them ceremoniously from group to group:

"Mrs. Buchanan . . . and Mr. Buchanan—" After an instant's hesitation he added: "the polo player."

"Oh, no," objected Tom quickly, "not me."

But evidently the sound of it pleased Gatsby, for Tom remained "the polo player" for the rest of the evening.

"I've never met so many celebrities," Daisy exclaimed. "I liked that man— what was his name?—with the sort of blue nose."

Gatsby identified him, adding that he was a small producer.

"Well, I liked him anyhow."

"I'd a little rather not be the polo player," said Tom pleasantly, "I'd rather look at all these famous people—in oblivion."

Daisy and Gatsby danced. I remember being surprised by his graceful, conservative fox-trot—I had never seen him dance before. Then they sauntered over to my house and sat on the steps for half an hour, while at her request I remained watchfully in the garden. "In case there's a fire or a flood," she explained, "or any act of God."

Tom appeared from his oblivion as we were sitting down to supper together. "Do you mind if I eat with some people over here?" he said. "A fellow's getting off some funny stuff."

"Go ahead," answered Daisy genially, "and if you want to take down any addresses here's my little gold pencil." . . . She looked around after a moment and told me the girl was "common but pretty," and I knew that except for the half-hour she'd been alone with Gatsby she wasn't having a good time.

We were at a particularly tipsy table. That was my fault—Gatsby had been called to the phone, and I'd enjoyed these same people only two weeks before. But what had amused me then turned septic on the air now.

"How do you feel, Miss Baedeker?"

The girl addressed was trying, unsuccessfully, to slump against my shoulder. At this inquiry she sat up and opened her eyes.

"Wha'?"

A massive and lethargic woman, who had been urging Daisy to play golf with her at the local club tomorrow, spoke in Miss Baedeker's defence:

"Oh, she's all right now. When she's had five or six cocktails she always starts screaming like that. I tell her she ought to leave it alone."

"I do leave it alone," affirmed the accused hollowly.

"We heard you yelling, so I said to Doc Civet here: 'There's somebody that needs your help, Doc.' "

"She's much obliged, I'm sure," said another friend, without gratitude, "but you got her dress all wet when you stuck her head in the pool."

"Anything I hate is to get my head stuck in a pool," mumbled Miss Baedeker. "They almost drowned me once over in New Jersey."

"Then you ought to leave it alone," countered Doctor Civet.

"Speak for yourself!" cried Miss Baedeker violently. "Your hand shakes. I wouldn't let you operate on me!"

It was like that. Almost the last thing I remember was standing with Daisy and watching the moving-picture director and his Star. They were still under the white-plum tree and their faces were touching except for a pale, thin ray of moonlight between. It occurred to me that he had been very slowly bending toward her all evening to attain this proximity, and even while I watched I saw him stoop one ultimate degree and kiss at her cheek.

"I like her," said Daisy, "I think she's lovely."

But the rest offended her—and inarguably, because it wasn't a gesture but an emotion. She was appalled by West Egg, this unprecedented "place" that Broadway had begotten upon a Long Island fishing village—appalled by its raw vigor that chafed under the old euphemisms and by the too obtrusive fate that herded its inhabitants along a short-cut from nothing to nothing. She saw something awful in the very simplicity she failed to understand.

I sat on the front steps with them while they waited for their car. It was dark here in front; only the bright door sent ten square feet of light volleying out into the soft black morning. Sometimes a shadow moved against a dressing-room blind above, gave way to another shadow, an indefinite procession of shadows, who rouged and powdered in an invisible glass.

"Who is this Gatsby anyhow?" demanded Tom suddenly. "Some big bootlegger?"

"Where'd you hear that?" I inquired.

"I didn't hear it. I imagined it. A lot of these newly rich people are just big bootleggers, you know."

"Not Gatsby," I said shortly.

He was silent for a moment. The pebbles of the drive crunched under his feet.

"Well, he certainly must have strained himself to get this menagerie together."

A breeze stirred the gray haze of Daisy's fur collar.

"At least they're more interesting than the people we know," she said with an effort.

"You didn't look so interested."

"Well, I was."

Tom laughed and turned to me.

"Did you notice Daisy's face when that girl asked her to put her under a cold shower?"

Daisy began to sing with the music in a husky, rhythmic whisper, bringing out a meaning in each word that it had never had before and would never have again. When the melody rose, her voice broke up sweetly, following it, in a way contralto voices[7] have, and each change tipped out a little of her warm human magic upon the air.

"Lots of people come who haven't been invited," she said suddenly. "That girl hadn't been invited. They simply force their way in and he's too polite to object."

"I'd like to know who he is and what he does," insisted Tom. "And I think I'll make a point of finding out."

"I can tell you right now," she answered. "He owned some drug-stores, a lot of drug-stores. He built them up himself."

The dilatory limousine came rolling up the drive.

"Good night, Nick," said Daisy.

Her glance left me and sought the lighted top of the steps, where "Three O'Clock in the Morning,"[8] a neat, sad little waltz of that year, was drifting out the open door. After all, in the very casualness of Gatsby's party there were romantic possibilities totally absent from her world. What was it up there in the song that seemed to be calling her back inside? What would happen now in the dim, incalculable hours? Perhaps some unbelievable guest would arrive, a person

[7]Women's singing voices of low pitch.

[8]A waltz published in 1919 and then introduced with lyrics in a musical review in 1921.

infinitely rare and to be marvelled at, some authentically radiant young girl who with one fresh glance at Gatsby, one moment of magical encounter, would blot out those five years of unwavering devotion.

I stayed late that night, Gatsby asked me to wait until he was free, and I lingered in the garden until the inevitable swimming party had run up, chilled and exalted, from the black beach, until the lights were extinguished in the guest-rooms overhead. When he came down the steps at last the tanned skin was drawn unusually tight on his face, and his eyes were bright and tired.

"She didn't like it," he said immediately.

"Of course she did."

"She didn't like it," he insisted. "She didn't have a good time."

He was silent, and I guessed at his unutterable depression.

"I feel far away from her," he said. "It's hard to make her understand."

"You mean about the dance?"

"The dance?" He dismissed all the dances he had given with a snap of his fingers. "Old sport, the dance is unimportant."

He wanted nothing less of Daisy than that she should go to Tom and say: "I never loved you." After she had obliterated four years with that sentence they could decide upon the more practical measures to be taken. One of them was that, after she was free, they were to go back to Louisville and be married from her house—just as if it were five years ago.

"And she doesn't understand," he said. "She used to be able to understand. We'd sit for hours——"

He broke off and began to walk up and down a desolate path of fruit rinds and discarded favors and crushed flowers.

"I wouldn't ask too much of her," I ventured. "You can't repeat the past."

"Can't repeat the past?" he cried incredulously. "Why of course you can!"

He looked around him wildly, as if the past were lurking here in the shadow of his house, just out of reach of his hand.

"I'm going to fix everything just the way it was before," he said, nodding determinedly. "She'll see."

He talked a lot about the past, and I gathered that he wanted to recover something, some idea of himself perhaps, that had gone into loving Daisy. His life had been confused and disordered since then, but if he could once return to a certain starting place and go over it all slowly, he could find out what that thing was. . . .

. . . One autumn night, five years before, they had been walking down the street when the leaves were falling, and they came to a place where there were no trees and the sidewalk was white with moonlight. They stopped here and turned toward each other. Now it was a cool night with that mysterious excitement in it which comes at the two changes of the year. The quiet lights in the house were humming out into the darkness and there was a stir and bustle among the stars. Out of the corner of his eye Gatsby saw that the blocks of the sidewalks really formed a ladder and mounted to a secret place above the trees— he could climb to it, if he climbed alone, and once there he could suck on the pap of life, gulp down the incomparable milk of wonder.

His heart beat faster and faster as Daisy's white face came up to his own. He knew that when he kissed this girl, and forever wed his unutterable visions to her perishable breath, his mind would never romp again like the mind of God. So he waited, listening for a moment longer to the tuning-fork that had been struck upon a star. Then he kissed her. At his lips' touch she blossomed for him like a flower and the incarnation was complete.

Through all he said, even through his appalling sentimentality, I was reminded of something—an elusive rhythm, a fragment of lost words, that I had heard somewhere a long time ago. For a moment a phrase tried to take shape in my mouth and my lips parted like a dumb man's, as though there was more struggling upon them than a wisp of startled air. But they made no sound, and what I had almost remembered was uncommunicable forever.

CHAPTER VII

IT was when curiosity about Gatsby was at its highest that the lights in his house failed to go on one Saturday night—and, as obscurely as it had begun, his career as Trimalchio[1] was over. Only gradually did I become aware that the automobiles which turned expectantly into his drive stayed for just a minute and then drove sulkily away. Wondering if he were sick I went over to find out—an unfamiliar butler with a villainous face squinted at me suspiciously from the door.

"Is Mr. Gatsby sick?"

"Nope." After a pause he added "sir" in a dilatory, grudging way.

"I hadn't seen him around, and I was rather worried. Tell him Mr. Carraway came over."

"Who?" he demanded rudely.

"Carraway."

"Carraway. All right, I'll tell him."

Abruptly he slammed the door.

My Finn informed me that Gatsby had dismissed every servant in his house a week ago and replaced them with half a dozen others, who never went into West Egg village to be bribed by the tradesmen, but ordered moderate supplies over the telephone. The grocery boy reported that the kitchen looked like a pigsty, and the general opinion in the village was that the new people weren't servants at all.

Next day Gatsby called me on the phone.

"Going away?" I inquired.

"No, old sport."

"I hear you fired all your servants."

"I wanted somebody who wouldn't gossip. Daisy comes over quite often—in the afternoons."

So the whole caravansary[2] had fallen in like a card house at the disapproval in her eyes.

"They're some people Wolfsheim wanted to do something for. They're all brothers and sisters. They used to run a small hotel."

"I see."

He was calling up at Daisy's request—would I come to lunch at her house tomorrow? Miss Baker would be there. Half an hour later Daisy herself telephoned and seemed relieved to find that I was coming. Something was up. And yet I couldn't believe that they would choose this occasion for a scene—especially for the rather harrowing scene that Gatsby had outlined in the garden.

---

[1]Vulgar, newly rich character satirized in the *Satyricon* by the Roman writer Petronius Arbiter (d. A.D. 66). Among the first titles for the novel tentatively proposed by Fitzgerald was *Trimalchio in West Egg.*

[2]In the Near East, a large building and its courtyards, where travelers and caravans stop temporarily for rest and entertainment.

The next day was broiling, almost the last, certainly the warmest, of the summer. As my train emerged from the tunnel into sunlight, only the hot whistles of the National Biscuit Company broke the simmering hush at noon. The straw seats of the car hovered on the edge of combustion; the woman next to me perspired delicately for a while into her white shirtwaist, and then, as her newspaper dampened under her fingers, lapsed despairingly into deep heat with a desolate cry. Her pocket-book slapped to the floor.

"Oh, my!" she gasped.

I picked it up with a weary bend and handed it back to her, holding it at arm's length and by the extreme tip of the corners to indicate that I had no designs upon it—but every one near by, including the woman, suspected me just the same.

"Hot!" said the conductor to familiar faces. "Some weather! . . . Hot! . . . Hot! . . . Hot! . . . Is it hot enough for you? Is it hot? Is it . . . ?"

My commutation ticket came back to me with a dark stain from his hand. That any one should care in this heat whose flushed lips he kissed, whose head made damp the pajama pocket over his heart!

. . . Through the hall of the Buchanans' house blew a faint wind, carrying the sound of the telephone bell out to Gatsby and me as we waited at the door.

"The master's body!" roared the butler into the mouthpiece. "I'm sorry, madame, but we can't furnish it—it's far too hot to touch this noon!"

What he really said was: "Yes . . . Yes . . . I'll see."

He set down the receiver and came toward us, glistening slightly, to take our stiff straw hats.

"Madame expects you in the salon!" he cried, needlessly indicating the direction. In this heat every extra gesture was an affront to the common store of life.

The room, shadowed well with awnings, was dark and cool. Daisy and Jordan lay upon an enormous couch, like silver idols weighing down their own white dresses against the singing breeze of the fans.

"We can't move," they said together.

Jordan's fingers, powdered white over their tan, rested for a moment in mine.

"And Mr. Thomas Buchanan, the athlete?" I inquired.

Simultaneously I heard his voice, gruff, muffled, husky, at the hall telephone.

Gatsby stood in the center of the crimson carpet and gazed around with fascinated eyes. Daisy watched him and laughed, her sweet, exciting laugh; a tiny gust of powder rose from her bosom into the air.

"The rumor is," whispered Jordan, "that that's Tom's girl on the telephone."

We were silent. The voice in the hall rose high with annoyance: "Very well, then, I won't sell you the car at all. . . . I'm under no obligations to you at all . . . and as for your bothering me about it at lunch time, I won't stand that at all!"

"Holding down the receiver," said Daisy cynically.

"No, he's not," I assured her. "It's a bona-fide deal. I happen to know about it."

Tom flung open the door, blocked out its space for a moment with his thick body, and hurried into the room.

"Mr. Gatsby!" He put out his broad, flat hand with well-concealed dislike. "I'm glad to see you, sir. . . . Nick. . . ."

"Make us a cold drink," cried Daisy.

As he left the room again she got up and went over to Gatsby and pulled his face down, kissing him on the mouth.

"You know I love you," she murmured.

"You forget there's a lady present," said Jordan.

Daisy looked around doubtfully.

"You kiss Nick too."

"What a low, vulgar girl!"

"I don't care!" cried Daisy, and began to clog[3] on the brick fireplace. Then she remembered the heat and sat down guiltily on the couch just as a freshly laundered nurse leading a little girl came into the room.

"Bles-sed pre-cious," she crooned, holding out her arms. "Come to your own mother that loves you."

The child, relinquished by the nurse, rushed across the room and rooted shyly into her mother's dress.

"The bles-sed pre-cious! Did mother get powder on your old yellowy hair? Stand up now, and say—How-de-do."

Gatsby and I in turn leaned down and took the small reluctant hand. Afterward he kept looking at the child with surprise. I don't think he had ever really believed in its existence before.

"I got dressed before luncheon," said the child, turning eagerly to Daisy.

"That's because your mother wanted to show you off." Her face bent into the single wrinkle of the small white neck. "You dream, you. You absolute little dream."

"Yes," admitted the child calmly. "Aunt Jordan's got on a white dress too."

"How do you like mother's friends?" Daisy turned her around so that she faced Gatsby. "Do you think they're pretty?"

"Where's Daddy?"

"She doesn't look like her father," explained Daisy. "She looks like me. She's got my hair and shape of the face."

Daisy sat back upon the couch. The nurse took a step forward and held out her hand.

"Come, Pammy."

"Good-by, sweetheart!"

With a reluctant backward glance the well-disciplined child held to her nurse's hand and was pulled out the door, just as Tom came back, preceding four gin rickeys[4] that clicked full of ice.

Gatsby took up his drink.

"They certainly look cool," he said, with visible tension.

We drank in long, greedy swallows.

"I read somewhere that the sun's getting hotter every year," said Tom genially. "It seems that pretty soon the earth's going to fall into the sun—or wait a minute—it's just the opposite—the sun's getting colder every year.

"Come outside," he suggested to Gatsby, "I'd like you to have a look at the place."

I went with them out to the veranda. On the green Sound, stagnant in the heat, one small sail crawled slowly toward the fresher sea. Gatsby's eyes followed it momentarily; he raised his hand and pointed across the bay.

"I'm right across from you."

"So you are."

Our eyes lifted over the rose-beds and the hot lawn and the weedy refuse of the dog-days[5] along-shore. Slowly the white wings of the boat moved against

---

[3]A stamping dance, traditionally performed in heavy shoes (clogs).

[4]Gin mixed with lime juice and soda water.

[5]The hot summer days of July, August, and September when Sirius, the Dog Star, is high in the sky.

the blue cool limit of the sky. Ahead lay the scalloped ocean and the abounding blessed isles.[6]

"There's sport for you," said Tom, nodding. "I'd like to be out there with him for about an hour."

We had luncheon in the dining-room, darkened too against the heat, and drank down nervous gayety with the cold ale.

"What'll we do with ourselves this afternoon?" cried Daisy, "and the day after that, and the next thirty years?"

"Don't be morbid," Jordan said. "Life starts all over again when it gets crisp in the fall."

"But it's so hot," insisted Daisy, on the verge of tears, "and everything's so confused. Let's all go to town!"

Her voice struggled on through the heat, beating against it, molding its senselessness into forms.

"I've heard of making a garage out of a stable," Tom was saying to Gatsby, "but I'm the first man who ever made a stable out of a garage."

"Who wants to go to town?" demanded Daisy insistently. Gatsby's eyes floated toward her. "Ah," she cried, "you look so cool."

Their eyes met, and they stared together at each other, alone in space. With an effort she glanced down at the table.

"You always look so cool," she repeated.

She had told him that she loved him, and Tom Buchanan saw. He was astounded. His mouth opened a little, and he looked at Gatsby, and then back at Daisy as if he had just recognized her as someone he knew a long time ago.

"You resemble the advertisement of the man,"[7] she went on innocently. "You know the advertisement of the man——"

"All right," broke in Tom quickly, "I'm perfectly willing to go to town. Come on—we're all going to town."

He got up, his eyes still flashing between Gatsby and his wife. No one moved.

"Come on!" His temper cracked a little. "What's the matter, anyhow? If we're going to town, let's start."

His hand, trembling with his effort at self-control, bore to his lips the last of his glass of ale. Daisy's voice got us to our feet and out on to the blazing gravel drive.

"Are we just going to go?" she objected. "Like this? Aren't we going to let any one smoke a cigarette first?"

"Everybody smoked all through lunch."

"Oh, let's have fun," she begged him. "It's too hot to fuss."

He didn't answer.

"Have it your own way," she said. "Come on, Jordan."

They went upstairs to get ready while we three men stood there shuffling the hot pebbles with our feet. A silver curve of the moon hovered already in the western sky. Gatsby started to speak, changed his mind, but not before Tom wheeled and faced him expectantly.

"Have you got your stables here?" asked Gatsby with an effort.

"About a quarter of a mile down the road."

[6]The paradisal islands described in classical Greek and Roman mythology.

[7]The "Arrow Man," portrayed from 1905 to 1930 in advertisements for Arrow shirts and collars, illustrated by the American artist Joseph Leyendecker (1874–1951). Leyendecker's "Arrow Man" became the subject of stories, poems, a Broadway show and, by the early 1920s, a national ideal of handsome American manhood.

"Oh."

A pause.

"I don't see the idea of going to town," broke out Tom savagely. "Women get these notions in their heads——"

"Shall we take anything to drink?" called Daisy from an upper window.

"I'll get some whiskey," answered Tom. He went inside.

Gatsby turned to me rigidly:

"I can't say anything in his house, old sport."

"She's got an indiscreet voice," I remarked. "It's full of—" I hesitated.

"Her voice is full of money," he said suddenly.

That was it. I'd never understood before. It was full of money—that was the inexhaustible charm that rose and fell in it, the jingle of it, the cymbals' song of it. . . . High in a white palace the king's daughter, the golden girl. . . .

Tom came out of the house wrapping a quart bottle in a towel, followed by Daisy and Jordan wearing small tight hats of metallic cloth and carrying light capes over their arms.

"Shall we all go in my car?" suggested Gatsby. He felt the hot, green leather of the seat. "I ought to have left it in the shade."

"Is it standard shift?" demanded Tom.

"Yes."

"Well, you take my coupé and let me drive your car to town."

The suggestion was distasteful to Gatsby.

"I don't think there's much gas," he objected.

"Plenty of gas," said Tom boisterously. He looked at the gauge. "And if it runs out I can stop at a drug-store. You can buy anything at a drug-store nowadays."

A pause followed this apparently pointless remark. Daisy looked at Tom frowning, and an indefinable expression, at once definitely unfamiliar and vaguely recognizable, as if I had only heard it described in words, passed over Gatsby's face.

"Come on, Daisy," said Tom, pressing her with his hand toward Gatsby's car. "I'll take you in this circus wagon."

He opened the door, but she moved out from the circle of his arm.

"You take Nick and Jordan. We'll follow you in the coupé."

She walked close to Gatsby, touching his coat with her hand. Jordan and Tom and I got into the front seat of Gatsby's car, Tom pushed the unfamiliar gears tentatively, and we shot off into the oppressive heat, leaving them out of sight behind.

"Did you see that?" demanded Tom.

"See what?"

He looked at me keenly, realizing that Jordan and I must have known all along.

"You think I'm pretty dumb, don't you?" he suggested. "Perhaps I am, but I have a—almost a second sight, sometimes, that tells me what to do. Maybe you don't believe that, but science——"

He paused. The immediate contingency overtook him, pulled him back from the edge of the theoretical abyss.

"I've made a small investigation of this fellow," he continued. "I could have gone deeper if I'd known——"

"Do you mean you've been to a medium?"[8] inquired Jordan humorously.

[8]A spiritualist, one who claims to summon the spirits of the dead to tell the secrets of the past.

"What?" Confused, he stared at us as we laughed. "A medium?"

"About Gatsby."

"About Gatsby! No, I haven't. I said I'd been making a small investigation of his past."

"And you found he was an Oxford man," said Jordan helpfully.

"An Oxford man!" He was incredulous. "Like hell he is! He wears a pink suit."

"Nevertheless he's an Oxford man."

"Oxford, New Mexico," snorted Tom contemptuously, "or something like that."

"Listen, Tom. If you're such a snob, why did you invite him to lunch?" demanded Jordan crossly.

"Daisy invited him; she knew him before we were married—God knows where!"

We were all irritable now with the fading ale, and aware of it we drove for a while in silence. Then as Doctor T. J. Eckleburg's faded eyes came into sight down the road, I remembered Gatsby's caution about gasoline.

"We've got enough to get us to town," said Tom.

"But there's a garage right here," objected Jordan. "I don't want to get stalled in this baking heat."

Tom threw on both brakes impatiently, and we slid to an abrupt dusty stop under Wilson's sign. After a moment the proprietor emerged from the interior of his establishment and gazed hollow-eyed at the car.

"Let's have some gas!" cried Tom roughly. "What do you think we stopped for—to admire the view?"

"I'm sick," said Wilson without moving. "Been sick all day."

"What's the matter?"

"I'm all run down."

"Well, shall I help myself?" Tom demanded. "You sounded well enough on the phone."

With an effort Wilson left the shade and support of the doorway and, breathing hard, unscrewed the cap of the tank. In the sunlight his face was green.

"I didn't mean to interrupt your lunch," he said. "But I need money pretty bad, and I was wondering what you were going to do with your old car."

"How do you like this one?" inquired Tom. "I bought it last week."

"It's a nice yellow one," said Wilson, as he strained at the handle.

"Like to buy it?"

"Big chance," Wilson smiled faintly. "No, but I could make some money on the other."

"What do you want money for, all of a sudden?"

"I've been here too long. I want to get away. My wife and I want to go West."

"Your wife does," exclaimed Tom, startled.

"She's been talking about it for ten years." He rested for a moment against the pump, shading his eyes. "And now she's going whether she wants to or not. I'm going to get her away."

The coupé flashed by us with a flurry of dust and the flash of a waving hand.

"What do I owe you?" demanded Tom harshly.

"I just got wised up to something funny the last two days," remarked Wilson. "That's why I want to get away. That's why I been bothering you about the car."

"What do I owe you?"

"Dollar twenty."

The relentless beating heat was beginning to confuse me and I had a bad moment there before I realized that so far his suspicions hadn't alighted on Tom. He had discovered that Myrtle had some sort of life apart from him in another world, and the shock had made him physically sick. I stared at him and then at Tom, who had made a parallel discovery less than an hour before—and it occurred to me that there was no difference between men, in intelligence or race, so profound as the difference between the sick and the well. Wilson was so sick that he looked guilty, unforgivably guilty—as if he had just got some poor girl with child.

"I'll let you have that car," said Tom. "I'll send it over tomorrow afternoon."

That locality was always vaguely disquieting, even in the broad glare of afternoon, and now I turned my head as though I had been warned of something behind. Over the ashheaps the giant eyes of Doctor T. J. Eckleburg kept their vigil, but I perceived, after a moment, that other eyes were regarding us with peculiar intensity from less than twenty feet away.

In one of the windows over the garage the curtains had been moved aside a little, and Myrtle Wilson was peering down at the car. So engrossed was she that she had no consciousness of being observed, and one emotion after another crept into her face like objects into a slowly developing picture. Her expression was curiously familiar—it was an expression I had often seen on women's faces, but on Myrtle Wilson's face it seemed purposeless and inexplicable until I realized that her eyes, wide with jealous terror, were fixed not on Tom, but on Jordan Baker, whom she took to be his wife.

There is no confusion like the confusion of a simple mind, and as we drove away Tom was feeling the hot whips of panic. His wife and his mistress, until an hour ago secure and inviolate, were slipping precipitately from his control. Instinct made him step on the accelerator with the double purpose of overtaking Daisy and leaving Wilson behind, and we sped along toward Astoria at fifty miles an hour, until, among the spidery girders of the elevated, we came in sight of the easy-going blue coupé.

"Those big movies around Fiftieth Street are cool," suggested Jordan, "I love New York on summer afternoons when every one's away. There's something very sensuous about it—overripe, as if all sorts of funny fruits were going to fall into your hands."

The word "sensuous" had the effect of further disquieting Tom, but before he could invent a protest the coupé came to a stop, and Daisy signalled us to draw up alongside.

"Where are we going?" she cried.

"How about the movies?"

"It's so hot," she complained. "You go. We'll ride around and meet you after." With an effort her wit rose faintly, "We'll meet you on some corner. I'll be the man smoking two cigarettes."

"We can't argue about it here," Tom said impatiently, as a truck gave out a cursing whistle behind us. "You follow me to the south side of Central Park, in front of the Plaza."

Several times he turned his head and looked back for their car, and if the traffic delayed them he slowed up until they came into sight. I think he was afraid they would dart down a side street and out of his life forever.

But they didn't. And we all took the less explicable step of engaging the parlor of a suite in the Plaza Hotel.

The prolonged and tumultuous argument that ended by herding us into that room eludes me, though I have a sharp physical memory that, in the course of it, my underwear kept climbing like a damp snake around my legs and intermittent beads of sweat raced cool across my back. The notion originated with Daisy's suggestion that we hire five bathrooms and take cold baths, and then assumed more tangible form as "a place to have a mint julep."[9] Each of us said over and over that it was a "crazy idea"—we all talked at once to a baffled clerk and thought, or pretended to think, that we were being very funny. . . .

The room was large and stifling, and, though it was already four o'clock, opening the windows admitted only a gust of hot shrubbery from the park. Daisy went to the mirror and stood with her back to us, fixing her hair.

"It's a swell suite," whispered Jordan respectfully, and every one laughed.

"Open another window," commanded Daisy, without turning around.

"There aren't any more."

"Well, we'd better telephone for an axe——"

"The thing to do is to forget about the heat," said Tom impatiently. "You make it ten times worse by crabbing about it."

He unrolled the bottle of whiskey from the towel and put it on the table.

"Why not let her alone, old sport?" remarked Gatsby. "You're the one that wanted to come to town."

There was a moment of silence. The telephone book slipped from its nail and splashed to the floor, whereupon Jordan whispered, "Excuse me"—but this time no one laughed.

"I'll pick it up," I offered.

"I've got it." Gatsby examined the parted string, muttered "Hum!" in an interested way, and tossed the book on a chair.

"That's a great expression of yours, isn't it?" said Tom sharply.

"What is?"

"All this 'old sport' business. Where'd you pick that up?"

"Now see here, Tom," said Daisy, turning around from the mirror, "if you're going to make personal remarks I won't stay here a minute. Call up and order some ice for the mint julep."

As Tom took up the receiver the compressed heat exploded into sound and we were listening to the portentous chords of Mendelssohn's Wedding March[10] from the ballroom below.

"Imagine marrying anybody in this heat!" cried Jordan dismally.

"Still—I was married in the middle of June," Daisy remembered, "Louisville in June! Somebody fainted. Who was it fainted, Tom?"

"Biloxi," he answered shortly.

"A man named Biloxi. 'Blocks' Biloxi, and he made boxes—that's a fact—and he was from Biloxi, Tennessee."

"They carried him into my house," appended Jordan, "because we lived just two doors from the church. And he stayed three weeks, until Daddy told him he had to get out. The day after he left Daddy died." After a moment she added as if she might have sounded irreverent, "There wasn't any connection."

"I used to know a Bill Biloxi from Memphis," I remarked.

"That was his cousin. I knew his whole family history before he left. He gave me an aluminum putter that I use today."

---

[9]Bourbon whiskey mixed with sugar, mint leaves, and ice, a favorite summertime drink in the South.

[10]Felix Mendelssohn (1809–1847), a German Romantic composer. His "Wedding March" (1843) is traditionally played at marriage ceremonies.

The music had died down as the ceremony began and now a long cheer floated in at the window, followed by intermittent cries of "Yea—ea—ea!" and finally a burst of jazz as the dancing began.

"We're getting old," said Daisy. "If we were young we'd rise and dance."

"Remember Biloxi," Jordan warned her. "Where'd you know him, Tom?"

"Biloxi?" He concentrated with an effort. "I didn't know him. He was a friend of Daisy's."

"He was not," she denied. "I'd never seen him before. He came down in the private car."

"Well, he said he knew you. He said he was raised in Louisville. Asa Bird brought him around at the last minute and asked if we had room for him."

Jordan smiled.

"He was probably bumming his way home. He told me he was president of your class at Yale."

Tom and I looked at each other blankly.

"Biloxi?"

"First place, we didn't have any president——"

Gatsby's foot beat a short, restless tattoo and Tom eyed him suddenly.

"By the way, Mr. Gatsby, I understand you're an Oxford man."

"Not exactly."

"Oh, yes, I understand you went to Oxford."

"Yes—I went there."

A pause. Then Tom's voice, incredulous and insulting:

"You must have gone there about the time Biloxi went to New Haven."

Another pause. A waiter knocked and came in with crushed mint and ice, but the silence was unbroken by his "thank you" and the soft closing of the door. This tremendous detail was to be cleared up at last.

"I told you I went there," said Gatsby.

"I heard you, but I'd like to know when."

"It was in nineteen-nineteen. I only stayed five months. That's why I can't really call myself an Oxford man."

Tom glanced around to see if we mirrored his unbelief. But we were all looking at Gatsby.

"It was an opportunity they gave to some of the officers after the armistice," he continued. "We could go to any of the universities in England or France."

I wanted to get up and slap him on the back. I had one of those renewals of complete faith in him that I'd experienced before.

Daisy rose, smiling faintly, and went to the table.

"Open the whiskey, Tom," she ordered, "and I'll make you a mint julep. Then you won't seem so stupid to yourself. . . . Look at the mint!"

"Wait a minute," snapped Tom, "I want to ask Mr. Gatsby one more question."

"Go on," Gatsby said politely.

"What kind of a row are you trying to cause in my house anyway?"

They were out in the open at last and Gatsby was content.

"He isn't causing a row." Daisy looked desperately from one to the other. "You're causing a row. Please have a little self-control."

"Self-control!" repeated Tom incredulously. "I suppose the latest thing is to sit back and let Mr. Nobody from Nowhere make love to your wife. Well, if that's the idea you can count me out. . . . Nowadays people begin by sneering at family life and family institutions, and next they'll throw everything overboard and have intermarriage between black and white."

Flushed with his impassioned gibberish, he saw himself standing alone on the last barrier of civilization.

"We're all white here," murmured Jordan.

"I know I'm not very popular. I don't give big parties. I suppose you've got to make your house into a pigsty in order to have any friends—in the modern world."

Angry as I was, as we all were, I was tempted to laugh whenever he opened his mouth. The transition from libertine to prig was so complete.

"I've got something to tell *you*, old sport—" began Gatsby. But Daisy guessed at his intention.

"Please don't!" she interrupted helplessly. "Please let's all go home. Why don't we all go home?"

"That's a good idea." I got up. "Come on, Tom. Nobody wants a drink."

"I want to know what Mr. Gatsby has to tell me."

"Your wife doesn't love you," said Gatsby. "She's never loved you. She loves me."

"You must be crazy!" exclaimed Tom automatically.

Gatsby sprang to his feet, vivid with excitement.

"She never loved you, do you hear?" he cried. "She only married you because I was poor and she was tired of waiting for me. It was a terrible mistake, but in her heart she never loved any one except me!"

At this point Jordan and I tried to go, but Tom and Gatsby insisted with competitive firmness that we remain—as though neither of them had anything to conceal and it would be a privilege to partake vicariously of their emotions.

"Sit down, Daisy," Tom's voice groped unsuccessfully for the paternal note. "What's been going on? I want to hear all about it."

"I told you what's been going on," said Gatsby. "Going on for five years—and you didn't know."

Tom turned to Daisy sharply.

"You've been seeing this fellow for five years?"

"Not seeing," said Gatsby. "No, we couldn't meet. But both of us loved each other all that time, old sport, and you didn't know. I used to laugh sometimes"— but there was no laughter in his eyes—"to think that you didn't know."

"Oh—that's all." Tom tapped his thick fingers together like a clergyman and leaned back in his chair.

"You're crazy!" he exploded. "I can't speak about what happened five years ago, because I didn't know Daisy then—and I'll be damned if I see how you got within a mile of her unless you brought the groceries to the back door. But all the rest of that's a God damned lie. Daisy loved me when she married me and she loves me now."

"No," said Gatsby, shaking his head.

"She does, though. The trouble is that sometimes she gets foolish ideas in her head and doesn't know what she's doing." He nodded sagely. "And what's more, I love Daisy too. Once in a while I go off on a spree and make a fool of myself, but I always come back, and in my heart I love her all the time."

"You're revolting," said Daisy. She turned to me, and her voice, dropping an octave lower, filled the room with thrilling scorn: "Do you know why we left Chicago? I'm surprised that they didn't treat you to the story of that little spree."

Gatsby walked over and stood beside her.

"Daisy, that's all over now," he said earnestly. "It doesn't matter any more. Just tell him the truth—that you never loved him—and it's all wiped out forever."

She looked at him blindly. "Why—how could I love him—possibly?"

"You never loved him."

She hesitated. Her eyes fell on Jordan and me with a sort of appeal, as though she realized at last what she was doing—and as though she had never, all along, intended doing anything at all. But it was done now. It was too late.

"I never loved him," she said, with perceptible reluctance.

"Not at Kapiolani?"[11] demanded Tom suddenly.

"No."

From the ballroom beneath, muffled and suffocating chords were drifting up on hot waves of air.

"Not that day I carried you down from the Punch Bowl[12] to keep your shoes dry?" There was a husky tenderness in his tone. . . . "Daisy?"

"Please don't." Her voice was cold, but the rancor was gone from it. She looked at Gatsby. "There, Jay," she said—but her hand as she tried to light a cigarette was trembling. Suddenly she threw the cigarette and the burning match on the carpet.

"Oh, you want too much!" she cried to Gatsby. "I love you now—isn't that enough? I can't help what's past." She began to sob helplessly. "I did love him once—but I loved you too."

Gatsby's eyes opened and closed.

"You loved me *too*?" he repeated.

"Even that's a lie," said Tom savagely. "She didn't know you were alive. Why—they're things between Daisy and me that you'll never know, things that neither of us can ever forget."

The words seemed to bite physically into Gatsby.

"I want to speak to Daisy alone," he insisted. "She's all excited now——"

"Even alone I can't say I never loved Tom," she admitted in a pitiful voice. "It wouldn't be true."

"Of course it wouldn't," agreed Tom.

She turned to her husband.

"As if it mattered to you," she said.

"Of course it matters. I'm going to take better care of you from now on."

"You don't understand," said Gatsby, with a touch of panic. "You're not going to take care of her any more."

"I'm not?" Tom opened his eyes wide and laughed. He could afford to control himself now. "Why's that?"

"Daisy's leaving you."

"Nonsense."

"I am, though," she said with a visible effort.

"She's not leaving me!" Tom's words suddenly leaned down over Gatsby. "Certainly not for a common swindler who'd have to steal the ring he put on her finger."

"I won't stand this!" cried Daisy. "Oh, please let's get out."

"Who are you, anyhow?" broke out Tom. "You're one of that bunch that hangs around with Meyer Wolfsheim—that much I happen to know. I've made a little investigation into your affairs—and I'll carry it further tomorrow."

"You can suit yourself about that, old sport," said Gatsby steadily.

"I found out what your 'drug-stores' were." He turned to us and spoke rapidly. "He and this Wolfsheim bought up a lot of side-street drug-stores here and in

---

[11]A park on the island of Oahu, Hawaii.

[12]A crater of an ancient volcano, in the city of Honolulu.

Chicago and sold grain alcohol over the counter. That's one of his little stunts. I picked him for a bootlegger the first time I saw him, and I wasn't far wrong."

"What about it?" said Gatsby politely. "I guess your friend Walter Chase wasn't too proud to come in on it."

"And you left him in the lurch, didn't you? You let him go to jail for a month over in New Jersey. God! You ought to hear Walter on the subject of *you*."

"He came to us dead broke. He was very glad to pick up some money, old sport."

"Don't you call me 'old sport'!" cried Tom. Gatsby said nothing. "Walter could have you up on the betting laws too, but Wolfsheim scared him into shutting his mouth."

That unfamiliar yet recognizable look was back again in Gatsby's face.

"That drug-store business was just small change," continued Tom slowly, "but you've got something on now that Walter's afraid to tell me about."

I glanced at Daisy, who was staring terrified between Gatsby and her husband, and at Jordan, who had begun to balance an invisible but absorbing object on the tip of her chin. Then I turned back to Gatsby—and was startled at his expression. He looked—and this is said in all contempt for the babbled slander of his garden—as if he had "killed a man." For a moment the set of his face could be described in just that fantastic way.

It passed, and he began to talk excitedly to Daisy, denying everything, defending his name against accusations that had not been made. But with every word she was drawing further and further into herself, so he gave that up, and only the dead dream fought on as the afternoon slipped away, trying to touch what was no longer tangible, struggling unhappily, undespairingly, toward that lost voice across the room.

The voice begged again to go.

"*Please*, Tom! I can't stand this any more."

Her frightened eyes told that whatever intentions, whatever courage she had had, were definitely gone.

"You two start on home, Daisy," said Tom. "In Mr. Gatsby's car."

She looked at Tom, alarmed now, but he insisted with magnanimous scorn.

"Go on. He won't annoy you. I think he realizes that his presumptuous little flirtation is over."

They were gone, without a word, snapped out, made accidental, isolated, like ghosts, even from our pity.

After a moment Tom got up and began wrapping the unopened bottle of whiskey in the towel.

"Want any of this stuff? Jordan? . . . Nick?"

I didn't answer.

"Nick?" He asked again.

"What?"

"Want any?"

"No . . . I just remembered that today's my birthday."

I was thirty. Before me stretched the portentous, menacing road of a new decade.

It was seven o'clock when we got into the coupé with him and started for Long Island. Tom talked incessantly, exulting and laughing, but his voice was as remote from Jordan and me as the foreign clamor on the sidewalk or the tumult of the elevated overhead. Human sympathy has its limits, and we were content to let all their tragic arguments fade with the city lights behind. Thirty—the promise of a decade of loneliness, a thinning list of single men to know, a thinning brief-case of enthusiasm, thinning hair. But there was Jordan beside me, who, unlike Daisy, was too wise ever to carry well-forgotten dreams from age to age. As we passed over the dark bridge her wan face fell lazily against my coat's shoulder and the formidable stroke of thirty died away with the reassuring pressure of her hand.

So we drove on toward death through the cooling twilight.

The young Greek, Michaelis, who ran the coffee joint beside the ashheaps was the principal witness at the inquest. He had slept through the heat until after five, when he strolled over to the garage, and found George Wilson sick in his office—really sick, pale as his own pale hair and shaking all over. Michaelis advised him to go to bed, but Wilson refused, saying that he'd miss a lot of business if he did. While his neighbor was trying to persuade him a violent racket broke out overhead.

"I've got my wife locked in up there," explained Wilson calmly. "She's going to stay there till the day after tomorrow, and then we're going to move away."

Michaelis was astonished; they had been neighbors for four years, and Wilson had never seemed faintly capable of such a statement. Generally he was one of these worn-out men: when he wasn't working, he sat on a chair in the doorway and stared at the people and the cars that passed along the road. When any one spoke to him he invariably laughed in an agreeable, colorless way. He was his wife's man and not his own.

So naturally Michaelis tried to find out what had happened, but Wilson wouldn't say a word—instead he began to throw curious, suspicious glances at his visitor and ask him what he'd been doing at certain times on certain days. Just as the latter was getting uneasy, some workmen came past the door bound for his restaurant, and Michaelis took the opportunity to get away, intending to come back later. But he didn't. He supposed he forgot to, that's all. When he came outside again, a little after seven, he was reminded of the conversation because he heard Mrs. Wilson's voice, loud and scolding, downstairs in the garage.

"Beat me!" he heard her cry. "Throw me down and beat me, you dirty little coward!"

A moment later she rushed out into the dusk, waving her hands and shouting—before he could move from his door the business was over.

The "death car" as the newspapers called it, didn't stop; it came out of the gathering darkness, wavered tragically for a moment, and then disappeared around the next bend. Michaelis wasn't even sure of its color—he told the first policeman that it was light green. The other car, the one going toward New York, came to rest a hundred yards beyond, and its driver hurried back to where Myrtle Wilson, her life violently extinguished, knelt in the road and mingled her thick dark blood with the dust.

Michaelis and this man reached her first, but when they had torn open her shirtwaist, still damp with perspiration, they saw that her left breast was swinging loose like a flap, and there was no need to listen for the heart beneath. The mouth was wide open and ripped at the corners, as though she had choked a little in giving up the tremendous vitality she had stored so long.

We saw the three or four automobiles and the crowd when we were still some distance away.

"Wreck!" said Tom. "That's good. Wilson'll have a little business at last."

He slowed down, but still without any intention of stopping, until, as we came nearer, the hushed, intent faces of the people at the garage door made him automatically put on the brakes.

"We'll take a look," he said doubtfully, "just a look."

I became aware now of a hollow, wailing sound which issued incessantly from the garage, a sound which as we got out of the coupé and walked toward the door resolved itself into the words "Oh, my God!" uttered over and over in a gasping moan.

"There's some bad trouble here," said Tom excitedly.

He reached up on tiptoes and peered over a circle of heads into the garage, which was lit only by a yellow light in a swinging wire basket overhead. Then he made a harsh sound in his throat, and with a violent thrusting movement of his powerful arms pushed his way through.

The circle closed up again with a running murmur of expostulation; it was a minute before I could see anything at all. Then new arrivals deranged the line, and Jordan and I were pushed suddenly inside.

Myrtle Wilson's body, wrapped in a blanket, and then in another blanket, as though she suffered from a chill in the hot night, lay on a work-table by the wall, and Tom, with his back to us, was bending over it, motionless. Next to him stood a motorcycle policeman taking down names with much sweat and correction in a little book. At first I couldn't find the source of the high, groaning words that echoed clamorously through the bare garage—then I saw Wilson standing on the raised threshold of his office, swaying back and forth and holding to the doorposts with both hands. Some man was talking to him in a low voice and attempting, from time to time, to lay a hand on his shoulder, but Wilson neither heard nor saw. His eyes would drop slowly from the swinging light to the laden table by the wall, and then jerk back to the light again, and he gave out incessantly his high, horrible call:

"Oh, my Ga-od! Oh, my Ga-od! Oh, Ga-od! Oh, my Ga-od!"

Presently Tom lifted his head with a jerk and, after staring around the garage with glazed eyes, addressed a mumbled incoherent remark to the policeman.

"M-a-v—" the policeman was saying, "—o——"

"No, r—" corrected the man, "M-a-v-r-o——"

"Listen to me!" muttered Tom fiercely.

"r—" said the policeman, "o——"

"g——"

"g—" He looked up as Tom's broad hand fell sharply on his shoulder. "What you want, fella?"

"What happened?—that's what I want to know."

"Auto hit her. Ins'antly killed."

"Instantly killed," repeated Tom, staring.

"She ran out ina road. Son-of-a-bitch didn't even stopus car."

"There was two cars," said Michaelis, "one comin', one goin', see?"

"Going where?" asked the policeman keenly.

"One goin' each way. Well, she"—his hand rose toward the blankets but stopped half way and fell to his side—"she ran out there an' the one comin' from N'York knock right into her, goin' thirty or forty miles an hour."

"What's the name of this place here?" demanded the officer.

"Hasn't got any name."

A pale well-dressed negro stepped near.

"It was a yellow car," he said, "big yellow car. New."

"See the accident?" asked the policeman.

"No, but the car passed me down the road, going faster'n forty. Going fifty, sixty."

"Come here and let's have your name. Look out now. I want to get his name."

Some words of this conversation must have reached Wilson, swaying in the office door, for suddenly a new theme found voice among his gasping cries:

"You don't have to tell me what kind of car it was! I know what kind of car it was!"

Watching Tom, I saw the wad of muscle back of his shoulder tighten under his coat. He walked quickly over to Wilson and, standing in front of him, seized him firmly by the upper arms.

"You've got to pull yourself together," he said with soothing gruffness.

Wilson's eyes fell upon Tom; he started up on his tiptoes and then would have collapsed to his knees had not Tom held him upright.

"Listen," said Tom, shaking him a little. "I just got here a minute ago, from New York. I was bringing you that coupé we've been talking about. That yellow car I was driving this afternoon wasn't mine—do you hear? I haven't seen it all afternoon."

Only the negro and I were near enough to hear what he said, but the policeman caught something in the tone and looked over with truculent eyes.

"What's all that?" he demanded.

"I'm a friend of his." Tom turned his head but kept his hands firm on Wilson's body. "He says he knows the car that did it. . . . It was a yellow car."

Some dim impulse moved the policeman to look suspiciously at Tom.

"And what color's your car?"

"It's a blue car, a coupé."

"We've come straight from New York," I said.

Someone who had been driving a little behind us confirmed this, and the policeman turned away.

"Now, if you'll let me have that name again correct——"

Picking up Wilson like a doll, Tom carried him into the office, set him down in a chair, and came back.

"If somebody'll come here and sit with him," he snapped authoritatively. He watched while the two men standing closest glanced at each other and went unwillingly into the room. Then Tom shut the door on them and came down the single step, his eyes avoiding the table. As he passed close to me he whispered: "Let's get out."

Self-consciously, with his authoritative arms breaking the way, we pushed through the still gathering crowd, passing a hurried doctor, case in hand, who had been sent for in wild hope half an hour ago.

Tom drove slowly until we were beyond the bend—then his foot came down hard, and the coupé raced along through the night. In a little while I heard a low husky sob, and saw that the tears were overflowing down his face.

"The God damned coward!" he whimpered. "He didn't even stop his car."

The Buchanans' house floated suddenly toward us through the dark rustling trees. Tom stopped beside the porch and looked up at the second floor, where two windows bloomed with light among the vines.

"Daisy's home," he said. As we got out of the car he glanced at me and frowned slightly.

"I ought to have dropped you in West Egg, Nick. There's nothing we can do tonight."

A change had come over him, and he spoke gravely, and with decision. As we walked across the moonlight gravel to the porch he disposed of the situation in a few brisk phrases.

"I'll telephone for a taxi to take you home, and while you're waiting you and Jordan better go in the kitchen and have them get you some supper—if you want any." He opened the door. "Come in."

"No, thanks. But I'd be glad if you'd order me the taxi. I'll wait outside."

Jordan put her hand on my arm.

"Won't you come in, Nick?"

"No, thanks."

I was feeling a little sick and I wanted to be alone. But Jordan lingered for a moment more.

"It's only half-past nine," she said.

I'd be damned if I'd go in; I'd had enough of all of them for one day, and suddenly that included Jordan too. She must have seen something of this in my expression, for she turned abruptly away and ran up the porch steps into the house. I sat down for a few minutes with my head in my hands, until I heard the phone taken up inside and the butler's voice calling a taxi. Then I walked slowly down the drive away from the house, intending to wait by the gate.

I hadn't gone twenty yards when I heard my name and Gatsby stepped from between two bushes into the path. I must have felt pretty weird by that time, because I could think of nothing except the luminosity of his pink suit under the moon.

"What are you doing?" I inquired.

"Just standing here, old sport."

Somehow, that seemed a despicable occupation. For all I knew he was going to rob the house in a moment; I wouldn't have been surprised to see sinister faces, the faces of "Wolfsheim's people," behind him in the dark shrubbery.

"Did you see any trouble on the road?" he asked after a minute.

"Yes."

He hesitated.

"Was she killed?"

"Yes."

"I thought so; I told Daisy I thought so. It's better that the shock should all come at once. She stood it pretty well."

He spoke as if Daisy's reaction was the only thing that mattered.

"I got to West Egg by a side road," he went on, "and left the car in my garage. I don't think anybody saw us, but of course I can't be sure."

I disliked him so much by this time that I didn't find it necessary to tell him he was wrong.

"Who was the woman?" he inquired.

"Her name was Wilson. Her husband owns the garage. How the devil did it happen?"

"Well, I tried to swing the wheel—" He broke off, and suddenly I guessed at the truth.

"Was Daisy driving?"

"Yes," he said after a moment, "but of course I'll say I was. You see, when we left New York she was very nervous and she thought it would steady her to drive—and this woman rushed out at us just as we were passing a car coming the other way. It all happened in a minute, but it seemed to me that she wanted to speak to us, thought we were somebody she knew. Well, first Daisy turned away from the woman toward the other car, and then she lost her nerve and turned back. The second my hand reached the wheel I felt the shock—it must have killed her instantly."

"It ripped her open——"

"Don't tell me, old sport." He winced. "Anyhow—Daisy stepped on it. I tried to make her stop, but she couldn't, so I pulled on the emergency brake. Then she fell over into my lap and I drove on.

"She'll be all right tomorrow," he said presently. "I'm just going to wait here and see if he tries to bother her about that unpleasantness this afternoon. She's locked herself into her room, and if he tries any brutality she's going to turn the light out and on again."

"He won't touch her," I said. "He's not thinking about her."

"I don't trust him, old sport."

"How long are you going to wait?"

"All night, if necessary. Anyhow, till they all go to bed."

A new point of view occurred to me. Suppose Tom found out that Daisy had been driving. He might think he saw a connection in it—he might think anything. I looked at the house; there were two or three bright windows downstairs and the pink glow from Daisy's room on the second floor.

"You wait here," I said. "I'll see if there's any sign of a commotion."

I walked back along the border of the lawn, traversed the gravel softly, and tiptoed up the veranda steps. The drawing-room curtains were open, and I saw that the room was empty. Crossing the porch where we had dined that June night three months before, I came to a small rectangle of light which I guessed was the pantry window. The blind was drawn, but I found a rift at the sill.

Daisy and Tom were sitting opposite each other at the kitchen table, with a plate of cold fried chicken between them, and two bottles of ale. He was talking intently across the table at her, and in his earnestness his hand had fallen upon and covered her own. Once in a while she looked up at him and nodded in agreement.

They weren't happy, and neither of them had touched the chicken or the ale—and yet they weren't unhappy either. There was an unmistakable air of natural intimacy about the picture, and anybody would have said that they were conspiring together.

As I tiptoed from the porch I heard my taxi feeling its way along the dark road toward the house. Gatsby was waiting where I had left him in the drive.

"Is it all quiet up there?" he asked anxiously.

"Yes, it's all quiet." I hesitated. "You'd better come home and get some sleep." He shook his head.

"I want to wait here till Daisy goes to bed. Good night, old sport."

He put his hands in his coat pockets and turned back eagerly to his scrutiny of the house, as though my presence marred the sacredness of the vigil. So I walked away and left him standing there in the moonlight—watching over nothing.

CHAPTER VIII

I COULDN'T sleep all night; a fog-horn was groaning incessantly on the Sound, and I tossed half-sick between grotesque reality and savage, frightening dreams. Toward dawn I heard a taxi go up Gatsby's drive, and immediately I jumped out of bed and began to dress—I felt that I had something to tell him, something to warn him about, and morning would be too late.

Crossing his lawn, I saw that his front door was still open and he was leaning against a table in the hall, heavy with dejection or sleep.

"Nothing happened," he said wanly. "I waited, and about four o'clock she came to the window and stood there for a minute and then turned out the light."

His house had never seemed so enormous to me as it did that night when we hunted through the great rooms for cigarettes. We pushed aside curtains that were like pavilions, and felt over innumerable feet of dark wall for electric light switches—once I tumbled with a sort of splash upon the keys of a ghostly piano. There was an inexplicable amount of dust everywhere, and the rooms were musty, as though they hadn't been aired for many days. I found the humidor on an unfamiliar table, with two stale, dry cigarettes inside. Throwing open the French windows of the drawing-room, we sat smoking out into the darkness.

"You ought to go away," I said. "It's pretty certain they'll trace your car."

"Go away *now*, old sport?"

"Go to Atlantic City for a week, or up to Montreal."

He wouldn't consider it. He couldn't possibly leave Daisy until he knew what she was going to do. He was clutching at some last hope and I couldn't bear to shake him free.

It was this night that he told me the strange story of his youth with Dan Cody—told it to me because "Jay Gatsby" had broken up like glass against Tom's hard malice, and the long secret extravaganza was played out. I think that he would have acknowledged anything now, without reserve, but he wanted to talk about Daisy.

She was the first "nice" girl he had ever known. In various unrevealed capacities he had come in contact with such people, but always with indiscernible barbed wire between. He found her excitingly desirable. He went to her house, at first with other officers from Camp Taylor, then alone. It amazed him—he had never been in such a beautiful house before. But what gave it an air of breathless intensity, was that Daisy lived there—it was as casual a thing to her as his tent out at camp was to him. There was a ripe mystery about it, a hint of bedrooms upstairs more beautiful and cool than other bedrooms, of gay and radiant activities taking place through its corridors, and of romances that were not musty and laid away already in lavender but fresh and breathing and redolent of this year's shining motor-cars and of dances whose flowers were scarcely withered. It excited him, too, that many men had already loved Daisy—it increased her value in his eyes. He felt their presence all about the house, pervading the air with the shades and echoes of still vibrant emotions.

But he knew that he was in Daisy's house by a colossal accident. However glorious might be his future as Jay Gatsby, he was at present a penniless young man without a past, and at any moment the invisible cloak of his uniform might slip from his shoulders. So he made the most of his time. He took what he could get, ravenously and unscrupulously—eventually he took Daisy one still October night, took her because he had no real right to touch her hand.

He might have despised himself, for he had certainly taken her under false pretenses. I don't mean that he had traded on his phantom millions, but he had deliberately given Daisy a sense of security; he let her believe that he was a person from much the same stratum as herself—that he was fully able to take care of her. As a matter of fact, he had no such facilities—he had no comfortable family standing behind him, and he was liable at the whim of an impersonal government to be blown anywhere about the world.

But he didn't despise himself and it didn't turn out as he had imagined. He had intended, probably, to take what he could and go—but now he found that he had committed himself to the following of a grail. He knew that Daisy was extraordinary, but he didn't realize just how extraordinary a "nice" girl could be. She vanished into her rich house, into her rich, full life, leaving Gatsby— nothing. He felt married to her, that was all.

When they met again, two days later, it was Gatsby who was breathless, who was, somehow, betrayed. Her porch was bright with the bought luxury of star-shine; the wicker of the settee squeaked fashionably as she turned toward him and he kissed her curious and lovely mouth. She had caught a cold, and it made her voice huskier and more charming than ever, and Gatsby was overwhelmingly aware of the youth and mystery that wealth imprisons and preserves, of the freshness of many clothes, and of Daisy, gleaming like silver, safe and proud above the hot struggles of the poor.

"I can't describe to you how surprised I was to find out I loved her, old sport. I even hoped for a while that she'd throw me over, but she didn't, because she was in love with me too. She thought I knew a lot because I knew different things from her . . . Well, there I was, 'way off my ambitions, getting deeper in love every minute, and all of a sudden I didn't care. What was the use of doing great things if I could have a better time telling her what I was going to do?"

On the last afternoon before he went abroad, he sat with Daisy in his arms for a long, silent time. It was a cold fall day, with fire in the room and her cheeks flushed. Now and then she moved and he changed his arm a little, and once he kissed her dark shining hair. The afternoon had made them tranquil for a while, as if to give them a deep memory for the long parting the next day promised. They had never been closer in their month of love, nor communicated more profoundly one with another, than when she brushed silent lips against his coat's shoulder or when he touched the end of her fingers, gently, as though she were asleep.

He did extraordinarily well in the war. He was a captain before he went to the front, and following the Argonne battles he got his majority and the com-mand of the divisional machine-guns. After the armistice he tried frantically to get home, but some complication or misunderstanding sent him to Oxford instead. He was worried now—there was a quality of nervous despair in Daisy's letters. She didn't see why he couldn't come. She was feeling the pressure of the world outside, and she wanted to see him and feel his presence beside her and be reassured that she was doing the right thing after all.

For Daisy was young and her artificial world was redolent of orchids and pleasant, cheerful snobbery and orchestras which set the rhythm of the year, summing up the sadness and suggestiveness of life in new tunes. All night the saxophones wailed the hopeless comment of the "Beale Street Blues"[1] while a hundred pairs of golden and silver slippers shuffled the shining dust. At the gray tea hour there were always rooms that throbbed incessantly with this low, sweet fever, while fresh faces drifted here and there like rose petals blown by the sad horns around the floor.

Through this twilight universe Daisy began to move again with the season; suddenly she was again keeping half a dozen dates a day with half a dozen men, and drowsing asleep at dawn with the beads and chiffon of an evening dress tangled among dying orchids on the floor beside her bed. And all the time something within her was crying for a decision. She wanted her life shaped now,

[1] A song written (1916) by the American composer W. C. Handy (1873–1958).

immediately—and the decision must be made by some force—of love, of money, of unquestionable practicality—that was close at hand.

That force took shape in the middle of spring with the arrival of Tom Buchanan. There was a wholesome bulkiness about his person and his position, and Daisy was flattered. Doubtless there was a certain struggle and a certain relief. The letter reached Gatsby while he was still at Oxford.

It was dawn now on Long Island and we went about opening the rest of the windows downstairs, filling the house with gray-turning, gold-turning light. The shadow of a tree fell abruptly across the dew and ghostly birds began to sing among the blue leaves. There was a slow, pleasant movement in the air, scarcely a wind, promising a cool, lovely day.

"I don't think she ever loved him," Gatsby turned around from a window and looked at me challengingly. "You must remember, old sport, she was very excited this afternoon. He told her those things in a way that frightened her—that made it look as if I was some kind of cheap sharper. And the result was she hardly knew what she was saying."

He sat down gloomily.

"Of course she might have loved him just for a minute, when they were first married—and loved me more even then, do you see?"

Suddenly he came out with a curious remark.

"In any case," he said, "it was just personal."

What could you make of that, except to suspect some intensity in his conception of the affair that couldn't be measured?

He came back from France when Tom and Daisy were still on their wedding trip, and made a miserable but irresistible journey to Louisville on the last of his army pay. He stayed there a week, walking the streets where their footsteps had clicked together through the November night and revisiting the out-of-the-way places to which they had driven in her white car. Just as Daisy's house had always seemed to him more mysterious and gay than other houses, so his idea of the city itself, even though she was gone from it, was pervaded with a melancholy beauty.

He left feeling that if he had searched harder, he might have found her—that he was leaving her behind. The day-coach—he was penniless now—was hot. He went out to the open vestibule and sat down on a folding-chair, and the station slid away and the backs of unfamiliar buildings moved by. Then out into the spring fields, where a yellow trolley raced them for a minute with people in it who might once have seen the pale magic of her face along the casual street.

The track curved and now it was going away from the sun, which, as it sank lower, seemed to spread itself in benediction over the vanishing city where she had drawn her breath. He stretched out his hand desperately as if to snatch only a wisp of air, to save a fragment of the spot that she had made lovely for him. But it was all going by too fast now for his blurred eyes and he knew that he had lost that part of it, the freshest and the best, forever.

It was nine o'clock when we finished breakfast and went out on the porch. The night had made a sharp difference in the weather and there was an autumn flavor in the air. The gardener, the last one of Gatsby's former servants, came to the foot of the steps.

"I'm going to drain the pool today, Mr. Gatsby. Leaves'll start falling pretty soon, and then there's always trouble with the pipes."

"Don't do it today," Gatsby answered. He turned to me apologetically. "You know, old sport, I've never used that pool all summer?"

I looked at my watch and stood up.

"Twelve minutes to my train."

I didn't want to go to the city. I wasn't worth a decent stroke of work, but it was more than that—I didn't want to leave Gatsby. I missed that train, and then another, before I could get myself away.

"I'll call you up," I said finally.

"Do, old sport."

"I'll call you about noon."

We walked slowly down the steps.

"I suppose Daisy'll call too." He looked at me anxiously, as if he hoped I'd corroborate this.

"I suppose so."

"Well, good-by."

We shook hands and I started away. Just before I reached the hedge I remembered something and turned around.

"They're a rotten crowd," I shouted across the lawn. "You're worth the whole damn bunch put together."

I've always been glad I said that. It was the only compliment I ever gave him, because I disapproved of him from beginning to end. First he nodded politely, and then his face broke into that radiant and understanding smile, as if we'd been in ecstatic cahoots on that fact all the time. His gorgeous pink rag of a suit made a bright spot of color against the white steps, and I thought of the night when I first came to his ancestral home, three months before. The lawn and drive had been crowded with the faces of those who guessed at his corruption—and he had stood on those steps, concealing his incorruptible dream, as he waved them good-by.

I thanked him for his hospitality. We were always thanking him for that—I and the others.

"Good-by," I called. "I enjoyed breakfast, Gatsby."

Up in the city, I tried for a while to list the quotations on an interminable amount of stock, then I fell asleep in my swivel-chair. Just before noon the phone woke me, and I started up with sweat breaking out on my forehead. It was Jordan Baker; she often called me up at this hour because the uncertainty of her own movements between hotels and clubs and private houses made her hard to find in any other way. Usually her voice came over the wire as something fresh and cool, as if a divot from a green golf-links had come sailing in at the office window, but this morning it seemed harsh and dry.

"I've left Daisy's house," she said. "I'm at Hempstead, and I'm going down to Southampton[2] this afternoon."

Probably it had been tactful to leave Daisy's house, but the act annoyed me, and her next remark made me rigid.

"You weren't so nice to me last night."

"How could it have mattered then?"

Silence for a moment. Then:

"However—I want to see you."

"I want to see you, too."

"Suppose I don't go to Southampton, and come into town this afternoon?"

"No—I don't think this afternoon."

"Very well."

[2]Hempstead: a village in eastern Long Island. Southampton: a village and fashionable summer resort on the southern shore of Long Island, on the Atlantic Ocean.

"It's impossible this afternoon. Various——"

We talked like that for a while, and then abruptly we weren't talking any longer. I don't know which of us hung up with a sharp click, but I know I didn't care. I couldn't have talked to her across a tea-table that day if I never talked to her again in this world.

I called Gatsby's house a few minutes later, but the line was busy. I tried four times; finally an exasperated central told me the wire was being kept open for long distance from Detroit. Taking out my time-table, I drew a small circle around the three-fifty train. Then I leaned back in my chair and tried to think. It was just noon.

When I passed the ashheaps on the train that morning I had crossed deliberately to the other side of the car. I supposed there'd be a curious crowd around there all day with little boys searching for dark spots in the dust, and some garrulous man telling over and over what had happened, until it became less and less real even to him and he could tell it no longer, and Myrtle Wilson's tragic achievement was forgotten. Now I want to go back a little and tell what happened at the garage after we left there the night before.

They had difficulty in locating the sister, Catherine. She must have broken her rule against drinking that night, for when she arrived she was stupid with liquor and unable to understand that the ambulance had already gone to Flushing.[3] When they convinced her of this, she immediately fainted, as if that was the intolerable part of the affair. Someone, kind or curious, took her in his car and drove her in the wake of her sister's body.

Until long after midnight a changing crowd lapped up against the front of the garage, while George Wilson rocked himself back and forth on the couch inside. For a while the door of the office was open, and every one who came into the garage glanced irresistibly through it. Finally someone said it was a shame, and closed the door. Michaelis and several other men were with him; first, four or five men, later two or three men. Still later Michaelis had to ask the last stranger to wait there fifteen minutes longer, while he went back to his own place and made a pot of coffee. After that, he stayed there alone with Wilson until dawn.

About three o'clock the quality of Wilson's incoherent muttering changed—he grew quieter and began to talk about the yellow car. He announced that he had a way of finding out whom the yellow car belonged to, and then he blurted out that a couple of months ago his wife had come from the city with her face bruised and her nose swollen.

But when he heard himself say this, he flinched and began to cry "Oh, my God!" again in his groaning voice. Michaelis made a clumsy attempt to distract him.

"How long have you been married, George? Come on there, try and sit still a minute and answer my questions. How long have you been married?"

"Twelve years."

"Ever had any children? Come on, George, sit still—I asked you a question. Did you ever have any children?"

The hard brown beetles kept thudding against the dull light, and whenever Michaelis heard a car go tearing along the road outside it sounded to him like the car that hadn't stopped a few hours before. He didn't like to go into the garage, because the work bench was stained where the body had been lying, so

---

[3]Formerly a separate village, now part of the borough of Queens in New York City.

he moved uncomfortably around the office—he knew every object in it before morning—and from time to time sat down beside Wilson trying to keep him more quiet.

"Have you got a church you go to sometimes, George? Maybe even if you haven't been there for a long time? Maybe I could call up the church and get a priest to come over and he could talk to you, see?"

"Don't belong to any."

"You ought to have a church, George, for times like this. You must have gone to church once. Didn't you get married in a church? Listen, George, listen to me. Didn't you get married in a church?"

"That was a long time ago."

The effort of answering broke the rhythm of his rocking—for a moment he was silent. Then the same half-knowing, half-bewildered look came back into his faded eyes.

"Look in the drawer there," he said, pointing at the desk.

"Which drawer?"

"That drawer—that one."

Michaelis opened the drawer nearest his hand. There was nothing in it but a small, expensive dog-leash, made of leather and braided silver. It was apparently new.

"This?" he inquired, holding it up.

Wilson stared and nodded.

"I found it yesterday afternoon. She tried to tell me about it, but I knew it was something funny."

"You mean your wife bought it?"

"She had it wrapped in tissue paper on her bureau."

Michaelis didn't see anything odd in that, and he gave Wilson a dozen reasons why his wife might have bought the dog-leash. But conceivably Wilson had heard some of these same explanations before, from Myrtle, because he began saying "Oh, my God!" again in a whisper—his comforter left several explanations in the air.

"Then he killed her," said Wilson. His mouth dropped open suddenly.

"Who did?"

"I have a way of finding out."

"You're morbid, George," said his friend. "This has been a strain to you and you don't know what you're saying. You'd better try and sit quiet till morning."

"He murdered her."

"It was an accident, George."

Wilson shook his head. His eyes narrowed and his mouth widened slightly with the ghost of a superior "Hm!"

"I know," he said definitely, "I'm one of these trusting fellas and I don't think any harm to *no*body, but when I get to know a thing I know it. It was the man in that car. She ran out to speak to him and he wouldn't stop."

Michaelis had seen this too, but it hadn't occurred to him that there was any special significance in it. He believed that Mrs. Wilson had been running away from her husband, rather than trying to stop any particular car.

"How could she of been like that?"

"She's a deep one," said Wilson, as if that answered the question. "Ah-h-h——"

He began to rock again, and Michaelis stood twisting the leash in his hand.

"Maybe you got some friend that I could telephone for, George?"

This was a forlorn hope—he was almost sure that Wilson had no friend: there was not enough of him for his wife. He was glad a little later when he noticed a change in the room, a blue quickening by the window, and realized that dawn wasn't far off. About five o'clock it was blue enough outside to snap off the light.

Wilson's glazed eyes turned out to the ashheaps, where small gray clouds took on fantastic shapes and scurried here and there in the faint dawn wind.

"I spoke to her," he muttered, after a long silence. "I told her she might fool me but she couldn't fool God. I took her to the window"—with an effort he got up and walked to the rear window and leaned with his face pressed against it—"and I said 'God knows what you've been doing, everything you've been doing. You may fool me, but you can't fool God!' "

Standing behind him, Michaelis saw with a shock that he was looking at the eyes of Doctor T. J. Eckleburg, which had just emerged, pale and enormous, from the dissolving night.

"God sees everything," repeated Wilson.

"That's an advertisement," Michaelis assured him. Something made him turn away from the window and look back into the room. But Wilson stood there a long time, his face close to the window pane, nodding into the twilight.

By six o'clock Michaelis was worn out, and grateful for the sound of a car stopping outside. It was one of the watchers of the night before who had promised to come back, so he cooked breakfast for three, which he and the other man ate together. Wilson was quieter now, and Michaelis went home to sleep; when he awoke four hours later and hurried back to the garage, Wilson was gone.

His movements—he was on foot all the time—were afterward traced to Port Roosevelt and then to Gad's Hill, where he bought a sandwich that he didn't eat, and a cup of coffee. He must have been tired and walking slowly, for he didn't reach Gad's Hill until noon. Thus far there was no difficulty in accounting for his time—there were boys who had seen a man "acting sort of crazy," and motorists at whom he stared oddly from the side of the road. Then for three hours he disappeared from view. The police, on the strength of what he said to Michaelis, that he "had a way of finding out," supposed that he spent that time going from garage to garage thereabout, inquiring for a yellow car. On the other hand, no garage man who had seen him ever came forward, and perhaps he had an easier, surer way of finding out what he wanted to know. By half-past two he was in West Egg, where he asked someone the way to Gatsby's house. So by that time he knew Gatsby's name.

At two o'clock Gatsby put on his bathing-suit and left word with the butler that if any one phoned word was to be brought to him at the pool. He stopped at the garage for a pneumatic mattress that had amused his guests during the summer, and the chauffeur helped him pump it up. Then he gave instructions that the open car wasn't to be taken out under any circumstances—and this was strange, because the front right fender needed repair.

Gatsby shouldered the mattress and started for the pool. Once he stopped and shifted it a little, and the chauffeur asked him if he needed help, but he shook his head and in a moment disappeared among the yellowing trees.

No telephone message arrived, but the butler went without his sleep and waited for it until four o'clock—until long after there was any one to give it to if it came. I have an idea that Gatsby himself didn't believe it would come, and perhaps he no longer cared. If that was true he must have felt that he had lost the old warm world, paid a high price for living too long with a single dream.

He must have looked up at an unfamiliar sky through frightening leaves and shivered as he found what a grotesque thing a rose is and how raw the sunlight was upon the scarcely created grass. A new world, material without being real, where poor ghosts, breathing dreams like air, drifted fortuitously about . . . like that ashen, fantastic figure gliding toward him through the amorphous trees.

The chauffeur—he was one of Wolfsheim's protégés—heard the shots—afterward he could only say that he hadn't thought anything much about them. I drove from the station directly to Gatsby's house and my rushing anxiously up the front steps was the first thing that alarmed any one. But they knew then, I firmly believe. With scarcely a word said, four of us, the chauffeur, butler, gardener, and I, hurried down to the pool.

There was a faint, barely perceptible movement of the water as the fresh flow from one end urged its way toward the drain at the other. With little ripples that were hardly the shadows of waves, the laden mattress moved irregularly down the pool. A small gust of wind that scarcely corrugated the surface was enough to disturb its accidental course with its accidental burden. The touch of a cluster of leaves revolved it slowly, tracing, like the leg of transit,[4] a thin red circle in the water.

It was after we started with Gatsby toward the house that the gardener saw Wilson's body a little way off in the grass, and the holocaust was complete.

CHAPTER IX

AFTER two years I remember the rest of that day, and that night and the next day, only as an endless drill of police and photographers and newspaper men in and out of Gatsby's front door. A rope stretched across the main gate and a policeman by it kept out the curious, but little boys soon discovered that they could enter through my yard, and there were always a few of them clustered openmouthed about the pool. Someone with a positive manner, perhaps a detective, used the expression "madman" as he bent over Wilson's body that afternoon, and the adventitious authority of his voice set the key for the newspaper reports next morning.

Most of those reports were a nightmare—grotesque, circumstantial, eager, and untrue. When Michaelis's testimony at the inquest brought to light Wilson's suspicions of his wife I thought the whole tale would shortly be served up in racy pasquinade[1]—but Catherine, who might have said anything, didn't say a word. She showed a surprising amount of character about it too—looked at the coroner with determined eyes under that corrected brow of hers, and swore that her sister had never seen Gatsby, that her sister was completely happy with her husband, that her sister had been into no mischief whatever. She convinced herself of it, and cried into her handkerchief, as if the very suggestion was more than she could endure. So Wilson was reduced to a man "deranged by grief" in order that the case might remain in its simplest form. And it rested there.

But all this part of it seemed remote and unessential. I found myself on Gatsby's side, and alone. From the moment I telephoned news of the catastrophe to West Egg village, every surmise about him, and every practical question, was referred to me. At first I was surprised and confused; then, as he lay in his house and didn't move or breathe or speak, hour upon hour, it grew upon me

[4]Fitzgerald later noted that he intended to correct "transit" to "compass."
[1]I.e., in the form of a satire, a lampoon, for public display.

that I was responsible, because no one else was interested—interested, I mean, with that intense personal interest to which every one has some vague right at the end.

I called up Daisy half an hour after we found him, called her instinctively and without hesitation. But she and Tom had gone away early that afternoon, and taken baggage with them.

"Left no address?"

"No."

"Say when they'd be back?"

"No."

"Any idea where they are? How I could reach them?"

"I don't know. Can't say."

I wanted to get somebody for him. I wanted to go into the room where he lay and reassure him: "I'll get somebody for you, Gatsby. Don't worry. Just trust me and I'll get somebody for you——"

Meyer Wolfsheim's name wasn't in the phone book. The butler gave me his office address on Broadway, and I called Information, but by the time I had the number it was long after five, and no one answered the phone.

"Will you ring again?"[2]

"I've rung them three times."

"It's very important."

"Sorry. I'm afraid no one's there."

I went back to the drawing-room and thought for an instant that they were chance visitors, all these official people who suddenly filled it. But, as they drew back the sheet and looked at Gatsby with unmoved eyes, his protest continued in my brain:

"Look here, old sport, you've got to get somebody for me. You've got to try hard. I can't go through this alone."

Someone started to ask me questions, but I broke away and going upstairs looked hastily through the unlocked parts of his desk—he'd never told me definitely that his parents were dead. But there was nothing—only the picture of Dan Cody, a token of forgotten violence, staring down from the wall.

Next morning I sent the butler to New York with a letter to Wolfsheim, which asked for information and urged him to come out on the next train. That request seemed superfluous when I wrote it. I was sure he'd start when he saw the newspapers, just as I was sure there'd be a wire from Daisy before noon—but neither a wire nor Mr. Wolfsheim arrived; no one arrived except more police and photographers and newspaper men. When the butler brought back Wolfsheim's answer I began to have a feeling of defiance, of scornful solidarity between Gatsby and me against them all.

Dear Mr. Carraway. This has been one of the most terrible shocks of my life to me I hardly can believe it that it is true at all. Such a mad act as that man did should make us all think. I cannot come down now as I am tied up in some very important business and cannot get mixed up in this thing now. If there is anything I can do a little later let me know in a letter by Edgar. I hardly know where I am when I hear about a thing like this and am completely knocked down and out.

Yours truly

MEYER WOLFSHEIM

and then hasty addenda beneath:

[2]In the 1920s, before the advent of dial telephones, calls were placed by operators who would "ring" the number requested by the caller.

Let me know about the funeral etc do not know his family at all.

When the phone rang that afternoon and Long Distance said Chicago was calling I thought this would be Daisy at last. But the connection came through as a man's voice, very thin and far away.

"This is Slagle speaking . . . "

"Yes?" The name was unfamiliar.

"Hell of a note, isn't it? Get my wire?"

"There haven't been any wires."

"Young Parke's in trouble," he said rapidly. "They picked him up when he handed the bonds over the counter. They got a circular from New York giving 'em the numbers just five minutes before. What d'you know about that, hey? You never can tell in these hick towns——"

"Hello!" I interrupted breathlessly. "Look here—this isn't Mr. Gatsby. Mr. Gatsby's dead."

There was a long silence on the other end of the wire, followed by an exclamation . . . then a quick squawk as the connection was broken.

I think it was on the third day that a telegram signed Henry C. Gatz arrived from a town in Minnesota. It said only that the sender was leaving immediately and to postpone the funeral until he came.

It was Gatsby's father, a solemn old man, very helpless and dismayed, bundled up in a long cheap ulster[3] against the warm September day. His eyes leaked continuously with excitement, and when I took the bag and umbrella from his hands he began to pull so incessantly at his sparse gray beard that I had difficulty in getting off his coat. He was on the point of collapse, so I took him into the music room and made him sit down while I sent for something to eat. But he wouldn't eat, and the glass of milk spilled from his trembling hand.

"I saw it in the Chicago newspaper," he said. "It was all in the Chicago newspaper. I started right away."

"I didn't know how to reach you."

His eyes, seeing nothing, moved ceaselessly about the room.

"It was a madman," he said. "He must have been mad."

"Wouldn't you like some coffee?" I urged him.

"I don't want anything. I'm all right now, Mr.——"

"Carraway."

"Well, I'm all right now. Where have they got Jimmy?"

I took him into the drawing-room, where his son lay, and left him there. Some little boys had come up on the steps and were looking into the hall; when I told them who had arrived, they went reluctantly away.

After a while Mr. Gatz opened the door and came out, his mouth ajar, his face flushed slightly, his eyes leaking isolated and unpunctual tears. He had reached an age where death no longer has the quality of ghastly surprise, and when he looked around him now for the first time and saw the height and splendor of the hall and the great rooms opening out from it into other rooms, his grief began to be mixed with an awed pride. I helped him to a bedroom upstairs; while he took off his coat and vest I told him that all arrangements had been deferred until he came.

"I didn't know what you'd want, Mr. Gatsby——"

"Gatz is my name."

"—Mr. Gatz. I thought you might want to take the body West."

---

[3]A loose-fitting, heavy overcoat.

He shook his head.

"Jimmy always liked it better down East. He rose up to his position in the East. Were you a friend of my boy's, Mr.——?"

"We were close friends."

"He had a big future before him, you know. He was only a young man, but he had a lot of brain power here."

He touched his head impressively, and I nodded.

"If he'd of lived, he'd of been a great man. A man like James J. Hill.[4] He'd of helped build up the country."

"That's true," I said, uncomfortably.

He fumbled at the embroidered coverlet, trying to take it from the bed, and lay down stiffly—was instantly asleep.

That night an obviously frightened person called up, and demanded to know who I was before he would give his name.

"This is Mr. Carraway," I said.

"Oh!" He sounded relieved. "this is Klipspringer."

I was relieved too, for that seemed to promise another friend at Gatsby's grave. I didn't want it to be in the papers and draw a sightseeing crowd, so I'd been calling up a few people myself. They were hard to find.

"The funeral's tomorrow," I said. "Three o'clock, here at the house, I wish you'd tell anybody who'd be interested."

"Oh, I will," he broke out hastily. "Of course I'm not likely to see anybody, but if I do."

His tone made me suspicious.

"Of course you'll be there yourself."

"Well, I'll certainly try. What I called up about is——"

"Wait a minute," I interrupted. "How about saying you'll come?"

"Well, the fact is—the truth of the matter is that I'm staying with some people up here in Greenwich,[5] and they rather expect me to be with them tomorrow. In fact, there's a sort of picnic or something. Of course I'll do my very best to get away."

I ejaculated an unrestrained "Huh!" and he must have heard me, for he went on nervously:

"What I called up about was a pair of shoes I left there. I wonder if it'd be too much trouble to have the butler send them on. You see, they're tennis shoes, and I'm sort of helpless without them. My address is care of B. F.——"

I didn't hear the rest of the name, because I hung up the receiver.

After that I felt a certain shame for Gatsby—one gentleman to whom I telephoned implied that he had got what he deserved. However, that was my fault, for he was one of those who used to sneer most bitterly at Gatsby on the courage of Gatsby's liquor, and I should have known better than to call him.

The morning of the funeral I went up to New York to see Meyer Wolfsheim; I couldn't seem to reach him any other way. The door that I pushed open, on the advice of an elevator boy, was marked "The Swastika Holding Company," and at first there didn't seem to be any one inside. But when I'd shouted "hello" several times in vain, an argument broke out behind a partition, and presently a lovely Jewess appeared at an interior door and scrutinized me with black hostile eyes.

"Nobody's in," she said. "Mr. Wolfsheim's gone to Chicago."

[4]America's greatest railroad builder (1838–1916), organizer of the Great Northern Railway linking the Middle West to the Pacific.

[5]Greenwich, Connecticut, wealthy suburb of New York City.

The first part of this was obviously untrue, for someone had begun to whistle "The Rosary,"[6] tunelessly, inside.

"Please say that Mr. Carraway wants to see him."

"I can't get him back from Chicago, can I?"

At this moment a voice, unmistakably Wolfsheim's, called "Stella!" from the other side of the door.

"Leave your name on the desk," she said quickly. "I'll give it to him when he gets back."

"But I know he's there."

She took a step toward me and began to slide her hands indignantly up and down her hips.

"You young men think you can force your way in here any time," she scolded. "We're getting sickantired of it. When I say he's in Chicago, he's in Chicago."

I mentioned Gatsby.

"Oh-h!" She looked at me over again. "Will you just—What was your name?"

She vanished. In a moment Meyer Wolfsheim stood solemnly in the doorway, holding out both hands. He drew me into his office, remarking in a reverent voice that it was a sad time for all of us, and offered me a cigar.

"My memory goes back to when first I met him," he said. "A young major just out of the army and covered over with medals he got in the war. He was so hard up he had to keep on wearing his uniform because he couldn't buy some regular clothes. First time I saw him was when he come into Winebrenner's poolroom at Forty-third Street and asked for a job. He hadn't eat anything for a couple of days. 'Come on have some lunch with me,' I sid. He ate more than four dollars' worth of food in half an hour."

"Did you start him in business?" I inquired.

"Start him! I made him."

"Oh."

"I raised him up out of nothing, right out of the gutter. I saw right away he was a fine-appearing, gentlemanly young man, and when he told me he was an Oggsford I knew I could use him good. I got him to join up in the American Legion and he used to stand high there. Right off he did some work for a client of mine up to Albany.[7] We were so thick like that in everything"—he held up two bulbous fingers—"always together."

I wondered if this partnership had included the World's Series transaction in 1919.

"Now he's dead," I said after a moment. "You were his closest friend, so I know you'll want to come to his funeral this afternoon."

"I'd like to come."

"Well, come then."

The hair in his nostrils quivered slightly, and as he shook his head his eyes filled with tears.

"I can't do it—I can't get mixed up in it," he said.

"There's nothing to get mixed up in. It's all over now."

"When a man gets killed I never like to get mixed up in it in any way. I keep out. When I was a young man it was different—if a friend of mine died, no matter how, I stuck with them to the end. You may think that's sentimental, but I mean it—to the bitter end."

I saw that for some reason of his own he was determined not to come, so I stood up.

[6]Popular song of the 1920s.
[7]The state capital of New York.

"Are you a college man?" he inquired suddenly.

For a moment I thought he was going to suggest a "gonnegtion," but he only nodded and shook my hand.

"Let us learn to show our friendship for a man when he is alive and not after he is dead," he suggested. "After that my own rule is to let everything alone."

When I left his office the sky had turned dark and I got back to West Egg in a drizzle. After changing my clothes I went next door and found Mr. Gatz walking up and down excitedly in the hall. His pride in his son and in his son's possessions was continually increasing and now he had something to show me.

"Jimmy sent me this picture." He took out his wallet with trembling fingers. "Look there."

It was a photograph of the house, cracked in the corners and dirty with many hands. He pointed out every detail to me eagerly. "Look there!" and then sought admiration from my eyes. He had shown it so often that I think it was more real to him now than the house itself.

"Jimmy sent it to me. I think it's a very pretty picture. It shows up well."

"Very well. Had you seen him lately?"

"He come out to see me two years ago and bought me the house I live in now. Of course we was broke up when he run off from home, but I see now there was a reason for it. He knew he had a big future in front of him. And ever since he made a success he was very generous with me."

He seemed reluctant to put away the picture, held it for another minute, lingeringly, before my eyes. Then he returned the wallet and pulled from his pocket a ragged old copy of a book called *Hopalong Cassidy*.[8]

"Look here, this is a book he had when he was a boy. It just shows you."

He opened it at the back cover and turned it around for me to see. On the last fly-leaf was printed the word SCHEDULE, and the date September 12, 1906. And underneath:

Rise from bed	6.00	A.M.
Dumbbell exercise and wall-scaling	6.15-6.30	"
Study electricity, etc.	7.15-8.15	"
Work . . . . :	8.30-4.30	P.M.
Baseball and sports	4.30-5.00	"
Practice elocution, poise and how to attain it	5.00-6.00	"
Study needed inventions	7.00-9.00	"

GENERAL RESOLVES

No wasting time at Shafters or [a name, indecipherable]
No more smokeing or chewing
Bath every other day
Read one improving book or magazine per week
Save $5.00 [crossed out] $3.00 per week
Be better to parents

"I come across this book by accident," said the old man. "It just shows you, don't it?"

"It just shows you."

"Jimmy was bound to get ahead. He always had some resolves like this or

---

[8]A western novel written by Clarence E. Mulford and published in 1910. Mulford's western stories with Hopalong Cassidy as hero were published in magazines as early as 1905.

something. Do you notice what he's got about improving his mind? He was always great for that. He told me I et like a hog once, and I beat him for it."

He was reluctant to close the book, reading each item aloud and then looking eagerly at me. I think he rather expected me to copy down the list for my own use.

A little before three the Lutheran minister arrived from Flushing, and I began to look involuntarily out the windows for other cars. So did Gatsby's father. And as the time passed and the servants came in and stood waiting in the hall, his eyes began to blink anxiously, and he spoke of the rain in a worried, uncertain way. The minister glanced several times at his watch, so I took him aside and asked him to wait for half an hour. But it wasn't any use. Nobody came.

About five o'clock our procession of three cars reached the cemetery and stopped in a thick drizzle beside the gate—first a motor hearse, horribly black and wet, then Mr. Gatz and the minister and I in the limousine, and a little later four or five servants and the postman from West Egg, in Gatsby's station wagon, all wet to the skin. As we started through the gate into the cemetery I heard a car stop and then the sound of someone splashing after us over the soggy ground. I looked around. It was the man with owl-eyed glasses whom I had found marvelling over Gatsby's books in the library one night three months before.

I'd never seen him since then. I don't know how he knew about the funeral, or even his name. The rain poured down his thick glasses, and he took them off and wiped them to see the protecting canvas unrolled from Gatsby's grave.

I tried to think about Gatsby then for a moment, but he was already too far away, and I could only remember, without resentment, that Daisy hadn't sent a message or a flower. Dimly I heard someone murmur "Blessed are the dead that the rain falls on," and then the owl-eyed man said "Amen to that," in a brave voice.

We straggled down quickly through the rain to the cars. Owl-eyes spoke to me by the gate.

"I couldn't get to the house," he remarked.

"Neither could anybody else."

"Go on!" He started. "Why, my God! they used to go there by the hundreds."

He took off his glasses and wiped them again, outside and in.

"The poor son-of-a-bitch," he said.

One of my most vivid memories is of coming back West from prep school and later from college at Christmas time. Those who went farther than Chicago would gather in the old dim Union Station at six o'clock of a December evening, with a few Chicago friends, already caught up into their own holiday gayeties, to bid them a hasty good-by. I remember the fur coats of the girls returning from Miss This-or-That's and the chatter of frozen breath and the hands waving overhead as we caught sight of old acquaintances, and the matchings of invitations: "Are you going to the Ordways'? the Herseys'? the Schultzes'?" and the long green tickets clasped tight in our gloved hands. And last the murkey yellow cars of the Chicago, Milwaukee & St. Paul railroad looking cheerful as Christmas itself on the tracks beside the gate.

When we pulled out into the winter night and the real snow, our snow, began to stretch out beside us and twinkle against the windows, and the dim lights of small Wisconsin stations moved by, a sharp wild brace came suddenly into the air. We drew in deep breaths of it as we walked back from dinner through the cold vestibules, unutterably aware of our identity with this country for one strange hour, before we melted indistinguishably into it again.

That's my Middle West—not the wheat or the prairies or the lost Swede towns, but the thrilling returning trains of my youth, and the street lamps and sleigh bells in the frosty dark and the shadows of holly wreaths thrown by lighted windows on the snow. I am part of that, a little solemn with the feel of those long winters, a little complacent from growing up in the Carraway house in a city where dwellings are still called through decades by a family's name. I see now that this has been a story of the West, after all—Tom and Gatsby, Daisy and Jordan and I, were all Westerners, and perhaps we possessed some deficiency in common which made us subtly unadaptable to Eastern life.

Even when the East excited me most, even when I was most keenly aware of its superiority to the bored, sprawling, swollen towns beyond the Ohio, with their interminable inquisitions which spared only the children and the very old—even then it had always for me a quality of distortion. West Egg, especially, still figures in my more fantastic dreams. I see it as a night scene by El Greco:[9] a hundred houses, at once conventional and grotesque, crouching under a sullen, overhanging sky and a lustreless moon. In the foreground four solemn men in dress suits are walking along the sidewalk with a stretcher on which lies a drunken woman in a white evening dress. Her hand, which dangles over the side, sparkles cold with jewels. Gravely the men turn in at a house—the wrong house. But no one knows the woman's name, and no one cares.

After Gatsby's death the East was haunted for me like that, distorted beyond my eyes' power of correction. So when the blue smoke of brittle leaves was in the air and the wind blew the wet laundry stiff on the line I decided to come back home.

There was one thing to be done before I left, an awkward, unpleasant thing that perhaps had better have been let alone. But I wanted to leave things in order and not just trust that obliging and indifferent sea to sweep my refuse away. I saw Jordan Baker and talked over and around what had happened to us together, and what had happened afterward to me, and she lay perfectly still, listening, in a big chair.

She was dressed to play golf, and I remember thinking she looked like a good illustration, her chin raised a little jauntily, her hair the color of an autumn leaf, her face the same brown tint as the fingerless glove on her knee. When I had finished she told me without comment that she was engaged to another man. I doubted that, though there were several she could have married at a nod of her head, but I pretended to be surprised. For just a minute I wondered if I wasn't making a mistake, then I thought it all over again quickly and got up to say good-by.

"Nevertheless you did throw me over," said Jordan suddenly. "You threw me over on the telephone. I don't give a damn about you now, but it was a new experience for me, and I felt a little dizzy for a while."

We shook hands.

"Oh, and do you remember"—she added—"a conversation we had once about driving a car?"

"Why—not exactly."

"You said a bad driver was only safe until she met another bad driver? Well, I met another bad driver, didn't I? I mean it was careless of me to make such a

[9]El Greco (Spanish: The Greek), Domenicos Theotocopoulos (c. 1541–1614), a painter born on Crete who lived and worked in Italy and Spain. His work is noted for its visionary scenes with elongated and distorted figures and vibrant colors.

wrong guess. I thought you were rather an honest, straightforward person. I thought it was your secret pride."

"I'm thirty," I said. "I'm five years too old to lie to myself and call it honor."

She didn't answer. Angry, and half in love with her, and tremendously sorry, I turned away.

One afternoon late in October I saw Tom Buchanan. He was walking ahead of me along Fifth Avenue in his alert, aggressive way, his hands out a little from his body as if to fight off interference, his head moving sharply here and there, adapting itself to his restless eyes. Just as I slowed up to avoid overtaking him he stopped and began frowning into the windows of a jewelry store. Suddenly he saw me and walked back, holding out his hand.

"What's the matter, Nick? Do you object to shaking hands with me?"

"Yes. You know what I think of you."

"You're crazy, Nick," he said quickly. "Crazy as hell. I don't know what's the matter with you."

"Tom," I inquired, "what did you say to Wilson that afternoon?"

He stared at me without a word, and I knew I had guessed right about those missing hours. I started to turn away, but he took a step after me and grabbed my arm.

"I told him the truth," he said. "He came to the door while we were getting ready to leave, and when I sent down word that we weren't in he tried to force his way upstairs. He was crazy enough to kill me if I hadn't told him who owned the car. His hand was on a revolver in his pocket every minute he was in the house—" He broke off defiantly. "What if I did tell him? That fellow had it coming to him. He threw dust into your eyes just like he did in Daisy's, but he was a tough one. He ran over Myrtle like you'd run over a dog and never even stopped his car."

There was nothing I could say, except the one unutterable fact that it wasn't true.

"And if you think I didn't have my share of suffering—look here, when I went to give up that flat and saw that damn box of dog biscuits sitting there on the sideboard, I sat down and cried like a baby. By God it was awful——"

I couldn't forgive him or like him, but I saw that what he had done was, to him, entirely justified. It was all very careless and confused. They were careless people, Tom and Daisy—they smashed up things and creatures and then retreated back into their money or their vast carelessness, or whatever it was that kept them together, and let other people clean up the mess they had made. . . .

I shook hands with him; it seemed silly not to, for I felt suddenly as though I were talking to a child. Then he went into the jewelry store to buy a pearl necklace—or perhaps only a pair of cuff buttons—rid of my provincial squeamishness forever.

Gatsby's house was still empty when I left—the grass on his lawn had grown as long as mine. One of the taxi drivers in the village never took a fare past the entrance gate without stopping for a minute and pointing inside; perhaps it was he who drove Daisy and Gatsby over to East Egg the night of the accident, and perhaps he had made a story about it all his own. I didn't want to hear it and I avoided him when I got off the train.

I spent my Saturday nights in New York because those gleaming, dazzling parties of his were with me so vividly that I could still hear the music and the laughter, faint and incessant, from his garden, and the cars going up and down his drive. One night I did hear a material car there, and saw its lights stop at his front steps. But I didn't investigate. Probably it was some final guest who had been away at the ends of the earth and didn't knew that the party was over.

On the last night, with my trunk packed and my car sold to the grocer, I went over and looked at that huge incoherent failure of a house once more. On the white steps an obscene word, scrawled by some boy with a piece of brick, stood out clearly in the moonlight, and I erased it, drawing my shoe raspingly along the stone. Then I wandered down to the beach and sprawled out on the sand.

Most of the big shore places were closed now and there were hardly any lights except the shadowy, moving glow of a ferryboat across the Sound. And as the moon rose higher the inessential houses began to melt away until gradually I became aware of the old island here that flowered once for Dutch sailors' eyes[10]— a fresh, green breast of the new world. Its vanished trees, the trees that had made way for Gatsby's house, had once pandered in whispers to the last and greatest of all human dreams; for a transitory enchanted moment man must have held his breath in the presence of this continent, compelled into an aesthetic contemplation he neither understood nor desired, face to face for the last time in history with something commensurate to his capacity for wonder.

And as I sat there brooding on the old, unknown world, I thought of Gatsby's wonder when he first picked out the green light at the end of Daisy's dock. He had come a long way to this blue lawn, and his dream must have seemed so close that he could hardly fail to grasp it. He did not know that it was already behind him, somewhere back in that vast obscurity beyond the city, where the dark fields of the republic rolled on under the night.

Gatsby believed in the green light, the orgastic future that year by year recedes before us. It eluded us then, but that's no matter—tomorrow we will run faster, stretch out our arms farther. . . . And one fine morning——

So we beat on, boats against the current, borne back ceaselessly into the past.

1922–1924   1925, 1989

Ernest Hemingway   *1899–1961*

Ernest Hemingway was born in Oak Park, Illinois, a suburb of Chicago. His father, a well-to-do physician, initiated his son into the rituals of hunting and fishing and bequeathed to him a way of life, and of death. In 1917, after graduation from high school, Ernest Hemingway went to work as a reporter for the Kansas City Star. Rejected for army service in World War I because of poor vision, he volunteered to serve as a driver for an American ambulance unit in France. Hemingway then transferred to duty on the Italian front, where he was seriously wounded in the explosion of a mortar shell. He was the first American to be wounded in Italy during World War I. After his recovery, and with decorations for valor which he believed he did not deserve, Hemingway returned home. He worked for the Toronto Star, covered the Graeco-Turkish War as a foreign correspondent, and then returned to Paris, which, after World War I, was a city full of intellectual life, creativity, and genius.

[10]Early in the seventeenth century, the Dutch established whaling and fishing villages on the coast of Long Island as part of the Colony of New Netherlands (established 1624), with New Amsterdam (modern-day New York City) as its capital.

In Paris, Hemingway—along with Gertrude Stein, Ezra Pound, T. S. Eliot, and James Joyce—helped create a revolution in literary style and language. He developed a spare, tight, reportorial prose based on deceptively simple sentence structure. He used a restricted vocabulary, precise imagery, and an impersonal, dramatic tone. His first book, Three Stories and Ten Poems, *appeared in 1923. Three years later, with the publication of* The Sun Also Rises, *Hemingway became the spokesman for the men and women that Gertrude Stein had called "a lost generation."*

*His works have sometimes been read as an essentially negative commentary on a modern world filled with sterility, failure, and death. Yet that nihilistic vision is repeatedly modified by Hemingway's affirmative assertion of the possibility of living with style and courage. His primary concern was an individual's "moment of truth" (a notion derived from bullfighting), and he was fascinated by the threat of physical, emotional, or psychic death, a fascination reflected in his lifelong preoccupation with stories of war (*A Farewell to Arms, *1929, and* For Whom the Bell Tolls, *1940), the bullfight (*Death in the Afternoon, *1932), and the hunt (*Green Hills of Africa, *1935). To Hemingway, man's greatest achievement is to show "grace under pressure," or what he described in* The Sun Also Rises *as holding the "purity of line through the maximum of exposure."*

Hemingway's stature as a writer was confirmed with the publication of A Farewell to Arms *in 1929. The novel portrays a farewell both to war and to love. Hemingway had rejected the romantic ideal of the ultimate unity of lovers. He suggested instead that all relationships must end in destruction and in death.*

In 1937 he became a foreign correspondent covering the Spanish Civil War. Three years later he published For Whom the Bell Tolls. *Set in Spain during the Civil War, the novel restates his view of love found and lost and describes the indomitable spirit of the common people. In 1952 the same judgment was reflected in his portrayal of the old fisherman, Santiago, triumphant even in defeat, in* The Old Man and the Sea.

For his novels and for his short stories, which include some of the finest in the English language, Hemingway received wide acclaim. In 1954 he was awarded a Nobel Prize for his "mastery of the art of modern narration." He became a public figure whose pronouncements and adventures were publicized and scrutinized throughout the world. Numerous parallels exist between the events of Hemingway's life and those of his characters, but few were closer than those of Richard Cantwell, the hero of Across the River and into the Trees *(1950), whose attempts at stoic control of physical and mental illness and whose eventual suicide foreshadow the struggles and defeats of Hemingway's final years, which ended when he, as his father had done some thirty years before, took his own life on July 2, 1961.*

FURTHER READING: *Ernest Hemingway, The Papers of a Writer,* ed. B. Oldsey, 1981; *Ernest Hemingway, Selected Letters,* ed. C. Baker, 1981; C. Fenton, *The Apprenticeship of Ernest Hemingway,* 1954; L. Ross, *Portrait of Hemingway,* 1961; A. Hotchner, *Papa Hemingway,* 1966; C. Baker, *Ernest Hemingway, A Life Story,* 1969; C. Baker, *Ernest Hemingway, The Writer as Artist,* 1952, 1956, 1963, 1972; P. Young, *Ernest Hemingway,* 1952, 1966; *Hemingway and His Critics,* ed. C. Baker, 1961; E. Rovit, *Ernest Hemingway,* 1963, 1986; S. Baker, *Ernest Hemingway,* 1967; E. Watts, *Ernest Hemingway and the Arts,* 1971; A. Waldhorn, *A Reader's Guide to Ernest Hemingway,* 1972; J. Bakker, *Ernest Hemingway, The Writer as a Man of Action,* 1972; *The Short Stories of Ernest Hemingway, Critical Essays,* ed. J. Benson, 1975; S. Donaldson, *By Force of Will, The Life and Art of Ernest Hemingway,* 1977; P. Griffin, *Along with Youth, Hemingway, The Early Years,* 1985; K. Lynn, *Hemingway, The Life and the Work,* 1987.

TEXT: *The Complete Short Stories of Ernest Hemingway,* 1987.

BIG TWO-HEARTED RIVER: PART I

THE TRAIN went on up the track out of sight, around one of the hills of burnt timber. Nick sat down on the bundle of canvas and bedding the baggage man had pitched out of the door of the baggage car. There was no town, nothing but the rails and the burned-over country. The thirteen saloons that had lined the one street of Seney had not left a trace. The foundations of the Mansion House hotel stuck up above the ground. The stone was chipped and split by the fire. It was all that was left of the town of Seney. Even the surface had been burned off the ground.

Nick looked at the burned-over stretch of hillside, where he had expected to find the scattered houses of the town and then walked down the railroad track to the bridge over the river. The river was there. It swirled against the log spiles[1] of the bridge. Nick looked down into the clear, brown water, colored from the pebbly bottom, and watched the trout keeping themselves steady in the current with wavering fins. As he watched them they changed their positions by quick angles, only to hold steady in the fast water again. Nick watched them a long time.

He watched them holding themselves with their noses into the current, many trout in deep, fast moving water, slightly distorted as he watched far down through the glassy convex surface of the pool, its surface pushing and swelling smooth against the resistance of the log-driven piles of the bridge. At the bottom of the pool were the big trout. Nick did not see them at first. Then he saw them at the bottom of the pool, big trout looking to hold themselves on the gravel bottom in a varying mist of gravel and sand, raised in spurts by the current.

Nick looked down into the pool from the bridge. It was a hot day. A kingfisher flew up the stream. It was a long time since Nick had looked into a stream and seen trout. They were very satisfactory. As the shadow of the kingfisher moved up the stream, a big trout shot upstream in a long angle, only his shadow marking the angle, then lost his shadow as he came through the surface of the water, caught the sun, and then, as he went back into the stream under the surface, his shadow seemed to float down the stream with the current, unre-sisting, to his post under the bridge where he tightened facing up into the current.

Nick's heart tightened as the trout moved. He felt all the old feeling.

He turned and looked down the stream. It stretched away, pebbly-bottomed with shallows and big boulders and a deep pool as it curved away around the foot of a bluff.

Nick walked back up the ties to where his pack lay in the cinders beside the railway track. He was happy. He adjusted the pack harness around the bundle, pulling straps tight, slung the pack on his back, got his arms through the shoulder straps and took some of the pull off his shoulders by leaning his forehead against the wide band of the tump-line[2]. Still, it was too heavy. It was much too heavy. He had his leather rod-case in his hand and leaning forward to keep the weight of the pack high on his shoulders he walked along the road that paralleled the railway track, leaving the burned town behind in the heat, and then turned off around a hill with a high, fire-scarred hill on either side onto a road that went

---

[1]Heavy support timbers, piles.
[2]A strap passed across the forehead to help support a backpack.

back into the country. He walked along the road feeling the ache from the pull of the heavy pack. The road climbed steadily. It was hard work walking up-hill. His muscles ached and the day was hot, but Nick felt happy. He felt he had left everything behind, the need for thinking, the need to write, other needs. It was all back of him.

From the time he had gotten down off the train and the baggage man had thrown his pack out of the open car door things had been different. Seney was burned, the country was burned over and changed, but it did not matter. It could not all be burned. He knew that. He hiked along the road, sweating in the sun, climbing to cross the range of hills that separated the railway from the pine plains.

The road ran on, dipping occasionally, but always climbing. Nick went on up. Finally the road after going parallel to the burnt hillside reached the top. Nick leaned back against a stump and slipped out of the pack harness. Ahead of him, as far as he could see, was the pine plain. The burned country stopped off at the left with the range of hills. On ahead islands of dark pine trees rose out of the plain. Far off to the left was the line of the river. Nick followed it with his eye and caught glints of the water in the sun.

There was nothing but the pine plain ahead of him, until the far blue hills that marked the Lake Superior height of land. He could hardly see them, faint and far away in the heat-light over the plain. If he looked too steadily they were gone. But if he only half-looked they were there, the far-off hills of the height of land.

Nick sat down against the charred stump and smoked a cigarette. His pack balanced on the top of the stump, harness holding ready, a hollow molded in it from his back. Nick sat smoking, looking out over the country. He did not need to get his map out. He knew where he was from the position of the river.

As he smoked, his legs stretched out in front of him, he noticed a grasshopper walk along the ground and up onto his woolen sock. The grasshopper was black. As he had walked along the road, climbing, he had started many grasshoppers from the dust. They were all black. They were not the big grasshoppers with yellow and black or red and black wings whirring out from their black wing sheathing as they fly up. These were just ordinary hoppers, but all a sooty black in color. Nick had wondered about them as he walked, without really thinking about them. Now, as he watched the black hopper that was nibbling at the wool of his sock with its fourway lip, he realized that they had all turned black from living in the burned-over land. He realized that the fire must have come the year before, but the grasshoppers were all black now. He wondered how long they would stay that way.

Carefully he reached his hand down and took hold of the hopper by the wings. He turned him up, all his legs walking in the air, and looked at his jointed belly. Yes, it was black too, iridescent where the black and head were dusty.

"Go on, hopper," Nick said, speaking out loud for the first time. "Fly away somewhere."

He tossed the grasshopper up into the air and watched him sail away to a charcoal stump across the road.

Nick stood up. He leaned his back against the weight of his pack where it rested upright on the stump and got his arms through the shoulder straps. He stood with the pack on his back on the brow of the hill looking out across the country, toward the distant river and then struck down the hillside away from the road. Underfoot the ground was good walking. Two hundred yards down the hillside the fire line stopped. Then it was sweet fern, growing ankle high, to walk through, and clumps of jack pines; a long undulating country with frequent rises and descents, sandy underfoot and the country alive again.

Nick kept his direction by the sun. He knew where he wanted to strike the river and he kept on through the pine plain, mounting small rises to see other rises ahead of him and sometimes from the top of a rise a great solid island of pines off to his right or his left. He broke off some sprigs of the heathery sweet fern, and put them under his pack straps. The chafing crushed it and he smelled it as he walked.

He was tired and very hot, walking across the uneven, shadeless pine plain. At any time he knew he could strike the river by turning off to his left. It could not be more than a mile away. But he kept on toward the north to hit the river as far upstream as he could go in one day's walking.

For some time as he walked Nick had been in sight of one of the big islands of pine standing out above the rolling high ground he was crossing. He dipped down and then as he came slowly up to the crest of the bridge he turned and made toward the pine trees.

There was no underbrush in the island of pine trees. The trunks of the trees went straight up or slanted toward each other. The trunks were straight and brown without branches. The branches were high above. Some interlocked to make a solid shadow on the brown forest floor. Around the grove of trees was a bare space. It was brown and soft underfoot as Nick walked on it. This was the over-lapping of the pine needle floor, extending out beyond the width of the high branches. The trees had grown tall and the branches moved high, leaving in the sun this bare space they had once covered with shadow. Sharp at the edge of this extension of the forest floor commenced the sweet fern.

Nick slipped off his pack and lay down in the shade. He lay on his back and looked up into the pine trees. His neck and back and the small of his back rested as he stretched. The earth felt good against his back. He looked up at the sky, through the branches, and then shut his eyes. He opened them and looked up again. There was a wind high up in the branches. He shut his eyes again and went to sleep.

Nick woke stiff and cramped. The sun was nearly down. His pack was heavy and the straps painful as he lifted it on. He leaned over with the pack on and picked up the leather rod-case and started out from the pine trees across the sweet fern swale, toward the river. He knew it could not be more than a mile.

He came down a hillside covered with stumps into a meadow. At the edge of the meadow flowed the river. Nick was glad to get to the river. He walked upstream through the meadow. His trousers were soaked with the dew as he walked. After the hot day, the dew had come quickly and heavily. The river made no sound. It was too fast and smooth. At the edge of the meadow, before he mounted to a piece of high ground to make camp, Nick looked down the river at the trout rising. They were rising to insects come from the swamp on the other side of the stream when the sun went down. The trout jumped out of water to take them. While Nick walked through the little stretch of meadow alongside the stream, trout had jumped high out of water. Now as he looked down the river, the insects must be settling on the surface, for the trout were feeding steadily all down the stream. As far down the long stretch as he could see, the trout were rising, making circles all down the surface of the water, as though it were starting to rain.

The ground rose, wooded and sandy, to overlook the meadow, the stretch of river and the swamp. Nick dropped his pack and rod-case and looked for a level piece of ground. He was very hungry and he wanted to make his camp before he cooked. Between two jack pines, the ground was quite level. He took the ax out of the pack and chopped out two projecting roots. That leveled a piece of ground large enough to sleep on. He smoothed out the sandy soil with his hand and pulled all the sweet fern bushes by their roots. His hands smelled good from the sweet fern. He smoothed the uprooted earth. He did not want anything making lumps under the blankets. When he had the ground smooth, he spread his three blankets. One he folded double, next to the ground. The other two he spread on top.

With the ax he slit off a bright slab of pine from one of the stumps and split it into pegs for the tent. He wanted them long and solid to hold in the ground. With the tent unpacked and spread on the ground, the pack, leaning against a jackpine, looked much smaller. Nick tied the rope that served the tent for a ridge-pole to the trunk of one of the pine trees and pulled the tent up off the ground with the other end of the rope and tied it to the other pine. The tent hung on the rope like a canvas blanket on a clothesline. Nick poked a pole he had cut up under the back peak of the canvas and then made it a tent by pegging out the sides. He pegged the sides out taut and drove the pegs deep, hitting them down into the ground with the flat of the ax until the rope loops were buried and the canvas was drum tight.

Across the open mouth of the tent Nick fixed cheescloth to keep out mosquitoes. He crawled inside under the mosquito bar with various things from the pack to put at the head of the bed under the slant of the canvas. Inside the tent the light came through the brown canvas. It smelled pleasantly of canvas. Already there was something mysterious and homelike. Nick was happy as he crawled inside the tent. He had not been unhappy all day. This was different though. Now things were done. There had been this to do. Now it was done. It had been a hard trip. He was very tired. That was done. He had made his camp. He was settled. Nothing could touch him. It was a good place to camp. He was there, in the good place. He was in his home where he had made it. Now he was hungry.

He came out, crawling under the cheesecloth. It was quite dark outside. It was lighter in the tent.

Nick went over to the pack and found, with his fingers, a long nail in a paper sack of nails, in the bottom of the pack. He drove it into the pine tree, holding it close and hitting it gently with the flat of the ax. He hung the pack up on the nail. All his supplies were in the pack. They were off the ground and sheltered now.

Nick was hungry. He did not believe he had ever been hungrier. He opened and emptied a can of pork and beans and a can of spaghetti into the frying pan.

"I've got a right to eat this kind of stuff, if I'm willing to carry it," Nick said. His voice sounded strange in the darkening woods. He did not speak again.

He started a fire with some chunks of pine he got with the ax from a stump. Over the fire he stuck a wire grill, pushing the four legs down into the ground with his boot. Nick put the frying pan on the grill over the flames. He was hungrier. The beans and spaghetti warmed. Nick stirred them and mixed them together. They began to bubble, making little bubbles that rose with difficulty to the surface. There was a good smell. Nick got out a bottle of tomato catchup and cut four slices of bread. The little bubbles were coming faster now. Nick sat down beside the fire and lifted the frying pan off. He poured about half the contents out into the tin plate. It spread slowly on the plate. Nick knew it was too hot. He poured on some tomato catchup. He knew the beans and spaghetti were still too hot. He looked at the fire, then at the tent, he was not going to spoil it all by burning his tongue. For years he had never enjoyed fried bananas because he had never been able to wait for them to cool. His tongue was very sensitive. He was very hungry. Across the river in the swamp, in the almost dark, he saw a mist rising. He looked at the tent once more. All right. He took a full spoonful from the plate.

"Chrise," Nick said, "Geezus Chrise," he said happily.

He ate the whole plateful before he remembered the bread. Nick finished the second plateful with the bread, mopping the pate shiny. He had not eaten since a cup of coffee and a ham sandwich in the station restaurant at St. Ignace. It had been a very fine experience. He had been that hungry before, but had not been able to satisfy it. He could have made camp hours before if he had wanted to. There were plenty of good places to camp on the river. But this was good.

Nick tucked two big chips of pine under the grill. The fire flared up. He had forgotten to get water for the coffee. Out of the pack he got a folding canvas bucket and walked down the hill, across the edge of the meadow, to the stream. The other bank was in the white mist. The grass was wet and cold as he knelt on the bank and dipped the canvas bucket into the stream. It bellied and pulled hard in the current. The water was ice cold. Nick rinsed the bucket and carried it full up to the camp. Up away from the stream it was not so cold.

Nick drove another big nail and hung up the bucket full of water. He dipped the coffee pot half full, put some more chips under the grill onto the fire and put the pot on. He could not remember which way he made coffee. He could remember an argument about it with Hopkins, but not which side he had taken. He decided to bring it to a boil. He remembered now that was Hopkin's way. He had once argued about everything with Hopkins. While he waited for the coffee to boil, he opened a small can of apricots. He liked to open cans. He emptied the can of apricots out into a tin cup. While he watched the coffee on the fire, he drank the juice syrup of the apricots, carefully at first to keep from spilling, then meditatively, sucking the apricots down. They were better than fresh apricots.

The coffee boiled as he watched. The lid came up and coffee and grounds ran down the side of the pot. Nick took it off the grill. It was a triumph for Hopkins. He put sugar in the empty apricot cup and poured some of the coffee out to cool. It was too hot to pour and he used his hat to hold the handle of the coffee pot. He would not let it steep in the pot at all. Not the first cup. It should be straight Hopkins all the way. Hop deserved that. He was a very serious coffee drinker. He was the most serious man Nick had ever known. Not heavy, serious. That was a long time ago. Hopkins spoke without moving his lips. He had played polo. He made millions of dollars in Texas. He had borrowed carfare to go to Chicago, when the wire came that his first big well had come in. He could have wired for money. That would have been too slow. They called Hop's girl the Blonde Venus. Hop did not mind because she was not his real girl. Hopkins said very confidently that none of them would make fun of his real girl. He was right. Hopkins went away when the telegram came. That was on the Black River. It took eight days for the telegram to reach him. Hopkins gave away his .22 caliber Colt automatic pistol to Nick. He gave his camera to Bill. It was to remember him always by. They were all going fishing again next summer. The Hop Head was rich. He would get a yacht and they would all cruise along the north shore of Lake Superior. He was excited but serious. They said good-bye and all felt bad. It broke up the trip. They never saw Hopkins again. That was a long time ago on the Black River.

Nick drank the coffee, the coffee according to Hopkins. The coffee was bitter. Nick laughed. It made a good ending to the story. His mind was starting to work. He knew he could choke it because he was tired enough. He spilled the coffee out of the pot and shook the grounds loose into the fire. He lit a cigarette and went inside the tent. He took off his shoes and trousers, sitting on the blankets, rolled the shoes up inside the trousers for a pillow and got in between the blankets.

Out through the front of the tent he watched the flow of the fire, when the night wind blew on it. It was a quiet night. The swamp was perfectly quiet. Nick stretched under the blanket comfortably. A mosquito hummed close to his ear. Nick sat up and lit a match. The mosquito was on the canvas, over his head. Nick moved the match quickly up to it. The mosquito made a satisfactory hiss in the flame. The match went out. Nick lay down again under the blanket. He turned on his side and shut his eyes. He was sleepy. He felt sleep coming. He curled up under the blanket and went to sleep.

BIG TWO-HEARTED RIVER: PART II

IN THE morning the sun was up and the tent was starting to get hot. Nick crawled out under the mosquito netting stretched across the mouth of the tent, to look at the morning. The grass was wet on his hands as he came out. He held his trousers and his shoes in his hands. The sun was just up over the hill. There was the meadow, the river and the swamp. There were birch trees in the green of the swamp on the other side of the river.

The river was clear and smoothly fast in the early morning. Down about two hundred yards were three logs all the way across the stream. They made the water smooth and deep above them. As Nick watched, a mink crossed the river on the logs and went into the swamp. Nick was excited. He was excited by the early morning and the river. He was really too hurried to eat breakfast, but he knew he must. He built a little fire and put on the coffee pot.

While the water was heating in the pot he took an empty bottle and went down over the edge of the high ground to the meadow. The meadow was wet with dew and Nick wanted to catch grasshoppers for bait before the sun dried the grass. He found plenty of good grasshoppers. They were at the base of the grass stems. Sometimes they clung to a grass stem. They were cold and wet with dew, and could not jump until the sun warmed them. Nick picked them up, taking only the medium-sized brown ones, and put them into the bottle. He turned over a log and just under the shelter of the edge were several hundred hoppers. It was a grasshopper lodging house. Nick put about fifty of the medium browns into the bottle. While he was picking up the hoppers the others warmed in the sun and commenced to hop away. They flew when they hopped. At first they made one flight and stayed stiff when they landed, as though they were dead.

Nick knew that by the time he was through with breakfast they would be as lively as ever. Without dew in the grass it would take him all day to catch a bottle full of good grasshoppers and he would have to crush many of them, slamming at them with his hat. He washed his hands at the stream. He was excited to be near it. Then he walked up to the tent. The hoppers were already jumping stiffly in the grass. In the bottle, warmed by the sun, they were jumping in a mass. Nick put in a pine stick as a cork. It plugged the mouth of the bottle enough, so the hoppers could not get out and left plenty of air passage.

He had rolled the log back and knew he could get grasshoppers there every morning.

Nick laid the bottle full of jumping grasshoppers against a pine trunk. Rapidly he mixed some buckwheat flour with water and stirred it smooth, one cup of flour, one cup of water. He put a handful of coffee in the pot and dipped a lump of grease out of a can and slid it sputtering across the hot skillet. On the smoking skillet he poured smoothly the buckwheat batter. It spread like lava, the grease spitting sharply. Around the edges the buckwheat cake began to firm, then brown, then crisp. The surface was bubbling slowly to porousness. Nick pushed under the browned under surface with a fresh pine chip. He shook the skillet sideways and the cake was loose on the surface. I won't try and flop it, he thought. He slid the chip of clean wood all the way under the cake, and flopped it over onto its face. It sputtered in the pan.

When it was cooked Nick regreased the skillet. He used all the batter. It made another big flapjack and one smaller one.

Nick ate a big flapjack and a smaller one, covered with apple butter. He put apple butter on the third cake, folded it over twice, wrapped it in oiled paper and put it in his shirt pocket. He put the apple butter jar back in the pack and cut bread for two sandwiches.

In the pack he found a big onion. He sliced it in two and peeled the silky outer skin. Then he cut one half into slices and made onion sandwiches. He wrapped them in oiled paper and buttoned them in the other pocket of his khaki shirt. He turned the skillet upside down on the grill, drank the coffee, sweetened and yellow brown with the condensed milk in it, and tidied up the camp. It was a good camp.

Nick took his fly rod out of the leather rod-case, jointed it, and shoved the rod-case back into the tent. He put on the reel and threaded the line through the guides. He had to hold it from hand to hand, as he threaded it, or it would slip back through its own weight. It was heavy, double tapered fly line. Nick had paid eight dollars for it a long time ago. It was made heavy to lift back in the air and come forward flat and heavy and straight to make it possible to cast a fly which has no weight. Nick opened the aluminum leader box. The leaders were coiled between the damp flannel pads. Nick had wet the pads at the water cooler on the train up to St. Ignace. In the damp pads the gut leaders had softened and Nick unrolled one and tied it by a loop at the end to the heavy fly line. He fastened a hook on the end of the leader. It was a small hook; very thin and springy.

Nick took it from his hook book, sitting with the rod across his lap. He tested the knot and the spring of the rod by pulling the line taut. It was a good feeling. He was careful not to let the hook bite into his finger.

He started down to the stream, holding his rod, the bottle of grasshoppers hung from his neck by a thong tied in half hitches around the neck of the bottle. His landing net hung by a hook from his belt. Over his shoulder was a long flour sack tied at each corner into an ear. The cord went over his shoulder. The sack flapped against his legs.

Nick felt awkward and professionally happy with all his equipment hanging from him. The grasshopper bottle swung against his chest. In his shirt the breast pockets bulged against him with the lunch and his fly book.

He stepped into the stream. It was a shock. His trousers clung tight to his legs. His shoes felt the gravel. The water was a rising cold shock.

Rushing, the current sucked against his legs. Where he stepped in, the water was over his knees. He waded with the current. The gravel slid under his shoes. He looked down at the swirl of water below each leg and tipped up the bottle to get a grasshopper.

The first grasshopper gave a jump in the neck of the bottle and went out

into the water. He was sucked under in a whirl by Nick's right leg and came
to the surface a little way down stream. He floated rapidly, kicking. In a quick
circle, breaking the smooth surface of the water, he disappeared. A trout had
taken him.

Another hopper poked his face out of the bottle. His antennæ wavered. He
was getting his front legs out of the bottle to jump. Nick took him by the head
and held him while he threaded the slim hook under his chin, down through
his thorax and into the last segments of his abdomen. The grasshopper took
hold of the hook with his front feet, spitting tobacco juice on it. Nick dropped
him into the water.

Holding the rod in his right hand he let out line against the pull of the
grasshopper in the current. He stripped off line from the reel with his left
hand and let it run free. He could see the hopper in the waves of the current.
It went out of sight.

There was a tug on the line. Nick pulled against the taut line. It was his first
strike. Holding the now living rod across the current, he brought in the line
with his left hand. The rod bent in jerks, the trout pumping against the current. Nick knew it was a small one. He lifted the rod straight up in the air. It
bowed in the pull.

He saw the trout in the water jerking with his head and body against the
shifting tangent of the line in the stream.

Nick took the line in his left hand and pulled the trout, thumping tiredly
against the current, to the surface. His back was mottled the clear, water-over-
gravel color, his side flashing in the sun. The rod under his right arm, Nick
stooped, dipping his right hand into the current. He held the trout, never still,
with his moist right hand, while he unhooked the barb from his mouth, then
dropped him back into the stream.

He hung unsteadily in the current, then settled to the bottom beside a stone.
Nick reached down his hand to touch him, his arm to the elbow under water.
The trout was steady in the moving stream, resting on the gravel, beside a stone.
As Nick's fingers touched him, touched his smooth, cool, underwater feeling he
was gone, gone in a shadow across the bottom of the stream.

He's all right, Nick thought. He was only tired.

He had wet his hand before he touched the trout, so he would not disturb
the delicate mucus that covered him. If a trout was touched with a dry hand, a
white fungus attacked the unprotected spot. Years before when he had fished
crowded streams, with fly fishermen ahead of him and behind him, Nick had
again and again come on dead trout, furry with white fungus, drifted against a
rock, or floating belly up in some pool. Nick did not like to fish with other men
on the river. Unless they were of your party, they spoiled it.

He wallowed down the stream, above his knees in the current, through the
fifty yards of shallow water above the pile of logs that crossed the stream. He
did not rebait his hook and held it in his hand as he waded. He was certain he
could catch small trout in the shallows, but he did not want them. There would
be no big trout in the shallows this time of the day.

Now the water deepened to his thighs sharply and coldly. Ahead was the
smooth dammed-back flood of water above the logs. The water was smooth and
dark; on the left, the lower edge of the meadow; on the right the swamp.

Nick leaned back against the current and took a hopper from the bottle. He
threaded the hopper on the hook and spat on him for good luck. Then he
pulled several yards of line from the reel and tossed the hopper out ahead onto
the fast, dark water. It floated down towards the logs, then the weight of the

line pulled the bait under the surface. Nick held the rod in his right hand, letting the line run out through his fingers.

There was a long tug. Nick struck and the rod came alive and dangerous, bent double, the line tightening, coming out of water, tightening, all in a heavy, dangerous, steady pull. Nick felt the moment when the leader would break if the strain increased and let the line go.

The reel ratcheted into a mechanical shriek as the line went out in a rush. Too fast. Nick could not check it, the line rushing out, the reel note rising as the line ran out.

With the core of the reel showing, his heart feeling stopped with the excitement, leaning back against the current that mounted icily his thighs, Nick thumbed the reel hard with his left hand. It was awkward getting his thumb inside the fly reel frame.

As he put on pressure the line tightened into sudden hardness and beyond the logs a huge trout went high out of water. As he jumped, Nick lowered the tip of the rod. But he felt, as he dropped the tip to ease the strain, the moment when the strain was too great; the hardness too tight. Of course, the leader had broken. There was no mistaking the feeling when all spring left the line and it became dry and hard. Then it went slack.

His mouth dry, his heart down, Nick reeled in. He had never seen so big a trout. There was a heaviness, a power not to be held, and then the bulk of him, as he jumped. He looked as broad as a salmon.

Nick's hand was shaky. He reeled in slowly. The thrill had been too much. He felt, vaguely, a little sick, as though it would be better to sit down.

The leader had broken where the hook was tied to it. Nick took it in his hand. He thought of the trout somewhere on the bottom, holding himself steady over the gravel, far down below the light, under the logs, with the hook in his jaw. Nick knew the trout's teeth would cut through the snell of the hook. The hook would imbed itself in his jaw. He'd bet the trout was angry. Anything that size would be angry. That was a trout. He had been solidly hooked. Solid as a rock. He felt like a rock, too, before he started off. By God, he was a big one. By God, he was the biggest one I ever heard of.

Nick climbed out onto the meadow and stood, water running down his trousers and out of his shoes, his shoes squelchy. He went over and sat on the logs. He did not want to rush his sensations any.

He wriggled his toes in the water, in his shoes, and got out a cigarette from his breast pocket. He lit it and tossed the match into the fast water below the logs. A tiny trout rose at the match, as it swung around in the fast current. Nick laughed. He would finish the cigarette.

He sat on the logs, smoking, drying in the sun, the sun warm on his back, the river shallow ahead entering the woods, curving into the woods, shallows, light glittering, big water-smooth rocks, cedars along the bank and white birches, the logs warm in the sun, smooth to sit on, without bark, gray to the touch; slowly the feeling of disappointment left him. It went away slowly, the feeling of disappointment that came sharply after the thrill that made his shoulders ache. It was all right now. His rod lying out on the logs, Nick tied a new hook on the leader, pulling the gut tight until it grimped into itself a hard knot.

He baited up, then picked up the rod and walked to the far end of the logs to get into the water, where it was not too deep. Under and beyond the logs was a deep pool. Nick walked around the shallow shelf near the swamp shore until he came out on the shallow bed of the stream.

On the left, where the meadow ended and the woods began, a great elm tree was uprooted. Gone over in a storm, it lay back into the woods, its roots clotted with dirt, grass growing in them, rising a solid bank beside the stream. The river cut to the edge of the uprooted tree. From where Nick stood he could see deep channels, like ruts, cut in the shallow bed of the stream by the flow of the current. Pebbly where he stood and pebbly and full of boulders beyond; where it curved near the tree roots, the bed of the stream was marly and between the ruts of deep water green weed fronds swung in the current.

Nick swung the rod back over his shoulder and forward, and the line, curving forward, laid the grasshopper down on one of the deep channels in the weeds. A trout struck and Nick hooked him.

Holding the rod far out toward the uprooted tree and sloshing backward in the current, Nick worked the trout, plunging, the rod bending alive, out of danger of the weeds into the open river. Holding the rod, pumping alive against the current, Nick brought the trout in. He rushed, but always came, the spring of the rod yielding to the rushes, sometimes jerking under water, but always bringing him in. Nick eased downstream with the rushes. The rod above his head he led the trout over the net, then lifted.

The trout hung heavy in the net, mottled trout back and silver sides in the meshes. Nick unhooked him; heavy sides, good to hold, big undershot jaw, and slipped him, heaving and big sliding, into the long sack that hung from his shoulders in the water.

Nick spread the mouth of the sack against the current and it filled, heavy with water. He held it up, the bottom in the stream, and the water poured out through the sides. Inside at the bottom was the big trout, alive in the water.

Nick moved downstream. The sack out ahead of him sunk heavy in the water, pulling from his shoulders.

It was getting hot, the sun hot on the back of his neck.

Nick had one good trout. He did not care about getting many trout. Now the stream was shallow and wide. There were trees along both banks. The trees of the left bank made short shadows on the current in the forenoon sun. Nick knew there were trout in each shadow. In the afternoon, after the sun had crossed toward the hills, the trout would be in the cool shadows on the other side of the stream.

The very biggest ones would lie up close to the bank. You could always pick them up there on the Black. When the sun was down they all moved out into the current. Just when the sun made the water blinding in the glare before it went down, you were liable to strike a big trout anywhere in the current. It was almost impossible to fish then, the surface of the water was blinding as a mirror in the sun. Of course, you could fish upstream, but in a stream like the Black, or this, you had to wallow against the current and in a deep place, the water piled up on you. It was no fun to fish upstream with this much current.

Nick moved along through the shallow stretch watching the banks for deep holes. A beech tree grew close beside the river, so that the branches hung down into the water. The stream went back in under the leaves. There were always trout in a place like that.

Nick did not care about fishing that hole. He was sure he would get hooked in the branches.

It looked deep though. He dropped the grasshopper so the current took it under water, back in under the overhanging branch. The line pulled hard and Nick struck. The trout threshed heavily, half out of water in the leaves and branches. The line was caught. Nick pulled hard and the trout was off. He reeled in and holding the hook in his hand, walked down the stream.

Ahead, close to the left bank, was a big log. Nick saw it was hollow; pointing up river the current entered it smoothly, only a little ripple spread each side of the log. The water was deepening. The top of the hollow log was gray and dry. It was partly in the shadow.

Nick took the cork out of the grasshopper bottle and a hopper clung to it. He picked him off, hooked him and tossed him out. He held the rod far out so that the hopper on the water moved into the current flowing into the hollow log. Nick lowered the rod and the hopper floated in. There was a heavy strike. Nick swung the rod against the pull. It felt as though he were hooked into the log itself, except for the live feeling.

He tried to force the fish out into the current. It came, heavily.

The line went slack and Nick thought the trout was gone. Then he saw him, very near, in the current, shaking his head, trying to get the hook out. His mouth was clamped shut. He was fighting the hook in the clear flowing current.

Looping in the line with his left hand, Nick swung the rod to make the line taut and tried to lead the trout toward the net, but he was gone, out of sight, the line pumping. Nick fought him against the current, letting him thump in the water against the spring of the rod. He shifted the rod to his left hand, worked the trout upstream, holding his weight, fighting on the rod, and then let him down into the net. He lifted him clear of the water, a heavy half circle in the net, the net dripping, unhooked him and slid him into the sack.

He spread the mouth of the sack and looked down in at the two big trout alive in the water.

Through the deepening water, Nick waded over to the hollow log. He took the sack off, over his head, the trout flopping as it came out of water, and hung it so the trout were deep in the water. Then he pulled himself up on the log and sat, the water from his trouser and boots running down into the stream. He laid his rod down, moved along to the shady end of the log and took the sandwiches out of his pocket. He dipped the sandwiches in the cold water. The current carried away the crumbs. He ate the sandwiches and dipped his hat full of water to drink, the water running out through his hat just ahead of his drinking.

It was cool in the shade, sitting on the log. He took a cigarette out and struck a match to light it. The match sunk into the gray wood, making a tiny furrow. Nick leaned over the side of the log, found a hard place and lit the match. He sat smoking and watching the river.

Ahead the river narrowed and went into a swamp. The river became smooth and deep and the swamp looked solid with cedar trees, their trunks close together, their branches solid. It would not be possible to walk through a swamp like that. The branches grew so low. You would have to keep almost level with the ground to move at all. You could not crash through the branches. That must be why the animals that lived in swamps were built the way they were, Nick thought.

He wished he had brought something to read. He felt like reading. He did not feel like going on into the swamp. He looked down the river. A big cedar slanted all the way across the stream. Beyond that the river went into the swamp.

Nick did not want to go in there now. He felt a reaction against deep wading with the water deepening up under his armpits, to hook big trout in places impossible to land them. In the swamp the banks were bare, the big cedars came together overhead, the sun did not come through, except in patches; in the fast deep water, in the half light, the fishing would be tragic. In the swamp fishing was a tragic adventure. Nick did not want it. He did not want to go down the stream any further today.

He took out his knife, opened it and stuck it in the log. Then he pulled up the sack, reached into it and brought out one of the trout. Holding him near the tail, hard to hold, alive, in his hand, he wacked him against the log. The trout quivered, rigid. Nick laid him on the log in the shade and broke the neck of the other fish the same way. He laid them side by side on the log. They were fine trout.

Nick cleaned them, slitting them from the vent to the tip of the jaw. All the insides and the gills and tongue came out in one piece. They were both males; long gray-white strips of milt, smooth and clean. All the insides clean and compact, coming out all together. Nick tossed the offal ashore for the minks to find.

He washed the trout in the stream. When he held them back up in the water they looked like live fish. Their color was not gone yet. He washed his hands and dried them on the log. Then he laid the trout on the sack spread out on the log, rolled them up in it, tied the bundle and put it in the landing net. His knife was still standing, blade stuck in the log. He cleaned it on the wood and put it in his pocket.

Nick stood up on the log, holding his rod, the landing net hanging heavy, then stepped into the water and splashed ashore. He climbed the bank and cut up into the woods, toward the high ground. He was going back to camp. He looked back. The river just showed through the trees. There were plenty of days coming when he could fish the swamp.

1924   1925, 1938

THE CAPITAL OF THE WORLD

MADRID is full of boys named Paco, which is the diminutive of the name Francisco, and there is a Madrid joke about a father who came to Madrid and inserted an advertisement in the personal columns of *El Liberal* which said: PACO MEET ME AT HOTEL MONTANA NOON TUESDAY ALL IS FORGIVEN PAPA and how a squadron of Guardia Civil[1] had to be called out to disperse the eight hundred young men who answered the advertisement. But this Paco, who waited on table at the Pension Luarca, had no father to forgive him, nor anything for the father to forgive. He had two older sisters who were chambermaids at the Luarca, who had gotten their place through coming from the same small village as a former Luarca chambermaid who had proven hardworking and honest and hence given her village and its products a good name; and these sisters had paid his way on the auto-bus to Madrid and gotten him his job as an apprentice waiter. He came from a village in a part of Extramadura[2] where conditions were incredibly primitive, food scarce, and comforts unknown and he had worked hard ever since he could remember.

He was a well built boy with very black, rather curly hair, good teeth and a skin that his sisters envied, and he had a ready and unpuzzled smile. He was fast on his feet and did his work well and he loved his sisters, who seemed beautiful and sophisticated; he loved Madrid, which was still an unbelievable

---

[1]Spanish: Civil Guard, the national police force.
[2]Rural region of western Spain, bordering on Portugal.

place, and he loved his work which, done under bright lights, with clean linen, the wearing of evening clothes, and abundant food in the kitchen, seemed romantically beautiful.

There were from eight to a dozen other people who lived at the Luarca and ate in the dining room but for Paco, the youngest of the three waiters who served at table, the only ones who really existed were the bull fighters.

Second-rate matadors[3] lived at that pension because the address in the Calle[4] San Jeronimo was good, the food was excellent and the room and board was cheap. It is necessary for a bull fighter to give the appearance, if not of prosperity, at least of respectability, since decorum and dignity rank above courage as the virtues most highly prized in Spain, and bull fighters stayed at the Luarca until their last pesetas[5] were gone. There is no record of any bull fighter having left the Luarca for a better or more expensive hotel; second-rate bull fighters never became first rate; but the descent from the Luarca was swift since any one could stay there who was making anything at all and a bill was never presented to a guest unasked until the woman who ran the place knew that the case was hopeless.

At this time there were three full matadors living at the Luarca as well as two very good picadors,[6] and one excellent banderillero.[7] The Luarca was luxury for the picadors and the banderilleros who, with their families in Seville,[8] required lodging in Madrid during the Spring season; but they were well paid and in the fixed employ of fighters who were heavily contracted during the coming season and the three of these subalterns would probably make much more apiece than any of the three matadors. Of the three matadors one was ill and trying to conceal it; one had passed his short vogue as a novelty; and the third was a coward.

The coward had at one time, until he had received a peculiarly atrocious horn wound in the lower abdomen at the start of his first season as a full matador, been exceptionally brave and remarkably skillful and he still had many of the hearty mannerisms of his days of success. He was jovial to excess and laughed constantly with and without provocation. He had, when successful, been very addicted to practical jokes but he had given them up now. They took an assurance that he did not feel. This matador had an intelligent, very open face and he carried himself with much style.

The matador who was ill was careful never to show it and was meticulous about eating a little of all the dishes that were presented at the table. He had a great many handkerchiefs which he laundered himself in his room and, lately, he had been selling his fighting suits. He had sold one, cheaply, before Christmas and another in the first week of April. They had been very expensive suits, had always been well kept and he had one more. Before he had become ill he had been a very promising, even a sensational, fighter and, while he himself could not read, he had clippings which said that in his debut in Madrid he had been better than Belmonte.[9] He ate alone at a small table and looked up very little.

The matador who had once been a novelty was very short and brown and

---

[3]The principal bullfighters, who kill the bull.
[4]Spanish: Street.
[5]Spanish coins of small value.
[6]Bullfighters who attack the bull with a lance, cutting and weakening its neck muscles.
[7]Bullfighter who places barbed darts (banderillos) in the bull's neck to enrage and further weaken him.
[8]City in southern Spain.
[9]Juan Belmonte (1892–1962), matador famous for his capework and for standing dangerously close to the bull's horns.

very dignified. He also ate alone at a separate table and he smiled very rarely
and never laughed. He came from Valladolid,[10] where the people are extremely
serious, and he was a capable matador; but his style had become old-fashioned
before he had ever succeeded in endearing himself to the public through his
virtues, which were courage and a calm capability, and his name on a poster
would draw no one to a bull ring. His novelty had been that he was so short that
he could barely see over the bull's withers,[11] but there were other short fighters,
and he had never succeeded in imposing himself on the public's fancy.

Of the picadors one was a thin, hawk-faced, gray-haired man, lightly built but
with legs and arms like iron, who always wore cattle-men's boots under his
trousers, drank too much every evening and gazed amorously at any woman in
the pension. The other was huge, dark, brown-faced, good-looking, with black
hair like an Indian and enormous hands. Both were great picadors although
the first was reputed to have lost much of his ability through drink and dissipation, and the second was said to be too headstrong and quarrelsome to stay
with any matador more than a single season.

The banderillero was middle-aged, gray, cat-quick in spite of his years and,
sitting at the table he looked a moderately prosperous business man. His legs
were still good for this season, and when they should go he was intelligent and
experienced enough to keep regularly employed for a long time. The difference
would be that when his speed of foot would be gone he would always be
frightened where now he was assured and calm in the ring and out of it.

On this evening every one had left the dining room except the hawk-faced
picador who drank too much, the birthmarked-faced auctioneer of watches at
the fairs and festivals of Spain, who also drank too much, and two priests from
Galicia[12] who were sitting at a corner table and drinking if not too much certainly
enough. At that time wine was included in the price of the room and board at
the Luarca and the waiters had just brought fresh bottles of Valdepeñas[13] to
the tables of the auctioneer, then to the picador and, finally, to the two priests.

The three waiters stood at the end of the room. It was the rule of the house
that they should all remain on duty until the diners whose tables they were
responsible for should all have left, but the one who served the table of the two
priests had an appointment to go to an Anarcho-Syndicalist[14] meeting and Paco
had agreed to take over his table for him.

Upstairs the matador who was ill was lying face down on his bed alone. The
matador who was no longer a novelty was sitting looking out of his window
preparatory to walking out to the café. The matador who was a coward had the
older sister of Paco in his room with him and was trying to get her to do something
which she was laughingly refusing to do. This matador was saying "Come on,
little savage."

"No," said the sister. "Why should I?"

"For a favor."

"You've eaten and now you want me for dessert."

"Just once. What harm can it do?"

"Leave me alone. Leave me alone, I tell you."

"It is a very little thing to do."

"Leave me alone, I tell you."

[10]Province of northwestern Spain.
[11]The top of an animal's shoulders.
[12]Region of northwest Spain, bordering on the Atlantic.
[13]A favorite wine in the cafés of Madrid, from Valdepeñas, a city 135 miles south of Madrid.
[14]Revolutionary anarchist labor organization.

Down in the dining room the tallest of the waiters, who was overdue at the meeting, said "Look at those black pigs drink."

"That's no way to speak," said the second waiter. "They are decent clients. They do not drink too much."

"For me it is a good way to speak," said the tall one. "There are the two curses of Spain, the bulls and the priests."

"Certainly not the individual bull and the individual priest," said the second waiter.

"Yes," said the tall waiter. "Only through the individual can you attack the class. It is necessary to kill the individual bull and the individual priest. All of them. Then there are no more."

"Save it for the meeting," said the other waiter.

"Look at the barbarity of Madrid," said the tall waiter. "It is now half-past eleven o'clock and these are still guzzling."

"They only started to eat at ten," said the other waiter. "As you know there are many dishes. That wine is cheap and these have paid for it. It is not a strong wine."

"How can there be solidarity of workers with fools like you?" asked the tall waiter.

"Look," said the second waiter who was a man of fifty. "I have worked all my life. In all that remains of my life I must work. I have no complaints against work. To work is normal."

"Yes, but the lack of work kills."

"I have always worked," said the older waiter. "Go on to the meeting. There is no necessity to stay."

"You are a good comrade," said the tall waiter. "But you lack all ideology."

"*Mejor si me falta eso que el otro,*" said the older waiter (meaning it is better to lack that than work). "Go on to the *mitin.*"

Paco had said nothing. He did not yet understand politics but it always gave him a thrill to hear the tall waiter speak of the necessity for killing the priests and the Guardia Civil. The tall waiter represented to him revolution and revolution also was romantic. He himself would like to be a good catholic, a revolutionary, and have a steady job like this, while, at the same time, being a bullfighter.

"Go on to the meeting, Ignacio," he said. "I will respond for your work."

"The two of us," said the older waiter.

"There isn't enough for one," said Paco. "Go on to the meeting."

"*Pues, me voy,*"[15] said the tall waiter. "And thanks."

In the meantime, upstairs, the sister of Paco had gotten out of the embrace of the matador as skillfully as a wrestler breaking a hold and said, now angry, "These are the hungry people. A failed bullfighter. With your ton-load of fear. If you have so much of that, use it in the ring."

"That is the way a whore talks."

"A whore is also a woman, but I am not a whore."

"You'll be one."

"Not through you."

"Leave me," said the matador who, now, repulsed and refused, felt the nakedness of his cowardice returning.

"Leave you? What hasn't left you?" said the sister. "Don't you want me to make up the bed? I'm paid to do that."

---

[15]Spanish: "Well, I'm leaving."

"Leave me," said the matador, his broad good-looking face wrinkled into a contortion that was like crying. "You whore. You dirty little whore."

"Matador," she said, shutting the door. "My matador."

Inside the room the matador sat on the bed. His face still had the contortion which, in the ring, he made into a constant smile which frightened those people in the first rows of seats who knew what they were watching. "And this," he was saying aloud. "And this. And this."

He could remember when he had been good and it had only been three years before. He could remember the weight of the heavy gold-brocaded fighting jacket on his shoulders on that hot afternoon in May when his voice had still been the same in the ring as in the café, and how he sighted along the point-dipping blade at the place in the top of the shoulders where it was dusty in the short-haired black hump of muscle above the wide, wood-knocking, splintered-tipped horns that lowered as he went in to kill, and how the sword pushed in as easy as into a mound of stiff butter with the palm of his hand pushing the pommel, his left arm crossed low, his left shoulder forward, his weight on his left leg, and then his weight wasn't on his leg. His weight was on his lower belly and as the bull raised his head the horn was out of sight in him and he swung over on it twice before they pulled him off it. So now when he went in to kill, and it was seldom, he could not look at the horns and what did any whore know about what he went through before he fought? And what had they been through that laughed at him? They were all whores and they knew what they could do with it.

Down in the dining room the picador sat looking at the priests. If there were women in the room he stared at them. If there were no women he would stare with enjoyment at a foreigner, *un inglés*,[16] but lacking women or strangers, he now stared with enjoyment and insolence at the two priests. While he stared the birth-marked auctioneer rose and folding his napkin went out, leaving over half the wine in the last bottle he had ordered. If his accounts had been paid up at the Luarca he would have finished the bottle.

The two priests did not stare back at the picador. One of them was saying, "It is ten days since I have been here waiting to see him and all day I sit in the ante-chamber and he will not receive me."

"What is there to do?"

"Nothing. What can one do? One cannot go against authority."

"I have been here for two weeks and nothing. I wait and they will not see me."

"We are from the abandoned country. When the money runs out we can return."

"To the abandoned country. What does Madrid care about Galicia? We are a poor province."

"One understands the action of our brother Basilio."

"Still I have no real confidence in the integrity of Basilio Alvarez."

"Madrid is where one learns to understand. Madrid kills Spain."

"If they would simply see one and refuse."

"No. You must be broken and worn out by waiting."

"Well, we shall see. I can wait as well as another."

At this moment the picador got to his feet, walked over to the priests' table and stood, gray-headed and hawk-faced, staring at them and smiling.

"A torero,"[17] said one priest to the other.

[16]Spanish: an Englishman.
[17]Spanish: bullfighter.

"And a good one," said the picador and walked out of the dining room, gray-jacketed, trim-waisted, bow-legged, in tight breeches over his high-heeled cattleman's boots that clicked on the floor as he swaggered quite steadily, smiling to himself. He lived in a small, tight, professional world of personal efficiency, nightly alcoholic triumph, and insolence. Now he lit a cigar and tilting his hat at an angle in the hallway went out to the café.

The priests left immediately after the picador, hurriedly conscious of being the last people in the dining room, and there was no one in the room now but Paco and the middle-aged waiter. They cleared the tables and carried the bottles into the kitchen.

In the kitchen was the boy who washed the dishes. He was three years older than Paco and was very cynical and bitter.

"Take this," the middle-aged waiter said, and poured out a glass of the Valdepeñas and handed it to him.

"Why not?" the boy took the glass.

"Tu,[18] Paco?" the older waiter asked.

"Thank you," said Paco. The three of them drank.

"I will be going," said the middle-aged waiter.

"Good night," they told him.

He went out and they were alone. Paco took a napkin one of the priests had used and standing straight, his heels planted, lowered the napkin and with head following the movement, swung his arms in the motion of a slow sweeping veronica.[19] He turned and advancing his right foot slightly, made the second pass, gained a little terrain on the imaginary bull and made a third pass, slow, perfectly timed and suave, then gathered the napkin to his waist and swung his hips away from the bull in a media-veronica.[20]

The dishwasher, whose name was Enrique, watched him critically and sneeringly.

"How is the bull?" he said.

"Very brave," said Paco. "Look."

Standing slim and straight he made four more perfect passes, smooth, elegant and graceful.

"And the bull?" asked Enrique standing against the sink, holding his wine glass and wearing his apron.

"Still has lots of gas," said Paco.

"You make me sick," said Enrique.

"Why?"

"Look."

Enrique removed his apron and citing the imaginary bull he sculptured four perfect, languid gypsy veronicas and ended up with a rebolera that made the apron swing in a stiff arc past the bull's nose as he walked away from him.

"Look at that," he said, "And I wash dishes."

"Why?"

"Fear," said Enrique. "*Miedo.* The same fear you would have in a ring with a bull."

"No," said Paco. "I wouldn't be afraid."

"*Leche!*"[21] said Enrique. "Every one is afraid. But a torero can control his fear

[18]Spanish: You.
[19]A pass in bullfighting, receiving the charge of the bull with the cape extended in both hands.
[20]A half-veronica, usually following a series of veronicas, in which the matador draws the cape around his hips as the bull passes.
[21]Spanish literally: "Milk"—often used as an expletive to express contemptuous disbelief.

so that he can work the bull. I went in an amateur fight and I was so afraid I couldn't keep from running. Every one thought it was very funny. So would you be afraid. If it wasn't for fear every bootblack in Spain would be a bullfighter. You, a country boy, would be frightened worse than I was."

"No," said Paco.

He had done it too many times in his imagination. Too many times he had seen the horns, seen the bull's wet muzzle, the ear twitching, then the head go down and the charge, the hoofs thudding and the hot bull pass him as he swung the cape, to re-charge as he swung the cape again, then again, and again, and again, to end winding the bull around him in his great media-veronica, and walk swingingly away, with bull hairs caught in the gold ornaments of his jacket from the close passes; the bull standing hypnotized and the crowd applauding. No, he would not be afraid. Others, yes. Not he. He knew he would not be afraid. Even if he ever was afraid he knew that he could do it anyway. He had confidence. "I wouldn't be afraid," he said.

Enrique said, *"Leche,"* again.

Then he said, "If we should try it?"

"How?"

"Look," said Enrique. "You think of the bull but you do not think of the horns. The bull has such force that the horns rip like a knife, they stab like a bayonet, and they kill like a club. Look," he opened a table drawer and took out two meat knives. "I will bind these to the legs of a chair. Then I will play bull for you with the chair held before my head. The knives are the horns. If you make those passes then they mean something."

"Lend me your apron," said Paco. "We'll do it in the dining room."

"No," said Enrique, suddenly not bitter. "Don't do it, Paco."

"Yes," said Paco. "I'm not afraid."

"You will be when you see the knives come."

"We'll see," said Paco. "Give me the apron."

At this time, while Enrique was binding the two heavy-bladed razor-sharp meat knives fast to the legs of the chair with two soiled napkins holding the half of each knife, wrapping them tight and then knotting them, the two chambermaids, Paco's sisters, were on their way to the cinema to see Greta Garbo in "Anna Christie."[22] Of the two priests, one was sitting in his underwear reading his breviary[23] and the other was wearing a nightshirt and saying the rosary. All the bullfighters except the one who was ill had made their evening appearance at the Café Fornos, where the big, dark-haired picador was playing billiards, the short, serious matador was sitting at a crowded table before a coffee and milk, along with the middle-aged banderillero and other serious workmen.

The drinking, gray-headed picador was sitting with a glass of cazalas brandy[24] before him staring with pleasure at a table where the matador whose courage was gone sat with another matador who had renounced the sword to become a banderillero again, and two very houseworn-looking prostitutes.

The auctioneer stood on the street corner talking with friends. The tall waiter was at the Anarcho-Syndicalist meeting waiting for an opportunity to speak. The middle-aged waiter was seated on the terrace of the Café Alvarez drinking a small beer. The woman who owned the Luarca was already asleep in her bed, where she lay on her back with the bolster between her legs; big, fat, honest, clean, easy-going, very religious and never having ceased to miss or pray daily

---

[22]Romantic motion picture (1930) starring Greta Garbo (1905–   ).
[23]A book of religious prayers, hymns, songs.
[24]Brandy flavored with anis seed.

for her husband, dead, now, twenty years. In his room, alone, the matador who was ill lay face down on his bed with his mouth against a handkerchief.

Now, in the deserted dining room, Enrique tied the last knot in the napkins that bound the knives to the chair legs and lifted the chair. He pointed the legs with the knives on them forward and held the chair over his head with the two knives pointing straight ahead, one on each side of his head.

"It's heavy," he said. "Look, Paco. It is very dangerous. Don't do it." He was sweating.

Paco stood facing him, holding the apron spread, holding a fold of it bunched in each hand, thumbs up, first finger down, spread to catch the eye of the bull.

"Charge straight," he said. "Turn like a bull. Charge as many times as you want."

"How will you know when to cut the pass?" asked Enrique. "It's better to do three and then a media."

"All right," said Paco. "But come straight. Huh, torito![25] Come on, little bull!"

Running with head down Enrique came toward him and Paco swung the apron just ahead of the knife blade as it passed close in front of his belly and as it went by it was, to him, the real horn, white-tipped, black, smooth, and as Enrique passed him and turned to rush again it was the hot, blood-flanked mass of the bull that thudded by, then turned like a cat and came again as he swung the cape slowly. Then the bull turned and came again and, as he watched the onrushing point, he stepped his left foot two inches too far forward and the knife did not pass, but had slipped in as easily as into a wineskin and there was a hot scalding rush above and around the sudden inner rigidity of steel and Enrique shouting. "Ay! Ay! Let me get it out! Let me get it out!" and Paco slipped forward on the chair, the apron cape still held, Enrique pulling on the chair as the knife turned in him, in him, Paco.

The knife was out now and he sat on the floor in the widening warm pool.

"Put the napkin over it. Hold it!" said Enrique. "Hold it tight. I will run for the doctor. You must hold in the hemorrhage."

"There should be a rubber cup,"[26] said Paco. He had seen that used in the ring.

"I came straight," said Enrique, crying. "All I wanted was to show the danger."

"Don't worry," said Paco, his voice sounding far away. "But bring the doctor."

In the ring they lifted you and carried you, running with you, to the operating room. If the femoral artery emptied itself before you reached there they called the priest.

"Advise one of the priests," said Paco, holding the napkin tight against his lower abdomen. He could not believe that this had happened to him.

But Enrique was running down the Carrera San Jeromino to the all-night first-aid station and Paco was alone, first sitting up, then huddled over, then slumped on the floor, until it was over, feeling his life go out of him as dirty water empties from a bathtub when the plug is drawn. He was frightened and he felt faint and he tried to say an act of contrition and he remembered how it started but before he had said, as fast as he could, "Oh, my God, I am heartily sorry for having offended Thee who art worthy of all my love and I firmly resolve . . . ," he felt too faint and he was lying face down on the floor and it was over very quickly. A severed femoral artery empties itself faster than you can believe.

As the doctor from the first-aid station came up the stairs accompanied by a

[25]Little bull!
[26]Applied with pressure to the wound, to stop the flow of blood, when a bullfighter is gored.

policeman who held on to Enrique by the arm, the two sisters of Paco were still in the moving-picture palace of the Gran Via, where they were intensely disappointed in the Garbo film, which showed the great star in miserable low surroundings when they had been accustomed to see her surrounded by great luxury and brilliance. The audience disliked the film thoroughly and were protesting by whistling and stamping their feet. All the other people from the hotel were doing almost what they had been doing when the accident happened, except that the two priests had finished their devotions and were preparing for sleep, and the gray-haired picador had moved his drink over to the table with the two houseworn prostitutes. A little later he went out of the café with one of them. It was the one for whom the matador who had lost his nerve had been buying drinks.

The boy Paco had never known about any of this nor about what all these people would be doing on the next day and on other days to come. He had no idea how they really lived nor how they ended. He did not even realize they ended. He died, as the Spanish phrase has it, full of illusions. He had not had time in his life to lose any of them, nor even, at the end, to complete an act of contrition.

He had not even had time to be disappointed in the Garbo picture which disappointed all Madrid for a week.

1936   1936, 1938

THE SHORT HAPPY LIFE OF
FRANCIS MACOMBER

It was now lunch time and they were all sitting under the double green fly of the dining tent pretending that nothing had happened.

"Will you have lime juice or lemon squash?" Macomber asked.

"I'll have a gimlet,"[1] Robert Wilson told him.

"I'll have a gimlet too. I need something," Macomber's wife said.

"I suppose it's the thing to do," Macomber agreed. "Tell him to make three gimlets."

The mess boy had started them already, lifting the bottles out of the canvas cooling bags that sweated wet in the wind that blew through the trees that shaded the tents.

"What had I ought to give them?" Macomber asked.

"A quid[2] would be plenty," Wilson told him. "You don't want to spoil them."

"Will the headman distribute it?"

"Absolutely."

Francis Macomber had, half an hour before, been carried to his tent from the edge of the camp in triumph on the arms and shoulders of the cook, the personal boys, the skinner and the porters. The gun-bearers had taken no part in the demonstration. When the native boys put him down at the door of his tent, he had shaken all their hands, received their congratulations, and then gone into the tent and sat on the bed until his wife came in. She did not speak to him when she came in and he left the tent at once to wash his face and hands in the portable wash basin outside and go over to the dining tent to sit in a comfortable canvas chair in the breeze and the shade.

[1] A cocktail made of gin and lime juice.
[2] A pound in English money.

"You've got your lion," Robert Wilson said to him, "and a damned fine one too."

Mrs. Macomber looked at Wilson quickly. She was an extremely handsome and well-kept woman of the beauty and social position which had, five years before, commanded five thousand dollars as the price of endorsing, with photographs, a beauty product which she had never used. She had been married to Francis Macomber for eleven years.

"He is a good lion, isn't he?" Macomber said. His wife looked at him now. She looked at both these men as though she had never seen them before.

One, Wilson, the white hunter, she knew she had never truly seen before. He was about middle height with sandy hair, a stubby mustache, a very red face and extremely cold blue eyes with faint white wrinkles at the corners that grooved merrily when he smiled. He smiled at her now and she looked away from his face at the way his shoulders sloped in the loose tunic he wore with the four big cartridges held in loops where the left breast pocket should have been, at his big brown hands, his old slacks, his very dirty boots and back to his red face again. She noticed where the baked red of his face stopped in a white line that marked the circle left by his Stetson hat that hung now from one of the pegs of the tent pole.

"Well, here's to the lion," Robert Wilson said. He smiled at her again and, not smiling, she looked curiously at her husband.

Francis Macomber was very tall, very well built if you did not mind that length of bone, dark, his hair cropped like an oarsman,[3] rather thin-lipped, and was considered handsome. He was dressed in the same sort of safari clothes that Wilson wore except that his were new, he was thirty-five years old, kept himself very fit, was good at court games, had a number of big-game fishing records, and had just shown himself, very publicly, to be a coward.

"Here's to the lion," he said. "I can't ever thank you for what you did."

Margaret, his wife, looked away from him and back to Wilson.

"Let's not talk about the lion," she said.

Wilson looked over at her without smiling and now she smiled at him.

"It's been a very strange day," she said. "Hadn't you ought to put your hat on even under the canvas at noon? You told me that, you know."

"Might put it on," said Wilson.

"You know you have a very red face, Mr. Wilson," she told him and smiled again.

"Drink," said Wilson.

"I don't think so," she said. "Francis drinks a great deal, but his face is never red."

"It's red today," Macomber tried a joke.

"No," said Margaret. "It's mine that's red today. But Mr. Wilson's is always red."

"Must be racial," said Wilson. "I say, you wouldn't like to drop my beauty as a topic, would you?"

"I've just started on it."

"Let's chuck it," said Wilson.

"Conversation is going to be so difficult," Margaret said.

"Don't be silly, Margot," her husband said.

"No difficulty," Wilson said. "Got a damn fine lion."

Margot looked at them both and they both saw that she was going to cry.

[3]I.e., a crew cut.

Wilson had seen it coming for a long time and he dreaded it. Macomber was past dreading it.

"I wish it hadn't happened. Oh, I wish it hadn't happened," she said and started for her tent. She made no noise of crying but they could see that her shoulders were shaking under the rose-colored, sun-proofed shirt she wore.

"Women upset," said Wilson to the tall man. "Amounts to nothing. Strain on the nerves and one thing'n another."

"No," said Macomber. "I suppose that I rate that for the rest of my life now."

"Nonsense. Let's have a spot of the giant killer,"[4] said Wilson. "Forget the whole thing. Nothing to it anyway."

"We might try," said Macomber. "I won't forget what you did for me though."

"Nothing," said Wilson. "All nonsense."

So they sat there in the shade where the camp was pitched under some wide-topped acacia trees with a boulder-strewn cliff behind them, and a stretch of grass that ran to the bank of a boulder-filled stream in front with a forest beyond it, and drank their just-cool lime drinks and avoided one another's eyes while the boys set the table for lunch. Wilson could tell that the boys all knew about it now and when he saw Macomber's personal boy looking curiously at his master while he was putting dishes on the table he snapped at him in Swahili. The boy turned away with his face blank.

"What were you telling him?" Macomber asked.

"Nothing. Told him to look alive or I'd see he got about fifteen of the best."

"What's that? Lashes?"

"It's quite illegal," Wilson said. "You're supposed to fine them."

"Do you still have them whipped?"

"Oh, yes. They could raise a row if they chose to complain. But they don't. They prefer it to the fines."

"How strange!" said Macomber.

"Not strange, really," Wilson said. "Which would you rather do? Take a good birching or lose your pay?"

Then he felt embarrassed at asking it and before Macomber could answer he went on, "We all take a beating every day, you know, one way or another."

This was no better. "Good God," he thought. "I am a diplomat, aren't I?"

"Yes, we take a beating," said Macomber, still not looking at him. "I'm awfully sorry about that lion business. It doesn't have to go any further, does it? I mean no one will hear about it, will they?"

"You mean will I tell it at the Mathaiga Club?" Wilson looked at him now coldly. He had not expected this. So he's a bloody four-letter man as well as a bloody coward, he thought. I rather liked him too until today. But how is one to know about an American?

"No," said Wilson. "I'm a professional hunter. We never talk about our clients. You can be quite easy on that. It's supposed to be bad form to ask us not to talk though."

He had decided now that to break would be much easier. He would eat, then, by himself and could read a book with his meals. They would eat by themselves. He would see them through the safari on a very formal basis—what was it the French called it? Distinguished consideration—and it would be a damn sight easier than having to go through this emotional trash. He'd insult him and make a good clean break. Then he could read a book with his meals and he'd still be drinking their whisky. That was the phrase for it when a safari went bad. You

[4]Whiskey.

ran into another white hunter and you asked, "How is everything going?" and he answered, "Oh, I'm still drinking their whisky," and you knew everything had gone to pot.

"I'm sorry," Macomber said and looked at him with his American face that would stay adolescent until it became middle-aged, and Wilson noted his crew-cropped hair, fine eyes only faintly shifty, good nose, thin lips and handsome jaw. "I'm sorry I didn't realize that. There are lots of things I don't know."

So what could he do, Wilson thought. He was all ready to break it off quickly and neatly and here the beggar was apologizing after he had just insulted him. He made one more attempt. "Don't worry about me talking," he said. "I have a living to make. You know in Africa no woman ever misses her lion and no white man ever bolts."

"I bolted like a rabbit," Macomber said.

Now what in hell were you going to do about a man who talked like that, Wilson wondered.

Wilson looked at Macomber with his flat, blue, machine-gunner's eyes and the other smiled back at him. He had a pleasant smile if you did not notice how his eyes showed when he was hurt.

"Maybe I can fix it up on buffalo," he said. "We're after them next, aren't we?"

"In the morning if you like," Wilson told him. Perhaps he had been wrong. This was certainly the way to take it. You most certainly could not tell a damned thing about an American. He was all for Macomber again. If you could forget the morning. But, of course, you couldn't. The morning had been about as bad as they come.

"Here comes the Memsahib,"[5] he said. She was walking over from her tent looking refreshed and cheerful and quite lovely. She had a very perfect oval face, so perfect that you expected her to be stupid. But she wasn't stupid. Wilson thought, no, not stupid.

"How is the beautiful red-faced Mr. Wilson? Are you feeling better, Francis, my pearl?"

"Oh, much," said Macomber.

"I've dropped the whole thing," she said, sitting down at the table. "What importance is there to whether Francis is any good at killing lions? That's not his trade. That's Mr. Wilson's trade. Mr. Wilson is really very impressive killing anything. You do kill anything, don't you?"

"Oh, anything," said Wilson. "Simply anything." They are, he thought, the hardest in the world; the hardest, the cruelest, the most predatory and the most attractive and their men have softened or gone to pieces nervously as they have hardened. Or is it that they pick men they can handle? They can't know that much at the age they marry, he thought. He was grateful that he had gone through his education on American women before now because this was a very attractive one.

"We're going after buff[6] in the morning," he told her.

"I'm coming," she said.

"No, you're not."

"Oh, yes, I am. Mayn't I Francis?"

"Why not stay in camp?"

"Not for anything," she said. "I wouldn't miss something like today for anything."

---

[5]A term of address used by natives in referring to white women.   [6]Buffalo.

When she left, Wilson was thinking, when she went off to cry, she seemed a hell of a fine woman. She seemed to understand, to realize, to be hurt for him and for herself and to know how things really stood. She is away for twenty minutes and now she is back, simply enamelled in that American female cruelty. They are the damnedest women. Really the damnedest.

"We'll put on another show for you tomorrow," Francis Macomber said.

"You're not coming," Wilson said.

"You're very mistaken," she told him. "And I want *so* to see you perform again. You were lovely this morning. That is if blowing things' heads off is lovely."

"Here's the lunch," said Wilson. "You're very merry, aren't you?"

"Why not? I didn't come out here to be dull."

"Well, it hasn't been dull," Wilson said. He could see the boulders in the river and the high bank beyond with the trees and he remembered the morning.

"Oh, no," she said. "It's been charming. And tomorrow. You don't know how I look forward to tomorrow."

"That's eland he's offering you," Wilson said.

"They're big cowy things that jump like hares, aren't they?"

"I suppose that describes them," Wilson said.

"It's very good meat," Macomber said.

"Did you shoot it, Francis?" she asked.

"Yes."

"They're not dangerous, are they?"

"Only if they fall on you," Wilson told her.

"I'm so glad."

"Why not let up on the bitchery just a little, Margot," Macomber said, cutting the eland steak and putting some mashed potato, gravy and carrot on the down-turned fork that tined through the piece of meat.

"I suppose I could," she said, "since you put it so prettily."

"Tonight we'll have champagne for the lion," Wilson said. "It's a bit too hot at noon."

"Oh, the lion," Margot said. "I'd forgotten the lion!"

So, Robert Wilson thought to himself, she *is* giving him a ride, isn't she? Or do you suppose that's her idea of putting up a good show? How should a woman act when she discovers her husband is a bloody coward? She's damn cruel but they're all cruel. They govern, of course, and to govern one has to be cruel sometimes. Still, I've seen enough of their damn terrorism.

"Have some more eland," he said to her politely.

That afternoon, late, Wilson and Macomber went out in the motor car with the native driver and the two gun-bearers. Mrs. Macomber stayed in the camp. It was too hot to go out, she said, and she was going with them in the early morning. As they drove off Wilson saw her standing under the big tree, looking pretty rather than beautiful in her faintly rosy khaki, her dark hair drawn back off her forehead and gathered in a knot low on her neck, her face as fresh, he thought, as though she were in England. She waved to them as the car went off through the swale of high grass and curved through the trees into the small hills of orchard bush.

In the orchard bush they found a herd of impala, and leaving the car they stalked one old ram with long, wide-spread horns and Macomber killed it with a very creditable shot that knocked the buck down at a good two hundred yards and sent the herd off bounding wildly and leaping over one another's backs in

long, leg-drawn-up leaps as unbelievable and as floating as those one makes
sometimes in dreams.

"That was a good shot," Wilson said. "They're a small target."

"Is it a worth-while head?" Macomber asked.

"It's excellent," Wilson told him. "You shoot like that and you'll have no
trouble."

"Do you think we'll find buffalo tomorrow?"

"There's a good chance of it. They feed out early in the morning and with
luck we may catch them in the open."

"I'd like to clear away that lion business," Macomber said. "It's not very pleasant
to have your wife see you do something like that."

I should think it would be even more unpleasant to do it, Wilson thought,
wife or no wife, or to talk about it having done it. But he said, "I wouldn't think
about that any more. Any one could be upset by his first lion. That's all over."

But that night after dinner and a whisky and soda by the fire before going to
bed, as Francis Macomber lay on his cot with the mosquito bar over him and
listened to the night noises it was not all over. It was neither all over nor was it
beginning. It was there exactly as it happened with some parts of it indelibly
emphasized and he was miserably ashamed at it. But more than shame he felt
cold, hollow fear in him. The fear was still there like a cold slimy hollow in all
the emptiness where once his confidence had been and it made him feel sick. It
was still there with him now.

It had started the night before when he had wakened and heard the lion
roaring somewhere up along the river. It was a deep sound and at the end there
were sort of coughing grunts that made him seem just outside the tent, and
when Francis Macomber woke in the night to hear it he was afraid. He could
hear his wife breathing quietly, asleep. There was no one to tell he was afraid,
nor to be afraid with him, and, lying alone, he did not know the Somali[7] proverb
that says a brave man is always frightened three times by a lion; when he first
sees his track, when he first hears him roar and when he first confronts him.
Then while they were eating breakfast by lantern light out in the dining tent,
before the sun was up, the lion roared again and Francis thought he was just at
the edge of camp.

"Sounds like an old-timer," Robert Wilson said, looking up from his kippers
and coffee. "Listen to him cough."

"Is he very close?"

"A mile or so up the stream."

"Will we see him?"

"We'll have a look."

"Does his roaring carry that far? It sounds as though he were right in camp."

"Carries a hell of a long way," said Robert Wilson. "It's strange the way it
carries. Hope he's a shootable cat. The boys said there was a very big one out
here."

"If I get a shot, where should I hit him," Macomber asked, "to stop him?"

"In the shoulders," Wilson said. "In the neck if you can make it. Shoot for
bone. Break him down."

"I hope I can place it properly," Macomber said.

"You shoot very well," Wilson told him. "Take your time. Make sure of him.
The first one in is the one that counts."

[7]Of Somalia (formerly Somaliland), in the Horn (the extreme eastern tip) of Africa.

"What range will it be?"

"Can't tell. Lion has something to say about that. Won't shoot unless it's close enough so you can make sure."

"At under a hundred yards?" Macomber asked.

Wilson looked at him quickly.

"Hundred's about right. Might have to take him a bit under. Shouldn't chance a shot at much over that. A hundred's a decent range. You can hit him wherever you want at that. Here comes the Memsahib."

"Good morning," she said. "Are we going after the lion?"

"As soon as you deal with your breakfast," Wilson said. "How are you feeling?"

"Marvellous," she said. "I'm very excited."

"I'll just go and see that everything is ready," Wilson went off. As he left the lion roared again.

"Noisy beggar," Wilson said. "We'll put a stop to that."

"What's the matter, Francis?" his wife asked him.

"Nothing," Macomber said.

"Yes, there is," she said. "What are you upset about?"

"Nothing," he said.

"Tell me," she looked at him. "Don't you feel well?"

"It's that damned roaring," he said. "It's been going on all night, you know."

"Why didn't you wake me," she said. "I'd love to have heard it."

"I've got to kill the damned thing," Macomber said, miserably.

"Well, that's what you're out here for, isn't it?"

"Yes, But I'm nervous. Hearing the thing roar gets on my nerves."

"Well then, as Wilson said, kill him and stop his roaring."

"Yes, darling," said Francis Macomber "It sounds easy, doesn't it?"

"You're not afraid, are you?"

"Of course not. But I'm nervous from hearing him roar all night."

"You'll kill him marvellously," she said. "I know you will. I'm awfully anxious to see it."

"Finish your breakfast and we'll be starting."

"It's not light yet," she said. "This is a ridiculous hour."

Just then the lion roared in a deep-chested moaning, suddenly guttural, ascending vibration that seemed to shake the air and ended in a sigh and a heavy, deep-chested grunt.

"He sounds almost here," Macomber's wife said.

"My God," said Macomber. "I hate that damned noise."

"It's very impressive."

"Impressive. It's frightful."

Robert Wilson came up then carrying his short, ugly shockingly big-bored .505 Gibbs and grinning.

"Come on," he said. "Your gun-bearer has your Springfield and the big gun. Everything's in the car. Have you solids?"[8]

"Yes."

"I'm ready," Mrs. Macomber said.

"Must make him stop that racket," Wilson said. "You get in front. The Memsahib can sit back here with me."

They climbed into the motor car and, in the gray first daylight, moved off up the river through the trees. Macomber opened the breech of his rifle and saw he had metal-cased bullets, shut the bolt and put the rifle on safety. He saw his

---

[8]Solid bullets.

hand was trembling. He felt in his pocket for more cartridges and moved his fingers over the cartridges in the loops of his tunic front. He turned back to where Wilson sat in the rear seat of the doorless, box-bodied motor car beside his wife, them both grinning with excitement, and Wilson leaned forward and whispered,

"See the birds dropping. Means the old boy has left his kill."

On the far bank of the stream Macomber could see, above the trees, vultures circling and plummeting down.

"Chances are he'll come to drink along here," Wilson whispered. "Before he goes to lay up. Keep an eye out."

They were driving slowly along the high bank of the stream which here cut deeply to its boulder-filled bed, and they wound in and out through big trees as they drove. Macomber was watching the opposite bank when he felt Wilson take hold of his arm. The car stopped.

"There he is," he heard the whisper. "Ahead and to the right. Get out and take him. He's a marvellous lion."

Macomber saw the lion now. He was standing almost broadside, his great head up and turned toward them. The early morning breeze that blew toward them was just stirring his dark mane, and the lion looked huge, silhouetted on the rise of bank in the gray morning light, his shoulders heavy, his barrel of a body bulking smoothly.

"How far is he? asked Macomber, raising his rifle.

"About seventy-five. Get out and take him."

"Why not shoot from where I am?"

"You don't shoot them from cars," he heard Wilson saying in his ear. "Get out. He's not going to stay there all day."

Macomber stepped out of the curved opening at the side of the front seat, onto the step and down onto the ground. The lion still stood looking majestically and coolly toward this object that his eyes only showed in silhouette, bulking like some super-rhino. There was no man smell carried toward him and he watched the object, moving his great head a little from side to side. Then watching the object, not afraid, but hesitating before going down the bank to drink with such a thing opposite him, he saw a man figure detach itself from it and he turned his heavy head and swung away toward the cover of the trees as he heard a cracking crash and felt the slam of a .30-06 220-grain solid bullet that bit his flank and ripped in sudden hot scalding nausea through his stomach. He trotted, heavy, big-footed, swinging wounded full-bellied, through the trees toward the tall grass and cover, and the crash came again to go past him ripping the air apart. Then it crashed again and he felt the blow as it hit his lower ribs and ripped on through, blood sudden hot and frothy in his mouth, and he galloped toward the high grass where he could crouch and not be seen and make them bring the crashing thing close enough so he could make a rush and get the man that held it.

Macomber had not thought how the lion felt as he got out of the car. He only knew his hands were shaking and as he walked away from the car it was almost impossible for him to make his legs move. They were stiff in the thighs, but he could feel the muscles fluttering. He raised the rifle, sighted on the junction of the lion's head and shoulders and pulled the trigger. Nothing happened though he pulled until he thought his finger would break. Then he knew he had the safety on and as he lowered the rifle to move the safety over he moved another frozen pace forward, the lion seeing his silhouette now clear of the silhouette of the car, turned and started off at a trot, and, as Macomber fired, he heard a whunk that meant that the bullet was home; but the lion kept on going. Macomber shot again and every one saw the bullet throw a spout of dirt beyond the trotting lion. He shot again, remembering to lower his aim, and they all heard the bullet hit, and the lion went into a gallop and was in the tall grass before he had the bolt pushed forward.

Macomber stood there feeling sick at his stomach, his hands that held the Springfield still cocked, shaking, and his wife and Robert Wilson were standing by him. Beside him too were the two gun-bearers chattering in Wakamba.[9]

"I hit him," Macomber said. "I hit him twice."

"You gut-shot him and you hit him somewhere forward," Wilson said without enthusiasm. The gun-bearers looked very grave. They were silent now.

"You may have killed him," Wilson went on. "We'll have to wait a while before we go in to find out."

"What do you mean?"

"Let him get sick before we follow him up."

"Oh," said Macomber.

"He's a hell of a fine lion," Wilson said cheerfully. "He's gotten into a bad place though."

"Why is it bad?"

"Can't see him until you're on him."

"Oh," said Macomber.

"Come on," said Wilson. "The Memsahib can stay here in the car. We'll go to have a look at the blood spoor."[10]

"Stay here, Margot," Macomber said to his wife. His mouth was very dry and it was hard for him to talk.

"Why?" she asked.

"Wilson says to."

"We're going to have a look," Wilson said. "You stay here. You can see even better from here."

"All right."

Wilson spoke in Swahili to the driver. He nodded and said, "Yes, Bwana."[11]

Then they went down the steep bank and across the stream, climbing over and around the boulders and up the other bank, pulling up by some projecting roots, and along it until they found where the lion had been trotting when Macomber first shot. There was dark blood on the short grass that the gun-bearers pointed out with grass stems, and that ran away behind the river bank trees.

"What do we do?" asked Macomber.

"Not much choice," said Wilson. "We can't bring the car over. Bank's too steep. We'll let him stiffen up a bit and then you and I'll go in and have a look for him."

"Can't we set the grass on fire?" Macomber asked.

"Too green."

"Can't we send beaters?"

Wilson looked at him appraisingly. "Of course we can," he said. "But it's just a touch murderous. You see we know the lion's wounded. You can drive an unwounded lion—he'll move on ahead of a noise—but a wounded lion's going to charge. You can't see him until you're right on him. He'll make himself

---

[9]A tribal dialect.
[10]Tracks.   [11]Swahili: Master, Boss.

perfectly flat in cover you wouldn't think would hide a hare. You can't very well send boys in there to that sort of a show. Somebody bound to get mauled."

"What about the gun-bearers?"

"Oh, they'll go with us. It's their *shauri*.[12] You see, they signed on for it. They don't look too happy though, do they?"

"I don't want to go in there," said Macomber. It was out before he knew he'd said it.

"Neither do I," said Wilson very cheerily. "Really no choice though." Then, as an afterthought, he glanced at Macomber and saw suddenly how he was trembling and the pitiful look on his face.

"You don't have to go in, of course," he said. "That's what I'm hired for, you know. That's why I'm so expensive."

"You mean you'd go in by yourself? Why not leave him there?"

Robert Wilson, whose entire occupation had been with the lion and the problem he presented, and who had not been thinking about Macomber except to note that he was rather windy, suddenly felt as though he had opened the wrong door in a hotel and seen something shameful.

"What do you mean?"

"Why not just leave him?"

"You mean pretend to ourselves he hasn't been hit?"

"No. Just drop it."

"It isn't done."

"Why not?"

"For one thing, he's certain to be suffering. For another, some one else might run onto him."

"I see."

"But you don't have to have anything to do with it."

"I'd like to," Macomber said. "I'm just scared, you know."

"I'll go ahead when we go in," Wilson said, "with Kongoni tracking. You keep behind me and a little to one side. Chances are we'll hear him growl. If we see him we'll both shoot. Don't worry about anything. I'll keep you backed up. As a matter of fact, you know, perhaps you'd better not go. It might be much better. Why don't you go over and join the Memsahib while I just get it over with?"

"No, I want to go."

"All right," said Wilson. "But don't go in if you don't want to. This is my *shauri* now, you know."

"I want to go," said Macomber.

They sat under a tree and smoked.

"Want to go back and speak to the Memsahib while we're waiting?" Wilson asked.

"No."

"I'll just step back and tell her to be patient."

"Good," said Macomber. He sat there, sweating under his arms, his mouth dry, his stomach hollow feeling, wanting to find courage to tell Wilson to go on and finish off the lion without him. He could not know that Wilson was furious because he had not noticed the state he was in earlier and sent him back to his wife. While he sat there Wilson came up. "I have your big gun," he said. "Take it. We've given him time, I think. Come on."

Macomber took the big gun and Wilson said:

"Keep behind me about five yards to the right and do exactly as I tell you."

[12]Business, duty.

Then he spoke in Swahili to the two gun-bearers who looked the picture of gloom.

"Let's go," he said.

"Could I have a drink of water?" Macomber asked. Wilson spoke to the older gun-bearer, who wore a canteen on his belt, and the man unbuckled it, unscrewed the top and handed it to Macomber, who took it noticing how heavy it seemed and how hairy and shoddy the felt covering was in his hand. He raised it to drink and looked ahead at the high grass with the flat-topped trees behind it. A breeze was blowing toward them and the grass rippled gently in the wind. He looked at the gun-bearer and he could see the gun-bearer was suffering too with fear.

Thirty-five yards into the grass the big lion lay flattened out along the ground. His ears were back and his only movement was a slight twitching up and down of his long, black-tufted tail. He had turned at bay as soon as he had reached this cover and he was sick with the wound through his full belly, and weakening with the wound through his lungs that brought a thin foamy red to his mouth each time he breathed. His flanks were wet and hot and flies were on the little openings the solid bullets had made in his tawny hide, and his big yellow eyes, narrowed with hate, looked straight ahead, only blinking when the pain came as he breathed, and his claws dug in the soft baked earth. All of him, pain, sickness, hatred and all of his remaining strength, was tightened into an absolute concentration for a rush. He could hear the men talking and he waited, gathering all of himself into this preparation for a charge as soon as the men would come into the grass. As he heard their voices his tail stiffened to twitch up and down, and, as they came into the edge of the grass, he made a coughing grunt and charged.

Kongoni, the old gun-bearer, in the lead watching the blood spoor, Wilson watching the grass for any movement, his big gun ready, the second gun-bearer looking ahead and listening, Macomber close to Wilson, his rifle cocked, they had just moved into the grass when Macomber heard the blood-choked coughing grunt, and saw the swishing rush in the grass. The next thing he knew he was running; runing wildly, in panic in the open, running toward the stream.

He heard the *ca-ra-wong!* of Wilson's big rifle, and again in a second crashing *carawong!* and turning saw the lion, horrible-looking now, with half his head seeming to be gone, crawling toward Wilson in the edge of the tall grass while the red-faced man worked the bolt on the short ugly rifle and aimed carefully as another blasting *carawong!* came from the muzzle, and the crawling, heavy, yellow bulk of the lion stiffened and the huge, mutilated head slid forward and Macomber, standing by himself in the clearing where he had run, holding a loaded rifle, while two black men and a white man looked back at him in contempt, knew the lion was dead. He came toward Wilson, his tallness all seeming a naked reproach, and Wilson looked at him and said:

"Want to take pictures?"

"No," he said.

That was all any one had said until they reached the motor car. Then Wilson had said:

"Hell of a fine lion. Boys will skin him out. We might as well stay here in the shade."

Macomber's wife had not looked at him nor he at her and he had sat by her in the back seat with Wilson sitting in the front seat. Once he had reached over and taken his wife's hand without looking at her and she had removed her hand from his. Looking across the stream to where the gun-bearers were skinning out the lion he could see that she had been able to see the whole thing. While they sat there his wife had reached forward and put her hand on Wilson's shoulder. He turned and she had leaned forward over the low seat and kissed him on the mouth.

"Oh, I say," said, Wilson, going redder than his natural baked color.

"Mr. Robert Wilson," she said. "The beautiful red-faced Mr. Robert Wilson."

Then she sat down beside Macomber again and looked away across the stream to where the lion lay, with uplifed, white-muscled tendon-marked naked forearms, and white bloating belly, as the black men fleshed away the skin. Finally the gun-bearers brought the skin over, wet and heavy, and climbed in behind with it, rolling it up before they got in, and the motor car started. No one had said anything more until they were back in camp.

That was the story of the lion. Macomber did not know how the lion had felt before he started his rush, nor during it when the unbelievable smash of the .505 with a muzzle velocity of two tons had hit him in the mouth, nor what kept him coming after that, when the second ripping crash had smashed his hind quarters and he had come crawling on toward the crashing, blasting thing that had destroyed him. Wilson knew something about it and only expressed it by saying, "Damned fine lion," but Macomber did not know how Wilson felt about things either. He did not know how his wife felt except that she was through with him.

His wife had been through with him before but it never lasted. He was very wealthy, and would be much wealthier, and he knew she would not leave him ever now. That was one of the few things that he really knew. He knew about that, about motor cycles—that was earliest—about motor cars, about duck-shooting, about fishing, trout, salmon and big-sea, about sex in books, many books, too many books, about all court games, about dogs, not much about horses, about hanging on to his money, about most of the other things his world dealt in, and about his wife not leaving him. His wife had been a great beauty and she was still a great beauty in Africa, but she was not a great enough beauty any more at home to be able to leave him and better herself and she knew it and he knew it. She had missed the chance to leave him and he knew it. If he had been better with women she would probably have started to worry about him getting another new, beautiful wife; but she knew too much about him to worry about him either. Also, he had always had a great tolerance which seemed the nicest thing about him if it were not the most sinister.

All in all they were known as a comparatively happily married couple, one of those whose disruption is often rumored but never occurs, and as the society columnist put it, they were adding more than a spice of *adventure* to their much envied and ever-enduring *Romance* by a *Safari* in what was known as *Darkest Africa* until the Martin Johnsons[13] lighted it on so many silver screens where they were pursuing *Old Simba* the lion, the buffalo, *Tembo* the elephant and as well collecting specimens for the Museum of Natural History. This same columnist had reported them *on the verge* at least three times in the past and they had been. But they always made it up. They had a sound basis of union. Margot was too beautiful for Macomber to divorce her and Macomber had too much money for Margot ever to leave him.

It was now about three o'clock in the morning and Francis Macomber, who had been asleep a little while after he had stopped thinking about the lion, wakened and then slept again, woke suddenly, frightened in a dream of the

---

[13]Osa and Martin Johnson, African explorers and wildlife photographers.

bloody-headed lion standing over him, and listening while his heart pounded, he realized that his wife was not in the other cot in the tent. He lay awake with that knowledge for two hours.

At the end of that time his wife came into the tent, lifted her mosquito bar and crawled cozily into bed.

"Where have you been?" Macomber asked in the darkness.

"Hello," she said. "Are you awake?"

"Where have you been?"

"I just went out to get a breath of air."

"You did, like hell."

"What do you want me to say, darling?"

"Where have you been?"

"Out to get a breath of air."

"That's a new name for it. You *are* a bitch."

"Well, you're a coward."

"All right," he said. "What of it?"

"Nothing as far as I'm concerned. But please let's not talk, darling, because I'm very sleepy."

"You think that I'll take anything."

"I know you will, sweet."

"Well, I won't."

"Please, darling, let's not talk. I'm so very sleepy."

"There wasn't going to be any of that. You promised there wouldn't be."

"Well, there is now," she said sweetly.

"You said if we made this trip that there would be none of that. You promised."

"Yes, darling. That's the way I meant it to be. But the trip was spoiled yesterday. We don't have to talk about it, do we?"

"You don't wait long when you have an advantage, do you?"

"Please let's not talk. I'm so sleepy, darling."

"I'm going to talk."

"Don't mind me then, because I'm going to sleep." And she did.

At breakfast they were all three at the table before daylight and Francis Macomber found that, of all the many men that he had hated, he hated Robert Wilson the most.

"Sleep well?" Wilson asked in his throaty voice, filling a pipe.

"Did you?"

"Topping," the white hunter told him.

You bastard, thought Macomber, you insolent bastard.

So she woke him when she came in, Wilson thought, looking at them both with his flat, cold eyes. Well, why doesn't he keep his wife where she belongs? What does he think I am, a bloody plaster saint? Let him keep her where she belongs. It's his own fault.

"Do you think we'll find buffalo?" Margot asked, pushing away a dish of apricots.

"Chance of it," Wilson said and smiled at her. "Why don't you stay in camp?"

"Not for anything," she told him.

"Why not order her to stay in camp?" Wilson said to Macomber.

"You order her," said Macomber coldly.

"Let's not have any ordering, nor," turning to Macomber, "any silliness, Francis," Margot said quite pleasantly.

"Are you ready to start?" Macomber asked.

"Any time," Wilson told him. "Do you want the Memsahib to go?"

"Does it make any difference whether I do or not?"

The hell with it, thought Robert Wilson. The utter complete hell with it. So this is what it's going to be like. Well, this is what it's going to be like, then.

"Makes no difference," he said.

"You're sure you wouldn't like to stay in camp with her yourself and let me go out and hunt the buffalo?" Macomber asked.

"Can't do that," said Wilson. "Wouldn't talk rot if I were you."

"I'm not talking rot. I'm disgusted."

"Bad word, disgusted."

"Francis, will you please try to speak sensibly!" his wife said.

"I speak too damned sensibly," Macomber said. "Did you ever eat such filthy food?"

"Something wrong with the food?" asked Wilson quietly.

"No more than with everything else."

"I'd pull yourself together, laddybuck," Wilson said very quietly. "There's a boy waits at table that understands a little English."

"The hell with him."

Wilson stood up and puffing on his pipe strolled away, speaking a few words in Swahili to one of the gun-bearers who was standing waiting for him. Macomber and his wife sat on at the table. He was staring at his coffee cup.

"If you make a scene I'll leave you, darling," Margot said quietly.

"No, you won't."

"You can try it and see."

"You won't leave me."

"No," she said. "I won't leave you and you'll behave yourself."

"Behave myself? That's a way to talk. Behave myself."

"Yes. Behave yourself."

"Why don't *you* try behaving?"

"I've tried it so long. So very long."

"I hate that red-faced swine," Macomber said. "I loathe the sight of him."

"He's really *very* nice."

"Oh, *shut up*," Macomber almost shouted. Just then the car came up and stopped in front of the dining tent and the driver and the two gun-bearers got out. Wilson walked over and looked at the husband and wife sitting there at the table.

"Going shooting?" he asked.

"Yes," said Macomber, standing up. "Yes."

"Better bring a woolly. It will be cool in the car," Wilson said.

"I'll get my leather jacket," Margot said.

"The boy has it," Wilson told her. He climbed into the front with the driver and Francis Macomber and his wife sat, not speaking, in the back seat.

Hope the silly beggar doesn't take a notion to blow the back of my head off, Wilson thought to himself. Women *are* a nuisance on safari.

The car was grinding down to cross the river at a pebbly ford in the gray daylight and then climbed, angling up the steep bank, where Wilson had ordered a way shovelled out the day before so they could reach the parklike wooded rolling country on the far side.

It was a good morning. Wilson thought. There was a heavy dew and as the wheels went through the grass and low bushes he could smell the odor of the crushed fronds. It was an odor like verbena and he liked this early morning smell of the dew, the crushed bracken and the look of the tree trunks showing black through the early morning mist, as the car made its way through the untracked, parklike country. He had put the two in the back seat out of his mind now and was thinking about buffalo. The buffalo that he was after stayed in the daytime in a thick swamp where it was impossible to get a shot, but in the night they fed out into an open stretch of country and if he could come between them and their swamp with the car, Macomber would have a good chance at them in the open. He did not want to hunt buff with Macomber in thick cover. He did not want to hunt buff or anything else with Macomber at all, but he was a professional hunter and he had hunted with some rare ones in his time. If they got buff today there would only be rhino to come and the poor man would have gone through his dangerous game and things might pick up. He'd have nothing more to do with the woman and Macomber would get over that too. He must have gone through plenty of that before by the look of things. Poor beggar. He must have a way of getting over it. Well, it was the poor sod's own bloody fault.

He, Robert Wilson, carried a double size cot on safari to accommodate any windfalls he might receive. He had hunted for a certain clientele, the international, fast, sporting set, where the woman did not feel they were getting their money's worth unless they had shared that cot with the white hunter. He despised them when he was away from them although he liked some of them well enough at the time, but he made his living by them; and their standards were his standards as long as they were hiring him.

They were his standards in all except the shooting. He had his own standards about the killing and they could live up to them or get some one else to hunt them. He knew, too, that they all respected him for this. This Macomber was an odd one though. Damned if he wasn't. Now the wife. Well, the wife. Yes, the wife. Hm, the wife. Well he'd dropped all that. He looked around at them. Macomber sat grim and furious. Margot smiled at him. She looked younger today, more innocent and fresher and not so professionally beautiful. What's in her heart God knows, Wilson thought. She hadn't talked much last night. At that it was a pleasure to see her.

The motor car climbed up a slight rise and went on through the trees and then out into a grassy prairie-like opening and kept in the shelter of the trees along the edge, the driver going slowly and Wilson looking carefully out across the prairie and all along its far side. He stopped the car and studied the opening with his field glasses. Then he motioned to the driver to go on and the car moved slowly along, the driver avoiding wart-hog holes and driving around the mud castles ants had built. Then, looking across the opening, Wilson suddenly turned and said,

"By God, there they are!"

And looking where he pointed, while the car jumped forward and Wilson spoke in rapid Swahili to the driver, Macomber saw three huge, black animals looking almost cylindrical in their long heaviness, like big black tank cars, moving at a gallop across the far edge of the open prairie. They moved at a stiff-necked, stiff bodied gallop and he could see the upswept wide black horns on their heads as they galloped heads out; the heads not moving.

"They're three old bulls," Wilson said. "We'll cut them off before they get to the swamp."

The car was going a wild forty-five miles an hour across the open and as Macomber watched, the buffalo got bigger and bigger until he could see the gray, hairless, scabby look of one huge bull and how his neck was a part of his shoulders and the shiny black of his horns as he galloped a little behind the others that were strung out in that steady plunging gait; and then, the car swaying as though it had just jumped a road, they drew up close and he could see the plunging hugeness of the bull, and the dust in his sparsely haired hide, the wide boss of horn and his outstretched, wide-nostrilled muzzle, and he was raising his rifle when Wilson shouted, "Not from the car, you fool!" and he had no fear, only hatred of Wilson, while the brakes clamped on and the car skidded, plowing sideways to an almost stop and Wilson was out on one side and he on the other, stumbling as his feet hit the still speeding-by of the earth, and then he was shooting at the bull as he moved away, hearing the bullets whunk into him, emptying his rifle at him as he moved steadily away, finally remembering to get his shots forward into the shoulder, and as he fumbled to re-load, he saw the bull was down. Down on his knees, his big head tossing, and seeing the other two still galloping he shot at the leader and hit him. He shot again and missed and he heard the *carawonging* roar as Wilson shot and saw the leading bull slide forward onto his nose.

"Get that other," Wilson said. "Now you're shooting!"

But the other bull was moving steadily at the same gallop and he missed, throwing a spout of dirt, and Wilson missed and the dust rose in a cloud and Wilson shouted, "Come on. He's too far!" and grabbed his arm and they were in the car again, Macomber and Wilson hanging on the sides and rocketing swayingly over the uneven ground, drawing up on the steady, plunging, heavy-necked, straight-moving gallop of the bull.

They were behind him and Macomber was filling his rifle, dropping shells onto the ground, jamming it, clearing the jam, then they were almost up with the bull when Wilson yelled "Stop," and the car skidded so that it amost swung over and Macomber fell forward onto his feet, slammed his bolt forward and fired as far forward as he could aim into the galloping, rounded black back, aimed and shot again, then again, then again, and the bullets, all of them hitting, had no effect on the buffalo that he could see. Then Wilson shot, the roar deafening him, and he could see the bull stagger. Macomber shot again, aiming carefully, and down he came, onto his knees.

"All right," Wilson said. "Nice work. That's the three."

Macomber felt a drunken elation.

"How many times did you shoot?" he asked.

"Just three," Wilson said. "You killed the first bull. The biggest one. I helped you finish the other two. Afraid they might have got into cover. You had them killed. I was just mopping up a little. You shot damn well."

"Let's go to the car" said Macomber. "I want a drink."

"Got to finish off that buff first." Wilson told him. The buffalo was on his knees and he jerked his head furiously and bellowed in pig-eyed, roaring rage as they came toward him.

"Watch he doesn't get up," Wilson said. Then, "Get a little broadside and take him in the neck just behind the ear."

Macomber aimed carefully at the center of the huge, jerking, rage-driven neck and shot. At the shot the head dropped forward.

"That does it," said Wilson. "Got the spine. They're a hell of a looking thing, aren't they?"

"Let's get the drink," said Macomber. In his life he had never felt so good.

In the car Macomber's wife sat very white faced. "You were marvellous, darling," she said to Macomber. "What a ride."

"Was it rough?" Wilson asked.

"It was frightful. I've never been more frightened in my life."

"Let's all have a drink," Macomber said.

"By all means," said Wilson. "Give it to the Memsahib." She drank the neat whisky from the flask and shuddered a little when she swallowed. She handed the flask to Macomber who handed it to Wilson.

"It was frightfully exciting," she said. "It's given me a dreadful headache. I didn't know you were allowed to shoot them from cars though."

"No one shot from cars," said Wilson coldly.

"I mean chase them from cars."

"Wouldn't ordinarily," Wilson said. "Seemed sporting enough to me though while we were doing it. Taking more chance driving that way across the plain full of holes and one thing and another than hunting on foot. Buffalo could have charged us each time we shot if he liked. Gave him every chance. Wouldn't mention it to any one though. It's illegal if that's what you mean."

"It seemed very unfair to me," Margot said, "chasing those big helpless things in a motor car."

"Did it?" said Wilson.

"What would happen if they heard about it in Nairobi?"[14]

"I'd lose my license for one thing. Other unpleasantnesses," Wilson said, taking a drink from the flask. "I'd be out of business."

"Really?"

"Yes, really."

"Well," said Macomber, and he smiled for the first time all day. "Now she has something on you."

"You have such a pretty way of putting things, Francis," Margot Macomber said. Wilson looked at them both. If a four-letter man marries a five-letter woman, he was thinking, what number of letters would their children be? What he said was, "We lost a gun-bearer. Did you notice it?"

"My God, no," Macomber said.

"Here he comes," Wilson said. "He's all right. He must have fallen off when we left the first bull."

Approaching them was the middle-aged gun-bearer, limping along in his knitted cap, khaki tunic, shorts and rubber sandals, gloomy-faced and disgusted looking. As he came up he called out to Wilson in Swahili and they all saw the change in the white hunter's face.

"What does he say?" asked Margot.

"He says the first bull got up and went into the bush," Wilson said with no expression in his voice.

"Oh," said Macomber blankly.

"Then it's going to be just like the lion," said Margot, full of anticipation.

"It's not going to be a damned bit like the lion," Wilson told her. "Did you want another drink, Macomber?"

"Thanks, yes," Macomber said. He expected the feeling he had had about the lion to come back but it did not. For the first time in his life he really felt wholly without fear. Instead of fear he had a feeling of definite elation.

"We'll go and have a look at the second bull," Wilson said. "I'll tell the driver to put the car in the shade."

"What are you going to do?" asked Margaret Macomber.

"Take a look at the buff," Wilson said.

"I'll come."

"Come along."

The three of them walked over to where the second buffalo bulked blackly in the open, head forward on the grass, the massive horns swung wide.

---

[14]Capital of Kenya, then part of British East Africa.

"He's a very good head," Wilson said. "That's close to a fifty-inch spread."

Macomber was looking at him with delight.

"He's hateful looking," said Margot. "Can't we go into the shade?"

"Of course," Wilson said. "Look," he said to Macomber, and pointed. "See that patch of bush?"

"Yes."

"That's where the first bull went in. The gun-bearer said when he fell off the bull was down. He was watching us helling along and the other two buff galloping. When he looked up there was the bull up and looking at him. Gun-bearer ran like hell and the bull went off slowly into that bush."

"Can we go in after him now?" asked Macomber eagerly.

Wilson looked at him appraisingly. Damned if this isn't a strange one, he thought. Yesterday he's scared sick and today he's a ruddy fire eater.

"No, we'll give him a while."

"Let's please go into the shade," Margot said. Her face was white and she looked ill.

They made their way to the car where it stood under a single, wide-spreading tree and all climbed in.

"Chances are he's dead in there," Wilson remarked. "After a little we'll have a look."

Macomber felt a wild unreasonable happiness that he had never known before.

"By God, that was a chase," he said. "I've never felt any such feeling. Wasn't it marvellous, Margot?"

"I hated it."

"Why?"

"I hated it," she said bitterly. "I loathed it."

"You know I don't think I'd ever be afraid of anything again," Macomber said to Wilson. "Something happened in me after we first saw the buff and started after him. Like a dam bursting. It was pure excitement."

"Cleans out your liver," said Wilson. "Damn funny things happen to people."

Macomber's face was shining. "You know something did happen to me," he said. "I feel absolutely different."

His wife said nothing and eyed him strangely. She was sitting far back in the seat and Macomber was sitting forward talking to Wilson who turned sideways talking over the back of the front seat.

"You know, I'd like to try another lion," Macomber said. "I'm really not afraid of them now. After all, what can they do to you?"

"That's it," said Wilson. "Worst one can do is kill you. How does it go? Shakespeare. Damned good. See if I can remember. Oh, damned good. Used to quote it to myself at one time. Let's see. 'By my troth, I care not; a man can die but once; we owe God a death and let it go which way it will he that dies this year is quit for the next.'[15] Damned fine, eh?"

He was very embarrassed, having brought out this thing he had lived by, but he had seen men come of age before and it always moved him. It was not a matter of their twenty-first birthday.

It had taken a strange chance of hunting, a sudden precipitation into action without opportunity for worrying beforehand, to bring this about with Macomber, but regardless of how it had happened it had most certainly happened. Look at the beggar now, Wilson thought. It's that some of them stay little boys so long, Wilson thought. Sometimes all their lives. Their figures stay boyish

---

[15]From *II Henry IV*, Act III, scene ii, lines 239–243.

when they're fifty. The great American boy-men. Damned strange people. But he liked this Macomber now. Damned strange fellow. Probably meant the end of cuckoldry too. Well, that would be a damned good thing. Damned good thing. Beggar had probably been afraid all his life. Don't know what started it. But over now. Hadn't had time to be afraid with the buff. That and being angry too. Motor car too. Motor cars made it familiar. Be a damn fire eater now. He'd seen it in the war work the same way. More of a change than any loss of virginity. Fear gone like an operation. Something else grew in its place. Main thing a man had. Made him into a man. Women knew it too. No bloody fear.

From the far corner of the seat Margaret Macomber looked at the two of them. There was no change in Wilson. She saw Wilson as she had seen him the day before when she had first realized what his great talent was. But she saw the change in Francis Macomber now.

"Do you have that feeling of happiness about what's going to happen?" Macomber asked, still exploring his new wealth.

"You're not supposed to mention it," Wilson said, looking in the other's face. "Much more fashionable to say you're scared. Mind you, you'll be scared too, plenty of times."

"But you *have* a feeling of happiness about action to come?"

"Yes," said Wilson. "There's that. Doesn't do to talk too much about all this. Talk the whole thing away. No pleasure in anything if you mouth it up too much."

"You're both talking rot," said Margot. "Just because you've chased some helpless animals in a motor car you talk like heroes."

"Sorry," said Wilson. "I have been gassing too much." She's worried about it already, he thought.

"If you don't know what we're talking about why not keep out of it?" Macomber asked his wife.

"You've gotten awfully brave, awfully suddenly," his wife said contemptuously, but her contempt was not secure. She was very afraid of something.

Macomber laughed, a very natural hearty laugh. "You know I *have*," he said. "I really have."

"Isn't it sort of late?" Margot said bitterly. Because she had done the best she could for many years back and the way they were together now was no one person's fault.

"Not for me," said Macomber.

Margot said nothing but sat back in the corner of the seat.

"Do you think we've given him time enough?" Macomber asked Wilson cheerfully.

"We might have a look," Wilson said. "Have you any solids left?"

"The gun-bearer has some."

Wilson called in Swahili and the older gun-bearer, who was skinning out one of the heads, straightened up, pulled a box of solids out of his pocket and brought them over to Macomber, who filled his magazine and put the remaining shells in his pocket.

"You might as well shoot the Springfield,"[16] Wilson said. "You're used to it. We'll leave the Mannlicher[17] in the car with the Memsahib. Your gun-bearer can carry your heavy gun. I've this damned cannon. Now let me tell you about them." He had saved this until the last because he did not want to worry

[16]United States military rifle, used in World War I, adapted for hunting.

[17]Light, hunting rifle named for its Austrian designer, Ferdinand von Mannlicher (1848–1904).

Macomber. "When a buff comes he comes with his head high and thrust straight out. The boss of the horns covers any sort of a brain shot. The only shot is straight into the nose. The only other shot is into his chest or, if you're to one side, into the neck or the shoulders. After they've been hit once they take a hell of a lot of killing. Don't try anything fancy. Take the easiest shot there is. They've finished skinning out that head now. Should we get started?"

He called to the gun-bearers, who came up wiping their hands, and the older one got into the back.

"I'll only take Kongoni," Wilson said. "The other can watch to keep the birds away."

As the car moved slowly across the open space toward the island of brushy trees that ran in a tongue of foliage along a dry water course that cut the open swale, Macomber felt his heart pounding and his mouth was dry again, but it was excitement, not fear.

"Here's where he went in," Wilson said. Then to the gun-bearer in Swahili, "Take the blood spoor."

The car was parallel to the patch of bush. Macomber, Wilson and the gun-bearer got down. Macomber, looking back, saw his wife, with the rifle by her side, looking at him. He waved to her and she did not wave back.

The brush was very thick ahead and the ground was dry. The middle-aged gun-bearer was sweating heavily and Wilson had his hat down over his eyes and his red neck showed just ahead of Macomber. Suddenly the gun-bearer said something in Swahili to Wilson and ran forward.

"He's dead in there," Wilson said. "Good work," and he turned to grip Macomber's hand as they shook hands, grinning at each other, the gun-bearer shouted wildly and they saw him coming out of the bush sideways, fast as a crab, and the bull coming, nose out, mouth tight closed, blood dripping, massive head straight out, coming in a charge, his little pig eyes bloodshot as he looked at them. Wilson, who was ahead was kneeling shooting, and Macomber, as he fired, unhearing his shot in the roaring of Wilson's gun, saw fragments like slate burst from the huge boss of the horns, and the head jerked, he shot again at the wide nostrils and saw the horns jolt again and fragments fly, and he did not see Wilson now and, aiming carefully, shot again with the buffalo's huge bulk almost on him and his rifle almost level with the on-coming head, nose out, and he could see the little wicked eyes and the head started to lower and he felt a sudden white-hot, blinding flash explode inside his head and that was all he ever felt.

Wilson had ducked to one side to get a shoulder shot. Macomber had stood solid and shot for the nose, shooting a touch high each time and hitting the heavy horns, splintering and chipping them like hitting a slate roof, and Mrs. Macomber, in the car, had shot at the buffalo with the 6.5 Mannlicher as it seemed about to gore Macomber and had hit her husband about two inches up and a little to one side of the base of his skull.

Francis Macomber lay now, face down, not two yards from where the buffalo lay on his side and his wife knelt over him with Wilson beside her.

"I wouldn't turn him over," Wilson said.

The woman was crying hysterically.

"I'd get back in the car," Wilson said. "Where's the rifle?"

She shook her head, her face contorted. The gun-bearer picked up the rifle.

"Leave it as it is," said Wilson. Then, "Go get Abdulla so that he may witness the manner of the accident."

He knelt down, took a handkerchief from his pocket, and spread it over

Francis Macomber's crew-cropped head where it lay. The blood sank into the dry, loose earth.

Wilson stood up and saw the buffalo on his side, his legs out, his thinly-haired belly crawling with ticks. "Hell of a good bull," his brain registered automatically. "A good fifty inches, or better. Better." He called to the driver and told him to spread a blanket over the body and stay by it. Then he walked over to the motor car where the woman sat crying in the corner.

"That was a pretty thing to do," he said in a toneless voice. "He *would* have left you too."

"Stop it," she said.

"Of course it's an accident," he said. "I know that."

"Stop it," she said.

"Don't worry," he said. "There will be a certain amount of unpleasantness but I will have some photographs taken that will be very useful at the inquest. There's the testimony of the gun-bearers and the driver too. You're perfectly all right."

"Stop it," she said.

"There's a hell of a lot to be done," he said. "And I'll have to send a truck off to the lake to wireless for a plane to take the three of us to Nairobi. Why didn't you poison him? That's what they do in England."

"Stop it. Stop it. Stop it," the woman cried.

Wilson looked at her with his flat blue eyes.

"I'm through now," he said. "I was a little angry. I'd begun to like your husband."

"Oh, please stop it," she said. "Please, please stop it."

"That's better," Wilson said. "Please is much better. Now I'll stop."

1936, 1938

William Faulkner   *1897–1962*

After he received the 1949 Nobel Prize for Literature, William Faulkner's reputation and influence spread throughout the world. But, ironically, the Nobel Prize was awarded largely for works that had been written years before and were so little recognized at the time of their publication that most of them were out of print by 1944. The only Faulkner novel that had come close to being a best seller in its day was Sanctuary, *a book more famous for its shock value than for its literary quality.*

Faulkner was born William Cuthbert Falkner (the "u" he added to his last name when he began to publish) in New Albany, Mississippi. When he was four or five years old, the family moved to Oxford, Mississippi, where he resided for the rest of his life. Oxford was, with some fictional modifications, a prototype of Jefferson, in the mythical county of Yoknapatawpha, the setting of Sartoris *and most of his subsequent works. His central theme, however, was not Oxford, or Mississippi, or even America. It was, as he put it, the universal theme of "the problems of the human heart in conflict with itself."*

Faulkner began his literary career as a poet rather than a fiction writer, but his poetry was undistinguished and commercially unsuccessful. He turned to the writing of prose in 1925, after meeting Sherwood Anderson in New Orleans. With Faulkner's third published novel, Sartoris, *which he completed in 1927 and which was printed in 1929, he "dis-*

*covered," as he said later, "that my own little postage stamp of native soil was worth
writing about and that I would never live long enough to exhaust it, and that by sublimating
the actual into the apocryphal I would have complete liberty to use whatever talent I might
have to its absolute top. It opened up a gold mine of other people, so I created a cosmos of
my own." Using his own cosmos to express his universal theme of "the problems of the
human heart," Faulkner created the novels for which he is now best known:* The Sound
and the Fury *(1929),* As I Lay Dying *(1936),* The Hamlet *(1940), and* Go Down,
Moses *(1942).*

*In 1948, after six years in which he published only a few short stories, he resumed his
career with* Intruder in the Dust. *Three years later* Requiem for a Nun, *a kind of
sequel to* Sanctuary, *appeared. His most ambitious single effort was, perhaps,* A Fable
*(1954), an allegorical novel, which took him at least nine years to write and which has so
far proved baffling to readers and critics alike.* The Town *(1957) and* The Mansion
(1959) complete the trilogy on the Snopes family which began with The Hamlet.
Faulkner's last novel, The Reivers, *was published on June 4, 1962. A month later he
died.*

*Faulkner also published about seventy short stories, some of which were later incorporated
into novels, such as "Wash" in* Absalom, Absalom!, *"Spotted Horses" in* The Hamlet,
and "The Bear" (with a long section added) in Go Down, Moses. *Collections of short
stories appeared in* These 13 *(1931),* Doctor Martino and Other Stories *(1934),*
Knight's Gambit *(1949),* Collected Stories of William Faulkner *(1950), and* Big
Woods *(1955).*

*Although his home was always Mississippi, Faulkner traveled extensively. He trained
as a pilot for the Royal Canadian Flying Corps during 1918, worked in New York City
in 1920 and 1921, spent most of 1925 in New Orleans and Europe, and labored off
and on for several years as a script writer in Hollywood. Like many other American writers,
he never graduated from college, but he read omnivorously a wide variety of literature:
the Bible, Greek and Roman classics, Shakespeare, the standard English and American
poets and novelists, and such modern writers as the French symbolist poets and Conrad,
James Joyce, and T. S. Eliot. Through the late 1920s and the 1930s his bold experiments
in the dislocation of narrative time and his use of stream-of-consciousness techniques placed
him in the forefront of the avant-garde. Faulkner's verbal innovations and the labyrinthine
organization of his novels make him difficult to read, but his popularity continues to grow,
and today is considered by many to have been the greatest writer of fiction that the United
States has yet produced.*

FURTHER READING: *Uncollected Short Stories of William Faulkner*, ed. J. Blotner, 1979;
Essays, Speeches and Public Letters by William Faulkner, ed. J. Meriwether, 1966; *Selected
Letters of William Faulkner*, ed. J. Blotner, 1977; *Faulkner in the University*, ed. F. Gwynn
and J. Blotner, 1959; J. Faulkner, *My Brother Bill*, 1963; J. Blotner, *Faulkner, A Biography*,
2 vols., 1974, 1 vol., 1982; S. Oates, *William Faulkner, The Man and Artist*, 1987; I. Howe,
William Faulkner, A Critical Study, 1952, 1962; H. Waggoner, *William Faulkner, From
Jefferson to the World*, 1959; O. Vickery, *The Novels of William Faulkner*, 1959, 1964; *William
Faulkner, Three Decades of Criticism*, ed. F. Hoffman and O. Vickery, 1960; F. Hoffman,
William Faulkner, 1961, 1966; C. Brooks, *William Faulkner, The Yoknapatawpha Country*,
1963; L. Thompson, *William Faulkner, An Introduction and Interpretation*, 1963, 1967; R.
Kirk and M. Klotz, *Faulkner's People*, 1963; E. Volpe, *A Reader's Guide to William Faulkner*,
1964; J. Hunt, *William Faulkner, Art in Theological Tension*, 1965; M. Millgate, *The Achievement of William Faulkner*, 1966; *Faulkner, A Collection of Critical Essays*, ed. R. Warren, 1966;
R. Adams, *Faulkner, Myth and Motion*, 1968; H. Richardson, *William Faulkner, The Journey
to Self-Discovery*, 1969; C. Brooks, *Toward Yoknapatawpha and Beyond*, 1978; D. Minter,
William Faulkner, His Life and Work, 1980; M. Kreisworth, *William Faulkner, The Making of
a Novelist*, 1983.

TEXTS: *Collected Stories of William Faulkner*, 1950.

THAT EVENING SUN

I

Monday is no different from any other weekday in Jefferson now. The streets are paved now, and the telephone and electric companies are cutting down more and more of the shade trees—the water oaks, the maples and locusts and elms—to make room for iron poles bearing clusters of bloated and ghostly and bloodless grapes, and we have a city laundry which makes the rounds on Monday morning, gathering the bundles of clothes into bright-colored, specially-made motor cars: the soiled wearing of a whole week now flees apparition-like behind alert and irritable electric horns, with a long di-minishing noise of rubber and asphalt like tearing silk, and even the Negro women who still take in white people's washing after the old custom, fetch and deliver it in automobiles.

But fifteen years ago, on Monday morning the quiet, dusty, shady streets would be full of Negro women with, balanced on their steady, turbaned heads, bundles of clothes tied up in sheets, almost as large as cotton bales, carried so without touch of hand between the kitchen door of the white house and the blackened washpot beside a cabin door in Negro Hollow.

Nancy would set her bundle on top of her head, then upon the bundle in turn she would set the black straw sailor hat which she wore winter and summer. She was tall, with a high, sad face sunken a little where her teeth were missing. Sometimes we would go a part of the way down the lane across the pasture with her, to watch the balanced bundle and the hat that never bobbed nor wavered, even when she walked down into the ditch and up the other side and stooped through the fence. She would go down on her hands and knees and crawl through the gap, her head rigid, uptilted, the bundle steady as a rock or a balloon, and rise to her feet again and go on.

Sometimes the husbands of the washing women would fetch and deliver the clothes, but Jesus never did that for Nancy, even before father told him to stay away from our house, even when Dilsey was sick and Nancy would come to cook for us.

And then about half the time we'd have to go down the lane to Nancy's cabin and tell her to come on and cook breakfast. We would stop at the ditch, because father told us to not have anything to do with Jesus—he was a short black man, with a razor scar down his face—and we would throw rocks at Nancy's house until she came to the door, leaning her head around it without any clothes on.

"What yawl mean, chunking my house?" Nancy said. "What you little devils mean?"

"Father says for you to come on and get breakfast," Caddy said. "Father says it's over a half an hour now, and you've got to come this minute."

"I aint studying no breakfast," Nancy said. "I going to get my sleep out."

"I bet you're drunk," Jason said. "Father says you're drunk. Are you drunk, Nancy?"

"Who says I is?" Nancy said. "I got to get my sleep out. I aint studying no breakfast."

So after a while we quit chunking the cabin and went back home. When she finally came, it was too late for me to go to school. So we thought it was whisky until that day they arrested her again and they were taking her to jail and they passed Mr Stovall. He was the cashier in the bank and a deacon in the Baptist church, and Nancy began to say:

"When you going to pay me, white man? When are you going to pay me, white man? It's been three times now since you paid me a cent—" Mr Stovall knocked her down, but she kept saying, "When you going to pay me, white man? It's been three times now since—" until Mr Stovall kicked her in the mouth with his heel and the marshall caught Mr Stovall back, and Nancy lying in the street, laughing. She turned her head and spat out some blood and teeth and said, "It's been three times now since he paid me a cent."

That was how she lost her teeth, and all that day they told about Nancy and Mr Stovall, and all that night the ones that passed the jail could hear Nancy singing and yelling. They could see her hands holding to the window bars, and a lot of them stopped along the fence, listening to her and to the jailer trying to make her stop. She didn't shut up until almost daylight, when the jailer began to hear a bumping and scraping upstairs and he went up there and found Nancy hanging from the window bar. He said that it was cocaine and not whisky, because no nigger would try to commit suicide unless he was full of cocaine, because a nigger full of cocaine wasn't a nigger any longer.

The jailer cut her down and revived her; then he beat her, whipped her. She had hung herself with her dress. She had fixed it all right, but when they arrested her she didn't have on anything except a dress and so she didn't have anything to tie her hands with and she couldn't make her hands let go of the window ledge. So the jailer heard the noise and ran up there and found Nancy hanging from the window, stark naked, her belly already swelling out a little, like a little balloon.

When Dilsey was sick in her cabin and Nancy was cooking for us, we could see her apron swelling out; that was before father told Jesus to stay away from the house. Jesus was in the kitchen, sitting behind the stove, with his razor scar on his black face like a piece of dirty string. He said it was a watermelon that Nancy had under her dress.

"It never come off your vine, though," Nancy said.

"Off of what vine?" Caddy said.

"I can cut down the vine it did come off of," Jesus said.

"What makes you want to talk like that before these children?" Nancy said. "Whyn't you go on to work? You done et. You want Mr Jason to catch you hanging around his kitchen, talking that way before these children?"

"Talking what way?" Caddy said. "What vine?"

"I cant hang around white man's kitchen," Jesus said. "But white man can hang around mine. White man can come in my house, but I cant stop him. When white man want to come in my house, I aint got no house. I cant stop him, but he cant kick me outen it. He cant do that."

Dilsey was still sick in her cabin. Father told Jesus to stay off our place. Dilsey was still sick. It was a long time. We were in the library after supper.

"Isn't Nancy through in the kitchen yet?" mother said. "It seems to me that she has had plenty of time to have finished the dishes."

"Let Quentin go and see," father said. "Go and see if Nancy is through, Quentin. Tell her she can go on home."

I went to the kitchen. Nancy was through. The dishes were put away and the fire was out. Nancy was sitting in a chair, close to the cold stove. She looked at me.

"Mother wants to know if you are through," I said.

"Yes," Nancy said. She looked at me. "I done finished." She looked at me.

"What is it?" I said. "What is it?"

"I aint nothing but a nigger," Nancy said. "It aint none of my fault."

She looked at me, sitting in the chair before the cold stove, the sailor hat on her head. I went back to the library. It was the cold stove and all, when you think of a kitchen being warm and busy and cheerful. And with a cold stove and the dishes all put away, and nobody wanting to eat at that hour.

"Is she through?" mother said.

"Yessum," I said.

"What is she doing?" mother said.

"She's not doing anything. She's through."

"I'll go and see," father said.

"Maybe she's waiting for Jesus to come and take her home." Caddy said.

"Jesus is gone," I said. Nancy told us how one morning she woke up and Jesus was gone.

"He quit me," Nancy said. "Done gone to Memphis, I reckon. Dodging them city *po*-lice for a while, I reckon."

"And a good riddance," father said. "I hope he stays there."

"Nancy's scaired of the dark," Jason said.

"So are you," Caddy said.

"I'm not," Jason said.

"Scairy cat," Caddy said.

"I'm not," Jason said.

"You, Candace!" mother said. Father came back.

"I am going to walk down the lane with Nancy," he said. "She says that Jesus is back."

'Has she seen him?" mother said.

"No. Some Negro sent her word that he was back in town. I wont be long."

"You'll leave me alone, to take Nancy home?" mother said. "Is her safety more precious to you than mine?"

"I wont be long," father said.

"You'll leave these children unprotected, with that Negro about?"

"I'm going too," Caddy said. "Let me go, Father."

"What would he do with them, if he were unfortunate enough to have them?" father said.

"I want go to, too," Jason said.

"Jason!" mother said. She was speaking to father. You could tell that by the way she said the name. Like she believed that all day father had been trying to think of doing the thing she wouldn't like the most, and that she knew all the time that after a while he would think of it. I stayed quiet, because father and I both knew that mother would want him to make me stay with her if she just thought of it in time. So father didn't look at me. I was the oldest. I was nine and Caddy was seven and Jason was five.

"Nonsense," father said. "We wont be long."

Nancy had her hat on. We came to the lane. "Jesus always been good to me." Nancy said. "Whenever he had two dollars, one of them was mine." We walked in the lane. "If I just get through the lane," Nancy said. "I be all right then."

The lane was always dark. "This is where Jason got scared on Hallowe'en," Caddy said.

"I didn't," Jason said.

"Cant Aunt Rachel do anything with him?" father said. Aunt Rachel was old. She lived in a cabin beyond Nancy's, by herself. She had white hair and she smoked a pipe in the door, all day long; she didn't work any more. They said she was Jesus' mother. Sometimes she said she was and sometimes she said she wasn't any kin to Jesus.

"Yes, you did," Caddy said. "You were scairder than Frony. You were scairder than T.P. even. Scairder than niggers."

"Cant nobody do nothing with him," Nancy said. "He say I done woke up the devil in him and aint but one thing going to lay it down again."

"Well, he's gone now," father said. "There's nothing for you to be afraid of now. And if you'd just let white men alone."

"Let what white men alone?" Caddy said. "How let them alone?"

"He aint gone nowhere," Nancy said. "I can feel him. I can feel him now, in this lane. He hearing us talk, every word, hid somewhere, waiting. I aint seen him, and I aint going to see him again but once more, with that razor in his mouth. That razor on that string down his back, inside his shirt. And then I aint going to be even surprised."

"I wasn't scaird," Jason said.

"If you'd behave yourself, you'd have kept out of this," father said. "But it's all right now. He's probably in St. Louis now. Probably got another wife by now and forgot all about you."

"If he has, I better not find out about it," Nancy said. "I'd stand there right over them, and every time he wropped her, I'd cut that arm off. I'd cut his head off and I'd slit her belly and I'd shove—"

"Hush," father said.

"Slit whose belly, Nancy?" Caddy said.

"I wasn't scaired," Jason said. "I'd walk right down this lane by myself."

"Yah," Caddy said. "You wouldn't dare to put your foot down in it if we were not here too."

II

Dilsey was still sick, so we took Nancy home every night until mother said, "How much longer is this going on? I to be left alone in this big house while you take home a frightened Negro?"

We fixed a pallet in the kitchen for Nancy. One night we waked up, hearing the sound. It was not singing and it was not crying, coming up the dark stairs. There was a light in mother's room and we heard father going down the hall, down the back stairs, and Caddy and I went into the hall. The floor was cold. Our toes curled away from it while we listened to the sound. It was like singing and it wasn't like singing, like the sounds that Negroes make.

Then it stopped and we heard father going down the back stairs, and we went to the head of the stairs. Then the sound began again, in the stairway, not loud, and we could see Nancy's eyes halfway up the stairs, against the wall. They looked like cat's eyes do, like a big cat against the wall, watching us. When we came down the steps to where she was, she quit making the sound again, and we stood there until father came back up from the kitchen, with his pistol in his hand. He went back down with Nancy and they came back with Nancy's pallet.

We spread the pallet in our room. After the light in mother's room went off, we could see Nancy's eyes again. "Nancy," Caddy whispered, "are you asleep, Nancy?"

Nancy whispered something. It was oh or no, I dont know which. Like nobody had made it, like it came from nowhere and went nowhere, until it was like

Nancy was not there at all; that I had looked so hard at her eyes on the stairs that they had got printed on my eyeballs, like the sun does when you have closed your eyes and there is no sun. "Jesus," Nancy whispered. "Jesus."

"Was it Jesus?" Caddy said. "Did he try to come into the kitchen?"

"Jesus," Nancy said. Like this: Jeeeeeeeeeeeeeeeesus, until the sound went out, like a match or a candle does.

"It's the other Jesus she means," I said.

"Can you see us, Nancy?" Caddy whispered. "Can you see our eyes too?"

"I aint nothing but a nigger," Nancy said. "God knows. God knows."

"What did you see down there in the kitchen?" Caddy whispered. "What tried to get in?"

"God knows," Nancy said. We could see her eyes. "God knows."

Dilsey got well. She cooked dinner. "You'd bettter stay in bed a day or two longer," father said.

"What for?" Dilsey said. "If I had been a day later, this place would be to rack and ruin. Get on out of here now, and let me get my kitchen straight again."

Dilsey cooked supper too. And that night, just before dark. Nancy came into the kitchen.

"How do you know he's back?" Dilsey said. "You aint seen him."

"Jesus is a nigger," Jason said.

"I can feel him," Nancy said. "I can feel him laying yonder in the ditch."

"Tonight?" Dilsey said. "Is he there tonight?"

"Dilsey's a nigger too," Jason said.

"You try to eat something," Dilsey said.

"I dont want nothing," Nancy said.

"I aint a nigger," Jason said.

"Drink some coffee." Dilsey said. She poured a cup of coffee for Nancy. "Do you know he's out there tonight? How come you know it's tonight?"

"I know," Nancy said. "He's there, waiting. I know. I done lived with him too long. I know what he is fixing to do fore he know it himself."

"Drink some coffee," Dilsey said. Nancy held the cup to her mouth and blew into the cup. Her mouth pursed out like a spreading adder's, like a rubber mouth, like she had blown all the color out of her lips with blowing the coffee.

"I aint a nigger," Jason said. "Are you a nigger, Nancy?"

"I hellborn, child," Nancy said. "I wont be nothing soon. I going back where I come from soon."

III

She began to drink the coffee. While she was drinking, holding the cup in both hands, she began to make the sound again. She made the sound into the cup and the coffee sploshed out onto her hands and her dress. Her eyes looked at us and she sat there, her elbows on her knees, holding the cup in both hands, looking at us across the wet cup, making the sound. "Look at Nancy," Jason said. "Nancy cant cook for us now. Dilsey's got well now."

"You hush up," Dilsey said. Nancy held the cup in both hands, looking at us, making the sound, like there were two of them: one looking at us and the other making the sound. "Whyn't you let Mr Jason telefoam the marshal?" Dilsey said. Nancy stopped then, holding the cup in her long brown hands. She tried to drink some coffee again, but it sploshed out of the cup, onto her hands and her dress, and she put the cup down. Jason watched her.

"I cant swallow it," Nancy said. "I swallows but it wont go down me."

"You go down to the cabin," Dilsey said. "Frony will fix you a pallet and I'll be there soon."

"Wont no nigger stop him," Nancy said.

"I aint a nigger," Jason said. "Am I, Dilsey?"

"I reckon not," Dilsey said. She looked at Nancy. "I dont reckon so. What you going to do, then?"

Nancy looked at us. Her eyes went fast, like she was afraid there wasn't time to look, without hardly moving at all. She looked at us, at all three of us at one time. "You member that night I stayed in yawls' room?" she said. She told about how we waked up early the next morning, and played. We had to play quiet, on her pallet, until father woke up and it was time to get breakfast. "Go and ask your maw to let me stay here tonight," Nancy said. "I wont need no pallet. We can play some more."

Caddy asked mother. Jason went too. "I cant have Negroes sleeping in the bedrooms," mother said. Jason cried. He cried until mother said he couldn't have any dessert for three days if he didn't stop. Then Jason said he would stop if Dilsey would make a chocolate cake. Father was there.

"Why dont you do something about it?" mother said. "What do we have officers for?"

"Why is Nancy afraid of Jesus?" Caddy said. "Are you afraid of father, mother?"

"What could the officers do?" father said. "If Nancy hasn't seen him, how could the officers find him?"

"Then why is she afraid?" mother said.

"She says he is there. She says she knows he is there tonight."

"Yet we pay taxes," mother said. "I must wait here alone in this big house while you take a Negro woman home."

"You know that I am not lying outside with a razor," father said.

"I'll stop if Dilsey will make a chocolate cake," Jason said. Mother told us to go out and father said he didn't know if Jason would get a chocolate cake or not, but he knew what Jason was going to get in about a minute. We went back to the kitchen and told Nancy.

"Father said for you to go home and lock the door, and you'll be all right," Caddy said. "All right from what, Nancy? Is Jesus mad at you?" Nancy was holding the coffee cup in her hands again, her elbows on her knees and her hands holding the cup between her knees. She was looking into the cup. "What have you done that made Jesus mad?" Caddy said. Nancy let the cup go. It didn't break on the floor, but the coffee spilled out, and Nancy sat there with her hands still making the shape of the cup. She began to make that sound again, not loud. Not singing and not unsinging. We watched her.

"Here," Dilsey said. "You quit that, now. You get aholt of yourself. You wait here. I going to get Versh to walk home with you." Dilsey went out.

We looked at Nancy. Her shoulders kept shaking, but she quit making the sound. We watched her. "What's Jesus going to do to you?" Caddy said. "He went away."

Nancy looked at us. "We had fun that night I stayed in yawls' room, didn't we?"

"I didn't," Jason said. "I didn't have any fun."

"You were asleep in mother's room," Caddy said. "You were not there."

'Let's go down to my house and have some more fun," Nancy said.

"Mother wont let us," I said. "It's too late now."

"Dont bother her," Nancy said. "We can tell her in the morning. She won't mind."

"She wouldn't let us," I said.

"Dont ask her now," Nancy said. "Dont bother her now."

"She didn't say we couldn't go," Caddy said.

"We didn't ask," I said.

"If you go, I'll tell," Jason said.

"We'll have fun," Nancy said. "They won't mind, just to my house. I been working for yawl a long time. They won't mind."

"I'm not afraid to go." Caddy said. "Jason is the one that's afraid. He'll tell."

"I'm not," Jason said.

"Yes, you are," Caddy said. "You'll tell."

"I won't tell," Jason said. "I'm not afraid."

"Jason ain't afraid to go with me," Nancy said. "Is you, Jason?"

"Jason is going to tell," Caddy said. The lane was dark. We passed the pasture gate. "I bet if something was to jump out from behind that gate, Jason would holler."

"I wouldn't," Jason said. We walked down the lane. Nancy was talking loud.

"What are you talking so loud for, Nancy?" Caddy said.

"Who; me?" Nancy said. "Listen at Quentin and Caddy and Jason saying I'm talking loud."

"You talk like there was five of us here," Caddy said. "You talk like father was here too."

"Who; me talking loud, Mr. Jason?" Nancy said.

"Nancy called Jason 'Mister,'" Caddy said.

"Listen how Caddy and Quentin and Jason talk," Nancy said.

"We're not talking loud," Caddy said. "You're the one that's talking like father—"

"Hush," Nancy said; "hush, Mr. Jason."

"Nancy called Jason 'Mister' aguh—"

"Hush," Nancy said. She was talking loud when we crossed the ditch and stooped through the fence where she used to stoop through with the clothes on her head. Then we came to her house. We were going fast then. She opened the door. The smell of the house was like the lamp and the smell of Nancy was like the wick, like they were waiting for one another to begin to smell. She lit the lamp and closed the door and put the bar up. Then she quit talking loud, looking at us.

"What're we going to do?" Caddy said.

"What do yawl want to do?" Nancy said.

"You said we would have some fun," Caddy said.

There was something about Nancy's house; something you could smell besides Nancy and the house. Jason smelled it, even. "I don't want to stay here." he said. "I want to go home."

"Go home, then," Caddy said.

"I don't want to go by myself," Jason said.

"We're going to have some fun," Nancy said.

"How?" Caddy said.

Nancy stood by the door. She was looking at us, only it was like she had emptied her eyes, like she had quit using them. "What do you want to do?" she said.

"Tell us a story," Caddy said. "Can you tell a story?"

"Yes," Nancy said.

"Tell it," Caddy said. We looked at Nancy. "You don't know any stories."

"Yes," Nancy said. "Yes I do."

She came and sat in a chair before the hearth. There was a little fire there. Nancy built it up, when it was already hot inside. She built a good blaze. She told a story. She talked like her eyes looked, like her eyes watching us and her voice talking to us did not belong to her. Like she was living somewhere else, waiting somewhere else. She was outside the cabin. Her voice was inside and the shape of her, the Nancy that could stoop under a barbed wire fence with a bundle of clothes balanced on her head as though without weight, like a balloon, was there. But that was all. "And so this here queen come walking up to the ditch, where that bad man was hiding. She was walking up to the ditch, and she say, 'If I can just get past this here ditch,' was what she say . . ."

"What ditch?" Caddy said. "A ditch like that one there? Why did a queen want to go into a ditch?"

"To get to her house," Nancy said. She looked at us. "She had to cross the ditch to get into her house quick and bar the door."

"Why did she want to go home and bar the door?" Caddy said.

IV

Nancy looked at us. She quit talking. She looked at us. Jason's legs stuck straight out of his pants where he sat on Nancy's lap. "I don't think that's a good story," he said. "I want to go home."

"Maybe we had better," Caddy said. She got up from the floor. "I bet they are looking for us right now." She went toward the door.

"No," Nancy said. "Don't open it." She got up quick and passed Caddy. She didn't touch the door, the wooden bar.

"Why not?" Caddy said.

"Come back to the lamp" Nancy said. "We'll have fun. You don't have to go."

"We ought to go," Caddy said. "Unless we have a lot of fun." She and Nancy came back to the fire, the lamp.

"I want to go home," Jason said. "I'm going to tell."

"I know another story," Nancy said. She stood close to the lamp. She looked at Caddy, like when your eyes look up at a stick balanced on your nose. She had to look down to see Caddy, but her eyes looked like that, like when you are balancing a stick.

"I won't listen to it," Jason said. "I'll bang on the floor."

"It's a good one," Nancy said. "It's better than the other one."

"What's it about?" Caddy said. Nancy was standing by the lamp. Her hand was on the lamp, against the light, long and brown.

"Your hand is on that hot globe," Caddy said. "Don't it feel hot to your hand?"

Nancy looked at her hand on the lamp chimney. She took her hand away, slow. She stood there, looking at Caddy, wringing her long hand as though it were tied to her wrist with a string.

"Let's do something else," Caddy said.

"I want to go home," Jason said.

"I got some popcorn," Nancy said. She looked at Caddy and then at Jason and then at me and then at Caddy again. "I got some popcorn."

"I don't like popcorn," Jason said. "I'd rather have candy."

Nancy looked at Jason. "You can hold the popper." She was still wringing her hand; it was long and limp and brown.

"All right," Jason said. "I'll stay a while if I can do that. Caddy can't hold it. I'll want to go home if Caddy holds the popper."

Nancy built up the fire. "Look at Nancy putting her hands in the fire," Caddy said. "What's the matter with you, Nancy.?"

"I got popcorn," Nancy said. "I got some." She took the popper from under the bed. It was broken. Jason began to cry.

"Now we can't have any popcorn," he said.

"We ought to go home, anyway," Caddy said. "Come on, Quentin."

"Wait," Nancy said; "wait. I can fix it. Don't you want to help me fix it?"

"I don't think I want any," Caddy said. "It's too late now."

"You help me, Jason," Nancy said. "Don't you want to help me?"

"No," Jason said. "I want to go home."

"Hush," Nancy said; "hush. Watch. Watch me. I can fix it so Jason can hold it and pop the corn." She got a piece of wire and fixed the popper.

"It won't hold good," Caddy said.

"Yes, it will," Nancy said. "Yawl watch. Yawl help me shell some corn."

The popcorn was under the bed too. We shelled it into the popper and Nancy helped Jason hold the popper over the fire.

"It's not popping," Jason said. "I want to go home."

"You wait," Nancy said. "It'll begin to pop. We'll have fun then." She was sitting close to the fire. The lamp was turned up so high it was beginning to smoke.

"Why don't you turn it down some?" I said.

"It's all right," Nancy said. "I'll clean it. Yawl wait. The popcorn will start in a minute."

"I don't believe it's going to start," Caddy said. "We ought to start home, anyway. They'll be worried."

"No," Nancy said. "It's going to pop. Dilsey will tell um yawl with me. I been working for yawl long time. They won't mind if yawl at my house. You wait, now. It'll start popping any minute now."

Then Jason got some smoke in his eyes and he began to cry. He dropped the popper into the fire. Nancy got a wet rag and wiped Jason's face, but he didn't stop crying.

"Hush," she said. "Hush." But he didn't hush. Caddy took the popper out of the fire.

"It's burned up," she said. "You'll have to get some more popcorn, Nancy."

"Did you put all of it in?" Nancy said.

"Yes," Caddy said. Nancy looked at Caddy. Then she took the popper and opened it and poured the cinders into her apron and began to sort the grains, her hands long and brown, and we watching her.

"Haven't you got any more?" Caddy said.

"Yes," Nancy said; "yes. Look. This here ain't burnt. All we need to do is—"

"I want to go home," Jason said. "I'm going to tell."

"Hush," Caddy said. We all listened. Nancy's head was already turned toward the barred door, her eyes filled with red lamplight. "Somebody is coming," Caddy said.

Then Nancy began to make that sound again, not loud, sitting there above the fire, her long hands dangling between her knees; all of a sudden water began to come out on her face in big drops, running down her face, carrying in each one a little turning ball of firelight like a spark until it dropped off her chin. "She's not crying," I said.

"I ain't crying," Nancy said. Her eyes were closed. "I ain't crying. Who is it?"

"I don't know," Caddy said. She went to the door and looked out. "We've got to go now," she said. "Here comes father."

"I'm going to tell," Jason said. "Yawl made me come."

The water still ran down Nancy's face. She turned in her chair. "Listen. Tell him. Tell him we going to have fun. Tell him I take good care of yawl until in the morning. Tell him to let me come home with yawl and sleep on the floor. Tell him I won't need no pallet. We'll have fun. You member last time how we had so much fun?"

"I didn't have fun," Jason said. "You hurt me. You put smoke in my eyes. I'm going to tell."

V

Father came in. He looked at us. Nancy did not get up.

"Tell him," she said.

"Caddy made us come down here," Jason said. "I didn't want to."

Father came to the fire. Nancy looked up at him. "Can't you go to Aunt Rachel's and stay?" he said. Nancy looked up at father, her hands between her knees. "He's not here," father said. "I would have seen him. There's not a soul in sight."

"He in the ditch," Nancy said. "He waiting in the ditch yonder."

"Nonsense," father said. He looked at Nancy. "Do you know he's there?"

"I got the sign," Nancy said.

"What sign?"

"I got it. It was on the table when I come in. It was a hogbone, with blood meat still on it, laying by the lamp. He's out there. When yawl walk out that door, I gone."

"Gone where, Nancy?" Caddy said.

"I'm not a tattletale," Jason said.

"Nonsense," father said.

"He out there," Nancy said. "He looking through that window this minute, waiting for yawl to go. Then I gone."

"Nonsense," father said. "Lock up your house and we'll take you on to Aunt Rachel's."

" 'Twon't do no good," Nancy said. She didn't look at father now, but he looked down at her, at her long, limp, moving hands. "Putting it off won't do no good."

"Then what do you want to do?" father said.

"I don't know," Nancy said. "I can't do nothing. Just put it off. And that don't do no good. I reckon it belong to me. I reckon what I going to get ain't no more than mine."

"Get what?" Caddy said. "What's yours?"

"Nothing," father said. "You all must get to bed."

"Caddy made me come," Jason said.

"Go on to Aunt Rachel's," father said.

"It won't do no good," Nancy said. She sat before the fire, her elbows on her knees, her long hands between her knees. "When even your own kitchen wouldn't do no good. When even if I was sleeping on the floor in the room with your children, and the next morning there I am, and blood—"

"Hush," father said. "Lock the door and put out the lamp and go to bed."

"I scared of the dark," Nancy said. "I scared for it to happen in the dark."

"You mean you're going to sit right here with the lamp lighted?" father said. Then Nancy began to make the sound again, sitting before the fire, her long hands between her knees. "Ah, damnation," father said. "Come along, chillen. It's past bedtime."

"When yawl go home, I gone," Nancy said. She talked quieter now, and her face looked quiet, like her hands. "Anyway, I got my coffin money saved up with Mr. Lovelady." Mr. Lovelady was a short, dirty man who collected the Negro insurance, coming around the the cabins or the kitchens every Saturday morning, to collect fifteen cents. He and his wife lived at the hotel. One morning his wife committed suicide. They had a child, a little girl. He and the child went away. After a week or two he came back alone. We would see him going along the lanes and the back streets on Saturday mornings.

"Nonsense," father said. "You'll be the first thing I'll see in the kitchen tomorrow morning."

"You'll see what you'll see, I reckon," Nancy said. "But it will take the Lord to say what that will be."

VI

We left her sitting before the fire.

"Come and put the bar up," father said. But she didn't move. She didn't look at us again, sitting quietly there between the lamp and the fire. From some distance down the lane we could look back and see her through the open door.

"What, Father?" Caddy said. "What's going to happen?"

"Nothing," father said. Jason was on father's back, so Jason was the tallest of all of us. We went down in to the ditch. I looked at it, quiet. I couldn't see much where the moonlight and the shadows tangled.

"If Jesus is hid here, he can see us, cant he?" Caddy said.

"He's not there," father said. "He went away a long time ago."

"You made me come," Jason said, high; against the sky it looked like father had two heads, a little one and a big one. "I didn't want to."

We went up out of the ditch. We could still see Nancy's house and the open door, but we couldn't see Nancy now, sitting before the fire with the door open, because she was tired. "I just done got tired," she said. "I just a nigger. It ain't no fault of mine."

But we could hear her, because she began just after we came up out of the ditch, the sound that was not singing and not unsinging. "Who will do our washing now, Father?" I said.

"I'm not a nigger," Jason said, high and close to father's head.

"You're worse," Caddy said, "you are a tattletale. If something was to jump out, you'd be scairder than a nigger."

"I wouldn't," Jason said.

"You'd cry," Caddy said.

"Caddy," father said.

"I wouldn't!" Jason said.

"Scairy cat," Caddy said.

"Candace!" father said.

1931

A ROSE FOR EMILY

I

When Miss Emily Grierson died, our whole town went to her funeral: the men through a sort of respectful affection for a fallen monument, the women mostly out of curiosity to see the inside of her house, which no one save an old manservant—a combined gardener and cook—had seen in at least ten years.

It was a big, squarish frame house that had once been white, decorated with cupolas and spires and scrolled balconies in the heavily lightsome style of the seventies, set on what had once been our most select street. But garages and cotton gins had encroached and obliterated even the august names of that neighborhood; only Miss Emily's house was left, lifting its stubborn and co-quettish decay above the cotton wagons and the gasoline pumps—an eyesore among eyesores. And now Miss Emily had gone to join the representatives of those august names where they lay in the cedar-bemused cemetery among the ranked and anonymous graves of Union and Confederate soldiers who fell at the battle of Jefferson.

Alive, Miss Emily had been a tradition, a duty, and a care; a sort of hereditary obligation upon the town, dating from that day in 1894 when Colonel Sartoris, the mayor—he who fathered the edict that no Negro woman should appear on the streets without an apron—remitted her taxes, the dispensation dating from the death of her father on into perpetuity. Not that Miss Emily would have accepted charity. Colonel Sartoris invented an involved tale to the effect that Miss Emily's father had loaned money to the town, which the town, as a matter of business, preferred this way of repaying. Only a man of Colonel Sartoris' generation and thought could have invented it, and only a woman could have believed it.

When the next generation, with its more modern ideas, became mayors and aldermen, this arrangement created some little dissatisfaction. On the first of the year they mailed her a tax notice. February came, and there was no reply. They wrote her a formal letter, asking her to call at the sheriff's office at her convenience. A week later the mayor wrote her himself, offering to call or to send his car for her, and received in reply a note on paper of an archaic shape, in a thin, flowery calligraphy in faded ink, to the effect that she no longer went out at all. The tax notice was also enclosed, without comment.

They called a special meeting of the Board of Aldermen. A deputation waited upon her, knocked at the door through which no visitor had passed since she ceased giving china-painting lessons eight or ten years earlier. They were ad-mitted by the old Negro into a dim hall from which a stairway mounted into still more shadow. It smelled of dust and disuse—a close, dank smell. The Negro led them into the parlor. It was furnished in heavy, leather-covered furniture. When the Negro opened the blinds of one window, they could see that the leather was cracked; and when they sat down, a faint dust rose sluggishly about their thighs, spinning with slow motes in the single sun-ray. On a tarnished gilt easel before the fireplace stood a crayon portrait of Miss Emily's father.

They rose when she entered—a small, fat woman in black, with a thin gold chain descending to her waist and vanishing into her belt, leaning on an ebony cane with a tarnished gold head. Her skeleton was small and spare; perhaps that was why what would have been merely plumpness in another was obesity in her. She looked bloated, like a body long submerged in motionless water, and of that pallid hue. Her eyes, lost in the fatty ridges of her face, looked like two small pieces of coal pressed into a lump of dough as they moved from one face to another while the visitors stated their errand.

She did not ask them to sit. She just stood in the door and listened quietly until the spokesman came to a stumbling halt. Then they could hear the invisible watch ticking at the end of the gold chain.

Her voice was dry and cold. "I have no taxes in Jefferson. Colonel Sartoris explained it to me. Perhaps one of you can gain access to the city records and satisfy yourselves."

"But we have. We are the city authorities, Miss Emily. Didn't you get a notice from the sheriff, signed by him?"

"I received a paper, yes," Miss Emily said. "Perhaps he considers himself the sheriff . . . I have no taxes in Jefferson."

"But there is nothing on the books to show that, you see. We must go by the—"

"See Colonel Sartoris. I have no taxes in Jefferson."

"But, Miss Emily—"

"See Colonel Sartoris." (Colonel Sartoris had been dead almost ten years.) "I have no taxes in Jefferson. Tobe!" The Negro appeared. "Show these gentlemen out."

II

So she vanquished them, horse and foot[1], just as she had vanquished their fathers thirty years before about the smell. That was two years after her father's death and a short time after her sweetheart—the one we believed would marry her—had deserted her. After her father's death she went out very little; after her sweetheart went away, people hardly saw her at all. A few of the ladies had the temerity to call, but were not received, and the only sign of life about the place was the Negro man—a young man then—going in and out with a market basket.

"Just as if a man—any man—could keep a kitchen properly," the ladies said; so they were not suprised when the smell developed. It was another link between the gross, teeming world and the high and mighty Griersons.

A neighbor, a woman, complained to the mayor, Judge Stevens, eighty years old.

"But what will you have me do about it, madam?" he said.

"Why, send her word to stop it," the woman said. "Isn't there a law?"

"I'm sure that won't be necessary," Judge Stevens said. It's probably just a snake or a rat that nigger of hers killed in the yard. I'll speak to him about it."

The next day he received two more complaints, one from a man who came in diffident deprecation. "We really must do something about it, Judge. I'd be the last one in the world to bother Miss Emily, but we've got to do something." That night the Board of Aldermen met—three graybeards and one younger man, a member of the rising generation.

"It's simple enough," he said. "Send her word to have her place cleaned up. Give her a certain time to do it in, and if she don't . . ."

"Dammit, sir," Judge Stevens said, "will you accuse a lady to her face of smelling bad?"

---

[1]I.e., totally—as in a victory over an army's cavalry (horse) and infantry (foot).

So the next night, after midnight, four men crossed Miss Emily's lawn and slunk about the house like burglars, sniffing along the base of the brickwork and at the cellar openings while one of them performed a regular sowing motion with his hand out of a sack slung from his shoulder. They broke open the cellar door and sprinkled lime there, and in all the outbuildings. As they recrossed the lawn, a window that had been dark was lighted and Miss Emily sat in it, the light behind her, and her upright torso motionless as that of an idol. They crept quietly across the lawn and into the shadow of the locusts that lined the street. After a week or two the smell went away.

That was when people had begun to feel really sorry for her. People in our town, remembering how old lady Wyatt, her great-aunt, had gone completely crazy at last, believed that the Griersons held themselves a little too high for what they really were. None of the young men were quite good enough for Miss Emily and such. We had long thought of them as a tableau, Miss Emily a slender figure in white in the background, her father a spraddled silhouette in the foreground, his back to her and clutching a horsewhip, the two of them framed by the back-flung front door. So when she got to be thirty and was still single, we were not pleased exactly, but vindicated; even with insanity in the family she wouldn't have turned down all of her chances if they had really materialized.

When her father died, it got about that the house was all that was left to her; and in a way, people were glad. At last they could pity Miss Emily. Being left alone, and a pauper, she had become humanized. Now she too would know the old thrill and the old despair of a penny more or less.

The day after his death all the ladies prepared to call at the house and offer condolence and aid, as is our custom. Miss Emily met them at the door, dressed as usual and with no trace of grief on her face. She told them that her father was not dead. She did that for three days, with the ministers calling on her, and the doctors, trying to persuade her to let them dispose of the body. Just as they were about to resort to law and force, she broke down, and they buried her father quickly.

We did not say she was crazy then. We believed she had to do that. We remembered all the young men her father had driven away, and we knew that with nothing left, she would have to cling to that which had robbed her, as people will.

III

She was sick for a long time. When we saw her again, her hair was cut short, making her look like a girl, with a vague resemblance to those angels in colored church windows—sort of tragic and serene.

The town had just let the contracts for paving the sidewalks, and in the summer after her father's death they began the work. The construction company came with niggers and mules and machinery, and a foreman named Homer Barron, a Yankee—a big, dark, ready man, with a big voice and eyes lighter than his face. The little boys would follow in groups to hear him cuss the niggers, and the niggers singing in time to the rise and fall of picks. Pretty soon he knew everybody in town. Whenever you heard a lot of laughing anywhere about the square, Homer Barron would be in the center of the group. Presently we began to see him and Miss Emily on Sunday afternoons driving in the yellow-wheeled buggy and the matched team of bays from the livery stable.

At first we were glad that Miss Emily would have an interest, because the ladies all said, "Of course a Grierson would not think seriously of a Northerner, a day laborer." But there were still others, older people, who said that even grief could not cause a real lady to forget *noblesse oblige*[1]—without calling it *noblesse oblige*. They just said, "Poor Emily. Her kinsfolk should come to her." She had some kin in Alabama; but years ago her father had fallen out with them over the estate of old lady Wyatt, the crazy woman, and there was no communication between the two families. They had not even been represented at the funeral.

And as soon as the old people said, "Poor Emily," the whispering began. "Do you suppose it's really so?" they said to one another. "Of course it is. What else could . . ." This behind their hands; rustling of craned silk and satin behind jalousies closed upon the sun of Sunday afternoon as the thin, swift clop-clop-clop of the matched team passed: "Poor Emily."

She carried her head high enough—even when we believed that she was fallen. It was as if she demanded more than ever the recognition of her dignity as the last Grierson; as if it had wanted that touch of earthliness to reaffirm her imperviousness. Like when she bought the rat poison, the arsenic. That was over a year after they had begun to say "Poor Emily," and while the two female cousins were visiting her.

"I want some poison," she said to the druggist. She was over thirty then, still a slight woman, though thinner than usual, with cold, haughty black eyes in a face the flesh of which was strained across the temples and about the eye-sockets as you imagine a lighthouse-keeper's face ought to look. "I want some poison," she said.

"Yes, Miss Emily. What kind? For rats and such? I'd recom—"

"I want the best you have. I don't care what kind."

The druggist named several. "They'll kill anything up to an elephant. But what you want is—"

"Arsenic," Miss Emily said. "Is that a good one?"

"Is . . . arsenic? Yes, ma'am. But what you want—"

"I want arsenic."

The druggist looked down at her. She looked back at him, erect, her face like a strained flag. "Why, of course," the druggist said. "If that's what you want. But the law requires you to tell what you are going to use it for."

Miss Emily just stared at him, her head tilted back in order to look him eye for eye, until he looked away and went and got the arsenic and wrapped it up. The Negro delivery boy brought her the package; the druggist didn't come back. When she opened the package at home there was written on the box, under the skull and bones: "For rats."

IV

So the next day we all said, "She will kill herself"; and we said it would be the best thing. When she had first begun to be seen with Homer Barron, we had said, "She will marry him." Then we said, "She will persuade him yet," because Homer himself had remarked—he liked men, and it was known that he drank with the younger men at the Elks' Club—that he was not a marrying man. Later we said, "Poor Emily" behind the jalousies as they passed on Sunday afternoon in the glittering buggy, Miss Emily with her head high and Homer Barron with his hat cocked and a cigar in his teeth, reins and whip in a yellow glove.

[1]French: duty obligates, i.e., the duties, obligations, and honorable behavior expected from people of high rank.

Then some of the ladies began to say that it was a disgrace to the town and a bad example to the young people. The men did not want to interfere, but at last the ladies forced the Baptist minister—Miss Emily's people were Episcopal— to call upon her. He would never divulge what happened during that interview, but he refused to go back again. The next Sunday they again drove about the streets, and the following day the minister's wife wrote to Miss Emily's relations in Alabama.

So she had blood-kin under her roof again and we sat back to watch developments. At first nothing happened. Then we were sure that they were to be married. We learned that Miss Emily had been to the jeweler's and ordered a man's toilet set in silver, with the letters H. B. on each piece. Two days later we learned that she had bought a complete outfit of men's clothing, including a nightshirt, and we said, "They are married." We were really glad. We were glad because the two female cousins were even more Grierson than Miss Emily had ever been.

So we were not surprised when Homer Barron—the streets had been finished some time since—was gone. We were a little disappointed that there was not a public blowing-off, but we believed that he had gone on to prepare for Miss Emily's coming, or to give her a chance to get rid of the cousins. (By that time it was a cabal, and we were all Miss Emily's allies to help circumvent the cousins.) Sure enough, after another week they departed. And, as we had expected all along, within three days Homer Barron was back in town. A neighbor saw the Negro man admit him at the kitchen door at dusk one evening.

And that was the last we saw of Homer Barron. And of Miss Emily for some time. The Negro man went in and out with the market basket, but the front door remained closed. Now and then we would see her at a window for a moment, as the men did that night when they sprinkled lime, but for almost six months she did not appear on the streets. Then we knew that this was to be expected too; as if that quality of her father which had thwarted her woman's life so many times had been too virulent and too furious to die.

When we next saw Miss Emily, she had grown fat and her hair was turning gray. During the next few years it grew grayer and grayer until it attained an even pepper-and-salt iron-gray, when it ceased turning. Up to the day of her death at seventy-four it was still that vigorous iron-gray, like the hair of an active man.

From that time on her front door remained closed, save for a period of six or seven years, when she was about forty, during which she gave lessons in china-painting. She fitted up a studio in one of the downstairs rooms, where the daughters and granddaughters of Colonie Sartoris' contemporaries were sent to her with the same regularity and in the same spirit that they were sent to church on Sundays with a twenty-five-cent piece for the collection plate. Meanwhile her taxes had been remitted.

Then the newer generation became the backbone and the spirit of the town, and the painting pupils grew up and fell away and did not send their children to her with boxes of color and tedious brushes and pictures cut from the ladies' magazines. The front door closed upon the last one and remained closed for good. When the town got free postal delivery, Miss Emily alone refused to let them fasten the metal numbers above her door and attach a mailbox to it. She would not listen to them.

Daily, monthly, yearly we watched the Negro grow grayer and more stooped, going in and out with the market basket. Each December we sent her a tax notice, which would be returned by the post office a week later, unclaimed. Now and then we would see her in one of the downstairs windows—she had evidently shut up the top floor of the house—like the carven torso of an idol in a niche, looking or not looking at us, we could never tell which. Thus she passed from generation to generation—dear, inescapable, impervious, tranquil, and perverse.

And so she died. Fell ill in the house filled with dust and shadows, with only a doddering Negro man to wait on her. We did not even know she was sick; we had long since given up trying to get any information from the Negro. He talked to no one, probably not even to her, for his voice had grown harsh and rusty, as if from disuse.

She died in one of the downstairs rooms, in a heavy walnut bed with a curtain, her gray head propped on a pillow yellow and moldy with age and lack of sunlight.

V

The Negro met the first of the ladies at the front door and let them in, with their hushed, sibilant voices and their quick, curious glances, and then he disappeared. He walked right through the house and out the back and was not seen again.

The two female cousins came at once. They held the funeral on the second day, with the town coming to look at Miss Emily beneath a mass of bought flowers, with the crayon face of her father musing profoundly above the bier and the ladies sibilant and macabre; and the very old men—some in their brushed Confederate uniforms—on the porch and the lawn, talking of Miss Emily as if she had been a contemporary of theirs, believing that they had danced with her and courted her perhaps, confusing time with its mathematical progression, as the old do, to whom all the past is not a diminishing road but, instead, a huge meadow which no winter ever quite touches, divided from them now by the narrow bottle-neck of the most recent decade of years.

Already we knew that there was one room in that region above stairs which no one had seen in forty years, and which would have to be forced. They waited until Miss Emily was decently in the ground before they opened it.

The violence of breaking down the door seemed to fill this room with pervading dust. A thin, acrid pall as of the tomb seemed to lie everywhere upon this room decked and furnished as for a bridal: upon the valance curtains of faded rose color, upon the rose-shaded lights, upon the dressing table, upon the delicate array of crystal and the man's toilet things backed with tarnished silver, silver so tarnished that the monogram was obscured. Among them lay a collar and tie, as if they had just been removed, which, lifted, left upon the surface a pale crescent in the dust. Upon a chair hung the suit, carefully folded; beneath it the two mute shoes and the discarded socks.

The man himself lay in the bed.

For a long while we just stood there, looking down at the profound and fleshless grin. The body had apparently once lain in the attitude of an embrace, but now the long sleep that outlasts love, that conquers even the grimace of love, had cuckolded him. What was left of him, rotted beneath what was left of the nightshirt, had become inextricable from the bed in which he lay; and upon him and upon the pillow beside him lay that even coating of the patient and biding dust.

Then we noticed that in the second pillow was the indentation of a head. One of us lifted something from it, and leaning forward, that faint and invisible dust dry and acrid in the nostrils, we saw a long strand of iron-gray hair.

1930, 1931

BARN BURNING

The store in which the Justice of the Peace's court was sitting smelled of cheese. The boy, crouched on his nail keg at the back of the crowded room, knew he smelled cheese, and more: from where he sat he could see the ranked shelves close-packed with the solid, squat, dynamic shapes of tin cans whose labels his stomach read, not from the lettering which meant nothing to his mind but from the scarlet devils and the silver curve of fish—this, the cheese which he knew he smelled and the hermetic meat which his intestines believed he smelled coming in intermittent gusts momentary and brief between the other constant one, the smell and sense just a little of fear because mostly of despair and grief, the old fierce pull of blood. He could not see the table where the Justice sat and before which his father and his father's enemy (*our enemy* he thought in that despair; *ourn! mine and hisn both! He's my father*) stood, but he could hear them, the two of them that is, because his father had said no word yet:

"But what proof have you, Mr. Harris?"

"I told you. The hog got into my corn. I caught it up and sent it back to him. He had no fence that would hold it. I told him so, warned him. The next time I put the hog in my pen. When he came to get it I gave him enough wire to patch up his pen. The next time I put the hog up and kept it. I rode down to his house and saw the wire I gave him still rolled on to the spool in his yard. I told him he could have the hog when he paid me a dollar pound fee. That evening a nigger came with the dollar and got the hog. He was a strange nigger. He said, 'He say to tell you wood and hay kin burn.' I said, 'What?' 'That whut he said to tell you,' the nigger said. 'Wood and hay kin burn.' That night my barn burned. I got the stock out but lost the barn."

"Where is the nigger? Have you got him?"

"He was a strange nigger, I tell you. I don't know what became of him."

"But that's not proof. Don't you see that's not proof?"

"Get that boy up here. He knows." For a moment the boy thought too that the man meant his older brother until Harris said, "Not him. The little one. The boy," and, crouching, small for his age, small and wiry like his father, in patched and faded jeans even too small for him, with straight, uncombed, brown hair and eyes gray and wild as storm scud, he saw the men between himself and the table part and become a lane of grim faces, at the end of which he saw the Justice, a shabby, collarless, graying man in spectacles, beckoning him. He felt no floor under his bare feet; he seemed to walk beneath the palpable weight of the grim turning faces. His father, stiff in his black Sunday coat donned not for the trial but for the moving, did not even look at him. *He aims for me to lie*, he thought, again with that frantic grief and despair. *And I will have to do hit.*

"What's your name, boy?" the Justice said.

"Colonel Sartoris Snopes," the boy whispered.

"Hey?" the Justice said. "Talk louder. Colonel Sartoris? I reckon anybody named for Colonel Sartoris in this country can't help but tell the truth, can they?" The boy said nothing. *Enemy! Enemy!* he thought; for a moment he could not even see, could not see that the Justice's face was kindly nor discern that his voice was troubled when he spoke to the man named Harris: "Do you want me to question this boy?" But he could hear, and during those subsequent long seconds while there was absolutely no sound in the crowded little room save that of quiet and intent breathing it was as if he had swung outward at the end of a grape vine, over a ravine, and at the top of the swing had been caught in a prolonged instant of mesmerized gravity, weightless in time.

"No!" Harris said violently, explosively. "Damnation! Send him out of here!" Now time, the fluid world, rushed beneath him again, the voices coming to him again through the smell of cheese and sealed meat, the fear and despair and the old grief of blood:

"This case is closed. I can't find against you, Snopes, but I can give you advice. Leave this country and don't come back to it."

His father spoke for the first time, his voice cold and harsh, level, without emphasis: "I aim to. I don't figure to stay in a country among people who . . ." he said something unprintable and vile, addressed to no one.

"That'll do," the Justice said. "Take your wagon and get out of this country before dark. Case dismissed."

His father turned, and he followed the stiff black coat, the wiry figure walking a little stiffly from where a Confederate provost man's musket ball had taken him in the heel on a stolen horse thirty years ago, followed the two backs now, since his older brother had appeared from somewhere in the crowd, no taller than the father but thicker, chewing tobacco steadily, between the two lines of grim-faced men and out of the store and across the worn gallery and down the sagging steps and among the dogs and half-grown boys in the mild May dust, where as he passed a voice hissed:

"Barn burner!"

Again he could not see, whirling; there was a face in a red haze, moonlike, bigger than the full moon, the owner of it half again his size, he leaping in the red haze toward the face, feeling no blow, feeling no shock when his head struck the earth, scrabbling up and leaping again, feeling no blow this time either and tasting no blood, scrabbling up to see the other boy in full flight and himself already leaping into pursuit as his father's hand jerked him back, the harsh, cold voice speaking above him: "Go get in the wagon."

It stood in a grove of locusts and mulberries across the road. His two hulking sisters in their Sunday dresses and his mother and her sister in calico and sunbonnets were already in it, sitting on and among the sorry residue of the dozen and more movings which even the boy could remember—the battered stove, the broken beds and chairs, the clock inlaid with mother-of-pearl, which would not run, stopped at some fourteen minutes past two o'clock of a dead and forgotten day and time, which had been his mother's dowry. She was crying, though when she saw him she drew her sleeve across her face and began to descend from the wagon. "Get back," the father said.

"He's hurt. I got to get some water and wash his . . ."

"Get back in the wagon," his father said. He got in too, over the tail-gate. His father mounted to the seat where the older brother already sat and struck the gaunt mules two savage blows with the peeled willow, but without heat. It was not even sadistic; it was exactly that same quality which in later years would cause his descendants to over-run the engine before putting a motor car into motion, striking and reining back in the same movement. The wagon went on, the store with its quiet crowd of grimly watching men dropped behind; a curve in the road hid it. *Forever* he thought. *Maybe he's done satisfied now, now that he has* . . . stopping himself, not to say it aloud even to himself. His mother's hand touched his shoulder.

"Does hit hurt?" she said.

"Naw," he said, "Hit don't hurt. Lemme be."

"Can't you wipe some of the blood off before hit dries?"

"I'll wash to-night," he said. "Lemme be, I tell you."

The wagon went on. He did not know where they were going. None of them ever did or ever asked, because it was always somewhere, always a house of sorts waiting for them a day or two days or even three days away. Likely his father had already arranged to make a crop on another farm before he . . . Again he had to stop himself. He (the father) always did. There was something about his wolflike independence and even courage when the advantage was at least neutral which impressed strangers, as if they got from his latent ravening ferocity not so much a sense of dependability as a feeling that his ferocious conviction in the rightness of his own actions would be of advantage to all whose interest lay with his.

That night they camped, in a grove of oaks and beeches where a spring ran. The nights were still cool and they had a fire against it, of a rail lifted from a nearby fence and cut into lengths—a small fire, neat, niggard almost, a shrewd fire; such fires were his father's habit and custom always, even in freezing weather. Older, the boy might have remarked this and wondered why not a big one; why should not a man who had not only seen the waste and extravagance of war, but who had in his blood an inherent voracious prodigality with material not his own, have burned everything in sight? Then he might have gone a step farther and thought that there was the reason: that niggard blaze was the living fruit of nights passed during those four years in the woods hiding from all men, blue or gray, with his strings of horses (captured horses, he called them). And older still, he might have divined the true reason: that the element of fire spoke to some deep mainspring of his father's being, as the element of steel or of powder spoke to other men, as the one weapon for the preservation of integrity, else breath were not worth the breathing, and hence to be regarded with respect and used with discretion.

But he did not think this now and he had seen those same niggard blazes all his life. He merely ate his supper beside it and was already half asleep over his iron plate when his father called him, and once more he followed the stiff back, the stiff and ruthless limp, up the slope and on to the starlit road where, turning, he could see his father against the stars but without face or depth—a shape black, flat, and bloodless as though cut from tin in the iron folds of the frockcoat which had not been made for him, the voice harsh like tin and without heat like tin:

"You were fixing to tell them. You would have told him." He didn't answer. His father struck him with the flat of his hand on the side of his head, hard but without heat, exactly as he had struck the two mules at the store, exactly as he would strike either of them with any stick in order to kill a horse fly, his voice still without heat or anger: "You're getting to be a man. You got to learn. You got to learn to stick to your own blood or you ain't going to have any blood to stick to you. Do you think either of them, any man there this morning, would? Don't you know all they wanted was a chance to get at me because they knew I had them beat? Eh?" Later, twenty years later, he was to tell himself, "If I had said they wanted only truth, justice, he would have hit me again." But now he said nothing. He was not crying. He just stood there. "Answer me," his father said.

"Yes," he whispered. His father turned.

"Get on to bed. We'll be there to-morrow."

To-morrow they were there. In the early afternoon the wagon stopped before a paintless two-room house identical almost with the dozen others it had stopped before even in the boy's ten years, and again, as on the other dozen occasions, his mother and aunt got down and began to unload the wagon, although his two sisters and his father and brother had not moved.

"Likely hit ain't fitten for hawgs," one of the sisters said.

"Nevertheless, fit it will and you'll hog it and like it," his father said. "Get out of them chairs and help your Ma unload."

The two sisters got down, big, bovine, in a flutter of cheap ribbons; one of them drew from the jumbled wagon bed a battered lantern, the other a worn broom. His father handed the reins to the older son and began to climb stiffly over the wheel. "When they get unloaded, take the team to the barn and feed them." Then he said, and at first the boy thought he was still speaking to his brother: "Come with me."

"Me?" he said.

"Yes," his father said. "You."

"Abner," his mother said. His father paused and looked back—the harsh level stare beneath the shaggy, graying, irascible brows.

"I reckon I'll have a word with the man that aims to begin to-morrow owning me body and soul for the next eight months."

They went back up the road. A week ago—or before last night, that is—he would have asked where they were going, but not now. His father had struck him before last night but never before had he paused afterward to explain why; it was as if the blow and the following calm, outrageous voice still rang, repercussed, divulging nothing to him save the terrible handicap of being young, the light weight of his few years, just heavy enough to prevent his soaring free of the world as it seemed to be ordered but not heavy enough to keep him footed solid in it, to resist it and try to change the course of its events.

Presently he could see the grove of oaks and cedars and the other flowering trees and shrubs where the house would be, though not the house yet. They walked beside a fence massed with honeysuckle and Cherokee roses and came to a gate swinging open between two brick pillars, and now, beyond a sweep of drive, he saw the house for the first time and at that instant he forgot his father and the terror and despair both, and even when he remembered his father again (who had not stopped) the terror and despair did not return. Because, for all the twelve movings, they had sojourned until now in a poor country, a land of small farms and fields and houses, and he had never seen a house like this before. *Hits big as a courthouse* he thought quietly, with a surge of peace and joy whose reason he could not have thought into words, being too young for that: *They are safe from him. People whose lives are a part of this peace and dignity are beyond his touch, he is no more to them than a buzzing wasp: capable of stinging for a little moment but that's all; the spell of this peace and dignity rendering even the barns and stable and cribs which belong to it impervious to the puny flames he might contrive . . .* this, the peace and joy, ebbing for an instant as he looked again at the stiff black back, the stiff and implacable limp of the figure which was not dwarfed by the house, for the reason that it had never looked big anywhere and which now, against the serene columned backdrop, had more than ever that impervious quality of something cut ruthlessly from tin, depthless, as though, sidewise to the sun, it would cast no shadow. Watching him, the boy remarked the absolutely undeviating course which his father held and saw the stiff foot come squarely down in a pile of fresh droppings where a horse had stood in the drive and which his father could have avoided by a simple change of stride. But it ebbed only for a moment, though he could not have thought this into words either, walking on in the spell of the house, which he could even want but without envy, without sorrow, certainly never with that ravening and jealous rage which unknown to him walked in the ironlike black coat before him: *Maybe he will feel it too. Maybe it will even change him now from what maybe he couldn't help but be.*

They crossed the portico. Now he could hear his father's stiff foot as it came down on the boards with clocklike finality, a sound out of all proportion to the displacement of the body it bore and which was not dwarfed either by the white door before it, as though it had attained to a sort of vicious and ravening minimum not to be dwarfed by anything—the flat, wide, black hat, the formal coat of broadcloth which had once been black but which had now that friction-glazed greenish cast of the bodies of old house flies, the lifted sleeve which was too large, the lifted hand like a curled claw. The door opened so promptly that the boy knew the Negro must have been watching them all the time, an old man with neat grizzled hair, in a linen jacket, who stood barring the door with his body, saying, "Wipe yo foots, white man, fo you come in here. Major ain't home nohow."

"Get out of my way, nigger," his father said, without heat too, flinging the door back and the Negro also entering, his hat still on his head. And now the boy saw the prints of the stiff foot on the doorjamb and saw them appear on the pale rug behind the machinelike deliberation of the foot which seemed to bear (or transmit) twice the weight which the body encompassed. The Negro was shouting "Miss Lula! Miss Lula!" somewhere behind them, then the boy, deluged as though by a warm wave by a suave turn of carpeted stair and a pendant glitter of chandeliers and a mute gleam of gold frames, heard the swift feet and saw her too, a lady—perhaps he had never seen her like before either—in a gray, smooth gown with lace at the throat and an apron tied at the waist and the sleeves turned back, wiping cake or biscuit dough from her hands with a towel as she came up the hall, looking not at his father at all but at the tracks on the blond rug with an expression of incredulous amazement.

"I tried," the Negro cried. "I tole him to . . ."

"Will you please go away?" she said in a shaking voice. "Major de Spain is not at home. Will you please go away?"

His father had not spoken again. He did not speak again. He did not even look at her. He just stood stiff in the center of the rug, in his hat, the shaggy iron-gray brows twitching slightly above the pebble-colored eyes as he appeared to examine the house with brief deliberation. Then with the same deliberation he turned; the boy watched him pivot on the good leg and saw the stiff foot drag round the arc of the turning, leaving a final long and fading smear. His father never looked at it, he never once looked down at the rug. The Negro held the door. It closed behind them, upon the hysteric and indistinguishable woman-wail. His father stopped at the top of the steps and scraped his boot clean on the edge of it. At the gate he stopped again. He stood for a moment, planted stiffly on the stiff foot, looking back at the house. "Pretty and white, ain't it?" he said. "That's sweat. Nigger sweat. Maybe it ain't white enough yet to suit him. Maybe he wants to mix some white sweat with it."

Two hours later the boy was chopping wood behind the house within which his mother and aunt and the two sisters (the mother and aunt, not the two girls, he knew that; even at this distance and muffled by walls the flat loud voices of the two girls emanated an incorrigible idle inertia) were setting up the stove to prepare a meal, when he heard the hooves and saw the linen-clad man on a fine sorrel mare, whom he recognized even before he saw the rolled rug in front of the Negro youth following on a fat bay carriage horse—a suffused, angry face vanishing, still at full gallop, beyond the corner of the house where his father and brother were sitting in the two tilted chairs; and a moment later, almost before he could have put the axe down, he heard the hooves again and watched the sorrel mare go back out of the yard, already galloping again. Then his father began to shout one of the sisters' names, who presently emerged backward from the kitchen door dragging the rolled rug along the ground by one end while the other sister walked behind it.

"If you ain't going to tote, go on and set up the wash pot," the first said.

"You, Sarty!" the second shouted. "Set up the wash pot!" His father appeared at the door, framed against that shabbiness, as he had been against that other bland perfection, impervious to either, the mother's anxious face at his shoulder.

"Go on," the father said. "Pick it up." The two sisters stooped, broad, lethargic; stooping, they presented an incredible expanse of pale cloth and a flutter of tawdry ribbons.

"If I thought enough of a rug to have to git hit all the way from France I wouldn't keep hit where folks coming in would have to tromp on hit," the first said. They raised the rug.

"Abner," the mother said. "Let me do it."

"You go back and git dinner," his father said. "I'll tend to this."

From the woodpile through the rest of the afternoon the boy watched them, the rug spread flat in the dust beside the bubbling wash-pot, the two sisters stooping over it with that profound and lethargic reluctance, while the father stood over them in turn, implacable and grim, driving them though never raising his voice again. He could smell the harsh homemade lye they were using; he saw his mother come to the door once and look toward them with an expression not anxious now but very like despair; he saw his father turn, and he fell to with the axe and saw from the corner of his eye his father raise from the ground a flattish fragment of field stone and examine it and return to the pot, and this time his mother actually spoke: "Abner. Abner. Please don't. Please, Abner."

Then he was done too. It was dusk; the whippoorwills had already begun. He could smell coffee from the room where they would presently eat the cold food remaining from the mid-afternoon meal, though when he entered the house he realized they were having coffee again probably because there was a fire on the hearth, before which the rug now lay spread over the backs of the two chairs. The tracks of his father's foot were gone. Where they had been were now long, water-cloudy scoriations resembling the sporadic course of a lilliputian mowing machine.

It still hung there while they ate the cold food and then went to bed, scattered without order or claim up and down the two rooms, his mother in one bed, where his father would later lie, the older brother in the other, himself, the aunt, and the two sisters on pallets on the floor. But his father was not in bed yet. The last thing the boy remembered was the depthless, harsh silhouette of the hat and coat bending over the rug and it seemed to him that he had not even closed his eyes when the silhouette was standing over him, the fire almost dead behind it, the stiff foot prodding him awake. "Catch up the mule," his father said.

When he returned with the mule his father was standing in the black door, the rolled rug over his shoulder. "Ain't you going to ride?" he said.

"No. Give me your foot."

He bent his knee into his father's hand, the wiry, surprising power flowed smoothly, rising, he rising with it, on to the mule's bare back (they had owned a saddle once; the boy could remember it though not when or where) and with the same effortlessness his father swung the rug up in front of him. Now in the starlight they retraced the afternoon's path, up the dusty road rife with honeysuckle, through the gate and up the black tunnel of the drive to the lightless house, where he sat on the mule and felt the rough warp of the rug drag across his thighs and vanish.

"Don't you want me to help?" he whispered. His father did not answer and now he heard again that stiff foot striking the hollow portico with that wooden and clocklike deliberation, that outrageous overstatement of the weight it carried. The rug, hunched, not flung (the boy could tell that even in the darkness) from his father's shoulder struck the angle of wall and floor with a sound unbelievably loud, thunderous, then the foot again, unhurried and enormous; a light came on in the house and the boy sat, tense, breathing steadily and quietly and just a little fast, though the foot itself did not increase its beat at all, descending the steps now; now the boy could see him.

"Don't you want to ride now?" he whispered. "We kin both ride now," the light within the house altering now, flaring up and sinking. *He's coming down the stairs now,* he thought. He had already ridden the mule up beside the horse block; presently his father was up behind him and he doubled the reins over and slashed the mule across the neck, but before the animal could begin to trot the hard, thin arm came round him, the hard, knotted hand jerking the mule back to a walk.

In the first red rays of the sun they were in the lot, putting plow gear on the mules. This time the sorrel mare was in the lot before he heard it at all, the rider collarless and even bareheaded, trembling, speaking in a shaking voice as the woman in the house had done, his father merely looking up once before stooping again to the hame he was buckling, so that the man on the mare spoke to his stooping back:

"You must realize you have ruined that rug. Wasn't there anybody here, any of your women . . ." he ceased, shaking, the boy watching him, the older brother leaning now in the stable door, chewing, blinking slowly and steadily at nothing apparently. "It cost a hundred dollars. But you never had a hundred dollars. You never will. So I'm going to charge you twenty bushels of corn against your crop. I'll add it in your contract and when you come to the commissary you can sign it. That won't keep Mrs. de Spain quiet but maybe it will teach you to wipe your feet off before you enter her house again."

Then he was gone. The boy looked at his father, who still had not spoken or even looked up again, who was now adjusting the logger-head in the hame.

"Pap," he said. His father looked at him—the inscrutable face, the shaggy brows beneath which the gray eyes glinted coldly. Suddenly the boy went toward him, fast, stopping as suddenly. "You done the best you could!" he cried. "If he wanted hit done different why didn't he wait and tell you how? He won't git no twenty bushels! He won't git none! We'll gather hit and hide hit! I kin watch . . ."

"Did you put the cutter back in that straight stock like I told you?"

"No, sir," he said.

"Then go do it."

That was Wednesday. During the rest of that week he worked steadily, at what was within his scope and some which was beyond it, with an industry that did not need to be driven nor even commanded twice; he had this from his mother, with the difference that some at least of what he did he liked to do, such as splitting wood with the half-size axe which his mother and aunt had earned, or saved money somehow, to present him with at Christmas. In company with the two older women (and on one afternoon, even one of the sisters), he built pens for the shoat and the cow which were a part of his father's contract with the landlord, and one afternoon, his father being absent, gone somewhere on one of the mules, he went to the field.

They were running a middle buster now, his brother holding the plow straight while he handled the reins, and walking beside the straining mule, the rich black soil shearing cool and damp against his bare ankles, he thought *Maybe this is the end of it. Maybe even that twenty bushels that seems hard to have to pay for just a rug will be a cheap price for him to stop forever and always from being what he used to be;* thinking, dreaming now, so that his brother had to speak sharply to him to mind the mule: *Maybe he even won't collect the twenty bushels. Maybe it will all add up and balance and vanish—corn, rug, fire; the terror and grief, the being pulled two ways like between two teams of horses—gone, done with for ever and ever.*

Then it was Saturday; he looked up from beneath the mule he was harnessing and saw his father in the black coat and hat. "Not that," his father said. "The wagon gear." And then, two hours later, sitting in the wagon bed behind his father and brother on the seat, the wagon accomplished a final curve, and he saw the weathered paintless store with its tattered tobacco and patent-medicine posters and the tethered wagons and saddle animals below the gallery. He mounted the gnawed steps behind his father and brother, and there again was the lane of quiet, watching faces for the three of them to walk through. He saw the man in spectacles sitting at the plank table and he did not need to be told this was a Justice of the Peace; he sent one glare of fierce, exultant, partisan defiance at the man in collar and cravat now, whom he had seen but twice before in his life, and that on a galloping horse, who now wore on his face an expression not of rage but of amazed unbelief which the boy could not have known was at the incredible circumstance of being sued by one of his own tenants, and came and stood against his father and cried at the Justice: "He ain't done it! He ain't burnt . . ."

"Go back to the wagon," his father said.

"Burnt?" the Justice said. "Do I understand this rug was burned too?"

"Does anybody here claim it was?" his father said. "Go back to the wagon." But he did not, he merely retreated to the rear of the room, crowded as that other had been, but not to sit down this time, instead, to stand pressing among the motionless bodies, listening to the voices:

"And you claim twenty bushels of corn is too high for the damage you did to the rug?"

"He brought the rug to me and said he wanted the tracks washed out of it. I washed the tracks out and took the rug back to him."

"But you didn't carry the rug back to him in the same condition it was in before you made the tracks on it."

His father did not answer, and now for perhaps half a minute there was no sound at all save that of breathing, the faint, steady suspiration of complete and intent listening.

"You decline to answer that, Mr. Snopes?" Again his father did not answer. "I'm going to find against you, Mr. Snopes. I'm going to find that you were responsible for the injury to Major de Spain's rug and hold you liable for it. But twenty bushels of corn seems a little high for a man in your circumstances to have to pay. Major de Spain claims it cost a hundred dollars. October corn will be worth about fifty cents. I figure that if Major de Spain can stand a ninety-five dollar loss on something he paid cash for, you can stand a five-dollar loss you haven't earned yet. I hold you in damages to Major de Spain to the amount of ten bushels of corn over and above your contract with him, to be paid to him out of your crop at gathering time. Court adjourned."

It had taken no time hardly, the morning was but half begun. He thought they would return home and perhaps back to the field, since they were late, far behind all other farmers. But instead his father passed on behind the wagon, merely indicating with his hand for the older brother to follow with it, and crossed the road toward the blacksmith shop opposite, pressing on after his father, overtaking him, speaking, whispering up at the harsh, calm face beneath the weathered hat: "He won't git no ten bushels neither. He won't git one. We'll . . ." until his father glanced for an instant down at him, the face absolutely calm, the grizzled eyebrows tangled above the cold eyes, the voice almost pleasant, almost gentle:

"You think so? Well, we'll wait till October anyway."

The matter of the wagon—the setting of a spoke or two and the tightening of the tires—did not take long either, the business of the tires accomplished by driving the wagon into the spring branch behind the shop and letting it stand there, the mules nuzzling into the water from time to time, and the boy on the seat with the idle reins, looking up the slope through the sooty tunnel of the shed where the slow hammer rang and where his father sat on an upended cypress bolt, easily, either talking or listening, still sitting there when the boy brought the dripping wagon up out of the branch and halted it before the door.

"Take them on to the shade and hitch," his father said. He did so and returned. His father and the smith and a third man squatting on his heels inside the door were talking, about crops and animals; the boy, squatting too in the ammoniac dust and hoof-parings and scales of rust, heard his father tell a long and unhurried story out of the time before the birth of the older brother even when he had been a professional horsetrader. And then his father came up beside him where he stood before a tattered last year's circus poster on the other side of the store, gazing rapt and quiet at the scarlet horses, the incredible poisings and convolutions of tulle and tights and the painted leers of comedians, and said, "It's time to eat."

But not at home. Squatting beside his brother against the front wall, he watched his father emerge from the store and produce from a paper sack a segment of cheese and divide it carefully and deliberately into three with his pocket knife and produce crackers from the same sack. They all three squatted on the gallery and ate, slowly, without talking; then in the store again, they drank from a tin dipper tepid water smelling of the cedar bucket and of living beech trees. And still they did not go home. It was a horse lot this time, a tall rail fence upon and along which men stood and sat and out of which one by one horses were led, to be walked and trotted and then cantered back and forth along the road while the slow swapping and buying went on the sun began to slant westward, they—the three of them—watching and listening, the older brother with his muddy eyes and his steady, inevitable tobacco, the father commenting now and then on certain of the animals, to no one in particular.

It was after sundown when they reached home. They ate supper by lamplight, then, sitting on the doorstep, the boy watched the night fully accomplish, listening to the whippoorwills and the frogs, when he heard his mother's voice: "Abner! No! No! Oh, God. Oh, God. Abner!" and he rose, whirled, and saw the altered light through the door where a candle stub now burned in a bottle neck on the table and his father, still in the hat and coat, at once formal and burlesque as though dressed carefully for some shabby and ceremonial violence, emptying the reservoir of the lamp back into the five-gallon kerosene can from which it had been filled, while the mother tugged at his arm until he shifted the lamp to the other hand and flung her back, not savagely or viciously, just hard, into the wall, her hands flung out against the wall for balance, her mouth open and in her face the same quality of hopeless despair as had been in her voice. Then his father saw him standing in the door.

"Go to the barn and get that can of oil we were oiling the wagon with," he said. The boy did not move. Then he could speak.

"What . . ." he cried. "What are you . . ."

"Go get that oil," his father said. "Go."

Then he was moving, running, outside the house, toward the stable; this the old habit, the old blood which he had not been permitted to choose for himself, which had been bequeathed him willy nilly and which had run for so long (and who knew where, battening on what of outrage and savagery and lust) before it came to him. *I could keep on,* he thought. *I could run on and on and never look back, never need to see his face again. Only I can't. I can't,* the rusted can in his hand now, the liquid sploshing in it as he ran back to the house and into it, into the sound of his mother's weeping in the next room, and handed the can to his father.

"Ain't you going to even send a nigger?" he cried. "At least you sent a nigger before!"

This time his father didn't strike him. The hand came even faster than the blow hand, the same hand which had set the can on the table with almost excruciating care flashing the can toward him too quick for him to follow it, gripping him by the back of his shirt and on to tiptoe before he had seen it quit the can, the face stooping at him in breathless and frozen ferocity, the cold, dead voice speaking over him to the older brother who leaned against the table, chewing with that steady, curious, sidewise motion of cows:

"Empty the can into the big one and go on. I'll catch up with you."

"Better tie him up to the bedpost," the brother said.

"Do like I told you," the father said. Then the boy was moving, his bunched shirt and the hard, bony hand between his shoulder-blades his toes just touching the floor, across the room and into the other one, past the sisters sitting with spread heavy thighs in the two chairs over the cold hearth, and to where his mother and aunt sat side by side on the bed, the aunt's arms about his mother's shoulders.

"Hold him," the father said. The aunt made a startled movement. "Not you," the father said. "Lennie. Take hold of him. I want to see you do it." His mother took him by the wrist. "You'll hold him better than that. If he gets loose don't you know what he is going to do? He will go up yonder." He jerked his head toward the road. "Maybe I'd better tie him."

"I'll hold him," his mother whispered.

"See you do then." Then his father was gone, the stiff foot heavy and measured upon the boards, ceasing at last.

Then he began to struggle. His mother caught him in both arms, he jerking and wrenching at them. He would be stronger in the end, he knew that. But he had no time to wait for it. "Lemme go!" he cried. "I don't want to have to hit you!"

"Let him go!" the aunt said. "If he don't go, before God, I am going up there myself!"

"Don't you see I can't?" his mother cried. "Sarty! Sarty! No! No! Help me, Lizzie!"

Then he was free. His aunt grasped at him but it was too late. He whirled, running, his mother stumbled forward on to her knees behind him, crying to the nearer sister: "Catch him, Net! Catch him!" But that was too late too, the sister (the sisters were twins, born at the same time, yet either of them now gave the impression of being, encompassing as much living meat and volume and weight of any other two of the family) not yet having begun to rise from the chair, her head, face, alone merely turned, presenting to him in the flying instant an astonishing expanse of young female features untroubled by any surprise even, wearing only an expression of bovine interest. Then he was out of the room, out of the house, in the mild dust of the starlit road and the heavy rifeness of honeysuckle, the pale ribbon unspooling with terrific slowness under his running feet, reaching the gate at last and turning in, running, his heart and lungs drumming, on up the drive toward the lighted house, the lighted door. He did not knock, he burst in, sobbing for breath, incapable for the moment of speech; he saw the astonished face of the Negro in the linen jacket without knowing when the Negro had appeared.

"De Spain!" he cried, panted. "Where's . . ." then he saw the white man too emerging from a white door down the hall. "Barn!" he cried. "Barn!"

"What?" the white man said. "Barn?"

"Yes!" the boy cried. "Barn!"

"Catch him!" the white man shouted.

But it was too late this time too. The Negro grasped his shirt, but the entire sleeve, rotten with washing, carried away, and he was out that door too and in the drive again, and had actually never ceased to run even while he was screaming into the white man's face.

Behind him the white man was shouting, "My horse! Fetch my horse!" and he thought for an instant of cutting across the park and climbing the fence into the road, but he did not know the park nor how high the vine-massed fence might be and he dared not risk it. So he ran on down the drive, blood and breath roaring; presently he was in the road again though he could not see it. He could not hear either: the galloping mare was almost upon him before he heard her, and even then he held his course, as if the very urgency of his wild grief and need must in a moment more find him wings, waiting until the ultimate instant to hurl himself aside and into the weed-choked roadside ditch as the horse thundered past and on, for an instant in furious silhouette against the stars, the tranquil early summer night sky which, even before the shape of the horse and rider vanished, strained abruptly and violently upward: a long, swirling roar incredible and soundless, blotting the stars, and he springing up and into the road again, running again, knowing it was too late yet still running even after he had heard the shot and, an instant later, two shots, pausing now without knowing he had ceased to run, crying "Pap! Pap!", running again before he knew he had begun to run, stumbling, tripping over something and scrabbling up again without ceasing to run, looking backward over his shoulder at the glare as he got up, running on among the invisible trees, panting, sobbing, "Father! Father!"

At midnight he was sitting on the crest of a hill. He did not know it was midnight and he did not know how far he had come. But there was no glare behind him now and he sat now, his back toward what he had called home for four days anyhow, his face toward the dark woods which he would enter when breath was strong again, small, shaking steadily in the chill darkness, hugging himself into the remainder of his thin, rotten shirt, the grief and despair now no longer terror and fear but just grief and despair. *Father. My father*, he thought. "He was brave!" he cried suddenly, aloud but not loud, no more than a whisper: "He was! He was in the war! He was in Colonel Sartoris' cav'ry!" not knowing that his father had gone to that war a private in the fine old European sense, wearing no uniform, admitting the authority of and giving fidelity to no man or army or flag, going to war as Malbrouck himself did: for booty—it meant nothing and less than nothing to him if it were enemy booty or his own.

The slow constellations wheeled on. It would be dawn and then sun-up after a while and he would be hungry. But that would be to-morrow and now he was only cold, and walking would cure that. His breathing was easier now and he decided to get up and go on, and then he found that he had been asleep because he knew it was almost dawn, the night almost over. He could tell that from the whippoorwills. They were everywhere now among the dark trees below him, constant and inflectioned and ceaseless, so that, as the instant for giving over to the day birds drew nearer and nearer, there was no interval at all between them. He got up. He was a little stiff, but walking would cure that too as it would the cold, and soon there would be the sun. He went on down the hill, toward the dark woods within which the liquid silver voices of the birds called unceasing—the rapid and urgent beating of the urgent and quiring heart of the late spring night. He did not look back.

1939, 1950

Langston Hughes   *1902–1967*

Although Langston Hughes became the leader of the Harlem writers who created the Black Literary Renaissance of the 1920s, he was born in Joplin, Missouri, and spent most of his youth in the American Middle West. He first came to New York in 1921 to attend Columbia University. A year later he shipped out as a seaman and cook's helper on a tramp steamer to Africa and Europe. He lived and worked in Paris and Italy and then returned to the United States, where he took a job as a busboy in a Washington, D.C., hotel. There, in 1925, he was "discovered" by the poet Vachel Lindsay, who praised Hughes's poems and advised him to devote himself to literature and to "Hide and write and study and think."

Hughes had begun writing long before. In grammar school he had been chosen class poet, and while still in high school he published two poems in national magazines. His first books, The Weary Blues *(1926) and* Fine Clothes to the Jew *(1927), won poetry prizes and brought him wide acclaim. His first novel,* Not Without Laughter, *appeared in 1930. Hughes had a wide-ranging talent. He was a successful humorist and a historian of the lives of blacks. He wrote novels, short stories, poems, children's books, song lyrics, and operas. He translated foreign writers and wrote numerous plays, three of which were produced on Broadway.*

Much of his best writing was journalistic. In 1937 he served as a foreign correspondent covering the Spanish Civil War for the Baltimore Afro-American *newspaper. His most popular works were newspaper sketches written for the* Chicago Defender *in the 1940s. The sketches recounted the adventures and opinions of an innocent, downtrodden Negro, "Simple," whose penetrating views of blacks and whites provided Hughes with the means for making broad satirical and critical commentary on society and government.*

Hughes was the first American black to support himself as a professional writer; in all, he produced more than sixty books. He was one of the first American writers to receive serious critical attention for realistic portrayals of blacks in the United States. Through his poetry, his fiction, and his essays, he became, in the latter half of the twentieth century, one of the dominant voices speaking out for black culture in white America.

FURTHER READING: *I Wonder as I Wander, An Autobiographical Journey*, 1956; *The Langston Hughes Reader*, 1958; J. Emanuel, *Langston Hughes*, 1967; D. Dickinson, *A Bio-Bibliography of Langston Hughes, 1902–1967*, 1967, 1972; M. Meltzer, *Langston Hughes, A Biography*, 1968; C. Rollins, *Black Troubadour*, 1970; A. Rampersand, *The Life of Langston Hughes*, Vol. I: *1902–1941*, 1986; *Langston Hughes, Black Genius*, ed. T. O'Daniel, 1971; O. Jemie, *Langston Hughes, An Introduction to the Poetry*, 1976: R. Barksdale, *Langston Hughes, The Poet and His Critics*, 1977; F. Berry, *Langston Hughes, Before and Beyond Harlem*, 1983.

TEXT: "Theme for English B," "Dream Boogie," and "Harlem" from *Montage of a Dream Deferred*, 1951. All other poems from *Selected Poems of Langston Hughes*, 1973. "On the Road" is from *Laughing to Keep from Crying*, 1952.

THE NEGRO SPEAKS OF RIVERS

I've known rivers:
I've known rivers ancient as the world and older than the
    flow of human blood in human veins.

My soul has grown deep like the rivers.

I bathed in the Euphrates[1] when dawns were young.
I built my hut near the Congo and it lulled me to sleep.
I looked upon the Nile and raised the pyramids above it.
I heard the singing of the Mississippi when Abe Lincoln
    went down to New Orleans, and I've seen its muddy
    bosom turn all golden in the sunset.   10

I've known rivers:
Ancient, dusky rivers.

My soul has grown deep like the rivers.
1920   1921, 1926

THE WEARY BLUES

Droning a drowsy syncopated tune,
Rocking back and forth to a mellow croon,

[1]Euphrates: river flowing through Turkey, Syria, and Iraq into the Persian Gulf. Congo, river flowing through west central Africa into the Atlantic. Nile: river flowing through Egypt into the Mediterranean. Each passes through lands where ancient civilizations once flourished.

I heard a Negro play.
Down on Lenox Avenue[1] the other night
By the pale dull pallor of an old gas light
    He did a lazy sway. . . .
    He did a lazy sway. . . .
To the tune o' those Weary Blues.
With his ebony hands on each ivory key
He made that poor piano moan with melody.   10
    O Blues!
Swaying to and fro on his rickety stool
He played that sad raggy tune like a musical fool.
    Sweet Blues!
Coming from a black man's soul.
    O Blues!
In a deep song voice with a melancholy tone
I heard that Negro sing, that old piano moan—
    "Ain't got nobody in all this world,
    Ain't got nobody but ma self.   20
    I's gwine to quit ma frownin'
    And put ma troubles on the shelf."
Thump, thump, thump, went his foot on the floor.
He played a few chords then he sang some more—
    "I got the Weary Blues
    And I can't be satisfied.
    Got the Weary Blues
    And can't be satisfied—
    I ain't happy no mo'
    And I wish that I had died."   30
And far into the night he crooned that tune.
The stars went out and so did the moon.
The singer stopped playing and went to bed
While the Weary Blues echoed through his head.
He slept like a rock or a man that's dead.

                          1926

YOUNG GAL'S BLUES

I'm gonna walk to the graveyard
'Hind ma friend Miss Cora Lee.
Gonna walk to the graveyard
'Hind ma dear friend Cora Lee
Cause when I'm dead some
Body'll have to walk behind me.

I'm goin' to the po' house
To see ma old Aunt Clew.
Goin' to the po' house
To see ma old Aunt Clew.   10

[1]Street in New York City's Harlem.

When I'm old an' ugly
I'll want to see somebody, too.

The po' house is lonely
An' the grave is cold.
O, the po' house is lonely,
The graveyard grave is cold.
But I'd rather be dead than
To be ugly an' old.

When love is gone what
Can a young gal do?   20
When love is gone, O,
What can a young gal do?
Keep on a-lovin' me, daddy,
Cause I don't want to be blue.

                    1927

I, TOO

I, too, sing America.

I am the darker brother.
They send me to eat in the kitchen
When company comes,
But I laugh,
And eat well,
And grow strong.

Tomorrow,
I'll be at the table
When company comes.   10
Nobody'll dare
Say to me,
"Eat in the kitchen,"
Then.

Besides,
They'll see how beautiful I am
And be ashamed—

I, too, am America.

                    1932

NOTE ON COMMERCIAL THEATRE

You've taken my blues and gone—
You sing 'em on Broadway

And you sing 'em in Hollywood Bowl,
And you mixed 'em up with symphonies
And you fixed 'em
So they don't sound like me.
Yep, you done taken my blues and gone.

You also took my spirituals and gone.
You put me in *Macbeth* and *Carmen Jones*
And all kinds of *Swing Mikados*[1]   10
And in everything but what's about me—
But someday somebody'll
Stand up and talk about me,
And write about me—
Black and beautiful—
And sing about me,
And put on plays about me!
I reckon it'll be
Me myself!

Yes, it'll be me.   20

                                        [1]949

DREAM BOOGIE

Good morning, daddy!
Ain't you heard
The boogie-woogie rumble
Of a dream deferred?

Listen closely:
You'll hear their feet
Beating out and beating out a——

        You think
        It's a happy beat?

Listen to it closely: 10
Ain't you heard
something underneath
like a——

        What did I say?

Sure,
I'm happy!
Take it away!

[1]Hughes refers to three Broadway shows produced with Negro casts.

Hey, pop!
Re-bop!
Mop!   20

Y-e-a-h!

1951

HARLEM

What happens to a dream deferred?

Does it dry up
like a raisin in the sun?
Or fester like a sore——
And then run?
Does it stink like rotten meat?
Or crust and sugar over——
like a syrupy sweet?

Maybe it just sags
like a heavy load.   10

Or does it explode?

1951

THEME FOR ENGLISH B

The instructor said,

Go home and write
a page tonight.
And let that page come out of you—
Then, it will be true.

I wonder if it's that simple?
I am twenty-one, colored, born in Winston-Salem.[1]
I went to school there, then Durham, then here
to this college[2] on the hill above Harlem.
I am the only colored student in my class.   10
The steps from the hill lead down into Harlem,
through a park, then I cross St. Nicholas,[3]
Eighth Avenue, Seventh, and I come to the Y,
the Harlem Branch Y, where I take the elevator
up to my room, sit down, and write this page:

[1]Winston-Salem, North Carolina; Durham, North Carolina.
[2]Columbia University in New York City.
[3]Street near Columbia University.

It's not easy to know what is true for you or me
at twenty-two, my age. But I guess I'm what
I feel and see and hear, Harlem, I hear you:
hear you, hear me—we two—you, me, talk on this page.
(I hear New York, too.) Me—who?   20
Well, I like to eat, sleep, drink, and be in love.
I like to work, read, learn, and understand life.
I like a pipe for a Christmas present,
or records—Bessie,[4] bop, or Bach.
I guess being colored doesn't make me *not* like
the same things other folks like who are other races.
So will my page be colored that I write?
Being me, it will not be white.
But it will be
a part of you, instructor.   30
You are white—
yet a part of me, as I am a part of you.
That's American.
Sometimes perhaps you don't want to be a part of me.
Nor do I often want to be a part of you.
But we are, that's true!
As I learn from you,
I guess you learn from me—
although you're older—and white—
and somewhat more free.   40

This is my page for English B.

                                                   1951

ON THE ROAD

He was not interested in the snow. When he got off the freight, one early evening during the depression, Sargeant never even noticed the snow. But he must have felt it seeping down his neck, cold, wet, sopping in his shoes. But if you had asked him, he wouldn't have known it was snowing. Sargeant didn't see the snow, not even under the bright lights of the main street, falling white and flaky against the night. He was too hungry, too sleepy, too tired.

The Reverend Mr. Dorset, however, saw the snow when he switched on his porch light, opened the front door of his parsonage, and found standing there before him a big black man with snow on his face, a human piece of night with snow on his face—obviously unemployed.

Said the Reverend Mr. Dorset before Sargeant even realized he'd opened his mouth: "I'm sorry. No! Go right on down this street four blocks and turn to your left, walk up seven and you'll see the Relief Shelter. I'm sorry, No!" He shut the door.

Sargeant wanted to tell the holy man that he had already been to the Relief Shelter, been to hundreds of relief shelters during the depression years, the

[4]Bessie Smith (c. 1898–1937), famous American blues singer.

beds were always gone and supper was over, the place was full, and they drew the color line anyhow. But the minister said, "No," and shut the door. Evidently he didn't want to hear about it. And he *had* a door to shut.

The big black man turned away. And even yet he didn't see the snow, walking right into it. Maybe he sensed it, cold, wet, sticking to his jaws, wet on his black hands, sopping in his shoes. He stopped and stood on the sidewalk hunched over—hungry, sleepy, cold—looking up and down. Then he looked right where he was—in front of a church. Of course! A church! Sure, right next to a parsonage, certainly a church.

It had *two* doors.

Broad white steps in the night all snowy white. Two high arched doors with slender stone pillars on either side. And way up, a round lacy window with a stone crucifix in the middle and Christ on the crucifix in stone. All this was pale in the street lights, solid and stony pale in the snow.

Sargeant blinked. When he looked up the snow fell into his eyes. For the first time that night he *saw* the snow. He shook his head. He shook the snow from his coat sleeves, felt hungry, felt lost, felt not lost, felt cold. He walked up the steps of the church. He knocked at the door. No answer. He tried the handle. Locked. He put his shoulder against the door and his long black body slanted like a ramrod. He pushed. With loud rhythmic grunts, like the grunts in a chain-gang song, he pushed against the door.

"I'm   tired . . . Huh! . . . Hongry . . . Uh! . . . I'm   sleepy . . . Huh!   I'm cold . . . I got to sleep somewheres," Sargeant said. "This here is a church, ain't it? Well, uh!"

He pushed against the door.

Suddenly, with an undue cracking and screaking, the door began to give way to the tall black Negro who pushed ferociously against the door.

By now two or three white people had stopped in the street, and Sargeant was vaguely aware of some of them yelling at him concerning the door. Three or four more came running, yelling at him.

"Hey!" they said. "Hey!"

'Uh-huh," answered the big tall Negro, "I know it's a white folks' church, but I got to sleep somewhere." He gave another lunge at the door. "Huh!"

And the door broke open.

But just when the door gave way, two white cops arrived in a car, ran up the steps with their clubs and grabbed Sargeant. But Sargeant for once had no intention of being pulled or pushed away from the door.

Sargeant grabbed, but not for anything so weak as a broken door. He grabbed for one of the tall stone pillars beside the door, grabbed at and caught it. And held it. The cops pulled and Sargeant pulled. Most of the people in the street got behind the cops and helped them pull.

"A big black unemployed Negro holding onto our church!" thought the people. "The idea!"

The cops began to beat Sargeant over the head, and nobody protested. But he held on.

And then the church fell down.

Gradually, the big stone front of the church fell down, the walls and the rafters, the crucifix and the Christ. Then the whole thing fell down, covering the cops and the people with bricks and stones and debris. The whole church fell down in the snow.

Sargeant got out from under the church and went walking on up the street with the stone pillar on his shoulder. He was under the impression that he had buried the parsonage and the Reverend Mr. Dorset who said, "No!" So he laughed, and threw the pillar six blocks up the street and went on.

Sargeant thought he was alone, but listening to the crunch, crunch, crunch on the snow of his own footsteps, he heard other footsteps, too, doubling his own. He looked around and there was Christ walking beside him, the same Christ that had been on the cross on the church—still stone with a rough stone surface, walking along beside him just like he was broken off the cross when the church fell down.

"Well, I'll be dogged," said Sargeant. "This here's the first time I ever seed you off the cross."

"Yes," said Christ, crunching his feet in the snow. "You had to pull the church down to get me off the cross."

"You glad?" said Sargeant.

"I sure am," said Christ.

They both laughed.

"I'm a hell of a fellow, ain't I?" said Sargeant. "Done pulled the church down!"

"You did a good job," said Christ. "They have kept me nailed on a cross for nearly two thousand years."

"Whee-ee-e!" said Sargeant. "I know you are glad to get off."

"I sure am," said Christ.

They walked on in the snow. Sargeant looked at the man of stone.

"And you been up there two thousand years?"

"I sure have," Christ said.

"Well, if I had a little cash," said Sargeant, "I'd show you around a bit."

"I been around," said Christ.

"Yeah, but that was a long time ago."

"All the same," said Christ, "I've been around."

They walked on in the snow until they came to the railroad yards. Sargeant was tired, sweating and tired.

"Where you goin'?" Sargeant said, stopping by the tracks. He looked at Christ. Sargeant said, "I'm just a bum on the road. How about you? Where you goin'?"

"God knows," Christ said, "but I'm leavin' here."

They saw the red and green lights of the railroad yard half veiled by the snow that fell out of the night. Away down the track they saw a fire in a hobo jungle.

"I can go there and sleep," Sargeant said.

"You can?"

"Sure," said Sargeant. "That place ain't got no doors."

Outside the town, along the tracks, there were barren trees and bushes below the embankment, snow-gray in the dark. And down among the trees and bushes there were makeshift houses made out of boxes and tin and old pieces of wood and canvas. You couldn't see them in the dark, but you knew they were there if you'd ever been on the road, if you had ever lived with the homeless and hungry in a depression.

"I'm side-tracking," Sargeant said. "I'm tired."

"I'm gonna make it on to Kansas City," said Christ.

"O.K.," Sargeant said. "So long!"

He went down into the hobo jungle and found himself a place to sleep. He never did see Christ no more. About six A.M. a freight came by. Sargeant scrambled out of the jungle with a dozen or so more hoboes and ran along the track, grabbing at the freight. It was dawn, early dawn, cold and gray.

"Wonder where Christ is by now?" Sargeant thought. "He must-a gone on way on down the road. He didn't sleep in this jungle."

Sargeant grabbed the train and started to pull himself up into a moving coal car, over the edge of a wheeling coal car. But strangely enough, the car was full of cops. The nearest cop rapped Sargeant soundly across the knuckles with his night stick. Wham! Rapped his big black hands for clinging to the top of the car. Wham! But Sargeant did not turn loose. He clung on and tried to pull himself into the car. He hollered at the top of his voice, "Damn it, lemme in this car!"

"Shut up," barked the cop. "You crazy coon!" He rapped Sargeant across the knuckles and punched him in the stomach. "You ain't out in no jungle now. This ain't no train. You in jail."

Wham! across his bare black fingers clinging to the bars of his cell. Wham! between the steel bars low down against his shins.

Suddenly Sargeant realized that he really was in jail. He wasn't on no train. The blood of the night before had dried on his face, his head hurt terribly, and a cop outside in the corridor was hitting him across the knuckles for holding onto the door, yelling and shaking the cell door.

"They must-a took me to jail for breaking down the door last night," Sargeant thought, "that church door."

Sargeant went over and sat on a wooden bench against the cold stone wall. He was emptier than ever. His clothes were wet, clammy cold wet, and shoes sloppy with snow water. It was just about dawn. There he was, locked up behind a cell door, nursing his bruised fingers.

The bruised fingers were his, but not the *door*.

Not the *club*, but the fingers.

"You wait," mumbled Sargeant, black against the jail wall. "I'm gonna break down this door, too."

"Shut up—or I'll paste you one," said the cop.

"I'm gonna break down this door," yelled Sargeant as he stood up in his cell.

Then he must have been talking to himself because he said, "I wonder where Christ's gone? I wonder if he's gone to Kansas City?"

                                                                                    1952

John Steinbeck   *1902–1968*

John Steinbeck was the foremost novelist of the American Depression of the 1930s. He was born in Salinas, California, the locale of much of his finest fiction. His sympathy for the migrant workers and the downtrodden, so evident in his writing, was the result of firsthand knowledge of their struggles. From his boyhood he was self-supporting; he worked as a laborer, a seaman on a cattle-boat (where he hoped and failed to become a writer), newspaper reporter, bricklayer, chemist's assistant, surveyor, and migratory fruitpicker. His writing reflected his concern with the rituals of manual labor, people "doing" rather than "being," and he believed that the writer's first duty was to "set down his time as nearly as he can understand it" and serve as "the watch-dog of society . . . to satirize its silliness, to attack its injustices, to stigmatize its faults."

The publication of Tortilla Flat *(1935), the tender, sentimental portrait of the inde-structibility of the California* paisanos, *brought him sudden fame. In the following year* In Dubious Battle *appeared. It was Steinbeck's most clearly "proletarian" novel of class struggle, depicting the lives of migrant workers and their resistance to exploitation by the entrenched forces of society. In* Of Mice and Men *(1937) he portrayed the friendship of two itinerant workers who yearn for a permanent home they will never find. In* The Long Valley *(1938) he described the fate of the lowly whose instinctive responses to life led only to destruction.* The Grapes of Wrath *(1939), generally regarded as his masterpiece, showed the migration of the "Okies" from the "Dust Bowls" to California, a migration that ended in broken dreams and misery but at the same time affirmed the ability of the common people to endure and prevail.*

Steinbeck's treatment of the social problems of his time, particularly the plight of the dispossessed farmer, earned him a Pulitzer Prize in 1940 and, in 1962, a Nobel Prize for Literature. At its best, Steinbeck's lyric prose vividly caught the qualities of speech, the character, the legends, and the humor of his native region. He was a superb storyteller whose reforming vision led him to contrast the conflicting moral codes of people in search of permanent ideals: "What we have always wanted," he wrote in The Sea of Cortez *(1941), "is an* unchangeable, *and we have found that only a compass point, a thought, an individual ideal, does not change."*

FURTHER READING: *Steinbeck, A Life in Letters,* ed. E. Steinbeck and R. Wallsten, 1975; N. Valjean, *John Steinbeck,* 1975; J. Benson, *The True Adventures of John Steinbeck, Writer,* 1984; H. Moore, *The Novels of John Steinbeck,* 1939, 1968; *Steinbeck and His Critics,* ed. E. Tedlock and C. Wicker, 1957; P. Lisca, *The Wide World of John Steinbeck,* 1958; W. French, *John Steinbeck,* 1961, 1975; J. Fontenrose, *John Steinbeck, An Introduction and Interpretation,* 1963; L. Marks, *Thematic Design in the Novels of John Steinbeck,* 1969; J. Gray, *John Steinbeck,* 1971; *Steinbeck, The Man and His Work,* ed. R. Astro and T. Hayashi, 1971; *John Steinbeck, A Collection of Critical Essays,* ed. R. Davis, 1972; R. Astro, *John Steinbeck and Edward F. Ricketts,* 1973; H. Levant, *The Novels of John Steinbeck,* 1974; P. Lisca, *John Steinbeck, Nature and Myth,* 1978; L. Owens, *John Steinbeck's Re-Vision of America,* 1985; J. Timmerman, *John Steinbeck's Fiction,* 1986.

TEXT: *The Long Valley,* 1938.

FLIGHT

About fifteen miles below Monterey, on the wild coast, the Torres family had their farm, a few sloping acres above a cliff that dropped to the brown reefs and to the hissing white waters of the ocean. Behind the farm the stone moun-tains stood up against the sky. The farm buildings huddled like little clinging aphids on the mountain skirts, crouched low to the ground as though the wind might blow them into the sea. The little shack, the rattling, rotting barn were grey-bitten with sea salt, beaten by the damp wind until they had taken on the color of the granite hills. Two horses, and a red cow and a red calf, half a dozen pigs and a flock of lean, multicolored chickens stocked the place. A little corn was raised on the sterile slope, and it grew short and thick under the wind, and all the cobs formed on the landward sides of the stalks.

Mama Torres, a lean, dry woman with ancient eyes, had ruled the farm for ten years, ever since her husband tripped over a stone in the field one day and fell full length on a rattlesnake. When one is bitten on the chest there is not much that can be done.

Mama Torres had three children, two undersized black ones of twelve and fourteen, Emilio and Rosy, whom Mama kept fishing on the rocks below the farm when the sea was kind and when the truant officer was in some distant part of Monterey County. And there was Pepé, the tall smiling son of nineteen, a gentle, affectionate boy, but very lazy. Pepé had a tall head, pointed at the top, and from its peak, coarse black hair grew down like a thatch all around. Over his smiling little eyes Mama cut a straight bang so he could see. Pepé had sharp Indian cheek bones and an eagle nose, but his mouth was as sweet and shapely as a girl's mouth, and his chin was fragile and chiseled. He was loose and gangling, all legs and feet and wrists, and he was very lazy. Mama thought him fine and brave, but she never told him so. She said, "Some lazy cow must have got into thy father's family, else how could I have a son like thee." And she said, "When I carried thee, a sneaking lazy coyote came out of the brush and looked at me one day. That must have made thee so."

Pepé smiled sheepishly and stabbed at the ground with his knife to keep the blade sharp and free from rust. It was his inheritance, that knife, his father's knife. The long heavy blade folded back into the black handle. There was a button on the handle. When Pepé pressed the button, the blade leaped out ready for use. The knife was with Pepé always, for it had been his father's knife.

One sunny morning when the sea below the cliff was glinting and blue and the white surf creamed on the reef, when even the stone mountains looked kindly, Mama Torres called out the door of the shack, "Pepé, I have a labor for thee."

There was no answer. Mama listened. From behind the barn she heard a burst of laughter. She lifted her full long skirt and walked in the direction of the noise.

Pepé was sitting on the ground with his back against a box. His white teeth glistened. On either side of him stood the two black ones, tense and expectant. Fifteen feet away a redwood post was set in the ground. Pepé's right hand lay limply in his lap, and in the palm the big black knife rested. The blade was closed back into the handle. Pepé looked smiling at the sky.

Suddenly Emilio cried, "Ya!"

Pepé's wrist flicked like the head of a snake. The blade seemed to fly open in mid-air, and with a thump the point dug into the redwood post, and the black handle quivered. The three burst into excited laughter. Rosy ran to the post and pulled out the knife and brought it back to Pepé. He closed the blade and settled the knife carefully in his listless palm again. He grinned self-consciously at the sky.

"Ya!"

The heavy knife lanced out and sunk into the post again. Mama moved forward like a ship and scattered the play.

"All day you do foolish things with the knife, like a toy-baby," she stormed. "Get up on thy huge feet that eat up shoes. Get up!" She took him by one loose shoulder and hoisted at him. Pepé grinned sheepishly and came half-heartedly to his feet. "Look!" Mama cried. "Big lazy, you must catch the horse and put on him thy father's saddle. You must ride to Monterey. The medicine bottle is empty. There is no salt. Go thou now, Peanut! Catch the horse."

A revolution took place in the relaxed figure of Pepé. "To Monterey, me? Alone? *Si*, Mama."

She scowled at him. "Do not think, big sheep, that you will buy candy. No, I will give you only enough for the medicine and the salt."

Pepé smiled. "Mama, you will put the hatband on the hat?"

She relented then. "Yes, Pepé. You may wear the hatband."

His voice grew insinuating. "And the green handkerchief, Mama?"

"Yes, if you go quickly and return with no trouble, the silk green handkerchief will go. If you make sure to take off the handkerchief when you eat so no spot may fall on it. . . . "

"*Si*, Mama. I will be careful. I am a man."

"Thou? A man? Thou art a peanut."

He went into the rickety barn and brought out a rope, and he walked agilely enough up the hill to catch the horse.

When he was ready and mounted before the door, mounted on his father's saddle that was so old that the oaken frame showed through torn leather in many places, then Mama brought out the round black hat with the tooled leather band, and she reached up and knotted the green silk handkerchief about his neck. Pepé's blue denim coat was much darker than his jeans, for it had been washed much less often.

Mama handed up the big medicine bottle and the silver coins. "That for the medicine," she said, "and that for the salt. That for a candle to burn for the papa. That for *dulces*[1] for the little ones. Our friend Mrs. Rodriguez will give you dinner and maybe a bed for the night. When you go to the church say only ten Paternosters and only twenty-five Ave Marias. Oh! I know, big coyote. You would sit there flapping your mouth over Aves all day while you looked at the candles and the holy pictures. That is not good devotion to stare at the pretty things."

The black hat, covering the high pointed head and black thatched hair of Pepé, gave him dignity and age. He sat the rangy horse well. Mama thought how handsome he was, dark and lean and tall. "I would not send thee now alone, thou little one, except for the medicine," she said softly. "It is not good to have no medicine, for who knows when the toothache will come, or the sadness of the stomach. These things are."

"Adios, Mama," Pepé cried. "I will come back soon. You may send me often alone. I am a man."

"Thou art a foolish chicken."

He straightened his shoulders, flipped the reins against the horse's shoulder and rode away. He turned once and saw that they still watched him, Emilio and Rosy and Mama. Pepé grinned with pride and gladness and lifted the tough buckskin horse to a trot.

When he had dropped out of sight over a little dip in the road, Mama turned to the black ones, but she spoke to herself. "He is nearly a man now," she said. "It will be a nice thing to have a man in the house again." Her eyes sharpened on the children. "Go to the rocks now. The tide is going out. There will be abalones to be found." She put the iron hooks into their hands and saw them down the steep trail to the reefs. She brought the smooth stone *metate* to the doorway and sat grinding her corn to flour and looking occasionally at the road over which Pepé had gone. The noonday came and then the afternoon, when the little ones beat the abalones on a rock to make them tender and Mama patted the tortillas to make them thin. They ate their dinner as the red sun was plunging

---

[1]Spanish: "sweets."

down toward the ocean. They sat on the doorsteps and watched the big white moon come over the mountain tops.

Mama said, "He is now at the house of our friend Mrs. Rodriguez. She will give him nice things to eat and maybe a present."

Emilio said, "Some day I too will ride to Monterey for medicine. Did Pepé come to be a man today?"

Mama said wisely, "A boy gets to be a man when a man is needed. Remember this thing. I have known boys forty years old because there was no need for a man."

Soon afterwards they retired, Mama in her big oak bed on one side of the room, Emilio and Rosy in their boxes full of straw and sheepskins on the other side of the room.

The moon went over the sky and surf roared on the rocks. The roosters crowed the first call. The surf subsided to a whispering surge against the reef. The moon dropped toward the sea. The roosters crowed again.

The moon was near down to the water when Pepé rode on a winded horse to his home flat. His dog bounced out and circled the horse yelping with pleasure. Pepé slid off the saddle to the ground. The weathered little shack was silver in the moonlight and the square shadow of it was black to the north and east. Against the east the piling mountains were misty with light; their tops melted into the sky.

Pepé walked wearily up the three steps and into the house. It was dark inside. There was a rustle in the corner.

Mama cried out from her bed. "Who comes? Pepé, is it thou?"

"*Si*, Mama."

"Did you get the medicine?"

"*Si*, Mama."

"Well, go to sleep, then. I thought you would be sleeping at the house of Mrs. Rodriguez." Pepé stood silently in the dark room. "Why do you stand there, Pepé? Did you drink wine?"

"*Si*, Mama."

"Well, go to bed then and sleep out the wine."

His voice was tired and patient, but very firm. "Light the candle, Mama. I must go away into the mountains."

"What is this, Pepé? You are crazy." Mama struck a sulphur match and held the little blue burr until the flame spread up the stick. She set light to the candle on the floor beside her bed. "Now, Pepé, what is this you say?" She looked anxiously into his face.

He was changed. The fragile quality seemed to have gone from his chin. His mouth was less full than it had been, the lines of the lips were straighter, but in his eyes the greatest change had taken place. There was no laughter in them any more, nor any bashfulness. They were sharp and bright and purposeful.

He told her in a tired monotone, told her everything just as it had happened. A few people came into the kitchen of Mrs. Rodriguez. There was wine to drink. Pepé drank wine. The little quarrel—the man started toward Pepé and then the knife—it went almost by itself. It flew, it darted before Pepé knew it. As he talked, Mama's face grew stern, and it seemed to grow more lean. Pepé finished. "I am a man now, Mama. The man said names to me I could not allow."

Mama nodded. "Yes, thou art a man, my poor little Pepé. Thou art a man. I have seen it coming on thee. I have watched you throwing the knife into the post, and I have been afraid." For a moment her face had softened, but now it grew stern again. "Come! We must get you ready. Go. Awaken Emilio and Rosy. Go quickly."

Pepé stepped over to the corner where his brother and sister slept among the sheepskins. He leaned down and shook them gently. "Come, Rosy! Come, Emilio! The mama says you must arise."

The little black ones sat up and rubbed their eyes in the candlelight. Mama was out of bed now, her long black skirt over her nightgown. "Emilio," she cried. "Go up and catch the other horse for Pepé. Quickly, now! Quickly." Emilio put his legs in his overalls and stumbled sleepily out the door.

"You heard no one behind you on the road?" Mama demanded.

"No, Mama. I listened carefully. No one was on the road."

Mama darted like a bird about the room. From a nail on the wall she took a canvas water bag and threw it on the floor. She stripped a blanket from her bed and rolled it into a tight tube and tied the ends with string. From a box beside the stove she lifted a flour sack half full of black stringy jerky. "Your father's black coat, Pepé. Here, put it on."

Pepé stood in the middle of the floor watching her activity. She reached behind the door and brought out the rifle, a long 38-56, worn shiny the whole length of the barrel. Pepé took it from her and held it in the crook of his elbow. Mama brought a little leather bag and counted the cartridges into his hand. "Only ten left," she warned. "You must not waste them."

Emilio put his head in the door. " *'Qui 'st 'l caballo,*[2] Mama."

"Put on the saddle from the other horse. Tie on the blanket. Here, tie the jerky to the saddle horn."

Still Pepé stood silently watching his mother's frantic activity. His chin looked hard, and his sweet mouth was drawn and thin. His little eyes followed Mama about the room almost suspiciously.

Rosy asked softly, "Where goes Pepé?"

Mama's eyes were fierce. "Pepé goes on a journey. Pepé is a man now. He has a man's thing to do."

Pepé straightened his shoulders. His mouth changed until he looked very much like Mama.

At last the preparation was finished. The loaded horse stood outside the door. The water bag dripped a line of moisture down the bay shoulder.

The moonlight was being thinned by the dawn and the big white moon was near down to the sea. The family stood by the shack. Mama confronted Pepé. "Look, my son! Do not stop until it is dark again. Do not sleep even though you are tired. Take care of the horse in order that he may not stop of weariness. Remember to be careful with the bullets—there are only ten. Do not fill thy stomach with jerky or it will make thee sick. Eat a little jerky and fill thy stomach with grass. When thou comest to the high mountains, if thou seest any of the dark watching men, go not near to them nor try to speak to them. And forget not thy prayers." She put her lean hands on Pepé's shoulders, stood on her toes and kissed him formally on both cheeks, and Pepé kissed her on both cheeks. Then he went to Emilio and Rosy and kissed both of their cheeks.

Pepé turned back to Mama. He seemed to look for a little softness, a little weakness in her. His eyes were searching, but Mama's face remained fierce. "Go now," she said. "Do not wait to be caught like a chicken."

---

[2]Spanish: "Here's the horse."

Pepé pulled himself into the saddle. "I am a man," he said.

It was the first dawn when he rode up the hill toward the little canyon which let a trail into the mountains. Moonlight and daylight fought with each other, and the two warring qualities made it difficult to see. Before Pepé had gone a hundred yards, the outlines of his figure were misty; and long before he entered the canyon, he had become a grey, indefinite shadow.

Mama stood stiffly in front of her doorstep, and on either side of her stood Emilio and Rosy. They cast furtive glances at Mama now and then.

When the grey shape of Pepé melted into the hillside and disappeared, Mama relaxed. She began the high, whining keen of the death wail. "Our beautiful— our brave," she cried. "Our protector, our son is gone." Emilio and Rosy moaned beside her. "Our beautiful—our brave, he is gone." It was the formal wail. It rose to a high piercing whine and subsided to a moan. Mama raised it three times and then she turned and went into the house and shut the door.

Emilio and Rosy stood wondering in the dawn. They heard Mama whimpering in the house. They went out to sit on the cliff above the ocean. They touched shoulders. "When did Pepé come to be a man?" Emilio asked.

"Last night," said Rosy. "Last night in Monterey." The ocean clouds turned red with the sun that was behind the mountains.

"We will have no breakfast," said Emilio. "Mama will not want to cook." Rosy did not answer him. "Where is Pepé gone?" he asked.

Rosy looked around at him. She drew her knowledge from the quiet air. "He has gone on a journey. He will never come back."

"Is he dead? Do you think he is dead?"

Rosy looked back at the ocean again. A little steamer, drawing a line of smoke sat on the edge of the horizon. "He is not dead," Rosy explained. "Not yet."

Pepé rested the big rifle across the saddle in front of him. He let the horse walk up the hill and he didn't look back. The stony slope took on a coat of short brush so that Pepé found the entrance to a trail and entered it.

When he came to the canyon opening, he swung once in his saddle and looked back, but the houses were swallowed in the misty light. Pepé jerked forward again. The high shoulder of the canyon closed in on him. His horse stretched out its neck and sighed and settled to the trail.

It was a well-worn path, dark soft leaf-mould earth strewn with broken pieces of sandstone. The trail rounded the shoulder of the canyon and dropped steeply into the bed of the stream. In the shallows the water ran smoothly, glinting in the first morning sun. Small round stones on the bottom were as brown as rust with sun moss. In the sand along the edges of the stream the tall, rich wild mint grew, while in the water itself the cress, old and tough, had gone to heavy seed.

The path went into the stream and emerged on the other side. The horse sloshed into the water and stopped. Pepé dropped his bridle and let the beast drink of the running water.

Soon the canyon sides became steep and the first giant sentinel redwoods guarded the trail, great round red trunks bearing foliage as green and lacy as ferns. Once Pepé was among the trees, the sun was lost. A perfumed and purple light lay in the pale green of the underbrush. Gooseberry bushes and blackberries and tall ferns lined the stream, and overhead the branches of the redwoods met and cut off the sky.

Pepé drank from the water bag, and he reached into the flour sack and brought out a black string of jerky. His white teeth gnawed at the string until the tough meat parted. He chewed slowly and drank occasionally from the water bag. His little eyes were slumberous and tired, but the muscles of his face were hard set. The earth of the trail was black now. It gave up a hollow sound under the walking hoofbeats.

The stream fell more sharply. Little waterfalls splashed on the stones. Five-fingered ferns hung over the water and dripped spray from their fingertips. Pepé rode half over in his saddle, dangling one leg loosely. He picked a bay leaf from a tree beside the way and put it into his mouth for a moment to flavor the dry jerky. He held the gun loosely across the pommel.

Suddenly he squared in his saddle, swung the horse from the trail and kicked it hurriedly up behind a big redwood tree. He pulled up the reins tight against the bit to keep the horse from whinnying. His face was intent and his nostrils quivered a little.

A hollow pounding came down the trail, and a horseman rode by, a fat man with red cheeks and a white stubble beard. His horse put down its head and blubbered at the trail when it came to the place where Pepé had turned off. "Hold up!" said the man and he pulled up his horse's head.

When the last sound of the hoofs died away, Pepé came back into the trail again. He did not relax in the saddle any more. He lifted the big rifle and swung the lever to throw a shell into the chamber, and then he let down the hammer to half cock.

The trail grew very steep. Now the redwood trees were smaller and their tops were dead, bitten dead where the wind reached them. The horse plodded on; the sun went slowly overhead and started down toward the afternoon.

Where the stream came out of a side canyon, the trail left it. Pepé dismounted and watered his horse and filled up his water bag. As soon as the trail had parted from the stream, the trees were gone and only the thick brittle sage and man-zanita and chaparral edged the trail. And the soft black earth was gone, too, leaving only the light tan broken rock for the trail bed. Lizards scampered away into the brush as the horse rattled over the little stones.

Pepé turned in his saddle and looked back. He was in the open now: he could be seen from a distance. As he ascended the trail the country grew more rough and terrible and dry. The way wound about the bases of great square rocks. Little grey rabbits skittered in the brush. A bird made a monotonous high creaking. Eastward the bare rock mountaintops were pale and powder-dry under the dropping sun. The horse plodded up and up the trail toward a little V in the ridge which was the pass.

Pepé looked suspiciously back every minute or so, and his eyes sought the tops of the ridges ahead. Once, on a white barren spur, he saw a black figure for a moment, but he looked quickly away, for it was one of the dark watchers. No one knew who the watchers were, nor where they lived, but it was better to ignore them and never to show interest in them. They did not bother one who stayed on the trail and minded his own business.

The air was parched and full of light dust blown by the breeze from the eroding mountains. Pepé drank sparingly from his bag and corked it tightly and hung it on the horn again. The trail moved up the dry shale hillside, avoiding rocks, dropping under clefts, climbing in and out of old water scars. When he arrived at the little pass he stopped and looked back for a long time. No dark watchers were to be seen now. The trail behind was empty. Only the high tops of the redwoods indicated where the stream flowed.

Pepé rode on through the pass. His little eyes were nearly closed with weari-ness, but his face was stern, relentless and manly. The high mountain wind coasted sighing through the pass and whistled on the edges of the big blocks of broken granite. In the air, a redtailed hawk sailed over close to the ridge and screamed angrily. Pepé went slowly through the broken jagged pass and looked down on the other side.

The trail dropped quickly, staggering among broken rock. At the bottom of the slope there was a dark crease, thick with brush, and on the other side of the crease a little flat, in which a grove of oak trees grew. A scar of green grass cut across the flat. And behind the flat another mountain rose, desolate with dead rocks and starving little black bushes. Pepé drank from the bag again for the air was so dry that it encrusted his nostrils and burned his lips. He put the horse down the trail. The hooves slipped and struggled on the steep way, starting little stones that rolled off into the brush. The sun was gone behind the westward mountain now, but still it glowed brilliantly on the oaks and on the grassy flat. The rocks and the hillsides still sent up waves of the heat they had gathered from the day's sun.

Pepé looked up to the top of the next dry withered ridge. He saw a dark form against the sky, a man's figure standing on top of a rock, and he glanced away quickly not to appear curious. When a moment later he looked up again, the figure was gone.

Downward the trail was quickly covered. Sometimes the horse floundered for footing, sometimes set his feet and slid a little way. They came at last to the bottom where the dark chaparral was higher than Pepé's head. He held up his rifle on one side and his arm on the other to shield his face from the sharp brittle fingers of the brush.

Up and out of the crease he rode, and up a little cliff. The grassy flat was before him, and the round comfortable oaks. For a moment he studied the trail down which he had come, but there was no movement and no sound from it. Finally he rode out over the flat, to the green streak, and at the upper end of the damp he found a little spring welling out of the earth and dropping into a dug basin before it seeped out over the flat.

Pepé filled his bag first, and then he let the thirsty horse drink out of the pool. He led the horse to the clump of oaks, and in the middle of the grove, fairly protected from sight on all sides, he took off the saddle and the bridle and laid them on the ground. The horse stretched his jaws sideways and yawned. Pepé knotted the lead rope about the horse's neck and tied him to a sapling among the oaks, where he could graze in a fairly large circle.

When the horse was gnawing hungrily at the dry grass, Pepé went to the saddle and took a black string of jerky from the sack and strolled to an oak tree on the edge of the grove, from under which he could watch the trail. He sat down in the crisp dry oak leaves and automatically felt for his big black knife to cut the jerky, but he had no knife. He leaned back on his elbow and gnawed at the tough strong meat. His face was blank, but it was a man's face.

The bright evening light washed the eastern ridge, but the valley was darkening. Doves flew down from the hills to the spring, and the quail came running out of the brush and joined them, calling clearly to one another.

Out of the corner of his eye Pepé saw a shadow grow out of the bushy crease. He turned his head slowly. A big spotted wildcat was creeping toward the spring, belly to the ground, moving like thought.

Pepé cocked his rifle and edged the muzzle slowly around. Then he looked apprehensively up the trail and dropped the hammer again. From the ground beside him he picked an oak twig and threw it toward the spring. The quail flew up with a roar and the doves whistled away. The big cat stood up: for a long moment he looked at Pepé with cold yellow eyes, and then fearlessly walked back into the gulch.

The dusk gathered quickly in the deep valley. Pepé muttered his prayers, put his head down on his arm and went instantly to sleep.

The moon came up and filled the valley with cold blue light, and the wind swept rustling down from the peaks. The owls worked up and down the slopes looking for rabbits. Down in the brush of the gulch a coyote gabbled. The oak trees whispered softly in the night breeze.

Pepé started up, listening. His horse had whinnied. The moon was just slipping behind the western ridge, leaving the valley in darkness behind it. Pepé sat tensely gripping his rifle. From far up the trail he heard an answering whinny and the crash of shod hooves on the broken rock. He jumped to his feet, ran to his horse and led it under the trees. He threw on the saddle and cinched it tight for the steep trail, caught the unwilling head and forced the bit into the mouth. He felt the saddle to make sure the water bag and the sack of jerky were there. Then he mounted and turned up the hill.

It was velvet dark. The horse found the entrance to the trail where it left the flat, and started up, stumbling and slipping on the rocks. Pepé's hand rose up to his head. His hat was gone. He had left it under the oak tree.

The horse had struggled far up the trail when the first exchange of dawn came into the air, a steel greyness as light mixed thoroughly with dark. Gradually the sharp snaggled edge of the ridge stood out above them, rotten granite tortured and eaten by the winds of time. Pepé had dropped his reins on the horn, leaving direction to the horse. The brush grabbed at his legs in the dark until one knee of his jeans was ripped.

Gradually the light flowed down over the ridge. The starved brush and rocks stood out in the half light, strange and lonely in high perspective. Then there came warmth into the light. Pepé drew up and looked back, but he could see nothing in the darker valley below. The sky turned blue over the coming sun. In the waste of the mountainside, the poor dry brush grew only three feet high. Here and there, big outcroppings of unrotted granite stood up like mouldering houses. Pepé relaxed a little. He drank from his water bag and bit off a piece of jerky. A single eagle flew over, high in the light.

Without warning Pepé's horse screamed and fell on its side. He was almost down before the rifle crash echoed up from the valley. From a hole behind the struggling shoulder, a stream of bright crimson blood pumped and stopped and pumped and stopped. The hooves threshed on the ground. Pepé lay half stunned beside the horse. He looked slowly down the hill. A piece of sage clipped off beside his head and another crash echoed up from side to side of the canyon. Pepé flung himself frantically behind a bush.

He crawled up the hill on his knees and one hand. His right hand held the rifle up off the ground and pushed it ahead of him. He moved with the instinctive care of an animal. Rapidly he wormed his way toward one of the big outcroppings of granite on the hill above him. Where the brush was high he doubled up and ran, but where the cover was slight he wriggled forward on his stomach, pushed the rifle ahead of him. In the last little distance there was no cover at all. Pepé poised and then he darted across the space and flashed around the corner of the rock.

He leaned panting against the stone. When his breath came easier he moved along behind the big rock until he came to a narrow slit that offered a thin section of vision down the hill. Pepé lay on his stomach and pushed the rifle barrel through the slit and waited.

The sun reddened the western ridges now. Already the buzzards were settling down toward the place where the horse lay. A small brown bird scratched in the dead sage leaves directly in front of the rifle muzzle. The coasting eagle flew back toward the rising sun.

Pepé saw a little movement in the brush far below. His grip tightened on the gun. A little brown doe stepped daintily out on the trail and crossed it and disappeared into the brush again. For a long time Pepé waited. Far below he could see the little flat and the oak trees and the slash of green. Suddenly his eyes flashed back at the trail again. A quarter of a mile down there had been a quick movement in the chaparral. The rifle swung over. The front sight nestled in the V of the rear sight. Pepé studied for a moment and then raised the rear sight a notch. The movement in the brush came again. The sight settled on it. Pepé squeezed the trigger. The explosion crashed down the mountain and up the other side, and came rattling back. The whole side of the slope grew still. No more movement. And then a white streak cut into the granite of the slit and a bullet whined away and a crash sounded up from below. Pepé felt a sharp pain in his right hand. A sliver of granite was sticking out from between his first and second knuckles and the point protruded from his palm. Carefully he pulled out the sliver of stone. The wound bled evenly and gently. No vein nor artery was cut.

Pepé looked into a little dusty cave in the rock and gathered a handful of spider web, and he pressed the mass into the cut, plastering the soft web into the blood. The flow stopped almost at once.

The rifle was on the ground. Pepé picked it up, levered a new shell into the chamber. And then he slid into the brush on his stomach. Far to the right he crawled, and then up the hill, moving slowly and carefully, crawling to cover and resting and then crawling again.

In the mountains the sun is high in its arc before it penetrates the gorges. The hot face looked over the hill and brought instant heat with it. The white light beat on the rocks and reflected from them and rose up quivering from the earth again, and the rocks and bushes seemed to quiver behind the air.

Pepé crawled in the general direction of the ridge peak, zig-zagging for cover. The deep cut between his knuckles began to throb. He crawled close to a rattlesnake before he saw it, and when it raised its dry head and made a soft beginning whirr, he backed up and took another way. The quick grey lizards flashed in front of him, raising a tiny line of dust. He found another mass of spider web and pressed it against his throbbing hand.

Pepé was pushing the rifle with his left hand now. Little drops of sweat ran to the end of his coarse black hair and rolled down his cheeks. His lips and tongue were growing thick and heavy. His lips writhed to draw saliva into his mouth. His little dark eyes were uneasy and suspicious. Once when a grey lizard paused in front of him on the parched ground and turned its head sideways he crushed it flat with a stone.

When the sun slid past noon he had not gone a mile. He crawled exhaustedly a last hundred yards to a patch of high sharp manzanita, crawled desperately, and when the patch was reached he wriggled in among the tough gnarly trunks and dropped his head on his left arm. There was little shade in the meager brush, but there was cover and safety. Pepé went to sleep as he lay and the sun beat on his back. A few little birds hopped close to him and peered and hopped away. Pepé squirmed in his sleep and he raised and dropped his wounded hand again and again.

The sun went down behind the peaks and the cool evening came, and then the dark. A coyote yelled from the hillside, Pepé started awake and looked about with misty eyes. His hand swollen and heavy; a little thread of pain ran up the inside of his arm and settled in a pocket in his armpit. He peered about and then stood up, for the mountains were black and the moon had not yet risen. Pepé stood up in the dark. The coat of his father pressed on his arm. His tongue was swollen until it nearly filled his mouth. He wriggled out of the coat and dropped it in the brush, and then he struggled up the hill, falling over rocks and tearing his way through the brush. The rifle knocked against stones as he went. Little dry avalanches of gravel and shattered stone went whispering down the hill behind him.

After a while the old moon came up and showed the jagged ridge top ahead of him. By moonlight Pepé traveled more easily. He bent forward so that his throbbing arm hung away from his body. The journey uphill was made in dashes and rests, a frantic rush up a few yards and then a rest. The wind coasted down the slope rattling the dry stems of the bushes.

The moon was at meridian when Pepé came at last to the sharp backbone of the ridge top. On the last hundred yards of the rise no soil had clung under the wearing winds. The way was on solid rock. He clambered to the top and looked down on the other side. There was a draw like the last below him, misty with moonlight, brushed with dry struggling sage and chaparral. On the other side the hill rose up sharply and at the top the jagged rotten teeth of the mountain showed against the sky. At the bottom of the cut the brush was thick and dark.

Pepé stumbled down the hill. His throat was almost closed with thirst. At first he tried to run, but immediately he fell and rolled. After that he went more carefully. The moon was just disappearing behind the mountains when he came to the bottom. He crawled into the heavy brush feeling with his fingers for water. There was no water in the bed of the stream, only damp earth. Pepé laid his gun down and scooped up a handful of mud and put it in his mouth, and then he spluttered and scraped the earth from his tongue with his finger, for the mud drew at his mouth like a poultice. He dug a hole in the stream bed with his fingers, dug a little basin to catch water; but before it was very deep his head fell forward on the damp ground and he slept.

The dawn came and the heat of the day fell on the earth, and still Pepé slept. Late in the afternoon his head jerked up. He looked slowly around. His eyes were slits of wariness. Twenty feet away in the heavy brush a big tawny mountain lion stood looking at him. Its long thick tail waved gracefully, its ears were erect with interest, not laid back dangerously. The lion squatted down on its stomach and watched him.

Pepé looked at the hole he had dug in the earth. A half inch of muddy water had collected in the bottom. He tore the sleeve from his hurt arm, with his teeth ripped out a little square, soaked it in the water and put it in his mouth. Over and over he filled the cloth and sucked it.

Still the lion sat and watched him. The evening came down but there was no movement on the hills. No birds visited the dry bottom of the cut. Pepé looked occasionally at the lion. The eyes of the yellow beast drooped as though he were about to sleep. He yawned and his long thin red tongue curled out. Suddenly his head jerked around and his nostrils quivered. His big tail lashed. He stood up and slunk like a tawny shadow into the thick brush.

A moment later Pepé heard the sound, the faint far crash of horses' hooves on gravel. And he heard something else, a high whining yelp of a dog.

Pepé took his rifle in his left hand and he glided into the brush almost as quietly as the lion had. In the darkening evening he crouched up the hill toward the next ridge. Only when the dark came did he stand up. His energy was short. Once it was dark he fell over the rocks and slipped to his knees on the steep slope, but he moved on and on up the hill, climbing and scrabbling over the broken hillside.

When he was far up toward the top, he lay down and slept for a little while. The withered moon, shining on his face, awakened him. He stood up and moved up the hill. Fifty yards away he stopped and turned back, for he had forgotten his rifle. He walked heavily down and poked about in the brush, but he could not find his gun. At last he lay down to rest. The pocket of pain in his armpit had grown more sharp. His arm seemed to swell out and fall with every heartbeat. There was no position lying down where the heavy arm did not press against his armpit.

With the effort of a hurt beast, Pepé got up and moved again toward the top of the ridge. He held his swollen arm away from his body with his left hand. Up the steep hill he dragged himself, a few steps and a rest, and a few more steps. At last he was nearing the top. The moon showed the uneven sharp back of it against the sky.

Pepé's brain spun in a big spiral up and away from him. He slumped to the ground and lay still. The rock ridge top was only a hundred feet above him.

The moon moved over the sky. Pepé half turned on his back. His tongue tried to make words, but only a thick hissing came from between his lips.

When the dawn came, Pepé pulled himself up. His eyes were sane again. He drew his great puffed arm in front of him and looked at the angry wound. The black line ran up from his wrist to his armpit. Automatically he reached in his pocket for the big black knife, but it was not there. His eyes searched the ground. He picked up a sharp blade of stone and scraped at the wound, sawed at the proud flesh and then squeezed the green juice out in big drops. Instantly he threw back his head and whined like a dog. His whole right side shuddered at the pain, but the pain cleared his head.

In the grey light he struggled up the last slope to the ridge and crawled over and lay down behind a line of rocks. Below him lay a deep canyon exactly like the last, waterless and desolate. There was no flat, no oak trees, not even heavy brush in the bottom of it. And on the other side a sharp ridge stood up, thinly brushed with starving sage, littered with broken granite. Strewn over the hill there were giant outcroppings, and on the top the granite teeth stood out against the sky.

The new day was light now. The flame of the sun came over the ridge and fell on Pepé where he lay on the ground. His coarse black hair was littered with twigs and bits of spider web. His eyes had retreated back into his head. Between his lips the tip of his black tongue showed.

He sat up and dragged his great arm into his lap and nursed it, rocking his body and moaning in his throat. He threw back his head and looked up into the pale sky. A big black bird circled nearly out of sight, and far to the left another was sailing near.

He lifted his head to listen, for a familiar sound had come to him from the valley he had climbed out of; it was the crying yelp of hounds, excited and feverish, on a trail.

Pepé bowed his head quickly. He tried to speak rapid words but only a thick hiss came from his lips. He drew a shaky cross on his breast with his left hand. It was a long struggle to get to his feet. He crawled slowly and mechanically to the top of a big rock on the ridge peak. Once there, he arose slowly, swaying to his feet, and stood erect. Far below he could see the dark brush where he had slept. He braced his feet and stood there, black against the morning sky.

There came a ripping sound at his feet. A piece of stone flew up and a bullet droned off into the next gorge. The hollow crash echoed up from below. Pepé looked down for a moment and then pulled himself straight again.

His body jarred back. His left hand fluttered helplessly toward his breast. The second crash sounded from below. Pepé swung forward and toppled from the rock. His body struck and rolled over and over, starting a little avalanche. And when at last he stopped against a bush, the avalanche slid slowly down and covered up his head.

1938

Katherine Anne Porter   *1890–1980*

Although she published only one novel and few short stories, Katherine Anne Porter enjoyed a reputation as one of America's finest stylists. Her writing is "disciplined" (one of her own terms), ironic, concentrated, and precise. Working within a narrow range and with limited subject matter she produced short stories of high distinction, an achievement which she suggested was the result of her dedication to art, "The substance of faith and the only reality."

Although she is known as a writer of great clarity, Katherine Anne Porter kept the details of her life obscure. She was born in Indian Creek, Texas, but the date is uncertain; at the end of her life she gave her birthdate as 1890, after saying for years that it was 1894. She told of being educated in Catholic convents as a child, but she rejected suggestions that her intellectual background was Roman Catholic. In the 1920s she went to Mexico to study art, and while there she became involved in left-wing revolutionary political movements. A journey from Mexico to Europe in the 1930s provided the background for her novel, Ship of Fools. *After the 1950s she spent much time lecturing and teaching in colleges and universities in the United States.*

Katherine Anne Porter was called "a maker of darkish parables" because of her portrayal of the impoverished spirit of mankind in the modern world and because of her repeated use of the themes of isolation, guilt, and spiritual denial. Many of her finest stories are set in the South, the Southwest, or in Mexico (she called Mexico "my familiar country"). They frequently turn on the conflicts between fixed social orders and movements for change. Her first story appeared in 1922 and her first book, Flowering Judas and Other Stories, *in 1930. Her second book of stories,* Pale Horse, Pale Rider, *was published in 1939; a third,* The Leaning Tower and Other Stories, *appeared in 1944. In explaining why she did not write more in the twenties and thirties Miss Porter was typically vague and cryptic: "I was not one of those who could flourish in the conditions of the past two decades." In her final years the quantity of her writing continued to remain small. A book of her critical essays,* The Days Before, *was published in 1952;* Ship of Fools *appeared in 1962 and was later made into an award-winning motion picture. Her most recent work,* The Never Ending Wrong (1977), *is a memoir of events surrounding the trial and execution of Sacco and Vanzetti in the 1920s. A biography of Cotton Mather, the great American Puritan, was promised for years, but only scattered excerpts were ever printed.*

FURTHER READING: *The Collected Essays and Occasional Writings of Katherine Anne Porter,* 1970; E. Lopez, *Conversations with Katherine Anne Porter,* 1981; J. Givner, *Katherine Anne Porter,* 1982; H. Mooney, *The Fiction and Criticism of Katherine Anne Porter,* 1957, 1962; R. West, *Katherine Anne Porter,* 1963; W. Nance, *Katherine Anne Porter and the Art of Rejection,* 1964; G. Hendrick, *Katherine Anne Porter,* 1965; W. Emmons, *Katherine Anne Porter, The Regional Stories,* 1967; *Katherine Anne Porter, A Critical Symposium,* ed. L. Hartley and G. Core, 1969; M. Liberman, *Katherine Anne Porter's Fiction,* 1971; J. Hardy, *Katherine Anne Porter,* 1973; *Katherine Anne Porter, A Collection of Critical Essays,* ed. R. Warren, 1979; J. De Mony, *Katherine Anne Porter's Women,* 1983; D. Unrue, *Truth and Vision in Katherine Anne Porter's Fiction,* 1985.

TEXT: *The Collected Stories of Katherine Anne Porter,* 1965.

FLOWERING JUDAS

Braggioni sits heaped upon the edge of a straight-backed chair much too small for him, and sings to Laura in a furry, mournful voice. Laura has begun to find reasons for avoiding her own house until the latest possible moment, for Braggioni is there almost every night. No matter how late she is, he will be sitting there with a surly, waiting expression, pulling at his kinky yellow hair, thumbing the strings of his guitar, snarling a tune under his breath. Lupe the Indian maid meets Laura at the door, and says with a flicker of a glance towards the upper room, "He waits."

Laura wishes to lie down, she is tired of her hairpins and the feel of her long tight sleeves, but she says to him, "Have you a new song for me this evening?" If he says yes, she asks him to sing it. If he says no, she remembers his favorite one, and asks him to sing it again. Lupe brings her a cup of chocolate and a plate of rice, and Laura eats at the small table under the lamp, first inviting Braggioni, whose answer is always the same: "I have eaten, and besides, chocolate thickens the voice."

Laura says, "Sing, then," and Braggioni heaves himself into song. He scratches the guitar familiarly as though it were a pet animal, and sings passionately off key, taking the high notes in a prolonged painful squeal. Laura, who haunts the markets listening to the ballad singers, and stops every day to hear the blind boy playing his reed-flute in Sixteenth of September Street,[1] listens to Braggioni with pitiless courtesy, because she dares not smile at his miserable performance. Nobody dares to smile at him. Braggioni is cruel to everyone, with a kind of specialized insolence, but he is so vain of his talents, and so sensitive to slights, it would require a cruelty and vanity greater than his own to lay a finger on the vast cureless wound of his self-esteem. It would require courage, too, for it is dangerous to offend him, and nobody has this courage.

Braggioni loves himself with such tenderness and amplitude and eternal charity that his followers—for he is a leader of men, a skilled revolutionist, and his skin has been punctured in horrible warfare—warm themselves in the reflected glow, and say to each other: "He has a real nobility, a love of humanity raised above mere personal affections." The excess of this self-love has flowed

---

[1] Street in Mexico City, named for the beginning date of the revolution for independence in 1810.

out, inconveniently for her, over Laura, who, with so many others, owes her comfortable situation and her salary to him. When he is in a very good humor, he tells her, "I am tempted to forgive you for being a *gringa*. *Gringita!*"[2] and Laura, burning, imagines herself leaning forward suddenly, and with a sound back-handed slap wiping the suety smile from his face. If he notices her eyes at these moments he gives no sign.

She knows what Braggioni would offer her, and she must resist tenaciously without appearing to resist, and if she could avoid it she would not admit even to herself the slow drift of his intention. During these long evenings which have spoiled a long month for her, she sits in her deep chair with an open book on her knees, resting her eyes on the consoling rigidity of the printed page when the sight and sound of Braggioni singing threaten to identify themselves with all her remembered afflictions and to add their weight to her uneasy premonitions of the future. The gluttonous bulk of Braggioni has become a symbol of her many disillusions, for a revolutionist should be lean, animated by heroic faith, a vessel of abstract virtues. This is nonsense, she knows it now and is ashamed of it. Revolution must have leaders, and leadership is a career for energetic men. She is, her comrades tell her, full of romantic error, for what she defines as cynicism in them is merely "a developed sense of reality." She is almost too willing to say, "I am wrong, I suppose I don't really understand the principles," and afterward she makes a secret truce with herself, determined not to surrender her will to such expedient logic. But she cannot help feeling that she has been betrayed irreparably by the disunion between her way of living and her feeling of what life should be, and at times she is almost contented to rest in this sense of grievance as a private source of consolation. Sometimes she wishes to run away, but she stays. Now she longs to fly out of this room, down the narrow stairs, and into the street where the houses lean together like conspirators under a single mottled lamp, and leave Braggioni singing to himself.

Instead she looks at Braggioni, frankly and clearly, like a good child who understands the rules of behavior. Her knees cling together under sound blue serge, and her round white collar is not purposely nun-like. She wears the uniform of an idea, and has renounced vanities. She was born Roman Catholic, and in spite of her fear of being seen by someone who might make a scandal of it, she slips now and again into some crumbling little church, kneels on the chilly stone, and says a Hail Mary on the gold rosary she bought in Tehuantepec.[3] It is no good and she ends by examining the altar with its tinsel flowers and ragged brocades, and feels tender about the battered doll-shape of some male saint whose white, lace-trimmed drawers hang limply around his ankles below the hieratic dignity of his velvet robe. She has encased herself in a set of principles derived from her early training, leaving no detail of gesture or of personal taste untouched, and for this reason she will not wear lace made on machines. This is her private heresy, for in her special group the machine is sacred, and will be the salvation of the workers. She loves fine lace, and there is a tiny edge of fluted cobweb on this collar, which is one of twenty precisely alike, folded in blue tissue paper in the upper drawer of her clothes chest.

Braggioni catches her glance solidly as if he had been waiting for it, leans forward, balancing his paunch between his spread knees, and sings with tremendous emphasis, weighing his words. He has, the song relates, no father and no mother, nor even a friend to console him; lonely as a wave of the sea he

[2]Spanish (contemptuous): "foreign girl. Little foreign girl!"
[3]Town in southern Mexico.

comes and goes, lonely as a wave. His mouth opens round and yearns sideways, his balloon cheeks grow oily with the labor of song. He bulges marvelously in his expensive garments. Over his lavender collar, crushed upon a purple necktie, held by a diamond hoop: over his ammunition belt of tooled leather worked in silver, buckled cruelly around his gasping middle: over the tops of his glossy yellow shoes Braggioni swells with ominous ripeness, his mauve silk hose stretched taut, his ankles bound with the stout leather thongs of his shoes.

When he stretches his eyelids at Laura she notes again that his eyes are the true tawny yellow cat's eyes. He is rich, not in money, he tells her, but in power, and this power brings with it the blameless ownership of things, and the right to indulge his love of small luxuries. "I have a taste for the elegant refinements," he said once, flourishing a yellow silk handkerchief before her nose. "Smell that? It is Jockey Club, imported from New York." Nonetheless he is wounded by life. He will say so presently. "It is true everything turns to dust in the hand, to gall on the tongue." He sighs and his leather belt creaks like a saddle girth. "I am disappointed in everything as it comes. Everything." He shakes his head. "You, poor thing, you will be disappointed too. You are born for it. We are more alike than you realize in some things. Wait and see. Some day you will remember what I have told you, you will know that Braggioni was your friend."

Laura feels a slow chill, a purely physical sense of danger, a warning in her blood that violence, mutilation, a shocking death, wait for her with lessening patience. She has translated this fear into something homely, immediate, and sometimes hesitates before crossing the street. "My personal fate is nothing, except as testimony of a mental attitude," she reminds herself, quoting from some forgotten philosophic primer, and is sensible enough to add, "Anyhow, I shall not be killed by an automobile if I can help it."

"It may be true I am as corrupt, in another way, as Braggioni," she thinks in spite of herself, "as callous, as incomplete," and if this is so, any kind of death seems preferable. Still she sits quietly, she does not run. Where could she go? Uninvited she has promised herself to this place; she can no longer imagine herself as living in another country, and there is no pleasure in remembering her life before she came here.

Precisely what is the nature of this devotion, its true motives, and what are its obligations? Laura cannot say. She spends part of her days in Xochimilco,[4] near by, teaching Indian children to say in English, "The cat is on the mat." When she appears in the classroom they crowd about her with smiles on their wise, innocent, clay-colored faces, crying, "Good morning my ticher!" in immaculate voices, and they make of her desk a fresh garden of flowers every day.

During her leisure she goes to union meetings and listens to busy important voices quarreling over tactics, methods, internal politics. She visits the prisoners of her own political faith in their cells, where they entertain themselves with counting cockroaches, repenting of their indiscretions, composing their memoirs, writing out manifestoes and plans for their comrades who are still walking about free, hands in pockets, sniffing fresh air. Laura brings them food and cigarettes and a little money, and she brings messages disguised in equivocal phrases from the men outside who dare not set foot in the prison for fear of disappearing into the cells kept empty for them. If the prisoners confuse night and day, and complain, "Dear little Laura, time doesn't pass in this infernal hole, and I won't know when it is time to sleep unless I have a reminder," she

---

[4]Town near Mexico City.

brings them their favorite narcotics, and says in a tone that does not wound them with pity, "Tonight will really be night for you," and though her Spanish amuses them, they find her comforting, useful. If they lose patience and all faith, and curse the slowness of their friends in coming to their rescue with money and influence, they trust her not to repeat everything, and if she inquires, "Where do you think we can find money, or influence?" they are certain to answer, "Well, there is Braggioni, why doesn't he do something?"

She smuggles letters from headquarters to men hiding from firing squads in back streets in mildewed houses, where they sit in tumbled beds and talk bitterly as if all Mexico were at their heels, when Laura knows positively they might appear at the band concert in the Alameda[5] on Sunday morning, and no one would notice them. But Braggioni says, "Let them sweat a little. The next time they may be careful. It is very restful to have them out of the way for a while." She is not afraid to knock on any door in any street after midnight, and enter in the darkness, and say to one of these men who is really in danger: "They will be looking for you—seriously—tomorrow morning after six. Here is some money from Vincente. Go to Vera Cruz[6] and wait."

She borrows money from the Roumanian agitator to give to his bitter enemy the Polish agitator. The favor of Braggioni is their disputed territory, and Braggioni holds the balance nicely, for he can use them both. The Polish agitator talks love to her over café tables, hoping to exploit what he believes is her secret sentimental preference for him, and he gives her misinformation which he begs her to repeat as the solemn truth to certain persons. The Roumanian is more adroit. He is generous with his money in all good causes, and lies to her with an air of ingenuous candor, as if he were her good friend and confidant. She never repeats anything they may say. Braggioni never asks questions. He has other ways to discover all that he wishes to know about them.

Nobody touches her, but all praise her gray eyes, and the soft, round under lip which promises gayety, yet is always grave, nearly always firmly closed: and they cannot understand why she is in Mexico. She walks back and forth on her errands, with puzzled eyebrows, carrying her little folder of drawings and music and school papers. No dancer dances more beautifully than Laura walks, and she inspires some amusing, unexpected ardors, which cause little gossip, because nothing comes of them. A young captain who had been a soldier in Zapata's[7] army attempted, during a horseback ride near Cuernavaca,[8] to express his desire for her with the noble simplicity befitting a rude folk-hero: but gently, because he was gentle. This gentleness was his defeat, for when he alighted, and removed her foot from the stirrup, and essayed to draw her down into his arms, her horse, ordinarily a tame one, shied fiercely, reared and plunged away. The young hero's horse careered blindly after his stable-mate, and the hero did not return to the hotel until rather late that evening. At breakfast he came to her table in full charro dress, gray buckskin jacket and trousers with strings of silver buttons down the leg, and he was in a humorous, careless mood. "May I sit with you?" and "You are a wonderful rider. I was terrified that you might be thrown and dragged. I should never have forgiven myself. But I cannot admire you enough for your riding!"

"I learned to ride in Arizona," said Laura.

"If you will ride with me again this morning, I promise you a horse that will

---

[5]A park in central Mexico City.   [6]On the Gulf of Mexico.
[7]Emiliano Zapata (1877?–1919), Mexican revolutionary leader.
[8]City south of Mexico City.

not shy with you," he said. But Laura remembered that she must return to Mexico City at noon.

Next morning the children made a celebration and spent their playtime writing on the blackboard, "We lov ar ticher," and with tinted chalks they drew wreaths of flowers around the words. The young hero wrote her a letter: "I am a very foolish, wasteful, impulsive man. I should have first said I love you, and then you would not have run away. But you shall see me again." Laura thought, "I must send him a box of colored crayons," but she was trying to forgive herself for having spurred her horse at the wrong moment.

A brown, shock-haired youth came and stood in her patio one night and sang like a lost soul for two hours, but Laura could think of nothing to do about it. The moonlight spread a wash of gauzy silver over the clear spaces of the garden, and the shadows were cobalt blue. The scarlet blossoms of the Judas tree were dull purple, and the names of the colors repeated themselves automatically in her mind, while she watched not the boy, but his shadow, fallen like a dark garment across the fountain rim, trailing in the water. Lupe came silently and whispered expert counsel in her ear: "If you will throw him one little flower, he will sing another song or two and go away." Laura threw the flower, and he sang a last song and went away with the flower tucked in the band of his hat. Lupe said, "He is one of the organizers of the Typographers Union, and before that he sold corridos[9] in the Merced market,[10] and before that, he came from Guanajuato, where I was born. I would not trust any man, but I trust least those from Guanajuato."

She did not tell Laura that he would be back again the next night and the next, or that he would follow her at a certain fixed distance around the Merced market, through the Zócalo,[11] up Francisco I. Madero Avenue,[12] and so along the Paseo de la Reforma to Chapultepec Park, and into the Philosopher's Footpath, still with that flower withering in his hat, and an indivisible attention in his eyes.

Now Laura is accustomed to him, it means nothing except that he is nineteen years old and is observing a convention with all propriety, as though it were founded on a law of nature, which in the end it might well prove to be. He is beginning to write poems which he prints on a wooden press, and he leaves them stuck like handbills in her door. She is pleasantly disturbed by the abstract, unhurried watchfulness of his black eyes which will in time turn easily towards another object. She tells herself that throwing the flower was a mistake, for she is twenty-two years old and knows better; but she refuses to regret it, and persuades herself that her negation of all external events as they occur is a sign that she is gradually perfecting herself in the stoicism she strives to cultivate against that disaster she fears, though she cannot name it.

She is not at home in the world. Every day she teaches children who remain strangers to her, though she loves their tender round hands and their charming opportunist savagery. She knocks at unfamiliar doors not knowing whether a friend or a stranger shall answer, and even if a known face emerges from the sour gloom of that unknown interior, still it is the face of a stranger. No matter what this stranger says to her, nor what her message to him, the very cells of her flesh reject knowledge and kinship in one monotonous word. No. No. No. She draws her strength from this one holy talismanic word which does not suffer

---

[9]Spanish: "ballads."   [10]Open air market in Mexico City.
[11]The popular name for Constitution Square in central Mexico City.
[12]Named for the revolutionary leader (1873–1913) who served as President of Mexico, 1911–1913.

her to be led into evil. Denying everything, she may walk anywhere in safety, she looks at everything without amazement.

No, repeats this firm unchanging voice of her blood; and she looks at Braggioni without amazement. He is a great man, he wishes to impress this simple girl who covers her great round breasts with thick dark cloth, and who hides long, invaluably beautiful legs under a heavy skirt. She is almost thin except for the incomprehensible fullness of her breasts, like a nursing mother's, and Braggioni, who considers himself a judge of women, speculates again on the puzzle of her notorious virginity, and takes the liberty of speech which she permits without a sign of modesty, indeed, without any sort of sign, which is disconcerting.

"You think you are so cold, *gringita!* Wait and see. You will surprise yourself some day! May I be there to advise you!" He stretches his eyelids at her, and his ill-humored cat's eyes waver in a separate glance for the two points of light marking the opposite ends of a smoothly drawn path between the swollen curve of her breasts. He is not put off by that blue serge, nor by her resolutely fixed gaze. There is all the time in the world. His cheeks are bellying with the wind of song. "O girl with the dark eyes," he sings, and reconsiders. "But yours are not dark. I can change all that. O girl with the green eyes, you have stolen my heart away!" then his mind wanders to the song, and Laura feels the weight of his attention being shifted elsewhere. Singing thus, he seems harmless, he is quite harmless, there is nothing to do but sit patiently and say "No," when the moment comes. She draws a full breath, and her mind wanders also, but not far. She dares not wander too far.

Not for nothing has Braggioni taken pains to be a good revolutionist and a professional lover of humanity. He will never die of it. He has the malice, the cleverness, the wickedness, the sharpness of wit, the hardness of heart, stipulated for loving the world profitably. *He will never die of it.* He will live to see himself kicked out from his feeding trough by other hungry world-saviors. Traditionally he must sing in spite of his life which drives him to bloodshed, he tells Laura, for his father was a Tuscany peasant who drifted to Yucatan and married a Maya woman: a woman of race, an aristocrat. They gave him the love and knowledge of music, thus: and under the rip of his thumbnail, the strings of the instrument complain like exposed nerves.

Once he was called Delgadito[13] by all the girls and married women who ran after him; he was so scrawny all his bones showed under his thin cotton clothing, and he could squeeze his emptiness to the very backbone with his two hands. He was a poet and the revolution was only a dream then; too many women loved him and sapped away his youth, and he could never find enough to eat anywhere, anywhere! Now he is a leader of men, crafty men who whisper in his ear, hungry men who wait for hours outside his office for a word with him, emaciated men with wild faces who waylay him at the street gate with a timid, "Comrade, let me tell you . . ." and they blow the foul breath from their empty stomachs in his face.

He is always sympathetic. He gives them handfuls of small coins from his own pocket, he promises them work, there will be demonstrations, they must join the unions and attend the meetings, above all they must be on the watch for spies. They are closer to him than his own brothers, without them he can do nothing—until tomorrow, comrade!

Until tomorrow. "They are stupid, they are lazy, they are treacherous, they would cut my thoat for nothing," he says to Laura. He has good food and

---

[13]Spanish: Skinny.

abundant drink, he hires an automobile and drives in the Paseo on Sunday morning, and enjoys plenty of sleep in a soft bed beside a wife who dares not disturb him; and he sits pampering his bones in easy billows of fat, singing to Laura, who knows and thinks these things about him. When he was fifteen, he tried to drown himself because he loved a girl, his first love, and she laughed at him. "A thousand women have paid for that," and his tight little mouth turns down at the corners. Now he perfumes his hair with Jockey Club, and confides to Laura: "One woman is really as good as another for me, in the dark. I prefer them all."

His wife organizes unions among the girls in the cigarette factories, and walks in picket lines, and even speaks at meetings in the evenings. But she cannot be brought to acknowledge the benefits of true liberty. "I tell her I must have my freedom, net. She does not understand my point of view." Laura has heard this many times. Braggioni scratches the guitar and meditates. "She is an instinctively virtuous woman, pure gold, no doubt of that. If she were not, I should lock her up, and she knows it."

His wife, who works so hard for the good of the factory girls, employs part of her leisure lying on the floor weeping because there are so many women in the world, and only one husband for her, and she never knows where nor when to look for him. He told her: "Unless you can learn to cry when I am not here, I must go away for good." That day he went away and took a room at the Hotel Madrid.

It is this month of separation for the sake of higher principles that has been spoiled not only for Mrs. Braggioni, whose sense of reality is beyond criticism, but for Laura, who feels herself bogged in a nightmare. Tonight Laura envies Mrs. Braggioni, who is alone, and free to weep as much as she pleases about a concrete wrong. Laura has just come from a visit to the prison, and she is waiting for tomorrow with a bitter anxiety as if tomorrow may not come, but time may be caught immovably in this hour, with herself transfixed, Braggioni singing on forever, and Eugenio's body not yet discovered by the guard.

Braggioni says: "Are you going to sleep?" Almost before she can shake her head, he begins telling her about the May-day disturbances coming on in Morelia,[14] for the Catholics hold a festival in honor of the Blessed Virgin, and the Socialists celebrate their martyrs on that day. "There will be two independent processions, starting from either end of town, and they will march until they meet, and the rest depends . . ." He asks her to oil and load his pistols. Standing up, he unbuckles his ammunition belt, and spreads it laden across her knees. Laura sits with the shells slipping through the cleaning cloth dipped in oil, and he says again he cannot understand why she works so hard for the revolutionary idea unless she loves some man who is in it. "Are you not in love with someone?" "No," says Laura. "And no one is in love with you?" "No." "Then it is your own fault. No woman need go begging. Why, what is the matter with you? The legless beggar woman in the Alameda has a perfectly faithful lover. Did you know that?"

Laura peers down the pistol barrel and says nothing, but a long, slow faintness rises and subsides in her; Braggioni curves his swollen fingers around the throat of the guitar and softly smothers the music out of it, and when she hears him again he seems to have forgotten her, and is speaking in the hypnotic voice he uses when talking in small rooms to a listening, close-gathered crowd. Some day this world, now seemingly so composed and eternal, to the edges of every

---

[14]City west of Mexico City.

sea shall be merely a tangle of gaping trenches, of crashing walls and broken bodies. Everything must be torn from its accustomed place where it has rotted for centuries, hurled skyward and distributed, cast down again clean as rain, without separate identity. Nothing shall survive that the stiffened hands of poverty have created for the rich and no one shall be left alive except the elect spirits destined to procreate a new world cleansed of cruelty and injustice, ruled by benevolent anarchy: "Pistols are good, I love them, cannon are even better, but in the end I pin my faith to good dynamite," he concludes, and strokes the pistol lying in her hands. "Once I dreamed of destroying this city, in case it offered resistance to General Ortíz,[15] but it fell into his hands like an overripe pear."

He is made restless by his own words, rises and stands waiting. Laura holds up the belt to him: "Put that on, and go kill somebody in Morelia, and you will be happier," she says softly. The presence of death in the room makes her bold. "Today, I found Eugenio going into a stupor. He refused to allow me to call the prison doctor. He had taken all the tablets I brought him yesterday. He said he took them because he was bored."

"He is a fool, and his death is his own business," says Braggioni, fastening his belt carefully.

"I told him if he had waited only a little while longer, you would have got him set free," says Laura. "He said he did not want to wait."

"He is a fool and we are rid of him," says Braggioni, reaching for his hat.

He goes away. Laura knows his mood has changed, she will not see him any more for a while. He will send word when he needs her to go on errands into strange streets, to speak to the strange faces that will appear, like clay masks with the power of human speech, to mutter their thanks to Braggioni for his help. Now she is free, and she thinks, I must run while there is time. But she does not go.

Braggioni enters his own house where for a month his wife has spent many hours every night weeping and tangling her hair upon her pillow. She is weeping now, and she weeps more at the sight of him, the cause of all her sorrows. He looks about the room. Nothing is changed, the smells are good and familiar, he is well acquainted with the woman who comes toward him with no reproach except grief on her face. He says to her tenderly: "You are so good, please don't cry any more, you dear good creature." She says, "Are you tired, my angel? Sit here and I will wash your feet." She brings a bowl of water, and kneeling, unlaces his shoes, and when from her knees she raises her sad eyes under her blackened lids, he is sorry for everything, and bursts into tears. "Ah, yes, I am hungry, I am tired, let us eat something together," he says, between sobs. His wife leans her head on his arm and says, "Forgive me!" and this time he is refreshed by the solemn, endless rain of her tears.

Laura takes off her serge dress and puts on a white linen nightgown and goes to bed. She turns her head a little to one side, and lying still, reminds herself that it is time to sleep. Numbers tick in her brain like little clocks, soundless doors close of themselves around her. If you would sleep, you must not remember anything, the children will say tomorrow, good morning, my teacher, the poor prisoners who come every day bringing flowers to their jailor. 1-2-3-4-5— it is monstrous to confuse love with revolution, night with day, life with death— ah, Eugenio!

The tolling of the midnight bell is a signal, but what does it mean? Get up,

[15]Pascual Ortiz Rubio (1877–1963), revolutionary leader of the 1920s and President of Mexico (1930–1932).

Laura, and follow me: come out of your sleep, out of your bed, out of this strange house. What are you doing in this house? Without a word, without fear she rose and reached for Eugenio's hand, but he eluded her with a sharp, sly smile and drifted away. This is not all, you shall see—Murderer, he said, follow me, I will show you a new country, but it is far away and we must hurry. No, said Laura, not unless you take my hand, no; and she clung first to the stair rail, and then to the topmost branch of the Judas tree that bent down slowly and set her upon the earth, and then to the rocky ledge of a cliff, and then to the jagged wave of a sea that was not water but a desert of crumbling stone. Where are you taking me, she asked in wonder but without fear. To death, and it is a long way off, and we must hurry, said Eugenio. No, said Laura, not unless you take my hand. Then eat these flowers, poor prisoner, said Eugenio in a voice of pity, take and eat: and from the Judas tree he stripped the warm bleeding flowers, and held them to her lips. She saw that his hand was fleshless, a cluster of small white petrified branches, and his eye sockets were without light, but she ate the flowers greedily for they satisfied both hunger and thirst. Murderer! said Eugenio, and Cannibal! This is my body and my blood. Laura cried No! and at the sound of her own voice, she awoke trembling, and was afraid to sleep again.

1930

James Thurber   *1894–1961*

James Thurber has been acclaimed as the best American humorist since Mark Twain. Like Twain, he saw literary humorists as despairing recorders of human folly and perverse fate. The notion that humorists "are gay of heart and carefree is curiously untrue," he once wrote. "The little wheels of their invention are set in motion by the damp hand of melancholy." As with Twain, Thurber's sense of melancholy and his awareness of the comedy of life grew out of his childhood experiences in the American Midwest. He was born and raised in Columbus, Ohio, at the turn of the century. At the age of six he lost his left eye in an accident. As a result of improper medical treatment he was constantly troubled by diminishing vision until, in the 1940s, he became blind. Handicapped by poor sight and a glass eye that always seemed out of alignment, Thurber grew up a shy and awkward youth, inept at games and suffering the taunts of schoolmates who called him "blinky."

Thurber's view of humanity was nourished by an array of eccentric and daft relatives whose antics he later portrayed in his best writing. His father was mild-mannered and meek, but his mother was lively and dramatic, a practical joker of local renown. Among the others was a grandfather who walked the streets of Columbus with a rose clamped in his teeth, a grandmother menaced by the fear that electricity dripped from empty light bulb sockets, and a distant uncle who died, Thurber claimed, of chestnut tree blight in spite of the fact that the local tree doctor had been called in to spray him.

In 1913, Thurber entered Ohio State University. Bashful and friendless, he was at first an indifferent student. But he was a talented writer and cartoonist, and he eventually became a campus personality and chief editor of the university humor and literary magazine. But he failed to graduate from the university: he could never satisfactorily perform the military drill required of male students, and—as he later recorded in "University Days," one of his best humorous pieces—he was unable to pass the required biology course because the only thing he could see in a microscope was the reflection of his own eyeball.

In *1918, Thurber left Ohio State without a degree and got a job with the U.S. State Department. Assigned to work as a code clerk in the American Embassy in Paris, he remained in Europe until 1920, when he returned to Columbus and began work as a newspaper reporter. In 1923 he sold his first short story. Hoping to make his way as a writer, he took his life savings and returned to France to write a novel, but in 1926, having recognized that he had no talent for novel writing, Thurber returned to the United States. He worked as a reporter for the New York* Evening Post *and began submitting humorous sketches to various journals, among them the newly established* New Yorker *magazine. In 1927, after many rejections,* The New Yorker *finally accepted one of Thurber's pieces, and in the same year the magazine's owner, Harold Ross, hired Thurber to work, first as an editor and later as a writer for the magazine. Thurber thus began the long and productive association with* The New Yorker *that he later described in his book* The Years with Ross *(1959).*

In *1929 Thurber published his first book,* Is Sex Necessary? *Written with E. B. White, another writer for* The New Yorker, *the book was a satire on the sex guides and self-help books that offer dubious advice on love and marriage to gullible readers. The volume was noteworthy for presenting the first Thurber drawings to appear in book form, cartoons that—like Thurber's writing—reveal men and women caught in the small catastrophes of life. Reprinted twenty-one times in its first year,* Is Sex Necessary? *became a best seller and brought Thurber his first international recognition as a writer and artist.*

In *1933 his humorous autobiography,* My Life and Hard Times, *appeared and presented memorable portraits of his relatives and his childhood in Ohio. But with the approach of World War II, Thurber's writing began to shift to political and social issues. He wrote parables, such as* The Last Flower *(1939), to describe the brutal destructiveness of war and human aggression. Working in collaboration with his friend, the actor and playwright Elliott Nugent, Thurber wrote a comedy,* The Male Animal. *Set in a midwestern university town resembling Columbus, the play presented the typical Thurber subject of matrimonial discord, but it also dealt with questions of academic and political freedom. Produced in 1940, the play had a successful Broadway run and was later adapted for the screen.*

In *all, Thurber wrote twenty-seven volumes—fantasies and farces, fables, sketches, reminiscences, essays, plays, fairy tales, and short stories. Among the most famous is "The Secret Life of Walter Mitty," the story of the harassed, shy little man who escapes his oppressors by living in a world of fantasy. First published in* The New Yorker *the story was an instantaneous success. It has since been reprinted innumerable times and adapted for the stage, radio, and motion pictures. The word "Mitty" has entered the English language as a term used to describe a meek and mild daydreamer. The "Walter Mitty Syndrome" has even become a medical designation for "daydreaming on a grand scale," and during the Watergate scandals in Washington, D.C., political commentators used the term "Walter Mitty Complex" to describe the mental derangements of government officials caught up in their own secret and fantastic schemes.*

Thurber's most memorable work portrayed the folly and weakness of insignificant men and women troubled by the dilemmas always lurking beneath the drab surface of their lives. His humor centered on characters like Walter Mitty who are intimidated by frowns and sharp remarks, by machines, by waiters, store clerks, and large, predatory wives. Thurber had little faith in the ultimate perfectibility of man, or woman. He insisted that he trusted animals, especially dogs, more than humans—particularly uplifters, do-gooders, and practical "realists." He saw the mass of humanity as a weak and endangered species whose best sanctuary is always to be found in fantasy and the joys of the imagination. And as for mankind's grandiose hope to reach an understanding of life, he concluded that man "is surely further away from the Answer than any other animal this side of the ladybug."

FURTHER READING: *The Selected Letters of James Thurber*, ed. H. Thurber and E. Weeks, 1981; R. Morsberger, *James Thurber*, 1964; R. Tobias, *The Art of James Thurber*, 1970; S. Black, *James Thurber, His Masquerade*, 1970; C. Holmes, *The Clocks of Columbus, The Literary Career of James Thurber*, 1972; *Thurber*, ed. C. Holmes, 1974; B. Bernstein, *Thurber, A Biography*, 1975; C. McGhee, *Thurber's Anatomy of Confusion*, 1984.

TEXT: *My World—and Welcome to It*, 1942.

THE SECRET LIFE OF WALTER MITTY

"WE'RE going through!" The Commander's voice was like thin ice breaking. He wore his full-dress uniform, with the heavily braided white cap pulled down rakishly over one cold gray eye. "We can't make it, sir. It's spoiling for a hurricane, if you ask me." "I'm not asking you, Lieutenant Berg," said the Commander. "Throw on the power lights! Rev her up to 8,500! We're going through!" The pounding of the cylinders increased: ta-pocketa-pocketa-pock-eta-*pocketa-pocketa*. The Commander stared at the ice forming on the pilot window. He walked over and twisted a row of complicated dials. "Switch on No. 8 auxiliary!" he shouted. "Switch on No. 8 auxiliary!" repeated Lieutenant Berg. "Full strength in No. 3 turret!" shouted the Commander. "Full strength in No. 3 turret!" The crew, bending to their various tasks in the huge, hurtling eight-engined Navy hydroplane, looked at each other and grinned. "The Old Man'll get us through," they said to one another. "The Old Man ain't afraid of Hell!" . . .

"Not so fast! You're driving too fast!" said Mrs. Mitty. "What are you driving so fast for?"

"Hmm?" said Walter Mitty. He looked at his wife, in the seat beside him, with shocked astonishment. She seemed grossly unfamiliar, like a strange woman who had yelled at him in a crowd. "You were up to fifty-five," she said. "You know I don't like to go more than forty. You were up to fifty-five." Walter Mitty drove on toward Waterbury in silence, the roaring of the SN202 through the worst storm in twenty years of Navy flying fading in the remote, intimate airways of his mind. "You're tensed up again," said Mrs. Mitty. "It's one of your days. I wish you'd let Dr. Renshaw look you over."

Walter Mitty stopped the car in front of the building where his wife went to have her hair done. "Remember to get those overshoes while I'm having my hair done," she said. "I don't need overshoes," said Mitty. She put her mirror back into her bag. "We've been all through that," she said, getting out of the car. "You're not a young man any longer." He raced the engine a little. "Why don't you wear your gloves? Have you lost your gloves?" Walter Mitty reached in a pocket and brought out the gloves. He put them on, but after she had turned and gone into the building and he had driven on to a red light, he took them off again. "Pick it up, brother!" snapped a cop as the light changed, and Mitty hastily pulled on his gloves and lurched ahead. He drove around the streets aimlessly for a time, and then he drove past the hospital on his way to the parking lot.

. . . "It's the millionaire banker, Wellington McMillan," said the pretty nurse. "Yes?" said Walter Mitty, removing his gloves slowly. "Who has the case?" "Dr.

Renshaw and R. Benbow, but there are two specialists here, Dr. Remington from New York and Mr. Pritchard-Mitford from London. He flew over." A door opened down a long, cool corridor and Dr. Renshaw came out. He looked distraught and haggard. "Hello, Mitty," he said. "We're having the devil's own time with McMillan, the millionaire banker and close personal friend of Roosevelt. Obstreosis[1] of the ductal tract. Tertiary.[2] Wish you'd take a look at him." "Glad to," said Mitty.

In the operating room there were whispered introductions: "Dr. Remington, Dr. Mitty. Mr. Pritchard-Mitford, Dr. Mitty." "I've read your book on streptothricosis," said Pritchard-Mitford, shaking hands. "A brilliant performance, sir." "Thank you," said Mitty. "Didn't know you were in the States, Mitty," grumbled Remington. "Coals to Newcastle, bringing Mitford and me up here for a tertiary." "You are very kind," said Mitty. A huge, complicated machine, connected to the operating table, with many tubes and wires, began at this moment to go picketa-pocketa-pocketa. "The new anesthetizer is giving way!" shouted an intern. "There is no one in the East who knows how to fix it!" "Quiet, man!" said Mitty, in a low, cool voice. He sprang to the machine, which was now going pocketa-pocketa-queep-pocketa-queep. He began fingering delicately a row of glistening dials. "Give me a fountain pen!" he snapped. Someone handed him a fountain pen. He pulled a faulty piston out of the machine and inserted the pen in its place. "That will hold for ten minutes," he said. "Get on with the operation." A nurse hurried over and whispered to Renshaw, and Mitty saw the man turn pale. "Coreopsis[3] has set in," said Renshaw nervously. "If you would take over, Mitty?" Mitty looked at him and at the craven figure of Benbow, who drank, and at the grave, uncertain faces of the two great specialists. "If you wish," he said. They slipped a white gown on him; he adjusted a mask and drew on thin gloves; nurses handed him shining . . .

"Back it up, Mac! Look out for that Buick!" Walter Mitty jammed on the brakes. "Wrong lane, Mac," said the parking-lot attendant, looking at Mitty closely. "Gee. Yeh," muttered Mitty. He began cautiously to back out of the lane marked "Exit only." "Leave her sit there," said the attendant. "I'll put her away." Mitty got out of the car. "Hey, better leave the key." "Oh," said Mitty, handing the man the ignition key. The attendant vaulted into the car, backed it up with insolent skill, and put it where it belonged.

They're so damn cocky, thought Walter Mitty, walking along Main Street; they think they know everything. Once he had tried to take his chains off, outside New Milford, and he had got them wound around the axles. A man had had to come out in a wrecking car and unwind them, a young, grinning garageman. Since then Mrs. Mitty always made him drive to a garage to have the chains taken off. The next time, he thought, I'll wear my right arm in a sling; they won't grin at me then. I'll have my right arm in a sling and they'll see I couldn't possibly take the chains off myself. He kicked the slush on the sidewalk. "Overshoes," he said to himself, and he began looking for a shoe store.

When he came out into the street again, with the overshoes in a box under his arm, Walter Mitty began to wonder what the other thing was his wife had told him to get. She had told him twice, before they set out from their house for Waterbury. In a way he hated these weekly trips to town—he was always getting something wrong. Kleenex, he thought, Squibb's, razor blades? No. Toothpaste, toothbrush, bicarbonate, carborundum, initiative and referendum?

---

[1]A meaningless term, as is "streptothricosis," below.
[2]Medical term meaning a third, hence advanced, stage of a disease.
[3]A genus of flower.

He gave it up. But she would remember it. "Where's the what's-its-name?" A
newsboy went by shouting something about the Waterbury trial.

. . . "Perhaps this will refresh your memory." The District Attorney suddenly
thrust a heavy automatic at the quiet figure on the witness stand. "Have you
ever seen this before?" Walter Mitty took the gun and examined it expertly.
"This is my Webley-Vickers 50.80," he said calmly. An excited buzz ran around
the courtroom. The judge rapped for order. "You are a crack shot with any
sort of firearms, I believe?" said the District Attorney, insinuatingly. "Objection!"
shouted Mitty's attorney. "We have shown that the defendant could not have
fired the shot. We have shown that he wore his right arm in a sling on the night
of the fourteenth of July." Walter Mitty raised his hand briefly and the bickering
attorneys were stilled. "With any known make of gun," he said evenly, "I could
have killed Gregory Fitzhurst at three hundred feet *with my left hand.*" Pandemonium broke loose in the courtroom. A woman's scream rose above the bedlam
and suddenly a lovely, dark-haired girl was in Walter Mitty's arms. The District
Attorney struck at her savagely. Without rising from his chair, Mitty let the man
have it on the point of the chin. "You miserable cur!" . . .

"Puppy biscuit," said Walter Mitty. He stopped walking and the buildings of
Waterbury rose up out of the misty courtroom and surrounded him again. A
woman who was passing laughed. "He said 'Puppy biscuit,'" she said to her
companion. "That man said 'Puppy biscuit' to himself." Walter Mitty hurried
on. He went into an A. & P., not the first one he came to but a smaller one
farther up the street. "I want some biscuit for small, young dogs," he said to the
clerk. "Any special brand, sir?" The greatest pistol shot in the world thought a
moment. "It says 'Puppies Bark for It' on the box," said Mitty.

His wife would be through at the hairdresser's in fifteen minutes, Mitty saw
in looking at his watch, unless they had trouble drying it; sometimes they had
trouble drying it. She didn't like to get to the hotel first; she would want him to
be there waiting for her as usual. He found a big leather chair in the lobby,
facing a window, and he put the overshoes and the puppy biscuit on the floor
beside it. He picked up an old copy of *Liberty*[4] and sank down into the chair.
"Can Germany Conquer the World Through the Air?" Walter Mitty looked at
the pictures of bombing planes and of ruined streets.

. . . "The cannonading has got the wind up in young Raleigh, sir," said the
sergeant. Captain Mitty looked up at him through tousled hair. "Get him to
bed," he said wearily. "With the others. I'll fly alone." "But you can't, sir," said
the sergeant anxiously. "It takes two men to handle that bomber and the Archies[5]
are pounding hell out of the air. Von Richtman's circus[6] is between here and
Saulier." "Somebody's got to get that ammunition dump," said Mitty. "I'm going
over. Spot of brandy?" He poured a drink for the sergeant and one for himself.
War thundered and whined around the dugout and battered at the door. There
was a rending of wood and splinters flew through the room. "A bit of a near
thing," said Captain Mitty carelessly. "The box barrage[7] is closing in," said the
sergeant. "We only live once, Sergeant," said Mitty, with his faint, fleeting smile.
"Or do we?" He poured another brandy and tossed it off. "I never see a man

[4]A popular weekly magazine (1924–1951).
[5]World War I slang term for anti-aircraft guns and their shell bursts.
[6]A battle group of World War I fighter squadrons organized to shift quickly to danger spots.
Because they moved frequently and thus resembled traveling circus troupes, they were called "flying
circuses." The most feared German "flying circus" was commanded by Manfred von Richthofen, the
"Red Baron."
[7]An artillery barrage in which shells are fired to the rear and sides of an enemy force so that it can
neither receive reinforcements nor retreat from frontal assault.

could hold his brandy like you, sir," said the sergeant. "Begging your pardon, sir." Captain Mitty stood up and strapped on his huge Webley-Vickers automatic. "It's forty kilometers through hell, sir," said the sergeant. Mitty finished one last brandy. "After all," he said softly, "what isn't?" The pounding of the cannon increased; there was the rat-tat-tatting of machine guns, and from somewhere came the menacing picketa-pocketa-pocketa of the new flame-throwers. Walter Mitty walked to the door of the dugout humming "Auprès de Ma Blonde."[8] He turned and waved to the sergeant. "Cheerio!" he said. . . .

Something struck his shoulder. "I've been looking all over this hotel for you," said Mrs. Mitty. "Why do you have to hide in this old chair? How did you expect me to find you?" "Things close in," said Walter Mitty vaguely. "What?" Mrs. Mitty said. "Did you get the what's-its-name? The puppy biscuit? What's in that box?" "Overshoes," said Mitty. "Couldn't you have put them on in the store?" "I was thinking," said Walter Mitty. "Does it ever occur to you that I am sometimes thinking?" She looked at him. "I'm going to take your temperature when I get you home," she said.

They went out through the revolving doors that made a faintly derisive whistling sound when you pushed them. It was two blocks to the parking lot. At the drugstore on the corner she said, "Wait here for me. I forgot something. I won't be a minute." She was more than a minute. Walter Mitty lighted a cigarette. It began to rain, rain with sleet in it. He stood up against the wall of the drugstore, smoking. . . . He put his shoulders back and his heels together. "To hell with the handkerchief," said Walter Mitty scornfully. He took one last drag on his cigarette and snapped it away. Then, with a faint, fleeting smile playing about his lips, he faced the firing squad; erect and motionless, proud and disdainful, Walter Mitty the Undefeated, inscrutable to the last.

1938–1939   1939

Eudora Welty   *1909–*

Eudora Welty was born and raised in Jackson, Mississippi. She attended Mississippi State College for Women for two years and then transferred to the University of Wisconsin, from which she graduated in 1929. The following year she entered Columbia University in New York to study advertising. Two years later she returned to Jackson, Mississippi, where she worked for a local radio station and wrote society news for a Memphis newspaper. She wrote publicity for the WPA, and she worked for a state commission to attract tourists to Mississippi.

She had begun serious attempts at writing after her return to Mississippi from New York in 1931, and in June 1936 her first story "Death of a Traveling Salesman," was published. Since that time she has written several novels, the last being Losing Battles *(1970) and* The Optimist's Daughter *(1972), and numerous short stories which have been widely anthologized, translated into numerous foreign languages, and dramatized on Broadway and on television.*

[8]French: "Near to My Blonde," the title of a French soldier's marching song popular during World War I.

Her work displays a strong sense of place. She has insisted that successful fiction depends in large measure on the appropriate location of the appropriate action. "It seems plain," she has observed, "that the art that speaks most clearly, explicitly, directly, and passionately from its place of origin will remain the longest understood." She exhibits a strong sense of her southern heritage, yet she is capable of a sustained detachment. Her fiction is largely concerned with the inner life, the mysteries of human beings confronting each other. She reveals the sharp eye of a painter or photographer, displaying an acute sense of light, color, and atmosphere.

As a southerner she has been compared to William Faulkner, a fellow Mississippian, but although she resembles Faulkner in her concern for the South and its landscape, and although she is similarly metaphorical and symbolic, she does not exhibit the tragic vision of Faulkner and his concern with the dissolution of a moribund society. And she is best in short stories—even her novels have the qualities of extended short tales—which present her ironic view of human beings struggling amid the follies of life and the menace of death.

FURTHER READING: *Selected Stories of Eudora Welty*, 1954; *The Eye of the Story, Selected Essays and Reviews*, 1978; *The Collected Stories of Eudora Welty*, 1980; *One Writer's Beginnings*, 1984; R. Vande Kieft, *Eudora Welty*, 1962, 1987; A. Appel, *A Season of Dreams, The Fiction of Eudora Welty*, 1965; J. Bryant, *Eudora Welty*, 1968; *Eudora Welty, Critical Essays*, ed. P. Prenshaw, 1979; M. Kreyling, *Eudora Welty's Achievement of Order*, 1980; E. Evans, *Eudora Welty*, 1981; A. Devlin, *Eudora Welty's Chronicle*, 1983; C. Manning, *Ears Opening Like Morning Glories, Eudora Welty and the Love of Story Telling*, 1985.

TEXT: *A Curtain of Green*, 1941.

DEATH OF A TRAVELING SALESMAN

R. J. Bowman, who for fourteen years had traveled for a shoe company through Mississippi, drove his Ford along a rutted dirt path. It was a long day! The time did not seem to clear the noon hurdle and settle into a soft afternoon. The sun, keeping its strength here even in winter, stayed at the top of the sky, and every time Bowman stuck his head out of the dusty car to stare up the road, it seemed to reach a long arm down and push against the top of his head, right through his hat—like the practical joke of an old drummer, long on the road. It made him feel all the more angry and helpless. He was feverish, and he was not quite sure of the way.

This was his first day back on the road after a long siege of influenza. He had had very high fever, and dreams, and had become weakened and pale, enough to tell the difference in the mirror, and he could not think clearly. . . . All afternoon, in the midst of his anger, and for no reason, he had thought of his dead grandmother. She had been a comfortable soul. Once more Bowman wished he could fall into the big feather bed that had been in her room. . . . Then he forgot her again.

This desolate hill country! And he seemed to be going the wrong way—it was as if he were going back, far back. There was not a house in sight. . . . There was no use wishing he were back in bed, though. By paying the hotel doctor his bill he had proved his recovery. He had not even been sorry when the pretty trained nurse said good-bye. He did not like illness, he distrusted it, as he distrusted the road without signposts. It angered him. He had given the nurse a really expensive bracelet, just because she was packing up her bag and leaving.

But now—what if in fourteen years on the road he had never been ill before and never had an accident? His record was broken, and he had even begun almost to question it. . . . He had gradually put up at better hotels, in the bigger towns, but weren't they all, eternally, stuffy in summer and drafty in winter? Women? He could only remember little rooms within little rooms, like a nest of Chinese paper boxes, and if he thought of one woman he saw the worn loneliness that the furniture of the room seemed built of. And he himself—he was a man who always wore rather wide-brimmed black hats, and in the wavy hotel mirrors he had looked something like a bullfighter, as he paused for that inevitable instant on the landing, walking downstairs to supper. . . . He leaned out of the car again, and once more the sun pushed at his head.

Bowman had wanted to reach Beulah by dark, to go to bed and sleep off his fatigue. As he remembered, Beulah was fifty miles away from the last town, on a graveled road. This was only a cow trail. How had he ever come to such a place? One hand wiped the sweat from his face, and he drove on.

He had made the Beulah trip before, but he had never seen this hill or this petering-out path before—or that cloud, he thought shyly, looking up and then down quickly—any more than he had seen this day before. Why did he not admit he was simply lost and had been for miles? . . . He was not in the habit of asking the way of strangers, and these people never knew where the very roads they lived on went to; but then he had not even been close enough to anyone to call out. People standing in the fields now and then, or on top of the haystacks, had been too far away, looking like leaning sticks or weeds, turning a little at the solitary rattle of his car across their countryside, watching the pale sobered winter dust where it chunked out behind like big squashes down the road. The stares of these distant people had followed him solidly like a wall, impenetrable, behind which they turned back after he had passed.

The cloud floated there to one side like the bolster on his grandmother's bed. It went over a cabin on the edge of a hill, where two bare chinaberry trees clutched at the sky. He drove through a heap of dead oak leaves, his wheels stirring their weightless sides to make a silvery melancholy whistle as the car passed through their bed. No car had been along this way ahead of him. Then he saw that he was on the edge of a ravine that fell away, a red erosion, and that this was indeed the road's end.

He pulled the brake. But it did not hold, though he put all his strength into it. The car, tipped toward the edge, rolled a little. Without doubt, it was going over the bank.

He got out quietly, as though some mischief had been done him and he had his dignity to remember. He lifted his bag and sample case out, set them down, and stood back and watched the car roll over the edge. He heard something—not the crash he was listening for, but a slow, unuproarious crackle. Rather distastefully he went to look over, and he saw that his car had fallen into a tangle of immense grapevines as thick as his arm, which caught it and held it, rocked it like a grotesque child in a dark cradle, and then, as he watched, concerned somehow that he was not still inside it, released it gently to the ground.

He sighed.

Where am I? he wondered with a shock. Why didn't I do something? All his anger seemed to have drifted away from him. There was the house, back on the hill. He took a bag in each hand and with almost childlike willingness went toward it. But his breathing came with difficulty, and he had to stop to rest.

It was a shotgun house, two rooms and an open passage between, perched on the hill. The whole cabin slanted a little under the heavy heaped-up vine that covered the roof, light and green, as though forgotten from summer. A woman stood in the passage.

He stopped still. Then all of a sudden his heart began to behave strangely. Like a rocket set off, it began to leap and expand into uneven patterns of beats which showered into his brain, and he could not think. But in scattering and falling it made no noise. It shot up with great power, almost elation, and fell gently, like acrobats into nets. It began to pound profoundly, then waited irresponsibly, hitting some sort of inward mockery first at his ribs, then against his eyes, then under his shoulder blades, and against the roof of his mouth when he tried to say, "Good afternoon, madam." But he could not hear his heart—it was as quiet as ashes falling. This was rather comforting; still, it was shocking to Bowman to feel his heart beating at all.

Stock-still in his confusion, he dropped his bags, which seemed to drift in slow bulks gracefully through the air and to cushion themselves on the gray prostrate grass near the doorstep.

As for the woman standing there, he saw at once that she was old. Since she could not possibly hear his heart, he ignored the pounding and now looked at her carefully, and yet in his distraction dreamily, with his mouth open.

She had been cleaning the lamp, and held it, half blackened, half clear, in front of her. He saw her with the dark passage behind her. She was a big woman with a weather-beaten but unwrinkled face; her lips were held tightly together, and her eyes looked with a curious dulled brightness into his. He looked at her shoes, which were like bundles. If it were summer she would be barefoot. . . . Bowman, who automatically judged a woman's age on sight, set her age at fifty. She wore a formless garment of some gray coarse material, rough-dried from a washing, from which her arms appeared pink and unexpectedly round. When she never said a word, and sustained her quiet pose of holding the lamp, he was convinced of the strength in her body.

"Good afternoon, madam," he said.

She stared on, whether at him or at the air around him he could not tell, but after a moment she lowered her eyes to show that she would listen to whatever he had to say.

"I wonder if you would be interested—" He tried once more. "An accident— my car . . ."

Her voice emerged low and remote, like a sound across a lake. "Sonny he ain't here."

"Sonny?"

"Sonny ain't here now."

Her son—a fellow able to bring my car up, he decided in blurred relief. He pointed down the hill. "My car's in the bottom of the ditch. I'll need help."

"Sonny ain't here, but he'll be here."

She was becoming clearer to him and her voice stronger, and Bowman saw that she was stupid.

He was hardly surprised at the deepening postponement and tedium of his journey. He took a breath, and heard his voice speaking over the silent blows of his heart. "I was sick. I am not strong yet. . . . May I come in?"

He stooped and laid his big black hat over the handle of his bag. It was a humble motion, almost a bow, that instantly struck him as absurd and betraying of all his weakness. He looked up at the woman, the wind blowing his hair. He might have continued for a long time in this unfamiliar attitude; he had never been a patient man, but when he was sick he had learned to sink submissively into the pillows, to wait for his medicine. He waited on the woman.

Then she, looking at him with blue eyes, turned and held open the door, and after a moment Bowman, as if convinced in his action, stood erect and followed her in.

Inside, the darkness of the house touched him like a professional hand, the doctor's. The woman set the half-cleaned lamp on a table in the center of the room and pointed, also like a professional person, a guide, to a chair with a yellow cowhide seat. She herself crouched on the hearth, drawing her knees up under the shapeless dress.

At first he felt hopefully secure. His heart was quieter. The room was enclosed in the gloom of yellow pine boards. He could see the other room, with the foot of an iron bed showing, across the passage. The bed had been made up with a red-and-yellow pieced quilt that looked like a map or a picture, a little like his grandmother's girlhood painting of Rome burning.

He had ached for coolness, but in this room it was cold. He stared at the hearth with dead coals lying on it and iron pots in the corners. The hearth and smoked chimney were of the stone he had seen ribbing the hills, mostly slate. Why is there no fire? he wondered.

And it was so still. The silence of the fields seemed to enter and move familiarly through the house. The wind used the open hall. He felt that he was in a mysterious, quiet, cool danger. It was necessary to do what? . . . To talk.

"I have a nice line of women's low-priced shoes . . ." he said.

But the woman answered, "Sonny'll be here. He's strong. Sonny'll move your car."

"Where is he now?"

"Farms for Mr. Redmond."

Mr. Redmond. Mr. Redmond. That was someone he would never have to encounter, and he was glad. Somehow the name did not appeal to him. . . . In a flare of touchiness and anxiety, Bowman wished to avoid even mention of unknown men and their unknown farms.

"Do you two live here alone?" He was surprised to hear his old voice, chatty, confidential, inflected for selling shoes, asking a question like that—a thing he did not even want to know.

"Yes. We are alone."

He was surprised at the way she answered. She had taken a long time to say that. She had nodded her head in a deep way too. Had she wished to affect him with some sort of premonition? he wondered unhappily. Or was it only that she would not help him, after all, by talking with him? For he was not strong enough to receive the impact of unfamiliar things without a little talk to break their fall. He had lived a month in which nothing had happened except in his head and his body—an almost inaudible life of heartbeats and dreams that came back, a life of fever and privacy, a delicate life which had left him weak to the point of—what? Of begging. The pulse in his palm leapt like a trout in a brook.

He wondered over and over why the woman did not go ahead with cleaning the lamp. What prompted her to stay there across the room, silently bestowing her presence upon him? He saw that with her it was not a time for doing little tasks. Her face was grave; she was feeling how right she was. Perhaps it was only politeness. In docility he held his eyes stiffly wide; they fixed themselves on the woman's clasped hands as though she held the cord they were strung on.

Then, "Sonny's coming," she said.

He himself had not heard anything, but there came a man passing the window and then plunging in at the door, with two hounds beside him. Sonny was a big enough man, with his belt slung low about his hips. He looked at least thirty. He had a hot, red face that was yet full of silence. He wore muddy blue pants and an old military coat stained and patched. World War? Bowman wondered. Great God, it was a Confederate coat. On the back of his light hair he had a wide filthy black hat which seemed to insult Bowman's own. He pushed down the dogs from his chest. He was strong, with dignity and heaviness in his way of moving. . . . There was the resemblance to his mother.

They stood side by side. . . . He must account again for his presence here.

"Sonny, this man, he had his car to run off over the prec'pice an' wants to know if you will git it out for him," the woman said after a few minutes.

Bowman could not even state his case.

Sonny's eyes lay upon him.

He knew he should offer explanations and show money—at least appear either penitent or authoritative. But all he could do was to shrug slightly.

Sonny brushed by him going to the window, followed by the eager dogs, and looked out. There was effort even in the way he was looking, as if he could throw his sight out like a rope. Without turning Bowman felt that his own eyes could have seen nothing: it was too far.

"Got me a mule out there an' got me a block an' tackle," said Sonny meaningfully. "I *could* catch me my mule an' git me my ropes, an' before long I'd git your car out the ravine."

He looked completely around the room, as if in meditation, his eyes roving in their own distance. Then he pressed his lips firmly and yet shyly together, and with the dogs ahead of him this time, he lowered his head and strode out. The hard earth sounded, cupping to his powerful way of walking—almost a stagger.

Mischievously, at the suggestion of those sounds, Bowman's heart leapt again. It seemed to walk about inside him.

"Sonny's goin' to do it," the woman said. She said it again, singing it almost, like a song. She was sitting in her place by the hearth.

Without looking out, he heard some shouts and the dogs barking and the pounding of hoofs in short runs on the hill. In a few minutes Sonny passed under the window with a rope, and there was a brown mule with quivering, shining, purple-looking ears. The mule actually looked in the window. Under its eyelashes it turned targetlike eyes into his. Bowman averted his head and saw the woman looking serenely back at the mule, with only satisfaction in her face.

She sang a little more, under her breath. It occurred to him, and it seemed quite marvelous, that she was not really talking to him, but rather following the thing that came about with words that were unconscious and part of her looking.

So he said nothing, and this time when he did not reply he felt a curious and strong emotion, not fear, rise up in him.

This time, when his heart leapt, something—his soul—seemed to leap too, like a little colt invited out of a pen. He stared at the woman while the frantic nimbleness of his feeling made his head sway. He could not move; there was nothing he could do, unless perhaps he might embrace this woman who sat there growing old and shapeless before him.

But he wanted to leap up, to say to her, I have been sick and I found out then, only then, how lonely I am. Is it too late? My heart puts up a struggle inside me, and you may have heard it, protesting against emptiness. . . . It should be full, he would rush on to tell her, thinking of his heart now as a deep lake, it should be holding love like other hearts. It should be flooded with love. There would be a warm spring day . . . Come and stand in my heart, whoever you are, and a whole river would cover your feet and rise higher and take your knees in whirlpools, and draw you down to itself, your whole body, your heart too.

But he moved a trembling hand across his eyes, and looked at the placid crouching woman across the room. She was still as a statue. He felt ashamed and exhausted by the thought that he might, in one more moment, have tried by simple words or embraces to communicate some strange thing—something which seemed always to have just escaped him . . .

Sunlight touched the furthest pot on the hearth. It was late afternoon. This time tomorrow he would be somewhere on a good graveled road, driving his car past things that happened to people, quicker than their happening. Seeing ahead to the next day, he was glad, and knew that this was no time to embrace an old woman. He could feel in his pounding temples the readying of his blood for motion and for hurrying away.

"Sonny's hitched up your car by now," said the woman. "He'll git it out the ravine right shortly."

"Fine!" he cried with his customary enthusiasm.

Yet it seemed a long time that they waited. It began to get dark. Bowman was cramped in his chair. Any man should know enough to get up and walk around while he waited. There was something like guilt in such stillness and silence.

But instead of getting up he listened. . . . His breathing restrained, his eyes powerless in the growing dark, he listened uneasily for a warning sound, forgetting in wariness what it would be. Before long he heard something—soft, continuous, insinuating.

"What's that noise?" he asked, his voice jumping into the dark. Then wildly he was afraid it would be his heart beating so plainly in the quiet room, and she would tell him so.

"You might hear the stream," she said grudgingly.

Her voice was closer. She was standing by the table. He wondered why she did not light the lamp. She stood there in the dark and did not light it.

Bowman would never speak to her now, for the time was past. I'll sleep in the dark, he thought, in his bewilderment pitying himself.

Heavily she moved on to the window. Her arm, vaguely white, rose straight from her full side and she pointed out into the darkness.

"That white speck's Sonny," she said, talking to herself.

He turned unwillingly and peered over her shoulder; he hesitated to rise and stand beside her. His eyes searched the dusky air. The white speck floated smoothly toward her finger, like a leaf on a river, growing whiter in the dark. It was as if she had shown him someting secret, part of her life, but had offered no explanation. He looked away. He was moved almost to tears, feeling for no reason that she had made a silent declaration equivalent to his own. His hand waited upon his chest.

Then a step shook the house, and Sonny was in the room. Bowman felt how the woman left him there and went to the other man's side.

"I done got your car out, mister," said Sonny's voice in the dark. "She's settin' a-waitin' in the road, turned to go back where she come from."

"Fine!" said Bowman, projecting his own voice to loudness. "I'm surely much obliged—I could never have done it myself—I was sick. . . ."

"I could do it easy," said Sonny.

Bowman could feel them both waiting in the dark, and he could hear the dogs panting out in the yard, waiting to bark when he should go. He felt strangely helpless and resentful. Now that he could go, he longed to stay. From what was he being deprived? His chest was rudely shaken by the violence of his heart. These people cherished something here that he could not see, they withheld some ancient promise of food and warmth and light. Between them they had a conspiracy. He thought of the way she had moved away from him and gone to Sonny, she had flowed toward him. He was shaking with cold, he was tired, and it was not fair. Humbly and yet angrily he stuck his hand into his pocket.

"Of course I'm going to pay you for everything—"

"We don't take money for such," said Sonny's voice belligerently.

"I want to pay. But do something more . . . Let me stay—tonight. . . ." He took another step toward them. If only they could see him, they would know his sincerity, his real need! His voice went on, "I'm not very strong yet, I'm not able to walk far, even back to my car, maybe, I don't know—I don't know exactly where I am—"

He stopped. He felt as if he might burst into tears. What would they think of him!

Sonny came over and put his hands on him. Bowman felt them pass (they were professional too) across his chest, over his hips. He could feel Sonny's eyes upon him in the dark.

"You ain't no revenuer come sneakin' here, mister, ain't got no gun?"

To this end of nowhere! And yet *he* had come. He made a grave answer. "No."

"You can stay."

"Sonny," said the woman, "you'll have to borrow some fire."

"I'll go git it from Redmond's," said Sonny.

"What?" Bowman strained to hear their words to each other.

"Our fire, it's out, and Sonny's got to borry some, because it's dark an' cold." she said.

"But matches—I have matches—"

"We don't have no need for 'em," she said proudly. "Sonny's goin' after his own fire."

"I'm goin' to Redmond's," said Sonny with an air of importance, and he went out.

After they had waited a while, Bowman looked out the window and saw a light moving over the hill. It spread itself out like a little fan. It zigzagged along the field, darting and swift, not like Sonny at all. . . . Soon enough, Sonny staggered in, holding a burning stick behind him in tongs, fire flowing in his wake, blazing light into the corridors of the room.

"We'll make a fire now," the woman said, taking the brand.

When that was done she lit the lamp. It showed its dark and light. The whole room turned golden-yellow like some sort of flower, and the walls smelled of it and seemed to tremble with the quiet rushing of the fire and the waving of the burning lampwick in its funnel of light.

The woman moved among the iron pots. With the tongs she dropped hot coals on top of the iron lids. They made a set of soft vibrations, like the sound of a bell far away.

She looked up and over at Bowman, but he could not answer. He was trembling. . . .

"Have a drink, mister?" Sonny asked. He had brought a chair from the other room and sat astride it with folded arms across the back. Now we are all visible to one another, Bowman thought, and cried, "Yes sir, you bet, thanks!"

"Come after me and do just what I do," said Sonny.

It was another excursion into the dark. They went through the hall, out to the back of the house, past a shed and a hooded well. They came to a wilderness of thicket.

"Down on your knees," said Sonny.

"What?" Sweat broke out on his forehead.

He understood when Sonny began to crawl through a sort of tunnel that the bushes made over the ground. He followed, startled in spite of himself when a twig or a thorn touched him gently without making a sound, clinging to him and finally letting him go.

Sonny stopped crawling and, crouched on his knees, began to dig with both his hands into the dirt. Bowman shyly struck matches and made a light. In a few minutes Sonny pulled up a jug. He poured out some of the whisky into a bottle from his coat pocket, and buried the jug again. "You never know who's liable to knock at your door," he said, and laughed. "Start back," he said, almost formally. "Ain't no need for us to drink outdoors, like hogs."

At the table by the fire, sitting opposite each other in their chairs, Sonny and Bowman took drinks out of the bottle, passing it across. The dogs slept; one of them was having a dream.

"This is good," said Bowman. "This is what I needed." It was just as though he were drinking the fire off the hearth.

"He makes it," said the woman with quiet pride.

She was pushing the coals off the pots, and the smells of corn bread and coffee circled the room. She set everything on the table before the men, with a bone-handled knife stuck into one of the potatoes, splitting out its golden fiber. Then she stood for a minute looking at them, tall and full above them where they sat. She leaned a little toward them.

"You all can eat now," she said, and suddenly smiled.

Bowman had just happened to be looking at her. He set his cup back on the table in unbelieving protest. A pain pressed at his eyes. He saw that she was not an old woman. She was young, still young. He could think of no number of years for her. She was the same age as Sonny, and she belonged to him. She stood with the deep dark corner of the room behind her, the shifting yellow light scattering over her head and her gray formless dress, trembling over her tall body when it bent over them in its sudden communication. She was young. Her teeth were shining and her eyes glowed. She turned and walked slowly and heavily out of the room, and he heard her sit down on the cot and then lie down. The pattern on the quilt moved.

"She's goin' to have a baby," said Sonny, popping a bite into his mouth.

Bowman could not speak. He was shocked with knowing what was really in this house. A marriage, a fruitful marriage. That simple thing. Anyone could have had that.

Somehow he felt unable to be indignant or protest, although some sort of joke had certainly been played upon him. There was nothing remote or mysterious here—only something private. The only secret was the ancient communication between two people. But the memory of the woman's waiting silently by the cold hearth, of the man's stubborn journey a mile away to get fire, and how they finally brought out their food and drink and filled the room proudly with all they had to show, was suddenly too clear and too enormous within him for response. . . .

"You ain't as hungry as you look," said Sonny.

The woman came out of the bedroom as soon as the men had finished, and ate her supper while her husband stared peacefully into the fire.

Then they put the dogs out, with the food that was left.

"I think I'd better sleep here by the fire, on the floor," said Bowman.

He felt that he had been cheated, and that he could afford now to be generous. Ill though he was, he was not going to ask them for their bed. He was through with asking favors in this house, now that he understood what was there.

"Sure, mister."

But he had not known yet how slowly he understood. They had not meant to give him their bed. After a little interval they both rose and looking at him gravely went into the other room.

He lay stretched by the fire until it grew low and dying. He watched every tongue of blaze lick out and vanish. "There will be special reduced prices on all footwear during the month of January," he found himself repeating quietly, and then he lay with his lips tight shut.

How many noises the night had! He heard the stream running, the fire dying, and he was sure now that he heard his heart beating, too, the sound it made under his ribs. He heard breathing, round and deep, of the man and his wife in the room across the passage. And that was all. But emotion swelled patiently within him, and he wished that the child were his.

He must get back to where he had been before. He stood weakly before the red coals and put on his overcoat. It felt too heavy on his shoulders. As he started out he looked and saw that the woman had never got through with cleaning the lamp. On some impulse he put all the money from his billfold under its fluted glass base, almost ostentatiously.

Ashamed, shrugging a little, and then shivering, he took his bags and went out. The cold air seemed to lift him bodily. The moon was in the sky.

On the slope he began to run, he could not help it. Just as he reached the road, where his car seemed to sit in the moonlight like a boat, his heart began to give off tremendous explosions like a rifle, bang bang bang.

He sank in fright onto the road, his bags falling about him. He felt as if all this had happened before. He covered his heart with both hands to keep anyone from hearing the noise it made.

But nobody heard it.

1936

Raymond Chandler   *1888–1959*

Little in the early life of Raymond Chandler suggested that he would create one of the most notable characters in modern American writing: the hard-boiled detective Philip Marlowe. Although Chandler's origins were American—he was born in Chicago in 1888—his parents were separated when he was seven, and his mother took him to her native Great Britain. There he received a traditional upper-class English education, was naturalized as a British citizen, and began working in the British Admiralty as a civil servant.

Although Chandler seemed destined to live the comfortable life of an English gentleman, he soon tired of his civil service career and set out to support himself as a free-lance journalist, writing essays, poems, and book reviews. But he failed to prosper as a member of the English literary establishment, and in 1912 he returned to America, where he settled in California and set out to make his way as a businessman.

Two years later the First World War began. Chandler, still a British citizen, enlisted in the Canadian Army and fought on the Western Front in France, once escaping as the only survivor of his entire unit. Returning to California after the end of the war, he worked in the oil industry and rose to a high corporate position, but in 1932, in the midst of the Great Depression, he was fired.

He was forty-four, had little money, and could find no way to earn a living in the business he knew best. To support himself he turned again to writing, first submitting stories and articles to the well-paying "slick" magazines of the day: Collier's, Liberty, The Saturday Evening Post—*but with no success. Desperate, he next tried his hand at writing the kind of detective stories published in the "pulps," popular magazines named for the cheap wood-pulp paper on which they were printed.*

The traditions and the formulas of American crime stories, filled with American characters speaking American criminal slang, were fundamentally alien to Chandler, the English public-school intellectual. But he studied them closely, and in 1933 he sold his first detective short story, "Blackmailers Don't Shoot," to Black Mask, *one of the best of the detective "pulps."*

Through the remainder of the 1930s, Chandler made a bare living by writing detective fiction, at a penny a word, for magazines such as Black Mask *and* Dime Detective. *In 1939 he combined the plots of three of his short stories and wrote his first novel,* The Big Sleep. *Its publication seemed to release a flood of creative energy in Chandler, and by 1953 he had published six novels, each with Philip Marlowe as its detective hero and each a classic of the hard-boiled school of detective fiction:* The Big Sleep (*1939*), Farewell My Lovely (*1940*), The High Window (*1942*), The Lady in the Lake (*1943*), The Little Sister (*1949*), *and* The Long Goodbye (*1953*).

Chandler's novels brought him widespread attention, and in the mid-1940's he went to work in Hollywood, as a script-writer for Paramount Pictures, earning the then grand sum of $750 a week, far more than his stories or novels had ever brought him. He worked on such notable movies as Double Indemnity (*1944*), The Blue Dahlia (*1946*), *and* Strangers on a Train (*1951*). *For his movie scripts he gained critical recognition, and he was nominated for an Academy Award, but nothing he wrote for the movies was the artistic equal of his detective novels.*

Chandler scorned the traditional English detective story, which he derided as "an affair of the upper class, the week-end house party, and the vicar's rose garden." He rejected the fake tradition of millionaire dilettante sleuths and playboy crime fighters. He argued that the crime story, if it would be more than a popular thriller, must be "credibly motivated."

He ruled out "trick endings" and called for stories that are "technically sound as to the methods of murder" and have "no fantastic poisons" and no "snakes climbing bellropes." He insisted that important facts "must not be concealed" and that writers should make every effort to portray "real people in a real world."

Chandler made a conscious attempt to rise above the outworn conventions of genteel detective fiction by writing of the social and political decay that he saw under the surface of American life. He portrayed disreputable men and women speaking authentic language. His criminals are unredeemable, and his police are hard, cynical, and corrupt. His women are self-indulgent, greedy, untrustworthy. And his famous hero, Philip Marlowe, moves through a world of cruelty and casual violence, taking a sour delight in recording what he, and Chandler himself, perceived as the sleazy glories of Southern California and Los Angeles.

Chandler acknowledged that Dashiell Hammett was the originator of the private detective crime story. But with the passage of time it has become clear that Chandler's stories of Philip Marlowe have had a greater influence on writers of detective fiction, ranging from Ross Macdonald all the way down to Mickey Spillane, whose hero, Mike Hammer, seems an exaggerated, almost parodic, version of Chandler's Philip Marlowe.

Chandler's work has inspired innumerable short stories, novels, television shows, and moving pictures—even comic strips—whose themes and plots are derived from Chandler, whose settings are modeled on his descriptions of shabby offices with cigarette-burned furniture and whiskey bottles hidden in the file drawers, and whose wise-cracking and battered detectives, like Marlowe, are both sustained and impeded by an old-fashioned code of justice, an outworn ideal of virtue that seems pointless in a dreary world filled with seedy crooks, conniving victims, and the spoils of drab venality.

FURTHER READING: *The Simple Art of Murder*, 1950; *Chandler Speaking*, ed. D. Gardiner and K. Walker, 1962; *Chandler Before Marlowe, Chandler's Early Prose and Poetry 1908–1912*, ed. M. Bruccoli, 1973; *The Notebooks of Raymond Chandler*, ed. F. MacShane, 1976; *Selected Letters of Raymond Chandler*, ed. F. MacShane, 1981; P. Durham, *Down These Mean Streets a Man Must Go*, 1963; F. MacShane, *The Life of Raymond Chandler*, 1976; S. Pendo, *Raymond Chandler, His Novels in Film*, 1976; *The World of Raymond Chandler*, ed. M. Gross, 1977; J. Speir, *Raymond Chandler*, 1981; D. Porter, *In Pursuit of Crime*, 1981; W. Luhr, *Raymond Chandler and Film*, 1982; A. Clark, *Chandler in Hollywood*, 1983; E. Thorpe, *Chandlertown, The Los Angeles of Philip Marlowe*, 1983; W. Marling, *Raymond Chandler*, 1986.
TEXT: "Red Wind," *Five Sinister Characters*, 1945.

RED WIND

1

There was a desert wind blowing that night. It was one of those hot dry Santa Anas[1] that come down through the mountain passes and curl your hair and make your nerves jump and your skin itch. On nights like that every booze party ends in a fight. Meek little wives feel the edge of the carving knife and study their husbands' necks. Anything can happen. You can even get a full glass of beer at a cocktail lounge.

I was getting one in a flossy new place across the street from the apartment house where I lived. It had been open about a week and it wasn't doing any business. The kid behind the bar was in his early twenties and looked as if he had never had a drink in his life.

There was only one other customer, a souse on a bar stool with his back to the door. He had a pile of dimes stacked neatly in front of him, about two dollars' worth. He was drinking straight rye in small glasses and he was all by himself in a world of his own.

I sat farther along the bar and got my glass of beer and said: "You sure cut the clouds off[2] them, buddy. I will say that for you."

"We just opened up," the kid said. "We got to build up trade. Been in before, haven't you, mister?"

---

[1] Hot, dry winds that blow from the desert, through the mountain passes, to Los Angeles.
[2] "Scrape the foam off." I.e., "serve a full glass."

"Uh-huh."

"Live around here?"

"In the Berglund Apartments across the street," I said. "And the name is Philip Marlowe."

"Thanks, mister. Mine's Lew Petrolle." He leaned close to me across the polished dark bar. "Know that guy?"

"No."

"He ought to go home, kind of. I ought to call a taxi and send him home. He's doing his next week's drinking too soon."

"A night like this," I said. "Let him alone."

"It's not good for him," the kid said, scowling at me.

"Rye!" the drunk croaked, without looking up. He snapped his fingers so as not to disturb his piles of dimes by banging on the bar.

The kid looked at me and shrugged. "Should I?"

"Whose stomach is it? Not mine."

The kid poured him another straight rye and I think he doctored it with water down behind the bar because when he came up with it he looked as guilty as if he'd kicked his grandmother. The drunk paid no attention. He lifted coins off his pile with the exact care of a crack surgeon operating on a brain tumor.

The kid came back and put more beer in my glass. Outside the wind howled. Every once in a while it blew the stained-glass door open a few inches. It was a heavy door.

The kid said: "I don't like drunks in the first place, and in the second place I don't like them getting drunk in here, and in the third place I don't like them in the first place."

"Warner Brothers[3] could use that," I said.

"They did."

Just then we had another customer. A car squeaked to a stop outside and the swinging door came open. A fellow came in who looked a little in a hurry. He held the door and ranged the place quickly with flat, shiny, dark eyes. He was well set up, dark, good-looking in a narrow-faced, tight-lipped way. His clothes were dark and a white handkerchief peeped coyly from his pocket and he looked cool as well as under a tension of some sort. I guessed it was the hot wind. I felt a bit the same myself only not cool.

He looked at the drunk's back. The drunk was playing checkers with his empty glasses. The new customer looked at me, then he looked along the line of half-booths at the other side of the place. They were all empty. He came on in— down past where the drunk sat swaying and muttering to himself—and spoke to the bar kid.

"Seen a lady in here, buddy? Tall, pretty, brown hair, in a print bolero jacket over a blue crêpe silk dress. Wearing a wide-brimmed straw hat with a velvet band." He had a tight voice I didn't like.

"No, sir. Nobody like that's been in," the bar kid said.

"Thanks. Straight Scotch. Make it fast, will you?"

The kid gave it to him and the fellow paid and put the drink down in a gulp and started to go out. He took three or four steps and stopped, facing the drunk. The drunk was grinning. He swept a gun from somewhere so fast that it was just a blur coming out. He held it steady and he didn't look any drunker than

----

[3]A motion picture production company.

I was. The tall dark guy stood quite still and then his head jerked back a little and then he was still again.

A car tore by outside. The drunk's gun was a .22 target automatic, with a large front sight. It made a couple of hard snaps and a little smoke curled—very little.

"So long, Waldo," the drunk said.

Then he put the gun on the barman and me.

The dark guy took a week to fall down. He stumbled, caught himself, waved one arm, stumbled again. His hat fell off, and then he hit the floor with his face. After he hit it he might have been poured concrete for all the fuss he made.

The drunk slid down off the stool and scooped his dimes into a pocket and slid towards the door. He turned sideways, holding the gun across his body. I didn't have a gun. I hadn't thought I needed one to buy a glass of beer. The kid behind the bar didn't move or make the slightest sound.

The drunk felt the door lightly with his shoulder, keeping his eyes on us, then pushed through it backwards. When it was wide a hard gust of air slammed in and lifted the hair of the man on the floor. The drunk said: "Poor Waldo. I bet I made his nose bleed."

The door swung shut. I started to rush it—from long practice in doing the wrong thing. In this case it didn't matter. The car outside let out a roar and when I got onto the sidewalk it was flicking a red smear of taillight around the nearby corner. I got its license number the way I got my first million.

There were people and cars up and down the block as usual. Nobody acted as if a gun had gone off. The wind was making enough noise to make the hard quick rap of .22 ammunition sound like a slammed door, even if anyone heard it. I went back into the cocktail bar.

The kid hadn't moved, even yet. He just stood with his hands flat on the bar, leaning over a little and looking down at the dark guy's back. The dark guy hadn't moved either. I bent down and felt his neck artery. He wouldn't move—ever.

The kid's face had as much expression as a cut of round steak and was about the same color. His eyes were more angry than shocked.

I lit a cigarette and blew smoke at the ceiling and said shortly: "Get on the phone."

"Maybe he's not dead," the kid said.

"When they use a twenty-two that means they don't make mistakes. Where's the phone?"

"I don't have one. I got enough expenses without that. Boy, can I kick eight hundred bucks in the face!"

"You own this place?"

"I did till this happened."

He pulled his white coat off and his apron and came around the inner end of the bar. "I'm locking this door," he said, taking the keys out.

He went out, swung the door to and juggled the lock from the outside until the bolt clicked into place. I bent down and rolled Waldo over. At first I couldn't even see where the shots went in. Then I could. A couple of tiny holes in his coat, over his heart. There was a little blood on his shirt.

The drunk was everything you could ask—as a killer.

The prowl-car boys came in about eight minutes. The kid, Lew Petrolle, was back behind the bar by then. He had his white coat on again and he was counting his money in the register and putting it in his pocket and making notes in a little book.

I sat at the edge of one of the half-booths and smoked cigarettes and watched Waldo's face get deader and deader. I wondered who the girl in the print coat was, why Waldo had left the engine of his car running outside, why he was in a hurry, whether the drunk had been waiting for him or just happened to be there.

The prowl-car boys came in perspiring. They were the usual large size and one of them had a flower stuck under his cap and his cap on a bit crooked. When he saw the dead man he got rid of the flower and leaned down to feel Waldo's pulse.

"Seems to be dead," he said, and rolled him around a little more. "Oh yeah, I see where they went in. Nice clean work. You two see him get it?"

I said yes. The kid behind the bar said nothing. I told them about it, that the killer seemed to have left in Waldo's car.

The cop yanked Waldo's wallet out, went through it rapidly and whistled. "Plenty of jack and no driver's license." He put the wallet away. "Okay, we didn't touch him, see? Just a chance we could find did he have a car and put it on the air."

"The hell you didn't touch him," Lew Petrolle said.

The cop gave him one of those looks. "Okay, pal," he said softly. "We touched him."

The kid picked up a clean highball glass and began to polish it. He polished it all the rest of the time we were there.

In another minute a homicide fast-wagon sirened up and screeched to a stop outside the door and four men came in, two dicks, a photographer and a laboratory man. I didn't know either of the dicks. You can be in the detecting business a long time and not know all the men on a big city force.

One of them was a short, smooth, dark, quiet, smiling man, with curly black hair and soft intelligent eyes. The other was big, raw-boned, long-jawed, with a veined nose and glassy eyes. He looked like a heavy drinker. He looked tough, but he looked as if he thought he was a little tougher than he was. He shooed me into the last booth against the wall and his partner got the kid up front and the bluecoats went out. The fingerprint man and photographer set about their work.

A medical examiner came, stayed just long enough to get sore because there was no phone for him to call the morgue wagon.

The short dick emptied Waldo's pockets and then emptied his wallet and dumped everything into a large handkerchief on a booth table. I saw a lot of currency, keys, cigarettes, another handkerchief, very little else.

The big dick pushed me back into the end of the half-booth. "Give," he said. "I'm Copernik, Detective Lieutenant."

I put my wallet in front of him. He looked at it, went through it, tossed it back, made a note in a book.

"Philip Marlowe, huh? A shamus.[4] You here on business?"

"Drinking business," I said. "I live just across the street in the Berglund."

"Know this kid up front?"

"I've been in here once since he opened up."

"See anything funny about him now."

---

[4]Slang: "a private detective."

"No."

"Takes it too light for a young fellow, don't he? Never mind answering. Just tell the story."

I told it—three times. Once for him to get the outline, once for him to get the details and once for him to see if I had it too pat. At the end he said: "This dame interests me. And the killer called the guy Waldo, yet didn't seem to be anyways sure he would be in. I mean, if Waldo wasn't sure the dame would be here, nobody could be sure Waldo would be here."

"That's pretty deep," I said.

He studied me. I wasn't smiling. "Sounds like a grudge job, don't it? Don't sound planned. No getaway except by accident. A guy don't leave his car unlocked much in this town. And the killer works in front of two good witnesses. I don't like that."

"I don't like being a witness," I said. "The pay's too low."

He grinned. His teeth had a freckled look. "Was the killer drunk really?"

"With that shooting? No."

"Me too. Well, it's a simple job. The guy will have a record and he's left plenty of prints. Even if we don't have his mug here we'll make him in hours. He had something on Waldo, but he wasn't meeting Waldo tonight. Waldo just dropped in to ask about a dame he had a date with and had missed connections on. It's a hot night and this wind would kill a girl's face. She'd be apt to drop in somewhere to wait. So the killer feeds Waldo two in the right place and scrams and don't worry about you boys at all. It's that simple."

"Yeah," I said.

"It's so simple it stinks," Copernik said.

He took his felt hat off and tousled up his ratty blond hair and leaned his head on his hands. He had a long mean horse face. He got a handkerchief out and mopped it, and the back of his neck and the back of his hands. He got a comb out and combed his hair—he looked worse with it combed—and put his hat back on.

"I was just thinking," I said.

"Yeah? What?"

"This Waldo knew just how the girl was dressed. So he must already have been with her tonight."

"So, what? Maybe he had to go to the can. And when he came back she's gone. Maybe she changed her mind about him."

"That's right," I said.

But that wasn't what I was thinking at all. I was thinking that Waldo had described the girl's clothes in a way the ordinary man wouldn't know how to describe them. Printed bolero jacket over blue crêpe silk dress. I didn't even know what a bolero jacket was. And I might have said blue dress or even blue silk dress, but never blue crêpe silk dress.

After a while two men came with a basket. Lew Petrolle was still polishing his glass and talking to the short dark dick.

We all went down to headquarters.

Lew Petrolle was all right when they checked on him. His father had a grape ranch near Antioch in Contra Costa County. He had given Lew a thousand dollars to go into business and Lew had opened the cocktail bar, neon sign and all, on eight hundred flat.

They let him go and told him to keep the bar closed until they were sure they didn't want to do any more printing. He shook hands all around and grinned and said he guessed the killing would be good for business after all, because nobody believed a newspaper account of anything and people would come to him for the story and buy drinks while he was telling it.

"There's a guy won't ever do any worrying," Copernik said, when he was gone. "Over anybody else."

"Poor Waldo," I said. "The prints any good?"

"Kind of smudged," Copernik said sourly. "But we'll get a classification and teletype it to Washington[5] some time tonight. If it don't click, you'll be in for a day on the steel picture racks[6] down stairs."

I shook hands with him and his partner, whose name was Ybarra, and left. They didn't know who Waldo was yet either. Nothing in his pockets told.

2

I got back to my street about 9 P.M. I looked up and down the block before I went into the Berglund. The cocktail bar was farther down on the other side, dark, with a nose or two against the glass, but no real crowd. People had seen the law and the morgue wagon, but they didn't know what had happened. Except the boys playing pinball games in the drugstore on the corner. They know everything, except how to hold a job.

The wind was still blowing, oven-hot, swirling dust and torn paper up against the walls.

I went into the lobby of the apartment house and rode the automatic elevator up to the fourth floor. I unwound the doors and stepped out and there was a tall girl standing there waiting for the car.

She had brown hair under a wide-brimmed straw hat with a velvet band and loose bow. She had wide eyes and eyelashes that didn't quite reach her chin. She wore a blue dress that might have been crêpe silk, simple in lines but not missing any curves. Over it she wore what might have been a print bolero jacket.

I said: "Is that a bolero jacket?"

She gave me a distant glance and made a motion as if to brush a cobweb out of the way.

"Yes. Would you mind—I'm rather in a hurry. I'd like—"

I didn't move. I blocked her off from the elevator. We stared at each other and she flushed very slowly.

"Better not go out on the street in those clothes," I said.

"Why, how dare you—"

The elevator clanked and started down again. I didn't know what she was going to say. Her voice lacked the edgy twang of a beer-parlor frill.[1] It had a soft light sound, like spring rain.

"It's not a make,"[2] I said. "You're in trouble. If they come to this floor in the elevator, you have just that much time to get off the hall. First take off the hat and jacket—and snap it up!"

She didn't move. Her face seemed to whiten a little behind the not-too-heavy make-up.

---

[5]To the Fingerprint Identification Department of the Federal Bureau of Investigation in Washington, D.C.

[6]Police department collection of photographs, mounted in metal racks, showing known criminals.   [1]Girl, woman.   [2]A "pass," a sexual proposition.

"Cops," I said, "are looking for you. In those clothes. Give me the chance and I'll tell you why."

She turned her head swiftly and looked back along the corridor. With her looks I didn't blame her for trying one more bluff.

"You're impertinent, whoever you are. I'm Mrs. Leroy in apartment thirty-one. I can assure—"

"That you're on the wrong floor," I said. "This is the fourth." The elevator had stopped down below. The sound of doors being wrenched open came up the shaft.

"Off!" I rapped. "Now!"

She switched her hat off and slipped out of the bolero jacket, fast. I grabbed them and wadded them into a mess under my arm. I took her elbow and turned her and we were going down the hall.

"I live in forty-two. The front one across from yours, just a floor up. Take your choice. Once again—I'm not on the make."

She smoothed her hair with that quick gesture, like a bird preening itself. Ten thousand years of practice behind it.

"Mine," she said, and tucked her bag under her arm and strode down the hall fast. The elevator stopped at the floor below. She stopped when it stopped. She turned and faced me.

"The stairs are back by the elevator shaft," I said gently.

"I don't have an apartment," she said.

"I didn't think you had."

"Are they searching for me?"

"Yes, but they won't start gouging the block stone by stone before tomorrow. And then only if they don't make Waldo."

She stared at me. "Waldo?"

"Oh, you don't know Waldo," I said.

She shook her head slowly. The elevator started down in the shaft again. Panic flicked in her blue eyes like a ripple on water.

"No," she said breathlessly, "but take me out of this hall."

We were almost at my door. I jammed the key in and shook the lock around and heaved the door inward. I reached in far enough to switch lights on. She went in past me like a wave. Sandalwood floated on the air, very faint.

I shut the door, threw my hat into a chair and watched her stroll over to a card table on which I had a chess problem set out that I couldn't solve. Once inside, with the door locked, her panic had left her.

"So you're a chess player," she said, in that guarded tone, as if she had come to look at my etchings. I wished she had.

We both stood still then and listened to the distant clang of the elevator doors and then steps—going the other way.

I grinned, but with strain, not pleasure, went out into the kitchenette and started to fumble with a couple of glasses and then realized I still had her hat and bolero jacket under my arm. I went into the dressing room behind the wall bed[3] and stuffed them into a drawer, went back out to the kitchenette, dug out some extra-fine Scotch and made a couple of highballs.

When I went in with the drinks she had a gun in her hand. It was a small automatic with a pearl grip. It jumped up at me and her eyes were full of horror.

I stopped, with a glass in each hand, and said: "Maybe this hot wind has got you crazy too. I'm a private detective. I'll prove it if you let me."

---

[3]A bed that folds up into the wall.

She nodded slightly and her face was white. I went over slowly and put a glass down beside her, and went back and set mine down and got a card out that had no bent corners. She was sitting down, smoothing one blue knee with her left hand, and holding the gun on the other. I put the card down beside her drink and sat with mine.

"Never let a guy get that close to you," I said. "Not if you mean business. And your safety catch is on."

She flashed her eyes down, shivered, and put the gun back in her bag. She drank half the drink without stopping, put the glass down hard and picked up the card.

"I don't give many people that liquor," I said. "I can't afford to."

Her lips curled. "I suppose you would want money."

"Huh?"

She didn't say anything. Her hand was close to her bag again.

"Don't forget the safety catch," I said. Her hand stopped. I went on: "This fellow I called Waldo is quite tall, say five-eleven, slim, dark, brown eyes with a lot of glitter. Nose and mouth too thin. Dark suit, white handkerchief showing, and in a hurry to find you. Am I getting anywhere?"

She took her glass again. "So that's Waldo," she said. "Well, what about him?" Her voice seemed to have a slight liquor edge now.

"Well, a funny thing. There's a cocktail bar across the street . . . Say, where have you been all evening?"

"Sitting in my car," she said coldly, "most of the time."

"Didn't you see a fuss across the street up the block?"

Her eyes tried to say no and missed. Her lips said: "I knew there was some kind of disturbance. I saw policemen and red searchlights. I supposed someone had been hurt."

"Someone was. And this Waldo was looking for you before that. In the cocktail bar. He described you and your clothes."

Her eyes were set like rivets now and had the same amount of expression. Her mouth began to tremble and kept on trembling.

"I was in there," I said, "talking to the kid that runs it. There was nobody in there but a drunk on a stool and the kid and myself. The drunk wasn't paying any attention to anything. Then Waldo came in and asked about you and we said no, we hadn't seen you and he started to leave."

I sipped my drink. I like an effect as well as the next fellow. Her eyes ate me.

"Just started to leave. Then this drunk that wasn't paying any attention to anyone called him Waldo and took a gun out. He shot him twice"—I snapped my fingers twice—"like that. Dead."

She fooled me. She laughed in my face. "So my husband hired you to spy on me," she said. "I might have known the whole thing was an act. You and your Waldo."

I gawked at her.

"I never thought of him as jealous," she snapped. "Not of a man who had been our chauffeur anyhow. A little about Stan, of course—that's natural. But Joseph Coates—"

I made motions in the air. "Lady, one of us has this book open at the wrong page," I grunted. "I don't know anybody named Stan or Joseph Coates. So help me, I didn't even know you had a chauffeur. People around here don't run to them. As for husbands—yeah, we do have a husband once in a while. Not often enough."

She shook her head slowly and her hand stayed near her bag and her blue eyes had glitters in them.

"Not good enough, Mr. Marlowe. No, not nearly good enough. I know you private detectives. You're all rotten. You tricked me into your apartment, if it is your apartment. More likely it's the apartment of some horrible man who will swear anything for a few dollars. Now you're trying to scare me. So you can blackmail me—as well as get money from my husband. All right," she said breathlessly, "how much do I have to pay."

I put my empty glass aside and leaned back. "Pardon me if I light a cigarette," I said. "My nerves are frayed."

I lit it while she watched me without enough fear for any real guilt to be under it. "So Joseph Coates is his name," I said. "The guy that killed him in the cocktail bar called him Waldo."

She smiled a bit disgustedly, but almost tolerantly. "Don't stall. How much?"

"Why were you trying to meet this Joseph Coates?"

"I was going to buy something he stole from me, of course. Something that's valuable in the ordinary way too. Almost fifteen thousand dollars. The man I loved gave it to me. He's dead. There! He's dead! He died in a burning plane. Now, go back and tell my husband that, you slimy little rat!"

"I'm not little and I'm not a rat," I said.

"You're still slimy. And don't bother about telling my husband. I'll tell him myself. He probably knows anyway."

I grinned. "That's smart. Just what was I supposed to find out?"

She grabbed her glass and finished what was left of her drink. "So he thinks I'm meeting Joseph. Well, perhaps I was. But not to make love. Not with a chauffeur. Not with a bum I picked off the front step and gave a job to. I don't have to dig down that far, if I want to play around."

"Lady," I said, "you don't indeed."

"Now I'm going," she said. "You just try and stop me." She snatched the pearl-handled gun out of he bag. I didn't move.

"Why, you nasty little string of nothing," she stormed. "How do I know you're a private detective at all? You might be a crook. This card you gave me doesn't mean anything. Anybody can have cards printed."

"Sure," I said. "And I suppose I'm smart enough to live here two years because you were going to move in today so I could blackmail you for not meeting a man named Joseph Coates who was bumped off across the street under the name of Waldo. Have you got the money to buy this something that cost fifteen grand?"

"Oh! You think you'll hold me up, I suppose!"

"Oh!" I mimicked her. "I'm a stick-up artist now, am I? Lady, will you please either put that gun away or take the safety catch off? It hurts my professional feelings to see a nice gun made a monkey of that way."

"You're a full portion of what I don't like," she said. "Get out of my way."

I didn't move. She didn't move. We were both sitting down—and not even close to each other.

"Let me in on one secret before you go," I pleaded. "What in hell did you take the apartment down on the floor below for? Just to meet a guy down on the street?"

"Stop being silly," she snapped. "I didn't. I lied. It's his apartment."

"Joseph Coates'?"

She nodded sharply.

"Does my description of Waldo sound like Joseph Coates?"

She nodded sharply again.

"All right. That's one fact learned at last. Don't you realize Waldo described your clothes before he was shot—when he was looking for you—that the description was passed on to the police—that the police don't know who Waldo is—and are looking for somebody in those clothes to help tell them? Don't you get that much?"

The gun suddenly started to shake in her hand. She looked down at it, sort of vacantly, slowly put it back in her bag.

"I'm a fool," she whispered, "to be even talking to you." She stared at me for a long time, then pulled in a deep breath. "He told me where he was staying. He didn't seem afraid. I guess blackmailers are like that. He was to meet me on the street, but I was late. It was full of police when I got here. So I went back and sat in my car for a while. Then I came up to Joseph's apartment and knocked. Then I went back to my car and waited again. I came up here three times in all. The last time I walked up a flight to take the elevator. I had already been seen twice on the third floor. I met you. That's all."

"You said something about a husband," I grunted. "Where is he?"

"He's at a meeting."

"Oh, a meeting," I said nastily.

"My husband's a very important man. He has lots of meetings. He's a hydroelectric engineer. He's been all over the world. I'd have you know—"

"Skip it," I said. "I'll take him to lunch some day and have him tell me himself. Whatever Joseph had on you is dead stock now. Like Joseph."

"He's really dead?" she whispered. "Really?"

"He's dead," I said. "Dead, dead, dead. Lady, he's dead."

She believed it at last. I hadn't thought she ever would somehow. In the silence, the elevator stopped at my floor.

I heard steps coming down the hall. We all have hunches. I put my finger to my lips. She didn't move now. Her face had a frozen look. Her big blue eyes were as black as the shadows below them. The hot wind boomed against the shut windows. Windows have to be shut when a Santa Ana blows, heat or no heat.

The steps that came down the hall were the casual ordinary steps of one man. But they stopped outside my door, and somebody knocked.

I pointed to the dressing room behind the wall bed. She stood up without a sound, her bag clenched against her side. I pointed again, to her glass. She lifted it swiftly, slid aross the carpet, through the door, drew the door quietly shut after her.

I didn't know just what I was going to all this trouble for.

The knocking sounded again. The backs of my hands were wet. I creaked my chair and stood up and made a loud yawning sound. Then I went over and opened the door—without a gun. That was a mistake.

3

I didn't know him at first. Perhaps for the opposite reason Waldo hadn't seemed to know him. He'd had a hat on all the time over at the cocktail bar and he didn't have one on now. His hair ended completely and exactly where his hat would start. Above that line was hard white sweatless skin almost as glaring as scar tissue. He wasn't just twenty years older. He was a different man.

But I knew the gun he was holding, the .22 target automatic with the big front sight. And I knew his eyes. Bright, brittle, shallow eyes like the eyes of a lizard.

He was alone. He put the gun against my face very lightly and said between his teeth: "Yeah, me. Let's go on in."

I backed in just far enough and stopped. Just the way he would want me to, so he could shut the door without moving much. I knew from his eyes that he would want me to do just that.

I wasn't scared. I was paralyzed.

When he had the door shut he backed me some more, slowly, until there was something against the back of my legs. His eyes looked into mine.

"That's a card table," he said. "Some goon here plays chess. You?"

I swallowed. "I don't exactly play it. I just fool around."

"That means two," he said with a kind of hoarse softness, as if some cop had hit him across the windpipe with a blackjack once, in a third-degree[1] session.

"It's a problem," I said. "Not a game. Look at the pieces."

"I wouldn't know."

"Well, I'm alone," I said, and my voice shook just enough.

"It don't make any difference," he said. "I'm washed up anyway. Some nose[2] puts the bulls on me tomorrow, next week, what the hell? I just didn't like your map, pal. And that smug-faced pansy in the bar coat that played left tackle for Fordham or something. To hell with guys like you guys."

I didn't speak or move. The big front sight raked my cheek lightly, almost caressingly. The man smiled.

"It's kind of good business too," he said. "Just in case. An old con like me don't make good prints, all I got against me is two witnesses. The hell with it."

"What did Waldo do to you?" I tried to make it sound as if I wanted to know, instead of just not wanting to shake too hard.

"Stooled[3] on a bank job in Michigan and got me four years. Got himself a nolle prosse.[4] Four years in Michigan ain't no summer cruise. They make you be good in them lifer states."[5]

"How'd you know he'd come in there?" I croaked.

"I didn't. Oh yeah, I was lookin' for him. I was wanting to see him all right. I got a flash of him on the street night before last but I lost him. Up to then I wasn't lookin' for him. Then I was. A cute guy, Waldo. How is he?"

"Dead," I said.

"I'm still good," he chuckled. "Drunk or sober. Well, that don't make no doughnuts for me now. They make me downtown yet?"

I didn't answer him quick enough. He jabbed the gun into my throat and I choked and almost grabbed for it by instinct.

"Naw," he cautioned me softly. "Naw. You ain't that dumb."

I put my hands back, down at my sides, open, the palms towards him. He would want them that way. He hadn't touched me, except with the gun. He didn't seem to care whether I might have one too. He wouldn't—if he just meant the one thing.

He didn't seem to care very much about anything, coming back on that block. Perhaps the hot wind did something to him. It was booming against my shut windows like the the surf under a pier.

"They got prints," I said. "I don't know how good."

---

[1]Harsh, brutal interrogation.   [2]Informer.   [3]Informed.
[4]Latin: *nolle prosequi*, unwilling to pursue; i.e., an agreement by the authorities not to prosecute.
[5]States in which life imprisonment is mandatory for repeat felons.

"They'll be good enough—but not for teletype work. Take 'em airmail time to Washington and back to check 'em right. Tell me why I came here, pal."

"You heard the kid and me talking in the bar. I told him my name, where I lived."

"That's how, pal. I said why." He smiled at me. It was a lousy smile to be the last one you might see.

"Skip it," I said. "The hangman won't ask you to guess why he's there."

"Say, you're tough at that. After you, I visit that kid. I tailed him home from headquarters, but I figure you're the guy to put the bee on first. I tail him home from the city hall, in the rent car Waldo had. From headquarters, pal. Them funny dicks. You can sit in their laps and they don't know you. Start runnin' for a streetcar and they open up with machine guns and bump two pedestrians, a hacker[6] asleep in his cab, and an old scrubwoman on the second floor workin' a mop. And they miss the guy they're after. Them funny lousy dicks."

He twisted the gun muzzle in my neck. His eyes looked madder than before.

"I got time," he said. "Waldo's rent car don't get a report right away. And they don't make Waldo very soon. I know Waldo. Smart he was. A smooth boy, Waldo."

"I'm going to vomit," I said, "if you don't take that gun out of my throat."

He smiled and moved the gun down to my heart. "This about right? Say when."

I must have spoken louder than I meant to. The door of the dressing room by the wall bed showed a crack of darkness. Then an inch. Then four inches. I saw eyes, but didn't look at them. I stared hard into the bald-headed man's eyes. Very hard. I didn't want him to take his eyes off mine.

"Scared?" he asked softly.

I leaned against his gun and began to shake. I thought he would enjoy seeing me shake. The girl came out through the door. She had her gun in her hand. I was sorry as hell for her. She'd try to make the door—or scream. Either way it would be curtains—for both of us.

"Well, don't take all night about it," I bleated. My voice sounded far away, like a voice on the radio on the other side of a street.

"I like this, pal," he smiled. "I'm like that."

The girl floated in the air, somewhere behind him. Nothing was ever more soundless than the way she moved. It wouldn't do any good though. He wouldn't fool around with her at all. I had known him all my life but I had been looking into his eyes for only five minutes.

"Suppose I yell," I said.

"Yeah, suppose you yell. Go ahead and yell," he said with his killer's smile.

She didn't go near the door. She was right behind him.

"Well—here's where I yell," I said.

As if that was the cue, she jabbed the little gun hard into his short ribs, without a single sound.

He had to react. It was like a knee reflex. His mouth snapped open and both his arms jumped out from his sides and he arched his back just a little. The gun was pointing at my right eye.

I sank and kneed him with all my strength, in the groin.

His chin came down and I hit it. I hit it as if I was driving the last spike on the first transcontinental railroad. I can still feel it when I flex my knuckles.

His gun raked the side of my face but it didn't go off. He was already limp.

[6]Cab driver.

He writhed down gasping, his left side against the floor. I kicked his right shoulder—hard. The gun jumped away from him, skidded on the carpet, under a chair. I heard the chessmen tinkling on the floor behind me somewhere.

The girl stood over him, looking down. Then her wide dark horrified eyes came up and fastened on mine.

"That buys me," I said. "Anything I have is yours—now and forever."

She didn't hear me. Her eyes were strained open so hard that the whites showed under the vivid blue iris. She backed quickly to the door with her little gun up, felt behind her for the knob and twisted it. She pulled the door open and slipped out.

The door shut.

She was bareheaded and without her bolero jacket.

She had only the gun, and the safety catch on that was still set so that she couldn't fire it.

It was silent in the room then, in spite of the wind. Then I heard him gasping on the floor. His face had a greenish pallor. I moved behind him and pawed him for more guns, and didn't find any. I got a pair of store cuffs out of my desk and pulled his arms in front of him and snapped them on his wrists. They would hold if he didn't shake them too hard.

His eyes measured me for a coffin, in spite of their suffering. He lay in the middle of the floor, still on his left side, a twisted, wizened, bald-headed little guy with drawn-back lips and teeth spotted with cheap silver fillings. His mouth looked like a black pit and his breath came in little waves, choked, stopped, came on again, limping.

I went into the dressing room and opened the drawer of the chest. Her hat and jacket lay there on my shirts. I put them underneath, at the back, and smoothed the shirts over them. Then I went out to the kitchenette and poured a stiff jolt of whiskey and put it down and stood a moment listening to the hot wind howl against the window glass. A garage door banged, and a power-line wire with too much play between the insulators thumped on the side of the building with a sound like somebody beating a carpet.

The drink worked on me. I went back into the living room and opened a window. The guy on the floor hadn't smelled her sandalwood, but somebody else might.

I shut the window again, wiped the palms of my hands and used the phone to dial headquarters.

Copernik was still there. His smart-aleck voice said: "Yeah? Marlowe? Don't tell me. I bet you got an idea."

"Make the killer yet?"

"We're not saying, Marlowe. Sorry as all hell and so on. You know how it is."

"Okay, I don't care who he is. Just come and get him off the floor of my apartment."

"Holy Christ!" Then his voice hushed and went down low. "Wait a minute, now. Wait a minute." A long way off I seemed to hear a door shut. Then his voice again. "Shoot," he said softly.

"Handcuffed," I said. "All yours. I had to knee him, but he'll be all right. He came here to eliminate a witness."

Another pause. The voice was full of honey. "Now listen, boy, who else is in this with you?"

"Who else? Nobody. Just me."

"Keep it that way, boy. All quiet. Okay?"

"Think I want all the bums in the neighborhood in here sight-seeing?"

"Take it easy, boy. Easy. Just sit tight and sit still. I'm practically there. No touch nothing. Get me?"

"Yeah." I gave him the address and apartment number again to save him time.

I could see his big bony face glisten. I got the .22 target gun from under the chair and sat holding it until feet hit the hallway outside my door and knuckles did a quiet tattoo on the door panel.

Copernik was alone. He filled the doorway quickly, pushed me back into the room with a tight grin and shut the door. He stood with his back to it, his hand under the left side of his coat. A big hard bony man with flat cruel eyes.

He lowered them slowly and looked at the man on the floor. The man's neck was twitching a little. His eyes moved in short stabs—sick eyes.

"Sure it's the guy?" Copernik's voice was hoarse.

"Positive. Where's Ybarra?"

"Oh, he was busy." He didn't look at me when he said that. "Those your cuffs?"

"Yeah."

"Key."

I tossed it to him. He went down swiftly on one knee beside the killer and took my cuffs off his wrists, tossed them to one side. He got his own off his hip, twisted the bald man's hands behind him and snapped the cuffs on.

"All right, you bastard," the killer said tonelessly.

Copernik grinned and balled his fist and hit the handcuffed man in the mouth a terrific blow. His head snapped back almost enough to break his neck. Blood dribbled from the lower corner of his mouth.

"Get a towel," Copernik ordered.

I got a hand towel and gave it to him. He stuffed it between the handcuffed man's teeth, viciously, stood up and rubbed his bony fingers through his ratty blond hair.

"All right. Tell it."

I told it—leaving the girl out completely. It sounded a little funny. Copernik watched me, said nothing. He rubbed the side of his veined nose. Then he got his comb out and worked on his hair just as he had done earlier in the evening, in the cocktail bar.

I went over and gave him the gun. He looked at it casually, dropped it into his side pocket. His eyes had something in them and his face moved in a hard bright grin.

I bent down and began picking up my chessmen and dropping them into the box. I put the box on the mantel, straightened out a leg of the card table, played around for a while. All the time Copernik watched me. I wanted him to think something out.

At last he came out with it. "This guy uses a twenty-two," he said. "He uses it because he's good enough to get by with that much gun. That means he's good. He knocks at your door, pokes that gat in your belly, walks you back into the room, says he's here to close your mouth for keeps—and yet you take him. You not having any gun. You take him alone. You're kind of good yourself, pal."

"Listen," I said, and looked at the floor. I picked up another chessman and twisted it between my fingers. "I was doing a chess problem," I said. "Trying to forget things."

"You got something on your mind, pal," Copernik said softly. "You wouldn't try to fool an old copper, would you, boy?"

"It's a swell pinch and I'm giving it to you," I said. "What the hell more do you want?"

The man on the floor made a vague sound behind the towel. His bald head glistened with sweat.

"What's the matter, pal? You been up to something?" Copernik almost whispered.

I looked at him quickly, looked away again. "All right," I said. "You know damn well I couldn't take him alone. He had the gun on me and he shoots where he looks."

Copernik closed one eye and squinted at me amiably with the other. "Go on, pal. I kind of thought of that too."

I shuffled around a little more, to make it look good. I said slowly: "There was a kid here who pulled a job over in Boyle Heights, a heist job. It didn't take. A two-bit service station stick-up. I know his family. He's not really bad. He was here trying to beg train money off me. When the knock came he sneaked in—there."

I pointed at the wall bed and the door beside. Copernik's head swiveled slowly, swiveled back. His eyes winked again. "And this kid had a gun," he said.

I nodded. "And he got behind him. That takes guts, Copernik. You've got to give the kid a break. You've got to let him stay out of it."

"Tag[7] out for this kid?" Copernik asked softly.

"Not yet, he says. He's scared there will be."

Copernik smiled. "I'm a homicide man," he said. "I wouldn't know—or care."

I pointed down at the gagged and handcuffed man on the floor. "You took him, didn't you?" I said gently.

Copernik kept on smiling. A big whitish tongue came out and massaged his thick lower lip. "How'd I do it?" he whispered.

"Get the slugs out of Waldo?"

"Sure. Long twenty-two's. One smashed rib, one good."

"You're a careful guy. You don't miss any angles. You know anything about me? You dropped in on me to see what guns I had."

Copernik got up and went down on one knee again beside the killer. "Can you hear me, guy?" he asked with his face close to the face of the man on the floor.

The man made some vague sound. Copernik stood up and yawned. "Who the hell cares what he says? Go on, pal."

"You wouldn't expect to find I had anything, but you wanted to look around my place. And while you were mousing around in there"—I pointed to the dressing room—"and me not saying anything, being a little sore, maybe, a knock came on the door. So he came in. So after a while you sneaked out and took him."

"Ah." Copernik grinned widely, with as many teeth as a horse. "You're on, pal. I socked him and kneed him and I took him. You didn't have no gun and the guy swiveled on me pretty sharp and I left-hooked him down the backstairs. Okay?"

"Okay," I said.

"You'll tell it like that downtown?"[8]

"Yeah," I said.

---

[7]Warrant for arrest.
[8]Police headquarters.

"I'll protect you, pal. Treat me right and I'll always play ball. Forget about that kid. Let me know if he needs a break."

He came over and held out his hand. I shook it. It was as clammy as a dead fish. Clammy hands and the people who own them make me sick.

"There's just one thing," I said. "This partner of yours—Ybarra. Won't he be a bit sore you didn't bring him along on this?"

Copernik tousled his hair and wiped his hatband with a large yellowish silk handkerchief.

"That guinea?"[9] he sneered. "To hell with him!" He came close to me and breathed in my face. "No mistakes, pal—about that story of ours."

His breath was bad. It would be.

4

There were just five of us in the chief of detectives' office when Copernik laid it before them. A stenographer, the chief, Copernik, myself, Ybarra. Ybarra sat on a chair tilted against the side wall. His hat was down over his eyes but their softness loomed underneath, and the small still smile hung at the corners of the clean-cut Latin lips. He didn't look directly at Copernik. Copernik didn't look at him at all.

Outside in the corridor there had been photos of Copernik shaking hands with me, Copernik with his hat on straight and his gun in his hand and a stern, purposeful look on his face.

They said they knew who Waldo was, but they wouldn't tell me. I didn't believe they knew, because the chief of detectives had a morgue photo of Waldo on his desk. A beautiful job, his hair combed, his tie straight, the light hitting his eyes just right to make them glisten. Nobody would have known it was a photo of a dead man with two bullet holes in his heart. He looked like a dance-hall sheik[1] making up his mind whether to take the blonde or the red-head.

It was about midnight when I got home. The apartment door was locked and while I was fumbling for my keys a low voice spoke to me out of the darkness.

All it said was "Please!" but I knew it. I turned and looked at a dark Cadillac coupe parked just off the loading zone. It had no lights. Light from the street touched the brightness of a woman's eyes.

I went over there. "You're a darn fool," I said.

She said: "Get in."

I climbed in and she started the car and drove it a block and a half along Franklin and turned down Kingsley Drive. The hot wind still burned and blustered. A radio lilted from an open, sheltered side window of an apartment house. There were a lot of parked cars but she found a vacant space behind a small brand-new Packard cabriolet[2] that had the dealer's sticker on the windshield glass. After she'd jockeyed us up to the curb she leaned back in the corner with her gloved hands on the wheel.

She was all in black now, or dark brown, with a small foolish hat. I smelled the sandalwood in her perfume.

"I wasn't very nice to you, was I?" she said.

"All you did was save my life."

[9]Slang: Italian.
[1]Handsome, smartly dressed male, a "Romeo."   [2]Convertible coupe.

"What happened?"

"I called the law and fed a few lies to a cop I don't like and gave him all the credit for the pinch and that was that. That guy you took away from me was the man who killed Waldo."

"You mean—you didn't tell them about me?"

"Lady," I said again, "all you did was save my life. What else do you want done? I'm ready, willing, and I'll try to be able."

She didn't say anything, or move.

"Nobody learned who you are from me," I said. "Incidentally, I don't know myself."

"I'm Mrs. Frank C. Barsaly, two-twelve Fremont Place, Olympia two-four-five-nine-six. Is that what you wanted?"

"Thanks," I mumbled, and rolled a dry unlit cigarette around in my fingers. "Why did you come back?" Then I snapped the fingers on my left hand. "The hat and jacket," I said. "I'll go up and get them."

"It's more than that," she said. "I want my pearls." I might have jumped a little. It seemed as if there had been enough without pearls.

A car tore by down the street going twice as fast as it should. A thin bitter cloud of dust lifted in the streetlights and whirled and vanished. The girl ran the window up quickly against it.

"All right," I said. "Tell me about the pearls. We have had a murder and a mystery woman and a mad killer and a heroic rescue and a police detective framed into making a false report. Now we will have pearls. All right—feed it to me."

"I was to buy them for five thousand dollars. From the man you call Waldo and I call Joseph Coates. He should have had them."

"No pearls," I said. "I saw what came out of his pockets. A lot of money, but no pearls."

"Could they be hidden in his apartment."

"Yes," I said. "So far as I know he could have had them hidden anywhere in California except in his pockets. How's Mr. Barsaly this hot night?"

"He's still downtown at his meeting. Otherwise I couldn't have come."

"Well, you could have brought him," I said. "He could have sat in the rumble seat."

"Oh, I don't know," she said. "Frank weighs two hundred pounds and he's pretty solid. I don't think he would like to sit in the rumble seat, Mr. Marlowe."

"What the hell are we talking about anyway?"

She didn't answer. Her gloved hands tapped lightly, provokingly on the rim of the slender wheel. I threw the unlit cigarette out the window, turned a little and took hold of her.

When I let go of her, she pulled as far away from me as she could against the side of the car and rubbed the back of her glove against her mouth. I sat quite still.

We didn't speak for some time. Then she said very slowly: "I meant you to do that. But I wasn't always that way. It's only been since Stan Phillips was killed in his plane. If it hadn't been for that, I'd be Mrs. Phillips now. Stan gave me the pearls. They cost fifteen thousand dollars, he said once. White pearls, forty-one of them, the largest about a third of an inch across. I don't know how many grains. I never had them appraised or showed them to a jeweler, so I don't know those things. But I loved them on Stan's account. I loved Stan. The way you do just the one time. Can you understand?"

"What's your first name?" I asked.

"Lola."

"Go on talking, Lola." I got another dry cigarette out of my pocket and fumbled it between my fingers just to give them something to do.

"They had a simple silver clasp in the shape of a two-bladed propeller. There was one small diamond where the boss would be. I told Frank they were store pearls I had bought myself. He didn't know the difference. It's not so easy to tell, I dare say. You see—Frank is pretty jealous."

In the darkness she came closer to me and her side touched my side. But I didn't move this time. The wind howled and the trees shook. I kept on rolling the cigarette around in my fingers.

"I suppose you've read that story," she said. "About the wife and the real pearls and her telling her husband they were false?"

"I've read it," I said, "Maugham."[3]

"I hired Joseph. My husband was in Argentina at the time. I was pretty lonely."

"*You* should be lonely," I said.

"Joseph and I went driving a good deal. Sometimes we had a drink or two together. But that's all. I don't go around—"

"You told him about the pearls," I said. "And when your two hundred pounds of beef came back from Argentina and kicked him out—he took the pearls, because he knew they were real. And then offered them back to you for five grand."

"Yes," she said simply. "Of course I didn't want to go to the police. And of course in the circumstance Joseph wasn't afraid of my knowing where he lived."

"Poor Waldo," I said. "I feel kind of sorry for him. It was a hell of a time to run into an old friend that had a down on you."

I struck a match on my shoe sole and lit the cigarette. The tobacco was so dry from the hot wind that it burned like grass. The girl sat quietly beside me, her hands on the wheel again.

"Hell with women—these fliers," I said. "And you're still in love with him, or think you are. Where did you keep the pearls?"

"In a Russian malachite jewelry box on my dressing table. With some other costume jewelry. I had to, if I ever wanted to wear them."

"And they were worth fifteen grand. And you think Joseph might have hidden them in his apartment. Thirty-one, wasn't it?"

"Yes," she said. "I guess it's a lot to ask."

I opened the door and got out of the car. "I've been paid." I said. "I'll go look. The doors in my apartment are not very obstinate. The cops will find out where Waldo lived when they publish his photo, but not tonight, I guess."

"It's awfully sweet of you," she said. "Shall I wait here?"

I stood with a foot on the running board, leaning in, looking at her. I didn't answer her question. I just stood there looking in at the shine of her eyes. Then I shut the car door and walked up the street towards Franklin.

Even with the wind shriveling my face I could still smell the sandalwood in her hair. And feel her lips.

I unlocked the Berglund door, walked through the silent lobby to the elevator, and rode up to 3. Then I soft-footed along the silent corridor and peered down at the sill of apartment 31. No light. I rapped—the old light, confidential tattoo of the bootlegger with the big smile and the extra-deep hip pockets. No answer. I took the piece of thick hard celluloid that pretended to be a window over the driver's license in my wallet, and eased it between the lock and the jamb, leaning

[3]William Somerset Maugham (1874–1965), English writer. The reference is to his short story "Mr. Know-All."

hard on the knob, pushing it towards the hinges. The edge of the celluloid caught the slope of the spring lock and snapped it back with a small brittle sound, like an icicle breaking. The door yielded and I went into near darkness. Street light filtered in and touched a high spot here and there.

I shut the door and snapped the light on and just stood. There was a queer smell in the air. I made it in a moment—the smell of dark-cured tobacco. I prowled over to a smoking stand by the window and looked down at four brown butts—Mexican or South American cigarettes.

Upstairs, on my floor, feet hit the carpet and somebody went into a bathroom. I heard the toilet flush. I went into the bathroom of apartment 31. A little rubbish, nothing, no place to hide anything. The kitchenette was a longer job, but I only half searched. I knew there were no pearls in that apartment. I knew Waldo had been on his way out and that he was in a hurry and that something was riding him when he turned and took two bullets from an old friend.

I went back to the living room and swung the wall bed and looked past its mirror side into the dressing room for signs of still current occupancy. Swinging the bed farther I was no longer looking for pearls. I was looking at a man.

He was small, middle-aged, iron-gray at the temples, with a very dark skin, dressed in a fawn-colored suit with a wine-colored tie. His neat little brown hands hung limply by his sides. His small feet, in pointed polished shoes, pointed almost at the floor.

He was hanging by a belt around his neck from the metal top of the bed. His tongue stuck out farther than I thought it possible for a tongue to stick out.

He swung a little and I didn't like that, so I pulled the bed shut and he nestled quietly between the two clamped pillows. I didn't touch him yet. I didn't have to touch him to know that he would be cold as ice.

I went around him into the dressing room and used my handkerchief on drawer knobs. The place was striped clean except for the light litter of a man living alone.

I came out of there and began on the man. No wallet. Waldo would have taken that and ditched it. A flat box of cigarettes, half full, stamped in gold:

> LOUIS TAPIA Y CIA
> CALLE DE PAYSANDÚ, 19
> MONTEVIDEO

Matches from the Spezzia Club. An underarm holster of dark-grained leather and in it a 9-millimeter Mauser.

The Mauser made him a professional, so I didn't feel so badly. But not a very good professional, or bare hands would not have finished him, with the Mauser— a gun you can blast through a wall with—undrawn in his shoulder holster.

I made a little sense of it, not much. Four of the brown cigarettes had been smoked, so there had been either waiting or discussion. Somewhere along the line Waldo had got the little man by the throat and held him in just the right way to make him pass out in a matter of seconds. The Mauser had been less useful to him than a toothpick. Then Waldo had hung him up by the strap, probably dead already. That would account for haste, cleaning out the apartment, for Waldo's anxiety about the girl. It would account for the car left unlocked outside the cocktail bar.

That is, it would account for these things if Waldo had killed him, if this was really Waldo's apartment—if I wasn't just being kidded.

I examined some more pockets. In the left trouser one I found a gold penknife, some silver. In the left hip pocket a handkerchief, folded, scented. On the right hip another, unfolded but clean. In the right leg pocket four or five tissue handkerchiefs. A clean little guy. He didn't like to blow his nose on his handkerchief. Under these there was a small new keytainer holding four new keys— car keys. Stampled in gold on the keytainer was:

COMPLIMENTS OF R. K. VOGELSANG, INC.
"THE PACKARD HOUSE."

I put everything as I had found it, swung the bed back, used my handkerchief on knobs and other projections, and flat surfaces, killed the light and poked my nose out the door. The hall was empty. I went down to the street and around the corner to Kingsley Drive. The Cadillac hadn't moved.

I opened the car door and leaned on it. She didn't seem to have moved, either. It was hard to see any expression on her face. Hard to see anything but her eyes and chin, but not hard to smell the sandalwood.

"That perfume," I said, "would drive a deacon nuts . . . no pearls."

"Well, thanks for trying," she said in a low, soft vibrant voice. "I guess I can stand it. Shall I . . . Do we . . . Or . . .?"

"You go on home now," I said. "And whatever happens you never saw me before. Whatever happens. Just as you may never see me again."

"I'd hate that."

"Good luck, Lola." I shut the car door and stepped back.

The lights blazed on, the motor turned over. Against the wind at the corner the big coupe made a slow contemptuous turn and was gone. I stood there by the vacant space at the curb where it had been.

It was quite dark there now. Windows had become blanks in the apartment where the radio sounded. I stood looking at the back of a Packard cabriolet which seemed to be brand-new. I had seen it before—before I went upstairs, in the same place, in front of Lola's car. Parked, dark, silent, with a blue sticker pasted to the right-hand corner of the shiny windshield.

And in my mind I was looking at something else, a set of brand-new car keys in a keytainer stamped "THE PACKARD HOUSE," upstairs, in a dead man's pocket.

I went up to the front of the cabriolet and put a small pocket flash on the blue slip. It was the same dealer all right. Written in ink below his name and slogan was a name and address—Eugénie Kolchenko, 5315 Arvieda Street, West Los Angeles.

It was crazy. I went back up to apartment 31, jimmied the door as I had done before, stepped in behind the wall bed and took the keytainer from the trousers pocket of the neat brown dangling corpse. I was back down on the street beside the cabriolet in five minutes. The keys fitted.

5

It was a small house, near a canyon rim out beyond Sawtelle, with a circle of writhing eucalyptus trees in front of it. Beyond that, on the other side of the street, one of those parties was going on where they come out and smash bottles on the sidewalk with a whoop like Yale making a touchdown against Princeton.

There was a wire fence at my number and some rose trees, and a flagged walk and a garage that was wide open and had no car in it. There was no car in front of the house either. I rang the bell. There was a long wait, then the door opened rather suddenly.

I wasn't the man she had been expecting. I could see it in her glittering kohl-rimmed eyes.[1] Then I couldn't see anything in them. She just stood and looked at me, a long, lean, hungry brunette, with rouged cheekbones, thick black hair parted in the middle, a mouth made for three-decker sandwiches, coral-and-gold pajamas, sandals—and gilded toenails. Under her ear lobes a couple of miniature temple bells gonged lightly in the breeze. She made a slow disdainful motion with a cigarette in a holder as long as a baseball bat.

"We-el, what ees it, little man? You want sometheeng? You are lost from the bee-ootiful party across the street, hein?"[2]

"Ha-ha," I said. "Quite a party, isn't it? No, I just brought your car home. Lost it, didn't you?"

Across the street somebody had delirium tremens in the front yard and a mixed quartet tore what was left of the night into small strips and did what they could to make the strips miserable. While this was going on the exotic brunette didn't move more than one eyelash.

She wasn't beautiful, she wasn't even pretty, but she looked as if things would happen where she was.

"You have said what?" she got out, at last, in a voice as silky as a burnt crust of toast.

"Your car." I pointed over my shoulder and kept my eyes on her. She was the type that uses a knife.

The long cigarette holder dropped very slowly to her side and the cigarette fell out of it. I stamped it out, and that put me in the hall. She backed away from me and I shut the door.

The hall was like the long hall of a railroad flat.[3] Lamps glowed pinkly in iron brackets. There was a bead curtain at the end, a tiger skin on the floor. The place went with her.

"You're Miss Kolchenko?" I asked, not getting any more action.

"Ye-es. I am Mees Kolchenko. What the 'ell you want?"

She was looking at me now as if I had come to wash the windows, but at an inconvenient time.

I got a card out with my left hand, held it out to her. She read it in my hand, moving her head just enough. "A detective?" she breathed.

"Yeah."

She said something in a spitting language. Then in English: "Come in! Theese damn wind dry up my skeen like so much teesue paper."

"We're in," I said. "I just shut the door. Snap out of it, Nazimova.[4] Who was he? The little guy?"

Beyond the bead curtain a man coughed. She jumped as if she had been stuck with an oyster fork. Then she tried to smile. It wasn't very successful.

"A reward," she said softly. "You weel wait 'ere? Ten dollars it is fair to pay, no?"

"No," I said.

I reached a finger towards her slowly and added: "He's dead."

She jumped about three feet and let out a yell.

A chair creaked harshly. Feet pounded beyond the bead curtain, a large hand plunged into view and snatched it aside, and a big hard-looking blond man was

---

[1]Eyelids made-up with kohl, a dark, cosmetic powder.   [2]French: "eh?"
[3]An apartment with rooms laid out in a line, like boxcars on a train.
[4]Stage name of Alla Leventon (1878–1945), Russian-born American actress.

with us. He had a purple robe over his pajamas, his right hand held something in his robe pocket. He stood quite still as soon as he was through the curtain, his feet planted solidly, his jaw out, his colorless eyes like gray ice. He looked like a man who would be hard to take out on an off-tackle play.

"What's the matter, honey?" He had a solid, burring voice, with just the right sappy tone to belong to a guy who would go for a woman with gilded toenails.

"I came about Miss Kolchenko's car," I said.

"Well, you could take your hat off," he said. "Just for a light work-out."

I took it off and apologized.

"Okay," he said, and kept his right hand shoved down hard in the purple pocket. "So you came about Miss Kolchenko's car. Take it from there."

I pushed past the woman and went closer to him. She shrank back against the wall and flattened her palms against it. Camille[5] in a high school play. The long holder lay empty at her toes.

When I was six feet from the big man he said easily: "I can hear you from there. Just take it easy. I've got a gun in this pocket and I've had to learn to use one. Now about the car?"

"The man who borrowed it couldn't bring it," I said, and pushed the card I was still holding towards his face. He barely glanced at it. He looked back at me.

"So what?" he said.

"Are you always this tough?" I asked. "Or only when you have your pajamas on?"

"So why couldn't he bring it himself?" he asked. "And skip the mushy talk."

The dark woman made a stuffed sound at my elbow.

"It's all right, honeybunch," the man said. "I'll handle this. Go on."

She slid past both of us and flicked through the bead curtain.

I waited a little while. The big man didn't move a muscle. He didn't look any more bothered than a toad in the sun.

"He couldn't bring it because somebody bumped him off," I said. "Let's see you handle that."

"Yeah?" he said. "Did you bring him with you to prove it?"

"No," I said. "But if you put your tie and crush hat[6] on, I'll take you down and show you."

"Who the hell did you say you were, now?"

"I didn't say. I thought maybe you could read." I held the card at him some more.

"Oh, that's right," he said. "Philip Marlowe, private investigator. Well, well. So I should go with you to look at who, why?"

"Maybe he stole the car," I said.

The big man nodded. "That's a thought. Maybe he did. Who?"

"The little brown guy who had the keys to it in his pocket, and had it parked around the corner from the Berglund Apartments."

He thought that over, without any apparent embarrassment. "You've got something there," he said. "Not much. But a little. I guess this must be the night of the Police Smoker. So you're doing all their work for them."

"Huh?"

"The card says private detective to me," he said. "Have you got some cops outside that were too shy to come in?"

"No, I'm alone."

[5]The lead role in *Camille; The Lady of the Camellias* (1852), a romantic tragedy by the French writer Alexandre Dumas, Fils (1824–1895).

[6]Fancy, soft felt hat.

He grinned. The grin showed white ridges in his tanned skin. "So you find somebody dead and take some keys and find a car and come riding out here—all alone. No cops. Am I right?"

"Correct."

He sighed. "Let's go inside," he said. He yanked the bed curtain aside and made an opening for me to go through. "It might be you have an idea I ought to hear."

I went past him and he turned, keeping his heavy pocket towards me. I hadn't noticed until I got quite close that there were beads of sweat on his face. It might have been the hot wind but I didn't think so.

We were in the living room of the house.

We sat down and looked at each other across a dark floor, on which a few Navajo rugs and a few dark Turkish rugs made a decorating combination with some well-used overstuffed furniture. There was a fireplace, a small baby grand, a Chinese screen, a tall Chinese lantern on a teakwood pedestal, and gold net curtains against lattice windows. The windows to the south were open. A fruit tree with a whitewashed trunk whipped about outside the screen, adding its bit to the noise from across the street.

The big man eased back into a brocaded chair and put his slippered feet on a footstool. He kept his right hand where it had been since I met him—on his gun.

The brunette hung around in the shadows and a bottle gurgled and her temple bells gonged in her ears.

"It's all right, honeybunch," the man said. "It's all under control. Somebody bumped somebody off and this lad thinks we're interested. Just sit down and relax."

The girl tilted her head and poured half a tumbler of whiskey down her throat. She sighed, said, "Goddam," in a casual voice, and curled up on a davenport. It took all of the davenport. She had plenty of legs. Her gilded toenails winked at me from the shadowy corner where she kept herself quiet from then on.

I got a cigarette out without being shot at, lit it and went into my story. It wasn't all true, but some of it was. I told them about the Berglund Apartments and that I had lived there and that Waldo was living there in apartment 31 on the floor below mine and that I had been keeping an eye on him for business reasons.

"Waldo what?" the blond man put in. "And what business reasons?"

"Mister," I said, "have you no secrets?" He reddened slightly.

I told him about the cocktail lounge across the street from the Berglund and what had happened there. I didn't tell him about the printed bolero jacket or the girl who had worn it. I left her out of the story altogether.

"It was an undercover job—from my angle," I said. "If you know what I mean." He reddened again, bit his teeth. I went on: "I got back from the City Hall without telling anybody I knew Waldo. In due time, when I decided they couldn't find out where he lived that night, I took the liberty of examining his apartment."

"Looking for what?" the big man said thickly.

"For some letters. I might mention in passing there was nothing there at all—except a dead man. Strangled and hanging by a belt to the top of the wall bed—well out of sight. A small man, about forty-five, Mexican or South American, well-dressed in a fawn-colored—"

"That's enough," the big man said. "I'll bite, Marlowe. Was it a blackmail job you were on?"

"Yeah. The funny part was this little brown man had plenty of gun under his arm."

"He wouldn't have five hundred bucks in twenties in his pocket, of course? Or are you saying?"

"He wouldn't. But Waldo had over seven hundred in currency when he was killed in the cocktail bar."

"Looks like I underrated this Waldo," the big man said calmly. "He took my guy and his pay-off money, gun and all. Waldo have a gun?"

"Not on him."

"Get us a drink, honeybunch," the big man said. "Yes, I certainly did sell this Waldo person shorter than a bargain-counter shirt."

The brunette unwound her legs and made two drinks with soda and ice. She took herself another gill[7] without trimmings, wound herself back on the davenport. Her big glittering black eyes watched me solemnly.

"Well, here's how," the big man said, lifting his glass in salute. "I haven't murdered anybody, but I've got a divorce suit on my hands from now on. You haven't murdered anybody, the way you tell it, but you laid an egg down at police headquarters. What the hell! Life's a lot of trouble, anyway you look at it. I've still got honeybunch here. She's a white Russian I met in Shanghai. She's safe as a vault and she looks as if she could cut your throat for a nickel. That's what I like about her. You get the glamour without the risk."

"You talk damn foolish," the girl spat him.

"You look okay to me." The big man went on ignoring her. "That is, for a keyhole peeper. Is there an out?"

"Yeah. But it will cost a little money."

"I expect that. How much?"

"Say another five hundred."

"Goddam, thees hot wind make me dry like the ashes of love," the Russian girl said bitterly.

"Five hundred might do," the blond man said. "What do I get for it?"

"If I swing it—you get left out of the story. If I don't—you don't pay."

He thought it over. His face looked lined and tired now. The small beads of sweat twinkled in his short blond hair.

"This murder will make you talk," he grumbled. "The second one, I mean. And I don't have what I was going to buy. And if it's a hush, I'd rather buy it direct."

"Who was the little brown man?" I asked.

"Name's Leon Valesanos, a Uruguayan. Another of my importations. I'm in a business that takes me a lot of places. He was working in the Spezzia Club in Chiseltown—you know, the strip of Sunset next to Beverly Hills. Working on roulette, I think. I gave him the five hundred to go down to this—this Waldo— and buy back some bills for stuff Miss Kolchenko had charged to my account and delivered here. That wasn't bright, was it? I had them in my briefcase and this Waldo got a chance to steal them. What's your hunch about what happened?"

I sipped my drink and looked at him down my nose. "Your Uruguayan pal probably talked cut and Waldo didn't listen good. Then the little guy thought maybe that Mauser might help his argument—and Waldo was too quick for him. I wouldn't say Waldo was a killer—not by intention. A blackmailer seldom is. Maybe he lost his temper and maybe he just held on to the little guy's neck too long. Then he had to take it on the lam. But he had another date, with more

---

[7]A drinking glass that holds a quarter of a pint.

money coming up. And he worked the neighborhood looking for the party. And accidentally he ran into a pal who was hostile enough and drunk enough to blow him down."

"There's a hell of a lot of coincidence in all this business," the big man said.

"It's the hot wind." I grinned. "Everybody's screwy tonight."

"For the five hundred you guarantee nothing? If I don't get my cover-up, you don't get your dough. Is that it?"

"That's it," I said, smiling at him.

"Screwy is right," he said, and drained his highball. "I'm taking you up on it."

"There are just two things," I said softly, leaning forward in my chair. "Waldo had a getaway car parked outside the cocktail bar where he was killed, unlocked with the motor running. The killer took it. There's always a chance of a kickback from that direction. You see, all Waldo's stuff must have been in that car."

"Including my bills, and your letters."

"Yeah. But the police are reasonable about things like that—unless you're good for a lot of publicity. If you're not, I think I can eat some stale dog[8] downtown and get by. If you are—that's the second thing. What did you say your name was?"

The answer was a long time coming. When it came I didn't get as much kick out of it as I thought I would. All at once it was too logical.

"Frank C. Barsaly," he said.

After a while the Russian girl called me a taxi. When I left, the party across the street was doing all that a party could do. I noticed the walls of the house were still standing. That seemed a pity.

6

When I unlocked the glass entrance door of the Berglund I smelled policeman. I looked at my wrist watch. It was nearly 3 A.M. In the dark corner of the lobby a man dozed in a chair with a newspaper over his face. Large feet stretched out before him. A corner of the paper lifted an inch, dropped again. The man made no other movement.

I went on along the hall to the elevator and rode up to my floor. I soft-footed along the hallway, unlocked my door, pushed it wide and reached for the light switch.

A chain switch tinkled and light glared from a standing lamp by the easy chair, beyond the card table on which my chessmen were still scattered.

Copernik sat there with a stiff unpleasant grin on his face. The short dark man, Ybarra, sat across the room from him, on my left, silent, half smiling as usual.

Copernik showed more of his big yellow horse teeth and said: "Hi. Long time no see. Been out with the girls?"

I shut the door and took my hat off and wiped the back of my neck slowly, over and over again. Copernik went on grinning. Ybarra looked at nothing with his soft dark eyes.

"Take a seat, pal," Copernik drawled. "Make yourself to home. We got pow-wow to make. Boy, do I hate this night sleuthing. Did you know you were low on hooch?"

"I could have guessed it," I said. I leaned against the wall.

[8]Eat crow, recant.

Copernik kept on grinning. "I always did hate private dicks," he said, "but I never had a chance to twist one like I got tonight."

He reached down lazily beside his chair and picked up a printed bolero jacket, tossed it on the card table. He reached down again and put a wide-brimmed hat beside it.

"I bet you look cuter than all hell with these on," he said.

I took hold of a straight chair, twisted it around and straddled it, leaned my folded arms on the chair and looked at Copernik.

He got up very slowly—with an elaborate slowness, walked across the room and stood in front of me smoothing his coat down. Then he lifted his open right hand and hit me across the face with it—hard. It stung but I didn't move.

Ybarra looked at the wall, looked at the floor, looked at nothing.

"Shame on you, pal," Copernik said lazily. "The way you was taking care of this nice exclusive merchandise. Wadded down behind your old shirts. You punk peepers always did make me sick."

He stood there over me for a moment. I didn't move or speak. I looked into his glazed drinker's eyes. He doubled a fist at his side, then shrugged and turned and went back to the chair.

"Okay," he said. "The rest will keep. Where did you get these things?"

"They belong to a lady."

"Do tell. They belong to a lady. Ain't you the lighthearted bastard! I'll tell you what lady they belong to. They belong to the lady a guy named Waldo asked about in a bar across the street—about two minutes before he got shot kind of dead. Or would that have slipped your mind?"

I didn't say anything.

"You was curious about her yourself," Copernik sneered on. "But you were smart, pal. You fooled me."

"That wouldn't make me smart," I said.

His face twisted suddenly and he started to get up. Ybarra laughed, suddenly and softly, almost under his breath. Copernik's eyes swung on him, hung there. Then he faced me again, bland-eyed.

"The guinea likes you," he said. "He thinks you're good."

The smile left Ybarra's face, but no expression took its place. No expression at all.

Copernik said: "You knew who the dame was all the time. You knew who Waldo was and where he lived. Right across the hall a floor below you. You knew this Waldo person had bumped a guy off and started to lam, only this broad came into his plans somewhere and he was anxious to meet up with her before he went away. Only he never got the chance. A heist guy from back east named Al Tessilore took care of that by taking care of Waldo. So you met the gal and hid her clothes and sent her on her way and kept your trap glued. That's the way guys like you make your beans. Am I right?"

"Yeah," I said. "Except that I only knew these things very recently. Who was Waldo?"

Copernik bared his teeth at me. Red spots burned high on his sallow cheeks. Ybarra, looking down at the floor, said very softly: "Waldo Ratigan. We got him from Washington by teletype. He was a two-bit porch climber with a few small terms[1] on him. He drove a car in a bank stick-up job in Detroit. He turned the gang in later and got a nolle prosse. One of the gang was this Al Tessilore. He

---

[1] I.e., he had served a few, brief terms in jail.

hasn't talked a word, but we think the meeting across the street was purely accidental."

Ybarra spoke in the soft quiet modulated voice of a man for whom sounds have a meaning. I said: "Thanks, Ybarra. Can I smoke—or would Copernik kick it out of my mouth?"

Ybarra smiled suddenly. "You may smoke, sure," he said.

"The guinea likes you all right," Copernik jeered. "You never know what a guinea will like, do you?"

I lit a cigarette. Ybarra looked at Copernik and said very softly: "The word guinea—you overwork it. I don't like it so well applied to me."

"The hell with what you like, guinea."

Ybarra smiled a little more. "You are making a mistake," he said. He took a pocket nail file out and began to use it, looking down.

Copernik blared: "I smelled something rotten on you from the start, Marlowe. So when we make these two mugs, Ybarra and me think we'll drift over and dabble a few more words with you. I bring one of Waldo's morgue photos—nice work, the light just right in his eyes, his tie all straight and a white hand-kerchief showing just right in his pocket. Nice work. So on the way up, just as a matter of routine, we rout out the manager here and let him lamp it. And he knows the guy. He's here as A. B. Hummel, apartment thirty-one. So we go in there and find a stiff. Then we go round and round with that. Nobody knows him yet, but he's got some swell finger bruises under that strap and I hear they fit Waldo's fingers very nicely."

"That's something," I said. "I thought maybe I murdered him."

Copernik stared at me a long time. His face had stopped grinning and was just a hard brutal face now. "Yeah. We got something else even," he said. "We got Waldo's getaway car—and what Waldo had in it to take with him."

I blew cigarette smoke jerkily. The wind pounded the shut windows. The air in the room was foul.

"Oh, we're bright boys," Copernik sneered. "We never figured you with that much guts. Take a look at this."

He plunged his bony hand into his coat pocket and drew something up slowly over the edge of the card table, drew it along the green top and left it there stretched out, gleaming. A string of white pearls with a clasp like a two-bladed propeller. They shimmered softly in the thick smoky air.

Lola Barsaly's pearls. The pearls the flier had given her. The guy who was dead, the guy she still loved.

I stared at them, but I didn't move. After a long moment Copernik said almost gravely: "Nice, ain't they? Would you feel like telling us a story about now, Mister Marlowe?"

I stood up and pushed the chair from under me, walked slowly across the room and stood looking down at the pearls. The largest was perhaps a third of an inch across. They were pure white, iridescent, with a mellow softness. I lifted them slowly off the card table from beside her clothes. They felt heavy, smooth, fine.

"Nice," I said. "A lot of trouble was about these. Yeah, I'll talk now. They must be worth a lot of money."

Ybarra laughed behind me. It was a very gentle laugh. "About a hundred dollars," he said. "They're good phonies—but they're phony."

I lifted the pearls again. Copernik's glassy eyes gloated at me. "How do you tell?" I asked.

"I know pearls," Ybarra said. "These are good stuff, the kind women very often have made on purpose, as a kind of insurance. But they are slick like glass. Real pearls are gritty between the edges of the teeth. Try."

I put two or three of them between my teeth and moved my teeth back and forth, then sideways. Not quite biting them. The beads were hard and slick.

"Yes. They are very good," Ybarra said. "Several even have little waves and flat spots, as real pearls might have."

"Would they cost fifteen grand—if they were real?" I asked.

"Sí. Probably. That's hard to say. It depends on a lot of things."

"This Waldo wasn't so bad," I said.

Copernik stood up quickly, but I didn't see him swing. I was still looking down at the pearls. His fist caught me on the side of the face, against the molars. I tasted blood at once. I staggered back and made it look like a worse blow than it was.

"Sit down and talk, you bastard!" Copernik almost whispered.

I sat down and used a handkerchief to pat my cheek. I licked at the cut inside my mouth. Then I got up again and went over and picked up the cigarette he had knocked out of my mouth. I crushed it out in a tray and sat down again.

Ybarra filed at his nails and held one up against the lamp. There were beads of sweat on Copernik's eyebrows, at the inner ends.

"You found the beads in Waldo's car," I said, looking at Ybarra. "Find any papers?"

He shook his head without looking up.

"I'd believe you," I said. "Here it is. I never saw Waldo until he stepped into the cocktail bar tonight and asked about the girl. I knew nothing I didn't tell. When I got home and stepped out of the elevator this girl, in the printed bolero jacket and the wide hat and the blue silk crêpe dress—all as he had described them—was waiting for the elevator, here on my floor. And she looked like a nice girl."

Copernik laughed jeeringly. It didn't make any difference to me. I had him cold. All he had to do was know that. He was going to know it now, very soon.

"I knew what she was up against as a police witness," I said. "And I suspected there was something else to it. But I didn't suspect for a minute that there was anything wrong with her. She was just a nice girl in a jam—and she didn't even know she was in a jam. I got her in here. She pulled a gun on me. But she didn't mean to use it."

Copernik sat up very suddenly and he began to lick his lips. His face had a stony look now. A look like wet gray stone. He didn't make a sound.

"Waldo had been her chauffeur," I went on. "His name was then Joseph Coates. Her name is Mrs. Frank C. Barsaly. Her husband is a big hydroelectric engineer. Some guy gave her the pearls once and she told her husband they were just store pearls. Waldo got wise somehow there was a romance behind them and when Barsaly came home from South America and fired him, because he was too good-looking, he lifted the pearls."

Ybarra lifted his head suddenly and his teeth flashed. "You mean he didn't know they were phony?"

"I thought he fenced the real ones and had imitations fixed up," I said.

Ybarra nodded. "It's possible."

"He lifted something else," I said. "Some stuff from Barsaly's briefcase that showed he was keeping a woman—out in Brentwood. He was blackmailing wife and husband both, without either knowing about the other. Get it so far?"

"I get it," Copernik said harshly, between his tight lips. His face was still wet gray stone. "Get the hell on with it."

"Waldo wasn't afraid of them," I said. "He didn't conceal where he lived. That was foolish, but it saved a lot of finagling, if he was willing to risk it. The girl came down here tonight with five grand to buy back her pearls. She didn't find Waldo. She came here to look for him and walked up a floor before she went back down. A woman's idea of being cagey. So I met her. So I brought her in here. So she was in that dressing room when Al Tessilore visited me to rub out a witness." I pointed to the dressing-room door. "So she came out with her little gun and stuck it in his back and saved my life," I said.

Copernik didn't move. There was something horrible in his face now. Ybarra slipped his nail file into a small leather case and slowly tucked it into his pocket.

"Is that all?" he said gently.

I nodded. "Except that she told me where Waldo's apartment was and I went in there and looked for the pearls. I found the dead man. In his pocket I found new car keys in a case from a Packard agency. And down on the street I found the Packard and took it to where it came from. Barsaly's kept woman. Barsaly had sent a friend from the Spezzia Cub down to buy something and he had tried to buy it with his gun instead of the money Barsaly gave him. And Waldo beat him to the punch."

"Is that all?" Ybarra said softly.

"That's all," I said, licking the torn place on the inside of my cheek.

Ybarra said slowly: "What do you want?"

Copernik's face convulsed and he slapped his long hard thigh. "This guy's good," he jeered. "He falls for a stray broad and breaks every law in the book and you ask him what does he want? I'll give him what he wants, guinea!"

Ybarra turned his head slowly and looked at him. "I don't think you will," he said. "I think you'll give him a clean bill of health and anything else he wants. He's giving you a lesson in police work."

Copernik didn't move or make a sound for a long minute. None of us moved. Then Copernik leaned forward and his coat fell open. The butt of his service gun looked out of his underarm holster.

"So what do you want?" he asked me.

"What's on the table there. The jacket and hat and the phony pearls. And some names kept away from the papers. Is that too much?"

"Yeah—it's too much," Copernik said almost gently. He swayed sideways and his gun jumped neatly into his hand. He rested his forearm on his thigh and pointed the gun at my stomach.

"I like better that you get a slug in the guts resisting arrest," he said. "I like that better, because of a report I made out on Al Tessilore's arrest and how I made the pinch. Because of some photos of me that are in the morning sheets going out about now. I like it better that you don't live long enough to laugh about that baby."

My mouth felt suddenly hot and dry. Far off I heard the wind booming. It seemed like the sound of guns.

Ybarra moved his feet on the floor and said coldly: "You've got a couple of cases all solved, policeman. All you do for it is leave some junk here and keep some names from the papers. Which means from the D.A. If he gets them anyway, too bad for you."

Copernik said: "I like the other way." The blue gun in his hand was like a rock. "And God help you, if you don't back me up on it."

Ybarra said: "If the woman is brought out into the open, you'll be a liar on the police report and a chiseler on your own partner. In a week they won't even speak your name at Headquarters. The taste of it would make them sick."

The hammer clicked back on Copernik's gun and I watched his big finger slide in farther around the trigger.

Ybarra stood up. The gun jumped at him. He said: "We'll see how yellow a guinea is. I'm telling you to put that gun up, Sam."

He started to move. He moved four even steps. Copernik was a man without a breath of movement, a stone man.

Ybarra took one more step and quite suddenly the gun began to shake.

Ybarra spoke evenly: "Put it up, Sam. If you keep your head everything lies the way it is. If you don't—you're gone."

He took one more step. Copernik's mouth opened wide and made a gasping sound and then he sagged in the chair as if he had been hit on the head. His eyelids dropped.

Ybarra jerked the gun out of his hand with a movement so quick it was no movement at all. He stepped back quickly, held the gun low at his side.

"It's the hot wind, Sam. Let's forget it," he said in the same even almost dainty voice.

Copernik's shoulders sagged lower and he put his face in his hands. "Okay," he said between his fingers.

Ybarra went softly across the room and opened the door. He looked at me with lazy, half-closed eyes. "I'm eating this dish, but as a cop you can't expect me to like it."

I said: "The little man in the bed is called Leon Valesanos. He was a croupier at the Spezzia Club."

Copernik got up heavily and walked across the room and out of the open door and out of my sight. Ybarra stepped through the door after him and started to close it.

I said: "Wait a minute."

He turned his head slowly, his left hand on the door, the blue gun hanging down close to his right side.

"I'm not in this for money," I said. "The Barsalys live at two-twelve Fremont Place. You can take the pearls to her. If Barsaly's name stays out of the paper, I get five C's. It goes to the Police Fund. I'm not so damn smart as you think. It just happened that way—and you had a heel for a partner."

Ybarra looked across the room at the pearls on the card table. His eyes glistened. "You take them," he said. "The five hundred's okay. I think the fund has it coming."

He shut the door quietly and in a moment I heard the elevator doors clang.

7

I opened a window and stuck my head out into the wind and watched the squad car tool off down the block. The wind blew in hard and I let it blow. A picture fell off the wall and two chessmen rolled off the card table. The material of Lola Barsaly's bolero jacket lifted and shook.

I went out to the kitchenette and drank some Scotch and went back into the living room and called her—late as it was.

She answered the phone herself, very quickly, with no sleep in her voice.

"Marlowe," I said. "Okay your end?"

"Yes . . . yes," she said. "I'm alone."

"I found something," I said. "Or rather the police did. But your dark boy gypped you. I have a string of pearls. They're not real. He sold the real ones, I guess, and made you up a string of ringers, with your clasp."

She was silent for a long time. Then, a little faintly: "The police found them?"

"In Waldo's car. But they're not telling. We have a deal. Look at the papers in the morning and you'll be able to figure out why."

"There doesn't seem to be anything more to say," she said. "Can I have the clasp?"

"Yes. Can you meet me tomorrow at four in the Club Esquire bar?"

"You're really rather sweet," she said in a dragged-out voice. "I can. Frank is still at his meeting."

"Those meetings—they take it out of a guy," I said. We said goodbye.

I called a West Los Angeles number. He was still there, with the Russian girl.

"You can send me a check for five hundred in the morning," I told him. "Made out to the Police Relief Fund, if you want to. Because that's where it's going."

Copernik made the third page of the morning papers with two photos and a nice half-column. The little brown man in apartment 31 didn't make the paper at all. The Apartment House Association has a good lobby too.

I went out after breakfast and the wind was all gone. It was soft, cool, a little foggy. The sky was close and comfortable and gray. I rode down to the boulevard and picked out the best jewelry store on it and laid a string of pearls on a black velvet mat under a daylight-blue lamp. A man in a wing collar and striped trousers looked down at them languidly.

"How good?" I asked.

"I'm sorry, sir. We don't make appraisals. I can give you the name of an appraiser."

"Don't kid me," I said. "They're Dutch."[1]

He focused the light a little and leaned down and toyed with a few inches of the string.

"I want a string just like them, fitted to that clasp, and in a hurry," I added.

"How, like them?" He didn't look up. "And they're not Dutch. They're Bohemian."

"Okay, can you duplicate them?"

He shook his head and pushed the velvet pad away as if it soiled him. "In three months, perhaps. We don't blow glass like that in this country. If you wanted them matched—three months at least. And this house would not do that sort of thing at all."

"It must be swell to be that snooty," I said. I put a card under his black sleeve. "Give me a name that will—and not in three months—and maybe not exactly like them."

He shrugged, went away with the card, came back in five minutes and handed it back to me. There was something written on the back.

The old Levantine had a shop on Melrose, a junk shop with everything in the window from a folding baby carriage to a French horn, from a mother-of-pearl lorgnette in a faded plush case to one of those .44 Special Single Action six-shooters they still make for Western peace officers whose grandfathers were tough.

---

[1] Fakes.

The old Levantine wore a skull cap and two pairs of glasses and a full beard. He studied my pearls, shook his head sadly, and said: "For twenty dollars, almost so good. Not so good, you understand. Not so good glass."

"How like will they look?"

He spread his firm strong hands. "I am telling you the truth," he said. "They would not fool a baby."

"Make them up," I said. "With this clasp. And I want the others back, too, of course."

"Yah. Two o'clock," he said.

Leon Valesanos, the little brown man from Uruguay, made the afternoon papers. He had been found hanging in an unnamed apartment. The police were investigating.

At four o'clock I walked into the long cool bar of the Club Esquire and prowled along the rows of booths until I found one where a woman sat alone. She wore a hat like a shallow soup plate with a very wide edge, a brown tailor-made suit with a severe mannish shirt and tie.

I sat down beside her and slipped a parcel along the seat. "You don't open that," I said. "In fact you can slip it into the incinerator as is, if you want to."

She looked at me with dark tired eyes. Her fingers twisted a thin glass that smelled of peppermint. "Thanks." Her face was very pale.

I ordered a highball and the waiter went away. "Read the papers?"

"Yes."

"You understand now about this fellow Copernik who stole your act? That's why they won't change the story or bring you into it."

"It doesn't matter now," she said. "Thank you, all the same. Please—please show them to me."

I pulled the string of pearls out of the loosely wrapped tissue paper in my pocket and slid them across to her. The silver propeller clasp winked in the light of the wall bracket. The little diamond winked. The pearls were as dull as white soap. They didn't even match in size.

"You were right," she said tonelessly. "They are not my pearls."

The waiter came with my drink and she put her bag on them deftly. When he was gone she fingered them slowly once more, dropped them into the bag and gave a dry mirthless smile.

"As you said—I'll keep the clasp."

I said slowly: "You don't know anything about me. You saved my life last night and we had a moment, but it was just a moment. You still don't know anything about me. There's a detective downtown named Ybarra, a Mexican of the nice sort, who was on the job when the pearls were found in Waldo's suitcase. That is in case you would like to make sure—"

She said: "Don't be silly. It's all finished. It was a memory. I'm too young to nurse memories. It may be for the best. I loved Stan Phillips—but he's gone—long gone."

I stared at her, didn't say anything.

She added quietly: "This morning my husband told me something I hadn't known. We are to separate. So I have very little to laugh about today."

"I'm sorry," I said lamely. "There's nothing to say. I may see you sometime. Maybe not. I don't move much in your circle. Good luck."

I stood up. We looked at each other for a moment. "You haven't touched your drink," she said.

"You drink it. That peppermint stuff will just make you sick."

I stood there a moment with a hand hard on the table.

"If anybody ever bothers you," I said, "let me know."

I went out of the bar without looking back at her, got into my car and drove west on Sunset and down all the way to the Coast Highway. Everywhere along the way gardens were full of withered and blackened leaves and flowers which the hot wind had burned.

But the ocean looked cool and languid and just the same as ever. I drove on almost to Malibu and then parked and went and sat on a big rock that was inside somebody's wire fence. It was about half-tide and coming in. The air smelled of kelp. I watched the water for a while and then I pulled a string of Bohemian glass imitation pearls out of my pocket and cut the knot at one end and slipped the pearls off one by one.

When I had them all loose in my left hand I held them like that for a while and thought. There wasn't really anything to think about. I was sure.

"To the memory of Mr. Stan Phillips," I said aloud. "Just another four-flusher."

I flipped her pearls out into the water one by one at the floating seagulls.

They made little splashes and the seagulls rose off the water and swooped at the splashes.

Richard Wright *1908–1960*

Of Richard Wright's greatest book, Irving Howe has said, "The day Native Son *appeared, American culture was changed forever. No matter how much qualifying the book might later need, it made impossible a repetition of the old lies." Racial attitudes in America may not, in fact, have been forever changed by the appearance of that one novel, but there is little doubt that the book and its author had a significant impact on American culture.*

Richard Wright experienced a troubled and frightening Southern boyhood. His father deserted his family and left his son to be raised in a oppressive atmosphere by his fundamentalist grandmother and stern mother. Although hindered by the limited educational opportunities for Negroes in the South in the 1920s, Wright still managed to distinguish himself in school. He graduated as valedictorian of his class. He read widely and even had a story published while still in high school. But his talents could not find recognition in his segregated society, and, like thousands of other Negroes of the time, he fled north, first Memphis, Tennessee, and then to Chicago. The story of his youth is recounted in his remarkable autobiography, Black Boy *(1945).*

In Chicago, Wright had several menial jobs. During the Depression he became involved with the Federal Negro Theatre (a WPA project) and with the Illinois Writers' Project. At this time, he began to attend meetings of the John Reed Club, a group supported by the Communist Party. Throughout the 1930s, under the sponsorship of the John Reed Club, Wright wrote and published stories and essays. Although leaders of the Communist Party complained of his failure to follow the party line in his writing, Wright continued to work within the party, and in 1937 he moved to New York to become Harlem editor of the Daily Worker. *His first book,* Uncle Tom's Children: Four Novellas, *was published in 1938, and he subsequently won a Guggenheim Fellowship which enabled him to complete and publish* Native Son *in 1940.*

The book won immediate acclaim and sold a quarter of a million copies in its first month of publication. Rewritten for the stage, it was produced in 1941 and became one of the first plays by a Negro playwright to be presented on Broadway. As Wright became a national figure, he grew increasingly distressed by the lack of racial progress in America. After a bitter fight he left the Communist Party in 1944. In 1945 Black Boy was published, and Wright again received great popular acclaim. He had become the first black American whose work appeared on national bestseller lists, but in 1947, embittered by the racial prejudice he encountered, he emigrated to Europe, where he was to live until his death. Wright published more novels, essays, and stories, but his later work never again achieved the popular or critical acclaim of Native Son *and* Black Boy. *He was at work on a novel when he died of a heart attack, in France, on November 28, 1960.*

In retrospect, much of Wright's work other than Native Son, Black Boy, *and a few early short stories seems thin and uneven. He was never able to repeat the power, intensity, and quality of his two finest books, and once having left America he lost contact with the American Negro experience, the source of much of his strength as a writer. Nevertheless, his dramatic and gripping picture of the black man in the United States and the impact his writing has had on Americans, both white and black, have assured Wright's place among the notable writers of twentieth-century America.*

FURTHER READING: *Richard Wright Reader*, ed. E. Wright and M. Fabre, 1978; *Richard Wright, Letters to Joe C. Brown*, ed. T. Knipp, 1968; C. Webb, *Richard Wright, A Biography*, 1968; J. Williams, *The Most Native of Sons, A Biography of Richard Wright*, 1970; A. Gayle, *Richard Wright, Ordeal of a Native Son*, 1980; D. McCall, *The Example of Richard Wright*, 1969; E. Margolies, *The Art of Richard Wright*, 1969; R. Bone, *Richard Wright*, 1969; R. Brignano, *Richard Wright, An Introduction to the Man and His Works*, 1970; R. Abcarian, *Richard Wright's "Native Son," A Critical Handbook*, 1970; *Richard Wright, Impressions and Perspectives*, ed. D. Ray and R. Farnsworth, 1973; K. Kinnamon, *The Emergence of Richard Wright*, 1973; M. Fabre, *The Unfinished Quest of Richard Wright*, 1979; R. Felgar, *Richard Wright*, 1980; *Critical Essays on Richard Wright*, ed. Y. Hakutani, 1982; M. Fabre, *The World of Richard Wright*, 1985; J. Joyce, *Richard Wright's Art of Tragedy*, 1986.

TEXT: *Eight Men*, 1961.

from *EIGHT MEN*

THE MAN WHO WAS ALMOST A MAN

Dave struck out across the fields, looking homeward through paling light. Whut's the use talkin wid em niggers in the field? Anyhow, his mother was putting supper on the table. Them niggers can't understan nothing. One of these days he was going to get a gun and practice shooting, then they couldn't talk to him as though he were a little boy. He slowed, looking at the ground. Shucks, Ah ain scareda them even ef they are biggern me! Aw, Ah know whut Ahma do. Ahm going to ol Joe's sto n git that Sears Roebuck catlog n look at them guns. Mebbe Ma will lemme buy one when she gits mah pay from ol man Hawkins. Ahma beg her t gimme some money. Ahm ol ernough to hava gun. Ahm seventeen. Almost a man. He strode, feeling his long loose-jointed limbs. Shucks, a man oughta hava little fun aftah he done worked hard all day.

He came in sight of Joe's store. A yellow lantern glowed on the front porch. He mounted steps and went through the screen door, hearing it bang behind him. There was a strong smell of coal oil and mackerel fish. He felt very confident until he saw fat Joe walk in through the rear door, then his courage began to ooze.

"Howdy Dave! Whutcha want?"

"How yuh, Mistah Joe? Aw, Ah don wanna buy nothing. Ah just wanted to see ef yuhd lemme look at tha catlog erwhile."

"Sure! You wanna see it here?"

"Nawsuh. Ah wans t take it home wid me. Ah'll bring it back termorrow when Ah come in from the fiels."

"You plannin on buyin something?"

"Yessuh."

"Your ma letting you have your own money now?"

"Shucks. Mistah Joe, Ahm gettin t be a man like anybody else!"

Joe laughed and wiped his greasy white face with a red bandanna.

"What you plannin on buyin?"

Dave looked at the floor, scratched his head, scratched his thigh, and smiled. Then he looked up shyly.

"Ah'll tell yuh, Mistah Joe, ef yuh promise yuh won't tell."

"I promise."

"Waal, Ahma buy a gun."

"A gun? Whut you want with a gun?"

"Ah wanna keep it."

"You ain't nothing but a boy. You don't need a gun."

"Aw, lemme have the catalog. Mistah Joe. Ah'll bring it back."

Joe walked through the rear door. Dave was elated. He looked around at barrels of sugar and flour. He heard Joe coming back. He craned his neck to see if he were bringing the book. Yeah, he's got it. Gawddog, he's got it!

"Here, but be sure you bring it back. It's the only one I got."

"Sho, Mistah Joe."

"Say, if you wanna buy a gun, why don't you buy one from me? I gotta gun to sell."

"Will it shoot?"

"Sure it'll shoot."

"Whut kind is it?"

"Oh, it's kinda old . . . a left-hand Wheeler. A pistol. A big one."

"Is it got bullets in it?"

"It's loaded."

"Kin Ah see it?"

"Where's your money?"

"Whut yuh wan fer it?"

"I'll let you have it for two dollars."

"Just two dollahs? Shucks, Ah could buy that when Ah git mah pay."

"I'll have it here when you want it."

"Awright, suh. Ah be in fer it."

He went through the door, hearing it slam again behind him. Ahma git some money from Ma n buy me a gun! Only two dollahs! He tucked the thick catalogue under his arm and hurried.

"Where yuh been, boy?" His mother held a steaming dish of black-eyed peas.

"Aw, Ma, Ah just stopped down the road to talk wid the boys."

"Yuh know bettah t keep suppah waitin."

He sat down, resting the catalogue on the edge of the table.

"Yuh git up from there and git to the well n wash yosef! Ah ain feedin no hogs in mah house!"

She grabbed his shoulder and pushed him. He stumbled out of the room, then came back to get the catalogue.

"Whut this?"

"Aw, Ma, it's jusa catlog."

"Who yuh got it from?"

"From Joe, down at the sto."

"Waal thas good. We kin use it in the outhouse."

"Naw, Ma." He grabbed for it. "Gimme ma catlog, Ma."

She held onto it and glared at him.

"Quit hollerin at me! Whut's wrong wid yuh? Yuh crazy?"

"But Ma, please. It ain mine! It's Joe's! He tol me t bring it back t im termorrow."

She gave up the book. He stumbled down the back steps, hugging the thick book under his arm. When he had splashed water on his face and hands, he groped back to the kitchen and fumbled in a corner for the towel. He bumped into a chair; it clattered to the floor. The catalogue sprawled at his feet. When he had dried his eyes he snatched up the book and held it again under his arm. His mother stood watching him.

"Now, ef yuh gonna act a fool over that ol book, Ah'll take it n burn it up."

"Naw, Ma, please."

"Waal, set down n be still!"

He sat down and drew the oil lamp close. He thumbed page after page, unaware of the food his mother set on the table. His father came in. Then his small brother.

"Whutcha got there, Dave?" his father asked.

"Jusa catlog," he answered, not looking up.

"Yeah, here they is!" His eyes glowed at blue-and-black revolvers. He glanced up, feeling sudden guilt. His father was watching him. He eased the book under the table and rested it on his knees. After the blessing was asked, he ate. He scooped up peas and swallowed fat meat without chewing. Buttermilk helped to wash it down. He did not want to mention money before his father. He would do much better by cornering his mother when she was alone. He looked at his father uneasily out of the edge of his eye.

"Boy, how come yuh don quit foolin wid tha book n eat yo suppah?"

"Yessuh."

"How you n ol man Hawkins gitten erlong?"

"Suh?"

"Can't yuh hear? Why don yuh lissen? Ah ast yuh how wuz yuh n ol man Hawkins gitten erlong?"

"Oh, swell, Pa. Ah plows mo lan than anybody over there."

"Waal, yuh oughta keep you mind on whut yuh doin."

"Yessuh."

He poured his plate full of molasses and sopped it up slowly with a chunk of cornbread. When his father and brother had left the kitchen, he still sat and looked again at the guns in the catalogue, longing to muster courage enough to present his case to his mother. Lawd, ef Ah only had that pretty one! He could almost feel the slickness of the weapon with his fingers. If he had a gun like that he would polish it and keep it shining so it would never rust. N Ah'd keep it loaded, by Gawd!

"Ma?" His voice was hesitant.

"Hunh?"

"Ol man Hawkins give yuh mah money yit?"

"Yeah, but ain no usa yuh thinkin bout throwin nona it erway. Ahm keepin tha money sos yuh kin have cloes to go to school this winter."

He rose and went to her side with the open catalogue in his palms. She was washing dishes, her head bent low over a pan. Shyly he raised the book. When he spoke, his voice was husky, faint.

"Ma, Gawd knows Ah wans one of these."

"One of whut?" she asked, not raising her eyes.

"One of these," he said again, not daring even to point. She glanced up at the page, then at him with wide eyes.

"Nigger, is yuh gone plumb crazy?"

"Aw, Ma—"

"Git outta here! Don yuh talk t me bout no gun! Yuh a fool!"

"Ma, Ah kin buy one fer two dollahs."

"Not ef Ah knows it, yuh ain!"

"But yuh promised me one—"

"Ah don care what Ah promised! Yuh ain nothing but a boy yit!"

"Ma, ef yuh lemme buy one Ah'll *never* ast yuh fer nothing no mo."

"Ah tol yuh to git outta here! Yuh ain gonna toucha penny of tha money fer no gun! Thas how come Ah has Mistah Hawkins t pay yo wages to me, cause Ah knows yuh ain got no sense."

"But, Ma, we needa gun. Pa ain got no gun. We needa gun in the house. Yuh kin never tell whut might happen."

"Now don yuh try to maka fool outta me, boy! Ef we did hava gun yuh wouldn't have it!"

He laid the catalogue down and slipped his arm around her waist.

"Aw, Ma, Ah done worked hard alla summer n ain ast yuh fer nothing, is Ah, now?"

"Thas whut yuh spose t do!"

"But Ma, Ah wans a gun. Yuh kin lemme have two dollahs outta mah money. Please, Ma. I kin give it to Pa . . . Please, Ma! Ah loves yuh, Ma."

When she spoke her voice came soft and low.

"Whut yu wan wida gun, Dave? Yuh don need no gun. Yuh'll git in trouble. N ef yo pa just thought Ah let yuh have money t buy a gun he'd hava fit."

"Ah'll hide it, Ma. It ain but two dollahs."

"Lawd, chil, whut's wrong wid yuh?"

"Ain nothin wrong, Ma. Ahm almos a man now. Ah wans a gun."

"Who gonna sell yuh a gun?"

"Ol Joe at the sto."

"N it don cos but two dollahs?"

"Thas all, Ma. Jus two dollahs. Please, Ma."

She was stacking the plates away; her hands moved slowly, reflectively. Dave kept an anxious silence. Finally, she turned to him.

"Ah'll let yuh git tha gun ef yuh promise me one thing."

"Whut's tha, Ma?"

"Yuh bring it straight back t me, yuh hear? It be fer Pa."

"Yessum! Lemme go now, Ma."

She stooped, turned slightly to one side, raised the hem of her dress, rolled down the top of he stocking, and came up with a slender wad of bills.

"Here," she said. "Lawd knows yuh don need no gun. But yer pa does. Yuh bring it right back t me, yuh hear? Ahma put it up. Now ef yuh don, Ahma have yuh pa lick yuh so hard yuh won fergit it."

"Yessum."

He took the money, ran down the steps, and across the yard.

"Dave! Yuuuuuh Daaaaave!"

He heard, but he was not going to stop now. "Naw, Lawd!"

The first movement he made the following morning was to reach under his pillow for the gun. In the gray light of dawn he held it loosely, feeling a sense of power. Could kill a man with a gun like this. Kill anybody, black or white. And if he were holding his gun in his hand, nobody could run over him; they would have to respect him. It was a big gun, with a long barrel and a heavy handle. He raised and lowered it in his hand, marveling at its weight.

He had not come straight home with it as his mother had asked; instead he had stayed out in the fields, holding the weapon in his hand, aiming it now and then at some imaginary foe. But he had not fired it; he had been afraid that his father might hear. Also he was not sure he knew how to fire it.

To avoid surrendering the pistol he had not come into the house until he knew that they were all asleep. When his mother had tiptoed to his bedside late that night and demanded the gun, he had first played possum; then he had told her that the gun was hidden outdoors, that he would bring it to her in the morning. Now he lay turning it slowly in his hands. He broke it, took out the cartridges, felt them, and put them back.

He slid out of bed, got a long strip of old flannel from a trunk, wrapped the gun in it, and tied it to his naked thigh while it was still loaded. He did not go in to breakfast. Even though it was not yet daylight, he started for Jim Hawkins' plantation. Just as the sun was rising he reached the barns where the mules and plows were kept.

"Hey! That you, Dave?"

He turned. Jim Hawkins stood eyeing him suspiciously.

"What're yuh doing here so early?"

"Ah didn't know Ah wuz gettin up so early, Mistah Hawkins. Ah wuz fixin t hitch up ol Jenny n taker her t the fiels."

"Good. Since you're so early, how about plowing that stretch down by the woods?"

"Suits me, Mistah Hawkins."

"O.K. Go to it!"

He hitched Jenny to a plow and started across the fields. Hot dog! This was just what he wanted. If he could get down by the woods, he could shoot his gun and nobody would hear. He walked behind the plow, hearing the traces creaking, feeling the gun tied to his thigh.

When he reached the woods, he plowed two whole rows before he decided to take out the gun. Finally, he stopped, looked in all directions, then untied the gun and held it in his hand. He turned to the mule and smiled.

"Know whut this is, Jenny? Naw, yuh wouldn know! Yuhs jusa ol mule! Anyhow, this is a gun, n it kin shoot, by Gawd!"

He held the gun at arm's length. Whut t hell, Ahma shoot this thing! He looked at Jenny again.

"Lissen here, Jenny! When Ah pull this ol trigger, Ah don wan yuh t run n acka fool now!"

Jenny stood with head down, her short ears pricked straight. Dave walked off about twenty feet, held the gun far out from him at arm's length and turned his head. Hell, he told himself. Ah ain afraid. The gun felt loose in his fingers; he waved it wildly for a moment. Then he shut his eyes and tightened his forefinger. Bloom! A report half deafened him and he thought his right hand was torn from his arm. He heart Jenny whinnying and galloping over the field, and he found himself on his knees, squeezing his fingers hard between his legs. His hand was numb; he jammed it into his mouth, trying to warm it, trying to stop the pain. The gun lay at his feet. He did not quite know what had happened. He stood up and stared at the gun as though it were a living thing. He gritted his teeth and kicked the gun. Yuh almos broke mah arm! He turned to look for Jenny; she was far over the fields, tossing her head and kicking wildly.

"Hol on there, ol mule!"

When he caught up with her she stood trembling, walling her big white eyes at him. The plow as far away; the traces had broken. Then Dave stopped short, looking, not believing. Jenny was bleeding. Her left side was red and wet with blood. He went closer. Lawd, have mercy! Wondah did Ah shoot this mule? He grabbed for Jenny's mane. She flinched, snorted, whirled, tossing her head.

"Hol on now! Hol on."

Then he saw the hole in Jenny's side, right between the ribs. It was round, wet, red. A crimson stream streaked down the front leg flowing fast. Good Gawd! Ah wuzn't shootin at that mule. He felt panic. He knew he had to stop that blood, or Jenny would bleed to death. He had never seen so much blood in all his life. He chased the mule for half a mile, trying to catch her. Finally she stopped, breathing hard, stumpy tail half arched. He caught her mane and led her back to where the plow and gun lay. Then he stopped and grabbed handfuls of damp black earth and tried to plug the bullet hole. Jenny shuddered, whinnied, and broke from him.

"Hol on! Hol on now!"

He tried to plug it again, but blood came anyhow. His fingers were hot and sticky. He rubbed dirt into his palms, trying to dry them. Then again he attempted to plug the bullet hole, but Jenny shied away, kicking her heels high. He stood helpless. He had to do something. He ran at Jenny; she dodged him. He watched a red stream of blood flow down Jenny's leg and form a bright pool at her feet.

"Jenny . . . Jenny," he called weakly.

His lips trembled. She's bleeding t death! He looked in the direction of home, wanting to go back, wanting to get help. But he saw the pistol lying in the damp black clay. He had a queer feeling that if he only did something, this would not be; Jenny would not be there bleeding to death.

When he went to her this time, she did not move. She stood with sleepy, dreamy eyes; and when he touched her she gave a low-pitched whinny and knelt to the ground, her front knees slopping in blood.

"Jenny . . . Jenny . . ." he whispered.

For a long time she held her neck erect; then her head sank, slowly. Her ribs swelled with a mighty heave and she went over.

Dave's stomach felt empty, very empty. He picked up the gun and held it gingerly between his thumb and forefinger. He buried it at the foot of a tree. He took a stick and tried to cover the pool of blood with dirt—but what was the use? There was Jenny lying with her mouth open and her eyes walled and glassy. He could not tell Jim Hawkins he had shot his mule. But he had to tell something. Yeah, Ah'll tell em Jenny started gittin wil n fell on the point of the plow. . . . But that would hardly happen to a mule. He walked across the field slowly, head down.

It was sunset. Two of Jim Hawkins' men were over near the edge of the woods digging a hole in which to bury Jenny. Dave was surrounded by a knot of people, all of whom were looking down at the dead mule.

"I don't see how in the world it happened," said Jim Hawkins for the tenth time.

The crowd parted and Dave's mother, father, and small brother pushed into the center.

"Where Dave?" his mother called.

"There he is," said Jim Hawkins.

His mother grabbed him.

"What happened, Dave? Whut yuh done?"

"Nothin."

"C mon, boy, talk," his father said.

Dave took a deep breath and told the story he knew nobody believed.

"Waal," he drawled, "Ah brung ol Jenny down here sos Ah could do mah plowin. Ah plowed bout two rows, jus like yuh see." He stopped and pointed at the long rows of upturned earth. "Then somethin musta been wrong wid ol Jenny. She wouldn't ack right a-tall. She started snortin n kickin her heels. Ah tried t hol her, but she pulled erway, rearin n goin in. Then when the point of the plow was stickin up in the air, she swung erroun n twisted herself back on it . . . She stuck herself n started t bleed. N fo Ah could do anything, she wuz dead."

"Did you ever hear of anything like that in all your life?" asked Jim Hawkins.

There were white and black standing in the crowd. They murmured. Dave's mother came close to him and looked hard into his face. "Tell the truth, Dave," she said.

"Looks like a bullet hole to me," said one man.

"Dave, whut yuh do wid the gun?" his mother said.

The crowd surged in, looking at him. He jammed his hands into his pockets, shook his head slowly from left to right, and backed away. His eyes were wide and painful.

"Did he hava gun?" asked Jim Hawkins.

"By Gawd, Ah tol yuh tha wuz a gun wound," said a man, slapping his thigh.

His father caught his shoulders and shook him till his teeth rattled.

"Tell whut happened, yuh rascal! Tell whut . . ."

Dave looked at Jenny's stiff legs and began to cry.

"Whut yuh do wid tha gun?" his mother asked.

"Whut wuz he doin wida gun?" his father asked.

"Come on and tell the truth," said Hawkins. "Ain't nobody going to hurt you . . ."

His mother crowded close to him.

"Did yuh shoot tha mule, Dave?"

Dave cried, seeing blurred white and black faces.

"Ahh ddinn gggo tt sshooot hher . . . Ah ssswear ffo Gawd Ahh ddin . . . Ah wuz a-tryin t sssee ef the old gggun would sshoot—"

"Where yuh git the gun from?" his father asked.

"Ah got it from Joe, at the sto."

"Where yuh git the money?"

"Ma give it to me."

"He kept worryin me, Bob. Ah had t. Ah tol im t bring the gun right back t me . . . It was fer yuh, the gun."

"But how yuh happen to shoot that mule?" asked Jim Hawkins.

"Ah wuzn shootin at the mule, Mistah Hawkins. The gun jumped when Ah pulled the trigger . . . N fo Ah knowed anythin Jenny was there a-bleedin."

Somebody in the crowd laughed. Jim Hawkins walked close to Dave and looked into his face.

"Well, looks like you have bought you a mule, Dave."

"Ah swear fo Gawd, Ah didn go t kill the mule, Mistah Hawkins!"

"But you killed her!"

All the crowd was laughing now. They stood on tiptoe and poked heads over one another's shoulders.

"Well, boy, looks like yuh done bought a dead mule! Hahaha!"

"Ain tha ershame."

"Hohohohoho."

Dave stood, head down, twisting his feet in the dirt.

"Well, you needn't worry about it, Bob," said Jim Hawkins to Dave's father. "Just let the boy keep on working and pay me two dollars a month."

"Whut yuh wan fer yo mule, Mistah Hawkins?"

Jim Hawkins screwed up his eyes.

"Fifty dollars."

"Whut yuh do wid tha gun?" Dave's father demanded.

Dave said nothing.

"Yuh wan me t take a tree n beat yuh till yuh talk!"

'Nawsuh!"

"Whut yuh do wid it?"

"Ah throwed it erway."

"Where?"

"Ah . . . Ah throwed it in the creek."

"Wall, c mon home. N firs thing in the mawnin git to that creek n fin tha gun."

"Yessuh."

"Whut yuh pay fer it?"

"Two dollahs."

"Take tha gun n git yo money back n carry it t Mistah Hawkins, yuh hear? N don fergit Ahma lam you black bottom good fer this! Now march yosef on home, suh!"

Dave turned and walked slowly. He heard people laughing. Dave glared, his eyes welling with tears. Hot anger bubbled in him. Then he swallowed and stumbled on.

That night Dave did not sleep. He was glad he had gotten out of killing the mule so easily, but he was hurt. Something hot seemed to turn over inside him each time he remembered how they had laughed. He tossed on his bed, feeling his hard pillow. N Pa says he's gonna beat me . . . He remembered other beatings, and his back quivered. Naw, naw, Ah sho don wan im to beat me that way no mo. Dam em all! Nobody ever gave him anything. All he did was work. They treat me like a mule, n then they beat me. He gritted his teeth. N Ma had t tell on me.

Well, if he had to, he would take old man Hawkins that two dollars. But that meant selling the gun. And he wanted to keep that gun. Fifty dollars for a dead mule.

He turned over, thinking how he had fired the gun. He had an itch to fire it again. Ef other men kin shoota gun, by Gawd, Ah kin! He was still listening. Mebbe they all sleepin now. The house was still. He heard the soft breathing of his brother. Yes, now! He would go down and get that gun and see if he could fire it! He eased out of bed and slipped into overalls.

The moon was bright. He ran almost all the way to the edge of the woods. He stumbled over the ground, looking for the spot where he had buried the gun. Yeah, here it is. Like a hungry dog scratching for a bone, he pawed it up. He puffed his black cheeks and blew dirt from the trigger and barrel. He broke it and found four cartridges unshot. He looked around; the fields were filled with silence and moonlight. He clutched the gun stiff and hard in his fingers. But, as soon as he wanted to pull the trigger, he shut his eyes and turned his head. Naw, Ah can't shoot wid mah eyes closed n mah head turned. With effort he held his eyes open; then he squeezed. *Blooooom!* He was stiff, not breathing. The gun was still in his hands. Dammit, he'd done it! He fired again. *Blooooom!* He smiled. *Blooooom! Blooooom! Click, click.* There! It was empty. If anybody could shoot a gun, he could. He put the gun into his hip pocket and started across the fields.

When he reached the top of a ridge he stood straight and proud in the moonlight, looking at Jim Hawkins' big white house, feeling the gun sagging in his pocket. Lawd, ef Ah had just one mo bullet Ah'd taka shot at tha house. Ah'd like to scare ol man Hawkins jusa little . . . Jusa enough t let im know Dave Saunders is a man.

To his left the road curved, running to the tracks of the Illinois Central. He jerked his head, listening. From far off came a faint *hoooof-hoooof; hoooof-hoooof; hoooof-hoooof.* . . . He stood rigid. Two dollahs a mont. Les see now . . . Tha means it'll take bout two years. Shucks! Ah'll be dam!

He started down the road, toward the tracks. Yeah, here she comes! He stood beside the track and held himself stiffly. Here she comes, erroun the ben . . . C mon, yuh slow poke! C mon! He had his hand on his gun; something quivered in his stomach. Then the train thundered past, the gray and brown box cars rumbling and clinking. He gripped the gun tightly; then he jerked his hand out of his pocket. Ah betcha Bill wouldn't do it! Ah betcha . . . The cars slid past, steel grinding upon steel. Ahm ridin yuh ternight, so help me Gawd! He was hot all over. He hesitated just a moment; then he grabbed, pulled atop a car, and lay flat. He felt his pocket; the gun was still there. Ahead the long rails were glinting in the moonlight, stretching away, away to somewhere, somewhere where he could be a man . . .

1961

Ralph Ellison   *1914–*

Ralph Ellison's novel, Invisible Man, *has won high praise ever since its publication in 1952. A poll of literary critics in 1965 selected his book as the most distinguished novel of the previous twenty years, but since this auspicious beginning Ellison has been strangely silent. He has published only occasional essays and stories, some of which are reportedly part of a second novel, but no successor to* Invisible Man *has yet appeared.*

Named after the nineteenth-century essayist and poet Emerson, Ralph Waldo Ellison was born in Oklahoma in 1914. He did well in school and won a scholarship to the Tuskegee Institute in 1933, where he studied music. Before graduating he went north to Harlem to study sculpture. In New York, where he was befriended and encouraged by

Richard Wright, Ellison began to write. Like many other intellectuals of the time, he became involved with the left-wing political movements of the Depression period, but Ellison's flirtation with communism was brief, and the party is bitingly satirized in Invisible Man. *In 1942 Ellison became editor of* Negro Quarterly *and, after service in the Merchant Marine in World War II, seriously began work on his novel. Since the completion of* Invisible Man *Ellison has held various academic positions while he has continued to work on his promised second novel. A collection of his essays,* Shadow and Act, *was published in 1964.*

Despite all the acclaim, Invisible Man *has been criticized as insufficiently militant. In a sense, the criticism is true, for the novel is both so subtle and so complex that it lacks the immediate emotional impact of, for example, Richard Wright's novel* Native Son. *Ellison's* Invisible Man *is based on a set of symbols, on the conscious use of myth, and on historical allusions. It presents the traditional theme of the development of youth into maturity and is concerned, in Ellison's words, with "the American theme," the search for identity.* Invisible Man *is not, therefore, merely a racial protest novel. Ellison's intellect and his artistic imagination are too complex to stop at the presentation merely of anger and militancy, no matter how justified. His aim was broader. Early in life he gained, he says, "a passion to link together all I loved within the Negro community and all those things I felt in the world which lay beyond."* Invisible Man *achieves such a linking. It equates the social maturation of a young black boy with the archetypal theme of self-realization; it portrays the Negro as the symbol of all men and their aspirations and frustrations, and it achieves Ellison's self-professed goal in art, the "universal."*

FURTHER READING: *Invisible Man, A Collection of Critical Essays*, ed. J. Reilly, 1970; R. O'Meally, *The Craft of Ralph Ellison*, 1980; R. List, *Dedalus in Harlem, The Joyce-Ellison Connection*, 1982; A. Nadel, *Invisible Criticism, Ralph Ellison and the American Canon*, 1988.
TEXT: *Invisible Man*, 1952.

from *INVISIBLE MAN*

CHAPTER I

It goes a long way back, some twenty years. All my life I had been looking for something, and everywhere I turned someone tried to tell me what it was. I accepted their answers too, though they were often in contradiction and even self-contradictory. I was naïve. I was looking for myself and asking everyone except myself questions which I, and only I, could answer. It took me a long time and much painful boomeranging of my expectations to achieve a realization everyone else appears to have been born with: That I am nobody but myself. But first I had to discover that I am an invisible man!

And yet I am no freak of nature, nor of history. I was in the cards, other things having been equal (or unequal) eighty-five years ago. I am not ashamed of my grandparents for having been slaves. I am only ashamed of myself for having at one time been ashamed. About eighty-five years ago they were told that they were free, united with others of our country in everything pertaining to the common good, and, in everything social, separate like the fingers of the hand. And they believed it. They exulted in it. They stayed in their place, worked hard, and brought up my father to do the same. But my grandfather is the one. He was an odd old guy, my grandfather, and I am told I take after him. It was he who caused the trouble. On his deathbed he called my father to him and said, "Son, after I'm gone I want you to keep up the good fight. I never told you, but our life is a war and I have been a traitor all my born days, a spy in the enemy's country ever since I give up my gun back in the Reconstruction. Live with your head in the lion's mouth. I want you to overcome 'em with yeses, undermine 'em with grins, agree 'em to death and destruction, let 'em swoller you till they vomit or bust wide open." They thought the old man had gone out of his mind. He had been the meekest of men. The younger children were rushed from the room, the shades drawn and the flame of the lamp turned so low that it sputtered on the wick like the old man's breathing. "Learn it to the younguns," he whispered fiercely; then he died.

But my folks were more alarmed over his last words than over his dying. It was as though he had not died at all, his words caused so much anxiety. I was warned emphatically to forget what he had said and, indeed, this is the first time it has been mentioned outside the family circle. It had a tremendous effect upon me, however. I could never be sure of what he meant. Grandfather had been a quiet old man who never made any trouble, yet on his deathbed he had called himself a traitor and a spy, and he had spoken of his meekness as a dangerous activity. It became a constant puzzle which lay unanswered in the back of my mind. And whenever things went well for me I remembered my grandfather and felt guilty and uncomfortable. It was as though I was carrying out his advice in spite of myself. And to make it worse, everyone loved me for it. I was praised by the most lily-white men of the town. I was considered an example of desirable conduct—just as my grandfather had been. And what puzzled me was that the old man had defined it as *treachery*. When I was praised for my conduct I felt a guilt that in some way I was doing something that was really against the wishes of the white folks, that if they had understood they would have desired me to act just the opposite, that I should have been sulky and mean, and that that really would have been what they wanted, even though they were fooled and thought they wanted me to act as I did. It made me afraid that some day they would look upon me as a traitor and I would be lost. Still I was more afraid to act any other way because they didn't like that at all. The old man's words were like a curse. On my graduation day I delivered an oration in which I showed that humility was the secret, indeed, the very essence of progress. (Not that I believed this—how could I, remembering my grandfather?—I only believed that it worked.) It was a great success. Everyone praised me and I was invited to give the speech at a gathering of the town's leading white citizens. It was a triumph for our whole community.

It was in the main ballroom of the leading hotel. When I got there I discovered that it was on the occasion of a smoker, and I was told that since I was to be there anyway I might as well take part in the battle royal to be fought by some of my schoolmates as part of the entertainment. The battle royal came first.

All of the town's big shots were there in their tuxedoes, wolfing down the buffet foods, drinking beer and whiskey and smoking black cigars. It was a large room with a high ceiling. Chairs were arranged in neat rows around three sides of a portable boxing ring. The fourth side was clear, revealing a gleaming space of polished floor. I had some misgivings over the battle royal, by the way. Not from a distaste for fighting, but because I didn't care too much for the other fellows who were to take part. They were tough guys who seemed to have no grandfather's curse worrying their minds. No one could mistake their toughness. And besides, I suspected that fighting a battle royal might detract from the dignity of my speech. In those pre-invisible days I visualized myself as a potential Booker T. Washington.[1] But the other fellows didn't care too much for me

---

[1] Negro educator (1856–1915), author of *Up from Slavery* (1901).

either, and there were nine of them. I felt superior to them in my way, and I didn't like the manner in which we were all crowded together into the servants' elevator. Nor did they like my being there. In fact, as the warmly lighted floors flashed past the elevator we had words over the fact that I, by taking part in the fight, had knocked one of their friends out of a night's work.

We were led out of the elevator through a rococo hall into an anteroom and told to get into our fighting togs. Each of us was issued a pair of boxing gloves and ushered out into the big mirrored hall, which we entered looking cautiously about us and whispering, lest we might accidentally be heard above the noise of the room. It was foggy with cigar smoke. And already the whiskey was taking effect. I was shocked to see some of the most important men of the town quite tipsy. They were all there—bankers, lawyers, judges, doctors, fire chiefs, teachers, merchants. Even one of the more fashionable pastors. Something we could not see was going on up front. A clarinet was vibrating sensuously and the men were standing up and moving eagerly forward. We were a small tight group, clustered together, our bare upper bodies touching and shining with anticipatory sweat; while up front the big shots were becoming increasingly excited over something we still could not see. Suddenly I heard the school superintendent, who had told me to come, yell, "Bring up the shines, gentlemen! Bring up the little shines!"

We were rushed up to the front of the ballroom, where it smelled even more strongly of tobacco and whiskey. Then we were pushed into place. I almost wet my pants. A sea of faces, some hostile, some amused, ringed around us, and in the center, facing us, stood a magnificent blonde—stark naked. There was dead silence. I felt a blast of cold air chill me. I tried to back away, but they were behind me and around me. Some of the boys stood with lowered heads, trembling. I felt a wave of irrational guilt and fear. My teeth chattered, my skin turned to goose flesh, my knees knocked. Yet I was strongly attracted and looked in spite of myself. Had the price of looking been blindness, I would have looked. The hair was yellow like that of a circus kewpie doll, the face heavily powdered and rouged, as though to form an abstract mask, the eyes hollow and smeared a cool blue, the color of a baboon's butt. I felt a desire to spit upon her as my eyes brushed slowly over her body. Her breasts were firm and round as the domes of East Indian temples, and I stood so close as to see the fine skin texture and beads of pearly perspiration glistening like dew around the pink and erected buds of her nipples. I wanted at one and the same time to run from the room, to sink through the floor, or go to her and cover her from my eyes and the eyes of the others with my body; to feel the soft thighs, to caress her and destroy her, to love her and murder her, to hide from her, and yet to stroke where below the small American flag tattooed upon her belly her thighs formed a capital V. I had a notion that of all in the room she saw only me with her impersonal eyes.

And then she began to dance, a slow sensuous movement; the smoke of a hundred cigars clinging to her like the thinnest of veils. She seemed like a fair bird-girl girdled in veils calling to me from the angry surface of some gray and threatening sea. I was transported. Then I became aware of the clarinet playing and the big shots yelling at us. Some threatened us if we looked and others if we did not. On my right I saw one boy faint. And now a man grabbed a silver pitcher from a table and stepped close as he dashed ice water upon him and stood him up and forced two of us to support him as his head hung and moans issued from his thick bluish lips. Another boy began to plead to go home. He was the largest of the group, wearing dark red fighting trunks much too small to conceal the erection which projected from him as though in answer to the insinuating low-registered moaning of the clarinet. He tried to hide himself with his boxing gloves.

And all the while the blonde continued dancing, smiling faintly at the big shots who watched her with fascination, and faintly smiling at our fear. I noticed a certain merchant who followed her hungrily, his lips loose and drooling. He was a large man who wore diamond studs in a shirtfront which swelled with the ample paunch underneath, and each time the blonde swayed her undulating hips he ran his hand through the thin hair of his bald head and, with his arms upheld, his posture clumsy like that of an intoxicated panda, wound his belly in a slow and obscene grind. This creature was completely hypnotized. The music had quickened. As the dancer flung herself about with a detached expression on her face, the men began reaching out to touch her. I could see their beefy fingers sink into the soft flesh. Some of the others tried to stop them and she began to move around the floor in graceful circles, as they gave chase, slipping and sliding over the polished floor. It was mad. Chairs went crashing, drinks were spilt, as they ran laughing and howling after her. They caught her just as she reached a door, raised her from the floor, and tossed her as college boys are tossed at a hazing, and above her red, fixed-smiling lips I saw the terror and disgust in her eyes, almost like my own terror and that which I saw in some of the other boys. As I watched, they tossed her twice and her soft breasts seemed to flatten against the air and her legs flung wildly as she spun. Some of the sober ones helped her to escape. And I started off the floor, heading for the anteroom with the rest of the boys.

Some were still crying and in hysteria. But as we tried to leave we were stopped and ordered to get into the ring. There was nothing to do but what we were told. All ten of us climbed under the ropes and allowed ourselves to be blind-folded with broad bands of white cloth. One of the men seemed to feel a bit sympathetic and tried to cheer us up as we stood with our backs against the ropes. Some of us tried to grin. "See that boy over there?" one of the men said. "I want you to run across at the bell and give it to him right in the belly. If you don't get him, I'm going to get you. I don't like his looks." Each of us was told the same. The blindfolds were put on. Yet even then I had been going over my speech. In my mind each word was as bright as flame. I felt the cloth pressed into place, and frowned so that it would be loosened when I relaxed.

But now I felt a sudden fit of blind terror. I was unused to darkness. It was as though I had suddenly found myself in a dark room filled with poisonous cottonmouths. I could hear the bleary voices yelling insistently for the battle royal to begin.

"Get going in there!"

"Let me at that big nigger!"

I strained to pick up the school superintendent's voice, as though to squeeze some security out of that slightly more familiar sound.

"Let me at those black sonsabitches!" someone yelled.

"No, Jackson, no!" another voice yelled. "Here, somebody, help me hold Jack."

I stood against the ropes trembling. For in those days I was what they called ginger-colored, and he sounded as though he might crunch me between his teeth like a crisp ginger cookie.

Quite a struggle was going on. Chairs were being kicked about and I could hear voices grunting as with a terrific effort. I wanted to see, to see more desperately than ever before. But the blindfold was tight as a thick skin-puck-

ering scab and when I raised my gloved hands to push the layers of white aside
a voice yelled, "Oh, no you don't, black bastard! Leave that alone!"

"Ring the bell before Jackson kills him a coon!" someone boomed in the
sudden silence. And I heard the bell clang and the sound of the feet scuffling
forward.

A glove smacked against my head. I pivoted, striking out stiffly as someone
went past, and felt the jar ripple along the length of my arm to my shoulder.
Then it seemed as though all nine boys had turned upon me at once. Blows
pounded me from all sides while I struck out as best I could. So many blows
landed upon me that I wondered if I were not the only blindfolded fighter in
the ring, or if the man called Jackson hadn't succeeded in getting me after all.

Blindfolded, I could no longer control my motions. I had no dignity. I
stumbled about like a baby or a drunken man. The smoke had become thicker
and with each new blow it seemed to sear and further restrict my lungs. My
saliva became like hot bitter glue. A glove connected with my head, filling my
mouth with warm blood. It was everywhere. I could not tell if the moisture I
felt upon my body was sweat or blood. A blow landed hard against the nape of
my neck. I felt myself going over, my head hitting the floor. Streaks of blue
light filled the black world behind the blindfold. I lay prone, pretending that I
was knocked out, but felt myself seized by hands and yanked to my feet. "Get
going, black boy! Mix it up!" My arms were like lead, my head smarting from
blows. I managed to feel my way to the ropes and held on, trying to catch my
breath. A glove landed in my mid-section and I went over again, feeling as
though the smoke had become a knife jabbed into my guts. Pushed this way and
that by the legs milling around me, I finally pulled erect and discovered that I
could see the black, sweat-washed forms weaving in the smoky-blue atmosphere
like drunken dancers weaving to the rapid drum-like thuds of blows.

Everyone fought hysterically. It was complete anarchy. Everybody fought
everybody else. No group fought together for long. Two, three, four, fought
one, then turned to fight each other, were themselves attacked. Blows landed
below the belt and in the kidney, with the gloves open as well as closed, and with
my eye partly opened now there was not so much terror. I moved carefully,
avoiding blows, although not too many to attract attention, fighting from group
to group. The boys groped about like blind, cautious crabs crouching to protect
their mid-sections, their heads pulled in short against their shoulders, their arms
stretched nervously before them, with their fists testing the smoke-filled air like
the knobbed feelers of hypersensitive snails. In one corner I glimpsed a boy
violently punching the air and heard him scream in pain as he smashed his hand
against a ring post. For a second I saw him bent over holding his hand, then
going down as a blow caught his unprotected head. I played one group against
the other, slipping in and throwing a punch then stepping out of range while
pushing the others into the melee to take the blows blindly aimed at me. The
smoke was agonizing and there were no rounds, no bells at three minute intervals
to relieve our exhaustion. The room spun round me, a swirl of lights, smoke,
sweating bodies sourrounded by tense white faces. I bled from both nose and
mouth, the blood spattering upon my chest.

The men kept yelling, "Slug him, black boy! Knock his guts out!"

"Uppercut him! Kill him! Kill that big boy!"

Taking a fake fall, I saw a boy going down heavily beside me as though we
were felled by a single blow, saw a sneaker-clad foot shoot into his groin as the
two who had knocked him down stumbled upon him. I rolled out of range,
feeling a twinge of nausea.

The harder we fought the more threatening the men became. And yet, I had begun to worry about my speech again. How would it go? Would they recognize my ability? What would they give me?

I was fighting automatically when suddenly I noticed that one after another of the boys was leaving the ring. I was surprised, filled with panic, as though I had been left alone with an unknown danger. Then I understood. The boys had arranged it among themselves. It was the custom for the two men left in the ring to slug it out for the winner's prize. I discovered this too late. When the bell sounded two men in tuxedoes leaped into the ring and removed the blindfold. I found myself facing Tatlock, the biggest of the gang. I felt sick at my stomach. Hardly had the bell stopped ringing in my ears than it clanged again and I saw him moving swiftly toward me. Thinking of nothing else to do I hit him smash on the nose. He kept coming, bringing the rank sharp violence of stale sweat. His face was a black blank of a face, only his eyes alive—with hate of me and aglow with a feverish terror from what had happened to us all. I became anxious. I wanted to deliver my speech and he came at me as though he meant to beat it out of me. I smashed him again and again, taking his blows as they came. Then on a sudden impulse I struck him lightly and as we clinched, I whispered, "Fake like I knocked you out, you can have the prize."

"I'll break your behind," he whispered hoarsely.

"For *them?*"

"For *me,* sonofabitch!"

They were yelling for us to break it up and Tatlock spun me half around with a blow, and as a joggled camera sweeps in a reeling scene, I saw the howling red faces crouching tense beneath the cloud of blue-gray smoke. For a moment the world wavered, unraveled, flowed, then my head cleared and Tatlock bounced before me. The fluttering shadow before my eyes was his jabbing left hand. Then falling forward, my head against his damp shoulder, I whispered,

"I'll make it five dollars more."

"Go to hell!"

But his muscles relaxed a trifle beneath my pressure and I breathed, "Seven?"

"Give it to your ma," he said, ripping me beneath the heart.

And while I still held him I butted him and moved away. I felt myself bombarded with punches. I fought back with hopeless desperation. I wanted to deliver my speech more than anything else in the world, because I felt that only these men could judge truly my ability, and now this stupid clown was ruining my chances. I began fighting carefully now, moving in to punch him and out again with my greater speed. A lucky blow to his chin and I had him going too—until I heard a loud voice yell, "I got my money on the big boy."

Hearing this, I almost dropped my guard. I was confused: Should I try to win against the voice out there? Would not this go against my speech, and was not this a moment for humility, for nonresistance? A blow to my head as I danced about sent my right eye popping like a jack-in-the-box and settled my dilemma. The room went red as I fell. It was a dream fall, my body languid and fastidious as to where to land, until the floor became impatient and smashed up to meet me. A moment later I came to. An hypnotic vice said FIVE emphatically. And I lay there, hazily watching a dark red spot of my own blood shaping itself into a butterfly, glistening and soaking into the soiled gray world of the canvas.

When the voice drawled TEN I was lifted up and dragged to a chair. I sat dazed. My eye pained and swelled with each throb of my pounding heart and I wondered if now I would be allowed to speak. I was wringing wet, my mouth still bleeding. We were grouped along the wall now. The other boys ignored me as they congratulated Tatlock and speculated as to how much they would be paid. One boy whimpered over his smashed hand. Looking up front, I saw attendants in white jackets rolling the portable ring away and placing a small square rug in the vacant space surrounded by chairs. Perhaps, I thought, I will stand on the rug to deliver my speech.

Then the M.C. called to us, "Come on up here boys and get your money."

We ran forward to where the men laughed and talked in their chairs, waiting. Everyone seemed friendly now.

"There it is on the rug," the man said. I saw the rug covered with coins of all dimensions and a few crumpled bills. But what excited me, scattered here and there, were the gold pieces.

"Boys, it's all yours," the man said. "You get all you grab."

"That's right, Sambo," a blond man said, winking at me confidentially.

I trembled with excitement, forgetting my pain. I would get the gold and the bills, I thought. I would use both hands. I would throw my body against the boys nearest me to block them from the gold.

"Get down on the rug now," the man commanded, "and don't anyone touch it until I give the signal."

"This ought to be good," I heard.

As told, we got around the square rug on our knees. Slowly the man raised his freckled hand as we followed it upward with our eyes.

I heard, "These niggers look like they're about to pray!"

Then, "Ready," the man said, "Go!"

I lunged for a yellow coin lying on the blue design of the carpet, touching it and sending a surprised shriek to join those rising around me. I tried frantically to remove my hand but could not let go. A hot, violent force tore through my body, shaking me like a wet rage. The rug was electrified. The hair bristled up on my head as I shook myself free. My muscles jumped, my nerves jangled, writhed. But I saw that this was not stopping the other boys. Laughing in fear and embarrassment, some were holding back and scooping up the coins knocked off by the painful contortions of the others. The men roared above us as we struggled.

"Pick it up, goddamnit, pick it up!" someone called like a bass-voiced parrot. "Go on, get it!"

I crawled rapidly around the floor, picking up the coins, trying to avoid the coppers and to get greenbacks and the gold. Ignoring the shock by laughing, as I brushed the coins off quickly, I discovered that I could contain the electricity—a contradiction, but it works. Then the men began to push us onto the rug. Laughing embarrassedly, we struggled out of their hands and kept after the coins. We were all wet and slippery and hard to hold. Suddenly I saw a boy lifted into the air, glistening with sweat like a circus seal, and dropped, his wet back landing flush upon the charged rug, heard him yell and saw him literally dance upon his back, his elbows beating a frenzied tattoo upon the floor, his muscles twitching like the flesh of a horse stung by many flies. When he finally rolled off, his face was gray and no one stopped him when he ran from the floor amid booming laughter.

"Get the money," the M.C. called. "That's good hard American cash!"

And we snatched and grabbed, snatched and grabbed. I was careful not to come too close to the rug now, and when I felt the hot whiskey breath descend upon me like a cloud of foul air I reached out and grabbed the leg of a chair. It was occupied and I held on desperately.

"Leggo, nigger! Leggo!"

The huge face wavered down to mine as he tried to push me free. But my body was slippery and he was too drunk. It was Mr. Colcord, who owned a chain of movie houses and "entertainment palaces." Each time he grabbed me I slipped out of his hands. It became a real struggle. I feared the rug more than I did the drunk, so I held on, surprising myself for a moment by trying to topple *him* upon the rug. It was such an enormous idea that I found myself actually carrying it out. I tried not to be obvious, yet when I grabbed his leg, trying to tumble him out of the chair, he raised up roaring with laughter, and, looking at me with soberness dead in the eye, kicked me viciously in the chest. The chair leg flew out of my hand and I felt myself going and rolled. It was as though I had rolled through a bed of hot coals. It seemed a whole century would pass before I would roll free, a century in which I was seared through the deepest levels of my body to the fearful breath within me and the breath seared and heated to the point of explosion. It'll all be over in a flash, I thought as I rolled clear. It'll all be over in a flash.

But not yet, the men on the other side were waiting, red faces swollen as though from apoplexy as they bent forward in their chairs. Seeing their fingers coming toward me, I rolled away as a fumbled football rolls off the receiver's fingertips, back into the coals. That time I luckily sent the rug sliding out of place and heard the coins ringing against the floor and the boys scuffling to pick them up and the M.C. calling, "All right, boys that's all. Go get dressed and get your money."

I was limp as a dish rag. My back felt as though it had been beaten with wires.

When we had dressed the M.C. came in and gave us each five dollars, except Tatlock, who got ten for being last in the ring. Then he told us to leave. I was not to get a chance to deliver my speech, I thought. I was going out into the dim alley in despair when I was stopped and told to go back. I returned to the ballroom, where the men were pushing back their chairs and gathering in groups to talk.

The M.C. knocked on a table for quiet. "Gentlemen," he said, "we almost forgot about an important part of the program. A most serious part, gentlemen. This boy was brought here to deliver a speech which he made at his graduation yesterday . . ."

"Bravo!"

"I'm told that he is the smartest boy we've got out there in Greenwood. I'm told that he knows more big words than a pocket-sized dictionary."

Much applause and laughter.

"So now, gentlemen, I want you to give him your attention."

There was still laughter as I faced them, my mouth dry, my eye throbbing. I began slowly, but evidently my throat was tense, because they began shouting, "Louder! Louder!"

"We of the younger generation extol the wisdom of that great leader and educator," I shouted, "who first spoke these flaming words of wisdom: 'A ship lost at sea for many days suddenly sighted a friendly vessel. From the mast of the unfortunate vessel was seen a signal: "Water, water; we die of thirst!" The answer from the friendly vessel came back: "Cast down your bucket where you are." The captain of the distressed vessel, at last heeding the injunction, cast down his bucket, and it came up full of fresh sparkling water from the mouth of the Amazon River.' And like him I say, and in his words, 'To those of my race who depend upon bettering their condition in a foreign land, or who underestimate the importance of cultivating friendly relations with the Southern white man, who is his next-door neighbor, I would say: "Cast down your bucket

where you are"—cast it down in making friends in every manly way of the people
of all races by whom we are surrounded . . ."

I spoke automatically and with such fervor that I did not realize that the men
were still talking and laughing until my dry mouth, filling up with blood from
the cut, almost strangled me. I coughed, wanting to stop and go to one of the
tall brass, sand-filled spittoons to relieve myself, but a few of the men, especially
the superintendent, were listening and I was afraid. So I gulped it down, blood,
saliva and all, and continued. (What powers of endurance I had during those
days! What enthusiasm! What a belief in the rightness of things!) I spoke even
louder in spite of the pain. But still they talked and still they laughed, as though
deaf with cotton in dirty ears. So I spoke with greater emotional emphasis. I
closed my ears and swallowed blood until I was nauseated. The speech seemed
a hundred times as long as before, but I could not leave out a single word. All
had to be said, each memorized nuance considered, rendered. Nor was that all.
Whenever I uttered a word of three syllables a group of voices would yell for
me to repeat it. I used the phrase "social responsibility" and they yelled:

"What's that word you say, boy?"

"Social responsibility," I said.

"What?"

"Social . . ."

"Louder."

". . . responsibility."

"More!"

"Respon—"

"Repeat!"

"—sibility."

The room filled with the uproar of laughter until, no doubt, distracted by
having to gulp down my blood, I made a mistake and yelled a phrase I had
often seen denounced in newspaper editorials, heard debated in private.

"Social . . ."

"What?" they yelled.

". . . equality—"

The laughter hung smokelike in the sudden stillness. I opened my eyes,
puzzled. Sounds of displeasure filled the room. The M.C. rushed forward. They
shouted hostile phrases at me. But I did not understand.

A small dry mustached man in the front row blared out, "Say that slowly,
son!"

"What, sir?"

"What you just said!"

"Social responsibility, sir," I said.

"You weren't being smart, were you, boy?" he said, not unkindly.

"No, sir!"

"You sure that about 'equality' was a mistake?"

"Oh, yes, sir," I said. "I was swallowing blood."

"Well, you had better speak more slowly so we can understand. We mean to
do right by you, but you've got to know your place at all times. All right, now,
go on with your speech."

I was afraid. I wanted to leave but I wanted also to speak and I was afraid
they'd snatch me down.

"Thank you, sir," I said, beginning where I had left off, and having them
ignore me as before.

Yet when I finished there was a thunderous applause. I was surprised to see the superintendent come forth with a package wrapped in white tissue paper, and, gesturing for quiet, address the men.

"Gentlemen, you see that I did not overpraise this boy. He makes a good speech and some day he'll lead his people in the proper paths. And I don't have to tell you that that is important in these days and times. This is a good, smart boy, and so to encourage him in the right direction, in the name of the Board of Education I wish to present him a prize in the form of this . . ."

He paused, removing the tissue paper and revealing a gleaming calfskin brief case.

". . . in the form of this first-class article from Shad Whitmore's shop."

"Boy," he said, addressing me, "take this prize and keep it well. Consider it a badge of office. Prize it. Keep developing as you are and some day it will be filled with important papers that will help shape the destiny of your people."

I was so moved that I could hardly express my thanks. A rope of bloody saliva forming a shape like an undiscovered continent drooled upon the leather and I wiped it quickly away. I felt an importance that I had never dreamed.

"Open it and see what's inside," I was told.

My fingers a-tremble, I complied, smelling the fresh leather and finding an official-looking document inside. It was a scholarship to the state college for Negroes. My eyes filled with tears and I ran awkwardly off the floor.

I was overjoyed; I did not even mind when I discovered that the gold pieces I had scrambled for were brass pocket tokens advertising a certain make of automobile.

When I reached home everyone was excited. Next day the neighbors came to congratulate me. I even felt safe from grandfather, whose deathbed curse usually spoiled my triumphs. I stood beneath his photograph with my brief case in hand and smiled triumphantly into his stolid black peasant's face. It was a face that fascinated me. The eyes seemed to follow everywhere I went.

That night I dreamed I was at a circus with him and that he refused to laugh at the clowns no matter what they did. Then later he told me to open my brief case and read what was inside and I did, finding an official envelope stamped with the state seal; and inside the envelope, I found another and another, endlessly, and I thought I would fall of weariness. "Them's years," he said. "Now open that one." And I did and in it I found an engraved document containing a short message in letters of gold. "Read it," my grandfather said. "Out loud!"

"To Whom It May Concern," I intoned. "Keep This Nigger-Boy Running."

I awoke with the old man's laughter ringing in my ears.

(It was a dream I was to remember and dream again for many years after. But at that time I had no insight into its meaning. First I had to attend college.)

1952

Tennessee Williams *1911–1983*

Tennessee Williams achieved his first great stage success with The Glass Menagerie. *Produced in New York City in 1945, it won the New York Drama Critics' Circle Prize as the best play of the year. Since that time, critics have recognized the play as the beginning of the new American drama that emerged at the end of World War II, free of domination by the theatrical traditions of Europe.*

The Glass Menagerie *portrays an American family struggling to survive physically and spiritually in the late 1930s. In writing the play, Williams drew heavily upon his own family experiences, describing the lives of his mother, his sister, and himself. He was born Thomas Lanier Williams in Columbus, Mississippi. His father, a traveling shoe-salesman, spent little time at home, and for the first years of his life, Williams and his mother lived with his mother's father, an Episcopal clergyman. In 1918, when Williams was seven, his father became a sales manager for a shoe company in St. Louis, Missouri, and seven-year-old Tom and his sister were uprooted and moved to the city. Timid and sickly, the boy found St. Louis a painful change from the happy life he had led while living in his grandfather's rectory in Mississippi. He found few friends; his mother and father quarrelled incessantly; and his father, who believed that his indulgent wife had "sissified" their son, taunted him with the name "Miss Nancy." Enveloped in an unhappy world, Williams, like his counterpart Tom Wingfield in* The Glass Menagerie, *found escape and adventure in the movies, which affected him so intensely, he later recalled, that he "used to want to climb into the screen and join the action."*

At fourteen he won first prize ($25.00) in an essay contest sponsored by a national magazine, The Smart Set. *When he was seventeen his first published story, a gothic tale named "The Vengeance of Nitrocris," appeared in the August 1928 issue of* Weird Tales. *The next year he entered the University of Missouri, but in 1932 he withdrew from the university and took a job in the shoe factory where his father was a sales manager. After three years working in the company warehouse, a period that Williams later described as a "living death," he had a nervous breakdown. Following a year's recuperation with his grandparents in Memphis, Tennessee, he returned to college, eventually graduating from the University of Iowa with a B.A., in 1938.*

Williams had begun writing plays at the University of Missouri, and after his graduation he continued to write while supporting himself with a variety of menial jobs. By 1939 he was calling himself "Tennessee"—plain "Tom Williams" being, he thought, "rather dull." In that same year he won a national drama award for a group of plays called American Blues. *The next year his first play to be produced by a major company,* Battle of Angels, *opened in Boston and failed, closing after only one performance. Two years later he managed to get hired as a screenwriter for Metro-Goldwyn-Mayer in Hollywood. None of his scripts was accepted, and after a few months he lost his job, but one of his rejected scripts* The Gentleman Caller, *he later rewrote, turning it into his first great success,* The Glass Menagerie.

Since that time, Williams averaged a play every two years. Of his most memorable dramas A Streetcar Named Desire (1947) *and* Cat on a Hot Tin Roof (1955) *each won a Pulitzer Prize as the year's best American play. In 1956 his controversial film* Baby Doll *was produced, and it was followed by such Broadway and motion picture successes as* Suddenly Last Summer (1958), Sweet Bird of Youth (1959), *and* Night of the Iguana (1961). *In all, fifteen moving pictures have been made from Williams's works. In addition to plays he wrote a novel,* The Roman Spring of Mrs. Stone (1950), *two volumes of poetry, and six volumes of prose, including three collections of short stories.*

Williams's plays have shocked audiences by confronting them with an array of depravities never presented before on the American stage: murder, rape, castration, drug addiction, homosexuality, alcoholism, fetishism, nymphomania, even cannibalism. By dealing with such subjects Williams helped break taboos long imposed on the American theater, preparing the way for dramatists such as Imamu Amiri Baraka (LeRoi Jones) and Edward Albee, who would follow with even harsher depictions of violence and sexuality.

Williams's writing has sometimes been dismissed as willful pandering to the prurient interests of theatergoers. Yet the popular and critical acclaim that his work continues to receive has come not simply because he writes of the bizarre and fantastic but also because his plays are filled with fascinating characters and compelling dialogue. They are illuminated, even gilded, by verbal, visual, and sound symbolism that is intended to convey meanings beyond those possible in what Williams has termed "the exhausted theater of realism." He employs an array of expressionistic literary and theatrical devices: special settings, musical themes, unusual sound and lighting effects—all as a means of leading his audience to see the truths that lurk beneath life's surface.

His characters and their actions are often exaggerated. They are made to resemble the characters and events of ancient myths. Certain character types recur frequently: the outsider, a man or woman who differs from the mass of mankind by seeing clearly the frightening horror of life; the physically and emotionally deformed; the neurotic and the insane; real or would-be artists; victims and victimizers; and foreigners—strangers like the Gentleman Caller in The Glass Menagerie—*who intrude into and disrupt the lives of others. His characters are commonly overwhelmed by one another and by a growing awareness that the universe is indifferent to their suffering.*

In Williams's view, "Whether or not we admit it to ourselves, we are all haunted by a truly awful sense of impermanence." To dramatize his dark and narrow vision of life, he wrote of faded men and women, consumed by time and decay. They attempt to escape by moving, by fleeing; they can resist time but never overcome it—for life in Williams's plays can only be attenuated, never triumphant. Yet he shows that for those who come to see clearly the frightening chaos of the world there is a kind of victory, for their vision brings release from guilt and from pointless despair. They can then achieve the kind of dignity Williams believed to be possible if one lives "steadfastly, as if he, too, like a character in a play, were immured against the corrupting rush of time."

FURTHER READING: *The Theatre of Tennessee Williams*, 5 vols. 1972–1976; *Memoirs*, 1975; *Tennessee Williams' Letters to Donald Windham, 1940–1965*, ed. D. Windham, 1977; E. Williams and L. Freeman, *Remember Me to Tom*, 1963; N. Tischler, *Tennessee Williams, Rebellious Puritan*, 1961; N. Benjamin, *Tennessee Williams, The Man and His Work*, 1961; S. Falk, *Tennessee Williams*, 1961, 1978; F. Donahue, *The Dramatic World of Tennessee Williams*, 1964; E. Jackson, *The Broken World of Tennessee Williams*, 1965; M. Gilbert, *Tennessee Williams and Friends*, 1965; M. Steen, *A Look at Tennessee Williams*, 1969; *Tennessee Williams, A Tribute*, ed. J. Tharpe, 1977; M. Yacowar, *Tennessee Williams and Film*, 1977; *The World of Tennessee Williams*, ed. R. Leavitt, 1978; *Twentieth-Century Interpretations of the Glass Menagerie*, 1983; H. Rasky, *Tennessee Williams*, 1986; *Tennessee Williams*, ed. H. Bloom, 1987; R. Bloxill, *Tennessee Williams*, 1987.

TEXT: *The Glass Menagerie*, 1945.

THE GLASS MENAGERIE

Nobody, not even the rain, has such small hands.[1]
E. E. CUMMINGS

SCENE: An Alley in St. Louis

Part I. Preparation for a Gentleman Caller.
Part II. The Gentleman calls.

Time: *Now and the Past.*

[1] From "[somewhere i have never travelled,gladly beyond]." See page 1209.

THE CHARACTERS

AMANDA WINGFIELD (*the mother*): A little woman of great but confused vitality clinging frantically to another time and place. Her characterization must be carefully created, not copied from type. She is not paranoiac, but her life is paranoia. There is much to admire in Amanda, and as much to love and pity as there is to laugh at. Certainly she has endurance and a kind of heroism, and though her foolishness makes her unwittingly cruel at times, there is tenderness in her slight person.

LAURA WINGFIELD (*her daughter*): Amanda, having failed to establish contact with reality, continues to live vitally in her illusions, but Laura's situation is even graver. A childhood illness has left her crippled, one leg slightly shorter than the other, and held in a brace. This defect need not be more than suggested on the stage. Stemming from this, Laura's separation increases till she is like a piece of her own glass collection, too exquisitely fragile to move from the shelf.

TOM WINGFIELD (*her son*): And the narrator of the play. A poet with a job in a warehouse. His nature is not remorseless, but to escape from a trap he has to act without pity.

JIM O'CONNOR (*the gentleman caller*): A nice, ordinary, young man.

SCENE ONE

The Wingfield apartment is in the rear of the building, one of those vast hive-like conglomerations of cellular living-units that flower as warty growths in overcrowded urban centers of lower middle-class population and are symptomatic of the impulse of this largest and fundamentally enslaved section of American society to avoid fluidity and differentiation and to exist and function as one interfused mass of automatism.

The apartment faces an alley and is entered by a fire escape, a structure whose name is a touch of accidental poetic truth, for all of these huge buildings are always burning with the slow and implaccable fires of human desperation. The fire escape is part of what we see—that is, the landing of it and steps descending from it.

The scene is memory and is therefore nonrealistic. Memory takes a lot of poetic license. It omits some details; others are exaggerated, according to the emotional value of the articles it touches, for memory is seated predominantly in the heart. The interior is therefore rather dim and poetic.

At the rise of the curtain, the audience is faced with the dark, grim rear wall of the Wingfield tenement. This building is flanked on both sides by dark, narrow alleys which run into murky canyons of tangled clotheslines, garbage cans, and the sinister latticework of neighboring fire escapes. It is up and down these side alleys that exterior entrances and exits are made during the play. At the end of Tom's opening commentary, the dark tenement wall slowly becomes transparent and reveals the interior of the ground-floor Wingfield apartment.

Nearest the audience is the living room, which also serves as a sleeping room for Laura, the sofa unfolding to make her bed. Just beyond, separated from the living room by a wide arch or second proscenium with transparent faded portieres (or second curtain), is the dining room. In an old-fashioned whatnot in the living room are seen scores of transparent glass animals. A blown-up photograph of the father hangs on the wall of the living room, to the left of the archway. It is the face of a very handsome young man in a doughboy's

First World War cap. He is gallantly smiling, ineluctably smiling, as if to say "I will be smiling forever."

Also hanging on the wall, near the photograph, are a typewriter keyboard chart and a Gregg shorthand diagram. An upright typewriter on a small table stands beneath the charts.

The audience hears and sees the opening scene in the dining room through both the transparent fourth wall of the building and the transparent gauze portiers of the dining-room arch. It is during this revealing scene that the fourth wall slowly ascends, out of sight. This transparent exterior wall is not brought down again until the very end of the play, during Tom's final speech.

The narrator is an undisguised convention of the play. He takes whatever license with dramatic convention is convenient to his purposes.

Tom enters, dressed as a merchant sailor, and strolls across to the fire escape. There he stops and lights a cigarette. He addresses the audience.

TOM: Yes, I have tricks in my pocket, I have things up my sleeve. But I am the opposite of a stage magician. He gives you illusion the appearance of truth. I give you truth in the pleasant disguise of illusion.

To begin with, I turn back time. I reverse it to that quaint period, the thirties, when the huge middle class of America was matriculating in a school for the blind. Their eyes had failed them, or they had failed their eyes, and so they were having their fingers pressed forcibly down on the fiery Braille alphabet of a dissolving economy.

In Spain there was a revolution. Here there was only shouting and confusion. In Spain there was Guernica.[2] Here there were disturbances of labor, sometimes pretty violent, in otherwise peaceful cities such as Chicago, Cleveland, Saint Louis . . .

This is the social background of the play.

[*Music begins to play*]

The play is memory. Being a memory play, it is dimly lighted, it is sentimental, it is not realistic. In memory everything seems to happen to music. That explains the fiddle in the wings.

I am the narrator of the play, and also a character in it. The other characters are my mother, Amanda, my sister, Laura, and a gentleman caller who appears in the final scenes. He is the most realistic character in the play, being an emissary from a world of reality that we were somehow set apart from. But since I have a poet's weakness for symbols, I am using this character also as a symbol; he is the long-delayed but always expected something that we live for.

There is a fifth character in the play who doesn't appear except in this larger-than-life-size photograph over the mantel. This is our father who left us a long time ago. He was a telephone man who fell in love with long distances; he gave up his job with the telephone company and skipped the light fantastic out of town . . .

The last we heard of him was a picture postcard from Mazatlan, on the Pacific coast of Mexico, containing a message of two words: "Hello—Goodbye!" and no address.

I think the rest of the play will explain itself. . . .

[*Amanda's voice becomes audible through the portieres.*]

---

[2]Town in northern Spain, bombed in April 1937 by German planes flying for the fascists during the Spanish Civil War.

[*Legend on screen:* "Ou sont les neiges d'antan?"[3]]

[*Tom divides the portieres and enters the dining room. Amanda and Laura are seated at a drop-leaf table. Eating is indicated by gestures without food or utensils. Amanda faces the audience. Tom and Laura are seated in Profile. The interior is lit up softly and through the scrim we see Amanda and Laura seated at the table.*]

AMANDA [*calling*]: Tom?

TOM: Yes, Mother.

AMANDA: We can't say grace until you come to the table!

TOM: Coming, Mother. [*He bows slightly and withdraws, reappearing a few moments later in his place at the table.*]

AMANDA [*to her son*]: Honey, don't *push* with your *fingers*. If you have to push with something, the thing to push with is a crust of bread. And chew—chew! Animals have secretions in their stomachs which enable them to digest food without mastication, but human beings are supposed to chew their food before they swallow it down. Eat food leisurely, son, and really enjoy it. A well-cooked meal has lots of delicate flavors that have to be held in the mouth for appreciation. So chew your food and give your salivary glands a chance to function!

[*Tom deliberately lays his imaginary fork down and pushes his chair back from the table.*]

TOM: I haven't enjoyed one bite of this dinner because of your constant directions on how to eat it. It's you that make me rush through meals with your hawklike attention to every bite I take. Sickening—spoils my appetite—all this discussion of—animals' secretion—salivary glands—mastication!

AMANDA [*lightly*]: Temperament like a Metropolitan star!

[*Tom rises and walks toward the living room.*]

You're not excused from the table.

TOM: I'm getting a cigarette.

AMANDA: You smoke too much.

[*Laura rises.*]

LAURA: I'll bring in the blanc mange.

[*Tom remains standing with his cigarette by the portieres.*]

AMANDA [*rising*]: No, sister, no, sister—you be the lady this time and I'll be the darky.

LAURA: I'm already up.

AMANDA: Resume your seat, little sister— I want you to stay fresh and pretty—for gentlemen callers!

LAURA: [*sitting down*]: I'm not expecting any gentlemen callers.

AMANDA: [*crossing out to the kitchenette, airily*]: Sometimes they come when they are least expected! Why, I remember one Sunday afternoon in Blue Mountain—

[*She enters the kitchenette.*]

TOM: I know what's coming!

LAURA: Yes. But let her tell it.

TOM: Again?

LAURA: She loves to tell it.

[*Amanda returns with a bowl of desert.*]

AMANDA: One Sunday afternoon in Blue Mountain—your mother received—*seventeen!*—gentlemen callers! Why, sometimes there weren't chairs enough to accommodate them all. We had to send the nigger over to bring in folding chairs from the parish house.

TOM: [*remaining at the portieres*]: How did you entertain those gentlemen callers?

[3]French: "Where are the snows of bygone years?" A refrain from "Ballade of the Ladies of Bygone Times" by François Villon (1431–1463?).

AMANDA: I understood the art of conversation!

TOM: I bet you could talk.

AMANDA: Girls in those days *knew* how to talk, I can tell you.

TOM: Yes?

[*Image on screen:* Amanda as a girl on a porch, greeting callers.]

AMANDA: They knew how to entertain their gentlemen callers. It wasn't enough for a girl to be possessed of a pretty face and a graceful figure—although I wasn't slighted in either respect. She also needed to have nimble wit and a tongue to meet all occasions.

TOM: What did you talk about?

AMANDA: Things of importance going on in the world! Never anything coarse or common or vulgar.

[*She addresses Tom as though he were seated in the vacant chair at the table though he remains by the portieres. He plays this scene as though reading from a script.*]

My callers were gentlemen—all! Among my callers were some of the most prominent young planters of the Mississippi Delta—planters and sons of planters!

[*Tom motions for music and a spot of light on Amanda. Her eyes lift, her face glows, her voice becomes rich and elegiac.*]

[*Screen legend:* "Ou sont les neiges d'antan?"]

There was young Champ Laughlin who later became vice-president of the Delta Planters Bank. Hadley Stevenson who was drowned in Moon Lake and left his widow one hundred and fifty thousand in Government bonds. There were the Cutrere brothers, Wesley and Bates. Bates was one of my bright particular beaux! He got in a quarrel with that wild Wainwright boy. They shot it out on the floor of Moon Lake Casino. Bates was shot through the stomach. Died in the ambulance on his way to Memphis. His widow was also well provided-for, came into eight or ten thousand acres, that's all. She married him on the rebound—never loved her—carried my picture on him the night he died! And there was that boy that every girl in the Delta had set her cap for! That beautiful, brilliant young Fitzhugh boy from Greene County!

TOM: What did he leave his widow?

AMANDA: He never married! Gracious, you talk as though all of my old admirers had turned up their toes to the daisies!

TOM: Isn't this the first you've mentioned that still survives?

AMANDA: That Fitzhugh boy went North and made a fortune—came to be known as the Wolf of Wall Street! He had the Midas touch, whatever he touched turned to gold! And I could have been Mrs. Duncan J. Fitzhugh, mind you! But—I picked your *father!*

LAURA: [*rising*]: Mother, let me clear the table.

AMANDA: No, dear, you go in front and study your typewriter chart. Or practice your shorthand a little. Stay fresh and pretty!—It's almost time for our gentlemen callers to start arriving. [*She flounces girlishly toward the kitchenette*] How many do you suppose we're going to entertain this afternoon?

[*Tom throws down the paper and jumps up with a groan.*]

LAURA: [*alone in the dining room*]: I don't believe we're going to receive any, Mother.

AMANDA: [*reappearing, airily*]: What? No one—not one? You must be joking! [*Laura nervously echoes her laugh. She slips in a fugitive manner through the half-open portieres and draws them gently behind her. A shaft of very clear light is thrown on her face against the faded tapestry of the curtains. Faintly the music of "The Glass Menagerie" is heard as she continues, lightly:*]

Not one gentleman caller? It can't be true! There must be a flood, there must have been a tornado!

LAURA: It isn't a flood, it's not a tornado, Mother. I'm just not popular like you were in Blue Mountain. . . .

[*Tom utters another groan. Laura glances at him with a faint, apologetic smile. Her voice catches a little:*]

Mother's afraid I'm going to be an old maid.

[*The scene dims out with the "Glass Menagerie" music.*]

SCENE TWO

On the dark stage the screen is lighted with the image of blue roses. Gradually Laura's figure becomes apparent and the screen goes out. The music subsides.

Laura is seated in the delicate ivory chair at the small claw-foot table. She wears a dress of soft violet material for a kimono—her hair is tied back from her forehead with a ribbon. She is washing and polishing her collection of glass. Amanda appears on the fire escape steps. At the sound of her ascent, Laura catches her breath, thrusts the bowl of ornaments away, and sets herself stiffly before the diagram of the typewriter keyboard as though it held her spellbound. Something has happened to Amanda. It is written in her face as she climbs to the landing: a look that is grim and hopeless and a little absurd. She has on one of those cheap or imitation velvety-looking cloth coats with imitation fur collar. Her hat is five or six years old, one of those dreadful cloche hats that were worn in the late Twenties, and she is clutching an enormous black patent-leather pocketbook with nickel clasps and initials. This is her full-dress outfit, the one she usually wears to the D.A.R.[1] Before entering she looks through the door. She purses her lips, opens her eyes very wide, rolls them upward and shakes her head. Then she slowly lets herself in the door. Seeing her mother's expression Laura touches her lips with a nervous gesture.

LAURA: Hello, Mother, I was—[*She makes a nervous gesture toward the chart on the wall. Amanda leans against the shut door and stares at Laura with a martyred look.*]

AMANDA: Deception? Deception? [*She slowly removes her hat and gloves, continuing the sweet suffering stare. She lets the hat and gloves fall on the floor—a bit of acting.*]

LAURA: [*shakily*]: How was the D.A.R. meeting?

[*Amanda slowly opens her purse and removes a dainty white handkerchief which she shakes out delicately and delicately touches to her lips and nostrils.*]

Didn't you go to the D.A.R. meeting, Mother?

AMANDA: [*faintly, almost inaudibly*]: —No.—No.[*then more forcibly:*] I did not have the strength—to go to the D.A.R. In fact, I did not have the courage! I wanted to find a hole in the ground and hide myself in it forever! [*She crosses slowly to the wall and removes the diagram of the typewriter keyboard. She holds it in front of her for a second, staring at it sweetly and sorrowfully—then bites her lips and tears it in two pieces.*]

LAURA: [*faintly*]: Why did you do that, Mother?

[*Amanda repeats the same procedure with the chart of the Gregg Alphabet.*]

Why are you—

AMANDA: Why? Why? How old are you, Laura?

LAURA: Mother, you know my age.

AMANDA: I thought that you were an adult; it seems that I was mistaken. [*She crosses slowly to the sofa and sinks down and stares at Laura.*]

[1] I.e., to a meeting of the Daughters of the American Revolution, a patriotic society dedicated to celebration of the participants of the American Revolution.

LAURA: Please don't stare at me, Mother.

[*Amanda closes her eyes and lowers her head. There is a ten-second pause.*]

AMANDA: What are we going to do, what is going to become of us, what is the future?

[*There is another pause.*]

LAURA: Has something happened, Mother?

[*Amanda draws a long breath, takes out the handkerchief again, goes through the dabbing process.*]

Mother, has—something happened?

AMANDA: I'll be all right in a minute, I'm just bewildered—[*She hesitates.*]—by life. . . .

LAURA: Mother, I wish that you would tell me what's happened!

AMANDA: As you know, I was supposed to be inducted into my office at the D.A.R. this afternoon.

[*Screen image:* A swarm of typewriters.]

But I stopped off at Rubicam's Business College to speak to your teachers about your having a cold and ask them what progress they thought you were making down there.

LAURA: Oh. . . .

AMANDA: I went to the typing instructor and introduced myself as your mother. She didn't know who you were. "Wingfield," she said, "We don't have any such student enrolled at the school!"

I assured her she did, that you had been going to classes since early in January. "I wonder," she said, "If you could be talking about that terribly shy little girl who dropped out of school after only a few days' attendance?"

"No," I said, "Laura, my daughter, has been going to school every day for the past six weeks!"

"Excuse me," she said. She took the attendance book out and there was your name, unmistakably printed, and all the dates you were absent until they decided you had dropped out of school.

I still said, "No, there must have been some mistake! There must have been some mix-up in the records!"

And she said, "No—I remember her perfectly now. Her hands shook so that she couldn't hit the right keys! The first time we gave a speed test, she broke down completely—was sick at the stomach and almost had to be carried into the wash room! After that morning she never showed up any more. We phoned the house but never got any answer"—While I was working at Famous-Barr, I suppose, demonstrating those—

[*She indicates a brassiere with her hands.*]

Oh! I felt so weak I could barely keep on my feet! I had to sit down while they got me a glass of water! Fifty dollars' tuition, all of our plans—my hopes and ambitions for you—just gone up the spout, just gone up the spout like that.

[*Laura draws a long breath and gets awkwardly to her feet. She crosses to the Victrola and winds it up.*]

What are you doing?

LAURA: Oh! [*She releases the handle and returns to her seat.*]

AMANDA: Laura, where have you been going when you've gone out pretending that you were going to business college?

LAURA: I've just been going out walking.

AMANDA: That's not true.

LAURA: It is. I just went walking.

AMANDA: Walking? Walking? In winter? Deliberately courting pneumonia in that light coat? Where did you walk to, Laura?

LAURA: All sorts of places—mostly in the park.

AMANDA: Even after you'd started catching that cold?

LAURA: It was the lesser of two evils, Mother.

[*Screen image:* Winter scene in a park.]

I couldn't go back there. I—threw up—on the floor!

AMANDA: From half past seven till after five every day you mean to tell me you walked around in the park, because you wanted to make me think that you were still going to Rubicam's Business College?

LAURA: It wasn't as bad as it sounds. I went inside places to get warmed up.

AMANDA: Inside where?

LAURA: I went in the art museum and the bird houses at the Zoo. I visited the penguins every day! Sometimes I did without lunch and went to the movies. Lately I've been spending most of my afternoons in the Jewel Box, that big glass house where they raise tropical flowers.

AMANDA: You did all this to deceive me, just for deception?

[*Laura looks down.*] Why?

LAURA: Mother, when you're disappointed, you get that awful suffering look on your face, like the picture of Jesus' mother in the museum!

AMANDA: Hush!

LAURA: I couldn't face it.

[*There is a pause. A whisper of strings is heard. Legend on screen:* "The Crust of Humility."]

AMANDA: [*hopelessly fingering the huge pocketbook*]: So what are we going to do the rest of our lives? Stay home and watch the parades go by? Amuse ourselves with the glass menagerie, darling? Eternally play those worn-out phonograph records your father left as a painful reminder of him? We won't have a business career—we've given that up because it gave us nervous indigestion! [*She laughs wearily.*] What is there left but dependency all our lives? I know so well what becomes of unmarried women who aren't prepared to occupy a position. I've seen such pitiful cases in the South—barely tolerated spinsters living upon the grudging patronage of sister's husband or brother's wife!—stuck away in some little mousetrap of a room—encouraged by one in-law to visit another—little birdlike women without any nest—eating the crust of humility all their life! Is that the future that we've mapped out for ourselves? I swear it's the only alternative I can think of! [*She pauses.*] It isn't a very pleasant alternative, is it? [*She pauses again.*] Of course—some girls *do marry*.

[*Laura twists her hands nervously.*]

Haven't you ever liked some boy?

LAURA: Yes. I liked one once. [*She rises.*] I came across his picture a while ago.

AMANDA: [*with some interest*]: He gave you his picture?

LAURA: No, it's in the yearbook.

AMANDA: [*disappointed*]: Oh—a high school boy.

[*Screen image:* Jim as the high school hero bearing a silver cup.]

LAURA: Yes. His name was Jim. [*She lifts the heavy annual from the claw-foot table.*] Here he is in *The Pirates of Penzance*.

AMANDA: [*absently*]: The what?

LAURA: The operetta the senior class put on. He had a wonderful voice and we sat across the aisle from each other Mondays, Wednesdays and Fridays in the Aud. Here he is with the silver cup for debating! See his grin?

AMANDA: [*absently*]: He must have had a jolly disposition.

LAURA: He used to call me—Blue Roses.

[*Screen image:* Blue roses.]

AMANDA: Why did he call you such a name as that?

LAURA: When I had that attack of pleurosis—he asked me what was the matter when I came back. I said pleurosis—he thought I said Blue Roses! So that's what he always called me after that. Whenever he saw me, he'd holler, "Hello, Blue Roses!" I didn't care for the girl that he went out with. Emily Meisenbach. Emily was the best-dressed girl at Soldan. She never struck me, though, as being sincere . . . It says in the Personal Section—they're engaged. That's—six years ago! They must be married by now.

AMANDA: Girls that aren't cut out for business careers usually wind up married to some nice man. [*She gets up with a spark of revival.*] Sister, that's what you'll do!

[*Laura utters a startled, doubtful laugh. She reaches quickly for a piece of glass.*]

LAURA: But, Mother—

AMANDA: Yes? [*She goes over to the phonograph.*]

LAURA: [*in a tone of frightened apology*]: I'm—crippled!

AMANDA: Nonsense! Laura, I've told you never, never to use that word. Why, you're not crippled, you just have a little defect—hardly noticeable, even! When people have some slight disadvantage like that, they cultivate other things to make up for it—develop charm—and vivacity—and—*charm!* That's all you have to do! [*She turns again to the phonograph.*] One thing your father had *plenty of*— was *charm!*

[*The scene fades out with music.*]

SCENE THREE

Legend on screen: "After the fiasco—"

Tom speaks from the fire escape landing.

TOM: After the fiasco at Rubicam's Business College, the idea of getting a gentleman caller for Laura began to play a more and more important part in Mother's calculations. It became an obsession. Like some archetype of the universal unconscious, the image of the gentleman caller haunted our small apartment. . . .

[*Screen image:* A young man at the door of a house with flowers.]

An evening at home rarely passed without some allusion to this image, this specter, this hope. . . . Even when he wasn't mentioned, his presence hung in Mother's preoccupied look and in my sister's frightened, apologetic manner— hung like a sentence passed upon the Wingfields!

Mother was a woman of action as well as words. She began to take logical steps in the planned direction. Late that winter and in the early spring—realizing that extra money would be needed to properly feather the nest and plume the bird— she conducted a vigorous campaign on the telephone, roping in subscribers to one of those magazines for matrons called *The Homemaker's Companion,* the type of journal that features the serialized sublimations of ladies of letters who think in terms of delicate cuplike breasts, slim, tapering waists, rich, creamy thighs, eyes like wood smoke in autumn, fingers that soothe and caress like strains of music, bodies as powerful as Etruscan sculpture.

[*Screen image:* The cover of a glamor magazine.]

[*Amanda enters with the telephone on a long extension cord. She is spotlighted in the dim stage.*]

AMANDA: Ida Scott? This is Amanda Wingfield! We *missed* you at the D.A.R. last Monday! I said to myself: She's probably suffering with that sinus condition! How is that sinus condition?

Horrors! Heaven have mercy!—You're a Christian martyr, yes, that's what you are, a Christian martyr!

Well, I just now happened to notice that your subscription to the *Companion's* about to expire! Yes, it expires with the next issue, honey!—just when that wonderful new serial by Bessie Mae Hopper is getting off to such an exciting start. Oh, honey, it's something that you can't miss! You remember how *Gone with the Wind* took everybody by storm? You simply couldn't go out if you hadn't read it. All everybody *talked* was Scarlett O'Hara. Well, this is a book that critics already compare to *Gone with the Wind*. It's the *Gone with the Wind* of the post-World-War generation!—What?—Burning?—Oh, honey, don't let them burn, go take a look in the oven and I'll hold the wire! Heavens—I think she's hung up!

[*The scene dims out.*]

[*Legend on screen:* "You think I'm in love with Continental Shoemakers?"]

[*Before the lights come up again, the violent voices of Tom and Amanda are heard. They are quarrelling behind the portieres. In front of them stands Laura with clenched hands and panicky expression. A clear pool of light is on her figure throughout this scene.*]

TOM: What in Christ's name am I—

AMANDA: [*shrilly*]: Don't you use that—

TOM: —supposed to do!

AMANDA: —expression! Not in my—

TOM: Ohhh!

AMANDA: —presence! Have you gone out of your senses?

TOM: I have, that's true, *driven* out!

AMANDA: What is the matter with you, you—big—big—IDIOT!

TOM: Look!—I've got *no thing*, no single thing—

AMANDA: Lower your voice!

TOM: —in my life here that I can call my OWN! Everything is—

AMANDA: Stop that shouting!

TOM: Yesterday you confiscated my books! You had the nerve to—

AMANDA: I took that horrible novel back to the library—yes! That hideous book by that insane Mr. Lawrence.

[*Tom laughs wildly.*]

I cannot control the output of diseased minds or people who cater to them—

[*Tom laughs still more wildly.*]

BUT I WON'T ALLOW SUCH FILTH BROUGHT INTO MY HOUSE! No, no, no, no, no!

TOM: House, house! Who pays rent on it, who makes a slave of himself to—

AMANDA: [*fairly screeching*]: Don't you DARE to—

TOM: No, no, *I* mustn't say things! *I've* got to just—

AMANDA: Let me tell you—

TOM: I don't want to hear any more!

[*He tears the portieres open. The dining-room area is lit with a turgid smoky red glow. Now we see Amanda; her hair is in metal curlers and she is wearing a very old bathrobe, much too large for her slight figure, a relic of the faithless Mr. Wingfield. The upright typewriter now stands on the drop-leaf table, along with a wild disarray of manuscripts. The quarrel was probably precipitated by Amanda's interruption of Tom's creative labor.*]

A chair lies overthrown on the floor. Their gesticulating shadows are cast on the ceiling by the fiery glow.]

AMANDA: You *will* hear more, you—

TOM: No, I won't hear more, I'm going out!

AMANDA: You come right back in—

TOM: Out, out, out! Because I'm—

AMANDA: Come back here, Tom Wingfield! I'm not through talking to you!

TOM; Oh, go—

LAURA: [*desperately*]:—Tom!

AMANDA: You're going to listen, and no more insolence from you! I'm at the end of my patience!

[*He comes back toward her.*]

TOM: What do you think I'm at? Aren't I supposed to have any patience to reach the end of, Mother? I know, I know. It seems unimportant to you, what I'm *doing*—what I *want* to do—having a little *difference* between them! You don't think that—

AMANDA: I think you've been doing things that you're ashamed of. That's why you act like this. I don't believe that you go every night to the movies. Nobody goes to the movies night after night. Nobody in their right minds goes to the movies as often as you pretend to. People don't go to the movies at nearly midnight, and movies don't let out at two A.M. Come in stumbling. Muttering to yourself like a maniac! You get three hours' sleep and then go to work. Oh, I can picture the way you're doing down there. Moping, doping, because you're in no condition.

TOM: [*wildly*]: No, I'm in no condition!

AMANDA: What right have you got to jeopardize your job? Jeopardize the security of us all? How do you think we'd manage if you were—

TOM: Listen! You think I'm crazy about the *warehouse*? [*He bends fiercely toward her slight figure.*] You think I'm in love with the Continental Shoemakers? You think I want to spend fifty-five *years* down there in that—*celotex interior!* with—*fluorescent—tubes!* I'd rather somebody picked up a crowbar and battered out my brains—than go back mornings! I *go!* Every time you come in yelling that Goddamn *"Rise and Shine!" "Rise and Shine!"* I say to myself. "How *lucky dead* people are!" But I get up. I *go!* For sixty-five dollars a month I give up all that I dream of doing and being *ever!* And you say self—*self's* all I ever think of. Why, listen, if self is what I thought of, Mother, I'd be where he is—GONE! [*He points to his father's picture.*] As far as the system of transportation reaches! [*He starts past her. She grabs his arm.*] Don't grab at me, Mother!

AMANDA: Where are you going?

TOM: I'm going to the *movies!*

AMANDA: I don't believe that lie!

[*Tom crouches toward her, overtowering her tiny figure. She backs away, gasping.*]

TOM: I'm going to opium dens! Yes, opium dens, dens of vice and criminals' hangouts, Mother. I've joined the Hogan Gang, I'm a hired assassin, I carry a tommy gun in a violin case! I run a string of cat houses in the Valley! They call me Killer, Killer Wingfield, I'm leading a double-life, a simple, honest warehouse worker by day, by night a dynamic *czar* of the *underworld, Mother.* I go to gambling casinos, I spin away fortunes on the roulette table! I wear a patch over one eye and a false mustache, sometimes I put on green whiskers. On those occasions they call me—*El Diablo!*[1] Oh, I could tell you many things to make you sleepless!

---

[1]Spanish: "The Devil!"

My enemies plan to dynamite this place. They're going to blow us all sky-high some night! I'll be glad, very happy, and so will you! You'll go up, up on a broomstick, over Blue Mountain with seventeen gentlemen callers! You ugly— babbling old—*witch*. . . .

[*He goes through a series of violent, clumsy movements, seizing his overcoat, lunging to the door, pulling it fiercely open. The women watch him, aghast. His arm catches in the sleeve of the coat as he struggles to pull it on. For a moment he is pinioned by the bulky garment. With an outraged groan he tears the coat off again, splitting the shoulder of it, and hurls it across the room. It strikes against the shelf of Laura's glass collection, and there is a tinkle of shattering glass. Laura cries out as if wounded.*]

[*Music.*]

[*Screen legend:* "The Glass Menagerie."]

LAURA: [*shrilly*]: My glass!—menagerie. . . . [*She covers her face and turns away.*]

[*But Amanda is still stunned and stupefied by the "ugly witch" so that she barely notices this occurrence. Now she recovers her speech.*]

AMANDA: [*in an awful voice*]: I won't speak to you—until you apologize!

[*She crosses through the portieres and draws them together behind her. Tom is left with Laura. Laura clings weakly to the mantel with her face averted. Tom stares at her stupidly for a moment. Then he crosses to the shelf. He drops awkwardly on his knees to collect the fallen glass, glancing at Laura as if he would speak but couldn't.*]

[*"The Glass Menagerie" music steals in as the scene dims out.*]

SCENE FOUR

The interior of the apartment is dark. There is a faint light in the alley. A deep-voiced bell in a church is tolling the hour of five.

Tom appears at the top of the alley. After each solemn boom of the bell in the tower, he shakes a little noisemaker or rattle as if to express the tiny spasm of man in contrast to the sustained power and dignity of the Almighty. This and the unsteadiness of his advance make it evident that he has been drinking. As he climbs the few steps to the fire escape landing light steals up inside. Laura appears in the front room in a nightdress. She notices that Tom's bed is empty. Tom fishes in his pockets for his door key, removing a motley assortment of articles in his search, including a shower of movie ticket stubs and an empty bottle. At last he finds the key, but just as he is about to insert it, it slips from his fingers. He strikes a match and crouches below the door.

TOM: [*bitterly*]: One crack—and it falls through!

[*Laura opens the door.*]

LAURA: Tom! Tom, what are you doing?

TOM: Looking for a door key.

LAURA: Where have you been all this time?

TOM: I have been to the movies.

LAURA: All this time at the movies?

TOM: There was a very long program. There was a Garbo picture and a Mickey Mouse and a travelogue and a newsreel and a preview of coming attractions. And there was an organ solo and a collection for the Milk Fund—simultane-ously—which ended up in a terrible fight between a fat lady and an usher!

LAURA: [*innocently*]: Did you have to stay through everything?

TOM: Of course! And, oh, I forgot! There was a big stage show! The headliner on this stage show was Malvolio the Magician. He performed wonderful tricks, many of them, such as pouring water back and forth between pitchers. First it turned to wine and then it turned to beer and then it turned to whisky. I know it was whisky it finally turned into because he needed somebody to come up out of the audience to help him, and I came up—both shows! It was Kentucky Straight Bourbon. A very generous fellow, he gave souvenirs. [*He pulls from his back pocket a shimmering rainbow-colored scarf.*] He gave me this. This is his magic scarf. You can have it, Laura. You wave it over a canary cage and you get a bowl of goldfish. You wave it over the goldfish bowl and they fly away canaries. . . . But the wonderfullest trick of all was the coffin trick. We nailed him into a coffin and he got out of the coffin without removing one nail. [*He has come inside.*] There is a trick that would come in handy for me—get me out of this two-by-four situation! [*He flops on the bed and starts removing his shoes.*]

LAURA: Tom—shhh!

TOM: What're you shushing me for?

LAURA: You'll wake up Mother.

TOM: Goody, goody! Pay'er back for all those "Rise an' Shines." [*He lies down, groaning.*] You know it don't take much intelligence to get yourself into a nailed-up coffin, Laura. But who the hell ever got himself out of one without removing one nail?

[*As if in answer, the father's grinning photograph lights up. The scene dims out.*]

[*Immediately following, the church bell is heard striking six. At the sixth stroke the alarm clock goes off in Amanda's room, and after a few moments we hear her calling: "Rise and Shine! Rise and Shine! Laura, go tell you brother to rise and shine!"*]

TOM: [*sitting up slowly*]: I'll rise—but I won't shine.

[*The light increases.*]

AMANDA: Laura, tell your brother his coffee is ready.

[*Laura slips into the front room.*]

LAURA: Tom!—It's nearly seven. Don't make Mother nervous.

[*He stares at her stupidly.*]

[*beseechingly:*] Tom, speak to Mother this morning. Make up with her, apologize, speak to her!

TOM: She won't to me. It's her that started not speaking.

LAURA: If you just say you're sorry she'll start speaking.

TOM: Her not speaking—is that such a tragedy?

LAURA: Please—please!

AMANDA: [*calling from the kitchenette*]: Laura, are you going to do what I asked you to do, or do I have to get dressed and go out myself?

LAURA: Going, going—soon as I get on my coat!

[*She pulls on a shapeless felt hat with a nervous, jerky movement, pleadingly glancing at Tom. She rushes awkwardly for her coat. The coat is one of Amanda's inaccurately made-over, the sleeves too short for Laura.*]

Butter and what else?

AMANDA: [*entering from the kitchenette*]: Just butter. Tell them to charge it.

LAURA: Mother, they make such faces when I do that.

AMANDA: Sticks and stones can break our bones, but the expression on Mr. Garfinkel's face won't harm us! Tell you brother his coffee is getting cold.

LAURA: [*at the door*]: Do what I asked you, will you, will you, Tom?

[*He looks sullenly away.*]

AMANDA: Laura, go now or just don't go at all!

LAURA: [*rushing out*]: Going—going!

[*A second later she cries out. Tom springs up and crosses to the door. Tom opens the door.*]

TOM: Laura?

LAURA: I'm all right. I slipped, but I'm all right.

AMANDA: [*peering anxiously after her*]: If anyone breaks a leg on those fire-escape steps, the landlord ought to be sued for every cent he possesses! [*She shuts the door. Now she remembers she isn't speaking to Tom and returns to the other room.*]

[*As Tom comes listlessly for his coffee, she turns her back to him and stands rigidly facing the window on the gloomy gray vault of the areaway. Its light on her face with its aged but childish features is cruelly sharp, satirical as a Daumier[1] print.*]

[*The music of "Ave Maria" is heard softly.*]

[*Tom glances sheepishly but sullenly at her averted figure and slumps at the table. The coffee is scalding hot; he sips it and gasps and spits it back in the cup. At his gasp, Amanda catches her breath and half turns. Then she catches herself and turns back to the window. Tom blows on his coffee, glancing sidewise at his mother. She clears her throat. Tom clears his. He starts to rise, sinks back down again, scratches his head, clears his throat again. Amanda coughs. Tom raises his cup in both hands to blow on it, his eyes staring over the rim of it at his mother for several moments. Then he slowly sets the cup down and awkwardly and hesitantly rises from the chair.*]

TOM: [*hoarsely*]: Mother. I—I apologize, Mother.

[*Amanda draws a quick, shuddering breath. Her face works grotesquely. She breaks into childlike tears.*]

I'm sorry for what I said, for everything that I said, I didn't mean it.

AMANDA: [*sobbingly*]: My devotion has made me a witch and so I make myself hateful to my children!

TOM: No, you *don't*.

AMANDA: I worry so much, don't sleep, it makes me nervous!

TOM: [*gently*]: I understand that.

AMANDA: I've had to put up a solitary battle all these years. But you're my right-hand bower! Don't fall down, don't fail!

TOM: [*gently*]: I try, Mother.

AMANDA: [*with great enthusiasm*]: Try and you will *succeed!* [*The notion makes her breathless.*] Why, you—you're just *full* of natural endowments! Both of my children—they're *unusual* children! Don't you think I know it? I'm so—*proud!* Happy and—feel I've—so much to be thankful for but—promise me one thing, son!

TOM: What, Mother?

AMANDA: Promise, son, you'll—never be a drunkard!

TOM: [*turns to her grinning*]: I will never be a drunkard, Mother.

AMANDA: That's what frightened me so, that you'd be drinking! Eat a bowl of Purina!

TOM: Just coffee, Mother.

AMANDA: Shredded wheat biscuit?

TOM: No. No, Mother, just coffee.

AMANDA: You can't put in a day's work on an empty stomach. You've got ten minutes—don't gulp! Drinking too-hot liquids makes cancer of the stomach. . . . Put cream in.

TOM: No, thank you.

AMANDA: To cool it.

TOM: No! No, thank you, I want it black.

AMANDA: I know, but it's not good for you. We have to do all that we can to build ourselves up. In these trying times we live in, all that we have to cling to

---

[1]Honoré Daumier (1808–1879), French caricaturist and painter.

is—each other. . . . That's why it's important to—Tom, I—I sent out your sister so I could discuss something with you. If you hadn't spoken I would have spoken to you. [*She sits down.*]

TOM: [*gently*]: What is it, Mother, that you want to discuss?

AMANDA: *Laura!*

[*Tom puts his cup down slowly.*]

[*Legend on screen:* "Laura." *Music:* "The Glass Menagerie."]

TOM: —Oh.—Laura . . .

AMANDA [*touching his sleeve*]: You know how Laura is. So quiet but—still water runs deep! She notices things and I think she—broods about them.

[*Tom looks up.*]

A few days ago I came in and she was crying.

TOM: What about?

AMANDA: You.

TOM: Me?

AMANDA: She has an idea that you're not happy here.

TOM: What gave her that idea?

AMANDA: What gives her any idea? However, you do act strangely. I—I'm not criticizing, understand *that!* I know your ambitions do not lie in the warehouse, that like everybody in the whole wide world—you've had to—make sacrifices, but—Tom—Tom—life's not easy, it calls for—Spartan endurance! There's so many things in my heart that I cannot describe to you! I've never told you but I—*loved* your father. . . .

TOM: [*gently*]: I know that, Mother.

AMANDA: And you—when I see you taking after his ways! Staying out late—and—well, you *had* been drinking the night you were in that—terrifying condition! Laura says that you hate the apartment and that you go out nights to get away from it! Is that true, Tom?

TOM: No. You say there's so much in your heart that you can't describe to me. That's true of me, too. There's so much in my heart that I can't describe to *you!* So let's respect each other's—

AMANDA: But, why—*why,* Tom—are you always so *restless?* Where do you *go* to, nights?

TOM: I—go to the movies.

AMANDA: Why do you go to the movies so much, Tom?

TOM: I go to the movies because—I like adventure. Adventure is something I don't have much of at work, so I go to the movies.

AMANDA: But, Tom, you go to the movies *entirely* too *much!*

TOM: I like a lot of adventure.

[*Amanda looks baffled, then hurt. As the familiar inquisition resumes, Tom becomes hard and impatient again. Amanda slips back into her querulous attitude toward him.*]

[*Image on screen:* A sailing vessel with Jolly Roger.]

AMANDA: Most young men find adventure in their careers.

TOM: Then most young men are not employed in a warehouse.

AMANDA: The world is full of young men employed in warehouses and offices and factories.

TOM: Do all of them find adventure in their careers?

AMANDA: They do or they do without it! Not everybody has a craze for adventure.

TOM: Man is by instinct a lover, a hunter, a fighter, and none of those instincts are given much play at the warehouse!

AMANDA: Man is by instinct! Don't quote instinct to me! Instinct is something that people have got away from! It belongs to animals! Christian adults don't want it!

TOM: What do Christian adults want, then, Mother?

AMANDA: Superior things! Things of the mind and the spirit! Only animals have to satisfy instincts! Surely your aims are somewhat higher than theirs! Than monkeys—pigs—

TOM: I reckon they're not.

AMANDA: You're joking. However, that isn't what I wanted to discuss.

TOM: [*rising*]: I haven't much time.

AMANDA: [*pushing his shoulders*]: Sit down.

TOM: You want me to punch in red at the warehouse, Mother?

AMANDA: You have five minutes. I want to talk about Laura.

[*Screen legend:* "Plans and Provisions."]

TOM: All right! What about Laura?

AMANDA: We have to be making some plans and provisions for her. She's older than you, two years, and nothing has happened. She just drifts along doing nothing. It frightens me terribly how she just drifts along.

TOM: I guess she's the type that people call home girls.

AMANDA: There's no such type, and if there is, it's a pity! That is unless the home is hers, with a husband!

TOM: What?

AMANDA: Oh, I can see the handwriting on the wall as plain as I see the nose in front of my face! It's terrifying! More and more you remind me of your father! He was out all hours without explanation!—Then *left! Goodbye!* And me with the bag to hold. I saw that letter you got from the Merchant Marine. I know what you're dreaming of. I'm not standing here blindfolded. [*She pauses.*] Very well, then. Then *do* it! But not till there's somebody to take your place.

TOM: What do you mean?

AMANDA: I mean that as soon as Laura has got somebody to take care of her, married, a home of her own, independent—why, then you'll be free to go wherever you please, on land, on sea, whichever way the wind blows you! But until that time you've got to look out for your sister. I don't say me because I'm old and don't matter! I say for your sister because she's young and dependent.

I put her in business college—a dismal failure! Frightened her so it made her stick at the stomach. I took her over to the Young People's League at the church. Another fiasco. She spoke to nobody, nobody spoke to her. Now all she does is fool with those pieces of glass and play those worn-out records. What kind of a life is that for a girl to lead?

TOM: What can I do about it?

AMANDA: Overcome selfishness! Self, self, self is all that you ever think of!

[*Tom springs up and crosses to get his coat. It is ugly and bulky. He pulls on a cap with earmuffs.*]

Where is your muffler? Put your wool muffler on!

[*He snatches it angrily from the closet, tosses it around his neck and pulls both ends tight.*]

Tom! I haven't said what I had in mind to ask you.

TOM: I'm too late to—

AMANDA: [*catching his arm—very importunately; then shyly*]: Down at the ware-house, aren't there some—nice young men?

TOM: No!

AMANDA: There *must* be—some . . .

TOM: Mother—[*He gestures.*]

AMANDA: Find out one that's clean-living—doesn't drink and ask him out for sister!

TOM: What?

AMANDA: For *sister!* To *meet!* Get *acquainted!*

TOM: [*stamping to the door*]: Oh, my go-osh!

AMANDA: Will you?

[*He opens the door. She says, imploringly:*]

Will you?

[*He starts down the fire escape.*]

Will you? *Will* you, dear?

TOM: [*calling back*]: Yes!

[*Amanda closes the door hesitantly and with a troubled but faintly hopeful expression.*]

[*Screen image:* The cover of a glamor magazine.]

[*The spotlight picks up Amanda at the phone.*]

AMANDA: Ella Cartwright? This is Amanda Wingfield!

How are you, honey?

How is that kidney condition?

[*There is a five-second pause.*]

Horrors!

[*There is another pause.*]

You're a Christian martyr, yes, honey, that's what you are, a Christian martyr! Well, I just now happened to notice in my little red book that your subscription to the *Companion* has just run out! I knew that you wouldn't want to miss out on the wonderful serial starting in this new issue. It's by Bessie Mae Hopper, the first thing she's written since *Honeymoon for Three.* Wasn't that a strange and interesting story? Well, this one is even lovelier, I believe. It has a sophisticated, society background. It's all about the horsey set on Long Island!

[*The light fades out.*]

SCENE FIVE

Legend on the screen: "Annunciation."

Music is heard as the light slowly comes on.

It is early dusk of a spring evening. Supper has just been finished in the Wingfield apartment. Amanda and Laura, in light-colored dresses, are removing dishes from the table in the dining room, which is shadowy, their movements formalized almost as a dance or ritual, their moving forms as pale and silent as moths. Tom, in white shirt and trousers, rises from the table and crosses toward the fire escape.

AMANDA: [*as he passes her*]: Son, will you do me a favor?

TOM: What?

AMANDA: Comb your hair! You look so pretty when your hair is combed!

[*Tom slouches on the sofa with the evening paper. Its enormous headline reads:* "Franco Triumphs."][1]

There is only one respect in which I would like you to emulate your father.

TOM: What respect is that?

AMANDA: The care he always took of his appearance. He never allowed himself to look untidy.

[1]A reference to a military victory of Francisco Franco, leader of the fascist forces in the Spanish Civil War.

[*He throws down the paper and crosses to the fire escape.*]
Where are you going?

TOM: I'm going out to smoke.

AMANDA: You smoke too much. A pack a day at fifteen cents a pack. How much would that amount to in a month? Thirty times fifteen is how much Tom? Figure it out and you will be astounded at what you could save. Enough to give you a night-school course in accounting at Washington U.! Just think what a wonderful thing that would be for you, son!

[*Tom is unmoved by the thought.*]

TOM: I'd rather smoke. [*He steps out on the landing, letting the screen door slam.*]

AMANDA: [*sharply*]: I know! That's the tragedy of it. . . . [*Alone, she turns to look at her husband's picture.*]

[*Dance music: "The World Is Waiting for the Sunrise!"*]

TOM: [*to the audience*]: Across the alley from us was the Paradise Dance Hall. On evenings in spring the windows and doors were open and the music came outdoors. Sometimes the lights were turned out except for a large glass sphere that hung from the ceiling. It would turn slowly about and filter the dusk with delicate rainbow colors. Then the orchestra played a waltz or a tango, something that had a slow and sensuous rhythm. Couples would come outside, to the relative privacy of the alley. You could see them kissing behind ash pits and telephone poles. This was the compensation for lives that passed like mine, without any change or adventure. Adventure and change were imminent in this year. They were waiting around the corner for all these kids. Suspended in the midst over Berchtesgaden, caught in the folds of Chamberlain's umbrella.[2] In Spain there was Guernica! But here there was only hot swing music and liquor, dance halls, bars, and movies, and sex that hung in the gloom like a chandelier and flooded the world with brief, deceptive rainbows. . . . All the world was waiting for bombardments!

[*Amanda turns from the picture and comes outside.*]

AMANDA: [*sighing*]: A fire escape landing's a poor excuse for a porch. [*She spreads a newspaper on a step and sits down, gracefully and demurely as if she were settling into a swing on a Mississippi veranda.*] What are you looking at?

TOM: The moon.

AMANDA: Is there a moon this evening?

TOM: It's rising over Garfinkel's Delicatessen.

AMANDA: So it is! A little silver slipper of a moon. Have you made a wish on it yet?

TOM: Um-hum.

AMANDA: What did you wish for?

TOM: That's a secret.

AMANDA: A secret, huh? Well, I won't tell mine either. I will be just as mysterious as you.

TOM: I bet I can guess what yours is.

AMANDA: Is my head so transparent?

TOM: You're not a sphinx.

AMANDA: No, I don't have secrets. I'll tell you what I wished for on the moon. Success and happiness for my precious children! I wish for that whenever there's a moon, and when there isn't a moon, I wish for it, too.

---

[2]Near Berchtesgaden, Germany, Neville Chamberlain, the Prime Minister of Great Britain (1937–1940), met with Adolf Hitler in a futile effort to avoid World War II. On his return to England, he declared that he had arranged for "peace in our time." Because of his folly, Chamberlain and the umbrella that he carried subsequently became symbols of the foolish appeasement of evil.

TOM: I thought perhaps you wished for a gentleman caller.

AMANDA: Why do you say that?

TOM: Don't you remember asking me to fetch one?

AMANDA: I remember suggesting that it would be nice for your sister if you brought home some nice young man from the warehouse. I think that I've made that suggestion more than once.

TOM: Yes, you have made it repeatedly.

AMANDA: Well?

TOM: We are going to have one.

AMANDA: *What?*

TOM: A gentleman caller!

[*The annunciation is celebrated with music.*]

[*Amanda rises.*]

[*Image on screen:* A caller with a bouquet.]

AMANDA: You mean you have asked some nice young man to come over?

TOM: Yep. I've asked him to dinner.

AMANDA: You really did?

TOM: I did!

AMANDA: You did, and did he—*accept?*

TOM: He did!

AMANDA: Well, well—well, well! That's—lovely!

TOM: I thought that you would be pleased.

AMANDA: It's definite then?

TOM: Very definite.

AMANDA: Soon?

TOM: Very soon.

AMANDA: For heaven's sake, stop putting on and tell me some things, will you?

TOM: What things do you want me to tell you?

AMANDA: *Naturally* I would like to know when he's *coming!*

TOM: He's coming tomorrow.

AMANDA: *Tomorrow?*

TOM: Yep. Tomorrow.

AMANDA: But, Tom!

TOM: Yes, Mother?

AMANDA: Tomorrow gives me no time!

TOM: Time for what?

AMANDA: Preparations! Why didn't you phone me at once, as soon as you asked him, the minute that he accepted? Then, don't you see, I could have been getting ready!

TOM: You don't have to make any fuss.

AMANDA: Oh, Tom, Tom, Tom, of course I have to make a fuss! I want things nice, not sloppy! Not thrown together. I'll certainly have to do some fast thinking, won't I?

TOM: I don't see why you have to think at all.

AMANDA: You just don't know. We can't have a gentleman caller in a pigsty! All my wedding silver has to be polished, the monogrammed table linen ought to be laundered! The windows have to be washed and fresh curtains put up. And how about clothes? We have to *wear* something, don't we?

TOM: Mother, this boy is no one to make a fuss over!

AMANDA: Do you realize he's the first young man we've introduced to your sister? It's terrible, dreadful, disgraceful that poor little sister has never received a single gentleman caller! Tom, come inside!

[*She opens the screen door.*]

TOM: What for?

AMANDA: I want to ask you some things.

TOM: If you're going to make such a fuss, I'll call it off, I'll tell him not to come!

AMANDA: You certainly won't do anything of the kind. Nothing offends people worse than broken engagements. It simply means I'll have to work like a Turk! We won't be brilliant, but we will pass inspection. Come on inside.

[*Tom follows her inside, groaning.*]

Sit down.

TOM: Any particular place you would like me to sit?

AMANDA: Thank heavens I've got that new sofa! I'm also making payments on a floor lamp I'll have sent out! And put the chintz covers on, they'll brighten things up! Of course I'd hoped to have these walls re-papered. . . . What is the young man's name?

TOM: His name is O'Connor.

AMANDA: That, of course, means fish—tomorrow is Friday! I'll have that salmon loaf—with Durkee's dressing! What does he do? He works at the warehouse?

TOM: Of course! How else would I—

AMANDA: Tom, he—doesn't drink?

TOM: Why do you ask me that?

AMANDA: Your father *did!*

TOM: Don't get started on that!

AMANDA: He *does* drink, then?

TOM: Not that I know of!

AMANDA: Make sure, be certain! The last thing I want for my daughter's a boy who drinks!

TOM: Aren't you being a little bit premature? Mr. O'Connor has not yet appeared on the scene!

AMANDA: But will tomorrow. To meet your sister, and what do I know about his character? Nothing! Old maids are better off than wives of drunkards!

TOM: Oh, my God!

AMANDA: Be still!

TOM [*leaning forward to whisper*]: Lots of fellows meet girls whom they don't marry!

AMANDA: Oh, talk sensibly, Tom—and don't be sarcastic! [*She has gotten a hairbrush.*]

TOM: What are you doing?

AMANDA: I'm brushing that cowlick down! [*She attacks his hair with the brush.*] What is this young man's position at the warehouse?

TOM [*submitting grimly to the brush and the interrogation*]: This young man's position is that of a shipping clerk, Mother.

AMANDA: Sounds to me like a fairly responsible job, the sort of a job *you* would be in if you just had more *get-up*. What is his salary? Have you any idea?

TOM: I would judge it to be approximately eighty-five dollars a month.

AMANDA: Well—not princely, but—

TOM: Twenty more than I make.

AMANDA: Yes, how well I know! But for a family man, eighty-five dollars a month is not much more than you can just get by on. . . .

TOM: Yes, but Mr. O'Connor is not a family man.

AMANDA: He might be, mightn't he? Some time in the future?

TOM: I see. Plans and provisions.

AMANDA: You are the only young man that I know of who ignores the fact that the future becomes the present, the present the past, and the past turns into everlasting regret if you don't plan for it!

TOM: I will think that over and see what I can make of it.

AMANDA: Don't be supercilious with your mother! Tell me some more about this—what do you call him?

TOM: James D. O'Connor. The D. is for Delaney.

AMANDA: Irish on *both* sides! *Gracious!* And doesn't drink?

TOM: Shall I call him up and ask him right this minute?

AMANDA: The only way to find out about those things is to make discreet inquiries at the proper moment. When I was a girl in Blue Mountain and it was suspected that a young man drank, the girl whose attentions he had been receiving, if any girl *was*, would sometimes speak to the minister of his church, or rather her father would if her father was living, and sort of feel him out on the young man's character. That is the way such things are discreetly handled to keep a young woman from making a tragic mistake!

TOM: Then how did you happen to make a tragic mistake?

AMANDA: That innocent look of your father's had everyone fooled! He *smiled*— the world was *enchanted!* No girl can do worse than put herself at the mercy of a handsome appearance! I hope that Mr. O'Connor is not too good-looking.

TOM: No, he's not too good-looking. He's covered with freckles and hasn't too much of a nose.

AMANDA: He's not right-down homely, though?

TOM: Not right-down homely. Just medium homely, I'd say.

AMANDA: Character's what to look for in a man.

TOM: That's what I've always said, Mother.

AMANDA: You've never said anything of the kind and I suspect you would never give it a thought.

TOM: Don't be so suspicious of me.

AMANDA: At least I hope he's the type that's up and coming.

TOM: I think he really goes in for self-improvement.

AMANDA: What reason have you to think so?

TOM: He goes to night school.

AMANDA: [*beaming*]: Splendid! What does he do, I mean study?

TOM: Radio engineering and public speaking!

AMANDA: Then he has visions of being advanced in the world! Any young man who studies public speaking is aiming to have an executive job some day! And radio engineering! A thing for the future! Both of these facts are very illuminating. Those are the sort of things that a mother should know concerning any young man who comes to call on her daughter. Seriously or—not.

TOM: One little warning. He doesn't know about Laura. I didn't let on that we had dark ulterior motives. I just said, why don't you come and have dinner with us? He said okay and that was the whole conversation.

AMANDA: I bet it was! You're eloquent as an oyster. However, he'll know about Laura when he gets here. When he sees how lovely and sweet and pretty she is, he'll thank his lucky stars he was asked to dinner.

TOM: Mother, you mustn't expect too much of Laura.

AMANDA: What do you mean?

TOM: Laura seems all those things to you and me because she's ours and we love her. We don't even notice she's crippled any more.

AMANDA: Don't say crippled! You know that I never allow that word to be used!

TOM: But face facts, Mother. She is and—that's not all—

AMANDA: What do you mean "not all"?

TOM: Laura is very different from other girls.

AMANDA: I think the difference is to her advantage.

TOM: Not quite all—in the eyes of others—strangers—she's terribly shy and lives in a world of her own and those things make her seem a little peculiar to people outside the house.

AMANDA: Don't say peculiar.

TOM: Face the facts. She is.

[*The dance hall music changes to a tango that has a minor and somewhat ominous tone.*]

AMANDA: In what way is she peculiar—may I ask?

TOM: [*gently*]: She lives in a world of her own—a world of little glass ornaments, Mother. . . .

[*He gets up. Amanda remains holding the brush, looking at him, troubled.*]

She plays old phonograph records and—that's about all—[*He glances at himself in the mirror and crosses to the door.*]

AMANDA: [*sharply*]: Where are you going?

TOM: I'm going to the movies. [*He goes out the screen door.*]

AMANDA: Not to the movies, every night to the movies! [*She follows quickly to the screen door.*] I don't believe you always go to the movies!

[*He is gone. Amanda looks worriedly after him for a moment. Then vitality and optimism return and she turns from the door, crossing the portieres.*]

Laura! Laura!

[*Laura answers from the kitchenette.*]

LAURA: Yes, Mother.

AMANDA: Let those dishes go and come in front!

[*Laura appears with a dish towel. Amanda speaks to her gaily.*]

Laura, come here and make a wish on the moon!

[*Screen image:* The Moon.]

LAURA [*entering*]: Moon—moon?

AMANDA: A little silver slipper of a moon. Look over your left shoulder, Laura, and make a wish!

[*Laura looks faintly puzzled as if called out of sleep. Amanda seizes her shoulders and turns her at an angle by the door.*]

Now! Now, darling, *wish!*

LAURA: What shall I wish for, Mother?

AMANDA [*her voice trembling and her eyes suddenly filling with tears*]: Happiness! Good fortune!

[*The sound of the violin rises and the stage dims out.*]

SCENE SIX

The light comes up on the fire escape landing. Tom is leaning against the grill, smoking.

[*Screen image:* The high school hero.]

TOM: And so the following evening I brought Jim home to dinner. I had known Jim slightly in high school. In high school Jim was a hero. He had tremendous Irish good nature and vitality with the scrubbed and polished look of white chinaware. He seemed to move in a continual spotlight. He was a star in basketball, captain of the debating club, president of the senior class and the glee club and he sang the lead in the annual light operas. He was always running or bounding, never just walking. He seemed always at the point of defeating the law of gravity. He was shooting with such velocity through his adolescence that you would logically expect him to arrive at nothing short of the White House by the time he was thirty. But Jim apparently ran into more interference after his graduation from Soldan. His speed had definitely slowed. Six years after he left high school he was holding a job that wasn't much better than mine.

[*Screen image:* The Clerk.]

He was the only one at the warehouse with whom I was on friendly terms. I was valuable to him as someone who could remember his former glory, who had seen him win basketball games and the silver cup in debating. He knew of my secret practice of retiring to a cabinet of the washroom to work on poems when business was slack in the warehouse. He called me Shakespeare. And while the other boys in the warehouse regarded me with suspicious hostility, Jim took a humorous attitude toward me. Gradually his attitude affected the others, their hostility wore off and they also began to smile at me as people smile at an oddly fashioned dog who trots across their path at some distance.

I knew that Jim and Laura had known each other at Soldan, and I had heard Laura speak admiringly of his voice. I didn't know if Jim remembered her or not. In high school Laura had been as unobtrusive as Jim had been astonishing. If he did remember Laura, it was not as my sister, for when I asked him to dinner, he grinned and said, "You know, Shakespeare, I never thought of you as having folks!"

He was about to discover that I did. . . .

[*Legend on screen:* "The accent of a coming foot."]

[*The light dims out on Tom and comes up in the Wingfield living room—a delicate lemony light. It is about five on a Friday evening of late spring which comes "scattering poems in the sky."*]

[*Amanda has worked like a Turk in preparation for the gentleman caller. The results are astonishing. The new floor lamp with its rose silk shade is in place, a colored paper lantern conceals the broken light fixture in the ceiling, new billowing white curtains are at the windows, chintz covers are on the chairs and sofa, a pair of new sofa pillows make their initial appearance. Open boxes and tissue paper are scattered on the floor.*]

[*Laura stands in the middle of the room with lifted arms while Amanda crouches before her, adjusting the hem of a new dress, devout and ritualistic. The dress is colored and designed by memory. The arrangement of Laura's hair is changed; it is softer and more becoming. A fragile, unearthly prettiness has come out in Laura: she is like a piece of translucent glass touched by light, given a momentary radiance, not actual, not lasting.*]

AMANDA [*impatiently*]: Why are you trembling?

LAURA: Mother, you've made me so nervous!

AMANDA: How have I made you nervous?

LAURA: By all this fuss! You make it seem so important!

AMANDA: I don't understand you, Laura. You couldn't be satisfied with just sitting home, and yet whenever I try to arrange something for you, you seem to resist it. [*She gets up.*] Now take a look at yourself. No, wait! Wait just a moment—I have an idea!

LAURA: What is it now?

[*Amanda produces two powder puffs which she wraps in handkerchiefs and stuffs in Laura's bosom.*]

LAURA: Mother, what are you doing?

AMANDA: They call them "Gay Deceivers"!

LAURA: I won't wear them!

AMANDA: You will!

LAURA: Why should I?

AMANDA: Because, to be painfully honest, your chest is flat.

LAURA: You make it seem like we were setting a trap.

AMANDA: All pretty girls are a trap, a pretty trap, and men expect them to be.
[*Legend on screen:* "A pretty trap."]
Now look at yourself, young lady. This is the prettiest you will ever be! [*She stands back to admire Laura.*] I've got to fix myself now! You're going to be surprised by your mother's appearance!
[*Amanda crosses through the portieres, humming gaily. Laura moves slowly to the long mirror and stares solemnly at herself. A wind blows the white curtains inward in a slow, graceful motion and with a faint, sorrowful sighing.*]

AMANDA: [*from somewhere behind the portieres*] It isn't dark enough yet.
[*Laura turns slowly before the mirror with a troubled look.*]
[*Legend on screen:* "This is my sister: Celebrate her with strings!" *Music plays.*]

AMANDA: [*laughing, still not visible*]: I'm going to show you something. I'm going to make a spectacular appearance!

LAURA: What is it, Mother?

AMANDA: Possess your soul in patience—you will see! Something I've resurrected from that old trunk! Styles haven't changed so terribly much after all. . . .
[*She parts the portieres.*] Now just look at your mother! [*She wears a girlish frock of yellowed voile with a blue silk sash. She carries a bunch of jonquils—the legend of her youth is nearly revived. Now she speaks feverishly:*] This is the dress in which I led the cotillion. Won the cakewalk twice at Sunset Hill, wore one Spring to the Governor's Ball in Jackson! See how I sashayed around the ballroom, Laura?
[*She raises her skirt and does a mincing step around the room.*] I wore it on Sundays for my gentlemen callers! I had it on the day I met your father. . . . I had malaria fever all that Spring. The change of climate from East Tennessee to the Delta—weakened resistance. I had a little temperature all the time—not enough to be serious—just enough to make me restless and giddy! Invitations poured in—parties all over the Delta! "Stay in bed," said Mother, "you have a fever!"—but I just wouldn't. I took quinine but kept on going, going! Evenings, dances! Afternoons, long, long rides! Picnics—lovely! So lovely, that country in May—all lacy with dogwood, literally flooded with jonquils! That was the spring I had the craze for jonquils. Jonquils became an absolute obsession. Mother said, "Honey, there's no more room for jonquils." And still I kept on bringing in more jonquils. Whenever, wherever I saw them, I'd say, "Stop! Stop! I see jonquils!" I made the young men help me gather the jonquils! It was a joke, Amanda and her jonquils. Finally there were no more vases to hold them, every available space was filled with jonquils. No vases to hold them? All right, I'll hold them myself! And then I—[*She stops in front of the picture. Music plays.*] met your father! Malaria fever and jonquils and then—this—boy. . . . [*She switches on the rose-colored lamp.*] I hope they get here before it starts to rain. [*She crosses the room and places the jonquils in a bowl on the table.*] I gave your brother a little extra change so he and Mr. O'Connor could take the service car home.

LAURA [*with an altered look*]: What did you say his name was?

AMANDA: O'Connor.

LAURA: What is his first name?

AMANDA: I don't remember. Oh, yes, I do. It was—Jim!
[*Laura sways slightly and catches hold of a chair.*]
[*Legend on screen:* "Not, Jim!"]

LAURA [*faintly*]: Not—Jim!

AMANDA: Yes, that was it, it was Jim! I've never known a Jim that wasn't nice! [*The music becomes ominous.*]

LAURA: Are you sure his name is Jim O'Connor?

AMANDA: Yes. Why?

LAURA: Is he the one that Tom used to know in high school?

AMANDA: He didn't say so. I think he just got to know him at the warehouse.

LAURA: There was a Jim O'Connor we both knew in high school—[*then, with effort*] If that is the one that Tom is bringing to dinner—you'll have to excuse me, I won't come to the table.

AMANDA: What sort of nonsense is this?

LAURA: You asked me once if I'd ever liked a boy. Don't you remember I showed you this boy's picture?

AMANDA: You mean the boy you showed me in the year-book?

LAURA: Yes, that boy.

AMANDA: Laura, Laura, were you in love with that boy?

LAURA: I don't know, Mother. All I know is I couldn't sit at the table if it was him!

AMANDA: It won't be him! It isn't the least bit likely. But whether it is or not, you will come to the table. You will not be excused.

LAURA: I'll have to be, Mother.

AMANDA: I don't intend to humor your silliness, Laura. I've had too much from you and your brother, both! So just sit down and compose yourself till they come. Tom has forgotten his key so you'll have to let them in, when they arrive.

LAURA [*panicky*]: Oh, Mother—*you* answer the door!

AMANDA [*lightly*]: I'll be in the kitchen—busy!

LAURA: Oh, Mother, please answer the door, don't make me do it!

AMANDA [*crossing into the kitchenette*]: I've got to fix the dressing for the salmon. Fuss, fuss—silliness!—over a gentleman caller!

[*The door swings shut. Laura is left alone.*]

[*Legend on screen:* "Terror!"]

[*She utters a low moan and turns off the lamp—sits stiffly on the edge of the sofa, knotting her fingers together.*]

[*Legend on screen:* "The Opening of a Door!"]

[*Tom and Jim appear on the fire escape steps and climb to the landing. Hearing their approach, Laura rises with a panicky gesture. She retreats to the portieres. The doorbell rings. Laura catches her breath and touches her throat. Low drums sound.*]

AMANDA [*calling*]: Laura, sweetheart! The door!

[*Laura stares at it without moving.*]

JIM: I think we just beat the rain.

TOM: Uh-huh. [*He rings again, nervously. Jim whistles and fishes for a cigarette.*]

AMANDA [*very, very gaily*]: Laura, that is your brother and Mr. O'Connor! Will you let them in, darling!

[*Laura crosses toward the kitchenette door.*]

LAURA [*breathlessly*]: Mother—you go to the door!

[*Amanda steps out of the kitchenette and stares furiously at Laura. She points imperiously at the door.*]

LAURA: Please, please!

AMANDA [*in fierce whisper*]: What is the matter with you, you silly thing?

LAURA [*desperately*]: Please, you answer it, *please!*

AMANDA: I told you I wasn't going to humor you, Laura. Why have you chosen this moment to lose your mind?

LAURA: Please, please, please, you go!

AMANDA: You'll have to go to the door because I can't!

LAURA [*despairingly*]: I can't either!

AMANDA: *Why?*

LAURA: I'm *sick!*

AMANDA: I'm sick, too—of your nonsense! Why can't you and your brother be normal people? Fantastic whims and behavior!

[*Tom gives a long ring.*]

Preposterous goings on! Can you give me one reason—[*She calls out lyrically.*] *Coming! Just one second!*—why should you be afraid to open a door? Now you answer it, Laura!

LAURA: Oh, oh, oh . . . [*She returns through the portieres, darts to the Victrola, winds it frantically and turns it on.*]

AMANDA: Laura Wingfield, you march right to that door!

LAURA: Yes—yes, Mother!

[*A faraway, scratchy rendition of "Dardanella" softens the air and gives her strength to move through it. She slips to the door and draws it cautiously open. Tom enters with the caller, Jim O'Connor.*]

TOM: Laura, this is Jim. Jim, this is my sister, Laura.

JIM [*stepping inside*]: I didn't know that Shakespeare had a sister!

LAURA [*retreating, stiff and trembling, from the door*]: How—how do you do?

JIM [*heartily, extending his hand*]: Okay!

[*Laura touches it hesitantly with hers.*]

JIM: Your hand's *cold*, Laura!

LAURA: Yes, well—I've been playing the Victrola. . . .

JIM: Must have been playing classical music on it! You ought to play a little hot swing music to warm you up!

LAURA: Excuse me—I haven't finished playing the Victrola. . . . [*She awkwardly hurries into the front room. She pauses a second by the Victrola. Then she catches her breath and darts through the portieres like a frightened deer.*]

JIM [*grinning*]: What was the matter?

TOM: Oh—with Laura? Laura is—terribly shy.

JIM: Shy, huh? It's unusual to meet a shy girl nowadays. I don't believe you ever mentioned you had a sister.

TOM: Well, now you know. I have one. Here is the *Post Dispatch.* You want a piece of it?

JIM: Uh-huh.

TOM: What piece? The comics?

JIM: Sports! [*He glances at it.*] Ole Dizzy Dean is on his bad behavior.

TOM [*uninterested*]: Yeah? [*He lights a cigarette and goes over to the fire-escape door.*]

JIM: Where are *you* going?

TOM: I'm going out on the terrace.

JIM [*going after him*]: You know, Shakespeare—I'm going to sell you a bill of goods!

TOM: What goods?

JIM: A course I'm taking.

TOM: Huh?

JIM: In public speaking! You and me, we're not the warehouse type.

TOM: Thanks—that's good news. But what has public speaking got to do with it?

JIM: It fits you for—executive positions!

TOM: Awww.

JIM: I tell you it's done a helluva lot for me.

[*Image on screen:* Executive at his desk.]

TOM: In what respect?

JIM: In every! Ask yourself what is the difference between you an' me and men in the office down front? Brains?—No!—Ability?—No! Then what? Just one little thing—

TOM: What is that one little thing?

JIM: Primarily it amounts to—social poise! Being able to square up to people and hold your own on any social level!   •

AMANDA [*from the kitchenette*]: Tom?

TOM: Yes, Mother?

AMANDA: Is that you and Mr. O'Connor?

TOM: Yes, Mother.

AMANDA: Well, you just make yourselves comfortable in there.

TOM: Yes, Mother.

AMANDA: Ask Mr. O'Connor if he would like to wash his hands.

JIM: Aw, no—no—thank you—I took care of that at the warehouse. Tom—

TOM: Yes?

JIM: Mr. Mendoza was speaking to me about you.

TOM: Favorably?

JIM: What do you think?

TOM: Well—

JIM: You're going to be out of a job if you don't wake up.

TOM: I am waking up—

JIM: You show no signs.

TOM: The signs are interior.

[*Image on screen:* The sailing vessel with the Jolly Roger again.]

TOM: I'm planning to change. [*He leans over the fire-escape rail, speaking with quiet exhilaration. The incandescent marquees and signs of the first-run movie houses light his face from across the alley. He looks like a voyager.*] I'm right at the point of committing myself to a future that doesn't include the warehouse and Mr. Mendoza or even a night-school course in public speaking.

JIM: What are you gassing about?

TOM: I'm tired of the movies.

JIM: Movies!

TOM: Yes, movies! Look at them—[*a wave toward the marvels of Grand Avenue*] All of those glamorous people—having adventures—hogging it all, gobbling the whole thing up! You know what happens? People go to the *movies* instead of *moving!* Hollywood characters are supposed to have all the adventures for everybody in America, while everybody in America sits in a dark room and watches them have them! Yes, until there's a war. That's when adventure becomes available to the masses! *Everyone's* dish, not only Gable's! Then the people in the dark room come out of the dark room to have some adventures themselves—goody, goody! It's our turn now, to go to the South Sea Island— to make a safari—to be exotic, far-off! But I'm not patient. I don't want to wait till then. I'm tired of the *movies* and I am *about* to move!

JIM [*incredulously*]: Move?

TOM: Yes.

JIM: When?

TOM: Soon!

JIM: Where? When?

[*The music seems to answer the question, while Tom thinks it over. He searches in his pockets.*]

TOM: I'm starting to boil inside. I know I seem dreamy, but inside—well, I'm boiling! Whenever I pick up a shoe, I shudder a little thinking how short life is and what I am doing! Whatever that means, I know it doesn't mean shoes— except as something to wear on a traveler's feet! [*He finds what he has been searching for in his pockets and holds out a paper to Jim.*] Look—

JIM: What?

TOM: I'm a member.

JIM [*reading*]: The Union of Merchant Seamen.

TOM: I paid my dues this month, instead of the light bill.

JIM: You will regret it when they turn the lights off.

TOM: I won't be here.

JIM: How about your mother?

TOM: I'm like my father. The bastard son of a bastard! Did you notice how he's grinning in his picture in there? And he's been absent going on sixteen years!

JIM: You're just talking, you drip. How does your mother feel about it?

TOM: Shhh! Here comes Mother! Mother is not acquainted with my plans!

AMANDA [*coming through the portieres*]: Where are you all?

TOM: On the terrace, Mother.

[*They start inside. She advances to them. Tom is distinctly shocked at her appearance. Even Jim blinks a little. He is making his first contact with girlish Southern vivacity and in spite of the night-school course in public speaking is somewhat thrown off the beam by the unexpected outlay of social charm. Certain responses are attempted by Jim but are swept aside by Amanda's gay laughter and chatter. Tom is embarrassed but after the first shock Jim reacts very warmly. He grins and chuckles, is altogether won over.*]

[*Image on screen: Amanda as a girl.*]

AMANDA [*coyly smiling, shaking her girlish ringlets*]: Well, well, well, so this is Mr. O'Connor. Introductions entirely unnecessary. I've heard so much about you from my boy. I finally said to him, Tom—good gracious!—why don't you bring this paragon to supper? I'd like to meet this nice young man at the warehouse!— instead of just hearing him sing your praises so much! I don't know why my son is so stand-offish—that's not Southern behavior!

Let's sit down and—I think we could stand a little more air in here! Tom, leave the door open. I felt a nice fresh breeze a moment ago. Where has it gone to? Mmm, so warm already! And not quite summer, even. We're going to burn up when summer really gets started. However, we're having—we're having a very light supper. I think light things are better fo' this time of year. The same as light clothes are. Light clothes an' light food are what warm weather calls fo'. You know our blood gets so thick during th' winter—it takes a while fo' us to *adjust* ou'selves—when the season changes . . . It's come so quick this year. I wasn't prepared. All of a sudden—heavens! Already summer! I ran to the trunk an' pulled out this light dress—terribly old! Historical almost! But feels so good— so good an' co-ol, y' know. . . .

TOM: Mother—

AMANDA: Yes, honey?

TOM: How about—supper?

AMANDA: Honey, you go ask Sister if supper is ready! You know that Sister is in full charge of supper! Tell her you hungry boys are waiting for it. [*to Jim*] Have you met Laura?

JIM: She—

AMANDA: Let you in? Oh, good, you've met already! It's rare for a girl as sweet an' pretty as Laura to be domestic! But Laura is, thank heavens, not only pretty but also very domestic. I'm not at all. I never was a bit. I never could make a thing but angel-food cake. Well, in the South we had so many servants. Gone, gone, gone. All vestiges of gracious living! Gone completely! I wasn't prepared for what the future brought me. All of my gentlemen callers were sons of planters and so of course I assumed that I would be married to one and raise my family on a large piece of land with plenty of servants. But man proposes— and woman accepts the proposal! To vary that old, old saying a little bit—I married no planter! I married a man who worked for the telephone company! That gallantly smiling gentleman over there! [*She points to the picture.*] A telephone man who—fell in love with long-distance! Now he travels and I don't even know where! But what am I going on for about my—tribulations? Tell me yours—I hope you don't have any! Tom?

TOM [*returning*]: Yes, Mother?

AMANDA: Is supper nearly ready?

TOM: It looks to me like supper is on the table.

AMANDA: Let me look—[*She rises prettily and looks through the portieres.*] Oh, lovely! But where is Sister?

TOM: Laura is not feeling well and says that she thinks she'd better not come to the table.

AMANDA: What? Nonsense! Laura? Oh, Laura!

LAURA [*from the kitchenette, faintly*]: Yes, Mother.

AMANDA: You really must come to the table. We won't be seated until you come to the table! Come in, Mr. O'Connor. You sit over there, and I'll. . . . Laura? Laura Wingfield! You're keeping us waiting, honey! We can't say grace until you come to the table!

[*The kitchenette door is pushed weakly open and Laura comes in. She is obviously quite faint, her lips trembling, her eyes wide and staring. She moves unsteadily toward the table.*]

[*Screen legend:* "Terror!"]

[*Outside a summer storm is coming on abruptly. The white curtains billow inward at the windows and there is a sorrowful murmur from the deep blue dusk.*]

[*Laura suddenly stumbles; she catches at a chair with a faint moan.*]

TOM: Laura!

AMANDA: Laura!

[*There is a clap of thunder.*]

[*Screen legend:* "Ah!"]

[*despairingly*] Why, Laura, you *are* ill, darling! Tom, help your sister into the living room, dear! Sit in the living room, Laura—rest on the sofa. Well! [*to Jim as Tom helps his sister to the sofa in the living room*] Standing over the hot stove made her ill! I told her that it was just too warm this evening, but—

[*Tom comes back to the table.*]

Is Laura all right now?

TOM: Yes.

AMANDA: What *is* that? Rain? A nice cool rain has come up! [*She gives Jim a frightened look.*] I think we may—have grace—now . . .

[*Tom looks at her stupidly.*] Tom, honey—you say grace!

TOM: Oh . . . "For these and all thy mercies—"

[*They bow their heads, Amanda stealing a nervous glance at Jim. In the living room*

Laura, stretched on the sofa, clenches her hand to her lips, to hold back a shuddering sob.]
God's Holy Name be praised—
[*The scene dims out.*]

SCENE SEVEN

It is half an hour later. Dinner is just being finished in the dining room. Laura is still huddled upon the sofa, her feet drawn under her, her head resting on a pale blue pillow, her eyes wide and mysteriously watchful. The new floor lamp with its shade of rose-colored silk gives a soft, becoming light to her face, bringing out the fragile, unearthly prettiness which usually escapes attention. From outside there is a steady murmur of rain, but it is slackening and soon stops; the air outside becomes pale and luminous as the moon breaks through the clouds. A moment after the curtain rises, the lights in both rooms flicker and go out.

JIM: Hey, there, Mr. Light Bulb!
[*Amanda laughs nervously.*]
[*Legend on screen:* "Suspension of public service."]
AMANDA: Where was Moses when the lights went out? Ha-ha. Do you know the answer to that one, Mr. O'Connor?
JIM: No, Ma'am, what's the answer?
AMANDA: In the dark!
[*Jim laughs appreciatively.*]
Everybody sit still. I'll light the candles. Isn't it lucky we have them on the table? Where's a match? Which of you gentlemen can provide a match?
JIM: Here.
AMANDA: Thank you, Sir.
JIM: Not at all, Ma'am!
AMANDA [*as she lights the candles*]: I guess the fuse has burnt out. Mr. O'Connor, can you tell a burnt-out fuse? I know I can't and Tom is a total loss when it comes to mechanics.
[*They rise from the table and go into the kitchenette, from where their voices are heard.*]
Oh, be careful you don't bump into something. We don't want our gentleman caller to break his neck. Now wouldn't that be a fine howdy-do?
JIM: Ha-ha! Where is the fuse-box?
AMANDA: Right here next to to the stove. Can you see anything?
JIM: Just a minute.
AMANDA: Isn't electricity a mysterious thing? Wasn't it Benjamin Franklin who tied a key to a kite? We live in such a mysterious universe, don't we? Some people say that science clears up all the mysteries for us. In my opinion it only creates more! Have you found it yet?
JIM: No, Ma'am. All these fuses look okay to me.
AMANDA: Tom!
TOM: Yes, Mother?
AMANDA: That light bill I gave you several days ago. The one I told you we got the notices about?
[*Legend on screen:* "Ha!"]
TOM: Oh—yeah.
AMANDA: You didn't neglect to pay it by any chance?

TOM: Why, I—

AMANDA: Didn't! I might have known it!

JIM: Shakespeare probably wrote a poem on that light bill, Mrs. Wingfield.

AMANDA: I might have known better than to trust him with it! There's such a high price for negligence in this world!

JIM: Maybe the poem will win a ten-dollar prize!

AMANDA: We'll just have to spend the remainder of the evening in the nineteenth century, before Mr. Edison made the Mazda lamp!

JIM: Candlelight is my favorite kind of light.

AMANDA: That shows you're romantic! But that's no excuse for Tom. Well, we got through dinner. Very considerate of them to let us get through dinner before they plunged us into everlasting darkness, wasn't it, Mr. O'Connor?

JIM: Ha-ha!

AMANDA: Tom, as a penalty for your carelessness you can help me with the dishes.

JIM: Let me give you a hand.

AMANDA: Indeed you will not!

JIM: I ought to be good for something.

AMANDA: Good for something? [*Her tone is rhapsodic.*] Why, Mr. O'Connor, nobody, *nobody's* given me this much entertainment in years—as you have!

JIM: Aw, now, Mrs. Wingfield!

AMANDA: I'm not exaggerating, not one bit! But Sister is all by her lonesome. You go keep her company in the parlor! I'll give you this lovely old candelabrum that used to be on the altar at the Church of the Heavenly Rest. It was melted a little out of shape when the church burnt down. Lightning struck it one spring. Gypsy Jones was holding a revival at the time and he intimated that the church was destroyed because the Episcopalians gave card parties.

JIM: Ha-ha.

AMANDA: And how about you coaxing Sister to drink a little wine? I think it would be good for her! Can you carry both at once?

JIM: Sure. I'm Superman!

AMANDA: Now, Thomas, get into this apron!

[*Jim comes into the dining room, carrying the candelabrum, its candles lighted, in one hand and a glass of wine in the other. The door of the kitchenette swings closed on Amanda's gay laughter; the flickering light approaches the portieres. Laura sits up nervously as Jim enters. She can hardly speak from the almost intolerable strain of being alone with a stranger.*]

[*Screen legend:* "I don't suppose you remember me at all!"]

[*At first, before Jim's warmth overcomes her paralyzing shyness, Laura's voice is thin and breathless, as though she had just run up a steep flight of stairs. Jim's attitude is gently humorous. While the incident is apparently unimportant, it is to Laura the climax of her secret life.*]

JIM: Hello there, Laura.

LAURA [*faintly*]: Hello.

[*She clears her throat.*]

JIM: How are you feeling now? Better?

LAURA: Yes. Yes, thank you.

JIM: This is for you. A little dandelion wine. [*He extends the glass toward her with extravagant gallantry.*]

LAURA: Thank you.

JIM: Drink it—but don't get drunk!

[*He laughs heartily. Laura takes the glass uncertainly; she laughs shyly.*]

Where shall I set the candles?

LAURA: Oh—oh, anywhere . . .

JIM: How about here on the floor? Any objections?

LAURA: No.

JIM: I'll spread a newspaper under to catch the drippings. I like to sit on the floor. Mind if I do?

LAURA: Oh, no.

JIM: Give me a pillow?

LAURA: What?

JIM: A pillow!

LAURA: Oh . . . [*She hands him one quickly.*]

JIM: How about you? Don't you like to sit on the floor?

LAURA: Oh—yes.

JIM: Why don't you, then?

LAURA: I—will.

JIM: Take a pillow!

[*Laura does. She sits on the floor on the other side of the candelabrum. Jim crosses his legs and smiles engagingly at her.*] I can't hardly see you sitting way over there.

LAURA: I can—see you.

JIM: I know, but that's not fair, I'm in the limelight.

[*Laura moves her pillow closer.*]

Good! Now I can see you! Comfortable?

LAURA: Yes.

JIM: So am I. Comfortable as a cow! Will you have some gum?

LAURA: No thank you.

JIM: I think that I will indulge, with your permission. [*He musingly unwraps a stick of gum and holds it up.*] Think of the fortune made by the guy that invented the first piece of chewing gum. Amazing, huh? The Wrigley Building is one of the sights of Chicago—I saw it when I went up to the Century of Progress. Did you take in the Century of Progress?

LAURA: No, I didn't.

JIM: Well, it was quite a wonderful exposition. What impressed me most was the Hall of Science. Gives you an idea of what the future will be in America, even more wonderful than the present time is! [*There is a pause. Jim smiles at her.*] Your brother tells me you're shy. Is that right, Laura?

LAURA: I—don't know.

JIM: I judge you to be an old-fashioned type of girl. Well, I think that's a pretty good type to be. Hope you don't think I'm being too personal—do you?

LAURA [*hastily, out of embarrassment*]: I believe I *will* take a piece of gum, if you—don't mind. [*clearing her throat*] Mr. O'Connor, have you—kept up with your singing?

JIM: Singing? Me?

LAURA: Yes. I remember what a beautiful voice you had.

JIM: When did you year me sing?

[*Laura does not answer, and in the long pause which follows a man's voice is heard singing offstage.*]

> VOICE:
> O blow, ye winds, heigh-ho,
> A-roving I will go!
> I'm off to my love
> With a boxing glove—

Ten thousand miles away!

JIM: You say you've heard me sing?

LAURA: Oh, yes! Yes, very often . . . I—don't suppose—you remember me—
at all?

JIM [*smiling doubtfully*]: You know I have an idea I've seen you before. I had
that idea as soon as you opened the door. It seemed almost like I was about to
remember your name. But the name that I started to call you—wasn't a name!
And so I stopped myself before I said it.

LAURA: Wasn't it—Blue Roses?

JIM [*springing up, grinning*]: Blue Roses! My gosh, yes—Blue Roses! That's
what I had on my tongue when you opened the door! Isn't it funny what tricks
your memory plays? I didn't connect you with high school somehow or other.
But that's where it was; it was high school. I didn't even know you were Shakespeare's sister! Gosh, I'm sorry.

LAURA: I didn't expect you to. You—barely knew me!

JIM: But we did have a speaking acquaintance, huh?

LAURA: Yes, we—spoke to each other.

JIM: When did you recognize me?

LAURA: Oh, right away!

JIM: Soon as I came in the door?

LAURA: When I heard your name I thought it was probably you. I knew that
Tom used to know you a little in high school. So when you came in the door—
well, then I was—sure.

JIM: Why didn't you *say* something, then?

LAURA [*breathlessly*]: I didn't know what to say, I was—too surprised!

JIM: For goodness sakes! You know, this sure is funny!

LAURA: Yes! Yes, isn't it, though . . .

JIM: Didn't we have a class in something together?

LAURA: Yes, we did.

JIM: What class was that?

LAURA: It was—singing—chorus!

JIM: Aw!

LAURA: I sat across the aisle from you in the Aud.

JIM: Aw.

LAURA: Mondays, Wednesdays, and Fridays.

JIM: Now I remember—you always came in late.

LAURA: Yes, it was so hard for me, getting upstairs. I had that brace on my
leg—it clumped so loud!

JIM: I never heard any clumping.

LAURA: [*wincing at the recollection*]: To me it sounded like—thunder!

JIM: Well, well, well, I never even noticed.

LAURA: And everybody was seated before I came in. I had to walk in front of
all those people. My seat was in the back row. I had to go clumping all the way
up the aisle with everyone watching!

JIM: You shouldn't have been self-conscious.

LAURA: I know, but I was. It was always such a relief when the singing started.

JIM: Aw, yes, I've placed you now! I used to call you Blue Roses. How was it
that I got started calling you that?

LAURA: I was out of school a little with pleurosis. When I came back you asked
me what was the matter. I said I had pleurosis—you thought I said *Blue Roses*.
That's what you always called me after that!

JIM: I hope you didn't mind.

LAURA: Oh, no—I liked it. You see, I wasn't acquainted with many—people. . . .

JIM: As I remember you sort of stuck by yourself.

LAURA: I—I—never have had much luck at—making friends.

JIM: I don't see why you wouldn't.

LAURA: Well, I—started out badly.

JIM: You mean being—

LAURA: Yes, it sort of—stood between me—

JIM: You shouldn't have let it!

LAURA: I know, but it did, and—

JIM: You were shy with people!

LAURA: I tried not to be but never could—

JIM: Overcome it?

LAURA: No, I—I never could!

JIM: I guess being shy is something you have to work out of kind of gradually.

LAURA: [*sorrowfully*]: Yes—I guess it—

JIM: Takes time!

LAURA: Yes—

JIM: People are not so dreadful when you know them. That's what you have to remember! And everybody has problems, not just you, but practically everybody has got some problems. You think of yourself as having the only problems, as being the only one who is disappointed. But just look around you and you will see lots of people as disappointed as you are. For instance, I hoped when I was going to high school that I would be further along at this time, six years later, than I am now. You remember that wonderfull write-up I had in *The Torch*?

LAURA: Yes![*She rises and crosses to the table.*]

JIM: It said I was bound to succeed in anything I went into!

[*Laura returns with the high school yearbook.*]

Holy Jeez! *The Torch!*

[*He accepts it reverently. They smile across the book with mutual wonder. Laura crouches beside him and they begin to turn the pages. Laura's shyness is dissolving in his warmth.*]

LAURA: Here you are in *The Pirates of Penzance!*

JIM: [*wistfully*]: I sang the baritone lead in that operetta.

LAURA: [*raptly*]: So—*beautifully!*

JIM: [*protesting*]: Aw—

LAURA: Yes, yes—beautifully—beautifully!

JIM: You heard me?

LAURA: All three times!

JIM: No!

LAURA: Yes!

JIM: All three performances?

LAURA: [*looking down*]: Yes.

JIM: Why?

LAURA: I—wanted to ask you to—autograph my program.

[*She takes the program from the back of the yearbook and shows it to him.*]

JIM: Why didn't you ask me to?

LAURA: You were always surrounded by your own friends so much that I never had a chance to.

JIM: You should have just—

LAURA: Well, I—thought you might think I was—

JIM: Thought I might think you was—what?

LAURA: Oh—

JIM: [*with reflective relish*]: I was beleaguered by females in those days.

LAURA: You were terribly popular!

JIM: Yeah—

LAURA: You had such a—friendly way—

JIM: I was spoiled in high school.

LAURA: Everybody—liked you!

JIM: Including you?

LAURA: I—yes, I—did, too—[*She gently closes the book in her lap.*]

JIM: Well, well, well! Give me that program, Laura.

[*She hands it to them. He signs it with a fluorish.*]
There you are—better late than never!

LAURA: Oh, I—what a—surprise!

JIM: My signature isn't worth very much right now. But some day—maybe—
it will increase in value! Being disappointed is one thing and being discouraged
is something else. I am disappointed but I am not discouraged. I'm twenty-three
years old. How old are you?

LAURA: I'll be twenty-four in June.

JIM: That's not old age!

LAURA: No, but—

JIM: You finished high school?

LAURA [*with difficulty*]: I didn't go back.

JIM: You mean you dropped out?

LAURA: I made bad grades in my final examinations. [*She rises and replaces the
book and the program on the table. Her voice is strained.*] How is—Emily Meisenbach
getting along?

JIM: Oh, that kraut-head!

LAURA: Why do you call her that?

JIM: That's what she was.

LAURA: You're not still—going with her?

JIM: I never see her.

LAURA: It said in the "Personal" section that you were—engaged!

JIM: I know, but I wasn't impressed by that—propaganda!

LAURA: It wasn't—the truth?

JIM: Only in Emily's optimistic opinion!

LAURA: Oh—

[*Legend:* "What have you done since high school?"]

[*Jim lights a cigarette and leans indolently back on his elbows smiling at Laura with a
warmth and charm which lights her inwardly with altar candles. She remains by the
table, picks up a piece from the glass menagerie collection, and turns it in her hands to
cover her tumult.*]

JIM [*after several reflective puffs on his cigarette*]: What have you done since high
school?

[*She seems not to hear him.*]
Huh?

[*Laura looks up.*]
I said what have you done since high school, Laura?

LAURA: Nothing much.

JIM: You must have been doing something these six long years.

LAURA: Yes.

JIM: Well, then, such as what?

LAURA: I took a business course at business college—
JIM: How did that work out?
LAURA: Well, not very—well—I had to drop out, it gave me—indigestion—
[*Jim laughs gently.*]
JIM: What are you doing now?
LAURA: I don't do anything—much. Oh, please don't think I sit around doing nothing! My glass collection takes up a good deal of time. Glass is something you have to take good care of.
JIM: What did you say—about glass?
LAURA: Collection I said—I have one—[*She clears her throat and turns away again, acutely shy.*]
JIM [*abruptly*]: You know what I judge to be the trouble with you? Inferiority complex! Know what that is? That's what they call it when someone low-rates himself! I understand it because I had it, too. Although my case was not so aggravated as yours seems to be. I had it until I took up public speaking, developed my voice, and learned that I had an aptitude for science. Before that time I never thought of myself as being outstanding in any way whatsoever! Now I've never made a regular study of it, but I have a friend who says I can analyze people better than doctors that make a profession of it. I don't claim that to be necessarily true, but I can sure guess a person's psychology, Laura! [*He takes out his gum.*] Excuse me, Laura. I always take it out when the flavor is gone. I'll use this scrap of paper to wrap it in. I know how it is to get it stuck on a shoe. [*He wraps the gum in paper and puts it in his pocket.*] Yep—that's what I judge to be your principal trouble. A lack of confidence in yourself as a person. You don't have the proper amount of faith in yourself. I'm basing that fact on a number of your remarks and also on certain observations I've made. For instance that clumping you thought was so awful in high school. You say that you even dreaded to walk into class. You see what you did? You dropped out of school, you gave up an education because of a clump, which as far as I know was practically nonexistent! A little physical defect is what you have. Hardly noticeable even! Magnified thousands of times by imagination! You know what my strong advice to you is? Think of yourself as *superior* in some way!
LAURA: In what way would I think?
JIM: Why, man alive, Laura! Just look about you a little. What do you see? A world full of common people! All of 'em born and all of 'em going to die! Which of them has one-tenth of your good points! Or mine! Or anyone else's, as far as that goes—gosh! Everybody excels in some one thing. Some in many! [*He unconsciously glances at himself in the mirror.*] All you've got to do is to discover in *what!* Take me, for instance. [*He adjusts his tie at the mirror.*] My interest happens to lie in electro-dynamics. I'm taking a course in radio engineering at night school, Laura, on top of a fairly responsible job at the warehouse. I'm taking that course and studying public speaking.
LAURA: Ohhhh.
JIM: Because I believe in the future of television! [*turning his back to her.*] I wish to be ready to go up right along with it. Therefore I'm planning to get in on the ground floor. In fact I've already made the right connections and all that remains is for the industry itself to get under way! Full steam—[*His eyes are starry.*] *Knowledge*—Zzzzzp! *Money*—Zzzzzzp!—*Power!* That's the cycle democracy is built on!
[*His attitude is convincingly dynamic. Laura stares at him, even her shyness eclipsed in her absolute wonder. He suddenly grins.*]
I guess you think I think a lot of myself?

LAURA: No—o-o-o, I—

JIM: Now how about you? Isn't there something you take more interest in than anything else?

LAURA: Well, I do—as I said—have my—glass collection—

[*A peal of girlish laughter rings from the kitchenette.*]

JIM: I'm not right sure I know what you're talking about. What kind of glass is it?

LAURA: Little articles of it, they're ornaments mostly! Most of them are little animals made out of glass, the tiniest little animals in the world. Mother calls them the glass menagerie! Here's an example of one, if you'd like to see it! This one is one of the oldest. It's nearly thirteen.

[*Music:* "The Glass Menagerie."]

Oh, be careful—if you breathe, it breaks!

JIM: I'd better not take it. I'm pretty clumsy with things.

LAURA: Go on, I trust you with him! [*She places the piece in his palm.*] There now—you're holding him gently! Hold him over the light, he loves the light! You see how the light shines through him?

JIM: It sure does shine!

LAURA: I shouldn't be partial, but he is my favorite one.

JIM: What kind of a thing is this one supposed to be?

LAURA: Haven't you noticed the single horn on his forehead?

JIM: A unicorn, huh?

LAURA: Mmmm-hmmm!

JIM: Unicorns—aren't they extinct in the modern world?

LAURA: I know!

JIM: Poor little fellow, he must feel sort of lonesome.

LAURA [*smiling*]: Well, if he does, he doesn't complain about it. He stays on a shelf with some horses that don't have horns and all of them seem to get along nicely together.

JIM: How do you know?

LAURA [*lightly*]: I haven't heard any arguments among them!

JIM [*grinning*]: No arguments, huh? Well, that's a pretty good sign! Where shall I set him!

LAURA: Put him on the table. They all like a change of scenery once in a while!

JIM: Well, well, well, well—[*He places the glass piece on the table, then raises his arms and stretches.*] Look how big my shadow is when I stretch!

LAURA: Oh, oh, yes—it stretches across the ceiling!

JIM [*crossing to the door*]: I think it's stopped raining. [*He opens the fire-escape door and the background music changes to a dance tune.*] Where does the music come from?

LAURA: From the Paradise Dance Hall across the alley.

JIM: How about cutting the rug a little, Miss Wingfield?

LAURA: Oh, I—

JIM: Or is your program filled up? Let me have a look at it. [*He grasps an imaginary card.*] Why, every dance is taken! I'll just have to scratch some out.

[*Waltz music:* "La Golondrina."]

Ahhh, a waltz! [*He executes some sweeping turns by himself, then holds his arms toward Laura.*]

LAURA [*breathlessly*]: I—can't dance!

JIM: There you go, that inferiority stuff!

LAURA: I've never danced in my life!

JIM: Come on, try!

LAURA: Oh, but I'd step on you!

JIM: I'm not made out of glass.

LAURA: How—how—how do we start?

JIM: Just leave it to me. You hold your arms out a little.

LAURA: Like this?

JIM [*taking her in his arms*]: A little bit higher. Right. Now don't tighten up, that's the main thing about it—relax.

LAURA [*laughing breathlessly*]: It's hard not to.

JIM: Okay.

LAURA: I'm afraid you can't budge me.

JIM: What do you bet I can't? [*He swings her into motion.*]

LAURA: Goodness, yes, you can!

JIM: Let yourself go, now, Laura, just let yourself go.

LAURA: I'm—

JIM: Come on!

LAURA: —trying!

JIM: Not so stiff—easy does it!

LAURA: I know but I'm—

JIM: Loosen th' backbone! There now, that's a lot better.

LAURA: Am I?

JIM: Lots, lots better! [*He moves her about the room in a clumsy waltz.*]

LAURA: Oh, my!

JIM: Ha-ha!

LAURA: Oh, my goodness!

JIM: Ha-ha-ha!

[*They suddenly bump into the table, and the glass piece on it falls to the floor. Jim stops the dance.*]

What did we hit on?

LAURA: Table.

JIM: Did something fall off it? I think—

LAURA: Yes.

JIM: I hope that it wasn't the little glass horse with the horn!

LAURA: Yes. [*She stoops to pick it up.*]

JIM: Aw, aw, aw. It is broken?

LAURA: Now it is just like all the other horses.

JIM: It's lost its—

LAURA: Horn! It doesn't matter. Maybe it's a blessing in disguise.

JIM: You'll never forgive me. I bet that that was your favorite piece of glass.

LAURA: I don't have favorites much. It's no tragedy, Freckles. Glass breaks so easily. No matter how careful you are. The traffic jars the shelves and things fall off them.

JIM: Still I'm awfully sorry that I was the cause.

LAURA [*smiling*]: I'll just imagine he had an operation. The horn was removed to make him feel less—freakish!

[*They both laugh.*]

Now he will feel more at home with the other horses, the ones that don't have horns.

JIM: Ha-ha, that's very funny! [*Suddenly he is serious.*] I'm glad to see that you have a sense of humor. You know—you're—well—very different! Surprisingly different from anyone else I know! [*His voice becomes soft and hesitant with a genuine feeling.*] Do you mind me telling you that?

[*Laura is abashed beyond speech.*]

I mean it in a nice way—

[*Laura nods shyly, looking away.*]

You make me feel sort of—I don't know how to put it! I'm usually pretty good at expressing things, but—this is something that I don't know how to say!

[*Laura touches her throat and clears it—turns the broken unicorn in her hands. His voice becomes softer.*]

Has anyone ever told you that you were pretty?

[*There is a pause, and the music rises slightly. Laura looks up slowly, with wonder, and shakes her head.*]

Well, you are! In a very different way from anyone else. And all the nicer because of the difference, too.

[*His voice becomes low and husky. Laura turns away, nearly faint with the novelty of her emotions.*]

I wish that you were my sister. I'd teach you to have some confidence in yourself. The different people are not like other people, but being different is nothing to be ashamed of. Because other people are not such wonderful people. They're one hundred times one thousand. You're one times one! They walk all over the earth. You just stay here. They're common as—weeds, but—you—well, you're—*Blue Roses!*

[*Image on screen:* Blue Roses.]

[*The music changes.*]

LAURA: But blue is wrong for—roses. . . .

JIM: It's right for you! You're—pretty!

LAURA: In what respect am I pretty?

JIM: In all respects—believe me! Your eyes—your hair—are pretty! Your hands are pretty! [*He catches hold of her hand.*] You think I'm making this up because I'm invited to dinner and have to be nice. Oh, I could do that! I could put on an act for you, Laura, and say lots of things without being very sincere. But this time I am. I'm talking to you sincerely. I happened to notice you had this inferiority complex that keeps you from feeling comfortable with people. Somebody needs to build your confidence up and make you proud instead of shy and turning away and—blushing. Somebody—ought to—*kiss* you, Laura!

[*His hand slips slowly up her arm to her shoulder as the music swells tumultuously. He suddenly turns her about and kisses her on the lips. When he releases her, Laura sinks on the sofa with a bright, dazed look. Jim backs away and fishes in his pocket for a cigarette.*]

[*Legend on screen:* "A souvenir."]

Stumblejohn!

[*He lights the cigarette, avoiding her look. There is a peal of girlish laughter from Amanda in the kitchenette. Laura slowly raises and opens her hand. It still contains the little broken glass animal. She looks at it with a tender, bewildered expression.*]

Stumblejohn! I shouldn't have done that—that was way off the beam. You don't smoke, do you?

[*She looks up, smiling, not hearing the question. He sits beside her rather gingerly. She looks at him speechlessly—waiting. He coughs decorously and moves a little farther aside as he considers the situation and senses her feelings, dimly, with perturbation. He speaks gently.*]

Would you—care for a—mint?

[*She doesn't seem to hear him but her look grows brighter even.*]

Peppermint? Life Saver? My pocket's a regular drugstore—wherever I go. . . .

[*He pops a mint in his mouth. Then he gulps and decides to make a clean breast of it. He speaks slowly and gingerly.*] Laura, you know, if I had a sister like you, I'd do the same thing as Tom. I'd bring out fellows and—introduce her to them. The right type of boys—of a type to—appreciate her. Only—well—he made a mistake about me. Maybe I've got no call to be saying this. That may not have been the idea in having me over. But what if it was? There's nothing wrong about that. The only trouble is that in my case—I'm not in a situation to—do the right thing. I can't take down your number and say I'll phone. I can't call up next week and—ask for a date. I thought I had better explain the situation in case you— misunderstood it and—I hurt your feelings. . . .

[*There is a pause. Slowly, very slowly, Laura's look changes, her eyes returning slowly from his to the glass figure in her palm. Amanda utters another gay laugh in the kitchenette.*]

LAURA [*faintly*]: You—won't—call again?

JIM: No, Laura, I can't. [*He rises from the sofa.*] As I was just explaining, I've— got strings on me. Laura, I've—been going steady! I go out all the time with a girl named Betty. She's a home-girl like you, and Catholic, and Irish, and in a great many ways we—get along fine. I met her last summer on a moonlight boat trip up the river to Alton, on the *Majestic*. Well—right away from the start it was—love!

[*Legend:* Love!]

[*Laura sways slightly forward and grips the arm of the sofa. He fails to notice, now enrapt in his own comfortable being.*]

Being in love has made a new man of me!

[*Leaning stiffly forward, clutching the arm of the sofa, Laura struggles visibly with her storm. But Jim is oblivious; she is a long way off.*]

The power of love is really pretty tremendous! Love is something that— changes the whole world, Laura!

[*The storm abates a little and Laura leans back. He notices her again.*]

It happened that Betty's aunt took sick, she got a wire and had to go to Centralia. So Tom—when he asked me to dinner—I naturally just accepted the invitation, not knowing that you—that he—that I—[*He stops awkwardly.*] Huh— I'm a stumblejohn!

[*He flops back on the sofa. The holy candles on the altar of Laura's face have been snuffed out. There is a look of almost infinite desolation. Jim glances at her uneasily.*]

I wish that you would—say something.

[*She bites her lip which was trembling and then bravely smiles. She opens her hand again on the broken glass figure. Then she gently takes his hand and raises it level with her own. She carefully places the unicorn in the palm of his hand, then pushes his fingers closed upon it.*]

What are you—doing that for? You want me to have him? Laura?

[*She nods.*]

What for?

LAURA: A—souvenir . . . .

[*She rises unsteadily and crouches beside the Victrola to wind it up.*]

[*Legend on screen:* "Things have a way of turning out so badly!" *Or image:* "Gentleman caller waving goodbye—gaily."]

[*At this moment Amanda rushes brightly back into the living room. She bears a pitcher of fruit punch in an old-fashioned cut-glass pitcher, and a plate of macaroons. The plate has a gold border and poppies painted on it.*]

AMANDA: Well, well, well! Isn't the air delightful after the shower! I've made you children a little liquid refreshment.

[*She turns gaily to Jim.*] Jim, do you know that song about lemonade?

> "Lemonade, lemonade
> Made in the shade and stirred with a spade—
> Good enough for any old maid!"

JIM [*uneasily*]: Ha-ha! No—I never heard it.

AMANDA: Why, Laura! You look so serious!

JIM: We were having a serious conversation.

AMANDA: Good! Now you're better acquainted!

JIM: [*uncertainly*]: Ha-ha! Yes.

AMANDA: You modern young people are much more serious-minded than my generation. I was so gay as a girl!

JIM: You haven't changed, Mrs. Wingfield.

AMANDA: Tonight I'm rejuvenated! The gaiety of the occasion, Mr. O'Connor! [*She tosses her head with a peal of laughter, spilling some lemonade.*] Oooo! I'm baptizing myself!

JIM: Here—let me—

AMANDA: [*setting the pitcher down*]: There now. I discovered we had some maraschino cherries. I dumped them in, juice and all!

JIM: You shouldn't have gone to that trouble, Mrs. Wingfield.

AMANDA: Trouble, trouble? Why, it was loads of fun! Didn't you hear me cutting up in the kitchen? I bet your ears were burning! I told Tom how outdone with him I was for keeping you to himself so long a time! He should have brought you over much, much sooner! Well, now that you've found your way, I want you to be a very frequent caller! Not just occasional but all the time. Oh, we're going to have a lot of gay times together! I see them coming! Mmm, just breathe that air! So fresh, and the moon's so pretty! I'll skip back out—I know where my place is when young folks are having a—serious conversation!

JIM: Oh, don't go out, Mrs. Wingfield. The fact of the matter is I've got to be going.

AMANDA: Going, now? You're joking! Why, it's only the shank of the evening, Mr. O'Connor.

JIM: Well, you know how it is.

AMANDA: You mean you're a young workingman and have to keep working-men's hours. We'll let you off early tonight. But only on the condition that next time you stay later. What's the best night for you? Isn't Saturday night the best night for you workingmen?

JIM: I have a couple of time-clocks to punch, Mrs. Wingfield. One at morning, another one at night!

AMANDA: My, but you *are* ambitious! You work at night, too?

JIM: No, Ma'am, not work but—Betty!

[*He crosses deliberately to pick up his hat. The band at the Paradise Dance Hall goes into a tender waltz.*]

AMANDA: Betty? Betty? Who's—Betty!

[*There is an ominous cracking sound in the sky.*]

JIM: Oh, just a girl. The girl I go steady with!

[*He smiles charmingly. The sky falls.*]

[*Legend:* "The Sky Falls."]

AMANDA [*a long-drawn exhalation*]: Ohhhh . . . Is it a serious romance, Mr. O'Connor?

JIM: We're going to be married the second Sunday in June.

AMANDA: Ohhhh—how nice! Tom didn't mention that you were engaged to be married.

JIM: The cat's not out of the bag at the warehouse yet. You know how they are. They call you Romeo and stuff like that. [*He stops at the oval mirror to put on his hat. He carefully shapes the brim and the crown to give a discreetly dashing effect.*] It's been a wonderful evening, Mrs. Wingfield. I guess this is what they mean by Southern hospitality.

AMANDA: It really wasn't anything at all.

JIM: I hope it don't seem like I'm rushing of. But I promised Betty I'd pick her up at the Wabash depot, an' by the time I get my jalopy down there her train'll be in. Some women are pretty upset if you keep 'em waiting.

AMANDA: Yes, I know—the tyranny of women! [*She extends her hand.*] Goodbye, Mr. O'Connor. I wish you luck—and happiness—and success! All three of them, and so does Laura! Don't you, Laura?

LAURA: Yes!

JIM [*taking Laura's hand*]: Goodbye, Laura. I'm certainly going to treasure that souvenir. And don't you forget the good advice I gave you. [*He raises his voice to a cheery shout.*] So long, Shakespeare! Thanks again, ladies. Good night!

[*He grins and ducks jauntily out. Still barely grimacing, Amanda closes the door on the gentleman caller. Then she turns back to the room with a puzzled expression. She and Laura don't dare to face each other. Laura crouches beside the Victrola to wind it.*]

AMANDA [*faintly*]: Things have a way of turning out so badly. I don't believe that I would play the Victrola. Well, well—well! Our gentleman caller was engaged to be married! [*She raises her voice.*] Tom!

TOM [*from the kitchenette*]: Yes, Mother?

AMANDA: Come in here a minute. I want to tell you something awfully funny.

TOM [*entering with a macaroon and a glass of the lemonade*]: Has the gentleman caller gotten away already?

AMANDA: The gentleman caller has made an early departure. What a wonderful joke you played on us!

TOM: How do you mean?

AMANDA: You didn't mention that he was engaged to be married.

TOM: Jim? Engaged?

AMANDA: That's what he just informed us.

TOM: I'll be jiggered! I didn't know about that.

AMANDA: That seems very peculiar.

TOM: What's peculiar about it?

AMANDA: Didn't you call him your best friend down at the warehouse?

TOM: He is, but how did I know?

AMANDA: It seems extremely peculiar that you wouldn't know your best friend was going to be married!

TOM: The warehouse is where I work, not where I know things about people!

AMANDA: You don't know things anywhere! You live in a dream; you manufacture illusions!

[*He crosses to the door.*]
Where are you going?

TOM: I'm going to the movies.

AMANDA: That's right, now that you've had us make such fools of ourselves. The effort, the preparations, all the expense! The new floor lamp, the rug, the clothes for Laura! All for what? To entertain some other girl's fiancé! Go to the movies, go! Don't think about us, a mother deserted, an unmarried sister who's crippled and has no job! Don't let anything interfere with your selfish pleasure! Just go, go, go—to the movies!

TOM: All right, I will! The more you shout about my selfishness to me the quicker I'll go, and I won't go to the movies!

AMANDA: Go, then! Go to the moon—you selfish dreamer!

[*Tom smashes his glass on the floor. He plunges out on the fire escape, slamming the door. Laura screams in fright. The dance-hall music becomes louder. Tom stands on the fire escape, gripping the rail. The moon breaks through the storm clouds, illuminating his face.*]

[*Legend on screen:* "And so goodbye . . ."]

[*Tom's closing speech is timed with what is happening inside the house. We see, as though through soundproof glass, that Amanda appears to be making a comforting speech to Laura, who is huddled upon the sofa. Now that we cannot hear the mother's speech, her silliness is gone and she has dignity and tragic beauty. Laura's hair hides her face until, at the end of the speech, she lifts her head to smile at her mother. Amanda's gestures are slow and graceful, almost dancelike, as she comforts her daughter. At the end of her speech she glances a moment at the father's picture—then withdraws through the portieres. At the close of Tom's speech, Laura blows out the candles, ending the play.*]

TOM: I didn't go to the moon, I went much further—for time is the longest distance between two places. Not long after that I was fired for writing a poem on the lid of a shoe-box. I left Saint Louis. I descended the steps of this fire escape for a last time and followed, from then on, in my father's footsteps, attempting to find in motion what was lost in space. I traveled around a great deal. The cities swept about me like dead leaves, leaves that were brightly colored but torn away from the branches. I would have stopped, but I was pursued by something. It always came upon me unawares, taking me altogether by surprise. Perhaps it was a familiar bit of music. Perhaps it was only a piece of transparent glass. Perhaps I am walking along a street at night, in some strange city, before I have found companions. I pass the lighted window of a shop where perfume is sold. The window is filled with pieces of colored glass, tiny transparent bottles in delicate colors, like bits of a shattered rainbow. Then all at once my sister touches my shoulder. I turn around and look into her eyes. Oh, Laura, Laura, I tried to leave you behind me, but I am more faithful than I intended to be! I reach for a cigarette, I cross the street, I run into the movies or a bar, I buy a drink, I speak to the nearest stranger—anything that can blow your candles out!

[*Laura bends over the candles.*]

For nowadays the world is lit by lightning! Blow out your candles, Laura—and so goodbye. . . .

[*She blows the candles out.*]

1945

Gwendolyn Brooks *1917–*

The first black writer to win a Pulitzer Prize, Gwendolyn Brooks is regarded as one of America's finest poets. For over twenty-five years she has been publishing poetry of exceptional intensity and high craftsmanship. Moreover, her poetic development precisely demonstrates a major aspect of twentieth-century writing: the conflict between commitment to a social ideal and commitment to art.

The Brooks family moved from Kansas to Illinois when Gwendolyn Brooks was an infant, and she has spent most of her life in the Chicago area. She began writing as a child, having her first poem published when she was thirteen. In 1945 her first book of poetry, A Street in Bronzeville, *appeared, bringing her immediate critical praise. Her second book of poems,* Annie Allen, *was published in 1949 and won a Pulitzer Prize for poetry. In 1953 she wrote a short novel,* Maud Martha, *the story of a young black girl growing up in Chicago.*

The Bean Eaters *was published in 1960,* Selected Poems *in 1963, and* In the Mecca (*poems based on life in a large, slum apartment building in Chicago's black ghetto*) *in 1968. These later poems reflect a growing racial consciousness. She has said, "poets who happen also to be Negroes are twice-tried. They have to write poetry, and they have to remember that they are Negroes." In more recent poems she has shown a movement away from her previous closely controlled forms, verbal wit and dexterity. Since the mid-1960s, in such volumes as* Riot (*1969*) *and* Family Pictures (*1970*)*, her general development has been toward a compressed, less formal, harsher, more urgent verse. In 1981* To Disembark *was published, an anthology of her writing from the 1960s to the 1980s.*

While teaching in colleges and universities in Illinois and Wisconsin, Gwendolyn Brooks has been instrumental in helping young black poets in their development. And in 1985 she was appointed Consultant in Poetry to the Library of Congress. But she will be remembered most, and most deservedly, for her poetic skill and her statements of compassionate understanding of the human dilemmas of her America.

FURTHER READING: *The World of Gwendolyn Brooks,* 1971; *Aloneness,* 1972; *Report from Part One,* 1972; H. Shaw, *Gwendolyn Brooks,* 1980; D. H. Melhem, *Gwendolyn Brooks,* 1987; *A Life Distilled, Gwendolyn Brooks, Her Poetry and Fiction,* eds. M. Mootry and G. Smith, 1987.

TEXTS: "The Blackstone Rangers" is from *In the Mecca,* 1968; all other poems are from *Selected Poems,* 1963.

KITCHENETTE BUILDING

We are things of dry hours and the involuntary plan,
Grayed in, and gray. "Dream" makes a giddy sound, not
   strong
Like "rent," "feeding a wife," "satisfying a man."

But could a dream send up through onion fumes
Its white and violet, fight with fried potatoes
And yesterday's garbage ripening in the hall,
Flutter, or sing an aria down these rooms

Even if we were willing to let it in,
Had time to warm it, keep it very clean,
Anticipate a message, let it begin?   10

We wonder. But not well! not for a mintue!
Since Number Five is out of the bathroom now,
We think of lukewarm water, hope to get in it.

1945

THE VACANT LOT

Mrs. Coley's three-flat brick
Isn't here any more.
All done with seeing her fat little form
Burst out of the basement door;
And with seeing her African son-in-law
(Rightful heir to the throne)
With his great white strong cold squares of teeth
And his little eyes of stone;
And with seeing the squat fat daughter
Letting in the men   10
When majesty has gone for the day—
And letting them out again.

1945

THE MOTHER

Abortions will not let you forget.
You remember the children you got that you did not get,
The damp small pulps with a little or with no hair,
The singers and workers that never handled the air.
You will never neglect or beat
Them, or silence or buy with a sweet.
You will never wind up the sucking-thumb
Or scuttle off ghosts that come.
You will never leave them, controlling your luscious sigh,
Return for a snack of them, with gobbling mother-eye.   10

I have heard in the voices of the wind the voices of my dim
        killed children.
I have contracted. I have eased
My dim dears at the breasts they could never suck.
I have said, Sweets, if I sinned, if I seized
Your luck
And your lives from your unfinished reach,
If I stole your births and your names,
Your straight baby tears and your games,
Your stilted or lovely loves, your tumults, your marriages,
        aches, and your deaths,
If I poisoned the beginnings of your breaths,   20
Believe that even in my deliberateness I was not deliberate.
Though why should I whine,
Whine that the crime was other than mine?—

Since anyhow you are dead.
Or rather, or instead,
You were never made.

But that too, I am afraid,
Is faulty: oh, what shall I say, how is the truth to be said?
You were born, you had body, you died.
It is just that you never giggled or planned or cried.   30

Believe me I loved you all.
Believe me, I knew you, though faintly, and I loved, I loved you
All   1945

SADIE AND MAUD

Maud went to college.
Sadie stayed at home.

Sadie scraped life
With a fine-tooth comb.

She didn't leave a tangle in.
Her comb found every strand.
Sadie was one of the livingest chits
In all the land.

Sadie bore two babies
Under her maiden name.   10
Maud and Ma and Papa
Nearly died of shame.
Every one but Sadie
Nearly died of shame.

When Sadie said her last so-long
Her girls struck out from home.
(Sadie had left as heritage
Her fine-tooth comb.)

Maud, who went to college,
Is a thin brown mouse.
She is living all alone
In this old house.   20

1945

THE CHILDREN OF THE POOR

1

People who have no children can be hard:
Attain a mail of ice and insolence:

Need not pause in the fire, and in no sense
Hesitate in the hurricane to guard.
And when wide world is bitten and bewarred
They perish purely, waving their spirits hence
Without a trace of grace or of offense
To laugh or fail, diffident, wonder-starred.
While through a throttling dark we others hear
The little lifting helplessness, the queer   10
Whimper-whine; whose unridiculous
Lost softness softly makes a trap for us.
And makes a curse. And makes a sugar of
The malocclusions, the inconditions of love.

2

What shall I give my children? who are poor,
Who are adjudged the leastwise of the land,
Who are my sweetest lepers, who demand
No velvet and no velvety velour;
But who have begged me for a brisk contour,
Crying that they are quasi, contraband   20
Because unfinished, graven by a hand
Less than angelic, admirable or sure.
My hand is stuffed with mode, design, device.
But I lack access to my proper stone.
And plenitude of plan shall not suffice,
Nor grief nor love shall be enough alone
To ratify my little halves who bear
Across an autumn freezing everywhere.

1949

BEVERLY HILLS, CHICAGO

"and the people live till they have white hair"
—E. M. PRICE

The dry brown coughing beneath their feet,
(Only a while, for the handyman is on his way)
These people walk their golden gardens.
We say ourselves fortunate to be driving by today.

That we may look at them, in their gardens where
The summer ripeness rots. But not raggedly.
Even the leaves fall down in lovelier patterns here.
And the refuse, the refuse is a neat brilliancy.

When they flow sweetly into their houses
With softness and slowness touched by that everlasting gold,   10
We know what they go to. To tea. But that does not mean
They will throw some little black dots into some water and add sugar
    and the juice of the cheapest lemons that are sold,

While downstairs that woman's vague phonograph bleats, "Knock me
    a kiss."
And the living all to be made again in the sweatingest physical manner
Tomorrow. . . . Not that anybody is saying that these people have
    no trouble.
Merely that it is trouble with a gold-flecked beautiful banner.

Nobody is saying that these people do not ultimately cease to be. And
Sometimes their passings are even more painful than ours.
It is just that so often they live till their hair is white.
They make excellent corpses, among the expensive flowers. . . .   20

Nobody is furious. Nobody hates these people.
At least, nobody driving by in this car.
It is only natural, however, that it should occur to us
How much more fortunate they are than we are.

It is only natural that we should look and look
At their wood and brick and stone
And think, while a breath of pine blows,
How different these are from our own.

We do not want them to have less.
But it is only natural that we should think we have not enough.   30
We drive on, we drive on.
When we speak to each other our voices are a little gruff.

1949

WE REAL COOL

The Pool Players.
Seven at the Golden Shovel.[1]

We real cool. We
Left school. We

Lurk late. We
Strike straight. We

Sing sin. We
Thin gin. We

Jazz June. We
Die soon.

1960

THE LOVERS OF THE POOR

                arrive. The Ladies from the Ladies' Betterment
    League
  Arrive in the afternoon, the late light slanting

---

[1]A pool hall in Chicago.

In diluted gold bars across the boulevard brag
Of proud, seamed faces with mercy and murder hinting
Here, there, interrupting, all deep and debonair,
The pink paint on the innocence of fear;
Walk in a gingerly manner up the hall.
Cutting with knives served by their softest care,
Served by their love, so barbarously fair.   10
Whose mothers taught: You'd better not be cruel!
You had better not throw stones upon the wrens!
Herein they kiss and coddle and assault
Anew and dearly in the innocence
With which they baffle nature. Who are full,
Sleek, tender-clad, fit, fiftyish, a-glow, all
Sweetly abortive, hinting at fat fruit,
Judge it high time that fiftyish fingers felt
Beneath the lovelier planes of enterprise.
To ressurect. To moisten with milky chill.   20
To be a random hitching-post or plush.
To be, for wet eyes, random and handy hem.
                    Their guild is giving money to the poor.
The worthy poor. The very very worthy
And beautiful poor. Perhaps just not too swarthy?
Perhaps just not too dirty nor too dim
Nor—passionate. In truth, what they could wish
Is—something less than derelict or dull.
Not staunch enough to stab, though, gaze for gaze!
God shield them sharply from the beggar-bold!   30
The noxious needy ones whose battle's bald
Nonetheless for being voiceless, hits one down.
                    But it's all so bad! and entirely too much for them.
The stench; the urine, cabbage, and dead beans,
Dead porridges of assorted dusty grains,
The old smoke, *heavy* diapers, and they're told,
Something called chitterlings. The darkness. Drawn
Darkness, or dirty light. The soil that stirs.
The soil that looks the soil of centuries.
And for that matter the *general* oldness. Old   40
Wood. Old marble. Old tile. Old old old.
Not homekind Oldness! Not Lake Forest, Glencoe.[1]
Nothing is sturdy, nothing is majestic,
There is no quiet drama, no rubbed glaze, no
Unkillable infirmity of such
A tasteful turn as lately they have left,
Glencoe, Lake Forest, and to which their cars
Must presently restore them. When they're done
With dullards and distortions of this fistic
Patience of the poor and put-upon.   50
                    They've never seen such a make-do-ness as
Newspaper rugs before! In this, this "flat,"
Their hostess is gathering up the oozed, the rich

---

[1]Fashionable suburbs of Chicago.

Rugs of the morning (tattered! the bespattered. . . .)
Readies to spread clean rugs for afternoon.
Here is a scene for you. The Ladies look,
In horror, behind a substantial citizeness
Whose trains clank out across her swollen heart.
Who, arms akimbo, almost fills a door.
All tumbling children, quilts dragged to the floor   60
And tortured thereover, potato peelings, soft-
Eyed kitten, hunched-up, haggard, to-be-hurt.
　　　　　　　Their League is allotting largesse to the Lost.
But to put their clean, their pretty money, to put
Their money collected from delicate rose-fingers
Tipped with their hundred flawless rose-nails seems . . .
　　　　　　　They own Spode, Lowestoft,² candelabra,
Mantels, and hostess gowns, and sunburst clocks,
Turtle soup, Chippendale,³ red satin "hangings,"
Aubussons⁴ and Hattie Carnegie.⁵ They Winter   70
In Palm Beach; cross the Water in June; attend,
When suitable, the nice Art Institute;
Buy the right books in the best bindings; saunter
On Michigan,⁶ Easter mornings, in sun or wind.
Oh Squalor! This sick four-story hulk, this fibre
With fissures everywhere! Why, what are bringings
Of loathe-love largesse? What shall peril hungers
So old old, what shall flatter the desolate?
Tin can, blocked fire escape and chitterling
And swaggering seeking youth and the puzzled wreckage   80
Of the middle passage,⁷ and urine and stale shames
And, again, the porridges of the underslung
And children children children. Heavens! That
Was a rat, surely, off there, in the shadows? Long
And long-tailed? Gray? The Ladies from the Ladies'
Betterment League agree it will be better
To achieve the outer air that rights and steadies,
To hie⁸ to a house that does not holler, to ring
Bells elsetime, better presently to cater
To no more Possibilities, to get   90
Away. Perhaps the money can be posted.
Perhaps they two may choose another Slum!
Some serious sooty half-unhappy home!—
Where loathe-love likelier may be invested.
　　　　　　　Keeping their scented bodies in the center
Of the hall as they walk down the hysterical hall,
They allow their lovely skirts to graze no wall,
Are off at what they manage of a canter,

²Expensive Chinaware made in England.
³Elegant and expensive furniture made in the style of the English furniture maker Thomas
Chippendale (1718?–1779).
⁴Scenic tapestries, used as wall-hangings.
⁵High-fashion dress designer.
⁶Chicago boulevard with expensive shops.
⁷The Atlantic route from Africa to America used by slave-traders.
⁸Speed.

And, resuming all the clues of what they were,
Try to avoid inhaling the laden air.   100

1960

THE CHICAGO DEFENDER[1] SENDS A MAN TO LITTLE ROCK[2]

Fall, 1957

In Little Rock the people bear
Babes, and comb and part their hair
And watch the want ads, put repair
To roof and latch. While wheat toast burns
A woman waters multiferns.

Time upholds or overturns
The many, tight, and small concerns.
In Little Rock the people sing
Sunday hymns like anything,
Through Sunday pomp and polishing.   10

And after testament and tunes,
Some often Sunday afternoons
With lemon tea and Lorna Doones.[3]

I forecast
And I believe
Come Christmas Little Rock will cleave
To Christmas tree and trifle, weave,
From laugh and tinsel, texture fast.

In Little Rock is baseball; Barcarolle.[4]
That hotness in July . . . the uniformed figure raw and im-
       placable   20
And not intellectual,
Batting the hotness or clawing the suffering dust.
The Open Air Concert, on the special twilight green. . . .
When Beethoven is brutal or whispers to lady-like air.
Blanket-sitters are solemn, as Johann troubles to lean
To tell them what to mean. . . .

There is love, too, in Little Rock. Soft women softly
Opening themselves in kindness.
Or, pitying one's blindness,
Awaiting one's pleasure   30

[1] A Chicago newspaper.
[2] Little Rock, Arkansas, the scene of racial disturbances over public school integration in 1957.
[3] A brand of cookies.
[4] A nineteenth-century song traditionally sung by Venetian gondoliers.

In azure
Glory with anguished rose at the root. . . .
To wash away old semi-discomfitures.
They re-teach purple and unsullen blue.
The wispy soils go. And uncertain
Half-havings have they clarified to sures.

In Little Rock they know
Not answering the telephone is a way of rejecting life,
That it is our business to be bothered, is our business
To cherish bores or boredom, be polite   40
To lies and love and many-faceted fuzziness.

I scratch my head, massage the hate-I-had.
I blink across my prim and pencilled pad.
The saga I was sent for is not down.
Because there is a puzzle in this town.
The biggest News I do not dare
Telegraph to the Editor's chair:
"They are like people everywhere."

The angry Editor would reply
In hundred harryings of Why.   50

And true, they are hurling spittle, rock,
Garbage and fruit in Little Rock.
And I saw coiling storm a-writhe
On bright madonnas. And a scythe
Of men harassing brownish girls.
(The bows and barrettes in the curls
And braids declined away from joy.)

I saw a bleeding brownish boy. . . .

The lariat lynch-wish I deplored.

The loveliest lynchee was our Lord.   60

1960

THE BLACKSTONE RANGERS[1]

I
AS SEEN BY DISCIPLINES

There they are.
Thirty at the corner.
Black, raw, ready.
Sores in the city
that do not want to heal.

[1]The name of a Chicago street gang.

II
THE LEADERS

Jeff. Gene. Geronimo. And Bop.
They cancel, cure and curry.
Hardly the dupes of the downtown thing
the cold bonbon,
the rhinestone thing. And hardly
in a hurry.
Hardly Belafonte, King,
Black Jesus, Stokely, Malcolm X or Rap.
Bungled trophies.
Their country is a Nation on no map.   10

Jeff, Gene, Geronimo and Bop
in the passionate noon,
in bewitching night
are the detailed men, the copious men.
They curry, cure,
they cancel, cancelled images whose Concerts
are not divine, vivacious; the different tins
are intense last entries; pagan argument;
translations of the night.

The Blackstone bitter bureaus   20
(bureaucracy is footloose) edit, fuse
unfashionable damnations and descent;
and exulting, monstrous hand on monstrous hand,
Construct, strangely, a monstrous pearl or grace.

III
GANG GIRLS

A Rangerette

Gang Girls are sweet exotics.
Mary Ann
uses the nutrients of her orient,
but sometimes sighs for Cities of blue and jewel
beyond her Ranger rim of Cottage Grove.[2]
(Bowery Boys, Disciples, Whip-Birds[3] will
dissolve no margins, stop no savory sanctities.)

Mary is
a rose in a whiskey glass.

Mary's   10
Februaries shudder and are gone. Aprils
fret frankly, lilac hurries on.
Summer is a hard irregular ridge.

[2]A Chicago street.   [3]Rival street gangs.

October looks away.
And that's the Year!
          Save for her bugle-love.
Save for the bleat of not-obese devotion.
Save for Somebody Terribly Dying, under
the philanthropy of robins. Save for her Ranger
bringing   20
an amount of rainbow in a string-drawn bag.
"Where did you get the diamond?" Do not ask:
but swallow, straight, the spirals of his flask
and assist him at your zipper; pet his lips
and help him clutch you.

Love's another departure.
Will there be any arrivals, confirmations?
Will there be gleaning?

Mary, the Shakedancer's child
from the rooming-flat, pants carefully, peers at   30
her laboring lover. . . .
            Mary! Mary Ann!
Settle for sandwiches! settle for stocking caps!
for sudden blood, aborted carnival,
the props and niceties of non-loneliness—
the rhymes of Leaning.

                                1968

Theodore Roethke   *1908–1963*

Although he died at the height of his creative powers, Theodore Roethke left a body of first-rate poetry sufficient to establish him as one of the finest American poets of the twentieth century. Recognition came while he still lived. After receiving Guggenheim Fellowships in 1946 and 1950, he was awarded the Pulitzer Prize in 1954 for The Waking: Poems, 1933–1953 *(1953).* Words for the Wind *(1958) received a Bollingen Prize in 1958 and the Edna St. Vincent Millay Prize in 1959. Acclaim for his work has continued since his death:* The Far Field, *published posthumously in 1964, won the National Book Award in 1965. Since the publication of his* Collected Poems *(1966), and as critics have looked more deeply into Roethke's poems, his reputation has continued to rise.*

Roethke was born in Saginaw, Michigan, where a dingy industrial atmosphere contrasted sharply with the loveliness of nearby lakes and streams, woods and farmlands, scenes that aroused in him a mystical reverence for nature. Roethke's father was a florist, and the strange paradoxes Roethke perceived in the plant world of his father's greenhouse—where death and life mingled in a weird, grotesque kind of beauty—helped shape Roethke's poetic sensibility and provided him with a rich source of imagery.

After taking his B.A. in *1929*, at the University of Michigan, Roethke began a career in college and university teaching that took him first to Lafayette College in Pennsylvania, from *1931* to *1935*, then, after he completed his M.A. at Michigan in *1936*, to Pennsylvania State College, where he remained until *1943*. During World War II he taught at Bennington College, and in *1947* he took a position at the University of Washington, Seattle, where he remained for the rest of his life.

Roethke's development as a poet began in his early twenties, soon after he graduated from the University of Michigan, but he was well into his thirties when his first volume, Open House, appeared in *1941*. His poems may be divided broadly into two groups: first, those that are orthodox in form, rational in theme, ironic in tone; and second, poems that utilize free forms, reflecting the influence of Whitman ("Be with me, Whitman, maker of catalogues") and the romantic transcendentalism of Emerson. The impact of T. S. Eliot on Roethke was chiefly formal and technical, evident particularly in Roethke's efforts to effect "something other than the usual in old forms." He shared Emerson's belief in the immanence of spirit in nature, but Roethke's poems display the individual stamp of their author. He saw the dark side of nature that Emerson tended to explain away, and from the whimsy of Roethke's delightful "Nonsense Poems" to the irony of the pieces in The Far Field, Roethke's vision of life and poetic style remained uniquely his own.

FURTHER READING: *On the Poet and His Craft, Selected Prose of Theodore Roethke*, ed. R. Mills, 1965; *Selected Letters of Theodore Roethke*, ed. R. Mills, 1968; *Straw from Fire, From the Notebooks of Theodore Roethke*, ed. D. Wagoner, 1972; A. Seagar, *The Glass House, The Life of Theodore Roethke*, 1968; R. Mills, *Theodore Roethke*, 1963; *Theodore Roethke, Essays on the Poetry*, ed. A. Stein, 1965; K. Malkoff, *Theodore Roethke, An Introduction to the Poetry*, 1966; R. Blessing, *Theodore Roethke's Dynamic Vision*, 1974; R. Sullivan, *Theodore Roethke, The Garden Master*, 1975; J. La Belle, *The Echoing Wood of Theodore Roethke*, 1976; H. Williams, "The Edge Is What I Have," *Theodore Roethke and After*, 1977; J. Parini, *Theodore Roethke*, 1979; G. Wolff, *Theodore Roethke*, 1981; N. Chaney, *Theodore Roethke, The Poetics of Wonder*, 1981; L. Ross-Bryant, *Theodore Roethke, Poetry of the Earth*, 1981; N. Bowers, *Theodore Roethke, The Journey from I to Otherwise*, 1982.

TEXT: *The Collected Poems of Theodore Roethke*, 1966.

DOLOR

I have known the inexorable sadness of pencils,
Neat in their boxes, dolor of pad and paper-weight,
All the misery of manila folders and mucilage,
Desolation in immaculate public places,
Lonely reception room, lavatory, switchboard,
The unalterable pathos of basin and pitcher,
Ritual of multigraph, paper-clip, comma,
Endless duplication of lives and objects.
And I have seen dust from the walls of institutions,
Finer than flour, alive, more dangerous than silica,   10
Sift, almost invisible, through long afternoons of tedium,
Dropping a fine film on nails and delicate eyebrows,
Glazing the pale hair, the duplicate grey standard faces.

                                                   1943, 1948

OPEN HOUSE

My secrets cry aloud.
I have no need for tongue.
My heart keeps open house,
My doors are widely swung.
An epic of the eyes
My love, with no disguise.

My truths are all foreknown,
This anguish self-revealed.
I'm naked to the bone,
With nakedness my shield.   10
Myself is what I wear:
I keep the spirit spare.

The anger will endure,
The deed will speak the truth
In language strict and pure.
I stop the lying mouth:
Rage warps my clearest cry
To witless agony.
1936   1941

ON THE ROAD TO WOODLAWN[1]

I miss the polished brass, the powerful black horses,
The drivers creaking the seats of the baroque hearses,
The high-piled floral offerings with sentimental verses,
The carriages reeking with varnish and stale perfume.

I miss the pallbearers momentously taking their places,
The undertaker's obsequious grimaces,
The craned necks, the mourners' anonymous faces,
—And the eyes, still vivid, looking up from a sunken room.
1939   1941

CUTTINGS

Sticks-in-a-drowse droop over sugary loam,
Their intricate stem-fur dries;
But still the delicate slips keep coaxing up water;
The small cells bulge;

[1]The name of a cemetery.

One nub of growth
Nudges a sand-crumb loose,
Pokes through a musty sheath
Its pale tendrilous horn.
1943–1944   1948

CUTTINGS

(Later)

This urge, wrestle, resurrection of dry sticks,
Cut stems struggling to put down feet,
What saint strained so much,
Rose on such lopped limbs to a new life?

I can hear, underground, that sucking and sobbing,
In my veins, in my bones I feel it,—
The small waters seeping upward,
The tight grains parting at last.
When sprouts break out,
Slippery as fish,   10
I quail, lean to beginnings, sheath-wet.
1943–1944   1948

ROOT CELLAR

Nothing would sleep in that cellar, dank as a ditch,
Bulbs broke out of boxes hunting for chinks in the dark,
Shoots dangled and drooped,
Lolling obscenely from mildewed crates,
Hung down long yellow evil necks, like tropical snakes.
And what a congress of stinks!—
Roots ripe as old bait,
Pulpy stems, rank, silo-rich,
Leaf-mold, manure, lime, piled against slippery planks.
Nothing would give up life: 10
Even the dirt kept breathing a small breath.
1943   1948

BIG WIND

Where were the greenhouses going,
Lunging into the lashing
Wind driving water
So far down the river

All the faucets stopped?—
So we drained the manure-machine
For the steam plant,
Pumping the stale mixture
Into the rusty boilers,
Watching the pressure gauge 10
Waver over to red,
As the seams hissed
And the live steam
Drove to the far
End of the rose-house,
Where the worst wind was,
Creaking the cypress window-frames,
Cracking so much thin glass
We stayed all night,
Stuffing the holes with burlap; 20
But she rode it out,
That old rose-house,
She hove into the teeth of it,
The core and pith of that ugly storm,
Ploughing with her stiff prow,
Bucking into the wind-waves
That broke over the whole of her,
Flailing her sides with spray,
Flinging long strings of wet across the roof-top,
Finally veering, wearing themselves out, merely 30
Whistling thinly under the wind-vents;
She sailed until the calm morning,
Carrying her full cargo of roses.
1946   1948

MY PAPA'S WALTZ

The whiskey on your breath
Could make a small boy dizzy;
But I hung on like death:
Such waltzing was not easy.

We romped until the pans
Slid from the kitchen shelf;
My mother's countenance
Could not unfrown itself.

The hand that held my wrist
Was battered on one knuckle; 10
At every step you missed
My right ear scraped a buckle.

You beat time on my head
With a palm caked hard by dirt,
Then waltzed me off to bed
Still clinging to your shirt.
1942   1948

THE LOST SON

1. *The Flight*

At Woodlawn I heard the dead cry:
I was lulled by the slamming of iron,
A slow drip over stones,
Toads brooding wells.
All the leaves stuck out their tongues;
I shook the softening chalk of my bones,
Saying,
Snail, snail, glister me forward,
Bird, soft-sigh me home,
Worm, be with me   10
This is my hard time.

Fished in an old wound,
The soft pond of repose;
Nothing nibbled my line,
Not even the minnows came.

Sat in an empty house
Watching shadows crawl,
Scratching.
There was one fly.

Voice, come out of the silence.   20
Say something.
Appear in the form of a spider
Or a moth beating the curtain.

Tell me:
Which is the way I take;
Out of what door do I go,
Where and to whom?

Dark hollows said, lee to the wind,
The moon said, back of an eel,
The salt said, look by the sea,   30
Your tears are not enough praise,
You will find no comfort here,
In the kingdom of bang and blab.

Running lightly over spongy ground,
Past the pasture of flat stones,
The three elms,
The sheep strewn on a field,
Over a rickety bridge
Toward the quick-water, wrinkling and rippling.

Hunting along the river,   40
Down among the rubbish, the bug-riddled foliage,
By the muddy pond-edge, by the bog-holes,
By the shrunken lake, hunting, in the heat of summer.

The shape of a rat?
    It's bigger than that.
    It's less than a leg
    And more than a nose,
    Just under the water
    It usually goes.

Is it soft like a mouse?   50
Can it wrinkle its nose?
Could it come in the house
On the tips of its toes?

    Take the skin of a cat
    And the back of an eel,
    The roll them in grease,—
    That's the way it would feel.

    It's sleek as an otter
    With wide webby toes
    Just under the water   60
    It usually goes.

2. *The Pit*

Where do the roots go?
    Look down under the leaves.
Who put the moss there?
    These stones have been here too long.
Who stunned the dirt into noise?
    Ask the mole, he knows.
I feel the slime of a wet nest.
    Beware Mother Mildew.
Nibble again, fish nerves.   70

3. *The Gibber*

At the wood's mouth,
By the cave's door,
I listened to something
I had heard before.

Dogs of the groin
Barked and howled,
The sun was against me,
The moon would not have me.

The weeds whined,
The snakes cried,   80
The cows and briars
Said to me: Die.

What a small song. What slow clouds. What dark water.
Hath the rain a father? All the caves are ice. Only the snow's here.
I'm cold. I'm cold all over. Rub me in father and mother.
Fear was my father, Father Fear.
His look drained the stones.

    What gliding shape
    Beckoning through halls,
    Stood poised on the stair,   90
    Fell dreamily down?

    From the mouths of jugs
    Perched on many shelves,
    I saw substance flowing
    That cold morning.

    Like a slither of eels
    That watery cheek
    As my own tongue kissed
    My lips awake.

Is this the storm's heart? The ground is unstilling itself.   100
My veins are running nowhere. Do the bones cast out their fire?
Is the seed leaving the old bed? These buds are live as birds.
Where, where are the tears of the world?
Let the kisses resound, flat like a butcher's palm;
Let the gestures freeze; our doom is already decided.
All the windows are burning! What's left of my life?
I want the old rage, the lash of primordial milk!
Goodbye, goodbye, old stones, the time-order is going,
I have married my hands to perpetual agitation,
I run, I run to the whistle of money.   110

    Money money money
    Water water water

    How cool the grass is.
    Has the bird left?
    The stalk still sways.
    Has the worm a shadow?
    What do the clouds say?

These sweeps of light undo me.
Look, look, the ditch is running white!
I've more veins than a tree!   120
Kiss me, ashes, I'm falling through a dark swirl.

4. *The Return*

The way to the boiler was dark,
Dark all the way,
Over slippery cinders
Through the long greenhouse.

The roses kept breathing in the dark.
They had many mouths to breathe with.
My knees made little winds underneath
Where the weeds slept.

There was always a single light   130
Swinging by the fire-pit,
Where the fireman pulled out roses,
The big roses, the big bloody clinkers.[1]

Once I stayed all night.
The light in the morning came slowly over the white
Snow.
There were many kinds of cool
Air.
Then came steam.

Pipe-knock.[2]   140

Scurry of warm over small plants.
Ordnung! ordnung![3]
Papa is coming!
    A fine haze moved off the leaves;
    Frost melted on far panes;
    The rose, the chrysanthemum turned toward the light.
    Even the hushed forms, the bent yellowy weeds
    Moved in a slow up-sway.

5. *"It Was Beginning Winter"*

It was beginning winter,
An in-between time,   150
The landscape still partly brown:
The bones of weeds kept swinging in the wind,
Above the blue snow.

[1]Slag, fused lumps of impurities left by a coal fire.
[2]I.e., the knocking of steam-radiator pipes.
[3]German: Order! order!

It was beginning winter,
The light moved slowly over the frozen field,
Over the dry seed-crowns,
The beautiful surviving bones
Swinging in the wind.

Light traveled over the wide field;
Stayed.   160
The weeds stopped swinging.
The mind moved, not alone,
Through the clear air, in the silence.

    Was it light?
    Was it light within?
    Was it light within light?
    Stillness becoming alive,
    Yet still?

A lively understandable spirit
Once entertained you.   170
It will come again.
Be still.
Wait.

1946   1948

THE WAKING

    I wake to sleep, and take my waking slow.
    I feel my fate in what I cannot fear.
    I learn by going where I have to go.

    We think by feeling. What is there to know?
    I hear my being dance from ear to ear.
    I wake to sleep, and take my waking slow.

    Of those so close beside me, which are you?
    God bless the Ground! I shall walk softly there,
    And learn by going where I have to go.

    Light takes the Tree; but who can tell us how?   10
    The lowly worm climbs up a winding stair;
    I wake to sleep, and take my waking slow.

    Great Nature has another thing to do
    To you and me; so take the lively air,
    And, lovely, learn by going where to go.

This shaking keeps me steady. I should know.
What falls away is always. And is near.
I wake to sleep, and take my waking slow.
I learn by going where I have to go.
1952   1953

I KNEW A WOMAN

I knew a woman, lovely in her bones,
When small birds sighed, she would sigh back at them;
Ah, when she moved, she moved more ways than one:
The shapes a bright container can contain!
Of her choice virtues only gods should speak,
Or English poets who grew up on Greek
(I'd have them sing in chorus, cheek to cheek).

How well her wishes went! She stroked my chin,
She taught me Turn, and Counter-turn, and Stand;
She taught me Touch, that undulant white skin;   10
I nibbled meekly from her proffered hand;
She was the sickle; I, poor I, the rake,
Coming behind her for her pretty sake
(But what prodigious mowing we did make).

Love likes a gander, and adores a goose:
Her full lips pursed, the errant note to seize;
She played it quick, she played it light and loose;
My eyes, they dazzled at her flowing knees;
Her several parts could keep a pure repose,
Or one hip quiver with a mobile nose   20
(She moved in circles, and those circles moved).

Let seed be grass, and grass turn into hay:
I'm martyr to a motion not my own;
What's freedom for? To know eternity.
I swear she cast a shadow white as stone.
But who would count eternity in days?
These old bones live to learn her wanton ways:
(I measure time by how a body sways).

                                            1958

IN A DARK TIME

I
In a dark time, the eye begins to see:
I meet my shadow in the deepening shade;

I hear my echo in the echoing wood,
A lord of nature weeping to a tree.
I live between the heron and the wren,
Beasts of the hill and serpents of the den.

II

What's madness but nobility of soul
At odds with circumstance? The day's on fire!
I know the purity of pure despair,
My shadow pinned against a sweating wall.   10
That place among the rocks—is it a cave
Or winding path? The edge is what I have.

III

A steady storm of correspondences!—
A night flowing with birds, a ragged moon,
And in broad day the midnight come again!
A man goes far to find out what he is—
Death of the self in a long tearless night,
All natural shapes blazing unnatural light.

IV

Dark, dark my light, and darker my desire.
My soul, like some heat-maddened fly,
Keeps buzzing at the sill. Which I is *I*?   20
A fallen man, I climb out of my fear.
The mind enters itself, and God the mind,
And one is One, free in the tearing wind.

                                          1960, 1963

WISH FOR A YOUNG WIFE

My lizard, my lively writher,
May your limbs never wither,
May the eyes in your face
Survive the green ice
Of envy's mean gaze;
May you live out your life
Without hate, without grief,
And your hair ever blaze,
In the sun, in the sun,
When I am undone,
When I am no one.
1963   1964

Randall Jarrell *1914–1965*

Randall Jarrell was renowned as a teacher, a critic, and a poet. He spent most of his adult life as a professor of literature and once remarked, "If I were a rich man, I would pay money for the privilege of being able to teach." His critical writings were renowned for their savage dissections of poetic mediocrity and their enthusiastic praise of poetic skill. Of Jarrell's own poetic talent, the American poet Robert Lowell observed: "His gifts, both by nature and by a lifetime of hard dedication and growth, were wit, pathos, and brilliance of intelligence. These qualities, in themselves, were often so well employed that he became, I think, the most heartbreaking English poet of his generation."

Jarrell spent his early years in California living with his paternal grandparents and great-grandparents. When he was twelve he moved to Tennessee, where he attended high school. Following his graduation, he was enrolled in a secretarial school to learn bookkeeping and shorthand in order to enter his uncle's candy firm. But Jarrell's indifference to business studies was so profound that his uncle finally agreed to send him to college instead. At Vanderbilt University he edited the literary magazine and studied under the poet-critic John Crowe Ransom. In 1939 Jarrell took an M.A. at Vanderbilt. He taught English at Kenyon College and at the University of Texas, and from 1942 to 1946 he served in the United States Army Air Force. From his military experiences came some of his finest writing, poems dealing with flying and the terrors of aerial warfare. In 1945, while still in the army, he published a volume of poems, Little Friend, Little Friend. *After his discharge from the Air Force, in 1946, he served for a short period as the literary editor of the* Nation. *In 1947 he accepted a position at the Women's College of the University of North Carolina, where he remained for the rest of his life.*

Jarrell wrote six volumes of poetry, a novel: Pictures from an Institution *(1954), and four volumes of critical essays:* Poetry and the Age *(1953),* A Sad Heart at the Supermarket *(1962),* The Third Book of Criticism *(1969), and* Kipling, Auden and Co., Essays and Reviews, 1935–1964 *(1980). Some of Jarrell's poetry was painfully realistic, some so extravagantly allusive as to resist interpretation. His dominant theme is change—change affecting women, children, and men in war and peace. His recurring motifs are journeys, dreams, fears, and death. He described human lives that fail to fulfill ideals, and he wrote of isolated people, suffering from loss and grieving at evil, men and women who could respond to life's agonies only by attempting, but failing, to escape them.*

FURTHER READING: *Randall Jarrell's Letters,* ed. M. Jarrell, 1985; *Randall Jarrell, 1914–1965,* ed. R. Lowell, P. Taylor, and R. Warren, 1967; K. Shapiro, *Randall Jarrell,* 1967; *The Achievement of Randall Jarrell,* ed. F. Hoffman, 1970; S. Ferguson, *The Poetry of Randall Jarrell,* 1971; M. Rosenthal, *Randall Jarrell,* 1972; H. Hagenbuchle, *The Black Goddess, A Study of the Archetypal Feminine in the Poetry of Randall Jarrell,* 1975; B. Quinn, *Randall Jarrell,* 1981; *Critical Essays on Randall Jarrell,* ed. S. Ferguson, 1983; J. Bryant, *Understanding Randall Jarrell,* 1986.

TEXT: *The Complete Poems,* 1969.

LOSSES

It was not dying: everybody died.
It was not dying: we had died before
In the routine crashes—and our fields

Called up the papers, wrote home to our folks,
And the rates rose, all because of us.
We died on the wrong page of the almanac,
Scattered on mountains fifty miles away;
Diving on haystacks, fighting with a friend,
We blazed up on the lines[1] we never saw.
We died like aunts or pets or foreigners.   10
(When we left high school nothing else had died
For us to figure we had died like.)

In our new planes, with our new crews, we bombed
The ranges by the desert or the shore,
Fired at towed targets, waited for our scores—
And turned into replacements and woke up
One morning, over England, operational.
It wasn't different: but if we died
It was not an accident but a mistake
(But an easy one for anyone to make).   20
We read our mail and counted up our missions—
In bombers named for girls, we burned
The cities we had learned about in school—
Till our lives wore out; our bodies lay among
The people we had killed and never seen.
When we lasted long enough they gave us medals;
When we died they said, "Our casualties were low."
They said, "Here are the maps": we burned the cities.

It was not dying—no, not ever dying;
But the night I died I dreamed that I was dead,   30
And the cities said to me: "Why are you dying?
We are satisfied, if you are; but why did I die?"

                                             1944, 1945

THE DEATH OF THE BALL TURRET GUNNER[1]

From my mother's sleep I fell into the State,
And I hunched in its belly till my wet fur froze.
Six miles from earth, loosed from its dream of life,
I woke to black flak[2] and the nightmare fighters.
When I died they washed me out of the turret with a hose.

                                             1945

---

[1]Electric power lines.
[1]"A ball turret was a plexiglass sphere set into the belly of a B-17 or B-24 and inhabited by two .50 caliber machine-guns and one man, a short small man. When this gunner tracked with his machine-guns a fighter attacking his bomber from below, he revolved with the turret; hunched upside-down in his little sphere, he looked like the foetus in the womb. The fighters which attacked him were armed with cannon firing explosive shells. The hose was a steam hose."—Jarrell's note.
[2]Anti-aircraft fire.

A CAMP IN THE PRUSSIAN FOREST[1]

I walk beside the prisoners to the road.
Load on puffed load,
Their corpses, stacked like sodden wood,
Lie barred or galled with blood

By the charred warehouse. No one comes today
In the old way
To knock the fillings from their teeth;
The dark, coned, common wreath

Is plaited for their grave—a kind of grief.
The living leaf   10
Clings to the planted profitable
Pine if it is able;

The boughs sigh, mile on green, calm, breathing mile,
From this dead file
The planners ruled for them. . . .[2] One year
They sent a million here:

Here men were drunk like water, burnt like wood.
The fat of good
And evil, the breast's star of hope
Were rendered into soap.   20

I paint the star I sawed from yellow pine—
And plant the sign
In soil that does not yet refuse
Its usual Jews

Their first asylum. But the white, dwarfed star—
This dead white star—
Hides nothing, pays for nothing; smoke
Fouls it, a yellow joke,

The needles of the wreath are chalked with ash,
A filmy trash   30
Litters the black woods with the death
Of men; and one last breath

[1] " 'A Camp in the Prussian Forest': An American soldier is speaking after the capture of one of the German death camps. Jews, under the Nazis, were made to wear a yellow star. The Star of David is set over Jewish graves as the Cross is set over Christian graves."—Jarrell's note.
[2] Here, and throughout, the ellipses points are Jarrell's.

Curls from the monstrous chimney. . . . I laugh aloud
Again and again;
The star laughs from its rotting shroud
Of flesh. O star of men!

1946, 1948

SEELE IM RAUM[1]

It sat between my husband and my children
A place was set for it—a plate of greens.
It had been there: I had seen it
But not somehow—but this was like a dream—
Not seen it so that I knew I saw it.
It was as if I could not know I saw it
Because I had never once in all my life
Not seen it. It was an eland.
An eland! *That* is why the children
Would ask my husband, for a joke, at Christmas: 10
"Father, is it Donner?" He would say, "No, Blitzen."
It had been there always. Now we put silver
At its place at meals, fed it the same food
We ourselves ate, and said nothing. Many times
When it breathed heavily (when it had tried
A long useless time to speak) and reached to me
So that I touched it—of a different size
And order of being, like the live hard side
Of a horse's neck when you pat the horse—
And looked with its great melting tearless eyes   20
Fringed with a few coarse wire-like lashes
Into my eyes, and whispered to me
So that my eyes turned backward in their sockets
And they said nothing—
                    many times
I have known, when they said nothing,
That it did not exist. If they had heard
They *could* not have been silent. And yet they heard;
Heard many times what I have spoken
When it could no longer speak, but only breathe—   30
When I could no longer speak, but only breathe.

And, after some years, the others came
And took it from me—it was ill, they told me—
And cured it, they wrote me: my whole city
Sent me cards like lilac-branches, mourning
As I had mourned—
                    and I was standing
By a grave in flowers, by dyed rolls of turf,
And a canvas marquee the last brown of earth.

[1]" 'Seele im Raum' is the title of one of Rilke's poems; 'Soul in Space' sounded so glib that I couldn't use it instead. An eland is the largest sort of African antelope—the males are as big as a horse, and you often see people gazing at them, at the zoo, an uneasy wonder."—Jarrell's note.

It is over. 40
It is over so long that I began to think
That it did not exist, that I have never—
And my son says, one morning, from the paper:
"An eland. Look, an eland!"
                    —It was so.

Today, in a German dictionary, I saw *elend*
And the heart in my breast turned over, it was—

It was a word one translates *wretched.*

It is as if someone remembered saying:
"This is an antimacassar that I grew from seed," 50
And this were true.
                    And, truly,
One could not wish for anything more strange—
For anything more. And yet it wasn't *interesting* . . .
—It was worse than impossible, it was a joke.

And yet when it was, I *was*—
Even to think that I once thought
That I could see it is to feel the sweat
Like needles at my hair-roots, I am blind

—It was not even a joke, not even a joke. 60

Yet how can I believe it? Or believe that I
Owned it, a husband, children? Is my voice the voice
Of that skin of being—of what owns, is owned
In honor or dishonor, that is borne and bears—
Or of that raw thing, the being inside it
That has neither a wife, a husband, nor a child
But goes at last as naked from this world
As it was born into it—

And the eland comes and grazes on its grave.

                    This is senseless? 70
Shall I make sense or shall I tell the truth?
Choose either—I cannot do both.

I tell myself that. And yet it is not so,
And what I say afterwards will not be so:
To be at all is to be wrong.
                    Being is being old
And saying, almost comfortably, across a table
From—
        from what I don't know—
                    in a voice 80

Rich with a kind of longing satisfaction:
"To own an eland! That's what I call life!"

                                                        1950, 1955

A GIRL IN A LIBRARY[1]

An object among dreams, you sit here with your shoes off
And curl your legs up under you; your eyes
Close for a moment, your face moves toward sleep . . .
You are very human.
                        But my mind, gone out in tenderness,
Shrinks from its object with a thoughtful sigh.
This is a waist the spirit breaks its arm on.
The gods themselves, against you, struggle in vain.[2]
This broad low strong-boned brow; these heavy eyes;
These calves, grown muscular with certainties;   10
This nose, three medium-sized pink strawberries
—But I exaggerate. In a little you will leave:
I'll hear, half squeal, half shriek, your laugh of greeting—
Then, *decrescendo*,[3] bars of that strange speech
In which each sound sets out to seek each other,
Murders its own father, marries its own mother,
And ends as one grand transcendental vowel.

(Yet for all I know, the Egyptian Helen[4] spoke so.)
As I look, the world contracts around you:
I see Brünnhilde[5] had brown braids and glasses   20
She used for studying; Salome[6] straight brown bangs,
A calf's brown eyes, and sturdy light-brown limbs
Dusted with cinnamon, an apple-dumpling's . . .
Many a beast has gnawn a leg off and got free,
Many a dolphin curved up from Necessity[7]—

---

[1] "'A Girl in a Library' is a poem about the New World and the Old: about a girl, a student of Home Economics and Physical Education, who has fallen asleep in the library of a Southern college; about a woman who looks out of one book, Pushkin's *Eugene Onegin*, at this girl asleep among so many; and about the *I* of the poem, a man somewhere between the two. A *blind date* is an unknown someone you accompany to something; if he promises to come for you and doesn't, he has *stood you up*. The Corn King and the Spring Queen went by many names; in the beginning they were the man and woman who, after ruling for a time, were torn to pieces and scattered over the fields in order that the grain might grow. . . ."—Jarrell's note.

[2] Jarrell's version of the phrase, "Against stupidity the very gods/Themselves contend in vain," from *The Maid of Orleans* (1801), by the German poet Johann Friedrich von Schiller (1759–1805).

[3] Decreasing in force or sound.

[4] According to one version of the legend, Helen of Troy was carried off to Egypt; it was her phantom that accompanied Paris to Troy.

[5] Daughter of the Teutonic god Wotan, portrayed in Richard Wagner's opera cycle, *The Ring of the Nibelungs* (1869–1874). She is put into a deep sleep until awakened by a kiss from the hero Siegfried.

[6] Temptress, niece of King Herod, who won the head of John the Baptist as a reward for her dancing. Matthew 14:6–11.

[7] The philosophical doctrine that the actions of all things are inevitably dictated by their being or nature.

The trap has closed about you, and you sleep.
If someone questioned you, *What doest thou here?*[8]
You'd knit your brows like an orangoutang
(But not so sadly; not so thoughtfully)
And answer with a pure heart, guilelessly: 30
I'm studying. . . .
                    If only you were not!
Assignments,
                    recipes,
                    the *Official Rulebook*
Of Basketball—ah, let them go; you needn't mind.
The soul has no assignments, neither cooks
Nor referees: it wastes its time.
                    It wastes its time.
Here in this enclave there are centuries   40
For you to waste: the short and narrow stream
Of Life meanders into a thousand valleys
Of all that was, or might have been, or is to be.
The books, just leafed through, whisper endlessly . . .
Yet it is hard. One sees in your blurred eyes
The "uneasy half-soul" Kipling[9] saw in dogs'.
One sees it, in the glass, in one's own eyes.
In rooms alone, in galleries, in libraries,
In tears, in searchings of the heart, in staggering joys
We memorize once more our old creation,   50
Humanity: with what yawns the unwilling
Flesh puts on its spirit, O my sister!

So many dreams! And not one troubles
Your sleep of life? no self stares shadowily
From these worn hexahedrons, beckoning
With false smiles, tears? . . .
                    Meanwhile Tatyana
Larina[10] (gray eyes nickel with the moonlight)
That falls through the willows onto Lensky's tomb;
Now young and shy, now old and cold and sure)   60
Asks, smiling: "But what is she dreaming of, fat thing?"
I answer: She's not fat. She isn't dreaming.
She purrs or laps or runs, all in her sleep;
Believes, awake, that she is beautiful;
She never dreams.
                    Those sunrise-colored clouds
Around man's head—that inconceivable enchantment
From which, at sunset, we come back to life
To find our graves dug, families dead, selves dying:

[8]Words spoken by the Lord to Elijah, who is then moved to higher levels of perception. I Kings 19:9.
[9]Rudyard Kipling (1865–1936), English poet and short story writer. His poem "Supplication of a Black Aberdeen" portrays a dog's "dim, distressed half-soul."
[10]A woman of beauty and sophistication in the verse drama *Eugene Onegin* (1833), by the Russian poet Alexander Pushkin (1799–1837), where she is saddened by the death of her friend Vladimir Lensky, killed in a duel.

Of all this, Tanya,[11] she is innocent.   70
For nineteen years she's faced reality:
They look alike already.
                                They say, man wouldn't be
The best thing in this world—and isn't he?—
If he were not too good for it. But she
—She's good enough for it.
                                And yet sometimes
Her sturdy form, in its pink strapless formal,
Is as if bathed in moonlight—modulated
Into a form of joy, a Lydian mode;[12]   80
This Wooden Mean's[13] a kind, furred animal
That speaks, in the Wild of things, delighting riddles
To the soul that listens, trusting . . .
                                Poor senseless Life:
When, in the last light sleep of dawn, the messenger
Comes with his message, you will not awake.
He'll give his feathery whistle, shake you hard,
You'll look with wide eyes at the dewy yard
And dream, with calm slow factuality:
"Today's Commencement. My bachelor's degree   90
In Home Ec., my doctorate of philosophy
In Phys. Ed.
                [Tanya, they won't even *scan*]
Are waiting for me. . . ."
                                Oh, Tatyana,
The Angel comes: better to squawk like a chicken
Than to say with truth, "But I'm a *good* girl,"
And Meet his Challenge with a last firm strange
Uncomprehending smile; and—then, then!—see
The blind date that has stood you up: your life.   100
(For all this, if it isn't perhaps, life,
Has yet, at least, a language of its own
Different from the books'; worse than the books'.)
And yet, the ways we miss our lives are life.
Yet . . . yet . . .
                        to have one's life add up to *yet!*

You sigh a shuddering sigh. Tatyana murmurs,
"Don't cry, little peasant"; leaves us with a swift
"Good-bye, good-bye . . . Ah, don't think ill of me . . ."
Your eyes open: you sit here thoughtlessly.   110
I love you—and yet—and yet—I love you.

Don't cry, little peasant. Sit and dream.
One comes, a finger's width beneath your skin,
To the braided maidens[14] singing as they spin;

[11]Diminutive form of "Tatyana."

[12]One of the modes of ancient Greek music, rich and sensual.

[13]A contemptuous contrast to the Golden Mean, the philosophical doctrine that virtue is achieved through moderation and use of the intellect.

[14]The "braided maidens," and the shepherd and watchman alluded to below, are minor characters in Wagnerian opera. Insignificant and dull-witted, they are unaware of what occurs around them.

There sound the shepherd's pipe, the watchman's rattle
Across the short dark distance of the years.
I am a thought of yours: and yet, you do not think . . .
The firelight of a long, blind, dreaming story
Lingers upon your lips; and I have seen
Firm, fixed forever in your closing eyes,   120
The Corn King beckoning to his Spring Queen.

                                          1951, 1955

IN MONTECITO

In a fashionable suburb of Santa Barbara,[1]
Montecito, there visited me one night at midnight
A scream with breasts. As it hung there in the sweet air
That was always the right temperature, the contractors
Who had undertaken to dismantle it, stripped off
The lips, let the air out of the breasts.
                                  People disappear
Even in Montecito. Greenie Taliaferro,[2]
In her white maillot,[3] her good figure almost firm,
Her old pepper-and-salt hair stripped by the hairdresser   10
To nothing and dyed platinum—Greenie has left her Bentley.[4]
They have thrown away her electric toothbrush, someone else slips
The key into the lock of her safety-deposit box
At the Crocker-Anglo Bank; her seat at the cricket matches
Is warmed by buttocks less delectable than hers.
Greenie's girdle is empty.
                          A scream hangs there in the night:
They strip off the lips, let the air out of the breasts,
And Greenie has gone into the Greater Montecito
That surrounds Montecito like the echo of a scream.   20

                                          1965

A WELL-TO-DO INVALID

When you first introduced me to your nurse
I thought: "She's like your wife." I mean, I thought:
"She's like your nurse—" it was your wife.

She gave this old friend of her husband's
A pale ingratiating smile; we talked
And she agreed with me about everything.
I thought: "She's quite agreeable."
You gave a pleased laugh—you were feeling good.

[1]In California.   [2]Pronounced "Tolliver."
[3]A tight-fitting gymnastic suit of stretch-knit fabric.
[4]An expensive, English automobile.

She laughed and agreed with you.
                                    I said to her   10
—That is, I didn't say to her: "You liar!"
She held out
Her deck of smiles, I cut, and she dealt.

Almost as the years have sprung up, fallen back,
I've seen you in and out of bed; meanwhile,
Hovering solicitously alongside,
This governess, this mother
In her off-whites—pretty as a nurse
Is thinly and efficiently and optimistically
Pretty—has spoken with an enthusiasm   20
Like winter sunlight, of the comprehensiveness of insurance.
If you want it to, it can cover anything.

Like the governor on an engine, she has governed
Your rashness. And how many sins
She has forgiven in her big child! How many times
She has telephoned in an emergency
For the right specialist!
After I'd left your bed she'd take me to the door
And tell me about your heart and bowels.
When you were up and talking she would listen   30
A long time, oh so long! but go to bed
Before we did, with a limp, wan, almost brave
"Goodnight!" You are a natural
Disaster she has made her own. Meanly
Clinging to you, taking care—all praise
And understanding outside, and inside all insurance—
She has stood by you like a plaster Joan of Arc.
Prematurely tired, prematurely
Mature, she has endured
Much, indulgently   40
Repeating like a piece of white carbon paper
The opinions of that boisterous, sick thing, a man.
I can see through her—but then, who can't?
Her dishonesty is so transparent
It has about it a kind of honesty.
She has never once said what she thought, done what she wanted,
But (as if invented by some old economist
And put on an island, to trade with her mate)
Has acted in impersonal self-interest.

Never to do one thing for its own sake!   50

Year in, year out, with what sincerity
You said anything, demanded everything,
And she, the liar!
Was good to you—oh, insincerely good,
Good for all the worst reasons. Good.
And she was nice to me, and I was nice

To her: I *wanted* to be nice to her.
She was wrong, and I was right, and I was sick of it.
It wasn't right for her always to be wrong
And work so hard and get so little: I felt guilty   60
Because I wasn't on her side. I was on her side.
It was a terrible shock to me when she died.
I saw her cheeks red for the first time
Among the snowdrifts covering her coffin;
And you were up and talking, well with grief.
As I realized how easily you'd fill
This vacancy, I was sorry
For you and for that pale self-sufficient ghost
That had tended so long your self-sufficiency.

1965

Elizabeth Bishop *1911–1979*

Elizabeth Bishop was born in Worcester, Massachusetts, and raised in Nova Scotia, Canada, and in Boston, Massachusetts. She attended Vassar College, where she majored in English literature, and in the year of her graduation, 1934, she met Marianne Moore, whose poetry of closely observed detail was a significant influence on Elizabeth Bishop's work. She traveled widely in Europe and South America (from 1952 to 1969 she lived in Brazil), and some of the themes and details of her poetry are responses to her travels and to her early childhood experiences in New England and Canada.

Her first volume, North and South, *appeared in 1946. For her* Poems (1955) *she received a Pulitzer Prize. A third volume of poetry,* A Question of Travel (1965), *was followed by* The Complete Poems (1969), *which received a National Book Award. Her last book of poems was* Geography III (1976). *In her poetry, Elizabeth Bishop often functioned as an impersonal observer capable of detachment and understanding at the same time. She used subtle rhythms, unlikely rhymes, and the impressionist's technique of implication and suggestion. She had a painter's eye for surfaces and appearances, yet her portrayals of the stark landscapes of the matter-of-fact world frequently evolved into dreamlike sequences, contrasting the commonsense world of everyday reality and the world of impressions and the imagination.*

FURTHER READING: *The Collected Prose*, 1984; A. Stevenson, *Elizabeth Bishop*, 1966; D. Kalstone, *Five Temperaments*, 1977; *Elizabeth Bishop and Her Art*, ed. L. Schwartz and S. Estes, 1983; *Elizabeth Bishop*, ed. H. Bloom, 1986.
TEXT: *The Complete Poems*, 1983.

A MIRACLE FOR BREAKFAST

At six o'clock we were waiting for coffee,
waiting for coffee and the charitable crumb

that was going to be served from a certain balcony,
—like kings of old, or like a miracle.
It was still dark. One foot of the sun
steadied itself on a long ripple in the river.

The first ferry of the day had just crossed the river.
It was so cold we hoped that the coffee
would be very hot, seeing that the sun
was not going to warm us; and that the crumb   10
would be a loaf each, buttered, by a miracle.
At seven a man stepped out on the balcony.

He stood for a minute alone on the balcony
looking over our heads toward the river.
A servant handed him the makings of a miracle,
consisting of one lone cup of coffee
and one roll, which he proceeded to crumb,
his head, so to speak, in the clouds—along with the sun.

Was the man crazy? What under the sun
was he trying to do, up there on his balcony!   20
Each man received one rather hard crumb,
which some flicked scornfully into the river,
and, in a cup, one drop of the coffee.
Some of us stood around, waiting for the miracle.

I can tell what I saw next; it was not a miracle.
A beautiful villa stood in the sun
and from its doors came the smell of hot coffee.
In front, a baroque white plaster balcony
added by birds, who nest along the river,
—I saw it with one eye close to the crumb—   30

and galleries and marble chambers. My crumb
my mansion, made for me by a miracle,
through ages, by insects, birds, and the river
working the stone. Every day, in the sun,
at breakfast time I sit on my balcony
with my feet up, and drink gallons of coffee.

We licked up the crumb and swallowed the coffee.
A window across the river caught the sun
as if the miracle were working, on the wrong balcony.

1946

ROOSTERS

At four o'clock
in the gun-metal blue dark

we hear the first crow of the first cock

just below
the gun-metal blue window
and immediately there is an echo

off in the distance,
then one from the backyard fence,
then one, with horrible insistence,

grates like a wet match   10
from the broccoli patch,
flares, and all over town begins to catch.

Cries galore
come from the water-closet door,
from the dropping-plastered henhouse floor,

where in the blue blur
their rustling wives admire,
the roosters brace their cruel feet and glare

with stupid eyes
while from their beaks there rise   20
the uncontrolled, traditional cries.

Deep from protruding chests
in green-gold medals dressed,
planned to command and terrorize the rest,

the many wives
who lead hens' lives
of being courted and despised;

deep from raw throats
a senseless order floats
all over town. A rooster gloats   30

over our beds
from rusty iron sheds
and fences made from old bedsteads,

over our churches
where the tin rooster perches,
over our little wooden northern houses,

making sallies
from all the muddy alleys,
marking out maps like Rand McNally's:

glass-headed pins,   40

oil-golds and copper greens,
anthracite blues, alizarins,[1]

each one an active
displacement in perspective;
each screaming, "This is where I live!"

Each screaming
"Get up! Stop dreaming!"
Roosters, what are you projecting?

You, whom the Greeks elected
to shoot at on a post, who struggled   50
when sacrificed, you whom they labeled

"Very combative . . ."[2]
what right have you to give
commands and tell us how to live,

cry "Here!" and "Here!"
and wake us here where are
unwanted love, conceit and war?

The crown of red
set on your little head
is charged with all your fighting blood.   60

Yes, that excrescence
makes a most virile presence,
plus all that vulgar beauty of iridescence.

Now in mid-air
by twos they fight each other.
Down comes a first flame-feather,

and one is flying,
with raging heroism defying
even the sensation of dying.

And one has fallen,   70
but still above the town
his torn-out, bloodied feathers drift down;

and what he sung
no matter. He is flung
on the gray ash-heap, lies in dung

with his dead wives
with open, bloody eyes,
while those metallic feathers oxidize.

[1]Dyes that produce various shades of red and brown.
[2]Here, and throughout, the ellipses are Bishop's.

St. Peter's sin
was worse than that of Magdalen[3]   80
whose sin was of the flesh alone;

of spirit, Peter's,
falling, beneath the flares,
among the "servants and officers."

Old holy sculpture
could set it all together
in one small scene, past and future:

Christ stands amazed,
Peter, two fingers raised
to surprised lips, both as if dazed.   90

But in between
a little cock is seen
carved on a dim column[4] in the travertine,

explained by *gallus canit;*
flet Petrus[5] underneath it.
There is inescapable hope, the pivot;

yes, and there Peter's tears
run down our chanticleer's
sides and gem his spurs.

Tear-encrusted thick   100
as a medieval relic
he waits. Poor Peter, heart-sick,

still cannot guess
those cock-a-doodles yet might bless,
his dreadful rooster come to mean forgiveness,

a new weathervane
on basilica and barn,
and that outside the Lateran[6]

there would always be
a bronze cock on a porphyry   110
pillar so the people and the Pope might see

[3]When Jesus was seized and brought to trial, the Apostle Peter was brought before the authorities where he, fearing for his life, three times denied that he was Jesus' disciple, thus fulfilling Jesus' prophecy: "this night, before the cock crow, thou shalt deny me thrice." Matthew 26:34. Mary Magdalene was a prostitute whose sins were forgiven by Jesus. Luke 7:37; 8:2.

[4]Peter's denial of Christ, a frequent subject of early Christian sculpture, is traditionally shown with the cock either at Peter's feet or atop a column placed between Jesus and Peter.

[5]Latin: "The Cock crows; Peter weeps," a reference to Matthew 26:75: "Peter remembered the word of Jesus, which said unto him, Before the cock crow, thou shalt deny me thrice. And he went out and wept bitterly."

[6]The church (basilica) of St. John Lateran in Rome, where a column, once thought to be the original from which the cock crowed, is preserved.

that even the Prince
of the Apostles long since
had been forgiven, and to convince

all the assembly
that "Deny deny deny"
is not all the roosters cry.

In the morning
a low light is floating
in the backyard, and gilding   120

from underneath
the broccoli, leaf by leaf;
how could the night have come to grief?

gilding the tiny
floating swallow's belly
and lines of pink cloud in the sky,

the day's preamble
like wandering lines in marble.
The cocks are now almost inaudible.

The sun climbs in,   130
following "to see the end,"
faithful as enemy, or friend.

                                        1946

THE FISH

I caught a tremendous fish
and held him beside the boat
half out of water, with my hook
fast in a corner of his mouth.
He didn't fight.
He hadn't fought at all.
He hung a grunting weight,
battered and venerable
and homely. Here and there
his brown skin hung in strips   10
like ancient wallpaper,
and its pattern of darker brown
was like wallpaper:
shapes like full-blown roses
stained and lost through age.
He was speckled with barnacles,

fine rosettes of lime,
and infested
with tiny white sea-lice,
and underneath two or three   20
rags of green weed hung down.
While his gills were breathing in
the terrible oxygen
—the frightening gills,
fresh and crisp with blood,
that can cut so badly—
I thought of the coarse white flesh
packed in like feathers,
the big bones and the little bones,
the dramatic reds and blacks   30
of his shiny entrails,
and the pink swim-bladder
like a big peony.
I looked into his eyes
which were far larger than mine
but shallower, and yellowed,
the irises backed and packed
with tarnished tinfoil
seen through the lenses
of old scratched isinglass.   40
They shifted a little, but not
to return my stare.
—It was more like the tipping
of an object toward the light.
I admired his sullen face,
the mechanism of his jaw,
and then I saw
that from his lower lip
—if you could call it a lip—
grim, wet, and weaponlike,   50
hung five old pieces of fish-line,
or four and a wire leader
with the swivel still attached,
with all their five big hooks
grown firmly in his mouth.
A green line, frayed at the end
where he broke it, two heavier lines,
and a fine black thread
still crimped from the strain and snap
when it broke and he got away.   60
Like medals with their ribbons
frayed and wavering,
a five-haired beard of wisdom
trailing from his aching jaw.
I stared and stared
and victory filled up
the little rented boat,
from the pool of bilge

where oil had spread a rainbow
around the rusted engine   70
to the bailer rusted orange,
the sun-cracked thwarts,
the oarlocks on their strings,
the gunnels—until everything
was rainbow, rainbow, rainbow!
And I let the fish go.

1946

OVER 2,000 ILLUSTRATIONS AND
A COMPLETE CONCORDANCE

Thus should have been our travels:
serious, engravable.
The Seven Wonders of the World are tired
and a touch familiar, but the other scenes,
innumerable, though equally sad and still,
are foreign. Often the squatting Arab,
or group of Arabs, plotting, probably,
against our Christian Empire,
while one apart, with outstretched arm and hand
points to the Tomb, the Pit, the Sepulcher.[1]   10
The branches of the date-palms look like files.
The cobbled courtyard, where the Well is dry,
is like a diagram, the brickwork conduits
are vast and obvious, the human figure
far gone in history or theology,
gone with its camel or its faithful horse.
Always the silence, the gesture, the specks of birds
suspended on invisible threads above the Site,
or the smoke rising solemnly, pulled by threads.
Granted a page alone or a page made up   20
of several scenes arranged in cattycornered rectangles
or circles set on stippled gray,
granted a grim lunette,[2]
caught in the toils of an initial letter,
when dwelt upon, they all resolve themselves.
The eye drops, weighted, through the lines
the burin[3] made, the lines that move apart
like ripples above sand,
dispersing storms, God's spreading fingerprint,
and painfully, finally, that ignite   30
in watery prismatic white-and-blue.

[1]The tomb, enclosed in the Church of the Holy Sepulcher in Jerusalem, where Jesus is said to
have been buried.
[2]A crescent-shaped or semicircular form.
[3]Engraver's tool.

Entering the Narrows at St. Johns[4]
the touching bleat of goats reached to the ship.
We glimpsed them, reddish, leaping up the cliffs
among the fog-soaked weeds and butter-and-eggs.
And at St. Peter's[5] the wind blew and the sun shone madly.
Rapidly, purposefully, the Collegians marched in lines,
crisscrossing the great square with black,[6] like ants.
In Mexico the dead man lay
in a blue arcade; the dead volcanoes   40
glistened like Easter lilies.
The jukebox went on playing "Ay, Jalisco!"[7]
And at Volubilis[8] there were beautiful poppies
splitting the mosaics; the fat old guide made eyes.
In Dingle[9] harbor a golden length of evening
the rotting hulks held up their dripping plush.
The Englishwoman poured tea, informing us
that the Duchess was going to have a baby.
And in the brothels of Marrakesh[10]
the little pockmarked prostitutes   50
balanced their tea-trays on their heads
and did their belly-dances; flung themselves
naked and giggling against our knees,
asking for cigarettes. It was somewhere near there
I saw what frightened me most of all:
A holy grave, not looking particularly holy,
one of a group under a keyhole-arched stone baldaquin[11]
open to every wind from the pink desert.
An open, gritty, marble trough, carved solid
with exhortation, yellowed   60
as scattered cattle-teeth;
half-filled with dust, not even the dust
of the poor prophet paynim[12] who once lay there.
In a smart burnoose[13] Khadour looked on amused.

Everything only connected by "and" and "and."
Open the book. (The gilt rubs off the edges
of the pages and pollinates the fingertips.)
Open the heavy book. Why couldn't we have seen
this old Nativity[14] while we were at it?   70
—the dark ajar, the rocks breaking with light,
an undisturbed, unbreathing flame,
colorless, sparkless, freely fed on straw,

[4]Entrance to St. John's Harbor in Newfoundland, Canada.
[5]Church in Rome.
[6]I.e., files of seminary students, wearing black robes, crossing St. Peter's Square, from their
residential colleges to their university classrooms.
[7]Jalisco: state in Mexico where mariachi music originated.
[8]Ancient Roman city in North Africa, now a ruin.
[9]Town in southwest Ireland.
[10]City in Morocco.
[11]Ornamental structure, resembling a canopy, built over a sacred object.
[12]A pagan, a nonbeliever—a term sometimes used by Christians to refer to a Muslim.
[13]Hooded cloak worn by Arabs.
[14]The birth of Christ.

and, lulled within, a family with pets,
—and looked and looked our infant sight away.

                                                                        1955

VISITS TO ST. ELIZABETHS[1]

1950

This is the house of Bedlam.

This is the man
that lies in the house of Bedlam.

This is the time
of the tragic man
that lies in the house of Bedlam.

This is a wristwatch
telling the time
of the talkative man
that lies in the house of Bedlam.   10

This is a sailor
wearing the watch
that tells the time
of the honored man
that lies in the house of Bedlam.

This is the roadstead all of board
reached by the sailor
wearing the watch
that tells the time
of the old, brave man   20
that lies in the house of Bedlam.

These are the years and the walls of the ward,
the winds and clouds of the sea of board
sailed by the sailor
wearing the watch
that tells the time
of the cranky man
that lies in the house of Bedlam.

This is a Jew in a newspaper hat
that dances weeping down the ward   30
over the creaking sea of board
beyond the sailor

[1]A hospital for the mentally ill, in Washington, D.C., where the poet Ezra Pound was confined
from 1946 to 1958.

winding his watch
that tells the time
of the cruel man
that lies in the house of Bedlam.

This is a world of books gone flat.
This is a Jew in a newspaper hat
that dances weeping down the ward
over the creaking sea of board   40
of the batty sailor
that winds his watch
that tells the time
of the busy man
that lies in the house of Bedlam.

This is a boy that pats the floor
to see if the world is there, is flat,
for the widowed Jew in the newspaper hat
that dances weeping down the ward
waltzing the length of a weaving board   50
by the silent sailor
that hears his watch
that ticks the time
of the tedious man
that lies in the house of Bedlam.

These are the years and the walls and the door
that shut on a boy that pats the floor
to feel if the world is there and flat.
This is a Jew in a newspaper hat
that dances joyfully down the ward   60
into the parting seas of board
past the staring sailor
that shakes his watch
that tells the time
of the poet, the man
that lies in the house of Bedlam.

This is the soldier home from the war.
These are the years and the walls and the door
that shut on a boy that pats the floor
to see if the world is round or flat.   70
This is a Jew in a newspaper hat
that dances carefully down the ward,
walking the plank of a coffin board
with the crazy sailor
that shows his watch
that tells the time
of the wretched man
that lies in the house of Bedlam.

                    1950, 1965

THE PRODIGAL

The brown enormous odor he lived by
was too close, with its breathing and thick hair,
for him to judge. The floor was rotten; the sty
was plastered halfway up with glass-smooth dung.
Light-lashed, self-righteous, above moving snouts,
the pigs' eyes followed him, a cheerful stare—
even to the sow that always ate her young—
till, sickening, he leaned to scratch her head.
But sometimes morning after drinking bouts
(he hid the pints behind a two-by-four),   10
the sunrise glazed the barnyard mud with red;
the burning puddles seemed to reassure.
And then he thought he almost might endure
his exile yet another year or more.

But evenings the first star came to warn.
The farmer whom he worked for came at dark
to shut the cows and horses in the barn
beneath their overhanging clouds of hay,
with pitchforks, faint forked lightnings, catching light,
safe and companionable as in the Ark.   20
The pigs stuck out their little feet and snored.
The lantern—like the sun, going away—
laid on the mud a pacing aureole.
Carrying a bucket along a slimy board,
he felt the bats' uncertain staggering flight,
his shuddering insights, beyond his control,
touching him. But it took him a long time
finally to make his mind up to go home.

                                                          ¹955

THE ARMADILLO

for ROBERT LOWELL[1]

This is the time of year
when almost every night
the frail, illegal fire balloons appear.
Climbing the mountain height,

rising toward a saint
still honored in these parts,[2]
the paper chambers flush and fill with light
that comes and goes, like hearts.

---

[1]Compare Robert Lowell's "Skunk Hour" on page 1710.
[2]In Rio de Janeiro, Brazil.

Once up against the sky it's hard
to tell them from the stars—   10
planets, that is—the tinted ones:
Venus going down, or Mars,

or the pale green one. With a wind,
they flare and falter, wobble and toss;
but if it's still they steer between
the kite sticks of the Southern Cross,[3]

receding, dwindling, solemnly
and steadily forsaking us,
or, in the downdraft from a peak,
suddenly turning dangerous.   20

Last night another big one fell.
It splattered like an egg of fire
against the cliff behind the house.
The flame ran down. We saw the pair

of owls who nest there flying up
and up, their whirling black-and-white
stained bright pink underneath, until
they shrieked up out of sight.

The ancient owls' nest must have burned.
Hastily, all alone,   30
a glistening armadillo left the scene,
rose-flecked, head down, tail down,

and then a baby rabbit jumped out,
short-eared, to our surprise.
So soft!—a handful of intangible ash
with fixed, ignited eyes.

Too pretty, dreamlike mimicry!
O falling fire and piercing cry
and panic, and a weak mailed fist
clenched ignorant against the sky!   40

                                                    1965

IN THE WAITING ROOM

In Worcester, Massachusetts,
I went with Aunt Consuelo
to keep her dentist's appointment
and sat and waited for her
in the dentist's waiting room.

---

[3]A constellation of the southern hemisphere.

It was winter, It got dark
early. The waiting room
was full of grown-up people,
arctics and overcoats,
lamps and magazines.   10
My aunt was inside
what seemed like a long time
and while I waited I read
the *National Geographic*
(I could read) and carefully
studied the photographs:
the inside of a volcano,
black, and full of ashes;
then it was spilling over
in rivulets of fire   20
Osa and Martin Johnson[1]
dressed in riding breeches,
laced boots, and pith helmets.
A dead man slung on a pole
—"Long Pig," the caption said.
Babies with pointed heads
wound round and round with string;
black, naked women with necks
wound round and round with wire
like the necks of light bulbs.   30
Their breasts were horrifying.
I read it right straight through.
I was too shy to stop.
And then I looked at the cover:
the yellow margins, the date.

Suddenly, from inside,
came an *oh!* of pain
—Aunt Consuelo's voice—
not very loud or long.
I wasn't at all surprised;   40
even then I knew she was
a foolish, timid woman.
I might have been embarrassed,
but wasn't. What took me
completely by surprise
was that it was *me:*
my voice, in my mouth.
Without thinking at all
I was my foolish aunt,
I—we—were falling, falling,   50
our eyes glued to the cover
of the *National Geographic,*
February, 1918.

[1]Man and wife explorers and wildlife photographers, famous for their expeditions to the South
Sea islands, Borneo, and Africa.

I said to myself: three days
and you'll be seven years old.
I was saying it to stop
the sensation of falling off
the round, turning world
into cold, blue-black space.
But I felt: you are an *I,*   60
you are an *Elizabeth,*
you are one of *them.*
Why should you be one, too?
I scarcely dared to look
to see what it was I was.
I gave a sidelong glance
—I couldn't look any higher—
at shadowy gray knees,
trousers and skirts and boots
and different pairs of hands   70
lying under the lamps.
I knew that nothing stranger
had ever happened, that nothing
stranger could ever happen.

Why should I be my aunt,
or me, or anyone?
What similarities—
boots, hands, the family voice
I felt in my throat, or even
the *National Geographic*   80
and those awful hanging breasts—
held us all together
or made us all just one?
How—I didn't know any
word for it—how "unlikely" . . .
How had I come to be here,
like them, and overhear
a cry of pain that could have
got loud and worse but hadn't?

The waiting room was bright   90
and too hot. It was sliding
beneath a big black wave,
another, and another.

Then I was back in it.
The War was on. Outside,
in Worcester, Massachusetts,
were night and slush and cold,
and it was still the fifth
of February, 1918.

1976

Robert Lowell   *1917–1977*

Robert Lowell was, by common agreement, one of the great American poets of the twentieth century. He was descended from distinguished New England families that included statesmen, soldiers, Mayflower *colonists, and the poets James Russell Lowell and Amy Lowell. He was educated at a fashionable New England prep school, St. Mark's. For two years he attended Harvard, and then he transferred to Kenyon College in Ohio, where he studied under the distinguished poet and critic John Crowe Ransom.*

In 1940 Lowell graduated from Kenyon as valedictorian of his class. Soon after the United States entered World War II, he tried to enlist, first in the army and then in the navy, but he was rejected. Later, as the war progressed, he became so opposed to the Allies' mass bombing of enemy civilian targets that he refused to serve when he was called up for the draft. As a result, in 1943 he was convicted of draft evasion and sentenced to a year and a day in a federal prison.

After serving five months of his sentence, Lowell was paroled. Shortly afterwards, he published Land of Unlikeness *(1944), his first book of poems. Two years later his fame as a poet was established with the publication of* Lord Weary's Castle, *for which he received a Pulitzer Prize for poetry. The volume is concerned with Lowell's New England background, his own ancestry, and especially with the moral and spiritual decline he saw in society. In both* Lord Weary's Castle *and his next book,* The Mills of the Kavanaughs *(1951), Lowell's despair is expressed in highly symbolic, richly allusive, rhetorical language.*

With the publication of Life Studies *(1959) a new direction in Lowell's poetry was confirmed. The poems deal, in a painfully candid way, with revelation of the self. Their descriptions of personal disturbances and confinement in a hospital for the insane marked the advent of a new school of "confessional poets" who were given to intense self-examination and emotional self-exposure.* Life Studies, *Lowell's finest work and one of the most influential volumes of poetry of the age, also exhibits a less formal and less rhetorical manner than his earlier poems, for, as he said in an interview, he chose not to get his new "experience into tight metrical forms."*

In his subsequent poetry (For the Union Dead, 1964, is especially notable) Lowell partially moved away from personal revelation, just as he had moved away from his New England background as a subject for his writing. He also worked with a variety of literary forms, writing verse dramas and translating poems into English. In his last years he turned increasingly to political activity: in protest over America's foreign policy he refused to attend a White House Fine Arts Festival in 1956, and in 1967 he was arrested during a march on the Pentagon to protest the Vietnam War. At the end of his life Lowell was reworking and republishing a unified series of poems under various titles; a recent version (History, 1973) shows that Lowell had sought a renewed mastery of blank verse. His last work, Day by Day, *was published in 1977, shortly before his death.*

Lowell's career presents two of the major developments of modern poetry: the search for the impersonal (the assumption of "masks," the reliance on allusion, reference, and translation) and its contrary, the open expression of self-revelation, the exposure of the "I." Robert Frost judged that much of Lowell's early poetry lacked "compression," and some of his late work has been criticized as "trivia," "organized jotting." But at its best Lowell's writing displays great technical craft and elegance, and in describing the instability of life and in portraying death, sin, and furtive guilt, Lowell achieved some of the finest poetry of our age.

FURTHER READING: I. Hamilton, *Robert Lowell, A Biography,* 1982; H. Staples, *Robert*

Lowell, The First Twenty Years, 1962; J. Mazzaro, *The Poetic Themes of Robert Lowell*, 1965; T. Parkinson, *Robert Lowell, A Collection of Critical Essays*, 1968; R. Meiners, *Everything to Be Endured, An Essay on Robert Lowell*, 1970; P. Cosgrave, *The Public Poetry of Robert Lowell*, 1970; J. Martin, *Robert Lowell*, 1970, 1979; P. Cooper, *The Autobiographical Myth of Robert Lowell*, 1970; R. Fein, *Robert Lowell*, 1970; M. Perloff, *The Poetic Art of Robert Lowell*, 1973; A. Williamson, *The Political Vision of Robert Lowell*, 1974; S. Yenser, *Circle to Circle, The Poetry of Robert Lowell*, 1975; S. Axelrod, *Robert Lowell, Life and Art*, 1978; C. Heymann, *American Aristocracy*, 1980; B. Raffel, *Robert Lowell*, 1981; V. Bell, *Robert Lowell, Nihilist as Hero*, 1983; M. Rudman, *Robert Lowell, An Introduction to the Poetry*, 1983; N. Procopiow, *Robert Lowell, The Poet and His Critics*, 1984; *Robert Lowell*, ed. H. Bloom, 1987; *R. Lowell, Interviews and Memoirs*, ed. J. Meyers, 1988.

TEXTS: "At a Bible House" is from *Lord Weary's Castle*, 1946; "Lady Ralegh's Lament" is from *For the Union Dead*, 1964; "For Theodore Roethke" is from *Near the Ocean*, 1967; all other selections are from *Selected Poems*, 1976.

IN MEMORY OF ARTHUR WINSLOW[1]

I

DEATH FROM CANCER

This Easter, Arthur Winslow, less than dead,
Your people set you up in Phillips' House,[2]
To settle off your wrestling with the crab[3]—
The claws drop flesh upon your yachting blouse
Until longshoreman Charon[4] come and stab
Through your adjusted bed
And crush the crab. On Boston Basin,[5] shells
Hit water by the Union Boat Club wharf:
You ponder why the coxes'[6] squeakings dwarf
The *resurrexit dominus*[7] of all the bells.   10

Grandfather Winslow, look, the swanboats[8] coast
That island in the Public Gardens, where
The bread-stuffed ducks are brooding, where with tub
And strainer the mid-Sunday Irish scare
The sun-struck shallows for the dusky chub[9]
This Easter, and the ghost
Of risen Jesus walks the waves to run
Arthur upon a trumpeting black swan
Beyond Charles River to the Acheron
Where the wide waters and their voyager are one.   20

[1]The poet's maternal grandfather (1861–1938).
[2]Part of Massachusetts General Hospital in Boston.
[3]Latin "cancer" means "crab."
[4]The boatman in Greek myth who ferried the spirits of the dead to Hades, across the rivers Styx and Acheron.
[5]A portion of the Charles River at Boston.
[6]Coxswains, the steersmen of racing shells.
[7]Latin: "the Lord has risen."
[8]Excursion boats in the lake of the Boston Public Garden.
[9]A carp-like fish.

II

DUNBARTON[10]

The stones are yellow and the grass is gray
Past Concord by the rotten lake and hill
Where crutch and trumpet meet the limousine
And half-forgotten Starks and Winslows fill
The granite plot and the dwarf pines are green
From watching for the day
When the great year of the little yeomen come
Bringing its landed Promise and the faith
That made the Pilgrim Makers take a lathe
And point their wooden steeples lest the Word be dumb.   30

O fearful witnesses, your day is done:
The minister from Boston waves your shades,
Like children, out of sight and out of mind.
The first selectman of Dunbarton spreads
Wreaths of New Hampshire pine cones on the lined
Casket where the cold sun
Is melting. But, at last, the end is reached;
We start our cars. The preacher's mouthings still
Deafen my poor relations on the hill:
their sunken landmarks echo what our fathers preached.   40

III

FIVE YEARS LATER

This Easter, Arthur Winslow, five years gone
I came to mourn you, not to praise the craft
That netted you a million dollars, late
Hosing out gold in Colorado's waste,[11]
Then lost it all in Boston real estate.
Now from the train, at dawn
Leaving Columbus in Ohio, shell
On shell of our stark culture strikes the sun
To fill my head with all our fathers won
When Cotton Mather wrestled with the fiends from hell.   50

You must have hankered for our family's craft:
The block-house Edward[12] made, the Governor,
At Marshfield, and the slight coin-silver spoons
The Sheriff[13] beat[14] to shame the gaunt Revere,[15]

[10]Town in New Hampshire where various Starks and Winslows, Lowell's ancestors, are buried.
[11]Arthur Winslow was a mining engineer in Colorado, where he used hydraulic mining to extract gold from the soil.
[12]Edward Winslow (1595–1655), three times Governor of the Plymouth Colony. In 1633 he was granted a section of land at Marshfield, Massachusetts, fifteen miles north of Plymouth.
[13]Edward Winslow (1669–1753), grandnephew of Governor Winslow and High Sheriff of the County of Suffolk. He was a noted silversmith.
[14]Formed by beating with a mallet.
[15]Paul Revere, of the "midnight ride," was a Boston silversmith.

And General Stark's[16] coarse bas-relief in bronze
Set on your granite shaft
In rough Dunbarton; for what else could bring
You, Arthur, to the veined and alien West
But devil's notions that your gold at least
Could give back life to men who whipped or backed the King?   60

IV

A PRAYER FOR MY GRANDFATHER
TO OUR LADY

Mother, for these three hundred years or more
Neither our clippers nor our slavers reached
The haven of your peace in this Bay State:
Neither my father nor his father. Beached
On these dry flats of fishy real estate,
O Mother, I implore
Your scorched, blue thunderbreasts of love to pour
Buckets of blessings on my burning head
Until I rise like Lazarus from the dead:[17]
Lavabis nos et super nivem dealbabor.[18]   70

"On Copley Square, I saw you hold the door
To Trinity,[19] the costly Church, and saw
The painted Paradise of harps and lutes[20]
Sink like Atlantis in the Devil's jaw
And knock the Devil's teeth out by the roots;
But when I strike for shore
I find no painted idols to adore:
Hell is burned out, heaven's harp-strings are slack.
Mother, run to the chalice, and bring back
Blood on your finger-tips for Lazarus who was poor."[21]   80

1943, 1944

THE QUAKER GRAVEYARD IN NANTUCKET

(For Warren Winslow,[1] Dead at Sea)

Let man have dominion over the fishes of the sea and the fowls of the air and the beasts and the whole earth, and every creeping creature that moveth upon the earth.[2]

[16]John Stark (1728–1822), Revolutionary War general and Lowell's ancestor.
[17]Jesus raised Lazarus from the dead. John II:1–44.
[18]Latin: "Wash us and I shall be made whiter than snow." A variant of the biblical "Wash me, and I shall be whiter than snow." Psalms 51:7.
[19]Trinity Episcopal Church on Copley Square in Boston.
[20]A phrase taken from "Ballade—Que Villon Feist à la Requeste de sa Mère, Pour Prier Nostre Dame" by the French poet François Villon (1431–1463?).
[21]The Lazarus of Jesus' parable of the rich man. Luke 16:19–31.
[1]The poet's cousin, killed during World War II.
[2]Genesis 1:26. Lowell quotes from the Douay Version of the Bible.

I

A brackish reach of shoal off Madaket,[3]—
The sea was still breaking violently and night
Had steamed into our north Atlantic Fleet,
When the drowned sailor clutched the drag-net. Light
Flashed from his matted head and marble feet,
He grappled at the net
With the coiled, hurdling muscles of his thighs:
The corpse was bloodless, a botch of reds and whites,
Its open, staring eyes
Were lustreless dead-lights[4]   10
Or cabin-windows on a stranded hulk
Heavy with sand. We weight the body, close
Its eyes and heave it seaward whence it came,
Where the heel-headed dogfish barks its nose
On Ahab's[5] void and forehead; and the name
Is blocked in yellow chalk.
Sailors, who pitch this portent at the sea
Where dreadnaughts shall confess
Its hell-bent deity,
When you are powerless   20
To sand-bag this Atlantic bulwark, faced
By the earth-shaker,[6] green, unwearied, chaste
In his steel scales: ask for no Orphean lute
To pluck life back.[7] The guns of the steeled fleet
Recoil and then repeat
The hoarse salute.

II

Whenever winds are moving and their breath
Heaves at the roped-in bulwarks of this pier,
The terns and sea-gulls tremble at your death
In these home waters. Sailor, can you hear   30
The Pequod's sea wings, beating landward, fall
Headlong and break on our Atlantic wall
Off 'Sconset,[8] where the yawing S-boats[9] splash
The bellbuoy, with ballooning spinnakers,
As the entangled, screeching mainsheet clears
The blocks: off Madaket, where lubbers lash
The heavy surf and throw their long lead squids
For blue-fish? Sea-gulls blink their heavy lids
Seaward. The winds' wings beat upon the stones,
Cousin, and scream for you and the claws rush   40
At the sea's throat and wring it in the slush

[3]Town and harbor at Nantucket Island, off the coast of Cape Cod.
[4]Heavy glass panes set into a ship's deck or side.
[5]The captain of the whaler *Pequod*, in Herman Melville's novel *Moby Dick* (1851), to which Lowell repeatedly alludes in the poem.
[6]Poseidon, Greek god of the sea and earthquakes.
[7]In Greek myth, Orpheus attempted to bring his bride, Eurydice, back from Hades by the power of his music.
[8]Siasconset, a town on Nantucket.   [9]A class of racing yacht.

Of this old Quaker graveyard where the bones
Cry out in the long night for the hurt beast
Bobbing by Ahab's whaleboats in the East.

III

All you recovered from Poseidon died
With you, my cousin, and the harrowed brine
Is fruitless on the blue beard of the god,
Stretching beyond us to the castles in Spain,
Nantucket's westward haven. To Cape Cod
Guns, cradled on the tide,   50
Blast the eelgrass about a waterclock
Of bilge and backwash, roil the salt and sand
Lashing earth's scaffold, rock
Our warships in the hand
Of the great God, where time's contrition blues
Whatever it was these Quaker sailors lost
In the mad scramble of their lives. They died
When time was open-eyed,
Wooden and childish; only bones abide
There, in the nowhere, where their boats were tossed   60
Sky-high, where mariners had fabled news
Of IS,[10] the whited monster. What it cost
Them is their secret. In the sperm-whale's slick
I see the Quakers drown and hear their cry:
"If God himself had not been on our side,
If God himself had not been on our side,
When the Atlantic rose against us, why,
Then it had swallowed us up quick."

IV

This is the end of the whaleroad[11] and the whale
Who spewed Nantucket bones on the thrashed swell   70
And stirred the troubled waters to whirlpools
To send the Pequod packing off to hell:
This is the end of them, three-quarters fools,
Snatching at straws to sail
Seaward and seaward on the turntail whale,
Spouting out blood and water as it rolls,
Sick as a dog to these Atlantic shoals:
Clamavimus,[12] O depths. Let the sea-gulls wail

For water, for the deep where the high tide
Mutters to its hurt self, mutters and ebbs.   80
Waves wallow in their wash, go out and out,
Leave only the death-rattle of the crabs,
The beach increasing, its enormous snout
Sucking the ocean's side.

[10]Perhaps a reference to Revelation 17:8: "Behold the beast that was and is not and yet is."
[11]The sea.
[12]Latin: "We have cried out," an allusion to Psalms 130:1, "Out of the depths I have cried unto thee, O Lord."

This is the end of running on the waves;
We are poured out like water. Who will dance
The mast-lashed master of Leviathans[13]
Up from this field of Quakers in their unstoned graves?

V

When the whale's viscera go and the roll
Of its corruption overruns this world   90
Beyond tree-swept Nantucket and Wood's Hole[14]
And Martha's Vineyard,[15] Sailor, will your sword
Whistle and fall and sink into the fat?
In the great ash-pit of Jehoshaphat[16]
The bones cry for the blood of the white whale,
The fat flukes arch and whack about its ears,
The death-lance churns into the sanctuary, tears
The gun-blue swingle,[17] heaving like a flail,
And hacks the coiling life out: it works and drags
And rips the sperm-whale's midriff into rags,   100
Gobbets of blubber spill to wind and weather,
Sailor, and gulls go round the stoven timbers
Where the morning stars sing out together
And thunder shakes the white surf and dismembers
The red flag hammered in the mast-head.[18] Hide
Our steel, Jonas Messias,[19] in Thy side.

VI

OUR LADY OF WALSINGHAM[20]

There once the penitents took off their shoes
And then walked barefoot the remaining mile;
And the small trees, a stream and hedgerows file
Slowly along the munching English lane,   110
Like cows to the old shrine, until you lose
Track of your dragging pain.
The stream flows down under the druid tree,[21]
Shiloah's[22] whirlpools gurgle and make glad
The castle of God. Sailor, you were glad
And whistled Sion[23] by that stream. But see:

Our Lady, too small for her canopy,
Sits near the altar. There's no comeliness

[13]Old Testament sea monsters.
[14]Town on the Atlantic coast of Massachusetts, opposite Martha's Vineyard.
[15]Island near Nantucket.
[16]The "valley of decision," the scene of the Lord's judgment of the world. Joel 3:11–16.
[17]A wooden, knifelike instrument.
[18]A reference to the flag nailed to the mast of the sinking *Pequod* at the end of *Moby Dick*.
[19]Jonah (Jonas) and the Messiah, Jesus, have frequently been compared in Christian writing, Jonah's experiences being considered prophetic of the Resurrection of Jesus.
[20]A shrine dedicated to the Virgin Mary, in Walsingham Priory, Norfolk, England.
[21]The oak tree held sacred among ancient pagan Celtic Druids.
[22]Shiloh, a town in ancient Palestine.
[23]Zion, a hill in Jerusalem that became a center of Hebrew government and life. Hence the term came later to be used to describe the Israelites, the church, and the heavenly city of God.

At all or charm in that expressionless
Face with its heavy eyelids. As before,   120
This face, for centuries a memory,
Non est species, neque decor,[24]
Expressionless, expresses God: it goes
Past castled Sion. She knows what God knows,
Not Calvary's Cross nor crib at Bethlehem
Now, and the world shall come to Walsingham.

VII

The empty winds are creaking and the oak
Splatters and splatters on the cenotaph,[25]
The boughs are trembling and a gaff
Bobs on the untimely stroke   130
Of the greased wash exploding on a shoal-bell
In the old mouth of the Atlantic. It's well;
Atlantic, you are fouled with the blue sailors,
Sea-monsters, upward angel, downward fish:
Unmarried and corroding, spare of flesh
Mart once of supercilious, wing'd clippers,
Atlantic, where your bell-trap guts its spoil
You could cut the brackish winds with a knife
Here in Nantucket, and cast up the time
When the Lord God formed man from the sea's slime   140
And breathed into his face the breath of life,
And blue-lung'd combers lumbered to the kill.
The Lord survives the rainbow of His will.

1945, 1946

AT A BIBLE HOUSE

At a Bible House
Where smoking is forbidden
By the Prophet's law,
I saw you wiry, bed-ridden,
Gone in the kidneys; raw
Onions and a louse
Twitched on the sheet before
The palsy of your white
Stubble—a Mennonite
Or die-hard Doukabor,[1]   10
God-rooted, hard. You spoke
Whistling gristle-words
Half inaudible
To us: of raw-boned birds
Migrating from the smoke

---

[24]Latin: "There is no form nor comeliness," adopted from Isaiah 53:2.
[25]A tomb monument built to honor one who is buried elsewhere.
[1]Two radical Protestant sects whose members are renowned for their fierce religious independence.

Of cities, of a gull
Perched on the redwood
Thrusting short awl-shaped leaves:
Three hundred feet of love
Where the Pacific heaves   20
The tap-root—wise above
Man's wisdom with the food
Squeezed from three thousand years'
Standing. It is all
A moment. The trees
Grow earthward: neither good
Nor evil, hopes nor fears,
Repulsion nor desire,
Earth, water, air or fire
Will serve to stay the fall.   30

1946

MR. EDWARDS[1] AND THE SPIDER

I saw the spiders marching through the air,
Swimming from tree to tree that mildewed day
   In latter August when the hay
   Came creaking to the barn. But where
      The wind is westerly,
Where gnarled November makes the spiders fly
Into the apparitions of the sky,
   They purpose nothing but their ease and die
Urgently beating east to sunrise and the sea;

What are we in the hands of the great God?   10
It was in vain you set up thorn and briar
   In battle array against the fire
   And treason crackling in your blood;
      For the wild thorns grow tame
And will do nothing to oppose the flame;
Your lacerations tell the losing game
   You play against a sickness past your cure.
How will the hands be strong? How will the heart
   endure?[2]

A very little thing, a little worm,
Or hourglass-blazoned spider,[3] it is said,   20
   Can kill a tiger. Will the dead
   Hold up his mirror and affirm

---

[1] A reference to Jonathan Edwards (1703–1758), the last great defender of American Puritanism. The poem derives from Edwards' renowned essay "The Flying Spider" and from his sermons, among them "Sinners in the Hands of an Angry God." See p. 251 of Volume I.

[2] "Can thine heart endure, or can thine hands be strong, in the days that I shall deal with thee?" Ezekiel 22:14. Edwards used this text for his sermon "Sinners in the Hands of an Angry God."

[3] The venomous female black widow spider has a red hourglass design on its underside.

To the four winds the smell
And flash of his authority? It's well
If God who holds you to the pit of hell,
Much as one holds a spider, will destroy,
Baffle and dissipate your soul. As a small boy

On Windsor Marsh,[4] I saw the spider die
When thrown into the bowels of fierce fire:
   There's no long struggle, no desire   30
   To get up on its feet and fly—
     It stretches out its feet
And dies. This is the sinner's last retreat;
Yes, and no strength exerted on the heat
Then sinews the abolished will, when sick
And full of burning, it will whistle on a brick.

But who can plumb the sinking of that soul?
Josiah Hawley,[5] picture yourself cast
   Into a brick-kiln where the blast
   Fans your quick vitals to a coal—   40
     If measured by a glass,
How long would it seem burning! Let there pass
A minute, ten, ten trillion; but the blaze
Is infinite, eternal: this is death,
To die and know it. This is the Black Widow, death.

                            1946

AFTER THE SURPRISING CONVERSIONS[1]

September twenty-second, Sir: today
I answer. In the latter part of May,
Hard on our Lord's Ascension,[2] it began
To be more sensible.[3] A gentleman[4]
Of more than common understanding, strict
In morals, pious in behavior, kicked
Against our goad. A man of some renown,
An useful, honored person in the town,
He came of melancholy parents; prone
To secret spells, for years they kept alone—   10
His uncle, I believe, was killed of it:
Good people, but of too much or little wit.
I preached one Sabbath on a text from Kings;

---

[4]Near East Windsor, Connecticut, Edwards' boyhood home.
[5]A relative of Edwards and a suicide whose death Edwards attributed to the devil. See "After the Surprising Conversions."
[1]On May 30, 1735, in reply to an inquiry from a Boston clergyman, Jonathan Edwards wrote "A Narrative of Surprising Conversions" to describe the revival of religion that Edwards was arousing in his Northampton, Massachusetts, church.
[2]Ascension Day, in May, forty days after Easter.   [3]Evident.
[4]Josiah Hawley, Jonathan Edwards' uncle by marriage.

He showed concernment for his soul. Some things
In his experience were hopeful. He
Would sit and watch the wind knocking a tree
And praise this countryside our Lord has made.
Once when a poor man's heifer died, he laid
A shilling on the doorsill; though a thirst
For loving shook him like a snake, he durst   20
Not entertain much hope of his estate
In heaven. Once we saw him sitting late
Behind his attic window by a light
That guttered on his Bible; through that night
He meditated terror, and he seemed
Beyond advice or reason, for he dreamed
That he was called to trumpet Judgment Day
To Concord. In the latter part of May
He cut his throat. And though the coroner
Judged him delirious, soon a noisome stir   30
Palsied our village. At Jehovah's nod
Satan seemed more let loose amongst us: God
Abandoned us to Satan, and he pressed
Us hard, until we thought we could not rest
Till we had done with life. Content was gone.
All the good work was quashed. We were undone.
The breath of God had carried out a planned
And sensible withdrawal from this land;
The multitude, once unconcerned with doubt,
Once neither callous, curious nor devout,   40
Jumped at broad noon, as though some peddler groaned
At it in its familiar twang: "My friend,
Cut your own throat. Cut your own throat. Now! Now!"
September twenty-second, Sir, the bough
Cracks with the unpicked apples, and at dawn
The small-mouth bass breaks water, gorged with spawn.

                                                                 1946

FALLING ASLEEP OVER THE AENEID[1]

An old man in Concord forgets to go to morning service. He falls asleep, while reading Virgil, and dreams that he is Aeneas at the funeral of Pallas, an Italian prince.

The sun is blue and scarlet on my page,
And *yuck-a, yuck-a, yuck-a, yuck-a,* rage
The yellowhammers[2] mating. Yellow fire
Blankets the captives dancing on their pyre,
And the scorched lictor[3] screams and drops his rod.

---

[1]The Latin epic by the Roman poet Virgil (70–19 B.C.) describing the escape and wanderings of Aeneas, after the fall of Troy, and the origin and growth of the Roman Empire.
[2]A variety of woodpecker.
[3]An attendant who walked before a Roman magistrate, carrying a rod as a symbol of high office.

Trojans are singing to their drunken God,
Ares.[4] Their helmets catch on fire. Their files
Clank by the body of my comrade—miles
Of filings! Now the scythe-wheeled chariot rolls
Before their lances long as vaulting poles,   10
And I stand up and heil the thousand men,
Who carry Pallas[5] to the bird-priest. Then
The bird-priest groans, and as his birds foretold,
I greet the body, lip to lip. I hold
The sword that Dido[6] used. It tries to speak,
A bird with Dido's sworded breast. Its beak
Clangs and ejaculates the Punic[7] word
I hear the bird-priest chirping like a bird.
I groan a little. "Who am I, and why?"
It asks, a boy's face, though its arrow-eye   20
Is working from its socket. "Brother, try,
O Child of Aphrodite,[8] try to die:
To die is life." His harlots hang his bed
With feathers of his long-tailed birds. His head
Is yawning like a person. The plumes blow;
The beard and eyebrows ruffle. Face of snow,
You are the flower that country girls have caught,
A wild bee-pillaged honey-suckle brought
To the returning bridegroom—the design
Has not yet left it, and the petals shine;   30
The earth, its mother, has, at last, no help:
It is itself. The broken-winded yelp
Of my Phoenician hounds, that fills the brush
With snapping twigs and flying, cannot flush
The ghost of Pallas. But I take his pall,
Stiff with its gold and purple, and recall
How Dido hugged it to her, while she toiled,
Laughing—her golden threads, a serpent coiled
In cypress. Now I lay it like a sheet;
It clinks and settles down upon his feet,   40
The careless yellow hair that seemed to burn
Beforehand. Left foot, right foot—as they turn,
More pyres are rising: armored horses, bronze,
And gagged Italians, who must file by ones
Across the bitter river, when my thumb
Tightens into their wind-pipes. The beaks drum;
Their headman's cow-horned death's-head bites its tongue,
And stiffens, as it eyes the hero slung
Inside his feathered hammock on the crossed
Staves of the eagles that we winged. Our cost   50
Is nothing to the lovers, whoring Mars
And Venus, father's lover. Now his car's

[4]A war god in Greek myth.
[5]A companion of Aeneas in the war against the Italians. He is killed by Turnus, king of the Rutuli, an Italian tribe.
[6]Queen of Carthage who committed suicide when Aeneas abandoned her.
[7]Carthaginian.   [8]Aeneas' mother was the goddess Aphrodite.

Plumage is ready, and my marshals fetch
His squire, Acoetes, white with age, to hitch
Aethon, the hero's charger, and its ears
Prick, and it steps and steps, and stately tears
Lather its teeth; and then the harlots bring
The hero's charms and baton—but the King,
Vain-glorious Turnus, carried off the rest.
"I was myself, but Ares thought it best   60
The way it happened." At the end of time,
He sets his spear, as my descendants climb
The knees of Father Time, his beard of scalps,
His scythe, the arc of steel that crowns the Alps.
The elephants of Carthage hold those snows,
Turms[9] of Numidian horse unsling their bows,
The flaming turkey-feathered arrows swarm
Beyond the Alps. "Pallas," I raise my arm
And shout, "Brother, eternal health. Farewell
Forever." Church is over, and its bell   70
Frightens the yellowhammers, as I wake
And watch the whitecaps wrinkle up the lake.
Mother's great-aunt, who died when I was eight,
Stands by our parlor sabre. "Boy, it's late.
Vergil must keep the Sabbath." Eighty years!
It all comes back. My Uncle Charles appears.
Blue-capped and bird-like. Phillips Brooks and Grant
Are frowning at his coffin, and my aunt,
Hearing his colored volunteers parade
Through Concord, laughs, and tells her English maid   80
To clip his yellow nostril hairs, and fold
His colors on him. . . .[10] It is I. I hold
His sword to keep from falling, for the dust
Of the stuffed birds is breathless, for the bust
Of young Augustus[11] weighs on Vergil's shelf:
It scowls into my glasses at itself.

                                        1948, 1950

COMMANDER LOWELL

1887–1950

There were no undesirables or girls in my set,
when I was a boy at Mattapoisett[1]—
only Mother, still her Father's daughter.
Her voice was still electric
with a hysterical, unmarried panic,
when she read to me from the Napoleon book.

[9]Cavalry groups.
[10]Here, and throughout the poetry, the ellipses are Lowell's.
[11]Augustus Caesar (63B.C.–A.D. 14), first Roman emperor, celebrated in the *Aenid*. Virgil read portions of the epic to him in 23 B.C.
[1]Summer resort on the Massachusetts coast, south of Boston.

Long-nosed Marie Louise
Hapsburg[2] in the frontispiece
had a downright Boston bashfulness,
where she grovelled to Bonaparte, who scratched his navel,[3]   10
and bolted his food—just my seven years tall![4]
And I, bristling and manic,
skulked in the attic
and got two hundred French generals by name,
from *A* to *V*—from Augereau to Vandamme.
I used to dope myself asleep,
naming those unpronounceables like sheep.

Having a naval officer
for my Father was nothing to shout
about to the summer colony at "Matt."   20
He wasn't at all "serious,"
when he showed up on the golf course,
wearing a blue serge jacket and numbly cut
white ducks he'd bought
at a Pearl Harbor commissariat. . . .
and took four shots with his putter to sink his putt.
"Bob," they said, "golf's a game you really ought to know how to
        play,
if you play at all."
They wrote him off as "naval,"
naturally supposed his sport was sailing.   30
Poor Father, his training was engineering!
Cheerful and cowed
among the seadogs at the Sunday yacht club,
he was never one of the crowd.

"Anchors aweigh," Daddy boomed in his bathtub,
"Anchors aweigh,"
when Lever Brothers offered to pay
him double what the Navy paid.
I nagged for his dress sword with gold braid,
and cringed because Mother, new   40
caps on all her teeth, was born anew
at forty. With seamanlike celerity,
Father left the Navy,
and deeded Mother his property.

He was soon fired. Year after year,
he still hummed "Anchors aweigh" in the tub—
whenever he left a job,
he bought a smarter car.
Father's last employer

---

[2]Wife of Napoleon I, Empress of France (1810–1815). She was the daughter of the Austrian emperor, Francis I of the royal house of Hapsburg.
[3]A reference to Napoleon's characteristic pose with his right hand inserted in the front of his coat.
[4]Napoleon's biographers frequently comment on his inelegant table manners and his short stature (five feet two inches).

was Scudder, Stevens and Clark, Investment Advisors,   50
himself his only client.
While Mother dragged to bed alone,
read Menninger,[5]
and grew more and more suspicious,
he grew defiant.
Night after night,
à la clarté déserte de sa lampe,[6]
he slid his ivory Annapolis slide rule
across a pad of graphs—
piker speculations! In three years   60
he squandered sixty thousand dollars.

Smiling on all,
Father was once successful enough to be lost
in the mob of ruling-class Bostonians.
As early as 1928,
he owned a house converted to oil,
and redecorated by the architect
of St. Mark's School[7]. . . . Its main effect
was a drawing room, "longitudinal as Versailles,"
its ceiling, roughened with oatmeal, was blue as the sea.   70
And once
nineteen, the youngest ensign in his class,
he was "the old man" of a gunboat on the Yangtze.

                                                    1958, 1959

MEMORIES OF WEST STREET AND LEPKE

Only teaching on Tuesdays, book-worming
in pajamas fresh from the washer each morning,
I hog a whole house on Boston's
"hardly passionate Marlborough Street,"[1]
where even the man
scavenging filth in the back alley trash cans,
has two children, a beach wagon, a helpmate,
and is a "young Republican."
I have a nine months' daughter,
young enough to be my granddaughter.   10
Like the sun she rises in her flame-flamingo infants' wear.

These are the tranquillized *Fifties,*
and I am forty. Ought I to regret my seedtime?

[5]Karl Menninger (1893–   ), American psychiatrist.
[6]French: "in the solitary light of his lamp," a quotation from the poem "Brise Marine" by the French poet Étienne Mallarmé (1842–1898).
[7]A private school for boys at Southborough, Massachusetts, near Boston.
[1]A phrase by Henry James describing a street in an elegant section of Boston. Lowell lived in a house on Marlborough Street from 1955 to 1958.

I was a fire-breathing Catholic C. O.,[2]
and made my manic statement,
telling off the state and president, and then
sat waiting sentence in the bull pen
beside a Negro boy with curlicues
of marijuana in his hair.

Given a year,
I walked on the roof of the West Street Jail, a short
enclosure like my school soccer court,
and saw the Hudson River once a day
through sooty clothesline entanglements
and bleaching khaki tenements.
Strolling, I yammered metaphysics with Abramowitz,
a jaundice-yellow ("it's really tan")
and fly-weight pacifist,
so vegetarian,
he wore rope shoes and preferred fallen fruit.
He tried to convert Bioff and Brown,[3]
the Hollywood pimps, to his diet.
Hairy, muscular, suburban,
wearing chocolate double-breasted suits,
they blew their tops and beat him black and blue.

I was so out of things, I'd never heard
of the Jehovah's Witnesses.[4]
"Are you a C.O.?" I asked a fellow jailbird.
"No," he answered, "I'm a J.W."
He taught me the "hospital tuck,"[5]
and pointed out the T shirted back
of *Murder Incorporated's* Czar Lepke,[6]
there piling towels on a rack,
or dawdling off to his little segregated cell full
of things forbidden the common man:
a portable radio, a dresser, two toy American
flags tied together with a ribbon of Easter palm.
Flabby, bald, lobotomized,
he drifted in a sheepish calm,
where no agonizing reappraisal[7]
jarred his concentration on the electric chair—

20

30

40

50

[2]In 1943 Lowell, a conscientious objector ("C.O.") was convicted of violating the Selective Service Act and sentenced to prison for a year and a day. While awaiting transfer to a federal prison he was held for ten days in the West Side Jail in New York City.

[3]William Bioff and George Browne, officials of a theatrical union, convicted in 1943 of extortion in Hollywood. In 1922 Browne had been convicted of pandering.

[4]Religious sect in the United States whose members refuse to participate in affairs of government or bear arms in wartime.

[5]Making a bed by tucking the loose ends of the bed clothes under the mattress.

[6]Louis "Lepke" Buchalter, a notorious racketeer convicted of murder in 1941. He had been the leader of "Murder Incorporated," a criminal assassination gang whose services were for hire. He was executed by electrocution in March 1944.

[7]In a speech given December 1953, John Foster Dulles, the United States Secretary of State, called for an "agonizing reappraisal" of American foreign policy.

hanging like an oasis in his air
of lost connections. . . .

                                                        1958

SKUNK HOUR

(For Elizabeth Bishop)[1]

Nautilus Island's hermit
heiress still lives through winter in her Spartan cottage;
her sheep still graze above the sea.
Her son's a bishop. Her farmer
is first selectman[2] in our village;
she's in her dotage.

Thirsting for
the hierarchic privacy
of Queen Victoria's century,
she buys up all   10
the eyesores facing her shore,
and lets them fall.

The season's ill—
we've lost our summer millionaire,
who seemed to leap from an L. L. Bean[3]
catalogue. His nine-knot yawl[4]
was auctioned off to lobstermen.
A red fox stain covers Blue Hill.[5]

And now our fairy
decorator brightens his shop for fall;   20
his fishnet's filled with orange cork,
orange, his cobbler's bench and awl;
there is no money in his work,
he'd rather marry.

One dark night,
my Tudor Ford climbed the hill's skull;
I watched for love-cars. Lights turned down,
they lay together, hull to hull,
where the graveyard shelves on the town. . . .
My mind's not right.   30

A car radio bleats,

---

[1]Lowell stated that "Skunk Hour" was modeled after Elizabeth Bishop's "Armadillo," pages 1690–1691.
[2]An official elected to administer town affairs.
[3]Mail-order clothing and sporting goods store in Freeport, Maine.
[4]Sailboat.   [5]A hill and coastal town near Bangor, Maine.

"Love, O careless Love. . . ."[6] I hear
my ill-spirit sob in each blood cell,
as if my hand were at its throat. . . .
I myself am hell;[7]
nobody's here—

only skunks, that search
in the moonlight for a bite to eat.
They march on their soles up Main Street:
white stripes, moonstruck eyes' red fire   40
under the chalk-dry and spar spire
of the Trinitarian Church.

I stand on top
of our back steps and breathe the rich air—
a mother skunk with her column of kittens swills the garbage pail.
She jabs her wedge-head in a cup
of sour cream, drops her ostrich tail,
and will not scare.

                                        1958, 1959

WAKING IN THE BLUE

The night attendant, a B.U.[1] sophomore,
rouses from the mare's-nest of his drowsy head
propped on *The Meaning of Meaning*.[2]
He catwalks down our corridor.
Azure day
makes my agonized blue window bleaker.
Crows maunder[3] on the petrified fairway.
Absence! My heart grows tense
as though a harpoon were sparring for the kill.
(This is the house for the "mentally ill.")   10

What use is my sense of humor?
I grin at Stanley, now sunk in his sixties,
once a Harvard all-American fullback,
(if such were possible!)
still hoarding the build of a boy in his twenties,
as he soaks, a ramrod
with the muscle of a seal
in his long tub,
vaguely urinous from the Victorian plumbing.

[6]A quotation from the lyrics of the folk song, "Careless Love."
[7]An adaptation of "Which way I fly is Hell; myself am Hell," the words of Satan in *Paradise Lost* (Book IV, line 75) by John Milton.
[1]Boston University.
[2]A book of philosophy and literary criticism by I. A. Richards and C. K. Ogden, published in 1923.
[3]Wander slowly.

A kingly granite profile in a crimson golf-cap,   20
worn all day, all night,
he thinks only of his figure,
of slimming on sherbet and ginger ale—
more cut off from words than a seal.

This is the way day breaks in Bowditch Hall at McLean's;[4]
the hooded night lights bring out "Bobbie,"
Porcellian '29,[5]
a replica of Louis XVI[6]
without the wig—
redolent and roly-poly as a sperm whale,   30
as he swashbuckles about in his birthday suit
and horses at chairs.

These victorious figures of bravado ossified young.

In between the limits of day,
hours and hours go by under the crew haircuts
and slightly too little nonsensical bachelor twinkle
of the Roman Catholic attendants.
(There are no Mayflower
screwballs in the Catholic Church.)

After a hearty New England breakfast,   40
I weigh two hundred pounds
this morning. Cock of the walk,
I strut in my turtle-necked French sailor's jersey
before the metal shaving mirrors,
and see the shaky future grow familiar
in the pinched, indigenous faces
of these thoroughbred mental cases,
twice my age and half my weight.
We are all old-timers,
each of us holds a locked razor.   50

1959

FOR THE UNION DEAD

"Relinquunt Omnia Servare Rem Publicam."[1]

The old South Boston Aquarium stands
in a Sahara of snow now. It's broken windows are boarded.
The bronze weathervane cod has lost half its scales.
The airy tanks are dry.

[4]McLean Hospital, an institution for the mentally ill, in Belmont, Massachusetts.
[5]A member, class of 1929, of Porcellian, an exclusive Harvard social club.
[6]King of France (1774–1792).
[1]Latin: "They give up everything to serve the republic."

Once my nose crawled like a snail on the glass;
my hand tingled
to burst the bubbles
drifting from the noses of the cowed, compliant fish.

My hand draws back. I often sigh still
for the dark downward and vegetating kingdom   10
of the fish and reptile. One morning last March,
I pressed against the new barbed and galvanized

fence on the Boston Common. Behind their cage,
yellow dinosaur steamshovels were grunting
as they cropped up tons of mush and grass
to gouge their underworld garage.

Parking spaces luxuriate like civic
sandpiles in the heart of Boston.
A girdle of orange, Puritan-pumpkin colored girders
braces the tingling Statehouse,   20

shaking over the excavations, as it faces Colonel Shaw[2]
and his bell-cheeked Negro infantry
on St. Gaudens' shaking Civil War relief,[3]
propped by a plank splint against the garage's earthquake.

Two months after marching through Boston,
half the regiment was dead;
at the dedication,
William James[4] could almost hear the bronze Negroes breathe.

Their monument sticks like a fishbone
in the city's throat.   30
Its Colonel is as lean
as a compass-needle.

He has an angry wrenlike vigilance,
a greyhound's gentle tautness;
he seems to wince at pleasure,
and suffocate for privacy.

He is out of bounds now. He rejoices in man's lovely,
peculiar power to choose life and die—
when he leads his black soldiers to death,
he cannot bend his back.   40

---

[2]Colonel Robert Shaw (1837–1863), commander of a Negro regiment, the 54th Massachusetts, in the Civil War.

[3]A monument by the American sculptor Augustus Saint-Gaudens (1848–1907), on the Boston Common across from the Boston State House.

[4]American philosopher (1842–1910), brother of the novelist Henry James. In his "Oration at the Dedication of the Monument" (May 1897) William James said, "There on foot go the dark outcasts, so true to nature that one can almost hear them breathing as they march."

On a thousand small town New England greens,
the old white churches hold their air
of sparse, sincere rebellion; frayed flags
quilt the graveyards of the Grand Army of the Republic.[5]

The stone statues of the abstract Union Soldier
grow slimmer and younger each year—
wasp-waisted they doze over muskets
and muse through their sideburns . . .

Shaw's father wanted no monument
except the ditch,   50
where his son's body was thrown
and lost with his "niggers."[6]

The ditch is nearer.
There are no statues for the last war[7] here;
on Boylston Street,[8] a commercial photograph
shows Hiroshima boiling

over a Mosler Safe, the "Rock of Ages"
that survived the blast. Space is nearer.
When I crouch to my television set,
the drained faces of Negro school-children rise like balloons.   60

Colonel Shaw
is riding on his bubble,
he waits
for the blessèd break.

The Aquarium is gone. Everywhere,
giant finned cars nose forward like fish;
a savage servility
slides by on grease.

                                                              1959, 1964

THE PUBLIC GARDEN[1]

Burnished, burned-out, still burning as the year
you lead me to our stamping ground.
The city and its cruising cars surround
the Public Garden. All's alive—
the children crowding home from school at five,
punting a football in the bricky air,

---

[5]Civil War veterans' organization of former members of the Union army and navy.
[6]The term used by a Confederate officer to describe Shaw's troops. Shaw and much of his regiment were killed in an assault on the Confederate Fort Wagner in South Carolina, 18 July 1863. They were buried in a common grave.
[7]World War II, 1939–1945.   [8]A street in Boston.
[1]Public park in Boston.

the sailors and their pick-ups under trees
with Latin labels.[2] And the jaded flock
of swanboats paddles to its dock.
The park is drying.   10
Dead leaves thicken to a ball
inside the basin of a fountain, where
the heads of four stone lions stare
and suck on empty fawcets. Night
deepens. From the arched bridge, we see
the shedding park-bound mallards, how they keep
circling and diving in the lanternlight,
searching for something hidden in the muck.
And now the moon, earth's friend, that cared so much
for us, and cared so little, comes again—   20
always a stranger! As we walk,
it lies like chalk
over the waters. Everything's aground.
Remember summer? Bubbles filled
the fountain, and we splashed. We drowned
in Eden, while Jehovah's grass-green lyre
was rustling all about us in the leaves
that gurgled by us, turned upside down . . .
The fountain's failing waters flash around
the garden. Nothing catches fire.   30

                                                                    1964

LADY RALEGH'S LAMENT[1]

1618

Sir Walter, oh, oh, my own Sir Walter—
the sour Tower and the Virgin Queen's garden close
are deflowered and gone now . . .
Horrible the connoisseur tyrant's[2] querulous strut;
an acorn dances in a girdle of green oak leaves
up the steps to the scaffold to the block,
square bastard of an oak. Clearly, clearly,
the Atlantic whitens to merge Sir Walter's head,
still dangling in its scarlet, tangled twine,
as if beseeching voyage. Voyage?   10
Down and down; the compass needle dead on terror.

                                                                    1964

WAKING EARLY SUNDAY MORNING

O to break loose, like the chinook
salmon jumping and falling back,

---

[2]Identification markers showing the trees' botanical classifications in Latin.
[1]Sir Walter Ralegh was imprisoned in the Tower of London and, in 1618, beheaded.
[2]King James I, who succeeded the Virgin Queen, Elizabeth I, in 1603.

nosing up to the impossible
stone and bone-crushing waterfall—
raw-jawed, weak-fleshed there, stopped by ten
steps of the roaring ladder, and then
to clear the top on the last try,
alive enough to spawn and die.

Stop, back off. The salmon breaks
water, and now my body wakes   10
to feel the unpolluted joy
and criminal leisure of a boy—
no rainbow smashing a dry fly
in the white run is free as I,
here squatting like a dragon on
time's hoard before the day's begun!

Vermin run for their unstopped holes;
in some dark nook a fieldmouse rolls
a marble, hours on end, then stops;
the termite in the woodwork sleeps—   20
listen, the creatures of the night
obsessive, casual, sure of foot,
go on grinding, while the sun's
daily remourseful blackout dawns.

Fierce, fireless mind, running downhill.
Look up and see the harbor fill:
business as usual in eclipse
goes down to the sea in ships—
wake of refuse, dacron rope,
bound for Bermuda or Good Hope,   30
all bright before the morning watch
the wine-dark hulls of yawl and ketch.

I watch a glass of water wet
with a fine fuzz of icy sweat,
silvery colors touched with sky,
serene in their neutrality—
yet if I shift, or change my mood,
I see some object made of wood,
background behind it of brown grain,
to darken it, but not to stain.   40

O that the spirit could remain
tinged but untarnished by its strain!
Better dressed and stacking birch,
or lost with the Faithful at Church—
anywhere, but somewhere else!
And now the new electric bells,
clearly chiming, "Faith of our fathers,"
and now the congregation gathers.

O Bible chopped and crucified

in hymns we hear but do not read,   50
none of the milder subtleties
of grace or art will sweeten these
stiff quatrains shovelled out four-square—
they sing of peace, and preach despair;
yet they gave darkness some control,
and left a loophole for the soul.

No, put old clothes on, and explore
the corners of the woodshed for
its dregs and dreck: tools with no handle,
ten candle-ends not worth a candle,   60
old lumber banished from the Temple,
damned by Paul's precept and example,
cast from the kingdom, banned in Israel,
the wordless sign, the tinkling cymbal.

When will we see Him face to face?
Each day, He shines through darker glass.
In this small town where everything
is known, I see His vanishing
emblems, His white spire and flag-
pole sticking out above the fog,   70
like old white china doorknobs, sad,
slight, useless things to calm the mad.

Hammering military splendor,
top-heavy Goliath in full armor—
little redemption in the mass
liquidations of their brass,
elephant and phalanx moving
with the times and still improving,
when that kingdom hit the crash:
a million foreskins stacked like trash . . .   80

Sing softer! But what if a new
diminuendo brings no true
tenderness, only restlessness,
excess, the hunger for success,
sanity of self-deception
fixed and kicked by reckless caution,
while we listen to the bells—
anywhere, but somewhere else!

O to break loose. All life's grandeur
is something with a girl in summer . . .   90
elated as the President
girdled by his establishment
this Sunday morning, free to chaff
his own thoughts with his bear-cuffed staff,
swimming nude, unbuttoned, sick
of his ghost-written rhetoric!

No weekends for the gods now. Wars
flicker, earth licks its open sores,
fresh breakage, fresh promotions, chance
assassinations, no advance.   100
Only man thinning out his kind
sounds through the Sabbath noon, the blind
swipe of the pruner and his knife
busy about the tree of life . . .

Pity the planet, all joy gone
from this sweet volcanic cone;
peace to our children when they fall
in small war on the heels of small
war—until the end of time
to police the earth, a ghost   110
orbiting forever lost
in our monotonous sublime.

                                              1967

NEAR THE OCEAN

(For E. H. L.)[1]

The house is filled. The last heartthrob
thrills through her flesh. The hero stands,
stunned by the applauding hands,
and lifts her head to please the mob . . .
No, young and starry-eyed, the brother
and sister wait before their mother,
old iron-bruises, powder, "Child,
these breasts . . ." He knows. And if she's killed

his treadmill heart will never rest—
his wet mouth pressed to some slack breast,   10
or shifting over on his back . . .
the severed radiance filters back,
athirst for nightlife—gorgon head,
fished up from the Aegean dead,
with all its stranded snakes uncoiled,
here beheaded and despoiled.

We hear the ocean. Older seas
and deserts give asylum, peace
to each abortion and mistake.
Lost in the Near Eastern dreck,[2]   20
the tyrant and tyrannicide
lie like the bridegroom and the bride;
the battering ram, abandoned, prone,
beside the apeman's phallic stone.

[1]Elizabeth Hardwick Lowell, the poet's former wife.
[2]Trash, rubbish.

Betrayals! Was it the first night?
They stood against a black and white
inland New England backdrop. No dogs
there, horse or hunter, only frogs
chirring from the dark trees and swamps.
Elms watching like extinguished lamps.
Knee-high hedges of black sheep 30
encircling them at every step.

Some subway-green coldwater flat,
its walls tattooed with neon light,
then high delirious squalor, food
burned down with vodka . . . menstrual blood
caking the covers, when they woke
to the dry, childless Sunday walk,
saw cars on Brooklyn Bridge descend
through steel and coal dust to land's end. 40

Was it years later when they met,
and summer's coarse last-quarter drought
had dried the hardveined elms to bark—
lying like people out of work,
dead sober, cured, recovered, on
the downslope of some gritty green,
all access barred with broken glass;
and dehydration browned the grass?

Is it this shore? Their eyes worn white
as moons from hitting bottom? Night, 50
the sandfleas scissoring their feet,
the sandbed cooling to concrete,
one borrowed blanket, lights of cars
shining down at them like stars? . . .
Sand built the lost Atlantis . . . sand,
Atlantic ocean, condoms, sand.

Sleep, sleep. The ocean, grinding stones,
can only speak the present tense;
nothing will age, nothing will last,
or take corruption from the past. 60
A hand, your hand then! I'm afraid
to touch the crisp hair on your head—
Monster loved for what you are,
till time, that buries us, lay bare.

                              1967

FOR THEODORE ROETHKE[1]

1908–1963

All night you wallowed through my sleep,
then in the morning you were lost

_____
[1]See page 1657.

in the Maine sky—close, cold and gray,
smoke and smoke-colored cloud.

Sheeplike, unsociable reptilian, two
hell-divers[1] splattered squawking on the water,
loons devolving to a monochrome.
You honored nature,

helpless, elemental creature.
The black stump of your hand   10
just touched the waters under the earth,
and left them quickened with your name. . . .

Now, you honor the mother,
Omnipresent,
she made you nonexistent,
the ocean's anchor, our high tide.

                                                    1967

WILL NOT COME BACK

[VOLVERAN][1]

Dark swallows will doubtless come back killing
the injudicious nightflies with a clack of the beak;
but these that stopped full flight to see your beauty
and my good fortune . . . as if they knew our names—
they'll not come back. The thick lemony honeysuckle,
climbing from the earthroot to your window,
will open more beautiful blossoms to the evening;
but these . . . like dewdrops, trembling, shining, falling,
the tears of day—they'll not come back. . . .
Some other love will sound his firework for you   10
and wake your heart, perhaps, from its cool sleep;
but silent, absorbed, and on his knees,
as men adore God at the altar, as I love you—
don't blind yourself, you'll not be loved like that.

                                                    1970, 1973

John Berryman *1914–1972*

*"I am interested only in people in crisis," Berryman once told a fellow poet. The remark
underscores the qualities in his poetry that brought him to prominence. From a poet of
technically competent, but undistinguished verse, fashionably derivative of Yeats and*

[1]Diving birds of the loon family.
[1]Spanish: they will return, the title given the poem in its first version, published in 1970.

Auden, he evolved into one of the most innovative poets of his generation. Well in advance of Robert Lowell's Life Studies *and the advent of "confessional" poetry, Berryman was turning from themes of political and social disillusionment—"the evil waste of history"— to an increasingly personal poetry focused upon his own deeply troubled and crisis-prone inner life.*

The overriding event in his life occurred in childhood. He was born in McAlester, Oklahoma, and named after his father, John Allyn Smith. When he was ten, the family moved to Tampa, Florida. A year later, outside his son's window, his father shot himself. The family then resettled in New York City, his mother remarried, and John acquired his stepfather's surname. The trauma of his father's suicide remained, however. In time it became

> *The inexhaustible ability of man*
> *Loved once, long lost, still to prevent my peace. . . .*

In his last years, thrice married and suffering from recurrent mental illness and alcoholism, Berryman was haunted by the notion that his own suicidal impulses were the legacy of a father who he felt had abandoned him. In 1972 Berryman committed suicide.

Berryman had received degrees from Columbia University and Clare College, Cambridge. At Columbia, he was a student of Mark Van Doren, who encouraged his decision to become a poet. His subsequent two years at Cambridge gave him the opportunity to meet William Butler Yeats, Dylan Thomas, and W. H. Auden. Back home, he taught English for a year at Wayne State University in Detroit, Michigan. He published his first group of "Twenty Poems" in Five Young American Poets *(1940). For the next ten years, the decade of the 'forties, he taught at Harvard and Princeton and produced, along with a critical biography of Stephen Crane, three collections of poetry:* Poems *(1942);* Berryman's Sonnets *(written in 1947 but withheld from publication until 1967); and* The Dispossessed *(1948). Of these,* Berryman's Sonnets, *a long, Petrarchan sonnet sequence about an illicit love affair—written while undergoing psychoanalysis—marked his first exploration of self-revelatory material.*

The publication of his first major poem, Homage to Mistress Bradstreet *(1953) became the literary event that made Berryman's reputation. Edmund Wilson called it "the most distinguished long poem by an American since* The Waste Land.*"*

His most ambitious undertaking, the work of some fifteen years, was The Dream Songs *(1969). Consisting of 385 poems, mostly of eighteen lines each, the series first appeared in two sections:* 77 Dream Songs *(1964), which won the Pulitzer Prize; and* His Toy, His Dream, His Rest *(1968), which won the National Book Award and a Bollingen Prize. Autobiographical, but not in chronological sequence, the "Songs" portray stages in a psychological history. They are united solely by the character of "Henry," Berryman's persona, who variously appears in first, second, and third person and adopts other identities, becoming a "rabbi" or a minstrel in blackface named "Mr. Bones." Henry's novel idiom is a Berryman trademark; it ranges from the formal to the colloquial in a mixture of garbled syntax, grammatical oddities, private allusions, puns, and off-rhymes. He emerges from* The Dream Songs *as a memorable creation, but Henry is a character of limited insight. Self-mocking, self-pitying, tormented, he is a fragmented personality at odds with his experience.*

In 1969, Berryman was named a Regents' Professor at the University of Minnesota, where he had held a teaching post for many years. He was a frequent visiting lecturer at other universities and the recipient of numerous awards that allowed him to travel and live abroad. In 1970 he published Love & Fame; *his last poems,* Delusions, *etc. (1972), and an unfinished autobiographical novel,* Recovery *(1973), were published posthumously.*

FURTHER READING: W. Martz, *John Berryman*, 1969; J. Linebarger, *John Berryman*, 1974; J. Conarroe, *John Berryman*, 1977; G. Arpin, *The Poetry of John Berryman*, 1978; J. Haffenden, *John Berryman, A Critical Commentary*, 1980; J. Haffenden, *The Life of John Berryman*, 1982; J. Bloom, *The Stock of Available Reality*, 1984; S. Matterson, *Berryman and Lowell, The Art of Living*, 1987.

TEXTS: "The Ball Poem" and "A Professor's Song" are from *The Dispossessed*, 1948; the "Dream Songs" are from *The Dream Songs*, 1969.

THE BALL POEM

What is the boy now, who has lost his ball,
What, what is he to do? I saw it go
Merrily bouncing, down the street, and then
Merrily over—there it is in the water!
No use to say 'O there are other balls':
An ultimate shaking grief fixes the boy
As he stands rigid, trembling, staring down
All his young days into the harbour where
His ball went. I would not intrude on him,
A dime, another ball, is worthless. Now   10
He senses first responsibility
In a world of possessions. People will take balls,
Balls will be lost always, little boy.
And no one buys a ball back. Money is external.
He is learning, well behind his desperate eyes,
The epistemology of loss, how to stand up
Knowing what every man must one day know
And most know many days, how to stand up.
And gradually light returns to the street,
A whistle blows, the ball is out of sight,   20
Soon part of me will explore the deep and dark
Floor of the harbour . . I am everywhere,
I suffer and move, my mind and my heart move
With all that move me, under the water
Or whistling, I am not a little boy.

                                                    1942

A PROFESSOR'S SONG

(. . rabid or dog-dull.) Let me tell you how
The Eighteenth Century couplet ended. Now
Tell me. Troll[1] me the sources of that Song—
Assigned last week—by Blake.[2] Come, come along,
Gentlemen. (Fidget and huddle, do. Squint soon.)
I want to end these fellows all by noon.

[1] Sing or chant heartily.   [2] William Blake (1757–1827), English poet.

"That deep romantic chasm"[3]—an early use;
The word is from the French, by our abuse
Fished out a bit. (Red all your eyes. O when?)
"A poet is a man speaking to men":[4]
But I am then a poet, am I not?—
Ha ha. The radiator, please. Well, what?

Alive now—no—Blake would have written prose,
But movement following movement crisply flows,
So much the better, better the much so,
As burbleth Mozart.[5] Twelve. The class can go.
Until I meet you, then, in Upper Hell
Convulsed, foaming immortal blood: farewell.

                                    1948

from *DREAM SONGS*

1

Huffy Henry[1] hid   the day,
unappeasable Henry sulked.
I see his point,—a trying to put things over.
It was the thought that they thought
they could *do* it made Henry wicked & away.
But he should have come out and talked.

All the world like a woolen lover
once did seem on Henry's side.
Then came a departure.
Thereafter nothing fell out as it might or ought.
I don't see how Henry, pried
open for all the world to see, survived.

What he has now to say is a long
wonder the world can bear & be.
Once in a sycamore I was glad
all at the top, and I sang.
Hard on the land wears the strong sea
and empty grows every bed.
1958   1959, 1964

---

[3]A quotation from *Kubla Khan* (1816), a poem by Samuel Taylor Coleridge (1772–1834), English poet.
[4]A quotation adapted from the preface to *Lyrical Ballads* (1802) by William Wordsworth (1770–1850), English poet.
[5]Wolfgang Amadeus Mozart (1756–1791), Austrian composer.
[1]In *Dream Songs* (1969) Berryman identifies Henry as "an imaginary character (not the poet, not me) named Henry, a white American in early middle age sometimes in blackface, who has suffered an irreversible loss and talks about himself sometimes in the first person, sometimes in the third, sometimes even in the second; he has a friend, never named, who addresses him as Mr. Bones and variants thereof. Requiescant in pace."

14

Life, friends, is boring. We must not say so.
After all, the sky flashes, the great sea yearns,
we ourselves flash and yearn,
and moreover my mother told me as a boy
(repeatingly) 'Ever to confess you're bored
means you have no

Inner Resources.' I conclude now I have no
inner resources, because I am heavy bored.
Peoples bore me,
literature bores me, especially great literature,   10
Henry bores me, with his plights & gripes
as bad as achilles,[1]

who loves people and valiant art, which bores me.
And the tranquil hills, & gin, look like a drag
and somehow a dog
has taken itself & its tail considerably away
into mountains or sea or sky, leaving
behind: me, wag.

                                                              1963, 1964

29

There sat down, once, a thing on Henry's heart
só heavy, if he had a hundred years
& more, & weeping, sleepless, in all them time
Henry could not make good.
Starts again always in Henry's ears
the little cough somewhere, an odour, a chime.

And there is another thing he has in mind
like a grave Sienese face[1] a thousand years
would fail to blur the still profiled reproach of. Ghastly,
with open eyes, he attends, blind.   10
All the bells say: too late. This is not for tears;
thinking.

But never did Henry, as he thought he did,
end anyone and hacks her body up
and hide the pieces, where they may be found.
He knows: he went over everyone, & nobody's missing.
Often he reckons, in the dawn, them up.
Nobody is ever missing.

                                                              1960, 1964

---

[1]Hero of *The Iliad*. Because of injured pride he sulked in his tent, refusing to fight the Trojans.
[1]As seen in religious paintings by artists of Siena, Italy, in the fourteenth and fifteenth centuries.

45

He stared at ruin. Ruin stared straight back.
He thought they was old friends. He felt on the stair
where her papa found them bare
they became familiar. When the papers were lost
rich with pals' secrets, he thought he had the knack
of ruin. Their paths crossed

and once they crossed in jail; they crossed in bed;
and over an unsigned letter their eyes met,
and in an Asian city
directionless & lurchy at two & three,   10
or trembling to a telephone's fresh threat,
and when some wired his head

to reach a wrong opinion, 'Epileptic'.
But he noted now that: they were not old friends.
He did not know this one.
This one was a stranger, come to make amends
for the imposters, and to make it stick.
Henry nodded, un-.
1962?   1963, 1964

48

He[1] yelled at me in Greek,[2]
my God![3]—It's not his language
and I'm no good at—his is Aramaic,
was—I am a monoglot[4] of English
(American version) and, say pieces from
a baker's dozen others: where's the bread?

but rising in the Second Gospel, pal:
The seed goes down,[5] god dies,
a rising happens,
some crust, and then occurs   an eating.[6] He said so,   10
a Greek idea,
troublesome to imaginary Jews,

[1]Jesus.
[2]The New Testament, originally written in Greek, translated the words of Jesus, who spoke Galilean Aramaic, a Semitic language similar to Hebrew.
[3]A reference to the words spoken by Jesus on the cross, "My God, My God, why has thou forsaken me?" Matthew 27:46 and Mark 15:34.
[4]One who speaks only a single language.
[5]A reference to the parable of the mustard seed which, like religious faith, "when it is sown, it groweth up and becometh greater than all herbs." Mark 4:31–32.
[6]A reference to the sacrament of the Lord's Supper and the eating of bread and wine.

like bitter Henry, full of the death of love,
Cawdor[7]-uneasy, disambitious, mourning
the whole implausible necessary thing.
He dropped his voice & sybilled[8] of
the death of the death of love.
I óught to get going.
1959   1963, 1964

53

He lay in the middle of the world, and twitcht.
More Sparine[1] for Pelides,[2]
human (half) & down here as he is,
with probably insulting mail to open
and certainly unworthy words to hear
and his unforgivable memory.

—I seldom *go* to *films*. They are too exciting,
said the Honourable Possum.[3]
—It takes me so long to read the 'paper,
said to me one day a novelist hot as a firecracker,[4]   10
because I have to identify myself with everyone in it,
including the corpses, pal.'

Kierkegaard[5] wanted a society, to refuse to read 'papers,
and that was not, friends, his worst idea.
Tiny Hardy,[6] toward the end, refused to say *anything*,
a programme adopted early on by young Housman,[7]
and Gottfried Benn[8]
said:—We are using our own skins for wallpaper and we cannot win.
1958   1960, 1964

75

Turning it over, considering, like a madman
Henry put forth a book.
No harm resullted from this.
Neither the menstruating   stars (nor man) was moved
at once.
Bare dogs drew closer for a second look

[7]A reference to Shakespeare's Macbeth, the thane (lord) of Cawdor.
[8]I.e., spoke in the manner of the sibyls, prophetesses of ancient Greece and Rome.
[1]A tranquilizing drug.
[2]Another name for the Greek hero Achilles. He was the son of King Peleus and the sea nymph Thetis and thus half human.
[3]A nickname of the poet T. S. Eliot.
[4]A reference to Berryman's friend, Saul Bellow, the American novelist.
[5]Søren Kierkegaard (1813–1855), Danish philosopher
[6]Thomas Hardy (1840–1928), English novelist.
[7]Alfred Edward Housman (1859–1936), English lyric poet noted for his economy of words.
[8]German poet (1886–1956).

and performed their friendly operations there.
Refreshed, the bark rejoiced.
Seasons went and came.
Leaves fell, but only a few.   10
Something remarkable about this
unshedding bulky bole-proud blue-green moist

thing made by savage & thoughtful
surviving Henry
began to strike the passers from despair
so that sore on their shoulders old men hoisted
six-foot sons and polished women called
small girls to dream awhile toward the flashing & bursting
  tree!
                                                        1959, 1964

76

Henry's Confession

Nothin very bad happened to me lately.
How you explain that? —I explain that, Mr Bones,[1]
terms o' your bafflin odd sobriety.
Sober as man can get, no girls, no telephones,
what could happen bad to Mr Bones?
—*If* life is a handkerchief sandwich,

in a modesty of death I join my father
who dared so long agone leave me.
A bullet on a concrete stoop
close by a smothering southern sea   10
spreadeagled on an island, by my knee.
—You is from hunger, Mr Bones,

I offers you this handkerchief, now set
your left foot by my right foot,
shoulder to shoulder, all that jazz,
arm in arm, by the beautiful sea,
hum a little, Mr Bones.
—I saw nobody coming, so I went instead.
1960?   1964

143

—That's enough of that, Mr Bones. *Some* lady you make.
Honour the burnt cork,[1] be a vaudeville man,

[1]Name traditionally given one of the characters in a blackface minstrel show who rhythmically rattled bones.
[1]Used as makeup by white actors playing blackface roles.

I'll sing you now a song
the like of whích may bring your heart to break:
he's gone! and we don't know where. When he began
taking the pistol out & along,

you was just a little; but gross fears
accompanied us along the beaches, pal.
My mother was scared almost to death.
He was going to swim out, with me, forevers,   10
and a swimmer strong he was in the phosphorescent   Gulf,
but he decided on lead.[2]

That mad drive wiped out my childhood. I put him down
while all the same on forty years I love him
stashed in Oklahoma
besides his brother Will. Bite the nerve of the town
for anyone so desperate. I repeat: I love him
until *I* fall into coma.
1967   1968

224

Eighty[1]

Lonely in his great age, Henry's old friend
leaned on his burning cane while hís old friend
was hymnéd out of living.
The Ábbey rang with sound. Pound white as snow
bowed to them with his thoughts—it's hard to know them though
for the old man sang no word.

Dry, ripe with pain, busy with loss, let's guess.
Gone. Gone them wine-meetings, gone green grasses
of the picnics of rising youth.
Gone all, slowly. Stately, not as the tongue   10
worries the loose tooth, wits as strong as young,
only the albino body failing.

Where the smother clusters pinpoint insights clear.
The tennis is over.[2] The last words are here.
What, in the world, will they be?
White is the hue of death & victory,

[2]Distressed over his marital difficulties, Berryman's father periodically threatened to drown himself and his son. In 1926, when the family moved from Oklahoma to Florida, Berryman's father committed suicide with a pistol.
[1]In February 1965, when he was eighty years old, Ezra Pound attended the memorial services held at Westminster Abbey in London for the poet T. S. Eliot, who had died January 4, 1965.
[2]Pound had been an avid tennis player.

all the old generosities dismissed
while the white years insist.

1965, 1968

382

At Henry's bier let some thing fall out well:
enter there none who somewhat has to sell,
the music ancient & gradual,
the voices solemn but the grief subdued,
no hairy jokes but everybody's mood
subdued, subdued,

until the Dancer comes, in a short short dress
hair black & long & loose, dark dark glasses,
uptilted face,
pallor & strangeness, the music changes   10
to 'Give!' & 'Ow!' and how! the music changes,
she kicks a backward limb

on tiptoe, pirouettes, & she is free
to the knocking music, sails, dips, & suddenly
returns to the terrible gay
occasion hopeless & mad, she weaves, it's hell,
she flings to her head a leg, bobs, all is well,
she dances Henry away.
1968   1968

384

The marker slants, flowerless, day's almost done,
I stand above my father's grave with rage,
often, often before
I've made this awful pilgrimage to one
who cannot visit me, who tore his page
out: I come back for more,

I spit upon this dreadful banker's grave
who shot his heart out in a Florida dawn
O ho alas alas
When will indifference come, I moan & rave   10
I'd like to scrabble till I got right down
away down under the grass

and ax the casket open ha to see
just how he's taking it, which he sought so hard
we'll tear apart
the mouldering grave clothes ha & then Henry
will heft the ax once more, his final card,
and fell it on the start.

1968

385

My daughter's heavier. Light leaves are flying.
Everywhere in enormous numbers turkeys will be dying
and other birds, all their wings.
They never greatly flew, Did they wish to?
I should know. Off away somewhere once I knew
such things.

Or good Ralph Hodgson[1] back then did, or does.
The man is dead whom Eliot praised. My praise
follows and flows too late.
Fall is grievy, brisk. Tears behind the eyes   10
almost fall. Fall comes to us as a prize
to rouse us toward our fate.

My house is made of wood and it's made well,
unlike us. My house is older than Henry;
that's fairly old.
If there were a middle   ground between things and the soul
or if the sky resembled more the sea,
I wouldn't have to scold

                                        my heavy daughter.
                                                 1965

Richard Wilbur   *1921–*

*Although Richard Wilbur was born in New York City, he has belonged by training as well
as by occupation to New England. He graduated from Amherst College in Massachusetts,
took his M.A. at Harvard, and then began a teaching career that has included positions
at Harvard, at Wellesley, and, since 1957, at Wesleyan University in Connecticut.
Wilbur's poetry, with its careful craftsmanship, verbal dexterity, and wide-ranging use of
traditional forms, is more akin to that of Edwin Arlington Robinson, Robert Frost, and
Robert Lowell than to the free verse effusiveness of Walt Whitman. Wilbur's concern with
the puzzling tangle of appearance and reality, his belief in the power of imagination to
perceive and create reality, and his love for and absorption with nature suggest a New
England literary kinship with Emerson, Thoreau, and Emily Dickinson. Wilbur's first
volumes of poetry,* The Beautiful Changes *(1947) and* Ceremony *(1950), brought
him immediate critical approval. His third,* Things of This World *(1956), won a
Pulitzer Prize and a National Book Award. Other volumes have followed:* Advice to a
Prophet *(1961);* The Poems of Richard Wilbur*(1963);* Walking to Sleep *(1969);*
Opposites *(1973);* The Mind-Reader, *(1976);* Responses *(1976), essays on poets
and poetry.*

  What most impresses Wilbur's readers, perhaps, is the freshness of his imagery, his

[1]English poet (1871–1962) who wrote of nature and animals.

mastery of a number of complex stanzaic forms, and the diversity of his themes. The rhythms of his poems are sometimes reminiscent of the hymn meters employed by Emily Dickinson, while his perceptions suggest her uses of the minutiae of nature and her fusion of images of life and death to convey a complex emotional experience. Wilbur's subjects range from the philosophical "Epistemology" to such down-to-earth pieces as "The Death of a Toad." He seeks "contact with the true sights and sounds of this world." In tone his poems vary from the light and comic to the tragic; in point of view they shift from the most subjectively lyrical to the detached and objective. But always within his admirable versatility and technical mastery lie a sharpness and freshness of figurative language that reveal his love of particularities, of colors and shapes and textures, and his conviction that the spirit is drawn to the actual things of the material world: "I like it," he has said, "when the ideas of a poem seem to be necessary aspects of the things or actions which it presents."

FURTHER READING: D. Hill, *Richard Wilbur*, 1967; H. Stevens, *Richard Wilbur*, 1977; *Richard Wilbur's Creation*, ed. W. Salinger, 1983.
    TEXT: *New and Collected Poems*, 1988.

MINED COUNTRY

They have gone into the gray hills quilled with birches,
Drag now their cannon up the chill mountains;
But it's going to be long before
Their war's gone for good.

I tell you it hits at childhood more than churches
Full up with sky or buried town fountains,
Rooms laid open or anything
Cut stone or cut wood,

Seeing the boys come swinging slow over the grass
(Like playing pendulum) their silver plates,[2]   10
Stepping with care and listening
Hard for hid metal's cry.

It's rightly-called-chaste Belphoebe[1] some would miss,
Some, calendar colts at Kentucky gates;
But the remotest would guess that
Some scheme's gone awry.

Danger is sunk in the pastures, the woods are sly.
Ingenuity's covered with flowers!
We thought woods were wise but never
Implicated, never involved.   20

Cows in mid-munch go splattered over the sky;
Roses like brush-whores smile from bowers;
Shepherds must learn a new language; this

[2]"Mine detectors."—Wilbur's note.
[1]The chaste huntress in Spenser's "Faerie Queene."

Isn't going to be quickly solved.

Sunshiny field grass, the woods floor, are so mixed up
With earliest trusts, you have to pick back
Far past all you have learned, to go
Disinherit the dumb child,

Tell him to trust things alike and never to stop
Emptying things, but not let them lack   30
Love in some manner restored; to be
Sure the whole world's wild.

                                                               1946, 1947

THE DEATH OF A TOAD

A toad the power mower caught,
Chewed and clipped of a leg, with a hobbling hop has got
   To the garden verge, and sanctuaried him
Under the cineraria leaves, in the shade
   Of the ashen heartshaped leaves, in a dim,
      Low, and a final glade.

The rare original heartsblood goes,
Spends on the earthen hide, in the folds and wizenings, flows
   In the gutters of the banked and staring eyes. He lies
As still as if he would return to stone,   10
   And soundlessly attending, dies
      Toward some deep monotone,

Toward misted and ebullient seas
And cooling shores, toward lost Amphibia's[1] emperies.[2]
   Day dwindles, drowning, and at length is gone
In the wide and antique eyes, which still appear
   To watch, across the castrate lawn,
      The haggard daylight steer.

                                                               1948, 1950

MUSEUM PIECE

The good gray guardians of art
Patrol the halls on spongy shoes,
Impartially protective, though
Perhaps suspicious of Toulouse.[1]

Here dozes one against the wall,

---

[1]The class of animals that includes toads.   [2]Empires.
[1]Henri de Toulouse-Lautrec (1864–1901), French painter.

Disposed upon a funeral chair.
A Degas[2] dancer pirouettes
Upon the parting of his hair.

See how she spins! The grace is there,
But strain as well is plain to see.   10
Degas loved the two together:
Beauty joined to energy.

Edgar Degas purchased once
A fine El Greco,[3] which he kept
Against the wall beside his bed
To hang his pants on while he slept.

1948, 1950

STILL, CITIZEN SPARROW

Still, citizen sparrow, this vulture which you call
Unnatural, let him but lumber again to air
Over the rotten office, let him bear
The carrion ballast up, and at the tall

Tip of the sky lie cruising. Then you'll see
That no more beautiful bird is in heaven's height,
No wider more placid wings, no watchfuller flight;
He shoulders nature there, the frightfully free,

The naked-headed one. Pardon him, you
Who dart in the orchard aisles, for it is he   10
Devours death, mocks mutability,
Has heart to make an end, keeps nature new.

Thinking of Noah, childheart, try to forget
How for so many bedlam hours his saw
Soured the song of birds with its wheezy gnaw,
And the slam of his hammer all the day beset

The people's ears. Forget that he could bear
To see the towns like coral under the keel,
And the fields so dismal deep. Try rather to feel
How high and weary it was, on the waters where   20

He rocked his only world, and everyone's.
Forgive the hero, you would have died

[2]Edgar Degas (1834–1917), French painter.
[3]Domenikos Theotokopoulos (1541–1614), Spanish painter born in Crete.

Gladly with all you knew; he rode that tide
To Ararat; all men are Noah's sons.

                                                                    1948, 1950

JUGGLER

A ball will bounce, but less and less. It's not
A light-hearted thing, resents its own resilience.
Falling is what it loves, and the earth falls
So in our hearts from brilliance,
Settles and is forgot.
It takes a sky-blue juggler with five red balls

To shake our gravity up. Whee, in the air
The balls roll round, wheel on his wheeling hands,
Learning the ways of lightness, alter to spheres
Grazing his finger ends,   10
Cling to their courses there,
Swinging a small heaven about his ears.

But a heaven is easier made of nothing at all
Than the earth regained, and still and sole within
The spin of worlds, with a gesture sure and noble
He reels that heaven in,
Landing it ball by ball,
And trades it all for a broom, a plate, a table.

Oh, on his toe the table is turning, the broom's
Balancing up on his nose, and the plate whirls   20
On the tip of the broom! Damn, what a show, we cry:
The boys stamp, and the girls
Shriek, and the drum booms
And all comes down, and he bows and says good-bye.

If the juggler is tired now, if the broom stands
In the dust again, if the table starts to drop
Through the daily dark again, and though the plate
Lies flat on the table top,
For him we batter our hands
Who has won for once over the world's weight.   30

                                                                    1949, 1950

EPISTEMOLOGY

I

Kick at the rock, Sam Johnson,[1] break your bones;
But cloudy, cloudy is the stuff of stones.

[1]Upon being told that one could not refute the theory that physical objects exist only in the mind of a perceiver, the English writer Samuel Johnson (1709–1784) kicked a large stone and announced, "I refute it thus!"

II
We milk the cow of the world, and as we do
We whisper in her ear, "You are not true."

1950

MARGINALIA

Things concentrate at the edges; the pond-surface
Is bourne to fish and man and it is spread
In textile scum and damask light, on which
The lily-pads are set; and there are also
   Inlaid ruddy twigs, becalmed pine-leaves,
   Air-baubles, and the chain mail of froth.

Descending into sleep (as when the night-lift
Falls past a brilliant floor), we glimpse a sublime
Décor and hear, perhaps, a complete music,
But this evades us, as in the night meadows   10
   The crickets' million roundsong dies away
   From all advances, rising in every distance.

Our riches are centrifugal; men compose
Daily, unwittingly, their final dreams,
And those are our own voices whose remote
Consummate chorus rides on the whirlpool's rim,
   Past which we flog our sails, toward which we drift,
   Plying our trades, in hopes of a good drowning.

1954, 1956

LAMARCK[1] ELABORATED

"The environment creates the organ"

The Greeks were wrong who said our eyes have rays;
Not from these sockets or these sparkling poles
Comes the illumination of our days.
It was the sun that bored these two blue holes.

It was the song of doves begot the ear
And not the ear that first conceived of sound:
That organ bloomed in vibrant atmosphere,
As music conjured Ilium[2] from the ground.

The yielding water, the repugnant stone,
The poisoned berry and the flaring rose   10

---

[1] Jean Baptiste Lamarck (1744–1829), French biologist. His theory of evolution asserts that all life is shaped by a need to adapt to the environment.
[2] Troy. Described in the poetry of Homer.

Attired in sense the tactless finger-bone
And set the taste-buds and inspired the nose.

Out of our vivid ambiance came unsought
All sense but that most formidably dim.
The shell of balance rolls in seas of thought.
It was the mind that taught the head to swim.

Newtonian[3] numbers set in cosmic lyres
Whelmed us in whirling worlds we could not know,
And by the imagined floods of our desires
The voice of Sirens[4] gave us vertigo.   20

1956

SOMEONE TALKING TO HIMSELF

Even when first her face,
Younger than any spring,
Older than Pharaoh's grain
And fresh as Phoenix-ashes,
Shadowed under its lashes
Every earthly thing,
There was another place
I saw in a flash of pain:
Off in the fathomless dark
Beyond the verge of love   10
I saw blind fishes move,
And under a stone shelf
Rode the recusant shark—
Cold, waiting, himself.

Oh, even when we fell,
Clean as a mountain source
And barely able to tell
Such ecstasy from grace,
Into the primal bed
And current of our race,   20
We knew yet must deny

To what we gathered head:
That music growing harsh,
Trees blotting the sky
Above the roaring course
That in the summer's drought
Slowly would peter out
Into a dry marsh.

Love is the greatest mercy,
A volley of the sun   30
That lashes all with shade,
That the first day be mended;
And yet, so soon undone,
It is the lover's curse
Till time be comprehended
And the flawed heart unmade.
What can I do but move
From folly to defeat,
And call that sorrow sweet
That teaches us to see   40
The final face of love
In what we cannot be?

1958, 1961

ADVICE TO A PROPHET

When you come, as you soon must, to the streets of our city,
Mad-eyed from stating the obvious,
Not proclaiming our fall but begging us
In God's name to have self-pity,

[3]Sir Isaac Newton (1642–1727), English mathematician and physicist.
[4]Sea nymphs in Greek myth. Their alluring songs drew listeners to their death.

Spare us all word of the weapons, their force and range,
The long numbers that rocket the mind;
Our slow, unreckoning hearts will be left behind,
Unable to fear what is too strange.

Nor shall you scare us with talk of the death of the race.
How should we dream of this place without us?—
The sun mere fire, the leaves untroubled about us,
A stone look on the stone's face?

Speak of the world's own change. Though we cannot conceive
Of an undreamt thing, we know to our cost
How the dreamt cloud crumbles, the vines are blackened by frost,
How the view alters. We could believe,

If you told us so, that the white-tailed deer will slip
Into perfect shade, grown perfectly shy,
The lark avoid the reaches of our eye,
The jack-pine lose its knuckled grip

On the cold ledge, and every torrent burn
As Xanthus[1] once, its gliding trout
Stunned in a twinkling. What should we be without
The dolphin's arc, the dove's return,

These things in which we have seen ourselves and spoken?
Ask us, prophet, how we shall call
Our natures forth when that live tongue is all
Dispelled, that glass obscured or broken

In which we have said the rose of our love and the clean
Horse of our courage, in which beheld
The singing locust of the soul unshelled,
And all we mean or wish to mean.

Ask us, ask us whether with the worldless rose
Our hearts shall fail us; come demanding
Whether they shall be lofty or long standing
When the bronze annals of the oak-tree close.

                                                    1959, 1961

A HOLE IN THE FLOOR

for René Magritte[1]

The carpenter's made a hole
In the parlor floor, and I'm standing
Staring down into it now

---

[1] A river god in Greek myth. Angered at the Greeks he caused a river at Troy to flood. Hephaestus, Greek god of fire, then punished the river by causing it to burn.

[1] French surrealist painter (1898–1967).

At four o'clock in the evening,
As Schliemann[2] stood when his shovel
Knocked on the crowns of Troy.

A clean-cut sawdust sparkles
On the grey, shaggy laths,
And here is a cluster of shavings
From the time when the floor was laid.   10
They are silvery-gold, the color
Of Hesperian apple-parings.[3]

Kneeling, I look in under
Where the joists go into hiding.
A pure street, faintly littered
With bits and strokes of light,
Enters the long darkness
Where its parallels will meet.

The radiator-pipe
Rises in middle distance   20
Like a shuttered kiosk, standing
Where the only news is night.
Here it's not painted green,
As it is in the visible world.

For God's sake, what am I after?
Some treasure, or tiny garden?
Or that untrodden place,
The house's very soul,
Where time has stored our footbeats
And the long skein of our voices?   30

Not these, but the buried strangeness
Which nourishes the known:
That spring from which the floor-lamp
Drinks now a wilder bloom,
Inflaming the damask love-seat
And the whole dangerous room.

                                                  1961

PLAYBOY

High on his stockroom ladder like a dunce
The stock-boy sits, and studies like a sage
The subject matter of one glossy page,
As lost in curves as Archimedes once.

---

[2]Heinrich Schliemann (1822–1890), German archeologist who discovered Troy.
[3]In Greek myth, one of the "labors" of Hercules was to obtain a golden apple from a tree guarded by a dragon and belonging to the Hesperides—"Daughters of the Evening."

Sometimes, without a glance, he feeds himself.
The left hand, like a mother-bird in flight,
Brings him a sandwich for a sidelong bite,
And then returns it to a dusty shelf.

What so engrosses him? The wild décor
Of this pink-papered alcove into which   10
A naked girl has stumbled, with its rich
Welter of pelts and pillows on the floor,

Amidst which, kneeling in a supple pose,
She lifts a goblet in her farther hand,
As if about to toast a flower-stand
Above which hovers an exploding rose

Fired from a long-necked crystal vase that rests
Upon a tasseled and vermilion cloth
One taste of which would shrivel up a moth?
Or is he pondering her perfect breasts?   20

Nothing escapes him of her body's grace
Or of her floodlit skin, so sleek and warm
And yet so strangely like a uniform,
but what now grips his fancy is her face,

And how the cunning picture holds her still
At just that smiling instant when her soul,
Grown sweetly faint, and swept beyond control,
Consents to his inexorable will.

                                                                1969

Howard Nemerov   *1920–*

*In his novels, short stories, literary criticism, and in his volumes of poetry Howard Nemerov
displays the virtues of honesty, craftsmanship, and the plain style. His subject is history,
public and private, seen through twentieth-century perspectives. From his first volume of
poems,* The Image and the Law *(1947), through* Inside the Onion *(1984) and* War
Stories *(1987), his variety of subjects has ranged widely: nature, urban life, contemporary
events, psychology, anthropology, astronomy, physics.*

*Nemerov, a graduate of Harvard University, fought in the R.A.F. during World War
II. In 1988 he was appointed Poet Laureate of the United States. He is now a professor
of English at Washington University in St. Louis, perhaps a partial explanation of the
scholarly tone of unruffled calm that is present in his verse and that sharply contrasts with
his puns and playfulness. But for all his controlled versification, much of Nemerov's poetry*

is an expression of opposing attitudes: romanticism and realism, belief and doubt, certainty and loss, and the puzzlement of any intelligent man or woman "gazing at the great inane like the rest of us."

FURTHER READING: P. Meinke, *Howard Nemerov*, 1968; *The Critical Reception of Howard Nemerov*, ed. D. Bowie, 1971; J. Bartholomay, *The Shield of Perseus, The Vision and Imagination of Howard Nemerov*, 1972; W. Mills, *The Stillness in Moving Things, The World of Howard Nemerov*, 1975; R. Labrie, *Howard Nemerov*, 1980.

TEXT: *Collected Poems*, 1977.

THE POND

At the long meadow's end, where the road runs
High on a bank, making a kind of wall,
The rains of last October slowly built
Us up this pond some hundred yards across
And deep maybe to the height of a man's thigh
At the deepest place. It was surprising how
Slowly the water gained across the land
All autumn, no one noticing, until
We had the pond where none had been before
To any memory—most surprising in   10
This country where we think of contours as
Fixed on a map and named and permanent,
Where even if a stream runs dry in summer
You have the stream-bed still to go by and
The chartered name—Red Branch, and Henry's Creek,
And Anthony's Race—for reassurance, though
The reason of those names be sunken with
The man who named them so, in the natural past
Before our history began to be
Written in book or map; our history,   20
Or the settled story that we give the world
Out of the mouths of crones and poachers
Remembering or making up our kinship
In the overgrown swamplands of the mind;
And precious little reassurance, if
You think of it, but enough about that.
Here was, at any rate, surprisingly,
This piece of water covering the ground:
Clear blue, and pale, and crisping up to black
Squalls when the north wind moved across its face;   30
The question whether it would go or stay
Never came up, and no one gave it a name—
Only the water-birds on their way south
Accepted it, and rested there at night,
Coming at dusk down the meadow on wide wings
And splashing up on beating wings at dawn.

By Christmastime the pond was frozen solid
Under a foot of snow, level and white
Across the meadow so you couldn't say
Except from memory where the water was   40
And where the land; and maybe no adult
Would have remembered, but the children did
And brought their skates, and someone's father patched
Together a plough from plank and two-by-four
That half-a-dozen kids could lean against
And clear the snow down to the glittering ice.
They skated all the darkening afternoons
Until the sun burnt level on the ice,
And built their fires all along the shore
To warm their hands and feet, and skated nights   50
Under the full moon or the dark; the ice
Mirrored the moon's light, or the fire's, cold.
There was a tragedy, if that is what
One calls it, the newspapers called it that:
"Pond Claims First Victim" (it still had no name),
As though a monster underneath the ice
Had been in wait to capture the little boy
Skating in darkness all alone, away
From the firelight—the others heard his cry
But he was gone before they found the place—,   60
Or else as though, a tribe of savages,
We sanctified our sports with sacrifice.
At any rate, the skating didn't stop
Despite the funeral and motherly gloom
And editorials; what happened was
The pond took the boy's name of Christopher.
And this was voted properly in meeting
For a memorial and would be so
On the next map, when the next map was drawn:
Christopher Pond: if the pond should still be there.   70

The winter set its teeth; near Eastertide
Before the pond was free of ice all night;
And by that time the birds were coming back
Leisurely, staying a day or so before
They rose and vanished in the northward sky;
Their lonely cries across the open water
Played on the cold, sweet virginal of spring
A chaste, beginning tune carried along
With a wind out of the east. Killdeer and plover
Came and were gone; grackle, starling and flicker   80
Settled to stay; and the sparrowhawk would stand
In the height of noon, a stillness on beating wings,
While close over the water swallows would trace
A music nearly visible in air,
Snapping at newborn flies. Slowly the pond
Warmed into life: cocoon and bud and egg,
All winter's seed and shroud, unfolded being

In the pond named for Christopher, who drowned.
By day the birds, and then the frogs at night,
Kept up a music there, part requiem,   90
Part hunting-song; among the growing reeds
The water boatman worked his oar, the strider
Walked between air and water, dragonfly
Climbed to be born, and dazzled on clear wings.
Then day by day, in the heat of June, the green
World raised itself to natural arrogance,
And the air sang with summer soon to come.

In sullen August, under the massy heat
Of the sun towering in the height, I sat
At the pond's edge, the indeterminate   100
Soft border of what no longer was a pond
But a swamp, a marsh, with here and there a stretch
Of open water, even that half spread
With lily pads and the rich flesh of lilies.
And elsewhere life was choking on itself
As though, in spite of all the feeding there,
Death could not keep the pace and had to let
Life curb itself: pondweed and pickerel-weed
And bladderwort, eel-grass and delicate
Sundew and milfoil, peopled thick the city   110
Of themselves; and dragonfly and damselfly
By hundreds darted among the clustering leaves,
Striders by hundreds skated among the stalks
Of pitcher-plant and catkin; breathless the air
Under the intense quiet whining of
All things striving to breathe; the gift of life
Turning its inward heat upon itself.
So, Christopher, I thought, this is the end
Of dedication, and of the small death
We sought to make a name and sacrifice.   120
The long year has turned away, and the pond
Is drying up, while its remaining life
Grasps at its own throat: the proud lilies wilt,
The milfoil withers, catkins crack and fall,
The dragonfly glitters over it all;
All that your body and your given name
Could do in accidental consecrations
Against nature, returns to nature now,
And so, Christopher, goodbye.
                                        But with these thoughts   130
There came a dragonfly and settled down
On a stem before my eyes, and made me think
How in nature too there is a history,
And that this winged animal of light,
Before it could delight the eye, had been
In a small way a dragon of the deep,
A killer and meat-eater on the floor
Beneath the April surface of the pond;

And that it rose and casts its kind in May
As though putting away costume and mask   140
In the bitter play, and taking a lighter part.
And thinking so, I saw with a new eye
How nothing given us to keep is lost
Till we are lost, and immortality
Is ours until we have no use for it
And live anonymous in nature's name
Though named in human memory and art.
Not consolation, Christopher, though rain
Fill up the pond again and keep your name
Bright as the glittering water in the spring;   150
Not consolation, but our acquiescence.
And I made this song for a memorial
Of yourself, boy, and the dragonfly together.

                                        1954, 1955

THE VACUUM

The house is so quiet now
The vacuum cleaner sulks in the corner closet
Its bag limp as a stopped lung, its mouth
Grinning into the floor, maybe at my
Slovenly life, my dog-dead youth.

I've lived this way long enough,
But when my old woman died her soul
Went into that vacuum cleaner, and I can't bear
To see the bag swell like a belly, eating the dust
And the woolen mice, and begin to howl   10

Because there is old filth everywhere
She used to crawl, in the corner and under the stair.
I know now how life is cheap as dirt,
And still the hungry, angry heart
Hangs on and howls, biting at air.

                                        1955

THE GOOSE FISH

On the long shore, lit by the moon
To show them properly alone,
Two lovers suddenly embraced
So that their shadows were as one.
The ordinary night was graced
For them by the swift tide of blood
That silently they took at flood,

And for a little time they prized
  Themselves emparadised.

Then, as if shaken by stage-fright   10
Beneath the hard moon's bony light,
They stood together on the sand
Embarrassed in each other's sight
But still conspiring hand in hand,
Until they saw, there underfoot,
As though the world had found them out,
The goose fish turning up, though dead,
  His hugely grinning head.

There in the china light he lay,
Most ancient and corrupt and grey.   20
They hesitated at his smile,
Wondering what it seemed to say
To lovers who a little while
Before had thought to understand,
By violence upon the sand,
The only way that could be known
  To make a world their own.

It was a wide and moony grin
Together peaceful and obscene;
They knew not what he would express,   30
So finished a comedian
He might mean failure or success,
But took it for an emblem of
Their sudden, new and guilty love
To be observed by, when they kissed,
  That rigid optimist.

So he became their patriarch,
Dreadfully mild in the half-dark.
His throat that the sand seemed to choke,
His picket teeth, these left their mark   40
But never did explain the joke
That so amused him, lying there
While the moon went down to disappear
Along the still and tilted track
  That bears the zodiac.

                                                    1955

THE TOWN DUMP

*"The art of our necessities is strange,
That can make vile things precious."*

A mile out in the marshes, under a sky
Which seems to be always going away
In a hurry, on that Venetian land threaded
With hidden canals, you will find the city
Which seconds ours (so cemeteries, too,
Reflect a town from hillsides out of town),
Where Being most Becomingly ends up
Becoming some more. From cardboard tenements,
Windowed with cellophane, or simply tenting
In paper bags, the angry mackerel eyes   10
Glare at you out of stove-in, sunken heads
Far from the sea; the lobster, also, lifts
An empty claw in his most minatory
Of gestures; oyster, crab, and mussel shells
Lie here in heaps, savage as money hurled
Away at the gate of hell. If you want results,
These are results.
                    Objects of value or virtue,
However, are also to be picked up here,
Though rarely, lying with bones and rotten meat,   20
Eggshells and mouldy bread, banana peels
No one will skid on, apple cores that caused
Neither the fall of man nor a theory
Of gravitation. People do throw out
The family pearls by accident, sometimes,
Not often; I've known dealers in antiques
To prowl this place by night, with flashlights, on
The off-chance of somebody's having left
Derelict chairs which will turn out to be
By Hepplewhite,[1] a perfect set of six   30
Going to show, I guess, that in any sty
Someone's heaven may open and shower down
Riches responsive to the right dream; though
It is a small chance, certainly, that sends
The ghostly dealer, heavy with fly-netting
Over his head, across these hills in darkness,
Stumbling in cut-glass goblets, lacquered cups,
And other products of his dreamy midden
Penciled with light and guarded by the flies.

For there are flies, of course. A dynamo   40
Composed, by thousands, of our ancient black
Retainers, hums here day and night, steady
As someone telling beads, the hum becoming
A high whine at any disturbance; then,
Settled again, they shine under the sun
Like oil-drops, or are invisible as night,
By night.
          All this continually smoulders,
Crackles, and smokes with mostly invisible fires

---

[1]George Hepplewhite (d. 1786), English furniture maker.

Which, working deep, rarely flash out and flare,   50
And never finish. Nothing finishes;
The flies, feeling the heat, keep on the move.

Among the flies, the purifying fires,
The hunters by night, acquainted with the art
Of our necessities, and the new deposits
That each day wastes with treasure, you may say
There should be ratios. You may sum up
The results, if you want results. But I will add
That wild birds, drawn to the carrion and flies,
Assemble in some numbers here, their wings   60
Shining with light, their flight enviably free,
Their music marvelous, though sad, and strange.

1957, 1958

BOOM!

SEES BOOM IN RELIGION, TOO

Atlantic City, June 23, 1957 (AP).—President Eisenhower's pastor said tonight that Americans are living in a period of "unprecedented religious activity" caused partially by paid vacations, the eight-hour day and modern conveniences.

"These fruits of material progress," said the Rev. Edward L. R. Elson of the National Presbyterian Church, Washington, "have provided the leisure, the energy, and the means for a level of human and spiritual values never before reached."

Here at the Vespasian-Carlton, it's just one
religious activity after another; the sky
is constantly being crossed by cruciform
airplanes, in which nobody disbelieves
for a second, and the tide, the tide
of spiritual progress and prosperity
miraculously keeps rising, to a level
never before attained. The churches are full,
the beaches are full, and the filling-stations
are full, God's great ocean is full   10
of paid vacationers praying an eight-hour day
to the human and spiritual values, the fruits,
the leisure, the energy, and the means, Lord,
the means for the level, the unprecedented level,
and the modern conveniences, which also are full.
Never before, O Lord, have the prayers and praises
from belfry and phonebooth, from ballpark and barbecue
the sacrifices, so endlessly ascended.

It was not thus when Job in Palestine
sat in the dust and cried, cried bitterly;   20

when Damien[1] kissed the lepers on their wounds
it was not thus; it was not thus
when Francis[2] worked a fourteen-hour day
strictly for the birds; when Dante took
a week's vacation without pay and it rained
part of the time, O Lord, it was not thus.

But now the gears mesh and the tires burn
and the ice chatters in the shaker and the priest
in the pulpit, and Thy Name, O Lord,
is kept before the public, while the fruits   30
ripen and religion booms and the level rises
and every modern convenience runneth over,
that it may never be with us as it hath been
with Athens and Karnak[3] and Nagasaki,
nor Thy sun for one instant refrain from shining
on the rainbow Buick by the breezeway
or the Chris Craft with the uplift life raft;
that we may continue to be the just folks we are,
plain people with ordinary superliners and
disposable diaperliners, people of the stop'n'shop   40
'n'pray as you go, of hotel, motel, boatel,
the humble pilgrims of no deposit no return
and please adjust thy clothing, who will give to Thee,
if Thee will keep us going, our annual
Miss Universe, for Thy Name's Sake, Amen.

                                              1958, 1960

THIRTIETH ANNIVERSARY REPORT
OF THE CLASS OF '41

We who survived the war and took to wife
And sired the kids and made the decent living,
And piecemeal furnished forth the finished life
Not by grand theft so much as petty thieving—

Who had the routine middle-aged affair
And made our beds and had to lie in them
This way or that because the beds were there,
And turned our bile and choler in for phlegm—

Who saw grandparents, parents, to the vault
And wives and selves grow wrinkled, grey and fat   10
And children through their acne and revolt
And told the analyst about all that—

[1] Joseph Damien (1841–1889), a Belgian priest who ministered to lepers in Hawaii.
[2] St. Francis of Assisi (1181?–1226). He is frequently portrayed as preaching to the birds.
[3] Present-day Egyptian village at the site of ancient Thebes.

Are done with it. What is there to discuss?
There's nothing left for us to say of us.

1973

FIGURES OF THOUGHT

To lay the logarithmic spiral on
Sea-shell and leaf alike, and see it fit,
To watch the same idea work itself out
In the fighter pilot's steepening, tightening turn
Onto his target, setting up the kill,
And in the flight of certain wall-eyed bugs
Who cannot see to fly straight into death
But have to cast their sidelong glance at it
And come but cranking to the candle's flame—

How secret that is, and how privileged   10
One feels to find the same necessity
Ciphered in forms diverse and otherwise
Without kinship—that is the beautiful
In Nature as in art, not obvious,
Not inaccessible, but just between.

It may diminish some our dry delight
To wonder if everything we are and do
Lies subject to some little law like that;
Hidden in nature, but not deeply so.

1975

Allen Ginsberg *1926–*

*"I saw the best minds of my generation destroyed by madness, starving hysterical naked, /
dragging themselves through the negro streets at dawn looking for an angry fix, / angelhead
hipsters burning for the ancient heavenly connection. . . ." Thus, in his best-known work,*
Howl *(1956), Allen Ginsberg described the alienated Americans of the postwar 1950s
whom his novelist friend Jack Kerouac named the "Beat Generation." Influenced chiefly
by Walt Whitman and William Blake, Ginsberg has bellowed his own "barbaric yawp,"
in lines far freer than Whitman's and with hallucinations far more frenzied than Blake's.*

*Ginsberg's aim is to provide a rationale for the "disaffiliation" of all who protest against
the official culture of the United States. His public readings, delivered in the style of the
bardic chant and featuring a hirsute Ginsberg in the pose of an Old Testament prophet,
have been given behind and before the Iron Curtain, from the Ganges to Galilee to*

California, and his language of "extra vagance" has made him one of the most widely known American poets of the age. He was born in Newark, New Jersey, the son of Louis Ginsberg, a teacher and lyric poet. After attending public schools in Paterson, New Jersey, Allen Ginsberg enrolled at Columbia University in 1943 at the age of seventeen. Two years later he was dismissed for allegedly scrawling an anti-Semitic obscenity on a classroom window and for making uncomplimentary remarks about the university president. After working at a number of odd jobs, Ginsberg was readmitted to Columbia, and following his graduation in 1948 he stayed on for graduate work.

Sometime during 1948–1949 he began to have mystical visions of William Blake, and later he spent eight months in a mental hospital undergoing psychiatric therapy. He worked for a time in 1950 as a book reviewer for Newsweek magazine and then took a job as a market research consultant. After a trip to Mexico in 1954 he settled in San Francisco, where, two years later, Lawrence Ferlinghetti's City Lights Books published Howl and Other Poems. The enormous success of that small volume—enhanced greatly by a widely publicized trial which eventually cleared the book of charges of obscenity—helped bring Ginsberg the fame he enjoys today.

The poems of Howl have been characterized by Ginsberg's followers as prophetic in the same sense that much of the Bible is prophetic, denouncing evil and "pointing the way out. . . ." Ginsberg has declared that his poetry was "adapted from prose seeds, journals, scratchings . . . according to ideas of measure of American speech picked up from W. C. Williams' imagist preoccupations." It exhibits Whitmanesque incantations and cataloging and is packed with stray thoughts and reflections on orgies and ecstasies. Although he is pacific in his social and political postures, he is militant in his wailing rhetoric. His poetry is uneven and effusive, and such volumes as Empty Mirror (1960), Kaddish (1960), Reality Sandwiches (1963), and The Fall of America (1973) are flooded with folly, rant, and spleen. But they are intense expressions of ideas passionately held and they have made Ginsberg a pop hero and a cult leader of great popularity. A poster of Ginsberg, posed in an Uncle Sam suit, has become one of the best sellers of all time. His stature as a poet is still subject to debate, but that he exemplifies a real tradition in American poetry is beyond dispute. And both his detractors and adherents can agree that his free verse and his intensity of expression clearly qualify him as the most conspicuous "sidewalk bard of America."

FURTHER READING: T. Merrill, *Allen Ginsberg*, 1969; J. Kramer, *Allen Ginsberg in America*, 1970; *Allen Verbatim, Lectures on Poetry, Politics, Consciousness*, ed. G. Ball, 1974; J. Tytell, *Naked Angels, The Lives and Literature of the Beat Generation*, 1976; R. Portugés, *The Visionary Poetics of Allen Ginsberg*, 1978; *On the Poetry of Allen Ginsberg*, ed. H. Lewis, 1984.

TEXTS: *Collected Poems, 1947–1980*, 1984.

HOWL

for Carl Solomon[1]

I

I saw the best minds of my generation destroyed by madness, starving hysterical naked,

dragging themselves through the negro streets at dawn looking for an angry fix,

[1] A friend of Ginsberg and a fellow patient in a psychiatric hospital in 1949.

angelheaded hipsters burning for the ancient heavenly connection to
     the starry dynamo in the machinery of night,
who poverty and tatters and hollow-eyed and high sat up smoking in
     the supernatural darkness of cold-water flats floating across the tops
     of cities contemplating jazz,
who bared their brains to Heaven under the El[2] and saw
     Mohammedan angels staggering on tenement roofs illuminated,
who passed through universities with radiant cool eyes hallucinating
     Arkansas and Blake-light[3] tragedy among the scholars of war,
who were expelled from the academies for crazy & publishing obscene
     odes on the windows[4] of the skull,
who cowered in unshaven rooms in underwear, burning their money
     in wastebaskets and listening to the Terror through the wall,
who got busted in their pubic beards returning through Laredo[5] with a
     belt of marijuana for New York,
who ate fire in paint hotels or drank turpentine in Paradise Alley,[6]
     death, or purgatoried their torsos night after night   10
with dreams, with drugs, with waking nightmares, alcohol and cock
     and endless balls,
incomparable blind streets of shuddering cloud and lightning in the
     mind leaping toward poles of Canada & Paterson,[7] illuminating all
     the motionless world of Time between,
Peyote solidities of halls, backyard green tree cemetery dawns, wine
     drunkenness over the rooftops, storefront boroughs of teahead
     joyride neon blinking traffic light, sun and moon and tree vibrations
     in the roaring winter dusks of Brooklyn, ashcan rantings and kind
     king light of mind,
who chained themselves to subways for the endless ride from Battery
     to holy Bronx[8] on benzedrine until the noise of wheels and children
     brought them down shuddering mouth-wracked and battered bleak
     of brain all drained of brilliance in the drear light of Zoo,
who sank all night in submarine light of Bickford's[9] floated out and sat
     through the stale beer afternoon in desolate Fugazzi's,[10] listening to
     the crack of doom on the hydrogen jukebox,
who talked continuously seventy hours from park to pad to bar to
     Bellevue[11] to museum to the Brooklyn Bridge,
a lost battalion of platonic conversationalists jumping down the stoops
     off fire escapes off windowsills off Empire State[12] out of the moon,
yacketayakking screaming vomiting whispering facts and memories

[2]Elevated railway in New York City.
[3]Ginsberg had had a mystical vision of the English poet William Blake (1757–1827).
[4]In 1945 Ginsberg was expelled from Columbia University for writing obscenities on university
windows.
[5]City in Texas, on the border of Mexico.
[6]"A slum courtyard N. Y. Lower East Side, site of Kerouac's *Subterraneans*, 1958."—Ginsberg's
note. Jack Kerouac (1922–1969), author of the Beat novel *The Subterraneans* (1958).
[7]Paterson, New Jersey, Ginsberg's hometown.
[8]The New York City subway line that runs north from the Battery at the south end of Manhattan
Island, to the Bronx Zoo.
[9]All-night cafeteria in New York City.
[10]Bar in New York City's Greenwich Village.
[11]Public hospital in New York City that treats persons suffering from mental disorders.
[12]The Empire State Building in New York City.

and anecdotes and eyeball kicks and shocks of hospitals and jails
and wars,
whole intellects disgorged in total recall for seven days and nights with
brilliant eyes, meat for the Synagogue cast on the pavement,
who vanished into nowhere Zen New Jersey leaving a trail of
ambiguous picture postcards of Atlantic City Hall,   20
suffering Eastern sweats and Tangerian bone-grindings and migraines
of China[13] under junk-withdrawal in Newark's bleak furnished room,
who wandered around and around at midnight in the railroad yard
wondering where to go, and went, leaving no broken hearts,
who lit cigarettes in boxcars boxcars boxcars racketing through snow
toward lonesome farms in grandfather night,
who studied Plotinus[14] Poe St. John of the Cross[15] telepathy and bop
kabbalah[16] because the cosmos instinctively vibrated at their feet in
Kansas,
who loned it through the streets of Idaho seeking visionary indian
angels who were visionary indian angels,
who thought they were only mad when Baltimore gleamed in
supernatural ecstasy,
who jumped in limousines with the Chinaman of Oklahoma on the
impulse of winter midnight streetlight smalltown rain,
who lounged hungry and lonesome through Houston seeking jazz or
sex or soup, and followed the brilliant Spaniard to converse about
America and Eternity, a hopeless task, and so took ship to Africa,
who disappeared into the volcanoes of Mexico leaving behind nothing
but the shadow of dungarees and the lava and ash of poetry
scattered in fireplace Chicago,
who reappeared on the West Coast investigating the FBI in beards and
shorts with big pacifist eyes sexy in their dark skin passing out
incomprehensible leaflets,   30
who burned cigarette holes in their arms protesting the narcotic
tobacco haze of Capitalism,
who distributed Supercommunist pamphlets in Union Square[17]
weeping and undressing while the sirens of Los Alamos[18] wailed
them down, and wailed down Wall, and the Staten Island ferry
also wailed,
who broke down crying in white gymnasiums naked and trembling
before the machinery of other skeletons,
who bit detectives in the neck and shrieked with delight in policecars
for committing no crime but their own wild cooking pederasty and
intoxication,
who howled on their knees in the subway and were dragged off the
roof waving genitals and manuscripts,
who let themselves be fucked in the ass by saintly motorcyclists, and
screamed with joy,

[13]Tangiers and China, in Africa and Asia: sources of drugs imported into the United States.
[14]Roman philosopher (105–170) who advocated the pursuit of ecstatic, visionary experiences.
[15]Spanish religious mystic and poet (1542–1591).
[16]The mystical interpretation of Hebrew scriptures (the Kaballa) presented in the Bop jazz style
of the late 1940s.
[17]In New York City, a meeting place for radical speakers and protesters.
[18]Los Alamos, New Mexico, where the atom bomb was developed.

who blew and were blown by those human seraphim, the sailors,
    caresses of Atlantic and Caribbean love,
who balled in the morning in the evenings in rosegardens and the
    grass of public parks and cemeteries scattering their semen freely to
    whomever come who may,
who hiccuped endlessly trying to giggle but wound up with a sob
    behind a partition in a Turkish Bath when the blond & naked angel
    came to pierce them with a sword,
who lost their loveboys to the three old shrews of fate[19] the one eyed
    shrew of the heterosexual dollar the one eyed shrew that winks
    out of the womb and the one eyed shrew that does nothing but
    sit on her ass and snip the intellectual golden threads of the
    craftsman's loom,
who copulated ecstatic and insatiate with a bottle of beer a sweetheart a   40
    package of cigarettes a candle and fell off the bed, and continued
    along the floor and down the hall and ended fainting on the wall
    with a vision of ultimate cunt and come eluding the last gyzym of
    consciousness,
who sweetened the snatches of a million girls trembling in the sunset,
    and were red eyed in the morning but prepared to sweeten the
    snatch of the sunrise, flashing buttocks under barns and naked in
    the lake,
who went out whoring through Colorado in myriad stolen night-cars,
    N.C.,[20] secret hero of these poems, cocksman and Adonis of
    Denver—joy to the memory of his innumerable lays of girls in empty
    lots & diner backyards, moviehouses' rickety rows, on mountaintops
    in caves or with gaunt waitresses in familiar roadside lonely petticoat
    upliftings & especially secret gas-station solipsisms[21] of johns, &
    hometown alleys too,
who faded out in vast sordid movies, were shifted in dreams, woke on
    a sudden Manhattan, and picked themselves up out of basements
    hungover with heartless Tokay[22] and horrors of Third Avenue iron
    dreams & stumbled to unemployment offices,
who walked all night with their shoes full of blood on the snowbank
    docks waiting for a door in the East River[23] to open to a room full of
    streamheat and opium,
who created great suicidal dramas on the apartment cliff-banks of the
    Hudson[24] under the wartime blue floodlight of the moon & their
    heads shall be crowned with laurel in oblivion,
who ate the lamb stew of the imagination or digested the crab at the
    muddy bottom of the rivers of Bowery,[25]
who wept at the romance of the streets with their pushcarts full of
    onions and bad music,

[19]In classical myth, the Fates are three goddesses of destiny. The first spins the individual's thread
of life, the second determines its length, and the third cuts it off.
    [20]Neal Cassady (1926–1968), Beat writer and friend of Ginsberg and Jack Kerouac.
    [21]Solipsism: the philosophical theory that the self is the only thing that exists, and all experience
is therefore subjective.
    [22]A potent, fortified, inexpensive wine traditionally used by alcoholic derelicts.
    [23]The river separating Brooklyn and Manhattan Island.
    [24]The Hudson River, at New York City, lined with high-rise apartment buildings.
    [25]Slum area at the southern tip of Manhattan Island.

who sat in boxes breathing in the darkness under the bridge, and rose
up to build harpsichords in their lofts,

who coughed on the sixth floor of Harlem crowned with flame under
the tubercular sky surrounded by orange crates of theology,   50

who scribbled all night rocking and rolling over lofty incantations
which in the yellow morning were stanzas of gibberish,

who cooked rotten animals lung heart feet tail borsht[26] & tortillas
dreaming of the pure vegetable kindgom,

who plunged themselves under that meat trucks looking for an egg,

who threw their watches off the roof to cast their ballot for Eternity
outside of Time, & alarm clocks fell on their heads every day for the
next decade,

who cut their wrists three times successively unsuccessfully, gave up
and were forced to open antique stores where they thought they
were growing old and cried,

who were burned alive in their innocent flannel suits on Madison
Avenue[27] amid blasts of leaden verse & the tanked-up clatter of the
iron regiments of fashion & the nitroglycerine shrieks of the fairies
of advertising & the mustard gas of sinister intelligent editors, or
were run down by the drunken taxicabs of Absolute Reality,

who jumped off the Brooklyn Bridge this actually happened and
walked away unknown and forgotten into the ghostly daze of
Chinatown soup alleyways & firetrucks, not even one free beer,

who sang out of their windows in despair, fell out of the subway
window, jumped in the filthy Passaic,[28] leaped on negroes, cried all
over the street, danced on broken wineglasses barefoot smashed
phonograph records of nostalgic European 1930s German jazz
finished the whiskey and threw up groaning into the bloody toilet,
moans in their ears and the blast of colossal steamwhistles,

who barreled down the highways of the past journeying to each other's
hotrod-Golgotha[29] jail-solitude watch or Birmingham jazz
incarnation,

who drove crosscountry seventytwo hours to find out if I had a vision
or you had a vision or he had a vision to find out Eternity,   60

who journeyed to Denver, who died in Denver, who came back to
Denver & waited in vain, who watched over Denver & brooded &
loned in Denver and finally went away to find out the Time, & now
Denver is lonesome for her heroes,

who fell on their knees in hopeless cathedrals praying for each other's
salvation and light and breasts, until the soul illuminated its hair for
a second,

who crashed through their minds in jail waiting for impossible
criminals with golden heads and the charm of reality in their hearts
who sang sweet blues to Alcatraz,

who retired to Mexico to cultivate a habit,[30] or Rocky Mount[31] to

---

[26]A soup made of beets.

[27]In New York City, a center of advertising and publishing firms where, it is said, middle-class conformists traditionally wear look-alike gray flannel suits.

[28]River, renowned for its pollution, that flows through the industrial section of New Jersey.

[29]Hebrew for "Calvary," the site of the crucifixion of Jesus.

[30]The homosexual Beat author and drug addict William Burroughs (1914–   ) had lived in Mexico and Tangiers in North Africa.

[31]Jack Kerouac (1922–1969), lived in Rocky Mount, North Carolina.

tender Buddha or Tangiers to boys or Southern Pacific[32] to the black
    locomotive or Harvard to Narcissus[33] to Woodlawn[34] to the
    daisychain or grave,
who demanded sanity trials accusing the radio of hypnotism & were
    left with their insanity & their hands & a hung jury,
who threw potato salad at CCNY[35] lecturers on Dadaism[36] and
    subsequently presented themselves on the granite steps of the
    madhouse with shaven heads and harlequin speech of suicide,
    demanding instantaneous lobotomy,[37]
and who were given instead the concrete void of insulin Metrazol[38]
    electricity hydrotherapy psychotherapy occupational therapy
    pingpong & amnesia,
who in humorless protest overturned only one symbolic pingpong
    table, resting briefly in catatonia,[39]
returning years later truly bald except for a wig of blood, and tears
    and fingers, to the visible madman doom of the wards of the
    madtowns of the East,
Pilgrim State's Rockland's and Greystone's[40] foetid halls, bickering with
    the echoes of the soul, rocking and rolling in the midnight solitude-
    bench dolmen-realms of love, dream of life a nightmare, bodies
    turned to stone as heavy as the moon,   70
with mother finally ******, and the last fantastic book flung out of the
    tenement window, and the last door closed at 4 A.M. and the last
    telephone slammed at the wall in reply and the last furnished room
    emptied down to the last piece of mental furniture, a yellow paper
    rose twisted on a wire hanger in the closet, and even that imaginary,
    nothing but a hopeful little bit of hallucination—
ah, Carl,[41] while you are not safe I am not safe, and now you're really
    in the total animal soup of time—
and who therefore ran through the icy street obsessed with a sudden
    flash of the alchemy of the use of the ellipse the catalog the meter &
    the vibrating plane,
who dreamt and made incarnate gaps in Time & Space through
    images juxtaposed, and trapped the archangel of the soul between 2
    visual images and joined the elemental verbs and set the noun and
    dash of consciousness together jumping with sensation of Pater
    Omnipotens Aeterna Deus[42]
to recreate the syntax and measure of poor human prose and stand
    before you speechless and intelligent and shaking with shame,

---

[32]Neal Cassady worked for the Southern Pacific Railroad.
[33]Figure in Greek myth who fell in love with his own reflection.
[34]Cemetery in the Bronx, New York.
[35]The City College of New York.
[36]A movement in art and literature that advocated deliberate absurdity and irrationality.
[37]Surgical incisions that sever nerves in the frontal lobes of the brain, to relieve acute mental disorders.
[38]A drug used in shock treatment for medical therapy.
[39]Severe mental disorder in which the patient loses the ability or the will to move.
[40]Three hospitals for the insane, near New York City. Ginsberg's mother died at Greystone in 1956.
[41]Carl Solomon
[42]Latin quotation taken from a letter written (April 1904) by the French impressionist painter Paul Cézanne (1839–1906): "Omnipotent Father, Eternal God." Ginsberg changed Cézanne's "Aeterne" ("Eternal") to "Aeterna," the feminine form of the word.

rejected yet confessing out the soul to conform to the rhythm of
thought in his naked and endless head,

the madman bum and angel beat in Time, unknown, yet putting down
here what might be left to say in time come after death,

and rose reincarnate in the ghostly clothes of jazz in the goldhorn
shadow of the band and blew the suffering of America's naked mind
for love into an eli eli lamma lamma sabacthani[43] saxophone cry that
shivered the cities down to the last radio

with the absolute heart of the poem of life butchered out of their own
bodies good to eat a thousand years.

II

What sphinx of cement and aluminum bashed open their skulls and
ate up their brains and imagination?

Moloch![1] Solitude! Filth! Ugliness! Ashcans and unobtainable dollars!
Children screaming under the stairways! Boys sobbing in armies!
Old men weeping in the parks! Moloch! Moloch! Nightmare of
Moloch! Moloch the loveless! Mental Moloch! Moloch the heavy
judger of men!

Moloch the incomprehensible prison! Moloch the crossbone soulless
jailhouse and Congress of sorrows! Moloch whose buildings are
judgment! Moloch the vast stone of war! Moloch the stunned
governments!

Moloch whose mind is pure machinery! Moloch whose blood is
running money! Moloch whose fingers are ten armies! Moloch whose
breast is a cannibal dynamo! Moloch whose ear is a smoking tomb!

Moloch whose eyes are a thousand blind windows! Moloch whose
skyscrapers stand in the long streets like endless Jehovahs! Moloch
whose factories dream and croak in the fog! Moloch whose
smokestacks and antennae crown the cities!

Moloch whose love is endless oil and stone! Moloch whose soul is
electricity and banks! Moloch whose poverty is the specter of genius!
Moloch whose fat is a cloud of sexless hydrogen! Moloch whose
name is the Mind!

Moloch in whom I sit lonely! Moloch in whom I dream Angels! Crazy
in Moloch! Cocksucker in Moloch! Lacklove and manless in Moloch!

Moloch who entered my soul early! Moloch in whom I am a
consciousness without a body! Moloch who frightened me out of my
natural ecstasy! Moloch whom I abandon! Wake up in Moloch! Light
streaming out of the sky!

Moloch! Moloch! Robot apartments! invisible suburbs! skeleton
treasuries! blind capitals! demonic industries! special nations!
invincible madhouses! granite cocks! monstrous bombs!   10

They broke their backs lifting Moloch to Heaven! Pavements, trees,
radios, tons! lifting the city to Heaven which exists and is everywhere
about us!

---

[43] An adaptation of the Aramaic "Eli, Eli, lama sabachthani?" "My God, My God, why has thou
forsaken me?" Jesus' last words on the cross. Matthew 27:46.

[1] "Or Molech, the Canaanite fire god, whose worship was marked by parents burning their children
as propitiatory sacrifice. 'And thou shalt not let any of thy seed pass through the fire to Molech'
(Leviticus 18:21)."—Ginsberg's note

Visions! omens! hallucinations! miracles! ecstasies! gone down the
  American river!
Dreams! adorations! illuminations! religions! the whole boatload of
  sensitive bullshit!
Breakthroughs! over the river! flips and crucifixions! gone down the
  flood! Highs! Epiphanies![2] Despairs! Ten years' animal screams and
  suicides! Minds! New loves! Mad generation! down on the rocks of
  Time!
Real holy laughter in the river! They saw it all! the wild eyes! the holy
  yells! They bade farewell! They jumped off the roof! to solitude!
  waving! carrying flowers! Down to the river! into the street!

III

Carl Solomon! I'm with you in Rockland
  where you're madder than I am
I'm with you in Rockland
  where you must feel very strange
I'm with you in Rockland
  where you imitate the shade of my mother
I'm with you in Rockland
  where you've murdered your twelve secretaries
I'm with you in Rockland
  where you laugh at this invisible humor
I'm with you in Rockland
  where we are great writers on the same dreadful typewriter
I'm with you in Rockland
  where your condition has become serious and is reported on
  the radio
I'm with you in Rockland
  where the faculties of the skull no longer admit the worms of the
  senses
I'm with you in Rockland
  where you drink the tea of the breasts of the spinsters of Utica
I'm with you in Rockland
  where you pun on the bodies of your nurses the harpies of
  the Bronx   10
I'm with you in Rockland
  where you scream in a straightjacket that you're losing the game of
  the actual pingpong of the abyss
I'm with you in Rockland
  where you bang on the catatonic piano the soul is innocent and
  immortal it should never die ungodly in an armed madhouse
I'm with you in Rockland
  where fifty more shocks[1] will never return your soul to its body
  again from its pilgrimage to a cross in the void
I'm with you in Rockland
  where you accuse your doctors of insanity and plot the Hebrew
  socialist revolution against the fascist national Golgotha
I'm with you in Rockland

[2]The manifestations or appearances of a divine being.
[1]Electric shocks administered as treatment for mental disorders.

where you will split the heavens of Long Island and resurrect your
living human Jesus from the superhuman tomb
I'm with you in Rockland
where there are twentyfive thousand mad comrades all together
singing the final stanzas of the Internationale[2]
I'm with you in Rockland
where we hug and kiss the United States under our bedsheets the
United States that coughs all night and won't let us sleep
I'm with you in Rockland
where we wake up electrified out of the coma by our own souls'
airplanes roaring over the roof they've come to drop angelic bombs
the hospital illuminates itself   imaginary walls collapse   O skinny
legions run outside   O starry-spangled shock of mercy the eternal
war is here   O victory forget your underwear we're free
I'm with you in Rockland
in my dreams you walk dripping from a sea-journey on the highway
across America in tears to the door of my cottage in the Western
night

1955–1956   1956

A SUPERMARKET IN CALIFORNIA

What thoughts I have of you tonight, Walt Whitman, for I walked
down the sidestreets under the trees with a headache self-conscious looking
at the full moon.

In my hungry fatigue, and shopping for images, I went into the neon
fruit supermarket, dreaming of your enumerations!

What peaches and what penumbras! Whole families shopping at
night! Aisles full of husbands! Wives in the avocados, babies in the tomatoes! —and you, García Lorca,[1] what were you doing down by the watermelons?

I saw you, Walt Whitman, childless, lonely old grubber, poking among
the meats in the refrigerator and eyeing the grocery boys.

I heard you asking questions of each: Who killed the pork chops?
What price bananas? Are you my Angel?

I wandered in and out of the brillant stacks of cans following you,
and followed in my imagination by the store detective.

We strode down the open corridors together in our solitary fancy
tasting artichokes, possessing every frozen delicacy, and never passing the
cashier.

Where are we going, Walt Whitman? The doors close in an hour.
Which way does your beard point tonight?

(I touch your book and dream of our odyssey in the supermarket and
feel absurd.)

Will we walk all night through solitary streets? The trees add shade
to shade, lights out in the houses, we'll both be lonely.   10

[2]National anthem of the Soviet Union from 1917 to 1944.
[1]Spanish poet and dramatist (1889–1937), author of "Ode to Walt Whitman."

Will we stroll dreaming of the lost America of love past blue automobiles in driveways, home to our silent cottage?

Ah, dear father, graybeard, lonely old courage-teacher, what America
did you have when Charon[2] quit poling his ferry and you got out on a
smoking bank and stood watching the boat disappear on the black waters
of Lethe?[3]

1955   1956

SUNFLOWER SUTRA[1]

I walked on the banks of the tincan banana dock and sat down under the
    huge shade of a Southern Pacific locomotive to look at the sunset over the
    box house hills and cry.
Jack Kerouac sat beside me on a busted rusty iron pole, companion, we
    thought the same thoughts of the soul, bleak and blue and sad-eyed,
    surrounded by the gnarled steel roots of trees of machinery.
The oily water on the river mirrored the red sky, sun sank on top of final
    Frisco peaks, no fish in that stream, no hermit in those mounts, just
    ourselves rheumy-eyed and hung-over like old bums on the riverbank,
    tired and wily.
Look at the Sunflower, he said, there was a dead gray shadow against the
    sky, big as a man, sitting dry on top of a pile of ancient sawdust—
—I rushed up enchanted—it was my first sunflower, memories of Blake—[2]
    my visions—Harlem
and Hells of the Eastern rivers, bridges clanking Joes Greasy Sandwiches,
    dead baby carriages, black treadless tires forgotten and unretreaded, the
    poem of the riverbank, condoms & pots, steel knives, nothing stainless,
    only the dank muck and the razor-sharp artifacts passing into the past—
and the gray Sunflower poised against the sunset, crackly bleak and dusty
    with the smut and smog and smoke of olden locomotives in its eye—
corolla[3] of bleary spikes pushed down and broken like a battered crown,
    seeds fallen out of its face, soon-to-be-toothless mouth of sunny air,
    sunrays obliterated on its hairy head like a dried wire spiderweb,
leaves stuck out like arms out of the stem, gestures from the sawdust root,
    broke pieces of plaster fallen out of the black twigs, a dead fly in its ear,
Unholy battered old thing you were, my sunflower O my soul, I loved you
    then!
The grime was no man's grime but death and human locomotives,
all that dress of dust, that veil darkened railroad skin, that smog of cheek,
    that eyelid of black mis'ry, that sooty hand or phallus or protuberance of
    artificial worse-than-dirt—industrial—modern—all that civilization spotting
    your crazy golden crown—
and those blear thoughts of death and dusty loveless eyes and ends and

[2]Boatman, in classical myth, who ferried the dead across the river Styx to Hades.
[3]River of forgetfulness in Hades, where the dead drink and forget their previous lives.
[1]A Sanskrit word meaning a collection of religious rules or aphorisms.
[2]William Blake (1757–1827), English poet. In 1948 Ginsberg had a mystical vision in which he
heard a voice he believed to be William Blake's reciting Blake's poem "Ah Sun-Flower" (from *Songs
of Experience*, 1794).
[3]The petals that encircle the center of a flower.

withered roots below, in the home-pile of sand and sawdust, rubber dollar
bills, skin of machinery, the guts and innards of the weeping coughing
car, the empty lonely tincans with their rusty tongues alack, what more
could I name, the smoked ashes of some cock cigar, the cunts of
wheelbarrels and the milky breasts of cars, wornout asses out of chairs &
sphincters of dynamos—all these
entangled in your mummied roots—and you there standing before me in
the sunset, all your glory in your form!
A perfect beauty of a sunflower! a perfect excellent lovely sunflower
existence! a sweet natural eye to the new hip moon, woke up alive and
excited grasping in the sunset shadow sunrise golden monthly breeze!
How many flies buzzed round you innocent of your grime, while you cursed
the heavens of the railroad and your flower soul?
Poor dead flower? when did you forget you were a flower? when did you
look at your skin and decide you were an impotent dirty old locomotive?
the ghost of a locomotive? the specter and shade of a once powerful mad
American locomotive?
You were never no locomotive, Sunflower, you were a sunflower!
And you Locomotive, you are a locomotive, forget me not!
So I grabbed up the skeleton thick sunflower and stuck it at my side like a
scepter,
and deliver my sermon to my soul, and Jack's soul too, and anyone who'll
listen,
—We're not our skin of grime, we're not our dread bleak dusty imageless
locomotive, we're all golden sunflowers inside, blessed by our own seed &
hairy naked accomplishment-bodies growing into mad black formal
sunflowers in the sunset, spied on by our eyes under the shadow of the
mad locomotive riverbank sunset Frisco hilly tincan evening sitdown
vision.
1955

1956

AMERICA

America I've given you all and now I'm nothing.
America two dollars and twentyseven cents January 17, 1956.
I can't stand my own mind.
America when will we end the human war?
Go fuck yourself with your atom bomb.
I don't feel good don't bother me.
I won't write my poem till I'm in my right mind.
America when will you be angelic?
When will you take off your clothes?
When will you look at yourself through the grave?
When will you be worthy of your million Trotskyites?[1]   10
America why are your libraries full of tears?
America when will you send your eggs to India?
I'm sick of your insane demands.

[1]Followers of the Russian Communist Leon Trotsky (1877–1940).

When can I go into the supermarket and buy what I need with my
    good looks?
America after all it is you and I who are perfect not the next world.
Your machinery is too much for me.
You made me want to be a saint.
There must be some other way to settle this argument.
Burroughs[2] is in Tangiers I don't think he'll come back it's sinister.   20
Are you being sinister or is this some form of practical joke?
I'm trying to come to the point.
I refuse to give up my obsession.
America stop pushing I know what I'm doing.
America the plum blossoms are falling.
I haven't read the newspapers for months, everyday somebody goes on
    trial for murder.
America I feel sentimental about the Wobblies.[3]
America I used to be a communist when I was a kid I'm not sorry.
I smoke marijuana every chance I get.
I sit in my house for days on end and stare at the roses in the closet.   30
When I go to Chinatown I get drunk and never get laid.
My mind is made up there's going to be trouble.
You should have seen me reading Marx.[4]
My psychoanalyst thinks I'm perfectly right.
I won't say the Lord's Prayer.
I have mystical visions and cosmic vibrations.
America I still haven't told you what you did to Uncle Max after he
    came over from Russia.

I'm addressing you.
Are you going to let your emotional life be run by Time Magazine?
I'm obsessed by Time Magazine   40
I read it every week.
Its cover stares at me every time I slink past the corner candystore.
I read it in the basement of the Berkeley Public Library.
It's always telling me about responsibility. Businessmen are serious.
    Movie producers are serious. Everybody's serious but me.
It occurs to me that I am America.
I am talking to myself again.

Asia is rising against me.
I haven't got a chinaman's chance.
I'd better consider my national resources.
My national resources consist of two joints of marijuana millions of
    genitals an unpublishable private literature that jetplanes 1400 miles
    an hour and twentyfive-thousand mental institutions.   50
I say nothing about my prisons nor the millions of underprivileged
    who live in my flowerpots under the light of five hundred suns.
I have abolished the whorehouses of France, Tangiers is the next
    to go.

[2]William Burroughs was then living in Morocco.
[3]Nickname for members of the Industrial Workers of the World, a radical organization of unions,
established in 1905.
[4]Karl Marx (1818–1883) German social philosopher, major theorist of socialism and communism,
author (with Friedrich Engels) of *The Communist Manifesto* (1848).

My ambition is to be President despite the fact that I'm a Catholic.

America how can I write a holy litany in your silly mood?
I will continue like Henry Ford my strophes are as individual as his
  automobiles more so they're all different sexes.
America I will sell you strophes $2500 apiece $500 down on your old
  strophe
America free Tom Mooney[5]
America save the Spanish Loyalists[6]
America Sacco & Vanzetti must not die[7]
America I am the Scottsboro boys.[8]
America when I was seven momma took me to Communist Cell
  meetings they sold us garbanzos[9] a handful per ticket a ticket costs a
  nickel and the speeches were free everybody was angelic and
  sentimental about the workers it was all so sincere you have no idea
  what a good thing the party was in 1935 Scott Nearing[10] was a grand
  old man a real mensch[11] Mother Bloor the Silk-strikers' Ewig-
  Weibliche[12] made me cry I once saw the Yiddish orator Israel Amter
  plain. Everybody must have been a spy.
America you don't really want to go to war.
America it's them bad Russians.
Them Russians them Russians and them Chinamen. And them
  Russians.
The Russia wants to eat us alive. The Russia's power mad. She wants to
  take our cars from out our garages.
Her wants to grab Chicago. Her needs a Red *Reader's Digest*. Her wants
  our auto plants in Siberia. Him big bureaucracy running our
  fillingstations.
That no good. Ugh. Him make Indians learn read. Him need big black
  niggers. Hah. Her makes us all work sixteen hours a day. Help.
America this is quite serious.
America this is the impression I get from looking in the television set.
America is this correct?   70
I'd better get right down to the job.
It's true I don't want to join the Army or turn lathes in precision parts
  factories, I'm nearsighted and psychopathic anyway.
America I'm putting my queer shoulder to the wheel.
1956   1956

---

[5]American labor leader imprisoned for murder in 1916 and pardoned in 1939.
[6]Supporters of the Spanish government against the insurgent armies of Francisco Franco in the
Spanish Civil War (1936–1939).
[7]Nicola Sacco and Bartolomeo Vanzetti, political radicals convicted of robbery and murder in
Massachusetts and executed in 1927. Their supporters argued that the two men were convicted
because of their unpopular political beliefs.
[8]Nine blacks indicted in 1931 at Scottsboro, Alabama, for the rape of two white women. Their
trials and convictions created a national uproar because of widespread belief that they were the
victims of racial bigotry. Eventually all regained freedom.
[9]Chick peas.
[10]Scott Nearing (1883–1983), Ella "Mother" Bloor (1862–1951), and Israel Amter (1881–1954),
American socialist and communist leaders.
[11]German: human being.
[12]German: Eternal Female.

TO AUNT ROSE

Aunt Rose—now—might I see you
with your thin face and buck tooth smile and pain
              of rheumatism—and a long black heavy shoe
                  for your bony left leg
limping down the long hall in Newark on the running carpet
              past the black grand piano
                  in the day room
                        where the parties were
      and I sang Spanish loyalist songs
          in a high squeaky voice   10
                  (hysterical) the committee listening
          while you limped around the room
              collected the money—
Aunt Honey, Uncle Sam, a stranger with a cloth arm
          in his pocket
              and huge young bald head
                  of Abraham Lincoln Brigade[1]

—your long sad face
          your tears of sexual frustration
              (what smothered sobs and bony hips   20
                  under the pillows of Osborne Terrace)
      —the time I stood on the toilet seat naked
          and you powdered my thighs with calamine
              against the poison ivy—my tender
                  and shamed first black curled hairs
what were you thinking in secret heart then
          knowing me a man already—
and I an ignorant girl of family silence on the thin pedestal
          of my legs in the bathroom—Museum of Newark.

                  Aunt Rose
                                                                               30
Hitler is dead, Hitler is in Eternity; Hitler is with
          Tamburlane and Emily Brontë
Though I see you walking still, a ghost on Osborne Terrace
          down the long dark hall to the front door
      limping a little with a pinched smile
              in what must have been a silken
                  flower dress
      welcoming my father, the Poet, on his visit to Newark
          —see you arriving in the living room
              dancing on your crippled leg   40
              and clapping hands his book
                  had been accepted by Liveright

---

[1]A brigade of American volunteers who fought against Franco in the Spanish Civil War.

Hitler is dead and Liveright's gone out of business
The Attic of the Past and Everlasting Minute[2] are out of print
    Uncle Harry sold his last silk stocking
   Claire quit interpretive dancing school
    Buba[3] sits a wrinkled monument in Old
      Ladies Home blinking at new babies

 last time I saw you was the hospital
   pale skull protruding under ashen skin
    blue veined unconscious girl   50
     in an oxygen tent
   the war in Spain has ended long ago
    Aunt Rose

1958
                1961

AMERICAN CHANGE

 The first I looked on, after a long time far from home in mid Atlantic
on a summer day
  Dolphins breaking the glassy water under the blue sky,
 a gleam of silver in my cabin, fished up out of my jangling new pocket
of coins and green dollars
 —held in my palm, the head of the feathered indian, old Buck-Rogers
eagle eyed face, a gash of hunger in the cheek
 gritted jaw of the vanished man begone like a Hebrew with hairlock[1]
combed down the side—O Rabbi Indian
 what visionary gleam 100 years ago on Buffalo prairie under the
molten cloud-shot sky, 'the same clear light 10000 miles in all directions'
 but now with all the violin music of Vienna, gone into the great slot
machine of Kansas City, Reno—
 The coin seemed so small after vast European coppers thick francs
leaden pesetas, lire endless and heavy,
 a miniature primeval memorialized in 5¢ nickel candy-store nostalgia
of the redskin, dead on silver coin,
 with shaggy buffalo on reverse, hump-backed little tail incurved, head
butting against the rondure of Eternity,
 cock forelock below, bearded shoulder muscle folded below muscle,   10
head of prophet, bowed,
 vanishing beast of Time, hoar body rubbed clean of wrinkles and
shining like polished stone, bright metal in my forefinger, ridiculous buffalo—Go to New York.[2]

 Dime next I found, Minerva, sexless cold & chill, ascending goddess
of money—and was it the wife of Wallace Stevens,[3] truly?

[2]Books of poetry written by Louis Ginsberg (1896–1976), the poet's father. *The Everlasting Minute*
was published by the Horace Liveright Company.
[3]Yiddish: Grandmother.
[1]The long side-lock of hair worn by Orthodox Jewish males.
[2]A pun on the saying, "Go West young man," usually attributed, mistakenly, to Horace Greeley.
[3]Elsie Stevens, wife of the American poet Wallace Stevens, served as the model for Minerva (Roman
goddess of wisdom) stamped on the dime.

and now from the locks flowing the miniature wings of speedy thought,

executive dyke,[4] Minerva, goddess of Madison Avenue, forgotten useless dime that can't buy hot dog, dead dime—

Then we've George Washington, less primitive, the snub-nosed quarter, smug eyes and mouth, some idiot's design of the sexless Father,

naked down to his neck, a ribbon in his wig, high forehead, Roman line down the nose, fat cheeked, still showing his falsetooth[5] ideas—
O Eisenhower & Washington—O Fathers—No movie star dark beauty—
O thou Bignoses—

Quarter, remembered quarter, 40¢ in all—What'll you buy me when I land—one icecream soda?—

poor pile of coins, original reminders of the sadness, forgotten money of America—

nostalgia of the first touch of those coins, American change,   20
the memory in my aging hand, the same old silver reflective there,
the thin dime hidden between my thumb and forefinger
All the struggles for those coins, the sadness of their reappearance
my reappearence on those fabled shores
and the failure of that Dream, that Vision of Money reduced to this haunting recollection
of the gas lot in Paterson where I found half a dollar gleaming in the grass—

I have a $5 bill in my pocket—it's Lincoln's sour black head moled wrinkled, forelocked too, big eared, flags at announcement flying over the bill, stamps in green and spiderweb black,

long numbers in racetrack green, immense promise, a girl, a hotel, a busride to Albany, a night of brilliant drunk in some faraway corner of Manhattan

a stick of several teas,[6] or paper or cap of Heroin, or a $5 strange present to the blind.

Money money, reminder, I might as well write poems to you—dear American money—O statue of Liberty I ride enfolded in money in my mind to you—and last   30

Ahhh! Washington again, on the Dollar, some poetic black print, dark words, The United States of America, innumerable numbers

R956422481 One Dollar This Certificate is Legal Tender (tender!) for all debts public and private

My God My God why have you forsaken me
Ivy Baker Priest[7] Series 1953 F

and over, the Eagle, wild wings outspread, halo of the Stars encircled by puffs of smoke & flame—

a circle the Masonic Pyramid, the sacred Swedenborgian Dollar America, bricked up to the top, & floating surreal above

the triangle of holy outstaring Eye sectioned out of the aire, shining

---

[4]An aggressive lesbian.
[5]George Washington's protruding cheeks and lips, portrayed in numerous portraits, are thought to have been the result of his ill-fitting false teeth.
[6]Marijuana cigarettes.
[7]Treasurer of the United States from 1953 to 1961, during which time her signature was printed on the nation's paper currency.

light emitted from the eyebrowless triangle—and a desert of cactus, scattered all around, clouds afar,

this being the Great Seal of our Passion, Annuit Coeptis,[8] Novus Ordo Seclorum,[9]

the whole surrounded by green spiderwebs designed by T-Men[10] to prevent foul counterfeit—

                              ONE   40

1958

                                                        1963

MUGGING

I

Tonite I walked out of my red apartment door on East tenth street's dusk—

Walked out of my home ten years, walked out in my honking neighborhood

Tonight at seven walked out past garbage cans chained to concrete anchors

Walked under black painted fire escapes, giant castiron plate covering a hole in ground

—Crossed the street, traffic lite red, thirteen bus roaring by liquor store,

past corner pharmacy iron grated, past Coca Cola & Mylai[1] posters fading scraped on brick

Past Chinese Laundry wood door'd, & broken cement stoop steps For Rent hall painted green & purple Puerto Rican style

Along E. 10th's glass splattered pavement, kid blacks & Spanish oiled hair adolescents' crowded house fronts—

Ah, tonite I walked out on my block NY City under humid summer sky Halloween,

thinking what happened Timothy Leary[2] joining brain police for a season?

thinking what's all this Weathermen,[3] secrecy & selfrighteousness beyond reason—F.B.I. plots?   10

Walked past a taxicab controlling the bottle strewn curb—

past young fellows with their umbrella handles & canes leaning against a ravaged Buick

—and as I looked at the crowd of kids on the stoop—a boy stepped up, put his arm around my neck

tenderly I thought for a moment, squeezed harder, his umbrella handle against my skull,

---

[8]Latin: "He favored our undertakings."
[9]Latin: "The new order of the world."
[10]Law enforcement agents of the U. S. Treasury.
[1]Site in Vietnam of a massacre of civilians by U.S. troops, Mar. 16, 1968.
[2]Harvard University professor (b. 1920) fired for advocating psychedelic-drug use.
[3]"Underground radical extreme confrontation-protest antiwar SDS [Students for a Democratic Society] splinter group. . . ."—Ginsberg's note.

and his friends took my arm, a young brown companion tripped his
    foot 'gainst my ankle—
as I went down shouting Om Ah Hūm[4] to gangs of lovers on the stoop
    watching
slowly appreciating, why this is a raid, these strangers mean strange
    business
with what—my pockets, bald head, broken-healed-bone leg, my
    softshoes, my heart—
Have they knives? Om Ah Hūm—Have they sharp metal wood to
    shove in eye ear ass? Om Ah Hūm   20
& slowly reclined on the pavement, struggling to keep my woolen bag
    of poetry address calendar & Leary-lawyer notes hung from my
    shoulder
dragged in my neat orlon shirt over the crossbar of a broken metal
    door
dragged slowly onto the fire-soiled floor an abandoned store, laundry
    candy counter 1929—
now a mess of papers & pillows & plastic car seat covers cracked
    cockroach-corpsed ground—
my wallet back pocket passed over the iron foot step guard
and fell out, stole by God Muggers' lost fingers, Strange—
Couldn't tell—snakeskin wallet actually plastic, 70 dollars my bank
    money for a week,
old broken wallet—and dreary plastic contents—Amex[5] card & Manf.
    Hanover Trust[6] Credit too—business card from Mr. Spears British
    Home Minister Drug Squad—my draft card—membership ACLU[7] &
    Naropa Institute[8] Instructor's identification
Om Ah Hūm I continued chanting Om Ah Hūm
Putting my palm on the neck of an 18 year old boy fingering my back
    pocket crying "Where's the money"   30
"Om Ah Hūm there isn't any"
My card Chief Boo-Hoo Neo American Church New Jersey & Lower
    East Side
Om Ah Hūm—what not forgotten crowded wallet—Mobile Credit,
    Shell? old lovers addresses on cardboard pieces, booksellers calling
    cards—
—"Shut up or we'll murder you"—"Om Ah Hūm take it easy"
Lying on the floor shall I shout more loud?—the metal door closed on
    blackness
one boy felt my broken healed ankle, looking for hundred dollar bills
    behind my stocking weren't even there—a third boy untied my Seiko
    Hong Kong watch rough from right wrist leaving a clasp-prick skin
    tiny bruise
"Shut up and we'll get out of here"—and so they left.

[4]"Trikaya mantra [Buddhist verbal spell or prayer chant] of body, speech and mind."—Ginsberg's note.

[5]American Express.

[6]Manufacturers Hanover Trust, a bank in New York City.

[7]American Civil Liberties Union.

[8]A school of arts, letters, and religious studies, part of a Tibetan Buddhist meditation center in Boulder, Colorado, where Ginsberg studied "crazy wisdom" in the early 1970s. Later Ginsberg served as a faculty member of the Jack Kerouac School of Disembodied Poetics, a school he established as part of the Naropa Institute in 1974.

as I rose from the cardboard mattress thinking Om Ah Hūṃ didn't
    stop em enough,
the tone of voice too loud—my shoulder bag with 10,000 dollars full of
    poetry left on the broken floor—
November 2, 1974

II

Went out the door dim eyed, bent down & picked up my glasses from
    step edge I placed them while dragged in the store—looked out—   40
Whole street a bombed-out face, building rows' eyes & teeth missing
burned apartments half the long block, gutted cellars, hallways'
    charred beams
hanging over trash plaster mounded entrances, couches & bedsprings
    rusty after sunset
Nobody home, but scattered stoopfuls of scared kids frozen in black
    hair
chatted giggling at house doors in black shoes, families cooked For
    Rent some six story houses mid the street's wreckage
Nextdoor Bodega,[1] a phone, the police? "I just got mugged" I said
to the man's face under fluorescent grocery light tin ceiling—
puffy, eyes blank & watery, sickness of beer kidney and language
    tongue
thick lips stunned as my own eyes, poor drunken Uncle minding the
    store!
O hopeless city of idiots empty eyed staring afraid, red beam top'd car
    at street curb arrived—   50
"Hey maybe my wallet's still on the ground got a flashlight?"
Back into the burnt-doored cave, & the policeman's gray flashlight
    broken no eyebeam—
"My partner all he wants is sit in the car never gets out Hey Joe bring
    your flashlight—"
a tiny throwaway beam, dim as a match in the criminal dark
"No I can't see anything here" . . . "Fill out this form"
Neighborhood street crowd behind a car "We didn't see nothing"
Stoop young girls, kids laughing "Listen man last time I messed with
    them see this—"
rolled up his skinny arm shirt, a white knife scar on his brown
    shoulder
"Besides we help you the cops come don't know anybody we all get
    arrested
go to jail I never help no more mind my business everytime"   60
"Agh!" upstreet think "Gee I don't know anybody here ten years lived
    half block crost Avenue C
and who knows who?"—passing empty apartments, old lady with
    frayed paper bags
sitting in the tin-boarded doorframe of a dead house.
December 10, 1974
    1977

---

[1]Spanish: Grocery store.

Adrienne Rich   *1929–*

Adrienne Rich has declared, "What we see, we see / and seeing is changing." Her writing is a presentation of a changing view of man and woman. It exhibits a growing hostility to what she calls "patriarchal politics and patriarchal civilization." She speaks from a feminist's viewpoint precisely, bluntly, stridently about human relationships and, particularly in her later poems, about the individual's search for sanctuary and release.

Her early life was spent in Baltimore, Maryland; she graduated from Radcliffe College in 1951, and has lived in Cambridge Massachusetts, in the Netherlands, and in New York City. Her first book, A Change of World, *published in her senior year at college, revealed her debts to Frost and Yeats and won praise from W. H. Auden, who spoke of her acute ear and her "intuitive grasp of much subtler and difficult matters like proportion, consistency of diction and tone, and the matching of these with the subject in hand." Subsequent volumes* The Diamond Cutters *(1955) and* Snapshots of a Daughter-in-Law *(1962) gave indication of her stylistic changes from a poetry of lapidary precision to a poetry of looser and more casual forms, revealing the influences of such poets as William Carlos Williams and Robert Lowell. In the course of her development she came to view the poem not as a commentary upon life but as life itsef, an artifact "created as experience, not as a reaction or defense against experience."*

Subsequent volumes, Necessities of Life *(1966),* Leaflets *(1969),* The Will to Change *(1971),* Diving into the Wreck *(1973),* On Lies, Secrets, and Silence *(1979), a collection of essays, and* The Fact of a Door, Poems Selected and New 1950–1984 *(1984) exhibit a mind increasingly focused on social protest, conditions in the ghetto, public complacency, and the political and psychological problems of the nation and of individuals. Sex for the individual and politics for the state are contraries that make up related modes of oppression in her poetry. As she sees it, they call for individual and social wholeness as a means of preserving the human ego that must itself remain "defenseless and unhoused—waiting it out."*

FURTHER READING: *The Dream of a Common Language, Poems 1974–1977; A Wild Patience Has Taken Me This Far, Poems 1978–1981; Adrienne Rich's Poetry,* ed. B. and A. Gelpi, 1975; *Reading Adrienne Rich,* ed. J. Cooper, 1984; C. Keyes, *The Aesthetics of Power,* 1986.

TEXTS: "Living in Sin" is from *The Diamond Cutters,* 1955; "Breakfast in a Bowling Alley in Utica, New York" is from *Necessities of Life,* 1966; "Integrity" is from *A Wild Patience Has Taken Me This Far,* 1981; all others are from *Poems Selected and New, 1950–1974,* 1975.

AT A BACH CONCERT

Coming by evening through the wintry city
We said that art is out of love with life.
Here we approach a love that is not pity.

This antique discipline, tenderly severe,
Renews belief in love yet masters feeling,
Asking of us a grace in what we bear.

Form is the ultimate gift that love can offer—
The vital union of necessity

With all that we desire, all that we suffer.

A too-compassionate art is half an art.   10
Only such proud restraining purity
Restores the else-betrayed, too-human heart.

1951

LIVING IN SIN

She had thought the studio would keep itself;
No dust upon the furniture of love.
Half heresy, to wish the taps less vocal,
The panes relieved of grime. A plate of pears,
A piano with a Persian shawl, a cat
Stalking the picturesque amusing mouse
Had been her vision when he pleaded "Come."
Not that at five each separate stair would writhe
Under the milkman's tramp; that morning light
So coldly would delineate the scraps   10
Of last night's cheese and blank sepulchral bottles;
That on the kitchen shelf among the saucers
A pair of beetle-eyes would fix her own—
Envoy from some black village in the mouldings . . .[1]
Meanwhile her night's companion, with a yawn
Sounded a dozen notes upon the keyboard,
Declared it out of tune, inspected whistling
A twelve hours' beard, went out for cigarettes;
While she, contending with a woman's demons,
Pulled back the sheets and made the bed and found   20
A fallen towel to dust the table-top,
And wondered how it was a man could wake
From night to day and take the day for granted.
By evening she was back in love again,
Though not so wholly but throughout the night
She woke sometimes to feel the daylight coming
Like a relentless milkman up the stairs.

1955

THE CELEBRATION IN THE PLAZA

The sentimentalist sends his mauve balloon
Meandering into air. The crowd applauds.
The mayor eats ices with a cardboard spoon.

See how that colour charms the sunset air;

[1]Here, and throughout, the ellipsis points are Rich's.

A touch of lavender is what was needed.—
Then, pop! no floating lavender anywhere.

Hurrah, the pyrotechnic engineer
Comes with his sparkling tricks, consults the sky,
Waits for the perfect instant to appear.

Bouquets of gold splash into bloom and pour   10
Their hissing pollen downwind on the dusk.
Nothing like this was ever seen before.

The viceroy of fireworks goes his way,
Leaving us with a sky so dull and bare
The crowd thins out: what conjures them to stay?

The road is cold with dew, and by and by
We see the constellations overhead.
But is that all? some little children cry.

All we have left, their pedagogues reply.

                                          1955

LUCIFER IN THE TRAIN

Riding the black express from heaven to hell
He bit his fingers, watched the countryside,
Vernal and crystalline, forever slide
Beyond his gaze: the long cascades that fell
Ribboned in sunshine from their sparkling height,
The fishers fastened to their pools of green
By silver lines; the birds in sudden flight—
All things the diabolic eye had seen
Since heaven's cockcrow. Imperceptibly
That landscape altered: now in paler air   10
Tree, hill and rock stood out resigned, severe,
Beside the strangled field, the stream run dry.

Lucifer, we are yours who stiff and mute
Ride out of worlds we shall not see again,
And watch from windows of a smoking train
The ashen prairies of the absolute.
Once out of heaven, to an angel's eye
Where is the bush or cloud without a flaw?
What bird but feeds upon mortality,
Flies to its young with carrion in its claw?   20
O foundered angel, first and loneliest
To turn this bitter sand beneath your hoe,
Teach us, the newly-landed, what you know;
After our weary transit, find us rest.

                                          1955

THE TREES

The trees inside are moving out into the forest,
the forest that was empty all these days
where no bird could sit
no insect hide
no sun bury its feet in shadow
the forest that was empty all these nights
will be full of trees by morning.

All night the roots work
to disengage themselves from the cracks
in the veranda floor.
The leaves strain toward the glass   10
small twigs stiff with exertion
long-cramped boughs shuffling under the roof
like newly discharged patients
half-dazed, moving
to the clinic doors.

I sit inside, doors open to the veranda
writing long letters
in which I scarcely mention the departure
of the forest from the house.   20
The night is fresh, the whole moon shines
in a sky still open
the smell of leaves and lichen
still reaches like a voice into the rooms.
My head is full of whispers
which tomorrow will be silent.

Listen. The glass is breaking.
The trees are stumbling forward
into the night. Winds rush to meet them.
The moon is broken like a mirror,   30
its pieces flash now in the crown
of the tallest oak.

1963

BREAKFAST IN A BOWLING ALLEY IN UTICA, NEW YORK

Smudged eyeballs,
mouth stale as air,
I'm newly dead, a corpse

so fresh the grave unnerves me.
Nobody here but me

and Hermes[1] behind the counter

defrosting sandwich steaks.
Paeans of *vox humana*[2]
sob from the walls. THIS LAND

IS MY LAND. . . . It sounds   10
mummified. Has no sex,
no liquor license.

I chew meat and bread
thinking of wheatfields—
a gold-beige ceinture[3]

and cattle like ghosts
of the buffalo, running
across plains, nearing

the abattoir.[4] Houses
dream old-fashionedly   20
in backwoods townships

while the land glitters
with temporary life
stuck fast by choice:

trailers put out taproots
of sewage pipe, suckers
of TV aerial—

but in one of them,
perhaps, a man
alone with his girl   30

for the first time.

                                        1963

[SEX, AS THEY HARSHLY CALL IT,]

Sex, as they harshly call it,
I fell into this morning
at ten o'clock, a drizzling hour
of traffic and wet newspapers.
I thought of him who yesterday
clearly didn't
turn me to a hot field
ready for plowing,

---

[1]Greek god who conducted the dead to Hades.
[2]Latin: the human voice.   [3]French: belt, sash.   [4]French: slaughterhouse.

and longing for that young man
piercéd me to the roots
bathing every vein,[1] etc.   10
All day he appears to me
touchingly desirable,
a prize one could wreck one's peace for.
I'd call it love if love
didn't take so many years
but lust too is a jewel
a sweet flower and what
pure happiness to know
all our high-toned questions   20
breed in a lively animal.

                                                    1964

CHARLESTON IN THE EIGHTEEN-SIXTIES

Derived from the diaries of Mary Boykin Chestnut[1]

He seized me by the waist and kissed my throat . . .
Your eyes, dear, are they grey or blue,
eyes of an angel?
The carts have passed already with their heaped
night-soil, we breathe again . . .
Is this what war is? Nitrate . . .
But smell the pear,
the jasmine, the violets.
Why does this landscape always sadden you?
Now the freshet is up on every side,   10
the river comes to our doors,
limbs of primeval trees dip in the swamp.

So we fool on into the black
cloud ahead of us.
Everything human glitters fever-bright—
the thrill of waking up
out of a stagnant life?
There seems a spell upon
your lovers,—all dead of wounds
or blown to pieces . . . Nitrate!   20
I'm writing, blind with tears of rage.
In vain. Years, death, depopulation, fears,
bondage—these shall all be borne.
No imagination to forestall woe.
1966   1969

[1]An adaptation of the opening lines of Chaucer's *Canterbury Tales.*
[1]"See Ben Ames Williams' selections from Mary Chestnut's diaries in *A Diary from Dixie.*"—Rich's note.

PLANETARIUM

Thinking of Caroline Herschel
(1750–1848)
astronomer, sister of William;[1] and others.

A woman in the shape of a monster
a monster in the shape of a woman
the skies are full of them

a woman   'in the snow
among the Clocks and instruments
or measuring the ground with poles'

in her 98 years to discover
8 comets[2]

she whom the moon ruled
like us   10
levitating into the night sky
riding the polished lenses

Galaxies of women, there
doing penance for impetuousness
ribs chilled
in those spaces   of the mind

An eye,
         'virile, precise and absolutely certain'
         from the mad webs of Uranusborg[3]

                                        encountering the NOVA   20

every impulse of light exploding
from the core
as life flies out of us

         Tycho whispering at last
         'Let me not seem to have lived in vain'[4]

What we see, we see
and seeing is changing

the light that shrivels a mountain
and leaves a man alive

[1]Caroline Lucretia Herschel and her brother William Herschel (1738–1822), famous English astronomers.
[2]Among the accomplishments of Caroline Herschel were the discoveries of eight comets and three nebulas.
[3]Uranienborg, the name of the castle built by Tycho Brahe (1546–1601), Danish astronomer. In his nearby observatory he studied a supernova, now called Tycho's star, in the constellation Cassiopeia.
[4]Reportedly the last words spoken by Tycho Brahe.

Heart beat of the pulsar[5]
heart sweating through my body

30

The radio impulse
pouring in from Taurus[6]

      I am bombarded yet   I stand

I have been standing all my life in the
direct path of a battery of signals
the most accurately transmitted most
untranslatable language in the universe
I am a galactic[7] cloud so deep   so invo-
luted that a light wave could take 15
years to travel through me   And has
taken   I am an instrument in the shape
of a woman trying to translate pulsations
into images   for the relief of the body
and the reconstruction of the mind.
1968

40

1971

DIVING INTO THE WRECK

First having read the book of myths,
and loaded the camera,
and checked the edge of the knife-blade,
I put on
the body-armor of black rubber
the absurd flippers
the grave and awkward mask.
I am having to do this
not like Cousteau[1] with his
assiduous team
aboard the sun-flooded schooner
but here alone.

10

There is a ladder.
The ladder is always there
hanging innocently
close to the side of the schooner.
We know what it is for,
we who have used it.
Otherwise
it's a piece of maritime floss
some sundry equipment.

20

[5]An object in stellar space that emits pulsating radio waves.
[6]Constellation in the northern hemisphere.
[7]Of some galaxy such as the Milky Way.
[1]Jacques Cousteau (1910–   ), French oceanographer and explorer.

I go down.
Rung after rung and still
the oxygen immerses me
the blue light
the clear atoms
of our human air.
I go down.
My flippers cripple me,
I crawl like an insect down the ladder   30
and there is no one
to tell me when the ocean
will begin.

First the air is blue and then
it is bluer and then green and then
black I am blacking out and yet
my mask is powerful
it pumps my blood with power
the sea is another story
the sea is not a question of power   40
I have to learn alone
to turn my body without force
in the deep element.

And now: it is easy to forget
what I came for
among so many who have always
lived here
swaying their crenellated[2] fans
between the reefs
and besides   50
you breathe differently down here.

I came to explore the wreck.
The words are purposes.
The words are maps.
I came to see the damage that was done
and the treasures that prevail.
I stroke the beam of my lamp
slowly along the flank
of something more permanent
than fish or weed   60

the thing I came for:
the wreck and not the story of the wreck
the thing itself and not the myth

[2]Notched.

the drowned face[3] always staring
toward the sun
the evidence of damage
worn by salt and sway into this threadbare beauty
the ribs of disaster
curing their assertion
among the tentative haunters.   70

This is the place.
And I am here, the mermaid whose dark hair
streams black, the merman in his armored body
We circle silently
about the wreck
we dive into the hold.
I am she: I am he

whose drowned face sleeps with open eyes
whose breasts still bear the stress
whose silver, copper, vermeil[4] cargo lies   80
obscurely inside barrels
half-wedged and left to rot
we are the half-destroyed instruments
that once held to a course
the water-eaten log
the fouled compass

We are, I am, you are
by cowardice or courage
the one who find our way
back to this scene   90
carrying a knife, a camera
a book of myths
in which
our names do not appear.
1972   1973

INTEGRITY[1]

the quality or state of being complete; unbroken condition; entirety
—Webster

A wild patience has taken me this far

as if I had to bring to shore
a boat with a spasmodic outboard motor
old sweaters, nets, spray-mottled books

[3]The ships figurehead.   [4]Gilded.
[1]To my knowledge, this word was first introduced in a feminist context by Janice Raymond in her essay "the Illusion of Androgyny," *Quest: A Feminist Quarterly* 2, no. 1 (Summer 1975)."—Rich's note.

tossed in the prow
some kind of sun burning my shoulder-blades.
Splashing the oarlocks. Burning through.
Your fore-arms can get scalded, licked with pain
in a sun blotted like unspoken anger
behind a casual mist.   10

The length of daylight
this far north, in this
forty-ninth year of my life
is critical.

The light is critical: of me, of this
long-dreamed, involuntary landing
on the arm of an inland sea.
The glitter of the shoal
depleting into shadow   20
I recognize: the stand of pines
violet-black really, green in the old postcard
but really I have nothing but myself
to go by; nothing
stands in the realm of pure necessity
except what my hands can hold.

Nothing but myself? . . . My selves.
After so long, this answer.
As if I had always known
I steer the boat in, simply.   30
The motor dying on the pebbles
cicadas taking up the hum
dropped in the silence.

Anger and tenderness: my selves.
And now I can believe they breathe in me
as angels, not polarities.
Anger and tenderness: the spider's genius
to spin and weave in the same action
from her own body, anywhere—
even from a broken web.

The cabin in the stand of pines   40
is still for sale. I know this. Know the print
of the last foot, the hand that slammed and locked that door,
then stopped to wreathe the rain-smashed clematis
back on the trellis
for no one's sake except its own.
I know the chart nailed to the wallboards
the icy kettle squatting on the burner.
The hands that hammered in those nails
emptied that kettle one last time
are these two hands   50
and they have caught the baby leaping

from between trembling legs
and they have worked the vacuum aspirator
and stroked the sweated temples
and steered the boat here through this hot
misblotted sunlight, critical light
imperceptibly scalding
the skin these hands will also salve.

1978

Denise Levertov   1923–

With the publication of her second volume of verse, Here and Now *(1957), Denise Levertov revealed a distinctiveness of style and observation that has made her one of the most respected poets of her generation. She was born and grew up in England and was educated at home. She wrote most of the poems in her first volume,* The Double Image *(1946), while working in London hospitals during World War II. In 1947 she married the American writer Mitchell Goodman and came to live in the United States, where she became a citizen in 1956.*

In America, Denise Levertov became interested in the poetry and prosody of such writers as Wallace Stevens, Ezra Pound, and William Carlos Williams, and during the interval between her first and second volumes of poetry her work underwent a transformation from the traditional versification of English poetry to the freer rhythms and colloquial diction of experimental American verse of the 1950s.

Her third volume of poems, Overland to the Islands, *appeared in 1958, and her fourth,* With Eyes at the Back of Our Heads, *two years later. In 1961 she became poetry editor for the* Nation, *and she published* The Jacob's Ladder. *In 1964* O Taste and See *was published, followed by* The Sorrow Dance *(1967),* Relearning the Alphabet *(1970),* To Stay Alive *(1971),* Footprints *(1972),* The Freedom of the Dust *(1973), and* Life in the Forest, *(1979). In 1973 she published a collection of essays,* The Poet in the World.

Denise Levertov's carefully controlled, exact lines and stanzas attest to the fact that she has not sacrificed form entirely for content in her poems. Although she has rejected traditional accent and meter and such poetic devices as alliteration, she has also avoided the opposite extreme of "spontaneous" writing. Her poems are constructed around the objects of this world at this time. Her aim is to render those objects in a fashion so precise that they convey at once the poet's innermost feelings and the moral and even political significance they suggest. The scope of Denise Levertov's themes is almost as broad as her range of imagery, and her emphasis on the essential identity of symbol and meaning is a conscious effort to give her poems a harmony "in utter contrast to the chaos in which they exist."

FURTHER READING: L. Wagner, *Denise Levertov*, 1967.

TEXT: "Beyond the End" is from *Here and Now*, 1957; "Pure Products" is from *Overland to the Islands*, 1958; "To the Reader" and "Come into Animal Presence" are from *The Jacob's Ladder*, 1961, "September 1961," "The Ground Mist," and "O Taste and See" are from *O Taste and See*, 1964; "A Day Begins" and "The Earth Worm" are from *The Sorrow Dance*, 1967; all other poems are from *Relearning the Alphabet*, 1970.

BEYOND THE END

In "nature" there's no choice—
                              flowers
swing their heads in the wind, sun & moon
        are as they are. But we seem
almost to have it (not just
        available death)

It's energy: a spider's thread: not to
"go on living" but to quicken, to activate: extend:
        Some have it, they force it—
with work or laughter or even   10
        the act of buying, if that's
all they can lay hands on—

            the girls crowding the stores, where light,
                colour, solid dreams are—what gay
            desire! It's their festival,
                ring game, wassail, mystery.

It has no grace like that of
the grass, the humble rhythms, the
falling & rising of leaf and star;
it's barely   20
a constant. Like salt:
take it or leave it

The "hewers of wood"[1] & so on; every damn
craftsman has it while he's working
        but it's not
a question of work: some
shine with it, in repose. (Maybe it is
response, the will to respond—'reason
can give nothing at all/like
the response to desire') maybe   30
a gritting of the teeth, to go
just that much further, beyond the end
beyond whatever ends: to begin, to be, to defy.
                                              1957

PURE PRODUCTS

To the sea they came—
2000 miles in an old bus
fitted with brittle shelves and makeshift beds

---

[1]"Let them live; but let them be hewers of wood and drawers of water." Joshua 9:21.

and cluttered with U.S. canned goods
                    —to the Sea!
on which they paddle
innertubes   —and the lowhovering Sun—
from which the old woman hides her head
under what looks like
a straw wastebasket.   10
                    "Yep, they cured me alright,
but see, it made my breasts grow like a woman's."
And she: "Something hurts him in his chest,
I think
          maybe it's his heart,"—and hers
I can see beating at the withered throat.

To the Sea some force has driven them—
                    away from a lifetime.
And in this windless heat they purpose
to walk the 3 miles of shadeless beach to the shore   20
to ask in Spanish (of which they know
only yes and no) for wholewheat flour
(which is unknown in the region) that she
may bake their bread!
                    They are dying
in their gentleness, adorned
with wrinkled apple smiles—nothing
remains for them
but to live a little, invoking   30
the old powers.

                                        1958

TO THE READER

As you read, a white bear leisurely
pees, dyeing the snow
saffron,

and as you read, many gods
lie among lianas: eyes of obsidian
are watching the generations of leaves,

and as you read
the sea is turning its dark pages,
turning
its dark pages.   10

                              1961

COME INTO ANIMAL PRESENCE

Come into animal presence.
No man is so guileless as

the serpent. The lonely white
rabbit on the roof is a star
twitching its ears at the rain.
The llama intricately
folding its hind legs to be seated
not disdains but mildly
disregards human approval.
What joy when the insouciant   10
armadillo glances at us and doesn't
quicken his trotting
across the track into the palm brush.

What is this joy? That no animal
falters, but knows what it must do?
That the snake has no blemish,
that the rabbit inspects his strange surroundings
in white star-silence? The llama
rests in dignity, the armadillo
has some intention to pursue in the palm-forest.   20
Those who were sacred have remained so,
holiness does not dissolve, it is presence
of bronze, only the sight that saw it
faltered and turned from it.
And old joy returns in holy presence.

                                                     1961

SEPTEMBER 1961

This is the year the old ones,
the old great ones
leave us alone on the road.

The road leads to the sea.
We have the words in our pockets,
obscure directions. The old ones

have taken away the light of their presence,
we see it moving away over a hill
off to one side.

They are not dying,   10
they are withdrawn
into a painful privacy

learning to live without words.
E.P.[1] "It looks like dying"—Williams:[2] "I can't
describe to you what has been

[1]Ezra Pound.   [2]William Carlos Williams.

happening to me"—
H.D.[3] "unable to speak."
The darkness

twists itself in the wind, the stars
are small, the horizon
ringed with confused urban light-haze.   20

They have told us
the road leads to the sea,
and given

the language into our hands.
We hear
our footsteps each time a truck

has dazzled past us and gone
leaving us new silence.
One can't reach   30

the sea on this endless
road to the sea unless
one turns aside at the end, it seems,

follows
the owl that silently glides above it
aslant, back and forth,

and away into deep woods.

But for us the road
unfurls itself, we count the
words in our pockets, we wonder   40

how it will be without them, we don't
stop walking, we know
there is far to go, sometimes

we think the night wind carries
a smell of the sea . . .

                                             1964

THE GROUND-MIST

In hollows of the land
in faults and valleys
                        the white fog
        bruised

[3]Hilda Doolittle (1886–1961), American imagist poet.

        by blue shadows
a mirage of lakes

and in the human
faults and depths
                        silences
floating   10
            between night and daybreak
illusion and substance.

But is illusion
so repeated, known
                        each dawn,
silence
        suspended in the
mind's shadow

always, not substance
of a sort?   20
            the white
bruised
            ground-mist the mirage
of a true lake.
                                1964

O TASTE AND SEE

The world is
not with us enough.[1]
O taste and see[2]

the subway Bible poster said,
meaning **The Lord,** meaning
if anything all that lives
to the imagination's tongue,

grief, mercy, language,
tangerine, weather, to   10
breathe them, bite,
savor, chew, swallow, transform

into our flesh our
deaths, crossing the street, plum, quince,
living in the orchard and being

hungry, and plucking
the fruit.
                                1964

[1]A reference to Wordsworth's sonnet "The World Is Too Much with Us" (1807).
[2]Psalms 34:8 "O taste and see that the Lord is good."

THE EARTH WORM

The worm artist
out of soil, by passage
of himself
constructing.
Castles of metaphor!
Delicate
         dungeon turrets!
He throws off
artifacts as he
contracts and expands the   10
muscle of his being,
ringed in himself,
tilling. He
is homage to
earth, aerates
the ground of his living.
         1967

A DAY BEGINS

A headless squirrel, some blood
oozing from the unevenly
chewed-off neck

lies in rainsweet grass
near the woodshed door.
Down the driveway

the first irises
have opened since dawn,
ethereal, their mauve

almost a transparent gray,   10
their dark veins
bruise-blue.
         1967

ADVENT 1966

Because in Vietnam the vision of a Burning Babe
is multiplied, multiplied,
         the flesh on fire
not Christ's, as Southwell[1] saw it, prefiguring
the Passion upon the Eve of Christmas,

[1]Robert Southwell (1561–1595), English poet and Jesuit martyr. His best-known poem, "The Burning Babe," describes his vision of the Christ-child burning for the sins of men.

but wholly human and repeated, repeated,
infant after infant, their names forgotten,
their sex unknown in the ashes,
set alight, flaming but not vanishing,
not vanishing as his vision but lingering,   10

cinders upon the earth or living on
moaning and stinking in hospitals three abed;

because of this my strong sight,
my clear caressive sight, my poet's sight I was given
that it might stir me to song,
is blurred.
        There is a cataract filming over
my inner eyes. Or else a monstrous insect
has entered my head, and looks out
from my sockets with multiple vision,   20

seeing not the unique Holy Infant
burning sublimely, an imagination of redemption,
furnace in which souls are wrought into new life,
but, as off a beltline, more, more senseless figures aflame.

And this insect (who is not there—
it is my own eyes do my seeing, the insect
is not there, what I see is there)
will not permit me to look elsewhere,

or if I look, to see except dulled and unfocused
the delicate, firm, whole flesh of the still unburned.   30

                    1970

WHAT WILD DAWNS THERE WERE

What wild dawns there were
    in our first years here
when we would run outdoors naked
to pee in the long grass behind the house
      and see over the hills such streamers,
        such banners of fire and blue (the blue
          that is Lilith[1] to full day's honest Eve)—
What feathers of gold under the morning star
      we saw from dazed eyes before
stumbling back to bed chilled with dew   10
    to sleep till the sun was high!

[1] In Jewish folklore, an evil spirit and Adam's first "wife."

Now if we wake early
    we don't go outdoors—or I don't—
    and you if you do go
    rarely call me to see the day break.
I watch the dawn through glass: this year
        only cloudless flushes of light, paleness
        slowly turning to rose,
        and fading subdued.
We have not spoken of these tired   20
risings of the sun.

                      1970

MAD SONG

My madness is dear to me.
I who was almost always the sanest among my friends,
one to whom others came for comfort,
now at my breasts (that look timid and ignorant,
        that don't look as if milk had flowed from them,
        years gone by)
cherish a viper.
        Hail, little serpent of useless longing
that may destroy me,
that bites me with such idle   10
needle teeth.

I who am loved by those who love me
for honesty,
to whom life was an honest breath
        taken in good faith,
I've forgotten how to tell joy from bitterness.

Dear to me, dear to me,
blue poison, green pain in the mind's veins.
How am I to be cured against my will?

                      1970

A HUNGER

Black beans, white sunlight.
These have sufficed.

Approval of mothers, of brothers,
of strangers—a plunge of the hands
in sifted flour, over the wrists.
It gives pleasure.

And being needed. Being loved for that.

Being forgiven.

What mountains there are
to border solitude and provide   10
limits, blue or
dark as raisins.

But hunger: a hunger there is
refuses. Refuses the earth.

                                                    1970

Anne Sexton   *1928–1974*

*Anne Sexton was one of America's most notable confessional poets: "I tell so much truth
in my poetry that I'm a fool if I say any more." She was born in Newton, Massachusetts,
attended private and public schools, worked simultaneously as a librarian and a fashion
model, and began writing poetry in 1957 when she studied at Boston University under
Robert Lowell.*

*Her best work has the quality of a succinct short story in verse. It reads like a forced
confession that is painfully direct and marked by witty irony, self-mockery, and sensitive
meditation. The subject matter of her first volume,* To Bedlam and Part Way Back
(1960), is apparent in the title—mental disturbance and psychic distress. Bedlam *grew
out of her own mental breakdown and her consequent commitment to an asylum, and it
charts with painful honesty her journeys into madness and her visions of death. Her views
of life and death were developed further in her second volume,* All My Pretty Ones
(1962), and in collections that followed: Live or Die *(1967), which won a Pulitzer
Prize,* Love Poems *(1969), and* Transformations *(1971), which offers macabre
reappraisals of familiar fairy tales. In* The Book of Folly *(1972) and in works published
after her death, such as* 45 Mercy Street *(1976), she continued her conversions of
experience into harsh metaphors expressing an awareness of victimization, guilt, chaos.
She was fascinated with death—with suicide as a rebuke of life and the living. Her later
work sometimes was uneven, emotionally indulgent. Yet with its irrationalism and violence
it was nonetheless compelling and piercing, just as she had wanted it to be. In an interview
before her death, by suicide, in 1974, she had said of poetry: "I think it should be a shock
to the senses. It should almost hurt."*

FURTHER READING: *Anne Sexton, A Self-Portrait in Letters,* ed. L. Sexton and L. Ames,
1977; *Anne Sexton, The Artist and Her Critics,* ed. J. McClatchy, 1978; *No Evil Star,* ed.
S. Colburn, 1985.
TEXTS: *The Complete Poems,* ed. L. Sexton, 1981.

HER KIND

I have gone out, a possessed witch,
haunting the black air, braver at night;

dreaming evil, I have done my hitch
over the plain houses, light by light:
lonely thing, twelve-fingered,[1] out of mind.
A woman like that is not a woman, quite.
I have been her kind.

I have found the warm caves in the woods,
filled them with skillets, carvings, shelves,
closets, silks, innumerable goods;   10
fixed the suppers for the worms and the elves:
whining, rearranging the disaligned.
A woman like that is misunderstood.
I have been her kind.

I have ridden in your cart, driver,
waved my nude arms at villages going by,
learning the last bright routes, survivor
where your flames still bite my thigh
and my ribs crack where your wheels wind.
A woman like that is not ashamed to die.   20
I have been her kind.

                                                    1960

THE FARMER'S WIFE

From the hodge porridge
of their country lust,
their local life in Illinois,
where all their acres look
like a sprouting broom factory,
they name just ten years now
that she has been his habit;
as again tonight he'll say
honey bunch let's go
and she will not say how there   10
must be more to living
than this brief bright bridge
of the raucous bed or even
the slow braille touch of him
like a heavy god grown light,
that old pantomime of love
that she wants although
it leaves her still alone,
built back again at last,
mind's apart from him, living   20
her own self in her own words

---

[1]In previous centuries, deformations, such as a sixth finger, were commonly accepted as evidence
of witchcraft and demonic possession.

and hating the sweat of the house
they keep when they finally lie
each in separate dreams
and then how she watches him,
still strong in the blowzy bag
of his usual sleep while
her young years bungle past
their same marriage bed
and she wishes him cripple, or poet,   30
or even lonely, or sometimes,
better, my lover, dead.

                                        1960

RINGING THE BELLS

        And this is the way they ring
the bells in Bedlam
and this is the bell-lady
who comes each Tuesday morning
to give us a music lesson
and because the attendants make you go
and because we mind by instinct,
like bees caught in the wrong hive,
we are the circle of the crazy ladies
who sit in the lounge of the mental house   10
and smile at the smiling woman
who passes us each a bell,
who points at my hand
that holds my bell, E flat,
and this is the gray dress next to me
who grumbles as if it were special
to be old, to be old,
and this is the small hunched squirrel girl
on the other side of me
who picks at the hairs over her lip,   20
who picks at the hairs over her lip all day,
and this is how the bells really sound,
as untroubled and clean
as a workable kitchen,
and this is always my bell responding
to my hand that responds to the lady
who points at me, E flat;
and although we are no better for it,
they tell you to go. And you do.

                                        1960

ALL MY PRETTY ONES

Father, this year's jinx rides us apart
where you followed our mother to her cold slumber;

a second shock boiling its stone to your heart,
leaving me here to shuffle and disencumber
you from the residence you could not afford:
a gold key, your half a woolen mill,
twenty suits from Dunne's, an English Ford,
the love of legal verbiage of another will,
boxes of pictures of people I do not know.
I touch their cardboard faces. They must go.   10

But the eyes, as thick as wood in this album,
hold me. I stop here, where a small boy
waits in a ruffled dress for someone to come . . .[1]
for this soldier who holds his bugle like a toy
or for this velvet lady who cannot smile.
Is this your father's father, this commodore
in a mailman suit? My father, time meanwhile
has made it unimportant who you are looking for.
I'll never know what these faces are all about.
I lock them into their book and throw them out.   20

This is the yellow scrapbook that you began
the year I was born; as crackling now and wrinkly
as tobacco leaves: clippings where Hoover outran
the Democrats, wiggling his dry finger at me
and Prohibition; news where the *Hindenburg* went
down[2] and recent years where you went flush
on war. This year, solvent but sick, you meant
to marry that pretty widow in a one-month rush.
Before you had that second chance, I cried
on your fat shoulder. Three days later you died.   30

These are the snapshots of marriage, stopped in places.
Side by side at the rail toward Nassau[3] now;
here, with the winner's cup at the speedboat races,
here, in tails at the Cotillion, you take a bow,
here, by our kennel of dogs with their pink eyes,
running like show-bred pigs in their chain-link pen;
here, at the horseshow where my sister wins a prize;
and here, standing like a duke among groups of men.
Now I fold you down, my drunkard, my navigator,
my first lost keeper, to love or look at later.   40

I hold a five-year diary that my mother kept
for three years, telling all she does not say
of your alcoholic tendency. You overslept,
she writes. My God, father, each Christmas Day
with your blood, will I drink down your glass
of wine? The diary of your hurly-burly years

---

[1]The ellipsis points are Sexton's.
[2]The dirigible airship *Hindenburg* crashed at Lakehurst, New Jersey, in 1937 with a loss of thirty-six lives.
[3]City in the Bahama Islands.

goes to my shelf to wait for my age to pass.
Only in this hoarded span will love persevere.
Whether you are pretty or not, I outlive you,
bend down my strange face to yours and forgive you.   50

1962

FOR GOD WHILE SLEEPING

Sleeping in fever, I am unfit
to know just who you are:
hung up like a pig on exhibit,
the delicate wrists,
the beard drooling blood and vinegar;
hooked to your own weight,
jolting toward death under your nameplate.

Everyone in this crowd needs a bath.
I am dressed in rags.
The mother wears blue. You grind your teeth   10
and with each new breath
your jaws gape and your diaper sags.
I am not to blame
for all this. I do not know your name.

Skinny man, you are somebody's fault.
You ride on dark poles—
a wooden bird that a trader built
for some fool who felt
that he could make the flight. Now you roll
in your sleep, seasick   20
on your own breathing, poor old convict.

1962

THE TRUTH THE DEAD KNOW

FOR MY MOTHER, BORN MARCH 1902, DIED MARCH 1959
AND MY FATHER, BORN FEBRUARY 1900, DIED JUNE 1959

Gone, I say and walk from church,
refusing the stiff procession to the grave,
letting the dead ride alone in the hearse.
It is June. I am tired of being brave.

We drive to the Cape.[1] I cultivate
myself where the sun gutters from the sky,

---
[1]Cape Cod, Massachusetts.

where the sea swings in like an iron gate
and we touch. In another country people die.

My darling, the wind falls in like stones
from the whitehearted water and when we touch   10
we enter touch entirely. No one's alone.
Men kill for this, or for as much.

And what of the dead? They lie without shoes
in their stone boats. They are more like stone
than the sea would be if it stopped. They refuse
to be blessed, throat, eye and knucklebone.

                                                1962

AND ONE FOR MY DAME

A born salesman,
my father made all his dough
by selling wool to Fieldcrest, Woolrich and Faribo.

A born talker,
he could sell one hundred wet-down bales
of that white stuff. He could clock the miles and sales

and make it pay.
At home each sentence he would utter
had first pleased the buyer who'd paid him off in butter.

Each word   10
had been tried over and over, at any rate,
on the man who was sold by the man who filled my plate.

My father hovered
over the Yorkshire pudding and the beef:
a peddler, a hawker, a merchant and an Indian chief.

Roosevelt! Willkie! and war!
How suddenly gauche I was
with my old-maid heart and my funny teenage applause.

Each night at home
my father was in love with maps   20
while the radio fought its battles with Nazis and Japs.

Except when he hid
in his bedroom on a three-day drunk,
he typed out complex itineraries, packed his trunk,

his matched luggage
and pocketed a confirmed reservation,
his heart already pushing over the red routes of the nation.

I sit at my desk
each night with no place to go,
opening the wrinkled maps of Milwaukee and Buffalo, 30

the whole U.S.,
its cemeteries, its arbitrary time zones,
through routes like small veins, capitals like small stones.

He died on the road,
his heart pushed from neck to back,
his white hanky signaling from the window of the Cadillac.

My husband,
as blue-eyed as a picture book, sells wool:
boxes of card waste, laps and rovings he can pull

to the thread 40
and say *Leicester, Rambouillet, Merino,*[1]
a half-blood, it's greasy and thick, yellow as old snow.

And when you drive off, my darling,
Yes, sir! Yes, sir! It's one for my dame,
your sample cases branded with my father's name,

your itinerary open,
its tolls ticking and greedy,
its highways built up like new loves, raw and speedy.
1962   1966

THE ADDICT

Sleepmonger,
deathmonger,
with capsules in my palms each night,
eight at a time from sweet pharmaceutical bottles
I make arrangements for a pint-sized journey.
I'm the queen of this condition.
I'm an expert on making the trip
and now they say I'm an addict.
Now they ask why.
Why! 10

Don't they know
that I promised to die!
I'm keeping in practice.
I'm merely staying in shape.
The pills are a mother, but better,
every color and as good as sour balls.

[1] Breeds of sheep.

I'm on a diet from death.

Yes, I admit
it has gotten to be a bit of a habit—
blows eight at a time, socked in the eye,   20
hauled away by the pink, the orange,
the green and the white goodnights.
I'm becoming something of a chemical
mixture.
That's it!

My supply
of tablets
has got to last for years and years.
I like them more than I like me.
Stubborn as hell, they won't let go.   30
It's a kind of marriage.
It's a kind of war
where I plant bombs inside
of myself.

Yes
I try
to kill myself in small amounts,
an innocuous occupation.
Actually I'm hung up on it.
But remember I don't make too much noise.   40
And frankly no one has to lug me out
and I don't stand there in my winding sheet.
I'm a little buttercup in my yellow nightie
eating my eight loaves in a row
and in a certain order as in
the laying on of hands
or the black sacrament.

It's a ceremony
but like any other sport
its full of rules.   50
It's like a musical tennis match where
my mouth keeps catching the ball.
Then I lie on my altar
elevated by the eight chemical kisses.

What a lay me down this is
with two pink, two orange,
two green, two white goodnights.
Fee-fi-fo-fum—
Now I'm borrowed.
Now I'm numb.   60
1966   1966

US

I was wrapped in black
fur and white fur and
you undid me and then
you placed me in gold light
and then you crowned me,
while snow fell outside
the door in diagonal darts.
While a ten-inch snow
came down like stars
in small calcium fragments,   10
we were in our own bodies
(that room that will bury us)
and you were in my body
(that room that will outlive us)
and at first I rubbed your
feet dry with a towel
because I was your slave
and then you called me princess.
Princess!

Oh then   20
I stood up in my gold skin
and I beat down the psalms
and I beat down the clothes
and you undid the bridle
and you undid the reins
and I undid the buttons,
the bones, the confusions,
the New England postcards,
the January ten o'clock night,
and we rose up like wheat,   30
acre after acre of gold,
and we harvested,
we harvested.

                                        1969

ROWING

A story, a story!
(Let it go. Let it come.)
I was stamped out like a Plymouth fender
into this world.
First came the crib
with its glacial bars.
Then dolls
and the devotion to their plastic mouths.
Then there was school,

the little straight rows of chairs,   10
blotting my name over and over,
but undersea all the time,
a stranger whose elbows wouldn't work.
Then there was life
with its cruel houses
and people who seldom touched—
though touch is all—
but I grew,
like a pig in a trenchcoat I grew,
and then there were many strange apparitions,   20
the nagging rain, the sun turning into poison
and all of that, saws working through my heart,
but I grew, I grew,
and God was there like an island I had not rowed to,
still ignorant of Him, my arms and my legs worked,
and I grew, I grew,
I wore rubies and bought tomatoes
and now, in my middle age,
about nineteen in the head I'd say,
I am rowing, I am rowing   30
though the oarlocks stick and are rusty
and the sea blinks and rolls
like a worried eyeball,
but I am rowing, I am rowing,
though the wind pushes me back
and I know that that island will not be perfect,
it will have the flaws of life,
the absurdities of the dinner table,
but there will be a door
and I will open it   40
and I will get rid of the rat inside of me,
the gnawing pestilential rat.
God will take it with his two hands
and embrace it.

As the African says:
This is my tale which I have told,
if it be sweet, if it be not sweet,
take somewhere else and let some return to me.
This story ends with me still rowing.
                                                                        1975

Sylvia Plath   *1932–1963*

The work of Sylvia Plath represents a romanticism in extremis, *intense private agonies made public with a grotesque clarity. Her poetry has been praised as a supreme example of the confessional mode in modern literature and disparaged as "the longest suicide note ever written."*

She was born in Boston, Massachusetts, the daughter of a German father and an Austrian mother whose attitudes and personalities were relentlessly exposed in their daughter's writing. As a child Sylvia Plath was brilliant but erratic. At seventeen she published her first poem and her first short story. She entered Smith College on a scholarship, but she became increasingly filled with apprehensions of horror and death and obsessed with a sense of isolation and entrapment: "I've gone around for most of my life as in the rarified atmosphere under a bell jar."

Unable to reconcile her inner and external worlds she was briefly hospitalized and underwent intense psychiatric therapy. The events of these years she later presented in The Bell Jar, *an autobiographical novel about personality disintegration, which she published in 1963 under the pseudonym Victoria Lucas.*

In 1955 she graduated from Smith with highest honors and received a fellowship to Cambridge University, where she took her M.A. degree in 1957. In England she met and married British poet Ted Hughes in 1956. After a temporary return to America she lived in England for the remainder of her life.

Sylvia Plath's first book of poetry, The Colossus, *was published in 1960 and acclaimed by critics for its range of language and stylistic brilliance. After the publication of* The Colossus *she began work on the poems that were later to appear in* Ariel, *but instead of writing in her usual laborious manner she wrote poems at "top speed, as one might write an urgent letter." The* Ariel *poems composed during this period reflect her renewed sense of ungovernable chaos of human experience and her frightening visions of violence and horror. On February 11, 1963, she committed suicide.*

The Ariel *poems, published posthumously in 1965, were followed by* Uncollected Poems *(1965),* Crossing the Water *(1971), and,* Winter Trees *(1972), works that reveal the painful intensity and desperation of a mind seeking to express, in hideous clarity, the visions of one trapped "in The Bell Jar" for whom "the world itself is a bad dream."*

FURTHER READING: *Letters from Home by Sylvia Plath, Correspondence 1950–1963,* ed. A. Roth, 1975; *Journals of Sylvia Plath,* ed. F. McCullough and T. Hughes, 1982; S. Basnett, *Sylvia Plath,* 1987; L. Wagner-Martin, *Sylvia Plath,* 1987. *The Art of Sylvia Plath,* ed. C. Newman, 1970; N. Steiner, *A Closer Look at Ariel, A Memory of Sylvia Plath,* 1973; R. Holbrook, *Sylvia Plath, Poetry and Existence,* 1976; E. Butscher, *Sylvia Plath, Method and Madness,* 1976; *Sylvia Plath, The Woman and Her Work,* ed. E. Butscher, 1977; C. Barnard, *Sylvia Plath,* 1978; *Sylvia Plath, New Views on the Poetry,* ed. G. Lane, 1979; M. Uroff, *Sylvia Plath and Ted Hughes,* 1979; J. Rosenblatt, *Sylvia Plath, The Poetry of Initiation,* 1979; M. Broe, *Protean Poetic, The Poetry of Sylvia Plath,* 1980; L. Bundtzen, *Plath's Incarnations,* 1983; *Critical Essays on Sylvia Plath,* ed. L. Wagner, 1984.

TEXTS: *The Collected Poems, Sylvia Plath,* ed. T. Hughes, 1981.

ALL THE DEAD DEARS

In the Archælogical Museum in Cambridge is a stone coffin of the fourth century A.D. *containing the skeletons of a woman, a mouse and a shrew. The ankle-bone of the woman has been slightly gnawn.*

Rigged poker-stiff on her back
With a granite grin
This antique museum-cased lady
Lies, companioned by the gimcrack
Relics of a mouse and a shrew
That battened for a day on her ankle-bone.

These three, unmasked now, bear
Dry witness
To the gross eating game
We'd wink at if we didn't hear   10
Stars grinding, crumb by crumb,
Our own grist down to its bony face.

How they grip us through thin and thick,
These barnacle dead!
This lady here's no kin
Of mine, yet kin she is: she'll suck
Blood and whistle my marrow clean
To prove it. As I think now of her head,

From the mercury-backed glass
Mother, grandmother, greatgrandmother   20
Reach hag hands to haul me in,
And an image looms under the fishpond surface
Where the daft father went down
With orange duck-feet winnowing his hair—

All the long gone darlings: they
Get back, though, soon,
Soon: be it by wakes, weddings,
Childbirths or a family barbecue:
Any touch, taste, tang's
Fit for those outlaws to ride home on,   30

And to sanctuary: usurping the armchair
Between tick
And tack of the clock, until we go,
Each skulled-and-crossboned Gulliver
Riddled with ghosts, to lie
Deadlocked with them, taking root as cradles rock.

                              1957, 1960

TWO VIEWS OF A CADAVER ROOM

1

The day she visited the dissecting room
They had four men laid out, black as burnt turkey,
Already half unstrung. A vinegary fume
Of death vats clung to them;
The white-smocked boys started working.
The head of his cadaver had caved in,
And she could scarcely make out anything
In that rubble of skull plates and old leather.
A sallow piece of string held it together.

In their jars the snail-nosed babies moon and glow.   10
He hands her the cut-out heart like a cracked heirloom.

                                  2
In Brueghel's panorama of smoke and slaughter[1]
Two people only are blind to the carrion army:
He, afloat in the sea of her blue satin
Skirts, sings in the direction
Of her bare shoulder, while she bends,
Fingering a leaflet of music, over him,
Both of them deaf to the fiddle in the hands
Of the death's-head shadowing their song.
The Flemish lovers flourish; not for long.   20

Yet desolation, stalled in paint, spares the little country
Foolish, delicate, in the lower right-hand corner.
                                                    1959, 1960

THE HANGING MAN

By the roots of my hair some god got hold of me.
I sizzled in his blue volts like a desert prophet.

The nights snapped out of sight like a lizard's eyelid:
A world of bald white days in a shadeless socket.

A vulturous boredom pinned me in this tree.
If he were I, he would do what I did.
1960   1960

MORNING SONG

Love set you going like a fat gold watch.
The midwife slapped your footsoles, and your bald cry
Took its place among the elements.

Our voices echo, magnifying your arrival. New statue.
In a drafty museum, your nakedness
Shadows our safety. We stand round blankly as walls.

I'm no more your mother
Than the cloud that distills a mirror to reflect its own slow
Effacement at the wind's hand.

[1]*The Triumph of Death* painted c. 1562 by the Flemish artist Peter Brueghel the Elder (1520?–1569) and showing the army of the dead as hordes of skeletons attacking the living.

All night your moth-breath   10
Flickers among the flat pink roses.[1] I wake to listen:
A far sea moves in my ear.

One cry, and I stumble from bed, cow-heavy and floral
In my Victorian nightgown.
Your mouth opens clean as a cat's. The window square

Whitens and swallows its dull stars. And now you try
Your handful of notes;
The clear vowels rise like balloons.
1961   1961

THE BEE MEETING

Who are these people at the bridge to meet me? They are the villagers——
The rector, the midwife, the sexton, the agent for bees.
In my sleeveless summery dress I have no protection,
And they are all gloved and covered, why did nobody tell me?
They are smiling and taking out veils tacked to ancient hats.

I am nude as a chicken neck, does nobody love me?
Yes, here is the secretary of bees with her white shop smock,
Buttoning the cuffs at my wrists and the slit from my neck to my knees.
Now I am milkweed silk, the bees will not notice.
They will not smell my fear, my fear, my fear.   10

Which is the rector now, is it that man in black?
Which is the midwife, is that her blue coat?
Everybody is nodding a square black head, they are knights in visors,
Breastplates of cheesecloth knotted under the armpits.
Their smiles and their voices are changing. I am led through a beanfield.

Strips of tinfoil winking like people,
Feather dusters fanning their hands in a sea of bean flowers,
Creamy bean flowers with black eyes and leaves like bored hearts.
Is it blood clots the tendrils are dragging up that string?
No, no, it is scarlet flowers that will one day be edible.   20

Now they are giving me a fashionable white straw Italian hat
And a black veil that molds to my face, they are making me one of them.
They are leading me to the shorn grove, the circle of hives.
Is it the hawthorn that smells so sick?
The barren body of hawthorn, etherizing its children.

Is it some operation that is taking place?
It is the surgeon my neighbors are waiting for,
This apparition in a green helmet,
Shining gloves and white suit.
Is it the butcher, the grocer, the postman, someone I know?   30

[1]Roses on the room's wallpaper.

I cannot run, I am rooted, and the gorse hurts me
With its yellow purses, its spiky armory.
I could not run without having to run forever.
The white hive is snug as a virgin,
Sealing off her brood cells, her honey, and quietly humming.

Smoke rolls and scarves in the grove.
The mind of the hive thinks this is the end of everything.
Here they come, the outriders, on their hysterical elastics.
If I stand very still, they will think I am cow-parsley,
A gullible head untouched by their animosity,   40

Not even nodding, a personage in a hedgerow.
The villagers open the chambers, they are hunting the queen.
Is she hiding, is she eating honey? She is very clever.
She is old, old, old, she must live another year, and she knows it.
While in their fingerjoint cells the new virgins

Dream of a duel they will win inevitably,
A curtain of wax dividing them from the bride flight,
The upflight of the murderess into a heaven that loves her.
The villagers are moving the virgins, there will be no killing.
The old queen does not show herself, is she so ungrateful?   50

I am exhausted, I am exhausted——
Pillar of white in a blackout of knives.
I am the magician's girl who does not flinch.
The villagers are untying their disguises, they are shaking hands.
Whose is that long white box in the grove, what have they accomplished,
          why am I cold.
1962   1962

LADY LAZARUS

I have done it again.
One year in every ten
I manage it——

A sort of walking miracle, my skin
Bright as a Nazi lampshade,
My right foot

A paperweight,
My face a featureless, fine
Jew linen.

Peel off the napkin   10
O my enemy.
Do I terrify?——

The nose, the eye pits, the full set of teeth?
The sour breath
Will vanish in a day.

Soon, soon the flesh
The grave cave ate will be
At home on me

And I a smiling woman.
I am only thirty.
And like the cat I have nine times to die.   20

This is Number Three.
What a trash
to annihilate each decade.

What a million filaments.
The peanut-crunching crowd
Shoves in to see

Them unwrap me hand and foot——
The big strip tease.
Gentleman, ladies,   30

These are my hands,
My knees.
I may be skin and bone,

Nevertheless, I am the same, identical woman.
The first time it happened I was ten.
It was an accident.

The second time I meant
To last it out and not come back at all.
I rocked shut

As a seashell.   40
They had to call and call
And pick the worms off me like sticky pearls.

Dying
Is an art, like everything else.
I do it exceptionally well.

I do it so it feels like hell.
I do it so it feels real.
I guess you could say I've a call.

It's easy enough to do it in a cell.
It's easy enough to do it and stay put.   50
It's the theatrical

Comeback in broad day
To the same place, the same face, the same brute
Amused shout:

"A miracle!"
That knocks me out.
There is a charge

For the eyeing of my scars, there is a charge
For the hearing of my heart——
It really goes.   60

And there is a charge, a very large charge,
For a word or a touch
Or a bit of blood

Or a piece of my hair or my clothes.
So, so, Herr Doktor.[1]
So, Herr Enemy.

I am your opus,
I am your valuable,
The pure gold baby

That melts to a shriek.   70
I turn and burn.
Do not think I underestimate your great concern.

Ash, ash—
You poke and stir.
Flesh, bone, there is nothing there——

A cake of soap,
A wedding ring,
A gold filling.

Herr God, Herr Lucifer,
Beware   80
Beware.

Out of the ash
I rise[2] with my red hair
And I eat men like air.
1962   1963, 1965

ARIEL[1]

Stasis in darkness.
Then the substanceless blue

---

[1]German: Mr. Doctor.
[2]In Near Eastern fable the Phoenix, a symbol of death and resurrection, is a red and gold bird that, at the end of life, burns itself to ashes on a funeral pyre and then rises from the ashes newly reborn.
[1]The poet's horse.

Pour of tor[2] and distances.

God's lioness,
How one we grow,
Pivot of heels and knees!—The furrow

Splits and passes, sister to
The brown arc
Of the neck I cannot catch,

Nigger-eye   10
Berries cast dark
Hooks——

Black sweet blood mouthfuls,
Shadows.
Something else

Hauls me through air——
Thighs, hair;
Flakes from my heels.

White
Godiva[3], I unpeel—
Dead hands, dead stringencies.

And now I
Foam to wheat, a glitter of seas.   20
The child's cry

Melts in the wall.
And I
Am the arrow,

The dew that flies
Suicidal, at one with the drive
Into the red   30

Eye, the cauldron of morning.
1962   1963, 1965

THE APPLICANT

First, are you our sort of a person?
Do you wear
A glass eye, false teeth or a crutch,
A brace or a hook,

[2]A high hill.   [3]Lady Godiva, eleventh-century wife of an English Earl, famous for her legendary ride naked through the city of Coventry, to win remission of heavy taxes on the people.

Rubber breasts or a rubber crotch,

Stitches to show something's missing? No, no? Then
How can we give you a thing?
Stop crying.
Open your hand.
Empty? Empty. Here is a hand   10

To fill it and willing
To bring teacups and roll away headaches
And do whatever you tell it.
Will you marry it?
It is guaranteed

To thumb shut your eyes at the end
And dissolve of sorrow.
We make new stock from the salt.
I notice you are stark naked.   20
How about this suit—

Black and stiff, but not a bad fit.
Will you marry it?
It is waterproof, shatterproof, proof
Against fire and bombs through the roof.
Believe me, they'll bury you in it.

Now your head, excuse me, is empty.
I have the ticket for that.
Come here, sweetie, out of the closet.
Well, what do you think of *that*?   30
Naked as paper to start

But in twenty-five years she'll be silver,
In fifty, gold.[1]
A living doll, everywhere you look.
It can sew, it can cook,
It can talk, talk, talk.

It works, there is nothing wrong with it.
You have a hole, it's a poultice.
You have an eye, it's an image.
My boy, it's your last resort.
Will you marry it, marry it, marry it.   40
1962   1962

DADDY

You do not do, you do not do
Any more, black shoe

[1]For the twenty-fifth (silver) and fiftieth (gold) wedding anniversaries.

In which I have lived like a foot
For thirty years, poor and white,
Barely daring to breathe or Achoo.

Daddy, I have had to kill you.
You died before I had time——
Marble-heavy, a bag full of God,
Ghastly statue with one grey toe[1]
Big as a Frisco seal   10

And a head in the freakish Atlantic
Where it pours bean green over blue
In the waters off beautiful Nauset.[2]
I used to pray to recover you.[3]
Ach, du.[4]

In the German tongue, in the Polish town[5]
Scraped flat by the roller
Of wars, wars, wars.
But the name of the town is common.
My Polack friend   20

Says there are a dozen or two.
So I never could tell where you
Put your foot, your root,
I never could talk to you.
The tongue stuck in my jaw.

It stuck in a barb wire snare.
Ich, ich, ich, ich,[6]
I could hardly speak.
I thought every German was you.
And the language obscene   30

An engine, an engine
Chuffing me off like a Jew.
A Jew to Dachau, Auschwitz, Belsen.[7]
I began to talk like a Jew.
I think I may well be a Jew.

The snows of the Tyrol[8], the clear beer of
   Vienna
Are not very pure or true.
With my gypsy ancestress and my weird luck
And my Taroc pack[9] and my Taroc pack
I may be a bit of a Jew.   40

[1]The toe of Plath's father was swollen and discolored from diabetic gangrene.
[2]Beach and harbor on Cape Cod.   [3]Plath's father died when she was a child.
[4]German: Ah, you.   [5]Plath's father was born in Poland to German parents.
[6]German: I, I, I, I.   [7]Nazi concentration camps in Germany and Poland.
[8]Mountain region of Austria.   [9]Tarot cards, used in fortune-telling.

I have always been scared of *you,*
With your Luftwaffe,[10] your gobbledygoo.
And your neat moustache
And your Aryan eye, bright blue.[11]
Panzer[12] man, panzer-man, O You——

Not God but a swastika
So black no sky could squeak through.
Every woman adores a Fascist,
The boot in the face, the brute
Brute heart of a brute like you.   50

You stand at the blackboard, daddy,
In the picture I have of you,
A cleft in your chin instead of your foot
But no less a devil for that, no not
Any less the black man who

Bit my pretty red heart in two.
I was ten when they buried you.
At twenty I tried to die
And get back, back, back to you.
I thought even the bones would do.   60

But they pulled me out of the sack,
And they stuck me together with glue.[13]
And then I knew what to do.
I made a model of you,
A man in black with a Meinkampf[14] look

And a love of the rack and the screw.
And I said I do, I do.
So daddy, I'm finally through.
The black telephone's off at the root,
The voices just can't worm through.   70

If I've killed one man, I've killed two——
The vampire who said he was you
And drank my blood for a year,
Seven years, if you want to know.
Daddy, you can lie back now.

There's a stake in your fat black heart
And the villagers never liked you.
They are dancing and stamping on you.
They always *knew* it was you.
Daddy, daddy, you bastard, I'm through.   80
1962   1963, 1965

[10]The name of the German air force in World War II.
[11]Reference to the Nazi theory of the superiority of the blond, blue-eyed Aryan race.
[12]German: armored, tank.
[13]A reference to Plath's recovery from her first suicide attempt.
[14]German: My struggle, the title of Adolf Hitler's political manifesto.

FEVER 103°

Pure? What does it mean?
The tongues of hell
Are dull, dull as the triple

Tongues of dull, fat Cerberus[1]
Who wheezes at the gate. Incapable
Of licking clean

The aguey tendon, the sin, the sin.
The tinder cries.
The indelible smell

Of a snuffed candle!   10
Love, love, the low smokes roll
From me like Isadora's scarves,[2] I'm in a fright

One scarf will catch and anchor in the wheel.
Such yellow sullen smokes
Make their own element. They will not rise,

But trundle round the globe
Choking the aged and the meek,
The weak

Hothouse baby in its crib,
The ghastly orchid   20
Hanging its hanging garden in the air,

Devilish leopard!
Radiation turned it white
And killed it in an hour.

Greasing the bodies of adulterers
Like Hiroshima ash and eating in.
The sin. The sin.

Darling, all night
I have been flickering, off, on, off, on.
The sheets grow heavy as a lecher's kiss.   30

Three days. Three nights.
Lemon water, chicken
Water, water make me retch.

I am too pure for you or anyone.
Your body
Hurts me as the world hurts God. I am a lantern——

[1]In classical myth, the three-headed dog that guarded the entrance to Hades.
[2]Isadora Duncan (1878–1927), American dancer who was strangled when her long scarf caught
in the wheel of the car in which she rode.

My head a moon
Of Japanese paper, my gold beaten skin
Infinitely delicate and infinitely expensive.

Does not my heat astound you. And my light.   40
All by myself I am a huge camellia
Glowing and coming and going, flush on flush.

I think I am going up,
I think I may rise——
The beads of hot metal fly, and I, love, I

Am a pure acetylene
Virgin
Attended by roses,

By kisses, by cherubim,[3]
By whatever these pink things mean.   50
Not you, nor him

Not him, nor him
(My selves dissolving, old whore petticoats)——
To Paradise.
1962   1965

James Dickey *1923–*

*James Dickey is everybody's notion of the muscular poet. A football player and track star
in college, he is an avid outdoorsman, archery expert, and guitarist; he served as a fighter
pilot in both World War II and the Korean War, and he gave up a successful business
career in advertising to write poetry. He was born in Atlanta, Georgia, on Ground Hog
Day, as he likes to point out, a suggestion perhaps of his affinity with the wilderness, which
is to Dickey "a subject of endless interest and rejoicing."*

    *Dickey came to poetry, in his own words, "comparatively late": he was twenty-four before
he began writing seriously, and in his late thirties before the publication of his first book
of poems,* Into the Stone *(1960). Most of the poems in Dickey's first three volumes of
poetry (*Into the Stone; Drowning with Others, *1962; and* Helmets, *1964) were
written mainly in short, three-beat lines; the syntax is usually clear and precise; stanzas
are organized around a cluster of images. The worlds of physicality, animals, and nature
are frequent subjects; the dominant themes are death and renewal and the transformation
possible for all living things. Even though Dickey often described dreams, memories, or*

---

[3]One of the orders of heavenly angels.

illusions—"hallucinatory" subjects, in the poet's phrase—his poetry was relatively straight-forward.

Dickey's next book, Buckdancer's Choice *(1965), marked the beginning of a change as he developed what he calls the "conclusionless" poem, which would "involve the reader in it, in all its imperfections and impurities, rather than offering him a (supposedly) perfected work for contemplation, judgment, and evaluation." Such later poems are more narrative in form, with irregular meter and with longer lines typographically set to replace conventional punctuation and denote accents. The style is lush, sometimes even woolly. The sense of the grotesque remains strong.*

In 1977 Dickey published The Bible: A New Vision, *a series of prose poems based on biblical texts. He has also written literary criticism and novels,* Deliverance *(1970), which was made into a successful motion picture, and* Alnilam *(1987) that parallels, as did* Deliverance, *ancient quest myths. Dickey has taught at several colleges and universities and has read his poetry and lectured throughout the country, and he has served as Consultant in Poetry to the Library of Congress. Poetry remains his primary vocation, and in such volumes as* Poems 1957–1967 *(1967)* The Eye-Beaters *(1970), and* The Zodiac, *(1974), Dickey has continued to demonstrate remarkable verbal energy, intensity, sympathy, and a sense of reconciliation unique in contemporary American poetry.*

FURTHER READING: *Babel to Byzantium,* 1968; *Self Interviews,* 1970; *Sorties, Journals and New Essays,* 1971; R. Calhoun, *James Dickey, The Expansive Imagination,* 1973; R. Calhoun and R. Hill, *James Dickey,* 1983; R. Baughman, *Understanding James Dickey,* 1985; R. Kirschsten, *James Dickey and the Gentle Easy of Earth,* 1987.

TEXTS: "Diabetes" is from *The Eye-Beaters,* 1970; all other poems are from *Poems 1957–1967,* 1967.

THE LIFEGUARD

In a stable of boats I lie still,
From all sleeping children hidden.
The leap of fish from its shadow
Makes the whole lake instantly tremble.
With my foot on the water, I feel
The moon outside

Take on the utmost of its power.
I rise and go out through the boats.
I set my broad sole upon silver,
On the skin of the sky, on the moonlight,   10
Stepping outward from earth onto water
In quest of the miracle

This village of children believed
That I could perform as I dived
For one who had sunk from my sight.
I saw his cropped haircut go under.
I leapt, and my steep body flashed
Once, in the sun.

Dark drew all the light from my eyes.
Like a man who explores his death   20
By the pull of his slow-moving shoulders,
I hung head down in the cold,
Wide-eyed, contained, and alone
Among the weeds,

And my fingertips turned into stone
From clutching immovable blackness.
Time after time I leapt upward
Exploding in breath, and fell back
From the change in the children's faces
At my defeat.   30

Beneath them I swam to the boathouse
With only my life in my arms
To wait for the lake to shine back
At the risen moon with such power
That my steps on the light of the ripples
Might be sustained.

Beneath me is nothing but brightness
Like the ghost of a snowfield in summer.
As I move toward the center of the lake,
Which is also the center of the moon,   40
I am thinking of how I may be
The savior of one

Who has already died in my care.
The dark trees fade from around me.
The moon's dust hovers together.
I call softly out, and the child's
Voice answers through blinding water.
Patiently, slowly,

He rises, dilating to break
The surface of stone with his forehead.   50
He is one I do not remember
Having ever seen in his life.
The ground I stand on is trembling
Upon his smile.

I wash the black mud from my hands.
On a light given off by the grave
I kneel in the quick of the moon
At the heart of a distant forest
And hold in my arms a child
Of water, water, water.   60

                    1961, 1962

REINCARNATION (I)

Still, passed through the spokes of an old wheel, on and around
The hub's furry rust in the weeds and shadows of the riverbank,
This one is feeling his life as a man move slowly away.
Fallen from that estate, he has gone down on his knees
And beyond, disappearing into the egg buried under the sand

And wakened the low world being born, consisting now
Of the wheel on its side not turning, but leaning to rot away
In the sun a few feet farther off than it is for any man.
The roots bulge directly under the earth beneath him;
With his tongue he can hear them in their concerted effort   10

To raise something, anything, out of the dark of the ground.
He has come by gliding, by inserting the head between stems.
Everything follows that as naturally as the creation
Of the world, leaving behind arms and legs, leaving behind
The intervals between tracks, leaving one long wavering step

In sand and none in grass: he moves through, moving nothing,
And the grass stands as never entered. It is in the new
Life of resurrection that one can come in one's own time
To a place like a rotting wheel, the white paint flaking from it,
Rust slowly emerging, and coil halfway through it, stopped   20

By a just administration of light and dark over the diamonds
Of the body. Here, also naturally growing, is a flat leaf
To rest the new head upon. The stem bends but knows the weight
And does not touch the ground, holding the snub, patterned face
Swaying with the roots of things. Inside the jaws, saliva

Has turned ice cold, drawn from bird eggs and thunderstruck rodents,
Dusty pine needles, blunt stones, horse dung, leaf mold,
But mainly, now, from waiting—all the time a symbol of evil—
Not for food, but for the first man to walk by the gentle river:
Minute by minute the head becomes more poisonous and poised.   30

Here in the wheel is the place to wait, with the eyes unclosable,
Unanswerable, the tongue occasionally listening, this time
No place in the body desiring to burn the tail away or to warn,
But only to pass on, handless, what yet may be transferred
In a sudden giving-withdrawing move, like a county judge striking a match.

1964, 1965

IN THE MOUNTAIN TENT

I am hearing the shape of the rain
Take the shape of the tent and believe it,

Laying down all around where I lie
A profound, unspeakable law.
I obey, and am free-falling slowly

Through the thought-out leaves of the wood
Into the minds of animals.
I am there in the shining of water
Like dark, like light, out of Heaven.

I am there like the dead, or the beast   10
Itself, which thinks of a poem—
Green, plausible, living, and holy—
And cannot speak, but hears,
Called forth from the waiting of things,

A vast, proper, reinforced crying
With the sifted, harmonious pause,
The sustained intake of all breath
Before the first word of the Bible.

At midnight water dawns
Upon the held skulls of the foxes   20
And weasels and tousled hares
On the eastern side of the mountain.
Their light is the image I make

As I wait as if recently killed,
Receptive, fragile, half-smiling,
My brow watermarked with the mark
On the wing of a moth

And the tent taking shape on my body
Like ill-fitting, Heavenly clothes.
From holes in the ground comes my voice   30
In the God-silenced tongue of the beasts.
"I shall rise from the dead," I am saying.
                                            1962

CHERRYLOG ROAD

Off Highway 106
At Cherrylog Road I entered
The '34 Ford without wheels,
Smothered in kudzu,[1]
With a seat pulled out to run
Corn whiskey down from the hills,

And then from the other side

[1]A rapid-growing, spreading vine used for ground cover.

Crept into an Essex[2]
With a rumble seat of red leather
And then out again, aboard
A blue Chevrolet, releasing   10
The rust from its other color,

Reared up on three building blocks.
None had the same body heat;
I changed with them inward, toward
The weedy heart of the junkyard,
For I knew that Doris Holbrook
Would escape from her father at noon

And would come from the farm
To seek parts owned by the sun   20
Among the abandoned chassis,
Sitting in each in turn
As I did, leaning forward
as in a wild stock-car race

In the parking lot of the dead.
Time after time, I climbed in
And out the other side, like
An envoy or movie star
Met at the station by crickets.
A radiator cap raised its head,   30

Become a real toad or a kingsnake
As I neared the hub of the yard,
Passing through many states,
Many lives, to reach
Some grandmother's long Pierce-Arrow
Sending platters of blindness forth

From its nickel hubcaps
And spilling its tender upholstery
On sleepy roaches,
The glass panel in between   40
Lady and colored driver
Not all the way broken out,

The back-seat phone
Still on its hook.
I got in as though to exclaim,
"Let us go to the orphan asylum,
John; I have some old toys
For children who say their prayers."

I popped with sweat as I thought
I heard Doris Holbrook scrape   50

[2]American automobile of the 1920s and 1930s, as is the Pierce-Arrow (line 35).

Like a mouse in the southern-state sun
That was eating the paint in blisters
From a hundred car tops and hoods.
She was tapping like code,

Loosening the screws,
Carrying off headlights,
Sparkplugs, bumpers,
Cracked mirrors and gear-knobs,
Getting ready, already,
To go back with something to show   60

Other than her lips' new trembling
I would hold to me soon, soon,
Where I sat in the ripped back seat
Talking over the interphone,
Praying for Doris Holbrook
To come from her father's farm

And to get back there
With no trace of me on her face
To be seen by her red-haired father
Who would change, in the squalling barn,   70
Her back's pale skin with a strop,
Then lay for me

In a bootlegger's roasting car
With a string-triggered 12-gauge shotgun
To blast the breath from the air.
Not cut by the jagged windshields,
Through the acres of wrecks she came
With a wrench in her hand,

Through dust where the blacksnake dies
Of boredom, and the beetle knows   80
The compost has no more life.
Someone outside would have seen
The oldest car's door inexplicably
Close from within:

I held her and held her and held her,
Convoyed at terrific speed
By the stalled, dreaming traffic around us,
So the blacksnake, stiff
With inaction, curved back
Into life, and hunted the mouse   90

With deadly overexcitement,
The beetles reclaimed their field
As we clung, glued together,
With the hooks of the seat springs
Working through to catch us red-handed
Amidst the gray, breathless batting

That burst from the seat at our backs.
We left by separate doors
Into the changed, other bodies
Of cars, she down Cherrylog Road   100
And I to my motorcycle
Parked like the soul of the junkyard

Restored, a bicycle fleshed
With power, and tore off
Up Highway 106, continually
Drunk on the wind in my mouth,
Wringing the handlebar for speed,
Wild to be wreckage forever.

                                          1964

THE SHARK'S PARLOR

Memory: I can take my head and strike it on a wall   on Cumberland
    Island
Where the night tide came crawling under the stairs   came up the first
Two or three steps   and the cottage stood on poles all night
With the sea-sprawled under it   as we dreamed of the great fin
    circling
Under the bedroom floor. In daylight there was my first brassy taste
    of beer
And Payton Ford and I came back from the Glynn County
    slaughterhouse
With a bucket of entrails and blood. We tied one end of a hawser
To a spindling porch pillar and rowed straight out of the house
Three hundred yards into the vast front yard of windless blue water
The rope outslithering its coil   the two-gallon jug stoppered and
    sealed   10
With wax   and a ten-foot chain leader   a drop-forged shark hook
    nestling.
We cast our blood on the waters   the land blood easily passing
For sea blood   and we sat in it for a moment with the stain
    spreading
Out from the boat   sat in a new radiance   in the pond of blood in
    the sea
Waiting for fins,   waiting to spill our guts also in the glowing water.
We dumped the bucket, and baited the hook with a run-over collie
    pup. The jug
Bobbed, trying to shake off the sun as a dog would shake off the sea.
We rowed to the house   feeling the same water lift the boat a new
    way,
All the time seeing where we lived rise and dip with the oars.
We tied up and sat down in rocking chairs, one eye or the other
    responding   20
to the blue-eye wink of the jug. Payton got us a beer and we sat

All morning sat there with blood on our minds   the red mark out
In the harbor slowly failing us   then   the house groaned   the rope
Sprang out of the water   splinters flew   we leapt from our chairs
And grabbed the rope   hauled   did nothing   the house coming
    subtly
Apart   all around us   underfoot   boards beginning to sparkle
    like sand
With the glinting of the bright hidden parts of ten-year-old nails
Pulling out   the tarred poles we slept propped-up on   leaning to sea
As in land wind   crabs scuttling from under the floor   as we took
    turns about
Two more porch pillars   and looked out and saw   something
    a fish-flash
An almighty fin in trouble   a moiling of secret forces   a false start
Of water   a round wave growing: in the whole of Cumberland
    Sound the one ripple.
Payton took off without a word   I could not hold him either

But clung to the rope anyway: it was the whole house bending
Its nails that held whatever it was   coming in a little and like a fool
I took up the slack on my wrist. The rope drew gently   jerked   I
    lifted
Clean off the porch and hit the water   the same water it was in
I felt in blue blazing terror at the bottom of the stairs and scrambled
Back up looking desperately into the human house as deeply as I
    could
Stopping my gaze before it went out the wire screen of the back
    door
Stopped it on the thistled rattan   the rugs I lay on and read
On my mother's sewing basket with next winter's socks spilling from
    it
The flimsy vacation furniture   a bucktoothed picture of myself.
Payton came back with three men from a filling station   and glanced
    at me
Dripping water   inexplicable   then we all grabbed hold like a
    tug-of-war.

We were gaining a little   from us a cry went up   from everywhere
People came running. Behind us the house filled with men and boys.
On the third step from the sea I took my place   looking down the
    rope
Going into the ocean, humming and shaking off drops. A houseful
Of people put their backs into it   going up the steps from me
Into the living room   through the kitchen   down the back stairs
Up and over a hill of sand   across a dust road   and onto a raised
    field
Of dunes   we were gaining   the rope in my hands began to be wet
With deeper water   all other haulers retreated through the house
But Payton and I on the stairs   drawing hand over hand on our
    blood
Drawing into existence by the nose   a huge body   becoming
A hammerhead   rolling in beery shallows   and I began to let up

But the rope still strained behind me   the town had gone
Pulling-mad in our house: far away in a field of sand they struggled
They had turned their backs on the sea   bent double   some on their
    knees   60
The rope over their shoulders like a bag of gold   they strove for the
    ideal
Esso station across the scorched meadow   with the distant fish
    coming up
The front stairs the   sagging boards   still coming in   up   taking
Another step   toward the empty house   where the rope stood
    straining
By itself through the rooms   in the middle of the air. "Pass the
    word,"
Payton said, and I screamed it: "Let up, good God, let up!"   to no
    one there.
The shark flopped on the porch, grating with salt-sand   driving
    back in
The nails he had pulled out   coughing chunks of his formless blood.
The screen door banged and tore off   he scrambled on his tail   slid
Curved   did a thing from another world   and was out of his
    element and in   70
Our vacation paradise   cutting all four legs from under the dinner
    table
With one deep-water move   he unwove the rugs in a moment
    throwing pints
Of blood over everything we owned   knocked the buck teeth out of
    my picture
His odd head full of crushed jelly-glass splinters and radio tubes
    thrashing
Among the pages of fan magazines   all the movie stars drenched in
    sea-blood.
Each time we thought he was dead   he struggled back and smashed
One more thing   in all coming back to die   three or four more
    times after death.
At last we got him out   log-rolling him   greasing his sandpaper skin
With lard to slide him   pulling on his chained lips as the tide came
Tumbled him down the steps as the first night wave went under the
    floor.   80
He drifted off   head back   belly white as the moon. What could I
    do but buy
That house   for the one black mark still there   against death   a
    forehead-
toucher in the room he circles beneath   and has been invited to
    wreck?
Blood hard as iron on the wall   black with time   still bloodlike
Can be touched whenever the brow is drunk enough: all changes:
    Memory:
Something like three-dimensional dancing in the limbs   with age
Feeling more in two worlds than one   in all worlds the growing
    encounters.

                          1965

DIABETES

I

Sugar

One night I thirsted like a prince
          Then like a king
        Then like an empire   like a world
        On fire. I rose and flowed away and fell
        Once more to sleep. In an hour I was back
In the kingdom   staggering, my belly going round with self-
          Made night-water, wondering what
          The hell. Months of having a tongue
        Of flame convinced me: I had better not go
          On this way. The doctor was young   10

        And nice. He said, I must tell you,
        My friend, that it is needles moderation
And exercise. You don't want to look forward
            To gangrene and kidney

    Failure   boils blindness infection skin trouble falling
    Teeth coma and death.
                          O.K.
                                  In sleep my mouth went dry
        With my answer   and in it burned the sands
        Of time with new fury. Sleep could give me no water   20
              But my own. Gangrene in white
            Was in my wife's hand at breakfast
        Heaped like a mountain. Moderation, moderation,
        My friend, and exercise. Each time the barbell
              Rose   each time a foot fell
              Jogging, it counted itself
    One death   two death   three death and resurrection
For a little while. Not bad! I always knew it would have to be
                                      somewhere around
            The house: the real
            Symbol of Time I could eat   30
      And live with, coming true when I opened my mouth:
        True in the coffee and the child's birthday
            Cake   helping sickness be fire-
              tongued, sleepless and water-
            logged   but not bad, sweet sand
        Of time, my friend, an everyday—
            A livable death at last.

II

Under Buzzards

                                  [for Robert Penn Warren]
Heavy summer. Heavy. Companion, if we climb our mortal bodies

High with great effort, we shall find ourselves
Flying with the life   40
Of the birds of death. We have come up
Under buzzards   they face us
Slowly   slowly circling   and as we watch them they turn us
Around, and you and I spin
Slowly, slowly rounding
Out the hill. We are level
Exactly on this moment: exactly on the same bird-

plane with those deaths. They are the salvation of our sense
Of glorious movement. Brother, it is right for us to face
Them every which way, and come to ourselves and come   50
From every direction
There is. Whirl and stand fast!
Whence cometh death, O Lord?
On the downwind, riding fire,

Of Hogback Ridge.
But listen: what is dead here?
They are not falling but waiting   but waiting
Riding, and they may know
The rotten, nervous sweetness of my blood.
Somewhere riding the updraft   60
Of a far forest fire, they sensed the city sugar
The doctors found in time.
My eyes are green as lettuce with my diet,
My weight is down,

One pocket nailed with needles and injections, the other dragging
With sugar cubes to balance me in life
And hold my blood
Level, level. Tell me, black riders, does this do any good?
Tell me what I need to know about my time
In the world. Out of the fiery   70

Furnace of pine-woods, in the sap-smoke and crownfire of needles,
Say when I'll die. When will the sugar rise boiling
Against me, and my brain be sweetened
to death?
In heavy summer, like this day.
All right! Physicians, witness! I will shoot my veins
Full of insulin. Let the needle burn
In. From your terrible heads
The flight-blood drains   and you are falling back
Back to the body-raising   80

Fire.
Heavy summer. Heavy. My blood is clear
For a time. Is it too clear? Heat waves are rising
Without birds. But something is gone from me,
Friend. This is too sensible. Really it is better

To know when to die   better for my blood
To stream with death-wish of birds.
You know, I had just as soon crush
This doomed syringe
Between two mountain rocks, and bury this needle in needles   90

Of trees. Companion, open that beer.
How the body works   how hard it works
For its medical books is not
Everything: everything is how
Much glory is in it: heavy summer is right

For a long drink of beer. Red sugar of my eyeballs
Feels them turn blindly
In the fire   rising   turning   turning
Back to Hogback Ridge, and it is all
Delicious, brother: my body is turning   is flashing unbalanced   100
Sweetness everywhere, and I am calling my birds.

                                                        1969, 1970

W. S. Merwin   *1927–*

W. S. Merwin was born in New York, the son of a clergyman. He attended Princeton University, where he studied medieval literature and romance languages. In 1948 he made his way to Europe, where he lived in France, Spain, and Portugal, worked as a tutor to the children of a Portuguese nobleman, and studied in Majorca under the English poet Robert Graves. He has written a number of translations: The Poem of the Cid *(1959),* The Satires of Persius *(1960),* Spanish Ballads *(1960), and* The Song of Roland *(1963). And he has written four plays, the first of which,* Darkling Child, *was produced in London in 1956.*

His first volume of verse, A Mask for Janus *(1952), won a Yale Younger Poets Award, and he has since published* The Dancing Bears *(1954),* The Drunk in the Furnace *(1960),* The Moving Target *(1963),* The Lice *(1967),* The Carriers of Ladders *(1970), which won a Pulitzer Prize,* The Compass Flower *(1977),* Finding the Islands *(1982),* Opening the Hand *(1983), and* Rain in the Trees *(1987). Merwin's poetry has been an effort not to portray experience but to re-create it. In his later work he has moved from the full discursiveness of his earlier poetry to an epigrammatic poetry of bare statement and "shrinking margins." His poetry presents an unsentimental portrait of humankind and the natural world. It is both urgent and lyrical, exhibiting the universalities of myth and perceiving emblems and messages in everyday objects and events.*

FURTHER READING: *W.S. Merwin,* The First Four Books of Poems, *1975; Regions of Memory, Uncollected Prose, 1949–1982, 1987; C. Davis, W. S. Merwin, 1981; W.S. Merwin, Essays on the Poetry, eds. C. Nelson and E. Folsom, 1987.*

TEXTS: "Grandfather in the Old Men's Home" and "The Drunk in the Furnace" are from *The Drunk in the Furnace*, 1960; "Noah's Raven" is from *The Moving Target*, 1963; "Direction" is from *Opening the Hand*, 1983; all other poems are from *The Lice*, 1967.

GRANDFATHER IN THE OLD MEN'S HOME

Gentle at last, and as clean as ever,
He did not even need drink any more,
And his good sons unbent and brought him
Tobacco to chew, both times when they came
To be satisfied he was well cared for.
And he smiled all the time to remember
Grandmother, his wife, wearing the true faith
Like an iron nightgown, yet brought to birth
Seven times and raising the family
Through her needle's eye while he got away   10
Down the green river, finding directions
For boats. And himself coming home sometimes
Well-heeled but blind drunk, to hide all the bread
And shoot holes in the bucket while he made
His daughters pump. Still smiled as kindly in
His sleep beside the other clean old men
To see Grandmother, every night the same,
Huge in her age, with her thumbed-down mouth, come
Hating the river, filling with her stare
His gliding dream, while he turned to water,   20
While the children they both had begotten,
With old faces now, but themselves shrunken
To child-size again, stood ranged at her side,
Beating their little Bibles till he died.

                                             1960

THE DRUNK IN THE FURNACE

For a good decade
The furnace stood in the naked gully, fireless
And vacant as any hat. Then when it was
No more to them than a hulking black fossil
To erode unnoticed with the rest of the junk-hill
By the poisonous creek, and rapidly to be added
To their ignorance.

They were afterwards astonished
To confirm, one morning, a twist of smoke like a pale
Resurrection, staggering out of its chewed hole,   10

And to remark then other tokens that someone,
Cosily bolted behind the eye-holed iron
Door of the drafty burner, had there established
      His bad castle.

      Where he gets his spirits
It's a mystery. But the stuff keeps him musical:
Hammer-and-anvilling with poker and bottle
To his jugged bellowings, till the last groaning clang
As he collapses onto the rioting
Springs of a litter of car-seats ranged on the grates,   20
      To sleep like an iron pig.

      In their tar-paper church
On a text about stoke-holes that are sated never
Their Reverend lingers. They nod and hate trespassers.
When the furnace wakes, though, all afternoon
Their witless offspring flock like piped rats to its siren
Crescendo, and agape on the crumbling ridge
      Stand in a row and learn.

               1960

NOAH'S RAVEN[1]

Why should I have returned?
My knowledge would not fit into theirs.
I found untouched the desert of the unknown,
Big enough for my feet. It is my home.
It is always beyond them. The future
Splits the present with the echo of my voice.
Hoarse with fulfilment, I never made promises.

               1963

THE DRY STONE MASON

The mason is dead the gentle drunk
Master of dry walls
What he made of his years crosses the slopes without wavering
Upright but nameless
Ignorant in the new winter
Rubbed by running sheep
But the age of mortar has come to him

Bottles are waiting like fallen shrines
Under different trees in the rain

---

[1]From the Ark, Noah sent forth a dove and a raven to learn if the Flood had subsided. The dove returned. The raven did not. Genesis 8:7–9.

And stones drip where his hands left them   10
Leaning slightly inwards
His thirst is past

As he had no wife
The neighbors found where he kept his suit
A man with no family they sat with him
When he was carried through them they stood by their own dead
And they have buried him among the graves of the stones

1967

THE ASIANS DYING

When the forests have been destroyed their darkness remains
The ash the great walker follows the possessors
Forever
Nothing they will come to is real
Nor for long
Over the watercourses
Like ducks in the time of the ducks
The ghosts of the villages trail in the sky
Making a new twilight

Rain falls into the open eyes of the dead   10
Again again with its pointless sound
When the moon finds them they are the color of everything

The nights disappear like bruises but nothing is healed
The dead go away like bruises
The blood vanishes into the poisoned farmlands
Pain the horizon
Remains
Overhead the seasons rock
They are paper bells
Calling to nothing living   20

The possessors move everywhere under Death their star
Like columns of smoke they advance into the shadows
Like thin flames with no light
They with no past
And fire their only future

1967

FLY

I have been cruel to a fat pigeon
Because he would not fly

All he wanted was to live like a friendly old man

He had let himself become a wreck filthy and confiding
Wild for his food beating the cat off the garbage
Ignoring his mate perpetually snotty at the beak
Smelling waddling having to be
Carried up the ladder at night content

Fly I said throwing him into the air
But he would drop and run back expecting to be fed   10
I said it again and again throwing him up
As he got worse
He let himself be picked up every time
Until I found him in the dovecote dead
Of the needless efforts

So that is what I am

Pondering his eye that could not
Conceive that I was a creature to run from

I who have always believed too much in words

                                                        1967

DIRECTION

All I remember of the long lecture
which is all I remember of one summer
are the veins of the old   old bald head
and the loose white sleeve   and bony finger pointing
beyond the listeners
over their heads

there was the dazzling   wall and the empty sunlight
and reaching out of his age he told them
for the last time
what to do when they got to the world   10
giving them his every breath   to take with them like water
as they vanished

nobody was coming back that way

                                                        1983

James Wright   *1927–1980*

*James Wright was born in Martins Ferry, Ohio. He went to Kenyon College and the
University of Washington, from which he received an M.A. and a Ph.D. He lived in
Europe and taught at the University of Minnesota and at Hunter College in New York*

City. His first book of poems, The Green Wall, *was published in 1957. A number of collections of his poetry followed, including* Saint Judas *(1959),* The Branch Will Not Break *(1963), and* Shall We Gather at the River *(1968). In addition he translated prose and poetry from German and Spanish. His* Collected Poems *(1971) won a Pulitzer Prize. Subsequently he published* Two Citizens *(1973) and* To A Blossoming Pear Tree *(1977).*

  Wright's poetic visions arose from his perceptions of a world populated by farm animals, grass, trees, and roots, Midwestern landscapes without nightmare or visions of life and death. He found universals in portraits of ordinary people and commonplace things. His poetry shows a compassion for outsiders, social outcasts, and it dwells on loneliness of which death is the ultimate form. His later poems are marked by image-filled spontaneity. Critics complain that his writing sometimes declined into sentimentality and easy self-indulgence. Yet his language is one of controlled simplicity moving from literal observations into the imagination and conveying the vitality and the importance of the ordinary and the mundane.

FURTHER READING: G. Lensing and R. Moran, *Four Poets and the Emotive Imagination,* 1976; *The Pure Clear Word, Essays on the Poetry of James Wright,* ed. D. Smith, 1982.

TEXTS: "Morning Hymn to a Dark Girl" is from *The Green Wall,* 1957; "Confession to J. Edgar Hoover" and "In Response to a Rumor . . ." are from *Shall We Gather at the River,* 1968; all other poems are from *The Branch Will Not Break,* 1963.

AUTUMN BEGINS IN MARTINS FERRY, OHIO

In the Shreve High football stadium,
I think of Polacks nursing long beers in Tiltonsville,
And gray faces of Negroes in the blast furnace at Benwood,
And the ruptured night watchman of Wheeling Steel,
Dreaming of heroes.

All the proud fathers are ashamed to go home.
Their women cluck like starved pullets,
Dying for love.

Therefore,
Their sons grow suicidally beautiful   10
At the beginning of October,
And gallop terribly against each other's bodies.

1963

DEPRESSED BY A BOOK OF BAD POETRY, I WALK TOWARD AN UNUSED PASTURE AND INVITE THE INSECTS TO JOIN ME

Relieved, I let the book fall behind a stone.
I climb a slight rise of grass.
I do not want to disturb the ants

Who are walking single-file up the fence post,
Carrying small white petals,
Casting shadows so frail that I can see through them.
I close my eyes for a moment, and listen.
The old grasshoppers
Are tired, they leap heavily now,
Their thighs are burdened.   10
I want to hear them, they have clear sounds to make.
Then lovely, far off, a dark cricket begins
In the maple trees.

                                                          1963

A PRAYER TO ESCAPE FROM THE MARKET PLACE

I renounce the blindness of the magazines.
I want to lie down under a tree.
This is the only duty that is not death.
This is the everlasting happiness
Of small winds.
Suddenly,
A pheasant flutters, and I turn
Only to see him vanishing at the damp edge
Of the road.

                                                          1963

A BLESSING

Just off the highway to Rochester, Minnesota,
Twilight bounds softly forth on the grass.
And the eyes of those two Indian ponies
Darken with kindness.
They have come gladly out of the willows
To welcome my friend and me.
We step over the barbed wire into the pasture
Where they have been grazing all day, alone.
They ripple tensely, they can hardly contain their
     happiness   10
That we have come.
They bow shyly as wet swans. They love each other.
There is no loneliness like theirs.
At home once more,
They begin munching the young tufts of spring in the
     darkness.
I would like to hold the slenderer one in my arms,
For she has walked over to me
And nuzzled my left hand.
She is black and white,   20

Her mane falls wild on her forehead,
And the light breeze moves me to caress her long ear
That is delicate as the skin over a girl's wrist.
Suddenly I realize
That if I stepped out of my body I would break
Into blossom.

1963

CONFESSION TO J. EDGAR HOOVER

Hiding in the church of an abandoned stone,
A Negro soldier
Is flipping the pages of the Articles of War,
That he can't read.

Our father,
Last evening I devoured the wing
Of a cloud.
And, in the city, I sneaked down
To pray with a sick tree.

I labor to die, father,   10
I ride the great stones,
I hide under stars and maples,
And yet I cannot find my own face.
In the mountains of blast furnaces,
The trees turn their backs on me.

Father, the dark moths
Crouch at the sills of the earth, waiting.

And I am afraid of my own prayers.
Father, forgive me.
I did not know what I was doing.   20

1968

IN RESPONSE TO A RUMOR THAT THE OLDEST WHOREHOUSE IN WHEELING, WEST VIRGINIA, HAS BEEN CONDEMNED

I will grieve alone,
As I strolled alone, years ago, down along
The Ohio shore.
I hid in the hobo jungle weeds
Upstream from the sewer main,
Pondering, gazing.

I saw, down river,
At Twenty-third and Water Streets
By the vinegar works,
The doors open in early evening.   10
Swinging their purses, the women
Poured down the long street to the river
And into the river.

I do not know how it was
They could drown every evening.
What time near dawn did they climb up the other shore,
Drying their wings?

For the river at Wheeling, West Virginia
Has only two shores:
The one in hell, the other   20
In Bridgeport, Ohio.

And nobody would commit suicide, only
To find beyond death
Bridgeport, Ohio.

                                                              1968

A. R. Ammons   *1926–*

Ammons's distinguishing characteristic is his awareness of the natural world, of the facts, forms, and conditions of existence. He entitled his first book Ommateum *(1955), meaning the compound eye of an insect—an appropriate metaphor for a poet whose vision of reality is of an "overwhelming multiplicity." With a background in science and an eye for minutiae, whether he is scrutinizing a spider web, strolling a beach, or considering a backyard elm tree, he approaches his subject with the patience of a naturalist on a field trip. As he explains in one poem, ". . . the way I think is / I think what I see."*

A Southerner, Ammons grew up on a backwoods farm near Whiteville, North Carolina. During World War II he worked in a shipyard and then served in the navy in the South Pacific. He returned home to enter Wake Forest College where he earned a Bachelor of Science degree. For a time he was a principal of an elementary school and then attended the University of California at Berkeley for three semesters. For the next 12 years he lived in New Jersey, where he became vice-president of a company manufacturing laboratory glass. His first book of poems, Ommateum, *went unnoticed, but his second,* Expressions of Sea Level *(1964), brought him a teaching appointment at Cornell University, a post he still holds. Thereafter, successive books appeared almost yearly:* Corsons Inlet *(1965),* Tape for the Turn of the Year *(1965);* Northfield Poems *(1966); Selected Poems (1968);* Uplands *(1970);* Briefings *(1971);* Collected Poems 1951–1971 *(1972), which received the National Book Award;* Sphere: The Form of a Motion *(1974), which won the Bollingen Prize;* Diversifications: Poems *(1975);* The Snow Poems

(1977); The Selected Poems; 1951–1977 (1977); and A Coast of Trees: Poems *(1981).*

The character of Ammons's poetry changed radically after his first book. In Ommateum, *he addressed the vast and indifferent forms of nature in rather melodramatic, figurative modes: he assumed the stance of the insignificant man who is longing to escape the finite and who is questing, like the poet Emerson, for an infinite "Beyond." In subsequent books, Ammons reversed directions, recognizing, as he says in the retrospective poem "Emerson," that Emerson needed "to get up and I down."*

Ammons's allegiance to reality has meant an immersion in discrete particulars, often in the most lowly forms—an insect, a crab, a weed; and his best known poems are probably those in which, in the tradition of William Carlos Williams and Marianne Moore, he presents a single perception in short, free-verse lyrics. Much of his work, however, deals with larger configurations. He is fascinated with the mystery of identity, with life cycles from generation to death, with the persistence of forms and species. His themes have evolved through a series of opposing abstractions: permanence and change, stasis and motion, form and formlessness, order and disorder. The early transcendental strain persists in a final opposition: the One and the many. Usually, he raises the subject only to dismiss it with the recognition that "the eternal will not lie down on any temporal hill," but there remains the tantalizing possibility of an ultimate unity existing behind the chaotic world of particulars.

Ammons's theories of poetry and language are recurrent subjects in his work. In the poem "Essay on Poetics," he offers a revision or expansion of the organic theory of poetry: he sees the poems as analogous to a living organism; it is both synthesis and process, changing, dissolving, reorganizing as it flows through time. Since it reflects reality best when it is open to the greatest possible complexity, without imposed restrictions, the poet's art becomes "the conscious preparation for the unconscious / event."

The emphasis upon flow, or linear movement, is apparent in Ammons's preference for free-verse, run-over lines, and light, on-going rhythms. He usually prefers minimal punctuation, but he savors the colon (a mark of anticipatory pause). His style tends to be casual, flattened toward the norm of prose, often with the literalness and factual quality of a report. In his long, experimental poems, he has been interested in opening poetry to less structured forms and broader ranges of subject.

Similarly, his recent book, The Snow Poems, *is an attempt to make the everyday life of car repairs and supermarket excursions into acceptable subject matter. Such poems might be described as a series of diary entries which range from the serious to the trivial and zany—to weather reports, shopping lists, menus, jingles, and word games. While there is some question as to when such "open" poetry becomes simply "non-poetry," Ammons's efforts to expand the acceptable limits of his art, to jar preconceptions, and to surprise, shock, even bore his readers, represent one of the most significant directions in contemporary poetry.*

FURTHER READING: R. Howard, *Alone With America*, 1969; A. Holder, *A. R. Ammons*, 1978.

TEXT: *Collected Poems, 1951–1971*, 1972.

SO I SAID I AM EZRA

So I said I am Ezra
and the wind whipped my throat
gaming for the sounds of my voice

I listened to the wind
go over my head and up into the night
Turning to the sea I said
            I am Ezra
but there were no echoes from the waves
The words were swallowed up
      in the voice of the surf   10
or leaping over the swells
lost themselves oceanward
      Over the bleached and broken fields
I moved my feet and turning from the wind
      that ripped sheets of sand
      from the beach and threw them
      like seamists across the dunes
swayed as if the wind were taking me away
and said
            I am Ezra   20
As a word too much repeated
falls out of being
so I Ezra went out into the night
like a drift of sand
and splashed among the windy oats
that clutch the dunes
of unremembered seas

                                                    1955

APOLOGIA PRO VITA SUA

I started picking up the stones
throwing them into one place
and by sunrise I was going far away
for the large ones
always turning to see never lost
the cairn's height
lengthening my radial reach:

the sun watched with deep concentration
and the heap through the hours grew
and became by nightfall   10
distinguishable from all the miles around
of slate and sand:

during the night the wind falling
turned earthward its lofty freedom and speed
and the sharp blistering sound muffled
toward dawn and the blanket was
drawn up over a breathless face:

even so you can see in full dawn
the ground there lifts
a foreign thing desertless in origin.   20

                                                    1955

GRAVELLY RUN

I don't know somehow it seems sufficient
to see and hear whatever coming and going is,
losing the self to the victory
    of stones and trees,
of bending sandpit lakes, crescent
round groves of dwarf pine:

for it is not so much to know the self
as to know it as it is known
    by galaxy and cedar cone,

as if birth had never found it
and death could never end it: 10

the swamp's slow water comes
down Gravelly Run fanning the long
    stone-held algal[1]
hair and narrowing roils[2] between
the shoulders of the highway bridge:

holly grows on the banks in the woods there,
and the cedars's gothic-clustered
    spires could make
green religion in winter bones: 20

so I look and reflect, but the air's glass
jail seals each thing in its entity:

no use to make any philosophies here:
    I see no
god in the holly, hear no song from
the snowbroken weeds: Hegel[3] is not the winter
yellow in the pines: the sunlight has never
heard of trees: surrendered self among
    unwelcoming forms: stranger,
hoist your burdens, get on down the road.   30

                                1965

COON SONG

I got one good look
    in the raccoon's eyes
        when he fell from the tree

[1]Of alga, algae-like.   [2]Swirls.
[3]Geoge Friedrich Hegel (1770–1831), German philosopher who asserted that the great unifying plan of the universe was evident in nature.

came to his feet
   and perfectly still
      seized the baying hounds
in his dull fierce stare,
   in that recognition all
      decision lost,
choice irrelevant, before the   10
   battle fell
      and the unwinding
of his little knot of time began:

      Dostoevsky[1] would think
it important if the coon
   could choose to
      be back up the tree:
or if he could choose to be
   wagging by a swamp pond,
      dabbling at scuttling   20
crawdads: the coon may have
   dreamed in fact of curling
      into the holed-out gall
of a fallen oak some squirrel
   had once brought
      high into the air
clean leaves to: but

      reality can go to hell
is what the coon's eyes said to me:
   and said how simple   30
      the solution to my
problem is: it needs only
   not to be: I thought the raccoon
      felt no anger,
saw none; cared nothing for cowardice,
   bravery; was in fact
      bored at
knowing what would ensue:
   the unwinding, the whirling growls,
      exposed tenders,   40
the wet teeth—a problem to be
   solved, the taut-coiled vigor
      of the hunt
ready to snap loose:

      you want to know what happened,
you want to hear me describe it,
   to placate the hound's mouth
      slobbering in your own heart:
I will not tell you: actually the coon

[1]Feodor Mikhailovich Dostoevsky (1821–1881), Russian novelist.

50

    possessing secret knowledge
      pawed dust on the dogs
and they disappeared, yapping into
  nothingness, and the coon went
    down to the pond
and washed his face and hands and beheld
  the world: maybe he didn't:
    I am no slave that I
should entertain you, say what you want
  to hear, let you wallow in
    your silt: one two three four five:
one two three four five six seven eight nine ten:

60

    (all this time I've been
      counting spaces
while you were thinking of something else)
  mess in your own sloppy silt:
    the hounds disappeared
yelping (the way you would at extinction)
    into—the order
    breaks up here—immortality:
I know that's where you think the brave
  little victims should go:
    I do not care what
you think: I do not care what you think:
  I do not care what you
    think: one two three four five
six seven eight nine ten: here we go
  round the here-we-go-round, the
    here-we-go-round, the here-we-
go-round: coon will end in disorder at the
  teeth of hounds: the situation
    will get him:
spheres roll, cubes stay put: now there
  one two three four five
    are two philosophies:
here we go round the mouth-wet of hounds:

70

80

    what I choose
    is youse:
    baby

1965

UNSAID

Have you listened for the things I have left out?
I am nowhere near the end yet and already
  hear
    the hum of omissions,

the chant of vacancies, din of

silences:

there is the other side of matter, antimatter,
        the antiproton:
    we
have measured the proton: it has mass: we   10
have measured the antiproton: it has negative mass:

you will not

hear me completely even at this early point
unless you hear my emptiness:
        go back:
        how can I
tell you what I have not said: you must look for it

yourself: that

side has weight, too, though words cannot bear it
out: listen for the things I have left out: 20
        I am
        aware
of them, as you must be, or you will miss

the non-song

in my singing: it is not that words *cannot* say
what is missing: it is only that what is missing
        cannot
        be missed if
spoken: read the parables of my unmaking:

feel the ris-

ing bubble's trembling walls: rush into the domes
these wordy arches shape: hear
        me
        when I am
silent: gather the boundaried vacancies:

                                                    1965

CORSONS INLET[1]

I went for a walk over the dunes again this morning
to the sea,

[1]In southeast New Jersey.

then turned right along
   the surf
            rounded a naked headland
            and returned

along the inlet shore:

it was muggy sunny, the wind from the sea steady and high,
crisp in the running sand,
     some breakthroughs of sun   10
   but after a bit

continuous overcast:

the walk liberating, I was released from forms,
from the perpendiculars,
    straight lines, blocks, boxes, binds
of thought
into the hues, shadings, rises, flowing bends and blends
       of sight:

               I allow myself eddies of meaning:
yield to a direction of significance   20
running
like a stream through the geography of my work:
  you can find
in my sayings
          swerves of action
          like the inlet's cutting edge:
      there are dunes of motion,
organizations of grass, white sandy paths of remembrance
in the overall wandering of mirroring mind:

but Overall is beyond me: is the sum of these events   30
I cannot draw, the ledger I cannot keep, the accounting
beyond the account:

in nature there are few sharp lines; there are areas of
primrose
    more or less dispersed;
disorderly orders of bayberry; between the rows
of dunes,
irregular swamps of reeds,
though not reeds alone, but grass, bayberry, yarrow, all . . .
predominantly reeds: 40

I have reached no conclusions, have erected no boundaries,
shutting out and shutting in, separating inside
    from outside, I have
    drawn no lines:
    as

manifold events of sand
change the dune's shape that will not be the same shape
tomorrow,

so I am willing to go along, to accept
the becoming   50
thought, to stake off no beginnings or ends, establish
          no walls:
by transitions the land falls from grassy dunes to creek
to undercreek: but there are no lines, though
      change in that transition is clear
   as any sharpness: but "sharpness" spread out,
allowed to occur over a wider range
than mental lines can keep:

the moon was full last night: today, low tide was low:
black shoals of mussels exposed to the risk   60
of air
and, earlier, of sun,
waved in and out with the waterline, waterline inexact,
caught always in the event of change:
      a young mottled gull stood free on the shoals
      and ate
to vomiting: another gull, squawking possession, cracked a crab,
picked out the entrails, swallowed the soft-shelled legs, a ruddy
turnstone[2] running in to snatch leftover bits:

risk is full: every living thing in   70
siege: the demand is life, to keep life: the small
white blacklegged egret, how beautiful, quietly stalks and spears
          the shadows, darts to shore
                    to stab—what? I couldn't
      see against the black mudflats—a frightened
      fiddler crab?

          the news to my left over the dunes and
reeds and bayberry clumps was
          fall: thousands of tree swallows
          gathering for flight: 80
          an order held
          in constant change: a congregation
rich with entropy: nevertheless, separable, noticeable
      as one event,
                not chaos: preparations for
flight from winter,
cheet, cheet, cheet, cheet, wings rifling the green clumps,
beaks
at the bayberries
   a perception full of wind, flight, curve,
   sound: 90
      the possibility of rule as the sum of rulelessness:
the "field" of action
with moving, incalculable center:

in the smaller view, order tight with shape:
blue tiny flowers on a leafless weed: carapace of crab:

[2]A migratory shore bird.

snail shell:
      pulsations of order
     in the bellies of minnows: orders swallowed,
broken down, transferred through membranes
to strengthen larger orders: but in the large view, no   100
lines or changeless shapes: the working in and out, together
     and against, of millions of events: this,
               so that I make
               no form
               formlessness:

orders as summaries, as outcomes of actions override
or in some way result, not predictably (seeing me gain
the top of a dune,
the swallows
could take flight—some other fields of bayberry   110
       could enter fall
berryless) and there is serenity:

       no arranged terror: no forcing of image, plan,
or thought:
no propaganda, no humbling of reality to precept:

terror pervades but is not arranged, all possibilities
of escape open: no route shut, except in
   the sudden loss of all routes:

       I see narrow orders, limited tightness, but will   120
not run to that easy victory:
     still around the looser, wider forces work:
     I will try
   to fasten into order enlarging grasps of disorder, widening
scope, but enjoying the freedom that
Scope eludes my grasp, that there is no finality of vision,
that I have perceived nothing completely,
     that tomorrow a new walk is a new walk.

                             1965

THE UNIFYING PRINCIPLE

Ramshackles, archipelagoes, loose constellations
are less fierce, subsidiary centers, with the
attenuations of interstices, roughing the salience,

jarring the outbreak of too insistent commonalty:
a board, for example, not surrendering the rectitude
of its corners, the island of the oaks an

admonishment to pines, underfigurings (as of the Bear)
that take identity on: this motion is against
the grinding oneness of seas, hallows distinction

into the specific: but less lovely, too, for how   10
is the mass to be amassed, by what sanction
neighbor touch neighbor, island bear resemblance,

how are distinction's hard lines to be dissolved
(and preserved): what may all the people turn to,
the old letters, the shaped, characteristic peak

generations of minds have deflected and kept:
a particular tread that sometimes unweaves, taking
more shape on, into dance: much must be

tolerated as out of timbre, out of step, as being not
in its time or mood (the hiatus of the unconcerned)   20
and much room provided for the wretched to find caves

to ponder way off in: what then can lift the people
and only when they choose to rise or what can make
them want to rise, though business prevents: the

unifying principle will be a
phrase shared, an old cedar long known, general
wind-shapes in a usual sand: those objects single,

single enough to be uninterfering, multiple by
the piling on of shared sight, touch, saying:
when it's found the people live the small wraths of ease.   30
1966

THE CITY LIMITS

When you consider the radiance, that it does not withhold
itself but pours its abundance without selection into every
nook and cranny not overhung or hidden; when you consider

that birds' bones make no awful noise against the light but
lie low in the light as in a high testimony; when you consider
the radiance, that it will look into the guiltiest

swervings of the weaving heart and bear itself upon them,
not flinching into disguise or darkening; when you consider
the abundance of such resource as illuminates the glow-blue

bodies and gold-skeined wings of flies swarming the dumped   10
guts of a natural slaughter or the coil of shit and in no
way winces from its storms of generosity; when you consider

that air or vacuum, snow or shale, squid or wolf, rose or lichen,
each is accepted into as much light as it will take, then
the heart moves roomier, the man stands and looks about, the

leaf does not increase itself above the grass, and the dark
work of the deepest cells is of a tune with May bushes
and fear lit by the breath of such calmly turns to praise.

1971

Louise Glück   *1943–*

*Louise Glück has been called "a poet of a fallen world"; her poems have been described
as "searing," "unforgiving," "relentless," a "succession of shocks." Her writing is stark,
unconsoling; it presents dreary landscapes of pain and loss. She writes of nature, of fields
and ponds and trees, but it is a hostile region, a barren world of ignoble human existence.
She writes of intense human relationships, of love, but it is failed love, cankered by betrayal
or withering in the aftermath of passion.*

Louise Glück began publishing her poems in her early twenties. Her first book, Firstborn
*(1968), appeared when she was twenty-five and brought her wide critical attention. Its
range was narrow, and its poems were brief, gnomic. They were ingrained with loneliness,
abandonment, and death. They spoke of "netted fish," "refuse," "poisoned air," "paralysis
preceding death," "waste," "senility." And they were filled with piercing, evocative images
that stunned her readers.*

Seven years later she published The House on the Marshland, *followed by* Descending Figure *(1980), books that revealed a broadening vision, a growing interest in longer
poetic forms, and a use of myth and Biblical metaphor to present more universal expression
of her themes than was possible in her earlier, terse and imagistic lines. With the publication
of her latest volume of poems,* The Triumph of Achilles *(1985), which received the
National Book Critics Circle prize for poetry, she has come to be recognized as one of the
most notable of recent American poets.*

*Her poems are usually brief, often of sonnet length and near sonnet form. Her diction
is sharp, understated, blunt. She commonly avoids the flourishes and rhetoric of regular
meter and rhyme, using near rhyme, internal rhyme, alliteration, and assonance to lend
her poems a strong cohesiveness. Her writing has been compared to that of the "confessional"
poets Robert Lowell and Sylvia Plath, but whereas Glück's poetry has some of the revelatory
quality of confessional poetry and displays a similar interest in tensions and discontent, it
does not depend so heavily on autobiographical details, nor does it seethe with the mad
fury or exhibit the historical themes that characterize the poetry of Plath or Lowell.*

*Glück writes with a detached objectivity. Her poetry is devoid of sentimentalism, devoid
of nostalgic celebrations of love, motherhood, and family, devoid of the conventional poetic
consolations for loss, devoid even of the romantic pleasure of despair and rage. Her poems
create an austere world where hope is a delusion and love a snare, a world pitilessly
revealed in sardonic images of the floating wool scarves of drowned children, of passion
"flushed down the refuse," and of a slatternly mother sprawled and oblivious to the lice
"rooted" in her baby's hair.*

TEXTS: "The Drowned Children" and "The Garden" are from *Descending Figure*, 1980. "Mock Orange" and "The Reproach" are from *The Triumph of Achilles*, 1985. All others are from *First Born*, 1968.

HESITATE TO CALL

Lived to see you throwing
Me aside. That fought
Like netted fish inside me. Saw you
     throbbing
In my syrups. Saw you sleep. And lived to see
That all that all flushed down
The refuse. Done?
It lives in me.
You live in me. Malignant.
Love, you ever want me, don't.

                                                    1966

THE CHICAGO TRAIN

Across from me the whole ride
Hardly stirred: just Mister with his barren
Skull across the arm-rest while the kid
Got his head between his mama's legs and slept. The poison
That replaces air took over.
And they sat—as though paralysis preceding death
Had nailed them there. The track bent south.
I saw her pulsing crotch . . . the lice rooted in that baby's hair.

                                                    1967

THE EDGE

Time and again, time and again I tie
My heart to that headboard
While my quilted cries
Harden against his hand. He's bored—
I see it. Don't I lick his bribes, set his bouquets
In water? Over Mother's lace I watch him drive into the gored
Roasts, deal slivers in his mercy . . . I can feel his thighs
Against me for the children's sakes. Reward?
Mornings, crippled with this house,
I see him toast his toast and test   10
His coffee, hedgingly. The waste's my breakfast.

                                                    1967

MY NEIGHBOR IN THE MIRROR

M. le professeur[1] in prominent senility
Across the hall tidies his collected prose
And poems. Returning from a shopping spree
Not long ago, I caught him pausing to pose
Before the landing mirror in grandiose semi-profile.
It being impossible to avoid encounter on the stairs
I thought it best to smile
Openly, as though we two held equal shares
In the indiscretion. But his performance of a nod
Was labored and the infinite *politesse*[2] of rose palm   10
Unfurled for salutation fraud-
ulent. At any rate, lately there's been some
Change in his schedule. He receives without zeal
Now, and judging by his refuse, eats little but oatmeal.

                                                    1967

THANKSGIVING

In every room, encircled by a name-
less Southern boy from Yale,
There was my younger sister singing a Fellini theme[1]
And making phone calls
While the rest of us kept moving her discarded boots
Or sat and drank. Outside, in twenty-
nine degrees, a stray cat
Grazed in our driveway,
Seeking waste. It scratched the pail.
There were no other sounds.
Yet on and on the preparation of that vast consoling meal   10
Edged toward the stove. My mother
Had the skewers in her hands.
I watched her tucking skin
As though she missed her young, while bits of onion
Misted snow over the pronged death.

                                                    1968

THE DROWNED CHILDREN

You see, they have no judgment.
So it is natural that they should drown,
first the ice taking them in

---

[1]French: Mr. professor.
[2]French: politeness.
[1]I.e., music from the soundtrack of a film by the Italian director Federico Fellini (1920–   ).

and then, all winter, their wool scarves
floating behind them as they sink
until at last they are quiet.
And the pond lifts them in its manifold dark arms.

But death must come to them differently,
so close to the beginning.
As though they had always been   10
blind and weightless. Therefore
the rest is dreamed, the lamp,
the good white cloth that covered the table,
their bodies.

And yet they hear the names they used
like lures slipping over the pond:
What are you waiting for
come home, come home, lost
in the waters, blue and permanent.

                                                        1980

THE GARDEN

1. The Fear of Birth

One sound. Then the hiss and whir
of houses gliding into their places.
And the wind
leafs through the bodies of animals—

But my body that could not content itself
with health—why should it be sprung back
into the chord of sunlight?

It will be the same again.
This fear, this inwardness,
until I am forced into a field   10
without immunity
even to the least shrub that walks
stiffly out of the dirt, trailing
the twisted signature of its root,
even to a tulip, a red claw.

And then the losses,
one after another,
all supportable.

2. The Garden

The garden admires you.
For your sake it smears itself with green pigment,   20

the ecstatic reds of the roses,
so that you will come to it with your lovers.

And the willows—
see how it has shaped these green
tents of silence. Yet
there is still something you need,
your body so soft, so alive, among the stone animals.

Admit that it is terrible to be like them,
beyond harm.

3. The Fear of Love

That body lying beside me like obedient stone—   30
once its eyes seemed to be opening,
we could have spoken.

At that time it was winter already.
By day the sun rose in its helmet of fire
and at night also, mirrored in the moon.
Its light passed over us freely,
as though we had lain down
in order to leave no shadows,
only these two shallow dents in the snow.
And the past, as always, stretched before us,   40
still, complex, impenetrable.

How long did we lie there
as, arm in arm in their cloaks of feathers,
the gods walked down
from the mountain we built for them?

4. Origins

As though a voice were saying
You should be asleep by now—
But there was no one. Nor
had the air darkened,
though the moon was there,   50
already filled in with marble.

As though, in a garden crowded with flowers,
a voice had said
How dull they are, these golds,
so sonorous, so repetitious
until you closed your eyes,
lying among them, all
stammering flame:

And yet you could not sleep,
poor body, the earth   60
still clinging to you—

5. The Fear of Burial

In the empty field, in the morning,
the body waits to be claimed.
The spirit sits beside it, on a small rock—
nothing comes to give it form again.

Think of the body's loneliness.
At night pacing the sheared field,
its shadow buckled tightly around.
Such a long journey.
And already the remote, trembling lights of the village   70
not pausing for it as they scan the rows.
How far away they seem,
the wooden doors, the bread and milk
laid like weights on the table.

                                                        1980

MOCK ORANGE

It is not the moon, I tell you.
It is these flowers
lighting the yard.

I hate them.
I hate them as I hate sex,
the man's mouth
sealing my mouth, the man's
paralyzing body—

and the cry that always escapes,
the low, humiliating   10
premise of union—

In my mind tonight
I hear the question and pursuing answer
fused in one sound
that mounts and mounts and then
is split into the old selves,
the tired antagonisms. Do you see?
We were made fools of.
And the scent of mock orange
drifts through the window.   20

How can I rest?
How can I be content
when there is still
that odor in the world?

1985

THE REPROACH

You have betrayed me, Eros.[1]
You have sent me
my true love.

On a high hill you made
his clear gaze;
my heart was not
so hard as your arrow.

What is a poet
without dreams?
I lie awake; I feel
actual flesh upon me,   10
meaning to silence me—
Outside, in the blackness
over the olive trees,
a few stars.

I think this is a bitter insult:
that I prefer to walk
the coiled paths of the garden,
to walk beside the river
glittering with drops
of mercury. I like to lie   20
in the wet grass beside the river,
running away, Eros,
not openly, with other men,
but discreetly, coldly—

All my life
I have worshiped the wrong
    gods.
When I watch the trees
on the other side,
the arrow in my heart   30
is like one of them,
swaying and quivering.

1985

[1]God of love, in Greek myth.

Amy Clampitt   *1920–*

Amy Clampitt was born in Iowa, a farmer's daughter, and her poetry often portrays the American midland, showing its scenes and people as if on "an ordinary evening," as if "seen from a Greyhound bus." She graduated with honors from Iowa's Grinnell College. Later she attended Columbia University and the New School for Social Research in New York City, where she now lives. She has worked for the National Audubon Society in New York, and she has been a free-lance writer and an editor for a publishing house. For her achievements as a poet she has received a Guggenheim Fellowship, an honorary degree from Grinnell College, and she has served as writer in residence at Amherst College, the University of Wisconsin, and the College of William and Mary in Virginia.

Amy Clampitt's poems began to appear in magazines and literary journals in the 1970s. Her first major collection of poetry, The Kingfisher, *was published in 1983. Its fifty poems, including "The Kingfisher," "Berceuse," and "Marginal Employment," dazzled the critics. She was described as "the most refreshing new American poet to appear in many years . . . one of the few poets of major ambition and major talent now writing in America." Since that time she has published, every two years, important collections of poetry:* What the Light as Like *(1985) and, her most recent book,* Archaic Figure *(1987).*

Her writing is ardent, complex, and rich with implication. She writes of love, death, the changes of time; she moves from descriptions of exalted moments and exalted scenes of the past to reflections on modern life and the crass, greedy quality of today's culture. Her vocabulary and images, often highly allusive and referential, are drawn from nature, from science, from the visual arts, from mythology, history, the classical world, and literature.

She prefers to write in regular stanzas, using enjambment, carrying the meaning beyond a single poetic line. As a result her sentences are often lengthy, richly ornamented and complex. Her poetry can be playful or solemn, and it moves from details and personal experiences to general observations on life. About the details of her own life, Amy Clampitt has remained reticent, saying: "I would prefer to have my work speak for itself."

TEXTS: "Witness" and "Burial in Cypress Hills" are from *What the Light Was Like,* 1985; "Archaic Figure" and "Man Feeding Pigeons" are from *Archaic Figure,* 1987. All others are from *The Kingfisher,* 1983.

THE KINGFISHER

In a year the nightingales were said to be so loud
they drowned out slumber, and peafowl strolled screaming
beside the ruined nunnery, through the long evening
of a dazzled pub crawl, the halcyon color, portholed
by those eye-spots' stunning tapestry, unsettled
the pastoral nightfall with amazements opening.

Months later, intermission in a pub on Fifty-fifth Street[1]
found one of them still breathless, the other quizzical,
acting the philistine, puncturing Stravinsky[2]—"Tell

[1] In New York City.
[2] Igor Fedorovich Stravinsky (1882–1971), Russian-American avant-garde composer whose works (such as *The Firebird,* 1910) departed radically from musical tradition.

me, what *was* that racket in the orchestra about?"—
hauling down the Firebird, harum-scarum, like a kite,
a burnished, breathing wreck that didn't hurt at all.

Among the Bronx Zoo's exiled jungle fowl, they heard
through headphones of a separating panic, the bellbird
reiterate its single *chong,* a scream nobody answered.
When he mourned, "The poetry is gone," she quailed,
seeing how his hands shook, sobered into feeling old.
By midnight, yet another fifth[3] would have been killed.

A Sunday morning, the November of their cataclysm
(Dylan Thomas brought in *in extremis* to St. Vincent's,[4]
that same week, a symptomatic datum) found them
wandering a downtown churchyard. Among its headstones,
while from unruined choirs the noise of Christendom
poured over Wall Street,[5] a benison[6] in vestments,

a late thrush paused, in transit from some grizzled
spruce bog to the humid equatorial fireside: berry-
eyed, bark-brown above, with dark hints of trauma
in the stigmata[7] of its underparts—or so, too bruised
just then to have invented anything so fancy,
later, re-embroidering a retrospect, she had supposed.

In gray England, years of muted recrimination (then
dead silence) later, she could not have said how many
spoiled takeoffs, how many entanglements gone sodden,
how many gaudy evenings made frantic by just one
insomniac nightingale, how many liaisons gone down
screaming in a stroll beside the ruined nunnery;

a kingfisher's burnished plunge, the color
of felicity afire, came glancing like an arrow
through landscapes of untended memory: ardor
illuminating with its terrifying currency
now no mere glimpse, no porthole vista
but, down on down, the uninhabitable sorrow.

1983

MARGINAL EMPLOYMENT

The Duc de Berry[1] usually wore a robe
the color of the Mediterranean, and listed

---

[3] A fifth of a gallon of whiskey or similar alcoholic drink.
[4] Dylan Thomas (1914–1953), Welsh-born English poet. He died, from alcoholism, at St. Vincent's Hospital in New York City.
[5] Commercial and banking center of New York City.
[6] Blessing, benediction.
[7] Scars or marks that resemble the wounds of Christ crucified.
[1] Jean, duc de Berry (1340–1416), French patron of the arts for whom the *Très Riches Heures* (French: *Very Rich Hours,* 1414–1416?) was created. A devotional book, it contained an illustrated calendar of months and prayers for set hours of the day.

two pots of salts of cobalt
along with apes and dromedaries.
a tooth of Charlemagne,[2] another
from a narwhal, and a charred snippet
from the mantel of the prophet,[3]
among his choicest curios.

Though unacquainted with the works
of Marx,[4] he added value   10
to the hours of no one knows
how many lapidaries,[5] couturiers,[6]
embroiderers of passementerie[7]
with gilt and pearls, and wielders
in gold leaf of the minutest
marginal punctilio.[8] The progress
of his *Très Riches Heures*
is burdened with a fossil gilding
not only of the lily but also of the even
finer flower of the grass, which goes   20

clothed nowadays in common purple—
nerve-nets of tressed fertility,
marginal fan-vaultings[9] scintillating
with a sequin rain: out of what matrix
of pounded relics, what impastos'[10]
thickened blood and mire, the scandal
of such squandered ornament, no less
than any artifice uniquely crafted
for an emperor's enjoyment, escapes
our mere totting-up. The earth's hours   30
are weightier, for all this lightness,
than the sum of human enterprise's
tumbledown fiascos, and the burden
of the oceans' robe, unlike the air
it takes the color of, is more ponderous
than greed, although
it flows, it flows, it flows.

                                                  1983

---

[2]Charles the Great (714–814), Holy Roman Emperor (800–814). His remains were sometimes thought to have miraculous powers.

[3]The robe of the prophet Muhammad, the greatest of the prophets of Islam.

[4]Karl Marx (1818–1883), German political and economic philosopher, chief theorist of socialism and communism. His "labor theory of value" argued that the actual value of a commodity was determined by the amount of labor required to make it.

[5]Those who cut or engrave precious stones, jewelers.

[6]Dress designers.

[7]Fancy trimming made of braid, beads, or metallic thread.

[8]Careful detail.

[9]Elaborate decorative tracery in which the vaulting ribs of a ceiling diverge like the rays of a fan.

[10]Thickened pigments used in paintings.

BERCEUSE[1]

Listen to Gieseking[2] playing a Berceuse
of Chopin[3]—the mothwing flutter
light as ash, perishable as burnt paper—

and sleep, now the furnaces of Auschwitz[4]
are all out, and tourists go there.
The purest art has slept with turpitude,

we all pay taxes. Sleep. The day of waking
waits, cloned from the phoenix—[5]
a thousand replicas in upright silos,[6]

nurseries of the ultimate enterprise.   10
Decay will undo what it can, the rotten
fabric of our repose connives with doomsday.

Sleep on, scathed felicity. Sleep, rare
and perishable relic. Imagining's no shutter
against the absolute, incorrigible sunrise.

                                              1983

WITNESS

An ordinary evening in Wisconsin
seen from a Greyhound bus—mute aisles
of merchandise the sole inhabitants
of the half-darkened Five and Ten,

the tables of the single lit café awash
with unarticulated pathos, the surface membrane
of the inadvertently transparent instant
when no one is looking : outside town

the barns, their red gone dark with sundown,
withhold the shudder of a warped terrain—   10
the castle rocks above, tree-clogged ravines
already submarine with nightfall, flocks

[1]A tranquil piece of music, a lullaby.
[2]Walter Gieseking (1895–1956), French-born German pianist. After World War II he was charged
with, but later cleared of, collaborating with the Nazis.
[3]Frederic Chopin (1810–1849), Polish pianist and composer.
[4]Nazi concentration camp and extermination center in Poland.
[5]Magical bird that, after its death by fire, rises reborn from its own ashes.
[6]Missile silos.

(like dark sheep) of toehold junipers,
the lucent arms of birches: purity
without a mirror, other than a mind bound
elsewhere, to tell it how it looks.

                                                              1985

BURIAL IN CYPRESS HILLS

For Beverly and Lloyd Barzey

Back through East Flatbush, a raw grave
littered by the trashing of the social contract,
to this motel of the dead, its plywood and acrylic
itching gimcrack Hebrew like a brand name.

Her case botched by a vandal of a Brooklyn doctor,
she'd readied everything, had all the old snapshots
sorted, down to the last mysterious interior
obliterated in the processes of coming clear.

Surprising, the amount of privacy that opens,
for all the lifetime rub of other people,   10
around a name uncertified by being in the papers—
one mainly of the bilked, who never formed a party—

and how unhandsome the nub of actual survival.
Nobody is ever ready for the feel of the raw edge
between being and nothing, the knowledge
that abrades the palm, refusing to lie easy.

Yet something in the way the sun shines even now,
out in the open, on that final nugget, makes
bereavement blithe. The undertaker's deputy,
getting the latest lot of mourners into cars,   20

barks like a sergeant, as though even limbo must
be some new sort of boot camp. "Brooklyn people"—
one of the cousins sums it all up, without rancor:
a way of doing business, part of the local color.

Burial in Cypress Hills, a place whose avenues
are narrower than anywhere in Brooklyn: dark-
boled gateposts crowded elbow to elbow,
the woodlot of innumerable burial societies,

each pair of verticals dense as a tenement
with names, or as a column in the *Daily Forward*.[1]   30

[1]The *Jewish Daily Forward*, Yiddish newspaper in New York City.

Whoever enters here to take up residence
arrives an immigrant, out of another country.

The cortege, one of many, inches forward, no more
to be hurried than at Ellis Island.[2] On foot now,
we find the yellow cellar hole, a window into clay,
without a sill, whose only view is downward.

Time, for the gravediggers, is unarguably money:
the cadence of their lifted shovelfuls
across the falling phrases of the Kaddish[3]
strikes on a rarely opened vein of metal   40

whose pure ore rings like joy, although that's not
the name we've been conditioned into giving it.
Around us, flowering trees hang their free fabric,
incorporeal as the act of absolution. At our feet

an unintended dandelion breaks the hasp
of the adjoining plot's neglected ivy
to spend ungrudgingly its single
fringed medallion, alms for the sun.

                                                    1985

ARCHAIC FIGURE

Headless in East Berlin, no goddess
but a named mere girl (Ornithe, "Little Bird")[1]
out of the rubble, six centuries underneath
        the plinth of what we quaintly call

Our Time, informs the foaming underside
of linden boulevards in bloom, sweet hide
laid open onto—sterile as an operating table,
        past the closed incision of the Wall[2]—

the treeless reach of Alexanderplatz,[3]
paved counterpart of the interior flatland,   10
halfway across the globe, we'd left behind:
        projection, factor, yield, the quantifiable

latitude; malls, runways, blacktop; tressed
cornsilk and alfalfa, drawn milk of the humdrum
nurture there were those of us who ran away
        from toward another, earlier, bonier

---

[2]Island in New York Bay, near Manhattan Island, from 1892 to 1943 the chief immigration center of the United States.

[3]A Jewish prayer recited by mourners of the dead.

[1]One of six draped, headless Greek statues (c. 560 B.C.), each inscribed with a name, from the island of Samos in the Aegean—now in a Berlin museum.

[2]The Berlin Wall (built in 1961) separating Communist East Berlin from West Berlin.

[3]Large square with stores and restaurants, the center of life in East Berlin.

one, another middle of the earth, yearned-
for stepmotherland of Hölderlin and Goethe:[4]
sunlight and grief, the cypress and the
    crucifix, the vivid poverty   20

of terraced slopes, of bread, wine, olives,
fig and pomegranate shade we stumbled into,
strolling the sad northern drizzle, in
    the uprooted Turks'[5] quasi-bazaar,

as here, among uprooted artifacts, we've come
upon this shape's just-lifted pleats, her
chitoned[6] stillness the cold chrism[7] of a time
    that saw—or so to us it seems—

with unexampled clarity to the black core
of what we are, of everything we were to be,   30
have since become. Who stands there headless.
    Barbar,[8] she would have called us all.

                              1987

MAN FEEDING PIGEONS

It was the form of the thing, the unmanaged
symmetry of it, of whatever it was
he convoked as he knelt on the sidewalk
and laid out from his unfastened briefcase
a benefaction of breadcrumbs—this band

arriving of the unhoused and opportune
we have always with us, composing
as they fed, heads together, wing tip
and tail edge serrated like chicory[1]
(that heavenly weed, that cerulean   10

commoner of waste places), but with a
glimmer in it, as though the winged
beings of all the mosaics of Ravenna[2]
had gotten the message somehow and come
flying in to rejoin the living: plump-

[4]Friedrich Hölderlin (1770–1843) and Johann Goethe (1749–1832), German poets much influenced by the ideals of classical Greece and Rome.
[5]A generic term for foreign laborers brought from southern Europe and the Near East to Germany during its industrial expansion following World War II.
[6]Dressed in a chiton, a draped tunic, usually of fine linen.
[7]A consecrated oil used in religious services such as baptism.
[8]Greek: Barbarian.
[1]Common, perennial herb with serrated (notched) leaves and cerulean (blue) flowers.
[2]Italian city, on the Adriatic coast, noted for its Byzantine mosaics.

contoured as the pomegranates and pears
in a Della Robbia holiday wreath[3] that had
put on the bloom, once again, of the soon
to perish, to begin to decay, to re-enter
that dance of freewheeling dervishes,[4]   20

the breakdown of order: it was the form
of the thing, if a thing is what it was,
and not the merest wisp of a part of
a process—this unraveling inkling
of the envisioned, of states of being

past alteration, of all that we've
never quite imagined except by way of
the body: the winged proclamations,
the wheelings, the stairways, the
vast, concentric, paradisal rose.[5]   30

1987

James Baldwin *1924–1987*

James Baldwin has been called the most important American black writer of the twentieth century. He was born in Harlem, the oldest of nine children. His childhood and adolescence were dominated by his father, a stern, authoritarian man who was the minister of a storefront church. When he was fourteen, James Baldwin underwent a deep religious experience and began to preach in competition with his father, a conflict of personal as well as religious significance. At the same time he began writing, and after his graduation from high school he continued to write, supporting himself in a succession of menial jobs.

In the winter of 1944–1945 Baldwin met Richard Wright, who encouraged him in his literary ambitions. Baldwin was to become literally and figuratively Wright's successor—his "native son" and heir as an American black writer. Like Wright, to escape American racial injustice, Baldwin left the United States for Europe, where he lived for nine years. While he was in Europe, Baldwin's books first began to be published in the United States. His novel Go Tell It on the Mountain *(1953), a thinly veiled account of his youth, is considered by many critics to be his best work. In 1955 he produced a collection of essays,* Notes of a Native Son, *and in 1956,* Giovanni's Room, *the story of a young, white expatriate in France attempting to come to terms with his homosexuality, a frequent subject of Baldwin's work.*

In 1957 he returned to America and immediately became involved in the civil rights struggle. His essays in this period, Nobody Knows My Name, More Notes of a Native Son *(1961) and* The Fire Next Time *(1963), are written with a force and a perceptiveness that have led many to consider Baldwin as one of the foremost essayists in recent*

---

[3]The Della Robbia family of Italian artists (fifteenth and sixteenth centuries) was famous for its brightly colored, glazed ceramic sculptures, often in circular form surrounded by a wreath.
[4]Members of a Muslim religious order who perform a whirling dance to induce religious trances.
[5]The rose, in literature and the arts, is frequently used as an emblem of perfection and paradise.

American literature. Baldwin's next novel, Another Country *(1962), reflects an increasing anxiety about race relations in America, as does a subsequent collection of short stories,* Going to Meet the Man *(1965). A later novel,* Tell Me How Long the Train's Been Gone *(1968), continues Baldwin's preoccupation with the subjects of homosexuality, interracial love, and racial conflict.*

In 1971 Baldwin published a collection of dialogues with the noted anthropologist Margaret Mead, under the title A Rap on Race, *and in 1972 a volume of observations,* No Name in the Street, *expressing a furious disillusionment with modern America and the world. In 1974 he published* If Beale Street Could Talk, *a bitter protest novel. And in 1979 he published* Just Above my Head, *a long and angry novel that is set in Harlem and tells the story of a famous gospel singer. In 1985 he published a collection of his nonfiction,* The Price of a Ticket. *Although Baldwin was fiercely attacked as insufficiently militant, he was nonetheless a forceful, brilliant voice, warning white America of the explosions to come and cautioning black America against the self-destructive excesses of racial hatred. Baldwin insisted that the American "complex fate" (a phrase he took from Henry James) necessarily makes the lives and the concerns of blacks and whites inseparable in twentieth-century America.*

FURTHER READING: F. Eckman, *The Furious Passage of James Baldwin,* 1966; *James Baldwin, a Critical Evaluation,* ed. T. O'Daniel, 1977; L. Pratt, *James Baldwin,* 1978; C. Sylvander, *James Baldwin,* 1980; *James Baldwin,* ed. H. Bloom, 1986.

TEXT: *Going to Meet the Man,* 1965.

SONNY'S BLUES

I read about it in the paper, in the subway, on my way to work. I read it, and I couldn't believe it, and I read it again. Then perhaps I just stared at it, at the newsprint spelling out his name, spelling out the story. I stared at it in the swinging lights of the subway car, and in the faces and bodies of the people, and in my own face, trapped in the darkness which roared outside.

It was not to be believed and I kept telling myself that, as I walked from the subway station to the high school. And at the same time I couldn't doubt it. I was scared, scared for Sonny. He became real to me again. A great block of ice got settled in my belly and kept melting there slowly all day long, while I taught my classes algebra. It was a special kind of ice. It kept melting, sending trickles of ice water all up and down my veins, but it never got less. Sometimes it hardened and seemed to expand until I felt my guts were going to come spilling out or that I was going to choke or scream. This would always be at a moment when I was remembering some specific thing Sonny had once said or done.

When he was about as old as the boys in my classes his face had been bright and open, there was a lot of copper in it; and he'd had wonderfully direct brown eyes, and great gentleness and privacy. I wondered what he looked like now. He had been picked up the evening before, in a raid on an apartment downtown, for peddling and using heroin.

I couldn't believe it: but what I mean by that is that I couldn't find any room for it anywhere inside me. I had kept it outside me for a long time. I hadn't wanted to know. I had had suspicions, but I didn't name them, I kept putting them away. I told myself that Sonny was wild, but he wasn't crazy. And he'd always been a good boy, he hadn't ever turned hard or evil or disrespectful, the way kids can, so quick, especially in Harlem. I didn't want to believe that I'd ever see my brother going down, coming to nothing, all that light in his face gone out, in the condition I'd already seen so many others. Yet it had happened and here I was, talking about algebra to a lot of boys who might, every one of them for all I knew, be popping off needles every time they went to the head. Maybe it did more for them than algebra could.

I was sure that the first time Sonny had ever had horse,[1] he couldn't have been much older than these boys were now. These boys, now, were living as we'd been living then, they were growing up with a rush and their heads bumped abruptly against the low ceiling of their actual possibilities. They were filled with rage. All they really knew were two darknesses, the darkness of their lives, which was now closing in on them, and the darkness of the movies, which had blinded them to that other darkness, and in which they now, vindictively, dreamed, at once more together than they were at any other time, and more alone.

When the last bell rang, the last class ended, I let out my breath. It seemed I'd been holding it for all that time. My clothes were wet—I may have looked as though I'd been sitting in a steam bath, all dressed up all afternoon. I sat alone in the classroom a long time. I listened to the boys outside, downstairs, shouting and cursing and laughing. Their laughter struck me for perhaps the first time. It was not the joyous laughter which—God knows why—one associates with children. It was mocking and insular, its intent was to denigrate. It was disenchanted, and in this, also, lay the authority of their curses. Perhaps I was listening to them because I was thinking about my brother and in them I heard my brother. And myself.

One boy was whistling a tune, at once very complicated and very simple, it seemed to be pouring out of him as though he were a bird, and it sounded very cool and moving through all that harsh, bright air, only just holding its own through all those other sounds.

I stood up and walked over to the window and looked down into the courtyard. It was the beginning of the spring and the sap was rising in the boys. A teacher passed through them every now and again, quickly, as though he or she couldn't wait to get out of that courtyard, to get those boys out of their sight and off their minds. I started collecting my stuff. I thought I'd better get home and talk to Isabel.

The courtyard was almost deserted by the time I got downstairs. I saw this boy standing in the shadow of a doorway, looking just like Sonny. I almost called his name. Then I saw that it wasn't Sonny, but somebody we used to know, a boy from around our block. He'd been Sonny's friend. He'd never been mine, having been too young for me, and, anyway, I'd never liked him. And now, even though he was a grown-up man, he still hung around that block, still spent hours on the street corners, was always high and raggy. I used to run into him from time to time and he'd often work around to asking me for a quarter or fifty cents. He always had some real good excuse too, and I always gave it to him, I don't know why.

But now, abruptly I hated him. I couldn't stand the way he looked at me, partly like a dog, partly like a cunning child. I wanted to ask him what the hell he was doing in the school courtyard.

He sort of shuffled over to me, and he said, "I see you got the papers. So you already know about it."

"You mean about Sonny? Yes, I already know about it. How come they didn't get you?"

[1]Heroin.

He grinned. It made him repulsive and it also brought to mind what he'd looked like as a kid. "I wasn't there. I stay away from them people."

"Good for you." I offered him a cigarette and I watched him through the smoke. "You come all the way down here just to tell me about Sonny?"

"That's right." He was sort of shaking his head and his eyes looked strange, as though they were about to cross. The bright sun deadened his damp dark brown skin and it made his eyes look yellow and showed up the dirt in his kinked hair. He smelled funky. I moved a little way away from him and I said, "Well, thanks. But I already know about it and I got to get home."

"I'll walk you a little ways," he said. We started walking. There were a couple of kids still loitering in the courtyard and one of them said goodnight to me and looked strangely at the boy beside me.

"What're you going to do?" he asked me. "I mean, about Sonny?"

"Look. I haven't seen Sonny for over a year. I'm not sure I'm going to do anything. Anyway, what the hell *can* I do?"

"That's right," he said quickly, "ain't nothing you can do. Can't much help old Sonny no more, I guess."

It was what I was thinking and so it seemed to me he had no right to say it.

"I'm surprised at Sonny, though," he went on—he had a funny way of talking, he looked straight ahead as though he were talking to himself—"I thought Sonny was a smart boy, I thought he was too smart to get hung."

"I guess he thought so too," I said sharply, "and that's how he got hung. And how about you? You're pretty goddamn smart, I bet."

Then he looked direclty at me, just for a minute. "I ain't smart," he said. "If I was smart, I'd have reached for a pistol a long time ago."

"Look. Don't tell *me* your sad story, if it was up to me, I'd give you one." Then I felt guilty—guilty, probably, for never having supposed that the poor bastard *had* a story of his own, much less a sad one, and I asked, quickly, "What's going to happen to him now?"

He didn't answer this. He was off by himself some place. "Funny thing," he said, and from his tone we might have been discussing the quickest way to get to Brooklyn, "when I saw the papers this morning, the first thing I asked myself was if I had anything to do with it. I felt sort of responsible."

I began to listen more carefully. The subway station was on the corner, just before us, and I stopped. He stopped, too. We were in front of a bar and he ducked slightly, peering in, but whoever he was looking for didn't seem to be there. The juke box was blasting away with something black and bouncy and I half watched the barmaid as she danced her way from the juke box to her place behind the bar. And I watched her face as she laughingly responded to something someone said to her, still keeping time to the music. When she smiled one saw the little girl, one sensed the doomed, still struggling woman beneath the battered face of the semi-whore.

"I never *give* Sonny nothing," the boy said finally, "but a long time ago I come to school high and Sonny asked me how it felt." He paused, I couldn't bear to watch him, I watched the barmaid, and I listened to the music which seemed to be causing the pavement to shake. "I told him it felt great." The music stopped, the barmaid paused and watched the juke box until the music began again. "It did."

All this was carrying me some place I didn't want to go. I certainly didn't want to know how it felt. It filled everything, the people, the houses, the music, the dark, quicksilver barmaid, with menace, and this menace was their reality.

"What's going to happen to him now?" I asked again.

"They'll send him away some place and they'll try to cure him." He shook his head. "Maybe he'll even think he's kicked the habit. Then they'll let him loose"—he gestured, throwing his cigarette into the gutter. "That's all."

"What do you mean that's *all*?"

But I knew what he meant.

"I *mean*, that's *all*." He turned his head and looked at me, pulling down the corners of his mouth. "Don't you know what I mean?" he asked, softly.

"How the hell *would* I know what you mean?" I almost whispered it, I don't know why.

"That's right," he said to the air, "how would *he* know what I mean?" He turned toward me again, patient and calm, and yet I somehow felt him shaking, shaking as though he were going to fall apart. I felt that ice in my guts again, the dread I'd felt all afternoon; and again I watched the barmaid, moving about the bar, washing glasses, and singing. "Listen. They'll let him out and then it'll just start all over again. "That's what I mean."

"You mean—they'll let him out. And then he'll just start working his way back in again. You mean he'll never kick the habit. Is that what you mean?"

"That's right," he said cheerfully. "*You* see what I mean."

"Tell me," I said at last, "why does he want to die? He must want to die, he's killing himself, why does he want to die?"

He looked at me in surprise. He licked his lips. "He don't want to die. He wants to live. Don't nobody want to die, ever."

Then I wanted to ask him—too many things. He could not have answered, or if he had, I could not have borne the answers. I started walking. "Well, I guess it's none of my business."

"It's going to be rough on old Sonny," he said. We reached the subway station. "This is your station?" he asked. I nodded. I took one step down. "Damn!" he said suddenly. I looked up at him. He grinned again. "Damn it if I didn't leave all my money home. You ain't got a dollar on you, have you? Just for a couple of days, is all."

All at once something inside gave and threatened to come pouring out of me. I didn't hate him any more. I felt that in another moment I'd start crying like a child.

"Sure," I said. "Don't sweat. "I looked in my wallet and didn't have a dollar, I only had five. "Here." I said. "That hold you?"

He didn't look at it—he didn't want to look at it. A terrible closed look came over his face, as though he were keeping the number on the bill a secret from him and me. "Thanks," he said, and now he was dying to see me go. "Don't worry about Sonny. Maybe I'll write him or something."

"Sure," I said. "You do that. So long."

"Be seeing you," he said. I went on down the steps.

And I didn't write Sonny or send him anything for a long time. When I finally did, it was just after my little girl died, he wrote me back a letter which made me feel like a bastard.

Here's what he said:

Dear brother,

You don't know how much I needed to hear from you. I wanted to write you many a time but I dug how much I must have hurt you and so I didn't write. But now I feel like a man who's been trying to climb up out of some deep, real deep and funky hole and just saw the sun up there, outside. I got to get outside.

I can't tell you much about how I got here. I mean I don't know how to tell you. I guess I was afraid of something or I was trying to escape from something and you know I have never been very strong in the head (smile). I'm glad Mama and Daddy are dead and can't see what's happened to their son and I swear if I'd known what I was doing I would never have hurt you so, you and a lot of other fine people who were nice to me and who believed in me.

I don't want you to think it had anything to do with me being a musician. It's more than that. Or maybe less than that. I can't get anything straight in my head down here and I try not to think about what's going to happen to me when I get outside again. Sometime I think I'm going to flip and *never* get outside and sometime I think I'll come straight back. I tell you one thing, though, I'd rather blow my brains out than go through this again. But that's what they all say, so they tell me. If I tell you when I'm coming to New York and if you could meet me, I sure would appreciate it. Give my love to Isabel and the kids and I was sure sorry to hear about little Gracie. I wish I could be like Mama and say the Lord's will be done, but I don't know it seems to me that trouble is the one thing that never does get stopped and I don't know what good it does to blame it on the Lord. But maybe it does some good if you believe it.

Your brother,
Sonny

Then I kept in constant touch with him and I sent him whatever I could and I went to meet him when he came back to New York. When I saw him many things I thought I had forgotten came flooding back to me. This was because I had begun, finally, to wonder about Sonny, about the life that Sonny lived inside. This life, whatever it was, had made him older and thinner and it had deepened the distant stillness in which he had always moved. He looked very unlike my baby brother. Yet, when he smiled, when we shook hands, the baby brother I'd never known looked out from the depths of his private life, like an animal waiting to be coaxed into the light.

"How you been keeping?" he asked me.

"All right. And you?"

"Just fine." He was smiling all over his face. "It's good to see you again."

"It's good to see you."

The seven years' difference in our ages lay between us like a chasm: I wondered if these years would ever operate between us as a bridge. I was remembering, and it made it hard to catch my breath, that I had been there when he was born; and I had heard the first words he had ever spoken. When he started to walk, he walked from our mother straight to me. I caught him just before he fell when he took the first steps he ever took in this world.

"How's Isabel?"

"Just fine. She's dying to see you."

"And the boys?"

"They're fine, too. They're anxious to see their uncle."

"Oh, come on. You know they don't remember me."

"Are you kidding? Of course they remember you."

He grinned again. We got into a taxi. We had a lot to say to each other, far too much to know how to begin.

As the taxi began to move, I asked, "You still want to go to India?"

He laughed. "You still remember that. Hell, no. This place is Indian enough for me."

"It used to belong to them," I said.

And he laughed again. "They damn sure knew what they were doing when they got rid of it."

Years ago, when he was around fourteen, he'd been all hipped on the idea of going to India. He read books about people sitting on rocks, naked, in all kinds of weather, but mostly bad, naturally, and walking barefoot through hot coals and arriving at wisdom. I used to say that it sounded to me as though they were getting away from wisdom as fast as they could. I think he sort of looked down on me for that.

"Do you mind," he asked, "if we have the driver drive alongside the park? On the west side—I haven't seen the city in so long."

"Of course not," I said. I was afraid that I might sound as though I were humoring him, but I hoped he wouldn't take it that way.

So we drove along, between the green of the park and the stony, lifeless elegance of hotels and apartment buildings, toward the vivid, killing streets of our childhood. These streets hadn't changed, though housing projects jutted up out of them now like rocks in the middle of a boiling sea. Most of the houses in which we had grown up had vanished, as had the stores from which we had stolen, the basements in which we had first tried sex, the rooftops from which we had hurled tin cans and bricks. But houses exactly like the houses of our past yet dominated the landscape, boys exactly like the boys we once had been found themselves smothering in these houses, came down into the streets for light and air and found themselves encircled by disaster. Some escaped the trap, most didn't. Those who got out always left something of themselves behind, as some animals amputate a leg and leave it in the trap. It might be said, perhaps, that I had escaped, after all, I was a school teacher; or that Sonny had, he hadn't lived in Harlem for years. Yet, as the cab moved uptown through streets which seemed, with a rush, to darken with dark people, and as I covertly studied Sonny's face, it came to me that what we both were seeking through our separate cab windows was that part of ourselves which had been left behind. It's always at the hour of trouble and confrontation that the missing member aches.

We hit 110th Street and started rolling up Lenox Avenue. And I'd known this avenue all my life, but it seemed to me again, as it had seemed on the day I'd first heard about Sonny's trouble, filled with a hidden menace which was its very breath of life.

"We almost there," said Sonny.

"Almost." We were both too nervous to say anything more.

We live in a housing project. It hasn't been up long. A few days after it was up it seemed uninhabitably new, now, of course, it's already rundown. It looks like a parody of the good, clean, faceless life—God knows the people who live in it do their best to make it a parody. The beat-looking grass lying around isn't enough to make their lives green, the hedges will never hold out the streets, and they know it. The big windows fool no one, they aren't big enough to make space out of no space. They don't bother with the windows, they watch the TV screen instead. The playground is most popular with the children who don't play at jacks, or skip rope, or roller skate, or swing, and they can be found in it after dark. We moved in partly because it's not too far from where I teach, and partly for the kids; but it's really just like the houses in which Sonny and I grew up. The same things happen, they'll have the same things to remember. The moment Sonny and I started into the house I had the feeling that I was simply bringing him back into the danger he had almost died trying to escape.

Sonny has never been talkative. So I don't know why I was sure he'd be dying to talk to me when supper was over the first night. Everything went fine, the oldest boy remembered him, and the youngest boy liked him, and Sonny had remembered to bring something for each of them; and Isabel, who is really much nicer than I am, more open and giving, had gone to a lot of trouble about dinner and was genuinely glad to see him. And she's always been able to tease Sonny in a way that I haven't. It was nice to see her face so vivid again and to hear her laugh and watch her make Sonny laugh. She wasn't, or, anyway, she didn't seem to be, at all uneasy or embarrassed. She chatted as though there were no subject which had to be avoided and she got Sonny past his first, faint stiffness. And thank God she was there, for I was filled with that icy dread again. Everything I did seemed awkward to me, and everything I said sounded freighted with hidden meaning. I was trying to remember everything I'd heard about dope addiction and I couldn't help watching Sonny for signs. I wasn't doing it out of malice. I was trying to find out something about my brother. I was dying to hear him tell me he was safe.

"Safe!" my father grunted, whenever Mamma suggested trying to move to a neighborhood which might be safer for children. "Safe, hell! Ain't no place safe for kids, nor nobody."

He always went on like this, but he wasn't, ever, really as bad as he sounded, not even on weekends, when he got drunk. As a matter of fact, he was always on the lookout for "something a little better," but he died before he found it. He died suddenly, during a drunken weekend in the middle of the war, when Sonny was fifteen. He and Sonny hadn't ever got on too well. And this was partly because Sonny was the apple of his father's eye. It was because he loved Sonny so much and was frightened for him, that he was always fighting with him. It doesn't do any good to fight with Sonny. Sonny just moves back, inside himself, where he can't be reached. But the principal reason that they never hit it off is that they were so much alike. Daddy was big and rough and loud-talking, just the opposite of Sonny, but they both had—that same privacy.

Mama tried to tell me something about this, just after Daddy died. I was home on leave from the army.

This was the last time I ever saw my mother alive. Just the same, this picture gets all mixed up in my mind with pictures I had of her when she was younger. The way I always see her is the way she used to be on a Sunday afternoon, say, when the old folks were talking after the big Sunday dinner. I always see her wearing pale blue. She'd be sitting on the sofa. And my father would be sitting in the easy chair, not far from her. And the living room would be full of church folks and relatives. There they sit, in chairs all around the living room, and the night is creeping up outside, but nobody knows it yet. You can see the darkness growing against the window-panes and you hear the street noises every now and again, or maybe the jangling beat of a tambourine from one of the churches close by, but it's real quiet in the room. For a moment nobody's talking, but every face looks darkening, like the sky outside. And my mother rocks a little from the waist, and my father's eyes are closed. Everyone is looking at something a child can't see. For a minute they've forgotten the children. Maybe a kid is lying on the rug, half asleep. Maybe somebody's got a kid in his lap and is absent-mindedly stroking the kid's head. Maybe there's a kid, quiet and big-eyed, curled up in a big chair in the corner. The silence, the darkness coming, and the darkness in the faces frightens the child obscurely. He hopes that the hand which strokes his forehead will never stop—will never die. He hopes that there will never come a time when the old folks won't be sitting around the living room, talking about where they've come from, and what they've seen, and what's happened to them and their kinfolk.

But something deep and watchful in the child knows that this is bound to end, is already ending. In a moment someone will get up and turn on the light. Then the old folks will remember the children and they won't talk any more that day. And when light fills the room, the child is filled with darkness. He knows that every time this happens he's moved just a little closer to that darkness outside. The darkness outside is what the old folks have been talking about. It's what they've come from. It's what they endure. The child knows that they won't talk any more because if he knows too much about what's happening to *them*, he'll know too much too soon, about what's going to happen to *him*.

The last time I talked to my mother, I remember I was restless. I wanted to get out and see Isabel. We weren't married then and we had a lot to straighten out between us.

There Mama sat, in black, by the window. She was humming an old church song, *Lord you brought me from a long ways off*. Sonny was out somewhere. Mama kept watching the streets.

"I don't know," she said, "if I'll ever see you again, after you go off from here. But I hope you'll remember the things I tried to teach you."

"Don't talk like that," I said, and smiled. "You'll be here a long time yet."

She smiled, too, but she said nothing. She was quiet for a long time. And I said, "Mama, don't you worry about nothing. I'll be writing all the time, and you be getting the checks. . . ."

"I want to talk to you about your brother," she said, suddenly. "If anything happens to me he ain't going to have nobody to look out for him."

"Mama," I said, "ain't nothing going to happen to you *or* Sonny. Sonny's all right. He's a good boy and he's got good sense."

"It ain't a question of his being a good boy," Mama said, "nor of his having good sense. It ain't only the bad ones, nor yet the dumb ones that gets sucked under." She stopped, looking at me. "Your Daddy once had a brother," she said, and she smiled in a way that made me feel she was in pain. "You didn't never know that, did you?"

"No," I said, "I never knew that," and I watched her face.

"Oh, yes," she said, "your Daddy had a brother. She looked out of the window again. "I know you never saw your Daddy cry. But *I* did—many a time, through all these years."

I asked her, "What happened to his brother? How come nobody's ever talked about him?"

This was the first time I ever saw my mother look old.

"His brother got killed," she said, "when he was just a little younger than you are now. I knew him. He was a fine boy. He was maybe a little full of the devil, but he didn't mean nobody no harm."

Then she stopped and the room was silent, exactly as it had sometimes been on those Sunday afternoons. Mama kept looking out into the streets.

"He used to have a job in the mill," she said, "and, like all young folks, he just liked to perform on Saturday nights. Saturday nights, him and your father would drift around to different places, go to dances and things like that, or just sit around with people they knew, and your father's brother would sing, he had a fine voice, and play along with himself on his guitar.

Well, this particular Saturday night, him and your father was coming home from some place, and they were both a little drunk and there was a moon that night, it was bright like day. Your father's brother was feeling kind of good, and he was whistling to himself, and he had his guitar slung over his shoulder. They was coming down a hill and beneath them was a road that turned off from the highway. Well, your father's brother, being always kind of frisky, decided to run down this hill, and he did, with that guitar banging and clanging behind him, and he ran across the road, and he was making water behind a tree. And your father was sort of amused at him and he was still coming down the hill, kind of slow. Then he heard a car motor and that same minute his brother stepped from behind the tree, into the road, in the moonlight. And he started to cross the road. And your father started to run down the hill, he says he don't know why. This car was full of white men. They was all drunk, and when they seen your father's brother they let out a great whoop and holler and they aimed the car straight at him. They was having fun, they just wanted to scare him, the way they do sometimes, you know. But they was drunk. And I guess the boy, being drunk, too, and scared, kind of lost his head. By the time he jumped it was too late. Your father says he heard his brother scream when the car rolled over him, and he heard the wood of that guitar when it give, and he heard them strings go flying, and he heard them white men shouting, and the car kept on a-going and it ain't stopped till this day. And, time your father got down the hill, his brother weren't nothing but blood and pulp."

Tears were gleaming on my mother's face. There wasn't anything I could say.

"He never mentioned it," she said, "because I never let him mention it before you children. Your Daddy was like a crazy man that night and for many a night thereafter. He says he never in his life seen anything as dark as that road after the lights of that car had gone away. Weren't nothing, weren't nobody on that road, just your Daddy and his brother and that busted guitar. Oh, yes. Your Daddy never did really get right again. Till the day he died he weren't sure but that every white man he saw was the man that killed his brother."

She stopped and took out her handkerchief and dried her eyes and looked at me.

"I ain't telling you all this," she said, "to make you scared or bitter or to make you hate nobody. I'm telling you this because you got a brother. And the world ain't changed."

I guess I didn't want to believe this. I guess she saw this in my face. She turned away from me, toward the window again, searching those streets.

"But I praise my Redeemer," she said at last, "that He called your Daddy home before me. I ain't saying it to throw no flowers at myself, but, I declare, it keeps me from feeling too cast down to know I helped your father get safely through this world. Your father always acted like he was the roughest, strongest man on earth. And everybody took him to be like that. But if he hadn't had *me* there—to see his tears!"

She was crying again. Still I couldn't move. I said, "Lord, Lord, Mama, I didn't know it was like that."

"Oh, honey," she said, "there's a lot that you don't know. But you are going to find it out." She stood up from the window and came over to me. "You got to hold on to your brother," she said, "and don't let him fall, no matter what it looks like is happening to him and no matter how evil you gets with him. You going to be evil with him many a time. But don't you forget what I told you, you hear?"

"I won't forget," I said. "Don't you worry, I won't forget. I won't let nothing happen to Sonny."

My mother smiled as though she were amused at something she saw in my face. Then, "You may not be able to stop nothing from happening. But you got to let him know you's *there*."

Two days later I was married, and then I was gone. And I had a lot of things on my mind and I pretty well forgot my promise to Mama until I got shipped home on a special furlough for her funeral.

And, after the funeral, with just Sonny and me alone in the empty kitchen, I tried to find out something about him.

"What do you want to do?" I asked him.

"I'm going to be a musician," he said.

For he had graduated, in the time I had been away, from dancing to the juke box to finding out who was playing what, and what they were doing with it, and he had bought himself a set of drums.

"You mean, you want to be a drummer?" I somehow had the feeling that being a drummer might be all right for other people but not for my brother Sonny.

"I don't think," he said, looking at me very gravely, "that I'll ever be a good drummer. But I think I can play a piano."

I frowned. I'd never played the role of the older brother quite so seriously before, had scarcely ever, in fact, *asked* Sonny a damn thing. I sensed myself in the presence of something I didn't really know how to handle, didn't understand. So I made my frown a little deeper as I asked: "What kind of musician do you want to be?"

He grinned. "How many kinds do you think there are?"

"Be *serious*," I said.

He laughed, throwing his head back, and then looked at me. "I *am* serious."

"Well, then, for Christ's sake, stop kidding around and answer a serious question. I mean, do you want to be a concert pianist, or want to play classical music and all that, or—or what?" Long before I finished he was laughing again. "For Christ's *sake*, Sonny!"

He sobered, but with difficulty. "I'm sorry. But you sound so—*scared!*" and he was off again.

"Well, you may think it's funny now, baby, but it's not going to be so funny when you have to make your living at it, let me tell you *that*." I was furious because I knew he was laughing at me and I didn't know why.

"No," he said, very sober now, and afraid, perhaps, that he'd hurt me, "I don't want to be a classical pianist. That isn't what interests me. I mean"—he paused, looking hard at me, as though his eyes would help me to understand, and then gestured helplessly, as though perhaps his hand would help— "I mean, I'll have a lot of studying to do, and I'll have to study *everything*, but, I mean, I want to play *with*—jazz musicians." He stopped. "I want to play jazz," he said.

Well, the word had never before sounded as heavy, as real, as it sounded that afternoon in Sonny's mouth. I just looked at him and I was probably frowning a real frown by this time. I simply couldn't see why on earth he'd want to spend his time hanging around nightclubs, clowning around on bandstands, while people pushed each other around a dance floor. It seemed—beneath him, somehow. I had never thought about it before, had never been forced to, but I suppose I had always put jazz musicians in a class with what Daddy called "good-time people."

"Are you *serious?*"

"Hell, *yes,* I'm serious."

He looked more helpless than ever, and annoyed, and deeply hurt.

I suggested helpfully: "You mean—like Louis Armstrong?"

His face closed as though I'd struck him. "No. I'm not talking about none of that old-time, down home crap."

"Well, look Sonny, I'm sorry, don't get mad. I just don't altogether get it, that's all. Name somebody—you know, a jazz musician you admire."

"Bird."

"Who?"

"Bird! Charlie Parker! Don't they teach you nothing in the god-damn army?"

I lit a cigarette. I was surprised and then a little amused to discover that I was trembling. "I've been out of touch," I said. "You'll have to be patient with me. Now. Who's this Parker character?"

"He's just one of the greatest jazz musicians alive," said Sonny, sullenly, his hands in his pockets, his back to me. "Maybe *the* greatest," he added, bitterly, "that's probably why *you* never heard of him."

"All right," I said, "I'm ignorant. I'm sorry. I'll go out and buy all the cat's records right away, all right?"

"It don't," said Sonny, with dignity, "make any difference to me. I don't care what you listen to. Don't do me no favors."

I was beginning to realize that I'd never seen him so upset before. With another part of my mind I was thinking that this would probably turn out to be one of those things kids go through and that I shouldn't make it seem important by pushing it too hard. Still, I didn't think it would do any harm to ask: "Doesn't all this take a lot of time? Can you make a living at it?"

He turned back to me and half leaned, half sat, on the kitchen table. "Everything takes time," he said, "and—well, yes, sure, I can make a living at it. But what I don't seem to be able to make you understand is that it's the only thing I want to do."

"Well, Sonny," I said gently, "you know people can't always do exactly what they *want* to do—"

"*No,* I don't know that," said Sonny, surprising me. "I think people *ought* to do what they want to do, what else are they alive for?"

"You are getting to be a big boy," I said desperately, "it's time you started thinking about your future."

"I'm thinking about my future," said Sonny, grimly. "I think about it all the time."

I gave up. I decided, if he didn't change his mind, that we could always talk about it later. "In the meantime," I said, "you got to finish school." We had already decided that he'd have to move in with Isabel and her folks. I knew this wasn't the ideal arrangement because Isabel's folks are inclined to be dicty[2] and they hadn't especially wanted Isabel to marry me. But I didn't know what else to do. "And we have to get you fixed up at Isabel's."

There was a long silence. He moved from the kitchen table to the window. "That's a terrible idea. You know it yourself."

"Do you have a *better* idea?"

He just walked up and down the kitchen for a minute. He was as tall as I was. He had started to shave. I suddenly had the feeling that I didn't know him at all.

---

[2]Snobbish.

He stopped at the kitchen table and picked up my cigarettes. Looking at me with a kind of mocking, amused defiance, he put one between his lips. "You mind?"

"You smoking already?"

He lit the cigarette and nodded, watching me through the smoke. "I just wanted to see if I'd have the courage to smoke in front of you." He grinned and blew a great cloud of smoke to the ceiling. "It was easy." He looked at my face. "Come on, now. I bet you was smoking at my age, tell the truth."

I didn't say anything but the truth was on my face, and he laughed. But now there was something very strained in his laugh. "Sure. And I bet that ain't all you was doing."

He was frightening me a little. "Cut the crap," I said. "We already decided that you was going to go and live at Isabel's. Now what's got into you all of a sudden?"

"*You* decided it," he pointed out. "*I* didn't decide nothing." He stopped in front of me, leaning against the stove, arms loosely folded. "Look, brother. I don't want to stay in Harlem no more, I really don't." He was very earnest. He looked at me, then over toward the kitchen window. There was something in his eyes I'd never seen before, some thoughtfulness, some worry all his own. He rubbed the muscle of one arm. "It's time I was getting out of here."

"Where do you want to *go*, Sonny?"

"I want to join the army. Or the navy, I don't care. If I say I'm old enough, they'll believe me."

Then I got mad. It was because I was so scared. "You must be crazy. You goddamn fool, what the hell do you want to go and join the *army* for?"

"I just told you. To get out of Harlem."

"Sonny, you haven't even finished *school*. And if you really want to be a musician, how do you expect to study if you're in the *army?*"

He looked at me, trapped, and in anguish. "There's ways. I might be able to work out some kind of deal. Anyway, I'll have the G.I. Bill when I come out."

"*If* you come out." We stared at each other. "Sonny, please. Be reasonable. I know the setup is far from perfect. But we got to do the best we can."

"I ain't learning nothing in school," he said. "Even when I go." He turned away from me and opened the window and threw his cigarette out into the narrow alley. I watched his back. "At least, I ain't learning nothing you'd want me to learn." He slammed the window so hard I thought the glass would fly out, and turned back to me. "And I'm sick of the stink of these garbage cans!"

"Sonny," I said, "I know how you feel, but if you don't finish school now, you're going to be sorry later that you didn't." I grabbed him by the shoulders. "And you only got another year. It ain't so bad. And I'll come back and I swear I'll help you do *whatever* you want to do. Just try to put up with it till I come back. Will you please do that? For me?"

He didn't answer and he wouldn't look at me.

"Sonny. You hear me?"

He pulled away. "I hear you. But you never hear anything *I* say."

I didn't know what to say to that. He looked out of the window and then back at me. "OK," he said, and sighed. "I'll try."

Then I said, trying to cheer him up a little, "They got a piano at Isabel's. You can practice on it."

And as a matter of fact, it did cheer him up for a minute. "That's right," he said to himself. "I forgot that." His face relaxed a little. But the worry, the thoughtfulness, played on it still, the way shadows play on a face which is staring into the fire.

But I thought I'd never hear the end of that piano. At first, Isabel would write me, saying how nice it was that Sonny was so serious about his music and how, as soon as he came in from school, or wherever he had been when he was supposed to be at school, he went straight to that piano and stayed there until suppertime. And, after supper, he went back to that piano and stayed there until everybody went to bed. He was at the piano all day Saturday and all day Sunday. Then he bought a record player and started playing records. He'd play one record over and over again, all day long sometimes, and he'd improvise along with it on the piano. Or he'd play one section of the record, one chord, one change, one progression, then he'd do it on the piano. Then back to the record. Then back to the piano.

Well, I really don't know how they stood it. Isabel finally confessed that it wasn't like living with a person at all, it was like living with sound. And the sound didn't make any sense to her, didn't make any sense to any of them—naturally. They began, in a way, to be afflicted by this presence that was living in their home. It was as though Sonny were some sort of god, or monster. He moved in an atmosphere which wasn't like theirs at all. They fed him and he ate, he washed himself, he walked in and out of their door; he certainly wasn't nasty or unpleasant or rude, Sonny isn't any of those things; but it was as though he were all wrapped up in some cloud, some fire, some vision all his own; and there wasn't any way to reach him.

At the same time, he wasn't really a man yet, he was still a child, and they had to watch out for him in all kinds of ways. They certainly couldn't throw him out. Neither did they dare to make a great scene about that piano because even they dimly sensed, as I sensed, from so many thousands of miles away, that Sonny was at that piano playing for his life.

But he hadn't been going to school. One day a letter came from the school board and Isabel's mother got it—there had, apparently, been other letters but Sonny had torn them up. This day, when Sonny came in, Isabel's mother showed him the letter and asked where he'd been spending his time. And she finally got it out of him that he'd been down in Greenwich Village, with musicians and other characters, in a white girls' apartment. And this scared her and she started to scream at him and what came up, once she began—though she denies it to this day—was what sacrifices they were making to give Sonny a decent home and how little he appreciated it.

Sonny didn't play the piano that day. By evening, Isabel's mother had calmed down but then there was the old man to deal with, and Isabel herself. Isabel says she did her best to be calm but she broke down and started crying. She says she just watched Sonny's face. She could tell, by watching him, what was happening with him. And what was happening was that they penetrated his cloud, they had reached him. Even if their fingers had been a thousand times more gentle than human fingers ever are, he could hardly help feeling that they had stripped him naked and were spitting on that nakedness. For he also had to see that his presence, that music, which was life or death to him, had been torture for them and that they had endured it, not at all for his sake, but only for mine. And Sonny couldn't take that. He can take it a little better today than he could then but he's still not very good at it and, frankly, I don't know anybody who is.

The silence of the next few days must have been louder than the sound of all the music ever played since time began. One morning, before she went to work,

Isabel was in his room for something and she suddenly realized that all of his records were gone. And she knew for certain that he was gone. And he was. He went as far as the navy would carry him. He finally sent me a postcard from some place in Greece and that was the first I knew that Sonny was still alive. I didn't see him any more until we were both back in New York and the war had long been over.

He was a man by then, of course, but I wasn't willing to see it. He came by the house from time to time, but we fought almost every time we met. I didn't like the way he carried himself, loose and dreamlike all the time, and I didn't like his friends, and his music seemed to be merely an excuse for the life he led. It sounded just that weird and disordered.

Then we had a fight, a pretty awful fight, and I didn't see him for months. By and by I looked him up, where he was living, in a furnished room in the Village, and I tried to make it up. But there were lots of other people in the room and Sonny just lay on his bed, and he wouldn't come downstairs with me, and he treated these other people as though they were his family and I weren't. So I got mad and then he got mad, and then I told him that he might just as well be dead as live the way he was living. Then he stood up and he told me not to worry about him any more in life, that he *was* dead as far as I was concerned. Then he pushed me to the door and the other people looked on as though nothing were happening, and he slammed the door behind me. I stood in the hallway, staring at the door. I heard somebody laugh in the room and then the tears came to my eyes. I started down the steps, whistling to keep from crying, I kept whistling to myself, *You going to need me, baby, one of these cold, rainy days.*

I read about Sonny's trouble in the spring. Little Grace died in the fall. She was a beautiful little girl. But she only lived a little over two years. She died of polio and she suffered. She had a slight fever for a couple of days, but it didn't seem like anything and we just kept her in bed. And we would certainly have called the doctor, but the fever dropped, she seemed to be all right. So we thought it had just been a cold. Then, one day, she was up, playing, Isabel was in the kitchen fixing lunch for the two boys when they'd come in from school, and she heard Grace fall down in the living room. When you have a lot of children you don't always start running when one of them falls, unless they start screaming or something. And, this time, Grace was quiet. Yet, Isabel says that when she heard that *thump* and then that silence, something happened in her to make her afraid. And she ran to the living room and there was little Grace on the floor, all twisted up, and the reason she hadn't screamed was that she couldn't get her breath. And when she did scream, it was the worst sound, Isabel says, that she'd ever heard in all her life, and she still hears it sometimes in her dreams. Isabel will sometimes wake me up with a low, moaning, strangled sound and I have to be quick to awaken her and hold her to me and where Isabel is weeping against me seems a mortal wound.

I think I may have written Sonny the very day that little Grace was buried. I was sitting in the living room in the dark, by myself, and I suddenly thought of Sonny. My trouble made his real.

One Saturday afternoon, when Sonny had been living with us, or, anyway, been in our house, for nearly two weeks, I found myself wandering aimlessly about the living room, drinking from a can of beer, and trying to work up the courage to search Sonny's room. He was out, he was usually out whenever I was home, and Isabel had taken the children to see their grandparents. Suddenly I was standing still in front of the living room window, watching Seventh Avenue. The idea of searching Sonny's room made me still. I scarcely dared to admit to myself what I'd be searching for. I didn't know what I'd do if I found it. Or if I didn't.

On the sidewalk across from me, near the entrance to a barbecue joint, some people were holding an old-fashioned revival meeting. The barbecue cook, wearing a dirty white apron, his conked hair reddish and metallic in the pale sun, and a cigarette between his lips, stood in the doorway, watching them. Kids and older people paused in their errands and stood there, along with some older men and a couple of very tough-looking women who watched everything that happened on the avenue, as though they owned it, or were maybe owned by it. Well, they were watching this, too. The revival was being carried on by three sisters in black, and a brother. All they had were their voices and their Bibles and a tambourine. The brother was testifying and while he testified two of the sisters stood together, seeming to say, amen, and the third sister walked around with the tambourine outstretched and a couple of people dropped coins into it. Then the brother's testimony ended and the sister who had been taking up the collection dumped the coins into her palm and transferred them to the pocket of her long black robe. Then she raised both hands, striking the tambourine against the air, and then against one hand, and she started to sing. And the two other sisters and the brother joined in.

It was strange, suddenly, to watch, though I had been seeing these street meetings all my life. So, of course, had everybody else down there. Yet, they paused and watched and listened and I stood still at the window. *"'Tis the old ship of Zion,"* they sang, and the sister with the tambourine kept a steady, jangling beat, *"it has rescued many a thousand!"* Not a soul under the sound of their voices was hearing this song for the first time, not one of them had been rescued. Nor had they seen much in the way of rescue work being done around them. Neither did they especially believe in the holiness of the three sisters and the brother, they knew too much about them, knew where they lived, and how. The woman with the tambourine, whose voice dominated the air, whose face was bright with joy, was divided by very little from the woman who stood watching her, a cigarette between her heavy, chapped lips, her hair a cuckoo's nest, her face scarred and swollen from many beatings, and her black eyes glittering like coal. Perhaps they both knew this, which was why, when, as rarely, they addressed each other, they addressed each other as Sister. As the singing filled the air the watching, listening faces underwent a change, the eyes focusing on something within; the music seemed to soothe a poison out of them; and time seemed, nearly, to fall away from the sullen, belligerent, battered faces, as though they were fleeing back to their first condition, while dreaming of their last. The barbecue cook half shook his head and smiled, and dropped his cigarette and disappeared into his joint. A man fumbled in his pockets for change and stood holding it in his hand impatiently, as though he had just remembered a pressing appointment further up the avenue. He looked furious. Then I saw Sonny, standing on the edge of the crowd. He was carrying a wide, flat notebook with a green cover, and it made him look, from where I was standing, almost like a schoolboy. The coppery sun brought out the copper in his skin, he was very faintly smiling, standing very still. Then the singing stopped, the tambourine turned into a collection plate again. The furious man dropped in his coins and vanished, so did a couple of the women, and Sonny dropped some change in the plate, looking directly at the woman with a little smile. He started across the avenue, toward the house. He has a slow, loping walk, something like the way Harlem hipsters walk, only he's imposed on this his own half-beat. I had never really noticed it before.

I stayed at the window, both relieved and apprehensive. As Sonny disappeared from my sight, they began singing again. And they were still singing when his key turned in the lock.

"Hey," he said.

"Hey, yourself. You want some beer?"

"No. Well, maybe." But he came up to the window and stood beside me, looking out. "What a warm voice," he said.

They were singing *If I could only hear my mother pray again!*

"Yes," I said, "and she can sure beat that tambourine."

"But what a terrible song," he said, and laughed. He dropped his notebook on the sofa and disappeared into the kitchen. "Where's Isabel and the kids?"

"I think they went to see their grandparents. You hungry?"

"No." He came back into the living room with his can of beer. "You want to come some place with me tonight?"

I sensed, I don't know how, that I couldn't possibly say no. "Sure. Where?"

He sat down on the sofa and picked up his notebook and started leafing through it. "I'm going to sit in with some fellows in a joint in the Village."

"You mean, you're going to play, tonight?"

"That's right." He took a swallow of his beer and moved back, to the window. He gave me a sidelong look. "If you can stand it."

"I'll try," I said.

He smiled to himself and we both watched as the meeting across the way broke up. The three sisters and the brother, heads bowed, were singing *God be with you till we meet again.* The faces around them were very quiet. Then the song ended. The small crowd dispersed. We watched the three women and the lone man walk slowly up the avenue.

"When she was singing before," said Sonny, abruptly, "her voice reminded me for a minute of what heroin feels like sometimes—when it's in your veins. It makes you feel sort of warm and cool at the same time. And distant. And— and sure." He sipped his beer, very deliberately not looking at me. I watched his face. "It makes you feel—in control. Sometimes you've got to have that feeling."

"Do you?" I sat down slowly in the easy chair.

"Sometimes." He went to the sofa and picked up his notebook again. "Some people do."

"In order," I asked, "to play?" And my voice was very ugly, full of contempt and anger.

"Well"—he looked at me with great, troubled eyes, as though, in fact, he hoped his eyes would tell me things he could never otherwise say—"they *think* so. And *if* they think so—!"

"And what do *you* think?" I asked.

He sat on the sofa and put his can of beer on the floor. "I don't know," he said, and I couldn't be sure if he were answering my question or pursuing his thoughts. His face didn't tell me. "It's not so much to *play*. It's to *stand* it, to be able to make it at all. On any level." He frowned and smiled: "In order to keep from shaking to pieces."

"But these friends of yours," I said, "they seem to shake themselves to pieces pretty goddamn fast."

"Maybe." He played with the notebook. And something told me that I should curb my tongue, that Sonny was doing his best to talk, that I should listen. "But of course you only know the ones that've gone to pieces. Some don't—or at least they haven't *yet* and that's just about all *any* of us can say." He paused. "And then there are some who just live, really, in hell, and they know it and they see what's happening, and they go right on. I don't know." He sighed, dropped the notebook, folded his arms. "Some guys, you can tell from the way they play, they on something *all* the time. And you can see that, well, it makes something real for them. But of course," he picked up his beer from the floor and sipped it and put the can down again, "they *want* to, too, you've got to see that. Even some of them that say they don't—*some*, not all."

"And what about you?" I asked—I couldn't help it. "What about you? Do *you* want to?"

He stood up and walked to the window and remained silent for a long time. Then he sighed. "Me," he said. Then: "While I was downstairs before, on my way here, listening to that woman sing, it struck me all of a sudden how much suffering she must have had to go through—to sing like that. It's *repulsive* to think you have to suffer that much."

I said: "But there's no way not to suffer—is there, Sonny?"

"I believe not," he said and smiled, "but that's never stopped anyone from trying." He looked at me. "Has it?" I realized, with this mocking look, that there stood between us, forever, beyond the power of time or forgiveness, the fact that I had held silence—so long!—when he had needed human speech to help him. He turned back to the window. "No, there's no way not to suffer. But you try all kinds of ways to keep from drowning in it, to keep on top of it, and to make it seem—well, like *you.* Like you did something, all right, and now you're suffering for it. You know?" I said nothing. "Well you know," he said, impatiently, "why *do* people suffer? Maybe it's better to do something to give it a reason, *any* reason."

"But we just agreed," I said, "that there's no way not to suffer. Isn't it better, then, just to—take it?"

"But nobody just takes it," Sonny cried, "that's what I'm telling you! *Everybody* tries not to. You're just hung up on the *way* some people try—it's not *your* way!"

The hair on my face began to itch, my face felt wet. "That's not true," I said, "that's not true. I don't give a damn what other people do, I don't even care how they suffer. I just care how *you* suffer." And he looked at me. "Please believe me," I said. "I don't want to see you—die—trying not to suffer."

"I won't," he said, flatly, "die trying not to suffer. At least, not any faster than anybody else."

"But there's no need," I said, trying to laugh, "is there? in killing yourself."

I wanted to say more, but I couldn't. I wanted to talk about will power and how life could be—well, beautiful. I wanted to say that it was all within; but was it? or, rather, wasn't that exactly the trouble? And I wanted to promise that I would never fail him again. But it would all have sounded—empty words and lies.

So I made the promise to myself and prayed that I would keep it.

"It's terrible sometimes, inside," he said, "that's what's the trouble. You walk these streets, black and funky and cold, and there's not really a living ass to talk to, and there's nothing shaking, and there's no way of getting it out—that storm inside. You can't talk it and you can't make love with it, and when you finally try to get with it and play it, you realize *nobody's* listening. So *you've* got to listen. You got to find a way to listen."

And then he walked away from the window and sat on the sofa again, as though all the wind had suddenly been knocked out of him. "Sometimes you'll do *anything* to play, even cut your mother's throat." He laughed and looked at me. "Or your brother's." Then he sobered. "Or your own." Then: "Don't worry. I'm all right now and I think I'll *be* all right. But I can't forget—where I've been. I don't mean just the physical place I've been, I mean where I've *been*. And *what* I've been."

"What have you been, Sonny?" I asked.

He smiled—but sat sideways on the sofa, his elbow resting on the back, his fingers playing with his mouth and chin, not looking at me. "I've been something I didn't recognize, didn't know I could be. Didn't know anybody could be." He stopped, looking inward, looking helplessly young, looking old. "I'm not talking about it now because I feel *guilty* or anything like that—maybe it would be better if I did, I don't know. Anyway, I can't really talk about it. Not to you, not to anybody," and now he turned and faced me. "Sometimes, you know and it was actually when I was most *out* of the world. I felt that I was in it, that I was *with* it, really, and I could play or I didn't really have to *play*, it just came out of me, it was there. And I don't know how I played, thinking about it now, but I know I did awful things, those times, sometimes, to people. Or it wasn't that I *did* anything to them—it was that they weren't real." He picked up the beer can; it was empty; he rolled it between his palms: "And other times—well, I needed a fix, I needed to find a place to lean, I needed to clear a space to *listen*—and I couldn't find it, and I—went crazy, I did terrible things to *me*, I was terrible *for* me." He began pressing the beer can between his hands, I watched the metal begin to give. It glittered, as he played with it, like a knife, and I was afraid he would cut himself, but I said nothing. "Oh well. I can never tell you. I was all by myself at the bottom of something, stinking and sweating and crying and shaking, and I smelled it, you know? *my* stink, and I thought I'd die if I couldn't get away from it and yet, all the same, I knew that everything I was doing was just locking me in with it. And I didn't know," he paused, still flattening the beer can, "I didn't know, I still *don't* know, something kept telling me that maybe it was good to smell your own stink, but I didn't think that *that* was what I'd been trying to do—and—who can stand it?" and he abruptly dropped the ruined beer can, looking at me with a small, still smile, and then rose, walking to the window as though it were the lodestone rock. I watched his face, he watched the avenue. "I couldn't tell you when Mama died—but the reason I wanted to leave Harlem so bad was to get away from drugs. And then, when I ran away, that's what I was running from—really. When I came back, nothing had changed, *I* hadn't changed, I was just—older." And he stopped drumming with his fingers on the windowpane. The sun had vanished, soon darkness would fall. I watched his face. "It can come again," he said, almost as though speaking to himself. Then he turned to me. "It can come again," he repeated. "I just want you to know that."

"All right," I said, at last. "So it can come again, All right."

He smiled, but the smile was sorrowful. "I had to try to tell you," he said.

"Yes," I said. "I understand that."

"You're my brother," he said, looking straight at me, and not smiling at all.

"Yes," I repeated, "yes. I understand that."

He turned back to the window, looking out. "All that hatred down there," he said, "all that hatred and misery and love. It's a wonder it doesn't blow the avenue apart."

We went to the only nightclub on a short, dark street, downtown. We squeezed through the narrow, chattering, jam-packed bar to the entrance of the big room, where the bandstand was. And we stood there for a moment, for the lights were very dim in this room and we couldn't see. Then, "Hello, boy," said a voice and an enormous black man, much older than Sonny or myself, erupted out of all that atmospheric lighting and put an arm around Sonny's shoulder. "I been sitting right here," he said, "waiting for you."

He had a big voice, too, and heads in the darkness turned toward us.

Sonny grinned and pulled a little away, and said, "Creole, this is my brother. I told you about him."

Creole shook my hand. "I'm glad to meet you, son," he said, and it was clear that he was glad to meet me *there,* for Sonny's sake. And he smiled, "You got a real musician in *your* family," and he took his arm from Sonny's shoulder and slapped him, lightly, affectionately, with the back of his hand.

"Well. Now I've heard it all," said a voice behind us. This was another musician, and a friend of Sonny's, a coal-black, cheerful-looking man, built close to the ground. He immediately began confiding to me, at the top of his lungs, the most terrible things about Sonny, his teeth gleaming like a lighthouse and his laugh coming up out of him like the beginning of an earthquake. And it turned out that everyone at the bar knew Sonny, or almost everyone; some were musicians, working there, or nearby, or not working, some were simply hangers-on, and some were there to hear Sonny play. I was introduced to all of them and they were all very polite to me. Yet, it was clear that, for them, I was only Sonny's brother. Here, I was in Sonny's world. Or, rather: his kingdom. Here, it was not even a question that his veins bore royal blood.

They were going to play soon and Creole installed me, by myself, at a table in a dark corner. Then I watched them, Creole, and the little black man, and Sonny, and the others, while they horsed around, standing just below the bandstand. The light from the bandstand spilled just a little short of them and, watching them laughing and gesturing and moving about, I had the feeling that they, nevertheless, were being most careful not to step into that circle of light too suddenly: that if they moved into the light too suddenly, without thinking, they would perish in flame. Then, while I watched, one of them, the small, black man, moved into the light and crossed the bandstand and started fooling around with his drums. Then—being funny and being, also, extremely ceremonious— Creole took Sonny by the arm and led him to the piano. A woman's voice called Sonny's name and a few hands started clapping. And Sonny, also being funny and being ceremonious, and so touched, I think, that he could have cried, but neither hiding it nor showing it, riding it like a man, grinned, and put both hands to his heart and bowed from the waist.

Creole then went to the bass fiddle and a lean, very bright-skinned brown man jumped up on the bandstand and picked up his horn. So there they were, and the atmosphere on the bandstand and in the room began to change and tighten. Someone stepped up to the microphone and announced them. Then there were all kinds of murmurs. Some people at the bar shushed others. The waitress ran around, frantically getting in the last orders, guys and chicks got closer to each other, and the lights on the bandstand, on the quartet, turned to a kind of indigo. Then they all looked different there. Creole looked about him for the last time, as though he were making certain that all his chickens were in the coop, and then he—jumped and struck the fiddle. And there they were.

All I know about music is that not many people ever really hear it. And even then, on the rare occasions when something opens within, and the music enters, what we mainly hear, or hear corroborated, are personal, private, vanishing evocations. But the man who creates the music is hearing something else, is dealing with the roar rising from the void and imposing order on it as it hits the air. What is evoked in him, then, is of another order, more terrible because it has no words, and triumphant, too, for that same reason. And his triumph, when he triumphs, is ours. I just watched Sonny's face. His face was troubled, he was working hard, but he wasn't with it. And I had the feeling that, in a way, everyone on the bandstand was waiting for him, both waiting for him and pushing him along. But as I began to watch Creole, I realized that it was Creole who held them all back. He had them on a short rein. Up there, keeping the beat with his whole body, wailing on the fiddle, with his eyes half closed, he was listening to everything, but he was listening to Sonny. He was having a dialogue with Sonny. He wanted Sonny to leave the shoreline and strike out for the deep water. He was Sonny's witness that deep water and drowning were not the same thing—he had been there, and he knew. And he wanted Sonny to know. He was waiting for Sonny to do the things on the keys which would let Creole know that Sonny was in the water.

And, while Creole listened, Sonny moved, deep within, exactly like someone in torment. I had never before thought of how awful the relationship must be between the musician and his instrument. He has to fill it, this instrument, with the breath of life, his own. He has to make it do what he wants it to do. And a piano is just a piano. It's made out of so much wood and wires and little hammers and big ones, and ivory. While there's only so much you can do with it, the only way to find this out is to try; to try and make it do everything.

And Sonny hadn't been near a piano for over a year. And he wasn't on much better terms with his life, not the life that stretched before him now. He and the piano stammered, started one way, got scared, stopped; started another way, panicked, marked time, started again; then seemed to have found a direction, panicked again, got stuck. And the face I saw on Sonny I'd never seen before. Everything had been burned out of it, and, at the same time, things usually hidden were being burned in, by the fire and fury of the battle which was occurring in him up there.

Yet, watching Creole's face as they neared the end of the first set, I had the feeling that something had happened, something I hadn't heard. Then they finished, there was scattered applause, and then, without an instant's warning, Creole started into something else, it was almost sardonic, it was *Am I Blue.* And, as though he commanded, Sonny began to play. Something began to happen. And Creole let out the reins. The dry, low, black man said something awful on the drums, Creole answered, and the drums talked back. Then the horn insisted, sweet and high, slightly detached perhaps, and Creole listened, commenting now and then, dry, and driving, beautiful and calm and old. Then they all came together again, and Sonny was part of the family again. I could tell this from his face. He seemed to have found, right there beneath his fingers, a damn brand-new piano. It seemed that he couldn't get over it. Then, for awhile, just being happy with Sonny, they seemed to be agreeing with him that brand-new pianos certainly were a gas.

Then Creole stepped forward to remind them that what they were playing was the blues. He hit something in all of them, he hit something in me, myself, and the music tightened and deepened, apprehension began to beat the air. Creole began to tell us what the blues were all about. They were not about anything very new. He and his boys up there were keeping it new, at the risk of ruin, destruction, madness, and death, in order to find new ways to make us listen. For, while the tale of how we suffer, and how we are delighted, and how we may triumph is never new, it always must be heard. There isn't any other tale to tell, it's the only light we've got in all this darkness.

And this tale, according to that face, that body, those strong hands on those strings, has another aspect in every country, and a new depth in every generation. Listen, Creole seemed to be saying, listen. Now these are Sonny's blues. He made the little black man on the drums know it, and the bright, brown man on the horn. Creole wasn't trying any longer to get Sonny in the water. He was wishing him Godspeed. Then he stepped back, very slowly, filling the air with the immense suggestion that Sonny speak for himself.

Then they all gathered around Sonny and Sonny played. Every now and again one of them seemed to say, amen. Sonny's fingers filled the air with life, his life. But that life contained so many others. And Sonny went all the way back, he really began with the spare, flat statement of the opening phrase of the song. Then he began to make it his. It was very beautiful because it wasn't hurried and it was no longer a lament. I seemed to hear with what burning he had made it his, with what burning we had yet to make it ours, how we could cease lamenting. Freedom lurked around us and I understood, at last, that he could help us to be free if we would listen, that he would never be free until we did. Yet, there was no battle in his face now. I heard what he had gone through, and would continue to go through until he came to rest in earth. He had made it his: that long line, of which we knew only Mama and Daddy. And he was giving it back, as everything must be given back, so that, passing through death, it can live forever. I saw my mother's face again, and felt, for the first time, how the stones of the road she had walked on must have bruised her feet. I saw the moonlit road where my father's brother died. And it brought something else back to me, and carried me past it, I saw my little girl again and felt Isabel's tears again, and I felt my own tears begin to rise. And I was yet aware that this was only a moment, that the world waited outside, as hungry as a tiger, and that trouble stretched above us, longer than the sky.

Then it was over. Creole and Sonny let out their breath, both soaking wet, and grinning. There was a lot of applause and some of it was real. In the dark, the girl came by and I asked her to take drinks to the bandstand. There was a long pause, while they talked up there in the indigo light and after awhile I saw the girl put a Scotch and milk on top of the piano for Sonny. He didn't seem to notice it, but just before they started playing again he sipped from it and looked toward me, and nodded. Then he put it back on top of the piano. For me, then, as they began to play again, it glowed and shook above my brother's head like the very cup of trembling.

1965

Flannery O'Connor   *1925–1964*

Flannery O'Connor's fiction presents what she called the "sacramental view of life," a perspective usually developed out of antitheses. Her characters confront a world of violence and unexplained evil, against which none of the traditional virtues of sincerity, hard work, and foresight avail.

Her style is noted for its simplicity, wit, and masterful reproduction of the colloquial speech of her native South. She was born in Savannah, Georgia, and grew up in the small town of Milledgeville, where she lived until she died, aged thirty-eight. She attended the Women's College of Georgia and while in college published a number of short stories. She then studied in the writer's program at the State University of Iowa, receiving an M.F.A. in 1947.

Flannery O'Connor's fiction is peopled with characters who have been described as haunted and grotesque, physical and emotional freaks who embrace a single and ferocious truth. They play out their lives against the backgrounds of the deepest, darkest South as in her novel Wise Blood *(1952), in which she used the setting of rural Tennessee to examine the character of a backwoods preacher both innocent and demonic, victim and assailant, who created a church without Christ, where violence substituted for religious faith.*

She is best known for short stories that exhibit an ironic, unsentimental acceptance of the human condition. They are filled with wry comedy and examples of satanic evil, and they are often concerned with what she called "the redemptive act" and a pervading "sense of Mystery which cannot be accounted for by human formula."

FURTHER READING: *Flannery O'Connor, The Complete Stories,* 1971; *The Habit of Being, Letters of Flannery O'Connor,* ed. S. Fitzgerald, 1979; C. Martin, *The True Country, Themes in the Fiction of Flannery O'Connor,* 1969; J. Hendin, *The World of Flannery O'Connor,* 1970; K. Seeley, *Flannery O'Connor, The Voice of the Peacock,* 1971; L. Driskell and J. Brittain, *The Eternal Crossroads, The Art of Flannery O'Connor,* 1971; M. Orvell, *Invisible Parade, The Fiction of Flannery O'Connor,* 1972; G. Muller, *Nightmares and Visions, Flannery O'Connor and the Catholic Grotesque,* 1972; D. Eggenschwiler, *The Christian Humanism of Flannery O'Connor,* 1972; D. Walters, *Flannery O'Connor,* 1973; M. Stephens, *The Question of Flannery O'Connor,* 1973; J. May, *The Pruning Word, The Parables of Flannery O'Connor,* 1976; B. McKenzie, *Flannery O'Connor's Georgia,* 1980; G. Schloss, *Flannery O'Connor's Dark Comedies,* 1980; F. Asals, *Flannery O'Connor, The Imagination of Extremity,* 1982; *Critical Essays on Flannery O'Connor,* eds. M. Friedman and B. Clark, 1985; E. Kessler, *Flannery O'Connor and the Language of Apocalypse,* 1986; J. Desmond, *Rise Sons, Flannery O'Connor's Vision of History,* 1987.

TEXT: *A Good Man Is Hard to Find,* 1955.

A GOOD MAN IS HARD TO FIND

The grandmother didn't want to go to Florida. She wanted to visit some of her connections in east Tennessee and she was seizing at every chance to change Bailey's mind. Bailey was the son she lived with, her only boy. He was sitting on the edge of his chair at the table, bent over the orange sports section of the *Journal.* "Now look here, Bailey," she said, "see here, read this," and she stood with one hand on her thin hip and the other rattling the newspaper at his bald head. "Here this fellow that calls himself the Misfit is aloose from the Federal Pen and headed toward Florida and you read here what it says he did to these people. Just you read it. I wouldn't take my children in any direction with a criminal like that aloose in it. I couldn't answer to my conscience if I did."

Bailey didn't look up from his reading so she wheeled around then and faced the children's mother, a young woman in slacks, whose face was as broad and innocent as a cabbage and was tied around with a green head-kerchief that had two points on the top like rabbit's ears. She was sitting on the sofa, feeding the baby his apricots out of a jar. "The children have been to Florida before," the old lady said. "You ought to take them somewhere else for a change so they would see different parts of the world and be broad. They never have been to east Tennessee."

The children's mother didn't seem to hear but the eight-year-old boy, John Wesley, a stocky child with glasses, said, "If you don't want to go to Florida, why dontcha stay at home?" He and the little girl, June Star, were reading the funny papers on the floor.

"She wouldn't stay at home to be queen for a day," June Star said without raising her yellow head.

"Yes and what would you do if this fellow, The Misfit, caught you?" the grandmother asked.

"I'd smack his face," John Wesley said.

"She wouldn't stay at home for a million bucks," June Star said. "Afraid she'd miss something. She has to go everywhere we go."

"All right, Miss," the grandmother said. "Just remember that the next time you want me to curl your hair."

June Star said her hair was naturally curly.

The next morning the grandmother was the first one in the car, ready to go. She had her big black valise that looked like the head of a hippopotamus in one corner, and underneath it she was hiding a basket with Pitty Sing, the cat, in it. She didn't intend for the cat to be left alone in the house for three days because he would miss her too much and she was afraid he might brush against one of the gas burners and accidentally asphyxiate himself. Her son, Bailey, didn't like to arrive at a motel with a cat.

She sat in the middle of the back seat with John Wesley and June Star on either side of her. Bailey and the children's mother and the baby sat in front and they left Atlanta at eight forty-five with the mileage on the car at 55890. The grandmother wrote this down because she thought it would be interesting to say how many miles they had been when they got back. It took them twenty minutes to reach the outskirts of the city.

The old lady settled herself comfortably, removing her white cotton gloves and putting them up with her purse on the shelf in front of the back window. The children's mother still had on slacks and still had her head tied up in a green kerchief, but the grandmother had on a navy blue straw sailor hat with a bunch of white violets on the brim and a navy blue dress with a small white dot in the print. Her collars and cuffs were white organdy trimmed with lace and at her neckline she had pinned a purple spray of cloth violets containing a sachet. In case of an accident, anyone seeing her dead on the highway would know at once that she was a lady.

She said she thought it was going to be a good day for driving, neither too hot nor too cold, and she cautioned Bailey that the speed limit was fifty-five miles an hour and that the patrolmen hid themselves behind billboards and small clumps of trees and sped out after you before you had a chance to slow down. She pointed out interesting details of the scenery: Stone Mountain; the blue granite that in some places came up to both sides of the highway; the brilliant red clay banks slightly streaked with purple; and the various crops that made rows of green lace-work on the ground. The trees were full of silver-white sunlight and the meanest of them sparkled. The children were reading comic magazines and their mother had gone back to sleep.

"Let's go through Georgia fast so we won't have to look at it much," John Wesley said.

"If I were a little boy," said the grandmother, "I wouldn't talk about my native state that way. Tennessee has the mountains and Georgia has the hills."

"Tennessee is just a hillbilly dumping ground," John Wesley said, "and Georgia is a lousy state too."

"You said it," June Star said.

"In my time," said the grandmother, folding her thin veined fingers, "children were more respectful of their native states and their parents and everything else. People did right then. Oh look at the cute little pickaninny!" she said and pointed to a Negro child standing in the door of a shack. "Wouldn't that make a picture, now?" she asked and they all turned and looked at the little Negro out of the back window. He waved.

"He didn't have any britches on," June Star said.

"He probably didn't have any," the grandmother explained. "Little niggers in the country don't have things like we do. If I could paint, I'd paint that picture," she said.

The children exchanged comic books.

The grandmother offered to hold the baby and the children's mother passed him over the front seat to her. She set him on her knee and bounced him and told him about the things they were passing. She rolled her eyes and screwed up her mouth and stuck her leathery thin face into his smooth bland one. Occasionally he gave her a faraway smile. They passed a large cotton field with five or six graves fenced in the middle of it, like a small island. "Look at the graveyard!" the grandmother said, pointing it out. "That was the old family burying ground. That belonged to the plantation."

"Where's the plantation?" John Wesley asked.

"Gone With the Wind," said the grandmother. "Ha. Ha."

When the children finished all the comic books they had brought, they opened the lunch and ate it. The grandmother ate a peanut butter sandwich and an olive and would not let the children throw the box and the paper napkins out the window. When there was nothing else to do they played a game by choosing a cloud and making the other two guess what shape it suggested. John Wesley took one the shape of a cow and June Star guessed a cow and John Wesley said, no, an automobile, and June Star said he didn't play fair, and they began to slap each other over the grandmother.

The grandmother said she would tell them a story if they would keep quiet. When she told a story, she rolled her eyes and waved her head and was very dramatic. She said once when she was a maiden lady she had been courted by a Mr. Edgar Atkins Teagarden from Jasper, Georgia. She said he was a very good-looking man and a gentleman and that he brought her a watermelon every Saturday afternoon with his initials cut in it, E. A. T. Well, one Saturday, she said, Mr. Teagarden brought the watermelon and there was nobody at home and he left it on the front porch and returned in his buggy to Jasper, but she never got the watermelon, she said, because a nigger boy ate it when he saw the initials, E. A. T.! This story tickled John Wesley's funny bone and he giggled and giggled but June Star didn't think it was any good. She said she wouldn't marry a man that just brought her a watermelon on Saturday. The grandmother said she would have done well to marry Mr. Teagarden because he was a gentleman and had bought Coca-Cola stock when it first came out and that he had died only a few years ago, a very wealthy man.

They stopped at The Tower for barbecued sandwiches. The Tower was a part stucco and part wood filling station and dance hall set in a clearing outside of Timothy. A fat man named Red Sammy Butts ran it and there were signs stuck here and there on the building and for miles up and down the highway saying, TRY RED SAMMY'S FAMOUS BARBECUE. NONE LIKE FAMOUS RED SAMMY'S! RED SAM! THE FAT BOY WITH THE HAPPY LAUGH. A VETERAN! RED SAMMY'S YOUR MAN!

Red Sammy was lying on the bare ground outside The Tower with his head under a truck while a gray monkey about a foot high, chained to a small chinaberry tree, chattered nearby. The monkey sprang back into the tree and got on the highest limb as soon as he saw the children jump out of the car and run toward him.

Inside, The Tower was a long dark room with a counter at one end and tables at the other and dancing space in the middle. They all sat down at a board table next to the nickelodeon and Red Sam's wife, a tall burnt-brown woman with hair and eyes lighter than her skin, came and took their order. The children's mother put a dime in the machine and played "The Tennessee Waltz," and the grandmother said that tune always made her want to dance. She asked Bailey if he would like to dance but he only glared at her. He didn't have a naturally sunny disposition like she did and trips made him nervous. The grandmother's brown eyes were very bright. She swayed her head from side to side and pretended she was dancing in her chair. June Star said play something she could tap to so the children's mother put in another dime and played a fast number and June Star stepped out onto the dance floor and did her tap routine.

"Ain't she cute?" Red Sam's wife said, leaning over the counter. "Would you like to come be my little girl?"

"No I certainly wouldn't," June Star said. "I wouldn't live in a broken-down place like this for a million bucks!" and she ran back to the table.

"Ain't she cute?" the woman repeated, stretching her mouth politely.

"Aren't you ashamed?" hissed the grandmother.

Red Sam came in and told his wife to quit lounging on the counter and hurry up with these people's order. His khaki trousers reached just to his hip bones and his stomach hung over them like a sack of meal swaying under his shirt. He came over and sat down at a table nearby and let out a combination sigh and a yodel. "You can't win," he said. "You can't win," and he wiped his sweating red face off with a gray handkerchief. "These days you don't know who to trust," he said. "Ain't that the truth?"

"People are certainly not nice like they used to be," said the grandmother.

"Two fellers come in here last week," Red Sammy said, "driving a Chrysler. It was a old beat-up car but it was a good one and these boys looked all right to me. Said they worked at the mill and you know I let them fellers charge the gas they bought? Now why did I do that?"

"Because you're a good man!" the grandmother said at once.

"Yes'm, I suppose so," Red Sam said as if he were struck with this answer.

His wife brought the orders, carrying the five plates all at once without a tray, two in each hand and one balanced on her arm. "It isn't a soul in this green world of God's that you can trust," she said. "And I don't count nobody out of that, not nobody," she repeated, looking at Red Sammy.

"Did you read about that criminal, The Misfit, that's escaped?" asked the grandmother.

"I wouldn't be a bit surprised if he didn't attact this place right here," said the woman. "If he hears about it being here, I wouldn't be none surprised to see him. If he hears it's two cent in the cash register, I wouldn't be a tall surprised if he . . ."

"That'll do," Red Sam said. "Go bring these people their Co'-Colas," and the woman went off to get the rest of the order.

"A good man is hard to find," Red Sammy said. "Everything is getting terrible. I remember the day you could go off and leave your screen door unlatched. Not no more."

He and the grandmother discussed better times. The old lady said that in her opinion Europe was entirely to blame for the way things were now. She said the way Europe acted you would think we were made of money and Red Sam said it was no use talking about it, she was exactly right. The children ran outside into the white sunlight and looked at the monkey in the lacy chinaberry tree. He was busy catching fleas on himself and biting each one carefully between his teeth as if it were a delicacy.

They drove off again into the hot afternoon. The grandmother took cat naps and woke up every few minutes with her own snoring. Outside of Toombsboro she woke up and recalled an old plantation that she had visited in this neighborhood once when she was a young lady. She said the house had six white columns across the front and that there was an avenue of oaks leading up to it and two little wooden trellis arbors on either side in front where you sat down with your suitor after a stroll in the garden. She recalled exactly which road to turn off to get to it. She knew that Bailey would not be willing to lose any time looking at an old house, but the more she talked about it, the more she wanted to see it once again and find out if the little twin arbors were still standing. "There was a secret panel in this house," she said craftily, not telling the truth but wishing that she were, "and the story went that all the family silver was hidden in it when Sherman came through but it was never found . . ."

"Hey!" John Wesley said. "Let's go see it! We'll find it! We'll poke all the woodwork and find it! Who lives there? Where do you turn off at? Hey Pop, can't we turn off there?"

"We never have seen a house with a secret panel!" June Star shrieked. "Let's go to the house with the secret panel! Hey Pop, can't we go see the house with the secret panel!"

"It's not far from here, I know," the grandmother said. "It wouldn't take over twenty minutes."

Bailey was looking straight ahead. His jaw was as rigid as a horseshoe. "No," he said.

The children began to yell and scream that they wanted to see the house with the secret panel. John Wesley kicked the back of the front seat and June Star hung over her mother's shoulder and whined desperately into her ear that they never had any fun even on their vacation, that they could never do what THEY wanted to do. The baby began to scream and John Wesley kicked the back of the seat so hard that his father could feel the blows in his kidney.

"All right!" he shouted and drew the car to a stop at the side of the road. "Will you all shut up? Will you all just shut up for one second? If you don't shut up, we won't go anywhere."

"It would be very educational for them," the grandmother murmured.

"All right," Bailey said, "but get this: this is the only time we're going to stop for anything like this. This is the one and only time."

"The dirt road that you have to turn down is about a mile back," the grandmother directed. "I marked it when we passed."

"A dirt road," Bailey groaned.

After they had turned around and were headed toward the dirt road, the grandmother recalled other points about the house, the beautiful glass over the front doorway and the candle-lamp in the hall. John Wesley said that the secret panel was probably in the fireplace.

"You can't go inside this house," Bailey said. "You don't know who lives there."

"While you all talk to the people in front, I'll run around behind and get in a window," John Wesley suggested.

"We'll all stay in the car," his mother said.

They turned onto the dirt road and the car raced roughly along in a swirl of pink dust. The grandmother recalled the times when there were no paved roads and thirty miles was a day's journey. The dirt road was hilly and there were sudden washes in it and sharp curves on dangerous embankments. All at once they would be on a hill, looking down over the blue tops of trees for miles around, then the next minute, they would be in a red depression with the dustcoated trees looking down on them.

"This place had better turn up in a minute," Bailey said, "or I'm going to turn around."

The road looked as if no one had traveled on it in months.

"It's not much farther," the grandmother said and just as she said it, a horrible thought came to her. The thought was so embarrassing that she turned red in the face and her eyes dilated and her feet jumped up, upsetting her valise in the corner. The instant the valise moved, the newspaper top she had over the basket under it rose with a snarl and Pitty Sing, the cat, sprang onto Bailey's shoulder.

The children were thrown to the floor and their mother, clutching the baby, was thrown out the door onto the ground; the old lady was thrown into the front seat. The car turned over once and landed right-side-up in a gulch off the side of the road. Bailey remained in the driver's seat with the cat—gray-striped with a broad white face and an orange nose—clinging to his neck like a caterpillar.

As soon as the children saw they could move their arms and legs, they scrambled out of the car, shouting, "We've had an ACCIDENT!" The grandmother was curled up under the dashboard, hoping she was injured so that Bailey's wrath would not come down on her all at once. The horrible thought she had had before the accident was that the house she had remembered so vividly was not in Georgia but in Tennessee.

Bailey removed the cat from his neck with both hands and flung it out the window against the side of a pine tree. Then he got out of the car and started looking for the children's mother. She was sitting against the side of a red gutted ditch, holding the screaming baby, but she only had a cut down her face and a broken shoulder. "We've had an ACCIDENT!" the children screamed in a frenzy of delight.

"But nobody's killed," June Star said with disappointment as the grandmother limped out of the car, her hat still pinned to her head but the broken front brim standing up at a jaunty angle and the violet spray hanging off the side. They all sat down in the ditch, except the children, to recover from the shock. They were all shaking.

"Maybe a car will come along," said the children's mother hoarsely.

"I believe I have injured an organ," said the grandmother, pressing her side, but no one answered her. Bailey's teeth were clattering. He had on a yellow sport shirt with bright blue parrots designed in it and his face was as yellow as the shirt. The grandmother decided that she would not mention that the house was in Tennessee.

The road was about ten feet above and they could see only the tops of the trees on the other side of it. Behind the ditch they were sitting in there were more woods, tall and dark and deep. In a few minutes they saw a car some distance away on top of a hill, coming slowly as if the occupants were watching them. The grandmother stood up and waved both arms dramatically to attract their attention. The car continued to come on slowly, disappeared around a bend and appeared again, moving even slower, on top of the hill they had gone over. It was a big black battered hearse-like automobile. There were three men in it.

It came to a stop just over them and for some minutes, the driver looked down with a steady expressionless gaze to where they were sitting, and didn't speak. Then he turned his head and muttered something to the other two and they got out. One was a fat boy in black trousers and a red sweat shirt with a silver stallion embossed on the front of it. He moved around on the right side of them and stood staring, his mouth partly open in a kind of loose grin. The other had on khaki pants and a blue striped coat and a gray hat pulled down very low, hiding most of his face. He came around slowly on the left side. Neither spoke.

The driver got out of the car and stood by the side of it, looking down at them. He was an older man than the other two. His hair was just beginning to gray and he wore silver-rimmed spectacles that gave him a scholarly look. He had a long creased face and didn't have on any shirt or undershirt. He had on blue jeans that were too tight for him and he was holding a black hat and a gun. The two boys also had guns.

"We've had an ACCIDENT!" the children screamed.

The grandmother had the peculiar feeling that the bespectacled man was someone she knew. His face was as familiar to her as if she had known him all her life but she could not recall who he was. He moved away from the car and began to come down the embankment, placing his feet carefully so that he wouldn't slip. He had on tan and white shoes and no socks, and his ankles were red and thin. "Good afternoon," he said. "I see you all had you a little spill."

"We turned over twice!" said the grandmother.

"Oncet," he corrected. "We seen it happen. Try their car and see will it run, Hiram," he said quietly to the boy with the gray hat.

"What you got that gun for?" John Wesley asked. "Whatcha gonna do with that gun?"

"Lady," the man said to the children's mother, "would you mind calling them children to sit down by you? Children make me nervous. I want all you all to sit down right together there where you're at."

"What are you telling US what to do for?" June Star asked.

Behind them the line of woods gaped like a dark open mouth. "Come here," said the mother.

"Look here now," Bailey began suddenly, "we're in a predicament! We're in . . ."

The grandmother shrieked. She scrambled to her feet and stood staring. "You're The Misfit!" she said. "I recognized you at once!"

"Yes'm," the man said, smiling slightly as if he were pleased in spite of himself to be known, "but it would have been better for all of you, lady, if you hadn't reckernized me."

Bailey turned his head sharply and said something to his mother that shocked even the children. The old lady began to cry and The Misfit reddened.

"Lady," he said, "don't you get upset. Sometimes a man says things he don't mean. I don't reckon he meant to talk to you that-away."

"You wouldn't shoot a lady, would you?" the grandmother said and removed a clean handkerchief from her cuff and began to slap at her eyes with it.

The Misfit pointed the toe of his shoe into the ground and made a little hole and then covered it up again. "I would hate to have to," he said.

"Listen," the grandmother almost screamed, "I know you're a good man. You don't look a bit like you have common blood. I know you must come from nice people!"

"Yes mam," he said, "finest people in the world." When he smiled he showed a row of strong white teeth. "God never made a finer woman than my mother and my daddy's heart was pure gold," he said. The boy with the red sweat shirt had come around behind them and was standing with his gun at his hip. The Misfit squatted down on the ground. "Watch them children, Bobby Lee," he said. "You know they make me nervous." He looked at the six of them huddled together in front of him and he seemed to be embarrassed as if he couldn't think of anything to say. "Ain't a cloud in the sky," he remarked, looking up at it. "Don't see no sun but don't see no cloud neither."

"Yes, it's a beautiful day," said the grandmother. "Listen," she said, "you shouldn't call yourself The Misfit because I know you're a good man at heart. I can just look at you and tell."

"Hush!" Bailey yelled. "Hush! Everybody shut up and let me handle this!" He was squatting in the position of a runner about to sprint forward but he didn't move.

"I pre-chate that, lady," The Misfit said and drew a little circle in the ground with the butt of his gun.

"It'll take a half a hour to fix this here car," Hiram called, looking over the raised hood of it.

"Well, first you Bobby Lee get him and that little boy to step over yonder with you," The Misfit said, pointing to Bailey and John Wesley. "The boys want to ast you something," he said to Bailey. "Would you mind stepping back in them woods there with them?"

"Listen," Bailey began, "we're in a terrible predicament! Nobody realizes what this is," and his voice cracked. His eyes were as blue and intense as the parrots in his shirt and he remained perfectly still.

The grandmother reached up to adjust her hat brim as if she were going to the woods with him but it came off in her hand. She stood staring at it and after a second she let it fall on the ground. Hiram pulled Bailey up by the arm as if he were assisting an old man. John Wesley caught hold of his father's hand and Bobby Lee followed. They went off toward the woods and just as they reached the dark edge, Bailey turned and supporting himself against a gray naked pine trunk, he shouted, "I'll be back in a minute, Mamma, wait on me!"

"Come back this instant!" his mother shrilled but they all disappeared into the woods.

"Bailey Boy!" the grandmother called in a tragic voice but she found she was looking at The Misfit squatting on the ground in front of her. "I just know you're a good man," she said desperately. "You're not a bit common!"

"Nome, I ain't a good man," The Misfit said after a second as if he had considered her statement carefully, "but I ain't the worst in the world neither. My daddy said I was a different breed of dog from my brothers and sisters.

'You know,' Daddy said, 'it's some that can live their whole life without asking about it and it's others has to know why it is, and this boy is one of the latters. He's going to be into everything!'" He put on his black hat and looked up suddenly and then away deep into the woods as if he were embarrassed again. "I'm sorry I don't have on a shirt before you ladies," he said, hunching his shoulders slightly. "We buried our clothes that we had on when we escaped and we're just making do until we can get better. We borrowed these from some folks we met," he explained.

"That's perfectly all right," the grandmother said. "Maybe Bailey has an extra shirt in his suitcase."

"I'll look and see terrectly," The Misfit said.

"Where are you taking him?" the children's mother screamed.

"Daddy was a card himself," The Misfit said. "You couldn't put anything over on him. He never got in trouble with the Authorities though. Just had the knack of handling them."

"You could be honest too if you'd only try," said the grandmother. "Think how wonderful it would be to settle down and live a comfortable life and not have to think about somebody chasing you all the time."

The Misfit kept scratching in the ground with the butt of his gun as if he were thinking about it. "Yes'm, somebody is always after you," he murmured.

The grandmother noticed how thin his shoulder blades were just behind his hat because she was standing up looking down on him. "Do you ever pray?" she asked.

He shook his head. All she saw was the black hat wiggle between his shoulder blades. "Nome," he said.

There was a pistol shot from the woods, followed closely by another. Then silence. The old lady's head jerked around. She could hear the wind move through the tree tops like a long satisfied insuck of breath. "Bailey Boy!" she called.

"I was a gospel singer for a while," The Misfit said. "I been most everything. Been in the arm service, both land and sea, at home and abroad, been twict married, been an undertaker, been with the railroads, plowed Mother Earth, been in a tornado, seen a man burnt alive oncet," and he looked up at the children's mother and the little girl who were sitting close together, their faces white and their eyes glassy. "I even seen a woman flogged," he said.

"Pray, pray," the grandmother began, "pray, pray . . ."

"I never was a bad boy that I remember of," The Misfit said in an almost dreamy voice, "but somewheres along the line I done something wrong and got sent to the penitentiary. I was buried alive," and he looked up and held her attention to him by a steady stare.

"That's when you should have started to pray," she said, "What did you do to get sent to the penitentiary that first time?"

"Turn to the right, it was a wall," The Misfit said, looking up again at the cloudless sky. "Turn to the left, it was a wall. Look up it was a ceiling, look down it was a floor. I forget what I done, lady. I set there and set there, trying to remember what it was I done and I ain't recalled it to this day. Oncet in a while, I would think it was coming to me, but it never come."

"Maybe they put you in by mistake," the old lady said vaguely.

"Nome," he said. "It wasn't no mistake. They had the papers on me."

"You must have stolen something," she said.

The Misfit sneered slightly. "Nobody had nothing I wanted," he said. "It was a head-doctor at the penitentiary said what I had done was kill my daddy but I

know that for a lie. My daddy died in nineteen ought nineteen of the epidemic
flu and I never had a thing to do with it. He was buried in the Mount Hopewell
Baptist churchyard and you can go there and see for yourself."

"If you would pray," the old lady said, "Jesus would help you."

"That's right," The Misfit said.

"Well then, why don't you pray?" she asked trembling with delight suddenly.

"I don't want no hep," he said. "I'm doing all right by myself."

Bobby Lee and Hiram came ambling back from the woods. Bobby Lee was
dragging a yellow shirt with bright blue parrots in it.

"Thow me that shirt, Bobby Lee," The Misfit said. The shirt came flying at
him and landed on his shoulder and he put it on. The grandmother couldn't
name what the shirt reminded her of. "No, lady," The Misfit said while he was
buttoning it up, "I found out the crime don't matter. You can do one thing or
you can do another, kill a man or take a tire off his car, because sooner or later
you're going to forget what it was you done and just be punished for it."

The children's mother had begun to make heaving noises as if she couldn't
get her breath. "Lady," he asked, "would you and that little girl like to step off
yonder with Bobby Lee and Hiram and join your husband?"

"Yes, thank you," the mother said faintly. Her left arm dangled helplessly
and she was holding the baby, who had gone to sleep, in the other. "Hep that
lady up, Hiram," The Misfit said as she struggled to climb out of the ditch, "and
Bobby Lee, you hold onto that little girl's hand."

"I don't want to hold hands with him," June Star said, "He reminds me of a
pig."

The fat boy blushed and laughed and caught her by the arm and pulled her
off into the woods after Hiram and her mother.

Alone with The Misfit, the grandmother found that she had lost her voice.
There was not a cloud in the sky nor any sun. There was nothing around her
but woods. She wanted to tell him that he must pray. She opened and closed
her mouth several times before anything came out. Finally she found herself
saying, "Jesus. Jesus," meaning, Jesus will help you, but the way she was saying
it, it sounded as if she might be cursing.

"Yes'm," The Misfit said as if he agreed. "Jesus thown everything off balance.
It was the same case with Him as with me except He hadn't committed any
crime and they could prove I had committed one because they had the papers
on me. Of course," he said, "they never shown me my papers. That's why I sign
myself now. I said long ago, you get you a signature and sign everything you
do and keep a copy of it. Then you'll know what you done and you can hold up
the crime to the punishment and see do they match and in the end you'll have
something to prove you ain't been treated right. I call myself The Misfit," he
said, "because I can't make what all I done wrong fit what all I gone through in
punishment."

There was a piercing scream from the woods, followed closely by a pistol
report. "Does it seem right to you, lady, that one is punished a heap and another
ain't punished at all?"

"Jesus!" the old lady cried. "You've got good blood! I know you wouldn't
shoot a lady! I know you come from nice people! Pray! Jesus, you ought not to
shoot a lady. I'll give you all the money I've got!"

"Lady," The Misfit said, looking beyond her far into the woods, "there never
was a body that give the undertaker a tip."

There were two more pistol reports and the grandmother raised her head like a parched old turkey hen crying for water and called, "Bailey Boy, Bailey Boy!" as if her heart would break.

"Jesus was the only One that ever raised the dead," The Misfit continued, "and He shouldn't have done it. He thown everything off balance. If He did what He said, then it's nothing for you to do but thow away everything and follow Him, and if He didn't, then it's nothing for you to do but enjoy the few minutes you got left the best way you can—by killing somebody or burning down his house or doing some other meanness to him. No pleasure but meanness," he said and his voice had become almost a snarl.

"Maybe He didn't raise the dead," the old lady mumbled, not knowing what she was saying and feeling so dizzy that she sank down in the ditch with her legs twisted under her.

"I wasn't there so I can't say He didn't," The Misfit said. "I wisht I had of been there," he said, hitting the ground with his fist. "It ain't right I wasn't there because if I had been there I would of known. Listen lady," he said in a high voice, "if I had of been there I would of known and I wouldn't be like I am now." His voice seemed about to crack and the grandmother's head cleared for an instant. She saw the man's face twisted close to her own as if he were going to cry and she murmured, "Why you're one of my babies. You're one of my own children!" She reached out and touched him on the shoulder. The Misfit sprang back as if a snake had bitten him and shot her three times through the chest. Then he put his gun down on the ground and took off his glasses and began to clean them.

Hiram and Bobby Lee returned from the woods and stood over the ditch, looking down at the grandmother who half sat and half lay in a puddle of blood with her legs crossed under her like a child's and her face smiling up at the cloudless sky.

Without his glasses, The Misfit's eyes were red-rimmed and pale and defense-less-looking. "Take her off and thow her where you thown the others," he said, picking up the cat that was rubbing itself against his leg.

"She was a talker, wasn't she?" Bobby Lee said, sliding down the ditch with a yodel.

"She would of been a good woman," The Misfit said, "if it had been somebody there to shoot her every minute of her life."

"Some fun!" Bobby Lee said.

"Shut up, Bobby Lee," The Misfit said. "It's no real pleasure in life."

1955

John Cheever   *1912–1982*

John Cheever was a satiric chronicler of upper-middle-class America. His ironic sketches of domestic and expatriate New Yorkers and New Englanders placed him in a literary tradition that concerns itself primarily with manners and only secondarily with morals. His prevailing interest as a writer is suggested by the title of his first collection of stories, The Way Some People Live *(1943), and he continued his portrayals of the dilemmas of American suburbia in subsequent volumes that include* The Enormous Radio (*1953*), The Housebreaker of Shady Hill (*1958*), The World of Apples (*1972*), Falconer (*1977*), *and* Oh What a Paradise it Seems (*1982*). *In Cheever country things are frequently awry. Cheever women exist in a world of faltering marriages and monumental boredom, their lives enlivened only by desperate dreams of phantom romances. Cheever men, in the manic throes of middle age, are attacked by demons and fantasies that drive them into one-man crime waves or ritualistic cross-country tours of suburban swimming pools.*

Cheever was born in New England, the locale of two of his novels, The Wapshot Chronicle (*1957*) *and* The Wapshot Scandal (*1964*), *witty stories of the social eccentricities and the latter-day disintegration of an ancient New England family. Cheever came to writing early. He published a number of sketches, entitled "Expelled," in the* New Republic *shortly after he was dismissed from prep school when he was seventeen. Since that time he wrote more than a hundred stories, most of which appeared first in the* New Yorker *and bear the stamp of that magazine's sophisticated detachment and ironic observance of prosperous and puzzled Americans. Cheever's novel,* Falconer (*1977*) *is set not in the suburbs but in a prison. Its hero is not a successful businessman but a murderer. Yet Cheever's prisoners, like his suburbanites, are constantly reduced and deflated, suffering estrangement and doomed to precarious, almost surrealistic, lives.*

FURTHER READING: L. Waldeland, *John Cheever*, 1979; *Critical Essays on John Cheever*, ed. R. Collins, 1982; S. Cheever, *Home before Dark, A Biographical Memoir of John Cheever by His Daughter*, 1984; *Conversations with John Cheever*, ed. S. Donaldson, 1987; S. Donaldson, *John Cheever*, 1988.

TEXT: *The Brigadier and the Golf Widow*, 1964.

THE SWIMMER

It was one of those midsummer Sundays when everyone sits around saying: "I *drank* too much last night." You might have heard it whispered by the parishioners leaving church, heard it from the lips of the priest himself, struggling with his cassock in the *vestiarium,* heard it from the golf links and the tennis courts, heard it from the wildlife preserve where the leader of the Audubon group was suffering from a terrible hangover. "I *drank* too much," said Donald Westerhazy. "We all *drank* too much," said Lucinda Merrill. "It must have been the wine," said Helen Westerhazy. "I *drank* too much of that claret."

This was at the edge of the Westerhazy's pool. The pool, fed by an artesian well with a high iron content, was a pale shade of green. It was a fine day. In the west there was a massive stand of cumulus cloud so like a city seen from a distance—from the bow of an approaching ship—that it might have had a name. Lisbon. Hackensack. The sun was hot. Neddy Merrill sat by the green water, one hand in it, one around a glass of gin. He was a slender man—he seemed to have the especial slenderness of youth—and while he was far from young he had slid down his banister that morning and given the bronze backside of Aphrodite on the hall table a smack, as he jogged toward the smell of coffee in his dining room. He might have been compared to a summer's day, particularly the last hours of one, and while he lacked a tennis racket or a sail bag the impression was definitely one of youth, sport, and clement weather. He had been swimming and now he was breathing deeply, stertorously as if he could gulp into his lungs the components of that moment, the heat of the sun, the intenseness of his pleasure. It all seemed to flow into his chest. His own house stood in Bullet Park, eight miles to the south, where his four beautiful daughters would have had their lunch and might be playing tennis. Then it occurred to him that by taking a dogleg to the southwest he could reach his home by water.

His life was not confining and the delight he took in this observation could not be explained by its suggestion of escape. He seemed to see, with a cartographer's eye, that string of swimming pools, that quasi-subterranean stream that curved across the county. He had made a discovery, a contribution to modern geography; he would name the stream Lucinda after his wife. He was not a practical joker nor was he a fool but he was determinedly original and had a vague and modest idea of himself as a legendary figure. The day was beautiful and it seemed to him that a long swim might enlarge and celebrate its beauty.

He took off a sweater that was hung over his shoulders and dove in. He had an inexplicable contempt for men who did not hurl themselves into pools. He swam a choppy crawl, breathing either with every stroke or every fourth stroke and counting somewhere well in the back of his mind the one-two one-two of a flutter kick. It was not a serviceable stroke for long distances but the domestication of swimming had saddled the sport with some customs and in his part of the world a crawl was customary. To be embraced and sustained by the light green water was less a pleasure, it seemed, than the resumption of a natural condition, and he would have liked to swim without trunks, but this was not possible, considering his project. He hoisted himself up on the far curb—he never used the ladder—and started across the lawn. When Lucinda asked where he was going he said he was going to swim home.

The only maps and charts he had to go by were remembered or imaginary but these were clear enough. First there were the Grahams, the Hammers, the Lears, the Howlands, and the Crosscups. He would cross Ditmar Street to the Bunkers and come, after a short portage, to the Levys, the Welchers, and the public pool in Lancaster. Then there were the Hallorans, the Sachses, the Biswangers, Shirley Adams, the Gilmartins, and the Clydes. The day was lovely, and that he lived in a world so generously supplied with water seemed like a clemency, a beneficence. His heart was high and he ran across the grass. Making his way home by an uncommon route gave him the feeling that he was a pilgrim, an explorer, a man with a destiny, and he knew that he would find friends all along the way; friends would line the banks of the Lucinda River.

He went through a hedge that separated the Westerhazy's land from the Grahams', walked under some flowering apple trees, passed the shed that housed their pump and filter, and came out at the Grahams' pool. "Why, Neddy," Mrs. Graham said, "what a marvelous surprise. I've been trying to get you on the phone all morning. Here, let me get you a drink." He saw then, like any explorer, that the hospitable customs and traditions of the natives would have to be handled with diplomacy if he was ever going to reach his destination. He did not want to mystify or seem rude to the Grahams nor did he have the time to linger there. He swam the length of their pool and joined them in the sun and was rescued, a few minutes later, by the arrival of two carloads of friends from Connecticut. During the uproarious reunions he was able to slip away. He went down by the front of the Grahams' house, stepped over a thorny hedge, and crossed a vacant lot to the Hammers'. Mrs. Hammer, looking up from her roses, saw him swim by although she wasn't quite sure who it was. The Lears heard him splashing past the open windows of their living room. The

Howlands and the Crosscups were away. After leaving the Howlands' he crossed
Ditmar Street and started for the Bunkers', where he could hear, even at that
distance, the noise of a party.

The water refracted the sound of voices and laughter and seemed to suspend
it in midair. The Bunkers' pool was on a rise and he climbed some stairs to a
terrace where twenty-five or thirty men and women were drinking. The only
person in the water was Rusty Towers, who floated there on a rubber raft. Oh
how bonny and lush were the banks of the Lucinda River! Prosperous men and
women gathered by the sapphire-colored waters while caterer's men in white
coats passed them cold gin. Overhead a red de Haviland trainer was circling
around and around and around in the sky with something like the glee of a
child in a swing. Ned felt a passing affection for the scene, a tenderness for the
gathering, as if it was something he might touch. In the distance he heard
thunder. As soon as Enid Bunker saw him she began to scream: "Oh look who's
here! What a marvelous surprise! When Lucinda said that you couldn't come I
thought I'd *die*." She made her way to him through the crowd, and when they
had finished kissing she led him to the bar, a progress that was slowed by the
fact that he stopped to kiss eight or ten other women and shake the hands of as
many men. A smiling bartender he had seen at a hundred parties gave him a
gin and tonic and he stood by the bar for a moment, anxious not to get stuck in
any conversation that would delay his voyage. When he seemed about to be
surrounded he dove in and swam close to the side to avoid colliding with Rusty's
raft. At the far end of the pool he bypassed the Tomlinsons with a broad smile
and jogged up the garden path. The gravel cut his feet but this was the only
unpleasantness. The party was confined to the pool, and as he went toward the
house he heard the brilliant, watery sound of voices fade, heard the noise of a
radio from the Bunkers' kitchen, where someone was listening to a ballgame.
Sunday afternoon. He made his way through the parked cars and down the
grassy border of their driveway to Alewives' Lane. He did not want to be seen
on the road in his bathing trunks but there was no traffic and he made the short
distance to the Levys' driveway, marked with a private property sign and a green
tube for the *New York Times*. All the doors and windows of the big house were
open but there were no signs of life; not even a dog barked. He went around
the side of the house to the pool and saw that Levys had only recently left.
Glasses and bottles and dishes of nuts were on a table at the deep end, where
there was a bathhouse or gazebo, hung with Japanese lanterns. After swimming
the pool he got himself a glass and poured a drink. It was his fourth or fifth
drink and he had swum nearly half the length of the Lucinda River. He felt
tired, clean, and pleased at that moment to be alone; pleased with everything.

It would storm. The stand of cumulus cloud—that city—had risen and darkened, and while he sat there he heard the percussiveness of thunder again. The
de Haviland trainer was still circling overhead and it seemed to Ned that he
could almost hear the pilot laugh with pleasure in the afternoon; but when there
was another peal of thunder he took off for home. A train whistle blew and he
wondered what time it had gotten to be. Four? Five? He thought of the provincial
station at that hour, where a waiter, his tuxedo concealed by a raincoat, a dwarf
with some flowers wrapped in newspaper, and a woman who had been crying
would be waiting for the local. It was suddenly growing dark; it was that moment
when the pin-headed birds seem to organize their song into some acute and
knowledgeable recognition of the storm's approach. Then there was a fine noise
of rushing water from the crown of an oak at his back, as if a spigot there had
been turned. Then the noise of fountains came from the crowns of all the tall

trees. Why did he love storms, what was the meaning of his excitement when the door sprang open and the rain wind fled rudely up the stairs, why had the simple task of shutting the windows of an old house seemed fitting and urgent, why did the first watery notes of a storm wind have for him the unmistakable sound of good news, cheer, glad tidings? Then there was an explosion, a smell of cordite, and rain lashed the Japanese lanterns that Mrs. Levy had bought in Kyoto the year before last, or was it the year before that?

He stayed in the Levys' gazebo until the storm had passed. The rain had cooled the air and he shivered. The force of the wind had stripped a maple of its red and yellow leaves and scattered them over the grass and the water. Since it was midsummer the tree must be blighted, and yet he felt a peculiar sadness at this sign of autumn. He braced his shoulders, emptied his glass, and started for the Welchers' pool. This meant crossing the Lindleys' riding ring and he was surprised to find it overgrown with grass and all the jumps dismantled. He wondered if the Lindleys had sold their horses or gone away for the summer and put them out to board. He seemed to remember having heard something about the Lindleys and their horses but the memory was unclear. On he went, barefoot through the wet grass, to the Welchers', where he found their pool was dry.

This breach in his chain of water disappointed him absurdly, and he felt like some explorer who seeks a torrential headwater and finds a dead stream. He was disappointed and mystified. It was common enough to go away for the summer but no one ever drained his pool. The Welchers had definitely gone away. The pool furniture was folded, stacked, and covered with a tarpaulin. The bathhouse was locked. All the windows of the house were shut, and when he went around to the driveway in front he saw a for-sale sign nailed to a tree. When had he last heard from the Welchers—when, that is, had he and Lucinda last regretted an invitation to dine with them. It seemed only a week or so ago. Was his memory failing or had he so disciplined it in the repression of unpleasant facts that he had damaged his sense of the truth? Then in the distance he heard the sound of a tennis game. This cheered him, cleared away all his apprehensions and let him regard the overcast sky and the cold air with indifference. This was the day that Neddy Merrill swam across the county. That was the day! He started off then for his most difficult portage.

Had you gone for a Sunday afternoon ride that day, you might have seen him, close to naked, standing on the shoulders of route 424, waiting for a chance to cross. You might have wondered if he was the victim of foul play, had his car broken down, or was he merely a fool. Standing barefoot in the deposits of the highway—beer cans, rags, and blowout patches—exposed to all kinds of ridicule, he seemed pitiful. He had known when he started that this was a part of his journey—it had been on his maps—but confronted with the lines of traffic, worming through the summery light, he found himself unprepared. He was laughed at, jeered at, a beer can was thrown at him, and he had no dignity or humor to bring to the situation. He could have gone back, back to the Wester-hazy's, where Lucinda would still be sitting in the sun. He had signed nothing, vowed nothing, pledged nothing not even to himself. Why, believing as he did, that all human obduracy was susceptible to common sense, was he unable to turn back? Why was he determined to complete his journey even if it meant putting his life in danger? At what point had this prank, this joke, this piece of horseplay become serious? He could not go back, he could not even recall with any clearness the green water at the Westerhazy's, the sense of inhaling the day's components, the friendly and relaxed voices saying that they had *drunk* too much. In the space of an hour, more or less, he covered a distance that made his return impossible.

An old man, tooling down the highway at fifteen miles an hour, let him go to the middle of the road, where there was a grass divider. Here he was exposed to the ridicule of the northbound traffic, but after ten or fifteen minutes he was able to cross. From here he had only a short walk to the Recreation Center at the edge of the Village of Lancaster, where there were some handball courts and a public pool.

The effect of the water on voices, the illusion of brilliance and suspense, was the same here as it had been at the Bunkers' but the sounds here were louder, harsher, and more shrill, and as soon as he entered the crowded enclosure he was confronted with regimentation. "ALL SWIMMERS MUST TAKE A SHOWER BEFORE USING THE POOL. ALL SWIMMERS MUST USE THE FOOTBATH. ALL SWIMMERS MUST WEAR THEIR IDENTIFICATION DISKS." He took a shower, washed his feet in a cloudy and bitter solution and made his way to the edge of the water. It stank of chlorine and looked to him like a sink. A pair of lifeguards in a pair of towers blew police whistles at what seemed to be regular intervals and abused the swimmers through a public address system. Neddy remembered the sapphire water at the Bunkers' with longing and thought that he might contaminate himself—damage his own prosperousness and charm—by swimming in this murk, but he reminded himself that he was an explorer, a pilgrim, and that this was merely a stagnant bend in the Lucinda River. He dove, scowling with distaste, into the chlorine and had to swim with his head above water to avoid collisions, but even so he was bumped into, splashed and jostled. When he got to the shallow end both lifeguards were shouting at him: "Hey, you, you without the identification disk, get outa the water." He did, but they had no way of pursuing him and he went thrugh the reek of suntan oil and chlorine out through the hurricane fence and passed the handball courts. By crossing the road he entered the wooded part of the Halloran estate. The woods were not cleared and the footing was treacherous and difficult until he reached the lawn and the clipped beech hedge that encircled their pool.

The Hallorans were friends, an elderly couple of enormous wealth who seemed to bask in the suspicion that they might be Communists. They were zealous reformers but they were not Communists, and yet when they were accused, as they sometimes were, of subversion, it seemed to gratify and excite them. Their beech hedge was yellow and he guessed this had been blighted like the Levys' maple. He called hullo, hullo, to warn the Hallorans of his approach, to palliate his invasion of their privacy. The Hallorans, for reasons that had never been explained to him, did not wear bathing suits. No explanations were in order, really. Their nakedness was a detail in their uncompromising zeal for reform and he stepped politely out of his trunks before he went through the opening in the hedge.

Mrs. Halloran, a stout woman with white hair and a serene face, was reading the *Times*. Mr. Halloran was taking beech leaves out of the water with a scoop. They seemed not surprised or displeased to see him. Their pool was perhaps the oldest in the county, a fieldstone rectangle, fed by a brook. It had no filter or pump and its waters were the opaque gold of the stream.

"I'm swimming across the county," Ned said.

"Why, I didn't know one could," exclaimed Mrs. Halloran.

"Well, I've made it from the Westerhazys'," Ned said. "That must be about four miles."

He left his trunks at the deep end, walked to the shallow end, and swam this stretch. As he was pulling himself out of the water he heard Mrs. Halloran say: "We've been *terribly* sorry to hear about all your misfortunes, Neddy."

"My misfortunes?" Ned asked. "I don't know what you mean."

"Why we heard that you'd sold the house and that your poor children . . ."

"I don't recall having sold the house," Ned said, "and the girls are at home."

"Yes," Mrs. Halloran sighed. "Yes . . ." Her voice filled the air with an unseasonable melancholy and Ned spoke briskly. "Thank you for the swim."

"Well, have a nice trip," said Mrs. Halloran.

Beyond the hedge he pulled on his trunks and fastened them. They were loose and he wondered if, during the space of an afternoon, he could have lost some weight. He was cold and he was tired and the naked Hallorans and their dark water had depressed him. The swim was too much for his strength but how could he have guessed this, sliding down the banister that morning and sitting in the Westerhazys' sun? His arms were lame. His legs felt rubbery and ached at the joints. The worst of it was the cold in his bones and the feeling that he might never be warm again. Leaves were falling down around him and he smelled woodsmoke on the wind. Who would be burning wood at this time of year?

He needed a drink. Whiskey would warm him, pick him up, carry him through the last of his journey, refresh his feeling that it was original and valorous to swim across the county. Channel swimmers took brandy. He needed a stimulant. He crossed the lawn in front of the Hallorans' house and went down a little path to where they had built a house for their only daughter Helen and her husband Eric Sachs. The Sachses' pool was small and he found Helen and her husband there.

"Oh, *Neddy*," Helen said. "Did you lunch at Mothers'?"

"Not *really*," Ned said. "I *did* stop to see your parents." This seemed to be explanation enough. "I'm terribly sorry to break in on you like this but I've taken a chill and I wonder if you'd give me a drink."

"Why, I'd *love* to," Helen said, "but there hasn't been anything in this house to drink since Eric's operation. That was three years ago."

Was he losing his memory, had his gift for concealing painful facts let him forget that he had sold his house, that his children were in trouble, and that his friend had been ill? His eyes slipped from Eric's face to his abdomen, where he saw three pale, sutured scars, two of them at least a foot long. Gone was his navel, and what, Neddy thought, would the roving hand, bed-checking one's gifts at 3 A.M. make of a belly with no navel, no link to birth, this breach in the succession?

"I'm sure you can get a drink at the Biswangers'," Helen said, "They're having an enormous do. You can hear it from here. Listen!"

She raised her head and from across the road, the lawns, the gardens, the woods, the fields, he heard again the brilliant noise of voices over water. "Well, I'll get wet," he said, still feeling that he had no freedom of choice about his means of travel. He dove into the Sachses' cold water and, gasping, close to drowning, made his way from one end of the pool to the other. "Lucinda and I want *terribly* to see you," he said over his shoulder, his face set toward the Biswangers'. "We're sorry it's been so long and we'll call you *very* soon."

He crossed some fields to the Biswangers' and the sounds of revelry there. They would be honored to give him a drink, they would be happy to give him a drink, they would in fact be lucky to give him a drink. The Biswangers invited him and Lucinda for dinner four times a year, six weeks in advance. They were always rebuffed and yet they continued to send out their invitations, unwilling to comprehend the rigid and undemocratic realities of their society. They were the sort of people who discussed the price of things at cocktails, exchanged market tips during dinner, and after dinner told dirty stories to mixed company. They did not belong to Neddy's set—they were not even on Lucinda's Christmas card list. He went toward their pool with feelings of indifference, charity, and some unease, since it seemed to be getting dark and these were the longest days of the year. The party when he joined it was noisy and large. Grace Biswanger was the kind of hostess who asked the optometrist, the veterinarian, the real-estate dealer and the dentist. No one was swimming and the twilight, reflected on the water of the pool, had a wintry gleam. There was a bar and he started for this. When Grace Biswanger saw him she came toward him, not affectionately as he had every right to expect, but bellicosely.

"Why, this party has everything," she said loudly, "including a gate crasher."

She could not deal him a social blow—there was no questions about this and he did not flinch. "As a gate crasher," he asked politely, "do I rate a drink?"

"Suit yourself," she said. "You don't seem to pay much attention to invitations."

She turned her back on him and joined some guests, and he went to the bar and ordered a whiskey. The bartender served him but he served him rudely. His was a world in which the caterer's men kept the social score, and to be rebuffed by a part-time barkeep meant that he had suffered some loss of social esteem. Or perhaps the man was new and uninformed. Then he heard Grace at his back say: "They went for broke overnight—nothing but income—and he showed up drunk one Sunday and asked us to loan him five thousand dollars. . . ." She was always talking about money. It was worse than eating your peas off a knife. He dove into the pool, swam its length and went away.

The next pool on his list, the last but two, belonged to his old mistress, Shirley Adams. If he had suffered any injuries at the Biswangers' they would be cured here. Love—sexual roughhouse in fact—was the supreme elixir, the painkiller, the brightly colored pill that would put the spring back into his step, the joy of life in his heart. They had had an affair last week, last month, last year. He couldn't remember. It was he who had broken it off, his was the upper hand, and he stepped through the gate of the wall that surrounded her pool with nothing so considered as self-confidence. It seemed in a way to be his pool as the lover, particularly the illicit lover, enjoys the possessions of his mistress with an authority unknown to holy matrimony. She was there, her hair the color of brass, but her figure, at the edge of the lighted, cerulean water, excited in him no profound memories. It had been, he thought, a lighthearted affair, although she had wept when he broke it off. She seemed confused to see him and he wondered if she was still wounded. Would she, God forbid, weep again?

"What do you want?" she said.

"I'm swimming across the county."

"Good Christ. Will you ever grow up?"

"What's the matter?"

"If you've come here for money," she said, "I won't give you another cent."

"You could give me a drink."

"I could but I won't. I'm not alone."

"Well, I'm on my way."

He dove and swam the pool, but when he tried to haul himself up onto the curb he found that the strength in his arms and shoulders had gone, and he paddled to the ladder and climbed out. Looking over his shoulder he saw, in the lighted bathhouse, a young man. Going out onto the dark lawn he smelled chrysanthemums or marigolds—some stubborn autumnal fragrance—on the night air, strong as gas. Looking overhead he saw that the stars had come out, but why should he seem to see Andromeda, Cepheus, and Cassiopeia? What had become of the constellations of midsummer? He began to cry.

It was probably the first time in his adult life that he had ever cried, certainly the first time in his life that he had ever felt so miserable, cold, tired, and bewildered. He could not understand the rudeness of the caterer's barkeep or the rudeness of a mistress who had come to him on her knees and showered his trousers with tears. He had swum too long, he had been immersed too long, and his nose and his throat were sore from the water. What he needed then was a drink, some company, and some clean dry clothes, and while he could have cut directly across the road to his home, he went to the Gilmartin's pool. Here, for the first time in his life, he did not dive but went down the steps into the icy water and swam a hobbled side stroke that he might have learned as a youth. He staggered with fatigue on his way to the Clydes' and paddled the length of their pool, stopping again and again with his hand on the curb to rest. He climbed up the ladder and wondered if he had the strength to get home. He had done what he wanted, he had swum the county, but he was so stupefied with exhaustion that his triumph seemed vague. Stooped, holding onto the gateposts for support, he turned up the driveway of his own house.

The place was dark. Was it so late that they had all gone to bed? Had Lucinda stayed at the Westerhazy's for supper? Had the girls joined her there or gone someplace else? Hadn't they agreed, as they usually did on Sunday, to regret all their invitations and stay at home? He tried the garage doors to see what cars were in but the doors were locked and rust came off the handles onto his hands. Going toward the house, he saw that the force of the thunderstorm had knocked one of the rain gutters loose. It hung down over the front door like an umbrella rib, but it could be fixed in the morning. The house was locked, and he thought that the stupid cook or the stupid maid must have locked the place up until he remembered that it had been some time since they had employed a maid or a cook. He shouted, pounded on the door, tried to force it with his shoulder, and then, looking in at the windows, saw that the place was empty.

1964

John Updike *1932–*

John Updike was born in the small town of Shillington, Pennsylvania, the son of a junior high school mathematics teacher. Growing up in what seemed to be a world of narrow horizons, John Updike came to an early awareness that he could escape only through his own wits. Encouraged by his ambitious mother, he wrote his first short story at the age of eight. In school he was an honor student, edited his school newspaper, was president of his high school class, and when he graduated from high school, he entered Harvard, the college selected by his mother because she believed that it somehow nurtured writers.

Updike graduated from Harvard summa cum laude in 1954. Later that year he sold his first short story to the New Yorker, *the magazine in which he would establish his reputation as a writer of short fiction in the 1950s and 60s. He spent a year on a fellowship studying art in England (later in life he confessed that his greatest unrealized aim was to be a graphic artist and cartoonist).*

In 1955 Updike got a job as a staff writer on the New Yorker *where he turned out poems, sketches, essays, short stories, and reviews. Within a short time he became known* as *"The Brilliant Young Writer,"* a title that has since stirred critics to argue that in his later work Updike has failed to fulfill his early promise.

In *1957* Updike left the New Yorker, *moved to Ipswich, Massachusetts, and became an independent writer. His first book,* The Carpentered Hen, *a collection of poems, appeared the next year. His first novel,* The Poorhouse Fair, *and his first collection of short stories,* The Same Door, *were published in 1959. In the years that have followed, Updike has become one of the most prolific writers in modern American literature, publishing numerous novels, articles and reviews, an opera libretto, a play, and dozens of short stories.*

Updike won his first widespread, popular recognition with Couples *(1968), a novel of suburban life that is filled with descriptions of compulsive adulteries. Its carnality caused it to be described as "unredeemed pornography" and made it a vast commercial success. Of greater artistic significance was* Centaur *(1963), a highly symbolic and allusive novel, drawing heavily on classical myth, that won the National Book Award.*

In *1978* Updike published the novel The Coup, *a dark comedy set in modern Africa and reporting the reminiscences of a one-time dictator of a newly emerged African nation. But Updike most frequently has set his fiction in small-town America—rural villages and prosperous suburbia—a landscape described in many of his short stories and in four notable novels:* Rabbit Run *(1960),* Rabbit Redux *(1971),* Rabbit Is Rich *(1981), and* The Witches of Eastwick *(1984). In his last two novels,* Roger's Version *(1986) and the witty, satirical* S. *(1988), Updike reworks themes and re-creates characters from Nathaniel Hawthorne's* The Scarlet Letter, *treating religious faith, marriage, love, and the abundant opportunities for self-delusion available to affluent "spiritual seekers" in modern-day America.*

Updike's America is often a mundane world of middle- and lower-class materialism, a land of sterile, empty, trivial lives centered on TV, movies, and fan mags for the riff raff— brand-name America whose inhabitants are sunk in installment buying, whose stomachs are bloated with franchised food, and whose minds are dulled by the soaps and by the trashy newspapers sold at checkout stands. Updike's characters are often searching for spiritual and religious meaning in life, but they often discover that, in their worlds, sentimental love is a trap and a deceit, happiness is brief, and life is as dull as their prepackaged meals.

Updike's critics have named him the *"sweet lonesome singer of Protestant mediocrity,"* and he, in turn, has compared his critics to *"pigs at a pastry cart."* They complain that he overburdens his prose by straining for elegance; that his work is suffused with nostalgia, *"mired in the realm of childhood";* that too often his characters are predictably autobiographical: the puzzled young man, the loyal but not-too-bright girlfriend, the strong, older woman who is animated by *"misplaced enthusiasms."*

But Updike's very strengths lie in his elegant prose, filled with balanced, rhythmic sentences; in his concern with the *"business of memory";* in his explorations of private feeling; in his writing of clothes, houses, cars, parents, and girlfriends; all as a means of portraying an America, in all its ugliness, where people hold on—an America he has celebrated in his poetry as a land of

> *your nothing streetcorners*
> *your ugly eateries*
> *your dear barbarities*
> *and vacant lots*
>
>   .   .   .
>
> *Don't read your reviews,*
> *A*M*E*R*I*C*A*
> *You are the only land.*

FURTHER READING: A. K. Hamilton, *The Elements of John Updike*, 1970; L. Taylor, *Pastoral and Anti-Pastoral Patterns in John Updike's Fiction*, 1971; R. Burchard, *John Updike, Yea Sayings*, 1971; R. Detewiler, *John Updike*, 1972; J. Markle, *John Updike's Fiction*, 1973; P. Vaughan, *John Updike's Images of America*, 1981; S. Uphaus, *John Updike*, 1980; *Critical Essays on John Updike*, ed. W. Macnaughton, 1982; D. Greiner, *The Other John Updike*, 1982; D. Greiner, *John Updike's Novels*, 1984; *John Updike*, ed. H. Bloom, 1987; J. Newman, *John Updike*, 1988.

TEXT: *Pigeon Feathers*, 1962.

FLIGHT

At the age of seventeen I was poorly dressed and funny-looking, and went around thinking about myself in the third person. "Allen Dow strode down the street and home." "Allen Dow smiled a thin sardonic smile." Consciousness of a special destiny made me both arrogant and shy. Years before, when I was eleven or twelve, just on the brink of ceasing to be a little boy, my mother and I, one Sunday afternoon—my father was busy, or asleep—hiked up to the top of Shale Hill, a child's mountain that formed one side of the valley that held our town. There the town lay under us, Olinger, perhaps a thousand homes, the best and biggest of them climbing Shale Hill toward us, and beyond them the blocks of brick houses, one- and two-family, the homes of my friends, sloping down to the pale thread of the Alton Pike, which strung together the high school, the tennis courts, the movie theatre, the town's few stores and gasoline stations, the elementary school, the Lutheran church. On the other side lay more homes, including our own, a tiny white patch placed just where the land began to rise toward the opposite mountain. Cedar Top. There were rims and rims of hills beyond Cedar Top, and looking south we could see the pike dissolving in other towns and turning out of sight amid the patches of green and brown farmland, and it seemed the entire county was lying exposed under a thin veil of haze. I was old enough to feel embarrassment at standing there alone with my mother, beside a wind-stunted spruce tree, on a long spine of shade. Suddenly she dug her fingers into the hair on my head and announced, "There we all are, and there we'll all be forever." She hesitated before the word "forever," and hesitated again before adding, "Except you, Allen. You're going to fly." A few birds were hung far out over the valley, at the level of our eyes, and in her impulsive way she had just plucked the image from them, but it felt like the clue I had been waiting all my childhood for. My most secret self had been made to respond, and I was intensely embarrassed, and irritably ducked my head out from under her melodramatic hand.

She was impulsive and romantic and inconsistent. I was never able to develop this spurt of reassurance into a steady theme between us. That she continued to treat me like an ordinary child seemed a betrayal of the vision she had made me share. I was captive to a hope she had tossed off and forgotten. My shy attempts to justify irregularities in my conduct—reading late at night or not coming back from school on time—by appealing to the image of flight were received with a startled blank look, as if I were talking nonsense. It seemed outrageously unjust. Yes, but, I wanted to say, yes, but it's *your* nonsense. And of course it was just this that made my appeal ineffective: her knowing that I had not made it mine, that I cynically intended to exploit both the privileges of being extraordinary and the pleasures of being ordinary. She feared my wish to be ordinary; once she did respond to my protest that I was learning to fly, by crying with red-faced ferocity, "You'll never learn, you'll stick and die in the dirt just like I'm doing. Why should you be better than your mother?"

She had been born ten miles to the south, on a farm she and her mother had loved. Her mother, a small fierce woman who looked more like an Arab than a German, worked in the fields with the men, and drove the wagon to market ten miles away every Friday. When still a tiny girl, my mother rode with her, and my impression of those rides is of fear—the little girl's fear of the gross and beery men who grabbed and hugged her, her fear of the wagon breaking, of the produce not selling, fear of her mother's possible humiliation and of her father's condition when at nightfall they returned. Friday was his holiday, and he drank. His drinking is impossible for me to picture; for I never knew him except as an enduring, didactic, almost Biblical old man, whose one passion was reading the newspapers and whose one hatred was of the Republican Party. There was something public about him; now that he is dead I keep seeing bits of him attached to famous politicians—his watch chain and his plump square stomach in old films of Theodore Roosevelt, his high-top shoes and the tilt of his head in a photograph of Alfalfa Bill Murray.[1] Alfalfa Bill is turning his head to talk, and holds his hat by the crown, pinching it between two fingers and a thumb, a gentle and courtly grip that reminded me so keenly of my grandfather that I tore the picture out of *Life* and put it in a drawer.

Laboring in the soil had never been congenial to my grandfather, though with his wife's help he prospered by it. Then, in an era when success was hard to avoid, he began to invest in stocks. In 1922 he bought our large white home in the town—its fashionable section had not yet shifted to the Shale Hill side of the valley—and settled in to reap his dividends. He believed to his death that women were foolish, and the broken hearts of his two must have seemed specially so. The dignity of finance for the indignity of farming must have struck him as an eminently advantageous exchange. It strikes me that way, too, and how to reconcile my idea of those fear-ridden wagon rides with the grief that my mother insists she and her mother felt at being taken from the farm? Perhaps prolonged fear is a ground of love. Or perhaps, and likelier, the equation is long and complex, and the few factors I know—the middle-aged woman's mannish pride of land, the adolescent girl's pleasure in riding horses across the fields, their common feeling of rejection in Olinger—are enclosed in brackets and heightened by coefficients that I cannot see. Or perhaps it is not love of land but its absence that needs explaining, in my grandfather's fastidiousness and pride. He believed that as a boy he had been abused, and bore his father a grudge that my mother could never understand. Her grandfather to her was a saintly slender giant, over six feet tall when this was a prodigy, who knew the names of everything, like Adam in Eden. In his old age he was blind. When he came out of the house, the dogs rushed forward to lick his hands. When he lay dying, he requested a Gravenstein apple from the tree on the far edge of the meadow, and his son brought him a Krauser from the orchard near the house. The old man refused it, and my grandfather made a second trip, but in my mother's eyes the outrage had been committed, a savage insult insanely without provocation. What had his father done to him? The only specific complaint I ever heard my grandfather make was that when he was a boy and had to fetch water for the men in the fields, his father would tell him sarcastically, "Pick up your feet; they'll come down themselves." How incongruous! As if each generation

---

[1]William Henry Murray (1869–1956), colorful Democratic politician, Governor of Oklahoma 1931–1935. His nickname came from his success as an alfalfa farmer.

of parents commits atrocities against their children which by God's decree remain invisible to the rest of the world.

I remember my grandmother as a little dark-eyed woman who talked seldom and who tried to feed me too much, and then as a hook-nosed profile pink against the lemon cushions of the casket. She died when I was seven. All the rest I know about her is that she was the baby of thirteen children, that while she was alive she made our yard one of the most beautiful in town, and that I am supposed to resemble her brother Pete.

My mother was precocious; she was fourteen when they moved, and for three years had been attending the county normal school. She graduated from Lake College, near Philadelphia, when she was only twenty, a tall handsome girl with a deprecatory smile, to judge from one of the curling photographs kept in a shoebox that I was always opening as a child, as if it might contain the clue to the quarrels in my house. My mother stands at the end of our brick walk, beside the elaborately trimmed end of our privet hedge—in shape a thick square column mounted by a rough ball of leaf. The ragged arc of a lilac bush in flower cuts into the right edge of the photograph, and behind my mother I can see a vacant lot where there had been a house ever since I can remember. She poses with a kind of country grace in a long fur-trimmed coat, unbuttoned to expose her beads and a short yet somehow demure flapper dress. Her hands are in her coat pockets, a beret sits on one side of her bangs, and there is a swank about her that seemed incongruous to me, examining this picture on the stained carpet of an ill-lit old house in the evening years of the thirties and in the dark of the warring forties. The costume and the girl in it look so up-to-date, so formidable. It was my grandfather's pleasure, in his prosperity, to give her a generous clothes allowance. My father, the penniless younger son of a Presbyterian minister in Passaic, had worked his way through Lake College by waiting on tables, and still speaks with mild resentment of the beautiful clothes that Lillian Baer wore. This aspect of my mother caused me some pain in high school; she was a fabric snob, and insisted on buying my slacks and sports shirts at the best store in Alton, and since we had little money, she bought me few, when of course what I needed was what my classmates had—a wide variety of cheap clothes.

At the time the photograph was taken, my mother wanted to go to New York. What she would have done there, or exactly what she wanted to do, I don't know; but her father forbade her. "Forbid" is a husk of a word today, but at that time, in that quaint province, in the mouth of an "indulgent father," it apparently was still viable, for the great moist weight of that forbidding continued to be felt in the house for years, and when I was a child, as one of my mother's endless harangues to my grandfather screamed toward its weeping peak, I could feel it around and above me, like a huge root encountered by an earthworm.

Perhaps in a reaction of anger my mother married my father, Victor Dow, who at least took her as far away as Wilmington, where he had made a beginning with an engineering firm. But the depression hit, my father was laid off, and the couple came to the white house in Olinger, where my grandfather sat reading the newspapers that traced his stocks' cautious decline into worthlessness. I was born. My grandmother went around as a cleaning lady, and grew things in our quarter-acre yard to sell. We kept chickens, and there was a large plot of asparagus. After she had died, in a frightened way I used to seek her in the asparagus patch. By midsummer it would be a forest of dainty green trees, some as tall as I was, and in their frothy touch a spirit seemed to speak, and in the soft thick net of their intermingling branches a promise seemed to be caught, as well as a menace. The asparagus trees were frightening; in the center of the patch, far from the house and the alley, I would fall under a spell, and become tiny, and wander among the great smooth green trunks expecting to find a little house with a smoking chimney, and in it my grandmother. She herself had believed in ghosts, which made her own ghost potent. Even now, sitting alone in my own house, a board creaks in the kitchen and I look up fearing she will come through the doorway. And at night, just before I fall asleep, her voice calls my name in a penetrating whisper, or calls, *"Pete."*

My mother went to work in an Alton department store, selling inferior fabric for $14 a week. During the daytime of my first year of life it was my father who took care of me. He has since said, flattering me as he always does, that it was having me on his hands that kept him from going insane. It may have been this that has made my affection for him so inarticulate, as if I were still a wordless infant looking up into the mothering blur of his man's face. And that same shared year helps account, perhaps, for his gentleness with me, for his willingness to praise, as if everything I do has something sad and crippled in it. He feels sorry for me; my birth coincided with the birth of a great misery, a national misery—only recently has he stopped calling me by the nickname "Young America." Around my first birthday he acquired a position teaching arithmetic and algebra in the Olinger high school, and though he was so kind and humorous he couldn't enter a classroom without creating uproarious problems of discipline, he endured it day by day and year by year, and eventually came to occupy a place in this alien town, so that I believe there are now one or two dozen ex-students, men and women nearing middle-age, who carry around with them some piece of encouragement my father gave them, or remember some sentence of his that helped shape them. Certainly there are many who remember the antics with which he burlesqued his discomfort in the classroom. He kept a confiscated cap pistol in his desk, and upon getting an especially stupid answer, he would take it out and, wearing a preoccupied, regretful expression, shoot himself in the head.

My grandfather was the last to go to work, and the most degraded by it. He was hired by the borough crew, men who went around the streets shoveling stones and spreading tar. Bulky and ominous in their overalls, wreathed in steam, and associated with dramatic and portentous equipment, these men had grandeur in the eyes of a child, and it puzzled me, as I walked to and from elementary school, that my grandfather refused to wave to me or confess his presence in any way. Curiously strong for a fastidious man, he kept at it well into his seventies, when his sight failed. It was my task then to read his beloved newspapers to him as he sat in his chair by the bay window, twiddling his high-top shoes in the sunshine. I teased him, reading too fast, then maddeningly slow, skipping from column to column to create one long chaotic story; I read him the sports page, which did not interest him, and mumbled the editorials. Only the speed of his feet's twiddling betrayed vexation. When I'd stop, he would plead mildly in his rather beautiful, old-fashioned, elocutionary voice, "Now just the obituaries, Allen. Just the names to see if anyone I know is there." I imagined, as I viciously barked at him the list of names that might contain the name of a friend, that I was avenging my mother; I believed that she hated him, and for her sake I tried to hate him also. From her incessant resurrection of mysterious grievances buried far back in the confused sunless earth of the time before I was born, I had been able to deduce only that he was an evil man, who had ruined her life, that fair creature in the beret. I did not understand. She fought with him not because she wanted to fight but because *she could not bear to leave him alone.*

Sometimes, glancing up from the sheet of print where our armies swarmed in retreat like harried insects, I would catch the old man's head in the act of lifting slightly to receive the warm sunshine on his face, a dry frail face ennobled by its thick crown of combed corn-silk hair. It would dawn on me then that his sins as a father were likely no worse than any father's. But my mother's genius was to give the people closest to her mythic immensity. I was the phoenix. My father and grandmother were legendary invader-saints, she springing out of some narrow vein of Arab blood in the German race and he crossing over from the Protestant wastes of New Jersey, both of them serving and enslaving their mates with their prodigious powers of endurance and labor. For my mother felt that she and her father alike had been destroyed by marriage, been made captive by people better yet less than they. It was true, my father had loved Mom Baer, and her death made him seem more of an alien than ever. He, and her ghost, stood to one side, in the shadows but separate from the house's dark core, the inheritance of frustration and folly that had descended from my grandfather to my mother to me, and that I, with a few beats of my grown wings, was destined to reverse and redeem.

At the age of seventeen, in the fall of my senior year, I went with three girls to debate at a high school over a hundred miles away. They were, all three, bright girls, A students; they were disfigured by A's as if by acne. Yet even so it excited me to be mounting a train with them early on a Friday morning, at an hour when our schoolmates miles away were slumping into the seats of their first class. Sunshine spread broad bars of dust down the length of the half-empty car, and through the windows Pennsylvania unravelled in a long brown scroll scribbled with industry. Black pipes raced beside the tracks for miles. At rhythmic intervals one of them looped upward, like the Greek letter Ω. "Why does it do that?" I asked. "Is it sick?"

"Condensation?" Judith Potteiger suggested in her shy, transparent voice. She loved science.

"No," I said. "It's in pain. It's writhing! It's going to grab the train! Look out!" I ducked, honestly a little scared. All the girls laughed.

Judith and Catharine Miller were in my class, and expected me to be amusing; the third girl, a plump small junior named Molly Bingaman, had not known what to expect. It was her fresh audience I was playing to. She was the best dressed of us four, and the most poised; this made me suspect that she was the least bright. She had been substituted at the last moment for a sick member of the debating team; I knew her just by seeing her in the halls and in assembly. From a distance she seemed dumpy and prematurely adult. But up close she was gently fragrant, and against the weary purple cloth of the train seats her skin seemed luminous. She had beautiful skin, heartbreaking skin a pencil dot would have marred, and large blue eyes equally clear. Except for a double chin, and a mouth too large and thick, she would have been perfectly pretty, in a little woman's compact and cocky way. She and I sat side by side, facing the two senior girls, who more and more took on the wan slyness of matchmakers. It was they who had forced the seating arrangements.

We debated in the afternoon, and won. Yes, the German Federal Republic *should* be freed of all Allied control. The school, a posh castle on the edge of a miserable coal city, was the site of a statewide cycle of debates that was to continue into Saturday. There was a dance Friday night in the gym. I danced with Molly mostly, though to my annoyance she got in with a set of Harrisburg boys while I conscientiously pushed Judith and Catharine around the floor. We were stiff dancers, the three of us; only Molly made me seem good, floating backward from my feet fearlessly as her cheek rumpled my moist shirt. The gym was hung with orange and black crepe paper in honor of Hallowe'en, and the pennants of all the competing schools were fastened to the walls, and a twelve-piece band pumped away blissfully on the year's sad tunes—"Heartaches,", "Near You," "That's My Desire." A great cloud of balloons gathered in the steel girders was released. There was pink punch, and a local girl sang.

Judith and Catharine decided to leave before the dance was over, and I made Molly come too, though she was in a literal sweat of pleasure; her perfect skin in the oval above her neckline was flushed and glazed. I realized, with a little shock of possessiveness and pity, that she was unused to attention back home, in competition with the gorgeous Olinger ignorant.

We walked together to the house where the four of us had been boarded, a large white frame owned by an old couple and standing with lonely decency in a semi-slum. Judith and Catharine turned up the walk, but Molly and I, with a diffident decision that I believe came from their initiative, contined, "to walk around the block." We walked miles, stopping off after midnight at a trolley-car-shaped diner. I got a hamburger, and she impressed me by ordering coffee. We walked back to the house and let ourselves in with the key we had been given; but instead of going upstairs to our rooms we sat downstairs in the living room and talked softly for more hours.

What did we say? I talked about myself. It is hard to hear, much less re-member, what we ourselves say, just as it might be hard for a movie projector, given life, to see the shadows its eye of light is casting. A transcript, could I produce it, of my monologue through the wide turning point of that night, with all its word-by-word conceit, would distort the picture: this living room miles from home, the street light piercing the chinks in the curtains and erect-ing on the wallpaper rods of light the size of yardsticks, our hosts and com-panions asleep upstairs, the incessant sigh of my voice, coffee-primed Molly on the floor beside my chair, her stockinged legs stretched out on the rug; and this odd sense in the room, a tasteless and odorless aura unfamiliar to me, as a pool of water widening.

I remember one exchange. I must have been describing the steep waves of fearing death that had come over me ever since early childhood, about one every three years, and I ended by supposing that it would take great courage to be an atheist. "But I bet you'll become one," Molly said. "Just to show yourself that you're brave enough." I felt she overestimated me, and was flattered. Within a few years, while I still remembered many of her words, I realized how touch-ingly gauche our assumption was that an atheist is a lonely rebel; for mobs of men are united in atheism, and oblivion—the dense lead-like sea that would occasionally sweep over me—is to them a weight as negligible as the faint pressure of their wallets in their hip pockets. This grotesque and tender misestimate of the world flares in my memory of our conversation like one of the innumerable matches we struck.

The room filled with smoke. Too weary to sit, I lay down on the floor beside her, and stroked her silver arm in silence, yet still was too timid to act on the wide and negative aura that I did not understand was of compliance. On the upstairs landing, as I went to turn into my room, Molly came forward with a prim look and kissed me. With clumsy force I entered the negative space that had been waiting. Her lipstick smeared in little unflattering flecks into the skin around her mouth; it was as if I had been given a face to eat, and the presence of bone—skull under skin, teeth behind lips—impeded me. We stood for a long time under the burning hall light, until my neck began to ache from bowing. My legs were trembling when we finally parted and sneaked into our rooms. In bed I thought, "Allen Dow tossed restlessly," and realized it was the first time that day I had thought of myself in the third person.

On Saturday morning, we lost our debate. I was sleepy and verbose and haughty, and some of the students in the audience began to boo whenever I opened my mouth. The principal came up on the stage and made a scolding speech, which finished me and my cause, untrammeled Germany. On the train back, Catharine and Judith arranged the seating so that they sat behind Molly and me, and spied on only the tops of our heads. For the first time, on that ride home, I felt what it was to bury a humiliation in the body of a woman. Nothing but the friction of my face against hers drowned out the echo of those boos. When we kissed, a red shadow would well under my lids and eclipse the hostile hooting faces of the debate audience, and when our lips parted, the bright inner sea would ebb, and there the faces would be again, more intense than ever. With a shudder of shame I'd hide my face on her shoulder and in the warm darkness there, while a frill of her prissy collar gently scratched my nose, I felt united with Hitler and all the villains, traitors, madmen, and failures who had managed to keep, up to the moment of capture or death, a woman with them. This had puzzled me. In high school females were proud and remote; in the newspapers they were fantastic monsters of submission. And now Molly administered reassurance to me with small motions and bodily adjustments that had about them a strange flavor of the practical.

Our parents met us at the station. I was startled at how tired my mother looked. There were deep blue dents on either side of her nose, and her hair seemed somehow dissociated from her head, as if it were a ragged, half-gray wig she had put on carelessly. She was a heavy woman and her weight, which she usually carried upright, like a kind of wealth, had slumped away from her ownership and seemed, in the sullen light of the railway platform, to weigh on the world. I asked, "How's Grandpa?" He had taken to bed several months before with pains in his chest.

"He still sings," she said rather sharply. For entertainment in his increasing blindness my grandfather had long ago begun to sing, and his shapely old voice would pour forth hymns, forgotten comic ballads, and camp-meeting songs at any hour. His memory seemed to improve the longer he lived.

My mother's irritability was more manifest in the private cavity of the car; her heavy silence oppressed me. "You look so tired, Mother," I said, trying to take the offensive.

"That's nothing to how you look," she answered. "What happened up there? You stoop like an old married man."

"Nothing happened," I lied. My cheeks were parched, as if her high steady anger had the power of giving sunburn.

"I remember that Bingaman girl's mother when we first moved to town. She was the smuggest little snip south of the pike. They're real old Olinger stock, you know. They have no use for hillbillies."

My father and I tried to change the subject. "Well, you won one debate, Allen, and that's more than I would have done. I don't see how you do it."

"Why, he gets it from you, Victor. I've never won a debate with you."

"He gets it from Pop Baer. If that man had gone into politics, Lillian, all the misery of his life would have been avoided."

"Dad was never a debater. He was a bully. Don't go with little women, Allen. It puts you too close to the ground."

"I'm not *going* with *anybody,* Mother. Really, you're so fanciful."

"Why, when she stepped off the train from the way her chins bounced I thought she had eaten a canary. And then making my poor son, all skin and bones, carry her bag. When she walked by me I honestly was afraid she'd spit in my eye."

"I had to carry somebody's bag. I'm sure she doesn't know who you are." Though it was true I had talked a good deal about my family the night before.

My mother turned away from me. "You see, Victor—he defends her. When I was his age that girl's mother gave me a cut I'm still bleeding from, and my own son attacks me on behalf of her fat little daughter. I wonder if her mother put her up to catching him."

"Molly's a nice girl," my father interceded. "She never gave me any trouble in class like some of those smug bastards." But he was curiously listless, for so Christian a man, in pronouncing this endorsement.

I discovered that nobody wanted me to go with Molly Bingaman. My friends— for on the strength of being funny I did have some friends, classmates whose love affairs went on over my head but whom I could accompany, as clown, on communal outings—never talked with me about Molly, and when I brought her to their parties gave the impression of ignoring her, so that I stopped taking her. Teachers at school would smile an odd tight smile when they saw us leaning by her locker or hanging around in the stairways. The eleventh-grade English instructor—one of my "boosters" on the faculty, a man who was always trying to "challenge" me, to "exploit" my "potential"—took me aside and told me how stupid she was. She just couldn't grasp the logical principles of syntax. He confided her parsing mistakes to me as if they betrayed—as indeed in a way they did—an obtuseness her social manner cleverly concealed. Even the Fabers, an ultra-Republican couple who ran a luncheonette near the high school, showed malicious delight whenever Molly and I broke up, and persistently treated my attachment as being a witty piece of play, like my pretense with Mr. Faber of being a Communist. The entire town seemed ensnarled in my mother's myth, that escape was my proper fate. It was as if I were a sport that the ghostly elders of Olinger had segregated from the rest of the livestock and agreed to donate in time to the air; this fitted with the ambiguous sensation I had always had in the town, of being simultaneously flattered and rejected.

Molly's parents disapproved because in their eyes my family was virtually white trash. It was so persistently hammered into me that I was too good for Molly that I scarcely considered the proposition that, by another scale, she was too good for me. Further, Molly herself shielded me. Only once, exasperated by some tedious, condescending confession of mine, did she state that her mother didn't like me. "Why not?" I asked, genuinely surprised. I admired Mrs Bingaman—she was beautifully preserved—and I always felt gay in her house, with its white woodwork and matching furniture and vases of iris posing before polished mirrors.

"Oh, I don't know. She thinks you're flippant."

"But that's not true. Nobody takes himself more seriously than I do."

While Molly protected me from the Bingaman side of the ugliness, I conveyed the Dow side more or less directly to her. It infuriated me that nobody allowed me to be proud of her. I kept, in effect, asking her, Why was she stupid in English? Why didn't she get along with my friends? Why did she look so dumpy and smug?—this last despite the fact that she often, especially in intimate moments, looked beautiful to me. I was especially angry with her because this affair had brought out an ignoble, hysterical, brutal aspect of my mother that I might never have had to see otherwise. I had hoped to keep things secret from her, but even if her intuition had not been relentless, my father, at school, knew everything. Sometimes, indeed, my mother said that she didn't care if I went with Molly; it was my father who was upset. Like a frantic dog tied by one leg, she snapped in any direction, mouthing ridiculous fancies—such that Mrs. Bingaman had sicked Molly on me just to keep me from going to college and giving the Dows something to be proud of—that would make us both suddenly start laughing. Laughter in that house that winter had a guilty sound. My grandfather was dying, and lay upstairs singing and coughing and weeping as the mood came to him, and we were too poor to hire a nurse, and too kind and cowardly to send him to a "home." It was still his house, after all. Any noise he made seemed to slash my mother's heart, and she was unable to sleep upstairs near him, and waited the nights out on the sofa downstairs. In her desperate state she would say unforgivable things to me even while the tears streamed down her face. I've never seen so many tears as I saw that winter.

Every time I saw my mother cry, it seemed I had to make Molly cry. I developed a skill at it; it came naturally to an only child who had been surrounded all his life by adults ransacking each other for the truth. Even in the heart of intimacy, half-naked each of us, I would say something to humiliate her. We never made love in the final, coital sense. My reason was a mixture of idealism and superstition; I felt that if I took her virginity she would be mine forever. I depended overmuch on a technicality; she gave herself to me anyway, and I had her anyway, and have her still, for the longer I travel in a direction I could not have taken with her, the more clearly she seems the one person who loved me without advantage. I was a homely, comically ambitious hillbilly, and I even refused to tell her I loved her, to pronounce the word "love"—an icy piece of pedantry that shocks me now that I have almost forgotten the context of confusion in which it seemed wise.

In addition to my grandfather's illness, and my mother's grief, and my waiting to hear if I had won a scholarship to the one college that seemed good enough for me, I was burdened with managing too many petty affairs of my graduating class. I was in charge of the yearbook writeups, art editor of the school paper, chairman of the Class Gift Committee, director of the Senior Assembly, and teachers' workhorse. Frightened by my father's tales of nervous breakdowns he had seen, I kept listening for the sounds of my brain snapping, and the image of that gray, infinitely interconnected mass seemed to extend outward, to become my whole world, one dense organic dungeon, and I felt I had to get out; if I could just get out of this, into June, it would be blue sky, and I would be all right for life.

One Friday night in spring, after trying for over an hour to write thirty-five affectionate words for the yearbook about a null girl in the Secretarial Course I had never spoken a word to, I heard my grandfather begin coughing upstairs with a sound like dry membrane tearing, and I panicked. I called up the stairs, "Mother! I must go out."

"It's nine-thirty."

"I know, but I have to. I'm going insane."

Without waiting to hear her answer or to find a coat, I left the house and got our old car out of the garage. The weekend before, I had broken up with Molly again. All week I hadn't spoken to her, though I had seen her once in Faber's, with a boy in her class, averting her face while I, hanging by the side of the pinball machine, made wisecracks in her direction. I didn't dare go up to her door and knock so late at night; I just parked across the street and watched the lit windows of her house. Through their living-room window I could see one of Mrs. Bingaman's vases of hothouse iris standing on the white mantel, and my open car window admitted the spring air, which delicately smelled of wet ashes. Molly was probably out on a date with that moron in her class. But then the Bingaman's door opened, and her figure appeared in the rectangle of light. Her back was toward me, a coat was on her arm, and her mother seemed to be screaming. Molly closed the door and ran off the porch and across the street and quickly got into the car, her eyes downcast in their sockets of shadow. *She came.* When I have finally forgotten everything else, her powdery fragrance, her lucid cool skin, the way her lower lip was like a curved pillow of two cloths, the dusty red outer and wet pink inner, I'll still be grieved by this about Molly, that she came to me.

After I returned her to her house—she told me not to worry, her mother enjoyed shouting—I went to the all-night diner just beyond the Olinger town line and ate three hamburgers, ordering them one at a time, and drank two glasses of milk. It was close to two o'clock when I got home, but my mother was still awake. She lay on the sofa in the dark, with the radio sitting on the floor murmuring Dixieland piped up from New Orleans by way of Philadelphia. Radio music was a steady feature of her insomniac life; not only did it help drown out the noise of her father upstairs but she seemed to enjoy it in itself. She would resist my father's pleas to come to bed by saying that the New Orleans program was not over yet. The radio was an old Philco we had always had; I had once drawn a fish on the orange disc of its celluloid dial, which looked to my child's eyes like a fishbowl.

Her loneliness caught at me; I went into the living room and sat on a chair with my back to the window. For a long time she looked at me tensely out of the darkness. "Well," she said at last, "how was little hotpants?" The vulgarity this affair had brought out in her language appalled me.

"I made her cry," I told her.

"Why do you torment the girl?"

"To please you."

"It doesn't please me."

"Well, then, stop nagging me."

"I'll stop nagging you if you'll solemnly tell me you're willing to marry her."

I said nothing to this, and after waiting she went on in a different voice, "Isn't it funny, that you should show this weakness."

"Weakness is a funny way to put it when it's the only thing that gives me strength."

"Does it really, Allen? Well. It may be. I forget, you were born here."

Upstairs, close to our heads, my grandfather, in a voice frail but still melodious, began to sing, "There is a happy land, far, far away, where saints in glory stand, bright, bright as day." We listened; and his voice broke into coughing, a terrible rending cough growing in fury, struggling to escape, and loud with fear he called my mother's name. She didn't stir. His voice grew enormous, a bully's voice, as he repeated, "Lillian! Lillian!" and I saw my mother's shape quiver with the force coming down the stairs into her; she was like a dam; and then the power, as my grandfather fell momentarily silent, flowed toward me in the darkness, and I felt intensely angry, and hated that black mass of suffering, even while I realized, with a rapid, light calculation, that I was too weak to withstand it.

In a dry tone of certainty and dislike—how hard my heart had become—I told her, "All right. You'll win this one, Mother; but it'll be the last one you'll win."

My pang of fright following this unprecedentedly cold insolence seemed to blot my senses; the chair ceased to be felt under me, and the walls and furniture of the room fell away—there was only the dim orange glow of the radio dial down below. In a husky voice that seemed to come across a great distance my mother said, with typical melodrama, "Goodbye, Allen."

1959   1962

Norman Mailer *1923*–

Norman Mailer was born in Long Branch, New Jersey, and grew up in Brooklyn, New York. He entered Harvard at age sixteen to study aeronautical engineering, but he became much more interested in writing, and in 1941 he won Story *magazine's annual award for college fiction. Shortly after graduation from Harvard with a B.S. in engineering, Mailer was drafted into the army and served as a rifleman with a reconnaissance unit in the Philippines during the Second World War.*

It was from his military experiences that Mailer drew in writing his first and most successful novel, The Naked and the Dead *(1948), the story of a U.S. Army platoon during the invasion of a Japanese-held island in the Pacific. Mailer's second novel,* Barbary Shore *(1951), portrays the limitations of political radicalism and questions the possibility of honor, virtue, and order in the modern world.* The Deer Park *(1955) uses a documentary style, directness, and humor to reveal Mailer's growing concern with the self rather than society, the inner world of dreams and fantasy rather than the outer world of action. It has been judged one of the finest novels ever written about the world of Hollywood, which Mailer presents as emblematic of American society.*

In 1956 Mailer began a newspaper column for The Village Voice, *in New York City, and his subsequent writings, including* The White Negro *(1958) and* Advertisements for Myself *(1959), reveal an increasingly subjective response to a world he sees as filled with chaos, violence, and irrationality, a view that he has continued to express in his later works, including* The Armies of the Night *(1968),* Miami and the Siege of Chicago *(1968),* The Prisoner of Sex *(1972), and* Marilyn *(1973), an essay on the film star Marilyn Monroe, whom Mailer sees as a symbol and an ideal of American culture. In 1980 he won a Pulitzer Prize for* The Executioner's Song. *His recent novels,* Ancient Evenings *(1983) and* Tough Guys Don't Dance *(1984), are by most accounts failures and partially confirm Gore Vidal's observation that Mailer has ceased to be a novelist and has become "a superb journalist, with himself as subject."*

Mailer is said to dwell in a hyperbolic world. He has been criticized as egocentric and pugnacious (Saul Bellow called him the Joe Louis of literature). Some critics think of him as one who cannot reconcile his role as public performer with the role of serious writer, as one whose writing is too often merely profitable literary swaggering. Yet, his novel The Naked and the Dead *continues to be praised as one of the finest novels written in America since World War II, and in his essays and occasional journalism he has expanded the traditional boundaries of American literature, all of which has inspired a tide of critical estimates of his work that place him among the most important writers of twentieth-century America.*

FURTHER READING: *The Long Patrol, Twenty-Five Years of Writing from the Work of Norman Mailer,* ed. R. Lucid, 1971; R. Foster, *Normal Mailer,* 1968; D. Kaufmann, *Norman Mailer, The Countdown,* 1969; B. Leeds, *The Structured Vision of Norman Mailer,* 1969; R. Lucid, *Norman Mailer, The Man and His Work,* 1971; R. Poirier, *Norman Mailer,* 1972; *Norman Mailer, A Collection of Critical Essays,* ed. L. Braudy, 1972; R. Solotaroff, *Down Mailer's Way,* 1974; J. Radford, *Norman Mailer, A Critical Study,* 1975; L. Adams, *Existential Battles, The Growth of Norman Mailer,* 1976; R. Merrill, *Norman Mailer,* 1978; H. Mills, *Mailer,* 1982; *Mailer, His Life and Times,* ed. P. Manso, 1985; *Critical Essays on Norman Mailer,* ed. J. Lennon, 1986; J. Wenke, *Mailer's America,* 1987.

TEXT: "The White Negro" is from *Advertisements for Myself,* 1959; other selections are from *The Armies of the Night,* 1968.

THE WHITE NEGRO

SUPERFICIAL REFLECTIONS ON THE HIPSTER

Our search for the rebels of the generation led us to the hipster. The hipster is an *enfant terrible*[1] turned inside out. In character with his time, he is trying to get back at the conformists by lying low . . . You can't interview a hipster because his main goal is to keep out of a society which, he thinks, is trying to make everyone over in its own image. He takes marijuana because it supplies him with experiences that can't be shared with "squares." He may affect a broad-brimmed hat or a zoot suit, but usually he prefers to skulk unmarked. The hipster may be a jazz musician; he is rarely an artist, almost never a writer. He may earn his living as a petty criminal, a hobo, a carnival roustabout or a free-lance moving man in Greenwich Village, but some hipsters have found a safe refuge in the upper income brackets as television comics or movie actors. (The late James Dean, for one, was a hipster hero.) . . . It is tempting to describe the hipster in psychiatric terms as infantile, but the style of his infantilism is a sign of the times. He does not try to enforce his will on others, Napoleon-fashion, but contents himself with a magical omnipotence never disproved because never tested. . . . As the only extreme nonconformist of his generation, he exercises a powerful if underground appeal for conformists, through newspaper accounts of his delinquencies, his structureless jazz, and his emotive grunt words.

> *"Born 1930: The Unlost Generation"*
> *by Caroline Bird*
> Harper's Bazaar, *Feb. 1957*

Probably, we will never be able to determine the psychic havoc of the concentration camps and the atom bomb upon the unconscious mind of almost everyone alive in these years. For the first time in civilized history, perhaps for the first time in all of history, we have been forced to live with the suppressed knowledge that the smallest facets of our personality or the most minor projection of our ideas, or indeed the absence of ideas and the absence of personality could mean equally well that we might still be doomed to die as a cipher in some vast statistical operation in which our teeth would be counted, and our hair would be saved, but our death itself would be unknown, unhonored, and unremarked, a death which could not follow with dignity as a possible consequence to serious actions

[1]French: unruly child.

we have chosen, but rather a death by *deus ex machina*[2] in a gas chamber or a radioactive city; and so if in the midst of civilization—that civilization founded upon the Faustian urge to dominate nature by mastering time, mastering the links of social cause and effect—in the middle of an economic civilization founded upon the confidence that time could indeed be subjected to our will, our psyche was subjected itself to the intolerable anxiety that death being causeless, life was causeless as well, and time deprived of cause and effect had come to a stop.

The Second World War presented a mirror to the human condition which blinded anyone who looked into it. For if tens of millions were killed in concentration camps out of the inexorable agonies and contractions of super-states founded upon the always insoluble contradictions of injustice, one was then obliged also to see that no matter how crippled and perverted an image of man was the society he had created, it was nonetheless his creation, his collective creation (at least his collective creation from the past) and if society was so murderous, then who could ignore the most hideous of questions about his own nature?

Worse. One could hardly maintain the courage to be individual, to speak with one's own voice, for the years in which one could complacently accept oneself as part of an elite by being a radical were forever gone. A man knew that when he dissented, he gave a note upon his life which could be called in a year of overt crisis. No wonder then that these have been the years of conformity and depression. A stench of fear has come out of every pore of American life, and we suffer from a collective failure of nerve. The only courage, with rare exceptions, that we have been witness to, has been the isolated courage of isolate⌐ people.

2

It is on this bleak scene that a phenomenon has appeared: the American existentialist—the hipster, the man who knows that if our collective condition is to live with instant death by atomic war, relatively quick death by the State as *l'univers concentrationnaire*,[3] or with a slow death by conformity with every creative and rebellious instinct stifled (at what damage to the mind and the heart and the liver and the nerves no research foundation for cancer will discover in a hurry), if the fate of twentieth-century man is to live with death as immediate danger, to divorce oneself from society, the only life-giving answer is to accept the terms of death, to live with death from adolescence to premature senescence, why then to exist without roots, to set out on that uncharted journey into the rebellious imperatives of the self. In short, whether life is criminal or not, the decision is to encourage the psychopath in oneself, to explore that domain of experience where security is boredom and therefore sickness, and one exists in the present, in that enormous present which is without past or future, memory or planned intention, the life where a man must go until he is beat, where he must gamble with his energies through all those small or large crises of courage and unforeseen situations which beset his day, where he must be with it or doomed not to swing. The unstated essence of Hip, its psychopathic brilliance, quivers with the knowledge that new kinds of victories increase one's power for

[2]Latin: a god from a machine.
[3]French: universal concentration camp.

new kinds of perception; and defeats, the wrong kind of defeats, attack the body and imprison one's energy until one is jailed in the prison air of other people's habits, other people's defeats, boredom, quiet desperation, and muted icy self-destroying rage. One is Hip or one is Square (the alternative which each new generation coming into American life is beginning to feel), one is a rebel or one conforms, one is a frontiersman in the Wild West of American night life, or else a Square cell, trapped in the totalitarian tissues of American society, doomed willy-nilly to conform if one is to succeed.

A totalitarian society makes enormous demands on the courage of men, and a partially totalitarian society makes even greater demands, for the general anxiety is greater. Indeed if one is to be a man, almost any kind of unconventional action often takes disproportionate courage. So it is no accident that the source of Hip is the Negro for he has been living on the margin between totalitarianism and democracy for two centuries. But the presence of Hip as a working philosophy in the sub-worlds of American life is probably due to jazz, and its knifelike entrance into culture, its subtle but so penetrating influence on an avant-garde generation—that postwar generation of adventurers who (some consciously, some by osmosis) had absorbed the lessons of disillusionment and disgust of the twenties, the depression, and the war. Sharing a collective disbelief in the words of men who had too much money and controlled too many things, they knew almost as powerful a disbelief in the socially monolithic ideas of the single mate, the solid family and the respectable love life. If the intellectual antecedents of this generation can be traced to such separate influences as D. H. Lawrence, Henry Miller, and Wilhelm Reich, the viable philosophy of Hemingway fit most of their facts: in a bad world, as he was to say over and over again (while taking time out from his parvenu snobbery and dedicated gourmandize), in a bad world there is no love nor mercy nor charity nor justice unless a man can keep his courage, and this indeed fitted some of the facts. What fitted the need of the adventurer even more precisely was Hemingway's categorical imperative that what made him feel good became therefore The Good.

So no wonder that in certain cities of America, in New York of course, and New Orleans, in Chicago and San Francisco and Los Angeles, in such American cities as Paris and Mexico, D.F., this particular part of a generation was attracted to what the Negro had to offer. In such places as Greenwich Village, a ménage-à-trois[4] was completed— the bohemian and the juvenile delinquent came face-to-face with the Negro, and the hipster was a fact in American life. If marijuana was the wedding ring, the child was the language of Hip for its argot gave expression to abstract states of feeling which all could share, at least all who were Hip. And in this wedding of the white and the black it was the Negro who brought the cultural dowry. Any Negro who wishes to live must live with danger from his first day, and no experience can ever be casual to him, no Negro can saunter down a street with any real certainty that violence will not visit him on his walk. The cameos of security for the average white: mother and the home, job and the family, are not even a mockery to millions of Negroes; they are impossible. The Negro has the simplest of alternatives: live a life of constant humility or ever-threatening danger. In such a pass where paranoia is as vital to survival as blood, the Negro had stayed alive and begun to grow by following the need of his body where he could. Knowing in the cells of his existence that life was war, nothing but war, the Negro (all exceptions admitted) could rarely afford the sophisticated inhibitions of civilization, and so he kept for his survival

[4]French: a household of three, a triangle.

the art of the primitive, he lived in the enormous present, he subsisted for his Saturday night kicks, relinquishing the pleasures of the mind for the more obligatory pleasures of the body, and in his music he gave voice to the character and quality of his existence, to his rage and the infinite variations of joy, lust, languor, growl, cramp, pinch, scream and despair of his orgasm. For jazz is orgasm, it is the music of orgasm, good orgasm and bad, and so it spoke across a nation, it had the communciation of art even where it was watered, perverted, corrupted, and almost killed, it spoke in no matter what laundered popular way of instantaneous existential states to which some whites could respond, it was indeed a communication by art because it said, "I feel this, and now you do too."

So there was a new breed of adventurers, urban adventurers who drifted out at night looking for action with a black man's code to fit their facts. The hipster had absorbed the existentialist synapses of the Negro, and for practical purposes could be considered a white Negro.

To be an existentialist, one must be able to feel oneself—one must know one's desires, one's rages, one's anguish, one must be aware of the character of one's frustration and know what would satisfy it. The overcivilized man can be an existentialist only if it is chic, and deserts it quickly for the next chic. To be a real existentialist (Sartre admittedly to the contrary) one must be religious, one must have one's sense of the "purpose"—whatever the purpose may be—but a life which is directed by one's faith in the necessity of action is a life committed to the notion that the substratum of existence is the search, the end meaningful but mysterious; it is impossible to live such a life unless one's emotions provide their profound conviction. Only the French, alienated beyond alienation from their unconscious, could welcome an existential philosophy without ever feeling it at all; indeed only a Frenchman by declaring that the unconscious did not exist could then proceed to explore the delicate involutions of consciousness, the microscopically sensuous and all but ineffable *frissons*[5] of mental becoming, in order finally to create the theology of atheism and so submit that in a world of absurdities the existential absurdity is most coherent.

In the dialogue between the atheist and the mystic, the atheist is on the side of life, rational life, undialectical life—since he conceives of death as emptiness, he can, no matter how weary or despairing, wish for nothing but more life; his pride is that he does not transpose his weakness and spiritual fatigue into a romantic longing for death, for such appreciation of death is then all too capable of being elaborated by his imagination into a universe of meaningful structure and moral orchestration.

Yet this masculine argument can mean very little for the mystic. The mystic can accept the atheist's description of his weakness, he can agree that his mysticism was a response to despair. And yet . . . and yet his argument is that he, the mystic, is the one finally who has chosen to live with death, and so death is his experience and not the atheist's, and the atheist by eschewing the limitless dimensions of profound despair has rendered himself incapable to judge the experience. The real argument which the mystic must always advance is the very intensity of his private vision—his argument depends from the vision precisely because what was left in the vision is so extraordinary that no rational argument, no hypotheses of "oceanic feelings" and certainly no skeptical reductions can explain away what has become for him the reality more real than the reality of closely reasoned logic. His inner experience of the possibilities within death is his logic. So, too, for the existentialist. And the psychopath. And

[5]French: shivers.

the saint and the bull-fighter and the lover. The common denominator for all of them is their burning consciousness of the present, exactly that incandescent consciousness which the possibilities within death has opened for them. There is a depth of desperation to the condition which enables one to remain in life only by engaging death, but the reward is their knowledge that what is happening at each instant of the electric present is good or bad for them, good or bad for their cause, their love, their action, their need.

It is this knowledge which provides the curious community of feeling in the world of the hipster, a muted cool religious revival to be sure, but the element which is exciting, disturbing, nightmarish perhaps, is that incompatibles have come to bed, the inner life and the violent life, the orgy and the dream of love, the desire to murder and the desire to create, a dialectical conception of existence with a lust for power, a dark, romantic, and yet undeniably dynamic view of existence for its sees every man and woman as moving individually through each moment of life forward into growth or backward into death.

3

It may be fruitful to consider the hipster a philosophical psychopath, a man interested not only in the dangerous imperatives of his psychopathy but in codifying, at least for himself, the suppositions on which his inner universe is constructed. By this premise the hipster is a psychopath, and yet not a psychopath but the negation of the psychopath, for he possesses the narcissistic detachment of the philosopher, that absorption in the recessive nuances of one's own motive which is so alien to the unreasoning drive of the psychopath. In this country where new millions of psychopaths are developed each year, stamped with the mint of our contradictory popular culture (where sex is sin and yet sex is paradise), it is as if there has been room already for the development of the antithetical psychopath who extrapolates from his own condition, from the inner certainty that his rebellion is just, a radical vision of the universe which thus separates him from the general ignorance, reactionary prejudice, and self-doubt of the more conventional psychopath. Having converted his unconscious experience into much conscious knowledge, the hipster has shifted the focus of his desire from immediate gratification toward that wider passion for future power which is the mark of civilized man. Yet with an irreducible difference. For Hip is the sophistication of the wise primitive in a giant jungle, and so its appeal is still beyond the civilized man. If there are ten million Americans who are more or less psychopathic (and the figure is most modest), there are probably not more than one hundred thousand men and women who consciously see themselves as hipsters, but their importance is that they are an elite with the potential ruthlessness of an elite, and a language most adolescents can understand instinctively, for the hipster's intense view of existence matches their experience and their desire to rebel.

Before one can say more about the hipster, there is obviously much to be said about the psychic state of the psychopath—or, clinically, the psychopathic personality. Now, for reasons which may be more curious than the similarity of the words, even many people with a psychoanalytical orientation often confuse the psychopath with the psychotic. Yet the terms are polar. The psychotic is legally insane, the psychopath is not; the psychotic is almost always incapable of discharging in physical acts the rage of his frustration, while the psychopath at his extreme is virtually as incapable of restraining his violence. The psychotic lives in so misty a world that what is happening at each moment of his life is not very real to him whereas the psychopath seldom knows any reality greater than the face, the voice, the being of the particular people among whom he may find himself at any moment. Sheldon and Eleanor Glueck describe him as follows:

The psychopath . . . can be distinguished from the person sliding into or clambering out of a "true psychotic" state by the long tough persistence of his anti-social attitude and behaviour and the absence of hallucinations, delusions, manic flight of ideas, confusion, disorientation, and other dramatic signs of psychosis.

The late Robert Lindner, one of the few experts on the subject, in his book *Rebel Without a Cause—The Hypnoanalysis of a Criminal Psychopath* presented part of his definition in this way:

. . . the psychopath is a rebel without a cause, an agitator without a slogan, a revolutionary without a program: in other words, his rebelliousness is aimed to achieve goals satisfactory to himself alone; he is incapable of exertions for the sake of others. All his efforts, hidden under no matter what disguise, represent investments designed to satisfy his immediate wishes and desires. . . . The psychopath, like the child, cannot delay the pleasures of gratification; and this trait is one of his underlying, universal characteristics. He cannot wait upon erotic gratification which convention demands should be preceded by the chase before the kill: he must rape. He cannot wait upon the development of prestige in society: his egoistic ambitions lead him to leap into headlines by daring performances. Like a red thread the predominance of this mechanism for immediate satisfaction runs through the history of every psychopath. It explains not only his behaviour but also the violent nature of his acts.

Yet even Lindner, who was the most imaginative and most sympathetic of the psychoanalysts who have studied the psychopathic personality, was not ready to project himself into the essential sympathy—which is that the psychopath may indeed be the perverted and dangerous front-runner of a new kind of personality which could become the central expression of human nature before the twentieth century is over. For the psychopath is better adapted to dominate those mutually contradictory inhibitions upon violence and love which civilization has exacted of us, and if it be remembered that not every psychopath is an extreme case, and that the condition of psychopathy is present in a host of people including many politicians, professional soldiers, newspaper columnists, entertainers, artists, jazz musicians, call-girls, promiscuous homosexuals and half the executives of Hollywood, television, and advertising, it can be seen that there are aspects of psychopathy which already exert considerable cultural influence.

What characterizes almost every psychopath and part-psychopath is that they are trying to create a new nervous system for themselves. Generally we are obliged to act with a nervous system which has been formed from infancy, and which carries in the style of its circuits the very contradictions of our parents and our early milieu. Therefore, we are obliged, most of us, to meet the tempo of the present and the future with reflexes and rhythms which come from the past. It is not only the "dead weight of the institutions of the past" but indeed the inefficient and often antiquated nervous circuits of the past which strangle our potentiality for responding to new possibilities which might be exciting for our individual growth.

Through most of modern history, "sublimation" was possible: at the expense of expressing only a small portion of oneself, that small portion could be expressed intensely. But sublimation depends on a reasonable tempo to history. If the collective life of a generation has moved too quickly, the "past" by which particular men and women of that generation may function is not, let us say, thirty years old, but relatively a hundred or two hundred years old. And so the nervous system is overstressed beyond the possibility of such compromises as sublimation, especially since the stable middle-class values so prerequisite to sublimation have been virtually destroyed in our time, at least as nourishing values free of confusion or doubt. In such a crisis of accelerated historical tempo and deteriorated values, neurosis tends to be replaced by psychopathy, and the success of psychoanalysis (which even ten years ago gave promise of becoming a direct major force) diminishes because of its inbuilt and characteristic incapacity to handle patients more complex, more experienced, or more adventurous than the analyst himself. In practice, psychoanalysis has by now become all too often no more than a psychic blood-letting. The patient is not so much changed as aged, and the infantile fantasies which he is encouraged to express are condemned to exhaust themselves against the analyst's nonresponsive reactions. The result for all too many patients is a diminution, a "tranquilizing" of their most interesting qualities and vices. The patient is indeed not so much altered as worn out—less bad, less good, less bright, less willful, less destructive, less creative. He is thus able to conform to that contradictory and unbearable society which first created his neurosis. He can conform to what he loathes because he no longer has the passion to feel loathing so intensely.

The psychopath is notoriously difficult to analyze because the fundamental decision of his nature is to try to live the infantile fantasy, and in this decision (given the dreary alternative of psychoanalysis) there may be a certain instinctive wisdom. For there is a dialectic to changing one's nature, the dialectic which underlies all psychoanalytic method: it is the knowledge that if one is to change one's habits, one must go back to the source of their creation, and so the psychopath exploring backward along the road of the homosexual, the orgiast, the drug-addict, the rapist, the robber and the murderer seeks to find those violent parallels to the violent and often hopeless contradictions he knew as an infant and as a child. For if he has the courage to meet the parallel situation of the moment when he is ready, then he has a chance to act as he has never acted before, and in satisfying the frustration—if he can succeed—he may then pass by symbolic substitute through the locks of incest. In thus giving expression to the buried infant in himself, he can lessen the tension of those infantile desires and so free himself to remake a bit of his nervous system. Like the neurotic he is looking for the opportunity to grow up a second time, but the psychopath knows instinctively that to express a forbidden impulse actively is far more beneficial to him than merely to confess the desire in the safety of a doctor's room. The psychopath is ordinately ambitious, too ambitious ever to trade his warped brilliant conception of his possible victories in life for the grim if peaceful attrition of the analyst's couch. So his associational journey into the past is lived out in the theatre of the present, and he exists for those charged situations where his senses are so alive that he can be aware actively (as the analysand is aware passively) of what his habits are, and how he can change them. The strength of the psychopath is that he knows (where most of us can only guess) what is good for him and what is bad for him at exactly those instants when an old crippling habit has become so attacked by experience that the potentiality exists to change it, to replace a negative and empty fear with an outward action, even if—and here I obey the logic of the extreme psychopath—even if the fear is of himself, and the action is to murder. The psychopath murders—if he has the courage—out of the necessity to purge his violence, for if he cannot empty his hatred then he cannot love, his being is frozen with implacable self-hatred for his cowardice. (It can of course be suggested that it takes little courage for two strong eighteen-year-old hoodlums, let us say, to beat in the brains of a candy-store keeper, and indeed the act—even by the logic of the psychopath— is not likely to prove very therapeutic, for the victim is not an immediate equal. Still, courage of a sort is necessary, for one murders not only a weak fifty-year-old man but an institution as well, one violates private property, one enters into a new relation with the police and introduces a dangerous element into one's life. The hoodlum is therefore daring the unknown, and so no matter how brutal the act, it is not altogether cowardly.)

At bottom, the drama of the psychopath is that he seeks love. Not love as the search for a mate, but love as the search for an orgasm more apocalyptic than the one which preceded it. Orgasm is his therapy—he knows at the seed of his being that good orgasm opens his possibilities and bad orgasm imprisons him. But in this search, the psychopath becomes an embodiment of the extreme contradictions of the society which formed his character, and the apocalyptic orgasm often remains as remote as the Holy Grail, for there are clusters and nests and ambushes of violence in his own necessities and in the imperatives and retaliations of the men and women among whom he lives his life, so that even as he drains his hatred in one act or another, so the conditions of his life create it anew in him until the drama of his movements bears a sardonic resemblance to the frog who climbed a few feet in the well only to drop back again.

Yet there is this to be said for the search after the good orgasm: when one lives in a civilized world, and still can enjoy none of the cultural nectar of such a world because the paradoxes on which civilization is built demand that there remain a cultureless and alienated bottom of exploitable human material, then the logic of becoming a sexual outlaw (if one's psychological roots are bedded in the bottom) is that one has at least a running competitive chance to be physically healthy so long as one stays alive. It is therefore no accident that psychopathy is most prevalent with the Negro. Hated from outside and therefore hating himself, the Negro was forced into the position of exploring all those moral wildernesses of civilized life which the Square automatically condemns as delinquent or evil or immature or morbid or self-destructive or corrupt. (Actually the terms have equal weight. Depending on the telescope of the cultural clique from which the Square surveys the universe, "evil" or "immature" are equally strong terms of condemnation.) But the Negro, not being privileged to gratify his self-esteem with the heady satisfactions of categorical condemnation, chose to move instead in that other direction where all situations are equally valid, and in the worst of perversion, promiscuity, pimpery, drug addiction, rape, razor-slash, bottle-break, what-have-you, the Negro discovered and elaborated the morality of the bottom, an ethical differentiation between the good and the bad in every human activity from the go-getter pimp (as opposed to the lazy one) to the relatively dependable pusher or prostitute. Add to this, the cunning of their language, the abstract ambiguous alternatives in which from the danger of their oppression they learned to speak ("Well, now, man, like I'm looking for a cat to turn me on . . ."), add even more the profound sensitivity of the Negro jazzman who was the cultural mentor of a people, and it is not too difficult to believe that the language of Hip which evolved was an artful language, tested and shaped by an intense experience and therefore different in kind from white slang, as different as the special obscenity of the soldier, which in its emphasis upon "ass" as the soul and "shit" as circumstance, was able to express the existential states of the enlisted man. What makes Hip a special language is that it cannot really be taught—if one shares none of the experiences of elation and exhaustion which it is equipped to describe, then it seems merely arch or vulgar or irritating. It is a pictorial language, but pictorial like non-objective art, imbued with the dialectic of small but intense change, a language of the micro-cosm, in this case, man, for it takes the immediate experiences of any passing man and magnifies the dynamic of his movements, not specifically but abstractly so that he is seen more as a vector in a network of forces than as a static character in a crystallized field. (Which latter is the practical view of the snob.) For example, there is real difficulty in trying to find a Hip substitute for "stubborn." The best possibility I can come up with is: "That cat will never come off his groove, dad." But groove implies movement, narrow movement but motion nonetheless. There is really no way to describe someone who does not move at all. Even a creep does move—if at a pace exasperatingly more slow than the pace of the cool cats.

4

Like children, hipsters are fighting for the sweet, and their language is a set of subtle indications of their success or failure in the competition for pleasure. Unstated but obvious is the social sense that there is not nearly enough sweet for everyone. And so the sweet goes only to the victor, the best, the most, the man who knows the most about how to find his energy and how not to lose it. The emphasis is on energy because the psychopath and the hipster are nothing without it since they do not have the protection of a position or a class to rely on when they have overextended themselves. So the language of Hip is a language of energy, how it is found, how it is lost.

But let us see. I have jotted down perhaps a dozen words, the Hip perhaps most in use and most likely to last with the minimum of variation. The words are man, go, put down, make, beat, cool, swing, with it, crazy, dig, flip, creep, hip, square. They serve a variety of purposes and the nuance of the voice uses the nuance of the situation to convey the subtle contextual difference. If the hipster moves through his life on a constant search with glimpses of Mecca in many a turn of his experience (Mecca being the apocalyptic orgasm) and if everyone in the civilized world is at least in some small degree a sexual cripple, the hipster lives with the knowledge of how he is sexually crippled and where he is sexually alive, and the faces of experience which life presents to him each day are engaged, dismissed or avoided as his need directs and his lifemanship makes possible. For life is a contest between people in which the vigor generally recuperates quickly and the loser takes long to mend, a perpetual competition of colliding explorers in which one must grow or else pay more for remaining the same (pay in sickness, or depression, or anguish for the lost opportunity), but pay or grow.

Therefore one finds words like go, and make it, and with it, and swing: "Go" with its sense that after hours or days or months or years of monotony, boredom, and depression one has finally had one's chance, one has amassed enough energy to meet an exciting opportunity with all one's present talents for the flip (up or down) and so one is ready to go, ready to gamble. Movement is always to be preferred to inaction. In motion a man has a chance, his body is warm, his instincts are quick, and when the crisis comes, whether of love or violence, he can make it, he can win, he can release a little more energy for himself since he hates himself a little less, he can make a little better nervous system, make it a little more possible to go again, to go faster next time and so make more and thus find more people with whom he can swing. For to swing is to communicate, is to convey the rhythms of one's own being to a lover, a friend, or an audience, and—equally necessary—be able to feel the rhythms of their response. To swing with the rhythms of another is to enrich oneself—the conception of the learning process as dug by Hip is that one cannot really learn until one contains within oneself the implicit rhythm of the subject or the person. As an example, I remember once hearing a Negro friend have an intellectual discussion at a party for half an hour with a white girl who was a few years out of college. The Negro literally could not read or write, but he had an extraordinary ear and a fine sense of mimicry. So as the girl spoke, he would detect the particular formal uncertainties in her argument, and in a pleasant (if slightly Southern) English accent, he would respond to one or another facet of her doubts. When she would finish what she felt was a particularly well-articulated idea, he would smile privately and say, "Other-direction . . . do you really believe in that?"

"Well . . . No," the girl would stammer, "now that you get down to it, there is something disgusting about it to me," and she would be off again for five more minutes.

Of course the Negro was not learning anything about the merits and demerits of the argument, but he was learning a great deal about a type of girl he had never met before, and that was what he wanted. Being unable to read or write, he could hardly be interested in ideas nearly as much as in lifemanship, and so he eschewed any attempt to obey the precision or lack of precision in the girl's language, and instead sensed her character (and the values of her social type) by swinging with the nuances of her voice.

So to swing is to be able to learn, and by learning take a step toward making it, toward creating. What is to be created is not nearly so important as the hipster's belief that when he really makes it, he will be able to turn his hand to anything, even to self-discipline. What he must do before that is find his courage at the moment of violence, or equally make it in the act of love, find a little more between his woman and himself, or indeed between his mate and himself (since many hipsters are bisexual), but paramount, imperative, is the necessity to make it because in making it, one is making the new habit, unearthing the new talent which the old frustration denied.

Whereas if you goof (the ugliest word in Hip), if you lapse back into being a frightened stupid child, or if you flip, if you lose your control, reveal the buried weaker more feminine part of your nature, then it is more difficult to swing the next time, your ear is less alive, your bad and energy-wasting habits are further confirmed, you are farther away from being with it. But to be with it is to have grace, is to be closer to the secrets of that inner unconscious life which will nourish you if you can hear it, for you are then nearer to that God which every hipster believes is located in the senses of his body, that trapped, mutilated and nonetheless megalomaniacal God who is It, who is energy, life, sex, force, the Yoga's *prana*,[6] the Reichian's orgone, Lawrence's "blood," Hemingway's "good," the Shavian life-force; "It,"; God; not the God of the churches but the unachievable whisper of mystery within the sex, the paradise of limitless energy and perception just beyond the next wave of the next orgasm.

To which a cool cat might reply, "Crazy, man!"

[6]Sanskrit: life power.

Because, after all, what I have offered above is an hypothesis, no more, and there is not the hipster alive who is not absorbed in his own tumultuous hypotheses. Mine is interesting, mine is way out (on the avenue of the mystery along the road to "It") but still I am just one cat in a world of cool cats, and everything interesting is crazy, or at least so the Squares who do not know how to swing would say.

(And yet crazy is also the self-protective irony of the hipster. Living with questions and not with answers, he is so different in his isolation and in the far reach of his imagination from almost everyone with whom he deals in the outer world of the Square, and meets generally so much enmity, competition, and hatred in the world of Hip, that his isolation is always in danger of turning upon itself, and leaving him indeed just that, crazy.)

If, however, you agree with my hypothesis, if you as a cat are way out too, and we are in the same groove (the universe now being glimpsed as a series of ever-extending radii from the center), why then you say simply, "I dig," because neither knowledge nor imagination comes easily, it is buried in the pain of one's forgotten experience, and so one must work to find it, one must occasionally exhaust oneself by digging into the self in order to perceive the outside. And indeed it is essential to dig the most, for if you do not dig you lose your superiority over the Square, and so you are less likely to be cool (to be in control of a situation because you have swung where the Square has not, or because you have allowed to come to consciousness a pain, a guilt, a shame or a desire which the other has not had the courage to face). To be cool is to be equipped, and if you are equipped it is more difficult for the next cat who comes along to put you down. And of course one can hardly afford to be put down too often, or one is beat, one has lost one's confidence, one has lost one's will, one is impotent in the world of action and so closer to the demeaning flip of becoming a queer, or indeed closer to dying, and therefore it is even more difficult to recover enough energy to try to make it again, because once a cat is beat he has nothing to give, and no one is interested any longer in making it with him. This is the terror of the hipster—to be beat—because once the sweet of sex has deserted him, he still cannot give up the search. It is not granted to the hipster to grow old gracefully—he has been captured too early by the oldest dream of power, the gold fountain of Ponce de León, the fountain of youth where the gold is in the orgasm.

To be beat is therefore a flip, it is a situation beyond one's experience, impossible to anticipate—which indeed in the circular vocabulary of Hip is still another meaning for flip, but then I have given just a few of the connotations of these words. Like most primitive vocabularies each word is a prime symbol and serves a dozen or a hundred functions of communication in the instinctive dialectic through which the hipster perceives his experience, that dialectic of the instantaneous differentials of existence in which one is forever moving forward into more or retreating into less.

5

It is impossible to conceive a new philosophy until one creates a new language, but a new popular language (while it must implicitly contain a new philosophy) does not necessarily present its philosophy overtly. It can be asked then what really is unique in the life-view of Hip which raises its argot above the passing verbal whimsies of the bohemian or the lumpenproletariat.

The answer would be in the psychopathic element of Hip which has almost no interest in viewing human nature, or better, in judging human nature, from a set of standards conceived a priori to the experience, standards inherited from the past. Since Hip sees every answer as posing immediately a new alternative, a new question, its emphasis is on complexity rather than simplicity (such complexity that its language without the illumination of the voice and the articulation of the face and body remains hopelessly incommunicative). Given its emphasis on complexity, Hip abdicates from any conventional moral responsibility because it would argue that the results of our actions are unforeseeable, and so we cannot know if we do good or bad, we cannot even know (in the Joycean sense of the good and the bad) whether we have given energy to another, and indeed if we could, there would still be no idea of what ultimately the other would do with it.

Therefore, men are not seen as good or bad (that they are good-and-bad is taken for granted) but rather each man is glimpsed as a collection of possibilities, some more possible than others (the view of character implicit in Hip) and some humans are considered more capable than others of reaching more possibilities within themselves in less time, provided, and this is the dynamic, provided the particular character can swing at the right time. And here arises the sense of context which differentiates Hip from a Square view of character. Hip sees the context as generally dominating the man, dominating him because his character is less significant than the context in which he must function. Since it is arbitrarily five times more demanding of one's energy to accomplish even an inconsequential action in an unfavorable context than a favorable one, man is then not only his character but his context, since the success or failure of an action in a given context reacts upon the character and therefore affects what the character will be in the next context. What dominates both character and context is the energy available at the moment of intense context.

Character being thus seen as perpetually ambivalent and dynamic enters then into an absolute relativity where there are no truths other than the isolated truths of what each observer feels at each instant of his existence. To take a perhaps unjustified metaphysical extrapolation, it is as if the universe which has usually existed conceptually as a Fact (even if the Fact were Berkeley's God) but a Fact which it was the aim of all science and philosophy to reveal, becomes instead a changing reality whose laws are remade at each instant by everything living, but most particularly man, man raised to a neo-medieval summit where the truth is not what one has felt yesterday or what one expects to feel tomorrow but rather truth is no more nor less than what one feels at each instant in the perpetual climax of the present.

What is consequent therefore is the divorce of man from his values, the liberation of the self from the Super-Ego of society. The only Hip morality (but of course it is an ever-present morality) is to do what one feels whenever and wherever it is possible, and—this is how the war of the Hip and the Square begins—to be engaged in one primal battle: to open the limits of the possible for oneself, for oneself alone, because that is one's need. Yet in widening the arena of the possible, one widens it reciprocally for others as well, so that the nihilistic fulfillment of each man's desire contains its antithesis of human cooperation.

If the ethic reduces to Know Thyself and Be Thyself, what makes it radically different from Socratic moderation with its stern conservative respect for the experience of the past is that the Hip ethic is immoderation, childlike in its adoration of the present (and indeed to respect the past means that one must also respect such ugly consequences of the past as the collective murders of the State). It is this adoration of the present which contains the affirmation of Hip, because its ultimate logic surpasses even the unforgettable solution of the Marquis de Sade to sex, private property, and the family, that all men and women have absolute but temporary rights over the bodies of all other men and women—the nihilism of Hip proposes as its final tendency that every social restraint and category be removed, and the affirmation implicit in the proposal is that man would then prove to be more creative than murderous and so would not destroy himself. Which is exactly what separates Hip from the authoritarian philosophies which now appeal to the conservative and liberal temper—what haunts the middle of the twentieth century is that faith in man has been lost, and the appeal of authority has been that it would restrain us from ourselves. Hip, which would return us to ourselves, at no matter what price in individual violence, is the affirmation of the barbarian, for it requires a primitive passion about human nature to believe that individual acts of violence are always to be preferred to the collective violence of the State; it takes literal faith in the creative possibilities of the human being to envisage acts of violence as the catharsis which prepares growth.

Whether the hipster's desire for absolute sexual freedom contains any genuinely radical conception of a different world is of course another matter, and it is possible, since the hipster lives with his hatred, that many of them are the material for an elite of storm troopers ready to follow the first truly magnetic leader whose view of mass murder is phrased in a language which reaches their emotions. But given the desperation of his condition as a psychic outlaw, the hipster is equally a candidate for the most reactionary and most radical of movements, and so it is just as possible that many hipsters will come—if the crisis deepens—to a radical comprehension of the horror of society, for even as the radical has had his incommunicable dissent confirmed in his experience by precisely the frustration, the denied opportunities, and the bitter years which his ideas have cost him, so the sexual adventurer deflected from his goal by the implacable animosity of a society constructed to deny the sexual radical as well, may yet come to an equally bitter comprehension of the slow relentless inhumanity of the conservative power which controls him from without and from within. And in being so controlled, denied, and starved into the attrition of conformity, indeed the hipster may come to see that his condition is no more than an exaggeration of the human condition, and if he would be free, then everyone must be free. Yes, this is possible, too, for the heart of Hip is its emphasis upon courage at the moment of crisis, and it is pleasant to think that courage contains within itself (as the explanation of its existence) some glimpse of the necessity of life to become more than it has been.

It is obviously not very possible to speculate with sharp focus on the future of the hipster. Certain possibilities must be evident, however, and the most central is that the organic growth of Hip depends on whether the Negro emerges as a dominating force in American life. Since the Negro knows more about the ugliness and danger of life than the white, it is probable that if the Negro can win his equality, he will possess a potential superiority, a superiority so feared that the fear itself has become the underground drama of domestic politics. Like all conservative political fear it is the fear of unforeseeable consequences, for the Negro's equality would tear a profound shift into the psychology, the sexuality, and the moral imagination of every white alive.

With this possible emergence of the Negro, Hip may erupt as a psychically armed rebellion whose sexual impetus may rebound against the antisexual foundation of every organized power in America, and bring into the air such animosities, antipathies, and new conflicts of interest that the mean empty hypocrisies of mass conformity will no longer work. A time of violence, new hysteria, confusion and rebellion will then be likely to replace the time of conformity. At that time, if the liberal should prove realistic in his belief that there is peaceful room for every tendency in American life, then Hip would end by being absorbed as a colorful figure in the tapestry. But if this is not the reality, and the economic, the social, the psychological, and finally the moral crises accompanying the rise of the Negro should prove insupportable, then a time is coming when every political guidepost will be gone, and millions of liberals will be faced with political dilemmas they have so far succeeded in evading, and with a view of human nature they do not wish to accept. To take the desegregation of the schools in the South as an example, it is quite likely that the reactionary sees the reality more closely than the liberal when he argues that the deeper issue is not desegregation but miscegenation. (As a radical I am of course facing in the opposite direction from the White Citizen's Councils— obviously I believe it is the absolute human right of the Negro to mate with the white, and matings there will undoubtedly be, for there will be Negro high school boys brave enough to chance their lives.) But for the average liberal whose mind has been dulled by the committee-ish cant of the professional liberal, miscegenation is not an issue because he has been told that the Negro does not desire it. So, when it comes, miscegenation will be a terror, comparable perhaps to the derangement of the American Communists when the icons to Stalin came tumbling down. The average American Communist held to the myth of Stalin for reasons which had little to do with the political evidence and everything to do with their psychic necessities. In this sense it is equally a psychic necessity for the liberal to believe that the Negro and even the reactionary Southern white are eventually and fundamentally people like himself, capable of becoming good liberals too if only they can be reached by good liberal reason. What the liberal cannot bear to admit is the hatred beneath the skin of a society so unjust that the amount of collective violence buried in the people is perhaps incapable of being contained, and therefore if one wants a better world one does well to hold one's breath, for a worse world is bound to come first, and the dilemma may well be this: given such hatred, it must either vent itself nihilistically or become turned into the cold murderous liquidations of the totalitarian state.

6

No matter what its horrors the twentieth century is a vastly exciting century for its tendency is to reduce all of life to its ultimate alternatives. One can well wonder if the last war of them all will be between the blacks and the whites, or between the women and the men, or between the beautiful and ugly, the pillagers and managers, or the rebels and the regulators. Which of course is carrying speculation beyond the point where speculation is still serious, and yet despair at the monotony and bleakness of the future have become so engrained in the radical temper that the radical is in danger of abdicating from all imagination. What a man feels is the impulse for his creative effort, and if an alien but nonetheless passionate instinct about the meaning of life has come so unexpectedly from a virtually illiterate people, come out of the most intense conditions of exploitation, cruelty, violence, frustration, and lust, and yet has succeeded as an instinct in keeping this tortured people alive, then it is perhaps possible that the Negro holds more of the tail of the expanding elephant of truth than the radical, and if this is so, the radical humanist could do worse than to brood upon the phenomenon. For if a revolutionary time should come again, there would be a crucial difference if someone had already delineated a neo-Marxian calculus aimed at comprehending every circuit and process of society from ukase to kiss as the communications of human energy—a calculus capable of translating the economic relations of man into his psychological relations and then back again, his productive relations thereby embracing his sexual relations as well, until the crises of capitalism in the twentieth century would yet be understood as the unconscious adaptations of a society to solve its economic imbalance at the expense of a new mass psychological imbalance. It is almost beyond the imagination to conceive of a work in which the drama of human energy is engaged, and a theory of its social currents and dissipations, its imprisonments, expressions, and tragic wastes are fitted into some gigantic synthesis of human action where the body of Marxist thought, and particularly the epic grandeur of *Das Kapital* (that first of the major *psychologies* to approach the mystery of social cruelty so simply and practically as to say that we are a collective body of humans whose life-energy is wasted, displaced, and proce-durally stolen as it passes from one of us to another)—where particularly the epic grandeur of *Das Kapital* would find its place in an even more God-like view of human justice and injustice, in some more excruciating vision of those intimate and institutional processes which lead to our creations and disasters, our growth, our attrition, and our rebellion.

1957   1959

from *THE ARMIES OF THE NIGHT*[1]

from Part II
FRIDAY AFTERNOON

THE HISTORIAN

To write an intimate history of an event which places its focus on a central figure who is not central to the event, is to inspire immediate questions about the competence of the historian. Or, indeed, his honorable motive. The figure he has selected may be convenient to him rather than critical to the history. Such cynical remarks obviously suggest themselves in the choice of our particular protagonist. It could be said that for this historian, there is no other choice. While that might not be necessarily inaccurate, nonetheless a presentation of his good motives had best be offered now.

The March on the Pentagon was an ambiguous event whose essential value or absurdity may not be established for ten or twenty yers, or indeed ever. So to place the real principals, the founders or designers of the March, men like David Dellinger, or Jerry Rubin, in the center of our portrait could prove misleading. They were serious men, devoted to hard detailed work; their po-

[1]Mailer's account (published 1968) of the 1967 peace march on the Pentagon to protest against the Vietnam War.

sition in these affairs, precisely because it was central, can resolve nothing of the ambiguity. For that, an eyewitness who is a participant but not a vested partisan is required, further he must be not only involved, but ambiguous in his own proportions, a comic hero, which is to say, one cannot happily resolve the emphasis of the category—is he finally comic, a ludicrous figure with mock-heroic associations; or is he not unheroic, and therefore embedded somewhat tragically in the comic? Or is he both at once, and all at once? These questions, which probably are not much more answerable than the very ambiguities of the event, at least help to recapture the precise feel of the ambiguity of the event and its monumental disproportions. Mailer[2] is a figure of monumental dispro-portions and so serves willy-nilly as the bridge—many will say the *pons asinorum*[3]—into the crazy house, the crazy mansion, of that historic moment when a mass of the citizenry—not much more than a mob—marched on a bastion which symbolized the military might of the Republic, marching not to capture it, but to wound it *symbolically*; the forces defending that bastion reacted as if a symbolic wound could prove as mortal as any other combative rent. In the midst of a technological century, close to its apogee, a medieval, nay, a primitive mode of warfare was reinvigorated, and the nations of the world stood in grave observation. Either the century was entrenching itself more deeply into the absurd, or the absurd was delivering evidence that it was possessed of some of the nutritive mysteries of a marrow which would yet feed the armies of the absurd. So if the event took place in one of the crazy mansions, or indeed *the* crazy house of history, it is fitting that any ambiguous comic hero of such a history should be not only off very much to the side of the history, but that he should be an egotist of the most startling misproportions, outrageously and often unhappily self-assertive, yet in command of a detachment classic in severity (for he was a novelist and so in need of studying every last lineament of the fine, the noble, the frantic, and the foolish in others and in himself). Such egotism being two-headed, thrusting itself forward the better to study itself, finds itself therefore at home in a house of mirrors, since it has habits, even the talent, to regard itself. Once History inhabits a crazy house, egotism may be the last tool left to History.

Let us then make our comic hero the narrative vehicle for the March on the Pentagon. Let us follow further. He is awakening Friday morning in his room at the Hay-Adams[4] after his night on the stage of the Ambassador[5] and the party thereafter. One may wonder if the Adams in the name of his hotel bore any relation to Henry; we need not be concerned with Hay who was a memorable and accomplished gentleman from the nineteenth century (then Secretary of State to McKinley and Roosevelt) other than to say that the hotel looked like its name, and was indeed the staunchest advocate of that happy if heavy style in Washington architecture which spoke of a time when men and events were solid, comprehensible, often obedient to a code of values, and resolutely non-electronic. Mailer awakening with a thunderous electronic headache began his morning revery with a conclusion that the Georgian period in architecture was not resolutely suited to himself.

[2]Mailer refers to himself in the third person.
[3]Latin: asses' bridge. A classical term for any learning device or aid to reasoning used by beginners or dullards.
[4]Washington, D.C., hotel, named for Henry Adams and John Hay (1838–1905), American statesman and author.
[5]Theater in Washington, D.C.

THE CITIZEN

All right, let us look into his mind. It has been burned out by the gouts of bourbon he has taken into himself the night before (in fact, one of the reasons he detests napalm[1] is that he assumes its effect on the countryside is comparable to the ravages of booze on the better foliage of his brain) however, one can make too much of a hangover, these are comic profits which should perhaps be reinvested—his headache is in truth not thunderous so much as definite and ineradicable until late afternoon, when whiskey wastes half-cleared, he will feel legitimized to take another drink. In the meantime, he must stir his stupefied message center into sufficient activity to give him a mind to meet the minds he would encounter this day, for this day, Friday, was—you will remember—the occasion on which he would lend the dubious substance of his name to those young men brave enough, idealistic enough, (and doubtless vegetarian enough!) to give their draft cards back to the government on the steps of the Department of Justice. Mailer detested the thought of getting through the oncoming hours. Under the best of circumstances the nature of these heroics was too dry, too dignified, too obviously severed from bravura to make the Novelist happy (not for nothing had an eminent critic once said that Mailer was as fond of his style as an Italian tenor is fond of his vocal cords) no, he liked good character when it issued into action which was visually tumultuous rather than inspiring awe in the legal mind. To the extent any revolution was legalistic, Mailer detested it, cursed those logics of commitment which carried him into such formal lines of protest.

Of course, the alternatives did not appeal to him on this morning either. His head delicate, he could not help remembering that these affairs were not always so dignified; there had been occasional small riots between pro- and anti-war demonstrators, and the past week had had its associated excitements in Oakland, Chicago, at the University of Wisconsin, Reed College, Brooklyn College, on Boston Common where four thousand demonstrators had massed at a draft-card burning. ("67 men," *Time* was later to report, "ignited their cards with a candlestick once owned by William Ellery Channing.")[2] In some of these places there had been violence with the police, broken heads, the use of Mace[3] by the Oakland police, a particularly nasty chemical spray which blinded people for a few hours. (Indeed its name was appropriate for Batman). Mailer's eyesight was not good—the thought of Mace in his hard-used eyes inspired a small horror. He did not expect the demonstrations to reach such proportions today, but on Saturday . . . well, he simply did not wish to get Mace in his eyes. As for broken heads—he had been struck once with a policeman's billy and it had opened a cut worth thirteen stitches; Mailer still remembered how disagreeable the subsequent hours in prison had been with his head bleeding, and his brain in the stupefactions of a near to overpowering headache. It was not inspirational to add the memory of the headache to his present one. Still, Mailer could hardly conceive of trouble in Washington on the steps of the Department of Justice—the police would doubtless be superior to their fine colleagues in Brooklyn, Oakland, and Wisconsin.

Revolutionaries-for-a-weekend should never get hangovers. Mailer detected that he was secretly comforted by the thought there would probably be no

---

[1]Highly incendiary jellied gasoline—used in firebombs.
[2]American clergyman and author (1780–1842).
[3]Nonlethal disabling spray, used to incapacitate attackers and subdue rioters.

violence today; even worse, he was comforted by the conclusion that the best police in Washington would be at the Department of Justice to maintain order. His exertions of the night before had been perfect for delivering him of some weeks of concentrated rage, perhaps even violence, at a variety of frustrations, he felt cleansed of the kind of hatred which leaves one leaden or tense, and his voice—which he did not dare to use yet, not even in an attempt to clear his throat—was clearly extinguished down to a whisper by last night's vocal exertions without a mike. Even his chest, chronic captive of a mysterious iron vise upon his lungs (which is why he had given up smoking) was relaxed this morning. Yelling on stage seemed literally to have loosened the screw of the vise. To his surprise, Mailer realized he felt gentle—in fact, this morning, he felt like a damn Quaker, which was no way for a revolutionary to feel, unless he was—mark this conjunction—going to consort with pacifists and draft-card burners.

The trouble with being gentle is that one has no defense against shame. Mailer was beginning to remember what he had said last night—he could not tell himself he was altogether happy about the confidential specifications concerning the men's room; if the memory of that was balmed by the recollection of presenting himself as Lyndon Johnson's[4] dwarf alter ego, well, the general memory of the evening (like a deep bruise which might yet prove languorous and not unpleasant in the intimations of its pain or, to the contrary, directly nauseating) was still a little too delicate to probe. Mailer left the memories alone. He was a suggestion uneasy about the newspapers.

They, however, could have been significantly worse. Reading *The Washington Post* downstairs, over breakfast, Mailer decided he had gotten away with it, and so enjoyed his food and ate with large appetite, an ability he almost always possessed no matter how much he had drunk the night before—the best reason perhaps why he never considered it possible to become an alcoholic.

In the dining room were friends and acquaintances, a political writer, Jack Newfield, who did a column for *The Village Voice*,[5] and Jacob Brackman, a young writer for *The New Yorker*. There were friends and wives and relatives about— a muted festivity was in the air, almost as if the hotel were headquarters for a small convention of gentle professionals, editors let us say, of numismatic magazines—something to offer small aggregations of security to one's years.

The program for the day was presented in a leaflet which Mailer had brought with him to Washington. In a typical anxiety at his essential lack of orientation to the protean forms of these protests he had put a folder of mailings, leaflets, programs, reprints, and associated letters for money in his attaché case—each morning he whipped through the folder selecting what seemed appropriate for the occasion. Even a protest against the 10 percent increase in income tax had gotten into this—Mailer had to put it aside each morning. Since he had taken the oath not to pay the 10 percent increase in the event it was passed (for the increase had been announced as a surtax to meet the costs of the war in Vietnam) he anticipated with no particular joy that the Department of Internal Revenue would examine his returns in the years ahead with no ordinary tolerance. (In fact he fully expected his financial tidbits to be fried.) Stating this supposition with his own variety of gallows humor had been the most direct pleasure in a letter he had written to James Baldwin, Bruce Jay Friedman, Philip Roth, Joseph Heller, Tennessee Williams, Edward Albee, Jack Richardson, Robert Lowell, Truman Capote, Nelson Algren, James Jones, Gore Vidal, Arthur Miller, Lillian

[4]President of the United States (1963–1969)
[5]Greenwich Village (New York City) newspaper.

Hellman, Lillian Ross, Vance Bourjaily, Mary McCarthy, and Jules Feiffer,[6] asking them to join this protest.

Actually, he had hated the thought of signing the protest, he had piped up every variety of the extraordinarily sound argument that his work was the real answer to Vietnam, and these mass demonstrations, sideshows, and bloody income tax protests just took energy and *money* away from the real thing—getting the work out. But for such an argument to succeed, it was necessary to have work which absorbed all one's effort, and a sense of happy status with oneself. Mailer had had neither for the last year or two. His work had been good—there were some who thought *Why Are We In Vietnam?*[7] was the best book he had ever written, but no project had seemed to cost him enough, and he had been suffering more and more in the past few years from the private conviction that he was getting a little soft, a hint curdled, perhaps an almost invisible rim of corruption was growing around the edges. His career, his legend, his idea of himself—were they stale? So he had no real alternative—he was not sufficiently virtuous to eschew the income tax protest, and had signed, and to his surprise had been repaid immediately by the abrupt departure of a measurable quantity of moral congestion, a noticeable lowering of his spiritual flatulence and a reduction in his New York fever, that ferocious inflammation which New York seemed always to encourage: envy, greed, claustrophobia, excitement, bourbon, broads, action, ego, jousts, cruelty and too-rich food in expensive hateful restaurants. Yes, signing the protest had been good for him. (He hoped he remembered in future years when the penalty might have to be paid.) But now, going through his attaché case, he could grin in the mirror, for if he had only known in September that shortly, so shortly, he was going to be an incometaxnik, he could have told Mitch Goodman[8] where to shove his RESISTANCE. (Or was it called RESIST?—even with the pamphlets Mailer could not get the names right, there were so many and they changed so rapidly.) "Yes, Mitch," he could have said, "I think your RESISTANCE is first rate! first rate! but I'm putting my energy these days into the income tax drive. You have your going-to-jail bag—now I have mine." Of course, on the other hand, if he had only joined RESIST? RESISTANCE? with a little good grace he could have told the tax protest people . . .

This was vast humor perhaps to no one else, but in the middle of his hangover, Mailer was still remotely delighted by the mock dialogue of all this: yessir, boss, we'se gonna get in all the jail bags before day is done.

So over the tag-ends of breakfast, he read once more right over the following literature:

WE ARE PLANNING AN ACT OF DIRECT CREATIVE RESISTANCE TO THE WAR AND THE DRAFT IN WASHINGTON ON FRIDAY, OCTOBER 20. The locale of our action will be the Department of Justice. We will gather at the First United Congregational Church of Christ, 10th and G Streets, N.W., Washington (near Pennsylvania Avenue), at 1 P.M. We will appear at the Justice Department together with 30 or 40 young men brought by us to Washington to represent the 24 Resistance groups from all over the country. There we will present to the Attorney General the draft cards turned in locally by these groups on October 16. (Those of us who want to include their own draft cards will be able to do so.) We will, in a clear, simple ceremony make concrete our affirmation of support for these young men who are the spearhead of direct resistance to the war and all of its machinery.

[6]Here and below, Mailer cites prominent literary and intellectual figures of America in the 1960s.
[7]The title of Mailer's previous book, his fifth novel (1967).
[8]American writer and friend of Mailer.

The draft law commands that we shall not aid, abet or counsel men to refuse the draft. But as a group of the clergy have recently said, when young men refuse to allow their conscience to be violated by an unjust law and a criminal war, then it is necessary for their elders—their teachers, ministers, friends—to make clear their commitment, in conscience, to *aid, abet, and counsel* them against conscription. Most of us have already done this privately. Now publicly we will demonstrate, side by side with these young men, our determination to continue to do so.

Mitchell Goodman, Henry Braun, Denise Levertov, Noam Chomsky, William Sloane Coffin, Dwight Macdonald

NOTE: Among the hundreds already committed to this action are Robert Lowell, Norman Mailer, Ashley Montagu, Arthur Waskow, and professors from most of the major colleges and universities in the East.

JUSTICE

Well, they were now at the steps—one of the set of steps in any case. It all seemed a hint undramatic. When he had first heard of the action from Mitch Goodman, pictures had crossed his mind of charged disagreeable encounters with FBI men in the corridors of the Department of Justice, now instead there was not a government man in sight if one did not count the number of FBI and CIA agents doubtless circulating among the press as photographers, newsreel men, TV cameramen, and newspapermen, there to mug and map every subversive face in sight. The nearest representative of any potential violence face to face was a stand of five American Nazis wearing swastikas for armbands, and kept by the police off to one side of the proceedings. All through the afternoon the Nazis kept chanting slogans. "We want dead Reds," was the clearest.

Here was the disposition of bodies: on a corner of the steps of the Department of Justice were gathered about fifteen men, most of whom were going to speak for a minute or two. Facing them, just below the steps, was a phalanx of mass-media representatives, and they were going through a preliminary boxing out and jockeying in for position between newsreel, still and television cameras. To the sides of them, and behind them, was a group of four or five hundred people who for the most part cheered politely although with distinct well-bred fervor at remarks they particularly liked.

Coffin[1] gave the main address. He began by speaking of the procedure to be followed. After a few short speeches, those students representing themselves or organizations of students who might wish to turn in their draft cards, would come forward one by one and deposit their cards in a bag. Then, any individuals in the audience, student, faculty, or onlookers who thought to hand in their draft cards as well could join. At that point, Mitch Goodman, Coffin, Dr. Spock,[2] and seven other demonstrators would "disappear for a while and enter the Department of Justice Building. Once inside," said Coffin, "we will proceed to the Office of the Attorney General and there hand over the cards and notify him of our intention which is that we hereby publicly counsel these young men to continue in their refusal to serve in the Armed Forces as long as the war in Vietnam continues, and we pledge ourselves to aid and abet them in all the ways we can." There were cheers. "At that point," Coffin went on, "depending on

[1]William Sloan Coffin, Jr., the chaplain of Yale University.
[2]Dr. Benjamin Spock, noted pediatrician and antiwar activist.

how we are received, we shall either leave, and rejoin you here to report our conversation, or if there are difficulties, we may be delayed." It was impossible to tell if he was hinting they might be arrested. "If we do not reappear quickly, I would ask you all to wait and divert yourselves with speeches"—small titter— "or song." More amusement. "If it takes too long, and we are not able to send word out, I would then suggest you disperse and those interested can come together tonight at the meeting already signified, for a full account."

Then he gave his prepared speech. It was reasonable in length, the points clearly made, his indignation kept nicely in leash but nonetheless vibrant. His sentences had a nonpoetic bony statement of meaning which made them exactly suitable for newspaper quotation.

". . . in our view it is not wild-eyed idealism but clear-eyed revulsion that brings us here. For as one of our number put it: 'If what the United States is doing in Vietnam is right, what is there left to be called wrong?'

"Many of us are veterans, and all of us have the highest sympathy for our boys in Vietnam. They know what a dirty, bloody war it is. But they have been told that the ends justify the means, and that the cleansing water of victory will wash clean their hands of all the blood and dirt. No wonder they hate us who say 'There must be no cleansing water.' But what they must strive to understand, hard as it is, is that there can be no cleansing water if military victory spells moral defeat.

"We have the highest sympathy also for those who back the war because their sons or lovers or husbands are fighting or have died in Vietnam. But they too must understand a very basic thing—that sacrifice in and of itself confers no sanctity. Even if half a million of our boys were to die in Vietnam that would not make the cause one whit more sacred. Yet we realize how hard that knowledge is to appropriate when one's husband is numbered among the sacrificed."

Had he, Mailer was ready to wonder, come from a long line of New England ministers whose pride resided partly in their ability to extract practical methods from working in the world? It was a Protestant discipline of which our Participant knew little, and it had made in his opinion for a great deal of waste in the world, since America's corporations were in Mailer's opinion more guilty than the Communists at polluting the air, fields, and streams, debasing the value of manufactured products, transmuting faith into science, technology, and medicine, while all embarked on scandalous foreign adventures with their eminently practical methods—yes, all that might have come by panning the homely practical silt out of the tumultuous rivers of Christian experience in the world. What was fascinating to Mailer is that the Yale Chaplain had one of those faces you expected to see on the cover of *Time* or *Fortune,* there as the candidate for Young Executive of the Year, he had that same flint of the eye, single-mindedness in purpose, courage to bear responsibility, that same hard humor about the details in the program under consideration, that same suggestion of an absolute lack of humor once the line which enclosed his true Wasp temper had been breached. He was one full example of the masculine principle at work in the cloth.

"As the law now stands, for a man to qualify as a conscientious objector he must believe in God. Could anything be more ethically absurd? Have humanists no conscience? Why,—and as a Christian I say this with contrition—some of the most outstanding humanists I know would think they were slipping from their high ideals were they to take steps towards conversion. As a Christian I am convinced it is a gross misfortune not to believe in God, but it is not automatically an ethical default.

"Then despite numerous appeals by numerous religious bodies, Congress last spring chose to provide alternative service only for the absolute pacifist. This too is absurd, for the rights of a man whose conscience forbids him to participate in a particular war are as deserving of respect as the rights of a man whose conscience forbids him to participate in any war at all."

This drew the largest applause of his speech. Just as in the thirties when the success of every Communist meeting was absolutely dependent upon the victory talk being given by a man with a fine Irish brogue—"Down with the doorty capitalist system say I!"—so the conscientious objection of the non-religious would be advanced consummately in the hands of a minister. Indeed, who else?

"The law of the land is clear. Section 12 of the National Selective Service Act declares that anyone 'who knowingly counsels, aids, or abets another to refuse or evade registration or service in the armed forces . . . shall be liable to imprisonment for not more than five years or a fine of ten thousand dollars or both.'

"We hereby publicly counsel these young men to continue in their refusal to serve in the armed forces as long as the war in Vietnam continues, and we pledge ourselves to aid and abet them in all the ways we can. This means that if they are now arrested for failing to comply with a law that violates their consciences, we too must be arrested, for in the sight of that law we are now as guilty as they."

There were a few more speeches, all short. Mitch Goodman made one, Dr. Spock made one, and then three or four other people whose names Mailer did not recognize and to whose speeches he hardly listened. It was turning cold, the sun had gone back of a cloud, and his hangover had settled in for a bout. It would not leave now until the proceedings were over, and he could go somewhere to get a drink. He had no idea if they would call upon him in a little while to speak, although he judged not. Probably Mitch Goodman had passed word that Mailer was attending, but with no especial good grace.

In the middle of these speakers, Robert Lowell was called up. He had been leaning against a wall in his habitual slumped over position, deep in revery at the side of the steps—and of course had been photographed as a figure of dejection—the call for him to say a few words caught him partly by surprise. He now held the portable hand microphone with a delicate lack of intimacy as if it were some valuable, huge, and rare tropical spider which he was obliged to examine but did not have to enjoy. "I was asked earlier today," he began in his fine stammering voice which gave the impression that life rushed at him like a series of hurdles and some he succeeded in jumping and some he did not, "I was asked earlier this afternoon by a reporter why I was not turning in my draft card," Lowell said with the beginnings of a pilgrim's passion, "and I did not tell him it was a stupid question, although I was tempted to. I thought he should have known that I am now too old to have a draft card, but that it makes no difference. When some of us pledge ourselves to counsel and aid and abet any young men who wish to turn in their cards, why then you may be certain we are aware of the possible consequences and do not try to hide behind the technicality of whether we literally have a draft card or not. So I'm now saying to the gentlemen of the press that unlike the authorities who are running this country, we are not searching for tricks, we try to think of ourselves as serious men, if the press, that is, can comprehend such an effort, and we will protest this war by every means available to our conscience, and therefore not try to avoid whatever may arise in the way of retribution."

It was said softly, on a current of intense indignation and Lowell had never looked more dignified nor more admirable. Each word seemed to come on a separate journey from the poet's mind to his voice, along a winding route or through an exorbitant gate. Each word cost him much—Lowell's fine grace was in the value words had for him, he seemed to emit a horror at the possibility of squandering them or leaving them abused, and political speeches had never seemed more difficult for him, and on the consequence, more necessary for statement.

So Mailer applauded when Lowell was done. And suddenly liked him enormously for his speech, and decided he liked him truly. Beneath all snobbery, affectations of weariness, literary logrollermanship, neutralsmanship, and whatever other fatal snob-infested baggage of the literary world was by now willy-nilly in the poet's system, worked down intimately close to all his best and most careful traditions and standards, all flaws considered, Lowell was still a fine, good, and honorable man, and Norman Mailer was happy to be linked in a cause with him.

But now much began to happen to Mailer on the aftermath of this speech. For shortly afterward students began to file up the steps to deposit their solitary or collective draft cards in the bag, and this procession soon became a ceremony. Each man came up, gave his name, and the state or area or college he represented, and then proceeded to name the number of draft cards he had been entrusted to turn in. The numbers were larger than one might have expected. There were almost two hundred from New York, there were much more than two hundred from Boston, and a good number from Yale. As these numbers were announced, the crowd being when all is said, good Americans, gave murmurs of pleasure, an academic distance from the cry they had given as children to the acrobats of the circus, but not entirely unrelated, for there was something of the flying trapeze in these maneuvers now; by handing in draft cards, these young men were committing their future either to prison, emigration, frustration, or at best, years where everything must be unknown, and that spoke of a readiness to take moral leaps which the acrobat must know when he flies off into space—one has to have faith in one's ability to react with grace en route, one has ultimately, it may be supposed, to believe in some kind of grace.

On the *a fortiori*[3] evidence, then, they were young men with souls of interesting dimension, and their faces did nothing to disprove this. None of them looked alike; they had a surprising individuality in their appearance. Some were scholarly and slight, dressed conservatively, and looked like clerks; others were in dungarees, and possessed, like Dickie Harris, the Negro on the grass, that private élan reminiscent of the old cavaliers of SNCC;[4] a few were sports and looked to have eight hobbies, custom cars, pot, draft cards, skiing, guitar, surfboard, chicks, and scuba—not many of these, but Mailer had been expecting none. One tall student from the West, California no doubt, even looked like one's image of the President of the Young Republicans at Stanford, he was handsome enough in conventional measure to have been Number 1 Deke in Delta Kappa Eps. After he dropped his card in the bag, he gave a little talk to the effect that many of these students had been scared when first they burned their cards, months ago—they had said goodbye to their girls and family and waited for the clang of the jail gate. But the jail gate never came. "Now we think the government might be afraid to go near us. That gets around. A lot of kids who were afraid to join us last year won't be afraid this year. So every bit helps. If we get arrested, we make our point, and people won't forget it—our point being that with good careers ahead of us, we still hate this war so much that we go to jail—if they

[3]Latin: with greater reason, with more convincing power.
[4]Student Non-Violent Coordinating Committee, group active in the black civil rights movement of the 1950s.

show they're reluctant to arrest us, then others are in more of a hurry to join us." He was almost too good to be true. The suspicion came up for a moment that the CIA had doubtless not stopped their recruiting in colleges, and would certainly be happy to infiltrate here, an unpleasant thought, but then (1) Mailer came from New York where unpleasant thoughts were common, and (2) the writer in him was intrigued at the thought of a short novel about a young American leading a double life in college as a secret policeman. What a good novel that could make! About once a week Mailer bypassed wistfully around the excitements of the new book which had just come into his head. He would leave it to his detractors to decide that the ones he did not write were better than the ones he did.

Another student came by, then another. One of them, slight, with a sharp face, wearing a sport shirt and dark glasses had the appearance of a Hollywood hustler, but that was misleading; he wore the dark glasses because his eyes were still weak from the Mace squirted in them by police at Oakland. This student had a Berkeley style which Mailer did not like altogether: it was cocky, knowledgeable, and quick to mock the generations over thirty. Predictably, this was about the first item on which the kid began to scold the multitude. "You want to come along with us," he told the Over-Thirties, "that's okay, that's your thing, but we've got our thing, and we're going to do it alone whether you come with us or not." Mailer always wanted to give a kick into the seat of all reflection when he was told he had his thing—one did not look forward to a revolution which would substitute "thing" for better words.

Still, the boy from Berkeley proved to have a fair wit. He had begun to tell about Mace. To correct the hint of self-pity in his voice (which had an adenoidal complacency reminiscent of any number of old-line Party speakers who were never so unbearable as when bona fire martyrs) he made the little point that while the suffering was great, the reporting, for once, had also been great. "You see," he said, "the reporters were on our side." He looked down boldly now on the fifty or more assorted media men in front of him, and said, "They didn't want to be particularly, but the cops were so dumb they couldn't tell the reporters from the demonstrators, so the reporters got the Mace in their eyes too. For once, instead of putting down our big threat to the American flag, the cops were the villains, that is: the cops were the villains as soon as the reporters could see well enough to go back and write their story, which took a couple of hours, I can assure you. That Mace is rough on the eyes."

On they came, twenty-four to thirty of them, one by one, making for the most part short dry single sentences for statement, as for example, "I am ready to turn in my draft card, but can't because I burned it in Kansas City several months ago so am here submitting an affidavit with my name and address so the government can find me."

In a little more than a half hour, the students were done. Now began the faculty. They too came up one by one, but now there was no particular sense offered of an internal organization. Unlike the students, they had not debated these matters in open forum for months, organized, proselyted, or been overcome by argument, no, most of them had served as advisers to the students, had counseled them, and been picked up, many of them, and brought along by the rush of this moral stream much as a small piece of river bank might separate from the shore and go down the line of the flood. It must have been painful for these academics. They were older, certainly less suited for jail, aware more precisely of how and where their careers would be diverted or impeded, they had families many of them, they were liberal academics, technologues, they were being forced to abdicate from the machines they had chosen for their life. Their decision to turn in draft cards must have come for many in the middle of the night; for others it must have come even last night, or as they stood here debating with themselves. Many of them seemed to stand irresolutely near the steps for long periods, then move up at last. Rogoff,[5] standing next to Mailer, hugging his thin chest in the October air, now cold, finally took out his card and, with a grin at Mailer, said, "I guess I'm going to turn this in. But you know the ridiculous part of it is that I'm 4-F." So they came up one by one, not in solidarity, but as individuals, each breaking the shield or the fence or the mold or the home or even the construct of his own security. And as they did this, a deep gloom began to work on Mailer, because a deep modesty was on its way to him, he could feel himself becoming more and more of a modest man as he stood there in the cold with his hangover, and he hated this because modesty was an old family relative, he had been born to a modest family, had been a modest boy, a modest young man, and he hated that, he loved the pride and the arrogance and the confidence and the egocentricity he had acquired over the years, that was his force and his luxury and the iron in his greed, the richest sugar of his pleasure, the strength of his competitive force, he had lived long enough to know that the intimation one was being steeped in a new psychical condition (like this oncoming modest grace) was never to be disregarded, permanent new states could come into one on just so light a breeze. He stood in the cold watching the faculty men come up, yes always one by one, and felt his hangover which had come in part out of his imperfectly swallowed contempt for them the night before, and in part out of his fear, yes now he saw it, fear of the consequences of this weekend in Washington, for he had known from the beginning it could disrupt his life for a season or more, and in some way the danger was there it could change him forever. He was forty-four years old, and it had taken him most of those forty-four years to begin to be able to enjoy his pleasures where he found them, rather than worry about those pleasures which eluded him—it was obviously no time to embark on ventures which could eventually give one more than a few years in jail. Yet, there was no escape. As if some final cherished rare innocence of childhood still preserved intact in him was brought finally to the surface and there expired, so he lost at that instant the last secret delight he retained in life as a game where finally you never got hurt if you played the game well enough. For years he had envisioned himself in some final cataclysm, as an underground leader in the city, or a guerrilla with a gun in the hills, and had scorned the organizational aspects of revolution, the speeches, mimeograph machines, the hard dull forging of new parties and programs, the dull maneuvering to keep power, the intolerable obedience required before the over-all intellectual necessities of each objective period, and had scorned it, yes, had spit at it, and perhaps had been right, certainly had been right, such revolutions were the womb and cradle of technology land, no the only revolutionary truth was a gun in the hills, and that would not be his, he would be too old by then, and too incompetent, yes, too incompetent said the new modesty, and too showboat, too lacking in essential judgment—besides, he was too well-known! He would pay for the pleasures of his notoriety in the impossibility of disguise. No gun in the hills, no taste for organization, no, he was a figurehead, and therefore he was expendable, said the new modesty—not a future leader, but a future victim: *there* would be his real value. He could go to jail for protest, and spend some years if it came to it, possibly his life, for if

[5]Yale University drama professor.

the war went on, and America put its hot martial tongue across the Chinese border, well, jail was the probable perspective, detention camps, dissociation centers, liquidation alleys, that would be his portion, and it would come about the time he had learned how to live.

The depth of this gloom and this modesty came down on Mailer, and he watched the delegation take the bag into the Department of Justice with 994 cards contained inside, and listened to the speeches while they waited, and was eventually called up himself to make a speech, and made a modest one in a voice so used by the stentorian demonstrations of the night before that he was happy for the mike since otherwise he might have communicated in a whisper. He said a little of what he had thought while watching the others: that he had recognized on this afternoon that the time had come when Americans, many Americans, would have to face the possibility of going to jail for their ideas, and this was a prospect with no cheer because prisons were unattractive places where much of the best in oneself was slowly extinguished, but it could be there was no choice. The war in Vietnam was an obscene war, the worst war the nation had ever been in, and so its logic might compel sacrifice from those who were not so accustomed. And, out of hardly more than a sense of old habit and old anger, he scolded the press for their lies, and their misrepresentation, for their guilt in creating a psychology over the last twenty years in the average American which made wars like Vietnam possible; then he surrendered the mike and stepped down and the applause was pleasant.

After a period, Coffin came out from the Department of Justice with his delegation. He made a short announcement. The draft cards had not been accepted. A game of bureaucratic evasion had been played. In fact, the Attorney General had not even been there, instead his assistant. "The assistant simply refused to take our cards," said Coffin. "Consider this! Here was an officer of the law facing clear evidence of an alleged crime, and refusing to accept that evidence. He was derelict in his duty." There was a contained anger in Coffin, much like lawyer's anger, as if some subtle game had been played in which a combination had been based on a gambit, but the government had refused the gambit, so now the combination was halted.

Further reports were given by Dr. Spock, and one or two other members of the delegation. Then the meeting dispersed. Macdonald, Lowell, and Mailer going off for well-earned drinks at the nearest bar, ended up having dinner together. For all his newly inherited modesty, Mailer had nonetheless a merry meal. Liquor, it seemed, was still given special dispensation by the new regime of discipline, ascetism, moderation and self-sacrifice. Yet before dinner was over, the three men had agreed they would go out together tomorrow on the March to the Pentagon, and that they would probably—all consideration given— seek to get arrested. Mailer's hangover was now about gone. The evening went its agreeable way.

from PART III
SATURDAY MATINEE

A CONFRONTATION BY THE RIVER

It was not much of a situation to study. The MPs stood in two widely spaced ranks. The first rank was ten yards behind the rope, and each MP in that row was close to twenty feet from the next man. The second rank, similarly spaced, was ten yards behind the first rank and perhaps thirty yards behind them a cluster appeared, every fifty yards or so, of two or three U.S. Marshals in white helmets and dark blue suits. They were out there waiting. Two moods confronted one another, two separate senses of a private silence.

It was not unlike being a boy about to jump from one garage roof to an adjoining garage roof. The one thing not to do was wait. Mailer looked at Macdonald and Lowell. "Let's go," he said. Not looking again at them, not pausing to gather or dissipate resolve, he made a point of stepping neatly and decisively over the low rope. Then he headed across the grass to the nearest MP he saw.

It was as if the air had changed, or light had altered; he felt immediately much more alive—yes, bathed in air—and yet disembodied from himself, as if indeed he were watching himself in a film where this action was taking place. He could feel the eyes of the people behind the rope watching him, could feel the intensity of their existence as spectators. And as he walked forward, he and the MP looked at one another with the naked stricken lucidity which comes when absolute strangers are for the moment absolutely locked together.

The MP lifted his club to his chest as if to bar all passage. To Mailer's great surprise—he had secretly expected the enemy to be calm and strong, why should they not? they had every power, all the guns—to his great surprise, the MP was trembling. He was a young Negro, part white, who looked to have come from some small town where perhaps there were not many other Negroes; he had at any rate no Harlem smoke, no devil swish, no black, no black power for him, just a simple boy in an Army suit with a look of horror in his eye, "Why, why did it have to happen to me?" was the message of the petrified marbles in his face.

"Go back," he said hoarsely to Mailer.

"If you don't arrest me, I'm going to the Pentagon."

"No. Go back."

The thought of a return—"since they won't arrest me, what can I do?"—over these same ten yards was not at all suitable.

As the MP spoke, the raised club quivered. He did not know if it quivered from the desire of the MP to strike him, or secret military wonder was he now possessed of a moral force which implanted terror in the arms of young soldiers? Some unfamiliar current, now gyroscopic, now a sluggish whirlpool, was evolving from that quiver of the club, and the MP seemed to turn slowly away from his position confronting the rope, and the novelist turned with him, each still facing the other until the axis of their shoulders was now perpendicular to the rope, and still they kept turning in this psychic field, not touching, the club quivering, and then Mailer was behind the MP, he was free of him, and he wheeled around and kept going in a half run to the next line of MPs and then on the push of a sudden instinct, sprinted suddenly around the nearest MP in the second line, much as if he were a back cutting around the nearest man in the secondary to break free—that was actually his precise thought—and had a passing perception of how simple it was to get past these MPs. They looked petrified. Stricken faces as he went by. They did not know what to do. It was his dark pinstripe suit, his vest, the maroon and blue regimental tie, the part in his hair, the barrel chest, the early paunch—he must have looked like a banker himself, a banker gone ape! And then he saw the Pentagon to his right across the field, not a hundred yards away, and a little to his left, the marshals, and he ran on a jog toward them, and came up, and they glared at him and shouted, "Go back."

He had a quick impression of hard-faced men with gray eyes burning some transparent fuel for flame, and said, "I won't go back. If you don't arrest me, I'm going on to the Pentagon," and knew he meant it, some absolute certainty had come to him, and then two of them leaped on him at once in the cold clammy murderous fury of all cops at the existential moment of making their bust—all cops who secretly expect to be struck at that instant for their sins— and a surprising force came to his voice, and he roared, to his own distant pleasure in new achievement and new authority—"Take your hands off me, can't you see? I'm not resisting arrest," and one then let go of him, and the other stopped trying to pry his arm into a lock, and contented himself with a hard hand under his armpit, and they set off walking across the field at a rabid intent quick rate, walking parallel to the wall of the Pentagon, fully visible on his right at last, and he was arrested, he had succeeded in that, and without a club on his head, the mountain air in his lungs as thin and fierce as smoke, yes, the livid air of tension on this livid side promised a few events of more interest than the routine wait to be free, yes he was more than a visitor, he was in the land of the enemy now, he would get to see their face.

1968

Philip Roth   *1933–*

Controversies swirl around Philip Roth and his work. He is seen as a major figure in the Jewish-American school of writers (along with Bernard Malamud and Saul Bellow), but his repeated emphasis on Jews and Jewish culture in America has been questioned both by literary critics, who feel that Roth has narrowly limited his literary range, and by many members of the Jewish community, who find Roth's satirical treatment of Judaism and Jews to be superficial, sometimes even demeaning.

Like the hero of his novel Goodbye, Columbus, *Roth was born and raised in Newark, New Jersey, and attended the Newark branch of Rutgers University. Later Roth transferred to Bucknell University, where he graduated* magna cum laude *in English. He moved on to graduate study at the University of Chicago, receiving an M.A. degree but never completing his doctoral studies. His short stories began to appear in the mid-1950s, and after the publication of* Goodbye, Columbus *(1959), awards, honors, and fellowships followed in rapid succession. They include a Guggenheim fellowship, the Jewish Book Council award, a* Paris Review *award. And in 1960* Goodbye, Columbus *earned for Roth the National Book Award as the most distinguished work of fiction published in 1959. Few literary careers have begun with such immediate, wide-spread, positive response.*

Letting Go (1962), a novel focusing on graduate school experiences, confirmed Roth's reputation as a writer of stature. The theme of the perils and rewards of human commitment—nearly always present in Roth's work—is central to that novel as it is to When She Was Good *(1967), a novel of American domestic manners and one of Roth's few works not centered on the lives of American Jews. With the sensational* Portnoy's Complaint *(1969), he not only received nation-wide attention (often from those who assumed that Roth was describing his own triumphs as a sexual acrobat), he also entered into a new stage: realistic novels of manners were replaced by a series of works that were highly comic, inventive, mythic, even surrealistic—but still controversial.* Portnoy's Complaint *was followed by* Our Gang *(1971), a timely but heavy-handed satire of the Nixon administration. In 1972 Roth published* The Breast, *a Kafka-like tale of a man who is transformed into a giant breast. In the next year* The Great American Novel *appeared, a "comic extravaganza" that uses baseball as a metaphor to describe much of the American culture. Later works have included* My Life as a Man *(1974),* The Professor of Desire *(1977), and a collection of illuminating critical essays,* Reading Myself and Others *(1975).* Zuckerman Unbound *(1981), his autobiographical novel, tells of the trials of a writer who seeks literary distinction but whose works are read merely for their steamy carnality. In 1985 Roth published* Zuckerman Bound, *a collection of four short novels, continuing the saga of his fictional counterpart, Nathan Zuckerman.*

Roth is a master of satiric wit which, in the case of Goodbye, Columbus, *has been transferred masterfully to the motion picture screen. He has a highly developed talent for presenting events that are both grotesque and funny. He writes of Jews struggling in Jewish and gentile worlds that threaten to suffocate them. He satirizes America's swollen prosperity and the puzzled young men who wander confusedly amid the glut of its riches. Although his works are humorous, his view of life is often harsh. Lives are surrounded by predictable miseries. Rapture is brief. Love is blunted. Even the act of sex declines into a form of protest—against parents and propriety.*

Roth is at his best in revealing the varieties of life in cities like Newark and the New York suburbs, where the poor overflow the urban centers and struggle to catch even a glimpse of beauty while the moneyed suburbanites wallow complacently in shallow materialism. It is the world that Roth dissects satirically by depicting crass parents and spoiled children, by presenting memorable scenes of vulgar display, and by revealing the anguish and confusion of true believers and puzzled doubters whose best advice is, "You should never hit anybody about God."

FURTHER READING: *A Philip Roth Reader,* 1980; J. McDaniel, *The Fiction of Philip Roth,* 1974; S. Pinsker, *The Comedy that "Hoits,"* 1975; B. Rodgers, *Philip Roth,* 1978; J. Jones and G. Nance, *Philip Roth,* 1981; *Critical Essays on Philip Roth,* ed. S. Pinsker, 1982; H. Lee, *Philip Roth,* 1982; G. Searles, *The Fiction of Philip Roth and John Updike,* 1984; *Philip Roth,* ed. H. Bloom, 1986; *Reading Philip Roth,* eds., Z. Milbauer and D. Watson, 1988.

TEXT: *Goodbye, Columbus,* 1959.

THE CONVERSION OF THE JEWS

"You're a real one for opening your mouth in the first place," Itzie said. "What do you open your mouth all the time for?"

"I didn't bring it up, Itz, I didn't," Ozzie said.

"What do you care about Jesus Christ for anyway?"

"I didn't bring up Jesus Christ. He did. I didn't even know what he was talking about. Jesus is historical, he kept saying. Jesus is historical." Ozzie mimicked the monumental voice of Rabbi Binder.

"Jesus was a person that lived like you and me," Ozzie continued. "That's what Binder said—"

"Yeah? . . . So what! What do I give two cents whether he lived or not. And what do you gotta open your mouth!" Itzie Lieberman favored closed-mouthedness, especially when it came to Ozzie Freedman's questions. Mrs. Freedman had to see Rabbi Binder twice before about Ozzie's questions and this Wednesday at four-thirty would be the third time. Itzie preferred to keep *his* mother in the kitchen; he settled for behind-the-back subtleties such as gestures, faces, snarls and other less delicate barnyard noises.

"He was a real person, Jesus, but he wasn't like God, and we don't believe he is God." Slowly, Ozzie was explaining Rabbi Binder's position to Itzie, who had been absent from Hebrew School the previous afternoon.

"The Catholics," Itzie said helpfully, "they believe in Jesus Christ, that he's God." Itzie Lieberman used "the Catholics" in its broadest sense—to include the Protestants.

Ozzie received Itzie's remark with a tiny head bob, as though it were a footnote, and went on. "His mother was Mary, and his father probably was Joseph," Ozzie said. "But the New Testament says his real father was God."

"His *real* father?"

"Yeah," Ozzie said, "that's the big thing, his father's supposed to be God."

"Bull."

"That's what Rabbi Binder says, that it's impossible—"

"Sure it's impossible. That stuff's all bull. To have a baby you gotta get laid," Itzie theologized. "Mary hadda get laid."

"That's what Binder says: 'The only way a woman can have a baby is to have intercourse with a man.' "

"He said *that*, Ozz?" For a moment it appeared that Itzie had put the theological question aside. "He said that, intercourse?" A little curled smile shaped itself in the lower half of Itzie's face like a pink mustache. "What you guys do, Ozz, you laugh or something?"

"I raised my hand."

"Yeah? Whatja say?"

"That's when I asked the question."

Itzie's face lit up. "Whatja ask about—intercourse?"

"No, I asked the question about God, how if He could create the heaven and earth in six days, and make all the animals and the fish and the light in six days—the light especially, that's what always gets me, that He could make the light. Making fish and animals, that's pretty good—"

"That's damn good." Itzie's appreciation was honest but unimaginative: it was as though God had just pitched a one-hitter.

"But making light . . . I mean when you think about it, it's really something," Ozzie said. "Anyway, I asked Binder if He could make all that in six days, and He could *pick* the six days he wanted right out of nowhere, why couldn't He let a woman have a baby without having intercourse."

"You said intercourse, Ozz, to Binder?"

"Yeah."

"Right in class?"

"Yeah."

Itzie smacked the side of his head.

"I mean, no kidding around," Ozzie said, "that'd really be nothing. After all that other stuff, that'd practically be nothing."

Itzie considered a moment. "What'd Binder say?"

"He started all over again explaining how Jesus was historical and how he lived like you and me but he wasn't God. So I said I under*stood* that. What I wanted to know was different."

What Ozzie wanted to know was always different. The first time he had wanted to know how Rabbi Binder could call the Jews "The Chosen People" if the

Declaration of Independence claimed all men to be created equal. Rabbi Binder tried to distinguish for him between political equality and spiritual legitimacy, but what Ozzie wanted to know, he insisted vehemently, was different. That was the first time his mother had to come.

Then there was the plane crash. Fifty-eight people had been killed in a plane crash at La Guardia. In studying a casualty list in the newspaper his mother had discovered among the list of those dead eight Jewish names (his grandmother had nine but she counted Miller as a Jewish name); because of the eight she said the plane crash was "a tragedy." During free-discussion time on Wednesday Ozzie had brought to Rabbi Binder's attention this matter of "some of his relations" always picking out the Jewish names. Rabbi Binder had begun to explain cultural unity and some other things when Ozzie stood up at his seat and said that what he wanted to know was different. Rabbi Binder insisted that he sit down and it was then that Ozzie shouted that he wished all fifty-eight were Jews. That was the second time his mother came.

"And he kept explaining about Jesus being historical, and so I kept asking him. No kidding, Itz, he was trying to make me look stupid."

"So what he finally do?"

"Finally he starts screaming that I was deliberately simple-minded and a wise guy, and that my mother had to come, and this was the last time. And that I'd never get bar-mitzvahed[1] if he could help it. Then, Itz, then he starts talking in that voice like a statue, real slow and deep, and he says that I better think over what I said about the Lord. He told me to go to his office and think it over." Ozzie leaned his body towards Itzie. "Itz, I thought it over for a solid hour, and now I'm convinced God could do it."

Ozzie had planned to confess his latest transgression to his mother as soon as she came home from work. But it was a Friday night in November and already dark, and when Mrs. Freedman came through the door she tossed off her coat, kissed Ozzie quickly on the face, and went to the kitchen table to light the three yellow candles, two for the Sabbath and one for Ozzie's father.

When his mother lit the candles she would move her two arms slowly towards her, dragging them through the air, as though persuading people whose minds were half made up. And her eyes would get glassy with tears. Even when his father was alive Ozzie remembered that her eyes had gotten glassy, so it didn't have anything to do with his dying. It had something to do with lighting the candles.

As she touched the flaming match to the unlit wick of a Sabbath candle, the phone rang, and Ozzie, standing only a foot from it, plucked it off the receiver and held it muffled to his chest. When his mother lit candles Ozzie felt there should be no noise; even breathing, if you could manage it, should be softened. Ozzie pressed the phone to his breast and watched his mother dragging whatever she was dragging, and he felt his own eyes get glassy. His mother was a round, tired, gray-haired penguin of a woman whose gray skin had begun to feel the tug of gravity and the weight of her own history. Even when she was dressed up she looked like a chosen person. But when she lit candles she looked like something better; like a woman who knew momentarily that God could do anything.

After a few mysterious minutes she was finished. Ozzie hung up the phone and walked to the kitchen table where she was beginning to lay the two places

---

[1] I.e., he would be denied the ceremony of bar mitzvah that initiates a Jewish boy of thirteen to his religious duties.

for the four-course Sabbath meal. He told her that she would have to see Rabbi Binder next Wednesday at four-thirty, and then he told her why. For the first time in their life together she hit Ozzie across the face with her hand.

All through the chopped liver and chicken soup parts of the dinner Ozzie cried; he didn't have any appetite for the rest.

On Wednesday, in the largest of the three basement classrooms of the synagogue, Rabbi Marvin Binder, a tall, handsome, broad-shouldered man of thirty with thick strong-fibered black hair, removed his watch from his pocket and saw that it was four o'clock. At the rear of the room Yakov Blotnik, the seventy-one-year-old custodian, slowly polished the large window, mumbling to himself, unaware that it was four o'clock or six o'clock, Monday or Wednesday. To most of the students Yakov Blotnik's mumbling, along with his brown curly beard, scythe nose, and two heel-trailing black cats, made him an object of wonder, a foreigner, a relic, towards whom they were alternately fearful and disrespectful. To Ozzie the mumbling had always seemed a monotonous, curious prayer; what made it curious was that old Blotnik had been mumbling so steadily for so many years, Ozzie suspected he had memorized the prayers and forgotten all about God.

"It is now free-discussion time," Rabbi Binder said. "Feel free to talk about any Jewish matter at all—religion, family, politics, sports—"

There was silence. It was a gusty, clouded November afternoon and it did not seem as though there ever was or could be a thing called baseball. So nobody this week said a word about that hero from the past, Hank Greenberg[2]—which limited free discussion considerably.

And the soul-battering Ozzie Freeman had just received from Rabbi Binder had imposed its limitation. When it was Ozzie's turn to read aloud from the Hebrew book the rabbi had asked him petulantly why he didn't read more rapidly. He was showing no progress. Ozzie said he could read faster but that if he did he was sure not to understand what he was reading. Nevertheless, at the rabbi's repeated suggestion Ozzie tried, and showed a great talent, but in the midst of a long passage he stopped short and said he didn't understand a word he was reading, and started in again at a drag-footed pace. Then came the soul-battering.

Consequently when free-discussion time rolled around none of the students felt too free. The rabbi's invitation was answered only by the mumbling of feeble old Blotnik.

"Isn't there anything at all you would like to discuss?" Rabbi Binder asked again, looking at his watch. "No questions or comments?"

There was a small grumble from the third row. The rabbi requested that Ozzie rise and give the rest of the class the advantage of his thought.

Ozzie rose. "I forget it now," he said, and sat down in his place.

Rabbi Binder advanced a seat towards Ozzie and poised himself on the edge of the desk. It was Itzie's desk and the rabbi's frame only a dagger's-length away from his face snapped him to sitting attention.

"Stand up again, Oscar," Rabbi Binder said calmly, "and try to assemble your thoughts."

Ozzie stood up. All his classmates turned in their seats and watched as he gave an unconvincing scratch to his forehead.

"I can't assemble any," he announced, and plunked himself down.

[2]American baseball player (1911–   ).

"Stand up!" Rabbi Binder advanced from Itzie's desk to the one directly in front of Ozzie; when the rabbinical back was turned Itzie gave it five-fingers off the tip of his nose, causing a small titter in the room. Rabbi Binder was too absorbed in squelching Ozzie's nonsense once and for all to bother with titters. "Stand up, Oscar. What's your question about?"

Ozzie pulled a word out of the air. It was the handiest word. "Religion."

"Oh, now you remember?"

"Yes."

"What is it?"

Trapped, Ozzie blurted the first thing that came to him. "Why can't He make anything He wants to make!"

As Rabbi Binder prepared an answer, a final answer, Itzie, ten feet behind him, raised one finger on his left hand, gestured it meaningfully towards the rabbi's back, and brought the house down.

Binder twisted quickly to see what had happened and in the midst of the commotion Ozzie shouted into the rabbi's back what he couldn't have shouted to his face. It was a loud, toneless sound that had the timbre of something stored inside for about six days.

"You don't know! You don't know anything about God!"

The rabbi spun back towards Ozzie. "What?"

"You don't know—you don't—"

"Apologize, Oscar, apologize!" It was a threat.

"You don't—"

Rabbi Binder's hand flicked out at Ozzie's cheek. Perhaps it had only been meant to clamp the boy's mouth shut, but Ozzie ducked and the palm caught him squarely on the nose.

The blood came in a short, red spurt on to Ozzie's shirt front.

The next moment was all confusion. Ozzie screamed, "You bastard, you bastard!" and broke for the classroom door. Rabbi Binder lurched a step backwards, as though his own blood had started flowing violently in the opposite direction, then gave a clumsy lurch forward and bolted out the door after Ozzie. The class followed after the rabbi's huge blue-suited back, and before old Blotnik could turn from his window, the room was empty and everyone was headed full speed up the three flights leading to the roof.

If one should compare the light of day to the life of man: sunrise to birth; sunset—the dropping down over the edge—to death; then as Ozzie Freedman wiggled through the trapdoor of the synagogue roof, his feet kicking backwards bronco-style at Rabbi Binder's outstretched arms—at that moment the day was fifty years old. As a rule, fifty or fifty-five reflects accurately the age of late afternoons in November, for it is in that month, during those hours, that one's awareness of light seems no longer a matter of seeing, but of hearing: light begins clicking away. In fact, as Ozzie locked shut the trapdoor in the rabbi's face, the sharp click of the bolt into the lock might momentarily have been mistaken for the sound of the heavier gray that had just throbbed through the sky.

With all his weight Ozzie kneeled on the locked door; any instant he was certain that Rabbi Binder's shoulder would fling it open, splintering the wood into shrapnel and catapulting his body into the sky. But the door did not move and below him he heard only the rumble of feet, first loud then dim, like thunder rolling away.

A question shot through his brain. "Can this be *me*?" For a thirteen-year-old who had just labeled his religious leader a bastard, twice, it was not an improper question. Louder and louder the question came to him—"Is it me? Is it me?"—until he discovered himself no longer kneeling, but racing crazily towards the edge of the roof, his eyes crying, his throat screaming, and his arms flying every-whichway as though not his own.

"Is it me? Is it me ME ME ME ME! It has to be me—but is it!"

It is the question a thief must ask himself the night he jimmies open his first window, and it is said to be the question with which bridegrooms quiz themselves before the altar.

In the few wild seconds it took Ozzie's body to propel him to the edge of the roof, his self-examination began to grow fuzzy. Gazing down at the street, he became confused as to the problem beneath the question: was it, is-it-me-who-called-Binder-a-bastard? or, is-it-me-prancing-around-on-the-roof? However, the scene below settled all, for there is an instant in any action when whether it is you or somebody else is academic. The thief crams the money in his pockets and scoots out the window. The bridegroom signs the hotel register for two. And the boy on the roof finds a streetful of people gaping at him, necks stretched backwards, faces up, as though he were the ceiling of the Hayden Planetarium.[3] Suddenly you know it's you.

"Oscar! Oscar Freedman!" A voice rose from the center of the crowd, a voice that, could it have been seen, would have looked like the writing on scroll. "Oscar Freedman, get down from there. Immediately!" Rabbi Binder was pointing one arm stiffly up at him; and at the end of that arm, one finger aimed menacingly. It was the attitude of a dictator, but one—the eyes confessed all—whose personal valet had spit neatly in his face.

Ozzie didn't answer. Only for a blink's length did he look towards Rabbi Binder. Instead his eyes began to fit together the world beneath him, to sort out people from places, friends from enemies, participants from spectators. In little jagged starlike clusters his friends stood around Rabbi Binder, who was still pointing. The topmost point on a star compounded not of angels but of five adolescent boys was Itzie. What a world it was, with those stars below, Rabbi Binder below . . . Ozzie, who a moment earlier hadn't been able to control his own body, started to feel the meaning of the word control: he felt Peace and he felt Power.

"Oscar Freedman, I'll give you three to come down."

Few dictators give their subjects three to do anything; but, as always, Rabbi Binder only looked dictatorial.

"Are you ready, Oscar?"

Ozzie nodded his head yes, although he had no intention in the world—the lower one of the celestial one he'd just entered— of coming down even if Rabbi Binder should give him a million.

"All right then," said Rabbi Binder. He ran a hand through his black Samson hair as though it were the gesture prescribed for uttering the first digit. Then, with his other hand cutting a circle out of the small piece of sky around him, he spoke. "One!"

There was no thunder. On the contrary, at that moment, as though "one" was the cue for which he had been waiting, the world's least thunderous person appeared on the synagogue steps. He did not so much come out the synagogue door as lean out, onto the darkening air. He clutched at the doorknob with one hand and looked up at the roof.

[3]Building in New York City that houses a device that projects a representation of the heavens onto a domed ceiling for viewing by spectators.

"Oy!"

Yakov Blotnik's old mind hobbled slowly, as if on crutches, and though he couldn't decide precisely what the boy was doing on the roof, he knew it wasn't good—that is, it wasn't-good-for-the-Jews. For Yakov Blotnik life had fractionated itself simply: things were either good-for-the-Jews or no-good-for-the-Jews.

He smacked his free hand to his in-sucked cheek, gently. "Oy, Gut!" And then quickly as he was able, he jacked down his head and surveyed the street. There was Rabbi Binder (like a man at an auction with only three dollars in his pocket, he had just delivered a shaky "Two!"); there were the students, and that was all. So far it-wasn't-so-bad-for-the-Jews. But the boy had to come down immediately, before anybody saw. The problem: how to get the boy off the roof?

Anybody who has ever had a cat on the roof knows how to get him down. You call the fire department. Or first you call the operator and you ask her for the fire department. And the next thing there is great jamming of brakes and clanging of bells and shouting of instructions. And then the cat is off the roof. You do the same thing to get a boy off the roof.

That is, you do the same thing if you are Yakov Blotnik and you once had a cat on the roof.

When the engines, all four of them, arrived, Rabbi Binder had four times given Ozzie the count of three. The big hook-and-ladder swung around the corner and one of the firemen leaped from it, plunging headlong towards the yellow fire hydrant in front of the synagogue. With a huge wrench he began to unscrew the top nozzle. Rabbi Binder raced over to him and pulled at his shoulder.

"There's no fire . . . ."

The fireman mumbled back over his shoulder and, heatedly, continued working at the nozzle.

"But there's no fire, there's no fire . . ." Binder shouted. When the fireman mumbled again, the rabbi grasped his face with both hands and pointed it up at the roof.

To Ozzie it looked as though Rabbi Binder was trying to tug the fireman's head out of his body, like a cork from a bottle. He had to giggle at the picture they made: it was a family portrait—rabbi in black skullcap, fireman in red fire hat, and the little yellow hydrant squatting beside like a kid brother, bareheaded. From the edge of the roof Ozzie waved at the portrait, a one-handed, flapping, mocking wave; in doing it his right foot slipped from under him. Rabbi Binder covered his eyes with his hands.

Firemen work fast. Before Ozzie had even regained his balance, a big, round, yellowed net was being held on the synagogue lawn. The firemen who held it looked up at Ozzie with stern, feelingless faces.

One of the firemen turned his head towards Rabbi Binder. "What, is the kid nuts or something?"

Rabbi Binder unpeeled his hands from his eyes, slowly, painfully, as if they were tape. Then he checked: nothing on the sidewalk, no dents in the net.

"Is he gonna jump, or what?" the fireman shouted.

In a voice not at all like a statue, Rabbi Binder finally answered. "Yes. Yes, I think so . . . He's been threatening to . . ."

Threatening to? Why, the reason he was on the roof, Ozzie remembered, was to get away; he hadn't even thought about jumping. He had just run to get away, and the truth was that he hadn't really headed for the roof as much as he'd been chased there.

"What's his name, the kid?"

"Freedman," Rabbi Binder answered. "Oscar Freedman."

The fireman looked up at Ozzie. "What is it with you, Oscar? You gonna jump, or what?"

Ozzie did not answer. Frankly, the question had just arisen.

"Look, Oscar, if you're gonna jump, jump—and if you're not gonna jump, don't jump. But don't waste our time, willya?"

Ozzie looked at the fireman and then at Rabbi Binder. He wanted to see Rabbi Binder cover his eyes one more time.

"I'm going to jump."

And then he scampered around the edge of the roof to the corner, where there was no net below, and he flapped his arms at his sides, swishing the air and smacking his palms to his trousers on the downbeat. He began screaming like some kind of engine, "Wheeeee . . . wheeeeee," and leaning way out over the edge with the upper half of his body. The firemen whipped around to cover the ground with the net. Rabbi Binder mumbled a few words to somebody and covered his eyes. Everything happened quickly, jerkily, as in a silent movie. The crowd, which had arrived with the fire engines, gave out a long, Fourth-of-July fireworks oooh-aahhh. In the excitement no one had paid the crowd much heed, except, of course, Yakov Blotnik, who swung from the doorknob counting heads. "Fier und tsvansik . . . finf und tsvantsik[4] . . . Oy, Gut!" It wasn't like this with the cat.

Rabbi Binder peeked through his fingers, checked the sidewalk and net. Empty. But there was Ozzie racing to the other corner. The firemen raced with him but were unable to keep up. Whenever Ozzie wanted to he might jump and splatter himself on the sidewalk, and by the time the firemen scooted to the spot all they could do with their net would be to cover the mess.

"Wheeeee . . . wheeeee . . ."

"Hey, Oscar," the winded fireman yelled. "What the hell is this, a game or something?"

"Wheeeee . . . wheeeee . . ."

"Hey, Oscar—"

But he was off now to the other corner, flapping his wings fiercely. Rabbi Binder couldn't take it any longer—the fire engines from nowhere, the screaming suicidal boy, the net. He fell to his knees, exhausted, and with his hands curled together in front of his chest like a little dome, he pleaded, "Oscar, stop it, Oscar. Don't jump, Oscar. Please come down . . . Please don't jump."

And further back in the crowd a single voice, a single young voice, shouted a lone word to the boy on the roof.

"Jump!"

It was Itzie. Ozzie momentarily stopped flapping.

"Go ahead, Ozz—jump!" Itzie broke off his point of the star and courageously, with the inspiration not of a wise-guy but of a disciple, stood alone. "Jump, Ozz, jump!"

Still on his knees, his hands still curled, Rabbi Binder twisted his body back. He looked at Itzie, then, agonizingly, back to Ozzie.

"OSCAR, DON'T JUMP! PLEASE, DON'T JUMP . . . please please . . ."

_____
[4]Yiddish: "twenty-four . . . twenty-five."

"Jump!" This time it wasn't Itzie but another point of the star. By the time Mrs. Freedman arrived to keep her four-thirty appointment with Rabbi Binder, the whole little upside down heaven was shouting and pleading for Ozzie to jump, and Rabbi Binder no longer was pleading with him not to jump, but was crying into the dome of his hands.

Understandably Mrs. Freedman couldn't figure out what her son was doing on the roof. So she asked.

"Ozzie, my Ozzie, what are you doing? My Ozzie, what is it?"

Ozzie stopped wheeeeeing and slowed his arms down to a cruising flap, the kind birds use in soft winds, but he did not answer. He stood against the low, clouded, darkening sky—light clicked down swiftly now, as on a small gear—flapping softly and gazing down at the small bundle of a woman who was his mother.

"What are you doing, Ozzie?" She turned towards the kneeling Rabbi Binder and rushed so close that only a paper-thickness of dusk lay between her stomach and his shoulders.

"What is my baby doing?"

Rabbi Binder gaped at her but he too was mute. All that moved was the dome of his hands; it shook back and forth like a weak pulse.

"Rabbi, get him down! He'll kill himself. Get him down, my only baby . . ."

"I can't," Rabbi Binder said, "I can't . . ." and he turned his handsome head towards the crowd of boys behind him. "It's them. Listen to them."

And for the first time Mrs. Freedman saw the crowd of boys, and she heard what they were yelling.

"He's doing it for them. He won't listen to me. It's them." Rabbi Binder spoke like one in a trance.

"For them?"

"Yes."

"Why for them?"

"They want him to . . ."

Mrs. Freedman raised her two arms upward as though she were conducting the sky. "For them he's doing it!" And then in a gesture older than pyramids, older than prophets and floods, her arms came slapping down to her sides. "A martyr I have. Look!" She tilted her head to the roof. Ozzie was still flapping softly. "My martyr."

"Oscar, come down, *please*," Rabbi Binder groaned.

In a startling even voice Mrs. Freedman called to the boy on the roof. "Ozzie, come down, Ozzie. Don't be a martyr."

"Gawhead, Ozz—*be* a Martin!" It was Itzie. "Be a Martin, be a Martin," and all the voices joined in singing for Martindom, whatever *it* was. "Be a Martin, be a Martin . . ."

Somehow when you're on a roof the darker it gets the less you can hear. All Ozzie knew was that two groups wanted two new things: his friends were spirited and musical about what they wanted; his mother and the rabbi were even-toned, chanting, about what they didn't want. The rabbi's voice was without tears now and so was his mother's.

The big net stared up at Ozzie like a sightless eye. The big, clouded sky pushed down. From beneath it looked like a gray corrugated board. Suddenly, looking up into that unsympathetic sky, Ozzie realized all the strangeness of what these people, his friends, were asking: they wanted him to jump, to kill himself; they were singing about it now—it made them that happy. And there was an even greater strangeness: Rabbi Binder was on his knees, trembling. If there was a question to be asked now it was not "Is it me?" but rather "Is it us? . . . Is it us?"

Being on the roof, it turned out, was a serious thing. If he jumped would the singing become dancing? Would it? What would jumping stop? Yearningly, Ozzie wished he could rip open the sky, plunge his hands through, and pull out the sun; and on the sun, like a coin, would be stamped JUMP or DON'T JUMP.

Ozzie's knees rocked and sagged a little under him as though they were setting him for a dive. His arms tightened, stiffened, froze, from shoulders to finger-nails. He felt as if each part of his body were going to vote as to whether he should kill himself or not—and each part as though it were independent of *him*.

The light took an unexpected click down and the new darkness, like a gag, hushed the friends singing for this and the mother and rabbi chanting for that.

Ozzie stopped counting votes, and in a curiously high voice, like one who wasn't prepared for speech, he spoke.

"Mamma?"

"Yes, Oscar."

"Mamma, get down on your knees, like Rabbi Binder."

"Oscar—"

"Get down on your knees," he said, "or I'll jump."

Ozzie heard a whimper, then a quick rustling, and when he looked down where his mother had stood he saw the top of a head beneath that circle of dress. She was kneeling beside Rabbi Binder.

He spoke again. "Everybody kneel." There was the sound of everybody kneeling.

Ozzie looked around. With one hand he pointed towards the synagogue entrance. "Make *him* kneel."

There was a noise, not of kneeling, but of body-and-cloth stretching. Ozzie could hear Rabbi Binder saying in a gruff whisper, ". . . or he'll *kill* himself," and when next he looked there was Yakov Blotnik off the doorknob and for the first time in his life upon his knees in the Gentile posture of prayer.

As for the firemen—it is not as difficult as one might imagine to hold a net taut while you are kneeling.

Ozzie looked around again; and then he called to Rabbi Binder.

"Rabbi?"

"Yes, Oscar."

"Rabbi Binder, do you believe in God?"

"Yes."

"Do you believe God can do Anything?" Ozzie leaned his head out into the darkness. "Anything?"

"Oscar, I think—"

"Tell me you believe God can do Anything."

There was a second's hesitation. Then: "God can do Anything."

"Tell me you believe God can make a child without intercourse."

"He can."

"Tell me!"

"God," Rabbi Binder admitted, "can make a child without intercourse."

"Mamma, you tell me."

"God can make a child without intercourse," his mother said.

"Make *him* tell me." There was no doubt who *him* was.

In a few moments Ozzie heard an old comical voice say something to the increasing darkness about God.

Next, Ozzie made everybody say it. And then he made them all say they believed in Jesus Christ—first one at a time, then all together.

When the catechizing was through it was the beginning of evening. From the street it sounded as if the boy on the roof might have sighed.

"Ozzie?" A woman's voice dared to speak. "You'll come down now?"

There was no answer, but the woman waited, and when a voice finally did speak it was thin and crying, and exhausted as that of an old man who has just finished pulling the bells.

"Mamma, don't you see—you shouldn't hit me. He shouldn't hit me. You shouldn't hit me about God, Mamma. You should never hit anybody about God—"

"Ozzie, please come down now."

"Promise me, promise me you'll never hit anybody about God."

He had asked only his mother, but for some reason everyone kneeling in the street promised he would never hit anybody about God.

Once again there was silence.

"I can come down now, Mamma," the boy on the roof finally said. He turned his head both ways as though checking the traffic lights. "Now I can come down . . ."

And he did, right into the center of the yellow net that glowed in the evening's edge like an overgrown halo.

1959

Joseph Heller   *1923–*

Joseph Heller was born and raised in Brooklyn, New York. During World War II he served in the United States Army Air Force and then attended New York University, Columbia University, and Oxford University in England. After a period of teaching at Pennsylvania State University he worked in the advertising business in New York City. Although he had published four or five short stories while still in college, Heller first came to the attention of the broad reading public in 1961 with the publication of Catch-22, *his sardonic novel of life in an air force squadron in World War II.*

Since the publication of Catch-22, *Heller has written a play,* We Bombed in New Haven (1968). *His second novel,* Something Happened, *was published in 1974. His most recent works are* Good as Gold (1979) *and* God Knows (1984). *Heller has announced "I don't write realism." And his novel* Catch-22 *is filled with lexical distortions and extravagant puns, incongruous details and misplaced events. It mocks the traditions of war fiction and the idealized concepts of patriotic heroism, mixing grisly horrors with comic absurdities to assail authority, hierarchies, and the madness of war.*

FURTHER READING: *Critical Essays on "Catch-22"*, ed. J. Nagel, 1974; *Critical Essays on Joseph Heller*, ed. J. Nagel, 1984.
TEXT: *Catch-22*, 1961.

from CATCH-22

XLI SNOWDEN

"Cut," said a doctor.

"You cut," said another.

"No cuts," said Yossarian with a thick, unwieldy tongue.

"Now look who's butting in," complained one of the doctors. "Another county heard from. Are we going to operate or aren't we?"

"He doesn't need an operation," complained the other. "It's a small wound. All we have to do is stop the bleeding, clean it out and put a few stitches in."

"But I've never had a chance to operate before. Which one is the scalpel? Is this one the scalpel?"

"No, the other one is the scalpel. Well, go ahead and cut already if you're going to. Make the incision."

"Like this?"

"Not there, you dope!"

"No incisions," Yossarian said, perceiving through the lifting fog of insensibility that two strangers were ready to begin cutting him.

"Another county heard from," complained the first doctor sarcastically. "Is he going to keep talking that way while I operate on him?"

"You can't operate on him until I admit him," said a clerk.

"You can't admit him until I clear him," said a fat, gruff colonel with a mustache and an enormous pink face that pressed down very close to Yossarian and radiated scorching heat like the bottom of a huge frying pan. "Where were you born?"

The fat, gruff colonel reminded Yossarian of the fat, gruff colonel who had interrogated the chaplain and found him guilty. Yossarian stared up at him through a glassy film. The cloying scents of formaldehyde and alcohol sweetened the air.

"On a battlefield," he answered.

"No, no. In what state were you born?"

"In a state of innocence."

"No, no, you don't understand."

"Let me handle him," urged a hatchet-faced man with sunken acrimonious eyes and a thin, malevolent mouth. "Are you a smart aleck or something?" he asked Yossarian.

"He's delirious," one of the doctors said. "Why don't you let us take him back inside and treat him?"

"Leave him right here if he's delirious. He might say something incriminating."

"But he's still bleeding profusely. Can't you see? He might even die."

"*Good* for him!"

"It would serve the finky bastard right," said the fat, gruff colonel. "All right, John, let's speak out. We want to get to the truth."

"Everyone calls me Yo-Yo."

"We want you to co-operate with us, Yo-Yo. We're your friends and we want you to trust us. We're here to help you. We're not going to hurt you."

"Let's jab our thumbs down inside his wound and gouge it," suggested the hatchet-faced man.

Yossarian let his eyes fall closed and hoped they would think he was unconscious.

"He's fainted," he heard a doctor say. "Can't we treat him now before it's too
late? He really might die."

"All right, take him. I hope the bastard does die."

"You can't treat him until I admit him," the clerk said.

Yossarian played dead with his eyes shut while the clerk admitted him by
shuffling some papers, and then he was rolled away slowly into a stuffy,
dark room with searing spotlights overhead in which the cloying smell of
formaldehyde and sweet alcohol was even stronger. The pleasant, permeating stink was intoxicating. He smelled ether too and heard glass tinkling. He
listened with secret, egotistical mirth to the husky breathing of the two doctors. It delighted him that they thought he was unconscious and did not
know he was listening. It all seemed very silly to him until one of the doctors
said:

"Well, do you think we should save his life? They might be sore at us if we
do."

"Let's operate," said the other doctor. "Let's cut him open and get to the inside
of things once and for all. He keeps complaining about his liver. His liver looks
pretty small on this X-ray."

"That's his pancreas, you dope. This is his liver."

"No it isn't. That's his heart. I'll bet you a nickel this is his liver. I'm going to
operate and find out. Should I wash my hands first?"

"No operations," Yossarian said, opening his eyes and trying to sit up.

"Another county heard from," scoffed one of the doctors indignantly. "Can't
we make him shut up?"

"We could give him a total. The ether's right here."

"No totals," said Yossarian.

"Another county heard from," said a doctor.

"Let's give him a total and knock him out. Then we can do what we want with
him."

They gave Yossarian total anesthesia and knocked him out. He woke up
thirsty in a private room, drowning in ether fumes. Colonel Korn was there at
his bedside, waiting calmly in a chair in his baggy, wool, olive-drab shirt and
trousers. A bland, phlegmatic smile hung on his brown face with its heavy-
bearded cheeks, and he was buffing the facets of his bald head gently with the
palms of both hands. He bent forward chuckling when Yossarian awoke, and
assured him in the friendliest tones that the deal they had made was still on if
Yossarian didn't die. Yossarian vomited, and Colonel Korn shot to his feet at
the first cough and fled in disgust, so it seemed indeed that there was a silver
lining to every cloud, Yossarian reflected, as he drifted back into a suffocating
daze. A hand with sharp fingers shook him awake roughly. He turned and
opened his eyes and saw a strange man with a mean face who curled his lip at
him in a spiteful scowl and bragged,

"We've got your pal, buddy. "We've got your pal."

Yossarian turned cold and faint and broke into a sweat.

"Who's my pal?" he asked when he saw the chaplain sitting where Colonel
Korn had been sitting.

"Maybe I'm your pal," the chaplain answered.

But Yossarian couldn't hear him and closed his eyes. Someone gave him water
to sip and tiptoed away. He slept and woke up feeling great until he turned his
head to smile at the chaplain and saw Aarfy there instead. Yossarian moaned

instinctively and screwed his face up with excruciating irritability when Aarfy chortled and asked how he was feeling. Aarfy looked puzzled when Yossarian inquired why he was not in jail. Yossarian shut his eyes to make him go away. When he opened them, Aarfy was gone and the chaplain was there. Yossarian broke into laughter when he spied the chaplain's cheerful grin and asked him what in the hell he was so happy about.

"I'm happy about you," the chaplain replied with excited candor and joy. "I heard at Group that you were very seriously injured and that you would have to be sent home if you lived. Colonel Korn said your condition was critical. But I've just learned from one of the doctors that your wound is really a very slight one and that you'll probably be able to leave in a day or two. You're in no danger. It isn't bad at all."

Yossarian listened to the chaplain's news with enormous relief. "That's good."

"Yes," said the chaplain, a pink flush of impish pleasure creeping into his cheeks. "Yes, that is good."

Yossarian laughed, recalling his first conversation with the chaplain. "You know, the first time I met you was in the hospital. And now I'm in the hospital again. Just about the only time I see you lately is in the hospital. Where've you been keeping yourself?"

The chaplain shrugged. "I've been praying a lot," he confessed. "I try to stay in my tent as much as I can, and I pray every time Sergeant Whitcomb leaves the area, so that he won't catch me."

"Does it do any good?"

"It takes my mind off my troubles," the chaplain answered with another shrug. "And it gives me something to do."

"Well, that's good, then, isn't it?"

"Yes," agreed the chaplain enthusiastically, as though the idea had not occurred to him before. "Yes, I guess that is good." He bent forward impulsively with awkward solicitude. "Yossarian, is there anything I can do for you while you're here, anything I can get you?"

Yossarian teased him jovially. "Like toys, or candy, or chewing gum?"

The chaplain blushed again, grinning self-consciously, and then turned very respectful. "Like books, perhaps, or anything at all. I wish there *was* something I could do to make you happy. You know, Yossarian, we're all very proud of you."

"Proud?"

"Yes, of course. For risking your life to stop that Nazi assassin. It was a very noble thing to do."

"What Nazi assassin?"

"The one that came here to murder Colonel Cathcart and Colonel Korn. And you saved them. He might have stabbed you to death as you grappled with him on the balcony. It's a lucky thing you're alive."

Yossarian snickered sardonically when he understood. "That was no Nazi assassin."

"Certainly it was. Colonel Korn said it was."

"That was Nately's girl friend. And she was after me, not Colonel Cathcart and Colonel Korn. She's been trying to kill me ever since I broke the news to her that Nately was dead."

"But how could that be?" the chaplain protested in livid and resentful confusion. "Colonel Cathcart and Colonel Korn both saw him as he ran away. The official report says you stopped a Nazi assassin from killing them."

"Don't believe the official report," Yossarian advised dryly. "It's part of the deal."

"What deal?"

"The deal I made with Colonel Cathcart and Colonel Korn. They'll let me go home a big hero if I say nice things about them to everybody and never criticize them to anyone for making the rest of the men fly more missions."

The chaplain was appalled and rose halfway out of his chair. He bristled with bellicose dismay. "But that's terrible! That's a shameful, scandalous deal, isn't it?"

"Odious," Yossarian answered, staring up woodenly at the ceiling with just the back of his head resting on the pillow. "I think 'odious' is the word we decided on."

"Then how could you agree to it?"

"It's that or a court-martial, Chaplain."

"Oh," the chaplain exclaimed with a look of stark remorse, the back of his hand covering his mouth. He lowered himself into his chair uneasily. "I shouldn't have said anything."

"They'd lock me in prison with a bunch of criminals."

"Of course. You must do whatever you think is right, then." The chaplain nodded to himself as though deciding the argument and lapsed into embarrassed silence.

"Don't worry" Yossarian said with a sorrowful laugh after several moments had passed. "I'm not going to do it."

"But you must do it," the chaplain insisted, bending forward with concern. "Really, you must. I had no right to influence you. I really had no right to say anything."

"You didn't influence me." Yossarian hauled himself over onto his side and shook his head in solemn mockery. "Christ, Chaplain! Can you imagine that for a sin? Saving Colonel Cathcart's life! That's one crime I don't want on my record."

The chaplain returned to the subject with caution. "What will you do instead? You can't let them put you in prison."

"I'll fly more missions. Or maybe I really will desert and let them catch me. They probably would."

"And they'd put you in prison. You don't want to go to prison."

"Then I'll just keep flying missions until the war ends, I guess. Some of us have to survive."

"But you might get killed."

"Then I guess I won't fly any more missions."

"What will you do?"

"I don't know."

"Will you let them send you home?"

"I don't know. Is it hot out? It's very warm in here."

"It's very cold out," the chaplain said.

"You know," Yossarian remembered, "a very funny thing happened—maybe I dreamed it. I think a strange man came in here before and told me he's got my pal. I wonder if I imagined it."

"I don't think you did," the chaplain informed him. "You started to tell me about him when I dropped in earlier."

"Then he really did say it, 'We've got your pal, buddy,' he said. 'We've got your pal.' He had the most malignant manner I ever saw. I wonder who my pal is."

"I like to think that I'm your pal, Yossarian," the chaplain said with humble sincerity. "And they certainly have got me. They've got my number and they've got me under surveillance, and they've got me right where they want me. That's what they told me at my interrogation."

"No, I don't think it's you he meant," Yossarian decided. "I think it must be someone like Nately or Dunbar. You know, someone who was killed in the war, like Clevinger, Orr, Dobbs, Kid Sampson or McWatt." Yossarian emitted a startled gasp and shook his head. "I just realized it," he exclaimed. "They've got all my pals, haven't they? The only ones left are me and Hungry Joe." He tingled with dread as he saw the chaplain's face go pale. "Chaplain, what is it?"

"Hungry Joe was killed."

"God, no! On a mission?"

"He died in his sleep while having a dream. They found a cat on his face."

"Poor bastard," Yossarian said, and began to cry, hiding his tears in the crook of his shoulder. The chaplain left without saying good-bye. Yossarian ate something and went to sleep. A hand shook him awake in the middle of the night. He opened his eyes and saw a thin, mean man in a patient's bathrobe and pajamas who looked at him with a nasty smirk and jeered,

"We've got your pal, buddy. We've got your pal."

Yossarian was unnerved. "What the *hell* are you talking about?" he pleaded in incipient panic.

"You'll find out, buddy. You'll find out."

Yossarian lunged for his tormentor's throat with one hand, but the man glided out of reach effortlessly and vanished into the corridor with a malicious laugh. Yossarian lay there trembling with a pounding pulse. He was bathed in icy sweat. He wondered who his pal was. It was dark in the hospital and perfectly quiet. He had no watch to tell him the time. He was wide-awake, and he knew he was a prisoner in one of those sleepless, bedridden nights that would take an eternity to dissolve into dawn. A throbbing chill oozed up his legs. He was cold, and he thought of Snowden, who had never been his pal but was a vaguely familiar kid who was badly wounded and freezing to death in the puddle of harsh yellow sunlight splashing into his face through the side gunport when Yossarian crawled into the rear section of the plane over the bomb bay after Dobbs had beseeched him on the intercom to help the gunner, please help the gunner. Yossarian's stomach turned over when his eyes first beheld the macabre scene; he was absolutely revolted, and he paused in fright a few moments before descending, crouched on his hands and knees in the narrow tunnel over the bomb bay beside the sealed corrugated carton containing the first aid kit. Snowden was lying on his back on the floor with his legs stretched out, still burdened cumbersomely by his flak suit, his flak helmet, his parachute harness and his Mae West. Not far away on the floor lay the small tail gunner in a dead faint. The wound Yossarian saw was in the outside of Snowden's thigh, as large and deep as a football, it seemed. It was impossible to tell where the shreds of his saturated coveralls ended and the ragged flesh began.

There was no morphine in the first-aid kit, no protection for Snowden against pain but the numbing shock of the gaping wound itself. The twelve syrettes of morphine had been stolen from their case and replaced by a cleanly lettered note that said: "What's good for M & M Enterprises is good for the country. Milo Minderbinder." Yossarian swore at Milo and held two aspirins out to ashen lips unable to receive them. But first he hastily drew a tourniquet around Snowden's thigh because he could not think what else to do in those first tumultuous moments when his senses were in turmoil, when he knew he must act competently at once and feared he might go to pieces completely. Snowden watched him steadily, saying nothing. No artery was spurting, but Yossarian pretended to absorb himself entirely into the fashioning of a tourniquet, because applying tourniquet was something he did know how to do. He worked with simulated skill and composure, feeling Snowden's lackluster gaze resting upon him. He recovered possession of himself before the tourniquet was finished and loosened it immediately to lessen the danger of gangrene. His mind was clear now, and he knew how to proceed. He rummaged through the first-aid kit for scissors.

"I'm cold," Snowden said softly. "I'm cold."

"You're going to be all right, kid," Yossarian reassured him with a grin. "You're going to be all right."

"I'm cold," Snowden said again in a frail, childlike voice. "I'm cold."

"There, there," Yossarian said, because he did not know what else to say. "There, there."

"I'm cold," Snowden whimpered. "I'm cold."

"There, there. There, there."

Yossarian was frightened and moved more swiftly. He found a pair of scissors at last and began cutting carefully through Snowden's coveralls high up above the wound, just below the groin. He cut through the heavy gabardine cloth all the way around the thigh in a straight line. The tiny tail gunner woke up while Yossarian was cutting with the scissors, saw him, and fainted again. Snowden rolled his head to the other side of his neck in order to stare at Yossarian more directly. A dim, sunken light glowed in his weak and listless eyes. Yossarian, puzzled, tried not to look at him. He began cutting downward through the coveralls along the inside seam. The yawning wound—was that a tube of slimy bone he saw running deep inside the gory scarlet flow behind the twitching, startling fibers of weird muscle?—was dripping blood in several trickles, like snow melting on eaves, but viscous and red, already thickening as it dropped. Yossarian kept cutting through the coveralls to the bottom and peeled open the severed leg of the garment. It fell to the floor with a plop, exposing the hem of khaki undershorts that were soaking up blotches of blood on one side as though in thirst. Yossarian was stunned at how waxen and ghastly Snowden's bare leg looked, how loathsome, how lifeless and esoteric the downy, fine, curled blond hairs on his odd, white shin and calf. The wound, he saw now, was not nearly as large as a football, but as long and wide as his hand, and too raw and deep to see into clearly. The raw muscles inside twitched like live hamburger meat. A long sigh of relief escaped slowly through Yossarian's mouth when he saw that Snowden was not in danger of dying. The blood was already coagulating inside the wound, and it was simply a matter of bandaging him up and keeping him calm until the plane landed. He removed some packets of sulfanilamide from the first-aid kit. Snowden quivered when Yossarian pressed against him gently to turn him up slightly on his side.

"Did I hurt you?"

"I'm cold," Snowden whimpered. "I'm cold."

"There, there," Yossarian said. "There, there."

"I'm cold. I'm cold."

"There, there. There, there."

"It's starting to hurt me," Snowden cried out suddenly with a plaintive, urgent wince.

Yossarian scrambled frantically through the first-aid kit in search of morphine again and found only Milo's note and a bottle of aspirin. He cursed Milo and held two aspirin tablets out to Snowden. He had no water to offer. Snowden rejected the aspirin with an almost imperceptible shake of his head. His face was pale and pasty. Yossarian removed Snowden's flak helmet and lowered his head to the floor.

"I'm cold," Snowden moaned with half-closed eyes. "I'm cold."

The edges of his mouth were turning blue. Yossarian was petrified. He wondered whether to pull the rip cord of Snowden's parachute and cover him with the nylon folds. It was very warm in the plane. Glancing up unexpectedly, Snowden gave him a wan, co-operative smile and shifted the position of his hips a bit so that Yossarian could begin salting the wound with sulfanilamide. Yossarian worked with renewed confidence and optimism. The plane bounced hard inside an air pocket, and he remembered with a start that he had left his own parachute up front in the nose. There was nothing to be done about that. He poured envelope after envelope of the white crystalline powder into the bloody oval wound until nothing red could be seen and then drew a deep, apprehensive breath, steeling himself with gritted teeth as he touched his bare hand to the dangling shreds of drying flesh to tuck them up inside the wound. Quickly he covered the whole wound with a large cotton compress and jerked his hand away. He smiled nervously when his brief ordeal had ended. The actual contact with the dead flesh had not been nearly as repulsive as he had anticipated, and he found excuse to caress the wound with his fingers again and again to convince himself of his own courage.

Next he began binding the compress in place with a roll of gauze. The second time around Snowden's thigh with the bandage, he spotted the small hole on the inside through which the piece of flak had entered, a round, crinkled wound the size of a quarter with blue edges and a black core inside where the blood had crusted. Yossarian sprinkled this one with sulfanilamide too and continued unwinding the gauze around Snowden's leg until the compress was secure. Then he snipped off the roll with the scissors and slit the end down the center. He made the whole thing fast with a tidy square knot. It was a good bandage, he knew, and he sat back on his heels with pride, wiping the perspiration from his brow, and grinned at Snowden with spontaneous friendliness.

"I'm cold," Snowden moaned. "I'm cold."

"You're going to be all right, kid," Yossarian assured him, patting his arm comfortingly. "Everything's under control."

Snowden shook his head feebly. "I'm cold," he repeated, with eyes as dull and blind as stone. "I'm cold."

"There, there," said Yossarian, with growing doubt and trepidation. "There, there. In a little while we'll be back on the ground and Doc Daneeka will take care of you."

But Snowden kept shaking his head and pointed at last, with just the barest movement of his chin, down toward his armpit. Yossarian bent forward to peer and saw a strangely colored stain seeping through the coveralls just above the armhole of Snowden's flak suit. Yossarian felt his heart stop, then pound so violently he found it difficult to breath. Snowden was wounded inside his flak suit. Yossarian ripped open the snaps of Snowden's flak suit and heard himself scream wildly as Snowden's insides slithered down to the floor in a soggy pile and just kept dripping out. A chunk of flak more than three inches big had shot into his other side just underneath the arm and blasted all the way through, drawing whole mottled quarts of Snowden along with it through the gigantic hole in his ribs it made as it blasted out. Yossarian screamed a second time and squeezed both hands over his eyes. His teeth were chattering in horror. He forced himself to look again. Here was God's plenty, all right, he thought bitterly as he stared—liver, lungs, kidneys, ribs, stomach and bits of the stewed tomatoes Snowden had eaten that day for lunch. Yossarian hated stewed tomatoes and turned away dizzily and began to vomit, clutching his burning throat. The tail gunner woke up while Yossarian was vomiting, saw him, and fainted again. Yossarian was limp with exhaustion, pain and despair when he finished. He turned back weakly to Snowden, whose breath had grown softer and more rapid, and whose face had grown paler. He wondered how in the world to begin to save him.

"I'm cold," Snowden whimpered. "I'm cold."

"There, there," Yossarian mumbled mechanically in a voice too low to be heard. "There, there."

Yossarian was cold, too, and shivering uncontrollably. He felt goose pimples clacking all over him as he gazed down despondently at the grim secret Snowden had spilled all over the messy floor. It was easy to read the message in his entrails. Man was matter, that was Snowden's secret. Drop him out a window and he'll fall. Set fire to him and he'll burn. Bury him and he'll rot like other kinds of garbage. The spirit gone, man is garbage. That was Snowden's secret. Ripeness was all.

"I'm cold," Snowden said. "I'm cold."

"There, there," said Yossarian. "There, there." He pulled the rip cord of Snowden's parachute and covered his body with the white nylon sheets.

"I'm cold."

"There, there."

1961

Bernard Malamud   *1914–1986*

Bernard Malamud was a recorder of the Jewish experience, with all its despair, possibility, and hope for redemption. He was born in Brooklyn, the son of Russian immigrant parents. After graduating from the City College of New York in 1936 he attended Columbia University from which he received an M.A. in 1942. He taught in a high school and then at Oregon State University from 1949 to 1961. While there he published The Natural *(1952), a comic novel that ironically mythologizes the American passion for "the national pastime," baseball. In 1957 he published* The Assistant, *a tragi-comedy of a young Italian-American living in the midst of a Jewish family, which many critics consider to be his most successful novel.* The Magic Barrel *(1958), a collection of short stories for which he received a National Book Award, similarly reveals the tragedy and comedy inherent in human life. In* A New Life *(1961), one of Malamud's best-selling works, he concentrated on the spiritual rebirth of a comically suffering and despairing English teacher trapped in an academic wilderness.*

In 1963 he published Idiots First, *a collection of short stories which was followed by* The Fixer *(1966), a parable of the plight of Russian Jews. In* Pictures of Fidelman *(1969), he presented a comic novel of a painter who travels to Europe and tries his hand at art criticism, imitation, forgery, and creation.* The Tenants *(1971) depicts the life of a middle-aged man living in a run-down tenement house and struggling to find mercy in a hostile world. In 1979 Malamud published his seventh and most ambitious novel, Dubin's Lives, a story of marriage and infidelity. The novel's hero, an aging writer, seeks rejuvenation and escape from a stale world. He finds, instead, a portion of the moral insight that can be gained from painful experience.*

Malamud's works often display the search for meaning made by a bereft, bewildered wanderer who yearns, but fails, to find the secret of life and happiness. Malamud revealed the relationships of comedy and terror, of failure and success, of weakness and courage; and he presented the individual as an emblem of modern man, confused, clinging to shattered dreams, and struggling for love and self-understanding in the midst of folly and threatening doom.

FURTHER READING: *The Stories of Bernard Malamud,* 1983; S. Richmond, *Bernard Malamud,* 1967; G. Meeter, *Bernard Malamud and Philip Roth, A Critical Essay,* 1968; R. Ducharme, *Art and Idea in the Novels of Bernard Malamud,* 1974; S. Cohen, *Bernard Malamud and the Trial by Love,* 1974; *Bernard Malamud,* ed. L. and J. Field, 1975; *The Fiction of Bernard Malamud,* ed. R. Astro and J. Benson, 1977; S. Hershinow, *Bernard Malamud,* 1980; I. Alter, *The Good Man's Dilemma, Social Criticism in the Fiction of Bernard Malamud,* 1981; J. Helterman, *Understanding Bernard Malamud,* 1985; *Bernard Malamud,* ed. H. Bloom, 1986..

TEXT: *The Magic Barrel,* 1958.

THE MAGIC BARREL

Not long ago there lived in uptown New York, in a small, almost meager room, though crowded with books, Leo Finkle, a rabbinical student in the Yeshivah University. Finkle, after six years of study, was to be ordained in June and had been advised by an acquaintance that he might find it easier to win himself a congregation if he were married. Since he had no present prospects of marriage, after two tormented days of turning it over in his mind, he called in Pinye Salzman, a marriage broker whose two-line advertisement he had read in the *Forward.*[1]

The matchmaker appeared one night out of the dark fourth-floor hallway of the graystone rooming house where Finkle lived, grasping a black, strapped portfolio that had been worn thin with use. Salzman, who had been long in the business, was of slight but dignified build, wearing an old hat, and an overcoat too short and tight for him. He smelled frankly of fish, which he loved to eat, and although he was missing a few teeth, his presence was not displeasing, because of an amiable manner curiously contrasted with mournful eyes. His voice, his lips, his wisp of beard, his bony fingers were animated, but give him a moment of repose and his mild blue eyes revealed a depth of sadness, a characteristic that put Leo a little at ease although the situation, for him, was inherently tense.

He at once informed Salzman why he had asked him to come, explaining that his home was in Cleveland, and that but for his parents, who had married comparatively late in life, he was alone in the world. He had for six years devoted himself almost entirely to his studies, as a result of which, understandably, he had found himself without time for a social life and the company of young women. Therefore he thought it the better part of trial and error—of embar-

[1] *The Jewish Daily Forward,* Yiddish newspaper in New York City.

rassing fumbling—to call in an experienced person to advise him on these matters. He remarked in passing that the function of the marriage broker was ancient and honorable, highly approved in the Jewish community, because it made practical the necessary without hindering joy. Moreover, his own parents had been brought together by a matchmaker. They had made, if not a financially profitable marriage—since neither had possessed any worldly goods to speak of—at least a successful one in the sense of their everlasting devotion to each other. Salzman listened in embarrassed surprise, sensing a sort of apology. Later, however, he experienced a glow of pride in his work, an emotion that had left him years ago, and he heartily approved of Finkle.

The two went to their business. Leo had led Salzman to the only clear place in the room, a table near a window that overlooked the lamp-lit city. He seated himself at the matchmaker's side but facing him, attempting by an act of will to suppress the unpleasant tickle in his throat. Salzman eagerly unstrapped his portfolio and removed a loose rubber band from a thin packet of much-handled cards. As he flipped through them, a gesture and sound that physically hurt Leo, the student pretended not to see and gazed steadfastly out the window. Although it was still February, winter was on its last legs, signs of which he had for the first time in years begun to notice. He now observed the round white moon, moving high in the sky through a cloud menagerie, and watched with half-open mouth as it penetrated a huge hen, and dropped out of her like an egg laying itself. Salzman, though pretending through eyeglasses he had just slipped on, to be engaged in scanning the writing on the cards, stole occasional glances at the young man's distinguished face, noting with pleasure the long, severe scholar's nose, brown eyes heavy with learning, sensitive yet ascetic lips, and a certain, almost hollow quality of the dark cheeks. He gazed around at shelves upon shelves of books and let out a soft, contented sigh.

When Leo's eyes fell upon the cards, he counted six spread out in Salzman's hand.

"So few?" he asked in disappointment.

"You wouldn't believe me how much cards I got in my office," Salzman replied. "The drawers are already filled to the top, so I keep them now in a barrel, but is every girl good for a new rabbi?"

Leo blushed at this, regretting all he had revealed of himself in a curriculum vitae he had sent to Salzman. He had thought it best to acquaint him with his strict standards and specifications, but in having done so, he felt he had told the marriage broken more than was absolutely necessary.

He hesitantly inquired, "Do you keep photographs of your clients on file?"

"First comes family, amount of dowry, also what kind promises," Salzman replied, unbuttoning his tight coat and settling himself in the chair. "After comes pictures, rabbi."

"Call me Mr. Finkle. I'm not yet a rabbi."

Salzman said he would, but instead called him doctor, which he changed to rabbi when Leo was not listening too attentively.

Salzman adjusted his horn-rimmed spectacles, gently cleared his throat and read in an eager voice the contents of the top card:

"Sophie P. Twenty four years. Widow one year. No children. Educated high school and two years college. Father promises eight thousand dollars. Has wonderful wholesale business. Also real estate. On the mother's side comes teachers, also one actor. Well known on Second Avenue."

Leo gazed up in surprise. "Did you say a widow?"

"A widow don't mean spoiled, rabbi. She lived with her husband maybe four months. He was a sick boy she made a mistake to marry him."

"Marrying a widow has never entered my mind."

"This is because you have no experience. A widow, especially if she is young and healthy like this girl, is a wonderful person to marry. She will be thankful to you the rest of her life. Believe me, if I was looking now for a bride, I would marry a widow."

Leo reflected, then shook his head.

Salzman hunched his shoulders in an almost imperceptible gesture of disappointment. He placed the card down on the wooden table and began to read another:

"Lily H. High school teacher. Regular. Not a substitute. Has savings and new Dodge car. Lived in Paris one year. Father is successful dentist thirty-five years. Interested in professional man. Well Americanized family. Wonderful opportunity."

"I knew her personally," said Salzman. "I wish you could see this girl. She is a doll. Also very intelligent. All day you could talk to her about books and theyater and what not. She also knows current events."

"I don't believe you mentioned her age?"

"Her age?" Salzman said, raising his brows. "Her age is thirty-two years."

Leo said after a while, "I'm afraid that seems a little too old."

Salzman let out a laugh. "So how old are you, rabbi?"

"Twenty-seven."

"So what is the difference, tell me, between twenty-seven and thirty-two? My own wife is seven years older than me. So what did I suffer?—Nothing. If Rothschild's a daughter wants to marry you, would you say on account her age, no?"

"Yes," Leo said dryly.

Salzman shook off the no in the yes. "Five years don't mean a thing. I give you my word that when you will live with her for one week you will forget her age. What does it mean five years—that she lived more and knows more than somebody who is younger? On this girl, God bless her, years are not wasted. Each one that it comes makes better the bargain."

"What subject does she teach in high school?"

"Languages. If you heard the way she speaks French, you will think it is music. I am in the business twenty-five years, and I recommend her with my whole heart. Believe me, I know what I'm talking, rabbi."

"What's on the next card?" Leo said abruptly.

Salzman reluctantly turned up the third card:

"Ruth K. Nineteen years. Honor student. Father offers thirteen thousand cash to the right bridegroom. He is a medical doctor. Stomach specialist with marvelous practice. Brother in law owns own garment business. Particular people."

Salzman looked as if he had read his trump card.

"Did you say nineteen?" Leo asked with interest.

"On the dot."

"Is she attractive?" He blushed. "Pretty?"

Salzman kissed his finger tips. "A little doll. On this I give my word. Let me call the father tonight and you will see what means pretty."

But Leo was troubled. "You're sure she's that young?"

"This I am positive. The father will show you the birth certificate."

"Are you positive there isn't something wrong with her?" Leo insisted.

"Who says there is wrong?"

"I don't understand why an American girl her age should go to a marriage broker."

A smile spread over Salzman's face.

"So for the same reason you went, she comes."

Leo flushed. "I am pressed for time."

Salzman, realizing he had been tactless, quickly explained. "The father came, not her. He wants she should have the best, so he looks around himself. When we will locate the right boy he will introduce him and encourage. This makes a better marriage than if a young girl without experience takes for herself. I don't have to tell you this."

"But don't you think this young girl believes in love?" Leo spoke uneasily.

Salzman was about to guffaw but caught himself and said soberly, "Love comes with the right person, not before."

Leo parted dry lips but did not speak. Noticing that Salzman had snatched a glance at the next card, he cleverly asked, "How is her health?"

"Perfect," Salzman said, breathing with difficulty. "Of course, she is a little lame on her right foot from an auto accident that it happened to her when she was twelve years, but nobody notices on account she is so brilliant and also beautiful."

Leo got up heavily and went to the window. He felt curiously bitter and upbraided himself for having called in the marriage broker. Finally, he shook his head.

"Why not?" Salzman persisted, the pitch of his voice rising.

"Because I detest stomach specialists."

"So what do you care what is his business? After you marry her do you need him? Who says he must come every Friday night in your house?"

Ashamed of the way the talk was going, Leo dismissed Salzman, who went home with heavy, melancholy eyes.

Though he had felt only relief at the marriage broker's departure, Leo was in low spirits the next day. He explained it as arising from Salzman's failure to produce a suitable bride for him. He did not care for his type of clientele. But when Leo found himself hesitating whether to seek out another matchmaker, one more polished than Pinye, he wondered if it could be—his protestations to the contrary, and although he honored his father and mother—that he did not, in essence, care for the match-making institution? This thought he quickly put out of mind yet found himself still upset. All day he ran around in the woods— missed an important appointment, forgot to give out his laundry, walked out of a Broadway cafeteria without paying and had to run back with the ticket in his hand; had even not recognized his landlady in the street when she passed with a friend and courteously called out, "A good evening to you, Doctor Finkle." By nightfall, however, he had regained sufficient calm to sink his nose into a book and there found peace from his thoughts.

Almost at once there came a knock on the door. Before Leo could say enter, Salzman, commercial cupid, was standing in the room. His face was gray and meager, his expression hungry, and he looked as if he would expire on his feet. Yet the marriage broker managed, by some trick of the muscles, to display a broad smile.

"So good evening. I am invited?

Leo nodded, disturbed to see him again, yet unwilling to ask the man to leave.

Beaming still, Salzman laid his portfolio on the table. "Rabbi, I got for you tonight good news."

"I've asked you not to call me rabbi. I'm still a student."

"Your worries are finished. I have for you a first-class bride."

"Leave me in peace concerning this subject." Leo pretended lack of interest.

"The world will dance at your wedding."

"Please, Mr. Salzman, no more."

"But first must come back my strength," Salzman said weakly. He fumbled with the portfolio straps and took out of the leather case an oily paper bag, from which he extracted a hard, seeded roll and a small, smoked white fish. With a quick motion of his hand he stripped the fish out of its skin and began ravenously to chew. "All day in a rush," he muttered.

Leo watched him eat.

"A sliced tomato you have maybe?" Salzman hesitantly inquired.

"No."

The marriage broker shut his eyes and ate. When he had finished he carefully cleaned up the crumbs and rolled up the remains of the fish, in the paper bag. His spectacled eyes roamed the room until he discovered, amid some piles of books, a one-burner gas stove. Lifting his hat he humbly asked, "A glass tea you got, rabbi?"

Conscience-stricken, Leo rose and brewed the tea. He served it with a chunk of lemon and two cubes of lump sugar, delighting Salzman.

After he had drunk his tea, Salzman's strength and good spirits were restored.

"So tell me, rabbi," he said amiably, "you considered some more the three clients I mentioned yesterday?"

"There was no need to consider."

"Why not?"

"None of them suits me."

"What then suits you?"

Leo let it pass because he could give only a confused answer.

Without waiting for a reply, Salzman asked, "You remember this girl I talked to you—the high school teacher?"

"Age thirty-two?"

But, surprisingly, Salzman's face lit in a smile. "Age twenty-nine."

Leo shot him a look. "Reduced from thirty-two?"

"A mistake," Salzman avowed. "I talked today with the dentist. He took me to his safety deposit box and showed me the birth certificate. She was twenty-nine years last August. They made her a party in the mountains where she went for her vacation. When her father spoke to me the first time I forgot to write the age and I told you thirty-two, but now I remember this was a different client, a widow."

"The same one you told me about? I thought she was twenty-four?"

"A different. Am I responsible that the world is filled with widows?"

"No, but I'm not interested in them, nor for that matter, in school teachers."

Salzman pulled his clasped hands to his breast. Looking at the ceiling he devoutly exclaimed, "Yiddishe kinder,[2] what can I say to somebody that he is not interested in high school teachers? So what then you are interested?"

Leo flushed but controlled himself.

"In what else will you be interested," Salzman went on, "if you not interested

[2]Yiddish: "Yiddish children."

in this fine girl that she speaks four languages and has personally in the bank ten thousand dollars? Also her father guarantees further twelve thousand. Also she has a new car, wonderful clothes, talks on all subjects, and she will give you a first-class home and children. How near do we come in our life to paradise?"

"If she's so wonderful, why wasn't she married ten years ago?"

"Why?" said Salzman with a heavy laugh. "—Why? Because she is *partikiler*. This is why. She wants the *best*."

Leo was silent, amused at how he had entangled himself. But Salzman had aroused his interest in Lily H., and he began seriously to consider calling on her. When the marriage broker observed how intently Leo's mind was at work on the facts he had supplied, he felt certain they would soon come to an agreement.

Late Saturday afternoon, conscious of Salzman, Leo Finkle walked with Lily Hirschorn along Riverside Drive. He walked briskly and erectly, wearing with distinction the black fedora that he had that morning taken with trepidation out of the dusty hat box on his closet shelf, and the heavy black Saturday coat he had thoroughly whisked clean. Leo also owned a walking stick, a present from a distant relative, but quickly put temptation aside and did not use it. Lily, petite and not unpretty, had on something signifying the approach of spring. She was au courant,[3] animatedly, with all sorts of subjects, and he weighed her words and found her surprisingly sound—score another for Salzman, whom he uneasily sensed to be somewhere around, hiding perhaps high in a tree along the street, flashing the lady signals with a pocket mirror; or perhaps a cloven-hoofed Pan, piping nuptial ditties as he danced his invisible way before them, strewing wild buds on the walk and purple grapes in their path, symbolizing fruit of a union, though there was of course still none.

Lily startled Leo by remarking, "I was thinking of Mr. Salzman, a curious figure, wouldn't you say?"

Not certain what to answer, he nodded.

She bravely went on, blushing, "I for one am grateful for his introducing us. Aren't you?"

He courteously replied, "I am."

"I mean," she said with a little laugh—and it was all in good taste, or at least gave the effect of being not in bad—"do you mind that we came together so?"

He was not displeased with her honesty, recognizing that she meant to set the relationship aright, and understanding that it took a certain amount of experience in life, and courage, to want to do it quite that way. One had to have some sort of past to make that kind of beginning.

He said that he did not mind. Salzman's function was traditional and honorable—valuable for what it might achieve, which, he pointed out, was frequently nothing.

Lily agreed with a sigh. They walked on for a while and she said after a long silence, again with a nervous laugh, "Would you mind if I asked you something a little bit personal? Frankly, I find the subject fascinating." Although Leo shrugged, she went on half embarrassedly, "How was it that you came to your calling? I mean was it a sudden passionate inspiration?"

Leo, after a time, slowly replied, "I was always interested in the Law."

"You saw revealed in it the presence of the Highest?"

He nodded and changed the subject. "I understand that you spent a little time in Paris, Miss Hirschorn?"

[3]Informed, up-to-date.

"Oh, did Mr. Salzman tell you, Rabbi Finkle?" Leo winced but she went on, "It was ages ago and almost forgotten. I remember I had to return for my sister's wedding."

And Lily would not be put off. "When," she asked in a trembly voice, "did you become enamored of God?"

He stared at her. Then it came to him that she was talking not about Leo Finkle, but of a total stranger, some mystical figure, perhaps even passionate prophet that Salzman had dreamed up for her—no relation to the living or dead. Leo trembled with rage and weakness. The trickster had obviously sold her a bill of goods, just as he had him, who'd expected to become acquainted with a young lady of twenty-nine, only to behold, the moment he laid eyes upon her strained and anxious face, a woman past thirty-five and aging rapidly. Only his self control had kept him this long in her presence.

"I am not,' he said gravely, "a talented religious person," and in seeking words to go on, found himself possessed by shame and fear. "I think," he said in a strained manner, "that I came to God not because I loved Him, but because I did not."

This confession he spoke harshly because its unexpectedness shook him.

Lily wilted. Leo saw a profusion of loaves of bread go flying like ducks high over his head, not unlike the winged loaves by which he had counted himself to sleep last night. Mercifully, then, it snowed, which he would not put past Salzman's machinations.

He was infuriated with the marriage broker and swore he would throw him out of the room the minute he reappeared. But Salzman did not come that night, and when Leo's anger had subsided, an unaccountable despair grew in its place. At first he thought this was caused by his disappointment in Lily, but before long it became evident that he had involved himself with Salzman without a true knowledge of his own intent. He gradually realized—with an emptiness that seized him with six hands—that he had called in the broker to find him a bride because he was incapable of doing it himself. This terrifying insight he had derived as a result of his meeting and conversation with Lily Hirschorn. Her probing questions had somehow irritated him into revealing—to himself more than her—the true nature of his relationship to God, and from that it had come upon him, with shocking force, that apart from his parents, he had never loved anyone. Or perhaps it went the other way, that he did not love God so well as he might, because he had not loved man. It seemed to Leo that his whole life stood starkly revealed and he saw himself for the first time as he truly was— unloved and loveless. This bitter but somehow not fully unexpected revelation brought him to a point of panic controlled only by extraordinary effort. He covered his face with his hands and cried.

The week that followed was the worst of his life. He did not eat and lost weight. His beard darkened and grew ragged. He stopped attending seminars and almost never opened a book. He seriously considered leaving the Yeshivah, although he was deeply troubled at the thought of the loss of all his years of study—saw them like pages torn from a book, strewn over the city—and at the devastating effect of this decision upon his parents. But he had lived without knowledge of himself, and never in the Five Books and all the Commentaries— mea culpa[4]—had the truth been revealed to him. He did not know where to turn, and in all this desolating loneliness there was no *to whom*, although he

---

[4]Latin: my fault, a ritual phrase spoken by sinners.

often thought of Lily but not once could bring himself to go downstairs and make the call. He became touchy and irritable, especially with his landlady, who asked him all manner of personal questions; on the other hand, sensing his own disagreeableness, he waylaid her on the stairs and apologized abjectly, until mortified, she ran from him. Out of this, however, he drew the consolation that he was a Jew and that a Jew suffered. But gradually, as the long and terrible week drew to a close, he regained his composure and some idea of purpose in life: to go on as planned. Although he was imperfect, the ideal was not. As for his quest of a bride, the thought of continuing afflicted him with anxiety and heartburn, yet perhaps with this new knowledge of himself he would be more successful than in the past. Perhaps love would now come to him and a bride to that love. And for this sanctified seeking who needed a Salzman?

The marriage broker, a skeleton with haunted eyes, returned that very night. He looked, withal, the picture of frustrated expectancy—as if he had steadfastly waited the week at Miss Lily Hirschorn's side for a telephone call that never came.

Casually coughing, Salzman came immediately to the point: "So how did you like her?"

Leo's anger rose and he could not refrain from chiding the matchmaker: "Why did you lie to me, Salzman?"

Salzman's pale face went dead white, the world had snowed on him.

"Did you not state that she was twenty-nine?" Leo insisted.

"I gave you my word—"

"She was thirty-five, if a day. *At least* thirty-five."

"Of this don't be too sure. Her father told me—"

"Never mind. The worst of it was that you lied to her."

"How did I lie to her, tell me?"

"You told her things about me that weren't true. You made me out to be more, consequently less than I am. She had in mind a totally different person, a sort of semimystical Wonder Rabbi."

"All I said, you was a religious man."

"I can imagine."

Salzman sighed. "This is my weakness that I have," he confessed. "My wife says to me I shouldn't be a salesman, but when I have two fine people that they would be wonderful to be married, I am so happy that I talk too much." He smiled wanly. "This is why Salzman is a poor man."

Leo's anger left him. "Well, Salzman, I'm afraid that's all."

The marriage broker fastened hungry eyes on him.

"You don't want any more a bride?"

"I do," said Leo, "but I have decided to seek her in a different way. I am no longer interested in an arranged marriage. To be frank, I now admit the necessity of premarital love. That is, I want to be in love with the one I marry."

"Love?" said Salzman, astounded. After a moment he remarked "For us, our love is our life, not for the ladies. In the ghetto they—"

"I know, I know," said Leo. "I've thought of it often. Love, I have said to myself, should be a by-product of living and worship rather than its own end. Yet for myself I find it necessary to establish the level of my need and fulfill it."

Salzman shrugged but answered, "Listen, rabbi, if you want love, this I can find for you also. I have such beautiful clients that you will love them the minute your eyes will see them."

Leo smiled unhappily. "I'm afraid you don't understand."

But Salzman hastily unstrapped his portfolio and withdrew a manila packet from it.

"Pictures," he said, quickly laying the envelope on the table.

Leo called after him to take the pictures away, but as if on the wings of the wind, Salzman had disappeared.

March came. Leo had returned to his regular routine. Although he felt not quite himself yet—lacked energy—he was making plans for a more active social life. Of course it would cost something, but he was an expert in cutting corners; and when there were no corners left he would make circles rounder. All the while Salzman's pictures had lain on the table, gathering dust. Occasionally as Leo sat studying, or enjoying a cup of tea, his eyes fell on the manila envelope, but he never opened it.

The days went by and no social life to speak of developed with a member of the opposite sex—it was difficult, given the circumstances of his situation. One morning Leo toiled up the stairs to his room and stared out the window at the city. Although the day was bright his view of it was dark. For some time he watched the people in the street below hurrying along and then turned with a heavy heart to his little room. On the table was the packet. With a sudden relentless gesture he tore it open. For a half-hour he stood by the table in a state of excitement, examining the photographs of the ladies Salzman had included. Finally, with a deep sigh he put them down. There were six, of varying degrees of attractiveness, but look at them long enough and they all became Lily Hirschorn; all past their prime, all starved behind bright smiles, not a true personality in the lot. Life, despite their frantic yoohooings, had passed them by; they were pictures in a brief case that stunk of fish. After a while, however, as Leo attempted to return the photographs into the envelope, he found in it another, a snapshot of the type taken by a machine for a quarter. He gazed at it a moment and let out a cry.

Her face deeply moved him. Why, he could at first not say. It gave him the impression of youth—spring flowers, yet age—a sense of having been used to the bone, wasted; this came from the eyes, which were hauntingly familiar, yet absolutely strange. He had a vivid impression that he had met her before, but try as he might he could not place her although he could almost recall her name, as if he had read it in her own handwriting. No, this couldn't be; he would have remembered her. It was not, he affirmed, that she had an extraordinary beauty—no, though her face was attractive enough; it was that *something* about her moved him. Feature for feature, even some of the ladies of the photographs could do better; but she leaped forth to his heart—had *lived*, or wanted to—more than just wanted, perhaps regretted how she had lived—had somehow deeply suffered: it could be seen in the depths of those reluctant eyes, and from the way the light enclosed and shone from her, and within her, opening realms of possibility: this was her own. Her he desired. His head ached and eyes narrowed with the intensity of his gazing, then as if an obscure fog had blown up in the mind, he experienced fear of her and was aware that he had received an impression, somehow, of evil. He shuddered, saying softly, it is thus with us all. Leo brewed some tea in a small pot and sat sipping it without sugar, to calm himself. But before he had finished drinking, again with excitement he examined the face and found it good: good for Leo Finkle. Only such a one could understand him and help him seek whatever he was seeking. She might, perhaps, love him. How she had happened to be among the discards in Salzman's barrel he could never guess, but he knew he must urgently go find her.

Leo rushed downstairs, grabbed up the Bronx telephone book, and searched for Salzman's home address. He was not listed, nor was his office. Neither was he in the Manhattan book. But Leo remembered having written down the address on a slip of paper after he had read Salzman's advertisement in the "personals" column of the *Forward*. He ran up to his room and tore through his papers, without luck. It was exasperating. Just when he needed the matchmaker he was nowhere to be found. Fortunately Leo remembered to look in his wallet. There on a card he found his name written and a Bronx address. No phone number was listed, the reason—Leo now recalled—he had originally communicated with Salzman by letter. He got on his coat, put a hat on over his skull cap and hurried to the subway station. All the way to the far end of the Bronx he sat on the edge of his seat. He was more than once tempted to take out the picture and see if the girl's face was as he remembered it, but he refrained, allowing the snapshot to remain in his coat pocket, content to have her so close. When the train pulled into the station he was waiting at the door and bolted out. He quickly located the street Salzman had advertised.

The building he sought was less than a block from the subway, but it was not an office building, nor even a loft, nor a store in which one could rent office space. It was a very old tenement house. Leo found Salzman's name in pencil on a soiled tag under the bell and climbed three dark flights to his apartment. When he knocked, the door was opened by a thin, asthmatic, gray-haired woman, in felt slippers.

"Yes?" she said, expecting nothing. She listened without listening. He could have sworn he had seen her, too, before but knew it was an illusion.

"Salzman—does he live here? Pinye Salzman," he said, "the matchmaker?"

She stared at him a long minute. "Of course."

He felt embarrassed. "Is he in?"

"No." Her mouth, though left open, offered nothing more.

"The matter is urgent. Can you tell me where his office is?"

"In the air." She pointed upward.

"You mean he has no office?" Leo asked.

"In his socks."

He peered into the apartment. It was sunless and dingy, one large room divided by a half-open curtain, beyond which he could see a sagging metal bed. The near side of a room was crowded with rickety chairs, old bureaus, a three-legged table, racks of cooking utensils, and all the apparatus of a kitchen. But there was no sign of Salzman or his magic barrel, probably also a figment of the imagination. An odor of frying fish made Leo weak to the knees.

"Where is he?" he insisted. "I've got to see your husband."

At length she answered, "So who knows where he is? Every time he thinks a new thought he runs to a different place. Go home, he will find you."

"Tell him Leo Finkle."

She gave no sign she had heard.

He walked downstairs, depressed.

But Salzman, breathless, stood waiting at his door.

Leo was astounded and overjoyed. "How did you get here before me?"

"I rushed."

"Come inside."

They entered. Leo fixed tea, and a sardine sandwich for Salzman. As they were drinking he reached behind him for the packet of pictures and handed them to the marriage broker.

Salzman put down his glass and said expectantly, "You found somebody you like?"

"Not among these."

The marriage broker turned away.

"Here is the one I want." Leo held forth the snapshot.

Salzman slipped on his glasses and took the picture into his trembling hand. he turned ghastly and let out a groan.

"What's the matter?" cried Leo.

"Excuse me. Was an accident this picture. She isn't for you."

Salzman frantically shoved the manila packet into his portfolio. He thrust the snapshot into his pocket and fled down the stairs.

Leo, after momentary paralysis, gave chase and cornered the marriage broker in the vestibule. The landlady made hysterical outcries but neither of them listened.

"Give me back the picture, Salzman."

"No." The pain in his eyes was terrible.

"Tell me who she is then."

"This I can't tell you. Excuse me."

He made to depart, but Leo, forgetting himself, seized the matchmaker by his tight coat and shook him frenziedly.

"Please," sighed Salzman. *"Please."*

Leo ashamedly let him go. "Tell me who she is," he begged. "It's very important for me to know."

"She is not for you. She is a wild one—wild, without shame. This is not a bride for a rabbi."

"What do you mean wild?"

"Like an animal. Like a dog. For her to be poor was a sin. This is why to me she is dead now."

"In God's name, what do you mean?"

"Her I can't introduce to you," Salzman cried.

"Why are you so excited?"

"Why, he asks," Salzman said, bursting into tears. "This is my baby, my Stella, she should burn in hell."

Leo hurried up to bed and hid under the covers. Under the covers he thought his life through. Although he soon fell asleep he could not sleep her out of his mind. He woke, beating his breast. Though he prayed to be rid of her, his prayers went unanswered. Through days of torment he endlessly struggled not to love her; fearing success, he escaped it. He then concluded to convert her to goodness, himself to God. The idea alternately nauseated and exalted him.

He perhaps did not know that he had come to a final decision until he encountered Salzman in a Broadway cafeteria. He was sitting alone at a rear table, sucking the bony remains of a fish. The marriage broker appeared haggard, and transparent to the point of vanishing.

Salzman looked up at first without recognizing him. Leo had grown a pointed beard and his eyes were weighted with wisdom.

"Salzman," he said, "love has at last come to my heart."

"Who can love from a picture?" mocked the marriage broker.

"It is not impossible."

"If you can love her, then you can love anybody. Let me show you some new clients that they just sent me their photographs. One is a little doll."

"Just her I want," Leo murmured.

"Don't be a fool, doctor. Don't bother with her."

"Put me in touch with her, Salzman," Leo said humbly. "Perhaps I can be of service."

Salzman had stopped eating and Leo understood with emotion that it was now arranged.

Leaving the cafeteria, he was, however, afflicted by a tormenting suspicion that Salzman had planned it all to happen this way.

Leo was informed by letter that she would meet him on a certain corner, and she was there one spring night, waiting under a street lamp. He appeared, carrying a small bouquet of violets and rosebuds. Stella stood by the lamp post, smoking. She wore white with red shoes, which fitted his expectations, although in a troubled moment he had imagined the dress red, and only the shoes white. She waited uneasily and shyly. From afar he saw that her eyes—clearly her father's—were filled with desperate innocence. He pictured, in her, his own redemption. Violins and lit candles revolved in the sky. Leo ran forward with flowers outthrust.

Around the corner, Salzman, leaning against a wall, chanted prayers for the dead.

1954, 1958

Tillie Olsen   *1913–*

Although she has published only a slight body of writing, Tillie Olsen has gained wide critical attention as a prose stylist and as a spokeswoman for the poor, the oppressed, the "despised people" of America. She has written of the lives of immigrants, western coal miners, middle-western farm laborers, sewer workers, slaughter house workers, merchant seamen, people she has known and lived with. She was born in Nebraska to Russian immigrant parents. Her formal education stopped at the eleventh grade, but she educated herself at the public library, and by the time she was eighteen she had begun to write. In her early twenties she had already won recognition as a writer of poems and short fiction about the difficult lives of workers, blacks, women, vagrants, strikers, and the poor.

She began work on her novel, Yonnondio, *in 1932, when she was only nineteen. But while she was still in her twenties, her career was interrupted as she married, raised children, and was forced to work at numerous jobs to help support her family. Her book* Silences *(1978) describes the interruptions imposed on her writing career and the burdens that most women must suffer in their efforts to give expression to their lives, how even the daily tasks of housekeeping and child rearing inevitably smother women's artistic creativity and breed "silences."*

Finally published in 1974, Yonnondio, *the story of a coal miner's family and its long struggle to endure, was praised as one of the best works of the proletarian movement in American literature. But her greatest fame came with the publication of* Tell Me a Riddle *(1978). Its stories, including "I Stand Here Ironing," have frequently been reprinted, adapted for readings, and presented in stage productions. Tillie Olsen has frequently been praised as a prose stylist, but her greatest achievement has been to catch "the downward movement of life," to portray eloquently the working-class men and women of America struggling to understand one another and to find lives of dignity and fulfillment.*

FURTHER READING: E. Orr, *Tillie Olsen and a Feminist Spiritual Vision*, 1987.
TEXT: *Tell Me a Riddle*, 1956.

I STAND HERE IRONING

I stand here ironing, and what you asked me moves tormented back and forth with the iron.

"I wish you would manage the time to come in and talk with me about your daughter. I'm sure you can help me understand her. She's a youngster who needs help and whom I'm deeply interested in helping."

"Who needs help." . . . Even if I came, what good would it do? You think because I am her mother I have a key, or that in some way you could use me as a key? She has lived for nineteen years. There is all that life that has happened outside of me, beyond me.

And when is there time to remember, to sift, to weigh, to estimate, to total? I will start and there will be an interruption and I will have to gather it all together again. Or I will become engulfed with all I did or did not do, with what should have been and what cannot be helped.

She was a beautiful baby. The first and only one of our five that was beautiful at birth. You do not guess how new and uneasy her tenancy in her now-loveliness. You did not know her all those years she was thought homely, or see her poring over her baby pictures, making me tell her over and over how beautiful she had been—and would be, I would tell her—and was now, to the seeing eye. But the seeing eyes were few or nonexistent. Including mine.

I nursed her. They feel that's important nowadays. I nursed all the children, but with her, with all the fierce rigidity of first motherhood, I did like the books then said. Though her cries battered me to trembling and my breasts ached with swollenness, I waited till the clock decreed.

Why do I put that first? I do not even know if it matters, or if it explains anything.

She was a beautiful baby. She blew shining bubbles of sound. She loved motion, loved light, loved color and music and textures. She would lie on the floor in her blue overalls patting the surface so hard in ecstasy her hands and feet would blur. She was a miracle to me, but when she was eight months old I had to leave her daytimes with the woman downstairs to whom she was no miracle at all, for I worked or looked for work and for Emily's father, who "could no longer endure" (he wrote in his good-bye note) "sharing want with us."

I was nineteen. It was the pre-relief, pre-WPA world of the depression. I would start running as soon as I got off the streetcar, running up the stairs, the place smelling sour, and awake or asleep to startle awake, when she saw me she would break into a clogged weeping that could not be comforted, a weeping I can hear yet.

After a while I found a job hashing at night so I could be with her days, and it was better. But it came to where I had to bring her to his family and leave her.

It took a long time to raise the money for her fare back. Then she got chicken pox and I had to wait longer. When she finally came, I hardly knew her, walking quick and nervous like her father, looking like her father, thin, and dressed in a shoddy red that yellowed her skin and glared at the pockmarks. All the baby loveliness gone.

She was two. Old enough for nursery school they said, and I did not know then what I know now—the fatigue of the long day, and the lacerations of group life in the kinds of nurseries that are only parking places for children.

Except that it would have made no difference if I had known. It was the only place there was. It was the only way we could be together, the only way I could hold a job.

And even without knowing, I knew. I knew the teacher that was evil because all these years it has curdled into my memory, the little boy hunched in the corner, her rasp, "why aren't you outside, because Alvin hits you? that's no reason, go out, scaredy." I knew Emily hated it even if she did not clutch and implore "don't go Mommy" like the other children, mornings.

She always had a reason why we should stay home. Momma, you look sick. Momma, I feel sick. Momma, the teachers aren't there today, they're sick. Momma, we can't go, there was a fire there last night. Momma, it's a holiday today, no school, they told me.

But never a direct protest, never rebellion. I think of our others in their three-, four-year-oldness—the explosions, the tempers, the denunciations, the demands—and I feel suddenly ill. I put the iron down. What in me demanded that goodness in her? And what was the cost, the cost to her of such goodness?

The old man living in the back once said in his gentle way: "You should smile at Emily more when you look at her." What *was* in my face when I looked at her? I loved her. There were all the acts of love.

It was only with the others I remembered what he said, and it was the face of joy, and not of care or tightness or worry I turned to them—too late for Emily. She does not smile easily, let alone almost always as her brothers and sisters do. Her face is closed and sombre, but when she wants, how fluid. You must have seen it in her pantomimes, you spoke of her rare gift for comedy on the stage that rouses a laughter out of the audience so dear they applaud and applaud and do not want to let her go.

Where does it come from, that comedy? There was none of it in her when she came back to me that second time, after I had had to send her away again. She had a new daddy now to learn to love, and I think perhaps it was a better time.

Except when we left her alone nights, telling ourselves she was old enough.

"Can't you go some other time, Mommy, like tomorrow?" she would ask. "Will it be just a little while you'll be gone? Do you promise?"

The time we came back, the front door open, the clock on the floor in the hall. She rigid awake. "It wasn't just a little while. I didn't cry. Three times I called you, just three times, and then I ran downstairs to open the door so you could come faster. The clock talked loud. I threw it away, it scared me what it talked."

She said the clock talked loud again that night I went to the hospital to have Susan. She was delirious with the fever that comes before red measles, but she was fully conscious all the week I was gone and the week after we were home when she could not come near the new baby or me.

She did not get well. She stayed skeleton thin, not wanting to eat, and night after night she had nightmares. She would call for me, and I would rouse from exhaustion to sleepily call back: "You're all right, darling, go to sleep, it's just a dream," and if she still called, in a sterner voice, "now go to sleep, Emily, there's nothing to hurt you." Twice, only twice, when I had to get up for Susan anyhow, I went in to sit with her.

Now when it is too late (as if she would let me hold and comfort her like I do the others) I get up and go to her at once at her moan or restless stirring. "Are you awake, Emily? Can I get you something?" And the answer is always the same: "No, I'm all right, go back to sleep, Mother."

They persuaded me at the clinic to send her away to a convalescent home in the country where "she can have the kind of food and care you can't manage for her, and you'll be free to concentrate on the new baby." They still send children to that place. I see pictures on the society page of sleek young women planning affairs to raise money for it, or dancing at the affairs, or decorating Easter eggs or filling Christmas stockings for the children.

They never have a picture of the children so I do not know if the girls still wear those gigantic red bows and the ravaged looks on the every other Sunday when parents can come to visit "unless otherwise notified"—as we were notified the first six weeks.

Oh it is a handsome place, green lawns and tall trees and fluted flower beds. High up on the balconies of each cottage the children stand, the girls in their red bows and white dresses, the boys in white suits and giant red ties. The parents stand below shrieking up to be heard and the children shriek down to be heard, and between them the invisible wall "Not To Be Contaminated by Parental Germs or Physical Affection."

There was a tiny girl who always stood hand in hand with Emily. Her parents never came. One visit she was gone. "They moved her to Rose Cottage" Emily shouted in explanation. "They don't like you to love anybody here."

She wrote once a week, the labored writing of a seven-year-old. "I am fine. How is the baby. If I write my leter nicly I will have a star. Love." There never was a star. We wrote every other day, letters she could never hold or keep but only hear read—once. "We simply do not have room for children to keep any personal possessions," they patiently explained when we pieced one Sunday's shrieking together to plead how much it would mean to Emily, who loved so to keep things, to be allowed to keep her letters and cards.

Each visit she looked frailer. "She isn't eating," they told us.

(They had runny eggs for breakfast or mush with lumps. Emily said later, I'd hold it in my mouth and not swallow. Nothing ever tasted good, just when they had chicken.)

It took us eight months to get her released home, and only the fact that she gained back so little of her seven lost pounds convinced the social worker.

I used to try to hold and love her after she came back, but her body would stay stiff, and after a while she'd push away. She ate little. Food sickened her, and I think much of life too. Oh she had physical lightness and brightness, twinkling by on skates, bouncing like a ball up and down up and down over the jump rope, skimming over the hill; but these were momentary.

She fretted about her appearance, thin and dark and foreign-looking at a time when every little girl was supposed to look or thought she should look a chubby blonde replica of Shirley Temple. The doorbell sometimes rang for her, but no one seemed to come and play in the house or be a best friend. Maybe because we moved so much.

There was a boy she loved painfully through two school semesters. Months later she told me how she had taken pennies from my purse to buy him candy. "Licorice was his favorite and I brought him some every day, but he still liked

Jennifer better'n me. Why, Mommy?" The kind of question for which there is no answer.

School was a worry to her. She was not glib or quick in a world where glibness and quickness were easily confused with ability to learn. To her overworked and exasperated teachers she was an overconscientious "slow learner" who kept trying to catch up and was absent entirely too often.

I let her be absent, though sometimes the illness was imaginary. How different from my now-strictness about attendance with the others. I wasn't working. We had a new baby, I was home anyhow. Sometimes, after Susan grew old enough, I would keep her home from school, too, to have them all together.

Mostly Emily had asthma, and her breathing, harsh and labored, would fill the house with a curiously tranquil sound. I would bring the two old dresser mirrors and her boxes of collections to her bed. She would select beads and single earrings, bottle tops and shells, dried flowers and pebbles, old postcards and scraps, all sorts of oddments; then she and Susan would play Kingdom, setting up landscapes and furniture, peopling them with action.

Those were the only times of peaceful companionship between her and Susan. I have edged away from it, that poisonous feeling between them, that terrible balancing of hurts and needs I had to do between the two, and did so badly, those earlier years.

Oh there are conflicts between the others too, each one human, needing, demanding, hurting, taking—but only between Emily and Susan, no, Emily toward Susan that corroding resentment. It seems so obvious on the surface, yet it is not obvious. Susan, the second child, Susan, golden- and curly-haired and chubby, quick and articulate and assured, everything in appearance and manner Emily was not; Susan, not able to resist Emily's precious things, losing or sometimes clumsily breaking them; Susan telling jokes and riddles to company for applause while Emily sat silent (to say to me later: that was *my* riddle, Mother, I told it to Susan); Susan, who for all the five years' difference in age was just a year behind Emily in developing physically.

I am glad for that slow physical development that widened the difference between her and her contemporaries, though she suffered over it. She was too vulnerable for that terrible world of youthful competition, of preening and parading, of constant measuring of yourself against every other, of envy, "If I had that copper hair," "If I had that skin. . . ." She tormented herself enough about not looking like the others, there was enough of the unsureness, the having to be conscious of words before you speak, the constant caring—what are they thinking of me? without having it all magnified by the merciless physical drives.

Ronnie is calling. He is wet and I change him. It is rare there is such a cry now. That time of motherhood is almost behind me when the ear is not one's own but must always be racked and listening for the child cry, the child call. We sit for a while and I hold him, looking out over the city spread in charcoal with its soft aisles of light. *"Shoogily,"* he breathes and curls closer. I carry him back to bed, asleep. *Shoogily.* A funny word, a family word, inherited from Emily, invented by her to say: *comfort.*

In this and other ways she leaves her seal, I say aloud. And startle at my saying it. What do I mean? What did I start to gather together, to try and make coherent? I was at the terrible, growing years. War years. I do not remember them well. I was working, there were four smaller ones now, there was not time for her. She had to help be a mother, and housekeeper, and shopper. She had to set her seal. Mornings of crisis and near hysteria trying to get lunches packed, hair combed, coats and shoes found, everyone to school or Child Care on time, the baby ready for transportation. And always the paper scribbled on by a smaller one, the book looked at by Susan then mislaid, the homework not done. Running out to that huge school where she was one, she was lost, she was a drop; suffering over the unpreparedness, stammering and unsure in her classes.

There was so little time left at night after the kids were bedded down. She would struggle over books, always eating (it was in those years she developed her enormous appetite that is legendary in our family) and I would be ironing, or preparing food for the next day, or writing V-mail to Bill, or tending the baby. Sometimes, to make me laugh, or out of her despair, she would imitate happenings or types at school.

I think I said once: "Why don't you do something like this in the school amateur show?" One morning she phoned me at work, hardly understandable through the weeping: "Mother, I did it. I won, I won; they gave me first prize; they clapped and clapped and wouldn't let me go."

Now suddenly she was Somebody, and as imprisoned in her difference as she had been in anonymity.

She began to be asked to perform at other high schools, even in colleges, then at city and statewide affairs. The first one we went to, I only recognized her that first moment when thin, shy, she almost drowned herself into the curtains. Then: Was this Emily? The control, the command, the convulsing and deadly clowning, the spell, then the roaring, stamping audience, unwilling to let this rare and precious laughter out of their lives.

Afterwards: You ought to do something about her with a gift like that—but without money or knowing how, what does one do? We have left it all to her, and the gift has as often eddied inside, clogged and clotted, has been used and growing.

She is coming. She runs up the stairs two at a time with her light graceful step, and I know she is happy tonight. Whatever it was that occasioned your call did not happen today.

"Aren't you ever going to finish the ironing, Mother? Whistler painted his mother in a rocker. I'd have to paint mine standing over an ironing board." This is one of her communicative nights and she tells me everything and nothing as she fixes herself a plate of food out of the icebox.

She is so lovely. Why did you want me to come in at all? Why were you concerned? She will find her way.

She starts up the stairs to bed. "Don't get me up with the rest in the morning." "But I thought you were having midterms." "Oh, those," she comes back in, kisses me, and says quite lightly, "in a couple of years when we'll all be atom-dead they won't matter a bit."

She has said it before. She *believes* it. But because I have been dredging the past, and all that compounds a human being is so heavy and meaningful in me, I cannot endure it tonight.

I will never total it all. I will never come in to say: She was a child seldom smiled at. Her father left me before she was a year old. I had to work her first six years when there was work, or I sent her home and to his relatives. There were years she had care she hated. She was dark and thin and foreign-looking in a world where the prestige went to blondeness and curly hair and dimples, she was slow where glibness was prized. She was a child of anxious, not proud, love. We were poor and could not afford for her the soil of easy growth. I was a young mother, I was a distracted mother. There were the other children pushing up, demanding. Her younger sister seemed all that she was not. There were years she did not want me to touch her. She kept too much in herself, her life was such she had to keep too much in herself. My wisdom came too late. She has much to her and probably nothing will come of it. She is a child of her age, of depression, of war, of fear.

Let her be. So all that is in her will not bloom—but in how many does it? There is still enough left to live by. Only help her to know—help make it so there is cause for her to know—that she is more than this dress on the ironing board, helpless before the iron.

1953–1954   1956

Tomás Rivera   *1935–1984*

Tomás Rivera was a pioneer in the development of modern Mexican-American literature. His writing drew upon his life as a Chicano in the United States, where he was born in the small farm-town of Crystal City, Texas, in 1935. His parents were migrant farm laborers who traveled, seasonally, through the Midwestern United States, following the crop harvests.

Rivera received his earliest formal education in Spanish-speaking schools, and he did not become fluent in English until he was in the fifth grade. He attended a junior college in Texas and later graduated from Southwest Texas State University. Rivera then enrolled in the graduate program in literature at the University of Oklahoma, from which he received a Ph.D. in 1969. Ten years later, after a career of teaching and administrative jobs in high schools and colleges in the Southwest, he was appointed Chancellor of the University of California at Riverside, a post he held until his death in 1984.

In his writing Rivera attempted to record the lives, the culture, and the heritage of Chicano men, women, and children in the United States. He wrote of migrant farmworkers and of those who live in urban barrios. *His poems and stories record the stresses of life of the kind that he himself experienced as a young Chicano isolated from the dominant "Anglo" world of affluence and position.*

But Rivera's primary aim was not to write social protest literature or propaganda for social causes. He wrote to portray realistically the lives of Mexican-Americans who are simultaneously linked to the ancient traditions of Mexico and confronted by the English-speaking world of North America. He wrote of the collective faults and strengths and of the individual misperceptions and apprehensions of a cultural minority that must struggle to understand its own traditions and that lives in the midst of a dominant "Anglo" culture from which it often stands alienated and separate.

FURTHER READING: *Introduction to Chicano Studies,* ed. L. Duran and B. Russell, 1973; C. Tatum, *Chicano Literature,* 1982.

TEXT: *. . . And the Earth Did Not Part,* 1971.

. . . AND THE EARTH DID NOT PART

The first time he felt hate and anger was when he saw his mother cry for his uncle and for his aunt. They had both gotten tuberculosis and each of them had been sent to different sanitoriums. The children had then been parceled out among their aunts and uncles and they had taken care of them as best they could. His aunt had later died and shortly afterward his uncle had been brought home from the sanitorium, but he was already spitting blood every time he coughed. It was then that he saw his mother crying all the time. He had become angry because he couldn't strike back at anyone. He felt the same way now. But this time it was on account of his father.

"You should have left right away, son. Couldn't you see that your father was sick? All of you knew very well that he had been sunstruck before. Why didn't you come home?"

"Well, I don't know. Since the rest of us were soaking wet with sweat we didn't realize it was so hot, but I guess when one has been sunstruck it's different. Anyway, I told him to sit under the tree that's at the end of the rows but he didn't want to. It was then that he started to vomit. Then we saw that he couldn't hoe and we had to drag him to get him under the tree. He didn't struggle anymore. He simply let us take him. He didn't put up a fuss or anything.

"Poor man, my poor husband. He hardly slept last night. Didn't you hear him outside the house? He was twisting and turning all night; it must be painful. God, how I pray he gets well. I've been giving him cool lemonade all day but his eyes are still glassy. If I had been in the field yesterday I assure you that he would not have had a sunstroke. Poor man, he'll have spasms all over his body for at least three days and three nights. Now all of you take care of yourselves. If it gets too hot, rest. Don't overwork yourselves. Don't pay attention to the boss if he hurries you. Since he is not the one breaking his back, he thinks its easy."

He became angrier when he heard his father moan outside the shack. His father didn't stay inside because he said that he was overcome with anxiety whenever he did. He had to be outside where he could get fresh air. There he could stretch out on the grass and roll around when the spasms hit him. Then he thought about whether his father was going to die from the sunstroke. From time to time he would hear his father pray and ask God for help. At first he had hoped that he would get well soon but the following day he felt his anger increase. And he felt it increase more when his mother or his father clamored for the mercy of God. And their father's moans had awakened them that night and also at dawn and their mother had gotten up and had taken off his scapularies from around his neck and had washed them for him. She had then lighted some small candles. But to no avail. It was the same as with his uncle and his aunt.

"What do you gain by doing that, mother? Don't tell me that you believe that sort of thing helped my uncle and my aunt? Why is it that we are here on earth as though buried alive? Either the germs eat us from the inside or the sun from the outside. Always some illness. And work, work, day in and day out. And for what? Poor father, he works just as hard as the rest of us, perhaps harder. He was born working, as he says. Barely five years old and he was already out there planting corn with his father. After feeding the earth and the sun for such a long time, . . . one day unexpectedly he is felled by the sun. And powerless to do anything. And to top it off, praying to God. God doesn't even remember us . . . There must not be a God. . . . No, better not to say it, what if father should worsen? Poor man, at least that must give him some hope."

His mother noticed how furious he was and in the morning she told him to calm down, that everything was in the hands of God and that his father would get well with God's help.

"Come now, do you really believe that? God, I am sure, doesn't give a damn about us.

Look, can you tell me if father is mean or without love? You tell me if he has ever hurt anyone?"

"Well, no."

"There you are. See? And my uncle and my aunt? You tell me. And now their poor children not knowing their parents. Why did He have to take them? So you see, God doesn't give a damn about us poor people. Look, why do we have to live under these conditions? Are we hurting anybody? You're such a good person and yet you have to suffer so much. Can't you see ? Tell me!"

"Oh, son, don't talk like that. Don't question the will of God. The ground might open up and devour you for talking like that. One must resign oneself to the will of God. Please don't talk like that, son. You frighten me. It seems that already the devil is in your very blood."

"Well, perhaps. At least the way I could release my anger. I'm tired of asking, why? Why you? Why father? Why my uncle? Why my aunt? Why their children? Can you tell me why? Why should we always be tied to the dirt, half buried in the earth like animals without any hope of any kind? You know that the only thing we can look forward to is coming over here every year. And as you yourself say, one does not rest until one dies. I guess that is the way my uncle and my aunt felt, and that's the way father will eventually feel!"

"That's the way it is, son. Only death can bring us rest."

"But, why us?"

"Well, it is said that . . . ."

"Don't say it! Don't tell me anything! I know what you're going to tell me!—that the poor will go to heaven."

The day started out cloudy and he felt the cool morning breeze brush his eyelashes as he and his brothers and sisters started to work. His mother had had to stay at home to take care of her husband. Thus he felt responsible for encouraging his brothers and sisters. In the morning, at least during the early hours, they were able to withstand the sun, but by ten-thirty the sun had suddenly completely cleared the sky and penetrated everything and everyone. They worked much slower because they would feel weakness and suffocation overcome them if they worked at a hurried pace. They then had to wipe the sweat from their eyes every few minutes because their eyes would become blurry.

"When you kids see blurry, stop working or slow down. When we get to the end of the rows we'll rest awhile to regain our strength. It's going to be hot today. I wish it would remain cloudy, as it was this morning. No one would complain then. But no, once the sun bears down not even a tiny cloud dares show itself out of sheer fright. The hell of it is, we'll be finished here by two and then we have to go to that field that is nothing but hills. It's ok on the top of the hill but when we're in the low parts it's suffocating. Not even the slightest breeze blows through there. Air almost doesn't enter. Remember?"

"Yes."

"That's where we'll spend the hottest part of the day. Just drink a lot of water every few minutes even if the boss gets angry. If not you'll get sick. And if you can't take it any longer, tell me right away, ok? We'll go home. You saw what happened to father for holding out. The sun can suck the life out of you."

Just as they had thought, they had had to move to the other field by early afternoon. By three o'clock they were already sopping wet with sweat. Not a single part of their clothing remained dry. Every few minutes they stopped. Sometimes they gasped for breath, then everything became blurred and the fear of sunstroke creeped into them, but they continued.

"How do you feel?"

"Man, it's hot! But we have to keep going. At least until six. Only thing is that the water we have is no longer good for our thirst. How I wish I had a glass of cool water, real cold, just pulled up from the well, or an icy coke."

"You're crazy, you'd sure get sunstroke that way. Just don't work too fast. Let's see if we can hold up until six. Can you take it?"

At four o'clock the youngest became sick. He was only nine years old but since he was paid as an adult he tried to keep up with the others. He started to vomit and sat down, then he lay down. Fear stricken they all rushed over to him. He appeared to have fainted and when they opened his eyelids they found his eyes turned around. The one next to him in age started to cry but he told him immediately to shut up and help take him home. Spasms were moving over his small body. He then threw him on his back and carried him by himself. Once again he began asking why?

"Why my father, and now my little brother? He is barely nine years old. Why? He has to work like an animal, tied to the ground. Father, Mother, and he, my little brother, how could they possibly be guilty of anything?"

Each step that he took toward the house brought forth the echo of the question "why?" Half way down the road he became furious and then he started to cry out of despair. His other brothers and sisters didn't know what to do and they also started to cry, but out of fear. He then began to swear. And he didn't know when, but what he said he had been wanting to say for a long time. He cursed God. Upon doing it he felt the fear instilled in him by time and by his parents. For a split second he saw the earth open up to devour him. But, although he didn't look down, he then felt himself walking on very solid ground; *it was harder than he had ever felt it*. Anger swelled up in him again and he released it by cursing God. Then he noticed that his little brother no longer appeared quite so ill. He didn't know if his other little brothers and sisters realized how serious his curse had been.

That evening he didn't go to sleep until very late. He was experiencing a peace that he had never known before. It seemed to him that he had completely detached himself from everything. He was no longer worried about his father nor about his brother. All that he looked forward to was the new day, the coolness of the morning. By dawn his father was better. He was on his way to recovery. His little brother was also almost completely free of spasms. Time after time he felt surprised at what he had done the previous afternoon. He had cursed God and the earth had not parted. He was going to tell his mother but he decided to keep it a secret. He only told her that the earth didn't devour anyone, and that the sun didn't destroy anyone either.

He left for work and he was faced with a very cool morning. There were clouds and for the first time he felt himself capable of doing and undoing whatever he chose. He looked toward the ground and he kicked it and said to it,

"Not yet, you can't eat me yet. Someday. But I won't know."

Imamu Amiri Baraka (LeRoi Jones)   *1934–*

He was born LeRoi Jones in Newark, New Jersey. In 1966, when he was thirty-two, he returned to Newark to serve as a leader, known as Imamu Amiri Baraka, of Spirit House, an African culture center. Jones had graduated from high school and attended Rutgers University in Newark. Later he transferred to Howard University, in Washington, D.C., from which he received a degree in English literature. For two years he served in the Air Force, stationed much of the time in Puerto Rico. Following his discharge he returned to the United States, to New York City, where he studied at Columbia University and at the New School for Social Research, from which he received an M.A. in German literature.

Jones taught at Columbia and at the New School, wrote newspaper and magazine articles, and in 1961 he published his first collection of poems, Preface to a Twenty Volume Suicide Note. *Three years later he published his second volume of poems,* The Dead Lecturer. *He has also written volumes of plays, fiction, and essays, including* Dutchman and The Slave *(1964);* The System of Dante's Hell *(1965), a partially autobiographical novel;* Home, Social Essays *(1966);* Tales *(1967); and two books on music:* Blues People, Negro Music in White America *(1963) and* Black Music *(1967). In 1971 he published* Raise Race Rays Raze, Essays Since 1965 *and in 1978* The Motion of History and Other Plays.

Jones's early poetry shows the influence of such poets as Ezra Pound and, especially, William Carlos Williams, whose "quantitative verse" Jones sought to duplicate. He wanted to bring his poems close to the rhythms of spoken English by relating line lengths, pauses, phrasings, and the arrangements of stanzas to the rhythms of breathing, thus giving the poet a measure of control over the voicing of verse in a manner similar to that of a director of a musical score.

In the last decade Jones's growing interest in the black revolution has made his poetry increasingly nonformal and nontraditional. He has sought to write authentically of his own experiences in a vital street style, free of orthodox diction, images, and received ideas— a rejection of what he considers to be "white" poetic tradition. His views are evident in his drama Dutchman, *a savage portrait of racial betrayal and of cynical violence. As Imamu Amiri Baraka he is both a Black Power advocate and a black visionary writer. He wants, in his words, to "reach some people, move some people"—not with mere "skin drama," the black, Broadway plays that lack revolutionary ideology, but with propaganda that is art: writing that unites art and politcis; literature with a "clear revolutionary edge to it."*

FURTHER READING: *The Selected Plays and Prose,* 1979; *Selected Poetry,* 1979; *The Autobiography of LeRoi Jones,* 1984; *Daggers and Javelins, Essays 1974–1979,* 1984; T. Hudson, *From LeRoi Jones to Amiri Baraka,* 1973; K. Benston, *Baraka, The Renegade and the Mask,* 1976; W. Sellors, *Amiri Baraka/LeRoi Jones, The Quest for a "Populist Modernism,"* 1978; L. Brown, *Amiri Baraka,* 1980.

TEXTS: "In Memory of Radio," "The Bridge," and "Notes for a Speech" are from *Preface to a Twenty Volume Suicide Note,* 1961; "An Agony. As Now.," "A Poem for Democrats," and "A Poem for Speculative Hipsters" are from *The Dead Lecturer,* 1964; all other poems are from *Black Magic,* 1969; *Dutchman* is from *Dutchman and The Slave,* 1964.

IN MEMORY OF RADIO

Who has ever stopped to think of the divinity of Lamont Cranston?[1]
(Only Jack Kerouac, that I know of: & me.
The rest of you probably had on WCBS and Kate Smith,
Or something equally unattractive.)

What can I say?
It is better to have loved and lost
Than to put linoleum in your living rooms?

Am I a sage or something?
Mandrake's hypnotic gesture of the week?[2]
(Remember, I do not have the healing powers of Oral
    Roberts . . .[3]
I cannot, like F. J. Sheen,[4] tell you how to get saved & *rich!*
I cannot even order you to gaschamber satori[5] like Hitler or
    Goody Knight[6]

& Love is an evil word.
Turn it backwards/see, see what I mean?
An evol word. & besides
who understands it?
I certainly wouldn't like to go out on that kind of limb.

Saturday mornings we listened to *Red Lantern* & his undersea folk.
At 11, *Let's Pretend*/& we did/& I, the poet, still do, Thank God!

What was it he used to say (after the transformation, when he was
safe & invisible & the unbelievers couldn't throw stones?) "Heh, heh,
heh,
Who knows what evil lurks in the hearts of men? The Shadow
    knows."[7]

O, yes he does
O, yes he does.
An evil word it is,
This Love.

1961

THE BRIDGE

(# for wieners & mcclure)

    I have forgotten the head

[1]The hero of the radio serial "The Shadow" (1931–1954), who had "the power to cloud men's minds" and make himself invisible.
[2]The comic-strip hero Mandrake the Magician used magic hypnotic powers to overcome evil.
[3]Here, and throughout, the ellipsis points are Jones's.
[4]Bishop Fulton J. Sheen (1895–1979), renowned for his radio sermons in the 1930s and 1940s.
[5]A state of sudden enlightenment in Zen Buddhism.
[6]Goodwin Knight, Governor of California (1953–1959) during controversies over the use of the gas chamber for capital punishment.
[7]Repeated signature phrase of "The Shadow."

of where I am. Here at the bridge. 2
bars, down the street, seeming
to warp themselves around my fingers, the day,
screams in me; pitiful like a little girl
you sense will be dead before the winter
is over.

I can't see the bridge now, I've past
it, its shadow, we drove through, headed out
along the cold insensitive roads to what   10
we wanted to call "ourselves."
"How does the bridge go?" Even tho
you find yourself in its length
strung out along its breadth, waiting
for the cold sun to tear out your eyes. Enamoured
of its blues, spread out in the silk clubs of
this autumn tune. The changes are difficult, when
you hear them, & know they are all in you, the chords

of your disorder meddle with your would be disguises.
Sifting in, down, upon your head, with the sun & the insects.   20

(Late feeling) Way down till it barely, after that rush of
wind & odor reflected from hills you have forgotten the color
when you touch the water, & it closes, slowly, around your head.

The bridge will be behind you, that music you know, that place,
you feel when you look up to say, it is me, & I have forgotten,
all the things, you told me to love, to try to understand, the
bridge will stand, high up in the clouds & the light, & you,

(when you have let the song run out) will be sliding through
unmentionable black.

                                                        1961

NOTES FOR A SPEECH

African blues
does not know me. Their steps, in sands
of their own
land. A country
in black & white, newspapers
blown down pavements
of the world. Does
not feel
what I am.
            Strength   10
in the dream, an oblique
suckling of nerve, the wind

throws up sand, eyes
are something locked in
hate, of hate, of hate, to
walk abroad, they conduct
their deaths apart
from my own. Those
heads, I call
my "people."   20
           (And who are they. People. To concern
myself, ugly man. Who
you, to concern
the white flat stomachs
of maidens, inside houses
dying. Black, Peeled moon
light on my fingers
move under
her clothes. Where
is her husband. Black   30
words throw up sand
to eyes, fingers of
their private dead. Whose
soul, eyes, in sand. My color
is not theirs. Lighter, white man
talk. They shy away. My own
dead souls, my, so called
people. Africa
is a foreign place. You are
as any other sad man here   40
american.

                     1961

AN AGONY. AS NOW.

I am inside someone
who hates me. I look
out from his eyes. Smell
what fouled tunes come in
to his breath. Love his
wretched women.

Slits in the metal, for sun. Where
my eyes sit turning, at the cool air
the glance of light, or hard flesh
rubbed against me, a woman, a man,   10
without shadow, or voice, or meaning.

This is the enclosure (flesh,
where innocence is a weapon. An
abstraction. Touch. (Not mine.

Or yours, if you are the soul I had
and abandoned when I was blind and had
my enemies carry me as a dead man
(if he is beautiful, or pitied.)

It can be pain. (As now, as all his
flesh hurts me.) It can be that. Or   20
pain. As when she ran from me into
that forest.
              Or pain, the mind
silver spiraled whirled against the
sun, higher than even old men thought
God would be. Or pain. And the other. The
yes. (Inside his books, his fingers. They
are withered yellow flowers and were never
beautiful.) The yes. You will, lost soul, say
'beauty.' Beauty, practiced, as the tree. The   30
slow river. A white sun in its wet sentences.

Or, the cold men in their gale. Ecstasy. Flesh
or soul. The yes. (Their robes blown. Their bowls
empty. They chant at my heels, not at yours.) Flesh
or soul, as corrupt. Where the answer moves too quickly.
Where the God is a self, after all.)

Cold air blown through narrow blind eyes. Flesh,
white hot metal. Glows as the day with its sun.
It is human love, I live inside. A bony skeleton
you recognize as words or simple feeling.   40

But it has no feeling. As the metal, is hot, it is not,
given to love.

It burns the thing
inside it. And that thing
screams.

                                        1964

A POEM FOR DEMOCRATS

          the city rises

                    in color, our sad
ness, blanket this wood place, single drop
of rain, blue image of
someone's love.
                    Net of rain. Crystal ice
glass strings, smash
(on such repertoire of memory
as:
      baskets   10

the long walk up harbor
& the insistence, rain, as they build

City, is wicked. Not
this one, where I am, where they
still move, go to, out of
(transporting your loved one
across the line is death
by drowning.

    Drowned love
hanged man, swung, cement on his feet.)   20
       But
the small filth of the small mind
short structures of
newark, baltimore, cincinnati, omaha. Distress,
europe has passed we are alone. Europe
frail woman dead, we are alone
        1964

A POEM FOR SPECULATIVE HIPSTERS

He had got, finally,
to the forest
of motives. There were no
owls, or hunters. No Connie Chatterleys[1]
resting beautifully
on their backs, having casually
brought socialism
to England.
    Only ideas,
and their opposites.   10
      Like,
   he was *really*
   nowhere.
        1964

A POEM SOME PEOPLE
WILL HAVE TO UNDERSTAND

Dull unwashed windows of eyes
and buildings of industry. What
industry do I practice? A slick
colored boy, 12 miles from his
home. I practice no industry.

[1]The heroine of D. H. Lawrence's novel *Lady Chatterley's Lover* (1928).

I am no longer a credit
to my race. I read a little,
scratch against silence slow spring
afternoons.
        I had thought, before, some years ago   10
that I'd come to the end of my life.
        Watercolor ego. Without the preciseness
a violent man could propose.
        But the wheel, and the wheels,
won't let us alone. All the fantasy
        and justice, and dry charcoal winters
All the pitifully intelligent citizens
        I've forced myself to love.

We have awaited the coming of a natural
phenomenon. Mystics and romantics, knowledgeable   20
workers
of the land.

But none has come.
(*Repeat*)
                  but none has come.

Will the machinegunners please step forward?

                                 1969

POEM FOR HALF-WHITE COLLEGE
STUDENTS

Who are you, listening to me, who are you
listening to yourself? Are you white or
black, or does that have anything to do
with it? Can you pop your fingers to no
music, except those wild monkies go on
in your head, can you jerk, to no melody,
except finger poppers get it together
when you turn from starchecking to checking
yourself? How do you sound, your words, are they
yours? The ghost you see in the mirror, is it really   10
you, can you swear you are not an imitation greyboy,
can you look right next to you in that chair, and swear,
that the sister you have your hand on is not really
so full of Elizabeth Taylor, Richard Burton is
coming out of her ears. You may even have to be Richard
with a white shirt and face, and four million negroes
think you cute, you may have to be Elizabeth Taylor, old lady,
if you want to sit up in your crazy spot dreaming about dresses,
and the sway of certain porters' hips. Check yourself, learn who it is
speaking, when you make some ultrasophisticated point, check

yourself 20
when you find yourself gesturing like Steve McQueen, check it out,
    ask
in your black heart who it is your are, and is that image black or
    white,

you might be surprised right out the window, whistling dixie on
    the way

1969

BIOGRAPHY

Hangs.
whipped
blood
striped
meat pulled
clothes ripped
slobber
feet dangled
pointing
noised 10
noise
churns
face
black sky
and moon
leather night
red
bleeds
drips
ground 20
sucks
blood
hangs
life wetting
sticky
mud

laughs
bonnets
wolfmoon
crazyteeth 30

hangs

hangs

granddaddy

granddaddy, they tore

his
neck

1969

DUTCHMAN

CHARACTERS

CLAY, twenty-year-old Negro
LULA, thirty-year-old white woman
RIDERS OF COACH, white and black
YOUNG NEGRO
CONDUCTOR

In the flying underbelly of the city. Steaming hot, and summer on top, outside. Under-ground. The subway heaped in modern myth.

Opening scene is a man sitting in a subway seat, holding a magazine but looking vacantly just above its wilting pages. Occasionally he looks blankly toward the window on his right. Dim lights and darkness whistling by against the glass. (Or paste the lights, as admitted props, right on the subway windows. Have them move, even dim and flicker. But give the sense of speed. Also stations, whether the train is stopped or the glitter and activity of these stations merely flashes by the windows.)

The man is sitting alone. That is, only his seat is visible, though the rest of the car is outfitted as a complete subway car. But only his seat is shown. There might be, for a time, as the play begins, a loud scream of the actual train. And it can recur throughout the play, or continue on a lower key once the dialogue starts.

The train slows after a time, pulling to a brief stop at one of the stations. The man looks idly up, until he sees a woman's face staring at him through the windows; when it realizes that the man has noticed the face, it begins very premeditatedly to smile. The man smiles, too, for a moment, without a trace of self-consciousness. Almost an instinctive though undesirable response. Then a kind of awkwardness or embarrassment sets in, and the man makes to look away, is further embarrassed, so he brings back his eyes to where the face was, but by now the train is moving again, and the face would seem to be left behind by the way the man turns his head to look back through the other windows at the slowly fading platform. He smiles then; more comfortably confident, hoping perhaps that his memory of this brief encounter will be pleasant. And then he is idle again.

SCENE I

Train roars. Lights flash outside the windows.

LULA *enters from the rear of the car in bright, skimpy summer clothes and sandals. She carries a net bag full of paper books, fruit, and other anonymous articles. She is wearing sunglasses, which she pushes up on her forehead from time to time.* LULA *is a tall, slender, beautiful woman with long red hair hanging straight down her back, wearing only loud lipstick in somebody's good taste. She is eating an apple, very daintily. Coming down the car toward* CLAY.

She stops beside CLAY'S *seat and hangs languidly from the strap, still managing to eat the apple. It is apparent that she is going to sit in the seat next to* CLAY, *and that she is only waiting for him to notice her before she sits.*

CLAY *sits as before, looking just beyond his magazine, now and again pulling the magazine slowly back and forth in front of his face in a hopeless effort to fan himself. Then he sees the woman hanging there beside him and he looks up into her face, smiling quizzically.*

LULA. Hello.

CLAY. Uh, hi're you?

LULA. I'm going to sit down. . . . O.K.?

CLAY. Sure.

LULA. (*Swings down onto the seat, pushing her legs straight out as if she is very weary*) Oooof! too much weight.

CLAY. Ha, doesn't look like much to me. (*Leaning back against the window, a little surprised and maybe stiff*)

LULA. It's so anyway. (*And she moves her toes in the sandals, then pulls her right leg up on the left knee, better to inspect the bottoms of the sandals and the back of her heel. She appears for a second not to notice that* CLAY *is sitting next to her or that she has spoken to him just a second before.* CLAY *looks at the magazine, then out the black window. As he does this, she turns very quickly toward him*) Weren't you staring at me through the window?

CLAY. (*Wheeling around and very much stiffened*) What?

LULA. Weren't you staring at me through the window? At the last stop?

CLAY. Staring at you? What do you mean?

LULA. Don't you know what staring means?

CLAY. I saw you through the window . . . if that's what it means. I don't know if I was staring. Seems to me you were staring through the window at me.

LULA. I was. But only after I'd turned around and saw you staring through that window down in the vicinity of my ass and legs.

CLAY. Really?

LULA. Really. I guess you were just taking those idle potshots. Nothing else to do. Run your mind over people's flesh.

CLAY. Oh boy. Wow, now I admit I was looking in your direction. But the rest of that weight is yours.

LULA. I suppose.

CLAY. Staring through train windows is weird business. Much weirder than staring very sedately at abstract asses.

LULA. That's why I came looking through the window . . . so you'd have more than that to go on. I even smiled at you.

CLAY. That's right.

LULA. I even got into this train, going some other way than mine. Walked down the aisle . . . searching you out.

CLAY. Really? That's pretty funny.

LULA.That's pretty funny. . . . God, you're dull.

CLAY. Well, I'm sorry, lady, but I really wasn't prepared for party talk.

LULA. No. You're not. What are you prepared for? (*Wrapping the apple core in a Kleenex and dropping it on the floor*)

CLAY. (*Takes her conversation as pure sex talk. He turns to confront her squarely with this idea*) I'm prepared for anything. How about you?

LULA. (*Laughing loudly and cutting it off abruptly*) What do you think you're doing?

CLAY. What?

LULA. You think I want to pick you up, get you to take me somewhere and screw me, huh?

CLAY. Is that the way I look?

LULA. You look like you been trying to grow a beard. That's exactly what you look like. You look like you live in New Jersey with your parents and are trying to grow a beard. That's what. You look like you've been reading Chinese poetry and drinking lukewarm sugarless tea. (*Laughs, uncrossing and recrossing her legs*) You look like death eating a soda cracker.

CLAY. (*Cocking his head from one side to the other, embarrassed and trying to make some comeback, but also intrigued by what the woman is saying . . . even the sharp city coarseness of her voice, which is still a kind of gentle sidewalk throb*) Really? I look like all that?

LULA. Not all of it. (*She feints a seriousness to cover an actual somber tone*) I lie a lot. (*Smiling*) It helps me control the world.

CLAY. (*Relieved and laughing louder than the humor*) Yeah, I bet.

LULA. But it's true, most of it, right? Jersey? Your bumpy neck?

CLAY. How'd you know all that? Huh? Really, I mean about Jersey . . . and even the beard. I met you before? You know Warren Enright?

LULA. You tried to make it with your sister when you were ten. (CLAY *leans back hard against the back of the seat, his eyes opening now, still trying to look amused*) But I succeeded a few weeks ago. (*She starts to laugh again*)

CLAY. What're you talking about? Warren tell you that? You're a friend of Georgia's?

LULA. I told you I lie. I don't know your sister. I don't know Warren Enright.

CLAY. You mean you're just picking these things out of the air?

LULA. Is Warren Enright a tall skinny black boy with a phony English accent?

CLAY. I figured you knew him.

LULA. But I don't. I just figured you would know somebody like that. (*Laughs*)

CLAY. Yeah, yeah.

LULA. You're probably on your way to his house now.

CLAY. That's right.

LULA. (*Putting her hand on* CLAY'S *closest knee, drawing it from the knee up to the thigh's hinge, then removing it, watching his face very closely, and continuing to laugh, perhaps more gently than before*) Dull, dull, dull. I bet you think I'm exciting.

CLAY. You're O.K.

LULA. Am I exciting you now?

CLAY. Right. That's not what's supposed to happen?

LULA. How do I know? (*She returns her hand, without moving it, then takes it away and plunges it in her bag to draw out an apple*) You want this?

CLAY. Sure.

LULA. (*She gets one out of the bag for herself*) Eating apples together is always the first step. Or walking up uninhabited Seventh Avenue in the twenties on weekends. (*Bites and giggles, glancing at* CLAY *and speaking in loose sing-song*) Can get you involved . . . boy! Get us involved. Um-huh. (*Mock seriousness*) Would you like to get involved with me, Mister Man?

CLAY. (*Trying to be as flippant as* LULA, *whacking happily at the apple*) Sure. Why not? A beautiful woman like you. Huh, I'd be a fool not to.

LULA. And I bet you're sure you know what you're talking about. (*Taking him a little roughly by the wrist, so he cannot eat the apple, then shaking the wrist*) I bet you're sure of almost everything anybody ever asked you about . . . right? (*Shakes his wrist harder*) Right?

CLAY. Yeah, right. . . . Wow, you're pretty strong, you know? Whatta you, a lady wrestler or something?

LULA. What's wrong with lady wrestlers? And don't answer because you never knew any. Huh (*Cynically*) That's for sure. They don't have any lady wrestlers in that part of Jersey. That's for sure.

CLAY. Hey, you still haven't told me how you know so much about me.

LULA. I told you I didn't know anything about *you* . . . you're a well-known type.

CLAY. Really?

LULA. Or at least I know the type very well. And your skinny English friend too.

CLAY. Anonymously?

LULA. (*Settles back in seat, single-mindedly finishing her apple and humming snatches of rhythm and blues song*) What?

CLAY. Without knowing us specifically?

LULA. Oh boy. (*Looking quickly at* CLAY) What a face. You know, you could be a handsome man.

CLAY. I can't argue with you.

LULA. (*Vague, off-center response*) What?

CLAY. *Raising his voice, thinking the train noise has drowned part of his sentence*) I can't argue with you.

LULA. My hair is turning gray. A gray hair for each year and type I've come through.

CLAY. Why do you want to sound so old?

LULA. But it's always gentle when it starts. (*Attention drifting*) Hugged against tenements, day or night.

CLAY. What?

LULA. (*Refocusing*) Hey, why don't you take me to that party you're going to?

CLAY. You must be a friend of Warren's to know about the party.

LULA. Wouldn't you like to take me to the party? (*Imitates clinging vine*) Oh, come on, ask me to your party.

CLAY. Of course I'll ask you to come with me to the party. And I'll bet you're a friend of Warren's.

LULA. Why not be a friend of Warren's? Why not? (*Taking his arm*) Have you asked me yet?

CLAY. How can I ask you when I don't know your name?

LULA. Are you talking to my name?

CLAY. What is it, a secret?

LULA. I'm Lena the Hyena.

CLAY. The famous woman poet?

LULA. Poetess! The same!

CLAY. Well, you know so much about me . . . what's my name?

LULA. Morris the Hyena.

CLAY. The famous woman poet?

LULA. The same. (*Laughing and going into her bag*) You want another apple?

CLAY. Can't make it, lady, I only have to keep one doctor away a day.

LULA. I bet your name is . . . something like . . . uh, Gerald or Walter. Huh?

CLAY. God, no.

LULA. Lloyd, Norman? One of those hopeless colored names creeping out of New Jersey? Leonard? Gag. . . .

CLAY. Like Warren?

LULA. Definitely. Just exactly like Warren. Or Everett.

CLAY. Gag. . . .

LULA. Well, for sure, it's not Willie.

CLAY. It's Clay.

LULA. Clay? Really? Clay what?

CLAY. Take your pick. Jackson, Johnson, or Williams.

LULA. Oh, really? Good for you. But it's got to be Williams. You're too pretentious to be a Jackson or Johnson.

CLAY. Thass right.

LULA. But Clay's O.K.

CLAY. So's Lena.

LULA. It's Lula.

CLAY. Oh?

LULA. Lula the Hyena.

CLAY. Very good.

LULA. (*Starts laughing again*) Now you say to me, "Lula, Lula, why don't you go to this party with me tonight?" It's your turn, and let those be your lines.

CLAY. Lula, why don't you go to this party with me tonight, Huh?

LULA. Say my name twice before you ask, and no huh's.

CLAY. Lula, Lula, why don't you go to this party with me tonight?

LULA. I'd like to go, Clay, but how can you ask me to go when you barely know me?

CLAY. That is strange, isn't it?

LULA. What kind of reaction is that? You're supposed to say, "Aw, come on, we'll get to know each other better at the party."

CLAY. That's pretty corny.

LULA. What are you into anyway? (*Looking at him half sullenly but still amused*) What thing are you playing at, Mister? Mister Clay Williams? (*Grabs his thigh, up near the crotch*) What are *you* thinking about?

CLAY. Watch it now, you're gonna excite me for real.

LULA. (*Taking her hand away and throwing her apple core through the window*) I bet. (*She slumps in the seat and is heavily silent*)

CLAY. I thought you knew everything about me? What happened? (LULA *looks at him, then looks slowly away, then over where the other aisle would be. Noise of the train. She reaches in her bag and pulls out one of the paper books. She puts it on her leg and thumbs the pages listlessly.* CLAY *cocks his head to see the title of the book. Noise of the train.* LULA *flips pages and her eyes drift. Both remain silent*) Are you going to the party with me, Lula?

LULA. (*Bored and not even looking*) I don't even know you.

CLAY. You said you know my type.

LULA. (*Strangely irritated*) Don't get smart with me, Buster. I know you like the palm of my hand.

CLAY. The one you eat the apples with?

LULA. Yeh. And the one I open doors late Saturday evening with. That's my door. Up at the top of the stairs. Five flights. Above a lot of Italians and lying Americans. And scrape carrots with. Also ... (*Looks at him*) the same hand I unbutton my dress with, or let my skirt fall down. Same hand. Lover.

CLAY. Are you angry about anything? Did I say something wrong?

LULA. Everything you say is wrong. (*Mock smile*) That's what makes you so attractive. Ha. In that funnybook jacket with all the buttons. (*More animate, taking hold of his jacket*) What've you got that jacket and tie on in all this heat for? And why're you wearing a jacket and tie like that? Did your people ever burn witches or start revolutions over the price of tea? Boy, those narrrow-shoulder clothes come from a tradition you ought to feel oppressed by. A three-button suit. What right do you have to be wearing a three-button suit and striped tie? Your grandfather was a slave, he didn't go to Harvard.

CLAY. My grandfather was a night watchman.

LULA. And you went to a colored college where everybody thought they were Averell Harriman.[1]

CLAY. All except me.

LULA. And who did you think you were? Who do you think you are now?

CLAY. (*Laughs as if to make light of the whole trend of the conversation*) Well, in college I thought I was Baudelaire.[2] But I've slowed down since.

LULA. I bet you never once thought you were a black nigger. (*Mock serious, then she howls with laughter.* CLAY *is stunned but after initial reaction, he quickly tries to appreciate the humor.* LULA *almost shrieks*) A black Baudelaire.

CLAY. That's right.

LULA. Boy, are you corny. I take back what I said before. Everything you say is not wrong. It's perfect. You should be on television.

CLAY. You act like you're on television already.

LULA. That's because I'm an actress.

CLAY. I thought so.

LULA. Well, you're wrong. I'm no actress. I told you I always lie. I'm nothing, honey, and don't you ever forget it. (*Lighter*) Although my mother was a Communist. The only person in my family ever to amount to anything.

CLAY. My mother was a Republican.

LULA. And your father voted for the man rather than the party.

CLAY. Right!

LULA. Yea for him. Yea, yea for him.

CLAY. Yea!

LULA. And yea for America where he is free to vote for the mediocrity of his choice! Yea!

CLAY. Yea!

LULA. And yea for both your parents who even though they differ about so crucial a matter as the body politic still forged a union of love and sacrifice that was destined to flower at the birth of the noble Clay ... what's your middle name?

CLAY. Clay.

LULA. A union of love and sacrifice that was destined to flower at the birth of the noble Clay Clay Williams. Yea! And most of all yea yea for you, Clay Clay. The Black Baudelaire! Yes (And with knife-like cynicism) My Christ. My Christ.

CLAY. Thank you, ma'am.

LULA. May the people accept you as a ghost of the future. And love you, that you might not kill them when you can.

[1]American banker and government official.
[2]Charles Pierre Baudelaire (1821–1867), decadent French poet.

CLAY. What?

LULA. You're a murderer, Clay, and you know it. (*Her voice darkening with significance*) You know goddamn well what I mean.

CLAY. I do?

LULA. So we'll pretend the air is light and full of perfume.

CLAY. And we'll pretend the people cannot see you. That is, the citizens. And that you are free of your own history. And I am free of my history. We'll pretend that we are both anonymous beauties smashing along through the city's entrails. (*She yells as loud as she can*) GROOVE!

Black

SCENE II

Scene is the same as before, though now there are other seats visible in the car. And throughout the scene other people get on the subway. There are maybe one or two seated in the car as the scene opens, though neither CLAY *nor* LULA *notices them.* CLAY'S *tie is open.* LULA *is hugging his arm.*

CLAY. The party!

LULA. I know it'll be something good. You can come in with me, looking casual and significant. I'll be strange, haughty, and silent, and walk with long slow strides.

CLAY. Right.

LULA. When you get drunk, pat me once, very lovingly on the flanks, and I'll look at you cryptically, licking my lips.

CLAY. It looks like something we can do.

LULA. You'll go around talking to young men about your mind, and to old men about your plans. If you meet a very close friend who is also with someone like me, we can stand together, sipping our drinks and exchanging codes of lust. The atmosphere will be slithering in love and half-love and very open moral decision.

CLAY. Great. Great.

LULA. And everyone will pretend they don't know your name, and then . . . (*She pauses heavily*) later, when they have to, they'll claim a friendship that denies your sterling character.

CLAY. (*Kissing her neck and fingers*) And then what?

LULA. Then? Well, then we'll go down the street, late night, eating apples and winding very deliberately toward my house.

CLAY. Deliberately?

LULA. I mean, we'll look in all the shopwindows, and make fun of the queers. Maybe we'll meet a Jewish Buddhist and flatten his conceits over some very pretentious coffee.

CLAY. In honor of whose God?

LULA. Mine.

CLAY. Who is . . . ?

LULA. Me . . . and you?

CLAY. A corporate Godhead.

LULA. Exactly. Exactly. (*Notices one of the other people entering*)

CLAY. Go on with the chronicle. Then what happens to us?

LULA. (*A mild depression, but she still makes her description triumphant and increasingly direct*) To my house, of course.

CLAY. Of course.

LULA. And up the narrow steps of the tenement.

CLAY. You live in a tenement?

LULA. Wouldn't live anywhere else. Reminds me specifically of my novel form of insanity.

CLAY. Up the tenement stairs.

LULA. And with my apple-eating hand I push open the door and lead you, my tender big-eyed prey, into my . . . God, what can I call it . . . into my hovel.

CLAY. Then what happens?

LULA. After the dancing and games, after the long drinks and long walks, the real fun begins.

CLAY. Ah, the real fun. (*Embarrassed, in spite of himself*) Which is . . . ?

LULA. (*Laughs at him*) Real fun in the dark house. Hah! Real fun in the dark house, high up above the street and the ignorant cowboys. I lead you in, holding your wet hand gently in my hand . . .

CLAY. Which is not wet?

LULA. Which is dry as ashes.

CLAY. And cold?

LULA. Don't think you'll get out of your responsibility that way. It's not cold at all. You Fascist! Into my dark living room. Where we'll sit and talk endlessly, endlessly.

CLAY. About what?

LULA. About what? About your manhood, what do you think? What do you think we've been talking about all this time?

CLAY. Well, I didn't know it was that. That's for sure. Every other thing in the world but that. (*Notices another person entering, looks quickly, almost involuntarily up and down the car, seeing the other people in the car*) Hey, I didn't even notice when those people got on.

LULA. Yeah, I know.

CLAY. Man, this subway is slow.

LULA. Yeah, I know.

CLAY. Well, go on. We were talking about my manhood.

LULA. We still are. All the time.

CLAY. We were in your living room.

LULA. My dark living room. Talking endlessly.

CLAY. About my manhood.

LULA. I'll make a map of it. Just as soon as we get to my house.

CLAY. Well, that's great.

LULA. One of the things we do while we talk. And screw.

CLAY. (*Trying to make his smile broader and less shaky*) We finally got there.

LULA. And you'll call my rooms black as a grave. You'll say, "This place is like Juliet's tomb.

CLAY. (*Laughs*) I might.

LULA. I know. You've probably said it before.

CLAY. And is that all? The whole grand tour?

LULA. Not all. You'll say to me very close to my face, many, many times, you'll say, even whisper, that you love me.

CLAY. Maybe I will.

LULA. And you'll be lying.

CLAY. I wouldn't lie about something like that.

LULA. Hah. It's the only kind of thing you will lie about. Especially if you think it'll keep me alive.

CLAY. Keep you alive? I don't understand.

LULA. (*Bursting out laughing, but too shrilly*) Don't understand? Well, don't look at me. It's the path I take, that's all. Where both feet take me when I set them down. One in front of the other.

CLAY. Morbid. Morbid. You sure you're not an actress. All that self-aggrandizement.

LULA. Well, I told you I wasn't an actress . . . but I also told you I lie all the time. Draw your own conclusions.

CLAY. And is that all of our lives together you've described? There's no more?

LULA. I've told you all I know. Or almost all.

CLAY. There's no funny parts?

LULA. I thought it was all funny.

CLAY. But you mean peculiar, not ha-ha.

LULA. You don't know what I mean.

CLAY. Well, tell me the almost part then. You said almost all. What else? I want the whole story.

LULA. (*Searching aimlessly through her bag. She begins to talk breathlessly, with a light and silly tone*) All stories are whole stories. All of 'em. Our whole story . . . nothing but change. How could things go on like that forever? Huh? (*Slaps him on the shoulder, begins finding things in her bag, taking them out and throwing them over her shoulder into the aisle*) Except I do go on as I do. Apples and long walks with the deathless intelligent lovers. But you mix it up. Look out the window, all the time. Turning pages. Change change change. Till, shit, I don't know you. Wouldn't, for that matter. You're too serious. I bet you're even too serious to be psychoanalyzed. Like all those Jewish poets from Yonkers, who leave their mothers looking for other mothers, or others' mothers, on whose baggy tits they lay their fumbling heads. Their poems are always funny, and all about sex.

CLAY. They sound great. Like movies.

LULA. But you change. (*Blankly*) And things work on till you hate them. (*More people come into the train. They come closer to the couple, some of them not sitting, but swinging drearily on the straps, staring at the two with uncertain interest*)

CLAY. Wow. All these people, so suddenly. They must all come from the same place.

LULA. Right. That they do.

CLAY. Oh? You know about them too?

LULA. Oh yeah. About them more than I know about you. Do they frighten you?

CLAY. Frighten me? Why should they frighten me?

LULA. 'Cause you're an escaped nigger.

CLAY. Yeah?

LULA. 'Cause you crawled through the wire and made tracks to my side.

CLAY. Wire?

LULA. Don't they have wire around plantations?

CLAY. You must be Jewish. All you can think about is wire. Plantations didn't have any wire. Plantations were big open whitewashed places like heaven, and everybody on 'em was grooved to be there. Just strummin' and hummin' all day.

LULA. Yes, yes.

CLAY. And that's how the blues was born.

LULA. Yes, yes. And that's how the blues was born. (*Begins to make up a song that becomes quickly hysterical. As she sings she rises from her seat, still throwing things out of her bag into the aisle, beginning a rhythmical shudder and twistlike wiggle, which she continues up and down the aisle, bumping into many of the standing people and tripping over the feet of those sitting. Each time she runs into a person she lets out a very vicious piece of profanity, wiggling and stepping all the time*) And that's how the blues was born. Yes. Yes. Son of a bitch, get out of the way. Yes. Quack. Yes. Yes. And that's how the blues was born. Ten little niggers sitting on a limb, but none of them ever looked like him. (*Points to* CLAY, *returns toward the seat, with her hands extended for him to rise and dance with her*) And that's how the blues was born. Yes. Come on, Clay. Let's do the nasty. Rub bellies. Rub bellies.

CLAY. (*Waves his hands to refuse. He is embarrassed, but determined to get a kick out of the proceedings*) Hey, what was in those apples? Mirror, mirror on the wall, who's the fairest one of all? Snow White, baby, and don't you forget it.

LULA. (*Grabbing for his hands, which he draws away*) Come on, Clay. Let's rub bellies on the train. The nasty. The nasty. Do the gritty grind, like your ol' rag-head mommy. Grind till you lose your mind. Shake it, shake it, shake it, shake it! OOOOweeee! Come on, Clay. Let's do the choo-choo train shuffle, the naval scratcher.

CLAY. Hey, you coming on like the lady who smoked up her grass skirt.

LULA. (*Becoming annoyed that he will not dance, and becoming more animated as if to embarrass him still further*) Come on, Clay . . . let's do the thing. Uhh! Uhh! Clay! Clay! You middle-class black bastard. Forget your social-working mother for a few seconds and let's knock stomachs. Clay, you liver-lipped white man. You would-be Christian. You ain't no nigger, you're just a dirty white man. Get up, Clay. Dance with me, Clay.

CLAY. Lula! Sit down, now. Be cool.

LULA. (*Mocking him, in wild dance*) Be cool. Be cool. That's all you know . . . shaking that wildroot cream-oil on your knotty head, jackets buttoning up to your chin, so full of white man's words. Christ. God. Get up and scream at these people. Like scream meaningless shit in these hopeless faces. (*She screams at people in train, still dancing*) Red trains cough Jewish underwear for keeps! Expanding smells of silence. Gravy snot whistling like sea birds. Clay. Clay, you got to break out. Don't sit here dying the way they want you to die. Get up.

CLAY. Oh, sit the fuck down. (*He moves to restrain her*) Sit down, goddamn it.

LULA. (*Twisting out of his reach*) Screw yourself, Uncle Tom. Thomas Woolly-head. (*Begins to dance a kind of jig, mocking* CLAY *with loud forced humor*) There is Uncle Tom . . . I mean, Uncle Thomas Woolly-Head. With old white matted mane. He hobbles on his wooden cane. Old Tom. Old Tom. Let the white man hump his ol' mama, and he jes' shuffle off in the woods and hide his gentle gray head. Ol' Thomas Woolly-Head. (*Some of the other riders are laughing now. A drunk gets up and joins* LULA *in her dance, singing, as best he can, her "song."* CLAY *gets up out of his seat and visibly scans the faces of the other riders*)

CLAY. Lula! Lula! (*She is dancing and turning, still shouting as loud as she can. The drunk too is shouting, and waving his hands wildly*) Lula . . . you dumb bitch. Why don't you stop it? (*He rushes half stumbling from his seat, and grabs one of her flailing arms*)

LULA. Let me go! You black son of a bitch. (*She struggles against him*) Let me go! Help! (CLAY *is dragging her towards her seat, and the drunk seeks to interfere. He grabs* CLAY *around the shoulders and begins wrestling with him.* CLAY *clubs the drunk to the floor without releasing* LULA, *who is still screaming.* CLAY *finally gets her to the seat and throws her into it*)

CLAY. Now you shut the hell up. (*Grabbing her shoulders*) Just shut up. You don't know what you're talking about. You don't know anything. So just keep your stupid mouth closed.

LULA. You're afraid of white people. And your father was. Uncle Tom Big Lip!

CLAY. (*Slaps her as hard as he can, across the mouth.* LULA'S *head bangs against the back of the seat. When she raises it again,* CLAY *slaps her again*) Now shut up and let me talk. (*He turns toward the other riders, some of whom are sitting on the edge of their seats. The drunk is on one knee, rubbing his head, and singing softly the same song. He shuts up too when he sees* CLAY *watching him. The others go back to newspapers or stare out the windows*) Shit, you don't have any sense, Lula, nor feelings either. I could murder you now. Such a tiny ugly throat. I could squeeze it flat, and watch you turn blue, on a humble. For dull kicks. And all these weak-faced ofays squatting around here, staring over their papers at me. Murder them too. Even if they expected it. That man there . . . (*Points to well-dressed man*) I could rip that *Times* right out of his hand, as skinny and middle-classed as I am, I could rip that paper out of his hand and just as easily rip out his throat. It takes no great effort. For what? To kill you soft idiots? You don't understand anything but luxury.

LULA. You fool!

CLAY. (*Pushing her against the seat*) I'm not telling you again, Tallulah Bankhead! Luxury. In your face and your fingers. You telling me what I ought to do. (*Sudden scream frightening the whole coach*) Well, don't! Don't you tell me anything! If I'm a middle-class fake white man . . . let me be. And let me be in the way I want. (*Through his teeth*) I'll rip your lousy breasts off! Let me be who I feel like being. Uncle Tom. Thomas. Whoever. It's none of your business. You don't know anything except what's there for you to see. An act. Lies. Device. Not the pure heart, the pumping black heart. You don't ever know that. And I sit here, in this buttoned-up suit, to keep myself from cutting all your throats. I mean wantonly. You great liberated whore! You fuck some black man, and right away you're an expert on black people. What a lotta shit that is. The only thing you know is that you come if he bangs you hard enough. And that's all. The belly rub? You want to do the belly rub? Shit, you don't even know how. You don't know how. That ol' dipty-dip shit you do, rolling your ass like an elephant. That's not my kind of belly rub. Belly rub is not Queens. Belly rub is dark places, with big hats and overcoats held up with one arm. Belly rub hates you, Old bald-headed four-eyed ofays popping their fingers . . . and don't know yet what they're doing. They say, "I love Bessie Smith." And don't even understand that Bessie Smith is saying, "Kiss my ass, kiss my black unruly ass." Before love, suffering, desire, anything you can explain, she's saying, and very plainly, "Kiss my black ass." And if you don't know that, it's you that's doing the kissing.

Charlie Parker? Charlie Parker. All the hip white boys scream for Bird. And Bird saying, "Up your ass, feeble-minded ofay! Up your ass." And they sit there talking about the tortured genius of Charlie Parker. Bird would've played not a note of music if he just walked up to East Sixty-seventh Street and killed the first ten white people he saw. Not a note! And I'm the great would-be poet. Yes. That's right! Poet. Some kind of bastard literature . . . all it needs is a simple knife thrust. Just let me bleed you, you loud whore, and one poem vanished. A whole people of neurotics, struggling to keep from being sane. And the only thing that would cure the neurosis would be your murder. Simple as that. I mean if I murdered you, then other white people would begin to understand me. You understand? No. I guess not. If Bessie Smith had killed some white people she wouldn't have needed that music. She could have talked very straight and plain about the world. No metaphors. No grunts. No wiggles in the dark of her soul. Just straight two and two are four. Money. Power. Luxury. Like that. All of them. Crazy niggers turning their backs on sanity. When all it needs is that simple act. Murder. Just murder! Would make us all sane. (*Suddenly weary*) Ahhh. Shit. But who needs it? I'd rather be a fool. Insane. Safe with my words, and no deaths, and clean, hard thoughts, urging me to new conquests. My people's madness. Hah! That's a laugh. My people. They don't need me to claim them. They got legs and arms of their own. Personal insanities. Mirrors. They don't need all those words. They don't need any defense. But listen, though, one more thing. And you tell this to your father, who's probably the kind of man who needs to know at once. So he can plan ahead. Tell him not to preach so much rationalism and cold logic to these niggers. Let them alone. Let them sing curses at you in code and see your filth as simple lack of style. Don't make the mistake, through some irresponsible surge of Christian charity, of talking too much about the advantages of Western rationalism, or the great intellectual legacy of the white man, or maybe they'll begin to listen. And then, maybe one day, you'll find they actually do understand exactly what you are talking about, all these fantasy people. All these blues people. And on that day, as sure as shit, when you really believe you can "accept" them into your fold, as half-white trusties late of the subject peoples. With no more blues, except the very old ones, and not a watermelon in sight, the great missionary heart will have triumphed, and all of those ex-coons will be stand-up Western men, with eyes for clean hard useful lives, sober, pious and sane, and they'll murder you. They'll murder you, and have very rational explanations. Very much like your own. They'll cut your throats, and drag you out to the edge of your cities so the flesh can fall away from your bones, in sanitary isolation.

LULA. (*Her voice takes on a different, more businesslike quality*) I've heard enough.

CLAY. (*Reaching for his books*) I bet you have. I guess I better collect my stuff and get off this train. Looks like we won't be acting out that little pageant you outlined before.

LULA. No. We won't. You're right about that, at least. (*She turns to look quickly around the rest of the car*) All right! (*The others respond*)

CLAY. (*Bending across the girl to retrive his belongings*) Sorry, baby, I don't think we could make it. (*As he is bending over her, the girl brings up a small knife and plunges it into* CLAY'S *chest. Twice. He slumps across her knees, his mouth working stupidly*)

LULA. Sorry is right. (*Turning to the others in the car who have already gotten up from their seats*) Sorry is the rightest thing you've said. Get this man off me! Hurry, now! (*The others come and drag* CLAY'S *body down the aisle*) Open the door and throw his body out. (*They throw him off*) And all of you get off at the next stop. (LULA *busies herself straightening her things. Getting everything in order. She takes out a notebook and makes a quick scribbling note. Drops it in her bag. The train apparently stops and all the others get off, leaving her alone in the coach.*

Very soon a young Negro of about twenty comes into the coach, with a couple of books under his arm. He sits a few seats in back of LULA. *When he is seated she turns and gives him a long slow look. He looks up from his books and drops the book on his lap. Then an old Negro conductor comes into the car, doing a sort of restrained soft shoe, and half mumbling the words of some song. He looks at the young man, briefly, with a quick greeting*)

CONDUCTOR. Hey, brother!

YOUNG MAN. Hey. (*The conductor continues down the aisle with his little dance and the mumbled song.* LULA *turns to stare at him and follows his movements down the aisle. The conductor tips his hat when he reaches her seat, and continues out the car*)

CURTAIN

1964

Edward Albee   *1928–*

In 1962, responding to critical reviews linking him to the traditions of the European Theatre of the Absurd, Edward Albee remarked, "Which theatre is the absurd one?" He was pointing scornfully at the commercial Broadway theater, which had fallen on dismal days and stood in sharp contrast to the vitality of Off-Broadway theater, the milieu from which Albee himself had come and for which he has written his finest work.

Edward Franklin Albee III was a foundling, adopted in infancy by a wealthy theatrical family. Expelled from two private schools, he did better at a third, where he had the opportunity to spend many hours writing poetry and fiction. Much of his real learning, as with Eugene O'Neill, came later from odd jobs: office boy, restaurant counterman, Western Union messenger. Except for one juvenile experiment, a three-act farce composed when he was twelve, Zoo Story *was Albee's first play. Written in 1958, it was first produced in September 1959 in Berlin. The first American staging was Off-Broadway in 1960, and like most Off-Broadway plays,* Zoo Story *is short, has a small cast, deals with human encounter and the search for communion. Its author's structural pattern is revealed: normal opening, increasing emotional tangle, peak of intensity, quick drop-off.*

Following Zoo Story *came a series of one-act plays:* The Death of Bessie Smith *(1960), a drama of social ostracism based on the life of a famous Negro jazz singer;* The Sandbox *(1960); and* The American Dream *(1961), which displayed a pattern increasingly familiar in Albee's plays: the middle-class American family living on illusion and dominated by an overbearing woman.*

Albee's first full-length play, and his greatest hit, was Who's Afraid of Virginia Woolf? *(1962), which ran on Broadway for two years, won many awards, and was made into a memorable and successful film. Since that time Albee has written an adaptation of Carson McCullers'* The Ballad of the Sad Café *(1963),* Tiny Alice *(1964),* Delicate Balance *(1966),* All Over *(1971), and more recently* Seascape *(1975) and* The Lady from Dubuque *(1978). Albee's later plays have been marred by dubious excursions into metaphysics and have failed to duplicate his earlier successes, yet they continue to reveal a talent for wit and penetrating dialogue, and they offer compelling portrayals of psychological and physical violence and of what Albee sees as the complacency and emptiness of contemporary life.*

FURTHER READING: G. Debusscher, *Edward Albee, Tradition and Renewal,* 1967; N. Dos, *Eugene Ionesco and Edward Albee, A Critical Essay,* 1968; R. Cohn, *Edward Albee,* 1969; M. Rutenberg, *Edward Albee, Playwright in Protest,* 1969; and R. Amacher, *Edward Albee,* 1969; A. Paolucci, *Edward Albee, And the Theater of Arrogance,* 1972; *Edward Albee, A Collection of Critical Essays,* ed. C. Bigsby, 1975; *Edward Albee, An Interview and Essays,* ed. J. Wasserman, 1983; *Critical Essays on Edward Albee,* eds. P. Kolin and J. Davis, 1986; *Edward Albee,* ed. H. Bloom, 1987; G. McCarthy, *Edward Albee,* 1987; M. Roudané, *Understanding Edward Albee,* 1987.

TEXT: *The Zoo Story,* 1960.

THE ZOO STORY

THE PLAYERS

PETER: *A man in his early forties, neither fat nor gaunt, neither handsome nor homely. He wears tweeds, smokes a pipe, carries hornrimmed glasses. Although he is moving into middle age, his dress and his manner would suggest a man younger.*

JERRY: *A man in his late thirties, not poorly dressed, but carelessly. What was once a trim and lightly muscled body has begun to go to fat; and while he is no longer handsome, it is evident that he once was. His fall from physical grace should not suggest debauchery; he has, to come closest to it, a great weariness.*

THE SCENE

It is Central Park; a Sunday afternoon in summer; the present. There are two park benches, one toward either side of the stage; they both face the audience. Behind them: foliage, trees, sky. At the beginning, Peter is seated on one of the benches.

Stage Directions: As the curtain rises, PETER *is seated on the bench stage-right. He is reading a book. He stops reading, cleans his glasses, goes back to reading.* JERRY *enters.*

JERRY. I've been to the zoo. (PETER *doesn't notice*) I said, I've been to the zoo. MISTER, I'VE BEEN TO THE ZOO!

PETER. Hm? . . .[1] What? . . . I'm sorry, were you talking to me?

JERRY. I went to the zoo, and then I walked until I came here. Have I been walking north?

PETER. (*Puzzled*) North? Why . . . I . . . I think so. Let me see.

JERRY. (*Pointing past the audience*) Is that Fifth Avenue?

PETER. Why yes; yes, it is.

JERRY. And what is that cross street there; that one, to the right?

PETER. That? Oh, that's Seventy-fourth Street.

JERRY. And the zoo is around Sixty-fifth Street; so, I've been walking north.

PETER. (*Anxious to get back to his reading*) Yes; it would seem so.

JERRY. Good old north.

PETER. (*Lightly, by reflex*) Ha, ha.

JERRY. (*After a slight pause*) But not due north.

PETER. I . . . well, no, not due north; but, we . . . call it north. It's northerly.

JERRY. (*Watches as* PETER, *anxious to dismiss him, prepares his pipe*) Well, boy; you're not going to get lung cancer, are you?

PETER. (*Looks up, a little annoyed, then smiles*) No, sir. Not from this.

JERRY. No, sir. What you'll probably get is cancer of the mouth, and then you'll have to wear one of those things Freud wore after they took one whole side of his jaw away. What do they call those things?

PETER. (*Uncomfortable*) A prosthesis?

JERRY. The very thing! A prosthesis. You're an educated man, aren't you? Are you a doctor?

PETER. Oh, no; no. I read about it somewhere; *Time* magazine, I think. (*He turns to his book*)

JERRY. Well, *Time Magazine* isn't for blockheads.

PETER. No, I suppose not.

JERRY. (*After a pause*) Boy, I'm glad that's Fifth Avenue there.

PETER. (*Vaguely*) Yes.

JERRY. I don't like the west side of the park much.

PETER. Oh? (*Then, slightly wary, but interested*) Why?

JERRY. (*Offhand*) I don't know.

PETER. Oh. (*He returns to his book*)

[1]Here, and throughout, the ellipsis points are Albee's.

JERRY. (*He stands for a few seconds, looking at* PETER, *who finally looks up again, puzzled*) Do you mind if we talk?

PETER. (*Obviously minding*) Why . . . no, no.

JERRY. Yes you do; you do.

PETER. (*Puts his book down, his pipe out and away, smiling*) No, really; I don't mind.

JERRY. Yes you do.

PETER. (*Finally decided*) No; I don't mind at all, really.

JERRY. It's . . . it's a nice day.

PETER. (*Stares unnecessarily at the sky*) Yes. Yes, it is; lovely.

JERRY. I've been to the zoo.

PETER. Yes, I think you said so . . . didn't you?

JERRY. You'll read about it in the papers tomorrow, if you don't see it on your TV tonight. You have TV, haven't you?

PETER. Why yes, we have two; one for the children.

JERRY. You're married!

PETER. (*With pleased emphasis*) Why, certainly.

JERRY. It isn't a law, for God's sake.

PETER. No . . . no, of course not.

JERRY. And you have a wife.

PETER. (*Bewildered by the seeming lack of communication*) Yes!

JERRY. And you have children.

PETER. Yes; two.

JERRY. Boys?

PETER. No, girls . . . both girls.

JERRY. But you wanted boys.

PETER. Well . . . naturally, every man wants a son, but . . .

JERRY. (*Lightly mocking*) But that's the way the cookie crumbles?

PETER. (*Annoyed*) I wasn't going to say that.

JERRY. And you're not going to have any more kids, are you?

PETER. (*A bit distantly*) No. No more. (*Then back, and irksome*) Why did you say that? How would you know about that?

JERRY. The way you cross your legs, perhaps; something in the voice. Or maybe I'm just guessing. Is it your wife?

PETER. (*Furious*) That's none of your business! (*A silence*) Do you understand? (JERRY *nods.* PETER *is quiet now*) Well, you're right. We'll have no more children.

JERRY. (*Softly*) That *is* the way the cookie crumbles.

PETER. (*Forgiving*) Yes . . . I guess so.

JERRY. Well, now; what else?

PETER. What were you saying about the zoo . . . that I'd read about it, or see . . .?

JERRY. I'll tell you about it, soon. Do you mind if I ask you questions?

PETER. Oh, not really.

JERRY. I'll tell you why I do it; I don't talk to many people—except to say like: give me a beer, or where's the john, or what time does the feature go on, or keep your hands to yourself, buddy. You know—things like that.

PETER. I must say I don't . . .

JERRY. But every once in a while I like to talk to somebody, really *talk;* like to get to know somebody, know all about him.

PETER. (*Lightly laughing, still a little uncomfortable*) And am I the guinea pig for today?

JERRY. On a sun-drenched afternoon like this? Who better than a nice married man with two daughters and . . . uh . . . a dog? (PETER *shakes his head*) No? Two dogs. (PETER *shakes his head again*) Hm. No dogs? (PETER *shakes his head, sadly*) Oh, that's a shame. But you look like an animal man. CATS? (PETER *nods his head, ruefully*) Cats! But, that can't be your idea. No, sir. Your wife and daughters? (PETER *nods his head*) Is there anything else I should know?

PETER. (*He has to clear his throat*) There are . . . there are two parakeets. One . . . uh . . . one for each of my daughters.

JERRY. Birds.

PETER. My daughters keep them in a cage in their bedroom.

JERRY. Do they carry disease? The birds?

PETER. I don't believe so.

JERRY. That's too bad. If they did you could set them loose in the house and the cats could eat them and die, maybe. (PETER *looks blank for a moment, then laughs*) And what else? What do you do to support your enormous household?

PETER. I . . . uh . . . I have an executive position with a . . . a small publishing house. We . . . uh . . . we publish textbooks.

JERRY. That sounds nice; very nice. What do you make?

PETER. (*Still cheerful*) Now look here!

JERRY. Oh, come on.

PETER. Well, I make around eighteen thousand a year, but I don't carry more than forty dollars at any one time . . . in case you're a . . . a holdup man . . .ha, ha, ha.

JERRY. (*Ignoring the above*) Where do you live? (PETER *is reluctant*) Oh, look; I'm not going to rob you, and I'm not going to kidnap your parakeets, your cats, or your daughters.

PETER. (*Too loud*) I live between Lexington and Third Avenue, on Seventy-fourth Street.

JERRY. That wasn't so hard, was it?

PETER. I didn't mean to seem . . . ah . . . it's that you don't really carry on a conversation; you just ask questions. And I'm . . . I'm normally . . . uh . . . reticent. Why do you just stand there?

JERRY. I'll start walking around in a little while, and eventually I'll sit down. (*Recalling*) Wait until you see the expression on his face.

PETER. What? Whose face? Look here; is this something about the zoo?

JERRY. (*Distantly*) The what?

PETER. The zoo; the zoo. Something about the zoo.

JERRY. The zoo?

PETER. You mentioned it several times.

JERRY. (*Still distant, but returning abruptly*) The zoo? Oh, yes; the zoo. I was there before I came here. I told you that. Say, what's the dividing line between upper-middle-class and lower-upper-middle-class?

PETER. My dear fellow, I . . .

JERRY. Don't my dear fellow me.

PETER. (*Unhappily*) Was I patronizing? I believe I was; I'm sorry. But, you see, your question about the classes bewildered me.

JERRY. And when you're bewildered you become patronizing?

PETER. I . . . I don't express myself too well, sometimes. (*He attempts a joke on himself*) I'm in publishing, not writing.

JERRY. (*Amused, but not at the humor*) So be it. The truth *is: I* was being patronizing.

PETER. Oh, now; you needn't say that. (*It is at this point that* JERRY *may begin to move about the stage with slowly increasing determination and authority, but pacing himself, so that the long speech about the dog comes at the high point of the arc*)

JERRY. All right. Who are your favorite writers? Baudelaire and J. P. Marquand?[2]

PETER. (*Wary*) Well, I like a great many writers; I have a considerable . . . catholicity of taste, if I may say so. Those two men are fine, each in his way. (*Warming up*) Baudelaire, of course . . . uh . . . is by far the finer of the two, but Marquand has a place . . . in our . . . uh . . . national . . .

JERRY. Skip it.

PETER. I . . . sorry.

JERRY. Do you know what I did before I went to the zoo today? I walked all the way up Fifth Avenue from Washington Square; all the way.

PETER. Oh; you live in the Village! (*This seems to enlighten* PETER)

JERRY. No, I don't. I took the subway down to the Village so I could walk all the way up Fifth Avenue to the zoo. It's one of those things a person has to do; sometimes a person has to go a very long distance out of his way to come back a short distance correctly.

PETER. (*Almost pouting*) Oh, I thought you lived in the Village.

JERRY. What were you trying to do? Make sense out of things? Bring order? The old pigeonhole bit? Well, that's easy; I'll tell you. I live in a four-story brownstone rooming-house on the upper West Side between Columbus Avenue and Central Park West. I live on the top floor; rear; west. It's a laughably small room, and one of my walls is made of beaverboard; this beaverboard separates my room from another laughably small room, so I assume that the two rooms were once one room, a small room, but not necessarily laughable. The room beyond my beaverboard wall is occupied by a colored queen who always keeps his door open; well, not always but *always* when he's plucking his eyebrows, which he does with Buddhist concentration. This colored queen has rotten teeth, which is rare, and he has a Japanese kimono, which is also pretty rare; and he wears this kimono to and from the john in the hall, which is pretty frequent. I mean, he goes to the john a lot. He never bothers me, and he never brings anyone up to his room. All he does is pluck his eyebrows, wear his kimono and go to the john. Now, the two front rooms on my floor are a little larger, I guess; but they're pretty small, too. There's a Puerto Rican family in one of them, a husband, a wife, and some kids; I don't know how many. These people entertain a lot. And in the other front room, there's somebody living there, but I don't know who it is. I've never seen who it is. Never. Never ever.

PETER. (*Embarrassed*) Why . . . why do you live there?

JERRY. (*From a distance again*) I don't know.

PETER. It doesn't sound like a very nice place . . . where you live.

JERRY. Well, no; it isn't an apartment in the East Seventies. But, then again, I don't have one wife, two daughters, two cats and two parakeets. What I do have, I have toilet articles, a few clothes, a hot plate that I'm not supposed to have, a can opener, one that works with a key, you know; a knife, two forks, and two spoons, one small, one large; three plates, a cup, a saucer, a drinking glass, two picture frames, both empty, eight or nine books, a pack of pornographic playing cards, regular deck, an old Western Union typewriter that prints nothing but capital letters, and a small strongbox without a lock which has in it . . . what?

[2]American popular novelist (1893–1960).

Rocks! Some rocks . . . sea-rounded rocks I picked up on the beach when I was a kid. Under which . . . weighed down . . . are some letters . . . please letters . . . please why don't you do this, and please when will you do that letters. And when letters, too. When will you write? When will you come? When? These letters are from more recent years.

PETER. (*Stares glumly at his shoes, then*) About those two empty picture frames . . . ?

JERRY. I don't see why they need any explanation at all. Isn't it clear? I don't have pictures of anyone to put in them.

PETER. Your parents . . . perhaps . . . a girl friend . . .

JERRY. You're a very sweet man, and you're possessed of a truly enviable innocence. But good old Mom and good old Pop are dead . . . you know? . . . I'm broken up about it, too . . . I mean really. BUT. That particular vaudeville act is playing the cloud circuit now, so I don't see how I can look at them, all neat and framed. Besides, or, rather, to be pointed about it, good old Mom walked out on good old Pop when I was ten and a half years old; she embarked on an adulterous turn of our southern states . . . a journey of a year's duration . . . and her most constant companion . . . among others, among many others . . . was a Mr. Barleycorn. At least, that's what good old Pop told me after he went down . . . came back . . . brought her body north. We'd received the news between Christmas and New Year's, you see, that good old Mom had parted with the ghost in some dump in Alabama. And, without the ghost . . . she was less welcome. I mean, what was she? A stiff . . . a northern stiff. At any rate, good old Pop celebrated the New Year for an even two weeks and then slapped into the front of a somewhat moving city omnibus, which sort of cleaned things out family-wise. Well no; then there was Mom's sister, who was given neither to sin nor the consolations of the bottle. I moved in on her, and my memory of her is slight excepting I remember still that she did all things dourly: sleeping, eating, working, praying. She dropped dead on the stairs to her apartment, my apartment then, too, on the afternoon of my high school graduation. A terribly middle-European joke, if you ask me.

PETER. Oh, my; oh, my.

JERRY. Oh, your what? But that was a long time ago, and I have no feeling about any of it that I care to admit to myself. Perhaps you can see, though, why good old Mom and good old Pop are frameless. What's your name? Your first name?

PETER. I'm Peter.

JERRY. I'd forgotten to ask you. I'm Jerry.

PETER. (*With a slight, nervous laugh*) Hello, Jerry.

JERRY. (*Nods his hello*) And let's see now; what's the point of having a girl's picture, especially in two frames? I have two picture frames, you remember. I never see the pretty little ladies more than once, and most of them wouldn't be caught in the same room with a camera. It's odd, and I wonder if it's sad.

PETER. The girls?

JERRY. No. I wonder if it's sad that I never see the little ladies more than once. I've never been able to have sex with, or, how is it put? . . . make love to anybody more than once. Once; that's it. . . . Oh, wait; for a week and a half, when I was fifteen . . . and I hang my head in shame that puberty was late . . . I was a h-o-m-o-s-e-x-u-a-l. I mean, I was queer . . . (*Very fast*) . . . queer, queer, queer . . . with bells ringing, banners snapping in the wind. And for those eleven days, I met at least twice a day with the park superintendent's son . . . a Greek boy, whose birthday was the same as mine, except he was a year older. I think I was very much in love . . . maybe just with sex. But that was the jazz of a very special hotel, wasn't it? And now; oh, do I love the little ladies; really, I love them. For about an hour.

PETER. Well, it seems perfectly simple to me. . . .

JERRY. (*Angry*) Look! Are you going to tell me to get married and have parakeets?

PETER. (*Angry himself*) Forget the parakeets! And stay single if you want to. It's no business of mine. I didn't start this conversation in the . . .

JERRY. All right, all right. I'm sorry. All right? You're not angry?

PETER. (*Laughing*) No, I'm not angry.

JERRY. (*Relieved*) Good. (*Now back to his previous tone*) Interesting that you asked me about the picture frames. I would have thought that you would have asked me about the pornographic playing cards.

PETER. (*With a knowing smile*) Oh, I've seen those cards.

JERRY. That's not the point. (*Laughs*) I suppose when you were a kid you and your pals passed them around, or you had a pack of your own.

PETER. Well, I guess a lot of us did.

JERRY. And you threw them away just before you got married.

PETER. Oh, now; look here. I didn't *need* anything like that when I got older.

JERRY. No?

PETER. (*Embarrassed*) I'd rather not talk about these things.

JERRY. So? Don't. Besides, I wasn't trying to plumb your postadolescent sexual life and hard times; what I wanted to get at is the value difference between pornographic playing cards when you're a kid, and pornographic playing cards when you're older. It's that when you're a kid you use the cards as a substitute for a real experience, and when you're older you use real experience as a substitute for the fantasy. But I imagine you'd rather hear about what happened at the zoo.

PETER. (*Enthusiastic*) Oh, yes; the zoo. (*Then, awkward*) That is . . . if you. . . .

JERRY. Let me tell you about why I went . . . well, let me tell you some things. I've told you about the fourth floor of the roominghouse where I live. I think the rooms are better as you go down, floor by floor. I guess they are; I don't know. I don't know any of the people on the third and second floors. Oh, wait! I do know that there's a lady living on the third floor, in the front. I know because she cries all the time. Whenever I go out or come back in, whenever I pass her door, I always hear her crying, muffled, but . . . very determined. Very determined indeed. But the one I'm getting to, and all about the dog, is the landlady. I don't like to use words that are too harsh in describing people. I don't like to. But the landlady is a fat, ugly, mean, stupid, unwashed, misanthropic, cheap, drunken bag of garbage. And you may have noticed that I very seldom use profanity, so I can't describe her as well as I might.

PETER. You describe her . . . vividly.

JERRY. Well, thanks. Anyway, she has a dog, and I will tell you about the dog, and she and her dog are the gatekeepers of my dwelling. The woman is bad enough; she leans around in the entrance hall, spying to see that I don't bring in things or people, and when she's had her midafternoon pint of lemon-flavored gin she always stops me in the hall, and grabs ahold of my coat or my arm, and she presses her disgusting body up against me to keep me in a corner so she can talk to me. The smell of her body and her breath . . . you can't imagine it . . . and somewhere, somewhere in the back of that pea-sized brain of hers, an organ developed just enough to let her eat, drink, and emit, she has some foul parody of sexual desire. And I, Peter, I am the object of her sweaty lust.

PETER. That's disgusting. That's . . . horrible.

JERRY. But I have found a way to keep her off. When she talks to me, when she presses herself to my body and mumbles about her room and how I should come there, I merely say: but, Love; wasn't yesterday enough for you, and the day before? Then she puzzles, she makes slits of her tiny eyes, she sways a little, and then, Peter . . . and it is at this moment that I think I might be doing some good in that tormented house . . . a simple-minded smile begins to form on her unthinkable face, and she giggles and groans as she thinks about yesterday and the day before; as she believes and relives what never happened. Then, she motions to that black monster of a dog she has, and she goes back to her room. And I am safe until our next meeting.

PETER. It's so . . . unthinkable. I find it hard to believe that people such as that really *are*.

JERRY. (*Lightly mocking*) It's for reading about, isn't it?

PETER. (*Seriously*) Yes.

JERRY. And fact is better left to fiction. You're right, Peter. Well, what I have been meaning to tell you about is the dog; I shall, now.

PETER. (*Nervously*) Oh, yes; the dog.

JERRY. Don't go. You're not thinking of going, are you?

PETER. Well . . . no, I don't think so.

JERRY. (*As if to a child*) Because after I tell you about the dog, do you know what then? Then . . . then I'll tell you about what happened at the zoo.

PETER. (*Laughing faintly*) You're . . . you're full of stories, aren't you?

JERRY. You don't *have* to listen. Nobody is holding you here; remember that. Keep that in your mind.

PETER. (*Irritably*) I know that.

JERRY. You do? Good. (*The following long speech, it seems to me, should be done with a great deal of action, to achieve a hypnotic effect on* PETER, *and on the audience, too. Some specific actions have been suggested, but the director and the actor playing* JERRY *might best work it out for themselves*) ALL RIGHT. (*As if reading from a huge billboard*) THE STORY OF JERRY AND THE DOG! (*Natural again*) What I am going to tell you has something to do with how sometimes it's necessary to go a long distance out of the way in order to come back a short distance correctly; or, maybe I only think that it has something to do with that. But, it's why I went to the zoo today, and why I walked north . . . northerly, rather . . . until I came here. All right. The dog, I think I told you, is a black monster of a beast: an oversized head, tiny, tiny ears, and eyes . . . bloodshot, infected, maybe; and a body you can see the ribs through the skin. The dog is black, all black; all black except for the bloodshot eyes, and . . . yes . . . and open sore on its . . . *right* forepaw; that is red, too. And, oh yes; the poor monster, and I do believe it's an old dog . . . it's certainly a misused one . . . almost always has an erection . . . of sorts. That's red, too. And . . . what else? . . . oh, yes; there's a gray-yellow-white color, too, when he bares his fangs. Like this: Grrrrrrr! Which is what he did when he saw me for the first time . . . the day I moved in. I worried about that animal the very first minute I met him. Now, animals don't take to me like Saint Francis had birds hanging off him all the time. What I mean is: animals are indifferent to me . . . like people (*He smiles slightly*) . . . most of the time. But this dog wasn't indifferent. From the very beginning he'd snarl and then go for me, to get one of my legs. Not like he was rabid, you know; he was sort of a stumbly dog, but he wasn't half-assed, either. It was a good, stumbly run; but I always got away. He got a piece of my trouser leg, look, you can see right here, where it's mended; he got that the second day I lived there; but, I kicked free and got upstairs fast, so that was that. (*Puzzles*) I still don't know to this day how the other roomers manage it, but you know what I *think:* I think it had to do only with me. Cozy. So. Anyway, this went on for over a week, whenever I came in; but never when I went out. That's funny. Or, it *was* funny. I could pack up and live in the street for all the dog cared. Well, I thought about it up in my room one day, one of the times after I'd bolted upstairs, and I made up my mind. I decided: First, I'll kill the dog with kindness, and if that doesn't work . . . I'll just kill him. (PETER *winces*) Don't react, Peter; just listen. So, the next day I went out and bought a bag of hamburgers, medium rare, no catsup, no onion; and on the way home I threw away the rolls and kept just the meat. (*Action for the following, perhaps*) When I got back to the roominghouse the dog was waiting for me. I half-opened the door that led into the entrance hall, and there he was; waiting for me. It figured. I went in, very cautiously, and I had the hamburgers, you remember; I opened the bag, and I set the meat down about twelve feet from where the dog was snarling at me. Like so! He snarled; stopped snarling; sniffed; moved slowly; then faster; then faster toward the meat. Well, when he got to it he stopped, and he looked at me. I smiled; but tentatively, you understand. He turned his face back to the hamburgers, smelled, sniffed some more, and then . . . RRRAAAAGGGGGHHHH, like that . . . he tore into them. It was as if he had never eaten anything in his life before, except like garbage. Which might very well have been the truth. I don't think the landlady ever eats anything but garbage. But. He ate all the hamburgers, almost all at once, making sounds in his throat like a woman. *Then,* when he'd finished the meat, the hamburger, and tried to eat the paper, too, he sat down and smiled. I think he smiled; I know cats do. It was a very gratifying few moments. Then, BAM, he snarled and made for me again. He didn't get me this time, either. So, I got upstairs, and I lay down on my bed and started to think about the dog again. To be truthful, I was offended, and I was damn mad, too. It was six perfectly good hamburgers with not enough pork in them to make it disgusting. I was offended. But, after a while, I decided to try it for a few more days. If you think about it, this dog had what amounted to an antipathy toward me; really. And, I wondered if I mightn't overcome this antipathy. So, I tried it for five more days, but it was always the same: snarl, sniff: move; faster; stare; gobble; RAAGGGHHH; smile; snarl; BAM. Well, now; by this time Columbus Avenue was strewn with hamburger rolls and I was less offended than disgusted. So, I decided to kill the dog. (PETER *raises a hand in protest*) Oh, don't be so alarmed, Peter; I didn't succeed. The day I tried to kill the dog I bought only one hamburger and what I thought was a murderous portion of rat poison. When I bought the hamburger I asked the man not to bother with the roll, all I wanted was the meat. I expected some reaction from him, like: we don't sell no hamburgers without rolls; or, wha' d'ya wanna do, eat it out'a ya han's? But no; he smiled benignly, wrapped up the hamburger in waxed paper, and said: A bite for ya pussy-cat? I wanted to say: No, not really; it's part of a plan to poison a dog I know. But, you can't say "a dog I know" without sounding funny; so I said, a little too loud, I'm afraid, and too formally: YES, A BITE FOR MY PUSSY-CAT. People looked up. It always happens when I try to simplify things; people look up. But that's neither hither nor thither. So. On my way back to the roominghouse, I kneaded the hamburger and the rat poison together between my hands, at that point feeling as much sadness as disgust. I opened the door to the entrance hall, and there the monster was, waiting to take the offering and then jump me. Poor bastard; he never learned that the moment he took to smile before he went for me gave me time enough to get out of range.

BUT, there he was; malevolence with an erection, waiting. I put the poison patty down, moved toward the stairs and watched. The poor animal gobbled the food down as usual, smiled, which made me almost sick, and then, BAM. But, I sprinted up the stairs, as usual, and the dog didn't get me, as usual. AND IT CAME TO PASS THAT THE BEAST WAS DEATHLY ILL. I knew this because he no longer attended me, and because the landlady sobered up. She stopped me in the hall the same evening of the attempted murder and confided the information that God had struck her puppy-dog a surely fatal blow. She had forgotten her bewildered lust, and her eyes were wide open for the first time. They looked like the dog's eyes. She sniveled and implored me to pray for the animal. I wanted to say to her: Madam, I have myself to pray for, the colored queen, the Puerto Rican family, the person in the front room whom I've never seen, the woman who cries deliberately behind her closed door, and the rest of the people in all roominghouses, everywhere; besides, Madam, I don't understand how to pray. But . . . to simplify things . . . I told her I would pray. She looked up. She said that I was a liar, and that I probably wanted the dog to die. I told her, and there was so much truth here, that I didn't want the dog to die. I didn't, and not just because I'd poisoned him. I'm afraid that I must tell you I wanted the dog to live so that I could see what our new relationship might come to. (PETER *indicates his increasing displeasure and slowly growing antagonism*) Please understand, Peter; that sort of thing is important. You must believe me; it *is* important. We have to know the effect of our actions. (*Another deep sigh*) Well, anyway; the dog recovered. I have no idea why, unless he was a descendant of the puppy that guarded the gates of hell or some such resort. I'm not up on my mythology. (*He pronounces the word myth-o-logy*) Are you? (PETER *sets to thinking, but* JERRY *goes on*) At any rate, and you've missed the eight-thousand-dollar question, Peter; at any rate, the dog recovered his health and the landlady recovered her thirst, in no way altered by the bow-wow's deliverance. When I came home from a movie that was playing on Forty-second Street, a movie I'd seen, or one that was very much like one or several I'd seen, after the landlady told me puppykins was better, I was so hoping for the dog to be waiting for me. I was . . . well, how would you put it . . . enticed? . . . fascinated? . . . no, I don't think so . . . heart-shatteringly anxious, that's it; I was heart-shatteringly anxious to confront my friend again. (PETER *reacts scoffingly*) Yes, Peter; friend. That's the only word for it. I was heart-shatteringly et cetera to confront my doggy friend again. I came in the door and advanced, unafraid, to the center of the entrance hall. The beast was there . . . looking at me. And, you know, he looked better for his scrape with the nevermind. I stopped; I looked at him; he looked at me. I think . . . I think we stayed a long time that way . . . still, stone-statue . . . just looking at one another. I looked more into his face than he looked into mine. I mean, I can concentrate longer at looking into a dog's face than a dog can concentrate at looking into mine, or into anybody else's face, for that matter. But during that twenty seconds or two hours that we looked into each other's face, we made contact. Now, here is what I had wanted to happen: I loved the dog now, and I wanted him to love me. I had tried to love, and I had tried to kill, and both had been unsuccessful by themselves. I hoped . . . and I don't really know why I expected the dog to understand anything, much less my motivations . . . I hoped that the dog would understand. (PETER *seems to be hypnotized*) It's just . . . it's just that . . . (JERRY *is abnormally tense, now*) . . . it's just that if you can't deal with people, you have to make a start somewhere. WITH ANIMALS! (*Much faster now, and like a conspirator*) Don't you see? A person has to have some way of dealing with SOMETHING. If not with people . . . if not with people . . . SOMETHING. With a bed, with a cockroach, with a mirror . . . no, that's too hard, that's one of the last steps. With a cockroach, with a . . . with a . . . with a carpet, a roll of toilet paper . . . no, not that, either . . . that's a mirror, too; always check bleeding. You see how hard it is to find things? With a street corner, and too many lights, all colors reflecting on the oily-wet streets . . . with a wisp of smoke, a wisp . . . of smoke . . . with . . . with pornographic playing cards, with a strongbox . . . WITHOUT A LOCK . . . with love, with vomiting, with crying, with fury because the pretty little ladies aren't pretty little ladies, with making money with your body which is an act of love and I could prove it, with howling because you're alive; with God. How about that? WITH GOD WHO IS A COLORED QUEEN WHO WEARS A KIMONO AND PLUCKS HIS EYEBROWS, WHO IS A WOMAN WHO CRIES WITH DETERMINATION BEHIND HER CLOSED DOOR . . . with God who, I'm told, turned his back on the whole thing some time ago . . . with . . . some day, with people. (JERRY *sighs the next word heavily*) People. With an idea; a concept. And where better, where ever better in this humiliating excuse for a jail, where better to communicate one single, simpleminded idea than in an entrance hall? Where? It would be A START! Where better to make a beginning . . . to understand and just possibly be understood . . . a beginning of an understanding, that with . . . (*Here* JERRY *seems to fall into almost grotesque fatigue*) . . . than with A DOG. Just that; a dog. (*Here there is a silence that might be prolonged for a moment or so; then* JERRY *wearily finishes his story*) A dog. It seemed like a perfectly sensible idea. Man is a dog's best friend, remember. So: the dog and I looked at each other. I longer than the dog. And what I saw then has been the same ever since. Whenever the dog and I see each other we both stop where we are. We regard each other with a mixture of sadness and suspicion, and then we feign indifference. We walk past each other safely; we have an understanding. It's very sad, but you'll have to admit that it is an understanding. We had made many attempts at contact, and we had failed. The dog has returned to garbage, and I to solitary but free passage. I have not returned. I mean to say, I have *gained* solitary free passage, if that much further loss can be said to be gain. I have learned that neither kindness nor cruelty by themselves, independent of each other, creates any effect beyond themselves; and I have learned that the two combined, together, at the same time, are the teaching emotion. And what is gained is loss. And what has been the result: the dog and I have attained a compromise; more of a bargain, really. We neither love nor hurt because we do not try to reach each other. And, *was* trying to feed the dog an act of love? And, perhaps, was the dog's attempt to bite me *not* an act of love? If we can so misunderstand, well then, why have we invented the word love in the first place? (*There is silence.* JERRY *moves to* PETER'S *bench and sits down beside him. This is the first time* JERRY *has sat down during the play*) The Story of Jerry and the Dog; the end. (PETER *is silent*) Well, Peter? (JERRY *is suddenly cheerful*) Well, Peter? Do you think I could sell that story to the *Reader's Digest* and make a couple of hundred bucks for *The Most Unforgettable Character I've Ever Met*? Huh? (JERRY *is animated, but* PETER *is disturbed*) Oh, come on now, Peter; tell me what you think.

PETER. (*Numb*) I . . . I don't understand what . . . I don't think I . . . (*Now, almost tearfully*) Why did you tell me all of this?

JERRY. Why not?

PETER. I DON'T UNDERSTAND!

JERRY. (*Furious, but whispering*) That's a lie.

PETER. No. No, it's not.

JERRY. (*Quietly*) I tried to explain it to you as I went along. I went slowly; it all has to do with . . .

PETER. I DON'T WANT TO HEAR ANY MORE. I don't understand you, or your landlady, or her dog. . . .

JERRY. *Her* dog! I thought it was my . . . No. No, you're right. It *is* her dog. (*Looks at* PETER *intently, shaking his head*) I don't know what I was thinking about; of course you don't understand. (*In a monotone, wearily*) I don't live in your block; I'm not married to two parakeets, or whatever your setup is. I am a *permanent transient*, and my home is the sickening roominghouses on the West Side of New York City, which is the greatest city in the world. Amen.

PETER. I'm . . . I'm sorry; I didn't mean to . . .

JERRY. Forget it. I suppose you don't quite know what to make of me, eh?

PETER. (*A joke*) We get all kinds in publishing. (*Chuckles*)

JERRY. You're a funny man. (*He forces a laugh*) You know that? You're a very . . . a richly comic person.

PETER. (*Modestly, but amused*) Oh, now, not really. (*Still chuckling*)

JERRY. Peter, do I annoy you, or confuse you?

PETER. (*Lightly*) Well, I must confess that this wasn't the kind of afternoon I'd anticipated.

JERRY. You mean, I'm not the gentleman you were expecting.

PETER. I wasn't expecting anybody.

JERRY. No, I don't imagine you were. But I'm here, and I'm not leaving.

PETER. (*Consulting his watch*) Well, you may not be, but I must be getting home soon.

JERRY. Oh, come on; stay a while longer.

PETER. I really should get home; you see . . .

JERRY. (*Tickles* PETER'S *ribs with his fingers*) Oh, come on.

PETER. (*He is very ticklish; as* JERRY *continues to tickle him his voice becomes falsetto*) No, I . . . OHHHHH! Don't do that. Stop, Stop. Ohhh, no, no.

JERRY. Oh, come on.

PETER. (*As* JERRY *tickles*) Oh, hee, hee, hee. I must go. I . . . hee, hee, hee. After all, stop, stop, hee, hee, hee, after all, the parakeets will be getting dinner ready soon. Hee, hee. And the cats are setting the table. Stop, stop, and, and . . . (PETER *is beside himself now*) . . . and we're having . . . hee, hee . . . uh . . . ho, ho, ho. (JERRY *stops tickling* PETER, *but the combination of the tickling and his own mad whimsy has* PETER *laughing almost hysterically. As his laughter continues, then subsides,* JERRY *watches him, with a curious fixed smile*)

JERRY. Peter?

PETER. Oh, ha, ha, ha, ha, ha. What? What?

JERRY. Listen, now.

PETER. Oh, ho, ho. What . . . what is it, Jerry? Oh, my.

JERRY. (*Mysteriously*) Peter, do you want to know what happened at the zoo?

PETER. Ah, ha, ha. The what? Oh, yes; the zoo. Oh, ho, ho. Well, I had my own zoo there for a moment with . . . hee, hee, the parakeets getting dinner ready, and the . . . ha, ha, whatever it was, the . . .

JERRY. (*Calmly*) Yes, that was very funny, Peter. I wouldn't have expected it. But do you want to hear about what happened at the zoo, or not?

PETER. Yes. Yes, by all means; tell me what happened at the zoo. Oh, my. I don't know what happened to me.

JERRY. Now I'll let you in on what happened at the zoo; but first, I should tell you why I went to the zoo. I went to the zoo to find out more about the way people exist with animals, and the way animals exist with each other, and with people too. It probably wasn't a fair test, what with everyone separated by bars from everyone else, the animals for the most part from each other, and always the people from the animals. But, if it's a zoo, that's the way it is. (*He pokes* PETER *on the arm*) Move over.

PETER. (*Friendly*) I'm sorry, haven't you enough room? (*He shifts a little*)

JERRY. (*Smiling slightly*) Well, all the animals are there, and all the people are there, and it's Sunday and all the children are there. (*He pokes* PETER *again*) Move over.

PETER. (*Patiently, still friendly*) All right. (*He moves some more, and* JERRY *has all the room he might need*)

JERRY. And it's a hot day, so all the stench is there, too, and all the balloon sellers, and all the ice cream sellers, and all the seals are barking, and all the birds are screaming. (*Pokes* PETER *harder*) Move over!

PETER. (*Beginning to be annoyed*) Look here, you have more than enough room! (*But he moves more, and is now fairly cramped at one end of the bench*)

JERRY. And I am there, and it's feeding time at the lions' house, and the lion keeper comes into the lion cage, one of the lion cages, to feed one of the lions. (*Punches* PETER *on the arm, hard*) MOVE OVER!

PETER. (*Very annoyed*) I can't move over any more, and stop hitting me. What's the matter with you?

JERRY. Do you want to hear the story? (*Punches* PETER'S *arm again*)

PETER. (*Flabbergasted*) I'm not so sure! I certainly don't want to be punched in the arm.

JERRY. (*Punches* PETER'S *arm again*) Like that?

PETER. Stop it! What's the matter with you?

JERRY. I'm crazy, you bastard.

PETER. That isn't funny.

JERRY. Listen to me, Peter. I want this bench. You go sit on the bench over there, and if you're good I'll tell you the rest of the story.

PETER. (*Flustered*) But . . . whatever for? What *is* the matter with you? Besides, I see no reason why I should give up this bench. I sit on this bench almost every Sunday afternoon, in good weather. It's secluded here; there's never anyone sitting here, so I have it all to myself.

JERRY. (*Softly*) Get off this bench, Peter; I want it.

PETER. (*Almost whining*) No.

JERRY. I said I want this bench, and I'm going to have it. Now get over there.

PETER. People can't have everything they want. You should know that; it's a rule; people can have some of the things they want, but they can't have everything.

JERRY. (*Laughs*) Imbecile! You're slow-witted!

PETER. Stop that!

JERRY. You're a vegetable! Go lie down on the ground.

PETER. (*Intense*) Now *you* listen to me. I've put up with you all afternoon.

JERRY. Not really.

PETER. LONG ENOUGH. I've put up with you long enough. I've listened to you because you seemed . . . well, because I thought you wanted to talk to somebody.

JERRY. You put things well; economically, and, yet . . . oh, what is the word I want to put justice to your . . . JESUS, you make me sick . . . get off here and give me my bench.

PETER. MY BENCH!

JERRY. (*Pushes* PETER *almost, but not quite, off the bench*) Get out of my sight.

PETER. (*Regarding his position*) God da . . . mn you. That's enough! I've had enough of you. I will not give up this bench; you can't have it, and that's that. Now, go away (JERRY *snorts but does not move*) Go away, I said. (JERRY *does not move*) Get away from here. If you don't move on . . . you're a bum . . . that's what you are. . . . If you don't move on, I'll get a policeman here and make you go. (JERRY *laughs, stays*) I warn you. I'll call a policeman.

JERRY. (*Softly*) You won't find a policeman around here; they're all over the west side of the park chasing fairies down from trees or out of the bushes. That's all they do. That's their function. So scream your head off; it won't do you any good.

PETER. POLICE! I warn you, I'll have you arrested. POLICE! (*Pause*) I said POLICE! (*Pause*) I feel ridiculous.

JERRY. You look ridiculous: a grown man screaming for the police on a bright Sunday afternoon in the park with nobody harming you. If a policeman *did* fill his quota and come sludging over this way he'd probably take you in as a nut.

PETER. (*With disgust and impotence*) Great God, I just came here to read, and now you want me to give up the bench. You're mad.

JERRY. Hey, I got news for you, as they say. I'm on your precious bench, and you're never going to have it for yourself again.

PETER. (*Furious*) Look, you; get off my bench. I don't care if it makes any sense or not. I want this bench to myself; I want you OFF IT!

JERRY. (*Mocking*) Aw . . . look who's mad.

PETER. GET OUT!

JERRY. No.

PETER. I WARN YOU!

JERRY. Do you know how ridiculous you look *now*?

PETER. (*His fury and self-consciousness have possessed him*) It doesn't matter. (*He is almost crying*) GET AWAY FROM MY BENCH!

JERRY. Why? You have everthing in the world you want; you've told me about your home, and your family, and *your own* little zoo. You have everything, and now you want this bench. Are these the things men fight for? Tell me, Peter, is this bench, this iron and this wood, is this your honor? Is this the thing in the world you'd fight for? Can you think of anything more absurd?

PETER. Absurd? Look, I'm not going to talk to you about honor, or even try to explain it to you. Besides, it isn't a question of honor; but even if it were, you wouldn't understand.

JERRY. (*Contemptuously*) You don't even know what you're saying, do you? This is probably the first time in your life you've had anything more trying to face than changing your cat's toilet box. Stupid! Don't you have any idea, not even the slightest, what other people *need*?

PETER. Oh, boy, listen to you; well, you don't need this bench. That's for sure.

JERRY. Yes; yes, I do.

PETER. (*Quivering*) I've come here for years; I have hours of great pleasure, great satisfaction, right here. And that's important to a man. I'm a responsible person, and I'm a GROWNUP. This is my bench, and you have no right to take it away from me.

JERRY. Fight for it, then. Defend yourself; defend your bench.

PETER. You've *pushed* me to it. Get up and fight.

JERRY. Like a man?

PETER. (*Still angry*) Yes, like a man, if you insist on mocking me even further.

JERRY. I'll have to give you credit for one thing; you *are* a vegetable, and a slightly nearsighted one, I think . . .

PETER. THAT'S ENOUGH.

JERRY. . . . but, you know, as they say on TV all the time—you know—and I mean this, Peter, you have a certain dignity; it surprises me. . . .

PETER. STOP!

JERRY. (*Rises lazily*) Very well, Peter, we'll battle for the bench, but we're not evenly matched. (*He takes out and clicks open an ugly-looking knife*)

PETER. (*Suddenly awakening to the reality of the situation*) You *are* mad! You're stark raving mad! YOU'RE GOING TO KILL ME! (*But before* PETER *has time to think what to do,* JERRY *tosses the knife at* PETER'S *feet*)

JERRY. There you go. Pick it up. You have the knife and we'll be more evenly matched.

PETER. (*Horrified*) No!

JERRY. (*Rushes over to* PETER, *grabs him by the collar;* PETER *rises; their faces almost touch*) Now you pick up that knife and you fight with me. You fight for your self-respect; you fight for that goddamned bench.

PETER. (*Struggling*) No! Let . . . let go of me! He . . . Help!

JERRY. (*Slaps* PETER *on each "fight"*) You fight, you miserable bastard; fight for that bench; fight for your parakeets; fight for your cats; fight for your two daughters; fight for your wife; fight for your manhood, you pathetic little vegetable. (*Spits in* PETER'S *face*) You couldn't even get your wife with a male child.

PETER. (*Breaks away, enraged*) It's a matter of genetics, not manhood, you . . . you monster. (*He darts down, picks up the knife and backs off a little; he is breathing heavily*) I'll give you one last chance; get out of here and leave me alone! (*He holds the knife with a firm arm, but far in front of him, not to attack, but to defend*)

JERRY. (*Sighs heavily*) So be it! (*With a rush he charges* PETER *and impales himself on the knife. Tableau: For just a moment, complete silence,* JERRY *impaled on the knife at the end of* PETER'S *still firm arm. Then* PETER *screams, pulls away, leaving the knife in* JERRY. JERRY *is motionless, on point. Then he, too, screams, and it must be the sound of an infuriated and fatally wounded animal. With the knife in him, he stumbles back to the bench that* PETER *had vacated. He crumbles there, sitting facing* PETER, *his eyes wide in agony, his mouth open*)

PETER. (*Whispering*) Oh my God, oh my God, oh my God. . . . (*He repeats these words many times, very rapidly*)

JERRY. (JERRY *is dying; but now his expression seems to change. His features relax, and while his voice varies, sometimes wrenched with pain, for the most part he seems removed from his dying. He smiles*) Thank you, Peter. I mean that, now; thank you very much. (PETER'S *mouth drops open. He cannot move; he is transfixed*) Oh, Peter, I was so afraid I'd drive you away. (*He laughs as best he can*) You don't know how afraid I was you'd go away and leave me. And now I'll tell you what happened at the zoo. I think . . . I think this is what happened at the zoo . . . I think. I think that while I was at the zoo I decided that I would walk north . . . northerly, rather . . . until I found you . . . or somebody . . . and I decided that I would talk to you . . . I would tell you things . . . and things that I would tell you would . . . Well, here we are. You see? Here we *are*. But . . . I don't know . . . could I have planned all this? No . . . no, I couldn't have. But I think I did. And now I've told you what you wanted to know, haven't I? And now you know all about what happened at the zoo. And now you know what you'll see in your TV, and the face I told you about . . . you remember . . . the face I told you about . . . my face, the face you see right now. Peter . . . Peter? . . . Peter . . . thank you. I came unto you (*He laughs, so faintly*) and you have comforted me. Dear Peter.

PETER. (*Almost fainting*) Oh my God!

JERRY. You'd better go now. Somebody might come by, and you don't want to be here when anyone comes.

PETER. (*Does not move, but begins to weep*) Oh my God, oh my God.

JERRY. (*Most faintly, now; he is very near death*) You won't be coming back here any more, Peter; you've been dispossessed. You've lost your bench, but you've defended your honor. And Peter, I'll tell you something now; you're not really a vegetable; it's all right, you're an animal. You're an animal, too. But you'd better hurry now, Peter. Hurry, you'd better go . . . see? (JERRY *takes a handkerchief and with great effort and pain wipes the knife handle clean of finger prints*) Hurry away, Peter. (PETER *begins to stagger away*) Wait . . . wait, Peter. Take your book . . . book. Right here . . . beside me . . . on your bench . . . my bench, rather. Come . . . take your book. (PETER *starts for the book, but retreats*) Hurry . . . Peter. (PETER *rushes to the bench, grabs the book, retreats*) Very good, Peter . . . very good. Now . . . hurry away. (PETER *hesitates for a moment, then flees, stage-left*) Hurry away . . . (*His eyes are closed now*) Hurry away, your parakeets are making the dinner . . . the cats . . . are setting the table . . .

PETER. (*Off stage*) (*A pitiful howl*) OH MY GOD!

JERRY. (*His eyes still closed, he shakes his head and speaks; a combination of scornful mimicry and supplication*) Oh . . . my . . . God. (*He is dead*)

CURTAIN

1958   1959, 1960

Saul Bellow *1915–*

The work of Saul Bellow is dominated by the figure of the marginal man, an alienated and absurd character caught between his own inadequacies and those imposed on him by his friends and society. Bellow's major themes were evident in his first novel, The Dangling Man (*1944*), which was based in part on the experiences of his early life. He was born of Russian immigrant parents in a small town in Quebec, Canada. He was raised in Chicago, Illinois, in a multilingual (English, French, Yiddish, and Hebrew), Orthodox Jewish household, an environment he recalls as deeply religious, almost superstitious. In *1937* Bellow graduated from Northwestern University, with honors in anthropology and sociology, and entered the University of Wisconsin on a graduate scholarship, but he soon withdrew to follow his consuming interest, the writing of fiction. For four years he supported himself by teaching in a Chicago teachers' college; he then served briefly in the Merchant Marine in World War II and later worked on the editorial staff of the Encyclopedia Britannica.

The Dangling Man *was published when Bellow was twenty-nine. Three years later he published his second novel,* The Victim. *In 1953 his picaresque novel,* The Adventures of Augie March, *appeared and won the first of his three National Book Awards. Bellow's fourth novel,* Seize the Day (*1956*), *has been followed by* Henderson the Rain King (*1958*), Herzog (*1964*) *and* Mr. Sammler's Planet (*1970*), *a grim novel of social turmoil. Bellow has also written numerous short stories, some of which are collected in* Mosby's Memories (*1968*), *and a number of plays, including* The Last Analysis, *which was produced in 1964. In 1975 Bellow published* Humboldt's Gift, *a "comedy*

of success and failure" that is Bellow's most humorous book. His latest novel, More Die
of Heartbreak *(1987), again deals with the dilemmas and follies of intellectuals struggling to flourish in materialist and mechanical America.*

*In 1976 Bellow won a Pulitzer Prize for literature, and in the same year he became
the seventh American to receive the Nobel Prize for literature. The Nobel Prize came in
recognition of his "exuberant ideas, flashing irony . . . and burning compassion," and for
his depiction of the modern anti-hero, the contemporary man "who keeps on trying to find
a foothold during his wanderings in our tottering world, one who can never relinquish
his faith that the value of life depends on its dignity, not its success."*

FURTHER READING: J. Clayton, *Saul Bellow, In Defense of Man,* 1967; K. Opdahl, *The
Novels of Saul Bellow,* 1967; H. Harper, *Desperate Faith,* 1967; *Saul Bellow and the Critics,*
ed. I. Malin, 1967; I Malin, *Saul Bellow's Fiction,* 1969; R. Dutton, *Saul Bellow,* 1971; B.
Scheer-Schäzler, *Saul Bellow,* 1972; M. Porter, *Whence the Power? The Artistry and Humanity
of Saul Bellow,* 1974; S. Blacher, *Saul Bellow's Enigmatic Laughter,* 1974; *Saul Bellow, A
Collection of Critical Essays,* ed. E. Rovit, 1975; C. Kulshrestha, *Saul Bellow, The Problem of
Affirmation,* 1978; J. Clayton, *Saul Bellow, In Defense of Man,* 1979; *Critical Essays on Saul
Bellow,* ed. S. Trachtenberg, 1979; M. Harris, *Saul Bellow, Drumlin Woodchuck,* 1980; R.
Dutton, *Saul Bellow,* 1982; D. Fuchs, *Saul Bellow, Vision and Revision,* 1984; J. Wilson, *On
Bellow's Planet,* 1985; *Saul Bellow,* ed. H. Bloom, 1986.
    TEXT: *Seize the Day,* 1956.

SEIZE THE DAY

I

When it came to concealing his troubles, Tommy Wilhelm was not less capable
than the next fellow. So at least he thought, and there was a certain amount of
evidence to back him up. He had once been an actor—no, not quite, an extra—
and he knew what acting should be. Also, he was smoking a cigar, and when a
man is smoking a cigar, wearing a hat, he has an advantage; it is harder to find
out how he feels. He came from the twenty-third floor down to the lobby on
the mezzanine to collect his mail before breakfast, and he believed—he hoped—
that he looked passably well: doing all right. It was a matter of sheer hope,
because there was not much that he could add to his present effort. On the
fourteenth floor he looked for his father to enter the elevator; they often met
at this hour, on the way to breakfast. If he worried about his appearance it was
mainly for his old father's sake. But there was no stop on the fourteenth, and
the elevator sank and sank. Then the smooth door opened and the great dark
red uneven carpet that covered the lobby billowed toward Wilhelm's feet. In
the foreground the lobby was dark, sleepy. French drapes like sails kept out the
sun, but three high, narrow windows were open, and in the blue air Wilhelm
saw a pigeon about to light on the great chain that supported the marquee of
the movie house directly underneath the lobby. For one moment he heard the
wings beating strongly.

Most of the guests at the Hotel Gloriana were past the age of retirement.
Along Broadway in the Seventies, Eighties, and Nineties, a great part of New
York's vast population of old men and women lives. Unless the weather is too
cold or wet they fill the benches about the tiny railed parks and along the subway
gratings from Verdi Square to Columbia University, they crowd the shops and
cafeterias, the dime stores, the tea-rooms, the bakeries, the beauty parlors, the

reading rooms and club rooms. Among these old people at the Gloriana, Wilhelm felt out of place. He was comparatively young, in his middle forties, large and blond, with big shoulders; his back was heavy and strong, if already a little stooped or thickened. After breakfast the old guests sat down on the green leather armchairs and sofas in the lobby and began to gossip and look into the papers; they had nothing to do but wait out the day. But Wilhelm was used to an active life and liked to go out energetically in the morning. And for several months, because he had no position, he had kept up his morale by rising early; he was shaved and in the lobby by eight o'clock. He bought the paper and some cigars and drank a Coca-Cola or two before he went in to breakfast with his father. After breakfast—out, out, out to attend to business. The getting out had in itself become the chief business. But he had realized that he could not keep this up much longer, and today he was afraid. He was aware that his routine was about to break up and he sensed that a huge trouble long presaged but till now formless was due. Before evening, he'd know.

Nevertheless he followed his daily course and crossed the lobby.

Rubin, the man at the newsstand, had poor eyes. They may not have been actually weak but they were poor in expression, with lacy lids that furled down at the corners. He dressed well. It didn't seem necessary—he was behind the counter most of the time—but he dressed very well. He had on a rich brown suit; the cuffs embarrassed the hairs on his small hands. He wore a Countess Mara painted necktie. As Wilhelm approached, Rubin did not see him: he was looking out dreamily at the Hotel Ansonia, which was visible from his corner, several blocks away. The Ansonia, the neighborhood's great landmark, was built by Stanford White.[1] It looks like a baroque palace from Prague or Munich enlarged a hundred times, with towers, domes, huge swells and bubbles of metal gone green from exposure, iron fretwork and festoons. Black television antennae are densely planted on its round summits. Under the changes of weather it may look like marble or like sea water, black as a slate in the fog, white as tufa[2] in sunlight. This morning it looked like the image of itself reflected in deep water, white and cumulous above, with cavernous distortions underneath. Together, the two men gazed at it.

Then Rubin said, "Your dad is in to breakfast already, the old gentleman."

"Oh, yes? Ahead of me today?"

"That's a real knocked-out shirt you got on," said Rubin. "Where's it from, Saks?"

"No, it's a Jack Fagman—Chicago."

Even when his spirits were low, Wilhelm could still wrinkle his forehead in a pleasing way. Some of the slow, silent movements of his face were very attractive. He went back a step, as if to stand away from himself and get a better look at his shirt. His glance was comic, a comment upon his untidiness. He liked to wear good clothes, but once he had put it on each article appeared to go its own way. Wilhelm, laughing, panted a little; his teeth were small; his cheeks when he laughed and puffed grew round, and he looked much younger than his years. In the old days when he was a college freshman and wore a raccoon coat and a beanie on his large blond head his father used to say that, big as he was, he could charm a bird out of a tree. Wilhelm had great charm still.

"I like this dove-gray color," he said in his sociable, good-natured way. "It isn't washable. You have to send it to the cleaner. It never smells as good as washed. But it's a nice shirt. It cost sixteen, eighteen bucks."

[1]American architect (1853–1906).   [2]A soft, porous stone.

This shirt had not been bought by Wilhelm; it was a present from his boss—his former boss, with whom he had a falling out. But there was no reason why he should tell Rubin the history of it. Although perhaps Rubin knew—Rubin was the kind of man who knew, and knew and knew. Wilhelm also knew many things about Rubin, for that matter, about Rubin's wife and Rubin's business, Rubin's health. None of these could be mentioned, and the great weight of the unspoken left them little to talk about.

"Well, y'lookin' pretty sharp today," Rubin said.

And Wilhelm said gladly, "Am I? Do you really think so?" He could not believe it. He saw his reflection in the glass cupboard full of cigar boxes, among the grand seals and paper damask and the gold-embossed portraits of famous men, García, Edward the Seventh, Cyrus the Great.[3] You had to allow for the darkness and deformations of the glass, but he thought he didn't look too good. A wide wrinkle like a comprehensive bracket sign was written upon his forehead, the point between his brows, and there were patches of brown on his dark blond skin. He began to be half amused at the shadow of his own marveling, troubled, desirous eyes, and his nostrils and his lips. Fair-haired hippopotamus!—that was how he looked to himself. He saw a big round face, a wide, flourishing red mouth, stump teeth. And the hat, too; and the cigar, too. I should have done hard labor all my life, he reflected. Hard honest labor that tires you out and makes you sleep. I'd have worked off my energy and felt better. Instead, I had to distinguish myself—yet.

He had put forth plenty of effort, but that was not the same as working hard, was it? And if as a young man he had got off to a bad start it was due to this very same face. Early in the nineteen-thirties, because of his striking looks, he had been very briefly considered star material, and he had gone to Hollywood. There for seven years, stubbornly, he had tried to become a screen artist. Long before that time his ambition or delusion had ended, but through pride and perhaps also through laziness he had remained in California. At last he turned to other things, but those seven years of persistence and defeat had unfitted him somehow for trades and businesses, and then it was too late to go into one of the professions. He had been slow to mature, and he had lost ground, and so he hadn't been able to get rid of his energy and he was convinced that this energy itself had done him the greatest harm.

"I didn't see you at the gin game last night," said Rubin.

"I had to miss it. How did it go?"

For the last few weeks Wilhelm had played gin[4] almost nightly, but yesterday he had felt that he couldn't afford to lose any more. He had never won. Not once. And while the losses were small they weren't gains, were they? They were losses. He was tired of losing, and tired also of the company, and so he had gone by himself to the movies.

"Oh," said Rubin, "it went okay. Carl made a chump of himself yelling at the guys. This time Doctor Tamkin didn't let him get away with it. He told him the psychological reason why."

"What was the reason?"

Rubin said, "I can't quote him. Who could? You know the way Tamkin talks. Don't ask me. Do you want the *Trib*?[5] Aren't you going to look at the closing quotations?"

---

[3]Diego Garcia (1471–1529), Portuguese explorer; Edward VII, King of England, (1901–1910); Cyrus the Great, King of Persia (550–529 B.C.).

[4]Gin rummy.

[5]New York *Herald Tribune* newspaper.

"It won't help much to look. I know what they were yesterday at three," said Wilhelm. "But I suppose I better had get the paper." It seemed necessary for him to lift one shoulder in order to put his hand into his jacket pocket. There, among little packets of pills and crushed cigarette butts and strings of cellophane, the red tapes of packages which he sometimes used as dental floss, he recalled that he had dropped some pennies.

"That doesn't sound so good," said Rubin. He meant to be conversationally playful, but his voice had no tone and his eyes, slack and lid-blinded, turned elsewhere. He didn't want to hear. It was all the same to him. Maybe he already knew, being the sort of man who knew and knew.

No, it wasn't good. Wilhelm held three orders of lard in the commodities market. He and Dr. Tamkin had bought this lard together four days ago at 12.96, and the price at once began to fall and was still falling. In the mail this morning there was sure to be a call for additional margin payment. One came every day.

The psychologist, Dr. Tamkin, had got him into this. Tamkin lived at the Gloriana and attended the card game. He had explained to Wilhelm that you could speculate in commodities at one of the uptown branches of a good Wall Street house without making the full deposit of margin legally required. It was up to the branch manager. If he knew you—and all the branch managers knew Tamkin—he would allow you to make short-term purchases. You needed only to open a small account.

"The whole secret of this type of speculation," Tamkin had told him, "is in the alertness. You have to act fast—buy it and sell it; sell it and buy in again. But quick! Get to the window and have them wire Chicago at just the right second. Strike and strike again! Then get out the same day. In no time at all you turn over fifteen, twenty thousand dollars' worth of soy beans, coffee, corn, hides, wheat, cotton." Obviously the doctor understood the market well. Otherwise he could not make it sound so simple. "People lose because they are greedy and can't get out when it starts to go up. They gamble, but I do it scientifically. This is not guesswork. You must take a few points and get out. Why, ye gods!" said Dr. Tamkin with his bulging eyes, his bald head, and his drooping lip. "Have you stopped to think how much dough people are making in the market?"

Wilhelm with a quick shift from gloomy attention to the panting laugh which entirely changed his face had said, "Ho, have I ever! What do you think? Who doesn't know it's way beyond nineteen-twenty-eight—twenty-nine[6] and still on the rise? Who hasn't read the Fulbright investigation?[7] There's money everywhere. Everyone is shoveling it in. Money is—is—"

"And can you rest—can you sit still while this is going on?" said Dr. Tamkin. "I confess to you I can't. I think about people, just because they have a few bucks to invest, making fortunes. They have no sense, they have no talent, they just have the extra dough and it makes them more dough. I get so worked up and tormented and restless, so restless! I haven't even been able to practice my profession. With all this money around you don't want to be a fool while everyone else is making. I know guys who make five, ten thousand a week just by fooling around. I know a guy at the Hotel Pierre. There's nothing to him, but he has a whole case of Mumm's champagne at lunch. I know another guy on Central Park South—But what's the use of talking. They make millions. They have smart lawyers who get them out of taxes by a thousand schemes."

[6]The years 1928 and 1929, when the stockmarket reached its highest peak before the Great Crash of October 1929.

[7]An investigation of stock market irregularities.

"Whereas I got taken," said Wilhelm. "My wife refused to sign a joint return.[8] One fairly good year and I got into the thirty-two-per-cent bracket and was stripped bare. What of all my bad years?"

"It's a business men's government," said Dr. Tamkin. "You can be sure that these men making five thousand a week—"

"I don't need that sort of money," Wilhelm had said. "But oh! if I could only work out a little steady income from this. Not much. I don't ask much. But how badly I need—! I'd be so grateful if you'd show me how to work it."

"Sure I will. *I* do it regularly. I'll bring you my receipts if you like. And do you want to know something? I approve of your attitude very much. You want to avoid catching the money fever. This type of activity is filled with hostile feeling and lust. You should see what it does to some of these fellows. They go on the market with murder in their hearts."

"What's that I once heard a guy say?" Wilhelm remarked. "A man is only as good as what he loves."

"That's it—just it," Tamkin said. "You don't have to go about it their way. There's also a calm and rational, a psychological approach."

Wilhelm's father, old Dr. Adler, lived in an entirely different world from his son, but he had warned him once against Dr. Tamkin. Rather casually—he was a very bland old man—he said, "Wilky, perhaps you listen too much to this Tamkin. He's interesting to talk to. I don't doubt it. I think he's pretty common but he's a persuasive man. However, I don't know how reliable he may be."

It made Wilhelm profoundly bitter that his father should speak to him with such detachment about his welfare. Dr. Adler liked to appear affable. Affable! His own son, his one and only son, could not speak his mind or ease his heart to him. I wouldn't turn to Tamkin, he thought, if I could turn to him. At least Tamkin sympathizes with me and tries to give me a hand, whereas Dad doesn't want to be disturbed.

Old Dr. Adler had retired from practice; he had a considerable fortune and could easily have helped his son. Recently Wilhelm had told him, "Father—it so happens that I'm in a bad way now. I hate to have to say it. You realize that I'd rather have good news to bring you. But it's true. And since it's true, Dad— What else am I supposed to say? It's true."

Another father might have appreciated how difficult this confession was—so much bad luck, weariness, weakness, and failure. Wilhelm had tried to copy the old man's tone and made himself sound gentlemanly, low-voiced, tasteful. He didn't allow his voice to tremble; he made no stupid gesture. But the doctor had no answer. He only nodded. You might have told him that Seattle was near Puget Sound, or that the Giants and Dodgers were playing a night game, so little was he moved from his expression of healthy, handsome, good-humored old age. He behaved toward his son as he had formerly done toward his patients, and it was a great grief to Wilhelm; it was almost too much to bear. Couldn't he see—couldn't he feel? Had he lost his family sense?

Greatly hurt, Wilhelm struggled however to be fair. Old people are bound to change, he said. They have hard things to think about. They must prepare for where they are going. They can't live by the old schedule any longer and all their perspectives change, and other people become alike, kin and acquaintances. Dad is no longer the same person, Wilhelm reflected. He was thirty-two when I was born, and now he's going on eighty. Furthermore, it's time I stopped feeling like a kid toward him, a small son.

---

[8]A money-saving, joint income tax return.

The handsome old doctor stood well above the other old people in the hotel. He was idolized by everyone. This was what people said: "That's old Professor Adler, who used to teach internal medicine. He was a diagnostician, one of the best in New York, and had a tremendous practice. Isn't he a wonderful-looking old guy? It's a pleasure to see such a fine old scientist, clean and immaculate. He stands straight and understands every single thing you say. He still has all his buttons. You can discuss any subject with him." The clerks, the elevator operators, the telephone girls and waitresses and chambermaids, the management flattered and pampered him. That was what he wanted. He had always been a vain man. To see how his father loved himself sometimes made Wilhelm madly indignant.

He folded over the *Tribune* with its heavy, black, crashing sensational print and read without recognizing any of the words, for his mind was still on his father's vanity. The doctor had created his own praise. People were primed and did not know it. And what did he need praise for? In a hotel where everyone was busy and contacts were so brief and had such small weight, how could it satisfy him? He could be in people's thoughts here and there for a moment; in and then out. He could never matter much to them. Wilhelm let out a long, hard breath and raised the brows of his round and somewhat circular eyes. He stared beyond the thick borders of the paper.

> . . . love that well which thou must leave ere long.[9]

Involuntary memory brought him this line. At first he thought it referred to his father, but then he understood that it was for himself, rather. *He* should love that well. "This thou perceivest, which makes *thy* love more strong."[10] Under Dr. Tamkin's influence Wilhelm had recently begun to remember the poems he used to read. Dr. Tamkin knew, or said he knew, the great English poets and once in a while he mentioned a poem of his own. It was a long time since anyone had spoken to Wilhelm about this sort of thing. He didn't like to think about his college days, but if there was one course that now made sense it was Literature I. The textbook was Lieder and Lovett's *British Poetry and Prose,* a black heavy book with thin pages. Did I read that? he asked himself. Yes, he had read it and there was one accomplishment at least he could recall with pleasure. He had read "Yet once more, O ye laurels."[11] How pure this was to say! It was beautiful.

> Sunk though he be beneath the wat'ry floor . . .[12]

Such things had always swayed him, and now the power of such words was far, far greater.

Wilhelm respected the truth, but he could lie and one of the things he lied often about was his education. He said he was an alumnus of Penn State; in fact he had left school before his sophomore year was finished. His sister Catherine had a B.S. degree. Wilhelm's late mother was a graduate of Bryn Mawr. He was the only member of the family who had no education. This was another sore point. His father was ashamed of him.

But he had heard the old man bragging to another old man, saying, "My son is a sales executive. He didn't have the patience to finish school. But he does all right for himself. His income is up in the five figures somewhere."

[9]From Shakespeare's Sonnet 73, line 14.   [10]From Shakespeare's Sonnet 73, line 13.
[11]From Milton's "Lycidas," line 1.   [12]From Milton's "Lycidas," line 167.

"What—thirty, forty thousand?" said his stooped old friend.

"Well, he needs at least that much for his style of life. Yes, he needs that."

Despite his troubles, Wilhelm almost laughed. Why, that boasting old hypocrite. He knew the sales executive was no more. For many weeks there had been no executive, no sales, no income. But how we love looking fine in the eyes of the world—how beautiful are the old men when they are doing a snow job! It's Dad, thought Wilhelm, who is the salesman. He's selling me. *He* should have gone on the road.

But what of the truth? Ah, the truth was that there were problems, and of these problems his father wanted no part. His father was ashamed of him. The truth, Wilhelm thought, was very awkward. He pressed his lips together, and his tongue went soft; it pained him far at the back, in the cords and throat, and a knot of ill formed in his chest. Dad never was a pal to me when I was young, he reflected. He was at the office or the hospital, or lecturing. He expected me to look out for myself and never gave me much thought. Now he looks down on me. And maybe in some respects he's right.

No wonder Wilhelm delayed the moment when he would have to go into the dining room. He had moved to the end of Rubin's counter. He had opened the *Tribune;* the fresh pages drooped from his hands; the cigar was smoked out and the hat did not defend him. He was wrong to suppose that he was more capable than the next fellow when it came to concealing his troubles. They were clearly written out upon his face. He wasn't aware of it.

There was the matter of the different names, which, in the hotel, came up frequently. "Are you Doctor Adler's son?" "Yes, but my name is Tommy Wilhelm." And the doctor would say, "My son and I use different monickers. I uphold tradition. He's for the new." The Tommy was Wilhelm's own invention. He adopted it when he went to Hollywood, and dropped the Adler. Hollywood was his own idea, too. He used to pretend that it had all been the doing of a certain talent scout named Maurice Venice. But the scout had never made him a definite offer of a studio connection. He had approached him, but the results of the screen tests had not been good. After the test Wilhelm took the initiative and pressed Maurice Venice until he got him to say, "Well, I suppose you might make it out there." On the strength of this Wilhelm had left college and had gone to California.

Someone had said, and Wilhelm agreed with the saying, that in Los Angeles all the loose objects in the country were collected, as if America had been tilted and everything that wasn't tightly screwed down had slid into Southern California. He himself had been one of these loose objects. Sometimes he told people, "I was too mature for college. I was a big boy, you see. Well, I thought, when do you start to become a man?" After he had driven a painted flivver and had worn a yellow slicker with slogans on it, and played illegal poker, and gone out on Coke dates, he had *had* college. He wanted to try something new and quarreled with his parents about his career. And then a letter came from Maurice Venice.

The story of the scout was long and intricate and there were several versions of it. The truth about it was never told. Wilhelm had lied first boastfully and then out of charity to himself. But his memory was good, he could still separate what he had invented from the actual happenings, and this morning he found it necessary as he stood by Rubin's showcase with his *Tribune* to recall the crazy course of the true events.

I didn't seem even to realize that there was a depression. How could I have been such a jerk as not to prepare for anything and just go on luck and inspiration? With round gray eyes expanded and his large shapely lips closed in severity toward himself he forced open all that had been hidden. Dad I couldn't affect one way or another. Mama was the one who tried to stop me, and we carried on and yelled and pleaded. The more I lied the louder I raised my voice, and charged—like a hippopotamus. Poor Mother! How I disappointed her. Rubin heard Wilhelm give a broken sigh as he stood with the forgotten *Tribune* crushed under his arm.

When Wilhelm was aware that Rubin watched him, loitering and idle, apparently not knowing what to do with himself this morning, he turned to the Coca-Cola machine. He swallowed hard at the Coke bottle and coughed over it, but he ignored his coughing, for he was still thinking, his eyes upcast and his lips closed behind his hand. By a peculiar twist of habit he wore his collar turned up always, as though there were a wind. It never lay flat. But on his broad back, stooped with its own weight, its strength warped almost into deformity, the collar of his sports coat appeared anyway to be no wider than a ribbon.

He was listening to the sound of his own voice as he explained, twenty-five years ago in the living room on West End Avenue, "But Mother, if I don't pan out as an actor I can still go back to school."

But she was afraid he was going to destroy himself. She said, "Wilky, Dad could make it easy for you if you wanted to go into medicine." To remember this stifled him.

"I can't bear hospitals. Besides, I might make a mistake and hurt someone or even kill a patient. I couldn't stand that. Besides, I haven't got that sort of brains."

Then his mother had made the mistake of mentioning her nephew Artie, Wilhelm's cousin, who was an honor student at Columbia in math and languages. That dark little gloomy Artie with his disgusting narrow face, and his moles and self-sniffing ways and his unclean table manners, the boring habit he had of conjugating verbs when you went for a walk with him. "Roumanian is an easy language. You just add a *tl* to everything." He was now a professor, this same Artie with whom Wilhelm had played near the soldiers' and sailors' monument on Riverside Drive. Not that to be a professor was in itself so great. How could anyone bear to know so many languages? And Artie also had to remain Artie, which was a bad deal. But perhaps success had changed him. Now that he had a place in the world perhaps he was better. Did Artie love his languages, and live for them, or was he also, in his heart, cynical? So many people nowadays were. No one seemed satisfied, and Wilhelm was especially horrified by the cynicism of successful people. Cynicism was bread and meat to everyone. And irony, too. Maybe it couldn't be helped. It was probably even necessary. Wilhelm, however, feared it intensely. Whenever at the end of the day he was unusually fatigued he attributed it to cynicism. Too much of the world's business done. Too much falsity. He had various words to express the effect this had on him. Chicken! Unclean! Congestion! he exclaimed in his heart. Rat race! Phony! Murder! Play the Game! Buggers!

At first the letter from the talent scout was nothing but a flattering sort of joke. Wilhelm's picture in the college paper when he was running for class treasurer was seen by Maurice Venice, who wrote to him about a screen test. Wilhelm at once took the train to New York. He found the scout to be huge and oxlike, so stout that his arms seemed caught from beneath in a grip of flesh and fat; it looked as though it must be positively painful. He had little hair. Yet he enjoyed a healthy complexion. His breath was noisy and his voice rather difficult and husky because of the fat in his throat. He had on a double-breasted suit of the type then known as pillbox; it was chalk-striped, pink on blue, the trousers hugged his ankles.

They met and shook hands and sat down. Together these two big men dwarfed the tiny Broadway office and made the furnishings look like toys. Wilhelm had the color of a Golden Grimes apple when he was well, and then his thick blond hair had been vigorous and his wide shoulders unwarped; he was leaner in the jaws, his eyes fresher and wider; his legs were then still awkward but he was impressively handsome. And he was about to make his first great mistake. Like, he sometimes thought, I was going to pick up a weapon and strike myself a blow with it.

Looming over the desk in the small office darkened by overbuilt midtown— sheer walls, gray spaces, dry lagoons of tar and pebbles—Maurice Venice proceeded to establish his credentials. He said, "My letter was on the regular stationery, but maybe you want to check on me?"

"Who, *me?*" said Wilhelm. "Why?"

"There's guys who think I'm in a racket and make a charge for the test. I don't ask a cent. I'm no agent. There ain't no commission."

"I never even thought of it," said Wilhelm. Was there perhaps something fishy about this Maurice Venice? He protested too much.

In his husky, fat-weakened voice he finally challenged Wilhelm, "If you're not sure, you can call the distributor and find out who I am, Maurice Venice."

Wilhelm wondered at him. "Why shouldn't I be sure? Of course I am."

"Because I can see the way you size me up, and because this is a dinky office. Like you don't believe me. Go ahead. Call. I won't care if you're cautious. I mean it. There's quite a few people who doubt me at first. They can't really believe that fame and fortune are going to hit 'em."

"But I tell you I do believe you," Wilhelm had said, and bent inward to accommodate the pressure of his warm, panting laugh. It was purely nervous. His neck was ruddy and neatly shaved about the ears—he was fresh from the barbershop; his face anxiously glowed with his desire to make a pleasing impression. It was all wasted on Venice, who was just as concerned about the impression *he* was making.

"If you're surprised, I'll just show you what I mean," Venice had said, "It was about fifteen months ago right in this identical same office when I saw a beautiful thing in the paper. It wasn't even a photo but a drawing, a brassière ad, but I knew right away that this was star material. I called up the paper to ask who the girl was, they gave me the name of the advertising agency; I phoned the agency and they gave me the name of the artist; I got hold of the artist and he gave me the number of the model agency. Finally, finally I got her number and phoned her and said, 'This is Maurice Venice, scout for Kaskaskia Films.' So right away she says, 'Yah, so's your old lady.' Well, when I saw I wasn't getting nowhere with her I said to her, 'Well, miss. I don't blame you. You're a very beautiful thing and must have a dozen admirers after you all the time, boy friends who like to call and pull your leg and give you a tease. But as I happen to be a very busy fellow and don't have the time to horse around or argue, I tell you what to do. Here's my number, and here's the number of the Kaskaskia Distributors, Inc. Ask them who am I, Maurice Venice. The scout.' She did it. A little while later she phoned me back, all apologies and excuses, but I didn't want to embarrass her and get off on the wrong foot with an artist. I know better than to do that. So I told her it was a natural precaution, never mind. I wanted to run a screen test right away. Because I seldom am wrong about talent. If I see it, it's there. Get that, please. And do you know who that little girl is today?"

"No," Wilhelm said eagerly. "Who is she?"

Venice said impressively, " 'Nita Christenberry."

Wilhelm sat utterly blank. This was failure. He didn't know the name, and Venice was waiting for his response and would be angry.

And in fact Venice had been offended. He said, "What's the matter with you! Don't you read a magazine? She's a starlet."

"I'm sorry," Wilhelm answered. "I'm at school and don't have time to keep up. If I don't know her, it doesn't mean a thing. She made a big hit, I'll bet."

"You can say that again. Here's a photo of her." He handed Wilhelm some pictures. She was a bathing beauty—short, the usual breasts, hips, and smooth thighs. Yes, quite good, as Wilhelm recalled. She stood on high heels and wore a Spanish comb and mantilla.[13] In her hand was a fan.

He had said, "She looks awfully peppy."

"Isn't she a divine girl? And what personality! Not just another broad in the show business, believe me." He had a surprise for Wilhelm. "I have found happiness with her," he said.

"You have?" said Wilhelm, slow to understand.

"Yes, boy, we're engaged."

Wilhelm saw another photograph, taken on the beach. Venice was dressed in a terry-cloth beach outfit, and he and the girl, cheek to cheek, were looking into the camera. Below, in white ink, was written "Love at Malibu Colony."

"I'm sure you'll be very happy. I wish you—"

"I *know*," said Venice firmly, "I'm going to be happy. When I saw that drawing, the breath of fate breathed on me. I felt it over my entire body."

"Say, it strikes a bell suddenly," Wilhelm had said. "Aren't you related to Martial Venice, the producer?"

Venice was either a nephew of the producer or the son of a first cousin. Decidedly he had not made good. It was easy enough for Wilhelm to see this now. The office was so poor, and Venice bragged so nervously and identified him so scrupulously—the poor guy. He was the obscure failure of an aggressive and powerful clan. As such he had the greatest sympathy from Wilhelm.

Venice had said, "Now I suppose you want to know where you come in. I seen your school paper, by accident. You take quite a remarkable picture."

"It can't be so much," said Wilhelm, more panting than laughing.

"You don't want to tell me my business," Venice said. "Leave it to me. I studied up on this."

"I never imagined— Well, what kind of roles do you think I'd fit?"

"All this time that we've been talking, I've been watching. Don't think I haven't. You remind me of someone. Let's see who it can be—one of the great old-timers. Is it Milton Sills? No, that's not the one. Conway Tearle, Jack Mulhall? George Bancroft?[14] No, his face was ruggeder. One thing I can tell you, though, a George Raft[15] type you're not—those tough, smooth, black little characters."

"No, I wouldn't seem to be."

"No, you're not that flyweight type, with the fists, from a nightclub, and the glamorous sideburns, doing the tango or the bolero. Not Edward G. Robinson, either—I'm thinking aloud. Or the Cagney[16] fly-in-your-face role, a cabbie, with that mouth and those punches."

[13] A light scarf worn over the head and shoulders.
[14] Early moving picture stars.
[15] Moving picture star of the 1930s and 1940s who acted the roles of gangsters and dancers.
[16] Edward G. Robinson and James Cagney, moving picture stars of the 1930s and 1940s, as were William Powell and Charles "Buddy" Rogers, (p. 2022).

"I realize that."

"Not suave like William Powell, or a lyric juvenile like Buddy Rogers. I suppose you don't play the sax? No. But—"

"But what?"

"I have you placed as the type that loses the girl to the George Raft type or the William Powell type. You are steady, faithful, you get stood up. The older women would know better. The mothers are on your side. With what they been through, if it was up to them, they'd take you in a minute. You're very sympathetic, even the young girls feel that. You'd make a good provider. But they go more for the older types. It's as clear as anything."

This was not how Wilhelm saw himself. And as he surveyed the old ground he recognized now that he had been not only confused but hurt. Why, he thought, he cast me even then for a loser.

Wilhelm had said, with half a mind to be defiant, "Is that your opinion?"

It never occurred to Venice that a man might object to stardom in such a role. "Here's your chance," he said. "Now you're just in college. What are you studying?" He snapped his fingers. "Stuff." Wilhelm himself felt this way about it. "You may plug along fifty years before you get anywheres. This way, in one jump, the world knows who you are. You become a name like Roosevelt, Swanson.[17] From east to west, out to China, into South America. This is no bunk. You become a lover to the whole world. The world wants it, needs it. One fellow smiles, a billion people also smile. One fellow cries, the other billion sob with him. Listen, bud—" Venice had pulled himself together to make an effort. On his imagination there was some great weight which he could not discharge. He wanted Wilhelm, too, to feel it. He twisted his large, clean, well-meaning, rather foolish features as though he were their unwilling captive, and said in his choked, fat-obstructed voice, "Listen, everywhere there are people trying hard, miserable, in trouble, downcast, tired, trying and trying. They need a break, right? A break through, a help, luck or sympathy."

"That certainly is the truth," said Wilhelm. He had seized the feeling and he waited for Venice to go on. But Venice had no more to say; he had concluded. He gave Wilhelm several pages of blue hectographed script, stapled together, and told him to prepare for the screen test. "Study your lines in front of a mirror," he said. "Let yourself go. The part should take ahold of you. Don't be afraid to make faces and be emotional. Shoot the works. Because when you start to act you're no more an ordinary person, and those things don't apply to you. You don't behave the same way as the average."

And so Wilhelm had never returned to Penn State. His roommate sent his things to New York for him, and the school authorities had to write to Dr. Adler to find out what had happened.

Still, for three months Wilhelm delayed his trip to California. He wanted to start out with the blessings of his family, but they were never given. He quarreled with his parents and his sister. And then, when he was best aware of the risks and knew a hundred reasons against going and had made himself sick with fear, he left home. This was typical of Wilhelm. After much thought and hesitation and debate he invariably took the course he had rejected innumerable times. Ten such decisions made up the history of his life. He had decided that it would be a bad mistake to go to Hollywood, and then he went. He had made up his mind not to marry his wife, but ran off and got married. He had resolved not to invest money with Tamkin, and then had given him a check.

[17]Franklin Delano Roosevelt (1882–1945), president of the United States, 1933–1945. Gloria Swanson (1899–1983), moving picture star.

But Wilhelm had been eager for life to start. College was merely another delay. Venice had approached him and said that the world had named Wilhelm to shine before it. He was to be freed from the anxious and narrow life of the average. Moreover, Venice had claimed that he never made a mistake. His instinct for talent was infallible, he said.

But when Venice saw the results of the screen test he did a quick about-face. In those days Wilhelm had a speech difficulty. It was not a true stammer, it was a thickness of speech which the sound track exaggerated. The film showed that he had many peculiarities, otherwise unnoticeable. When he shrugged, his hands drew up within his sleeves. The vault of his chest was huge, but he really didn't look strong under the lights. Though he called himself a hippopotamus, he more nearly resembled a bear. His walk was bearlike, quick and rather soft, toes turned inward, as though his shoes were an impediment. About one thing Venice had been right. Wilhelm was photogenic, and his wavy blond hair (now graying) came out well, but after the test Venice refused to encourage him. He tried to get rid of him. He couldn't afford to take a chance on him, he had made too many mistakes already and lived in fear of his powerful relatives.

Wilhelm had told his parents, "Venice says I owe it to myself to go." How ashamed he was now of this lie! He had begged Venice not to give him up. He had said, "Can't you help me out? It would kill me to go back to school now."

Then when he reached the Coast he learned that a recommendation from Maurice Venice was the kiss of death. Venice needed help and charity more than he, Wilhelm, ever had. A few years later when Wilhelm was down on his luck and working as an orderly in a Los Angeles hospital, he saw Venice's picture in the papers. He was under indictment for pandering. Closely following the trial, Wilhelm found out that Venice had indeed been employed by Kaskaskia Films, but that he had evidently made use of the connection to organize a ring of call girls. Then what did he want with me? Wilhelm had cried to himself. He was unwilling to believe anything very bad about Venice. Perhaps he was foolish and unlucky, a fall guy, a dupe, a sucker. You didn't give a man fifteen years in prison for that. Wilhelm often thought that he might write him a letter to say how sorry he was. He remembered the breath of fate and Venice's certainty that he would be happy. 'Nita Christenberry was sentenced to three years. Wilhelm recognized her although she had changed her name.

By that time Wilhelm too had taken his new name. In California he became Tommy Wilhelm. Dr. Adler would not accept the change. Today he still called his son Wilky, as he had done for more than forty years. Well, now, Wilhelm was thinking, the paper crowded in disarray under his arm, there's really very little that a man can change at will. He can't change his lungs, or nerves, or constitution or temperament. They're not under his control. When he's young and strong and impulsive and dissatisfied with the way things are he wants to rearrange them to assert his freedom. He can't overthrow the government or be differently born; he only has a little scope and maybe a foreboding, too, that essentially you can't change. Nevertheless, he makes a gesture and becomes Tommy Wilhelm. Wilhelm had always had a great longing to be Tommy. He had never, however, succeeded in feeling like Tommy, and in his soul had always remained Wilky. When he was drunk he reproached himself horribly as Wilky. "You fool, you clunk, you Wilky!" he called himself. He thought that it was a good thing perhaps that he had not become a success as Tommy since that would not have been a genuine success. Wilhelm would have feared that not he but Tommy had brought it off, cheating Wilky of his birthright. Yes, it had been a stupid thing to do, but it was his imperfect judgment at the age of twenty which should be blamed. He had cast off his father's name, and with it his father's opinion of him. It was, he knew it was, his bid for liberty, Adler being in his mind the title of the species, Tommy the freedom of the person. But Wilky was his inescapable self.

In middle age you no longer thought such thoughts about free choice. Then it came over you that from one grandfather you had inherited such and such a head of hair which looked like honey when it whitens or sugars in the jar; from another, broad thick shoulders; an oddity of speech from one uncle, and small teeth from another, and the gray eyes with darkness diffused even into the whites, and a wide-lipped mouth like a statue from Peru. Wandering races have such looks, the bones of one tribe, the skin of another. From his mother he had gotten sensitive feelings, a soft heart, a brooding nature, a tendency to be confused under pressure.

The changed name was a mistake, and he would admit it as freely as you liked. But this mistake couldn't be undone now, so why must his father continually remind him how he had sinned? It was too late. He would have to go back to the pathetic day when the sin was committed. And where was that day? Past and dead. Whose humiliating memories were these? His and not his father's. What had he to think back on that he could call good? Very, very little. You had to forgive. First, to forgive yourself, and then general forgiveness. Didn't he suffer from his mistakes far more than his father could?

"Oh, God," Wilhelm prayed. "Let me out of my trouble. Let me out of my thoughts, and let me do something better with myself. For all the time I have wasted I am very sorry. Let me out of this clutch and into a different life. For I am all balled up. Have mercy."

II

The mail.

The clerk who gave it to him did not care what sort of appearance he made this morning. He only glanced at him from under his brows, upward, as the letters changed hands. Why should the hotel people waste courtesies on him? They had his number. The clerk knew that he was handing him, along with the letters, a bill for his rent. Wilhelm assumed a look that removed him from all such things. But it was bad. To pay the bill he would have to withdraw money from his brokerage account, and the account was being watched because of the drop in lard. According to the *Tribune's* figures lard was still twenty points below last year's level. There were government price supports. Wilhelm didn't know how these worked but he understood that the farmer was protected and that the SEC[1] kept an eye on the market and therefore he believed that lard would rise again and he wasn't greatly worried as yet. But in the meantime his father might have offered to pick up his hotel tab. Why didn't he? What a selfish old man he was! He saw his son's hardships; he could so easily help him. How little it would mean to him, and how much to Wilhelm! Where was the old man's heart? Maybe, thought Wilhelm, I was sentimental in the past and exaggerated his kindliness—warm family life. It may never have been there.

Not long ago his father had said to him in his usual affable, pleasant way, "Well, Wilky, here we are under the same roof again, after all these years."

Wilhelm was glad for an instant. At last they would talk over old times. But

[1]Securities and Exchange Commission.

he was also on guard against insinuations. Wasn't his father saying, "Why are you here in a hotel with me and not at home in Brooklyn with your wife and two boys? You're neither a widower nor a bachelor. You have brought me all your confusions. What do you expect me to do with them?"

So Wilhelm studied the remark for a bit, then said, "The roof is twenty-six stories up. But how many years has it been?"

"That's what I was asking you."

"Gosh, Dad, I'm not sure. Wasn't it the year Mother died? What year was that?"

He asked this question with an innocent frown on his Golden Grimes, dark blond face. *What year was it!* As though he didn't know the year, the month, the day, the very hour of his mother's death.

"Wasn't it nineteen-thirty-one?" said Dr. Adler.

"Oh, was it?" said Wilhelm. And in hiding the sadness and the overwhelming irony of the question he gave a nervous shiver and wagged his head and felt the ends of his collar rapidly.

"Do you know?" his father said. "You must realize, an old fellow's memory becomes unreliable. It was in winter, that I'm sure of. Nineteen-thirty-two?"

Yes, it was age. Don't make an issue of it, Wilhelm advised himself. If you were to ask the old doctor in what year he had interned, he'd tell you correctly. All the same, don't make an issue. Don't quarrel with your own father. Have pity on an old man's failings.

"I believe the year was closer to nineteen-thirty-four, Dad," he said.

But Dr. Adler was thinking, Why the devil can't he stand still when we're talking? He's either hoisting his pants up and down by the pockets or jittering with his feet. A regular mountain of tics, he's getting to be. Wilhelm had a habit of moving his feet back and forth as though, hurrying into a house, he had to clean his shoes first on the doormat.

Then Wilhelm had said, "Yes, that was the beginning of the end, wasn't it, Father?"

Wilhelm often astonished Dr. Adler. Beginning of the end? What could he mean—what was he fishing for? Whose end? The end of family life? The old man was puzzled but he would not give Wilhelm an opening to introduce his complaints. He had learned that it was better not to take up Wilhelm's strange challenges. So he merely agreed pleasantly, for he was a master of social behavior, and said, "It was an awful misfortune for us all."

He thought, What business has he to complain to *me* of his mother's death?

Face to face they had stood, each declaring himself silently after his own way. It was: it was not, the beginning of the end—*some* end.

Unaware of anything odd in his doing it, for he did it all the time, Wilhelm had pinched out the coal of his cigarette and dropped the butt in his pocket, where there were many more. And as he gazed at his father the little finger of his right hand began to twitch and tremble; of that he was unconscious, too.

And yet Wilhelm believed that when he put his mind to it he could have perfect and even distinguished manners, outdoing his father. Despite the slight thickness in his speech—it amounted almost to a stammer when he started the same phrase over several times in his effort to eliminate the thick sound—he could be fluent. Otherwise he would never have made a good salesman. He claimed also that he was a good listener. When he listened he made a tight mouth and rolled his eyes thoughtfully. He would soon tire and begin to utter short, loud, impatient breaths, and he would say, "Oh yes . . . yes . . . yes. I couldn't agree more." When he was forced to differ he would declare, "Well,

I'm not sure. I don't really see it that way. I'm of two minds about it." He would never willingly hurt any man's feelings.

But in conversation with his father he was apt to lose control of himself. After any talk with Dr. Adler, Wilhelm generally felt dissatisfied, and his dissatisfaction reached its greatest intensity when they discussed family matters. Ostensibly he had been trying to help the old man to remember a date, but in reality he meant to tell him, "You were set free when Ma died. You wanted to forget her. You'd like to get rid of Catherine, too. Me, too. You're not kidding anyone"—Wilhelm striving to put this across, and the old man not having it. In the end he was left struggling, while his father seemed unmoved.

And then once more Wilhelm had said to himself, "But man! you're not a kid. Even then you weren't a kid!" He looked down over the front of his big, indecently big, spoiled body. He was beginning to lose his shape, his gut was fat, and he looked like a hippopotamus. His younger son called him "a hum-muspotamus"; that was little Paul. And here he was still struggling with his old dad, filled with ancient grievances. Instead of saying, "Good-by, youth! Oh, good-by those marvelous, foolish wasted days. What a big clunk I was—I *am*."

Wilhelm was still paying heavily for his mistakes. His wife Margaret would not give him a divorce, and he had to support her and the two children. She would regularly agree to divorce him, and then think things over again and set new and more difficult conditions. No court would have awarded her the amounts he paid. One of today's letters, as he had expected, was from her. For the first time he had sent her a postdated check, and she protested. She also enclosed bills for the boy's educational insurance policies, due next week. Wilhelm's mother-in-law had taken out these policies in Beverly Hills, and since her death two years ago he had to pay the premiums. Why couldn't she have minded her own business! They were his kids, and he took care of them and always would. He had planned to set up a trust fund. But that was on his former expectations. Now he had to rethink the future, because of the money problem. Meanwhile, here were the bills to be paid. When he saw the two sums punched out so neatly on the cards he cursed the company and its IBM equipment. His heart and his head were congested with anger. Everyone was supposed to have money. It was nothing to the company. It published pictures of funerals in the magazines and frightened the suckers, and then punched out little holes, and the customers would lie awake to think out ways to raise the dough. They'd be ashamed not to have it. They couldn't let a great company down, either, and they got the scratch. In the old days a man was put in prison for debt, but there were subtler things now. They made it a shame not to have money and set everybody to work.

Well, and what else had Margaret sent him? He tore the envelope open with his thumb, swearing that he would send any other bills back to her. There was, luckily, nothing more. He put the hole-punched cards in his pocket. Didn't Margaret know that he was nearly at the end of his rope? Of course. Her instinct told her that this was her opportunity, and she was giving him the works.

He went into the dining room, which was under Austro-Hungarian management at the Hotel Gloriana. It was run like a European establishment. The pastries were excellent, especially the strudel. He often had apple strudel and coffee in the afternoon.

As soon as he entered he saw his father's small head in the sunny bay at the farther end, and heard his precise voice. It was with an odd sort of perilous expression that Wilhelm crossed the dining room.

Dr. Adler liked to sit in a corner that looked across Broadway down to the Hudson and New Jersey. On the other side of the street was a supermodern cafeteria with gold and purple mosaic columns. On the second floor a private-eye school, a dental laboratory, a reducing parlor, a veteran's club, and a Hebrew school shared the space. The old man was sprinkling sugar on his strawberries. Small hoops of brilliance were cast by the water glasses on the white tablecloth, despite a faint murkiness in the sunshine. It was early summer, and the long window was turned inward; a moth was on the pane; the putty was broken and the white enamel on the frames was streaming with wrinkles.

"Ha, Wilky," said the old man to his tardy son. "You haven't met our neighbor Mr. Perls, have you? From the fifteenth floor."

"How d'do," Wilhelm said. He did not welcome this stranger; he began at once to find fault with him. Mr. Perls carried a heavy cane with a crutch tip. Dyed hair, a skinny forehead—these were not reasons for bias. Nor was it Mr. Perls's fault that Dr. Adler was using him, not wishing to have breakfast with his son alone. But a gruffer voice within Wilhelm spoke, asking, "Who is this damn frazzle-faced herring with his dyed hair and his fish teeth and this drippy mustache? Another one of Dad's German friends. Where does he collect all these guys? What is the stuff on his teeth? I never saw such pointed crowns. Are they stainless steel, or a kind of silver? How can a human face get into this condition. Uch!" Staring with his widely spaced gray eyes, Wilhelm sat, his broad back stooped under the sports jacket. He clasped his hands on the table with an implication of suppliance. Then he began to relent a little toward Mr. Perls, beginning at the teeth. Each of those crowns represented a tooth ground to the quick, and estimating a man's grief with his teeth as two per cent of the total, and adding to that his flight from Germany and the probable origin of his wincing wrinkles, not to be confused with the wrinkles of his smile, it came to a sizable load.

"Mr. Perls was a hosiery wholesaler," said Dr. Adler.

"Is this the son you told me was in the selling line?" said Mr. Perls.

Dr. Adler replied, "I have only this one son. One daughter. She was a medical technician before she got married—anesthetist. At one time she had an important position in Mount Sinai."[2]

He couldn't mention his children without boasting. In Wilhelm's opinion, there was little to boast of. Catherine, like Wilhelm, was big and fair-haired. She had married a court reporter who had a pretty hard time of it. She had taken a professional name, too—Philippa. At forty she was still ambitious to become a painter.

Wilhelm didn't venture to criticize her work. It didn't do much to him, he said, but then he was no critic. Anyway, he and his sister were generally on the outs and he didn't often see her paintings. She worked very hard, but there were fifty thousand people in New York with paints and brushes, each practically a law unto himself. It was the Tower of Babel[3] in paint. *He* didn't want to go far into this. Things were chaotic all over.

Dr. Adler thought that Wilhelm looked particularly untidy this morning—unrested, too, his eyes red-rimmed from excessive smoking. He was breathing through his mouth and he was evidently much distracted and rolled his red-shot eyes barbarously. As usual, his coat collar was turned up as though he had had to go out in the rain. When he went to business he pulled himself together a little; otherwise he let himself go and looked like hell.

[2]Mount Sinai Hospital in New York City.
[3]Confusion, chaos—from the biblical Tower of Babel, Genesis 11:1–9.

"What's the matter, Wilky, didn't you sleep last night?"

"Not very much."

"You take too many pills of every kind—first stimulants and then depressants, anodynes followed by analeptics,[4] until the poor organism doesn't know what's happened. Then the luminal won't put people to sleep, and the Pervitin or Benzedrine won't wake them. God knows! These things get to be as serious as poisons, and yet everyone puts all their faith in them."

"No, Dad, it's not the pills. It's that I'm not used to New York any more. For a native, that's very peculiar, isn't it? It was never so noisy at night as now, and every little thing is a strain. Like the alternate parking. You have to run out at eight to move your car. And where can you put it? If you forget for a minute they tow you away. Then some fool puts advertising leaflets under your windshield wiper and you have heart failure a block away because you think you've got a ticket. When you do get stung with a ticket, you can't argue. You haven't got a chance in court and the city wants the revenue."

"But in your line you have to have a car, eh?" said Mr. Perls.

"Lord knows why any lunatic would want one in the city who didn't need it for his livelihood."

Wilhelm's old Pontiac was parked in the street. Formerly, when on an expense account, he had always put it up in a garage. Now he was afraid to move the car from Riverside Drive lest he lose his space, and he used it only on Saturdays when the Dodgers were playing in Ebbets Field and he took his boys to the game. Last Saturday, when the Dodgers were out of town, he had gone out to visit his mother's grave.

Dr. Adler had refused to go along. He couldn't bear his son's driving. Forgetfully, Wilhelm traveled for miles in second gear; he was seldom in the right lane and he neither gave signals nor watched for lights. The upholstery of his Pontiac was filthy with grease and ashes. One cigarette burned in the ashtray, another in his hand, a third on the floor with maps and other waste paper and Coca-Cola bottles. He dreamed at the wheel or argued and gestured, and therefore the old doctor would not ride with him.

Then Wilhelm had come back from the cemetery angry because the stone bench between his mother's and his grandmother's graves had been overturned and broken by vandals. "Those damn teen-age hoodlums get worse and worse," he said. "Why, they must have used a sledge-hammer to break the seat smack in half like that. If I could catch one of them!" He wanted the doctor to pay for a new seat, but his father was cool to the idea. He said he was going to have himself cremated.

Mr. Perls said, "I don't blame you if you get no sleep up where you are." His voice was tuned somewhat sharp, as though he were slightly deaf. "Don't you have Parigi the singing teacher there? God, they have some queer elements in this hotel. On which floor is that Estonian woman with all her cats and dogs? They should have made her leave long ago."

"They've moved her down to twelve," said Dr. Adler.

Wilhelm ordered a large Coca-Cola with his breakfast. Working in secret at the small envelopes in his pocket, he found two pills by touch. Much fingering had worn the weakened the paper. Under cover of a napkin he swallowed a Phenaphen sedative and a Unicap, but the doctor was sharp-eyed and said, "Wilky, what are you taking now?"

---

[4]Anodynes: pain relievers. Analeptics: drugs that stimulate the nervous system.

"Just my vitamin pills." He put his cigar butt in an ashtray on the table behind him, for his father did not like the odor. Then he drank his Coca-Cola.

"That's what you drink for breakfast, and not orange juice?" said Mr. Perls. He seemed to sense that he would not lose Dr. Adler's favor by taking an ironic tone with his son.

"The caffeine stimulates brain activity," said the old doctor. "It does all kinds of things to the respiratory center."

"It's just a habit of the road, that's all," Wilhelm said. "If you drive around long enough it turns your brains, your stomach, and everything else."

His father explained, "Wilky used to be with the Rojax Corporation. He was their northeastern sales representative for a good many years but recently ended the connection."

"Yes," said Wilhelm, "I was with them from the end of the war." He sipped the Coca-Cola and chewed the ice, glancing at one and the other with his attitude of large, shaky, patient dignity. The waitress set two boiled eggs before him.

"What kind of line does this Rojax company manufacture?" said Mr. Perls.

"Kiddies' furniture. Little chairs, rockers, tables, Jungle-Gyms, slides, swings, seesaws."

Wilhelm let his father do the explaining. Large and stiff-backed, he tried to sit patiently, but his feet were abnormally restless. All right! His father had to impress Mr. Perls? He would go along once more, and play his part. Fine! He would play along and help his father maintain his style. Style was the main consideration. That was just fine!

"I was with the Rojax Corporation for almost ten years," he said. "We parted ways because they wanted me to share my territory. They took a son-in-law into the business—a new fellow. It was his idea."

To himself, Wilhelm said, Now God alone can tell why I have to lay my whole life bare to this blasted herring here. I'm sure nobody else does it. Other people keep their business to themselves. Not me.

He continued, "But the rationalization was that it was too big a territory for one man. I had a monopoly. That wasn't so. The real reason was that they had gotten to the place where they would have to make me an officer of the corporation. Vice presidency. I was in line for it, but instead this son-in-law got in, and—"

Dr. Adler thought Wilhelm was discussing his grievances much too openly and said, "My son's income was up in the five figures."

As soon as money was mentioned, Mr. Perls's voice grew eagerly sharper. "Yes? What, the thirty-two-per-cent bracket? Higher even, I guess?" He asked for a hint, and he named the figures not idly but with a sort of hugging relish. Uch! How they love money, thought Wilhelm. They adore money! Holy money! Beautiful money! It was getting so that people were feeble-minded about everything except money. While if you didn't have it you were a dummy, a dummy! You had to excuse yourself from the face of the earth. Chicken! that's what it was. The world's business. If only he could find a way out of it.

Such thinking brought on the usual congestion. It would grow into a fit of passion if he allowed it to continue. Therefore he stopped talking and began to eat.

Before he struck the egg with his spoon he dried the moisture with his napkin. Then he battered it (in his father's opinion) more than was necessary. A faint grime was left by his fingers on the white of the egg after he had picked away the shell. Dr. Adler saw it with silent repugnance. What a Wilky he had given to the world! Why, he didn't even wash his hands in the morning. He used an electric razor so that he didn't have to touch water. The doctor couldn't bear Wilky's dirty habits. Only once—and never again, he swore—had he visited his room. Wilhelm, in pajamas and stockings had sat on his bed, drinking gin from a coffee mug and rooting for the Dodgers on television. "That's two and two on you, Duke.[5] Come on—hit it, now." He came down on the mattress—bam! The bed looked kicked to pieces. Then he drank the gin as though it were tea, and urged his team on with his fist. The smell of dirty clothes was outrageous. By the bedside lay a quart bottle and foolish magazines and mystery stories for the hours of insomnia. Wilhelm lived in worse filth than a savage. When the Doctor spoke to him about this he answered, "Well, I have no wife to look after my things." And who—*who!*—had done the leaving? Not Margaret. The Doctor was certain that she wanted him back.

Wilhelm drank his coffee with a trembling hand. In his full face his abused bloodshot gray eyes moved back and forth. Jerkily he set his cup back and put half the length of a cigarette into his mouth; he seemed to hold it with his teeth, as though it were a cigar.

"I can't let them get away with it," he said. "It's also a question of morale."

His father corrected him. "Don't you mean a moral question, Wilky?"

"I mean that, too. I have to do something to protect myself. I was promised executive standing." Correction before a stranger mortified him, and his dark blond face changed color, more pale, and then more dark. He went on talking to Perls but his eyes spied on his father. "I was the one who opened the territory for them. I could go back for one of their competitors and take away their customers. *My* customers. Morale enters into it because they've tried to take away my confidence."

"Would you offer a different line to the same people?" Mr. Perls wondered.

"Why not? I know what's wrong with the Rojax product."

"Nonsense," said his father. "Just nonsense and kid's talk, Wilky. You're only looking for trouble and embarrassment that way. What would you gain by such a silly feud? You have to think about making a living and meeting your obligations."

Hot and bitter, Wilhelm said with pride, while his feet moved angrily under the table, "I don't have to be told about my obligations. I've been meeting them for years. In more than twenty years I've never had a penny of help from anybody. I preferred to dig a ditch on the WPA[6] but never asked anyone to meet my obligations for me."

"Wilky has had all kinds of experiences," said Dr. Adler.

The old doctor's face had a wholesome reddish and almost translucent color, like a ripe apricot. The wrinkles beside his ears were deep because the skin conformed so tightly to his bones. With all his might, he was a healthy and fine small old man. He wore a white vest of a light check pattern. His hearing-aid doodad was in the pocket. An unusual shirt of red and black stripes covered his chest. He bought his clothes in a college shop farther uptown. Wilhelm thought he had no business to get himself up like a jockey, out of respect for his profession.

"Well," said Mr. Perls. "I can understand how you feel. You want to fight it out. By a certain time of life, to have to start all over again can't be a pleasure, though a good man can always do it. But anyway you want to keep

[5]Duke Snider, outfielder for the Brooklyn Dodgers baseball team, 1947–1957.
[6]The Works Progress Administration created jobs for the unemployed during the 1930s depression.

on with a business you know already, and not have to meet a whole lot of new contacts."

Wilhelm again thought, Why does it have to be me and my life that's discussed, and not him and his life? He would never allow it. But I am an idiot. I have no reserve. To me it can be done. I talk. I must ask for it. Everybody wants to have intimate conversations, but the smart fellows don't give out, only the fools. The smart fellows talk intimately about the fools, and examine them all over and give them advice. Why do I allow it? The hint about his age had hurt him. No, you can't admit it's as good as ever, he conceded. Things do give out.

"In the meanwhile," Dr. Adler said, "Wilky is taking it easy and considering various propositions. Isn't that so?"

"More or less," said Wilhelm. He suffered his father to increase Mr. Perls's respect for him. The WPA ditch had brought the family into contempt. He was a little tired. The spirit, the peculiar burden of his existence lay upon him like an accretion, a load, a hump. In any moment of quiet, when sheer fatigue prevented him from struggling, he was apt to feel this mysterious weight, this growth or collection of nameless things which it was the business of his life to carry about. That must be what a man was for. This large, odd, excited, fleshy, blond, abrupt personality named Wilhelm, or Tommy, was here, present, in the present—Dr. Tamkin had been putting into his mind many suggestions about the present moment, the here and now—this Wilky, or Tommy Wilhelm, forty-four years old, father of two sons, at present living in the Hotel Gloriana, was assigned to be the carrier of a load which was his own self, his characteristic self. There was no figure or estimate for the value of this load. But it is probably exaggerated by the subject. T. W. Who is a visionary sort of animal. Who has to believe that he can know why he exists. Though he has never seriously tried to find out why.

Mr. Perls said, "If he wants time to think things over and have a rest, why doesn't he run down to Florida for a while? Off season it's cheap and quiet. Fairyland. The mangoes are just coming in. I got two acres down there. You'd think you were in India."

Mr. Perls utterly astonished Wilhelm when he spoke of fairyland with a foreign accent. Mangoes—India? What did he mean, India?

"Once upon a time," said Wilhelm, "I did some public-relations work for a big hotel down in Cuba. If I could get them a notice in Leonard Lyons[7] or one of the other columns it might be good for another holiday there, gratis. I haven't had a vacation for a long time, and I could stand a rest after going so hard. You know that's true, Father." He meant that his father knew how deep the crisis was becoming; how badly he was strapped for money; and that he could not rest but would be crushed if he stumbled; and that his obligations would destroy him. He couldn't falter. He thought, The money! When I had it, I flowed money. They bled it away from me. I hemorrhaged money. But now it's almost gone, and where am I supposed to turn for more?

He said, "As a matter of fact, Father, I am tired as hell."

But Mr. Perls began to smile and said, "I understand from Doctor Tamkin that you're going into some kind of investment with him, partners."

"You know, he's a very ingenious fellow," said Dr. Adler. "I really enjoy hearing him go on. I wonder if he really is a medical doctor."

"Isn't he?" said Perls. "Everybody thinks he is. He talks about his patients. Doesn't he write prescriptions?"

[7]Newspaper gossip columnist in New York City.

"I don't really know what he does," said Dr. Adler.. "He's a cunning man."

"He's a psychologist, I understand," said Wilhelm.

"I don't know what sort of psychologist or psychiatrist he may be," said his father. "He's a little vague. It's growing into a major industry, and a very expensive one. Fellows have to hold down very big jobs in order to pay those fees. Anyway, this Tamkin is clever. He never said he practiced here, but I believe he was a doctor in California. They don't seem to have much legislation out there to cover these things, and I hear a thousand dollars will get you a degree from a Los Angeles correspondence school. He gives the impression of knowing something about chemistry, and things like hypnotism. I wouldn't trust him, though."

"And why wouldn't you?" Wilhelm demanded.

"Because he's probably a liar. Do you believe he invented all the things he claims?"

Mr. Perls was grinning.

"He was written up in *Fortune*," said Wilhelm. "Yes, in *Fortune* magazine. He showed me the article. I've seen his clippings."

"That doesn't make him legitimate," said Dr. Adler. "It might have been another Tamkin. Make no mistake, he's an operator. Perhaps even crazy."

"Crazy, you say?"

Mr. Perls put in, "He could be both sane and crazy. In these days nobody can tell for sure which is which."

"An electrical device for truck drivers to wear in their caps," said Dr. Adler, describing one of Tamkin's proposed inventions. "To wake them with a shock when they begin to be drowsy at the wheel. It's triggered by the change in blood-pressure when they start to doze."

"It doesn't sound like such an impossible thing to me," said Wilhelm.

Mr. Perls said, "To me he described an underwater suit so a man could walk on the bed of the Hudson in case of an atomic attack. He said he could walk to Albany in it."

"Ha, ha, ha, ha, ha!" cried Dr. Adler in his old man's voice. "Tamkin's Folly. You could go on a camping trip under Niagara Falls."

"This is just his kind of fantasy," said Wilhelm. "It doesn't mean a thing. Inventors are supposed to be like that. I get funny ideas myself. Everybody wants to make something. Any American does."

But his father ignored this and said to Perls, "What other inventions did he describe?"

While the frazzle-faced Mr. Perls and his father in the unseemly, monkey-striped shirt were laughing, Wilhelm could not restrain himself and joined in with his own panting laugh. But he was in despair. They were laughing at the man to whom he had given a power of attorney over his last seven hundred dollars to speculate for him in the commodities market. They had bought all that lard. It had to rise today. By ten o'clock, or half-past ten, trading would be active, and he would see.

III

Between white tablecloths and glassware and glancing silverware, through overfull light, the long figure of Mr. Perls went away into the darkness of the lobby. He thrust with his cane, and dragged a large built-up shoe which Wilhelm had not included in his estimate of troubles. Dr. Adler wanted to talk about him. "There's a poor man," he said, "with a bone condition which is gradually breaking him up."

"One of those progressive diseases?" said Wilhelm.

"Very bad. I've learned," the doctor told him, "to keep my sympathy for the real ailments. This Perls is more to be pitied than any man I know."

Wilhelm understood that he was being put on notice and did not express his opinion. He ate and ate. He did not hurry but kept putting food on his plate until he had gone through the muffins and his father's strawberries, and then some pieces of bacon that were left; he had several cups of coffee, and when he was finished he sat gigantically in a state of arrest and didn't seem to know what he should do next.

For a while father and son were uncommonly still. Wilhelm's preparations to please Dr. Adler had failed completely, for the old man kept thinking, You'd never guess he had a clean upbringing, and, What a dirty devil this son of mine is. Why can't he try to sweeten his appearance a little? Why does he want to drag himself like this? And he makes himself look so idealistic.

Wilhelm sat, mountainous. He was not really so slovenly as his father found him to be. In some aspects he even had a certain delicacy. His mouth, though broad, had a fine outline, and his brow and his gradually incurved nose, dignity, and in his blond hair there was white but there were also shades of gold and chestnut. When he was with the Rojax Corporation Wilhelm had kept a small apartment in Roxbury, two rooms in a large house with a small porch and garden, and on mornings of leisure, in late spring weather like this, he used to sit expanded in a wicker chair with the sunlight pouring through the weave, and sunlight through the slug-eaten holes of the young hollyhocks and as deeply as the grass allowed into small flowers. This peace (he forgot that that time had had its troubles, too), this peace was gone. It must not have belonged to him, really, for to be here in New York with his old father was more genuinely like his life. He was well aware that he didn't stand a chance of getting sympathy from his father, who said he kept his for real ailments. Moreover, he advised himself repeatedly not to discuss his vexatious problems with him, for his father, with some justice, wanted to be left in peace. Wilhelm also knew that when he began to talk about these things he made himself feel worse, he became congested with them and worked himself into a clutch. Therefore he warned himself, Lay off, pal. It'll only be an aggravation. From a deeper source, however, came other promptings. If he didn't keep his troubles before him he risked losing them altogether, and he knew by experience that this was worse. And furthermore, he could not succeed in excusing his father on the ground of old age. No. No, he could not. I am his son, he thought. He is my father. He is as much father as I am son—old or not. Affirming this, though in complete silence, he sat, and, sitting, he kept his father at the table with him.

"Wilky," said the old man, "have you gone down to the baths here yet?"

"No, Dad, not yet."

"Well, you know the Gloriana has one of the finest pools in New York. Eighty feet, blue tile. It's a beauty."

Wilhelm had seen it. On the way to the gin game you passed the stairway to the pool. He did not care for the odor of the wall-locked and chlorinated water.

"You ought to investigate the Russian and Turkish baths, and the sunlamps and massage. I don't hold with sunlamps. But the massage does a world of good, and there's nothing better than hydrotherapy when you come right down to it. Simple water has a calming effect and would do you more good than all the barbiturates and alcohol in the world."

Wilhelm reflected that this advice was as far as his father's help and sympathy would extend.

"I thought," he said, "that the water cure was for lunatics."

The doctor received this as one of his son's jokes and said with a smile, "Well, it won't turn a sane man into a lunatic. It does a great deal for me. I couldn't live without my massages and steam."

"You're probably right. I ought to try it one of these days. Yesterday, late in the afternoon, my head was about to bust and I just had to have a little air, so I walked around the reservoir, and I sat down for a while in a playground. It rests me to watch the kids play potsy[1] and skiprope."

The doctor said with approval, "Well, now, that's more like the idea."

"It's the end of the lilacs," said Wilhelm. "When they burn it's the beginning of summer. At least, in the city. Around the time of year when the candy stores take down the windows and start to sell sodas on the sidewalk. But even though I was raised here, Dad, I can't take city life any more, and I miss the country. There's too much push here for me. It works me up too much. I take things too hard. I wonder why you never retired to a quieter place."

The doctor opened his small hand on the table in a gesture so old and so typical that Wilhelm felt it like an actual touch upon the foundations of his life. "I am a city boy myself, you must remember," Dr. Adler explained. "But if you find the city so hard on you, you ought to get out."

"I'll do that," said Wilhelm, "as soon as I can make the right connection. Meanwhile—"

His father interrupted, "Meanwhile I suggest you cut down on drugs."

"You exaggerate that, Dad. I don't really—I give myself a little boost against—" He almost pronounced the word "misery" but he kept his resolution not to complain.

The doctor, however, fell into the error of pushing his advice too hard. It was all he had to give his son and he gave it once more. "Water and exercise," he said.

He wants a young, smart, successful son, thought Wilhelm, and he said, "Oh, Father, it's nice of you to give me this medical advice, but steam isn't going to cure what ails me."

The doctor measurably drew back, warned by the sudden weak strain of Wilhelm's voice and all that the droop of his face, the swell of his belly against the restraint of his belt intimated.

"Some new business?" he asked unwillingly.

Wilhelm made a great preliminary summary which involved the whole of his body. He drew and held a long breath, and his color changed and his eyes swam. "New?" he said.

"You make too much of your problems," said the doctor. "They ought not to be turned into a career. Concentrate on real troubles—fatal sickness, accidents." The old man's whole manner said, Wilky, don't start this on me. I have a right to be spared.

Wilhelm himself prayed for restraint; he knew this weakness of his and fought it. He knew, also, his father's character. And he began mildly, "As far as the fatal part of it goes, everyone on this side of the grave is the same distance from death. No, I guess my trouble is not exactly new. I've got to pay premiums on two policies for the boys. Margaret sent them to me. She unloads everything on

[1]The children's game hopscotch.

me. Her mother left her an income. She won't even file a joint tax return. I get stuck. Etcetera. But you've heard the whole story before."

"I certainly have," said the old man. "And I've told you to stop giving her so much money."

Wilhelm worked his lips in silence before he could speak. The congestion was growing. "Oh, but my kids, Father. My kids. I love them. I don't want them to lack anything."

The doctor said with a half-deaf benevolence, "Well, naturally. And she, I'll bet, is the beneficiary of that policy."

"Let her be. I'd sooner die myself before I collected a cent of such money."

"Ah, yes." The old man sighed. He did not like the mention of death. "Did I tell you that your sister Catherine—Philippa—is after me again."

"What for?"

"She wants to rent a gallery for an exhibition."

Stiffly fair-minded, Wilhelm said, "Well, of course that's up to you, Father."

The round-headed old man with his fine, feather-white, ferny hair said, "No, Wilky. There's not a thing on those canvases. I don't believe it; it's a case of the emperor's clothes. I may be old enough for my second childhood, but at least the first is well behind me. I was glad enough to buy crayons for her when she was four. But now she's a woman of forty and too old to be encouraged in her delusions. She's no painter."

"I wouldn't go so far as to call her a born artist," said Wilhelm, "but you can't blame her for trying something worth while."

"Let her husband pamper her."

Wilhelm had done his best to be just to his sister, and he had sincerely meant to spare his father, but the old man's tight, benevolent deafness had its usual effect on him. He said, "When it comes to women and money, I'm completely in the dark. What makes Margaret act like this?"

"She's showing you that you can't make it without her," said the doctor. "She aims to bring you back by financial force."

"But if she ruins me, Dad, how can she expect me to come back? No, I have a sense of honor. What you don't see is that she's trying to put an end to me."

His father stared. To him this was absurd. And Wilhelm thought, Once a guy starts to slip, he figures he might as well be a clunk. A real big clunk. He even takes pride in it. But there's nothing to be proud of—hey, boy? Nothing. I don't blame Dad for his attitude. And it's no cause for pride.

"I don't understand that. But if you feel like this why don't you settle with her once and for all?"

"What do you mean, Dad?" said Wilhelm, surprised. "I thought I told you. Do you think I'm not willing to settle? Four years ago when we broke up I gave her everything—goods, furniture, savings. I tried to show good will, but I didn't get anywhere. Why when I wanted Scissors, the dog, because the animal and I were so attached to each other—it was bad enough to leave the kids—she absolutely refused me. Not that she cared a damn about the animal. I don't think you've seen him. He's an Australian sheep dog. They usually have one blank or whitish eye which gives a misleading look, but they're the gentlest dogs and have unusual delicacy about eating or talking. Let me at least have the companionship of this animal. Never." Wilhelm was greatly moved. He wiped his face at all corners with his napkin. Dr. Adler felt that his son was indulging himself too much in his emotions.

"Whenever she can hit me, she hits, and she seems to live for that alone. And she demands more and more, and still more. Two years ago she wanted to go back to college and get another degree. It increased my burden but I thought it would be wiser in the end if she got a better job through it. But still she takes as much from me as before. Next thing she'll want to be a Doctor of Philosophy. She says the women in her family live long, and I'll have to pay and pay for the rest of my life."

The doctor said impatiently, "Well, these are details, not principles. Just details which you can leave out. The dog! You're mixing up all kinds of irrelevant things. Go to a good lawyer."

"But I've already told you, Dad. I got a lawyer, and she got one, too, and both of them talk and send me bills, and I eat my heart out. Oh, Dad, Dad, what a hole I'm in!" said Wilhelm in utter misery. "The lawyers—see?—draw up an agreement, and she says okay on Monday and wants more money on Tuesday. And it begins again."

"I always thought she was a strange kind of woman," said Dr. Adler. He felt that by disliking Margaret from the first and disapproving of the marriage he had done all that he could be expected to do.

"Strange, Father? I'll show you what she's like." Wilhelm took hold of his broad throat with brown-stained fingers and bitten nails and began to choke himself.

"What are you doing?" cried the old man.

"I'm showing you what she does to me."

"Stop that—stop it!" the old man said and tapped the table commandingly.

"Well, Dad, she hates me. I feel that she's strangling me. I can't catch my breath. She just has fixed herself on me to kill me. She can do it at a long distance. One of these days I'll be struck down by suffocation or apoplexy because of her. I just can't catch my breath."

"Take your hands off your throat, you foolish man," said his father. "Stop this bunk. Don't expect me to believe in all kinds of voodoo."

"If that's what you want to call it, all right." His face flamed and paled and swelled and his breath was laborious.

"But I'm telling you that from the time I met her I've been a slave. The Emancipation Proclamation was only for colored people. A husband like me is a slave, with an iron collar. The churches go up to Albany and supervise the law. They won't have divorces. The court says, 'You want to be free. Then you have to work twice as hard—twice, at least! Work! you bum.' So then guys kill each other for the buck, and they may be free of a wife who hates them but they are sold to the company. The company knows a guy has got to have his salary, and takes full advantage of him. Don't talk to me about being free. A rich man may be free on an income of a million net. A poor man may be free because nobody cares what he does. But a fellow in my position has to sweat it out until he drops dead."

His father replied to this, "Wilky, it's entirely your own fault. You don't have to allow it."

Stopped in his eloquence, Wilhelm could not speak for a while. Dumb and incompetent, he struggled for breath and frowned with effort into his father's face.

"I don't understand your problems," said the old man. "I never had any like them."

By now Wilhelm had lost his head and he waved his hands and said over and over, "Oh, Dad, don't give me that stuff, don't give me that. Please don't give me that sort of thing."

"It's true," said his father. "I come from a different world. Your mother and I led an entirely different life."

"Oh, how can you compare Mother," Wilhelm said. "Mother was a help to you. Did she harm you ever?"

"There's no need to carry on like an opera, Wilky," said the doctor. "This is only your side of things."

"What? It's the truth," said Wilhelm.

The old man could not be persuaded and shook his round head and drew his vest down over the gilded shirt, and leaned back with a completeness of style that made this look, to anyone out of hearing, like an ordinary conversation between a middle-aged man and his respected father. Wilhelm towered and swayed, big and sloven, with his gray eyes red-shot and his honey-colored hair twisted in flaming shapes upward. Injustice made him angry, made him beg. But he wanted an understanding with his father, and he tried to capitulate to him. He said, "You can't compare Mother and Margaret, and neither can you and I be compared, because you, Dad, were a success. And a success—is a success. I never made a success."

The doctor's old face lost all of its composure and became hard and angry. His small breast rose sharply under the red and black shirt and he said, "Yes. Because of hard work. I was not self-indulgent, not lazy. My old man sold dry goods in Williamsburg. We were nothing, do you understand? I knew I couldn't afford to waste my chances."

"I wouldn't admit for one minute that I was lazy," said Wilhelm. "If anything, I tried too hard. I admit I made many mistakes. Like I thought I shouldn't do things you had done already. Study chemistry. You had done it already. It was in the family."

His father continued, "I didn't run around with fifty women, either. I was not a Hollywood star. I didn't have time to go to Cuba for a vacation. I stayed at home and took care of my children."

Oh, thought Wilhelm, eyes turning upward. Why did I come here in the first place, to live near him? New York is like a gas. The colors are running. My head feels so tight, I don't know what I'm doing. He thinks I want to take away his money or that I envy him. He doesn't see what I want.

"Dad," Wilhelm said aloud, "you're being very unfair. It's true the movies was a false step. But I love my boys. I didn't abandon them. I left Margaret because I had to."

"Why did you have to?"

"Well—" said Wilhelm, struggling to condense his many reasons into a few plain words. "I had to—I had to."

With sudden and surprising bluntness his father said, "Did you have bed-trouble with her? Then you should have stuck it out. Sooner or later everyone has it. Normal people stay with it. It passes. But you wouldn't, so now you pay for your stupid romantic notions. Have I made my view clear?"

It was very clear. Wilhelm seemed to hear it repeated from various sides and inclined his head different ways, and listened and thought. Finally he said, "I guess that's the medical standpoint. You may be right, I just couldn't live with Margaret. I wanted to stick it out, but I was getting very sick. She was one way and I was another. She wouldn't be like me, so I tried to be like her, and I couldn't do it."

"Are you sure she didn't tell *you* to go?" the doctor said.

"I wish she had. I'd be in a better position now. No, it was me. I didn't want to leave, but I couldn't stay. Somebody had to take the initiative. I did. Now I'm the fall guy too."

Pushing aside in advance all the objections that his son would make, the doctor said, "Why did you lose your job with Rojax?"

"I didn't, I've told you."

"You're lying. You wouldn't have ended the connection. You need the money too badly. But you must have got into trouble." The small old man spoke concisely and with great strength. "Since you have to talk and can't let it alone, tell the truth. Was there a scandal—a woman?"

Wilhelm fiercely defended himself. "No, Dad, there wasn't any woman. I told you how it was."

"Maybe it was a man, then," the old man said wickedly.

Shocked, Wilhelm stared at him with burning pallor and dry lips. His skin looked a little yellow. "I don't think you know what you're talking about," he answered after a moment. "You shouldn't let your imagination run so free. Since you've been living here on Broadway you must think you understand life, up to date. You ought to know your own son a little better. Let's drop that, now."

"All right, Wilky, I'll withdraw it. But something must have happened in Roxbury nevertheless. You'll never go back. You're just talking wildly about representing a rival company. You won't. You've done something to spoil your reputation, I think. But you've got girl friends who are expecting you back, isn't that so?"

"I take a lady out now and then while on the road," said Wilhelm. "I'm not a monk."

"No one special? Are you sure you haven't gotten into complications?"

He had tried to unburden himself and instead, Wilhelm thought, he had to undergo an inquisition to prove himself worthy of a sympathetic word. Because his father believed that he did all kinds of gross things.

"There is a woman in Roxbury that I went with. We fell in love and wanted to marry, but she got tired of waiting for my divorce. Margaret figured that. On top of which the girl was a Catholic and I had to go with her to the priest and make an explanation."

Neither did this last confession touch Dr. Adler's sympathies or sway his calm old head or affect the color of his complexion.

"No, no, no, no; all wrong," he said.

Again Wilhelm cautioned himself. Remember his age. He is no longer the same person. He can't bear trouble. I'm so choked up and congested anyway I can't see straight. Will I ever get out of the woods, and recover my balance? You're never the same afterward. Trouble rusts out the system.

"You really *want* a divorce?" said the old man.

"For the price I pay I should be getting something."

"In that case," Dr. Adler said, "It seems to me no normal person would stand for such treatment from a woman."

"Ah, Father, Father!" said Wilhelm. "It's always the same thing with you. Look how you lead me on. You always start out to help me with my problems, and be sympathetic and so forth. It gets my hopes up and I begin to be grateful. But before we're through I'm a hundred times more depressed than before. Why is that? You have no sympathy. You want to shift all the blame on to me. Maybe you're wise to do it." Wilhelm was beginning to lose himself. "All you seem to think about is your death. Well, I'm sorry. But I'm going to die too. And I'm your son. It isn't my fault in the first place. There ought to be a right way to do this, and be fair to each other. But what I want to know is, why do you start up with me if you're not going to help me? What do you want to know about my problems for, Father? So you can lay the whole responsibility on me—so that you won't have to help me? D'you want me to comfort you for having such a son?" Wilhelm had a great knot of wrong tied tight within his chest, and tears approached his eyes but he didn't let them out. He looked shabby enough as it was. His voice was thick and hazy, and he was stammering and could not bring his awful feelings forth.

"You have some purpose of your own," said the doctor, "in acting so unreasonable. What do you want from me? What do you expect?"

"What do I expect?" said Wilhelm. He felt as though he were unable to recover something. Like a ball in the surf, washed beyond reach, his self-control was going out. "I expect *help!*" The words escaped him in a loud, wild, frantic cry and startled the old man, and two or three breakfasters within hearing glanced their way. Wilhelm's hair, the color of whitened honey, rose dense and tall with the expansion of his face, and he said, "When I suffer—you aren't even sorry. That's because you have no affection for me, and you don't want any part of me."

"Why must I like the way you behave? No, I don't like it." said Dr. Adler.

"All right. You want me to change myself. But suppose I could do it—what would I become? What could I? Let's suppose that all my life I have had the wrong ideas about myself and wasn't what I thought I was. And wasn't even careful to take a few precautions, as most people do—like a woodchuck has a few exits to his tunnel. But what shall I do now? More than half my life is over. More than half. And now you tell me I'm not even normal."

The old man too had lost his calm. "You cry about being helped," he said. "When you thought you had to go into the service I sent a check to Margaret every month. As a family man you could have had an exemption. But no! The war couldn't be fought without you and you had to get yourself drafted and be an office-boy in the Pacific theater. Any clerk could have done what you did. You could find nothing better to become than a GI."

Wilhelm was going to reply, and half raised his bearish figure from the chair, his fingers spread and whitened by their grip on the table, but the old man would not let him begin. He said, "I see other elderly people here with children who aren't much good, and they keep backing them and holding them up at a great sacrifice. But I'm not going to make that mistake. It doesn't enter your mind that when I die—a year, two years from now—you'll still be here. I do think of it."

He had intended to say that he had a right to be left in peace. Instead he gave Wilhelm the impression that he meant it was not fair for the better man of the two, and the more useful, the more admired, to leave the world first. Perhaps he meant that, too—a little; but he would not under other circumstances have come out with it so flatly.

"Father," said Wilhelm with an unusual openness of appeal. "Don't you think I know how you feel? I have pity. I want you to live on and on. If you outlive me, that's perfectly okay by me." As his father did not answer this avowal and turned away his glance, Wilhelm suddenly burst out, "No, but you hate me. And if I had money you wouldn't. By God, you have to admit it. The money makes the difference. Then we would be a fine father and son, if I was a credit to you—so you could boast and brag about me all over the hotel. But I'm not the right type of son. I'm too old, I'm too old and unlucky."

His father said, "I can't give you any money. There would be no end to it if

I started. You and your sister would take every last buck from me. I'm still alive, not dead. I am still here. Life isn't over yet. I am as much alive as you or anyone. And I want nobody on my back. Get off! And I give you the same advice, Wilky. Carry nobody on your back."

"Just keep your money," said Wilhelm miserably. "Keep it and enjoy it yourself. That's the ticket!"

IV

Ass! Idiot! Wild boar! Dumb mule! Slave! Lousy, wallowing hippopotamus! Wilhelm called himself as his bending legs carried him from the dining room. His pride! His inflamed feelings! His begging and feebleness! And trading insults with his old father—and spreading confusion over everything. Oh, how poor, contemptible, and ridiculous he was! When he remembered how he had said, with great reproof, "You ought to know your own son"—why, how corny and abominable it was.

He could not get out of the sharply brilliant dining room fast enough. He was horribly worked up; his neck and shoulders, his entire chest ached as though they had been tightly tied with ropes. He smelled the salt odor of tears in his nose.

But at the same time, since there were depths in Wilhelm not unsuspected by himself, he received a suggestion from some remote element in his thoughts that the business of life, the real business—to carry his peculiar burden, to feel shame and impotence, to taste these quelled tears—the only important business, the highest business was being done. Maybe the making of mistakes expressed the very purpose of his life and the essence of his being here. Maybe he was supposed to make them and suffer from them on this earth. And though he had raised himself above Mr. Perls and his father because they adored money, still they were called to act energetically and this was better than to yell and cry, pray and beg, poke and blunder and go by fits and starts and fall upon the thorns of life. And finally sink beneath that watery floor—would that be tough luck, or would it be good riddance?

But he raged once more against his father. Other people with money, while they're still alive, want to see it do some good. Granted, he shouldn't support me. But have I ever asked him to do that? Have I ever asked for dough at all, either for Margaret or for the kids or for myself? It isn't the money, but only the assistance; not even assistance, but just the feeling. But he may be trying to teach me that a grown man should be cured of such feeling. Feeling got me in dutch at Rojax. I had the *feeling* that I belonged to the firm, and my *feelings* were hurt when they put Gerber in over me. Dad thinks I'm too simple. But I'm not so simple as he thinks. What about his feelings? He doesn't forget death for one single second, and that's what makes him like this. And not only is death on his mind but through money he forces me to think about it, too. It gives him power over me. He forces me that way, he himself, and then he's sore. If he was poor, I could care for him and show it. The way I *could* care, too, if I only had a chance. He'd see how much love and respect I had in me. It would make him a different man, too. He'd put his hands on me and give me his blessing.

Someone in a gray straw hat with a wide cocoa-colored band spoke to Wilhelm in the lobby. The light was dusky, splotched with red underfoot; green, the leather furniture; yellow, the indirect lighting.

"Hey, Tommy. Say, there."

"Excuse me," said Wilhelm, trying to reach a house phone. But this was Dr. Tamkin, whom he was just about to call.

"You have a very obsessional look on your face," said Dr. Tamkin.

Wilhelm thought, Here he is, Here he is. If I could only figure this guy out.

"Oh," he said to Tamkin. "Have I got such a look? Well, whatever it is, you name it, and I'm sure to have it."

The sight of Dr. Tamkin brought his quarrel with his father to a close. He found himself flowing into another channel.

"What are we doing?" he said. "What's going to happen to lard today?"

"Don't worry yourself about that. All we have to do is hold on to it and it's sure to go up. But what's made you so hot under the collar, Wilhelm?"

"Oh, one of those family situations." This was the moment to take a new look at Tamkin, and he viewed him closely but gained nothing by the new effort. It was conceivable that Tamkin was everything that he claimed to be, and all the gossip false. But was he a scientific man, or not? If he was not, this might be a case for the district attorney's office to investigate. Was he a liar? That was a delicate question. Even a liar might be trustworthy in some ways. Could he trust Tamkin—could he? He feverishly, fruitlessly sought an answer.

But the time for this question was past, and he had to trust him now. After a long struggle to come to a decision, he had given him the money. Practical judgment was in abeyance. He had worn himself out, and the decision was no decision. How had this happened? But how had his Hollywood career begun? It was not because of Maurice Venice, who turned out to be a pimp. It was because Wilhelm himself was ripe for the mistake. His marriage, too, had been like that. Through such decisions somehow his life had taken form. And so, from the moment when he tasted the peculiar flavor of fatality in Dr. Tamkin, he could no longer keep back the money.

Five days ago Tamkin had said, "Meet me tomorrow, and we'll go to the market." Wilhelm, therefore, had had to go. At eleven o'clock they had walked to the brokerage office. On the way, Tamkin broke the news to Wilhelm that though this was an equal partnership he couldn't put up his half of the money just yet; it was tied up for a week or so in one of his patents. Today he would be two hundred dollars short; next week, he'd make it up. But neither of them needed an income from the market, of course. This was only a sporting proposition anyhow, Tamkin said. Wilhelm had to answer, "Of course." It was too late to withdraw. What else could he do? Then came the formal part of the transaction, and it was frightening. The very shade of green of Tamkin's check looked wrong; it was a false, disheartening color. His handwriting was peculiar, even monstrous; the e's were like i's, the t's and l's the same, and the h's like wasps' bellies. He wrote like a fourth-grader. Scientists, however, dealt mostly in symbols; they printed. This was Wilhelm's explanation.

Dr. Tamkin had given him his check for three hundred dollars. Wilhelm, in a blinded and convulsed aberration, pressed and pressed to try to kill the trembling of his hand as he wrote out his check for a thousand. He set his lips tight, crouched with his huge back over the table, and wrote with crumbling, terrified fingers, knowing that if Tamkin's check bounced his own would not be honored either. His sole cleverness was to set the date ahead by one day to give the green check time to clear.

Next he had signed a power of attorney, allowing Tamkin to speculate with his money, and this was an even more frightening document. Tamkin had never said a word about it, but here they were and it had to be done.

After delivering his signatures, the only precaution Wilhelm took was to come back to the manager of the brokerage office and ask him privately, "Uh, about Doctor Tamkin. We were in here a few minutes ago, remember?"

That day had been a weeping, smoky one and Wilhelm had gotten away from Tamkin on the pretext of having to run to the post office. Tamkin had gone to lunch alone, and here was Wilhelm, back again, breathless, his hat dripping, needlessly asking the manager if he remembered.

"Yes, sir, I know," the manager had said. He was a cold, mild, lean German who dressed correctly and around his neck wore a pair of opera glasses with which he read the board. He was an extremely correct person except that he never shaved in the morning, not caring, probably, how he looked to the fumblers and the old people and the operators and the gamblers and the idlers of Broadway uptown. The market closed at three. Maybe, Wilhelm guessed, he had a thick beard and took a lady out to dinner later and wanted to look fresh-shaven.

"Just a question," said Wilhelm. "A few minutes ago I signed a power of attorney so Doctor Tamkin could invest for me. You gave me the blanks."

"Yes, sir, I remember."

"Now this is what I want to know," Wilhelm had said. "I'm no lawyer and I only gave the paper a glance. Does this give Doctor Tamkin power of attorney over any other assets of mine—money, or property?"

The rain had dribbled from Wilhelm's deformed, transparent raincoat; the buttons of his shirt, which always seemed tiny, were partly broken, in pearly quarters of the moon, and some of the dark, thick golden hairs that grew on his belly stood out. It was the manager's business to conceal his opinion of him; he was shrewd, gray, correct (although unshaven) and had little to say except on matters that came to his desk. He must have recognized in Wilhelm a man who reflected long and then made the decision he had rejected twenty separate times. Silvery, cool, level, long-profiled, experienced, indifferent, observant, with unshaven refinement, he scarcely looked at Wilhelm, who trembled with fearful awkwardness. The manager's face, low-colored, long-nostriled, acted as a unit of perception; his eyes merely did their reduced share. Here was a man, like Rubin, who knew and knew and knew. He, a foreigner, knew; Wilhelm, in the city of his birth, was ignorant.

The manager had said, "No, sir, it does not give him."

"Only over the funds I deposited with you?"

"Yes, that is right, sir."

"Thank you, that's what I wanted to find out," Wilhelm had said, grateful.

The answer comforted him. However, the question had no value. None at all. For Wilhelm had no other assets. He had given Tamkin his last money. There wasn't enough of it to cover his obligations anyway, and Wilhelm had reckoned that he might as well go bankrupt now as next month. "Either broke or rich," was how he had figured, and that formula had encouraged him to make the gamble. Well, not rich; he did not expect that, but perhaps Tamkin might really show him how to earn what he needed in the market. By now, however, he had forgotten his own reckoning and was aware only that he stood to lose his seven hundred dollars to the last cent.

Dr. Tamkin took the attitude that they were a pair of gentlemen experimenting with lard and grain futures. The money, a few hundred dollars, meant nothing much to either of them. He said to Wilhelm, "Watch. You'll get a big kick out of his and wonder why more people don't go into it. You think the Wall Street guys are so smart—geniuses? That's because most of us are psychologically afraid to think about the details. Tell me this. When you're on the road, and you don't understand what goes on under the hood of your car, you'll worry what'll happen if something goes wrong with the engine. Am I wrong?" No, he was right. "Well," said Dr. Tamkin with an expression of quiet triumph abut his mouth, almost the suggestion of a jeer. "It's the same psychological principle, Wilhelm. They are rich because you don't understand what goes on. But it's no mystery, and by putting in a little money and applying certain principles of observation, you begin to grasp it. It can't be studied in the abstract. You have to take a specimen risk so that you feel the process, the money-flow, the whole complex. To know how it feels to be a seaweed you have to get in the water. In a very short time we'll take out a hundred-per-cent profit." Thus Wilhelm had had to pretend at the outset that his interest in the market was theoretical.

"Well," said Tamkin when he met him now in the lobby, "what's the problem, what is this family situation? Tell me." He put himself forward as the keen mental scientist. Whenever this happened Wilhelm didn't know what to reply. No matter what he said or did it seemed that Dr. Tamkin saw through him.

"I had some words with my dad."

Dr. Tamkin found nothing extraordinary in this. "It's the eternal same story," he said. "The elemental conflict of parent and child. It won't end, ever. Even with a fine old gentleman like your dad."

"I don't suppose it will. I've never been able to get anywhere with him. He objects to my feelings. He thinks they're sordid. I upset him and he gets mad at me. But maybe all old men are alike."

"Sons, too. Take it from one of them," said Dr. Tamkin. "All the same, you should be proud of such a fine old patriarch of a father. It should give you hope. The longer he lives, the longer your life-expectancy becomes."

Wilhelm answered, brooding, "I guess so. But I think I inherit more from my mother's side, and she died in her fifties."

"A problem arose between a young fellow I'm treating and his dad—I just had a consultation," said Dr. Tamkin as he removed his dark gray hat.

"So early in the morning?" said Wilhelm with suspicion.

"Over the telephone, of course."

What a creature Tamkin was when he took off his hat! The indirect light showed the many complexities of his bald skull, his gull's nose, his rather handsome eyebrows, his vain mustache, his deceiver's brown eyes. His figure was stocky, rigid, short in the neck, so that the large ball of the occiput touched his collar. His bones were peculiarly formed, as though twisted twice where the ordinary human bone turned only once, and his shoulders rose in two pagoda-like points. At midbody he was thick. He stood pigeon-toed, a sign perhaps that he was devious or had much to hide. The skin of his hands was aging, and his nails were moonless, concave, clawlike, and they appeared loose. His eyes were as brown as beaver fur and full of strange lines. The two large brown naked balls looked thoughtful—but were they? And honest—but was Dr. Tamkin honest? There was a hypnotic power in his eyes, but this was not always of the same strength, nor was Wilhelm convinced that it was completely natural. He felt that Tamkin tried to make his eyes deliberately conspicuous, with studied art, and that he brought forth his hypnotic effect by an exertion. Occasionally it failed or drooped, and when this happened the sense of his face passed downward to his heavy (possibly foolish?) red underlip.

Wilhelm wanted to talk about the lard holdings, but Dr. Tamkin said, "This father-and-son case of mine would be instructive to you. It's a different psychological type completely than your dad. This man's father thinks that he isn't his son."

"Why not?"

"Because he has found out something about the mother carrying on with a friend of the family for twenty-five years."

"Well, what do you know!" said Wilhelm. His silent thought was, Pure bull. Nothing but bull!

"You must note how interesting the woman is, too. She has two husbands. Whose are the kids? The fellow detected her and she gave a signed confession that two of the four children were not the father's."

"It's amazing," said Wilhelm, but he said it in a rather distant way. He was always hearing such stories from Dr. Tamkin. If you were to believe Tamkin, most of the world was like this. Everybody in the hotel had a mental disorder, a secret history, a concealed disease. The wife of Rubin at the newsstand was supposed to be kept by Carl, the yelling, loud-mouthed gin-rummy player. The wife of Frank in the barbershop had disappeared with a GI while he was waiting for her to disembark at the French Lines pier. Everyone was like the faces on a playing card, upside down either way. Every public figure had a character-neurosis. Maddest of all were the businessmen, the heartless, flaunting, boisterous business class who ruled this country with their hard manners and their bold lies and their absurd words that nobody could believe. They were crazier than anyone. They spread the plague. Wilhelm, thinking of the Rojax Corporation, was inclined to agree that many businessmen were insane. And he supposed that Tamkin, for all his peculiarities, spoke a kind of truth and did some people a sort of good. It confirmed Wilhelm's suspicions to hear that there was a plague, and he said, "I couldn't agree with you more. They trade on anything, they steal everything, they're cynical right to the bones."

"You have to realize," said Tamkin, speaking of his patient, or his client, "that the mother's confession isn't good. It's a confession of duress. I try to tell the young fellow he shouldn't worry about a phony confession. But what does it help him if I am rational with him?"

"No?" said Wilhelm, intensely nervous. "I think we ought to go over to the market. It'll be opening pretty soon."

"Oh, come on," said Tamkin. "It isn't even nine o'clock, and there isn't much trading the first hour anyway. Things don't get hot in Chicago until half-past ten, and they're an hour behind us, don't forget. Anyway, I say lard will go up, and it will. Take my word. I've made a study of the guilt-aggression cycle which is behind it. I ought to know *something* about that. Straighten your collar."

"But meantime," said Wilhelm, "we have taken a licking this week. Are you sure your insight is at its best? Maybe when it isn't we should lay off and wait."

"Don't you realize," Dr. Tamkin told him, "you can't march in a straight line to the victory? You fluctuate toward it. From Euclid to Newton there was straight lines. The modern age analyzes the wavers.[1] On my own accounts, I took a licking in hides and coffee. But I have confidence. I'm sure I'll outguess them." He gave Wilhelm a narrow smile, friendly, calming, shrewd, and wizard-like, patronizing, secret, potent. He saw his fears and smiled at them. "It's something," he remarked, "to see how the competition-factor will manifest itself in different individuals."

"So? Let's go over."

"But I haven't had my breakfast yet."

[1]Euclid, ancient Greek geometrician. Sir Isaac Newton (1642–1727), English mathematician and natural scientist. Their theories have been superseded by the modern quantum theory of physics and its application (wave mechanics) to the movement of material particles.

"I've had mine."

"Come, have a cup of coffee."

"I wouldn't want to meet my dad." Looking through the glass doors, Wilhelm saw that his father had left by the other exit. Wilhelm thought, He didn't want to run into me, either. He said to Dr. Tamkin, "Okay, I'll sit with you, but let's hurry it up because I'd like to get to the market while there's still a place to sit. Everybody and his uncle gets in ahead of you."

"I want to tell you about this boy and his dad. It's highly absorbing. The father was a nudist. Everybody went naked in the house. Maybe the woman found men *with* clothes attractive. Her husband didn't believe in cutting his hair, either. He practiced dentistry. In his office he wore riding pants and a pair of boots, and he wore a green eyeshade."

"Oh, come off it," said Wilhelm.

"This is a true case history."

Without warning, Wilhelm began to laugh. He himself had had no premonition of his change of humor. His face became warm and pleasant, and he forgot his father, his anxieties; he panted bearlike, happily, through his teeth. "This sounds like a horse-dentist. He wouldn't have to put on pants to treat a horse. Now what else are you going to tell me? Did the wife play the mandolin? Does the boy join the cavalry? Oh, Tamkin, you really are a killer-diller."

"Oh, you think I'm trying to amuse you," said Tamkin. "That's because you aren't familiar with my outlook. I deal in facts. Facts always are sensational. I'll say that a second time. Facts *always!* are sensational."

Wilhelm was reluctant to part with his good mood. The doctor had little sense of humor. He was looking at him earnestly.

"I'd bet you any amount of money," said Tamkin, "that the facts about you are sensational."

"Oh—ha, ha! You want them? You can sell them to a true confession magazine."

"People forget how sensational the things are that they do. They don't see it on themselves. It blends into the background of their daily life."

Wilhelm smiled. "Are you sure this boy tells you the truth?"

"Yes, because I've known the whole family for years."

"And you do psychological work with your own friends? I didn't know that was allowed."

"Well, I'm a radical in the profession. I have to do good wherever I can."

Wilhelm's face became ponderous again and pale. His whitened gold hair lay heavy on his head, and he clasped uneasy fingers on the table. Sensational, but oddly enough, dull, too. Now how do you figure that out? It blends with the background. Funny but unfunny. True but false. Casual but laborious, Tamkin was. Wilhelm was most suspicious of him when he took his driest tone.

"With me," said Dr. Tamkin, "I am at my most efficient when I don't need the fee. When I only love. Without a financial reward. I remove myself from the social infuence. Especially money. The spiritual compensation is what I look for. Bringing people into the here-and-now. The real universe. That's the present moment. The past is no good to us. The future is full of anxiety. Only the present is real—the here-and-now. Seize the day."

"Well," said Wilhelm, his earnestness returning. "I know you are a very unusual man. I like what you say about here-and-now. Are all the people who come to see you personal friends and patients too? Like that tall handsome girl, the one who always wears those beautiful broomstick skirts and belts?"

"She was an epileptic, and a most bad and serious pathology, too. I'm curing her successfully. She hasn't had a seizure in six months, and she used to have one every week."

"And that young cameraman, the one who showed us those movies from the jungles of Brazil, isn't he related to her?"

"Her brother. He's under my care, too. He has some terrible tendencies, which are to be expected when you have an epileptic sibling. I came into their lives when they needed help desperately, and took hold of them. A certain man forty years older than she had her in his control and used to give her fits by suggestion whenever she tried to leave him. If you only knew one per cent of what goes on in the city of New York! You see, I understand what it is when the lonely person begins to feel like an animal. When the night comes and he feels like howling from his window like a wolf. I'm taking complete care of that young fellow and his sister. I have to steady him down or he'll go from Brazil to Australia the next day. The way I keep him in the here-and-now is by teaching him Greek."

This was a complete surprise! "What, do you know Greek?"

"A friend of mine taught me when I was in Cairo. I studied Aristotle with him to keep from being idle."

Wilhelm tried to take in these new claims and examine them. Howling from the window like a wolf when night comes sounded genuine to him. That was something really to think about. But the Greek! He realized that Tamkin was watching to see how he took it. More elements were continually being added. A few days ago Tamkin had hinted that he had once been in the underworld, one of the Detroit Purple Gang. He was once head of a mental clinic in Toledo. He had worked with a Polish inventor on an unsinkable ship. He was a technical consultant in the field of television. In the life of a man of genius, all of these things might happen. But had they happened to Tamkin? Was he a genius? He often said that he had attended some of the Egyptian royal family as a psychiatrist. "But everybody is alike, common or aristocrat," he told Wilhelm. "The aristocrat knows less about life."

An Egyptian princess whom he had treated in California, for horrible disorders he had described to Wilhelm, retained him to come back to the old country with her, and there he had had many of her friends and relatives under his care. They turned over a villa on the Nile to him. "For ethical reasons, I can't tell you many of the details about them," he said—but Wilhelm had already heard all these details, and strange and shocking they were, if true. *If* true—he could not be free from doubt. For instance, the general who had to wear ladies' silk stockings and stand otherwise naked before the mirror—and all the rest. Listening to the doctor when he was so strangely factual, Wilhelm had to translate his words into his own language, and he could not translate fast enough or find terms to fit what he heard.

"Those Egyptian big shots invested in the market, too, for the heck of it. What did they need extra money for? By association, I almost became a millionaire myself, and if I had played it smart there's no telling what might have happened. I could have been the ambassador." The American? The Egyptian ambassador? "A friend of mine tipped me off on the cotton. I made a heavy purchase of it. I didn't have that kind of money, but everybody there knew me. It never entered their minds that a person of their social circle didn't have dough. The sale was made on the phone. Then, while the cotton shipment was at sea, the price tripled. When the stuff suddenly became so valuable all hell broke loose on the world cotton market, they looked to see who was the owner of this big shipment. Me! They investigated my credit and found out I was a mere doctor, and they canceled. This was illegal. I sued them. But as I didn't have the money to fight them I sold the suit to a Wall Street lawyer for twenty thousand dollars. He fought it and was winning. They settled with him out of court for more than a million. But on the way back from Cairo, there was a crash. All on board died. I have this guilt on my conscience, of being the murderer of that lawyer. Although he was a crook."

Wilhelm thought, I must be a real jerk to sit and listen to such impossible stories. I guess I am a sucker for people who talk about the deeper things of life, even the way he does.

"We scientific men speak of irrational guilt, Wilhelm," said Dr. Tamkin, as if Wilhelm were a pupil in his class. "But in such a situation, because of the money, I wished him harm. I realize it. This isn't the time to describe all the details, but the money made me guilty. *M*oney and *M*urder both begin with *M*. Machinery. Mischief."

Wilhelm, his mind thinking for him at random, said, "What about *M*ercy? Milk-of-human-kindness?"

"One fact should be clear to you by now. Money-making is aggression. That's the whole thing. The functionalistic explanation is the only one. People come to the market to kill. They say, 'I'm going to make a killing.' It's not accidental. Only they haven't got the genuine courage to kill, and they erect a symbol of it. The money. They make a killing by a fantasy. Now, counting any number is always a sadistic activity. Like hitting. In the Bible, the Jews wouldn't allow you to count them. They knew it was sadistic."

"I don't understand what you mean," said Wilhelm. A strange uneasiness tore at him. The day was growing too warm and his head felt dim. "What makes them want to kill?"

"By and by, you'll get the drift," Dr. Tamkin assured him. His amazing eyes had some of the rich dryness of a brown fur. Innumerable crystalline hairs or spicules of light glittered in their bold surfaces. "You can't understand without first spending years on the study of the ultimates of human and animal behavior, the deep chemical, organismic, and spiritual secrets of life. I am a psychological poet."

"If you're this kind of poet," said Wilhelm, whose fingers in his pocket were feeling in the little envelopes for the Phenaphen capsules, "what are you doing on the market?"

"That's a good question. Maybe I am better at speculation because I don't care. Basically, I don't wish hard enough for money, and therefore I come with a cool head to it."

Wilhelm thought, Oh, sure! That's an answer, is it? I bet that if I took a strong attitude he'd back down on everything. He'd grovel in front of me. The way he looks at me on the sly, to see if I'm being taken in! He swallowed his Phenaphen pill with a long gulp of water. The rims of his eyes grew red as it went down. And then he felt calmer.

"Let me see if I can give you an answer that will satisfy you," said Dr. Tamkin. His flapjacks were set before him. He spread the butter on them, poured on brown maple syrup, quartered them, and began to eat with hard, active, muscular jaws which sometimes gave a creak at the hinges. He pressed the handle of his knife against his chest and said, "In here, the human bosom—mine, yours, everybody's—there isn't just one soul. There's a lot of souls. But there are two main ones, the real soul and a pretender soul. Now! Every man realizes that he has to love something or somebody. He feels that he must go outward. 'If thou canst not love, what art thou?' Are you with me?"

"Yes, Doc, I think so," said Wilhelm listening—a little skeptically but nonetheless hard.

" 'What art thou?' Nothing. That's the answer. Nothing. In the heart of hearts—Nothing; So of course you can't stand that and want to be Something, and you try. But instead of being this Something, the man puts it over on everybody instead. You can't be that strict to yourself. You love a *little*. Like you have a dog" (*Scissors!*) "or give some money to a charity drive. Now that isn't love, is it? What is it? Egotism, pure and simple. It's a way to love the pretender soul. Vanity. Only vanity, is what it is. And social control. The interest of the pretender soul is the same as the interest of the social life, the society mechanism. This is the main tragedy of human life. Oh, it is terrible! Terrible! You are not free. Your own betrayer is inside of you and sells you out. You have to obey him like a slave. He makes you work like a horse. And for what? For who?"

"Yes, for what?" The doctor's words caught Wilhelm's heart. "I couldn't agree more," he said. "When do we get free?"

"The purpose is to keep the whole thing going. The true soul is the one that pays the price. It suffers and gets sick, and it realizes that the pretender can't be loved. Because the pretender is a lie. The true soul loves the truth. And when the true soul feels like this, it wants to kill the pretender. The love has turned into hate. Then you become dangerous. A killer. You have to kill the deceiver."

"Does this happen to everybody?"

The doctor answered simply, "Yes, to everybody. Of course, for simplification purposes, I have spoken of the soul; it isn't a scientific term, but it helps you to understand it. Whenever the slayer slays, he wants to slay the soul in him which has gypped and deceived him. Who is his enemy? Him. And his lover? Also. Therefore, all suicide is murder, and all murder is suicide. It's the one and identical phenomenon. Biologically, the pretender soul takes away the energy of the true soul and makes it feeble, like a parasite. It happens unconsciously, unawaringly, in the depths of the organism. Ever take up parasitology?"

"No, it's my dad who's the doctor."

"You should read a book about it."

Wilhelm said, "But this means that the world is full of murderers. So it's not the world. It's a kind of hell."

"Sure," the doctor said. "At least a kind of purgatory. You walk on the bodies. They are all around. I can hear them cry *de profundis*[2] and wring their hands. I hear them, poor human beasts. I can't help hearing. And my eyes are open to it. I have to cry, too. This is the human tragedy-comedy."

Wilhelm tried to capture his vision. And again the doctor looked untrustworthy to him, and he doubted him. "Well," he said, "there are also kind, ordinary, helpful people. They're—out in the country. All over. What kind of morbid stuff do you read, anyway?" The doctor's room was full of books.

"I read the best of literature, science and philosophy," Dr. Tamkin said. Wilhelm had observed that in his room even the TV aerial was set upon a pile of volumes. "Korzybski,[3] Aristotle, Freud, W.H. Sheldon,[4] and all the great

---

[2]Latin: "out of the depths," from Psalm 130, "Out of the depths I have cried unto thee O Lord."

[3]Alfred Korzybski (1879–1950), Polish-American scientist and writer, author of *Science and Sanity* (1933).

[4]American psychologist and physician (1898–1977).

poets. You answer me like a layman. You haven't applied your mind strictly to this."

"Very interesting," said Wilhelm. He was aware that he hadn't applied his mind strictly to anything. "You don't have to think I'm a dummy, though. I have ideas, too." A glance at the clock told him that the market would soon open. They could spare a few minutes yet. There were still more things he wanted to hear from Tamkin. He realized that Tamkin spoke faultily, but then scientific men were not always striclty literate. It was the description of the two souls that had awed him. In Tommy he saw the pretender. And even Wilky might not be himself. Might the name of his true soul be the one by which his old grandfather had called him—Velvel? The name of a soul, however, must be only that—soul. What did it look like? Does my soul look like me? Is there a soul that looks like Dad? Like Tamkin? Where does the true soul get its strength? Why does it have to love truth? Wilhelm was tormented, but tried to be oblivious to his torment. Secretly, he prayed the doctor would give him some useful advice and transform his life. "Yes, I understand you," he said. "It isn't lost on me."

"I never said you weren't intelligent, but only you just haven't made a study of it all. As a matter of fact you're a profound personality with very profound creative capacities but also disturbances. I've been concerned with you, and for some time I've been treating you."

"Without my knowing it? I haven't felt you doing anything. What do you mean? I don't think I like being treated without my knowledge. I'm of two minds. What's the matter, don't you think I'm normal?" And he really was divided in mind. That the doctor cared about him pleased him. This was what he craved, that someone should care about him, wish him well. Kindness, mercy, he wanted. But—and here he retracted his heavy shoulders in his peculiar way, drawing his hands up into his sleeves; his feet moved uneasily under the table—but he was worried, too, and even somewhat indignant. For what right had Tamkin to meddle without being asked? What kind of privileged life did this man lead? He took other people's money and speculated with it. Everybody came under his care. No one could have secrets from him.

The doctor looked at him with his deadly brown, heavy, impenetrable eyes, his naked shining head, his red hanging underlip, and said, "You have lots of guilt in you."

Wilhelm helplessly admitted, as he felt the heat rise to his wide face, "Yes, I think so too. But personally," he added, "I don't feel like a murderer. I always try to lay off. It's the others who get me. You know—make me feel oppressed. And if you don't mind, and it's all the same to you, I would rather know it when you start to treat me. And now, Tamkin, for Christ's sake, they're putting out the lunch menus already. Will you sign the check, and let's go!"

Tamkin did as he asked, and they rose. They were passing the bookkeeper's desk when he took out a substantial bundle of onionskin papers and said, "These are receipts of the transactions. Duplicates. You'd better keep them as the account is in your name and you'll need them for income taxes. And here is a copy of a poem I wrote yesterday."

"I have to leave something at the desk for my father," Wilhelm said, and he put his hotel bill in an envelope with a note. *Dear Dad, Please carry me this month, Yours, W.* He watched the clerk with his sullen pug's profile and his stiff-necked look push the envelope into his father's box.

"May I ask you really why you and your dad had words?" said Dr. Tamkin, who had hung back, waiting.

"It was about my future," said Wilhelm. He hurried down the stairs with swift steps, like a tower in motion, his hands in his trousers pockets. He was ashamed to discuss the matter. "He says there's a reason why I can't go back to my old territory, and there is. I told everybody I was going to be an officer of the corporation. And I was supposed to. It was promised. But then they welshed because of the son-in-law. I bragged and made myself look big."

"If you was humble enough, you could go back. But it doesn't make much difference. We'll make you a good living on the market."

They came into the sunshine of upper Broadway, not clear but throbbing through the dust and fumes, a false air of gas visible at eye-level as it spurted from the bursting buses. From old habit, Wilhelm turned up the collar of his jacket.

"Just a technical question," Wilhelm said. "What happens if your losses are bigger than your deposit?"

"Don't worry. They have ultra-modern electronic bookkeeping machinery, and it won't let you get in debt. It puts you out automatically. But I want you to read this poem. You haven't read it yet."

Light as a locust, a helicopter bringing mail from Newark Airport to La Guardia sprang over the city in a long leap.

The paper Wilhelm unfolded had ruled borders in red ink. He read:

MECHANISM VS FUNCTIONALISM
ISM VS HISM

If thee thyself couldst only see
Thy greatness that is and yet to be,
Thou would feel joy-beauty-what ecstasy.
They are at thy feet, earth-moon-sea, the trinity.

Why-forth then dost thou tarry
And partake thee only of the crust
And skim the earth's surface narry
When all creations art thy just?

Seek ye then that which art not there
In thine own glory let thyself rest.
Witness. Thy power is not bare.
Thou art King. Thou art at thy best.

Look then right before thee.
Open thine eyes and see.
At the foot of Mt. Serenity
Is thy cradle to eternity.

Utterly confused, Wilhelm said to himself explosively, What kind of mish-mash, claptrap is this! What does he want from me? Damn him to hell, he might as well hit me on the head, and lay me out, kill me. What does he give me this for? What's the purpose? Is it a deliberate test? Does he want to mix me up? He's already got me mixed up completely. I was never good at riddles. Kiss those seven hundred bucks good-by, and call it one more mistake in a long line of mistakes—Oh, Mama, what a line! He stood near the shining window of a fancy fruit store, holding Tamkin's paper, rather dazed, as though a charge of photographer's flash powder had gone up in his eyes.

But he's waiting for my reaction. I have to say something to him about his poem. It really is no joke. What will I tell him? Who is this King? The poem is written *to* someone. But who? I can't even bring myself to talk. I feel too choked and strangled. With all the books he reads, how come the guy is so illiterate? And why do people just naturally assume that you'll know what they're talking about? No. I don't know, and nobody knows. The planets don't, the stars don't, infinite space doesn't. It doesn't square with Planck's Constant[5] or anything else. So what's the good of it? Where's the need of it? What does he mean here by Mount Serenity? Could it be a figure of speech for Mount Everest? As he says people are all committing suicide, maybe those guys who climbed Everest were only trying to kill themselves, and if we want peace we should stay at the foot of the mountain. In the here-and-now. But it's also here-and-now on the slope, and on the top, where they climbed to seize the day. Surface narry is something he can't mean, I don't believe. I'm about to start foaming at the mouth. "Thy cradle . . ." *Who* is resting in his cradle—in his glory? My thoughts are at an end. I feel the wall. No more. So ——k it all! The money and everything. Take it away! When I have the money they eat me alive, like those piranha fish in the movie about the Brazilian jungle. It was hideous when they ate up that Brahma bull in the river. He turned pale, just like clay, and in five minutes nothing was left except the skeleton still in one piece, floating away. When I haven't got it any more, at least they'll let me alone.

"Well, what do you think of this?" said Dr. Tamkin. He gave a special sort of wise smile, as though Wilhelm must now see what kind of man he was dealing with.

"Nice. Very nice. Have you been writing long?"

"I've been developing this line of thought for years and years. You follow it all the way?"

"I'm trying to figure out who this Thou is."

"Thou? Thou is you."

"Me! Why? This applies to *me*?"

"Why shouldn't it apply to you? You were in my mind when I composed it. Of course, the hero of the poem is sick humanity. If it would open its eyes it would be great."

"Yes, but how do I get into this?"

"The main idea of the poem is *con*struct or *de*struct. There is no ground in between. Mechanism is *de*struct. Money of course is *de*struct. When the last grave is dug, the gravedigger will have to be paid. If you could have confidence in nature you would not have to fear. It would keep you up. Creative is nature. Rapid. Lavish. Inspirational. It shapes leaves. It rolls the waters of the earth. Man is the chief of this. All creations are his just inheritance. You don't know what you've got within you. A person either creates or he destroys. There is no neutrality . . ."

"I realized you were no beginner," said Wilhelm with propriety. "I have only one criticism to make. I think 'why-forth' is wrong. You should write 'Wherefore then dost thou . . .'" And he reflected, So? I took a gamble. It'll have to be a miracle, though, to save me. My money will be gone, then it won't be able to destruct me. He can't just take and lose it, though. He's in it, too. I think he's

---

[5] A law of physics formulated by Max Planck (1858–1947), German physicist.

in a bad way himself. He must be. I'm sure because, come to think of it, he sweated blood when he signed that check. But what have I let myself in for? The waters of the earth are going to roll over me.

V

Patiently, in the window of the fruit store, a man with a scoop spread crushed ice between his rows of vegetables. There were also Persian melons, lilacs, tulips with radiant black at the middle. The many street noises came back after a little while from the caves of the sky. Crossing the tide of Broadway traffic, Wilhelm was saying to himself, the reason Tamkin lectures me is that somebody has lectured him, and the reason for the poem is that he wants to give me good advice. Everybody seems to know something. Even fellows like Tamkin. Many people know what to do, but how many can do it?

He believed that he must, that he could and would recover the good things, the happy things, the easy tranquil things of life. He had made mistakes, but he could overlook these. He had been a fool, but that could be forgiven. The time wasted—must be relinquished. What else could one do about it? Things were too complex, but they might be reduced to simplicity again. Recovery was possible. First he had to get out of the city. No, first he had to pull out his money. . . .

From the carnival of the street—pushcharts, accordion and fiddle, shoeshine, begging, the dust going round like a woman on stilts—they entered the narrow crowded theater of the brokerage office. From front to back it was filled with the Broadway crowd. But how was lard doing this morning? From the rear of the hall Wilhelm tried to read the tiny figures. The German manager was looking through his binoculars. Tamkin placed himself on Wilhelm's left and covered his conspicuous bald head. "The guy'll ask me about the margin," he muttered. They passed, however, unobserved. "Look, the lard has held its place," he said.

Tamkin's eyes must be very sharp to read the figures over so many heads and at this distance—another respect in which he was unusual.

The room was always crowded. Everyone talked. Only at the front could you hear the flutter of the wheels within the board. Teletyped news items crossed the illuminated screen above.

"Lard. Now what about rye?" said Tamkin, rising on his toes. Here he was a different man, active and impatient. He parted people who stood in his way. His face turned resolute, and on either side of his mouth odd bulges formed under his mustache. Already he was pointing out to Wilhelm the appearance of a new pattern on the board. "There's something up today," he said.

"Then why'd you take so long with breakfast?" said Wilhelm.

There were no reserved seats in the room, only customary ones. Tamkin always sat in the second row, on the commodities side of the aisle. Some of his acquaintances kept their hats on the chairs for him.

"Thanks. Thanks," said Tamkin, and he told Wilhelm, "I fixed it up yesterday."

"That was a smart thought," said Wilhelm. They sat down.

With folded hands, by the wall, sat an old Chinese businessman in a seersucker coat. Smooth and fat, he wore a white Vandyke.[1] One day Wilhelm had seen him on Riverside Drive pushing two little girls along in a baby carriage—his

---

[1]Short, pointed beard.

grandchildren. Then there were two women in their fifties, supposed to be sisters, shrewd and able money-makers, according to Tamkin. They had never a word to say to Wilhelm. But they would chat with Tamkin. Tamkin talked to everyone.

Wilhelm sat between Mr. Rowland, who was elderly, and Mr. Rappaport, who was very old. Yesterday Rowland had told him that in the year 1908, when he was a junior at Harvard, his mother had given him twenty shares of steel for his birthday, and then he had started to read the financial news and had never practiced law but instead followed the market for the rest of his life. Now he speculated only in soy beans, of which he had made a specialty. By his conservative method, said Tamkin, he cleared two hundred a week. Small potatoes, but then he was a bachelor, retired, and didn't need money.

"Without dependents," said Tamkin. "He doesn't have the problems that you and I do."

Did Tamkin have dependents? He had everything that it was possible for a man to have—science, Greek, chemistry, poetry, and now dependents too. That beautiful girl with epilepsy, perhaps. He often said that she was a pure, marvelous, spiritual child who had no knowledge of the world. He protected her, and, if he was not lying, adored her. And if you encouraged Tamkin by believing him, or even if you refrained from questioning him, his hints became more daring. Sometimes he said that he paid for her music lessons. Sometimes he seemed to have footed the bill for the brother's camera expedition to Brazil. And he spoke of paying for the support of the orphaned child of a dead sweetheart. These hints, made dully as asides, grew by repetition into sensational claims.

"For myself, I don't need much," said Tamkin. "But a man can't live for himself and I need the money for certain important things. What do you figure you have to have, to get by?"

"Not less than fifteen grand, after taxes. That's for my wife and the two boys."

"Isn't there anybody else?" said Tamkin with a shrewdness almost cruel. But his look grew more sympathetic as Wilhelm stumbled, not willing to recall another grief.

"Well—there was. But it wasn't a money matter."

"I should hope!" said Tamkin. "If love is love, it's free. Fifteen grand, though, isn't too much for a man of your intelligence to ask out of life. Fools, hardhearted criminals, and murderers have millions to squander. They burn up the world—oil, coal, wood, metal, and soil, and suck even the air and the sky. They consume, and they give back no benefit. A man like you, humble for life, who wants to feel and live, has trouble—not wanting," said Tamkin in his parenthetical fashion, "to exchange an ounce of soul for a pound of social power—he'll never make it without help in a world like this. But don't you worry." Wilhelm grasped at this assurance. "Just you never mind. We'll go easily beyond your figure."

Dr. Tamkin gave Wilhelm comfort. He often said that he had made as much as a thousand a week in commodities. Wilhelm had examined the receipts, but until this moment it had never occurred to him that there must be debit slips too; he had been shown only the credits.

"But fifteen grand is not an ambitious figure," Tamkin was telling him. "For that you don't have to wear yourself out on the road, dealing with narrow-minded people. A lot of them don't like Jews, either, I suppose?"

"I can't afford to notice. I'm lucky when I have my occupation. Tamkin, do you mean you can save our money?"

"Oh, did I forget to mention what I did before closing yesterday? You see, I closed out one of the lard contracts and bought a hedge of December rye. The rye is up three points already and takes some of the sting out. But lard will go up, too."

"Where? God, yes, you're right," said Wilhelm, eager, and got to his feet to look. New hope freshened his heart. "Why didn't you tell me before?"

And Tamkin, smiling like a benevolent magician, said, "You must learn to have trust. The slump in lard can't last. And just take a look at eggs. Didn't I predict they couldn't go any lower? They're rising and rising. If we had taken eggs we'd be far ahead."

"Then why didn't we take them?"

"We were just about to. I had a buying order in at .24, but the tide turned at .26¼ and we barely missed. Never mind. Lard will go back to last year's levels."

Maybe. But when? Wilhelm could not allow his hopes to grow too strong. However, for a little while he could breathe more easily. Late-morning trading was getting active. The shining numbers whirred on the board, which sounded like a huge cage of artificial birds. Lard fluctuated between two points, but rye slowly climbed.

He closed his strained, greatly earnest eyes briefly and nodded his Buddha's head, too large to suffer such uncertainties. For several moments of peace he was removed to his small yard in Roxbury.

He breathed in the sugar of the pure morning.

He heard the long phrases of the birds.

No enemy wanted his life.

Wilhelm thought, I will get out of here. I don't belong in New York any more. And he sighed like a sleeper.

Tamkin said, "Excuse me," and left his seat. He could not sit still in the room but passed back and forth between the stocks and commodities sections. He knew dozens of people and was continually engaging in discussions. Was he giving advice, gathering information, or giving it, or practicing—whatever mysterious profession he practiced? Hypnotism? Perhaps he could put people in a trance while he talked to them. What a rare, peculiar bird he was, with those pointed shoulders, that bare head, his loose nails, almost claws, and those brown, soft, deadly, heavy eyes.

He spoke of things that mattered, and as very few people did this he could take you by surprise, excite you, move you. Maybe he wished to do good, maybe give himself a lift to a higher level, maybe believe his own prophecies, maybe touch his own heart. Who could tell? He had picked up a lot of strange ideas; Wilhelm could only suspect, he could not say with certainty, that Tamkin hadn't made them his own.

Now Tamkin and he were equal partners, but Tamkin had put up only three hundred dollars. Suppose he did this not only once but five times; then an investment of fifteen hundred dollars gave him five thousand to speculate with. If he had power of attorney in every case, he could shift the money from one account to another. No, the German probably kept an eye on him. Nevertheless it was possible. Calculations like this made Wilhelm feel ill. Obviously Tamkin was a plunger. But how did he get by? He must be in his fifties. How did he support himself? Five years in Egypt; Hollywood before that; Michigan; Ohio; Chicago. A man of fifty has supported himself for at least thirty years. You could be sure that Tamkin had never worked in a factory or in an office. How did he make it? His taste in clothes was horrible, but he didn't buy cheap things. He wore corduroy or velvet shirts from Clyde's, painted neckties, striped socks.

There was a slightly acid or pasty smell about his person; for a doctor, he didn't bathe much. Also, Dr. Tamkin had a good room at the Gloriana and had had it for about a year. But so was Wilhelm himself a guest, with an unpaid bill at present in his father's box. Did the beautiful girl with the skirts and belts pay him? Was he defrauding his so-called patients? So many questions impossible to answer could not be asked about an honest man. Nor perhaps about a sane man. Was Tamkin a lunatic, then? That sick Mr. Perls at breakfast had said that there was no easy way to tell the sane from the mad, and he was right about that in any big city and especially in New York—the end of the world, with its complexity and machinery, bricks and tubes, wires and stones, holes and heights. And was everybody crazy here? What sort of people did you see? Every other man spoke a language entirely his own, which he had figured out by private thinking; he had his own ideas and peculiar ways. If you wanted to talk about a glass of water, you had to start back with God creating the heavens and earth; the apple; Abraham; Moses and Jesus; Rome; the Middle Ages; gunpowder; the Revolution; back to Newton; up to Einstein; then war and Lenin and Hitler. After reviewing this and getting it all straight again you could proceed to talk about a glass of water. "I'm fainting, please get me a little water." You were lucky even then to make yourself understood. And this happened over and over and over with everyone you met. You had to translate and translate, explain and explain, back and forth, and it was the punishment of hell itself not to understand or be understood, not to know the crazy from the sane, the wise from the fools, the young from the old or the sick from the well. The fathers were no fathers and the sons no sons. You had to talk with yourself in the daytime and reason with yourself at night. Who else was there to talk to in a city like New York?

A queer look came over Wilhelm's face with its eyes turned up and his silent mouth with its higher upper lip. He went several degrees further—when you are like this, dreaming that everybody is outcast, you realize that this must be one of the small matters. There is a larger body, and from this you cannot be separated. The glass of water fades out. You do not go from simple a and simple b to the great x and y, nor does it matter whether you agree about the glass but, far beneath such details, what Tamkin would call the real soul says plain and understandable things to everyone. There sons and fathers are themselves, and a glass of water is only an ornament; it makes a hoop of brightness on the cloth; it is an angel's mouth. There truth for everybody may be found, and confusion is only—only temporary, thought Wilhelm.

The idea of this larger body had been planted in him a few days ago beneath Times Square, when he had gone downtown to pick up tickets for the baseball game on Saturday (a double-header at the Polo Grounds). He was going through an underground corridor, a place he had always hated and hated more than ever now. On the walls between the advertisements were words in chalk: "Sin No More," and "Do Not Eat the Pig," he had particularly noticed. And in the dark tunnel, in the haste, heat, and darkness which disfigure and make freaks and fragments of nose and eyes and teeth, all of a sudden, unsought, a general love for all these imperfect and lurid-looking people burst out in Wilhelm's breast. He loved them. One and all, he passionately loved them. They were his brothers and his sisters. He was imperfect and disfigured himself, but what difference did that make if he was united with them by his blaze of love? And as he walked he began to say, "Oh my brothers—my brothers and my sisters," blessing them all as well as himself.

So what did it matter how many languages there were, or how hard it was to describe a glass of water? Or matter that a few minutes later he didn't feel anything like a brother toward the man who sold him the tickets?

On that same afternoon he didn't hold so high an opinion of this same onrush of loving kindness. What did it come to? As they had the capacity and must use it once in a while, people were bound to have such involuntary feelings. It was only another one of those subway things. Like having a hard-on at random. But today, his day of reckoning, he consulted his memory again and thought, I must go back to that. That's the right clue and may do me the most good. Something very big. Truth, like.

The old fellow on the right, Mr. Rappaport, was nearly blind and kept asking Wilhelm, "What's the new figure on November wheat? Give me July soy beans too." When you told him he didn't say thank you. He said, "Okay," instead, or, "Check," and turned away until he needed you again. He was very old, older even than Dr. Adler, and if you believed Tamkin he had once been the Rockefeller of the chicken business and had retired with a large fortune.

Wilhelm had a queer feeling about the chicken industry, that it was sinister. On the road, he frequently passed chicken farms. Those big, rambling, wooden buildings out in the neglected fields; they were like prisons. The lights burned all night in them to cheat the poor hens into laying. Then the slaughter. Pile all the coops of the slaughtered on end, and in one week they'd go higher than Mount Everest or Mount Serenity. The blood filling the Gulf of Mexico. The chicken shit, acid, burning the earth.

How old—old this Mr. Rappaport was! Purple stains were buried in the flesh of his nose, and the cartilage of his ear was twisted like a cabbage heart. Beyond remedy by glasses, his eyes were smoky and faded.

"Read me that soy-bean figure now, boy," he said, and Wilhelm did. He thought perhaps the old man might give him a tip, or some useful advice or information about Tamkin. But, no. He only wrote memoranda on a pad, and put the pad in his pocket. He let no one see what he had written. And Wilhelm thought this was the way a man who had grown rich by the murder of millions of animals, little chickens, would act. If there was a life to come he might have to answer for the killing of all those chickens. What if they all were waiting? But if there was a life to come, everybody would have to answer. But if there was a life to come, the chickens themselves would be all right.

Well! What stupid ideas he was having this morning. Phooey!

Finally old Rappaport did address a few remarks to Wilhelm. He asked him whether he had reserved his seat in the synagogue for Yom Kippur.[2]

"No," said Wilhelm.

"Well, you better hurry up if you expect to say *Yiskor*[3] for your parents. I never miss."

And Wilhelm thought, Yes, I suppose I should say a prayer for Mother once in a while. His mother had belonged to the Reform congregation. His father had no religion. At the cemetery Wilhelm had paid a man to say a prayer for her. He was among the tombs and he wanted to be tipped for the *El molai rachamin*. "Thou God of Mercy," Wilhelm thought that meant. *B'gan Aden*—"in Paradise." Singing, they drew it out, *B'gan Ay–den*. The broken bench beside the grave made him wish to do something. Wilhelm often prayed in his own manner. He did not go to the synagogue but he would occasionally perform certain devotions, according to his feelings. Now he reflected, In Dad's eyes I

[2]Hebrew: "Day of Atonement," a Jewish religious holiday.
[3]Jewish religious service for the dead.

am the wrong kind of Jew. He doesn't like the way I act. Only he is the right kind of Jew. Whatever you are, it always turns out to be the wrong kind."

Mr. Rappaport grumbled and whiffed at his long cigar, and the board, like a swarm of electrical bees, whirred.

"Since you were in the chicken business, I thought you'd speculate in eggs, Mr. Rappaport." Wilhelm, with his warm, panting laugh, sought to charm the old man.

"Oh. Yeah. Loyalty, hey?" said old Rappaport. "I should stick to them. I spent a lot of time amongst chickens. I got to be an expert chicken-sexer. When the chick hatches you have to tell the boys from the girls. It's not easy. You need long, long experience. What do you think it's a joke? A whole industry depends on it. Yes, now and then I buy a contract eggs. What have you got today?"

Wilhelm said anxiously, "Lard, Rye."

"Buy? Sell?"

"Bought."

"Uh," said the old man. Wilhelm could not determine what he meant by this. But of course you couldn't expect him to make himself any clearer. It was not in the code to give information to anyone. Sick with desire, Wilhelm waited for Mr. Rappaport to make an exception in his case. Just this once! Because it was critical. Silently, by a sort of telephathic concentration, he begged the old man to speak the single word that would save him, give him the merest sign. "Oh, please—please help," he nearly said. If Rappaport would close one eye, or lay his head to one side, or raise his finger and point to a column in the paper or to a figure on his pad. A hint! A hint!

A long perfect ash formed on the end of the cigar, the white ghost of the leaf with all its veins and its fainter pungency. It was ignored, in its beauty, by the old man. For it was beautiful. Wilhelm he ignored as well.

Then Tamkin said to him, "Wilhelm, look at the jump our rye just took."

December rye climbed three points as they tensely watched; the tumblers raced and the machine's lights buzzed.

"A point and a half more, and we can cover the lard losses," said Tamkin. He showed him his calculations on the margin of the *Times.*

"I think you should put in the selling order now. Let's get out with a small loss."

"Get out now? Nothing doing."

"Why not? Why should we wait?"

"Because," said Tamkin with a smiling, almost openly scoffing look, "you've got to keep your nerve when the market starts to go places. Now's when you can make something."

"I'd get out while the getting's good."

"No, you shouldn't lose your head like this. It's obvious to me what the mechanism is, back in the Chicago market. There's a short supply of December rye. Look, it's just gone up another quarter. We should ride it."

"I'm losing my taste for the gamble," said Wilhelm. "You can't feel safe when it goes up so fast. It's liable to come down again just as quick."

Dryly, as though he were dealing with a child, Tamkin told him in a tone of tiring patience, "Now, listen, Tommy. I have it diagnosed right. If you wish I should sell I can give the sell order. But this is the difference between healthiness and pathology. One is objective, doesn't change his mind every minute, enjoys the risk element. But that's not the neurotic character. The neurotic character—"

"Damn it, Tamkin!" said Wilhelm roughly. "Cut that out. I don't like it. Leave my character out of consideration. Don't pull any more of that stuff on me. I tell you I don't like it."

Tamkin therefore went no further; he backed down. "I meant," he said, softer, "that as a salesman you are basically an artist type. The seller is in the visionary sphere of the business function. And then you're an actor, too."

"No matter what type I am—" An angry and yet weak sweetness rose into Wilhelm's throat. He coughed as though he had the flu. It was twenty years since he had appeared on the screen as an extra. He blew the bagpipes in a film called *Annie Laurie*. Annie had come to warn the young Laird; he would not believe her and called the bagpipers to drown her out. He made fun of her while she wrung her hands. Wilhelm, in a kilt, barelegged, blew and blew and blew and not a sound came out. Of course all the music was recorded. He fell sick with the flu after that and still suffered sometimes from chest weakness.

"Something stuck in your throat?" said Tamkin. "I think maybe you are too disturbed to think clearly. You should try some of my 'here-and-now' mental exercises. It stops you from thinking so much about the future and the past and cuts down confusion."

"Yes, yes, yes, yes," said Wilhelm, his eyes fixed on December rye.

"Nature only knows one thing, and that's the present. Present present, eternal present, like a big, huge, giant wave—colossal, bright and beautiful, full of life and death, climbing into the sky, standing in the seas. You must go along with the actual, the Here-and-Now, the glory—"

. . . chest weakness, Wilhelm's recollection went on. Margaret nursed him. They had had two rooms of furniture, which was later seized. She sat on the bed and read to him. He made her read for days, and she read stories, poetry, everything in the house. He felt dizzy, stifled when he tried to smoke. They had him wear a flannel vest.

> Come then, Sorrow!
> Sweetest Sorrow!
> Like an own babe I nurse thee on my breast!

Why did he remember that? Why?

"You have to pick out something that's in the actual, immediate present moment," said Tamkin. "And say to yourself here-and-now, here-and-now. 'Where am I?' 'Here.' 'When is it?' 'Now.' Take an object or a person. Anybody. 'Here and now I see a person.' 'Here and now I see a man.' 'Here and now I see a man sitting on a chair.' Take me, for instance. Don't let your mind wander. 'Here and now I see a man in a brown suit. Here and now I see a corduroy shirt.' You have to narrow it down, one item at a time, and not let your imagination shoot ahead. Be in the present. Grasp the hour, the moment, the instant."

Is he trying to hypnotize or con me? Wilhelm wondered. To take my mind off selling? But even if I'm back at seven hundred bucks, then where am I?

As if in prayer, his lids coming down with raised veins, frayed out, on his significant eyes, Tamkin said, " 'Here and now I see a button. Here and now I see the thread that sews the button. Here and now I see the green thread.' " Inch by inch he contemplated himself in order to show Wilhelm how calm it would make him. But Wilhelm was hearing Margaret's voice as she read, somewhat unwillingly,

> Come then, Sorrow!
> .   .   .   .
> I thought to leave thee,

And deceive thee,
But now of all the world I love thee best.[4]

Then Mr. Rappaport's old hand pressed his thigh, and he said, "What's my wheat? Those damn guys are blocking the way. I can't see."

VI

Rye was still ahead when they went out to lunch, and lard was holding its own.

They ate in the cafeteria with the gilded front. There was the same art inside as outside. The food looked sumptuous. Whole fishes were framed like pictures with carrots, and the salads were like terraced landscapes or like Mexican pyramids; slices of lemon and onion and radishes were like sun and moon and stars; the cream pies were about a foot thick and the cakes swollen as if sleepers had baked them in their dreams.

"What'll you have?" said Tamkin.

"Not much. I ate a big breakfast. I'll find a table. Bring me some yogurt and crackers and a cup of tea. I don't want to spend much time over lunch."

Tamkin said, "You've got to eat."

Finding an empty place at this hour was not easy. The old people idled and gossiped over their coffee. The elderly ladies were rouged and mascaraed and hennaed and used blue hair rinse and eye shadow and wore costume jewelry, and many of them were proud and stared at you with expressions that did not belong to their age. Were there no longer any respectable old ladies who knitted and cooked and looked after their grandchildren? Wilhelm's grandmother had dressed him in a sailor suit and danced him on her knee, blew on the porridge for him and said, "Admiral, you must eat." But what was the use of remembering this so late in the day?

He managed to find a table, and Dr. Tamkin came along with a tray piled with plates and cups. He had Yankee pot roast, purple cabbage, potatoes, a big slice of watermelon, and two cups of coffee. Wilhelm could not even swallow his yogurt. His chest pained him still.

At once Tamkin involved him in a lengthy discussion. Did he do it to stall Wilhelm and prevent him from selling out the rye—or to recover the ground lost when he had made Wilhelm angry by hints about the neurotic character? Or did he have no purpose except to talk?

"I think you worry a lot too much about what your wife and your father will say. Do they matter so much?"

Wilhelm replied, "A person can become tired of looking himself over and trying to fix himself up. You can spend the entire second half of your life recovering from the mistakes of the first half."

"I believe your dad told me he had some money to leave you."

"He probably does have something."

"A lot?"

"Who can tell," said Wilhelm guardedly.

"You ought to think over what you'll do with it."

"I may be too feeble to do anything by the time I get it. If I get anything."

"A thing like this you ought to plan out carefully. Invest it properly." He began to unfold schemes whereby you bought bonds, and used the bonds as

[4]From *Endymion* (1817–1818), Book IV, lines 279–284, by the English poet John Keats (1795–1821).

security to buy something else and thereby earned twelve per cent safely on your money. Wilhelm failed to follow the details. Tamkin said, "If he made you a gift now, you wouldn't have to pay the inheritance taxes."

Bitterly, Wilhelm told him, "My father's death blots out all other considerations from his mind. He forces me to think abut it, too. Then he hates me because he succeeds. When I get desperate—of course I think about money. But I don't want anything to happen to him. I certainly don't want him to die." Tamkin's brown eyes glittered shrewdly at him. "You don't believe it. Maybe it's not psychological. But on my word of honor. A joke is a joke, but I don't want to joke about stuff like this. When he dies, I'll be robbed, like. I'll have no more father."

"You love your old man?"

Wilhelm grasped at this. "Of course, of course I love him. My father. My mother—" As he said this there was a great pull at the very center of his soul. When a fish strikes the line you feel the live force in your hand. A mysterious being beneath the water, driven by hunger, has taken the hook and rushes away and fights, writhing. Wilhelm never identified what struck within him. It did not reveal itself. It got away.

And Tamkin, the confuser of the imagination, began to tell, or to fabricate, the strange history of *his* father. "He was a great singer," he said. "He left us five kids because he fell in love with an opera soprano. I never held it against him, but admired the way he followed the life-principle. I wanted to do the same. Because of unhappiness, at a certain age, the brain starts to die back." (True, true! thought Wilhelm) "Twenty years later I was doing experiments in Eastman Kodak, Rochester, and I found the old fellow. He had five more children." (False, false!) "He wept; he was ashamed. I had nothing against him. I naturally felt strange."

"My dad is something of a stranger to me, too," said Wilhelm, and he began to muse. Where is the familiar person he used to be? Or I used to be? Catherine— she won't even talk to me any more, my own sister. It may not be so much my trouble that Papa turns his back on as my confusion. It's too much. The ruins of life, and on top of that confusion—chaos and old night. Is it an easier farewell for Dad if we don't part friends? He should maybe do it angrily—"Blast you with my curse!" And why, Wilhelm further asked, should he or anybody else pity me; or why should I be pitied sooner than another fellow? It is my childish mind that thinks people are ready to give it just because you need it.

Then Wilhelm began to think about his own two sons and to wonder how he appeared to them, and what they would think of him. Right now he had an advantage through baseball. When he went to fetch them, to go to Ebbets Field,[1] though, he was not himself. He put on a front but he felt as if he had swallowed a fistful of sand. The strange, familiar house, horribly awkward; the dog, Scissors, rolled over on his back and barked and whined. Wilhelm acted as if there were nothing irregular, but a weary heaviness came over him. On the way to Flatbush he would think up anecdotes about old Pigtown and Charlie Ebbets for the boys and reminiscences of the old stars, but it was very heavy going. They did not know how much he cared for them. No. It hurt him greatly and he blamed Margeret for turning them against him. She wanted to ruin him, while she wore the mask of kindness. Up in Roxbury he had to go and explain to the priest, who was not sympathetic. They don't care about individuals, their

---

[1]Home field (1913–1958) for the Brooklyn Dodgers baseball team. Built in "Pigtown," a slum area near the former village of Flatbush, the field was named after Charles Ebbets, long-time owner of the Dodgers.

rules come first. Olive said she would marry him outside the Church when he was divorced. But Margaret would not let go. Olive's father was a pretty decent old guy, an osteopath, and he understood what it was all about. Finally he said, "See here, I have to advise Olive. She is asking me. I am mostly a freethinker myself, but the girl has to live in this town." And by now Wilhelm and Olive had had a great many troubles and she was beginning to dread his days in Roxbury, she said. He trembled at offending this small, pretty, dark girl whom he adored. When she would get up late on Sunday morning she would wake him almost in tears at being late for Mass. He would try to help her hitch her garters and smooth out her slip and dress and even put on her hat with shaky hands; then he would rush her to church and drive in second gear in his forgetful way, trying to apologize and to calm her. She got out a block from church to avoid gossip. Even so she loved him, and she would have married him if he had obtained the divorce. But Margaret must have sensed this. Margaret would tell him he did not really want a divorce; he was afraid of it. He cried. "Take everything I've got, Margaret. Let me go to Reno. Don't you want to marry again?" No. She went out with other men, but took his money. She lived in order to punish him.

Dr. Tamkin told Wilhelm, "Your dad is jealous of you."

Wilhelm smiled. "Of *me*? That's rich."

"Sure. People are always jealous of a man who leaves his wife."

"Oh," said Wilhelm scornfully. "When it comes to wives he wouldn't have to envy me."

"Yes, and your wife envies you, too. She thinks, He's free and goes with young women. Is she getting old?"

"Not exactly old," said Wilhelm, whom the mention of his wife made sad. Twenty years ago, in a neat blue wool suit, in a soft hat made of the same cloth— he could plainly see her. He stooped his yellow head and looked under the hat at the clear, simple face, her living eyes moving, her straight small nose, her jaw beautifully, painfully clear in its form. It was a cool day, but he smelled the odor of pines in the sun, in the granite canyon. Just south of Santa Barbara, this was.

"She's forty-some years old," he said.

"I was married to a lush, said Tamkin. "A painful alcoholic. I couldn't take her out to dinner because she'd say she was going to the ladies' toilet and disappear into the bar. I'd ask the bartenders they shouldn't serve her. But I loved her deeply. She was the most spiritual woman of my entire experience."

"Where is she now?"

"Drowned," said Tamkin. "At Provincetown, Cape Cod. It must have been a suicide. She was that way—suicidal. I tried everything in my power to cure her. Because," said Tamkin, "my real calling is to be a healer. I get wounded. I suffer from it. I would like to escape from the sicknesses of others, but I can't. I am only on loan to myself, so to speak. I belong to humanity."

Liar! Wilhelm inwardly called him. Nasty lies. He invented a woman and killed her off and then called himself a healer, and made himself so earnest he looked like a bad-natured sheep. He's a puffed-up little bogus and humbug with smelly feet. A doctor! A doctor would wash himself. He believes he's making a terrific impression, and he practically invites you to take off your hat when he talks about himself; and he thinks he has an imagination, but he hasn't, neither is he smart.

Then what am I doing with him here, and why did I give him the seven hundred dollars? thought Wilhelm.

Oh, this was a day of reckoning. It was a day, he thought, on which, willing or not, he would take a good close look at the truth. He breathed hard and his misshapen hat came low upon his congested dark blond face. A rude look. Tamkin was a charlatan, and furthermore he was desperate. And furthermore, Wilhelm had always known this about him. But he appeared to have worked it out at the back of his mind that Tamkin for thirty of forty years had gotten through many a tight place, that he would get through this crisis too and bring him, Wilhelm, to safety also. And Wilhelm realized that he was on Tamkin's back. It made him feel that he had virtually left the ground and was riding upon the other man. He was in the air. It was for Tamkin to take the steps.

The doctor, if he was a doctor, did not look anxious. But then the face did not have much variety. Talking always about spontaneous emotion and open receptors and free impulses, he was about as expressive as a pincushion. When his hypnotic spell failed, his big underlip made him look weak-minded. Fear started from his eyes, sometimes, so humble as to make you sorry for him. Once or twice Wilhelm had seen that look. Like a dog, he thought. Perhaps he didn't look it now, but he was very nervous. Wilhelm knew, but he could not afford to recognize this too openly. The doctor needed a little room, a little time. He should not be pressed now. So Tamkin went on, telling his tales.

Wilhelm said to himself, I am on his back—his back. I gambled seven hundred bucks, so I must take this ride. I have to go along with him. It's too late. I can't get off.

"You know," Tamkin said, "that blind old man Rappaport—he's pretty close to totally blind—is one of the most interesting personalities around here. If you could only get him to tell his true story. It's fascinating. This is what he told me. You often hear about bigamists with a secret life. But this old man never hid anything from anybody. He's a regular patriarch. Now, I'll tell you what he did. He had two whole families, separate and apart, one in Williamsburg and the other in the Bronx. The two wives knew about each other. The wife in the Bronx was younger; she's close to seventy now. When he got sore at one wife he went to live with the other. Meanwhile he ran his chicken business in New Jersey. By one wife he had four kids, and by the other six. They're all grown, but they never have met their half-brothers and sisters and don't want to. The whole bunch of them are listed in the telephone book."

"I can't believe it," said Wilhelm.

"He told me this himself. And do you know what else? While he had his eyesight he used to read a lot, but the only books he would read were by Theodore Roosevelt. He had a set in each of the places where he lived, and he brought his kids up on those books."

"Please," said Wilhelm, "don't feed me any more of this stuff, will you? Kindly do not—"

"In telling you this," said Tamkin with one of his hypnotic subtleties, "I do have a motive. I want you to see how some people free themselves from morbid guilt feelings and follow their instincts. Innately, the female knows how to cripple by sickening a man with guilt. It is a very special *de*struct, and she sends her curse to make him feel impotent. As if she says, 'Unless I allow it, you will never more be a man.' But men like my old dad or Mr. Rappaport answer, 'Woman, what art thou to me?' You can't do that yet. You're a half way case. You want to follow your instinct, but you're too worried still. For instance, about your kids—"

"Now, look here," said Wilhelm, stamping his feet. "One thing! Don't bring up my boys. Just lay off."

"I was only going to say that they are better off than with conflicts in the home."

"I'm deprived of my children." Wilhelm bit his lip. It was too late to turn away. The anguish struck him. "I pay and pay. I never see them. They grow up without me. She makes them like herself. She'll bring them up to be my enemies. Please let's not talk about this."

But Tamkin said, "Why do you let her make you suffer so? It defeats the original object in leaving her. Don't play her game. Now, Wilhelm, I'm trying to do you some good. I want to tell you, don't marry suffering. Some people do. They get married to it, and sleep and eat together, just as husband and wife. If they go with joy they think it's adultery."

When Wilhelm heard this he had, in spite of himself, to admit that there was a great deal in Tamkin's words. Yes, thought Wilhelm, suffering is the only kind of life they are sure they can have, and if they quit suffering they're afraid they'll have nothing. He knows it. This time the faker knows what he's talking about.

Looking at Tamkin he believed he saw all this confessed from his usually barren face. Yes, yes, he too. One hundred falsehoods, but at last one truth. Howling like a wolf from the city window. No one can bear it any more. Everyone is so full of it that at last everybody must proclaim it. It! It!

Then suddenly Wilhelm rose and said, "That's enought of this Tamkin, let's go back to the market."

"I haven't finished my melon."

"Never mind that. You've had enough to eat. I want to go back."

Dr. Tamkin slid the two checks across the table. "Who paid yesterday? It's your turn, I think."

It was not until they were leaving the cafeteria that Wilhelm remembered definitely that he had paid yesterday too. But it wasn't worth arguing about.

Tamkin kept repeating as they walked down the street that there were many who were dedicated to suffering. But he told Wilhelm, "I'm optimistic in your case, and I have seen a world of maladjustment. There's hope for you. You don't really want to destroy yourself. You're trying hard to keep your feelings open, Wilhelm. I can see it. Seven per cent of this country is committing suicide by alcohol. Another three, maybe, narcotics. Another sixty just fading away into dust by boredom. Twenty more who have sold their souls to the devil. Then there's a small percentage of those who want to live. That's the only significant thing in the whole world of today. Those are the only two classes of people there are. Some want to live, but the great majority don't." This fantastic Tamkin began to surpass himself. "They don't. Or else, why these wars? I'll tell you more," he said. "The love of the dying amounts to one thing; they want you to die with them. It's because they love you. Make no mistake."

True, true! thought Wilhelm, profoundly moved by these revelations. How does he know these things? How can he be such a jerk, and even perhaps an operator, a swindler, and understand so well what gives? I believe what he says. It simplifies much—everything. People are dropping like flies. I am trying to stay alive and work too hard at it. That's what's turning my brains. This working hard defeats its own end. At what point should I start over? Let me go back a ways and try once more.

Only a few hundred yards separated the cafeteria from the broker's, and within that short space Wilhelm turned again, in measurable degrees, from these wide considerations to the problems of the moment. The closer he approached to the market, the more Wilhelm had to think about money.

They passed the newsreel theater where the ragged shoeshine kids called after them. The same old bearded man with his bandaged beggar face and his tiny ragged feet and the old press clipping on his fiddle case to prove he had once been a concert violinist, pointed his bow at Wilhelm, saying, "You!" Wilhelm went by with worried eyes, bent on crossing Seventy-second Street. In full tumult the great afternoon current raced for Columbus Circle, where the mouth of midtown stood open and the skyscrapers gave back the yellow fire of the sun.

As they approached the polished stone front of the new office building, Dr. Tamkin said, "Well, isn't that old Rappaport by the door? I think he should carry a white cane, but he will never admit there's a single thing the matter with his eyes."

Mr. Rappaport did not stand well; his knees were sunk, while his pelvis only half filled his trousers. His suspenders held them, gaping.

He stopped Wilhelm with an extended hand, having somehow recognized him. In his deep voice he commanded him, "Take me to the cigar store."

"You want me—? Tamkin!" Wilhelm whispered, "You take him."

Tamkin shook his head. "He wants you. Don't refuse the old gentleman." Significantly he said in a lower voice. "This minute is another instance of the 'here-and-now.' You have to live in this very minute, and you don't want to. A man asks you for help. Don't think of the market. It won't run away. Show your respect to the old boy. Go ahead. That may be more valuable."

"Take me," said the old chicken merchant again.

Greatly annoyed, Wilhelm wrinkled his face at Tamkin. He took the old man's big but light elbow at the bone. "Well, let's step on it," he said. "Or wait—I want to have a look at the board first to see how we're doing."

But Tamkin had already started Mr. Rappaport forward. He was walking, and he scolded Wilhelm, saying, "Don't leave me standing in the middle of the sidewalk. I'm afraid to get knocked over."

"Let's get a move on. Come," Wilhelm urged him as Tamkin went into the broker's.

The traffic seemed to come down Broadway out of the sky, where the hot spokes of the sun rolled from the south. Hot, stony odors rose from the subway grating in the street.

"The teen-age hoodlums worry me. I'm ascared of these Puerto Rican kids, and these young characters who take dope," said Mr. Rappaport. "They go around all hopped up."

"Hoodlums?" said Wilhelm. "I went to the cemetery and my mother's stone bench was split. I could have broken somebody's neck for that. Which store do you go to?"

"Across Broadway. That La Magnita sign next door to the Automat."

"What's the matter with this store here on this side?"

"They don't carry my brand, that's what's the matter."

Wilhelm cursed, but checked the words.

"What are you talking?"

"Those damn taxis," said Wilhelm. "They want to run everybody down."

They entered the cool, odorous shop. Mr. Rappaport put away his large cigars with great care in various pockets while Wilhelm muttered, "Come on, you old creeper. What a poky old character! The whole world waits on him." Rappaport did not offer Wilhelm a cigar, but, holding one up, he asked, "What do you say at the size of these, huh? They're Churchill-type cigars."[2]

---

[2]Winston Churchill, prime minister of Great Britain (1940–1945, 1951–1955), was noted for smoking large cigars.

He barely crawls along, thought Wilhelm. His pants are dropping off because he hasn't got enough flesh for them to stick to. He's almost blind, and covered with spots, but this old man still makes money in the market. Is loaded with dough, probably. And I bet he doesn't give his children any. Some of them must be in their fifties. This is what keeps middle-aged men as children. He's master over the dough. Think—just think! Who controls everything? Old men of this type. Without needs. They don't need therefore they have. I need, therefore I don't have. That would be too easy.

"I'm older even than Churchill," said Rappaport.

Now he wanted to talk! But if you asked him a question in the market, he couldn't be bothered to answer.

"I bet you are," said Wilhelm. "Come, let's get going."

"I was a fighter, too, like Churchill," said the old man. "When we licked Spain[3] I went into the Navy. Yes, I was a gob[4] that time. What did I have to lose? Nothing. After the battle of San Juan Hill, Teddy Roosevelt[5] kicked me off the beach."

"Come, watch the curb," said Wilhelm.

"I was serious and wanted to see what went on. I didn't have no business there, but I took a boat and rowed myself to the beach. Two of our guys was dead, layin' under the American flag to keep the flies off. So I says to the guy on duty, there, who was the sentry, 'Let's have a look at these guys. I want to see what went on here,' and he says, 'Naw,' but I talked him into it. So he took off the flag and there were these two tall guys, both gentlemen, lying in their boots. They was very tall. The two of them had long mustaches. They were high-society boys. I think one of them was called Fish, from up the Hudson, a big-shot family. When I looked up, there was Teddy Roosevelt, with his hat off, and he was looking at these fellows, the only ones who got killed there. Then he says to me, "What's the Navy want here? Have you got orders?' 'No, sir,' I says to him. 'Well, get the hell off the beach, then.' "

Old Rappaport was very proud of this memory. "Everything he said had such snap, such class. Man! I love that Teddy Roosevelt," he said, "I love him!"

Ah, what people are! He is almost not with us, and his life is nearly gone, but T. R. once yelled at him, so he loves him. I guess it is love, too. Wilhelm smiled. So maybe the rest of Tamkin's story was true, about the ten children and the wives and the telephone directory.

He said, "Come on, come on, Mr. Rappaport," and hurried the old man back by the large hollow elbow; he gripped it through the thin cotton cloth. Re-entering the brokerage office where under the lights the tumblers[6] were speeding with the clack of drumsticks upon wooden blocks, more than ever resembling a Chinese theater, Wilhelm strained his eyes to see the board.

The lard figures were unfamiliar. That amount couldn't be lard! They must have put the figures in the wrong slot. He traced the line back to the margin. It was down to .19, and had dropped twenty points since noon. And what about the contract of rye? It had sunk back to its earlier position, and they had lost their chance to sell.

Old Mr. Rappaport said to Wilhelm, "Read me my wheat figure."

---

[3]In the Spanish-American War (April–December 1898).

[4]Slang: sailor in the U.S. Navy.

[5]Theodore Roosevelt (1858–1919), president of the United States (1901–1909). On July 1–2, 1898, Roosevelt led a force of Rough Riders in the Battle of San Juan Hill during the invasion of Cuba in the Spanish-American War.

[6]Revolving numerals on a display board that show stock market prices.

"Oh, leave me alone for a minute," he said, and positively hid his face from the old man behind one hand. He looked for Tamkin, Tamkin's bald head, or Tamkin with his gray straw and the cocoa-colored band. He couldn't see him. Where was he? The seats next to Rowland were taken by strangers. He thrust himself over the one on the aisle, Mr. Rappaport's former place, and pushed at the back of the chair until the new occupant, a red-headed man with a thin, determined face, leaned forward to get out of his way but would not surrender the seat. "Where's Tamkin?" Wilhelm asked Rowland.

"Gee, I don't know. Is anything wrong?"

"You must have seen him. He came in a while back."

"No, but I didn't."

Wilhelm fumbled out a pencil from the top pocket of his coat and began to make calculations. His very fingers were numb, and in his agitation he was afraid he made mistakes with the decimal points and went over the subtraction and multiplication like a schoolboy at an exam. His heart, accustomed to many sorts of crisis, was now in a new panic. And, as he had dreaded, he was wiped out. It was unnecessary to ask the German manager. He could see for himself that the electronic bookkeeping device must have closed him out. The manager probably had known that Tamkin wasn't to be trusted, and on that first day he might have warned him. But you couldn't expect him to interfere.

"You get hit?" said Mr. Rowland.

And Wilhelm, quite coolly, said, "Oh, it could have been worse I guess." He put the piece of paper into his pocket with its cigarette butts and packets of pills. The lie helped him out—although, for a moment, he was afraid he would cry. But he hardened himself. The hardening effort made a violent, vertical pain go through his chest, like that caused by a pocket of air under the collar bones. To the old chicken millionaire, who by this time had become acquainted with the drop in rye and lard, he also denied that anything serious had happened. "It's just one of those temporary slumps. Nothing to be scared about," he said, and remained in possession of himself. His need to cry, like someone in a crowd, pushed and jostled and abused him from behind, and Wilhelm did not dare turn. He said to himself, I will not cry in front of these people. I'll be damned if I'll break down in front of them like a kid, even though I never expect to see them again. No! No! And yet his unshed tears rose and rose and he looked like a man about to drown. But when they talked to him, he answered very distinctly. He tried to speak proudly.

". . . going away?" he heard Rowland ask.

"What?"

"I thought you might be going away too. Tamkin said he was going to Maine this summer for his vacation."

"Oh, going away?"

Wilhelm broke off and went to look for Tamkin in the men's toilet. Across the corridor was the room where the machinery of the board was housed. It hummed and whirred like mechanical birds, and the tubes glittered in the dark. A couple of businessmen with cigarettes in their fingers were having a conversation in the lavatory. At the top of the closet door sat a gray straw hat with a cocoa-colored band. "Tamkin," said Wilhelm. He tried to identify the feet below the door. "Are you in there, Doctor Tamkin?" he said with stifled anger. "Answer me. It's Wilhelm."

The hat was taken down, the latch lifted, and a stranger came out who looked at him with annoyance.

"You waiting?" said one of the businessmen. He was warning Wilhelm that he was out of turn.

"Me? Not me," said Wilhelm. "I'm looking for a fellow."

Bitterly angry, he said to himself that Tamkin would pay him the two hundred dollars at least, his share of the original deposit. "And before he takes the train to Maine, too. Before he spends a penny on vacation—that liar! We went into this as equal partners."

VII

I was the man beneath; Tamkin was on my back, and I thought I was on his. He made me carry him, too, besides Margaret. Like this they ride on me with hoofs and claws. Tear me to pieces, stamp on me and break my bones.

Once more the hoary old fiddler pointed his bow at Wilhelm as he hurried by. Wilhelm rejected his begging and denied the omen. He dodged heavily through traffic and with his quick, small steps ran up the lower stairway of the Gloriana Hotel with its dark-tinted mirrors, kind to people's defects. From the lobby he phoned Tamkin's room, and when no one answered he took the elevator up. A rouged woman in her fifties with a mink stole led three tiny dogs on a leash, high-strung creatures with prominent black eyes, like dwarf deer, and legs like twigs. This was the eccentric Estonian lady who had been moved with her pets to the twelfth floor.

She identified Wilhelm, "You are Doctor Adler's son," she said.

Formally, he nodded.

"I am a dear friend of your father."

He stood in the corner and would not meet her glance, and she thought he was snubbing her and made a mental note to speak of it to the doctor.

The linen-wagon stood at Tamkin's door, and the chambermaid's key with its big brass tongue was in the lock.

"Has Doctor Tamkin been here?" he asked her.

"No, I haven't seen him."

Wilhelm came in, however, to look around. He examined the photos on the desk, trying to connect the faces with the strange people in Tamkin's stories. Big, heavy volumes were stacked under the double-pronged TV aerial. *Science and Sanity*, he read, and there were several books of poetry. The *Wall Street Journal* hung in separate sheets from the bed-table under the weight of the silver water jug. A bathrobe with lightning streaks of red and white was laid across the foot of the bed with a pair of expensive batik pajamas. It was a box of a room, but from the windows you saw the river as far uptown as the bridge, as far downtown as Hoboken. What lay between was deep, azure, dirty, complex, crystal, rusty, with the red bones of new apartments rising on the bluffs of New Jersey, and huge liners in their berths, the tugs with matted beards of cordage. Even the brackish tidal river smell rose this high, like the smell of mop water. From every side he heard pianos, and the voices of men and women singing scales and opera, all mixed, and the sounds of pigeons on the ledges.

Again Wilhelm took the phone. "Can you locate Doctor Tamkin in the lobby for me?" he asked. And when the operator reported that she could not, Wilhelm gave the number of his father's room, but Dr. Adler was not in either. "Well, please give me the masseur. I say the massage room. Don't you understand me?

The men's health club. Yes, Max Schilper's—how am I suppose to know the name of it?"

There a strange voice said, "Toktor Adler?" It was the old Czech prizefighter with the deformed nose and ears who was attendant down there and gave out soap, sheets, and sandals. He went away. A hollow endless silence followed. Wilhelm flickered the receiver with his nails, whistled into it, but could not summon either the attendant or the operator.

The maid saw him examining the bottles of pills on Tamkin's table and seemed suspicious of him. He was running low on Phenaphen pills and was looking for something else. But he swallowed one of his own tablets and went out and rang again for the elevator. He went down to the health club. Through the steamy windows, when he emerged, he saw the reflection of the swimming pool swirling green at the bottom of the lowest stairway. He went through the locker-room curtains. Two men wrapped in towels were playing Ping-pong. They were awkward and the ball bounded high. The Negro in the toilet was shining shoes. He did not know Dr. Adler by name, and Wilhelm descended to the massage room. On the tables naked men were lying. It was not a brightly lighted place, and it was very hot, and under the white faint moons of the ceiling shone pale skins. Calendar pictures of pretty girls dressed in tiny fringes were pinned on the wall. On the first table, eyes deeply shut in heavy silent luxury lay a man with a full square beard and short legs, stocky and black-haired. He might have been an orthodox Russian. Wrapped in a sheet, waiting, the man beside him was newly shaved and red from the steambath. He had a big happy face and was dreaming. And after him was an athlete, strikingly muscled, powerful and young, with a strong white curve to his genital and a half-angry smile on his mouth. Dr. Adler was on the fourth table, and Wilhelm stood over his father's pale, slight body. His ribs were narrow and small, his belly round, white, and high. It had its own being, like something separate. His thighs were weak, the muscles of his arms had fallen, his throat was creased.

The masseur in his undershirt bent and whispered in his ear, "It's your son," and Dr. Adler opened his eyes to Wilhelm's face. At once he saw the trouble in it, and by an instantaneous reflex he removed himself from the danger of contagion, and he said serenely, "Well, have you taken my advice, Wilky?"

"Oh, Dad," said Wilhelm.

"To take a swim and get a massage?"

"Did you get my note?" said Wilhelm.

"Yes, but I'm afraid you'll have to ask somebody else, because I can't. I had no idea you were low on funds. How did you let it happen? Didn't you lay anything aside?"

"Oh, please, Dad," said Wilhelm, almost bringing his hands together in a clasp.

"I'm sorry," said the doctor. "I really am. But I have set up a rule. I've thought about it, I believe it is a good rule, and I don't want to change it. You haven't acted wisely. What's the matter?"

"Everything. Just everything. What isn't? I did have a little, but I haven't been very smart."

"You took some gamble? You lost it? Was it Tamkin? I told you, Wilky, not to build on that Tamkin. Did you? I suspect—"

"Yes, Dad, I'm afraid I trusted him."

Dr. Adler surrendered his arm to the masseur, who was using wintergreen oil. "Trusted! And got taken?"

"I'm afraid I kind of—" Wilhelm glanced at the masseur but he was absorbed in his work. He probably did not listen to conversations. "I did. I might as well say it. I should have listened to you."

"Well, I won't remind you how often I warned you. It must be very painful."

"Yes, Father, it is."

"I don't know how many times you have to be burned in order to learn something. The same mistakes, over and over."

"I couldn't agree with you more," said Wilhelm with a face of despair. "You're so right, Father. It's the same mistakes, and I get burned again and again. I can't seem to—I'm stupid, Dad, I just can't breathe. My chest is all up—I feel choked. I just simply can't catch my breath."

He stared at his father's nakedness. Presently he became aware that Dr. Adler was making an effort to keep his temper. He was on the verge of an explosion. Wilhelm hung his face and said, "Nobody likes bad luck, eh Dad?"

"So! It's bad luck, now. A minute ago it was stupidity."

"It is stupidity—it's some of both. It's true that I can't learn. But I—"

"I don't want to listen to the details," said his father. "And I want you to understand that I'm too old to take on new burdens. I'm just too old to do it. And people who will just wait for help—must *wait* for help. They have got to stop waiting."

"It isn't all a question of money—there are other things a father can give to a son." He lifted up his gray eyes and his nostrils grew wide with a look of suffering appeal that stirred his father even more deeply against him.

He warningly said to him, "Look out, Wilky, you're tiring my patience very much."

"I try not to. But one word from you, just one word, would go a long way. I've never asked you for very much. But you are not a kind man, Father. You don't give the little bit I beg you for."

He recognized that his father was now furiously angry. Dr. Adler started to say something, and then raised himself and gathered the sheet over him as he did so. His mouth opened, wide, dark, twisted, and he said to Wilhelm, "You want to make yourself into my cross. But I am not going to pick up a cross. I'll see you dead, Wilky, by Christ, before I let you do that to me."

"Father, listen! Listen!"

"Go away from me now. It's torture for me to look at you, you slob!" cried Dr. Adler.

Wilhelm's blood rose up madly, in anger equal to his father's, but then it sank down and left him helplessly captive to misery. He said stiffly, and with a strange sort of formality, "Okay, Dad. That'll be enough. That's about all we should say." And he stalked out heavily by the door adjacent to the swimming pool and the steam room, and labored up two long flights from the basement. Once more he took the elevator to the lobby on the mezzanine.

He inquired at the desk for Dr. Tamkin.

The clerk said, "No, I haven't seen him. But I think there's something in the box for you."

"Me? Give it here," said Wilhelm and opened a telephone message from his wife. It read, "Please phone Mrs. Wilhelm on return. Urgent."

Whenever he received an urgent message from his wife he was always thrown into a great fear for the children. He ran to the phone booth, spilled out the change from his pockets onto the little curved steel shelf under the telephone, and dialed the Digby number.

"Yes?" said his wife. Scissors barked in the parlor.

"Margaret?"

"Yes, hello." They never exchanged any other greeting. She instantly knew his voice.

"The boys all right?"

"They're out on their bicycles. Why shouldn't they be all right? Scissors, quiet!"

"Your message scared me," he said. "I wish you wouldn't make 'urgent' so common."

"I had something to tell you."

Her familiar unbending voice awakened in him a kind of hungry longing, not for Margaret but for the peace he had once known.

"You sent me a postdated check," she said. "I can't allow that. It's already five days past the first. You dated your check for the twelfth."

"Well, I have no money. I haven't got it. You can't send me to prison for that. I'll be lucky if I can raise it by the twelfth."

She answered, "You better get it, Tommy."

"Yes? What for?" he said. "Tell me. For the sake of what? To tell lies about me to everyone? You—"

She cut him off. "You know what for. I've got the boys to bring up."

Wilhelm in the narrow booth broke into a heavy sweat. He dropped his head and shrugged while with his fingers he arranged nickels, dimes, and quarters in rows. "I'm doing my best," he said. "I've had some bad luck. As a matter of fact, it's been so bad that I don't know where I am. I couldn't tell you what day of the week this is. I can't think straight. I'd better not even try. This has been one of those days, Margaret. May I never live to go through another like it. I mean that with all my heart. So I'm not going to try to do any thinking today. Tomorrow I'm going to see some guys. One is a sales manager. The other is in television. But not to act," he hastily added. "On the business end."

"That's just some more of your talk, Tommy," she said. "You ought to patch things up with Rojax Corporation. They'd take you back. You've got to stop thinking like a youngster."

"What do you mean?"

"Well," she said, measured and unbending, remorselessly unbending, "you still think like a youngster. But you can't do that any more. Every other day you want to make a new start. But in eighteen years you'll be eligible for retirement. Nobody wants to hire a new man of your age."

"I know. But listen, you don't have to sound so hard. I can't get on my knees to them. And really you don't have to sound so hard. I haven't done you so much harm."

"Tommy, I have to chase you and ask for money that you owe us, and I hate it." She hated also to be told that her voice was hard.

"I'm making an effort to control myself," she told him.

He could picture her, her graying bangs cut with strict fixity above her pretty, decisive face. She prided herself on being fair-minded. We could not bear, he thought, to know what we do. Even though blood is spilled. Even though the breath of life is taken from someone's nostrils. This is the way of the weak; quiet and fair. And then smash! They smash!

"Rojax take me back? I'd have to crawl back. They don't need me. After so many years I should have got stock in the firm. How can I support the three of you, and live myself, on half the territory? And why should I even try when you won't lift a finger to help? I sent you back to school, didn't I? At that time you said—"

His voice was rising. She did not like that and intercepted him. "You misunderstood me," she said.

"You must realize you're killing me. You can't be as blind as all that. Thou shalt not kill! Don't you remember that?"

She said, "You're just raving now. When you calm down it'll be different. I have great confidence in your earning ability."

"Margaret, you don't grasp the situation. You'll have to get a job."

"Absolutely not. I'm not going to have two young children running loose."

"They're not babies," Wilhelm said. "Tommy is fourteen. Paulie is going to be ten."

"Look," Margaret said in her deliberate manner. "We can't continue this conversation if you're going to yell so, Tommy. They're at a dangerous age. There are teen-aged gangs—the parents working, or the families broken up."

Once again she was reminding him that it was he who had left her. She had the bringing up of the children as her burden, while he must expect to pay the price of his freedom.

Freedom! he thought with consuming bitterness. Ashes in his mouth, not freedom. Give me my children. For they are mine too.

Can you be the woman I lived with? he started to say. Have you forgotten that we slept so long together? Must you now deal with me like this, and have no mercy?

He would be better off with Margaret again than he was today. This was what she wanted to make him feel, and she drove it home. "Are you in misery?" she was saying. "But you have deserved it." And he could not return to her any more than he could beg Rojax to take him back. If it cost him his life, he could not. Margaret had ruined him with Olive. She hit him and hit him, beat him, battered him, wanted to beat the very life out of him.

"Margaret, I want you please to reconsider about work. You have that degree now. Why did I pay your tuition?"

"Because it seemed practical. But it isn't. Growing boys need parental authority and a home."

He begged her, "Margaret, go easy on me. You ought to. I'm at the end of my rope and feel that I'm suffocating. You don't want to be responsible for a person's destruction. You've got to let up. I feel I'm about to burst." His face had expanded. He struck a blow upon the tin and wood and nails of the wall of the booth. "You've got to let me breathe. If I should keel over, what then? And it's something I can never understand about you. How you can treat someone like this whom you lived with so long. Who gave you the best of himself. Who tried. Who loved you." Merely to pronounce the word "love" made him tremble.

"Ah," she said with a sharp breath. "Now we're coming to it. How did you imagine it was going to be—big shot? Everything made smooth for you? I thought you were leading up to this."

She had not, perhaps, intended to reply as harshly as she did, but she brooded a great deal and now she could not forbear to punish him and make him feel pains like those she had to undergo.

He struck the wall again, this time with his knuckles, and he had scarcely enough air in his lungs to speak in a whisper, because his heart pushed upward with a frightful pressure. He got up and stamped his feet in the narrow enclosure.

"Haven't I always done my best?" he yelled, though his voice sounded weak and thin to his own ears. "Everything comes from me and nothing back again to me. There's no law that'll punish this, but you are committing a crime against me. Before God—and that's no joke. I mean that. Before God! Sooner or later the boys will know it."

In a firm tone, levelly, Margaret said to him, "I won't stand to be howled at.

When you can speak normally and have something sensible to say I'll listen. But not to this." She hung up.

Wilhelm tried to tear the apparatus from the wall. He ground his teeth and seized the black box with insane digging fingers and made a stifled cry and pulled. Then he saw an elderly lady staring through the glass door, utterly appalled by him, and he ran from the booth, leaving a large amount of change on the shelf. He hurried down the stairs and into the street.

On Broadway it was still bright afternoon and the gassy air was almost motionless under the leaden spokes of sunlight, and sawdust footprints lay about the doorways of butcher shops and fruit stores. And the great, great crowd, the inexhaustible current of millions of every race and kind pouring out, pressing round, of every age, of every genius, possessors of every human secret, antique and future, in every face the refinement of one particular motive or essence—*I labor, I spend, I strive, I design, I love, I cling, I uphold, I give way, I envy, I long, I scorn, I die, I hide, I want.* Faster, much faster than any man could make the tally. The sidewalks were wider than any causeway; the street itself was immense, and it quaked and gleamed and it seemed to Wilhelm to throb at the last limit of endurance. And although the sunlight appeared like a broad tissue, its actual weight made him feel like a drunkard.

"I'll get a divorce if it's the last thing I do," he swore. "As for Dad—As for Dad—I'll have to go sell the car for junk and pay the hotel. I'll have to go on my knees to Olive and say, 'Stand by me a while. Don't let her win. Olive!' " And he thought, I'll try to start again with Olive. In fact, I must. Olive loves me. Olive—

Beside a row of limousines near the curb he thought he saw Dr. Tamkin. Of course he had been mistaken before about the hat with the cocoa-colored band and didn't want to make the same mistake twice. But wasn't that Tamkin who was speaking so earnestly, with pointed shoulders, to someone under the canopy of the funeral parlor? For this was a huge funeral. He looked for the singular face under the dark gray, fashionable hatbrim. There were two open cars filled with flowers, and a policeman tried to keep a path open to pedestrians. Right at the canopy-pole, now wasn't that that damned Tamkin talking away with a solemn face, gesticulating with an open hand?

"Tamkin!" shouted Wilhelm, going forward. But he was pushed to the side by a policeman clutching his nightstick at both ends, like a rolling pin. Wilhelm was even farther from Tamkin now, and swore under his breath at the cop who continued to press him back, back, belly and ribs, saying, "Keep it moving there, please," his face red with impatient sweat, his brows like red fur. Wilhelm said to him haughtily, "You shouldn't push people like this."

The policeman, however, was not really to blame. He had been ordered to keep a way clear. Wilhelm was moved forward by the pressure of the crowd.

He cried, "Tamkin!"

But Tamkin was gone. Or rather, it was he himself who was carried from the street into the chapel. The pressure ended inside, where it was dark and cool. The flow of fan-driven air dried his face, which he wiped hard with his handkerchief to stop the slight salt itch. He gave a sigh when he heard the organ notes that stirred and breathed from the pipes and he saw people in the pews. Men in formal clothes and black homburgs[1] strode softly back and forth on the cork floor, up and down the center aisle. The white of the stained glass was like mother-of-pearl, the blue of the Star of David like velvet ribbon.

---

[1]Men's elegant hat with the crown creased lengthwise.

Well, thought Wilhelm, if that was Tamkin outside I might as well wait for him here where it's cool. Funny, he never mentioned he had a funeral to go to today. But that's just like the guy.

But within a few minutes he had forgotten Tamkin. He stood along the wall with others and looked toward the coffin and the slow line that was moving past it, gazing at the face of the dead. Presently he too was in this line, and slowly, slowly, foot by foot, the beating of his heart anxious, thick, frightening, but somehow also rich, neared the coffin and paused for his turn, and gazed down. He caught his breath when he looked at the corpse, and his face swelled, his eyes shone hugely with instant tears.

The dead man was gray-haired. He had two large waves of gray hair at the front. But he was not old. His face was long, and he had a bony nose, slightly, delicately twisted. His brows were raised as though he had sunk into the final thought. Now at last he was with it, after the end of all distractions, and when his flesh was no longer flesh. And by this meditative look Wilhelm was so struck that he could not go away. In spite of the tinge of horror, and then the splash of heartsickness that he felt, he could not go. He stepped out of line and remained beside the coffin; his eyes filled silently and through his still tears he studied the man as the line of visitors moved with veiled looks past the satin coffin toward the standing bank of lilies, lilacs, roses. With great stifling sorrow, almost admiration, Wilhelm nodded and nodded. On the surface, the dead man with his formal shirt and tie and silk lapels and his powdered skin looked so proper; only a little beneath so—black, Wilhelm thought, so fallen in the eyes.

Standing a little apart, Wilhelm began to cry. He cried at first softly and from sentiment, but soon from deeper feeling. He sobbed loudly and his face grew distorted and hot, and the tears stung his skin. A man—another human creature, was what first went through his thoughts, but other and different things were torn from him. What'll I do? I'm stripped and kicked out. . . . Oh, Father, what do I ask of you? What'll I do about the kids—Tommy, Paul? My children. And Olive? My dear! Why, why, why—you must protect me against that devil who wants my life. If you want it, then kill me. Take, take it, take it from me."

Soon he was past words, past reason, coherence. He could not stop. The source of all tears had suddenly sprung open within him, black, deep, and hot, and they were pouring out and convulsed his body, bending his stubborn head, bowing his shoulders, twisting his face, crippling the very hands with which he held the handkerchief. His efforts to collect himself were useless. The great knot of ill and grief in his throat swelled upward and he gave in utterly and held his face and wept. He cried with all his heart.

He, alone of all the people in the chapel, was sobbing. No one knew who he was.

One woman said, "Is that perhaps the cousin from New Orleans they were expecting?"

"It must be somebody real close to carry on so."

"Oh my, oh my! To be mourned like that," said one man and looked at Wilhelm's heavy shaken shoulders, his clutched face and whitened fair hair, with wide, glinting, jealous eyes.

"The man's brother, maybe?"

"Oh, I doubt that very much," said another bystander. "They're not alike at all. Night and day."

The flowers and lights fused ecstatically in Wilhelm's blind, wet eyes; the heavy sea-like music came up to his ears. It poured into him where he had hidden himself in the center of a crowd by the great and happy oblivion of tears.

He heard it and sank deeper than sorrow, through torn sobs and cries toward
the consummation of his heart's ultimate need.

1956

Joyce Carol Oates   *1938–*

*Joyce Carol Oates is one of the most prolific of modern American writers. Since the
appearance of her first book,* By the North Gate *(1963), a collection of short stories,
she has published more than thirty volumes—short stories, novels, poems, plays, and
essays—an average of two books each year. She began telling stories at an early age:
"Before I could write," she has said, "I drew pictures to tell my stories." Her first
published fiction appeared in* Mademoiselle *magazine in 1959, when she was twenty-
one. Since that time her writing has gained wide critical acclaim. She has received
awards from the Guggenheim Foundation and the National Institute of Arts and Letters, and her novel* them *(1969) won the National Book Award as the best American
Novel of the year.*

*She has said that "all art is autobiographical," but nothing in the outward events of
her own life parallels the terror-filled and violent lives that exist in her fiction. She was
born in Lockport, New York, and raised in a middle-class family. She attended Syracuse
University on a scholarship, and after her graduation in 1960 she received a fellowship
at the University of Wisconsin. One year later she graduated with an M.A., and for the
next six years she taught literature at the University of Detroit. In 1967 she moved to
Canada where she was a faculty member of the University of Windsor, in Ontario. In
recent years she has been teaching at Princeton University.*

*As a writer she is praised not merely for her phenomenal productivity on her wide-
ranging talents but because of her power to depict the torments and frightening derangements suffered by ordinary people in the modern world. She writes of factory workers,
school girls, businessmen, teachers, preachers. They live in a middle-class world centered
on their houses, large and small; on back-yard barbecues; shopping centers; drive-in
restaurants; automobiles; and television. Outwardly her characters seem commonplace
and predictable. Inwardly they are complex, often terrorized by others, by cruel fate, or by
their own corrosive fears. Her works repeatedly portray frightening violence: murder,
suicide, rape, riots, arson, beatings. Her use of sudden horrors and grotesque experiences
has been described as "gothic," like tales by Washington Irving, Edgar Allan Poe, and
their contemporaries who wrote of graveyards, ancient ruins, and mysterious forces of
demonic evil. To Joyce Carol Oates, today's "gothic" world is not one of ghosts in ancient
ruined castles but of haunted lives in modern ruined cities. To perceive our situation as
fundamentally grotesque and "gothic," she has said, is nothing more than to make "a fairly
realistic assessment of modern life."*

*Her writing has been compared with that of Flannery O'Connor and William Faulkner,
whose characters also confront violence and enigmatic malice, yet Oates has been accused
of taking excessive delight in showing only the frightening destinies that await us. For the
unrelieved sense of dread that pervades much of her writing, for the gloomy view of life
it expresses, she has been called "The Dark Lady of American Letters." But from the brutal
eruptions that she describes there often comes an affirmation, a revelation of the world
behind—or beneath—the apparent world, a redeeming insight imposed on characters and
readers alike by the very nightmarish experiences that she describes.*

At a time when modern literature increasingly seems to move toward antirealism, away from depiction of the world of everyday things seen and heard and felt, Joyce Carol Oates continues to write primarily in the realistic tradition, rejecting the fragmentary and surrealistic quality of much avant-garde fiction. At times she does use narrative techniques common to experimental writers, as in "How I Contemplated the World from the Detroit House of Correction and Began My Life Over Again"; but from her early work to her recent Solstice *(1985) and* You Must Remember This *(1988), the impact of her writing has depended not on the mode of story-telling but on her ability to reveal the extraordinary behind the façade of the ordinary and on her vision of urban America as a swirling, nightmarish world of obsessions, neurotic fears, and grotesque brutality.*

FURTHER READING: M. Grant, *The Tragic Vision of Joyce Carol Oates*, 1978; G. Waller, *Dreaming America, Obsession and Transcendence in the Fiction of Joyce Carol Oates*, 1979; *Critical Essays on Joyce Carol Oates*, ed. L. Wagner, 1979; J. Creighton, *Joyce Carol Oates*, 1979; E. Friedman, *Joyce Carol Oates*, 1980; *Joyce Carol Oates*, ed. H. Bloom, 1987; E. Bender, *Artist in Residence, The Phenomenon of Joyce Carol Oates*; 1987; G. Johnson, *Understanding Joyce Carol Oates*, 1987.

TEXT: *The Wheel of Love and Other Stories*, 1970.

HOW I CONTEMPLATED THE WORLD FROM THE DETROIT HOUSE OF CORRECTION AND BEGAN MY LIFE OVER AGAIN

NOTES FOR AN ESSAY FOR AN ENGLISH CLASS AT BALDWIN COUNTRY DAY SCHOOL; POKING AROUND IN DEBRIS; DISGUST AND CURIOSITY; A REVELATION OF THE MEANING OF LIFE; A HAPPY ENDING . . .

I EVENTS

1. The girl (myself) is walking through Branden's, that excellent store. Suburb of a large famous city that is a symbol for large famous American cities. The event sneaks up on the girl, who believes she is herding it along with a small fixed smile, a girl of fifteen, innocently experienced. She dawdles in a certain style by a counter of costume jewelry. Rings, earrings, necklaces. Prices from $5 to $50, all within reach. All ugly. She eases over to the glove counter, where everything is ugly too. In her close-fitted coat with its black fur collar she contemplates the luxury of Branden's, which she has known for many years: its many mild pale lights, easy on the eye and the soul, its elaborate tinkly decorations, its women shoppers with their excellent shoes and coats and hairdos, all dawdling gracefully, in no hurry.

Who was ever in a hurry here?

2. The girl seated at home. A small library, paneled walls of oak. Someone is talking to me. An earnest, husky, female voice drives itself against my ears, nervous, frightened, groping around my heart, saying, "If you wanted gloves, why didn't you say so? Why didn't you ask for them?" That store, Branden's is owned by Raymond Forrest who lives on Du Maurier Drive. We live on Sioux Drive. Raymond Forrest. A handsome man? An ugly man? A man of fifty or sixty, with gray hair, or a man of forty with earnest, courteous eyes, a good golf game; who is Raymond Forrest, this man who is my salvation? Father has been

talking to him. Father is not his physician; Dr. Berg is his physician. Father and Dr. Berg refer patients to each other. There is a connection. Mother plays bridge with . . . On Mondays and Wednesdays our maid Billie works at . . . The strings draw together in a cat's cradle, making a net to save you when you fall. . . .

3. *Harriet Arnold's.* A small shop, better than Branden's. Mother in her black coat, I in my close-fitted blue coat. Shopping. Now look at this, isn't this cute, do you want this, why don't you want this, try this on, take this with you to the fitting room, take this also, what's wrong with you, what can I do for you, why are you so strange . . .? "I wanted to steal but not to buy," I don't tell her. The girl droops along in her coat and gloves and leather boots, her eyes scan the horizon, which is pastel pink and decorated like Branden's, tasteful walls and modern ceilings with graceful glimmering lights.

4. Weeks later, the girl at a bus stop. Two o'clock in the afternoon, a Tuesday; obviously she has walked out of school.

5. The girl stepping down from a bus. Afternoon, weather changing to colder. Detroit. Pavement and closed-up stores; grill-work over the windows of a pawnshop. What is a pawnshop, exactly?

II CHARACTERS

1. The girl stands five feet five inches tall. An ordinary height. Baldwin Country Day School draws them up to that height. She dreams along the corridors and presses her face against the Thermoplex glass. No frost or steam can ever form on that glass. A smudge of grease from her forehead . . . could she be boiled down to grease? She wears her hair loose and long and straight in suburban teen-age style, 1968. Eyes smudged with pencil, dark brown. Brown hair. Vague green eyes. A pretty girl? An ugly girl? She sings to herself under her breath, idling in the corridor, thinking of her many secrets (the thirty dollars she once took from the purse of a friend's mother, just for fun, the basement window she smashed in her own house just for fun) and thinking of her brother who is at Susquehanna Boys' Academy, an excellent preparatory school in Maine, remembering him unclearly . . . he has long manic hair and a squeaking voice and he looks like one of the popular teen-age singers of 1968, one of those in a group. *The Certain Forces, The Way Out, The Maniacs Responsible.* The girl in her turn looks like one of those fieldsful of girls who listen to the boys' singing, dreaming and mooning restlessly, breaking into high sullen laughter, innocently experienced.

2. The mother. A Midwestern woman of Detroit and suburbs. Belongs to the Detroit Athletic Club. Also the Detroit Golf Club. Also the Bloomfield Hills Country Club. The Village Women's Club at which lectures are given each winter on Genet and Sartre[1] and James Baldwin,[2] by the Director of the Adult Education Program at Wayne State University. . . . The Bloomfield Art Association. Also the Founders Society of the Detroit Institute of Arts. Also . . . Oh,

---

[1]Jean Genet (b. 1910), French dramatist; Jean-Paul Sartre (b. 1905), French philosopher and novelist.
[2]American novelist.

she is in perpetual motion, this lady, hair like blown-up gold and finer than gold, hair and fingers and body of inestimable grace. Heavy weighs the gold on the back of her hairbrush and hand mirror. Heavy heavy the candlesticks in the dining room. Very heavy is the big car, a Lincoln, long and black, that on one cool autumn day split a squirrel's body in two unequal parts.

3. The father. Dr.   . He belongs to the same clubs as #2. A player of squash and golf; he has a golfer's umbrella of stripes. Candy stripes. In his mouth nothing turns to sugar, however; saliva works no miracles here. His doctoring is of the slightly sick. The sick are sent elsewhere (to Dr. Berg?), the deathly sick are sent back for more tests and their bills are sent to their homes, the unsick are sent to Dr. Coronet (Isabel, a lady), an excellent psychiatrist for unsick people who angrily believe they are sick and want to do something about it. If they demand a male psychiatrist, the unsick are sent by Dr.   (my father) to Dr. Lowenstein, a male psychiatrist, excellent and expensive, with a limited practice.

4. Clarita. She is twenty, twenty-five, she is thirty or more? Pretty, ugly, what? She is a woman lounging by the side of a road, in jeans and a sweater, hitchhiking, or she is slouched on a stool at a counter in some roadside diner. A hard line of jaw. Curious eyes. Amused eyes. Behind her eyes processions move, funeral pageants, cartoons. She says, "I never can figure out why girls like you bum around down here. What are you looking for anyway?" An odor of tobacco about her. Unwashed underclothes, or no underclothes, unwashed skin, gritty toes, hair long and falling into strands, not recently washed.

5. Simon. In this city the weather changes abruptly, so Simon's weather changes abruptly. He sleeps through the afternoon. He sleeps through the morning. Rising, he gropes around for something to get him going, for a cigarette or a pill to drive him out to the street, where the temperature is hovering around 35°. Why doesn't it drop? Why, why doesn't the cold clean air come down from Canada; will he have to go-up into Canada to get it? will he have to leave the Country of his Birth and sink into Canada's frosty fields . . .? Will the F.B.I. (which he dreams about constantly) chase him over the Canadian border on foot, hounded out in a blizzard of broken glass and horns . . .?

"Once I was Huckleberry Finn," Simon says, "but now I am Roderick Usher."[3] Beset by frenzies and fears, this man who makes my spine go cold, he takes green pills, yellow pills, pills of white and capsules of dark blue and green . . . he takes other things I may not mention, for what if Simon seeks me out and climbs into my girl's bedroom here in Bloomfield Hills and strangles me, what then . . .? (As I write this I begin to shiver. Why do I shiver? I am now sixteen and sixteen is not an age for shivering.) It comes from Simon, who is always cold.

III   WORLD EVENTS

Nothing.

[3]Tormented character in "The Fall of the House of Usher," by Edgar Allan Poe. See Volume I.

IV PEOPLE & CIRCUMSTANCES
CONTRIBUTING TO THIS DELINQUENCY

Nothing.

V SIOUX DRIVE

George, Clyde G. 240 Sioux. A manufacturer's representative; children, a dog, a wife. Georgian with the usual columns. You think of the White House, then of Thomas Jefferson, then your mind goes blank on the white pillars and you think of nothing. Norris, Ralph W. 246 Sioux. Public relations. Colonial Bay window, brick, stone, concrete, wood, green shutters, sidewalk, lantern, grass, trees, blacktop drive, two children, one of them my classmate Esther (Esther Norris) at Baldwin. Wife, cars. Ramsey, Michael D. 250 Sioux. Colonial. Big living room, thirty by twenty-five, fireplaces in living room, library, recreation room, paneled walls wet bar five bathrooms five bedrooms two lavatories central air conditioning automatic sprinkler automatic garage door three children one wife two cars a breakfast room a patio a large fenced lot fourteen trees a front door with a brass knocker never knocked. Next is our house. Classic contemporary. Traditional modern. Attached garage, attached Florida room, attached patio, attached pool and cabana, attached roof. A front door mail slot through which pour *Time Magazine, Fortune, Life, Business Week,* the *Wall Street Journal,* the *New York Times,* the *New Yorker,* the *Saturday Review, M.D., Modern Medicine, Disease of the Month* . . . and also. . . . And in addition to all this, a quiet sealed letter from Baldwin saying: *Your daughter is not doing work compatible with her performance on the Stanford-Binet.*[4] . . . And your son is not doing well, not well at all, very sad. Where is your son anyway? Once he stole trick-and-treat candy from some six-year-old kids, he himself being a robust ten. The beginning. Now your daughter steals. In the Village Pharmacy she made off with, yes she did, don't deny it, she made off with a copy of *Pageant Magazine* for no reason, she swiped a roll of Life Savers in a green wrapper and was in no need of saving her life or even in need of sucking candy; when she was no more than eight years old she stole, don't blush, she stole a package of Tums only because it was out on the counter and available, and the nice lady behind the counter (now dead) said nothing. . . . Sioux Drive. Maples, oaks, elms. Diseased elms cut down. Sioux Drive runs into Roosevelt Drive. Slow, turning lanes, not streets, all drives and lanes and ways and passes. A private police force. Quiet private police, in unmarked cars. Cruising on Saturday evenings with paternal smiles for the residents who are streaming in and out of houses, going to and from parties, a thousand parties, slightly staggering, the women in their furs alighting from automobiles bought of Ford and General Motors and Chrysler, very heavy automobiles. No foreign cars. Detroit. In 275 Sioux, down the block in that magnificent French-Normandy mansion, lives   himself, who has the C   account itself, imagine that! Look at where he lives and look at the enormous trees and chimneys, imagine his many fireplaces, imagine his wife and children, imagine his wife's hair, imagine her fingernails, imagine her bathtub of smooth clean glowing pink, imagine their embraces, his trouser pockets filled with odd coins and keys and dust and peanuts, imagine their ecstasy on Sioux Drive, imagine their income tax returns, imagine their little

[4]An intelligence test.

boy's pride in his experimental car, a scaled-down C , as he roars around the neighborhood on the sidewalks frightening dogs and Negro maids, oh imagine all these things, imagine everything, let your mind roar out all over Sioux Drive and Du Maurier Drive and Roosevelt Drive and Ticonderoga Pass and Burning Bush Way and Lincolnshire Pass and Lois Lane.

When spring comes, its winds blow nothing to Sioux Drive, no odors of hollyhocks or forsythia, nothing Sioux Drive doesn't already possess, everything is planted and performing. The weather vanes, had they weather vanes, don't have to turn with the wind, don't have to contend with the weather. There is no weather.

VI DETROIT

There is always weather in Detroit. Detroit's temperature is always 32°. Fast-falling temperatures. Slow-rising temperatures. Wind from the north-northeast four to forty miles an hour, small craft warnings, partly cloudy today and Wednesday changing to partly sunny through Thursday . . . small warnings of frost, soot warnings, traffic warnings, hazardous lake conditions small craft and swimmers, restless Negro gangs, restless cloud formations, restless temperatures aching to fall out the very bottom of the thermometer or shoot up over the top and boil everything over in red mercury.

Detroit's temperature is 32°. Fast-falling temperatures. Slow-rising temperatures. Wind from the north-northeast four to forty miles an hour. . . .

VII EVENTS

1. The girl's heart is pounding. In her pocket is a pair of gloves! In a plastic bag! Airproof breathproof plastic bag, gloves selling for twenty-five dollars on Branden's counter! In her pocket! Shoplifted! . . . In her purse is a blue comb, not very clean. In her purse is a leather billfold (a birthday present from her grandmother in Philadelphia) with snapshots of the family in clean plastic windows, in the billfold are bills, she doesn't know how many bills. . . . In her purse is an ominous note from her friend Tykie *What's this about Joe H. and the kids hanging around at Louise's Sat. night? You heard anything?* . . . passed in French class. In her purse is a lot of dirty yellow Kleenex, her mother's heart would break to see such very dirty Kleenex, and at the bottom of her purse are brown hairpins and safety pins and a broken pencil and a ballpoint pen (blue) stolen from somewhere forgotten and a purse-size compact of Cover Girl Make-Up, Ivory Rose. . . . Her lipstick is Broken Heart, a corrupt pink; her fingers are trembling like crazy; her teeth are beginning to chatter; her insides are alive; her eyes glow in her head; she is saying to her mother's astonished face *I want to steal but not to buy.*

2. At Clarita's Day or night? What room is this? A bed, a regular bed, and a mattress on the floor nearby. Wallpaper hanging in strips. Clarita says she tore it like that with her teeth. She was fighting a barbaric tribe that night, high from some pills; she was battling for her life with men wearing helmets of heavy iron and their faces no more than Christian crosses to breathe through, every one of those bastards looking like her lover Simon, who seems to breathe with great difficulty through the slits of mouth and nostrils in his face. Clarita has never

heard of Sioux Drive. Raymond Forrest cuts no ice with her, nor does the C account and its millions; Harvard Business School could be at the corner of Vernor and 12th Street[5] for all she cares, and Vietnam might have sunk by now into the Dead Sea under its tons of debris, for all the amazement she could show . . . her face is overworked, overwrought, at the age of twenty (thirty?) it is already exhausted but fanciful and ready for a laugh. Clarita says mournfully to me *Honey somebody is going to turn you out let me give you warning.* In a movie shown on late television Clarita is not a mess like this but a nurse, with short neat hair and a dedicated look, in love with her doctor and her doctor's patients and their diseases, enamored of needles and sponges and rubbing alcohol. . . . Or no: she is a private secretary. Robert Cummings is her boss. She helps him with fantastic plots, the canned audience laughs, no, the audience doesn't laugh because nothing is funny, instead her boss is Robert Taylor and they are not boss and secretary but husband and wife, she is threatened by a young starlet, she is grim, handsome, wifely, a good companion for a good man. . . . She is Claudette Colbert. Her sister too is Claudette Colbert. They are twins, identical. Her husband Charles Boyer is a very rich handsome man and her sister, Claudette Colbert, is plotting her death in order to take her place as the rich man's wife, no one will know because they are *twins.* . . . All these marvelous lives Clarita might have lived, but she fell out the bottom at the age of thirteen. At the age when I was packing my overnight case for a slumber party at Toni Deshield's she was tearing filthy sheets off a bed and scratching up a rash on her arms. . . . Thirteen is uncommonly young for a white girl in Detroit, Miss Brock of the Detroit House of Correction said in a sad newspaper interview for the *Detroit News;* fifteen and sixteen are more likely. Eleven, twelve, thirteen are not surprising in colored . . . they are more precocious. What can we do? Taxes are rising and the tax base is falling. The temperature rises slowly but falls rapidly. Everything is falling out the bottom, Woodward Avenue is filthy, Livernois Avenue[6] is filthy! Scraps of paper flutter in the air like pigeons, dirt flies up and hits you right in the eye, oh Detroit is breaking up into dangerous bits of newspaper and dirt, watch out. . . .

Clarita's apartment is over a restaurant. Simon her lover emerges from the cracks at dark. Mrs. Olesko, a neighbor of Clarita's, an aged white wisp of a woman, doesn't complain but sniffs with contentment at Clarita's noisy life and doesn't tell the cops, hating cops, when the cops arrive. I should give more fake names, more blanks, instead of telling all these secrets. I myself am a secret; I am a minor.

3. My father reads a paper at a medical convention in Los Angeles. There he is, on the edge of the North American continent, when the unmarked detective put his hand so gently on my arm in the aisle of Branden's and said, "Miss, would you like to step over here for a minute?"

And where was he when Clarita put her hand on my arm, that wintry dark sulphurous aching day in Detroit, in the company of closed-down barber shops, closed-down diners, closed-down movie houses, homes, windows, basements, faces . . . she put her hand on my arm and said, "Honey, are you looking for somebody down here?"

And was he home worrying about me, gone for two weeks solid, when they carried me off . . .? It took three of them to get me in the police cruiser, so they said, and they put more than their hands on my arm.

[5]Downtown Detroit.
[6]Main streets in Detroit.

4. I work on this lesson. My English teacher is Mr. Forest, who is from Michigan State. Not handsome, Mr. Forest, and his name is plain, unlike Raymond Forrest's, but he is sweet and rodentlike, he has conferred with the principal and my parents, and everything is fixed . . . treat her as if nothing has happened, a new start, begin again, only sixteen years old, what a shame, how did it happen?—nothing happened, nothing could have happened, a slight physiological modification known only to a gynecologist or to Dr. Coronet. I work on my lesson. I sit in my pink room. I look around the room with my sad pink eyes. I sigh, I dawdle, I pause, I eat up time, I am limp and happy to be home, I am sixteen years old suddenly, my head hangs heavy as a pumpkin on my shoulders, and my hair has just been cut by Mr. Faye at the Crystal Salon and is said to be very becoming.

(Simon too put his hand on my arm and said, "Honey, you have got to come with me," and in his six-by-six room we got to know each other. Would I go back to Simon again? Would I lie down with him in all that filth and craziness? Over and over again.

a Clarita is being betrayed as in front of a Cunningham Drug Store she is nervously eyeing a colored man who may or may not have money, or a nervous white boy of twenty with sideburns and an Appalachian look, who may or may not have a knife hidden in his jacket pocket, or a husky red-faced man of friendly countenance who may or may not be a member of the Vice Squad out for an early twilight walk.)

I work on my lesson for Mr. Forest. I have filled up eleven pages. Words pour out of me and won't stop. I want to tell everything . . . what was the song Simon was always humming, and who was Simon's friend in a very new trench coat with an old high school graduation ring on his finger . . . ? Simon's bearded friend? When I was down too low for him, Simon kicked me out and gave me to him for three days, I think, on Fourteenth Street in Detroit, an airy room of cold cruel drafts with newspapers on the floor. . . . Do I really remember that or am I piecing it together from what they told me? Did they tell the truth? Did they know much of the truth?

VIII CHARACTERS

1. Wednesdays after school, at four; Saturday mornings at ten. Mother drives me to Dr. Coronet. Ferns in the office, plastic or real, they look the same. Dr. Coronet is queenly, an elegant nicotine-stained lady who would have studied with Freud had circumstances not prevented it, a bit of a Catholic, ready to offer you some mystery if your teeth will ache too much without it. Highly recommended by Father! Forty dollars an hour, Father's forty dollars! Progress! Looking up! Looking better! That new haircut is so becoming, says Dr. Coronet herself, showing how normal she is for a woman with an I.Q. of 180 and many advanced degrees.

2. Mother. A lady in a brown suede coat. Boots of shiny black material, black gloves, a black fur hat. She would be humiliated could she know that of all the people in the world it is my ex-lover Simon who walks most like her . . . self-conscious and unreal, listening to distant music, a little bowlegged with craftiness. . . .

3. Father. Tying a necktie. In a hurry. On my first evening home he put his hand on my arm and said, "Honey, we're going to forget all about this."

4. Simon. Outside, a plane is crossing the sky, in here we're in a hurry. Morning. It must be morning. The girl is half out of her mind, whimpering and vague; Simon her dear friend is wretched this morning . . . he is wretched with morning itself . . . he forces her to give him an injection with that needle she knows is filthy, she has a dread of needles and surgical instruments and the odor of things that are to be sent into the blood, thinking somehow of her father. . . . This is a bad morning, Simon says that his mind is being twisted out of shape, and so he submits to the needle that he usually scorns and bites his lip with his yellowish teeth, his face going very pale. *Ah baby!* he says in his soft mocking voice, which with all women is a mockery of love, *do it like this—Slowly—* And the girl, terrified, almost drops the precious needle but manages to turn it up to the light from the window . . . is it an extension of herself then? She can give him this gift then? *I wish you wouldn't do this to me,* she says, wise in her terror, because it seems to her that Simon's danger—in a few minutes he may be dead— is a way of pressing her against him that is more powerful than any other embrace. She has to work over his arm, the knotted corded veins of his arm, her forehead wet with perspiration as she pushes and releases the needle, staring at that mixture of liquid now stained with Simon's bright blood. . . . When the drug hits him she can feel it herself, she feels that magic that is more than any woman can give him, striking the back of his head and making his face stretch as if with the impact of a terrible sun. . . . She tries to embrace him but he pushes her aside and stumbles to his feet. *Jesus Christ,* he says. . . .

5. Princess, a Negro girl of eighteen. What is her charge? She is closed-mouthed about it, shrewd and silent, you know that no one had to wrestle her to the sidewalk to get her in here; she came with dignity. In the recreation room she sits reading *Nancy Drew and the Jewel Box Mystery,* which inspires in her face tiny wrinkles of alarm and interest: what a face! Light brown skin, heavy shaded eyes, heavy eyelashes, a serious sinister dark brow, graceful fingers, graceful wristbones, graceful legs, lips, tongue, a sugar-sweet voice, a leggy stride more masculine than Simon's and my mother's, decked out in a dirty white blouse and dirty white slacks; vaguely nautical is Princess' style. . . . At breakfast she is in charge of clearing the table and leans over me, saying, *Honey you sure you ate enough?*

6. The girl lies sleepless, wondering. Why here, why not there? Why Bloom-field Hills and not jail? Why jail and not her pink room? Why downtown Detroit and not Sioux Drive? What is the difference? Is Simon all the difference? The girl's head is a parade of wonders. She is nearly sixteen, her breath is marvelous with wonders, not long ago she was coloring with crayons and now she is smearing the landscape with paints that won't come off and won't come off her fingers either. She says to the matron *I am not talking about anything,* not because everyone has warned her not to talk but because, because she will not talk; because she won't say anything about Simon, who is her secret. And she says to the matron, *I won't go home,* up until that night in the lavatory when everything was changed. . . . "No, I won't go home I want to stay here," she says, listening to her own words with amazement, thinking that weeds might climb everywhere over that marvelous $180,000 house and dinosaurs might return to muddy the beige carpeting, but never never will she reconcile four o'clock in the morning in

Detroit with eight o'clock breakfasts in Bloomfield Hills. . . . oh, she aches still for Simon's hands and his caressing breath, though he gave her little pleasure, he took everything from her (five-dollar bills, ten-dollar bills, passed into her numb hands by men and taken out of her hands by Simon) until she herself was passed into the hands of other men, police, when Simon evidently got tired of her and her hysteria. . . . *No, I won't go home, I don't want to be bailed out.* The girl thinks as a *Stubborn and Wayward Child* (one of several charges lodged against her), and the matron understands her crazy white-rimmed eyes that are seeking out some new violence that will keep her in jail, should someone threaten to let her out. Such children try to strangle the matrons, the attendants, or one another . . . they want the locks locked forever, the doors nailed shut . . . and this girl is no different up until that night her mind is changed for her. . . .

IX THAT NIGHT

Princess and Dolly, a little white girl of maybe fifteen, hardy however as a sergeant and in the House of Correction for armed robbery, corner her in the lavatory at the farthest sink and the other girls look away and file out to bed, leaving her. God, how she is beaten up! Why is she beaten up? Why do they pound her, why such hatred? Princess vents all the hatred of a thousand silent Detroit winters on her body, this girl whose body belongs to me, fiercely she rides across the Midwestern plains on this girls' tender bruised body . . . revenge on the oppressed minorities of America! revenge on the slaughtered Indians! revenge on the female sex, on the male sex, revenge on Bloomfield Hills, revenge revenge. . . .

X DETROIT

In Detroit, weather weighs heavily upon everyone. The sky looms large. The horizon shimmers in smoke. Downtown the buildings are imprecise in the haze. Perpetual haze. Perpetual motion inside the haze. Across the choppy river is the city of Windsor, in Canada. Part of the continent has bunched up here and is bulging outward, at the tip of Detroit; a cold hard rain is forever falling on the expressways. . . . Shoppers shop grimly, their cars are not parked in safe places, their windshields may be smashed and graceful ebony hands may drag them out through their shatterproof smashed windshields, crying *Revenge for the Indians!* Ah, they all fear leaving Hudson's[7] and being dragged to the very tip of the city and thrown off the parking roof of Cobo Hall,[8] that expensive tomb, into the river. . . .

XI CHARACTERS WE ARE
FOREVER ENTWINED WITH

1. Simon drew me into his tender rotting arms and breathed gravity into me. Then I came to earth, weighed down. He said, *You are such a little girl,* and he weighed me down with his delight. In the palms of his hands were teeth marks from his previous life experiences. He was thirty-five, they said. Imagine Simon

---

[7]Detroit department store.   [8]Exhibition hall in Detroit.

in this room, in my pink room: he is about six feet tall and stoops slightly, in a feline cautious way, always thinking, always on guard, with his scuffed light suede shoes and his clothes that are anyone's clothes, slightly rumpled ordinary clothes that ordinary men might wear to not-bad jobs. Simon has fair long hair, curly hair, spent languid curls that are like . . . exactly like the curls of wood shavings to the touch, I am trying to be exact . . . and he smells of unheated mornings and coffee and too many pills coating his tongue with a faint green-white scum. . . . Dear Simon, who would be panicked in this room and in this house (right now Billie is vacuuming next door in my parents' room; a vacuum cleaner's roar is a sign of all good things), Simon who is said to have come from a home not much different from this, years ago, fleeing all the carpeting and the polished banisters . . . Simon has a deathly face, only desperate people fall in love with it. His face is bony and cautious, the bones of his cheeks prominent as if with the rigidity of his ceaseless thinking, plotting, for he has to make money out of girls to whom money means nothing, they're so far gone they can hardly count it, and in a sense money means nothing to him either except as a way of keeping on with his life. *Each Day's Proud Struggle,* the title of a novel we could read at jail. . . . Each day he needs a certain amount of money. He devours it. It wasn't love he uncoiled in me with his hollowed-out eyes and his courteous smile, that remnant of a prosperous past, but a dark terror that needed to press itself flat against him, or against another man . . . but he was the first, he came over to me and took my arm, a claim. We struggled on the stairs and I said, *Let me loose, you're hurting my neck, my face,* it was such a surprise that my skin hurt where he rubbed it, and afterward we lay face to face and he breathed everything into me. In the end I think he turned me in.

2. Raymond Forrest. I just read this morning that Raymond Forrest's father, the chairman of the board at,   died of a heart attack on a plane bound for London. I would like to write to Raymond Forrest a note of sympathy. I would like to thank him for not pressing charges against me one hundred years ago, saving me, being so generous . . . well, men like Raymond Forrest are generous men, not like Simon. I would like to write him a letter telling of my love, or of some other emotion that is positive and healthy. Not like Simon and his poetry, which he scrawled down when he was high and never changed a word . . . but when I try to think of something to say, it is Simon's language that comes back to me, caught in my head like a bad song, it is always Simon's language:

> *There is no reality only dreams*
> *Your neck may get snapped when you wake*
> *My love is drawn to some violent end*
> *She keeps wanting to get away*
> *My love is heading downward*
> *And I am heading upward*
> *She is going to crash on the sidewalk*
> *And I am going to dissolve into the clouds*

XII EVENTS

1. Out of the hospital, bruised and saddened and converted, with Princess' grunts still tangled in my hair . . . and Father in his overcoat looking like a prince

himself, come to carry me off. Up the expressway and out north to home. Jesus Christ, but the air is thinner and cleaner here. Monumental houses. Heartbreaking sidewalks, so clean.

2. Weeping in the living room. The ceiling is two stories high and two chandeliers hang from it. Weeping, weeping, though Billie the maid is *probably listening*. I will never leave home again. Never. Never leave home. Never leave this home again, never.

3. Sugar doughnuts for breakfast. The toaster is very shiny and my face is distorted in it. Is that my face?

4. The car is turning in the driveway. Father brings me home. Mother embraces me. Sunlight breaks in movieland patches on the roof of our traditional-contemporary home, which was designed for the famous automotive stylist whose identity, if I told you the name of the famous car he designed, you would all know, so I can't tell you because my teeth chatter at the thought of being sued . . . or having someone climb into my bedroom with a rope to strangle me. . . . The car turns up the blacktop drive. The house opens to me like a doll's house, so lovely in the sunlight, the big living room beckons to me with its walls falling away in a delirium of joy at my return. Billie the maid is *no doubt* listening from the kitchen as I burst into tears and the hysteria Simon got so sick of. Convulsed in Father's arms, I say I will never leave again, never, why did I leave, where did I go, what happened, my mind is gone wrong, my body is one big bruise, my backbone was sucked dry, it wasn't the men who hurt me and Simon never hurt me but only those girls . . . my God, how they hurt me . . . I will never leave home again. . . . The car is perpetually turning up the drive and I am perpetually breaking down in the living room and we are perpetually taking the right exit from the expressway (Lahser Road) and the wall of the rest room is perpetually banging against my head and perpetually are Simon's hands moving across my body and adding everything up and so too are Father's hands on my shaking bruised back, far from the surface of my skin on the surface of my good blue cashmere coat (dry-cleaned for my release). . . . I weep for all the money here, for God in gold and beige carpeting, for the beauty of chandeliers and the miracle of a clean polished gleaming toaster and faucets that run both hot and cold water, and I tell them, *I will never leave home, this is my home, I love everything here, I am in love with everything here. . . .*

I am home.

1970

Alice Walker   *1944–*

Alice Walker was born in Georgia, the eighth child of impoverished black sharecroppers. Encouraged by her mother, who supported her desire to gain an education and become a writer, Alice Walker graduated at the top of her high school class and received a scholarship to Spelman College for women in Atlanta, Georgia. After two years at Spelman, she transferred to Sarah Lawrence College in New York, graduating with a B.A. in 1965.

Returning to the South, to Mississippi, she taught writing and black literature and joined in efforts to improve welfare rights and increase voter registration among southern blacks. Her first publication appeared in 1966, an essay on the civil rights movement. Two years later she published her first book, Once *(1968), a collection of poems. Her first collection of short fiction,* In Love and Trouble *(1973), won an award from the National Institute of Arts and Letters for its unflinching portrayals of black women who exist as the wretched victims of racial and sexual oppression. Her second volume of stories,* You Can't Keep a Good Woman Down, *(1981) brought her additional recognition as a short-story writer, but her greatest recognition has come as a writer of novels.*

The Third Life of Grange Copeland *(1970), Alice Walker's first novel, presented themes that appear in much of her writing: the dehumanizing racism and sexism that black women experience at the hands of whites and blacks alike. Her second novel,* Meridian *(1976), won praise as the finest novel of the civil rights movement of the 1960s. With her third novel,* The Color Purple *(1982), she received worldwide acclaim. Set in the first half of the twentieth century and written in the black English of the American South, the novel covers thirty years in the life of a semiliterate, downtrodden black woman who triumphs over black male oppression and demonstrates the power of women to join together and liberate themselves from sexual abuse and violence.* The Color Purple *won for its author a Pulitzer Prize and was made into an award-winning motion picture. By 1988 the novel had been translated into twenty-two languages and had sold more than six million copies.*

Walker has dealt unflinchingly with violence and sexuality, with abortion, sadism, rape, pornography, and the impact of racial and sexual stereotypes on the relations of black men and women. Some critics have objected that her stories are too often melodramatic, that her characterizations are simplistic, a repetitious portrayal of good women suffering at the hands of bad men. And Walker has acknowledged that as a black feminist (she prefers the word "womanist"), her sympathies lie almost entirely with black women.

But in her most recent collection of essays, Living by the Word, Selected Writings *1973–1987 (1988), and in a film documentary on her life and work,* Visions of the Spirit *(1988), Alice Walker reveals a vision that has grown beyond black feminism to a sympathy for the oppressed in all life, a sympathy for all human beings, for all living things on a planet that is itself increasingly and dangerously oppressed by greed, ignorance, and the threat of nuclear war. Nevertheless, her greatest achievement remains her portrayal of the lives of black women, often grotesque and inarticulate like the heroine of "Her Sweet Jerome," who suffer from white racism and the sexism of black men and who struggle to deliver themselves from what Alice Walker has described as the black woman's demeaning life as "the mule of the world."*

TEXT: *In Love and Trouble*, 1973.

HER SWEET JEROME

1

Ties she had bought him hung on the closet door, which now swung open as she hurled herself again and again into the closet. Glorious ties, some with birds and dancing women in grass skirts painted on by hand, some with little polka dots with bigger dots dispersed among them. Some red, lots red and green, and one purple, with a golden star, through the center of which went his gold mustang stickpin, which she had also given him. She looked in the pockets of the black leather jacket he had reluctantly worn the night before. Three of his suits, a pair of blue twill work pants, an old gray sweater with a hood and pockets lay thrown across the bed. The jacket leather was sleazy and damply clinging to her hands. She had bought it for him, as well as the three suits: one light blue with side vents, one gold with green specks, and one reddish that had a silver imitation-silk vest. The pockets of the jacket came softly outward from the lining like skinny milktoast rats. Empty. Slowly she sank down on the bed and began to knead, with blunt anxious fingers, all the pockets in all the clothes piled around her. First the blue suit, then the gold with green, then the reddish one that he said he didn't like most of all, but which he would sometimes wear if she agreed to stay home, or if she promised not to touch him anywhere at all while he was getting dressed.

She was a big awkward woman, with big bones and hard rubbery flesh. Her short arms ended in ham hands, and her neck was a squat roll of fat that protruded behind her head as a big bump. Her skin was rough and puffy, with plump molelike freckles down her cheeks. Her eyes glowered from under the mountain of her brow and were circled with expensive mauve shadow. They were nervous and quick when she was flustered and darted about at nothing in particular while she was dressing hair or talking to people.

Her troubles started noticeably when she fell in love with a studiously quiet schoolteacher, Mr. Jerome Franklin Washington III, who was ten years younger than her. She told herself that she shouldn't want him, he was so little and cute and young, but when she took into account that he was a schoolteacher, well, she just couldn't seem to get any rest until, as she put it, "I were Mr. and Mrs. Jerome Franklin Washington the third, *and that's the truth!*"

She owned a small beauty shop at the back of her father's funeral home, and they were known as "colored folks with money." She made pretty good herself, though she didn't like standing on her feet so much, and her father let anybody know she wasn't getting any of his money while he was alive. She was proud to say she had never asked him for any. He started relenting kind of fast when he heard she planned to add a schoolteacher to the family, which consisted of funeral directors and bootleggers, but she cut him off quick and said she didn't want anybody to take care of her man but her. She had learned how to do hair from an old woman who ran a shop on the other side of town and was proud to say that she could make her own way. And much better than some. She was fond of telling schoolteachers (women schoolteachers) that she didn't miss her "eddicashion" as much as some did who had no learning and no money both together. She had a low opinion of women schoolteachers, because before and after her marriage to Jerome Franklin Washington III, they were the only females to whom he cared to talk.

The first time she saw him he was walking past the window of her shop with an armful of books and his coat thrown casually over his arm. Looking so neat and *cute*. What popped into her mind was that if he was hers the first thing she would get him was a sweet little red car to drive. And she worked and went into debt and got it for him, too—after she got him—but then she could tell he didn't like it much because it was only a Chevy. She had started right away to save up so she could make a down payment on a brand-new white Buick deluxe, with automatic drive and whitewall tires.

Jerome was dapper, every inch a gentleman, as anybody with half an eye could see. That's what she told everybody before they were married. He was beating her black and blue even then, so that every time you saw her she was sporting her "shades." She could not open her mouth without him wincing and pretending he couldn't stand it, so he would knock her out of the room to keep her from talking to him. She tried to be sexy and stylish, and was, in her fashion, with a predominant taste for pastel taffetas and orange shoes. In the summertime she paid twenty dollars for big umbrella hats with bows and flowers on them and when she wore black and white together she would liven it up with elbow-length gloves of red satin. She was genuinely undecided when she woke up in the morning whether she really outstripped the other girls in town for beauty, but could convince herself that she was equally good-looking by the time she had breakfast on the table. She was always talking with a lot of extra movement to her thick coarse mouth, with its hair tufts at the corners, and when she drank coffee she held the cup over the saucer with her little finger sticking out, while she crossed her short hairy legs at the knees.

If her husband laughed at her high heels as she teetered and minced off to church on Sunday mornings, with her hair greased and curled and her new dress bunching up at the top of her girdle, she pretended his eyes were approving. Other times, when he didn't bother to look up from his books and only muttered curses if she tried to kiss him good-bye, she did not know whether to laugh or cry. However, her public manner was serene.

"I just don't know how some womens can stand it, honey," she would say slowly, twisting her head to the side and upward in an elegant manner. "One thing my husband does not do," she would enunciate grandly, "he don't beat me!" And she would sit back and smile in her pleased oily fat way. Usually her listeners, captive women with wet hair, would simply smile and nod in sympathy and say, looking at one another or at her black eye, "You say he don't? Hummmm, well, hush your mouf." And she would continue curling or massaging or straightening their hair, fixing her face in a steamy dignified mask that encouraged snickers.

2

It was in her shop that she first heard the giggling and saw the smirks. It was at her job that gossip gave her to understand, as one woman told her, "Your cute little man is sticking his finger into somebody else's pie." And she was not and could not be surprised, as she looked into the amused and self-contented face, for she had long been aware that her own pie was going—and for the longest time had been going—strictly untouched.

From that first day of slyly whispered hints, "Your old man's puttin' something *over* on you, sweets," she started trying to find out who he was fooling around with. Her sources of gossip were malicious and mean, but she could think of nothing else to do but believe them. She searched high and she searched low. She looked in taverns and she looked in churches. She looked in the school where he worked.

She went to whorehouses and to prayer meetings, through parks and outside the city limits, all the while buying axes and pistols and knives of all descriptions. Of course she said nothing to her sweet Jerome, who watched her maneuverings from behind the covers of his vast supply of paperback books. This hobby of his she heartily encouraged, relegating reading to the importance of scanning the funnies; and besides, it was something he could do at home, if she could convince him she would be completely silent for an evening, and, of course, if he would stay.

She turned the whole town upside down, looking at white girls, black women, brown beauties, ugly hags of all shades. She found nothing. And Jerome went on reading, smiling smugly as he shushed her with a carefully cleaned and lustred finger. "Don't interrupt me," he was always saying, and he would read some more while she stood glowering darkly behind him, muttering swears in her throaty voice, and then tramping flatfooted out of the house with her collection of weapons.

Some days she would get out of bed at four in the morning after not sleeping a wink all night, throw an old sweater around her shoulders, and begin the search. Her firm bulk became flabby. Her eyes were bloodshot and wild, her hair full of lint, nappy at the roots and greasy on the ends. She smelled bad from mouth and underarms and elsewhere. She could not sit still for a minute without jumping up in bitter vexation to run and search a house or street she thought she might have missed before.

"You been messin' with my Jerome?" she would ask whomever she caught in her quivering feverish grip. And before they had time to answer she would have them by the chin in a headlock with a long knife pressed against their necks below the ear. Such blood-chilling questioning of its residents terrified the town, especially since her madness was soon readily perceivable from her appearance. She had taken to grinding her teeth and tearing at her hair as she walked along. The townspeople, none of whom knew where she lived—or anything about her save the name of her man, "Jerome"—were waiting for her to attempt another attack on a woman openly, or, better for them because it implied less danger to a resident, they hoped she would complete her crack-up within the confines of her own home, preferably while alone; in that event anyone seeing or hearing her would be obliged to call the authorities.

She knew this in her deranged but cunning way. But she did not let it interfere with her search. The police would never catch her, she thought; she was too clever. She had a few disguises and a thousand places to hide. A final crack-up in her own home was impossible, she reasoned contemptuously, for she did not think her husband's lover bold enough to show herself on his wife's own turf.

Meanwhile, she stopped operating the beauty shop, and her patrons were glad, for before she left for good she had had the unnerving habit of questioning a woman sitting underneath her hot comb—"You the one ain't you?!"—and would end up burning her no matter what she said. When her father died he proudly left his money to "the schoolteacher" to share or not with his wife, as he had "learnin' enough to see fit." Jerome had "learnin' enough" not to give his wife one cent. The legacy pleased Jerome, though he never bought anything with the money that his wife could see. As long as the money lasted Jerome spoke of it as "insurance." If she asked insurance against what, he would say fire and theft. Or burglary and cyclones. When the money was gone, and it seemed to her it vanished overnight, she asked Jerome what he had bought. He said, Something very big. She said, Like what? He said, Like a tank. She did not ask any more questions after that. By that time she didn't care about the money anyhow, as long as he hadn't spent it on some woman.

As steadily as she careened downhill, Jerome advanced in the opposite direction. He was well known around town as a "shrewd joker" and a scholar. An "intellectual," some people called him, a word that meant nothing whatever to her. Everyone described Jerome in a different way. He had friends among the educated, whose talk she found unusually trying, not that she was ever invited to listen to any of it. His closest friend was the head of the school he taught in and had migrated south from some famous university in the North. He was a small slender man with a ferociously unruly beard and large mournful eyes. He called Jerome "brother." The women in Jerome's group wore short kinky hair and large hoop earrings. They stuck together, calling themselves by what they termed their "African" names, and never went to church. Along with the men, the women sometimes held "workshops" for the young toughs of the town. She had no idea what went on in these; however, she had long since stopped believing they had anything to do with cabinetmaking or any other kind of woodwork.

Among Jerome's group of friends, or "comrades," as he sometimes called them jokingly (or not jokingly, for all she knew), were two or three whites from the community's white college and university. Jerome didn't ordinarily like white people, and she could not understand where they fit into the group. The principal's house was the meeting place, and the whites arrived looking backward over their shoulders after nightfall. She knew, because she had watched this house night after anxious night, trying to rouse enough courage to go inside. One hot night, when a drink helped stiffen her backbone, she burst into the living room in the middle of the evening. The women, whom she had grimly "suspected," sat together in debative conversation in one corner of the room. Every once in a while a phrase she could understand touched her ear. She heard "slave trade" and "violent overthrow" and "off de pig," an expression she'd never heard before. One of the women, the only one of this group to acknowledge her, laughingly asked if she had come to "join the revolution." She had stood shaking by the door, trying so hard to understand she felt she was going to faint. Jerome rose from among the group of men, who sat in a circle on the other side of the room, and, without paying any attention to her, began reciting some of the nastiest-sounding poetry she'd every heard. She left the room in shame and confusion, and no one bothered to ask why she'd stood so long staring at them, or whether she needed anyone to show her out. She trudged home heavily, with her head down, bewildered, astonished, and perplexed.

3

And now she hunted through her husband's clothes looking for a clue. Her hands were shaking as she emptied and shook, pawed and sometimes even lifted to her nose to smell. Each time she emptied a pocket, she felt there was something, *something*, some little thing that was escaping her.

Her heart pounding, she got down on her knees and looked under the bed. It was dusty and cobwebby, the way the inside of her head felt. The house was filthy, for she had neglected it totally since she began her search. Now it seemed that all the dust in the world had come to rest under her bed. She saw his shoes; she lifted them to her perspiring cheeks and kissed them. She ran her fingers inside them. Nothing.

Then, before she got up from her knees, she thought about the intense blackness underneath the headboard of the bed. She had not looked there. On her side of the bed on the floor beneath the pillow there was nothing. She hurried around to the other side. Kneeling, she struck something with her hand on the floor under his side of the bed. Quickly, down on her stomach, she raked it out. Then she raked and raked. She was panting and sweating, her ashen face slowly coloring with the belated rush of doomed comprehension. In a rush it came to her: "It ain't no woman." Just like that. It had never occurred to her there could be anything more serious. She stifled the cry that rose in her throat.

Coated with grit, with dust sticking to the pages, she held in her crude, indelicate hands, trembling now, a sizable pile of paperback books. Books that had fallen from his hands behind the bed over the months of their marriage. She dusted them carefully one by one and looked with frowning concentration at their covers. Fists and guns appeared everywhere. "Black" was the one word that appeared consistently on each cover. *Black Rage, Black Fire, Black Anger, Black Revenge, Black Vengeance, Black Hatred, Black Beauty, Black Revolution*. Then the word "revolution" took over. *Revolution in the Streets, Revolution from the Rooftops, Revolution in the Hills, Revolution and Rebellion, Revolution and Black People in the United States, Revolution and Death*. She looked with wonder at the books that were her husband's preoccupation, enraged that the obvious was what she had never guessed before.

How many times had she encouraged his light reading? How many times been ignorantly amused? How many times had he laughed at her when she went out looking for "his" women? With a sob she realized she didn't even know what the word "revolution" meant, unless it meant to go round and round, the way her head was going.

With quiet care she stacked the books neatly on his pillow. With the largest of her knives she ripped and stabbed them through. When the brazen and difficult words did not disappear with the books, she hastened with kerosene to set the marriage bed afire. Thirstily, in hopeless jubilation, she watched the room begin to burn. The bits of words transformed themselves into luscious figures of smoke, lazily arching toward the ceiling. "Trash!" she cried over and over, reaching through the flames to strike out the words, now raised from the dead in glorious colors. "I kill you! I kill you!" she screamed against the roaring fire, backing enraged and trembling into a darkened corner of the room, not near the open door. But the fire and the words rumbled against her together, overwhelming her with pain and enlightenment. And she hid her big wet face in her singed then sizzling arms and screamed and screamed.

1973

Donald Barthelme *1931–*

Donald Barthelme is one of the notable literary innovators of recent American literature. Since his first short story appeared in the New Yorker, *in 1963, his stories and novels have won national literary prizes and a growing audience of readers and critics who have been attracted to his artful and dazzling "linguistic games" and his mocking portraits of the lives and feelings of modern Americans.*

Barthelme has been categorized as one of the "celebrants of unreason, chaos, and inexorable decay," a writer suited best for the "far outs." His writing, with its puzzles and fragmentary structures, has been called "postmodernism," "anti-traditional," and "metafiction" because he has often abandoned the familiar literary devices of plot and characterization. He makes little attempt to mirror reality. Instead, he uses conventional settings and situations for the display of ludicrous and paradoxical events, striving for

*what is "sometimes spoken of as the ineffable. . . . somewhere probably between mathematics
and religion, in which what may fairly be called truth exists."*

*In two novels—*Snow White *(1967) and* The Dead Father *(1975)—and in more
than one hundred and fifty short stories, including his recent* Forty Stories, *1987,
Barthelme has used fragments of popular song lyrics, sayings, advertising slogans, and
the stereotyped phrases of the day. He has rewritten well-known fairy tales in which expected
and familiar events are warped and "they lived happily ever after" is not to be.*

*The conventional world, for Barthelme, is a thicket of arbitrary follies, overgrown with
unrecognized paradoxes and infested by characters whose minds swarm with the pictures
of pop advertising and the ideas of pop thought. Barthelme questions received truths, the
conventions that our dulled senses automatically accept. His brief stories show how modern
consciousness is often a state of foolish innocence and modern life a series of mordant
experiences needlessly repeated.*

*In the comic turns of his deft prose Barthelme exposes America's most cherished insti-
tutions: its businesses, homes, and—in "The School"—its classrooms, where dim-witted
teachers grope for clichés with which to express the formulaic thought that clutters their
brains and where grade-school children, just out of infancy, speak in high-flown rhetoric
about the "taken-for-granted mundanity of the everyday."*

FURTHER READING: L. Gordon, *Donald Barthelme*, 1981; M. Couturier and R. Durand,
Donald Barthelme, 1982; C. Molesworth, *Donald Barthelme's Fiction*, 1982; L. McCaffrey,
The Metafictional Muse, 1982.
TEXT: *Sixty Stories*, 1981.

THE SCHOOL

Well, we had all these children out planting trees, see, because we figured
that . . . that was part of their education, to see how, you know, the root systems
. . . and also the sense of responsibility, taking care of things, being individually
responsible. You know what I mean. And the trees all died. They were orange
trees. I don't know why they died, they just died. Something wrong with the soil
possibly or maybe the stuff we got from the nursery wasn't the best. We complained about it. So we've got thirty kids there, each kid had his or her own little
tree to plant, and we've got these thirty dead trees. All these kids looking at
these little brown sticks, it was depressing.

It wouldn't have been so bad except that just a couple of weeks before the
thing with the trees, the snakes all died. But I think that the snakes—well, the
reason that the snakes kicked off was that . . . you remember, the boiler was
shut off for four days because of the strike, and that was explicable. It was
something you could explain to the kids because of the strike. I mean, none of
their parents would let them cross the picket line and they knew there was a
strike going on and what it meant. So when things got started up again and we
found the snakes they weren't too disturbed.

With the herb gardens it was probably a case of overwatering, and at least
now they know not to overwater. The children were very conscientious with the
herb gardens and some of them probably . . . you know, slipped them a little
extra water when we weren't looking. Or maybe . . . well, I don't like to think
about sabotage, although it did occur to us. I mean, it was something that crossed
our minds. We were thinking that way probably because before that the gerbils

had died, and the white mice had died, and the salamander . . . well, now they know not to carry them around in plastic bags.

Of course we *expected* the tropical fish to die, that was no surprise. Those numbers, you look at them crooked and they're belly-up on the surface. But the lesson plan called for a tropical-fish input at that point, there was nothing we could do, it happens every year, you just have to hurry past it.

We weren't even supposed to have a puppy.

We weren't even supposed to have one, it was just a puppy the Murdoch girl found under a Gristede's truck one day and she was afraid the truck would run over it when the driver had finished making his delivery, so she stuck it in her knapsack and brought it to school with her. So we had this puppy. As soon as I saw the puppy I thought, Oh Christ, I bet it will live for about two weeks and then . . . And that's what it did. It wasn't supposed to be in the classroom at all, there's some kind of regulation about it, but you can't tell them they can't have a puppy when the puppy is already there, right in front of them, running around on the floor and yap yap yapping. They named it Edgar—that is, they named it after me. They had a lot of fun running after it and yelling, "Here, Edgar! Nice Edgar!" Then they'd laugh like hell. They enjoyed the ambiguity. I enjoyed it myself. I don't mind being kidded. They made a little house for it in the supply closet and all that. I don't know what it died of. Distemper, I guess. It probably hadn't had any shots. I got it out of there before the kids got to school. I checked the supply closet each morning, routinely, because I knew what was going to happen. I gave it to the custodian.

And then there was this Korean orphan that the class adopted through the Help the Children program, all the kids brought in a quarter a month, that was the idea. It was an unfortunate thing, the kid's name was Kim and maybe we adopted him too late or something. The cause of death was not stated in the letter we got, they suggested we adopt another child instead and sent us some interesting case histories, but we didn't have the heart. The class took it pretty hard, they began (I think, nobody ever said anything to me directly) to feel that maybe there was something wrong with the school. But I don't think there's anything wrong with the school, particularly, I've seen better and I've seen worse. It was just a run of bad luck. We had an extraordinary numer of parents passing away, for instance. There were I think two heart attacks and two suicides, one drowning, and four killed together in a car accident. One stroke. And we had the usual heavy mortality rate among the grandparents, or maybe it was heavier this year, it seemed so. And finally the tragedy.

The tragedy occurred when Matthew Wein and Tony Mavrogordo were playing over where they're excavating for the new federal office building. There were all these big wooden beams stacked, you know, at the edge of the excavation. There's a court case coming out of that, the parents are claiming that the beams were poorly stacked. I don't know what's true and what's not. It's been a strange year.

I forgot to mention Billy Brandt's father, who was knifed fatally when he grappled with a masked intruder in his home.

One day, we had a discussion in class. They asked me, where did they go? The trees, the salamander, the tropical fish, Edgar, the poppas and mommas, Matthew and Tony, where did they go? And I said, I don't know, I don't know. And they said, who knows? and I said, nobody knows. And they said, is death that which gives meaning to life? And I said, no, life is that which gives meaning to life. Then they said, but isn't death, considered as a fundamental datum, the means by which the taken-for-granted mundanity of the everyday may be transcended in the direction of—

I said, yes, maybe.

They said, we don't like it.

I said, that's sound.

They said, it's a bloody shame!

I said, it is.

They said, will you make love now with Helen (our teaching assistant) so that we can see how it is done? We know you like Helen.

I do like Helen but I said that I would not.

We've heard so much about it, they said, but we've never seen it.

I said I would be fired and that it was never, or almost never, done as a demonstration. Helen looked out of the window.

They said, please, please make love with Helen, we require an assertion of value, we are frightened.

I said that they shouldn't be frightened (although I am often frightened) and that there was value everywhere. Helen came and embraced me. I kissed her a few times on the brow. We held each other. The children were excited. Then there was a knock on the door, I opened the door, and the new gerbil walked in. The children cheered wildly.

Anne Beattie   *1947–*

Ann Beattie writes of middle-class American suburbanites who grew up in the turbulent 1960s, who saw themselves as part of the with-it generation of the counterculture, and who now have lost their way and don't know what to do. They collect grievances and ruined marriages; they suffer from tepid depressions and self-pitying nihilism; like the hero of "The Lawn Party," they seem to enjoy "feeling blue" and "being rotten." Their world has, outwardly at least, rewarded them; they dwell in an affluent limbo; they have mastered the social rituals and tribal rites of their class, but their lives are cluttered with former wives, former lovers, and former friends.

Literary Beattie-land is the suburbia of eastern America extending from New England to Virginia, where she herself has spent her life. She was born and raised in Washington, D.C., graduated from American University, did graduate work in English at the University of Connecticut, and has taught at Harvard and the University of Virginia. In 1972 she published her first significant short story, in the Atlantic Monthly. *The next year one of her stories appeared in the* New Yorker, *a magazine to which she has now become a regular and honored contributor. In 1976 her first novel,* Chilly Scenes of Winter, *and her first collection of short stories,* Distortions, *were published. Since then she has published two more novels and three collections of short stories, the last,* Where You'll Find Me, and Other Stories, *appearing in 1986.*

Her fiction is often compared to the New Yorker *stories of John Cheever and John Updike. Like them she writes of white, middle-class Americans who are disoriented, anxious, and isolated. Her stories have a narrow range, and some critics have complained that she fails to present a clear meaning or conventionally plotted narrative action with a clear resolution at the end of a story. She responds that it is not necessarily her duty to hand her readers appropriate meanings and clear resolutions, that she is more interested in showing the situation of a group of characters at a particular moment in their lives.*

Ann Beattie uses simple declarative sentences, almost without metaphor or musical rhythm. She says, "I write in those flat simple sentences because that's the way I think." Using unemotional, unadorned prose, and with a masterful control of tone, she has become the most notable chronicler of a generation of Americans, men and women in their twenties and thirties whose yearnings and disillusionments are revealed in the words they say, the clothes they wear, the games they play, and the memories they have of such bypassed phenomena as Woodstock, Janis Joplin, and "Heartbreak Hotel."

FURTHER READING: C. Murphy, *Ann Beattie*, 1986.
TEXT: *Secrets and Surprises*, 1978.

THE LAWN PARTY

I said to Lorna last night, "Do you want me to tell you a story?" "No," she said. Lorna is my daughter. She is ten and a great disbeliever. But she was willing to hang around my room and talk. "Regular dry cleaning won't take that out," Lorna said when she saw the smudges on my suede jacket. "Really," she said. "You have to take it somewhere special." In her skepticism, Lorna assumes that everyone else is also skeptical.

According to the Currier & Ives calendar hanging on the back of the bedroom door, and according to my watch, and according to my memory, which would be keen without either of them, Lorna and I have been at my parents' house for three days. Today is the annual croquet game that all our relatives here in Connecticut gather for (even some from my wife's side). It's the Fourth of July, and damn hot. I have the fan going. I'm sitting in a comfortable chair (moved upstairs, on my demand, by my father and the maid), next to the window in my old bedroom. There is already a cluster of my relatives on the lawn. Most of them are wearing little American flags pinned somewhere on their shirts or blouses or hanging from their ears. A patriotic group. Beer (forgive them: Heineken's) and wine (Almadén Chablis) drinkers. My father loves this day better than his own birthday. He leans on his mallet and gives instructions to my sister Eva on the placement of the posts. Down there, he can see the American flags clearly. But if he is already too loaded to stick the posts in the ground, he probably isn't noticing the jewelry.

Lorna has come into my room twice in the last hour—once to ask me when I am coming down to join what she calls "the party," another time to say that I am making everybody feel rotten by not joining them. A statement to be dismissed with a wave of the hand, but I have none. No right arm, either. I have a left hand and a left arm, but I have stopped valuing them. It's the right one I want. In the hospital, I rejected suggestions of a plastic arm or a claw. "Well, then, what do you envision?" the doctor said. "Air," I told him. This needed amplification. "Air where my arm used to be," I said. He gave a little "Ah, so" bow of the head and left the room.

I intend to sit here at the window all day, watching the croquet game. I will drink the Heineken's Lorna has brought me, taking small sips because I am unable to wipe my mouth after good foamy sips. My left hand is there to wipe with, but who wants to set down his beer bottle to wipe his mouth?

Lorna's mother has left me. I think of her now as Lorna's mother because she has made it clear that she no longer wants to be my wife. She has moved to another apartment with Lorna. She, herself, seems to be no happier for having left me and visits me frequently. Mention is no longer made of the fact that I am her husband and she is my wife. Recently Mary (her name) took the ferry to the Statue of Liberty. She broke in on me on my second day here in the room, explaining that she would not be here for the croquet game, but with the news that she had visited New York yesterday and had taken the ferry to the Statue of Liberty. "And how was the city?" I asked. "Wonderful," she assured me. She went to the Carnegie Delicatessen and had cheese cake. When she does not visit, she writes. She has a second sense about when I have left my apartment for my parents' house. In her letters she usually tells me something about Lorna, although no mention is made of the fact that Lorna is my child. In fact, she once slyly suggested in a bitter moment that Lorna was not—but she backed down about that one.

Lorna is a great favorite with my parents, and my parents are rich. This, Mary always said jokingly, was why she married me. Actually, it was my charm. She thought I was terrific. If I had not fallen in love with her sister, everything would still be fine between us. I did it fairly; I fell in love with her sister before the wedding. I asked to have the wedding delayed. Mary got drunk and cried. Why was I doing this? How could I do it? She would leave me, but she wouldn't delay the wedding. I asked her to leave. She got drunk and cried and would not. We were married on schedule. She had nothing more to do with her sister. I, on the other hand—strange how many things one cannot say anymore—saw her whenever possible. Patricia—that was her name—went with me on business trips, met me for lunches and dinners, and was driving my car when it went off the highway.

When I came to, Mary was standing beside my hospital bed, her face distorted, looking down at me. "My sister killed herself and tried to take you with her," she said.

I waited for her to throw herself on me in pity.

"You deserved this," she said, and walked out of the room.

I was being fed intravenously in my left arm. I looked to see if my right arm was hooked up to anything. It hurt to move my head. My right arm was free— how free I didn't know at the time. I swear I saw it, but it had been amputated when I was unconscious. The doctor spoke to me at length about this later, insisting that there was no possibility that my arm was there when my wife was in the room and gone subsequently—gone when she left. No, indeed. It was amputated at once, in surgery, and when I saw my wife I was recovering from surgery. I tried to get at it another way, leaving Mary out of it. Wasn't I conscious before Mary was there? Didn't I see the arm? No, I was unconscious and didn't see anything. No, indeed. The physical therapist, the psychiatrist and the chaplain the doctor had brought with him nodded their heads in fast agreement. But soon I would have an artificial arm. I said that I did not want one. It was then that we had the discussion about air.

Last Wednesday was my birthday. I was unpleasant to all. Mrs. Bates, the cook, baked me chocolate-chip cookies with walnuts (my favorite), but I didn't eat any until she went home. My mother gave me a red velour shirt, which I hinted was unsatisfactory. "What's wrong with it?" she said. I said, "It's got one too many arms." My former student Banks visited me in the evening, not knowing that it was my birthday. He is a shy, thin, hirsute individual of twenty— a painter, a true *artiste*. I liked him so well that I had given him the phone number at my parents' house. He brought with him his most recent work, a canvas of a nude woman, for my inspection. While we were all gathered around the birthday cake, Banks answered my question about who she was by saying that she was a professional model. Later, strolling in the backyard, he told me that he had picked her up at a bus stop, after convincing her that she did not want to spend her life waiting for buses, and brought her to his apartment, where he fixed a steak dinner. The woman spent two days there, and when she left, Banks gave her forty dollars, although she did not want any money. She thought the painting he did of her was ugly, and wanted to be reassured that she wasn't really that heavy around the hips. Banks told her that it was not a representational painting; he said it was an Impressionist painting. She gave him her phone number. He called; there was no such number. He could not understand it. He went back to the bus stop, and eventually he found her again. She told him to get away or she'd call the police.

Ah, Banks. Ah, youth—to be twenty again, instead of thirty-two. In class, Banks used to listen to music on his cassette player through earphones. He would eat candy bars while he nailed frames together. Banks was always chewing food or mouthing songs. Sometimes he would forget and actually sing in class—an eerie wail, harmonizing with something none of the rest of us heard. The students who did not resent Bank's talent resented his chewing or singing or his success with women. Banks had great success with Lorna. He told her she looked like Bianca Jagger and she was thrilled. "Why don't you get some platform shoes like hers?" he said, and her eyes shriveled with pleasure. He told her a couple of interesting facts about Copernicus; she told him about the habits of gypsy moths. When he left, he kissed her hand. It did my heart good to see her so happy. I never delight her at all, as Mary keeps telling me.

They have written me from the college where I work, saying that they hope all is well and that I will be back teaching in the fall. It is not going to be easy to teach painting, with my right arm gone. Still, one remembers Matisse in his last years. Where there's a will, et cetera. My department head has sent flowers twice (mixed and tulips), and the dean himself has written a message on a get-well card. There is a bunny on the card, looking at a rainbow. Banks is the only one who really tempts me to go back to work. The others, Banks tells me, are "full of it."

Now I have a visitor. Danielle, John's wife, has come up to see me. John is my brother. She brings an opened beer and sets it on the windowsill without comment. Danielle is wearing a white dress with small porpoises on it, smiling as they leap. Across that chest, no wonder.

"Are you feeling blue today or just being rotten?" she asks.

The beginnings of many of Danielle's sentences often put me in mind of trashy, romantic songs. Surely someone has written a song called "Are You Feeling Blue?"

"Both," I say. I usually give Danielle straight answers. She tries to be nice. She has been nice to my brother for five years. He keeps promising to take her back to France, but he never does.

She sits on the rug, next to my chair. "Their rotten lawn parties," she says. Danielle is French, but her English is very good.

"Pull up a chair and watch the festivities," I say.

"I have to go back," she says, pouting. "They want you to come back with me."

Champagne glasses clinking, white tablecloth, single carnation, key of A: "They Want You Back with Me."

"Who sent you?" I ask.

"John. But I think Lorna would like it if you were there."

"Lorna doesn't like me anymore. Mary's turned her against me."

"Ten is a difficult age," Danielle says.

"I thought the teens were difficult."

"How would I know? I don't have children."

She has a drink of beer, and then puts the bottle in my hand instead of back on the window sill.

"You have beautiful round feet," I say.

She tucks them under her. "I'm embarrassed," she says.

"Our talk is full of the commonplace today," I say, sighing.

"You're insulting me," she says. "That's why John wouldn't come up. He says he gets tired of your insults."

"I wasn't trying to be insulting. You've got beautiful feet. Raise one up here and I'll kiss it."

"Don't make fun of me," Danielle says.

"Really," I say.

Danielle moves her leg, unstraps a sandal and raises her right foot. I take it in my hand and bend over to kiss it across the toes.

"Stop it," she says, laughing. "Someone will come in."

"They won't," I say. "John isn't the only one tired of my insults."

I have been taking a little nap. Waking up, I look out the window and see Danielle below. She is sitting in one of the redwood chairs, accepting a drink from my father. One leg is crossed over the other, her beautiful foot dangling. They all know I am watching but they refuse to look up. Eventually my mother does. She makes a violent sweep with her arm—like a coach motioning the defensive team onto the field. I wave. She turns her back and rejoins the group—Lorna, John, Danielle, my Aunt Rosie, Rosie's daughter Elizabeth, my father, and some others. Wednesday was also Elizabeth's birthday—her eighteenth. My parents called and sang to her. When Janis Joplin died Elizabeth cried for six days. "She's an emotional child," Rosie said at the time. Then, forgetting that, she asked everyone in the family why Elizabeth had gone to pieces. "Why did you feel so bad about Janis, Elizabeth?" I said. "I don't know," she said. "Did her death make you feel like killing yourself?" I said. "Are you unhappy the way she was?" Rosie now speaks to me only perfunctorily. On her get-well card to me (no visit) she wrote: "So sorry." They are all sorry. They have been told by the doctor to ignore my gloominess, so they ignore me. I ignore them because even before the accident I was not very fond of them. My brother, in particular, bores me. When we were kids, sharing a bedroom, John would talk to me at night. When I fell asleep he'd come over and shake my mattress. One night my father caught him doing it and hit him. "It's not my fault," John hollered. "He's a goddamn snob." We got separate bedrooms. I was eight and John was ten.

Danielle comes back, looking sweatier than before. Below they are playing the first game. My father's brother Ed pretends to be a majorette and struts with his mallet, twirling it and pointing his knees.

"Nobody sent me this time," Danielle says. "Are you coming down to dinner? They're grilling steaks."

"He's so cheap he'll serve Almadén with them," I say. "You grew up in France. How can you drink that stuff?"

"I just drink one glass," she says.

"Refuse to do it," I say.

She shrugs, "You're in an awful mood," she says.

"Give back that piggy," I say.

She frowns. "I came to have a serious discussion. Why aren't you coming to dinner?"

"Not hungry."

"Come down for Lorna."

"Lorna doesn't care."

"Maybe you're mean to her."

"I'm the same way I always was with her."

"Be a little extra nice, then."

"Give back that piggy," I say, and she puts her foot up. I unbuckle her sandal with my left hand. There are strap marks on the skin. I lick down her baby toe and kiss it, at the very tip. In turn, I kiss all the others.

•　　•　　•　[1]

It's evening, and the phone is ringing. I think about answering it. Finally someone else in the house picks it up. I get up and then sit on the bed and look around. My old bedroom looks pretty much the way it looked when I left for college, except that my mother has added a few things that I never owned, which seem out of place. Two silver New Year's Eve hats rest on the bedposts, and a snapshot of my mother in front of a Mexican fruit stand (I have never been to Mexico) that my father took on their "second honeymoon" is on my bureau. I pull open a drawer and take out a pack of letters. I pull out one of the letters at random and read it. It is from an old girl friend of mine. Her name was Alison, and she once loved me madly. In the letter she says she is giving up smoking so that when we are old she won't be repulsive to me. The year I graduated from college, she married an Indian and moved to India. Maybe now she has a little red dot in the middle of her forehead.

I try to remember loving Alison. I remember loving Mary's sister, Patricia. She is dead. That doesn't sink in. And she can't have meant to die, in spite of what Mary said. A woman who meant to die wouldn't buy a big wooden bowl and a bag of fruit, and then get in the car and drive it off the highway. It is a fact, however, that as the car started to go sideways I looked at Patricia, and she was whipping the wheel to the right. Maybe I imagined that. I remember putting my arm out to brace myself as the car started to turn over. If Patricia were alive, I'd have to be at the croquet game. But if she were alive, she and I could disappear for a few minutes, have a kiss by the barn.

I said to Lorna last night that I would tell her a story. It was going to be a fairy tale, all about Patricia and me but disguised as the prince and the princess, but she said no, she didn't want to hear it, and walked out. Just as well. If it had ended sadly it would have been an awful trick to pull on Lorna, and if it had ended happily, it would have depressed me even more. "There's nothing wrong with coming to terms with your depression," the doctor said to me. He kept urging me to see a shrink. The shrink came, and urged me to talk to him. When he left, the chaplain came in and urged me to see *him*. I checked out.

Lorna visits a third time. She asks whether I heard the phone ringing. I did. She says that—well, she finally answered it. "When you were first walking, one of your favorite things was to run for the phone," I said. I was trying to be nice to her. "Stop talking about when I was a baby," she says, and leaves. On the way

---

[1]Beattie's ellipsis points.

out, she says, "It was your friend who came over the other night. He wants you to call him. His number is here." She comes back with a piece of paper, then leaves again.

"I got drunk," Banks says on the phone, "and I felt sorry for you."

"The hell with that, Banks," I say, and reflect that I sound like someone talking in *The Sun Also Rises*.[2]

"Forget it, old Banks," I say, enjoying the part.

"You're not loaded too, are you?" Banks says.

"No, Banks," I say.

"Well, I wanted to talk. I wanted to ask if you wanted to go out to a bar with me. I don't have any more beer or money."

"Thanks, but there's a big rendezvous here today. Lorna's here. I'd better stick around."

"Oh," Banks says. "Listen. Could I come over and borrow five bucks?"

Banks does not think of me in my professional capacity.

"Sure," I say.

"Thanks," he says.

"Sure, old Banks. Sure," I say, and hang up.

Lorna stands in the doorway. "Is he coming over?" she asks.

"Yes. He's coming to borrow money. He's not the man for you, Lorna."

"You don't have any money either," she says. "Grandpa does."

"I have enough money," I say defensively.

"How much do you have?"

"I make a salary, you know, Lorna. Has your mother been telling you I'm broke?"

"She doesn't talk about you."

"Then why did you ask how much money I had?"

"I wanted to know."

"I'm not going to tell you," I say.

"They told me to come talk to you," Lorna says. "I was supposed to get you to come down."

"Do you want me to come down?" I ask.

"Not if you don't want to."

"You're supposed to be devoted to your daddy," I say.

Lorna sighs. "You won't answer any of my questions, and you say silly things."

"What?"

"What you just said—about my daddy?"

"I am your daddy," I say.

"I know it," she says.

There seems nowhere for the conversation to go.

"You want to hear that story now?" I ask.

"No. Don't try to tell me any stories. I'm ten."

"I'm thirty-two," I say.

My father's brother William is about to score a victory over Elizabeth. He puts his foot on the ball, which is touching hers, and knocks her ball down the hill. He pretends he has knocked it an immense distance and cups his hand over his brow to squint after it. William's wife will not play croquet; she sits on the grass

---

[2]Novel by Ernest Hemingway.

and frowns. She is a dead ringer for the woman behind the cash register in Edwar Hopper's "Tables for Ladies."[3]

"How's it going?" Danielle asks, standing in the doorway.

"Come on in," I say.

"I just came upstairs to go to the bathroom. The cook is in the one downstairs."

She comes in and looks out the window.

"Do you want me to get you anything?" she asks. "Food?"

"You're just being nice to me because I kiss your piggies."

"You're horrible," she says.

"I tried to be nice to Lorna, and all she wanted to talk about was money."

"All they talk about down there is money," she says.

She leaves and then comes back with her hair combed and her mouth pink again.

"What do you think of William's wife?" I ask.

"I don't know, she doesn't say much." Danielle sits on the floor, with her chin on her knees. "Everybody always says that people who only say a few dumb things are sweet."

"What dumb things has she said?" I say.

"She said, 'Such a beautiful day,' and looked at the sky."

"You shouldn't be hanging out with these people, Danielle," I say.

"I've got to go back," she says.

Banks is here. He is sitting next to me as it gets dark. I am watching Danielle out on the lawn. She has a red shawl that she winds around her shoulders. She looks tired and elegant. My father has been drinking all afternoon. "Get the hell down here!" he hollered to me a little while ago. My mother rushed up to him to say that I had a student with me. He backed down. Lorna came up and brought us two dishes of peach ice cream (handmade by Rosie), giving the larger one to Banks. She and Banks discussed *The Hobbit*[4] briefly. Banks kept apologizing to me for not leaving, but said he was too strung out to drive. He went into the bathroom and smoked a joint and came back and sat down and rolled his head from side to side. "You make sense," Banks says now, and I am flattered until I realize that I have not been talking for a long time.

"It's too bad it's so dark," I say. "That woman down there in the black dress looks just like somebody in an Edward Hopper painting. You'd recognize her."

"Nah," Banks says, head swaying. "Everything's basically different. I get so tired of examining things and finding out they're different. This crappy nature poem isn't at all like that crappy nature poem. That's what I mean," Banks says.

"Do you remember your accident?" he says.

"No," I say.

"Excuse me," Banks says.

"I remember thinking of *Jules and Jim*."[5]

"Where she drove off the cliff?" Banks says, very excited.

"Umm."

"When did you think that?"

"As it was happening."

"Wow," Banks says. "I wonder if anybody else flashed on that before you?"

"I couldn't say."

Banks sips his iced gin. "What do you think of me as an artist?" he says.

[3]Painting by the American realist Edward Hopper (1882–1967).
[4]Novel (1937) by the English writer J. R. R. Tolkien.
[5]French motion picture (1961).

"You're very good, Banks."

It begins to get cooler. A breeze blows the curtains toward us.

"I had a dream that I was a raccoon," Banks says. "I kept trying to look over my back to count the rings of my tail, but my back was too high, and I couldn't count past the first two."

Banks finishes his drink.

"Would you like me to get you another drink?" I ask.

"That's an awful imposition," Banks says, extending his glass.

I take the glass and go downstairs. A copy of *The Hobbit* is lying on the rose brocade sofa. Mrs. Bates is sitting at the kitchen table, reading *People*.

"Thank you very much for the cookies," I say.

"It's nothing," she says. Her earrings are on the table. Her feet are on a chair.

"Tell them we ran out of gin if they want more," I say. "I need this bottle."

"Okay," she says. "I think there's another bottle, anyway."

I take the bottle upstairs in my armpit, carrying a glass with fresh ice in it in my hand.

"You know," Banks says, "they say that if you face things—if you just get them through your head—you can accept them. They say you can accept anything if you can once get it through your head."

"What's this about?" I say.

"Your arm," Banks says.

"I realize that I don't have an arm," I say.

"I don't mean to offend you," Banks says, drinking.

"I know you don't."

"If you ever want me to yell at you about it, just say the word. That might help—help it sink in."

"I already realize it, Banks," I say.

"You're a swell guy," Banks says. "What kind of music do you listen to?"

"Do you want to hear music?"

"No. I just want to know what you listen to."

"Schoenberg,"[6] I say. I have not listened to Schoenberg for years.

"Ahh," Banks says.

He offers me his glass. I take a drink and hand it back.

"You know how they always have cars—car ads—you ever notice . . . I'm all screwed up," Banks says.

"Go on," I say.

"They always put the car on the beach?"

"Yeah."

"I was thinking about doing a thing with a great big car in the background and a little beach up front." Banks chuckles.

Outside, the candles have been lit. A torch flames from a metal holder—one of the silliest things I have ever seen—and blue lanterns have been lit in the trees. Someone has turned on a radio, and Elizabeth and some man, not recognizable, dance to "Heartbreak Hotel."

"There's Schoenberg," Banks says.

"Banks," I say, "I want you to take this the right way. I like you, and I'm glad you came over. Why did you come over?"

"I wanted you to praise my paintings." Banks plays church and steeple with his hands. "But also, I just wanted to talk."

"Was there anything particularly—"

[6]Arnold Schoenberg (1874–1951), Austrian-born American composer.

"I thought you might want to talk to me."

"Why don't you talk to me, instead?"

"I've got to be a great painter," Banks says. "I paint and then at night I smoke up or go out to some bar, and in the morning I paint . . . All night I pray until I fall asleep that I will become great. You must think I'm crazy. What do you think of me?"

"You make me feel old," I say.

The gin bottle is in Banks's crotch, the glass resting on the top of the bottle.

"I sensed that," Banks says, "before I got too wasted to sense anything."

"You want to hear a story?" I say.

"Sure."

"The woman who was driving the car I was in—the Princess . . . " I laugh, but Banks only nods, trying hard to follow. "I think the woman must have been out to commit suicide. We had been out buying things. The back seat was loaded with nice antiques, things like that, and we had had a nice afternoon, eaten ice cream, talked about how she would be starting school again in the fall—"

"Artist?" Banks asks.

"A linguistics major."

"Okay. Go on."

"What I'm saying is that all was well in the kingdom. Not exactly, because she wasn't my wife, but she should have been. But for the purpose of the story, what I'm saying is that we were in fine shape, it was a fine day—"

"Month?" Banks says.

"March," I say.

"That's right," Banks says.

"I was going to drop her off at the shopping center, where she'd left her car, and she was going to continue on to her castle and I'd go to mine . . . "

"Continue," Banks says.

"And then she tried to kill us. She did kill herself."

"I read it in the papers," Banks says.

"What do you think?" I ask.

"Banks's lesson," Banks says. "Never look back. Don't try to count your tail rings."

Danielle walks into the room. "I have come for the gin," she says. "The cook said you had it."

"Danielle, this is Banks."

"How do you do," Banks says.

Danielle reaches down and takes the bottle from Banks. "You're missing a swell old time," she says.

"Maybe a big wind will come along and blow them all away," Banks says.

Danielle is silent a moment, then laughs—a laugh that cuts through the darkness. She ducks her head down by my face and kisses my cheek, and turns in a wobbly way and walks out of the room.

"Jesus," Banks says. "Here we are sitting here and then this weird thing happens."

"Her?" I say.

"Yeah."

Lorna comes, very sleepy, carrying a napkin with cookies on it. She obviously wants to give them to Banks, but Banks has passed out, upright, in the chair next to mine. "Climb aboard," I say, offering my lap. Lorna hesitates, but then does, putting the cookies down on the floor without offering me any. She tells me that her mother has a boyfriend.

"What's his name?" I ask.

"Stanley," Lorna says.

"Maybe a big wind will come and blow Stanley away," I say.

"What's wrong with him?" she says, looking at Banks.

"Drunk," I say. "Who's drunk downstairs?"

"Rosie," she says. "And William, and, uh, Danielle."

"Don't drink," I say.

"I won't," she says. "Will he still be here in the morning?"

"I expect so," I say.

Banks has fallen asleep in an odd posture. His feet are clamped together, his arms are limp at his sides, and his chin is jutting forward. The melting ice cubes from the overturned glass have encroached on the cookies.

At the lawn party, they've found a station on the radio that plays only songs from other years. Danielle begins a slow, drunken dance. Her red shawl has fallen to the grass. I stare at her and imagine her dress disappearing, her shoes kicked off, beautiful Danielle dancing naked in the dusk. The music turns to static, but Danielle is still dancing.

Reference Works, Bibliographies

Atlick, Richard D., and Wright, Andrew. *Selective Bibliography for the Study of English and American Literature,* 6th edition, 1979.

Blanck, Jacob. *Bibliography of American Literature,* Vols. I–, 1955–.

Bryer, J. R., ed. *Sixteen Modern American Authors: A Survey of Research and Criticism,* 1973.

Burke, W. J., and Howe, W. D. *American Authors and Books,* revised by Irving Weiss, 1962.

Clark, H. H. *American Literature: Poe through Garland,* 1971.

Davis, R. B. *American Literature through Bryant,* 1969.

Duke, Maurice, and others, eds. *American Women Writers: Bibliographical Essays,* 1983.

Erisman, Fred, and Etulain, Richard, eds. *Fifty Western Writers: A Bio-Bibliographical Sourcebook,* 1982.

Etulain, Richard. *A Bibliographical Guide to the Study of Western American Literature,* 1982.

Gerstenberger, Donna, and Hendrick, George. *The American Novel: A Checklist of Twentieth-Century Criticism on Novels Written Since 1789,* 2 vols., 1961, 1970.

Gohdes, Clarence. *Literature and Theater in the States and Regions of the U.S.A.: An Historical Bibliography,* 1967.

Gohdes, Clarence, and Marovitz, Sanford. *Bibliographical Guide to the Study of the Literature of the U.S.A.,* 5th edition, 1983.

Handlin, Oscar, and others. *Harvard Guide to American History,* 1954.

Hanna, Archibald. *A Mirror for the Nation: An Annotated Bibliography of American Social Fiction, 1901–1950,* 1985.

Hart, J. D. *The Oxford Companion to American Literature,* 5th edition, 1983.

Havelice, Patricia. *Index to American Author Bibliographies,* 1971.

Herzberg, M. J., and others. *The Reader's Encyclopedia of American Literature,* 1961.

Hoffman, Daniel, ed. *Harvard Guide to Contemporary American Writing,* 1979.

Holman, C. H. *The American Novel through Henry James,* 1966.

Jones, H. M., and Ludwig, R. M. *Guide to American Literature and Its Backgrounds Since 1890,* 4th edition, 1972.

Kolb, Harold. *A Field Guild to the Study of American Literature,* 1976.

Kunitz, S. J., and Haycraft, Howard, eds. *American Authors, 1600–1900,* 1944.

——. *Twentieth Century Authors,* 1942. 1st supplement, 1955.

Kuntz, Joseph. *Poetry Explication,* 1953. Revised 1962.

——. *American Literature: A Study and Research Guide,* 1976.

Leary, Lewis. *Articles on American Literature, 1900–1950,* 1954.

——. *Articles on American Literature, 1950–1967,* 1970.

——. *Articles on American Literature, 1968–1975,* 1979.

Long, E. H. *American Drama from Its Beginning to the Present,* 1970.

Ludwig, R. M., ed. *Bibliographical Supplement, Literary History of the United States,* 4th edition, revised, 1974.

Mainiero, Lina. *American Women Writers: A Critical Reference Guide from Colonial Times to the Present,* 4 vols., 1979–1982.

Malkoff, Karl. *Crowell's Handbook of Contemporary American Poetry,* 1973.

Millet, F. B. *Contemporary American Authors: A Critical Survey and 219 Biographies,* 1940.

Morris, R. B., ed. *Encyclopedia of American History,* 1953.

Myerson, Joel, and Helterman, J. eds. *Dictionary of Literary Biographies,* 9 vols., 1978–1983.

Nadel, I. B. *Jewish Writers of North America: A Guide to Information Sources,* 1981.

Nevius, Blake. *The American Novel: Sinclair Lewis to the Present,* 1970.

Nilon, Charles. *Bibliography of Bibliographies of American Literature*, 1970.

Page, James, and Min Roh, Joe. *Selected Black American, African, and Caribbean Authors: A Bio-Bibliography*, 1985.

Palmer, Helen, and Dyson, Jane. *American Drama Criticism*, 1967. Supplement 1970.

Parker, Patricia. *Early American Fiction: A Reference Guide*, 1984.

Rees, Robert, and Harbert, Earl, eds. *Fifteen American Authors Before 1900*, 1984.

Rock, Roger. *The Native American in American Literature: A Selectively Annotated Bibliography*, 1985.

Rubin, Louis, ed. *A Bibliographical Guide to the Study of Southern Literature*, 1969.

Rush, T. G., and others, eds. *Black American Writers Past and Present: A Biographical and Bibliographical Dictionary*, 1975.

Sabin, Joseph, and others. *A Dictionary of Books Relating to America from Its Discovery to the Present Time*, 29 vols., 1868–1936.

Schweik, Robert, and Riesner, Dieter. *Reference Sources in English and American Literature*, 1977.

Thurston, Jarvis, and others. *Short Fiction Criticism*, 1960.

Tompkins, Jane. *Sensational Designs: The Cultural Work of American Fiction, 1790–1860*, 1985.

Turner, Darwin. *Afro-American Writers*, 1970.

Tyler, Gary. *Drama Criticism*, 1966.

Ungar, Leonard. *American Writers: A Collection of Literary Biographies*, 8 vols., 1974–1979.

Vinson, James, ed. *Contemporary Dramatists*, 2nd. ed., 1977.

———. *Contemporary Novelists*, 3rd. ed., 1980.

———. *Contemporary Poets*, 3rd. ed., 1980.

Vinson, James, and Kirkpatrick, D. L. *Twentieth-Century Western Writers*, 1982.

Vrana, Stan. *Interviews and Conversations with Twentieth-Century Authors Writing in English: An Index*, 1982.

Walker, Warren, *Twentieth-Century Short Story Explication*, 3rd edition, 1977; Supplement I, 1980; Supplement II, 1983.

Weixlmann, Joe. *American Short-Fiction Criticism and Scholarship, 1959–1977*, 1982.

White, B. A. *American Women Writers: An Annotated Bibliography of Criticism*, 1977.

William, Jerry. *Southern Literature, 1968–1975: A Checklist of Scholarship*, 1978.

Woodress, James. *Dissertations in American Literature, 1891–1966*, 1968.

———, ed. *American Literary Scholarship: An Annual*, 1965–.

———, ed. *Eight American Authors: A Review of Research and Criticism*, revised edition, 1971.

Wright, Lyle. *American Fiction, 1774–1850*, 1948. 2nd edition, 1969.

———. *American Fiction, 1851–1875*, 1957.

———. *American Fiction, 1876–1900*, 1966.

Criticism, Literary and Cultural History

Aaron, Daniel. *Writers on the Left: Episodes in American Literary Communism*, 1961.
——————. *The Unwritten War: American Writers and the Civil War*, 1973.
Ahnebrink, Lars. *The Beginnings of Naturalism in American Fiction*, 1961.
Aldridge, John. *After the Lost Generation: A Critical Study of the Writers of Two Wars*, 1951.
Aldridge, Owen. *Early American Literature: A Comparatist Approach*, 1983.
Allen, G. W. *American Prosody*, 1935.
Altieri, Charles. *Enlarging the Temple: New Directions in American Poetry during the 1960s*, 1979.
Anderson, Quentin, *The Imperial Self*, 1971.
Auchincloss, Louis. *Pioneers and Caretakers: A Study of Nine American Women Novelists*, 1965.
Baumbach, Jonathan. *The Landscape of Nightmare: Studies in the Contemporary American Novel*, 1965.
Beach, J. W. *American Fiction: 1920–1940*, 1941.
Bercovitch, Sacvan, ed. *The Revaluation of Puritanism*, 1974.
——————. *The Puritan Origins of the American Self*, 1975.
Berthoff, Warner. *The Ferment of Realism: American Literature, 1884–1919*, 1965.
——————. *A Literature without Qualities: American Writers since 1945*, 1979.
Bewley, Marius. *The Complex Fate*, 1954.
——————. *The Eccentric Design*, 1959.
Bigsby, C. W. E. *A Critical Introduction to Twentieth Century American Drama*, Vol. I, 1900–1940, 1982.
Blair, Walter, ed. *Native American Humor*, 2nd edition, 1960.
Bogan, Louise. *Achievement in American Poetry, 1900–1950*, 1951.
Bone, R. A. *The Negro Novel in America*, revised edition, 1965.
Bordman, Gerald. *The Oxford Companion to American Theatre*, 1984.
Bradbury, John. *Renaissance in the South*, 1963.
Bridgman, Richard. *The Colloquial Style in America*, 1966.
Brooks, Peter. *Reading for the Plot: Design and Intention in Narrative*, 1985.
Brooks, Van Wyck. *The Flowering of New England, 1815–1865*, 1937.
——————. *New England: Indian Summer, 1865–1915*, 1940.
——————. *The Times of Melville annd Whitman*, 1947.
——————. *The Confident Years: 1885–1915*, 1955.
Brown, H. R. *The Sentimental Novel in America, 1789–1860*, 1940.
Brown, Sterling. *Negro Poetry and Drama*, 1937.
Buell, Lawrence. *Literary Transcendentalism*, 1973.
Byerman, Keith. *Fingering the Jagged Grain: Tradition and Form in Recent Black Fiction*, 1985.
Cady, E. H. *The Light of Common Day: Realism in American Fiction*, 1971.
Canby, H. S. *Classic Americans*, 1958.
Cargill, Oscar. *Intellectual America: Ideas on the March*, 1941.
Carter, Everett. *The American Idea*, 1977.
Chase, Richard. *The American Novel and Its Tradition*, 1957.
Clark, H. H., ed. *Transitions in American Literary History*, 1954.
Commager, H. S. *The American Mind*, 1950.
Cowie, Alexander. *The Rise of the American Novel*, 1948.
Cowley, Malcolm. *After the Genteel Tradition: American Writers, 1910–1930*, revised edition, 1964.
——————. *A Second Flowering: Works and Days of the Lost Generation*, 1973.

Cunliffe, Marcus. *The Literature of the United States,* 3rd edition, 1967.

Curti, Merle. *The Growth of American Thought,* 3rd edition, 1964.

Davis, Richard. *Intellectual Life in the Colonial South, 1585–1763,* 1977.

Davis, Thadious, and Harris, Trudier. *Afro-American Literary Critics: An Introduction,* 1984.

Dembo, L. S. *Conceptions of Reality in Modern American Poetry,* 1966.

Edel, Leon. *The Psychological Novel, 1900–1950,* 1955.

Eisinger, Chester. *Fiction of the Forties,* 1963.

Elder, John. *Imagining the Earth: Poetry and the Vision of Nature,* 1985.

Elliott, Emory. *American Colonial Writers, 1735–1781,* 1984.

————. *American Writers of the Early Republic,* 1984.

————. *Colonial Writers, 1606–1734,* 1984.

Elliott, Emory, and others, eds., *Columbia Literary History of the United States,* 1988.

Emerson, Everett, ed. *Major Writers of Early American Literature,* 1972.

————. ed. *American Literature 1764–1789: The Revolutionary Years,* 1977.

————. *Puritanism in America, 1620–1750,* 1977.

Falk, Robert. *The Victorian Mode in American Fiction, 1865–1885,* 1965.

Feidelson, Charles. *Symbolism and American Literature,* 1959.

Felperin, Howard. *Beyond Deconstruction: The Uses and Abuses of Literary Theory,* 1985.

Fiedler, Leslie. *Love and Death in the American Novel,* 1960.

Fisher, Philip. *Hard Facts: Setting and Form in the American Novel,* 1985.

Fishkin, Shelley. *From Fact to Fiction: Journalism and Imaginative Writing in America,* 1985.

French, Warren. *The Social Novel at the End of an Era,* 1966.

Frohock, W. M. *The Novel of Violence in America,* revised edition, 1957.

Fryer, Judith. *The Faces of Eve: Women in the Nineteenth-Century American Novel,* 1976.

Fussell, Edwin. *Frontier: American Literature and the American West,* 1965.

Galloway, David. *The Absurd Hero in American Fiction,* 1966.

Geismar, Maxwell. *Rebels and Ancestors: The American Novel, 1890–1915,* 1953.

————. *The Last of the Provincials: The American Novel, 1915–1925,* 1947.

————. *Writers in Crisis: The American Novel between Two Wars,* 1942.

————. *American Moderns: From Rebellion to Conformity,* 1958.

Gelpi, Albert. *The Tenth Muse: The Psyche of the American Poet,* 1975.

Gregory, Horace, and Zaturenska, Marya. *A History of American Poetry, 1900–1940,* 1946, 1969.

Gross, S. L., and Hardy, J. E., eds. *Images of the Negro in American Literature,* 1966.

Hart, J. D. *The Popular Book: A History of America's Literary Taste,* 1950.

Hassan, Ihab. *Radical Innocence, Studies in the Contemporary American Novel,* 1961.

————. *Contemporary American Literature 1945–1972,* 1973.

Hoffman, Daniel. *Form and Fable in American Fiction,* 1961.

————. *Harvard Guide to American Writing,* 1979.

Hoffman, Frederick. *The Art of Southern Fiction,* 1967.

————. *The Twenties: American Writing in the Postwar Decade,* 1955.

Horton, R. W., and Edwards, Herbert. *Backgrounds of American Literary Thought,* 1952.

Howard, Leon. *Literature and the American Tradition,* 1960.

Hubbell, Jay B. *The South in American Literature, 1607–1900,* 1954.

Huggins, R. I. *Harlem Renaissance,* 1971.

Hughes, Glenn. *A History of the American Theater, 1700–1950,* 1951.

Jones, Howard Mumford. *O Strange New World: American Culture, The Formative Years,* 1964.

————. *The Theory of American Literature,* 2nd edition, 1965.

————. *The Age of Energy: Varieties of American Experience, 1865–1915,* 1971.

Kalstone, David. *Five Temperaments,* 1977.

Kammer, Michael. *A Season of Youth*, 1978.
Kartiganer, Donald M., and Griffith, Malcolm A. *Theories of American Literature*, 1972.
Kaul, A. N. *The American Vision: Actual and Ideal Society in Nineteenth-Century Fiction*, 1963.
Kazin, Alfred. *On Native Grounds: An Interpretation of Modern American Prose Literature*, 1942.
————. *Bright Book of Life: American Novelists and Storytellers from Hemingway to Mailer*, 1973.
Kenner, Hugh. *A Homemade World: The American Modernist Writers*, 1975.
Klein, Marcus. *After Alienation: American Novels in Mid-Century*, 1964.
Knight, Grant. *The Critical Period in American Literature, 1890–1900*, 1951.
————. *The Strenuous Age in American Literature, 1900–1910*, 1954.
Kolb, Harold. *The Illusion of Life: American Realism as a Literary Form*, 1970.
Kramer, Dale. *Chicago Renaissance: The Literary Life in the Midwest, 1900–1930*, 1966.
Krutch, J. W. *The American Drama Since 1918*, 1939.
Lawrence, D. H. *Studies in Classic American Literature*, 1923.
Leisy, E. E. *The American Historical Novel*, 1950.
Levin, David. *In Defense of Historical Literature*, 1967.
Levin, Harry. *The Power of Blackness: Hawthorne, Poe, Melville*, 1958.
Lewis, R. W. B. *The American Adam; Innocence, Tragedy, and Tradition in the Nineteenth Century*, 1955.
Lively, Robert. *Fiction Fights the Civil War*, 1956.
Lynen, J. F. *The Design of the Present; Essays on Time and Form in American Literature*, 1969.
McGiffert, Michael. *Puritanism and the American Experience*, 1969.
Malin, Irving. *New American Gothic*, 1962.
Margolies, Edward. *Native Sons: A Critical Study of Twentieth-Century Negro American Authors*, 1968.
Martin, Jay. *Harvests of Change: American Literature, 1865–1914*, 1967.
Marx, Leo. *The Machine in the Garden: Technology and the Pastoral Ideal in America*, 1964.
Matthiessen, F. O. *American Renaissance: Art and Expression in the Age of Emerson and Whitman*, 1941.
May, Henry. *The End of American Innocence: The First Years of Our Own Time, 1912–1917*, 1959.
————. *The Enlightenment in America*, 1976.
Mazzaro, Jerome. *Postmodern American Poetry*, 1980.
Mencken, H. L. *The American Language: An Inquiry into the Development of English in the United States*, revised edition, 1936. Supplement I, 1945; Supplement II, 1948.
Meserve, Walter. *An Emerging Entertainment: The Drama of the American People from the Beginnings to 1828*, 1977.
Miller, Perry. *The New England Mind: The Seventeenth Century*, 1939.
————. *The New England Mind: From Colony to Province*, 1953.
————. *The Raven and the Whale: The War of Words and Wits in the Era of Poe and Melville*, 1956.
Miller, Ruth. *Backgrounds to Black American Literature*, 1971.
Millgate, Michael. *American Social Fiction*, 1967.
Morgan, E. S. *Visible Saints: The History of a Puritan Idea*, 1963.
Morison, S. E. *The Intellectual Life of Colonial New England*, 1956.
Mott, F. L. *Golden Multitudes: The Story of Best Sellers in the United States*, 1947.
————. *American Journalism: A History of Newspapers in the United States through 250 Years, 1690 to 1940*, 1941, revised 1951.
————. *A History of American Magazines*, 4 vols., 1938–1957.
Mumford, Lewis. *The Golden Day*, 1926.

Murdock, K. B. *Literature and Theology in Colonial New England*, 1949.

Myerson, Joel, ed. *The Transcendentalists: A Review of Research and Criticism*, 1984.

Newman, Charles. *The Post-Modern Aura: The Act of Fiction in an Age of Inflation*, 1985.

Nye, Russel. *The Cultural Life of the New Nation*, 1960.

Olderman, Raymond. *Beyond the Wasteland: The American Novel in the 1960s*, 1972.

Parrington, V. L. *Main Currents in American Thought: An Interpretation of American Literature from the Beginnings to 1920*, 3 vols., 1927–1930.

Pattee, F. L. *A History of American Literature since 1870*, 1915.

————. *The Development of the American Short Story*, 1923, 1966.

Pearce, R. H. *The Continuity of American Poetry*, 1961.

Peden, William. *The American Short Story: Continuity and Change 1940–1975*, 2nd edition, 1975.

Perkins, David. *A History of Modern Poetry*, 2 vols., 1976, 1987.

Person, Stow. *American Minds: A History of Ideas*, 1958.

Phillips, Robert. *The Confessional Poets*, 1963.

Pinsky, Robert. *The Situation of Poetry: Contemporary Poetry and Its Traditions*, 1977.

Pizer, Donald. *Realism and Naturalism in Nineteenth-Century American Literature*, 1966.

————, and Harbert, Earl. *American Realists and Naturalists*, 1982.

Pochmann, H. A. *German Culture in America: Philosophical and Literary Influences, 1600–1900*, 1961.

Poirier, Richard. *A World Elsewhere: The Place of Style in American Literature*, 1966.

Porte, Joel. *The Romance in America*, 1969.

Quinn, A. H. *A History of the American Drama from the Civil War to the Present Day*, revised edition, 1936.

————. *American Fiction: An Historical and Critical Survey*, 1936.

————. *A History of the American Drama from the Beginning to the Civil War*, revised edition, 1943.

————, and others. *The Literature of the American People*, 1951.

Quinones, Ricardo. *Mapping Literary Modernism: Time and Development*, 1985.

Rideout, Walter. *The Radical Novel in the United States, 1900–1954*, 1956.

Riley, I. W. *American Thought from Puritanism to Pragmatism and Beyond*, 1923, 1959.

Rourke, Constance. *American Humor: A Study of the National Character*, 1931.

Rubin, Louis. *Writers of the Modern South*, 1963.

————, ed. *The History of Southern Literature*, 1985.

Ruland, Richard. *The Rediscovery of American Literature: Premises of Critical Taste, 1900–1940*, 1967.

————, ed. *The Native Muse: Theories of American Literature*, Vol. I, 1972.

————, ed. *A Stories Land: Theories of American Literature*. Vol. II, 1976.

Schneider, H. W. *The Puritan Mind*, 1930, 1958.

Seelye, John. *Prophetic Waters: The River in Early American Life and Literature*, 1977.

Silverman, Kenneth. *A Cultural History of the American Revolution*, 1976.

Slotkin, Richard. *Regeneration Through Violence: The Mythology of the American Frontier, 1600–1860*, 1973.

Smith, H. N. *Virgin Land: The American West as Symbol and Myth*, 1950.

————. *Democracy and The Novel*, 1979.

Spencer, Benjamin. *The Quest for Nationality: An American Literary Campaign*, 1957.

Spengermann, William C. *The Adventurous Muse: The Poetics of American Fiction: 1789–1900*, 1977.

Spiller, R. E. *The Cycle of American Literature*, 1960.

————, and others. *Literary History of the United States*, 4th edition, revised, 1974.

Stepanchev, Stephen. *American Poetry Since 1945*, 1965.

Stewart, Randall. *American Literature and the Christian Tradition*, 1958.

Stipes, Emily. *The Poetry of American Women from 1632 to 1945*, 1977.

Tanner, Tony. *The Reign of Wonder*, 1965.

————. *The City of Words*, 1971.

Taubmann, Howard. *The Making of the American Theatre*, 1965.

Taylor, W. F. *The Economic Novel in America*, 1942.

Trachtenberg, Stanley. *American Humorists, 1800–1950*, 1982.

————. *Colonial Writers, 1606–1734*, 1984.

Trent, W. P., and others. *Cambridge History of American Literature*, 4 vols., 1917–1933.

Tyler, M. C. *A History of American Literature, 1607–1765*, 2 vols., 1878.

————. *The Literary History of the American Revolution, 1763–1783*, 2 vols., 1897, 1957.

Van Doren, Carl. *The American Novel, 1789–1939*, 1940.

Vogel, Dan. *The Three Masks of American Tragedy*, 1976.

von Hallberg, Robert. *American Poetry and Culture, 1945–1980*, 1985.

Wagenknecht, Edward. *Cavalcade of the American Novel*, 1952.

Waggoner, H. H. *American Poets: From the Puritans to the Present Day*, 1968.

Walcutt, C. C. *American Literary Nationalism, A Divided Stream*, 1956.

Weales, Gerald. *American Drama Since World War Two*, 1962.

————. *The Jumping-off Place: American Drama in the 1960s*, 1969.

West, Ray. *The Short Story in America 1900–1950*, 1952.

White, Peter, ed. *Puritan Poets and Poetics: Seventeenth-Century Poetry in Theory and Practice*, 1985.

Williams, S. T. *The Spanish Background of American Literature*, 1955.

Wilson, Edmund. *Patriotic Gore: Studies in the Literature of the American Civil War*, 1962.

Wood, James. *Magazines in the United States*, 2nd edition, 1956.

Ziff, Larzer. *The American 1890's*, 1966.

————. *Puritanism in America: New Culture in a New World*, 1973.

Chronology

1600

1600 Spaniards explore American Southwest
1607 Jamestown settlers arrive in Virginia in April. First permanent British settlement in North America
1603–1613 Champlain explores Saint Lawrence River. Founds Quebec

1609–1610 Henry Hudson discovers Hudson River and Hudson's Bay
1611 First Virginia tobacco crop

1620 Pilgrims found Plymouth
1621 Dutch found New Amsterdam
1622 Indians massacre Jamestown settlers
1624 Dutch settle Manhattan

1628 Fifty Puritans led by John Endecott settle at Salem
1630–1643 "Great Migration" of the Puritans to Massachusetts

1633 Maryland founded

1636 Roger Williams founds Providence

1639 First colonial printing press, established at Cambridge, Massachusetts

1558–1603 Elizabeth I reigns in England

1603–1625 James I reigns in England

1619 America's first legislature convenes in Virginia
1621 William Bradford succeeds John Carver as governor of Plymouth Colony

1625–1649 Charles I reigns in England
1625 Colonial Office established at London
1628 Charles I dissolves Parliament

1637 Pequot War
1637 Anne Hutchinson banished from Massachusetts Bay Colony

1642–1646 English Civil War

1649 Charles I executed

1653–1658 Oliver Cromwell rules England as Lord Protector

1650

1656 First Quakers arrive in Massachusetts

1664 English take New Amsterdam from the Dutch

1608 John Smith publishes *A True Relation,* earliest first-hand account of
Virginia settlement.

1616 John Smith publishes *A Description of New England*
1619 African Negroes first sold as
slaves, in Virginia
1621 First Thanksgiving at Plymouth

1624 John Smith publishes *General
History of Virginia*

1630–1649 John Winthrop writes his
Journal
1630–1651 William Bradford writes
History of Plymouth Plantation
1635 Boston Latin School establishes.
First American public school
1636 Harvard College founded
1637 Thomas Morton publishes *The
New English Canaan*
1639 First printing press established
in Massachusetts
1640 Colonial population estimated
at 28,000
1640 *Bay Psalm Book,* first book published in North American colonies
1643 Roger Williams publishes *A Key
into the Language of America*
1650 Anne Bradstreet's Book of poems
The Tenth Muse published in London
1656 First Quakers arrive in Massachusetts
1662 Michael Wigglesworth's *Day of
Doom* published

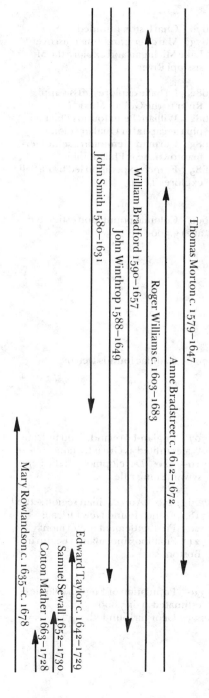

John Smith 1580–1631

William Bradford 1590–1657

John Winthrop 1588–1649

Thomas Morton c. 1579–1647

Roger Williams c. 1603–1683

Anne Bradstreet c. 1612–1672

Mary Rowlandson c. 1635–c. 1678

Edward Taylor c. 1642–1729

Samuel Sewall 1652–1730

Cotton Mather 1663–1728

1670   Charleston founded
1673   Marquette and Joliet discover
Lake Michigan and explore the Mississippi River

1675–1678   King Philip's War in New
England
1680   New Hampshire made a royal
colony, separate from Massachusetts

1682   La Salle explores Mississippi
River to the Gulf of Mexico
1682   William Penn founds Philadelphia as capital of Quaker colony
1683   German Mennonites settle Germantown, near Philadelphia
1685   French expedition led by La Salle
explores Texas

1685–1688   James II reigns in England

1688—"Glorious Revolution" ends
reign of James II. William and
Mary begin reign as king and queen
of England
1689   Boston colonists rebel against
Governor Andros

1690   Colonial population estimated
at 213,500

1691   Massachusetts receives a new
charter and a royal governor. The
Plymouth Colony is absorbed by
Massachusetts

1700   1701   Cadillac founds Detroit

1702   New Jersey becomes a royal
colony

1707   England, Ireland, Scotland, and
Wales united as Great Britain
1710–1740   Development of the Pennsylvania long rifle

1713   Carolina divided into North and
South Carolina

1716–1750   Appalachian region settled
1718   French found New Orleans
1720   First settlement in Vermont
1721   Smallpox inoculation begun in
Boston

1729   North and South Carolina become separate royal colonies

1730   Population of English colonies
estimated at 655,000
1733   Georgia founded

Society and Culture	Lives of Authors

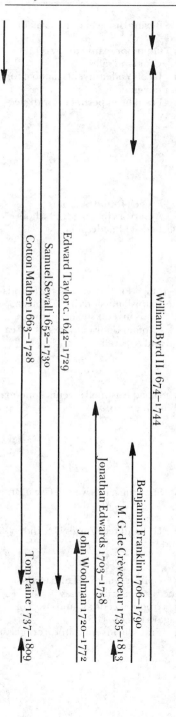

1669   Nathaniel Morton publishes *New England's Memorial*

1682   Mary Rowlandson publishes her *Narrative of Captivity*

c. 1683   *New England Primer* published

1687   First Church of England service held in Boston

1690   *New England Primer* published
1690   First newspaper published, in Boston

1692   Salem witch trials
1693   College of William and Mary founded in Virginia
1701   Yale College established
1702   Cotton Mather's *Magnalia Christi Americana* published
1704   First weekly newspaper, *Boston News-Letter*
1704   First organ built, in Philadelphia
1709–1712   William Byrd writes his *Secret Diary*

1714   Tea is introduced into the colonies

1726–1756   Great Awakening. Religious revivalism throughout the colonies
1730   First art exhibition, in Boston
1732–1757   Benjamin Franklin publishes *Poor Richard's Almanack*
1738   Painters John Singleton Copley and Benjamin West born

Cotton Mather 1663–1728

Samuel Sewall 1652–1730

Edward Taylor c. 1642–1729

William Byrd II 1674–1744

Benjamin Franklin 1706–1790

M. G. de Crèvecoeur 1735–1813

Jonathan Edwards 1703–1758

John Woolman 1720–1772

Tom Paine 1737–1809

1750

1741   Bering discovers Alaska mainland
1749   Ohio Company surveys Ohio Valley for land sales
1750   Jacob Yoder invents flatboat for river navigation
1752   Franklin experiments with electricity

1764   French found St. Louis
1765   America's first medical school established at Philadelphia

1769–1784   Fr. Junipero Serra founds nine Spanish missions in California
1769   Watts invents steam engine
1770   Captain Cook explores New Zealand and Australia

1775   David Bushnell invents a one-man submarine

1779   Spain declares war on Great Britain

1782   Holland recognizes U.S. independence

1784   Congress adopts Land Ordinance to create new states
1784   Iroquois cede all lands west of Niagara river to U.S.
1784   Franklin invents bifocal eyeglasses

1745   New Englanders capture French fortress at Louisburg, Cape Breton Island, Canada

1754–1763   French and Indian War. Victorious British gain all French Canada

1764   Sugar Act, Currency Act
1765   Stamp Act, Sons of Liberty formed
1766   Repeal of Stamp Act
1767   Townshend Acts tax tea, paper, etc.
1768   British troops land in Boston

1773   Boston Tea Party
1774   First Continental Congress meets in Philadelphia
1775–1781   War for American Independence
1775   Battles at Lexington, Concord, Ticonderoga, Bunker Hill
1775   England hires German mercenaries to fight in America
1776   France sends aid to American revolutionaries

1781   Cornwallis surrenders at Yorktown

1783   Treaty of Paris formally ends American Revolution

1787   Constitutional Convention meets in Philadelphia

1752 First general hospital, Philadelphia
1754 Jonathan Edwards publishes
Freedom of the Will
1754 Franklin publishes first American political cartoon, calling for
action against the French
1761 First musical society founded, in
Charleston, South Carolina

1767 First American play professionally produced: Thomas Godfrey's *The
Prince of Parthia*
1769 American Philosophical Society
founded

1771–1790 Benjamin Franklin writes
his *Autobiography*
1774–1781 Crèvecoeur writes *Letters
from an American Farmer*
1775 Quakers establish first antislavery society
1775 "Yankee Doodle" written

1776 Tom Paine publishes *Common
Sense and The American Crisis I*

1782–1783 Jefferson writes *Notes on the
State of Virginia*
1783 Noah Webster publishes *The
American Spelling Book*

1787 First native comedy professionally produced, Royall Tyler's *The
Contrast*

William Byrd II 1674–1744

Benjamin Franklin 1706–1790

M. G. de Crèvecoeur 1735–1813

Philip Freneau 1752–1832

Tom Paine 1737–1809

Thomas Jefferson 1743–1826

Washington Irving 1783–1859

	1789 Constitution ratified by states. Washington elected first President
	1789 French revolution begins
1790 First census. Population 3,929,214	
1791 Washington, D.C. established	1791 Bill of Rights adopted
1792 Kentucky statehood	1792 Congress establishes decimal system of coinage. Washington reelected for second term
1793 Eli Whitney invents the cotton gin	
1797 Cast-iron plow invented	1796 Washington's Farewell Address. John Adams elected President
	1799 Death of Washington
1800 National census, population 5,308,483	1800 Thomas Jefferson elected President. Re-elected 1804.
1803 U.S. buys Louisiana from France for $15 million	
1804–1806 Lewis and Clark expedition explores Far West	1808 James Madison elected President. Re-elected 1812
1810 New York becomes the most populous city	
1812 Louisiana statehood	1812–1815 War with Great Britain
	1814 Washington, D.C. burned by British troops
	1815 Battle of New Orleans. Andrew Jackson defeats British troops
	1816 James Monroe elected President
1818 Tin can first introduced in America	
1818 First steamboat on the Great Lakes	
1819 U.S. acquires Florida from Spain	
1820 National census, population 9,638,453, 7% city, 93% rural	1820 Missouri compromise
1821 Santa Fe Trail opens	
	1823 Monroe Doctrine proclaimed
1825 Erie Canal opens, connecting Great Lakes region with the Atlantic	
1828 Baltimore and Ohio Railroad, first passenger railroad in U.S.	1828 Andrew Jackson defeats John Quincy Adams for Presidency
1830 Fur trappers explore the Rockies	
1831 McCormick invents the reaper	

1800

1787–1788   Hamilton, Madison, and
Jay write *The Federalist*
1789   William Hill Brown publishes
the first American novel, *The Power
of Sympathy*
1789   University of North Carolina,
first state university to begin instruction

1794   Charles Wilson Peale opens first
museum
1794–1796   Tom Paine publishes *The
Age of Reason*

1800   Library of Congress founded

1803   First American piano built

1809   Washington Irving publishes
Knickerbocker's History of New York

1814   Francis Scott Key writes "The
Star Spangled Banner"

1819–1820   Irving publishes *The Sketch
Book*

1823   James Fenimore Cooper begins
"The Leatherstocking Tales"
1825   Thomas Cole begins the Hudson
River School of painting
1827   John James Audubon publishes
his *Birds of America*
1828   Noah Webster publishes *An
American Dictionary of the English Language*

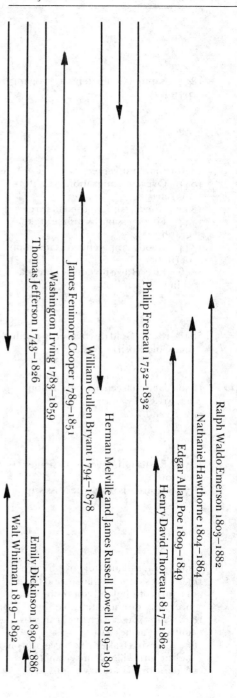

Thomas Jefferson 1743–1826

Washington Irving 1783–1859

James Fenimore Cooper 1789–1851

William Cullen Bryant 1794–1878

Herman Melville and James Russell Lowell 1819–1891

Philip Freneau 1752–1832

Edgar Allan Poe 1809–1849

Henry David Thoreau 1817–1862

Nathaniel Hawthorne 1804–1864

Ralph Waldo Emerson 1803–1882

Walt Whitman 1819–1892

Emily Dickinson 1830–1886

	1832 Jackson re-elected
1835 Samuel Colt patents a revolving pistol	
	1836 Martin Van Buren elected President
	1836 Republic of Texas established
	1838 Underground Railway begins transport of slaves to Canada
1840 Bicycle invented	1841 William Henry Harrison first President to die in office, succeeded by John Tyler
1841 Overland migration to California starts	
1842 Anesthesia first used in surgery	
1844 First message by Morse's telegraph	
1844 Goodyear patents vulcanization of rubber	
1846 Elias Howe invents sewing machine	1845 Texas admitted to the Union
	1846–1848 War with Mexico
	1846–1850 Bear Flag Revolt, California joins U.S.
	1847 Battles of Monterey, Buena Vista, and Chapultepec
1848–1849 Gold discovered in California. Gold Rush begins	1848 Treaty of Guadalupe Hidalgo ends Mexican War
	1848 Women's Rights Convention at Seneca, New York
1850 National census, population 23,191,876	1850 Compromise of 1850, with Fugitive Slave Act, passed by Congress

1850

1852 Elisha Otis invents passenger elevator	1852 Democrat Franklin Pierce elected President
1854 Railroads reach the Mississippi	1854 Republican Party formed
	1857 Supreme Court makes Dred Scott decision
1858 Transatlantic telegraph cable	1858 Lincoln-Douglas Debates
1858 President Buchanan and Queen Victoria of England communicate over first transatlantic cable	1858 Lincoln-Douglas Debates during Illinois senatorial race
1858 First stagecoach line from Missouri to Pacific coast.	
1859 Edwin Drake drills successful oil well at Titusville, Pennsylvania; American oil industry begins	1859 John Brown raids Harpers Ferry

Society and Culture	Lives of Authors

1833 American Anti-Slavery society formed

1833 Oberlin College founded, first coeducational college

1836 American Temperance Union established

1836 Ralph Waldo Emerson publishes *Nature*

1837 Mount Holyoke, first women's college, established

1841–1847 Brook Farm

1844 Poe publishes "The Raven"

1845 Thoreau moves to Walden Pond

1846 Congress founds the Smithsonian Institution

1848 Stephen Foster's "Oh! Susanna" becomes a popular song

1850 *Harper's Magazine* founded

1850 Hawthorne publishes *The Scarlet Letter*

1851 *New York Times* established

1851 Herman Melville publishes *Moby Dick*

1852 Harriet Beecher Stowe publishes *Uncle Tom's Cabin*

1855 Walt Whitman publishes *Leaves of Grass*

1855 First kindergarten opens, in Wisconsin

1858 Longfellow publishes "The Courtship of Miles Standish"

Walt Whitman 1819–1892

Emily Dickinson 1830–1886

William Cullen Bryant 1794–1878

Herman Melville and James Russell Lowell 1819–1891

Mark Twain 1835–1910

Edgar Allan Poe 1809–1849

Henry David Thoreau 1817–1862

Henry James 1843–1916

Nathaniel Hawthorne 1804–1864

Ralph Waldo Emerson 1803–1882

1859   Oregon statehood
1859   Gold discovered in Colorado
and Nevada
1860   Pony Express runs from Missouri to California
1860   Oliver Winchester develops the
repeating rifle

1861   Telegraph links East and West
coasts

1862   Richard Gatling perfects the revolving machine gun

1867   Typewriter invented
1867   U.S. buys Alaska from Russia
for $7.2 million
1867   British establish The Dominion
of Canada. Alfred Nobel patents
dynamite
1868   First commercial typewriter patented

1869   Vacuum cleaner invented
1869   Transcontinental railroad completed
1870   National census: population
39,818,494
1876   General Custer and 265 men
killed at Little Bighorn, Montana
1876   Alexander Graham Bell patents
the telephone

1860   Southern states assert right to
secede
1860   Abraham Lincoln elected President
1860   South Carolina secedes from the
Union
1861   Mississippi, Florida, Alabama,
Georgia, Louisiana, Virginia, Arkansas, Tennessee, North Carolina, and
Texas secede
1861   West Virginia separates from
Virginia, remains loyal to the Union
1861–1865   American Civil War
1862   First Federal income tax
1862   Lincoln issues Emancipation
Proclamation
1863   Lincoln delivers Gettysburg Address
1864   Lincoln re-elected
1865   Lee surrenders at Appomatox
1865   Lincoln assassinated. Andrew
Johnson becomes President
1865   13th Amendment abolishes
slavery
1867   U.S. buys Alaska for $7,200,000

1868   Congress approves 8-hour day
for federal employees
1868   14th Amendment grants Negroes
citizenship
1868   U.S. Grant elected President.
Re-elected 1872
1869   Wyoming passes first U.S.
woman-suffrage law

1870   Virginia, Mississippi, Texas, and
Georgia readmitted to the Union

1877   Reconstruction ends. All federal
troops withdrawn from the South

1862 Julia Ward Howe publishes
      "The Battle Hymn of the Republic"

1865 Mark Twain publishes "The
      Celebrated Jumping Frog of Calave-
      ras County"

1866 Whittier publishes *Snow-Bound*

1869 First professional baseball team,
      Cincinnati Red Stockings, established
1869 First intercollegiate football
      game. Rutgers defeats Princeton

1876 National Baseball League
      founded
1876 Mark Twain publishes *Tom Saw-
      yer*
1877 American Museum of Natural
      History opens in New York City
1877 Philadelphia Conservatory of Mu-
      sic founded

Nathaniel Hawthorne 1804–1864

Henry David Thoreau 1817–1862

Ralph Waldo Emerson 1803–1882

Henry James 1843–1916

Mark Twain 1835–1910

Herman Melville and James Russell Lowell 1819–1891

William Cullen Bryant 1794–1878

Emily Dickinson 1830–1886

Walt Whitman 1819–1892

Edwin Arlington Robinson 1869–1935

Stephen Crane 1871–1900

Theodore Dreiser 1871–1945

Robert Frost 1874–1963

1878   Bicycles first manufactured
in U.S.
1878   Edison patents phonograph
1879   Edison invents workable incandescent lightbulb

1880   First important gold strike in
Alaska

                               1881   President Garfield assassinated.
Chester Arthur becomes President

1882   Indian chief Geronimo captured;
Plains Indian warfare ends
1883   Brooklyn Bridge completed

1884   Steam turbine invented

1885   Automobile invented

                               1884–1888   Woman Suffragettes form
Equal Rights party, nominate
woman candidate for President

1888   First successful electric trolley
line opened. First Kodak hand camera developed
1890   As settlement expands, American frontier disappears. National
census 62,947,714
1891   Edison patents motion-picture
camera

                               1889   Indian Territory (Oklahoma)
opened to white settlement

                               1892   Grover Cleveland elected Presi-
dent. Re-elected second time
1893   Cherokee Strip in Oklahoma   1894   Coxey's Army of protesters
opened for settlement   marches on Washington, D.C.

1895   King Gillette invents safety
razor
1896   First public exhibition of motion
pictures
1897   First American subway opens,
Boston
1897–1898   Gold Rush to the Canadian Klondike
1898   Spain cedes Guam, Puerto Rico,
and the Philippines to the U.S. for
$20 million

                               1898   U.S. Battleship *Maine* blows up
in Havana, Cuba harbor
1898–1899   Spanish-American War
1898   U.S. annexes Hawaii

Society and Culture

1879 Henry James publishes *Daisy Miller*

1879 Henry George publishes *Progress and Poverty*

1880 Salvation Army established in U.S.

1880 Metropolitan Museum of New York City opens

1880 Joel Chandler Harris publishes *Uncle Remus*

1881 American Red Cross formed

1883 Railroads establish standard time zones

1883 New York Metropolitan Opera House opens

1884 Mark Twain publishes *Huckleberry Finn*

1885 First "skyscraper" built, in Chicago

1886 Statue of Liberty dedicated

1886 American Federation of Labor formed

1889 First All-American football team selected

1891 James Naismith invents basketball

1891 International Copyright Law established

1893 Chicago World's Columbian Exposition

1894 Labor Day declared legal holiday

1895 Stephen Crane publishes *The Red Badge of Courage*

1897 Library of Congress completed

1898 First show of American Impressionist painters

Lives of Authors

Ralph Waldo Emerson 1803–1882

Edwin Arlington Robinson 1869–1935

Stephen Crane 1871–1900

Henry James 1843–1916

Mark Twain 1835–1910

Robert Frost 1874–1963

Theodore Dreiser 1871–1945

Wallace Stevens 1879–1955

Ezra Pound 1885–1972

Ernest Hemingway 1898–1961

T. S. Eliot 1888–1965

William Faulkner 1897–1962

F. Scott Fitzgerald 1896–1940

1900

1900   Hawaii granted territorial status. National census: population 75,994,575
1901   United States Steel Corporation founded

1903   Ford Motor Company founded
1903   Wright brothers make first airplane flight
1904–1914   Panama Canal built

1907   Electric washing machine invented

1910   Ford Model T first produced

1913   First assembly line begins to operate at Ford

1914   Robert Goddard gets first U.S. patent for multistage rockets
1914–1918   World War I
1917   U.S. buys Virgin Islands from Denmark
1918   Armistice, World War I ends
1918–1919   World-wide influenza epidemic kills millions, 500,000 die in U.S.
1919–1921   Civil war in Russia

1900   Socialist Party formed.

1901   Anti-saloon leader Carrie Nation makes first raid on a saloon, Wichita, Kansas
1901   President McKinley assassinated. Theodore Roosevelt becomes President
1901   Socialist Party of America formed

1904   Theodore Roosevelt elected President
1906   Federal Pure Food and Drug Act passed
1907–1909   Georgia, Oklahoma, Mississippi, North Carolina, Tennessee, Alabama enact "dry" laws

1912   Woodrow Wilson elected President. Re-elected 1916

1917   U.S. declares war on Germany. First U.S. troops land in France

1919   U.S. Senate fails to approve the Versailles Treaty ending World War I
1919   Communist party, American Legion, and RCA established in U.S.

Society and Culture

1899   Scott Joplin introduces ragtime to white Americans
1899   Coca-Cola first bottled
1899   Sigmund Freud publishes *The Interpretation of Dreams*
1900   Theodore Dreiser publishes *Sister Carrie*

1901   Connecticut passes first law regulating auto speed

1902   First Rose Bowl football game
1903   *The Great Train Robbery* exhibited, first film telling a story

1907   First Mother's Day celebration
1907   Henry Adams publishes *The Education of Henry Adams*
1908   Works by American Ash Can School of painters exhibited
1909   National Association for the Advancement of Colored People founded
1910   Boy Scouts of America founded
1911   Irving Berlin publishes "Alexander's Ragtime Band"
1913   Armory Show opens in New York. First large exhibit of modern art in America
1913   Mack Sennett begins making movie comedies

1917   Pulitzer Prize awards inaugurated. First jazz band recording made

1919–1926   Jack Dempsey heavyweight boxing champion of the world

Lives of Authors

F. Scott Fitzgerald 1896–1940

T.S. Eliot 1888–1965

Robert Frost 1874–1963

Theodore Dreiser 1871–1945

Wallace Stevens 1879–1955

William Faulkner 1897–1962

Henry James 1843–1916

Edwin Arlington Robinson 1869–1935

Ezra Pound 1885–1972

Ernest Hemingway 1898–1961

Bernard Malamud 1914–1986

Robert Lowell 1917–1978

Saul Bellow 1915–

1920   National census: population
105,710,620. Urban population exceeds rural population for the first
time

1920   League of Nations organized.
U.S. Senate refuses to vote for membership

1921   Albert Einstein wins Nobel Prize
for physics

1922   Mussolini forms Fascist government in Italy

1922   Union of Soviet Socialist Republics established

1924   Adolf Hitler writes *Mein Kampf*

1926   Hirohito becomes emperor of
Japan

1927   Charles Lindbergh flies the Atlantic alone

1928   Television tube developed

1930   Jet propulsion engine developed

1931   Japanese invade Manchuria

1933   Hitler voted into power in Germany

1934   S.S. *Normandie*, French ocean
liner, crosses Atlantic in 107 hours

1935   Anti-semitic laws passed in Germany

1935–1936   Italy invades Ethiopia

1936   King Edward VIII of Great
Britain abdicates

1936–1939   Spanish Civil War

1938   Germany absorbs Austria

1939   Scientists inform President Roosevelt of the possibility of making an
atomic bomb

1920   Prohibition (18th) Amendment
goes into effect

1920   Transcontinental airmail begins.
19th Amendment gives women the
vote

1920   Warren G. Harding elected President

1920–1933   Sale of intoxicating beverages prohibited in U.S.

1923   Harding dies. Calvin Coolidge
becomes President

1924   Calvin Coolidge elected President

1928   Congress appropriates
$32,000,000 to enforce Prohibition
laws

1928   Herbert Hoover defeats Al
Smith for the Presidency

1929   Stock market crash. The Great
Depression begins

1932   Franklin Roosevelt elected President. Re-elected 1936, 1940, 1944

1933–1936   Severe drought. Plains
states become "Dust Bowl"

1933   Twenty-first Amendment repeals
Prohibition

1939–1945   World War II brings economic boom to U.S.

Society and Culture

1920 Sinclair Lewis publishes *Main Street*. F. Scott Fitzgerald publishes his first novel, *This Side of Paradise*

1921 KDKA, Cincinnati transmits first regular radio broadcasts in U.S.

1922 Lincoln Memorial dedicated in Washington, D.C.

1922 T. S. Eliot publishes *The Waste Land*

1922 *Reader's Digest* founded

1924 Premiere of "Rhapsody in Blue" by George Gershwin

1925 F. Scott Fitzgerald publishes *The Great Gatsby*

1926 Ernest Hemingway publishes *The Sun Also Rises*

1927 *The Jazz Singer*, first full-length sound movie

1929 William Faulkner publishes *The Sound and the Fury*

1930 Sinclair Lewis, first American to win the Nobel Prize for literature

1933 Film *King Kong* released

1935 Premiere of George Gershwin's *Porgy and Bess*

1936 Eugene O'Neill receives Nobel Prize for literature

1936 Margaret Mitchell publishes *Gone With the Wind*

1939 John Steinbeck publishes *The Grapes of Wrath*

Lives of Authors

- F. Scott Fitzgerald 1896–1940
- T. S. Eliot 1888–1965
- Robert Frost 1874–1963
- Theodore Dreiser 1871–1945
- Wallace Stevens 1879–1955
- William Faulkner 1897–1962
- Saul Bellow 1915–
- Robert Lowell 1917–1978
- Edwin Arlington Robinson 1869–1935
- Ezra Pound 1885–1972
- Norman Mailer 1923–
- Bernard Malamud 1914–1986
- Ernest Hemingway 1898–1961
- Joyce Carol Oates 1938–
- James Baldwin 1924–1987

International Affairs, Exploration, Settlement and Science

1939   Russia invades Finland

1939   Germany invades Poland, September. World War II begins

1940   German "blitzkrieg" conquers Norway, Denmark, Low Countries, and France

Dec. 1941   Japan bombs Pearl Harbor. U.S. declares war on Japan, Germany, and Italy

1942   Atomic Age begins with first self-sustaining nuclear chain reaction

June 1944   D-Day; Allies invade France

May 1945   Germany surrenders

Aug. 1945   Atomic bombs dropped on Hiroshima and Nagasaki. Japan surrenders

1948   Transistor invented

1948   Israel gains independence

1949   Chinese communists proclaim People's Republic of China

1950

1950   National Census: 150,697,361 population

1950–1953   Korean War

1953   Mount Everest climbed

1956–1959   Cuban civil war. Victory for Castro forces

1957   Russia successfully launches "Sputnik," first man-made satellite

1961   Berlin Wall seals Iron Curtain

1961   Soviet cosmonaut first man to orbit earth

1962   Russian missiles withdrawn from Cuba after America threatens action

Politics and Government

1940   Alien Registration Act

1940   Franklin Roosevelt reelected President

1941   Selective Service Systems extends draftees' service to 18 months

1945   FDR dies. Harry S. Truman becomes President

1945   Rationing of shoes, butter, and tires ends

1946   Inflation rate rises to 18.2 percent

1950   Senator Joseph McCarthy begins his attacks on Communism in government

1952   Eisenhower elected President. Reelected 1956

1957   Civil Rights Act

1958–1959   Alaska and Hawaii become states

1960   John F. Kennedy elected president

Society and Culture
1940 Ernest Hemingway publishes *For Whom the Bell Tolls*
1940 Color television first shown
1941 Orson Wells directs and stars in the film *Citizen Kane*
1943 Jitterbug dancing becomes popular
1943 Rogers and Hammerstein's *Oklahoma!* opens
1945 Tennessee Williams' *The Glass Menagerie* opens in New York City
1948 Kinsey report, *Sexual Behavior in the Human Male* published
1948 T. S. Eliot wins Nobel Prize for literature. Ezra Pound publishes *The Pisan Cantos*
1949 William Faulkner wins Nobel Prize for literature
1954 Elvis Presley releases first record on Sun label. Rock music begins
1954 Ernest Hemingway wins Nobel Prize for literature
1954 Supreme Court decision bans segregation in schools
1956 Rev. Martin Luther King leads Montgomery, Alabama bus boycott
1956 Grace Metalious publishes *Peyton Place*
1960 Presidential debates appear on TV
1962 John Steinbeck wins Nobel Prize for literature

Lives of Authors:

F. Scott Fitzgerald 1896–1940

Theodore Dreiser 1871–1945

Wallace Stevens 1879–1955

Robert Frost 1874–1963

T. S. Eliot 1888–1965

William Faulkner 1897–1962

Saul Bellow 1915–

Robert Lowell 1917–1978

Joyce Carol Oates 1938–

Norman Mailer 1923–

Ezra Pound 1885–1972

Bernard Malamud 1914–1986

Ernest Hemingway 1898–1961

James Baldwin 1924–1987

1963   John F. Kennedy assassinated.
Lyndon B. Johnson becomes President

1965–1979   Annual inflation rate rises
from 2% to 13%

1967   Six-Day War between Israel and
Arab nations
1967   Christian Bernard performs first
human heart transplant

1968   Robert Kennedy and Rev. Martin Luther King assassinated
1968   Richard M. Nixon elected 37th
President. Reelected 1972
1969   First U.S. troops withdrawn
from Vietnam. Anti-Vietnam-war
demonstrations increase

1969   World population estimated at
3.5 billion
1969   U.S. astronauts land on the moon

1969–1979   Average annual household
income rises from $8,000 to $16,000
1971   26th Amendment gives 18-year-olds the vote
1971–1979   Price of gold rises from
$40 to $340 per ounce
1971   Supreme Court upholds decision
requiring the busing of school children for racial balance
1972   Watergate scandal emerges
1972   U.S. military conscription ends
1973   Spiro Agnew resigns as Vice-President

1973   OPEC quintuples oil prices
1973   U.S. forces withdraw from Vietnam

1974   July, U.S. House of Representatives recommends impeachment of
President Nixon. August, Nixon resigns

1976   Supersonic jet transport between
U.S. and Europe—4 hours
1976   Mao Tse-tung, Chairman of
Chinese Communist party, dies

1976   Jimmy Carter elected President

1978   Three American balloonists
make first successful Atlantic crossing
1978   Over 900 die in mass suicide in
Guyana religious commune
1979   Mob seizes U.S. Embassy in Iran

1978   Panama Canal Treaty gives control of canal to Panama in 1999

1979   U.S. and China establish full
diplomatic relations
1979   OPEC nations continue to raise
oil prices. Gas shortage and inflation
strike U.S.

1980   National Census, population
226,545,805
1980   Mt. St. Helens volcano eruption
kills thirty-four

1980   Ronald Reagan elected president

1964   Beatles and Rolling Stones release their first albums
1965   Hippie phenomenon begins in San Francisco

1968   78 million TV sets in the U.S.

1969   Pants suits become stylish for women
1969   The Woodstock Festival

1971   "Fiddler on the Roof" becomes longest running musical in Broadway history

1976   Saul Bellow wins Nobel Prize for literature
1976   U.S. celebrates Bicentennial
1977   "Star Wars" becomes biggest box office draw to date
1978   Isaac Bashevis Singer wins Nobel prize for literature

1980   TV show "Dallas" claims 300,000,000 viewers world-wide

T. S. Eliot 1888–1965

Robert Frost 1874–1963

Ezra Pound 1885–1972

Robert Lowell 1917–1978

Norman Mailer 1923–

Joyce Carol Oates 1938–

Saul Bellow 1915–

Bernard Malamud 1914–1986

James Baldwin 1924–1987

Imamu Amira Baraka (LeRoi Jones) 1934–

Edward Albee 1928–

International Affairs, Exploration, Settlement and Science	Politics and Government

1981   Iran releases U.S. hostages

1984   Reagan proposes budget with record deficit of $180,000,000,000

1985   Ronald Reagan sworn in for 2nd
term. Oldest man ever elected President

1986   Nuclear accident at Chernobyl
power plant in the Soviet Union

1986   Irangate scandal exposed secret
sale of arms to Iran

1987   U.S. Stock Market crash. Inves-
tors lose $500,000,000,000

1987   U.S. celebrates 200-year anniversary of the Constitution

1984   Summer Olympics held at Los Angeles

1986   National battle against AIDS begins

1987   Scandals stir criticism of TV evangelism

Edward Albee 1928–

Imamu Amira Baraka (LeRoi Jones) 1934–

James Baldwin 1924–1987

Bernard Malamud 1914–1986

Norman Mailer 1923–

Joyce Carol Oates 1938–

Saul Bellow 1915–

Index to Authors, Titles, and First Lines

Note: First lines are set in roman type; all titles are italicized except titles of short works when listed under authors' names.